Britain

written and researched by

Robert Andrews, Jules Brown, Rob Humphreys, Tom Hutton, Phil Lee and Donald Reid

ROUGH GUIDES

NEW YORK • LONDON • DELHI

www.roughguides.com

A
TOY

Contents

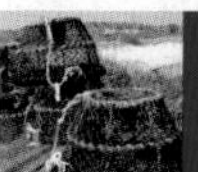

Coastal Britain colour section following p.360

Literary Britain colour section following p.632

Festivals and events colour section following p.968

◀◀ Dancing in the rain ◀ Brighton fairground

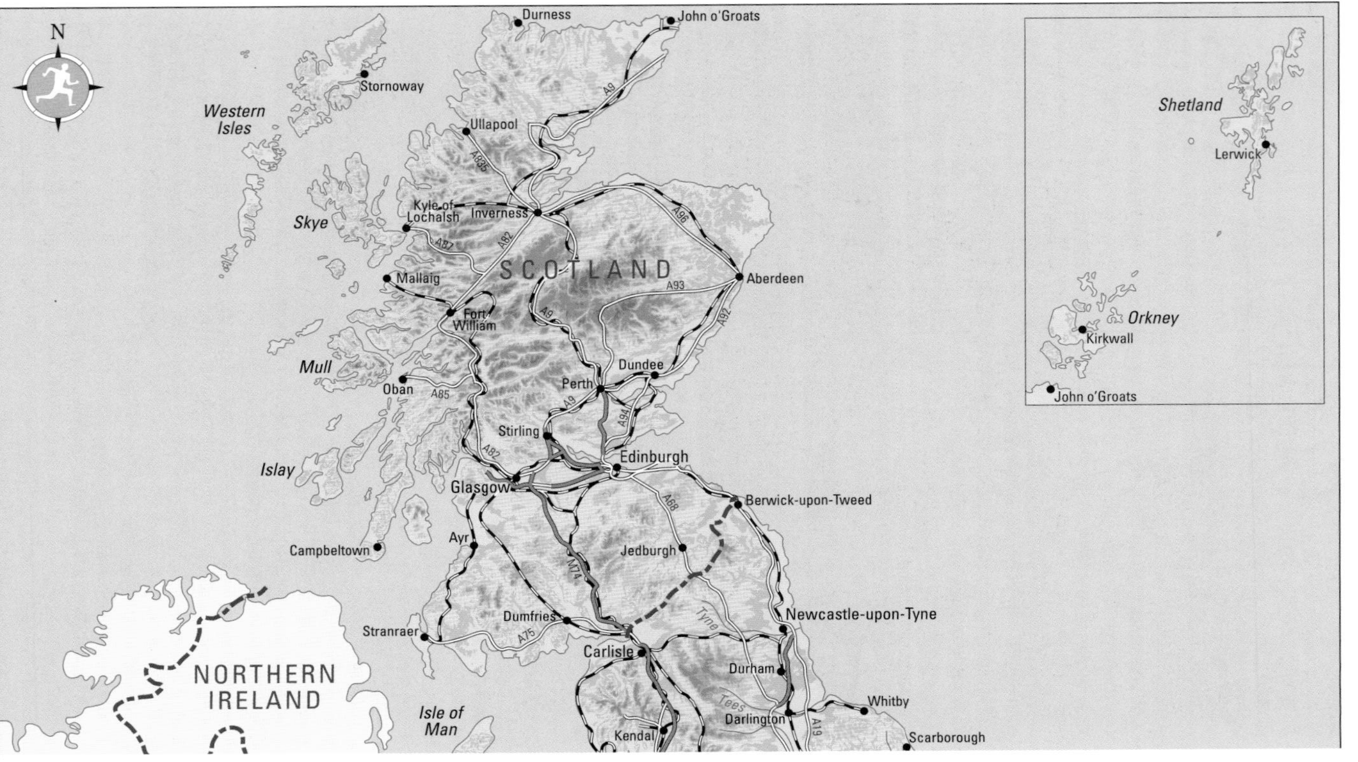
N
Shetland
Lerwick
Orkney
Kirkwall
John o'Groats
Durness
John o'Groats
Stornoway
Western Isles
Ullapool
A9
A835
Kyle of Lochalsh
Inverness
A96
Skye
A87
A82
SCOTLAND
Aberdeen
Mallaig
A93
Fort William
A9
A92
Mull
Dundee
Oban
Perth
A85
A9
A94
Stirling
Edinburgh
Islay
A82
Glasgow
Berwick-upon-Tweed
A68
Ayr
Campbeltown
Jedburgh
M74
Tyne
Newcastle-upon-Tyne
Dumfries
Stranraer
A75
Carlisle
Durham
NORTHERN IRELAND
Tees
Whitby
Isle of Man
Darlington
A19
Kendal
Scarborough

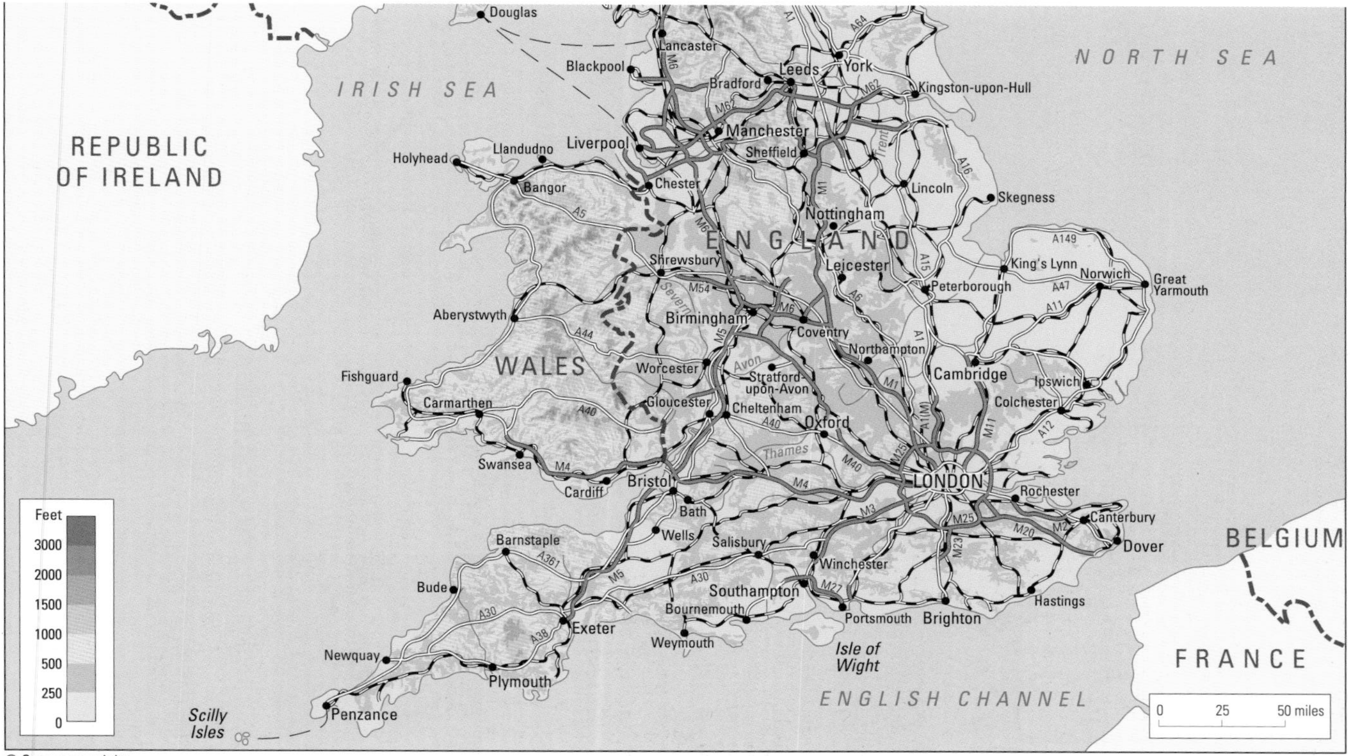

NORTH SEA
IRISH SEA
REPUBLIC OF IRELAND
ENGLAND
WALES
BELGIUM
FRANCE
ENGLISH CHANNEL
Douglas
Lancaster
Blackpool
Leeds
York
Bradford
Kingston-upon-Hull
Manchester
Liverpool
Sheffield
Llandudno
Holyhead
Bangor
Chester
Lincoln
Skegness
Nottingham
Shrewsbury
Leicester
King's Lynn
Norwich
Great Yarmouth
Peterborough
Aberystwyth
Birmingham
Coventry
Northampton
Cambridge
Ipswich
Colchester
Fishguard
Worcester
Stratford-upon-Avon
Carmarthen
Gloucester
Cheltenham
Oxford
Swansea
Cardiff
Bristol
LONDON
Rochester
Canterbury
Dover
Bath
Wells
Salisbury
Winchester
Barnstaple
Bude
Southampton
Bournemouth
Weymouth
Exeter
Portsmouth
Brighton
Hastings
Isle of Wight
Newquay
Plymouth
Penzance
Scilly Isles
Severn
Avon
Thames
Trent
M6
M62
M1
M54
M5
M4
M40
M25
A1(M)
M11
M3
M23
M20
M2
M27
A1
A64
A16
A149
A15
A47
A11
A6
A12
A5
A44
A40
A361
A30
A38

Feet
3000
2000
1500
1000
500
250
0

0
25
50 miles

Introduction to

Britain

If you were building a country from scratch, you would never try to force England, Scotland and Wales together into a single United Kingdom. Britain is not one country but three, with three capitals (London, Cardiff and Edinburgh), three national identities and myriad accent shifts. The three countries have had centuries to get used to each other, but it often feels like there's little love lost: Wales has long been resentful of English dominance; Scotland is happiest as far away from both as possible; northern England is contemptuous of the south; and Londoners are convinced they're in a league of their own.

All this regional diversity means there's enough in Britain for months of travels if you have the time: start in dynamic, cosmopolitan London and head up to the remotest Scottish fishing villages; stop by England's post-industrial heartland and explore the former mining regions of the Welsh valleys; or even walk or cycle from Land's End to John O'Groats, the longest journey in the country, as charity-fundraisers often do. Travelling around Britain is not without its idiosyncrasies. Public transport, especially the railway system, is in disarray, and commuters and long-distance travellers are in an almost permanent state of delay and revolt. Drivers will find the motorways and ring roads aren't much better, and are often gridlocked around major cities. And those who have just arrived clutching euros from a tour of "The Continent" will be swiftly disabused of the notion that Britain is an integral part of Europe.

Britain has dithered for decades about its role in the world: having ruled the roost for several hundred years, Brits are still uncertain about their place in the new world order. Paradoxically, it's the Welsh and the Scots, for so long under the English thumb, who have emerged with their national identities intact and tangible political power embodied in their own parliamentary assemblies. The English, still without a regional voice, are left unsure of how to modernize their institutions, ever-fearful of conflict erupting between town and country, north and south, rich and poor, blacks, Asians and whites, and increasingly lagging behind the social and political change that is being wrought as effectively in Edinburgh as in Brussels. England remains the dominant and most urbanized member of the British partnership, but crossing the border

▲ British icons

Fact file

- **Britain** (or Great Britain) is a geographical term referring to the largest of the British Isles. "United Kingdom" is a political term indicating the state comprising England, Scotland, Wales and Northern Ireland.
- The **population** of Britain is about 58 million: 50 million in England, 5 million in Scotland and 3 million in Wales. The biggest city is London, with some 7.4 million inhabitants. **Ethnic minorities** represent about six percent of the total population, the largest groups being those of Caribbean or African descent (875,000 people), Indians (840,000), and Pakistanis and Bangladeshis (640,000). The official **language** is English, though Welsh also has official status in Wales. Scottish Gaelic is used in parts of Scotland.
- The **lowest point** is in the Fens of eastern England, at 13ft below sea level; the **highest point** is the summit of Ben Nevis at 4406ft. From the south coast of England to the extreme north of Scotland is about 600 miles; the **longest journey**, from Land's End to John O'Groats, is nearer 850 miles.
- The UK, comprising Britain and Northern Ireland, is a **constitutional monarchy**, whose head of state is Queen Elizabeth II. The bicameral parliament is composed of the directly elected House of Commons and the unelected **House of Lords**. There is no written constitution, and real power is concentrated in the hands of the **Prime Minister**, head of the largest party in the House of Commons.

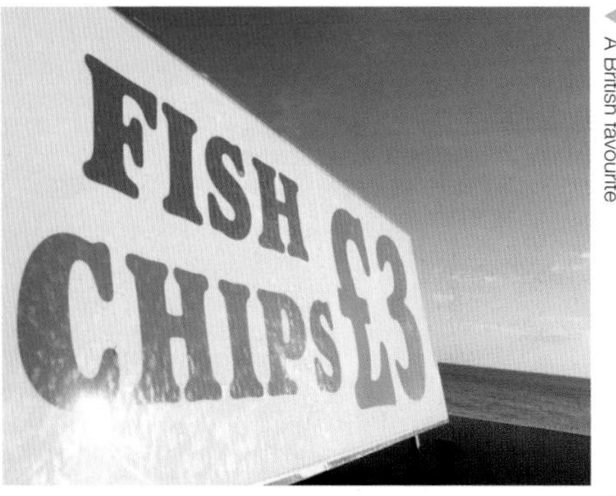

A British favourite

into predominantly rural Wales brings you into an unmistakeably Celtic land, while in Scotland (a nation whose absorption into the state was rather more recent) the presence of a profoundly non-English world-view is striking.

If ever a nation were both hostage to and beneficiary of its history, it's Britain. Across the country, virtually every town bears a mark of former wealth and power, whether it be a Gothic cathedral financed from a monarch's treasury, a parish church funded by the tycoons of medieval trade, or a triumphalist Victorian civic building raised

Understanding the British

As a glance at the popular papers will confirm, Britain is a nation of overweight, binge-drinking reality TV addicts, obsessed with toffs and C-list celebs. But it's also a nation of animal-loving, tea-drinking, charity donors, where queuing remains a national pastime and bastions of civilization, like Radio 4, are jealously protected. It's a place where accent and vocabulary can stamp a person's identity like a brand, but, despite pockets of racism and xenophobia, it's also a genuine haven for refugees, with immigrants from more than 100 ethnic backgrounds. Britain has perhaps the most dynamic media in the world and journalists are brazenly provocative – to the point where cynicism has become the entry price for intelligent conversation. Yet millions of Britons will stand in silence to honour the dead of the country's great wars, and the duties of public office are still accorded immense respect – the merest whiff of corrupt practice draws down immediate scandal and legal action.

Ask any Briton to comment on all this and – assuming you're not trying to talk to a stranger in a public place, which in London at least, can be seen as tantamount to physical assault – you will get an entertaining range of views. There is no national identity, no national day and no national dress – and nobody can agree on what it means to be British. Or whether it even matters.

British pub

with the income of the British Empire. Elsewhere, you'll find old dockyards from which the Royal Navy patrolled the oceans, and mills that employed the populations of entire towns. Meanwhile, Britain's museums and galleries – several ranking among the world's finest and most of the major ones with free admission – are full of treasures trawled from its imperial conquests. Heritage is big business in Britain, with everyone from the Queen in Buckingham Palace to the seedy tourist shops in John O'Groats cashing in on whatever assets are available. At times, the wheels of the heritage industry grind a bit too hard for comfort.

Where Britain seems to feel most at ease with itself is in the urbane world of arts and city life. Although the hearts of many towns – and increasingly their outskirts – consist of identikit retail zones, pockmarked with car parks, the vibrant music scenes of London, Bristol, Cardiff and a dozen other cities, the fashionable restaurants and bars of Manchester and Glasgow, and the outstanding contemporary architecture of Liverpool and Newcastle all provide a palpable buzz and confidence. Indeed, there's always been an innovative flair to British popular culture, which contrasts sharply with the bucolic image of Britain favoured by many tourist boards. The countryside may yield all manner of delights, from walkers' trails around the hills and lakes, through prehistoric stone circles, to traditional village pubs, but Britain's urban culture is fast becoming as popular a draw as its countryside and history.

Britain is not one country, but three, with three capitals and three national identities.

Standing stones

Why the prehistoric peoples of Britain built circles of standing stones may never be fully known. The theories are as diverse as the sites themselves: perhaps they were places of sacrifice and celebration, or erected for an astronomical function. But two things remain obvious, even at a distance of five thousand years. Firstly, each series of standing stones represents a highly organized effort by ancient peoples once thought of as unsophisticated. And secondly, whatever their function, the circles retain a powerful presence even today, recognized by the disparate bands of druids and New Age travellers who still seek solace in the stones. Mass tourism has dragged famous sites like Stonehenge into the embrace of the heritage industry, but there are other sites that retain their sense of mystery and isolation. At Castlerigg in the Lake District, Calanais in western Scotland or Holy Island in North Wales, you can still wander alone, forming your own theories as the early morning mist rises above the stones.

Where to go

England

London is the place to start. Nowhere in the country can match the scope and innovation of the captial, a colossal, frenetic city, perhaps not as immediately attractive as its European counterparts, but with so much variety that the only obstacle to having a great time is the shockingly high cost of everything. It's here that you'll find Britain's best spread of nightlife, cultural events, museums, galleries, pubs and restaurants. Other large cities, such as **Birmingham**, **Newcastle**, **Leeds**, **Manchester** and **Liverpool**, each have their strengths too. Birmingham has a resurgent arts scene, for example, while people travel for miles to sample Newcastle's nightlife. Manchester these days can match the capital for glamour in cafés and clubs, and also boasts the inimitable draw of the world's best-known football team, while its near-neighbour Liverpool earned the title of European Capital of Culture 2008.

England's ancient cathedral cities, such as **Lincoln**, **York**, **Salisbury**, **Durham** and **Winchester**, cannot be equalled for sheer physical beauty, and wherever you're based, you're never more than a few miles from a ruined castle, a majestic country house, a secluded chapel or a monastery. In the southwest there are remnants of a Celtic culture that was all but eradicated elsewhere by the Romans, and everywhere you can find traces of prehistoric settlers – most famously the megalithic circles of **Stonehenge** and **Avebury**.

▲ London underground

Most beguiling of all are the long-established villages of England, hundreds of which amount to nothing more than a pub, a shop, a gaggle of cottages and a farmhouse offering bed and breakfast. **Devon**, **Cornwall**, the **Cotswolds** and the **Yorkshire Dales** harbour some especially picturesque specimens, but every county can boast a decent showing. Then, of course, there's the English countryside, an extraordinarily diverse terrain from which Constable, Turner, Wordsworth, Emily Brontë and a host of other writers and artists took inspiration. **Exmoor**, **Dartmoor**, **Bodmin Moor**, the **North York Moors** and the **Lake District** are the most dramatic and best known of the national parks, each offering an array of landscapes criss-crossed with walking routes.

Wales

Although **Cardiff** boasts most of Wales's national institutions, including the National Museum, the appeal of a visit lies outside the towns, where there's ample evidence of the warmongering that shaped the country's development. Castles are everywhere, from the little stone keeps of the early Welsh princes and the mighty **Carreg Cennan** to Edward I's doughty fortresses such as Beaumaris, **Conwy** and Harlech. Passage graves and stone circles (such as on **Holy Island**) offer a link to the pre-Roman era when the priestly order of druids ruled over early Celtic peoples, and great medieval monastic houses, like ruined **Tintern Abbey**, are easily accessible.

Where Britain seems to feel most at ease with itself is in the urbane world of arts and city life.

All these attractions are enhanced by the beauty of the wild Welsh countryside. The backbone of the Cambrian Mountains terminates in the soaring peaks of **Snowdonia National Park** and the angular ridges of the **Brecon**

Tintern Abbey, Monmouthshire

Beacons; both are superb walking country, as is the **Pembrokeshire coast** in the southwest. Much of the rest of the coast remains unspoilt, though long sweeps of sand are often backed by traditional British seaside resorts, such as **Llandudno** in the north or **Tenby** in the south.

Scotland

The Scottish capital, **Edinburgh**, is a handsome and ancient city, famous for its magnificent **castle** and **Palace of Holyroodhouse** as well as for an acclaimed international arts festival and some excellent museums – not least the outstanding **National Museum of Scotland**. A short journey west is **Glasgow**, a sprawling industrial metropolis that has done much to improve its image in recent years and can now boast a range of fine museums and galleries and dynamic nightlife to complement the impressive architectural legacy of its eighteenth- and nineteenth-century heyday.

Red deer stag

Southern Scotland, often underrated, features some gorgeous scenery, but nothing quite to compare with the shadowy glens and well-walked hills of the **Trossachs**, or with the **Highlands**, whose multitude of mountains, sea cliffs, glens and lochs cover the northern two-thirds of the country. **Inverness** is an obvious base here, although **Fort William**, near **Ben Nevis**, Britain's highest mountain, is an alternative.

Some of Britain's most thrilling wilderness experiences are to be had on the Scottish islands, the most accessible of which extend in a long rocky chain off the Atlantic coast, from **Arran** through **Skye** (the most visited of the Hebrides) to the **Western Isles**, where the remarkably hostile terrain harbours some of the last bastions of the Gaelic language. At Britain's northern extreme lie the sea- and wind-buffeted **Orkney** and **Shetland** islands, whose rich Norse heritage makes them distinct in dialect and culture from mainland Scotland, while their wild scenery offers some of Britain's finest bird-watching and some stunning archeological remains.

When to go

Considering the temperate nature of the British **climate**, it's amazing how much mileage the locals get out of the subject: a two-day cold snap is discussed as if it were the onset of a new Ice Age, and a week in the upper 70s starts rumours of a heatwave. The fact is that summers rarely get hot and the winters don't get very cold, except in the north of Scotland and on the highest points of the Welsh and Scottish uplands. Rainfall is fairly even, though again mountainous areas get higher quantities throughout the year (the west coast of Scotland is especially damp, and Llanberis, at the foot of Snowdon, gets more than twice as much rainfall as Caernarfon, seven miles away).

▲ Inclement weather

In general, the south is warmer and sunnier than the north, but the bottom line is that it's impossible to say with any degree of certainty what the weather will be like. May might be wet and grey one year and gloriously sunny the next; November stands an equal chance of being crisp and clear or foggy and grim. If you're planning to lie on a beach, or camp in the dry, you'll want to visit between June and September – a period when you shouldn't go anywhere without booking your accommodation in advance. Otherwise, if you're balancing the clemency of the weather against the density of the crowds, the best months to explore are April, May, September and October.

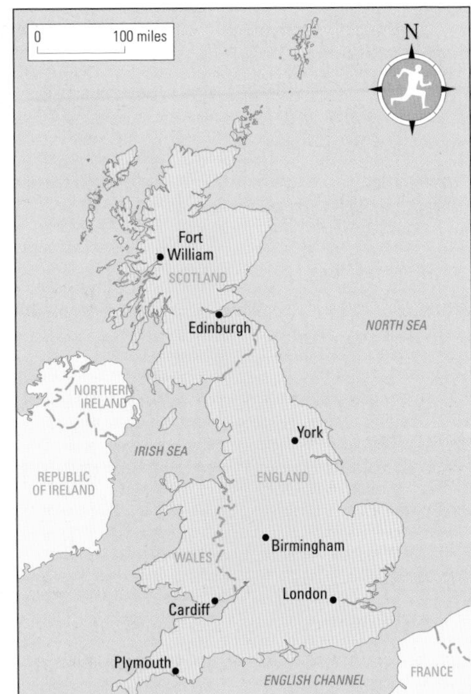

Average daily maximum temperatures

	Jan	Feb	Mar	Apr	May	Jun	Jul	Aug	Sep	Oct	Nov	Dec
Birmingham												
°F	42	43	48	54	61	66	68	68	63	55	48	44
°C	5	6	9	12	16	19	20	20	17	13	9	7
Cardiff												
°F	45	45	50	56	60	68	69	69	64	58	51	46
°C	7	7	10	13	16	20	21	21	18	14	11	8
Edinburgh												
°F	42	43	46	51	56	64	65	64	61	54	48	44
°C	5	6	8	11	13	18	18	18	16	12	9	7
Fort William												
°F	43	44	48	52	58	61	62	63	61	54	49	45
°C	6	7	9	11	14	16	17	17	16	12	9	7
London												
°F	43	44	50	56	62	69	71	71	65	58	50	45
°C	6	7	10	13	17	21	22	22	19	14	10	7
Plymouth												
°F	47	47	50	54	59	64	66	67	64	58	52	49
°C	8	8	10	12	15	18	19	19	18	14	11	9
York												
°F	43	44	49	55	61	67	70	69	64	57	49	45
°C	6	7	10	13	16	19	21	21	18	14	9	7

34

things not to miss

It's not possible to see everything that Britain has to offer in one trip – and we don't suggest you try. What follows is a selective taste of the highlights of England, Wales and Scotland: beautiful scenery, awe-inspiring buildings, fantastic activities and delicious food and drink. They're arranged in five colour-coded categories, which you can browse through to find the very best things to see and experience. All entries have a page reference to take you straight into the Guide, where you can find out more.

01 **West Highland Railway** Page **978** • Take one of the great railway journeys of the world.

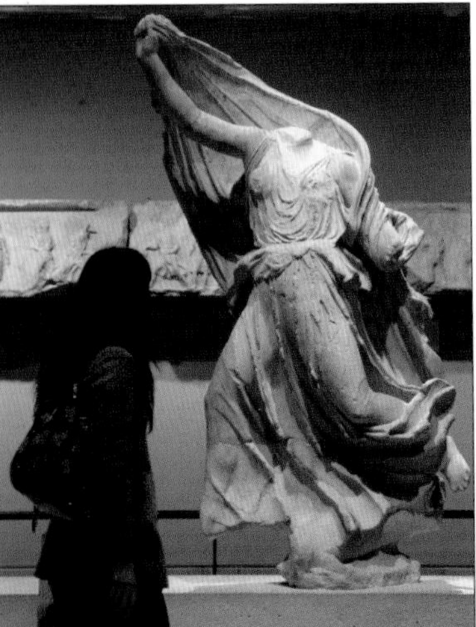

02 British Museum Page **106** • In parts controversial and generally not British, the collections of the BM are still the greatest in the world.

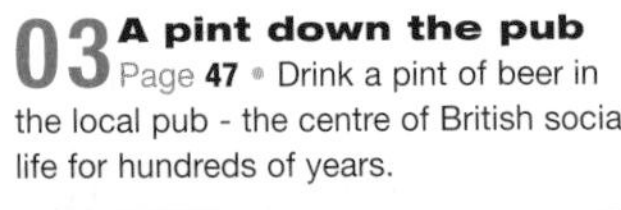

03 A pint down the pub Page **47** • Drink a pint of beer in the local pub - the centre of British social life for hundreds of years.

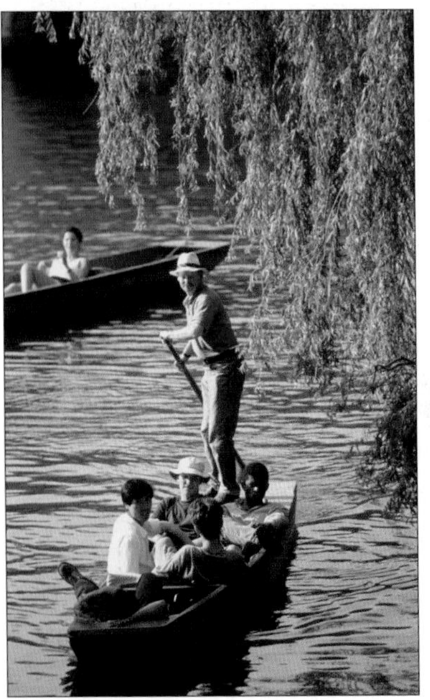

04 Punting on the Cam Page **393** • Pack a picnic and take a trip down the river by punt in the handsome university town of Cambridge.

05 York Minster Page **568** • See the world's largest medieval stained-glass window at Britain's biggest and most dramatic Gothic church.

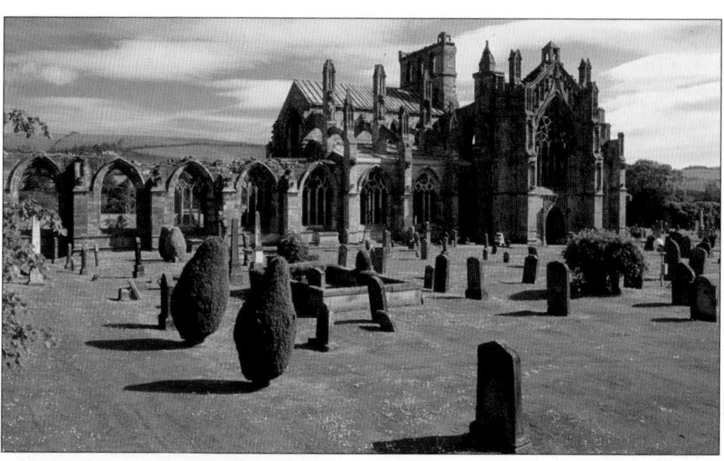

06 Melrose Abbey Page **804** • Melrose and its fine abbey ruins are reason enough for visiting the Scottish Borders region.

07 Whale- and dolphin-watching Page **983** • Take a boat trip in the Cromarty Firth to see these beautiful marine creatures.

08 Iona Page **901** • The home of Celtic Christian spirituality, an island of pilgrimage today as in antiquity.

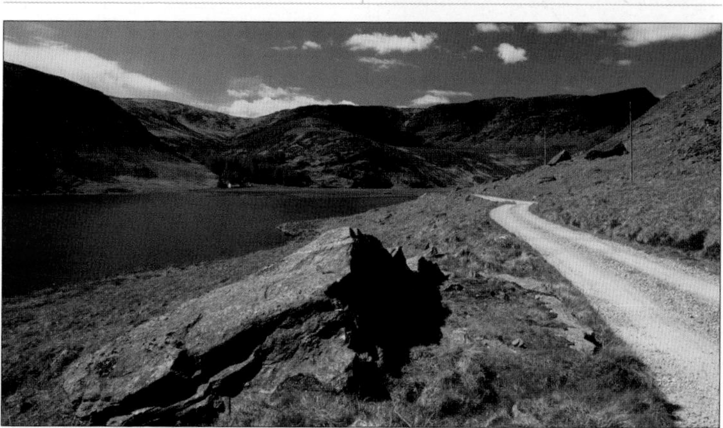

09 Cairngorms National Park Page **984** • The most extensive mountain range in Britain offers unmatched walking and water-sports opportunities.

10 Whitby fish and chips Page **585** • Sample Yorkshire's most delicious rough-and-ready cuisine, at its best with mushy peas.

11 Tobermory Page **899** • Scotland's most picturesque fishing port, bar none.

12 Stately homes and castles Page **62** • For tangible proof of Britain's history, the country's many castles and stately homes – like Castle Howard in Yorkshire – can't be bettered.

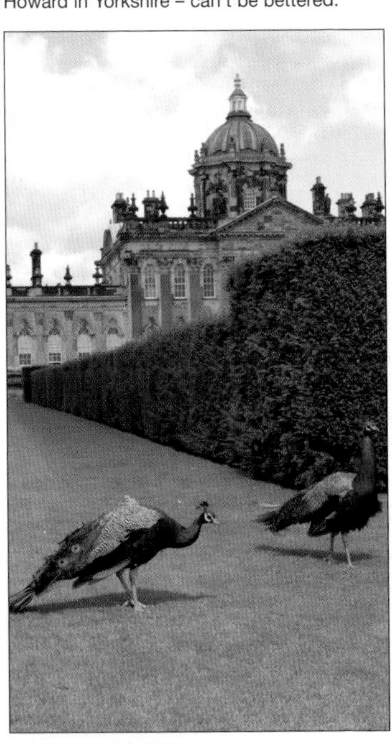

13 Kinloch Castle, Rùm Page **928** • Stay in the servants' quarters of this Edwardian Scottish-island hideaway or in a four-poster bed.

14 Hadrian's Wall Page **611** • Once the frontier against Britain's northern tribes, the Roman wall today is remarkably well preserved – and you can walk its length along the 84-mile Hadrian's Wall Path.

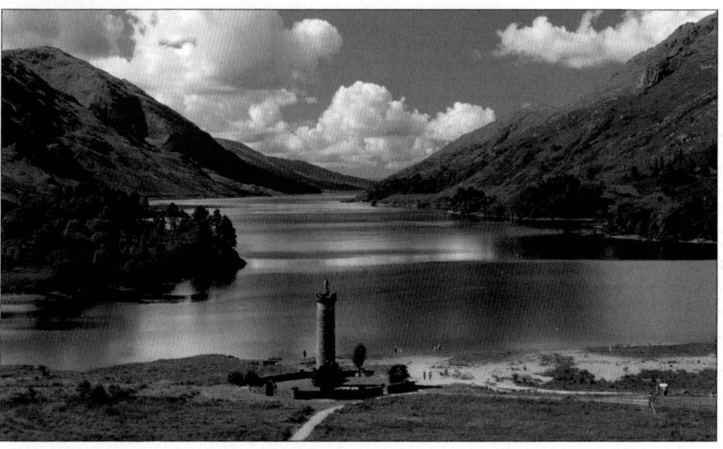

15 Loch Shiel Page **998** • Among Scotland's myriad lochs, Shiel stands out for its serene beauty and compelling history.

16 Mountain-biking Page **700** • Wales is home to some of the most exhilarating mountain-biking in the world – superior tracks, fantastic downhills and stupendous views.

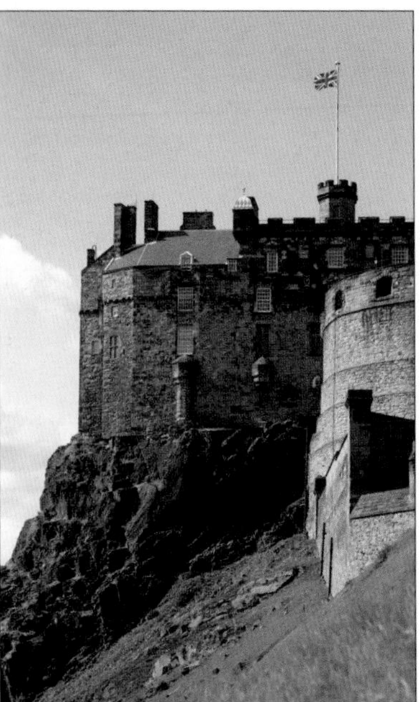

17 Edinburgh Castle Page **764** • Dominating Scotland's capital, this fortress-cum-royal palace is intimately linked to the country's history.

18 Ullswater Page **532** • Serene Ullswater is many people's favourite Lake District lake, overlooked by the heights of Helvellyn and by Wordsworth's dancing daffodils.

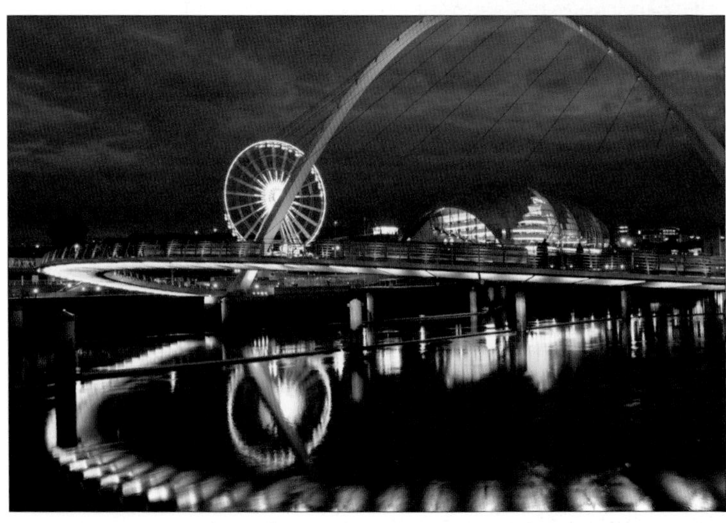

19 A night on the town, Newcastle upon Tyne Page **607** • Northeastern England's premier arts and nightlife destination has a scintillating quayside of bridges, bars, galleries and concert halls.

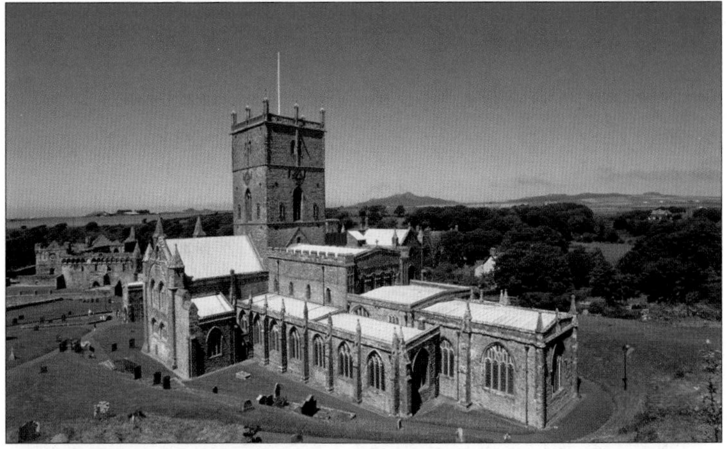

20 St David's Cathedral Page **669** • Serene cathedral set in a quiet village that has drawn pilgrims to this westernmost tip of Wales for well over a thousand years.

21 National Museum of Wales Page **646** • Find out everything you ever wanted to know about Wales in Cardiff's National Museum and Gallery.

22 London's markets Page **160** • From Borough's foodie treats to Columbia Road's flowers and the arty, boho clothes of Greenwich, London's markets have something for everyone.

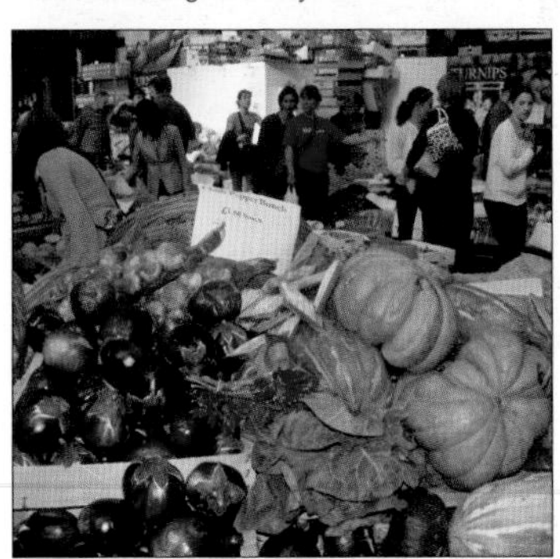

23 Snowdonia Page **721** • One of Britain's finest national parks, a wedge of mountainous Welsh territory focused on the Snowdon massif.

24 Surfing, Newquay Page **353** • The beaches strung along the north coast of Devon and Cornwall offer some great breaks, and Newquay is still the place to see and be seen.

25 Whisky Page **967** • Sup a dram in northeast Scotland's "whisky triangle", whose Malt Whisky Trail showcases the best distilleries.

26 Oxford Page **255** • One of the world's finest academic cities glories in its dreaming spires, honey-coloured stone and manicured quadrangles.

27 Bath Page **292** • Whether you're visiting the Roman baths, England's most elegant Georgian terrace, or the new high-tech spa, Bath has it all.

28 Harlech Page **697** • An evocative castle and twisting narrow streets make this town a highlight of the Cambrian coast.

29 Glasgow School of Art Page **838** • The finest example of the unique style of Glasgow architect and designer Charles Rennie Mackintosh.

30 Shopping in Leeds Page **549** • Glorious Victorian arcades packed with designer labels, plus indoor markets and Harvey Nick's – there's no better place to blow your budget.

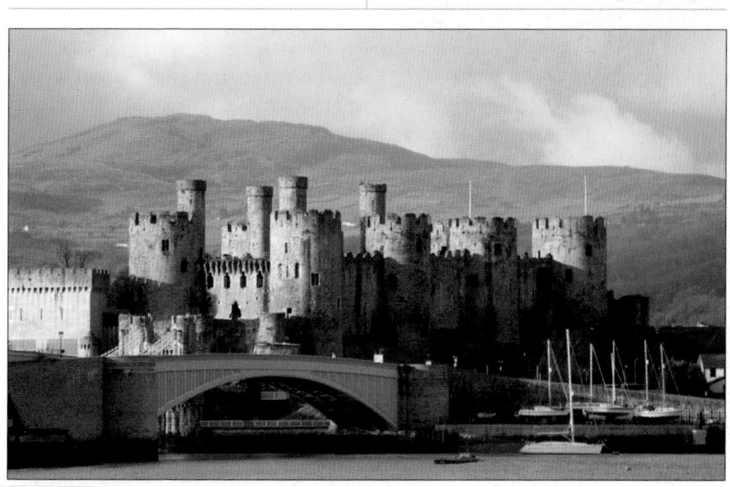

31 Conwy Page **743** • Conwy is commonly agreed to be the most spectacular of Edward I's Iron Ring of monumental fortresses.

32 Avebury Page **244** • Avebury's stone circle rivals Stonehenge in aspect and interest, and its function is as hotly debated.

33 Tate St Ives, Cornwall Page **351** • Southwest England's best art collection occupies a superb site overlooking Porthmeor Beach.

34 Eden Project, Cornwall Page **343** • Spectacular and refreshingly ungimmicky display of the planet's plant life, mainly housed in vast geodesic "biomes".

Basics

Basics

Getting there

For most travellers to Britain, the range of options will be greatest – and the fares usually the lowest – flying into London, one of the world's busiest transport hubs. However, if you're planning to tour the north of England or Scotland, you should consider a nonstop flight into one of the country's regional airports instead, such as Manchester, Birmingham or Glasgow. It's also possible to connect in London to many other regional airports around England, Wales or Scotland on a domestic carrier.

London's biggest airports – **Heathrow** and **Gatwick** – take the bulk of transatlantic and long-haul flights into the UK, and are about equal in terms of convenient access to the capital. London's three smaller airports – **Stansted**, **Luton** and **City** – are well served by low-cost flights from mainland Europe, as are other regional airports, including **Manchester** in the northwest, **Birmingham** in the West Midlands, **Bristol** in the West Country, **Leeds/Bradford** in Yorkshire, **Newcastle** in Northeast England, **Nottingham East Midlands** in the East Midlands, and **Edinburgh**, **Glasgow** and **Aberdeen** in Scotland and **Cardiff** in Wales.

Airfares to Britain are highest from early June to mid-September, at Easter, and at Christmas and New Year; fares drop during the "shoulder" seasons – mid-September to early November and mid-April to early June – and it's usually cheapest during the low season, November through to April. Note that flying at **weekends** is generally more expensive, and that quoted prices are often exclusive of **taxes and fees**, which can add significantly to the cost.

Tickets are available either direct from the airlines or from a **discount travel agent**, which sometimes offers student and youth fares as well as a range of other travel-related services. Many airline and **travel websites** can now also book package holidays, accommodation and car rental. You can turn up some great online deals, but always check the small print as many tickets are nonchangeable and nonrefundable.

Travelling from mainland **Europe**, drivers and foot and rail passengers can either cross the Channel by **ferry** or go under it, by **Eurotunnel** (the drive-on drive-off shuttle train for vehicles) or **Eurostar** (the high-speed passenger train from Paris and Brussels to London). If you're on a very tight budget, you might consider picking up a **bus** from any of the major European cities. **From Ireland**, it's quickest to fly, but there are also plenty of **ferry** crossings – especially useful if you're planning to tour around Scotland, Wales or the west of England.

Package tours of Britain, where all flights, accommodation and ground transport are arranged for you, take the hassle out of travel and can sometimes be cheaper than organizing things yourself. Many outfits in the UK and overseas offer standard **coach-tour** itineraries of Britain's historic highlights, or help you explore some aspect of the country's heritage, such as art and architecture, gardens and stately homes, culture and sports. Some companies offer budget versions of their holidays, staying in hostels or B&Bs, as well as hotel packages. For activity holidays, see p.59.

Flights from the US and Canada

Many airlines fly direct **from the US** to London and some also to regional airports, including Continental Airlines with flights from New York to Bristol, Birmingham, Manchester, Glasgow and Edinburgh. New York has the most nonstop services, though there are also nonstop flights from Washington DC, Boston, Chicago, Miami, Orlando, Las Vegas, San Francisco and Los Angeles. Flights with a connection, usually on mainland European airlines, are often cheaper but tend to route through their European hubs, adding (sometimes significantly) to your journey time. Depending on the airline, low-season midweek fares from New York cost under $500, from Los Angeles more like $600–700, but bear in mind that the very cheapest deals tend to have little or no flexibility, and that taxes and fees can add up to $100 to any quoted price.

From **Canada**, airlines like Air Canada and bmi fly nonstop from the gateway cities of Toronto, Montréal and Vancouver to London and Manchester. Low-season fares from Toronto start at around CAN$550 return, from Vancouver more like CAN$900. Zoom Airlines offer budget fares to London and Manchester from Ottawa, Montréal, Toronto, Halifax, Winnipeg, Calgary, and Vancouver, while the charter operator Air Transat has good-value flights to London, Manchester, Newcastle, Birmingham and Exeter, mainly from Toronto, but also from Vancouver.

Flying time to any British airport from New York or Toronto is around seven hours, and from LA or Vancouver more like ten hours (it's an hour extra coming the other way, due to headwinds).

Flights from Ireland

Stiff competition on routes between Ireland and England keeps the cost of flights low. **From the Republic**, a number of budget airlines offer very cheap deals, sometimes even offering free flights, with passengers paying just the taxes (around €30). Otherwise, you can usually expect to pay from around €70 return. The chief budget airlines are: Aer Arann, from Dublin, Galway, Waterford, Cork, Sligo and Kerry to Birmingham, Bristol, Cardiff, London Luton, Leeds/Bradford, Manchester, Newcastle, Edinburgh, Inverness, and the Isle of Man; bmibaby, from Cork and Knock to Birmingham and Manchester; and Ryanair from Dublin, Cork, Kerry, Knock and Shannon to fourteen airports in England and three in Scotland. Aer Lingus and British Airways also offer cut-price deals, and fly from Dublin, Cork and Shannon to Birmingham, Manchester, Newcastle, London, Glasgow and Edinburgh.

The cheapest options **from Belfast** are easyJet to Bristol, Liverpool, London, Newcastle, Glasgow and Edinburgh; Flybe, which serves eight English and four Scottish airports; Ryanair to Glasgow, East Midlands, Liverpool and London, and bmibaby to Manchester, East Midlands, Birmingham and Cardiff. Ryanair also flies from Derry to Bristol, Liverpool, London, East Midlands and Glasgow. Return flights cost from around £50, though much cheaper deals are possible.

Flights from Australia, New Zealand and South Africa

The route **from Australia and New Zealand** to London is highly competitive, with the lowest return fares usually in the range of A$1500–2500 from Australia, NZ$2000–3000 from New Zealand. The main departure points are Sydney, Melbourne, Perth and Auckland. The very cheapest tickets rarely have much, if any, flexibility and you might want to pay more to be able to change your dates or to travel with one of the major airlines like Qantas, British Airways, Air New Zealand or Singapore Airlines. These airlines also tend to be able to arrange things like fly-drive and accommodation packages or onward travel to other British destinations – flights to Manchester, for example, are sometimes available at no extra cost. To reach Scotland, you'll have to change planes either in London – the most popular choice – or in another European gateway such as Paris or Amsterdam.

Travel time from Australia or New Zealand to England is over twenty hours, even with the best connections, so you might want to consider a stopover – most airlines will let you do this for no extra charge. Some of the cheapest flights on Asian and Middle Eastern airlines involve a stop in any case, for example at Hong Kong or Dubai. Most New Zealand flights involve a connection, whether in Asia or the US; there's little to choose between the two routes in terms of journey time.

Flights from Johannesburg in **South Africa** usually cost ZAR6000–8000 return and take over eleven hours nonstop, though some of the cheapest, operated by Emirates, involve lengthy connections in Dubai. There are fewer direct flights from Cape Town, and they take slightly longer and cost a bit more.

Fly less – stay longer! Travel and climate change

Climate change is the single biggest issue facing our planet. It is caused by a build-up in the atmosphere of carbon dioxide and other greenhouse gases, which are emitted by many sources – including planes. Already, flights account for around 3–4 percent of human-induced global warming: that figure may sound small, but it is rising year on year and threatens to counteract the progress made by reducing greenhouse emissions in other areas.

Rough Guides regard travel, overall, as a global benefit, and feel strongly that the advantages to developing economies are important, as are the opportunities for greater contact and awareness among peoples. But we all have a responsibility to limit our personal "carbon footprint". That means giving thought to how often we fly and what we can do to redress the harm that our trips create.

Flying and climate change

Pretty much every form of motorized travel generates CO_2, but planes are particularly bad offenders, releasing large volumes of greenhouse gases at altitudes where their impact is far more harmful. Flying also allows us to travel much further than we would contemplate doing by road or rail, so the emissions attributable to each passenger become truly shocking. For example, one person taking a return flight between Europe and California produces the equivalent impact of 2.5 tonnes of CO_2 – similar to the yearly output of the average UK car.

Less harmful planes may evolve but it will be decades before they replace the current fleet – which could be too late for avoiding climate chaos. In the meantime, there are limited options for concerned travellers: to reduce the amount we travel by air (take fewer trips, stay longer!), to avoid night flights (when plane contrails trap heat from Earth but can't reflect sunlight back to space), and to make the trips we do take "climate neutral" via a carbon offset scheme.

Carbon offset schemes

Offset schemes run by **climatecare.org**, **carbonneutral.com** and others allow you to "neutralize" the greenhouse gases that you are responsible for releasing. Their websites have simple calculators that let you work out the impact of any flight. Once that's done, you can pay to fund projects that will reduce future carbon emissions by an equivalent amount (such as the distribution of low-energy lightbulbs and cooking stoves in developing countries). Please take the time to visit our website and make your trip climate neutral.

Ⓦ www.roughguides.com/climatechange

Flights from mainland Europe

Low-cost airlines have not only reduced the cost of flying to Britain considerably, but have opened up access to many regional airports. Ryanair, easyJet, bmibaby, Flybe, VLM, Brussels Airlines and others fly to regional British airports from all over the continent. There are airports at Manchester, Liverpool, Newcastle, Durham Tees Valley and Leeds/Bradford for northern England; Bournemouth and Southampton for the south coast; Nottingham for the Midlands; Stansted and Norwich for East Anglia; Bristol, Newquay and Exeter for the southwest; Cardiff and Swansea for Wales; and Aberdeen, Edinburgh and Glasgow for Scotland.

Ferries from mainland Europe and Ireland

Ferries cross from several European countries to ports in Britain. The quickest, cheapest services are on the traditional cross-Channel routes **from France** (Calais, Boulogne, Dieppe and Dunkerque) to Dover, Folkestone and Newhaven in the southeast. However, other services might be more convenient, depending on your departure point and destination: you can reach Ramsgate in northern Kent from **Belgium**

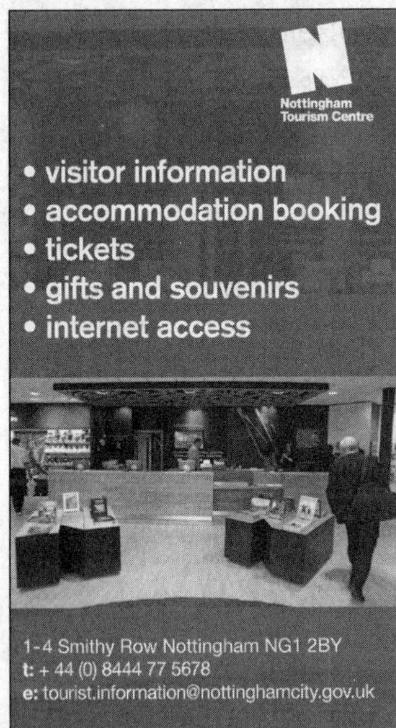

(Ostend); Portsmouth, Poole and Weymouth in the south and Plymouth in the southwest from Brittany (Roscoff, St Malo), Normandy (Caen, Cherbourg) and **Spain** (Bilbao and Santander); Harwich in Essex from **Denmark** (Esbjerg) and **Holland** (Hook of Holland); Hull in Yorkshire from Belgium (Zeebrugge) and Holland (Rotterdam); Newcastle in the northeast from Holland (Amsterdam), **Norway** (Stavanger, Bergen) and **Sweden** (Gothenburg), or Lerwick in the Shetlands from Bergen in Norway. As an alternative to the ferry crossing, drivers can load their cars aboard trains at Calais for the Eurotunnel crossing to Folkestone (see below).

Unless you're bringing your own vehicle to the UK, there's little incentive in coming by ferry from either the **Republic or Northern Ireland**, as crossings tend to take longer and are often more expensive than flying. The main **direct services to England** are from Dublin and Belfast to Liverpool (P&O and Norfolk Line) and Douglas, Isle of Man (Isle of Man Steam Packet), and from Larne to Fleetwood (Stena Line). As for **ferries to Wales** from Ireland, there are car ferries from Dun Laoghaire to Holyhead (Stena Line), from Dublin to Holyhead (Irish ferries and Stena Line), and from Rosslare to Fishguard (Stena Line) and Pembroke (Irish Ferries). **To Scotland by ferry**, there are services from Belfast to Stranraer (Stena Line), and from Larne to Troon and Cairnryan (both P&O).

Fares on all routes vary according to the time of year, time and type of crossing, while sleeping accommodation is often obligatory on night crossings from the continent. Consult Ⓦwww.directferries.com to compare all the options.

Trains from mainland Europe and Ireland

Direct **Eurostar trains** run roughly hourly through the Channel Tunnel to London St Pancras International from Lille (1hr 25min), Paris (2hr 20min) and Brussels (2hr). Return fares start from around €75 return from Paris or Lille, €95 from Brussels, though these rates come with many restrictions. More flexible tickets can cost around €200 return, though discounted flexible youth (for under-26s) and senior (over-60s) fares are available. If you are intending to tour Kent, you might consider disembarking at Ashford (for mid-Kent) or Ebbsfleet (for North Kent) rather than London.

For drivers, **Eurotunnel** operates drive-on-drive-off shuttle trains through the Channel Tunnel from Calais/Coquelles to Folkestone. The 24-hour service runs every 20–30 minutes throughout the day (every 90min or so at night) and takes 35 minutes. Although you can just turn up, booking is advised, especially at weekends, or if you want the best deals. Off-peak return fares for a car and passengers booked at least 14 days in advance start at around €140 return, though fully flexible fares allowing changes cost much more than this.

From Ireland, you can book integrated train and ferry services from almost any station in Ireland to any English station. The quickest Dublin–London route takes 7hr 20min, with one-way fares around €44; contact Irish Ferries (see p.33) for details.

Buses from mainland Europe and Ireland

Eurolines is Europe's largest international bus network, coordinating independent coach services to London from dozens of **mainland European cities**, including Amsterdam, Brussels, Frankfurt, Hamburg, Madrid, Paris and Rome. Prices are around €70 return from Paris, though this often offers no saving over a low-cost airline. Eurolines also operate bus and ferry services **from Dublin** (connections can be booked from other major towns in Ireland), to a number of British cities from €35 return. National Express offers a bus/ferry route **from Belfast** to London (around £50 return). The downside is that from both north and south the trip involves an overnight ferry crossing to Holyhead, arriving in England at the crack of dawn.

Airlines, agents and operators

Online booking

Ⓦ **www.expedia.com** (in US), Ⓦ **www.expedia.ca** (in Canada)
Ⓦ **www.lastminute.com.au** (in Australia), Ⓦ **www.lastminute.ie** (in Republic of Ireland), Ⓦ **www.us.lastminute.com** (in US)
Ⓦ **www.orbitz.com** (in US)
Ⓦ **www.travelocity.com** (in US), Ⓦ **www.travelocity.ca** (in Canada)
Ⓦ **www.zuji.com.au** (in Australia), Ⓦ **www.zuji.co.nz** (in New Zealand)

Airlines

Aer Arann Republic of Ireland Ⓣ 0818/210210, Ⓦ www.aerarann.com.
Air Canada Canada & US Ⓣ 1-888/247-2262, Ⓦ www.aircanada.com.
Air New Zealand Australia Ⓣ 0800/132 476, US Ⓣ 1-800/262-1234, New Zealand Ⓣ 0800/737000; Ⓦ www.airnz.co.nz.
Air Transat Canada Ⓣ 1-866/847-1112, Ⓦ www.airtransat.com.
American Airlines Canada & US Ⓣ 1-800/433-7300, Ⓦ www.aa.com.
bmi US Ⓣ 1-800/788-0555, Republic of Ireland Ⓣ 01/407 3036; Ⓦ www.flybmi.com.
bmibaby Republic of Ireland Ⓣ 1890/340 122, Ⓦ www.bmibaby.com.
British Airways US & Canada Ⓣ 1-800/AIRWAYS, Republic of Ireland Ⓣ 1890/626747, Australia Ⓣ 1300/767 177, New Zealand Ⓣ 09/966 9777, South Africa Ⓣ 114/418 600; Ⓦ www.ba.com.
Brussels Airlines Belgium Ⓣ 0902/51600, Ⓦ www.brusselsairlines.com.
Continental Airlines Australia Ⓣ 02/9244 2242, Canada & US Ⓣ 1-800/523-3273, New Zealand Ⓣ 09/308 3350, Republic of Ireland Ⓣ 1890/925252; Ⓦ www.continental.com.
Delta Canada & US Ⓣ 1-800/221-1212, Ⓦ www.delta.com.
easyJet Ⓦ www.easyjet.com.
Flybe Republic of Ireland/International Ⓣ +44/1392 268529, Ⓦ www.flybe.com.
Qantas Airways Australia Ⓣ 13 13 13, Canada & US Ⓣ 1-800/227-4500, New Zealand Ⓣ 0800/808 767 or 09/357 8900; Ⓦ www.qantas.com.
Ryanair Republic of Ireland Ⓣ 0818/303030, Ⓦ www.ryanair.com.
Singapore Airlines Australia Ⓣ 13 10 11, New Zealand Ⓣ 0800/808 909; Ⓦ www.singaporeair.com.
South African Airways South Africa Ⓣ 11/978 1111, Ⓦ www.flysaa.com.
United Airlines US Ⓣ 1-800/UNITED-1, Ⓦ www.united.com.
Virgin Atlantic South Africa Ⓣ 11/340 3400, US Ⓣ 1-800/821-5438; Ⓦ www.virgin-atlantic.com.
VLM Airlines Belgium Ⓣ 032/878080, Holland Ⓣ 0900/450 5050; Ⓦ www.flyvlm.com.
Zoom Airlines Canada & US Ⓣ 1-866/359-9666, Ⓦ www.flyzoom.com.

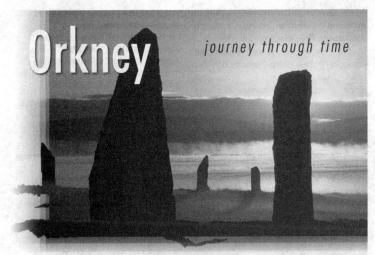

Agents and operators

Abercrombie & Kent US ⓣ1-800/554-7016, ⓦwww.abercrombiekent.com. Classy travel specialist, with no-expense-spared escorted and independent trips.

British Airways Holidays US ⓣ1-877/428-2228, ⓦwww.baholidays.com. Flight-inclusive vacations and sightseeing itineraries, including London city breaks.

British Travel International US ⓣ1-727/643-5710, ⓦwww.britishtravel.com. Agent for all independent arrangements: rail and bus passes, car rental, hotels and a comprehensive accommodation reservation service.

Carry On Tours UK ⓣ0208748 9197, ⓦwww.carryontours.com. One-, two- and three-day minibus tours out of London on a variety of themes, from Eccentric Britain to *Harry Potter* locations. A 6-day tour of Britain's highlights takes in Snowdonia and Edinburgh.

Contiki Holidays UK ⓣ020/8290 6422, ⓦwww.contiki.com. Lively adventure tours for 18–35s, in particular 3- and 5-day London trips or an 8-day all-Britain tour.

Delta Vacations US ⓣ1-800/654-6559, ⓦwww.deltavacations.com. General tour operator with city breaks in London, Manchester, Edinburgh and Glasgow.

ebookers Republic of Ireland ⓣ01/488 3507, ⓦwww.ebookers.ie. Low fares on an extensive selection of scheduled flights and package deals.

English Experience US ⓣ1-800/892-9317, ⓦwww.english-experience.com. Small-group, customized tours in B&Bs or hotels, covering the historic sights in Sussex, Kent, the Cotswolds, Lake District, Yorkshire Dales, Devon and Cornwall, and East Anglia.

Explore Holidays Australia ⓣ02/9423 8080, ⓦwww.exploreholidays.com.au. Organizes customized London packages and tours all over Britain that include accommodation, passes to sights, car rental and the like.

Flightcentre US ⓣ1-866/967-5351, ⓦwww.flightcentre.us; Canada ⓣ1-877/967-5302, ⓦwww.flightcentre.ca; Australia ⓣ133 133, ⓦwww.flightcentre.com.au; New Zealand ⓣ0800/243 544, ⓦwww.flightcentre.co.nz. Discount flight agent.

Martin Randall Travel UK ⓣ020/8742 3355, ⓦwww.martinrandall.com. All-inclusive historical and cultural tours led by experts – for example, tours of West Country churches, or concert tours of northern England.

Maupintour US ⓣ1-800/255-4266, ⓦwww.maupintour.com. Quality, all-inclusive, themed escorted tours – London at Christmas, or lakes and literature, for example.

Road Trip UK ⓣ0845/200 6791, ⓦwww.roadtrip.co.uk. Inclusive, activity-filled budget bus tours, departing from London, using mainly hostel accommodation. Two- or three-day weekend tours to Bath and Stonehenge, Cornwall, Devon (murder mystery), or York and Sherwood Forest; longer tours touch on Scotland, Wales and Ireland.

STA Travel Australia ⓣ134 STA, New Zealand ⓣ0800/474 400, South Africa ⓣ0861/781 781, US & Canada ⓣ1-800/781-4040; ⓦwww.statravel.com. Worldwide specialists in independent travel; also student IDs, travel insurance, car rental, rail passes, and more. Good discounts for students and under-26s.

Thomas Cook UK ⓣ0870/750 5711, ⓦwww.thomascook.co.uk. Wide range of UK breaks, plus hotel and theatre-ticket bookings.

Trailfinders Australia ⓣ1300/780 212, ⓦwww.trailfinders.com.au. One of the best-informed and most efficient agents for independent travellers.

Travel Cuts US ⓣ1-800/592-CUTS, Canada ⓣ1-800/246-9762; ⓦwww.travelcuts.com. Efficient, easy-to-use flightfinder for budget and student travel.

Rail contacts

BritRail Travel US ⓣ1-866/BRITRAIL, Canada ⓣ1-514/733-5247; ⓦwww.britrail.com.

Europrail International Canada ⓣ1-888/667-9734, ⓦwww.europrail.net.

Eurostar outside UK ⓣ+44 1233/617575, ⓦwww.eurostar.com.

Eurotunnel Belgium ⓣ070/223210, France ⓣ08.10.63.03.04; ⓦwww.eurotunnel.com.

The Man in Seat Sixty-One ⓦwww.seat61.com. The world's finest train travel website, with more detail than you ever wanted to know about train travel in the UK (and worldwide), but full of useful tips and links.

Rail Europe US ⓣ1-877/257-2887, ⓦwww.raileurope.com/us; Canada ⓣ1-800/361-RAIL, ⓦwww.raileurope.ca; Australia ⓦwww.railplus.com.au; New Zealand ⓦwww.railplus.co.nz.

Bus contacts

Eurolines UK ⓣ0870/580 8080, ⓦwww.nationalexpress.com/eurolines.

Ferry contacts

Brittany Ferries UK ⓣ0870/366 5333, Republic of Ireland ⓣ021/4277 801; ⓦwww.brittanyferries.co.uk.

DFDS Seaways UK ⓣ0870/252 0524, ⓦwww.dfdsseaways.co.uk.

Irish Ferries Northern Ireland ⓣ0818/300 400, Republic of Ireland ⓣ0818/300 400, UK ⓣ0870/517 1717; ⓦwww.irishferries.com.

Isle of Man Steam Packet UK ⓣ0871/222 1333, ⓦwww.steam-packet.com.

Norfolkline France ⓣ03.28.59.01.01, Republic of Ireland ⓣ01/819 2999, UK ⓣ0871/870 1020 for English Channel, ⓣ0870/600 4321 for Irish Sea; ⓦwww.norfolkline.com.

P&O Ferries France ⓣ02.85.12.01.56, Spain ⓣ902 020 461, UK ⓣ0870/598 0333; ⓦwww.poferries.com.

Sea France France ⓣ08.25.08.25.05, UK ⓣ0871/663 2546; ⓦwww.seafrance.com.

SpeedFerries France ⓣ03.21.10.50.00, UK ⓣ0870/220 0570; ⓦwww.speedferries.com.

Stena Line Northern Ireland ⓣ0870/520 4204, Republic of Ireland ⓣ01/204 7777, UK ⓣ0870/570 7070; ⓦwww.stenaline.co.uk.

Transmanche France ⓣ0800/650 100, UK ⓣ0800/917 1201; ⓦwww.transmancheferries.com.

Getting around

Almost every town and village across the UK can be reached by train and/or bus, but costs are among the highest in Europe and travelling around can eat up a large part of your budget. It pays to investigate all the train and bus passes and special deals on offer, though note that some are only available outside the UK and must be purchased before you arrive. It's often cheaper to drive yourself around (certainly if you're sharing costs), though fuel and car rental tariffs are again among the highest in Europe. Congestion around the main cities can be bad, and even the motorways are liable to sporadic gridlock, especially on public holidays. Principal train and bus routes and schedules are indicated at the end of every chapter in "Travel details".

By air

For longer journeys across the country such as London–Inverness or Manchester–Newquay, you might consider using **domestic flights**, operated by such airlines as British Airways, easyJet, Ryanair, Flybe and bmibaby. You can often find lower prices than the equivalent train fares, though you won't always save much on total travel time.

However, flying is particularly useful for places such as the Isle of Man and in the **Scottish Highlands and Islands**, where a flight can save a day of travel by local bus and ferry. The remoter parts of Scotland have numerous minor airports – though some are little more than gravel strips – and fares are pretty reasonable. Most flights within Scotland are operated by British Airways or Loganair (a BA partner), who combine to offer a number of discount air passes, but new companies are emerging all the time, for example **Highland Airways**, which flies a few routes from Inverness.

Airlines within Britain

bmibaby ⓣ 0871/224 0224, ⓦ www.bmibaby.com.
British Airways ⓣ 0870/850 9850, ⓦ www.ba.com.
easyJet ⓦ www.easyjet.com.
Flybe ⓣ 0871/700 2000, ⓦ www.flybe.com.
Highland Airways ⓣ 0845/450 2245, ⓦ www.highlandairways.co.uk.
Loganair ⓣ 0844/800 2855, ⓦ www.loganair.co.uk.
Ryanair ⓦ www.ryanair.com.
Scot Airways ⓦ www.scotairways.com.

By rail

The **British rail network** does not compare favourably with other European systems either in terms of efficiency or cost, at least in part because the national network was privatized and broken up into a number of different companies several years ago – still a real sore point for many Brits. That said, few major towns in **England** lack rail links and mainline routes out of London are fast and frequent – York or Exeter, for instance, can be reached in around two hours – though travelling cross-country, east to west, can be a lengthy business, often involving two or more train changes. **Scotland**, on the other hand, has a more modest rail network, at its densest in the central belt between Edinburgh and Glasgow, at its most skeletal in the Highlands, and all but nonexistent in the Islands. The West Highland Line, from Glasgow to Fort William, is probably the most scenic train ride in Britain. In **Wales**, there are only two main lines, one in the north from Chester to Holyhead, the other in the south running from Newport to Fishguard.

Ticket prices are relatively high. The various train-operating companies offer a bewildering variety of ticket options, all with Byzantine restrictions and weird anomalies (for instance, two single tickets are often cheaper than a return). As a rule, the earlier you book, the cheaper your ticket will be. Just turning up and buying a ticket at the station is the most expensive way to go, especially during peak periods or at any time on a Friday. An open, fully flexible London to

Manchester return ticket can cost up to £220, while booking at least one day in advance, travelling off-peak and accepting certain restrictions (no refund, no amendments) can bring the return fare as low as £25. However, as only limited numbers of the cheapest tickets are issued, they sell out quickly, and should be booked one to four weeks in advance. **Megatrain** offer a limited number of budget fares on certain routes, though you'll need to be fairly flexible regarding departure time and journey time (trains on these routes tend to be slower) to take advantage of these.

A **seat reservation** is usually included with the ticket – vital if you want to ensure a seat and not a perch in the corridor next to the toilets. At weekends and on public holidays, many long-distance services let you upgrade your ticket by buying a **first-class supplement** for around £15, worth paying if you're facing a five-hour journey on a popular route. If the station's ticket office is closed or does not have a vending machine, you may buy your ticket on the train. Otherwise, **boarding without a ticket** will render you liable to paying the most expensive fare to your destination.

You can buy through tickets at any station, though advance credit-card **reservations** can also be made through the rail companies themselves (National Rail Enquiries can supply the necessary contact name and number), or through an **online booking** service, such as The Train Line. In all instances, the **National Rail Enquiries** information line or website is an essential first call for timetable and route information.

Useful rail contacts

Megatrain ⓣ0900/160 0900, ⓦwww.megatrain.com.
National Rail Enquiries ⓣ0845/748 4950, ⓦwww.nationalrail.co.uk.
Train line ⓦwww.thetrainline.com.

Rail passes

For overseas visitors planning to travel widely by train, a **BritRail pass** might be a wise investment. It gives unlimited travel throughout Britain and is valid for varied periods of up to one month (consecutive days travel) or two months (flexi-travel). The pass is available in a wide variety of types, with first- and second-class versions,

Mileage chart

	Birmingham	Bristol	Edinburgh	London
Birmingham	-	90	298	121
Bristol	90	-	380	120
Edinburgh	298	380	-	413
London	121	120	413	-
Manchester	89	171	221	204
Newcastle	207	298	106	285
Penzance	274	193	565	310
York	133	224	193	211

discounted Youth Passes and Senior Passes (first-class only). Other BritRail combo passes are tailored to families or small groups. Note that BritRail passes have to be bought before you enter the UK. Any good travel agent or tour operator can supply up-to-date information, or consult any of the BritRail or Rail Europe websites listed under Rail contacts, p.33.

Eurail passes (ⓦwww.eurail.com) are not valid in the UK, though they do provide discounts on the Eurostar service to England and some ferry routes. However, European residents (proof of residency required) can buy an **InterRail** pass (ⓦwww.raileurope.co.uk/inter-rail), which provides free, unlimited train travel in the UK, as well as discounts on Eurostar and certain cross-Channel ferries.

In Britain itself, a variety of **regional rail "Rover" passes** can be purchased by both locals and visitors, offering unlimited travel in multi-day or flexi-day formats, from around £40 for four days' train travel. You need to check restrictions and validity carefully before buying – all the information is on ⓦwww.nationalrail.co.uk.

Alternatively, there's a whole raft of UK **discount passes** including the **Young Person's Railcard** (£20), available to full-time students and those aged between 16 and 25, and **Senior Railcard** for people over 60 (£20), both of which give a third off most fares. Locals and visitors can buy the passes from most UK stations – take along two passport photographs and proof of age or status. Those with children can buy a **Family Railcard** (£20), which entitles up to four adults to a 33 percent discount, and up to four children to a sixty percent reduction of the child's full fare. No photos are needed, and not all adults and children need to be related.

Buses

Long-distance bus services duplicate many rail routes, very often at half the price of the train or less. Services between major towns and cities are frequent and the buses – often referred to as coaches – are modern and comfortable. However, journeys take much longer than the equivalent train ride, partly due to traffic congestion.

By far the biggest countrywide operator is **National Express** (ⓣ0870/580 8080, ⓦwww.nationalexpress.com), whose network extends to every corner of England as well as parts of Wales; its sister company **Scottish Citylink** (ⓣ0870/550 5050, ⓦwww.citylink.co.uk) takes over north of the border. On busy routes, and on any route at weekends and during holidays, it's advisable to book ahead, rather than just turn up. Fares are very reasonable, with big discounts for under-26s, over-60s and families, while advance-purchase fares and special deals are common – "fun fares" from £1 from London to other major cities, for example. Overseas passport holders can buy a **BritXplorer** pass (in 7-, 14- or 28-day versions) in the UK, from National Express travel shops or at major ports and airports, though you'd have to do a lot of bus travelling to make it pay.

Megabus (ⓣ0900/160 0900, ⓦwww.megabus.com) also operates low-budget coach services between some 35 towns in England, three in Wales and eight in Scotland. Some routes have frequent

Manchester	Newcastle	Penzance	York
89	207	274	133
171	298	193	224
221	106	565	193
204	285	310	211
-	145	356	71
145	-	482	89
356	482	-	408
71	89	408	-

services, though most have one to three departures a day, often at inconvenient times. Again, fares are generally cheaper the further in advance you book them.

Local bus services are run by a huge array of companies. In many cases, timetables and routes are well integrated, but it's increasingly the case that private companies duplicate the busiest routes in an attempt to undercut the commercial opposition, leaving the more remote spots neglected. As a rule, the further away from urban areas you get, the less frequent and more expensive bus services become, but there are very few rural areas which aren't served by at least an occasional minibus.

In the spring and summer, many national park areas support a network of **weekend and bank holiday buses**, taking visitors to beauty spots, villages and hiking trailheads. In addition, some rural areas not covered by other forms of public transport are served by inexpensive weekday **Postbus** minibuses (ⓣ0845/774 0740, ⓦwww.royalmail.com/postbus), that carry mail and fare-paying passengers, usually early in the morning.

For up-to-date information, the website and phone service **Traveline** (ⓣ0871/200 2233, ⓦwww.traveline.org.uk) has details of all national and local bus routes and schedules.

By car or motorbike

In order to drive in the UK you need a current full driving licence. If you're bringing your own vehicle into the country you should also carry your vehicle registration, ownership and insurance documents at all times. Motorbikers and their passengers are obliged to wear a helmet while riding.

In the UK you **drive on the left**. Motorways – "M" roads – and main "A" roads may have up to four lanes in each direction, but even these can get very congested, with long tailbacks a regular occurrence, especially at peak travel times and on public holidays. In the country, on "B" roads and minor roads, there might only be one lane (single track) for both directions. Keep your speed down, and be prepared for abrupt encounters with tractors, sheep, ponies and other hazards in remote spots.

Don't underestimate the British weather – snow, ice, fog and wind cause havoc every year, and driving conditions on motorways as much as in rural areas can deteriorate quickly. Local radio stations and national Radio Five Live (693/909 MW) feature constantly updated traffic bulletins.

Speed limits are 20–40mph in built-up areas, 70mph on motorways and dual carriageways (freeways) and 60mph on most other roads. As a rule, assume that in any area with street lighting the speed limit is 30mph unless otherwise stated. Britain has so far resisted toll roads (apart from one or two minor examples), but the principle has been broached by the success of **congestion charging** in London – if you intend to drive a car into central London, it will cost you (see p.84 for more).

Fuel is expensive – unleaded petrol (gasoline) and diesel cost over £1 per litre. Out-of-town supermarkets usually have the lowest prices, while the highest prices are charged by motorway stations.

The AA (Automobile Association; Ⓦwww.theaa.com), RAC (Ⓦwww.rac.co.uk) and Green Flag (Ⓦwww.greenflag.co.uk) all operate **24-hour emergency breakdown** services, and offer useful online route plans. You may be entitled to free assistance through a reciprocal arrangement with a motoring organization in your home country – check before setting out. You can make use of these emergency services if you are not a member of the organization, but you will need to join at the roadside and will incur a hefty surcharge too.

Distances, weights and measures

Distances (and speeds) on British signposts are in miles, and beer is still served in pints. For everything else – money, weights and measures – a confusing mixture of metric and imperial systems is used: fuel is dispensed by the litre, while meat, milk and vegetables may be sold in either or both systems.

Parking

Car parking in towns, cities and popular tourist spots can be a nightmare and often costs a small fortune. If you're in a tourist city for a day, look out for **park-and-ride schemes** in which you park on the outskirts and take a cheap or free bus to the centre. Parking in long- or short-stay **car parks** will be cheaper than using on-street meters, which often restrict parking time to one or two hours at the most. As a rule, the smaller the town, the cheaper the parking. Some towns operate free **disc-zone parking**, which allows limited-hours town-centre parking in designated areas: if that's what roadside signs indicate, you need to pick up a cardboard disc from any local shop and display it in your windscreen. A yellow line along the edge of the road indicates **parking restrictions**; check the nearest sign to see exactly what they are. A double-yellow line means no parking at any time, though you can stop briefly to unload or pick up people or goods, while a red line signifies no stopping at all.

Vehicle rental

Car rental is usually cheaper arranged in advance from home through one of the large multinational chains or through your tour operator as part of a fly-drive package.

If you rent a car from a company in the UK (see below), expect to pay around £30 per day, £50 for a weekend, or from £120 per week. You can sometimes find last-minute or web fares of under £20 per day, though you'll need to book well in advance for the cheapest rates and be prepared for extra charges (like cleaning fees). Otherwise, small **local agencies** often undercut the major chains – we've highlighted some in the "Listings" sections of certain towns and cities. Few companies will rent to drivers with less than one year's experience and most will only rent to people between 21 and 75 years of age.

For **camper van** rental, Just Go (Ⓣ0870/240 1918, from outside UK Ⓣ+44 1582/842888, Ⓦwww.justgo.uk.com), can supply quality vehicles sleeping four to six people, equipped with CD/DVD, full bathrooms, kitchenette and bike racks. Rates range from £300 to £950 per week, depending on the vehicle and season; minimum hire is five days (winter) or seven days (summer).

Car rental agencies

Avis UK Ⓣ0870/606 0100, Republic of Ireland Ⓣ021/428 1111, US & Canada Ⓣ1-800/331-1212, Australia Ⓣ13 63 33 or 02/9353 9000, New Zealand Ⓣ09/526 2847 or 0800/655 111; Ⓦwww.avis.com.

Budget UK Ⓣ0870/156 5656, US Ⓣ1-800/527-0700, Canada Ⓣ1-800/268-8900, Australia Ⓣ1300/362 848, New Zealand Ⓣ0800/283 438; Ⓦwww.budget.com.

easyCar UK Ⓣ0871/050 0444, Ⓦwww.easycar.com.

Europcar UK Ⓣ0870/607 5000, Republic of Ireland Ⓣ01/614 2800, US & Canada Ⓣ1-877/940-6900, Australia Ⓣ393/306 160; Ⓦwww.europcar.com.

Hertz UK Ⓣ020/7026 0077, Republic of Ireland Ⓣ01/870 5777, US & Canada Ⓣ1-800/654-3131, Australia Ⓣ133 039, New Zealand Ⓣ0800/654 321; Ⓦwww.hertz.com.

National UK Ⓣ0870/400 4581, US Ⓣ1-800/CAR-RENT, Australia Ⓣ0870/600 6666, New Zealand Ⓣ03/366 5574; Ⓦwww.nationalcar.com.

Suncars UK Ⓣ0870/902 8021, Republic of Ireland Ⓣ1850/201 416; Ⓦwww.suncars.com.

Thrifty UK Ⓣ01494/751 500, Republic of Ireland Ⓣ01/844 1950, US & Canada Ⓣ1-800/847-4389, Australia Ⓣ1300/367 227, New Zealand Ⓣ09/256 1405; Ⓦwww.thrifty.com.

Cycling

No one would choose to get around Britain by **cycling** on the main "A" roads – there's simply too much traffic and cyclists are given scant regard by many motorists. If you have to use the roads, it's far better to stick to the quieter "B" roads and country lanes; best of all, however, is to follow one of the **traffic-free trails** of the extensive National Cycle Network (see "Sports and outdoor activities", p.58).

Surprisingly, **cycle helmets** are not compulsory in the UK – but if you're hell-bent on tackling the congestion, pollution and aggression of city traffic, you're well advised to wear one. You do have to have a **rear reflector** and front and back **lights** when riding at night, and you are not allowed to carry children without a special **child seat**. It is also illegal to cycle on pavements and in most public parks, while **off-road** cyclists must stick to bridleways and byways designated for their use.

Bike rental is available at cycle shops in most large towns, and at villages within national parks and other scenic areas; contact details are given in the Guide. Expect to pay around £10–15 per day, with discounts for longer periods; you may need to provide credit card details, or leave a passport as a deposit.

Accommodation

Accommodation in Britain ranges from motorway lodges to country retreats, and from budget guesthouses and hostels to swish boutique hotels. There are plenty of characterful and well-refurbished old buildings – former coaching inns in towns, converted mansions and manor houses in rural areas – with heaps of historic atmosphere.

Nearly all tourist offices will **reserve rooms** for you. In some areas you pay a deposit that's deducted from your first night's bill (usually ten percent); in others the office will take a percentage or flat-rate commission – usually around £3. Also useful is the "Book-a-bed-ahead" scheme, which reserves accommodation in your next destination – again for a small charge.

A nationwide **grading system** awards stars to hotels (five stars is the top rank), guesthousess and B&Bs. There's no hard and fast correlation between rank and price, but the grading system does lay down minimum levels of standards and service. On the whole, British people don't tend to insist on **seeing a room before taking it**, but you shouldn't be afraid to ask – any place worth its salt, be it designer hotel or humble B&B, should have no objection.

Hotels

Hotels vary wildly in size, style, comfort and price. The starting price for a one-star establishment is around £60 per night for a double/twin room, breakfast usually included; two- and three-star hotels can easily cost £100 a night, while four-and five-star properties may charge around £200 a night, often considerably more in London or in resort or country-house hotels. Many city hotels offer cut-price **weekend rates** to fill the rooms vacated by the weekday business trade. It's worth noting that many upper-end urban hotels charge a room-rate only – breakfast can be another whopping £10 or £15 on top.

Several **budget hotel chains** – including Premier Travel Inn (Ⓦwww.premierinn.com), Holiday Inn Express (Ⓦwww.hiexpress.com), Jurys Inn (Ⓦwww.jurysinns.com), Travel Lodge (Ⓦwww.travelodge.co.uk) – have properties usefully located in city centres across the country. Their style tends towards the no-frills (with breakfast charged extra), but with rates starting at £60–70 for an en-suite room (often sleeping up to four), they're a good deal for families and people travelling in small groups. Travel Lodge has rooms on selected dates and booked online far enough in advance for around £10.

B&Bs and guesthouses

At its most basic, the typical British **bed-and-breakfast** (**B&B**) is an ordinary private house with a couple of bedrooms set aside for paying guests. Larger establishments with more rooms, particularly in resorts, style themselves **guesthouses**, but they are pretty much the same thing. Many B&Bs have raised their game in recent years – some are truly excellent – and we've highlighted the best choices in every area.

Single travellers tend not to get as good a deal as couples, since many B&Bs and small hotels don't have single rooms – establishments often charge well over half the room rate for sole occupancy of a double/twin room. Finally, don't assume that a B&B is no good if it's ungraded: many places choose not to enter into a grading scheme, and in the rural backwaters some of the best accommodation is to be found in **farmhouses** and other properties whose facilities may technically fall short of official standards.

In towns and villages, many **pubs** also offer B&B, again often not graded. Standards vary wildly – some are great, others truly awful – but at best you'll be staying in a friendly spot with a sociable bar on hand, and you'll rarely pay more than £70 a room.

Accommodation price codes

Throughout this guide, accommodation is graded on a scale of ❶ to ❾, the number indicating the lowest price you could expect to pay per night in that establishment for a **double room in high season**. Breakfast is included unless otherwise stated. We've given the starting high-season price (current at time of writing) for **dorm accommodation** in youth and backpackers' hostels, as well as price codes for those hostels that have private double rooms.

❶ £40 or under
❷ £41–50
❸ £51–60
❹ £61–70
❺ £71–90
❻ £91–110
❼ £111–150
❽ £151–200
❾ over £200

At the lower end of this scale (❶–❸) – almost always B&Bs rather than hotels – you'll normally experience small rooms, spartan facilities and shared bathrooms, though above £50 you can expect a little more space and comfort all round. Even in the most basic of places, you should get a washbasin, a TV and a kettle in the room, and the use of a guest lounge. You'll pay a few pounds more for en-suite shower and toilet facilities – but don't expect a great deal of space (or indeed a bath) in these "bathrooms". Some properties located in rural or unfashionable localities, however, will have cheaper rates without sacrificing comfort.

Most accommodation in England falls into categories ❹–❻, which usually guarantees a good location, decent en-suite rooms, and a few trimmings. Parking should be available, and often dining facilities too. Credit-card payments will often be accepted at these establishments. At the higher end of the range you can expect a range of services and facilities such as fresh flowers, gourmet breakfasts, king-sized beds and quality bathrooms. Many top-notch B&Bs in this category offer more luxury and better value pound for pound than more impersonal hotels. Paying the top rates (❼–❾), usually in superior hotels in city centres, in seaside villas or in rural mansions, you can expect to be properly pampered, with first-class facilities – there may be a gym, pool and other leisure activities on hand – and spacious rooms. Almost always, there will be a good restaurant on the premises.

Useful contacts

B&B My Guest ⓣ0870/444 3840, ⓦwww.beduk.co.uk. Online bookings at 300 traditional or historic B&B properties.

Distinctly Different ⓣ01225/866842, ⓦwww.distinctlydifferent.co.uk. Stay the night in converted buildings across the country, from old brothel to Baptist chapel, windmill to lighthouse.

Farm Stay UK ⓣ024/7669 6909, ⓦwww.farmstay.co.uk. The largest network of farm-based accommodation in the UK.

Wolsey Lodges ⓣ01473/822058, ⓦwww.wolseylodges.com. Superior B&B in inspected properties across England, from Elizabethan manor houses to Victorian rectories.

Hostels, camping barns and student halls

The **Youth Hostels Association** (YHA; ⓣ0870/770 8868, ⓦwww.yha.org.uk) has over 220 properties in England and Wales, and the **Scottish Youth Hostels Association** (SYHA; ⓣ0870/155 3255, ⓦwww.syha.org.uk) has more than 70 properties in Scotland. Both are affiliated to Hostelling International (HI) and are responsible for a wide range of premises ranging from mansions to thatched cottages, offering bunk-bed accommodation in single-sex dormitories or smaller rooms of two, four or six beds. Some hostels also offer tipi accommodation, and some have pitches for camping. In cities, resorts and national park areas the facilities are often every bit as good as some budget hotels. Indeed, most hostels have moved well away from their old-fashioned, institutional ambience, and many boast laundry facilities, Internet access, a sitting room, cycle stores, cafés and bike rental.

You no longer have to be a member to use a YHA/SYHA hostel, though non-members pay a small supplement. Otherwise, adult **membership** of the YHA costs around £16

per year, £23 for joint/family, or £10 for under-26s, while the SYHA charges just £8 per adult with children under 16 given free membership when their parent/guardian joins. Overseas members of **International Youth Hostel Federation** (IYHF) have automatic membership of the YHA; if you aren't an IYHF member, you can join the YHA/SYHA in person at any affiliated hostel on your first night's stay.

Prices at YHA/SYHA hostels are calculated according to season and demand, with most charging around £14–21 for members, a little less in simpler places and slightly more in cities such as York, Bristol and London. Many hostels also have private twin/double and family rooms available (£35–65). Length of stay is normally unlimited and the hostel will provide bed linen, pillows and duvet. Hostel **meals** – breakfast, packed lunch or dinner – are always good value (around £5), while nearly all hostels also have self-catering kitchens.

It's always best to book well in advance, especially as many hostels operate irregular opening days, and it's well nigh essential during school holidays (Easter, late July to early September and the Christmas period, plus half-terms). Note that very few hostels are open year-round, with some only open to group bookings for long periods of the year, and many closed at least one day a week, even in high season. Always check – we've given the phone number and email for every hostel mentioned. You can book online, and many places accept payment by credit card.

A growing number of independent **backpacker hostels** offer similar facilities to the YHA, generally at lower prices. They tend to attract a more youthful, backpacking (rather than the YHA/SYHA's family/hiker) crowd, and they usually don't have membership requirements or curfews. A useful publication is the annually updated **Independent Hostel Guide** (Backpackers Press; ⓦwww.backpackerspress.com). The website ⓦwww.backpackers.co.uk also gives the lowdown on independent hostels and budget accommodation.

More institutional **YMCAs** (ⓦwww.ymca.org.uk) are often good options in towns and cities – they're usually well maintained, with dormitories (£13–18) and private rooms (around £40 for two), plus good sports facilities. Not all are suitable for short-term holiday accommodation however – check first.

In the wilder parts of England and Wales – for example in the north Pennines, Snowdonia, the Lake District, Peak District, Dartmoor and Exmoor – walkers and other hardy types can book accommodation in **camping barns**, mostly administered by the YHA (and members get discounts), but open to all. Housing up to twenty people, these agricultural outbuildings are often unheated and sparsely furnished, with wooden sleeping platforms – or bunks if you're lucky – a couple of tables, a toilet and cold-water supply, but they are weatherproof and extremely good value (from £5 a night); the thirteen Lake District barns have their own website, ⓦwww.lakelandcampingbarns.co.uk. The SYHA's equivalent is its chain of Rustic Hostels, often old crofters' cottages, also in isolated places and similarly frugal and inexpensive. Many parts of the UK also have privately run barns, also known as **bunkhouses** (or **bothies** in Scotland), with prices starting at around £8–10 per night.

In the UK's university towns you can sometimes find out-of-term accommodation

(Easter and Christmas hols, plus July–Sept) in **student halls of residence**, in one-bedded rooms either with their own or shared bathrooms, or in self-contained flats with self-catering facilities. Prices start at around £20 per night, not always including breakfast. For a list of everything that's on offer, contact the Summer Village (Ⓣ0870/712 5002, Ⓦwww.thesummervillage.com) or Venuemasters (Ⓣ0114/249 3090, Ⓦwww.venuemasters.co.uk).

Camping and caravanning

There are hundreds of **campsites** in the UK, charging from £6 per tent per night in simple, family-run places in low season to around £18 a night on large sites with laundries, shops and sports facilities. Some hostels also have small campsites on their property, charging half the indoor overnight price per person.

Between October and Easter, you'll often have to travel several miles to find a campsite that's open, though if you're desperate it's always worth asking at places nominally closed – they'll sometimes give you a pitch with minimal facilities for a small fee. In addition to official sites, **farmers** may offer pitches for around £5 per night, but don't expect tiled bathrooms and hair dryers for that kind of money. Even farmers without a reserved camping area may let you pitch in a field if you ask first; setting up a tent without asking will not be well received. **Camping rough** is illegal in national parks and nature reserves.

Campervans and caravans are well served at sites throughout Britain. Many campsites in the most popular parts of rural and coastal Britain have caravans to rent, usually by the week, the majority of them large, fully-equipped units permanently stationed at their sites. If you've got a tent, however, you may prefer to look for a site that's exclusively for tents.

Detailed, annually revised **guides** to Britain's camping and caravan sites include the official *Caravan and Camping Parks in Britain*, available in all major bookshops. The website Ⓦwww.ukcampsite.co.uk lists thousands of sites, and includes helpful user-written reviews.

Self-catering accommodation

Holiday properties for rent in the UK range from city penthouses to secluded cottages. **Studios and apartments**, available by the night in an increasing number of British cities, offer an attractive alternative to hotel stays, with prices from around £100 a night, or from £140 in London. Rural self-catering **cottages and houses** work out cheaper, though the minimum rental period is usually a week. The least you can expect to pay for a small cottage sleeping four people in mid-winter would be around £250 per week, but in summer for a sizeable house near the Cornwall coast or in the Lake District you should budget for £650 and upwards.

We've listed the main **agencies** on p.44, but every regional tourist board has details of cottage rentals in its area. Otherwise, Stilwell's (Ⓣ0870/197 6964, Ⓦwww.stilwell.co.uk) can send you their free annual guide, *Cottages Direct*, where you select your property and then book direct with the cottage owners.

Houses and cottages

Cornish Cottage Holidays ⓣ01326/573808, ⓦwww.cornishcottageholidays.co.uk. Lots of thatched cottages and seaside places.

Country Holidays ⓣ0870/078 1200, ⓦwww.country-holidays.co.uk. A range of graded properties all over the UK.

Heart of the Lakes ⓣ01539/432321, ⓦwww.heartofthelakes.co.uk. Excellent choice of over 300 quality properties in the Lake District.

Helpful Holidays ⓣ01647/433593, ⓦwww.helpfulholidays.com. Everything from cottage rentals to a castle, throughout the West Country.

Hoseasons Holidays ⓣ01502/502588, ⓦwww.hoseasons.co.uk. Holiday lodges and country cottages throughout Britain.

Landmark Trust ⓣ01628/825925, ⓦwww.landmarktrust.org.uk. Their handbook (£11.50 – refundable on first booking) lists over 180 converted historic properties, ranging from restored forts and Martello towers to a tiny radio shack used in World War II.

Mackay's Agency ⓣ0131/550 1180, ⓦwww.mackays-self-catering.co.uk. A huge range of self-catering cottages in Scotland.

National Trust ⓣ0870/458 4422, ⓦwww.nationaltrustcottages.co.uk. The NT owns 350 cottages, houses and farmhouses, most set in their own gardens or grounds.

Rural Retreats ⓣ01386/701177, ⓦwww.ruralretreats.co.uk. Upmarket accommodation in restored old buildings, many of them listed.

Scottish Country Cottages ⓣ0870/078 1100, ⓦwww.scottish-country-cottages.co.uk. Superior cottages with lots of character scattered across Scotland.

Wales Holidays ⓣ01686/628200, ⓦwww.wales-holidays.co.uk. A varied selection of 500 properties all over Wales.

Studios and apartments

Apartment Service ⓣ020/8944 1444, ⓦwww.apartmentservice.com. Studios and apartments in towns and cities all over the UK.

Holiday Serviced Apartments ⓣ0845/470 4477, from overseas +44 1923/820077, ⓦwww.holidayapartments.co.uk. Available in London, Cambridge, Manchester, Edinburgh and Glasgow.

Serviced Stays ⓣ0871/226 1902, from overseas +44 29/2079 5800, ⓦwww.servicedstays.com. Apartments in London, Manchester, Bristol, Cardiff, Edinburgh and Glasgow.

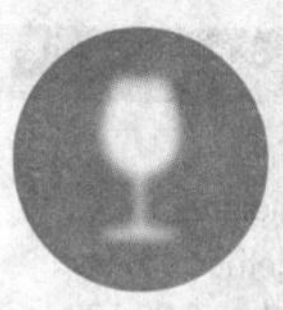

Food and drink

Though the British still tend to regard eating as a functional necessity rather than a sociable pleasure, things are improving. Over the last decade, changing popular tastes have transformed both supermarket shelves and café/restaurant menus, while there's an increasing importance placed on "ethical" eating, whether free-range, organic, humanely produced or locally sourced. London continues to be the gourmet's main destination, while good, moderately priced restaurants and, increasingly, "gastropubs" can be found across Britain. Thankfully, some more traditional pubs remain, and for tourists and locals alike the old-fashioned "local" remains an enduring social institution, and is often the best introduction to town or village life.

Specialities and regional food

In many hotels and B&Bs you'll be offered an "**English breakfast**" – or Welsh or Scottish in the respective countries – which is basically sausage, tomatoes, mushrooms, bacon and eggs plus tea/coffee and toast. Places offering a vegetarian version might substitute soya/tofu sausages or similar for the meat, while travellers in northern England may be offered black pudding, a blend of onions, pork fat, oatmeal and congealed blood. This breakfast used to be the typical working-class start to the day, but these days most British people have adopted the cereal alternative – and the majority of places will give you this option as well. Traditionally, a "**Scottish breakfast**" includes oatmeal porridge eaten with salt (though sugar is always on offer too). You may also be served kippers or Arbroath smokies (delicately smoked haddock with butter), or a large piece of haddock with a poached egg on top. Oatcakes (plain savoury biscuits) and a "buttery" – not unlike a French croissant – will often feature; kippers (smoked herring) and haddock are common on English and Welsh breakfast menus too. (If you don't want a big fry-up every morning you can generally ask for scrambled, boiled or poached eggs instead, while the better establishments might offer dishes like homemade muesli and yoghurt, fresh fruit salad, and pancakes.)

For most overseas visitors the quintessential British meal is **fish and chips** (known in Scotland as a "fish supper", even at lunchtime), a dish that can vary from the succulently fresh to the indigestibly greasy: local knowledge is the key, as most towns, cities and resorts have at least one first-rate fish-and-chip shop/restaurant – like Whitby's *Magpie Café* (see p.583) or *Stein's Fish & Chips* in Padstow (see p.354).

Other **traditional British dishes** are just as ubiquitous – steak and kidney pie, liver and onions, lamb chops, roast beef and roast chicken all figure on menu after menu in cafés, pubs and restaurants across the land. Unfortunately, though, far too many places churn out very average examples that conform to every negative stereotype about **British cooking** – overcooked meat, soggy veg, frozen chips and lumpy gravy. However, for every dismal meal served, there's a local café or restaurant somewhere providing excellent food at reasonable prices, from fresh soup using local, seasonal ingredients to home-made ice cream.

There's a new emphasis, too, on the importance of local growers and suppliers, and many cafés and restaurants now boast locally sourced or organic ingredients. The increasing interest in regional authenticity, however, can make ordering problematic – a simple bread roll, for example, is referred to as a roll, cob, bap, barmcake, teacake or bread-bun, depending on which part of Britain you're in; see p.46 for more oddly named dishes.

Many mid-range and top-end restaurants present what, for the want of a better term,

Some traditional British dishes and foods

Bara brith – a fruit bread found in all Welsh teashops

Black pudding – blood sausage, particularly popular in the north of England

Bread and butter pudding – slices of buttered white bread layered together, covered in milk or custard, sprinkled liberally with sugar and sultanas, and baked until golden

Bubble and squeak – fried leftover potato and cabbage (and sometimes other veg)

Chip butty – a chip sandwich

Cornish pasty – steak, turnip and potatoes in a wedge-shaped pie (though there are countless variations)

Crumble – a dessert of stewed fruit topped with a crunchy cooked mix of butter, flour and sugar. Can also refer to savoury, usually vegetable, dishes (without the sugar)

Faggot – an offal meatball

Haggis – a sheep's stomach stuffed with spiced liver, offal, oatmeal and onion, traditionally eaten with bashed neeps (mashed turnips) and chappit tatties (mashed potatoes). The quintessential Scottish dish

Lancashire hot-pot – lamb and potato stew

Laver bread (*bara lawr*) – a thoroughly tasty seaweed and oatmeal cake often included in a traditional fried breakfast in Wales

Mushy peas – soaked and boiled marrowfat peas, almost a paste, served with fish and chips

Piccalilli – a mustard pickle

Ploughman's lunch – a cheese (or sometimes ham), pickle, bread and salad plate

Shepherds' pie – savoury minced lamb topped with mashed potato (when made with minced beef, it's a cottage pie)

Spotted dick – a dessert of suet pudding with currants

Sticky toffee pudding – wedge of steamed sponge drenched in a caramelized hot-toffee sauce

Stovies – a Scottish favourite, comprising a tasty mash of onion and fried potato heated up with minced beef

Toad-in-the-hole – sausages baked in Yorkshire pudding

Trifle – a wobbly, semi-solid concoction of biscuits or cake soaked in brandy with layers of fruit jelly, everything topped with custard, crystallized fruits and sugary icing

Yorkshire pudding – baked batter, usually served with gravy as part of a traditional Sunday roast

is generally known as **Modern British** cuisine. This can be code for "mix and match", sometimes to disastrous effect, but at its best this inventive feel for food marries local, seasonal produce with Mediterranean, Asian or even Pacific Rim ingredients and techniques.

Vegetarians are fairly well catered for in Britain. Away from London and the big cities, specialist vegetarian places are thin on the ground, but most restaurants and pubs have at least one vegetarian option on their menus, while Italian, Indian and Chinese restaurants usually provide a decent choice of meat-free dishes. For a list of vegetarian establishments across the UK, check the Veg Dining website (Ⓦwww.vegdining.com). Gluten-free options on menus are still rare.

Cafés and restaurants

Every town, city and resort has a plethora of cheap **cafés**, characteristically unassuming places offering non-alcoholic drinks, all-day breakfasts, snacks and meals. Most are only open during the daytime (8am–5pm), and tend to be cash-only establishments with few airs and graces. **Teashops** or **tearooms** tend to be more genteel, and serve a range of sandwiches, cakes and light meals throughout the day, as well, of course, as tea.

Old-fashioned chrome-and-formica **coffee bars** – almost always Italian in origin – still cling on in London and a few other towns. Most, however, have been replaced by American-style chain coffee shops, such as *Starbucks*, *Costa* and *Caffè Nero*.

Licensed **café-bars** on the European model are now commonplace, too – although primarily places to drink, an increasing number serve reasonably priced food. Given the challenge posed by the newcomers, **pubs** that serve food have had to raise their game over the last few years, and many have embraced the change in British tastes – indeed, the **gastropub** (more of an informal restaurant) is now a recognized fixture in many villages, towns and cities.

Half-jokingly, Britain's national dish was recently proclaimed to be **chicken tikka masala** (chicken in a creamy, spicy, tomato sauce) – a reflection of the extent that Britain's postwar immigrant communities have contributed to the country's dining experience. Even the smallest town these days boasts an Indian (more properly Bangladeshi or Pakistani, in most cases), Thai or Chinese (mostly Cantonese) restaurant, the majority relatively inexpensive. The best – and most authentic examples – of these are in ethnic enclaves in London and the industrial cities of the Midlands (Birmingham, Leicester) and the Northwest (Manchester, Liverpool). Most small towns also have Italian trattorias and pizza places, while Spanish tapas bars and French chain bistros are well represented too.

It goes without saying that London has the best selection of **top-class restaurants**, and the widest choice of cuisines, but visitors to Manchester, Birmingham, Bristol, Leeds and other major cities hardly suffer these days. Indeed, wherever you are in the UK you're never more than half an hour's drive from a really good meal – and some of the very best dining experiences are just as likely to be found in a suburban back street or quiet village rather than a metropolitan hotspot. Heston Blumenthal's Michelin-starred *Fat Duck*, for example – often touted as the world's best restaurant – is in the small Berkshire village of Bray.

The biggest deterrent to enjoying the UK's gastronomic delights is the expense.

Restaurant prices

Where individual prices are not given, restaurants listed in the Guide may be described according to one of four price categories:

Inexpensive under £12.50

Moderate £12.50–20

Expensive £20–35

Very expensive over £35

This is the price you can expect to pay per person for a three-course meal or equivalent, *excluding* drinks and service.

While a great curry in London's Brick Lane or a Cantonese feast in Manchester's Chinatown can still be had for under £15 a head, the going rate for a full meal with drinks in most modest restaurants is more like £20–25 per person. Even in a decent pub, with main courses averaging £8–10 the price soon mounts up. If a restaurant has any sort of reputation, you can expect to be spending £30–40 each, and much, much more for the services of a top chef – tasting menus at the best-known Michelin-starred restaurants cost £75–100 per person.

Restaurants generally open for **lunch** (usually noon–2/3pm) and **dinner** (7–10/11pm); in the reviews in the Guide we've stated any significant variations from this rule. Pub kitchens often close in the afternoon – between about 2pm and 6pm – and on one or two evenings a week, often Sunday and Monday; few serve after about 9pm. **Reservations** are recommended for all popular restaurants, especially at weekends – and the most celebrated places will require advance reservations weeks (or months) in advance. **Credit cards**, in particular American Express and Diners, are not always accepted, especially at small places or out in the sticks.

Pubs and bars

Originating as wayfarers' hostelries and coaching inns, **pubs** have outlived the church and marketplace as the focal points of many a British town and village. They are as varied as the townscapes: in larger market towns you'll find huge oak-beamed inns with open fires and polished brass fittings; in remoter upland villages there are stone-built pubs no larger than a two-bedroomed cottage. At its best, the pub can be as welcoming as the full name – "public house" – suggests. Sometimes, particularly in the more inward-looking parts of industrial Britain, you might have to dig deeper for a welcome, especially in those no-nonsense pubs where something of the old division of the sexes still holds sway. In such places, the "spit and sawdust" **public bar** is where working men can bond over a pint or two; the plusher **saloon bar**, with a separate entrance, is the preferred haunt of couples and women.

In many towns and cities, and especially in areas with a younger population, the traditional pub faces a challenge from the contemporary **bar and café-bar**. The majority are owned and operated by chains – for example All Bar One and Pitcher & Piano – though there are a few honourable independent exceptions, many of which we've listed in the Guide.

After almost a century, British **licensing hours** have been liberalized, with pubs and bars in theory now able to open 24 hours a day, provided they have the necessary permission. In practice, hours in most pubs are still 11am to 11pm, though cities and resorts all now have a growing number of places with extended licenses, especially at weekends – it isn't that difficult these days to get a drink after 11pm somewhere, at least in urban areas. "Last orders" are called five to ten minutes before closing and you then have thirty minutes to drink up before you are chucked out. The legal **drinking age** is 18 and unless there's a special family room or a beer garden, children are not always welcome.

No smoking

In the UK, **smoking** is banned outright in all public buildings and offices, restaurants and pubs, and on all public transport, and the vast majority of hotels and B&Bs no longer allow it.

Beer and wine

The most widespread type of English and Welsh beer is **"bitter"**, a dark, uncarbonated brew which should be pumped by hand from the cellar and served at cellar temperature. If it comes out of an electric pump (and especially if it's labelled "smoothflow" or similar), it isn't the real thing. Controversy exists over the head of foam on top: in southern England, people prefer their pint without a head, and brimming to the top of the glass; in the North and Scotland, flat beer is frowned on and drinkers prefer a short head of foam. Sweeter, darker **mild** and stronger **porter** are quite common in Welsh pubs, though virtually extinct in England. Traditional Scottish beer is a thick, dark ale known as **heavy**, graded by a shilling mark (/-) and served with a full head. Nevertheless, cold, blonde, fizzy **lager** is now more popular than bitter just about everywhere: every pub will have at least two or three brands on offer, but rarely is it a patch on bitter – as **CAMRA**, the influential Campaign for Real Ale (Ⓦwww.camra.org.uk), has long been at pains to point out. Many pubs are owned by large breweries who favour their own beers, though there should also be one or two "guest ales" available. For the best choice, however, you generally need to find a **free house** – an independently run pub that can sell whichever brand of beer it pleases.

The big breweries do distribute some good bitters – Boddington's, Directors, John Smith's, Tetley's and Bass are commonplace – but the real glory of British beer is in the local detail. Hundreds of medium-sized and small breweries still produce what are known as **"real ales"** to traditional recipes. Alongside beer, you'll also find cider, made from fermented apples, and – particularly in England's West Country and Shropshire – **scrumpy**, a potent and cloudy beverage, usually flat, dry and very apple-y. **Guinness**, a dark, creamy Irish stout, is popular worldwide and is on sale in hundreds of UK pubs, though purists will tell you that it doesn't compare with the stuff sold in Ireland.

The British also consume an enormous quantity of **wine**, though the wine sold in pubs can vary enormously in quality – wine bars will always have a decent range, and usually sell a food accompaniment too. Recent years have seen a significant improvement in home-produced wines, the product of better knowledge and management. The majority of the UK's vineyards are located in the southern half of England, where conditions can be similar to those in Germany and northern France – however, the variable climate means that some years produce far better crops than others.

Whisky

Scotland's national drink is **whisky** – *uisge beatha*, the "water of life" in Gaelic (and almost never referred to as "scotch") – traditionally drunk in pubs with a half-pint of beer on the side, a combination known as a "nip and a hauf". There are two types of whisky: **single malt**, made from malted barley, and **grain whisky**, which is made from maize and a little malted barley in a continuous still. **Blended whisky**, which accounts for more than ninety percent of all sales, is a mixture of the two types, with each brand's distinctive flavour coming from the malt whisky which is added to the grain in different quantities: the more expensive the blend, the higher the proportion of malts that have gone into it. Johnnie Walker, Bells, Teachers and The Famous Grouse are some of the best-known blended whiskies. All have a similar flavour, and are drunk neat or with water, sometimes with mixers such as soda or lemonade (though these additions may horrify your fellow drinkers).

Single malt whisky is infinitely superior, and, as a result, a great deal more expensive. It is best drunk neat or with a splash of water to release its distinctive flavours. Single malts vary enormously depending on the amount of peat used for drying the barley, the water used for mashing, and the type of oak cask used in the maturing process. The two most important whisky regions are **Speyside**, which produces famous varieties such as Glenlivet, Glenfiddich and Macallan, and **Islay**, which produces distinctively peaty whiskies such as Laphroaig, Lagavulin and Ardbeg.

The media

The British are fond of their daily newspapers and there are a lot to choose from, though most are drearily conservative in tone and substance. As well as the nationals, most regions have their own local titles, and newsagents' shelves are stacked high with magazines of every description. As regards TV, there are five terrestrial channels – three commercial, and two state subsidized, run by the British Broadcasting Corporation (BBC) – as well as a plethora of satellite and cable channels. The BBC also runs an extensive network of radio stations, competing against a slew of independent, mostly local, commercial stations.

Newspapers and magazines

From Monday to Saturday, four **daily newspapers** occupy the "quality" end of the English market: the Rupert Murdoch-owned *Times*, the staunchly Conservative *Daily Telegraph*, and the left-of-centre *Independent* and *Guardian*. Among the high-selling **tabloid titles**, the most popular is the *Sun*, a muck-raking right-wing Murdoch paper whose chief rival is the traditionally left-leaning *Daily Mirror*. The middlebrow daily tabloids – the *Daily Mail* and the *Daily Express* – are noticeably (some would say rabidly) xenophobic and right-wing. England's oldest **Sunday newspaper** is *The Observer*, now in the same stable as the *Guardian* and with a similar stance, while all the other major papers publish their own Sunday editions.

In **Scotland**, the principal English papers are widely available, often as specific Scottish editions. The Scottish press produces two major daily papers, the liberal-left *Scotsman* and the slightly less-so *Herald*. Scotland's best-selling daily paper is the downmarket *Daily Record*. Many national Sunday newspapers include a Scottish section, but Scotland's own Sunday "quality" is *Scotland on Sunday*. Far more fun is the tabloid *Sunday Post*, read by over half the population. In **Wales**, where again English papers are widely available, the only quality Welsh daily is the *Western Mail*, a mix of local, Welsh, British and international news. There is also one quality Sunday offering, *Wales on Sunday*. Meanwhile, an army of **local newspapers** – at least one in every major town and city – provide insights into British life, with local news, events and personalities to the fore.

Newsagents offer a range of **specialist magazines and periodicals** covering just about every subject, with motoring, music, sport, computers, gardening and home improvements leading the way. *The Economist* is essential reading in many a boardroom; the left-wing *New Statesman* concentrates on social issues, while the satirical bi-weekly *Private Eye* prides itself on printing the stories the rest of the press won't touch, and on riding the consequent stream of libel suits.

Australians, New Zealanders and South Africans in London should look out for the weekly free magazine *TNT*, which provides a résumé of news from home as well as jobs, accommodation and events in the capital. Otherwise, the *Wall Street Journal*, *USA Today* and the *International Herald Tribune* are widely distributed, as are the magazines *Time* and *Newsweek*.

Television

There are five main terrestrial **television channels** in the UK. These are divided between the state-funded BBC (ⓦwww.bbc.co.uk), which operates BBC1 and BBC2, and three independent commercial channels, ITV, Channel 4 and Channel 5 (the latter still not available everywhere in the UK). Broadcasting standards leave a lot to be desired, with much of the output imported from the US, but despite regular complaints about falling standards and periodic mutterings about the licence fee (paid by all British viewers), there's still more than enough quality to keep the **BBC** in good repute both at home and abroad. Of the two BBC channels, BBC2 is the more offbeat and heavyweight, BBC1 more avowedly populist. Various regional companies together form the **ITV** network, and they're united by a more tabloid approach to programme-making – necessarily so, because if they don't get the advertising they don't survive. **Channel 4** is similarly influenced, but is the home of hit (and hip) US comedies and serials, as well as a fair slice of sleaze and cheese, and has some of the best investigative and internationalist news programmes. The newer **Channel 5** is slowly offering a better range of programmes following a tawdry and much-mocked start.

The UK's **satellite** and **cable** TV companies are mounting a strong challenge

The Big Issue

On shopping streets all around Britain, you'll come across people selling **The Big Issue** magazine (ⓦwww.bigissue.com) for £1.50. Buy it, if you can. The "big issue" of its title is homelessness, and the magazine represents an admirable way of combating social exclusion: vendors – who are all either homeless or at risk of becoming homeless – buy bundles of the magazine at around forty percent of the cover price. They then sell the magazine and keep the difference as a way to help themselves off the streets. Apart from its laudable social aims, the magazine is itself consistently good, covering social and political stories with intelligence and insight, and often scooping big interviews. There are five versions sold in the UK – one each for Scotland, Northern England, London and the Southeast, the Southwest and Wales (Cymru).

to the erstwhile dominance of the terrestrial channels. Live sport, in particular, is increasingly in the hands of Rupert Murdoch's Sky, the major satellite provider, whose 24-hour rolling Sky News programme rivals that of CNN. In response, both the BBC and the other commercial channels have launched their own digital ventures, including the BBC's News 24 (rolling news), BBC3 (young adult) and BBC4 (arts and culture), ITV's entertainment channel ITV2, and Channel 4's film channel Film4, entertainment channel E4 and more serious More4.

Radio

The BBC's **radio network** (Ⓦwww.bbc.co.uk/radio) has five nationwide stations. These are **Radio 1**, which is almost exclusively devoted to new chart music and specialist DJs; **Radio 2** (Britain's most listened-to radio station), a combination of light pop and specialist music, with a sprinkling of arts programmes and documentaries; **Radio 3**, which focuses on classical music; the speech-based **Radio 4**, a blend of current affairs, arts and drama; and **Five Live**, a 24-hour rolling sports and news channel.

All have faced tough challenges for market share in recent years, the hardest hit being Radio 1, whose rivals include a range of local commercial stations, most notably London's **Capital Radio** (95.8 FM) and **Heart** (106.2 FM), though Radio 3 has had to struggle hard against **Classic FM** (100 to 102 FM). The BBC also operates a full roster of **local radio stations**, mostly featuring local news, chat and mainstream pop.

Festivals and events

Many of the showpiece events in the British festival calendar have indelible associations with the ruling class – from the military pageant of the Trooping of the Colour to the displays at the Royal Tournament – but these say little about the country's folk history and even less about contemporary Britain. Better to catch London's exuberant Notting Hill Carnival or a wacky village celebration for a more instructive idea of what makes the British tick. Every major town and city has at least one prime event, some dating back centuries, others more recent concoctions, from medieval jousting through to contemporary performing arts. The May and August bank holiday weekends, and the summer school holidays (July and Aug) are the favoured times for events to be held.

The festival and events calendar below picks out the annual highlights, but for exhaustive lists of events contact local tourist offices. See also the *Festival and events* colour section.

January/February

London Parade (Jan 1). A procession of floats, marching bands, clowns, American cheerleaders and classic cars wends its way from Parliament Square at noon, through the centre of London, to Berkeley Square.

Celtic Connections (mid- to late Jan). A major celebration of Celtic and folk music held in venues across Glasgow.

Burns Night (Jan 25). Scots worldwide get stuck into haggis, whisky and vowel-grinding poetry to commemorate Scotland's greatest poet, Robert Burns.

Chinese New Year (Jan 26, 2009; Feb 14, 2010). Processions, fireworks and festivities in the country's two main Chinatowns in London and Manchester.

Shrove Tuesday (47 days before Easter Sunday, so usually in Feb). The last day before Lent is also known as "Pancake Day" – eating them and racing with them are traditional pastimes. The most famous race is held in Olney (Buckinghamshire).

Shrovetide Football (Shrove Tuesday & Ash Wednesday). The world's oldest, largest, longest, maddest football game takes place in and around Ashbourne, Derbyshire. See p.435.

March

St David's Day (March 1). Celebrations all over Wales.
Whuppity Scourie (March 1). Local children race round Lanark church beating each other with home-made paper weapons in a representation (it's thought) of the chasing away of winter or the warding off of evil spirits. See p.855

Easter

British and World Marbles Championship (Good Friday). Held at Tinsley Green, near Crawley, Sussex.
Bacup Nutters Dance (Easter Saturday). Blacked-up Lancashire clog dancers mark the Bacup town boundaries.
Hare Pie Scramble and Bottle-Kicking (Easter Monday). Barmy and chaotic village bottle-kicking contest at Hallaton, Leicestershire.
World Coal-Carrying Championship (Easter Monday). Gawthorpe, near Ossett, West Yorkshire, sees an annual race to carry 50kg of coal a mile through the village and be crowned "King of the Coil Humpers".
Easter Parade (Easter Monday). One of England's largest parades (since 1885) is held in London's Battersea Park.

April/May

Ulverston Walking Festival (April/May). Cumbria's "Festival Town" celebrates the great outdoors with hikes and events. See p.533.
Padstow Obby Oss (May 1). Processions, music and dancing through the streets of Padstow, Cornwall; an equally raucous Obby Oss festival takes place in Minehead, Somerset. See p.354.
Helston Furry Dance (May 8). A courtly procession and dance through the Cornish town by men in top hats and women in formal dresses. See p.347.
Bath International Music Festival (mid-May to 1st week June). Arts jamboree, with a concurrent fringe festival. See pp.292–299.
Glyndebourne Opera Festival (mid-May to end Aug). One of the classiest arts festivals in the country, in East Sussex. See p.192.
Brockworth Cheese Rolling (late May bank holiday Mon). Pursuit of a cheese wheel down a murderous Gloucestershire incline – one of the weirdest knees-ups in England.
Chelsea Flower Show (3rd or 4th week). Essential event for England's green-fingered legions at the Royal Hospital, Chelsea, in London.
Hay Festival of Literature and the Arts (last week). The nation's literary types descend on this Welsh border town for a big bookish shindig. See p.416.

June

Shinty Camanachd Cup Final (June). The climax of the season for Scotland's own stick-and-ball game, normally held in one of the main Highland towns. Also marks the beginning of the Highland Games season across the Highlands, Northeast and Argyll.
Aldeburgh Festival (June). Suffolk jamboree of classical music, established by Benjamin Britten. See p.376.
Eisteddfod Genedlaethol Urdd (1st week). The largest youth festival in Europe, alternating between North and South Wales.
Beating Retreat (early June). Soldiers on foot and horseback provide a colourful, very British ceremony on Horse Guards Parade over three evenings, marking the old military custom of drumming and piping the troops back to base at dusk.
Strawberry Fair (1st Sat). Free festival of music, arts and crafts held on Midsummer Common in Cambridge. See pp.392–401.
Appleby Horse Fair (2nd week). The country's most important gypsy gathering at Appleby-in-Westmorland, Cumbria. See p.536.
Trooping the Colour (2nd Sat). Massed bands, equestrian pageantry, gun salutes and fly-pasts for the Queen's Official Birthday on Horse Guards Parade, London. See p.96.
Cardiff Singer of the World (mid-June). Huge week-long biennial music festival, with a star-studded list of international competitors.
Glastonbury Festival (last week). Top-class music and comedy line-up – the rain nearly always turns it into a mud bath, but nothing dampens the trippy-hippy vibe. See p.304 and the *Festival and events* colour section.
World Worm-Charming Championships (end June). Annual world championships of worm-charming and other zany pastimes, held at Willaston, Cheshire.

July

Llangollen International Music Eisteddfod (early July). Over 12,000 participants from all over the world, including choirs, dancers, folk singers, groups and instrumentalists. See pp.718–720 and the *Festival and events* colour section.
Urban Games (dates vary June/July). Skater-chic comes to Clapham Common, London, for a weekend of boarding, BMXing and freestyling.
Rushbearing Festival (1st week). Symbolic procession of crosses and garlands at Ambleside in the Lake District, dating back centuries. See p.522.
York Early Music Festival (1st/2nd week). The country's premier early music festival, spread out over ten days. See p.572.

Great Yorkshire Show (2nd week). England's biggest region celebrates its heritage, culture and cuisine in a huge three-day agricultural bash at Harrogate, North Yorkshire. See p.563.
Gŵyl Werin y Cnapan Ffostrasol, near Lampeter, Ceredigion (2nd weekend). The best folk and Celtic music festival in the world. See p.710.
Swan Upping (3rd week). Ceremonial registering of the River Thames cygnets, during which liveried rowers search for swans, marking them as belonging to either the Queen, the Dyers' or the Vintners' City liveries.
Cambridge Folk Festival (last week). Biggest event of its kind in England, with lots more than just folk music. See pp.392–401.
Whitstable Oyster Festival (late July & early Aug). Oysters are washed down with champagne and Guinness, with parades and diverse musical accompaniments. See p.170.
WOMAD (late July). Renowned three-day world music festival at Charlton Park, outside Malmesbury, Wiltshire.
The Proms (July to early Sept). Top-flight international classical music festival at the Royal Albert Hall, London, with very cheap standing-room tickets, ending in the famously patriotic Last Night of the Proms. See p.159.
Royal Tournament (last week). Precision military displays at Earls Court Exhibition Centre, London.
Pride London (dates vary). Encompassing a rally in Trafalgar Square, a whistle-blowing march through the city streets, plus cabaret stage and Drag Idol contest in Leicester Square.

August

Edinburgh Festival (Aug). One of the world's great arts jamborees. See p.789.
Brighton Pride (1st week). A week of events celebrating lesbian, gay, bisexual and transgender culture, culminating in the country's biggest gay carnival parade on the final Saturday. See pp.193–199.
Cowes Week (1st week). Full-blown sailing extravaganza in the Isle of Wight, with partying aplenty and star-studded entertainment for land lubbers. See p.218.
Royal National Eisteddfod (1st week). Wales's biggest single annual event: fun, very impressive and worth seeing if only for the pageantry.
Sidmouth Folk Week (1st week). Folk and roots performers at a variety of venues. See p.317.
Whitby Regatta (1st week). The country's oldest regatta – sea races, funfair and fireworks on the windy North Yorkshire coast. See p.583.
Lammas Fair (early Aug). The two-day fair at St Andrews; the oldest medieval market in the country. See p.873.
Grasmere Lakeland Sports and Show (3rd/4th week). Wrestling, fell-running, ferret-racing and other curious Lake District pastimes. See p.523.
Notting Hill Carnival (last Sun & bank holiday Mon). Vivacious celebration led by London's Caribbean community but including everything from Punjabi drummers to Brazilian salsa, plus music, food and floats. See p.153 and the *Festival and events* colour section.
Leeds West Indian Carnival (bank holiday Mon). England's oldest carnival, featuring processions, dancing and barbecues. See p.551.
World Bog Snorkelling Championships (bank holiday Mon). Held in Llanwrtyd Wells in Wales, the festivities include a mountain-bike bog-leaping contest. See p.687.
Whitby Folk Week (bank holiday week). One of England's most traditional folk meets, a week's worth of morris and sword dancing, finger-in-your-ear singing, storytelling and more. See p.583.
Reading Festival (bank holiday weekend). Berkshire's annual three-day rock and contemporary music jamboree. See p.253.

September

Blackpool Illuminations (early Sept to early Nov). Five miles of extravagantly kitsch light displays on the Blackpool seafront. See pp.503–506.
Abbots Bromley Horn Dance (1st Mon after Sept 4). Vaguely pagan mass dance in mock-medieval costume – one of the most famous of England's ancient customs, at Abbots Bromley, Staffordshire.
St Ives September Festival (2 weeks mid-Sept). Eclectic Cornish festival of art, poetry, literature, jazz, folk, rock and world music. See p.351.
Open House (3rd weekend). A once-a-year opportunity to peek inside hundreds of buildings, many of which don't normally open their doors to the public. Takes place in London and, to a lesser extent, elsewhere in the country.

October

Swansea Festival of Music and the Arts (early to mid-Oct). Concerts, jazz, drama, opera, ballet and art events throughout the city over two weeks. See p.652.
World Conker Championship (2nd Sun). Thousands flock to Ashton, Northamptonshire, to watch modern-day gladiators fight for glory armed only with a nut and twelve inches of string.
Glenfiddich Piping Championships (late Oct). Held at Blair Atholl for the world's top ten solo pipers. See p.889.
State Opening of Parliament (late Oct). The Queen arrives in a fancy coach accompanied by the Household Cavalry to give a speech in the House of Lords and officially open Parliament at 11am. It also

takes place whenever a new government is sworn in. See p.96

Halloween (Oct 31). Last day of the Celtic calendar and All Hallows Eve: pumpkins, plus a lot of ghoulish dressing-up, trick-or-treating and parties.

November

London to Brighton Veteran Car Rally (1st Sun). Ancient machines lumbering the 57 miles down the A23 to the seafront.

Guy Fawkes Night/Bonfire Night (Nov 5). Nationwide fireworks and bonfires commemorating the foiling of the Gunpowder Plot in 1605 – most notably at York (Fawkes' birthplace), Ottery St Mary in Devon, and at Lewes, East Sussex (see p.91). See also the *Festival and events* colour section.

Lord Mayor's Show (2nd Sat). Celebrations held since 1215, featuring a daytime cavalcade and nighttime fireworks, to mark the inauguration of the new Lord Mayor of the City of London.

December

Tar Barrels Parade (Dec 31). Locals in Allendale Town, Northumberland turn up with trays of burning pitch on their heads to parade round a large communal bonfire.

Hogmanay and Ne'er Day (Dec 31 & Jan 1). Traditionally more important to the Scots than Christmas, known for the custom of "first-footing", when groups of revellers troop into neighbours' houses at midnight bearing gifts. More popular these days are huge and highly organized street parties, most notably in Edinburgh, but also in Aberdeen, Glasgow and other Scottish cities. See p.787 and the *Festival and events* colour section.

New Year's Eve (Dec 31). In London, there's a massive fireworks display over the Thames, and thousands of inebriates in Trafalgar Square; also a huge bash on Newcastle's Quayside.

Sports and outdoor activities

As the birthplace of football, cricket, rugby and tennis – to name just four sports – Britain can boast a series of sporting events that attract a world audience. If you prefer participating to spectating, the UK caters for just about every outdoor activity, too: we've concentrated below on walking, cycling and water sports, but there are also opportunities for anything from rock-climbing to pony-trekking. The Guide highlights recommended operators in every region, or contact any local tourist office.

Spectator sports

Football (soccer) is the national game in both Scotland and England, with a wide programme of professional league matches taking place every Saturday afternoon from early August to early May, with plenty of Sunday and midweek fixtures too. It's very difficult to get tickets to Premier League matches involving the most famous teams (Chelsea, Arsenal, Manchester United, Liverpool, Rangers and Celtic), but tours of their grounds are feasible or you can try one of the lower-league games. The two annual showpieces are the English **FA Cup Final**, the culmination of the country's biggest domestic knock-out football competition and the **Scottish Cup Final**, played on consecutive weekends in May – though again, tickets are virtually unobtainable: you're best advised to find a lively bar and watch it on TV with the rest of the country.

Rugby comes in two codes – 15-a-side **Rugby Union** and 13-a-side **Rugby League**, both fearsomely brutal contact sports that can make entertaining viewing even if you don't understand the rules. In England, rugby is much less popular than football, but Rugby League has a loyal and dedicated fan base in the North – especially Yorkshire and Lancashire – whilst Union has traditionally been popular with the English middle class. Rugby League has never taken off in Wales and Scotland, but Rugby Union is popular in the Scottish Borders and is effectively the **national sport in Wales**. Key Rugby Union and League games are sold out months in advance, but ordinary fixtures present few ticketing problems. The Rugby Union season runs from September to May, Rugby League February to September.

The game of **cricket** is British idiosyncrasy at its finest. Foreigners – and most Britons for that matter – marvel at a game that can last five days and still end in a draw, while few people have the faintest idea about its rules or tactics. A plethora of competitions and matches between the 18 "first-class" English counties (played April–Sept) means visitors can easily experience the sport – if the four-day County Championship matches or the five-day **Test matches** seem like too much of a commitment, there are also one-day National League matches, a one-day knockout cup competition (the C&G Trophy) and the highly popular three-hour matches of the Twenty20 Cup.

Another traditional British sporting passion that doubles as a social (and gambling) event is **horse racing**. Meetings at the country's most famous race courses have become national events and, while every big race is shown live on TV, there's no substitute for being there and tipping a winner. The grandest race in the horse-racing calendar is the **Grand National**, the "World's Greatest Steeplechase", held the last Saturday in March or the first in April and run at Liverpool's Aintree course.

Finally, if you're in England at the end of June or early July, you won't be able to miss the country's annual fixation with **tennis** in the shape of the Wimbledon championships. No one gives a hoot about the sport for the other fifty weeks of the year, but as long as one plucky Brit endures, the entire country gets caught up with tennis fever.

Sporting events calendar

Six Nations Rugby Union (Feb–March). Hotly contested tournament between Scotland, England, Wales, Ireland, France and Italy.

National Hunt Festival, Cheltenham (mid-March). The country's premier steeplechase (fence-jumping) meeting, including the Cheltenham Gold Cup. See p.277.

University Boat Race (Sat in late March/early April). Two eight-man crews race down the Thames in London.

Grand National, Aintree (1st Sat April). Thrills and lots of spills in the steeplechase to end them all. See p.503.

London Marathon (April). The country's biggest running race, as vicars and people dressed as teapots trail in behind the speedy pros.

FA Cup Final and the Scottish Cup Final (May). Football's two biggest domestic games.

Derby week, Epsom (1st week June). The world's most expensive horseflesh competing in the 200-year-old Derby, the Coronation Cup and the Oaks.

Royal Ascot (mid-June). High-class horse racing attended by the wealthy and well-connected.

Wimbledon Lawn Tennis Championships (last week June & 1st week July). England's annual bout of tennis fever.

Henley Royal Regatta (1st week July). Glamorous Oxfordshire rowing tournament, with tons of toffs and strawberries.

British Open Golf Championship (mid-July). The season's last Grand Slam golf tournament; variable venue.

Scottish Open Golf Championship (July). Held at a different venue each year.

Twenty20 Cup Finals Day (early Aug). Two semi-finals and the final take place in one fast-and-furious day of cricket.

Rugby League Challenge Cup Final (last Sat Aug). Held since 1896, this is the culmination of the biggest knock-out competition for Rugby League clubs.

Walking

Walking routes track across many of Britain's wilder areas, amid landscapes varied enough to suit any taste. We've highlighted local walks, climbs, rambles and trails throughout the Guide, but it goes without saying that even for short hikes you need to be **properly equipped**, follow local advice and listen out for local weather reports – British weather is notoriously changeable. You will also need a good **map** (see p.67). In England and Wales you should keep to established routes as you'll often be crossing private land, even within the national parks; Scotland, in contrast, has a tradition of **free public access** to most of the countryside, restricted only at certain times of the year. For details of operators specializing in **organized walking holidays**, see p.59.

Walking in England

England's finest **walking areas** are the granite moorlands and spectacular coastlines of Devon and Cornwall in the Southwest, and the highlands of the North – notably the Peak District, the Yorkshire Dales, the North York Moors, and the Lake District. Keen hikers might want to tackle one of England's dozen or so **National Trails** (ⓦwww.nationaltrail.co.uk), which amount to some 2500 miles of waymarked path and track. Perhaps the most famous – certainly the toughest – is the **Pennine Way** (268 miles; usual walking time 16 days), stretching from the Derbyshire Peak District to the Scottish Borders, while the challenging **South West Coast Path** (630 miles; 56 days) through Cornwall, Devon, Somerset and Dorset tends to be tackled in shorter sections. Other trails are less gung-ho in character, like the **South Downs Way** (101 miles; 8 days) or the fascinating **Hadrians's Wall Path** (84 miles; 7 days). You'll find more details on all these walks in the Guide; excellent guides to all National Trails are published by Aurum Press.

Britain's national parks

Britain has fourteen national parks, ranging from Dartmoor in the southwest to the Cairngorms in the north. The Norfolk and Suffolk Broads has equivalent legal status and is effectively a ninth, while a tenth – the South Downs – is awaiting official designation. Check out the round-up below for the best things to do and see in each park, and click on ⓦwww.nationalparks.gov.uk for more information and links.

Brecon Beacons See pp.680–684. In southern Wales, this low-profile range of grassy hills covers 520 square miles, with a striking sandstone scarp at the head of the South Wales coalfield, and lush, cave-riddled limestone valleys to the south. Don't miss: the climb up Pen y Fan (p.682).

The Broads See p.384. The best place for a boating holiday – the rivers, marshes, fens and canals of Norfolk and Suffolk make up one of the important wetlands in Europe, and are also ideal for birdwatching. It's the one park where a car isn't much use – cyclists and walkers have the best of it. Don't miss: a wildlife-viewing trip on the Electric Eel (p.384).

Cairngorms See p.984. In the Scottish Highlands, this is Britain's biggest national park, which includes its highest mountain massif. It includes some marvellous walking around Aviemore, and a gamut of sports and recreational facilities, not least skiing. Don't miss: the RSPB Reserve at Loch Garten (p.987).

Dartmoor See pp.325–331. England's largest wilderness attracts back-to-nature hikers and tripped-out stone-chasers to Devon in equal measure – the open moorland walking can be pretty hardcore, while Dartmoor is famous for its standing stones, Stone Age hut circles and hill-forts. Don't miss: Grimspound Bronze Age village (p.327).

Exmoor See pp.335–339. A slightly tamer version of Dartmoor but similar in feel, Exmoor straddles the Somerset/Devon border and on its northern edge overlooks the sea from high, hogback hills. Crisscrossed by trails and also accessible from the South West Coast Path, it's ideal for walking and pony-trekking. Don't miss: Tarr Steps, a 17-span medieval bridge.

Lake District See pp.517–533. The biggest and, for many, the best national park, the Lake District (in Cumbria, in the northwest) is an almost alpine landscape of glacial lakes and rugged mountains. It's great for hiking, rock-climbing and water sports, but also has strong literary connections and thriving cultural traditions. Don't miss: Honister's hard-hat mine tour and mountain traverse (p.530).

Loch Lomond and the Trossachs See pp.870–873. Scotland's first national park incorporates a stretch of the West Highland Way along the loch itself, the park's

Walking in Scotland

The whole of **Scotland** offers good opportunities for gentle hill walking, from the smooth, grassy hills and moors of the **Southern Uplands** to the wild and rugged country of the northwest. Scotland has five main **Long Distance Footpaths (LDPs)**, each of which takes days to walk, though you can of course just cover sections of them. The **Southern Upland Way** crosses Scotland from coast to coast in the south, and is the country's longest at 212 miles; the best known is the **West Highland Way**, a 95-mile hike from Glasgow to Fort William via Loch Lomond and Glen Coe; and the gentler **Speyside Way**, in Aberdeenshire, is a mere thirty miles. The green signposts of the Scottish Rights of Way Society point to these and many other cross-country routes, while in the wilder parts the accepted freedom to roam allows extensive mountain walking, rock climbing, orienteering and allied activities.

Walking in Wales

Wales's best **walking country** is to be found within its national parks (see box below). One of these includes the **Pembrokeshire Coast Path,** one of Wales's three

centrepiece. The wild glens of the Trossach range – a sort of miniature Highlands – are also highly scenic. Don't miss: the ascent of Ben Lomond.

New Forest See pp.223–224. In the predominantly domesticated landscape of Hampshire, the country's best surviving example of a medieval hunting forest can be surprisingly wild. The majestic woodland is interspersed by tracts of heath, and a good network of paths and bridleways offers plenty of scope for biking and pony rides. Don't miss: an off-road bike-ride from Brockenhurst (p.223).

Northumberland See pp.614–617. Where England meets Scotland, remote Northumberland in England's northeast is adventure country. The long-distance Pennine Way runs the length of the park, while the Romans left their mark in the shape of Hadrian's Wall, along which you can hike or bike. Don't miss: the Chillingham cattle wildlife safari (p.617).

North York Moors See pp.576–581. A stunning mix of heather moorland, gentle valleys, ruined abbeys and wild coastline. Walking and mountain-biking are the big outdoor activities here in North Yorkshire, but you can also tour the picturesque stone villages or hang out with Goths in Whitby. Don't miss: a day out at Ryedale Folk Museum (p.579).

Peak District See pp.433–442. England's first national park (1951) is also the most visited, because it sits between the major population centres of the Midlands and the northwest. It's rugged outdoors country, with some dramatic underground caverns, tempered by stately homes and spa and market towns. Don't miss: a trip down Speedwell Cavern (p.438).

Pembrokeshire Coast See p.665. One hundred and seventy miles of Wales's southwestern peninsula make up this park, best explored along the Pembrokeshire Coast Path that traverses the cliff tops, frequently dipping down into secluded coves. Don't miss: the hike round St Bride's Bay (p.665).

Snowdonia National Park See pp.721–732. Occupying almost the whole of the northwestern corner of Wales, this park incorporates a dozen of the country's highest peaks separated by dramatic glacial valleys and laced with hundreds of miles of ridge and moorland paths. Don't miss: a ride on the Snowdon Mountain Railway (p.728).

Yorkshire Dales See pp.553–564. Probably the best choice for walking, cycling and pony-trekking, Yorkshire's second national park spreads across twenty dales, or valleys, at the heart of the Pennines. But England's most scenic railway – the Settle to Carlisle line – is another great draw, while caves, waterfalls and castles provide the backdrop. Don't miss: taking the train across Ribblehead Viaduct.

National Trails – the other two are the 168-mile-long **Offa's Dyke Path** that traces the England–Wales border and **Glyndŵr's Way**, which weaves through mid-Wales for 120 miles. The other long-distance route of special note is the 274-mile **Cambrian Way**, cutting north–south over the Cambrian Mountains.

Cycling

The **National Cycle Network** is made up of 10,000 miles of signed cycle route, a third on traffic-free paths (including disused railways and canal towpaths), the rest mainly on country roads. You're never very far from one of the numbered routes, all of which are detailed on the Sustrans website (Ⓣ0845/113 0065, Ⓦwww.sustrans.org.uk), a charitable trust devoted to the development of environmentally sustainable transport.

Major routes include the well-known **C2C** (Sea-to-Sea), 140 miles between Whitehaven/Workington on the northwest coast and Newcastle/Sunderland on the northeast. There's also the **Cornish Way** (123 miles), from Bude to Land's End, and routes that cut through the very heart of England, such as from Derby to York (154 miles) or along the rivers Severn and Thames (128 miles; Gloucester to Reading). The classic cross-Britain route, however, is from Land's End, in the far southwest of England, to John O'Groats, on the northeast tip of Scotland – roughly a thousand miles, which can be covered in two to three weeks, depending on which of the three CTC-recommended routes you choose.

Most local tourist offices and good bookshops stock a range of **cycling guides**, with maps and detailed route descriptions. You can also get maps and guidance (some free) from Sustrans and from the Cyclists Touring Club (Ⓣ0870/873 0060, Ⓦwww.ctc.org.uk). For **cycling holiday operators**, see p.59.

Water sports

With hundreds of miles of coastline and inland waterways, not to mention an entire district of lakes, it's hardly surprising that Britain offers excellent water sports opportunities.

Sailing and **windsurfing** are especially popular along the south coast (particularly the Isle of Wight and Solent) and in the southwest (around Falmouth in the Carrick Roads estuary, Cornwall, and around Salcombe and Dartmouth, both in South Devon). Here, and up in the Lake District, on Windermere, Derwent Water and Ullswater, you'll be able to rent boards, dinghies and boats, either by the hour or for longer periods of instruction – from around £25 for a couple of hours of windsurfing to around £140 for a two-day non-residential sailing course. The UK Sailing Academy (Ⓣ01983/294941, Ⓦwww.uk-sail.org.uk) in Cowes on the Isle of Wight is England's finest instruction centre for windsurfing, dinghy sailing, kayaking and kitesurfing and offers non-residential and residential courses.

Newquay in Cornwall is the country's undisputed **surfing** centre, whose main break, Fistral, regularly hosts international contests. But there are quieter spots all along the north coast of Cornwall and Devon, as well a growing scene on the more isolated northeast coast from Yorkshire to Northumberland. The coastline here is often spectacular, especially in Northumberland, and although the more popular breaks, such as Cayton Bay and Saltburn, are now crowded, you can find greater isolation with ease. In England's southwest (less so in the northeast) there are plenty of places where you can rent or buy equipment, which means that prices are kept down to reasonable levels, say around £10 per day each for board and wetsuit.

Surfing in **Wales** tends to be concentrated on the south coast, around the Gower Peninsula, which boasts a good variety of beach and reef breaks, but the most consistent surf beach in Wales is Freshwater West in Pembrokeshire. **Scotland** is fast gaining a reputation for the high quality of its breaks with the number-one spot being Thurso on the north coast. Many other good breaks lie within easy reach of large cities (eg Pease Bay, near Edinburgh, and Fraserburgh, near Aberdeen), while the spectacular west coast has numerous possibilities: try

Sandwood Bay, the most isolated beach in Britain, or the waves of the Outer Hebrides.

Activity holiday operators

Most operators offering **activity holidays** tend to have two types of trip: escorted (or guide-led) and self-guided, the latter usually slightly cheaper. On all holidays you can expect luggage transfer each night, pre-booked accommodation, detailed route instructions, a packed lunch and back-up support. Some companies offer budget versions of their holidays, staying in hostels or B&Bs, as well as hotel packages.

Boating and sailing

Blakes Holiday Boating ⓣ0870/220 2498, ⓦwww.blakes.co.uk. Cruisers, yachts and narrowboats on the Norfolk Broads, the River Thames and various English canals.

Classic Sailing ⓣ01872/580022, ⓦwww.classic-sailing.co.uk. Hands-on sailing holidays on traditional wooden boats and tall ships, including Devon, Cornwall and the Isles of Scilly. Women-only weekends available.

Hoseasons Holidays ⓣ01502/502588, ⓦwww.hoseasons.co.uk. Self-drive cruisers on the Norfolk Broads and River Thames, as well as traditional narrowboats on inland waterways.

Le Boat US ⓣ1-800/992-0291, ⓦwww.leboat.com. Hire a hotel-barge or self-drive cruiser on the River Thames (3 days or 1 week) or the Norfolk Broads (1 week).

Cycling

Capital Sport ⓣ01296/631671, ⓦwww.capital-sport.co.uk. Gentle self-guided cycling tours in Kent, Oxford and the Cotswolds, in either B&B or "fine" accommodation.

Country Lanes ⓣ01425/655022, ⓦwww.countrylanes.co.uk. Ranging from day-trips to week-long outings, mainly in the Lake District and New Forest.

Holiday Lakeland ⓣ01697/371871, ⓦwww.holiday-lakeland.co.uk. Offers 3- to 5-day tours in Northumberland and the Pennines, including coast-to-coast, Pennine Cycleway and Hadrian's Wall Cycleway routes; also a 4-day, self-guided Lake District tour.

Saddle Skedaddle ⓣ0191/265 1110, ⓦwww.skedaddle.co.uk. Biking adventures and classic road rides – includes guided and self-guided tours in Cornwall, the Cotswolds, Northumberland, the New Forest, Wales and Scotland, from a weekend to a week.

Surfing

Big Friday ⓣ01637/872512, ⓦwww.bigfriday.com. Surf weekend packages from London to Newquay, with accommodation, travel and tuition laid on. Also women-only weekends.

Global Boarders ⓣ0845/330 9303, ⓦwww.globalboarders.com. Tailor-made surf packages in Cornwall, with a variety of accommodation options and transport to wherever the best breaks are.

Surfers World ⓣ01271/871224, ⓦwww.surfersworld.co.uk. Short breaks with surfing courses in Woolacombe, north Devon, or on the north Cornwall coast.

Walking

Above The Line ⓣ019467/26229, ⓦwww.wasdale.com. Mountain courses (hill walking for softies, guided ascents, navigation and so on), with accommodation in the *Wasdale Head Inn*, the Lake District birthplace of British mountaineering.

Backroads ⓣ1-800/462-2848, ⓦwww.backroads.com. World hiking specialists offering a 6-day ramble round the Scottish Highlands and the Isle of Skye, staying in elegant country-house hotels.

Classic Journeys ⓣ1-800/200-3887, ⓦwww.classicjourneys.com. Upmarket guided (walking) tours of classic English and Scottish destinations, including the Cotswolds, the Cornish coast, Edinburgh and the Highlands.

Contours Walking Holidays ⓣ01768/480451, ⓦwww.contours.co.uk. Short breaks or longer walking holidays and self-guided hikes in every region, north and south, from famous trails to little-known local routes.

English Lakeland Ramblers US ⓣ1-800/724-8801, ⓦwww.ramblers.com. Escorted walking tours in the Lake District and the Cotswolds, as well as the Welsh Borders and the Scottish Highlands and islands, either inn-to-inn or based in a country hotel.

Footpath Holidays ⓣ01985/840049, ⓦwww.footpath-holidays.com. Guided and self-guided walking packages to various hill and coastal areas, from the West Highland Way to Cornwall, most with 5 or 7 nights B&B.

Ramblers Countrywide Holidays ⓣ01707/386800, ⓦwww.ramblersholidays.co.uk. Sociable guided walking tours (scenic, themed or special interest) all over the UK, graded from "leisurely" to "challenging".

REI Adventures ⓣ1-800/622-2236, ⓦwww.rei.com. Week-long hiking tours in the Highlands.

Sherpa Expeditions ⓣ020/8577 2717, ⓦwww.sherpa-walking-holidays.co.uk. At-your-own-pace, self-guided walks (and cycle tours) between country pubs. Places include Yorkshire, the Lakes and

St Cuthbert's Way, straddling England and Scotland, and most trips last 8–10 days between April and October.

Walkabout Scotland ⓣ0131/661 7168, ⓦwww.walkaboutscotland.com. A great way to get a taste of hiking in Scotland, with guided hill-walking holidays, tours and day-trips with all transport included.

Walking Women ⓣ0845/644 5335, ⓦwww.walkingwomen.co.uk. Popular, year-round women-only walking breaks in such areas as Snowdonia, the Lake District, the Yorkshire Dales, the Cotswolds and the South Downs, mainly 3–5 days.

Wilderness Travel US ⓣ1-800/368-2794, ⓦwww.wildernesstravel.com. Inn-to-inn hiking packages, including the Lake District, Yorkshire Dales (both 10 days), coast-to-coast (2 weeks) and the West Highland Way (9 days).

Miscellaneous

Doone Valley Trekking ⓣ01598/741234, ⓦwww.doonevalleytrekking.co.uk. Short breaks and week-long holidays on Exmoor, for all ages and levels, with self-catering farmhouse accommmodation.

Explore Britain ⓣ01740/650900, ⓦwww.xplorebritain.com. Escorted and independent walking and cycling holidays including coast-to-coast, the Thames Valley, the Cotswolds, the Lake District, Anglesey, Offa's Dyke and the Scottish Highlands.

Mountain Water Experience ⓣ01548/550675, ⓦwww.mountainwaterexperience.com. Kayaking, caving, coasteering and other adventure pursuits, based in Dartmoor and south Devon.

Outward Bound ⓣ0870/242 3028, ⓦwww.outwardbound-uk.org. Residential courses and activity holidays in the Lake District, including climbing, caving, sailing and canoeing, geared towards under-25s, but family weekends also available.

YHA ⓣ0870/770 8868, ⓦwww.yha.org.uk. Huge range of good-value hostel-based activity weekends and holidays, from walking, climbing and biking to surfing, kayaking and caving.

Shopping

Although it is now one of the chief leisure activities of the Brits, shopping can be a rather soulless experience in towns and cities. High streets up and down the country feature the same bland chain stores selling very similar ranges of mass-produced items. But while out-of-town shopping centres and supermarkets have sucked much of the life out of town centres, it is still possible to track down neighbourhoods, stores and the occasional oddity that make for a more enjoyable retail experience.

Most places, for example, have a **market** at least once a week, which may vary from a sprawling sea of stalls, as in London's Camden, Portobello and Spitalfields (see p.160), to sedate local village affairs. Street markets or covered markets are often the best places to pick up craft items, though you may have to wade among a proliferation of candles, t-shirts and twee bric-a-brac to find anything truly original. Markets are also the only places (apart from antique shops and some second-hand shops) where **haggling** is acceptable. Look on ⓦwww.country-markets.co.uk to find where and when a market takes place close to you. Many towns also have a weekly or monthly **farmers' market** (see ⓦwww.farmersmarkets.net), where local foodstuffs and artisan products are offered – the biggest of these is in Winchester, with over 90 producers. You'll also find similarly authentic local items in rural **farmshops**, usually signposted by the side of the road.

If you're looking for specific items, you'll want to seek out particular districts and towns which specialize in them: Birmingham's Jewellery Quarter for silver and gold, for example, or Hay-on-Wye (see p.416) for

Clothing and shoe sizes

Women's dresses and skirts

American	4	6	8	10	12	14	16	18	
British	8	10	12	14	16	18	20	22	
Continental	38	40	42	44	46	48	50	52	

Women's blouses and sweaters

American	6	8	10	12	14	16	18	
British	30	32	34	36	38	40	42	
Continental	40	42	44	46	48	50	52	

Women's shoes

American	5	6	7	8	9	10	11
British	3	4	5	6	7	8	9
Continental	36	37	38	39	40	41	42

Men's suits

American	34	36	38	40	42	44	46	48
British	34	36	38	40	42	44	46	48
Continental	44	46	48	50	52	54	56	58

Men's shirts

American	14	15	15.5	16	16.5	17	17.5	18
British	14	15	15.5	16	16.5	17	17.5	18
Continental	36	38	39	41	42	43	44	45

Men's shoes

American	7	7.5	8	8.5	9.5	10	10.5	11	11.5
British	6	7	7.5	8	9	9.5	10	11	12
Continental	39	40	41	42	43	44	44	45	46

books, while almost every Cotswold hamlet sports an antiques shop or two.

On the whole, though, Britain is not an especially cheap place to shop. Most goods in the UK, with the chief exceptions of books and food, are subject to 17.5-percent **Value Added Tax** (VAT), which is included in the marked price. Visitors from non-EU countries can save a lot of money through the **Retail Export Scheme** (tax-free shopping), which allows a refund of VAT on goods to be taken out of the country. (Savings will usually be minimal for EU nationals because of the rates at which the goods will be taxed upon import to the home country.) Note that not all shops participate in this scheme (those doing so will display a sign to this effect), and that you cannot reclaim VAT charged on hotel bills or other services.

Travel essentials

Costs

Britain is an expensive place to visit. Even if you're camping or hostelling, using public transport, buying picnic lunches and eating in pubs and cafés your minimum expenditure will be around £35/US$70/€50 per person per day. Couples staying in B&Bs, eating at unpretentious restaurants and visiting a fair number of tourist attractions, are looking at £60–70/US$125–145/€85–100 per person, while if you're renting a car, staying in hotels and eating well, budget for at least £120/US$245/€170 each. This last figure, of course, won't even cover your accommodation if you're staying in stylish city or grand country-house hotels, while on any visit to London work on the basis that you'll need an extra £25/US$50/€35 per day to get the best out of the city.

Many of Britain's **historic attractions** – from castles to stately homes – are owned and/or operated by either the **National Trust** (Ⓣ0870/458 4000, Ⓦwww.nationaltrust.org.uk), covering England and Wales, or the **National Trust for Scotland** (Ⓣ0844/493 2100, Ⓦwww.nts.org.uk) – whose properties are denoted in the Guide with "NT" or "NTS". Many other historic sites are operated by **English Heritage** (Ⓣ0870/333 1181, Ⓦwww.english-heritage.org.uk), whose properties are denoted in the Guide with "EH", **Historic Scotland** (HS; Ⓣ0131/668 8600, Ⓦwww.historic-scotland.gov.uk), and **CADW Welsh Historic Monuments** (CADW; Ⓣ01443/336000, Ⓦwww.cadw.wales.gov.uk). All three organizations charge entry fees for most of their sites (usually £4–8), though some are free. If you plan to visit more than half a dozen places owned by any of them, it's worth considering an annual membership (around £40), which allows unlimited entry to each organization's respective properties – and you can join on your first visit to any attraction. US members of the Royal Oak Foundation (Ⓦwww.royal-oak.org) get free admission to all National Trust properties. For further details concerning membership fees and special deals, consult the respective websites.

Many **stately homes** remain privately owned, in the hands of the landed gentry, who tend to charge £8–12 for admission to edited highlights of their domain. Other old buildings are owned by local authorities, which generally charge lower admission charges or allow free access.

Municipal art galleries and museums across the UK often have free admission, as do the great **state museums** in London and the provinces, such as the British Museum, National Gallery, Cardiff's National Museum of Wales, and the National Museum of Scotland and National Gallery of Scotland in Edinburgh. Private museums and other collections usually charge for entrance, but rarely more than £6. Several of the country's **cathedrals** charge admission – of around £4 – but most ask for voluntary donations, as do many churches.

Tipping

Although there are no fixed rules for **tipping**, a ten to fifteen percent tip is anticipated by restaurant waiters and expected by taxi drivers. Some restaurants levy a "discretionary" or "optional" **service charge** of 10 or 12.5 percent. If they've done this, it should be clearly stated on the menu and on the bill. However, you are not obliged to pay the charge, and certainly not if the food or service wasn't what you expected. It is not normal to leave tips in pubs, but the bar staff are sometimes offered drinks, which they may accept in the form of money. The only other occasions when you'll be expected to tip are at the hairdressers, and in upmarket hotels where porters, bell boys and table waiters expect and usually get a pound or two.

Britain on a budget

Faced with another £2.50 pint, a £30 theatre ticket and a £20 taxi ride back to your £100-a-night hotel, you might feel that Britain is the most expensive place in Europe. However, there are ways to stick to a **budget** and still get the most out of your stay.

- Entry is free to many of Britain's showpiece **museums and galleries**, including some of the world's finest art and historical collections in London, Leeds, York, Birmingham, Manchester, Liverpool and Edinburgh.
- **Beer** is cheaper in the north of England, and cheapest of all in Lancashire, according to the peerless *Good Pub Guide*.
- Take every **discount card/ID** you're entitled to, as students, young travellers, youth hostellers and seniors all get free or discounted entry to many sights and attractions.
- Go to the **cinema** during the day; it's nearly always cheaper before 5pm.
- Set meals can be a real steal, even at the poshest of **restaurants**, where a limited-choice two- or three-course lunch or a "pre-theatre" menu might only cost 40 percent of the usual price.
- Book **transport** tickets as far in advance as possible, and always ask about Day Rovers and other special deals.
- Don't drive – **walk**. In places like the Yorkshire Dales, the Lake District, or along the Cornish coastal path, the easiest and most enjoyable way to get from village to village is on your own two feet.
- Give the big-ticket **festivals** (Glastonbury, Glyndebourne) a miss; there are thousands of others throughout the year that are free and fun, from Derbyshire well-dressing to the Notting Hill Carnival.
- Visit the **markets** – from grungy Camden in London to Welsh farmers' markets, you can browse for free and pick up some bargains along the way.

The admission charges given in the Guide are the full adult rate, unless otherwise stated. Concessionary rates for **senior citizens** (over 60), under-26s and **children** (from 5 to 17) apply almost everywhere, from fee-paying attractions to public transport, and typically give around fifty percent discount; you'll need official identification as proof of age. The unemployed and full-time students are often entitled to discounts too, and under-5s are rarely charged.

Students and under-26s can benefit from an International Student ID Card or International Youth Travel Card, while teachers qualify for the **International Teacher Card**, all giving special air, rail and bus fares and discounts at museums, theatres and other attractions. All cost around £10/US$22/€14 from ISIC (Ⓦwww.isiccard.com) or ISTC (Ⓦwww.isic.org). Several other travel organizations and accommodation groups (including the youth hostel organization, IYHF) have their own cards providing various discounts. Specialist travel agencies in your home country (including STA worldwide) can provide more information and application forms.

Non-UK residents can buy a **Great British Heritage Pass** (4 days £28/US$54/€42/; 7 days £39/US$75/€58; 15 days £52/US$99/€76; 30 days £70/US$133/€102), which gives free entry into 600 cultural and historic properties, including those operated by the National Trust and English Heritage. You can buy it (at equivalent local rates) from travel agents in your own country before you come, or at major tourist offices in the UK on arrival – see Ⓦwww.visitbritain.com or www.britishheritagepass.com for more details.

Crime and personal safety

Terrorist attacks in England and Scotland may have changed the general perception of how safe Britain feels, with heightened **security** at airports, major train stations and other transport termini; however, it's still highly unlikely that you'll be at any risk as you travel around the country.

While Britain is far from crime-free, the vast majority of tourists experience few, if any, problems, at least in part because they are unlikely to visit the inner-city estates where crime flourishes. You can walk around most areas of London and the larger cities without fear of harassment or assault, though all the big conurbations have their edgy districts and it's always better to err on the side of caution late at night, when – for instance – badly lit streets and drunken groups should be avoided. If possible, always leave your passport and valuables in a hotel or hostel safe (carrying **ID** is not yet compulsory in the UK), and exercise the usual caution on the tube, trains and buses. After public transport shuts down for the night, take a licensed taxi to your destination. If you are robbed, you need to report it to the police, not least because your insurance company will require a **crime report number** – make sure you get one.

Other than asking for directions, most visitors rarely come into close contact with the British **police**, who as a rule are approachable and helpful – though they can get tetchy at football matches, demonstrations and in the evenings when pubs close and clubs open. Most wear chest guards and carry batons, though street officers do not normally carry guns.

Being caught in possession of a small quantity of "soft" **drugs** – mainly marijuana and cannabis – will probably result in a police caution. If, on the other hand, the police suspect you are dealing, you can expect to be held in custody and ultimately prosecuted. Finally, making "jokes" about bombs or **suspicious packages** in check-in lines or at security barriers is not advised, and can result in serious trouble, heavy delays and possibly prosecution.

Customs

Travellers coming into Britain directly **from most other EU countries** can bring almost as many cigarettes and as much wine or beer into the country as they can carry. The guidance levels are 10 litres of spirits, 90 litres of wine and 110 litres of beer – any more than this and you'll have to provide proof that it's for personal use only. The general guidelines for tobacco are 3200 cigarettes, 400 cigarillos, 200 cigars or 3kg of loose tobacco – note that the limits from some new EU member countries are lower than this.

If you're travelling to or from a non-EU country, you can still buy a limited amount of **duty-free goods**, but within the EU, this perk no longer exists. If you need any clarification on British import regulations, contact **HM Revenue and Customs** (ⓣ0845/010 9000 or +44 292/050 1261 for international callers; ⓦcustoms.hmrc.gov.uk).

Electricity

In the UK, the **current** is 240V AC. North American appliances will need a transformer and adaptor; those from Europe, Australia and New Zealand only need an adaptor.

Entry requirements

EU citizens have the right of free movement and residence throughout the UK, with just a passport or identity card. US, Canadian, South African, Australian and New Zealand citizens can stay in the country for up to six months without a visa, provided they have a valid passport. Most other nationalities – but not citizens of Switzerland or EEA countries like Norway – require a visa, obtainable from the British consular office in the country of application. Incidentally, the Channel Islands and the Isle of Man have their own immigration laws and policies, but UK visa offices can issue visas for these islands. For current details about entry and visa requirements, consult the UK's Foreign and Commonwealth Office's visa website, ⓦwww.ukvisas.gov.uk.

Citizens of EU countries who want to stay in the UK other than as a short-term visitor or tourist can apply for a residence permit. Non-EU citizens can apply to extend their visas, though this must be done before the current visa expires. In both cases, you should first contact the **Border and Immigration Agency**, Lunar House, 40 Wellesley Rd, Croydon CR9 2BY (ⓣ0870/606 7766, ⓦwww.ind.homeoffice.gov.uk); there are other offices in Liverpool and Birmingham. US, Canadian, South African, Australian and New Zealand citizens who want to stay longer than six months will need an **entry clearance certificate**, available from the British consular office at the embassy/high commission in their own country.

British embassies and high commissions abroad

Australia British High Commission, Commonwealth Ave, Yarralumla, Canberra, ACT 2600 ⓣ02/6270 6666, ⓦwww.britaus.net.
Canada British High Commission, 80 Elgin St, Ottawa, ON K1P 5K7 ⓣ613/237-1530, ⓦwww.britainincanada.org.
Ireland British Embassy, 29 Merrion Rd, Ballsbridge, Dublin 4 ⓣ01/205 3700, ⓦwww.britishembassy.ie.
New Zealand British High Commission, 44 Hill St, Thorndon, Wellington 6011 ⓣ04/924 2888, ⓦwww.britain.org.nz.
South Africa British High Commission, 255 Hill St, Arcadia 0002, Pretoria ⓣ202/421-7500, ⓦwww.britain.org.za.
USA British Embassy, 3100 Massachusetts Ave, Washington DC 20008 ⓣ202/588-7800, ⓦwww.britainusa.com.

Gay and lesbian travellers

Britain offers one of the most diverse and accessible **lesbian** and **gay** scenes anywhere in Europe. Nearly every town of any size has some kind of organized gay life – from bars and clubs to community groups – with the major scenes found in London, Manchester, Brighton, Edinburgh, Glasgow, Cardiff, Swansea and Newport. Many gay and lesbian venues are listed in this book, and most major towns will have a free local listings sheet. Other listings and news can be found in the fortnightly *Pink Paper* (ⓦwww.pinkpaper.com) and the glossy monthly *Gay Times* (ⓦwww.gaytimes.co.uk), available from many newsagents and alternative bookstores. The Gay Britain Network (ⓦwww.gaybritain.co.uk) has comprehensive information and links for events, restaurants, bars, clubs, and services across the UK, while ⓦwww.gaytravel.co.uk lists over 400 gay and lesbian hotels and travel establishments from Brighton to Blackpool. The age of consent in England, Scotland and Wales for both homosexual and heterosexual acts is 16.

Health

No vaccinations are required for entry into Britain. Citizens of all EU and EEA countries are entitled to free medical treatment within the UK's National Health Service (NHS), which includes the vast majority of hospitals and doctors, on production of their **European Health Insurance Card** (EHIC) or, in extremis, their passport or national identity card. The same applies to those Commonwealth countries that have reciprocal healthcare arrangements with the UK – for example Australia and New Zealand. If you don't fall into either of these categories, you will be charged for all medical services, so health insurance is strongly advised.

Pharmacies and medical treatment

Pharmacists (known as **chemists** in Britain) can dispense only a limited range of drugs without a doctor's prescription. Most chemists are open standard shop hours, though in large towns some stay open until 10pm – local newspapers carry lists of late-opening "duty" pharmacies, and the information will also be posted on pharmacy doors. For generic, off-the-shelf pain-relief tablets, cold cures and the like, the local supermarket is usually the cheapest option.

Minor complaints and injuries can be dealt with at a **doctor's (GP's) surgery** – any tourist office or hotel should be able to point you in the right direction. For complaints that require immediate attention, you can turn up at the 24-hour casualty (A&E) department of the local **hospital** (detailed in our main city and town accounts). In an **emergency**, call an ambulance on ⓣ999 or 112.

NHS Direct (ⓣ0845/4647, ⓦwww.nhsdirect.nhs.uk) provides 24-hour medical advice by phone, and also runs an increasing number of walk-in centres (usually daily 7.30am–9pm) in the bigger towns and cities.

Insurance

Visitors are advised to take out an **insurance policy** before travelling to the UK to cover against theft, loss and illness or injury. A typical policy will provide cover for loss of baggage, tickets and – up to a certain limit – cash or traveller's cheques, as well as cancellation or curtailment of your journey. Most exclude so-called dangerous sports unless an extra premium is paid: in Britain this can mean most water sports, rock-climbing and mountaineering, though hiking, kayaking and jeep safaris would probably be covered.

Medical coverage is strongly advised, though you should always ascertain beforehand whether benefits will be paid as treatment proceeds or only after you return home, and whether there is a 24-hour medical emergency number. When securing **baggage cover**, make sure that the per-article limit will cover your most valuable possession. If you need to make a claim, you should keep receipts for medicines and medical treatment, and in the event you have anything stolen you must obtain an official statement from the police – we've noted the contact details for police stations in all major towns and cities.

Internet access

There are **Internet cafés** in virtually every town and resort in Britain, mainly open daytime only, though you can find late-night and 24-hour access in London and other major centres. Charges vary wildly, but average around £2–3 an hour. An increasing number of hotels, guesthouses, hostels, cafés and tourist offices have Internet terminals for public use, and many have a **Wi-Fi** facility (branches of McDonald's and Starbucks, for example, are Wi-Fi-enabled). Almost every **public library** in the country also offers Internet access, usually for free (though you may be limited to thirty minutes or so) – where there is a charge it's always almost cheaper than the alternative. You may have to wait for a free terminal, though slots can usually be booked.

Laundry

Coin-operated **laundries** (launderettes) are commonplace in every large city and town. Most operate extended opening hours – usually about twelve hours a day – and many offer "service washes", with your laundry washed and dried for you in just a few hours; this costs around £6 for a bagful of clothes. Using a hotel laundry service is always far more expensive.

Living in Britain

Provided you have fulfilled the visa requirements (see Entry requirements, p.64), there are numerous opportunities to extend your stay in the UK. **Student exchange** programmes, **work exchange** schemes and **volunteer programmes** organized in advance allow you to set up home in different parts of the country, usually with a back-up apparatus in place to provide accommodation and assist with the bureaucracy. Without this kind of support, finding a home and a job are the main challenges for those intending to stay on. For **accommodation**, seek out estate agencies and rental agencies, and scour the small ads section of local newspapers as well as cards advertising rooms displayed in some news-agents and food shops. In towns and cities, job centres will try to match you up with suitable **employment**. Again, ads in news-papers and shop windows are best for casual work. Temporary jobs are most commonly available in hotels, pubs, bars and restaurants, especially in holiday destinations – though this kind of work is usually seasonal. Obviously, a good knowledge of English is a big advantage.

Study and work programmes

AFS Intercultural Programs US ⓣ1-800/AFS-INFO, Canada ⓣ1-800/361-7248 or 514/288-3282, UK ⓣ0113/242 6136, Australia

Rough Guides travel insurance

Rough Guides has teamed up with Columbus Direct to offer you **travel insurance** that can be tailored to suit your needs. Products include a low-cost **backpacker** option for long stays, a **short-break** option for city getaways, a typical **holiday package** option, and others. There are also annual **multi-trip** policies for those who travel regularly. Different sports and activities (trekking, skiing, etc) can be usually be covered if required.

See our website (ⓦwww.roughguides.com/website/shop) for eligibility and purchasing options. Alternatively, UK residents should call ⓣ0870/033 9988; Australians should call ⓣ1300/669 999 and New Zealanders should call ⓣ0800/55 9911. All other nationalities should call ⓣ+44 870/890 2843.

Ⓣ1300/131 736 or 02/9215 0077, New Zealand Ⓣ0800/600 300 or 04/494 6020, South Africa Ⓣ11/447 2673, international enquiries Ⓣ1-212/807-8686; Ⓦwww.afs.org. Study and volunteer programmes in England, mainly for under-30s.

American Institute for Foreign Study US Ⓣ1-866/906-2437, Ⓦwww.aifs.com. Intercultural exchange organization which arranges arts and business courses in London for a semester, summer or a whole year.

BTCV (British Trust for Conservation Volunteers) Ⓣ01302/388 888, Ⓦwww.btcv.org.uk. One of the largest environmental charities in Britain, with a programme of working holidays (as a paying volunteer) throughout the country.

BUNAC US Ⓣ1-800/GO-BUNAC, UK Ⓣ020/7251 3472, Republic of Ireland Ⓣ01/477 3027; Ⓦwww.bunac.org. Organizes working holidays for students in a range of destinations, including London, York, Manchester and Edinburgh.

Council on International Educational Exchange (CIEE) US Ⓣ1-800/40-STUDY or 1-207/533-7600, UK Ⓣ020/8939 9057; Ⓦwww.ciee.org. Leading NGO offering study programmes in London.

Earthwatch Institute US Ⓣ1-800/776-0188 or 978/461-0081, UK Ⓣ01865/318 838, Australia Ⓣ03/9682 6828; Ⓦwww.earthwatch.org. Scientific expedition project that includes environmental and archeological ventures in Britain, such as excavating in the Yorkshire Dales, or surveying for whales and dolphins in the Moray Firth and Hebrides.

Mail

The national **postal system** is operated by **Royal Mail** (Ⓣ0845/774 0740, Ⓦwww.royalmail.com), whose customer service line and website details postal services and current postage costs, and can help you find individual post offices. Virtually all **post offices** are open Monday to Friday from 9am to 5.30pm, and on Saturdays from 9am to 12.30 or 1pm, with smaller branches closing on Wednesday afternoons too. In major cities main offices stay open all day Saturday, while in small and rural communities you'll find sub-post offices operating out of general stores, though post office facilities are only available during the hours above even if the shop itself is open for longer.

Stamps are on sale at post offices, though if you know which ones you want, you can avoid queues by buying them instead at newsagents and other stores advertising them. Postage rates depend on the size and weight of the envelope or package, and when you want it to arrive. For UK destinations, postcards and letters up to 100g in weight and of a size no greater than 240mm length, 165mm width and 5mm thickness can be sent either first-class (theoretically for next-day delivery), costing 34p, or second-class (for delivery within three working days), costing 24p. A post office will have a full list of prices for letters exceeding these dimensions. For non-UK destinations, postcards and letters up to 20g cost 48p to Europe, those sent outside Europe cost 54p up to 10g, or 78p 10–20g. Above 20g, rates rise incrementally. Airmail to European destinations should arrive within three working days, and to countries outside Europe within five. Slower "surface mail" and express delivery services are also available.

Maps

For an overview of the **whole of Britain** on one (double-sided) map, Collins' 1:550,000 and Ordnance Survey's 1:625,000 maps are probably the best; both include some city plans. Ordnance Survey (OS; Ⓦwww.ordnancesurvey.co.uk) and Michelin also produce useful regional maps at a scale of 1:250,000 and 1:400,000 respectively, while Philips, in conjunction with OS, produce detailed county maps at a scale of 1:18,000. Otherwise, for general route-finding the most useful resources are the road atlases produced by AA, RAC, Geographers' A–Z and Collins, among others, at a scale of around 1:250,000.

The **National Cycle Network** of cross-country routes along country lanes and traffic-free paths is covered by a series of excellent waterproof maps (1:100,000) published by Sustrans (Ⓦwww.sustrans.org.uk). For **hikers**, the large-scale topographic maps produced by OS are renowned for their accuracy and clarity. The maps in their 1:50,000 (pink) Landranger series show enough detail to be useful for most walkers and cyclists, and there's more detail still in the full-colour 1:25,000 (orange) Explorer series – both cover the whole of Britain.

Finally, **Rough Guides' London map** (1:5000/25,000), on waterproof, tearproof paper, and with full city listings, is invaluable for exploring the capital.

Most of these maps are available from large bookshops or **specialist map and travel stores** in your own country. Alternatively, try a general online bookstore or a world map specialist like Ⓦwww.randmcnally.com. **In the UK** main bookshops and tourist offices usually stock a good range of local/regional maps, while visitors to London or Bristol should call in at **Stanfords** (Ⓦwww.stanfords.co.uk), England's premier map and travel specialist.

Online maps include Ⓦwww.multimap.com, which has town plans and area maps with scales up to 1:3600, plus an address search, traffic information and more, and Ⓦwww.visitmap.com, with clickable A–Z maps covering cities and large and small towns.

Money

Britain's currency is the **pound sterling** (£), divided into 100 pence (p). Coins come in denominations of 1p, 2p, 5p, 10p, 20p, 50p and £1 and £2. Notes are in denominations of £5, £10, £20 and £50. Scottish and Northern Irish banknotes are legal tender throughout Britain, though some traders may be unwilling to accept them.

Every sizeable town and village has a branch of at least one of the main high-street **banks**: Barclays, Halifax, HSBC, Lloyds-TSB and NatWest. The easiest way to get hold of cash is to use your **debit card** in an **ATM**; there's usually a daily withdrawal limit of £250. You'll find ATMs outside banks, at all major points of arrival and motorway service areas, at most large supermarkets, some petrol stations and even in some pubs, rural post offices and village shops (though a charge may be levied on cash withdrawals at small, stand-alone ATMs). Depending on your bank and your debit card, you may also be able to ask for "cash back" when you shop at supermarkets.

Some overseas travellers still prefer sterling **traveller's cheques**, at least as a back-up. The most commonly accepted are issued by American Express, followed by Visa. American Express will not charge commission if you exchange cheques at their own offices, nor will some banks (such as NatWest) – otherwise you will be charged 2–3 percent commission. Note that in the UK you are unlikely to be able to use your traveller's cheques as cash – you'll always have to cash them first, making them an unreliable source of funds in more remote areas.

Outside banking hours, you can change cheques or cash at **post offices** (locations are detailed in the Guide) and **bureaux de change** – the latter tend to be open longer hours and are found in most city centres, and at major airports and train stations. Avoid changing cash or cheques in hotels, where the rates are normally poor.

Finally, **credit cards** can be used widely either in ATMs or over the counter. MasterCard and Visa are accepted in most hotels, shops and restaurants in Britain, American Express and Diners Club less so. Plastic is less useful in rural areas, and smaller establishments all over the country, such as B&Bs, will often accept cash only. Remember that cash advances from ATMs using your credit card are treated as loans, with interest accruing daily from the date of withdrawal. You can avoid interest fees by depositing money into your credit card account before leaving (though some companies will not allow this).

At time of writing, £1 was equivalent to €1.40 and US$2.05; €1 was 72p, and US$1 was 49p.

Opening hours and public holidays

General **business hours** for most businesses, shops and offices are Monday to Saturday 9am to 5.30 or 6pm, although the **supermarket** chains tend to stay open until 8 or 9pm from Monday to Saturday, with larger ones staying open round the clock. Many major stores and supermarkets now **open on Sundays**, too, usually from 11am or noon to 4pm, though some provincial towns still retain an **early-closing day** (usually Wednesday) when most shops close at 1pm. **Banks** are usually open Monday to Friday from 9am to 4pm, with some branches also open on Saturday mornings. You can usually get fuel any time of the day or night in larger towns and cities (though note that not all motorway **service stations** open for 24 hours). Full opening hours for specific museums, galleries and other tourist attractions are given in the Guide – where

Public holidays

Britain's public holidays are:

January 1

January 2 (Scotland only)

Good Friday

Easter Monday (not Scotland)

First Monday in May

Last Monday in May

Last Monday in August

November 30 (or nearest Mon if weekend; Scotland only)

December 25

December 26

Note that if January 1, December 25 or December 26 falls on a Saturday or Sunday, the next weekday becomes a public holiday.

these are seasonal (summer hours are usually Easter–Oct, winter Nov–Easter), they are shown in the format 9/10am–5/6pm. For the usual opening hours of cafés, restaurants and pubs, see Food and drink, p.45.

Banks, businesses and most shops close on **public holidays**, though large supermarkets, small corner shops and many tourist attractions don't. However, nearly all museums, galleries and other attractions are closed on Christmas Day and New Year's Day, with many also closed on Boxing Day (Dec 26). Confusingly, several of Britain's public holidays are usually referred to as **bank holidays** (though it's not just the banks who have a day off).

Phones

The UK's telephone network has been privatized, though one company, British Telecom (BT), still operates the bulk of the system. **Peak period** (Mon–Fri 8am–6pm) calls are more expensive than at the weekend or in the evening – and the same applies to **international calls**. Most hotel rooms have telephones, but there is almost always an exorbitant surcharge for their use. Public pay-phone rates for national and international calls are higher than those applied to private phones. Kiosks or **phone boxes** are plentiful: most take coins (with a minimum charge of 40p), and most also accept phone and credit cards. You can make direct-dial **international calls** from any telephone box, though it's usually cheaper to buy an **international phonecard**, available from many newsagents in denominations of £5, £10 and upwards. You dial the company's local access number, key in the pin number on the card and then dial your number. Your phone company back home may also provide a **telephone charge card**, with which calls can be charged to your own telephone account. Bear in mind, however, that rates aren't necessarily cheaper than making an ordinary call.

Every British landline number has a prefix, which, if beginning ⓣ01 or 02 represents an **area code**. However, some prefixes relate to the cost of calls rather than the location of the subscriber, including: ⓣ0800 and ⓣ0808 prefixes, which are free of charge to the caller; ⓣ0845 numbers, which are charged at local rates; and ⓣ0870 numbers, where callers are charged at national rates irrespective of where they call from. Beware of **premium-rate numbers**, which are common for pre-recorded information services (including some tourist authorities), and usually have the prefix ⓣ0906 or 0909; these are charged at anything up to £1.50 a minute. The prefix ⓣ07 is for mobile phones.

For domestic and international **directory enquiries**, there are numerous competing information lines, all of them expensive. BT's domestic service, on ⓣ118 500, is as good as any (and it's free online at ⓦwww.bt.com); its international directory assistance number is ⓣ118 505. Or you can look up business and service numbers for free in public libraries or on the very useful ⓦwww.yell.com.

Across the UK, **mobile phone** access is routine in all the major cities and in most of the countryside. There are occasional blind spots, and coverage can be patchy in rural and hill areas, but generally you should have few problems.

If you want to use your own mobile phone in the UK, check with your phone provider before you set out – some networks need to have international roaming activated, others do it automatically. Phones bought for use in the US, however, rarely work outside the States. If you do bring your own phone, note that you are likely to be charged extra for incoming calls or texts when abroad as the people calling or texting you will be paying the usual domestic rate. It might be simplest, certainly if you're staying in Britain for any length of time, to **buy a mobile** in the UK – basic non-contract "pay as you go" models start at around £50, usually including a few pounds' worth of free calls.

In the UK, dial ⓣ100 for the **operator**, ⓣ155 for the international operator. To call Britain **from abroad**, dial your international access code + ⓣ44 + area code minus initial zero + number.

Time

Greenwich Mean Time (GMT) is used from late October to late March, when the clocks go forward an hour for British Summer Time (BST). GMT is five hours ahead of the US Eastern Standard Time and ten hours behind Australian Eastern Standard Time.

Tourist information

Britain's tourism authority, VisitBritain, has offices worldwide, while regional tourism boards within the UK concentrate on particular areas. The official national websites, ⓦwww.visitbritain.com, ⓦwww.enjoyengland.com, ⓦwww.visitscotland.com and ⓦwww.visitwales.com are very useful, covering everything from local accommodation to festival dates, and there is a large number of regional and other specialist websites dedicated to the UK that are worth consulting.

Calling home from abroad

Note that the initial zero is omitted from the area code when dialling the countries listed here from abroad.

Australia international access code + 61 + city code.

New Zealand international access code + 64 + city code.

US and Canada international access code + 1 + area code.

Republic of Ireland international access code + 353 + city code.

South Africa international access code + 27 + city code.

Tourist offices (also called Tourist Information Centres, or "TICs" for short) exist in virtually every British town. They tend to follow standard shop hours (Mon–Sat 9am–5.30pm), though sometimes also open on Sundays, with hours curtailed during the winter season (Nov–Easter).

Staff at tourist offices will nearly always be able to book accommodation, reserve space on guided tours, and sell guidebooks, maps and walk leaflets. They can also provide lists of local cafés, restaurants and pubs, though they aren't supposed to recommend particular places. An increasing number of offices have Internet access for visitors, but rarely have the space to look after baggage while you scoot around town.

Areas designated as **national parks** usually have their own dedicated information centres, which offer similar services to TICs but can also provide expert guidance on local walks and outdoor pursuits.

English regional tourism organizations

East of England Tourism ⓣ01284/727470, ⓦwww.visiteastofengland.com. Bedfordshire, Cambridgeshire, Hertfordshire, Essex, Norfolk and Suffolk.

East Midlands Tourism ⓦwww.enjoyeastmidlands.com. Derbyshire, Lincolnshire, Nottinghamshire, Leicestershire, Rutland and Northamptonshire.

England's Northwest ⓦwww.visitenglandsnorthwest.com. Cumbria and the Lake District, Cheshire, Lancashire, Manchester, Liverpool and Merseyside.

Heart of England Tourism ⓦwww.visittheheart.co.uk. Birmingham, Worcestershire, Herefordshire, Shropshire, Staffordshire and Warwickshire.

North East England Tourism ⓦwww.visitnortheastengland.com. County Durham, Northumberland, Tees Valley and Tyne and Wear.

South West Tourism ⓣ0870/442 0880, ⓦwww.visitsouthwest.co.uk. Bath, Bristol, Devon, Cornwall, Dorset, Gloucestershire and the Cotswolds, Somerset and Wiltshire.

Tourism South East ⓦwww.visitsoutheastengland.com. Sussex, Kent, Surrey, Berkshire, Hampshire, Oxfordshire, Buckinghamshire and the Isle of Wight.

Visit London ⓦwww.visitlondon.com. Greater London.

Yorkshire Tourist Board ⓦwww.yorkshire.com.

Scottish regional tourism organizations

Aberdeen and Grampian ⓣ01224/288828, ⓦwww.agtb.org.
Angus and Dundee ⓣ01382/527527, ⓦwww.angusanddundee.co.uk.
Argyll, the Isles, Loch Lomond, Stirling and Trossachs ⓣ0845/225 5121, ⓦwww.visitscottishheartlands.com.
Ayrshire and Arran ⓣ0845/225 5121, ⓦwww.ayrshire-arran.com.
Dumfries and Galloway ⓣ01387/253862, ⓦwww.visitdumfriesandgalloway.co.uk.
Edinburgh and the Lothians ⓣ0845/225 5121, ⓦwww.edinburgh.org.
Fife ⓣ0845/225 5121, ⓦwww.standrews.co.uk.
Greater Glasgow and Clyde Valley ⓣ0141/204 4400, ⓦwww.seeglasgow.com.
Hebrides ⓣ0845/225 5121, ⓦwww.visithebrides.com.
Highlands of Scotland ⓣ0845/225 5121, ⓦwww.visithighlands.com.
Orkney ⓣ0845/225 5121, ⓦwww.visitorkney.com.
Perthshire ⓣ0845/225 5121, ⓦwww.perthshire.co.uk.
Scottish Borders ⓣ0845/225 5121, ⓦwww.scot-borders.co.uk.
Shetland ⓣ0870/199 9440, ⓦwww.visitshetland.com.

Welsh regional tourism organizations

Mid Wales Tourism ⓦwww.visitmidwales.co.uk.
North Wales Tourism ⓣ01492/531731, ⓦwww.nwt.co.uk.
South Wales Tourism ⓦwww.visitsouthwales.com.

Travellers with disabilities

In many ways, the UK is ahead of the field in terms of facilities for travellers with disabilities. All new public buildings – including museums, galleries and cinemas – are obliged to provide **wheelchair access**, train stations and airports are generally fully accessible, many buses have easy-access boarding ramps, while dropped kerbs and signalled crossings are the rule in every city and town. The number of accessible hotels and restaurants is also growing, and reserved parking bays are available almost everywhere, from shopping malls to museums.

If you have specific requirements, it's always best to talk first to your travel agent, chosen hotel or tour operator.

Useful organizations

abletogo ⓦwww.abletogo.com. Accommodation in Britain for disabled and elderly travellers, rated for accessibility.
Access-Able ⓦwww.access-able.com. US-based resource for travellers with disabilities, with links to UK operators and organizations.
All Go Here ⓦwww.allgohere.com. Information on airline services, accommodation and other hospitality-related matters for disabled travellers throughout the UK.
Capability Scotland ⓣ0131/313 5510, ⓦwww.capability-scotland.org.uk. Well-run, well-connected organization for all disability issues and information.
Door-to-Door ⓦwww.dptac.gov.uk/door-to-door. Transport and travel website offering information and advice on UK transport for those with a mobility problem.
Holiday Care ⓣ0845/124 9971, ⓦwww.holidaycare.org.uk. Holiday and travel information service for disabled and older travellers, offering advice on accessible accommodation, attractions and activity holidays in the UK.
RADAR (Royal Association for Disability and Rehabilitation) ⓦwww.radar.org.uk. National network of disability organizations whose website has links to holiday and travel services in the UK. Also publish the excellent *Holidays in Britain and Ireland.*

Travelling with children

On the whole, facilities in the UK for travellers with children are no worse than in the rest of Europe. **Baby-changing** apparatus is usually available in shopping centres and train stations, while pharmacies and supermarkets stock a useful range of products (shops in rural areas will have less choice). Children aren't allowed in certain **licensed (alcohol-serving) premises**, though this doesn't apply to restaurants, and many pubs and inns have family rooms or beer gardens where children are welcome. Some **B&Bs and hotels** won't accept children under a certain age (usually 12). Under-5s generally travel free on public transport and get in free to attractions; 5–16-year-olds are usually entitled to concessionary rates of up to half the adult rate/fare.

The **websites** ⓦwww.travellingwithchildren.co.uk and www.babygoes2.com offer advice and services.

England

England

London

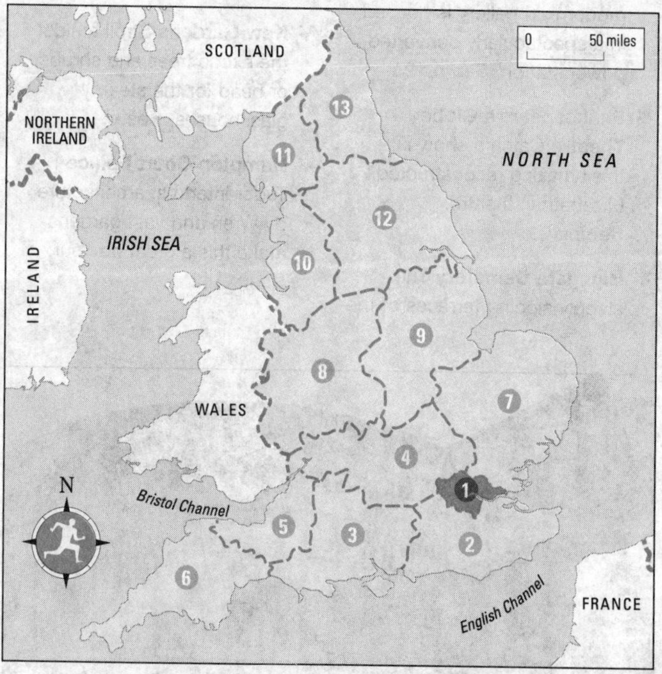

CHAPTER 1

Highlights

* **British Museum** Quite simply one of the world's greatest museums. See p.106
* **London Eye** The universally loved observation wheel is now a key London landmark. See p.121
* **Tate Modern** London's huge modern-art gallery is housed in a spectacularly converted power station. See p.123
* **Shakespeare's Globe Theatre** Catch a show in this amazing reconstructed Elizabethan theatre. See p.123
* **Highgate Cemetery** The steeply sloping terraces of the West Cemetery's overgrown graves are the last word in Victorian Gothic gloom. See p.135
* **Greenwich** Picturesque riverside spot, boasting a weekend market, the National Maritime Museum and old Royal Observatory. See p.136
* **Kew Gardens** Stroll amidst the exotic trees and shrubs, or head for the steamy glasshouses. See p.141
* **Hampton Court Palace** Tudor interiors, architecture by Wren and vast gardens make this a great day out. See p.142

▲ The Globe Theatre

1

London

What strikes visitors more than anything about **LONDON** is the sheer size of the place. Stretching for more than thirty miles east to west, on either side of the River Thames, and with an ethnically diverse population of several million, it's one of the largest cities in Europe. Londoners tend to cope with all this by compartmentalizing the city, identifying with the neighbourhoods in which they work or live, and just making occasional forays into the "centre of town" or "up West", to the West End, London's shopping and entertainment heartland.

Despite Scottish, Welsh and Northern Irish devolution, London still dominates the national horizon, too: this is where the country's news and money are made, it's where the central government resides and, as far as its inhabitants are concerned, provincial life begins beyond the circuit of the city's orbital motorway. Londoners' sense of superiority causes enormous resentment in the regions, yet it's undeniable that the capital has a unique aura of excitement and success – in most walks of British life, if you want to get on, you've got to do it in London.

And it's looking better than it has done for some time, thanks to an investment that has seen virtually all London's world-class **museums**, **galleries** and **institutions** reinvented, from the Royal Opera House to the British Museum. The city boasts the ultramodern art gallery in Tate Modern, the enormous observation wheel, the London Eye, and two fantastic pedestrian bridges that have helped transform the south bank of the Thames into a magnet for visitors and Londoners alike. London's running more smoothly too, thanks to the efforts of Ken Livingstone, mayor since 2000, who's determined to try and solve one of the city's biggest problems – transport. He was also instrumental in helping London win the right to stage the Olympics in 2012, something that will see a large slice of the city's East End transformed over the next five years.

In the meantime, London's **traditional sights** – Big Ben, Westminster Abbey, Buckingham Palace, St Paul's Cathedral and the Tower of London – continue to draw in millions of tourists every year. Monuments from the capital's more glorious past are everywhere to be seen, from medieval banqueting halls and the great churches of Christopher Wren to the eclectic Victorian architecture of the triumphalist British Empire. There is also much enjoyment to be had from the city's quiet Georgian squares, the narrow alleyways of the City of London, the riverside walks, and the quirks of what is still identifiably a collection of villages. Even London's heavy traffic is offset by surprisingly large **expanses of greenery**: Hyde Park, Green Park and St James's Park are all within a few minutes' walk of the West End, while, further afield, you can enjoy the more expansive parklands of Hampstead Heath and Richmond Park.

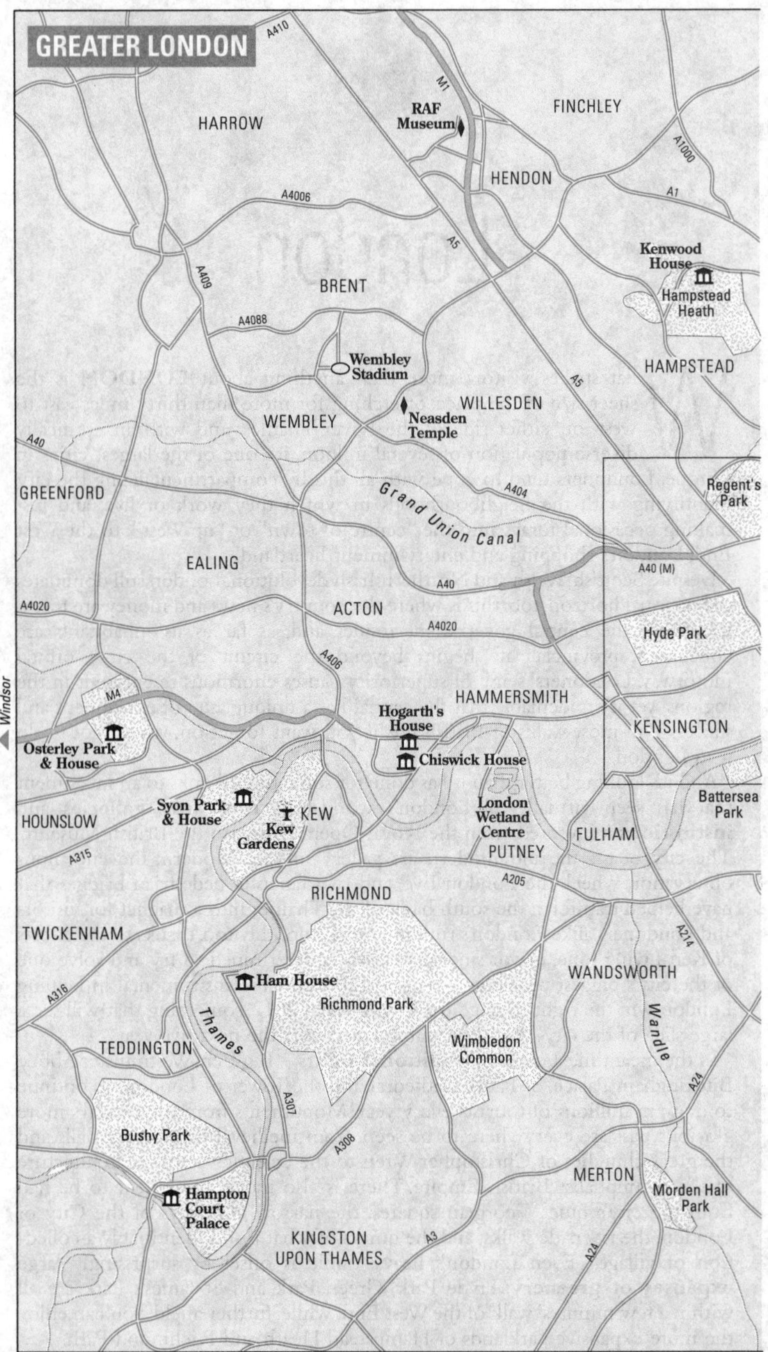
GREATER LONDON
A410
M1
RAF Museum
FINCHLEY
HARROW
A1000
HENDON
A1
A4006
A5
Kenwood House
Hampstead Heath
A409
BRENT
A4088
HAMPSTEAD
Wembley Stadium
A5
WILLESDEN
Neasden Temple
WEMBLEY
A40
Regent's Park
GREENFORD
A404
Grand Union Canal
EALING
A40 (M)
A40
A4020
ACTON
A4020
Hyde Park
A406
Windsor
M4
HAMMERSMITH
Hogarth's House
KENSINGTON
Osterley Park & House
Chiswick House
Syon Park & House
KEW
Kew Gardens
London Wetland Centre
Battersea Park
HOUNSLOW
FULHAM
A315
PUTNEY
A205
RICHMOND
TWICKENHAM
A214
WANDSWORTH
Ham House
A316
Richmond Park
Wandle
Thames
Wimbledon Common
TEDDINGTON
A24
A307
Bushy Park
A308
MERTON
Hampton Court Palace
Morden Hall Park
KINGSTON UPON THAMES
A3
A24

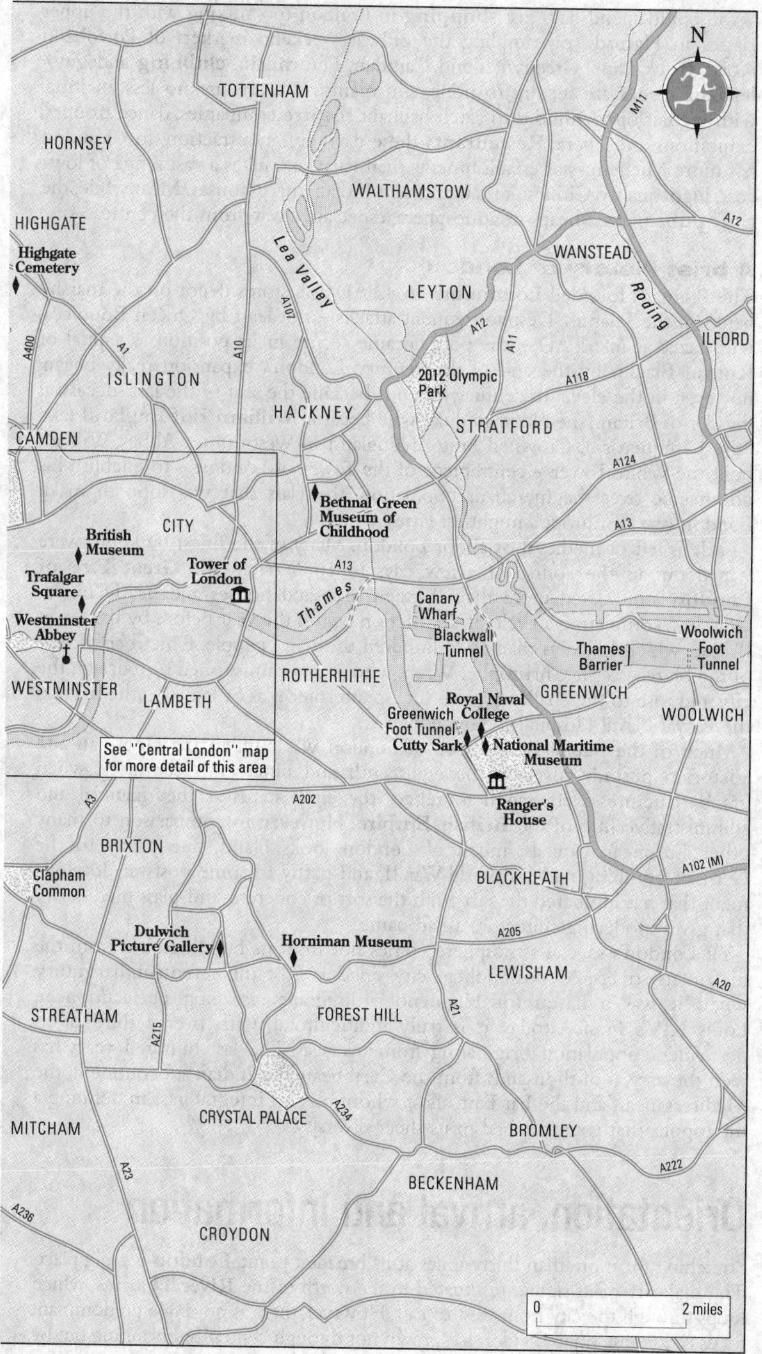
N
TOTTENHAM
HORNSEY
WALTHAMSTOW
HIGHGATE
Highgate Cemetery
Lea Valley
WANSTEAD
Roding
LEYTON
ILFORD
ISLINGTON
2012 Olympic Park
HACKNEY
STRATFORD
CAMDEN
Bethnal Green Museum of Childhood
CITY
British Museum
Tower of London
Trafalgar Square
Thames
Canary Wharf
Westminster Abbey
Blackwall Tunnel
Thames Barrier
Woolwich Foot Tunnel
ROTHERHITHE
WESTMINSTER
LAMBETH
GREENWICH
Royal Naval College
WOOLWICH
Greenwich Foot Tunnel
Cutty Sark
National Maritime Museum
See "Central London" map for more detail of this area
Ranger's House
BRIXTON
BLACKHEATH
Clapham Common
Dulwich Picture Gallery
Horniman Museum
LEWISHAM
STREATHAM
FOREST HILL
MITCHAM
CRYSTAL PALACE
BROMLEY
BECKENHAM
CROYDON
M11
A12
A107
A11
A118
A400
A1
A10
A124
A13
A202
A3
A102 (M)
A205
A20
A21
A215
A234
A222
A23
A236
0
2 miles

You could spend days just **shopping** in London too, mixing with the upper classes in Harrods, or sampling the offbeat weekend markets of Portobello Road, Brick Lane, Greenwich and Camden. The **music**, **clubbing** and **gay/lesbian** scenes are second to none, and mainstream arts are no less exciting, with regular opportunities to catch brilliant **theatre** companies, dance troupes, exhibitions and opera. **Restaurants** these days, are an attraction, too. London has more Michelin-star establishments than Paris, as well as a vast range of low-cost, high-quality Chinese restaurants and Indian curry houses. Meanwhile, the city's **pubs** possess heaps of atmosphere, especially away from the centre.

A brief history of London

The Romans founded **Londinium** in 43 AD as a stores depot on the marshy banks of the Thames. Despite frequent attacks – not least by Queen Boudicca, who razed it in 61 AD – the port became secure in its position as capital of Roman Britain by the end of the century. London's expansion really began, however, in the eleventh century, when it became the seat of the last successful invader of Britain, the Norman duke who became **William I of England** (aka "the Conqueror"). Crowned king of England in Westminster Abbey, William built the White Tower – centrepiece of the Tower of London – to establish his dominance over the merchant population, the class that was soon to make London one of Europe's mightiest cities.

Little is left of medieval or Tudor London. Many of the finest buildings were wiped out in the course of a few days in 1666 when the **Great Fire of London** annihilated more than thirteen thousand houses and nearly ninety churches, completing a cycle of destruction begun the year before by the Great Plague, which killed as many as a hundred thousand people. Chief beneficiary of the blaze was Sir Christopher Wren, who was commissioned to redesign the city and rose to the challenge with such masterpieces as St Paul's Cathedral and the Royal Naval Hospital in Greenwich.

Much of the public architecture of London was built in the Georgian and Victorian periods covering the eighteenth and nineteenth centuries, when grand structures were raised to reflect the city's status as the financial and administrative hub of the **British Empire**. However, in comparison to many other European capitals, much of London looks bland, due partly to the German bombing raids in World War II, and partly to some postwar development that has lumbered the city with the sort of concrete-and-glass mediocrity that gives modern architecture a bad name.

Yet London's special atmosphere comes not from its buildings, but from the life on its streets. A cosmopolitan city since at least the seventeenth century, when it was a haven for Huguenot immigrants escaping persecution in Louis XIV's France, today it is truly multicultural, with over a third of its permanent population originating from overseas. The last hundred years has seen the arrival of thousands from the Caribbean, the Indian subcontinent, the Mediterranean and the Far East, all of whom play an integral part in defining a metropolis that is unmatched in its sheer diversity.

Orientation, arrival and information

Stretching for more than thirty miles at its broadest point, **London** is a big place. The majority of its sights are situated to the north of the **River Thames**, which loops through the city from west to east. However, there is no single predominant focus of interest, since London has grown not through centralized planning but by a process of agglomeration – villages and urban developments that once surrounded the core are now lost within the amorphous mass of Greater London.

Westminster, the country's royal, political and ecclesiastical power base for centuries, was once a separate city. The grand streets and squares to the north of Westminster, from **St James's** to **Covent Garden**, were built as residential suburbs after the Restoration, and are now the city's shopping and entertainment zones known collectively as the **West End**. To the east, is the original City of London – known simply as **The City** – founded by the Romans, and now one of the world's great financial centres.

It's worth exploring south of the Thames: including the **London Eye**, the **South Bank Centre**, London's concrete culture bunker and the **Tate Modern** art gallery. In the suburbs, the **museums** of South Kensington are a must, as are literary Hampstead and Highgate, either side of half-wild **Hampstead Heath**, and **Greenwich**, with its nautical associations, royal park and observatory. Finally, there are plenty of rewarding day-trips along the Thames from **Chiswick** to **Windsor**, most notably to Hampton Court Palace and Windsor Castle.

Arrival

Flying into London, you'll arrive at one of the capital's five **international airports**: Heathrow, Gatwick, Stansted, Luton or City Airport, all of which are less than an hour from the city centre.

Heathrow (Ⓣ0870/000 0123, Ⓦwww.baa.co.uk), fifteen miles west of the city centre, has five terminals and three train/tube stations: one for terminals 1, 2 and 3, and separate ones for terminals 4 and 5. The high-speed **Heathrow Express** (Ⓦwww.heathrowexpress.com) trains travel non-stop to Paddington Station (every 15min; 15–20min) for £28 return (£1 less if you book online, £2 more if you buy your ticket on board). A much cheaper alternative is to take the **Piccadilly Underground line** into central London (every 5–9min; 50min) for £4 one-way. If you plan to make several sightseeing journeys on your arrival day, buy a Travelcard or top up an Oyster card at the station (see p.83). National Express run **bus services** (Ⓦwww.nationalexpress.com) from Heathrow direct to Victoria Coach Station (daily every 20–30min 5am–9.30pm; 40min–1hr), which cost £4 single, £8 return. From midnight, you can take **night bus** #N9 (every 30min; 1hr) from Heathrow to Trafalgar Square for £2.

Gatwick (Ⓣ0870/000 2468, Ⓦwww.baa.co.uk) is around thirty miles to the south of London: the non-stop **Gatwick Express** (Ⓦwww.gatwickexpress.com) trains run between the airport's South Terminal and Victoria Station (every 15min; 30min) for £27 return. Other train options include the **Southern** services to Victoria (every 15–20min; 40min) for £9 one-way, or **Thameslink** to King's Cross (every 15–30min; 30min) for around £10 one-way.

Stansted (Ⓣ0870/000 0303, Ⓦwww.baa.co.uk) lies roughly 35 miles northeast of the capital, and is served by the **Stansted Express** (Ⓦwww.stanstedexpress.co.uk) to Walthamstow Station and Liverpool Street (every 15–30min; 45min to Liverpool Street), which costs £25.50 return. National Express **Airbus #6** runs 24 hours a day to Victoria Coach Station (every 30min; 1hr 30min), and costs £10 single, £15 return; Terravision (Ⓦwww.lowcostcoach.com) also run coaches to Victoria and Liverpool Street, (every 30min) for £8 single, £14 return.

Luton (Ⓣ01582/405100, Ⓦwww.london-luton.com) is roughly thirty miles north of the city centre, and mostly handles charter flights. A **free shuttle bus** takes five minutes to transport passengers to Luton Airport Parkway station, connected by train (every 15min; 30–40min) to St Pancras, King's Cross and other stations in central London; tickets cost £10 single. Alternatively, **Green Line** bus #757 and Terravision run from Luton to

Victoria Station (every 30min; 1hr 15min), costing around £10 single. From late spring to early autumn, **Easybus** (ⓦwww.easybus.co.uk) also runs coach services every 45 minutes to near Baker Street tube for a bargain fare of just £8 single, or as little as £2 if you book in advance online.

City Airport (ⓣ020/7646 0000, ⓦwww.londoncityairport.com), London's smallest, used primarily by business folk, is situated in Docklands, ten miles east of central London. The **Docklands Light Railway** (DLR) will take you straight to Bank in the City (20min), where you can change to the tube; tickets cost around £4.

Eurostar trains arrive at **St Pancras International**, north of the centre, next door to King's Cross. Arriving by train (ⓣ08457/484950, ⓦwww.nationalrail.co.uk) from elsewhere in Britain, you'll come into one of London's numerous main-line stations, all of which have adjacent Underground stations linking into the city centre's tube network. Coming into London **by coach** (ⓣ0870/580 8080, ⓦwww.nationalexpress.com), you're most likely to arrive at **Victoria Coach Station**, a couple of hundred yards south down Buckingham Palace Road from the train and Underground stations of the same name.

Information

The main tourist office in London is the **London Visitor Centre**, near Piccadilly Circus at 1 Regent St (Mon 9.30am–6.30pm, Tues–Fri 9am–6.30pm, Sat & Sun 10am–4pm; June–Sept same times except Sat 9am–5pm; ⓦwww.visitbritain.com); there's also a tiny information window in the tickets kiosk on Leicester Square (Mon–Fri 8am–11pm, Sat & Sun 11am–6pm; ⓦwww.visitlondon.com). Individual boroughs also run tourist offices, the most central one is on the south side of St Paul's Cathedral (May–Sept daily 9.30am–5pm; Oct–April Mon–Fri 9.30am–5pm; ⓣ020/7332 1456, ⓦwww.cityoflondon.gov.uk).

London: The Rough Guide Map is a comprehensive full-colour, waterproof and non-tearable map detailing restaurants, bars, shops and visitor attractions. If you want to find your way around every nook and cranny of the city you'll need to invest in either an *A–Z Atlas* or a *Nicholson Streetfinder*, both of which have a street index covering every street in the capital. You can get them at most bookshops and newsagents for less than £5.

The only comprehensive and critical weekly **listings** magazine is *Time Out*, which costs £2.80 and comes out every Tuesday afternoon. In it you'll find details of all the latest exhibitions, shows, films, music, sport, guided walks and events in and around the capital.

City transport

London's transport network is among the most complex and expensive in the world. **Transport for London** (TfL) provides excellent free maps and details of bus and tube services from its **travel information** offices: the main one is at Piccadilly Circus tube station (Mon–Sat 7.15am–9pm, Sun 8.15am–8pm), and there are other desks at Heathrow and various tube and train stations. There's also a 24-hour phone line for information on all bus and tube services ⓣ020/7222 1234 and a website ⓦwww.tfl.gov.uk. One word of warning – avoid travelling during the **rush hour** (Mon–Fri 8–9.30am & 5–7pm), when tubes become unbearably crowded (the lack of air conditioning doesn't help), and some buses get so full they literally won't let you on.

Travelcards

To get the best value out of the transport system, buy a **Travelcard**. Available from machines and booths at all tube and train stations, and at some newsagents (look for the sign), these are valid for the bus, tube, Docklands Light Railway, Tramlink and suburban rail networks. **Day Travelcards** come in two varieties: Off-Peak – which are valid after 9.30am on weekdays and all day during the weekend – and Peak. A Day Travelcard (Off-Peak), costs £5.10 for the central zones 1 and 2, rising to £6.70 for zones 1–6 (including Heathrow); the Day Travelcard (Peak) starts at £6.60 for zones 1 and 2. A **3-Day Travelcard** costs £16.40 for zones 1 and 2, but is obviously only worth it if you need to travel during peak hours; **Weekly Travelcards** are much more economical, beginning at £23.20 for zones 1 and 2. **Children** under 5 travel free at all times; under-11s travel free on all forms of transport (off-peak) and under-14s travel free on all buses and trams. All-zone Off-Peak Day Travelcards for under-16s cost £2, or if they're traveling with an adult, just £1.

Since the introduction of the **Oyster card**, London's transport smartcard, most Londoners don't bother with paper tickets any more. However, they are only really worth it if you are staying in London longer than a week; for more details see the TfL website.

Except for very short journeys, the fastest way of moving around the city is by **Underground** or tube, as it's known to all Londoners. The eleven different tube lines cross much of the metropolis, although London south of the river is not very well covered. Each line has its own colour and name – all you need to know is which direction you're travelling in: northbound, eastbound, southbound or westbound. Services operate from around 5.30am Monday to Saturday, until 12.30am and from 7.30am on Sundays until 11.30pm; you rarely have to wait more than five minutes for a train from central stations. **Tickets** must be bought in advance; if you're caught without a valid ticket, you'll be charged an on-the-spot Penalty Fare of £20. A single journey in the central zone costs an unbelievable £4, so if you're intending to travel about a bit, a Travelcard is a much better bet (see box above).

London's famous red **double-decker buses** are fun to ride on, but tend to get stuck in traffic jams, which prevent them running to a regular timetable. In central London, and on all the extra-long "bendy buses", you must **have a valid ticket before boarding** either a Travelcard, Oyster card or one from the machines at the bus stop. Tickets for all bus journeys cost a flat fare of £2. Another option is a **One-Day Bus Pass**, which costs £3.50 for adults and can be used on all buses anytime anywhere in London. Some buses run a 24-hour service, but most run between about 5am and midnight, with a network of **Night Buses** (prefixed with the letter "N") operating outside this period. Night bus routes radiate out from Trafalgar Square at approximately twenty-to thirty-minute intervals, more frequently on some routes and on Friday and Saturday nights. All stops are treated as request stops, so you must signal to get the bus to stop, and press the bell in order to get off.

Large areas of London's suburbs are best reached by the **suburban train** network (Travelcards valid). Wherever a sight can only be reached by overground train, we've indicated the nearest train station and the central terminus from which you can depart.

Boat services on the Thames are much improved, but they still do not form part of an integrated public transport system. As a result fares are quite expensive, with Travelcards currently only giving the holders a 33 percent discount on tickets. Typical **fares** are £6 single, £7 return Westminster to the Tower or £7 single,

Congestion charge

All vehicles entering central London on weekdays between 7am and 6.30pm are liable to a **congestion charge** of £8 per vehicle. Drivers can pay for the charge online, over the phone and at garages and shops, and must do so before 10pm the same day or incur a surcharge. The congestion-charging zone is bounded by Marylebone and Euston roads in the north, Commercial Street and Tower Bridge in the east, Kennington Lane and the river in the south, and Earl's Court Road in the west. For the latest visit Ⓦwww.cclondon.com.

£9 return Westminster to Greenwich – £9.50 will buy you an unlimited hop-on, hop-off ticket. **Timetables** and services are complex, and there are numerous companies and small charter operators – for a full list pick up a booklet from a TfL information office, phone Ⓣ020/7222 1234 or visit Ⓦwww.tfl.gov.uk.

Compared to many capital cities, London's metered **black cabs** are an expensive option unless there are three or more of you – a ride from Euston to Victoria, for example, costs around £12–15 (Mon–Fri 6am–8pm). After 8pm on weekdays and all day during the weekend, a higher tariff applies, and after 10pm, a much higher one. A yellow light over the windscreen tells you if the cab is available – just stick your arm out to hail it. To order a black cab in advance, phone Ⓣ0871/871 8710, and be prepared to pay an extra £2.

Minicabs look just like regular cars and are considerably cheaper than black cabs, but the best way to pick a company is to take the advice of the place you're at, unless you want to be certain of a woman driver, in which case call Ladycabs (Ⓣ020/7272 3300), or a gay/lesbian-friendly driver, in which case call Liberty Cars (Ⓣ020/7734 1313).

Last, and definitely least, there are usually plenty of **bicycle taxis** available for hire in the West End. The oldest and biggest of the bunch are Bugbugs (Ⓣ020/7620 0500, Ⓦwww.bugbugs.co.uk), who have over fifty rickshaws operating Monday to Saturday from 7pm until the early hours of the morning. The rickshaws take up to three passengers and fares are negotiable, though they should work out at around £5 per person per mile.

Accommodation

There's no getting away from the fact that **accommodation** in London is expensive. The city's hostels are among the most costly in the world, while venerable institutions such as the *Ritz*, the *Dorchester* and the *Savoy* charge guests the very top international prices – from £300 per luxurious night.

The cheapest places to stay are the city's **campsites**, some of which also have dormitories, charging as little as £6 a night. A dorm bed in an independent

London postcodes

A brief word on **London postcodes**: the name of each street is followed by a letter giving the geographical location (E for "east", WC for "west central" and so on) and a number that specifies the postal area. However, this is not a reliable indication of the remoteness of the locale – W5, for example, lies beyond the more remote sounding NW10 – so it's always best to check a map before taking a room in what may sound like a fairly central area.

hostel will cost you double that, while official YHA hostels will charge £20 or more. Even the most basic **B&Bs** struggle to bring their tariffs down to £45 for a double with shared facilities, and you're more likely to find yourself paying £60 or more. For a decent **hotel** room, you shouldn't expect much change out of £100 a night.

All London tourist offices (listed on p.82) operate a room-booking service, for which a small fee is levied (they also take the first night's fee in advance). The **British Hotel Reservation Centre** (BHRC; Ⓦwww.bhrc.co.uk) desks at Heathrow, Gatwick and Victoria train and coach stations don't charge a fee for booking rooms, and most of their offices are open daily from 6am till midnight. You can also book for free **online** at Ⓦwww.londontown.com; payment is made directly to the hotel on checking out and they can offer discounts of up to fifty percent.

Hotels and B&Bs

With **hotels** you get less for your money in London than elsewhere in the country – generally breakfasts are more meagre and rooms more spartan than in similarly priced places in the provinces. Whatever the time of year, you should phone as far in advance as you can if you want to stay within a couple of tube stops of the West End. When choosing your **area**, bear in mind that the West End – Soho, Covent Garden, St James's, Mayfair and Marylebone – and the western districts of Knightsbridge and Kensington are dominated by expensive, upmarket hotels, whereas Bloomsbury is both inexpensive and very central. For cheaper rooms, the widest choice is close to the main train termini of Victoria and Paddington, and amongst the budget B&Bs of Earl's Court. Where possible, we've marked the following on the maps in this chapter.

St James's, Mayfair and Marylebone

Edward Lear 28–30 Seymour St, W1 Ⓣ020/7402 5401, Ⓦwww.edlear.com; Marble Arch tube. See map, pp.132–133. Lear's former home enjoys a great location close to Oxford St and Hyde Park, with lovely flower boxes and a plush foyer. Rooms themselves need a bit of a makeover, but the low prices reflect both this and the fact that most only have shared facilities. ④

Lincoln House 33 Gloucester Place, W1 Ⓣ020/7486 7630, Ⓦwww.lincoln-house-hotel.co.uk; Marble Arch or Baker Street tube. See map, pp.132–133. Dark wood panelling gives this Georgian B&B in Marylebone a ship's-cabin feel, while all the rooms are en suite and well equipped. Rates vary according to the size of the bed and length of stay. ⑤

Wigmore Court 23 Gloucester Place, W1 Ⓣ020/7935 0928, Ⓦwww.wigmore-court-hotel.co.uk; Marble Arch or Baker Street tube. See map, pp.132–133. The decor may not be to everyone's taste, but this Georgian townhouse is a better-than-average B&B, boasting a high tally of returning clients. Comfortable rooms with en-suite facilities, plus two cheaper doubles with shared facilities. Also a laundry and basic kitchen for guests' use. ⑦

Soho, Covent Garden and Holborn

The Fielding 4 Broad Court, Bow St, WC2 Ⓣ020/7836 8305, Ⓦwww.the-fielding-hotel.co.uk; Covent Garden tube. See map, pp.92–93. Quietly and perfectly situated on a traffic-free and gaslit court, this excellent hotel is one of Covent Garden's hidden gems. Its en-suite rooms are a firm favourite with visiting performers, since it's just a few yards from the Royal Opera House. Breakfast is extra. ⑥

Hazlitt's 6 Frith St, W1 Ⓣ020/7434 1771, Ⓦwww.hazlittshotel.com; Tottenham Court Road tube. See map, pp.92–93. Located off the south side of Soho Square, this early eighteenth-century building is a hotel of real character and charm, offering en-suite rooms decorated and furnished as close to period style as convenience and comfort allow. There's a small sitting room, but no dining room; continental breakfast (served in the rooms) is extra. ⑨

St Martin's Lane 45 St Martin's Lane, WC2 Ⓣ020/7300 5500, Ⓦwww.morganshotelgroup.com; Leicester Square tube. See map, pp.92–93. This self-consciously chic boutique hotel, with a bafflingly anonymous glassed facade, is a big hit with the media crowd. The *Light Bar* is the most startling of the hotel's eating and drinking outlets.

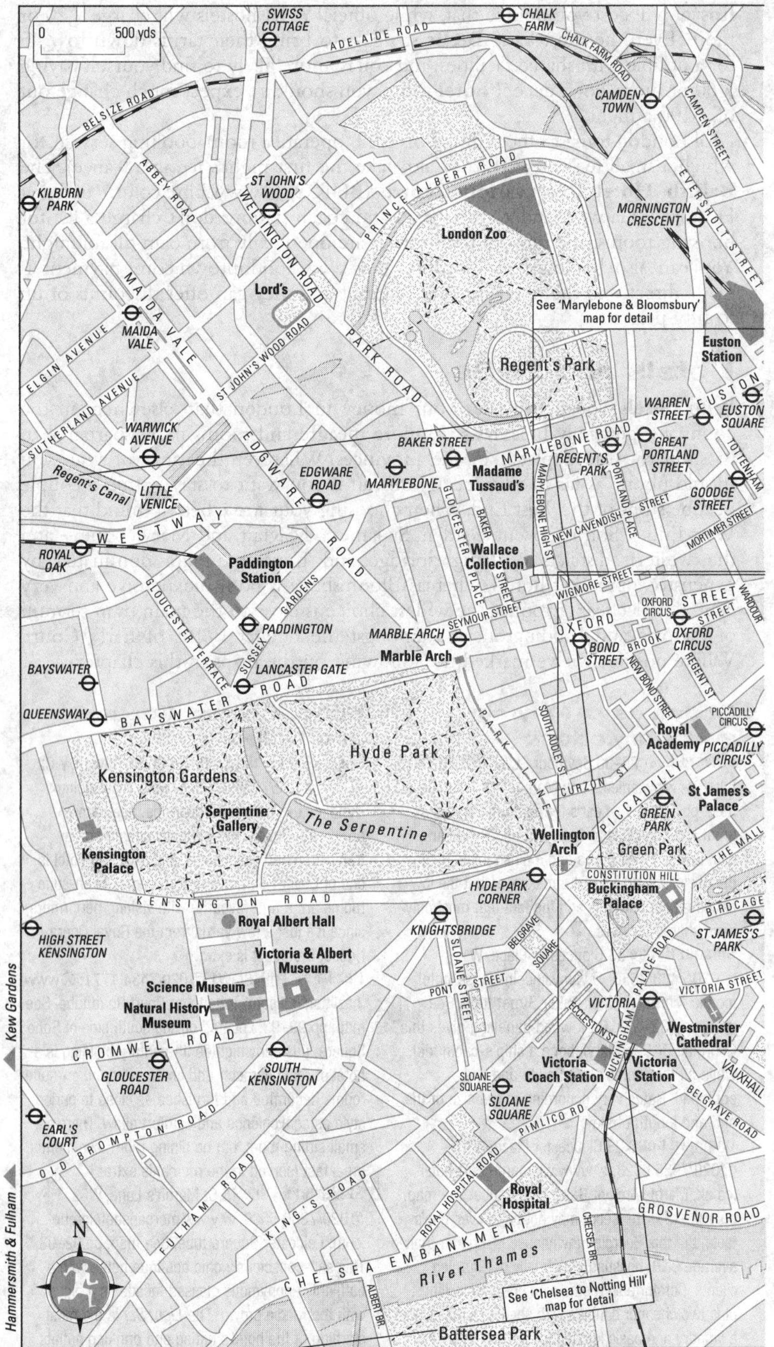
0 500 yds
SWISS COTTAGE
CHALK FARM
ADELAIDE ROAD
CHALK FARM ROAD
CAMDEN TOWN
CAMDEN STREET
BELSIZE ROAD
ABBEY ROAD
PRINCE ALBERT ROAD
EVERSHOLT STREET
KILBURN PARK
ST JOHN'S WOOD
WELLINGTON ROAD
London Zoo
MORNINGTON CRESCENT
MAIDA VALE
Lord's
See 'Marylebone & Bloomsbury' map for detail
ELGIN AVENUE
ST JOHN'S WOOD ROAD
PARK ROAD
Regent's Park
Euston Station
SUTHERLAND AVENUE
WARREN STREET
EUSTON
EUSTON SQUARE
WARWICK AVENUE
BAKER STREET
MARYLEBONE ROAD
GREAT PORTLAND STREET
TOTTENHAM
Regent's Canal
EDGWARE
Madame Tussaud's
REGENT'S PARK
LITTLE VENICE
EDGWARE ROAD
MARYLEBONE
GLOUCESTER PLACE
MARYLEBONE HIGH ST
PORTLAND PLACE
GOODGE STREET
WESTWAY
BAKER STREET
NEW CAVENDISH STREET
MORTIMER STREET
ROYAL OAK
Paddington Station
ROAD
Wallace Collection
GLOUCESTER TERRACE
GARDENS
WIGMORE STREET
OXFORD CIRCUS
OXFORD STREET
WARDOUR
PADDINGTON
SEYMOUR STREET
MARBLE ARCH
OXFORD
Marble Arch
BOND STREET
BROOK STREET
OXFORD CIRCUS
SUSSEX GARDENS
BAYSWATER
LANCASTER GATE
REGENT ST
NEW BOND STREET
BAYSWATER ROAD
QUEENSWAY
PARK LANE
SOUTH AUDLEY ST
PICCADILLY CIRCUS
Royal Academy
PICCADILLY CIRCUS
Hyde Park
Kensington Gardens
CURZON ST
PICCADILLY
St James's Palace
Serpentine Gallery
The Serpentine
GREEN PARK
Wellington Arch
Green Park
THE MALL
Kensington Palace
CONSTITUTION HILL
HYDE PARK CORNER
Buckingham Palace
KENSINGTON ROAD
BIRDCAGE
Royal Albert Hall
KNIGHTSBRIDGE
ST JAMES'S PARK
HIGH STREET KENSINGTON
SLOANE STREET
BELGRAVE SQUARE
Victoria & Albert Museum
PALACE ROAD
Science Museum
PONT STREET
VICTORIA STREET
Natural History Museum
VICTORIA
ECCLESTON ST
BUCKINGHAM
Westminster Cathedral
CROMWELL ROAD
Victoria Coach Station
Victoria Station
VAUXHALL
SOUTH KENSINGTON
GLOUCESTER ROAD
SLOANE SQUARE
SLOANE SQUARE
BELGRAVE ROAD
EARL'S COURT
OLD BROMPTON ROAD
PIMLICO RD
ROYAL HOSPITAL ROAD
Royal Hospital
FULHAM ROAD
KING'S ROAD
GROSVENOR ROAD
CHELSEA BR.
N
CHELSEA EMBANKMENT
River Thames
ALBERT BR.
See 'Chelsea to Notting Hill' map for detail
Battersea Park
Kew Gardens
Hammersmith & Fulham

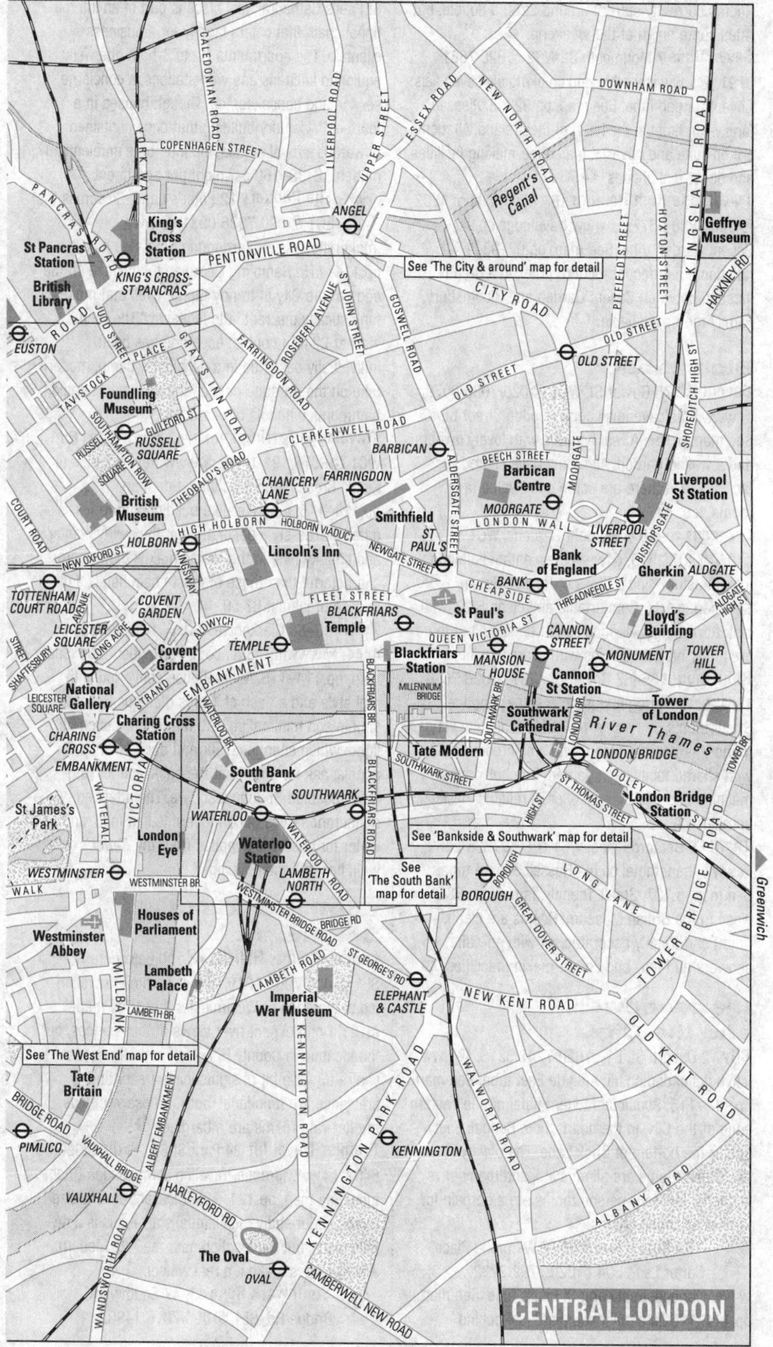
CALEDONIAN ROAD
LIVERPOOL ROAD
UPPER STREET
ESSEX ROAD
NEW NORTH ROAD
DOWNHAM ROAD
KINGSLAND ROAD
COPENHAGEN STREET
YORK WAY
PANCRAS ROAD
Regent's Canal
ANGEL
King's Cross Station
St Pancras Station
KING'S CROSS-ST PANCRAS
British Library
PENTONVILLE ROAD
See 'The City & around' map for detail
Geffrye Museum
PITFIELD STREET
HOXTON STREET
HACKNEY RD
CITY ROAD
ST JOHN STREET
GOSWELL ROAD
ROSEBERY AVENUE
FARRINGDON ROAD
OLD STREET
SHOREDITCH HIGH ST
EUSTON
ROAD
JUDD STREET
PLACE
TAVISTOCK
GRAY'S INN ROAD
Foundling Museum
GUILFORD ST
SOUTHAMPTON ROW
RUSSELL SQUARE
CLERKENWELL ROAD
BARBICAN
BEECH STREET
MOORGATE
Barbican Centre
Liverpool St Station
THEOBALD'S ROAD
CHANCERY LANE
FARRINGDON
ALDERSGATE STREET
British Museum
COURT ROAD
Smithfield
LONDON WALL
LIVERPOOL STREET
BISHOPSGATE
HIGH HOLBORN
HOLBORN VIADUCT
HOLBORN
ST PAUL'S
NEWGATE STREET
Lincoln's Inn
KINGSWAY
NEW OXFORD ST
Bank of England
Gherkin
ALDGATE
ALDGATE HIGH ST
TOTTENHAM COURT ROAD
FLEET STREET
BANK
CHEAPSIDE
THREADNEEDLE ST
COVENT GARDEN
LEICESTER SQUARE
AVENUE
LONG ACRE
BLACKFRIARS
Temple
St Paul's
Lloyd's Building
ALDWYCH
QUEEN VICTORIA ST
CANNON STREET
SHAFTESBURY
TEMPLE
Covent Garden
Blackfriars Station
MANSION HOUSE
MONUMENT
TOWER HILL
EMBANKMENT
National Gallery
STRAND
BLACKFRIARS BR.
MILLENNIUM BRIDGE
Cannon St Station
SOUTHWARK BR.
LONDON BR.
Tower of London
Charing Cross Station
WATERLOO BR.
Southwark Cathedral
River Thames
CHARING CROSS
LONDON BRIDGE
TOWER BR.
Tate Modern
EMBANKMENT
VICTORIA
SOUTHWARK STREET
TOOLEY ST
South Bank Centre
ST THOMAS STREET
London Bridge Station
WHITEHALL
BLACKFRIARS ROAD
SOUTHWARK
HIGH ST
St James's Park
WATERLOO
WATERLOO ROAD
See 'Bankside & Southwark' map for detail
London Eye
Waterloo Station
See 'The South Bank' map for detail
Greenwich
WESTMINSTER
LAMBETH NORTH
BOROUGH
LONG LANE
WALK
WESTMINSTER BR.
WESTMINSTER BRIDGE ROAD
GREAT DOVER STREET
Houses of Parliament
BRIDGE RD
TOWER BRIDGE ROAD
Westminster Abbey
MILLBANK
Lambeth Palace
LAMBETH ROAD
ST GEORGE'S RD
Imperial War Museum
ELEPHANT & CASTLE
NEW KENT ROAD
LAMBETH BR.
See 'The West End' map for detail
KENNINGTON ROAD
OLD KENT ROAD
Tate Britain
WALWORTH ROAD
BRIDGE ROAD
PIMLICO
VAUXHALL BRIDGE
ALBERT EMBANKMENT
KENNINGTON PARK ROAD
KENNINGTON
VAUXHALL
HARLEYFORD RD
ALBANY ROAD
The Oval
OVAL
WANDSWORTH ROAD
CAMBERWELL NEW ROAD
CENTRAL LONDON
Lambeth

Rooms currently start at around £250 a double, but rates come down at the weekend. ⑨

Seven Dials 7 Monmouth St, WC2 ⓣ020/7681 0791, ⓦwww.smoothhound.co.uk/hotels/sevendials; Covent Garden tube. See map, pp.92–93. Pleasant family-run hotel in the heart of theatreland. All rooms are en suite and have TV, tea/coffee-making facilities and direct-dial phones. ④

Travelodge High Holborn 166 High Holborn, WC2 ⓣ020/7836 0877, ⓦwww.travelodge.co.uk; Covent Garden tube. See map, pp.92–93. A functional but decent modern hotel, in a dream location between Covent Garden and Bloomsbury. Family rooms available. ⑥

Bloomsbury

Cavendish 75 Gower St, WC1 ⓣ020/7636 9079, ⓦwww.hotelcavendish.com; Goodge Street tube. See map, p.107. A real bargain, with lovely owners and a walled garden. All rooms have shared facilities, and there are some good-value family rooms, too. ②

Crescent 49–50 Cartwright Gardens, WC1 ⓣ020/7387 1515, ⓦwww.crescenthoteloflondon.com; Euston, King's Cross or Russell Square tube. See map, p.107. Comfortable and clean B&B, with pink furnishings. All doubles are en suite, but there are a few bargain singles with shared facilities. ⑥

Ridgemount 65–67 Gower St, WC1 ⓣ020/7636 1141, ⓦwww.ridgemounthotel.co.uk; Goodge Street tube. See map, p.107. Old-fashioned, very friendly, family-run place, with small rooms, half with shared facilities, a garden, free hot-drinks machine and a laundry service. A reliable, basic bargain. ③

Thanet 8 Bedford Place, WC1 ⓣ020/7636 2869, ⓦwww.thanethotel.co.uk; Russell Square tube. See map, p.107. Small, friendly, family-run B&B close to the British Museum. Rooms are clean, bright and freshly decorated, all with en-suite showers and tea- and coffee-making facilities. ⑥

Clerkwenwell and the City

City 12 Osborn St, E1 ⓣ020/7247 3313, ⓦwww.cityhotellondon.co.uk; Aldgate East tube. See map, pp.114–115. Spacious modern hotel on the eastern edge of the City, in the heart of the Bengali East End at the bottom of Brick Lane. The plainly decorated rooms are all en suite, and many have kitchens, too; four-person rooms are a bargain for families or small groups. ⑤

The King's Wardrobe 6 Wardrobe Place, Carter Lane EC4 ⓣ020/7792 2222, ⓦwww.bridgestreet.com; St Paul's tube. See map, pp.114–115. In a quiet courtyard just behind St Paul's Cathedral, this place is part of an international chain that caters largely for a business clientele. The apartments (1- to 3-bed) offer fully equipped kitchens and workstations, a concierge service and housekeeping. Though housed in a fourteenth-century building that once contained Edward III's royal regalia, the interior is unrelentingly modern. £130–160 per night per apartment. ⑦

The Rookery 12 Peter's Lane, Cowcross St, EC1 ⓣ020/7336 0931, ⓦwww.rookeryhotel.com; Farringdon tube. See map, pp.114–115. Rambling Georgian townhouse on the edge of the City in trendy Clerkenwell that makes a fantastically discreet little hideaway. The rooms start at £245 a double; each one has been individually designed in a deliciously camp, modern take on the Baroque period, and all have splendid bathrooms with lots of character. ⑨

Travelodge Farringdon 10–42 King's Cross Rd, WC1 ⓣ0870/191 1774, ⓦwww.travelodge.co.uk; King's Cross/Farringdon tube. See map, pp.114–115. A bunker-like building and rather dated 1970s-style decor, though the swirly plaster and chunky pine in the rooms makes them more characterful than those of most chain hotels. Full English breakfast £7.50. ④

Zetter 86–88 Clerkenwell Rd, EC1 ⓣ020/7324 4444, ⓦwww.thezetter.com; Farringdon tube. See map, pp.114–115. A warehouse converted with real style and a dash of 1960s glamour. Rooms are simple and minimalist, with fun touches such as lights which change colour and decorative floral panels; ask for a room at the back, overlooking quiet, cobbled St John's Square. The attached restaurant serves good modern Italian food, and water for guests is supplied from the *Zetter's* own well, beneath the building. ⑦

South Bank and Southwark

London County Hall Travel Inn Belvedere Rd, SE1 ⓣ020/7902 1619, ⓦwww.premiertravelinn.com; Waterloo or Westminster tube. See map, p.121. Don't expect river views at these prices, but the location in County Hall itself is pretty good if you're up for a bit of sightseeing. Decor and ambience are functional, but for those with kids, the flat-rate rooms are a bargain. ⑥

Premier Travel Inn 34 Park St SE1 ⓣ0870/990 6402, ⓦwww.premiertravelinn.com; London Bridge tube. See map, pp.124–125. Pleasant decent-sized rooms and friendly multilingual staff – this is a no-frills place, but the location near the Tate Modern and low rates make it a real winner. ⑤

Southwark Rose 43–47 Southwark Bridge Rd, SE1 ⓣ020/7015 1490,

ⓦwww.southwarkrosehotel.co.uk; London Bridge tube. See map, pp.124–125. The *Southwark Rose* markets itself as a budget hotel with boutique style, and nice design touches raise the rooms several notches above the bland chain hotels in the area. Giant aluminium lamps hover over the lobby, which is lined with funky photographs, while the penthouse restaurant offers breakfast with a rooftop view and free Internet access. ⑦

Victoria

B&B Belgravia 64–66 Ebury St, SW1 ⓣ020/7823 4928, ⓦwww.bb-belgravia.com; Victoria tube. See map, pp.92–93. A real rarity in this neck of the woods – a B&B with flair, very close to the train and coach station. The 17 rooms are of boutique-hotel quality, with original cornicing and large sash windows and have stylish modern touches – all have flat-screen TVs and funky bathrooms with mosaic tiling. Staff are welcoming and enthusiastic. Free in-room Internet access. ⑥

Morgan House 107 & 120 Ebury St, SW1 ⓣ020/7730 2384, ⓦwww.morganhouse.co.uk; Victoria tube. See map, pp.132–133. An above-average B&B, run by a vivacious couple. Great breakfasts, patio garden, and a fridge for guests to use. Most rooms are en suite. ⑤

Sanctuary House 33 Tothill St, SW1 ⓣ020/7799 4044, ⓦwww.fullershotels.co.uk; St James's Park tube. See map, pp.92–93. Run by Fuller's Brewery, situated above a Fuller's pub, and decked out like one too, in gaudy pseudo-Victoriana. Breakfast is extra, and is served in the pub, but the location right by St James's Park is terrific. Ask about the weekend deals. ⑦

Paddington, Bayswater and Notting Hill

Columbia 95–99 Lancaster Gate, W2 ⓣ020/7402 0021, ⓦwww.columbiahotel.co.uk; Lancaster Gate tube. See map, pp.132–133. This large hotel, once five Victorian houses, offers simply decorated rooms, some with views over Hyde Park, as well as a spacious public lounge with a vaguely Art Deco feel and a cocktail bar. Rooms are en suite. ⑤

The Pavilion 34–36 Sussex Gardens, W2 ⓣ020/7262 0905, ⓦwww.pavilionhoteluk.com; Paddington tube. See map, pp.132–133. A decadent rock star's home from home, with outrageously over-the-top decor and every room individually themed, from "honky tonk Afro" to "Highland Fling". ⑥

Portobello Gold 95–97 Portobello Rd, W11 ⓣ020/7460 4900, ⓦwww.portobellogold.com; Notting Hill Gate or Holland Park tube. See map, pp.132–133. A fun and friendly option – six rooms and an apartment above a cheery modern pub. Rooms are plain and some are tiny, with miniature en-suite bathrooms, but all are fairly priced. The apartment is a brilliant option for a group – it sleeps 6 (at a bit of a pinch) and costs £170 a night. ④

St David's 14–20 Norfolk Square, W2 ⓣ020/7723 3856 or 4963, ⓦwww.stdavidshotels.com; Paddington tube. See map, pp.132–133. A friendly welcome is assured at this inexpensive B&B, famed for its substantial English breakfast. Most rooms are en suite. The large rooms make it a good option for families on a budget. Basic singles start at £35, family rooms at £130. ③

Vancouver Studios 30 Prince's Square, W2 ⓣ020/7243 1270, ⓦwww.vancouverstudios.co.uk; Bayswater tube. See map, pp.132–133. Part of a growing trend away from standard hotel accommodation, *Vancouver Studios* offers self-contained apartments in a grand Victorian townhouse, with fully equipped kitchens and hotel-style porterage and maid service. Decor is to a high standard and mixes modern trends with traditional period touches. ⑥

Knightsbridge, Kensington and Chelsea

Abbey House 11 Vicarage Gate, W8 ⓣ020/7727 2594, ⓦwww.abbeyhousekensington.com; High St Kensington tube. See map, pp.132–133. Inexpensive Victorian B&B in a quiet street just north of Kensington High St, maintained to a very high standard by its attentive owners. Rooms are large and bright – prices are kept down by sharing facilities. Full English breakfast, with free tea and coffee available all day. Cash only. ⑤

Aster House 3 Sumner Place, SW7 ⓣ020/7581 5888, ⓦwww.asterhouse.com; South Kensington tube. See map, pp.132–133. Pleasant award-winning B&B in a luxurious South Ken white-stuccoed street; there's a lovely garden at the back and a large conservatory, where breakfast is served. Singles with shared facilities start at around £120 a night. ⑧

The Gore 189 Queen's Gate, SW7 ⓣ020/7584 6601, ⓦwww.gorehotel.com; South Kensington, Gloucester Road or High Street Kensington tube. See map, pp.132–133. Popular, privately owned century-old hotel, a step away from Hyde Park and awash with oriental rugs, rich mahogany, walnut panelling and other Victoriana. Rooms, some with four-poster beds, from £190. ⑧

Hotel 167 167 Old Brompton Rd, SW5 ⓣ020/7373 3221, ⓦwww.hotel167.com; Gloucester Road tube. See map, pp.132–133. Small, stylishly furnished B&B with en-suite facilities, double glazing and a fridge in all rooms.

Continental buffet-style breakfast is served in the attractive morning room/reception. 6

Vicarage 10 Vicarage Gate, W8 ⓣ020/7229 4030, ⓦwww.londonvicaragehotel.com; Notting Hill Gate or Kensington High Street tube. See map, pp.132–133. Ideally located B&B a step away from Hyde Park. Clean and smart floral rooms with shared facilities, and a full English breakfast included in the rates. Cash or traveller's cheques only. 5

Earl's Court

Mayflower 26–28 Trebovir Rd, SW5 ⓣ020/7370 0991, ⓦwww.mayflower-group.co.uk; Earl's Court tube. In a street of bog-standard B&Bs, this is a real winner, decked out in bold warm colours, strewn with Indian antiques, and featuring parrots in the lounge. Rooms are en suite, comfortable and appealing. Singles from £75, and there are also apartments from £109, which are economical if you're in a group. 7

Merlyn Court 2 Barkston Gardens, SW5 ⓣ020/7370 1640, ⓦwww.merlyncourthotel.com; Earl's Court tube. Well-appointed and popular B&B in a quiet leafy street close to the tube. Some rooms with en-suite facilities; English breakfast is included. 3

Hampstead

Hampstead Village Guesthouse 2 Kemplay Rd, NW3 ⓣ020/7435 8679, ⓦwww.hampsteadguesthouse.com; Hampstead tube. Lovely B&B in a freestanding Victorian house on a quiet backstreet between Hampstead village and the Heath. Rooms (most en suite) are wonderfully characterful, crammed with books, pictures and handmade and antique furniture. Cute cabin-like single for £48, and a self-contained studio for £90. Meals to order. 5

La Gaffe 107–111 Heath St, NW3 ⓣ020/7435 8965, ⓦwww.lagaffe.co.uk; Hampstead tube. Small hotel situated above a long-established Italian restaurant and bar in the heart of Hampstead village. All rooms are en suite and there's a roof terrace for use in fine weather. 6

Hostels and campsites

London's official **Youth Hostel Association (YHA) hostels** (ⓦwww.yha.org.uk) are generally the cleanest, most efficiently run hostels in the capital. However, they charge around fifty percent or more above the rates of private hostels, and tend to get booked up several months in advance. **Independent hostels** are cheaper and more relaxed, but can be less reliable in terms of facilities. A good **website** for booking independent places online is ⓦwww.hostellondon.com. London's **campsites** are all on the perimeter of the city, though they are without doubt the cheapest accommodation available.

Where possible we've marked the location of hostels on one of the maps in this chapter.

YHA hostels

London Earl's Court 38 Bolton Gardens, SW5 ⓣ0870/770 5804, ⓔearlscourt@yha.org.uk; Earl's Court tube. See map, pp.114–115. Better than a lot of accommodation in Earl's Court, offering dorms of mostly four or six beds, plus ten twins. Kitchen, café and patio garden. No groups. £24.50 per person. 2

Holland Park Hostel Holland Walk, W8 ⓣ0870/770 5866, ⓔhollandpark@yha.org.uk; Holland Park or High Street Kensington tube. See map, pp.132–133. Idyllically situated in the wooded expanse of Holland Park and fairly convenient for the centre, this extensive hostel offers a decent kitchen and an inexpensive café, but tends to be popular with school groups. Dorms only (most with over ten beds) at £22 per person.

London St Pauls 36 Carter Lane, EC4 ⓣ0870/770 5764, ⓔstpauls@yha.org.uk; St Paul's tube. Large 200-bed hostel in a superb location opposite St Paul's Cathedral. Some twins at £50 a room, but mostly four- to eight-bed dorms for £25 per person. There's no kitchen, but it has a café for dinner. No groups. Breakfast included. 2

London Thameside 20 Salter Rd, SE16 ⓣ0870 770 6010, ⓔrotherhithe@yha.org.uk; Rotherhithe or Canada Water tube. London's largest purpose-built hostel can feel a little out of things, but is well connected to central London. Often has space when more central places are full. Breakfast, packed lunch and evening meals available. Rooms have 2, 4, 6 or 10 beds and cost from £24 per person. 2

Private hostels

Ashlee House 261–265 Gray's Inn Rd, WC1 ⓣ020/7833 9400, ⓦwww.ashleehouse.co.uk; King's Cross tube. Clean and friendly hostel in a converted office block near King's Cross Station.

Internet access, laundry and kitchen facilities are provided. Dorms, which vary in size from four to sixteen beds, start at £9 if you book online; there are also a few private singles and twins, starting at £25 per person. Breakfast is included. ❷

Generator Compton Place, off Tavistock Place, WC1 ⓣ020/7388 7666, ⓦwww.the-generator.co.uk; Russell Square or Euston tube. See map, p.107. A huge, funky 800-bed hostel, with post-industrial decor and prices starting at just £12.50 a night for a dorm bed and breakfast. Continental breakfast (included in the room rate) and evening meals from just £3.50. Room prices range from £35 for a single, £46 for a twin and £60 for a triple. ❷

Leinster Inn 7–12 Leinster Square, W2 ⓣ020/7229 9641, ⓦwww.astorhostels.com; Queensway or Notting Hill Gate tube. See map, pp.132–133. With 360 beds, this is the biggest and liveliest of the *Astor* chain, with a party atmosphere, and two bars open until the small hours. Some rooms in all categories have their own shower. Dorm beds (4–8 per room) £12–18 per person, singles £26.50, doubles from £41. ❷

Museum Inn 27 Montague St, W1 ⓣ020/7580 5360, ⓦwww.astorhostels.com; Holborn tube. See map, p.107. In a lovely Georgian house by the British Museum, this is the quietest of the *Astor* hostels. There's no bar, though it's still a sociable, laid-back place, and well situated. There are 75 beds in dorms of four to ten for £16–19, plus some twins at £50, including breakfast. Decent-sized kitchen and TV lounge, plus laundry and Internet access. ❷

St Christopher's Village 161–165 Borough High St, SE1 ⓣ020/7407 1856, ⓦwww.st-christophers.co.uk; Borough tube. See map, pp.124–125. Flagship of a chain of independent hostels, with branches on Borough High St, in Camden, Greenwich and Shepherd's Bush. The decor is upbeat and cheerful, the place is efficiently run and there's a party-animal ambience, fuelled by the neighbouring bar and the rooftop hot tub and sauna. Beds in dorms of four to fourteen £14–22, twins £44. ❷

Campsites

Crystal Palace Crystal Palace Parade, SE19 ⓣ020/8778 7155; Crystal Palace train station from Victoria or London Bridge. All-year Caravan Club site; some traffic noise.

Lea Valley Leisure Centre Caravan Park Meridian Way, N9 ⓣ020/8803 6900; Ponders End train station from Liverpool St. Well-equipped site, situated behind the leisure centre at Pickett's Lock, backing on to a vast reservoir.

Westminster and Whitehall

Political, religious and regal power has emanated from **Westminster** and **Whitehall** for almost a millennium. It was Edward the Confessor (1042–66) who first established Westminster as London's royal and ecclesiastical power base, some three miles west of the City of London. The embryonic English parliament used to meet in the abbey and eventually took over the old royal palace of Westminster. In the nineteenth century, Whitehall became the "heart of the Empire", its ministries ruling over a quarter of the world's population. Even now, though the UK's world status has diminished, the institutions that run the country inhabit roughly the same geographical area: Westminster for the politicians, Whitehall for the civil servants.

The monuments and buildings in and around Whitehall and Westminster also span the millennium, and include some of London's most famous landmarks – **Nelson's Column**, **Big Ben** and the **Houses of Parliament**, **Westminster Abbey**, plus two of the city's finest permanent art collections, the **National Gallery** and **Tate Britain**. This is a well-trodden tourist circuit since it's also one of the easiest parts of London to walk round, with all the major sights within a mere half-mile of each other, linked by one of London's most majestic streets, **Whitehall**.

Trafalgar Square

Despite the persistent noise of traffic, **Trafalgar Square** is still one of London's grandest architectural set pieces. John Nash designed the basic layout in the 1820s, but died long before the square took its present form. The Neoclassical

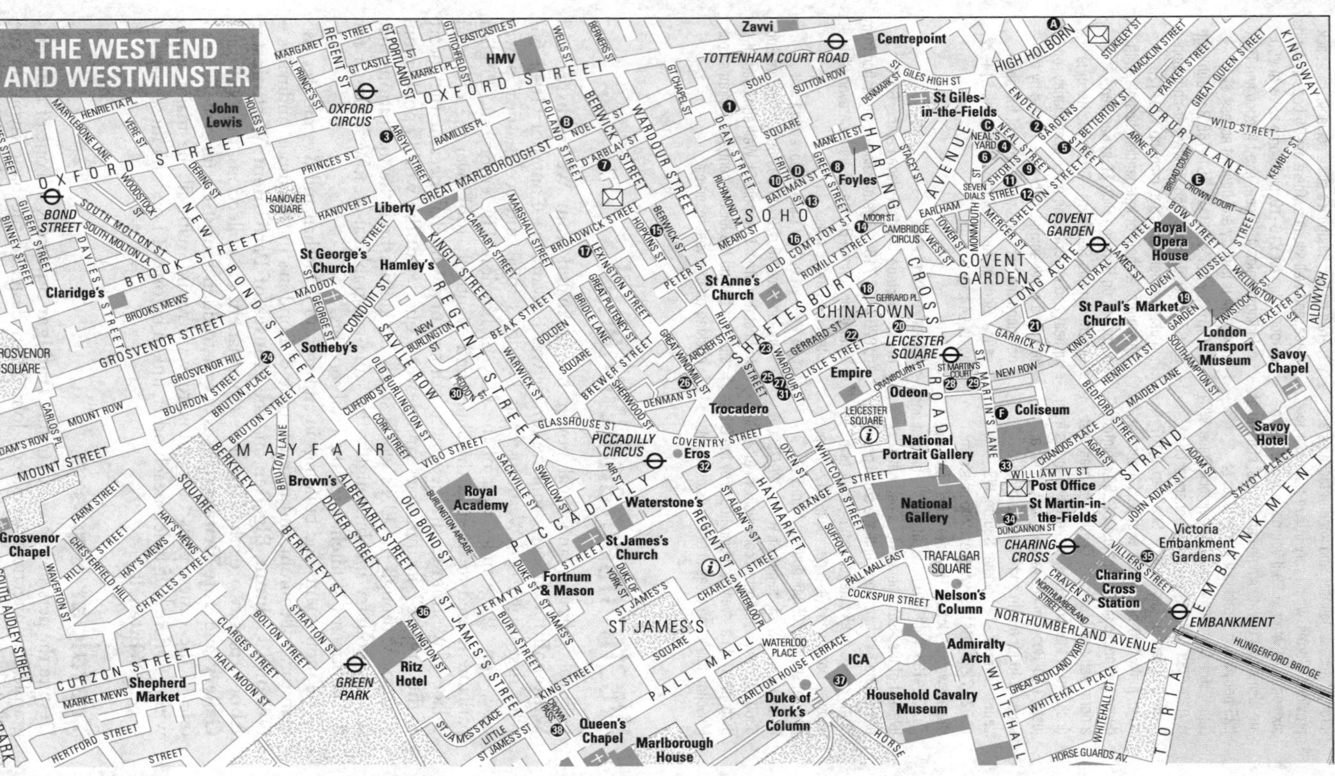
THE WEST END AND WESTMINSTER
Zavvi
Centrepoint
TOTTENHAM COURT ROAD
HMV
John Lewis
OXFORD CIRCUS
BOND STREET
St Giles-in-the-Fields
Neal's Yard
Seven Dials
Foyles
SOHO
COVENT GARDEN
Royal Opera House
Liberty
Hamley's
St George's Church
Claridge's
Sotheby's
St Anne's Church
CHINATOWN
LEICESTER SQUARE
Empire
Odeon
Trocadero
Coliseum
National Portrait Gallery
St Paul's Church
Market
London Transport Museum
Savoy Chapel
Savoy Hotel
PICCADILLY CIRCUS
Eros
MAYFAIR
Brown's
Royal Academy
Waterstone's
St James's Church
Fortnum & Mason
ST JAMES'S
National Gallery
Post Office
St Martin-in-the-Fields
TRAFALGAR SQUARE
Nelson's Column
CHARING CROSS
Charing Cross Station
Victoria Embankment Gardens
EMBANKMENT
HUNGERFORD BRIDGE
Admiralty Arch
ICA
Household Cavalry Museum
Duke of York's Column
Marlborough House
Queen's Chapel
Ritz Hotel
GREEN PARK
Shepherd Market
Grosvenor Chapel
GROSVENOR SQUARE
OXFORD STREET
REGENT STREET
PICCADILLY
SHAFTESBURY AVENUE
CHARING CROSS ROAD
STRAND
PALL MALL
WHITEHALL
NORTHUMBERLAND AVENUE
HAYMARKET
DRURY LANE
LONG ACRE
KINGSWAY
HIGH HOLBORN
EMBANKMENT
NEW BOND STREET
BERKELEY SQUARE
CURZON STREET
SOUTH AUDLEY STREET
ALDWYCH

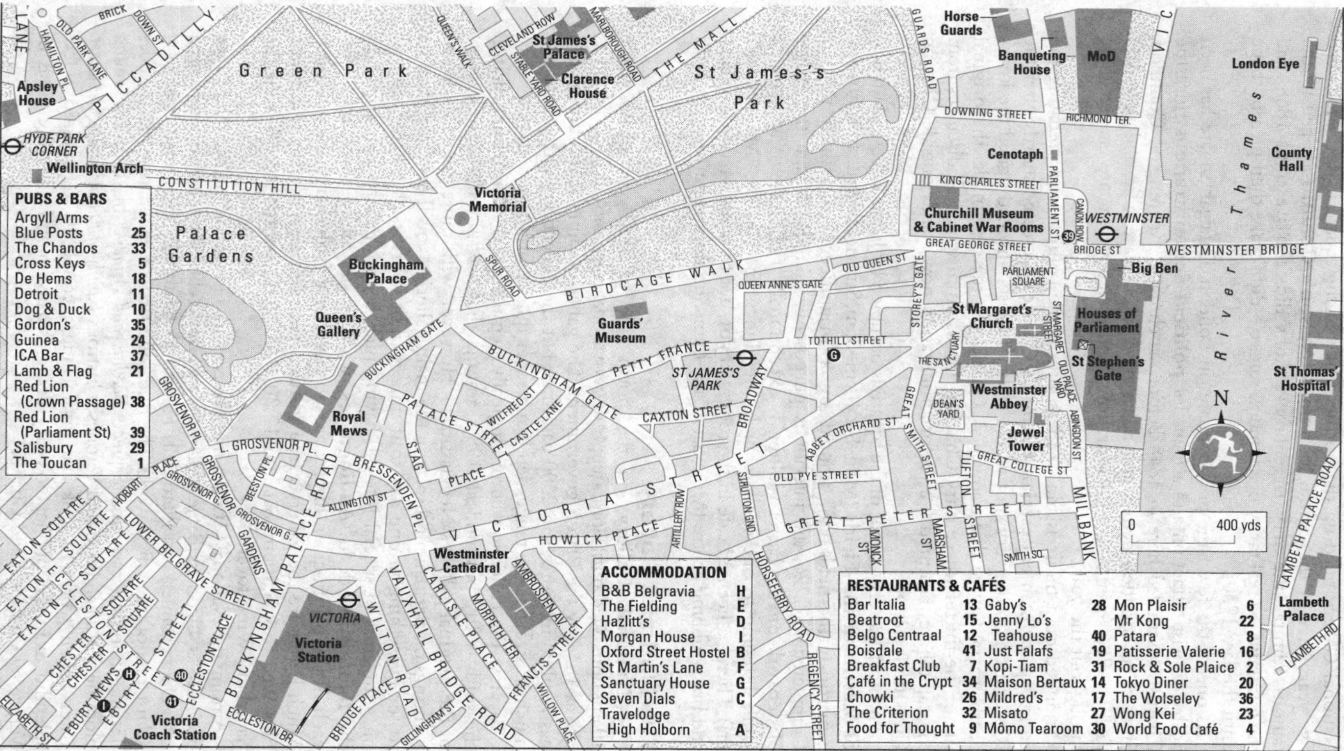
PUBS & BARS
Argyll Arms 3
Blue Posts 25
The Chandos 33
Cross Keys 5
De Hems 18
Detroit 11
Dog & Duck 10
Gordon's 35
Guinea 24
ICA Bar 37
Lamb & Flag 21
Red Lion (Crown Passage) 38
Red Lion (Parliament St) 39
Salisbury 29
The Toucan 1
ACCOMMODATION
B&B Belgravia H
The Fielding E
Hazlitt's D
Morgan House I
Oxford Street Hostel B
St Martin's Lane F
Sanctuary House G
Seven Dials C
Travelodge High Holborn A
RESTAURANTS & CAFÉS
Bar Italia 13
Beatroot 15
Belgo Centraal 12
Boisdale 41
Breakfast Club 7
Café in the Crypt 34
Chowki 26
The Criterion 32
Food for Thought 9
Gaby's 28
Jenny Lo's
Teahouse 40
Just Falafs 19
Kopi-Tiam 31
Maison Bertaux 14
Mildred's 17
Misato 27
Mômo Tearoom 30
Mon Plaisir 6
Mr Kong 22
Patara 8
Patisserie Valerie 16
Rock & Sole Plaice 2
Tokyo Diner 20
The Wolseley 36
Wong Kei 23
World Food Café 4
Green Park
St James's Park
Palace Gardens
River Thames
Apsley House
HYDE PARK CORNER
Wellington Arch
PICCADILLY
LANE
HAMILTON PL.
OLD PARK LANE
BRICK
DOWN ST
CONSTITUTION HILL
QUEEN'S WALK
CLEVELAND ROW
St James's Palace
STABLE YARD ROAD
Clarence House
MARLBOROUGH ROAD
THE MALL
Victoria Memorial
Buckingham Palace
Queen's Gallery
Royal Mews
SPUR ROAD
BIRDCAGE WALK
Guards' Museum
BUCKINGHAM GATE
PETTY FRANCE
ST JAMES'S PARK
PALACE STREET
WILFRED ST
CASTLE LANE
CAXTON STREET
BROADWAY
TOTHILL STREET
QUEEN ANNE'S GATE
OLD QUEEN ST
STOREY'S GATE
GUARDS ROAD
Horse Guards
Banqueting House
MoD
DOWNING STREET
RICHMOND TER.
Cenotaph
KING CHARLES STREET
PARLIAMENT ST
Churchill Museum & Cabinet War Rooms
GREAT GEORGE STREET
CANON ROW
WESTMINSTER
BRIDGE ST
WESTMINSTER BRIDGE
London Eye
County Hall
Big Ben
PARLIAMENT SQUARE
St Margaret's Church
ST MARGARET STREET
Houses of Parliament
St Stephen's Gate
OLD PALACE YARD
ABINGDON ST
THE SANCTUARY
Westminster Abbey
DEAN'S YARD
Jewel Tower
GREAT COLLEGE ST
GREAT SMITH STREET
TUFTON STREET
MILLBANK
St Thomas' Hospital
LAMBETH PALACE ROAD
Lambeth Palace
LAMBETH RD
N
0 400 yds
ABBEY ORCHARD ST
OLD PYE STREET
GREAT PETER STREET
MONCK ST
MARSHAM ST
SMITH SQ.
STRUTTON GND
ARTILLERY ROW
HORSEFERRY ROAD
REGENCY STREET
VICTORIA STREET
HOWICK PLACE
STAG PLACE
BRESSENDEN PL.
ALLINGTON ST
Westminster Cathedral
AMBROSDEN AV.
MORPETH TER.
CARLISLE PLACE
FRANCIS STREET
WILLOW PLACE
VAUXHALL BRIDGE ROAD
GILLINGHAM ST
WILTON ROAD
BRIDGE PLACE
VICTORIA
Victoria Station
ECCLESTON BR.
BUCKINGHAM PALACE ROAD
GROSVENOR PL.
L. GROSVENOR PL.
BEESTON PL.
GROSVENOR G.
GROSVENOR GARDENS
HOBART PLACE
LOWER BELGRAVE STREET
EATON SQUARE
ECCLESTON SQUARE
CHESTER SQUARE
ECCLESTON STREET
EBURY STREET
EBURY MEWS
ECCLESTON PLACE
ELIZABETH ST
Victoria Coach Station
Tate Britain

National Gallery filled up the northern side of the square in 1838, followed five years later by the central focal point, **Nelson's Column**, topped by the famous admiral; the very large bronze lions didn't arrive until 1868, and the fountains – a real rarity in a London square – didn't take their present shape until the late 1930s.

As one of the few large public squares in London, Trafalgar Square has been both a tourist attraction and a focus for **political demonstrations** since the Chartists assembled here in 1848 before marching to Kennington Common. Since then countless demos and rallies have taken place here, and nowadays various free events, commemorations and celebrations are staged here throughout the year.

Stranded on a traffic island to the south of the column, and predating the entire square, is an **equestrian statue of Charles I**, erected shortly after the Restoration on the very spot where eight of those who had signed the king's death warrant were disembowelled. Charles's statue also marks the original site of the thirteenth-century **Charing Cross**, from where all distances from the capital are measured – a Victorian imitation now stands outside Charing Cross train station.

The northeastern corner of the square is occupied by James Gibbs's church of **St Martin-in-the-Fields** (Mon–Sat 10am–8pm, Sun noon–8pm; free; Ⓦwww.stmartin-in-the-fields.org), fronted by a magnificent Corinthian portico. Completed in 1726, the interior is purposefully simple, though the Italian plasterwork on the barrel vaulting is exceptionally rich; it's best appreciated while listening to one of the church's free lunchtime concerts (Mon, Tues & Fri). There's a licensed café in the roomy **crypt**, not to mention a shop, gallery and brass-rubbing centre (Mon–Sat 10am–6pm, Sun noon–6pm).

The National Gallery

The **National Gallery**, on the north side of Trafalgar Square (daily 10am–6pm, Wed until 8pm; free; Ⓦwww.nationalgallery.org.uk) was begun as late as 1824 by the British government. The gallery's canny acquisition policy has resulted in more than 2300 paintings, but the collection's virtue is not so much its size, but the range, depth and sheer quality of its contents.

To view the collection chronologically, begin with the **Sainsbury Wing**, the softly-softly, postmodern 1980s adjunct that playfully imitates elements of the original gallery's Neoclassicism. However, with more than a thousand paintings on permanent display in the main galleries, you'll need real stamina to see everything in one day, so if time is tight your best bet is to home in on your areas of special interest, having picked up a gallery plan at one of the information desks. **Audioguides**, with a brief audio commentary on each of the paintings on display are available for a "voluntary contribution". Much better are the gallery's **free guided tours** (daily 11.30am & 2.30pm, plus Wed 6 & 6.30pm, Sat also 12.30 & 3.30pm), which set off from the Sainsbury Wing foyer.

Among the National's **Italian** masterpieces are Leonardo's melancholic *Virgin of the Rocks*, Uccello's *Battle of San Romano*, Botticelli's *Venus and Mars* (inspired by a Dante sonnet) and Piero della Francesca's beautifully composed *Baptism of Christ*, one of his earliest works. The fine collection of Venetian works includes Titian's colourful early masterpiece *Bacchus and Ariadne*, his very late, much gloomier *Death of Acteon*, and Veronese's lustrous *Family of Darius before Alexander*. Later Italian works to look out for include a couple by Caravaggio, a few splendid examples of Tiepolo's airy draughtsmanship and glittering vistas of Venice by Canaletto and Guardi.

From **Spain** there are dazzling pieces by El Greco, Goya, Murillo and Velázquez, among them the provocative *Rokeby Venus*. From the **Low Countries**, standouts include van Eyck's *Arnolfini Marriage*, Memlinc's perfectly poised *Donne Triptych*, and a couple of typically serene Vermeers. There are numerous genre paintings, such as Frans Hals' *Family Group in a Landscape*, and some superlative landscapes, most notably Hobbema's *Avenue, Middleharnis*. An array of Rembrandt paintings that features some of his most searching portraits – two of them self-portraits – is followed by abundant examples of Rubens' expansive, fleshy canvases.

Holbein's masterful *Ambassadors* and several of van Dyck's portraits were painted for the English court; and there's home-grown **British** art, too, represented by important works such as Hogarth's satirical *Marriage à la Mode*, Gainsborough's translucent *Morning Walk*, Constable's ever-popular *Hay Wain*, and Turner's *Fighting Téméraire*. Highlights of the **French** contingent include superb works by Poussin, Claude, Fragonard, Boucher, Watteau and David.

Finally, there's a particularly strong showing of **Impressionists** and **Post-Impressionists** in rooms 43–46 of the East Wing. Among the most famous works are Manet's unfinished *Execution of Maximilian*, Renoir's *Umbrellas*, Monet's *Thames below Westminster*, Van Gogh's *Sunflowers*, Seurat's pointillist *Bathers at Asnières*, a Rousseau junglescape, Cézanne's proto-Cubist *Bathers* and Picasso's Blue Period *Child with a Dove*.

The National Portrait Gallery

Around the east side of the National Gallery lurks the **National Portrait Gallery** (daily 10am–6pm, Thurs & Fri till 9pm; free; Ⓦwww.npg.org.uk), founded in 1856 to house uplifting depictions of the good and the great. Though it undoubtedly has some fine works among its collection of ten thousand portraits, many of the studies are of less interest than their subjects. Nevertheless, it's interesting to trace who has been deemed worthy of admiration at any one time: aristocrats and artists in previous centuries, warmongers and imperialists in the early decades of the twentieth century, writers and poets in the 1930s and 1940s, and, latterly, retired footballers, and film and pop stars. The NPG's **Sound Guide** gives useful biographical background information and costs £2.

Whitehall

Whitehall, the unusually broad avenue connecting Trafalgar Square to Parliament Square, is synonymous with the faceless, pinstriped bureaucracy charged with the day-to-day running of the country, who inhabit the governmental ministries which line the street. The statues dotted about recall the days when Whitehall stood at the centre of an empire on which the sun never set.

During the sixteenth and seventeenth centuries, however, Whitehall was the permanent residence of the kings and queens of England, and was actually synonymous with royalty. The original **Whitehall Palace** was the London seat of the Archbishop of York, confiscated and greatly extended by Henry VIII after a fire at Westminster forced him to find alternative accommodation. The chief section of the old palace to survive the fire of 1698 was the **Banqueting House** (Mon–Sat 10am–5pm; £4.50; Ⓦwww.hrp.org.uk), begun by Inigo Jones in 1619 and the first Palladian building to be built in England. The one room open to the public has no original furnishings, but is well worth seeing for the superlative Rubens ceiling paintings glorifying the Stuart dynasty, commissioned by Charles I in the 1630s. Charles himself walked through the room for the last time in 1649 when he stepped onto the executioner's scaffold from one of its windows.

The Changing of the Guard

The Queen is colonel-in-chief of the seven **Household Regiments**: the Life Guards (who dress in red and white) and the Blues and Royals (who dress in blue and white) are the two Household Cavalry regiments; while the Grenadier, Coldstream, Scots, Irish and Welsh Guards make up the Foot Guards.

The **Changing of the Guard** takes place at two separate locations in London:the two Household Cavalry regiments take it in turns to stand guard at Horse Guards on Whitehall (Mon–Sat 11am, Sun 10am, with inspection daily at 4pm), while the Foot Guards take care of Buckingham Palace (April–Aug daily 11.30am; Sept–March alternate days; no ceremony if it rains). A ceremony also takes place regularly at Windsor Castle (see p.142).

Across the road, two mounted sentries of the Queen's Household Cavalry and two horseless colleagues, all in ceremonial uniform, are posted daily from 10am to 4pm. Ostensibly they are protecting the **Horse Guards** building, originally the main gateway to St James's Park and Buckingham Palace. The mounted guards are changed hourly; those standing every two hours. Try to coincide your visit with the Changing of the Guard (see box above).

Further down this west side of Whitehall is London's most famous address, **Number 10 Downing Street** (Ⓦwww.number-10.gov.uk), the seventeenth-century terraced house that has been the residence of the prime minister since it was presented to Sir Robert Walpole, Britain's first PM, by George II in 1732. Facing Downing Street's locked gates, in the middle of the road, stands Edwin Lutyens' **Cenotaph**, eschewing any kind of Christian imagery, and inscribed simply with the words "The Glorious Dead". The memorial remains the focus of the Remembrance Sunday ceremony in November.

In 1938, in anticipation of Nazi air raids, the basements of the civil service buildings on the south side of King Charles Street, south of Downing Street, were converted into the **Cabinet War Rooms** (daily 9.30am–6pm; £11; Ⓦcwr.iwm.org.uk). It was here that Winston Churchill directed operations and held Cabinet meetings for the duration of World War II and the rooms have been left pretty much as they were when they were finally abandoned on VJ Day 1945, making for an atmospheric underground trot through wartime London. Also in the basement is the excellent **Churchill Museum**. You can hear snippets of Churchill's most famous speeches and check out his trademark bowler, spotted bow tie and half-chewed Havana, not to mention his wonderful burgundy zip-up "romper suit".

The Houses of Parliament

Clearly visible at the south end of Whitehall is one of London's best-known monuments, the Palace of Westminster, better known as the **Houses of Parliament** (Ⓦwww.parliament.uk). The city's finest Victorian Gothic Revival building and symbol of a nation once confident of its place at the centre of the world, it's distinguished above all by the ornate, gilded clocktower popularly known as **Big Ben**, after the thirteen-ton main bell that strikes the hour (and is broadcast across the world by the BBC).

The original medieval palace burned down in 1834, and everything you see now – save for **Westminster Hall**, the westernmost building – dates from Victorian times. You get a glimpse of the hall en route to the public galleries; its huge oak hammerbeam roof makes it one of the most magnificent secular medieval halls in

Europe. The **Jewel Tower** (daily: April–Oct 10am–5pm; Nov–March 10am–4pm; £2.70; EH), across the road from parliament, is another remnant of the medieval palace, now housing an excellent exhibition on the history of parliament – worth visiting before you queue up to get into the Houses of Parliament.

To watch the proceedings in either the House of Commons or the Lords, simply join the queue for the **public galleries** outside St Stephen's Gate. The public are let in slowly from about 4pm onwards on Mondays and Tuesdays, from around 1pm Wednesdays & Thursdays, and from 10am on Fridays. If you want to avoid the queues, turn up an hour or more later, when the crowds have usually thinned. Recesses (holiday closures) of both Houses occur at Christmas, Easter, and from August to the middle of October; phone ⓣ020/7219 4272 for more information or visit ⓦwww.parliament.uk.

Question Time – when the House is at its most raucous and entertaining – takes place at 2.30pm (Mon & Tues), 11.30am (Wed) and 10.30am (Thurs); **Prime Minister's Question Time** is on Wednesday from noon until 12.30pm. UK citizens can attend either session by booking a **ticket** (several weeks in advance) from their local MP; they can also organize a free guided tour of the building and Big Ben (no under-11s) through their MP. For part of the summer recess, there are **guided tours** (Aug & Sept Mon–Sat; £7) for foreign and domestic tourists, lasting an hour and fifteen minutes; visitors can book in advance by phoning ⓣ0870/906 3773, or simply head for the ticket office on Abingdon Green, opposite Victoria Tower at the southern end of the palace.

Westminster Abbey

The Houses of Parliament dwarf their much older neighbour, **Westminster Abbey** (Mon–Fri 9.30am–3.45pm, Wed until 6pm, Sat 9.30am–1.45pm; £10; ⓦwww.westminster-abbey.org), yet this single building embodies much of the history of England: it has been the venue for all coronations since the time of William the Conqueror, and the site of more or less every royal burial for some five hundred years between the reigns of Henry III and George II. Scores of the nation's most famous citizens are honoured here, too (though many of the stones commemorate people buried elsewhere), and the interior is crammed with hundreds of monuments and statues.

Entry is via the north transept, cluttered with monuments to politicians and traditionally known as **Statesmen's Aisle**, shortly after which you come to the abbey's most dazzling architectural set piece, the **Lady Chapel**, added by Henry VII in 1503 as his future resting place. With its intricately carved vaulting and fan-shaped gilded pendants, the chapel represents the final spectacular gasp of the English Perpendicular style. The public are no longer admitted to the **Shrine of Edward the Confessor**, the sacred heart of the building (except on a guided verger tour; £4) though you do get to inspect Edward I's **Coronation Chair**, a decrepit oak throne dating from around 1300 and still used for coronations.

Nowadays, the abbey's royal tombs are upstaged by **Poets' Corner**, in the south transept, though the first occupant, Geoffrey Chaucer, was in fact buried here not because he was a poet, but because he lived nearby. By the eighteenth century this zone had become an artistic pantheon, and since then, the transept has been filled with tributes to all shades of talent. From the south transept, you can view the central sanctuary, site of the coronations, and the wonderful **Cosmati floor mosaic**, constructed in the thirteenth century by Italian craftsmen, and often covered by a carpet to protect it.

Doors in the south choir aisle (plus a separate entrance from Dean's Yard) lead to the Great Cloisters (daily 8am–6pm; free), rebuilt after a fire in 1298.

At the eastern end of the cloisters lies the octagonal Chapter House (daily 10.30am–4pm; free), where the House of Commons met from 1257. The thirteenth-century decorative paving tiles and apocalyptic wall paintings have survived intact. Also worth a look is the Abbey Museum (daily 10.30am–4pm; free), filled with generations of lifelike (but bald) royal funereal effigies.

It's only after exploring the cloisters that you get to see the **nave** itself: narrow, light and, at over a hundred feet in height, by far the tallest in the country. The most famous monument in this section is the **Tomb of the Unknown Soldier**, by the west door, which now serves as the main exit.

Tate Britain

A purpose-built gallery half a mile south of parliament, founded in 1897 with money from Henry Tate, inventor of the sugar cube, **Tate Britain** (daily 10am–5.50pm, first Fri of month until 10pm; free; Ⓦwww.tate.org.uk) is devoted exclusively to British art. As well as the collection covering 1500 to the present, the gallery also puts on large-scale temporary exhibitions (for which there is a charge) that showcase British artists and continues to sponsor the Turner Prize, the country's most prestigious modern-art prize.

The pictures are rehung more or less annually, but always include a fair selection of works by British artists such as Hogarth, Constable, Gainsborough, Reynolds and Blake, plus foreign artists like van Dyck who spent much of their career over here. The ever-popular **Pre-Raphaelites** are always well represented, as are established twentieth-century greats such as Stanley Spencer and Francis Bacon alongside living artists such as David Hockney and Lucien Freud. Lastly, don't miss the Tate's outstanding **Turner collection**, displayed in the Clore Gallery.

Westminster Cathedral

Halfway down Victoria Street, which runs southwest from Westminster Abbey, you'll find one of London's most surprising churches, the stripey neo-Byzantine

▲ Tate Britain

concoction of the Roman Catholic **Westminster Cathedral** (Mon–Fri 7am–7pm, Sat 8am–7pm, Sun 8am–8pm; free; Ⓦwww.westminstercathedral.org.uk). Begun in 1895, and thus one of the last and wildest monuments to the Victorian era, it's constructed from more than twelve million terracotta-coloured bricks, decorated with hoops of Portland stone, and culminating in a magnificent tapered campanile which rises to 274 feet, served by a lift (daily 9.30am–12.30pm & 1–5pm; £3). The **interior** is only half finished, so to get an idea of what the place will look like when it's finally completed, explore the series of **side chapels** whose rich, multicoloured decor makes use of over one hundred different marbles from around the world.

St James's

St James's, the exclusive little enclave sandwiched between St James's Park and Piccadilly, was laid out in the 1670s close to St James's Palace. Regal and aristocratic residences overlook Green Park, gentlemen's clubs cluster along Pall Mall and St James's Street, while jacket-and-tie restaurants and expense-account gentlemen's outfitters line Jermyn Street. Hardly surprising then that most Londoners rarely stray into this area. Plenty of folk, however, frequent **St James's Park**, with large numbers heading for the Queen's chief residence, **Buckingham Palace**, and the adjacent Queen's Gallery and Royal Mews.

The Mall and St James's Park

The tree-lined sweep of **The Mall** is at its best on Sundays, when it's closed to traffic. It was laid out in the first decade of the twentieth century as a memorial to Queen Victoria, and runs from Trafalgar Square to Buckingham Palace. The bombastic **Admiralty Arch** was erected to mark the entrance at the Trafalgar Square end of The Mall, while at the other end stands the ludicrous **Victoria Memorial**, Edward VII's overblown 2300-ton marble tribute to his mother, which is topped by a gilded statue of Victory, while the six outlying allegorical groups in bronze confidently proclaim the great achievements of her reign.

Flanking nearly the whole length of the Mall, **St James's Park** is the oldest of the royal parks, having been drained and enclosed for hunting purposes by Henry VIII. It was landscaped by Nash in the 1820s, and today its lake is a favourite picnic spot for the civil servants of Whitehall. Pelicans can still be seen at the eastern end of the lake, and there are exotic ducks, swans and geese aplenty.

Buckingham Palace

The graceless colossus of **Buckingham Palace** (Aug–Sept daily 9.30am–3.45pm; £15; Ⓦwww.royal.gov.uk), popularly known as "Buck House", has served as the monarch's permanent London residence only since the accession of Victoria. Bought by George III in 1762, the building was overhauled in the late 1820s by Nash and again in 1913, producing a palace that's as bland as it's possible to be.

For two months of the year, the hallowed portals are grudgingly nudged open; timed tickets are sold from the box office on the south side of the palace – to avoid queuing, you must book in advance (for an extra £1.25 per ticket) on Ⓣ020/7766 7300 or online. The interior, however, is a bit of an anticlimax: of the palace's 660 rooms you're permitted to see twenty or so, and there's little sign of life, as the Queen decamps to Scotland every summer. For the other ten months of the year there's little to do here – not that this deters the crowds who mill around the railings, and gather in some force to watch the **Changing of the Guard** (see p.96), in which a detachment of the Queen's Foot Guards marches to appropriate martial music from St James's Palace (unless it rains, that is).

The public can also pay through the nose to view a small portion of the Royal Collection, at the rebuilt **Queen's Gallery** (daily 10am–5.30pm; £7.50), on the south side of the palace. Exhibitions change regularly, drawn from a collection which is three times larger than the National Gallery, and includes masterpieces by Michelangelo, Reynolds, Gainsborough, Vermeer, van Dyck, Rubens, Rembrandt and Canaletto, as well as the odd Fabergé egg and heaps of Sèvres china.

There's more pageantry on show at the Nash-built **Royal Mews** (March–July & Oct daily except Fri 11am–4pm; Aug & Sept daily 10am–5pm; £7), further along Buckingham Palace Road. The royal carriages, lined up under a glass canopy in the courtyard, are the main attraction, in particular the Gold Carriage, made for George III in 1762, smothered in 22-carat gilding and weighing four tons, its axles supporting four life-size figures.

Waterloo Place to St James's Palace

St James's does, however, contain some interesting architectural set pieces, such as **Waterloo Place**, at the centre of which stands the Guards' Crimean Memorial, fashioned from captured Russian cannon and featuring a statue of Florence Nightingale. Clearly visible, beyond, is the "Grand Old" **Duke of York's Column**, erected in 1833, ten years before Nelson's more famous one in Trafalgar Square.

Cutting across Waterloo Place, Pall Mall leads west to **St James's Palace**, whose main red-brick gate-tower is pretty much all that remains of the Tudor palace erected here by Henry VIII. When Whitehall Palace burned down in 1698, St James's became the principal royal residence and, in keeping with tradition, an ambassador to the UK is still accredited to the "Court of St James's", even though the court has since moved down the road to Buckingham Palace. The modest, rambling, crenellated complex is off-limits to the public, with the exception of the **Chapel Royal** (Oct to Good Friday Sun 8.30am & sometimes 11.15am), situated within the palace, and the **Queen's Chapel** (Easter–July Sun 8.30am & sometimes 11.15am), on the other side of Marlborough Road; both are open for services only. **Clarence House** (Aug & Sept daily 10am–5.30pm; £7.50; ⓦwww.royal.gov.uk), connected to the palace's southwest wing, was home to the Queen Mother, and now serves as the official London home of Charles and his second wife Camilla; the public are allowed to view a handful of unremarkable rooms on the ground floor by guided tour only; tours are popular so you'll need to book ahead.

Mayfair and Marylebone

Mayfair and **Marylebone** emerged in the late seventeenth century as London's first real suburbs, characterized by grid-plan streets feeding into grand, formal squares. This expansion set the westward trend for middle-class migration, and as London's wealthier consumers moved west, so too did the city's more upmarket shops and luxury hotels, which are still a feature of the area.

Piccadilly, which forms the southern border of **Mayfair**, is no longer the fashionable promenade it once was, but a whiff of exclusivity still pervades **Bond Street** and its tributaries. **Regent Street** was created as a new "Royal Mile", but, along with **Oxford Street**, it has since become London's busiest shopping district – it's here that Londoners mean when they talk of "going shopping up the West End".

Marylebone, which lies to the north of Oxford Street, is another grid-plan Georgian development, a couple of social and real-estate leagues below Mayfair, but a wealthy area nevertheless. It boasts a very fine art gallery, the **Wallace Collection**, and, in its northern fringes, one of London's biggest tourist attractions, **Madame Tussaud's**, the oldest and largest wax museum in the world.

Piccadilly Circus and Regent Street

Anonymous and congested it may be, but **Piccadilly Circus** is, for many Londoners, the nearest their city comes to having a centre. A much-altered product of Nash's grand 1812 Regent Street plan and now a major traffic interchange, it may not be a picturesque place, but thanks to its celebrated aluminium statue, popularly known as **Eros**, it's prime tourist territory. The fountain's archer is one of the city's top attractions, a status that baffles all who live here. Despite the bow and arrow, it's not the god of love at all but his brother, Anteros, depicted as the *Angel of Christian Charity*, and erected to commemorate the Earl of Shaftesbury, a Bible-thumping social reformer who campaigned against child labour.

Regent Street, leading north off Piccadilly Circus, is reminiscent of one of Haussmann's Parisian boulevards without the trees. Drawn up by John Nash in 1812 as both a luxury shopping street and a triumphal way between George IV's Carlton House and Regent's Park, it was the city's earliest attempt at dealing with traffic congestion, slum clearance and planned social segregation, which would later be perfected by the Victorians. The increase in the purchasing power of the city's middle classes in the last century brought the tone of the street "down" and heavyweight stores catering for the masses now predominate. Among the best known are **Hamley's**, reputedly the world's largest toyshop, and **Liberty**, the department store that popularized Arts and Crafts designs in the early 1900s.

Piccadilly

Piccadilly apparently got its name from the ruffs or "pickadills" worn by the dandies who used to promenade here in the late seventeenth century. Despite its fashionable pedigree, it's no place for promenading in its current state, with traffic careering down it nose to tail most of the day and night. Infinitely more pleasant places to window-shop are the various **nineteenth-century arcades** on Piccadilly, originally built to protect shoppers from the mud and horse-dung on the streets, but now equally useful for escaping exhaust fumes.

The **Royal Academy of Arts** (daily 10am–6pm, Fri until 10pm; £7–10; Ⓦwww.royalacademy.org.uk) occupies one of the few surviving aristocratic mansions that once lined the north side of Piccadilly. The country's first-ever formal art school, the RA was founded in 1768 by a group of English painters including Thomas Gainsborough and Joshua Reynolds. The Academy hosts a wide range of art exhibitions, and an annual **Summer Exhibition** that remains a stop on the social calendar of upper-middle-class England. Anyone can enter paintings in any style, and the lucky winners get hung, in rather close proximity, and sold. RA "Academicians" are allowed to display six of their own works – no matter how awful. The result is a bewildering display, which gets panned annually by highbrow critics.

Bond Street

While Oxford Street, Regent Street and Piccadilly have all gone downmarket, **Bond Street**, which runs parallel with Regent Street, has carefully maintained its exclusivity. It is, in fact, two streets rolled into one: the southern half, laid out in the 1680s, is known as Old Bond Street; its northern extension, which followed less than fifty years later, is known as New Bond Street. They are both pretty unassuming streets architecturally, yet the shops that line them are among the flashiest in London, dominated by perfumeries, **jewellers** and designer clothing stores. In addition to fashion, Bond Street is also renowned for its fine art galleries and its **auction houses**, the oldest of which is Sotheby's, 34–35 New Bond St (Ⓦwww.sothebys.com), whose viewing galleries are open free of charge.

Oxford Street and around

As wealthy Londoners began to move out of the City in the eighteenth century in favour of the newly developed West End, so **Oxford Street** (Ⓦwww.oxfordstreet.co.uk) – the old Roman road to Oxford – gradually became London's main shopping thoroughfare. Today, despite successive recessions and sky-high rents, this two-mile hotchpotch of shops is still probably England's busiest street, and is home to (often several) flagship branches of Britain's major retailers (see p.159). The street's only real landmark store is **Selfridge's**, opened in 1909 with a facade featuring the Queen of Time riding the ship of commerce and supporting an Art Deco clock.

The Wallace Collection

Immediately north of Oxford Street, on Manchester Square, stands Hertford House, a miniature eighteenth-century French chateau which holds the splendid **Wallace Collection** (daily 10am–5pm; free; Ⓦwww.wallacecollection.org), a museum-gallery best known for its eighteenth-century French paintings, Franz Hals' *Laughing Cavalier*, Titian's *Perseus and Andromeda*, Velázquez's *Lady with a Fan* and Rembrandt's affectionate portrait of his teenage son, Titus. There's a modern café in the glassed-over courtyard, but at heart, the Wallace Collection remains an old-fashioned place, with exhibits piled high in glass cabinets, and paintings covering every inch of wall space. The fact that these exhibits are set amidst period fittings – and a bloody great armoury – makes the place even more remarkable.

Madame Tussaud's

Madame Tussaud's (Mon–Fri 9.30am–5.30pm, Sat & Sun 9am–6pm; £23; Ⓣ0870/400 3000, Ⓦwww.madame-tussauds.co.uk), on Marylebone Road, has been pulling in the crowds ever since the good lady arrived in London from Paris in 1802 bearing the sculpted heads of guillotined aristocrats. The entrance fee might be extortionate, the waxwork likenesses of the famous occasionally dubious and the attempts to relieve you of yet more cash relentless, but you can still rely on finding London's biggest queues here. The only way to avoid joining the line is to book a timed entry ticket in advance over the phone or on the Internet. Visitors can choose to opt out of Chamber of Horrors Live which features live actors trained to frighten the living daylights out of tourists.

Soho

Soho gives you the best and worst of London: the porn joints that proliferated from the mid-1960s onwards still have a strong presence, but the area also boasts a lively fruit and vegetable market on Berwick Street and a nightlife that has attracted writers and ravers of every sexual persuasion since the eighteenth century. The area's most recent transformation has seen it become Europe's leading gay centre, with bars and cafés bursting out from the Old Compton Street area. Despite regeneration, it has retained an unorthodox and slightly raffish air, born of an immigrant history as rich as that of the East End (see p.119).

Bounded by Regent Street to the west, Oxford Street to the north and Charing Cross Road to the east, Soho remains very much the heart of London and one of the capital's most diverse and spicy areas. Conventional sights are few and far between, yet it's a great area to wander through, with probably more streetlife than anywhere else in London – whatever hour you wander through, there's always something going on. Most folk head here to visit one of the big movie houses on **Leicester Square**, to drink in the latest designer bar or to grab a bite to eat at the innumerable cafés and restaurants, ranging from the inexpensive Chinese places that pepper the tiny enclave of **Chinatown**, to exclusive, Michelin-starred establishments in the backstreets of central Soho and its adjunct, **Fitzrovia**, to the north of Oxford Street.

Leicester Square and Chinatown

By night, when the big cinemas and discos are doing good business, and the buskers are entertaining the crowds, **Leicester Square** is one of the most crowded places in London, particularly on a Friday or Saturday when huge numbers of tourists and half the youth of the suburbs seem to congregate here. It wasn't until the mid-nineteenth century that the square actually began to emerge as an entertainment zone; cinema moved in during the 1930s, a golden age evoked by the sleek black lines of the Odeon on the east side, and maintains its grip on the area.

Chinatown, hemmed in between Leicester Square and Shaftesbury Avenue, is a self-contained jumble of shops, cafés and restaurants that makes up one of London's most distinct and popular ethnic enclaves. **Gerrard Street**, Chinatown's main drag, has been endowed with ersatz touches – telephone kiosks rigged out as pagodas and fake oriental gates or *paifang* – though few of London's 80,000 or so Chinese actually live in the three small blocks of Chinatown. Nonetheless, it remains a focus for the community, a place to do business or the weekly shopping, celebrate a wedding, or just meet up for meals, particularly on Sundays, when the restaurants overflow with Chinese families tucking into *dim sum*.

Old Compton Street

If Soho has a main drag, it has to be **Old Compton Street**, which runs parallel with Shaftesbury Avenue. The corner shops, peep shows, boutiques and trendy cafés here are typical of the area and a good barometer of the latest fads. Soho has been a permanent fixture on the **gay scene** for the better part of a century, but the approach is much more upfront nowadays, with gay bars, clubs and cafés jostling for position on Old Compton Street and round the corner in Wardour Street.

The streets round here are lined with Soho institutions past and present. One of the best known is London's longest-running jazz club, *Ronnie Scott's*, on Frith Street, founded in 1958 and still capable of pulling in the big names. Opposite is *Bar Italia*, an Italian café with late-night hours popular with Soho's clubbers. It was in this building, appropriately enough for such a media-saturated area, that John Logie Baird made the world's first public television transmission in 1926.

▲Old Compton Street

Covent Garden and the Strand

Covent Garden's transformation from a workaday fruit and vegetable market into a fashionable *quartier* is one of the most miraculous and enduring developments of the 1980s. More sanitized and brazenly commercial than neighbouring Soho, it's a far cry from the district's heyday when the piazza was the great playground (and red-light district) of eighteenth-century London. The buskers in front of St Paul's Church, the theatres round about, and the **Royal Opera House** on Bow Street are survivors of this tradition, and on a balmy summer evening, **Covent Garden Piazza** is still an undeniably lively place to be. Another positive side effect of the market development has been the renovation of the run-down warehouses to the north of the piazza, especially around the Neal Street area, which now boasts some of the West End's trendier shops, selling everything from shoes to skateboards.

As its name suggests, the **Strand**, just to the south of Covent Garden, once lay along the riverbank: it achieved its present-day form when the Victorians shored up the banks of the Thames to create the Embankment. The Strand's most intriguing sight is **Somerset House**, sole survivor of the street's grandiose river palaces, now housing several museums and galleries as well as a lovely fountain courtyard.

Covent Garden Piazza

London's oldest planned square, laid out in the 1630s by Inigo Jones, **Covent Garden Piazza** was initially a great success, its novelty value alone attracting a rich and aristocratic clientele, but over the next century the tone of the place fell as the fruit and vegetable market expanded, and theatres and coffee houses began to take over the peripheral buildings. When the market closed in 1974, the piazza narrowly survived being turned into an office development. Instead, the elegant Victorian market hall and its environs were restored to house shops, restaurants and arts-and-crafts stalls. Of Jones's original piazza, the only remaining parts are the two rebuilt sections of north-side arcading, and **St Paul's Church**, facing the west side of the market building.

London Transport Museum

A former flower-market shed on the piazza's east side is now home to the **London Transport Museum** (daily 10am–6pm, Fri 11am–9pm; £8; Ⓦwww.ltmuseum.co.uk), a glorious celebration of the city's transport system over the last two centuries. The reconstructed 1829 Shillibeer's Horse Omnibus, which provided the city's first regular horse-bus service, is dwarfed by several wonderful double-decker electric trams, which, in the 1930s, formed part of the world's largest electric tram system. By 1952 the whole network had been dismantled, to be superseded by trolleybuses, of which the museum has several examples – these, in turn, bit the dust in the following decade. Look out, too, for the first "tube train", whose lack of windows earned it the nickname "the padded cell".

The Royal Opera House

The arcading on the northeast side of the piazza was rebuilt as part of the recent redevelopment of the **Royal Opera House** (Ⓦwww.royaloperahouse.org), whose main Neoclassical facade dates from 1811 and opens onto Bow Street. Now, however, you can reach the opera house from a passageway in the corner of the arcading. The spectacular wrought-iron **Floral Hall** (daily 10am–3pm) serves as the opera house's main foyer, and is open to the public, as is the *Amphitheatre* bar/restaurant (from one and a half hours before performance to the end of the last interval), which has a glorious terrace overlooking the piazza. For backstage tours of the opera house, it's best to book in advance (Mon–Fri 10.30am, 12.30 & 2.30pm, Sat also 11.30am; £9; Ⓣ020/7304 4000).

Strand

Once famous for its riverside mansions, and later its music halls, the **Strand** – the main road connecting Westminster to the City – is a shadow of its former self. One of the few vestiges of glamour is **The Savoy**, London's grandest hotel, built in 1889 on the site of the medieval Savoy Palace on the south side of the street. César Ritz was the original manager, Guccio Gucci started out as a dishwasher here, and the list of illustrious guests is endless: Monet painted the Thames from one of the south-facing rooms, Sarah Bernhardt nearly died here, and Strauss the Younger arrived with his own orchestra.

Somerset House

Further east along the Strand, **Somerset House** (Ⓦwww.somerset-house.org.uk) is the sole survivor of the grand edifices which once lined the riverfront, its four wings enclosing a large **courtyard** (daily 7.30am–11pm; free) featuring a wonderful 55-jet fountain that spouts straight from the cobbles; in winter, an ice rink is set up in its place. The present building was begun in 1776 by William Chambers as a purpose-built governmental office development, but now also houses a series of museums and galleries.

The south wing, overlooking the Thames, is home to the **Hermitage Rooms** (daily 10am–6pm; £5; Ⓦwww.hermitagerooms.com), featuring changing displays drawn from St Petersburg's Hermitage Museum, and the **Gilbert Collection** (daily 10am–6pm; £5; Ⓦwww.gilbert-collection.org.uk), a museum of decorative arts displaying gaudy European silver and gold nick-nacks, micro-mosaics, clocks, portrait miniatures and snuffboxes. Alternatively, save yourself some money and go and admire the Royal Naval Commissioners' gilded eighteenth-century barge in the **King's Barge House**, at ground level in the south wing.

In the north wing are the **Courtauld Institute galleries** (daily 10am–6pm; £5; free Mon 10am–2pm; Ⓦwww.courtauld.ac.uk), chiefly known for their dazzling collection of Impressionist and Post-Impressionist paintings. Among the most celebrated works is a small-scale version of Manet's *Déjeuner sur l'herbe*, Renoir's *La Loge*, and Degas's *Two Dancers*, plus a whole heap of Cézanne's canvases, including one of his series of *Card Players*. The Courtauld also boasts a fine selection of works by the likes of Rubens, van Dyck, Tiepolo and Cranach the Elder. The collection has recently been augmented by the long-term loan of a hundred topnotch twentieth-century paintings and sculptures by, among others, Kandinksy, Matisse, Dufy, Derain, Rodin and Henry Moore.

Bloomsbury

Bloomsbury was built over in grid-plan style from the 1660s onwards, and the formal bourgeois Georgian squares laid out then remain the area's main distinguishing feature. In the twentieth century, Bloomsbury acquired a reputation as the city's most learned quarter, dominated by the dual institutions of the **British Museum** and **London University**, and home to many of London's chief book publishers, but perhaps best known for its literary inhabitants, among them T.S. Eliot and Virginia Woolf. Today, the British Museum is clearly the star attraction, but there are other minor sights, such as the **Foundling Museum** and the **Dickens House Museum**. Only in its northern fringes does the character of the area change dramatically, becoming steadily seedier as you near the main-line train stations of **Euston**, **St Pancras** and **King's Cross**.

The British Museum

The **British Museum** (daily 10am–5.30pm, Thurs & Fri until 8.30pm; free; Ⓦwww.britishmuseum.ac.uk) is one of the great museums of the world. With seventy thousand exhibits ranged over two and a half miles of galleries, the museum boasts a huge and comprehensive collection of antiquities, prints and drawings – over thirteen million at the last count (a number increasing daily with the stream of new acquisitions, discoveries and bequests). Its assortment of Roman and Greek art is unparalleled, its Egyptian collection is the most significant outside Egypt and, in addition, there are fabulous treasures from Anglo-Saxon and Roman Britain, from China, Japan, India and Mesopotamia – not to mention an enormous collection of prints and drawings, only a fraction of which can be displayed at any one time.

The building itself, begun in 1823, is the grandest of London's Greek Revival edifices, dominated by the giant Ionian colonnade and portico that forms the main entrance. At the heart of the museum is the **Great Court** (daily 9am–6pm, Thurs–Sat until 11pm), with its remarkable, curving glass-and-steel roof, designed by Norman Foster. At the centre stands the copper-domed former **Round Reading Room**, built in the 1850s to house the British Library. It was here, reputedly at desk O7, that Karl Marx penned *Das Kapital*. The building is now a public study area, and features a multimedia guide to the museum's displays.

You'll never manage to see everything in one visit, so the best advice is to concentrate on one or two areas of interest, or else sign up with one of the museum's **guided tours**. One place you could start is the collection of **Roman**

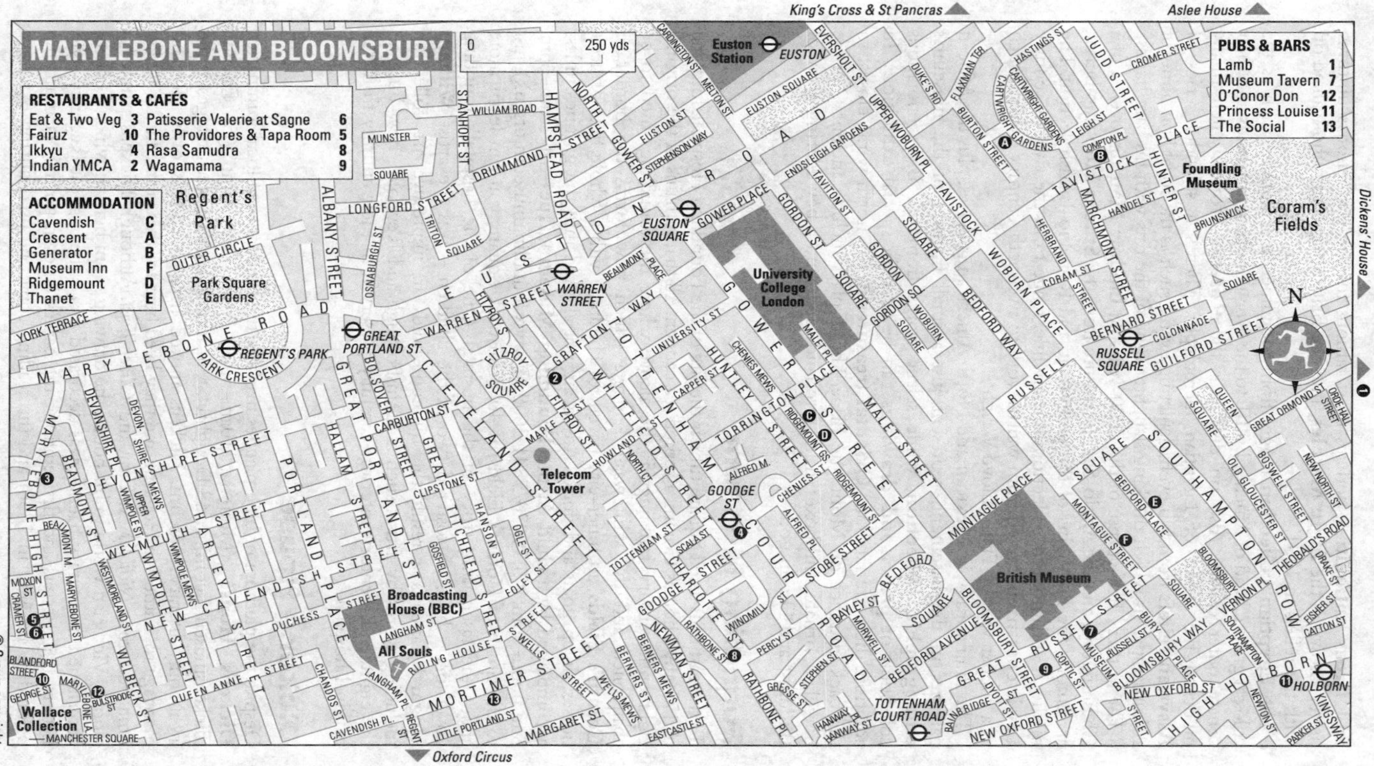

MARYLEBONE AND BLOOMSBURY

0 250 yds

RESTAURANTS & CAFÉS

Eat & Two Veg	3	Patisserie Valerie at Sagne	6
Fairuz	10	The Providores & Tapa Room	5
Ikkyu	4	Rasa Samudra	8
Indian YMCA	2	Wagamama	9

ACCOMMODATION

Cavendish	C
Crescent	A
Generator	B
Museum Inn	F
Ridgemount	D
Thanet	E

PUBS & BARS

Lamb	1
Museum Tavern	7
O'Conor Don	12
Princess Louise	11
The Social	13

King's Cross & St Pancras
Aslee House
Dickens' House
Oxford Circus

Euston Station
EUSTON
EUSTON SQUARE
WARREN STREET
GREAT PORTLAND ST
REGENT'S PARK
GOODGE ST
RUSSELL SQUARE
TOTTENHAM COURT ROAD
HOLBORN
Regent's Park
Park Square Gardens
University College London
Telecom Tower
Broadcasting House (BBC)
All Souls
British Museum
Foundling Museum
Coram's Fields
Wallace Collection

and Greek antiquities, perhaps most famous for the Parthenon sculptures, better known as the **Elgin Marbles**, after the British aristocrat who walked off with the reliefs in 1801.

The **Egyptian collection** ranges from monumental sculptures, such as the colossal granite head of Amenophis III, to the ever-popular **mummies** and their ornate outer caskets. Also on display is the **Rosetta Stone**, which finally unlocked the secret of Egyptian hieroglyphs. There's a splendid series of **Assyrian reliefs** from Nineveh, depicting events such as the royal lion hunts of Ashurbanipal, in which the king slaughters one of the cats with his bare hands.

The leathery half-corpse of the 2000-year-old **Lindow Man**, discovered in a Cheshire bog, and the Anglo-Saxon treasure from the **Sutton Hoo** ship burial, are among the highlights of the prehistoric and Romano-British section. The medieval and modern collections, meanwhile, range from the twelfth-century **Lewis chessmen**, carved from walrus ivory, to twentieth-century exhibits such as a copper vase by Frank Lloyd Wright.

The dramatically lit Mexican and North American galleries, plus the African galleries in the basement, represent just a small fraction of the museum's **ethnographic collection**, while select works from the BM's enormous collection of **prints and drawings** can be seen in special exhibitions. In addition, there are fabulous **Oriental treasures** in the north wing, closest to the back entrance on Montague Place. The displays include ancient Chinese porcelain, ornate snuffboxes, miniature landscapes, and a bewildering array of Buddhist and Hindu gods.

Foundling Museum

To the east of Russell Square tube is the site of the Foundling Hospital, founded in 1756 by Thomas Coram, a retired sea captain. All that remains of the original eighteenth-century buildings is the alcove where the foundlings used to be abandoned and the whitewashed loggia which now forms the border to **Coram's Fields**, an inner-city haven for children, with a whole host of hens, horses, sheep, goats and ducks. Adults are not allowed into the grounds unless accompanied by a child. At the **Foundling Museum** (Tues–Sat 10am–6pm, Sun noon–6pm; £5; ⓣ020/7841 3600, ⓦwww.foundlingmuseum.org.uk), just to the north of Coram's Fields, at 40 Brunswick Square, you can learn more about the fascinating story of the hospital. One of the hospital's founding governors – he even fostered two of the children – was the artist **William Hogarth**, and as a result the museum holds an impressive art collection including works by artists such as Gainsborough and Reynolds, now hung in the eighteenth-century interiors carefully preserved in their entirety from the original hospital.

Dickens House

Despite the plethora of blue plaques marking the residences of local luminaries, **Dickens House** (Mon–Sat 10am–5pm, Sun 11am–5pm; £5; ⓦwww.dickensmuseum.com), at 48 Doughty St, in Bloomsbury's eastern fringes, is the area's only literary museum. Dickens moved here in 1837 shortly after his marriage to Catherine Hogarth, and they lived here for two years, during which time he wrote *Nicholas Nickleby* and *Oliver Twist*. Although Dickens painted a gloomy Victorian world in his books, the drawing room here, in which Dickens entertained his literary friends, was decorated in a rather upbeat Regency style. Letters, manuscripts and first editions, the earliest known portrait (a miniature painted by his aunt in 1830) and the reading copies he used during extensive lecture tours in Britain and the States are the rewards for those with more than a passing interest in the novelist. You can also watch a half-hour film of his life.

The British Library

The **British Library** (Mon & Wed–Fri 9.30am–6pm, Tues 9.30am–8pm, Sat 9.30am–5pm, Sun 11am–5pm; free; Ⓦ www.bl.uk), located on the busy Euston Road on the northern fringes of Bloomsbury, opened to the public in 1998. As the country's most expensive public building it was hardly surprising that the place drew fierce criticism from all sides. Yet while it's true that the building's red-brick brutalism is horribly out of fashion, and compares unfavourably with its cathedralesque Victorian neighbour, the former *Midland Grand Hotel*, the interior of the library has met with general approval, and the high-tech exhibition galleries are superb.

With the exception of the reading rooms, the library is open to the general public. The three exhibition galleries are to the left as you enter; straight ahead is the spiritual heart of the BL, a multistorey glass-walled tower housing the vast **King's Library**, collected by George III, and donated to the museum by George IV in 1823; to the side of the King's Library are the pull-out drawers of the **philatelic collection**. If you want to explore the parts of the building not normally open to the public, you must sign up for a **guided tour** (Mon, Wed & Fri 3pm, Sat 10.30am & 3pm; £6; or Sun 11.30am & 3pm if you want to see the reading rooms; £7).

The first of the three exhibition galleries to head for is the dimly lit John Ritblat Gallery, where a superlative selection of the BL's ancient manuscripts, maps, documents and precious books, including the richly illustrated Lindisfarne Gospels, is displayed. One of the most appealing innovations is that you can turn the pages of various texts – from the Mercator's 1570s atlas of Europe to Leonardo da Vinci's notebook – "virtually" on the touch-screen computers, thus allowing you to see much more than the double page displayed in the glass cabinets. The Pearson Gallery of Living Words puts on excellent temporary exhibitions, for which there is sometimes an admission charge.

Holborn to Hoxton

Holborn (pronounced "Ho-bun"), on the periphery of the financial district of the City, has long been associated with the law, and its **Inns of Court** make for an interesting stroll, their archaic, cobbled precincts exuding the rarefied atmosphere of an Oxbridge college, and sheltering one of the city's oldest churches, the twelfth-century **Temple Church**. Close by the Inns, in Lincoln's Inn Fields, is the **Sir John Soane's Museum**, one of the most memorable and enjoyable of London's small museums, packed with architectural illusions and an eclectic array of curios.

Clerkenwell, to the northeast, is definitely off the conventional tourist trail, but harbours a host of good pubs, bars and restaurants. Neighbouring **Hoxton** (aka Shoreditch) to the east, has acquired a certain cache over the last decade or so, due to the high density of artists and architects who currently live and work here. Visually, Hoxton, a slum area badly damaged in the Blitz, remains harsher on the eye than Clerkenwell, though it, too, has more than its fair share of trendy bars, restaurants and clubs. Several of London's contemporary art dealers now have Hoxton outlets, and there's the excellent **Geffrye Museum** of furniture design to aim for too.

Temple and the Royal Courts of Justice

Temple is the largest and most complex of the Inns of Court, where every barrister in England must study before being called to the Bar. A few very old buildings survive here and the maze of courtyards and passageways is fun to explore. Medieval students ate, attended lectures and slept in the **Middle Temple Hall** (Mon–Fri 10–11.30am & 3–4pm; free), across the courtyard, still the Inn's main dining room. The present building was constructed in the 1560s and provided the setting for many great Elizabethan masques and plays – probably including Shakespeare's *Twelfth Night*, which is believed to have been premiered here in 1602. The hall is worth a visit for its fine hammerbeam roof, wooden panelling and decorative Elizabethan screen.

The two Temple Inns share the use of the complex's oldest building, **Temple Church** (daily 11am–4pm, though hours do vary; Ⓦwww.templechurch.com), built in 1185 by the Knights Templar. An oblong chancel was added in the thirteenth century, and the whole building was damaged in the Blitz, but the original round church – modelled on the Church of the Holy Sepulchre in Jerusalem – still stands, with its striking Purbeck marble piers, recumbent marble effigies of knights and tortured grotesques grimacing in the spandrels of the blind arcading.

Lincoln's Inn Fields

To the north of Temple, on the far side of the Royal Courts of Justice lies **Lincoln's Inn Fields**, laid out in the early 1640s with **Lincoln's Inn** (Mon–Fri 9am–6pm; Ⓦwww.lincolnsinn.org.uk), the first – and in many ways the prettiest – of the Inns of Court on its east side. The Inn's fifteenth-century **Old Hall** is open by appointment only (Ⓣ020/7405 1393), but you can view the early seventeenth-century **chapel** (Mon–Fri noon–2pm), with its unusual fan-vaulted open undercroft and, on the first floor, its late Gothic nave, hit by a zeppelin in World War I and much restored since.

The south side of Lincoln's Inn Fields is occupied by the gigantic Royal College of Surgeons, home to the **Hunterian Museum** (Tues–Sat 10am–5pm; free; Ⓦwww.rcseng.ac.uk), a fascinating collection of pickled skeletons and body pieces. Also on view are the skeleton of the "Irish giant", Charles Byrne (1761–83), who was seven feet ten inches tall, and, in the adjacent McCrae Gallery, the Sicilian midget Caroline Crachami (1815–24), who stood at only one foot ten and a half inches when she died at the age of nine.

A group of buildings on the north side of Lincoln's Inn Fields house **Sir John Soane's Museum** (Tues–Sat 10am–5pm; first Tues of the month also 6–9pm; free; Ⓦwww.soane.org), one of London's best-kept secrets. The chief architect of the Bank of England, Soane (1753–1837) was an avid collector who designed this house not only as a home and office, but also as a place to stash his large collection of art and antiquities. Arranged much as it was in his lifetime, the ingeniously planned house has an informal, treasure-hunt atmosphere, with surprises in every alcove; the museum has also begun to exhibit contemporary art. At 2.30pm every Saturday, a fascinating, hour-long **guided tour** (£3) takes you round the museum and the enormous research library, next door, containing architectural drawings, books and exquisitely detailed cork and wood models.

Hoxton

Until recently, **Hoxton** was an unpleasant amalgam of wholesale clothes and shoe shops, striptease pubs and roaring traffic. Over the last decade, however, it has been colonized by artists, designers and architects and transformed itself into the city's most vibrant artistic enclave, peppered with contemporary art galleries and a whole host of very cool bars and clubs.

On City Road stands one of Hoxton's few formal sights, the Georgian ensemble of **Wesley's Chapel and House** (Mon–Sat 10am–4pm, Sun 12.30–2pm; free; Ⓦwww.wesleyschapel.org.uk). A place of pilgrimage for Methodists, the uncharacteristically ornate chapel, built in 1777, heralded the coming of age of Wesley's sect. The **Museum of Methodism** (same hours) in the basement tells the story of Wesley and Methodism. Wesley lived his last two years in the Georgian **house** to the right of the main gates, and inside you can see bits of his furniture and his deathbed, plus an early shock-therapy machine with which he used to treat members of his congregation. Wesley's **grave** is round the back of the chapel, in the shadow of a modern office block.

The geographical focus of the area's transformation is **Hoxton Square**, situated northeast of Old Street tube, a strange and not altogether happy mixture of light industrial units and artists' studios arranged around a leafy, formal square. Despite the lack of aesthetic charm, the area has become an increasingly fashionable place to live and work and several leading West End **art galleries** have opened up premises here, among them Jay Jopling's White Cube at the south end of the square.

Hoxton's one other conventional tourist sight is the **Geffrye Museum** (Tues–Sat 10am–5pm, Sun noon–5pm; free; Ⓦwww.geffrye-museum.org.uk), a museum of furniture design, set back from Kingsland Road in a peaceful little enclave of eighteenth-century ironmongers' almshouses. A series of period living rooms, ranging from the oak-panelled seventeenth-century through refined Georgian and cluttered Victorian, leads to the excellent twentieth-century section and a pleasant café/restaurant. To get to the museum, take bus #149 or #242 from Liverpool Street tube.

The City

The City is where London began. Long established as the financial district, it stretches from Temple Bar in the west to the Tower of London in the east – administrative boundaries that are only slightly larger than those marked by the Roman walls and their medieval successors. However, in this Square Mile (as the City is sometimes referred to), you'll find few leftovers of London's early days, since four-fifths of the area burnt down in the Great Fire of 1666. Rebuilt in brick and stone, the City gradually lost its centrality as London swelled westwards, though it has maintained its position as Britain's financial heartland. What you see on the ground is mostly the product of three fairly recent building phases: the Victorian construction boom of the latter half of the nineteenth century; the overzealous postwar reconstruction following the Blitz; and the building frenzy that began in the 1980s, and which has seen fifty percent of the City's office space rebuilt.

When you consider what has happened here, it's amazing that so much has survived to pay witness to the City's two-thousand-year history. Wren's spires still punctuate the skyline here and there and his masterpiece, **St Paul's Cathedral**, remains one of London's geographical pivots. At the eastern edge of the City, the **Tower of London** still stands protected by some of the best-preserved medieval fortifications in Europe. Other relics, such as the City's few surviving medieval alleyways, Wren's **Monument** to the Great Fire and London's oldest synagogue and church, are less conspicuous, and even locals have problems finding the more modern attractions of the **Museum of London** and the **Barbican** arts complex.

Fleet Street

In 1500 a certain Wynkyn de Worde, a pupil of William Caxton, moved the Caxton presses from Westminster to **Fleet Street**, to be close to the lawyers of the Inns of Court and to the clergy of St Paul's. However, the street really boomed two hundred years later when, in 1702, the now-defunct *Daily Courant*, Britain's first daily newspaper, was published here. By the nineteenth century all the major national and provincial dailies had their offices and printing presses in the Fleet Street district, a situation that prevailed until the 1980s, when the press barons relocated their operations elsewhere. The best source of information about the old-style Fleet Street is the so-called "journalists' and printers' cathedral", the church of **St Bride's** (Mon–Fri 9am–5pm, Sat 11am–3pm; Ⓦ www.stbrides.com), which boasts Wren's tallest and most exquisite spire (said to be the inspiration for the tiered wedding cake), and whose crypt contains a little museum of Fleet Street history.

The western section of Fleet Street was spared the Great Fire, which stopped just short of **Prince Henry's Room** (Mon–Fri 11am–2pm; free; Ⓦ www.cityoflondon.gov.uk/phr), a fine Jacobean house with timber-framed bay windows. The first-floor room now contains material relating to the diarist **Samuel Pepys**, who was born nearby in Salisbury Court in 1633 and baptized in St Bride's. Even if you've no interest in Pepys, the wooden-panelled room is worth a look – it contains one of the finest Jacobean plasterwork ceilings in London, and a lot of original stained glass.

Numerous narrow alleyways lead off the north side of Fleet Street, two of which – Bolt Court and Hind Court – eventually open out into Gough Square, on which stands **Dr Johnson's House** (May–Sept Mon–Sat 11am–5.30pm; Oct–April

The City churches

The City of London boasts over forty churches (Ⓦ www.london-city-churches.org), the majority of them built or rebuilt by Wren after the Great Fire. As a general rule, weekday lunchtimes are the best time to visit these churches, many of which put on free lunchtime concerts. Below is a list of six of the most varied and interesting churches within the Square Mile:

St Bartholomew-the-Great Cloth Fair; Barbican tube. The oldest surviving church in the City and by far the most atmospheric; a fascinating building. St Paul's aside, if you visit just one church in the City, it should be this one.

St Mary Abchurch Abchurch Lane, Cannon Street; Cannon Street or Bank tube. Uniquely for Wren's City churches, the interior features a huge painted domed ceiling, plus the only authenticated Gibbons reredos.

St Mary Aldermary Queen Victoria Street; Mansion House tube. Wren's most successful stab at Gothic, with fan vaulting in the aisles and a panelled ceiling in the nave.

St Mary Woolnoth Lombard Street; Bank tube. Hawksmoor's only City church, sporting an unusually broad, bulky tower and a Baroque clerestory that floods the church with light from its semicircular windows.

St Olave Hart Street; Tower Hill tube. Built in the fifteenth century, and one of the few pre-Fire Gothic churches in the City.

St Stephen Walbrook Walbrook; Bank tube. Wren's dress rehearsal for St Paul's, with a wonderful central dome and plenty of original woodcarving.

Mon–Sat 11am–5pm; £4.50; Ⓦwww.drjohnsonshouse.org). The great savant, writer and lexicographer lived here from 1747 to 1759, whilst compiling the 41,000 entries for the first dictionary of the English language, two first editions of which can be seen in the grey-panelled rooms of the house. You can also view the open-plan attic, in which Johnson and his six helpers put together the dictionary.

St Paul's Cathedral

Designed by Christopher Wren and completed in 1711, **St Paul's Cathedral** (Mon–Sat 8.30am–4pm; £9.50; Ⓦwww.stpauls.co.uk), remains a dominating presence in the City, despite the encroaching tower blocks. Topped by an enormous lead-covered dome, its showpiece west facade is particularly magnificent. Westminster Abbey has the edge, however, when it comes to celebrity corpses, pre-Reformation sculpture, royal connections and sheer atmosphere. St Paul's, by contrast, is a soulless but perfectly calculated architectural set piece, a burial place for captains rather than kings, though it does contain more artists than Westminster Abbey.

The best place from which to appreciate the glory of St Paul's is beneath the **dome**, decorated (against Wren's wishes) with Thornhill's trompe l'oeil frescoes. The most richly decorated section of the cathedral, however, is the Quire or **chancel**, where the mosaics of birds, fish, animals and greenery, only dating from the 1890s, are particularly spectacular. The intricately carved oak and limewood **choir stalls**, and the imposing organ case, are the work of Wren's master carver, Grinling Gibbons.

A series of stairs, beginning in the south aisle, lead to the dome's three **galleries**, the first of which is the internal **Whispering Gallery**, so called because of its acoustic properties – words whispered to the wall on one side are distinctly audible over one hundred feet away on the other, though the place is often so busy you can't hear much above the hubbub. The other two galleries are exterior: the wide **Stone Gallery**, around the balustrade at the base of the dome, and ultimately the tiny **Golden Gallery**, below the golden ball and cross which top the cathedral.

Although the nave is crammed full of overblown monuments to military types, burials in St Paul's are confined to the whitewashed **crypt**, reputedly the largest in Europe. Immediately to your right is Artists' Corner, which boasts as many painters and architects as Westminster Abbey has poets, including Christopher Wren himself, who was commissioned to build the cathedral after its Gothic predecessor, Old St Paul's, was destroyed in the Great Fire. The crypt's two other star tombs are those of **Nelson** and **Wellington**, both occupying centre stage and both with more fanciful monuments upstairs.

Museum of London and the Barbican

Despite London's long pedigree, very few of its ancient structures are now standing. However, numerous Roman, Saxon and Elizabethan remains have been discovered during the City's various rebuildings, and many of these finds are now displayed at the **Museum of London** (Mon–Sat 10am–5.50pm, Sun noon–5.50pm; free; Ⓦwww.museumoflondon.org.uk), hidden above the western end of London Wall, in the southwestern corner of the Barbican complex. The museum's permanent exhibition is basically an educational trot through London's past from prehistory to the present day; hence the large number of school groups who pass through. The new displays are imaginatively set out, but half the museum (from Tudor times onwards) is undergoing refurbishment until 2009. In the meantime, you can still visit the museum's

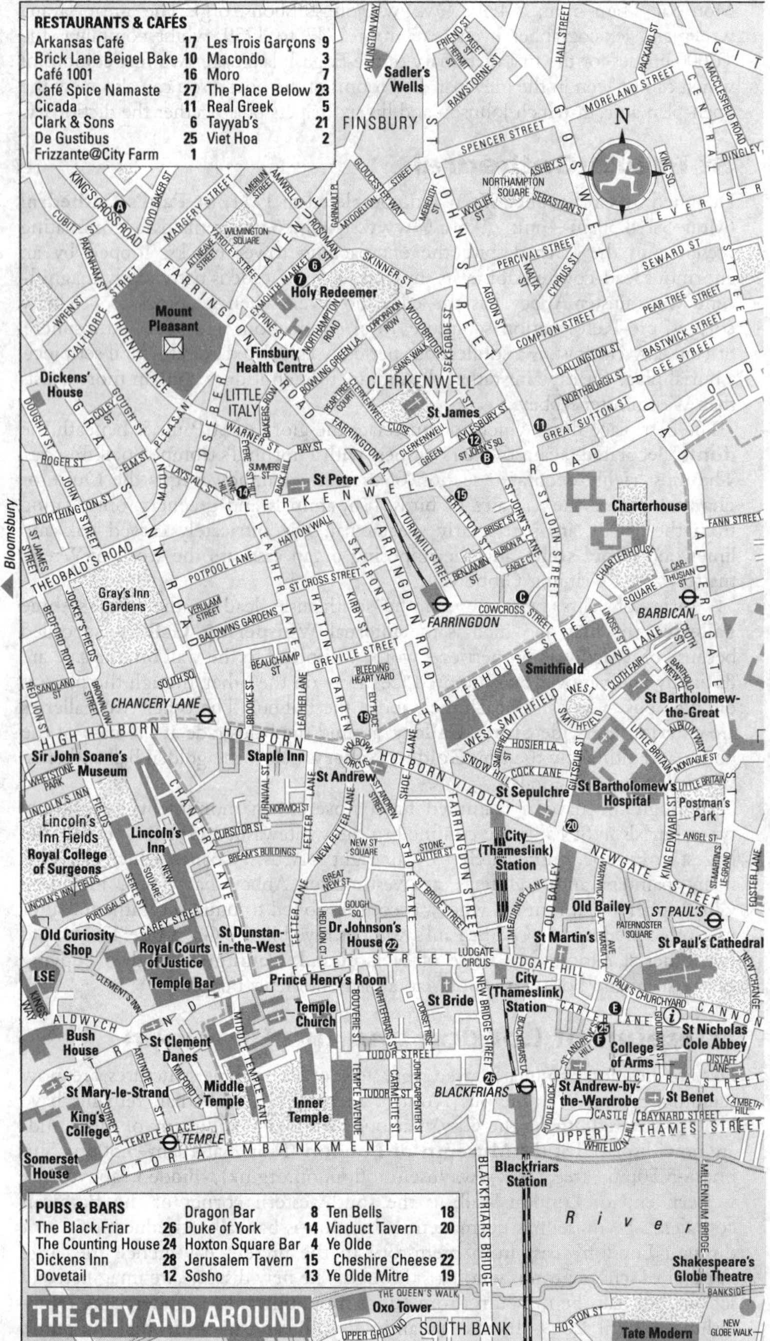
RESTAURANTS & CAFÉS
Arkansas Café 17
Brick Lane Beigel Bake 10
Café 1001 16
Café Spice Namaste 27
Cicada 11
Clark & Sons 6
De Gustibus 25
Frizzante@City Farm 1
Les Trois Garçons 9
Macondo 3
Moro 7
The Place Below 23
Real Greek 5
Tayyab's 21
Viet Hoa 2
PUBS & BARS
The Black Friar 26
The Counting House 24
Dickens Inn 28
Dovetail 12
Dragon Bar 8
Duke of York 14
Hoxton Square Bar 4
Jerusalem Tavern 15
Sosho 13
Ten Bells 18
Viaduct Tavern 20
Ye Olde Cheshire Cheese 22
Ye Olde Mitre 19
THE CITY AND AROUND
Sadler's Wells
FINSBURY
NORTHAMPTON SQUARE
Mount Pleasant
Holy Redeemer
Finsbury Health Centre
Dickens' House
LITTLE ITALY
CLERKENWELL
St James
St Peter
Charterhouse
Gray's Inn Gardens
FARRINGDON
BARBICAN
Smithfield
St Bartholomew-the-Great
CHANCERY LANE
Staple Inn
Sir John Soane's Museum
St Andrew
St Sepulchre
St Bartholomew's Hospital
Postman's Park
Lincoln's Inn Fields
Royal College of Surgeons
Lincoln's Inn
City (Thameslink) Station
Old Bailey
ST PAUL'S
St Martin's
St Paul's Cathedral
Old Curiosity Shop
Royal Courts of Justice
St Dunstan-in-the-West
Dr Johnson's House
LSE
Temple Bar
Prince Henry's Room
St Bride
Temple Church
Bush House
St Clement Danes
College of Arms
St Nicholas Cole Abbey
St Mary-le-Strand
Middle Temple
Inner Temple
BLACKFRIARS
St Andrew-by-the-Wardrobe
St Benet
King's College
TEMPLE
Somerset House
Blackfriars Station
River
Shakespeare's Globe Theatre
Oxo Tower
SOUTH BANK
Tate Modern
Bloomsbury

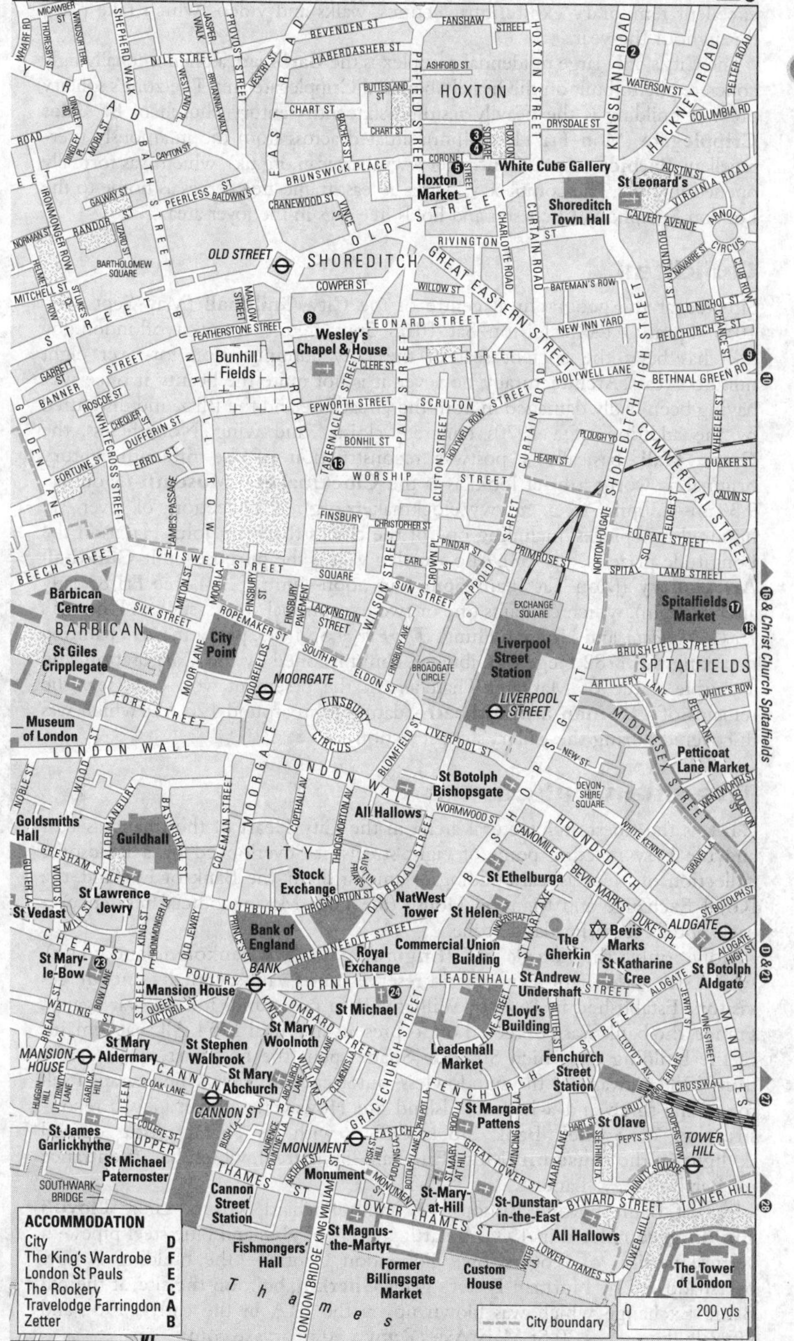
HOXTON
SHOREDITCH
BARBICAN
SPITALFIELDS
CITY
White Cube Gallery
Hoxton Market
St Leonard's
Shoreditch Town Hall
OLD STREET
Wesley's Chapel & House
Bunhill Fields
Barbican Centre
St Giles Cripplegate
City Point
MOORGATE
Liverpool Street Station
LIVERPOOL STREET
Spitalfields Market
Museum of London
Petticoat Lane Market
St Botolph Bishopsgate
All Hallows
Goldsmiths' Hall
Guildhall
Stock Exchange
NatWest Tower
St Ethelburga
St Helen
St Lawrence Jewry
St Vedast
Bank of England
Royal Exchange
Commercial Union Building
The Gherkin
Bevis Marks
St Katharine Cree
ALDGATE
St Botolph Aldgate
St Andrew Undershaft
St Mary-le-Bow
BANK
Mansion House
St Michael
Lloyd's Building
St Mary Woolnoth
St Mary Aldermary
MANSION HOUSE
St Stephen Walbrook
St Mary Abchurch
CANNON ST
Leadenhall Market
Fenchurch Street Station
St James Garlickhythe
St Michael Paternoster
MONUMENT
Monument
St Margaret Pattens
St Olave
TOWER HILL
Cannon Street Station
St-Mary-at-Hill
St-Dunstan-in-the-East
All Hallows
Fishmongers' Hall
St Magnus-the-Martyr
Former Billingsgate Market
Custom House
The Tower of London
Thames
SOUTHWARK BRIDGE
LONDON BRIDGE
15 & Christ Church Spitalfields
ACCOMMODATION
City D
The King's Wardrobe F
London St Pauls E
The Rookery C
Travelodge Farringdon A
Zetter B
City boundary
0 200 yds
© Crown copyright

excellent temporary exhibitions, lectures, walks and videos which take place throughout the year.

The City's only large residential complex is the **Barbican**, a phenomenally ugly concrete ghetto built on the heavily bombed Cripplegate area. The zone's solitary pre-war building is the heavily restored sixteenth-century church of **St Giles Cripplegate** (Mon–Fri 11am–4pm), situated across from the infamously user-repellent **Barbican Arts Centre** (Ⓦwww.barbican.org.uk), which was formally opened in 1982. The complex, which is at least traffic-free, serves as home to the London Symphony Orchestra and holds free gigs in the foyer area.

Guildhall

Situated at the geographical centre of the City, **Guildhall** (May–Sept daily 10am–5pm; Oct–April Mon–Sat 10am–5pm; free; Ⓦwww.cityoflondon.gov.uk) has been the ancient seat of the City administration for over eight hundred years. Architecturally, however, it is not quite the beauty it once was, having been badly damaged in both the Great Fire and the Blitz, and disfigured by the addition of a 1970s concrete cloister and wing. Nonetheless, the **Great Hall**, basically a postwar reconstruction of the fifteenth-century original, is worth a brief look, as is the **Clockmakers' Museum** (Mon–Sat 9.30am–4.30pm; free; Ⓦwww.clockmakers.org), a collection of over six hundred timepieces, including one of the clocks that won John Harrison the Longitude prize (see p.138). Also worth a visit is the purpose-built **Guildhall Art Gallery** (Mon–Sat 10am–5pm, Sun noon–4pm; £2.50, free Fri & daily after 3.30pm), which contains one or two exceptional works, such as Rossetti's *La Ghirlandata*, and Holman Hunt's *The Eve of St Agnes*, plus a massive painting depicting the 1782 Siege of Gibraltar, commissioned by the Corporation, and a marble statue of Margaret Thatcher. In the basement, you can view the remains of a **Roman amphitheatre**, dating from around 120 AD, which was discovered during the gallery's construction.

The financial centre

Bank is the finest architectural arena in the City. Heart of the finance sector and the busy meeting point of eight streets, it's overlooked by a handsome collection of Neoclassical buildings – among them, the Bank of England, the Royal Exchange and Mansion House (the Lord Mayor's official residence) – each one faced in Portland Stone.

Sadly, only the **Bank of England** (Ⓦwww.bankofengland.co.uk), which stores the nation's vast gold reserves in its vaults, actually encourages visitors. Established in 1694 by William III to raise funds for the war against France, the bank wasn't erected on its present site until 1734. All that remains of the building on which Sir John Soane spent the best part of his career from 1788 onwards is the windowless, outer curtain wall, which wraps itself round the three-and-a-half-acre island site. However, you can view a reconstruction of Soane's Bank Stock Office, with its characteristic domed skylight, in the **museum** (Mon–Fri 10am–5pm; free), which has its entrance on Bartholomew Lane.

East of Bank, beyond Bishopsgate, stands Richard Rogers' glitzy **Lloyd's Building**, completed in 1984. A startling array of glass and blue steel pipes – a vertical version of Rogers' own Pompidou Centre – the building is now overshadowed by Norman Foster's giant **Gherkin**, built on the site of the old Baltic Exchange which was blown up by the IRA in the early 1990s, and officially known as 30 St Mary Axe (Ⓦwww.30stmaryaxe.com).

Hidden away behind a modern red-brick office block in a little courtyard off Bevis Marks, north up St Mary Axe from the Lloyd's building, the **Bevis Marks Synagogue** (guided tours Wed & Fri noon, Sun 11.15am; £2; Ⓦ www.sandp.org) was built in 1701 by Sephardic Jews who had fled the Inquisition in Spain and Portugal. This is the country's oldest surviving synagogue, and its roomy, rich interior gives an idea of just how wealthy the congregation was at the time. Nowadays, the Sephardic community has dispersed across London and the congregation has dwindled, though the magnificent array of chandeliers makes it popular for candlelit Jewish weddings.

Just south of the Lloyd's building you'll find the picturesque **Leadenhall Market**, whose richly painted, graceful Victorian cast-ironwork dates from 1881. Inside, the traders cater mostly for the lunchtime City crowd, their barrows laden with exotic seafood and game, fine wines, champagne and caviar.

London Bridge and Monument

Until 1750, **London Bridge** was the only bridge across the Thames. The Romans were the first to build a permanent crossing here, but it was the medieval bridge that achieved world fame: built of stone and crowded with timber-framed houses, it became one of the great attractions of London – there's a model in the nearby church of St Magnus the Martyr (Tues–Fri 9.30am–4pm, Sun 10am–1pm). The houses were finally removed in the mid-eighteenth century, and a new stone bridge erected in 1831; that one now stands in the middle of the Arizona desert, having been bought for $2.4 million in the late 1960s by a gentleman who, so the story goes, was under the impression he had purchased Tower Bridge. The present concrete structure, without doubt the ugliest yet, dates from 1972.

The only reason to go anywhere near London Bridge is to see the **Monument** (daily 9.30am–5.30pm; £2), which was designed by Wren to commemorate the Great Fire of 1666. Crowned with spiky gilded flames, this plain Doric column stands 202 feet high; if it were laid out flat it would touch the bakery where the Fire started, east of Monument. The bas-relief on the base, now in very bad shape, depicts Charles II and the Duke of York in Roman garb conducting the emergency relief operation. The 311 steps to the viewing gallery once guaranteed an incredible view; nowadays it is somewhat dwarfed by the buildings around it.

The Tower of London

One of Britain's main tourist attractions, the **Tower of London** (March–Oct Mon & Sun 10am–6pm, Tues–Sat 9am–6pm; Nov–Feb closes 5pm; £16; Ⓦ www.hrp.org.uk), overlooks the river at the eastern boundary of the old city walls. Despite all the hype and heritage claptrap, it remains one of London's most remarkable buildings, site of some of the goriest events in the nation's history, and somewhere all visitors and Londoners should explore at least once. Chiefly famous as a place of imprisonment and death, it has variously been used as a royal residence, armoury, mint, menagerie, observatory and – a function it still serves – a safe-deposit box for the Crown Jewels.

It's a good idea to get your bearings by taking one of the free **guided tours**, given every thirty minutes or so by one of the Tower's **Beefeaters** (officially known as Yeoman Warders). Visitors today enter the Tower along Water Lane, but in times gone by most prisoners were delivered through **Traitors' Gate**, on the waterfront. The nearby **Bloody Tower**, which forms the main entrance to the Inner Ward, is where the 12-year-old Edward V and his 10-year-old brother

▲ Tower Bridge

were accommodated "for their own safety" in 1483 by their uncle, the future Richard III, and later murdered. It's also where **Walter Raleigh** was imprisoned on three separate occasions, including a thirteen-year stretch.

The **White Tower**, at the centre of the Inner Ward, is the original "Tower", begun in 1076, and now home to displays from the **Royal Armouries**. Even if you've no interest in military paraphernalia, you should at least pay a visit to the **Chapel of St John**, a beautiful Norman structure on the second floor that was completed in 1080 – making it the oldest intact church building in London. To the west of the White Tower is the execution spot on **Tower Green** where seven highly placed but unlucky individuals were beheaded, among them Anne Boleyn and her cousin Catherine Howard (Henry VIII's second and fifth wives).

The Waterloo Barracks, to the north of the White Tower, hold the **Crown Jewels**, perhaps the major reason so many people flock to the Tower; however, the moving walkways are disappointingly swift, allowing you just 28 seconds' viewing during peak periods. The oldest piece of regalia is the twelfth-century **Anointing Spoon**, but the vast majority of exhibits postdate the Commonwealth (1649–60), when many of the royal riches were melted down for coinage or sold off. Among the jewels are the three largest cut diamonds in the world, including the legendary **Koh-i-Noor**, set into the Queen Mother's Crown in 1937.

Tower Bridge

Tower Bridge ranks with Big Ben as the most famous of all London landmarks. Completed in 1894, its neo-Gothic towers are clad in Cornish granite and Portland stone, but conceal a steel frame, which, at the time, represented a considerable engineering achievement, allowing a road crossing that could be raised to give tall ships access to the upper reaches of the Thames. The raising of the bascules (from the French for "see-saw") remains an impressive sight – phone ahead to find out when the bridge is opening (Ⓣ020/7940 3984). If you buy a ticket (daily: April–Sept 10am–6.30pm; Oct–March 9.30am–6pm; £5.50; Ⓦwww.towerbridge.org.uk), you get to walk across the elevated walkways linking the summits of the towers and visit the Tower's Engine Room, on the south side of the bridge, where you can see the now defunct giant coal-fired boilers which drove the hydraulic system until 1976, and play some interactive engineering games.

The East End and Docklands

Few places in London have engendered so many myths as the **East End** (a catch-all title which covers just about everywhere east of the City). Its name is synonymous with slums, sweatshops and crime, as epitomized by antiheroes such as Jack the Ripper and the Kray Twins, but also with the rags-to-riches careers of the likes of Harold Pinter and Vidal Sassoon, and whole generations of Jews who were born in the most notorious of London's cholera-ridden quarters and have now moved to wealthier pastures.

The area's first immigrants were French Protestant Huguenots, fleeing religious persecution in the late seventeenth century. Within three generations the Huguenots were entirely assimilated, and the Irish became the new immigrant population, but it was the influx of Jews escaping pogroms in eastern Europe and Russia that defined the character of the East End in the late nineteenth century. The East End remains at the bottom of the pile; even the millions poured into the neighbouring **Docklands** development have failed to make much impression on local unemployment and housing problems. Racism is still a problem, and is directed, for the most part, against the large Bengali community, who came here from the poor rural area of Sylhet in Bangladesh in the 1960s and 1970s.

As the area is not an obvious place for sightseeing, and certainly no beauty spot – Victorian slum clearances, Hitler's bombs and postwar tower blocks have all left their mark – most visitors to the East End come for its famous **Sunday markets** (Ⓦwww.eastlondonmarkets.com). As for Docklands, most of it can be gawped at from the overhead light railway, including the vast and awesome **Canary Wharf** redevelopment.

Spitalfields and Bethnal Green

Spitalfields, within sight of the sleek tower blocks of the financial sector, lies at the old heart of the East End, where the French Huguenots settled in the seventeenth century, where the Jewish community was at its strongest in the late nineteenth century, and where today's Bengali community eats, sleeps, works and prays. If you visit just one area in the East End, it should be this zone, which preserves mementos from each wave of immigration.

The easiest approach is from Liverpool Street Station, a short stroll west of **Spitalfields Market**, the red-brick and green-gabled market hall built in 1893, half of which was demolished in order to make way for yet more City offices. The dominant architectural presence in Spitalfields, however, is **Christ Church** (Tues 11am–4pm, Sun 1–4pm), built in 1714–29 to a characteristically bold design by Nicholas Hawksmoor, and now facing the market hall. Best viewed from Brushfield Street, the church's main features are its huge 225-foot-high spire and a giant Tuscan portico, raised on steps and shaped like a Venetian window (a central arched opening flanked by two smaller rectangles), a motif repeated in the tower and doors.

The East End's most popular museum is the **V&A Museum of Childhood** (daily 10am–5.50pm; free; Ⓦwww.vam.ac.uk/moc), situated opposite Bethnal Green tube station. The open-plan, wrought-iron hall, originally part of (and still a branch of) the V&A (see p.128), was transported here in the 1860s to bring art to the East End. On the ground floor there are clockwork **toys**, everything from classic robots to a fully functioning model railway, marionettes and puppets, teddies and Smurfs and even Inuit dolls. The most famous exhibits are the remarkable antique **dolls' houses** dating back to 1673, now displayed upstairs, where you'll also find a play area for very small kids and the museum's space for temporary exhibitions.

Docklands

Built in the nineteenth century to cope with the huge volume of goods shipped along the Thames from all over the Empire, **Docklands** was once the largest enclosed cargo-dock system in the world. No one thought the area could be rejuvenated when the docks closed in the 1960s, but over the last twenty years, warehouses have been converted into luxury flats, waterside penthouse apartments have been built and a huge high-rise office development has sprung up around Canary Wharf. Although Canary Wharf is on the Jubilee line, the best way to view Docklands is either from one of the boats that course up and down the Thames (see p.83), or from the driverless, overhead **Docklands Light Railway** or DLR (Ⓦwww.tfl.gov.uk/dlr), which sets off from Bank, or from Tower Gateway, close to Tower Hill tube.

The only really busy bit of the new Docklands, Canary Wharf is best known as the home of Britain's tallest building, Cesar Pelli's landmark tower, officially known as **One Canada Square**. The world's first skyscraper to be clad in stainless steel, it's an undeniably impressive sight, both from a distance (its flashing pinnacle is a feature of the horizon at numerous points in London) and close up. However, it no longer stands alone, having been joined by several other skyscrapers that stop just short of Pelli's stumpy pinnacle.

One of the few original warehouses left to the north of Canary Wharf has been converted into the **Museum in Docklands** (daily 10am–6pm; £5; Ⓦwww.museumindocklands.org.uk), an excellent stab at charting the history of the area from Roman times to the present day. Highlights include a great model of old London Bridge, an eight-foot-long watercolour and a soft play area for kids. Unless you're keen to visit the museum, though, there's little point in getting off the DLR at Canary Wharf. Instead, stay on the train as it cuts right through the middle of the office buildings under a parabolic steel-and-glass canopy and keep going until you reach Greenwich (see p.136).

The South Bank

The **South Bank** – the area immediately opposite Victoria Embankment – is best known for the **London Eye**, one of the capital's most popular millennium projects. The arrival of the Eye helped kick-start the renovation of the **South Bank Centre**, London's much unloved concrete culture bunker of theatres and galleries, built, for the most part, in the 1960s. After decades in the doldrums, the centre is now under inspired artistic direction and the whole area is enjoying something of a renaissance.

It's also worth visiting the **Imperial War Museum**, a short walk inland from the river, which contains the most detailed exhibition on the Holocaust in Britain.

The South Bank Centre

The modern development of the South Bank dates back to the 1951 **Festival of Britain**, when the South Bank Exhibition was held on derelict land south of the Thames. The festival was an attempt to revive postwar morale by celebrating the centenary of the Great Exhibition (when Britain really did rule over half the world). The most striking features of the site were the Royal Festival Hall (which still stands), the ferris wheel (inspiration for the current London Eye), the saucer-shaped Dome of Discovery (disastrously revisited in the guise of the Millennium Dome), and the cigar-shaped Skylon tower.

The Festival of Britain's success provided the impetus for the eventual creation of the **South Bank Centre** (Ⓦ www.southbankcentre.co.uk), home to artistic institutions such as the Royal Festival Hall, the Hayward Gallery, the arts cinema BFI Southbank (formerly the NFT), London IMAX Cinema, and lastly Denys Lasdun's National Theatre (Ⓦ www.nationaltheatre.org.uk). Its unprepossessing appearance is softened, too, by its riverside location, its avenue of trees, its fluttering banners, its occasional buskers and skateboarders and the secondhand bookstalls outside the BFI Southbank.

The London Eye

South of the South Bank Centre proper is the **London Eye** (daily: June–Sept 10am–9pm; Oct–May 10am–8pm; £15; Ⓣ 0870/5000 600, Ⓦ www.ba-londoneye.com), the magnificently graceful millennium wheel which spins slowly and silently over the Thames. Standing 443ft high, the wheel is constantly in slow motion – a full-circle "flight" in one of its 32 pods takes around thirty

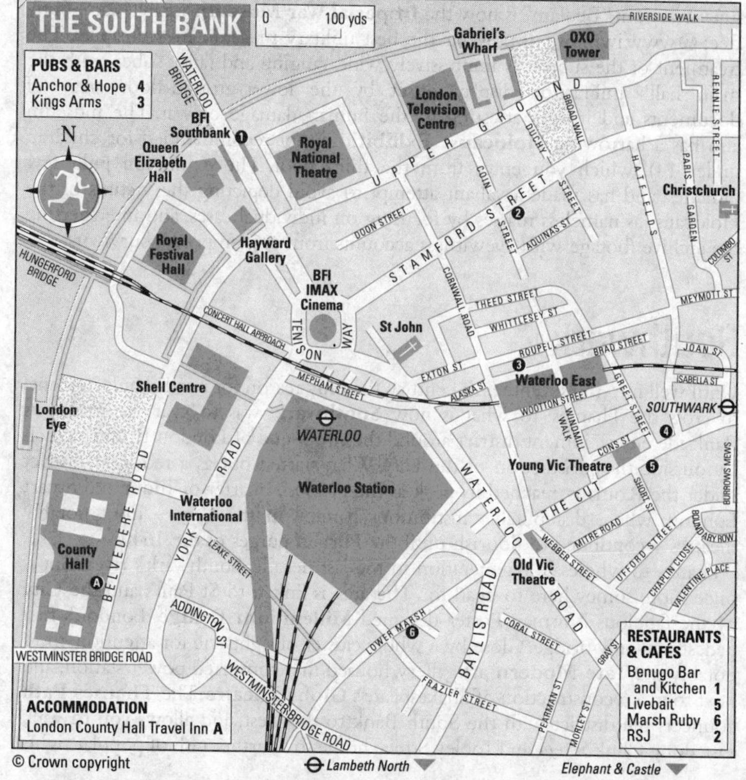

minutes, and lifts you high above the city. It's one of the few places (apart from a plane window) from which London looks a manageable size, as you can see right out to where the suburbs slip into the countryside. Ticket prices are outrageously high, and queues can be very bad at the weekend, so book in advance over the phone or online.

County Hall

Next to the London Eye is the only truly monumental building on the South Bank, **County Hall**, with its colonnaded crescent. Completed in 1933, it housed the LCC (London County Council), and later the GLC (Greater London Council), until 1986, and is now home to, among other things, two hotels, several restaurants, a giant aquarium, a glorified amusement arcade called Namco Station and a couple of art galleries.

County Hall's most popular attraction is the **London Aquarium** (daily 10am–6pm or later; £9.75; Ⓦwww.londonaquarium.co.uk), laid out across three floors of the basement. With some super-large, multi-floor tanks, and everything from dog-face puffers to piranhas, this is somewhere that's pretty much guaranteed to please younger kids. The Touching Pool where children can actually stroke the (non-sting) rays, is particularly popular.

Imperial War Museum

The domed building at the east end of Lambeth Road, formerly the infamous lunatic asylum "Bedlam" is now the **Imperial War Museum** (daily 10am–6pm; free; Ⓦwww.iwm.org.uk), by far the best military museum in the capital. The treatment of the subject is impressively wide-ranging and fairly sober, with the main hall's militaristic display offset by the lower-ground-floor array of documents and images attesting to the human damage of war. The museum also has a harrowing **Holocaust Exhibition** (not recommended for children under 14), which you enter from the third floor. The exhibition pulls few punches, and has made a valiant attempt to avoid depicting the victims of the Holocaust as nameless masses by focusing on individual cases, and interspersing the archive footage with eyewitness accounts from contemporary survivors.

Southwark

Until well into the seventeenth century, the only reason for north-bank residents to cross the Thames, to what is now **Southwark**, was to visit the infamous Bankside entertainment district around the south end of London Bridge, which lay outside the jurisdiction of the City. What started out as a red-light district under the Romans, reached its peak as the pleasure quarter of Tudor and Stuart London, where disreputable institutions banned in the City – most notably theatres – continued to flourish until the Puritan purges of the 1640s.

Thanks to wholesale regeneration in the last decade, Southwark's riverfront is once more somewhere to head for. The area is linked to St Paul's and the City by the fabulous Norman Foster-designed **Millennium Bridge**, London's first pedestrian-only bridge. Close by, a whole cluster of sights vie for attention, most notably the **Tate Modern** art gallery, housed in a converted power station, and next to it, a reconstruction of Shakespeare's **Globe Theatre**. The **Thames Path** connects the district with the South Bank to the west, and allows you to walk east along Clink Street and Tooley Street, home to a further rash of popular sights such as the **London Dungeon**. Further east still, Butler's Wharf is a thriving little warehouse development centred on the excellent **Design Museum**.

Tate Modern

The masterful conversion of the austere Bankside power station into the **Tate Modern** (daily 10am–6pm; Fri & Sat until 10pm; free; Ⓦwww.tate.org.uk) has left plenty of the original, industrial feel, while providing wonderfully light and spacious galleries in which to show off the Tate's vast international twentieth-century art collection. The best way to enter is down the ramp from the west, so you get the full effect of the stupendously large turbine hall. It's easy enough to find your way around the galleries, with levels 3 and 5 displaying the permanent collection, level 4 used for fee-paying temporary exhibitions, and level 7 home to a café with a great view over the Thames.

Given that Tate Modern is the largest modern art gallery in the world, you need to spend the best part of a day here to do justice to the place, or be very selective. Pick up a plan (and, for an extra £2, a multimedia guide), and take the escalator to level 3. The curators have eschewed the usual chronological approach through the "isms", preferring to group works together thematically. On the whole this works very well, though the early twentieth-century canvases, in their gilded frames do struggle when made to compete with contemporary installations.

Although the displays change every six months or so, you're still pretty much guaranteed to see at least some works by **Monet** and Bonnard, Cubist pioneers **Picasso** and Braque, Surrealists such as **Dalí**, abstract artists like **Mondrian**, Bridget Riley and Pollock, and Pop supremos **Warhol** and Lichtenstein. There are seminal works such as a replica of **Duchamp**'s urinal, entitled *Fountain* and signed "R. Mutt" and Yves Klein's totally blue paintings. And such is the space here that several artists get whole rooms to themselves, among them Joseph Beuys and his shamanistic wax and furs, and **Mark Rothko**, whose abstract "Seagram Murals", originally destined for a posh restaurant in New York, have their own shrine-like room in the heart of the collection.

From the Globe to Southwark Cathedral

Dwarfed by the Tate Modern but equally spectacular is **Shakespeare's Globe Theatre** (Ⓦwww.shakespeares-globe.org), a reconstruction of the polygonal playhouse where most of the Bard's later works were first performed, and which was originally erected on nearby Park Street in 1598. To find out more about Shakespeare and the history of Bankside, the Globe's stylish **exhibition** (daily: May–Sept 9am–noon & 12.30–5pm; Oct–April 10am–5pm; £9) is well worth a visit. It begins by detailing the long campaign by American actor Sam Wanamaker to have the Globe rebuilt, but it's the imaginative hands-on exhibits that really hit the spot. You can have a virtual play on medieval instruments such as the crumhorn or sackbut, prepare your own edition of Shakespeare, and feel the thatch, hazelnut-shell and daub used to build the theatre. There's also an informative **guided tour** round the theatre itself; during the summer season, you get to visit the exhibition and the remains of the nearby Rose Theatre instead.

An exact replica of the **Golden Hinde** (daily 10am–5.30pm, but phone ahead; £5.50; Ⓣ0870/011 8700, Ⓦwww.goldenhinde.org), the galleon in which Francis Drake sailed around the world from 1577 to 1580, nestles in St Mary Overie Dock, at the eastern end of Clink Street. The ship is surprisingly small, and its original crew of eighty-plus must have been cramped to say the least. There's a lack of interpretive panels, so it's worth paying the little bit extra and getting a guided tour from one of the folk in period garb – ring ahead to check a group hasn't booked the place up.

Close by the *Golden Hinde* stands **Southwark Cathedral** (Mon–Fri 7.30am–6pm, Sat & Sun 8.30am–6pm; free; ⓦwww.southwark.anglican.org/cathedral), built as the medieval Augustinian priory church of St Mary Overie, and given cathedral status only in 1905. Of the original thirteenth-century church, only the choir and retrochoir now remain, separated by a tall and beautiful stone Tudor screen, making them probably the oldest Gothic structures left in London. The nave was entirely rebuilt in the nineteenth century, but the cathedral contains numerous interesting monuments, from a thirteenth-century oak effigy of a knight to an early twentieth-century memorial to Shakespeare.

Borough Market (ⓦwww.boroughmarket.org.uk), squeezed underneath the railway arches by the cathedral, is one of the few wholesale fruit and vegetable markets still trading under its original Victorian wrought-iron shed. It's transformed from scruffy obscurity to a small foodie haven, with permanent outlets such as Neal's Yard Dairy and Konditor & Cook, joined by gourmet daytime market stalls on Thursdays (11am–5pm), Fridays (noon–6pm) and, particularly, Saturdays (9am–4pm).

From London Bridge to Butler's Wharf

The most educative and strangest of Southwark's many museums, the **Old Operating Theatre, Museum and Herb Garret** on St Thomas Street (daily 10.30am–5pm; £5.25; ⓦwww.thegarret.org.uk) is located to the east of the cathedral on St Thomas Street, on the other side of Borough High Street. Built in 1821 up a spiral staircase at the top of a church tower, where the hospital apothecary's herbs were stored, this women's operating theatre dates from the pre-anaesthetic era. Despite being entirely gore-free, the museum is as stomach-churning as the London Dungeon (see p.125). The surgeons who used this room would have concentrated on speed and accuracy (most amputations took less than a minute), but there was still a thirty percent

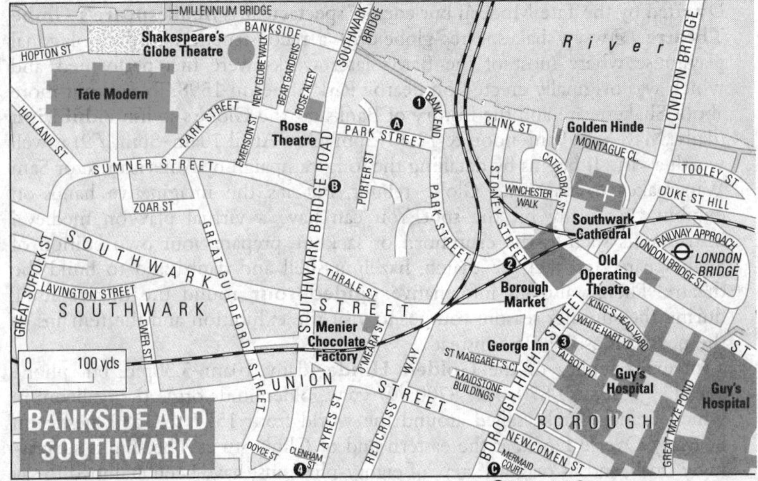

mortality rate, with many patients simply dying of shock, and many more from bacterial infection.

There's usually an impressive queue beside the railway arches of London Bridge train station, on the south side of Tooley Street, home to the ever-popular **London Dungeon** (daily: March to mid-July & Sept/Oct 10.30am–5.30pm; mid-July to Aug 9.30am–7.30pm; Nov–Feb 10.30am–5pm; £17; ⓣ020/7403 7221, ⓦwww.thedungeons.com) – to avoid the inevitable queue, buy your ticket online. Young teenagers and the credulous probably get the most out of the life-sized waxwork tableaux of folk being hanged, drawn, quartered and tortured, the general hysteria boosted by actors dressed as top-hatted Victorian vampires, executioners and monks pouncing out of the darkness. Visitors are led into the labyrinth, an old-fashioned mirror maze, before being herded through a series of live action scenarios, passing through the exploitative "Jack the Ripper Experience", and ending with a walk through a revolving tunnel of flames.

There's more World War II history at **HMS Belfast** (daily: March–Oct 10am–6pm; Nov–Feb 10am–5pm; £10; ⓦwww.iwm.org.uk), a World War II cruiser, permanently moored between London Bridge and Tower Bridge. Armed with six torpedoes, and six-inch guns with a range of over fourteen miles, the *Belfast* spent over two years of the war in the Royal Naval shipyards after being hit by a mine in the Firth of Forth at the beginning of hostilities. It later saw action in the Barents Sea during World War II and during the Korean War, before being decommissioned. The maze of cabins is fun to explore but if you want to find out more about the *Belfast*, head for the exhibition rooms in zone 5.

A short stroll east of the *Belfast* is Norman Foster's startling glass-encased **City Hall** (Mon–Fri 8am–8pm; ⓦwww.london.gov.uk), the new Greater London Authority headquarters that looks like a giant car headlight. Visitors are welcome to stroll around the building and watch the London Assembly proceedings from the second floor.

In contrast to the brash offices on Tooley Street, **Butler's Wharf**, east of Tower Bridge, has retained its historical character. **Shad Thames**, the narrow street at

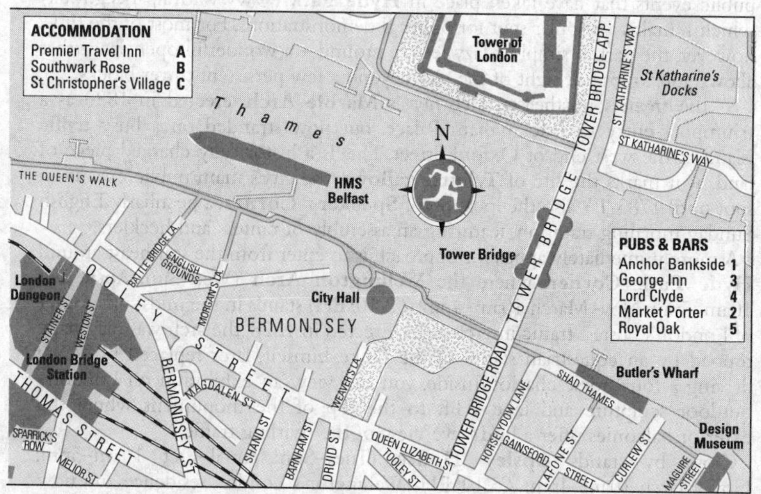

© Crown copyright

the back of Butler's Wharf, has kept the wrought-iron overhead gangways by which the porters used to transport goods from the wharves to the warehouses further back from the river, and is one of the most atmospheric alleyways in the whole of the district. The chief attraction of Butler's Wharf is the superb riverside **Design Museum** (daily 10am–5.45pm; £7; Ⓦwww.designmuseum.org), a stylish, Bauhaus-like conversion of a 1950s warehouse at the eastern end of Shad Thames. The museum has no permanent display, but instead hosts a series of temporary exhibitions (up to four at any one time) on important designers, movements or single products. The small coffee bar in the foyer is a great place to relax, and there's a pricier restaurant on the top floor.

Hyde Park, Kensington and Chelsea

Hyde Park, together with its westerly extension, Kensington Gardens, covers a distance of two miles from Oxford Street in the northeast to Kensington Palace, set in the Royal Borough of **Kensington** and **Chelsea**. Other districts go in and out of fashion, but this area has been in vogue ever since royalty moved into **Kensington Palace** in the late seventeenth century.

Aside from the shops around Harrods in Knightsbridge, however, the popular tourist attractions lie in **South Kensington**, where three of London's top **museums** – the Victoria and Albert, Natural History and Science museums – stand on land bought with the proceeds of the Great Exhibition of 1851. Chelsea, to the south, has a slightly more bohemian pedigree. In the 1960s, the **King's Road** carved out its reputation as London's catwalk, while in the late 1970s it was the epicentre of the punk explosion. Nothing so rebellious goes on in Chelsea now, though its residents like to think of themselves as rather more artistic and intellectual than the purely moneyed types of Kensington.

Hyde Park and Kensington Gardens

Hangings, muggings, duels and the Great Exhibition of 1851 are just some of the public events that have taken place in **Hyde Park** (Ⓦwww.royalparks.gov.uk) which remains a popular spot for political demonstrations. For most of the time, however, the park is simply a lazy leisure ground – a wonderful open space that allows you to lose all sight of the city beyond a few persistent tower blocks.

At the treeless northeastern corner is **Marble Arch**, erected in 1828 as a triumphal entry to Buckingham Palace, but now stranded on a busy traffic island at the west end of Oxford Street. This is a historically charged piece of land, as it marks the site of **Tyburn gallows**, the city's main public execution spot until 1783. It's also the location of **Speakers' Corner**, a peculiarly English Sunday morning tradition, featuring an assembly of ranters and hecklers.

A more immediately appealing approach is to enter from the southeast around **Hyde Park Corner**, where the **Wellington Arch** (Wed–Sun: April–Oct 10am–5pm; Nov–March 10am–4pm; £3.10; EH) stands in the midst of another of London's busiest traffic interchanges. Erected in 1828, the arch was originally topped by an equestrian statue of the Duke himself, later replaced by Peace driving a four-horse chariot. Inside, you can view an exhibition on London's outdoor sculpture and take a lift to the top of the monument where the exterior balconies offer a bird's-eye view of the swirling traffic.

Close by stands **Apsley House** (Tues–Sun: April–Oct 10am–5pm; Nov–March 10am–4pm; £5.10; EH), Wellington's London residence and now a museum to the "Iron Duke". Unless you're a keen fan of the Duke, the highlight of the museum is the **art collection**, much of which used to belong to the King of Spain. Among the best pieces, displayed in the Waterloo Gallery on the first floor, are works by de Hooch, van Dyck, Velázquez, Goya, Rubens and Murillo. The famous, more than twice life-size, nude statue of Napoleon by Antonio Canova stands at the foot of the main staircase.

Back outside, Hyde Park is divided in two by the **Serpentine Lake**, which has a popular **Lido** (mid-June to mid-Sept daily 10am–6pm; £3.75) on its south bank and a pretty upper section known as the **Long Water**, which narrows until it reaches a group of four fountains.

The western half of the park is officially known as **Kensington Gardens** (daily 6am to dusk), and its two most popular attractions are the **Serpentine Gallery** (daily 10am–6pm; free; Ⓦwww.serpentinegallery.org), which hosts contemporary art exhibitions, and the richly decorated, High Gothic **Albert Memorial** (guided tours Sun 2 & 3pm; £4.50), clearly visible to the west. Erected in 1876, the memorial is as much a hymn to the glorious achievements of Britain as to its subject, Queen Victoria's husband (who died of typhoid in 1861). Albert occupies the central canopy, gilded from head to toe and clutching a catalogue for the 1851 Great Exhibition that he helped to organize.

The Exhibition's most famous feature, the gargantuan glasshouse of the Crystal Palace, no longer exists, but the profits were used to buy a large tract of land south of the park, now home to South Kensington's remarkable cluster of museums and colleges, plus the vast **Royal Albert Hall** (Ⓦwww.royalalberthall.com), a splendid iron-and-glass-domed concert hall, with an exterior of red brick, terracotta and marble that became the hallmark of South Ken architecture. The hall is the venue for Europe's most democratic music festival, the Henry Wood Promenade Concerts, better known as the **Proms**, which take place from July to September, with standing-room tickets for £4.

Kensington Palace

On the western edge of Kensington Gardens stands **Kensington Palace** (daily: March–Oct 10am–6pm; Nov–Feb 10am–5pm; £12; Ⓦwww.hrp.org.uk), a modestly proportioned Jacobean brick mansion bought by William and Mary in 1689, and the chief royal residence for the next fifty years. KP, as it's fondly known in royal circles, is best known today as the place where **Princess Diana** lived until her death in 1997. Visitors don't get to see Diana's apartments, which were on the west side of the palace, where various minor royals still live. Instead, they get to view some of Diana's frocks – and also several worn by the Queen – and then the sparsely furnished state apartments. The highlights are the trompe l'oeil ceiling paintings by William Kent, in particular the Cupola Room, and the oil paintings in the King's Gallery. En route, you also see the tastelessly decorated rooms in which the future Queen Victoria spent her unhappy childhood. To recover from the above, take tea in the exquisite **Orangery** (times as for palace).

Leighton House

A number of wealthy Victorian artists rather self-consciously founded an artists' colony in the streets that lay to the west of Kensington Gardens. It's possible to visit one of the most remarkable of these artist pads, **Leighton House**, 12 Holland Park Rd (daily except Tues; 11am–5.30pm; guided tours Wed & Thurs 2.30pm; £3; Ⓦwww.rbkc.gov.uk/leightonhousemuseum). "It will be opulence, it will be sincerity", Lord Leighton opined before starting work on the house in the 1860s – he later became President of the Royal Academy and was ennobled on his deathbed. The big attraction is the domed Arab Hall, decorated with Saracen tiles, gilded mosaics and woodwork drawn from all over the Islamic world. The other rooms are less spectacular but, in compensation, are hung with paintings by Lord Leighton and his Pre-Raphaelite chums.

Knightsbridge and Harrods

South of Hyde Park lies the irredeemably snobbish **Knightsbridge**, revelling in its reputation as the swankiest shopping area in London, a status epitomized by **Harrods** (Mon–Sat 10am–8pm, Sun noon–6pm; Ⓦwww.harrods.com) on Brompton Road. London's most famous department store started out as a family-run grocery store in 1849, with a staff of two. The current 1905 terracotta building is owned by the Egyptian Mohammed Al Fayed and employs in excess of 3000 staff. The store even has a few sections that are architectural sights in their own right: the Food Hall, with its exquisite Arts and Crafts tiling; the Egyptian Hall, with its pseudo-hieroglyphs and sphinxes; and the fountain at the foot of the Egyptian Escalators dedicated to Di and Dodi. Note that the store has a draconian **dress code**: no ripped jeans, no flip-flops or thong sandals, no shorts, no vest T-shirts, and backpacks either have to be carried in the hand or placed in the store's left luggage (£2.50).

Victoria and Albert Museum (V&A)

In terms of sheer variety and scale, the **Victoria and Albert Museum**, on Cromwell Road (daily 10am–5.45pm, Fri until 10pm; free; Ⓦwww.vam.ac.uk), popularly known as the V&A, is the greatest museum of applied arts in the world. The range of exhibits on display here means that, whatever your taste, there's bound to be something to grab your attention. If you're flagging, there's an edifying café in the museum's period-piece Morris, Gamble & Poynter Rooms.

The most celebrated of the V&A's numerous exhibits are the **Raphael Cartoons**, seven vast biblical paintings that served as designs for a set of tapestries destined for the Sistine Chapel. Close by, you can view highlights from the country's largest dress collection, and the world's largest collection of Indian art outside India. In addition, there are galleries devoted to British, Chinese, Islamic, Japanese and Korean art, as well as costume jewellery, glassware, metalwork and photography. Wading through the huge collection of European sculpture, you come to the surreal **Cast Courts**, filled with copies of European art's greatest hits, from Michelangelo's *David* to Trajan's Column (sawn in half to make it fit).

If you've energy left after your visit, stop by London's most flamboyant Roman Catholic church, the **Brompton Oratory**, built in Neo-Baroque style in the 1880s, which lies just next door to the museum on Brompton Road.

Science Museum

Established as a technological counterpart to the V&A, the **Science Museum**, on Exhibition Road (daily 10am–6pm; free; Ⓦwww.sciencemuseum.org.uk), is undeniably impressive, filling seven floors with items drawn from every conceivable area of science, including space travel, digital technology, steam engines and carbon emissions. Keen to dispel the enduring image of museums devoted to its subject as boring and full of dusty glass cabinets, the Science Museum has modern galleries with interactive displays, and puts on daily demonstrations to show that not all science teaching has to be deathly dry.

First stop inside should be the **information desk**, where you can pick up a museum plan and find out what events and demonstrations are taking place; you can also sign up for a free **guided tour** on a specific subject. Most people will want to head for the **Wellcome Wing**, full of state-of-the-art interactive computers and an IMAX cinema, and geared to appeal to even the most museum-phobic teenager. To get there, you must first pass by the world's first steam engines in the Energy Hall, through the Space gallery, to the far side of the Making of the Modern World, a display of iconic inventions from Robert Stephenson's *Rocket* train of 1829 to the Ford Model T, the world's first mass-produced car.

Make for the popular Launch Pad, one of the first hands-on displays aimed at kids, on Level 3. The Materials gallery, on Level 1, is aimed more at adults, and is an extremely stylish exhibition covering the use of materials ranging from aluminium to zerodur (used for making laser gyroscopes), while Energy, on the second floor, has a great "do not touch" electric-shock machine that absolutely fascinates kids.

Natural History Museum

Alfred Waterhouse's purpose-built mock-Romanesque colossus ensures the **Natural History Museum** (daily 10am–5.50pm, last Fri of Month closes 9.30pm; free; ⓦwww.nhm.ac.uk) its status as London's most handsome museum. The museum has been massively redeveloped over the last decade or so, and is now, by and large, imaginatively designed, though there are still one or two sections that remain little changed since the original opening in 1881. The museum's dinosaur collection is a real hit with the kids, but its collections are also an important resource for serious zoologists.

The main entrance leads to what are now known as the **Life Galleries**, which include the ever-popular Dinosaur gallery, with its grisly life-sized animatronic dinosaur tableau, currently a roaring Tyrannosaurus rex. Other popular sections include the Creepy-Crawlies, the Mammals gallery with its life-size model of a blue whale, and the excellent **Investigate** gallery (Mon–Fri 2.30–5pm, Sat & Sun 11am–5pm; during school holidays daily 11am–5pm), where children aged 7 to 14yrs get to play at being scientists (you need to obtain a timed ticket).

Visitors can view more of the museum's millions of zoological specimens in the **Darwin Centre**. To see the rest of the building, however, you need to sign up for an **Explore tour** (book on the day at the information desk or by phoning ⓣ020/7942 6128; free). The tours last about 45 minutes, allowing visitors to get a closer look at the specimens. You also get to see behind the scenes at the labs, and even talk to one of the museum's scientists about their work.

If the queues for the museum are long (as they can be at weekends and during school holidays), you might be better off heading for the side entrance on Exhibition Road, which leads into the former Geology Museum, now known as the **Red Zone**, a visually exciting romp through the earth's evolution. The most popular sections are the slightly tasteless Kobe earthquake simulator, and the spectacular display of gems and crystals in the Earth's Treasury.

Chelsea

From the Swinging Sixties and even up to the Punk era, **Chelsea** had a slightly bohemian pedigree; these days, it's just another wealthy west London suburb. Among the most nattily attired of all those parading down the King's Road nowadays are the scarlet- or navy-blue-clad Chelsea Pensioners, army veterans

▲ A T-Rex at the Natural History Museum

from the nearby **Royal Hospital** (Mon–Sat 10am–noon & 2–4pm; April–Sept also Sun 2–4pm; free; ⓦ www.chelsea-pensioners.co.uk), founded by Charles II in 1681. The hospital's majestic red-brick wings and grassy courtyards became a blueprint for institutional and collegiate architecture all over the English-speaking world. The public are allowed to view the austere hospital chapel, and the equally grand, wood-panelled dining hall, opposite, which has a vast allegorical mural of Charles II.

The concrete bunker next door to the Royal Hospital, on Royal Hospital Road, houses the **National Army Museum** (daily 10am–5.30pm; free; Ⓦ www.national-army-museum.ac.uk). The militarily obsessed are unlikely to be disappointed by the succession of uniforms and medals, but there's little here for non-enthusiasts.

North London

Almost all of **North London**'s suburbs are easily accessible by tube from the centre – indeed it was the expansion of the tube which encouraged the forward march of bricks and mortar into many of these areas – though just a handful of these satellite villages, now subsumed into the general mass of the city, are worth bothering with.

First off, is one of London's finest parks, **Regent's Park**, framed by Nash-designed architecture and home of London Zoo. Close by is **Camden Town**, where the weekend market is one of the city's big attractions – a warren of stalls selling street fashion, books, records and ethnic goods. The real highlights of north London, though, for visitors and residents alike, are the village-like suburbs of **Hampstead** and **Highgate**, which have the added advantage of proximity to one of London's wildest patches of greenery, **Hampstead Heath**.

Regent's Park

According to John Nash's masterplan, devised in 1811 for the Prince Regent (later George IV), **Regent's Park** (daily 5am to dusk; Ⓦ www.royalparks.org.uk) was to be girded by a continuous belt of terraces, and sprinkled with a total of 56 villas, including a magnificent pleasure palace for the Prince himself. The plan was never fully realized, due to lack of funds, but enough was built to create something of the idealized garden city that Nash and the Prince Regent envisaged.

Prominent on the park's skyline is the shiny copper dome of **London Central Mosque** at 146 Park Rd (Ⓦ www.iccuk.org), an entirely appropriate addition given the Prince Regent's taste for the Orient. Within the Inner Circle is the **Open Air Theatre** (Ⓦ www.openairtheatre.org), which puts on summer performances of Shakespeare, opera and ballet, and **Queen Mary's Gardens**, by far the prettiest section of the park.

The northeastern corner of the park is occupied by **London Zoo** (daily: March–Oct 10am–5.30pm; Nov–Feb 10am–4pm; £12; Ⓦ www.zsl.org/london-zoo). Founded in 1826 with the remnants of the royal menagerie, the zoo has had to change with the times, and now bills itself as an eco-conscious place whose prime purpose is to save species under threat of extinction. It's still not the most uplifting spot for animal-lovers, though the enclosures are as humane as any inner-city zoo could make them, and kids usually love the place. Most are particularly taken by the children's enclosure, where they can actually handle the animals, and the regular "Animals in Action" live shows. The invertebrate house, now known as BUGS, the gorilla kingdom and the walk-through rainforest and monkey forest are all guaranteed winners.

Camden Town

For all its tourist popularity, **Camden Market** remains a genuinely offbeat place. More than 100,000 shoppers turn up here each weekend, and parts of the market now stay open week-long, alongside a similarly oriented crop of shops, cafés and

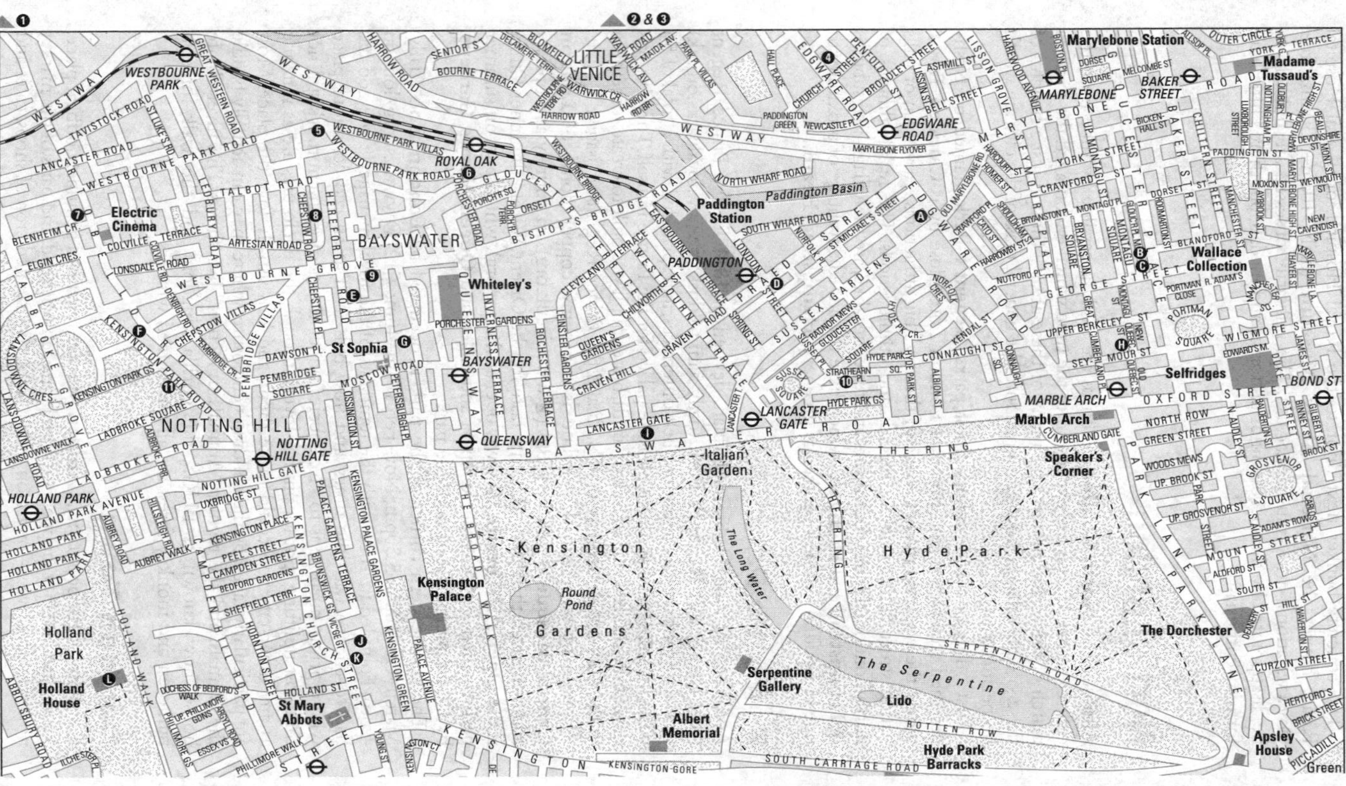
1
2 & 3
Marylebone Station
Madame Tussaud's
MARYLEBONE
BAKER STREET
EDGWARE ROAD
LITTLE VENICE
WESTBOURNE PARK
ROYAL OAK
Paddington Station
Paddington Basin
PADDINGTON
Electric Cinema
BAYSWATER
Whiteley's
Wallace Collection
Selfridges
BOND ST
MARBLE ARCH
Marble Arch
Speaker's Corner
LANCASTER GATE
QUEENSWAY
St Sophia
NOTTING HILL
NOTTING HILL GATE
HOLLAND PARK
Italian Garden
Kensington Gardens
Round Pond
The Long Water
Kensington Palace
Hyde Park
The Serpentine
Serpentine Gallery
Lido
Albert Memorial
Hyde Park Barracks
The Dorchester
Apsley House
Holland Park
Holland House
St Mary Abbots
WESTWAY
HARROW ROAD
EDGWARE ROAD
MARYLEBONE ROAD
BAYSWATER ROAD
OXFORD STREET
PARK LANE
KENSINGTON GORE
SOUTH CARRIAGE ROAD
ROTTEN ROW
SERPENTINE ROAD
THE RING
THE BROAD WALK
KENSINGTON CHURCH STREET
KENSINGTON HIGH STREET
HOLLAND PARK AVENUE
LADBROKE GROVE
WESTBOURNE GROVE
PORCHESTER ROAD
PRAED STREET
SUSSEX GARDENS
BAKER STREET
GLOUCESTER PLACE
PICCADILLY

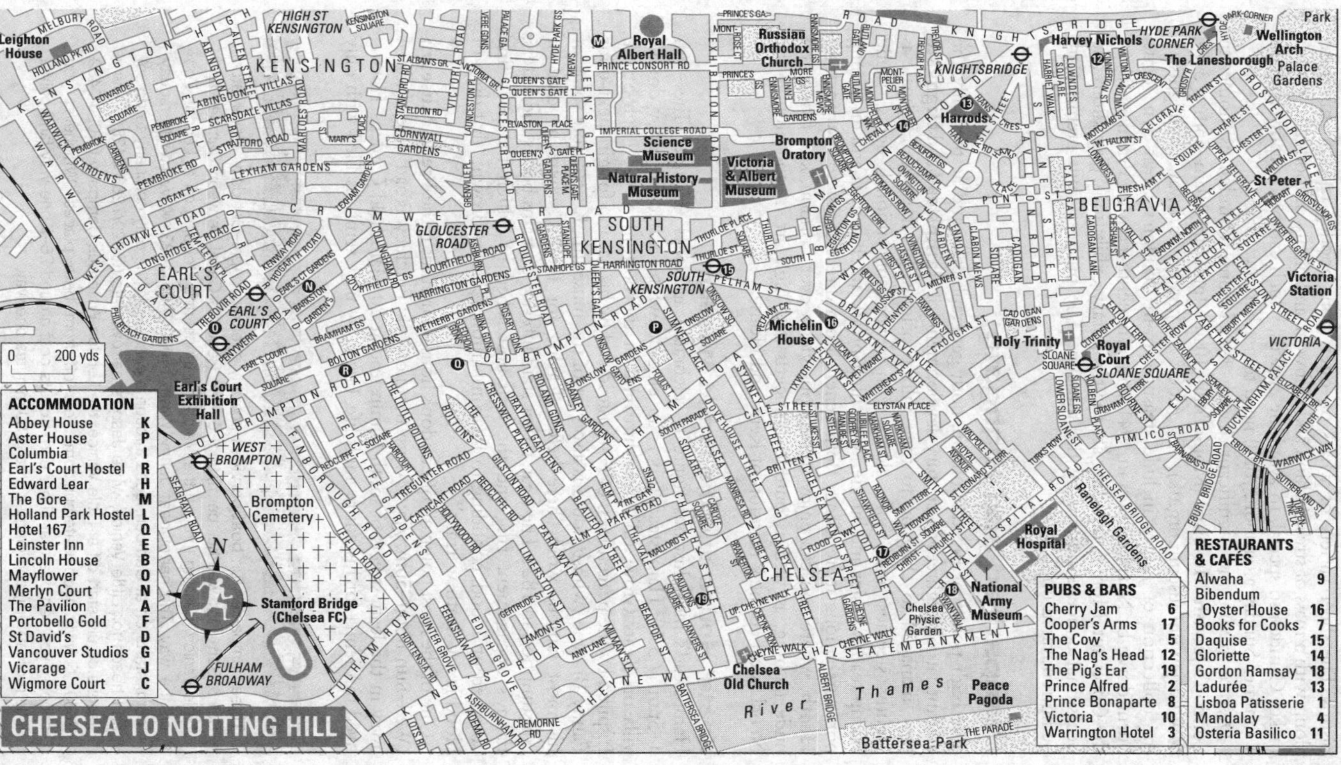
CHELSEA TO NOTTING HILL
ACCOMMODATION
Abbey House K
Aster House P
Columbia I
Earl's Court Hostel R
Edward Lear H
The Gore M
Holland Park Hostel L
Hotel 167 Q
Leinster Inn E
Lincoln House B
Mayflower O
Merlyn Court N
The Pavilion A
Portobello Gold F
St David's D
Vancouver Studios G
Vicarage J
Wigmore Court C
PUBS & BARS
Cherry Jam 6
Cooper's Arms 17
The Cow 5
The Nag's Head 12
The Pig's Ear 19
Prince Alfred 2
Prince Bonaparte 8
Victoria 10
Warrington Hotel 3
RESTAURANTS & CAFÉS
Alwaha 9
Bibendum Oyster House 16
Books for Cooks 7
Daquise 15
Gloriette 14
Gordon Ramsay 18
Ladurée 13
Lisboa Patisserie 1
Mandalay 4
Osteria Basilico 11
0 200 yds
KENSINGTON
SOUTH KENSINGTON
BELGRAVIA
CHELSEA
EARL'S COURT
River Thames
Battersea Park
Leighton House
Royal Albert Hall
Russian Orthodox Church
Harvey Nichols
Wellington Arch
The Lanesborough
Palace Gardens
Harrods
Science Museum
Natural History Museum
Victoria & Albert Museum
Brompton Oratory
St Peter
Victoria Station
Michelin House
Holy Trinity
Royal Court
Earl's Court Exhibition Hall
Brompton Cemetery
Stamford Bridge (Chelsea FC)
Royal Hospital
Ranelagh Gardens
National Army Museum
Chelsea Physic Garden
Chelsea Old Church
Peace Pagoda
HIGH ST KENSINGTON
HYDE PARK CORNER
KNIGHTSBRIDGE
GLOUCESTER ROAD
SOUTH KENSINGTON
SLOANE SQUARE
VICTORIA
EARL'S COURT
WEST BROMPTON
FULHAM BROADWAY

bistros. The sheer variety of what's on offer: from bootleg tapes to furniture, along with a mass of street fashion and clubwear, and plenty of foodstalls, is what makes Camden so special. To avoid the crowds, which can be overpowering on a summer Sunday afternoon, you'll need to get here by 10am.

Despite having no significant Jewish associations, Camden is home to London's **Jewish Museum** (Mon–Thurs 10am–4pm, Sun 10am–5pm; £3.50; ⓦwww.jewishmuseum.org.uk), 129 Albert St, just off Parkway. Highlights of the collection of *Judaica* include treasures from London's Great Synagogue, burnt down by Nazi bombers in 1941, and a sixteenth-century Venetian Ark of the Covenant. More compelling are the temporary exhibitions, discussions and occasional concerts put on by the museum. The purpose-built premises are being renovated until 2009.

Hampstead and Highgate

The high points of North London, both geographically and aesthetically, the elegant, largely eighteenth-century developments of **Hampstead** and **Highgate** have managed to cling on to their village origins. Of the two, Highgate is slightly sleepier and more aloof, with fewer conventional sights, while Hampstead is busier and buzzier, with high-profile intelligentsia and discerning pop stars among its residents. Both benefit from direct access to **Hampstead Heath**, where you can enjoy stupendous views over London, kite flying and nude bathing, as well as outdoor concerts and high art in and around the Neoclassical country mansion of Kenwood House.

Keats' House and the Freud Museum

Hampstead's most lustrous figure is celebrated at **Keats' House** (Tues–Sun 1–5pm; £3.50; Hampstead tube), an elegant, whitewashed Regency double villa on Keats Grove, off Downshire Hill, at the bottom of the High Street. Inspired by the peacefulness of Hampstead and by his passion for girl-next-door Fanny Brawne (whose house is also part of the museum), Keats wrote some of his most famous works here before leaving for Rome, where he died of consumption in 1821. The neat, rather staid interior contains books and letters, Fanny's engagement ring and the four-poster bed in which the poet first coughed up blood, confiding to his companion, Charles Brown, "that drop of blood is my death warrant".

One of the most poignant of London's house museums is the **Freud Museum** (Wed–Sun noon–5pm; £5; ⓦwww.freud.org.uk; Finchley Road tube), hidden away in the leafy streets of south Hampstead at 20 Maresfield Gardens. Having lived in Vienna for his entire adult life, Freud, by now semi-disabled with only

Regent's Canal by boat

Three companies run **boat services** (roughly speaking: April–Oct daily; Nov–March Sat & Sun only, weather permitting) on the Regent's Canal between Camden and Little Venice, passing through the Maida Hill tunnel and stopping off at London Zoo on the way. The narrowboat *Jenny Wren* (ⓣ020/7485 4433, ⓦwww.walkersquay.com) starts off at Camden, goes through a canal lock (the only company to do so) and heads for Little Venice, while Jason's narrowboats (ⓣ020/7286 3428, ⓦwww.jasons.co.uk) start off at Little Venice; the London Waterbus Company (ⓣ020/7482 2660, ⓦwww.londonwaterbus.com) sets off from both places. Whichever you choose, you can board at either end; **tickets** cost around £6–7 one-way (and only a little more return) and journey time is 50 minutes one way.

a year to live, was forced to flee the Nazis, arriving in London in the summer of 1938. The ground-floor study and library look exactly as they did when Freud lived here; the collection of erotic antiquities and the famous couch, sumptuously draped in Persian carpets, were all brought here from Vienna. Upstairs, home movies of family life in Vienna are shown continually, and a small room is dedicated to his daughter, Anna, herself an influential child analyst, who lived in the house until her death in 1982.

Hampstead Heath and Kenwood

North London's "green lung", **Hampstead Heath** is the city's most enjoyable public park. It may not have much of its original heathland left, but it packs a wonderful variety of bucolic scenery into its 800 acres. At its southern end are the rolling green pastures of **Parliament Hill**, north London's premier spot for kite flying. On either side are numerous ponds, three of which – one for men, one for women and one mixed – you can swim in for free. The thickest woodland is to be found in the **West Heath**, beyond Whitestone Pond, also the site of the most formal section, **Hill Garden**, a secretive and romantic little gem with eccentric balustraded terraces and a ruined pergola. Beyond lies **Golders Hill Park**, where you can gaze at pygmy goats and fallow deer, and inspect the impeccably maintained aviaries, home to flamingos, cranes and other exotic birds.

Finally, don't miss the landscaped grounds of Kenwood, in the north of the Heath, which are focused on the whitewashed Neoclassical mansion of **Kenwood House** (daily: April–Oct 11am–5pm; Nov–March 11am–4pm; free; EH; Hampstead tube or bus #210 from Archway tube). The house is now home to a collection of seventeenth- and eighteenth-century art, including a handful of real masterpieces by the likes of Vermeer, Rembrandt, Boucher, Gainsborough and Reynolds. Of the house's period interiors, the most spectacular is Robert Adam's sky-blue and gold library, its book-filled apses separated from the central entertaining area by paired columns.

Highgate Cemetery

Receiving far more visitors than Highgate itself, **Highgate Cemetery** (Ⓦwww.highgate-cemetery.org; Highgate tube), ranged on both sides of Swain's Lane, is London's best-known graveyard. The most illustrious incumbent of the **East Cemetery** (April–Oct Mon–Fri 10am–5pm, Sat & Sun 11am–5pm; Nov–March closes 4pm; £2) is **Karl Marx**. Marx himself asked for a simple grave topped by a headstone, but by 1954 the Communist movement decided to move his grave to a more prominent position and erect the vulgar bronze bust that now surmounts a granite plinth. Close by lies the much simpler grave of the author George Eliot.

What the East Cemetery lacks in atmosphere is in part compensated for by the fact that you can wander at will through its maze of circuitous paths, whereas to visit the more atmospheric and overgrown **West Cemetery**, with its spooky Egyptian Avenue and sunken catacombs, you must go round with a guided tour (March–Nov Mon–Fri 2pm, Sat & Sun hourly 11am–4pm; Dec–Feb Sat & Sun hourly 11am–3pm; £3; no under-8s). Among the prominent graves usually visited are those of artist Dante Gabriel Rossetti, and lesbian novelist Radclyffe Hall.

Hendon: The RAF Museum

A world-class assembly of historic military aircraft can be seen at the **RAF Museum** (daily 10am–6pm; free; Ⓦwww.rafmuseum.org.uk; Colindale tube), located in a godforsaken part of north London beside the M1 motorway.

Enthusiasts won't be disappointed, but those looking for a balanced account of modern aerial warfare will – the overall tone is unashamedly militaristic, not to say jingoistic. Those with children should head for the hands-on Aeronauts gallery; those without might prefer to explore the often overlooked display galleries, ranged around the edge of the Main Aircraft Hall, which contain an art gallery and an exhibition on the history of flight, accompanied by replicas of some of the deathtraps of early aviation.

Neasden: the Shri Swaminarayan temple

Perhaps the most remarkable building in the whole of London lies just off the North Circular, in the glum suburb of **Neasden**. Here, rising majestically above the surrounding semi-detached houses like a mirage, is the **Shri Swaminarayan Mandir** (daily 9am–6pm; free, Ⓦwww.mandir.org; Neasden tube), a traditional Hindu temple topped with domes and shikharas, erected in 1995 in a style and scale unseen outside of India for more than a millennium. To reach the temple, you must enter through the adjacent Haveli, or cultural complex, with its carved wooden portico and balcony. After taking off your shoes, you can proceed to the Mandir (temple) itself, carved entirely out of Carrara marble, with every possible surface transformed into a honeycomb of arabesques, flowers and seated gods. Beneath the Mandir, an **exhibition** (£2) explains the basic tenets of Hinduism and details the life of Lord Swaminarayan, and includes a video about the history of the building.

South London

Now largely built-up into a patchwork of Victorian terraces, **South London** nevertheless boasts one outstanding area for sightseeing, and that is **Greenwich**, with its fantastic ensemble of the Royal Naval College and the Queen's House, courtesy of Christopher Wren and Inigo Jones respectively. Most visitors, it has to be said, come to see the National Maritime Museum, the Royal Observatory, and the beautifully landscaped royal park, though Greenwich also pulls in an ever-increasing volume of Londoners in search of bargains at its Sunday **market**.

The only other suburban sights that stand out are the **Dulwich Picture Gallery**, a public art gallery even older than the National Gallery, and the eclectic **Horniman Museum**, in neighbouring Forest Hill.

Greenwich

Greenwich is one of London's most beguiling spots, but Greenwich town centre, laid out in the 1820s with Nash-style terraces, is nowadays plagued with heavy traffic. To reach Greenwich, you can take a **train** from London Bridge (every 30min), a **boat** from one of the piers in central London, or the **DLR** to Cutty Sark station, named after the **Cutty Sark** (Ⓦwww.cuttysark.org.uk), the world's last surviving tea clipper, built in 1869 and currently lying in a dry dock and being restored after a devastating fire in 2007. To escape the busy streets, head for the **Old Royal Naval College** (daily 10am–5pm; free; Ⓦwww.oldroyalnavalcollege.org), Wren's beautifully symmetrical Baroque ensemble which makes the most of its riverbank location. Initially built as a royal palace, but eventually converted into a hospital for disabled seamen, the complex was home to the Royal Naval College from 1873 until 1998, but now houses the

University of Greenwich and the Trinity College of Music. The two grandest rooms, situated underneath Wren's twin domes, are open to the public and well worth visiting. The **Chapel**, in the east wing, has exquisite pastel-shaded plasterwork and spectacular, decorative detailing on the ceiling, all designed by James "Athenian" Stuart after a fire in 1799 destroyed the original interior. Opposite the chapel is the magnificent **Painted Hall** in the west wing, which is dominated by James Thornhill's gargantuan allegorical ceiling painting, and his trompe l'oeil fluted pilasters.

National Maritime Museum

The main entrance to the excellent **National Maritime Museum** (daily 10am–5pm; July & Aug closes 6pm; free; Ⓦwww.nmm.ac.uk), which occupies the old Naval Asylum, is on Romney Road. From here, you enter the spectacular glass-roofed central courtyard, which houses the museum's largest artefacts, among them the splendid 63-foot-long gilded **Royal Barge**, designed in Rococo style by William Kent for Prince Frederick, the much unloved eldest son of George II.

The various themed galleries are superbly designed to appeal to visitors of all ages. In **Explorers**, on Level 1, you get to view some Titanic relics; **Passengers** re-lives the glory days of transatlantic shipping, which officially came to an end in 1957 when more people went by air than by sea; **Oceans of Discovery**, on Level 3, displays Captain Cook's sextant and K1 marine clock, Shackleton's compass, and **Captain Scott**'s overshoes, watch and funky sledging goggles.

Level 3 also boasts two hands-on galleries: **The Bridge**, where you can attempt to navigate a catamaran, a paddle steamer and a rowing boat to shore; and **All Hands**, where children can have a go at radio transmission, loading miniature cargo, firing a cannon and so forth. **Nelson's Navy** boasts lots of nineteenth-century Nelson kitsch, a video replay of the Battle of Trafalgar, and the great man's diminutive "undress coat", worn during the battle, with a tiny bullet hole made by the musket shot that killed him.

Inigo Jones's **Queen's House**, originally built amidst a rambling Tudor royal palace, is now the focal point of the Greenwich ensemble, and is an integral part of the Maritime Museum. As royal residences go, it's an unassuming country house, but as the first Neoclassical building in the country, it has enormous architectural significance. The interior is currently used for temporary exhibitions and very few features survive from Stuart times. Off the Great Hall, a perfect cube, lies the beautiful Tulip Staircase, Britain's earliest cantilevered spiral staircase – its name derives from the floral patterning in the wrought-iron balustrade.

Royal Observatory

Perched on the crest of Greenwich Park's highest hill, the **Royal Observatory** (daily 10am–5pm; July & Aug closes 6pm; free; Ⓦwww.nmm.ac.uk) is housed in a rather dinky Wren-built red-brick building, whose northeastern turret sports a bright-red time-ball that climbs the mast at 12.58pm and drops at 1pm GMT precisely; it was added in 1833 to allow ships to set their clocks.

Greenwich's greatest claim to fame, of course, is as the home of Greenwich Mean Time (GMT) and the Prime Meridian. Since 1884, Greenwich has occupied zero longitude – hence the world sets its clocks by GMT. The observatory itself was established in 1675 by Charles II to house the first Astronomer Royal, John Flamsteed, whose chief task was to study the night sky in order to discover an astronomical method of finding the longitude of a ship at sea. Astronomers continued to work here at Greenwich until the postwar smog forced them to decamp; the old observatory, meanwhile, is now a very popular museum.

The oldest part of the observatory is the Wren-built **Flamsteed House**, containing the Octagon Room, where the king used to show off to his guests. The Time galleries, beyond, focus on the search for the precise measurement of longitude, and display four of the clocks designed by **John Harrison**, including "H4", which helped win the Longitude Prize in 1763.

The observatory has also recently updated its **Astronomy** galleries and built a state-of-the-art **Planetarium** in the South Building, with regular shows presented by a Royal Observatory astronomer (Mon–Fri 1, 2, 3 & 4pm, Sat & Sun noon, 1, 3 & 4pm; £6).

The Ranger's House and the Fan Museum

Southwest of the observatory, and backing onto Greenwich Park's rose garden, is the **Ranger's House** (April–Sept Mon–Wed & Sun 10am–5pm; £5.50; EH), a red-brick Georgian villa that houses an art collection amassed by Julius Wernher, the German-born millionaire who made his money by exploiting the diamond deposits of South Africa. His taste in art is eclectic, ranging from medieval ivory miniatures to Iznik pottery, though he was definitely a man who placed technical virtuosity above artistic merit. The high points of the collection are Memlinc's *Virgin and Child* and the pair of sixteenth-century majolica dishes decorated with mythological scenes for Isabella d'Este (all located upstairs), and the Reynolds portraits and de Hooch interior (located downstairs).

Croom's Hill, running down the west side of the park, has some of Greenwich's finest Georgian buildings, one of which houses the **Fan Museum** at no. 12 (Tues–Sat 11am–5pm, Sun noon–5pm; £3.50; Ⓦwww.fan-museum.org). It's a fascinating little place (and an extremely beautiful house), revealing the importance of the fan as a social and political document. The permanent exhibition on the ground floor traces the history of the materials employed, from peacock feathers to straw, while temporary exhibitions on the first floor explore such subjects as techniques of production and changing fashion.

Dulwich Picture Gallery and the Horniman Museum

Dulwich Picture Gallery (Tues–Fri 10am–5pm, Sat & Sun 11am–5pm; £4; Ⓦwww.dulwichpicturegallery.org.uk; West Dulwich train station from Victoria), on College Road, is the nation's oldest public art gallery, designed by John Soane and opened in 1817. Soane created a beautifully spacious building, awash with natural light and crammed with superb paintings – elegiac landscapes by Cuyp, one of the world's finest Poussin series, and splendid works by Hogarth, Gainsborough, van Dyck, Canaletto and Rubens, plus **Rembrandt**'s tiny *Portrait of a Young Man*, a top-class portrait of poet, playwright and Royalist, the future Earl of Bristol. At the centre of the museum is a tiny mausoleum designed by Soane for the sarcophagi of the gallery's founders.

To the southeast of Dulwich Park, on the busy South Circular road, is the wacky **Horniman Museum** (daily 10.30am–5.30pm; free; Ⓦwww.horniman.ac.uk; Forest Hill train station from Victoria or London Bridge), purpose-built in 1901 by Frederick Horniman, a tea trader with a passion for collecting. In addition to the museum's natural history collection of stuffed birds and animals, there's an amazingly eclectic ethnographic collection, and a musical department with more than 1500 instruments from Chinese gongs to electric guitars. Don't miss the aquarium in the basement, and look out for the special sessions at the

Hands on Base, which allow you to handle and learn more about a whole range of the museum's artefacts.

Out west: Chiswick to Windsor

Most people experience **west London** en route to or from Heathrow Airport, either from the confines of the train or tube (which runs overground at this point), or the motorway. The city and its satellites seem to continue unabated, with only fleeting glimpses of the countryside. However, in the five-mile stretch from Chiswick to Osterley there are several former country retreats, now surrounded by suburbia, which are definitely deserved of discovery.

The Palladian villa of **Chiswick House** is perhaps the best known of these attractions. However, it draws nothing like as many visitors as **Syon House**, most of whom come for the gardening centre rather than for the house itself, a showcase for the talents of Robert Adam, who also worked at **Osterley House**, another Elizabethan conversion.

Running through much of the area is the **River Thames**, once known as the "Great Highway of London" and still the most pleasant way to travel in these parts during the summer. Boats plough up the Thames all the way from central London via the **Royal Botanic Gardens** at **Kew** and the picturesque riverside at **Richmond**, as far as **Hampton Court**, home of the country's largest royal residence and the famous maze. To reach the heavily touristed royal outpost of **Windsor Castle**, however, you need to take the train.

Chiswick

Chiswick House (April–Oct Wed–Fri & Sun 10am–5pm, Sat 10am–2pm; £4.20; EH Chiswick train station from Waterloo), is a perfect little Neoclassical villa, designed in the 1720s by the Earl of Burlington, and set in one of the most beautifully landscaped gardens in London. Like its prototype, Palladio's Villa Rotonda near Vicenza, the house was purpose-built as a "temple to the arts" where, amid his fine-art collection, Burlington could entertain artistic friends such as Swift, Handel and Pope. Entertaining took place on the **upper floor**, a series of cleverly interconnecting rooms, each enjoying a wonderful view out onto the gardens – all, that is, except the Tribunal, the domed octagonal hall at the centre of the villa, where the earl's finest paintings and sculptures would have been displayed.

If you leave Chiswick House gardens by the northernmost exit, beyond the Italian garden, it's just a short walk along the thunderous A4 road to **Hogarth's House** (Tues–Fri 1–4/5pm, Sat & Sun 1–5/6pm; closed Jan; free), where the artist spent each summer with his wife, sister and mother-in-law from 1749 until his death in 1764. Nowadays it's difficult to believe Hogarth came here for "peace and quiet", but in the eighteenth century the house was almost entirely surrounded by countryside. In addition to scores of Hogarth's engravings, you can see copies of his satirical series *An Election*, *Marriage à la Mode* and *A Harlot's Progress*, and compare the modern view from the parlour with the more idyllic scene in *Mr Ranby's House*.

Around Kew Bridge

Difficult to miss thanks to its stylish Italianate standpipe tower, **Kew Bridge Steam Museum** (daily 11am–5pm; Mon–Fri £4.25, Sat & Sun £5.75;

ⓦwww.kbsm.org; Kew Bridge train station from Waterloo; or bus #237 or #267 from Gunnersbury tube) occupies a former pumping station, on the corner of Kew Bridge Road and Green Dragon Lane, 100m west of the bridge itself. At the heart of the museum is the Steam Hall, which contains a triple expansion steam engine and four gigantic nineteenth-century Cornish beam engines. The museum also has a hands-on **Water for Life** gallery in the basement, devoted to the history of the capital's water supply. The best time to visit is at weekends, when each of the museum's industrial dinosaurs is put through its paces, and the small **narrow-gauge steam railway** runs back and forth round the yard (March–Nov Sun).

Syon House

Across the water from Kew stands **Syon Park** (ⓦwww.syonpark.co.uk), seat of the Duke of Northumberland since Elizabethan times, now as much a working commercial concern as a family home, embracing a garden centre, a wholefood shop, an aquatic centre stocked with tropical fish, a mini-zoo and a butterfly house, as well as the old aristocratic mansion and its gardens.

From its rather plain castellated exterior, you'd never guess that **Syon House** (April–Oct Wed, Thurs & Sun 11am–5pm; £8; bus #237 or #267 from Gunnersbury tube or Kew Bridge train station) contains the most opulent eighteenth-century interiors in the whole of London. The splendour of Robert Adam's refurbishment is immediately revealed, however, in the pristine **Great Hall**, an apsed double cube with a screen of Doric columns at one end and classical statuary dotted around the edges. There are several more Adam-designed rooms to admire in the house, plus a smattering of works by van Dyck, Lely, Gainsborough and Reynolds.

While Adam beautified Syon House, Capability Brown laid out its **gardens** (daily: March–Oct 10.30am–5pm or dusk; Nov–Feb Sat & Sun 10.30am–4pm; £4) around an artificial lake, surrounding it with oaks, beeches, limes and cedars. The gardens' chief focus now, however, is the crescent-shaped **Great Conservatory**, an early nineteenth-century addition which is said to have inspired Joseph Paxton, architect of the Crystal Palace.

Osterley Park and House

Robert Adam redesigned another colossal Elizabethan mansion three miles northwest of Syon at **Osterley Park** (daily 9am–7.30pm or dusk; free), which maintains the impression of being in the middle of the countryside, despite the presence of the M4 to the north of the house. The park itself is well worth exploring, and there's a great café in the Tudor stables, but anyone with a passing interest in Adam's work should pay a visit to **Osterley House** (mid-March to Oct Wed–Sun 1–4.30pm; Dec Sat & Sun 12.30–3.30pm; £7.50; NT; Osterley tube). From the outside, Osterley bears some similarity to Syon, the big

River transport

Westminster Passenger Services (ⓣ020/7930 2062, ⓦwww.wpsa.co.uk) runs four boats from Westminster Pier to Kew, and two boats to Richmond and Hampton Court daily from April to September. The full trip takes 3hr one way, and costs £13.50 single, £19.50 return. In addition, **Turks** (ⓣ020/8546 2434, ⓦwww.turks.co.uk) run a regular service from Richmond to Hampton Court (April to mid-Sept, Tues–Sun) which costs £5.50 single or £7 return.

difference being Adam's grand entrance portico, with its tall, Ionic colonnade. From here, you enter a characteristically cool **Entrance Hall**, followed by the so-called State Rooms of the south wing. Highlights include the **Drawing Room**, with Reynolds portraits on the damask walls and a coffered ceiling centred on a giant marigold, and the **Etruscan Dressing Room**, in which every surface is covered in delicate painted trelliswork, sphinxes and urns, a style that Adam (and Wedgwood) dubbed "Etruscan", though it is in fact derived from Greek vases found at Pompeii.

Kew Gardens

Established in 1759, the **Royal Botanic Gardens** (daily 9.30am–7.30pm or dusk; £12.25; ⓦwww.kew.org; Kew Gardens tube) have grown from their original eight acres into a three-hundred-acre site in which more than 33,000 species are grown in plantations and glasshouses, a display that attracts over a million visitors every year, most of them with no specialist interest at all. There's always something to see, whatever the season, but to get the most out of the place, come sometime between spring and autumn, bring a picnic and stay for the day.

Of all the glasshouses, by far the most celebrated is the **Palm House**, a curvaceous mound of glass and wrought-iron, designed by Decimus Burton in the 1840s. Its drippingly humid atmosphere nurtures most of the known palm species, while in the basement there's a small but excellent tropical aquarium. Kew's origins as an eighteenth-century royal pleasure garden are evident in the numerous follies dotted about Kew, the most conspicuous of which is the ten-storey, 163-foot-high **Pagoda**.

The three-storey red-brick mansion of Kew Palace (Easter–Oct Tues–Sun 10am–5pm; £5), to the northwest of the Palm House, was bought by George II as a nursery and schoolhouse for his umpteen children. Later, George III was confined to the palace and subjected to the dubious attentions of doctors who attempted to find a cure for his "madness". There are one or two bits and bobs belonging to the royals, like the much-loved dolls' house, on the ground floor, which belonged to George III's daughters. Upstairs, you can view the chair in which Queen Charlotte passed away in 1818, while the top floor has been left pretty much untouched since those days.

Richmond Park and Ham House

Richmond, upriver from Kew, basked for centuries in the glow of royal patronage, with Plantagenet kings and Tudor monarchs frequenting the riverside palace. Although most of the courtiers and aristocrats have gone, **Richmond** is still a wealthy district, with two theatres and highbrow pretensions. Richmond's greatest attraction though, is the enormous **Richmond Park** (daily: March–Sept 7am–dusk; Oct–Feb 7.30am–dusk; free; ⓦwww.royalparks.gov.uk), at the top of Richmond Hill – 2500 acres of undulating grassland and bracken, dotted with coppiced woodland and as wild as anything in London. Eight miles across at its widest point, this is Europe's largest city park, famed for its red and fallow deer, which roam freely, and for its ancient oaks. For the most part untamed, the park does have a couple of deliberately landscaped plantations that feature splendid springtime azaleas and rhododendrons, in particular the Isabella Plantation.

Back down the hill, if you continue along the towpath beyond Richmond Bridge, after a mile or so, you leave the rest of London far behind and arrive at **Ham House** (April–Oct Mon–Wed, Sat & Sun 1–5pm; £9; NT; Richmond tube), home to the earls of Dysart for nearly three hundred years. Expensively furnished in the seventeenth century, but little altered since then, the house is blessed with one of the finest Stuart interiors in the country, from the stupendously ornate Great Staircase to the Long Gallery, featuring six "Court Beauties" by Peter Lely. Elsewhere, there are several fine Verrio ceiling paintings, some exquisite parquet flooring and works by van Dyck and Reynolds. Another bonus are the formal seventeenth-century **gardens** (Mon–Wed, Sat & Sun 11am–6pm; £3, free with ticket for house), especially the Cherry Garden, laid out with a pungent lavender parterre, surrounded by yew hedges and pleached hornbeam arbours. The Orangery, overlooking the original kitchen garden, currently serves as a tearoom.

Hampton Court

Hampton Court Palace (daily: April–Oct 10am–6pm; Nov–March 10am–4.30pm; £13; Ⓦwww.hrp.org.uk; Hampton Court train station from Waterloo), a sprawling red-brick ensemble on the banks of the Thames, thirteen miles southwest of London, is the finest of England's royal abodes. Built in 1516 by the upwardly mobile **Cardinal Wolsey**, Henry VIII's Lord Chancellor, it was purloined by Henry himself after Wolsey fell from favour. In the second half of the seventeenth century, Charles II laid out the gardens, inspired by what he had seen at Versailles, while William and Mary had large sections of the palace remodelled by Wren a few years later.

The **Royal Apartments** are divided into six thematic walking tours. There's not a lot of information in any of the rooms, but guided tours, each lasting 45 minutes, are available at no extra charge and led by period-costumed historians, who do a fine job of bringing the place to life. If your energy is lacking – and Hampton Court is huge – the most rewarding sections are: **Henry VIII's State Apartments**, which feature the glorious double-hammerbeamed Great Hall; the **King's Apartments** (remodelled by William III); and the vast **Tudor Kitchens**. The last two are also served by audio tours. Part of the Royal Collection is housed in the **Renaissance Picture Gallery** and is chock-full of treasures, among them paintings by Tintoretto, Lotto, Titian, Cranach, Bruegel and Holbein.

Tickets to the Royal Apartments cover entry to the rest of the sites in the grounds. Those who don't wish to visit the apartments are free to wander around the gardens and visit the curious **Royal Tennis Courts** (April–Oct), but have to pay extra to try out the palace's famously tricky yew-hedge **Maze** (£3.50), and visit the **Privy Garden** (£4.50), where you can view Andrea Mantegna's colourful, heroic canvases, *The Triumphs of Caesar*, housed in the Lower Orangery, and the celebrated **Great Vine**, whose grapes are sold at the palace each year in September.

Windsor and Eton

Every weekend trains from Waterloo and Paddington are packed with people heading for **WINDSOR**, the royal enclave 21 miles west of London, where they join the human conveyor belt round **Windsor Castle** (daily: March–Oct 9.45am–5.15pm; Nov–Feb 9.45am–4.15pm; £14.20; Ⓦwww.royal.gov.uk; Paddington to Windsor & Eton Central via Slough, or Waterloo to Windsor & Eton Riverside – note that you must arrive and depart from the same station, as tickets are not interchangeable). Towering above the town on a steep chalk bluff, the castle is an undeniably awesome sight, its chilly grey walls, punctuated by mighty medieval bastions, continuing as far as the eye can see. Inside, most visitors just gape in awe at the monotonous, gilded grandeur of the **State**

Apartments, while the real highlights – the paintings from the Royal Collection that line the walls – are rarely given a second glance. More impressive is **St George's Chapel** (Mon–Sat 10am–4pm), a glorious Perpendicular structure ranking with Henry VII's chapel in Westminster Abbey (see p.97), and the second most important resting place for royal corpses after the Abbey. On a fine day, it pays to put aside some time for exploring Windsor Great Park, which stretches for several miles to the south of the castle.

Crossing the bridge at the end of Thames Avenue in Windsor town brings you to **ETON**, a one-street village lined with bookshops and antique dealers, but famous all over the world for **Eton College** (Easter, July & Aug daily 10.30am–4.30pm; after Easter to June & Sept daily 2–4.30pm; £4; ⓦwww.etoncollege.com), a ten-minute walk from the river. When the school was founded in 1440, its aim was to give free education to seventy poor scholars and choristers; how times have changed. The original fifteenth-century **schoolroom**, gnarled with centuries of graffiti, survives, but the real highlight is the **College Chapel**, completed in 1482, a wonderful example of English Perpendicular architecture. The self-congratulatory **Museum of Eton Life**, where you're deposited at the end of the tour, can be missed unless you have a fascination with flogging, fagging and bragging about the school's facilities and alumni – Percy Bysshe Shelley is a rare rebellious figure in the roll call of Establishment greats.

Eating

London is an exciting (though often expensive) place in which to eat out. You can pretty much sample any kind of cuisine here, from Georgian to Peruvian; indeed, London is now home to some of the best **Cantonese** restaurants in the whole of Europe, is a noted centre for **Indian** and **Bangladeshi** food, and has numerous French, Greek, Italian, Japanese, Spanish and Thai restaurants. Traditional and modern **British** food is available all over town, and some of the best venues are reviewed below.

▲ Windsor Castle

Cafés and snacks

There are plenty of **cafés** and small, basic restaurants all over London that can fill you up for under £10, including tea or coffee. It's worth bearing in mind that most **pubs** (which are covered in the following section) serve meals, and many take their food quite seriously.

Whitehall and Westminster

Café in the Crypt St Martin-in-the-Fields, Duncannon St, WC2; Charing Cross tube. See p.92. The self-service buffet food is nothing special, but there are regular veggie dishes, and the handy (and atmospheric) location makes this an ideal spot.

Jenny Lo's Teahouse 14 Ecclestone St, SW1; Victoria tube. See p.92. Bright, bare and utilitarian yet somehow stylish and fashionable too, *Jenny Lo's* serves good Chinese food at low prices. Be sure to check out the therapeutic teas. Closed Sun.

Mayfair and Marylebone

Eat & Two Veg 50 Marylebone High St, W1; Bond Street tube. See p.107. A lively and modern veggie restaurant, with some vegan and soya protein choices. The menu is eclectic, with Thai, Greek and Italian dishes.

Indian YMCA 41 Fitzroy Square, W1; Warren Street tube. See p.107. Don't take any notice of the signs saying the canteen is only for students – this place is open to all; just press the bell and pile in. The entire menu is portioned up into pretty little bowls; go and collect what you want and pay at the till. The food is great and the prices unbelievably low.

Mômo Tearoom 25 Heddon St, W1; Piccadilly Circus tube. See p.92. The ultimate Arabic pastiche, and a successful one at that. The adjacent restaurant is pricey, but the tearoom serves delicious snacks and is a great place to hang out, with tables and hookahs spilling out onto the pavement of this little Mayfair alleyway behind Regent St.

Patisserie Valerie at Sagne 105 Marylebone High St, W1; Bond Street tube. See p.107. Founded as Swiss-run *Maison Sagne* in the 1920s, and preserving its wonderful decor from those days, the café is now run by Soho's fab patisserie makers, and is without doubt Marylebone's finest.

The Wolseley 160 Piccadilly, W1; Green Park tube. See p.92. The lofty and stylish 1920s interior of this brasserie/restaurant (built as the showroom for Wolseley cars) is a big draw, and service is attentive and non-snooty. Given the glamour levels it's surprisingly affordable and the Viennese-inspired food delivers too. A great place for breakfast or a cream tea (£7.75).

Soho

Bar Italia 22 Frith St, W1; Leicester Square tube. See p.92. A tiny café that's a Soho institution, serving coffee, croissants and sandwiches more or less around the clock – as it has done since 1949.

Beatroot 92 Berwick St, W1; Piccadilly Circus tube. See p.92. Great little veggie café by the market, doling out hot savoury bakes, stews and salads (plus delicious cakes) in boxes of varying sizes.

Breakfast Club 33 D'Arblay St, W1; Oxford Circus tube. See p.92. Small, laid-back Aussie-style place, with substantial toasted sarnies, fresh juice, great coffee, free Wi-Fi and two computers. Closed Sun.

Gaby's 30 Charing Cross Rd, WC2; Leicester Square tube. See p.92. Busy café and takeaway joint that stays open till late serving a wide range of home-cooked veggie and Middle Eastern specialities. Hard to beat for value or choice and it's licensed, too. Closed Sun.

Maison Bertaux 28 Greek St, W1; Leicester Square tube. See p.92. Long-standing, old-fashioned and terribly French patisserie, with tables on two floors (and one or two outside) and a loyal clientele that keeps things busy.

Patisserie Valerie 44 Old Compton St, W1; Leicester Square or Piccadilly Circus tube. See p.92. Popular coffee, croissant and cake emporium dating from the 1950s and attracting a loud-talking, arty Soho crowd.

Chinatown

Kopi-Tiam 9 Wardour St, W1; Leicester Square tube. See p.92. Bright, cheap Malaysian café serving up curries, coconut rice, juices and "herbal soups" to local Malays, all for around a fiver.

Misato 11 Wardour St, W1; Leicester Square tube. See p.92. Modern, canteen-style Japanese café serving stomach-filling rice and noodle dishes for around a fiver, plus miso soup, sushi and bento boxes.

Tokyo Diner 2 Newport Place, WC2; Leicester Square tube. See p.92. Friendly place on the edge of Chinatown that shuns elaboration for fast food, Tokyo style. Minimalist decor lets the sushi and sumo do the talking.

Covent Garden and Bloomsbury

Food for Thought 31 Neal St, WC2; Covent Garden tube. See p.92. Long-established but minuscule, bargain veggie restaurant and takeaway counter – the food is good, with the menu changing twice daily. Expect to queue and don't expect to linger at peak times.

Just Falafs 27b Covent Garden Piazza, WC2; Covent Garden tube. See p.92. Mainly takeaway joint at the southeast corner of the piazza – wholesome falafels, mainly organic salad, yoghurt and seasonal beans rolled in a flatbread.

Rock & Sole Plaice 47 Endell St, WC2; Covent Garden tube. See p.92. A rare survivor: a traditional fish and chip shop in central London. Takeaway, eat in or out at one of the pavement tables.

Wagamama 4 Streatham St, WC1; Tottenham Court Road tube. See p.107. Much copied since, *Wagamama* was the pioneer when it comes to austere, minimalist, canteen-style noodle bars. Branches around central London.

World Food Café 14 Neal's Yard, WC2; Covent Garden tube. See p.92. First-floor veggie café that comes into its own in summer, when the windows are flung open and you can gaze down upon trendy humanity as you tuck into pricey but tasty dishes from all corners of the globe. Closed Sun.

Clerkenwell and Hoxton

Clark & Sons 46 Exmouth Market, EC1; Angel or Farringdon tube. See p.114. Exmouth Market has undergone something of a transformation, so it's all the more surprising to find this genuine eel and pie shop still going strong. Closed Sun.

Macondo 8–9 Hoxton Square, N1; Old Street tube. See p.114. Really relaxing Spanish café where you can hang out for hours, fuelling yourself with great tortilla and huge and delicious home-made cakes.

The City and the East End

Arkansas Café Unit 12, Old Spitalfields Market, E1; Liverpool Street tube. See p.114. American barbecue fuel stop, using only the very best free-range ingredients. Closed Sat.

Brick Lane Beigel Bake 159 Brick Lane, E1; Shoreditch or Whitechapel tube. See p.114. Classic 24hr bagel takeaway shop in the heart of the East End – unbelievably cheap, even for your top-end filling, smoked salmon and cream cheese.

Café 1001 1 Dray's Lane, E1; Whitechapel tube. See p.114. Off Brick Lane, tucked in by the Truman Brewery, this café has a beaten-up studenty look, with lots of sofas to crash in, and dishes out simple sandwiches and delicious cakes.

De Gustibus 53–55 Carter Lane, EC2; St Paul's or Blackfriars tube. See p.114. Award-winning bakery that creates a wide variety of sandwiches, bruschetta, *croque monsieur* and quiche to eat in or takeaway. Closed Sat & Sun.

Frizzante@City Farm 1a Goldsmith's Row, E2; Bethnal Green tube. See p.114. Hackney City Farm's café serves up home-made family-friendly generous all-day "Big Farm" or veggie breakfasts, risottos and delicious pizza-like *piadinas*, all for around a fiver.

The Place Below St Mary-le-Bow, Cheapside, EC2; St Paul's or Bank tube. See p.114. City café serving imaginative vegetarian dishes and delicious breakfast pastries, in a wonderful Norman crypt. Closed Sat & Sun.

The South Bank and Southwark

Benugo bar & kitchen BFI Southbank, SE1; Waterloo tube. See p.121. Former NFT bar is now a welcoming and glamorous option, with cosy armchairs in vibrant colours and free Wi-Fi. Pricey but delicious sarnies and a range of bar snacks, from chunky chips to a pint of sausage rolls.

Marsh Ruby 30 Lower Marsh, SE1; Waterloo tube. See p.121. Terrific filling lunchtime curries for under a fiver: the food is organic/free range and there's a basic but cheery communal dining area at the back. Closed Sat & Sun.

Kensington, Chelsea and Notting Hill

Books for Cooks 4 Blenheim Crescent, W11; Ladbroke Grove or Notting Hill Gate tube. See p.132. Tiny café/restaurant within London's top cookery bookshop – just wander in and have a coffee while browsing, or get there in time to grab a table for the set menu lunch. No smoking. Closed Mon & Sun & three weeks in Aug.

Daquise 20 Thurloe St, SW7; South Kensington tube. See p.132. This old-fashioned Polish café right by the tube is something of a South Ken institution, serving Polish home cooking or simple coffee, tea and cakes depending on the time of day.

Gloriette 128 Brompton Rd, SW7; South Kensington or Knightsbridge tube. See p.132. Long-established Viennese café that makes a perfect post-museum halt for coffee and outrageous cakes; also serves sandwiches, Wiener Schnitzel, pasta dishes, goulash and fish and chips.

Ladurée Harrods, 87/135 Brompton Rd, SW1; Knightsbridge tube. See p.132. This pretty white marble corner of Harrods has been taken over by Parisian tearoom *Ladurée*, in a corner of Harrods, with pyramids of coloured macaroons, sumptuous cakes, scented teas and a mirrored champagne bar.

Lisboa Patisserie 57 Golborne Rd, W10; Ladbroke Grove tube. Authentic and friendly Portuguese pastelaria, with coffee and cakes, including the best custard tarts this side of Lisbon. The *O'porto*, at 62a Golborne Rd, is a good fallback if this place is full.

Camden and Hampstead

Brew House Kenwood, Hampstead Lane, NW3; Bus #210 from Archway tube or a walk across the Heath from Hampstead tube. Everything from full English breakfast to lunches, cakes and teas, all served in the old laundry at Kenwood, or enjoyed on the terrace overlooking the lake.

Café Mozart 17 Swains Lane, N6; Gospel Oak train station. Conveniently located on the southeast side of Hampstead Heath, the best thing about this café is the Viennese cake selection and soothing classical music.

Louis Patisserie 32 Heath St, NW3; Hampstead tube. Popular Hungarian tearoom serving sticky cakes to a mix of Heath-bound hordes and elderly locals.

Marine Ices 8 Haverstock Hill, NW3; Chalk Farm tube. See p.86. Situated halfway between Camden and Hampstead, this is a splendid and justly famous old-fashioned Italian ice-cream parlour; pizza and pasta are served in a kiddie-friendly restaurant.

Greenwich

Goddard's 45 Greenwich Church St, SE10; Cutty Sark DLR. Established in 1890, *Goddard's* serves traditional pies (including veggie ones), eels and mash in an emerald green-tiled interior, with crumble and custard for afters.

Tai Won Mein 39 Greenwich Church St, SE10; Cutty Sark DLR or Greenwich DLR and train station. Good quality fast-food noodle bar that gets very busy at weekends. Decor is functional and minimalist; choose between rice, soup or various fried noodles, all for under a fiver.

Restaurants

London is an exciting – though often expensive – place in which to eat out, and as it's home to people from all over the globe, you can sample pretty much any kind of cuisine here. Many of the restaurants we've listed will be busy on most nights of the week, particularly on Thursday, Friday and Saturday, and it's best to **reserve a table**. As for **prices**, you can pay an awful lot for a meal in London, and if you're used to North American portions, you're not going to be particularly impressed by the volume in most places. For cheaper eats, see the section above. Where possible we've marked the following options on the maps in this chapter.

Afternoon tea

The classic English **afternoon tea** – assorted sandwiches, scones and cream, cakes and tarts, and, of course, lashings of tea – is available all over London. The best venues are the capital's top hotels and most fashionable department stores; a selection of the best is given below. To avoid disappointment it's essential to book ahead. Expect to spend £15–30 a head, and leave your jeans and trainers at home – most hotels will expect "smart casual attire", though only *The Ritz* insists on jacket and tie.

Brown's 33–34 Albemarle St, W1 ⓣ020/7493 6020, ⓦwww.brownshotel.com; Green Park tube. Daily 2–6pm.

Claridge's Brook St, W1 ⓣ020/7629 8860, ⓦwww.savoy-group.co.uk; Bond Street tube. Daily 3–5.30pm.

The Dorchester 54 Park Lane, W1 ⓣ020/7629 8888, ⓦwww.dorchesterhotel.com; Hyde Park Corner tube. Daily 3–6pm.

Fortnum & Mason 181 Piccadilly, W1 ⓣ020/7734 8040, ⓦwww.fortnumandmason.com; Green Park or Piccadilly Circus tube. Daily 3–5.30pm.

Lanesborough Hyde Park Corner, SW1 ⓣ020/7259 5599, ⓦwww.lanesborough.com; Green Park tube. Mon–Sat 3.30–6pm, Sun 4–6pm.

The Ritz Piccadilly, W1 ⓣ020/7493 8181, ⓦwww.theritzhotel.co.uk; Green Park tube. Daily 11.30am, 1.30, 3.30 & 5.30pm.

The Wolseley 160 Piccadilly, W1 ⓣ020/7499 699, ⓦwww.thewolseley.com; Green Park tube. Mon–Fri 3–5.30pm, Sat & Sun 3.30–6pm.

St James's, Mayfair and Marylebone

The Criterion 224 Piccadilly, W1 ⓣ020/7930 0488; Piccadilly Circus tube. See p.92. The predominately French food doesn't come cheap at this Marco Pierre White restaurant (though lunch is more of a bargain), but it is one of the city's most beautiful eating places, with a sparkling gold mosaic ceiling. Closed Sun. Very expensive.

Fairuz 3 Blandford St, W1 ⓣ020/7486 8108; Bond Street tube. See p.107. One of London's more accessible Middle Eastern restaurants, with an epic list of meze, a selection of charcoal grills and one or two oven-baked dishes. Moderate.

Mandalay 444 Edgware Rd, W2 ⓣ020/7258 3696; Edgware Road tube. See p.132. Pure and unexpurgated Burmese cuisine – a melange of Thai, Malaysian and a lot of Indian. The portions are huge, the service friendly and the prices relatively low. Closed Sun. Moderate.

The Providores & Tapa Room 109 Marylebone High St, W1 ⓣ020/7935 6175; Green Park tube. See p.107. Outstanding fusion restaurant run by an amiable New Zealander and split into two: snacky *Tapa Room* downstairs and an elegant restaurant upstairs. The food at both is original and wholly satisfying. *Tapa Room*: Inexpensive; *Providores*: Very expensive.

Soho and Chinatown

Chowki 2–3 Denman St, W1 ⓣ020/7439 1330; Piccadilly Circus tube. See p.92. Cheap Indian restaurant serving authentic food in stylish surroundings. The menu changes every month to feature three different regions of India – the regional feast for around £12.95 is great value. Inexpensive.

Mildred's 45 Lexington St, W1 ⓣ020/7494 1634; Oxford Circus or Piccadilly Circus tube. See p.92. This has a stylish feel than many veggie restaurants. The stir-fries, pasta dishes and burgers are wholesome, delicious and inexpensive. No bookings or credit cards. Moderate.

Mr Kong 21 Lisle St, WC2 ⓣ020/7437 7923; Leicester Square tube. See p.92. One of Chinatown's finest. Sample the restaurant's more unusual dishes from the "Today's" and "Chef's Specials" menu, and don't miss the mussels in black-bean sauce or the fresh razor clam with garlic. Inexpensive.

Patara 15 Greek St, W1 ⓣ020/7437 1071; Leicester Square tube. See p.92. A dimly lit and glamorous place, with orchids on the tables. Wonderful fresh ingredients and fine Thai cooking. Set lunch is around £12. Moderate.

Rasa Samudra 5 Charlotte St, W1 ⓣ020/7637 0222; Goodge Street tube. See p.107. The food served at *Rasa Samudra* would be more at home in Mumbai than in London, consisting as it does of sophisticated Southern Indian fish dishes – a million miles from curry-house staples. Moderate.

Wong Kei 41–43 Wardour St, W1 ⓣ020/7437 8408; Leicester Square tube. See p.92. A restaurant renowned for rudeness may not seem like much of a recommendation, but if you want quick, cheap Chinese then this is the place. Communal seating; have a look at the Art Noveau exterior on the way in. Inexpensive.

Covent Garden

Belgo Centraal 50 Earlham St, WC2 ⓣ020/7813 2233; Covent Garden tube. See p.92. Massive metal-minimalist cavern off Neal St, serving excellent kilo buckets of *moules marinières*, with *frites* and mayonnaise, a bewildering array of Belgian beers to choose from, and waffles for dessert. The £6.50 lunchtime specials are a bargain for central London. Moderate.

Ikkyu 67a Tottenham Court Rd, W1 ⓣ020/7636 9280; Goodge Street tube. See p.107. Busy basement Japanese restaurant, good for a quick lunch or a more elaborate dinner. Either way, prices are infinitely more reasonable than elsewhere in the capital, and the food is tasty and authentic. Closed all Sat & Sun lunch. Moderate.

Mon Plaisir 21 Monmouth St, WC2 ⓣ020/7836 7243; Covent Garden tube. See p.92. An atmospheric and sometimes formidably French restaurant with an intimate vintage feel, while the classic French meat and fish dishes are reliably excellent. The pre- and post-theatre menu is a bargain at £12.50 for two courses, £14.50 for three. Closed Sat eve & Sun. Moderate.

Clerkenwell and Hoxton

Cicada 132 St John St, EC1 ⓣ020/7608 1550; Farringdon tube. See p.114. Bar-restaurant set back from the street with alfresco eating and a pan-Asian menu. Closed Sat lunch & Sun. Expensive.

Real Greek 15 Hoxton Market, N1 ⓣ020/7739 8212; Old Street tube. See p.114. Modern, attractive with excellent service and a menu that shows off authentic dishes of Greece. Set lunch and early-doors dinner are a bargain. Neighbouring *Mezedopolio*, in a sympathetically converted mission building, serves *mezedes* and has a glamorous marble bar. Closed Sun. Moderate.

Moro 34–36 Exmouth Market, EC1 ⓣ020/7833 8336; Farringdon or Angel tube. See p.114. Spartan restaurant that's a place of pilgrimage for disciples of the wood-fired oven and those who love food that is both Moorish and more-ish. Expensive.

Viet Hoa 72 Kingsland Rd, E2 ⓣ020/7729 8293; Old Street tube. See p.114. Inexpensive, light and airy Vietnamese café not far from the Geffrye Museum, serving splendid "meals in a bowl" – soups and noodle dishes with everything from spring rolls to tofu. Inexpensive.

East End

Café Spice Namaste 16 Prescot St, E1 ⓣ020/7488 9242; Tower Hill tube. See p.114. Very popular Indian on the fringe of the City that is definitely not your average curry house. Goan and Kashmiri dishes are often included – and the tandoori specials, in particular, are awesome. Closed Sat lunch & Sun. Expensive.

Les Trois Garcons 1 Club Row, E1 ⓣ020/7613 1924; Shoreditch tube. See p.114. Wildly camp decor, with a bejewelled stuffed tiger to greet you at the door, handbags hanging from the ceilings, ornate tiles and glittering mirrors. The opulence is reflected in the prices and the dishes, with scallops, foie gras and oysters a regular feature. Expensive.

Tayyab's 83–89 Fieldgate St, E1 ⓣ020/7247 9543; Aldgate East or Whitechapel tube. See p.114. Smart, designer restaurant serving straightforward Pakistani fare: good, freshly cooked and served without pretension. Booking is essential and service is speedy and slick. Inexpensive.

South Bank and Southwark

Livebait The Cut, SE1 ⓣ020/7928 7211; Waterloo tube. See p.121. This bustling restaurant dishes up seafood galore, from classic fish'n'chips to heaped platters of lobster, crab and prawns. Expensive.

RSJ 13a Coin St, SE1 ⓣ020/7928 4554, ⓦwww.rsj.uk.com; Waterloo tube. See p.121. Regularly high standards of Anglo-French cooking make this a good spot for a meal after or before an evening at a South Bank theatre or concert hall. The set meals for around £17 are particularly popular. Closed Sat lunch & Sun. Moderate.

Kensington and Chelsea

Bibendum Oyster House Michelin House, 81 Fulham Rd, SW3 ⓣ020/7589 1480; South Kensington tube. See p.132. Built in 1911, this former garage is one of the prettiest places to eat shellfish in London – if you're really hungry, go for the "Plateau de Fruits de Mer". Expensive.

Boisdale 15 Eccleston St, SW1 ⓣ020/7730 6922; Victoria tube. See p.92. Owned by Ranald MacDonald, son of the Chief of Clanranald, this is a very Scottish place, strong on hospitality, and fresh Scottish produce. Live jazz every evening. Closed Sun. Expensive.

Gordon Ramsay 68–69 Royal Hospital Rd, SW3 ⓣ020/7352 4441; Sloane Square tube. See p.132. To order successfully here, just pick a dish or even an ingredient you like and see how it arrives; you won't be disappointed. Gordon Ramsay's Chelsea restaurant is a class act through and through; you have to book ahead to eat here. Closed Sat & Sun. Very expensive.

Bayswater and Notting Hill

Alwaha 75 Westbourne Grove, W2 ⓣ020/7229 0806; Queensway or Bayswater tube. See p.132. Arguably London's best Lebanese restaurant; meze-obsessed, but also painstaking in its preparation of the main-course dishes, where spanking fresh and accurately cooked grills predominate. Moderate.

Osteria Basilico 29 Kensington Park Rd, W11 ⓣ020/7727 9372; Ladbroke Grove tube. See p.132. A pretty, traditional Italian restaurant on a picturesque street just off Portobello Rd. It's a good place for the full Italian monty – antipasto, home-made pasta and then a fish or meat dish – or just for a pizza. Moderate.

Camden and Hampstead

Jin Kichi 73 Heath St, NW3 ⓣ020/7794 6158; Hampstead tube. Eschewing the slick minimalism and sushi-led cuisine of most Japanese restaurants, *Jin Kichi* is cramped, homely and very busy (so book ahead) and specializes in grilled skewers of meat. Closed Mon. Moderate.

Manna 4 Erskine Rd, NW3 ⓣ020/7722 8028; Chalk Farm tube. See p.86. Old-fashioned, casual vegetarian restaurant with 1970s decor, serving large portions of very good food. Closed Mon–Sat lunch. Moderate.

Trojka 101 Regent's Park Rd, NW1 ⓣ020/7483 3765; Chalk Farm tube. See p.86. A pleasant neighbourhood restaurant with filling and tasty eastern European food: the menu has a whole section on blinis and caviar, plus there are sturdy standbys such as stroganoff, and grills served with *Trojka*'s own tartare sauce. Moderate.

Chiswick to Richmond

Chez Lindsay 11 Hill Rise, Richmond ⓣ020/8948 7473; Richmond tube. Small, bright, authentic Breton creperie, with a "Cider with Lindsay" fixed menu (£15.75) offering three courses plus a cup of Breton cider. Choose between galettes, crepes or more formal French main courses, including lots of fresh fish and shellfish. Moderate.

The Gate 51 Queen Caroline St, W4 ⓣ020/8748 6932; Hammersmith tube. Tucked away behind the Hammersmith Apollo, this is a vegetarian restaurant that eschews healthy, wholefood eating. It's as rich, colourful, calorific and naughty as anywhere in town, just without meat. Closed Sat lunch & Sun. Expensive.

Drinking

London's **drinking** establishments run the whole gamut from grand Victorian gin palaces to funky modern bars with resident DJs catering to a pre-club crowd. Where possible, we've marked the places below on the maps in this chapter.

Whitehall and Westminster

The Chandos 29 St Martin's Lane, WC2; Leicester Square tube. See p.92. If you can get one of the booths downstairs, or the leather sofas upstairs in the more relaxed Opera Room Bar, then you'll find it difficult to leave, especially given the cheap Sam Smith's beer.

Red Lion 48 Parliament St, SW1; Westminster tube. See p.92. Good old pub, convenient for Westminster Abbey and Parliament. Popular with MPs, who are called to votes by a division bell in the bar.

St James's, Mayfair and Marylebone

Guinea 30 Bruton Place, W1; Bond Street or Green Park tube. See p.92. Pretty, old-fashioned, flower-strewn mews pub, serving good Young's bitter and excellent steak-and-kidney pies. Invariably packed to its tiny rafters. Closed Sun.

ICA Bar 94 The Mall, SW1; Piccadilly Circus or Charing Cross tube. See p.92. You have to be a member to drink at the *ICA Bar* – but anyone can join on the door (Mon–Fri £2, Sat & Sun £3). It's a cool drinking venue, with a noir dress code observed by the arty crowd and staff. Occasional club nights.

O'Conor Don 88 Marylebone Lane, W1; Bond Street tube. See p.107. A stripped-bare, stout-loving pub that's a cut above the average, with excellent Guinness, a pleasantly measured pace and Irish food on offer. Closed Sat & Sun.

Red Lion 23 Crown Passage, SW1; Green Park tube. See p.92. Hidden away in a narrow passageway off Pall Mall, this is a genuinely warm and cosy local, with a distinctive country-inn feel and super-friendly bar staff. Closed Sun.

Soho and Fitzrovia

Argyll Arms 18 Argyll St, W1; Oxford Circus tube. See p.92. A stone's throw from Oxford Circus, this is a great Victorian pub, which has preserved many of its original features and serves good real ales.

Blue Posts 28 Rupert St, W1; Piccadilly Circus tube or Oxford Circus tube. See p.92. Colourful, welcoming local with a relaxed vibe, frequented by a cheerful, hardy array of punters. The upstairs bar is frequently used for art exhibitions.

De Hems 11 Macclesfield St, W1; Leicester Square tube. See p.92. Probably your best bet in Chinatown, this is London's official Dutch pub, and has been since the 1890s; a simple wood-panelled affair with Oranjeboom on tap and Belgian beers in bottles.

Dog & Duck 18 Bateman St, W1; Leicester Square or Tottenham Court Road tube. See p.92. Tiny Soho pub that retains much of its old character, beautiful Victorian tiling and mosaics, and a loyal clientele.

The Social 5 Little Portland St, W1; Oxford Circus tube. See p.107. Industrial club-bar with great DJs playing everything from rock to rap, a truly hedonistic-cum-alcoholic crowd and the ultimate snacks – beans on toast and fish-finger sarnies – for when you get an attack of the munchies.

The Toucan 19 Carlisle St; Tottenham Court Road tube. See p.92. Small bar serving excellent Guinness and a wide range of Irish whiskeys, plus cheap, wholesome and filling food. So popular it can get mobbed. Closed Sun lunch.

Covent Garden and Strand

Cross Keys 31 Endell St, WC2; Covent Garden tube. See p.92. Stuffed with copper pots, brass instruments, paintings and other curios, this welcoming West End pub attracts an appealing blend of local residents, young workers and tourists – you'll do well to find a seat.

Detroit 35 Earlham St, WC2; Covent Garden tube. See p.92. Cavernous underground venue with an open-plan bar area, secluded Gaudíesque booths and a huge range of spirits. DJs take over at the weekends. Closed Sun.

Gordon's 47 Villiers St, WC2; Charing Cross or Embankment tube. See p.92. Cavernous, shabby, atmospheric wine bar specializing in ports, right next door to Charing Cross Station. The excellent and varied wine list, decent buffet food and genial atmosphere make this a favourite with local office workers, who spill outdoors in the summer.

Lamb & Flag 33 Rose St, WC2; Leicester Square tube. See p.92. Undeniably showing its age (more than 350 years old), this agreeably tatty yet much revered pub, tucked away down an alley between Garrick St and Floral St.

Salisbury 90 St Martin's Lane, WC2; Leicester Square tube. See p.92. Easily one of the most beautifully preserved Victorian pubs in the capital – and certainly the most central – with cut, etched and engraved windows, bronze figures, red velvet seating and a fine lincrusta ceiling.

Bloomsbury and Holborn

Lamb 94 Lamb's Conduit St, WC1; Russell Square tube. See p.107. Fine Young's pub with a marvellously well-preserved Victorian interior of mirrors, polished wood and etched glass "snob" screens gracing the bar.

Museum Tavern 49 Great Russell St, WC1; Tottenham Court Road or Russell Square tube. See p.107. Characterful old pub, opposite the British Museum, erstwhile drinking hole of Karl Marx.

Princess Louise 208 High Holborn, WC1; Holborn tube. See p.107. Architecturally, this is one of London's most impressive pubs, featuring gold-trimmed mirrors, gorgeous mosaics and a fine moulded ceiling. The Sam Smith's beer is very reasonably priced and there's always a lively crowd.

Ye Olde Mitre 1 Ely Court, off Ely Place, EC1; Farringdon tube. See p.114. Hidden down a tiny alleyway off Ely Place, this wonderfully atmospheric pub dates back to 1546, although it was actually rebuilt in the eighteenth century. Closed Sat & Sun.

Clerkenwell

Dovetail 9 Jerusalem Passage, EC1; Farringdon tube. See p.114. Marvellous, understated Belgian bar offering dozens of beers. The curious decor comprises pew-style seating, green-tiled tables and kitchen-style wall tiling. First-rate Belgian food, too. Closed Sun.

Duke of York 156 Clerkenwell Rd, EC1; Chancery Lane tube. See p.114. Just the basics you need for a good pub – clear glass windows, bare boards, bold red and blue paintwork, table football, pool, TV sport, mixed clientele and groovy tunes – and a lot less posey than most of Clerkenwell. Thai food available (except Sun).

Jerusalem Tavern 55 Britton St, EC1; Farringdon tube. See p.114. Converted Georgian coffee house that has retained much of its original character. Better still is the range of draught beers from the St Peter's Brewery in Suffolk. Closed Sat & Sun.

Hoxton

Dragon 5 Leonard St, EC2; Old Street tube. See p.114. Discreetly signed clubby pub with bare-brick walls and crumbling leather sofas, that attracts a mixed crowd happy to listen to whatever takes the resident DJ's fancy.

Hoxton Square Bar and Kitchen 2–4 Hoxton Square, N1; Old Street tube. See p.114. This *Blade Runner-esque* concrete bar attracts trendy types with its mix of modern European food, kitsch-to-club soundtracks, worn leather sofas, and temporary painting and photography exhibitions.

Sosho 2 Tabernacle St, EC2; Old Street tube. See p.114. Trendy club-bar with good cocktails and decent food; the ambience is chilled until the very popular DJs kick in (Wed–Sun), playing house, disco and electronica: there's a charge at the weekend. Closed Mon.

The City

The Black Friar 174 Queen Victoria St, EC4; Blackfriars tube. See p.114. A gorgeous, utterly original pub, with Art Nouveau marble friezes of boozy monks and a wonderful highly decorated alcove, all dating from 1905.

The Counting House 50 Cornhill, EC2; Bank tube. See p.114. A bank conversion, the magnificent interior features high ceilings, marble walls and mosaic flooring. The large, oval island bar – above which is an enormous glass dome – offers the full range of Fuller's ales. Closed Sat & Sun.

Viaduct Tavern 126 Newgate St, EC1; St Paul's tube. See p.114. Glorious gin palace built in 1869 opposite what was then Newgate Prison and is now the Old Bailey. Ask to see the old cells now used for storing beer. The walls are adorned with oils of faded ladies representing Commerce, Agriculture and the Arts. Closed Sat & Sun.

Ye Old Cheshire Cheese Wine Office Court, 145 Fleet St, EC4; Blackfriars tube. See p.114. A famous seventeenth-century watering hole, with several snug, dark panelled bars and real fires. Popular with tourists, but by no means exclusively so. Closed Sun eve.

East End and Docklands

Dickens Inn St Katharine's Way, E1; Tower Hill tube. See p.114. Eighteenth-century timber-framed warehouse transported on wheels from its original site, with a great view over the docks, but very firmly on the tourist trail.

The Gun 27 Cold Harbour, E14; South Quay or Blackwall DLR, or Canary Wharf tube. See p.124. Refurbished old dockers' pub with a classy restaurant, a cosy back bar with a couple of snugs, and an outside deck offering an unrivalled view of the Dome.

Prospect of Whitby 57 Wapping Wall, E1; Wapping tube. London's most famous riverside pub, with a pewter bar, flagstone floor, ancient timber beams and stacks of maritime memorabilia. Terrific views out across the Thames.

Ten Bells 84 Commercial St, E1; Liverpool Street or Shoreditch tube. See p.114. This plain and pleasantly ramshackle pub has Jack the Ripper associations, but the interior has some great Victorian tiling and the crowd these days is a trendy, relaxed bunch. DJs play Fri–Sun.

Town of Ramsgate 62 Wapping High St, E1; Wapping tube. Dark, narrow medieval pub where Captain Blood was discovered with the crown jewels under his cloak, and Admiral Bligh and Fletcher Christian were regular drinking partners in pre-mutiny days.

South Bank and Southwark

Anchor & Hope 36 The Cut, SE1; Waterloo tube; See p.121. The *Anchor* is a welcoming and unfussy gastropub, dishing up truly excellent grub: soups, salads and mains such as slow-cooked pork with *choucroute*, as well as mouthwatering puds. Closed Sun.

Anchor Bankside 34 Park St, SE1; London Bridge, Southwark or Blackfriars tube. See p.124. While the rest of Bankside has changed almost beyond all recognition, this pub still looks much as it did when first built in 1770 (on the inside, at least). Good for alfresco drinking by the river.

George Inn 77 Borough High St, SE1; Borough or London Bridge tube. See p.124. London's only surviving coaching inn – dating from the seventeenth century and now owned by the National Trust – serving a good range of real ales.

Kings Arms 25 Roupell St, SE1; Waterloo tube. See p.121. Terrific hideaway divided into two; the front part is a traditional drinking area, while the rear is a tastefully cluttered, glass and wood conservatory-style space featuring a large open fire and long wooden table.

Lord Clyde 27 Clenham St, SE1; Borough or London Bridge tube. See p.124. A genuinely hospitable, family-run boozer, with a good choice of ales, and obliging staff. Before entering, take a look at the superb frontage, with its cream and green glazed earthenware dating from 1913.

Market Porter 9 Stoney St, SE1; London Bridge tube. See p.124. Handsome semicircular pub with early opening hours for workers at the Borough Market, and a seriously huge range of real ales.

Royal Oak 44 Tabard St, SE1; Borough or London Bridge tube. See p.124. Beautiful, lovingly restored Victorian pub that eschews jukeboxes and one-armed bandits and opts simply for serving real ales from Lewes in Sussex. Closed Sat lunch & Sun eve.

Kensington and Chelsea

Cooper's Arms Bar 87 Flood St, SW3; Sloane Square tube. See p.132. An attractively understated interior, with quirky decor (vintage travel posters, grandfather clocks), first-rate beer and food, and an easy-going atmosphere, all contrive to give this very fine neighbourhood pub its deservedly popular reputation.

The Nag's Head 53 Kinnerton St, SW1; Hyde Park Corner or Knightsbridge tube. See p.132. A convivial, quirky and down-to-earth little pub tucked down a posh cobbled mews, with dark wood-panelling and nineteenth-century china handpumps. The unusual sunken backroom has a flagstone floor and fires in winter.

The Pig's Ear 35 Old Church St SW1; Sloane Square tube. See p.132. Deep in Chelsea village, *The Pig's Ear* is a sympathetically converted and stylish place. Enjoy a leisurely boardgame and a pint of Pig's Ear in the panelled downstairs bar, where classy pub grub is served, or head upstairs to the posh dining room.

Notting Hill

Cherry Jam 52 Porchester Rd, W2; Royal Oak tube. See p.132. Owned by Ben Watt (house DJ and half of pop group Everything But The Girl), this smart intimate basement place mixes a decadent cocktail bar with top-end West London DJs. Eve only.

The Cow 89 Westbourne Park Rd, W2; Westbourne Park or Royal Oak tube. See p.132. This pub pulls in the beautiful W11 types thanks to its spectacular food, including a daily supply of fresh oysters, and excellent Guinness.

Prince Bonaparte 80 Chepstow Rd, W2. Notting Hill Gate or Royal Oak tube. See p.132. Pared-down, minimalist pub, with acres of space for sitting and supping or enjoying the excellent Brit or Med food.

Victoria 10a Strathern Place, W2; Lancaster Gate tube. See p.132. Fabulously ornate corner pub, with two open fires, much Victorian brass and tilework, and gold-trimmed mirrors.

Maida Vale

Prince Alfred 9 Formosa St, W9; Warwick Avenue tube. See p.132. A fantastic period-piece Victorian pub with all its original 1862 fittings intact, right down to the glazed snob screens that divide the bar into a series of snugs, and a surprisingly young and funky clientele.

Warrington Hotel 93 Warrington Crescent, W9 Warwick Avenue or Maida Vale tube. See p.132. Yet another architectural gem – this time flamboyant Art Nouveau – in an area replete with them. The interior is rich and satisfying, as are the draught beers and the Thai restaurant upstairs.

Camden Town

Bar Vinyl 6 Inverness St, NW1; Camden Town tube. See p.86. Small, funky glass-bricked place with a record shop downstairs (open noon–8pm) and nightly DJs providing a breakbeat, funky house or electro vibe.

Bartok 78–79 Chalk Farm Rd, NW1; Chalk Farm or Camden Town tube. See p.86. Stylish bar where punters can sink into a sofa and listen to a varied programme of classical music. Eve only.

The Engineer 65 Gloucester Ave, NW1; Chalk Farm tube. See p.86. Classy Victorian pub and restaurant for the Primrose Hill posse. The food is excellent though quite pricey, and it's popular, so get here early to eat in the pub, or book a table in the restaurant or lovely garden out back.

Hampstead and Highgate

The Flask 14 Flask Walk, NW3; Hampstead tube. Convivial Hampstead local that retains much of its original Victorian interior, tucked down one of Hampstead's more atmospheric lanes.

The Flask 77 Highgate West Hill, N6; Highgate tube. Ideally situated at the heart of Highgate village green – with a rambling, low-ceilinged interior and a summer terrace – and as a result, very popular.

Hollybush 22 Holly Mount, NW3; Hampstead tube. A lovely old pub, with a real fire in winter, tucked away in the steep backstreets of Hampstead village, which can get a bit too mobbed at weekends.

Dulwich and Greenwich

Crown & Greyhound 73 Dulwich Village, SE21; West Dulwich train station from Victoria. Grandiose Victorian pub, convenient for the Picture Gallery, with an ornate plasterwork ceiling and a nice summer beer garden.

Cutty Sark Ballast Quay, off Lassell St, SE10; Cutty Sark DLR or Maze Hill train station. This Georgian pub is the nicest place for a riverside pint in Greenwich, and much less touristy than the *Trafalgar Tavern* (it's a couple of minutes' walk further east, following the river).

Chiswick to Richmond

Dove 19 Upper Mall, W6; Ravenscourt Park tube. Wonderful old riverside pub with literary associations, the smallest bar in the UK (4ft by 7ft), and very popular Sun roast dinners.

White Cross Hotel Water Lane, Richmond; Richmond tube. With a longer pedigree and more character than its rivals, the *White Cross* has a very popular, large garden.

Nightlife

On any night of the week London offers a bewildering range of things to do after dark, ranging from top-flight opera and theatre to clubs with a lifespan of a couple of nights. The **listings magazine** *Time Out* (see p.82) is essential if you want to get the most out of this city.

Live music venues

The **live music** scene remains extremely diverse, encompassing all variations of rock, blues, roots and world music; and although London's jazz clubs aren't on a par with those in the big American cities, there's a highly individual scene of home-based artists, supplemented by top-name visiting players.

General venues

100 Club 100 Oxford St, W1 ⓣ020/7636 0933, ⓦwww.the100club.co.uk; Tottenham Court Road tube. An unpretentious, inexpensive and fun venue with an incredible vintage – expect anything from jazz to indie.

Cargo 83 Rivington St, EC2 ⓣ020/7739 3440, ⓦwww.cargo-london.com. Old St tube. Small but upmarket club/venue that hosts a wide variety of interesting live acts, including jazz, Latin, hip-hop, indie and folk, which are often part of their excellent line-up of club nights.

Brixton Academy 211 Stockwell Rd, SW9 ⓣ020/7771 3000, ⓦwww.brixton-academy.co.uk; Brixton tube. This refurbished Victorian hall, complete with Neoclassical decorations, can hold four thousand but still manages to seem small and friendly.

Forum 9–17 Highgate Rd, NW5 ⓣ0844/847 2405, ⓦwww.kentishtownforum.com; Kentish Town tube. This is one of the capital's best medium-sized venues: it's large enough to attract established bands, but also promotes less well-known and interesting ones.

Hammersmith Apollo Queen Caroline St, W6 ⓣ08448/444748, ⓦwww.hammersmithapollo.net; Hammersmith tube. The former Hammersmith Odeon is a cavernous, theatre-style venue which, for the most part, tends to host safe, middle-of-the-road bands. If you don't like sitting, there's a large and atmospheric standing area at the front.

Roundhouse Chalk Farm Rd, NW1 ⓣ020/7424 9991, ⓦwww.roundhouse.org.uk; Chalk Farm tube. Magnificently restored Victorian engine house now one of London's premier performing arts centres; its wide-ranging programme includes regular appearances by both mainstream and world music stars.

Shepherd's Bush Empire Shepherds Bush Green, W12 ⓣ020/8354 3300, ⓦwww.shepherds-bush-empire.co.uk; Shepherd's Bush tube. Grand old West London theatre that regularly draws the finest cross-section of mid-league UK and US bands.

Union Chapel Compton Terrace, N1 ⓣ020/7226 1686, ⓦwww.unionchapel.org.uk; Highbury & Islington tube. Wonderful, intimate venue that doubles as a church, hence the pew-style seating arrangements; the eclectic array of artists ranges from international contemporary stars to world music legends.

Rock, blues and indie

12 Bar Club Denmark St, WC2 ⓣ020/7240 2120, ⓦwww.12barclub.com; Tottenham Court Road tube. Tiny, atmospheric bar, café and venue offering blues, contemporary country and acoustically driven pop and folk.

Borderline Orange Yard, off Manette St, W1 ⓦwww.meanfiddler.com; Tottenham Court Road tube. Small basement joint with a great sound and a diverse musical policy, though it's particularly strong on Americana and alt-country acts.

Metro 19–23 Oxford St, W1 ⓣ020/7437 0964, ⓦwww.blowupmetro.com; Tottenham Court Road tube. An intimate venue with a forward-thinking booking policy that makes it a good place to head to for new bands just before they get big. Also has club nights Mon–Sat till late.

Neighbourhood 12 Acklam Rd, W10 ⓣ0871 971 3995; Ladbroke Grove tube. Run by Ben Watt of Everything But the Girl, this is a live-music/club crossover venue in an arch under a flyover, where the crowd is as trendy as the house-oriented music.

Underworld 174 Camden High St, NW1 ⓣ020/7482 1932 ⓦwww.theunderworldcamden.co.uk; Camden Town tube. Popular grungy venue under the *World's End* pub, that's a great place to check out metal, hard core, ska, punk and heavy rock bands.

Jazz, world music and roots

606 Club 90 Lots Rd, SW10 ⓣ020/7352 5953, ⓦwww.606club.co.uk; Fulham Broadway tube. A rare all-jazz venue, off the end of the King's Rd. You can book a table, and if you're a non-member you must eat if you want to drink.

Jazz Café 5 Parkway, NW1 ⓣ020/7916 6060, ⓦwww.meanfiddler.com; Camden Town tube. Excellent, chilled-out venue with an adventurous booking policy exploring Latin, rap, funk, hip-hop and musical fusions. Restaurant upstairs with a few prime tables overlooking the stage (book ahead if you want one).

Pizza Express 10 Dean St, W1 ⓦwww.pizzaexpresslive.com; Tottenham Court Road tube. Also known as *Jazz Club Soho*, this restaurant hosts the best in both established and new jazz artists, and serves a good pizza, too.

Ronnie Scott's 47 Frith St, W1 ⓣ020/7439 0747, ⓦwww.ronniescotts.co.uk; Leicester Square tube. The most famous jazz club in London, great for top-line names, who play two sets – one at around 10pm, the other after midnight, except on Sun when the club shuts at midnight. Book a table, or you'll have to stand.

Clubs

London remains *the* place to come if you want to party after dark. The relaxation of late-night licensing laws has encouraged many of London's **dance clubs** to keep serving until 6am or even later. Some are open six or seven nights a week, some keep irregular days, others just open at the weekend – and very often a venue will host a different club on each night of the week; for up-to-the-minute listings, pop into one of Soho's many record shops to pick up flyers or check *Time Out*.

Admission charges vary enormously, with small midweek nights starting at around £3–5 and large weekend events charging as much as £25; around

Notting Hill Carnival

The two-day free **festival** (ⓦwww.rbkc.gov.uk) in Notting Hill is the longest-running, best-known and biggest street party in Europe. Dating back forty years, Carnival is a tumult of imaginatively decorated floats, eye-catching costumes, thumping sound systems, live bands, irresistible food and huge crowds. It takes place on the last weekend of August.

£10–15 is the average, but bear in mind that profit margins at the bar are even more outrageous than at live music venues.

93 Feet East 150 Brick Lane, E2 ⓣ020 7247 3293, ⓦwww.93feeteast.co.uk; Old Street tube. An old East End brewery with four rooms across two levels, as well as an excellent rooftop balcony and outdoor space that's well worth a visit in the summer.

333 333 Old St, EC1 ⓣ0207/739 5949 ⓦwww.333mother.com; Old Street tube. One of London's best clubs for new dance music; three floors of drum'n'bass, twisted disco and breakbeat madness.

Bar Rumba 36 Shaftesbury Ave, W1 ⓣ020/7287 6933, ⓦwww.barrumba.co.uk; Piccadilly Circus tube. Fun, smallish West End venue with an adventurous mix of nights ranging from salsa, R&B and dance to popular drum'n'bass.

Cuba 11–13 Kensington High St, W8 ⓣ020/7938 4137, ⓦwww.fiestahavana.com; Kensington High Street tube. Grab a cocktail upstairs in the sociable bar before heading below for club nights that focus around Latin, salsa and Brazilian bossa nova.

The End 18 West Central St, WC1 ⓣ020/7419 9199, ⓦwww.endclub.com; Tottenham Court Road or Holborn tube. Designed for clubbers by clubbers, *The End* is large and spacious, with chrome minimalist decor and a devastating sound system.

Fabric 77a Charterhouse St, EC1 ⓣ020/7336 8898, ⓦwww.fabriclondon.com; Farringdon tube. If you're a serious dance music fan then there really isn't a better weekend venue than *Fabric*, a cavernous, underground brewery-like space with three rooms. Get there early to avoid a night of queuing.

Fridge Town Hall Parade, Brixton Hill, SW2 ⓣ0871/223 2845, ⓦwww.fridgerocks.com; Brixton tube. Weekends alternate between pumping mixed/gay nights, and trance favourites with a psychedelic vibe.

Herbal 12–14 Kingsland Rd, E2 ⓣ020/7613 4462 ⓦwww.herbaluk.com; Old Street tube. An intimate two-floored venue comprising a cool loft and sweaty ground-floor club – a great place to check out drum'n'bass and breaks.

Ministry of Sound 103 Gaunt St, SE1 ⓦwww.ministryofsound.com; Elephant & Castle tube. A vast, state-of-the-art club, with an exceptional sound system. Corporate clubbing and full of tourists, but it still draws the top talent.

Notting Hill Arts Club 21 Notting Hill Gate, W11 ⓣ020/7460 4459, ⓦwww.nottinghillartsclub.com; Notting Hill Gate tube. Basement club that's popular for everything from Latin-inspired funk, jazz and disco through to soul, house and garage, and famed for its Sun afternoon/evening deep-house session and "concept visuals".

Plastic People 147–149 Curtain Rd, EC2 ⓣ020/739 6471, ⓦwww.plasticpeople.co.uk; Old Street tube. A state-of-the-art sound system and an interesting mix of nights, ranging from punk, and rock'n'roll to latin, Afro-jazz and hip-hop.

Rhythm Factory 16–18 Whitechapel Rd ⓣ020/7375 3774, ⓦwww.rhythmfactory.co.uk; Aldgate East or Whitechapel tube. This former textile factory turned club houses a bar area serving Thai food and two medium-sized rooms which usually see a range of excellent monthly shenanigans at the weekends.

Turnmills 63 Clerkenwell Rd, EC1 ⓣ0207/250 3409, ⓦwww.turnmills.co.uk. Farringdon tube. The place to come if you want to sweat to trance and house from dusk till dawn, with an alien-invasion-style bar and funky split-level dance floor in the main room.

Gay and lesbian London

London's **lesbian and gay scene** is so huge and well established that it's easy to forget just how much – and how fast – it has grown over the last couple of decades. **Soho** is the obvious place to start exploring, with a mix of traditional gay pubs, designer café-bars and a range of gay-run services. Details of most events appear in *Time Out*, while another excellent source of information is the London **Lesbian and Gay Switchboard** (ⓣ020/7837 7324, ⓦwww.queery.org.uk), which operates around the clock. The **outdoor event** of the year is **Pride London** (ⓦwww.pridelondon.org) in July, a colourful, whistleblowing march through the city streets followed at the end of the month by a huge, ticketed party in a central London park.

Bars and clubs

There are loads of lesbian and gay **cafés**, **bars and pubs** in London. Our list is by no means exhaustive as every corner of London has its own gay local. Many cafés and bars transform themselves into **drinking dens** at night and, as some open beyond licensing hours, they can be a cheap alternative to some **clubs**, which open up and shut down with surreal frequency – it's a good idea to check the gay press and listings mags before you set out. Bear in mind that although more and more lesbian bars admit gay men, mixed, as ever, tends to mean mostly men.

Mixed bars

The Black Cap 171 Camden High St, NW1; Camden Town tube. Venerable North London institution offering cabaret of wildly varying quality almost every night. Laugh, sing and lip-synch along, and then dance to 1980s tunes until the early hours.

The Box 32–34 Monmouth St, WC2; Covent Garden or Leicester Square tube. Popular, bright café/bar serving good food for a mixed gay/straight crowd during the day, and becoming queerer as the night draws in.

The Edge 11 Soho Square, W1; Tottenham Court Rd tube. Busy, style-conscious and pricey Soho café/bar spread over several floors, and (in summer) onto the pavement. Food daily, DJs most nights.

First Out 52 St Giles High St, WC2; Tottenham Court Rd tube. The West End's original gay café-bar, and still permanently packed, serving good veggie food at reasonable prices. Girl Friday (Fri) is a busy pre-club session for grrrls; gay men are welcome as guests.

Freedom 60–66 Wardour St, W1; Piccadilly Circus tube. Hip, busy, late-opening place, popular with a straight/gay Soho crowd. The basement transforms itself at night into a funky, intimate basement club, complete with pink banquettes and masses of glitter balls.

Retro Bar 2 George Court (off Strand), WC2; Charing Cross tube. Friendly, indie/retro bar playing 1970s, 80s, rock, pop, goth and alternative sounds, and featuring regular DIY DJ nights.

The Yard 57 Rupert St, W1; Piccadilly Circus tube. Attractive bar with courtyard, loft areas and a laid-back, sociable atmosphere – one of the best in Soho for alfresco drinking.

Lesbian bars

Candy Bar 4 Carlisle St, WC2; Tottenham Court Road tube. Now re-established at its original venue but still with the same crucial, cruisey vibe that made it the hottest girl bar in central London.

The Glass Bar West Lodge, Euston Square Gardens, 190 Euston Rd, NW1; Euston tube. Difficult to find (and hard to forget), you knock on the door and become a member to enter this friendly and intimate late-opening women-only bar. Closed Sat & Sun.

Star at Night 22 Great Chapel St, W1; Tottenham Court Rd tube. Comfortable new venue open from 6pm Tues–Sat, popular with a slightly older crowd who want somewhere to sit, a good glass of wine and good conversation.

Gay men's bars

79CXR 79 Charing Cross Rd, WC2; Leicester Square tube. Busy, cruisey men's den on two floors, with industrial decor, late licence and a no-messing atmosphere.

Central Station 37 Wharfdale Rd, N1; King's Cross tube. Award-winning, late-opening community pub on three floors, offering cabaret, cruisey club nights, and the UK's only gay sports bar. Not strictly men-only, but mostly so.

Compton's of Soho 53 Old Compton St, W1; Leicester Square or Piccadilly tube. This large, traditional-style pub is a Soho institution, always busy with a butch crowd, but still a relaxed place to cruise or just hang out. The upstairs Club Lounge is more chilled and attracts a younger crowd.

Kings Arms 23 Poland St, W1; Oxford Circus tube. London's best-known and perennially popular bear bar, with a traditional London pub atmosphere, DJ on Sat and karaoke night Sun.

Clubs

Area 67–68 Albert Embankment, SE1 Ⓦ www.areaclub.Info; Vauxhall tube. Stylish club with two dancefloors, several bars and chic decor. It hosts the long-running Coco Latte, as well as offering a London venue for big-name international DJs. Second Sat of the month is Bootylicious, devoted to urban dance music.

Crash 66 Goding St, SE11 Ⓦ www.crashlondon.com; Vauxhall tube. Four bars, two dancefloors, chill-out areas and hard bodies make this weekly Saturday-nighter busy, buzzy and sexy.

Duckie *Royal Vauxhall Tavern*, 372 Kennington Lane, SE11 Ⓣ 0207/7737 4043, Ⓦ www.duckie.co.uk; Vauxhall tube. Modern, rock-based hurdy-gurdy provides a creative and cheerfully ridiculous antidote to the dreary forces of gay house domination.

Exilio Latino *UCL*, Houghton St, WC2 ⓣ07931/374391, ⓦwww.exilio.co.uk; Holborn tube. Every Sat night, *Exilio* erupts in a lesbian and gay Latin frenzy, spinning salsa, cumbias and merengue, and also features live acts.

G.A.Y. *The Astoria*, 157 Charing Cross Rd, WC2; Tottenham Court Road tube. Widely considered as the launch venue for new (and ailing) boy and girl bands, this huge, unpretentious and fun-loving dance night is where the young crowd gathers.

Heaven *Under the Arches* Villiers St, WC2 ⓣ020/7930 2020, ⓦwww.heaven-london.com; Charing Cross or Embankment tube. Widely regarded as the UK's most popular gay club, this legendary, 2000-capacity venue continues to reign supreme. More Muscle Mary than Diesel Doris.

Popstarz *Scala*, 27 Pentonville Rd, N1 ⓦwww.popstarz.org; King's Cross tube. Groundbreaking Friday-night indie club, *Popstarz* has had to enforce a gay and lesbian majority door policy as its still-winning formula of alternative toons, 70s and 80s trash, cheap beer and no attitude attracts a growing straight, studenty crowd.

Theatre

The **West End** is the heart of London's "Theatreland", with Shaftesbury Avenue its most congested drag, but the term is more of a conceptual pigeon-hole than a geographical term. West End theatres tend to be dominated by tourist-magnet musicals, but others offer more intriguing productions. The **Royal Shakespeare Company** and the **National Theatre** often put on extremely original productions of mainstream masterpieces, while some of the most exciting work is performed in what have become known as the **Off-West End** theatres. Further down the financial ladder still are the **Fringe** theatres, more often than not pub venues, where ticket prices are lower, and quality more variable.

Tickets for £10 are restricted to the Fringe; the box-office average is closer to £20–25, with £30–50 the usual top whack. Ticket agencies such as Ticketmaster (ⓣ0161/385 3211, ⓦwww.ticketmaster.co.uk) or First Call (ⓣ0870/840 1111, ⓦwww.firstcalltickets.com) can get seats for most West End shows, but add up to twenty percent on the ticket price. The cheapest way to buy your ticket is to go to the theatre box office in person; if you book over the phone or online, you're likely to be charged a booking fee. Students, senior citizens and the unemployed can get **concessionary rates** on tickets for many shows, and several theatres offer reductions on standby tickets to these groups. Whatever you do, avoid the touts and the ticket agencies that abound in the West End.

The Society of London Theatre (ⓦwww.officiallondontheatre.co.uk) runs the **Half Price Ticket Booth** in Leicester Square, now known as **tkts** (Mon–Sat 10am–7pm, Sun noon–3pm), which sells on-the-day tickets for all the West End shows at discounts of up to fifty percent, though they tend to be in the top end of the price range, are limited to four per person, and carry a service charge of £2.50 per ticket.

Venues

What follows is a list of those West End theatres that offer a changing roster of good plays, along with the most consistent of the Off-West End and Fringe venues. This by no means represents the full tally of London's stages, as there are scores of fringe places that present work on an intermittent basis – the weekly listings mag *Time Out* provides the most comprehensive and detailed up-to-the-minute survey.

Almeida Almeida St, N1 ⓣ020/7359 4404, ⓦwww.almeida.co.uk; Angel or Highbury & Islington tube. Deservedly popular Off-West End venue in Islington that continues to premiere excellent new plays and excitingly reworked classics, and has attracted some big Hollywood names.

Barbican Centre Silk St, EC2 ⓣ020/7638 8891, ⓦwww.barbican.org.uk; Barbican or Moorgate tube. The Barbican's two venues – the excellently designed

Barbican Theatre and the much smaller Pit – put on a wide variety of theatrical spectacles from puppetry and musicals to new drama works, and of course Shakespeare, courtesy of the Royal Shakespeare Company who perform here (and elsewhere in London) on and off from autumn to spring each year.

Battersea Arts Centre 176 Lavender Hill, SW11 ⓣ020/7223 2223, ⓦwww.bac.org.uk; Clapham Junction train station from Victoria or Waterloo. The BAC is a triple-stage building, housed in an old town hall in south London, and has acquired a reputation for excellent Fringe productions, from straight theatre to comedy and cabaret.

Bush Shepherd's Bush Green, W12 ⓣ020/7610 4224; Goldhawk Road or Shepherd's Bush tube. This minuscule above-pub theatre is London's most reliable venue for new writing after the *Royal Court*, and it has turned out some great stuff.

Donmar Warehouse Thomas Neal's, Earlham St, WC2 ⓣ020/7369 1732, ⓦwww.donmar-warehouse.com; Covent Garden tube. An intimate central performance space that's noted for new plays and top-quality reappraisals of the classics.

Drill Hall 16 Chenies St, WC1 ⓣ020/7307 5060, ⓦwww.drillhall.co.uk; Goodge Street tube. This studio-style venue specializes in gay, lesbian, feminist and all-round politically correct new work.

ICA Nash House, The Mall, SW1 ⓣ020/7930 3647, ⓦwww.ica.org.uk; Piccadilly Circus or Charing Cross tube. The Institute of Contemporary Arts attracts the most innovative practitioners in all areas of performance. It also attracts a fair quantity of modish junk, but the hits generally outweigh the misses.

Menier Chocolate Factory 51–53 Southwark St, SE1 ⓣ020/7907 7060, ⓦwww.menierchocolatefactory.com; London Bridge tube. Great name, great new fringe venue in an old Victorian factory; consistently good shows and has a great bar and restaurant attached.

National Theatre South Bank Centre, South Bank, SE1 ⓣ020/7452 3000, ⓦwww.nationaltheatre.org.uk; Waterloo tube. The Royal National Theatre, as it's now officially known, consists of three separate theatres. The country's top actors and directors perform here in a programme ranging from Greek tragedies to Broadway musicals. Twenty to thirty cheap tickets go on sale on the morning of each performance – get there by 8am for the popular shows.

Open Air Theatre Regent's Park, Inner Circle, NW1 ⓣ020/7486 2431, ⓦwww.openairtheatre.org; Baker Street tube. If the weather's good, there's nothing quite like a dose of alfresco drama. This beautiful space in Regent's Park hosts a tourist-friendly summer programme of Shakespeare, musicals, plays and concerts.

Royal Court Sloane Square, SW1 ⓣ020/7565 5000, ⓦwww.royalcourttheatre.com; Sloane Square tube. The Royal Court is one of the best places in London to catch radical new writing, either in the proscenium arch Theatre Downstairs, or the smaller-scale Theatre Upstairs studio space.

Shakespeare's Globe New Globe Walk, SE1 ⓣ020/7401 9919, ⓦwww.shakespeares-globe.org; London Bridge, Blackfriars or Southwark tube. This thatch-roofed replica Elizabethan theatre uses only natural light and the minimum of scenery, and currently puts on solid, fun Shakespearean shows from mid-May to mid-Sept, with "groundling" tickets (standing-room only) for around a fiver.

Tricycle Theatre 269 Kilburn High Rd, NW6 ⓣ020/7328 1000, ⓦwww.tricycle.co.uk; Kilburn tube. One of London's most dynamic fringe venues, showcasing a mixed bag of new plays, often aimed at the theatre's multicultural neighbourhood, and often with a sharp political focus.

Comedy

The **comedy scene** continues to thrive in London, with the leading funny-persons catapulted to unlikely stardom on both stage and screen. The Comedy Store is the best known and most central venue on the circuit, but just about every London suburb has a pub stage giving a platform to young hopefuls (full listings appear on ⓦwww.chortle.co.uk and in *Time Out*). Note that many venues operate only on Friday and Saturday nights, and that August is a lean month, as much of London's talent heads north for the Edinburgh Festival. **Tickets** at smaller venues can be had for £5–7, but in the more established places, you're looking at £10 or more.

Backyard Comedy Club 231 Cambridge Heath Rd, E2 ⓣ020/7739 3122, ⓦwww.leehurst.com; Bethnal Green tube. Purpose-built club in Bethnal Green established by comedian Lee Hurst, who has successfully managed to attract a consistently strong line-up. Thurs–Sat.

Canal Café Theatre Delamere Terrace, W2 ⓣ020/7289 6054, ⓦwww.canalcafetheatre.com;

Warwick Avenue tube. Perched on the water's edge in Little Venice, this venue is good for improvisation acts and is home to the *Newsrevue* team of topical gagsters; there's usually something going on from Thurs–Sun.

Comedy Café 66 Rivington St, EC2 ⓣ020/7739 5706, ⓦwww.comedycafe.co.uk; Old Street tube. Long-established, purpose-built club in Shoreditch/Hoxton, often with impressive line-ups, and free admission for the new-acts slot on Wed nights. Wed–Sat.

Comedy Store Haymarket House, 1a Oxendon St, SW1 ⓣ020/7344 0234, ⓦwww.thecomedystore.co.uk; Piccadilly Circus tube. Widely regarded as the birthplace of alternative comedy, the Comedy Store has thrown many a stand-up onto primetime TV. Improvisation by in-house comics on Wed and Sun, in addition to a stand-up bill; Fri and Sat are the busiest nights, with two shows, at 8pm and midnight – book ahead.

Jongleurs Camden Lock, Dingwalls Building, 36 Camden Lock Place, Chalk Farm Rd, NW1 ⓣ0870/787 0707, ⓦwww.jongleurs.com for branches; Camden tube. Jongleurs is the chain store of comedy, doling out high-quality stand-up and post-revelry disco-dancing nightly on Fri. Book well in advance.

Cinema

There are an awful lot of **cinemas** in the West End, but very few places committed to independent films, and even fewer repertory cinemas programming serious films from the back catalogue. November's **London Film Festival** (ⓦwww.lff.org.uk), which occupies half a dozen West End cinemas, is now a huge event, and so popular that many of the films sell out soon after publication of the festival's programme. Below is a selection of the cinemas that put on the most interesting programmes.

Cinemas

BFI Imax South Bank, SE1 ⓣ0870/787 2525, ⓦwww.bfi.org.uk; Waterloo tube. The BFI's remarkable glazed drum houses Europe's largest screen. It's stunning, state-of-the-art stuff all right, showing 2D and 3D films on a massive screen, but like all IMAX cinemas, it suffers from the paucity of good material that's been shot in the format.

BFI Southbank Belvedere Rd, South Bank, SE1 ⓣ020/7928 3232, ⓦwww.bfi.org.uk; Waterloo tube. Known for its attentive audiences and an exhaustive, eclectic programme that includes directors' seasons and thematic series. Around six films daily are shown in the vast NFT1 and the smaller NFT2 and 3.

Electric 191 Portobello Rd, W11 ⓣ020/7908 9696, ⓦwww.the-electric.co.uk; Notting Hill Gate or Ladbroke Grove tube. One of the oldest cinemas in the country (opened 1910), the Electric has been filled out with luxury leather armchairs, footstools and sofas. Most seats cost £12.50.

Everyman Hollybush Vale, NW3 ⓣ0870/066 4777, ⓦwww.everymancinema.com; Hampstead tube. The city's oldest rep cinema, and still one of its best, with strong programmes of classics, cultish crowd-magnets and directors' seasons. Two screens and some very plush seating.

ICA Cinema Nash House, The Mall, SW1 ⓣ020/7930 3647, ⓦwww.ica.org.uk; Piccadilly Circus or Charing Cross tube. Vintage and underground movies shown on one of two tiny screens in the avant-garde HQ of the Institute of Contemporary Arts.

Prince Charles 2–7 Leicester Place, WC2 ⓣ020/7494 3654, ⓦwww.princecharlescinema.com; Leicester Square or Piccadilly Circus tube. The bargain basement of London's cinemas (entry for most shows is just £4.50), with a programme of new movies, classics and cult favourites, plus participatory "singalong" romps.

Classical music, opera and dance

London is spoilt for choice when it comes to **orchestras**. On most days you'll be able to catch a concert by the London Symphony Orchestra, the London Philharmonic, the Royal Philharmonic, the Philharmonia or the BBC Symphony Orchestra, or a smaller-scale performance from the English Chamber Orchestra or the Academy of St Martin-in-the-Fields. During the week, there are also **free lunchtime concerts** by students or professionals in numerous London churches, particularly in the City; performances in the Royal College of Music and Royal Academy of Music are of an amazingly high standard, and the choice of work is often a lot riskier than in commercial venues.

The principal **large-scale venue** is the South Bank Centre (Ⓣ02871/663 2500, Ⓦwww.southbankcentre.org.uk), where the biggest names appear at the Royal Festival Hall, with more specialized programmes staged in the Queen Elizabeth Hall and Purcell Room. With the outstanding London Symphony Orchestra as its resident orchestra, and with top foreign orchestras and big-name soloists in regular attendance, the Barbican (Ⓣ020/7638 8891, Ⓦwww.barbican.org.uk) is one of the capital's best arenas for classical music. For **chamber music**, the intimate and elegant Wigmore Hall, 36 Wigmore St, W1 (Ⓣ020/7935 2141, Ⓦwww.wigmore-hall.org.uk), is many a Londoner's favourite.

From July to September each year, **the Proms** at the Royal Albert Hall (Ⓦwww.bbc.co.uk/proms) feature at least one concert daily, with hundreds of standing tickets sold for just £4 on the night. The acoustics aren't the world's best, but the calibre of the performers is unbeatable and the programme is a fascinating mix of standards and new or obscure works. The hall is so vast that if you turn up half an hour before the show starts there should be little risk of being turned away.

The city is well served for **opera**, with two opera houses, both of which have recently been refurbished. The **Royal Opera House** (Ⓣ020/7304 4000, Ⓦwww.royaloperahouse.org), in Covent Garden, is the pricier and more conservative of the two, with a fairly standard repertoire performed in the original language (with surtitles), while **English National Opera** at the Coliseum on St Martin's Lane (Ⓣ0870/145 0200, Ⓦwww.eno.org) puts on lively, radical productions, sung in English.

From the time-honoured showpieces of the **Royal Ballet** (Ⓣ020/7304 4000, Ⓦwww.royaloperahouse.org) to the diverse and exciting range of British and international dance that goes on at Sadler's Wells (Ⓣ0844/412 4300, Ⓦwww.sadlers-wells.com), Rosebery Avenue and at the much smaller venue, The Place (Ⓣ020/7121 1000, Ⓦwww.theplace.org.uk), 17 Duke's Rd, there's always a **dance performance** of some kind afoot in London, and the city also has a good reputation for international dance festivals showcasing the work of a spread of ensembles. The biggest of the annual events is the **Dance Umbrella** (Ⓣ020/8741 4040, Ⓦwww.danceumbrella.co.uk), a six-week season (Sept–Nov) of new work from bright young choreographers and performance artists at venues across the city.

Shopping

Whether you've got time to kill or money to burn, London is one big **shopper's playground**. Although chains and superstores predominate along the high streets, you're never too far from the kind of oddball, one-off establishment that makes shopping an adventure rather than a routine. From the *folie de grandeur* that is Harrods to the frenetic street markets of the East End, there's probably nothing you can't find in some corner of the capital.

In the centre of town, **Oxford Street** is the city's hectic chain-store mecca, and, together with **Regent Street**, offers pretty much every mainstream clothing label you could wish for. Just off Oxford Street you can find expensive designer outlets in **St Christopher's Place** and **South Molton Street**, and even pricier designers and jewellers on the very chic **Bond Street**.

Tottenham Court Road is the place to go for stereos, computers, electrical goods and, in its northern section, furniture and design shops. **Charing Cross**

Road is the centre of London's book trade, both new and secondhand. At its north end, and particularly on **Denmark Street**, you can find music shops selling everything from instruments to sound equipment and sheet music. **Soho** offers an offbeat mix of sex boutiques, specialist record shops and fabric stores, while the streets surrounding **Covent Garden** yield art and design shops, mainstream fashion chains, designer wear, camping gear; Neal Street is the place to go to indulge a shoe-shopping habit.

Just off Piccadilly, **St James's** is the natural habitat of the quintessential English gentleman, with **Jermyn Street** in particular harbouring shops dedicated to his grooming. **Knightsbridge**, further west, is home to Harrods, and the big-name fashion stores of **Sloane Street** and **Brompton Road**.

Books

The biggest bookstore in the capital is Waterstones' Piccadilly branch (Piccadilly Circus tube), but the largest choice of bookshops is still on **Charing Cross Road**, where you'll not only find all the **chain stores** but also the long-established and idiosyncratic Foyles at no. 113–119, and other smaller **independent shops** such as art specialists Zwemmer at no. 80 and numerous **second hand stores**, including Any Amount of Books at no. 62.

Department stores

Fortnum & Mason, 181 Piccadilly (Green Park or Piccadilly Circus tube), is the place to go for fabulous, gorgeously presented and pricey food, plus upmarket clothes, furniture and stationery. **Harrods**, Knightsbridge (Knightsbridge tube), is famous for its fantastic Art Nouveau tiled food hall, obscenely huge toy department and supremely tasteless memorial to Di and Dodi; beware the draconian dress code (see p.128). Nearby, **Harvey Nichols**, 109–125 Knightsbridge, offers all the latest designer collections and famously frivolous and pricey luxury foods. Over at Oxford Circus, several major stores are close at hand, among them: **John Lewis**, 278–306 Oxford St (Oxford Circus tube), which offers everything from buttons to stockings to furniture and household goods; **Liberty**, 210–220 Regent St (Oxford Circus tube), founded as a retail outlet for the Victorian Arts and Crafts Movement, and still the place to go for regal fabrics and decorative household goods; and **Selfridge's**, 400 Oxford St (Bond Street tube), London's first great department store, which has a wide range of clothing, food and furnishings.

Markets

Camden, running from Camden High Street to Chalk Farm Road (daily; Camden Town tube), is top of the list for market shopping on most tourist itineraries; the atmosphere is a studenty mix of clubby and grungy and the stuff on sale is mainly cheap clothes and jewellery, though the stalls around Camden Lock are generally more interesting; weekends are the best – and busiest – times to visit. For a real foody experience, head for **Borough Market** (Fri & Sat; London Bridge or Borough tube). **Spitalfields**, Commercial Street (Sun; Liverpool Street tube), also offers organic fruit and veg, but is otherwise more of an arty-crafty market similar to Camden. Nearby, **Brick Lane** (Sun; Aldgate East, Shoreditch or Liverpool Street tube) has everything from sofas and antiques to cheap junk. **Bermondsey** (New Caledonian) Market, Bermondsey Square (Fri; Borough, London Bridge or Bermondsey tube), is a huge, unglamorous but highly regarded antique market that kicks off at 5am; while **Portobello**, Portobello Rd (Fri–Sun; Notting Hill or Ladbroke Grove tube), is mostly boho-chic clothes and (Sat only) portable antiques. South of the river,

Greenwich, Market Square (Sat & Sun; Cutty Sark DLR or Greenwich train station), is another small arty-crafty market, with second hand clothing and antiques on sale, too.

Music

The **megastores** are: HMV, 150 Oxford St (Oxford Circus tube); Tower Records, 1 Piccadilly Circus (Piccadilly Circus tube); Zavvi, 14–16 Oxford St (Tottenham Court Road tube). For **jazz**, try Ray's on the first floor of Foyles, 113–119 Charing Cross Rd (Tottenham Court Road tube). For **indie music**, there's Sister Ray, 94 Berwick St (Oxford Circus or Piccadilly Circus tube). For **African and world music**, head to Stern's, 293 Euston Rd, NW1 (Euston Square tube). **Hip-hop** is available at Mr Bongo 44 Poland St (Oxford Circus tube). For **house**, **techno** and **trance** go to Eukatech, 49 Endell St (Covent Garden tube).

Listings

Bike rental London Bicycle Tour Company, 1a Gabriel's Wharf SE1 ⓣ020/7928 6838, ⓦwww.londonbicycle.com Waterloo or Southwark tube; On Your Bike, 52–54 Tooley St, SE1 ⓣ020/7378 6669, ⓦwww.onyourbike.com; London Bridge tube.

Car rental For the most competitive rates, ring round a few local firms from the Yellow Pages (ⓦwww.yell.com) before you try your luck with the usual suspects.

Consulates and embassies Australia, Australia House, Strand, WC2 ⓣ020/7379 4334, ⓦwww.australia.org.uk; Canadian High Commission 1 Grosvenor Square, W1 ⓣ020/7528 6600, ⓦwww.canada.org.uk; Ireland, 17 Grosvenor Place, SW1 ⓣ020/7235 2171, ⓦwww.irlgov.ie; New Zealand, New Zealand House, 80 Haymarket, SW1 ⓣ020/7930 8422, ⓦwww.nzembassy.com; South Africa, South Africa House, Trafalgar Square, WC2 ⓣ020/7451 7299, ⓦwww.southafricahouse.com; USA, 24 Grosvenor Square, W1 ⓣ020/7499 9000, ⓦwww.usembassy.org.uk.

Cricket Two Test matches are played in London each summer: one at Lord's (ⓣ020/7432 1000, ⓦwww.lords.org; St John's Wood tube), the home of English cricket; the other at The Oval (ⓣ020/7582 6660, ⓦwww.surreycricket.com; Oval tube) in south London. In tandem with the full-blown five-day Tests, there's also a series of one-day internationals, two of which are usually held in London.

Football Despite the recent successes of Chelsea (ⓣ020/7386 9373, ⓦwww.chelseafc.com; Fulham Broadway tube), for the last decade or so Arsenal (ⓣ020/7704 4040, ⓦwww.arsenal.com; Arsenal tube) has been London's most successful club; their closest rivals (geographically) are Tottenham Hotspur (ⓣ0870/420 5000, ⓦwww.tottenhamhotspur.com; White Hart Lane train station from Liverpool St). Tickets for most Premiership games start at £30–35 and are virtually impossible to get hold of on a casual basis; you're more likely to have success if you try one of the smaller London sides, such as Fulham (ⓣ0870/442 1234, ⓦwww.fulhamfc.com; Putney Bridge tube), West Ham (ⓣ0870/112 2700, ⓦwww.whufc.co.uk; Upton Park tube) or Charlton Athletic (ⓣ0871/226 1905, ⓦwww.cafc.co.uk; Charlton train station from Charing Cross).

Hospitals For 24hr accident and emergency: St Mary's Hospital, Praed St, W2 ⓣ020/7886 6666; University College London Hospital, Grafton Way, WC1 ⓣ020/7387 9300.

Laundry Regent Dry Cleaners, 18 Embankment Place WC2 ⓣ020/7839 6775; Embankment or Charing Cross tube.

Left luggage Left luggage is available at all airports and major train terminals.

Maps Stanfords 12–14 Long Acre, WC2 ⓣ020/7836 1321, ⓦwww.stanfords.co.uk.

Motorbike rental Raceways, 201–203 Lower Rd, SE16 ⓣ020/7237 6494 (Surrey Quays tube) and 17 The Vale, Uxbridge Rd, W3 ⓣ020/8749 8181 (Shepherd's Bush tube), ⓦwww.raceways.net. Mon–Sat 9am–5pm.

Police Central police stations include: Charing Cross, Agar St, WC2 ⓣ020/7240 1212; Holborn, 10 Lambs Conduit St, WC1 ⓣ020/7704 1212; Marylebone, 1–9 Seymour St W1 ⓣ020/7486 1212; West End Central, 27 Savile Row, W1 ⓣ020/7437 1212, ⓦwww.met.police.uk; City of London Police, Bishopsgate, EC2 ⓣ020/7601 2222 ⓦwww.cityoflondon.police.uk.

Post offices The only (vaguely) late-opening post office is the Trafalgar Square branch at 24–28 William IV St, WC2 4DL ⓣ020/7930 9580

(Mon 8.30am–6.30pm, Tues 9.15am–6.30pm, Wed–Fri 8.30am–6.30pm, Sat 9am–5pm); it's also the city's poste restante collection point. For general postal enquiries phone ⓣ0845/7740 740 (Mon–Fri 8am–7.30pm, Sat 8am–2.30pm), or visit the website ⓦwww.royalmail.com.

Tennis Tennis in England is synonymous with Wimbledon (ⓣ020/8971 2473, ⓦwww.wimbledon.com), the only Grand Slam tournament in the world to be played on grass, and for many players the ultimate goal of their careers. To buy tickets on the day, you must arrive by around 7am for tickets on Centre, No. 1 & No. 2 courts, or by around 9am for the outside courts (and avoid the middle Sat of the tournament); alternatively, if you start queuing around 2pm, you should get in to see some play in the evening.

Train stations and information As a rough guide, Charing Cross handles services to Kent; Euston to the Midlands, northwest England and Glasgow; Fenchurch Street south Essex; King's Cross northeast England and Edinburgh; Liverpool Street eastern England; Marylebone the Midlands; Paddington southwest England; St Pancras Eurostar, East Midlands and South Yorkshire; Victoria and Waterloo southeast England. For information, contact national rail enquiries ⓣ08457/484950, ⓦwww.rail.co.uk.

Travel details

Buses

For information on all local and national bus services, contact Traveline ⓣ0871/200 2233 (daily 7am–10.30pm), ⓦwww.traveline.org.uk.

London Victoria Coach Station to: Bath (every 1–2hr; 3hr 30min); Birmingham (hourly; 2hr 40min); Brighton (hourly; 2hr 10min); Bristol (hourly; 2hr 30min); Cambridge (hourly; 2hr); Canterbury (hourly; 2hr); Dover (hourly; 2hr 30min–3hr); Exeter (every 2hr; 4hr 15min); Gloucester (hourly; 3hr 20min); Liverpool (6 daily; 4hr 50min–5hr 30min); Manchester (9 daily; 4hr 15min–5hr 20min); Newcastle (5 daily; 6hr 25min–7hr 45min); Oxford (every 15min; 1hr 50min); Plymouth (6 daily; 5hr 20min); Stratford (4 daily; 3hr).

Trains

For information on all local and national rail services, contact National Rail Enquiries ⓣ08457/484950, ⓦwww.nationalrail.co.uk.

London Charing Cross to: Canterbury West (hourly; 1hr 40min); Dover Priory (Mon–Sat every 30min; 1hr 40min–1hr 50min).

London Euston to: Birmingham New St (every 30min; 1hr 30min–2hr 10min); Carlisle (hourly; 3hr 30min 4hr); Lancaster (hourly; 2hr 50min); Liverpool Lime St (hourly; 2hr 30min); Manchester Piccadilly (hourly; 2hr 20min).

London King's Cross to: Brighton (Thameslink; every 15–30min; 1hr 15min); Cambridge (every 30min; 50min); Durham (hourly; 2hr 40min–3hr); Leeds (hourly; 2hr 25min); Newcastle (every 30min; 3hr); Peterborough (every 30min; 45min); York (every 30min; 2hr).

London Liverpool Street to: Cambridge (every 30min; 1hr 20min); Norwich (every 30min; 1hr 55min).

London Paddington to: Bath (every 30min–hourly; 1hr 30min–1hr 40min); Bristol (every 30–45min; 1hr 20min); Cheltenham (every 2hr; 2hr 15min); Exeter (hourly; 2hr 15min); Gloucester (every 2hr; 2hr); Oxford (every 30min–hourly; 55min); Penzance (every 1–2hr; 5hr 30min); Plymouth (hourly; 3hr 15min–3hr 40min); Windsor (change at Slough; Mon–Fri every 20min; Sat & Sun every 30min; journey time 30–40min); Worcester (hourly; 2hr 20min).

London St Pancras to: Leicester (every 30min; 1hr 10min); Nottingham (every 30min; 1hr 40min–2hr); Sheffield (hourly; 2hr 20min).

London Victoria to: Brighton (every 30min; 50min); Canterbury East (every 30min–hourly; 1hr 25min); Dover Priory (Mon–Sat every 30min; 1hr 40min–1hr 55min).

London Waterloo to: Portsmouth Harbour (every 30min; 1hr 35min); Southampton Central (every 30min; 1hr 15min); Winchester (every 30min; 1hr); Windsor (Mon–Sat every 30min; Sun hourly; 50min).

2

Surrey, Kent and Sussex

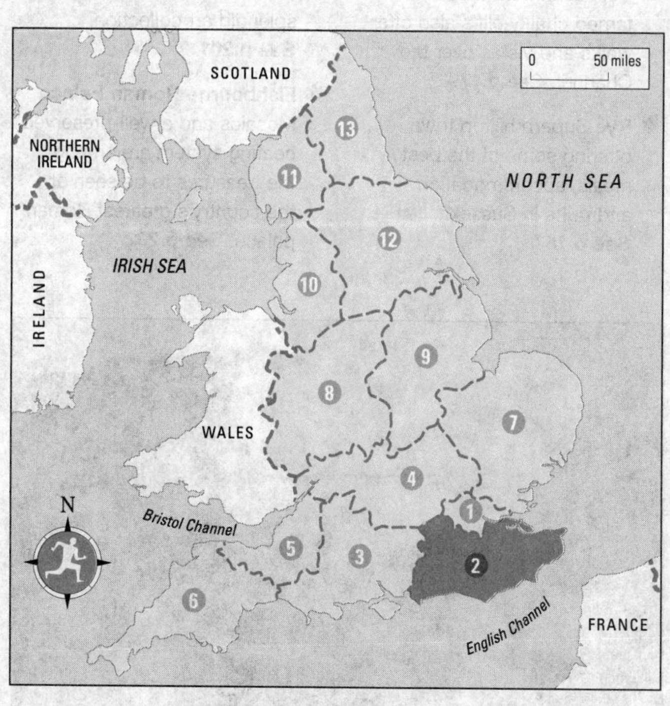

CHAPTER 2

Highlights

* **Canterbury Cathedral** The destination of the pilgrims in Chaucer's *Canterbury Tales*, with a magnificent sixteenth-century interior that includes a shrine to the murdered Thomas à Becket. See p.174

* **The White Cliffs of Dover** Best seen from a boat, the famed chalky cliffs also offer walks and vistas over the Channel. See p.179

* **Rye** Superb hilltop town offering some of the best meals, accommodation and pubs in Sussex. See p.187

* **The Royal Pavilion, Brighton** George IV's pleasure dome, designed by Nash, is the supreme (and only) example of Oriental Gothic architecture. See p.194

* **Petworth House** As well as being one of the country's most attractive stately homes, this place is home to a splendid art collection. See p.201

* **Fishbourne Roman Palace** Mosaics and a well-preserved heating system are among the treasures to be seen at the country's greatest Roman palace. See p.202

▲The White Cliffs of Dover

2

Surrey, Kent and Sussex

The southeast corner of England was traditionally where London went on holiday. In the past, trainloads of Eastenders were shuttled to the hop fields and orchards of **Kent** for a working break from the city; boats ferried people down the Thames to the beaches of north Kent; while everyone from royalty to cuckolding couples enjoyed the seaside at Brighton, a blot of decadence in the otherwise sedate county of **Sussex**. The home of wealthy metropolitan commuters, **Surrey** is the least pastoral and historically significant of the three counties, though it does have a couple of places worth visiting.

Although many of the old seaside resorts have struggled to keep their tourist custom in the face of ever more accessible foreign destinations, the region still boasts considerable charm, its narrow country lanes and verdant meadows appearing in places almost untouched by modern life.

The proximity of Kent and Sussex to the continent has dictated the history of this region, which has served as a gateway for an array of invaders. **Roman** remains dot the coastal area – most spectacularly at **Bignor** in Sussex and **Lullingstone** in Kent – and many roads, including the main A2 London to Dover road, follow the arrow-straight tracks laid by the legionaries. When **Christianity** spread through Europe, it arrived in Britain on the **Isle of Thanet** – the northeast tip of Kent, since rejoined to the mainland by silting and subsiding sea levels. In 597 AD Augustine moved inland and established a monastery at **Canterbury**, still the home of the Church of England and the county's prime historic attraction.

The last successful invasion of England took place in 1066, when the **Normans** overran King Harold's army near **Hastings**, on a site now marked by **Battle Abbey**. The Normans left their mark all over this corner of the kingdom, and Kent remains unmatched in its profusion of medieval castles, among them **Dover**'s sprawling cliff-top fortress guarding against continental invasion and **Rochester**'s huge, box-like citadel, close to the old dockyards of **Chatham**, power base of the formerly invincible British navy.

Away from the great historic sites, you can spend unhurried days in elegant old towns such as **Royal Tunbridge Wells**, **Rye** and **Lewes**, or enjoy the less elevated charms of the traditional resorts, of which fashionable **Brighton** is far and away the best, combining the buzz of a university town with a good-time atmosphere and an excellent range of eating options. Dramatic scenery may be in short supply hereabouts, but in places the **South Downs Way** offers an expanse of rolling chalk uplands that, as much as anywhere in the crowded Southeast, gets you away from it all. Kent, Sussex and Surrey also harbour some of the country's finest **gardens**, ranging from the lush flowerbeds of **Sissinghurst** to the great landscaped estate of **Petworth House**.

Almost everywhere of interest in this corner of England is close to a **train** station. National Express services from London and other main towns are pretty good, though local **bus** services are less impressive.

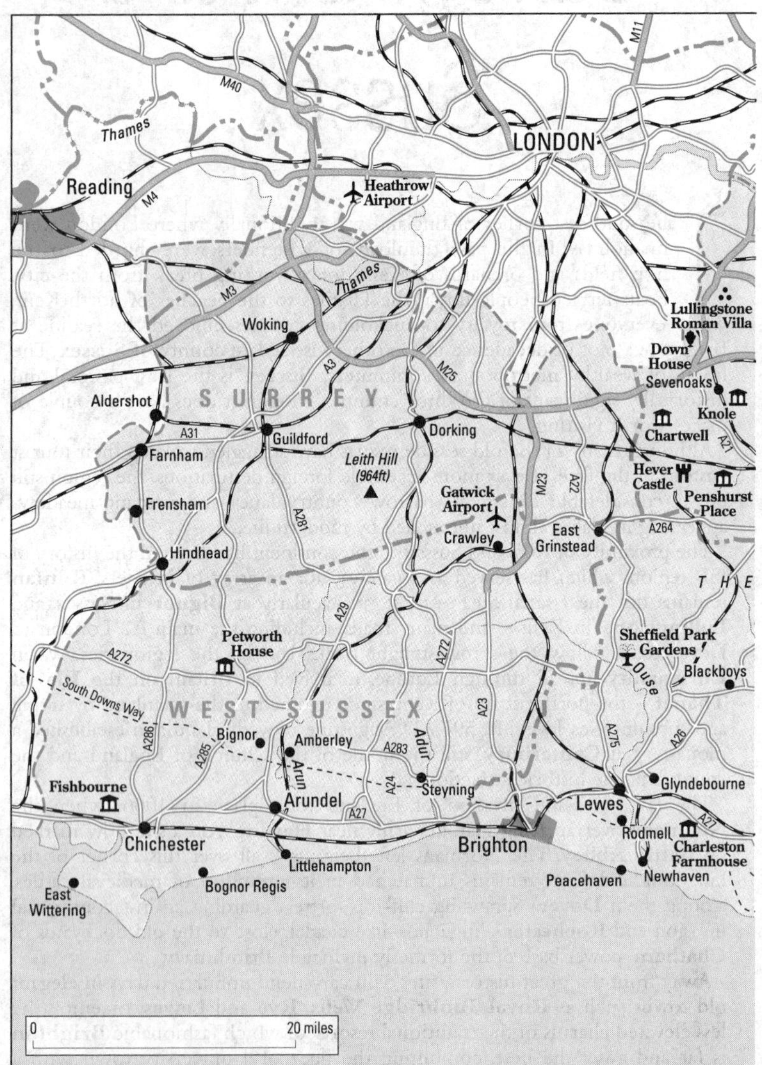

Guildford and Farnham

Thirty-five miles southwest of London, **GUILDFORD**, county town of Surrey, has little immediate appeal, though its sloping **High Street** retains plenty of architectural interest. Marked by a wonderful gilded clock projecting over the street, the **Guildhall** (guided tours Tues & Thurs 2 & 3pm; free) has an elaborate Restoration facade disguising Tudor foundations, while further up the street, you can take a peek at the pretty courtyard of **Archbishop Abbot's Hospital**, a hospice built for the elderly in 1619 and fronted by a palatial

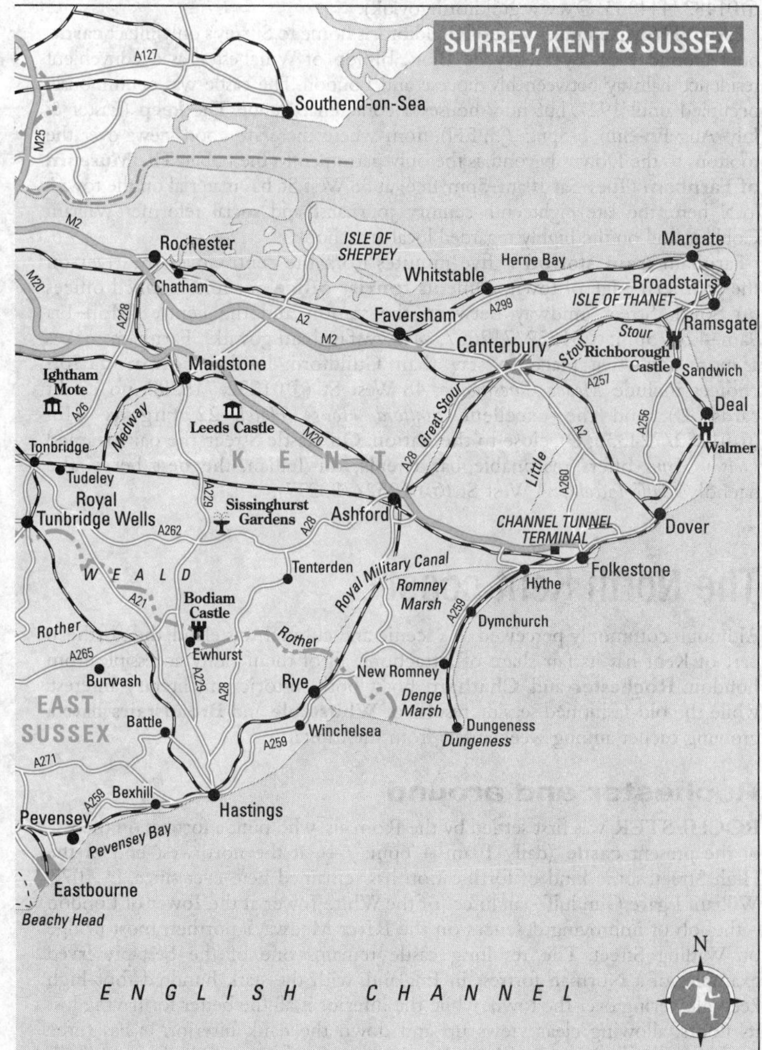

red-brick Tudor gateway. Back down towards the river, on the left at no. 72 is the **Undercroft**, a well-preserved thirteenth-century basement of vaulted arches.

Guildford **Castle**'s Norman keep (March & Oct Sat & Sun 11am–5pm; April–Sept daily 11am–5pm; £2.40) sits on its motte behind the High Street. Beneath the castle, **Guildford Museum** (Mon–Sat 11am–5pm; free) displays mementos of the writer Lewis Carroll (aka the Reverend Charles Dodgson), author of *Alice's Adventures in Wonderland* and *Alice Through the Looking Glass*.

Guildford's **train station** lies just over the river to the west of the town centre, and the **bus station** is nearby at the western end of North Street. The **tourist office** is at 14 Tunsgate, near the Guildhall, just off the High Street (Mon–Sat 9/9.30am–5/5.30pm, May–Sept also Sun 10am–4.30pm; ⓣ01483/444333, ⓦwww.guildford.gov.uk).

FARNHAM, ten miles west of Guildford, is home to Surrey's only intact **castle**, built around 1138 by Henry de Blois, Bishop of Winchester, as a convenient residence halfway between his diocese and London. The castle was continuously occupied until 1927, but now houses a conference venue. The **keep** (Easter & July–Aug Fri–Sun 1–5pm; £3; EH), from where there are good views over the rooftops to the Downs beyond, is the only part open to the public. The **Museum of Farnham** (Tues–Sat 10am–5pm; free) at 38 West St, has material on the town's local hero, the late eighteenth-century journalist and social reformer William Cobbett, and on the highly regarded local art school.

Farnham **train station** is five minutes from the centre, over the river on the southern edge of town, while its **tourist office** occupies council offices on South Street, midway between the station and the centre (Mon–Fri 9am–4.30/5pm; ⓣ01252/712667, ⓦwww.farnham.gov.uk). Farnham makes a more attractive place to stay than Guildford: local **accommodation** choices include *Meads Guesthouse*, 48 West St (ⓣ01252/715298; no credit cards; ❸), and the excellent *Stafford House Hotel*, 22 Firgrove Hill (ⓣ01252/724336; ❸), close to the station. On Castle Street, the oak-beamed *Nelson Arms* offers reasonable bar **meals**; for Italian, the best bet is the friendly *Caffé Piccolo*, 84 West St (ⓣ01252/723277).

The North Kent coast

Although commonly perceived as a scenic and cultural wasteland, the northern part of Kent has its fair share of attractions, all of them easily accessible from London. **Rochester** and **Chatham** boast both historic and literary interest, while the old-fashioned seaside resorts of **Whitstable** and **Broadstairs** have a growing cachet among weekenders from the capital.

Rochester and around

ROCHESTER was first settled by the Romans, who built a fortress on the site of the present **castle** (daily 10am–4/6pm; £4), at the northwest end of the High Street; some kind of fortification has remained here ever since. In 1077, William I gave Gundulf – architect of the White Tower at the Tower of London – the job of improving defences on the River Medway's northernmost bridge on Watling Street. The resulting castle remains one of the best-preserved examples of a Norman fortress in England, with the stark hundred-foot-high keep glowering over the town, while the interior is all the better for having lost its floors, allowing clear views up and down the dank interior. It has three square towers and a cylindrical one, the southwest tower, which was rebuilt following its collapse during the siege of 1215, when the bankrupt King John eventually wrested the castle from its archbishop. The outer walls and two of the towers retain their corridors and spiral stairwells, allowing access to the uppermost battlements.

The foundations of the adjacent **cathedral** (daily 8.30am–6pm; donation) were also Gundulf's work, but the building has been much modified over the past nine hundred years. Plenty of Norman touches have endured, however, particularly in the cathedral's west front, with pencil-shaped towers, blind arcading and a richly carved portal and tympanum. Some fine paintings survived the Dissolution, most notably the thirteenth-century depiction of the Wheel of Fortune on the walls of the choir (only half of which survives).

Charles Dickens spent his youth in Rochester, but would seem to have been less than impressed by the place – it appears as "Mudfog" in *The Mudfog Papers*, and "Dullborough" in *The Uncommercial Traveller*. Many of the buildings feature in his novels: the *Royal Victoria and Bull Hotel*, at the top of the High Street, became the *Bull* in *Pickwick Papers* and the *Blue Boar* in *Great Expectations*, while most of his last book, the unfinished *The Mystery of Edwin Drood*, was set in the town.

At the northwest end of the High Street, Rochester's excellent **Guildhall Museum** (daily 10am–4.30pm; free) holds a vivid model of the siege of the castle by King John in 1215 and a chilling exhibition on the prison ships or hulks used to house convicts and prisoners of war in the late eighteenth century.

Practicalities

Rochester **train station** is at the southeastern end of the High Street, and the **tourist office** is halfway along the High Street, opposite the cathedral at no. 95 (Mon–Fri 9am–5pm, Sat 10am–5pm, Sun 10.30am–5pm; ⓣ01634/843666, ⓦwww.medway.gov.uk). **Accommodation** is available at the ghost-ridden *Royal Victoria and Bull Hotel*, 16–18 High St (ⓣ01634/846266, ⓦwww.rvandb.co.uk; ⑤), while decent B&Bs include the *Grayling House*, 54 St Margaret's St (ⓣ01634/826593, ⓔgraylinghouse@aol.com; no credit cards; ②), further up the hill behind the castle. The nearest YHA **hostel** (ⓣ0870/770 5964, ⓔmedway@yha.org.uk; from £14, rooms ①) is at Capstone Farm, Gillingham, two miles southeast of Chatham (bus #114). The best **eating** options are all on the High Street: the Italian *Don Vincenzo*, 108 High St (ⓣ01634/408373), and the *Cumin Club* at no. 188 (ⓣ01634/400880) for contemporary Indian cuisine. Alternatively, the *Coopers Arms*, on St Margaret's Street, serves good lunches in its small beer garden.

Chatham

CHATHAM, less than two miles east of Rochester, has none of the charms of its neighbour. Its chief attraction is its **Historic Dockyard** (mid-Feb to Oct daily 10am–6pm or dusk; Nov Sat & Sun 10am–4pm, last entry 2hr before closing; £12.50), originally founded by Henry VIII, and once the major base of the Royal Navy, many of whose vessels were built, stationed and victualled here. By the time of Charles II it was England's largest naval base, but the shipbuilding era ended when the dockyards were closed in 1984, reopening soon afterwards as a tourist attraction.

The dockyard, with its array of historically and architecturally fascinating eighteenth-century buildings, occupies a vast eighty-acre site about one mile north of the town centre along the Dock Road (buses from Chatham Station, or the Dockside Shuttle Bus from the bus station); there's a free vintage-bus service to take you around. There's also the **Ocelot submarine**, the last warship built at Chatham, whose crew endured unbelievably cramped conditions – a major deterrent to visiting claustrophobes – and a newly restored Victorian sloop, the *Gannet*. The main part of the exhibition, however, consists of the **Ropery** complex, including the former rope-making room.

Following Dock Road further up to Leviathan Way, you'll come to **Dickens World** (daily 10am–5.30pm, closes 7pm during school hols; last admission 90min before closing; £12.50, or £9.75 after 3pm), devoted to recreating Dickensian London. Here, you can spend a couple of hours exploring lanes packed with references to scenes from Dickens and peopled by over-enthusiastic cockney staff in period garb.

Whitstable

Peculiarities of silt and salinity have made **WHITSTABLE** an oyster-friendly environment since classical times, when the Romans feasted on the region's marine delicacies. Indeed, production grew to such levels during the Middle Ages that **oysters** were exported all over Europe – but the whole industry collapsed during the twentieth century. Oysters are once more farmed in the area, but Whitstable is now more dependent on its commercial port, fishing and seaside tourism, while small-scale boat-building and a mildly bohemian ambience have made this one of the most agreeable spots along the North Kent coast to spend any time.

Follow the signs at the top of Whitstable's busy High Street to reach the seafront, a quiet shingle beach backed by some pretty weatherboard cottages. Local maritime history is illustrated in the **Whitstable Museum and Gallery** (Mon–Sat 10am–4pm, plus Sun 1–4pm in July & Aug; free), heralded by its eye-catching entrance on Oxford Street (the southern continuation of the High Street), with displays on diving and some good photographs and old film footage of the town's heyday.

Whitstable's **train station** is five minutes' walk along Cromwell Road, east of Oxford Street, while the **tourist office** is next to the museum at 7 Oxford St (Mon–Sat 10am–4/5pm; ⓣ01227/275482, ⓦwww.canterbury.co.uk). For **accommodation** along the seafront, try *Copeland House*, 4 Island Wall (ⓣ01227/266207, ⓦwww.copelandhouse.co.uk; no credit cards; ⑤), west of the High Street, or the Art Deco *Hotel Continental*, 29 Beach Walk (ⓣ01227/280280, ⓦwww.hotelcontinental.co.uk; ⑤), off the northern tip of Harbour Street, which also has accommodation in wooden fishermen's huts close to the beach. For **campsites**, head to *Seaview Caravan Park* (ⓣ01227/792246; closed Nov–March), which backs onto the beach towards Herne Bay.

Appropriate to the town's history, **eating** places feature lots of seafood: from fish-and-chip outlets along the High Street and Harbour Street to the very popular and famous *Whitstable Oyster Fishery Restaurant*, The Horsebridge (ⓣ01227/276856; closed Mon). For topnotch Italian food, head for *Giovanni's*, 49–55 Canterbury Rd (ⓣ01227/273034: closed Mon), while for a **drink** in excellent atmosphere check out the *Old Neptune*, standing alone in its white weatherboards on the beach.

The Thanet resorts

The **Isle of Thanet**, a featureless plain fringed by low chalk cliffs and the odd sandy bay, became part of the mainland when the navigable Wantsum Channel began silting up around the time of the first Roman invasion. The island is named after the "tenets", or fire beacons, which used to warn local residents of Saxon raids. The evangelist Augustine arrived here in 597 on a divine mission to end Anglo-Saxon paganism, and is supposed to have preached his first sermon at a spot three miles west of Ramsgate – a cross marks the location at Ebbsfleet, next to St Augustine's Golf Club.

Over the next thousand years or so, civilization advanced to the point at which, in 1751, a local resident, one Mr Benjamin Beale, invented the bathing machine, a wheeled cubicle that enabled people to slip into the sea without undue exhibitionism. It heralded the birth of sea bathing as a recreational and recuperative activity, and by the mid-twentieth century the Isle's intermittent expanses of sand had become fully colonized as the "bucket and spade" resorts of the capital's leisure-seeking proletariat.

Broadstairs

Said to have been established on the profits of shipbuilding and smuggling, today **BROADSTAIRS** is the smallest, quietest and most pleasant of Thanet's resort towns, overlooking the pretty little Viking Bay from its cliff-top setting. Its main claim to fame is as Dickens' holiday retreat: throughout his most productive years he stayed in various hostelries here, and eventually rented an "airy nest" overlooking Viking Bay from Fort Road, since renamed **Bleak House**, where he planned the eponymous novel as well as finishing *David Copperfield*. The building Dickens used as a model for Betsey Trotwood's house, on the main cliff-top seafront at 2 Victoria Parade, is now the **Dickens House Museum** (daily: Easter–June & Oct 2–5pm, July–Sept 10am–5pm; £2.50). It also houses the town's **tourist office** (April–Sept daily 9am–5pm; Oct–March Mon–Sat 9am–4.30pm; ⓣ0870/264 6111, ⓦwww.visitthanet.co.uk) – though plans are afoot for a move to a separate building in 2008, with the same contacts. In June, the town's **Dickens Festival** features lectures, dramatizations of the author's works and a nightly Victorian music hall.

It's a ten-minute walk from the **train station** to Broadstairs' seafront along the High Street. **Stay** at the comfortable, family-run *Royal Albion Hotel*, 6–12 Albion St (ⓣ01843/868071, ⓦwww.albionbroadstairs.co.uk; ⑥), where Dickens wrote part of *Nicholas Nickleby*. Alternatively, there's the modest *East Horndon Hotel* (ⓣ01843/868306, ⓦwww.easthorndonhotel.com; ①), on the Eastern Esplanade.

There are plenty of fish-and-chip outlets and **cafés** along Albion Street and Harbour Street, but for a more congenial setting, head for *Harpers Wine Bar*, also on Harbour Street (ⓣ01843/602494; eve only), which serves moderately priced seafood dishes. As for **pubs**, the *Tartar Frigate* on Harbour Street is a solid, sociable English tavern with its own seafood restaurant upstairs, while *Neptune's Hall* at the top of Harbour Street serves great beer.

Ramsgate

If Thanet had a capital, it would be **RAMSGATE**, a handsome resort, rich in robust Victorian red brick, mostly set high on a cliff linked to the seafront and harbour by broad, sweeping ramps. Housed in the harbour's nineteenth-century Clock House on the quayside, the **Ramsgate Maritime Museum** (Easter–Sept Tues–Sun 10am–5pm; Oct–Easter Thurs–Sun 11am–4.30pm; £1.50) chronicles municipal life from Roman times onwards; its most illuminating section focuses on the Goodwin Sands sandbanks, six miles southeast of Ramsgate – the occasional playing field of the eccentric Goodwin Sands Cricket Club.

Ramsgate's **train station** is about a mile northwest of the centre, at the end of Wilfred Road, at the top of the High Street. The **tourist office** is at 17 Albert Court, York Street (Tues–Sat 10am–4/6pm; ⓣ0870/264 6111, ⓦwww.visitthanet.co.uk). For an overnight **stay**, book into the attractive seafront

Crescent, 19 Wellington Crescent (ⓣ01843/591419, ⓦwww.ramsgate-uk.com; ②). For **food**, the reasonably priced *Surin Thai* at 30 Harbour St (ⓣ01843/592001; closed Sun) scores highly for its Cambodian, Lao and Thai food, while the gaudy *Peter's Fish Factory* at 96 Harbour Parade is the best for fish and chips. For traditional **pubs**, try the ornately tiled *Queen's Head* on Harbour Parade, and for harbour views, real ales and live music, head for the *Churchill Tavern* on The Paragon.

Canterbury

One of England's most venerable cities, **CANTERBURY** offers a rich slice through two thousand years of history, with Roman and early Christian ruins, a Norman castle and a famous cathedral that dominates a medieval warren of time-skewed Tudor dwellings. The city that began as a Belgic settlement was known as **Durovernum** to the Romans, who established a garrison and supply base here, and renamed **Cantwarabyrig** by the Saxons. In 597 the Saxon King Ethelbert welcomed Augustine, despatched by the pope to convert the British Isles to Christianity; one of the two Benedictine monasteries founded by Augustine – Christ Church, raised on the site of the Roman basilica – was to become England's first cathedral.

At the turn of the first millennium Canterbury suffered repeated sackings by the Danes, and Christ Church was eventually destroyed by fire a year before the Norman invasion. A struggle for power later developed between the archbishops, the abbots from the nearby Benedictine abbey and King Henry II, culminating in the assassination of Archbishop Thomas à Becket in 1170, a martyrdom that established this as one of Christendom's greatest shrines. Geoffrey Chaucer's *Canterbury Tales*, written towards the end of the fourteenth century, portrays the unexpectedly festive nature of pilgrimages to Becket's tomb, which was later plundered and destroyed on the orders of Henry VIII.

In 1830 a pioneering passenger railway service linked Canterbury to the sea and prosperity grew until the city suffered extensive German bombing on June 1, 1942, in one of the notorious **Baedeker Raids** – the Nazi plan to destroy Britain's most treasured historic sites as described in the eponymous German travel guides. Today the cathedral and compact town centre, enclosed on three sides by medieval walls, remain the focus for leisure-motivated pilgrims from across the globe.

Arrival, information and accommodation

Canterbury has two **train stations** – Canterbury East for services from London Victoria and Dover Priory, and Canterbury West for services from London Charing Cross and the Isle of Thanet – each a ten-minute walk from the cathedral. The bus station is just inside the city walls on St George's Lane. The busy **tourist office** is at the Butter Market at 12–13 Sun St (Easter–June Mon–Sat 9.30am–5pm, Sun 10am–4pm; July & Aug Mon–Sat 9.30am–6pm, Sun 10am–4pm; Sept–Easter Mon–Sat 10am–4pm; ⓣ01227/378100, ⓦwww.canterbury.co.uk), opposite the main entrance to the cathedral. For **Internet** access, go to *Dot Café*, 21 St Dunstans St (daily 9am–9pm).

Accommodation consists mostly of B&Bs and small hotels and can be difficult to secure in July and August – the tourist office can help, though they charge for the service.

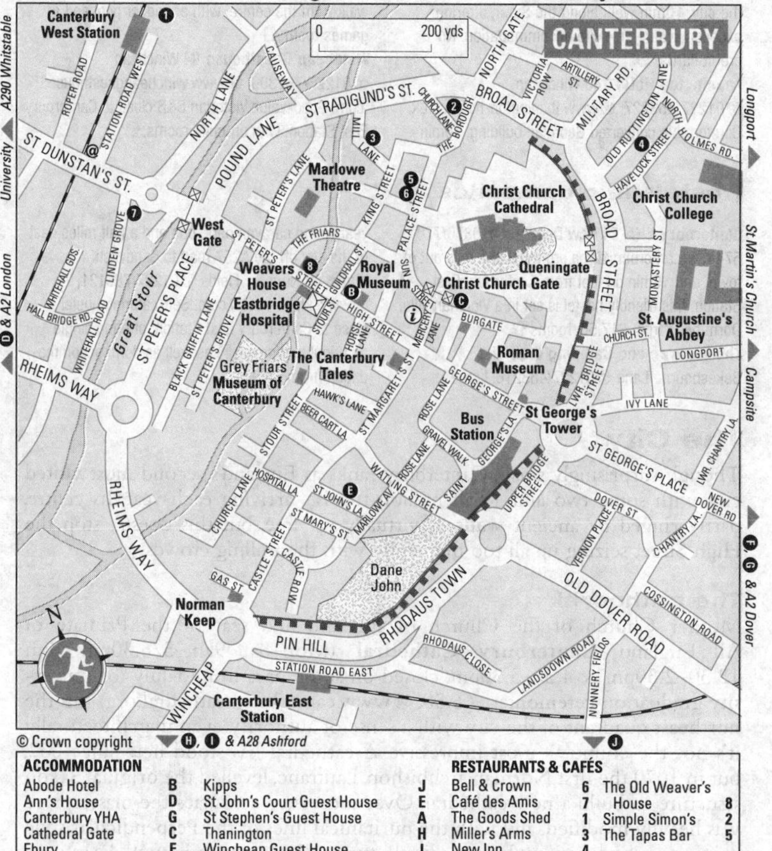

ACCOMMODATION				RESTAURANTS & CAFÉS			
Abode Hotel	B	Kipps	J	Bell & Crown	6	The Old Weaver's House	8
Ann's House	D	St John's Court Guest House	E	Café des Amis	7	Simple Simon's	2
Canterbury YHA	G	St Stephen's Guest House	A	The Goods Shed	1	The Tapas Bar	5
Cathedral Gate	C	Thanington	H	Miller's Arms	3		
Ebury	F	Wincheap Guest House	I	New Inn	4		

Hotels and B&Bs

Abode Hotel 30 High St ⓣ01227/766266, ⓦwww.abodehotels.co.uk/canterbury. Luxurious and stylish, this state-of-the-art hotel has spacious rooms with contemporary designs, the more expensive rooms with balconies overlooking the cathedral. There's also a topnotch restaurant. 7

Ann's House 63 London Rd ⓣ01227/768767, ⓦwww.annshousecanterbury.co.uk. Traditional Victorian villa offering comfortable rooms, most of which are en suite, a 10min walk from the centre. 2

Cathedral Gate 36 Burgate ⓣ01227/464381, ⓦwww.cathgate.co.uk. Built in 1438 and set in the city's medieval heart, this venerable pilgrims' hostelry features crooked floors and exposed timber beams alongside more modern amenities and fantastic views of the cathedral. 4

Ebury Hotel 65–67 New Dover Rd ⓣ01227/768433, ⓦwww.eburyhotel.co.uk. Very comfortable and spacious family-owned Victorian hotel, 15min walk from the centre, with an indoor pool. 5

St John's Court Guesthouse St John's Lane ⓣ01227/456425, ⓦwww.s-h-systems.co.uk. Obliging and good-value B&B in a quiet but central location, just south of the old town. Vegan break-fasts available. No credit cards. 1

St Stephen's Guesthouse 100 St Stephen's Rd ⓣ01227/767644, ⓦwww.st-stephens.fsnet.co.uk. A mock-Tudor house on the northern side of the city, 10min walk along the Stour, offering excellent-value en-suite accommodation. No credit cards. ❸

Thanington Hotel 140 Wincheap ⓣ01227/453227, ⓦwww.thanington-hotel.co.uk. Comfortable converted Georgian building, 10min walk from the centre, with an indoor pool and a games room. ❺

Wincheap Guesthouse 94 Wincheap ⓣ01227/762309, ⓦwww.wincheapguesthouse.com. Good-value Victorian B&B close to Canterbury East Station, with en-suite rooms. ❸

Hostels and campsites

Canterbury YHA 54 New Dover Rd ⓣ0870/770 5744, ⓔcanterbury@yha.org.uk. Half a mile out of town, and 15min on foot from Canterbury East Station, this friendly hostel is set in a Victorian villa. Dorm beds from £17.50, rooms ❶

The Caravan and Camping Club Site Bekesbourne Lane ⓣ01227/463216. Large year-round caravan park, one and a half miles east of the city off the A257 road to Sandwich.

Kipps 40 Nunnery Fields ⓣ01227/786121, ⓦwww.kipps-hostel.com. Self-catering hostel close to Canterbury East Station, offering single and double rooms (❶) as well as dorm accommodation (from £15).

The City

Though surprisingly small, Canterbury ranks as England's second most visited city, with some two and a half million tourists arriving each year. Its centre, partly ringed by ancient **walls**, is virtually car-free, but this doesn't stop the High Street seizing up all too frequently with the milling crowds.

The cathedral

Mother Church of the Church of England and seat of the Primate of All England, **Canterbury Cathedral** (Mon–Sat 9am–5/6.30pm, Sun 12.30–2.30pm & 4.30–5.30pm; closed on some days in mid-July for university graduation ceremonies; £6.50; ⓦwww.canterbury-cathedral.org) fills the northeast quadrant of the city with a sense of authority, even if architecturally it's not the country's most impressive. A cathedral has stood here since 602, but in 1070 the first Norman archbishop, Lanfranc, levelled the original Saxon structure to build a new cathedral. Over successive centuries the masterpiece was heavily modified, and with the puritanical lines of the Perpendicular style gaining ascendancy in late medieval times, the cathedral now derives its distinctiveness from the thrust of the 235-foot-high Bell Harry Tower, completed in 1505. The precincts (daily 9am–5.30pm) are entered through the superbly ornate early sixteenth-century **Christ Church Gate**, where Burgate and St Margaret's Street meet. This junction, the city's medieval core, is known as the Butter Market, where religious relics were once sold to pilgrims hoping to prevent an eternity in damnation. Once through the gatehouse, you can enjoy one of the best views of the cathedral, foreshortened and crowned with soaring towers and pinnacles.

In the magnificent **interior**, look for the tomb of Henry IV and his wife, Joan of Navarre, and for the gilded effigy of Edward III's son, the Black Prince, all of them in the Trinity Chapel, behind the main altar. Also here, until demolished in 1538, was the shrine of Thomas à Becket; the actual spot where he died, known as "The Martyrdom", is marked in the northwest transept by the **Altar of the Sword's Point**, where a jagged sculpture of the assassins' weapons is suspended on the wall. Steps from here descend to the low, Romanesque arches of the **crypt**, one of the few remaining relics of the Norman cathedral and considered the finest such structure in the country, with some amazingly well-preserved carvings on the capitals of the columns. Particularly vivid is the medieval **stained glass**, notably in the Trinity Chapel, where the life and

▲ Canterbury Cathedral

miraculous works ofThomas à Becket are depicted. Look out too for an animal-skin-clad Adam delving in the west window and Jonah and the whale in the Corona (the eastern end of the cathedral, beyond the Trinity Chapel). The thirteenth-century white marble **St Augustine's Chair**, on which all archbishops of Canterbury are enthroned, is located in the choir at the top of the steps beyond the high altar.

On the cathedral's north flank are the fan-vaulted colonnades of the **Great Cloister**, from where you enter the **Chapter House**, with its intricate web of fourteenth-century tracery supporting the roof and a wall of stained glass.

St Augustine's Abbey and St Martin's Church

Exiting the cathedral grounds at the Queningate, you come to the vestigial remains of **St Augustine's Abbey** (April–June Wed–Sun 10am–5pm; July & Aug daily 10am–6pm; Sept–March Sat & Sun 11am–5pm; £4.20; EH), occupying the site of the church founded by Augustine in 598. Built outside the city because of a Christian tradition forbidding burials within the walls, it became the final resting place of Augustine, Ethelbert and successive archbishops and kings of Kent, although no trace remains either of them or of the original Saxon church. Shortly after the Normans arrived, the church was demolished and replaced by a much larger abbey, most of which was destroyed in the Dissolution so that today only the ruins and foundations remain.

Nearby, on the corner of North Holmes Road and St Martin's Lane, **St Martin's Church** (Easter–Sept Tues, Thurs & Sat 10am–4pm; free) is one of England's oldest churches, built on the site of a Roman villa or temple and used by the earliest Christians. Although medieval additions obscure the original Saxon structure, this is perhaps the earliest Christian site in Canterbury – it was here that Queen Bertha welcomed St Augustine in 597, and her husband King Ethelbert was baptized.

The Roman Museum, The Canterbury Tales and the Museum of Canterbury

South of the Cathedral, the redevelopment of the Longmarket area between Burgate and the High Street in the early 1990s exposed Roman foundations and mosaics that are now part of the **Roman Museum** (Mon–Sat 10am–5pm; also open Sun 1.30–5pm June–Oct; £3.10). The display of recovered artefacts and general design of the museum are tasteful, with re-created Roman domestic scenes and a computer-generated view of Durovernum.

St Margaret's Street holds the former church that's now **The Canterbury Tales** (daily 9.30/10am–4.30/5pm; £7.50), a quasi-educational show based on Geoffrey Chaucer's book. In the odour-enhanced galleries, mannequins occupy idealized fourteenth-century tableaux and recount five of Chaucer's tales. Genuinely educational and better value is the **Museum of Canterbury**, round the corner in Stour Street (Mon–Sat 10.30am–5pm, also June–Oct Sun 1.30–5pm; £3.40), an interactive exhibition spanning local history from the splendour of Durovernum through to the more recent literary figures of Joseph Conrad and local-born Mary Tourtel, creator of the check-trousered philanthropist Rupert Bear. An excellent thirty-minute video on the Becket story details the intriguing personalities and events that led up to his assassination.

Along the High Street and St Peter's Street

Off the top of Stour Street on the High Street, the **Royal Museum and Art Gallery** (Mon–Sat 10am–5pm; free) is housed on the first floor of an awesome mock-Tudor building. The museum will be closing for a three-year refurbishment at the end of 2008.

Eastbridge Hospital, standing where the High Street passes over a branch of the River Stour (Mon–Sat 10am–5pm; £1), was founded in the twelfth century to provide poor pilgrims with shelter. Inside you can visit a refectory, a gallery showing the history of the hospital and sleeping quarters restored to their original medieval state. Over the road is the wonky, half-timbered **Weavers' House**, built around 1500 – once inhabited by Huguenot textile workers, it's now a café.

West of here, St Peter's Street terminates at the massive crenellated towers of the medieval **West Gate**, the only one of the town's seven city gates to have survived intact. Its prison cells and guard chambers house a small weaponry **museum** (Mon–Sat 11am–12.30pm & 1.30–3.30pm; £1.25).

Eating, drinking and nightlife

Canterbury has a good selection of **places to eat**, many of them in old and atmospheric settings. **Nightlife** keeps a low profile, though there are some great **pubs** worth seeking out.

University gigs and arthouse **films** take place at Cinema 3, and **plays** at the Gulbenkian Theatre (Ⓣ01227/769075, Ⓦwww.kent.ac.uk/gulbenkian). In town, the Marlowe Theatre in The Friars (Ⓣ01227/787787, Ⓦwww.marlowetheatre.com) is the main venue for drama. Taking place over two weeks in October, the **Canterbury Festival** (Ⓣ01227/452853, Ⓦwww.canterburyfestival.co.uk) has an international mix of music, theatre and arts. For all events, see the free *What, Where and When* **listings magazine** available at the tourist office.

Restaurants and cafés

Café des Amis 93–95 St Dunstan's St Ⓣ01227/464390. Popular Mexican place where you can sample sizzling chicken fajitas or delicious paella. Moderate.

The Goods Shed Station Rd West Ⓣ01227/459153. A large range of dishes: from a sandwich or bowl of soup to a first-class full meal, with ingredients fresh from the adjacent farmers' market. Closed Sun eve & all day Mon. Inexpensive to moderate.

The Old Weaver's House 1 St Peter's St Ⓣ01227/464660. With cosy, old-fashioned decor and an outdoor terrace overlooking the River Stour, this place dishes up both traditional British food and slap-up curries. Inexpensive.

The Tapas Bar 13 Palace St Ⓣ01227/762637. Tasty Spanish tapas (£4–8), accompanied by occasional live music. Inexpensive.

Pubs and bars

Bell & Crown 10 Palace St. Authentic and cramped medieval hostelry.

Miller's Arms 1–2 Mill Lane. A pleasant weir-side spot for a summertime pint whose splendid bar snacks and meals ensure its continued popularity.

New Inn 19 Havelock St. One of Canterbury's tiniest pubs, popular with students and locals, with a decent selection of real ale.

Simple Simon's Radigund's Hall, 1–9 Church Lane. Old hostelry that's popular with the university and King's School crowd; live music Tues–Sat.

The Channel ports

Dover, just 21 miles from mainland Europe (Calais' low cliffs are visible on a clear day), is Britain's principal cross-Channel port. It's an not immensely appealing town, even though its key position has left it with a clutch of historic attractions. To the north lie **Sandwich**, once the most important of the Cinque Ports but now no longer even on the coast, and the pleasant resort towns of **Deal** and **Walmer**, each with its own set of distinctive fortifications as well as a smattering of traditional seaside B&Bs.

Sandwich

SANDWICH, situated on the River Stour four miles north of Deal, is best known nowadays for giving rise to England's favourite culinary contribution

The Cinque Ports

In 1278 Edward I formalized the unofficial confederation of defensive coastal settlements – Dover, Hythe, Sandwich, New Romney and Hastings – as the **Cinque Ports** (pronounced "sink", despite its French origin). In return for providing England with maritime support, chiefly in the transportation of troops and supplies during times of war, the five ports were granted trading privileges and other liberties. Later, Rye, Winchelsea and a few other "limb" ports on the southeast coast were added to the confederation. The ports' privileges were revoked in 1685; their maritime services had become increasingly unnecessary after Henry VIII had founded a professional navy and, due to a shifting coastline, several of the ports' harbours had silted up anyway, leaving some of them several miles inland. Nowadays, only Dover is still a major working port.

when, in 1762, the Fourth Earl of Sandwich, passionately absorbed in a game of cards, ate his meat between two bits of bread for a quick snack. Until the Stour silted up, the town was chief among the **Cinque Ports** (see box above). The river still flows through town, however, its grassy willow-lined banks adding to the once-great medieval port's present charm.

By the bridge over the Stour stands Sandwich's best-known feature, the sixteenth-century **Barbican**, a stone gateway where tolls were once collected. In the town centre, a fine sixteenth-century edifice, the **Guildhall**, houses a small **museum** recounting the town's history (April–Nov Tues, Wed, Fri & Sat 10.30am–12.30pm & 2–4pm, Thurs & Sun 2–4pm; £1). The genteel town, with its crooked half-timbered facades, is separated from the sandy beaches of Sandwich Bay by the **Royal St George Golf Course** – frequent venue of the British Open tournament – and a mile of nature reserves. Most ornithologists head three miles north of town to the **Gazen Salts Nature Reserve**, renowned for its diversity of sea birds.

Sandwich's **tourist office**, housed in the Guildhall (April–Oct daily 10am–4pm; Ⓣ01304/613565, Ⓦwww.whitecliffscountry.org.uk), can provide a list of local **hotels** and **guesthouses**. Try the *Fleur de Lis*, an old coaching inn near the Guildhall at 6–8 Delf St (Ⓣ01304/611131, Ⓦwww.thefleur-sandwich.co.uk; ⑤), or the cheaper *Le Trayas* bungalow, 10 Poulders Rd (Ⓣ01304/611056, Ⓦwww.letrayas.co.uk; no credit cards; ③), a ten-minute walk from The Quay.

For **food,** *Fisherman's Wharf* on the quayside (Ⓣ01304/613636) serves burgers and huge deli sandwiches as well as excellent but pricey seafood. Alternatively, the pubs by the Barbican or *The Haven*, 20a King St, are good for coffee and snacks. The twee *Little Cottage Tearooms* on The Quay serves the definitive Sandwich sandwich.

Deal and Walmer Castle

One of the most unusual of Henry VIII's forts is the diminutive castle at **DEAL**, six miles southeast of Sandwich and site of Julius Caesar's first successful landfall in Britain in 55 BC. The **castle** (Easter–Sept Mon–Fri & Sun 10am–6pm, Sat 10am–5pm; £4.20; EH) is situated off The Strand at the south end of town. It owes its unusual shape – viewed from the air it looks like a Tudor rose – to the premise that the rounded walls would be better at deflecting missiles. Inside, the comprehensive display on the other similar forts built during Henry VIII's reign is well worth a visit.

A mile south of Deal, reachable either on hourly buses or, if the weather's good, on foot along the seafront, **Walmer Castle** (March & Oct Wed–Sun 10am–4pm; April–Sept Mon–Fri & Sun 10am–6pm, Sat 10am–4pm;

£6.50; EH) is another rotund Tudor-rose-shaped affair, commissioned when the castle became the official residence of the Lord Warden of the Cinque Ports in 1730. Now it resembles a heavily fortified stately home more than a military stronghold. The best-known resident was the Duke of Wellington, who died here in 1842, and not surprisingly, the house is devoted primarily to his life and times. Busts and portraits of the Iron Duke crowd the rooms and corridors, where you'll also find the armchair in which he expired and the original Wellington boots in which he triumphed at Waterloo.

Deal's **tourist office** is situated in the Landmark Centre on the High Street (Mon–Fri 10am–4pm, Sat 10am–noon; ⓣ01304/369576, ⓦwww.whitecliffscountry.org.uk). There's a whole host of places offering **accommodation** on Beach Street: try the winsome *King's Head* pub at no. 9 (ⓣ01304/368194, ⓦwww.kingsheaddeal.co.uk; ③), or the nearby townhouse, *Channel View*, at no. 17 (ⓣ01304/368194; ③), run by the same proprietor. Next door at no. 19, *Dunkerley's* (ⓣ01304/375016) has Deal's finest (and priciest) **restaurant**, where seafood is the speciality.

Dover

Badly bombed during World War II, **DOVER**'s town centre and seafront just don't have what it takes to induce many travellers to linger. Dover Castle is still by far the most interesting of the port's attractions, while entertainment of a saltier nature is offered by Dover's legendary White Cliffs, which dominate the town and have long been a source of inspiration for lovers, travellers and soldiers sailing off to war.

Dover Castle

It was in 1168, a century after the Conquest, that the Normans constructed the keep that now presides over the bulk of **Dover Castle** (Feb & March daily 10am–4pm; April–July & Sept daily 10am–6pm; Aug daily 9.30am–6pm; Oct daily 10am–5pm; Nov–Jan Mon & Thurs–Sun 10am–4pm; £10.30; EH), a superbly positioned defensive complex that was in continuous use as a military installation until the 1980s. Much earlier, the Romans had put Dover on the map when they chose the harbour as the base for their northern fleet, and erected a **lighthouse** (*pharos*) here to guide the ships into the river mouth. Beside the chunky hexagonal remains of this stands a Saxon-built church, **St Mary-in-Castro**, dating from the seventh century, with motifs graffitied by irreverent Crusaders still visible near the pulpit.

Further up the hill is the impressive, well-preserved **Norman Keep**, built by Henry II as a palace. The interior has an interactive exhibition on spying, and you can climb to the lofty battlements for views over the sea to France. The castle's other main attraction is its network of **Secret Wartime Tunnels** dug during the Napoleonic Wars and extended during World War II; free fifty-minute guided tours leave every twenty minutes.

The town and Dover's cliffs

Postwar rebuilding has made Dover **town centre** a rather unprepossessing place, though the **Roman Painted House** on New Street (April–Sept Tues–Sat 10am–5pm, Sun 1–4.30pm; £2), once a hotel for official guests, possesses some reasonable Roman wall paintings, the remains of an underground Roman heating system and some mosaics. The nearby **Dover Museum** on the Market Square (April–Sept Mon–Sat 10am–5.30pm, Sun noon–5pm; £2.50) has three floors packed with informative displays on Dover's past,

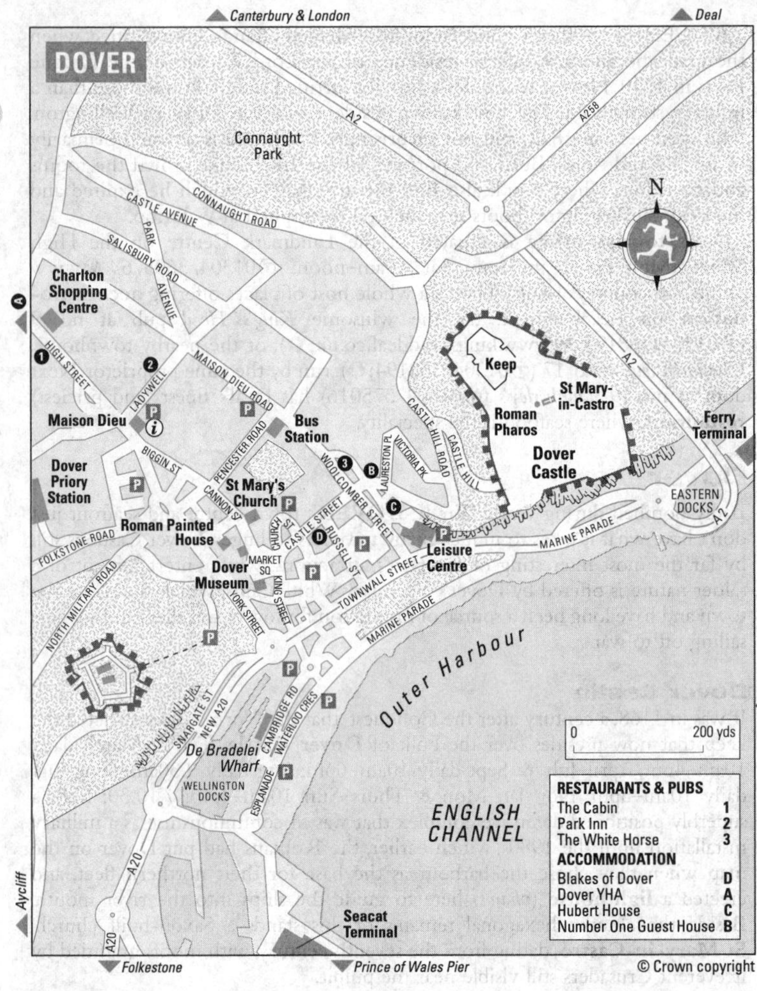

including a Bronze Age boat discovered in the town in 1992. In Biggin Street, the **Maison Dieu** was founded in the thirteenth century as a place for pilgrims en route to Canterbury. After the Reformation, it was turned into a naval storehouse, and in the last century became part of the town hall. The Stone Hall, with its fine timber roof, dates from 1253.

There are some superb **walks** along Dover's cliffs: to reach Shakespeare Cliff, catch bus #D2A from Worthington Street towards Aycliff; alternatively, there's a steep two-and-a-half-mile climb from North Military Road, off York Street, taking you by the **Western Heights**, a series of defensive battlements built into the cliff in the nineteenth century.

Practicalities

Dover Priory **train station** is situated off Folkestone Road, a ten-minute walk west of the centre; there are regular shuttle buses to the Eastern and Western docks. Buses from London run to the Eastern Docks and the town-centre **bus station** on Pencester Road. The **tourist office**, in the Old Town Gaol in Biggin Street (June–Aug daily 9am–5.30pm; Sept–May Mon–Fri 9am–5.30pm, Sat & Sun 10am–4pm; Oct–March closed Sun; ⓣ01304/205108, ⓦwww.whitecliffscountry.org.uk), has a free *White Cliffs Trails* pamphlet that outlines coastal and inland walks near Dover.

Dover's best **B&Bs** include *Hubert House*, 9 Castle Hill Rd (ⓣ01304/202253, ⓦwww.huberthouse.co.uk; ❷), convenient for the Eastern Dock; the smart, good-value *Number One Guesthouse*, opposite, at 1 Castle St (ⓣ01304/202007, ⓦwww.number1guesthouse.co.uk; ❷); and *Blakes of Dover*, 52 Castle St (ⓣ01304/202194, ⓦwww.blakesofdover.co.uk; ❷). There's a very busy YHA **hostel** in a Georgian house at 306 London Rd (ⓣ0870/770 5798, ⓔdover@yha.org.uk; dorm beds from £17.50, doubles ❶), a mile up the High Street from Dover Priory station.

Dover's culinary offerings are poor, though *Blakes* (see above) has a lovely wood-panelled wine bar and **restaurant**, and *The Cabin*, 91 High St, has good-value set-price menus. Dover's **pubs** are characterful, however: try the *Park Inn*, a big revamped old boozer at 1–2 Park Place, Ladywell, or *The White Horse* on St James Street, a fine old eighteenth-century pub at the foot of the castle.

Hythe to Dungeness: the Romney and Denge marshes

In Roman times, the **Romney and Denge marshes** – now the southernmost part of Kent – were submerged beneath the English Channel. The lowering of the sea levels in the Middle Ages and later reclamation created a forty-square-mile area of shingle and marshland which, until the nineteenth century, was afflicted by malaria and various other malaises. Contrasting strongly with the wooded pastures of Kent's interior, the sheep-speckled marshes have an eerie, forlorn appearance, as if still haunted by their maritime origins.

On the eastern edge of the reclaimed marshes, the ancient town of **HYTHE** is a sedate seaside resort bisected by the disused waterway of the **Royal Military Canal**, built as a defensive obstacle during the threat of Napoleonic invasion and linked with Rye in East Sussex (see p.187), on the marsh's western edge. Hythe's receding shoreline reduced its usefulness as a port and the nearby coast is now just a sweep of beach punctuated by **Martello Towers**, part of the chain of 74 such defensive towers built along the south and east coasts in the early nineteenth century.

West of Hythe's centre on the south bank of the canal lies the station for the fifteen-inch-gauge **Romney, Hythe and Dymchurch Railway** (April–Sept daily; March & Oct Sat & Sun, plus school hols throughout the year; £11.20 return; ⓣ01797/362353, ⓦwww.rhdr.demon.co.uk), which runs fourteen miles south to **DUNGENESS**. This shingly, somewhat spooky expanse is home to a nuclear power station, as well as huge colonies of gulls, terns, smews and gadwalls: information on the birdlife can be found at the **RSPB visitor centre** (daily: March–Oct 10am–5pm; Nov–Feb 10am–4pm; £3), off the road from Dungeness to Lydd.

The Kent Weald

The Weald is usually taken to refer to the region around the spa town of **Royal Tunbridge Wells**, but in fact it stretches across a much larger area between the North and South Downs and includes parts of both Kent and Sussex. During Saxon times, much of the Weald was covered in thick forest – the word itself derives from the Germanic word *Wald*, meaning forest, and the suffixes -hurst (meaning wood) and -den (meaning clearing) are commonly found in Wealden village names. Now, however, the region is epitomized by gentle hills, sunken country lanes and somnolent villages as well as some of England's most beautiful gardens – **Sissinghurst**, fifteen miles east of Tunbridge Wells, being the best known – and a scattering of highly picturesque historical sites, including **Leeds Castle**, north of Sissinghurst, and **Hever Castle**, northwest of Tunbridge Wells.

Royal Tunbridge Wells and around

Most associated with whingeing right-wing letter-writers, **ROYAL TUNBRIDGE WELLS** – not to be confused with the more mundane Tonbridge, a few miles to the north – was established after a bubbling spring discovered here in 1606 was claimed to have curative properties. A prosperous spa town evolved, reaching its height of popularity during the Regency period when such restorative cures were in vogue. In late July, the five-day **Georgian Festivities** sees the townsfolk relive the era, taking to the streets in eighteenth-century garb.

The icon of those genteel times is the **Pantiles**, an elegant colonnaded parade of shops, ten minutes' walk south of the train station, where the fashionable once gathered to promenade and take the waters. Hub of the Pantiles is the original **Chalybeate Spring** (pronounced with the emphasis on the "be") in the Bath House (Easter–Sept daily 10am–5pm), where a "Dipper" has been employed since the late eighteenth century to serve the ferrous waters. A period-dressed incumbent will fetch you a glass from the cool spring for 40p – or, with your own cup, you can help yourself for free from the adjacent source.

Tunbridge Wells' **train station** is located where the High Street becomes Mount Pleasant Road. The **tourist office** is housed in the Old Fish Market in the Pantiles (Mon–Sat 9am–5pm, Sun 10am–4/5pm; ⓣ01892/515675, ⓦwww.visittunbridgewells.com). The town has a number of plush **hotels**, such as the chic *Hotel du Vin* in Crescent Road (ⓣ01892/526455, ⓦwww.hotelduvin.com; ⑥), with an excellent bistro. For cheaper lodgings, there's an attractive Regency-style **B&B** at 40 York Rd (ⓣ01892/531342, ⓦwww.yorkroad.co.uk; ③).

Among the cluster of topnotch **restaurants** are *Thackeray's House*, one-time home of the writer, at 85 London Rd (ⓣ01892/511921; closed Sun eve & Mon), which offers a bargain three-course set menu at lunchtime, and the *Hotel du Vin* (see above). *Sankey's*, at 39 Mount Ephraim, is a popular wine bar with a garden that also serves fantastic seafood, while you'll find great veggie options at the *Trinity Arts Centre Café* in a converted church on Church Road (lunch & pre-theatre deals only; closed Sun).

Penshurst Place and Hever Castle

Tudor timber-framed houses and shops line the high street of the attractive village of **PENSHURST**, five miles northwest of Tunbridge Wells (bus #231 or #233; not Sun). The main reason for coming here is to visit **Penshurst Place** (daily noon–4pm, grounds 10.30am–6pm; £7.50, grounds only £6), home to the Sidney family since 1552 and birthplace of the Elizabethan soldier and poet, Sir Philip Sidney. The fourteenth-century Barons Hall, built for Sir John de Pulteney, four times Mayor of London, is the chief glory of the interior, with its sixty-foot-high chestnut roof still in place.

The moated **Hever Castle**, three miles further west (Easter–Oct daily 10.45am–6pm, Nov & Dec Thurs–Sun 10.45am–4pm; March–Easter Wed–Sun 10.45am–4pm; last entry 1hr before closing; £11.50, gardens only £9.30), is the childhood home of Anne Boleyn, second wife of Henry VIII, and where Anne of Cleves, Henry's fourth wife, lived after their divorce. In 1903, having fallen into disrepair, the castle was bought by William Waldorf-Astor, American millionaire-owner of *The Times*, who had the house assiduously restored. In the Inner Hall hangs a fine portrait of Henry VIII by Holbein; a further Holbein painting of Elizabeth I hangs on the middle floor. Upstairs, Anne of Cleves' room holds an unusually well-preserved tapestry illustrating the marriage of Henry's sister to King Louis XII of France, with Anne Boleyn as one of the ladies-in-waiting.

Outside in the grounds, next to the gift shop, is the absorbing **Guthrie Miniature Model Houses Collection**, showing the development of aristocratic seats from feudal times on. However, the best feature of the grounds is Waldorf-Astor's beautiful **Italian Garden**, built on reclaimed marshland and decorated with Roman statuary.

Sissinghurst and Leeds Castle

Sissinghurst, twelve miles east of Tunbridge Wells (late March to Oct Mon, Tues & Fri–Sun 11am–6.30pm or dusk; £8.60; NT), was described by Vita Sackville-West as "a garden crying out for rescue" when she and her husband took it over in the 1920s. Spread over the site of a medieval moated manor (which was rebuilt into an Elizabethan mansion of which only one wing remains today), the five-acre gardens were designed around the linear pattern of the former buildings' walls. The gardens' major appeal derives from the way that the flowers are allowed to spill over onto the narrow walkways, defying the classical formality of the great gardens that preceded it. The brick tower that Vita had restored and used as her study acts as a focal point and offers the best views of the walled gardens. Most impressive are the **White Garden**, composed solely of white flowers and silvery-grey foliage, and the **Cottage Garden**, featuring flora in shades of orange, yellow and red. **Bus** #5 stops in Sissinghurst village on its run between Maidstone and Hastings.

Leeds Castle, fifteen miles north of Sissinghurst off the A20 (daily: April–Oct 10am–7pm; Nov–March 10am–5pm; last admission 2hr before closing; castle, park & gardens £14), more closely resembles a fairy-tale palace than a defensively efficient fortress. Work on the castle began around 1120, half on an island in the middle of a lake and half on the mainland surrounded by landscaped parkland. Following centuries of regal and noble ownership (and, less glamorously, service as a prison) the castle now hosts conferences and sporting and cultural events. Its interior fails to match the castle's stunning external appearance and, in places, modern renovations have quashed its historical charm. The most unusual feature inside is the dog-collar museum in the gatehouse, while the grounds hold a fine aviary with some superb and colourful exotic specimens, as well as manicured gardens and a mildly challenging maze.

Sevenoaks and around

Set among the green sand ridges of west Kent, 25 miles from London, **SEVENOAKS** lost all but one of the ageing oaks from which it derives its

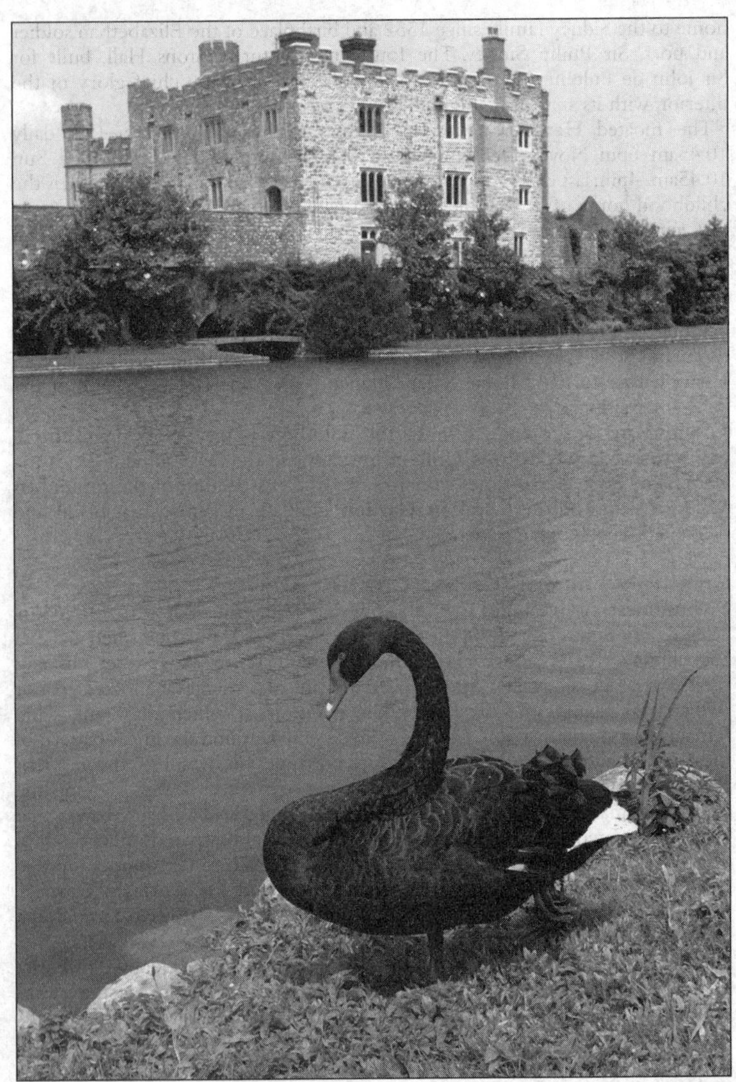

▲Leeds Castle

name in a freakish storm that struck southern England in October 1987. With mere saplings having taken their place, the only real reason to visit the town is for the immense baronial estate of **Knole** (mid-March to Oct Wed–Sun noon–4pm; garden late March to Oct Wed 11am–4pm; £8.50, garden £2; NT), entered from the south end of Sevenoaks High Street. Numerically designed to match the calendar with 365 rooms, 7 courtyards and 52 staircases, the palace was created in 1456 as a residence for the archbishops of Canterbury, and was appropriated by Henry VIII, who lavished further expense on it and hunted in the thousand acres of **parkland** (free access throughout the year), still home to several hundred deer. Henry's daughter, Elizabeth I, passed the estate on to her cousin, Thomas Sackville, who remodelled the house in 1605; it has remained in the family's hands ever since, with its Jacobean exterior preserved. Vita Sackville-West was brought up here, and her one-time lover Virginia Woolf derived inspiration for her novel *Orlando* from her frequent visits. An array of fine, if well-worn, furnishings and tapestries are on display, together with paintings by Gainsborough, Reynolds and van Dyck.

Sevenoaks' **tourist office** is in the library (Mon–Sat 9.30am–4.30/5pm; ⓣ01732/450305, ⓦwww.visitheartofkent.com), just beyond the **bus station** in Buckhurst Lane; the **train station** is north of the centre on London Road. The town's smartest **accommodation** is at the excellent *Royal Oak Hotel*, a seventeenth-century coaching inn at the south end of the High Street (ⓣ01732/451109, ⓦwww.brook-hotels.co.uk/royaloak; ❻), beyond the entrance to Knole. Alternatively, there's *4 Old Timber Top Cottages*, Bethel Road (ⓣ01732/460506, ⓦwww.timbertopcottage.co.uk; ❹); breakfast is included in the nightly rate, though the cottage also has self-catering facilities.

For top-class, but expensive, **meals**, try the *Royal Oak*'s restaurant, *No. 5* (ⓣ01732/455555). Among the **pubs**, there are good bar menus at the *Dorset Arms* on Dorset Street and *The Black Boy* on Bank Street.

Around Sevenoaks

Seven miles north of Sevenoaks and three-quarters of a mile along the river west of the village of Eynsford, **Lullingstone Roman Villa** (April–Sept daily 10am–6pm; Oct, Nov, Feb & March daily 10am–4pm; Dec & Jan Wed–Sun 10am–4pm; £5.50; EH) has some of the best-preserved Roman mosaics in southeast England on show. Believed to have been the first-century residence of a farmer, the site has yielded some fine marble busts now on display in the British Museum in London, but a superb floor remains, depicting the killing of the Chimera, a mythical fire-breathing beast with a lion's head, goat's body and a serpent's tail. Excavation in a nearby chamber has revealed early Christian iconography, which suggests that the villa may have become a Romano-Christian chapel in the third century, pre-empting the official arrival of that religion by three hundred years and making Lullingstone one of the earliest sites of clandestine Christian worship in England. From Sevenoaks there are hourly trains to Eynsford, from where it's a fifteen-minute walk.

Six miles west of Sevenoaks, **Chartwell** (mid-March to Oct Wed–Sun 11am–5pm; July & Aug also Tues; £9.80; NT) was the residence of Winston Churchill from 1924 until his death in 1965. It's an unremarkable, heavily restored Tudor building whose main appeal is the wartime premier's memorabilia, including his paintings, which show an unexpectedly contemplative side to the famously gruff statesman. Entry to the house is by timed ticket at peak times – expect long queues. A direct bus service runs to Chartwell from Sevenoaks bus station four times daily on Sundays and public holidays.

Hastings and around

During the twelfth and thirteenth centuries, **Hastings** flourished as an influential Cinque Port (see p.178), but in 1287 its harbour creek was silted up by the same storm that washed away nearby Winchelsea (see p.188). These days, Hastings is a curious mixture of unpretentious fishing port, traditional seaside resort and arty retreat popular with painters (there's even a street and quarter named Bohemia). In 1066, William, Duke of Normandy, landed at Pevensey Bay, a few miles west of town, and made Hastings his base, but his forces met Harold's army – exhausted after quelling a Nordic invasion near York – at **Battle**, six miles northwest of Hastings. Battle today boasts a magnificent abbey built by William in thanks for his victory. Further north, **Batemans**, once the home of Rudyard Kipling, and the classic **Bodiam Castle** are both easily reached from Hastings in a day-trip, as are the ancient Cinque Ports of **Rye** and **Winchelsea**, to the east.

Hastings

Hastings **old town**, east of the pier, holds most of the appeal of this part-tacky, part-pretty seaside resort. With the exception of the oddly neglected Regency architecture of **Pelham Crescent**, directly beneath the castle ruins, **All Saints Street** is by far the most evocative thoroughfare, punctuated with the odd, rickety, timber-framed dwelling from the fifteenth century. In the parallel High Street, the thirteenth-century **St Clement's Church** displays, at the top of its tower, a cannonball lodged by a Dutch galleon in the 1600s – its poignancy rather dispelled by a companion fitted in the eighteenth century for the sake of symmetry.

Down by the seafront, the area known as **The Stade** is characterized by its tall, black weatherboard **net shops**, most dating from the mid-nineteenth century (and still in use), but which first appeared here in Tudor times.

Castle Hill, separating the old town from the less interesting modern quarter, can be ascended by the **West Hill Cliff Railway**, from George Street, off Marine Parade. It's one of two Victorian funicular railways in Hastings, the other being the **East Cliff Railway**, on Rock-a-Nore Road (both daily: April–Oct 10am–5.30pm; Nov–March 11am–4pm; £1.60). Castle Hill is where William the Conqueror erected his first **Castle** in 1066, built on the site of an existing fort, probably of Saxon origins. It was soon replaced by a more permanent stone structure, but in the thirteenth century storms caused the cliffs to subside, tipping most of the castle into the sea; the surviving ruins, however, offer an excellent prospect of the town. The castle is home to **The 1066 Story** (daily: April–Sept 10am–5pm; Oct–May 11am–3pm; £3.75), in which the events of the last successful invasion of the British mainland are described inside a mock-up of a siege tent.

Practicalities

Hastings' **train station** is a ten-minute walk from the seafront along Havelock Road; National Express **bus** services operate from the station at the junction of Havelock and Queen's roads. The **tourist office** is in the Town Hall on Queen's Road (Mon–Fri 8.30am–6.15pm, Sat 9am–5pm, Sun 10.30am–4.30pm; ⓣ0845/274 1001, ⓦwww.visit1066country.com); there's also a smaller seafront office (Easter–Oct daily 10am–6pm; Nov–Easter Sun 10am–4.30pm; ⓣ01424/781120) near the Boating Lake on East Parade by the old town.

The best **accommodation** options are in the old town, such as cosy, timber-framed *Lavender and Lace*, 106 All Saints St (ⓣ01424/716290, ⓦwww.lavenderlace1066.co.uk; closed Jan & Feb; no credit cards; ④); alternatively, near the station at 32 Cambridge Gardens, there's the friendly *Argyle Guesthouse*, (ⓣ01424/421294; ①). Hastings has a few affordable places for a **meal**, including *Harris*, 58 High St (ⓣ01424/437221; closed Sun eve & Mon), where you can enjoy tapas in a wood-panelled setting, and *Pissarro's*,

10 South Terrace (☎01424/421363), offering a variety of bistro food with live jazz and blues accompaniment. The best fish and chips in town are served at *Mermaid*, 2 Rock-a-Nore, right by the beach.

The local fishermen's favourite **pub** is the *Lord Nelson*, right by the front on The Bourne. On George Street, you can hear blues every Monday at *The Hastings Arms*, and jazz on Tuesdays at *The Anchor*.

Battle

The town of **BATTLE** – a ten-minute train ride from Hastings – occupies the site of the most famous land battle in British history. Here, on October 14, 1066, the invading Normans swarmed up the hillside from Senlac Moor and overcame the Anglo-Saxon army of King Harold, who is thought to have been killed not by an arrow through the eye – a myth resulting from the misinterpretation of the Bayeux Tapestry – but by a workaday clubbing about the head. Before the battle took place, William vowed that, should he win the engagement, he would build a religious foundation on the very spot of Harold's slaying to atone for the bloodshed, and, true to his word, **Battle Abbey** (daily: Easter–Sept 10am–6pm; Oct–Easter 10am–4pm; £6.50; EH) was built four years later and subsequently occupied by a fraternity of Benedictines. The magnificent structure, though partially destroyed in the Dissolution and much rebuilt and revised over the centuries, still dominates the town. You can wander through the ruins of the abbey to the spot where Harold was killed – the site of the high altar of William's abbey, now marked by a memorial stone – while a visitor centre holds an interactive exhibition and an auditorium showing a dramatic re-enactment of the battle using film and computer simulations.

Though nothing can match the resonance of the abbey, the rest of the town is worth a stroll. At the far end of High Street, the fourteenth-century **Almonry** – the present town hall – holds a **museum** (April–Oct Mon–Sat 10am–4.30pm, Sun noon–5pm; £1) that contains the only battle-axe discovered at Battle and the oldest Guy Fawkes in the country. Every year, on the Saturday nearest to November 5, this 300-year-old effigy is paraded along High Street at the head of a torchlit procession culminating at a huge bonfire in front of the abbey gates – similar celebrations occur in Lewes (see p.190).

The **tourist office** is situated in the Gatehouse at Battle Abbey (daily: April–Sept 9.30am–5.30pm; Oct 9am–5pm; Nov–March 10am–4pm; ☎01424/773721, Ⓦwww.battle-sussex.co.uk). Battle's **accommodation** tends to be expensive; less pricey B&Bs include the central and cosy *White Lodge*, 42 Hastings Rd (☎01424/772122, Ⓦwww.bedandbreakfastbattle.co.uk; ④), with a heated outdoor pool in the summer, and *Jempson's Café*, 78 High St (☎01424/772856; ②), which has en-suite rooms upstairs.

For **food**, try the excellent *Pilgrims* restaurant, 1 High St (☎01424/772314; closed Sun eve), a fifteenth-century hall next to the abbey which offers good-value set-price meals (not weekends) as well as afternoon tea, while decent town-centre **pubs** include the fifteenth-century *Old King's Head* on Mount Street and the *Chequers Inn* at Lower Lake, on High Street.

Rye and Winchelsea

Ten miles northeast of Hastings, perched on a hill overlooking the Romney Marshes, the ancient town of **RYE** was added as a "limb" to the original Cinque Ports (see p.178), but was subsequently marooned two miles inland by the retreat of the sea and the silting-up of the River Rother. It is now one of the most visited places in East Sussex – half-timbered, skew-roofed and quintessentially English, but also very commercialized.

From Strand Quay, head up The Deals to Rye's most picturesque street, the sloping cobbled **Mermaid Street**. At its eastern end, **Lamb House** (March–Oct Thurs & Sat 2–6pm; £3.30; NT) was the home of the authors Henry James and (subsequently) E.F. Benson, while a blue plaque in the High Street testifies that Radclyffe Hall, author of the seminal lesbian novel, *The Well of Loneliness*, was also once a resident of the town. At the top of Mermaid Street is the peaceful oasis of Church Square, where **St Mary's Church** boasts the oldest functioning pendulum clock in the country; the ascent of the church tower offers fine views over the clay-tiled roofs. In the far corner of the square stands the **Ypres Tower** (April–Oct Mon & Thurs–Sun 10.30am–5pm; £2.95), formerly used to keep watch for cross-Channel invaders, and now a part of the **Rye Castle Museum** on nearby East Street (same times; £2.50, or £5 for both sites). Both places house a number of relics from Rye's past, including an eighteenth-century fire engine.

WINCHELSEA, sited on a hill two miles southwest of Rye and easily reached by train, bus, foot or bike, shares Rye's indignity of having become detached from the sea, but has a very different character. Rye gets all the visitors, whereas Winchelsea feels positively deserted, an impression augmented as you pass through the medieval Strand Gate and see the ghostly ruined **Church of St Thomas à Becket**, pillaged by the French in the fourteenth and fifteenth centuries. Head south for a mile and a half and you get to **Winchelsea beach**, a long expanse of pebbly sand.

Practicalities

Rye's **train station** is at the bottom of Station Approach, off Cinque Ports Street, while Winchelsea's is a mile north of the town. **Bus** #711 runs into the centre of both towns from Hastings. Rye's **tourist office** is on Strand Quay (daily 10am–4/5pm; ⓣ01797/226696, ⓦwww.visitrye.co.uk).

Rye's popularity with weekending Londoners gives it an excellent, but pricey, choice of **accommodation**. The most luxurious option is the atmospheric, fifteenth-century *Mermaid Inn* (ⓣ01797/223065, ⓦwww.mermaidinn.com; ❽), on Mermaid Street, while the Georgian *Durrant House Hotel*, 2 Market St (ⓣ01797/223182, ⓦwww.durranthouse.com; ❺), has a garden looking out towards Dungeness and the marshes. In Winchelsea, book in at the fourteenth-century *Strand House* (ⓣ01797/226276, ⓦwww.thestrandhouse.co.uk; ❸), at the foot of the cliff below Strand Gate.

Rye's **restaurants** offer excellent seafood, for example the expensive *Flushing Inn* on Market Street (ⓣ01797/223292; closed Mon eve & all Tues). The daytime *Peacock Tearooms*, 8 Lion St, serves up snacks, cream teas and full meals in a suitably ancient setting. The fifteenth-century *Mermaid* on Mermaid Street is Rye's most famous **pub**, with heavy exposed timbers throughout, though an excellent alternative is the *Ypres Castle* in Gun Gardens, down the steps behind the Ypres Tower.

Bodiam Castle

Bodiam Castle, nine miles north of Hastings (Feb–Oct daily 10am–6pm or dusk; Nov–Jan Sat & Sun 10.30am–4pm or dusk; £4.50; NT), is a classically stout square block with rounded corner turrets, battlements and a wide moat. When it was built in 1385 to guard what were the lower reaches of the River Rother, Bodiam was state-of-the-art military architecture, but during the Civil

War, a company of Roundheads breached the fortress and removed its roof to reduce its effectiveness as a possible stronghold for the king. Over the next 250 years Bodiam fell into neglect until restoration in the last century by Lord Curzon. The extremely steep spiral staircases, leading to the crenellated battlements, will test all but the strongest of thighs. An absorbing fifteen-minute video portrays medieval life in a castle. You can get here from Hastings by regular bus #349.

Burwash and Bateman's

Fifteen miles northwest of Hastings on the A265, halfway to Tunbridge Wells, **BURWASH**, with its red-brick and weatherboarded cottages and Norman church tower, exemplifies the pastoral idyll of inland Sussex. Half a mile south of the village lies the main attraction, **Bateman's** (house: mid-March to Oct Mon–Wed, Sat & Sun 11am–5pm; garden: early March Sat & Sun 11am–4pm, mid-March to Oct Mon–Wed, Sat & Sun 11am–5.30pm; Nov & Dec Wed–Sun 11am–4pm; £6.20, garden free in Nov & Dec; NT), home of the writer and journalist Rudyard Kipling from 1902 until his death in 1936. Built by a local ironmaster in the seventeenth century and set amid attractive gardens, the house features a working watermill converted by Kipling to generate electricity. Inside, the house displays Kipling's letters, early editions of his work and mementos from his travels on display. Getting to Bateman's without your own transport involves a three-mile walk from Etchingham Station, which is served by regular trains from Hastings.

Eastbourne and around

Like so many of the Southeast's seaside resorts, **EASTBOURNE** was kick-started into life in the 1840s, when the Brighton, Lewes and Hastings Rail Company built a branch line from Lewes to the sea. Nowadays Eastbourne has a solid reputation as a retirement town by the sea, with one of the grandest piers on the south coast jutting out from its long Promenade. The one lively exception to the prevailing sedateness is the **Towner Art Gallery and Museum** (Tues–Sat

The South Downs Way

Following the undulating crest of the South Downs, between the city of Winchester and the spectacular cliffs at Beachy Head, the **South Downs Way** extends over eighty miles along the chalk uplands, offering the Southeast's finest walks. If undertaken in its entirety, the bridle path is best traversed from west to east, taking advantage of the prevailing wind, Eastbourne's better transport services and accommodation, and the psychological appeal of ending at the sea. **Steyning**, the halfway point, marks a transition between predominantly wooded sections and more exposed chalk uplands – to the east of here you'll pass the modern YHA **hostel** at Truleigh Hill (Ⓣ0870/770 6078, Ⓔtruleigh@yha.org.uk; dorms from £14; ➊). Other hostels along the way are at Telscombe and Alfriston (see p.190), where a southern loop can be taken which brings you to Eastbourne along the cliffs of the Seven Sisters. There's also a bunkhouse at Gumber Farm (Ⓣ01243/814484; closed Nov–Easter; £9), near Bignor Hill.

The OS *Landranger* **maps** #198 and #199 cover the eastern end of the route; you'll need #185 and #197 as well to cover the lot. Check the website Ⓦwww.nationaltrail.co.uk/southdowns.

noon–5pm, Sun 2–5pm; free), a ten-minute walk northwest of the train station on High Street, Old Town, complete with refreshingly contemporary works of art and a **"How We Lived Then" Museum of Shops**, just down from the tourist office at 20 Cornfield Terrace (daily 10am–5.30pm; £4), where a range of artefacts – old packages, coronation cups, toys – from the last hundred years of consumerism is crammed into mock-up shops spread over several floors.

The real reason to visit Eastbourne, however, is for expeditions onto the **South Downs**. A short walk west from Eastbourne takes you out along the most dramatic stretch of coastline in Sussex, where the chalk uplands are cut by the sea into a sequence of splendid cliffs. The most spectacular of all, **Beachy Head**, is 575ft high, with a diminutive-looking lighthouse, but no beach – the headland's name derives from the French *beau chef* meaning "beautiful head". The beauty certainly went to Friedrich Engels' head; he insisted his ashes be scattered here, and depressed individuals regularly try to join him by leaping to their doom from this well-known suicide spot. An open-top bus runs half-hourly (late April to Oct; £7) from Eastbourne Pier to the top of Beachy Head.

West of the headland the scenery softens into a diminishing series of chalk cliffs, a landmark known as the **Seven Sisters**. The eponymous country park provides some of the most impressive walks in the county, taking in the cliff-top path and the lower valley of the meandering River Cuckmere, into which the Seven Sisters subside.

Practicalities

Eastbourne's **train station** is a splendid Italianate terminus ten minutes' walk from the seafront up Terminus Road; the **bus station** is on Cavendish Place right by the pier. The **tourist office** is at 3 Cornfield Rd, just off Terminus Road (July to early Sept Mon–Fri 9.30am–5.30pm, Sat 9.30am–4.30pm, Sun 10am–1pm; mid-Sept to June closed Sun; Ⓣ0871/663 0031, Ⓦwww.visiteastbourne.com).

The best **accommodation** options are *Sea Beach House Hotel*, 39–40 Marine Parade (Ⓣ01323/410458, Ⓦwww.seabeachhouse.co.uk; ❸), right on the seafront, and *Sea Breeze Guesthouse*, 6 Marine Rd (Ⓣ01323/725440, Ⓦwww.seabreezeguesthouse.co.uk; no credit cards; ❷), just a hundred yards from the sea. *Birling Gap Hotel* (Ⓣ01323/423197, Ⓦwww.birlinggaphotel.co.uk; ❹) is a Victorian villa overlooking the dramatic cliffs between Seven Sisters and Beachy Head, or there's the Frog Firle YHA **hostel** (Ⓣ0870/770 5666, Ⓔalfriston@yha.org.uk; from £13.75), in a traditional Sussex flint building a couple of miles south of Alfriston.

The best **restaurant** is the *Café Belge* on the seafront at 11–23 Grand Parade, good for *moules et frites* and snack lunches. Otherwise head for the concentration of moderately priced places in the Terminus Road area, between the train station and the sea. If you're in need of a large ice-cream sundae, go to *Fusciardi's* on Marine Parade. The most amenable **pubs** are some distance from the seafront: the *Lamb* on the High Street and the *Hurst Arms* at 76 Willingdon Rd, a ten-minute walk inland from the station up Upperton Road.

Lewes and around

LEWES, the county town of East Sussex, straddles the River Ouse as it carves a gap through the South Downs on its final stretch to the sea. Though there's

The bonfire societies

Each November 5, while the rest of Britain lights small domestic bonfires or attends municipal firework displays to commemorate the 1605 foiling of a Catholic plot to blow up the Houses of Parliament, Lewes puts on a more dramatic show, whose origins lie in the deaths of the town's Protestant martyrs. By the end of the eighteenth century, Lewes's **Bonfire Boys** had become notorious for the boisterousness of their anti-Catholic demonstrations, in which they set off fireworks indiscriminately and dragged rolling tar barrels through the streets – a tradition still practised today, although with a little more caution. In 1845 events came to a head when the incorrigible pyromaniacs of Lewes had to be read the Riot Act, instigating a night of violence between the police and Bonfire Boys. Lewes's first **bonfire societies** were established soon afterwards to instil some discipline into the proceedings, and in the early twentieth century they were persuaded to move their street fires to the town's perimeters.

Today's tightly knit bonfire societies spend much of the year organizing the Bonfire Night shenanigans, when their members dress up in traditional costumes and parade through the town carrying flaming torches, before marching off onto the Downs for their society's big fire. At each of the fires, effigies of Guy Fawkes and the pope are burned alongside contemporary, but equally reviled, figures – chancellors of the exchequer and prime ministers are popular choices.

been some rebuilding, the core of Lewes remains remarkably good-looking: replete with crooked older dwellings, narrow lanes – or "Twittens" – and Georgian houses. With some of England's most appealing chalkland close by and numerous traces of its long history still visible, Lewes is a worthwhile stopover on any tour of the Southeast – and an easy one, with good rail connections with London and along the coast.

Following the Norman Conquest, William's son-in-law, William de Warenne, built a priory and castle here, the latter still dominating the High Street. In 1264 Henry III's incompetence caused a baronial revolt led by Simon de Montfort which culminated in the king's surrender at the Battle of Lewes, although de Montfort and his reduced force were annihilated within a year at the Battle of Evesham. De Montfort's name crops up all over the town, as do references to the Lewes Martyrs, the seventeen Protestants burned here in 1556, at the height of Mary Tudor's militant revival of Catholicism – an event commemorated in spectacular fashion every November 5 (see box above).

Within a few miles of Lewes lies a pair of places worth visiting: **Charleston**, associated with the Bloomsbury group, and **Glyndebourne**, the mecca for picnicking opera-lovers.

The Town

From the train station, walk up Station Road and turn left into the High Street to find Lewes's **Castle** (Tues–Sat 10am–5.30pm, Sun & Mon 11am–5.30pm; closed Mon in Jan; winter closes at dusk; £4.70), hidden from view behind the houses on your right. Inside the castle complex – unusual for being built on two mottes, or mounds – the shell of the eleventh-century keep remains, and both the towers can be climbed for excellent views over the town to the surrounding Downs. Tickets for the castle include admission to the **museum** (same hours as castle), by the castle entrance, where exhibits include archeological artefacts and a town model.

Further west along the High Street, past St Michael's Church with its unusual twin towers, one wooden and the other flint, you'll come to the steep, cobbled and much photographed **Keere Street**, down which the reckless Prince Regent is alleged to have driven his carriage. Keere Street leads to **Southover Grange** (daily dawn–dusk; free), with its lovely gardens. Built in 1572 from the priory's remains, the Grange was the childhood home of the diarist John Evelyn. Past the gardens, a right turn down Southover High Street leads to the Tudor-built **Anne of Cleves House** (Tues–Sat 10am–5pm; also March–Oct Mon & Sun 11am–5pm; £3.50, combined ticket with the castle £7), given to her in settlement after her divorce from Henry VIII – though she never actually lived there. The magnificent oak-beamed Tudor bedroom is impressive, with a 400-year-old Flemish four-poster and a cumbersome "bed wagon", a bed-warming brazier which would fail the slackest of fire regulations.

On the opposite side of the road and closer to the train station is the church of **St John the Baptist**, with its squat, brick tower capped by a six-foot shark for a weather vane; inside there's some superb stained glass and a tiny chapel with the lead coffins of William de Warenne and his wife Gundrada, William I's daughter. Behind the church are the ruins of de Warenne's **St Pancras Priory**, once one of Europe's principal Cluniac institutions, with a church the size of Westminster Abbey, now an evocative ruin surrounded by playing fields.

At the east end of the High Street, School Hill descends towards **Cliffe Bridge**, built in 1727 and entrance to the commercial centre of the medieval settlement. For the energetic, a path leads up onto the Downs from the end of Cliffe High Street.

Practicalities

The **train station** lies south of High Street down Station Road, and the **bus station** is on Eastgate Street, near the foot of School Hill. The **tourist office** is at the junction of the High Street and Fisher Street (April–Sept Mon–Fri 9am–5pm, Sat 10am–5pm, Sun 10am–2pm; Oct–March Mon–Fri 9am–5pm, Sat 10am–2pm; ⓣ01273/483448, ⓦwww.lewes.gov.uk).

For **accommodation**, try *Castle Banks Cottage*, 4 Castle Banks (ⓣ01273/476291, ⓦwww.castlebankscottage.co.uk; no credit cards; ③), a beamed period house with great views, tucked away off West Street, or *The Crown Inn*, 191 High St, close to the tourist office (ⓣ01273/480670, ⓦwww.crowninn-lewes.co.uk; ③). The nearest YHA **hostel** is in the hamlet of Telscombe, six miles south of Lewes (ⓣ0870/770 6062; from £12), whose simple accommodation is in 200-year-old cottages; there's also a YHA **bunkhouse** – a rustic wooden cabin with basic facilities – eleven miles northeast of town at Blackboys, near Uckfield (ⓣ01825/890607; dorm bed from £13).

Lewes is home to the excellent Harvey's brewery and most of the **pubs** serve its wares. On the outskirts of town, the lively *Snowdrop Inn* at South Street also serves excellent **food** including vegetarian and vegan options, while *Circa* is a stylish brasserie serving eclectic, contemporary dishes on St Andrew's Lane (ⓣ01273/471333).

Around Lewes: Glyndebourne and Charleston

Glyndebourne, Britain's only unsubsidized opera house, is situated near the village of Glynde, three miles east of Lewes. Founded in 1934, the Glyndebourne season (mid-May to Aug) is an indispensable part of the high-society calendar, with ticket prices and a distribution system that excludes all but the most devoted opera-lovers. While the spectacle of lawns thronged with gentry and corporate bigwigs ingesting champagne and smoked salmon may put you off, the musical values at Glyndebourne are the highest in the country, using young talent rather than expensive star names, and taking the sort of risks Covent Garden wouldn't dream of. An award-winning theatre (seating 1200) has broadened this exclusive venue to a wider audience, and there are tickets available at reduced prices for dress rehearsals or for standing-room-only; call ⓣ01273/813813 or check ⓦwww.glyndebourne.com.

Six miles east of Lewes, off the A27, is **Charleston Farmhouse** (March–Oct Thurs, Fri, Sun & public hols 2–6pm, Wed & Sat 11.30am–6pm; July & Aug also Thurs & Fri opens 11.30am; £6.50; guided tours Wed–Sat; last entry 5pm), home to Virginia Woolf's sister Vanessa Bell, Vanessa's husband, Clive Bell, and her lover, Duncan Grant. As conscientious objectors, the trio moved here during World War I so that the men could work on local farms (farm labourers were exempted from military service). Almost every surface of the farmhouse interior is painted and the walls are hung with paintings by Picasso, Renoir and Augustus John, alongside the work of the markedly less talented residents.

Brighton

Recorded as the tiny fishing village of Brithelmeston in the Domesday Book, **BRIGHTON** seems to have slipped unnoticed through history until the mid-eighteenth century, when the new trend for sea-bathing established it as a resort. The fad received royal approval in the 1780s, after the decadent Prince of Wales (the future George IV) began patronizing the town in the company of his mistress, thus setting a precedent for the "dirty weekend". Trying to shake off this blowsy reputation, Brighton – which was granted city status in 2000 – now highlights its Georgian charm, its upmarket shops and classy restaurants, and its thriving conference industry. Despite these efforts, however, the essence of Brighton's appeal is its faintly bohemian vitality, a buzz that comes from a mix of English holiday-makers, foreign-language students, a thriving gay community and an energetic local student population from the art college and two universities.

Arrival, information and accommodation

Brighton **train station** is at the head of Queen's Road, which descends to the Clocktower and then becomes West Street, eventually leading to the seafront. The **bus station** is just in from the seafront on the south side of the Old Steine. The **tourist office** is opposite the Royal Pavilion at 4–5 Pavilion Buildings (daily 9.30am–5pm; ⓣ0906/711 2255, ⓦwww.visitbrighton.com).

You'll find most budget **accommodation** clustered around the **Kemp Town** district, to the east of Brighton Pier, with the more elegant and expensive hotels west of the town centre around Regency Square. Brighton's official **campsite** is the *Sheepcote Valley* site (ⓣ01273/626546), just north of Brighton Marina; take bus #1 or #1a to Wilson Avenue, or take the Volks railway and walk up Arundel Road to Wilson Avenue.

Hotels and B&Bs

Adelaide 51 Regency Square ⓣ01273/205286, ⓦwww.adelaidehotel.co.uk. Topnotch guesthouse on five floors (no lift), with sea views from some rooms. Veggies and vegans catered for. ❹

Ainsley House 28 New Steine ⓣ01273/605310, ⓦwww.ainsleyhotel.com. Friendly, rather old-fashioned guesthouse in an attractive Regency terrace. ❺

Hotel du Vin Ship St ⓣ01273/718588, ⓦwww.hotelduvin.com. A Gothic Revival building in a contemporary style, luxuriously furnished in subtle seaside colours, with an excellent bar and bistro. 7

Legends 31–34 Marine Parade ⓣ01273/624462, ⓦwww.legendsbrighton.com. Large, buzzing, gay hotel on the seafront, with late bar and regular cabaret nights. 4

Lichfield House 30 Waterloo St ⓣ01273/777740, ⓦwww.fieldhousehotels.co.uk. Stylish and colourfully furnished townhouse. 4

Pelirocco 10 Regency Square ⓣ01273/327055, ⓦwww.hotelpelirocco.co.uk. Self-styled rock'n'roll hang-out with themed rooms, a bohemian atmosphere and a late-opening bar. 5

The Twenty One 21 Charlotte St, off Marine Parade ⓣ01273/686450, ⓦwww.thetwentyone.co.uk. Classy Kemp Town B&B in an ornate, early-Victorian house where the comfortable rooms have fridges. 5

Urban House 20–21 New Steine ⓣ01273/688085, ⓦwww.urbanhouse.uk.com. Plusher than average choice in New Steine, with sleek, modern rooms fitted with flat-screen TVs and Wi-Fi, and there's a relaxation centre with sauna and steam room. 6

Hostels

Baggies Backpackers 33 Oriental Place ⓣ01273/733740. Spacious house a little west of the West Pier with large bright dorms (from £13 a night) and decent showers. No credit cards. Rooms 1

The Grapevine 29–30 North Rd ⓣ01273/703985, ⓦwww.grapevinewebsite.co.uk. Friendly, modern hostel in the heart of the North Laine area, with Internet access and free bike and luggage storage. No credit cards. Dorm beds from £15, rooms 1

The City

A visit to Brighton inevitably begins with a visit to its two most famous landmarks – the exuberant **Royal Pavilion** and the wonderfully tacky **Brighton Pier**, a few minutes away – followed by a stroll along the seafront promenade or the pebbly beach. Just as interesting, though, is an exploration of Brighton's car-free **Lanes** – the maze of narrow alleys marking the old town – where some of the town's diverse restaurants, bars and tiny bric-a-brac, jewellery and antique shops can be found, or a meander through the quaint, but more bohemian streets of **North Laine**.

The Royal Pavilion and Brighton Museum

In any survey to find England's most loved building, there's always a bucketful of votes for Brighton's exotic extravaganza, the **Royal Pavilion** (daily: April–Sept 9.30am–5.45pm; Oct–March 10am–5.15pm; last entry 45min before closing; £7.70), which flaunts itself in the middle of the main thoroughfare of Old Steine. The building was a conventional farmhouse until 1787, when the fun-loving Prince of Wales converted it into something more regal, and for a couple of decades the prince's south-coast pied-à-terre was a Palladian villa, with mildly Oriental embellishments. Upon becoming Prince Regent, however, George commissioned John Nash, architect of London's Regent Street, to build an extraordinary confection of slender minarets, twirling domes, pagodas, balconies and miscellaneous motifs imported from India and China. Supported on an innovative cast-iron frame, the result defined a genre of its own – Oriental Gothic. The dour Queen Victoria was not amused by George's taste in architecture, however, and all the Pavilion's valuable fittings were carted off to her London palaces. The gutted building has now been brilliantly restored, its exuberant compendium of Regency exotica enhanced by the return of many of the objects that Victoria had taken away.

Approached via the restrained Long Gallery, the **Banqueting Room** erupts with ornate splendour and is dominated by a one-ton chandelier hung from the jaws of a massive dragon cowering in a plantain tree. Next door, the huge, high-ceilinged kitchen, fitted with the most modern appliances of its time, has iron columns disguised as palm trees. The stunning **Music Room**, the first sight of which reduced George to tears of joy, has a huge dome lined with more than twenty-six thousand individually gilded scales and hung with exquisite umbrella-like glass lamps. After climbing the famous cast-iron staircase with its bamboo-look banisters, you can go into Victoria's sober and seldom-used bedroom and the North Gallery where the king's portrait hangs, along with a selection of satirical cartoons. More notable, though, is the **South Gallery**, decorated in sky-blue with trompe l'oeil bamboo trellises and a carpet that appears to be strewn with flowers.

Across the gardens from the Pavilion stands the **Dome**, once the royal stables and now the town's main concert hall. Adjoining it is the refurbished **Brighton Museum and Art Gallery** (Tues 10am–7pm, Wed–Sat & public hols 10am–5pm, Sun 2–5pm; free), which is entered just around the corner on Church Street. It houses an eclectic mix of modern fashion and design, archeology, painting and local history, including a large collection of pottery from basic Neolithic earthenware to delicate eighteenth-century porcelain figurines. The highlight of the collection of classic Art Deco and Art Nouveau furniture is Dalí's famous sofa based on Mae West's lips. The *Balcony Café* is the perfect setting for a coffee or tea.

The rest of the town

Tucked between the Pavilion and the seafront is a warren of narrow, pedestrianized thoroughfares known as **the Lanes** – the core of the old fishing village from which Brighton evolved. Long-established antiques shops, designer outlets and several bars, pubs and restaurants generate a lively and intimate atmosphere in this part of town.

North Laine, which spreads north of North Street along Kensington, Sydney, Gardner and Bond streets, is more bohemian than the Lanes, with its hub along pedestrianized Kensington Gardens. Here the eclectic shops, selling secondhand records, clothes, bric-a-brac and New Age objects, mingle with earthy coffee shops and funky cafés.

Off North Road on Jubilee Street, the **Jubilee Library** (Mon & Tues 10am–7pm, Wed & Fri 10am–2pm, Thurs 10am–8pm, Sat 10am–4pm), opened in 2005, has become an icon of Brighton's new metropolitan image. The generous glass front complemented by blue ceramic tiling gives access to its lofty interior, in which modern sculptures mingle with state-of-the-art technology, including free **Internet** points.

Much of Brighton's **seafront** is an ugly mix of shops, entertainment complexes and hotels such as the impressively pompous *Grand Hotel* – scene of the IRA's attempted assassination of the Conservative Cabinet in October 1984. To soak up the tackier side of Brighton, take a stroll along **Brighton Pier**, completed in 1899, whose every inch is devoted to cacophonous fun and money-making. Half a mile west along the seafront, the architecturally superior West Pier, dating from 1866, has been virtually destroyed by storms and fires, though there are plans to fund what amounts to a total reconstruction by erecting a "vertical pier", or viewing mast, 183m tall, known as the i360 and scheduled to open in 2009.

Just east of Brighton Pier, the antiquated locomotives of **Volk's Electric Railway** (Easter to mid-Sept Mon–Fri 10am–5pm, Sat & Sun 10am–6pm; £2.50 return) – the first electric train in the country – run eastward towards the Marina and the nudist beach, usually the preserve of just a few thick-skinned souls.

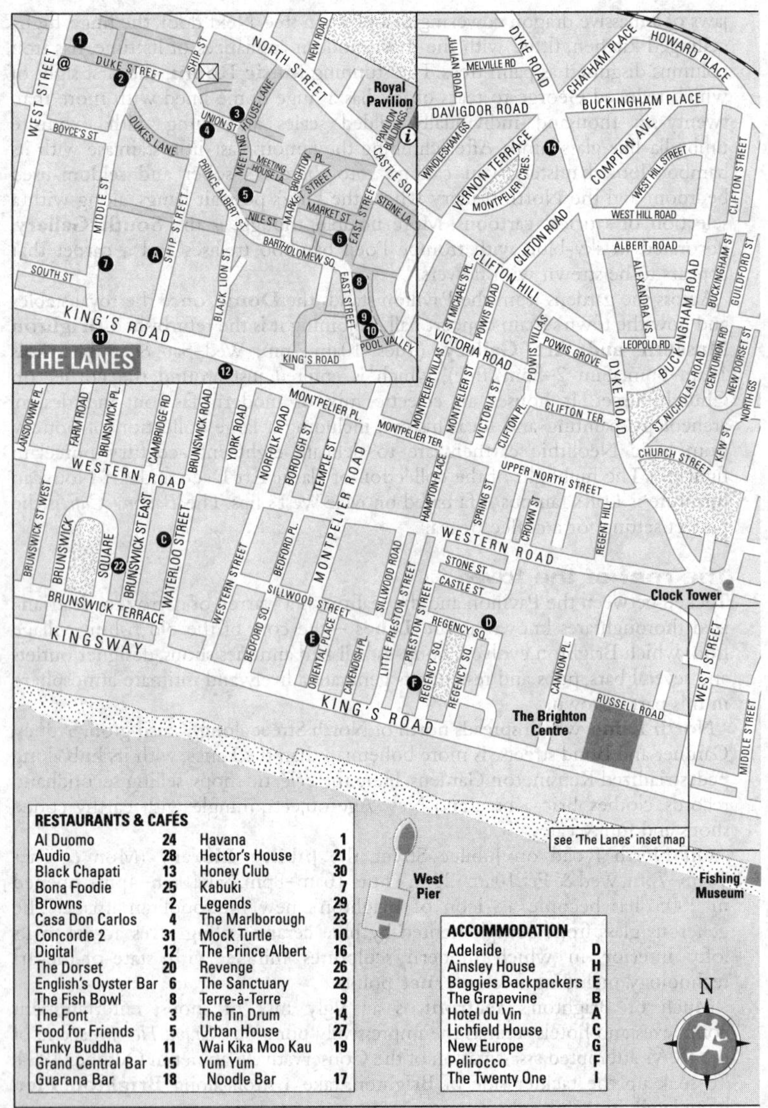

In Brighton's northern suburbs, the **Booth Museum of Natural History** (Mon–Sat 10am–5pm, Sun 2–5pm; free), a mile up Dyke Road from the centre of town (bus #27, #27A or #27B), is worth seeking out – a wonderfully fusty old Victorian museum with beetles, butterflies and animal skeletons galore, as well as some imaginative temporary exhibitions.

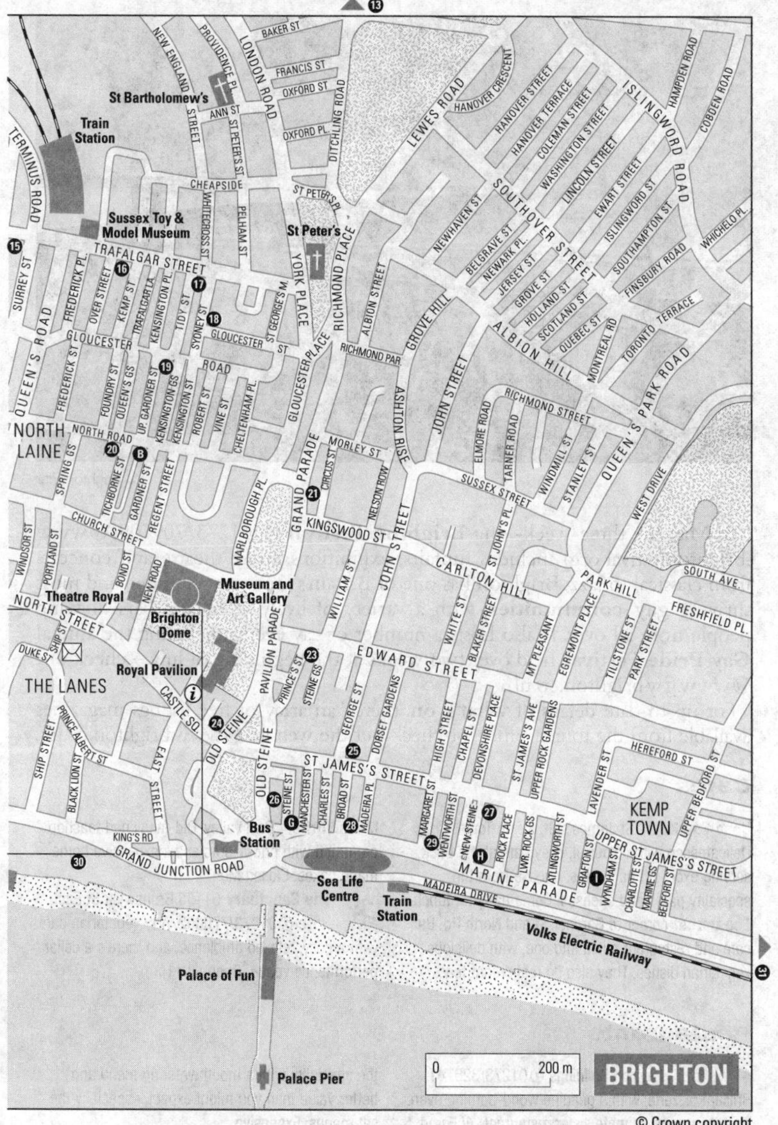

Eating, drinking and nightlife

Brighton has the greatest concentration of **restaurants** in the Southeast after London. Around North Laine are some great, inexpensive cafés, while for classier establishments head to the Lanes and out towards Hove. **Nightlife** is hectic and compulsively pursued throughout the year: as well as the mainstream **theatre** and **concert** venues, there are myriad **clubs**, lots of **live music** and plenty of cinemas.

▲ Brighton Pier

In May, the three-week-long **Brighton Festival** (Ⓣ01273/709709, Ⓦwww.brightonfestival.org) includes funfairs, exhibitions, street theatre and concerts from classical to jazz. Brighton has one of Britain's longest-established and most thriving **gay communities**, with a variety of lively clubs and bars drawing people from all over. It also hosts a number of gay events including the annual **Gay Pride Festival**, held over two weeks at the beginning of July – check out Ⓦwww.gay.brighton.co.uk.

For up-to-date details of **what's on**, there's an array of free listings magazines available from the tourist office, or check out the website Ⓦwww.brighton.co.uk.

Cafés

Bona Foodie 21 St James's St, Kemp Town. Delicatessen with colourful, cosy café at the back, serving excellent baguettes; choose from the speciality pâtés and cheeses. Come early for lunch.

The Dorset corner of Gardner St and North Rd. Bar, café and restaurant rolled into one, with delicious vegetarian dishes. They also do real cream teas.

Mock Turtle 4 Pool Valley. Old-fashioned teashop crammed with bric-a-brac and inexpensive home-made cakes. Closed Mon.

The Sanctuary 51–55 Brunswick St East, Hove Ⓣ01273/770002. Arty vegetarian café with a cosy, relaxed ambience, and there's a cellar performance venue. Open till 11pm.

Restaurants

Al Duomo 7 Pavilion Buildings Ⓣ01273/326741. Brilliant pizzeria, with a genuine wood-burning oven. There's a more intimate sister restaurant, *Al Forno*, at 36 East St (Ⓣ01273/324905). Inexpensive.

Casa Don Carlos 5 Union St Ⓣ01273/327177. Small, long-established tapas bar in the Lanes with outdoor seating and daily specials. Also serves more substantial Spanish dishes and drinks. Inexpensive.

English's Oyster Bar 29–31 East St Ⓣ01273/327980. Three fishermen's cottages knocked together to house a marble and brass oyster bar and a red velvet dining room. Seafood's the speciality with a mouthwatering menu and better value than you might expect, especially the set menus. Expensive.

Food for Friends 18 Prince Albert St Ⓣ01273/202310. Brighton's ever-popular wholefood veggie eatery is imaginative enough to please die-hard meat-eaters too. It's usually busy, but well worth the squeeze. Moderate.

Havana 32 Duke St Ⓣ01273/773388. Stylish continental brasserie with just a hint of colonial ambience. The menu is French-influenced – the lunchtime deal is particularly good value. Expensive.

Terre-à-Terre 71 East St ⓣ01273/729051. Inspired global veggie cuisine in a modern arty setting. Closed Mon lunch. Moderate–expensive.

The Tin Drum 43 St James's St ⓣ01273/777575. Buzzing continental-style café-bar and restaurant with a taste for Baltic-rim cooking and a blend of Eastern European influences; fresh seasonal ingredients and speciality vodkas. One of four around the city, similarly styled. Moderate.

Wai Kika Moo Kau 11 Kensington Gardens ⓣ01273/671117. Global veggie café/restaurant, very popular, with award-winning veggie burgers among more eclectic choices – all for around £5. Inexpensive.

Yum Yum Noodle Bar 22–23 Sydney St ⓣ01273/606777. Lunch-only place serving anything Southeast Asian – Chinese, Thai, Indonesian and Malaysian – at good-value prices. Located above a Chinese supermarket. Inexpensive.

Pubs and bars

The Fish Bowl 74 East St ⓣ01273/777505. Popular pre-club choice for its range of music – sometimes better than the clubs themselves – and a good daytime menu.

The Font Union St ⓣ01273/747727. Spacious converted chapel with a bar in place of the altar and occasional live music.

Grand Central Bar 29–30 Surrey St ⓣ01273/329086. Cool, light and comfy bar opposite the station. Well-priced breakfasts and snacks, live jazz and funk at weekends and a theatre upstairs.

Guarana Bar 36 Sydney St. Brazilian-style daytime bar in the North Laine quarter serving herbal cocktails and shakes made with guarana (extract of Amazonian vine).

Hector's House 52 Grand Parade ⓣ01273/681228. Big bare-boards-and-sofa student pub that has nightly pre-club music (except Mon) with in-house DJs and occasional live bands.

Kabuki 8–12 Middle St. Designer-cool Pacific-rim bar with DJs spinning R&B and hip-hop.

The Marlborough 4 Princes St ⓣ01273/570028. Friendly pub with good food, just off Old Steine, popular with a lesbian and student crowd, and there's a small theatre upstairs.

The Prince Albert 48 Trafalgar St ⓣ01273/730499. By the train station, this place is often crowded with students drawn to the real ales, live rock, theme nights and big-screen football.

Nightlife

Audio 10 Marine Parade ⓣ01273/606906, ⓦwww.audiobrighton.com. Brighton's trendiest nightclub packs them in night after night, specializing in funk and house.

Concorde 2 Madeira Shelter, Madeira Drive ⓣ01273/673311, ⓦwww.concorde2.co.uk. Live music venue, with an admirable booking policy; also has club nights at the weekend.

Digital 180–192 King's Rd Arches ⓣ01273/202407. Formerly *The Zap*, this is a big-name venue where DJs spin a range of sounds from breaks to rock/indie, and there are regular live bands. Expect laser shows.

Funky Buddha Lounge 169 King's Rd Arches ⓣ01273/725541, ⓦwww.funkybuddhabrighton.co.uk. Tiny venue renowned for progressive house, breakbeats and soul.

Honey Club 214 King's Rd Arches ⓣ07000/446639, ⓦwww.thehoneyclub.co.uk. Garage, trance, house, hip-hop, you name it, this club has a night for it – and big name DJs.

Revenge 32 Old Steine ⓣ01273/606064, ⓦwww.revenge.co.uk. The south's largest gay club with Mon night cabarets plus upfront dance and retro boogie on two floors.

Arundel and around

The hilltop town of **ARUNDEL**, eighteen miles west of Brighton, has for seven centuries been the seat of the dukes of Norfolk, whose fine **castle** looks over the valley of the River Arun. The medieval town's well-preserved appearance and picturesque setting draws in the crowds on summer weekends, but at any other time a visit reveals one of West Sussex's least spoilt old towns. North of here lie two contrasting sites: **Bignor Roman Villa**, containing some of the best Roman mosaics in the country, and the grand seventeenth-century **Petworth House**, replete with an impressive collection of paintings.

Despite its medieval appearance, most of what you see of **Arundel Castle** (April–Oct Tues–Sun noon–5pm; castle, keep, grounds & chapel £12; keep, grounds & chapel only £6.50) is little more than a century old, the result of a lavish reconstruction from 1718 onwards, following the original Norman structure that was destroyed during the Civil War. From the top of the keep, you can see the current duke's spacious residence and the pristine castle grounds. Inside the castle, the renovated quarters include the impressive **Barons Hall** and the **library**, which boasts paintings by Gainsborough, Holbein and van Dyck. On the edge of the castle grounds, the fourteenth-century **Fitzalan Chapel** houses tombs of past dukes of Norfolk including twin effigies of the seventh duke – one as he looked when he died and, underneath, one of his emaciated corpse. The Catholic chapel belongs to the Norfolk estate, but is actually physically joined to the **Church of St Nicholas**, the parish church, whose entrance is on London Road. Although traditionally Catholics, the dukes of Norfolk have shrewdly played down their papal allegiance in sensitive times – such as during the Tudor era when two of the third duke's nieces, Anne Boleyn and Catherine Howard, became Henry VIII's wives.

West of the parish church, further along London Road, is the towering Gothic bulk of **Arundel Cathedral** (daily 9am–6pm or dusk). Constructed in the 1870s by the fifteenth duke of Norfolk over the town's former Catholic church, the cathedral's spire was designed by John Hansom, inventor of the hansom cab, the earliest taxi. Inside are the enshrined remains of St Philip Howard, the fourth duke's son, who returned to the Catholic fold at a time when the Armada's defeat saw anti-Catholic feelings soar, and spent a decade in the Tower of London, where he died. The rest of Arundel is pleasant to wander round, with the antique-shop-lined Maltravers and Arun streets being the most attractive thoroughfares.

Practicalities

Arundel's **train station** is half a mile south of the town centre over the river on the A27, with **buses** arriving either on High Street or River Road. The **tourist office** is at 1–3 River Rd (Easter–Sept Mon–Sat 10am–6pm, Sun 10am–4pm; Oct–Easter daily 10am–3pm; ⓣ01903/882268, ⓦwww.sussexbythesea.com).

The best **accommodation** options are the ornate rooms of the Georgian *Town House*, 65 High St (ⓣ01903/883847, ⓦwww.thetownhouse.co.uk; ⑤), and the elegant eighteenth-century *Byass House*, 59 Maltravers St (ⓣ01903/882129, ⓦwww.byasshouse.com; no credit cards; ⑤). Alternatively, there's the modern *Woodpeckers*, 15 Dalloway Rd (ⓣ01903/883948; no credit cards; ④), on the outskirts of town. Arundel's YHA **hostel** (ⓣ0870/770 5676, ⓔarundel@yha.org.uk; from £20) is in a large Georgian house by the river at Warningcamp, a mile and a half northeast of town.

If your pocket is up to it, first choice for **food** is the *Town House* (see above; closed Mon) where you dine under a spectacular Italian gilded ceiling. Otherwise try the restaurant attached to the *White Hart* pub over the river at 3 Queen St (ⓣ01903/882374). At 36 Tarrant St, the *King's Arms* is the best real-ale **pub** in town. During the last week in August, Arundel's **festival** (ⓦwww.arundelfestival.co.uk) features everything from open-air theatre to salsa bands.

Bignor and Petworth

Six miles north of Arundel (with no public transport links), the excavated second-century ruins of the **Bignor Roman Villa** (March & April Tues–Sun 10am–5pm; May & Oct daily 10am–5pm; June–Sept daily 10am–6pm; £4.50) include some well-preserved mosaics, of which the Ganymede is the most outstanding. The site is superbly situated at the base of the South Downs and features the longest extant section of mosaic in England, as well as the remains of a hypocaust, the underfloor heating system developed by the Romans.

Adjoining the pretty little village of **PETWORTH**, eleven miles north of Arundel, **Petworth House** (mid-March to Oct 11am–4/5pm; park daily 8am–dusk; £8.10, park free; NT) is one of the Southeast's most impressive stately homes. Built in the late seventeenth century, the house contains an outstanding art collection, with paintings by van Dyck, Titian, Gainsborough, Bosch, Reynolds, Blake and Turner – the last a frequent guest here. The extensive **Servants' Quarters**, connected by a tunnel to the main house, contain an impressive series of kitchens bearing the latest technological kitchenware of the 1870s, while the seven-hundred-acre grounds were landscaped by Capability Brown and are considered one of his finest achievements.

To get to Petworth by **public transport** from Arundel involves a train journey to Pulborough station from where you can pick up the regular Stagecoach Coastline #1 bus. Petworth's **tourist office** is on Golden Square (April–Sept Mon–Fri 9.30am–4.30pm, Sat 10am–5pm, Sun 11am–3.30pm; Oct–March Mon–Fri 9.30am–4.30pm, Sat 10am–2pm; ⓣ01798/343523, ⓦwww.chichester.gov.uk). For a memorable night's **stay**, book in at the converted *Old Railway Station* (ⓣ01798/342346, ⓦwww.old-station.co.uk; ❺), two miles south of Petworth on the A285 Chichester road.

Chichester and around

The market town of **CHICHESTER** began life as a Roman settlement, and its Roman cruciform street plan is still evident in the four-quadrant symmetry of the town centre. The main streets lead off from the Gothic **Market Cross**, a bulky octagonal rotunda topped by ornate finials and a crown lantern spire, built in 1501 to provide shelter for the market traders. A short stroll down West Street brings you to Chichester's chief attraction, its Gothic **Cathedral** (daily 7.15am–6/7pm). Building began in the 1070s, but the church was extensively rebuilt following a fire a century later and has been only minimally modified since about 1300, except for the slender spire and the unique, freestanding fifteenth-century bell tower. The **interior** is renowned for its contemporary devotional art; there's also a sixteenth-century painting in the north transept of the past bishops of Chichester, and the fourteenth-century Fitzalan tomb which inspired a poem by Philip Larkin, *An Arundel Tomb*. However, the highlight is a pair of reliefs in the south aisle, close to the tapestry – created around 1140, they show the raising of Lazarus and Christ at the gate of Bethany. Originally highly coloured, with semiprecious stones set in the figures' eyes, the reliefs are among the finest Romanesque stone carvings in England.

Off South Street, in the well-preserved Georgian quadrant of the city known as the Pallants, you'll find **Pallant House Gallery**, 9 North Pallant (Tues, Wed, Fri & Sat 10am–5pm, Thurs 10am–8pm, Sun 12.30–5pm; £6.50). Stone dodos stand guard over the gates of this fine mansion, which houses artefacts and furniture from the early eighteenth century, as well as more modern pieces including works by Henry Moore, Barbara Hepworth and Graham Sutherland.

At the north end of Little London, the **Guildhall** (June to mid-Sept Sat noon–4pm; free), a branch museum within a thirteenth-century Franciscan church in the middle of Priory Park, has some well-preserved medieval frescoes. It was formerly a town hall and court of law, where the poet, painter and visionary William Blake was tried for sedition in 1804.

Chichester is one of southern England's major cultural centres, well known for its **Festival Theatre** in Oaklands Park (Ⓣ01243/784437, Ⓦwww.cft.org.uk), with a season running roughly between Easter and October. **Chichester Festivities** (Ⓣ01243/785718, Ⓦwww.chifest.org.uk), taking place at a range of venues over two weeks in late June and early July, features music from blues to classical, plus talks and other events.

Practicalities

Chichester's **train station** lies on Stockbridge Road, with the **bus station** across the road at South Street. From either station it's a ten-minute walk north to the Market Cross, passing the **tourist office** at 29a South St (April–Sept Mon 10.15am–5.15pm, Tues–Sat 9.15am–5.15pm, Sun 11am–3.30pm; Oct–March closed Sun; Ⓣ01243/775888, Ⓦwww.chichester.gov.uk).

Finding **accommodation** is easy, except during the festival. Central B&B options include *Litten House*, with an attractive walled garden at 148 St Pancras, just off East Street (Ⓣ01243/774503; ❷), and the 200-year-old *Friary Close*, Friary Lane (Ⓣ01243/527294, Ⓦwww.friaryclose.co.uk; ❸), just inside the city wall.

For something to **eat**, *Sadlers Wine Bar and Restaurant* at 42 East St (Ⓣ01243/778261) serves up innovative meals, while *Purchase's Wine Bar*, 31 North St (Ⓣ01243/537532; closed Sun), dishes up a good selection of Danish open sandwiches, pâtés and salads. *The Ship*, also on North Street, is a good place for a **drink**.

Fishbourne Roman Palace

Fishbourne, two miles west of Chichester and easily accessible by bus and train, is the largest and best-preserved Roman palace in the country (March–July, Sept & Oct daily 10am–5pm; Aug daily 10am–6pm; Nov to mid-Dec & mid-Jan to Feb daily 10am–4pm; mid-Dec to mid-Jan Sat & Sun 10am–4pm; £6.80). Roman relics have long been turning up hereabouts, and in 1960 a workman unearthed their source – the site of a depot used by the invading Romans in 43 AD, which is thought later to have become the vast, hundred-room palace of a Romanized Celtic aristocrat. The north wing of the remains displays floor mosaics depicting Fishbourne's famous dolphin-riding cupid as well as the more usual geometric patterns. The underfloor heating system has also been well restored, and an audiovisual programme portrays the palace as it was in Roman times. The extensive gardens attempt to re-create the appearance of the palace grounds as they would have been then.

Travel details

Buses

For information on all local and national bus services, contact Traveline ⓣ0871/200 2233 (daily 7am–9pm), ⓦwww.traveline.org.uk.

Arundel to: Brighton (Mon–Sat every 30min; Sun 1; 50min–2hr 10min); Chichester (Mon–Sat hourly; Sun 1; 35min).

Battle to: Hastings (Mon–Sat hourly; Sun 1; 15–30min).

Brighton to: Chichester (Mon–Sat every 30min, Sun hourly; 2hr 30min); Eastbourne (every 20min; 1hr 10min); Lewes (Mon–Sat every 15min; Sun hourly; 25–30min); London Victoria (1–2 hourly; 2hr 20min); Portsmouth (Mon–Sat every 30min; Sun hourly; 3hr 30min); Tunbridge Wells (Mon–Sat every 30min; Sun hourly; 1hr 35min).

Broadstairs to: Ramsgate (every 10min; 15min).

Canterbury to: Deal (Mon–Fri 1–3 hourly; Sat hourly; Sun 5; 1hr 5min); Dover (Mon–Sat 1–2 hourly; Sun 6; 35min); London Victoria (hourly; 2hr); Ramsgate (Mon–Sat hourly; 45min); Sandwich (Mon–Sat 1–3 hourly; Sun 5; 40min); Whitstable (Mon–Sat every 5–15min; Sun every 30min; 30min).

Chatham to: Rochester (every 5min; 5min).

Chichester to: Arundel (Mon–Sat 4–6 daily; Sun 1; 20–35min), Brighton (Mon–Sat every 30min; Sun hourly; 2hr 30min); Portsmouth (Mon–Sat every 30min; Sun hourly; 55min).

Deal to: Canterbury (hourly; 1hr 10min); Dover (Mon–Sat hourly; Sun every 2hr; 40min); Sandwich (Mon–Sat 2 hourly; Sun every 2hr; 30min).

Dover to: Canterbury (Mon–Sat hourly; Sun every 2hr; 35min); Deal (Mon–Sat 1–2 hourly; Sun every 2hrs; 30min); Hastings (Mon–Sat hourly; Sun every 2hr; 2hr 40min); Hythe (Mon–Sat every 30min; Sun hourly; 50min); London Victoria (hourly; 2hr 30min–3hr); Sandwich (Mon–Sat 8 daily; 55min).

Eastbourne to: Brighton (2–3 hourly; 1hr 15min); Hastings (Mon–Sat every 20min; Sun hourly; 1hr 10min); London Victoria (2 daily; 3–4hr).

Guildford to: Farnham (Mon–Sat 1–2 hourly; 25min or 1hr); London Victoria (8 daily; 1hr 30min).

Hastings to: Dover (Mon–Sat hourly; Sun 6; 2hr 50min); Eastbourne (Mon–Sat every 20–30min; Sun hourly; 1hr 15min); London Victoria (2 daily; 2hr 50min–3hr 50min); Rye (Mon–Sat 2 hourly; Sun 6; 40min).

Hythe to: Dover (Mon–Sat every 30min; Sun hourly; 55min); Rye (Mon–Sat 2 hourly; Sun 6; 1hr–1hr 15min).

Lewes to: Brighton (Mon–Sat every 15min; Sun hourly; 30min); Tunbridge Wells (Mon–Sat every 30min; Sun hourly; 1hr 10min).

Ramsgate to: Broadstairs (every 10–20min; 10min); Canterbury (Mon–Sat hourly; 45min); London Victoria (4 daily; 3hr); Margate (every 10min; 30min).

Rochester to: Chatham (every 5min; 5min).

Rye to: Hastings (Mon–Sat 1–2 hourly; Sun 6; 30–45min); Hythe (Mon–Sat hourly; Sun 6; 1hr 10min).

Sandwich to: Canterbury (Mon–Sat every 30min; Sun 6; 45min); Deal (Mon–Sat 1–2 hourly; Sun 5; 25min); Dover (Mon–Sat hourly; Sun every 2hr; 55min).

Sevenoaks to: Tunbridge Wells (Mon–Sat 2 hourly; Sun every 2hr; 40–55min).

Tunbridge Wells to: Brighton (Mon–Sat every 30min; Sun 9; 1hr 40min); Lewes (Mon–Sat every 30min; Sun 9; 1hr 10min); London Victoria (1 daily; 1hr 30min); Sevenoaks (Mon–Sat 2 hourly; Sun every 2hr; 40–50min).

Whitstable to: Canterbury (every 15–30min; 30min).

Trains

For information on all local and national rail services, contact National Rail Enquiries: ⓣ08457/484950, ⓦwww.nationalrail.co.uk.

Arundel to: Chichester (Mon–Sat 2 hourly; Sun hourly; 20min); London Victoria (Mon–Sat every 30min; Sun hourly; 1hr 30min); Portsmouth Harbour (hourly; 55min); Pulborough (Mon–Sat 2 hourly; Sun hourly; 10min).

Battle to: Hastings (2 hourly; 15–30min); London Charing Cross (2 hourly; 1hr 30min); Tunbridge Wells (2–3 hourly; 30min).

Brighton to: Chichester (Mon–Sat every 30min; Sun hourly; 50min); Eastbourne (2 hourly; 35min); Hastings (Mon–Sat 2 hourly; Sun hourly; 1hr–1hr 20min); Lewes (every 10–20min; 15min); London Bridge (Mon–Sat 4 hourly; 1hr); London King's Cross (Mon–Sat 2–4 hourly; 1hr 15min); London Victoria (1–2 hourly; 55min–1hr 20min); Portsmouth Harbour (Mon–Sat hourly; 1hr 30min).

Broadstairs to: London Victoria (Mon–Sat every 30min; Sun hourly; 1hr 50min).

Canterbury East to: Dover Priory (Mon–Sat every 30min; Sun hourly; 30min); London Victoria (Mon–Sat every 30min; 1hr 35min).

Canterbury West to: London Charing Cross (Mon–Sat every 30min; Sun hourly; 1hr 45min).

Chatham to: Dover Priory (Mon–Sat every 30min; Sun hourly; 1hr 10min); London Victoria (every 15min; 45min–1hr).
Chichester to: Arundel (Mon–Sat 2 hourly; Sun hourly; 20min); London Victoria (Mon–Sat 3 hourly; Sun hourly; 2hr–2hr 20min); Portsmouth Harbour (Mon–Sat every 30min; Sun hourly; 40min).
Dover Priory to: London Charing Cross (Mon–Sat 2 hourly; 1hr 40min); London Victoria (Mon–Sat 2 hourly; Sun hourly; 1hr 50min).
Eastbourne to: Brighton (2 hourly; 35min); Hastings (every 20–30min; 30min); Lewes (every 20–30min; 20–30min); London Victoria (Mon–Sat every 30min; Sun hourly; 1hr 35min).
Farnham to: London Waterloo (every 30min; 1hr).
Hastings to: London Victoria (hourly; 2hr–2hr 15min); Rye (hourly; 20min).
Lewes to: Brighton (every 15–20min; 15min); Eastbourne (every 20–30min; 20–30min); London Victoria (Mon–Sat every 30min; Sun hourly; 1hr 10min).
Ramsgate to: London Victoria (Mon–Sat hourly; 1hr 45min).
Rochester to: Dover Priory (Mon–Sat every 30min; Sun hourly; 1hr–1hr 15min); London Charing Cross (every 30min; 1hr 10min); London Victoria (Mon–Sat every 30min; Sun 2 hourly; 45min).
Rye to: Hastings (hourly; 20min).
Sandwich to: Dover Priory (hourly; 25min).
Sevenoaks to: London Blackfriars (Mon–Sat every 30min; London Charing Cross (3–5 hourly; 35min); 1hr); London Victoria (Sun hourly; 1hr); Tunbridge Wells (2 hourly; 20min).
Tunbridge Wells to: London Charing Cross (2 hourly; 55min).
Whitstable to: London Victoria (Mon–Sat every 30min; 1hr 20min).

3 Hampshire, Dorset and Wiltshire

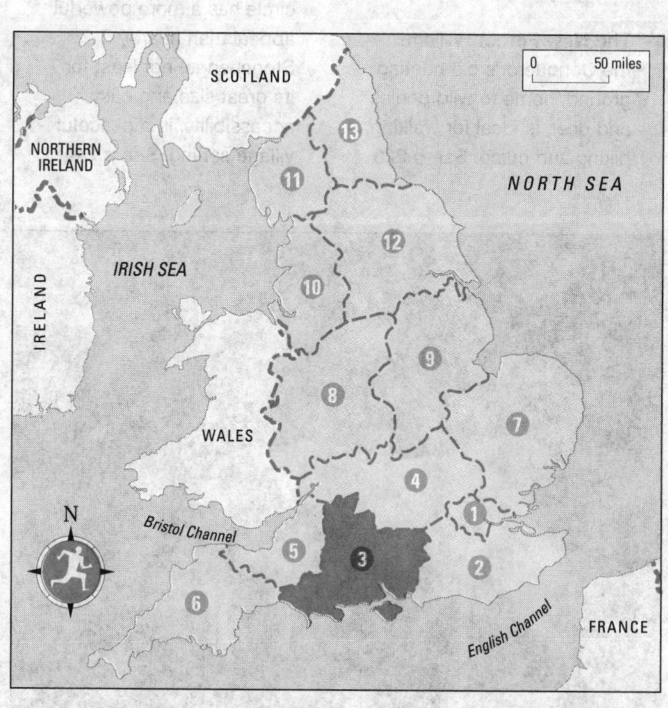

CHAPTER 3

Highlights

* **Cowes Week, Isle of Wight** This yachting jamboree draws thousands, infecting even the staunchest landlubbers. See p.218
* **Wykeham Arms, Winchester** Ancient tavern serving gourmet-standard food alongside the real ales. See p.222
* **The New Forest** William the Conqueror's old hunting ground, home to wild ponies and deer, is ideal for walking, biking and riding. See p.223
* **Corfe Castle** Picturesque ruins with a weathered, romantic charm. See p.229
* **Durdle Door** This crumbling natural arch stands at the end of a splendid beach – a great place for walkers and swimmers alike. See p.231
* **Avebury** This crude stone circle has a more powerful appeal than nearby Stonehenge, not least for its great size and easy accessibility, in a peaceful village setting. See p.244

▲ New Forest ponies

3

Hampshire, Dorset and Wiltshire

The distant past is perhaps more tangible in **Hampshire** (often abbreviated to "Hants"), **Dorset** and **Wiltshire** than in any other part of England. Predominantly rural, these three counties overlap substantially with the ancient kingdom of **Wessex**, whose most famous ruler, Alfred, repulsed the Danes in the ninth century and came close to establishing the first unified state in England. Before Wessex came into being, however, many earlier civilizations had left their stamp on the region. The chalky uplands of Wiltshire boast several of Europe's greatest Neolithic sites, including **Stonehenge** and **Avebury**, while in Dorset you'll find **Maiden Castle**, the most striking Iron Age hill fort in the country, and the **Cerne Abbas Giant**, source of many a legend. The Romans tramped all over these southern counties, leaving the most conspicuous signs of their occupation at the amphitheatre of **Dorchester** – though that town is more closely associated with the novels of Thomas Hardy and his distinctively gloomy vision of Wessex.

None of the landscapes of this region could be described as grand or wild, but the countryside is consistently seductive, not least the crumbling fossil-bearing cliffs around **Lyme Regis**, the managed woodlands of the **New Forest** and the gentle, open curves of **Salisbury Plain**. Its towns are also generally modest and slow-paced, with the notable exceptions of the two great maritime bases of **Portsmouth** and **Southampton**, a fair proportion of whose visitors are simply passing through on their way to the more genteel pleasures of the **Isle of Wight**. The two great cathedral cities in these parts, **Salisbury** and **Winchester**, and the seaside resort of **Bournemouth** see most tourist traffic, and the great houses of **Wilton**, **Stourhead**, **Longleat** and **Kingston Lacy** also attract the crowds; but you don't have to wander far off the beaten track to encounter medieval churches, manor houses and unspoilt country inns a-plenty.

Portsmouth

Britain's foremost naval station, **PORTSMOUTH** occupies the bulbous peninsula of Portsea Island, on the eastern flank of a huge, easily defended harbour. The ancient Romans raised a fortress on the northernmost edge of this

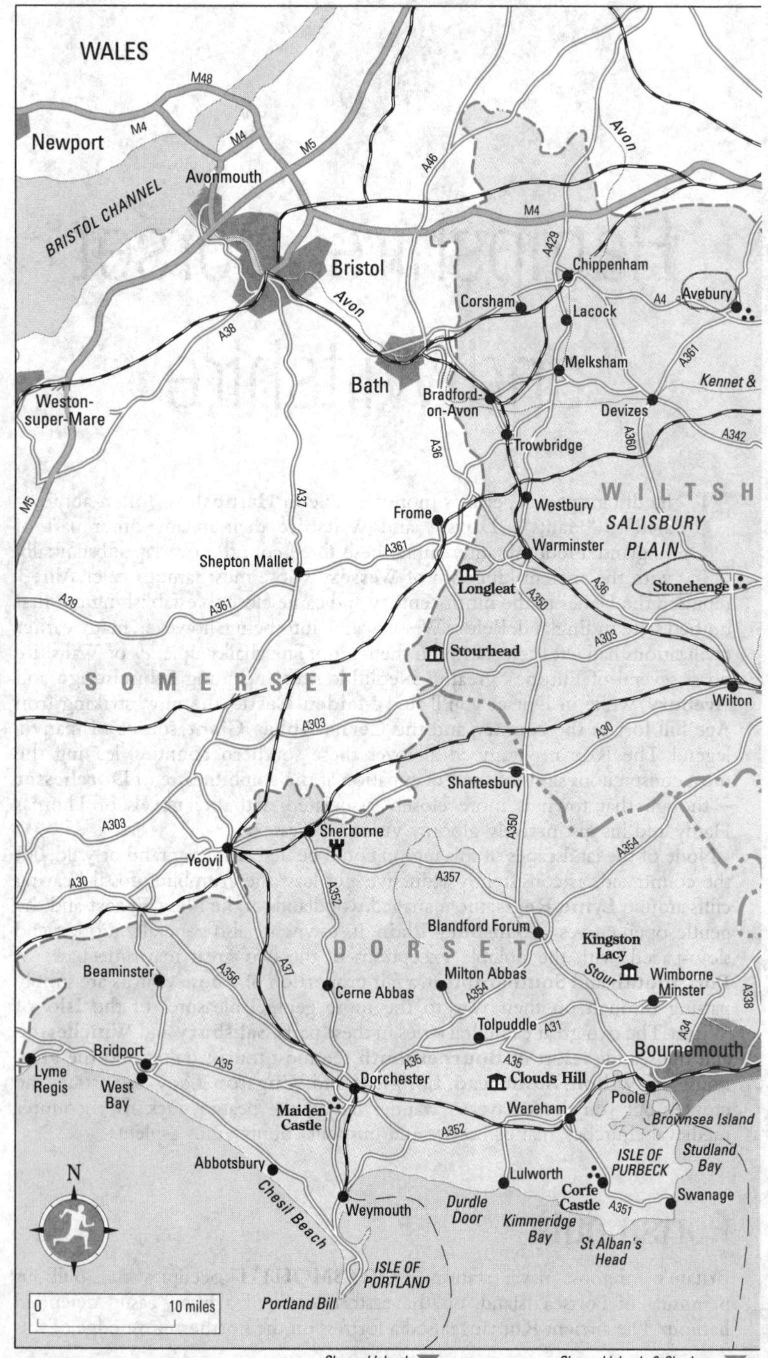
WALES
Newport
BRISTOL CHANNEL
Avonmouth
Bristol
Bath
Weston-super-Mare
M48
M4
M5
A38
A37
A36
A46
A429
A4
A361
A360
A342
A350
A303
A30
A39
A357
A352
A356
A354
A35
A31
A34
A338
A351
Avon
Chippenham
Corsham
Lacock
Avebury
Melksham
Kennet &
Bradford-on-Avon
Devizes
Trowbridge
WILTSH
SALISBURY PLAIN
Westbury
Frome
Warminster
Shepton Mallet
Longleat
Stonehenge
Stourhead
SOMERSET
Wilton
Shaftesbury
Sherborne
Yeovil
Blandford Forum
DORSET
Kingston Lacy
Stour
Wimborne Minster
Beaminster
Milton Abbas
Cerne Abbas
Tolpuddle
Bournemouth
Bridport
Lyme Regis
West Bay
Dorchester
Clouds Hill
Poole
Maiden Castle
Wareham
Brownsea Island
ISLE OF PURBECK
Studland Bay
Abbotsbury
Lulworth
Corfe Castle
Swanage
Chesil Beach
Weymouth
Durdle Door
Kimmeridge Bay
St Alban's Head
ISLE OF PORTLAND
Portland Bill
N
0
10 miles
Channel Islands
Channel Islands & Cherbourg

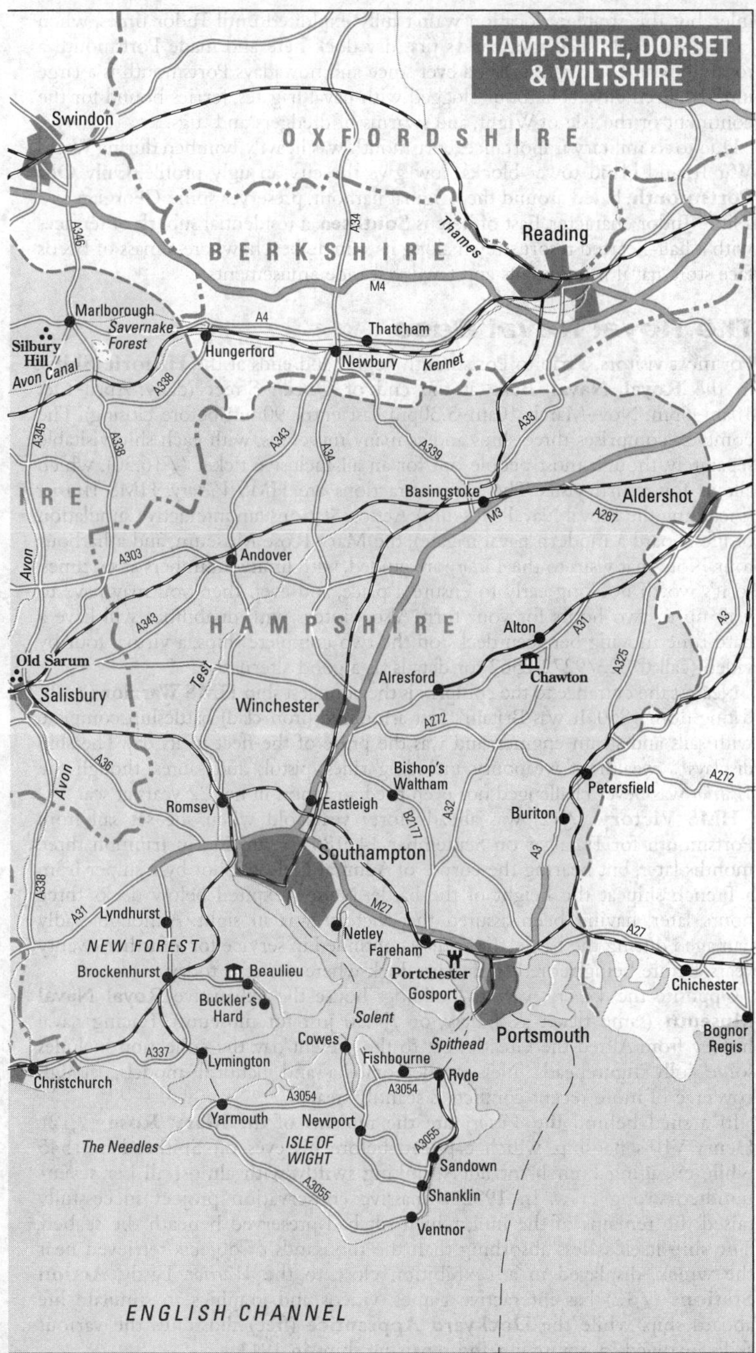
HAMPSHIRE, DORSET & WILTSHIRE
Swindon
OXFORDSHIRE
BERKSHIRE
Thames
Reading
M4
A346
A34
Marlborough
Savernake Forest
Silbury Hill
A4
Thatcham
Hungerford
Newbury
Kennet
Avon Canal
A338
A345
A343
A339
A33
Basingstoke
M3
Aldershot
A287
RE
A303
Andover
Avon
HAMPSHIRE
A343
Alton
A31
A3
Old Sarum
Test
Chawton
A325
Salisbury
Alresford
Winchester
A272
A36
Bishop's Waltham
Petersfield
A272
Avon
Romsey
Eastleigh
B2177
A32
Buriton
Southampton
A3
A338
A31
Lyndhurst
M27
Netley
NEW FOREST
Fareham
A27
Brockenhurst
Beaulieu
Portchester
Chichester
Buckler's Hard
Gosport
Solent
Bognor Regis
Cowes
Spithead
Portsmouth
A337
Lymington
Fishbourne
Christchurch
Ryde
A3054
A3054
Yarmouth
Newport
The Needles
ISLE OF WIGHT
A3055
Sandown
A3055
Shanklin
Ventnor
ENGLISH CHANNEL
Caen, St Malo, Bilbao, Cherbourg & Le Havre
© Crown copyright

inlet, but this strategic location wasn't fully exploited until Tudor times, when Henry VII established the world's first dry dock here and made Portsmouth a royal dockyard. It has flourished ever since and nowadays Portsmouth is a large industrialized city, its harbour clogged with naval frigates, ferries bound for the continent or the Isle of Wight, and swarms of dredgers and tugs.

Due to its military importance, Portsmouth was heavily bombed during World War II, and bland tower blocks now give the city an ugly profile. Only **Old Portsmouth**, based around the original harbour, preserves some Georgian and a little Tudor character. East of here is **Southsea**, a residential suburb of terraces with a half-hearted resort strewn along its shingle beach, where a mass of B&Bs face stoic naval monuments and tawdry seaside amusements.

The Royal Naval Base

For most visitors, a trip to Portsmouth begins and ends at the **Historic Ships**, in the **Royal Naval Base** at the end of Queen Street (daily: April–Oct 10am–6pm; Nov–March 10am–5.30pm; last entry 90min before closing). The complex comprises three ships and as many museums, with each ship visitable separately, though most people opt for an all-inclusive ticket (£16.50), which allows for return visits. The main attractions are HMS *Victory*, HMS *Warrior* (including the Royal Naval Museum), Action Stations (an interactive simulation of life aboard a modern naval frigate), the Mary Rose Museum, and a harbour tour. Note that visits to the *Victory* are guided, with limited numbers at set times, so it's worth booking early to ensure a place, and even then you may have to wait up to two hours for your turn. Also, visitors with disabilities will have a hard time moving between decks on the two complete ships; a virtual tour by video (call ⓣ023/9272 2562 for details) is a good alternative.

Nearest the entrance to the complex is the youngest ship, **HMS Warrior** (£12), dating from 1860. It was Britain's first armoured (iron-clad) battleship, complete with sails and steam engines, and was the pride of the fleet in its day. The ship displays a wealth of weaponry, including rifles, pistols and sabres, though the *Warrior* was never challenged nor even fired a cannon in her 22 years at sea.

HMS Victory (£12) was already forty years old when she set sail from Portsmouth for Trafalgar on September 14, 1805, returning in triumph three months later, but bearing the corpse of Admiral Nelson. Shot by a sniper from a French ship at the height of the battle, Nelson expired below decks three hours later, having been assured that victory was in sight. Although badly damaged during the battle, the *Victory* continued in service for a further twenty years, before being retired to the dry dock where she rests today.

Opposite the *Victory*, various buildings house the exhaustive **Royal Naval Museum** (same ticket as *Victory*, or £4.50 just for museum). Tracing naval history from Alfred the Great's fleet to the present day, the collection includes some jolly figureheads, Nelson memorabilia and nautical models, though coverage of more recent conflicts is scantily treated.

In a shed behind the *Victory* are the remains of the **Mary Rose** (£12), Henry VIII's flagship, which capsized before his eyes off Spithead in 1545 while engaging French intruders, sinking swiftly with almost all her seven-hundred-strong crew. In 1982 a massive conservation project successfully raised the remains of the hull, which silt had preserved beneath the seabed. The ship itself is less absorbing than the thousands of objects retrieved near the wreck, displayed in an exhibition close to the *Warrior*. Lastly, **Action Stations** (£12) has interactive games, videos and graphics to simulate life aboard ship, while the **Dockyard Apprentice** (free) illustrates the various skills involved in equipping and repairing ships in 1911.

Gosport

The naval theme is continued across the harbour in **Gosport**, reached by taking the passenger ferry from Harbour train station jetty (daily 5.30am–midnight; £2.10 return). Here, the **Submarine Museum** on Haslar Jetty (daily 10am–4.30/5.30pm; last tour 1hr before closing; £7.50) illustrates the long history of submersible craft, and a guided tour inside HMS *Alliance* gives you an insight into life on board.

Nearby, housed in the old armaments depot at Priddy's Hard, **Explosion! The Museum of Naval Firepower** (Sat & Sun 10am–4pm; last entry at 3pm; £4) tells the story of naval warfare from the days of gunpowder to the present with the aid of computer animations.

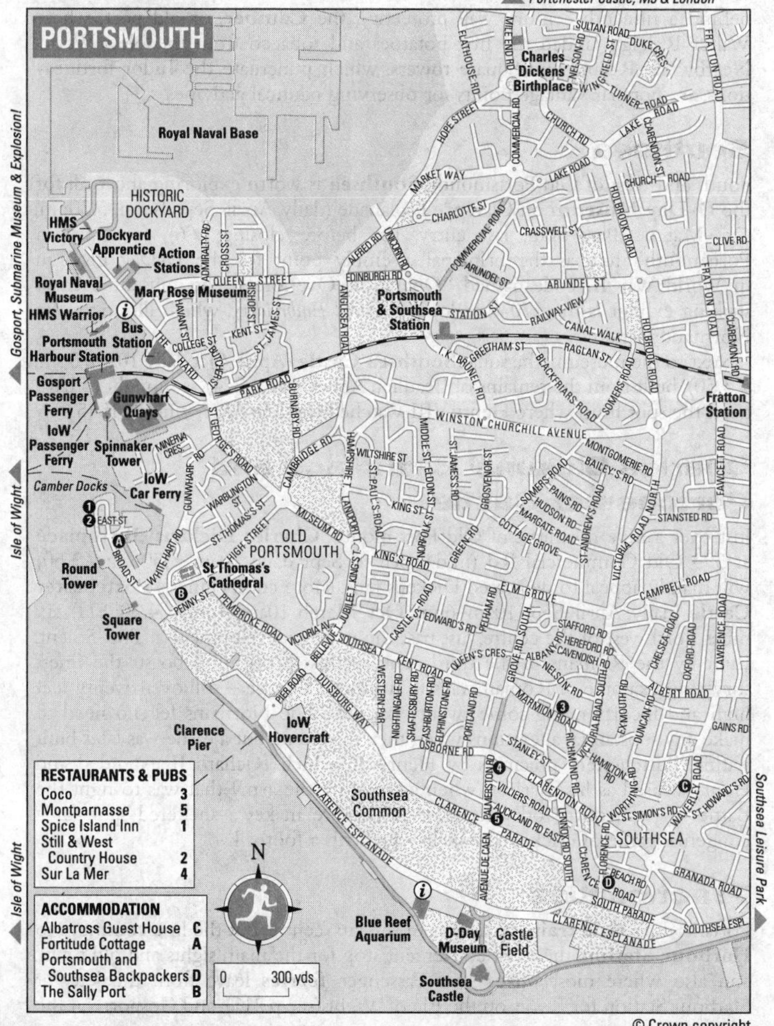

The waterfront and Old Portsmouth

Back at the Portsmouth's Harbour train station, it's a short walk along the historic waterfront to the sleek **Gunwharf Quays** development, which hosts a myriad of cafés, restaurants, nightspots and retail outlets. It's also home to the **Spinnaker Tower** (Mon–Fri & Sun 10am–5/6pm, Sat 10am–10pm; Aug daily 10am–10pm; £6.20). The elegant, sail-like structure rises 170m above the city, offering stunning vistas for up to twenty miles over land and sea. The two viewing decks can be reached by either a high-speed lift or a slower glass lift (£2).

It's a well-signposted fifteen-minute walk south of the tower to what remains of **Old Portsmouth**. Along the way, you pass the simple **Cathedral of St Thomas** on the High Street, whose original twelfth-century features have been obscured by rebuilding after the Civil War and again in the twentieth century. The High Street ends at a maze of cobbled Georgian streets huddling behind a fifteenth-century wall protecting the **Camber**, or old port, where Walter Raleigh landed the first potatoes and tobacco from the New World. Nearby, the Round and Square towers, which punctuate the Tudor fortifications, are popular vantage points for observing nautical activities.

Southsea

South and west of Old Portsmouth, **Southsea** is worth exploring above all for the **D-Day Museum** on Clarence Esplanade (daily: April–Sept 10am–5.30pm; Oct–March 10am–5pm; last entry 1hr before closing; £6), focusing on Portsmouth's role as the principal assembly point for the D-Day invasion in World War II, code-named "Operation Overlord". The museum's most striking exhibit is the 270-foot-long *Overlord Embroidery*, which illustrates the Normandy landings.

Next to the museum, the squat **Southsea Castle** (April–Oct daily 10am–5pm; £3.50), built from the remains of Beaulieu Abbey (see p.224), is thought to have been the spot from where Henry VIII watched the *Mary Rose* sink in 1545.

Charles Dickens' Birthplace and Portchester Castle

Just over a mile northeast of Old Portsmouth, **Charles Dickens' Birthplace** at 393 Old Commercial Rd (mid-April to Sept daily 10am–5.30pm; £3.50) will mainly appeal to dedicated Dickens fans. More compelling is **Portchester Castle** (daily: April–Sept 10am–6pm; Oct–March 10am–4pm; £4.20; EH), six miles northwest of the centre, just past the marina development at Port Solent. Built by the Romans in the third century this fortification boasts the finest surviving example of Roman walls in northern Europe – still over twenty feet high and incorporating some twenty bastions. The Normans felt no need to make any substantial alterations when they moved in, but a castle was later built within Portchester's precincts by Henry II, which Richard II extended and Henry V used as his garrison when assembling the army that was to fight the Battle of Agincourt. Today its grassy enclosure makes a sheltered spot for a congenial game of cricket or a kickabout with a football.

Practicalities

Portsmouth's main **train station** is in the city centre, but the line continues to **Harbour Station**, the most convenient stop for the main sights and old town, and also where most **buses** stop. Passenger **ferries** leave from the jetty at Harbour Station for Ryde, on the Isle of Wight (see p.215), and Gosport, on the other side of Portsmouth Harbour. Wightlink car ferries depart from the ferry port off Gunwharf Road for Fishbourne on the Isle of Wight (see p.214). There are two **tourist offices** in Portsmouth, one on The Hard, the other on Southsea's seafront, next to the Blue Reef Aquarium (both daily 9.30am–5.15/5.45pm; ⓣ023/9282 6722, ⓦwww.visitportsmouth.co.uk).

The main concentration of **hotels and B&Bs** is south of the centre in Southsea, where you'll find the *Albatross Guesthouse*, 51 Waverley Rd (ⓣ023/9282 8325, ⓦwww.albatrossguesthouse.co.uk; no credit cards; ❷), dating from the 1860s and with nautically themed rooms. In Old Portsmouth, *Fortitude Cottage* overlooks the quayside at 51 Broad St (ⓣ023/9282 3748, ⓦwww.fortitudecottage.co.uk; ❹). There's an independent **hostel**, *Portsmouth and Southsea Backpackers*, at 4 Florence Rd, Southsea (ⓣ023/9283 2495, ⓦwww.portsmouthbackpackers.co.uk; £12), with full facilities and some doubles (❶). **Campers** should head to *Southsea Leisure Park*, Melville Rd, Southsea (ⓣ023/9273 5070, ⓦwww.southsealeisurepark.com) – bus #15 or #16A from the Harbour station.

Places to eat are surprisingly scarce in the old town, though you'll find good food at the adjacent waterside hostelries in Bath Square, the *Spice Island Inn* and the *Still & West Country House*. In Southsea, try *Sur La Mer*, 69 Palmerston Rd (ⓣ023/9287 6678; closed Sun), serving inexpensive French and seafood dishes, or *Coco*, 59 Marmion Rd (ⓣ023/9281 9647; closed Sun), a patisserie that also serves full lunches and, on Friday and Saturday, tasty evening meals (closed Sun).

Southampton

A glance at the map gives some idea of the strategic maritime importance of **SOUTHAMPTON**, which stands on a triangular peninsula formed at the place where the rivers Itchen and Test flow into Southampton Water, an eight-mile inlet from the Solent. Sure enough, Southampton has figured in numerous stirring events: it witnessed the exodus of Henry V's Agincourt-bound army, the Pilgrim Fathers' departure in the *Mayflower* in 1620 and the maiden voyages of such ships as the *Queen Mary* and the *Titanic*. Unfortunately, since its pummelling by the Luftwaffe and some disastrous postwar planning, the thousand-year-old city is now a sprawling conurbation, with little to justify more than a fleeting visit.

Core of the modern town is the **Civic Centre**, a short walk east of the train station and home to an excellent **art gallery** that's particularly strong on twentieth-century British artists such as Sutherland, Piper and Spencer (Tues–Sat 10am–5pm, Sun 1–4pm; free). The **Western Esplanade**, curving southward from the station, runs alongside the best remaining bits of the old city **walls**. Rebuilt after a French attack in 1338, they incorporate **God's House Tower**, at the southern end of the old town in Winkle Street, where there's a **Museum of Archeology** (Tues–Fri 10am–4pm, Sat 10am–1pm & 2–4pm, Sun 1–4pm; free).

Best preserved of the city's seven gates is **Bargate**, at the opposite end of the old town, at the head of the High Street; it's an elaborate structure, cluttered with lions, classical figures and defensive apertures. By the seafront, the **Wool House**, a fine fourteenth-century stone warehouse formerly used as a jail for Napoleonic prisoners, now holds a **Maritime Museum** (same hours as Museum of Archeology; £2), recounting the heyday of the ocean liners.

Practicalities

Southampton's central **train station** is in Blechynden Terrace, west of the Civic Centre; the **bus** and **coach stations** are immediately south and north of the Civic Centre. The **tourist office** is at 9 Civic Centre Rd (Mon–Sat 9.30am–5pm, Sun 10am–3.30pm; ⓣ023/8083 3333, ⓦwww.visit-southampton.co.uk).

Accommodation options include two, four-hundred-year-old hotels, both halfway down the High Street: the *Star* (ⓣ023/8033 9939, ⓦwww.thestarhotel.com; ❺) and the *Dolphin* (ⓣ023/8033 9955, ⓦwww.thedolphin.co.uk; ❼). Alternatively, there's *Alcantara House,* 20 Howard Rd (ⓣ02380/332966, ⓦwww.alcantaraguesthouse.co.uk; ❹), a B&B a mile north of the train station off Shirley Road, with bright, en-suite rooms.

Oxford Street, off Bernard Street from the High Street, has a cluster of **eating** places including *The Olive Tree* at no. 29 (ⓣ023/8034 3333), which serves moderately priced Mediterranean dishes and brunches at weekends. As for **pubs**, try the tiny old *Platform Tavern* in Winkle Street, at the south end of the High Street, or the twelfth-century *Red Lion*, complete with minstrels' gallery at 55 High St.

The Isle of Wight

The lozenge-shaped **ISLE OF WIGHT** is shaking off its image as a tidy and unadventurous adjunct of rural southern England and instead attracting a younger, livelier crowd, with a couple of major annual rock festivals and a scattering of fashionable hotels. Despite measuring less than 23 miles at its widest point, the island packs in a surprising variety of landscapes and coastal scenery. Its beaches have long attracted holiday-makers, and the island was a favourite of such eminent Victorians as Tennyson, Dickens, Swinburne, Julia Margaret Cameron and Queen Victoria herself, who made **Osborne House**, near Cowes, her permanent home after Albert died.

Sea routes to the Isle of Wight

Hovertravel ⓣ023/9281 1000 or 01983/811000, ⓦwww.hovertravel.co.uk. Year-round hovercraft service from **Southsea to Ryde** for foot passengers only: from 7.10am (8.45am Sat, 9.15am Sun) until 8.10pm (or 8.45pm late July to Aug); every 30min; 10min; £14.40.

Red Funnel ⓣ0870/444 8898, ⓦwww.redfunnel.co.uk. Year-round ferries on two routes: **Southampton–East Cowes** hourly (every 2hr at night); 55min; £12.40 for foot passengers; £54 for car, driver and up to three passengers; **Southampton–West Cowes** high-speed foot-passenger service from 5.45am (6.45am Sat & Sun, but first sailing at 6.15am Sat Easter to early Oct) until 10.45pm (last sailing at 11.45pm Thurs–Sat & daily Easter–Aug); 1–2 hourly; 25min; £17.90.

Wightlink Ferries ⓣ0870/582 0202, ⓦwww.wightlink.co.uk. Three routes: **Portsmouth–Ryde** year-round high-speed catamaran for foot passengers only; 1–2 hourly; 20min; £17; **Portsmouth–Fishbourne** year-round ferry runs once or twice hourly; 40min; £14 for foot passengers; about £130 for car and driver, plus £14 per passenger; **Lymington–Yarmouth** ferry (Easter–Dec) 4am–midnight; 2 hourly; 30min; same fares as Portsmouth–Fishbourne ferry.

All the prices quoted are for a ninety-day (Wightlink and Red Funnel) or one-year (Hovertravel) standard return ticket in high season. Wightlink and Red Funnel offer cheaper day-returns as well as a range of discounted short-break deals for vehicles. Online booking and off-peak sailings are also cheaper.

Information and getting around

There are **tourist offices** in Ryde, Sandown, Shanklin, Yarmouth, Ventnor Cowes and Newport, open more or less the same hours: Mon–Sat 9.30/10am–4.30/5pm, Sun 10am–3.30pm; ⓣ01983/813813 (may close an hour earlier and Sun in winter). All share the same telephone number, ⓣ01983/813813, and website, ⓦwww.islandbreaks.co.uk.

For information on local **buses** (ⓣ0871/200 2233, ⓦwww.islandbuses.info), pick up a route map and timetable from any tourist or ferry office or the bus station. A Rover Ticket gives unlimited travel on the whole network, costing £10 for one day or £15 for two days, while the Freedom Pass is valid for seven days, costing £20 (tickets available on board any bus, from a bus station or travel shop). You might also make use of the useful east-coast **train** line linking Ryde, Brading, Sandown and Shanklin.

Cycling is a popular way of getting around the Isle of Wight, though in summer the island's narrow lanes can get very busy. For bike **rental**, contact Wight Offroad (ⓣ01983/408587 or 07976/740736, ⓦwww.wightoffroad.co.uk), which, with a day's notice, can deliver and collect bikes anywhere on the island (£10 per half-day, £16 per day, discounts for longer rents), and also organizes guided rides.

Ryde and around

As a major ferry terminal, **RYDE** is the first landfall many visitors make on the island, but one where few choose to linger, despite some grand nineteenth-century architecture and decent beach amusements. The **tourist office** (see above for details), **bus station**, **Hovercraft terminal** and **Esplanade train station** (the northern terminus of the Island Line train line) are all located near the base of the pier.

Accommodation is available right in the town centre at *Yelf's Hotel* on Union Street (ⓣ01983/564062, ⓦwww.yelfshotel.com; ❺), one of Ryde's oldest hotels, or try the less expensive *Trentham Guesthouse*, 38 The Strand (ⓣ01983/563418, ⓦwww.trentham-guesthouse.co.uk; no credit cards; ❶), just south of the Esplanade. Union Street offers the best **eating** opportunities, with *Room 4*, at no. 30, good for light snacks, while *Kasbah* at no. 76 offers a more exotic ambience for its tapas and daily specials.

Two miles west of Ryde, outside the village of Binstead, one of the island's earliest Christian relics, **Quarr Abbey**, was founded in 1132 by Richard de Redvers as one of the first Cistercian monasteries in Britain; its name was derived from the quarries nearby, where stone was mined for use in the construction of Winchester and Chichester cathedrals. Only stunted ruins survived the Dissolution and ensuing plunder of ready-cut stone, although an ivy-clad archway still hangs picturesquely over a farm track. In 1907 a new abbey was founded just west of the ruins, a striking rose-brick building with Byzantine overtones (daily 9am–9pm).

Just south of the ancient village of **Brading**, on the busy Ryde to Sandown A3055 (bus #2 or #3), the remains of **Brading Roman Villa** lie on Morton Old Road (daily 9.30am–5pm; £4.25), and are renowned for the superbly preserved mosaics, including intact images of Medusa and depictions of Orpheus. It's one of two such villas on the island, both of which were probably sites of bacchanalian worship.

Sandown and Shanklin

The two eastern resorts of Sandown and Shanklin merge into each other across the sandy reach of Sandown Bay, representing the island's holiday-making epicentre. **SANDOWN**, a traditional 1960s bucket-and-spade resort, appropriately possesses the island's only surviving pleasure **pier**, bedecked with various traditional amusements and a large theatre with nightly entertainment in season. At the northern end of the Esplanade, the **Isle of Wight Zoo** (daily: mid-Feb to March & Oct 10am–4pm; April–Sept 10am–6pm; Nov Sat & Sun 10am–4pm, weather permitting; ⓣ01983/403883; £5.95) contains several species of tigers, panthers and other big cats, as well as some frisky lemurs and an exhaustive selection of spiders and snakes.

SHANKLIN, with its auburn cliffs, Old Village and scenic Chine, has a marginally more sophisticated aura than its northern neighbour. The rose-clad, thatched **Old Village** may be syrupy, but the adjacent **Shanklin Chine** (daily: April to late May & mid-Sept to Oct 10am–5pm; late May to mid-Sept 10am–10pm; £3.75), a twisting pathway descending a mossy ravine and decorated on summer nights with fairy lights, is undeniably picturesque; local resident John Keats once drew inspiration from the environs.

Sandown's **tourist office** is located at 8 High St, while Shanklin's is at 67 High St (see p.215 for details). Both towns have Island Line train stations about half a mile inland from their beachfront centres. For **accommodation in Shanklin**, try *Pink Beach*, 20 Esplanade (ⓣ01983/862501, ⓦwww.pink-beach-hotel.co.uk; ④), a Victorian hotel just a stone's throw from the beach, or *Ryedale*, 3 Atherley Rd (ⓣ01983/862375, ⓦwww.ryedale-hotel.co.uk; ③), a family-run B&B just steps from the train station, also near the beach. In **Sandown**, try *The Montpelier*, Pier Street (ⓣ01983/403964, ⓦwww.themontpelier.co.uk), with some rooms overlooking the beach and pier.

As for **meals and refreshment**, Sandown's *Fat Harry's*, 53 High St, offers superior fish and chips as well as pies, burgers and vegetarian dishes, while on Shanklin's Appley Beach, at the southern end of the Esplanade, try the *Fisherman's Cottage*, an atmospheric seafaring pub serving wholesome food (no credit cards; closed Nov–Feb).

Ventnor and around

The seaside resort of **VENTNOR** and its two village suburbs of **Bonchurch** and **St Lawrence** sit at the foot of St Boniface Down, the island's highest point at 787ft. The Down periodically disintegrates into landslides, creating the jumbled terraces known locally as the **Undercliff**, whose sheltered, south-facing aspect, mild winter temperatures and thick carpet of undergrowth have contributed to the former fishing village becoming a fashionable health spa. Thanks to these unique factors, the town possesses rather more character than the island's other resorts, its Gothic Revival buildings clinging dizzily to zigzagging bends.

The floral terraces of the Cascade curve down to the slender Esplanade and narrow beach, where former boat-builders' cottages now provide more recreational services. From the Esplanade, it's a pleasant mile-long stroll to Ventnor's **Botanical Gardens**.

Ventnor's **tourist office** is at 34 High St (see p.215 for details). For **accommodation**, try the *Spyglass Inn* on Ventnor's Esplanade (ⓣ01983/855338; ④), which has a few self-contained rooms with balconies and also serves good pub grub. Better choices are in Bonchurch, however, where *Horseshoebay House*, Horseshoe Bay, has sea views from all rooms right on the beach (ⓣ01983/856800, ⓦwww.horseshoebayhouse.co.uk; ④). It also has a nice **café** with outdoor tables (closed Nov–Easter), though for a quality **meal** you can't beat the *Pond Café*, Bonchurch Village Rd (Ⓣ01983/855666; closed Mon), a stylish restaurant in a picturesque spot.

St Catherine's Point and the southwest coast

The western Undercliff begins to recede at the village of Niton, where a footpath continues to the most southerly tip of the island, **St Catherine's Point**, marked by a modern lighthouse. A prominent landmark on the downs behind is **St Catherine's Oratory**, known locally as the "Pepper Pot", and originally a lighthouse, reputedly built in 1325.

Seven miles northwest along the coast, Military Road ascends the flank of Compton Down before descending into Freshwater Bay. If you're walking this way, you might stop off at the National Trust-owned **Compton Bay**, a splendid spot for a swim or a picnic, frequented by local surfers and accessed by a steep path leading down from the dark red cliffs.

Yarmouth and the western tip

Linked to Lymington in the New Forest by car ferry, the pleasant town of **YARMOUTH**, on the northern coast of the Isle of Wight, is the best base for exploring the western tip of the island. Although razed by the French in 1377, the port prospered after **Yarmouth Castle** (Easter–Sept Mon–Thurs & Sun 11am–4pm; £3.50; EH), tucked between the quay and the pier, was commissioned by Henry VIII. The top attractions hereabouts, however, lie four miles west of Yarmouth, around the isle's westernmost point, reachable in summer on a half-hourly **open-top bus**: from the multichrome cliffs at **Alum Bay**, a chair lift (£4 return) runs down to ochre-hued sands, which were used as pigments for painting local landscapes in the Victorian era. From here, it's a twenty-minute walk to the lookout on top of the three tall chalk stacks known as **The Needles**, best seen from a boat trip leaving from Alum Bay (April–Oct; Needles Pleasure Cruises; Ⓣ01983/761587; £4).

Between the Needles and Freshwater Bay, the breezy four-mile ridge of **Tennyson Down** is one of the island's most satisfying walks, with vistas onto rolling downs and vales. There's a monument here to the poet and local resident after whom it's named. On the coastal road at Freshwater Bay, **Dimbola Lodge** (Tues–Sun: Feb–Oct 10am–5pm, daily during school summer hols; Nov–Jan 10am–4pm; £4) was the home of pioneer photographer Julia Margaret Cameron, who settled here after visiting Tennyson in 1860. The building now houses a gallery of her work and changing exhibitions, as well as a bookshop and tearoom/restaurant.

Yarmouth's **tourist office** is just back from the harbour (see p.215 for details). Affordable **accommodation** in town includes *Harvey's* in St James's Square (Ⓣ01983/760738, Ⓦwww.harveysbandb.co.uk; ❷), offering contemporary rooms, varied breakfasts (Ⓣ01983/760513; closed Nov–Easter; ❸), and bike hire. If you're flush, you can't do better than the seventeenth-century *George*, right by the ferry dock on Quay Street (Ⓣ01983/760331, Ⓦwww.thegeorge.co.uk; ❽), with elegantly furnished rooms: Charles II was once a guest here. There's a YHA **hostel** a short walk northeast from the Needles, at Totland Bay (Ⓣ0870/770 6070, Ⓔtotland@yha.org.uk; closed Nov–Jan; dorms from £16.50).

The George is the place to **eat** well, with a pleasant panelled bar, and a separate restaurant serving (expensive) seafood meals.

Cowes and around

COWES, at the island's northern tip, is inextricably associated with sailing craft and boat building: Henry VIII installed a castle here to defend the Solent's expanding naval dockyards from the French and Spanish, and in the 1950s the world's first hovercraft made its test runs here. In 1820 the Prince Regent's patronage of the yacht club gave the port its cachet with the Royal Yacht Squadron, now one of the world's most exclusive sailing clubs. The first week of August sees the international yachting festival known as **Cowes Week** (Ⓦwww.skandiacowesweek.co.uk), where serious sailors mingle with visiting royalty. There are dozens of organized events, including a spectacular fireworks display on the Friday night, and a great party atmosphere. In addition to Cowes Week, most summer weekends see some form of nautical event taking place in or around town.

The town is bisected by the River Medina, with West Cowes being the older, more interesting half, and holding the **tourist office** at the Arcade, Fountain Quay (see p.215 for details; extended hours during Cowes Week). At the bottom of the meandering High Street, **boat trips** around the harbour and the Solent leave from Thetis Wharf, near the Parade (Ⓣ01983/564602, Ⓦwww.solentcruises.co.uk). The more industrial East Cowes, where you'll find Osborne House, is connected to West Cowes by a "floating bridge", or chain ferry (pedestrians free, cars £1.40).

Accommodation options in West Cowes include the *Union Inn* in Watch House Lane, off High Street (Ⓣ01983/293163; ⑤), and *Halcyone Villa*, Grove Road, up Mill Hill Road from the east end of the High Street (Ⓣ01983/291334, Ⓔsandraonwight@btinternet.com; no credit cards; ③). In East Cowes, try the *Crossways House Hotel* (Ⓣ01983/298282, Ⓦwww.bedbreakfast-cowes.co.uk; ④), opposite Osborne House on Crossways Road, with four-poster beds and a

▲ Sailing during Cowes Week

garden. Prices rise steeply during Cowes Week, when most places are booked up well in advance.

For a quick bite to **eat** you can't beat the *Octopus's Garden*, 63 High St, a café/bistro filled with Beatles memorabilia (daytime only). Traditional **pub** meals are served at the *Union Inn* as well as the *Anchor* on the High Street, which has a garden and live music (Wed, Fri & Sat).

Osborne House

The only place of interest in East Cowes is Queen Victoria's family home, **Osborne House** (Easter–Sept daily 10am–6pm; Oct daily 10am–4pm; Nov–Easter Wed–Sun 10am–4pm; pre-booked tours only ☎01983/200022; house and grounds £10, grounds only £6; EH), signposted one mile southeast of town (bus #4 from Ryde or #5 from Newport, or either from East Cowes). The house was built in the late 1840s by Prince Albert and Thomas Cubitt as an Italianate villa, with balconies and large terraces overlooking the landscaped gardens towards the Solent. The state rooms, used for entertaining visiting dignitaries, exude an expected formality, while the private apartments feel more homely, like the affluent family holiday residence that Osborne was. Following Albert's death, the desolate Victoria spent much of her time here, and it's where she eventually died in 1901. Since then, according to her wishes, the house has remained virtually unaltered, allowing an unexpectedly intimate glimpse into Victoria's family life.

Newport and Carisbrooke Castle

NEWPORT, the capital of the Isle of Wight, sits at the centre of the island at a point where the River Medina's commercial navigability ends. The town isn't particularly engaging, though is worth a visit for the hilltop fortress of **Carisbrooke Castle** (daily: Easter–Sept 10am–5pm; Oct–Easter 10am–4pm; £6.50; EH), on the southwest outskirts (bus #6, #7 or #11 from Newport). This austere Norman keep's most famous visitor was Charles I, detained here (and caught one night ignominiously jammed between his room's bars while attempting escape) prior to his execution in London. The **museum** in the centre of the castle features many relics from his incarceration, as well as those of the last royal resident, Princess Beatrice, Queen Victoria's youngest daughter. The castle's other notable curiosity is the sixteenth-century well-house, where donkeys still trudge inside a huge treadmill to raise a barrel 160ft up the well shaft.

Newport's **tourist office** is in the centre of town at the Guildhall, High Street (see p.215, for details).

Winchester

Nowadays a tranquil, handsome market town, **WINCHESTER** was once one of the mightiest settlements in England. Under the Romans it was Venta Belgarum, the fifth largest town in Britain, but it was **Alfred the Great** who really put Winchester on the map when he made it the capital of his Wessex kingdom in the ninth century. For the next couple of centuries Winchester ranked alongside London, its status affirmed by William the Conqueror's coronation in both cities and by his commissioning of the local monks to prepare the **Domesday Book**. It wasn't until after the Battle of Naseby in 1645, when Cromwell took the city, that Winchester began its decline into provinciality.

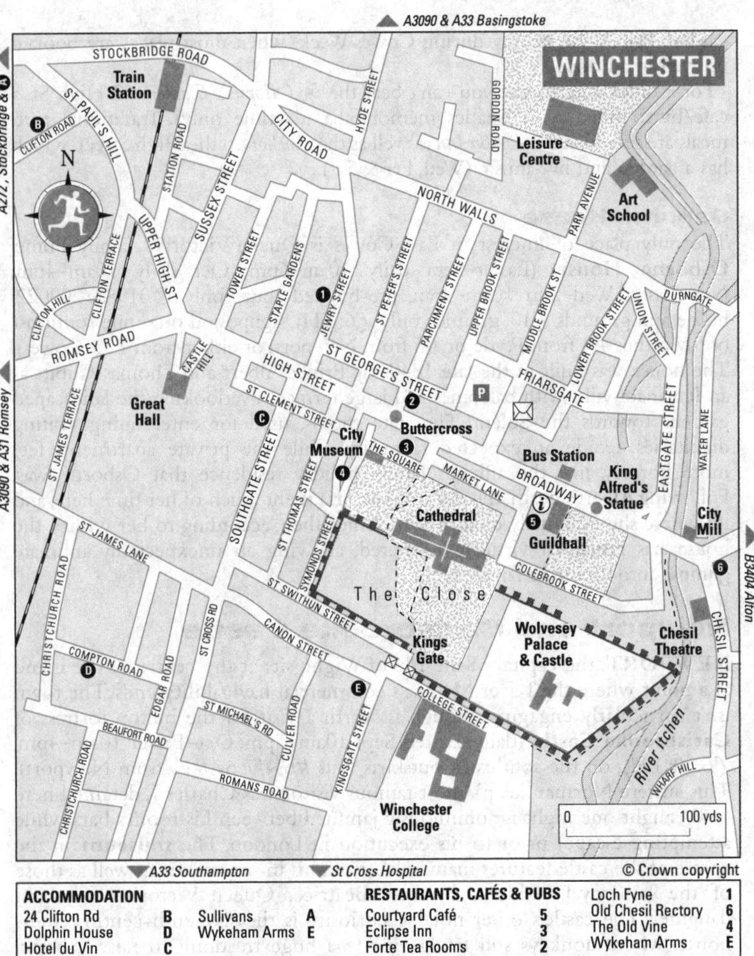

Hampshire's county town now has a scholarly and slightly anachronistic air, embodied by the ancient almshouses that still provide shelter for senior citizens of "noble poverty" – the pensioners can be seen wandering round the town in medieval black or mulberry-coloured gowns with silver badges.

The City

The first minster to be built in Winchester was raised by Cenwalh, the Saxon king of Wessex in the mid-seventh century, and traces of this building have been unearthed near the present **cathedral** (Mon–Sat 8.30am–6pm, Sun 8.30am–5.30pm; £5 donation requested), which was begun in 1079 and completed some three hundred years later. The exterior is not its best feature – squat and massive, the cathedral crouches stumpily over the tidy lawns of the Cathedral Close. The interior is rich and complex, however, and its 556-foot **nave** makes this Europe's longest medieval church. Outstanding features include its carved Norman font of black Tournai marble, the fourteenth-century misericords (the choir stalls are the oldest complete set in the country) and some amazing monuments – **William of Wykeham's Chantry**, halfway down the nave on the right, is one of the best. Jane Austen, who died in Winchester, is commemorated close to the font by a memorial brass and slab beneath which she's interred, though she's recorded simply as the daughter of a local clergyman. Above the high altar lie the mortuary chests of pre-Conquest kings, including Canute (though the bones were mixed up after Cromwell's Roundheads broke up the chests in 1645); William Rufus, killed while hunting in the New Forest in 1100, lies in the presbytery. Behind the impressive Victorian screen at the end of the presbytery, look out for the memorial shrine to St Swithun. Originally buried outside in the churchyard, his remains were later interred inside the cathedral where the "rain of heaven" could no longer fall on him, whereupon he took revenge and the heavens opened for forty days – hence the legend that if it rains on St Swithun's Day (July 15) it will continue for another forty. His exact burial place is unknown. Accessible from the north transept, the Norman **crypt** is only rarely open, since it's flooded for much of the time – the cathedral's original foundations were dug in marshy ground, and at the beginning of last century a steadfast diver, William Walker, spent five years replacing the rotten timber foundations with concrete.

Outside the cathedral, the **City Museum**, a basic local history display, sits on the Square (April–Oct Mon–Sat 10am–5pm, Sun noon–5pm; Nov–March Tues–Sat 10am–4pm, Sun noon–4pm; free). Walk west along the High Street from here to reach the **Great Hall** on Castle Street (daily 10am–4/5pm; free), the vestigial remains of a thirteenth-century castle destroyed by Cromwell. Sir Walter Raleigh heard his death sentence here in 1603, though he wasn't finally dispatched until 1618, and Judge Jeffreys held one of his Bloody Assizes (see p.232) in the castle after Monmouth's rebellion in 1685. The main interest now is a large, brightly painted disc slung on one wall like some curious antique dartboard. This is alleged to be King Arthur's Round Table, but the woodwork is probably fourteenth-century, later repainted as a PR exercise for the Tudor dynasty – the portrait of Arthur at the top of the table bears an uncanny resemblance to Henry VIII.

Head east along the High Street, past the Guildhall and the august bronze statue of King Alfred on the Broadway, to reach the River Itchen and the eighteenth-century **City Mill** (March, mid-April to June & mid-Sept to late Oct Wed–Sun 11am–5pm; early April, July to early Sept & late Oct daily 11am–5pm; Nov Wed–Sun 11am–4.30pm; Dec daily 11am–4.30pm; £3.40; NT), where you can see restored mill machinery. Turning right before the bridge you pass what remains of the Saxon walls, which bracket the ruins of the twelfth-century **Wolvesey Castle** (early April to Sept daily 10am–5pm; free; EH) and the Bishop's Palace, built by Christopher Wren. Immediately to the west up College Street stand the buildings of **Winchester College**, the oldest public school in England – established in 1382 by William of Wykeham for "poor scholars", it now educates few but the wealthy and privileged. The cloisters and chantry are open during term time and the chapel is open all year. Jane Austen moved to the house at 8 College St from Chawton in 1817, when she was already ill with Addison's Disease, dying there later the same year. The thirteenth-century **Kings Gate**, at the top of College Street, is one of the city's original medieval gateways, housing the tiny St Swithun's Church.

About a mile south of College Walk, reached by a pleasant stroll across the watermeadows of the Itchen, lies **St Cross Hospital** (April–Oct Mon–Sat

9.30am–5pm, Sun 1–5pm; Nov–March Mon–Sat 10.30am–3.30pm; £2.50). Founded in 1136 as a hostel for poor brethren, it boasts a fine church, begun in that year and completed a century or so later, where you can see a triptych by the Flemish painter Mabuse. Needy wayfarers may still apply for the "dole" at the Porter's Lodge – a tiny portion of bread and beer.

Practicalities

Winchester **train station** is about a mile northwest of the cathedral on Stockbridge Road. If you arrive by **bus**, you'll find yourself on the Broadway, conveniently opposite the **tourist office** in the imposing Guildhall (May–Sept Mon–Sat 9.30am–5.30pm, Sun 11am–4pm; Oct–April Mon–Sat 10am–5pm; ⓣ01962/840500, ⓦwww.visitwinchester.co.uk).

Good **accommodation** options include the B&Bs at 24 Clifton Rd (ⓣ01962/851620, ⓔa.williams1997@btinternet.com; ❷) and *Sullivans*, 29 Stockbridge Rd (ⓣ01962/862027, ⓔsullivans_bandb@hotmail.com; ❷), both convenient for the train station, while *Dolphin House*, 3 Compton Rd (ⓣ01962/853284, ⓦwww.dolphinhousestudios.co.uk; ❸), has two spacious en-suite rooms. None of the above takes credit cards. For character, however, it's hard to beat the *Wykeham Arms*, 75 Kingsgate St (ⓣ01962/853834, ⓔwykehamarms@fullers.co.uk; ❻), an antique inn with beamed, quirkily shaped rooms, or the designer-chic *Hotel du Vin*, Southgate Street (ⓣ01962/841414, ⓦwww.hotelduvin.com; ❼), a converted Georgian townhouse with a champagne bar, bistro and walled garden.

You can have daytime **snacks** and full **meals** at the relaxed *Courtyard Café*, behind the Guildhall and tourist office, or the animated *Forte Tea Rooms*, 78 Parchment St (closed Sun), which also serves evening meals Thurs–Sat. For gourmet English cuisine, there's the *Old Chesil Rectory*, 1 Chesil St (ⓣ01962/851555; closed Sun, Mon & daytime Tues), with set-price menus (£23 for lunch, £49 for supper), while *Loch Fyne*, 18 Jewry St (ⓣ01962/872930), a converted jailhouse, offers scrumptious breakfasts and quality seafood meals. The richly atmospheric *Wykeham Arms* (see above) also has first-class food and is the best place for a drink. Other good **pubs** include the sixteenth-century *Eclipse Inn*, 25 The Square, which has some outdoor seating, and, close by, *The Old Vine*, 8 Great Minster St, with oak beams, a log fire in winter and a patio in summer; both also serve food.

The Watercress Line and Chawton

ALRESFORD, six miles east of Winchester, is the departure-point for the **Mid-Hants Watercress Line** (March, April, Oct & Dec Sat & Sun; May–Sept & school hols daily; ⓣ01962/733810, ⓦwww.watercressline.co.uk; £10), a steam-powered train so named because it passes through the former watercress beds that once flourished here. The train chuffs ten miles to Alton, with gourmet dinners on Saturday evenings and traditional Sunday lunches served on board.

A mile southwest of Alton lies the village of **CHAWTON**, where Jane Austen lived from 1809 to 1817, during the last and most prolific years of her life, and where she wrote or revised almost all of her six books, including *Sense and Sensibility* and *Pride and Prejudice*. **Jane Austen's House** (daily 10.30am–4.30/5pm; Jan & Feb Sat & Sun only; £5), in the centre of the village, is a plain red-brick building, containing first editions of some of her greatest works.

The New Forest

Covering about 220 square miles, the **NEW FOREST** is one of southern England's favourite rural playgrounds, attracting some 13.5 million day-visits annually. The forest was requisitioned by William the Conqueror in 1079 as a game reserve, and the rights of its inhabitants soon became subservient to those of his precious deer. Fences to impede their progress were forbidden and terrible punishments were meted out to those who disturbed the animals – hands were lopped off, eyes put out. Later monarchs less passionate about hunting than the Normans gradually restored the forest-dwellers' rights, and today the New Forest enjoys a unique patchwork of ancient laws and privileges alongside the regulations applying to its National Park status.

The **trees** of the forest are now much more varied than they were in pre-Norman times, with birch, holly, yew, Scots pine and other conifers interspersed with the ancient oaks and beeches. One of the most venerable trees is the much-visited **Knightwood Oak**, just a few hundred yards north of the A35 three miles southwest of Lyndhurst, which measures about 22ft in circumference at shoulder height. The most conspicuous species of New Forest **fauna** is the New Forest **pony** – you'll see them grazing nonchalantly by the roadsides and ambling through some villages. The local deer are less visible now that some of the faster roads are fenced, although several species still roam the woods, including the tiny **sika deer**, descendants of a pair that escaped from nearby Beaulieu in 1904.

To get the best from the region, you need to **walk** or **ride** through it, avoiding the places cars can reach. There are 150 miles of car-free gravel roads in the forest, making **cycling** an appealing prospect – pick up a book of route maps from tourist offices or bike rental shops. The Ordnance Survey *Leisure Map 22* of the New Forest is best for exploring, and in Lyndhurst you'll find numerous specialist walking books and natural history guides.

Lyndhurst and nearby **Brockenhurst**, both on train lines, have bus connections to most parts of the forest, and both have plenty of reasonably priced accommodation. **Campsites** in the forest include nine run by the Forestry Commission (Ⓣ0845/130 8224, Ⓦwww.forest-holidays.com), and there's a YHA **hostel** in Cottesmore House, Cott Lane, Burley, in the west of the Forest (Ⓣ0870/770 5734, Ⓔburley@yha.org.uk; closed Nov–March; from £18), where tents and tipis can be rented.

Lyndhurst and Brockenhurst

LYNDHURST, its town centre skewered by an agonizing one-way system, isn't a particularly interesting place, though the brick **parish church** is worth a glance for its William Morris glass and the grave of Mrs Reginald Hargreaves, better known as Alice Liddell, Lewis Carroll's model for Alice. The town is of most interest to visitors for the **New Forest Museum and Visitor Centre** in the central car park off the High Street (daily 10am–5pm; Ⓣ023/8028 2269, Ⓦwww.thenewforest.co.uk), and the adjoining **museum** (£3), which focuses on the history, wildlife and industries of the forest. Nearby in Gosport Lane, AA Bike Hire (Ⓣ023/8028 3349) rents **bikes**.

For **accommodation** try *Forest Cottage*, at the west end of the High Street (Ⓣ023/8028 3461, Ⓦwww.forestcottage.co.uk; ③), with a well-stocked natural history library, or *Burwood Lodge*, 27 Romsey Rd (Ⓣ023/8028 2445, Ⓦwww.burwoodlodge.co.uk; ④), a large old house a few minutes from the High Street – neither takes credit cards. The *Parisien* café, at 64 High St, sells **snacks** that you can eat in its small garden in summer; for larger **meals**, head for the *Crown Hotel* further up the High Street.

The forest's most visited site, the **Rufus Stone**, stands three miles northwest of Lyndhurst. Erected in 1745, it marks the putative spot where the Conqueror's son and heir, **William II** – aka William Rufus after his ruddy complexion – was killed by a crossbow bolt in 1100.

BROCKENHURST, four miles south of Lyndhurst, has **bikes for rent** at Cycle Experience, by the level-crossing (ⓣ01590/624204, ⓦwww.cyclex.co.uk). Local **accommodation** choices include the *Cottage Hotel* on Sway Road (ⓣ01590/622296, ⓦwww.cottagehotel.org; ❻), and, just north of here on Grigg Lane, the quiet *Seraya* (ⓣ01590/622426, ⓦwww.serayanewforest.co.uk; no credit cards; ❸), where two of the three neat, cottagey rooms share a bathroom. There's fine **dining** at *Simply Poussin*, The Courtyard, Brookley Rd (ⓣ01590/623063; closed Sun & Mon), and *The Snakecatcher* **pub** on Lyndhurst Road serves decent bar meals.

Beaulieu and Buckler's Hard

The village of **BEAULIEU** (pronounced "Bewley"), in the southeast corner of the New Forest, was the site of one of England's most influential monasteries, a Cistercian house founded in 1204 by King John – in remorse, it is said, for ordering a group of supplicating monks to be trampled to death. Built using stone ferried from Caen in northern France and Quarr on the Isle of Wight, the **abbey** managed a self-sufficient estate of ten thousand acres, but was dismantled soon after the Dissolution. Its refectory now forms the parish church, which, like everything else in Beaulieu, has been subsumed by the Montagu family who have owned a large chunk of the New Forest since one of Charles II's illegitimate progeny was created duke of the estate.

Beaulieu's (daily: late May to Sept 10am–6pm; Oct to late May 10am–5pm; £15.25, or £8.40 excluding Motor Museum; ⓦwww.beaulieu.co.uk) complex comprises **Palace House**, the attractive if unexceptional family home, the abbey and the main attraction, Lord Montagu's **National Motor Museum**. An under-sized monorail and an old London bus ease the ten-minute walk between the entry point and Palace House. The latter, formerly the abbey's gatehouse, contains masses of Montagu-related memorabilia while the undercroft of the adjacent abbey houses an exhibition depicting medieval monastic life. The Motor Museum's collection of 250 cars and motorcycles includes spindly antiques, James Bond vehicles and star-owned cars, as well as a quartet of svelte land-speed racers.

Buckler's Hard, a couple of miles downstream on the River Beaulieu (daily 10am–4.30/5.30pm; £5.90), has a wonderful setting. It doesn't look much like a shipyard now, but from Elizabethan times onwards dozens of men o' war were assembled here from giant New Forest oaks. Several of Nelson's ships were launched here, to be towed carefully by rowing boats past the sandbanks and across the Solent to Portsmouth. The largest house in this hamlet of shipwrights' cottages, which forms part of the Montagu estate, belonged to Henry Adams, the master builder responsible for most of the Trafalgar fleet; it's now an upmarket hotel and restaurant. At the top of the village, the **Maritime Museum** traces the history of the great ships and incorporates buildings preserved in their eighteenth-century form.

Lymington

The most pleasant point of access for the Isle of Wight (for ferry details, see p.214) is **LYMINGTON**, a sheltered haven that's become one of the busiest leisure harbours on the south coast. Rising from the quay area, the old town is full of cobbled streets and Georgian houses and has one unusual building – the partly thirteenth-century church of **St Thomas the Apostle**, with a cupola-topped tower built in 1670.

Information is available in summer from the local **visitor centre** in New Street, off the High Street (Mon–Sat 10am–4pm; ⓣ01590/689000). Places to **stay** in town include *Durlston House*, Gosport St (ⓣ01590/677364, ⓦwww.durlstonhouse.co.uk; ④), a smart and clean townhouse, and *The Angel Inn*, 108 High St (ⓣ01590/672050, ⓦwww.roomattheinn.info; ⑤), an old coaching stop with functional rooms. Among Lymington's excellent **pubs**, all of which serve decent bar meals, try *Chequers* on Ridgeway Lane, on the west side of town, the *Bosun's Chair*, Station Rd, and the harbourfront *Ship Inn*, with seats outside looking over the water.

Bournemouth and around

Renowned for its clean sandy beaches, the resort of **Bournemouth** has a single-minded holiday-making atmosphere, though neighbouring **Poole** and **Christchurch** are more interesting historically. North of this unbroken coastal sprawl, the pleasant old market town of **Wimborne** has one of the area's most striking churches, while the stately home of **Kingston Lacy** contains an outstanding collection of old masters and other paintings.

The Town

BOURNEMOUTH dates only from 1811, when a local squire, Louis Tregonwell, built a summerhouse on the wild, unpopulated heathland that once occupied this stretch of coast, and planted the first of the pine trees that now characterize the area. The mild climate, sheltered site and glorious sandy beach encouraged the rapid growth of the resort, though today Bournemouth has acquired an unshakably genteel, elderly image. However, its geriatric nursing homes are counterbalanced by burgeoning numbers of language schools and a nightclub scene fuelled by a transient youthful population.

Apart from its pristine sandy beach (one of southern England's cleanest) Bournemouth is famed for its unusually high proportion of green space – a sixth of the town is given over to horticultural displays. Its most enthralling attraction, however, is the **Russell-Cotes Art Gallery and Museum** on East Cliff Promenade (Tues–Sun 10am–5pm; free), one of the region's best collections of Victoriana. The motley assortment of artworks and Oriental souvenirs was gathered from around the world by the Russell-Cotes family, hoteliers who grew wealthy during Bournemouth's late-Victorian tourist boom. There's also a cliff-top landscaped garden, and a decent café.

In the centre of town, there's the graveyard of **St Peter's** church, just east of the Square, where Mary Shelley, author of the Gothic horror tale *Frankenstein*, is buried, together with the heart belonging to her husband, the Romantic poet Percy Bysshe Shelley. The tombs of Mary's parents – radical thinker William Godwin and early feminist Mary Wollstonecraft – are also here.

Practicalities

The **train station** and **bus station** opposite lie about a mile east of the centre, connected by frequent buses. The **tourist office** is centrally located on

Westover Road (mid-July to mid-Sept daily 9.30am–6pm; mid-Sept to mid-July Mon–Sat 10am–5/5.30pm; ⓣ0845/051 1701, ⓦwww.bournemouth.co.uk). The town has **accommodation** to suit all budgets: try *Tudor Grange*, 31 Gervis Rd, East Cliff (ⓣ01202/291472, ⓦwww.tudorgrangehotel.co.uk; ⑤), with an attractive interior and gardens, or *Earlham Lodge*, 91 Alumhurst Rd, Alum Chine (ⓣ01202/761943, ⓦwww.earlhamlodge.com; ④), a friendly guesthouse near the beach. The small *Bournemouth Backpackers*, 3 Frances Rd (ⓣ01202/299491, ⓦwww.bournemouthbackpackers.co.uk), three minutes from the train and bus stations, takes non-UK nationals only, and has dormitory accommodation (£16) and one double (①).

Centrally located on the Promenade by the pier, *West Beach* (ⓣ01202/587785) is a sleek, modern seafood **restaurant** with great views and weekly live jazz, while *Bistro on the Beach*, by the sea at the Southbourne end of the Esplanade (ⓣ01202/431473), is an informal café by day and a good-value bistro in the evening (closed Mon & Tues in winter). The *Goat and Tricycle* **pub**, 27 West Hill Rd, is worth the uphill trek for the real ales and home-made food.

The biggest and best known of Bournemouth's **nightclubs** is *Elements*, centrally located on Firvale Road (ⓣ01202/311178, ⓦwww.elements-nightclub.com), though the flamboyant *Opera House*, 570 Christchurch Rd, Boscombe, has more character.

Christchurch

CHRISTCHURCH, five miles east of Bournemouth, is best known for its colossal parish church, **Christchurch Priory** (Mon–Sat 9.30am–5pm, Sun 2.15–5.30pm; £2 donation requested), bigger than most cathedrals. Built on the site of a Saxon minster dating from 650 AD, it is reputedly the longest parish church in England, at 311ft, and its fan-vaulted North Porch is the country's biggest. Fine views can be gained from the top of the 120-foot tower (ask at desk; £2).

The area round the old town quay has a carefully preserved charm, with the **Red House Museum and Gardens** on Quay Road (Tues–Sat 10am–5pm, Sun 2–5pm; free) containing an affectionate collection of local memorabilia. **Boat trips** (Easter–Oct daily; ⓣ01202/429119) leave from the grassy banks of the riverside quay east to Mudeford (30min; £5.50 return) or upriver to the *Tuckton Tea Rooms* (15min; £2.50 return).

Christchurch's **tourist office** is at 23 High St (Mon–Fri 9.30am–5/5.30pm, Sat 9.30am–4.30/5pm; ⓣ01202/471780, ⓦwww.visitchristchurch.info). Local **accommodation** can be fairly pricey, though Barrack and Stour roads, northwest of the centre, are lined with unexciting but reliable guesthouses. Alternatively, head out to the Highcliffe area, three miles east of town on the A337, where the airy, Art Deco *Beechcroft Place*, 106 Lymington Rd (ⓣ01425/277171, ⓦwww.beachmeetsforest.co.uk; ④), offers more stylish B&B, with organic breakfasts served in private lounges. For **food**, *La Mamma*, 51 Bridge St (ⓣ01202/471608; closed Sun lunch & Mon), serves cheap and cheerful Italian classics (including pizzas), with alfresco eating in summer, while *The Boathouse* on the Quay (ⓣ01202/480033; closed eves Sun, Mon & Tues in winter) offers everything from breakfasts to full evening meals and has great views. Christchurch's oldest **pub**, *Ye Olde George Inn* at 2a Castle St, has an attractive courtyard and decent food.

Poole

West of Bournemouth, **POOLE** is an ancient seaport on a huge, almost landlocked harbour. The town developed in the thirteenth century and was successively colonized by pirates, fishermen and timber traders. The old quarter by the quayside contains over a hundred historic buildings, as well as **Poole Museum**, at the bottom of Old High Street (Easter–Oct Mon–Sat 10am–5pm, Sun noon–5pm; Nov–Easter Tues–Sat 10am–4pm, Sun noon–4pm; free), which traces Poole's development over the centuries, with displays of local ceramics and tiles and a rare Iron Age log boat.

From Poole's quay, you can catch one of the frequent ferries (£7.50 return) to **Brownsea Island** (Easter to late July & Sept daily 10am–5pm; late July to Aug daily 10am–6pm; Oct daily 10am–4pm; £4.70; NT), famed for its red squirrels, wading birds and other wildlife, which you can spot along themed trails that reveal a surprisingly diverse landscape.

One of the area's most famous gardens lies on the outskirts of Poole, **Compton Acres** (daily: March–Oct 9am–6pm; Nov–Feb 10am–4pm; last entry 1hr before closing; £6.95), signposted off the A35 Poole Road, towards Bournemouth (buses #150 and #151). Each of the seven gardens here has a different international theme, the best of which is the elegantly understated Japanese Garden.

Poole's **train station** is on Serpentine Lane and the **bus station** close by on Kingland Road, both about a fifteen-minute walk from the waterfront along the High Street. The **tourist office** is on Poole Quay (April–June, Sept & Oct daily 10am–5pm; July & Aug daily 9.15am–6pm; Nov–March Mon–Fri 10am–5pm, Sat 10am–4pm; Ⓣ01202/253253, Ⓦwww.pooletourism.com). Central **accommodation** choices include *Corkers* (Ⓣ01202/681393, Ⓦwww.corkers.co.uk; ④), a café-restaurant at the bottom of the High Street with five rooms upstairs, two with panoramic roof balconies; and the handsome old *Antelope Hotel*, 8 High St (Ⓣ01202/672029; ⑥).

Apart from *Corkers*, Poole has a good selection of **restaurants** on the High Street, including *Storm*, a moderately priced seafood bistro at no. 16 (Ⓣ01202/674970; closed Sun lunch), and, at the top of the street, *Alcatraz* (Ⓣ01202/660244), a relaxed Italian eatery with outdoor tables. Among the **pubs**, try the *King Charles* on Thames Street, with leather armchairs.

Wimborne Minster

An ancient town on the banks of the Stour, just a few minutes' drive north from the suburbs of Bournemouth, **WIMBORNE MINSTER**, as the name suggests, is mainly of interest for its great church, the **Minster of St Cuthberga** (Mon–Sat 9.30am–5.30pm, Sun 2.30–5.30pm; free). Built on the site of an eighth-century monastery, its massive twin towers of mottled grey and tawny stone dwarf the rest of the town, and at one time the church was even more imposing – its spire crashed down during morning service in 1602. What remains today is basically Norman with later features added such as the Perpendicular west tower, which bears a figure dressed as a grenadier of the Napoleonic era, who strikes every quarter-hour with a hammer. Inside, the church is crowded with memorials and eye-catching details – look out for the orrery clock inside the west tower, with the sun marking the hours and the moon marking the days of the month, and for the organ with trumpets pointing out towards the congregation instead of pipes. The **Chained Library** above the choir vestry (Easter–Oct Mon–Fri 10.30am–12.30pm & 2–4pm, Sat 10.30am–12.30pm; Nov–Easter Sat 10.30am–12.30pm; free), dating from 1686, is Wimborne's most prized possession and one of the oldest public libraries in the country.

Wimborne's older buildings stand around the main square near the minster, and are mostly from the late eighteenth or early nineteenth century. The **Priest's House** on the High Street started life as lodgings for the clergy, then became a stationer's shop. Now it is a **museum** (April–Oct 10am–4.30pm; also open two weeks after Christmas; £3), with each room furnished in the style of a different period, such as a working Victorian kitchen, a Georgian parlour and an ironmonger's shop. There's also a display of items relating to local archeology and history, while the walled garden at the rear provides an excellent spot for summer teas.

Kingston Lacy

Kingston Lacy (house Easter–Oct Wed–Sun 11am–4pm; grounds Feb to mid-March Sat & Sun 10.30am–4pm; Easter–Oct daily 10.30am–6pm or dusk; Nov to mid-Dec Fri–Sun 10.30am–4pm; house & grounds £10, grounds only £5; NT), one of the country's finest seventeenth-century country houses, lies two miles northwest of Wimborne Minster, in 250 acres of parkland grazed by a herd of Red Devon cattle. Designed for the Bankes family, who were exiled from Corfe Castle (see p.229) after the Roundheads reduced it to rubble, the brick building was clad in grey stone during the nineteenth century by Sir Charles Barry, co-architect of the Houses of Parliament. William Bankes, then owner of the house, was a great traveller and collector, and the **Spanish Room** is a superb scrapbook of his Grand Tour souvenirs, lined with gilded leather and surmounted by a Venetian ceiling. Kingston Lacy's **picture collection** is also outstanding, featuring Titian, Rubens, Velázquez and many other old masters. The place can get swamped with visitors, so entry is by timed tickets on busy weekends.

The Isle of Purbeck

Though not actually an island, the **ISLE OF PURBECK** – a promontory of low hills and heathland jutting out beyond Poole Harbour – does have an insular and distinctive feel. Reached from the east by the **ferry from Sandbanks** (7am–11pm every 20min; pedestrians 90p, bikes 80p, cars £3), at the narrow mouth of Poole Harbour, or by a long and congested landward journey via the bottleneck of **Wareham**, Purbeck can be a difficult destination to reach, but its villages are immensely pretty, none more so than **Corfe Castle**, with its majestic ruins. From **Swanage**, a low-key seaside resort, the Dorset Coast Path provides access to the oily shales of Kimmeridge Bay, the spectacular cove at Lulworth and the much-photographed natural arch of **Durdle Door**.

The whole coast from Purbeck to Exmouth in Devon – dubbed the **Jurassic Coast** (Ⓦ www.jurassiccoast.com) – is a World Heritage Site on account of its geological significance and fossil remains; walkers can access it along the South West Coast Path.

Wareham and around

The grid pattern of its streets indicates the Saxon origins of **WAREHAM**, and the town is surrounded by even older earth ramparts known as the Walls. A riverside setting adds greatly to its charms, though the place gets fairly overrun in summer. Nearby lies an enclave of quaint houses around **Lady St Mary's Church**, which contains the marble coffin of Edward the Martyr, murdered at Corfe Castle in 978 by his stepmother, to make way for her son Ethelred. **St Martin's Church**, at the north end of town, dates from Saxon times and holds a faded twelfth-century mural of St Martin offering his cloak to a beggar. The church's most striking feature, however, is a romantic effigy of T.E. Lawrence in Arab dress, which was originally destined for Salisbury Cathedral, but was rejected by the dean there who disapproved of Lawrence's sexual proclivities. Lawrence was killed in 1935 in a motorbike accident on the road from Bovington (6 miles west); his simply furnished cottage is at **Clouds Hill**, seven miles northwest of Wareham (mid-March to Oct Thurs–Sun noon–5pm or dusk; £4; NT). The small **museum** next to Wareham's town hall in East Street (Easter–Oct Mon–Sat 10am–4pm; free) focuses on local history and displays some of Lawrence's memorabilia.

Wareham's **train station** lies north of the centre, a fifteen-minute walk (and connected by buses). Holy Trinity Church, on South Street, contains the **tourist office** (Easter–Oct Mon–Sat 9.30am–5pm, also Sun in summer school hols 9.30am–5pm; Nov–Easter Mon–Sat 9.30am–4pm; ⓣ01929/552740, ⓦwww.purbeck.gov.uk). The best **accommodation** option is *Anglebury House*, 15 North St (ⓣ01929/552988; ③), whose previous guests have included Thomas Hardy and T.E. Lawrence, while *Harry's*, 21 South St (closed Sun), offers filling **snacks**.

Corfe Castle

The romantic ruins crowning the hill behind the village of **CORFE CASTLE** (daily: March & Oct 10am–5pm; April–Sept 10am–6pm; Nov–Feb 10am–4pm; £5.30; NT) are perhaps the most evocative in England. The family seat of Sir John Bankes, Attorney General to Charles I, this Royalist stronghold withstood a Cromwellian siege for six weeks, gallantly defended by Lady Bankes. One of her own men, Colonel Pitman, eventually betrayed the castle to the Roundheads, after which it was reduced to its present gap-toothed state by gunpowder. Apparently the victorious Roundheads were so impressed by Lady Bankes's courage that they allowed her to take the keys to the castle with her – they can still be seen in the library at the Bankes's subsequent home, Kingston Lacy (see p.228).

The village is well stocked with tearooms and gift shops and has a couple of good **pubs** too: the *Fox* on West Street, and, below the castle ramparts, the *Greyhound*. There's comfortable **accommodation** at *Westaway*, 88 West St (ⓣ01929/480188, ⓦwww.westaway-corfecastle.co.uk; no credit cards; ③), a B&B five minutes from the castle, with a garden and views of the Purbeck Hills.

Swanage and around

Purbeck's largest town, **SWANAGE**, is a traditional seaside resort with a pleasant sandy beach and an ornate town hall. The town's station is the southern terminus of the **Swanage Steam Railway** (April–Oct daily; Nov, Dec & mid-Feb to March Sat & Sun; £7.50 all day; ⓣ01929/425800, ⓦwww.swanagerailway.co.uk), which runs for six miles to Norden, just north of Corfe Castle. On foot, you can walk north out of Swanage, past the Foreland promontory to the broad sweep of **Studland Bay**. Its most northerly stretch, **Shell Bay**, is a magnificent beach of icing-sugar sand backed by a remarkable heathland ecosystem that's home to all six British species of reptile – adders are quite common, so be careful.

Swanage's **tourist office** is by the beach on Shore Road (Easter–Oct daily 10am–5pm; Nov–Easter closed Sun; ⓣ01929/422885, ⓦwww.swanage.gov.uk). **Accommodation** includes a cluster of B&Bs on King's Road near the train station and along Park Road just off the High Street, including the spacious Victorian *Clare House*, 1 Park Rd (ⓣ01929/422855, ⓦwww.clare-house.com; ⑤), 200m from the beach. There's a YHA **hostel**, with good views across the bay, on Cluny Crescent (ⓣ0870/770 6058, ⓔswanage@yha.org.uk;

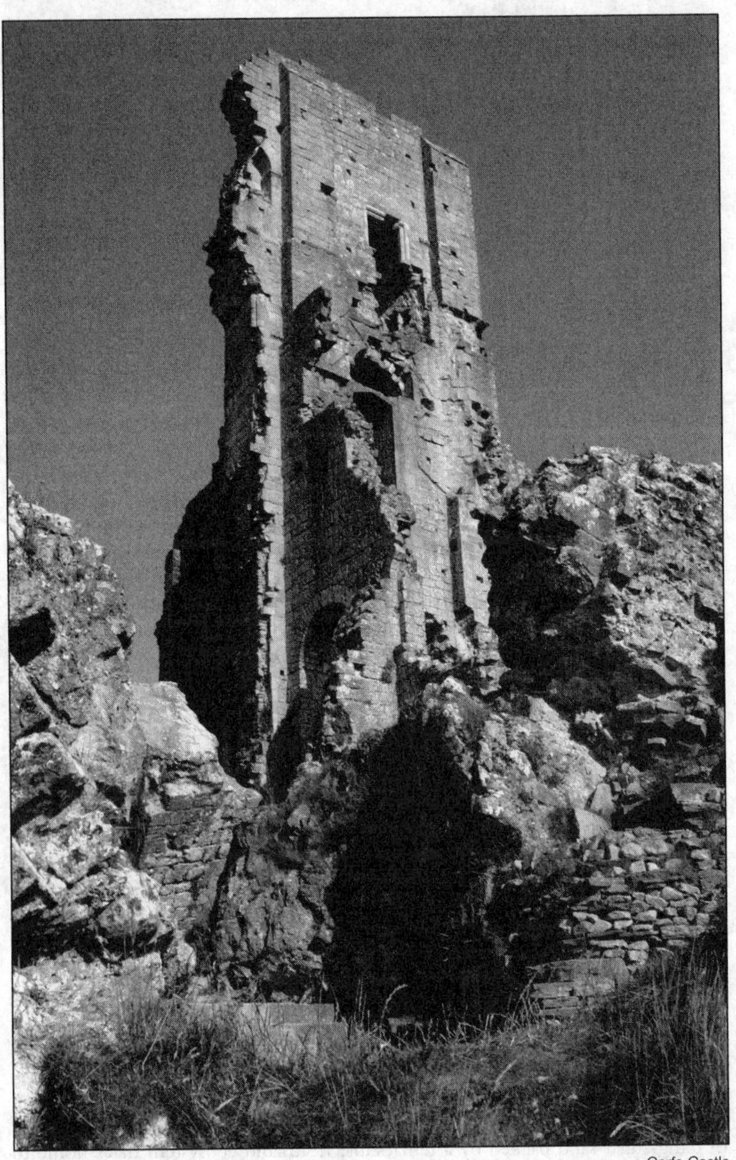

▲ Corfe Castle

open mainly during school hols, closed Dec & Jan; dorm beds from £22, private rooms ❶).

For a **meal**, head for the cosy *Trattoria*, 12 High St (☎01929/423784), a popular, moderately priced Italian restaurant; during the day, cappuccinos and baguettes are served next door at *Forte's Caffé Tratt*. **Bikes** can be rented from Bikeabout, 71 High St (☎01929/425050).

Durlstone Head to Durdle Door

Highlights of the coast beyond Swanage are the cliffs of **Durlstone Head** and the coastal path to **St Alban's Head**. West of this headland, **Kimmeridge Bay** shelters a remarkable marine wildlife reserve – and there's a Dorset Wildlife Trust **information centre** by the slipway (Easter–Sept daily 10am–5pm; Oct–Easter Sat & Sun 11.30am–4.30pm; Ⓣ01929/481044, Ⓦwww.dorsetwildlife.co.uk). The quaint thatch-and-stone villages of East and West Lulworth form a prelude to **Lulworth Cove**, a perfect shell-shaped bite formed when the sea broke through a weakness in the cliffs and then gnawed away at them from behind, forming a circular cave which eventually collapsed to leave a bay enclosed by sandstone cliffs. The mysteries of the local geology are explained at the **Lulworth Heritage Centre** (daily 10am–4/6pm; free).

Immediately west of the cove, **Stair Hole** is a roofless sea cave riddled with arches that will eventually collapse to form another Lulworth. A couple of miles west is the famous limestone arch of **Durdle Door**: most people take the uphill route to the arch which starts from the car park at Lulworth Cove, but you can avoid the steep climb by walking from the *Durdle Door Holiday Park*, on the road to East Chaldon from West Lulworth.

WEST LULWORTH is the obvious **place to stay** or **eat** hereabouts. The *Castle Inn* (Ⓣ01929/400311, Ⓦwww.thecastleinn-lulworthcove.co.uk; ➄), *Cromwell House Hotel* (Ⓣ01929/400253, Ⓦwww.lulworthcove.co.uk; ➅), right on the coast path, and the seventeenth-century *Ivy Cottage* (Ⓣ01929/400509, Ⓦwww.ivycottage.biz; no credit cards; ➂) all make for good stopoffs. There's a YHA **hostel** at the end of School Lane (Ⓣ0870/770 5940, Ⓔlulworth@yha.org.uk; closed Dec–Feb, also Sun & Mon in low season; dorm beds from £16), a stone's throw from the Dorset Coast Path. **Campers** can find a pitch at the above-mentioned *Durdle Door Holiday Park* (Ⓣ01929/400200, Ⓦwww.lulworth.com; closed Nov–Feb). *The Castle* in West Lulworth and the similarly thatched *Weld Arms* in East Lulworth offer refreshments and **meals**.

Dorchester and around

The county town of Dorset, **Dorchester** still functions as the main agricultural centre for the region, and is liveliest on Wednesdays – market day. The town has strong historical and literary associations, and the surrounding area also has its share of ancient sites, notably at prehistoric **Maiden Castle** and **Cerne Abbas**, whose rumbustious chalk-carved giant is the county's most photographed site. Further afield, Dorchester makes a useful base for exploring such picturesque rural centres as **Sherborne** and **Shaftesbury**, both imbued with a strong medieval flavour.

Dorchester

For many, **DORCHESTER** is essentially **Thomas Hardy**'s town; he was born at Higher Bockhampton, three miles east of here, his heart is buried in Stinsford, a couple of miles northeast (the rest of him is in Westminster Abbey), and he spent much of his life in Dorchester itself, where his statue now stands on High West Street. The town appears in his novels as Casterbridge, and the countryside all around is evocatively depicted, notably the wild heathland of the east (Egdon Heath) and the eerie yew forest of Cranborne Chase.

The real Dorchester has a pleasant central core of mostly seventeenth-century and Georgian buildings, though the town's origins go back to the Romans, who founded "Durnovaria" in about 70 AD. The Roman walls were replaced in the eighteenth century by tree-lined avenues called "Walks", but some traces of the Roman period have survived. On the southeast edge of town you'll find **Maumbury Rings**, where the Romans held vast gladiatorial combats in an amphitheatre adapted from a Stone Age site.

Dorchester is also associated with the notorious **Judge Jeffreys**, who, after the ill-fated rebellion of the Duke of Monmouth (another of Charles II's illegitimate offspring) against James II, held his "Bloody Assizes" in the Oak Room of the **Antelope Hotel** on Cornhill in 1685. A total of 292 men were sentenced to death, though most got away with a flogging and transportation to the West Indies, while 74 were hung, drawn and quartered, their heads stuck on pikes throughout Dorset and Somerset. Judge Jeffreys lodged just round the corner from the *Antelope* in High West Street, in what is now a half-timbered Italian restaurant.

In 1834 the **Shire Hall**, further down High West Street, witnessed another *cause célèbre*, when six men from the nearby village of Tolpuddle were sentenced to transportation for banding together to form the Friendly Society of Agricultural Labourers, in order to petition for a small wage increase on the grounds that their families were starving. After a public outcry the men were pardoned, and the **Tolpuddle Martyrs** passed into history as founders of the trade union movement. The room in which they were tried is preserved as a memorial to the martyrs, and you can find out more about them in Tolpuddle itself, eight miles east on the A35, where there's a fine little **museum** (April–Oct Tues–Sat 10am–5pm, Sun 11am–5pm; Nov–March Thurs–Sat 10am–4pm, Sun 11am–4pm; free).

The best place to find out about Dorchester's history is the engrossing **Dorset County Museum** on High West Street (daily 10am–5pm, closed Sun Oct–June; £6), where archeological and geological displays trace Celtic and Roman history, including a section on Maiden Castle. Pride of place goes to the re-creation of Thomas Hardy's study, where his pens are inscribed with the names of the books he wrote with them. Other museums in town include the formidably turreted **Keep Military Museum** (April–Sept Mon–Sat 9.30am–5pm; Oct–March Tues–Sat 9.30am–5pm; last entry 4pm; £5), at the top of High West Street, which traces the fortunes of the Dorset and Devonshire regiments over three hundred years and offers sweeping views.

Practicalities

Dorchester has two **train stations**, both south of the centre: trains from Weymouth and London arrive at Dorchester South, while Bath and Bristol trains use the Dorchester West station. Most **buses** stop on Trinity Street, off the High Street. The **tourist office** is in Antelope Walk (Mon–Sat 9am–4/5pm; ⓣ01305/267992, ⓦwww.westdorset.com). **Bikes** can be rented at Dorchester Cycles, 31 Great Western Rd (ⓣ01305/268787).

Central **accommodation** options in Dorchester include the superior Georgian *Casterbridge Hotel*, 49 High East St (ⓣ01305/264043, ⓦwww.casterbridgehotel.co.uk; ❻), and *Westwood House*, 29 High West St ⓣ01305/268018, ⓦwww.westwoodhouse.co.uk; ❹), an elegant B&B. Three miles west of town, *The Old Rectory* in Winterbourne Steepleton (ⓣ01305/889468, ⓦwww.theoldrectorybandb.co.uk; ❺) is a tranquil retreat surrounded by lawns. The nearest YHA **hostel** is at Litton Cheney (ⓣ0870/770 5922; closed Nov–Easter; from £14), halfway between Dorchester and Bridport: take bus #31 to Whiteway, then walk for a mile and a half.

For **food**, there are Mediterranean dishes and tasty desserts on offer at *Café Jagos*, 8 High West St (ⓣ01305/266056); alternatively, good **pub** meals are served at the *King's Arms* on High East Street, and the *Royal Oak* and the *Old Ship Inn*, both on High West Street.

Maiden Castle

One of southern England's finest prehistoric sites, **MAIDEN CASTLE** (free) stands on a hill two miles or so southwest of Dorchester. Covering about 115 acres, it was first developed around 3000 BC by a Stone Age farming community and then used during the Bronze Age as a funeral mound. Iron Age dwellers expanded it into a populous settlement and fortified it with a daunting series of ramparts and ditches, just in time for the arrival of Vespasian's Second Legion. The ancient Britons' slingstones were no match for the more sophisticated weapons of the Roman invaders, however, and Maiden Castle was stormed in a bloody massacre in 43 AD.

What you see today is a massive series of grassy concentric ridges about sixty feet high, creasing the surface of the hill. The main finds from the site are displayed in the Dorset County Museum (see p.232).

Cerne Abbas

Seven miles north of Dorchester, just off the A352 (and on the #D12 Dorchester–Sherborne bus route), **CERNE ABBAS** has bags of charm, with gorgeous Tudor cottages and abbey ruins, but its main attraction is the enormously priapic **giant** carved in the chalk hillside just north of the village, standing 180 feet high and flourishing a club over his disproportionately small head. The age of the monument is disputed, some authorities believing it to be pre-Roman, others thinking it might be a Romano-British figure of Hercules. Either way, in view of his prominent feature it's probable that the giant originated as some primeval fertility symbol. Folklore has it that lying on the outsize member will induce conception, but the National Trust, who now own the site, do their best to stop people wandering over it and eroding the two-foot trenches that form the outlines.

Sherborne

Tucked away in the northwest corner of Dorset, ten miles north of Cerne Abbas, the pretty town of **SHERBORNE** (bus #D12 from Dorchester) was once the capital of Wessex, its church having cathedral status until Old Sarum (see p.240) usurped the bishopric in 1075. This former glory is embodied by the magnificent **Abbey Church** (daily 8am–4/6pm; free), founded in 705 and later a Benedictine abbey. Most of its extant parts date from a rebuilding in the fifteenth century. Among the abbey church's many tombs are those of Alfred the Great's two brothers, Ethelred and Ethelbert, and the Elizabethan poet Thomas Wyatt, all located in the northeast corner. The **almshouse** on the opposite side of the Abbey Close was built in 1437 and is a rare example of a medieval hospital; another wing provides accommodation for Sherborne's well-known public school.

The town also has two "castles", both associated with Sir Walter Raleigh. Queen Elizabeth I first leased, then gave, Raleigh the twelfth-century **Old Castle** (Easter–June & Sept daily 10am–5pm; July & Aug daily 10am–6pm; Oct daily 10am–4pm; £2.50; EH), but it seems that he despaired of feudal accommodation and built himself a more comfortably domesticated house, **Sherborne Castle**, in adjacent parkland (Easter–Oct Wed–Fri & Sun 11am–5pm, Sat 2–5pm; castle & gardens £8.50, gardens only £4). When Sir Walter fell from the queen's favour by seducing her maid of honour, the Digby family acquired the house and have lived there ever since. The Old Castle fared less happily, and was pulverized by Cromwellian cannon fire for the obstinately Royalist leanings of its occupants. The **museum** near the abbey on Church Lane (April–Oct Tues–Sat 10.30am–4.30pm, some Suns 2.30–4.30pm;

£2, free on Wed) includes a model of the Old Castle and photographs of parts of the fifteenth-century Sherborne Missal, a richly illuminated tome weighing nearly fifty pounds, now housed in the British Library.

The **tourist office** is at 3 Tilton Court, Digby Rd (Mon–Sat: April–Oct 9am–5pm; Nov–March 10am–3pm; ⓣ01935/815341, ⓦwww.westdorset.com). For an **overnight stay** try the *Half Moon*, Half Moon Street (ⓣ01935/812017; ⑤). *Oliver's*, 19 Cheap St, is good for teas and light lunches, while the *Cross Keys Hotel*, 88 Cheap St, is a cosy **pub** with a few tables out front.

Shaftesbury

Fifteen miles east of Sherborne on the A30, **SHAFTESBURY** perches on a spur of lumpy hills, with severe gradients on three sides of the town. On a clear day, views from the town are terrific – one of the best vantage points is **Gold Hill**, quaint, cobbled and very steep. At its crest, the local history **museum** (April–Oct daily 10.30am–4.30pm; £2.50, or £4 with Abbey) displays items ranging from locally made buttons, for which the area was once renowned, to a mummified cat.

Pilgrims used to flock to Shaftesbury to pay homage to the bones of Edward the Martyr, which were brought to the **Abbey** in 978, though now only the footings of the abbey church survive, just off the main street (April–Oct daily 10am–5pm; £2.50, or £4 with museum). **St Peter's Church** on the market place is one of the few reminders of Shaftesbury's medieval grandeur, when it boasted a castle, twelve churches and four market crosses.

Shaftesbury has limited **bus** services from Sherborne, Salisbury (both Mon–Sat) and Dorchester (via Blandford Forum, Mon–Fri). The **tourist office** is on Bell Street (Mon–Sat 10am–3/5pm; ⓣ01747/853514, ⓦwww.ruraldorset.com). **Accommodation** options include the eco-friendly *Chalet* on Christy's Lane (ⓣ01747/853945, ⓦwww.thechalet.biz; no under-12s; no credit cards; ④), and, three miles south of town in Compton Abbas, *The Old Forge* (ⓣ01747/811881, ⓦwww.theoldforgedorset.co.uk; no under-8s; no credit cards; ④), a restored eighteenth-century cottage on Chapel Hill. In Shaftesbury, the *Salt Cellar* at the top of Gold Hill is a panoramic spot for a daytime **snack**.

Weymouth to West Bay

Whether George III's passion for sea bathing was a symptom of his eventual madness is uncertain, but it was at **Weymouth** that in 1789 he became the first reigning monarch to follow the craze. Sycophantic gentry rushed into the waves behind him, and soon the town, formerly a workaday harbour, took on the elegant Georgian stamp that it bears today. A lively family holiday destination in summer, Weymouth reverts to a more sedate rhythm out of season.

Just south of the town stretch the giant arms of Portland Harbour, and a long causeway links Weymouth to the odd excrescence of the **Isle of Portland**. The causeway stands on the easternmost section of the eighteen-mile bank of pebbles known as **Chesil Beach**, running northwest towards the fishing port of **West Bay**.

Weymouth

WEYMOUTH had long been a port before the Georgians popularized it as a resort. It's possible that a ship unloading a cargo here in 1348 first brought the Black Death to English shores, and it was from Weymouth that John Endicott sailed in 1628 to found Salem in Massachusetts. A few buildings survive from these pre-Georgian times: the restored **Tudor House** on Trinity Street (Feb–May & Oct–Dec first Sun of month 2–4pm; June–Sept Tues–Fri 1–4pm; £3) and the ruins of **Sandsfoot Castle** (free access), built by Henry VIII, overlooking Portland Harbour. But Weymouth's most imposing architectural heritage stands along the Esplanade, a dignified range of bow-fronted and porticoed buildings gazing out across the graceful bay. The more intimate quayside of the Old Harbour is linked to the Esplanade by the main pedestrianized thoroughfare St Mary's Street.

Weymouth boasts a number of "all-weather" attractions, notably **Sea Life Park** in Lodmoor Country Park, east of the Esplanade (daily 10am–4/6pm; last admission 1hr before closing; £12.95, or £9 from tourist office), where you can get close to sharks and rays; **Deep Sea Adventure** at the Old Harbour (daily 9.30am–5.30pm, closes later in summer; last entry 90min before closing; £3.95), which describes the origins of modern diving and the *Titanic* disaster, and, over the river on Hope Square, **Timewalk** (March–Oct daily 10am–4pm; summer school hols closes 9pm; last entry 1hr before closing; £4.75, or £4 from tourist office), holding an entertaining and educational walk-through exhibition of Weymouth's maritime and brewing past.

Practicalities

Weymouth's **train station** and **bus station** are next to each other off King Street, just steps away from the **tourist office** on the Esplanade (daily: April–Oct 9.30am–5pm; Nov–March 10am–4pm; ⓣ01305/785747, ⓦwww.visitweymouth.co.uk). **Accommodation** options lie at the south end of the Esplanade, for instance *The Chatsworth* at no. 14 (ⓣ01305/785012, ⓦwww.thechatsworth.co.uk; ❻), which has a garden terrace, and the Georgian *Cavendish House*, at no. 5 (ⓣ01305/782039; no credit cards; ❸), overlooking the bay with harbour views at the back. Nearer the bus and train stations and 150m from the seafront, try *Wilton Guesthouse*, 5 Gloucester St (ⓣ01305/782820, ⓦwww.thewiltonguesthouse.co.uk; ❹), the former home of George III's butler.

As for **restaurants**, the best seafood in town is served at *Perry's*, overlooking the quayside at 4 Trinity Rd (ⓣ01305/785799; closed Sat lunch & Mon). Less pricey fish dishes can also be enjoyed at most of the waterfront **pubs** lining the Old Harbour. Elsewhere, you'll find good bar meals with views from the garden at the amenable *Nothe Tavern*, buried among Nothe Gardens, south of the harbour on Barrack Road.

Portland

Stark, wind-battered and treeless, the **Isle of Portland** is famed above all for its hard white limestone, which has been quarried here for centuries – Wren used it for St Paul's Cathedral, and it clads the UN headquarters in New York. It was also used for the six-thousand-foot breakwater that protects Portland Harbour – the largest artificial harbour in Britain, built by convicts in the nineteenth century and still surveyed by **Portland Castle** (Easter–June & Sept daily 10am–5pm; July & Aug daily 10am–6pm; Oct daily 10am–4pm; £4; EH), commissioned by Henry VIII. Southeast of here, the craggy limestone of the Isle rises to 496ft at Verne Hill. At **Portland Bill**, the southern tip of the island, you can climb the 153 steps of **Portland Lighthouse** (Easter–Sept Mon–Fri & Sun 11am–5pm; £2), dating from 1906, for superb views. A **tourist office** is also housed here (Easter–Sept daily 11am–5pm; Oct–Easter Sat & Sun 11am–4pm; ⓣ01305/861233).

Accommodation options in the area include *Brackenbury House* (ⓣ01305/826509, ⓦwww.brackenburyhouse.co.uk; no credit cards; ❷; closed Dec & Jan), a converted vicarage in Fortuneswell, near Portland Castle, and a **youth hostel** just south of the castle on Castle Road (ⓣ0870/770 6000, ⓔportland@yha.org.uk; closed Nov–Easter, also Sun & Mon in low season; dorm beds from £20).

Chesil Beach to West Bay

Chesil Beach is the strangest feature of the Dorset coast, a two-hundred-yard-wide, fifty-foot-high bank of pebbles that extends for eighteen miles, its component stones gradually decreasing in size from fist-like pebbles at Portland to "pea gravel" at Burton Bradstock in the west. This sorting is an effect of the powerful coastal currents, which make this one of the most dangerous beaches in Europe – churchyards in the local villages display plenty of evidence of wrecks and drownings. Though not a swimming beach, Chesil is popular with sea anglers, and its wild, uncommercialized atmosphere makes an appealing antidote to the south-coast resorts. Behind the beach, **The Fleet**, a brackish lagoon, was the setting for J. Meade Faulkner's classic smuggling tale, *Moonfleet*.

At the point where the shingle beach attaches itself to the shore is the pretty village of **ABBOTSBURY**, all tawny ironstone and thatch. The three main attractions here draw people from far and wide (all open daily: mid-March to Sept 10am–6pm; Oct 10am–5pm; last admission 1hr before closing), and can be visited separately or on a passport ticket for £15. The most absorbing is the village **Swannery** (£8.50), a wetland reserve for mute swans dating back to medieval times, when presumably it formed part of the abbot's larder. The eel-grass reeds through which the swans paddle were once harvested to thatch roofs throughout the region. One example can be seen on the fifteenth-century Tithe Barn, the last remnant of the abbey and today housing the **Children's Farm** (£7), whose highlights include goat-racing and pony rides. Lastly, in the **Subtropical Gardens** (£8.50), delicate species thrive in the microclimate created by Chesil's stones, which act as a giant radiator to keep out all but the worst frosts. In the village centre, the handsome *Ilchester Arms* offers fine **food** as well as comfortable **accommodation** (ⓣ01305/871243, ⓦwww.ilchester-arms.co.uk; ❺).

Ten miles west of Abbotsbury, majestic red cliffs rear up above the peaceful fishing resort of **West Bay**. Here you'll find the area's best **place to eat**, the *Riverside Restaurant*, a renowned and pricey but informal fish place with good views over the river, worth booking ahead (ⓣ01308/422011; closed Sun eve, Mon, Thurs eve in winter & Dec to mid-Feb). You can eat and drink well for considerably less just across the road at *The George*, which also has comfortable **rooms** (ⓣ01308/423191; ❹).

Lyme Regis and around

LYME REGIS, Dorset's most westerly town, shelters snugly between steep, fossil-filled cliffs. Its intimate size and photogenic qualities make this a popular and congested spot in high summer, with some upmarket literary associations – Jane Austen summered in a seafront cottage and set part of *Persuasion* in Lyme (the town appears in the 1995 film version), while novelist John Fowles lived here until his death in 2005 (the film adaptation of his book, *The French Lieutenant's Woman*, was shot here).

Colourwashed cottages and elegant Regency and Victorian villas line its seafront and flanking streets, but Lyme's best-known feature is a practical reminder of its commercial origins: **The Cobb**, a curving harbour wall first constructed in the thirteenth century. It has suffered many alterations since, most notably in the nineteenth century, when its massive boulders were clad in neater blocks of Portland stone.

As you walk along the seafront and out towards The Cobb, look for the outlines of ammonites in the walls and paving stones. The cliffs around Lyme are made up of a complex layer of limestone, greensand and unstable clay, a perfect medium for preserving fossils, which are exposed by landslips of the waterlogged clays. In 1811, after a fierce storm caused parts of the cliffs to collapse, 12-year-old Mary Anning, a keen fossil-hunter, discovered an almost complete dinosaur skeleton, a 30-foot ichthyosaurus now displayed in London's Natural History Museum.

Hammering fossils out of the cliffs is frowned on by today's conservationists, and in any case is rather hazardous. Hands-off inspection of the area's complex geology can be enjoyed on both sides of town: to the west lies the **Undercliff**, a fascinating jumble of overgrown landslips, now a nature reserve. East of Lyme, the Dorset Coast Path is closed as far as jaded **Charmouth** (Jane Austen's favourite resort), but at low tide you can walk for two miles along the beach, then, just past Charmouth, rejoin the coastal path to the headland of **Golden Cap**, whose brilliant outcrop of auburn sandstone is crowned with gorse.

On Bridge Street, the excellent **Lyme Regis Museum** (Easter–Oct Mon–Sat 10am–5pm, Sun 11am–5pm; Nov–Easter Wed–Sun, daily in school holidays, 11am–4pm; £3) provides a crash course in local history and geology, while **Dinosaurland** on Coombe Street (Jan & Feb Sat & Sun 10am–4.30pm; March–Dec daily 10am–4.30/6pm; £4.50) fills out the story of ammonites and other local fossils. Also worth seeing are the small **Marine Aquarium** on The Cobb (March–Oct 10am–5pm, closes later in July & Aug; call for winter opening Ⓣ01297/444230; £4), where local fishermen bring unusual catches, and the fifteenth-century **parish church** of St Michael the Archangel, up Church Street, which contains a seventeenth-century pulpit and a massive chained Bible.

Practicalities

Lyme's nearest **train station** is in Axminster, five miles north (bus #31). The **tourist office** is on Church Street (May–Oct Mon–Sat 10am–5am, Sun 10am–4pm; Nov–April Mon–Sat 10am–3pm; Ⓣ01297/442138, Ⓦwww.lymeregistourism.co.uk).

Central **accommodation** choices in Lyme include *Coombe House*, 41 Coombe St (Ⓣ01297/443849, Ⓦwww.coombe-house.co.uk; no credit cards; ❸), a friendly B&B with large rooms and a self-catering appartment, and the *Old Monmouth Hotel*, 12 Church St (Ⓣ01297/442456, Ⓦwww.lyme-regis-hotel.co.uk; ❹). If you want to stay right next to the sea, book in at the *Cobb Arms*, Marine Parade (Ⓣ01297/443242; ❺).

For a daytime snack or **meal**, drop in at the bustling *Bell Cliff Restaurant* at 5–6 Broad St, also open until 9pm between Easter and September, or the *Town Mill Bakery* on Mill Lane (off Coombe St), offering delicious vegetable soup and spinach pancakes, and pizzas on Friday and Saturday evenings. The best **pubs** are the *Royal Standard*, near The Cobb at 25 Marine Parade, and the *Pilot Boat* on Bridge Street, both also serving food.

Salisbury

SALISBURY, huddled below Wiltshire's chalky plain in the converging valleys of the Avon and Nadder, looks from a distance very much as it did when Constable painted his celebrated view of it from across the water meadows.

The town sprang into existence in the early thirteenth century, when the bishopric was moved from **Old Sarum**, an ancient Iron Age hillfort settled by the Romans and their successors. The deserted remnant of Salisbury's precursor now stands on the northern fringe of the town.

The City

Begun in 1220, **Salisbury Cathedral** (daily 7.15am–6.15pm, mid-June to late Aug Mon–Sat closes 7.15pm; £5 suggested donation) was mostly completed within forty years and is thus unusually consistent in its style, with one extremely prominent exception – the **spire**, which was added a century later and at 404ft is the highest in England. Its survival is something of a miracle, for the foundations penetrate only about six feet into marshy ground, and when Christopher Wren surveyed it he found the spire to be leaning almost two and a half feet out of true. He added further tie-rods, which finally arrested the movement.

The interior is over-austere after James Wyatt's brisk eighteenth-century tidying, but there's an amazing sense of space and light in its high nave, despite the sombre pillars of grey Purbeck marble, which are visibly bowing beneath the weight they bear. Monuments and carved tombs line the walls, where they were neatly placed by Wyatt. Other features not to miss are the vaulted colonnades of the **cloisters**, and the octagonal **chapter house** (March to mid-June Mon–Sat 9.30am–5.30pm, Sun noon–5.30pm; mid-June to Aug Mon–Sat 9.30am–6.45pm, Sun noon–5.30pm; Sept & Oct Mon–Sat 9.30am–5.30pm, Sun 12.45–5.30pm; Nov–Feb Mon–Sat 10am–4.30pm, Sun 12.45–4.30pm), which displays a rare original copy of the Magna Carta, and whose walls are decorated with a frieze of scenes from the Old Testament. On most days, you can join a free 45-minute **tour** of the church leaving two or more times a day, and there are also tours to the roof and tower (£5.50).

Surrounding the cathedral is the **Close**, a peaceful precinct of lawns and mellow old buildings. Most of the houses have seemly Georgian facades, though some, like the Bishop's Palace and the deanery, date from the thirteenth century. **Mompesson House** (Easter–Oct Mon–Wed, Sat & Sun 11am–5pm; £4.70, garden only £1; NT), built by a wealthy merchant in 1701, contains some beautifully furnished eighteenth-century rooms and a superbly carved staircase. Also in the Close is the **King's House**, home to the **Salisbury and South Wiltshire Museum** (Mon–Sat 10am–5pm; £5) – an absorbing account of local history. It includes a good section on Stonehenge and also focuses on the life and times of General Pitt-Rivers, the father of modern archeology, who excavated many of Wiltshire's prehistoric sites, including Avebury (see p.244).

The Close's **North Gate** opens onto the centre's older streets, where narrow pedestrianized alleyways bear names like Fish Row and Salt Lane, indicative of their trading origin. Many half-timbered houses and inns have survived all over the centre, and the last of four market crosses, **Poultry Cross**, stands on stilts in Silver Street, near the Market Square. The market, held on Tuesdays and Saturdays, still serves a large agricultural area, as it did in earlier times when the city grew wealthy on wool. Nearby, the church of **St Thomas** – named after Thomas à Becket – is worth a look inside for its carved timber roof and

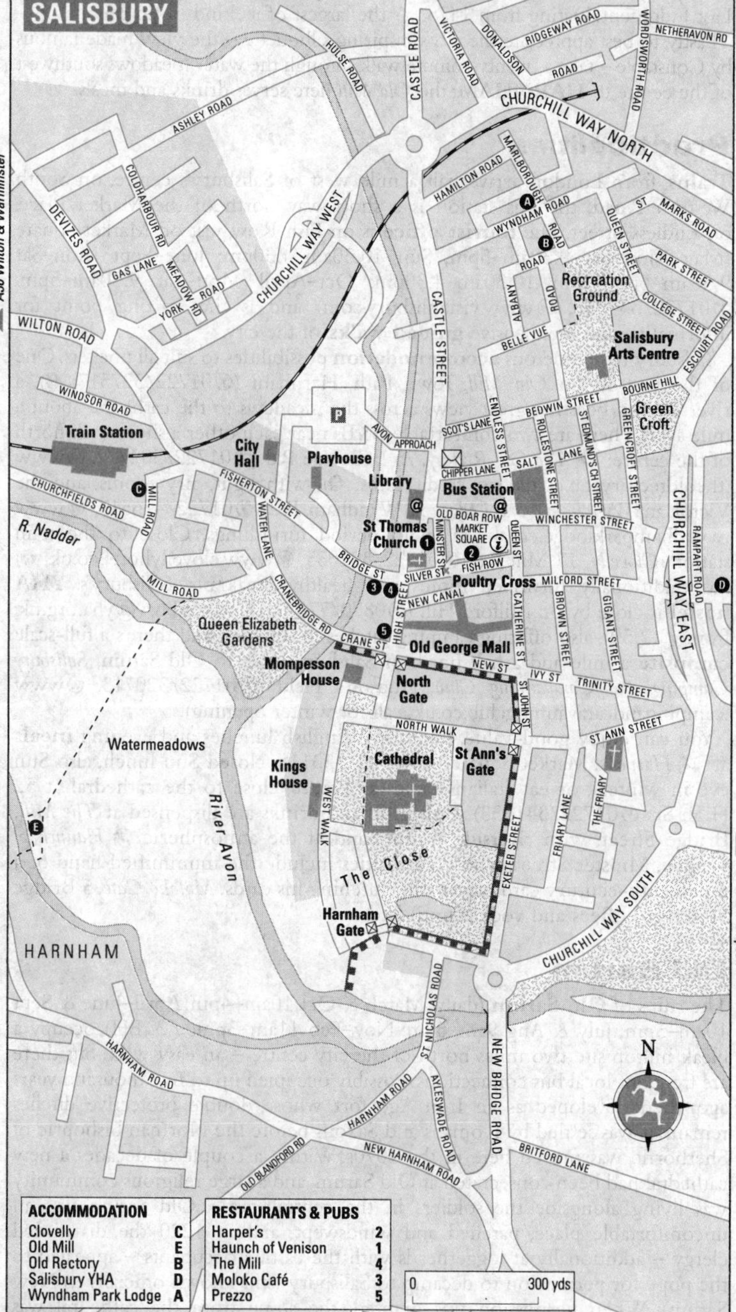
SALISBURY
Old Sarum, Stonehenge (A345) & Campsite
A36 Wilton & Warminster
A30 Marlborough
A36 Southampton
A338 Bournemouth
CASTLE ROAD
VICTORIA ROAD
DONALDSON ROAD
RIDGEWAY ROAD
WORDSWORTH ROAD
NETHERAVON RD
HULSE ROAD
CHURCHILL WAY NORTH
ASHLEY ROAD
HAMILTON ROAD
MARLBOROUGH ROAD
WYNDHAM ROAD
ST MARKS ROAD
QUEEN STREET
PARK STREET
COLLEGE STREET
ESCOURT ROAD
DEVIZES ROAD
COLDHARBOUR RD
GAS LANE
MEADOW RD
YORK ROAD
CHURCHILL WAY WEST
CASTLE STREET
ALBANY ROAD
Recreation Ground
BELLE VUE
Salisbury Arts Centre
WILTON ROAD
WINDSOR ROAD
ENDLESS STREET
BOURNE HILL
BEDWIN STREET
Green Croft
Train Station
City Hall
P
AVON APPROACH
SCOT'S LANE
Playhouse
ROLLESTONE STREET
ST EDMUND'S CH STREET
GREENCROFT STREET
SALT LANE
CHIPPER LANE
Library
Bus Station
CHURCHFIELDS ROAD
MILL ROAD
FISHERTON STREET
WATER LANE
OLD BOAR ROW
MARKET SQUARE
WINCHESTER STREET
CHURCHILL WAY EAST
RAMPART ROAD
R. Nadder
St Thomas Church
MINSTER ST
FISH ROW
QUEEN ST
BRIDGE ST
SILVER ST
Poultry Cross
MILFORD STREET
MILL ROAD
CRANEBRIDGE RD
HIGH STREET
NEW CANAL
CATHERINE ST
BROWN STREET
GIGANT STREET
Queen Elizabeth Gardens
CRANE ST
Old George Mall
NEW ST
Mompesson House
North Gate
IVY ST
ST JOHN ST
TRINITY STREET
NORTH WALK
ST ANN STREET
Watermeadows
Cathedral
St Ann's Gate
Kings House
WEST WALK
River Avon
FRIARY LANE
THE FRIARY
EXETER STREET
The Close
Harnham Gate
HARNHAM
CHURCHILL WAY SOUTH
ST NICHOLAS ROAD
NEW BRIDGE ROAD
HARNHAM ROAD
HARNHAM ROAD
AYLESWADE ROAD
NEW HARNHAM ROAD
BRITFORD LANE
OLD BLANDFORD RD
N
ACCOMMODATION
Clovelly C
Old Mill E
Old Rectory B
Salisbury YHA D
Wyndham Park Lodge A
RESTAURANTS & PUBS
Harper's 2
Haunch of Venison 1
The Mill 4
Moloko Café 3
Prezzo 5
0 300 yds

"Doom painting" over the chancel arch, depicting Christ presiding over the Last Judgment. Dating from 1475, it's the largest of its kind in England.

Lastly, to best appreciate the city's inspiring silhouette – the view made famous by Constable – take a twenty-minute walk through the water meadows southwest of the centre to **HARNHAM**; the *Old Mill* here serves drinks and meals.

Practicalities

Trains from London arrive half a mile west of Salisbury's centre, on South Western Road; the bus station is a short way north of the Market Place, on Endless Street. The **tourist office** is on Fish Row, just off Market Square (May Mon–Sat 9.30am–5pm, Sun 10.30am–4.30pm; June–Sept Mon–Sat 9.30am–6pm, Sun 10.30am–4.30pm; Oct–April Mon–Sat 9.30am–5pm; ⓣ01722/334956, ⓦwww.visitsalisbury.com) and is the starting point for informative and inexpensive **guided walks** of the city.

Salisbury has numerous **accommodation** possibilities to suit all pockets. One of the best is the *Old Mill*, Town Path, Harnham (ⓣ01722/327517; ❻), a riverside inn boasting great views across the meadows to the cathedral about a mile away. There are two comfortable B&Bs near each other a short walk north of the centre: *The Old Rectory*, 75 Belle Vue Rd (ⓣ01722/502702, ⓦwww.theoldrectory-bb.co.uk; no credit cards; ❹), with light, airy rooms, and the Victorian *Wyndham Park Lodge*, 51 Wyndham Rd (ⓣ01722/416517, ⓦwww.wyndhamparklodge.co.uk; ❸), with period furnishings. Close to the train station, *Clovelly*, 17 Mill Rd (ⓣ01722/322055, ⓦwww.clovellyhotel.co.uk; ❺) has traditionally furnished rooms and healthy breakfasts. Salisbury's **YHA hostel** is close by on Milford Hill (ⓣ0870/770 6018, ⓔsalisbury@yha.org.uk; from £17.50), also offering camping pitches in summer, and there's a full-scale **campsite** a mile and a half north of Salisbury close to Old Sarum, *Salisbury Camping and Caravanning Club*, Hudson's Field (ⓣ01722/320713, ⓦwww.campingandcaravanningclub.co.uk; call for winter opening).

You can enjoy good-value, traditional English lunches and evening **meals** at *Harper's*, Market Square (ⓣ01722/333118; closed Sun lunch, also Sun eve in winter), or eat Italian staples at *Prezzo*, close to the cathedral at 52 High St (ⓣ01722/341333). **Pub** grub and drinks are dispensed at *The Mill*, Bridge Street, with riverside seating, and at the atmospheric *Haunch of Venison*, Minster Street, whose curiosities include the mummified hand of a nineteenth-century card player still clutching his cards. *Moloko Café*, 5 Bridge St, serves coffees and vodkas until late.

Old Sarum

The ruins of **Old Sarum** (daily: March & Oct 10am–4pm; April–June & Sept 10am–5pm; July & Aug 9am–6pm; Nov–Feb 11am–3pm; £3; EH) occupy a bleak hilltop site two miles north of the city centre – an easy walk, but there are frequent local bus connections. Possibly occupied up to five thousand years ago, then developed as an Iron Age fort whose double protective ditches remain, it was settled by Romans and Saxons before the Norman bishopric of Sherborne was moved here in the 1070s. Within a couple of decades a new cathedral had been consecrated at Old Sarum, and a large religious community was living alongside the soldiers in the central castle. Old Sarum was an uncomfortable place, parched and windswept, and in 1220 the dissatisfied clergy – additionally at loggerheads with the castle's occupants – appealed to the pope for permission to decamp to Salisbury (still known officially as New Sarum). When permission was granted, the stone from the cathedral was commandeered for Salisbury's gateways, and once the church had gone the population waned. By the nineteenth century Old Sarum was deserted, and today the dominant features of the site are huge earthworks, banks and ditches, with a broad trench encircling the rudimentary remains of the Norman palace, castle and cathedral.

West of Salisbury: Wilton, Stourhead and Longleat

Just outside Salisbury, the village of **Wilton** is renowned for its carpet industry and, in **Wilton House**, holds one of Wiltshire's great houses. On the western edge of the county lie the landscaped grounds of **Stourhead** and the brasher stately home at **Longleat**, an unlikely hybrid of safari park and historic monument. Wilton is well connected to the county town by frequent buses, but you'll really need your own transport to visit the other, more far-flung attractions.

Wilton

WILTON, five miles west of Salisbury, draws in coach parties a-plenty for the splendid **Wilton House** (11am–5.30pm: April–Aug Mon–Thurs, Sun & occasional Sat; Sept Tues–Thurs; last entry 4.30pm; £12, grounds only £5), which dominates the village. The original Tudor house, built for the First Earl of Pembroke on the site of a dissolved Benedictine abbey, was ruined by fire in 1647 and rebuilt by Inigo Jones, whose classic hallmarks can be seen in the sumptuous Single Cube and Double Cube rooms, so called because of their precise dimensions.

The easel **paintings** are what makes Wilton really special, however – the collection includes paintings by van Dyck, Rembrandt, two of the Brueghel family, Poussin, Andrea del Sarto and Tintoretto. In the grounds, the famous **Palladian Bridge** has been joined by various ancillary attractions including an adventure playground and an audiovisual show on the colourful earls of Pembroke.

Stourhead

Landscape gardening was a favoured mode of display among the grandest eighteenth-century landowners, and **Stourhead**, 25 miles west of Salisbury, is one of the most accomplished examples of the genre (house Easter–Oct Mon, Tues & Fri–Sun 11.30am–4.30pm or dusk; garden daily 9am–7pm or dusk; house & garden £11.60, house £7, garden £7; NT). The Stourton estate was bought in 1717 by Henry Hoare, who commissioned Colen Campbell to build a new villa in the Palladian style. Hoare's heir, another Henry, returned from his Grand Tour in 1741 with his head full of the paintings of Claude and Poussin, and determined to translate their images of well-ordered, wistful classicism into real life. He dammed the Stour to create a lake, then planted the terrain with blocks of trees, domed temples, stone bridges, grottoes and statues, all mirrored vividly in the water. In 1772 the folly of **King Alfred's Tower** (Easter–Oct daily 11.30am–4.30pm or dusk; £2.40) was added and today affords fine views across the estate and into neighbouring counties. The house, in contrast, is fairly run-of-the-mill, though it has some good Chippendale furniture.

Longleat

If Stourhead is an unexpected outcrop of Italy in Wiltshire, the African savannah intrudes even more bizarrely at **Longleat** (house Easter–Oct Mon–Fri 10am–5pm, Sat & Sun 10am–5.30pm; Oct–March guided tours once or twice hourly 11am–3pm; safari park Easter–Oct Mon–Fri 10am–4pm, Sat, Sun & school holidays 10am–5pm; house £10; safari park £11, plus £4 for the safari bus; all attractions £20), some eight miles north of Stourhead and two and a half miles south of the road from Warminster to Frome. In 1946 the sixth marquess of Bath became the first stately-home owner to open his house to the paying public on a regular basis, and in 1966 he caused even more amazement when Longleat's Capability Brown landscapes were turned into England's first drive-through **safari park**. Other attractions followed, including a large hedge maze, a Doctor Who exhibition, a high-tech simulation of the world's most dangerous modes of travel, and the seventh marquess's steamy murals encapsulating his interpretation of life and the universe (children not admitted). Beyond the brazen razzmatazz, though, there's an exquisitely furnished Elizabethan house, built for Sir John Thynne, Elizabeth's High Treasurer, with an enormous library and a fine collection of pictures, including Titian's *Holy Family*.

Longleat is about four miles from the train stations of Frome and Warminster; the #53 bus (Mon–Sat) shuttles roughly every hour between the two stations – though be prepared to walk the two and a half miles to the house from the entrance of the grounds.

Salisbury Plain and northwards

The Ministry of Defence is the landlord of much of **Salisbury Plain**, the hundred thousand acres of chalky upland to the north of Salisbury. Flags warn casual trespassers away from MoD firing ranges and tank training grounds, while rather stricter security cordons off such secretive establishments as the research centre at Porton Down, Britain's centre for chemical and biological warfare.

Though now largely deserted except by forces' families living in ugly barracks quarters, Salisbury Plain once positively throbbed with communities. Stone Age, Bronze Age and Iron Age settlements left hundreds of burial mounds scattered over the chalklands, as well as major complexes at Danebury, Badbury, Figsbury, Old Sarum, and, of course, the great circle of **Stonehenge**. North of Salisbury Plain lies the softer Vale of Pewsey, traversed by the Kennet Canal, with another cluster of ancient sites to the north of the Vale, including the huge stone circle of **Avebury**, the mysterious grassy mound of **Silbury Hill** and the chamber graves of **West Kennet**.

Stonehenge

No ancient structure in England arouses more controversy than **Stonehenge** (daily: mid-March to May & Sept to mid-Oct 9.30am–6pm; June–Aug 9am–7pm; mid-Oct to mid-March 9.30am–4pm; £6.50; NT & EH), a mysterious ring of monoliths nine miles north of Salisbury. While archeologists argue over whether it was a place of ritual sacrifice and sun-worship, an astronomical calculator or a royal palace, the guardians of the site struggle to accommodate its year-round crowds. Conservation of Stonehenge is an urgent priority, and unless you arrange for special access (book at ⑦01722/343834 or through the website), you must be content with walking round rather than among the stones, equipped with handsets that dispense a range of information.

What exists today is only a small part of the original prehistoric complex, as many of the outlying stones were probably plundered by medieval and later farmers for building materials. The **construction** of Stonehenge is thought to have taken place in several stages. In about 3000 BC the outer circular bank and ditch were built, just inside which was dug a ring of 56 pits, which at a later date were filled with a mixture of earth and human ash. Around 2500 BC the first stones were raised within the earthworks, comprising approximately forty great blocks of dolerite (bluestone), whose ultimate source was Preseli in Wales. Some archeologists have suggested that these monoliths were found lying on Salisbury Plain, having been borne down from the Welsh mountains by a glacier in the last Ice Age, but the lack of any other glacial debris on the plain would seem to disprove this theory. It really does seem to be the case that the stones were cut from quarries in Preseli and dragged or floated here on rafts, a prodigious task which has defeated recent attempts to emulate it.

The crucial phase in the creation of the site came during the next six hundred years, when the incomplete bluestone circle was transformed by the construction of a circle of twenty-five **trilithons** (two uprights crossed by a lintel) and an inner horseshoe formation of five trilithons. Hewn from Marlborough Downs sandstone, these colossal stones (called sarsens), ranging from 13ft to 21ft in height and weighing up to thirty tons, were carefully dressed and worked – for example, to compensate for perspectival distortion the uprights have a slight swelling in the middle, the same trick as the builders of the Parthenon were to employ hundreds of years later. More bluestones were arranged in various patterns within the outer circle over this period. The purpose of all this work remains baffling, however. The symmetry and location of the site (a slight rise in a flat valley with even views of the horizon in all directions) as well as its alignment towards the points of sunrise and sunset on the summer and winter solstices tend to support the supposition that it was some sort of observatory or time-measuring device. The site ceased to be used at around 1600 BC, and by the Middle Ages it had become a "landmark". Recent excavations have revealed

▲ Stonehenge

istence of a much larger settlement here than had previously been thought – fact the most substantial Neolithic village of this period to be found on the ish mainland – covering a wide area. Nothing is to be seen of the new finds yet, though there are plans to re-create a part of the ancient complex.

There's a lot less charisma about the reputedly significant Bronze Age site of **Woodhenge** (dawn–dusk; free), two miles northeast of Stonehenge. The site consists of a circular bank about 220ft in diameter enclosing a ditch and six concentric rings of post holes, which would originally have held timber uprights, possibly supporting a roofed building of some kind. The holes are now marked more durably if less romantically by concrete pillars. A child's grave was found at the centre of the rings, suggesting that it may have been a place of ritual sacrifice.

Silbury Hill, West Kennet and Avebury

The neat green mound of **Silbury Hill**, sixteen miles north of Stonehenge, is probably overlooked by the majority of drivers whizzing by on the A4. At 130ft it's no great height, but when you realize it's the largest prehistoric artificial mound in Europe, and was made by a people using nothing more than primitive spades, it commands more respect. It was probably constructed around 2600 BC, but like so many of the sites of Salisbury Plain, no one knows quite what it was for, though the likelihood is that it was a burial mound. You can't actually walk on the hill – so having admired it briefly from the car park, cross the road to the footpath that leads half a mile to the **West Kennet Long Barrow** (free access; NT & EH). Dating from about 3250 BC, this was definitely a chamber tomb – nearly fifty burials have been discovered here.

Immediately to the west, the village of **AVEBURY** stands in the midst of a **stone circle** (free access) that rivals Stonehenge – the individual stones are generally smaller, but the circle itself is much wider and more complex. A massive earthwork 20ft high and 1400ft across encloses the main circle, which is approached by four causeways across the inner ditch, two of them leading into wide avenues stretching over a mile beyond the circle. The best guess is that it was built soon after 2500 BC, and presumably had a similar ritual or religious function to Stonehenge. The structure of Avebury's diffuse circle is quite difficult to grasp, but there are plans on the site, and you can get an excellent overview at the **Alexander Keiller Museum**, at the western entrance to the site (daily: April–Oct 10am–6pm or dusk; Nov–March 10am–4pm; £4.20, including Barn Gallery; NT & EH), while the nearby **Barn Gallery** holds a permanent exhibition on Avebury and the surrounding country. To the southeast of the circle, an avenue of standing stones leads half a mile beyond West Kennet towards a spot known as the Sanctuary, though there is little left to see here.

There's a **tourist office** (Easter–Oct Tues–Sun 9.30am–5pm; Nov–Easter Wed–Sun 9.30am–4.30pm; Ⓣ01380/734669, Ⓦwww.visitkennet.co.uk) in the Avebury Chapel Centre on Green Street. You can have a **snack** or cream tea at *The Circle* restaurant, next to the Barn Gallery, or a drink in the *Red Lion* **pub**, which also serves reasonable **meals** and has en-suite **rooms** (Ⓣ01672/539266; ⑤). Alternatively, you can wake up to views of the stones at *Manor Farm*, a B&B on the High Street (Ⓣ01672/539294; no credit cards; ⑤), which has a private guests' sitting room.

Lacock

LACOCK, twelve miles west of Avebury, is the perfect English feudal village, albeit one much gentrified by the National Trust and besieged by tourists all summer. Appropriately for so photogenic a spot, and one used as a location for several films (it features in the *Harry Potter* series), it has a fascinating museum dedicated to the founding father of photography, Henry Fox Talbot, a member of the dynasty which has lived in the local **abbey** since it passed to Sir William Sharington on the Dissolution of the Monasteries in 1539. Sir William's descendant, William Henry Fox Talbot, was the first to produce a photographic negative, and the **Fox Talbot Museum**, in a sixteenth-century barn by the abbey gates (Jan to mid-Feb & Nov to mid-Dec Sat & Sun 11am–4pm; March–Oct daily 11am–5.30pm; £5.10, including abbey garden and cloisters, £3.60 in winter; NT), captures something of the excitement he must have experienced as the dim outline of an oriel window in the abbey imprinted itself on a piece of silver nitrate paper. The **abbey** itself (April–Oct daily except Tues 1–5.30pm; £6.70, £8.30 including museum; NT) preserves a few monastic fragments amid the eighteenth-century Gothic, while the church of **St Cyriac** (free access) contains the opulent tomb of Sir William Sharington, buried beneath a splendid barrel-vaulted roof.

The village's delightfully Chaucerian-sounding hostelry, *At the Sign of the Angel*, is a good, if expensive, **hotel** and **restaurant** (ⓣ01249/730230, ⓦwww.lacock.co.uk; ⑥).

Travel details

Buses

For information on all local and national bus services, contact Traveline ⓣ0871/200 2233 (daily 7am–10pm), ⓦwww.traveline.org.uk.

Bournemouth to: Dorchester (4–5 daily; 50min–1hr 45min); London (hourly; 2hr 40min); Salisbury (Mon–Sat every 30min, Sun 7 daily; 1hr 10min); Southampton (11–14 daily; 45min–1hr 50min); Weymouth (5 daily; 1hr 20min); Winchester (6 daily; 1hr 15min–2hr).

Dorchester to: Bournemouth (2–4 daily; 1hr 10min–1hr 40min); London (1 daily; 4hr); Weymouth (3–6 hourly; 30min).

Portsmouth to: London (15 daily; 2hr 15min–3hr 50min); Salisbury (1 daily; 1hr 35min); Southampton (Mon–Sat 13 daily, Sun 6 daily; 40–50min).

Salisbury to: Bournemouth (Mon–Sat every 30min, Sun 7; 1hr 10min); London (3 daily; 2hr 50min–4hr); Portsmouth (1 daily; 1hr 30min); Southampton (Mon–Sat 1–2 hourly, Sun 6 daily; 45min–1hr); Winchester (Mon–Sat 5–7 daily; 1hr 20min).

Southampton to: Bournemouth (11–14 daily; 45min–1hr 50min); London (hourly; 2hr 35min–3hr); Portsmouth (Mon–Sat 13 daily, Sun 6 daily; 40–50min); Salisbury (Mon–Sat 1–2 hourly, Sun 6 daily; 45min–1hr); Weymouth (2 daily; 2hr 40min); Winchester (every 15–30min; 45min).

Winchester to: Alton (Mon–Sat hourly, Sun every 2hr; 40min); Bournemouth (3 daily; 1hr 15min–1hr 35min); London (9 daily; 2hr); Salisbury (Mon–Sat 5–7 daily; 1hr 20min); Southampton (every 15–30min; 45min).

Trains

For information on all local and national rail services, contact National Rail Enquiries ⓣ08457/484950, ⓦwww.nationalrail.co.uk.

Bournemouth to: Brockenhurst (3–4 hourly; 15–25min); Dorchester (1–2 hourly; 45min); London Waterloo (2 hourly; 2hr); Poole (3 hourly; 10min); Southampton (3 hourly; 30–50min); Weymouth (hourly; 55min); Winchester (2–3 hourly; 45min–1hr).

Dorchester to: Bournemouth (hourly; 45min); Brockenhurst (hourly; 1hr); London Waterloo (hourly; 2hr 40min); Weymouth (1–2 hourly; 10–15min).

Poole to: Bournemouth (2–3 hourly; 10–15min); Weymouth (hourly; 45min).

Portsmouth to: London Waterloo (3–4 hourly; 1hr 35min–2hr 15min); Salisbury (hourly; 1hr 20min); Southampton (2 hourly; 45min–1hr); Winchester (hourly; 1hr).

Ryde (Isle of Wight) to: Shanklin (Mon–Sat every 20–40min, Sun hourly; 25min).

Salisbury to: Bath (hourly; 1hr); Bristol (hourly; 1hr 20min); London Waterloo (2 hourly; 1hr 30min); Portsmouth (hourly; 1hr 20min); Southampton (1–2 hourly; 30min).

Southampton to: Bournemouth (3 hourly; 30–50min); Brockenhurst (2–3 hourly; 15–30min); London Waterloo (2–3 hourly; 1hr 20min); Portsmouth (2 hourly; 45min–1hr); Salisbury (1–2 hourly; 30min); Weymouth (hourly; 1hr 40min); Winchester (3–4 hourly; 15–30min).

Weymouth to: Bournemouth (hourly; 55min); London Waterloo (hourly; 2hr 50min–3hr 35min); Poole (hourly; 45min).

Winchester to: Bournemouth (3 hourly; 45min–1hr); London Waterloo (3–4 hourly; 1hr–1hr 15min); Portsmouth (hourly; 1hr); Southampton (4 hourly; 15–20min).

Oxfordshire, The Cotswolds and around

SCOTLAND
0 50 miles
NORTHERN IRELAND
NORTH SEA
IRISH SEA
IRELAND
WALES
N
Bristol Channel
English Channel
FRANCE

CHAPTER 4

Highlights

* **Chiltern Hills** The best base for exploring the lovely wooded scenery of the Chiltern Hills is Henley-on-Thames, site of the famous Henley Regatta. See pp.250–253

* **The Vale of White Horse** Takes its name from the huge, prehistoric horse cut into the chalk of the Berkshire Downs. See pp.253–255

* **Christ Church College, Oxford** Oxford boasts many beautiful old buildings, with Christ Church holding several of the most fascinating. See p.260

* **Chipping Campden, Gloucestershire** Perhaps the most handsome of the Cotswolds towns, with honey-coloured stone houses flanking the superb church of St James. See p.275

▲ The White Horse

Oxfordshire, The Cotswolds and around

Arching around the peripheries of London, beyond the orbital M25, the "Home Counties" of England form London's commuter belt. Beyond the suburban sprawl, however, there is plenty to entice. The north-western Home Counties – **Berkshire**, **Buckinghamshire** and **Hertfordshire** – are at their most appealing amidst the **Chiltern Hills**, a picturesque band of chalk uplands whose wooded ridges rise near Luton, beside the M1, and stretch southwest. The hills provide an exclusive setting for many of the capital's wealthiest commuters, but for the casual visitor the obvious target is **Henley-on-Thames**, an attractive old town famous for its Regatta; it's a handy base for further explorations, with the village of **Cookham** – and its Stanley Spencer gallery – leading the way.

Traversing the Chilterns is the 85mile-long **Ridgeway**, a prehistoric track – and now a national trail possessing a string of prehistoric sites, the most extraordinary being the gigantic chalk horse that gives the **Vale of White Horse** its name. The Vale is dotted with pleasant little villages, though the star is the nearby university city of **Oxford**, with its superb architecture, museums and lively student population. It's also close to **Woodstock**, the handsome little town abutting one of England's most imposing country homes, **Blenheim Palace**.

Beyond Oxford lie the rolling hills and ridges of the **Cotswolds**, covering much of **Oxfordshire** and **Gloucestershire**. Dotted with picturesque villages made from the local honey-coloured stone, the Cotswolds became rich from the medieval wool trade, whose evidence is all around in a multitude of beautiful old churches and handsome mansions. Be sure to visit the engaging market town of **Chipping Campden**, the delightful village of **Northleach** and bustling **Cirencester**. Ultimately, however, the Cotswolds' subtle charms only really reveal themselves when you take to the hills and valleys along its dense network of footpaths and trails, in particular the **Cotswold Way**, a hundred-mile national trail that runs along the edge of the Cotswold escarpment from Chipping Campden in the northeast to Bath in the southwest.

Heading west is **Cheltenham**, an appealing Regency spa town famous for its horse racing. It's a good base for visits to **Gloucester**, with its superb cathedral and rejuvenated harbour area.

The area covered in this chapter is threaded by four **motorways**, the M4, M40, M1 and A1(M). These give swift access from all directions, though drivers will need a detailed map to explore successfully its rural nooks and crannies. Long-distance **buses** mostly stick to the motorways, too, providing an efficient service to all the larger towns, but local services between the villages are patchy, sometimes non-existent. There are **mainline train** services from London's Paddington Station to Oxford, Reading, Cheltenham, Gloucester and Bristol, and trains from London's Paddington Station stop at several Cotswold towns en route to Worcester and Hereford. These main routes are supplemented by a number of branch lines.

The Chiltern Hills and Reading

The **Chiltern Hills** extend southwest from the workaday town of Luton, beside the M1, bumping across Buckinghamshire and Oxfordshire as far as the River Thames, just to the west of Reading. At their best, the hills offer handsome countryside, comprising a band of forested chalk hills with steep ridges and deep valleys interrupted by easy, rolling farmland. For non-residents, **Henley-on-Thames** is the draw, a pleasant riverside town within easy striking distance of the area's key attractions and with a reasonable range of accommodation. Nearby highlights include the village of **Cookham**, home to the fascinating Stanley Spencer gallery. Crossing the Chilterns to the north and west of Henley, the **Ridgeway National Trail** offers splendid hiking, though the most diverting part of the trail is further to the west, beyond the Chilterns and the Thames, amongst the more open scenery of the Berkshire and Oxfordshire downs, especially in the **Vale of White Horse** (see p.253).

Henley and Reading are well served from London by train and there's a branch line up to Cookham from Maidenhead.

Henley-on-Thames

Three counties – Oxfordshire, Berkshire and Buckinghamshire – meet at **HENLEY-ON-THAMES**, long a favourite stopping place for travellers between London and Oxford. Nowadays, Henley is a good-looking, affluent commuter town at its prettiest among the old brick and stone buildings that flank the short main drag, **Hart Street**. At one end of Hart Street is the Market Place and its large and fetching **Town Hall**, at the other stands the easy Georgian curves of **Henley Bridge**. Overlooking the bridge is the parish church of **St Mary**, whose sturdy square tower sports a set of little turrets worked in chequerboard flint and stone. Several operators run **boat trips** out along the Thames from the jetties just south of the bridge, including Hobbs & Sons (Ⓣ01491/572 035, Ⓦwww.hobbs-of-henley.com), who offer hour-long jaunts from April to September for £6.50. There's an imaginative **River and Rowing Museum** (daily 10am–5pm; £3.50; Ⓦwww.rrm.co.uk), a five- to ten-minute walk south along the riverbank from the foot of Hart Street via Thames Side. Inside the museum, a supplementary exhibition (£3.50 extra) is devoted to Kenneth Grahame's children's book *Wind in the Willows*. The book was set near Henley where Grahame (1859–1932) was sent to live with his grandmother, after his mother died from scarlet fever.

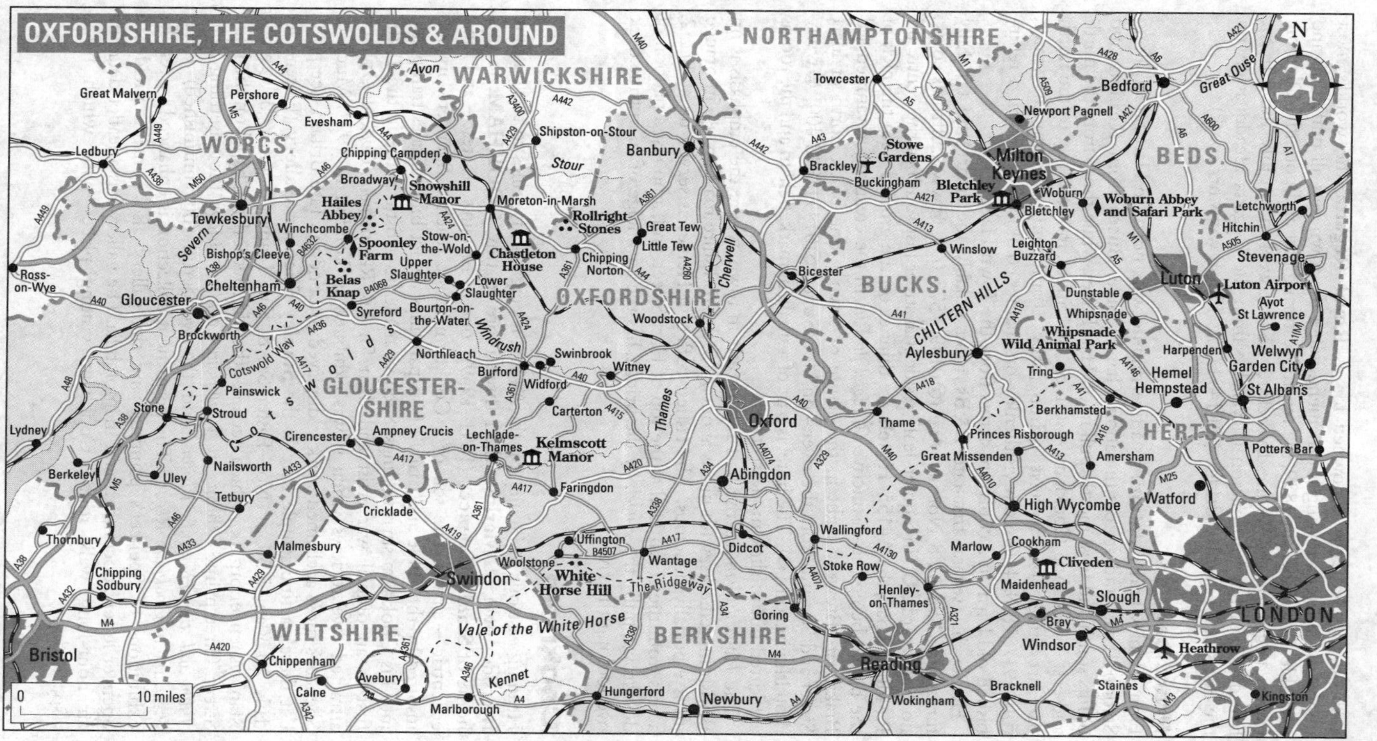

© Crown copyright

Above all, Henley is renowned for its **Royal Regatta**, the world's most important amateur rowing tournament, when the town gets all puffed up and excitable. Established in 1839, the regatta, featuring past and potential Olympic rowers, begins on the Wednesday before the first weekend in July and runs for five days. Further information is available from the Regatta Headquarters on the east side of Henley Bridge (Ⓣ01491/572 153, Ⓦwww.hrr.co.uk).

Practicalities

From Henley **train station**, it's a five-minute walk north to Hart Street, along Station Road and its continuation Thames Side. **Buses** from Reading and points south and west mostly pull in on Hart Street, while those from the north and east – including Cookham – stop on Bell Street, immediately to the north of Hart Street. The **tourist office** (daily 10am–5pm, till 4pm in winter; Ⓣ01491/578 034, Ⓦwww.visithenley-on-thames.co.uk) is located in a refurbished old barn, in a courtyard across from the Town Hall.

Henley has several first-rate **B&Bs**, most notably the smart and tastefully furnished *Alftrudis*, 8 Norman Ave (Ⓣ01491/573 099, Ⓦwww.alftrudis.co.uk; no credit cards; ❹), in a quiet, leafy residential street just south of the centre off Reading Road, the A4155. **Hotels** are thinner on the ground with the pick of the bunch being the distinctive *Hotel du Vin*, in the creatively revamped old Brakspears Brewery, right in the centre of town – one block north of Hart Street and 50 yards from the river - on New Street (Ⓣ01491/848 400, Ⓦwww.hotelduvin.com; ❼). The hotel is part of a small, upmarket chain and the rooms are kitted out in slick modern style.

The *Hotel du Vin* has the best **restaurant** in town, where the emphasis is on British ingredients, with mains about £15; the Yorkshire roast grouse in orange jus is especially delicious. The tastiest coffee in Henley is served up at *Bloc 2*, across from the Town Hall at the top of Hart Street, and, amongst a platoon of downtown pubs, the *Angel*, by the bridge, has the advantage of an outside deck overlooking the river.

Cookham

Heading east out of Henley on the A4155, it's eight leafy miles to the bustling riverside town of **Marlow**, then three more to tiny **COOKHAM**, former home of **Stanley Spencer** (1891–1959), one of Britain's greatest – and most eccentric – artists. The son of a Cookham music teacher, Spencer's art was inspired by the Bible and many of his paintings depict biblical tales transposed into his Cookham surroundings. Spencer made his artistic name in the 1920s, first as an official war artist and then for his *Resurrection: Cookham*, which attracted rave reviews when it was exhibited in London in 1927. Much of Spencer's most acclaimed work is displayed in London's Tate Britain (see p.98), but there's a fine sample here at the **Stanley Spencer Gallery** (Easter–Oct daily 10.30am–5.30pm; Nov–Easter Sat & Sun 11am–4.30pm; £3; Ⓦwww.stanleyspencer.org.uk), which occupies the old Methodist Chapel on the High Street. Three prime exhibits are *View from Cookham Bridge*, the unsettling *Sarah Tubb and the Heavenly Visitors*, and the wonderful (but unfinished) *Christ Preaching at Cookham Regatta*. The permanent collection is enhanced by regular exhibitions of Spencer's paintings and the gallery also contains incidental Spencer letters, documents and memorabilia. The gallery has a leaflet detailing an hour-long walk round Cookham, visiting places with which he is associated.

Practicalities

From **Cookham train station**, which is on the Maidenhead to Marlow branch line, it's a fifteen-minute walk east along the High Street to the gallery. Maidenhead is on the London Paddington to Reading line. From Henley, you have to change trains twice to reach Marlow (at Twycross and Maidenhead). The antique, half-timbered *Bel & The Dragon* **pub**, just across the street from the Spencer Gallery, is a good spot for a pint, though Cookham is also a short drive from one of England's most acclaimed and proclaimed restaurants, Heston Blumenthal's *Fat Duck*, on the High Street in **BRAY** (ⓣ01628/580 333, ⓦwww.fatduck.co.uk; Tues–Sat noon–2.30pm & 7–10.30pm, Sun noon–2.30pm). It's vastly expensive, but it's here you can taste extraordinary delights such as pig's trotter and truffle, snail porridge and egg and bacon ice cream; reservations are essential.

Reading

READING, ten miles south of Henley, is a modern, prosperous town on the south bank of the River Thames.

Reading boasts a couple of Victorian curiosities: the **prison** (no public access), a severe-looking structure on Forbury Road, where Oscar Wilde was incarcerated in the 1890s and wrote his poignant *Ballad of Reading Gaol*; and a replica of the **Bayeux Tapestry** recording William the Conqueror's invasion of England in 1066. The original is in France, but in the 1880s no less than thirty-five embroiderers worked on this 70m-long copy, now displayed in a purpose-built gallery at the **Museum of Reading**, in the Town Hall, on the northeast side of the main shopping precinct (Tues–Sat 10am–4pm, Sun 11am–4pm; free; ⓦwww.readingmuseum.org.uk).

Reading boasts a flourishing **arts scene**, with both the Reading Film Theatre (ⓣ0118/378 7151, ⓦwww.readingfilmtheatre.co.uk) and the Hexagon Theatre (ⓣ0118/960 6060, ⓦwww.readingarts.com) offering a good programme of concerts and shows, though the town's cultural highlight is the **Reading Festival** (ⓦwww.readingfestival.com), a three-day event held at the back end of August and featuring many of the big names of contemporary music.

With fast and frequent services from London Paddington, Reading **train station** is on the north side of town, a five- to ten-minute walk from the centre.

The Vale of White Horse

The **Vale of White Horse**, running east–west between Wantage, a modest market town about twenty-five miles northwest of Reading, and Faringdon, seventeen miles southwest of Oxford, is a shallow valley, whose fertile farmland is studded with tiny villages. It takes its name from the prehistoric figure cut into the chalk downs above two of its smaller hamlets – Uffington and Woolstone. Carved in the first century BC, the horse is the most conspicuous of the prehistoric remains – such as burial mounds and Iron Age forts – punctuating these open downs. The **Ridgeway National Trail**, running along – or near – the top of the downs, links several of these sites, offering wonderful, breezy views over the vale and skirting the White Horse itself. The Vale most readily lends itself to day-trips, but you might opt to stay locally in the attractive hostel on the ridge above **Wantage**, or in one of the Vale's quaint villages – tiny **Woolstone** is perhaps the most appealing.

As for public transport, there's an intermittent local **bus** service between the towns and villages of the Vale, but you'll need to plan ahead (call Traveline ⓣ0871/200 2233, or check ⓦwww.traveline.org.uk).

Wantage

WANTAGE is an unassuming, somewhat care-worn market town, whose crowded Market Place is overseen by a statue of its most famous son, Alfred the Great (849–99), the most distinguished of England's Saxon kings. From the south side of the Market Place a couple of alleys lead through to Church Street and to the **tourist office** (Mon–Sat 10am–4.30pm; ⓣ01235/771 447, ⓦwww.wantage.com), which sells local hiking maps, and a modest **museum**.

From Wantage, it's a couple of miles south to the **Ridgeway** at the point where it begins one of its finest stretches, running seven miles west along the downs to White Horse Hill (see below). There is B&B **accommodation** in the villages below White Horse Hill (see below), or you could head for the *Court Hill Centre* **hostel** (ⓣ01235/760 253, ⓦwww.courthill.org.uk; dorm beds £16.50, doubles ❶; Easter–Oct), in a prime position just off the A338 two miles south of Wantage. The hostel consists of several converted timber barns set around a courtyard, with sixty beds in two- to thirteen-bedded rooms; advance reservations are strongly recommended.

White Horse Hill and around

White Horse Hill, overlooking the B4507 six miles west of Wantage, follows close behind Stonehenge (see p.242) and Avebury (see p.244) in the hierarchy of Britain's ancient sites, though it attracts nothing like the same number of visitors. Carved into the north-facing slope of the downs above the villages of Uffington and Woolstone, the 374-foot-long **horse** looks like something created with a few swift strokes of an immense brush; there's been no lack of weird and wonderful theories as to its origins, but in fact burial sites excavated in the surrounding area point to the horse having some kind of sacred function, though frankly no one knows quite what. The first written record of the horse's existence dates from the time of Henry II, but it was cut much earlier, probably in the first century BC, making it one of the oldest chalk figures in Britain.

Just below the horse is **Dragon Hill**, a small flat-topped hillock that has its own legend. Locals long asserted that this was where St George killed and buried the dragon, a theory proved, so they argued, by the bare patch at the top and the channel down the side, where blood trickled from the creature's wounds. Here also, at the top of the hill, is the Iron Age earthwork of **Uffington Castle**, which provides wonderful views over the Vale.

The Ridgeway runs alongside the horse and continues west to reach, after one and a half miles, **Wayland's Smithy**, a 5000-year-old burial mound encircled by trees. It is one of the best Neolithic remains along the Ridgeway, though heavy restoration has rather detracted from its mystery. In ignorance of its original function, the invading Saxons named it after Weland (hence Wayland), an invisible smith who, according to their legends, made invincible armour and shod horses without ever being seen.

The B4507 passes the narrow lane that leads - after 500 yards – to the car park just below the White Horse. There are no regular buses.

Woolstone and Uffington

About three-quarters of a mile below the White Horse car park, on the north side of the B4057, is the minuscule hamlet of **WOOLSTONE**, where the attractive *White Horse Inn* (ⓣ01367/820 726, ⓦwww.whitehorsewoolstone.co.uk; ④) occupies a half-timbered, partly thatched old building. The inn offers both good-quality pub food and straightforward **accommodation**, mostly in a modern annexe. A mile or so to the north of Woolstone, the much larger village of **UFFINGTON** has an outstanding **B&B**, *The Craven*, on Fernham Road (ⓣ01367/820 449, ⓦwww.thecraven.co.uk; ④), in a delightful thatched cottage with the dinkiest of front doors. There are five infinitely cosy guest rooms and breakfast is served in the old farmhouse kitchen. Uffington's most famous son was Thomas Hughes (1823–96), the author of *Tom Brown's School Days* – hence the village's pocket-sized Tom Brown's School Museum.

Oxford

When they think of **OXFORD**, visitors almost always imagine its **university**, revered as one of the world's great academic institutions. But, although the university dominates central Oxford both physically and mentally, the wider city has an entirely different character, its economy built on the **car plants** of Cowley to the south of the centre. It was here that Britain's first mass-produced cars were produced in the 1920s and, although there have been more downs than ups in recent years, the plants are still vitally important to the area.

Oxford started late, in Anglo-Saxon times, and blossomed even later, under the Normans, when the cathedral was constructed and Oxford was chosen as a royal residence. The origins of the university are obscure, but it seems that the reputation of **Henry I**, the so-called "Scholar King", helped attract students in the early twelfth century. The first **colleges**, founded mostly by rich bishops, were essentially ecclesiastical institutions and this was reflected in collegiate rules and regulations – until 1877 lecturers were not allowed to marry and women were not granted degrees until 1920. There are common architectural features, too, with the private rooms of the students arranged around quadrangles (quads), as are most of the communal rooms – the chapels, halls (dining rooms) and libraries. Though they share a similar history, each of the university's 39 colleges has its own character and often a particular label, whether it's the richest (St John's), most left-wing (Wadham) or most public-school-dominated (Christ Church). Collegiate rivalries are long established, usually revolving around sports, and tension between the university and the city – "Town" and Gown" – has existed as long as the university itself.

Oxford should be high on anyone's itinerary, and can keep you occupied for several days. The university buildings include some of England's finest architecture, and the city can also boast some excellent museums and a good range of bars and restaurants. Getting there is easy, too: from London Paddington the journey takes just an hour by train, a little longer by bus.

Arrival

From Oxford **train station**, it's a five- to ten-minute walk east to the centre via Park End Street and its continuation Hythe Bridge Street. Long-distance and many county-wide buses terminate at the Gloucester Green **bus station**, in the city centre adjoining George Street. Most local and city buses terminate on the High Street and St Giles. There's also a **Park-and-Ride** scheme, with buses (daily Mon–Sat 6am–11pm, Sun 9am–7pm) travelling into the centre every fifteen minutes at peak times (every thirty minutes to an hour in the evening), from five large and clearly signed car parks on the main approach roads into the city. Parking costs are minimal, whereas parking in the city centre is – by municipal design – both inordinately expensive and hard to find.

Information and guided tours

The **tourist office** is in the centre of town at 15 Broad St (Mon–Sat 9.30am–5pm & Sun 10am–4pm; ⓣ01865/252 200, ⓦwww.visitoxford.org); they can supply the free listings booklet, *This Month in Oxford*. The tourist office also offers excellent **guided walking tours**, principally a two-hour gambol round the city centre and its colleges (several tours daily; £6.50). Further along Broad Street, the main Blackwell's bookshop (ⓣ01865/333 606) also runs specialist walking tours at £6.50 per adult. Their main offering is a Literary Tour of Oxford (2 weekly), but there are other, more infrequent offerings, like their Inklings Tour – Inklings being the group of writers, Tolkien and C.S. Lewis included, who met regularly in Oxford in the 1930s. In all cases, advance booking is recommended.

Accommodation

Oxford's central **hotels** are almost invariably expensive, though nowhere near as pricey as those in London. There are one or two inexpensive hotels in or near the centre, but by and large they are far from inspiring and at the budget end of the market – you're better off choosing a **guesthouse** or **B&B**, which are in healthy supply, though most are some way from the centre. Wherever you stay, book ahead in high season either direct or through the tourist office (see above), which operates an efficient accommodation-booking service. Note also that hotels almost always cost less during the week than on the weekend.

Hotels

Bath Place Hotel 4 Bath Place ⓣ01865/791 812, ⓦwww.bathplace.co.uk. This unusual, pink and blue hotel is tucked away down an old cobbled courtyard flanked by ancient buildings with higgledy-piggledy roofs. There are fourteen rooms, each individually decorated in attractive, antique style – canopied beds, bare stone walls and so forth. The location is excellent – in the centre, off Holywell St. ⑥

Old Bank Hotel 92 High St ⓣ01865/799 599, ⓦwww.oldbank-hotel.co.uk. Great location for a slick and sleek hotel comprising a glistening conversion of an old bank. Over forty bedrooms decorated in crisp, modern style – all pastel shades and whites. Some of the rooms have great views over All Souls College. ⑧

Old Parsonage Hotel 1 Banbury Rd ⓣ01865/310 210, ⓦwww.oldparsonage-hotel.co.uk. Arguably the best hotel in town, this lovely hotel occupies a charming, wisteria-clad stone former-parsonage by the church at the top of St Giles. The thirty-odd rooms are tastefully furnished in a bright modern manner, the only problem being the noise of the traffic. ⑧

Parklands Hotel 100 Banbury Rd ⓣ01865/554 374, ⓦwww.oxfordcity.co.uk. Pleasant fourteen-room hotel in a large Victorian house with a garden and bar. North of the centre, but connected to it by a frequent bus service. Good value. ⑤

The Randolph Hotel 1 Beaumont St ⓣ0870/400 8200, ⓦwww.randolph-hotel.com. The most famous hotel in the city, long the favoured choice of the well-heeled visitor, the *Randolph* occupies a large and well-proportioned brick building with a distinctive neo-Gothic interior – the carpeted staircase is especially handsome. Now part of a chain, but with impeccable service and well-appointed bedrooms with all mod cons. The rooms on the top floor are the quietest. Discounts are available at slack periods, but otherwise it's ⑧

Guesthouses and B&Bs

Becket House 5 Becket St ⓣ01865/724 675. Modest but proficient bay-windowed guesthouse in a plain terrace close to the train station. Most rooms en suite. ③

Isis Guesthouse 45–53 Iffley Rd ⓣ01865/248 894, ⓦwww.isisguesthouse.co.uk. From July to September, this college hall becomes a guesthouse with around forty single (£30, en-suite £38) and double rooms, about half of which are en suite.

Located within easy walking distance of Magdalen Bridge. Good value, with rooms decorated in a brisk if frugal modern style. 3

Newton House 82–84 Abingdon Rd ⓣ01865/240 561, ⓦwww.oxfordcity.co.uk. Appealing, family-run guesthouse in two good-looking and well-kept Victorian townhouses about 10min walk south of the centre – well placed for evening strolls along the Thames. The guest rooms are decorated in a smart, traditional style. Thirteen rooms, mostly en suite. 3

St Michael's Guesthouse 26 St Michael's St ⓣ01865/242 101. Often full, this friendly, well-kept B&B, in a cosy three-storey terrace house, has unsurprising furnishings and fittings, but a charming, central location. A real snip. 3

Hostels

Oxford Backpackers Hostel 9a Hythe Bridge St ⓣ01865/721 761. Independent hostel with quads and dorms. Fully equipped kitchen and laundry plus Internet facilities. Handy location between the train station and the centre; 24-hour access. Dorm beds £15–16.

Oxford Youth Hostel 2a Botley Rd ⓣ0870/770 5970, ⓦwww.yha.org.uk. In a clumpy modern block next door to the train station, this popular YHA hostel has 187 beds divided into two-, four- and six-bedded rooms. There's 24-hour access, laundry, Internet access, and an inexpensive café. Open daily all year. Dorm beds including breakfast £17.

The City

Central Oxford's principal point of reference is **Carfax**, a busy junction from where three of the city's main thoroughfares begin: the **High Street** runs east to Magdalen Bridge and the River Cherwell; **St Aldates** south to the Thames; and **Cornmarket** north to the broad avenue of St Giles. Many of the oldest **colleges** face onto the High Street or the side streets adjoining it, their mellow stonework combining to create the most beautiful part of Oxford, though the most stunning college of them all is **Christ Church**. Here, as elsewhere in the city, all of the more visited colleges have restricted opening hours and some impose an admission charge, while others permit no regular public access at all. Of those that do open their doors, **college opening hours** are fairly consistent throughout the year, but there are sporadic term-time variations, especially at weekends. It's also worth noting that during the exam season, which stretches from late April to early June, all the colleges have periods when they are closed to the public entirely. For more specific information, contact the relevant college – contact details are given in the text below.

On the river

Punting is a favourite summer pastime amongst both students and visitors, but handling a punt – a flat-bottomed boat ideal for the shallow waters of the Thames and Cherwell rivers – requires some practise. The punt is propelled and steered with a long pole, which beginners inevitably get stuck in riverbed mud: if this happens, let go and paddle back, otherwise you're likely to be pulled overboard. The Cherwell, though much narrower than the Thames and, therefore, trickier to navigate, provides more opportunities for pulling to the side for a picnic, an essential part of the punting experience.

There are two central **boat rental** places: Magdalen Bridge boathouse (ⓣ01865/202 643), beside the Cherwell at the east end of the High Street; and the Thames boat station at Folly Bridge (ⓣ01865/243 421), a five- to ten-minute stroll south of the centre along St Aldates. In summer, the queues soon build up at both, so try to get there early in the morning – at around 10am. At both boathouses, expect **to pay** about £12 per hour for a boat plus a £30 deposit; sometimes ID is required. Punts can take a maximum of five passengers – four sitting and one punting. Call the boathouses for opening times – which vary – or if there are any doubts about the weather. Both boathouses also rent out **chauffeured punts** (about £20 for 30min) and **pedaloes**, which cost less, but aren't as much fun.

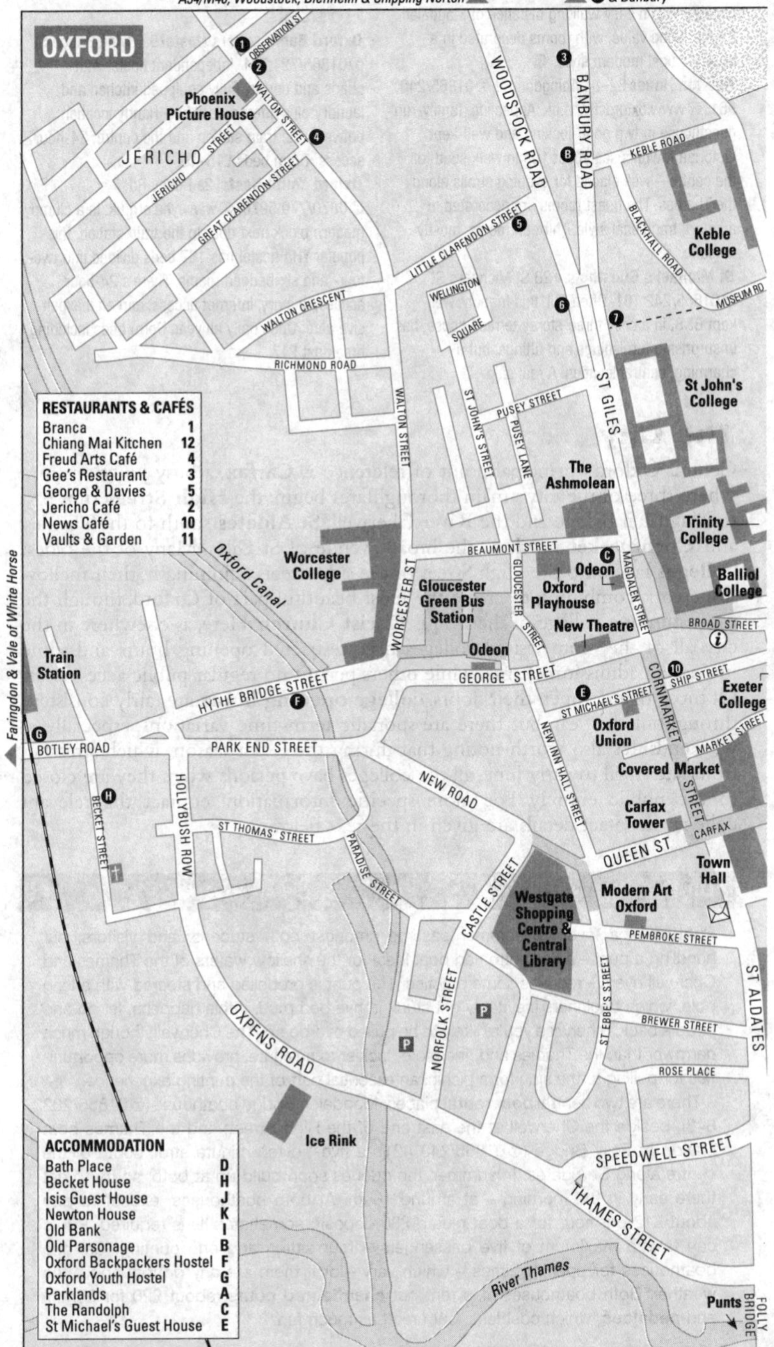
OXFORD
A34/M40, Woodstock, Blenheim & Chipping Norton
A & Banbury
Faringdon & Vale of White Horse
RESTAURANTS & CAFÉS
Branca 1
Chiang Mai Kitchen 12
Freud Arts Café 4
Gee's Restaurant 3
George & Davies 5
Jericho Café 2
News Café 10
Vaults & Garden 11
ACCOMMODATION
Bath Place D
Becket House H
Isis Guest House J
Newton House K
Old Bank I
Old Parsonage B
Oxford Backpackers Hostel F
Oxford Youth Hostel G
Parklands A
The Randolph C
St Michael's Guest House E
Observation St
Walton Street
Phoenix Picture House
JERICHO
Jericho Street
Great Clarendon Street
Woodstock Road
Banbury Road
Keble Road
Blackhall Road
Keble College
Museum Rd
Little Clarendon Street
Wellington Square
Walton Crescent
Richmond Road
St Giles
St John's College
Pusey Street
St John's Street
Pusey Lane
The Ashmolean
Trinity College
Beaumont Street
Magdalen Street
Odeon
Oxford Playhouse
Balliol College
Worcester College
Oxford Canal
Worcester St
Gloucester Green Bus Station
Gloucester Street
New Theatre
Broad Street
Train Station
George Street
Hythe Bridge Street
St Michael's Street
Ship Street
Cornmarket
Exeter College
Oxford Union
Market Street
Botley Road
Park End Street
Covered Market
New Road
New Inn Hall Street
Carfax Tower
Becket Street
Hollybush Row
St Thomas' Street
Paradise Street
Queen St
Carfax
Town Hall
Castle Street
Westgate Shopping Centre & Central Library
Modern Art Oxford
Pembroke Street
St Aldates
St Ebbe's Street
Brewer Street
Norfolk Street
Oxpens Road
Rose Place
Ice Rink
Speedwell Street
Thames Street
River Thames
Punts
Folly Bridge

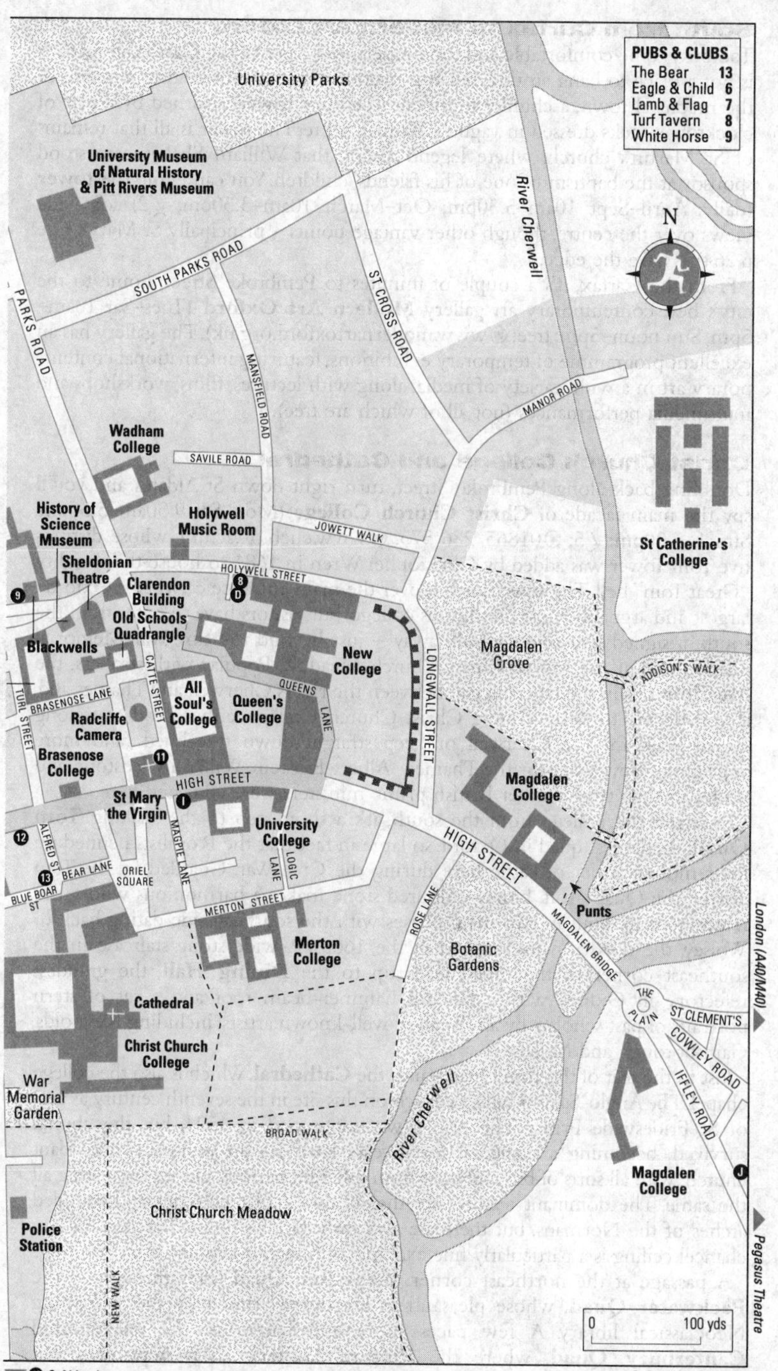
PUBS & CLUBS
The Bear 13
Eagle & Child 6
Lamb & Flag 7
Turf Tavern 8
White Horse 9
University Parks
University Museum of Natural History & Pitt Rivers Museum
River Cherwell
N
SOUTH PARKS ROAD
PARKS ROAD
ST CROSS ROAD
MANSFIELD ROAD
MANOR ROAD
Wadham College
SAVILE ROAD
St Catherine's College
History of Science Museum
Holywell Music Room
JOWETT WALK
Sheldonian Theatre
Clarendon Building
HOLYWELL STREET
Old Schools Quadrangle
Blackwells
New College
Magdalen Grove
ADDISON'S WALK
LONGWALL STREET
QUEENS LANE
CATTE STREET
TURL STREET
BRASENOSE LANE
All Soul's College
Queen's College
Radcliffe Camera
Brasenose College
HIGH STREET
St Mary the Virgin
Magdalen College
University College
ALFRED ST
MAGPIE LANE
LOGIC LANE
BEAR LANE
ORIEL SQUARE
BLUE BOAR ST
MERTON STREET
HIGH STREET
ROSE LANE
Punts
MAGDALEN BRIDGE
Merton College
Botanic Gardens
Cathedral
Christ Church College
THE PLAIN
ST CLEMENT'S
COWLEY ROAD
IFFLEY ROAD
London (A40/M40)
War Memorial Garden
BROAD WALK
River Cherwell
Magdalen College
Christ Church Meadow
Police Station
NEW WALK
Pegasus Theatre
0 100 yds
& Abingdon
© Crown copyright

South from Carfax to Modern Art Oxford

Too busy to be comfortable and too modern to be pretty, the **Carfax** crossroads is not a place to hang around, but it is overlooked by an interesting remnant of the medieval town, a chunky fourteenth-century **tower**, adorned by a pair of clocktower jacks dressed in vaguely Roman attire. The tower is all that remains of St Martin's church, where legend asserts that William Shakespeare stood sponsor at the baptism of one of his friends' children. You can climb the **tower** (daily: April–Sept 10am–5.30pm; Oct–March 10am–3.30pm; £2) for wide views over the centre, though other vantage points – principally St Mary's (see p.264) – have the edge.

From the Carfax, it's a couple of minutes to Pembroke Street, home to the city's best contemporary art gallery, **Modern Art Oxford** (Tues–Sat 10am–5pm, Sun noon–5pm; free; Ⓦwww.modernartoxford.org.uk). The gallery has an excellent programme of temporary exhibitions, featuring international contemporary art in a wide variety of media, along with lectures, films, workshops and multimedia performances (not all of which are free).

Christ Church College and Cathedral

Doubling back along Pembroke Street, turn right down St Aldates and you'll spy the main facade of **Christ Church College** (Mon–Sat 9.30am–5.30pm, Sun 1–5.30pm; £5; Ⓣ01865/286 573, Ⓦwww.chch.ox.ac.uk), whose distinctive Tom Tower was added by Christopher Wren in 1681 to house the weighty "Great Tom" bell. The tower lords it over the main entrance of what is Oxford's largest and arguably most prestigious college, but visitors have to enter from the south, a signed five-minute walk away – just beyond the tiny War Memorial Garden and at the top of Christ Church Meadow. Popular with strollers, the **Meadow** fills in the tapering gap between the rivers Cherwell and Thames and, if you decide to delay visiting Christ Church College, either head east along Broad Walk for the Cherwell or keep straight down tree-lined (and more appealing) New Walk for the Thames. Albert Einstein, William Gladstone and no fewer than twelve other British prime ministers were educated here.

Entering the college from the south, it's a short step to the striking **Tom Quad**, the largest quad in Oxford, so large in fact that the Royalists penned up their mobile larder of cattle here during the Civil War. Guarded by the Tom Tower, the Quad's soft, honey-coloured stone makes a harmonious whole, but it was actually built in two main phases with the southern side dating back to Wolsey, the north finally finished in the 1660s. A wide stone staircase in the southeast corner of the Quad leads up to the **Dining Hall**, the grandest refectory in Oxford with a fanciful hammer-beam roof and a set of stern portraits of past scholars by a roll call of well-known artists, including Reynolds, Gainsborough and Millais.

Just to the rear of the Tom Quad stands the **Cathedral**, which is also the college chapel. The Anglo-Saxons built a church on this site in the seventh century as part of St Frideswide Priory. The priory was suppressed in 1524, but the church survived, becoming a cathedral forty years later. It's an unusually discordant church, with all sorts of bits and bobs from different periods, but it's fascinating all the same. The dominant features are the sturdy circular columns and rounded arches of the Normans, but there are also early Gothic pointed arches and the chancel ceiling is a particularly fine example of fifteenth-century stone vaulting.

A passage at the northeast corner of the Tom Quad leads through to the **Peckwater Quad**, whose pleasantries are overwhelmed by the whopping Neoclassical library. A few paces more and you're in the pocket-sized **Canterbury Quad**, where the **Picture Gallery** (May–Sept Mon–Sat

10.30am–5pm, Sun 2–5pm; Oct–April Mon–Sat 10.30am–1pm & 2–4.30pm; £2) is home to fine works by artists from Italy and the Netherlands, including Leonardo da Vinci, Michelangelo, van Dyck and Frans Hals. The Canterbury Quad abuts **Oriel Square** with Merton College beckoning just beyond.

Merton College

Just a few yards from Christ Church, on Merton Street, stands **Merton College** (Mon–Fri 2–4pm, Sat & Sun 10am–4pm; free; Ⓣ01865/276 310, Ⓦwww.merton.ox.ac.uk), historically the city's most important college. Balliol and University colleges may have been founded earlier, but it was Merton – opened in 1264 – which set the model for colleges in both Oxford and Cambridge, being the first to gather its students and tutors together in one place. Furthermore, unlike the other two, Merton retains some of its original medieval buildings, with the best of the thirteenth-century architecture clustered around **Mob Quad**, a charming courtyard with mullioned windows and Gothic doorways to the right of the Front Quad. From the Mob Quad, an archway leads through to the **Chapel**, which dates from 1290. The chapel has never had a nave, leaving the choir as the main body of the church and the transepts as ante-chapels. In the latter is the curious funerary plaque of Thomas Bodley – founder of Oxford's most important library (see p.263) – his bust surrounded by ungainly, boyish-looking women in classical garb. Famous Merton alumni include T.S. Eliot, Angus Wilson, Louis MacNeice and Kris Kristofferson.

University and Queen's colleges

From Merton, narrow Magpie Lane cuts through to the west end of **University College** (no set opening times; Ⓣ01865/276 602, Ⓦwww.univ.ox.ac.uk), whose long sweeping facade and twin gateway towers spread along the High Street. Known as "Univ", the college claims Alfred the Great as its founder, but things really got going with a formal endowment in 1249, making it Oxford's oldest college – though nothing of that period survives. The college's most famous recent alumnus was Rhodes Scholar Bill Clinton, and Steven Hawking also studied here.

Across the High Street from Univ stands **Queen's College** (no set opening times; Ⓣ01865/279 120, Ⓦwww.queens.ox.ac.uk), whose handsome Baroque buildings cut an impressive dash. The only Oxford college to have been built in one period (1682–1765), Queen's benefited from the skills of several talented architects, most notably Nicholas Hawksmoor and Christopher Wren. Wren designed (or at least influenced the design of) the college's most diverting building, the **Chapel**, whose ceiling is filled with cherubs amidst dense foliage.

Magdalen College and the University Botanic Gardens

Heading east along the High Street from Queen's, it's a short hop to **Magdalen College** (pronounced "Maudlin"; late June to Sept daily noon–6pm, Oct to late June daily 1–6pm or dusk; £3; Ⓣ01865/276 000, Ⓦwww.magd.ox.ac.uk), whose gaggle of stone buildings is overshadowed by its chunky medieval bell tower. Steer right from the entrance and you soon reach the **Chapel**, which has a handsome reredos, though you have to admire it through the windows of an ungainly stone screen. The adjacent **cloisters** are adorned by standing figures, some biblical and others folkloric, most notably a tribe of grotesques. Magdalen also boasts better **grounds** than most other colleges, with a bridge – at the back of the cloisters – spanning the River Cherwell to join **Addison's Walk**.

Magdalen's alumni include Oscar Wilde, C.S. Lewis, John Betjeman, Julian Barnes and A.J.P. Taylor.

Across the High Street from Magdalen lie the **University of Oxford Botanic Gardens** (daily: March–April & Sept–Oct 9am–5pm; May–Aug 9am–6pm; Nov–Feb 9am–4.30pm; £3; Ⓦwww.botanic-garden.ox.ac.uk), whose greenery

▲ Sculpture on Magdalen College

is bounded by a graceful curve of the Cherwell. First planted in 1621, the gardens comprise several different zones, from a lily pond, a bog garden and a rock garden through to borders of bearded irises and variegated plants. There are also six large **glasshouses** featuring tropical and desert species.

The gardens are next to **Magdalen Bridge**, where you can rent punts (see box, p.257).

New College

Doubling back along the High Street, cut up **Queen's Lane** and you'll dog-leg your way north to **New College** (daily: Easter to early Oct 11am–5pm; £2; mid-Oct to Easter 2–4pm; free; ⓣ01865/279 555, ⓦwww.new.ox.ac.uk). Founded in 1379, the college kicks off with an attractive **Front Quad**, though the splendid Perpendicular Gothic architecture of the original was spoiled by the addition of an extra storey in 1674. The adjoining **Chapel** has been mucked about too, yet it can still lay claim to being the finest in Oxford, not so much for its design as its contents. The ante-chapel contains some superb fourteenth-century stained glass and the west window – of 1778 – holds an intriguing (if somewhat unsuccessful) Nativity scene based on a design by Sir Joshua Reynolds. Beneath it stands the wonderful *Lazarus* by Jacob Epstein; Khrushchev, after a visit to the college, claimed that the memory of this haunting sculpture kept him awake at night. An archway on the east side of the Front Quad leads through to the modest **Garden Quad**, with the thick flowerbeds of the **College Garden** beckoning beyond. The north side of the garden is flanked by the largest and best-preserved section of Oxford's medieval **city wall**, but the conspicuous earthen **mound** in the middle is a later decorative addition and not, disappointingly, medieval at all. Notable New College alumni include Tony Benn, the author John Fowles and the actor Hugh Grant.

From the entrance to New College, it's the briefest of walks to the east end of Broad Street.

The Sheldonian Theatre and the Clarendon Building

The east end of Broad Street abuts much of Oxford's most monumental architecture, beginning with the **Sheldonian Theatre** (Mon–Sat 10am–12.30pm & 2–4.30pm; Nov–Feb closes 3.30pm; £2; ⓦwww.sheldon.ox.ac.uk), ringed by a series of glum-looking, pop-eyed classical heads. The Sheldonian was Christopher Wren's first major work, a reworking of the Theatre of Marcellus in Rome, semicircular at the back and rectangular at the front. It was conceived in 1663, when the 31-year-old Wren's main job was as professor of astronomy. Designed as a stage for university ceremonies, nowadays it also functions as a concert hall, but the interior lacks any sense of drama, and even the views from the cupola are disappointing.

Wren's colleague, Nicholas Hawksmoor, designed the **Clarendon Building**, a domineering, solidly symmetrical edifice topped by allegorical figures that is set at right angles to – and lies immediately east of – the Sheldonian. The Clarendon was erected to house the University Press, but is now part of the **Bodleian Library** – the UK's largest after the British Library in London – with an estimated eighty miles of shelves distributed among its several buildings. The heart of the Bodleian is located straight across from the Clarendon in the Old Schools Quadrangle.

The Old Schools Quadrangle

Occupied by the Bodleian Library, the beautifully proportioned **Old Schools Quadrangle** was built in the early seventeenth century in ornate

Jacobean-Gothic style. On the quad's east side is the handsome **Tower of the Five Orders**, with tiers of columns built according to the five classical styles – Tuscan, Doric, Ionic, Corinthian and Composite. On the west side is the library's main entrance and, although most of the complex is out of bounds to the general public, you can pop into the **Divinity School** (Mon–Fri 9am–5pm, Sat 9am–4.30pm; £2), one large room where, until the nineteenth century, degree candidates were questioned in detail about their subject by two interlocutors, with a professor acting as umpire. Begun in 1424, and sixty years in the making, the Divinity School boasts an extravagant vaulted ceiling, a riot of pendants and decorative bosses, altogether an exquisite example of late-Gothic architecture. However, this elaborate design was never carried right through – funding was a constant problem – and parts of the school were finished off in a much plainer style with the change being especially pronounced on the south wall.

The Radcliffe Camera

Behind the Old Schools Quadrangle rises Oxford's most imposing – or vainglorious – building, the Bodleian's **Radcliffe Camera** (formerly the Radcliffe Library; no public access), a mighty rotunda, built between 1737 and 1748 by James Gibbs, architect of London's St Martin-in-the-Fields church. There's no false modesty here. Dr John Radcliffe was, according to a contemporary diarist, "very ambitious of glory" and when he died in 1714 he bequeathed a mountain of money for the construction of a library – the "Radcliffe Mausoleum" as one wag termed it. Gibbs was one of the few British architects of the period to have been trained in Rome and his rotunda is thoroughly Italian in style, its limestone columns ascending to a delicate balustrade, decorated with pinprick urns and encircling a lead-sheathed dome.

St Mary the Virgin

Flanking the High Street just behind the Radcliffe Camera, **St Mary the Virgin** (daily 9am–5pm; free) is a hotchpotch of architectural styles, but mostly dates from the fifteenth century. The church's saving graces are its elaborate, thirteenth-century pinnacled spire and its distinctive Baroque **porch**, flanked by chunky corkscrewed pillars – and paid for by one of Archbishop Laud's friends in 1637. The church's interior is disappointingly mundane, though the carved poppy heads on the choir stalls are of some historical interest: the tips were brusquely flattened off when a platform was installed here in 1554 to stage the heresy trial of Cranmer, Latimer and Ridley, leading Protestants who had run foul of Queen Mary. The church's other diversion is the **tower** (same times; £2.50), with wonderful views across to the Radcliffe Camera (see above) and east over **All Souls College** (Mon–Fri 2–4pm; free; ⓣ01865/279 379, ⓦwww.all-souls.ox.ac.uk), with its twin mock-Gothic towers (the work of Hawksmoor) and conspicuous, brightly decorated sundial designed by Wren.

History of Science Museum and Trinity College

Back on Broad Street, the classical heads that shield the Sheldonian (see p.263) continue along the front of the **History of Science Museum** (Tues–Fri noon–5pm, Sat 10am–5pm & Sun 2–5pm; free; ⓦwww.mhs.ox.ac.uk), whose two floors display an amazing clutter of antique microscopes and astrolabes, sundials, quadrants and sextants. The highlights are Elizabeth I's own astrolabe and Einstein's blackboard.

Across the street, **Trinity College** (no set opening times; free; ⓣ01865/279 900, ⓦwww.trinity.ox.ac.uk) is fronted by three dinky lodge-cottages. Behind them the manicured lawn of the Front Quad stretches back to the richly decorated **Chapel**, awash with Baroque stucco work. Its high altar is flanked by an exquisite example of the work of Grinling Gibbons – a distinctive performance, with cherubs' heads peering out from delicate foliage. Behind the chapel stands **Durham Quad**, an attractive ensemble of old stone buildings begun at the end of the seventeenth century. Trinity alumni include Francis Bacon, Alfred Lord Tennyson and Richard Burton.

Exeter College

From the south side of Broad Street, take Turl Street and you'll soon reach – on the left – the entrance to **Exeter College** (daily 2–5pm; free; ⓣ01865/279 600, ⓦwww.exeter.ox.ac.uk), another medieval foundation whose original buildings were chopped about in the nineteenth century. On this occasion, however, the Victorians did create something of interest in the elaborate, neo-Gothic **Chapel**, whose intricate, almost fussy detail was conceived by Gilbert Scott in the 1850s. The chapel contains a fine set of stained-glass windows illustrating scores of biblical stories – St Paul on the Road to Damascus and Samson bringing down the pillars of the Philistine temple for example – but their deep colours put the nave in permanent shade. The chapel also holds a superb Pre-Raphaelite tapestry, the *Adoration of the Magi*, a fine collaboration between William Morris and Edward Burne-Jones. Morris and Burne-Jones were both students here, as were J.R.R. Tolkien, Alan Bennett and Imogen Stubbs.

Cornmarket and the Ashmolean

Broad Street leads into the **Cornmarket**, a busy pedestrianized shopping strip lined by major stores. There's precious little here to fire the imagination, but it's only a few yards more to the **Ashmolean** (Tues–Sat 10am–5pm, Sun noon–5pm; free; ⓦwww.ashmolean.org), the university's principal museum, which occupies a mammoth Neoclassical building on the corner of Beaumont Street and St Giles. The museum grew from the collections of the magpie-like **John Tradescant**, gardener to Charles I, and an energetic traveller, and today it possesses a vast and far-reaching collection covering everything from English glass and Russian icons to Egyptian mummies. In order to display the full collection, the museum is undergoing a major expansion, which will create thirty new galleries. The redevelopment will not be completed until 2010 and in the meantime visitors have to take pot luck as to what is on display and what isn't, though the Western Art and Egyptology sections should be largely unaffected. Pick up a **plan** at reception for the latest state of affairs.

The University and Pitt-Rivers museums

From the Ashmolean, it's a brief walk north up St Giles to the *Lamb & Flag* pub, beside which an alley cuts through to the **University Museum of Natural History** (daily 10am–5pm; free; ⓦwww.oum.ox.ac.uk) on Parks Road. Exhibits include some impressive fossil dinosaurs, though the museum's natural history displays are outdone by the **Pitt-Rivers Museum** (Tues–Sun 10am–4.30pm, Mon noon–4.30pm; free; ⓦwww.prm.ox.ac.uk), reached through a door at the far end. Founded in 1884, this is one of the world's finest ethnographic museums and an extraordinary relic of the Victorian Age, arranged like an exotic junk shop with each bulging cabinet labelled meticulously by hand. The exhibits, brought to England by several explorers, Captain Cook among them, range from totem poles and mummified crocodiles to African fetishes and gruesome shrunken heads.

Eating and drinking

For a midday bite, one of the city's numerous **cafés** is ideal and there's also a sprinkling of first-rate **restaurants**. Reasonable food is served at most **pubs**, but those listed have been singled out for their ambience or selection of beers rather than for their menus.

Cafés

George & Davies Little Clarendon St. Great little place offering everything from ice cream to bagels and full breakfasts. The cow mural is good fun too. Daily 8am to midnight.

News Café 1 Ship St. Breakfasts, bagels and daily specials, plus beer and wine; also, as the name suggests, local and international newspapers. Daily 9am–10pm.

Vaults & Garden Radcliffe Square. In an atmospheric stone-vaulted room attached to the church of St Mary the Virgin, this café serves up good-quality coffee and cake, as well as quiche-and-salad lunches. There's a small outside area, but it's a tad glum. Daily 10am–5pm.

Restaurants

Branca 111 Walton St ⓣ01865/556 111. Large and informal brasserie-restaurant in proto-industrial premises offering a wide-ranging menu, though Italian dishes predominate. Excellent daily specials from £13. Main courses from as little as £6. Open daily from 11am till late.

Gee's Restaurant 61 Banbury Rd ⓣ01865/553 540. Chic conservatory setting for this well-established restaurant, where the inventive menu includes such items as chargrilled vegetables with polenta, roasted beetroot, a variety of steaks and a wide choice of breads. Strong on fish, too, with seafood main courses for around £16. Open daily for lunch and dinner plus Sat and Sun noon–10.30pm.

Chiang Mai Kitchen 130a High St ⓣ01865/202 233. Best and most authentic Thai restaurant in town serving all the classics and then some. Particularly strong on vegetarian dishes. Smart little place down an alley bang in the centre off the High St. Mains average around £8. Open daily for lunch and dinner.

Freud Arts Café 119 Walton St. Occupying a grand building in the style of a Roman temple, this fashionable café-bar serves straightforward Italian/Mediterranean food. Live music some nights too.

Jericho Café 112 Walton St ⓣ01865/310 840. Relaxed and relaxing neighbourhood café-restaurant, whose creative menu is strong on eastern Mediterranean dishes – try the lip-smacking mezes (from £11). Next door to the *Branca* (see above). Open daily for lunch and dinner.

Pubs

The Bear 6 Alfred St. Tucked away down a narrow side street in the centre of town, this popular pub has not been themed up – and a good job too. Offers a wide range of beers amidst and amongst its traditional decor.

Eagle & Child 49 St Giles. Known variously as the "Bird & Baby", "Bird & Brat" or "Bird & Bastard", this pub was once the haunt of J.R.R. Tolkien and C.S. Lewis. It still attracts an interesting crowd, but the modern extension at the back rather detracts from the cloistered rooms at the front.

Lamb & Flag St Giles. Generations of university students have hung out in this old pub, which comes complete with low-beamed ceilings and a series of cramped but cosy rooms.

Turf Tavern Bath Place, off Holywell St. Small, atmospheric seventeenth-century pub with a fine range of beers, and mulled wine in winter. Abundant seating outside.

White Horse 52 Broad St. A tiny, old pub with snug rooms, pictures of old university sports teams on the walls and real ales. It was used as a set for the *Inspector Morse* TV series.

Entertainment and nightlife

Oxford does not rate highly when it comes to contemporary **live music**, though devotees of **classical music** are well catered for, with the city's main concert halls and certain college chapels – primarily Christ Church, Merton and New College – offering a wide-ranging programme of concerts and recitals. As regards **theatre**, student productions dominate the city repertoire, but the quality of acting varies, particularly when they tackle Shakespeare, the favourite for the open-air college productions put on for tourists during the summer.

For classical music and theatre **listings**, consult *This Month in Oxford*, available free from the tourist office. The daily *Oxford Mail* newspaper also carries information on gigs and events. For more adventurous stuff – special club nights etc – watch out for flyers.

Live music and clubs

OFS (Old Fire Station) 40 George St ⓣ01865/297 170. Multipurpose venue hosting musicals and theatre, plus a separate café-bar featuring one-off DJ club nights.

Carling Academy 190 Cowley Rd ⓣ01865/813 500, ⓦwww.oxford-academy.co.uk. Far and away Oxford's liveliest indie and dance venue, with a fast-moving programme of live bands and guest DJs.

Classical music and theatre

Holywell Music Room 32 Holywell St. This small, plain, Georgian building was opened in 1748 as the first public music hall in England. It offers a varied programme, from straight classical to experimental, with occasional bouts of jazz. Programme details are posted outside and are available at the Oxford Playhouse (see below), which also sells its tickets.

Oxford Playhouse 11 Beaumont St ⓣ01865/305 305, ⓦwww.oxfordplayhouse.com. Professional touring companies perform a mixture of plays, opera and concerts at what is generally regarded as the city's best theatre.

Pegasus Theatre Magdalen Rd ⓣ01865/722 851, ⓦwww.pegasustheatre.org.uk. Low-budget, avant-garde productions dominate the programme of this adventurous theatre.

Sheldonian Theatre Broad St ⓣ01865/277 299. Some have criticized the acoustics here, but this is still Oxford's top concert hall and its resident symphony orchestra is the Oxford Philomusica (ⓣ01865/736 202, ⓦwww.oxfordphil.com).

Listings

Bike rental Bikezone, 6 Lincoln House, Market St, off Cornmarket (ⓣ01865/728 877, ⓦwww.bikezoneoxford.co.uk).

Bookshops The leading university bookshop is Blackwells (ⓦwww.blackwell.co.uk), with several outlets including three shops on Broad St: Blackwells Music, Blackwells Art & Posters, and the main bookshop at 48–51 Broad St (ⓣ01865/792 792).

Buses Most local buses, including Park-and-Ride, are operated by the Oxford Bus Company (ⓣ01865/785 400, ⓦwww.oxfordbus.co.uk), which also – amongst several companies – offers fast and frequent services to London Gatwick and Heathrow airports. Other local services are mostly in the hands of Stagecoach (ⓣ01865/772 250, ⓦwww.stagecoach-oxford.co.uk).

Car rental Avis ⓣ0870/153 9102; National ⓣ01865/240 471.

Cinema The Odeon cinemas on Magdalen and George streets (both ⓣ0871/224 4007, ⓦwww.odeon.co.uk) show the latest blockbusters, while the best art-house cinema is the Ultimate Picture Palace (UPP) on Jeune St, off Cowley Rd (ⓣ01865/245 288, ⓦwww.ultimatepicturepalace.co.uk). The Phoenix Picture House, 57 Walton St (ⓣ01865/512 526, ⓦwww.picturehouses.co.uk), shows mainstream and arts films, and regularly screens foreign-language films too.

Pharmacies Boots, 6 Cornmarket, ⓣ01865/247 461.

Post office At the top of St Aldates, near the corner with the High St.

Taxis Taxi ranks are liberally distributed across the city centre, with taxis lining up at the train station and on the High St. Alternatively, call Radio Taxis ⓣ01865/242 424.

Around Oxford

From Oxford, it's a short trip west to the Cotswolds (see pp.269–277) and a brief haul south to both the Vale of White Horse (see pp.253–255) and the Chiltern Hills (see pp.250–253). Nearer still – a brief bus ride north – is the charming little town of **Woodstock** and its imperious neighbour, **Blenheim Palace**, birthplace of Winston Churchill.

Woodstock

WOODSTOCK, eight miles north of Oxford, has royal associations going back to Saxon times, with a string of kings attracted by its excellent hunting. The Royalists used Woodstock as a base during the Civil War, but, after their defeat, Cromwell never got round to destroying either the town or the palace: the latter was ultimately given to (and flattened by) the Duke of Marlborough in 1704 when work started on the palace of today. Long dependent on royal and then ducal patronage, Woodstock is now both a well-heeled commuter town for Oxford and a provider of food, drink and beds for visitors to Blenheim. It is also an extremely pretty little place, its handsome stone buildings gathered around the main square, at the junction of Market and High streets. This is also where you'll find the town's one specific sight, the **Oxfordshire Museum** (Tues–Sat 10am–5pm, Sun 2–5pm; free), a well-composed review of the county's archeology, social history and industry.

The museum shares its premises with the town's **tourist office** (March–Oct Mon–Sat 9.30am–5.30pm, Sun 2–5pm; Nov–Feb Mon–Sat 10am–5pm; Ⓣ01993/813 276, Ⓦwww.oxfordshirecotswolds.org). Woodstock has several good **pubs**, but the bar of the *Bear Hotel*, an old coaching inn across from the museum with low-beamed ceilings and an open fire, is the most atmospheric. The *Bear* (Ⓣ0870/400 8202, Ⓦwww.bearhotelwoodstock.co.uk; ❻) has fifty or so luxurious rooms kitted out in an attractive, country-house style. Just as appealing, maybe more so, is the nearby *King's Arms*, 19 Market St (Ⓣ01993/813 636, Ⓦwww.kings-hotel-woodstock.co.uk; ❼), with fifteen chic, pastel-painted rooms, and a great **restaurant**, with main courses starting at about £11. The baked nut loaf with mushroom and watercress sauce is especially tasty.

Stagecoach **bus #20** leaves Oxford bus station bound for Woodstock every thirty minutes or so (hourly on Sun); thereafter it continues onto Chipping Norton in the Cotswolds (see p.275).

Blenheim Palace

Nowadays, successful British commanders get medals and titles, but in 1704, as a thank-you for his victory over the French at the Battle of Blenheim, Queen Anne gave **John Churchill, Duke of Marlborough** (1650–1722) the royal estate of Woodstock, along with the promise of enough cash to build himself a gargantuan palace.

Work started promptly on **Blenheim Palace** (mid-Feb to Oct daily 10.30am–5.30pm, last admission 4.45pm; Nov to mid-Dec Wed–Sun same hours; £16.50 including park, gardens & parking, £14 in winter; Ⓦwww.blenheimpalace.com) with the principal architect being Sir John Vanbrugh, who was also responsible for Castle Howard in Yorkshire (see p.573). However, the duke's formidable wife, Sarah Jennings, who had wanted Christopher Wren as architect, was soon at loggerheads with Vanbrugh, while Queen Anne had second thoughts, stifling the flow of money. Construction work was halted and the house was only finished after the duke's death at the instigation of his widow, who ended up paying most of the bills and designing much of the interior herself. The end result is the country's grandest example of Baroque civic architecture, an Italianate palace of finely worked yellow stone that is more a monument than a house – just as Vanbrugh intended.

The **interior** of the main house is stuffed with paintings and tapestries, plus all manner of objets d'art, including furniture from Versailles and carvings by Grinling Gibbons. Churchill fans may find more of interest in the **Churchill Exhibition**, which provides a brief introduction to Winston, accompanied by live recordings of some of his more famous speeches. Born here at Blenheim, Churchill (1874–1965) now lies buried alongside his wife in the graveyard of Bladon church just outside the estate.

Blenheim's formal **gardens** (same hours as house; £7.50–9.50 gardens, park & parking only), to the rear of the house, are divided into several distinct areas, including a rose garden and an arboretum, though the open **parkland** (daily 9am–5.30pm or dusk, last admission 45min before closing) is more enticing, leading from the front of the house down to an artificial lake, **Queen Pool**. Vanbrugh's splendid Grand Bridge crosses the lake to the **Column of Victory**, erected by Sarah Jennings and topped by a statue of her husband posing heroically in a toga.

There are two **entrances** to Blenheim, one just south of Woodstock on the Oxford road and another through the Triumphal Arch at the end of Park Street in Woodstock itself. Stagecoach bus #20 runs to Blenheim Palace from Oxford's bus stations every half-hour (hourly on Sun).

The Cotswolds

The limestone hills that make up the **Cotswolds** are preposterously photogenic, dotted with a string of picture-book villages, many of them built by wealthy cloth merchants in between the fourteenth and sixteenth centuries. Largely bypassed by the Industrial Revolution, which heralded the area's commercial decline, much of the Cotswolds is technically speaking a relic, its architecture beautifully preserved. Numerous churches are decorated with beautiful carving, for which the local limestone was ideal: soft and easy to carve when first quarried, but hardening after long exposure to the sunlight.

The Cotswolds have become one of the country's main tourist attractions, with many towns afflicted by plagues of tearooms and souvenir and antiques shops – this is Morris Dancing country. To see the Cotswolds at their best, you should visit off season or perhaps avoid the most popular towns and instead escape into the hills themselves, though even in high season the charms of towns like Chipping Campden – "Chipping"'as in *ceapen*, the Old English for market – Winchcombe and Northleach are evident. As for walking, this might be a tamed landscape, but there's good scope for exploring the byways, either in the gentler valleys that are most typical of the Cotswolds or along the dramatic escarpment that marks the boundary with the Severn Valley. A national trail, the **Cotswold Way,** runs along the top of the ridge, stretching about one hundred miles from Chipping Campden past Cheltenham, and Gloucester as far as Bath. A number of prehistoric sites provide added interest along the route, with some – such as Belas Knap near Winchcombe – being well worth a diversion.

There are also a few larger towns hereabouts, the biggest true Cotswold town being Cirencester, a buzzing community dating back to the Romans. On the western edge, there's also Cheltenham, but this has a very different feel, predominantly Regency in tone.

As for public transport, the train network comes close to ignoring the Cotswolds, the main exception being the Oxford to Worcester service, on which the slower trains stop at half a dozen of the region's villages and the town of Moreton-in-Marsh, though none of these are prime targets. As for the rest, you'll be reliant on the bus network, which does a good job connecting all the larger towns and villages, but not the smaller, more isolated places and nothing much at all on Sundays. All the region's tourist offices carry timetables and the larger ones sell an excellent synopsis of train and bus services in their *Explore the Cotswolds* brochure, with Oxfordshire County Council's *Public Transport Guide* filling in the gaps.

Burford

Twenty miles west of Oxford you get your first real taste of the Cotswolds at **BURFORD**, where the long and wide High Street, which slopes down to the bridge over the River Windrush, is simply magnificent – despite all the juggernauts. The street is flanked by a remarkable – and amazingly homogeneous – line of old buildings that exhibit almost every type of peccadillo known to the Cotswolds, from wonky mullioned windows and half-timbered facades with bendy beams, through to spiky brick chimneys, fancy bow-fronted, stone houses and grand horse and carriage gateways. What's more, Burford also possesses the fascinating church of **St John the Baptist**, by the river and down a lane off the High Street. Of all the Cotswold churches, this has the most historical resonance with architectural bits and pieces surviving from every phase of its construction, beginning with the Normans and ending in the wool boom of the seventeenth century. Thereafter, it was pretty much left alone and, most unusually, its clutter of mausoleums, chapels and chantries survived the Reformation to create the jingle and jangle of today.

Practicalities

Buses to Burford pull in along the High Street. The **tourist office** is located just off the High Street on Sheep Street (March–Oct Mon–Sat 9.30am–5.30pm, Nov–Feb Mon–Sat 9.30am–4pm; ⓣ01993/823 558, ⓦwww.oxfordshirecotswolds.org).

Burford has two first-class hotels, kicking off with *The Bay Tree*, Sheep Street (ⓣ01993/822 791, ⓦwww.cotswold-inns-hotels.co.uk; ❽), which occupies a wisteria-clad stone house dating from the seventeenth century. The rooms are both in the main house and in a couple of annexes, and each is done out in a modern, sometime lavish rendition of period style. The *Lamb Inn*, just along Sheep Street (ⓣ01993/823 155, ⓦwww.cotswold-inns-hotels.co.uk; ❼), is another great choice and is, if anything, a tad more traditional than its neighbour. For something less expensive, head for *The Angel*, just off the High Street at 14 Witney St (ⓣ01993/822 714, ⓦwww.theangelatburford.co.uk; ❻), where they have just three traditional guest rooms situated in a very old stone house. The *Angel* is also where you should **eat**: they serve from a lively, creative menu with mains from £14; the roasted monkfish with mussels is fantastic.

Cirencester and around

CIRENCESTER, some nineteen miles southwest of Burford, is a somewhat old-fashioned town on the southern fringes of the Cotswolds. As Corinium, it became a provincial capital and a centre of trade under the **Romans**. The town flourished for three centuries, and even had one of the largest forums north of the Alps, but the Saxons destroyed almost all of the Roman city, and the town only revived with the wool boom of the Middle Ages. Nowadays, Cirencester, with its handsome stone buildings, is an affluent little place of 19,000 souls that lays claim to be the "Capital of the Cotswolds"; it's also within easy striking distance of Malmesbury, where the big deal is the Norman abbey.

The Town

Cirencester's heart is the delightful, swirling **Market Place**, packed with traders' stalls on Mondays and Fridays. An irregular line of eighteenth-century facades along the north side contrasts with the heavier Victorian structures opposite, but the parish church of **St John the Baptist** (Mon–Sat 9.30am–5pm, Sun 2.15–5pm; £2 suggested donation), built in stages during the fifteenth century, dominates. The extraordinary flying buttresses that support the tower had to be added when it transpired that the church had been constructed over a filled-in ditch. The church contains a colourful wineglass **pulpit**, carved in stone around 1450 and one of the few pre-Reformation pulpits to have survived in Britain. Outside, one of the best views of the church is from the **Abbey Grounds**; site of the Saxon abbey, it's now a small park skirted by the modest River Churn and a fragment of the Roman city wall.

Few medieval buildings other than the church have survived in Cirencester. The houses along the town's most handsome streets – Park, Thomas and Coxwell – date mostly from the seventeenth and eighteenth centuries. One of those on Park Street, just to the west of the Market Place, houses the sleek **Corinium Museum** (Mon–Sat 10am–5pm, Sun 2–5pm; £3.90), which mostly devotes itself to Roman and Saxon artefacts, including several wonderful **mosaic pavements**.

The **Brewery Arts Centre** (Mon–Fri 10am–5pm, Sat 9.30am–5.30pm; free; Ⓣ01285/657181, Ⓦwww.breweryarts.org.uk), just south of the Market Place off Cricklade Street, is occupied by more than a dozen resident artists, whose studios you can visit and whose work you can buy in the shop. The centre's theatre hosts high-calibre plays and concerts (from jazz to classical), and there is a busy café on the first floor.

Practicalities

Despite nine roads converging on Cirencester – five of them Roman – **bus** services to the town could be better. All bus services to Cirencester stop in the Market Place, where the **tourist office** (Mon 9.45am–5.30pm, Tues–Sat 9.30am–5.30pm; Dec closes 5pm; Ⓣ01285/654 180, Ⓦwww.cotswold.gov.uk), in the Corn Hall, has a list of local **accommodation** pinned outside. The choicest **B&B** is in an old and attractively furnished Georgian house down a narrow alley just north of the Market Place, 107 Gloucester St (Ⓣ01285/657 861; no cards; ④). Alternatively, a string of **B&Bs** line up along Victoria Road, a short walk east of the Market Place, including *The Ivy House*, in high-gabled Victorian premises at no. 2 (Ⓣ01285/656 626, Ⓦwww.ivyhousecotswolds.com; ④); there are four guest rooms here, all en suite, and each is decorated in a modest but homely manner.

For **snacks,** you can't do much better than *Keith's Coffee Shop* on Black Jack Street, where they serve the best coffee in town, and the inexpensive *Coffee House*, in the Brewery Centre, which serves interesting vegetarian dishes (no credit cards; closed Sun). The best choice for a relaxing evening meal is *Harry Hare's*, 3 Gosditch St (Ⓣ01285/652 375), just behind the church, which offers moderately expensive wholesome English dishes, with a classy twist.

Malmesbury

The small hilltown of **MALMESBURY,** on the periphery of the Cotswolds twelve miles south of Cirencester, may have lost most of its good looks with a rash of modern development, but there's no gainsaying the stirring beauty of its partly ruinous Norman abbey, a majestic structure boasting some of the finest Romanesque sculpture in the country. Malmesbury's local celebrities include **Elmer the Monk**, who in 1005 attempted to fly from the abbey tower with the aid of wings: he limped for the rest of his life, but won immortal fame as the "flying monk".

Malmesbury's High Street begins at the bottom of the hill by the old silk mills and heads north across the river and up past a jagged row of ancient cottages on its way to the octagonal **Market Cross**, built around 1490 to provide shelter from the rain. Nearby, the eighteenth-century **Tolsey Gate** leads through to the **Abbey** (daily 10am–4pm; free), which was once a rich and powerful Benedictine monastery. The first abbey burnt down in about 1050, the second was roughed up during the Dissolution, but the beautiful Norman **nave of the abbey church** has survived, its south porch sporting a multitude of exquisite if badly worn figures. To the left of the high altar, the pulpit virtually hides the **tomb of King Athelstan**, grandson of Alfred the Great and the first Saxon to be recognized as king of England; the tomb, however, is empty and the location of the king's body is unknown. The abbey's greatest surviving treasures are housed in the *parvis* (room above the porch), reached via a narrow spiral staircase right of the main doorway, where pride of place is given to four Flemish **medieval Bibles**, written on parchment and sumptuously illuminated with gilt ink and exquisite miniature paintings.

Buses to Malmesbury pull into the Market Place, a short walk from the **tourist office**, on the corner of Cross Hayes and Market Lane (Mon–Thurs 9am–4.50pm, Fri 9am–4.20pm, Easter–Sept also Sat 10am–4pm; ⓣ01666/823 748, ⓦwww.visitwiltshire.co.uk). There's no real reason to **stay the night**, though the *Old Bell* in Abbey Row (ⓣ01666/822 344, ⓦwww.oldbellhotel.com; ❼) provides a strong incentive: originally built as a guesthouse for the abbey, it has loads of atmosphere, pleasantly appointed rooms, and a good **restaurant**.

Northleach

Secluded in a shallow depression some ten miles north of Cirencester, **NORTHLEACH** is one of the most appealing and least developed villages in the Cotswolds – a great base to explore the Cotswolds. Rows of immaculate late-medieval cottages cluster around the village's Market Place with more of the same framing the adjoining Green, but the most outstanding feature is the handsome Perpendicular Church of St Peter and St Paul, erected in the fifteenth century at the height of the wool boom. The porch of St Peter and St Paul is a suitably ostentatious affair overseen by a set of finely carved corbel heads and beyond the beautifully proportioned nave is lit by wide clerestory windows. The floor of the nave is inlaid with an exceptional collection of memorial brasses, marking the tombs of the merchants whose endowments paid for the church. On several, you can make out the woolsacks laid out beneath the corpse's feet – a symbol of wealth and power that features to this day in the House of Lords, where a woolsack is placed on the Lord Chancellor's seat.

Two minutes' walk up along the High Street from the Market Place is Northleach's other main attraction, **Keith Harding's World of Mechanical Music** (daily 10am–6pm; £7.50; ⓦwww.mechanicalmusic.co.uk), comprising a bewildering collection of antique musical boxes, automata, barrel organs and mechanical instruments all stuffed into one room. The entrance fee includes an hour-long demonstration tour, of which the highlight is hearing the likes of Rachmaninov, Gershwin or Paderewski playing their own masterpieces on piano rolls. Finally, **walking trails** radiate out from Northleach in all directions either across the grassy hills or along the river.

Practicalities

Buses pull into the centre of the village beside the green. There is no tourist office and two smashing places to **stay** – one B&B and one hotel. The B&B is *Cotteswold House* (ⓣ01451/860 493, ⓦwww.cotteswoldhouse.com; ④), a wonderfully well-preserved stone cottage with exposed stone arches and antique oak panelling right in the centre of the village on the Market Place. Alternatively, head for the excellent *Wheatsheaf Hotel* (ⓣ01451/860 244, ⓦwww.wheatsheaf.cotswoldsinns.com; ⑥), a former coaching inn just along from the Market Place on West End. The hotel's old stone exterior has been left intact, but the public rooms have been remodelled in a bright and brisk modern style and the same applies to the eight, en-suite guest rooms, though here the design is softened by period furniture. The *Wheatsheaf's* **restaurant** is first-rate too, offering delicious British cuisine – roast rack of lamb, cod in beer and so forth – with mains averaging around £14.

Stow-on-the-Wold and around

Ambling over a steep hill some ten miles north of Northleach, **STOW-ON-THE-WOLD** sucks in a disproportionate number of visitors for its size and attractions, which essentially comprise an old **marketplace** surrounded by cafés, pubs, antique and souvenir shops. The narrow walled alleyways, or "tunes", running into the square were designed for funnelling sheep into the market, which is itself dominated by an imposing Victorian hall – but architecturally that is pretty much it.

Stow is, however, easy to reach by bus from the likes of Cheltenham and Cirencester, with buses pulling in on the High Street, just off the main square, where the **tourist office** (April–Oct Mon–Sat 9.30am–5.30pm; Nov–March Mon–Sat 9.30am–4.30pm; ⓣ01451/831 082, ⓦwww.cotswold.gov.uk) carries oodles of local information. They will also book **accommodation**, of which there is a reasonable supply, including the *Tall Trees B&B* (ⓣ01451/831 296; no credit cards; ③), on the edge of town off the Oddington road (A436), which has sweeping views and a cosy wood burner in its modern sitting room annexe. There's only one **youth hostel** in the Cotswolds and it's here, in a good-looking Georgian townhouse on the main square (ⓣ0870/770 6050, ⓦwww.yha.org.uk; dorm beds £16). The hostel has fifty beds in four- to eight-bedded rooms (no doubles) and is open all year.

For **food**, *The Royalist Hotel*, just off the main square on the corner of Park and Digbeth streets, offers light meals in its *Eagle & Child* bar and also possesses the more formal but extremely good *947AD* restaurant (ⓣ01451/830 670), where a main course costs about £14. The best teashop in town is the *Cotswold Garden Tearoom*, yards from the *Royalist* on Digbeth Street and offers tasty home-made cakes and snacks.

Bourton-on-the-Water

If anywhere can be described as the epicentre of Cotswold tourism, it has to be **BOURTON-ON-THE-WATER**, some four miles south of Stow just to the east of the A429. The reason for all the fuss is the five (allegedly very

▲ Stow-on-the-Wold

picturesque) mini-bridges that straddle the River Windrush as it courses through the centre of the village. Add to this a few purpose-built attractions – a Model Village here, a Dragonfly Maze there – and you have enough to attract an army of tourist coaches.

Chipping Norton and around

The bustling market town of **CHIPPING NORTON**, eight miles east of Stow, is not the prettiest of the Cotswold towns by any means, but it is flanked to the east by one of the least explored and most scenic corners of the region, where the limestone uplands are patterned by long dry-stone walls and sprinkled with tiny stone hamlets. It was King John who granted a wool fair charter to Chipping Norton in the twelfth century, but the town reached its peak three hundred years later, when it acquired many of the stalwart stone buildings that now line up along the market square, though the lumpy Town Hall arrived later. Also paid for by wealthy wool merchants, St Mary's Parish Church, just below the square – and beyond a row of handsome almshouses – looks every inch the country church, the modesty of its tower offset by the long and slender windows of its beautiful Perpendicular Gothic nave.

Buses to Chipping Norton pull in on West Street, a few yards from the Town Hall. **Accommodation** is thin on the ground, but there are well-appointed rooms behind the Georgian facade of the *Crown and Cushion* (Ⓣ01608/642 533, Ⓦwww.crown-cushion.co.uk; ❺), a few yards from the Town Hall on the main square; curiously enough, the hotel was once owned by Keith Moon of The Who. More distinctively, *The Forge B&B* (Ⓣ01608/658 173, Ⓦwww.cotswolds-accommodation.com; ❹) offers a handful of en-suite rooms in tastefully converted old stone premises, three miles southwest of town along the B4450 in the middle of tiny Churchill. The best – or at least the most authentic – **pub** in Chipping Norton is the *Chequers*, just down from the main square near St Mary's.

Chipping Campden

CHIPPING CAMPDEN, some fifteen miles northwest of Chipping Norton, gives a better idea than anywhere else in the Cotswolds as to what a prosperous wool town might have looked like in the Middle Ages. The short High Street is hemmed in by ancient houses, whose undulating, weather-beaten roofs jag against each other, while down below are twisted beams and mullioned windows. The seventeenth-century **Market Hall** has survived too, a barn-like affair in the middle of the High Street, where farmers once gathered to sell their harvests. From the High Street, it's a brief walk east past a splendid sequence of old stone houses to the **church of St James** (April–Oct Mon–Fri 10am–5pm, Sat 11am–5pm & Sun 2–5pm; Nov–March Mon–Sat 11am–3pm, Sun 2–4pm; free), the archetypal Cotswold wool church built on the economic back of its sheep in the fifteenth century, the zenith of the town's wool-trading days. Inside, the light and airy nave is bathed in light from the clerestory windows.

Practicalities

Inevitably, Chipping Campden heaves with day-trippers in the summer, so try to stay overnight and explore in the evening or at dawn, when the streets are empty and the golden hues of the stone at their richest. Getting here by bus is relatively easy from Cheltenham, Moreton-in-Marsh (for Chipping Norton and Oxford) and Stratford-upon-Avon, but other places usually require more effort. The town's **tourist office** is bang in the middle of town, on the High Sreet (daily 10am–5.30pm; Ⓣ01386/841 206, Ⓦwww.chipping-campden.net). They will book accommodation on your behalf, a useful service in the height of the summer when rooms are in short supply. The town's best **B&B** by a long chalk is *Badgers Hall* (Ⓣ01386/840 839, Ⓦwww.badgershall.com; ❻), in an old stone house on the High Street, above their own tearoom. All the guest rooms are en suite and come complete with period detail – beamed ceilings and so forth; advance bookings are advised.

Badgers Hall is the best teashop in town and the pick of the **pubs** is the *Eight Bells Inn* (T01386/840 371, W www.eightbellsinn.co.uk), a particularly cosy spot in a charming old stone building on the way up to the church. The restaurant here is first-rate, trying wherever possible to source things locally; expect dishes like wild mushroom risotto with egg, and lamb shank in garlic jus. Main courses start at £9, less in the bar; the kitchen is open daily for lunch and dinner. If there's no room at the inn, try the half-timbered *Red Lion*, a pub and restaurant on the High Street, where a good range of English dishes is on offer, with main courses at about £12.

Broadway

BROADWAY, five miles from Chipping Campden, is a particularly handsome little village at the foot of the steep escarpment that rolls along the western edge of the Cotswolds. It seems likely that the Romans were the first to settle here, but Broadway's high times were as a stagecoach stop on the route from London to Worcester. It's this former function, which has defined much of its present appearance – its long and wide main street framed by stone cottages and shaded by chestnut trees. The village attracts more visitors than is good for it, but things quieten down in the evening and *The Olive Branch*, 78 High St (T01386/853 440, W www.theolivebranch-broadway.com; 5), is an extremely pleasant **B&B** in an old stone house and with half a dozen homely guest rooms. There are **bus** services to Broadway from Chipping Campden and Winchcombe (see below).

Winchcombe

From Broadway, it's about eight miles southwest to **WINCHCOMBE**, whose long main street is flanked by a fetching medley of stone and half-timbered buildings. The town was once an important Saxon town and one-time capital of the kingdom of Mercia; it flourished during the medieval cloth boom too, one of the results being **St Peter's**, the town's main church, a mainly fifteenth-century structure distinguished by the forty, striking gargoyles that ring the exterior, a mixed crew of devils, beasts and the insane.

Three or four buses a day arrive at Winchcombe from Cheltenham and Broadway (Mon–Sat); passengers arriving from Chipping Campden have to change at Broadway, though this can mean an awful long wait. Winchcombe **tourist office**, in the Town Hall on the High Sreet (Mon–Sat 10am–5pm, Sun 10am–4pm; T01242/602 925, W www.visitcotswoldsandsevernvale.gov.uk), has information on local hikes and attractions; they will also book accommodation.

Of the town's many B&Bs, one of the best is the excellent *Gower House*, 16 North St (T01242/602 616; no credit cards; 3), which offers three extremely comfortable rooms – two en suite – in an attractively modernized, seventeenth-century house in the town centre. Alternatively, the *White Hart Inn*, in a good-looking old building on the High Street (T01242/602 359, W www.wineandsausage.co.uk; 4), has eight spick-and-span rooms decorated in cosy, traditional-meets-folksy manner.

For food, the *White Hart Inn* is the place to go, its speciality being simple, British dishes in general and sausages in particular – not just any old sausage, but delicious gourmet versions, like venison and red wine or lamb, mint and apricot; you can eat either in the restaurant, where main courses start at about £8, or at the bar (from £4).

Drained by the sinuous River Isbourne, the valley around Wincombe is criss-crossed with rewarding and well-marked trails, one of the finest being a section of the **Cotswold Way** (see p.269), which cuts through the town before climbing to **Belas Knap** (see below) and the plateau of Cleve Common and West Down. From the edge of the escarpment, reached after a stiff one- to two-hour hike, the views over Cheltenham and the Severn Valley to the distant Malverns are superb.

Belas Knap

Up on the ridge overlooking Winchcombe to the south, the Neolithic long barrow of **Belas Knap** occupies one of the wildest spots in the Cotswolds. Dating from around 3000 BC, this is the best-preserved burial chamber in England, stretching out like a strange sleeping beast cloaked in green velvet. The best way to get there is to walk, undertaking the two-mile climb up the Cotswold Way from Winchcombe. The path strikes off to the right near the entrance to Sudeley Castle and afterwards, when you reach the country lane at the top, turn right and then left for the ten-minute hike to the barrow. It's also possible to drive to the Belas Knap along this same country lane, just follow the signs to the roadside pull-in where you can park before setting off for the briefest of hikes.

If you continue south past Belas Knap, the country lane scuttles over the hills and through dense woods bound for Syreford with the A40 (for Northleach, see p.272) a little further on.

Cheltenham

Until the eighteenth century **CHELTENHAM** was like any other Cotswold town, but then the discovery of a spring in 1716 transformed it into Britain's most popular **spa**. During Cheltenham's heyday, a century or so later, the royal, the rich and the famous descended in droves to take the waters, which were said to cure anything from constipation to worms. These days, the town has a lively, bustling atmosphere, lots of good restaurants and some of England's best-preserved Regency architecture.

The town is also a thriving arts centre, famous for its festivals of **folk** (Feb), **jazz** (April/May), **science** (June), **classical music** (July) and **literature** (April & Oct) – for information on any of these check Ⓦwww.cheltenhamfestivals.co.uk – and, of course, the races (see box below).

Cheltenham races

Cheltenham racecourse, on the north side of town, a ten-minute walk from Pittville Park at the foot of Cleeve Hill, is Britain's main steeplechasing venue. The principal event of the season, the three-day **National Hunt Festival** in March, attracts forty thousand people a day. Other meetings take place in January, April, October, November and December: a list of fixtures is posted up at the tourist office. For the cheapest but arguably the best view, pay £8 (rising to £15 during the Festival, £25 on Gold Cup Day) for entry to the Best Mate Enclosure, as the pen in the middle is known. For schedules and other information, call Ⓣ01242/226 226 or consult Ⓦwww.cheltenham.co.uk. For the National Hunt Festival it's essential to buy tickets in advance.

Arrival and information

All long-distance **buses** arrive at the bus station in Royal Well Road, just west off the main drag, the Promenade. Cheltenham Spa **train station** is on Queen's Road, southwest of the centre; local buses run into town every fifteen minutes, otherwise it's a twenty-minute walk. The **tourist office** is at 77 Promenade (Mon, Tues & Thurs–Sat 9.30am–5.15pm, Wed 10am–5.15pm; ⓣ01242/522 878, ⓦwww.visitcheltenham.co.uk).

Accommodation

Hotels and **guesthouses** abound, many of them in fine Regency houses, and rooms are easy to come by – except during the races and festivals, when you should book weeks in advance.

Abbey Hotel 14–16 Bath Parade ⓣ01242/516 053, ⓦwww.abbeyhotel-cheltenham.com. Rooms here are attractively and individually furnished and wholesome breakfasts are taken overlooking the garden. Friendly service. 5

Brennan 21 St Luke's Rd ⓣ01242/525 904. This is a good-value option in a small Regency building, on a quiet square. No credit cards. 3

Crossways 57 Bath Rd ⓣ01242/527 683, ⓦwww.crosswaysguesthouse.com. Very central, this comfortable Regency house has period trimmings and well-equipped rooms. 5

Kandinsky Bayshill Rd, Montpellier ⓣ01242/527 788, ⓦwww.hotelkandinsky.com. With colourful and stylish bedrooms, Oriental decor and basement cocktail-bar/nightclub, this hotel is good value for the price. 7

Lypiatt House Lypiatt Rd ⓣ01242/224 994, ⓦwww.lypiatt.co.uk. Victorian villa set in its own grounds, with open fires and a conservatory with a small bar. 5

Willoughby House 1 Suffolk Square ⓣ01242/522 798, ⓦwww.willoughbyhouse.com. South of the centre, in a handsome Regency building, this hotel has ornately opulent rooms and a restaurant. 7

The Town

The focus of Cheltenham, the broad **Promenade**, sweeps majestically south from the High Street, lined with some of the town's grandest houses and smartest shops. It leads into Imperial Square, whose greenery is surrounded by proud Regency terraces that herald the handsome and harmonious terraces and squares of the Montpellier district, which stretches south in a narrow block to Suffolk Road, making a delightful detour.

Back in the centre, just to the north of the Promenade on Clarence Street, the enjoyable **Cheltenham Art Gallery and Museum** (Mon–Sat 10am–5.20pm; free; ⓦwww.cheltenhammuseum.org.uk) has a room dedicated to the Arts and Crafts Movement, an array of rare Chinese ceramics, works by artists such as Stanley Spencer and Vanessa Bell, and a section devoted to Edward Wilson, a local man who died on Scott's ill-fated expedition to the Antarctic.

From the gallery, it's a brief stroll north to the **Holst Birthplace Museum**, at 4 Clarence Rd (Tues–Sat 10am–4pm, but closed mid-Dec to mid-Jan; £2.50; ⓦwww.holstmuseum.org.uk). Once the home of the composer of *The Planets*, the intimate rooms hold plenty of Holst memorabilia – including his piano – and also give a good insight into Victorian family life.

Pressing on, it's about ten minutes' walk to the Pittville district, where a certain Joseph Pitt planned to build his own spa. Work began on Pitt's grand scheme in the 1820s, but he went bust and most of Pittville is now parkland, though he did manage to complete the domed **Pump Room** (Mon & Wed–Sun 10am–4pm) before he hit the skids. A lovely Classical structure with an imposing colonnaded facade, the Pump Room is now used as a concert hall,

▲ The Pump Room

but you can still sample the spa waters from the marble fountain in the main auditorium for free – and very pungent they are too.

Eating, drinking and nightlife

Cheltenham caters for all tastes and pockets and possesses some of the best restaurants, bars and **pubs** in the area, drawing in the punters from nearby Gloucester as well as the Cotswolds.

Restaurants

Boogaloos 16 Regent St. Coffee house that's good for salads and sandwiches while chilling out in the relaxed sofa basement or the buzzing, brightly coloured upstairs rooms. Mon–Sat 8am–5pm.

Le Champignon Sauvage Suffolk Rd ⓣ01242/573 449, ⓦwww.lechampignonsauvage.co.uk. Topnotch French cuisine – including scrumptious desserts – at this chic and intimate restaurant. Two-course set menu £39, three-course £48. Book well ahead. Closed Sun & Mon.

The Daffodil 18–20 Suffolk Parade ⓣ01242/700 055, ⓦwww.thedaffodil.co.uk. Eat in the circle bar or auditorium of this former cinema, where the screen has been replaced with a hubbub of chefs. Great atmosphere and great modern-British food with main courses hovering around £15.

Pie and Mash 10 Bennington St ⓣ01242/702 785. As well as pie and mash, a range of other traditional English dishes is served here, and they're all organic. Local art in the upstairs bar and Nelly the singing Jack Russell provide entertainment. Closed daytime Tues & Wed, and all Sun & Mon.

Upstairs at the Beehive 1–3 Montpellier Villas ⓣ01242/702 270. Friendly ambience and great French food in a lofty, blue-draped room above the pub (see below) make this a popular dining spot. Mains from £13. Reservations advised; closed Sun eve.

Pubs and bars

The Beehive 1–3 Montpellier Villas. Easy-going Cheltenham institution with games shed, courtyard garden and cosy snug.

J's Vodka Bar 6 Regent St. Killer drinks from a range of 24 vodkas, served to the accompaniment of DJs playing house and funk.

Montpellier Wine Bar Bayshill Lodge, Montpellier St. Stylish wine bar and restaurant, with lovely bow-fronted windows. Good breakfasts are also served, and Friday's fish night.

The Retreat 10–11 Suffolk Parade. Lively venue which caters to the business fraternity at lunch-times and a Cheltenham Ladies College set in the evening. Good lunches too. Closed Sun.

Gloucester

For centuries life was good for **GLOUCESTER**, just ten miles west of Cheltenham. The Romans chose this spot for a garrison to guard the River Severn and spy on Wales, and later for a *colonia* or home for retired soldiers. Commercial success came with trade up the Severn, which developed into one of the busiest trade routes in Europe, and the city's political importance hit its peak under the Normans, with William the Conqueror a regular visitor. Gloucester became a religious centre too, as exemplified by the construction of what is now the cathedral, but by the fifteenth century it was on the skids: navigating the Severn as far up as Gloucester was so difficult that most trade gradually shifted south to Bristol. In a brave attempt to reverse the city's decline, a canal was opened in 1827 to link Gloucester to Sharpness, on a broader stretch of the Severn further south. Trade picked up for a time, but it was only a temporary stay of economic execution.

Today, the **canal** is busy once again, though this time with pleasure boats, and the Victorian **docks** have undergone a facelift, their assorted warehouses turned into offices, apartments, a large antiques centre and a museum. The main reason for a visit, however, is Gloucester's magnificent **cathedral**, which is the city's one and only outstanding attraction. Neither is there any strong reason to overnight here – a day-trip (from Cheltenham) is sufficient.

Arrival, information and accommodation

Gloucester's bus and train stations are opposite one another on Bruton Way, a five-minute walk east of the city centre. The **tourist office** is handily located at 28 Southgate St (Mon–Sat 9.30am–5pm, also Sun in July & Aug 11am–3pm; Ⓣ01452/396 572, Ⓦwww.gloucester.gov.uk/tourism). There's limited **accommodation** in the city centre, but you might consider the *Albert Hotel*, near the train station off Northgate at 56 Worcester St (Ⓣ01452/502 081, Ⓦwww.alberthotel.com; ④). The hotel occupies a listed red-brick building from the 1830s and has homely modern rooms.

The City

Gloucester lies on the east bank of the Severn, its centre spread around a curve in the river. **The Cross**, once the entrance to the Roman forum, marks the heart of the city and the meeting point of Northgate, Southgate, Eastgate and Westgate streets, all Roman roads. **St Michael's Tower**, the remains of an old church, overlooks it. The main shopping area lies east of the Northgate–Southgate axis, with the **cathedral** and the **docks**, the focus of interest, to the west.

The Cathedral

The superb condition of Gloucester **Cathedral** (daily 7.30am–6pm; suggested donation £3; Ⓦwww.gloucestercathedral.org.uk) is striking in a city that has lost so much of its history. The Saxons founded an abbey here, but four centuries later, in 1089, Benedictine monks arrived intent on building their own church;

work began in 1089. As a place of worship it shot to importance after the murder of King Edward II in 1327: Bristol and Malmesbury supposedly refused to take his body, but Gloucester did, and the king's shrine became a major place of pilgrimage. The money generated helped finance the conversion of the church into the country's first and greatest example of the **Perpendicular style**: the magnificent 225-foot tower crowns the achievement.

Beneath the reconstructions of the fourteenth and fifteenth centuries, some Norman aspects remain, best seen in the **nave**, which is flanked by sturdy pillars and arches adorned with immaculate zigzag carvings. Moving on, the **choir** provides the best vantage point for admiring the **east window** completed in around 1350 and – at almost 80 feet tall – the largest medieval window in Britain. Beneath it, to the left (as you're facing the east window) is the **tomb of Edward II**, immortalized in alabaster and marble. In the nearby **Lady Chapel**, delicate carved tracery holds a staggering patchwork of windows, a stunning cliff face of stained glass. The innovative nature of the cathedral's design can also be appreciated in the beautiful **cloisters**, completed in 1367 and featuring the first fan vaulting in the country. The setting was used to represent the corridors of Hogwart's School of Witchcraft and Wizardry in the *Harry Potter* films.

The Gloucester Docks

From the museum, it's about 600 yards to the Gloucester **Docks**, whose fourteen capacious **warehouses** were built for storing grain following the opening of the Sharpness canal to the River Severn in 1827. Most of these warehouses have been turned into offices and shops, but the southernmost Llanthony Warehouse is now occupied by the **National Waterways Museum** (daily: April–Oct 10am–5pm, Nov–March 11am–4pm; £7.50, £8.50 including boat trip; Ⓦwww.nwm.org.uk), which delves into every watery nook and cranny, from the engineering of the locks to the lives of the horses that trod the towpaths.

Eating and drinking

You'll find reliable if undemanding fare at the **café-bar** in the Guildhall on Eastgate Street – open until 11pm and always lively (closed Sun & Mon) - and well-prepared British and European dishes at *Bearlands*, a smart restaurant on Longsmith Street (Ⓣ01452/419 966, closed Sun & Mon), where a two-course meal will set you back £23. Alternatively, head for *Café René*, Greyfriars, 31 Southgate St (Ⓣ01452/309 340), whose walls and ceilings are covered with bottles: Desperate Dan Burgers and other more substantial dishes are on the menu and the Sunday barbecues in summer are worth going out of your way for.

Gloucester's best **pubs** are all within spitting distance of the Cross. The rambling fifteenth-century *New Inn* in Northgate Street has a good atmosphere, a splendid galleried courtyard and inexpensive meals, but for really tasty hot food at rock-bottom prices go to the *Fountain Inn*, down a narrow alley off Westgate Street; this pub pulls a sublime pint of Abbot ale and has tables in an adjacent courtyard – ideal for a sunny day. *Café René* (see above) hosts live blues, jazz and acoustic **music** in its cellar bar (Thurs–Sun).

Painswick

Heading south from Cheltenham on the A46, it's ten miles to the congenial, old wool town of **PAINSWICK**, where ancient buildings jostle for space on narrow streets running downhill off the busy main street. The fame of

Painswick's **church** stems not so much from the building itself as from the surrounding **graveyard**, where 99 yew trees, cut into bizarre bulbous shapes resembling lollipops, surround a collection of eighteenth-century table-tombs unrivalled in the Cotswolds. However, it's the **Rococo Garden** (mid-Jan to Oct daily 11am–5pm; £5.50; Ⓦwww.rococogarden.co.uk), about half a mile north up the Gloucester road – and attached to Painswick House (no access) – that ranks as the town's main attraction. Created in the early eighteenth century and later abandoned, the garden has been restored to its original form with the aid of a painting dated 1748. It's a beautiful example – and the country's only one – of Rococo garden design, a short-lived fashion typified by a mix of formal geometrical shapes and more naturalistic, curving lines. With a vegetable patch as an unusual centrepiece, the Painswick garden spreads across a sheltered gully – for the best vistas, walk around anticlockwise.

Bus #46 (Mon–Sat hourly, Sun 6 daily) links Cheltenham with Painswick, where the **tourist office** is housed in the library on the main street (April–Oct Tues–Sat 10am–5pm, Sun 10am–1pm; Ⓣ01452/813 552, Ⓦwww.painswick-pc.gov.uk). The best hotel is *Cardynham House* on St Mary's Street (Ⓣ01452/814 006, Ⓦwww.cardynham.co.uk; ⑤), which has themed rooms, most with four-posters and one with its own lounge and even its own private pool. You can eat well at the *Royal Oak* **pub**, also on St Mary's Street, which has a flowery courtyard and real ales.

Travel details

Buses

For information on all local and national bus services, contact Traveline Ⓣ0871/200 2233, Ⓦwww.traveline.org.uk.

Cheltenham to: Gloucester (Mon–Sat every 15min, Sun 2 hourly; 15–40min); London (11–13 daily; 2hr 35min–3hr 20min); Painswick (Mon–Sat hourly; Sun 6 daily; 30min).

Cirencester to: Cheltenham (Mon–Sat hourly; 45min); Gloucester (Mon–Sat 5 daily; 40min–1hr); Moreton-in-Marsh (Mon–Sat every 2–3hr; 1hr); Northleach (Mon–Sat every 2–3hr.)

Cotswolds: Swanbrook bus (Ⓣ01452/712386, Ⓦwww.swanbrook.co.uk) operates a particularly useful bus service linking Oxford with Gloucester via Burford, Northleach and Cheltenham (Mon–Sat 3–4 daily, Sun 1 daily).

Gloucester to: Cheltenham (Mon–Sat hourly; 15min–40min); Cirencester (6 daily; 1hr 40min); London (12 daily; 3hr 20min–3hr 50min).

Henley to: Oxford (hourly; 50min); London (every 30mon; 45min direct or 1hr, changing at Twyford); Reading (hourly; 20min); Wantage (hourly; 1hr 40min).

Oxford to: Buckingham (hourly; 1hr 30min); Henley (hourly; 50min); London (up to 3 hourly; 1hr 15min); Reading (every 2hr; 1hr 30min); Wantage (hourly; 1hr).

Reading to: Henley (hourly; 20min); Oxford (every 2hr; 1hr 30min).

Wantage to: Henley (hourly; 1hr 40min); Oxford (hourly; 1hr).

Trains

For information on all local and national rail services, contact National Rail Enquiries Ⓣ0845/748 4950, Ⓦwww.nationalrail.co.uk.

Cheltenham to: Bristol (3 hourly; 45min–1hr); Gloucester (2–3 hourly; 10min–15min); London (every 2hr; 2hr 10min).

Gloucester to: Bristol (hourly; 50min); Cheltenham (2–3 hourly; 10min–15min); London (every 2hr; 1hr 50min).

Henley to: London (every 30min with 1 or 2 changes; 1hr).

Oxford to: Bedford (hourly; 2hr 30min); Birmingham (hourly; 1hr 30min); London (1–2 hourly; 1hr).

5

Bristol, Bath and Somerset

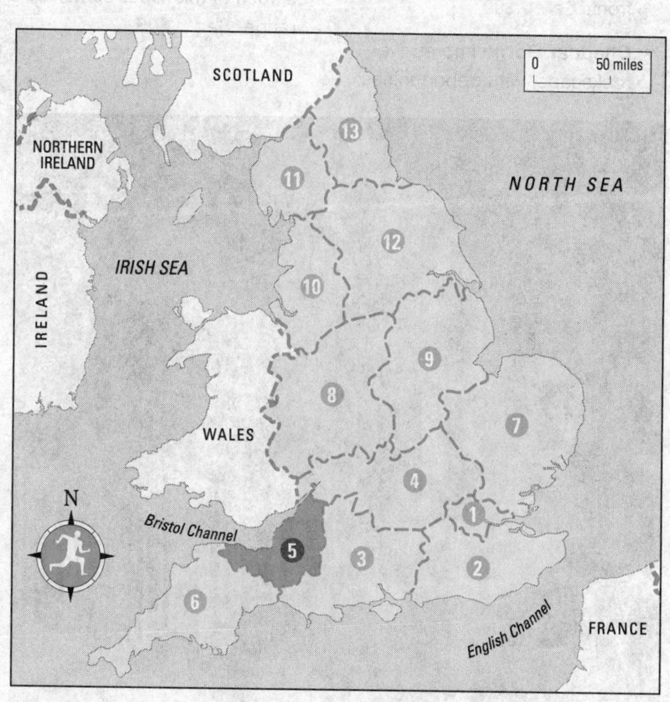

CHAPTER 5

Highlights

- **Clifton Suspension Bridge** Brunel's iconic construction rears above the impressive Aron Gorge. See p.291
- **Building of Bath Museum** Get to grips with how Bath came to assume its present appearance. See p.297
- **Wells Cathedral** A gem of medieval masonry, not least for its richly ornamented west front. See p.299
- **Cheddar Gorge** Impressive rockscape, with opportunities for wild walks in the Mendips. See p.301
- **Glastonbury Abbey** Evocative and picturesque ruins are a fitting setting for a complexity of Christian legends and Arthurian myths. See p.303
- **Quantock Hills** Follow in the footsteps of Coleridge and Wordsworth on the wooded slopes of this West Somerset range. See p.305

▲Wells Cathedral

5

Bristol, Bath and Somerset

The undulating green swards of **Somerset** encapsulate rural England at its best. The landscape is always varied, with tidy cricket greens and well-kept country pubs contrasting with wilder, more dramatic landscapes. A world away from this bucolic charm, the main city hereabouts is **Bristol**, one of the most dynamic and cosmopolitan centres outside London. The city's dense traffic and some hideous postwar architecture are more than compensated for by the surviving traces of its long maritime history, not to mention a great range of pubs, clubs and restaurants.

Just a few miles away, the graceful, Georgian, honey-toned terraces of **Bath** combine with the city's beautifully preserved Roman baths and a mellow café culture to make an unmissable stop on any itinerary. Within easy reach to the south lie the exquisite cathedral city of **Wells** and the ancient town of **Glastonbury**, a site steeped in Christian lore, Arthurian legend and New Age mysticism. The nearby **Mendip Hills** are pocked by cave systems, as at **Wookey Hole** and **Cheddar Gorge**, while to the west, **Bridgwater** makes a useful base for exploring the Quantocks.

The line from London's Paddington Station to Bristol, Bath and Bridgwater provides the **rail transport** through this region. From these centres, a network of **bus routes** connects with nearly all the places covered in this chapter – though the Mendip and **Quantock hills** are more easily explored with your own transport. The M4 and M5 motorways, which meet outside Bristol, are useful through-routes.

Bristol and around

On the borders of Gloucestershire and Somerset, **BRISTOL** has harmoniously blended its mercantile roots with an innovative, modern culture, fuelled by technology-based industries, a large student population and a lively arts and media community. As well as its vibrant nightlife, the city's sights range from medieval churches to cutting-edge attractions highlighting its scientific achievements.

Weaving through its centre, the River Avon forms part of a system of waterways that made Bristol a great inland port, in later years booming on the

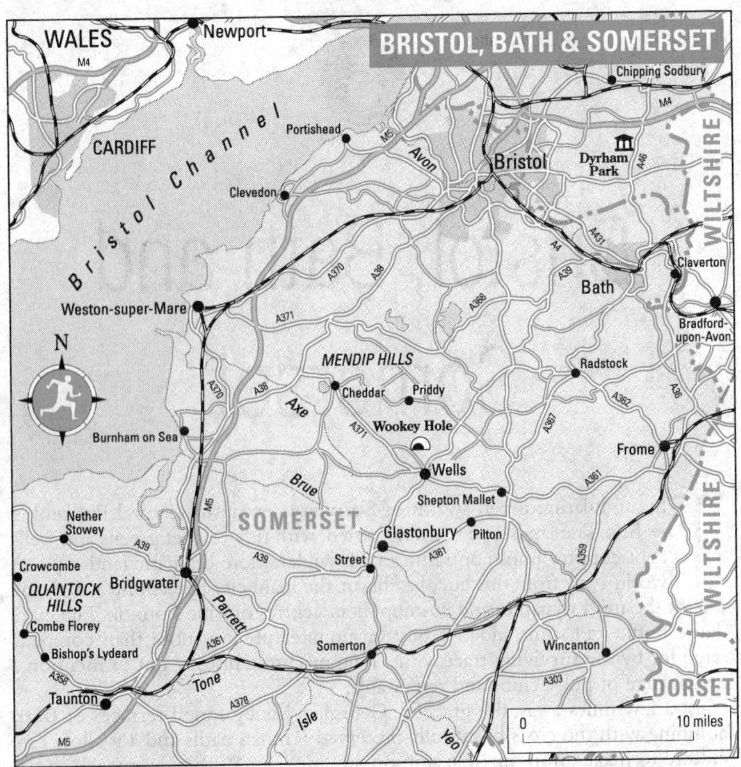

transatlantic trafficking of rum, tobacco and slaves. In the nineteenth century the illustrious **Isambard Kingdom Brunel** laid the foundations of a tradition of engineering, creating two of Bristol's greatest monuments – the SS *Great Britain* and the lofty Clifton Suspension Bridge.

Arrival, information and accommodation

Bristol's Temple Meads **train station** is a twenty-minute walk east of the city centre, served by frequent buses #8, #8A and #9, which pass through the centre on their way to Clifton. Alternatively, from behind the train station you can make use of the cycle-way into town or the river ferry that leaves for the centre every forty minutes. The **bus station** is centrally located off Marlborough Street, though Megabus services from London stop opposite Colston Hall, off The Centre – the name given to the busy traffic intersection at the heart of the modern city, where most **local buses** stop.

The main **tourist office** is in the at-Bristol complex, Harbourside (Mon–Fri during school terms 10am–5pm, Sat, Sun & daily in school hols 10am–6pm; ⓣ0906/711 2191, ⓦwww.visitbristol.co.uk).

Bristol has a range of **accommodation** in the centre and the leafy Clifton area, popular with students.

Arches 132 Cotham Brow ⓣ0117/924 7398, ⓦwww.arches-hotel.co.uk. In an attractive area of town (bus #9 from the centre), this eco-friendly place has small but comfortable rooms with or without bath, and vegan or vegetarian breakfasts only. ③

Bristol Backpackers 17 St Stephen's St ⓣ0117/925 7900, ⓦwww.bristolbackpackers.co.uk. Friendly independent hostel with a late bar, good showers and cheap Internet access. The area can be noisy at night. Dorm beds £14, doubles ①

Bristol YHA 14 Narrow Quay ⓣ0870/770 5726, ⓔbristol@yha.org.uk. Located in a refurbished warehouse on the quayside; most dorms have four beds (from £23, including breakfast). ②

Downs View 38 Upper Belgrave Rd ⓣ0117/973 7046, ⓦwww.downsviewguesthouse.co.uk. As the name implies, this B&B enjoys a good vista over Clifton Downs, though the city views from the back are even better. ③

Hotel du Vin Narrow Lewins Mead ⓣ0117/925 5577, ⓦwww.hotelduvin.co.uk. Chic, warehouse conversion, centrally located, with solid comforts, contemporary decor and excellent food and wine. ⑦

Victoria Square Victoria Square ⓣ0117/973 9058, ⓦwww.vicsquare.com. Some of the rooms in this Georgian hotel are on the small side, but the location is great, on a leafy square near Clifton Village. ⑤–⑥

The City

A good place to start exploring, **The Centre** was once a quay-lined dock but is now the traffic-ridden nucleus of the city. Just a few steps from here are the cathedral and the oldest quarter of town, and the nearby Quayhead is linked by water-taxi to the sights around the Floating Harbour, the waterway network that runs through the southern part of town and connects with the River Avon.

From the Cathedral to the City Museum

Just up from The Centre to the west, the grassy expanse of College Green is dominated by the crescent-shaped Council House and by the contrastingly medieval lines of **Bristol Cathedral** (daily 8am–5pm; free). Founded around 1140 as an abbey on the supposed spot of St Augustine's convocation with Celtic Christians in 603, it became a cathedral church with the Dissolution of the Monasteries. The two towers on the west front were erected in the nineteenth century in a faithful act of homage to Edmund Knowle, architect and abbot at the start of the fourteenth century. The cathedral's interior offers a unique example among Britain's cathedrals of a German-style hall church, in which the aisles, nave and choir rise to the same height. Abbot Knowle's **choir** offers one of the country's most exquisite illustrations of the early Decorated style of Gothic, while the adjoining **Elder Lady Chapel**, dating from the early thirteenth century, contains some fine tombs and eccentric carvings of animals, including a monkey playing the bagpipes accompanied by a ram on the violin. The ornate **Eastern Lady Chapel** has some of England's finest examples of heraldic glass. From the south transept, a door leads through to the **Chapter House**, a richly carved piece of late Norman architecture.

Elegant Georgian streets lead off the shop-lined **Park Street**, climbing steeply up from College Green. On Great George Street, the **Georgian House** (Mon–Wed, Sat & Sun 10am–5pm; free) is the faithfully restored former home of a local sugar merchant. From Great George Street, or from Berkeley Square further up the hill, you can gain access to **Brandon Hill Park**, home to the 105-foot **Cabot Tower** (open daily until dusk; free), built in 1897 to commemorate the 400th anniversary of John Cabot's voyage to America, and providing the city's best panorama.

At the top of Park Street, on Queen's Road, the **City Museum and Art Gallery** (daily 10am–5pm; free) has sections on local archeology,

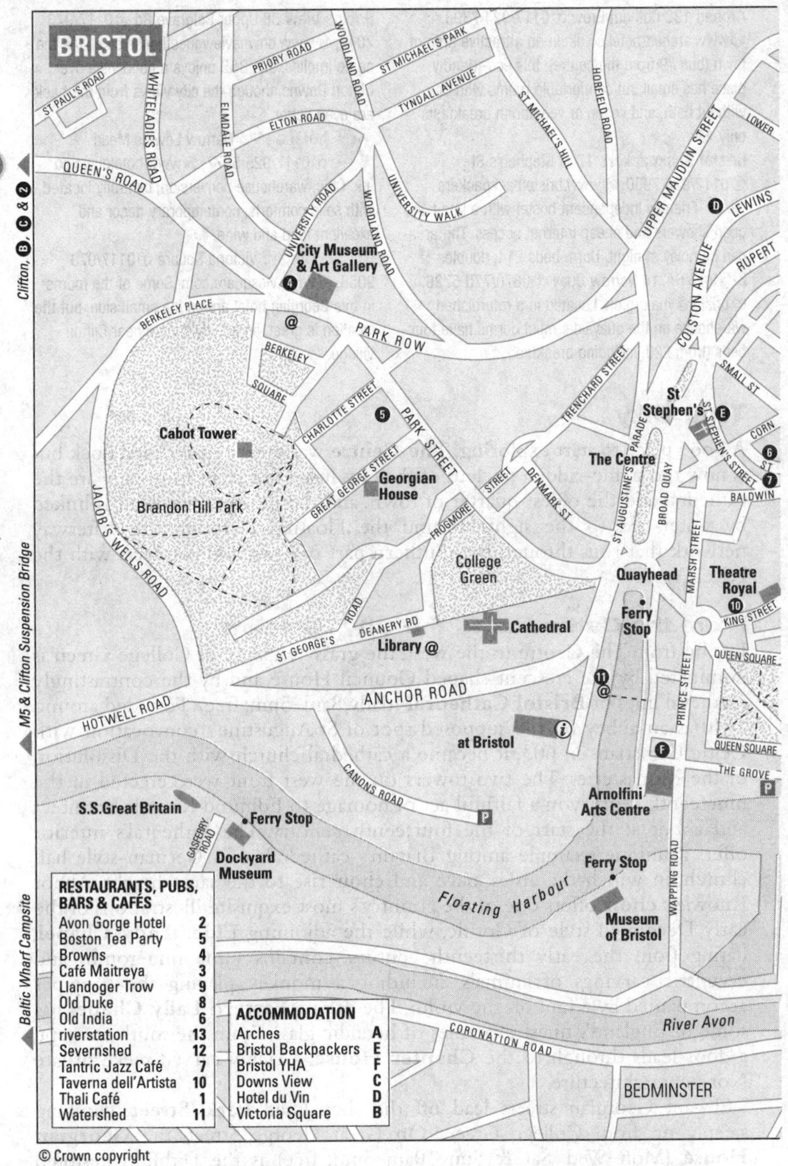

geology and natural history, as well as an important collection of Chinese porcelain, glassware, stoneware and ivory, and some magnificent eighth-century BC Assyrian reliefs. Art works by English Pre-Raphaelites and French Impressionists are mixed in with some choice older pieces, including a portrait of Martin Luther by Cranach and Giovanni Bellini's unusual *Descent into Limbo*.

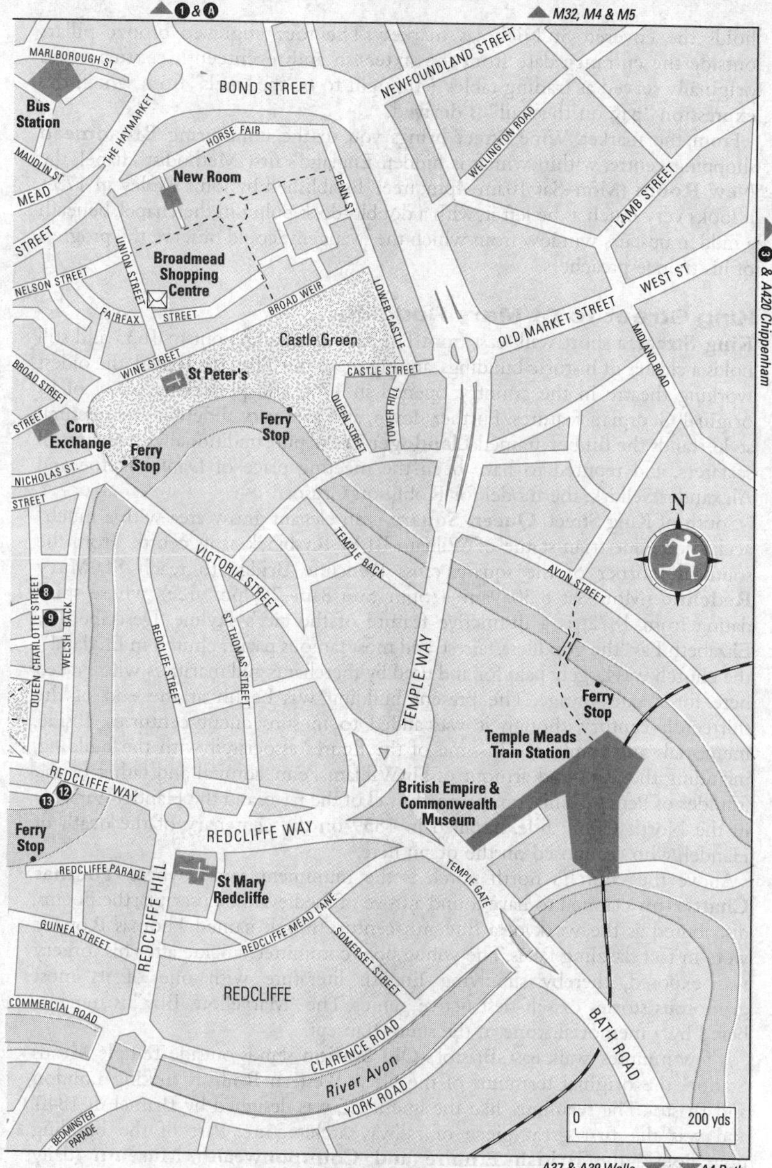

From The Centre to Broadmead

One of Bristol's oldest churches, **St Stephen's**, stands just east of The Centre. Established in the thirteenth century, rebuilt in the fifteenth and thoroughly restored with plenty of neo-Gothic trimmings in 1875, the parish church has some flamboyant tombs inside. On nearby **Corn Street**, the Georgian Corn Exchange was designed by John Wood of Bath and now holds the covered St Nicholas markets. The four engraved bronze pillars outside the entrance date from the sixteenth and seventeenth centuries and originally served as trading tables – thought to be the "nails" from which the expression "pay on the nail" is derived.

From the market, Wine Street brings you to the uninspiring **Broadmead** shopping centre, within which is hidden England's first Methodist chapel, the **New Room** (Mon–Sat 10am–4pm; free). Established by John Wesley in 1739, it looks very much as he left it, with a double-deck pulpit in the chapel, beneath a hidden upstairs window from which the evangelist could observe the progress of his trainee preachers.

King Street to St Mary Redcliffe

King Street, a short walk east from The Centre, was laid out in 1633 and still holds a cluster of historic buildings, among them the **Theatre Royal**, the oldest working theatre in the country, opened in 1766 and preserving many of its original Georgian features. Further down, and in a very different architectural style, stands the timber-framed **Llandoger Trow** pub, traditionally the haunt of seafarers, and reputed to have been the meeting place of Daniel Defoe and Alexander Selkirk, the model for Robinson Crusoe.

South of King Street, **Queen Square** is an elegant grassy area with a much-acclaimed equestrian statue of William III by Rysbrack at its centre. From the southeast corner of the square, cross Redcliffe Bridge to reach **St Mary Redcliffe** (Mon–Sat 8.30/9am–4/5pm, Sun 8am–7.30pm; free), whose spire, dating from 1872, is a distinctive feature of the city's skyline. Described by Elizabeth I as "the goodliest, fairest, and most famous parish church in England", the church was largely paid for and used by merchants and mariners who prayed here for a safe voyage. The present building was begun at the end of the thirteenth century, though it was added to in subsequent centuries. Inside, memorials and tombs recall some of the figures associated with the building, including the arms and armour of Sir William Penn, admiral and father of the founder of Pennsylvania, on the north wall of the nave, and the Handel Window in the North Choir aisle, installed in 1859 on the centenary of the death of Handel, who composed on the organ here.

Above the church's north porch is the muniment room, where **Thomas Chatterton** claimed to have found a trove of medieval manuscripts; the poems, distributed as the work of a fifteenth-century monk named Thomas Rowley, were in fact dazzling fakes. The young poet committed suicide after his forgery was exposed, thereby supplying English literature with one of its most glamorous stories of self-destructive genius. The "Marvellous Boy" is remembered by a memorial stone in the south transept.

A few minutes' walk east, Bristol's **Old Station** stands outside Temple Meads Station, the original terminus of the Great Western Railway linking London and Bristol. The terminus, like the line itself, was designed by Brunel in 1840, and was the first great piece of railway architecture. Part of the building now houses the **British Empire and Commonwealth Museum** (daily 10am–5pm; £7.95), which focuses on the history of the empire and the Commonwealth that succeeded it, covering trade, slavery and culture.

Around Bristol's waterways

At the southern end of The Centre, **St Augustine's Reach**, part of the Floating Harbour, is flanked by pubs, clubs, and the **Arnolfini** and **Watershed** arts centres. Opposite the Arnolfini is the site for the new Museum of Bristol, due to open in 2010. Behind the **Watershed**, cross Millennium Square to reach

at-Bristol (daily: Mon–Fri during school terms 10am–5pm; Sat, Sun & school hols 10am–6pm; last entry 1hr before closing; £9), consisting of the interactive science exhibition Explore, and a spherical, stainless-steel planetarium. Although chiefly aimed at children, there's enough scientific wizardry here to entertain and inform everyone; the planetarium has shows every 45 minutes (11am–2pm on weekdays during school terms, 11am–5pm on weekends & school hols), which should be booked when you buy your Explore tickets.

To explore further afield, a **ferry** connects the various parts of the Floating Harbour, leaving every forty minutes from St Augustine's Reach (10.30am–5.50pm; £1.50 single fare; £4.80 forty-minute round trip; £7 all-day ticket). The major attraction on the Harbour, and one of Bristol's iconic sights, is the **SS Great Britain** (daily: April–Oct 10am–6pm; Nov–March 10am–4.30pm; last entry 1hr before closing; £10.50), the first propeller-driven, ocean-going iron ship, built in 1843 by Brunel. She initially ran between Liverpool and New York, then between Liverpool and Melbourne, circumnavigating the globe 32 times over a period of 26 years. Her ocean-going days ended in 1886 when she was caught in a storm off Cape Horn, and she was eventually recovered and returned to Bristol in 1968. On board you can see restored cabins and peer into the immense engine room. The same ticket allows you admission to the much smaller **Matthew**, moored close by and to the adjoining **Dockyard Museum**, which gives the background of both vessels, of Cabot and his exploits, and of Bristol's long shipbuilding history.

Clifton

North and west of the City Museum (see p.287), **Clifton** was once an aloof spa resort, and is now Bristol's most elegant quarter. The select enclave of Clifton Village is centred on the Mall, close to **Royal York Crescent**, the longest Georgian crescent in the country, offering splendid views over the steep drop to the River Avon below.

A few minutes' walk from the Crescent is Bristol's most famous symbol, **Clifton Suspension Bridge**, 702ft long and poised 245ft above high water. Money was first put forward for a bridge to span the Avon Gorge by a Bristol wine merchant in 1753, though it was not until 1829 that a competition was held for a design, won by Isambard Brunel on a second round, and not until 1864 that the bridge was completed, five years after Brunel's death. Hampered by financial difficulties, the bridge never quite matched the engineer's original ambitious design, which included Egyptian-style towers topped by sphinxes at each end. You can see copies of his plans in the temporary **Visitor Centre**, located at the far side of the bridge (daily 10am–5pm; free), alongside designs proposed by Brunel's rivals, some of them frankly bizarre.

The wide green expanse of **Clifton Downs** stretches right up to the edge of the Gorge, a popular spot for picnickers, joggers and kite-flyers. Adjacent to the Downs, **Bristol Zoo** (daily 9am–5/5.30pm; £11.50) is renowned for its animal conservation work, and also features a collection of rare trees and shrubs.

Eating, drinking and nightlife

Bristol's numerous **pubs** and **restaurants** are nearly always buzzing – especially those around King Street and Corn Street. Nightlife is equally lively: to check out the **clubs**, pick up a copy of *Venue*, the weekly listings magazine (£1.50), or consult Ⓦ www.whatsonbristol.co.uk for details of events.

Restaurants

Browns 38 Queen's Rd ⓣ0117/930 4777. Spacious and relaxed place for a cocktail, hamburger or fisherman's pie, housed in the Venetian-style former university refectory. Moderate.

Café Maitreya 89 St Mark's Rd ⓣ0117/951 0100. Tucked away in the multicultural Easton neighbourhood (bus #48/49 from the centre), this easy-going place is rated one of the country's best vegetarian restaurants. Set menus are £17.50 and £21. Closed daytime and all Sun & Mon.

Old India 34 St Nicholas St ⓣ0117/922 1136. Housed in the old Stock Exchange building, this moderately priced restaurant has classy curries to match the sumptuous surroundings.

riverstation The Grove ⓣ0117/914 4434. In a former river-police station, two great restaurants with dockside views: deli-type snacks downstairs, and a more formal upstairs area serving modern European dishes (mains £14–19).

Severnshed The Grove ⓣ0117/925 1212. Right next to *riverstation* with a waterside terrace, this serves light, tasty dishes, and offers a two-course meal for under £10 (Mon–Sat noon–3pm & 6–7pm only).

Thali Café 12 York Rd ⓣ0117/942 6687. Dhaba-style Asian food in the villagey Montpelier quarter (half a mile north of bus station), with live music (Sun). Dishes cost £7. Closed Mon.

Pubs, bars and cafés

Avon Gorge Hotel Sion Hill. On the edge of the Gorge in Clifton Village, this modern bar has magnificent views from its broad terrace. Meals also available.

Boston Tea Party 75 Park St. Cosy place for teas, coffees, soups and pies, with seating on two floors and a heated terrace garden.

Llandoger Trow King St. Seventeenth-century tavern full of historical resonance, with cosy nooks and armchairs.

Old Duke King St. Trad-jazz pub with live bands most nights.

Tantric Jazz Café 39–41 St Nicholas St ⓣ0117/940 2304. Relaxed coffee stop that serves Mediterranean-style meals in the evenings, when there's live jazz and blues until late. Closed Sun.

Taverna dell'Artista King St. A haunt of theatrical folk, this Anglo-Italian bar has pizzas and pasta, and drinks until late. Closed Sun & Mon.

Watershed St Augustine's Reach. Café-bar in an arts complex overlooking the boats, with food available until 9pm (7pm on Sun).

Clubs and music venues

The Academy Frogmore St ⓣ0905/020 3999, ⓦwww.bristol-academy.co.uk. Near The Centre, this spacious, multi-level place stages almost nightly live gigs as well as club nights. Thurs is student night.

Bierkeller All Saints St, off Broadmead ⓣ0117/926 8514, ⓦwww.bristolbierkeller.co.uk. Sweaty cellar venue playing everything from thrash metal to revival bands.

Blue Mountain Stokes Croft. Excellent non-mainstream club featuring the best funk, hip-hop and drum'n'bass in town.

Colston Hall Colston Ave ⓣ0117/922 3686, ⓦwww.colstonhall.org. Major names appear in this stalwart mainstream venue. Hosts most of the events in the classical Proms Festival in late May.

Fiddlers Willway St, Bedminster ⓣ0117/987 3403, ⓦwww.fiddlers.co.uk. Mainly live folk and world music at this relaxed venue south of the river, off Bedminster Parade.

The Fleece 12 St Thomas St ⓣ0117/945 0996. Stone-flagged ex-wool warehouse, now a loud, sweaty pub for live rock and comedy.

St George's Great George St ⓣ0845/402 4001, ⓦwww.stgeorgesbristol.co.uk. Lunchtime and evening concerts of classical, world and jazz music are staged in this elegant Georgian church.

Thekla The Grove ⓣ0117/929 3301, ⓦwww.theklabristol.co.uk. Riverboat venue popular with students, staging regular live bands plus dub, funky house and indie club nights.

Bath and around

Though only twelve miles from Bristol, **BATH** has a very different feel from its neighbour – more harmonious, compact, leisurely and complacent. The city's elegant crescents and Georgian buildings are studded with plaques naming Bath's eminent inhabitants from its heyday as a spa resort; it was here that Jane Austen set *Persuasion* and *Northanger Abbey*, and where Gainsborough established himself as a portraitist and landscape painter. Nowadays Bath ranks as one of Britain's top tourist cities, yet the place has never lost the exclusive air those names evoke.

Bath owes its name and fame to its **hot springs** – the only ones in the country – which made it a place of reverence for the local Celtic population, though it had to wait for Roman technology to create a fully fledged bathing establishment. The baths fell into decline with the departure of the Romans, but the town later regained its importance under the Saxons, its abbey seeing the coronation of the **first king of all England**, Edgar, in 973. A new bathing complex was built in the sixteenth century, popularized by the visit of Elizabeth I in 1574, and the city reached its fashionable zenith in the eighteenth century, when **Beau Nash** ruled the town's social scene (see box, p.294). It was at this time that Bath acquired its ranks of Palladian mansions and Regency townhouses, all of them built in the local **Bath stone**, which is still the city's leitmotif today.

The swathes of parkland between Bath's Georgian terraces lend the city a spacious feel, but the sheer weight of traffic pouring through the central streets can be a major turn-off. Drivers are advised to use one of the **Park-and-Ride** car parks around the periphery – and if you're coming from Bristol, you can **cycle** all the way along a cycle-path that follows the route of a disused railway line and the course of the Avon.

Arrival, information and accommodation

Bath Spa **train station** and the city's **bus station** are both a short walk south of the centre. The **tourist office** is right next to the abbey in Abbey Churchyard (Mon–Sat 9.30am–5/6pm, Sun 10am–4pm; Ⓣ0906/711 2000, Ⓦwww.visitbath.co.uk). Most places offering **accommodation** are small (so always phone ahead), and most demand a two-night minimum stay at weekends.

Hotels and B&Bs

Bath Paradise House 88 Holloway Ⓣ01225/317723, Ⓦwww.paradise-house.co.uk. Georgian villa an uphill trudge from the centre, but with wonderful views. Open fires in winter, four-posters in three of the rooms and two rooms opening straight onto the lush garden are further attractions. 7

Belmont 7 Belmont, Lansdown Rd Ⓣ01225/423082, Ⓦwww.belmontbath.co.uk. Huge doubles, some with en-suite shower, in a centrally located B&B in a house designed by John Wood. No credit cards. 2

Cranleigh 159 Newbridge Hill Ⓣ01225/310197, Ⓦwww.cranleighguesthouse.com. A mile or so west of the centre (with frequent bus connections), this period Victorian house has fine views from the back rooms, two four-posters and a variety of breakfast options. 5

Harington's Queen St Ⓣ01225/461728, Ⓦwww.haringtons.co.uk. Very central hotel with small but well-equipped and quiet rooms, and friendly service. 7

Three Abbey Green 3 Abbey Green Ⓣ01225/428558, Ⓦwww.threeabbeygreen.com. Top-class B&B in a beautifully renovated Georgian house just steps from the abbey. The more spacious rooms overlooking a peaceful square are in a higher price category. 5

Hostels

Bath Backpackers Hostel 13 Pierrepoint St Ⓣ01225/446787, Ⓦwww.hostels.co.uk. Aussie-run place, with no curfew, no lockout, a kitchen, Internet access and a "party dungeon". Breakfast is included in the price. Beds in 4 to 10-bed dorms cost £14–18.

Bath YHA Bathwick Hill ⓣ0870/770 5688, ⓔbath@yha.org.uk. An Italianate mansion a mile above the centre, with gardens and panoramic views. Dorm beds (from £12.50) and double rooms (❶) available, also evening meals. Bus #18, #410 or #418.

White Hart Widcombe Hill ⓣ01225/313985, ⓦwww.whitehartbath.co.uk. The comfiest of Bath's hostels has a kitchen, a first-class restaurant and a sunny courtyard. Dorm beds are £15, and there's a range of neat doubles and twins (❷). Midnight curfew.

YMCA International House, Broad St ⓣ01225/325900, ⓦwww.bathymca.co.uk. Clean and central, with lots of room, this place charges £13–15 for dorm beds, £25–29 for singles and £38–46 for doubles, with reductions for weekly stays; all prices include breakfast (but there's no kitchen). ❶–❷

The City

Although Bath could easily be seen on a day-trip from Bristol, it really deserves a stay of a couple of days. The city itself is chock-full of museums, but some of the greatest enjoyment comes simply from wandering the streets, with their pale gold architecture and sweeping vistas.

The Roman Baths

Bath's focal point is the pedestrianized Abbey Church Yard, two interlocking squares usually busy with buskers, tourists and traders, and site of both the Baths and the Abbey. Although ticket prices are high for the **Roman Baths** (daily: March–June, Sept & Oct 9am–6pm; July & Aug 9am–9pm; Nov–Feb 9.30am–5.30pm; last entry 1hr before closing; £10.25, £11.25 in July & Aug, £13.50 combined ticket with Fashion Museum), there's two or three hours' worth of

Beau Nash and Bath's Golden Age

Richard "Beau" Nash was an ex-army officer, ex-lawyer, dandy and gambler, who became Bath's Master of Ceremonies in 1704, conducting public balls of an unprecedented splendour. Wielding dictatorial powers over dress and behaviour, Nash orchestrated the social manners of the city and even extended his influence to cover road improvements and the design of buildings. In an early example of health awareness, he banned smoking in Bath's public rooms at a time when pipe-smoking was a general pastime among men, women and children. Less philanthropically, he also encouraged gambling and even took a percentage of the bank's takings. Nonetheless, he was generally held in high esteem and succeeded in establishing rules such as the setting of specific hours and procedure for all social functions. Balls were to begin at six and end at eleven and every ball had to open with a minuet "danced by two persons of the highest distinction present". White aprons were banned, gossipers and scandalmongers were shunned, and, most radical of all, the wearing of swords in public places was forbidden.

As for Bath's distinctive Georgian style of architecture, this was largely the work of **John Wood** ("the elder", *c*.1704–54) and his son, also called John Wood ("the younger", 1727–81), both champions of the Neoclassical Palladianism that originated in Renaissance Italy. Their "speculative developments", designed to cater to the seasonal floods of fashionable visitors, were constructed in the soft oolitic limestone from local quarries belonging to **Ralph Allen** (*c*.1694–1764), another prominent figure of the period, and remembered for Prior Park.

Lastly, the name of **William Oliver** should not be forgotten in the story of Georgian Bath. A physician and philanthropist, Oliver did more than anyone to boost the city's profile as a therapeutic centre and founded the Bath General Hospital to enable the poor to make use of the waters. He is remembered today by the Bath Oliver biscuit, which he invented.

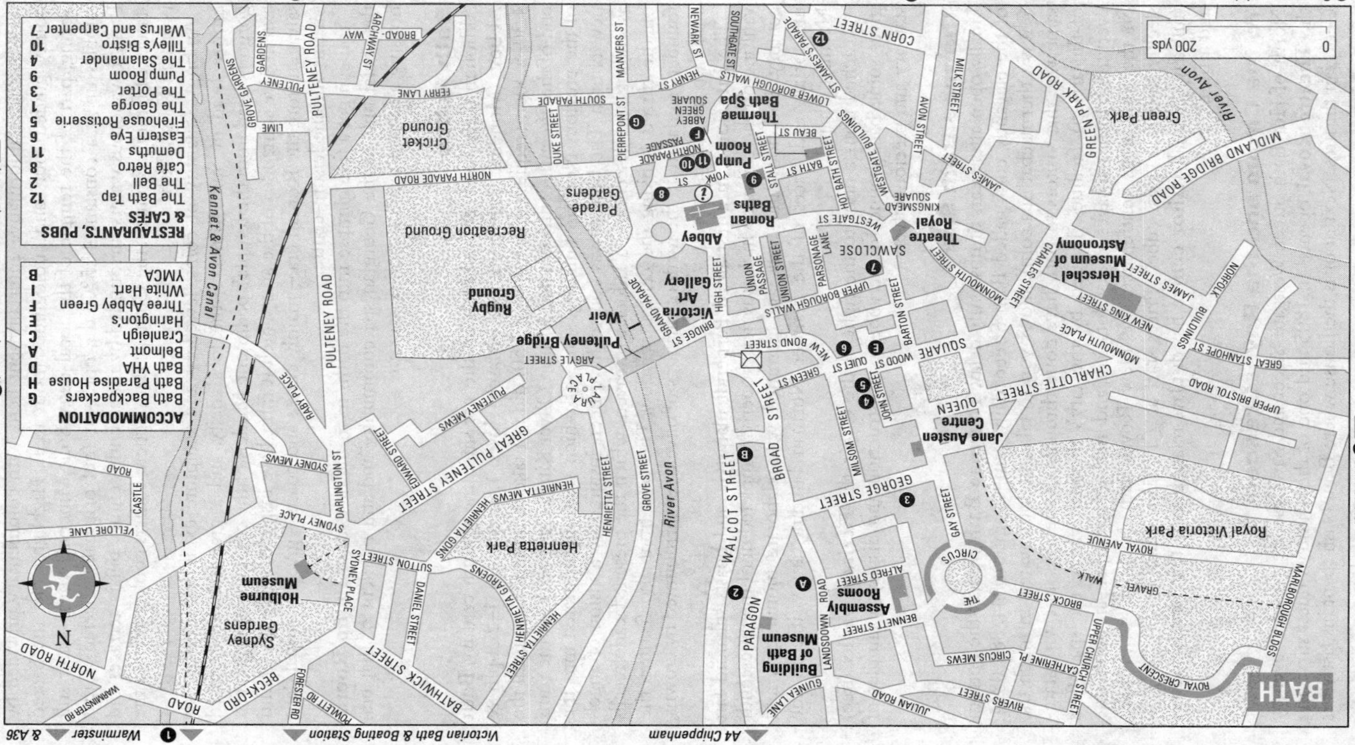
BATH
ACCOMMODATION
Bath Backpackers G
Bath Paradise House H
Bath YHA D
Belmont A
Cranleigh C
Harington's E
Three Abbey Green F
White Hart I
YMCA B
RESTAURANTS, PUBS & CAFÉS
The Bath Tap 12
The Bell 2
Café Retro 8
Demuths 11
Eastern Eye 6
Firehouse Rotisserie 5
The George 1
The Porter 3
Pump Room 9
The Salamander 4
Tilley's Bistro 10
Walrus and Carpenter 7
D (1 mile) & American Museum (3 miles)
Bus & train stations & @
I
H
© Crown copyright
A36 Tiverton
G & A4 Bristol
A4 Chippenham
Victorian Bath & Boating Station
1 Warminster & A36
0 200 yds
Kennet & Avon Canal
River Avon
Sydney Gardens
Holburne Museum
Henrietta Park
Rugby Ground
Recreation Ground
Cricket Ground
Parade Gardens
Pulteney Bridge
Weir
Victoria Art Gallery
Abbey
Roman Baths
Pump Room
Thermae Bath Spa
Theatre Royal
Herschel Museum of Astronomy
Jane Austen Centre
Assembly Rooms
Building of Bath Museum
Royal Victoria Park
Green Park
NORTH ROAD
BECKFORD ROAD
WARMINSTER RD
CASTLE ROAD
VELLORE LANE
SYDNEY MEWS
RABY PLACE
PULTENEY ROAD
GROVE GARDENS
GARDENS
LIME
PULTENEY
ARCHWAY ST
BROAD-WAY
FERRY LANE
NORTH PARADE ROAD
DUKE STREET
SOUTH PARADE
PIERREPONT ST
MANVERS ST
HENRY ST
NEWARK ST
SOUTHGATE ST
ST JAMES'S PARADE
CORN STREET
LOWER BOROUGH WALLS
ABBEY GREEN SQUARE
NORTH PARADE PASSAGE
YORK ST
BEAU ST
BATH ST
STALL STREET
HOT BATH STREET
WESTGATE BUILDINGS
WESTGATE ST
KINGSMEAD SQUARE
SAWCLOSE
AVON STREET
MILK STREET
JAMES STREET
GREEN PARK ROAD
MIDLAND BRIDGE ROAD
CHARLES STREET
JAMES STREET
NEW KING STREET
NORFOLK BUILDINGS
MONMOUTH STREET
MONMOUTH PLACE
GREAT STANHOPE ST
UPPER BRISTOL ROAD
CHARLOTTE STREET
QUEEN SQUARE
WOOD ST
QUIET ST
JOHN STREET
BARTON STREET
UPPER BOROUGH WALLS
PARSONAGE LANE
UNION STREET
UNION PASSAGE
HIGH STREET
BRIDGE ST
GRAND PARADE
NEW BOND STREET
GREEN ST
MILSOM STREET
BROAD STREET
WALCOT STREET
GEORGE STREET
GAY STREET
THE CIRCUS
ALFRED STREET
BENNETT STREET
LANDSDOWN ROAD
PARAGON
GUINEA LANE
JULIAN ROAD
RIVERS STREET
CATHERINE PL
CIRCUS MEWS
UPPER CHURCH STREET
BROCK STREET
GRAVEL WALK
ROYAL AVENUE
ROYAL CRESCENT
MARLBOROUGH BLDGS
ARGYLE STREET
LAURA PLACE
PULTENEY MEWS
GREAT PULTENEY STREET
EDWARD STREET
DARLINGTON ST
SYDNEY PLACE
SUTTON STREET
DANIEL STREET
HENRIETTA GDNS
HENRIETTA MEWS
HENRIETTA GARDENS
HENRIETTA STREET
GROVE STREET
BATHWICK STREET
FORESTER RD
POWLETT RD
N

well-balanced, informative entertainment here, with commentary provided by hourly guided tours and audioguides (both free). Highlights are: the Sacred Spring, part of the temple of the local deity Sulis Minerva, where water still bubbles up at a constant 46.5°C; the open-air (but originally covered) Great Bath, its vaporous waters surrounded by nineteenth-century pillars, terraces and statues of famous Romans; the Circular Bath, where bathers cooled off, and the Norman King's Bath.

Among a quantity of coins, jewellery and sculpture exhibited are the gilt bronze head of Sulis Minerva, the local deity, and a grand, Celtic-inspired gorgon's head from the temple's pediment. Models of the complex at its greatest extent give some idea of the awe which it must have inspired, while the graffiti salvaged from the Roman era – mainly curses and boasts – give a personal slant on this antique leisure-centre.

You can get a free glimpse into the baths from the next-door **Pump Room**, the social hub of the Georgian spa community and still redolent of that era, housing a formal tearoom and restaurant.

Bath Abbey

Although there has been a church on the site since the seventh century, **Bath Abbey** (Mon–Sat 9am–6pm, Nov–March closes 4.30pm; Sun 1–2.30pm & 4.30–5.30pm; requested donation £2.50) did not take its present form until the end of the fifteenth century, when Bishop Oliver King began work on the ruins of the previous Norman building, some of which were incorporated into the new church. The bishop was said to have been inspired by a vision of angels ascending and descending a ladder to heaven, which the present facade recalls on the turrets flanking the central window. The west front also features the founder's signature in the form of carvings of olive trees surmounted by crowns, a play on his name.

The **interior** is in a restrained Perpendicular style, and boasts splendid fan vaulting on the ceiling, which was not properly completed until the nineteenth century. The floor and walls are crammed with elaborate monuments and memorials, and traces of the grander Norman building are visible in the Norman Chapel.

Reached from a door to the right of the Choir, the **Heritage Vaults** (free) gives some background to the abbey's construction and displays examples of statuary and precious silver.

Thermae Bath Spa

Finally open after years of unseemly delay, **Thermae Bath Spa**, at the bottom of the elegantly colonnaded Bath Street (daily 9am–10pm; ⓣ0844/888 0844, ⓦwww.thermaebathspa.com), allows you to take the local waters in much the same way that visitors to Bath have done throughout the ages, but with state-of-the-art spa facilities. Heated by the city's thermal waters, the spa offers everything from massages to dry flotation, and includes two open-air pools, one on the roof of its centrepiece, the New Royal Bath, Nicholas Grimshaw's sleekly futuristic "glass cube". Prices start at £12 (1hr 30min), rising to £50 (full day). A small **visitor centre** has displays relating to Bath's thermal waters and a film.

To the Circus and the Royal Crescent

North of Hot Bath Street, Westgate Street and Sawclose are presided over by the **Theatre Royal**, opened in 1805 and one of the country's finest surviving Georgian theatres. Next door is the house where Beau Nash spent his last years (now a restaurant). Up from the Theatre Royal, off Barton Street, **Queen Square** was the first Bath venture of the architect **John Wood** (see box, p.294), who lived at no. 24.

West of Queen Square, the small **Herschel Museum of Astronomy** (Feb to mid-Dec Mon, Tues, Thurs & Fri 1–5pm, Sat & Sun 11am–5pm; £3.50) at 19 New King St, was the former home of the musician and astronomer Sir William Herschel and his sister Caroline, who together discovered the planet Uranus in 1781. Among the contemporary furnishings, musical instruments and various knick-knacks from the Herschels' life, you can see a replica of the telescope with which Uranus was identified. Just north of the square, at 40 Gay St, the **Jane Austen Centre** (March–Oct daily 9.45am–5.30pm, July & Aug Thurs–Sat open till 8.30pm; Nov–Feb Mon–Fri & Sun 11am–4.30pm, Sat 9.45am–5.30pm; £6.50) provides a superficial overview of the author's connections with the city, illustrated by extracts from her writings, contemporary costumes, furnishings and household items.

At the top of Gay Street, the elder John Wood's masterpiece, **The Circus**, consists of three crescents arranged in a tight circle of three-storey houses, with a carved frieze running round the entire circle. Wood died soon after laying the foundation stone for this enterprise, and the job was finished by his son. The painter Thomas Gainsborough lived at no. 17 from 1760 to 1774.

The Circus is connected by Brock Street to the **Royal Crescent**, grandest of Bath's crescents, begun by the younger John Wood in 1767. The stately arc of thirty houses is set off by a spacious sloping lawn from which a magnificent vista extends to green hills and distant ribbons of honey-coloured stone. The interior of **No. 1 Royal Crescent**, on the corner with Brock Street, has been restored to reflect as nearly as possible its original Georgian appearance (Tues–Sun: mid-Feb to Oct 10.30am–5pm; Nov 10.30am–4pm; £5).

At the bottom of the Crescent, Royal Avenue leads onto **Royal Victoria Park**, the city's largest open space, containing an aviary and botanical gardens.

The Assembly Rooms, the Paragon and Milsom Street

The younger John Wood's **Assembly Rooms**, east of the Circus on Bennett Street, were, with the Pump Room, the centre of Bath's social scene. A fire virtually destroyed the building in 1942, but it has now been perfectly restored and houses a **Fashion Museum** (daily: March–Oct 11am–5pm; Nov–Feb 11am–4pm; £6.75, or £13.50 with the Baths), an entertaining collection of clothing from the Stuart era to modern Milanese designs.

From the Assembly Rooms, Alfred Street leads to the area known as the **Paragon**. Here, accessed from the raised pavement, the Georgian-Gothic Countess of Huntingdon's Chapel houses the **Building of Bath Museum** (Tues–Sun 10.30am–5pm; £4), a fascinating exploration of the construction and architecture of Bath. At the bottom of the Paragon, off George Street, lies **Milsom Street**, a wide shopping strand designed by the elder Wood as the main thoroughfare of Georgian Bath.

The river and Great Pulteney Street

East of the abbey, Grand Parade looks down onto the formal Parade Gardens and the River Avon. The flow of the river here is interrupted by a graceful V-shaped weir just below the shop-lined **Pulteney Bridge**, an Italianate structure designed by Robert Adam. The bridge was intended to link the city centre with **Great Pulteney Street**, a handsome avenue originally planned as the nucleus of a large residential quarter on the eastern bank. The work ran into financial difficulties, however, so the roads running off it now stop short after a few yards, though there is a lengthy vista to the imposing classical facade of the **Holburne Museum** at the end of the street (Feb to mid-Dec Tues–Sat 10am–5pm, Sun 11am–5pm; £4.50). The three-storey building contains an impressive range of decorative and fine art, including work by Stubbs and the famous *Byam Family* by Gainsborough.

When Holburne House was a bustling hotel, the pleasure gardens behind it, now **Sydney Gardens**, were the venue for concerts and fireworks, as witnessed by Jane Austen, a frequent visitor here – the family had lodgings across the street at 4 Sydney Place. Today, the slopes are cut through by the railway and the Kennet and Avon Canal. From here, it's a pleasant one-and-a-half-mile saunter along the canal to the *George* pub (see p.299).

If you want to explore the river itself, rent a skiff, punt or canoe from the **Victorian Bath Boating Station** at the end of Forester Road, behind the Holburne Museum (Easter–Sept; £7 per person for 1hr, then £2 per hour). Organized **river trips** can be made from Pulteney Bridge and weir, and there are cruises on the Kennet and Avon Canal from Sydney Wharf, near Bathwick Bridge.

Eating, drinking and nightlife

Bath has a huge range of **eating** outlets, from expensive gourmet cuisine to decent, inexpensive cafés. Booking in the evening is advised at most places. Numerous congenial **pubs** also offer good-value fare in atmospheric surroundings.

Best of Bath's **clubs** is *Moles* (☎01225/404445, www.moles.co.uk) on George Street, a local institution which has live music and DJs; the next-door *Porter* also has free gigs, DJs and comedy nightly in its *Cellar Bar*. Other clubs include the *Fez Club*, The Paragon (☎01225/444162), and *Po Na Na*, 8 North Parade (☎01225/424952), both Moroccan-themed with largely student crowds, hosting indie, commercial, hip-hop and cheese nights.

For **events listings**, refer to the weekly *Venue* (£1.50), or *Bath Quarterly*, available free from the tourist office. **Theatre** and ballet fans should check out what's showing at the Theatre Royal on Sawclose (☎01225/448844), which stages more experimental productions in its Ustinov Studio.

There's a great range of festivals throughout the year, notably the **Bath International Music Festival** (www.bathmusicfest.org.uk), held between mid-May and June and featuring jazz, classical and world music; the **Bath Fringe Festival** (late May to early June; www.bathfringe.co.uk), with the accent on art and performance; and **Bath Literature Festival** (10 days in Feb/March; www.bathlitfest.org.uk). For further information on these and other festivals, call ☎01225/463362, www.bathfestivals.org.uk, or visit the festivals office at 2 Church St, Abbey Green.

Restaurants and cafés

Café Retro 18 York St. A cosy place near the abbey for a cappuccino or a meal. Also open Thurs–Sat eves for inventive international dishes for around £12. The adjacent *Retro-to-Go* takeaway sells rolls and salads.

Demuths 2 North Parade Passage ☎01225/446059. Bath's favourite eatery for veggies and vegans offers original and delicious moderate-to-expensive dishes from around the world, as well as organic beers, wines and coffees in a smooth and civilized ambience.

Eastern Eye 8 Quiet St ☎01225/422323. Just off Milsom St, this designer curry-house occupies a Georgian bank, with a spectacular vaulted ceiling and great food (mains around £8).

Firehouse Rotisserie 2 John St ☎01225/482070. Delicious, outsized Californian pizzas and grills (both £10–15) are the main items in this busy place with a pleasant wooden interior. Closed Sun.

Pump Room Abbey Church Yard ☎01225/444477. Splash out on an Eggs Benedict brunch, try the excellent lunchtime menu, or succumb to a Bath bun or a range of cream teas, all accompanied by a pianist or a classical trio. It's a bit hammy, and you may have to queue, but you get a good view of the Baths. Open daytime only, plus eves during the Bath Festival, Aug and Christmas, when three-course menus are around £21.

Tilley's Bistro 3 North Parade Passage ☎01225/484200. Informal, rather cramped French restaurant with different-sized portions (small £5–7, medium £6–9, large £10–17) to allow more samplings, and good set-price lunchtime menus. Closed Sun.

Walrus and Carpenter 28 Barton St ☎01225/314864. You'll find an extensive vegetarian menu in this warren of small rooms near the Theatre Royal – though organic meat dishes are also available (£10–14). The atmosphere is friendly and funky.

Pubs

The Bath Tap 19–20 St James's Parade. Home of Bath's gay and lesbian scene, lively but relaxed, with a mixed crowd. Open until 2am for club nights Thurs–Sat.

The Bell 103 Walcot St. Easy-going tavern with a beer garden and live music (Mon & Wed eve, plus Sun lunchtime).

The George Mill Lane, Bathampton. Popular canal-side pub 20min walk from the centre, with better than average bar food.

The Porter Miles Buildings, George St. Part of *Moles* club (see p.298), serving good beer and veggie food in a grungy setting. There are tables outside and pool and table football in the *Cellar Bar*, where, in the evenings, there's free live music (Mon–Thurs), DJs (Fri & Sat) and comedy (Sun).

The Salamander 3 John St. Real-ale pub with wooden decor, a laid-back atmosphere and good food available at the bar or in the upstairs restaurant.

Wells, the Mendips and Glastonbury

Wells, twenty miles south of Bristol across the Somerset border and the same distance southwest from Bath, is a miniature cathedral city that has not significantly altered in eight hundred years. You might decide to make it an accommodation stop for visiting nearby attractions in the **Mendip Hills**, such as the **Wookey Hole** caves and **Cheddar Gorge**. On the southern edge of the range, the town of **Glastonbury** has for centuries been one of the main Arthurian sites of the West Country, and is now the country's most enthusiastic centre of New Age cults.

Wells

WELLS owes its celebrity entirely to its **cathedral** (daily 7am–6/7pm; suggested donation £5.50). Hidden from sight until you pass into its spacious close from the central Market Place, the building presents a majestic spectacle, the broad lawn of the former graveyard providing a perfect foreground. The west front teems with some three hundred thirteenth-century figures of saints and kings, once brightly painted and gilded, though their present honey tint has a subtle splendour of its own. The facade was constructed about fifty years after work on the main building was begun in 1180. The **interior** is a supreme example of early English Gothic, the long nave punctuated by a dramatic "scissor arch", one of three that were constructed in 1338 to take the extra weight of the newly built tower. Beyond the arch, there are some gnarled old tombs to be seen in the aisles of the **Quire**, at the end of which is the richly coloured stained glass of the fourteenth-century **Lady Chapel**. The **capitals and corbels** of the transepts hold some amusing narrative carvings – look out for the men with toothache and an old man caught pilfering an orchard – and, in the north transept, there's a 24-hour astronomical clock dating from 1390. From his seat high up on the right of the clock, a figure known as Jack Blandiver kicks a couple of bells every quarter-hour, heralding the appearance of a pair of jousting knights charging at each other, and on the hour he strikes the bell in front of him. Opposite the clock, a doorway leads to a graceful, much-worn flight of steps rising to the **Chapter House**, an octagonal room elaborately ribbed in the Decorated style.

The row of clerical houses on the north side of the cathedral green are mainly seventeenth- and eighteenth-century, though one, the **Old Deanery**, shows traces of its fifteenth-century origins. The chancellor's house is now a **museum** (Easter–Oct Mon–Sat 10am–5.30pm, Sun 11am–4pm; Nov–Easter daily 11am–4pm; £3), displaying some of the cathedral's original statuary as well as a good geological section with fossils from the surrounding area.

Beyond the arch, a little further along the street, the cobbled medieval **Vicars' Close** holds more clerical dwellings, linked to the cathedral by the Chain Gate and fronted by small gardens. The cottages were built in the mid-fourteenth century – though only no. 22 has not undergone outward alterations – and have been continuously occupied by members of the cathedral clergy ever since.

On the other side of the cathedral – and accessible through the cathedral shop – are the cloisters, from which you can enter the tranquil grounds of the **Bishop's Palace** (April–Oct daily except Sat 10.30am–6pm; Aug daily 10.30am–6pm; last entry at 5pm; £4), also reachable from Market Place through the Bishop's Eye archway. The residence of the Bishop of Bath and Wells, the palace was walled and moated as a result of a rift with the borough in the fourteenth century, and the imposing gatehouse still displays the grooves of the portcullis and a chute for pouring oil and molten lead on would-be assailants. Its tranquil gardens contain the springs from which the city takes its name and the scanty but impressive remains of the **Great Hall**, built at the end of the thirteenth century and despoiled during the Reformation. Across the lawn stands the square **Bishop's Chapel** and the **Undercroft**, holding displays relating to the history of the site, state rooms and a café.

Practicalities

Wells' **bus station** is off Market Street, and its **tourist office** is on Market Place (April & Oct 10am–5pm, Sun 10am–4pm; May–Sept Mon–Sat 9am–5pm, Sun 10am–4pm; Nov–March Mon–Sat 10am–4pm; ⓣ01749/672552, ⓦwww.wellstourism.com). You can **hire bikes** – useful for visiting Wookey Hole – from Bike City, 38 Market St (ⓣ01749/671711).

Good, central **accommodation** choices include *Canon Grange*, whose spacious rooms face the cathedral's west front (ⓣ01749/671800, ⓦwww.canongrange.co.uk; ❸), and two old coaching inns full of antique atmosphere: the *Crown*, Market Place (ⓣ01749/673457, ⓦwww.crownatwells.co.uk; ❻), where William Penn was arrested in 1695 for illegal preaching, and the rambling *Swan*, on Sadler Street (ⓣ01749/836300, ⓦwww.swanhotelwells.co.uk; ❼).

The best **food** in town is at *Goodfellows*, both patisserie (open daily), good for superb sandwiches and pastries, and innovative but pricey seafood restaurant (ⓣ01749/673866; closed Tues eve and all Sun & Mon). Excellent wholefood is on hand at the *Good Earth* on Priory Road, near the bus station (closed eves & Sun), also with delicious takeaway items. Alternatively, head for the *City Arms*, a pub on Cuthbert Street, formerly the town gaol.

The Mendips

North of Wells, the **Mendip Hills** are chiefly famous for **Wookey Hole** – the most impressive of many caves in this narrow limestone chain – and for **Cheddar Gorge**, where a walk through the narrow cleft makes a starting point for more adventurous trips across the Mendips. Both can be reached on regular buses from Wells.

Wookey Hole

Hollowed out by the River Axe a couple of miles outside Wells, **Wookey Hole** is a stunning cave complex of deep pools and intricate rock formations, but it's folklore rather than geology that takes precedence on the guided tours (daily 10am–4/5pm; £12.50). Highlight of the hour-long tour is the alleged petrified remains of the Witch of Wookey, a "blear-eyed hag" who was said to turn her evil eye on crops, young lovers and local farmers. To finish off the tour, there's a functioning Victorian paper mill, rooms containing speleological exhibits and a range of amusements including a collection of Edwardian fairground pieces.

The *Wookey Hole Inn* (ⓣ01749/676677, ⓦwww.wookeyholeinn.com; ⑥), just along the street from the caves, is a great place to **stay the night**, with contemporary, fully equipped guest rooms, or for a good **meal**. The bar serves a great selection of Belgian beers, while the **restaurant** (booking essential; closed Sun eve) cooks up expensive but memorable dishes, and there's regular live music.

Cheddar Gorge

Six miles west of Wookey on the A371, the rather plain village of Cheddar has given its name to Britain's best-known cheese – most of it now mass-produced far from here – and is also renowned for the **Cheddar Gorge**, lying beyond the neighbourhood of Tweentown about a mile to the north.

Cutting a jagged gash across the Mendip Hills, the limestone gorge is an amazing geological phenomenon, though its natural beauty is undermined by the minor road running through it and by the Lower Gorge's mile of shops and parking areas. Few trippers venture further than the first few curves of the gorge, which admittedly holds its most dramatic scenery, though each turn of the two-mile length presents new, sometimes startling vistas, which can be viewed from the open-top bus that plies up and down between March and October (free to Cheddar Caves ticket-holders). At its narrowest the road squeezes between cliffs towering almost five hundred feet above. Those in a state of honed fitness can climb the 274 steps of **Jacob's Ladder** to a cliff-top viewpoint looking towards Glastonbury Tor, with occasional glimpses of Exmoor and the sea – or you can reach the same spot more easily via the narrow lane winding up behind the cliffs. There's a circular three-mile cliff-top Gorge Walk, and you can branch off along marked paths to such secluded spots as **Black Rock**, just two miles from Cheddar, or **Black Down**, at 1067ft the Mendips' highest point. The tourist office can provide details of the **West Mendip Way**, a forty-mile route extending from Uphill, near Weston-super-Mare, to Wells and Shepton Mallet.

Beneath the gorge, the **Cheddar Caves** (daily: July & Aug 10am–5.30pm; Sept–June 10.30am–5pm; £14) were scooped out by underground rivers in the wake of the Ice Age, and subsequently occupied by primitive communities. Today the caves are floodlit to pick out the subtle tones of the rock, and the array of tortuous rock formations that resemble organ pipes, waterfalls and giant birds.

The **tourist office** is at the bottom of the Gorge (Easter to mid-Sept daily 10am–5pm; mid-Sept to Oct daily 10.30am–4.30pm; Nov–Easter Sun 11am–4pm; ⓣ01934/744071, ⓦwww.visitsomerset.co.uk). Among Cheddar's handful of **B&Bs**, try *Chedwell Cottage*, Redcliffe St (ⓣ01934/743268; no credit cards; ②). There's a **youth hostel** off the Hayes (ⓣ0870/770 5760, ⓔcheddar@yha.org.uk; dorm bed from £14; call to check opening), and a central **campsite**, *Cheddar Bridge Park,* opposite the church on Draycott Road (ⓣ01934/743048, ⓦwww.cheddarbridge.co.uk; no under-18s; closed Dec–Feb).

Glastonbury

Six miles south of Wells, **GLASTONBURY** lies at the centre of the so-called **Isle of Avalon**, a region rich with mystical associations. At the heart of it all is the early Christian legend that the young Jesus once visited this site, a story that is not as far-fetched as it sounds. The Romans had a heavy presence in the area, mining lead in the Mendips, and one of these mines was owned by **Joseph of Arimathea**, a well-to-do merchant said to have been related to Mary. It's not completely impossible that the merchant took his kinsman on one of his many visits to his property, in a period of Christ's life of which nothing is recorded. It was this possibility to which William Blake referred in his *Glastonbury Hymn*, better known as *Jerusalem*: – "And did those feet in ancient times/Walk upon England's mountains green?"

Another legend relates how Joseph was imprisoned for twelve years after the Crucifixion, miraculously kept alive by the **Holy Grail**, the chalice of the Last Supper, in which the blood was gathered from the wound in Christ's side. The Grail, along with the spear which had caused the wound, were later taken by Joseph to Glastonbury, where he founded the abbey and commenced the conversion of Britain.

▲ Glastonbury Festival

Glastonbury Abbey

Aside from its mythological origins, **Glastonbury Abbey** (daily: March & Oct 9.30am–5.30pm; April–Sept 9.30am–6pm; Nov 9.30am–4.30pm; Dec–Feb 10am–4.30/5pm; £4.50) can claim to be the country's oldest Christian foundation, dating back to the seventh century and possibly earlier. Enlarged by St Dunstan in the tenth century, it became the richest Benedictine abbey in the country; three Anglo-Saxon kings (Edmund, Edgar and Edmund Ironside) were buried here, and the library had a far-reaching fame. Further expansion took place under the Normans, though most of the additions were destroyed by fire in 1184. Rebuilt, the abbey was later a casualty of the Dissolution of the Monasteries in the 1530s, and the ruins, now hidden behind walls and nestled among grassy parkland, can only hint at its former extent. The most prominent remains are the transept piers and the shell of the Lady Chapel, with its carved figures of the Annunciation, the Magi and Herod.

The abbey's **choir** introduces another strand to the Glastonbury story, for it holds what is alleged to be the tomb of **Arthur and Guinevere**. The story relates how, after being mortally wounded in battle, King Arthur sailed to Avalon where he was buried alongside his queen. The discovery of two bodies in an ancient cemetery outside the abbey in 1191 – from which they were transferred here in 1278 – was taken to confirm the popular identification of Glastonbury with Avalon. In the grounds, the fourteenth-century **abbot's kitchen** is the only monastic building to survive intact, with four huge corner fireplaces and a great central lantern above.

Behind the main entrance to the grounds, look out for the thorn-tree that is supposedly a descendant of the original **Glastonbury Thorn** said to have sprouted from the staff of Joseph of Arimathea.

The town and Glastonbury Tor

At the bottom of Glastonbury's High Street, abbots once presided over legal cases in the fourteenth-century **Tribunal**; it later became a hotel for pilgrims, and now holds the tourist office and the small **Glastonbury Lake Village Museum** (same hours as tourist office, see below; £2, free to EH members), which displays finds from the Iron Age villages that fringed the former marshland below the Tor. Further up the High Street, the fifteenth-century church of **St John the Baptist** has one of Somerset's finest towers, while its interior has a superb oak roof and stained glass illustrating the legend of St Joseph of Arimathea. The Glastonbury thorn in the churchyard is the biggest in town.

At the top of the High Street, walk down Lambrook and Chilkwell streets to find, at the southeastern edge of the abbey grounds, the fourteenth-century Abbey Barn, centrepiece of the engaging **Somerset Rural Life Museum** (April–Oct Tues–Fri 10am–5pm, Sat & Sun 2–6pm; Nov–March Tues–Sat 10am–5pm; free), focusing on a range of local rural occupations, from cheese- and cider-making to peat-digging, thatching and farming. Further down Chilkwell Street, the **Chalice Well** (daily: April–Oct 10am–5.30pm; Nov–March 10am–4pm; £3) stands amid a lush garden intended for quiet contemplation. The iron-red waters of the well – which is fondly supposed to be the hiding-place of the Holy Grail – were considered to have curative properties, making the town a spa for a brief period in the eighteenth century, and they are still prized (there's a tap in Wellhouse Lane).

From Chilkwell Street, turn left into Wellhouse Lane and immediately right for the footpath that leads up to **Glastonbury Tor**, at 521ft a landmark for miles around. The conical hill – topped by the dilapidated **St Michael's Tower**, sole remnant of a fourteenth-century church – commands stupendous views.

Glastonbury Festival

Glastonbury is, of course, best known for its **music festival**, which takes place most years over three days at the end of June outside the nearby village of Pilton. Having started in the 1970s, the festival has become one of the biggest in the country, without shedding too much of its alternative feel. Bands range from huge acts such as The Killers to up-and-coming indie groups, via old hands such as The Who. Though **tickets** cost around £150, they are snapped up almost instantaneously: for information call ⓣ01458/834596 or see ⓦwww.glastonburyfestivals.co.uk.

Pilgrims once embarked on the stiff climb here with hard peas in their shoes as penance – nowadays people come to feel the vibrations of crossing ley-lines. You can save some legwork by taking advantage of the **Glastonbury Tor Bus** (daily: April–Sept 9.30am–7pm; Oct–March 10am–3pm; £2 valid all day), from the abbey car park to the base of the Tor, with stops at the Rural Life Museum and Chalice Well.

Practicalities

Frequent buses #375, #376 and #377 connect Glastonbury with Wells. The **tourist office** is housed in the Tribunal on the High Street (April–Sept Mon–Thurs & Sun 10am–5pm, Fri & Sat 10am–5.30pm; Oct–March closes 1hr earlier; ⓣ01458/832954, ⓦwww.glastonburytic.co.uk).

Glastonbury's **accommodation** takes in everything from medieval hostelry to backpacker hostel, with most places within a brief walk of the Tor and town centre.

1 Park Terrace Street Rd ⓣ01458/835845, ⓦwww.no1parkterrace.co.uk. Large Victorian house, with Internet access and evening meals available. ③

3 Magdalene St ⓣ01458/832129, ⓦwww.numberthree.co.uk. Beautifully furnished bedrooms make for a stylish stay in this Georgian house with a large walled garden, right next to the abbey. ⑥

George & Pilgrims High St ⓣ01458/831146, ⓦwww.georgeandpilgrims.activehotels.com. This fifteenth-century oak-panelled inn brims with antique atmosphere. ④

Glastonbury Backpackers 4 Market Place ⓣ01458/833353, ⓦwww.glastonburybackpackers.com. Central ex-coaching inn with lively café/bar, pool room and no curfew. Dorm beds £14, doubles ①

Meadow Barn Middlewick Farm, Wick Lane ⓣ01458/832351, ⓦwww.middlewickholidaycottages.co.uk. A mile and a half north of town, this Canadian-run place offers peace and quiet in rural surroundings, with steam room and indoor pool. Minimum two-night stay. ③

Street YHA Ivythorn Hill, St ⓣ0870/770 6056, ⓔstreet@yha.org.uk. The nearest YHA lies a couple of miles south of Glastonbury (bus #375 or #376; alight at Marshalls Elm crossroads and follow signs). Dorm beds from £12. Call for opening details.

Eating, drinking and entertainment

Wedged between the esoteric shops of Glastonbury's High Street are several decent **cafés** serving inexpensive meals, including the *Blue Note Café* at no. 4, with some courtyard seating and evening meals in summer, and *Hundred Monkeys* at no. 52 (ⓣ01458/833386; closed Sun), which stays open Thursday–Saturday evenings for meals and live music. The eclectic menu at *Hawthorns*, 8 Northload St (ⓣ01458/831225), includes a lunchtime curry buffet, "Ethnic English" dishes and vegetarian options.

Across the road at 17 Northload St, the *Who'd a Thought It* is one of the best **pubs** locally, with decent food and a garden. *Glastonbury Backpackers* (see above) is also good for ales, atmosphere and live music, while the Assembly Rooms (ⓦwww.assemblyrooms.org.uk) host talks and musical and theatrical

performances, usually at weekends. Big-name concerts and drama productions take place in the abbey grounds in summer – call ⓣ01458/832267 or check ⓦwww.glastonburyabbey.com for details.

Bridgwater and the Quantocks

Travelling west from Glastonbury, your route could take you through **Bridgwater**, a handy starting point for excursions into the gently undulating **Quantock Hills**, dotted with snug villages set in scenic wooded valleys or "combes". Public transport is fairly minimal around here, but you can see quite a lot on the **West Somerset Railway** between Bishops Lydeard and the coastal resort of Minehead, with stops at some of the thatched, typically English villages along the west flank of the Quantocks.

Bridgwater

Sedate **BRIDGWATER** has seen little excitement since it was embroiled in the Civil War and its aftermath, in particular the events surrounding the **Monmouth Rebellion** of 1685. Having landed from his base in Holland, the Protestant Duke of Monmouth, an illegitimate son of Charles II, was enthusiastically proclaimed king and, having failed to take Bristol, attempted to surprise the forces of the Catholic James II on **Sedgemoor**, three miles outside Bridgwater. However, the disorganized rebel army was mown down by the royal artillery, Monmouth was captured and later beheaded, and a campaign of bloody repression was unleashed under the infamous Judge Jeffreys.

Despite some ugly outskirts, Bridgwater retains some handsome red-brick buildings in its centre, notably the thirteenth- to fourteenth-century **St Mary's Church**, identifiable by its polygonal, angled steeple soaring above the town centre. Features inside include an oak pulpit and a seventeenth-century Italian altarpiece. On Blake Street – round the corner from the red-brick Christ Church where Coleridge preached in 1797 and 1798 – Bridgwater's **Blake Museum** (Tues–Sat 10am–4pm; free) shows relics, models and a video relating to the Battle of Sedgemoor. The sixteenth-century building is reputedly the birthplace of local hero Robert Blake, admiral under Oliver Cromwell, whose swashbuckling career is chronicled and illustrated here.

Bridgwater's **tourist office** is on King's Square (Mon–Fri 8.45am–5pm; ⓣ01278/436438, ⓦwww.somersetbythesea.co.uk). Central **accommodation** choices include the *Old Vicarage*, opposite St Mary's Church (ⓣ01278/458891, ⓦwww.theoldvicaragebridgwater.com; ❻), one of the town's oldest buildings, and the more up-to-date *Tudor Hotel*, 27 St Mary St (ⓣ01278/422093; ❸). Both places serve teas, light lunches and full meals, while the *Tudor* also hosts live jazz on Thursday evenings. On Castle Street, the **Bridgwater Arts Centre** (ⓣ01278/422700, ⓦwww.bridgwaterartscentre.co.uk) has films, plays, concerts and comedy.

The Quantock Hills

The **Quantock Hills** extend just twelve miles in length, and rise to 800–900ft. Watered by clear streams and grazed by red deer, the range is enclosed by a triangle of roads leading up from Bridgwater and Taunton, within which narrow lanes connect the secluded hamlets.

Eight miles west of Bridgwater on the A39, on the edge of the hills, the pretty village of **NETHER STOWEY** is best known for its association with **Samuel Taylor Coleridge**, who in 1796 walked here from Bristol to join his wife and child at their new home. This "miserable cottage", as Sara Coleridge called it, was visited six months later by William Wordsworth and his sister Dorothy, who soon afterwards moved into the grander Alfoxden House, a couple of miles down the road near Holford. The year that Coleridge and Wordsworth spent as neighbours was extraordinarily productive – Coleridge composed some of his best poetry at this time, including *The Rime of the Ancient Mariner* and *Kubla Khan*, and the two poets collaborated on the *Lyrical Ballads*, the poetic manifesto of early English Romanticism. **Coleridge Cottage** (April–Sept Thurs–Sun 2–5pm; £3.90; NT) reveals the poet's parlour and reading room, and, upstairs, his bedroom and an exhibition room containing various letters and first editions. You can pick up leaflets here (or consult Ⓦwww.coleridgeway.co.uk) on the **Coleridge Way**, a walking route that supposedly follows the poet's footsteps between Nether Stowey and Porlock on the Exmoor coast (see p.338); waymarked with quill signs, the 36-mile hike passes through some of the most scenic parts of the Quantocks and Exmoor.

The village's **accommodation** choices are both on Castle Street: the handsomely furnished *Stowey Brooke House*, at no. 18 (Ⓣ01278/733356, Ⓦwww.stoweybrookehouse.co.uk; no credit cards; ❸), and the *Old Cider House* at no. 25 (Ⓣ01278/732228, Ⓦwww.theoldciderhouse.co.uk; ❸), which also serves quality evening meals. The *Rose & Crown* on St Mary Street provides ales and bar meals, as does the *George* next door. A couple of miles east of Nether Stowey, outside the village of Fiddington, *Mill Farm* offers **camping** (Ⓣ01278/732286, Ⓦwww.millfarm.biz), horse riding, indoor and outdoor pools, and **bike hire**.

South of Nether Stowey, a minor road winds off the A39 to the highest point on the Quantocks at **Wills Neck** (1260ft); drivers can park at Triscombe Stone, on the edge of Quantock Forest, from where a footpath leads to the summit about a mile distant. Stretching between Wills Neck and the village of Aisholt, the moorland plateau of **Aisholt Common** is the heart of the Quantocks, best explored from **West Bagborough**, where a five-mile path starts at Birches Corner. Lower down the slopes, outside Aisholt, the banks of **Hawkridge Reservoir** make a lovely picnic stop.

The other main road route fringing the Quantocks – the A358 heading northwest from Taunton – is accompanied for most of the way by the **West Somerset Railway** (Ⓣ01643/704996, Ⓦwww.west-somerset-railway.co.uk), a restored branch line running some twenty miles between the village of Bishops Lydeard, five miles out of Taunton, to Minehead on the Somerset coast (see p.337). Steam and diesel trains depart up to eight times daily between mid-March and October (plus some dates in Dec & Feb), stopping at renovated stations on the way; the full ticket to Minehead costs £8.80 single, £13 return. A special bus service links the terminus with Taunton's train station, or take bus #23 or #28A (both Mon–Sat).

BISHOPS LYDEARD itself is worth a wander, not least for **St Mary's** church, with a splendid tower and carved bench-ends inside. A couple of miles north, **COMBE FLOREY** is almost exclusively built of the pink-red sandstone characteristic of Quantock villages. For over fifteen years (1829–45), the local rector was the unconventional cleric Sydney Smith, called "the greatest master of ridicule since Swift" by Macaulay; more recently it was home to Evelyn Waugh. A little over three miles further along the A358, **CROWCOMBE** is another typical cob-and-thatch Quantock village, with a well-preserved Church House from 1515.

Travel details

Buses

For information on all local and national bus services, contact Traveline ⓣ0871/200 2233 (daily 7am–9pm), ⓦwww.traveline.org.uk.

Bath to: Bristol (Mon–Sat every 12min, Sun every 30min; 55min); London (10 daily; 3hr–3hr 50min); Salisbury (Mon–Sat 10 daily, Sun 1 daily; 1hr 15min); Wells (Mon–Sat hourly, Sun 7 daily; 1hr 15min).

Bridgwater to: Glastonbury (Mon–Sat hourly, Sun 4; 50min–1hr 10min); Nether Stowey (6 daily; 40min); Taunton (Mon–Sat every 30min, Sun every 2hr; 45min); Wells (Mon–Sat hourly, Sun 4 daily; 1hr 10min–1hr 25min).

Bristol to: Bath (Mon–Sat every 12min, Sun every 30min; 50min); Glastonbury (hourly; 1hr 15min); London (1–2 hourly; 2hr 30min); Wells (1–2 hourly; 1hr).

Glastonbury to: Bridgwater (Mon–Sat hourly, Sun 4 daily; 50min–1hr 10min); Bristol (hourly; 1hr 10min); Wells (2–4 hourly; 15min).

Wells to: Bath (Mon–Sat hourly, Sun 7 daily; 1hr 15min); Bridgwater (Mon–Sat hourly, Sun 4 daily; 1hr 10min–1hr 25min); Bristol (1–2 hourly; 1hr); Glastonbury (2–4 hourly; 15min); Wookey Hole (Mon–Sat 9 daily, Sun 4 daily; 10min).

Trains

For information on all local and national rail services, contact National Rail Enquiries ⓣ08457/484950, ⓦwww.nationalrail.co.uk.

Bath to: Bristol (2–3 hourly; 15min); London (1–2 hourly; 1hr 30min); Salisbury (1–2 hourly; 1hr).

Bristol to: Bath (2–3 hourly; 15min); Birmingham (every 30min; 1hr 30min); Bridgwater (hourly; 45min); Cheltenham (2–3 hourly; 40min–1hr); Exeter (1–2 hourly; 1hr); Gloucester (hourly; 50min); London (every 30min; 1hr 45min).

6 Devon and Cornwall

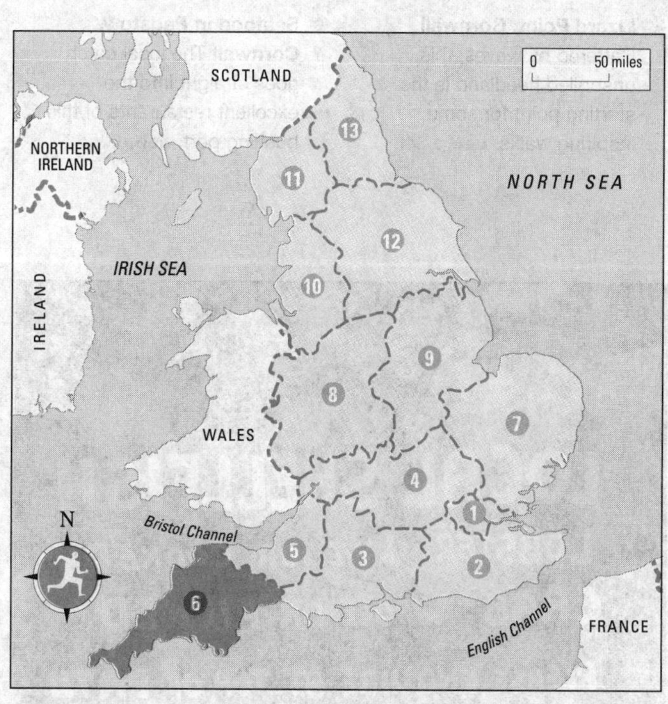

CHAPTER 6

Highlights

* **South West Coast Path** Ever-changing vistas ensure variety on Britain's longest waymarked path. See p.336
* **Eden Project, Cornwall** A disused clay pit is home to a fantastic array of exotic plants and crops. See p.343
* **Lizard Point, Cornwall** Battered by waves, this unspoiled headland is the starting point for some inspiring walks. See p.346
* **Tate St Ives, Cornwall** Local artists showcase their works at this modern gallery. See p.351
* **Surfing in Newquay** Endless ranks of rollers draw enthusiasts from far and wide. See p.353
* **Seafood in Padstow, Cornwall** The local catch goes straight into the excellent restaurants of this bustling port. See p.355

▲ Try the delicious seafood

Devon and Cornwall

At the western extremity of England, the counties of **Devon and Cornwall** encompass everything from genteel, cosy villages to vast Atlantic-facing strands of golden sand and wild expanses of granite moorland. The combination of rural peace and first-class beaches has made the peninsula perennially popular with tourists, so much so that tourism has replaced the traditional occupations of fishing and farming as the main source of employment and income. Enough remains of these beleaguered communities to preserve the region's authentic character, however – even if this can be occasionally obscured during the summer season. Avoid the peak periods and you'll be seduced by the genuine appeal of this area, which beckons ever westwards into rural backwaters where increasingly exotic place-names and idiosyncratic pronunciations recall that this was once England's last bastion of Celtic culture.

Straddling the border between Devon and Somerset, **Exmoor** is one of the peninsula's three great moors, its heathery slopes much favoured by hunting parties as well as by hikers. For wilderness, however, nothing can beat the remoter tracts of **Dartmoor**, the greatest of the West Country's granite massifs, much of which retains its solitude despite its proximity to the region's only major cities. Of the two, **Exeter** is by far the more interesting, dominated by the twin towers of its medieval cathedral and offering a rich selection of restaurants and nightlife. As for **Plymouth**, much of this great naval port was destroyed by bombing during World War II, and bland postwar development has blemished much of the rest, although enough of the city's Elizabethan core has survived to merit a visit.

The coastline on either side of Exeter and Plymouth is within easy reach. Enjoying more hours of sunshine than virtually anywhere else in England, this part of the country can sometimes come fairly close to the atmosphere of the Mediterranean, and indeed Devon's principal resort, **Torquay**, styles itself the capital of the "English Riviera". St Tropez it ain't, but there's no denying a certain glamour, alloyed with an old-fashioned charm which the seaside towns of **East Devon** and the cliff-backed resorts of the county's northern littoral also share.

Cornwall too has its pockets of concentrated tourist development – chiefly at **Falmouth** and **Newquay**, the first of these a sailing centre, the second a mecca for surfers drawn to its choice of west-facing beaches. **St Ives** is another crowd-puller, though the town has a separate identity as a magnet for the arts. Further up Cornwall's long northern coast, the rock-walled harbours of **Port Isaac** and **Boscastle** and the fortified site of **Tintagel** have an almost embattled character in the face of the turbulent Atlantic. However, the full elemental power of the

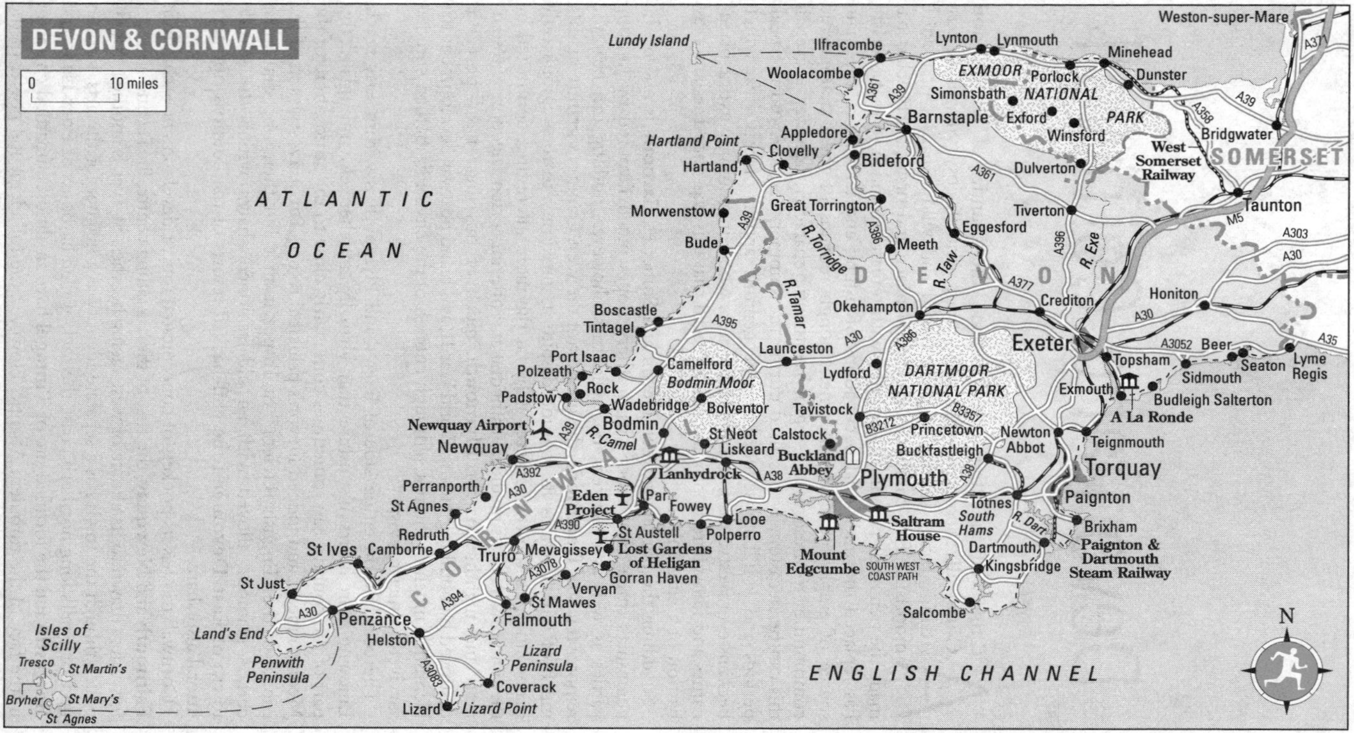

DEVON & CORNWALL

0 10 miles

ATLANTIC OCEAN
ENGLISH CHANNEL
N

Lundy Island
Ilfracombe
Woolacombe
Lynton
Lynmouth
EXMOOR NATIONAL PARK
Porlock
Minehead
Dunster
Simonsbath
Exford
Winsford
Barnstaple
Appledore
Bideford
Hartland Point
Clovelly
Hartland
Dulverton
West Somerset Railway
Bridgwater
Weston-super-Mare
SOMERSET
Taunton
Tiverton
Great Torrington
Morwenstow
Bude
Eggesford
Meeth
R. Torridge
R. Taw
R. Exe
R. Tamar
DEVON
Crediton
Honiton
Okehampton
Boscastle
Tintagel
Launceston
Exeter
Topsham
Beer
Seaton
Lyme Regis
Sidmouth
Budleigh Salterton
Exmouth
A La Ronde
Port Isaac
Polzeath
Camelford
Bodmin Moor
Lydford
DARTMOOR NATIONAL PARK
Rock
Padstow
Wadebridge
Bolventor
Tavistock
Princetown
Newquay Airport
Bodmin
R. Camel
St Neot
Calstock
Buckland Abbey
Newton Abbot
Teignmouth
Newquay
Liskeard
Buckfastleigh
Torquay
Lanhydrock
Plymouth
CORNWALL
Perranporth
Eden Project
Par
Fowey
Looe
Totnes
Paignton
St Agnes
St Austell
Polperro
Saltram House
South Hams
R. Dart
Brixham
Redruth
Camborne
St Ives
Truro
Mevagissey
Lost Gardens of Heligan
Gorran Haven
Mount Edgcumbe
SOUTH WEST COAST PATH
Dartmouth
Kingsbridge
Paignton & Dartmouth Steam Railway
St Just
Veryan
St Mawes
Salcombe
Penzance
Falmouth
Land's End
Helston
Lizard Peninsula
Penwith Peninsula
Coverack
Lizard
Lizard Point
Isles of Scilly
Tresco
St Martin's
Bryher
St Mary's
St Agnes

A371 A39 A358 A361 A303 A30 M5 A386 A396 A377 A395 A3052 A35 A38 B3357 B3212 A392 A390 A3078 A394 A3083 ocean can best be appreciated on the western headlands of **Lizard Point** and **Land's End**, where the cliffs resound to the constant thunder of the waves.

A disused clay pit is the site of the **Eden Project**, which imaginatively highlights the diversity of the planet's plant systems with the help of science-fiction "biomes", where tropical and Mediterranean climates and conditions have been re-created.

The best way of exploring the coast of Devon and Cornwall is along the **South West Coast Path**, Britain's longest waymarked footpath, which extends for over six hundred miles from Minehead in Somerset to Poole in Dorset. Getting around by **public transport** in the West Country can be a convoluted and lengthy process, especially if you're relying on the often deficient bus network. By train, you can reach Exeter, Plymouth and Penzance, with a handful of branch lines wandering off to the major coastal resorts.

Devon

With its rolling meadows, narrow lanes and remote thatched cottages, **Devon** has long been idealized as a vision of a pre-industrial, "authentic" England. But while many of its cosy, gentrified villages are inhabited largely by retired folk and urban refugees, at least the stereotyped image has helped to preserve the countryside and coast in the undeveloped condition for which they are famous, and the county offers an abundance of genuine tranquillity, from moorland villages to quiet coves on the cliff-hung coastline.

Reminders of Devon's leading role in the country's **maritime history** are never far away, particularly in the two cities of **Exeter** and **Plymouth**. These days the nautical tradition is perpetuated on a domesticated scale by yachts-people taking advantage of Devon's numerous creeks and bays, especially on its southern coast, where ports such as **Dartmouth** and **Salcombe** are awash with amateur sailors. Land-bound tourists flock to the sandy beaches and seaside resorts, of which **Torquay**, on the south coast, and **Ilfracombe**, on the north, are the busiest. The most attractive are those which have retained traces of their nineteenth-century elegance, such as **Sidmouth**, in East Devon. Inland, Devon is characterized by swards of lush pasture and a scattering of sheltered villages, the county's low population density dropping to almost zero on **Dartmoor**, the wildest and bleakest of the West's moors, and **Exmoor**, whose seaboard constitutes one of the West Country's most scenic littorals.

Exeter and Plymouth are on the main **rail** lines from London and the Midlands, with branch lines from Exeter linking the north coast at Barnstaple and the south-coast towns of Exmouth and Torquay. **Buses** from the chief stations fan out along the coasts and into the interior, though the service can be rudimentary for the smaller villages.

Exeter and around

EXETER's sights are richer than those of any other town in Devon or Cornwall, the legacy of an eventful history since its Celtic foundation and the

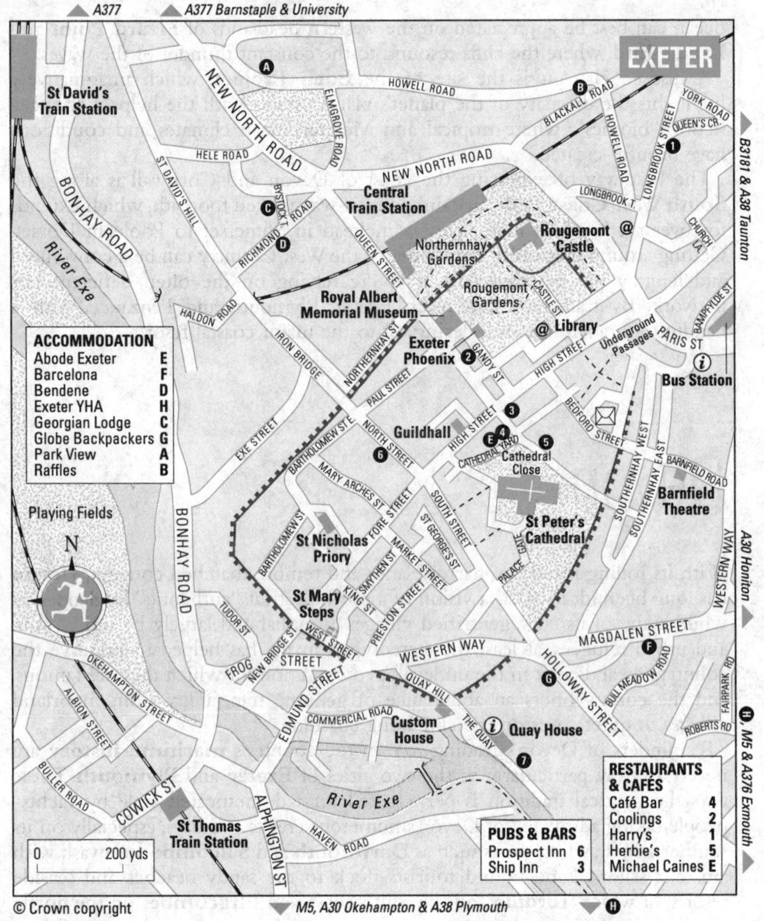

establishment here of the most westerly Roman outpost. After the Roman withdrawal, Exeter was refounded by Alfred the Great and by the time of the Norman Conquest had become one of the largest towns in England, profiting from its position on the banks of the River Exe. The expansion of the wool trade in the Tudor period sustained the city until the eighteenth century, and Exeter has maintained its status as commercial centre and county town, and, despite having much of its ancient centre gutted by World War II bombing, enough has survived to justify a lengthy exploration.

Arrival, information and accommodation

Exeter has two **train stations**, Exeter Central and St David's, the latter a little further out from the centre of town, and connected by frequent city buses. South West trains from Salisbury stop at both, as do trains on the branch lines to Barnstaple and Exmouth, but most long-distance trains stop at St David's only. The **bus station** is on Paris Street, opposite the main **tourist office** at

Dix's Field, off Princesshay (Mon–Sat 9am–5pm, also Sun 10am–4pm in July & Aug; ⓣ01392/665700, ⓦwww.exeterandessentialdevon.com).

Accommodation

Most of Exeter's cheaper **accommodation** lies north of the centre, near the two stations, though you can also find bargains more centrally.

Bendene 15 Richmond Rd ⓣ01392/213526, ⓦwww.bendene.co.uk. A heated outdoor swimming pool and low rates are the chief attractions of this central B&B. No credit cards. 3

Globe Backpackers 71 Holloway St ⓣ01392/215521, ⓦwww.exeterbackpackers.co.uk. Clean and central, with good showers and Internet access. Dorm beds £15, and a spacious double also available. 1

Hotel Barcelona Magdalen St ⓣ01392/281000, ⓦwww.aliashotels.com. Great place for a stylish splurge, in a red-brick former Victorian eye hospital. Light, spacious rooms, Gaudí-esque decor and a good bistro. 7

Park View 8 Howell Rd ⓣ01392/271772, ⓦwww.parkviewhotel.freeserve.co.uk. In a quiet location overlooking a park, this Georgian B&B has airy rooms overlooking a park. 3

Raffles 11 Blackall Rd ⓣ01392/270200, ⓦwww.raffles-exeter.co.uk. Elegant Victorian house with period furnishings and organic garden produce at breakfast. 4

YHA hostel 47 Countess Wear Rd ⓣ0870/770 5826, ⓔexeter@yha.org.uk. In a country house two miles outside the centre – take minibus #K or #T, or bus #57 or #85, or walk along the Exe. Dorm beds from £16.

The City

The most distinctive feature of Exeter's skyline, **St Peter's Cathedral** (daily 9.30am–5pm; £3.50 suggested donation) is a stately monument made conspicuous by the two great Norman towers flanking the nave. Close up, it's the facade's ornate Gothic screen that commands attention: its three tiers of sculpted (and very weathered) figures – including Alfred, Athelstan, Canute, William the Conqueror and Richard II – were begun around 1360, part of a rebuilding programme which left only the Norman towers from the original construction.

Entering the cathedral, you're confronted by the longest unbroken **Gothic ceiling** in the world, its **bosses** vividly painted – one, towards the west front, shows the murder of Thomas à Becket. The **Lady Chapel** and **Chapter House** – respectively at the far end of the building and off the right transept – are thirteenth-century, but the main part of the nave, including the lavish rib-vaulting dates from a century later. There are many fine examples of sculpture from this period, including, in the minstrels' gallery high up on the left side, angels playing musical instruments, and, below them, figures of Edward III and Queen Philippa. In the **Choir** don't miss the sixty-foot **bishop's throne** or the **misericords** – decorated with mythological figures around 1260, they are thought to be the oldest in the country. Outside, a graceful statue of the theologian Richard Hooker surveys the **Cathedral Close**, a motley mixture of architectural styles from Tudor to Regency, though most display Exeter's trademark red brickwork.

Some older buildings are still standing amid the banal concrete of the modern town centre, including, on the pedestrianized High Street, Exeter's finest civic building, the fourteenth-century **Guildhall** (Mon–Fri 11am–1pm & 2–4.30pm, Sat 10am–12.30pm; sometimes closed for functions, call ⓣ01392/265500 to check; free), claimed to be England's oldest municipal building in regular use. It's fronted by an elegant Renaissance portico, and merits a glance inside for its main chamber, whose arched roof timbers rest on carved bears holding staves, symbols of the Yorkist cause during the Wars of the Roses.

Around the corner from the High Street on Queen Street, the **Royal Albert Memorial Museum** is the closest thing in Devon to a county museum, but remains closed for a major refit until 2010. Off the top end of the High Street, the Princesshay shopping precinct holds the entrance to a network of **underground passages** (June–Sept & school hols Mon–Sat 9.30am–5.30pm, Sun 10.30am–4pm; Oct–May Tues–Fri 11.30am–5.30pm, Sat 9.30am–5.30pm, Sun 11.30am–4pm; £5), first excavated in the thirteenth century to bring water to the cathedral precincts, and now visitable on a guided **tour** – not recommended to claustrophobes.

On the west side of Fore Street, the continuation of the High Street, a turning leads to **St Nicholas Priory** (Mon–Sat 10am–5pm; free), part of a small Benedictine foundation that became a merchant's home after the Dissolution; the interior has been restored to what it might have looked like in the Tudor era. On the other side of Fore Street, trailing down towards the river, cobbled **Stepcote Hill** was once the main road into Exeter from the west, though it is difficult to imagine this steep and narrow lane as a main thoroughfare.

Exeter's centre is bounded to the southwest by the River Exe, where the port area is now mostly devoted to leisure activities, particularly around the old **Quayside**. Pubs, shops and cafés share the space with handsomely restored nineteenth-century warehouses and the smart **Custom House**, built in 1681, its opulence reflecting the former importance of the cloth trade. The area comes into its own at night, but is worth a wander at any time. You can **rent bikes** and **canoes** at Saddles & Paddles on the quayside (ⓣ01392/424241, ⓦwww.sadpad.com) to explore the **Exeter Canal**, which runs five miles to Topsham and beyond.

Eating and drinking

Exeter is well supplied with **eateries** to suit every pocket. Good **pubs** are harder to find, though the Quay makes a lively spot to while away an evening over a pint or two.

Restaurants and cafés

Café Bar Cathedral Yard ⓣ01392/223626. Opposite the cathedral, a modish spot for a coffee, lunch (toasties, salads, burgers and pastas) or full evening meal (set menus for £12.50 and £15.50). There's live music on Fri, DJs on Sat, for which booking is advised.

Coolings Gandy St. Popular wine bar and bistro serving tasty lunches (around £7) – it's also open until late evening with a cellar bar open for cocktails on Fri & Sat.

Harry's 86 Longbrook St ⓣ01392/202234. In a converted church, this place offers good-value Mexican, Italian and American staples (most about £11) and usually attracts a cheery crowd.

Herbie's 15 North St ⓣ01392/258473. Serves up great wholefood dishes (average £8) and organic beers, wines and ice cream. Closed all Sun & Mon eve.

Michael Caines *Abode Exeter Hotel*, Cathedral Yard ⓣ01392/223638. Exeter's classiest restaurant offers sophisticated modern European cuisine in sleek surroundings. Prices are fairly high (mains around £22), but there are reasonable fixed-price menus (£13 and £17.50) at lunchtime. Closed Sun.

Pubs

Prospect Inn The Quay. You can eat and drink sitting outside at this seventeenth-century waterside pub, which was the setting for TV drama *The Onedin Line*.

Ship Inn St Martin's Lane. Claiming to have once been Francis Drake's local, this pub also serves food (jacket potatoes, baps and French sticks) in the low-ceilinged bar adorned with knots and clay pipes, and main meals in the bistro upstairs.

Nightlife and entertainment

An alternative to the brash **club complexes** on Exeter's Quay is the mellower *Timepiece* on Little Castle Street (ⓣ01392/493096), occupying a former prison, or the club nights at the subterranean *Cavern Club* (ⓣ01392/495370, ⓦwww.cavernclub.co.uk), with entrances on Queen and Gandy streets – though the latter is best known for **live bands**, mainly post-punk, dub, electro and indie. Off Gandy Street, live music is among the cultural pursuits at **Exeter Phoenix** (ⓣ01392/667080, ⓦwww.exeterphoenix.org.uk), an arts centre which also hosts art-house films, exhibitions and readings.

Around Exeter: A La Ronde

Five miles south of Exeter off the A376 (bus #57), the Gothic folly of **A La Ronde** (Easter–Oct Mon–Wed, Sat & Sun 11am–5pm; £5.20; NT) was the creation of two cousins, Jane and Mary Parminter, who in the 1790s were inspired by their European Grand Tour to build a sixteen-sided house possibly based on the Byzantine basilica of San Vitale in Ravenna. The end product is filled with mementos of the Parminters' tour as well as a number of their more offbeat creations, such as a frieze made of feathers culled from game birds and chickens. In the upper rooms are a gallery and staircase completely covered in shells, too fragile to be visited, though part can be glimpsed from the completely enclosed octagonal room on the first floor. From the dormer windows on the second floor, there are superb views over the Exe estuary.

Sidmouth

Set amidst a shelf of crumbling red sandstone, **SIDMOUTH** is the chief resort on the east Devon coast (bus #52A or #52B from Exeter). The cream-and-white town boasts nearly five hundred buildings listed as having special historic or architectural interest, among them the stately Georgian homes of **York Terrace** behind the Esplanade. Both the mile-long main town beach and Jacob's Ladder, a cliff-backed shingle and sand strip to the west of town, are easily accessible and well tended. To the east, the coast path climbs steep Salcombe Hill to follow cliffs that give sanctuary to a range of birdlife including yellowhammers, green woodpeckers and the rarer grasshopper warbler. Further on, the path descends to meet one of the most isolated and attractive beaches in the area, **Weston Mouth**.

Practicalities

The **tourist office** is on Ham Lane, off the eastern end of the Esplanade (March & April Mon–Thurs 10am–4pm, Fri & Sat 10am–5pm, Sun 10am–1pm; May–July & Sept–Oct Mon–Sat 10am–5pm, Sun 10am–4pm; Aug Mon–Sat 10am–6pm, Sun 10am–5pm; Nov–Feb Mon–Sat 10am–1.30pm; ⓣ01395/516441, ⓦwww.visitsidmouth.co.uk). Of the **B&Bs**, *Rock Cottage* on Peak Hill Road (ⓣ01395/514253, ⓦwww.rockcottage.co.uk; no credit cards; ➎) offers unrivalled sea views and access to the beach at the quieter, western end of the Esplanade. A short walk from here, there's the friendly *Rose Cottage* on Coburg Road (ⓣ01395/577179, ⓦwww.rosecottage-sidmouth.co.uk; ➍). For **meals** in town, try the range of dishes at *Mocha Restaurant* on The Esplanade (daytime only, eves in summer), or the daily specials at *Brown's Wine Bar & Bistro*, 33 Fore St (ⓣ01395/516724; closed Mon & Tues in winter). *The Dove* on Fore Street and the *Swan Inn*, near the tourist office at 37 York St, are the pick of the pubs.

Beer

Eight miles east along the coast, the fishing village of **BEER** lies huddled within a small sheltered cove between gleaming white headlands. A stream rushes along a deep channel dug into Beer's main street, and if you can ignore the crowds in high summer much of the village looks unchanged since the time when it was a smugglers' eyrie. The area is best known for its quarries, which were worked from Roman times until the nineteenth century: **Beer stone** was used in many of Devon's churches and houses, and as far afield as London. You can visit the complex of **underground quarries** (April–Sept 10am–6pm; Oct 11am–5pm; last entry 1hr before closing; £5.50) a mile or so west of the village on a guided tour, along with a small exhibition of pieces carved by medieval masons.

Bay View (Ⓣ01297/20489, Ⓦwww.bayviewbeer.com; no credit cards; ❷), overlooking the sea on Fore Street, is the best of the **B&Bs**, and there's a YHA **hostel** half a mile northwest, at Bovey Combe, Townsend (Ⓣ0870/770 5690, Ⓔbeer@yha.org.uk; from £14). For **food**, the *Barrel o' Beer* pub (Ⓣ01297/20099), on the main street, serves local delicacies such as Devon oysters and home-smoked fish.

The "English Riviera" region

The wedge of land between Dartmoor and the sea contains fertile pastures, backing onto some of Devon's most popular coastal resorts. Chief of these is **Torbay**, an amalgam of **Torquay**, **Paignton** and **Brixham**, together forming the nucleus of an area optimistically known as "**The English Riviera**". To the south, the estuary port of **Dartmouth** is linked by riverboat to historic and almost unspoiled **Totnes**. West of the River Dart, the rich agricultural district of **South Hams** extends as far as Plymouth, cleft by a web of rivers flowing off Dartmoor. The main town here is **Kingsbridge**, at the head of an estuary down which a ferry runs to the sailing resort of **Salcombe**.

Torquay

Sporting a mini-corniche and promenades landscaped with flowerbeds, **TORQUAY** comes closest to living up to the self-styled "English Riviera" sobriquet. The much-vaunted palm trees and the coloured lights that festoon the harbour by night contribute to the town's unique flavour, a blend of the mildly exotic with classic English provincialism. Torquay's transformation from a fishing village began with its establishment as a fashionable haven for invalids, among them the consumptive Elizabeth Barrett Browning, who spent three years here.

The town is focused on the small **harbour** and marina, separated by limestone cliffs from Torquay's main beach, **Abbey Sands**, which takes its name from **Torre Abbey**, sited in ornamental gardens behind the beachside road (daily 10am–5/6pm; £5.90). The Norman church that once stood here was razed by Henry VIII, though a gatehouse, tithe barn, chapter house and tower escaped demolition. The present **Abbey Mansion** now contains a good museum, with collections of silver and glass, window designs by Edward Burne-Jones, illustrations by William Blake, and nineteenth-century and contemporary works of art.

Just up from the marina, **Torquay Museum**, 529 Babbacombe Rd (Easter–Oct Mon–Sat 10am–5pm, also Sun 1.30–5pm in summer; £3.95), has some interesting material on Agatha Christie, who was born and raised in

Torquay, as well as local history and natural history collections. At the northern end of the harbour, **Living Coasts** (daily: Easter–Sept 10am–5.30pm; Oct–Easter 10am–4.30pm; £6.75, or £14.50 with Paignton Zoo) is home to a variety of fauna and flora found on British shores, including puffins, penguins and seals. The rooftop café and restaurant have splendid panoramic views.

Beyond here, the coast path leads round a promontory to some good sand beaches: **Meadfoot Beach**, one of the busiest, is reached by crossing Daddyhole Plain, named after a large chasm in the adjacent cliff caused by a landslide, but locally attributed to the devil ("Daddy"). North of the Hope's Nose promontory, the coast path leads to a string of less-crowded beaches, including **Babbacombe Beach** and, beyond, **Watcombe** and **Maidencombe**.

Practicalities

Torquay's main **train station** is off Rathmore Road, southwest of Torre Abbey Gardens; most **buses** stop near the marina, close to the **tourist office** on Vaughan Parade (Easter–Sept Mon–Sat 9.30am–5.30pm, also June–Sept Sun 10am–4pm; Oct–Easter Mon–Sat 9.30am–5pm; ⓣ01803/211211, ⓦwww.englishriviera.co.uk). Most of Torquay's budget **accommodation** lies around Belgrave Road and Avenue Road, including the small, quiet *Exton*, 12 Bridge Rd (ⓣ01803/293561, ⓦwww.extonhotel.co.uk; ❸), ten minutes from the train station. For views and stately surroundings, try the *Allerdale Hotel*, Croft Rd (ⓣ01803/292667, ⓦwww.allerdalehotel.co.uk; ❹), with a long, lawned garden. The friendly *Torquay Backpackers* **hostel**, 119 Abbey Rd (ⓣ01803/299924, ⓦwww.torquaybackpackers.co.uk; £12), has some doubles (❶), and is a ten-minute walk from the station, with a free pick-up service.

One of the best **restaurants** in Torquay is the award-winning *Elephant*, 3 Beacon Terrace, right on the harbour (ⓣ01803/200044), where you can enjoy fine dining in the intimate upstairs area (open eves Tues–Sat; closed Jan), or more rough-and-ready fare in the ground-floor brasserie (Tues–Sat all day, plus Sun lunch). Cheaper options include *Al Beb*, 64 Torwood St (ⓣ01803/211755; closed lunchtime Mon, Wed, Thurs & Sun), for a North African ambience and belly dancing (Fri & Sat). Also strong on atmosphere is the *Hole in the Wall* **pub** on Park Lane, which serves bar meals.

Paignton and Brixham

Lacking Torquay's gloss, **PAIGNTON** is the least attractive of the Riviera's resorts, though it is home to **Paignton Zoo** (daily: summer 10am–6pm; winter 10am–4.30pm or dusk; last entry 1hr before closing; £9.35, or £14.50 with Living Coasts in Torquay), a mile out on Totnes Road. Paignton's Queen's Park train station, near the harbour, is also the terminus of the **Paignton & Dartmouth Steam Railway** (Easter–Oct, plus a few dates in Dec; ⓣ01803/555872, ⓦwww.paignton-steamrailway.co.uk), which connects with **Goodrington Sands** beach before following the Dart to Kingswear, seven miles south. You could make a day of it by taking the ferry from Kingswear to Dartmouth (see p.321), then taking a riverboat up the Dart to Totnes, from where you can take any bus back to Paignton – a "Round Robin" ticket (£14.50) lets you do this.

From Paignton, it's a fifteen-minute bus ride to **BRIXHAM**, a major fishing port and the prettiest of the Torbay towns. Among the trawlers on Brixham's quayside is moored a full-size reconstruction of the **Golden Hind** (March–Oct daily 9am–4pm, longer hours in summer; £3), the surprisingly small vessel in which Francis Drake circumnavigated the world. The harbour is overlooked by an unflattering statue of William III, who landed in Brixham to claim the crown of England in 1688. From the harbour, climb King Street and follow Berry Head Road to reach the promontory at the southern limit of Torbay, **Berry Head**, now a conservation area attracting colonies of nesting sea birds. There are fabulous views, and you can see the remains of fortifications built during the Napoleonic Wars.

Brixham's **tourist office** is on the quayside (Easter–Sept Mon–Sat 9.30am–5.30pm, also June–Sept Sun 10am–4pm; Oct–Easter Mon–Sat 9.30am–5pm; ⓣ01803/211211). For harbour views, the best **accommodation** is on King Street, including *Sampford House* at no. 57 (ⓣ01803/857761, ⓦwww.sampfordhouse.com; ③), a B&B with smallish but smart en-suite rooms, and the classy *Quayside Hotel* (ⓣ01803/855751, ⓦwww.quaysidehotel.co.uk; ⑥), with two bars and a restaurant. There's a YHA **hostel** four miles away outside the village of Galmpton, on the banks of the Dart (ⓣ0870/770 5962, ⓔriverdart@yha.org.uk; check opening; from £14), a two-mile walk from Churston Bridge (bus #12 or #12A, or the Paignton & Dartmouth Steam Railway).

For **food**, Brixham offers fish and more fish – from the harbourside stalls selling cockles, whelks and mussels to the moderately expensive *Yard Arms* (ⓣ01803/858266; closed Mon lunch), a semi-formal bar and bistro on Beach Approach, off the quayside. For a relaxed pint, try the *Blue Anchor* on Fore Street, with coal fires and low beams.

Totnes

Most of the Plymouth buses from Paignton and Torquay stop at **TOTNES**, on the west bank of the River Dart. The town has an ancient pedigree, its period of greatest prosperity occurring in the sixteenth century when this inland port exported cloth to France and brought back wine. Some handsome sixteenth-century structures from that era remain, and there is still a working port down on the river, but these days Totnes has mellowed into a residential market town, popular with the alternative and New Age crowd.

The town centres on the long main street that starts off as Fore Street, site of the town's **museum** (mid-March to Oct Mon–Fri 10.30am–5pm; £2), occupying a four-storey Elizabethan house at no. 70. Showing how wealthy clothiers lived at the peak of Totnes's fortunes, it's packed with domestic objects and furniture, and also has a room devoted to local mathematician Charles Babbage, whose "analytical engine" was the forerunner of the computer. Fore Street becomes the **High Street** at the East Gate, a much retouched medieval arch. Beneath it, Rampart Walk trails off along the old city walls, curving round the fifteenth-century church of **St Mary**, a red-sandstone building containing an exquisitely carved rood screen. Behind the church, the eleventh-century **Guildhall** (daily 10am–4.30pm; £1) was originally the refectory and kitchen of a Benedictine priory. Granted to the city corporation in 1553, the building still houses the town's Council Chamber, which you can see together with the former gaol cells and courtroom.

Totnes **Castle** (daily: late March to June & Sept 10am–5pm; July & Aug 10am–6pm; Oct 10am–4pm; £2.50; EH) on Castle Street – leading off the High Street – is a classic Norman structure of the motte and bailey design, its simple crenellated keep atop a grassy mound offering wide views of the town and Dart valley. Totnes is the highest navigable point on the **River Dart** for seagoing vessels, and the starting point for **cruises to Dartmouth**, leaving from Steamer Quay (1hr 15min; £9 return; ⓣ01803/834488, ⓦwww.riverlink.co.uk). Riverside walks in either direction pass some congenial pubs, and near the railway bridge you can board a steam train of the **South Devon Railway**

(April–Oct; ⓣ0845/345 1420, ⓦwww.southdevonrailway.org), which runs along the Dart to Buckfastleigh, on the edge of Dartmoor (£9 return).

Practicalities

Totnes's **tourist office** is in The Town Mill, near the Morrisons car park (Mon–Sat 9.30am–5pm; ⓣ01803/863168, ⓦwww.totnesinformation.co.uk). The best-value **accommodation** is at the friendly B&B, 3 Plymouth Rd, off the High Street, with simple rooms (ⓣ01803/866917, ⓦwww.mlfen.freeserve.co.uk; no credit cards; closed Nov–Feb; ②); for more character, try the nearby *Great Grubb*, Fallowfields, Plymouth Rd (ⓣ01803/849071, ⓦwww.thegreatgrubbw.co.uk; ④), offering healthy breakfasts, or the atmospheric *Royal Seven Stars Hotel* on The Plains (ⓣ01803/862125, ⓦwww.royalsevenstars.co.uk; ⑤).

The High Street has several good **places to eat** including *Willow*, at no. 87 (ⓣ01803/862605; closed Sun), with inexpensive vegetarian snacks, evening meals (Wed, Fri & Sat) and live music (Fri), and *The Barrel House* at no. 58–59 (ⓣ01803/863000), a café at street level, and a former ballroom upstairs where you can eat salads, burgers and moderately priced full meals. Local **pubs** include the *Steampacket*, by the riverside on St Peter's Quay (reached by walking west along The Plains), which is also good for meals.

A walkable couple of miles north of Totnes, **Dartington Hall** features a constant programme of films, performances and workshops – for details, call ⓣ01803/847070 or see ⓦwww.dartington.org.

Dartmouth and around

South of Torbay, and eight miles downstream from Totnes, **DARTMOUTH** has thrived since the Normans recognized the trading potential of this deepwater port. Today its activities embrace fishing, freight and a booming leisure industry, as well as the education of the senior service's officer class at the Royal Naval College, on a hill overlooking the port. Coming from Torbay, visitors to Dartmouth can save time and a long detour through Totnes by using the frequent ferries crossing over the Dart's estuary from Kingswear (£1; £2.50 or £3.30 for cars), the last one at around 10.45pm.

Behind the enclosed boat basin at the heart of town, the four-storey **Butterwalk**, built in the seventeenth century for a local merchant, is richly decorated with woodcarvings. The timber-framed construction was restored after bombing in World War II, though still looks precarious as it overhangs the street on eleven granite columns. This arcade now holds shops and Dartmouth's small **museum** (Mon–Sat: April–Oct 10am–4pm; Nov–March noon–3pm; £1.50), mainly devoted to maritime curios, including old maps, prints and models of ships. Nearby **St Saviour's**, rebuilt in the 1630s from a fourteenth-century church, has long been a landmark for boats sailing upriver. The building stands at the head of Higher Street, the old town's central thoroughfare and the site of another tottering medieval structure, the *Cherub* inn. More impressive is **Agincourt House** on the parallel Lower Street, originally built by a merchant after the battle for which it is named.

Lower Street leads down to **Bayard's Cove**, a short cobbled quay lined with eighteenth-century houses, where the Pilgrim Fathers stopped en route to the New World. A twenty-minute walk from here along the river takes you to **Dartmouth Castle** (late March to June & Sept daily 10am–5pm; July & Aug daily 10am–6pm; Oct daily 10am–4pm; Nov–March Sat & Sun 10am–4pm; £4; EH), one of two fortifications on opposite sides of the estuary dating from the fifteenth century. The castle was the first in England to be constructed specifically to withstand artillery, though was never tested in action, and consequently is excellently preserved. If you don't relish the return walk, you can take a **ferry** back to town (Easter–Oct continuous service 10am–4/5pm; £1.80).

Continuing south along the coastal path brings you through the pretty hilltop village of **Stoke Fleming** to **Blackpool Sands**, the best beach in the area. The unspoilt cove, flanked by steep, wooded cliffs, was the site of a battle in 1404 in which Devon archers repulsed a Breton invasion force sent to punish the privateers of Dartmouth for their cross-Channel raiding.

From Dartmouth there are regular ferries across the river to **Kingswear**, terminus of the Paignton & Dartmouth Steam Railway (see p.319). Various **cruises** from Dartmouth's quay up the River Dart are the best way to see the deep creeks and the various houses overlooking the river, among them the **Royal Naval College** and **Greenway House** (early March to mid-Oct Wed–Sat 10.30am–5pm; £5.20, or £4.40 if arriving by river; NT), birthplace of Walter Raleigh's three seafaring half-brothers, the Gilberts, and later rebuilt for Agatha Christie.

Practicalities

Dartmouth's **tourist office** is opposite the car park at Mayor's Avenue (Mon–Sat 9.30am–5pm; Easter–Oct also Sun 10am–2pm; ⓣ01803/834224, ⓦwww.discoverdartmouth.com). The less expensive **accommodation** is strung along Victoria Road, a continuation of Duke Street, but the hilltop choices are preferable for their views, for example the spacious and elegant *Avondale* at 5 Vicarage Hill (ⓣ01803/835831, ⓦwww.avondaledartmouth.co.uk; no credit cards; ⑤). More centrally, the rooms above *Café Alf Resco* on Lower Street (ⓣ01803/835880, ⓦwww.cafealfresco.co.uk; no credit cards; ⑤) have character and charm, while the **café** itself is good for all-day breakfasts, steaming coffees and occasional live music in summer.

Dartmouth's top **restaurant** is the *New Angel*, at 2 South Embankment (ⓣ01803/839425; closed Sun eve & all Mon), run by celebrity chef John Burton-Race and offering quality seafood in an informal atmosphere, with great riverside views. The ancient *Cherub Inn*, 13 Higher St, is one of the most atmospheric **pubs** in town, and serves meals in a small restaurant upstairs.

Salcombe and around

The area between the Dart and Plym estuaries, the **South Hams**, holds some of Devon's comeliest villages and most striking coastline. The "capital" of the region, **Kingsbridge**, is a useful transport hub but lacks the appeal of **SALCOMBE**, reachable on a summer ferry from Kingsbridge. Once a nondescript fishing village, Devon's southernmost resort is now a full-blown sailing and holiday centre, its calm waters strewn with small pleasure-craft.

You can swot up on boating and local history at **Salcombe Maritime Museum** on Market Street, off the north end of the central Fore Street (Easter–Oct 10.30am–12.30pm & 2.30–4.30pm; £1.50). From a quay off Fore Street, you can take a **ferry** down to the beach at South Sands (Easter–Oct; £2.70), from where it's a fifteen-minute climb to the excellent **Overbeck's Museum** (mid-March to mid-July & Sept Mon–Fri & Sun 11am–5.30pm; mid-July to Aug daily 11am–5.30pm; Oct Mon–Thurs & Sun 11am–4pm; garden open Mon–Thurs & Sun 10/11am–4/5.30pm; £5.80; NT), which focuses on the area's natural history. There's great coastal walking south and west of here, eventually leading to sandy **beaches** at Thurlestone and, across the Avon estuary, Bigbury-on-Sea, while the path eastwards from **East Portlemouth** – accessible by ferry from Salcombe's quay – takes in some craggily photogenic scenery around Gammon Point and Prawle Point.

Salcombe's **tourist office** is on Market Street (Easter to late July and early Sept to Oct daily 10am–5pm; mid-July to early Sept daily 9am–6pm; Nov–March Mon–Sat 10am–3pm; Ⓣ01548/843927, Ⓦwww.salcombeinformation.co.uk). Many of the town's **B&Bs** enjoy excellent estuary views, including *Rocarno* on Grenville Road (Ⓣ01548/842732, Ⓔrocarno@aol.com; ②), and *Ria View*, Devon Rd (Ⓣ01548/842965, Ⓦwww.salcombebandb.co.uk; closed Dec–Easter; ④) – neither takes credit cards. Part of Overbeck's Museum (see above) houses a YHA **hostel** (Ⓣ0870/770 6016, Ⓔsalcombe@yha.org.uk; call to check opening; from £14).

For a lively **restaurant** in Salcombe, try *Captain Flint's*, 82 Fore St, which specializes in pastas and pizzas (closed in winter); in Kingsbridge, drop in to the boldly coloured *Pig Finca Café*, The Quay (Ⓣ01548/855777; closed Tues eve and all Sun & Mon), serving Mediterranean dishes and weekly live music.

Plymouth and around

PLYMOUTH's predominantly bland and modern face belies its great historic role as a naval base and, in the sixteenth century, the stamping ground of such national heroes as John Hawkins and Francis Drake. It was from here that Drake sailed to defeat the Spanish Armada in 1588, and 32 years later the port was the last embarkation point for the Pilgrim Fathers, whose New Plymouth colony became the nucleus for the English settlement of North America. The importance of the city's Devonport dockyards made the city a target in World War II, when the Luftwaffe reduced most of the old centre to rubble. Subsequent reconstruction has done little to improve the place, though it would be difficult to spoil the glorious vista over **Plymouth Sound**, the basin of calm water at the mouth of the combined Plym, Tavy and Tamar estuaries, largely unchanged since Drake played his famous game of bowls on the Hoe before joining battle with the Armada.

One of the best local excursions from Plymouth is to **Mount Edgcumbe**, where woods and meadows provide a welcome antidote to the urban bustle,

Sir Francis Drake

Born around 1540 near Tavistock, **Francis Drake** worked in the domestic coastal trade from the age of 13, but was soon taking part in the first English slaving expeditions between Africa and the West Indies, led by his Plymouth kinsman John Hawkins. Later, Drake was active in the secret war against Spain, raiding and looting merchant ships in actions unofficially sanctioned by Elizabeth I. In 1572 he became the first Englishman to sight the Pacific, and soon afterwards, on board the *Golden Hind*, became the first to **circumnavigate the world**, for which he received a knighthood on his return in 1580. The following year Drake was made mayor of Plymouth, settling in Buckland Abbey (see p.325), but was back in action before long – in 1587 he "singed the king of Spain's beard" by entering Cadiz harbour and destroying 33 vessels that were to have formed part of Philip II's **armada**. When the replacement invasion fleet appeared in the English Channel in 1588, Drake – along with Raleigh, Hawkins and Frobisher – played a leading role in wrecking it. The following year he set off on an unsuccessful expedition to help the Portuguese against Spain, but otherwise most of the next decade was spent in relative inactivity in Plymouth, Exeter and London. Finally, in 1596 Drake left with Hawkins for a raid on Panama, a venture that cost the lives of both captains.

and are within easy reach of some fabulous sand. East of Plymouth, the aristocratic opulence of **Saltram House** includes some fine art and furniture, while to the north you can visit Drake's old residence at **Buckland Abbey**.

The City

A good place to start a tour of the city is **Plymouth Hoe**, an immense esplanade with glorious views over the sea. Here, alongside various war memorials stands a rather portly statue of Sir Francis Drake, gazing grandly out to the sea. Appropriately, there's a bowling green back from the brow. In front of the memorials, the red-and-white-striped **Smeaton's Tower** (Tues–Sat: 10am–noon & 1–3/4.30pm; £2) was erected in 1759 by John Smeaton on the treacherous Eddystone Rocks, fourteen miles out to sea. When replaced by a larger lighthouse in 1882, it was reassembled here, where it gives lofty views over Plymouth Sound.

Following the seafront round to the west, you'll reach the old town's quay at **Sutton Harbour**, where the **Mayflower Steps** commemorate the sailing of the Pilgrim Fathers, with a plaque listing the names and professions of the 102 Puritans on board. Edging the harbour, the **Barbican** district is the heart of old Plymouth: most of the buildings are now shops and restaurants, but off the quayside, New Street holds most of the oldest buildings, among them the **Elizabethan House** (mid-Feb to March Tues–Sat 10am–1pm & 1–3pm; April–Sept Tues–Sat 10am–5pm; £1.50), a captain's dwelling retaining most of the original architectural features. Cross the bridge over Sutton Harbour to reach the **National Marine Aquarium** (daily 10am–5/6pm; last entry 1hr before closing; £9.50), a grand complex on four levels where a range of marine environments have been re-created, from moorland stream to coral reef and deep-sea ocean.

Practicalities

Plymouth's **train station** is a mile north of The Hoe off Saltash Road (connected to the centre by bus #25); the **bus station** is at Bretonside, just over St Andrew's Cross from Royal Parade; and the **tourist office** is off Sutton Harbour at 3 The Barbican (April–Oct Mon–Sat 9am–5pm, Sun 10am–4pm; Nov–March Mon–Fri 9am–5pm, Sat 10am–4pm; ⓣ01752/306330, ⓦwww.visitplymouth.co.uk).

The city's **accommodation** includes a row of B&Bs edging the Hoe on Citadel Road, including *The Beeches*, at no. 175 (ⓣ01752/266475; no credit cards; ❷), and, around the corner, the easy-going *Brittany Guesthouse*, 28 Athenaeum St (ⓣ01752/262247, ⓦwww.brittanyguesthouse.co.uk; ❸). Facing the west side of the Hoe, the smart *Bowling Green Hotel*, 9–10 Osborne Place, Lockyer St (ⓣ01752/209090, ⓦwww.bowlingreenhotel.com; ❹), overlooks Francis Drake's fabled haunt. There's also an independent **hostel** at 172 Citadel Rd, *Globe Backpackers* (ⓣ01752/225158, ⓦwww.plymouthbackpackers.co.uk; from £13), with double rooms (❶).

Plymouth's Barbican area has an eclectic range of **restaurants**: one of the best is *Piermasters*, 3 Southside St (ⓣ01752/229345; closed Sun), whose seafood is supplied straight from the harbour, while tasty bistro dishes draw the crowds at the more casual *Barbican Kitchen,* 60 Southside St (ⓣ01752/604448), housed in the ancient Black Friars Distillery. Plymouth Arts Centre, 38 Looe St, has a vegetarian restaurant (closed all Sun & Mon eve), as well as exhibitions, films and live performances (ⓣ01752/206114, ⓦwww.plymouthac.org.uk). The *Dolphin* **pub** by Sutton Harbour has an authentic atmosphere and good ales.

Mount Edgcumbe

Lying on the Cornish side of Plymouth Sound and visible from the Hoe, **MOUNT EDGCUMBE** house (Easter–Sept Mon–Thurs & Sun 11am–4.30pm; £5) is a reconstruction of the bomb-damaged Tudor original, though inside the predominant note is eighteenth-century, the rooms elegantly restored with authentic Regency furniture. Far more enticing are the impeccable **gardens** divided into French, Italian and English sections – the first two a blaze of flower-beds adorned with classical statuary, the last an acre of sweeping lawn shaded by exotic trees – while the **park**, which is free and open all year, gives access to the coastal path. You can reach Edgcumbe by passenger **ferry** to Cremyll, leaving at least hourly from Admiral's Hard, in Plymouth's Stonehouse district (bus #34 from Royal Parade), or, in summer, by direct motor launch from the Mayflower Steps to **Cawsand**, an old smugglers' haunt two hours' walk from the house. Cawsand itself is just a mile from the huge **Whitsand Bay**, the best bathing beach for miles around, though subject to dangerous shifting sands and fierce currents.

Saltram House

The remodelled Tudor **SALTRAM HOUSE** (daily except Fri: mid-March to Sept noon–4.30pm: £8.40 including garden; NT), two miles east of Plymouth off the A38, is Devon's largest country house, featuring work by architect Robert Adam and fourteen portraits by **Joshua Reynolds**, who was born nearby in Plympton. The showpiece is the Saloon, a fussy but exquisitely furnished room dripping with gilt and plaster, and set off by a huge Axminster carpet especially woven for it in 1770. Saltram's landscaped **garden** (daily except Fri 11am–4/4.30pm; £4.20) provides a breather from this riot of interior design, though it's marred by the proximity of the road. You can get here on the hourly #22 bus (not Sun) from Royal Parade to Merafield Road, from where it's a fifteen-minute signposted walk.

Buckland Abbey

Six miles north of Plymouth, close to the River Tavy and on the edge of Dartmoor, **BUCKLAND ABBEY** (mid-Feb to mid-March & Nov Sat & Sun 2–5pm; mid-March to Oct daily except Thurs 10.30am–5.30pm; Dec Thurs–Sun 11am–5pm; £7.40, grounds only £3.90; NT) was once the most westerly of England's Cistercian abbeys. After its dissolution, Buckland was converted to a family home by the privateer Richard Grenville (cousin of Walter Raleigh), from whom the estate was acquired by Francis Drake in 1582, the year after he became mayor of Plymouth. It remained his home until his death, though the house reveals few traces of Drake's residence. There are, however, numerous maps, portraits and mementos of his buccaneering exploits on show, most famous of which is Drake's Drum, which was said to beat a supernatural warning of impending danger to the country. More eye-catching are the oak-panelled **Great Hall**, previously the nave of the abbey, and, in the majestic grounds, a fine fourteenth-century **monastic barn**. To get here from Plymouth, take any bus to Tavistock, changing at Yelverton for the hourly #55, or, on Sunday, take the #48 direct from Royal Parade.

Dartmoor

Occupying the main part of the county between Exeter and Plymouth, **DARTMOOR** is southern England's greatest expanse of wilderness, some 365 square miles of raw granite, barren bogland, sparse grass and heather-grown moor. It was not always so desolate, as testified by the remnants of scattered Stone Age settlements and the ruined relics of the area's nineteenth-century tin-mining industry. Today desultory flocks of sheep and groups of ponies are virtually the only living creatures to be seen wandering over the central fastnesses of the National Park, with solitary birds – buzzards, kestrels, pipits, stonechats and wagtails – wheeling and hovering high above.

The core of Dartmoor, characterized by tumbling streams and high tors chiselled by the elements, is **Dartmoor Forest**, which has belonged to the Duchy of Cornwall since 1307, though there is almost unlimited public access. Networks of signposts or painted stones exist to guide **walkers**, but map-reading abilities are a prerequisite for any but the shortest walks, and considerable experience is essential for longer distances. Overnight parking is only allowed in authorized places, and no vehicles are permitted beyond fifteen yards from the road; camping should be out of sight of houses and roads, and fires are strictly forbidden. Information on **guided walks** and riding facilities is available from National Park visitor centres in Dartmoor's major towns and villages, and from information points in smaller villages.

A significant portion of northern Dartmoor, containing the moor's highest tors and some of its most famous beauty spots, is run by the **Ministry of Defence**, whose firing ranges are marked by red and white posts; when firing is in progress, red flags or red lights signify that entry is prohibited. Generally, if no warning flags are flying by 9am between April and September, or by 10am from October to March, there will be no firing on that day; alternatively, check at ⓣ0800/458 4868 or ⓦwww.dartmoor-ranges.co.uk.

Scattered accommodation options include several **camping barns**, which it's always wise to book ahead, particularly at weekends: call the numbers given, or else the YHA, which administers them (ⓣ0870/770 8868, ⓔcampingbarns@yha.org.uk).

Princetown and the central moor

PRINCETOWN owes its growth to the proximity of Dartmoor Prison, a high-security jail originally constructed for POWs captured in the Napoleonic Wars. The grim presence seeps into the village, which has a somewhat oppressed air and functional grey stone houses, some of which – as well as the parish church of St Michael – were built by French and American prisoners. What Princetown lacks in beauty is amply compensated for by the surrounding countryside, the best of which lies immediately to the north.

Information on all of Dartmoor is given by the main **National Park information centre**, on the village's central green (10am–4/5pm; ⓣ01822/890414, ⓦwww.dartmoor-npa.gov.uk). One of the best **places to stay** locally is *Duchy House* on Tavistock Road (ⓣ01822/890552, ⓔduchyhouse@aol.com; no credit cards; closed Nov; ❷). In Princetown's central square the *Plume of Feathers* (ⓣ01822/890240; ❺), which claims to be the oldest building in town, offers B&B as well as dormitory accommodation in two bunkhouses (£12) and a **campsite**. Standard bar **food** is available here and from the neighbouring *Railway Inn*.

Northeast of Princetown, two miles north of the crossroads at Two Bridges, the dwarfed and misshapen oaks of **Wistman's Wood** are an evocative relic of the original Dartmoor Forest, cluttered with lichen-covered boulders and a dense undergrowth of ferns. The gnarled old trees are alleged to have been the site of druidic gatherings, a story unsupported by any evidence but quite plausible in this solitary spot.

▲ Dartmoor ponies

At Two Bridges you can see one of Dartmoor's **clapper bridges**: used by tin miners and farmers since medieval times, these simple structures consist of huge slabs of granite supported by piers of the same material. The largest and best preserved of these is three miles northeast at **POSTBRIDGE**, close to the **tourist office** (Easter–Oct 10am–5pm; Nov & Dec Sat & Sun 10am–4pm; ⓣ01822/880272). From here, you can head south through **Bellever Forest** to the open moor, where **Bellever Tor** (1453ft) affords outstanding views.

On the edge of the forest, a mile or so south of Postbridge on the banks of the East Dart River, lies one of Dartmoor's two YHA **hostels** (ⓣ0870/770 5692, ⓔbellever@yha.org.uk; from £14), accessible on the rare #98 from Tavistock or else on foot from Postbridge. There's also a **camping barn** close to Bellever Forest at Runnage Farm (ⓣ01822/880222, ⓦwww.runnagecampingbarns.co.uk), with a bunkhouse (£10) and camping facilities as well as bikes to rent. Two miles northeast of Postbridge, the solitary *Warren House Inn* offers warm, firelit comfort and **meals** in an unutterably bleak tract of moorland.

To the east of the B3212, reachable on a right turn towards Widecombe-in-the-Moor, the Bronze Age village of **Grimspound** lies below Hameldown Tor, about a mile off the road. Inhabited some three thousand years ago, this is the most complete example of Dartmoor's prehistoric settlements, consisting of 24 circular huts scattered within a four-acre enclosure. The site is thought to have been the model for the Stone Age settlement in which Sherlock Holmes camped in *The Hound of the Baskervilles*; while **Hound Tor**, an outcrop three miles to the southwest, was the inspiration for Conan Doyle's tale – according to local legend, phantom hounds were sighted racing across the moor to hurl themselves on the tomb of a hated squire following his death in 1677. There's a **camping barn** here, *Great Houndtor*, with a cooking area and showers (ⓣ01647/221202; £5).

Widecombe-in-the-Moor and the southeastern moor

Four miles east of the crossroads at Two Bridges, crowds home in on the beauty spot of **Dartmeet**, where the valley is memorably lush and you don't need to walk far to leave the car park and ice-cream vans behind. From here the Dart pursues a leisurely course, joined by the River Webburn near the pretty moorland village of **BUCKLAND-IN-THE-MOOR**, one of a cluster of moorstone-and-thatched hamlets on this southeastern side of the moor.

Four miles north, **WIDECOMBE-IN-THE-MOOR** is set in a hollow amid high granite-strewn ridges. Its church of **St Pancras** provides a famous local landmark, its pinnacled tower dwarfing the fourteenth-century main building, whose interior boasts a beautiful painted rood screen. The nearby **Church House** was built in the fifteenth century for weary churchgoers from outlying districts, and was later converted into almshouses. Widecombe's other claim to fame is the traditional song, *Widdicombe Fair*: the **fair** is still held annually on the second Tuesday of September. You could **stay** in Widecombe at the elegant *Old Rectory* (Ⓣ01364/621231, Ⓔrachel.belgrave@care4free.net; no credit cards; ③), opposite the post office and with a lovely garden, or, half a mile south, at *Higher Venton Farm* (Ⓣ01364/621235, Ⓦwww.ventonfarm.com; no credit cards; ③), a peaceful thatched longhouse where evening meals are served.

South of Buckland, the village of **HOLNE** is another rustic idyll surrounded on three sides by wooded valleys. The vicarage here was the birthplace of Charles Kingsley, author of *The Water Babies*.

The northeastern moor

On the northeastern edge of the moor, the market town of **MORETON-HAMPSTEAD** makes an attractive entry point from Exeter. There's a **tourist office** at 10 The Square (Easter–Oct daily 9.30am–5pm; Nov–Easter Fri–Sun 10am–4.30pm; Ⓣ01647/440043), and classy **accommodation** in Court Street on the western edge of the village: the *Old Post House* at no. 18 (Ⓣ01647/440900, Ⓦwww.theoldposthouse.com; no credit cards; ③), and *Cookshayes*, at no. 33 (Ⓣ01647/440374, Ⓦwww.cookshayes.co.uk; ②; closed Nov–Feb). The village also has a first-rate vegetarian **hostel**, *Sparrowhawk Backpackers*, at 45 Ford St (Ⓣ01647/440318, Ⓦwww.sparrowhawkbackpackers.co.uk; £14), with some private rooms (①).

Moretonhampstead has a historic rivalry with neighbouring **CHAGFORD**, a Stannary town (a chartered centre of the tin trade) that also enjoyed prosperity as a centre of the wool industry. It stands on a hillside overlooking the River Teign, with a fine fifteenth-century church and some good **accommodation** options, including the ancient *Three Crowns Hotel* (Ⓣ01647/433444, Ⓦwww.chagford-accom.co.uk; ⑤), facing the church, and the sixteenth-century *Cyprian's Cot*, 47 New St (Ⓣ01647/432256, Ⓦwww.cyprianscot.co.uk; no credit cards; ③). There's also a renowned and very expensive **restaurant**, *22 Mill Street* (Ⓣ01647/432244; closed Sun eve and all Mon), which offers top-quality European cuisine, and has two en-suite rooms for diners (⑤).

Numerous **walks** can be made in the immediate vicinity: downstream along the Teign to the twentieth-century extravaganza of **Castle Drogo** (early to mid-March Sat & Sun 11am–4pm; mid-March to early Nov daily except Tues 11am–4/5pm; Dec Sat & Sun noon–4pm; grounds early to mid-March Sat & Sun 10.30am–4.30pm; mid-March to early Nov daily 10.30am–4.30/5.30pm; early Nov to late Dec Fri–Sun 11am–4pm; £7.40, grounds only £4.75; NT), stupendously sited above the Teign gorge. Having retired at the age of 33,

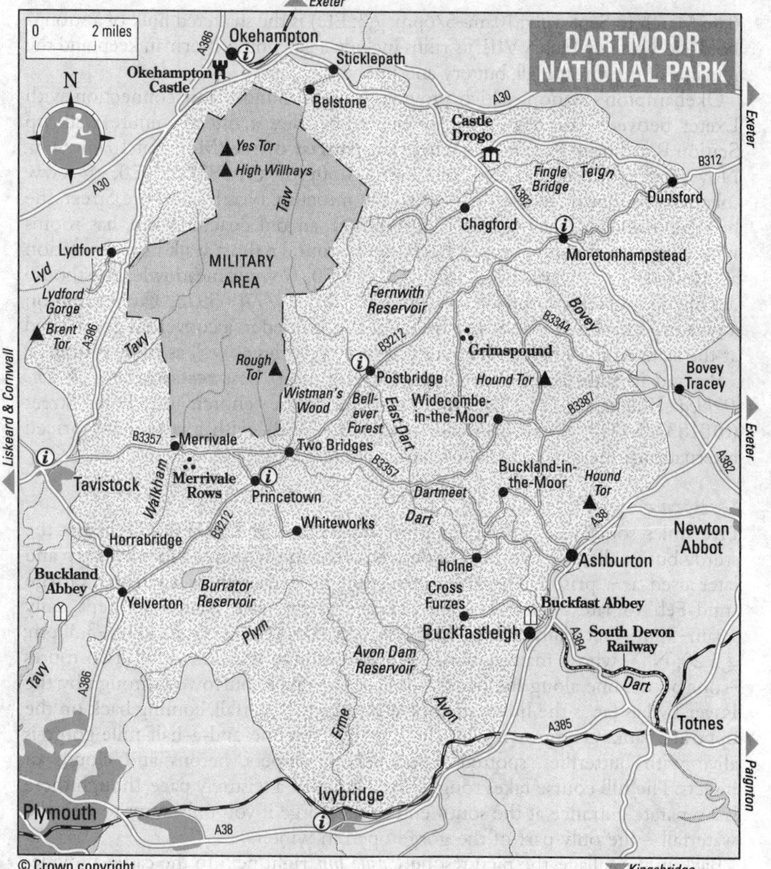

grocery magnate Julius Drewe unearthed a link that suggested his descent from a Norman baron, and set about creating a castle befitting his pedigree. Begun in 1910, to a design by **Edwin Lutyens**, it was not completed until 1930, but the result was an unsurpassed synthesis of medieval and modern elements.

Paths lead from Drogo east to **Fingle Bridge**, a lovely spot, where shaded green pools shelter trout and the occasional salmon. The *Fingle Bridge Inn* here has an adjoining **restaurant**.

The northern and western moor

The main centre on the northern fringes of Dartmoor, **OKEHAMPTON** grew prosperous as a market town for the medieval wool trade, and some fine old buildings survive between the two branches of the River Okement that meet here, among them the prominent fifteenth-century tower of the **Chapel of St James**. Across the road from the seventeenth-century town hall, a granite archway leads into the **Museum of Dartmoor Life** (Easter–Sept Mon–Sat 10.15am–4.30pm; £3), an excellent overview of habitation on the moor since the earliest times. Perched above the West Okement southwest of the centre, **Okehampton Castle** (late March to Sept daily: 10am–5/6pm; £3; EH) is the shattered hulk of a stronghold laid waste by Henry VIII; its ruins include a gatehouse, Norman keep, and the remains of the Great Hall, buttery and kitchens.

Okehampton's station, which provides a useful Sunday **rail** connection with Exeter between late May and late September, lies a fifteen-minute walk up Station Road from Fore Street, where the **tourist office** (Mon–Sat 10am–5pm; Nov–Easter Mon, Fri & Sat 10am–4.30pm; ⓣ01837/53020, ⓦwww.okehamptondevon.co.uk) sits next to the museum. Nearby on Fore Street, the beamed *Fountain Hotel* (ⓣ01837/53900; ③), an old coaching inn, has rooms with character, though cheaper **B&B** can be found a short walk near the station at *Meadowlea*, 65 Station Rd (ⓣ01837/53200, ⓦwww.meadowleaguesthouse.co.uk; ②). Okehampton's YHA **hostel** (ⓣ0870/770 5978, ⓔokehampton@yha.org.uk; closed Dec & Jan; from £14) is housed in a converted goods shed at the station, and offers a range of outdoor activities as well as **bike rental**.

Beyond its pubs and coffee shops, Okehampton's best **restaurant** is *The Pickled Walnut*, in a cellar hidden behind the church on Fore Street (ⓣ01837/54242; closed Sun, also eves Mon–Wed), with a reasonably priced international menu and a mellow atmosphere.

Lydford

Five miles southwest of Okehampton, the village of **LYDFORD** boasts the sturdy but small-scale Lydford Castle, a Saxon outpost, then a Norman keep and later used as a prison. The chief attraction here, though, is **Lydford Gorge** (mid-Feb to late March Fri–Sun 11am–3.30pm; late March to Sept daily 10am–5pm; Oct daily 10am–4pm; Nov & Dec Sat & Sun 11am–3.30pm; £5.20; NT), whose main entrance is a five-minute walk downhill. Two routes – one above, one along the banks – follow the ravine burrowed through by the River Lyd as far as the hundred-foot White Lady Waterfall, coming back on the opposite bank. Overgrown with thick woods, the one-and-a-half-mile gorge is alive with butterflies, spotted woodpeckers, dippers, herons and clouds of insects. The full course takes roughly two hours at a leisurely pace, though there is a separate entrance at the south end of the gorge if you only want to visit the waterfall – the only part of the gorge open in winter.

Back in the village, the picturesque *Castle Inn*, right next to the castle, provides **accommodation** in oak-beamed rooms (ⓣ01822/820242; ④), as well as a fire-lit sixteenth-century bar for drinks and snacks, a beer garden and a **restaurant**. Alternatively, you can eat well at the renowned *Dartmoor Inn* (ⓣ01822/820221; closed Sun eve & Mon lunchtime), on the A386 opposite the Lydford turning, which serves superior bar food and pricey meals that need booking.

Tavistock

The main town of the western moor, **TAVISTOCK** owes its distinctive Victorian appearance to the building boom that followed the discovery of copper deposits here in 1844. Originally, however, this market and Stannary town on the River Tavy grew around what was once the West Country's most important Benedictine abbey, established in the eleventh century. Some scant remnants survive in the churchyard of **St Eustace**, a mainly fifteenth-century building with stained glass from William Morris's studio in the south aisle.

Tavistock's **tourist office** is in the town hall on Bedford Square (April–Oct daily 9.30am–5pm; Nov–March Mon, Tues, Fri & Sat 10am–4.30pm; ⓣ01822/612938). Local **accommodation** includes *Kingfisher Cottage*, Mount Tavy Rd (ⓣ01822/613801, ⓔkingfisher.cott@fsnet.co.uk; no credit cards; ③), and, about half a mile east off the B3357 Princetown Road, *Mount Tavy Cottage*

The Tarka Line and the Tarka Trail

North Devon makes no secret of its association with Henry Williamson's *Tarka the Otter* (1927), one of the finest pieces of nature writing in the English language that relates the trails and travails of Tarka the otter. With parts of the book set in the Taw valley, it was inevitable that the Exeter to Barnstaple rail route – which follows the Taw for half of its length – should be dubbed the **Tarka Line**. Barnstaple itself forms the centre of the figure-of-eight traced by the **Tarka Trail**, which tracks the otter's wanderings for a distance of over 180 miles. To the north, the trail penetrates Exmoor then follows the coast back, passing through Williamson's home village of **Georgeham** on its return to Barnstaple. South, the path takes in Bideford (see p.333), and continues as far as Okehampton (see p.329), before swooping up via Eggesford, the point at which the Tarka Line joins the Taw valley.

Twenty-three miles of the trail follow a former rail line that's ideally suited to **bicycles**, and there are bike rental shops at Barnstaple and Bideford. You can pick up a *Tarka Trail* booklet and free leaflets on individual sections of the trail from tourist offices.

(Ⓣ01822/614253, Ⓦwww.mounttavy.freeserve.co.uk; ④), set in a lush garden and offering organic breakfasts.

North of Tavistock, a four-mile lane wanders up to **Brent Tor**, 1130 feet high and dominating Dartmoor's western fringes. Access to its conical summit is easiest along a path gently ascending through gorse on its southwestern side, leading to the small church of St Michael at the top. Bleak, treeless moorland extends in every direction, wrapped in silence that's occasionally pierced by the shrill cries of stonechats and wheatears. A couple of miles eastwards, **Gibbet Hill** looms over Black Down and the ruined stack of the abandoned Wheal Betsy silver and lead mine.

North Devon

From Exeter the A377 runs alongside the scenic Tarka Line railway to **North Devon**'s major town, **Barnstaple**. Within easy reach of here, the resorts of **Ilfracombe** and **Woolacombe** draw the crowds, though the fine sandy beaches surrounding the latter give ample opportunity to find your own space. The river port of **Bideford** gives its name to a long bay that holds the precipitous village of **Clovelly**, a famous beauty spot. Away from the coast, there is plenty of scope for walking and cycling along the Tarka Trail, passing through some of the region's loveliest countryside. For a complete break, the tiny island of **Lundy** provides further opportunities for stretching the legs and clearing the lungs.

Barnstaple

BARNSTAPLE, at the head of the Taw estuary, makes an excellent North Devon base, being well connected to the resorts of Bideford Bay, Ilfracombe and Woolacombe, as well as to the western fringes of Exmoor. The town's centuries-old role as a marketplace is perpetuated in the daily bustle around the huge timber-framed **Pannier Market** off the High Street, alongside which runs **Butchers Row**, its 33 archways now converted to a variety of uses. At the end of Boutport Street, the **Museum of North Devon** (Mon–Sat 9.30am–5pm; free) holds a lively miscellany that includes a collection of the eighteenth-century pottery for which the region was famous. The museum lies alongside the Taw, where footpaths make for a pleasant riverside stroll, with the colonnaded eighteenth-century **Queen Anne's Walk** – built as a merchants' exchange – providing some architectural interest and housing the **Barnstaple Heritage Centre** (April–Oct Tues–Sat 10am–5pm; Nov–March Tues–Fri 10am–4.30pm, Sat 10am–3.30pm; £3.50), which traces the town's social history by means of reconstructions and touch-screen computers.

Barnstaple's **tourist office** is at the Museum of North Devon (same times; ⓣ01271/375000, ⓦwww.staynorthdevon.co.uk). Local **accommodation** includes *The Old Post Office*, 22 Pilton St (ⓣ01271/859439, ⓦwww.theoldpostoffice-pilton.co.uk; no credit cards; ④), half a mile north of the centre, and, a couple of miles southeast of the centre on Landkey Road, *Mount Sandford* (ⓣ01271/342354; no credit cards; ③), an elegant, porticoed Regency building. Outside town at Muddiford, signposted two miles north of Barnstaple off the A39, *Broomhill Art Hotel* is a striking combination of gallery, restaurant and hotel (ⓣ01271/850262, ⓦwww.broomhillart.co.uk; no credit cards; ⑤), where the rooms look onto a sculpture garden. Half-board only is available at weekends. You can also **eat** well here, either snacks or Mediterranean-style fixed-price lunches and dinners (closed Mon & Tues). Otherwise, back in town, the seventeenth-century *Old School Coffee House* on Church Lane, near St Anne's Chapel, offers coffees and lunches (closed Sun).

Ilfracombe, Woolacombe and around

The most popular resort on Devon's northern coast, **ILFRACOMBE** is essentially little changed since its evolution into a Victorian and Edwardian tourist centre. In summer, if the crowds of holiday-makers become oppressive, you can escape on a coastal tour, a fishing trip or the fifteen-mile cruise to Lundy Island (see p.334), all available at the small harbour. On foot, you can explore the attractive stretch of coast running east out of Ilfracombe and beyond the grassy cliffs of Hillsborough, where a succession of undeveloped coves and inlets is surrounded by jagged slanting rocks and heather-covered hills. There are sandy **beaches** here, though many prefer those beyond **Morte Point**, five miles west of Ilfracombe, from where the view takes in Lundy. Below the promontory, the pocket-sized **Barricane Beach** is famous for the tropical shells washed up by Atlantic currents from the Caribbean. It's a popular swimming spot, though there's more space just south of here on the two miles of **Woolacombe Sands**, a broad, west-facing expanse much favoured by surfers and families alike. At the beach's more crowded northern end, a cluster of hotels, villas and retirement homes makes up the summer resort of **WOOLACOMBE**. At the quieter southern end lies the choice swimming spot of **Putsborough Sands** and the promontory of **Baggy Point**, where gannets, shags, cormorants and shearwaters gather from September to November. South of here, **Croyde Bay** is another surfers' delight, more compact than Woolacombe, with stalls on the sand renting surfboards and wet suits, while **Saunton Sands** is a magnificent long stretch of coast pummelled by endless ranks of classic breakers.

Practicalities

Ilfracombe's **tourist office** is at the Landmark on the seafront (Easter–Oct daily 10am–5pm; Nov–Easter Mon–Fri 10am–5pm, Sat 10am–4pm; ⓣ01271/863001, ⓦwww.visitilfracombe.co.uk), while Woolacombe's is on the Esplanade (Easter–Oct Mon–Sat 10am–5pm, Sun 10am–3pm; Nov–Easter Mon–Sat 10am–1pm; ⓣ01271/870553, ⓦwww.woolacombetourism.co.uk). Smartest choice among Ilfracombe's numerous **accommodation** choices is *Westwood*,

Torrs Park (Ⓣ01271/867443, Ⓦwww.west-wood.co.uk; ⑤), a boutique B&B west of the centre. On the east side of town, off Hillsborough Road, try *The Towers*, Chambercombe Park (Ⓣ01271/862809, Ⓦwww.thetowers.co.uk; no credit cards; ④), a roomy Victorian villa with sea views from most of its rooms. There's also an excellent **hostel**, *Ocean Backpackers*, near the bus station and harbour at 29 St James Place (Ⓣ01271/867835, Ⓦwww.oceanbackpackers.co.uk; £12), also offering double rooms (①). In Woolacombe, *Sandunes* is one of a number of B&Bs on Beach Road (Ⓣ01271/870661, Ⓦwww.sandwool.fsnet.co.uk; no credit cards; ⑤), with sea views. For **camping**, try *North Morte Farm*, near Morte Point (Ⓣ01271/870381, Ⓦwww.northmortefarm.co.uk; closed Nov–March).

At the harbour, Ilfracombe's most famous **restaurant**, *The Quay* (Ⓣ01271/868091; closed Sun eve and all Mon & Tues), is a quality seafood eatery owned by artist Damien Hirst, with a relaxed ground-floor bar (open daily) serving tapas. In Woolacombe, head for *West Beach*, Beach Rd (Ⓣ01271/870877; in winter open eves Fri & Sat only), for good seafood, occasional live music and summer barbecues.

Bideford Bay

Like Barnstaple, nine miles to the east, the estuary town of **BIDEFORD** formed an important link in north Devon's trade network in the Middle Ages, mainly due to its **bridge**, which still straddles the River Torridge. A couple of miles downstream, the old shipbuilding port of **APPLEDORE**, lined with pastel-coloured Georgian houses, is worth a wander and a drink in one of its cosy pubs.

Bideford's **tourist office** is in Victoria Park at the northern end of town (Easter–Sept Mon–Sat 10am–5pm, Sun 10am–1/4pm; Oct–Easter Mon, Tues, Thurs & Fri 10am–4.30pm, Wed & Sat 10am–1pm; Ⓣ01237/477676, Ⓦwww.torridge.gov.uk). The town's best **B&B** is the Georgian *Mount* on Northdown Road (Ⓣ01237/473748, Ⓦwww.themountbideford.co.uk; ④), set in its own walled garden and linked to the centre by a footpath. For a daytime **snack** or Mediterranean-style evening **meal**, head for *Cafecino Plus*, 26 Mill St (closed Mon eve & Sun), a lively café/bistro. Appledore has a pair of first-class **pubs** on Irsha Street: the *Royal George* and *Beaver Inn*, serving great seafood and with wonderful estuary views.

Clovelly

West along Bideford Bay, picturesque **CLOVELLY** was put on the map in the second half of the nineteenth century by two books: Charles Dickens' *A Message From the Sea* and *Westward Ho!* by Charles Kingsley, whose father was rector here for six years. The antique tone of the village has been preserved by strict regulations limiting hotel and holiday accommodation, but its excessive quaintness and the streams of visitors on summer days make it impossible to see beyond the artifice.

Past the **visitor centre** (daily 9/9.30am–4/6pm; Ⓦwww.clovelly.co.uk; £5.50), the cobbled, traffic-free main street plunges down past neat, flower-smothered cottages where sledges are tethered for transporting goods, the only way to carry supplies since the use of donkeys ended. At the bottom, Clovelly's stony beach and tiny harbour snuggle under a cleft in the cliff wall. If you can't face the return climb to the top of the village, there's a Land Rover service leaving every fifteen minutes or so from behind the *Red Lion* (Easter–Oct 9am–5.30pm; £2.20). From the visitor centre, a more level walk is possible along **Hobby Drive**, through woods of sycamore, oak, beech, rowan and holly, with grand views over the village.

Lundy Island

There are fewer than twenty full-time residents on **Lundy**, a tiny windswept island twelve miles north of Hartland Point. Now a refuge for thousands of marine birds, Lundy has no cars, just one pub and one shop – indeed little has changed since the Marisco family established itself here in the twelfth century, making use of the shingle beaches and coves to terrorize shipping along the Bristol Channel. The family's fortunes only fell in 1242 when one of their number, William de Marisco, was found to be plotting against the king, whereupon he was hung, drawn and quartered at Tower Hill in London. The castle erected by Henry III on Lundy's southern end dates from this time.

Today the island is managed by the Landmark Trust. Unless you're on a specially arranged diving or climbing expedition, **walking** along the interweaving tracks and footpaths is really the only thing to do here. The shores – mainly cliffy on the west, softer and undulating on the east – shelter a rich variety of **birdlife**, including kittiwakes, fulmars, shags and Manx shearwaters, which often nest in rabbit burrows. The most famous birds, though, are the **puffins** after which Lundy is named – from the Norse *Lunde* (puffin) and *ey* (island). They can only be sighted in April and May, when they come ashore to mate. Offshore, **grey seals** can be seen all the year round.

Between April and October, the MS *Oldenburg* sails to Lundy up to four times a week from Ilfracombe, less frequently from Bideford, taking around two hours from both places. Day-return tickets cost £29, open returns around £50; to reserve a place, call ⓣ01271/863636 (day-returns can also be booked from local tourist offices). **Accommodation** in a range of idiosyncratic properties on the island can be booked up months in advance. B&B-only bookings have to be made within two weeks of the proposed visit. Outside the holiday season, it's still possible to find a double room for under £60 per night. **Bookings** for weekly rentals must be made through the Landmark Trust's office (ⓣ01628/825925, ⓦwww.landmarktrust.org.uk), or call ⓣ01271/863636 for shorter B&B stays. There's also a **campsite** on the island open April–Oct. More information can be found on the website ⓦwww.lundyisland.co.uk.

Of the old village's two pricey **hotels**, the luxurious *Red Lion* enjoys the best position, right on the harbour (ⓣ01237/431237, ⓦwww.clovelly.co.uk; ❼). Halfway down the main street, *Donkey Shoe Cottage* (ⓣ01237/431601, ⓦwww.donkeyshoecottage.co.uk; no credit cards; ❷) offers more modest **B&B** accommodation, and there's a greater selection of guesthouses in Higher Clovelly, including *East Dyke Farmhouse* (ⓣ01237/431216, ⓔsteve.goaman@virgin.net; no credit cards; ❷), near the A39 junction.

West to Hartland Point

You could drive along minor roads to **Hartland Point**, ten miles west of Clovelly, but the best approach is on foot along the coast path. The headland presents one of Devon's most dramatic sights, its jagged black rocks battered by the sea and overlooked by a solitary lighthouse 350ft up. South of Hartland Point, the saw-toothed rocks and near-vertical escarpments defiantly confront the waves, with spectacular waterfalls tumbling over the cliffs. Inland, **HARTLAND** itself holds little appeal, but **Hartland Abbey** (Easter to late May Wed, Thurs & Sun 2–5pm; late May to early Oct also Mon & Tues; grounds Easter to early Oct daily except Sat noon–5pm; £8.50, grounds only £6.50) deserves a linger, an eighteenth-century country house incorporating the ruins of an abbey dissolved in 1539. Displaying fine furniture, old photographs and frescoes, it's surrounded by gardens and lush woodland.

There's a solitary pub and **hotel** surrounded by beautiful slate cliffs at Hartland Quay, *Hartland Quay Hotel* (ⓣ01237/441218, ⓦwww.hartlandquayhotel.com; ⑤), while, in Hartland, you can stay at the small, friendly **B&B** at 2 Harton Manor, The Square, off Fore Street (ⓣ01237/441670, ⓦwww.twohartonmanor.co.uk; no credit cards; ③). Basic **camping** is available at *Stoke Barton Farm* (ⓣ01237/441238; closed Nov–Easter), right by the fourteenth-century church of **St Nectan's** in the village of Stoke, half a mile west of Harland Abbey; tea and scones are also served here (closed Mon & Fri).

Exmoor

A high bare plateau sliced by wooded combes and splashing streams, **EXMOOR** can be one of the most forbidding landscapes in England, especially when shrouded in a sea mist. When it's clear, though, the moorland of this National Park reveals rich swathes of colour and an amazing diversity of wildlife, from buzzards to the unique **Exmoor ponies**, a species closely related to prehistoric horses. In the treeless heartland of the moor in particular, it's not difficult to spot these short and stocky animals, though fewer than twelve hundred are registered, and of these only about two hundred are free-living on the moor. Much more elusive are the **red deer**, England's largest native wild animal, of which Exmoor supports the country's only wild population, currently around two and half thousand.

Endless **walking routes** are possible along a network of some six hundred miles of footpaths and bridleways, and **horseback riding** is another option for getting the most out of Exmoor's desolate beauty – visitor centres can supply details of guided walks and local stables. Whether walking or riding, bear in mind that over seventy percent of the National Park is privately owned and that access is theoretically restricted to public rights of way; special permission should certainly be sought before camping, canoeing, fishing or similar. Check the website ⓦwww.activeexmoor.com for **organized activity** operators on Exmoor.

Inland, there are four obvious bases for walks, all on the Somerset side of the county border: **Dulverton** in the southeast, site of the main information facilities; **Simonsbath** in the centre; **Exford**, near Exmoor's highest point of Dunkery Beacon; and the attractive village of **Winsford**, close to the A396 on the east of the moor. Exmoor's coastline offers an alluring alternative to the open moorland, all of it accessible via the **South West Coast Path**, which embarks on its long coastal journey at **Minehead**, though there is more charm to be found further west at the sister villages of **Lynmouth** and **Lynton**, just over the Devon border.

Dulverton

The village of **DULVERTON**, on the southern edge of the National Park, is the Park Authority's headquarters and so makes a good introduction to Exmoor. Information on the whole moor is available at the **visitor centre** on Fore Street (daily: April–Oct 10am–5pm; Nov–March 10.30am–3pm; ⓣ01398/323841, ⓦwww.exmoor-nationalpark.gov.uk). Dulverton's best **accommodation** is *Town Mills* (ⓣ01398/323124, ⓦwww.townmillsdulverton.co.uk; ④), an old mill house in the centre of the village; alternatively try the *Lion Hotel* in Bank Square (ⓣ01398/323444; ⑤), or *Tongdam*, a Thai restaurant off 26 High St (ⓣ01398/323397) with two doubles (③) and a suite (⑤). A mile north of Dulverton, *Northcombe Farm* has two **camping barns** (£7.50) as well

The South West Coast Path

The South West Coast Path, Britain's longest footpath, starts at Minehead and tracks the coastline along Devon's northern seaboard, round Cornwall, back into Devon, and on to Dorset, where it finishes close to the entrance to Poole Harbour. The path was conceived in the 1940s, but it was just over 25 years ago that – barring a few significant gaps – the full **630-mile route** opened, much of it on land owned by the National Trust, and all of it well signposted.

The relevant Ordnance Survey **maps** can be found at most village shops en route, while Aurum Press (Ⓦwww.aurumpress.co.uk) publishes four *National Trail Guides* covering the route, and the **South West Coast Path Association** (Ⓣ01752/896237, Ⓦwww.swcp.org.uk) publishes an annual guide (£9.50) to the whole path, including accommodation lists, ferry timetables and transport details.

as basic camping facilities (Ⓣ01398/323602). Both the *Lion* and *Tongdam* offer moderately priced **meals**.

Winsford, Exford and Dunkery Beacon

Just west of the A396 five miles north of Dulverton, **WINSFORD** lays justified claim to being the moor's prettiest village. A scattering of thatched cottages ranged around a sleepy green, it is watered by a confluence of streams and rivers – one of them the Exe – giving it no fewer than seven bridges. The *Royal Oak*, a thatched and rambling old inn, has drinks, snacks and full restaurant **meals**, as well as plush **accommodation** (Ⓣ01643/851455, Ⓦwww.royaloak-somerset.co.uk; ❻–❼). Behind it on Halse Lane, *Karslake House* (Ⓣ01643/851242, Ⓦwww.karslakehouse.co.uk; ❺) offers excellent B&B and evening meals (not Sun or Mon).

The hamlet of **EXFORD**, an ancient crossing point on the River Exe, is popular with hunting folk as well as with walkers for the four-mile hike to **Dunkery Beacon**, Exmoor's highest point at 1700ft. Local **accommodation** includes *Exmoor Lodge*, a friendly B&B on Chapel Street (Ⓣ01643/831694, Ⓦwww.smoothhound.co.uk; ❸), and Exmoor's main YHA **hostel**, a rambling Victorian house (Ⓣ0870/770 5828, Ⓔexford@yha.org.uk; from £13).

Exmoor Forest and Simonsbath

At the heart of the National Park lies **Exmoor Forest**, the barest part of the moor, scarcely populated except by roaming sheep and a few red deer – the word "forest" denotes simply that it was a hunting reserve. In the middle of it stands the village of **SIMONSBATH** (pronounced "Simmonsbath"), home to the Knight family, who bought the forest in 1818 and, by introducing tenant farmers, building roads and importing sheep, brought systematic agriculture to an area that had never before produced any income.

Simonsbath makes a good base for hikes on the moor, though **accommodation** is limited to the *Exmoor Forest Inn* (Ⓣ01643/831341, Ⓦwww.exmoorforestinn.co.uk; ❺), studded with hunting trophies, and the *Simonsbath House Hotel* (Ⓣ01643/831259, Ⓦwww.simonsbathhouse.co.uk; ❻), former home of the Knights and now a cosy bolt hole offering elegant rooms and a good but expensive **restaurant**. In a converted barn next to the hotel, *Boevey's* offers coffees and lunches (closed Dec & Jan), while a couple of miles outside the village on the Brayford Road, the *Poltimore Arms* at **Yarde Down** is a classic country **pub** serving excellent food.

Minehead and Dunster

The Somerset port of **MINEHEAD** quickly became a favourite Victorian watering hole with the arrival of the railway, and it has preserved an upbeat holiday-town atmosphere ever since. Steep lanes link the two quarters of **Higher Town**, on North Hill, containing some of the oldest houses, and **Quay Town**, the harbour area.

The **tourist office** is midway between Higher Town and Quay Town at 17 Friday St, off the Parade (Mon–Sat 10am–12.30pm & 1.30–4/5pm, also Sun 10am–1pm in July & Aug; ⓣ01643/702624, ⓦwww.minehead.co.uk). **Accommodation** options include the *Old Ship Aground* right by the harbour on Quay Road (ⓣ01643/702087; ③) and, a few minutes' walk from the tourist office, *Kildare Lodge* on Townsend Road (ⓣ01643/702009; ④), a reconstructed Tudor inn. There's a YHA **hostel** a couple of miles southeast, outside the village of Alcombe (ⓣ0870/770 5968, ⓔminehead@yha.org.uk; from £12), in a secluded combe on the edge of Exmoor.

Minehead is a terminus for the **West Somerset Railway**, which curves eastwards into the Quantocks as far as Bishops Lydeard (see p.306). The area's major attraction, the old village of **DUNSTER**, is about a mile from the line's first stop, three miles inland. Dunster's main street is dominated by the towers and turrets of its **castle** (late March to Oct Mon–Wed, Sat & Sun 11am–4/5pm; grounds daily: March–Dec 10/11am–4/5pm; £7.80, grounds only £4.30; NT), most of whose fortifications were demolished after the Civil War. The castle then became something of an architectural showpiece, and subject to a thorough Victorian restoration. Tours take in various portraits of the Luttrells, owners of the house for six hundred years; a bedroom once occupied by Charles I; a fine seventeenth-century carved staircase, and a richly decorated banqueting hall. The grounds include terraced gardens and riverside walks, all overlooked by a hilltop folly, **Conygar Tower**, dating from 1776.

Below the castle, relics of Dunster's wool-making heyday include the octagonal **Yarn Market** in the High Street, dating from 1609, while the three-hundred-year-old **water mill** at the end of Mill Lane is still used commercially for milling the various grains which go to make the flour and muesli sold in the shop (April–May & Oct daily except Fri 11am–4.45pm;

Walks from Lynton and Lynmouth

In addition to the coastal path, there are several popular walks inland in this region. The one-and-a-half-mile tramp to **Watersmeet**, for example, follows the East Lyn River to where it's joined by Hoar Oak Water, a tranquil spot transformed into a roaring torrent after a bout of rain. From the fishing lodge here – now open as a café and shop in summer – you can branch off on a range of less-trodden paths, such as the three-quarters-of-a-mile route south to **Hillsford Bridge**, the confluence of Hoar Oak and Farley Water.

North of Watersmeet, a path climbs up **Countisbury Hill** and the higher **Butter Hill** (nearly 1000ft), affording great views of Lynton, Lynmouth and the north Devon coast, and there's also a track leading to the lighthouse at **Foreland Point**, close to the coastal path. East from Lynmouth you can reach the point via a fine sheltered shingle beach at the foot of Countisbury Hill – one of a number of tiny coves that are easily accessible on either side of the estuary.

From Lynton, an undemanding expedition takes you west along the North Walk, a mile-long path leading to the **Valley of the Rocks**, where the steep heathland is dominated by rugged rock formations and grazed by herds of wild goats.

June–Sept daily 11am–4.45pm; £2.85; NT) – the **café**, overlooking its riverside garden, is a good spot for lunch. There's a **National Park Centre** at the top of Dunster Steep by the main car park (Easter–Oct daily 10am–5pm, some weekends in winter 10.30am–3pm; ⓣ01643/821835), and **accommodation** at the traditional *Yarn Market Hotel*, 25–31 High St (ⓣ01643/821425, ⓦwww.yarnmarkethotel.co.uk; ⑤).

Porlock

Six miles west of Minehead and cupped on three sides by the hogbacked hills of Exmoor, the thatch-and-cob houses and distinctive charm of **PORLOCK** draws armies of tourists. Many come in search of the village's literary links: according to Coleridge's own less-than-reliable testimony, it was a "man from Porlock" who broke the opium trance in which he was composing *Kubla Khan*, while the High Street's beamed *Ship Inn* features prominently in the Exmoor romance *Lorna Doone* and, in real life, sheltered the poet Robert Southey. Two miles west over reclaimed marshland, the tiny harbour of **PORLOCK WEIR** is a tranquil spot for a breath of sea air and a drink.

Porlock's **tourist office** is at West End, High St (April–Oct Mon–Sat 10am–5pm, Sun 10am–1pm; Nov–Easter Tues–Fri 10.30am–1pm, Sat 10am–4pm; ⓣ01643/863150, ⓦwww.porlock.co.uk). The best **accommodation**, is on the High Street, including the Victorian *Lorna Doone Hotel* (ⓣ01643/862404, ⓦwww.lornadoonehotel.co.uk; ②) and the thatched, sixteenth-century *Myrtle Cottage* (ⓣ01643/862978, ⓦwww.myrtleporlock.co.uk; ③). The *Lorna Doone* serves snacks, **meals** and teas as does the *Whortleberry Tearoom*, also on the High Street (closed Mon & Tues).

Lynton and Lynmouth

Nine miles west of Porlock, just inside Devon, the Victorian resort of **LYNTON** perches above a lofty gorge with splendid views over the sea. Almost completely cut off from the rest of the country for most of its history, the village struck lucky during the Napoleonic Wars, when frustrated Grand Tourists – unable to visit their usual continental haunts – discovered in Lynton a domestic piece of Swiss landscape. Coleridge and Hazlitt trudged over to Lynton from the Quantocks, but the greatest spur to the village's popularity came with the publication in 1869 of R.D. Blackmore's Exmoor melodrama *Lorna Doone*, a book based on the outlaw clans who inhabited these parts in the seventeenth century.

Lynton is connected by **cliff railway** (daily 10am–5/7pm; £3 return) with **LYNMOUTH**, five hundred feet below at the junction and estuary of the East and West Lyn rivers. Shelley spent nine weeks here with his 16-year-old bride Harriet Westbrook, during which time he wrote his polemical *Queen Mab* (two different houses claim to have been the Shelleys' love nest). At the top of the village, you can explore the walks, waterfalls and an exhibition on the uses of waterpower in the wooded **Glen Lyn Gorge** (Easter–Oct daily 10am–3/6pm; £4). There are also details here of various **boat trips** that depart from the harbour (Easter–Sept; ⓣ01598/753207).

Practicalities

The local **tourist office** is in Lynton's town hall on Lee Road (Mon–Sat 9.30/10am–4/5pm, Sun 10am–2/4pm; ⓣ0845/660 3232, ⓦwww.lynton-lynmouth-tourism.co.uk). Lynton has the better choice of budget **accommodation**, including the friendly, Victorian B&B *The Turret*, 33 Lee Rd

(Ⓣ01598/753284, Ⓦwww.turrethotel.co.uk; ③), as well as the area's best option, the whitewashed, Georgian *St Vincent House*, Castle Hill (Ⓣ01598/752244, Ⓦwww.st-vincent-hotel.co.uk; closed Nov–March; ⑤), with beautifully furnished rooms and a renowned and expensive **restaurant** that specializes in French and Belgian recipes (eves only; closed Mon).

In Lynmouth, central accommodation choices include the posh *Shelley's*, right next to the Glen Lyn Gorge (Ⓣ01598/753219, Ⓦwww.shelleyshotel.co.uk; ⑤), where you can sleep in the room supposed to have been occupied by the poet, and *Tregonwell*, 1 Tors Rd (Ⓣ01598/753369, Ⓦwww.smoothhound.co.uk; ③), a Victorian B&B overlooking the East Lyn.

Cornwall

When D.H. Lawrence wrote that being in **Cornwall** was "like being at a window and looking out of England", he wasn't just thinking of its geographical extremity. Virtually unaffected by the Roman conquest, Cornwall was for centuries the last haven for a **Celtic culture** elsewhere eradicated by the Saxons. Primitive granite crosses and a crop of Celtic saints remain as traces of this formative period, and though the Cornish language had ebbed away by the eighteenth century, it is recalled in Celtic place-names that in many cases have grown more exotic as they have mutated over time.

Cornwall's formerly thriving **industrial economy** is far more conspicuous than in neighbouring Devon. Its more westerly stretches in particular are littered with the derelict stacks and castle-like ruins of the engine-houses that once powered the region's **copper** and **tin mines**, while deposits of **china clay** continue to be mined in the area around St Austell, as witnessed by the conical spoil heaps thereabouts. Also prominent throughout the county are the grey nonconformist chapels that reflect the impact of Methodism on Cornwall's mining communities.

Nowadays, of course, Cornwall's most flourishing industry is tourism. The repercussions of the holiday business have been uneven, for instance cluttering **Land's End** with a tacky leisure complex but leaving Cornwall's other great headland, **Lizard Point**, undeveloped. The thronged resorts of **Falmouth**, site of the National Maritime Museum, and **Newquay**, the West's chief surfing centre, have successfully adapted to the demands of mass tourism, but its effects have been more destructive in smaller, quainter places, such as **Mevagissey**, **Polperro** and **Padstow**, whose genuine charms can be hard to make out in full season. Other villages, such as **Fowey**, **Charlestown, Port Isaac** and **Boscastle**, still preserve an authentic feel, however, while you couldn't wish for anything more remote than **Bodmin Moor**, a tract of wilderness in the heart of Cornwall, or the **Isles of Scilly**, idyllically free of development. It would be hard to compromise the sense of desolation surrounding **Tintagel**, site of what is fondly known as King Arthur's Castle, or the appeal of the seaside resorts of **St Ives** and **Bude** – both with great surfing beaches – while, near **St Austell**, the spectacular **Eden Project**, located in an abandoned clay pit, celebrates environmental diversity with visionary style.

From Looe to Veryan Bay

The southeast strip of the Cornish coast holds a string of compact harbour towns interspersed with long stretches of magnificent coastline. The main rail stop is **St Austell**, and there's a rail link from Liskeard to touristy **Looe**. **Polperro** is easily accessible by bus from Plymouth, while the estuary town of **Fowey**, in a niche of Cornwall closely associated with the author Daphne Du Maurier, is most easily reached by bus from St Austell and Par, as is **Mevagissey**, to the west.

Looe

LOOE was drawing crowds as early as 1800, when the first "bathing-machines" were wheeled out, but the arrival of the railway in 1879 was what really packed its beaches. Though the river-divided town now touts itself as something of a shark-fishing centre, most people come here for the sand, the handiest stretch being the beach in front of East Looe. Away from the river-mouth, you'll find cleaner water a mile eastwards at **Millendreath**. The **Old Guildhall Museum** on Higher Market Street (Easter & late May to Sept Mon–Fri & Sun 11.30am–4.30pm; £1.50) includes a collection of maritime models among its exhibits; equally interesting are the fifteenth-century building's preserved prison cells and raised magistrates' benches.

East Looe's **tourist office** is at the New Guildhall, on Fore Street (Easter–Sept daily 10am–5pm; Oct–Easter unstaffed Mon–Fri 10am–noon; Ⓣ01503/262072, Ⓦwww.looecornwall.com). The best **accommodation** here enjoys lofty views: on East Cliff, try the friendly *Marwinthy* (Ⓣ01503/264382, Ⓦwww.marwinthy.co.uk; no credit cards; ❷), with old-fashioned rooms, some en suite, or on Barbican Hill there's the more up-to-date *Haven House* on (Ⓣ01503/264160, Ⓦwww.bedbreakfastlooe.co.uk; ❸). The town abounds in inexpensive **places to eat**, including the *Grapevine* on Fore Street (Ⓣ01503/263913; closed Sun eve & all Mon), which has a pleasant secluded courtyard.

Polperro

POLPERRO is linked to Looe by frequent buses – it's smaller and quainter than it's neighbour, but has a similar feel. From the bus stop and car park at the top of the village, it's a five- or ten-minute walk alongside the River Pol to the pretty harbour. The surrounding cliffs and the tightly packed houses rising on each side of the stream have an undeniable charm, and the tangle of lanes is little changed since the village's heyday of pilchard fishing and smuggling, but the tourist stream has also ruined it, and its straggling main street – the Coombes – is now an unbroken row of tacky shops and food outlets. The best places to **stay** include *The Cottles* on Longcoombe Lane, above the car park at the top of the village (Ⓣ01503/272578, Ⓦwww.cottles-polperro.co.uk; ❹), with a conservatory and decking, and the central but relatively secluded *Old Mill House*, an agreeable pub on Mill Hill (Ⓣ01503/272362, Ⓦwww.oldmillhouseinn.co.uk; ❸). There's a separate **restaurant** at the *Old Mill*, and you can get chunky crab sandwiches at the snug *Blue Peter* **pub** on The Quay, where there's live music at weekends.

Fowey and around

The ten miles west from Polperro to Polruan are among south Cornwall's best stretches of the coastal path, giving access to some beautiful secluded sand beaches. There are frequent ferries across the River Fowey from Polruan, affording a fine prospect of **FOWEY** (pronounced "Foy"), a cascade of neat, pale terraces at the mouth of one of the peninsula's greatest rivers. The major port on the county's south coast in the fourteenth century, Fowey finally became so ambitious that it provoked Edward IV to strip the town of its military capability, though it continued to thrive commercially, becoming the leading port for china clay shipments in the nineteenth century.

Fowey's steep layout centres on the distinctive fifteenth-century church of **St Fimbarrus**. Below the church, the **Ship Inn**, sporting some fine Elizabethan panelling and plaster ceilings, held the local Roundhead HQ during the Civil War. From here, Fore Street, Lostwithiel Street and the Esplanade fan out, the **Esplanade** leading to a footpath that gives access to some splendid coastal walks. Past the remains of a blockhouse that once supported a defensive chain hung across the river's mouth, the small beach of **Readymoney Cove** is soon reached, close to the ruins of **St Catherine's Castle**, built on the orders of Henry VIII and offering fine views across the estuary.

Coastwalkers can trace the rocky shore westwards to **Gribbin Head** (less than four miles), near which stands Menabilly House, where Daphne Du Maurier lived for 24 years – it was the model for the "Manderley" of *Rebecca*. The house is not open to the public, but the coast path takes you down to the twin coves of **Polridmouth**, where Rebecca met her watery end.

Practicalities

Separated from eastern routes by its river, Fowey is most accessible by #25 and #25B **buses** from St Austell and Par train stations. The **tourist office**, at 5 South St (Mon–Sat 9.30am–5.30pm, Sun 10am–4.30pm; ⓣ01726/833616, ⓦwww.fowey.co.uk), houses a small exhibition of the life and work of Daphne Du Maurier, and can provide information on the nine-day **Daphne Du Maurier Festival** (ⓣ0845/094 0428, ⓦwww.dumaurierfestival.co.uk), which takes place each May.

Most of the town's pubs offer **B&B**; try the *Ship Inn* on Trafalgar Square (ⓣ01726/832230; ❸) or the *Safe Harbour*, at the town's bus stop on Lostwithiel Street (ⓣ01726/833379, ⓦwww.cornwall-safeharbour.co.uk; ❹), which has less character but good views. Outside Fowey, *Coombe Farm*, at the end of a lane off the B3269 (ⓣ01726/833123, ⓦwww.coombefarmbb.co.uk; no credit cards; ❸), provides perfect rural isolation twenty minutes' walk from town and close to a beach. Two miles north of Fowey near Golant, there's a YHA **hostel** at the Georgian mansion *Penquite House*, with views over the valley (ⓣ0870/770 5832, ⓔgolant@yha.org.uk; from £15.50); tipis and bikes are available.

Fore Street is the place for **restaurants**: *Sam's* at no. 20 (no booking; no credit cards) has an eclectic menu from burgers to bouillabaisse, and at no. 41 *The Other Place* has takeaway items on the ground floor and a smart restaurant upstairs (ⓣ01726/833636; in winter closed Mon–Thurs & Sun). The area is also well provided with good **pubs** – the *Ship Inn* and the *King of Prussia* on the quayside are both worth a lingering drink or meal.

St Austell Bay

It was the discovery of china clay, or kaolin, in the downs to the north of **St Austell Bay** that spurred the area's growth in the eighteenth century. An essential ingredient in the production of porcelain, kaolin had until then only been produced in northern China. Still a vital part of Cornwall's economy, the clay is now mostly exported for use in the manufacture of paper, as well as paint and medicines. The conical spoil heaps left by the mines are a feature of the local landscape, the great green and white mounds making an eerie sight.

The town of **ST AUSTELL** itself is fairly unexciting, but makes a useful stop for trips in the surrounding area. Its nearest link to the sea is at **CHARLESTOWN**, an easy downhill walk from the centre of town. This unspoilt port is still used for china clay shipments, and provides a backdrop for the location filming that frequently takes place here. Behind the harbour, the **Shipwreck & Heritage Centre** (March–Oct daily 10am–5/6pm; £5.95) is entered through tunnels once used to convey the clay to the docks, and shows a good collection of photos and relics as well as tableaux of historical scenes. On either side of the dock, the coarse sand and stone **beaches** have small rock pools, above which cliff walks lead around the bay.

Charlestown is the most attractive **place to stay** hereabouts: try *T'Gallants* (Ⓣ01726/70203; ④), a smart Georgian B&B at the back of the harbour, or *Broad Meadow House*, behind the Shipwreck Centre on Quay Road (Ⓣ01726/76636, Ⓦwww.broadmeadowhouse.com; no credit cards; ③), which, as well as B&B, offers "tent and breakfast", with family-size tents in a meadow by the sea. Behind *T'Gallants* in Charlestown, the *Rashleigh Arms* serves real ale and a lunchtime carvery, and the *Harbourside Inn*, Harbourfront, also has a range of **food**.

Mevagissey to Veryan Bay

MEVAGISSEY was once known for the construction of fast vessels, used for carrying contraband as well as pilchards. Today the tiny port might display a few stacks of lobster pots, but the real business is tourism, and in summer the maze of backstreets is saturated with day-trippers, converging on the inner harbour and overflowing onto the large sand beach at **Pentewan** a mile to the north. A couple of miles north of Mevagissey lie the **Lost Gardens of Heligan** (daily 10am–5/6pm; last entry 90min before closing; £8.50), a fascinating Victorian garden which had fallen into neglect and was resurrected by Tim Smit, the visionary instigator of the Eden Project (see p.343). A boardwalk takes you through a jungle and under a canopy of bamboo and ferns down to the Lost Valley, where there are lakes, woods and wild-flower meadows.

Four miles south of Mevagissey juts the striking headland of **Dodman Point**, cause of many a wreck and topped by a stark granite cross built by a local parson as a seamark in 1896. The promontory holds the substantial remains of an Iron Age fort, with an earthwork bulwark cutting right across the point. Curving away to the west, elegant **Veryan Bay** holds a string of exquisite inlets and coves, such as **Hemmick Beach**, a fine place for a dip with rocky outcrops affording a measure of privacy, and **Porthluney Cove**, a crescent of sand whose centrepiece is the battlemented **Caerhays Castle** (mid-March to May Mon–Fri noon–4pm; gardens mid-Feb to May daily 10am–5pm; last entry 1hr before closing; house £5.50, garden £5.50, combined ticket £9.50), built in 1808 by John Nash and surrounded by beautiful gardens. A little further on, minuscule and whitewashed **Portloe** is fronted by jagged black rocks that throw up fountains of seaspray, giving it a good, end-of-the-road feel.

Practicalities

From St Austell's bus and train station, **buses** #26, #25B (Sun only, not Heligan) and #526 leave for Mevagissey and Heligan; Portloe is reachable on #T51 from Truro (not Sun). There's an independent **tourist office** on St George's Square (Easter–May, Sept & Oct Mon–Fri 10am–3pm; June–Aug Mon–Sat 10am–5pm, Sun 11am–4pm; Ⓣ0870/443 2928, Ⓦwww.mevagissey-cornwall.co.uk). In the heart of Mevagissey, the best **accommodation** option is the

The Eden Project

A disused clay pit four miles northeast of St Austell holds Cornwall's highest-profile attraction, the **Eden Project** (April–Oct daily 9.15am–6pm, may close later late July to early Sept; Nov–March Mon–Thurs 10am–4.30pm, Fri & Sat 10am–9pm, Sun 10am–6pm; last entry 90min before closing; £14; Ⓦwww.edenproject.com). Occupying a 160-foot-deep crater whose awesome scale only reveals itself once you have passed the entrance at its lip, the project showcases the diversity of the planet's plant life in an imaginative, sometimes wacky, but refreshingly ungimmicky style. The whole site is stunningly landscaped with an array of various crops and flowerbeds, but at centre stage are the geodesic "biomes" – vast conservatories made up of eco-friendly Teflon-coated, hexagonal panels. One biome holds groves of olive and citrus trees, cacti and other plants more usually found in the warm, temperate zones of the Mediterranean, southern Africa and southwestern USA, while the larger one contains plants from the tropics, including teak and mahogany trees, and there's a waterfall and river gushing through. Plans are afoot to add a third biome, using cutting-edge design and technology, dedicated to the warm desert regions and the impact of climate change. Equally impressive are the external grounds, where plantations of bamboo, tea, hops, hemp and tobacco are interspersed with brilliant swathes of flowers. The whole "living theatre" presents a constantly changing spectacle, and should ideally be visited in different seasons.

Allow at least half a day for a full exploration, but arrive early to avoid congestion. In summer, the grassy arena sees performances of a range of music – from Peter Gabriel to Hot Chip – and in winter a skating rink is set up; consult the website for details.

The most useful **bus routes** to Eden are #T9, #27B (Sun only) and #527 from St Austell station all year. Bus #27B also links the site with Truro, and #527 connects it with Newquay, as does #T10 in summer, and there's also the summer-only #T11 from Truro and Falmouth (Mon–Fri once-daily). Drivers will find the site signposted on most roads in the area, and there's a useful network of routes for walkers and cyclists, who can claim a £4 reduction off the adult entry fee.

fifteenth-century *Fountain Inn* on Cliff Street, off East Quay (Ⓣ01726/842320, Ⓦwww.staustellbrewery.co.uk; ❸); alternatively there's the *Old Parsonage*, 58 Church St (Ⓣ01726/843709, Ⓦwww.oldparsonage.net; ❹), a B&B with simply furnished rooms. The YHA **hostel** (Ⓣ0870/770 5712, Ⓔboswinger@yha.org.uk; from £13) is in a former farmhouse at **Boswinger**, a remote spot half a mile from Hemmick Beach and served infrequently by bus #526.

Mevagissey's **restaurants** specialize in fish – try the Portuguese *Alvorada*, 17 Church St (closed daytime, plus all Mon–Wed & Sun Oct–Feb; Ⓣ01726/842055), offering an inventive menu (fixed-price in winter: £21 for five courses). The *Fountain Inn* and the *Ship Inn* on Fore Street both do pub grub.

Truro, Falmouth and St Mawes

Lush tranquillity collides with frantic tourist activity around the estuary basin of **Carrick Roads**. Connected by river to the estuary, **Truro** is a stop on the main rail line to Penzance and the region's main transport hub. At the mouth of Carrick Roads, **Falmouth** is a major resort, and the site of one of Cornwall's mightiest castles, Pendennis. Its sister fort lies across the estuary in **St Mawes**, the main settlement on the **Roseland** peninsula, a luxuriant backwater of woods and sheltered creeks between the River Fal and the sea.

Truro

TRURO, one of Cornwall's two capitals (the other is Bodmin), presents a mixture of different styles, from its graceful Georgian architecture that came with the tin-mining boom of the 1800s to its modern shopping centre. Further blurring the town's overall identity, and its dominant feature, is its faux-medieval **Cathedral** (Mon–Sat 7.30am–6pm, Sun 9am–7pm; free), at the bottom of Pydar Street. Completed in 1910, it incorporates part of the fabric of the old parish church that previously occupied the site. In the airy interior, the neo-Gothic baptistry commands attention, complete with emphatically pointed arches and elaborate roof vaulting.

Truro's other unmissable attraction is the **Royal Cornwall Museum** (Mon–Sat 10am–5pm; free) on River Street, whose exhibits include minerals, Celtic inscriptions and paintings by Cornish artists.

The town's **tourist office** is on Boscawen Street (Mon–Fri 9am–5pm, Easter–Oct also Sat 9am–5pm; Ⓣ01872/274555, Ⓦwww.truro.gov.uk). Buses stop nearby at Lemon Quay, or near the train station on Richmond Hill. Best hotel **accommodation** in the centre of town is the *Royal Hotel* at the bottom of Lemon Street (Ⓣ01872/270345, Ⓦwww.royalhotelcornwall.co.uk; ❻), with a bright, modern feel. Among the **B&Bs**, try *Bay Tree*, a restored Georgian house at 28 Ferris Town (Ⓣ01872/240274, Ⓦwww.baytree-guesthouse.co.uk; no credit cards; ❸). The comfortable **hostel**, *Truro Backpackers Lodge*, is at 10 The Parade (Ⓣ01872/260857 or 0781/375 5210, Ⓦwww.trurobackpackers.co.uk), with dorm beds (£15) and single and double rooms (❶).

Truro's **restaurants** are also centrally located. For coffees, vegetarian lunches and a choice of organic wines and Belgian beers, head for *Lettuce & Lovage*, 15 Kenwyn St (Ⓣ01872/272546; closed eves & all Sun), while *Saffron*, 5 Quay St (Ⓣ01872/263771; closed Sun, also Mon eve Jan–May), serves inexpensive lunches and a good-value early-evening menu. The *One Eyed Cat*, in a converted church at 116 Kenwyn St (Ⓣ01872/222122), has pastas, pizzas and seafood dishes on the menu, and DJs at weekends. Among the **pubs**, you'll find good ales and bar food at the *Wig and Pen*, on the corner of Frances and Castle streets, and at the next-door *Globe Inn*.

Falmouth

The construction of Pendennis Castle on the southern point of Carrick Roads in the sixteenth century prepared the ground for the growth of **FALMOUTH**, then no more than a fishing village. Its prosperity was assured with the building of a deepwater harbour and with the port's establishment in 1689 as the base of the fast Falmouth Packets, which sped mail to the Americas.

Along with the beaches, its chief attraction is the **National Maritime Museum Cornwall** (daily 10am–5pm; £6.50): vessels from all over the world are exhibited on three levels, many of them suspended in midair in the cavernous Flotilla Gallery. Smaller galleries examine specific aspects of boat-building, seafaring history and Falmouth's packet ships.

A few minutes' walk west of the museum, **Pendennis Castle** (late March to June & Sept Mon–Fri & Sun 10am–5pm, Sat 10am–4pm; July & Aug Mon–Fri & Sun 10am–6pm, Sat 10am–4pm; Oct–March daily 10am–4pm; £5.50; EH) stands sentinel at the tip of the promontory that separates Carrick Roads from Falmouth Bay. The extensive fortification shows little evidence of its five-month siege by the Parliamentarians during the Civil War, which ended only when half its defenders had died and the rest had been starved into submission. Though this is a less-refined contemporary of the castle at St Mawes (see below), its site wins hands down, the stout ramparts offering the best all-round views of Carrick Roads and Falmouth Bay. Round Pendennis Point, south of the centre, a long sandy bay holds a succession of sheltered **beaches**: from the popular **Gyllyngvase Beach**, you can reach the more attractive **Swanpool Beach** by cliff path, or walk a couple of miles further on to **Maenporth**, from where there are some fine cliff-top walks.

Practicalities

Falmouth's **tourist office** is off the Prince of Wales Pier at 11 Market Strand (March–Oct Mon–Sat 9.30am–5.15pm; July & Aug also Sun 10.15am–1.45pm; Nov–Feb Mon–Fri 9.30am–5.15pm; ⓣ01326/312300, ⓦwww.acornishriver.co.uk). Most of the town's **accommodation** is near the train station and beach, including the Victorian *Melvill House Hotel*, 52 Melvill Rd (ⓣ01326/316645, ⓦwww.melvill-house-falmouth.co.uk; ③), with sea or harbour views. More centrally, the *Arwenack Hotel*, 27 Arwenack St (ⓣ01326/311185, ⓦwww.falmouthtownhotels.co.uk; no credit cards; ③), offers basic, good-value accommodation, with a great view from the top rooms. The clean and friendly *Falmouth Lodge* backpackers' **hostel** is near the beach at 9 Gyllyngvase Terrace (ⓣ01326/319996, ⓦwww.falmouthbackpackers.co.uk; from £16, doubles ①), with a kitchen and Internet access.

Arwenack Street has a range of **restaurants**, including *South Side* at no. 35–37 (ⓣ01326/212122), which has comfy sofas and everything from tapas to burgers and steaks on the menu, and the cool, contemporary *Hunky Dory* at no. 46 (ⓣ01326/212997; closed daytime). On Gyllyngvase Beach, you can tuck into grills and pizzas at the *Gylly Beach Café*, which has occasional live music. The *Quayside Inn*, on Arwenack Street, is the pick of the **pubs**, with outdoor tables overlooking the harbour.

St Mawes and the Roseland peninsula

At the end of a prong of land at the bottom of Carrick Roads, the secluded, unhurried town of **ST MAWES** is accessible by frequent **ferry** from Falmouth's Prince of Wales Pier. At the end of the walled seafront stands the small and pristine **St Mawes Castle** (late March to June & Sept Mon–Fri & Sun 10am–5pm; July & Aug Mon–Fri & Sun 10am–6pm; Oct daily 10am–4pm; Nov–March Fri–Mon 10am–4pm; £4; EH), built during the reign of Henry VIII to a cloverleaf design. The castle owes its excellent condition to its early surrender to Parliamentary forces during the Civil War in 1646. The dungeons and gun installations contain various artillery exhibits as well as some background on local social history.

Outside St Mawes, you could spend a pleasant afternoon poking around the **Roseland peninsula** between the Percuil River and Carrick Roads. In summer, there's a **ferry** from St Mawes to the southern arm of the Roseland Peninsula, which holds the charming twelfth- to thirteenth-century church of **St Anthony-in-Roseland**, while two and a half miles north of St Mawes, in the scattered hamlet of **ST JUST-IN-ROSELAND**, the strikingly picturesque church of St Just is surrounded by palms and subtropical shrubbery, its gravestones tumbling down to the edge of a creek.

Practicalities

St Mawes makes an attractive – if pricey – **place to stay**. The best budget choices are a ten-minute walk up from the seafront on Newton Road, all run by the same family: *Newton Farm* (ⓣ01326/270427; ③), *Little Newton* (ⓣ01326/270664; ③) and *Lower Meadow* (ⓣ01326/270036; ⑤) – each has spacious rooms and views. For location – and very steep rates – book in at the *Tresanton Hotel* (Ⓣ01326/270055, Ⓦwww.tresanton.com; ❾), an exclusive Mediterranean-style retreat. You can eat and drink at the *Victory Inn*, a fine old oak-beamed **pub** just off the seafront.

The Lizard peninsula

The **Lizard peninsula** – from the Celtic *lys ardh*, or "high point" – preserves a thankfully undeveloped appearance. If this flat and treeless expanse can be said to have a centre, it's **Helston**, a junction for **buses** running from Falmouth and Truro and for services to the spartan villages of the peninsula's interior and coast: #T2 to **St Keverne** and **Coverack**, #T3 to St Keverne, Coverack and **Helford**, and #T34 to **Mullion** and **The Lizard**.

The east coast to Lizard Point

To the north of the peninsula, the snug hamlets dotted around the **River Helford** are a complete contrast to the rugged character of most of the Lizard. On the river's south side, **Frenchman's Creek**, one of a splay of arcane inlets, was the inspiration for Daphne Du Maurier's novel of the same name.

From Helford Passage you can take a seasonal ferry to reach **Helford** on the south bank, an agreeable old smugglers' haunt worth a snack stop – the *Shipwright's Arms* has pub lunches and a garden overlooking the river. South of here, on the B3293, the broad, windswept plateau of Goonhilly Downs is interrupted by the futuristic saucers of Goonhilly Satellite Station and the nearby ranks of wind turbines. East, the road splits: left to **ST KEVERNE**, an inland village whose tidy square is flanked by two inns and a church, right to **COVERACK**, a fishing port in a sheltered bay. There's a handful of **places to stay** here, including the friendly *Fernleigh* (Ⓣ01326/280626, Ⓔsudan-ann03@hotmail.co.uk; no credit cards; ❸) on Chymbloth Way, a turn-off from Harbour Road, and the *Paris Hotel* (Ⓣ01326/280258 Ⓦwww.pariscoverack.com; ❹), right above the harbour. A YHA **hostel** just west of Coverack overlooks the bay (Ⓣ0870/770 5780, Ⓔcoverack@yha.org.uk; £18). For **eating**, the *Lifeboat House Seafood Restaurant* (Ⓣ01326/280899; closed Mon & Oct–Easter) is pricey and often fully booked, but the fish is superb, and you can pick up first-class fish and chips from the attached takeaway.

Beyond the safe and clean swimming spot of **Kennack Sands**, the south tip of the promontory and mainland Britain's southernmost point, **Lizard Point**, is marked by a plain lighthouse above a tiny cove and a ceaselessly churning sea. From the point, a road and footpath lead a mile inland to the nondescript village called simply **THE LIZARD**, with several central **accommodation** options, including *Caerthillian*, a comfortable Victorian guesthouse (Ⓣ01326/290019, Ⓦwww.thecaerthillian.co.uk; no credit cards; ❸), *Parc Brawse House* (Ⓣ01326/290466, Ⓦwww.cornwall-online.co.uk/parcbrawsehouse; ❸), and *Penmenner House* (Ⓣ01326/290370, Ⓦwww.cornwall-online.co.uk/penmennerhouse-thelizard; no credit cards; ❸). Signposted from The Lizard, a Victorian villa houses a YHA **hostel** right on the coast, with majestic views (Ⓣ0870/770 6120, Ⓔlizard@yha.org.uk; closed Nov–March; £18). In the village, the *Top House* pub provides **snacks**.

A mile west, the peninsula's best-known beach, **Kynance Cove**, has sheer hundred-foot cliffs, stacks and arches of serpentine rock and offshore outcrops. The water quality here is excellent – but take care not to be stranded by the tide.

The west coast

Four miles north of Kynance Cove, the inland village of **MULLION** has a fifteenth- to sixteenth-century church dedicated to the Breton **St Mellane** (or Malo), with a dog-door for canine churchgoers. A lane leads a mile and a quarter west to **Mullion Cove**, where a tiny beach is sheltered behind harbour walls and rock stacks, though the neighbouring sands at **Polurrian** and **Poldhu**, to the north, are better and attract surfers. At the cliff edge at Poldhu, the Marconi Monument marks the spot from which the first transatlantic radio transmission was made in 1901.

Back in Mullion, behind an enclosed garden at the top of Nansmellyon Road, *The Old Vicarage* (Ⓣ01326/240898, Ⓦwww.cornwall-online.co.uk/mullionoldvicarage; no credit cards; ⑤) provides elegant **accommodation**, while *Campden House*, just north of the village on The Commons (Ⓣ01326/240365; no credit cards; ③), lies ten minutes' walk from the sea and serves snacks and evening meals.

Another three or four miles up the coast, tin ore from inland mines was once shipped from **PORTHLEVEN**. Good **beaches** lie to either side: the best for swimming are around **Rinsey Head**, three miles north along the coast, including the sheltered **Praa Sands**. One and a quarter miles south of Porthleven, strong currents make it unsafe to swim at **Loe Bar**, a strip of shingle which separates the freshwater **Loe Pool** from the sea. The elongated Pool is one of two places claiming to be where the sword Excalibur was restored to its watery source (the other is on Bodmin Moor).

The path running along the western edge of Loe Pool makes a fine entry to **HELSTON**, five miles north and the main centre on the Lizard peninsula. The town is best known for its **Furry Dance** (or Flora Dance), which dates from the seventeenth century. Held on May 8 (unless this falls on Sun or Mon, when the procession takes place on the nearest Sat), it's a stately procession of top-hatted men and summer-frocked women performing a solemn dance through the town's streets and gardens. You can learn something about it and absorb plenty of other local history in the eclectic **Helston Folk Museum** (Mon–Sat 10am–1pm, closes 4pm school hols; £2, free on Sat), housed in former market buildings behind the Guildhall on Church Street.

For a drink in Helston, head for the *Blue Anchor*, 50 Coinagehall St, a fifteenth-century monastery rest house, now a snug **pub** with Spingo beer brewed on the premises. Next door, *No. 52* provides **meals** (closed daytime & Sun) as well as **B&B** (Ⓣ01326/569334, Ⓦwww.spingoales.com; ③) – ask in the pub if there's no reply.

The Penwith peninsula

Though more densely populated than the Lizard, the **Penwith peninsula** is a more rugged landscape, with a raw appeal that is still encapsulated by **Land's End**, despite the commercial paraphernalia superimposed on that headland. The seascapes, the quality of the light and the slow tempo of the local fishing communities made this area a hotbed of artistic activity towards the end of the nineteenth century, when the painters of Newlyn, near **Penzance**, established a distinctive school of painting. More innovative figures – among them Ben Nicholson, Barbara Hepworth and Naum Gabo – were soon afterwards to make **St Ives** one of England's liveliest cultural communities, and their enduring influence is illustrated in the St Ives branch of the Tate Gallery, showcasing the modern artists associated with the locality.

Penwith is far more easily toured than the Lizard, with a road circling its coastline and a better network of public transport from the two main towns, St Ives and Penzance, which also have most of the accommodation.

Penzance and around

Occupying a sheltered position at the northwest corner of Mount's Bay, **PENZANCE** has always been a major port, but most traces of the medieval town were obliterated at the end of the sixteenth century by a Spanish raiding party. At the top of **Market Jew Street** (from *Marghas Jew*, meaning "Thursday Market"), which climbs from the harbour and the train and bus stations, stands a statue of **Humphry Davy** (1778–1829), the local woodcarver's son who pioneered the science of electrochemistry and invented the life-saving miners' safety-lamp which his statue holds.

Turn left here into **Chapel Street**, which has some of the town's finest buildings, including the flamboyant **Egyptian House**, built in 1835 to contain a geological museum but subsequently abandoned until its restoration thirty years ago. Across the street, the seventeenth-century **Union Hotel** originally held the town's assembly rooms, where news of Admiral Nelson's victory at Trafalgar and the death of Nelson himself was first announced in 1805.

Off Chapel and Market Jew streets in Princes Street, a former telephone exchange houses a modern art gallery and education centre, **The Exchange** (Mon–Sat 10am–5pm, Sun 11am–4pm, closed Mon & Tues in winter; free), worth a visit for its sleek design and regular exhibitions. Off Morrab Road, west of Chapel Street, you'll find a more traditional collection of art at **Penlee House Gallery and Museum** (Mon–Sat: Easter–Sept 10am–5pm; Oct–April 10.30am–4.30pm; £3, free on Sat), notably works of the Newlyn School – impressionistic harbour scenes, frequently sentimentalized but often bathed in an evocatively luminous light.

Practicalities

Penzance's **tourist office** (May–Sept Mon–Fri 9am–5pm, Sat 9am–4pm, Sun 10am–2pm; Oct–April Mon–Fri 9am–5pm; ⓣ01736/362207, ⓦwww.visit-westcornwall.com) is right next to the train and bus stations on the seafront. **Accommodation** choices on Chapel Street include the historic *Union Hotel* (ⓣ01736/362319, ⓦwww.unionhotel.co.uk; ❹), and the Bohemian *Penzance Arts Club* (ⓣ01736/363761, ⓦwww.penzanceartsclub.co.uk; ❺). The tidy and friendly *Penzance Backpackers* **hostel** (ⓣ01736/363836, ⓦwww.pzbackpack.com; £14), which also has private rooms (❶), is on Alexandra Road, parallel to Morrab Road, and there's a YHA hostel at Castle Horneck, Alverton (ⓣ0870/770 5992, ⓔpenzance@yha.org.uk; from £15.50), a two-mile walk or take bus #5 or #6 from Penzance station to the *Pirate Inn*, from where it's signposted.

Among the town's **restaurants**, *Coco's* on Chapel Street is good for coffees, cakes, beer and tapas, while vegetarians will be happy at *Archie Browns*, above a health shop in Bread Street, open daytime and for occasional theme nights (closed Sun). Chapel Street has a couple of characterful **pubs**: the *Admiral Benbow*, crammed with gaudy ships' figureheads and other nautical items, and the *Turk's Head*, the town's oldest inn, reputed to date back to the thirteenth century.

St Michael's Mount

Frequent buses from Penzance leave for Marazion, five miles east, the access point to **St Michael's Mount** (late March to Oct Mon–Fri & Sun

The Isles of Scilly

The **Isles of Scilly** are a compact archipelago of about a hundred islands, 28 miles southwest of Land's End. None is bigger than three miles across, and only five of them are inhabited – **St Mary's**, **Tresco**, **Bryher**, **St Martin's** and **St Agnes**. In the annals of folklore, the Scillies are the peaks of the submerged land of Lyonnesse, a fertile plain that extended west from Penwith before the ocean broke in, drowning the land and leaving only one survivor to tell the tale. In fact they form part of the same granite mass as Land's End, Bodmin Moor and Dartmoor, and despite rarely rising above a hundred feet, they possess a remarkable variety of landscape. Points of interest include irresistible **beaches**, such as Par Beach on St Martin's; the Southwest's greatest concentration of **prehistoric remains**; some fabulous **rock formations**, and the exuberant **Tresco Abbey Gardens** (daily 10am–4pm; £9). Along with tourism, the main source of income is flower-growing, for which the equable climate and the long hours of sunshine – their name means "Sun Isles" – make the islands ideal. The profusion of **wild flowers** is even more noticeable than the fields of narcissi and daffodils, and the heaths and pathways are often dense with marigolds, gorse, sea thrift, trefoil and poppies, not to mention a host of more exotic varieties introduced by visiting foreign vessels. The waters hereabouts are held to be among the country's best for **diving**, while between May and September, on a Wednesday or Friday evening, islanders gather for **gig races**, performed by six-oared vessels – some over a hundred years old and thirty feet in length.

Free of traffic, theme parks and amusement arcades, the islands are a welcome respite from the tourist trail, the main drawbacks being the high cost of reaching them and the shortage of **accommodation**, most of which is on the main isle of St Mary's. All the islands except Tresco have campsites, though these usually close in the winter; camping rough is not allowed. The islands are accessible by sea or air. **Boats** to St Mary's, operated by Isles of Scilly Travel (Ⓣ0845/710 5555, Ⓦwww.islesofscilly-travel.co.uk), depart from Penzance's South Pier between Easter and October, the crossing lasting about two and three-quarter hours. The main departure points for **flights** (also run by Isles of Scilly Travel) are Land's End, near St Just, Newquay, Exeter, Bristol and Southampton; in winter, there are departures only from Land's End and Newquay. British International (Ⓣ01736/363871, Ⓦwww.islesofscillyhelicopter.com) also runs **helicopter** flights (20min) to St Mary's and Tresco from the heliport a mile east of Penzance. Launches link each of the inhabited islands, though these are sporadic in winter. The **tourist office** is in Hugh Town, St Mary's (Easter–Oct Mon–Fri 8.30am–6pm, Sat 8.30am–5pm, Sun 9am–2pm; Nov–Easter Mon–Fri 9am–5pm; Ⓣ01720/422536, Ⓦwww.simplyscilly.co.uk).

10.30am–5/5.30pm; Nov to late March guided tours Tues & Fri at 11am & 2pm, book at Ⓣ01736/710507; £6.40; NT), a couple of hundred yards offshore. A vision of the archangel Michael led to the building of a church on this granite pile around the fifth century, and within three centuries a Celtic monastery had been founded here. The present building derives from a chapel raised in the eleventh century by Edward the Confessor, who handed it over to the Benedictine monks of Brittany's Mont St Michel, whose island abbey was the model for this one. Following the Civil War, it became the residence of the St Aubyn family, who still inhabit the castle. Some of the buildings date from the twelfth century, but the later additions are more interesting, such as the battlemented **chapel** and the seventeenth-century decorations of the **Chevy Chase Room**, the former refectory. At low tide the promontory can be approached on foot via a cobbled causeway; at high tide there are boats from Marazion (£1.50).

Mousehole to Land's End

Accounts vary as to the derivation of the name of **MOUSEHOLE** (pronounced "Mowzle"), though it may be from a smugglers' cave just to the south. In any case, the name evokes perfectly this minuscule fishing port cradled in the arms of a granite breakwater, three miles south of Penzance. The village attracts more visitors than it can handle, so hang around until the crowds have departed before exploring its tight tangle of lanes, where you'll come across Mousehole's oldest house, the fourteenth-century **Keigwin House**, a survivor of the sacking of the village by Spaniards in 1595. Finish off with a drink at the harbourside *Ship Inn*, which also has **meals** and **rooms** (ⓣ01736/731234; ⑤).

Eight miles west, one of Penwith's best beaches lies at **PORTHCURNO**. Steep steps lead up from the beach of tiny white shells to the **Minack Theatre**, hewn out of the cliff in the 1930s and since enlarged to hold 750 seats, though retaining the basic Greek-inspired design. The spectacular backdrop of Porthcurno Bay makes this one of the country's most inspiring theatres – providing the weather holds. From May to September, a range of plays, operas and musicals are presented, with tickets at £7–8.50 (ⓣ01736/810181, ⓦwww.minack.com); bring a cushion and a rug. The attached **Exhibition Centre** (daily: Easter–Sept 9.30am–5.30pm; Oct–Easter 10am–4pm; closed during performances; £3) gives access to the theatre and explains the story of its creation.

On the shore to the east of Porthcurno, a white pyramid marks the spot where the first transatlantic cables were laid in 1880. On the headland beyond lies an Iron Age fort, **Treryn Dinas**, close to the famous rocking stone called **Logan Rock**, a seventy-ton monster that was knocked off its perch in 1824 by a gang of sailors, among them a nephew of playwright Oliver Goldsmith. Somehow they replaced the stone, but it never rocked again.

The extreme western tip of England, **Land's End**, lies four miles west of Porthcurno. Best approached on foot along the coastal path, the 60ft turf-covered cliffs provide a platform to view the Irish Lady, the Armed Knight, Dr Syntax Head and the rest of the Land's End outcrops, beyond which you can spot the Longships lighthouse, a mile and a half out to sea, and sometimes the Wolf Rock lighthouse, nine miles southwest, or even the Isles of Scilly, 28 miles away. Although nothing can completely destroy the potency of this majestic headland, the **Land's End Experience** theme park (daily from 10am; closing times vary: call ⓣ0870/458 0099 to check; £10), on an extensive site just behind, violates the spirit of the place, its trivializing array of lasers and sound effects no substitute for the real open-air experience.

Whitesand Bay to Zennor

To the north of Land's End the rounded granite cliffs fall away at **Whitesand Bay** to reveal a glistening mile-long shelf of beach that offers the best swimming on the Penwith peninsula. The rollers make for good surfing and boards can be rented at **Sennen Cove**, the more popular southern end of the beach. There are a few places to **stay** around here, including *Myrtle Cottage* (ⓣ01736/871698; no credit cards; ③), whose cosy teashop is also open to non-residents, and, inland on the A30, *Whitesands Hotel* (ⓣ01736/871776, ⓦwww.whitesandshotel.co.uk; ⑤), with a hammock on its deck and barbecues in summer. The **restaurant** here is open to all and has pizzas, pastas, and meat and seafood dishes.

Cape Cornwall, a highly scenic headland three miles northwards, is dominated by the chimney of the Cape Cornwall Mine, which closed in

1870. Half a mile inland the grimly grey village of **ST JUST-IN-PENWITH** was a centre of the tin and copper industry, with rows of cottages radiating out from Bank Square. The tone is somewhat lightened by a grassy open-air theatre where miracle plays were once staged, later used by Methodist preachers and Cornish wrestlers. St Just has limited **accommodation**, though the *Commercial Hotel* on Market Square (Ⓣ01736/788455; Ⓦwww.commercial-hotel.co.uk; ④) has en-suite rooms, and there's a YHA **hostel** (Ⓣ0870/770 5906, Ⓔlandsend@yha.org.uk; from £14) three-quarters of a mile south (take the left fork past the post office). A secluded **campsite** is close by, outside the hamlet of Kelynack, *Kelynack Caravan and Camping Park* (Ⓣ01736/787633, Ⓦwww.kelynackcaravans.co.uk; closed Nov–Easter), one of the few sheltered sites on Penwith, which also has bunks in small dorms available all year (£12). In St Just, *Kegen Teg*, 12 Market Square, offers coffees, teas and **meals** (closed eves also Jan & Feb).

Eight miles northeast of St Just, set in a landscape of rolling granite moorland, **ZENNOR** is where D.H. Lawrence came to live with his wife Frieda in 1916. "It is a most beautiful place," he wrote, "lovelier even than the Mediterranean". The Lawrences stayed a year and a half in the village – long enough for him to write *Women in Love* – before being given notice to quit by the local constabulary, who suspected them of unpatriotic sympathies (their Cornish experiences were later described in *Kangaroo*). Zennor's fascinating **Wayside Museum** is dedicated to Cornish life from prehistoric times (Easter–Oct daily 10.30/11am–5/5.30pm; £3). At the top of the lane, the church of **St Sennen** displays a sixteenth-century bench-carving of a mermaid who, according to local legend, was so entranced by the singing of a chorister that she lured him down to the sea, from where he never returned – though his singing can still occasionally be heard. Next to the church, the *Tinners Arms* is a cosy place to **drink** and **eat**, while the *Old Chapel Backpackers Hostel*, next to the Wayside Museum, is the place **to stay** (Ⓣ01736/798307, Ⓦwww.zennorbackpackers.co.uk; dorm beds from £15, family room ②), and its café provides snacks and evening meals.

Located on a windy hillside a couple of miles inland from Zennor, off the minor road to Penzance, the Iron Age village of **Chysauster** (late March to June & Sept daily 10am–5pm; July & Aug 10am–6pm; Oct daily 10am–4pm; £2.50; EH) is the best-preserved ancient settlement in the Southwest. Dating from about the first century BC, it contains two rows of four buildings, each consisting of a courtyard with small chambers leading off it, and a garden that was presumably used for growing vegetables.

St Ives

East of Zennor, the road runs four hilly miles on to the steeply built town of **ST IVES**. By the time the pilchard reserves dried up around the early 1900s, the town was beginning to attract a vibrant **artists' colony**, precursors of the wave later headed by Ben Nicholson, Barbara Hepworth, Naum Gabo and the potter Bernard Leach, who in the 1960s were followed by a third wave including Terry Frost and Patrick Heron.

The place to view the best work created in St Ives is the **Tate St Ives**, overlooking Porthmeor Beach on the north side of town (March–Oct daily 10am–5.20pm; Nov–Feb Tues–Sun 10am–4.20pm; closes two or three times a year for about ten days – call Ⓣ01736/796226 to check; £5.75, or £8.75 with Hepworth Museum). Most of the paintings, sculptures and ceramics displayed within the airy, gleaming-white building date from 1925 to 1975, with specially commissioned contemporary works also on view as well as exhibitions. The gallery's rooftop **café** is one of the best places in town for a coffee and snack.

A short distance away on Barnoon Hill, the **Barbara Hepworth Museum** (same times as Tate; £4.75, or £8.75 with the Tate) provides a further insight into the local arts scene. One of the foremost nonfigurative sculptors of her time, Hepworth lived in the building from 1949 until her death in a studio fire in 1975. Apart from the sculptures, which are arranged in positions chosen by Hepworth in the house and garden, the museum has background on her art, from photos and letters to catalogues and reviews.

Porthmeor Beach dominates the northern side of St Ives, its excellent water quality and surfer-friendly rollers drawing a regular crowd, while the broader **Porthminster Beach**, south of the station, is usually less busy.

Practicalities

St Ives **train station** is off Porthminster Beach, just below the **bus station** on Station Hill. The **tourist office** is in the narrow Street-an-Pol, five minutes' walk away (June–Sept Mon–Fri 9am–5.30pm, Sat 9am–5pm, Sun 10am–4pm; Oct–May Mon–Fri 9am–5pm, Sat 10am–1pm; ⓣ01736/796297, ⓦwww.visit-westcornwall.com).

Among the numerous **accommodation** choices near the stations and Porthminster Beach, try *Kynance*, 24 The Warren (ⓣ01736/796636, ⓦwww.kynance.com; closed mid-Oct to mid-April; ④), a B&B with a two-night minimum stay, and *Primrose Valley*, Porthminster Beach (ⓣ01736/794939, ⓦwww.primroseonline.co.uk; ⑦), an Edwardian villa with fresh and light rooms – both require a one-week minimum stay in July and August. More centrally, there's *Tre-pol-pen*, Street-an-pol (ⓣ01736/794996, ⓦwww.trepolpen.co.uk; ⑤), and *Cornerways*, The Square (ⓣ01736/796706, ⓦwww.cornerwaysstives.com; no credit cards; ⑤), both tasteful and modern cottage conversions. The *St Ives Backpackers* **hostel** at The Stennack (ⓣ01736/799444, ⓦwww.backpackers.co.uk/st-ives; £17, double rooms ①), occupies an old Wesleyan chapel school.

St Ives has a dazzling range of **restaurants**. With its sun deck and beach location, *Porthminster Café*, on Porthminster Beach (ⓣ01736/795352; Nov–Easter closed all Mon and eves Sun, Tues & Wed), makes a superb spot for coffees, snack lunches and fairly expensive dinners; under the same management, the *Porthgwidden Beach Café* in the Downalong area of town offers similar but cheaper fare (closed in winter). *Alba*, on the harbourfront (ⓣ01736/797222), is a sleekly modern restaurant with top-class seafood – set-price menus are available until 7.30pm – while *Peppers*, 22 Fore St (ⓣ01736/794014; eves only), is the place for a simple pizza or pasta in mellow surroundings. On Tregenna Place, *Isobar* is a cocktail and tapas bar with DJs on the decks and a separate club upstairs.

The north Cornish coast to Bude

The north Cornish coast is punctuated by some of the finest beaches in England, the most popular of which are to be found around **Newquay**, the surfers' capital, and **Padstow**, also renowned for its gourmet seafood restaurants. North of the Camel estuary, the cliffy coast is an almost unbroken line of cliffs as far as the Devon border, the gaunt, exposed terrain making a melodramatic setting for **Tintagel**, though there are more beaches at **Bude**, attracting both surfers and families.

Newquay and around

It is difficult to imagine a lineage for **NEWQUAY** that extends more than a few decades, but the "new quay" was built in the fifteenth century in what was already a long-established fishing port, up to then more colourfully known as Towan Blistra. The town was given a boost in the nineteenth century when a railway was constructed across the peninsula for china clay shipments. With the trains came a swelling stream of seasonal visitors, drawn to the town's superb position on a knuckle of cliffs overlooking fine golden sands and Atlantic rollers, natural advantages which have made Newquay the premier resort of north Cornwall. Try to coincide your visit to Newquay with one of the **surfing competitions** and events that run right through the summer – contact the tourist office for details.

The centre of town is a somewhat tacky parade of shops and restaurants from which lanes lead to ornamental gardens and cliff-top lawns. At the bottom of Beach Road, adjacent to the small harbour, the **Blue Reef Aquarium** (daily 10am–4/5pm; £7.95) allows you to view tropical fish from an underwater tunnel. Below the aquarium, in the crook of the massive Towan Head, **Towan Beach** is the most central of the seven miles of firm sandy beaches that line the coast. You can reach all of them on foot, or take bus #556 or the summer-only #T10 for some of the further ones, such as **Porth Beach**, with its grassy headland, and the extensive **Watergate Bay**. The beaches can get very busy in high season, and are popular with surfers all year, particularly Watergate and – west of Towan Head – **Fistral Bay**, the largest of the town beaches. On the other side of East Pentire Head from Fistral, **Crantock Beach** – reachable over the Gannel River by ferry or upstream footbridge – is usually less crowded, and has a lovely backdrop of dunes and undulating grassland. South of Crantock, **Holywell Bay** and the three-mile expanse of **Perran Beach**, enhanced by caves and natural rock arches, are also very popular with surfers.

Practicalities

Newquay's **train station** is off Cliff Road and the **bus station** on Manor Road, close to the **tourist office** on Marcus Hill (June–Aug Mon–Sat

▲Surfers at Newquay

9.30am–5.30pm, Sun 9.30am–3.30pm; Sept–May Mon–Fri 9.30am–4.30pm, also Sat 9.30am–12.30pm Easter–May & Sept; ⓣ01637/854020, ⓦwww.newquay.co.uk). You can rent or buy **surfing equipment** from beach stalls or from various outlets around town.

Newquay's **accommodation** is plentiful but can still be booked solid in July and August. Phone ahead for *Rockpool Cottage*, 92 Fore St (ⓣ01637/870848, ⓦwww.rockpoolcottage.co.uk; closed Jan–Easter; ❸), convenient for Fistral Beach, or *Trewinda Lodge*, 17 Eliot Gardens (ⓣ01637/877533, ⓦwww.trewindalodge.co.uk; no credit cards; ❸), close to Tolcarne Beach; both B&Bs can give informed advice to surfers. For a more upmarket option, try the *Harbour Hotel*, North Quay Hill (ⓣ01637/873040, ⓦwww.theharbour.uk.com; ❼), a small, luxurious hotel with fantastic views from its stylish rooms.

Among the town's plethora of independent **hostels**, there's the modern and fully equipped *Reef Surf Lodge*, centrally located at 10–12 Berry Rd (ⓣ01637/879058, ⓦwww.reefsurflodge.info; £30), with food, live entertainment and a surf centre, or *Matt's Surf Lodge*, 110 Mount Wise Rd (ⓣ01637/874651, ⓦwww.matts-surf-lodge.co.uk), slightly further out, with free tea and coffee and a licensed bar; dorm beds are from £20 in summer, and en-suite double rooms ❷. On the cliff top outside **Perranporth**, at the southern end of Perran Beach, there's a YHA **hostel** housed in a former coastguard station (ⓣ0870/770 5994, ⓔperranporth@yha.org.uk; from £15). Newquay's numerous **campsites** include *Trevelgue* (ⓣ0845/130 1515, ⓦwww.trevelgue.co.uk), a mile east of Porth Beach on Trevelgue Road.

Among Newquay's **eateries**, *The Chy* is worth finding, a modern café/restaurant on Beach Road, with a spacious terrace for seafood lunches and DJs at weekends. For a snack lunch or, in summer, an evening meal, check out the laid-back *Café Irie* at 38 Fore St (closed Mon–Thurs Nov–Easter; no credit cards), with a mellow music soundtrack. For the best food, however, head to **Watergate Bay**, where the *Beach Hut* provides surf food and full meals, and *Fifteen Cornwall*, run by celebrity chef Jamie Oliver, showcases the culinary talents of trainee chefs with an Italian-slanted set menu for £24.50 at lunchtime, £50 in the evening; breakfasts are also worth tucking into.

For a **night out**, have a drink in the Aussie-themed *Walkabout Inn* on Beachfield Avenue, with great waterside views, before hitting one of the town's **clubs**; the current hot spots are *Berties* on East Street (ⓣ01637/872255, ⓦwww.bertiesclub.com), *Sailors* on Fore Street (ⓣ01637/872838, ⓦwww.sailorsnightclub.com), and, on Beach Road, *The Beach* (ⓣ01637/872194, ⓦwww.beachclubnewquay.com) and the *Koola Club* (ⓣ01637/873415, ⓦwww.thekoola.com).

Padstow and around

The small fishing port of **PADSTOW** is nearly as popular as Newquay, but has a very different feel. Enclosed within the estuary of the Camel – the only river outlet of any size on Cornwall's north coast – the town has long retained its position as North Cornwall's principal fishing port, and can boast the best seafood restaurants. Padstow is also known for its annual **Obby Oss** festival, a May Day romp when a local in horse costume prances through the town preceded by a masked and club-wielding "teaser", in a spirited re-enactment of an old fertility rite.

On the hill overlooking Padstow, the church of **St Petroc** is dedicated to Cornwall's most important saint, a Welsh or Irish monk who landed here in the sixth century, died in the area and gave his name to the town – "Petrock's Stow". The building has a fine fifteenth-century font, an Elizabethan pulpit and some amusing carved bench-ends. The walls are lined with monuments to the local Prideaux family, who still occupy nearby **Prideaux Place**, an Elizabethan manor house with grand staircases, richly furnished rooms full of portraits, fantastically ornate ceilings and formal gardens (Easter & mid-May to early Oct Mon–Thurs & Sun 1.30–5pm, last tour at 4pm; grounds open from 12.30pm; £7, grounds only £2).

The harbour is jammed with launches and boats offering cruises in Padstow Bay, while a regular **ferry** (summer daily 8am–7.30pm; winter Mon–Sat 8am–4.30pm; £3 return) carries people across the river to **ROCK** – close to the isolated church of **St Enodoc** (John Betjeman's burial place) and to the good beaches around Polzeath (see below). At low water, the ferry leaves from near the war memorial downstream.

The coast on the **west side** of the estuary has more beaches and some terrific walks. Round **Stepper Point** you can reach the sandy and secluded Harlyn Bay and, turning the corner southwards, **Constantine Bay**, the area's best surfing beach. The dunes backing the beach and the rock pools skirting it make this one of the most appealing bays on this coast, though the tides can be treacherous and bathing hazardous near the rocks. Three or four miles further south, the slate outcrops of **Bedruthan Steps** were traditionally held to be the stepping-stones of a giant called Bedruthan; they can be readily viewed from the cliff-top path and the B3276, with steps descending to the broad beach below (not advised for swimming).

Padstow is also the start of an excellent **cycle-track** converted from the old rail line to Wadebridge, forming part of the **Camel Trail**, a fifteen-mile traffic-free path that follows the river up as far as Bodmin Moor. You can **rent bikes** from Trail Bike Hire (ⓣ01841/532594) and Padstow Cycle Hire (ⓣ01841/533533), both on South Quay, by the start of the Trail.

Practicalities

Padstow's **tourist office** is on the harbour (Easter–Oct Mon–Sat 9.30am–5pm, Sun 10am–4pm; Nov–Easter Mon–Fri 10am–4pm, Sat & Sun 10am–2pm; ⓣ01841/533449, ⓦwww.padstowlive.com). Local **accommodation** includes *Cullinans*, a B&B at 4 Riverside (ⓣ01841/532383, ⓔcullinan@madasafish.com; no credit cards; ③), also on the harbour, and *Treverbyn House*, Treverbyn Rd (ⓣ01841/532855, ⓦwww.treverbynhouse.com; ⑤), an elegant Edwardian house with great views. The nearest YHA **hostel** is well sited at Treyarnon Bay (ⓣ0870/770 6076, ⓔtreyarnon@yha.org.uk; from £15.50); take bus #556 to Constantine, then walk half a mile.

Padstow is well known for its **restaurants**, particularly those associated with star chef Rick Stein, whose *Seafood Restaurant*, at Riverside, is one of Britain's top places for fish. Its success has led to the opening of two offshoots, *St Petroc's Bistro* at 4 New St, offering a lighter version of its parent's menu, and, nearby at 10 Middle St, the cool and casual *Rick Stein's Café*. In addition, there's *Stein's Fish and Chips* on South Quay and his **deli** next door. All three of the main places also offer classy accommodation (⑥–⑧); for restaurants and accommodation reservations, call ⓣ01841/532700 or go to ⓦwww.rickstein.com.

Outside the Stein empire, you can get bar food from Padstow's **pubs**: try the *Shipwright's* on the harbour's north side, or the eighteenth-century *Old Ship* on Mill Square, both with outdoor seating.

Polzeath and Port Isaac

Facing west into Padstow Bay, the beaches around **POLZEATH** are the finest in the vicinity, pelted by rollers that make this one of the best surfing sites in the West Country (tuition and gear to rent are available from stalls and shops). The next settlement of any size is **PORT ISAAC**, wedged in a gap in the precipitous cliff wall and dedicated to the crab and lobster trade. Narrow lanes lead down to the seafront, where there are a couple of pubs and a pebble beach and rock pools exposed by the low tide. Among the **accommodation** choices here, you can enjoy wonderful views from both *The Gallery*, 44 Fore St (ⓣ01208/881032, ⓦwww.bed-and-breakfast-port-isaac.co.uk; ④), with stylish, contemporary rooms and a large garden, and the elegant Victorian *Bay Hotel*, 1 The Terrace (ⓣ01208/880380, ⓦwww.bayhotelportisaac.co.uk; ⑤). Local seafood can be sampled from the excellent **restaurant** at the *Slipway Hotel* on the quayside. The bar here is a congenial place for a pint, as is the neighbouring *Golden Lion*, which has a cellar bistro.

Tintagel

East of Port Isaac, the coast is wild and unspoiled, making for some steep and strenuous walking, and providing an appropriate backdrop for the forsaken ruins of **Tintagel Castle** (daily 10am–4/6pm; £4.70; EH). It was the twelfth-century chronicler Geoffrey of Monmouth who first popularized the notion that this was the **birthplace of King Arthur**, son of Uther Pendragon and Ygrayne. Tintagel is certainly a plausible candidate, though the **castle** ruins in fact belong to a Norman stronghold occupied by the earls of Cornwall, who after sporadic spurts of rebuilding allowed it to decay, most of it having been washed into the sea by the sixteenth century. The remains of a sixth-century **Celtic monastery** are also visible on the headland, and have provided important insights into how the country's earliest monastic houses were organized.

The easiest access to the site is from the village of **TINTAGEL**, a dreary collection of cafés and B&Bs where the only item of note is the **Old Post Office** (Easter to Sept daily 11am–5.30pm; Oct daily 11am–4pm; £2.70; NT), a rickety-roofed slate-built construction dating from the fourteenth century, now restored to its appearance in the Victorian era.

Buses stop on the main Fore Street close to Tintagel's **tourist office** on Bossiney Road (daily 10/10.30am–4/5pm; ⓣ01840/779084, ⓦwww.visittintagelandboscastle.com). Most of the **B&Bs** are a few minutes' walk along Atlantic Road, with the best being *Pendrin House* (ⓣ01840/770560, ⓦwww.pendrinhouse.co.uk; ③) and *Bosayne* (ⓣ01840/770514, ⓦwww.bosayne.co.uk; ④). Three-quarters of a mile west of Tintagel at Dunderhole Point, the offices of a former slate quarry now house a YHA **hostel** with great views of the coastline (ⓣ0870/770 6068; closed Nov–March; from £12). On Fore Street, both the *Old Malt House* and the *Tintagel Arms Hotel* have **restaurants**.

Boscastle

Three miles east of Tintagel, the port of **BOSCASTLE** lies compressed within a narrow ravine drilled by the rivers Jordan and Valency, and ending in a twisty harbour. The tidy riverfront bordered by thatched and lime-washed cottages was the scene of a devastating flash flood in 2004, but most of the damage has now been repaired. Above and behind, you can see more seventeenth- and eighteenth-century cottages on a circular walk that traces the valley of the Valency for about a mile to reach Boscastle's graceful **parish church**, tucked away in a peaceful glen.

Boscastle's **tourist office** is in the car park at the bottom of the main road into the village (daily 10/10.30am–4/5pm; ⓣ01840/250010, ⓦwww.visittintagelandboscastle.com). *St Christopher's Hotel* (ⓣ01840/250412,

King Arthur in Cornwall

Did **King Arthur** really exist? If he did, it's likely that he was an amalgam of two people: a sixth-century Celtic warlord who united the local tribes in a series of successful battles against the invading Anglo-Saxons, and a local Cornish saint. Whatever his origins, his role was recounted and inflated by poets and troubadours in later centuries. The Arthurian legends were elaborated by the medieval chroniclers Geoffrey of Monmouth and William of Malmesbury and in Thomas Malory's epic, *Morte d'Arthur* (1485), further romanticized in Tennyson's *Idylls of the King* (1859) and resurrected in T.H. White's saga, *The Once and Future King* (1958).

Although there are places throughout Britain and Europe that claim some association with Arthur, it's England's West Country, and **Cornwall** in particular, that has the greatest concentration of places boasting a link. Here, the myths, enriched by fellow Celts from Brittany and Wales, have established deep roots, so that, for example, the spirit of Arthur is said to be embodied in the Cornish chough – a bird now almost extinct. Cornwall's most famous Arthurian site is his supposed birthplace, **Tintagel**, where Merlin apparently lived in a cave under the castle (he also resided on a rock near Mousehole, south of Penzance, according to some sources). Nearby **Bodmin Moor** is littered with places with names such as "King Arthur's Bed" and "King Arthur's Downs", while Camlan, the battlefield where Arthur was mortally wounded fighting against his nephew Mordred, is associated with Slaughterbridge, on the northern reaches of the moor near **Camelford** (which is also sometimes identified as Camelot itself). At **Dozmary Pool**, the knight Bedivere was dispatched by the dying Arthur to return the sword Excalibur to the mysterious hand emerging from the water – though Loe Pool in Mount's Bay also claims this honour. Arthur's body, it is claimed, was carried after the battle to **Boscastle**, on Cornwall's northern coast, from where a funeral barge transported it to Avalon (identified with Glastonbury in Somerset).

Ⓦwww.st-christophers-boscastle.co.uk; no credit cards; ⑤) is a restored Georgian manor house at the top of the High Street with first-rate **accommodation**, but for a real Thomas Hardy experience, head for the *Old Rectory*, on the road to St Juliot (Ⓣ01840/250225, Ⓦwww.stjuliot.fsnet.co.uk; closed Dec to mid-Feb; ⑤), where you can stay in the author's bedroom and roam the extensive grounds. There's also a fine old YHA **hostel** on the harbourside (Ⓣ0870/770 5710, Ⓔboscastle@yha.org.uk; closed Nov–March; from £15.50).

You can eat at one of the village's excellent **pubs**: in the upper part of town, the *Napoleon* has a good seafood bistro, while the atmospheric *Cobweb* down near the harbour serves bar food; both have live music evenings.

Bude and around

Just four miles from the Devon border, Cornwall's northernmost town of **BUDE** is built around an estuary surrounded by a fine expanse of sands. The town has sprouted a crop of hotels and holiday homes, though these have not unduly spoilt the place nor the magnificent cliffy coast surrounding it.

Of the excellent beaches hereabouts, the central **Summerleaze** is clean and wide, while the mile-long **Widemouth Bay**, south of town, is the main focus of the holiday crowds (though bathing can be dangerous near the rocks at low tide). Surfers also congregate five miles down the coast at **Crackington Haven**, wonderfully situated between 430-foot crags at the mouth of a lush valley. The cliffs on this stretch are characterized by remarkable zigzagging strata of shale, limestone and sandstone, a mixture which erodes into vividly contorted detached formations. To the **north** of Bude, acres-wide **Crooklets** is the scene

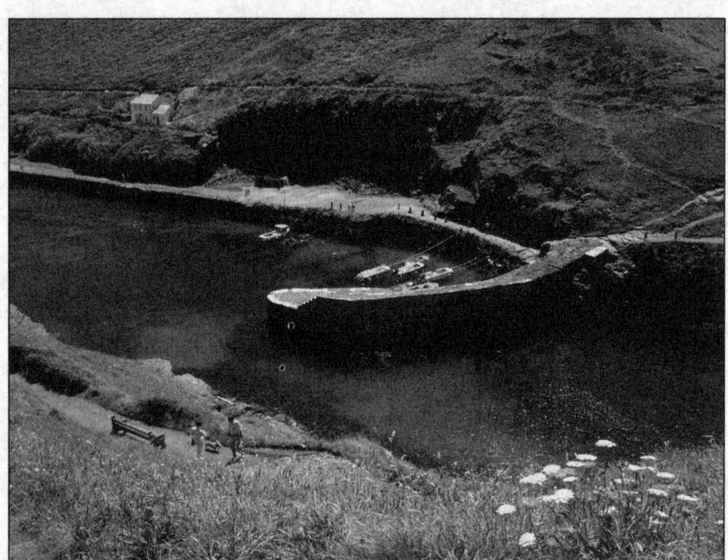

▲ Boscastle harbour

of **surfing** and life-saving demonstrations and competitions. A couple of miles further on, **Sandy Mouth** holds a pristine expanse of sand with rock pools beneath the encircling cliffs. It's a short walk from here to another surfers' delight, **Duckpool**, a tiny sandy cove flanked by jagged reefs at low tide, and dominated by the three-hundred-foot **Steeple Point**.

Bude's **tourist office** is in the car park off the Crescent (April–Sept Mon–Fri 10am–5pm, Sat 10am–5pm, Sun 10am–4pm; Oct–March Mon–Fri 10am–4pm, Sat 10am–1pm; Ⓣ01288/354240, Ⓦwww.visitbude.info). The town's cheaper **accommodation** includes a cluster of B&Bs overlooking the golf course on Burn View, among them *Palms* at no. 17 (Ⓣ01288/353962, Ⓦwww.palms-bude.co.uk; no credit cards; ③). Near Widemouth Bay, you can stay in spacious, beautifully designed modern rooms at *Bangors Organic*, a stylish B&B a mile inland at Poundstock (Ⓣ01288/361297, Ⓦwww.bangorsorganic.co.uk; ⑦). There's a backpackers' **hostel** at 57 Killerton Rd (Ⓣ01288/354256, Ⓦwww.northshorebude.com; £12), with a large garden, **Internet** access and some double rooms (①).

For style, location and cuisine, Bude's best **restaurant** is *Life's a Beach*, right on Summerleaze Beach, a café by day and a romantic (and expensive) bistro in the evening (Ⓣ01288/355222; closed winter weekday lunch and all Mon & Tues). In town, try the *Atlantic Diner*, 5–7 Belle Vue (closed Mon, plus most eves in winter; no credit cards), popular with shoppers and surfers alike for its inexpensive burgers, steaks, curries and ice creams. **Surfing equipment** can be rented from various outlets in town.

Bodmin and Bodmin Moor

Bodmin Moor, the smallest of the West Country's great moors, has some beautiful tors, torrents and rock formations, but much of its fascination lies in the strong human imprint, particularly the wealth of relics left behind by its **Bronze Age** population. Separated from these by some three millennia, the churches in the villages of **St Neot**, **Blisland** and **Altarnun** are among the region's finest examples of fifteenth-century art and architecture.

Bodmin

BODMIN's position on the western edge of Bodmin Moor, equidistant from the north and south Cornish coasts and the Fowey and Camel rivers, encouraged its growth as a trading town. It was also an important ecclesiastical centre after the establishment of a priory by St Petroc, who moved here from Padstow in the sixth century. The priory disappeared but Bodmin retained its prestige through its church of **St Petroc**, at the end of Fore Street, built in the fifteenth century and still the largest in Cornwall (open for services and April–Sept Mon–Sat 11am–3pm; free; at other times call ⓣ01208/73867). Inside, there's an extravagantly carved twelfth-century font and an ivory casket that once held the bones of the saint, while the southwest corner of the churchyard holds a sacred well. West of here on Berrycoombe Road, the notorious **Bodmin Jail** (daily 10am–dusk; £5) is redolent of the public executions that were once guaranteed crowd-pullers here. You can visit part of the original eighteenth-century structure, including the condemned cell and some grisly exhibits chronicling the lives of the inmates. There's a good café and **bike hire** here (ⓣ01208/74170).

From the train station (see below), it's less than two miles' walk to one of Cornwall's most celebrated country houses, **Lanhydrock** (house mid-March to Oct Tues–Sun 11am–5/5.30pm; gardens open daily 10am–6pm or dusk; £9.40, grounds only £5.30; NT), originally seventeenth-century but totally rebuilt after a fire in 1881. Within the granite exterior, the 50 rooms include a long picture gallery with a plaster ceiling depicting scenes from the Old Testament, and servants' quarters that fascinatingly reveal the daily workings of a Victorian manor house. The grounds have magnificent beds of magnolias, azaleas and rhododendrons, and a huge area of wooded parkland bordering onto the River Fowey.

Practicalities

Three miles outside town, Bodmin Parkway **train station** has a regular bus connection to the centre. All **buses** stop on Mount Folly, site of Bodmin's **tourist office** (Easter–Oct Mon–Sat 10am–5pm; Nov–Easter Mon–Fri 10am–5pm; ⓣ01208/76616, ⓦwww.bodminlive.com), which also offers **Internet** access. There's comfortable **B&B** at *Higher Windsor Cottage*, 18 Castle St (ⓣ01208/76474, ⓦwww.higherwindsorcottage.co.uk; no credit cards; ③), and at *Bedknobs*, further up the same street at Polgwyn (ⓣ01208/77553, ⓦwww.bedknobs.co.uk; ⑤), a Victorian villa in an acre of wooded garden.

Off Fore Street, the *Hole in the Wall* **pub** in Crockwell Street has bar lunches, an upstairs **restaurant** and a courtyard. Wholesome snacks are served at the tiny *Bara Café* at 14 Honey St (closed Sun except during summer school hols), just across from St Petroc's.

Blisland and the western moor

BLISLAND stands in the Camel valley on the western slopes of Bodmin Moor, three miles northeast of Bodmin. Georgian and Victorian houses cluster around a village green and a church whose well-restored interior has an Italianate altar and a startlingly painted screen. On **Pendrift Common** above the village, the gigantic **Jubilee Rock** is inscribed with various patriotic insignia commemorating the jubilee of George III's coronation in 1809. From this seven-hundred-foot vantage point you look eastward over the De Lank gorge and the boulder-crowned knoll of **Hawk's Tor**, three miles away. On the shoulder of the tor stand the Neolithic **Stripple Stones**, a circular platform once holding 28 standing stones, of which just four are still upright. On Blisland's village green, you can sample good **ales and food** at the *Blisland Inn*, with outdoor tables.

Camelford and the northern tors

The northern half of Bodmin Moor is dominated by its two highest tors, both of them easily accessible from **CAMELFORD**, which offers a couple of diverting museums. The **British Cycling Museum** (Mon–Thurs & Sun 10am–5pm, phone ahead for Fri & Sat ⓣ01840/212811; £3.35), housed in the old station one mile north of town on the Boscastle Road, is a cyclophile's dream, containing some four hundred examples of bikes through the ages. More conventionally, the **North Cornwall Museum** (April–Sept Mon–Sat 10am–5pm; £2.50) in the village itself, displays domestic items and exhibits relating to the local slate industry, and also houses the **tourist office** (same hours; ⓣ01840/212954). Among Camelford's **accommodation**, try the thirteenth-century, slate-hung *Darlington Inn* on Fore Street (ⓣ01840/213314; ❸), or the *Countryman Hotel*, at 7 Victoria Rd (ⓣ01840/212250, ⓦwww.thecountrymanhotel.co.uk; ❹), close to the National Cycle Way. The *Mason's Arms* on Market Place, with bar food and a beer garden, makes a good **refreshment** stop.

Rough Tor, the second highest peak on Bodmin Moor at 1311ft, is four miles' walk southeast from Camelford. A short distance to the east stand Little Rough Tor, where there are the remains of an Iron Age camp, and Showery Tor, capped by a prominent formation of piled rocks. Easily visible to the southeast, **Brown Willy** is, at 1375ft, the highest peak in Cornwall, as its original name signified – Bronewhella, or "highest hill". Like Rough Tor, Brown Willy shows various faces, its sugarloaf appearance from the north sharpening into a long multi-peaked crest as you approach. The tor is accessible by continuing from the summit of Rough Tor across the valley of the De Lank, or, from the south, by footpath from Bolventor.

Bolventor and Altarnun

The village of **BOLVENTOR**, lying at the centre of the moor midway between Bodmin and Launceston, is an uninspiring place close to one of the moor's chief focuses for walkers and sightseers alike – **Jamaica Inn** (ⓣ01566/86250, ⓦwww.jamaicainn.co.uk; ❺). A staging post even before the precursor of the A30 road was laid here in 1769, the inn was described as being "alone in glory, four square to the winds" by Daphne Du Maurier, who stayed here in 1930, soaking up inspiration for her smugglers' yarn, *Jamaica Inn*. Adjacent to the rather bland hotel, the **Smuggler's Museum** (daily 9/11am–4/6pm; £3.75) shows the diverse ruses used for concealing contraband.

The inn's car park makes a useful place to leave your vehicle and venture forth on foot. Just a mile south, **Dozmary Pool** is another link in the West Country's Arthurian mythologies – after Arthur's death Sir Bedivere hurled Excalibur, the king's sword, into the pool, where it was seized by an arm raised from the depths. Despite its proximity to the A30, the diamond-shaped lake usually preserves an ethereal air, though it's been known to run dry in summer, dealing a bit of a blow to the legend that it is bottomless.

Coastal Britain

With nowhere in Britain more than 75 miles from the coast, the sea – bulwark against the Spanish Armada, Napoleon and Hitler, among others – occupies an integral part of the national psyche. Poets, painters and photographers have been inspired through the centuries by the bays and beaches, cliffs and creeks, sand dunes and shingle of Britain's richly diverse coastline, which, at over 7700 miles in length (including more than a thousand islands), ranges from stark wilderness to traditional seaside resorts.

The Pembrokeshire Coast Path ▲

Windsurfing in Dorset ▼

Coastal paths

Almost every stretch of British coast is walkable, from the **Norfolk Coast Path** to the **Cleveland Way** along the Yorkshire coast (for both see Ⓦwww.nationaltrail.co.uk). In the southeast of England, revitalizing excursions can be made over the lovely **Seven Sisters** cliffs around Brighton, and over the iconic **White Cliffs of Dover**.

The longest National Trail is the 630-mile **South West Coast Path** (Ⓦwww.southwestcoastpath.com), which extends from Minehead in Somerset around the peninsula to Poole in Dorset. Wales's dramatic **Pembrokeshire Coast Path** (Ⓦwww.pcnpa.org.uk) is much shorter, at 186 miles, but it's arguably even more dramatic; while the 80-mile **Fife Coastal Path** in Scotland (Ⓦwww.fifecoastalpath.com) takes in the golden beaches between the Forth Rail Bridge and St Andrews' coastal golf links.

Water sports

Britain's **surf scene** is concentrated along the southwest coast of England, though the Welsh coast and the northeastern coast of Scotland are both increasing in popularity – see p.58. **Windsurfers** and **sailors** fare best on the more sheltered English south and southwest coasts, notably Hampshire, the Isle of Wight, and Devon and Cornwall, with Devon's pretty town of Salcombe a particular favourite for sailing. Cowes Week (see p.218) is an annual focus for keen sailors. Scotland also boasts some excellent cruising grounds on the Firth of Clyde and the rugged west coast. For **kayaking** and **canoeing**, the best places are Britain's lakes and rivers, particularly the Lake District National Park in northwest England.

Beaches

Britain's beaches can compare with the best in the world in terms of sheer natural beauty. For a combination of decent climate and good sand, the coasts of **Cornwall** and **Devon** are hard to beat. The Gulf Stream warms the northwest coast of Scotland, making the lonely beaches of the **Hebrides** a tempting proposition, while in **Wales** the best areas are the Gower peninsula, the Pembrokeshire coast, the Llýn and the southwest coast of Anglesey. England's south and east coasts are less picturesque, though the gravel beaches of East Anglia's shoreline give way to a string of wide sandy beaches along the **north Norfolk coast**. But it's northern Britain that can champion the finest strands, notably in **north Yorkshire**, in **Northumberland**, and along the coast of **northeast Scotland** from Aberdeen to Inverness.

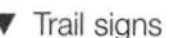

Britain's top five beaches

▸▸ **Par Beach**, St Martin's, Isles of Scilly. Hugely scenic and usually empty, despite the perfect sands. See p.349.

▸▸ **Ardudwy**, Harlech, Mid-Wales. Eight miles of wide sands and dunes, including Wales's only official naturist section. See p.698.

▸▸ **Porthcurno**, Cornwall. Surrounded by cliffs, with an open-air theatre nearby. See p.350.

▸▸ **Kiloran Bay**, Isle of Colonsay, Argyll. Unspoiled sandy beach pounded by Atlantic breakers. See p.904.

▸▸ **South Harris**, Western Isles, Scotland. Glorious golden sands framed by mountains and a turquoise sea. See p.934.

▲ St Martin's beach, Isles of Scilly

▼ Trail signs

▼ Lobster pots

Scarborough ▲

Esha Ness ▼

Seaside resorts

Any Brit can describe the quintessential seaside resort – the piercing screech of gulls, the ubiquitous smell of fish and chips, lobster-red flesh at every turn, rollicking fairgrounds, donkey rides, amusement arcades, rock pools and sand castles. **Blackpool** in Lancashire is the brilliant apotheosis of the genre – utterly compelling, enormously entertaining. No other British resort comes close, though many have an equally strong independent, contemporary identity, like fashionable **Brighton** in Sussex or the lively Welsh town of **Aberystwyth**. Others hark back to Victorian times: **Scarborough** in north Yorkshire, deemed to be England's oldest resort, is a classic example, with the Welsh equivalent found at **Llandudno**. Meanwhile, both **Bournemouth** (Dorset) and **Torquay** (Devon) combine traditional resort pursuits with an energetic club scene.

Top coastal beauty spots

▸▸ **Esha Ness**, Shetland. See p.1039. The full might of the Atlantic crashes against the sea stacks and blowholes of this dramatic headland.

▸▸ **Hartland Point**, Devon. See p.334. Fantastic slate cliffs give this remote place an otherworldly feel.

▸▸ **Lizard Point**, Cornwall. See p.346. Raging seas surround this rocky promontory.

▸▸ **The Needles**, Isle of Wight. See p.217. Spectacular pinnacles of rock thrust up from the sea.

▸▸ **Holy Island**, Northumberland. See p.621. A castle, priory ruins and abandoned hulks of boats add to the brooding character of this ancient spot.

Four miles northeast of Bolventor, **ALTARNUN** is a pleasant, granite-grey village snugly sheltered beneath the eastern heights of the moor. Its prominent **church**, St Nonna's, contains a fine Norman font and 79 bench-ends carved at the beginning of the sixteenth century, depicting saints, musicians and clowns. The *King's Head* here has beams, saggy ceilings and **rooms** (⊕01566/86241; ❷), as well as a range of **food and drink**.

St Neot and the southeastern moor

Approached through a lush wooded valley, **ST NEOT** is one of the moor's prettiest villages. Its fifteenth-century **church** contains some of the most impressive stained-glass windows of any parish church in the country, the oldest glass being the fifteenth-century **Creation Window**, at the east end of the south aisle.

One of the moor's most attractive spots lies a couple of miles east, below Draynes Bridge, where the Fowey tumbles through the **Golitha Falls**, less a waterfall than a series of rapids. Dippers and wagtails flit through the trees, and there's a pleasant woodland walk to Siblyback Lake reservoir just over a mile away. North and east of Siblyback Lake are some of Bodmin Moor's grandest landscapes. The quite modest elevations of Hawk's Tor (1079ft) and the lower Trewartha Tor appear enormous from the north, though they are overtopped by **Kilmar**, highest of the hills on the moor's eastern flank at 1280ft. **Stowe's Hill** is the site of the moor's most famous stone pile, **The Cheesewring**, a precarious pillar of balancing granite slabs, marvellously eroded by the wind. A mile or so south down Stowe's Hill stands an artificial rock phenomenon, **The Hurlers**, a wide complex of three circles dating from about 1500 BC. The purpose of these stark upright stones is not known, though they owe their name to the legend that they were men turned to stone for playing the Celtic game of hurling on the Sabbath.

The Hurlers are easily accessible just outside **MINIONS**, Cornwall's highest village, three miles south of which stands another Stone Age survival, **Trethevy Quoit**, a chamber tomb nearly nine feet high, surmounted by a massive capstone. Originally enclosed in earth, the stones have been stripped by centuries of weathering to create Cornwall's most impressive megalithic monument.

Travel details

Buses

For information on all local and national bus services, contact Traveline ⊕0871/200 2233 (daily 7am–9pm), ⓦwww.travelinesw.com.

Bodmin to: Newquay (4 daily; 30–50min); Padstow (Mon–Sat hourly, Sun 6 daily; 55min); Plymouth (3 daily; 1hr); St Austell (Mon–Sat hourly, Sun 5 daily; 50min).

Exeter to: Newquay (3–6 daily; 3hr 20min); Penzance (3–4 daily; 4hr 30min–5hr); Plymouth (Mon–Sat hourly, Sun every 1–2hr; 1hr 15min); Sidmouth (Mon–Sat 2–3 hourly, Sun 1–2 hourly; 40–50min); Torquay (Mon–Sat 8 daily, Sun 3 daily; 50min); Truro (3–4 daily; 3hr–3hr 50min).

Falmouth to: Helston (Mon–Sat hourly, Sun 2–4 daily; 25min–1hr 10min); Penzance (Mon–Sat 7–8 daily, Sun 1 daily; 1–2hr); St Austell (2 daily; 1hr 10min); Truro (Mon–Sat 3–4 hourly, Sun hourly; 35–50min).

Newquay to: Bodmin (4 daily; 30–50min); Padstow (Mon–Sat hourly, Sun 5 daily; 1hr 20min); Plymouth (3–4 daily; 1hr 30min–2hr); St Austell (every 1–2hr; 1hr); Truro (Mon–Sat 6–7 hourly, Sun 2 hourly; 50min–1hr 25min).

Penzance to: Falmouth (Mon–Sat 7–8 daily, Sun 1 daily; 1hr–1hr 45); Helston (Mon–Sat hourly, Sun 6 daily; 50min); Plymouth (7 daily; 2hr 35min–3hr 30min); St Austell (5 daily; 1hr 35min–2hr 15min); St Ives (Mon–Sat 3–5 hourly, Sun hourly;

30–50min); Truro (Mon–Sat 1–2 hourly, Sun 5 daily; 1hr–1hr 30min).

Plymouth to: Bodmin (3 daily; 1hr); Exeter (Mon–Sat hourly, Sun every 1–2hr; 1hr 15min); Falmouth (2 daily; 2hr 30min); Newquay (3–4 daily; 1hr 30min–1hr 50min); Penzance (7 daily; 3hr 15min); St Austell (6 daily; 1hr 20min); St Ives (4 daily; 2hr 45min); Torquay (Mon–Sat every 30min, Sun 6 daily; 1hr 40min–2hr); Truro (6 daily; 1hr 50min).

St Austell to: Bodmin (Mon–Sat hourly, Sun 5 daily; 50min); Exeter (3 daily; 2hr 50min); Falmouth (2 daily; 1hr); Newquay (every 1–2hr; 1hr 10min); Penzance (5 daily; 2hr); Plymouth (6 daily; 1hr 20min); St Ives (2 daily; 1hr 30min); Truro (Mon–Sat 1–2 hourly, Sun every 2hr; 40min).

St Ives to: Penzance (Mon–Sat 3–5 hourly, Sun hourly; 30–50min); Plymouth (4 daily; 3hr); St Austell (2 daily; 1hr 45min); Truro (Mon–Sat hourly, Sun 6 daily; 1hr 10min–1hr 40min).

Torquay to: Exeter (Mon–Sat 8 daily, Sun 3 daily; 50min); Plymouth (Mon–Sat every 30min, Sun 6 daily; 1hr 50min–2hr 10min).

Truro to: Exeter (3–4 daily; 3hr 10min–4hr); Falmouth (Mon–Sat 3–4 hourly, Sun hourly; 35–50min); Newquay (Mon–Sat 6–7 hourly, Sun 2 hourly; 50min–1hr 25min); Penzance (Mon–Sat 1–2 hourly, Sun 5 daily; 1hr–1hr 30min); Plymouth (6 daily; 2hr); St Austell (Mon–Sat hourly, Sun every 2hr; 40min); St Ives (Mon–Sat hourly, Sun 6 daily; 1hr–1hr 35min); St Mawes (Mon–Sat hourly, Sun 3 daily; 1hr).

Trains

For information on all local and national rail services, contact National Rail Enquiries ⓣ08457/484950, ⓦwww.nationalrail.co.uk.

Barnstaple to: Exeter (Mon–Sat 11 daily, Sun 6 daily; 1hr–1hr 30min).

Bodmin to: Exeter (1–2 hourly; 1hr 40min); Penzance (1–2 hourly; 1hr 25min); Plymouth (1–2 hourly; 45min).

Exeter to: Barnstaple (Mon–Sat hourly, Sun 6 daily; 1hr–1hr 30min); Bodmin (1–2 hourly; 1hr 45min); Liskeard (every 1–2hr; 1hr 30min); London (1–2 hourly; 2–3hr); Par (hourly; 2hr); Penzance (every 1–2hr; 3hr 10min); Plymouth (1–2 hourly; 1hr); Torquay (1–2 hourly; 30min–1hr); Totnes (1–2 hourly; 40min); Truro (hourly; 2hr 15min).

Falmouth to: Truro (hourly; 25min).

Liskeard to: Exeter (every 1–2hr; 1hr 30min); Looe (hourly, not Sun in winter; 30min); Penzance (1–2 hourly; 1hr 35min); Plymouth (1–2 hourly; 30min); Truro (hourly; 50min).

Newquay to: Par (4–8 daily, not Sun in winter; 50min).

Par to: Exeter (hourly; 2hr); Newquay (4–8 daily, not Sun in winter; 50min); Penzance (hourly; 1hr 15min); Plymouth (1–2 hourly; 50min).

Penzance to: Bodmin (1–2 hourly; 1hr 25min); Exeter (every 1–2hr; 3hr); Plymouth (1–2 hourly; 2hr); St Ives (most via St Erth; 1–2 hourly, not Sun in winter; 25–45min); Truro (1–2 hourly; 40min).

Plymouth to: Bodmin (1–2 hourly; 40min); Exeter (1–2 hourly; 1hr); Liskeard (1–2 hourly; 30min); Par (1–2 hourly; 50min); Penzance (1–2 hourly; 2hr); Truro (hourly; 1hr 15min).

St Ives to: Penzance (via St Erth; 1–2 hourly, not Sun in winter; 30min–1hr).

Torquay to: Exeter (1–2 hourly; 45min).

Truro to: Exeter (1–2 hourly; 2hr 15min); Falmouth (hourly; 25min); Liskeard (1–2 hourly; 50min); Penzance (1–2 hourly; 45min); Plymouth (hourly; 1hr 20min).

East Anglia

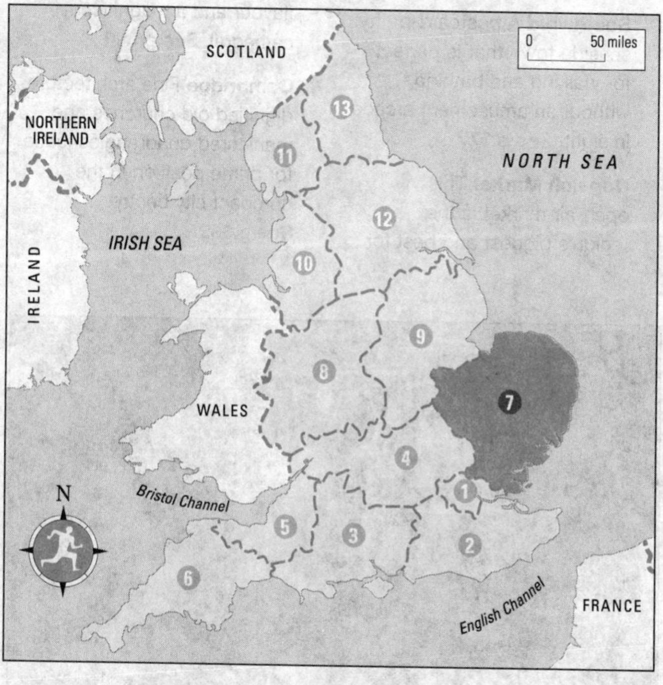

CHAPTER 7

Highlights

* **Orford** Solitary hamlet with a splendid coastal setting that makes for a wonderful weekend away. See p.374

* **The Aldeburgh Festival** The region's prime classical music festival washes over the ears every June for two and a half weeks. See p.376

* **Southwold** A postcard-pretty seaside town that is perfect for walking and bathing – without an amusement arcade in sight. See p.377

* **Norwich Market** This open-air market is the region's biggest and best for everything from whelks to wellies. See p.381

* **Holkham Bay and beach** This wide bay holds Norfolk's finest beach, acres of golden sand set against hilly dunes. See p.388

* **Ely** Isolated Cambridgeshire town, with a true fenland flavour and a magnificent cathedral. See p.390

* **Cambridge** Fine architecture, dignified old churches and manicured quadrangles jostle for prime position in the compact city centre. See p.392

▲ Biscuit stall at Norwich market

7

East Anglia

Strictly speaking, **East Anglia** is made up of just three counties – Suffolk, Norfolk and Cambridgeshire – which were settled by Angles from Schleswig-Holstein in present-day Germany in the fifth century, though in more recent times it's come to be loosely applied to parts of Essex too. As a region it's renowned for its wide skies and flat landscapes, and of course such generalizations always contain more than a grain of truth – if you're looking for mountains, you've come to the wrong place.

Heading into East Anglia from the south takes you through **Essex**, whose proximity to London has turned much of the county into an unappetizing commuter strip. Amidst the suburban gloom, there are, however, several worthwhile destinations, most notably **Colchester**, once a major Roman town and now a likeable place with an imposing castle, and the handsome hamlets of the bucolic **Stour River Valley** on the Essex–Suffolk border. Essex's **Dedham** is one of the prettiest of these villages, but the prime attraction hereabouts is Suffolk's **Flatford Mill**, famous for its associations with the painter John Constable.

Pushing on deeper into **Suffolk**, the county boasts a string of extremely pretty little towns – **Lavenham** is the prime example – that enjoyed immense prosperity from the thirteenth to the sixteenth century, the heyday of the wool trade. Elsewhere, the much maligned county town of **Ipswich** has more to offer than it's generally given credit for, but still, for many visitors it's the north Suffolk coast that steals the local show. With its comely Georgian high street, **Southwold** possesses a delightful seaside resort, elegant and relaxing in equal measure, while neighbouring **Aldeburgh** hosts one of the best music festivals in the country.

Norfolk, as everyone knows thanks to Noël Coward, is very flat. It's also one of the most sparsely populated and tranquil counties in England, a remarkable turnaround from the days when it was an economic and political powerhouse – until, that is, the Industrial Revolution simply passed it by. Its capital, **Norwich**, is still East Anglia's largest city, renowned for its Norman cathedral and castle, and for its high-tech Sainsbury Centre, exhibiting a challenging collection of twentieth-century art. The most visited part of Norfolk is, however, the **Broads**, a unique landscape of reed-ridden waterways that has been intensively exploited by boat-rental companies. Similarly popular, the **Norfolk coast** holds a string of busy, very English seaside resorts – **Cromer**, **Sheringham** and **Hunstanton** to name but three – but for the most part it's a charmingly unspoilt coast, whose marshes, creeks and tidal flats are studded with tiny flintstone villages, most enjoyably **Blakeney** and **Cley**.

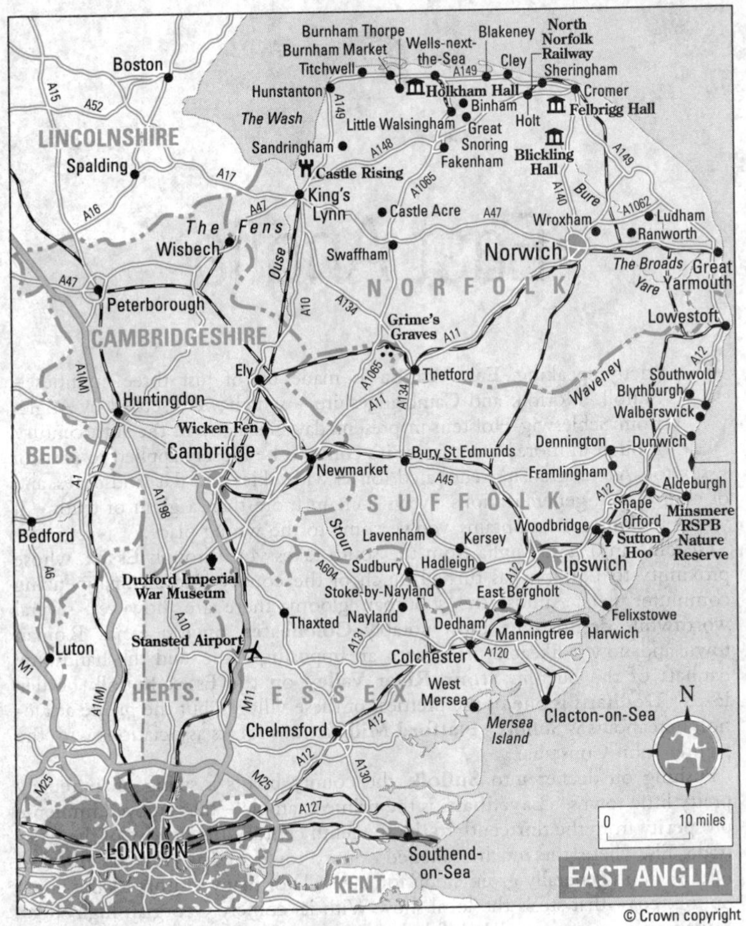

Cambridge is much visited, principally because of its world-renowned university, whose ancient colleges boast some of the finest medieval and early-modern architecture in the country. The rest of Cambridgeshire is pancake-flat **fenland**, for centuries an inhospitable marshland, but now rich alluvial farming land. The cathedral town of **Ely**, settled on one of the few areas of raised ground in the fens, is an easy and popular day-trip from Cambridge.

Getting around

East Anglia's **train** network is at its best to and from London, with quick and frequent services from the capital to all of the region's major towns. One main line links Colchester, Ipswich and Norwich, another Cambridge and Ely. These main-line services are supplemented by a number of cross-country branch lines, most usefully between Peterborough, Ely and Norwich and Ipswich. Once you get away from the major towns, however, you'll have to rely on local **buses**, whose services, run by a multitude of companies, are very patchy. Indeed, in parts of north Norfolk and inland Suffolk, you may find the only way to get about is by your own transport. The largest regional bus operator is **First** (Ⓦwww.firstgroup.com), which sells several sorts of **bus pass**, valid for unlimited travel on all their Norfolk and Suffolk bus routes. Their one-day Network Ticket costs £10, seven days £25. These are available at major bus stations and from bus drivers.

Given the prevailing flatness of the terrain, **hiking** in East Anglia is less strenuous than in most other English regions, and there are several **long-distance footpaths**. The main one is the **Peddars Way** (Ⓦwww.nationaltrail.co.uk), which runs north from Knettishall Heath, near Thetford, to the coast at Holme, near Hunstanton, where it continues east as the **Norfolk Coast Path** to Cromer – 93 miles in total.

Colchester

If you visit anywhere in Essex, it should be **COLCHESTER**, a busy sort of place with a castle, a university and a large army base, fifty miles or so northeast of London. More than anything else, Colchester prides itself on being England's oldest town and there is indeed documentary evidence of a settlement here as early as the fifth century BC. By the first century AD, the town was the region's capital under **King Cunobelin** – better known as Shakespeare's Cymbeline – and when the **Romans** invaded Britain in 43 AD they chose Colchester (Camulodunum) as their new capital, though it was soon eclipsed by London, becoming a retirement colony for legionaries instead. The first Roman temple in the country was erected here, and in 60 AD the colony was the target of Boudicca's abortive revolt. The conquering Normans built one of their mightiest strongholds in Colchester, but the conflict that most marked the town was the **Civil War**. In 1648, Colchester was subjected to a gruelling siege by the Parliamentarian army led by Lord Fairfax; after three months, during which the population ate every living creature within the walls, the town finally surrendered and the Royalist leaders were promptly executed for their pains.

Today, Colchester makes a potential base for further explorations of the surrounding countryside – particularly the Stour valley towns of Constable country (see pp.368–370), within easy reach a few miles to the north.

Arrival, information and accommodation

Colchester has two **train stations**, one for local services and the other, Colchester North, for main-line trains from London, Ipswich and Harwich ferry port. From this main-line station, it's a fifteen-minute walk south into town – follow the ring road, then take North Station Road and its continuation North Hill until you reach the west end of the High Street. The **bus station** is off Queen Street, a couple of minutes' walk from the High Street and yards from both the castle and the **tourist office**, at 1 Queen St (Mon–Sat 10am–5pm; Ⓣ01206/282 920, Ⓦwww.visitcolchester.com), who can book accommodation.

Colchester has its fair share of city-centre **hotels**, including the dependable, half-timbered *Best Western Rose & Crown*, on East Street (Ⓣ01206/866 677, Ⓦwww.bw-roseandcrown.co.uk; ④), a ten-minute walk east of the tourist office, via the High Street and East Hill. The hotel dates back to the fourteenth century and guests choose between the oak-beamed rooms in the original building or the attractively furnished rooms in the modern wing. The pick of the town's **B&Bs** is the *Old Manse*, 15 Roman Rd (Ⓣ01206/545 154; ②), with three pleasant guest rooms, set in a well-maintained, bay-windowed Victorian house on a quiet cul-de-sac; it's on the east side of the castle, a couple of minutes' walk from the tourist office.

The Town

At the heart of Colchester is the remains of its **castle**, a ruggedly imposing, honey-coloured keep, set in attractive parkland stretching down to the River Colne. Begun less than ten years after the Battle of Hastings, the keep was the largest in Europe at the time, and was built on the site of the Temple of Claudius. Inside the keep, a **museum** (Mon–Sat 10am–5pm, Sun 11–5pm; £5.10) holds an excellent collection of Romano-British archeological finds, including a miscellany of coins and tombstones. The museum also runs regular **guided tours** (45min; £2), giving access to the Roman vaults, the Norman chapel and the castle roof, which are otherwise out of bounds. Outside, down towards the river in Castle Park, is a section of the old **Roman walls**, whose battered remains are still visible around much of the town centre. They were erected after Boudicca had sacked the city and, as such, are a case of too little too late.

The castle stands at the eastern end of the wide and largely pedestrianized **High Street**, which follows pretty much the same route as it did in Roman times. The most arresting building here is the flamboyant **Town Hall**, built in 1902 and topped by a statue of St Helena, mother of Constantine the Great and daughter of "Old King Cole" of nursery-rhyme fame – after whom, some say, the town was named.

Looming above the western end of the High Street is the town landmark, "**Jumbo**", a disused nineteenth-century water tower, considerably more imposing than the nearby **Balkerne Gate**, which marked the western entrance to Roman Colchester. Built in 50 AD, this is the largest surviving Roman gateway in the country, though with the remains at only a touch over six feet in height, it's far from spectacular.

Eating and drinking

One of Colchester's best **restaurants** is *The Hub*, 19 Head St, which is at the west end of the High Street (ⓣ01206/564 977), offering contemporary Mediterranean dishes with main courses from around £13. Alternatively, try the *The Lemon Tree*, 48 St John's St (ⓣ01206/767 337; closed Sun), for a delicious dish such as marinated chicken with aubergine; mains hover around £13.

Colchester's **oysters** have been highly prized since Roman times: for top-quality seafood, head south out of town to the oyster fisheries at **West Mersea**, home of *The Company Shed*, 129 Coast Rd, (ⓣ01206/382 700), where the freshest of oysters are served without any frills at rickety tables. **Mersea Island**, home to both West and East Mersea, is located about six miles south of Colchester; the season runs from September to May.

The Stour Valley and the old wool towns of south Suffolk

Five miles or so north of Colchester, the **Stour River Valley** forms the border between Essex and Suffolk, and signals the beginning of East Anglia proper. The valley is dotted with lovely little villages, where rickety, half-timbered Tudor houses and elegant Georgian dwellings cluster around medieval churches, proud buildings with square, self-confident towers. The Stour's prettiest villages are concentrated along its lower reaches – to the east of the A134 – in Dedham Vale, with **Stoke-by-Nayland** and **Dedham** arguably the most appealing of them all. The vale is also known as "**Constable Country**", as it was the home of John Constable (1776–1837), one of England's greatest artists, and the subject of his most famous works. Inevitably, there's a Constable shrine – the much-visited complex of old buildings down by the river at **Flatford Mill**.

The villages along the River Stour and its tributaries were once busy little places at the heart of East Anglia's weaving trade, which boomed from the thirteenth to the fifteenth century. By the 1490s, the region produced more cloth than any other part of the country, but in Tudor times production shifted to Colchester, Ipswich and Norwich and, although most of the smaller settlements continued spinning cloth for the next three hundred years or so, their importance slowly dwindled. Bypassed by the Industrial Revolution, **south Suffolk** had, by the late nineteenth century, become a remote rural backwater, an impoverished area whose decline had one unforeseen consequence: with few exceptions, the towns and villages were never prosperous enough to modernize, and the architectural legacy of medieval and Tudor times survived. The best-preserved village is **Lavenham**. Nearby **Sudbury** is also attractive and boasts an excellent museum devoted to the work of Thomas Gainsborough, another talented English artist who spent much of his time painting the local landscape.

Seeing the region by **public transport** is problematic – distances are small (Dedham Vale is only about ten miles long), but **buses** between the villages are infrequent and you'll find it difficult to get away from the towns. Several **rail** lines cross south Suffolk, the most useful being the London Liverpool Street–Colchester–Sudbury route.

East Bergholt and Flatford Mill

"I associate my careless boyhood to all that lies on the banks of the Stour", wrote **John Constable**, who was born the son of a miller in **EAST BERGHOLT**, nine miles northeast of Colchester in 1776. The house in which he was born has long since disappeared, so it has been left to **Flatford Mill**, a mile or so to the south, to take up the painter's cause. The mill was owned by his father and was where Constable painted his most famous canvas, *The Hay Wain* (now in London's National Gallery, see p.94), which created a sensation when it was exhibited in 1824. To the chagrin of many of his contemporaries, Constable turned away from the landscape-painting conventions of the day, rendering his scenery with a realistic directness that harked back to the Dutch landscape painters of the seventeenth century. The mill itself – not the one he painted, but a Victorian replacement – is not open to the public, but the sixteenth-century thatched **Bridge Cottage** (March & April Wed–Sun 11am–5pm; May–Sept daily 10am–5.30pm; Oct daily 11am–4pm; Nov & Dec Wed–Sun 11am–3.30pm; Jan & Feb Sat & Sun 11am–3.30pm; free, except for parking; NT), which overlooks the scene, has been painstakingly restored and stuffed full of Constabilia. Unfortunately, none of the artist's paintings is displayed here, but there's a pleasant riverside tearoom to take in the view. Beyond stands **Willy Lott's Cottage** (also closed to the public), which does actually feature in *The Hay Wain*. In summer, the National Trust organizes **guided walks** around the sites of Constable's paintings (£2.50; call ⓣ01206/298 260 for details), but there are many other pleasant walks to be had along this deeply rural bend in the Stour. There's a **B&B** here too, *Flatford Granary* (ⓣ01206/298 111, ⓦwww.granaryflatford.co.uk; ③), in the annexe to the old granary which was once owned by Constable's father. The en-suite rooms are cottage-style affairs with beamed ceilings.

Dedham

Constable went to school in **DEDHAM**, just upriver from Flatford Mill and one of the region's most attractive villages, with a string of ancient timber-framed houses lining its wide main street. The only sights as such are **St Mary's Church**, an early sixteenth-century structure that Constable painted on several occasions, and the **Sir Alfred Munnings Art Museum**, in Castle House (Easter–July & Sept Wed & Sun 2–5pm; Aug Wed, Thurs, Sat & Sun 2–5pm; £4; Ⓦwww.siralfredmunnings.co.uk), just south of the village on the road to Ardleigh. A locally born academician, Munnings (1875–1959) is barely remembered today, but in his time he was well known for his portraits of horses.

There's a twice-daily Network Colchester **bus** (Mon–Sat; Ⓣ01206/764 029) from Colchester to Dedham, though both services depart in the late afternoon; on Sundays, First buses (Ⓣ01206/366 911) run the same route every couple of hours. Dedham possesses a fantastic **pub**, *The Sun Inn*, on the High Street (Ⓣ01206/323 351; Ⓦwww.thesuninndedham.com; ⑤, weekends ⑦), an ancient place with panelled walls and plank floors, where they serve real ales and delicious British food – for example, shin of veal roasted in red wine vinegar and gremolata; main courses begin at about £9. They also have five immaculate en-suite **rooms** with gorgeous four-poster beds.

Stoke-by-Nayland

Heading northwest from Dedham, the B1029 dips beneath the A12 to reach the byroad to **Higham**, an unremarkable hamlet where you pick up the road to **STOKE-BY-NAYLAND**, four miles further west. This is the most picturesque of villages, where a knot of half-timbered, pastel-painted cottages snuggle up to one of Constable's favourite subjects, **St Mary's Church** (daily 9am–5pm; free), with its pretty brick and stone-trimmed tower. The village also has a pair of great old **pubs**, beginning with *The Angel* (Ⓣ01206/263 245, Ⓦwww.theangelinn.net; ④), where there's real ale, quality bar food and six, cosy, en-suite guest **rooms**. The food at *The Crown* (Ⓣ01206/262 001, Ⓦwww.eoinns.co.uk; ⑤) is even better – try the smoked haddock with horseradish mash; main courses cost in the region of £12–15. At time of writing, *The Crown* does not have accommodation, but this is about to change with the construction of eleven new rooms.

Sudbury

With a population of around 12,000, **SUDBURY** has doubled in size in the last thirty years, to become by far the most important town in this part of the Stour Valley. A handful of timber-framed houses harks back to its days of wool-trade prosperity, but its three Perpendicular churches were underwritten by another local industry, **silk weaving**, which survives on a small scale to this day. Sudbury's most famous export, however, is **Thomas Gainsborough** (1727–1788), the leading English portraitist of the eighteenth century, whose **statue**, with brush and palette, stands on Market Hill, the town's predominantly Victorian marketplace. A superb collection of the artist's work is on display a few yards away in the house where he was born – **Gainsborough's House**, at 46 Gainsborough St (Mon–Sat 10am–5pm; £4; Ⓦwww.gainsborough.org). Gainsborough left Sudbury when he was just 13, moving to London where he was apprenticed to an engraver, but it seems he was soon moonlighting and the earliest of his surviving portrait paintings – his *Boy and Girl*, a remarkably self-assured work dated to 1744 – is displayed here. In 1752, Gainsborough moved on to Ipswich, where he quickly established himself as a portrait painter, thanks to his wonderful "**conversation pieces**", so called because the sitters engage in polite chitchat – or genteel activity – with a landscape as the backdrop. Seven years in Ipswich was followed by a move upmarket to Bath, where he painted high-society figures. During his years in Bath, Gainsborough developed a fluid style that was flattering for his aristocratic subjects, who posed in becoming postures painted in soft, evanescent colours. Gainsborough never bothered with assistants, with one exception, his nephew **Gainsborough Dupont**, who has a room devoted to his work on the top floor.

Practicalities

Sudbury is just seven miles northwest of Stoke-by-Nayland along the A134. It's accessible by **train** from Colchester, 14 miles away (for some services, change at Marks Tey), and is the hub of **bus** services to and from neighbouring towns and villages including Colchester and Ipswich. Once you've seen Gainsborough's house, there's little reason to spend the night, but if you do decide to stay, the **tourist office** in the town hall at the east end of Market Hill (April–Sept Mon–Fri 9am–5pm & Sat 10am–4.45pm; Oct–March Mon–Fri 9am–5pm & Sat 10am–2.45pm; ⓣ01787/881 320, ⓦwww.visit-suffolk.org.uk) can provide **accommodation** details.

Lavenham

LAVENHAM, some eight miles northeast of Sudbury off the A134, was once a centre of the region's wool trade and is now one of the most visited villages in Suffolk. The whole place has changed little since the demise of the wool industry, owing in part to a zealous local preservation society, which has carefully maintained the village's antique appearance.

The village is at its most beguiling in the triangular **Market Place**, an airy spot flanked by pastel-painted, medieval dwellings whose beams have been bent into all sorts of wonky angles by the passing of the years. It's here you'll find Lavenham's most celebrated building, the pale-white, timber-framed **Guildhall of Corpus Christi** (March–Oct Tues–Sun 11am–5pm; early to late Nov Sat & Sun 11am–4pm; £3.75; NT), erected in the sixteenth century as the headquarters of one of Lavenham's four guilds. In the much-altered interior (used successively as a prison and workhouse), there are exhibitions on timber-framed buildings and the wool industry, though most visitors head straight for the walled garden and the teashop. The other building worthy of special notice is the Perpendicular **church of St Peter and St Paul** (daily: May–Sept 8.30am–5.30pm; Oct–April 8.30am–3.30pm; free), sited a short walk southwest of the centre, at the top of Church Street. Local merchants endowed the church with a nave of majestic proportions and a mighty flint tower, at 141ft the highest for miles around, partly to celebrate the Tudor victory at the Battle of Bosworth in 1485, but mainly to vaunt their wealth.

Practicalities

There's an hourly **bus service which** links Colchester, Bury St Edmunds, Lavenham and Sudbury (Mon–Sat). Lavenham **tourist office** is plumb in the centre, just south off the Market Place on Lady Street (April–Oct daily 10am–5pm; Nov–March Sat & Sun 11am–3pm; ⓣ01787/248 207, ⓦwww.visit-suffolk.org.uk). They can help with **accommodation** – rooms get mighty

▲ Lavenham

tight in the high season – and sell a detailed, street-by-street walking guide. To cater for its many visitors, Lavenham has a veritable battery of **B&Bs** and one of the most luxurious is *Lavenham Priory*, in a rambling old house – and former priory – on Water Street (ⓣ01787/247 404, ⓦwww.lavenhampriory.co.uk; ❻). There are half a dozen en-suite guest rooms here and each is kitted out in a fancy period style. Less expensive B&Bs include the dinky *Angel Gallery*, 17 Market Place (ⓣ01787/248 417, ⓦwww.lavenham.co.uk/angelgallery; ❺), with three straightforward guest rooms situated above an art shop; and *The Guinea House*, 16 Bolton St (no cards; ⓣ01787/249 046, ⓦwww.guineahouse.co.uk; ❺), with two cosy, low-beamed guest rooms; there are great breakfasts here too – don't stint on the sausages. Amongst several **hotels**, the ancient *Angel Hotel*, on the Market Place (ⓣ01787/247 388, ⓦwww.theangelhotel-lavenham.co.uk; ❺), has eight, en-suite guest rooms.

The *Angel Hotel* serves excellent **food** in its bar and in its restaurant – tasty, unpretentious cuisine with dishes such as steak and ale pie, a snip at just £8. Alternatively, the chic and smart *Great House* restaurant, on Market Place (ⓣ01787/247 431; closed Sun eve & Mon), specializes in classic French cuisine, with main courses around £17. It's received rave reviews all over the place – so book ahead.

Ipswich

IPSWICH, situated at the head of the Orwell estuary some twenty miles east of Lavenham, was a rich trading port in the Middle Ages, but its appearance today is mainly the result of a revival of fortunes in the Victorian era – give or take some clumsy postwar development. The two surviving reminders of old Ipswich – **Christchurch Mansion** and the splendid **Ancient House** – plus the recently renovated **quayside** are all reason enough to spend at least an afternoon here.

The Town

Cornhill, the ancient Saxon marketplace, is still the town's focal point, an agreeable urban space flanked by a bevy of imposing Victorian edifices – the Italianate town hall, the old Neoclassical Post Office and the pseudo-Jacobean Lloyds building. From here, it's just a couple of minutes' walk south to Ipswich's most famous building, the **Ancient House**, on Buttermarket, just north of St Stephen's Lane, whose exterior was decorated around 1670 in extravagant style, a riot of pargeting and stucco work that together make it one of the finest examples of Restoration artistry in the country.

From the Ancient House, it's a short hop north to the gates of **Christchurch Mansion** (daily 10am–5pm; free), a handsome, if much-restored Tudor building, sporting seventeenth-century Dutch-style gables and set in 65 acres of parkland – an area larger than the town centre itself. The mansion's labyrinthine interior is worth exploring, with period furnishings and a good assortment of paintings by Constable and Gainsborough, as well as more contemporary art exhibitions.

On the other side of the town centre, about half a mile southeast of Cornhill, the **Wet Dock** was the largest dock in Europe when it opened in 1845. Today, after an imaginative refurbishment, it's flanked by apartments and offices, pubs, hotels and restaurants, many converted from the old marine warehouses. Walking round the Wet Dock is a pleasant way to pass an hour or so – look out, in particular, for the proud Neoclassical **Customs House** on Neptune Quay. Once weekly in July and August, **boat trips** run from Orwell Quay beside the Wet Dock down the River Orwell to Pin Mill, a rural picnic spot on the west bank of the river (Orwell River Cruises; ⓣ01473/836 680, ⓦwww.orwellrivercruises.com), the trips last two and a half hours and cost £9.

Practicalities

Ipswich **train station** is on the south bank of the river, about ten minutes' walk from Cornhill along Princes Street. The **bus station** is more central, located a short walk from Cornhill - and near the **tourist office**, in the converted St Stephen's church, off St Stephen's Lane (Mon–Sat 9am–5pm; ⓣ01473/258 070, ⓦwww.visit-suffolk.org.uk).

Ipswich has one really good **hotel**, the *Salthouse Harbour*, in a fantastically converted old warehouse, down by the Wet Dock at 1 Neptune Quay (ⓣ01473/226 789, ⓦwww.salthouseharbour.com; ⑦). It has great views over the docks from its upper floors and the rooms are decorated in modern, minimalist style. The hotel **brasserie** is good too, with a varied menu – from chicken liver and duck parfait to baked loin of rabbit with asparagus: main courses average around £12.

The Suffolk coast

The **Suffolk coast** feels detached from the rest of the county: the road and rail lines from Ipswich to the seaport of Lowestoft funnel traffic a few miles inland for most of the way, and patches of marsh and woodland make the separation still more complete. The coast has long been plagued by erosion and this has contributed to the virtual extinction of the local fishing industry, and, in the case of **Dunwich**, almost destroyed the whole town. What is left, however, is undoubtedly one of the most unspoilt shorelines in the country – if, that is, you set aside the Sizewell nuclear power station. Highlights include the sleepy isolation of minuscule **Orford** and several genteel resorts, most notably **Southwold**, which has evaded the lurid fate of so many English seaside towns. There are scores of delightful **walks** hereabouts too, easy routes along the coast that are best followed with either the appropriate OS *Explorer Map* or the simplified *Footpath Maps* available at most tourist offices. The Suffolk coast is also host to East Anglia's most compelling cultural gathering, the three-week-long **Aldeburgh Festival**, which takes place each and every June.

Local **buses** shunt up and down the coast linking Ipswich and Norwich with all of Suffolk's coastal towns and villages, but services are infrequent – just two or three times daily and nothing on Sundays – and time-consuming as you often have to change buses at least once: for example, it takes three hours and two changes to get from Orford to Southwold.

Orford and Orford Ness

Some twenty miles from Ipswich, on the far side of Tunstall Forest, two medieval buildings dominate the tiny, eminently appealing village of **ORFORD**. The more impressive is the twelfth-century **Castle** (April–Sept daily 10am–6pm; Oct–March Thurs–Mon 10am–4pm; £4.70; EH), built on high ground by Henry II, and under siege within months of its completion from Henry's rebellious sons. Most of the castle disappeared centuries ago, but the lofty keep remains, its striking stature hinting at the scale of the original fortifications. Orford's other medieval edifice is **St Bartholomew's church**, where Benjamin Britten premiered his most successful children's work, *Noye's Fludde*, as part of the 1958 Aldeburgh Festival (see box, p.376).

From the top of the castle keep, there's a great view across **Orford Ness National Nature Reserve**, a six-mile-long shingle spit that has all but blocked Orford from the sea since Tudor times. The National Trust offers **boat trips** (early April to June & Oct Sat only; July–Sept Tues–Sat; outward boats between 10am–2pm, last ferry back 5pm; £6.50, NT members £3.70; ⓣ01394/450 057) across to the Ness from Orford Quay, four hundred yards down the road from the church, and a five-mile hiking trail threads its way along the spit. There are also plenty of **walks** to be had around Orford itself. One of the best is the five-mile hike north along the river wall that guards the west bank of the River Alde, returning via Ferry Road, a narrow country lane.

Orford's gentle and unhurried air is best experienced by staying overnight at the stylish *Crown & Castle Hotel*, in a modest-looking building on the main square, Market Hill (ⓣ01394/450 205, ⓦwww.crownandcastlehotel.co.uk; ⑥). Replete with pastel-painted guest rooms and comfortable beds, there's a superb **restaurant**; main courses – grilled plaice with toasted almonds and grapes, for example – average around £13 and reservations are advised. The village is also home to the *Butley Orford Oysterage* (ⓣ01394/450 277; ⓦwww.butleyorfordoysterage.co.uk), where they catch and smoke their own fish and shellfish. The end results can be bought at their shop and sampled at their down-to-earth **café/restaurant** (daily noon–2pm, plus April–May & mid-Sept to Oct Wed–Sat 6.30–9pm; June to mid-Sept daily 6.30–9pm; Nov–March Fri & Sat 6.30–9pm), which is especially famous for its fresh oysters. For a **pint**, it's the *Crown & Castle* again or the *Jolly Sailor Inn*, down near the quay.

Aldeburgh

Well-heeled **ALDEBURGH**, just along the coast from Orford, is best known for its annual arts festival, the brainchild of composer **Benjamin Britten**

(1913–76), who is buried in the village churchyard alongside the tenor Peter Pears, his lover and musical collaborator. They lived by the seafront in Crag House on Crabbe Street – named after the poet, George Crabbe, who provided Britten with his greatest inspiration (see box, p.376). Outside of June, when the festival takes place, Aldeburgh is the quietest of places, with just a small fishing fleet selling its daily catch from wooden shacks along the pebbled shore, but there was an almighty rumpus – Barbours at dawn – when Maggi Hambling's thirteen-foot-high *Scallop* sculpture appeared on the beach in 2003. Made of steel, Hambling described her *Scallop* as a conversation with the sea and a suitable memorial to Britten; others compared it to a mantelpiece ornament gone wrong.

Aldeburgh's wide High Street and its narrow side streets run close to the beach, but this was not always the case – hence their garbled appearance. The sea swallowed most of what was once an extensive medieval town long ago and today Aldeburgh's oldest remaining building, the sixteenth-century, red-brick, flint and timber **Moot Hall**, which began its days in the centre of town, now finds itself on the seashore. Several **footpaths** radiate out from Aldeburgh, with the most obvious trail leading north along the coast to Thorpeness, and others leading southwest to the winding estuary of the **River Alde**, an area rich in wildfowl.

Practicalities

Aldeburgh's festival box office (see box, p.376) shares its High Street premises with the village **tourist office** (April–Sept daily 9am–5.30pm; Oct–March Mon–Sat 9am–5pm; ⓣ01728/453 637, ⓦwww.suffolkcoastal.gov.uk/tourism). They have local bus timetables and can book **accommodation**, though during the festival you'll need to reserve well in advance. The town boasts several **hotels**, including the family-owned *Wentworth* (ⓣ01728/452 312, ⓦwww.wentworth-aldeburgh.com; ⑦), which occupies a good-looking Edwardian mansion just along the seafront from the Moot Hall. The hotel has thirty-five well-appointed guest rooms. Amongst local **B&Bs**, the pick is *Ocean House*, 25 Crag Path (ⓣ01728/452 094, ⓦwww.oceanhousealdeburgh.co.uk; ⑤), in an immaculately maintained Victorian dwelling right on the seafront in the centre of town; there are just two guest rooms here – so advance booking is essential – and both have period furnishings. Delicious breakfasts too, full English with home-made bread. Finally, there's a **YHA hostel** in the old village school on Heath Walk in the hamlet of **Blaxhall** (ⓣ0870/770 5702, ⓔblaxhall@yha.org.uk; dorm beds £14, doubles ①). The hostel has forty beds in two- to six-bedded rooms, a self-catering kitchen, a café and a laundry. Blaxhall is a couple of miles southwest of the concert facilities at Snape Maltings (see box, p.376).

Pride of the gastronomic crop is *The Lighthouse*, 77 High St (ⓣ01728/453 377), a relaxed and informal **restaurant** in cosy premises that serves breakfast, lunch and dinner daily. The menu features both British and Mediterranean-style dishes, from cod with a cheese sauce to venison tagine with couscous; a set two-course lunch costs £12.50, a tad more in the evening. Aldeburgh also has two outstanding **fish and chip shops** – the original *Fish & Chip Shop* at 226 High St, and its sister, *The Golden Galleon*, just along the street at no. 137.

Dunwich

One-time seat of the kings of East Anglia, a bishopric and formerly the largest port on the Suffolk coast, the ancient city of **DUNWICH**, about twelve miles up the coast from Aldeburgh, reached its peak of prosperity in the twelfth century. Over the last millennium, however, something like a mile of land has been lost to the sea, a process that continues at the rate of about

Benjamin Britten and the Aldeburgh Festival

Born in Lowestoft in 1913, **Benjamin Britten** was closely associated with Suffolk for most of his life. The main break was during World War II when, as a conscientious objector, Britten exiled himself to the USA. Ironically enough, it was here that Britten first read the work of the nineteenth-century Suffolk poet, George Crabbe, whose **The Borough**, a grisly portrait of the life of the fishermen of Aldeburgh, was the basis of the libretto of Britten's best-known opera, **Peter Grimes**. The latter premiered in London in 1945 to great acclaim.

In 1947 Britten founded the English Opera Group and the following year launched the **Aldeburgh Festival** as a showpiece for his own works and those of his contemporaries. He lived in the village for the next ten years and it was during this period that he completed much of his best work as a conductor and pianist. For the rest of his life he composed many works specifically for the festival, including his masterpiece for children, **Noye's Fludde** and the last of his fifteen operas, **Death in Venice**.

By the mid-1960s, the festival had outgrown the parish churches in which it began, and moved into a collection of disused malthouses, five miles west of Aldeburgh on the River Alde, just south of the small village of **Snape**. **Snape Maltings** (Ⓦwww.snapemaltings.co.uk) were subsequently converted into one of the finest concert venues in the country and, in addition to the concert hall, there's now a recording studio, a music school, various craft shops and galleries, a tearoom, and a pub, the *Plough & Sail*.

The Aldeburgh Festival takes place every June for two and a half weeks. Core performances are still held at the Maltings, but a string of other local venues are pressed into service as well. Throughout the rest of the year, the Maltings hosts a wide-ranging programme of musical and theatrical events with showcase events including the three-day Britten Festival in October. For more information, contact **Aldeburgh Music** (Ⓣ01728/687 110, Ⓦwww.aldeburgh.co.uk), which operates two box offices, one at Snape Maltings, the other on Aldeburgh High Street. **Tickets** for the Aldeburgh Festival itself usually go on sale to the public towards the end of March, and sell out fast for the big-name recitals.

a yard a year. As a result, the whole of the medieval city now lies underwater, including all twelve churches, the last of which toppled over the cliffs in 1919. All that survives today are fragments of the Greyfriars monastery, which originally lay to the west of the city and now dangles at the sea's edge. For a potted history of the lost city, head for the **museum** (April–Sept daily 11.30am–4.30pm; Oct daily noon–4pm; free) in what's left of Dunwich – little more than one small street of terraced houses built by the local landowner in the nineteenth century.

A sprawling coastline **car park** gives ready access to this part of the seashore. From the car park, it's a short stroll to the village and the remains of Greyfriars, beyond which you can hike along the coast to **Dunwich Heath**, where the coastguard cottages house a National Trust shop and tearoom (times vary, call Ⓣ01728/648 501 for details). The heath is itself next to the **Minsmere RSPB Nature Reserve** (daily 9am–9pm or dusk; £5), home to a number of tern, avocet, marsh harrier and the very rare bittern. In the autumn, it's a gathering place for masses of wading birds and waterfowl. You can rent binoculars from the RSPB **visitor centre** (daily 9am–4pm or 5pm; Ⓣ01728/648 281) and strike out on the trails to the birdwatching hides.

Dunwich's one remaining **pub**, the *Ship Inn* (Ⓣ01728/648 219; Ⓦwww.shipinndunwich.co.uk), with its low wooden beams and open fire, is a good place for a drink; the inn also has a few rooms (❺).

Southwold

Perched on robust cliffs just to the north of the River Blyth, **SOUTHWOLD** gained what Dunwich lost, and by the sixteenth century it had overtaken all its local rivals to become a busy fishing port. In its turn, Southwold lost most of its fishery to Lowestoft and today, although a small fleet still brings in herring, sprats and cod, the town is primarily a seaside resort, a genteel and eminently appealing little place with none of the crassness of many of its competitors. There are fine old buildings, a long sandy beach, open heathland, a dinky harbour and even a little industry – in the shape of the Adnams brewery – but no burger bars and certainly no amusement arcades. This gentility was not to the liking of **George Orwell**, who lived for a time at his parents' house at 36 High St (a plaque marks the spot). Orwell heartily disliked the town's airs and graces, and has left no trace of his time here – apart from disguised slights in a couple of early novels.

The Town

Southwold's breezy **High Street** is framed by attractive, mainly Georgian buildings, which culminate in the pocket-sized Market Place. From here, it's a brief stroll along East Street to the curious **Sailors' Reading Room** (daily: April–Sept 9am–5pm; Oct–March 9am–3.30pm; free), decked out with model ships and nautical texts, and the bluff above the **beach**, where row upon row of candy-coloured huts face the sea. Queen Street begins at the Market Place too, quickly leading to **South Green**, the prettiest of several greens dotted across town. In 1659, a calamitous fire razed much of Southwold and when the town was rebuilt the greens were left to act as firebreaks. Beyond South Green, both Ferry Road and the ferry footpath lead down to the **harbour**, at the mouth of the River Blyth, an idyllic spot, where fishing smacks rest against old wooden jetties and nets are spread out along the banks to dry. A harbourside footpath leads to a tiny, **passenger ferry** (Easter–May Sat & Sun 10am–12.30pm & 2–4.30pm; June–Aug daily 10am–12.30pm & 2–4.30pm; 40p), which crosses the river to Walberswick. Turn right after the *Harbour Inn* and right again to walk back into town across **Southwold Common**. The whole circular walk takes about thirty minutes.

Back on Market Place, it's a couple of hundred yards north along Church Street to East Green, with **Adnams Brewery** on one side and the stumpy lighthouse on another. Close by is Southwold's architectural pride and joy, the **church of St Edmund** (daily: June–Aug 9am–6pm; Sept–May 9am–4pm; free), a handsome fifteenth-century structure whose solid symmetries are balanced by its long and elegantly carved windows. Inside, the slender, beautifully proportioned nave is distinguished by its panelled roof, embellished with praying angels, and its intricate rood screen.

Practicalities

Apart from on Sunday, Southwold is easy to reach by **bus**, with services from the likes of Norwich and Aldeburgh. Buses pull into the Market Place, yards from the **tourist office**, at 69 High St (April–Oct Mon–Fri 10am–5pm, Sat 10am–5.30pm, Sun 11am–4pm; Nov–March Mon–Fri 10.30am–3pm, Sat 10am–4.30pm; ⓣ01502/724 729, ⓦwww.visit-southwold.co.uk). The town has two well-known **hotels** beside the Market Place, both owned and run by Adnams. The smarter of the two is *The Swan* (ⓣ01502/722 186, ⓦwww.adnams.co.uk; ⑦), which occupies a splendid Georgian building with lovely period rooms in both the main house and in the garden annexe behind, though some are a little on the small side. *The Crown*, just along the High Street

(Ⓣ01502/722 275, Ⓦwww.adnams.co.uk; ⑦), costs slightly less and has fourteen spick-and-span bedrooms, all en suite, decorated in contemporary style. Alternatively, a string of **guesthouses** line up along the seafront, including the attractive *Home @ 21*, in a well-kept Victorian house at 21 North Parade (Ⓣ01502/722 573, Ⓦwww.northparade.southwold.info; ⑤).

Southwold has two outstanding **places to eat**. *The Crown*'s front bar serves delicious informal meals, with daily fish and meat specials and a great wine list. Expect to pay £14 or so for a main course – tope fillet baked in saffron yogurt for example; you'll have to make a booking if you want to eat in the adjacent restaurant, which is pricier, slightly more adventurous and just as terrific. The main gastronomic competitor is *Sutherland House*, in antique premises at 56 High St (Ⓣ01502/724 544; closed Mon); main courses start at £10. For a **drink**, sample Adnams' brews in *The Crown*'s wood-panelled back-bar or stroll along to the *Red Lion* on South Green.

Norwich

One of the five largest cities in Norman England, **NORWICH** once served a vast hinterland of East Anglian **cloth producers**, whose work was brought here by river and then exported elsewhere. Its isolated position beyond the Fens meant that it enjoyed closer links with the Low Countries than with the rest of England. By 1700, Norwich was the second richest city in the country after London.

With the onset of the Industrial Revolution, however, Norwich lost ground to the northern manufacturing towns – the city's famous mustard company, Colman's, is one of its few industrial success stories – and this, together with its continuing geographical isolation, has helped preserve much of the ancient street plan and many of the city's older buildings. Pride of place goes to the beautiful **cathedral** and the sterling **castle**, but the city's hallmark is its medieval **churches**, thirty or so squat flintstone structures with sturdy towers and sinuous stone tracery round the windows. Many are no longer in regular use and are now in the care of the **Norwich Historic Churches Trust** (Ⓦwww.norwichchurches.co.uk), whose excellent website describes each church in precise detail and gives opening times.

Norwich's relative isolation has also meant that the population has never swelled to any great extent and today, with just 130,000 inhabitants, it remains an easy and enjoyable city to negotiate. Yet Norwich is no provincial backwater. In the 1960s, the foundation of the **University of East Anglia** (UEA) made it more **cosmopolitan** and bolstered its arts scene, while in the 1980s it attracted new high-tech companies, who created something of a mini-boom, making the city one of England's wealthiest. As East Anglia's unofficial capital, Norwich also lies at the hub of the region's **transport** network, serving as a useful base for visiting the Broads and as a springboard for the north Norfolk coast.

Arrival and information

Norwich's grandiose **train station** is on the east bank of the River Wensum, ten minutes' walk from the city centre along Prince of Wales Road. Long-distance **buses** terminate at the Surrey Street Station, also little more than ten minutes' walk from the town centre, but this time to the south off Surrey Street (though some stop in the centre on Castle Meadow too). The **tourist office** is in the glassy Forum building overlooking the Market Place (April–Oct

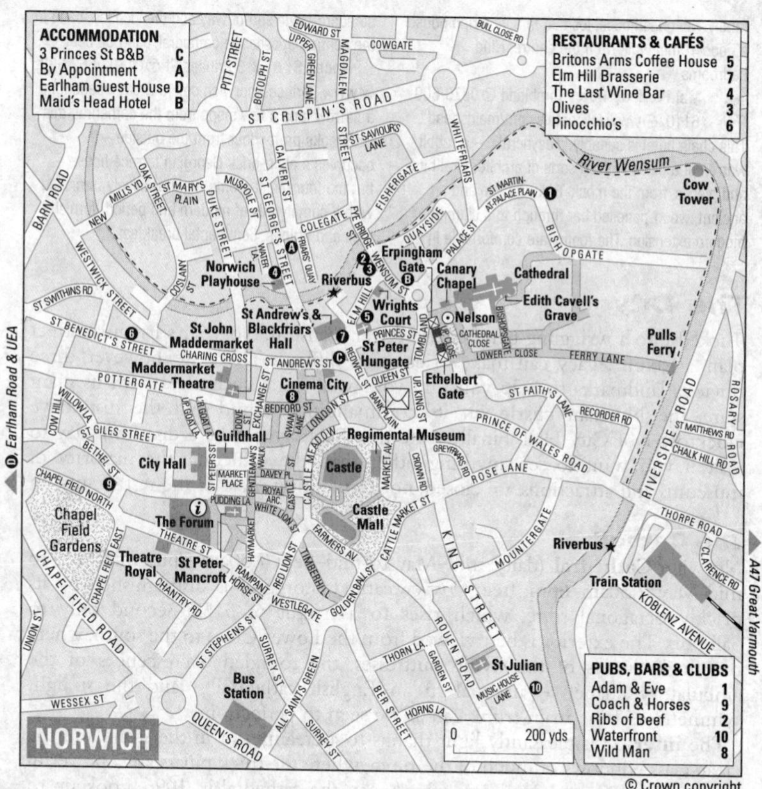

© Crown copyright

Mon–Sat 9.30am–6pm & Sun 10.30am–4.30pm; Nov–March Mon–Sat 9.30am–5.30pm; ⓣ01603/727 927, ⓦwww.visitnorwich.co.uk).

The best way to see the city is on **foot**, or by **riverbus** (April–Sept 4 daily; £4 return). The latter runs from the Thorpe Road Quay, opposite the train station, to the Elm Hill Quay near the cathedral, providing an inexpensive means of cruising Norwich's central waterway. The journey takes about fifteen minutes and the boats are operated by City Boats (ⓣ01603/701 701, ⓦwww.cityboats.co.uk), who also offer longer cruises out from Norwich and into the Norfolk Broads.

Accommodation

Norwich has **accommodation** to suit all budgets, though there's precious little in the town centre. Most **B&Bs** and **guesthouses** are strung along **Earlham Road**, a tedious, mostly Victorian street running west towards the university, UEA.

By Appointment 25 St George's St ⓣ01603/630 730, ⓦwww.byappointmnentnorwich.co.uk. Norwich's most unusual hotel – really a restaurant with five en-suite rooms up above; the bedrooms have beamed ceilings and heavy-drape curtains and the whole caboodle is jam-packed with antiques. ❻

Earlham Guesthouse 147 Earlham Rd ⓣ01603/454 169, ⓦwww.earlham-guesthouse.co.uk. Homely, spick-and-span rooms at this family-run guesthouse, located in a Victorian house a good 10min walk from the centre. Nine bedrooms. ③

Maid's Head Hotel Tombland ⓣ0870/609 6110, ⓦwww.foliohotels.com/maidshead. This chain hotel is suitably idiosyncratic – a rabbit warren of a place with all sorts of architectural bits and pieces, from the mock-Tudor facade and an ancient, wood-panelled bar through to a clumpy modern extension. The rooms are comfortable in a standard-issue sort of way and the location, bang in the centre opposite the cathedral, can't be beat. ⑤

3 Princes St B&B 3 Princes St ⓣ01603/662 693, ⓦwww.3princes-norwich.co.uk. Great location, up a narrow lane a few steps from the cathedral, this B&B looks pretty dour from the outside – it occupies a plain-brick Georgian terrace house – but the four guest rooms are attractively furnished with a comely mix of modern and period furnishings and fittings. Continental breakfast. ⑤

The City

Tucked into a wriggling bend of the River Wensum, Norwich's irregular street plan, a Saxon legacy, can make orientation difficult. There are, however, three obvious landmarks to help you find your way – the **cathedral** with its giant spire, the Norman **castle** on its commanding mound and the distinctive clocktower of City Hall. Finally, note that **Sunday** can be a disastrous day to visit if you want to see anything other than the cathedral: the majority of museums and attractions are closed, not to mention most of the restaurants.

The Cathedral

Norwich **Cathedral** (daily: mid–May to mid–Sept 7.30am–7pm; mid-Sept to mid-May 7.30am–6pm; free; ⓦwww.cathedral.org.uk) is distinguished by its prickly octagonal spire, which rises to a height of 315ft, second only to Salisbury. The exterior is best viewed from the Lower Close to the south, where the thick curves of the flying buttresses, the rounded excrescences of the ambulatory chapels – unusual in an English cathedral – and the straight symmetries of the main trunk can all be seen to perfection.

The **interior** is pleasantly light thanks to a creamy tint in the stone and the clear-glass windows of much of the **nave**, where the thick pillars are a powerful legacy of the Norman builders who began the cathedral in 1096. Look up to admire the nave's fan vaulting, delicate and geometrically precise carving adorned by several hundred roof **bosses** recounting – from east to west – the story of the Old and New Testaments from the Creation to the Last Judgement. Pushing on down the south (right) side of the ambulatory, you soon reach **St Luke's Chapel** where the cathedral's finest work of art, the *Despenser Reredos*, is a superb painted panel commissioned to celebrate the crushing of the Peasants' Revolt of 1381. Accessible from the south aisle of the nave are the cathedral's unique **cloisters**. Built between 1297 and 1450, and the only two-storey cloisters left standing in England, they contain a remarkable set of sculpted **bosses**, similar to the ones in the main nave, but here they are close enough to be scrutinized without binoculars. The carving is fabulously intricate and the dominant theme is the **Apocalypse**, but look out also for the bosses depicting green men, originally pagan fertility symbols.

The cathedral precincts

Outside, in front of the main entrance, stands the medieval **Canary Chapel**. This is the original building of Norwich School, whose blue-blazered pupils are often visible during term time – the rambling school buildings are adjacent. A statue of the school's most famous boy, **Horatio Nelson**, faces the chapel, standing on the green of the **Upper Close**, which is guarded by two ornate and imposing medieval gates, **Erpingham** and, a few yards to the south, **Ethelbert**. Beside the Erpingham gate is a memorial to **Edith Cavell**, a local woman who was a nurse in occupied Brussels during World War I. She was shot by the Germans in 1915 for helping allied prisoners to escape, a fate that made her an instant folk hero; her grave is outside the cathedral ambulatory. Both gates lead onto the old Saxon marketplace, **Tombland**, a wide and busy thoroughfare whose name derives from the Saxon word for an open space.

From Tombland to Elm Hill and St Andrew's Hall

At the north end of Tombland, fork left into Wensum Street and cobbled **Elm Hill**, more a gentle slope than a hill, soon appears on the left. While you're here take a look at **Wright's Court**, down a passageway at no. 43, one of the few remaining enclosed courtyards which were once a feature of the city.

Turn right at the top of Elm Hill and it's just a few yards to **St Andrew's Hall** and **Blackfriars Hall**, two adjoining buildings that were originally the nave and chancel, respectively, of a Dominican monastery church. Imaginatively recycled, the two halls are now used for a variety of public events, including concerts, weddings and antique fairs; the crypt of the former now serves as a **café** (Mon–Sat 10am–4.30pm).

The Market Place

From **Blackfriars Hall**, it's a short walk through to the city's **Market Place**, site of one of the country's largest open-air markets (closed Sun), with stalls selling everything from bargain-basement clothes to local mussels and whelks. Four very different but equally distinctive buildings oversee the market's stripy awnings, the oldest of them being the fifteenth-century **Guildhall**, a capacious flint and stone structure begun in 1407. Opposite, commanding the heights of the marketplace, are the austere **City Hall**, a lumbering brick pile with a landmark clocktower that was built in the 1930s in a Scandinavian style and **The Forum**, a large and flashy, glassy structure completed in 2001. The latter is home to the city's main library and the tourist office (see p.378).

On the south side of Market Place is the finest of the four buildings, **St Peter Mancroft** (Mon–Sat 10am–3.30pm; free), whose long and graceful nave leads to a mighty stone tower, an intricately carved affair surmounted by a spiky little spire. The church once delighted John Wesley, who declared "I scarcely ever remember to have seen a more beautiful parish church", a fair description of what remains an exquisite example of the Perpendicular style with the slender columns of the nave reaching up towards the delicate groining of the roof.

Back outside and just below the church is **Gentlemen's Walk**, the town's main promenade, which runs along the bottom of the marketplace and abuts the **Royal Arcade**, an Art Nouveau extravagance from 1899. The arcade has been beautifully restored to reveal the swirling tiling, ironwork and stained glass.

The Castle

Perched high on a grassy mound in the centre of town – and with a modern shopping mall drilled into its side – the stern walls of **Norwich Castle** date from the twelfth century. Formerly a reminder of Norman power and then a prison, the castle holds the **Castle Museum and Art Gallery** (Mon–Fri 10am–4.30pm, Sat 10am–5pm & Sun 1–5pm; £6.50 all zones, £4.50 per zone), which is divided into three zones. The **Art and Exhibitions** zone is the pick, scoring well with its temporary displays and boasting an outstanding selection of work by the **Norwich School**. Founded in 1803, and in existence for just thirty years, this school of landscape painters produced – for the most part – richly coloured, formally composed land- and seascapes in oil and watercolour, paintings whose realism harked back to the Dutch landscape painters of the seventeenth century. The leading figures were **John Crome** (1768–1821) – aka "Old Crome" – and **John Sell Cotman** (1782–1842), who is generally acknowledged as one of England's finest watercolourists. Both have a gallery to themselves and, helpfully, there's also a gallery given over to those Dutch painters who influenced them.

The **castle keep** itself is no more than a shell, its gloomy walls towering above a scattering of local archeological finds and some gory examples of traditional forms of punishment. More unusual is a bloated model **dragon**, known as Snap, which was paraded round town on the annual guilds' day procession – a folkloric hand-me-down from the dragon St George had so much trouble finishing off. To see more of the keep, join one of the regular **guided tours** that explore the battlements and the dungeons.

Finally, a long, dark (and one-way) tunnel leads down from the Castle Museum to the **Royal Norfolk Regimental Museum** (Tues–Fri 10am–4.30pm, Sat 10am–5pm; £3.10, but included in the all-zone castle ticket), which tracks through the history of the regiment with remarkable candour – including an even-handed account of the regiment's police-keeping role in Northern Ireland. The exit leaves you below the castle on Market Avenue.

The University

The **University of East Anglia** (UEA) occupies a sprawling campus on the western outskirts of the city beside the B1108. Its buildings are resolutely modern, an assortment of concrete-and-glass blocks of varying designs, some quite ordinary, others like the prize-winning "ziggurat" halls of residence, designed by Denys Lasdun, eminently memorable. The main reason to visit is the high-tech **Sainsbury Centre for Visual Arts** (Tues–Sun 10am–5pm, Wed till 8pm; free; Ⓦwww.scva.org.uk), built by Norman Foster in the 1970s. The interior houses one of the most varied collections of sculpture and painting in the country; Degas, Seurat, Picasso, Giacometti, Bacon and Henry

▲ Norwich Castle

Moore rub shoulders with Mayan and Egyptian antiquities. The centre also runs a first-rate programme of temporary exhibitions (for which admission may be charged).

Buses #25, #26 and #27 run frequently to UEA from Castle Meadow.

Eating and drinking

There are plenty of good-value **cafés and restaurants** in the city centre. Decent **pubs**, though, are harder to find, partly because previously serviceable places have been turned into ersatz "traditional" drinking dens for students.

Cafés and restaurants

Britons Arms Coffee House 9 Elm Hill. Home-made quiches, tarts, cakes and scones plus pies and salads in quaint Elm Hill premises. Mon–Sat 9.30am–5pm, but closed Mon in winter.

Elm Hill Brasserie 2 Elm Hill ⓣ01603/624 847. New kid on the gastronomic block, this intimate, one-room bistro-brasserie, housed in an old shop, offers a creative menu with a French twist. Daily specials, written on a blackboard, are well considered and reasonably priced at around £12 per main course. Closed Sun & Mon.

The Last Wine Bar 70 St George's St ⓣ01603/626 626. Imaginatively converted old shoe factory, holding a relaxed and very amenable wine bar in one section and an excellent restaurant in the other serving delicioius dishes like braised lamb shank with carrots and parsnips in a rosemary jus costing in the region of £13. Mon–Sat lunch and dinner. A couple of minutes' walk north of the river.

Olives 40 Elm Hill. In antique, half-timbered premises, this agreeable café serves up a good line in salads and light meals. Mon–Fri 8am–4.30pm & Sat 9am–4.30pm.

Pinocchio's 11 St Benedict's St ⓣ01603/613 318. Relaxed Italian restaurant in a bright and lively conversion of what was once a general store. The menu covers all the classics and then some, and prices are very reasonable with pizzas from as little as £8. Closed Sun.

Pubs, bars and clubs

Adam & Eve Bishopgate. There's been a pub on this site for seven hundred years and it's still a top spot for the discerning drinker with a changing range of real ales and an eclectic wine list supplied by Adnams.

Coach & Horses Bethel St. Pleasant city-centre pub with lived-in furnishings and fittings. Good for a quiet drink.

Ribs of Beef 24 Wensum St. Boisterous riverside drinking haunt popular with students and townies alike.

Waterfront 139–41 King St ⓣ01603/508 050, ⓦwww.waterfrontnorwich.com. Norwich's principal club and alternative music venue, with gigs and DJs most nights. Sponsored by UEA's Student Union.

Wild Man 29 Bedford St. Long-established, city-centre watering hole – a popular student hang-out.

Entertainment

As well as its fair share of multi-screen **cinemas** showing Hollywood blockbusters, Norwich has the excellent art-house **Cinema City**, in Suckling House on St Andrew's Plain (ⓣ01603/622 047, ⓦwww.cinemacity.co.uk). The city also has several noteworthy **theatres**: the Theatre Royal, on Theatre Street (ⓣ01603/630 000, ⓦwww.theatreroyal.co.uk), has a wide-ranging programme of mainstream and more adventurous plays and dance; the amateur Maddermarket, St John's Alley, off Pottergate (ⓣ01603/620 917, ⓦwww.maddermarket.co.uk), offers an interesting range of modern theatre; and Norwich Playhouse, on St George's Street (ⓣ01603/612 580, ⓦwww.norwichplayhouse.co.uk) chips in with just about everything from blues concerts to panto.

The north Norfolk coast

The first place of any note on the **north Norfolk coast** is **Cromer**, a seaside town whose bleak and blustery cliffs have drawn tourists for over a century. A few miles to the west is another well-established resort, **Sheringham**, but thereafter the shoreline becomes a ragged patchwork of salt marshes, dunes and shingle spits which form a series of nature reserves, supporting a fascinating range of flora and fauna. It's a lovely stretch of coast and the villages bordering it, principally **Cley**, **Blakeney** and **Wells-next-the-Sea** are prime targets for an overnight stay.

Cromer and Sheringham are the only places accessible by **train**, with an hourly service (every 2 hours on winter Sundays) from Norwich on the Bittern

The Norfolk Broads

Three **rivers** – the Yare, Waveney and Bure – meander across the flatlands to the east of Norwich, converging on Breydon Water before flowing into the sea at Great Yarmouth. In places these rivers swell into wide expanses of water known as **"broads"**, which for years were thought to be natural lakes. In fact they're the result of extensive peat cutting, several centuries of accumulated diggings made in a region where wood was scarce and peat a valuable source of energy. The pits flooded when sea levels rose in the thirteenth and fourteenth centuries to create the **Norfolk Broads**, now one of the most important wetlands in Europe – a haven for many birds such as kingfishers, grebes and warblers – and the county's major tourist attraction. Looking after the Broads is the **Broads Authority** (ⓦwww.broads-authority.gov.uk), which maintains a series of information centres throughout the region. At any of these, you can pick up a free copy of the *Broadcaster*, a useful newspaper guide to the area as a whole.

The region is crisscrossed by roads and rail lines, but the best – really the only – way to see the Broads is **by boat**, and you could happily spend a week or so exploring the 125 miles of lock-free navigable waterways, visiting the various churches, pubs and windmills en route. Of the many **boat rental** companies, Blakes Holiday Boating (ⓣ0870/220 2498, ⓦwww.blakes.co.uk) and Broads Tours Ltd (ⓣ01603/782 207, ⓦwww.broads.co.uk), are both well established and have rental outlets at **Wroxham**, seven miles to the northeast of Norwich – and easy to reach by train, bus and car. Prices for cruisers start at around £700 a week for four people in peak season, but less expensive, short-term rentals are widely available too. **Houseboats** are much cheaper than cruisers, but they are, of course, static.

Trying to explore the Broads by car is pretty much a waste of time, but cyclists and walkers can take advantage of the region's network of footpaths and cycle trails. There are Broads Authority **bike rental** points dotted around the region and **walkers** might consider the 56-mile Weavers' Way, a long-distance footpath that winds through the best parts of the Broads on its way from Cromer to Great Yarmouth, though there are many shorter options too. As for **specific sights** for landlubbers and boaters alike, one prime target is **Toad Hole Cottage** (June–Sept daily 9.30am–6pm; April, May & Oct Mon–Fri 10.30am–1pm & 1.30–5pm, Sat & Sun 10.30am–5pm; free), an old eel catcher's cottage holding a small exhibit on the history of the trade, which was common hereabouts until the 1940s. The cottage is at How Hill, close to the hamlet of **Ludham**, six miles east of Wroxham on the A1062. Behind the cottage is the narrow River Ant, where there are hour-long, wildlife-viewing **boat trips** in the *Electric Eel* (June–Sept daily 10am–5pm, every hour; £4.50; reservations on ⓣ01692/678 763). Another enjoyable boat trip is on the *Helen of Ranworth*, a former reed lighter that makes two-hour excursions (Easter–Oct 1 daily; £5.50; reservations on ⓣ01603/270 453) out into the Broads from **Ranworth**, a tiny hamlet about twelve miles east of Norwich via the A1151 and B1140. Most trips visit the isolated ruins of **St Benet's Abbey** (open access; free).

Line. Local **bus** services fill in (most of) the gaps, connecting all the towns and many of the villages. There's also the **Coasthopper bus** (Mon–Sat hourly, Sun 4 daily), operated by Norfolk Green (Ⓣ01553/776 980; Ⓦwww.norfolkgreen.co.uk), which runs the length of the coast from Cromer to Hunstanton. The Coasthopper Rover ticket (£7) gives a day's unlimited travel on the route.

Cromer

Dramatically poised on a high bluff, **CROMER** should be the most memorable of the Norfolk coastal resorts, but its fine aspect is undermined by a shabbiness in its streets and shopfronts. The tower of **St Peter and St Paul**, at 160ft the tallest in Norfolk, attests to the port's medieval wealth, but it was the advent of the railway in the 1880s that heralded the most frenetic flurry of building activity. A bevy of grand Edwardian hotels was constructed along the seafront and for a moment Cromer became the most fashionable of resorts, but the gloss soon wore off and only the dishevelled **Hotel de Paris** has survived as a reminder of all the bustles and top hats. While you're here, don't forget to grab a **crab** – J.W.H. Jonas, in the centre at 7 Chapel St (Ⓣ01263/514 121), has some fine specimens.

Somewhat miraculously Cromer has managed to retain its rail link with Norwich; the **train station** is a five-minute walk west of the centre. **Buses** terminate on Cadogan Road, next to the **tourist office** (daily 10am–4pm; Nov to mid-March closed 1–2pm; Ⓣ01263/512 497, Ⓦwww.visitnorthnorfolk.com), which is itself just 200 yards from the cliff-top promenade. An hour or two in Cromer is probably enough, though the **beach** is first-rate and the cliff-top walk exhilarating. There's no shortage of inexpensive **accommodation** – the tourist office has all the details – but it's hard to beat the enticing *Beachcomber B&B*, a cosy place with five en-suite rooms conveniently located near the centre at 17 Macdonald Rd (Ⓣ01263/513 398, Ⓦwww.beachcomber-guesthouse.co.uk; no credit cards; ❸).

Sheringham

SHERINGHAM, a popular seaside town four miles west of Cromer, has an amiable, easy-going air and makes a reasonable overnight stop, before hitting the more appealing places further to the west. One of the distinctive features of the town is the smooth beach pebbles that face and decorate the houses, a **flinting technique** used frequently in this part of Norfolk – the best examples here are just off the High Street. The downside is that the power of the waves, which makes the pebbles smooth, has also forced the local council to spend thousands rebuilding the sea defences. The resultant mass of reinforced concrete makes for a less than pleasing seafront – one reason to head, instead, for **Sheringham Park** (daily dawn to dusk; free, but parking extra; NT), the 770-acre woodland park a couple of miles southwest of the town, laid out by Humphrey Repton in the early 1800s. The park boasts wonderful battalions of rhododendrons and azaleas, at their best in late May to early June, and a series of lookout posts from which you can admire the view down to the coast.

Practicalities

Sheringham's **train station**, the terminus of the Bittern Line from Norwich, is yards from the **tourist office** (March–Oct Mon–Sat 10am–5pm, Sun 10am–4pm; Ⓣ01263/824 329, Ⓦwww.visitnorthnorfolk.com), which is itself a five-minute walk from the seafront, down Station Road and its continuation, the High Street. There are plenty of **B&Bs**; one of the best is the unassuming *Two Lifeboats*,

2 High St (Ⓣ01263/822 401, Ⓦwww.twolifeboats.co.uk; ❹), a small, traditional hotel on the promenade – most of the ten, en-suite bedrooms have sea views.

The tastiest **fish and chips** for miles around are served up at *Dave's*, at 50 High St and 7 Cooperative St. The *Sweet Shop*, 14 High St, sells Ronaldo's ice cream in a mouthwatering battery of flavours, from chocolate and ginger to cinnamon and lavender.

Cley and Blakeney Point

Travelling west from Sheringham, the **A149** meanders through a pretty rural landscape offering occasional glimpses of the sea and a shoreline protected by a giant shingle barrier erected after the catastrophic flood of 1953. After seven miles you reach **CLEY-NEXT-THE-SEA**, once a busy wool port but now little more than a row of flint cottages and Georgian mansions set beside a narrow, marshy inlet that (just) gives access to the sea. The original village was destroyed in a fire in 1612, which explains why Cley's fine medieval **church of St Margaret** is located half a mile inland at the very southern edge of the current village, overlooking the green. Cley's other draw – housed in an old forge on the main street – is the excellent **Cley Smoke House**, selling local smoked fish amongst other delicacies, while nearby **Picnic Fayre** has long been one of the finest delis in East Anglia.

It's about 400 yards east from the village to the mile-long byroad that leads to the shingle mounds of **Cley beach**. This is the starting point for the four-mile hike west out along the spit to **Blakeney Point**, a National Nature Reserve famed for its colonies of terns and seals. The seal colony is made up of several hundred common and grey seals, and the old lifeboat house, at the end of the spit, is now a National Trust information centre. The shifting shingle can make walking difficult, so keep to the low-water mark – which also means that you won't accidentally trample any nests. The easier alternative is to take one of the boat trips to the point from Blakeney or Morston (see below).

As for a **place to stay**, the outstanding *Cley Mill B&B* (Ⓣ01263/740 209, Ⓦwww.cleymill.co.uk; ❼) occupies a converted windmill complete with sails and a balcony offering wonderful views over the surrounding salt marshes and seashore. The guest rooms, both in the windmill and the adjoining outhouses, are decorated in attractive period style and the best, like the Stone Room, have splendid beamed ceilings; at peak times, there's a minimum two-night stay and self-catering arrangements are possible as well.

Blakeney

A mile west of Cley, delightful **BLAKENEY** was once a bustling port exporting fish, corn and salt, and is now a lovely little place of pebble-covered cottages sloping up from a narrow harbour just a mile west of Cley. Crab sandwiches are sold from stalls at the quayside, the meandering high street is flanked by family-run shops, and footpaths stretch out along the sea wall to east and west, allowing long, lingering looks over the salt marshes.

Blakeney **harbour** is linked to the sea by a narrow channel, which wriggles its way through the salt marshes. The channel is, however, only navigable for a few hours at high tide – at low tide the harbour is no more than a muddy creek (ideal for a bit of quayside crabbing and mud sliding). Depending on the tides, there are **boat trips** from either Blakeney or **Morston quay**, a mile or two to the west, to both Blakeney Point (see above) – where passengers have a couple of hours at the point before being ferried back – and to the seal colony just off the point. The main operators advertise departure times on blackboards by the quayside or you can reserve in advance with Beans Boats (ⓣ01263/740 505, ⓦwww.beansboattrips.co.uk) or Bishop's Boats (ⓣ01263/740 753, ⓦwww.norfolksealtrips.co.uk). Both the seal trips and those to Blakeney Point cost £7.50.

Practicalities

For **accommodation**, the quayside *Blakeney Hotel* (ⓣ01263/740 797, ⓦwww.blakeney-hotel.co.uk; ❽) is one of the most charming seaside hotels in Norfolk, a rambling building with high-pitched gables and pebble-covered walls. The hotel has a heated indoor swimming pool, a secluded garden, and cosy lounges with exquisite sea views; it also serves outstanding **food**. Less expensive options include the *Manor Hotel* (ⓣ01263/740 376, ⓦwww.blakeneymanor.co.uk; ❻), which occupies a low-lying courtyard complex a few yards to the east of the harbour; the *King's Arms* (ⓣ01263/740 341, ⓦwww.blakeneykingsarms.co.uk; ❹), a traditional pub with low, beamed ceilings and seven, modest, modern en-suite bedrooms just back from the quay on Westgate; and the *White Horse* (ⓣ01263/740 574, ⓦwww.blakeneywhitehorse.co.uk; ❺), an old pub in the centre of the village just up from the quay with nine bright and cheerful guest rooms.

Both the *White Horse* and the *King's Arms* serve first-rate **bar food** with local seafood the speciality; the former also has an excellent **restaurant**, where the menu features such delights as haddock fish cakes with red onion and caper salad; main courses average £12.

Wells-next-the-Sea

Despite its name, **WELLS-NEXT-THE-SEA**, some eight miles west of Blakeney, is situated a good mile or so from open water. In Tudor times, before the harbour silted up, this was one of the great ports of eastern England, a major player in the trade with the Netherlands. Today it's the only commercially viable port on the north Norfolk coast, but more importantly, Wells is one of the county's more attractive towns. Even though there are no specific sights among its narrow lanes, it does make a very good base for exploring the surrounding coastline.

The town divides into three distinct areas, starting with **The Buttlands**, a broad rectangular green on the south side of town, lined with oak and beech trees and framed by a string of fine Georgian houses. North from here, across Station Road, lie the narrow lanes of the town centre with **Staithe Street**, the minuscule main drag, flanked by quaint old-fashioned shops. Staithe Street leads down to the **quay**, a somewhat forlorn affair inhabited by a couple of amusement arcades and fish-and-chip shops, and the mile-long byroad that scuttles north to the **beach**, a handsome sandy tract backed by pine-clad dunes. The beach road is shadowed by a high flood defence and a tiny narrow-gauge **railway**, which scoots down to the beach every twenty minutes or so from 10.30am, Easter to October (90p each way).

Practicalities

Buses to Wells stop on The Buttlands, a short stroll from the **tourist office** at the foot of Staithe Street (mid-March to late May & mid-Sept to Oct daily 10am–2pm; late May to mid-Sept daily 10am–5pm; ⓣ01328/710 885, ⓦwww.visitnorthnorfolk.com). Several of the best **B&Bs** are along Standard Road, which runs up from the eastern end of the quayside. First choice here is *The Normans* (ⓣ01328/710 657, ⓦwww.thenormansatwells.co.uk; ❺), in a handsome Georgian red-brick mansion; the sitting room has a log fire and racks of games and the first-floor lookout window provides a wide view over the marshes – binoculars are provided. Similarly enticing, and also on Standard Road, is *Fern Cottage* (ⓣ01328/710 306, ⓦwww.ferncottage.co.uk; ⑤), a dinky little Georgian house with two immaculate period guest rooms; there is a minimum stay of two nights. There's also a **campsite**, the sprawling and extremely popular *Pinewoods Caravan and Camping Park*, right by the beach (ⓣ01328/710 439, ⓦwww.pinewoods.co.uk; closed Nov to mid-March).

Two smashing **pubs** serving bar food include *The Crown* and *The Globe*, both on The Buttlands; *The Globe* also has a restaurant.

Holkham Hall and Holkham Bay

One of the most popular outings from Wells is to **Holkham Hall** (June–Sept Mon–Thurs & Sun noon–5pm; £7; ⓦwww.holkham.co.uk), three miles to the west and a stop on the Coasthopper bus (see p.402). This grand and self-assured (or vainglorious) stately home was designed by the eighteenth-century architect William Kent for the first earl of Leicester and is still owned by the family. The severe sandy-coloured Palladian exterior belies the warmth and richness of the interior, which retains much of its original decoration, notably the much-admired marble hall, with its fluted columns and intricate reliefs. The rich colours of the state rooms are an appropriate backdrop for a fabulous selection of **paintings**, including canvases by van Dyck, Rubens, Gainsborough and Gaspar Poussin.

The **grounds** (Easter–Oct Mon–Sat 7am–7pm & Sun 9am–7pm; Nov–Easter Mon, Wed & Fri 7am–7pm, Tues & Thurs 10am–7pm; free) are laid out on sandy, saline land, much of it originally salt marsh. The focal point is an eighty-foot-high obelisk, atop a grassy knoll, from where you can view both the hall to the north and the triumphal arch to the south. In common with the rest of the north Norfolk coast, there's plenty of **birdlife** to observe – Holkham's lake attracts Canada geese, herons and grebes and several hundred deer graze the open pastures.

The **footpaths** latticing the estate stretch as far as the A149, from where a half-mile byroad – Lady Anne's Drive – leads north across the marshes from opposite the *Victoria Hotel* to **Holkham Bay**, which boasts one of the finest beaches on this stretch of coast, with golden sand and pine-studded sand dunes. Warblers, flycatchers and redstarts inhabit the drier coastal reaches, while waders paddle about the mud and salt flats.

Burnham Market

Heading west from Wells on the A149, it's about five miles to the pretty little village of **BURNHAM MARKET**, where a medley of Georgian and Victorian houses surrounds a dinky little green. The village attracts a well-heeled, north London crowd, in no small measure because of the *Hoste Arms* (ⓣ01328/738 777, ⓦwww.hostearms.co.uk; ⑦), an old coaching inn overlooking the green that has been intelligently and sympathetically modernized to offer some of the best restaurant and bar **food** on the coast. The seafood is the big deal here and main courses average around £16, less at lunch times. The guest rooms are round the back and range from the small-verging-on-the-cramped to the much more expansive (and expensive). The same people also own the village's *Railway Inn*, in the old station on Creake Road (same details), and several local cottages.

Burnham Deepdale, Brancaster Staithe and Titchwell

From Burnham Market, it's a couple of miles west to tiny **BURNHAM DEEPDALE**, where *Deepdale Farm* (Ⓣ01485/210 256, Ⓦwww.deepdalefarm.co.uk; dorm beds from £12.50, doubles ❷), situated just off the A149, is a lively and very amiable set-up, operating a combined campsite, café, art gallery and eco-friendly **hostel** in creatively renovated former stables. Behind the hamlet to the north stretches a tract of lagoon, sandspit and creek that pokes its head out into the ocean, attracting thousands of wildfowl. This is prime **walking** territory and Deepdale Farm's information centre sells hiking maps and will advise on routes. There's also a smashing pub-cum-hotel nearby, *The White Horse* (Ⓣ01485/210 262, Ⓦwww.whitehorsebrancaster.co.uk; ❻), just west along the A149 in the hamlet of **BRANCASTER STAITHE**. A dapper little place, there are great views across the marshes from the rear of the premises and the food – especially the fish – is excellent with main courses starting at around £10. There are fifteen, en-suite bedrooms here and each is kitted out in smart modern style with a scattering of nautical knick-knacks – model boats and so forth.

Pushing on west from Brancaster Staithe, it's a couple of miles more to minuscule **TITCHWELL**, the site of the **Titchwell Marsh RSPB Reserve** (Ⓦwww.rspb.org.uk) and the roadside *Titchwell Manor Hotel* (Ⓣ01485/210 221, Ⓦwww.titchwellmanor.com; ❻), whose thirty ultramodern rooms occupy a rambling Victorian brick house and an adjacent garden complex.

From Titchwell, it's just six miles more to Hunstanton.

Hunstanton

The Norfolk coast pretty much ends at **HUNSTANTON**, a Victorian seaside resort that grew up to the southwest of the original fishing village – now **Old Hunstanton**. The place has its fair share of amusement arcades, crazy golf, and entertainment complexes – not to mention England's largest joke shop "The World of Fun" – but it has also hung onto its genteel origins, and its sandy **beaches**, backed by stripy gateau-like cliffs, are among the cleanest in the county.

Hunstanton **tourist office** is in the town hall (daily: April–Sept 10am–5pm; Oct–March 10.30am–4pm; Ⓣ01485/532 610) on the wide sloping green that serves as the resort's focal point. They have a long list of **B&Bs** with the nicest (and priciest) among the cottages of Old Hunstanton. There's also a **YHA hostel** in a pair of Victorian townhouses at 15 Avenue Rd (Ⓣ0870/770 5872, Ⓔhunstanton@yha.org.uk; dorm beds £14, doubles ❶), a brief walk south of Hunstanton green. It has forty beds, in two- to eight-bedded rooms, a cycle store, garden and self-catering kitchen; advance booking is advised.

Sandringham House

Built in 1870 on land purchased by Queen Victoria for her son, the future Edward VII, **Sandringham House** (April–Oct daily 11am–last entry at 4.45pm, 4pm in Oct; closed for 2 weeks late July or early Aug; £9; Ⓦwww.sandringhamestate.co.uk) is located off the A149 about eight miles south of Hunstanton. The house is billed as a private home, but few families have a drawing room crammed with Russian silver and Chinese jade. The **museum** (same times), housed in the old coach and stable block, contains an exhibition of royal memorabilia from dolls to cars, but much more arresting are the beautifully maintained **gardens** (same dates daily 10.30am to last entry at 5pm,

4pm in Oct), a mass of rhododendrons and azaleas in spring and early summer. The estate's sandy soil is also ideal for game birds, which was the attraction of the place for the terminally bored Edward.

Local **buses** #40 and #41 make the journey to Sandringham from Hunstanton, as does the Coasthopper (see p.402).

Ely and around

Perched on a mound of clay above the River Great Ouse about thirty miles south of King's Lynn, the attractive little town of **ELY** – literally "eel island" – was to all intents and purposes a true island until the draining of the fens in the seventeenth century. Up until then, the town was encircled by treacherous marshland, which could only be crossed with the help of the local "fen-slodgers" who knew the firm tussock paths. In 1070, **Hereward the Wake** turned this inaccessibility to military advantage, holding out against the Normans and forcing William the Conqueror to undertake a prolonged siege – and finally to build an improvised road floated on bundles of sticks. Centuries later, the Victorian writer Charles Kingsley resurrected this obscure conflict in his novel *Hereward the Wake*. He presented the protagonist as the Last of the English who "never really bent their necks to the Norman yoke and … kept alive those free institutions which were the germs of our British liberty" – a heady mixture of nationalism and historical poppycock that went down a storm.

Since then, Ely has always been associated with Hereward, which is really rather ridiculous as Ely is, above all else, a Norman, ecclesiastical town. The Normans built the **cathedral**, a towering structure visible for miles across the flat fenland landscape and Ely's main sight. It's easy to see the town on a day-trip from Cambridge, but Ely does make a pleasant night's stop in its own right.

Ely Cathedral

Ely **Cathedral** (June–Sept daily 7am–7pm; Oct–May Mon–Sat 7.30am–6pm & Sun 7.30am–5pm; Mon–Sat £5.20, free on Sun; Ⓦwww.cathedral.ely.anglican.org) is one of the most impressive churches in England, but the west facade, where visitors enter, has been an oddly lopsided affair ever since one of the transepts collapsed in a storm in 1701. Nonetheless, the remaining transept, which was completed in the 1180s, is an imposing structure, its dog-tooth windows, castellated towers and blind arcading possessing all the rough, almost brutal charm of the Normans.

The first things to strike you as you enter the **nave** are the sheer length of the building and the lively nineteenth-century painted ceiling, largely the work of amateur volunteers. The nave's procession of plain late-Norman arches leads to the architectural feature that makes Ely so special, the **octagon** – the only one of its kind in England – built in 1322 to replace the collapsed central tower. Its construction, employing the largest oaks available in England to support some four hundred tons of glass and lead, remains one of the wonders of the medieval world, and the effect, as you look up into this Gothic dome, is simply breathtaking. From April to October, **Octagon Tower tours** (£3.20 extra; reservations & schedule Ⓣ01353/660 344) depart two to four times daily from the desk at the entrance, venturing up into the octagon itself.

When the central tower collapsed, it fell eastwards onto the **choir**, the first three bays of which were rebuilt at the same time as the octagon in the Decorated style – in contrast to the plainer Early English of the choir bays beyond. The other marvel is the **Lady Chapel**, a separate building accessible via the north transept. It lost its sculpture and its stained glass during the Reformation, but its fan vaulting remains, an exquisite example of English Gothic. Retracing your steps, the south triforium near the main entrance holds the **Stained Glass Museum** (Easter–Oct Mon–Fri 10.30am–5pm, Sat 10.30am–5.30pm & Sun noon–6pm; Nov–Easter Mon–Sat 10.30am–5pm & Sun noon–4.30pm; £3.50), an Anglican money-spinner exhibiting examples of this applied art from 1200 to the present day.

The rest of the town

The rest of Ely is pleasant and pretty enough, but hardly compelling after the wonders of the cathedral. To the north of the church is the **High Street**, a slender thoroughfare lined by Georgian buildings and old-fashioned shops that makes for an enjoyable browse. If you push on past the Market Place at its east end, then Forehill and its continuation Waterside lead down to the riverside Babylon Gallery (Tues–Sat 10am–4pm, Sun 11am–4pm; free; ⓣ01353/616 375, ⓦwww.babylongallery.co.uk), where an imaginative programme of temporary exhibitions featuring contemporary art and craft is displayed in an attractively renovated old brewery warehouse. Alternatively, head west from the cathedral entrance across the Palace Green to **Oliver Cromwell's House** at 29 St Mary's St (April–Oct daily 10am–5.30pm; Nov–March Sun–Fri 11am–4pm & Sat 10am–5pm; £4), a timber-framed former vicarage, which holds a small exhibition on the Protector's ten-year sojourn in Ely, when he was employed as a tithe collector.

Practicalities

Ely is a major rail intersection, receiving direct **trains** from as far afield as Liverpool, Norwich and London King's Cross, as well as from Cambridge, just twenty minutes to the south. From Ely **train station**, it's a ten-minute walk to the cathedral, straight up Station Road and its continuation Back Hill and then The Gallery. **Buses** (from King's Lynn and Cambridge) stop on Market Street immediately north of the cathedral. The **tourist office**, in Oliver Cromwell's House at 29 St Mary's St (April–Oct daily 10am–5.30pm; Nov–March Sun–Fri 11am–4pm & Sat 10am–5pm; ⓣ01353/662 062, ⓦwww.eastcambs.gov.uk/tourism) will help with accommodation.

Ely has several appealing **B&Bs**, with first choice being *Cathedral House*, in an attractive Georgian townhouse a brief stroll from the cathedral at 17 St Mary's St (ⓣ01353/662 124, ⓦwww.cathedralhouse.co.uk; no credit cards; ④). All the guest rooms here are en suite and each comes complete with period details, though they all tend to be a tad spartan. *Sycamore House* occupies an attractive and well-maintained detached house on the southwest edge of town at 91 Cambridge Rd (ⓣ01353/662 139, ⓦwww.sycamoreguesthouse.co.uk; no credit cards; ④); they have four en-suite, guest rooms and all are cheerfully decorated.

Amongst a battalion of **tearooms**, the most engaging is *The Almonry*, on the High Street (Mon–Sat 10am–5pm & Sun 11am–5pm), which offers smashing views of the cathedral from its outside area and good snacks and light meals. The best **restaurant** in town is *The Boathouse*, an expansive modern place down by the river at 5 Annesdale (ⓣ01353/664 388; daily noon–2.30pm & 6.30–9pm, 8.30pm Sun). The menu is great, thanks to the likes of pheasant and skate, mutton and – the house speciality – sausages and mash; mains average £13.

Ely has two excellent **pubs** on Silver Street, a right turn off The Gallery, which runs south from the cathedral's main entrance. These are the relaxed and welcoming *Fountain* at no. 1, and the infinitely cosy *Prince Albert*, at no. 62. Both serve real ales.

Cambridge

On the whole, **CAMBRIDGE** is a much quieter and more secluded place than Oxford, though for the visitor what really sets it apart from its scholarly rival is "**The Backs**" – the green sward of land that straddles the languid River Cam, providing exquisite views over the backs of the old colleges. At the front, the handsome facades of these same colleges dominate the layout of the town centre, lining up along the main streets. Most of the older colleges date back to the late thirteenth and early fourteenth centuries and are designed to a **similar plan** with the main gate leading through to a series of "courts," typically a carefully manicured slab of lawn surrounded on all four sides by college residences or offices. Many of the buildings are extraordinarily beautiful, but the most famous is **King's College**, whose magnificent **King's College Chapel** is one of the great statements of late Gothic architecture. There are 31 university colleges in total, each an independent, self-governing body, proud of its achievements and attracting – for the most part at least – a close loyalty from its students.

Cambridge is an extremely compact place, and you can **walk** round the centre, visiting the most interesting colleges, in an afternoon. A more thorough exploration, covering more of the colleges, a visit to the fine art of the Fitzwilliam Museum and a leisurely afternoon on a **punt**, will however take at least a couple of days. Note also that the most visited colleges have restricted their **opening times** and sometimes impose admission charges and that during the exam period (late April to early June), most colleges close their doors to the public at least some of the time.

Arrival

Cambridge **train station** is a mile or so to the southeast of the city centre, off Hills Road. It's an easy but tedious twenty-minute walk into the centre, or take local **bus** #3 to the bus stop on Emmanuel Street, which is itself yards from the Drummer Street long-distance **bus station**. Arriving by **car**, you'll find much of the city centre closed to traffic and on-street parking impossible to find; for a day-trip, at least, the best option is a **Park-and-Ride** car park; they are signposted on all major approaches.

Information and getting around

Cambridge's well-equipped **tourist office** is bang in the centre of town in the old library, on Wheeler Street, off King's Parade (April–Sept Mon–Fri 10am–5.30pm, Sat 10am–5pm & Sun 11am–3pm; Oct–March Mon–Fri 10am–5.30pm & Sat 10am–5pm; ⓣ0871/226 8006, accommodation line ⓣ01223/457 581; ⓦwww.visitcambridge.org). They issue free city maps, have lots of leaflets on local attractions and have an accommodation booking service (see opposite).

Cycling is an enjoyable way of getting around the city and has long been popular with locals and students alike. There are **bike rental** outlets dotted all over town (see p.401), but when and wherever you leave your bike, padlock it to something immovable as bike theft is not infrequent. The tourist office also runs very popular **walking tours** of the centre and its key colleges (1–4 daily; 2hr; £10; reservations on ⓣ01223/457 574); book well in advance in summer.

Messing about on the water

Punting is the quintessential Cambridge activity, though it is, in fact, a good deal harder than it looks. First-timers find themselves zigzagging across the water and "punt jams" are very common on the stretch of the River Cam beside The Backs in summer. **Punt rental** is available at several points, including the boatyard at Mill Lane (beside the Silver Street bridge), at Magdalene Bridge, and at the Garret Hostel Lane bridge at the back of Trinity College. It costs around £14 an hour (and most places charge a deposit), with up to six people in each punt. Alternatively, you can hire a **chauffeured punt** from any of the rental places for about £10 per person per hour.

Cambridge is also famous for its **rowing clubs**, which are clustered along the north bank of the river across from Midsummer Common. For their convenience, this stretch of water is punt-free. The most important inter-college races are the **May Bumps**, which, confusingly, take place in June.

Accommodation

Cambridge is short of central accommodation and those few **hotels** that do occupy prime locations are expensive. That said, Chesterton Lane and its continuation, Chesterton Road, the busy street running east from the top of Magdalene Street, have several reasonably priced hotels and guesthouses. There are lots of **B&Bs** on the outskirts of town, with several near the train station, and it's here you'll also find the **YHA hostel**. In high season, when vacant rooms are often thin on the ground, the tourist office's efficient **accommodation booking service** can be very useful (Ⓣ01223/457 581, Ⓦwww.visitcambridge.org).

Arundel House Hotel 53 Chesterton Rd Ⓣ01223/367 701, Ⓦwww.arundelhousehotels.co.uk. A converted row of late-Victorian houses overlooking the river and Jesus Green makes this one of the better mid-range hotel choices. Neat and tidy rooms, but mundane modern furnishings. ❻

Cambridge Garden House Hotel Granta Place, Mill Lane Ⓣ01223/259 988, Ⓦwww.cambridgegardenhouse.com. Outstanding hotel, the city's best, in a strikingly modern 1960s building a couple of minutes' walk from the centre. The foyer is wide and open; the breakfasts are first-rate; and some rooms have balconies overlooking the river (though the views are hardly riveting). ❼

Cambridge YHA 97 Tenison Rd Ⓣ0870/770 5742, Ⓔcambridge@yha.org.uk. This well-equipped hostel has laundry and self-catering facilities, a cycle store, a games room and a small courtyard garden. There are one hundred beds in two- to eight-bedded rooms and advance reservations are advised. It's located close to the train station – Tenison Rd is a right turn a couple of hundred yards down Station Rd. Dorm beds £17.50, doubles ❶

City Roomz Hotel Station Rd Ⓣ01223/304 050, Ⓦwww.cityroomz.com. This popular hotel is in an imaginatively converted granary warehouse, right outside the train station. Most of the rooms are bunk-style affairs done out in the manner of a ship's cabin, and there are a few doubles too. All rooms are en suite, with shower and TV. ❸

Crowne Plaza Hotel Cambridge 20 Downing St Ⓣ0870/400 9180, Ⓦwww.ichotelsgroup.com. Immaculately tailored behind a dignified facade, this sleek and slick hotel is first-rate. The rooms are resolutely modern in efficient chain-hotel style. Great central location too. ❼

Lensfield Hotel 53 Lensfield Rd Ⓣ01223/355 017, Ⓦwww.lensfieldhotel.co.uk. Well-kept, medium-sized hotel in Victorian premises on the inner ring road, just round the corner from the Fitzwilliam Museum. The hotel's pleasantly appointed guest rooms are decorated in frilly retro style. ❻

Worth House 152 Chesterton Rd Ⓣ01223/316 074, Ⓦwww.worth-house.co.uk. Pleasant B&B in a tastefully upgraded Victorian house, about 20min walk from the centre. Four bedrooms are all en suite. ❸

The City

The university developed on the land west of this latter route along the banks of the River Cam, and now forms a continuous half-mile parade of **colleges** from Peterhouse to Magdalene, with sundry others scattered about the periphery. The **Fitzwilliam Museum**, holding the city's finest art collection, is just along Trumpington Street south of Peterhouse. The account below starts with **King's College**, whose **chapel** is the university's most celebrated attraction, and covers the rest of the town in a broadly clockwise direction.

King's College and King's College Chapel

Henry VI founded **King's College** (term time: Mon–Fri 9.30am–3.30pm, Sat 9.30am–3.15pm & Sun 1.15–2.15pm; rest of year: Mon–Sat 9.30am–4.30pm & Sun 10am–5pm; free; Ⓣ01223/331 100, Ⓦwww.kings.cam.ac.uk) in 1441, but he was disappointed with his initial efforts. So, four years later he cleared away half of medieval Cambridge to make room for a much grander foundation. His plans were ambitious, but the Wars of the Roses – and bouts of royal insanity – intervened and by the time of his death in 1471 very little had been finished and work on what was intended to be Henry's **Great Court** hadn't even started. This part of the site remained empty for no less than three hundred years and the Great Court complex of today – facing King's Parade from behind a long stone screen – is largely neo-Gothic, built in the 1820s to a design by William Wilkins.

Henry's workmen did, however, start on the college's finest building, the much-celebrated **King's College Chapel** (same times; £4.50), on the north side of today's Great Court. Committed to canvas by Turner and Canaletto, and eulogized in no less than three sonnets by Wordsworth, it's now best known for its **boys' choir**, whose members process across the college grounds during term time in their antiquated garb to sing evensong (Tues–Sat at 5.30pm) and carols on Christmas Eve. The building seems impossibly slender, its streamlined buttresses channelling up to a dainty balustrade and four spiky turrets, but the exterior was, in a sense at least, a happy accident – its design predicated by the carefully composed interior. Here, the high and handsome **nave** boasts an exquisite ceiling, whose fan-tail tracery is a complex geometry of extraordinary complexity and delicacy, as well as magnificent stained-glass windows. Paid for by Henry VIII, the **glass** was largely the work of Flemish glaziers, with the lower windows portraying scenes from the New Testament and the Apocrypha, and the upper windows the Old Testament. Above the **altar** hangs Rubens' tender *Adoration of the Magi* and an exhibition in the side **chantries** puts more historical flesh on Henry's grand plans.

King's enjoyed an exclusive supply of students from the public school, Eton, and until 1851 claimed the right to award its students degrees without taking any examinations. The first non-Etonians were only accepted in 1873. Times have changed since those days, and, if anything, King's is now one of the more progressive colleges, having been one of the first to admit women in 1972. Among its most famous alumni are E.M. Forster, who described his experiences in *Maurice*, film director Derek Jarman, poet Rupert Brooke and John Maynard Keynes, whose economic theories did much to improve the college's finances when he became the college bursar.

From King's Parade to Gonville and Caius College

Originally the town's medieval High Street, **King's Parade** is dominated by King's College and Chapel, but the higgledy-piggledy shops and cafés opposite are an attractive foil to William Wilkins's architectural screen. At the northern end of King's Parade is **Great St Mary's** (daily 9am–6pm except during services; free), the university's pet church, a sturdy Gothic structure dating from the fifteenth century. Its tower (Mon–Sat 9.30am–4.30pm, Sun noon–4.30pm; £2.50) offers a good overall view of the colleges and a bird's-eye view of **Market Hill**, east of the

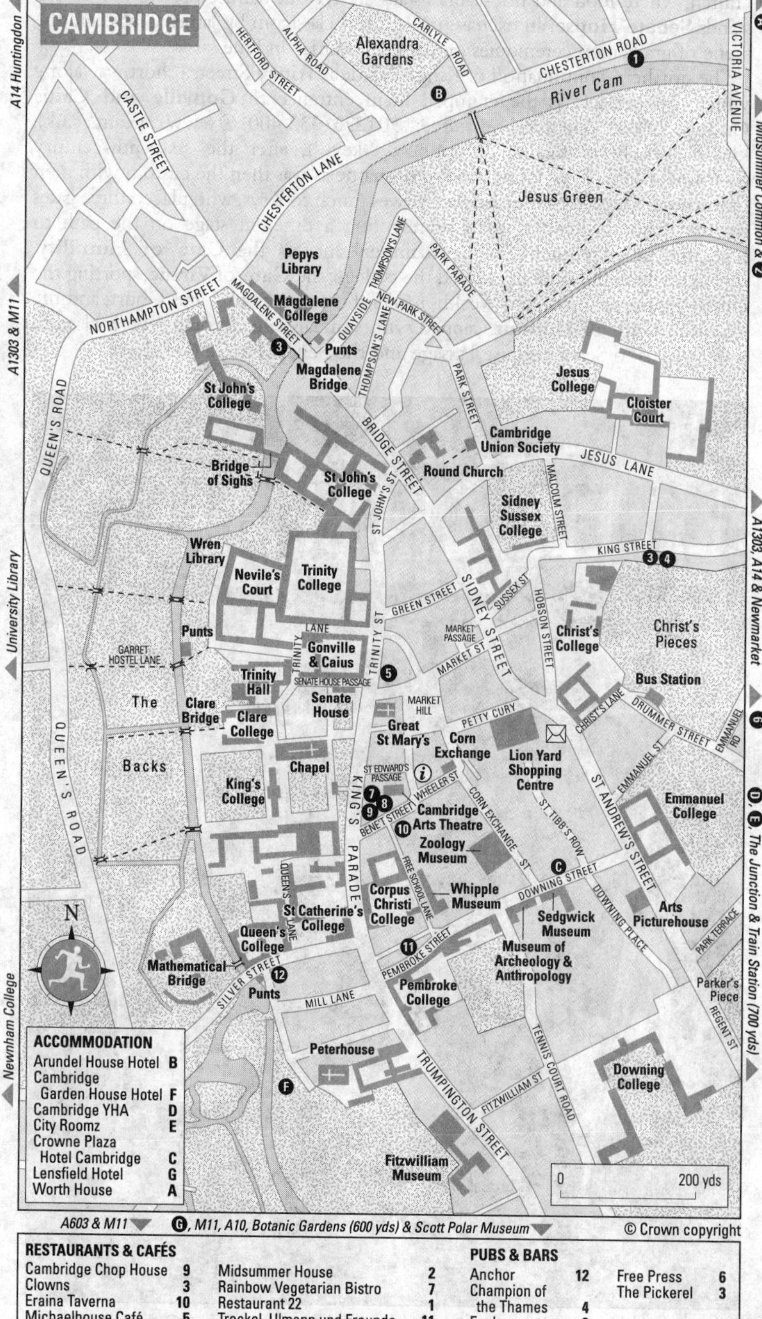
CAMBRIDGE
A14 Huntingdon
A1303 & M11
University Library
Newnham College
Midsummer Common & 2
A1303, A14 & Newmarket
6
D, E, The Junction & Train Station (700 yds)
A603 & M11
G, M11, A10, Botanic Gardens (600 yds) & Scott Polar Museum
© Crown copyright
A
B
C
F
1
2
3
4
5
6
7
8
9
10
11
12
Alexandra Gardens
Carlyle Road
Alpha Road
Hertford Street
Castle Street
Chesterton Road
Chesterton Lane
River Cam
Victoria Avenue
Jesus Green
Pepys Library
Magdalene College
Magdalene Street
Northampton Street
Quayside
Thompson's Lane
Park Parade
New Park Street
Punts
Magdalene Bridge
St John's College
Queen's Road
Park Street
Jesus College
Cloister Court
Cambridge Union Society
Bridge Street
Jesus Lane
Bridge of Sighs
St John's College
Round Church
Malcolm Street
Sidney Sussex College
St John's St
Wren Library
Nevile's Court
Trinity College
King Street
Green Street
Sidney Street
Sussex St
Hobson Street
Christ's Pieces
Punts
Trinity Lane
Market Passage
Christ's College
Garret Hostel Lane
Gonville & Caius
Trinity Street
Market St
Trinity Hall
Senate House Passage
Bus Station
The Backs
Clare Bridge
Senate House
Market Hill
Petty Cury
Christ's Lane
Drummer Street
Emmanuel Rd
Clare College
Great St Mary's
Corn Exchange
Lion Yard Shopping Centre
Chapel
St Edward's Passage
Wheeler St
Emmanuel St
King's College
St Andrew's Street
Emmanuel College
Cambridge Arts Theatre
Bene't Street
King's Parade
Corn Exchange St
St Tibb's Row
Zoology Museum
Free School Lane
Queen's Lane
Corpus Christi College
Whipple Museum
Downing Street
Sedgwick Museum
Downing Place
Arts Picturehouse
St Catherine's College
Queen's College
Park Terrace
Mathematical Bridge
Silver Street
Pembroke Street
Museum of Archeology & Anthropology
Parker's Piece
Punts
Mill Lane
Pembroke College
Regent St
Peterhouse
Trumpington Street
Tennis Court Road
Fitzwilliam St
Downing College
Fitzwilliam Museum
0
200 yds
N
ACCOMMODATION
Arundel House Hotel B
Cambridge Garden House Hotel F
Cambridge YHA D
City Roomz E
Crowne Plaza Hotel Cambridge C
Lensfield Hotel G
Worth House A
RESTAURANTS & CAFÉS
Cambridge Chop House 9
Clowns 3
Eraina Taverna 10
Michaelhouse Café 5
Midsummer House 2
Rainbow Vegetarian Bistro 7
Restaurant 22 1
Trockel, Ulmann und Freunde 11
PUBS & BARS
Anchor 12
Champion of the Thames 4
Eagle 8
Free Press 6
The Pickerel 3

church, where food and bric-a-brac stalls are set out daily. Opposite the church stands **Senate House**, an exercise in Palladian classicism by James Gibbs, and the scene of graduation ceremonies on the last Saturday in June.

The northern continuation of King's Parade is Trinity Street, a short way along which, on the left, is the cramped main entrance to **Gonville and Caius College** (no set opening hours; free; ⓣ01223/332 400, ⓦwww.cai.cam.ac.uk), known simply as Caius (pronounced "keys"), after the sixteenth-century co-founder John Keys, who latinized his name as was then the custom with men of learning. The design of the college owes much to Keys, who placed three gates on two adjoining courts, each representing a different stage on the path to academic enlightenment: at the main entrance is the **Gate of Humility**, through which the student entered the college; the **Gate of Virtue**, sporting the female figures of Fame and Wealth, marks the entrance to Caius Court; and the exquisite **Gate of Honour**, capped with sundials and decorated with classical motifs, leads to Senate House Passage and the Senate House (see above).

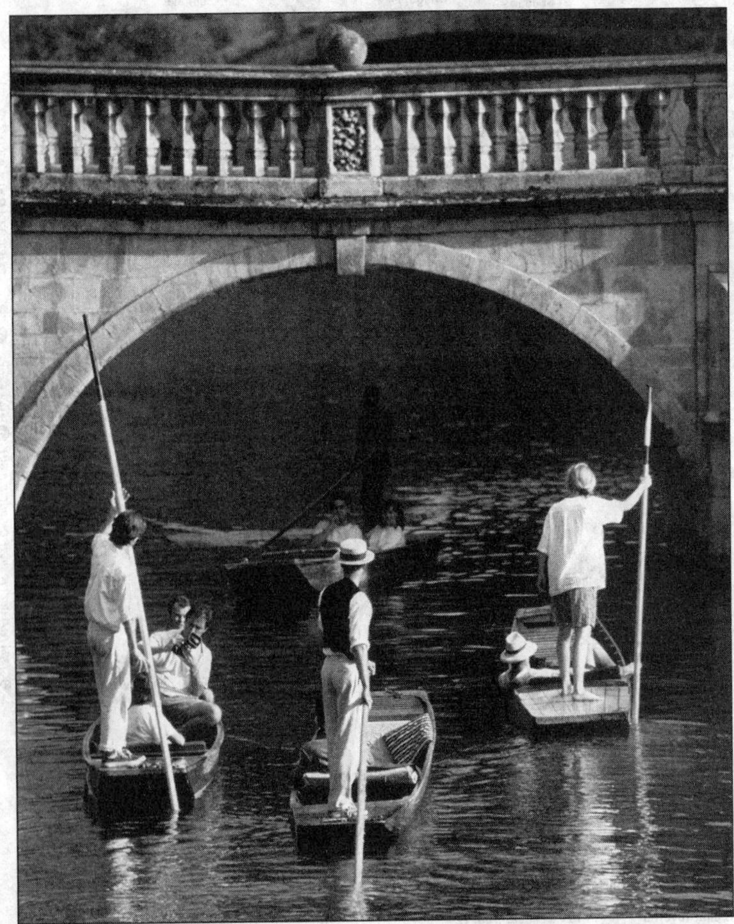

▲ Punting down the Cam

Clare College

Senate House Passage continues west beyond Caius College's Gate of Honour (see above) to Trinity Lane and **Trinity Hall** (daily 9.15am–noon & 2–5.30pm; free; ⓣ01223/332 500, ⓦwww.trinhall.cam.ac.uk) – not to be confused with Trinity College (see below) – where the Elizabethan library retains several of its original chains, designed to prevent students from purloining the texts. A few yards to the south is the much more diverting **Clare College** (daily 10.30am–4.30pm; free, but £2 in summer; ⓣ01223/333 200, ⓦwww.clare.cam.ac.uk), whose alumni include David Attenborough and Siegfried Sassoon. The college's plain period-piece courtyards, completed in the early eighteenth century, lead to one of the most picturesque of all the bridges over the Cam, **Clare Bridge**. Beyond lies the Fellows' Garden, one of the loveliest college gardens open to the public (times as college). Back at the entrance to Clare, it's a few steps more to the North Gate of King's College, beside King's College Chapel (see p.394).

Trinity College

Trinity College, on Trinity Street (daily 10am–5pm; Nov–Feb free, but otherwise £2.20; ⓣ01223/338 400, ⓦwww.trin.cam.ac.uk), is the largest of the Cambridge colleges and it also has the largest courtyard. It comes as little surprise then that its list of famous alumni is probably longer than any of its rivals: literary greats, including Dryden, Byron, Tennyson and Vladimir Nabokov; the Cambridge spies Blunt, Burgess and Philby; two prime ministers, Balfour and Baldwin; William Thackeray, Isaac Newton, Vaughan Williams, Pandit Nehru, Bertrand Russell and Ludwig Wittgenstein, not to mention a trio of (much less talented) royals, Edward VII, George VI and Prince Charles.

A statue of Henry VIII, who founded the college in 1546, sits in majesty over Trinity's **Great Gate**, his sceptre replaced long ago with a chair leg by a student wit. Beyond lies the vast asymmetrical expanse of **Great Court**, which displays a fine range of Tudor buildings, the oldest of which is the fifteenth-century clocktower. The centrepiece of the court is a delicate fountain, in which, legend has it, Lord Byron used to bathe naked with his pet bear – the college forbade students from keeping dogs.

On the far side of the Great Court, walk through "**the screens**" – the narrow passage separating the Hall from the kitchens – to reach **Nevile's Court**, where Newton first calculated the speed of sound. The west end of Nevile's Court is enclosed by one of the university's most famous buildings, the **Wren Library**, (Mon–Fri noon–2pm, plus Sat during term time 10.30am–12.30pm; free). Viewed from the outside, it's impossible to appreciate the scale of the interior thanks to Wren's clever device of concealing the internal floor level by means of two rows of stone columns. In contrast to many modern libraries, natural light pours into the white stuccoed interior, which contrasts wonderfully with the dark lime-wood bookcases, also Wren-designed.

St John's College

Next door to Trinity, **St John's College**, on St John's Street (March–Oct daily 10am–5.30pm; Nov–Feb Sat & Sun 10am–5.30pm; £2.80; ⓣ01223/338 600, ⓦwww.joh.cam.ac.uk), sports a grandiloquent Tudor gatehouse, which is distinguished by the coat of arms of the founder, Lady Margaret Beaufort, the mother of Henry VII, held aloft by two spotted, mythical beasts. Beyond, three successive courts lead to the river, but there's an excess of dull reddish brickwork here – enough for Wordsworth, who lived above the kitchens on F staircase, to describe the place as "gloomy". The arcade on the far side of Third Court leads through to the **Bridge of Sighs**, a chunky, covered bridge built in 1831 but in most respects very unlike its Venetian namesake. The bridge is best viewed from the much older – and much more stylish – Wren-designed bridge a few yards to the south. The Bridge of Sighs links the old college with the fanciful nineteenth-century **New Court**, a crenellated neo-Gothic extravaganza topped by a feast of dinky stone chimneys and pinnacles.

From the Round Church to Magdalene College

Back on St John's Street, it's a few seconds' walk to Bridge Street and the **Round Church** (Tues–Sat 10am–5pm, Sun 1–5pm; £2), built in the twelfth century on the model of the Holy Sepulchre in Jerusalem. It's a curious-looking structure, squat with an ill-considered late medieval extension to the rear, but the Norman pillars of the original church remain, overseen by sturdy arcading and a ring of finely carved faces.

From the Round Church, it takes a minute or two to stroll up to **Magdalene Bridge** and then **Magdalene College** (no set opening hours; free; ⓣ01223/332 100, ⓦwww.magd.cam.ac.uk) – pronounced "maudlin" – which was founded as a hostel by the Benedictines, became a university college in 1542 and was the last of the colleges to admit women, finally succumbing in 1988. The main focus of attention is the **Pepys Library** (Oct, Nov & mid-Jan to mid-March Mon–Sat 2.30–3.30pm; late April to Aug Mon–Sat 11.30am–12.30pm & 2.30–3.30pm; free), in the second of the college's ancient courtyards. Samuel Pepys, a Magdalene student, bequeathed his entire library to the college, where it has been displayed ever since in its original red-oak bookshelves. His famous diary also resides here.

Jesus College

Doubling back down Bridge Street, take Jesus Lane, the first left after the Round Church, to get to **Jesus College** (daily 10am–5pm; free; ⓣ01223/339 339, ⓦwww.jesus.cam.ac.uk), whose intimate cloisters are reminiscent of a monastery – appropriately, as the Bishop of Ely founded the college on the grounds of a suppressed Benedictine nunnery in 1496. The main red-brick gateway is approached via a distinctive walled walkway strewn with bicycles and known as "the Chimney". Beyond, much of the ground plan of the nunnery has been preserved, especially around **Cloister Court**, the first court on the right after the entrance and the prettiest part of the college, dripping with ivy and, in summer, overflowing with hanging baskets. Entered from the Cloister Court, the college **chapel** occupies the former priory chancel and looks like a medieval parish church; it was imaginatively restored in the nineteenth century, using ceiling designs by William Morris and Pre-Raphaelite stained glass. The poet Samuel Taylor Coleridge was the college's most famously bad student, absconding in his first year to join the Light Dragoons, and returning only to be kicked out for a combination of bad debts and unconventional opinions.

Sidney Sussex College

Near Jesus, Malcolm Street cuts off Jesus Lane to reach King Street and its continuation **Hobson Street**, named after the owner of a Cambridge livery stable, who would only allow customers to take the horse nearest the door – hence "Hobson's choice". Leading off Hobson Street is the pleasant shopping **arcade** that occupies the Victorian red bricks of tiny Sussex Street. The arcade leads through to **Sidney Sussex College** (no set opening times; free; ⓣ01223/338 800, ⓦwww.sid.cam.ac.uk), whose sombre, mostly mock-Gothic facade glowers over Sidney Street. The interior is fairly unexciting too, though the long, slender **chapel** is noteworthy for its fancy marble floor, hooped roof and Baroque wood panelling, as well as for being the last resting place of the skull of its most famous alumnus, Oliver Cromwell, though the exact location is a closely guarded secret.

Emmanuel College

Just to the south of Sidney Sussex College, on St Andrew's Street, you hit the hustle and bustle of the town's central shopping area and then **Emmanuel College**, which dates from 1584 (no set opening times; free; ⓣ01223/334 200, ⓦwww.emma.cam.ac.uk). The college's stolid Neoclassical facade hides a neat and trim Front Court, where the **chapel** was designed by Wren in a simple Classical style, its wood-panelled nave set beneath a fancy stucco ceiling. **Emmanuel** trained a new generation of Protestant clergy on the heels of the Reformation, and its recruits numbered among the Pilgrims who settled New England, which not only explains the derivation of the place-name Cambridge in Massachusetts but also accounts for Harvard University – **John Harvard**, another alumnus, is remembered by a memorial window in the chapel.

Queens' College

A short walk from Emmanuel, at the west end of Pembroke Street, turn right up King's Parade and then first left along Silver Street to get to Queens' College, (mid-March to mid-May Mon–Fri 11am–3pm, Sat & Sun 10am–4.30pm; late June to Sept daily 10am–4.30pm; Oct Mon–Fri 1.45–4.30pm, Sat & Sun 10am–4.30pm; Nov to mid-March daily 1.45–4.30pm; £2 in summer, otherwise free; ⓣ01223/335 511, ⓦwww.queens.cam.ac.uk), which is accessed through the visitors' gate on Queens' Lane.

This is one of the most popular colleges with university applicants, and it's not difficult to see why. In the **Old Court** and the **Cloister Court**, Queens' possesses two fairy-tale Tudor courtyards, with the first of the two the perfect illustration of the original collegiate ideal with kitchens, library, chapel, hall and rooms all set around a tiny green. Cloister Court is flanked by the Long Gallery of the President's Lodge, the last remaining half-timbered building in the university, and, in its southeast corner, by the tower where Erasmus is thought to have beavered away during his four years here, probably from 1510 to 1514. Be sure to pay a visit to the college **Hall**, off the screens passage between the two courts, which holds mantel tiles by William Morris, and portraits of Erasmus and one of the college's co-founders, Elizabeth Woodville, wife of Edward IV. Equally eye-catching is the wooden **Mathematical Bridge** over the River Cam (visible for free from the Silver Street Bridge), a copy of the mid-eighteenth-century original, which – so it was claimed – would stay in place even if the nuts and bolts were removed.

The Fitzwilliam Museum

Of all the museums in Cambridge, the **Fitzwilliam Museum**, on Trumpington Street (Tues–Sat 10am–5pm, Sun noon–5pm; free; ⓦwww.fitzmuseum.cam.ac.uk), stands head and shoulders above the rest. The building itself is an interpretation of Neoclassicism, built in the mid-nineteenth century to house the vast collection bequeathed by Viscount Fitzwilliam in 1816. Since then, the museum has been gifted a string of private collections, most of which are focused on a particular specialism, and consequently depicts the changing tastes of the British upper class. The **Lower Galleries,** on the ground floor, contain a wealth of antiquities including Egyptian sarcophagi and mummies, fifth-century BC black-and-red-figure Greek vases, plus a bewildering display of early European ceramics. Further on, there are sections dedicated to armour, glass and pewterware, medals, portrait miniatures and illuminated manuscripts, and – right at the far end – galleries devoted to Far Eastern applied arts and Korean ceramics.

The **Upper Galleries** concentrate on painting and sculpture, with an eclectic assortment of mostly nineteenth- and early twentieth-century European paintings. There are two rooms of French paintings – Monet, Renoir and Degas, among others, are represented – and two rooms of Italian works by the likes of Fra Filippo Lippi, Titian and Veronese. Two rooms feature British canvases by William Blake, Constable, Hogarth, and Gainsborough. The Dutch rooms display paintings by Frans Hals and Ruisdael. The twentieth-century gallery is packed with Lucian Freud, David Hockney, Henry Moore, Ben Nicholson and Barbara Hepworth.

Scott Polar Research Museum and Botanic Gardens

Past the Fitzwilliam Museum, turn left along busy Lensfield Road for the **Scott Polar Research Museum** (Tues–Fri 11am–1pm & 2–4pm, Sat noon–4pm; free), founded in 1920 in memory of the explorer, Captain Robert Falcon Scott (1868–1912), with displays from the expeditions of various polar adventurers, plus exhibitions on native cultures of the Arctic. There's more of general interest near at hand in the shape of the **University Botanic Gardens** (daily: Feb, March & Oct 10am–5pm; April–Sept 10am–6pm; Nov–Jan 10am–4pm; £3; ⓦ www.botanic.cam.ac.uk), whose entrance is on Bateman Street, about 500 yards to the south of Lensfield Road via Panton Street. Founded in 1760 and covering forty acres, the gardens are filled with glasshouses as well as bountiful outdoor displays. The outdoor beds are mostly arranged by natural order, but there's also a particularly interesting series of chronological beds, showing when different plants were introduced into Britain.

Eating and drinking

Even at Cambridge, students are not the world's greatest restaurant-goers, so although the downtown **takeaway** and **café** scene is fine, decent **restaurants** are a little thin on the ground. The myriad Italian places will stand you in good stead; otherwise, choose carefully, particularly in the more touristy areas, where quality isn't always all it should be. Happily, Cambridge abounds in excellent **pubs**.

Cafés and restaurants

Cambridge Chop House 2 King's Parade ⓣ01223/359 506. The cafés facing King's College have always been low-key and downbeat, but this flashy place stands out – and is perhaps the face of things to come. Large, bistro-style premises and a menu with an emphasis on locally produced, seasonal ingredients. Mains, such as mutton Barnsley chop wth winter greens, cost £13–20. Open daily for lunch and dinner.

Clowns 54 King St. Cappuccino and cakes, sandwiches and snacks, plus newspapers to browse. Off the tourist route and not part of a chain – bonuses in anyone's books. Daily 8am–late.

Eraina Taverna 2 Free School Lane ⓣ01223/368 786. Packed Greek taverna, which satisfies the hungry hordes with huge platefuls of stews and grills, as well as pizzas, curries and a whole host of other menu madness. Try to avoid getting stuck in the basement, though at weekends (when you'll probably have to queue) you'll be lucky to get a seat anywhere. Mains from £6.

Michaelhouse Café Trinity St. Good-quality café food – snacks, salads and so forth – in an attractively renovated medieval church. Great central location too. Mon–Sat 9.30am–5pm.

Midsummer House Midsummer Common ⓣ01223/369 299. Lovely riverside restaurant with conservatory, specializing in topnotch French-Mediterranean cuisine. Reservations essential. Main courses such as braised turbot with peanuts and pistachios, squash and asparagus begin at about £18. On the south side of the river, beside the footbridge just to the east of Victoria Ave. Tues 7–9.30pm & Wed–Sat noon–1.30pm & 7–9.30pm.

Rainbow Vegetarian Bistro 9a King's Parade ⓣ01223/321 551. Vegetarian restaurant with main courses – ranging from couscous to lasagna and Indonesian *gado-gado* – for around £8. Organic wines served with meals. Handy location, opposite King's College. Tues–Sat 10am–10pm.

Restaurant 22 22 Chesterton Rd ⓣ01223/351 880. One of the best restaurants in Cambridge, a candlelit townhouse which offers a good-value, fixed-price menu (at around £27). Expect dishes like sautéed squid with chorizo and a steamed sea bream and shellfish broth. Tues–Sat 7–9.45pm.

Trockel, Ulmann und Freunde 13 Pembroke St. Café food at its best in bright, creatively decorated premises. The baguettes have tasty, wholesome fillings – humous and avocado, for example; the soups are hot and tasty; and the cakes are simply delicious. Tends to get jam-packed during term time. Mon–Fri 9am–5pm, Sat 10am–5pm.

Pubs and bars

Anchor 12 Silver St. Very popular riverside tourist haunt with an outdoor deck – and adjacent punt rental.

Champion of the Thames 68 King St. Gratifyingly old-fashioned central pub with decent beer and a student/academic clientele.

Eagle 8 Bene't St. An ancient inn with a cobbled courtyard where Crick and Watson sought inspiration in the 1950s, at the time of their discovery of DNA. It's been tarted up since and gets horribly crowded, but is still worth a pint of anyone's time.

Free Press 7 Prospect Row. Classic, superbly maintained backstreet local with real-ale brews and delicious bar food: freshly prepared grub, from sandwiches and snacks at lunchtimes to heartier meals at night. To get there, proceed south down St Andrew's St, turn left along Park Terrace, which runs beside the grassy expanse of Parker's Piece; then, turn right onto Parkside, cross over the road and take Melbourne Place, a narrow, pedestrian alley that intersects with Prospect Row.

The Pickerel 30 Magdalene St. Once a brothel and now one of several pubs competing for the title of the oldest pub in town, the *Pickerel* has a lively atmosphere and offers a good range of beers beneath its low beams.

Entertainment

The **performing arts** scene is at its busiest and best during the university's term time with numerous student **drama** productions, **classical concerts** and **gigs** culminating in the traditional whizzerama of excess following the exam season. Apart from the places highlighted below, each college and several churches contribute to the performing arts scene too, with the **King's College choir** being, of course, the most famous attraction (see p.394), though the choral scholars who perform at the chapels of St John's and Trinity are also exceptionally good. For upcoming events, ask for details at the tourist office (see p.392), which issues free **listings** leaflets and brochures.

Arts Picturehouse 38–39 St Andrew's St ⓣ0871/704 2050, ⓦwww.picturehouses.co.uk. Art-house cinema with a wide-ranging programme.

Cambridge Arts Theatre 6 St Edward's Passage, off King's Parade ⓣ01223/503 333, ⓦwww.cambridgeartstheatre.com. The city's main repertory theatre, founded by John Maynard Keynes, and launch pad of a thousand-and-one famous careers; offers a topnotch range of cutting-edge and classic productions.

Cambridge Corn Exchange Wheeler St ⓣ01223/357 851, ⓦwww.cornex.co.uk. Revamped nineteenth-century trading hall, now the main city-centre venue for opera, ballet, musicals and comedy as well as regular rock and folk gigs.

Junction Clifton Rd ⓣ01223/511 511, ⓦwww.junction.co.uk. Rock, indie, jazz, reggae or soul gigs, plus theatre, comedy and dance at this popular arts and entertainments venue. Near the train station.

Listings

Bike rental Mikes Bikes, 28 Mill Rd (ⓣ01223/312 591); and H. Drake, near the train station at 56–60 Hills Rd (ⓣ01223/363 468).

Bookshops Cambridge University Press has a shop at 1 Trinity St; Borders is at 12–13 Market St; and Waterstones at 22 Sidney St. For secondhand books try the shops down St Edward's Passage off King's Parade: G. David, at no.16, is an antiquarian's and hard-back-hunter's paradise; the Haunted Bookshop, at no. 9, is better for first editions, travel and illustrated books.

Car rental Europcar ⓣ01223/233 644; Hertz ⓣ01223/309 842.
Pharmacies Boots: 4 St Andrews St ⓣ01223/321 459; 28 Petty Cury ⓣ01223/350 213.
Post office The main office is at 9–11 St Andrew's St (Mon–Sat 9am–5.30pm).

Around Cambridge: Duxford Imperial War Museum

Just eight miles south of Cambridge, and clearly visible from the M11 (Junction #10), the giant hangars of the **Duxford Imperial War Museum** dominate the eponymous airfield (daily: mid-March to late Oct 10am–6pm; late Oct to mid-March 10am–4pm; £16; ⓣ01223/835 000, ⓦwww.duxford.iwm.org.uk). Throughout World War II, East Anglia was a centre of operations for the RAF and the USAF, with the region's flat, unobstructed landscape dotted by dozens of airfields, amongst which Duxford was one of the more important. In total, the museum holds over 150 historic aircraft, a wide-ranging collection of civil and military planes from the Sunderland flying boat to Concorde and the Vulcan B2 bombers, which were used for the first and last time in the 1982 Falklands conflict; the Spitfires, however, remain the most enduringly popular. Most of the planes are kept in full working order and are taken out for a spin several times a year at **Duxford Air Shows**, which attract thousands of visitors. There are usually four air shows a year and advance bookings are strongly recommended – call ahead or consult the museum website, as you should also for details of the bus service linking Duxford with Cambridge bus station.

Travel details

Buses

For information on all local and national bus services, contact Traveline ⓣ0871/200 2233, ⓦwww.traveline.org.uk.
The Norfolk **Coasthopper bus** runs from Cromer to Hunstanton via a whole gaggle of coastal towns and villages, including Blakeney, Sheringham, Wells and the Burnhams. Frequencies vary on different stretches of the route and there are more buses in the summer than in the winter, but on the more popular stretches buses appear mostly every half-hour or hour, much less frequently on Sundays. The operator is Norfolk Green (ⓣ01553/776 980, ⓦwww.norfolkgreen.co.uk).
Cambridge to: Colchester (7 daily; 3hr 30min); Ely (every 30min; 50min); Ipswich (8 daily; 3–4hr); London (hourly; 2hr); Stansted Airport (hourly; 50min).
Colchester to: Cambridge (7 daily; 3hr 30min); Ipswich (hourly; 1–2hr); Sudbury (hourly; 50min).
Ely to: Cambridge (every 30min; 50min).
Ipswich to: Aldeburgh (hourly; 1hr 30min); Colchester (hourly; 1–2hr); Orford (every 2hr; 1hr 20min).
Norwich to: Sheringham (every 30min; 1hr 20min).
Peterborough to: Cambridge (hourly; 2hr 20min); Ely (every 2hr; 2hr); King's Lynn (hourly; 1hr 20min).

Trains

For information on all local and national rail services, contact National Rail Enquiries ⓣ0845/748 4950, ⓦwww.nationalrail.co.uk.
Cambridge to: Ely (hourly; 15min); Ipswich (6 daily; 1hr 20min); King's Lynn (hourly; 45min); London (every 30min; 1hr); Norwich (hourly; 1hr); Stansted Airport (10 daily; 40min).
Colchester to: Ipswich (2 hourly; 25min); London (2 hourly; 50min); Norwich (hourly; 1hr).
Ely to: King's Lynn (hourly; 30min); Nottingham (hourly; 1hr 45min).
Ipswich to: Ely (7 daily; 1hr); London (every 30min; 1hr 10min); Norwich (hourly; 45min).
Norwich to: Cromer (every 1–2hr; 50min); Ely (hourly; 50min); Ipswich (hourly; 45min); London (hourly; 2hr); Sheringham (every 1–2hr; 1hr).

8

The West Midlands and the Peak District

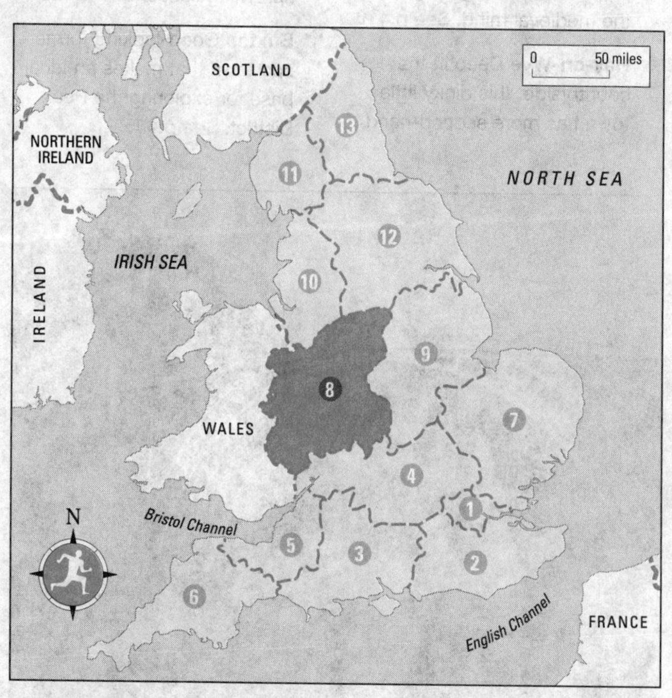

CHAPTER 8

Highlights

- **The theatres, Stratford-upon-Avon** The place to see Shakespeare's plays performed by the pre-eminent Royal Shakespeare Company. See p.411
- **Mappa Mundi, Hereford Cathedral** This antique map, dating to around 1000 AD, provides a riveting insight into the medieval mind. See p.416
- **Hay-on-Wye** Deep in the countryside, this dinky little town has more second-hand bookshops than anywhere else in the world. See p.416
- **Ironbridge Gorge** The first iron bridge ever constructed arches high above the River Severn. See p.419
- **Ludlow** A postcard-pretty country town with half-timbered houses and a sprawling castle. See p.423
- **Buxton** Good-looking former spa town that makes an ideal base for exploring the Peak District. See p.435

▲ The Ironbridge

8

The West Midlands and the Peak District

With justification, the small country towns and untrammelled scenery of the **West Midlands** are the apple of the tourist eye, but there's no disputing the urban epicentre of the region – **Birmingham**, Britain's second city, once the world's greatest industrial metropolis with a slew of factories that powered the Industrial Revolution. Long saddled with a reputation as a culture-hating, car-loving backwater, Birmingham has redefined its image in recent years, initiating some ambitious architectural and environmental schemes, jazzing up its museums and industrial heritage sites and giving itself a higher profile on the nation's cultural and nightlife map than it's ever had before.

The counties to the south and west of Birmingham and beyond the Black Country – **Warwickshire**, **Worcestershire**, **Herefordshire** and **Shropshire** – comprise a rural stronghold that maintains an emotional and political distance from the conurbation. Of the four counties, **Warwickshire** is the least obviously scenic, but draws by far the largest number of visitors, for – as the road signs declare at every entry point – this is "Shakespeare Country". The prime target is, of course, **Stratford-upon-Avon**, with its handful of Shakespeare-related sites and world-class theatre, but spare time also for the diverting town of Warwick, which has a superb church and a whopping castle.

Neighbouring **Worcestershire**, which stretches southwest from the urban fringes of the West Midlands, holds one principal place of interest, **Great Malvern**, a mannered inland resort spread along the rolling contours of the **Malvern Hills** – prime walking territory. From here, it's west again for **Herefordshire**, a large and sparsely populated county that's home to several charming market towns, most notably **Hay-on-Wye**, which boasts the largest concentration of second-hand bookshops in the world, and **Hereford**, where the remarkable medieval Mappa Mundi map is displayed. Next door, to the north, rural **Shropshire** weighs in with **Ludlow**, one of the region's prettiest towns, awash with antique half-timbered buildings, and the amiable county town of **Shrewsbury**, which is also close to the hiking trails of the **Long Mynd**. Shropshire has a fascinating industrial history, too, for it was here in the **Ironbridge Gorge** that British industrialists built the world's first iron bridge and pioneered the use of coal as a smelting fuel. These were two key events in

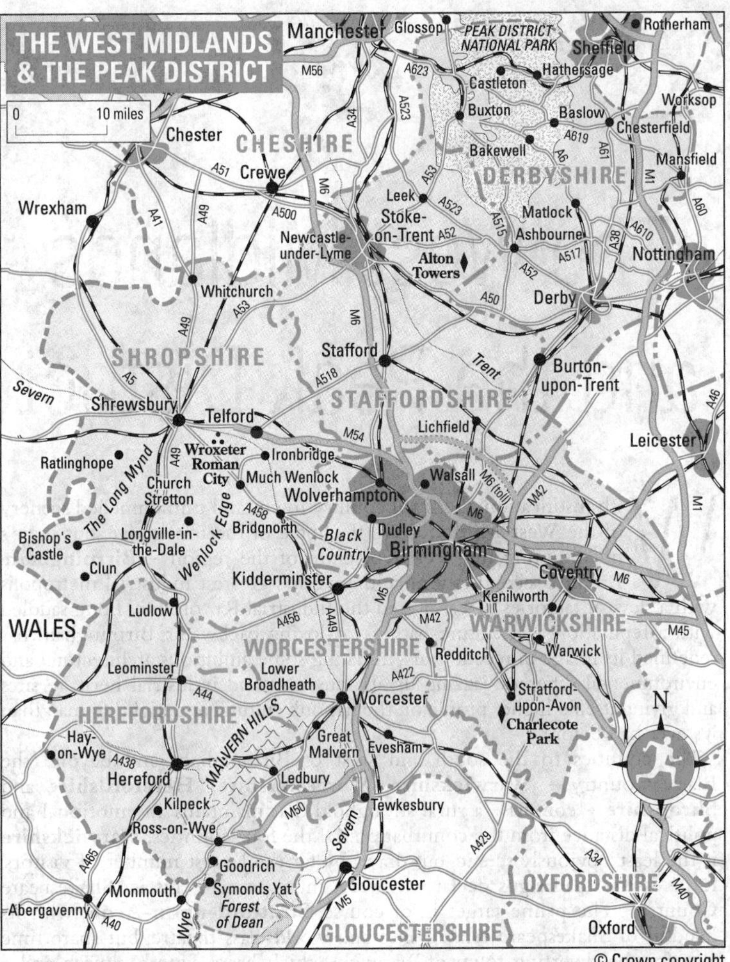

© Crown copyright

the Industrial Revolution and, appropriately, the gorge's industrial heyday is recalled by a phalanx of museums.

To the north of the sprawling Birmingham conurbation, is **Derbyshire**, whose northern reaches incorporate the region's finest scenery in the rough landscapes of the **Peak District National Park**. The latter offers great opportunities for moderately strenuous walks, as well as the comely former spa town of **Buxton**, the limestone caverns of **Castleton** and the so-called "Plague Village" of **Eyam**, not to mention the grandiose stately pile of **Chatsworth House**, a real favourite hereabouts.

Birmingham, the region's **public transport hub**, is easily accessible by **train** from London Euston, Liverpool, Manchester, Leeds, York and a score of other towns. It is also well served by the National Express **bus** network, with dozens of buses leaving every hour for destinations all over Britain. Local **bus** services are excellent around the West Midlands conurbation and very good in the Peak District, but fade away in amongst the villages of Herefordshire and Shropshire.

Stratford-upon-Avon

Despite its worldwide fame, **STRATFORD-UPON-AVON** is at heart an unassuming market town with an unexceptional pedigree. Its first settlers forded, and later bridged, the River Avon, and developed commercial links with the farmers who tilled the surrounding flatlands. A charter for Stratford's weekly market was granted in the twelfth century, a tradition continued to this day, and the town later became an important stopping-off point for stagecoaches between London, Oxford and the north. Like all such places, Stratford had its clearly defined class system and within this typical milieu John and Mary **Shakespeare** occupied the middle rank, and would have been forgotten long ago had their first son, **William**, not turned out to be the greatest writer ever to use the English language. A consequence of their good fortune is that this ordinary little town is nowadays all but smothered by package-tourist hype and, in the summer at least, its central streets groan under the weight of thousands of tourists. Don't let that deter you: the **Royal Shakespeare Company** offers superb theatre and dodging the multitudes is possible by avoiding the busiest attractions at peak times.

Arrival, information and getting around

Stratford **train station** is on the northwest edge of town, ten minutes' walk from the centre. Central Trains run hourly services from Birmingham (Moor Street and Snow Hill stations), and Chiltern Railways operate a regular service from London Marylebone (via Warwick). Local **bus services** arrive and depart from Bridge Street bang in the centre; National Express services and most other long-distance and regional buses pull into the Riverside station on the east side of the town centre, off Bridgeway.

The **tourist office** (April–Sept Mon–Sat 9am–5.30pm, Sun 10.30am–4pm, Oct–March Mon–Sat 9am–5pm & Sun 10am–3pm; Ⓣ0870/160 7930, Ⓦwww.shakespeare-country.co.uk) is handily located by the bridge at the junction of Bridgeway and Bridgefoot. They sell the all-in ticket for all five **Shakespeare Birthplace Trust** properties (£14), or a **Three In-Town Shakespeare Property Ticket** (£11) for the three Trust properties in the town centre; both tickets are also available from the sites themselves.

Accommodation

Stratford's **accommodation** is a tad pricey and often gets booked up well in advance. The town has a dozen or so **hotels**, the pick of which occupy old half-timbered buildings right in the centre of town, but most visitors choose to stay in a **B&B**, which are concentrated to the southwest of the centre around Grove Road, Evesham Place and Broad Walk. The tourist office operates an efficient and extremely useful **Accommodation Booking Hotline** (Ⓣ0870/160 7930, Ⓦwww.shakespeare-country.co.uk).

Hotels

Best Western Grosvenor Warwick Rd Ⓣ01789/269 213, Ⓦwww.bwgh.co.uk. Close to the canal, just a couple of minutes' walk from the town centre, the *Grosvenor* occupies a row of pleasant, two-storey Georgian houses. The

ACCOMMODATION				RESTAURANTS & CAFÉS		PUBS	
Best Western Grosvenor	C	The Shakespeare	G	Kingfisher Fish Bar	2	Dirty Duck	7
Falcon	F	Stratford-upon-Avon Youth Hostel	H	Lamb's Restaurant	3	Windmill Inn	6
Moonraker Guest House	A	Woodstock Guest House	D	Malbec Restaurant	1		
Payton	B			The Oppo	4		
Quilt and Croissants Guest House	E			Russons	5		

interior is crisp and modern and there's ample parking at the back. Discounted short-break deals available. ⑥

Falcon Chapel St ⓣ0870/832 9905, ⓦwww.legacy-hotels.co.uk. Handily situated in the middle of town, this hotel has a half-timbered facade dating from the sixteenth century, though most of the rest is an unremarkable modern rebuild. Substantial discounts are commonplace, but the rack rate is ⑦

Payton 6 John St ⓣ01789/266 442, ⓦwww.payton.co.uk. On the north side of the town centre, a couple of minutes' walk from the Birthplace Museum (see p.409), this comfortable hotel occupies an attractive Georgian townhouse on a quiet residential street. Family-run, the hotel has five comfortable rooms, all en suite. A good bet and very affordable. ⑤

The Shakespeare Chapel St ⓣ01789/294 997, ⓦwww.mercure.com. Now part of a chain, this old hotel, with its mullion windows and half-timbered facade, is one of Stratford's best known. The interior has low beams and open fires and represents a fairly successful amalgamation of the old and new. Right in the centre of town. ⑥

Guesthouses and B&Bs

Moonraker Guesthouse 40 Alcester Rd ⓣ01789/268 774, ⓦwww.moonrakerhouse.com. This amenable place, in a large suburban house, has seven en-suite guest rooms, each decorated in smart modern-meets-period style (canopied beds, mini-chandeliers and so forth). Great breakfasts too – either full English or vegetarian. Just beyond the train station, about 900 yards from the centre. ⑤

Quilt and Croissants Guesthouse 33 Evesham Place ⓣ01789/267 629, ⓦwww.quiltcroissants.co.uk. Amiable B&B in a bow-windowed, Victorian terrace house a short walk from the centre. Seven neat and trim single and double rooms, most en suite. Delicious home-made breakfasts. ②

Woodstock Guesthouse 30 Grove Rd ⓣ01789/299 881, ⓦwww.woodstock-house.co.uk. A smart and neatly kept B&B 5min walk from the centre, by the start of the path to Anne Hathaway's Cottage (see p.411). It has five extremely comfortable bedrooms, all en suite. No credit cards. ❸

Hostel

Stratford-upon-Avon Youth Hostel Hemmingford House, Alveston ⓣ0870/770 6052, ⓦwww.yha.org.uk. This hostel occupies a rambling Georgian mansion on the edge of the pretty village of Alveston. There are dormitories, double and family rooms, some of which are en suite, plus laundry, cycle hire, Internet access, car parking and self-catering facilities. Breakfasts and evening meals are on offer too. It's located two miles east of the town centre on the B4086 and served by regular bus from Stratford's Riverside bus station. Open all year. Dorm beds £20, doubles ❶

The Town

Stratford's **town centre** is flat and compact, its mostly modern buildings filling out a simple gridiron just two blocks deep and four blocks long. Running along the northern edge of the centre is **Bridge Street**, the main thoroughfare lined with shops and chock-a-block with local buses. At its west end Bridge Street divides into Henley Street, home of the **Birthplace Museum**, and Wood Street, which leads up to the marketplace. It also intersects with High Street. The latter, and its continuation Chapel and Church streets, cuts south to pass most of the old buildings that the town still possesses, most notably **Nash's House** and, on neighbouring Old Town Street, **Hall's Croft**. From here, it's a short hop to the charming **Holy Trinity Church**, where Shakespeare lies buried, and then only a few minutes back along the river past the **theatres** to the foot of Bridge Street. In itself, this circular walk only takes about fifteen minutes, but it takes all day if you potter around the attractions. In addition, there are two outlying Shakespearean properties, **Anne Hathaway's Cottage** in Shottery and **Mary Arden's House** in Wilmcote – though you have to be a really serious sightseer to want to see them all.

The Birthplace Museum

Top of everyone's itinerary is the **Birthplace Museum**, on Henley Street (June–Aug Mon–Sat 9am–5pm, Sun 9.30am–5pm; April–May & Sept–Oct daily 10am–5pm; Nov–March Mon–Sat 10am–4pm, Sun 10.30am–4pm; £7), comprising a modern visitor centre and the heavily restored, half-timbered building where the great man was born. The visitor centre pokes into every corner of Shakespeare's life and times, making the most of what little hard evidence there is. Next door, the half-timbered birthplace dwelling is actually two buildings knocked into one. The northern, much smaller and later part was the house of Joan, Shakespeare's sister, and it adjoins the main family home, bought by John Shakespeare in 1556 and now returned to something like its original appearance.

Nash's House and New Place

Follow **High Street** south from the junction of Bridge and Henley streets, and you'll soon come to another Birthplace Trust property, **Nash's House** on Chapel Street (June–Aug Mon–Sat 9.30am–5pm, Sun 10am–5pm; April–May & Sept–Oct daily 11am–5pm; Nov–March daily 11am–4pm; £3.75). Once the property of Thomas Nash, first husband of Shakespeare's granddaughter, Elizabeth Hall, the house's ground floor is kitted out with a pleasant assortment of period furnishings. Upstairs, the main display provides a potted history of Stratford. The adjacent gardens contain the bare foundations of **New Place** (same hours), Shakespeare's last residence, which was demolished long ago. A gated path leads from New Place into the assorted flowerbeds of the **Great Garden**, but the main entrance is on Chapel Lane.

On the other side of Chapel Lane stands the **Guild Chapel**, whose chunky tower and sturdy stonework shelter a plain interior enlivened by some rather crude stained-glass windows and a faded mural above the triumphal arch. The adjoining King Edward VI **Grammar School**, where it's assumed Shakespeare was educated, incorporates a creaky line of fifteenth-century **almshouses** running along Church Street.

Hall's Croft

At the end of Church Street, turn left along Old Town Street for Stratford's most impressive medieval house, the Birthplace Trust's **Hall's Croft** (June–Aug Mon–Sat 9.30am–5pm, Sun 10am–5pm; April–May & Sept–Oct daily 11am–5pm; Nov–March daily 11am–4pm; £3.75). The former home of Shakespeare's elder daughter, Susanna, and her doctor husband, John Hall, the immaculately maintained Croft, with its creaking wooden floors, beamed ceilings and fine kitchen range, holds a good-looking medley of period furniture and a fascinating display on **Elizabethan medicine**.

Holy Trinity Church

Beyond Hall's Croft, Old Town Street steers right to reach the handsome **Holy Trinity Church** (March & Oct Mon–Sat 9am–5pm & Sun 12.30–5pm; April–Sept Mon–Sat 8.30am–6pm & Sun 12.30–5pm; Nov–Feb Mon–Sat 9am–4pm & Sun 12.30–5pm free), whose mellow, honey-coloured stonework dates from the thirteenth century. Enhanced by its riverside setting, the dignified proportions of this quintessentially English church are the result of several centuries of chopping and changing, culminating in the replacement of the original wooden spire with today's stone version in 1763. Inside, the nave is flanked by a fine set of stained-glass windows, some of which are medieval, and bathed in light from the clerestory windows up above. William Shakespeare lies buried in the **chancel** (£1.50), his remains overseen by a sedate and studious memorial plaque and effigy added just seven years after his death.

The theatres

Doubling back from the church, turn right into the **park** just before you reach Southern Lane and you can stroll along – or at least near – the river bank, past the dinky little **chain ferry** (50p) across the Avon, en route to the Royal Shakespeare Company's two main **theatres** – the Swan Theatre and the Royal Shakespeare Theatre – though both are currently being rebuilt. There was no theatre in Stratford in Shakespeare's day and indeed the first home-town festival in his honour was only held in 1769 at the behest of London-based David Garrick. Thereafter, the idea of building a permanent home in which to perform Shakespeare's works slowly gained momentum, and finally, in 1879, the first Memorial Theatre was opened on land donated by local beer baron Charles Flower. A fire in 1926 necessitated the construction of a new theatre, and the ensuing architectural competition, won by Elisabeth Scott, produced the **Royal Shakespeare Theatre**, a cinema-like, red-brick edifice that lasted until 2007, when work started on the creation of a much grander structure. This new theatre is to be completed in 2010 and the revamped **Swan**, a replica "in-the-round" Elizabethan stage just round the back, will be reopened at the same time. In the meantime, a third RSC auditorium, **The Courtyard Theatre**, a few yards away on Southern Lane, will host all the major performances.

Tickets for the RSC

As the **Royal Shakespeare Company** (ⓣ01789/403 444, ⓦwww.rsc.org.uk) works on a repertory system, you could stay in Stratford for a few days and see three or four different plays. Neither would they all have to be Shakespearean: the RSC does indeed focus on the great man's plays, but it offers other productions too, from new modern writing through to plays written by Shakespeare's contemporaries. The RSC currently performs in the **Courtyard Theatre** (see p.410), where tickets start at £5 for a restricted view, rising to £30 for the best seats in the house. Tickets can be bought online (ⓦwww.rsc.org.uk); by phone (ⓣ0844 800 1110); at Stratford tourist office (see p.407); and in person at the Courtyard Theatre box office. Many performances are sold out months in advance and although there's always the off-chance of a last-minute return or stand-by ticket (for unsold seats), don't bet on it. Finally, some people find the Courtyard Theatre's seats very uncomfortable – take a cushion.

In front of the Royal Shakespeare Theatre, the manicured lawns of a small riverside park stretch north as far as **Bancroft Basin**, where the Stratford canal meets the river. The basin is usually packed with narrowboats. To round things off, stroll over to the Boathouse, on Swan's Nest Lane, where **Avon Boating** (April–Oct 9am till dusk; ⓣ01789/267 073, ⓦwww.avon-boating.co.uk) hires out rowing boats, punts and canoes for a couple of pounds a time; they also offer thirty-minute river trips (£4).

Anne Hathaway's Cottage

Anne Hathaway's Cottage (April–Oct Mon–Sat 9/9.30am–5pm, Sun 9.30/10am–5pm; Nov–March daily 10am–4pm; £5.50), also operated by the Birthplace Trust, is located just over a mile west of the centre in the well-heeled suburb of **Shottery**. The cottage – actually an old farmhouse – is an immaculately maintained, half-timbered affair with a thatched roof and diminutive chimneys. This was the home of Anne Hathaway before she married Shakespeare in 1582, and the interior holds a comely combination of period furniture, including a superb, finely carved four-poster bed. The garden is splendid too, crowded with bursting blooms in the summertime. The adjacent orchard and **Shakespeare Tree Garden** features a scattering of modern sculptures and over forty trees, shrubs and roses mentioned in the plays, with each bearing the appropriate quotation inscribed on a plaque. The most agreeable way to get to the cottage from the town centre is on the signposted **footpath** from Evesham Place, at the south end of Rother Street.

Mary Arden's House

The Birthplace Trust also owns **Mary Arden's House** (daily: April & May 10am–5pm; June–Aug 9.30am–5pm; Sept–Oct 11am–5pm; Nov–March 10am–4pm; £6), three miles northwest of the town centre in the village of **Wilmcote**. Mary was Shakespeare's mother and the only unmarried daughter of her father, Robert, at the time of his death in 1556. Unusually for the period, Mary inherited the house and land, thus becoming one of the neighbourhood's most eligible women – John Shakespeare, eager for self-improvement, married her within a year. The house is a well-furnished example of an Elizabethan farmhouse and, though the labelling is rather scant, a platoon of guides fills in the details of family life and traditions.

Eating and drinking

Stratford is used to feeding and watering thousands of visitors, so finding refreshment is never difficult. There's a scattering of very good **restaurants**, and a handful of **pubs** and **cafés** offer good food, too. The best restaurants are concentrated along Sheep Street, running up from Waterside.

Restaurants and cafés

Kingfisher Fish Bar 13 Ely St. The best fish-and-chip shop in town. Takeaway and sit-down. A 5min walk from the theatres. Closed Sun.

Lamb's Restaurant 12 Sheep St ⓣ01789/292 554. Chic and immensely appealing restaurant serving a mouthwatering range of stylish English and continental dishes in antique premises – beamed ceilings and so forth. Daily specials at around £8, other main courses £14–16. The best place in town. Mon 6–10pm, Tues–Sun noon–2pm & 6–10pm.

Malbec Restaurant 6 Union St ⓣ01789/269 106. Smart and intimate restaurant serving top-quality seafood and meat dishes, often with a Mediterranean slant. Mains around £15.

The Oppo 13 Sheep St ⓣ01789/269 980. International cuisine in a busy but amiable atmosphere and pleasant old premises. The dishes of the day, chalked up on a board inside, are good value at around £7, otherwise mains average £12.

Russons 8 Church St ⓣ01789/268 822. Excellent, good-value cuisine, featuring interesting meat and vegetarian dishes on the main menu and an extensive blackboard of daily specials. Cosy little place too. Main courses around £11. Closed Sun & Mon.

Pubs

Dirty Duck 53 Waterside. The archetypal actors' pub, stuffed to the gunwales every night with a vocal entourage of RSC employees and hangers-on. Traditional beers in somewhat spartan premises plus a terrace for hot-weather drinking.

Windmill Inn Church St. Popular pub with rabbit-warren rooms and low-beamed ceilings. Flowers beers too.

Warwick

Pocket-sized **WARWICK**, just eight miles northeast of Stratford and easily reached by bus and train, is famous for its massive **castle**, but it also possesses several charming streetscapes erected in the aftermath of a great fire in 1694. An hour or two is quite enough time to nose around the town centre, though you'll need the whole day if, braving the crowds and the medieval musicians, you're also set on exploring the castle and its extensive grounds: either way, Warwick is the perfect day-trip from Stratford.

The Castle

Towering above the River Avon at the foot of the town centre, **Warwick Castle** (daily: April–Sept 10am–6pm; Oct–March 10am–5pm; £17.95; parking £2.50–5; ⓦwww.warwick-castle.co.uk) is often proclaimed the "greatest medieval castle in Britain". This claim is valid enough if bulk equals greatness, though even so, much of the existing structure is the result of extensive nineteenth-century tinkering.

The **entrance** to the castle is through the old stable block at the bottom of Castle Street. Beyond, a footpath leads round to the imposing moated and mounded **East Gate**. Over the footbridge – and beyond the protective towers – is the main **courtyard**. You can stroll along the ramparts and climb the towers, but most visitors head straight for one or other of the special displays installed inside the castle's many chambers and towers. One of the most popular of these displays is the "Royal Weekend Party, 1898", an extravaganza of waxwork nobility hobnobbing in the private apartments which were rebuilt in the 1870s after fire damage. The **grounds** are much more enjoyable, acres of woodland and lawn inhabited by peacocks and including a large glass **conservatory**. A footbridge leads over the River Avon to **River Island**, the site of jousting tournaments and other such medieval hoopla.

The town centre

Re-emerging from the castle at the stables, **Castle Street** leads up the hill for a few yards to its junction with the High Street. Turn left and it's a brief stroll to another remarkable building, the **Lord Leycester Hospital** (April–Oct Tues–Sun 10am–5pm; Nov–March Tues–Sun 10am–4pm; £4.90), a tangle of half-timbered buildings that lean at fairy-tale angles against the old West Gate. The complex represents one of Britain's best-preserved examples of domestic Elizabethan architecture and it was established as a hostel for old soldiers by Robert Dudley, the Earl of Leicester, a favourite of Queen Elizabeth I.

Doubling back along the High Street, turn left up Church Street – opposite Castle Street – for **St Mary's Church** (daily: April–Oct 10am–6pm, Nov–March 10am–4.30pm; £1 donation suggested), which was rebuilt in a weird Gothic-Renaissance amalgam after the fire of 1694. One part remained untouched, however – the **chancel**, a glorious illustration of the Perpendicular style with a splendid vaulted ceiling of flying and fronded ribs. On the right-hand side of the chancel is the **Beauchamp Chapel**, which contains several beautiful tombs, exquisite works of art beginning with that of Richard Beauchamp, Earl of Warwick, who is depicted in an elaborate suit of armour of Italian design from the tip of his swan helmet down to his mailed feet.

Practicalities

From Warwick **train station**, on the northern edge of town, it's about ten minutes' walk to the centre via Station and Coventry roads. **Buses** stop on Market Street, close to the Market Square, from where it's a couple of minutes' walk east to St Mary's Church. The **tourist office** is in the old Courthouse at the corner of Castle and Jury streets (daily 9.30am–4.30pm; ⓣ01926/492 212, ⓦwww.warwick-uk.co.uk). They have a list of local hotels and B&Bs, but with Stratford so near and easy to reach, there's no special reason to stay, although *Forth House*, 44 High St (ⓣ01926/401 512, ⓦwww.forthhouseuk.co.uk; ❺), is an excellent **B&B** with two en-suite and very comfortable guest rooms in a listed sixteenth-century property a short walk from the tourist office.

For a bite to **eat**, try the *Catalan*, 6 Jury St (kitchen open: Mon–Sat noon–3pm plus Mon & Wed–Sat 6pm–10pm), a slick, modern café-restaurant, which offers tasty tapas and light lunches during the day, and Mediterranean-inspired food at night, with main courses from £10; it's located just along from the tourist office.

Worcestershire

Worcestershire is saucer-shaped, with the low-lying plains of the Severn Valley and the Vale of Evesham, Britain's foremost fruit-growing area, rising to a lip of hills, principally the Malverns in the west and the Cotswolds (see pp.269–277) to the south. To the north lie the industrial and overspill towns – Redditch for instance – that have much in common with the Birmingham conurbation, while the south is predominantly rural and holds the county's finest scenery in the **Malvern Hills**, excellent walking territory much loved by that most English of composers, **Edward Elgar**, and home to the amiable former spa town of **Great Malvern**.

The proximity of Birmingham ensures Worcestershire has a good network of **trains** and **buses**, though services are spasmodic amongst the villages in the south of the county. There's an excellent regional public transport information line covering all of the West Midlands – Centro (ⓣ0121/200 2787, ⓦwww.centro.org.uk) – or you can resort to the usual national numbers for bus (ⓣ0871/200 2233, ⓦwww.traveline.org.uk) and rail (ⓣ0845/748 4950, ⓦwww.nationalrail.co.uk).

Great Malvern and the Malvern Hills

One of the most exclusive and prosperous areas of the Midlands, **The Malverns** is the generic name for a string of towns and villages stretched along the eastern lower slopes of the **Malvern Hills**, which rise spectacularly out of the flatlands a few miles to the southwest of Worcester. About nine miles from north to south – between the A44 and the M50 – and never more than five miles wide, the hills straddle the Worcestershire–Herefordshire boundary. It's easy if energetic walking country, with great views, and there's an excellent network of **hiking trails**, most of which can be completed in a day or half-day.

Amongst The Malverns, it's **GREAT MALVERN** that grabs the attention, its pocket-sized centre clambering up the hillside with the crags of North Hill beckoning beyond. The Benedictines chose this hilly setting for one of their abbeys and although Henry VIII closed the place down in 1538, the **Priory Church** (daily: 9am–5pm; free) has survived, the crisp symmetries and elaborate decoration of its exterior witnessing the priory's former wealth.

A couple of minutes' walk away, hard by the top of Church Street, the modest **Malvern Museum** (Easter–Oct daily except for Wed 10.30am–5pm; £1) is housed in the delicately proportioned Priory Gatehouse, and concentrates on Great Malvern's days as a **spa town**, when the local spring waters packed the place out. You can still sample the waters at *St Ann's Well Café* (July & Aug Mon–Fri 11.30am–3.30pm, Sat & Sun 10am–4pm; May–June & Sept Tues–Fri 11.30am–3.30pm, Sat & Sun 10am–4pm; Oct–May Sat & Sun 11.30am–3.30pm, ⓣ01684/560 285, ⓦwww.stannswell.co.uk), a cosy little vegetarian café in an attractive Georgian building a steep fifteen-minute walk up the wooded hillside from the top of town; the signposted path begins on the far side of the main road across from the *Foley Arms Hotel*.

Back at the museum, it's a short walk down the hill to Grange Road, where the **Malvern Theatres** (ⓣ01684/892 277 ⓦwww.malvern-theatres.co.uk) is the key venue for the wide range of special events the town puts on each year.

Practicalities

Great Malvern's infinitely rustic **train station** has fast and frequent connections with Birmingham and Worcester. It's located half a mile or so from the town centre – take Avenue Road and then **Church Street**, the steeply sloping main drag. The **tourist office** is at the top of Church Street, across from the Priory Church (daily 10am–5pm; ⓣ01684/892 289, ⓦwww.malvernhills.gov.uk/tourism).

Amongst the **hotels**, the pick is *The Abbey* (ⓣ01684/892 332, ⓦwww.sarova.com; ⑥), a rambling, creeper-clad Victorian hotel with mock-Tudor timbering and plush rooms, all set behind the Priory Church on

Abbey Road – but note that the hotel's lumpy modern wing is unappetizing; the hotel is part of a small chain. A great **B&B** is *The Copper Beech House*, in a large Victorian house near the train station at 32 Avenue Rd (ⓣ01684/565 013, ⓦwww.copperbeechhouse.co.uk; ④), and offering a handful of well-appointed en-suite rooms.

For **food**, try the smart and chic *Anupam Asian* restaurant at 85 Church St (ⓣ01684/573 814; Mon–Sat 12.30–2pm & 5.30pm–midnight, plus Sun 12.30pm–midnight), where main courses average around £10.

Herefordshire

Over the Malvern Hills from Worcestershire, the rolling agricultural landscapes of **Herefordshire** have an easy-going charm, but the finest scenery hereabouts is along the banks of the **River Wye**. Plonked in the middle of the county on the Wye is **Hereford**, a sleepy, rather old-fashioned sort of place whose proudest possession, the remarkable Mappa Mundi map, was almost flogged off in a round of ecclesiastical budget cuts back in the 1980s. To the west of Hereford, hard by the Welsh border, the key attraction is **Hay-on-Wye**, which – thanks to the purposeful industry of the entrepreneurial Richard Booth – has become the world's largest repository of **second-hand books**, on sale in around thirty bookshops.

Herefordshire possesses one **rail line**, linking Hereford with points north to Shrewsbury and east to Great Malvern and Worcester. Otherwise, you'll be restricted to the tender mercies of the county's **buses**, which provide a reasonable service between the villages and towns, except on Sundays when there's almost nothing at all. All the local tourist offices have bus timetables and there's **bus information** on ⓣ0870/608 2608 and/or ⓦwww.herefordshire-buses.tbctimes.co.uk.

Hereford

HEREFORD – literally "army ford" – was long a border garrison town held against the Welsh, its military importance guaranteed by its strategic position beside the River Wye. Today, with the fortifications that once girdled the city all but vanished, it's the **cathedral,** which forms the main focus of architectural interest. It lies just to the north of the River Wye at the heart of the city centre, whose compact tangle of narrow streets and squares is clumsily boxed in by the ring road. Taken as a whole, Hereford makes for a pleasant – if not exactly riveting – overnight stay.

The Cathedral

Hereford **Cathedral** (daily 9.15am–5.30pm; £4 donation suggested; ⓦwww.herefordcathedral.org) is a curious building, an uncomfortable amalgamation of architectural styles, with bits and pieces added to the eleventh-century original by a string of bishops and culminating in an extensive – and not especially sympathetic – Victorian refit. From the outside, the sandstone **tower** is the dominant feature, constructed in the early fourteenth century to eclipse the Norman western tower, which subsequently collapsed under its own weight in 1786. The crashing masonry mauled the **nave** and its replacement lacks the grandeur of most other English cathedrals, though the forceful symmetries of the long rank of surviving Norman arches and piers more than hints at what went before.

In the 1980s, the cathedral's finances were so stretched that a plan was drawn up to sell its most treasured possession, the **Mappa Mundi**. Luckily, the government and John Paul Getty Jnr rode to the rescue, with the oil tycoon stumping up a million pounds to keep the map here and install it in a new building. Made of sandstone, this New Library – located next to the cathedral at the west end of the cloisters – blends in seamlessly with the other, older buildings close by. It contains the Mappa Mundi and Chained Library Exhibition (April–Oct Mon–Sat 10am–4.30pm, plus May–Sept Sun 11am–3.30pm; Nov–March Mon–Sat 10am–3.30pm, but some closures for maintenance in Jan; £4.50), which begins with a series of interpretative panels that lead to the Mappa, displayed in a dimly lit room. Dating to about 1300, and 64 by 52 inches in size (1.58 x 1.33 metres), the map is quite simply remarkable: it is indeed a map (as we know it) in so far as it suggests the general geography of the world – with Asia at the top and Europe and Africa below, to left and right respectively – but it also squeezes in history, mythology and theology.

Practicalities

From Hereford **train station**, it's about half a mile southwest to the main square, High Town – via Station Approach, Commercial Road and its continuation Commercial Street. The long-distance **bus station** is just off Commercial Road, but most local and some regional buses stop in St Peter's Square, at the east end of High Town. The **tourist office** is directly opposite the cathedral, at 1 King St (Mon–Sat 9am–5pm, plus mid-May to mid-Sept Sun 10am–4pm; ⓣ01432/268 430, ⓦwww.visitherefordshire.co.uk).

Easily the best **hotel** in town is the *Castle House*, an immaculate refurbished Georgian mansion just a couple of minutes' walk from the cathedral on Castle Street (ⓦwww.castlehse.co.uk; ❽). The hotel has a chic waterside terrace at the rear. Hereford also has a substantial number of **B&Bs**, the pick of which is *Charades*, 34 Southbank Rd (ⓣ01432/269 444, ⓦwww.charadeshereford.co.uk; ❹), with five comfortable, en-suite guest rooms in a large Victorian house a ten- to fifteen-minute walk northeast from the centre.

There are several appealing places to **eat** just north of the cathedral on pedestrianized **Church Street**: try *Nutters* (Mon–Sat 9am–5pm), a vegetarian café just off Church Street on Capuchin Yard. The smartest restaurant in town is at the *Castle House Hotel* (see above), where the emphasis is on local ingredients – Hereford beef and Gloucestershire pork for instance; main courses start at £13.

Don't leave town without sampling the favourite local tipple, **cider**. Every pub in town serves the stuff with one of the most enjoyable being *The Barrels*, five minutes' walk southeast of High Town, at 69 St Owen's St. *The Barrels* is also the home pub of the local Wye Valley Brewery (ⓦwww.wyevalleybrewery.co.uk), whose trademark **bitters** are much acclaimed.

Hay-on-Wye

Straddling the Anglo-Welsh border some twenty miles west of Hereford, the hilly little town of **HAY-ON-WYE** is known to most people for one thing – **books**. Hay saw its first bookshop open in 1961 and has since become a bibliophile's paradise, with just about every spare inch of the town being given over to the trade, including the old cinema and the ramshackle stone castle. As a consequence, many of Hay's inhabitants are now outsiders, which means that it has little indigenous feel, but there again when the hill farmers come into town on the razzle Hay gets a bit of a (welcome) jolt. The prestigious **Hay Festival of literature and the arts** (ⓣ0870/990 1299,

▲ Bookshop in Hay-on-Wye

Ⓦwww.hayfestival.com), is held over ten days at the back end of May, when London's literary world decamps here en masse.

Arrival and information

Buses to Hay stop yards from the centre of town on Oxford Road beside the main car park. The adjacent **tourist office** (daily: Easter–Oct 10am–1pm &

2–5pm; Nov–Easter 11am–1pm & 2–4pm; ⓣ01497/820 144, ⓦwww.hay-on-wye.co.uk) issues free town maps and free leaflets outlining what, in general terms at least, each of the town's bookshops stock and their specialisms, if any. The tourist office also sells an exhaustive range of hiking books and maps, and will arrange accommodation.

Accommodation

Accommodation gets booked up long in advance during the Hay Festival (see p.416). There are a handful of **hotels**, but the town's **B&Bs and guesthouses** are far more numerous. There are also several **campsites**, the handiest of which is the no-frills *Radnors End* (ⓣ01497/820 780), in a pleasant setting five minutes' walk from the town centre across the Wye bridge on the Clyro road.

La Fosse Guesthouse Oxford Rd, Hay ⓣ01497/820 613, ⓦwww.lafosse.co.uk. This agreeable B&B is in an old three-storey cottage a brief walk east of the tourist office at the junction of Lion and Oxford roads. All four cosy guest rooms are en suite. ③

Old Post Office B&B Llanigon ⓣ01497/820 008, ⓦwww.oldpost-office.co.uk. First-rate B&B in a seventeenth-century former post office, complete with wood floors and beamed ceilings. There are three rooms here, two en suite, and the vegetarian breakfasts are delicious; Llanigon is a couple of miles south of Hay along a country lane – take the Brecon Rd and watch for the signs. No credit cards; two nights' minimum stay on the weekend. ④

Start Bed and Breakfast Hay-on-Wye ⓣ01497/821 391, ⓦwww.the-start.net. One of the best B&Bs in town, occupying a modernized old house, beside the river just across the bridge from the town centre. There are three en-suite guest rooms here, each decorated in a bright and breezy manner. ③

The Town

Hay has an attractive riverside **setting** and its narrow, bendy streets are lined with a particularly engaging assortment of old stone houses, but before you start ambling round the town, visit the tourist office (see p.417) to pick up the free leaflet that gives the lowdown on all of Hay's **bookshops** together with a street plan. Across the street from the tourist office, a signed footpath leads up the slope to the **castle**, a careworn Jacobean mansion built into the walls of an earlier medieval fortress. The bookseller Richard Booth owns the castle, and its southern extremities are given over to a pair of bookshops: **Castle Street Books** (daily 10.30am–5pm; ⓣ01497/820 160), which has a large stock of remaindered books, and **Hay Castle Bookshop** (daily 9.30am–5.30pm; ⓣ01497/820 503 ⓦwww.richardbooth.demon.co.uk), a trusty collection focused on fine art, cinema, antiquarian and photography. From here, the footpath twists its way round the western flank of the castle to meet the steps that lead down to Castle Street, home to **The Pound Bookshop**, at no. 9 (daily 9am–5.30pm; ⓣ01497/821 572, ⓦwww.bookends.uk.com), where all the books cost £1.

Castle Street slopes up to the main square, High Town, just beyond which is Lion Street, where **Richard Booth's Bookshop**, at no. 44 (April–Oct daily 9am–7pm, Nov–March Mon–Sat 9am–5.30pm, Sun 11am–3.30pm; ⓣ01497/820 322, ⓦwww.richardbooth.demon.co.uk) is a huge, musty, bookish warehouse of a place offering almost unlimited browsing potential. At the foot of Lion Street is the town's main landmark, the ornate, somewhat Ruritanian Victorian **clocktower**.

Eating and drinking

For **food**, *Shepherds*, 9 High Town (Mon–Sat 9.30am–5.30pm, Sun 10.30am–5.30pm), is an appealing café with a good line in snacks and mouthwatering, locally made ice cream. There's also the hard-to-beat *Granary* (daily till 9pm; ⓣ01497/820 790), a combined café, bar and restaurant opposite the clocktower on Broad Street. Here they serve delicious wholefood snacks and soups as well as filling main meals (£7–9) with the emphasis on local organic produce; they have a roadside terrace, too, where hikers can kick off their boots and sink a leisurely pint. For something more formal, head for the restaurant of the *Old Black Lion*, Lion St; main courses start at about £12 – half that in the adjoining bar. The pub also serves up its own **beer** – Black Lion bitter.

Shropshire

One of England's largest and least populated counties, **Shropshire** (ⓦwww.shropshiretourism.com) stretches from its long and winding border with Wales to the very edge of the urban Black Country. The Industrial Revolution made a huge stride forward here, with the spanning of the River Severn by the very first **iron bridge**. The assorted industries that subsequently squeezed into the **Ironbridge Gorge** are long gone, but a series of **museums** celebrate their craftsmanship – from tiles through to iron. The River Severn also flows through the county town of **Shrewsbury**, whose antique centre holds dozens of old half-timbered buildings, though **Ludlow**, further to the south, has the edge when it comes to handsome Tudor and Jacobean architecture. In between the two lie some of the most beautiful parts of Shropshire, primarily the **Long Mynd**, a prime hiking area that is readily explored from the attractive little town of **Church Stretton**.

Yet, for all its attractions, Shropshire remains well off the main tourist routes, and one reason for this is the paucity of **public transport**. Shrewsbury and Telford are connected to Birmingham, whilst Ludlow and Church Stretton are connected to Shrewsbury on the Hereford line, but that's about the limit of the **train** services, whilst rural **buses** tend to connect the county's outlying villages on just a few days of the week. One useful service is the **Shropshire Hills Shuttle bus** service (ⓦwww.shropshirehillsshuttles.co.uk), aimed at the tourist market, and operating every weekend from April to October. The shuttle has two routes, the more useful of which noses round the Long Mynd and the Stiperstones and drops by Church Stretton; buses are hourly and an adult Day Rover ticket, valid on the whole route, costs just £4. Bus timetables are available at most Shropshire tourist offices and on the website.

Ironbridge Gorge

Ironbridge Gorge was the crucible of the Industrial Revolution, a process encapsulated by its famous span across the Severn – the world's first **iron bridge**, engineered by Abraham Darby and opened on New Year's Day, 1781. The area's factories once churned out engines, rails, wheels and other heavy-duty iron pieces in quantities unmatched anywhere else in the world, but manufacturing has now all but vanished and the surviving monuments make the gorge the most extensive **industrial heritage sight** in England – and one that has been granted World Heritage Site status by UNESCO.

The gorge contains several **museums** and an assortment of other industrial attractions spread along a five-mile stretch of the River Severn Valley. A thorough exploration takes a couple of days, but the **highlights** – the iron bridge itself, the Museum of Iron and the Jackfield Tile Museum – are easily manageable on a day-trip. Each museum and attraction charges its own admission fee, but if you're intending to visit several, then buy a **passport ticket** (£14), which allows access to each of them once in any calendar year. Passport tickets are available at all the main sights and at the tourist office (see below), which also issues local maps and information. **Parking** is free at most of the sights, but not in Ironbridge village itself.

Arrival, getting around and information

Every two hours or so, Monday to Saturday, there's a **bus** from Shrewsbury bus station to Ironbridge village, at the heart of the gorge; the journey takes an hour and a half. The problem is that once you have reached Ironbridge village, there are no connecting buses along the gorge except at the weekend (April–Oct), when the **Gorge Connect bus** shuttles along the gorge from Coalbrookdale in the west to Coalport (for Telford) in the east, taking in Ironbridge village on the way. Departures are every half-hour (9am–5pm) and each journey you make, no matter how short or long, costs 50p. Alternatively, **bike rental** is available from the Bicycle Hub (Tues–Sat 10am–5pm; ⓣ01952/883 249, ⓦwww.thebicyclehub.co.uk) in the same complex as Jackfield Tile Museum (see p.421).

The **Ironbridge Visitor Information Centre** (Mon–Fri 9am–5pm, Sat & Sun 10am–5pm; ⓣ01952/884 391, ⓦwww.ironbridge.org.uk) is located in the old toll house at the south end of the iron bridge in Ironbridge village.

Accommodation

Most visitors to the gorge come for the day, but there are several pleasant **B&Bs** in Ironbridge village, which is where you want to be.

Bridge View 10 Tontine Hill, Ironbridge village ⓣ01952/432 541, ⓦwww.ironbridgeview.co.uk. Sympathetically updated eighteenth-century house a stone's throw from the bridge with neat and trim rooms. ❸

Coalbrookdale Villa 17 Paradise, Coalbrookdale ⓣ01952/433 450, ⓦwww.coalbrookdalevilla.co.uk. This B&B occupies an attractive Victorian ironmaster's house about half a mile up the hill from the west end of Ironbridge village in the tiny hamlet of Paradise, close to Coalbrookdale iron foundry (see p.421). Sedately decorated en-suite bedrooms. In its own grounds. No cards. ❹

The Library House 11 Severn Bank, Ironbridge village ⓣ01952/432 299, ⓦwww.libraryhouse.com. Enjoyable B&B in a charming Georgian villa just yards from the iron bridge. Has three well-appointed double bedrooms decorated in a modern rendition of period style. ❺

Eating and drinking

Don't miss the *Coalbrookdale Inn*, a smashing traditional **pub** on the main road across from the Coalbrookdale iron foundry. It offers a tasty selection of real ales and delicious bar food (Mon–Sat noon–3pm & 6–9pm, Sun noon–3pm). The best **restaurant** hereabouts is *Restaurant Severn*, near the bridge at 33 High St (ⓣ01952/432 233), where the menu features mains like venison in a cognac and cranberry sauce; they average around £16.

Ironbridge village

There must have been an awful lot of nail-biting during the construction of the **iron bridge** over the River Severn in the late 1770s. No one was quite sure how the new material would wear and although the single-span design looked sound, many feared the bridge would simply tumble into the river. To compensate, Abraham Darby used more iron than was strictly necessary, but the end result still manages to appear stunningly graceful, arching between the steep banks with the river far below. The settlement at the north end of the span was promptly renamed **IRONBRIDGE**, and today its brown-brick houses climb prettily up the hill from the bridge. The village is also home to the **Museum of the Gorge** (daily 10am–5pm; £2.75), located in a neo-Gothic old riverside warehouse about 500yd west of the bridge along the main road. This provides an introduction to the industrial history of the gorge and provides a few environmental pointers too.

Coalbrookdale iron foundry

At the roundabout just to the **west** of the Museum of the Gorge, turn right for the half-mile trip up to what was once the gorge's big industrial deal, the **Coalbrookdale iron foundry**, which boomed throughout the eighteenth and early nineteenth century, employing up to four thousand men and boys. The foundry has been imaginatively converted into the **Museum of Iron** (daily 10am–5pm; £5.25), with a wide range of displays on iron-making in general and the history of the company in particular.

The Tar Tunnel and Jackfield

Heading **east** from the iron bridge, it's a third of a mile along the river to the battered brick-and-stone remains of the **Bedlam furnace** (open access; free), one of the first furnaces to use coke rather than charcoal. It was kept alight round-the-clock and at night its fiery silhouette scared passers-by half to death – hence the name. From here, it's a mile to the turning for Blists Hill (see below) and another 500yd or so to the **Tar Tunnel** (April–Oct daily 10am–5pm; £1.75), built to transport coal from one part of the gorge to another, but named for the bitumen that oozes naturally from its walls.

Beside the Tar Tunnel, a **footbridge** crosses the Severn to reach **JACKFIELD**, now a sleepy little hamlet whose brown-brick cottages string prettily along the river, but once a sooty, grimy place that hummed to the tune of two large tile factories, Maws and Craven Dunnill. Both were built in the middle of the nineteenth century to the latest industrial design, a fully integrated manufacturing system that produced literally thousands of tiles at breakneck speed. From the footbridge, it's a couple of minutes walk west to the first of the two, now the **Maws Craft Centre** (Ⓦ www.mawscraftcentre.co.uk), holding over twenty arts, craft and specialist shops. A short walk away, the former Craven Dunnill factory has become the excellent **Jackfield Tile Museum** (daily 10am–5pm; £5.25), whose exhibits include the superb "Style Gallery", where cabinet after cabinet illustrates the different styles of tile produced here, from Art Deco and Art Nouveau through to Arts and Crafts and the Aesthetic Movement.

Coalport

Back at the Tar Tunnel, a canal towpath leads east in a couple of minutes to **Coalport China works**, a large brick complex holding the **Coalport China Museum** (daily 10am–5pm; £5.25), crammed full with gaudy Coalport wares. There's also a workshop, where potters demonstrate their skills, and two **bottle-kilns**, those distinctive conical structures that were long the hallmark of the pottery industry. In the base of one is a small display of Coalport pieces, whilst the other explains how the kilns worked – though quite how the firers survived the conditions defies the imagination.

Blists Hill Victorian Town

Doubling back along the river, it's a third of a mile west from Coalport to the clearly signed, mile-long side road that cuts up to the gorge's most popular attraction, the rambling **Blists Hill Victorian Town** (daily 10am–5pm; £9.50).

This encloses a substantial number of reconstructed Victorian buildings, most notably a school, a candle-maker's, a doctor's surgery, a gaslit pub, and wrought-iron works. Jam-packed on most summer days, it's especially popular with school parties, who keep the period-dressed employees very busy.

Shrewsbury

SHREWSBURY, the county town of Shropshire, sits in a tight and narrow loop of the River Severn. It would be difficult to design a better defensive site and the Britons were quick to erect a fort here once the Roman legions had hot-footed it out of their colony in the fifth century. In Georgian times, Shrewsbury became a fashionable staging post on the busy London to Holyhead route and has since evolved into an easy-going, middling market town. It's the overall feel of the place that is its main appeal, though St Mary's Church and its immediate environs are particularly pleasing.

Arrival and information

Shrewsbury **train station** stands at the narrow neck of the loop in the river that holds the town centre; long-distance **buses** mostly pull into the Raven Meadows bus station, off the Smithfield Road, five minutes' walk southwest from the train station, further into the centre. The **tourist office** is a five-minute walk south up the hill from the train station, off High Street and on The Square (May–Sept Mon–Sat 9.30am–5.30pm, Sun 10am–4pm; Oct–April Mon–Sat 10am–5pm; ⓣ01743/281 200, ⓦwww.visitshrewsbury.com).

Accommodation

The best **hotel** in town is the *Prince Rupert*, which occupies an old building bang in the centre on Butcher Row, off Pride Hill (ⓣ01743/499 955, ⓦwww.prince-rupert-hotel.co.uk; ❻). There are over seventy bedrooms here and although some are a tad too fancy for most tastes – ornate bed-head canopies and so forth – the rooms are very comfortable. Among central **B&Bs**, one good choice is the *College Hill Guesthouse*, in a well-maintained Georgian townhouse at 11 College Hill, just south of The Square (ⓣ01743/365 744; no credit cards; ❸).

The Town

Poking up above the mansion-like train station, the careworn ramparts of Shrewsbury **castle** are but a pale reminder of the mighty medieval fortress that once dominated the town, largely because the illustrious Thomas Telford turned the castle into the private home of a local bigwig in the 1780s. **Castle Gates** winds up the hill from the station into the heart of the river loop where the medieval town took root. Here, off Pride Hill, several half-timbered buildings are dotted along **Butcher Row**, which leads into the quiet precincts of **St Alkmund's Church**, from where there's a charming view of the fine old buildings of **Fish Street**. Close by is the most interesting of the town's churches, **St Mary the Virgin** (Mon–Fri 10am–4/5pm, Sat 10am–4pm; free), whose interior boasts a splendid panelled roof, featuring angels with musical instruments, and a wonderful east window.

From St Mary's, it's the briefest of walks to the High Street, on the far side of which, in the narrow confines of The Square, is the **Old Market House**, a heavy-duty stone structure built in 1596. From The Square, High Street snakes down the hill to become **Wyle Cop**, lined with higgledy-piggledy ancient buildings and leading to the **English Bridge**, which sweeps across the Severn in grand Georgian style. Beyond the bridge, on Abbey Foregate, is the stumpy redstone mass of the **Abbey Church** (Mon–Sat 10am–4pm &

Sun 11.30am–2.30pm; free), all that remains of the Benedictine abbey that was a major political and religious force hereabouts until the Dissolution.

Eating and drinking

For **daytime food**, try the inexpensive *Goodlife Wholefood Restaurant* (Mon–Sat 9.30am–4pm), on Barracks Passage, just off – and about halfway along – Wyle Cop; they specialize in salads and vegetarian dishes with main courses costing around £5. In the **evening**, many locals swear by *Osteria da Paolo*, a homely Italian place offering mouthwatering dishes from its premises down a narrow alley off Hills Lane near the Welsh Bridge on the north side of the town centre (Mon–Sat from 6pm, plus Thurs–Sat noon–2pm; ⓣ01743/243 336); main courses here average around £10.

One of the most distinctive **pubs** is the *Loggerheads*, an ancient place with several small rooms and great real ales; it's located near St Alkmund's Place at 1 Church St. Other recommendable **pubs** include the *Three Fishes*, in an ancient building on Fish Street, and the cosy *Coach & Horses*, on Swan Hill just south of The Square.

The Long Mynd and Church Stretton

Beginning about ten miles south of Shrewsbury, the upland heaths of the **Long Mynd**, some ten miles long and between two and four miles wide, run parallel to and just to the west of the A49. This is prime walking territory and the heathlands are latticed with footpaths, the pick of which offer sweeping views over the border to the Black Mountains of Wales. Nestled at the foot of the Mynd beside the A49 is **CHURCH STRETTON**, a tidy little village and popular day-trippers' destination that makes an ideal base for hiking the area.

Church Stretton is easy to reach from Shrewsbury and Ludlow by **train** or **bus**. Most buses stop in the centre of the village along the High Street, but some pull in beside the train station, close to the A49 – and about 600yd east of the High Street. The helpful **tourist office** is on Church Street (April–Sept Mon–Sat 9.30am–5pm, Oct–March Mon–Sat 9.30am–12.30pm & 1.30–5pm; ⓣ01694/723 133, ⓦwww.churchstretton.co.uk), one block west of the High Street – they can book accommodation.

For **accommodation**, *Brookfields Guesthouse*, Watling Street North (ⓣ01694/722 314, ⓦwww.churchstretton-guesthouse.co.uk; ❹) is a comfortable B&B in a large bay-windowed Edwardian house with seven, well-appointed en-suite guest rooms. It's situated a five-minute walk east then north of the train station – Watling Street runs parallel to – and just to the east of – the A49. One mile north of Church Stretton, the lovely **B&B** *Jinlye* (ⓣ01694/723 243, ⓦwww.jinlye.co.uk; ❺), is an attractive stone cottage on Castle Hill on the edge of All Stretton; they have six splendid, homely guest rooms. **Hostellers** should head for **Bridges Long Mynd** (ⓣ01588/650 656, ⓦwww.yha.org.uk; dorm beds £13), a small hostel along country lanes in a converted village school just five miles west of Church Stretton on the western edge of the hamlet of **Ratlinghope**. The hostel has thirty-seven beds in five- to ten-bedded rooms, a café, camping facilities and a self-catering kitchen; it also makes a splendid base for hiking the Long Mynd and the **Stiperstones**, a remote range of boggy heather dotted with ancient cairns and earthworks.

Ludlow

LUDLOW, perched on a hill nearly thirty miles south of Shrewsbury, is one of the most picturesque towns in the West Midlands – a gaggle of beautifully preserved black-and-white half-timbered buildings packed around a craggy stone castle, with rural Shropshire forming a drowsy backdrop. The town is also something of a gastronomic hideyhole, with a clutch of outstanding restaurants.

Ludlow's immense **Castle** (Jan Sat & Sun 10am–4pm; Feb–July & Sept–Dec daily 10am–4/5pm; Aug daily 10am–7pm; £4; Ⓦwww.ludlowcastle.com), mostly dates from Norman times, its rambling remains incorporating towers and turrets, gatehouses and concentric walls. The castle also makes a fine open-air auditorium during the **Ludlow Festival** (Ⓣ01584/872 150, Ⓦwww.ludlowfestival.co.uk), two weeks of assorted musical and theatrical fun running from the end of June to early July.

The castle entrance abuts **Castle Square**, an airy rectangle, whose eastern side leads into four narrow lanes – take the one on the left, Church Street, and you'll soon reach the gracefully proportioned **Church of St Laurence**, whose interior is distinguished by its fineness of its stained-glass windows and the intricacy of its misericords. Back outside the church, it's a few paces to the **Bull Ring**, home of the **Feathers Hotel**, a fine Jacobean building with the fanciest wooden facade imaginable.

It's the town's general appearance that appeals rather than any special sight, but steeply sloping **Broad Street** is particularly attractive, flanked by many of Ludlow's five hundred half-timbered Tudor and red-brick Georgian listed buildings, its north end framed by the high and mighty **Butter Cross**, a Neoclassical extravagance from 1744. At the foot of Broad Street is Ludlow's only surviving medieval **gate**, which was turned into a house in the eighteenth century.

Practicalities

From Ludlow **train station**, which is on the Shrewsbury–Hereford line, it's a fifteen-minute walk southwest to the castle – just follow the signs. Most buses stop on Mill Street, just off Castle Square. Ludlow's **tourist office** is on Castle Square (April–Sept Mon–Sat 10am–5pm, Sun 10.30am–5pm; Oct–March Mon–Sat 10am–5pm; Ⓣ01584/875 053, Ⓦwww.ludlow.org.uk).

One excellent **accommodation** choice is *Dinham Hall Hotel*, handily located close to the castle in a rambling, bow-windowed eighteenth-century stone mansion that has previously seen service as a boarding house for Ludlow School (Ⓣ01584/876 464, Ⓦwww.dinhamhall.co.uk; ❼). Similarly enticing is *Mr Underhill's*, Dinham Weir (Ⓣ01584/874 431, Ⓦwww.mr-underhills.co.uk; ❼), in the jumble of old riverside buildings below and behind the castle walls beside the River Teme. The six smooth, calming guest rooms here have great river views. One other, less expensive option in the town centre is the *Wheatsheaf Inn*, a quaint little pub with five en-suite rooms at the foot of Broad Street (Ⓣ01584/872 980, Ⓦwww.wheatsheaf-ludlow.co.uk; ❸). During the festival, you must book accommodation well in advance.

Amongst a string of much lauded **restaurants**, one of the best is the Michelin-starred *Mr Underhill's* (see hotels above; reservations essential), where the menu is carefully crafted; set menus kick off at around £40 and offer delights such as chestnut custard with crispy smoked duck and greengage crumble with verbena ice cream. If that sounds too wallet-wilting, head for the popular *Olive Branch*, in the centre on the Bull Ring (Mon–Sat 10am–4pm, Sun 11am–3pm), whose speciality is inexpensive light meals and salads, or the superior pub food (Mon–Sat noon–2pm & 6–9pm) at the antique *Unicorn Inn*, on the north side of town on Lower Corve Street, a continuation of the Bull Ring; main courses here begin at £9.

Birmingham

If anywhere can be described as the first purely industrial conurbation, it has to be **BIRMINGHAM**. Unlike the more specialist industrial towns that grew up across the north and the Midlands, "Brum" – and its "Brummies" – turned its hand to every kind of manufacturing, gaining the epithet "the city of 1001 trades". It was here also that the pioneers of the Industrial Revolution – James Watt, Matthew Boulton, William Murdock, Josiah Wedgwood, Joseph Priestley and Erasmus Darwin (grandfather of Charles) – formed the **Lunar Society**, an extraordinary melting-pot of scientific and industrial ideas. They conceived the world's first purpose-built factory, invented gas lighting and pioneered both the distillation of oxygen and the mass production of the steam engine. Thus, a modest Midlands market town mushroomed into the nation's economic dynamo with the population to match: in 1841 there were 180,000 inhabitants, three times that number just fifty years later.

Now the second largest city in Britain, with a population of over one million, Birmingham has long outgrown the squalor and misery of its boom years and today its industrial supremacy is recalled in a crop of excellent **heritage museums** and an extensive network of **canals**. It also boasts a thoroughly multi-racial population. The recent shift to a post-manufacturing economy has provided for a revamp of the city centre that has included the construction of a glitzy **Convention Centre** and an extravagant face-lift to the **Bull Ring**, while the enormous **National Exhibition Centre** (NEC) now inhabits the outskirts near the international airport. Birmingham has also launched a veritable raft of cultural initiatives, enticing a division of the **Royal Ballet** to take up residence here, and building a fabulous new concert hall for the **City of Birmingham Symphony Orchestra**. Nevertheless, there's no pretending that Birmingham is packed with interesting sights – it isn't – though along with its first-rate restaurant scene and nightlife, it's well worth at least a couple of days.

Arrival, information and city transport

New Street train station, right in the heart of the city, is where all inter-city and the vast majority of local services go, though trains on the Stratford-upon-Avon, Warwick, Worcester and Malvern lines mostly use **Snow Hill** and **Moor Street stations**, both about ten minutes' signposted walk from New Street to the north and east respectively. National Express **coach** travellers are dumped in the grim surroundings of **Digbeth coach station**, from where it's a ten-minute uphill walk to the Bull Ring.

The main **tourist office** is located beside the Bull Ring at 150 New St, (Mon–Sat 9.30am–5.30pm & Sun 10.30am–4.30pm; ⓣ0870/225 0127, ⓦwww.beinbirmingham.com). A second, smaller office occupies a kiosk in front of New Street station, at the junction of New Street and Corporation Street (Mon–Sat 9am–5pm & Sun 10am–4pm; same number). Both tourist offices operate a hotel bed booking service at no charge. There's also a dedicated **Ticket Hotline** ⓣ0121/202 5000.

Birmingham has an excellent transport system, whose **trains**, **metro** and **buses** delve into almost every urban nook and cranny. Various companies provide these services, but they are co-ordinated by **Centro**, which operates a regional public transport information line (ⓣ0121/200 2787, ⓦwww.centro.org.uk). A **One Day Network Card**, valid on all services, can be purchased from bus drivers and at train and metro stations at a cost of £5.80; if you avoid peak-time travel, the price drops to £4.70, but then it's known as the **Daytripper**.

Accommodation

Central Birmingham is liberally sprinkled with chain **hotels**, from glitzy tower blocks through to more modest red-brick, but it's in the vicinity of the Gas Street Basin and Centenary Square that you really want to stay. The prize for originality goes to the National Trust, who rent out three reasonably priced "**cottages**" – actually restored old terrace houses – in the city centre on the edge of the Chinese Quarter. The tourist office (see p.425) publishes a free booklet detailing all of the city's hotels.

Hotels

Copthorne Birmingham Paradise Circus ⓣ0121/200 2727, ⓦwww.millenniumhotels.co.uk. It may look rather like a Rubik cube from the outside, but this is a great hotel, partly because its 212 modern bedrooms are spruce, and partly because its location – plumb in the centre beside Centenary Square – can't be bettered. It's expensive during the week, but weekends bring prices down to more affordable levels. 7, weekends 6

Hyatt Regency Birmingham 2 Bridge St ⓣ0121/643 1234 ⓦwww.hyatt.com. The sleek, black skyrise that towers above Centenary Square is a luxury *Hyatt* hotel. The central location is hard to beat, the city views from the guest rooms on the upper floors are superlative, and the public area has some pleasant Art Deco touches – and may have been feng-shuied. Less positively, the rooms are decorated in uninspiring chain-hotel style and you can't open the windows. Discounts are commonplace, but rack rate 9, weekends 7

Malmaison Hotel 1 Wharfside St, The Mailbox ⓣ0121/246 5000, ⓦwww.malmaison-birmingham.com. This impeccably stylish, designer hotel offers first-class accommodation of wit and substance – no wonder it's next door to Harvey Nichols. Every convenience and a central location. 7

Radisson SAS 12 Holloway Circus ⓣ0121/654 6000, ⓦwww.birmingham.radissonsas.com. Smart new hotel in a tall and glossy skyrise within a few minutes' walk of the centre. The interior is designed in routine modern-minimalist style, but the green amoebas etched onto the acres of glass add an air of distinction as do the floor-to-ceiling windows of many of the bedrooms. 6

Travelodge 230 Broad St ⓣ0871/984 6064, ⓦwww.travelodge.co.uk. Central chain hotel; prices are very reasonable and it's within easy walking distance of lots of restaurants, bars and clubs. 4

National Trust Cottages

Back to Backs Houses 52 Inge St ⓣ0870/458 4422, ⓦwww.nationaltrustcottages.co.uk. The National Trust has refurbished a small block of nineteenth-century back-to-back workers' houses just to the south of the city centre along Hurst St. In part of the complex, it has installed three small "cottages" – really terrace houses – and kitted them out with en-suite facilities. The cottages have a convenient, central location and make for the most distinctive place to stay in town. Each accommodates two guests and can be rented out for two nights or longer. Costs vary with the season: a two-night stay costs £125 in Jan, rising to £275 in Aug.

The City Centre

Many visitors get their first taste of central Birmingham at **New Street Station**, whose unreconstructed ugliness makes a dispiriting start, though there are plans afoot to give the place a thoroughgoing face lift. Things do, however, improve if you cut up east from the station to the **Bull Ring**, once itself a 1960s eyesore, but now a gleaming new shopping mall distinguished by the startling design of its leading store, **Selfridges**. Head west along pedestrianized **New Street** from here and it's brief stroll to the elegantly revamped **Victoria Square**, with its tumbling water fountain, and the adjacent **Chamberlain Square**, where pride of place goes to the **Birmingham Museum and Art Gallery**, the city's finest museum, complete with a stunning collection of Pre-Raphaelite art. Beyond, further west still, is the glossy **International Convention Centre**, from where it's another short hop to the **Gas Street Basin**, the prettiest part of the city's serpentine canal system. Close by is canalside **Brindley Place**, a smart brick and

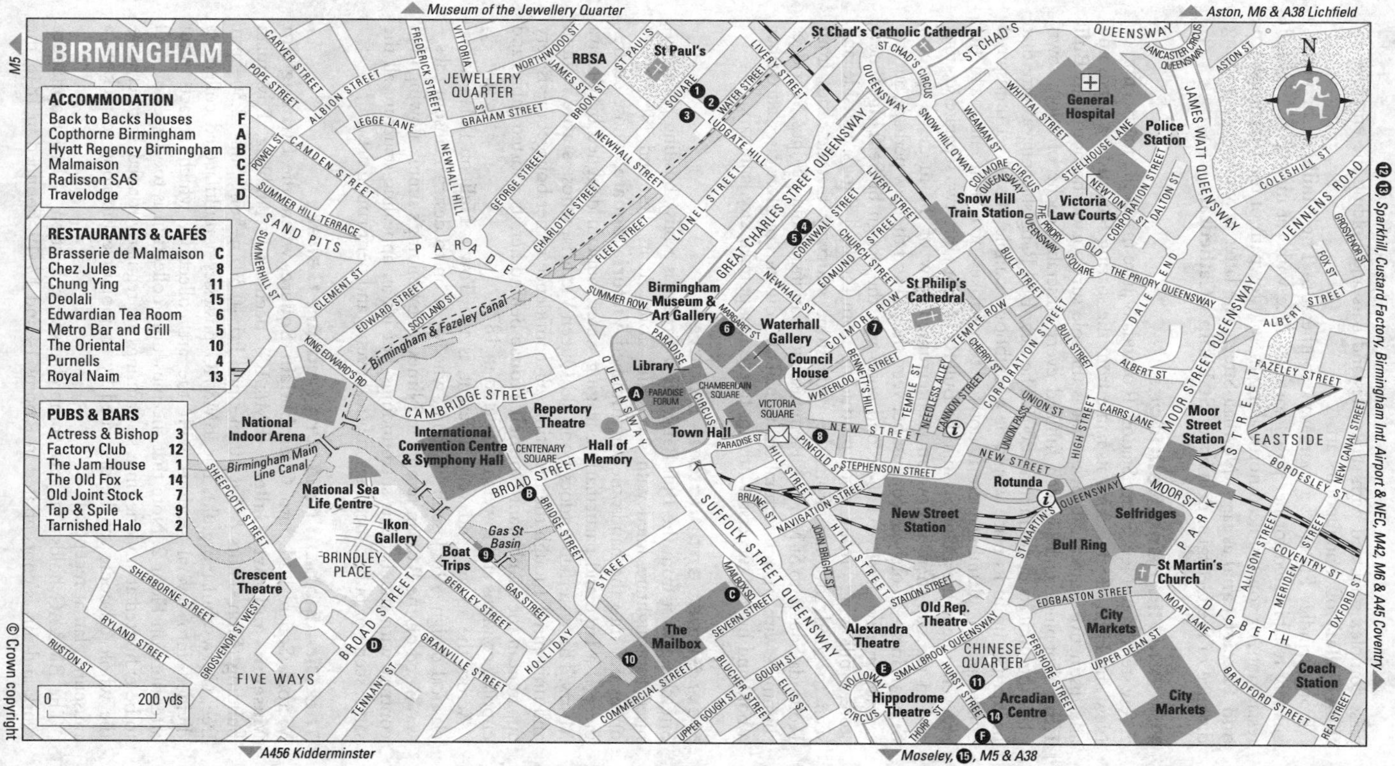

Museum of the Jewellery Quarter
Aston, M6 & A38 Lichfield
M5
⑫, ⑬, Sparkhill, Custard Factory, Birmingham Intl. Airport & NEC, M42, M6 & A45 Coventry
A456 Kidderminster
Moseley, ⑮, M5 & A38
BIRMINGHAM
ACCOMMODATION
Back to Backs Houses F
Copthorne Birmingham A
Hyatt Regency Birmingham B
Malmaison C
Radisson SAS E
Travelodge D
RESTAURANTS & CAFÉS
Brasserie de Malmaison C
Chez Jules 8
Chung Ying 11
Deolali 15
Edwardian Tea Room 6
Metro Bar and Grill 5
The Oriental 10
Purnells 4
Royal Naim 13
PUBS & BARS
Actress & Bishop 3
Factory Club 12
The Jam House 1
The Old Fox 14
Old Joint Stock 7
Tap & Spile 9
Tarnished Halo 2
0 200 yds
© Crown copyright
St Chad's Catholic Cathedral
General Hospital
Police Station
St Paul's
RBSA
JEWELLERY QUARTER
Snow Hill Train Station
Victoria Law Courts
St Philip's Cathedral
Birmingham Museum & Art Gallery
Waterhall Gallery
Council House
Library
Town Hall
Repertory Theatre
Hall of Memory
International Convention Centre & Symphony Hall
National Indoor Arena
National Sea Life Centre
Ikon Gallery
BRINDLEY PLACE
Boat Trips
Gas St Basin
Crescent Theatre
FIVE WAYS
The Mailbox
Alexandra Theatre
Old Rep. Theatre
CHINESE QUARTER
Hippodrome Theatre
Arcadian Centre
New Street Station
Rotunda
Bull Ring
Selfridges
St Martin's Church
City Markets
Moor Street Station
EASTSIDE
Coach Station
Birmingham & Fazeley Canal
Birmingham Main Line Canal

glass complex sprinkled with slick cafés and bars and holding the enterprising **Ikon Gallery** of contemporary art.

From Brindley Place, it's a short walk southeast to **The Mailbox**, the immaculately rehabilitated former postal sorting office with yet more chic bars and restaurants, or you can head north along the old towpath of the **Birmingham and Fazeley canal** as far as Newhall Street. The latter is within easy walking distance of the Georgian delights of **St Philip's Cathedral**.

The Bull Ring and Selfridges

A few steps from New Street Station, Rotunda Square marks the intersection of New and High streets, taking its name from the soaring **Rotunda**, a handsome and distinctive cylindrical tower that is the sole survivor of the notorious **Bull Ring** shopping centre, which fulfilled every miserable cliché of 1960s town planning until its demolition in 2001. The new Bull Ring shopping centre that has sprung up in its place would be a textbook example of safe yet uninspired contemporary planning were it not for two strokes of real invention. In the redevelopment, the architects split the Bull Ring shops into two separate sections and in the gap there is now an uninterrupted view of the medieval spire of **St Martin's** – an obvious contrast between the old and the new perhaps, but still extraordinarily effective. The second coup was the design of **Selfridges**' new store, a billowing organic swell protruding from the Bull Ring's east side, and seen to good advantage from the wide stone **stairway** that descends from Rotunda Square to St Martin's. Reminiscent of an inside-out octopus, Selfridges shimmers with an architectural chain mail of thousands of silver discs, altogether a bold and hugely successful attempt to create a popular city landmark.

New Street and Victoria Square

Stretching west from the Bull Ring, **New Street** is a busy, bustling pedestrianised thoroughfare, lined with shops and stores. At its west end, New Street opens out into the handsomely refurbished **Victoria Square**, whose centrepiece is a large and particularly engaging water fountain designed by Dhruva Mistry. The waterfall outdoes poor old Queen Victoria, whose **statue** is glum and uninspired, though the thrusting self-confidence of her bourgeoisie is very apparent in the flamboyant **Council House** behind her, its assorted gables and cupolas, columns and towers completed in 1879.

Across the square, and very different, is the **Town Hall** of 1834, whose classical design – by Joseph Hansom, who went on to design Hansom cabs – was based on the Roman temple in Nîmes. The building's simple, flowing lines contrast with much of its surroundings, but it's an appealing structure all the same, scene of public meetings, musical events and performing arts.

The Birmingham Museum and Art Gallery

Victoria Square leads into **Chamberlain Square**, where the **Birmingham Museum and Art Gallery** (BM&AG) occupies a rambling, Edwardian building (Mon–Thurs & Sat 10am–5pm, Fri 10.30am–5pm, Sun 12.30–5pm; free; Ⓦwww.bmag.org.uk). The BM&AG possesses a multifaceted collection divided into several sections with the art collection, which attracts most attention, on Floor 2. Note that the museum's collection is too large for it all to be exhibited at any one time, so paintings are regularly rotated. Furthermore, the whole caboodle can be disturbed by temporary exhibitions, so pick up a museum plan at reception.

The BM&AG holds a hugely comprehensive collection of **Pre-Raphaelite** work and this is concentrated in Rooms 14 and 17–19. Founded in 1848, the

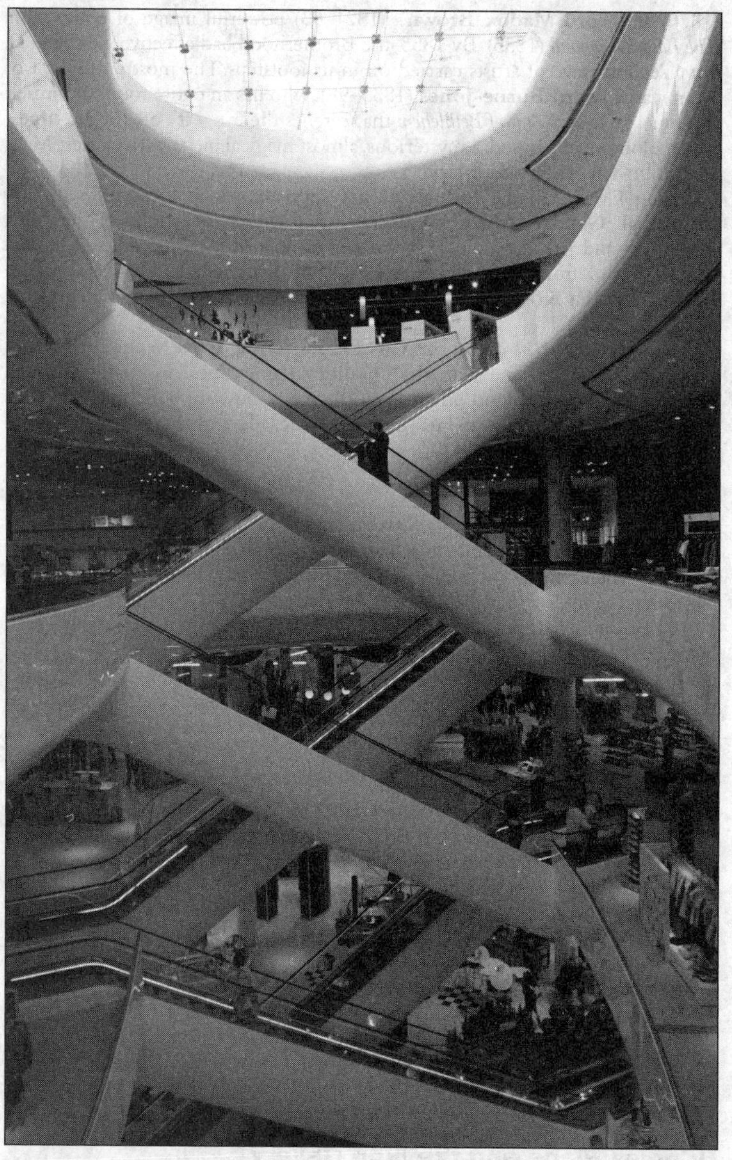

▲ Selfridges

Pre-Raphaelite Brotherhood consisted of seven young artists, of whom Rossetti, Holman Hunt, Millais and Madox Brown are the best known. The name of the group was selected to express their commitment to honest observation, which they thought had been lost with the Renaissance. Many of the Brotherhood's most important paintings are (usually) displayed here in these rooms, including **Dante Gabriel Rossetti**'s (1828–82) seminal *Beata Beatrix*

(1870) and **Ford Madox Brown**'s (1821–93) powerful image of emigration, *The Last of England* (1855). By 1853, the Brotherhood had effectively disbanded, but a second wave of artists carried on in its footsteps. The most prominent of them was **Edward Burne-Jones** (1833–98), who has an entire room to himself (Room 14). It's his *Star of Bethlehem* that catches the eye – it's one of the largest watercolours ever painted, a mysterious, almost magical piece with earnest Magi and a film-star-like Virgin Mary.

Sharing Floor 2 is the **industrial art section**, which kicks off with the **Industrial Gallery**, which holds small but choice selections of ceramics, metalwork and jewellery, plus a wonderful sample of locally produced stained glass retrieved from defunct churches across Birmingham. Here also is the **Edwardian Tea Room**, one of the more pleasant places in Birmingham for a cuppa (see p.432).

Moving on, Floor 1's cavernous **Gas Hall** is an impressive venue for touring art exhibitions, while the **Waterhall Gallery** (same times), inside the Council House, just across Edmund Street from the main museum building, showcases modern and contemporary art including the likes of Francis Bacon and Bridget Riley.

Centenary Square

From the north side of Chamberlain Square, walk through the hideously ugly **Paradise Forum** shopping and fast-food complex to get to **Centenary Square**, where there's an unusual World War I war memorial, the **Hall of Memory** (Mon–Sat 10am–4pm; free). Erected in 1923, to commemorate those 13,000 Brummies who had died in World War I, the memorial is an architectural hybrid, a delightful mix of Art Deco and Neoclassical features, whose centrepiece is a domed Remembrance chamber. From the memorial, a grassy lawn stretches over to the showpiece **Symphony Hall** and **International Convention Centre** (ICC) with the **Birmingham Repertory Theatre** on the right.

Gas Street Basin and The Mailbox

From the ICC, it's a brief stroll along Broad Street to Gas Street, on the left, which leads down to **Gas Street Basin**, the hub of Birmingham's intricate canal system. There are eight canals within the city's boundaries, comprising no less than 32 miles of canal, and although much of Birmingham's surviving canal network slices through the city's grimy, industrial bowels, certain sections have been immaculately restored with Gas Street Basin leading the way. At the junction of the Worcester and Birmingham and Birmingham Main Line canals, the Basin, with its herd of brightly painted narrowboats, is edged by a delightful medley of old brick buildings.

Follow the towpath along the canal southeast from the Basin and you soon reach **The Mailbox**, a talented reinvention of Birmingham's old postal sorting office complete with restaurants, hotels, and some of the snazziest shops in the city – including Jaeger and Harvey Nichols.

Brindley Place and the Ikon Gallery

Doubling back to the Basin, it's a short walk northwest along the canal towpath to the bars, shops and offices of waterside **Brindley Place**, named after James Brindley the eighteenth-century engineer who was responsible for many of Britain's early canals. It's an aesthetically pleasing development where you'll also find the city's celebrated **Ikon Gallery** (Tues–Sun 11am–6pm; free; Ⓦwww.ikon-gallery.co.uk), housed in a rambling Victorian building and one of the country's most imaginative venues for touring exhibitions of contemporary art.

Along the Birmingham & Fazeley canal to St Paul's Square

Just beyond Brindley Place, in front of the huge dome of the National Indoor Arena (NIA), the **canal forks**: the Birmingham & Fazeley leads northeast (to the right) and the Birmingham Main Line canal cuts west (to the left). Also beside the main canal junction is the shell-like **National Sea Life Centre** (daily 10am–5/6pm; £15.95, under 14s £10.95; Ⓣ0121/643 6777, Ⓦwww.sealifeeurope.com), an educational venture offering Birmingham's landlubbers an opportunity to view and even touch many unusual varieties of fish and sea life.

Beyond the main canal fork, the first part of the **Birmingham & Fazeley canal** has been attractively restored, its antique brick buildings cleaned of accumulated grime and leading past the quaint **Scotland Street Locks**. Further on, however, things take a grittier aspect as the canal bores beneath the city centre amidst its industrial tangle. Emerging at **Newhall Street** by means of a flight of (unsigned) steps, about half a mile from the main canal junction, you're a stone's throw from **St Paul's Square**, where an good-looking ensemble of old houses flank the Neoclassical **church of St Paul's**.

St Philip's Cathedral

A few minutes' walk southeast of St Paul's Square, on the other side of the ring road, is **Colmore Row**, where a string of fancily carved High Victorian stone buildings provide a suitable backdrop for **St Philip's Cathedral** (early Sept to late July Mon–Fri 7.30am–6.30pm, Sat & Sun 8.30am–5pm; late July to early Sept Mon–Fri 7.30am–5pm, Sat & Sun 8.30am–5pm; free; Ⓦwww.birminghamcathedral.com). Consecrated in 1715, St Philips is a handsome affair, its graceful, galleried interior all balance and poise, its harmonies unruffled by the Victorians, who enlarged the original church in the 1880s, when four new stained-glass windows were commissioned from local boy **Edward Burne-Jones**, a leading light of the Pre-Raphaelite movement (see p.428). The windows are typical of his style – intensely coloured, fastidiously detailed and distinctly sentimental. Three – the *Nativity*, *Crucifixion* and *Ascension* – are at the east end of the church beyond the high altar, the fourth – the *Last Judgement* – is directly opposite.

St Philip's Cathedral lies just to the west of the city centre's pedestrianized core with chain stores and shopping precincts bunching up along Corporation, New and High streets before reaching some sort of retail climax at the Bull Ring (see p.428).

Eating and drinking

Central Birmingham has a bevy of first-rate **restaurants** with a string of smart venues springing up in and around The Mailbox. There's also a concentration of decent, reasonably priced restaurants in the Chinese Quarter, just south of New Street Station, on and around Hurst Street. Birmingham's gastronomic speciality is the **balti**, a delicious and inexpensive Kashmiri stew cooked and served in a small wok-like dish called a **karahi**, with nan bread instead of cutlery: the original and arguably the best balti houses are in the gritty suburbs of **Balsall Heath/Moseley**, a couple of miles to the south of the centre, and **Sparkhill**, about three miles to the southeast. A few of these are listed here – but note that many are unlicensed, so you may want to take your own booze.

City-centre **pubs** vary as much as you'd expect. The liveliest, catering for a mixed bag of conference delegates and Brummies-out-on-the-ale, are liberally sprinkled along Broad Street, in the immediate vicinity of the Convention Centre, and in Brindley Place. Most of these are decorated in sharp, modern style, but there are more traditional places hereabouts as well – as there are in other parts of the city centre.

Cafés and restaurants

Brasserie de Malmaison The Mailbox, 1 Wharfside St ⓣ0121/246 5000. Slick and smart brasserie offering a varied menu of both French and English dishes. Part of the *Malmaison Hotel* (see p.426). Mains £11–18.

Chez Jules 5a Ethel St, off New St ⓣ0121/633 4664. Cosy, very recommendable, medium-priced French restaurant in the city centre, with especially good lunchtime deals. The lamb dishes are particularly tasty. A two-course lunch costs £8, main courses £10–15 in the evening. Closed Sun.

Chung Ying 16–18 Wrottesley St ⓣ0121/622 5669. Arguably the best Cantonese dishes in the Chinese Quarter, and always busy. Mains £8–11.

Deolali 23a St Mary's Row, Moseley ⓣ0121/442 2222. No flock wallpaper here in this slick Indian restaurant with its beamed dealings and bare brick walls. Excellent food with the emphasis on southern India dishes. Mains from £10. Closed Sun.

Edwardian Tea Room The Birmingham Museum and Art Gallery, Chamberlain Square. This café has a great location in one of the large and fancily decorated halls of the museum's industrial section – hence all the cast-iron columns – but the food is canteen-style routine.

Metro Bar and Grill 73 Cornwall St ⓣ0121 200 1911. Slick, modern Brummie bar-cum-restaurant serving Modern British cuisine with bar plates at just £6. Mains from £14. Closed Sun.

The Oriental The Mailbox, 128 Wharfside St ⓣ0121/633 9988. Large and smart restaurant decorated in pan-Asian style and with a smashing location, down by the canal in The Mailbox. Has a wide-ranging menu featuring Malay, Thai and Chinese dishes. A place to experiment – the Malay cuisine is the least familiar to most Brits. Main courses average a very reasonable £9.

Purnells 55 Cornwall St ⓣ0121/212 9799. Smooth and polished restaurant recently opened by much lauded chef, Glynn Purnell. The premises are Victorian red-brick, but the interior is all modernist – prestige dining with a three-course a la carte meal costing £40. Brill cooked in coconut milk with Indian red lentils gives the flavour of the menu. Closed Sun & Mon. Reservations essential.

Royal Naim 417 Stratford Rd, Sparkhill ⓣ0121/766 7849. Twice named Brum's best balti house – as good as it gets. Main courses from £6. Daily from noon.

Pubs and bars

Actress & Bishop 35 Ludgate Hill ⓣ0121/236 7426, ⓦwww.surgemusic.com. Popular bar in a fashionable part of town with a strong line-up of local bands.

Factory Club Custard Factory, Gibb St, off Digbeth. Great bar located in a laid-back arts complex that was once a custard factory. Turns into a club late at night – see p.433.

The Jam House 3 St Paul's Square ⓣ0121/200 3030, ⓦwww.thejamhouse.com. Jazz, funk, blues and swing joint pulling in artists from every corner of the globe. Daily except Mon from 6pm.

The Old Fox Hurst St. Over-modernized but popular pub, with an excellent selection of beers and a boisterous atmosphere. At least the great long windows (of 1891) have survived the updaters.

Old Joint Stock 4 Temple Row West. This delightful pub has the fanciest decor in town – with busts and a balustrade, a balcony and chandeliers, all dating from its days as a bank. A stone's throw from St Philip's Cathedral.

Tap & Spile 10 Gas St. Charming traditional pub with rickety rooms and low-beamed ceilings beside the canal on Gas St Basin. Once the hang-out of weathered canal men, it now attracts tourists and locals in equal measure.

Tarnished Halo 21 Ludgate Hill. Great name for this jam-packed bar where students hang out in numbers.

Nightlife and entertainment

Birmingham's **club scene** is recognized as one of Britain's best, spanning everything from word-of-mouth underground parties to meat-market mainstream clubs. **Live music** is strong in the city, too, with big-name concerts at several major venues and other, often local, bands appearing at some clubs and pubs. Birmingham's showpiece **Symphony Orchestra** and **Royal Ballet** are the spearheads of the city's **classical scene**.

For current **information** on all events, performances and exhibitions, pick up a free copy of the excellent, fortnightly **What's On**, Birmingham's definitive listings guide – or consult ⓦhttp://icbirmingham.icnetwork.co.uk/wow. The guide is available at all city tourist offices and many public venues.

Clubs

Air Heath Mill Lane, off Digbeth ⓣ0845/009 8888, ⓦwww.airbirmingham.com. Shiny, high-tech superclub host to hundreds of house- and trance-hungry clubbers.

Factory Club Custard Factory, Gibb Square, off Digbeth, ⓣ0121/224 7502, ⓦwww.factoryclub.co.uk. Eclectic and frequently impeccable music policy, plus juicy live events. One of the best nights out in town. Part of the arts complex that inhabits the old Alfred Bird Custard Factory (ⓦwww.custardfactory.com). There are a couple of cool cafés and bars here too.

The Nightingale Essex House, Kent St ⓣ0121/622 1718, ⓦwww.nightingaleclub.co.uk. The king of Brum's gay clubs, but popular with straights too. Five bars, three levels, two discos, a café-bar and even a garden. Just south of The Mailbox (see p.430).

Classical music, theatre and dance

Birmingham Repertory Theatre Centenary Square, Broad St ⓣ0121/236 4455, ⓦwww.birmingham-rep.co.uk. Mixed diet of classics and new work, featuring local and experimental writing.

Hippodrome Theatre Hurst St ⓣ0870/730 1234, ⓦwww.birminghamhippodrome.com. The Hippodrome is home to the Birmingham Royal Ballet, but also features touring plays and big pre- and post-West End productions, plus a splendiferous Christmas pantomime.

National Exhibition Centre (NEC) Bickenhill Parkway ⓣ0871/945 6000, ⓦwww.necgroup.co.uk. The NEC's arena hosts major pop concerts. Ten miles east of the centre beside the M42; train from New St to Birmingham International Station.

Symphony Hall International Convention Centre, Broad St ⓣ0121/780 3333, ⓦwww.thsh.co.uk. Acoustically one of the most advanced concert halls in Europe, home of the acclaimed City of Birmingham Symphony Orchestra (CBSO), as well as a venue for touring music and opera.

Town Hall Broad St ⓣ0121/780 3333, ⓦwww.thsh.co.uk. The old Town Hall offers a very programme of pop, classical and jazz music through to modern dance and ballet.

Listings

Public transport Centro Hotline ⓣ0121/200 2787, ⓦwww.centro.org.uk.

Pharmacy Boots, 65 High St ⓣ0121/212 1330.

Post office 1 Pinfold St at Victoria Square (Mon–Sat 9am–5.30pm).

Taxis Toa Taxis ⓣ0121/427 8888.

The Peak District

In 1951, the **Peak District**, at the southern tip of the Pennine range, became Britain's first National Park. Wedged between **Derby**, Manchester and Sheffield, it is effectively the backyard for the fifteen million people who live within an hour's drive of its boundaries, though somehow it accommodates the huge influx with minimum fuss.

Landscapes in the Peak District come in two forms: the brooding high moorland tops of **Dark Peak**, fifteen miles east of central Manchester, take their name from the underlying gritstone, known as millstone grit for its former use – a function commemorated in the millstones demarcating the park boundary. Windswept, mist-shrouded and inhospitable, the flat tops of these peaks are nevertheless a firm favourite with walkers on the **Pennine Way**, which meanders north from the tiny village of **Edale** to the Scottish border (see box, p.439); more forgiving, the southern limestone hills of the **White Peak** have been eroded into deep forested dales populated by small stone villages and often threaded by walking trails. The limestone is riddled with complex cave systems around **Castleton** and near the region's largest centre, **Buxton**, a charming former spa town just outside the park's boundaries. The Peak District also holds one of the country's most distinctive manorial piles, **Chatsworth House**, just outside modest **Baslow**, and the old lead-mining village of **Eyam**, which was ravaged by the plague in the seventeenth century.

As for a **base**, Buxton is your best bet by a (fairly) long chalk, though if you're after the hiking and cycling you'll probably prefer one of the area's villages.

Public transport

There are frequent **trains** (www.nationalrail.co.uk) south from Manchester to end-of-the-line Buxton and Manchester–Sheffield trains cut through Edale. The main **bus** access is via the Trent Barton bus company's TransPeak (www.transpeak.co.uk) service from Nottingham to Manchester via Derby, Matlock, Bakewell and Buxton; otherwise First (www.firstgroup.com) bus #272 runs regularly from Sheffield to Castleton and TM Travel (www.tmtravel.co.uk) bus #65 connects Sheffield to Buxton via Eyam every hour or two. If you're not planning on walking or driving between towns and villages, you'll need the essential, encyclopedic *Peak District Bus Timetable* as well as the free *Derbyshire Train Times* booklet, both of which are available at local tourist and National Park information offices. Buses are widespread, though there are limited winter and Sunday services, and often only sporadic links between the smaller villages. Various **one-day bus passes** allow unlimited travel to and within specified zones. It's a complicated system, but broadly speaking the South Yorkshire Peak Explorer (£7.50) covers the chunk of the park in Yorkshire; the Peak Wayfarer (£8.80), and the Derbyshire Wayfarer (£8.80) cover the rest. For all Peak District bus **timetable** information call 0871 200 2233.

The Peak District has a wide network of dedicated cycle lanes and trails, and the National Park Authority (for contact details, see below) operates three **cycle rental** outlets – at Ashbourne (01335/343 156); Derwent (01433/651 261); and Parsley Hay, Buxton (01298/84493).

Information

The main **Peak District National Park Authority** (01629/816 200, www.peakdistrict.gov.uk) operates a string of **visitor centres**, whose services supplement a host of town and village tourist offices. A variety of **maps** and **trail guides** is widely available across the Peaks, but for the non-specialist it's hard to beat the **Grate Little Guides**, a series of leaflets which provide hiking suggestions and trail descriptions for a dozen or so localities. They cost £1.80 each and are on sale at almost every tourist office and information centre, but note that the maps printed on the leaflets are best used in conjunction with an OS map. Be sure also to pick up a copy of the free and official **Peak District paper**, crammed with useful information and local news. Finally, there are two official Peak District **websites**, www.visitpeakdistrict.com and www.peak-experience.org.uk.

Accommodation

There's a plethora of **accommodation** in and around the National Park, mostly in B&Bs, though one of the area's distinctive features is the quality of its **country hotels** – like the ones in Baslow (see p.441). The greatest concentration of first-rate hotels and B&Bs is, however, in the town of Buxton. The Peak District also holds numerous **campsites** and half a dozen or so **youth hostels** as well as a network of YHA-operated **camping barns**. These are located in converted farm buildings and provide simple and inexpensive self-catering facilities. For further details, consult Ⓦwww.yha.org.uk.

Ashbourne

Twelve miles northwest of Derby, **ASHBOURNE** is an amiable little town, whose stubby, cobbled **Market Place** is flanked by a happy ensemble of old stone buildings. Hikers tramp into town from the neighbouring dales to hang around the square's cafés and pubs, and stroll down the hill to take a peek at the suspended wooden beam spanning Church Street. Once a common feature of English towns, but now a rarity, these **gallows** were not warnings to malcontents, but advertising hoardings. Walk west along **Church Street** from here and you soon leave the bustling centre for a quieter part of town, all set beneath the soaring spire of **St Oswald's Church**, an imposing lime- and ironstone structure dating from the thirteenth century.

There are no trains to Ashbourne, but the town is easy to reach by **bus** from Derby, Buxton and Manchester. From the bus station, it's a couple of minutes' walk to the Market Place. The **tourist office** is on the Market Place (March–Oct daily 10am–5pm; Nov–Feb Mon–Sat 10am–4pm; Ⓣ01335/343 666, Ⓦwww.visitpeakdistrict.com). They can also advise on accommodation, though Ashbourne is best regarded as a pit-stop rather than as a base for further wanderings. For **food**, Ashbourne boasts a first-rate delicatessen, Patrick & Brooksbank, 22 Market Place (Mon–Sat 9am–5pm; Ⓣ01335 342631), which has a superb selection of takeaway food, including local cheeses and hams – perfect for a picnic. The best café in town is inside the Bennetts store, at 19 St John St (closed Sun).

Buxton

BUXTON, twenty miles north of Ashbourne, holds a string of excellent hotels and B&Bs, making it a perfect base for exploring much of the Peaks National Park. It also boasts the outstanding **Buxton Festival** (Ⓣ01298/70395; Ⓦwww.buxtonfestival.co.uk), featuring classical music and opera and running for two weeks in July as well as the **Gilbert & Sullivan Festival** (Ⓦwww.gs-festival.co.uk, Ⓣ01422/323 252), a three-week affair in August mainly featuring amateur troupes and attracting an enthusiastic audience.

Buxton has a long history as a **spa**, beginning with the Romans, who happened upon a spring from which 1500 gallons of pure water gushed every hour at a constant 28°C. Impressed by the recuperative qualities of the water, the Romans came here by the chariot load, setting a trend that was to last hundreds of years. The spa's salad days came at the end of the eighteenth century with the **fifth Duke of Devonshire**'s grand design to create a northern answer to Bath or Cheltenham, a plan ultimately thwarted by the climate, but not before some distinguished buildings had been erected, most memorably The Crescent. Neither was Victorian Buxton a laggard, for although it may not have had quite the elan of its more southerly rivals, it still flourished, creating the raft of handsome stone houses that edge the town centre today. The stickiest years came after the town's thermal baths were closed for lack of custom in 1972, but Buxton hung on to emerge as the most appealing town in the Peaks.

Arrival and information

Hourly trains from Manchester Piccadilly to Buxton with trains pull into the **train station**, two minutes' walk from The Crescent on Station Road. The

TransPeak bus, running every two hours between Manchester and Nottingham, stops in Buxton's Market Place, as do buses from Sheffield. Buxton **tourist office** is in The Crescent (April–Oct daily 9.30am–5pm; Nov–March daily 10am–4pm; ⓣ01298/25106, ⓦwww.visitbuxton.co.uk) in what used to be the old Mineral Baths – hence the small display on Buxton's mineral water. They operate an accommodation booking service.

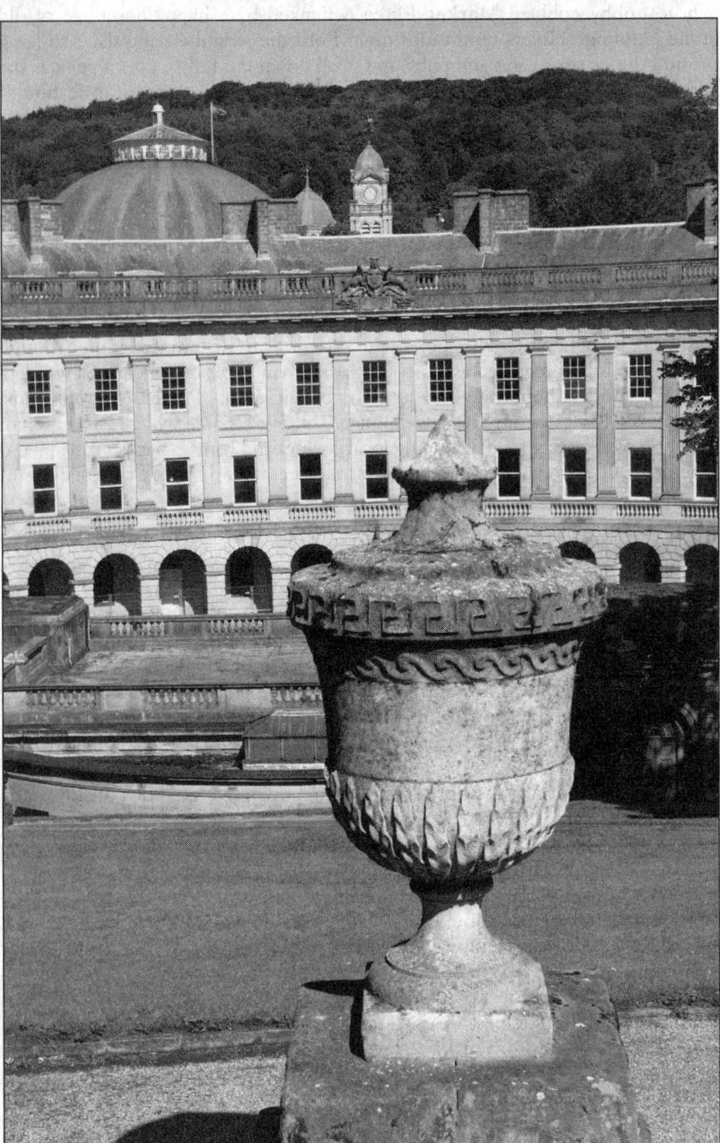

▲ The Crescent, Buxton

Accommodation

Several of the best **hotels** and **B&Bs** are located on the pedestrianized Broad Walk, where a string of distinguished Edwardian and Victorian stone houses face out onto the Pavilion Gardens. Finding somewhere to stay is rarely a problem, except during the Buxton Festival (see p.435), when advance reservations are well-nigh essential.

Buxton's Victorian Guesthouse 3a Broad Walk ⓣ01298/78759, ⓦwww.buxtonvictorian.co.uk. Cosy B&B with a handful of well-appointed rooms. Breakfasts feature local produce wherever feasible; the sausages and bacon are delicious. Occupies one of the grand Victorian houses flanking Broad Walk. ❺

Palace Hotel Palace Rd ⓣ01298/22001, ⓦwww.paramount-hotels.co.uk/palace. Built to impress, the *Palace* was the pride of the Victorian spa, its sweeping stone facade, with its pediments, pilasters, balconies and imposing central tower, lording it over the town centre from the high ground of Palace Rd. The hotel is a little careworn today, but there's no gainsaying the grandness of the entrance lobby and the soaring staircase beyond. The bedrooms are very comfortable and although the decor is modern, many have a quirky antique charm, as do the long, echoing corridors. Substantial discounts are commonplace – ring ahead to check. ❻

Roseleigh Hotel 19 Broad Walk ⓣ01298/24904, ⓦwww.roseleighhotel.co.uk. This classic three-storey gritstone Victorian townhouse, overlooking Pavilion Gardens, is an excellent place to stay, its neat and trim public rooms decorated in attractive Victorian style, the en-suite bedrooms beyond are similarly well appointed. Family-run and very competitively priced. ❹

The town centre

The centrepiece of Buxton's hilly, compact centre is **The Crescent**, a broad sweep of Georgian stonework commissioned by the fifth Duke of Devonshire in 1780 and modelled on the Royal Crescent in Bath. It's recently been refurbished, but remains empty while the townsfolk discuss its future, one idea being the creation of a new thermal baths. Facing The Crescent, the old **Pump Room** of 1894 provides space for art and crafts exhibitions, while the adjacent water **fountain**, supplied by St Ann's Well, is still used to fill many a local water bottle.

At the west end of The Crescent, the appealing old stone buildings of **The Square** – though square it isn't – nudge up to the grandly refurbished **Buxton Opera House**, an Edwardian extravagance whose twin towers, cherubs and tiffany glass date from 1903. Clearly visible here is the enormous **dome** of what was originally the Duke of Devonshire's stables and riding school, erected in 1789. For decades, the building was used as a hospital, but it's now part of Derby University.

Stretching back from the Opera House are the Pavilion Gardens, a slender string of connected buildings distinguished by their wrought-iron work and culminating in a large and glassy dome. The pavilions are actually a good deal more interesting from outside than from within, reason enough to wander off into the adjoining park, also known as the **Pavilion Gardens**, whose immaculate lawns and neat borders are graced by a bandstand, ponds, dinky little footbridges and fountains.

The Market Place and the Museum and Art Gallery

From the south end of The Square, **Hall Bank** scuttles up to the wide and breezy **Market Place**, from where it's only a few yards back down the hill along Terrace Road to the first-rate **Buxton Museum and Art Gallery** (Tues–Fri 9.30am–5.30pm, Sat 9.30am–5pm & Easter–Sept Sun 10.30am–5pm; free). The museum holds enterprising contemporary art exhibitions and features the large and proficient "Wonders of the Peak" display, which tracks through the history of the region from its geological construction through the Romans and on to the Victorians. Best of all, however, is the section dealing with the **petrifactioners**, who turned local semiprecious stones into ornaments and jewellery designed to tickle the fancy of the visitors who arrived here in numbers after the duke had put Buxton on the tourist map.

Eating and drinking

Buxton has several good places to eat, but the best **restaurant** in town is the *Columbine*, a small and intimate place in the centre at 7 Hall Bank (Mon–Sat 7–10pm, but closed most Tues in winter; ⓣ01298/78752). The menu here is short and imaginative, with main courses – such as saddle of monkfish with crab risotto – averaging £12; pre-theatre dinners are available by prior reservation from about 5pm. An excellent second choice is the *Sun Inn*, a fine old pub with antique beamed rooms just south of the Market Place at 33 High St. They offer fine ales and first-rate bar food – beef in ale, for instance, at £7.50, and chicken and ham pies at £8. The *Sun Inn* is also the best place for a **pint**.

Castleton

The agreeable little village of **CASTLETON**, ten miles northeast of Buxton, lies on the northern edge of the White Peak, its huddle of old stone cottages ringed by hills and set beside a babbling brook. As a base for local walks, the place is hard to beat. Overseeing the whole caboodle is **Peveril Castle** (April–Oct daily 10am–5pm; Nov–March Thurs–Mon 10am–4pm; £3.50; EH), from which the village takes its name. William the Conqueror's illegitimate son William Peveril raised the first fortifications here to protect the king's rights to the forest that then covered the district, but most of the remains – principally the ruinous square keep – date to the 1170s.

The limestone hills pressing in on Castleton are peppered with water-worn **cave systems**, and four of them – **Peak Cavern, Speedwell Cavern, Blue John** and **Treak Cliff Cavern** – have been developed as tourist attractions. They can all be reached by car or on foot, the latter by means of a three-and-a-half-mile circular trail that begins in the village and takes two hours. Contact the tourist office (see below) for details on this. Most visitors settle for just one set of caves – the deepest, **Speedwell Cavern** (daily 10am–5pm; £7.25; ⓦwww.speedwellcavern.co.uk). Located about 700 yards or so west of the village, the cavern is entered via a hundred dripping steps; the tour includes a boat trip through a quarter-mile-long claustrophobic tunnel that was blasted out in search of lead. At the end lies the Bottomless Pit, a pool where 40,000 tons of mining rubble were once dumped without raising the water level one iota.

Practicalities

The principal **bus** service to Castleton arrives from the east – from Sheffield (First bus #272). In the opposite direction, several operators combine to link Buxton with Castleton, but buses are few and far between, one or two a day if that. The nearest **train station** is at Hope, a couple of miles or so to the east of Castleton along the valley. The station is on the Manchester Piccadilly–Sheffield line and there are trains every hour or two; bus #272 links Hope with Castleton. The **Castleton Information Centre** (daily 9.30/10am–5pm, ⓣ01433/620 679; ⓦwww.visitpeakdistrict.com), a combined museum, community centre and tourist office, stands beside the car park on the west side of the village, just off the main street, which dog-legs through the village doubling as the A6187.

Cream of the **B&B** crop is *Bargate Cottage*, in a modernized old cottage at the top end of the Market Place (ⓣ01433/620 201, ⓦwww.bargatecottage.co.uk; no credit cards; ③). They have three well-kept en-suite rooms, and the breakfasts are first-rate. Another inexpensive option is the *Cryer House*, just off the Market Place, opposite the church on Castle Street (Ⓣ01433/620 244; ❸). This B&B occupies a former rectory and has just two guest rooms, plus a pleasant conservatory. Finally, the **youth hostel** (Ⓣ0870/770 5758, Ⓦwww.yha.org.uk; dorm beds £13, doubles ❶) is housed in Castleton Hall, a capacious old stone mansion on the Market Place. The hostel is well equipped with a self-catering kitchen, a café, cycle store and drying room, and its 140 beds are parcelled up into two- to six-bedded rooms, many of which are en suite.

For **food**, Castleton's pubs are its gastronomic mainstay and there's nowhere better than *The George*, on Castle Street, yards from the Market Place, which offers tasty bar food at affordable prices.

Edale village

There's almost nothing to **EDALE village**, some five miles from Castleton, except for a slender, half-mile trail of stone houses, which march up the main street from the train station with a couple of pubs, an old stone church and a scattering of B&Bs on the way – and it's this somnambulant air that is of immediate appeal. Walkers arrive in droves throughout the year to set off on the 268-mile **Pennine Way** (see box below) across England's backbone to Kirk Yetholm on the Scottish border; the route's starting point is signposted from outside the *Old Nag's Head* at the head of the village.

There are regular **trains** from Manchester and Sheffield to Edale station and there is also a patchy **bus** service from Castleton. From Edale train station, it's 400 yards or so up the road to the **Peak National Park's Moorland Centre** (April–Sept Mon–Fri 9.30am–5.30pm, Sat & Sun 9.30am–5pm; Oct–March Mon–Fri 10am–3pm, Sat & Sun 9.30am–4.30pm; Ⓣ01433/670 207), who sell all manner of trail leaflets and hiking guides and can advise about local accommodation. The nearest **youth hostel**, the *Edale YHA Activity Centre* (Ⓣ0870/770 5808, Ⓦwww.yha.org.uk; dorm beds £12.50, doubles ❶), lies two miles east of Edale train station at Rowland Cote, Nether Booth. It's clearly signed from the road into Edale or you can hoof it there across the fields from behind the information centre. There are 150 beds in two- to ten-bedded rooms and a good range of facilities from a laundry and a café through to a self-catering kitchen. They also offer an extensive programme of outdoor pursuits; these need to be booked in advance. Naturally enough, the hostel is popular with Pennine Way walkers – as is the **camping barn** not far from Edale at Upper Booth Farm

The Pennine Way

The 268-mile-long **Pennine Way** (Ⓦwww.nationaltrail.co.uk) was the country's first long-distance footpath, officially opened in 1965. It stretches north from the boggy plateau of the Peak District's Kinder Scout, through the Yorkshire Dales and Teesdale, crossing Hadrian's Wall and the Northumberland National Park, before entering Scotland to fizzle out at the village of Kirk Yetholm.

Now one of the most popular walks in the country, either taken in sections or completed in two to three weeks, depending on your level of fitness and experience, the Pennine Way is a challenge in the best of weather, since it passes through some of the wildest countryside in England. You must certainly be properly equipped and able to use a map and compass. The National Trail Guides *Pennine Way: South* and *Pennine Way: North*, are essential, though some still prefer to stick to Wainwright's *Pennine Way Companion*. Information centres along the route – like the one at Edale village – stock a selection of guides and associated trail leaflets and can offer advice.

(Ⓣ01433/670 250, Ⓦwww.upperboothcamping.co.uk). Those without hair shirts, or with more money, will do better at one of Edale's several **B&Bs**, the pick of which is *Stonecroft*, a detached Victorian house with two comfortable guest rooms in the village near the church (Ⓣ01433/670 262, Ⓦwww.stonecroftguesthouse.co.uk; ④). As for **food**, the hiker-friendly *Rambler*, yards from the train station at the bottom of the village, serves filling bar food.

Eyam

Within a year of September 7, 1665, the lonely lead-mining settlement of **EYAM** (pronounced "Eem"), nine miles southeast of Edale, had lost almost half of its population of 750 to the bubonic plague, a calamity that earned it the enduring epithet "**The Plague Village**". The first victim was one George Vicars, a journeyman tailor who is said to have released some infected fleas into his lodgings from a package of cloth he had brought here from London. Acutely conscious of the danger to neighbouring villages, **William Mompesson**, the village rector, speedily organized a self-imposed quarantine, arranging for food to be left at places on the parish boundary. Payment was made with coins left in pools of disinfecting vinegar in holes chiselled into the old boundary stones – and these can still be seen at **Mompesson's Well**, half a mile up the hill to the north of the village and accessible by footpath. Mompesson himself survived the plague, though his wife did not – poor reward for a man whose endeavours prevented the plague from spreading across the Peaks.

Long, thin and hilly, Eyam comprises one main street – Church and then Main Street – which trails west up from **The Square**, which is itself really no more than a crossroads overlooked by a few old stone houses. First up of interest along Church Street is the comely **church of St Lawrence**, of medieval foundation but extensively revamped in the nineteenth century. In the church graveyard a few feet from the entrance stands a conspicuous, eighth-century carved **Celtic cross** and close by is the distinctive **table-tomb** of Mompesson's wife, whose sterling work nursing sick villagers is recalled every Remembrance Day when red roses are left beside her tomb. Inside the church, informative panels reveal more of the village's plague history, highlighting a number of associated sites in and around the place.

Immediately to the west of the church are the so-called **plague cottages**, where plaques explain who died where and when – it was here that Vicars met his maker. Another short hop brings you to **Eyam Hall** (guided tours: July–Aug Wed, Thurs & Sun noon–4pm; £6.25; Ⓦwww.eyamhall.co.uk), which was built for a certain Thomas Wright a few years after the plague ended, possibly in an attempt to secure his position as the squire of the depleted village. Wright's heirs have lived in it ever since, building up a mildly diverting collection of furnishings, family portraits, tapestries, costumes and incidental bygones.

From the hall, it's a few minutes' walk along Main Street and up Hawkhill Road – follow the signs – to the modest Methodist chapel that now houses the **Eyam Museum** (mid-March to Oct Tues–Sun 10am–4.30pm; £1.75). This explains the history of the village and has a good section on the bubonic plague – its transmission, symptoms and social aftermath.

Practicalities

Buses to Eyam all stop on The Square, and one or two also run along Main/Church Street. There are surprisingly few places to stay, the pick of a handful of **B&Bs** being *Crown Cottage*, in a pleasant old stone building on Main Street (Ⓣ01433/630 858, Ⓦwww.crown-cottage.co.uk; ③). There are four homely guest rooms here, three doubles and one twin. The best alternative is the well-equipped **youth hostel** (ⓣ0870/770 5830, ⓦwww.yha.org.uk; £14, doubles ❶), which occupies an idiosyncratic Victorian house, whose ersatz medieval towers and turrets overlook Eyam from amidst wooded grounds on Hawkhill Road, a stiff, half-mile ramble up from Eyam Museum (see p.440). The hostel has a café, self-catering facilities, a cycle store and a lounge; the sixty beds are divided up into two- to ten-bedded rooms and advance reservations are recommended.

The best place **to eat** is the *Miner's Arms*, in antique premises just off The Square on Water Lane, which serves filling bar meals as well as very enjoyable and moderately priced traditional dinners in its restaurant (closed Sun).

Baslow

BASLOW, some four miles southeast of Eyam, is an inconclusive little village, whose oldest stone cottages string prettily along the River Derwent. The only building of note is **St Anne's Church** whose stone spire pokes up above the Victorian castellations of its nave in between the river and the busy junction of the A623/A619. Baslow may be inconsequential, but it is handy for the nearby Chatsworth estate (see below), especially if you're travelling by bus, and it possesses one of the Peak's finest **hotels**, *Fischer's Baslow Hall* (ⓣ01246/583 259, ⓦwww.fischers-baslowhall.co.uk; ❽), a mile or so out of the village back towards Eyam along the A623. In its own grounds, the hall is picture-postcard perfect, a handsome Edwardian building made of local stone with matching gables and a dinky canopy over the front door. The interior is suitably lavish and the service attentive with rooms both in the main building and in the Garden House annexe next door. The **restaurant** is superb too, and has won several awards for its imaginative cuisine – caramelized pork belly with peanut brittle and escabeche salad, for instance – set meals cost £65. Alternatively, you can pop back into Baslow for a bite at the excellent *Avant Garde Café* (daily 10am–5pm), where they serve a delicious range of salads and light meals in bright, modern surroundings; the café is opposite St Anne's Church.

Chatsworth House

Fantastically popular, **Chatsworth House** (mid-March to late Dec daily 11am–5.30pm, last admission 4.30pm; gardens till 6pm, last admission 5pm; house & gardens £13.50, gardens only £7.45; ⓦwww.chatsworth.org), just south of Baslow via the A619, was built in the seventeenth century by the first Duke of Devonshire and has been owned by the family ever since. The house is seen to best advantage from the **B6012**, which meanders across the estate to the west of the house, giving a full view of its vast Palladian frontage, whose clean lines are perfectly balanced by the undulating partly wooded **parkland**, which rolls in from the south and west.

Many visitors forgo the house altogether, concentrating on the gardens instead – an understandable decision given the predictability of the assorted baubles accumulated by the family over the centuries. Nonetheless, amongst the maze of grandiose rooms and staircases, there are several noteworthy highlights, including the showpiece **Great Dining Room**, which has its table set as it was for the visit of George V and Queen Mary in 1933. And then there are the paintings. Amongst many, Frans Hals, Tintoretto, Veronese and van Dyck all have a showing and there's even a Rembrandt – *A Portrait of an Old Man* – hanging in the chapel.

Back outside, the **gardens** are a real treat and owe much to the combined efforts of Capability Brown, who designed them in the 1750s, and Joseph

Paxton (designer of London's Crystal Palace), who had a bash seventy years later. Amongst all sorts of fripperies, there are water fountains, a rock garden, an artificial waterfall, a grotto and a folly as well as a nursery and greenhouses. Afterwards, you can wend your way to the café in the handsomely converted former Stables.

The best way to get to Chatsworth House is on foot along one of the footpaths that lattice the estate. It's easy walking and the obvious departure point is Baslow on the northern edge of the estate. The "Grate Little Guide" (see p.434) to Chatsworth describes an especially pleasant four-mile loop, taking in the house and beginning and ending in Baslow. There are no buses to Chatsworth House itself and the nearest you'll get is the village estate of Edensor, from where it's about one mile walk east across the park to the house – but buses are few and far between.

Travel details

Buses

For information on all local and national bus services, contact Traveline ⓣ0871/200 2233, ⓦwww.traveline.org.uk.

The TransPeak

Operated by the Trent Barton bus company, the TransPeak bus service (ⓦwww.transpeak.co.uk) runs from Nottingham to Manchester via Derby, Matlock, Bakewell and Buxton every 2 hours daily. The whole journey takes 3.5 hours.

Birmingham to: Buxton (2 daily; 4hr); Great Malvern (2 daily; 1hr 30min); Hereford (2 daily; 2hr 20min); Liverpool (6 daily: 3hr); London (hourly; 3hr); Ludlow (hourly; 2hr 10min); Manchester (hourly; 2hr 30min); Shrewsbury (2 daily; 1hr 20min); Stratford-upon-Avon (every 2hr; 1hr).
Buxton to: Ashbourne (4 daily; 2hr); Birmingham (2 daily; 4hr); Derby (3 daily; 1hr 30min).
Derby to: Buxton (3 daily; 1hr 30min).
Great Malvern to: Birmingham (2 daily; 1hr 30min); Hereford (1 daily; 40min); Stratford-upon-Avon (5 daily; 3hr 50min).
Hay-on-Wye to: Hereford (4 daily; 1hr).
Hereford to: Birmingham (2 daily; 2hr 20min); Great Malvern (1 daily; 40min); Hay-on-Wye (4 daily; 1hr); Ludlow (4 daily; 4hr); Shrewsbury (2 daily; 3hr 30min).
Ludlow to: Birmingham (hourly; 2hr 10min); Hereford (4 daily; 4hr); Shrewsbury (6 daily; 1hr 20min).
Shrewsbury to: Birmingham (2 daily; 1hr 20min); Hereford (2 daily; 3hr 30min); Ludlow (6 daily; 1hr 20min); Stratford-upon-Avon (2 daily; 2hr 30min).
Stratford-upon-Avon to: Birmingham (every 2hr; 1hr); Great Malvern (5 daily; 3hr 50min); Shrewsbury (2 daily; 2hr 30min).

Trains

For information on all local and national rail services, contact National Rail Enquiries ⓣ0845/748 4950, ⓦwww.nationalrail.co.uk.

Birmingham New Street to: Great Malvern (every 30min; 1hr); Hereford (hourly; 1hr 50min); London (every 30min; 1hr 30min); Shrewsbury (hourly; 1hr 20min).
Birmingham Snow Hill to: Stratford-upon-Avon (Mon–Sat hourly; 50min); Warwick (Mon–Sat hourly; 40min).
Hereford to: Birmingham (hourly; 1hr 40min); Great Malvern (hourly; 30min); London (hourly; 2hr 40min); Ludlow (hourly; 30min); Shrewsbury (hourly; 1hr).
Shrewsbury to: Birmingham (hourly; 1hr 20min); Church Stretton (every 30min; 15min); Hereford (hourly; 1hr); Ludlow (hourly; 30min); Telford (every 30min; 20min).
Stratford-upon-Avon to: Birmingham Snow Hill (Mon–Sat hourly; 50min); London Marylebone (every 2hr; 2hr 25min); Warwick (Mon–Sat hourly; 30min).
Worcester to: Birmingham (every 30min; 40min–1hr); Hereford (hourly; 50min).

The East Midlands

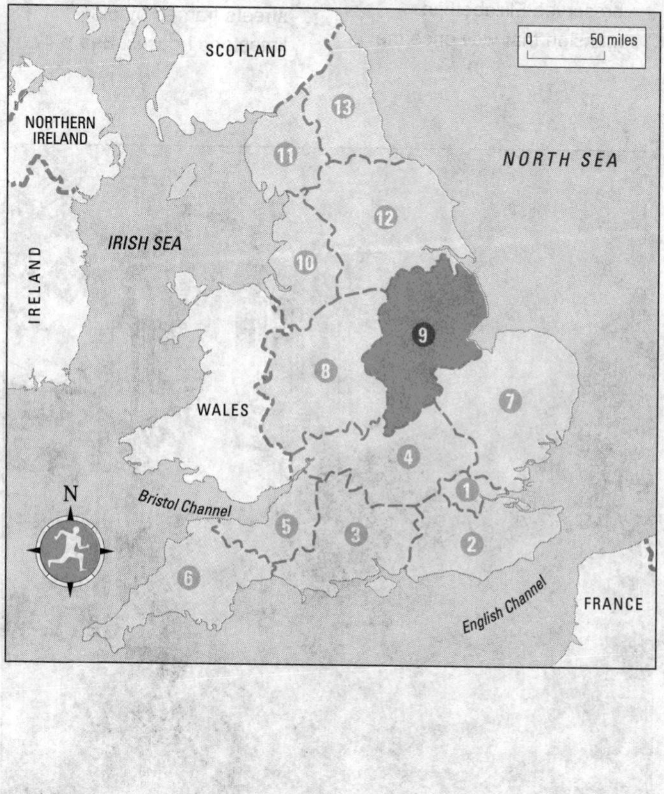

CHAPTER 9 Highlights

* **Rufford Abbey Country Park** Well off the usual tourist track, Rufford offers a ceramic gallery, a bird sanctuary, a mill and a sculpture garden with lots of relaxed strolling in between. See p.454
* **Hardwick Hall** A beautifully preserved Elizabethan mansion that was once the home of the illustrious Bess of Hardwick. See p.454
* **Lincoln Cathedral** One of the finest medieval cathedrals in the land, seen to fine advantage on a rooftop guided tour. See p.465
* **Stamford** Lincolnshire's prettiest town, with narrow streets framed by old limestone houses. See p.471

▲ Stamford

The East Midlands

Many tourists bypass the four major counties of the **East Midlands** – Nottinghamshire, Leicestershire, Northamptonshire and Lincolnshire – on their way to more obvious destinations, an understandable mistake given that the region is short on star attractions. The most obvious targets are **Nottingham**, **Leicester** and **Northampton** – three of the four county towns – but although they share a long and eventful history, they have all been badly bruised by postwar town planning and industrial development. Nevertheless, embedded in the modernity are a few historical landmarks – an especially fine church in Northampton, the castle in Nottingham and traces of Roman baths in Leicester – though **Nottingham** has enough character to give it an aesthetic edge. Furthermore, the countryside surrounding them can be delightful, with rolling farmland punctuated by wooded ridges and flowing hills, all sprinkled with prestigious country homes, pretty villages and old market towns.

In Nottinghamshire, there's the added bonus of Byron's **Newstead Abbey** and, just over the border in Derbyshire, **Hardwick Hall**, an especially beautiful Elizabethan country home built by the redoubtable Bess of Hardwick. East of Leicestershire, the easy countryside rolls over into **Rutland**, the region's fifth and smallest county, and here you'll find two more pleasant country towns, **Oakham** and **Uppingham**. Rutland benefits from the use of limestone as the traditional building material, as does **Northamptonshire**, whose selection of handsome, old stone villages and small towns includes **Fotheringhay** and **Oundle** – not to mention several large country estates, the best known of which is **Althorp**, the final resting place of Princess Diana.

Lincolnshire is very different in character from the rest of the region, an agricultural backwater that remains surprisingly remote. This was not always the case: throughout medieval times the county flourished as a centre of the wool trade with Flanders, its merchants and landowners becoming some of the wealthiest in England. Reminders of the high times are legion, beginning with the majestic cathedral that graces **Lincoln**, in part at least a dignified old city which, with its cobbled lanes and ancient buildings, well deserves an overnight stay. Equally enticing is the splendidly intact stone town of **Stamford**, but the county's urban attractions pretty much end there. Out in the sticks, the most distinctive feature is **The Fens**, whose pancake-flat fields, filling out much of the south of the county and extending deep into East Anglia (see Chapter 7), have been regained from the marshes and the sea. Fenland villages are generally short of charm, but their **parish churches**, whose spires regularly interrupt the wide-skied landscape, are simply stunning, the most impressive of the lot being St Botolph's in **Boston**.

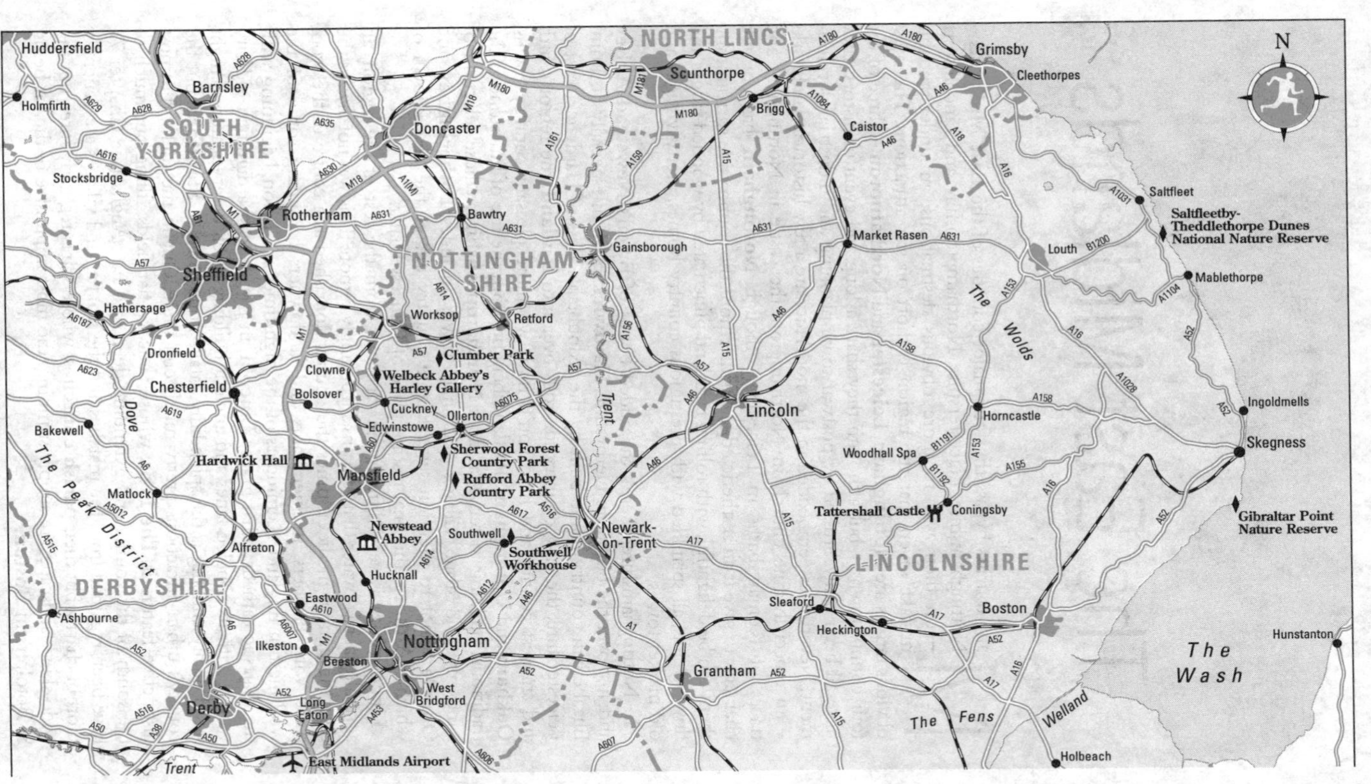
N
NORTH LINCS
SOUTH YORKSHIRE
NOTTINGHAMSHIRE
DERBYSHIRE
LINCOLNSHIRE
The Peak District
The Wolds
The Fens
The Wash
Trent
Dove
Welland
Huddersfield
Holmfirth
Barnsley
Stocksbridge
Doncaster
Rotherham
Sheffield
Hathersage
Dronfield
Chesterfield
Bakewell
Matlock
Alfreton
Ashbourne
Derby
Scunthorpe
Brigg
Grimsby
Cleethorpes
Caistor
Market Rasen
Louth
Saltfleet
Saltfleetby-Theddlethorpe Dunes National Nature Reserve
Mablethorpe
Ingoldmells
Skegness
Gibraltar Point Nature Reserve
Hunstanton
Holbeach
Boston
Sleaford
Heckington
Grantham
Lincoln
Horncastle
Woodhall Spa
Coningsby
Tattershall Castle
Gainsborough
Bawtry
Worksop
Retford
Clumber Park
Welbeck Abbey's Harley Gallery
Clowne
Bolsover
Cuckney
Ollerton
Edwinstowe
Sherwood Forest Country Park
Rufford Abbey Country Park
Hardwick Hall
Mansfield
Newstead Abbey
Southwell
Southwell Workhouse
Newark-on-Trent
Hucknall
Eastwood
Ilkeston
Nottingham
Beeston
West Bridgford
Long Eaton
East Midlands Airport

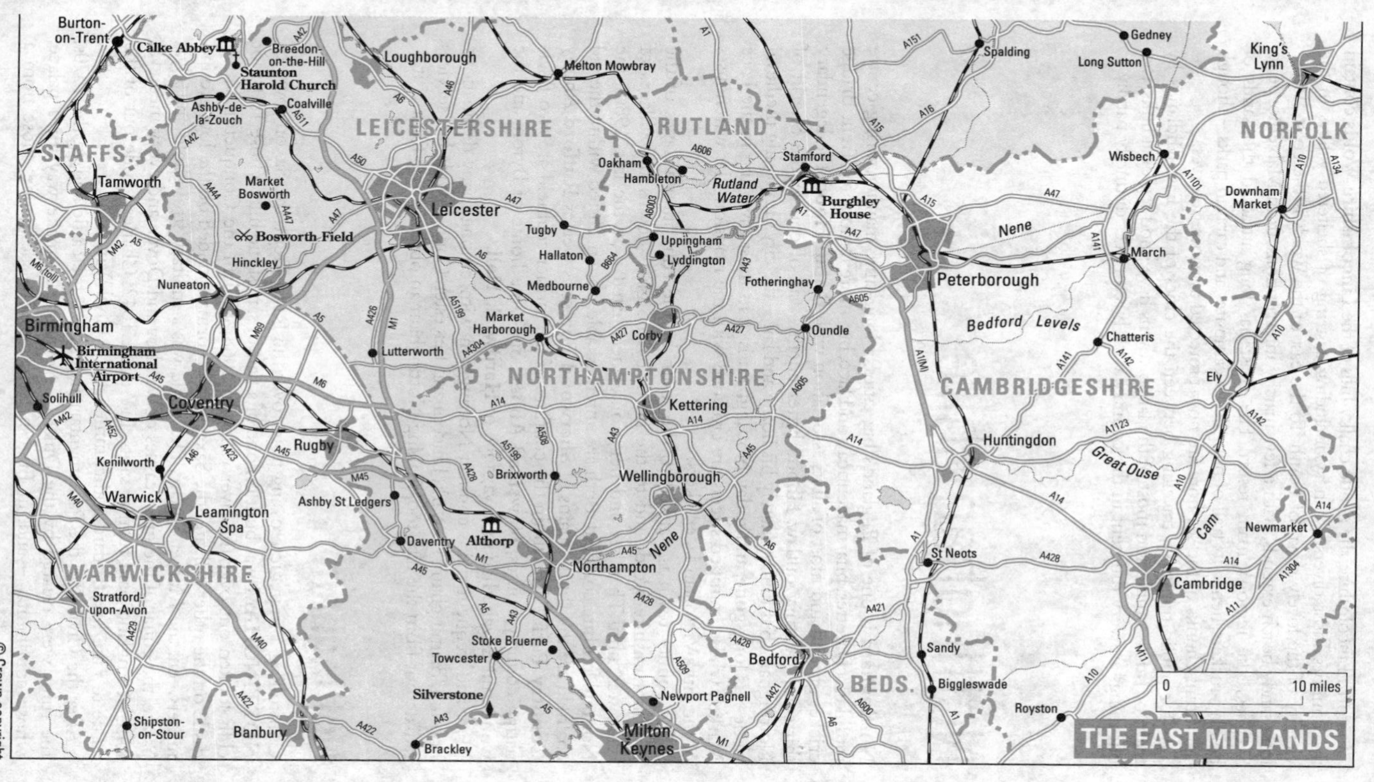
THE EAST MIDLANDS
0
10 miles
Burton-on-Trent
Calke Abbey
Breedon-on-the-Hill
Staunton Harold Church
Ashby-de-la-Zouch
Coalville
Loughborough
Melton Mowbray
Spalding
Gedney
Long Sutton
King's Lynn
LEICESTERSHIRE
RUTLAND
NORFOLK
STAFFS.
Tamworth
Market Bosworth
Bosworth Field
Hinckley
Nuneaton
Leicester
Tugby
Hallaton
Medbourne
Oakham
Hambleton
Rutland Water
Uppingham
Lyddington
Stamford
Burghley House
Fotheringhay
Oundle
Peterborough
Nene
Wisbech
Downham Market
March
Bedford Levels
Chatteris
Ely
Birmingham
Birmingham International Airport
Solihull
Coventry
Lutterworth
Market Harborough
Corby
NORTHAMPTONSHIRE
Kettering
CAMBRIDGESHIRE
Huntingdon
Great Ouse
Rugby
Kenilworth
Warwick
Leamington Spa
Ashby St Ledgers
Brixworth
Wellingborough
Daventry
Althorp
Northampton
St Neots
Cam
Newmarket
Cambridge
WARWICKSHIRE
Stratford-upon-Avon
Stoke Bruerne
Towcester
Silverstone
Bedford
Sandy
Biggleswade
BEDS.
Royston
Shipston-on-Stour
Banbury
Brackley
Newport Pagnell
Milton Keynes
A1
A6
A10
A14
A15
A16
A42
A43
A45
A46
A47
A50
A151
A134
A1101
A141
A142
A1123
A1(M)
A605
A606
A6003
A427
A4304
A5199
A508
A426
A428
A444
A447
A511
A5
A452
A423
A421
A429
A422
A509
A600
A1304
A11
B664
M1
M6
M6 (toll)
M11
M40
M42
M45
M69

In north Lincolnshire, the gentle chalky hills of the **Lincolnshire Wolds** contain the county's most diverse scenery, including a string of sheltered valleys in the vicinity of the lovely town of Louth. To the east of the Wolds is the coast, whose long sandy beach extends, with a few marshy interruptions, from Mablethorpe to Skegness, the region's main resort. The coast has long attracted thousands of holiday-makers, hence its trail of bungalows, campsites and caravan parks – though significant chunks of the seashore are now protected as nature reserves.

As for public transport, travelling between the cities of the East Midlands by **train** or **bus** is simple and most of the larger towns have good regional links, too; but things are very different in the country with bus services distinctly patchy.

Nottinghamshire

Nottingham is one of England's big cities, a long-time manufacturing centre for bikes, cigarettes, pharmaceuticals and lace, but more famous for Trent Bridge cricket ground and most of all its association with **Robin Hood**, the legendary thirteenth-century outlaw. Hood's bitter enemy was, of course, the Sheriff of Nottingham, but unfortunately his home and lair – the city's imposing medieval castle – is long gone, and today Nottingham is at its most diverting in the Lace Market, whose cramped streets are crowded with the mansion-like warehouses of the city's Victorian lacemakers.

The county town is flanked to the south by the commuter villages of the Nottinghamshire Wolds and to the north by the gritty towns and villages of what was, until Thatcher and her cronies decimated it in the late 1980s, the Nottinghamshire coalfield. Both are unremarkable, but encrusted within the old coalfield are the thin remains of **Sherwood Forest** as well as **Rufford Abbey Country Park**. Also within the confines of the former coalfield are two fascinating country houses, **Newstead Abbey**, one-time home of Byron, and the wonderful Elizabethan extravagance of **Hardwick Hall**.

Fast and frequent trains connect Nottingham with, among many destinations, London, Birmingham, Newark, Lincoln and Leicester. County-wide bus services radiate out from the city, too, making Nottingham an obvious base for a visit.

Nottingham

Controlling a strategic crossing point over the River Trent, the Saxon town of **NOTTINGHAM** was built on one of a pair of sandstone hills whose 130-foot cliffs looked out over the river valley. In 1068, William the Conqueror built a castle on the other hill, and the Saxons and Normans traded on the low ground in between, the Market Square. The castle was a military stronghold and royal palace, the equal of the great castles of Windsor and Dover, and every medieval king of England paid regular visits. In August 1642, Charles I rode out of the castle to raise his standard and commence the Civil War.

After the Civil War, the Parliamentarians slighted the castle and, in the 1670s, the ruins were cleared by the Duke of Newcastle to make way for a palace, whose continental – and, in English terms, novel – design he chose from a

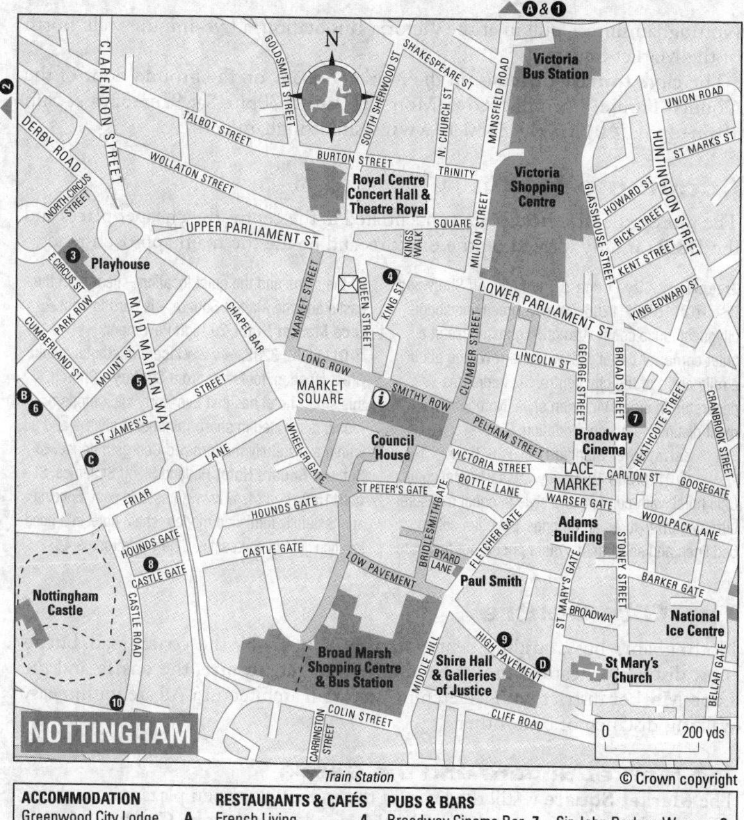

ACCOMMODATION		RESTAURANTS & CAFÉS		PUBS & BARS			
Greenwood City Lodge	A	French Living	4	Broadway Cinema Bar	7	Sir John Borlase Warren	2
Harts Hotel	B	Harts	6	Cast	3	Ye Olde Trip to Jerusalem Inn	10
Lace Market Hotel	D	Memsaab	5	Cock and Hoop	9		
Rutland Square Hotel	C	World Service	8	Lincolnshire Poacher	1		

pattern book, probably by Rubens. Beneath the castle lay a handsome, well-kept market town. In the second half of the eighteenth century, however, the city was transformed by the expansion of the lace and hosiery industries, and within the space of fifty years, Nottingham's population increased from ten thousand to fifty thousand, the resulting slum becoming a hotbed of radicalism.

The worst of Nottingham's slums were cleared in the early twentieth century, when the city centre assumed its present structure, with the main commercial area ringed by alternating industrial and residential districts. Thereafter, crass postwar development, adding tower blocks, shopping centres and a ring road, ensconced the remnants of the city's past.

Arrival and information

Nottingham **train station** is on the south side of the city centre, a five- to ten-minute walk from the Market Square – follow the signs. Most long-distance buses arrive at the Broad Marsh Bus Station, down the street from the train station on the way to the centre, but some – including services to north

Nottinghamshire – pull in at the Victoria Bus Station, a five-minute walk north of the Market Square.

The city's **tourist office** is on the Market Square, on the ground floor of the Council House, 1 Smithy Row (Mon–Fri 9am–5.30pm, Sat 9am–5pm & Sun 10am–4pm; ⓣ0115/915 5330, ⓦwww.visitnottingham.com).

Accommodation

The more expensive **hotels** are concentrated in the centre, the cheaper places and the **B&Bs** mostly located on the outskirts and beside the main approach roads.

Greenwood City Lodge 5 Third Ave, off Sherwood Rise ⓣ0115/962 1206, ⓦwww.greenwoodlodgecityguesthouse.co.uk. Attractive guesthouse in a quiet corner of the city, down a narrow lane about a mile north of the city centre. Six bedrooms decorated in smart Victorian style. Nottingham's most distinctive accommodation. ⑤

Harts Hotel Standard Hill, Park Row ⓣ0115/988 1900, ⓦwww.hartshotel.co.uk. Chic hotel, with comfort and style in equal measure: ultramodern fixtures and fittings, Egyptian cotton bed linen and so forth. It's quite pricey, but first-rate all the same and the quiet location – near both the castle and the Market Square – is hard to beat. ⑦

Lace Market Hotel 29 High Pavement ⓣ0115/852 3232, ⓦwww.lacemarkethotel.co.uk. Great location, footsteps from St Mary's Church, this smart hotel has just over forty slick modern rooms decorated in sharp minimalist style – and all within a tastefully modernized Georgian house. ⑦

Rutland Square Hotel Rutland St, off St James' St ⓣ0115/941 1114, ⓦwww.forestdale.com. Enticing and tastefully furnished modern chain hotel in a good location, just by the castle. Ninety-odd rooms. ⑥

The City Centre

Nottingham's busy, bustling centre attracts shoppers by the coach-load, but its most distinctive features are its handsome **Market Square**, the **castle** and the **Lace Market** district with its fetching Victorian architecture. All are within easy walking distance of each other.

The Market Square and the Castle

The **Market Square** is still the heart of the city, an airy open plaza whose shops, offices and fountain are overlooked by the grand neo-Baroque **Council House**. From here, it's a five-minute walk west up Friar Lane to **Nottingham Castle** (daily: March–Sept 10am–5pm, Oct–Feb 11am–4pm; £3.50), whose heavily restored medieval gateway leads into the gardens, which slope up to the squat, seventeenth-century ducal **palace**. The mansion occupies the site of the medieval castle's upper bailey, and round the back, just outside the main entrance, two sets of steps lead down into the maze of ancient caves that honeycomb the cliff beneath. One set is open for guided tours (Mon–Sat 2–3 daily; call ⓣ0115/915 3676 for times; £2), and this leads into **Mortimer's Hole**, a three-hundred-foot shaft along which, so the story goes, the young Edward III and his chums crept in October 1330 to capture the queen mother, Isabella, and her lover, Roger Mortimer. The couple had already polished off Edward III's father, the hapless Edward II, and were intent on usurping the crown, but the young Edward proved too shrewd for them and Mortimer came to a sticky end.

The interior of the ducal mansion holds the **Castle Museum and Art Gallery**, where a particular highlight is the "Story of Nottingham", a lively, well-presented and entertaining account of the city's development. In particular, look out for a small but exquisite collection of late medieval **alabaster carvings**, an art form for which Nottingham once had an international reputation. It's worth walking up to the top floor too, for a turn round the main **picture gallery**, a handsome and spacious room, which displays a curious assortment of mostly English nineteenth-century Romantic paintings.

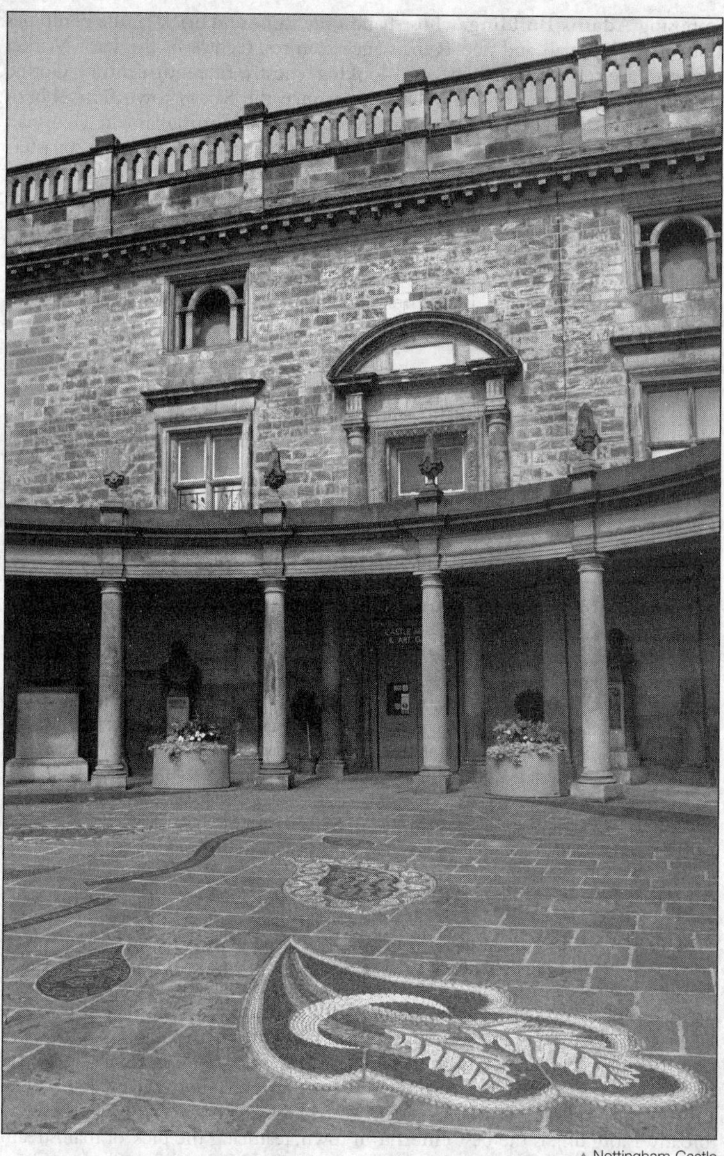

▲ Nottingham Castle

The Lace Market

A few minutes' walk away, on the east side of the Market Square up along Victoria Street, is the **Lace Market**, where the narrow lanes and alleys are flanked by an attractive assortment of Victorian factories and warehouses – a particular shame then that the spaceship-like National Ice Centre (Ⓦwww.national-ice-centre.com) interrupts the area's architectural flow. **Stoney Street** is the Lace Market at its most appealing, with pride of place going to the imposing **Adams Building**, whose handsome stone and brick facade combines both neo-Georgian and neo-Renaissance features. Centre of the Lace Market is the church of **St Mary**, a good-looking, mostly fifteenth-century Gothic structure built on top of the hill that was once the Saxon town. The church abuts High Pavement, the administrative centre of Nottingham in Georgian times, and here you'll find **Shire Hall**, whose Neoclassical columns, pilasters and dome date from 1770. The Shire Hall now houses the **Galleries of Justice** (April to early Sept Tues–Sun 10am–4pm; early Sept to March Tues–Fri 10am–3pm, Sat & Sun 11am–4pm; also Mon 10am–3/4pm in school holidays; £8.95; Ⓦwww.nccl.org.uk), whose child-friendly "Crime and Punishment" tour features lots of role-play.

Nearby, on Byard Lane, is the first shop of local lad **Paul Smith**, a major success story of contemporary British fashion.

Eating

Nottingham boasts at least half a dozen top-quality **restaurants**, where the elaborate menus attempt to balance unusual ingredients in unusual combinations. There are lots of more straightforward places too – primarily Italian and Asian – plus a slew of cafés and café-bars.

French Living 27 King St Ⓣ0115/958 5885. Authentic French cuisine served in an intimate, candlelit basement. Daytime snacks and baguettes in the ground-floor café too. Evening main courses from £10. Closed Sun & Mon.

Harts Standard Court, Park Row Ⓣ0115/947 7694. One of the city's most acclaimed restaurants, occupying part of the old general hospital and serving an international menu of carefully presented meals. Attractive, contemporary decor and attentive service. Reservations essential. Mains from £15.

Memsaab 12 Maid Marian Way Ⓣ0115/957 0009. One of a new breed of Indian restaurants (to Nottingham at least) – crisp, modern decor and bags of space. The food is exquisite, canny amalgamations of different Indian cooking styles from different regions. A large and imaginative menu with main courses starting from as little as £10.

World Service Newdigate House, Castle Gate Ⓣ0115/847 5587. Chic restaurant with bags of (vaguely Asiatic) flair in charming premises up near the castle. Try out tasty dishes such as monkfish in honey breadcrumbs and Nottinghamshire pork cutlet with onion marmalade. In the evenings, main courses start at around £16, but there are great deals at lunchtimes with two-course set meals costing £12, £16 for three.

Pubs and nightlife

Nottingham's **nightclub** scene is boisterous with places coming in and out of fashion all the time; a current hot spot is *Stealth*, in the centre on Goldsmith Street (Ⓦwww.stealthattack.com). **Pubs** around Market Square have a tough edge to them, especially on the weekend, but within a few minutes' walk there are several lively and more enjoyable drinking-holes. For **live music**, both popular and classical, most big names play at the Royal Centre Concert Hall on South Sherwood Street (Ⓣ0115/989 5555, Ⓦwww.royalcentre-nottingham.co.uk). The Broadway, in the Lace Market at 14 Broad St (Ⓣ0115/952 6611, Ⓦwww.broadway.org.uk), is the best **cinema** in town, featuring the pick of mainstream and avant-garde films, and there's theatre at the Nottingham Playhouse, on Wellington Circus (Ⓣ0115/941 9419, Ⓦwww.nottinghamplayhouse.co.uk)

Pubs and bars

Broadway Cinema Bar Broadway Cinema, 14 Broad St. Informal, fashionable (in an arty sort of way) bar that serves an eclectic assortment of bottled beers to a cinema-keen clientele. The bar food is, however, very average.

Cast Wellington Circus. The bar of the Nottingham Playhouse is a popular, easy-going spot with courtyard seating on summer nights. Patrons have the advantage of looking at a piece of modern art too – Anish Kapoor's whopping, reflective "Sky Mirror". There's also an attached deli and (pretty average) restaurant.

Cock and Hoop 25 High Pavement, Lace Market. One of the few pubs in the centre to have avoided being made over for a younger clientele – a curious little split-level bar that verges on the smart with its thick carpets and comfortable chairs. Real ales too.

Lincolnshire Poacher 161 Mansfield Rd. Popular and relaxed pub, popular with an older clientele, offering a wide selection of bottled and real ales.

Sir John Borlase Warren 1 Ilkeston Rd, Canning Circus. Pulling in a mixed bag of students and locals, this rambling old pub has character and a lively, (usually) friendly atmosphere. Half a mile up the hill from the city centre along Derby Rd.

Ye Olde Trip to Jerusalem Inn Below the castle in Brewhouse Yard. Carved into the castle rock, this ancient inn may well have been a meeting point for soldiers gathering for the Third Crusade. Its cave-like bars, with their rough sandstone ceilings, are delightfully secretive.

Northern Nottinghamshire

Rural **northern Nottinghamshire**, with its gentle rolling landscapes and large ducal estates, was transformed in the nineteenth century by **coal** – deep, wide seams of the stuff that spawned dozens of collieries, and colliery towns, stretching north across the county and on into Yorkshire. Almost without exception, the mines have closed, their passing marked only by the old pithead winding wheels left, bleak and solitary, to commemorate the thousands of men who laboured here. The suddenness of the pit closure programme imposed by the Conservative government in the 1980s knocked the stuffing out of the area but one prop of its recent revival has been the tourist industry: the countryside in between these former mining communities holds several enjoyable attractions, the best-known of which is **Sherwood Forest** – or at least the patchy remains of it – supposedly the one-time haunt of Robin Hood. Byron is a pipsqueak in the celebrity stakes by comparison, but his family home – **Newstead Abbey** – is here too, and then there's **Hardwick Hall**, a stunningly handsome Elizabethan mansion, not to mention the exemplary **Rufford Abbey Country Park**.

With the exception of Hardwick Hall, all these attractions are easy to reach by **bus** from Nottingham.

Newstead Abbey

In 1539, **Newstead Abbey**, ten miles north of Nottingham on the A60 (house April–Sept daily noon–5pm: grounds daily 9am–6pm or dusk; £6, grounds only £3; Ⓦ www.newsteadabbey.org.uk), was granted by Henry VIII to Sir John Byron, who demolished most of the church and converted the monastic buildings into a family home. In 1798, **Lord Byron** inherited the estate, then little more than a ruin. He restored part of the complex during his six-year residence (1808–14), but most of the present structure dates from later renovations, which maintained much of the shape and feel of the medieval original while creating the warren-like mansion that exists today. Inside, a string of intriguing period rooms includes everything from a neo-Gothic Great Hall to the Henry VII bedroom, fitted with carved panels and painted house screens imported from Japan. Some of the rooms are pretty much as they were when Byron lived here – notably his bedroom and dressing room – and in the library is a small collection of the poet's possessions. The surrounding **gardens** are delightful, a secretive and subtle combination of walled garden, lake, Gothic waterfalls, yew tunnels and Japanese-style rockeries, complete with idiosyncratic pagodas.

There's a fast and frequent **bus** service leaving every twenty minutes or so from Nottingham's Victoria Bus Station to the gates of Newstead Abbey, a mile from the house; the journey takes about 25 minutes.

Rufford Abbey Country Park

Council-run country parks may be ten-a-penny, but **Rufford Abbey Country Park** (daily dawn–dusk; main facilities daily 10.30am–5pm; free, but weekend car parking fee £3) shows just how things should be done. The remains of the original twelfth-century Cistercian abbey and the country house built in its stead – but largely demolished in 1956 – are neither very substantial nor especially interesting, but the old buildings are all pleasantly maintained and the former stable block now holds a café, a much better-than-average craft shop and a first-rate ceramics gallery. At the back of the stables are the gardens, both informal and formal, and an outstanding **Sculpture Garden**, which manages to be both accessible and contemporary with sculptures such as the eerily lifelike, concrete *Man and Sheep on a Bench*. Further afield is a lake and a mill, a bird sanctuary and a wetland area, all reachable via footpaths.

Rufford is right beside the A614 about eighteen miles north of Nottingham and reached on hourly Stagecoach **bus** #33 from Nottingham's Victoria Bus Station.

Sherwood Forest Country Park

Most of **Sherwood Forest**, once a vast royal woodland of oak, birch and bracken covering all of northern Nottinghamshire, was cleared in the eighteenth century and nowadays it's difficult to imagine the protection it provided for generations of outlaws, the most famous of whom was **Robin Hood**. There's no "true story" of Robin's life – the earliest reference to him, in Langland's *Piers Plowman* of 1377, treats him as a fiction – but to the balladeers of fifteenth-century England, who invented most of Hood's folklore, this was hardly the point. For them, Robin was a symbol of yeoman decency, a semi-mythological opponent of corrupt clergymen and evil officers of the law; in the early tales, although Robin shows sympathy for the peasant, he has rather more respect for the decent nobleman, and he's never credited with robbing the rich to give to the poor. This and other parts of the legend, such as Maid Marian and Friar Tuck, were added later.

Robin Hood may lack historical authenticity, but it hasn't discouraged the county council from spending thousands of pounds sustaining the **Major Oak**, the creaky tree where Maid Marian and Robin are supposed to have plighted their troth. The Major Oak is on a pleasant one-mile trail that begins beside the visitor centre at the main entrance to **Sherwood Forest Country Park** (daily dawn–dusk; free, weekend car parking fee £3), which comprises 450 acres of oak and silver birch crisscrossed with footpaths. The visitor centre is half a mile north of the village of Edwinstowe, itself just two miles northwest of Rufford Park and twenty-odd miles north of Nottingham via the A614.

Stagecoach **bus** #33 runs hourly from Nottingham's Victoria Bus Station to Edwinstowe via Rufford.

Hardwick Hall

Born the daughter of a minor Derbyshire squire, Elizabeth, Countess of Shrewsbury (1527–1608) – aka **Bess of Hardwick** – became one of the leading figures of Elizabethan England, renowned for her political and business acumen. She also had a penchant for building and her major achievement, **Hardwick Hall** (mid-March to Oct: house Wed, Thurs, Sat & Sun noon–4.30pm; gardens

Wed–Sun 11am–5.30pm; house & gardens £9, gardens only £4.50; NT), begun when she was 62, has survived in amazingly good condition. The house was the epitome of fashionable taste, a balance of symmetry and ingenious detail in which the rectangular lines of the building are offset by line upon line of window – there's actually more glass than stone – whilst up above her giant-sized initials (E.S.) hog every roof line. Inside, on the top floor, the **High Great Chamber**, where Bess received her most distinguished guests, boasts an extraordinary plaster frieze, a brightly painted, finely worked affair celebrating the goddess Diana, the virgin huntress – it was, of course, designed to please the virgin queen herself. Next door, the **Long Gallery** is simply breathtaking, like an indoor cricket pitch only with exquisite furnishings and fittings from the splendid chimneypieces and tapestries through to a fine set of portraits.

Outside, the **garden** makes for a pleasant wander and, beyond the ha-ha (the animal-excluding ditch and low wall), rare breeds of cattle and sheep graze the surrounding **parkland** (daily 8am–6pm; free). Finally – and rather confusingly – Hardwick Hall is next to **Hardwick Old Hall** (mid-March to Oct Wed, Thurs, Sat & Sun 10am–6pm; £3.90; EH), Bess's previous home, but now little more than a broken-down if substantial ruin.

The easiest way to reach Hardwick is along the M1; come off at Junction #29 and follow the signs from the roundabout at the top of the slip road – a three-mile trip. Note, however, that Hardwick is not signed from the motorway itself.

Leicestershire and Rutland

The compact county of **Leicestershire** is one of the more anonymous of the English shires, though **Leicester** itself is saved from mediocrity by its role as a focal point for Britain's Asian community. The county's rolling landscapes are blemished by a series of industrial settlements, but things pick up markedly at **Ashby-de-la-Zouch**, a pleasing little town graced by the substantial remains of its medieval castle. To the east of Leicestershire lies England's smallest county, **Rutland**, with two places of note – **Oakham**, the county town, and **Uppingham**, both rural centres with some elegant Georgian architecture.

Train lines radiate out from Leicester, most usefully to Oakham, and there's a good network of **bus** services between the market towns.

Leicester

At first glance, **LEICESTER** seems a resolutely modern city, but further inspection reveals traces of its medieval and Roman past, situated immediately to the west of the downtown shopping area near the River Soar. The Romans developed Leicester's precursor, Ratae Coritanorum, and the **Emperor Hadrian** kitted it out with huge public buildings. In the eighth century, the Danes colonized the town and later still its medieval castle became the base of the earls of Leicester, the most distinguished of whom was **Simon de Montfort**, who forced Henry III to convene the first English Parliament in 1265. Since the late seventeenth century, Leicester has been a centre of the hosiery trade and it was this industry that attracted hundreds of Asian immigrants to settle here in the 1950s and 1960s. Today, about a third of Leicester's population is **Asian** and the city elected England's first Asian MP, Keith Vaz, in 1987. Leicester's Hindus celebrate two massive autumn **festivals**, Navrati and Diwali.

Arrival and information

With frequent services from London St Pancras, Leicester **train station** is on London Road just to the southeast of the city centre. **St Margaret's bus station** is on the north side of the centre, just off Gravel Street. The centre is signed from both – the large Haymarket Shopping Centre between the two is an easy landmark. The **tourist office** is a short walk to the south of the Haymarket at 7–9 Every St, on Town Hall Square (Mon–Wed & Fri 9am–5.30pm, Thurs 10am–5.30pm, Sat 9am–5pm; premium-rate line ⓣ0906/294 1113, ⓦwww.goleicestershire.com); they will help you find accommodation.

Accommodation

With other more enticing cities nearby, there's no strong reason to overnight here, but Leicester does have a good crop of business **hotels** close to the centre, within walking distance of the train station. It's important to book ahead during the Navrati and Diwali festivals.

Best Western Belmont House Hotel De Montfort St ⓣ0116/254 4773, ⓦwww.belmonthotel.co.uk. Proficient chain hotel in a modernized and extended Georgian property about 300 yards south of the train station via London Rd. Popular with business folk. Weekend discounts. ⑦

Holiday Inn 129 St Nicholas Circle ⓣ0870/400 9048, ⓦwww.holiday-inn.com/leicester. Smart chain hotel, which manages to overcome its unfortunate location – in the middle of the ring road – by creating a relaxed and self-enclosed environment. Comfortable rooms, indoor pool and extensive fitness facilities. Weekend discounts. ⑦

Spindle Lodge Hotel 2 West Walk ⓣ0116/233 8801, ⓦwww.spindlelodge.com. Well-maintained hotel in a pleasantly converted, three-storey, ivy-clad Victorian townhouse on a quiet residential street. 10min walk from the train station – head south on London Rd, turn right onto De Montfort St and then left onto Regent Rd; *Spindle Lodge* is at the junction of Regent Rd and West Walk. ④

The city centre

The most conspicuous building in Leicester's crowded centre is undoubtedly the large, modern **Haymarket Shopping Centre**, but the proper landmark is the Victorian **clocktower** of 1868, standing in front of the Haymarket and marking the spot where seven streets meet. One of the seven is Cheapside, which leads to Leicester's open-air **market** (Mon–Sat), one of the best of its type in the country and the place where the young Gary Lineker, now the UK's best-known football pundit, worked on the family stall. Good-hearted Gary remains a popular figure hereabouts and has been made a freeman of the city, which gives him the right to graze his sheep in front of the town hall. Another of the seven streets is Silver Street (subsequently Guildhall Lane), which leads to **St Martin's Cathedral**, a much modified, eleventh-century structure incorporating a fine, ornately carved medieval entrance porch. Next door is the **Guildhall** (Feb–Nov Mon–Wed & Sat 11am–4.30pm, Sun 1–4.30pm; free), a half-timbered building that has served, variously, as the town hall, prison and police station. The most interesting part of a visit is the rickety Great Hall, its beams bent with age, but there are a couple of old cells too, plus the town gibbet on which the bodies of the hanged were publicly displayed up until the 1840s.

The Jewry Wall

From the Guildhall, it's a short walk west to St Nicholas Circle, a large roundabout that is part of the ring road. Go round it to the right – there's a walkway – and on the right behind the church is the **Jewry Wall**, a chunk of Roman masonry some 18ft high and 73ft long that was originally part of Hadrian's public baths. The project was a real irritation to the emperor: Hadrian's grand scheme was spoilt by the engineers, who miscalculated the line of the aqueduct that was to pipe in the water, and so bathers had to rely on a hand-filled cistern replenished from the river – which wasn't what he had in mind at all.

New Walk Museum and Art Gallery

From the Haymarket, it's about ten minutes' walk south to the **New Walk Museum and Art Gallery**, 55 New Walk (Mon–Sat 10am–5pm, Sun 11am–5pm; free), easily the best of the city's several museums. The museum covers a lot of ground, from the natural world to geology and beyond, but one highlight is its extensive collection of Ancient Egyptian artefacts, featuring mummies and hieroglyphic tablets brought back to Leicester in the 1880s. It also holds an enjoyable collection of paintings, including works by British artists such as Hogarth, Francis Bacon, Stanley Spencer and Lowry as well as a whole raft of mawkishly Romantic Victorian paintings, such as Charles Green's *The Girl I left behind Me* (1880). In addition, and this is something of a surprise, there's an outstanding collection of German Expressionist works, mostly sketches, woodcuts and lithographs by the likes of Otto Dix and George Grosz.

Belgrave

Beginning about a mile to the northeast of the centre, the cramped terraced houses of the **Belgrave** neighbourhood are the focus of Leicester's Asian community. Both Belgrave Road and its northerly continuation, Melton Road, are lined with Indian and Pakistani goldsmiths and jewellers, sari shops, Hindi music stores and curry houses. It's never dull down here, but Sunday afternoons are particularly enjoyable, when locals stroll the streets in their finest gear. Belgrave celebrates two major Hindu festivals: **Diwali**, the Festival of Light, held in October or November, when six thousand lamps are strung out along the Belgrave Road and thousands of people come to watch the switch-on alone; and **Navrati**, an eight-day celebration in October held in honour of the goddess Ambaji.

On the edge of Belgrave, just off the A6 two miles north of the city centre, the **National Space Centre** (Tues–Sun 10am–5pm; school holidays daily 10am–5pm; last entry 90min before closing; £12, children (5–16 years) £10; ⓣ0116/261 0261, ⓦwww.spacecentre.co.uk) is devoted to space, science and astronomy, with a string of themed galleries exploring everything from the planets to orbiting earth. The emphasis is on the interactive, which makes the place very popular with children. Bus #54 links the train station and the Haymarket with Abbey Lane, a five-minute walk from the centre.

Eating, drinking and entertainment

People come from miles around to eat at the **Indian restaurants** along Belgrave Road. The pick are clustered at the start of the road, just beyond the flyover to the northeast of the centre, and it's here you'll find the most famous, *Bobby's*, at no. 154 (ⓣ0116/266 0106; Tues–Sun noon–10pm). Run by Gujaratis, this bright, modern restaurant and takeaway is strictly vegetarian and uses no garlic or onions; try their delicious house speciality, the multi-flavoured

Bobby's Special Chaat. Alternatively, the *Sayonara Thali*, at no. 49 (☎0116/266 5888; daily noon–9.30/10pm), specializes in set thali meals, with several different dishes, breads and pickles served together on large steel plates, while the *Chaat House*, opposite the *Sayonara* at no. 108 (☎0116/266 0513), does wonderful *masala dosas* and other south Indian snacks. The best restaurant in the city centre is the *Opera House*, 10 Guildhall Lane (☎0116/223 6666), in lovely old premises and with a creative menu featuring dishes such as ravioli with wild mushrooms (mains from £13–20).

Leicester's excellent Phoenix Arts Centre, in the city centre on Newarke Street (☎0116/255 4854, Ⓦwww.phoenix.org.uk), features a first-rate mix of comedy, **music**, **theatre** and dance, whilst doubling up as an independent **cinema**.

Around Leicester

Give or take the odd industrial blip, most of **Leicestershire** is rural, its small towns and villages dotted over undulating countryside. The key attractions here, both of which are best visited as day-trips, comprise the castle at **Ashby-de-la-Zouch** and the hilltop church of neighbouring **Breedon-on-the-Hill**.

Ashby-de-la-Zouch

ASHBY-DE-LA-ZOUCH, fourteen miles northwest of Leicester, takes its fanciful name from two sources – the town's first Norman overlord was Alain de Parrhoet la Souche and the rest means "place by the ash trees". Nowadays, Ashby is far from rustic, but it's still an amiable little place with its principal attraction, the **Castle** (April–June & Sept–Oct Thurs–Mon 10am–5pm; July–Aug daily 10am–6pm; Nov–March Thurs–Mon 10am–4pm; £3.50; EH) standing just off the town's main drag, Market Street. Originally a Norman manor house, the stronghold was the work of Edward IV's chancellor, Lord Hastings, who received his "licence to crenellate" in 1474. Today, the rambling ruins include substantial leftovers from the old fortifications, but the star turn is the hundred-foot-high **Hastings Tower**, a self-contained four-storey stronghold which has survived in reasonably good nick: it provided a secure inner fastness for Hastings and his retinue both against any outside enemy and his own mercenaries – who, experience had shown elsewhere, were often a threat to their employer – and it also provided much better accommodation than was previously available.

There are regular **buses** to Ashby's Market Street from Leicester.

Breedon-on-the-Hill

It's five miles northeast from Ashby to the village of **BREEDON-ON-THE-HILL**, which sits in the shadow of the large, partly quarried hill from which it takes its name. A steep footpath and a winding, half-mile lane lead up from the village to the summit, where the fascinating church of **St Mary and St Hardulph** (daily 9.30am–4pm, sometimes later in summer; free) occupies the site of an Iron Age hill fort and an eighth-century Anglo-Saxon monastery. Mostly dating from the thirteenth century, the church is kitted out with Georgian pulpit and pews as well as a large and distinctly rickety box pew. Much rarer are a number of **Anglo-Saxon carvings**, both individual saints and prophets and wall friezes, where a dense foliage of vines is inhabited by a tangle of animals and humans. The friezes are quite extraordinary, and the fact that the figures look Byzantine rather than Anglo-Saxon has fuelled much academic debate.

Most **buses** from Ashby pull into the village at the bottom of the hill.

Rutland

Reinstated in 1997 as England's smallest county following 23 unpopular years of merger with its larger neighbour, Rutland boasts more gentle scenery and a couple of pleasant little towns – **Oakham** and **Uppingham**. Oakham is easily reached on the Leicester–Peterborough **train** line, or by regular **bus**, and there's an hourly bus service linking Oakham and Uppingham too.

Oakham

Some twenty miles east of Leicester, prosperous **OAKHAM** is Rutland's county town. The town's stone terraces and Georgian villas are too often interrupted by the mundanely modern to assume much grace, but Oakham does have its architectural moments – particularly in the L-shaped **Market Place**, where a brace of sturdy awnings shelter the old water pump and town stocks. A few steps from the north side of the Market Place stands **Oakham Castle** (Mon–Sat 10.30am–1pm & 1.30–5pm, Sun 2–4pm; free), consisting of a banqueting hall that was originally part of a fortified house dating back to 1191. Surrounded by the grassy banks of what was once a motte and bailey castle, the hall is a good example of Norman domestic architecture, and inside the white-washed walls are covered with horseshoes, the result of an ancient custom by which every lord or lady, king or queen, is obliged to present an ornamental horseshoe when they first set foot in the town.

The town's prosperity is bolstered by **Oakham School**, a late sixteenth-century foundation that's now one of the country's more exclusive private schools: it's housed in a series of impressive ironstone buildings that frame the west edge of the Market Place. On the right-hand side of the school, a narrow lane allows you to see a little more of the buildings on the way to **All Saints'** church, whose airy interior is distinguished by the intense medieval carvings along the columns of the nave and choir.

Practicalities

Oakham **train station** lies on the west side of town, a five-minute walk from the Market Place. **Buses** connect the town with Leicester, Nottingham and Melton Mowbray, and arrive on John Street, west of the Market Place. A thorough exploration of Oakham only takes an hour or so, but if you do decide to stay, the best **hotel** in town is the distinctive *Lord Nelson's House Hotel*, 11 Market Place (Ⓣ01572/723 199, Ⓦwww.nicksrestaurant.co.uk; ❺), with a handful of bedrooms decorated in attractive Georgian style. One of the best places to eat is *Don Paddy Sanchez*, 8 Market Place (Ⓣ01572/822 255, a combined craft shop and café-restaurant, where the cured-fish platter is especially tasty and good value (at £7). For a **drink**, the *Wheatsheaf* is a traditional pub with a good range of beers (and a garden) across from All Saints' church at 2–4 Northgate.

Uppingham

The town of **UPPINGHAM**, seven miles south of Oakham, has the uniformity of style Oakham lacks, its narrow, meandering High Street flanked by bow-fronted shops and ironstone houses, mostly dating from the eighteenth century. It's the general appearance that pleases, rather than any individual sight, but the town is famous as the home of **Uppingham School**, a bastion of privilege whose imposing, fortress-like building stands at the west end of the High Street.

Uppingham has one especially good **hotel**, the *Lake Isle*, in a tastefully modernized eighteenth-century townhouse at 16 High St East (Ⓣ01572/822 951, Ⓦwww.lakeislehotel.com; ❺). The hotel **restaurant** is outstanding too, offering a superb and varied menu from guinea fowl to local venison, with main courses averaging around £15. For a **drink**, head for *The Vaults*, on the tiny Market Place.

Northamptonshire

Northamptonshire is one of the region's most diverse counties – so diverse in fact that even many Midlanders can't recall what is actually in it and what isn't. Even so, its superabundance of stately homes and historic churches has given it a tag as the "County of Spires and Squires" and there's also a good scattering of charming unspoilt villages, the most picturesque of which are built of local limestone. By contrast, however, three of the county's four big towns – Wellingborough, Corby and Kettering – are primarily industrial and whatever charms they offer to their inhabitants, there's not much to attract the regular tourist. Yet the fourth town, **Northampton**, does something to bridge the gap, its busy centre possessed of several fine old buildings and an excellent museum devoted to shoe-making, the industry that long made the place tick.

Gentle hills, farmland and patchy woodland stretch right across the county, with the prime tourist attraction being **Althorp**, family home of the Spencers and the burial place of Diana, Princess of Wales. East Northamptonshire's star turn is the good-looking country town of **Oundle**, which makes the best base for visiting the delightful hamlet of **Fotheringhay**. The county also has a notable **long-distance footpath**, the seventy-mile Nene Valley Way, which follows the looping course of the river right across the county. Nene Way brochures are available at or from Northampton Tourist Office (see p.461).

Getting to Northampton by **public transport** is no problem, but to reach the villages and stately homes, you'll mostly need your own vehicle – or some careful planning around patchy bus services.

Northampton

Spreading north from the banks of the River Nene, **NORTHAMPTON** is a workaday modern town whose appearance largely belies its ancient past. Throughout the Middle Ages, this was one of central England's most important towns, a flourishing commercial centre whose now demolished castle was a popular stopping-off point for travelling royalty. A fire in 1675 burnt most of the medieval city to a cinder, and the Georgian town that grew up in its stead was itself swamped by the Industrial Revolution, when Northampton swarmed with boot- and shoemakers, whose products shod almost everyone in the empire.

Northampton's compact **centre** is at its most appealing on and around its main plaza, Market Square, which is where you'll find the town's finest buildings, notably All Saints' Church and the Guildhall. Half a day is enough for a quick gambol round the sights, but if you're tempted to stay the night there's one good hotel near the centre (see below).

The Town

Northampton's expansive, cobbled **Market Square** has a bustling, self-confident air, its sides flanked by a comparatively harmonious mixture of the old and the new. From here, either of a couple of narrow lanes leads through to the church of **All Saints** (Mon–Fri 9.30am–1pm; free), whose unusually secular appearance stems from its finely proportioned, pillared portico as well as its towered cupola. A statue of a bewigged Charles II in Roman attire surmounts the portico, a (flattering) thank-you for his donation of a thousand tons of timber after the Great Fire of 1675 had incinerated the earlier church. Inside, the elegant interior looks more like a ballroom than a church, from the sweep of its timber galleries through to its Neoclassical pillars and a ceiling coated in delicately sculpted plasterwork.

Just beyond that, in St Giles' Square, is the **Guildhall**, a flamboyant Victorian edifice constructed in the 1860s to a design by Edward Godwin. Godwin was one of the period's most inventive architects and his Gothic exterior, with its high-pointed windows and dinky turrets and towers, sports kings and queens plus scenes central to the county's history.

The **Northampton Museum and Art Gallery** (Mon–Sat 10am–5pm, Sun 2–5pm; free), a few yards south of the Guildhall on Guildhall Road, celebrates the town's industrial heritage with a fabulous collection of **shoes**. Along with silk slippers, clogs and high-heeled nineteenth-century court shoes, there's one of the four boots worn by an elephant during the British Expedition of 1959, which retraced Hannibal's putative route over the Alps into Italy. There's celebrity footwear too, such as the giant DMs Elton John wore in *Tommy*, plus whole cabinets of heavy-duty riding boots, pearl-inlaid raised wooden sandals from Ottoman Turkey, and a couple of cabinets showing just how long high heels have been in fashion.

Practicalities

From Northampton **train station**, which has regular services from Birmingham and London Euston, it's a ten-minute walk east to the Market Square. Buses pull into the **bus station** on Greyfriars, behind the over-large Grosvenor Shopping Centre, immediately to the north of the Market Square. At time of writing, the **tourist office** is in transit, but it will end up across from All Saints' church on George Row (Ⓣ01604/838 800, Ⓦwww.explorenorthamptonshire.co.uk).

For **accommodation**, the *Best Western Lime Trees Hotel*, 8 Langham Place, Barrack Rd (Ⓣ01604/632 188, Ⓦwww.limetreeshotel.co.uk; ❺), occupies attractive Georgian premises a little more than half a mile north of the centre on the A508.

The rest of Northamptonshire

The verdant countryside of **Northamptonshire** is dotted with stately homes, amongst which the most diverting is **Althorp**, the last resting place of Diana, Princess of Wales. The county also holds a string of postcard-pretty villages – **Oundle**, about 30 miles northeast of Northampton, is the most agreeable. Historic **Fotheringhay**, a few miles further along the River Nene, runs a close second.

Althorp

Some six miles northwest of Northampton off the A428, the ritzy mansion of **Althorp** (July–Aug daily 11am–5pm, last admission 4pm; £12.50; ⓣ01604/770 107, ⓦwww.althorp.com) is the focus of the Spencer estate. The Spencers have lived here for centuries, but this was no big deal until one of the tribe, **Diana**, married Prince Charles in 1981. The disintegration of the marriage and Diana's elevation to sainthood is a story known to millions – and most perceptively analysed by B. Campbell in her book, *Diana, Princess of Wales: How Sexual Politics Shook the Monarchy*. The public outpouring of grief following Diana's death in 1997 was quite astounding, and Althorp became the focus of massive media attention as the coffin was brought up the M1 motorway from London to be buried on an island in the grounds of the family estate. Today, visitors troop round the **Diana exhibition**, in the old stable block, as well as the adjacent Althorp house, where there's a large collection of priceless paintings, including works by Gainsborough, van Dyck and Rubens. From the house, a footpath leads round a lake in the middle of which is the islet (no access) where Diana is buried.

There are no scheduled **buses** from Northampton to Althorp – you need a car to get here.

Oundle

Arguably Northamptonshire's prettiest town, pocket-sized **OUNDLE** slopes up gently from the River Nene, its congregation of old limestone houses zeroing in on the congenial **Market Place**. Preserving much of its medieval layout, Oundle boasts some of the finest seventeenth- and eighteenth-century streetscapes in the Midlands, and is a suitably exclusive setting for one of England's better-known private schools, **Oundle School**. Above all it's the general appearance of the place that appeals rather than anything in particular, the exception being the parish church of **St Peter** (Mon–Sat 9am–5pm, Sun between services; free), whose magnificent two-hundred-foot Decorated spire soars high above the centre, though the interior – give or take the odd stained-glass window – is unremarkable.

Buses from Peterborough and Northampton stop on the Market Place, a short walk from the **tourist office**, at 14 West St (Mon–Sat 9am–5pm, plus Easter–Aug Sun 1–4pm; ⓣ01832/274 333, ⓦwww.explorenorthamptonshire.co.uk). The best place **to stay** in town is the seventeenth-century *Talbot Hotel*, just along from the Market Place on New Street (ⓣ01832/273 621, ⓦwww.thetalbot-oundle.com; ⑥). The hotel has thirty-five plush bedrooms, but its main claim to fame is the oak staircase, which was brought here from Fotheringhay Castle (see p.463) and is thought to be the very one that Mary, Queen of Scots, walked down on the way to her execution. Apparently the queen's executioner stayed at the *Talbot* and both his and Mary's ghost are said to wander the upper floor. To avoid an apparition – and save some money – try the immaculate *Ashworth House*, a spick-and-span little stone guesthouse, five minutes' walk from the Market Place at 75 West St (ⓣ01832/275 312, ⓦwww.ashworthhouse.co.uk; ③).

The *Talbot* has the best restaurant in town – try the beef & Ruddles ale pie for just £8 – and there's a first-rate deli too, *Trendalls* (closed Sun), on the Market Place, which is great for baguettes and sandwiches of all descriptions.

Fotheringhay

Nestling by the River Nene just four miles northeast of Oundle, the tiny hamlet of **FOTHERINGHAY** has long been left to its own devices, but its medieval heyday is recalled by the magnificent church of **St Mary and All Saints** (dawn–dusk; free), which rises mirage-like above the green meadows. Begun in 1411 and a hundred and fifty years in the making, the church is a paradigm of the Perpendicular, its exterior sporting wonderful arching buttresses, its nave lit by soaring windows and the whole caboodle topped by a splendid octagonal lantern tower. The interior is quite bare, but there are two fancily carved medieval pieces to inspect – a painted pulpit and a sturdy stone font.

Fotheringhay **castle** witnessed two key events – the birth of Richard III in 1452 and the beheading of Mary, Queen of Scots, in 1587. On the orders of Elizabeth I, Mary was executed in the castle's Great Hall with no one to stand in her defence – apart, that is, from her dog, who is said to have rushed from beneath her skirts as her head hit the deck. Not long afterwards, the castle fell into disrepair and nowadays only a grassy **mound** and ditch remain to mark its position; it's signposted down a short and narrow lane on the bend of the road as you come into the village from Oundle.

Fotheringhay has an excellent **pub-restaurant**, *The Falcon* (Ⓣ01832/226 254), which occupies a neat stone building with a modern patio. They offer a delicious menu here – pan-fried duck breast with pak choi, sechuan pepper and pineapple, for example – with main courses costing around £13.

Lincolnshire

The obvious place to start a visit to **Lincolnshire** is **Lincoln** itself, an old and easy-paced city whose cathedral, the third largest in England, remains the county's outstanding attraction. Northeast and east of here, the Lincolnshire **Wolds** band the county, their gentle green hills harbouring the pleasant market town of **Louth**. The Wolds are flanked by the coast, so different from the rest of Lincolnshire, its brashness encapsulated by the resort of **Skegness**, though there are unspoilt stretches too, most notably at the **Gibraltar Point Nature Reserve**.

Stamford, in the southwest corner of the county, makes an alternative base: it's an attractive town, whose narrow streets are flanked by a handsome ensemble of antique stone buildings, and on its doorstep stands one of the great monuments of Elizabethan England, **Burghley House**. From here, it's a short hop east into **The Fens**, where you'll find some of the country's finest medieval churches. The most exquisite, however, is **St Botolph's** in the old fenland port of **Boston**, now Lincolnshire's second town.

Getting around Lincolnshire by public transport can be difficult. Lincoln is the hub of the county's limited **rail** network, with regular services east to Heckington, Boston and Skegness. There are also links west to Grantham, in southwest Lincolnshire, and Newark, in Nottinghamshire, both of which are on the main line from London to the Northeast. In addition, reasonable **bus** services run between Lincoln and the county's larger market towns, like Louth and Boston, but you'll struggle to get to the villages without your own transport. For **information** on all aspects of the county, check the Lincolnshire's tourist board's very helpful website (Ⓦwww.visitlincolnshire.com).

Lincoln

Reaching high into the sky from the top of a steep hill, the triple towers of mighty **LINCOLN** cathedral are visible for miles across the surrounding flatlands. This conspicuous spot was first fortified by the Celts, who called their settlement Lindon, "hillfort by the lake", a reference to the pools formed by the River Witham in the marshy ground below. In 47 AD the Romans occupied Lindon and built a fortified town, which subsequently became Lindum Colonia, one of the four regional capitals of Roman Britain.

Today, only fragments of the Roman city survive, mostly pieces of the third-century town wall, and these are outdone by reminders of Lincoln's medieval heyday, which began during the reign of William the Conqueror with the construction of the **castle** and **cathedral**. Lincoln flourished, first as a Norman power base and then as a centre of the wool trade with Flanders until 1369, when the wool market was transferred to neighbouring Boston. It was almost five hundred years before the town revived, the recovery based upon its manufacture of agricultural machinery and drainage equipment for the neighbouring fenlands. As the nineteenth-century town spread south down the hill and out along the old Roman road – the Fosse Way – so Lincoln became a place of precise class distinctions: the **Uphill** area, spreading north from the cathedral,

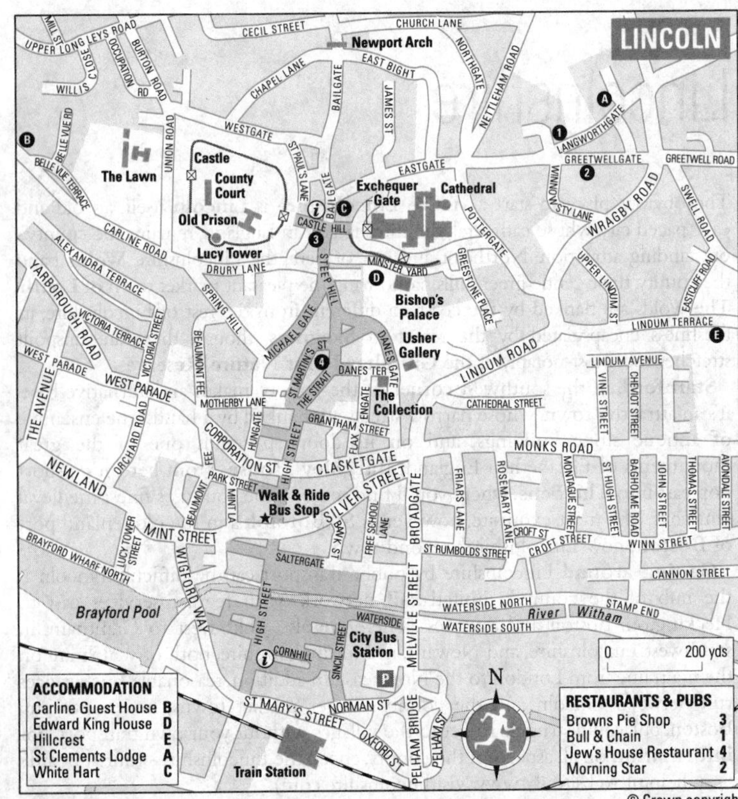

became synonymous with middle-class respectability, **Downhill** with the proletariat. It's a distinction that remains – locals selling anything and everything still put Uphill in brackets to signify a better quality of merchandise.

For the visitor, almost everything of interest is confined to the Uphill part of town, and it's here you'll also find the town's best **pubs** and **restaurants**.

Arrival and information

Both Lincoln **train station**, on St Mary's Street, and the **bus station**, close by off Melville Street, are located Downhill in the city centre. From either, it's a very steep, fifteen-minute walk up to the cathedral, or you can take the **Walk & Ride electric minibus** (Mon–Sat 10am–5pm & Sun noon–5pm; 3 hourly; £1 each way, £2.50 all-day pass); the nearest stop to the bus and train stations is on the High Street at the corner of Silver Street. There are two **tourist offices** (Mon–Thurs 9.30am–5.30pm, Fri 9.30am–5pm, Sat 10am–5pm; ⓣ01522/873 800; ⓦwww.lincoln.gov.uk), one on the corner of Cornhill and the High Street, the other at 9 Castle Hill, between the cathedral and the castle (also opens Sun 10am–5pm); both can book accommodation and guided city tours.

Accommodation

Lincoln has a good supply of competitively priced **hotels** and **B&Bs**. The best location is "Uphill", which is where you'll find all the places detailed below, with the exception of the youth hostel.

Carline Guesthouse 1–3 Carline Rd ⓣ01522/530 422, ⓦwww.carlineguesthouse.co.uk. One of the best B&Bs in the city, *Carline* occupies a neat and trim Edwardian house about 10min walk down from the cathedral – take Drury Lane from in front of the castle and keep going. Breakfasts are first-rate, and the rooms smart and tastefully furnished. No credit cards. ③

Edward King House The Old Palace, Minster Yard ⓣ01522/504 050, ⓦwww.ekhs.org.uk. This distinctive B&B, located immediately below the cathedral in a former residence of the bishops of Lincoln, is currently closed for a revamp – but check it out when it reopens in 2008. Some of the bedrooms have charming views over the medieval Bishop's Palace.

Hillcrest Hotel 15 Lindum Terrace ⓣ01522/510 182, ⓦwww.hillcrest-hotel.com. Traditional, very English hotel in a large red-brick house that was originally a Victorian rectory. Sixteen comfortable rooms with all mod cons plus a large, sloping garden. About 10min walk from the cathedral. ⑤

St Clements Lodge 21 Langworth Gate ⓣ01522/521 532. In a brisk, modern house a short walk from the cathedral, this comfortable and very friendly B&B has three pleasant, en-suite rooms. No credit cards. Home-made breakfasts – great haddock and kippers. ③

White Hart Hotel Bailgate ⓣ01522/526 222 ⓦwww.whitehart-lincoln.co.uk. Antique former coaching inn with charming public rooms, all with hidden nooks and crannies. The bedrooms are not quite as distinctive, but they're comfortable enough and many overlook the cathedral. Great Uphill location. Weekend deals can slash the normal price. ⑥

The Cathedral

Not a hill at all, **Castle Hill** is a wide, short and level cobbled street that links Lincoln's castle and cathedral. It's a charming spot and its east end is marked by the arches of the medieval **Exchequergate**, beyond which soars the glorious west front of **Lincoln Cathedral** (May–Sept Mon–Fri 7.15am–8pm, Sat & Sun 7.15am–6pm; Oct–April Mon–Sat 7.15am–6pm, Sun 7.15am–5pm; access restricted during services; £4 including guided tour – see box, p.467; ⓦwww.lincolncathedral.com), a sheer cliff face of blind arcading mobbed by decorative carving. Most striking of all is the extraordinary band of twelfth-century carved panels that depict biblical themes with passionate intimacy. The west front's apparent homogeneity is, however, deceptive, and further inspection reveals two phases of construction – the small stones and thick mortar of much of the facade belong to the original church, completed in 1092, whereas the longer stones and finer courses date from the early thirteenth century.

The cavernous interior is a fine example of Early English architecture, with the nave's pillars conforming to the same general design yet differing slightly, their varied columns and bands of dark Purbeck marble contrasting with the limestone that is the building's main material. Looking back up the nave from beneath the central tower, you can also observe a major medieval cock-up: Bishop Hugh's roof is out of alignment with the earlier west front, and the point where they meet has all the wrong angles. It's possible to pick out other irregularities, too – the pillars have bases of different heights, and there are ten windows in the nave's north wall and nine in the south – but these are deliberate features, reflecting a medieval aversion to the vanity of symmetry.

Beyond the rood screen lies St Hugh's Choir, its fourteenth-century misericords carrying an eccentric range of carvings, with scenes from the life of Alexander the Great and King Arthur mixed up with biblical characters and folkloric parables. Further on is the open and airy Angel Choir, completed in 1280 and dotted with stone table-tombs, its roof embellished by dozens of finely carved statuettes, including the tiny Lincoln Imp (see p.468). Finally, a corridor off the choir's north aisle leads to the wooden-roofed cloisters and the polygonal chapter house, where Edward I and Edward II convened gatherings that pre-figured the creation of the English Parliament.

The Bishop's Palace

Hidden behind a gated wall immediately to the south of the cathedral on Minster Yard are the ruins of what would, in its day, have been the city's most impressive building. This, the medieval **Bishop's Palace** (April–Oct daily 10am–5pm; Nov–March Mon & Thurs–Sun 10am–4pm; £3.60; EH), once consisted of two grand halls, a lavish chapel, kitchens and ritzy private chambers, but today the most coherent survivor is the battered and bruised

▲ Lincoln Cathedral

Guided tours of Lincoln cathedral

The cathedral offers two main sorts of **guided tour** free with the price of admission. The first – the **Floor Tour** (Mon–Sat 2–3 daily) – is a quick gambol round the cathedral's salient features, while the second, the 90min **Roof Tour** (Mon–Sat 1–2 daily), takes in parts of the church otherwise out of bounds. Both are very popular, so it's a good idea to book in advance on ☎01522/561 600.

Alnwick Tower – where the entrance is. The damage was done during the Civil War when a troupe of Roundheads occupied the palace until they themselves had to evacuate the place after a fierce fire. Nonetheless, the ruins are suitably fetching, with wide views over the surrounding flatlands. The adjoining gardens are immaculate, and abut an elevated terrace holding one of Europe's most northern vineyards.

The Castle

From the west front of the cathedral, it's a quick stroll across Castle Hill to **Lincoln Castle** (April–Sept Mon–Sat 9.30am–5.30pm, Sun 11am–5.30pm; Oct–March Mon–Sat 9.30am–4pm, Sun 11am–4pm; £3.90). Intact and forbidding, the castle walls incorporate bits and pieces from the twelfth to the nineteenth century with the wall walkway offering great views over town. The castle wall encloses a large central courtyard, part of which is occupied by the old prison, a dour red-brick structure that holds one of the four surviving copies of the Magna Carta as well as a truly remarkable prison **chapel**. Here, the prisoners were locked in high-sided cubicles, where they could see the preacher and his pulpit but not their fellow inmates. Neither was this approach just applied to chapel visits: the prisoners were kept in perpetual solitary confinement, and were compelled to wear masks when they took to the exercise yard. This system was founded on the pseudo-scientific theory that defined crime as a contagious disease, but unfortunately for the theorists, their so-called Pentonville System of "Separation and Silence", which was introduced here in 1846, drove so many prisoners crazy that it had to be abandoned thirty years later; nobody ever bothered to dismantle the chapel.

The rest of the city

As for the rest of Uphill Lincoln, it's scattered with historic remains, notably several chunks of Roman wall, the most prominent of which is the second-century **Newport Arch** straddling Bailgate and once the main north gate into the city. There's also a bevy of medieval stone houses, at their best on and around the aptly named Steep Hill as it cuts down from the cathedral to the city centre. In particular, look out for the tidily restored twelfth-century **Jew's House**, a reminder of the Jewish community that flourished in medieval Lincoln. A rare and superb example of domestic Norman architecture, it now houses the *Jew's House Restaurant* (see p.468).

Straddling Danesgate just below the Bishop's Palace, **The Collection** (daily 10am–5pm; free) occupies two buildings – a striking modern structure built to display the city's extensive collection of archeological artefacts, and a good-looking 1920s edifice, the **Usher Gallery**, which focuses on fine art. The gallery also holds an eclectic collection of coins, porcelain, watches and clocks. Dating from the seventeenth century, the timepieces were given to the gallery by its benefactor, James Ward Usher, a local jeweller and watchmaker who made a fortune on the back of the **Lincoln Imp**. First, in the 1880s, he devised the legend and then he sold the little trinkets and novelties to match – with such success that the imp became the city's emblem. His story has a couple of imps hopping around the cathedral, until one of them is turned to stone for trying to talk to the angels carved into the roof of the Angel Choir. His chum made a hasty exit on the back of a witch, but the wind is still supposed to haunt the cathedral awaiting their return.

Eating and drinking

There are a couple of excellent **restaurants** within shouting distance of the cathedral. First stop must be *Browns Pie Shop*, yards from the cathedral at 33 Steep Hill (☎01522/527 330), not a pie shop at all, but an excellent restaurant; a main course here will cost you about £12, but save room for the earth-shattering puddings. A second spot, just beyond the foot of Steep Hill, is the smart – and marginally more expensive – *Jew's House Restaurant*, 15 The Strait (☎01522/524 851); dishes include roast venison saddle with red onion marmalade and sloe gin sauce.

As for pubs, there are a pair of amiable and traditional locals near the cathedral – the *Bull & Chain*, on Langworthgate, and the *Morning Star*, close by on Greetwellgate. The former has a garden; the latter has real ales. For somewhere rowdier, there's a whole string of places on Bailgate.

The Wolds and the coast

The rolling hills and gentle valleys of the **Lincolnshire Wolds**, a narrow band of chalky land running southeast from Caistor to just outside Skegness, stand out amidst the more mundane agricultural landscapes of north Lincolnshire. A string of particularly appealing valleys is concentrated in the vicinity of **Louth**, which, with its striking church and antique centre, is easily the most enticing of the region's towns – with the added advantage of being fairly close to the coast. A few miles to the south of Louth, the Wolds dip down to the fens, pancake-flat and creating a wide and deep arch round the intrusive stump of The Wash. In the other direction, east of the Wolds, lies the coast, with its bungalows, campsites and caravans parked beside a sandy beach that extends, with a few marshy interruptions, north from **Skegness**, the main resort, to Mablethorpe and ultimately Cleethorpes. South of Skegness, the **Gibraltar Point Nature Reserve** is a welcome diversion from the bucket-and-spade and amusement-arcade commercialism.

Louth and around

Henry VIII described the county of Lincolnshire as "one of the most brutal and beestlie of the whole realm", his contempt based on the events of 1536, when thousands of northern peasants rebelled against his religious reforms. In Lincolnshire, this insurrection, the **Pilgrimage of Grace**, began in the northeast of the county at **LOUTH**, 25 miles from Lincoln, under the leadership of the local vicar, who was subsequently hung, drawn and quartered for his pains. There's a commemorative plaque in honour of the rebels beside Louth's church of **St James** (April–Christmas Mon–Sat 10.30am–4pm, Christmas–March Mon, Wed, Fri & Sat 8am–12pm; free), which is the town's one outstanding building, its soaring spire, buttresses, battlements and pinnacles set on a grassy knoll just to the west of the centre. The interior is delightful too, the sweeping symmetries of the nave illuminated by slender windows and capped by a handsome Georgian timber roof decorated with dinky little angels. Finally, don't forget the church's café (April–Dec Mon–Sat 10.30am–4pm) and its home-made cakes – locals set out early to get a slice of lemon-drizzle.

Next to the church, the well-tended gardens and Georgian houses of **Westgate** make it one of Louth's prettiest streets; you can grab a drink here at the antique *Wheatsheaf Inn*. Afterwards, it doesn't take long to explore the rest of the town centre, whose cramped lanes and alleys – focusing on the **Cornmarket** – are flanked by red-brick buildings mostly dating from the nineteenth century.

Practicalities

With regular weekday services from Boston and Lincoln, Louth's **bus station** is at the east end of Queen Street, a couple of minutes' walk from the Cornmarket: walk west along Queen Street and turn right onto the Market Place to get there. The **tourist office** is in the New Market Hall off Cornmarket (Mon–Sat 9am–4.30pm; ⓣ01507/609 289). The best **hotel** by a long chalk is the excellent, family-run *Priory*, 149 Eastgate (ⓣ01507/602 930, ⓦwww.theprioryhotel.com; ❺), in a handsomely maintained Georgian villa, with extensive gardens; the hotel is located east of the centre, about ten minutes' walk from the Cornmarket. Its **restaurant** (Mon–Sat; non-residents Fri & Sat only) is also the best place in town to eat, serving good-quality cuisine, with main courses from £13.

The Saltfleetby-Theddlethorpe dunes

An enjoyable short excursion from Louth takes you east along the **B1200** across about nine miles of fen farmland to the **coast**. This byroad is built over an old Roman road that was used to transport salt inland from the seashore salt pans, once a lucrative source of income for local traders. At the coast, turn right along the main A1031 and, after about half a mile, take the (poorly signed) gravel track on the left through the dunes of the **Saltfleetby-Theddlethorpe Dunes National Nature Reserve**. Comprising over five miles of sand dune, salt and freshwater marsh, the reserve is at its prettiest in midsummer, when the dunes sprout buckthorn bushes and sea heather flowers, forming a carpet of violet spreading down towards the ocean. A network of trails navigates the dunes and lagoons, with the latter attracting hundreds of migratory wildfowl in spring and autumn.

Skegness

SKEGNESS, south along the coast from Saltfleetby-Theddlethorpe, has been a busy resort ever since the railways reached the Lincolnshire coast in 1875. Its heyday was pre-1960s, when the Brits began to take themselves off to sunnier climes, but it still attracts tens of thousands of city-dwellers who come for the wide, sandy beaches and for a host of attractions ranging from nightclubs to bowling greens. Every inch the traditional English seaside town, Skegness outdoes its rivals by keeping its beaches sparklingly clean and its parks spick-and-span. That said, the seafront, with its rows of souvenir shops and amusement arcades, can be dismal, especially on rainy days, and you may well decide to sidestep the whole caboodle by heading south three miles along the coastal road to the **Gibraltar Point National Nature Reserve** (daily dawn–dusk; free), where, a network of clearly signed footpaths patterns a narrow strip of salt and freshwater marsh, sand dune and beach that attracts an inordinate number of birds.

Skegness' **bus** and **train stations** are next door to each other about ten minutes' walk from the seashore – cut across Lumley Square and go straight up the High Street to the landmark clocktower. The **tourist office** (April–Oct daily 9.30am–5pm; Nov–March Mon–Fri 9.30am–4.30pm; Ⓣ01754/899 887, Ⓦwww.visitlincolnshire.com) is only yards from the clocktower, on Grand Parade. Skegness has scores of **hotels**, **B&Bs** and **guesthouses**: one of the most appealing is the *Best Western Vine Hotel*, Vine Rd (Ⓣ01754/610 611, Ⓦwww.thevinehotel.com; ❹), a rambling, ivy-clad old house set in its own grounds on a quiet residential street about three-quarters of a mile from the clocktower.

The Lincolnshire Fens

The Lincolnshire section of **The Fens**, that great chunk of eastern England extending from Boston to Cambridge, encompasses some of the most productive farmland in Europe. With the exception of the occasional hillock, this dead-flat, treeless terrain has been painstakingly reclaimed from the marshes and swamps that once drained into The Wash, a process that has taken almost two thousand years. In earlier times, outsiders were often amazed by the dreadful conditions hereabouts, but they did spawn the distinctive culture of the so-called **fen slodgers**, who embanked small portions of marsh to create pastureland and fields, supplementing their diets by catching fish and fowl and gathering reed and sedge for thatching and fuel. Their economy was threatened by the large-scale land reclamation schemes of the late fifteenth and sixteenth centuries, and time and again the fenlanders sabotaged progress by breaking down the banks and dams. But the odds were stacked against the saboteurs, and a succession of great landowners eventually drained huge tracts of the fenland; by the end of the eighteenth century the fen slodgers' way of life had all but disappeared. Nonetheless, the Lincolnshire Fens remain a distinctive area of introverted little villages, with just one significant settlement, the old port of **Boston**.

Boston

As it approaches The Wash, the muddy River Witham weaves its way through **BOSTON**, England's second largest seaport for much of the medieval period, when its flourishing economy was dependent on the wool trade with Flanders. Local merchants, revelling in their success, decided to build a church that demonstrated their wealth and the result was the magnificent church of **St Botolph**. The church was completed in the early sixteenth century, but by then Boston was in decline as trade drifted west towards the Atlantic and the Witham silted up. The town's fortunes only revived in the late eighteenth century when, after the nearby fens had been drained, it became a minor agricultural centre with a modest port that has, in recent times, been modernized for trade with the EU. A singular mix of fenland town and seaport, Boston is an unusual little place that is at its liveliest on **market days** – Wednesday and Saturday.

The Town

Mostly flanked by Victorian red-brick buildings, the mazy streets of Boston's cramped and compact centre, on the east side of the River Witham, radiate out from the **Market Place**, a dishevelled square of irregular shape. Just to the west looms the massive bulk of **St Botolph's** (daily 8.30am–4.30pm; free), whose exterior masonry is embellished by the high-pointed windows and elaborate tracery of the Decorated style. Most of the structure dates from the fourteenth century, but the 272-foot **tower**, whose lack of a spire earned the church the nickname the "Boston Stump", is of later construction. The octagonal lantern is later still, added in the sixteenth century and graced by flying buttresses and pointy pinnacles. A tortuous 365-step spiral **staircase** (closed Sun) leads to a balcony near the top, from where the panoramic views over Boston and the fens amply repay both the price of the ticket (£2.50) and the effort of the climb. Down below, St Botolph's light and airy **nave** is all soaring columns and high windows. The sheer purity of design is stunning, its virtuosity heightened by the narrowness of the annexe-like chancel and the elegance of the Decorated arch that partly screens it from view.

The church's most famous vicar was **John Cotton** (1584–1652), who helped stir the Puritan stew during his twenty-year tenure, encouraging a stream of Lincolnshire dissidents to head off to the colonies of New England to found their "New Jerusalem". Cotton emigrated himself in 1633 and soon became the leading light among the Puritans of Boston, Massachusetts. The Cotton connection was finally commemorated here in the Stump by the creation of the **Cotton Chapel**, at the west end of the nave, in 1857. The most interesting relic from Cotton's sojourn here is not, however, in the chapel at all, but in the nave in the form of the ornate **pulpit** from which he pounded out his three-hour sermons.

Practicalities

It's ten minutes' walk east from Boston **train station** to the town centre – head straight out of the station along Station Street and keep going until you hit the river and cross the bridge. The **bus station** is also to the west of the river, just five minutes' walk away from the Market Place on Lincoln Lane. The **tourist office** (Mon–Sat 9.30am–5pm; ⓣ01205/356 656, ⓦwww.boston.gov.uk) is in the new Haven Gallery, a brief walk south of the Market Place along the river at 2 South Square. They have a list of **B&Bs** (❷), amongst which the *Bramley House*, 267 Sleaford Rd (ⓣ01205/354 538; ❷) occupies an attractively converted eighteenth-century farmhouse, a mile west of town beyond the train station. Another good choice is the *Fairfield Guesthouse*, 101 London Rd (ⓣ01205/362 869; no credit cards; ❷), about two miles south of the centre: it has sixteen guest rooms (mostly en suite), all decorated in bright and cheerful style.

Stamford

Delightful **STAMFORD** is a handsome little limestone town of yellow-grey seventeenth- and eighteenth-century buildings edging narrow streets that slope up from the River Welland. The town's salad days were as a centre of the medieval wool and cloth trade and it was then that its wealthy merchants built the medley of stone churches and houses. Stamford was also the home of **William Cecil**, Elizabeth's chief minister, who built his splendid mansion, **Burghley House**, close by. The town survived the collapse of the wool trade, prospering as an inland port after the Welland was made navigable to the sea in 1570, and, in the eighteenth century, as a staging point on the Great North Road from London. More recently, Stamford escaped the three main threats to old English towns – the Industrial Revolution, wartime bombing and postwar development – and was designated the country's first Conservation Area in 1967.

The Town

Above all, it's the harmony of Stamford's architecture that pleases, rather than any specific sight. There are, nevertheless, a handful of buildings of some special interest amongst the web of narrow streets that make up the town's compact centre.

Around the centre

The church of **St Mary** (no regular opening hours), set beside a pristine close of proud Georgian buildings just above the main bridge on St Mary's Place. The church, with its splendid spire, has a small, airy interior, which incorporates the Corpus Christi chapel, whose intricately embossed, painted and panelled roof dates from the 1480s.

Across the street from St Mary's, several lanes thread up to the carefully preserved **High Street**, from where Ironmonger Street leads north again to the wide and handsome Broad Street, the site of **Browne's Hospital** (June–Sept Sat & Sun 11am–4pm; £2.50), the most extensive of the town's almshouses, dating from the late fifteenth century. Not all of the complex is open to the public, but it's still worth visiting with the first room – the old dormitory – capped by a splendid wood-panelled ceiling. The adjacent chapel holds some delightfully folksy misericords and then it's upstairs for the audit room, which is illuminated by a handsome set of stained-glass windows.

From Browne's, it's a few paces more to Red Lion Square, which is overlooked by the church of **All Saints** (daily dawn–dusk; free). Entry is via the south porch, itself an ornate structure with a fine – if badly weathered – crocketted gable, and, although much of the interior is routinely Victorian, the carved capitals are of great delicacy. There's also an engaging folkloric carving of the Last Supper behind the high altar.

Down the slope from St Mary's, across the reedy River Welland on **High Street St Martin's**, is the **George Hotel**, a splendid old coaching inn whose Georgian facade supports one end of the gallows that span the street – not a warning to criminals, but a traditional advertising hoarding. Along – and across – the street, the sombre, late fifteenth-century church of **St Martin** (daily 9.30am–4pm; free) shelters the magnificent tombs of the lords Burghley, with a recumbent William Cecil carved beneath twin canopies, holding his rod of office and with a lion at his feet. Just behind, the early eighteenth-century effigies of John Cecil and his wife show the couple as Roman aristocrats, propped up on their elbows, she to gaze at him, John to stare across the nave commandingly.

Burghley House

Burghley House (late March to late Oct daily except Fri 11am–5pm, last admission 4.30pm; £10.40, including grounds; Ⓦwww.burghley.co.uk), an extravagant Elizabethan mansion standing in parkland landscaped by Capability Brown, is located a mile and a half or so to the east of Stamford, either out along the Barnack Road or by footpath from High Street St Martin's. Completed in 1587 after 22 years' work, the house sports a mellow-yellow ragstone exterior, embellished by dainty cupolas, a pyramidal clocktower and skeletal balustrading, all to a plan by **William Cecil**, the long-serving adviser to Elizabeth I. The grounds are at their busiest during the prestigious **Burghley Horse Trials** (Ⓦwww.burghley-horse.co.uk), held over four days in September.

With the notable exception of the Tudor kitchen, little remains of Burghley's Elizabethan interior. Instead, the house bears the heavy hand of John, fifth Lord Burghley, who toured France and Italy in the late seventeenth century, buying paintings and commissioning furniture, statuary and tapestries. To provide a suitable setting for his old masters, John brought in Antonio Verrio and his assistant Louis Laguerre, who between them covered many of Burghley's walls and ceilings with frolicking gods and goddesses. These gaudy and gargantuan murals are at their most engulfing in the **Heaven Room**, an artfully painted classical temple that adjoins the **Hell Staircase**, where the entrance to the inferno is through the gaping mouth of a cat.

Practicalities

From Stamford **train station**, which has frequent services from Cambridge, Leicester and Oakham, it's a five-minute walk north to the town centre, on the other side of the River Welland. The **bus station** is in the centre, on the north side of the river, on Sheepmarket, off All Saints' Street. The **tourist office** is also bang in the centre, in the Stamford Arts Centre at 27 St Mary's St (Mon–Sat 9.30am–5pm, April–Oct also Sun 10.30am–4pm; ⓣ01780/755 611, ⓦwww.southwestlincs.com). They have a full list of local accommodation, including a battery of **B&Bs** (❷), though most of these are on the outskirts of town.

The most celebrated of Stamford's **hotels** is the *George Hotel*, 71 High St St Martin's (ⓣ01780/750 750, ⓦwww.georgehotelofstamford.com; ❼), an old coaching inn with flagstone floors and antique furnishings, whose most appealing rooms overlook a cobbled courtyard. Further up the street, the attractive *Garden House Hotel* (ⓣ01780/763 359, ⓦwww.gardenhousehotel.com; ❻) occupies a tastefully modernized eighteenth-century building with twenty smart bedrooms.

For food, it has to be the *George Hotel* – either in the smart and polished **restaurant** (daily 12.30–2.15pm & 7.30–9.30pm), where the emphasis is on British ingredients served in imaginative ways with main courses costing around £13, or in the moderately priced and informal *Garden Lounge* (daily noon–10pm). The *York Bar* serves inexpensive and delicious **bar food**, but only at lunchtimes (Mon–Sat noon–2.30pm).

In summer (June–Aug), Tolethorpe Hall, a graceful Elizabethan mansion not far from town, hosts the **Stamford Shakespeare Company**'s open-air performances (ⓣ01780/756 133, ⓦwww.stamfordshakespeare.co.uk), though the audience is protected from the elements by a vast marquee.

Travel details

Buses

For information on all local and national bus services, contact Traveline ⓣ0871/200 2233, ⓦwww.traveline.org.uk.

Leicester to: Lincoln (hourly; 1hr 40min); Northampton (hourly; 1hr); Nottingham (every 30min; 1hr 40min); Oakham (hourly; 1hr 10min); Stamford (hourly; 2hr).

Lincoln to: Boston (hourly; 1hr 30min); Leicester (hourly; 1hr 30min); Louth (every 1–2hr; 40min); Northampton (hourly; 3hr); Nottingham (hourly; 2hr 30min); Oakham (hourly; 2hr 20min); Skegness (hourly; 1hr 45min).

Northampton to: Leicester (hourly; 1hr); Lincoln (hourly; 3hr); Nottingham (hourly; 2hr); Oundle (every 1–2hr; 2hr); Stamford (hourly; 2hr 30–50min).

Nottingham to: Leicester (every 30min; 1hr 40min); Lincoln (hourly; 2hr 30min); Newark (hourly; 30min); Northampton (hourly; 2hr).

Oakham to: Leicester (hourly; 1hr 10min); Lincoln (hourly; 2hr 20min); Nottingham (every 1–2hr; 1hr 30min); Stamford (every 30min; 20min).

Stamford to: Leicester (hourly; 2hr); Northampton (hourly; 2hr 30–50min); Oakham (every 30min; 20min).

Trains

For information on all local and national rail services, contact National Rail Enquiries ⓣ0845/748 4950, ⓦwww.nationalrail.co.uk.

Leicester to: Birmingham (every 30min; 1hr); Lincoln (hourly; 1hr 40min); London (every 30min; 1hr 30min); Melton Mowbray (hourly; 15min); Nottingham (every 30min; 20min); Oakham (hourly; 30min); Stamford (hourly; 50min).

Lincoln to: Boston (hourly; 1hr); Cambridge (hourly; 1hr); Heckington (every 2hr; 1hr); Leicester (hourly; 1hr 40min); London (hourly; 2hr 15min); Newark (hourly; 25min); Nottingham (hourly; 45min); Peterborough (hourly; 1hr 20min); Skegness (hourly; 1hr 40min).

Northampton to: Birmingham (every 30min; 1hr); London Euston (every 30min; 1hr 10min–1hr 40min).

Nottingham to: Birmingham (2–3 hourly; 1hr 20min); Leicester (every 30min; 20min); Lincoln (hourly; 1hr 15min); London (hourly; 1hr 40min); Newark (hourly; 30min); Oakham (hourly; 1hr, change at Leicester).

Stamford to: Cambridge (hourly; 1hr 20min); Leicester (hourly; 40min); Oakham (hourly; 10min); Peterborough (hourly; 15min).

10

The Northwest

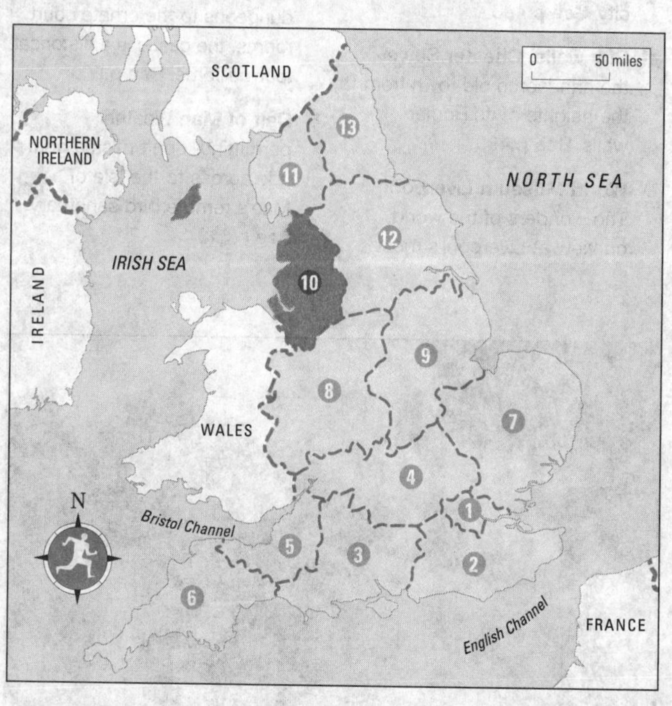

CHAPTER 10 Highlights

* **Imperial War Museum North, Manchester** A startlingly modern exploration of the reasons for, and effects of, war. See p.487

* **Café society, Manchester** Legendary café-bars set the tone for England's second city. See p.488

* **City walls, Chester** Survey the handsome old town from the heights of its Roman walls. See p.493

* **World Museum Liverpool** The wonders of the world, on view at Liverpool's most family-friendly museum. See p.499

* **Blackpool Tower** Blackpool's bold answer to the Eiffel Tower lights up the skyline of the UK's favourite resort. See p.505

* **Lancaster Castle** From the dungeons to the ornate court rooms, the castle is a historical *tour-de-force*. See p.506

* **Calf of Man** Weather permitting, don't miss a boat ride across to the Isle of Man's remote bird sanctuary. See p.513

▲ Chester's city walls

10

The Northwest

Within the **northwest** of England lie some of the ugliest and some of the most beautiful parts of the country. The least attractive zones are to be found in the urban sprawl linking the country's third and sixth largest conurbations, Manchester and Liverpool, but even here the picture isn't unrelievedly bleak, as the cities themselves are appealing. Where once only a handful of Victorian Gothic buildings lent any grace to the place, **Manchester** has been transformed in recent years by a rebuilding programme that puts it in the vanguard of modern British urban design. Quite apart from a clutch of top-class visitor attractions – including The Lowry and the Imperial War Museum North – where Manchester really scores is in the buzz of its thriving café and club scene. **Liverpool**, set on the Mersey estuary, is perhaps less appealing at first glance, though its revitalized dockside, Georgian townhouses, grand civic buildings and museums, and burgeoning café and restaurant scene soon change perceptions.

The southern suburbs of Manchester bump up into the steep hills of the Pennine range, and to the southwest the city slides into undulating, pastoral **Cheshire**, a county of rolling green countryside, whose dairy farms churn out the crumbly, white Cheshire cheese. The county town, **Chester**, with its complete circuit of town walls and partly Tudor centre, is especially alluring.

Lancashire, which historically lay directly to the north of Cheshire, reached industrial prominence in the nineteenth century, primarily due to the cotton-mill towns around Manchester. Along the coast to the west and north stretches a line of resorts that once formed the mainstay of the northern British holiday trade. Only **Blackpool** is really worth visiting for its own sake, a rip-roaring

Getting around

Manchester's international **airport** picks the city out as a major UK point of arrival, and there are direct train services from the airport to Liverpool, Blackpool, Lancaster, Leeds and York, as well as to Manchester itself. Both Manchester and Liverpool are well served by **trains**, with plentiful connections to the Midlands and London, and up the west coast to Scotland. There's also a frequent rail and bus service between both cities, and from each to Chester, allowing an easy triangular loop between Greater Manchester, Merseyside and Cheshire. The major east–west rail lines in the region are the direct routes between Manchester, Leeds and York, and between Blackpool, Bradford, Leeds and York. Regional **rover tickets** are available for unlimited travel between Liverpool, Manchester, the Peak District, Lancashire and Cumbria – the validity varies from pass to pass (Ⓦwww.nationalrail.co.uk) but flexi-tickets (4 days travel in 8) start at £52.

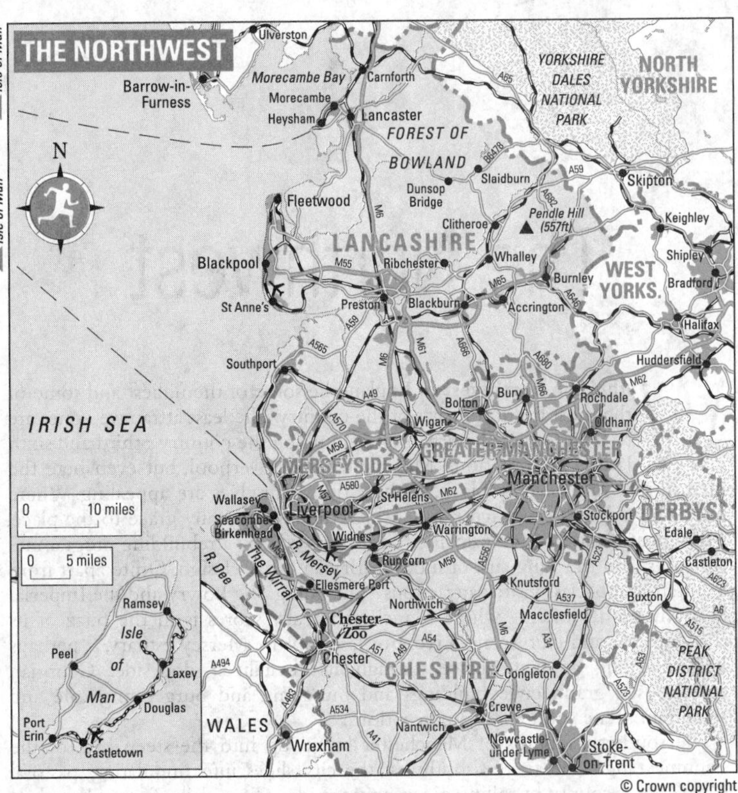

© Crown copyright

resort which has stayed at the top of its game by supplying undemanding entertainment with more panache than its neighbours. For anything more culturally invigorating you'll have to continue north to the historically important city of **Lancaster**, with its Tudor castle. Finally, the semi-autonomous **Isle of Man**, only 25 miles off the coast, provides a terrain almost as rewarding as that of the Lake District but without the seasonal overcrowding.

Manchester

Few cities in the world have embraced social change so heartily as **MANCHESTER**. From engine of the Industrial Revolution to test-bed of contemporary urban design, the city has no realistic English rival outside of London. Its pre-eminence expresses itself in various ways, most swaggeringly in the success of Manchester United, the richest football club in the world, but also in a thriving music and cultural scene that has given birth to world-beaters as diverse as the Hallé Orchestra and Oasis. The city's cutting-edge concert halls, theatres, clubs and café society are boosted by one of England's largest student populations and a blooming gay community, whose spending power has created a pioneering **Gay Village**.

Some history

Despite a **history** stretching back to Roman times, and pockets of surviving medieval and Georgian architecture, Manchester is first and foremost a **Victorian manufacturing city**. Its rapid growth was the equal of any flowering of the Industrial Revolution anywhere – from little more than a village in 1750 to the world's major cotton centre in only a hundred years. The spectacular rise of **Cottonopolis**, as it became known, arose from the manufacture of vast quantities of competitively priced imitations of expensive Indian calicoes, using water and then steam-driven machines developed in the late eighteenth and nineteenth centuries. This rapid industrialization brought immense wealth for a few but a life of misery for the majority. The discontent this engendered amongst the working class came to a head in 1819 when eleven people were killed at **Peterloo**, in what began as a peaceful demonstration against the oppressive **Corn Laws**. Things were, however, even worse when the 23-year-old Friedrich Engels came here in 1842 to work in his father's cotton plant: the grinding poverty he recorded in his *Condition of the Working Class in England* was a seminal influence on his later collaboration with **Karl Marx** in the *Communist Manifesto*.

The **Manchester Ship Canal** was constructed in 1894 to entice ocean-going vessels into Manchester and away from burgeoning Liverpool, playing a crucial part in sustaining Manchester's competitiveness. From the late 1950s, however, the docks, mills, warehouses and canals were in dangerous decline, undergoing sporadic efforts to pull the city out of the economic doldrums. The main engine of change turned out to be the devastating **IRA bomb**, which exploded outside the Arndale shopping centre in June 1996, wiping out a fair slice of the city's commercial infrastructure. Rather than simply patching things up, the city council embarked on an ambitious rebuilding scheme. It's very much work in progress, but it's impossible not to admire the drive and vision behind it all.

Specific attractions may be a little thin on the ground, but the city centre does possess the enjoyable **Manchester Art Gallery** as well as the extensive **Museum of Science and Industry**. Further out, to the west, are the revamped **Salford Quays**, home to a pair of prestigious museums, the **Lowry arts centre**, complete with a handsome selection of L.S. Lowry paintings, and the stirring and stunning **Imperial War Museum North**.

Arrival

Manchester **airport** is located ten miles south of the city centre. From the airport, there is an excellent train service to Manchester Piccadilly; tickets cost £2.80 single, £2.90 return; the taxi fare to the city centre is around £18.

Manchester has three main **train stations**: most long-distance services pull into **Piccadilly Station**, facing London Road, on the east side of the centre, with some services continuing onto **Oxford Road Station** just to the south of the centre. Trains from Lancashire and Yorkshire mostly terminate at **Victoria Station** on the north side of the centre. All three stations are connected to central Manchester via the **Metroshuttle** free bus service; Piccadilly and Victoria are also on the **Metrolink** tram line (see p.482).

Most long-distance **buses** use **Chorlton Street Coach Station**, about half-way between Piccadilly train station and Albert Square, though some regional buses drop passengers in nearby Piccadilly Gardens instead.

Information

The **Manchester Visitor Centre** is in the back of the Town Hall, bang in the centre of town on St Peter's Square (Mon–Sat 10am–5.30pm,

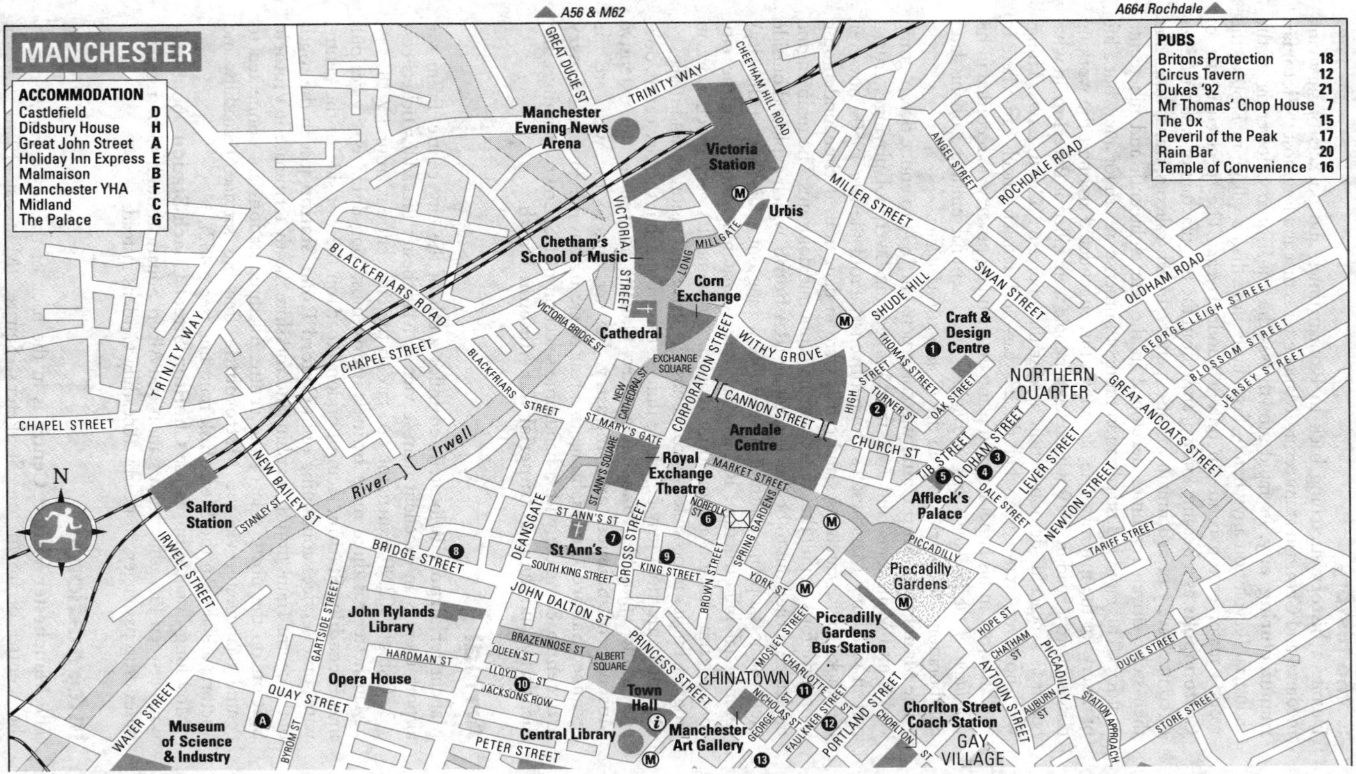

MANCHESTER

A56 & M62

A664 Rochdale

ACCOMMODATION

Castlefield	D
Didsbury House	H
Great John Street	A
Holiday Inn Express	E
Malmaison	B
Manchester YHA	F
Midland	C
The Palace	G

PUBS

Britons Protection	18
Circus Tavern	12
Dukes '92	21
Mr Thomas' Chop House	7
The Ox	15
Peveril of the Peak	17
Rain Bar	20
Temple of Convenience	16

Manchester Evening News Arena
Victoria Station
Urbis
Chetham's School of Music
Corn Exchange
Cathedral
Exchange Square
Craft & Design Centre
Northern Quarter
Arndale Centre
Royal Exchange Theatre
Affleck's Palace
Salford Station
St Ann's
Piccadilly Gardens
Piccadilly Gardens Bus Station
John Rylands Library
Opera House
Albert Square
Chinatown
Town Hall
Central Library
Manchester Art Gallery
Museum of Science & Industry
Chorlton Street Coach Station
Gay Village
River Irwell
N

Great Ducie St
Trinity Way
Cheetham Hill Road
Angel Street
Rochdale Road
Miller Street
Victoria Street
Long Millgate
Swan Street
Oldham Road
George Leigh Street
Blossom Street
Jersey Street
Blackfriars Road
Shude Hill
Victoria Bridge St
Withy Grove
Thomas Street
Oak Street
Chapel Street
Blackfriars Street
New Cathedral St
Corporation Street
High Street
Turner St
Great Ancoats Street
Cannon Street
St Mary's Gate
Church St
Tib Street
Oldham Street
Lever Street
Newton Street
Market Street
Dale Street
New Bailey St
Stanley St
St Ann's Square
Deansgate
St Ann's St
Cross Street
Norfolk St
Spring Gardens
Piccadilly
Tariff Street
Irwell Street
Bridge Street
South King Street
King Street
Brown Street
York St
John Dalton St
Mosley Street
Hope St
Gartside Street
Princess Street
Brazennose St
Queen St
Hardman St
Lloyd St
Jacksons Row
Charlotte St
Chatham St
Ducie Street
Water Street
Quay Street
Nicholas St
George St
Faulkner Street
Portland Street
Aytoun Street
Auburn St
Station Approach
Store Street
Byrom St
Peter Street
Chorlton St

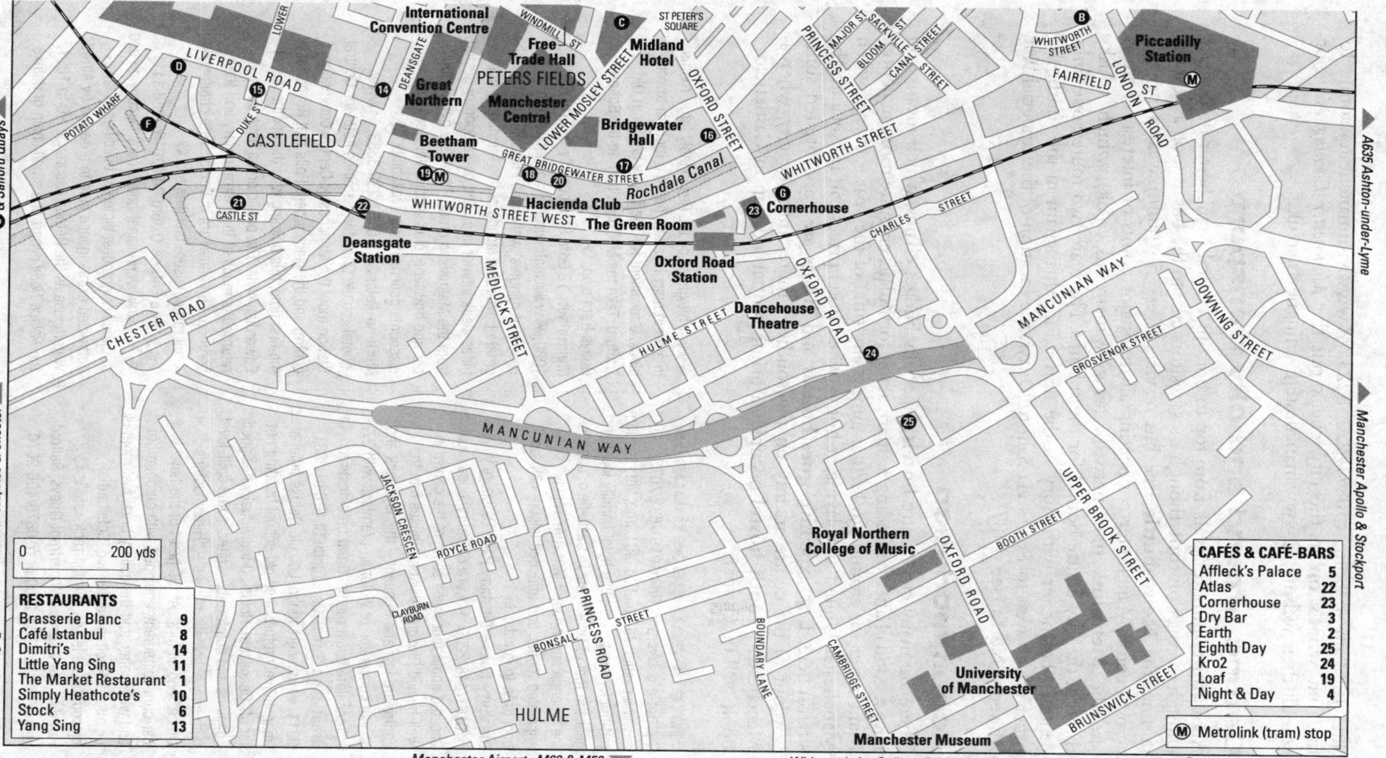
E & Salford Quays
A635 Ashton-under-Lyme
Old Trafford, A56 & Chester
Manchester Apollo & Stockport
Manchester Airport, M63 & M56
Whitworth Art Gallery, Rusholme, Didsbury, Contact Theatre & H
International Convention Centre
Lower
Windmill St
St Peter's Square
Free Trade Hall
Midland Hotel
Liverpool Road
Deansgate
Great Northern
Peters Fields
Manchester Central
Lower Mosley Street
Oxford Street
Princess Street
Major St
Bloom St
Sackville St
Canal Street
Whitworth Street
Piccadilly Station
Fairfield St
London Road
Potato Wharf
Duke St
Castlefield
Beetham Tower
Bridgewater Hall
Great Bridgewater Street
Rochdale Canal
Whitworth Street
Castle St
Hacienda Club
Cornerhouse
Whitworth Street West
The Green Room
Charles Street
Deansgate Station
Oxford Road Station
Medlock Street
Chester Road
Hulme Street
Dancehouse Theatre
Oxford Road
Mancunian Way
Downing Street
Grosvenor Street
Mancunian Way
Jackson Crescen
Royce Road
Clayburn Road
Bonsall Street
Princess Road
Boundary Lane
Cambridge Street
Royal Northern College of Music
Booth Street
Upper Brook Street
Oxford Road
University of Manchester
Brunswick Street
Manchester Museum
Hulme
0 200 yds
RESTAURANTS
Brasserie Blanc 9
Café Istanbul 8
Dimitri's 14
Little Yang Sing 11
The Market Restaurant 1
Simply Heathcote's 10
Stock 6
Yang Sing 13
CAFÉS & CAFÉ-BARS
Affleck's Palace 5
Atlas 22
Cornerhouse 23
Dry Bar 3
Earth 2
Eighth Day 25
Kro2 24
Loaf 19
Night & Day 4
M Metrolink (tram) stop
© Crown copyright

Sun 10.30am–4.30pm; ⓣ0871/222 8223, ⓦwww.visitmanchester.com). To find out **what's on** in the city, check out the *Manchester Evening News* or consult their website, ⓦwww.manchestereveningnews.co.uk.

Getting around and city transport

About thirty minutes' walk from top to bottom, central Manchester is compact enough to cover on **foot**, though most visitors take to the bus as soon as it starts raining: the **Metroshuttle** free bus service (every 5–10min) weaves its way across central Manchester connecting all the major points of interest. There is also the **Metrolink** tram network (ⓦwww.metrolink.co.uk), which whisks through the city centre bound for the suburbs. There are two routes: one links central Manchester with Bury in the north and Altrincham in the south, the other travels west to Eccles via Salford Quays, the location of the Imperial War Museum North (see p.487).

Accommodation

There are many city-centre **hotels**, especially budget chains, which means you have a good chance of finding a smart, albeit formulaic, en-suite room in central Manchester for around £60–70 at almost any time of the year – except when Manchester United are playing at home, when hotel prices can rocket into the stratosphere. Less expensive **guesthouses** and **B&Bs** are concentrated some way out of the centre, mainly on the southern routes into the city, whereas Manchester's **youth hostel** occupies a prime central location in Castlefield – book well in advance.

Hotels and guesthouses

Castlefield Liverpool Rd ⓣ0161/832 7073, ⓦwww.castlefield-hotel.co.uk. Large, very modern, red-brick, warehouse-style hotel handily located near the foot of Deansgate in Castlefield, opposite the Science and Industry Museum. Nicely appointed rooms, and attached leisure club and pool (free to guests). 7

Didsbury House Didsbury Park, Didsbury Village ⓣ0161/448 2200, ⓦwww.didsburyhouse.co.uk. Located about four miles south of the centre in well-heeled Didsbury Village – buses into the centre are fast and frequent – this is a slick and stylish conversion of Victorian premises with 27 immaculate guest rooms. Great breakfasts too. 7

Great John Street Great John St ⓣ0161/831 3211, ⓦwww.greatjohnst.co.uk. Deluxe hotel in an imaginatively refurbished old school building not far off Deansgate. Holds 30 individually designed, spacious and comfortable suites, some split-level, with nifty scholastic names – "Headmaster's Office" and so forth. At the heart of the hotel is a bar-cum-restaurant, equipped with an open fire and wide sofas, and the gallery breakfast room is up above. Rooftop garden too. Substantial discounts are legion, but the rack-rate is 9

Holiday Inn Express Waterfront Quays, Salford Quays ⓣ0161/868 1000 or ⓣ0870/400 9670, ⓦwww.hiexpress.co.uk. Reasonably large rooms in a great quay location, but in a modern tower block. Convenient for The Lowry and even Old Trafford. Take the Metrolink tram to the Salford Quays tram stop. 5

Malmaison 12 Gore St, Piccadilly ⓣ0161/278 1000, ⓦwww.malmaison-manchester.com. A couple of minutes' walk from Piccadilly Station, the ornate Edwardian facade of this handsome hotel hides sleek interior lines and contemporary design from the Malmaison group. There's a gym, sauna, bar and brasserie, plus substantial weekend discounts depending on availability. 7

Midland Peter St ⓣ0161/236 3333, ⓦwww.qhotels.co.uk. Once the terminus hotel for Central Station (now the Manchester Central convention centre) and the place where Rolls met Royce for the first time, this building was the apotheosis of Edwardian style. The public areas have been returned to much of their former glory and the bedrooms up above are in immaculate chain style. A full raft of leisure facilities too. 7

The Palace Oxford Rd ⓣ0161/288 1111, ⓦwww.principal-hotels.com. Occupying one of the city's grandest Victorian buildings, a terra-cotta-clad extravagance built to a design by Alfred Waterhouse as the Refuge Assurance HQ in 1891, the *Palace Hotel* is part of a small chain of deluxe

English hotels. The public rooms have all the stately grandeur you might expect, the foyer coming complete with ersatz Roman pillars and columns. Great location too, opposite the Cornerhouse arts centre. Has 250 plush rooms and suites. From ❻

Hostel

Manchester YHA Potato Wharf, Castlefield ⓣ0161/839 9960, ⓦwww.yhamanchester.org.uk. Excellent hostel overlooking the canal that runs close to the Museum of Science and Industry. There are thirty-four rooms in total (thirty, four-bunk and four, six-bunk rooms) and all of them are en suite. Facilities include Internet access, laundry, self-catering and a café. You can pay a little extra to use one of the four-bunk rooms as a double. Dorm beds £20.50, doubles ❷

The City Centre

If Manchester can be said to have a centre, it's **Albert Square** and the cluster of buildings surrounding it – the Town Hall, the Central Library and the *Midland Hotel*, originally built in the railway age to host visitors to Britain's greatest industrial city. South of here, the former Central Station now functions as the **Manchester Central** convention centre, with the Hallé Orchestra's home, **Bridgewater Hall**, just opposite. **Chinatown** and the **Gay Village** are just a short walk to the east, while to the northeast, the revamped **Piccadilly Gardens** provides access to the funky **Northern Quarter**. To the southwest is the **Castlefield** district, site of the **Museum of Science and Industry**. The central spine of the city is **Deansgate**, which runs from Castlefield to the cathedral and, in its northern environs, displays the most dramatic core of urban regeneration in the country, centred on the unalloyed modernity of **Exchange Square**.

Albert Square

Until recently at least, Manchester's only real claim to architectural merit was its panoply of **neo-Gothic** buildings and monuments, most of which date from the city's salad days in the second half of the nineteenth century. One of the more fanciful is the shrine-like, canopied **monument** to Prince Albert, Queen Victoria's husband, perched prettily in the middle of the trim little square that bears his name – **Albert Square**. The monument was erected in 1867, six years after Albert's death, supposedly because the prince had always shown an interest in industry, but perhaps more to curry favour with the grieving queen. Overlooking the prince is Alfred Waterhouse's magnificent, neo-Gothic **Town Hall** (Mon–Fri 9am–5pm; free), whose mighty clocktower, completed in 1877, pokes a sturdy finger into the sky, soaring high above its complementary gables, columns and arcaded windows.

St Peter's Square and around

Just to the south of the Town Hall, facing **St Peter's Square**, the circular **Central Library** (Mon–Thurs 10am–8pm, Fri & Sat 9am–5pm; free) was built in 1934 as the largest municipal library in the world, a self-consciously elegant, classical construction with a domed reading room.

Footsteps away, over on Peter Street, the **Free Trade Hall** was the home of the city's Hallé Orchestra for over a century – until Bridgewater Hall was completed in 1996. The Italianate facade of the Free Trade Hall survived intense wartime bombing and is now a protected part of the *Radisson Edwardian Hotel*, whose modern tower block rises up behind at a (fairly) discreet distance.

Manchester Art Gallery

Presiding over the northeast corner of St Peter's Square on Mosley Street is the **Manchester Art Gallery** (Tues–Sun 10am–5pm; free; ⓦwww.manchestergalleries.org), holding an invigorating collection of eighteenth- and nineteenth-century art spread over **Floor 1**. The paintings on this floor are divided by theme – Face and Place, Expressing Passion and so on – rather than by artist (or indeed school of artists), which makes it difficult to appreciate the strength of the collection, especially when it comes to its forte, the Pre-Raphaelite Brotherhood. There's much else – views of Victorian Manchester, a Turner or two, a pair of Gainsboroughs, the preposterous historicism of Alexander Wagner and last but not least Stubbs' famous *Cheetah and Stag with Two Indians*. **Floor 2** features temporary exhibitions and a Gallery of Craft and Design, while the **Ground Floor**'s Manchester Gallery is devoted to a visual history of the city.

South to Bridgewater Hall and Deansgate train station

South of St Peter's Square, **Lower Mosley Street** runs past the **Manchester Central** convention complex, the main part of which occupies what was, until 1969, a train station. Across the street from the complex rises **Bridgewater Hall**, Britain's finest concert hall, balanced on shock-absorbing springs to guarantee the clarity of the sound.

Pressing on, the apartment block at the corner of Lower Mosley Street and Whitworth Street West bears the name of the site's previous occupant, the fabulously famous – and musically seminal – **Hacienda Club**, the spiritual home of Factory Records, which closed in 1997.

Turn right along Whitworth Street West and you'll soon spot the string of café-bars and restaurants that have been shoehorned along the Rochdale canal's **Deansgate Locks**, a pattern repeated along and across the street in the old railway arches abutting Deansgate Station. Look up and you can't miss the striking **Beetham Tower**, easily the tallest skyscraper in Manchester and home to a glitzy *Hilton Hotel*.

The Museum of Science and Industry

From Deansgate station, it's a short stroll north to the extremely popular **Museum of Science and Industry**, whose several different sections spread out along Liverpool Road (daily 10am–5pm; free, but admission charge for special exhibitions; ⓣ0161/832 2244; ⓦwww.msim.org.uk). One of the most impressive museums of its type in the country, it mixes technological displays and special blockbuster exhibitions with trenchant analysis of the social impact of industrialization. A free map of the museum is issued at the entrance, with key points of interest including the **Power Hall**, which trumpets the region's remarkable technological contribution to the Industrial Revolution by means of a hall full of steam engines, some of which are fired up daily. There's more steam just outside the Power Hall in the shape of a working replica of Robert Stephenson's *Planet*, whose original design was based on the *Rocket*, the work of Robert's father George. Built in 1830, the *Planet* reliably attained a scorching 30mph but had no brakes; the museum's version does, and uses them at weekends (noon–4pm), dropping passengers a couple of hundred yards away at the **Station Building**, the world's oldest passenger railway station. It was here that the *Rocket* arrived on a rainy September 15, 1830, after fatally injuring Liverpool MP William Huskisson at the start of the inaugural passenger journey from Liverpool.

Elsewhere, the **1830 Warehouse** features a sound-and-light show that delves into the history of the city's warehouses whose immense storage capacity was essential to Manchester's economy, whilst the **Air and Space Hall**, which barely touches on Manchester at all, features vintage planes, cutaway engines and space exploration displays.

North along Deansgate to the John Rylands Library

Deansgate cuts through the city centre from the Rochdale canal to the cathedral (see below), its architectural reference points ranging from Victorian industrialism to post-millennium pouting. The first major point of interest is the former **Great Northern Railway Company's Goods Warehouse**, a great sweep of brickwork dating back to the 1890s, flanking Deansgate between Great Bridgewater and Peter streets. Now incorporated into a retail and leisure development called "Great Northern", the warehouse was originally an integral part of a large and ambitious trading depot with road and rail links up above and a canal way down below street level.

Continuing north along Deansgate, you soon reach the **John Rylands Library** (Mon–Sat 10am–5pm & Sun noon–5pm; free), the city's supreme example of Victorian Gothic, though recent refurbishment has added an unbecoming modern entrance wing to the original building. The architect who won the original commission, Basil Champneys, opted for a cloistered neo-Gothicism of narrow stone corridors, delicately crafted stonework, stained-glass windows and burnished wooden panelling. The library has survived in superb condition, but it's no longer a general-purpose library, housing instead specialist collections of rare books and manuscripts.

St Ann's Square, the Royal Exchange and Exchange Square

Slender **St Ann's Square** is tucked away off the eastern side of Deansgate, a couple of blocks up from the Rylands Library. Flanking the square's southern side is **St Ann's Church** (daily 9.45am–4.45pm; free), a trim sandstone structure whose Neoclassical symmetries date from 1709, though the stained-glass windows are firmly Victorian. At the other end of the square is the **Royal Exchange**, which houses the much lauded **Royal Exchange Theatre**. Formerly the Cotton Exchange, this building employed seven thousand people until trading finished on December 31, 1968 – the old trading board still shows the last day's prices for American and Egyptian cotton.

A pedestrian high street – **New Cathedral Street** – runs north from St Ann's Square to **Exchange Square**, which, with its water features, public sculptures and massive department stores (primarily Selfridges and Harvey Nichols), has been the focus of the ambitious city-centre rebuilding programme that followed the IRA bomb of 1996. On the southeast side of the square stands the whopping **Arndale Centre**, once a real Sixties eyesore, but now a modern shopping precinct, clad in glass.

Manchester Cathedral and Chetham's School of Music

Manchester Cathedral (Mon–Sat 10am–4.30pm, plus May–Sept Sun 11.30am–4pm; free), standing just beyond Exchange Square from the end of New Cathedral Street, dates back to the fifteenth century, though its Gothic lines have been hacked about too much to have any real architectural coherence. Actually, it's surprising it's still here at all: in 1940, a 1000lb bomb all but destroyed the interior, knocking out most of the stained glass, which is why it's so light inside today.

The cathedral's choristers are trained in **Chetham's School of Music** (Ⓣ0161/834 7961; Ⓦwww.chethams.org.uk), on the far side of the cathedral on Long Millgate. This fifteenth-century manor house became a school and a free public library in 1653 and was turned into a music school in 1969. There are free recitals during term time and, although there's no public access to most of the complex, you can visit the oak-panelled **Library** (Mon–Fri 9am–12.30pm & 1.30–4.30pm; free) with its handsome carved eighteenth-century bookcases. Along the side corridor is the main **Reading Room**, where Marx and Engels beavered away on the square table that still stands in the windowed alcove.

Urbis and Victoria Train Station

Directly opposite Chetham's – you can hardly miss it – is the six-storey glasswork of **Urbis** (Sun–Wed 10am–6pm, Thurs–Sat 10am–8pm; free except for special exhibitions; Ⓦwww.urbis.org.uk), a huge and distinctive sloping structure completed in 2002 as a museum and exhibition centre. The emphasis here is very much on urban life and modern culture – from punk through to graffiti and beyond. Manchester, as the world's first industrial city, is given due prominence.

Behind Urbis, down the slope, is **Victoria Station**, the most likeable of the city's several stations with its long, gently curving stone facade. Pop inside for a look at the Art Deco ticket booths and the immaculate tiled map of the Lancashire and Yorkshire Railway network as it was in the 1920s.

Piccadilly Gardens and the Northern Quarter

For years, the bleak expanse of **Piccadilly Gardens**, to the east of the Arndale Centre and about ten minutes' walk from Victoria Station, interrupted the architectural flow of the city centre, but a recent beautification by Japanese architects has dramatically enhanced its character, adding trees, a fountain and water jets, and a pavilion at one end to screen off the traffic. The gardens remain a major local transport hub and gateway to the still shabby but improving **Oldham Street**, which has been adopted by "alternative" entrepreneurs who have dubbed it the **Northern Quarter**. Traditionally, this is Manchester's garment district and you'll still find shops and wholesalers selling high-street fashions, shop fittings, mannequins and hosiery, but there are also new design outlets, lots of music stores, and some cool bars and cafés. For offbeat contemporary shopping, pop into Affleck's Palace, 52 Church St (closed Sun; Ⓦwww.afflecks-palace.co.uk). There are more skills and crafts on display in the excellent **Manchester Craft and Design Centre**, 17 Oak St (Mon–Sat 10am–5.30pm, plus Sun in Dec 10am–5.30pm; free; Ⓦwww.craftanddesign.com) – a great place to pick up ceramics, fabrics, earthenware, jewellery and decorative art, or just sip a drink in the café.

Chinatown and the Gay Village

From Piccadilly Gardens, it's a short walk to **Chinatown**, whose grid of narrow streets stretch north–south from Charlotte to Princess Street between Portland and Mosley streets, with the inevitable **Dragon Arch**, at Faulkner and Nicolas, providing the focus for the annual Chinese New Year celebrations. Close by, just to the southeast, the side roads off Portland Street lead down to the Rochdale canal, where Canal Street is the heart of Manchester's thriving **Gay Village**: the pink pound has filled this part of the city with canalside cafés, clubs, bars and businesses.

One block west of the Gay Village, at the junction of Oxford Road and Whitworth Street, stands the **Cornerhouse** (Ⓣ0161/200 1500, Ⓦwww.cornerhouse.org), the dynamo of the Manchester arts scene. In addition to screening art-house films, the Cornerhouse has three floors of gallery space devoted to contemporary and local artists' work as well as a popular café and bar. From the stops across the road, buses plough south down Oxford Road bound for the university and the suburbs beyond.

Salford Quays

After the Manchester Ship Canal opened in 1894, **Salford docks** played a pivotal role in turning Manchester into one of Britain's busiest seaports. By the 1970s, however, trade had well-nigh collapsed and the docks were forced to close in 1982, leaving a slew of post-industrial mess just a couple of miles to the west of the city centre. Since then, an extraordinarily ambitious redevelopment has transformed **Salford Quays**, as it was rebranded, into a hugely popular waterfront residential and leisure complex, with its own gleaming new apartment blocks, shopping mall and arts centre, **The Lowry**, amongst whose various delights are art galleries that feature the works of the centre's namesake, L.S. Lowry. Also on the quays is the much praised **Imperial War Museum North**, with its splendidly thoughtful displays on war in general and its effects on the individual in particular.

To get to the quays by public transport, take the **Metrolink** tram (Eccles line; see p.482) from the city centre to the Harbour City tram stop, from where it is a five-minute walk to both The Lowry and the Imperial War Museum.

The Lowry

Perched on the water's edge, **The Lowry** (Ⓣ0870/787 5780, Ⓦwww.thelowry.com) is the quays' shiny steel arts centre, where you seem to be able to do just about anything, from going to the theatre to getting married. A small part of The Lowry, the **Galleries** (Sun–Fri 11am–5pm, Sat 10am–5pm; free, but donation requested), is devoted to displays of fine art. There are some sixteen different exhibitions held here each year, but most of them showcase a selection of **Lowry paintings**, quite rightly given that no artist is more closely associated with Salford. The earlier paintings of **Lawrence Stephen Lowry** (1887–1976) have a sense of desolation and melancholia in their portrayal of Manchester mill workers, but later he modified his outlook, repeating earlier paintings but changing the greys and sullen browns for lively reds and pinks. Lowry also expanded his repertoire as he grew older, capturing mountain scenes and seascapes in broad sweeps of his brush, and painting full-bodied realistic portraits that are far less known than his internationally famous matchstick crowds. A twenty-minute **film** – "Meet Mr Lowry" – puts further flesh on the artistic bones.

Imperial War Museum North

A footbridge spans the Manchester Ship Canal to link The Lowry with the startling **Imperial War Museum North** (March–Oct daily 10am–6pm, Nov–Feb daily 10am–5pm; free; Ⓦwww.north.iwm.org.uk), which raises a giant steel fin into the air, all to the design of Daniel Libeskind. The interior is just as striking, its angular lines serving as a dramatic backdrop to the displays, which kick off with the Big Picture, when the walls of the main hall are transformed into giant screens to show regularly rotated, fifteen-minute, surround-sound films. In addition, there are all sorts of themed displays in six separate exhibition areas – the "Silos" – focusing on everything from women's work in the two world wars to war reporting and the build-up to the Iraq conflict of 2003. It's an ambitious and carefully conceived museum with a mixture of the personal and the general that is nothing less than superb.

Old Trafford

From the War Museum, it's about three-quarters of a mile southeast to **Old Trafford**, the self-styled "Theatre of Dreams" and home of **Manchester**

United (Ⓦ www.manutd.com), arguably the most famous football team in the world. The club's following is such that only season-ticket holders can ever attend games, but **guided tours** of Old Trafford and its museum (daily 9.30am–4.30pm; advance booking essential; £10) placate out-of-town fans who want to gawp at the silverware and sit in the dug-out. To get here by public transport, take the Metrolink tram to Old Trafford Station and walk up Warwick Road to Sir Matt Busby Way.

Eating and drinking

Second only to London in the breadth and scope of its **cafés** and **restaurants**, Manchester has something to suit everyone, from a cheap curry to a night out in a celebrity-chef hot spot. The bulk of Manchester's eating and drinking places are scattered around the **city centre**, but the **Rusholme** district, a couple of miles south of the centre, possesses the city's widest and best selection of Asian restaurants along the main drag, **Wilmslow Road**. From Rusholme, it's another couple of miles, again along the Wilmslow Road, to **Didsbury**, a leafy, well-heeled suburb very different from Rusholme and equipped, along with nearby **West Didsbury**, with several excellent restaurants.

Most city-centre **pubs** dish up something filling at lunchtime, but for a more modish snack or drink, European-style **café-bars** are everywhere, especially in the **Northern Quarter**, and in the **Gay Village** on the Rochdale canal.

Cafes and café-bars

Affleck's Palace 52 Church St, Northern Quarter. Five floors of hip/alternative/indie boutiques, with the pick of the cafés on the top floor, where you can grab a coffee and a grilled sandwich. Mon–Fri 10.30am–6pm, Sat 10am–6pm.

Atlas 376 Deansgate. In an old red-brick building that pokes its nose out from beneath a railway arch, *Atlas* is kitted out in slick, modern style, complete with large patio. Justly known for its quality focaccia sandwiches, it's also the place for Sun brunch, a bottle of beer or a decent glass of wine. Light meals and lunches from £4.

Cornerhouse 70 Oxford St. Slick ground-floor bar and first-floor café-bar in Manchester's premier art-house cinema and arts centre. Tasty, inexpensive snacks and light meals – from around £5 – though the service is patchy.

Dry Bar 28–30 Oldham St. The earliest of the designer café-bars on the scene, started by Factory records and the catalyst for much of what has happened since in the Northern Quarter. Still as cool (sometimes tough) as they come.

Earth 16–20 Turner St. Gourmet vegan and organic food in a stylish Northern Quarter pit-stop with Buddhist leanings – stuffed pancakes, pies, bakes, juices and deli delights. Tues–Fri 10am–7pm & Sat 10am–5pm.

Eighth Day 107–111 Oxford Rd. Manchester's oldest organic-vegetarian café has got spanking new premises on its old Oxford Rd site – shop, takeaway and juice bar upstairs, café/restaurant downstairs. Mon–Fri 8.30am–7pm, Sat 9.30am–7pm.

Kro2 Oxford House, Oxford Rd. Half the students in Manchester crowd into this good-natured café-bar, sited in glassy modern premises close to the Mancunian Way overpass and opposite the university. Offers imaginative value-for-money food and on a sunny day you'll struggle to find table space outside. There are four other *Kro* outlets in the city, three further out along Oxford Rd.

Loaf Deansgate Locks, Whitworth St West. Large queues at the weekend for this designer-industrial café-bar, not nearly so crowded during the day when you can grab an outdoor table underneath the arches and soak up the weak Manchester sun.

Manto 46 Canal St. Gay Village stalwart that has gone through several incarnations since it was established in 1990. *Manto* attracts a chic crowd, which laps up the cool sounds and club nights. Inexpensive fusion dishes served daily from noon till 8pm.

Night & Day 26 Oldham St. Unpretentious café-bar with a late licence and live music most nights from local musicians; club nights too. Details at Ⓦ www.nightnday.org.

Restaurants

Café Istanbul 79 Bridge St ⓣ 0161/833 9942. Delicious Turkish dishes, including a great meze selection, and an extensive wine list (including a powerful Turkish red). Main courses average around £12. Open daily from noon.

Dimitri's 1 Campfield Arcade, Deansgate Ⓣ0161/839 3319. Pick and mix from the Greek /Spanish/Italian menu (particularly good for vegetarians), or grab a sandwich, a drink and an arcade table. Snacks around £4, tapas £5.

Brasserie Blanc 55 King St Ⓣ0161/832 1000. Raymond Blanc's mid-range brasserie, housed in sleek modern premises near the Royal Exchange, is the city's best spot for reasonably priced classic and regional French cooking. Mains average around £13. Mon–Fri noon–2.45pm & 5.30–10.30pm, Sat & Sun noon–10pm.

Lime Tree 8 Lapwing Lane, West Didsbury Ⓣ0161/445 1217. Serves up a menu that chargrills and oven-roasts as if its life depended on it. Organic salmon is a signature dish, or else you could be chowing down on such delights as crispy duckling or courgette and leek cheesecake. Reservations recommended. Main courses cost from £13, less at lunch times. Mon & Sat 6–10.15pm, Tues–Fri & Sun noon–2.30pm & 6–10.15pm.

Little Yang Sing 17 George St Ⓣ0161/228 7722. Celebrated basement restaurant (forerunner to the larger Yang Sing) where the emphasis is on *dim sum*, rice or noodle dishes, and down-to-earth Cantonese cooking, with lots of choice under £8.

The Market Restaurant 104 High St Ⓣ0161/834 3743. First-rate Northern Quarter restaurant with a regularly changing menu featuring adventurous and eclectic dishes. Main courses go for around £13–18. Also a very good wine and beer list. Reservations absolutely essential. Open Wed–Sat 6.30–10pm & Wed–Fri noon–2pm.

No.4 4 Warburton St, Didsbury Ⓣ0161/445 0448. Tucked away off the main road, this little bolt hole has two floors of intimate dining. Omelettes and open sandwiches at lunch (around £5) give way to seasonally changing dinners, with main courses from £12. Tues–Sun noon–2pm & Tues–Sat 7–10pm.

Royal Darbar 65–67 Wilmslow Rd, Rusholme Ⓣ0161/224 4392. Award-winning Asian food in plain but friendly surroundings. The house speciality is *nihari*, a slow-cooked lamb dish, while other homestyle choices appear on Sun. Take your own booze. Main courses from as little as £9.

Sanam 145–151 Wilmslow Rd, Rusholme Ⓣ0161/224 8824. One of Rusholme's earliest Asian arrivals, now over thirty years old, the *Sanam* serves all the usual dishes plus award-winning *gulab juman*. Drop by the *Sanam* takeaway sweet centre, at 169 Wilmslow Rd, on the way home. No alcohol allowed. Mains from £9.

Simply Heathcote's Jackson's Row Ⓣ0161/835 3536. This large and popular first-floor restaurant occupies part of an old and classily revamped warehouse. Minimalist decor sets the tone, and the menu, the handiwork of Lancastrian chef Paul Heathcote, mixes Mediterranean and local flavours and ingredients, so expect updated working-class dishes alongside the parmesan shavings. Mains before 7pm hover around (a very reasonable) £9, £13 later on.

Stock 4 Norfolk St Ⓣ0161/839 6644. Superior Italian cooking – the fish is renowned – accompanied by a wine list of serious intent. It's housed in the city's old stock exchange, hence the name. Dress smartly. Main courses average £18, less at lunchtimes and from 5–7pm. Mon–Sat noon–2.30pm & 5.30–10.30pm.

Yang Sing 34 Princess St Ⓣ0161/236 2200. The *Yang Sing* is one of the best Cantonese restaurants in the country, with thoroughly authentic food, from a lunchtime plate of fried noodles to the full works. Stray from the printed menu for the most interesting dishes; ask the friendly staff for advice. Main courses from £10.

Pubs

Britons Protection 50 Great Bridgewater St. Cosy, old pub with a couple of small rooms and all sorts of Victorian decorative detail – most splendidly the tiles. Also has a backyard beer garden.

Circus Tavern 86 Portland St. Manchester's smallest pub – a Victorian drinking-hole that's many people's favourite city-centre pit-stop. You may have to knock on the door to get in; once you do, you're confronted by the landlord in the corridor pulling pints.

Dukes '92 Castle St. Classily revamped former stable block (for canal horses) with art on the walls, terrace seating and a good selection of beers. Serves great-value food too, including a wide range of pâtés and cheeses.

Mr Thomas' Chop House 52 Cross St. Victorian classic with a Dickensian feel to its nooks and crannies. Office workers, hardcore daytime drinkers, old goats and students all call it home. There's good-value, traditional English "chop-house" food (oysters, bubble and squeak, etc) served in the ornate dining-and-drinking room at the rear.

The Ox 71 Liverpool Rd. Pleasant and popular old boozer that dates back to Victorian times – as does some of the tilework. Good range of cask ales along with well-above-average bar food.

Peveril of the Peak 127 Great Bridgewater St. The pub that time forgot – one of Manchester's best real-ale houses, with a youthful crowd and some superb Victorian glazed tilework outside.

Rain Bar 80 Great Bridgewater St. Pub or bar? Experience both, drinking inside the stripped-wood pubby interior, up in the swish bar, or out on the canalside terrace. Good range of beers, a decent menu and summer barbecues.

Temple of Convenience Great Bridgewater St. Subterranean public toilet – yes that's right – turned into a cramped and crowded bar. Lots of students love it; others find it rather gruesome. At the intersection of Great Bridgewater and Oxford streets.

Nightlife

Manchester has a vivid **nightlife**, spearheaded by the success of its musical exports. Banks of fly-posters advertise what's going on in the numerous **clubs**, which, as elsewhere, frequently change names and styles on different nights of the week. The most enduring clubs are listed below and you can expect to pay £5–15 cover depending on what's on; many of the city's groovier café-bars also host regular club nights.

Manchester also has an excellent pub and club **live music** scene, with tickets for local bands usually under £5, more like £10–15 for someone well known. Star gigs take place either at one of the city's major venues, also listed below. For the broadest coverage of Manchester's musical happenings, check out the local daily, the *Manchester Evening News*.

Small live music and club venues

Band on the Wall 25 Swan St ⓣ0161/834 1786, ⓦwww.bandonthewall.org. Legendary Northern Quarter joint with a great reputation for its live bands – from world and folk to jazz and reggae – plus tasty club nights to boot. Currently closed for a thoroughgoing revamp – should reopen in 2009.

Manchester Roadhouse 8 Newton St, Piccadilly ⓣ0161/237 9789, ⓦwww.theroadhouselive.co.uk. Regular and varied gigs by local bands plus a succession of club nights.

Sankey's Soap Beehive Mill, Jersey St, Ancoats ⓣ0161/236 5444, ⓦwww.tribalgathering.co.uk. Many people's favourite night out, brought to you by the legendary Tribal Gathering crew, popular for their sleazy house music; other club night specials too. Ancoats is an inner-city suburb about half a mile north of Piccadilly Station.

Stadium venues

Manchester Apollo Stockport Rd, Ardwick Green ⓣ08709/913 913, ⓦwww.alive.co.uk/apollo. Huge theatre auditorium for all kinds of concerts.

Manchester Central Petersfield ⓣ0161/834 2700, ⓦwww.manchestercentral.co.uk. Mid-sized city-centre indoor stadium.

Manchester Evening News Arena 21 Hunt's Bank, beside Victoria Station ⓣ0844/847 8000, ⓦwww.menarena.com. Indoor stadium seating 20,000 and hosting all the big names.

Arts and culture

Manchester is blessed with the North's most highly prized **orchestra**, the Hallé, which is resident at Bridgewater Hall. Other acclaimed names include the BBC Philharmonic and the Manchester Camerata chamber orchestra (ⓦwww.manchestercamerata.com), who perform **concerts** at a variety of venues across the city. The Cornerhouse is the local "alternative" **arts** mainstay and the best art-house **cinema** in town, while a full range of mainstream and fringe **theatres** produces a lively, year-round programme of events.

Concerts and music

Bridgewater Hall Lower Mosley St ⓣ0161/907 9000, ⓦwww.bridgewater-hall.co.uk. Home of the Hallé Orchestra and the Manchester Camerata; also sponsors a full programme of chamber, pop, classical and jazz concerts.

Opera House Quay St ⓣ0161/828 1700, ⓦwww.ticketmaster.co.uk. Major venue for touring West End musicals, drama, comedy and concerts.

Royal Northern College of Music (RNCM) 124 Oxford Rd ⓣ0161/907 5555, ⓦwww.rncm.ac.uk. Stages top-quality classical and modern-jazz concerts, including performances by Manchester Camerata.

Theatre and the arts

Cornerhouse 70 Oxford St ⓣ0161/200 1500, ⓦwww.cornerhouse.org. Engaging centre for contemporary arts, with three cinema screens, changing art exhibitions, recitals, talks, bookshop, café and bar.

Dancehouse Theatre 10 Oxford Rd ⓣ0161/237 9753, ⓦwww.thedancehouse.co.uk. Home of the Northern Ballet School and the eponymous theatre troupe; venue for dance, drama and comedy.

Royal Exchange Theatre St Ann's Square ⓣ0161/833 9833, ⓦwww.royalexchange.co.uk. The theatre-in-the-round in the Royal Exchange is the most famous stage in the city, and there's a Studio Theatre (for works by new writers) alongside the main stage.

Cinema

Cornerhouse 70 Oxford St ⓣ0161/200 1500, ⓦwww.cornerhouse.org. The three screens at the Cornerhouse are your best bet for art-house releases, special screenings and cinema-related talks and events. Highly recommended.

Listings

Airport ⓣ0161/489 3000 ⓦwww.manchesterairport.co.uk.

Bus information For all Greater Manchester bus services, call GMPTE on ⓣ0871/200 2233, ⓦwww.gmpte.com.

Pharmacy Boots, 11–13 Piccadilly Gardens (ⓣ0161/834 8244) and 20 St Ann's St (ⓣ0161/839 1798).

Post office 26 Spring Gardens.

Taxis Mantax ⓣ0161/230 3333; Taxifone ⓣ0161/236 9974.

Train information For all Greater Manchester train services, contact GMPTE on ⓣ0871/200 2233, ⓦwww.gmpte.com.

Chester

CHESTER, forty miles southwest of Manchester across the Cheshire Plain, is home to a glorious two-mile ring of medieval and Roman walls that encircles a kernel of Tudor and Victorian buildings, all overhanging eaves, mini-courtyards, and narrow cobbled lanes, which culminate in the unique raised arcades called the "**Rows**". Taken altogether, Chester has enough in the way of sights, restaurants and atmosphere to make it an enjoyable base for a day or two.

Arrival and information

Most long-distance and regional **buses** pull in at the stops on Vicar's Lane, opposite one of the town's two tourist offices (see below) and a five-minute walk from the city centre. Local buses use the Bus Exchange right in the centre of town, between Princess and Hunter streets, off Northgate Street. From the **train station**, to the northeast of the centre, it's a good ten-minute walk down City Road and Foregate Street to the central Eastgate Clock. A shuttle bus (Mon–Sat 8am–6pm, free with rail ticket; every 15min) links the train station with the Bus Exchange. Drivers should note that city-centre parking is thin on the ground, which makes Chester's **Park-and-Ride** scheme attractive – just follow the signs on any of the major approach roads.

Chester has two **tourist offices**, one bang in the centre in the Town Hall on Northgate Street (April–Sept Mon–Sat 9.30am–5.30pm, Sun 10am–4pm; Oct–March Mon–Fri 10am–4pm, Sat 10am–5pm), a second – the Chester Visitor Centre – on Vicar's Lane, just to the east of the town centre (April–Sept

Mon–Sat 9.30am–5.30pm, Sun 10am–4pm; Oct–March Mon–Fri 10am–4pm, Sat 10–5 & Sun 10am–4pm). They share the same telephone number and website (Ⓣ01244/351 609, Ⓦwww.visitchester.co.uk).

Accommodation

Chester is a popular tourist destination and although most of its visitors are day-trippers, enough of them stay overnight to sustain dozens of **B&Bs** and a slew of **hotels**. At the height of the summer and on high days and holidays – like Chester Races – advance booking is strongly recommended either direct or via the tourist office.

Hotels and B&Bs

The Chester Grosvenor Eastgate St Ⓣ01244/324 024, Ⓦwww.chestergrosvenor.co.uk. Superbly appointed luxury hotel in an immaculately maintained Victorian building plumb in the centre of town. Extremely comfortable bedrooms and a whole host of facilities, not least a full-blown spa. Discounts common at the weekend. 8

Chester Town House B&B 23 King St Ⓣ01244/350 021, Ⓦwww.chestertownhouse.co.uk. High-standard B&B in a comfortably furnished seventeenth-century townhouse on a cobbled central street off Northgate St. There are five en-suite rooms and private parking. 4

The Green Bough 60 Hoole Rd Ⓣ01244/326 241, Ⓦwww.greenbough.co.uk. Award-winning, small and friendly family-run hotel with all sorts of thoughtful details – soft carpeting, comfortable beds, and plasma TV screens in each guest room or suite. Great breakfasts too, plus three-course evening meals for £45 and a rooftop garden. One mile northeast of the city centre en route to the M53/M56. 7

Hostel

Chester Youth Hostel Hough Green House, 40 Hough Green Ⓣ0870/770 5762, Ⓔchester@yha.org.uk. 20min walk southwest of the centre, this Victorian house has a cafeteria, self-catering and laundry facilities, and a shop. Over 100 beds in two- to ten-bedded rooms; dorm beds £17.50 including breakfast.

The City

Central Chester is full of easy charms that can be explored on foot. There are two special highlights, **The Rows**, the picturesque galleries that run above the central shops, and the ancient **city wall**, from the top of which there are fetching views of Chester's environs.

The Rows

Intersecting at **The Cross**, the four main thoroughfares of central Chester are lined by **The Rows**, galleried shopping arcades that run along the first floor of a wonderful set of half-timbered buildings with another set of shops down below at street level. This engaging tableau, which extends for the first 200 or 300 yards of each of the four main streets, is a blend of genuine Tudor houses and Victorian imitations. There's no clear explanation of the origin of The Rows – they were first recorded shortly after a fire wrecked Chester in 1278 – but it seems likely that the hard bedrock that lies underneath the town centre prevented its shopkeepers and merchants from constructing the cellars they required, so they built upwards instead. The finest Tudor buildings are on **Watergate Street**, though **Bridge Street** is perhaps more picturesque. From The Cross, it's also a brief walk along **Eastgate Street** to one of the old town gates, above which is perched the filigree **Eastgate Clock**, raised in honour of Queen Victoria's Diamond Jubilee.

The Town Hall and the Cathedral

North of The Cross, along **Northgate Street**, rises the neo-Gothic **Town Hall**, whose acres of red and grey sandstone look over to the **Cathedral**

(Mon–Sat 9am–5pm & Sun 12.30–4pm; £4), a much modified red sandstone structure dating back to the Normans. The **nave**, with its massive medieval pillars, is suitably imposing, and on one side it sports a splendid sequence of Victorian Pre-Raphaelite mosaic panels that illustrate Old Testament stories in melodramatic style. Close by, the **north transept** is the oldest and most Norman part of the church – hence the round-headed arch and arcade – and the adjoining **choir** holds an intricately carved set of fourteenth-century choir stalls with some especially beastly misericords.

Around the city walls

East of the cathedral, steps provide access to the top of **city walls** – a two-mile girdle of medieval and Roman handiwork that's the most complete in Britain, though in places the wall is barely above street level. You can walk past all its towers, turrets and gateways in an hour or so, and most have a tale or two to tell. The fifteenth-century **King Charles Tower** in the northeast corner is so named because Charles I stood here in 1645 watching his troops being beaten on Rowton Moor, two miles to the southeast, while the earlier **Water Tower** at the northwest corner, once stood in the river – evidence of the changes brought about by the gradual silting of the River Dee. South from the Water Tower you'll see the **Roodee**, England's oldest racecourse, laid out on a silted tidal pool where Roman ships once unloaded wine, figs and olive oil from the Mediterranean and slate, lead and silver from their mines in North Wales. Races are still held here throughout the year – the tourist office has the details.

The Roman Gardens and the Roman Amphitheatre

Immediately to the east of one of the old city gates, **Newgate**, a footpath leads into the **Roman Gardens** (open access), where a miscellany of Roman stonework – odd bits of pillar, coping stones and incidental statuary – is on display amidst the surrounding greenery. Footsteps away, along Little St John Street, is the shallow, partly excavated bowl that marks the site of the **Roman Amphitheatre** (open access); it is estimated to have held seven thousand spectators, making it the largest amphitheatre in Britain, but frankly it's not much to look at today.

Eating and drinking

You can't walk more than a few paces in downtown Chester without coming across somewhere to **eat and drink**, as often as not housed in a medieval or Tudor building.

Cafés and restaurants

Boulevard de la Bastille 39 Bridge St Row. One of the nicest of the arcade cafés, with tables looking over the street and doing a roaring trade in breakfasts, pastries and sandwiches. Sandwiches from as little as £1.70.

Chez Jules 71 Northgate St ☎01244/400 014. Classic brasserie menu – salade nicoise to vegetable cassoulet, Toulouse sausage to rib-eye steak – at this popular spot, housed in an attractive black-and-white, half-timbered building. In the evenings, main courses begin at about £9, but they also do a terrific-value, two-course lunch for £7.90. Mon–Sat noon–3pm & 6–10.30pm, Sun noon–4.30pm.

Three Kings Tearoom 90 Lower Bridge St. Behind the cutest of antique shops, an amenable little tearoom with pleasantly fuddy-duddy decor and tasty food – a filling salad and sandwich combo costs about £4. Open Tues–Sun 10am–4pm.

Pubs and bars

Albion Inn corner of Albion and Park sts. A true English Victorian terraced pub in the shadow of the city wall – no fruit machines or muzak. Good old fashioned decor too, plus tasty bar food and a great range of ales.

Mill Hotel Milton St. Ale-lovers flock to this converted Victorian corn mill to sample an excellent range of brews in a lively atmosphere.

Old Harkers Arms 1 Russell St, below the City Rd bridge. Canalside real-ale pub imaginatively sited in a former warehouse about 500 yards northeast of Foregate St. Quality bar food too.

Liverpool and around

Once the empire's second city, **LIVERPOOL** spent too many of the twentieth-century postwar years struggling against adversity. Things are looking up, as economic and social regeneration brightens the centre and old docks, and the city's stint as European Capital of Culture for 2008 has transformed the view from outside. Some may sneer at the very concept of Liverpudlian "culture", but this is a city with a Tate Gallery of its own, a series of innovative museums and a fascinating social history. Acerbic wit and loyalty to one of the city's two football teams (Liverpool and Everton) are the linchpins of Scouse culture, although Liverpool also makes great play of its musical heritage, which is reasonable enough from the city that produced The Beatles.

Some history

Liverpool gained its charter from King John in 1207, but remained a humble fishing village for half a millennium until the booming slave trade prompted the building of the first dock in 1715. From then until the abolition of slavery in Britain in 1807, Liverpool was the apex of the **slaving triangle** in which firearms, alcohol and textiles were traded for African slaves, who were then shipped to the Caribbean and America where they were in turn exchanged for tobacco, raw cotton and sugar. After the abolition of the trade, the port continued to grow into a seven-mile chain of docks, not only for freight but also to cope with wholesale European emigration, which saw nine million people leave for the Americas and Australasia between 1830 and 1930. During the 1970s and 1980s Liverpool became a byword for British economic malaise, but the waterfront area of the city was granted **UNESCO World Heritage** status in 2004, and there has been major subsequent refurbishment of the city's magnificent municipal and industrial buildings.

Visitors have to plan ahead if they are to get around the sights in two or three days. The **River Mersey** provides one focus, whether crossing on the famous ferry to the **Wirral** peninsula or on a tour of the attractions in Albert Dock. The associated Beatles' sights can easily occupy another day. If you want a cathedral, they've "got one to spare" as the song goes; plus there's a fine showing of British art in the celebrated **Walker Art Gallery**, a multitude of exhibits in the terrific **World Museum Liverpool**, and a revitalized arts and nightlife urban quarter centred on **FACT**, Liverpool's showcase for film and the media arts.

Arrival, information and city transport

Main-line **trains** pull in to Lime Street Station, while the suburban **Merseyrail** system (for trains from Chester) calls at four underground stations in the city, including Lime Street and James Street (for Pier Head and the Albert Dock). National Express **buses** use the station on Norton Street, just northeast of Lime Street, and local buses depart from Queen Square and Paradise Street. Liverpool **airport** – officially named after John Lennon – is eight miles southeast of the city centre and from outside the main entrance the Airlink #500 bus (every 20–30min: 5.10am–midnight; £2) runs into the city, or a taxi to Lime Street costs around £12. Most **ferries** – from the Isle of Man, Dublin and Belfast – dock at the terminals just north of Pier Head, not far from James Street Merseyrail station, though Norfolkline arrivals are over the water on the Wirral at Twelve Quays, near Woodside ferry terminal (ferry or Merseyrail to Liverpool).

The central **tourist office**, currently named The 08 Place, is at 36–38 Whitechapel (Mon–Sat 9/10am–6pm, Sun 11am–4pm; ⓣ0151/233 2008 or 0151/233 2459, accommodation line ⓣ0844/370 0123; ⓦwww.visitliverpool.com, ⓦwww.liverpool08.com). There are smaller offices in the Anchor Courtyard at the **Albert Dock** (daily 10am–5/5.30pm) and at the **airport** (daily 5am to midnight; ⓣ0151/907 1057). Other **websites** include ⓦwww.liverpoolmuseums.org.uk, ⓦwww.artinliverpool.com and ⓦwww.liverpool.com.

The local transport authority is **Merseytravel** (ⓣ0871/200 2233, ⓦwww.merseytravel.gov.uk), which has travel centres at Queen Square and the Paradise Street Interchange. If you're here for any length of time, consider buying a "Your Ticket for Liverpool" **visitor card** (£19.99; ⓣ0844 870 0123, ⓦwww.yourticketforliverpool.com), which gives free and discounted tickets to attractions over three days. The tourist offices have details of guided **walking tours** of the city (most Easter–Sept; from £3), and you shouldn't miss a trip on the amphibious half-truck-half-boat **Yellow Duckmarine** (daily from 10.30/11am; peak time £11.95, off-peak £9.95; ⓣ0151/708 7799, ⓦwww.theyellowduckmarine.co.uk), which departs from Gower Street, in front of Albert Dock.

Accommodation

Budget chains are well represented, with Premier Travel Inn, Ibis, Express by Holiday Inn, Campanile and others all with convenient city-centre locations, including down by Albert Dock. Both **universities** – John Moores University (ⓣ0151/231 3511, ⓦwww.ljmu.ac.uk/conferences; from around £17.50 room only) and the University of Liverpool (ⓣ0151/794 6440, ⓦwww.liv.ac.uk/conferenceservices; £34 with breakfast) – have hundreds of good-value single rooms available during the Easter holidays and from late June to early September.

Hotels and guesthouses

Aachen 89–91 Mount Pleasant ⓣ0151/709 3477, ⓦwww.aachenhotel.co.uk. The best of the Mount Pleasant budget choices, a range of value-for-money rooms (with and without en-suite showers), big "eat-as-much-as-you-like" breakfasts, and a late bar. ❸

Feathers 113–125 Mount Pleasant ⓣ0151/709 9655, ⓦwww.feathers.uk.com. A converted terrace of Georgian houses, with a variety of refurbished rooms in warm tones. Late bar, 24hr reception, and help-yourself hot-and-cold buffet breakfast included in the price. The *Alicia*, overlooking Sefton Park, around 3 miles southeast of the centre, is part of the same group. Both ❺

Hard Day's Night North John St ⓣ0151/236 1964, ⓦwww.harddaysnighthotel.com. Up-to-the-minute four-star close to Mathew St. Splashes of vibrant colour and artful lighting enhance the elegant decor. The Lennon and McCartney suites are the tops. Breakfast not included. ❼ suites ❾

Hope Street 40 Hope St (entrance on Hope Place) ⓣ0151/709 3000, ⓦwww.hopestreethotel.co.uk. This former Victorian warehouse still retains its original elegant brickwork and cast-iron columns but is now replete with hardwood floors, huge beds, TVs and luxurious bathrooms. Breakfast not included. ❼, suites ❾

Racquet Club Hargreaves Building, 5 Chapel St ⓣ0151/236 6676, ⓦwww.racquetclub.org.uk. Boutique-style townhouse hotel with just eight rooms, each mixing good linen and traditional furniture with contemporary art and all mod cons. Breakfast is not in the price, but is available courtesy of *Ziba*, the hotel's cutting-edge restaurant. ❼

Hostels

International Inn 4 South Hunter St, off Hardman St ⓣ0151/709 8135, ⓦwww.internationalinn.co.uk. Converted Victorian warehouse in a great location, with modern accommodation in en-suite rooms sleeping two to ten people. Dorm beds from £15, twin rooms ❶

Liverpool YHA 25 Tabley St, off Wapping ⓣ0870/770 5924, ⓔliverpool@yha.org.uk. One of the YHA's best, just south of Albert Dock. Accommodation is in smart en-suite two-, three-, four- or six-bed rooms, with licensed café and breakfast in the price. Dorms £16.50–24.50, twin rooms ❷–❹

The City

The main sights are scattered throughout the centre of Liverpool but you can easily walk between most of them, through cityscapes ranging from revamped shopping arcades and restyled city squares to the surviving regal Georgian

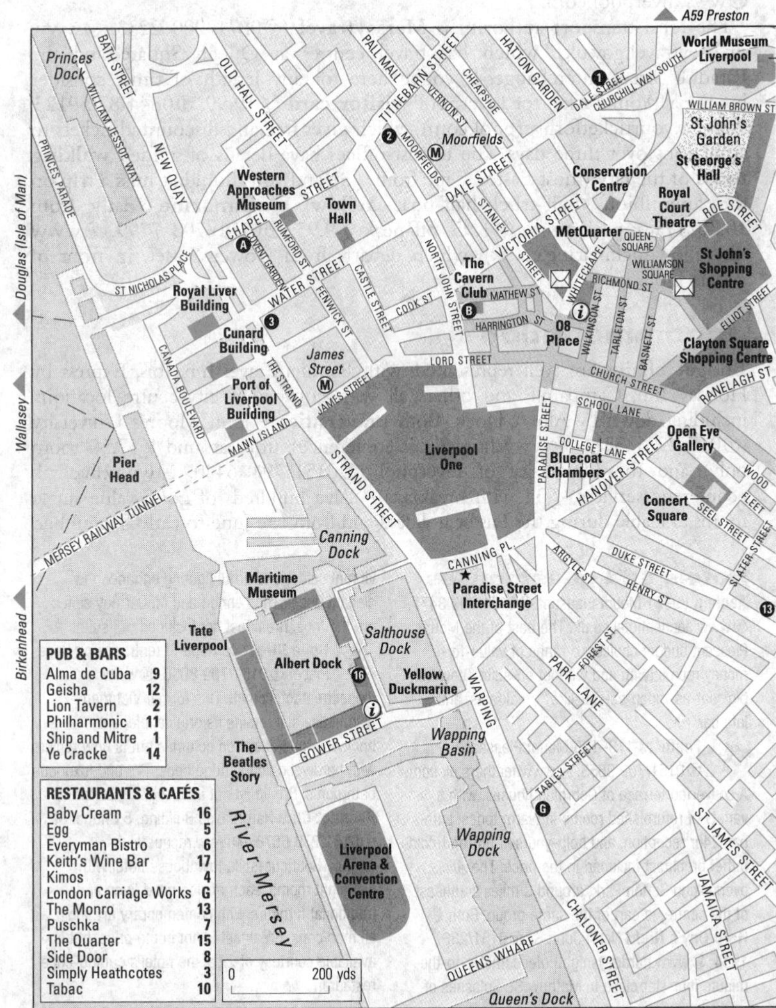

terraces around Rodney and Hope streets. If you're short on time, the two **cathedrals**, **Albert Dock** and the **World Museum Liverpool** are the stand-out highlights, with both the **Walker Art Gallery** and **Tate Liverpool** essential for art fans.

Lime Street and St George's Hall

Emerging from Lime Street Station, you can't miss **St George's Hall**, one of Britain's finest Greek Revival buildings and a testament to the wealth generated from transatlantic trade. Now primarily an exhibition venue, but once Liverpool's premier concert hall and crown court, its vaulted Great Hall features a floor tiled with thirty thousand precious Minton tiles (usually covered over), while the Willis organ is the third largest in Europe. You can take a self-guided

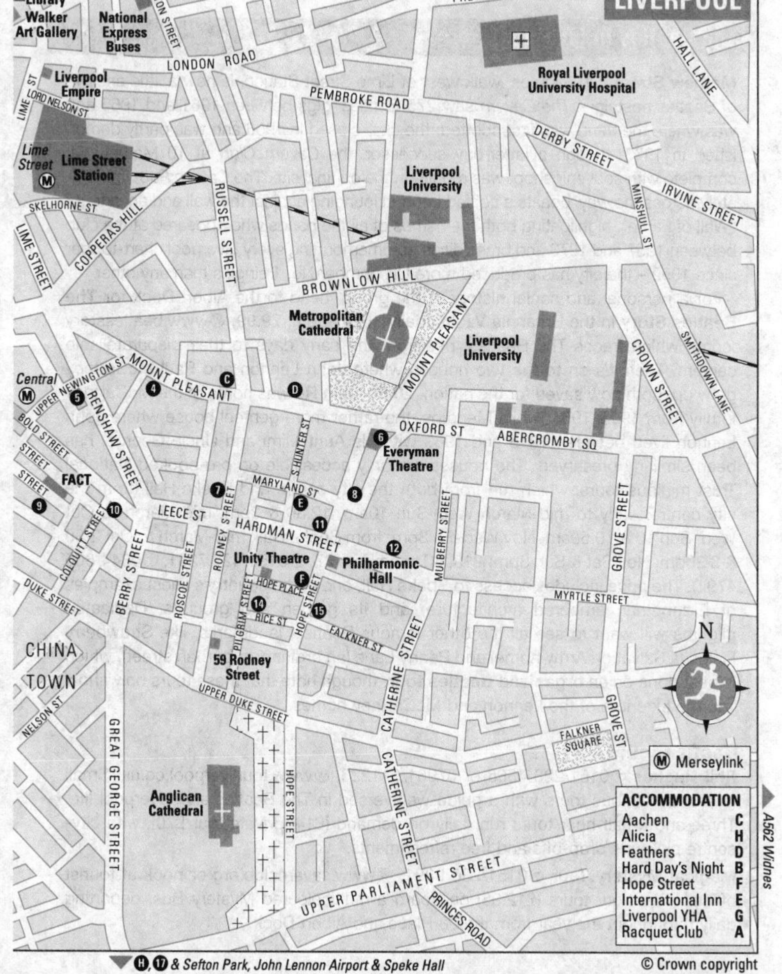

tour (Tues–Sat 10am–5pm, Sun 1–5pm; free) or call (Ⓣ0151/225 6909) for details of the guided tours.

Walker Art Gallery

Liverpool's **Walker Art Gallery** on William Brown Street (daily 10am–5pm; free; Ⓦwww.thewalker.org.uk) houses one of the country's best provincial art collections. The art is up on the first floor, but don't miss the ground-floor Sculpture Gallery, nor the Craft and Design Gallery, which displays changing exhibits from a large applied-art collection – glassware, ceramics, fabrics, precious metals and furniture, largely retrieved from the homes of the city's early industrial businessmen. Liverpool's explosive economic growth in the eighteenth and nineteenth centuries is reflected in much of the Walker's collection, as British painting begins to occupy centre stage – notably works by George Stubbs, England's greatest animal painter (and native Liverpudlian). Impressionists and Post-Impressionists, including Degas,

The Beatles in Liverpool

Mathew Street, ten minutes' walk west of Lime Street Station, is now a little enclave of Beatles nostalgia. *The Cavern* saw 275 Beatles' gigs between 1961 and 1963 and was where the band was first spotted; the club closed in 1966 and was partly demolished in 1973, though a latter-day successor, the *Cavern Club* at 10 Mathew St, complete with souvenir shop, was rebuilt on the original site. The *Cavern Pub*, immediately across the way, boasts a coiffed Lennon lounging against the wall and an exterior "Wall of Fame", highlighting both the names of all the bands who appeared at the club between 1957 and 1973 and brass discs commemorating every Liverpool chart-topper since 1952 – the city has produced more UK number No. 1 singles than any other.

For a personal and social history of the group, head to the Albert Dock for **The Beatles Story** in the Britannia Vaults (daily 10am–6pm; £9.99; Ⓦwww.beatlesstory.com), which traces The Beatles' rise from the early days to their disparate solo careers. Then it's on to the two houses where John Lennon and Paul McCartney grew up, both now saved for the nation. **20 Forthlin Rd** was home of the McCartney family from 1955–1964, while Mendips, the rather more genteel house where John Lennon lived between 1945 and 1963 with his Aunt Mimi and Uncle George, has been similarly preserved. The houses are only accessible on pre-booked National Trust minibus tours, which run from both the city centre and Speke Hall (from the city centre: early to mid-March Wed–Sun 10am, 12.30 & 3pm, mid-March to Oct Wed–Sun 10 & 10.50am, Nov Wed–Fri 3pm; from Speke Hall: mid-March to Oct 2.30 & 3.20pm; Nov Sat & Sun 3pm; £15, NT members £7; Ⓣ0151/427 7231, Ⓣ0844/800 4791). The price includes access to Speke Hall, one of the country's finest examples of Elizabethan timbered architecture, and its garden and grounds. Dedicated pilgrims will want to see all the other famous Beatles' landmarks, like Strawberry Fields (a Salvation Army home) and Penny Lane (an ordinary suburban street), which is best done on an **organized Beatles tour**, though note that these tours only show you the exteriors of the Lennon and McCartney homes.

Beatles tours

Phil Hughes Ⓣ0151/228 4565 or 07961/511223, Ⓦwww.tourliverpool.co.uk. Small (8-seater) minibus tours with a guide well versed in The Beatles and Liverpool life. Three-and-a-half-hour tours run daily on demand (£14; private tour £70), with city-centre pick-ups/drop-offs and free refreshments.

Magical Mystery Tour Ⓣ0151/236 9091, Ⓦwww.cavernclub.org or book at tourist offices. Two-hour tours (£12.95) on board a multicoloured Mystery Bus, departing daily throughout the year from the 08 Place and Albert Dock.

Sickert, Cézanne and Monet, drag the collection into more modern times and tastes, before the final round of galleries of contemporary British art. Paul Nash, Lucian Freud, Ben Nicholson, David Hockney and John Hoyland all have work here, much of it first displayed in the Walker's biennial John Moores Exhibition.

World Museum Liverpool

Further along William Brown Street the **World Museum Liverpool** (daily 10am–5pm; free; Ⓦwww.worldmuseumliverpool.org.uk) is the city's major family attraction. The dramatic six-storey atrium provides access to an eclectic series of themed exhibits of broad appeal – from natural history to ethnographical collections, insects to antiquities, dinosaurs to space rockets. Great sections for children include the Bug House (no explanation required), plus excellent hands-on natural history and archeology discovery centres. The planetarium and theatre have free daily shows, with times posted at the information desk.

The cathedrals

On the hill behind Lime Street, off Mount Pleasant, rises the idiosyncratically shaped Catholic **Metropolitan Cathedral** of Christ the King (daily 8am–5/6pm; donation requested; Ⓦwww.liverpoolmetrocathedral.org.uk), denigratingly known as "Paddy's Wigwam" or the "Mersey Funnel". Built in the wake of the revitalizing Second Vatican Council, it was raised on top of the tentative beginnings of Sir Edwin Lutyens' grandiose project to outdo St Peter's in Rome. Ceremonial steps mark the approach from Mount Pleasant/Hope Street, with a café-bar at the bottom and four huge bells at the top.

At the other end of Hope Street, the Anglican **Liverpool Cathedral** (daily 8am–6pm; donation requested; Ⓦwww.liverpoolcathedral.org.uk) looks much more ancient but was actually completed eleven years later, in 1978, after 74 years in construction. The last of the great British neo-Gothic structures, Sir Giles Gilbert Scott's masterwork claims a smattering of superlatives: Britain's largest and the world's fifth-largest cathedral, the world's tallest Gothic arches and the highest and heaviest bells. On a clear day, a trip up the 330-foot tower (£4.25, £6.75 combined ticket with film and audio-tour) is rewarded by views to the Welsh hills.

The city centre

After years of neglect, Liverpool's city centre is slowly being refashioned, often to quite dramatic effect. Some of the most strident changes have been made in the former warehouse and factory district between Bold Street and Duke Street (an area now known as the **Ropewalks**), where apartments, urban spaces, café-bars and shops have sprouted. **FACT** at 88 Wood St (Ⓦwww.fact.co.uk) – that's Film, Art and Creative Technology – provides a cultural anchor for the neighbourhood with its galleries for art, video and new media exhibitions (Tues–Sun 11am–6pm; free), community projects, cinema screens, café and bar. Nearby School Lane throws up the beautifully proportioned Bluecoat Chambers, originally built in 1717 as an Anglican boarding school for orphans. An integral part of Liverpool's cultural life for years, it has now been enlarged as **The Bluecoat** (Ⓦwww.thebluecoat.org.uk) to incorporate artists' studios and retail units.

Diverting towards Queen Square, one of the city centre's surviving Victorian warehouses, on the corner of Whitechapel and Queen Square, is occupied by the **Conservation Centre** (Mon–Sat 10am–5pm, Sun noon–5pm; free;

Ⓦwww.conservationcentre.org.uk). This is where Liverpool's museums and galleries undertake their restoration work and give visitors a chance to identify fabrics and furniture beetles or learn how to get the rust off a gold disc.

En route to Pier Head, the **Western Approaches Museum** at 1 Rumford St, off Chapel Street (Mon–Thurs & Sat 10.30am–4.30pm; £4.75; Ⓦwww.liverpoolwarmuseum.co.uk) reveals an underground labyrinth of rooms, formerly headquarters for the Battle of the Atlantic during World War II. The massive Operations Room vividly displays all the technology of a 1940s nerve centre – wooden pushers and model boats, chalkboards and ladders.

Pier Head, Mersey Ferry and the Three Graces

Though the tumult of shipping which once fought the current here has gone, the **Pier Head** landing stage remains the embarkation point for the Mersey Ferry (Ⓣ0151/330 1444, Ⓦwww.merseyferries.co.uk) to Woodside (for Birkenhead) and Seacombe (Wallasey). Straightforward ferry shuttles (£2.20 return) operate during the morning and evening rush hours. At other times the boats run circular fifty-minute "river explorer" **cruises** (hourly: Mon–Fri 10am–3pm, Sat & Sun 10am–6pm; £5.10), which you can combine with a visit to the Spaceport space exploration visitor attraction at Seacombe (£8.50, with ferry £11.50; closed Mon; Ⓦwww.spaceport.org.uk).

Dominating the waterfront are the so-called **Three Graces** – namely the Port of Liverpool Building (1907), Cunard Building (1913) and, most prominently, the 322-feet-high Royal Liver Building (1910), topped by the "Liver Birds", a couple of cormorants which have become the symbol of the city. Development of the waterfront area is ongoing – a new Mersey ferry terminal should be operational by the end of 2008, boats will be travelling the extension to the Leeds and Liverpool canal in 2009, and the following year will see opening of the new Museum of Liverpool.

Albert Dock

Albert Dock, five minutes' walk south of Pier Head, was built in 1846 when Liverpool's port was a world leader. It started to decline at the beginning of the twentieth century, as the new deep-draught ships were unable to berth here, and last saw service in 1972. A decade later the site was given a complete refit, emerging as a type of rescued urban heritage that's been copied throughout the country, but rarely as successfully as here.

The **Merseyside Maritime Museum** (all museums and galleries daily 10am–5pm; free; Ⓦwww.liverpoolmuseums.org.uk/maritime) fills one wing of the Dock; allow at least two hours to peruse the various galleries. The basement houses **Seized**, giving the lowdown on smuggling and revenue collection, along with **Emigrants to a New World**, an illuminating display detailing Liverpool's pivotal role as a springboard for over nine million emigrants. Other galleries tell the story of the Battle of the Atlantic and of the three ill-fated liners – the *Titanic*, *Lusitania* and *Empress of Ireland*. Finally, the unmissable **International Slavery Museum** on the third floor manages to be both challenging and chilling, telling both dehumanizing stories of slavery while examining contemporary issues of equality, freedom and racial injustice.

Also on the Dock, **Tate Liverpool** (June–Aug daily 10am–5.50pm; Sept–May Tues–Sun 10am–5.50pm; free, special exhibitions usually £5; Ⓦwww.tate.org.uk/liverpool) is the country's national collection of modern art in the north. Popular retrospectives and an ever-changing display of individual works are its bread and butter, and there's also a full programme of events, talks and tours – the daily tour at noon is free.

Eating, drinking and nightlife

Most **eating** choices are in three distinct areas – at Albert Dock, around Hardman and Hope streets, and along Berry and Nelson streets, heart of Liverpool's Chinatown. Failing those, take a short taxi ride out to Lark Lane in Aigburth, close to Sefton Park, where a dozen eating and drinking spots pack into one short street. The **Heritage Market** at Stanley Dock attracts around 200 stalls, including delicious food (along with retro clothing and antiques) every Sunday. In the Ropewalks area, Fleet Street, Slater Street and Wood Street have seen most development, with the action centred on Concert Square. Victoria Street in the business district is another fast-developing area for bars and nightlife, as is Albert Dock. The evening paper, the *Liverpool Echo* and the monthly *Liverpool.com* (Ⓦ www.liverpool.com) have events listings.

Cafés, bistros and café-bars

Baby Cream Edward Pavilion, Albert Dock. Hedonistic lounge bar that's always fun – a stylish crowd nibbles the "tear-and-share" food and sips cocktails.

Egg 16 Newington St. Up on the third floor, this informal and rather purple café serves excellent vegan and vegetarian food, with good set-meal deals.

Everyman Bistro 5–9 Hope St. Long-standing theatre-basement hang-out with home-made quiche, pies and bakes, pizza and salad-type meals, at around a tenner for two courses. The bar closes at midnight, or 2am on Fri & Sat. Closed Sun.

Keith's Wine Bar 107 Lark Lane Ⓣ 0151/728 7688. An old favourite, as much for its good-value bistro food (pasta, salads, risotto) as its wine selection. Moderate.

The Quarter 7 Falkner St Ⓣ 0151/707 1965. A great lunch place between the two cathedrals, with some seats outside on the Georgian terrace. Serves an Italian bistro menu, including gourmet pizza, but you can just stop by for coffee and cake.

Tabac 126 Bold St. Contemporary café-bar, serving a wide-ranging menu from breakfast onwards.

Restaurants

London Carriage Works 40 Hope St Ⓣ 0151/705 2222. One of Liverpool's finest, a see-and-be-seen restaurant in the city's coolest designer hotel. You'll need a reservation (book well in advance for weekends). Expensive.

The Monro 92–94 Duke St Ⓣ 0151/707 9933. A gastropub makeover for one of the city's oldest hostelries means this is now a place for serious British eating at a reasonable price. Moderate.

Puschka 16 Rodney St Ⓣ 0151/708 8698. Contemporary English dining from a seasonally changing menu – locals like its relaxed atmosphere and there's usually a good vegetarian choice. Closed Mon, and for lunch Tues–Fri. Expensive.

Side Door 29a Hope St Ⓣ 0151/707 7888. The intimate Georgian townhouse restaurant has settled on a winning combination of Mediterranean food and reasonable prices – with a bargain pre-theatre menu of £14.95. Closed Sun. Expensive.

Simply Heathcotes Beetham Plaza, 25 The Strand Ⓣ 0151/236 3536. Lancastrian magic behind a wall of glass – locally sourced ingredients, light lunches, grills, Sun brunch and other delights, in many people's favourite Liverpool restaurant. Expensive.

Pubs and bars

Alma de Cuba St Peter's Church, Seel St. Far more candles than when it was a church, but the mirrored altar is still the focus of this bar's rich and dark Cuban-themed interior. The mezzanine restaurant has even more dripping candles.

Geisha 7 Myrtle St. Luxurious quasi-industrial venue on an Eastern theme, with huge curving bar. *Dim sum*, sushi and noodles downstairs and balcony restaurant.

Lion Tavern 67 Moorfields. Real ale in superbly restored Victorian surroundings, from the tiles to the stained-glass rotunda. Also excellent cheese and pâté lunches (Mon–Fri).

Philharmonic 36 Hope St. Liverpool's finest traditional watering-hole where the main attractions – the beer aside – are the mosaic floors, tiling, gilded wrought-iron gates and the marble decor in the gents.

Ship and Mitre 133 Dale St. For the biggest real ale choice in Liverpool – twelve guest beers, plus ciders and imported lagers – visit this renowned Art Deco free house.

Ye Cracke 13 Rice St. Crusty backstreet pub off Hope St, much loved by the young Lennon, and with a great jukebox, and cheap-as-chips food (daytime only).

Clubs and live music

Barfly 90 Seel St ⓣ0870/907 0999, ⓦwww.barflyclub.com. Great indie/rock gigs and a wide variety of club nights – Chibuku and Circus are the big nights out.

Carling Academy 11–13 Hotham St ⓣ0151/707 3200, ⓦwww.liverpool-academy.co.uk. A good roster of contemporary, indie and rock gigs.

Cavern Club 10 Mathew St ⓣ0151/236 1965, ⓦwww.cavernclub.org. The self-styled "most famous club in the world" has live bands Wed–Sun.

Entertainment

The **Royal Liverpool Philharmonic Orchestra**, ranked with Manchester's Hallé as the northwest's best, dominates the city's classical music scene. Popular annual **festivals** include Beatles Week (last week of August) and the Mathew Street Festival (Aug bank hol; ⓦwww.mathewstreetfestival.co.uk), with half a million visitors dancing to hundreds of local, national and tribute bands.

Everyman Theatre and Playhouse 5–9 Hope St ⓣ0151/709 4776, ⓦwww.everymanplayhouse.com. A launchpad of local talent, presenting everything from Shakespeare to Jarman, plus concerts, exhibitions, dance and music.

Liverpool Empire Lime St ⓣ0870/606 3536, ⓦwww.liverpool-empire.co.uk. The city's largest theatre, a venue for touring West End shows, and large-scale opera and ballet productions – Welsh National Opera and English National Ballet both perform regularly.

Philharmonic Hall Hope St ⓣ0151/709 3789, ⓦwww.liverpoolphil.com. Home of the Royal Liverpool Philharmonic Orchestra, and with a full programme of other concerts. Shows classic films once a month.

Picturehouse at FACT Wood St ⓣ0871/704 2063, ⓦwww.picturehouses.co.uk. The city's only independent cinema screens, for new films, re-runs and festivals.

Royal Court Theatre Roe St ⓣ0870/787 1866, ⓦwww.royalcourtliverpool.co.uk. Art Deco theatre and concert hall, which sees regular plays, music and comedy acts.

▲ Nightlife in Liverpool

This sporting life

Liverpool's most popular recreational activity, bar none, is **football**. The team plays at Anfield (information ⓣ0844/844 0844, ⓦwww.liverpoolfc.tv) in front of some of the nation's most loyal supporters. You're unlikely to get a ticket for a game, but there are popular daily tours (not on match days) around the well-stocked museum, trophy room and dressing rooms (museum and tour £10, museum only £5; booking essential ⓣ0151/260 6677). Everton, the city's less glamorous side, command equally intense devotion at Goodison Park (information line ⓣ0870/442 1878; tours Mon, Wed, Fri & Sun ⓣ0151/330 2212; £8.50; ⓦwww.evertonfc.com).

The first Saturday in April is **Grand National Day** at Aintree – the "World's Greatest Steeplechase". The race is the culmination of a meeting that starts on the previous Thursday, with tickets starting from £17, £35 on Saturday. Catch the Merseyrail to Aintree, and book well ahead on ⓣ0151/522 2929. The "Grand National Experience" (May–Oct Mon–Fri; £7; individuals may join booked group tours, call ⓣ0151/523 2600, ⓦwww.aintree.co.uk) shows you the stables, weighing room and museum, before letting you ride the National on a race simulator.

Listings

Airport ⓣ0870/129 8484, ⓦwww.liverpooljohnlennonairport.com.
Car rental Avis ⓣ0870/608 6311; Europcar ⓣ0151/486 7111; Hertz ⓣ0151/486 7444.
Ferries Isle of Man Steam Packet Company for ferries/Sea Cats to Isle of Man ⓣ0871/222 1333, ⓦwww.steam-packet.com; Mersey Ferries ⓣ0151/330 1444, ⓦwww.merseyferries.co.uk; Norfolkline ⓣ0870/600 4321, ⓦwww.norfolkline-ferries.co.uk.
Hospital Royal Liverpool University Hospital, Prescot St ⓣ0151/706 2000; NHS Walk-in Centre 52 Great Charlotte Row ⓣ0151/285 3535.
Pharmacy Boots, Clayton Square Shopping Centre ⓣ0151/709 4711; Moss Pharmacy, 68–70 London Rd ⓣ0151/709 5271 (daily until 11pm).
Police Canning Place ⓣ0151/709 6010.
Post office City-centre office at St John's Precinct.

Blackpool

Shamelessly brash **BLACKPOOL** is the archetypal British seaside resort, its "Golden Mile" of piers, fortune-tellers, amusement arcades, tram and donkey rides, fish-and-chip shops, candyfloss stalls, fun pubs and bingo halls making no concessions to anything but lowbrow fun-seeking of the finest kind. It was the coming of the railway in 1846 that made Blackpool what it is today: Blackpool's own "Eiffel Tower" on the seafront and other refined diversions were built to cater to the tastes of the first influx of visitors, but it was the Central Pier's "open-air dancing for the working classes" that heralded the crucial change of accent. Suddenly Blackpool was favoured destination for the "Wakes Weeks", when whole Lancashire mill towns descended for their annual holiday.

Where other British holiday resorts have suffered from the rivalry of cheap foreign packages, Blackpool has gone from strength to strength. Underneath the populist veneer there's a sophisticated marketing approach, which balances ever more elaborate rides and attractions with well-grounded traditional entertainment. And when other resorts begin to close up for the winter, Blackpool's main season is just beginning, as over half a million light bulbs are used to create the **Illuminations** which decorate the promenade from the beginning of September to early November. Lately, Blackpool has been looking to extend its attractions further, with plans underway to transform the seafront promenade into a "people's playground" and bestow new entertainment complexes and leisure parks upon the town.

Arrival, information and accommodation

Blackpool's main **train station** is Blackpool North (direct trains from Manchester and Preston), with the **bus station** just a few steps away down Talbot Road; alternatively, trains also run hourly from Preston direct to Blackpool Pleasure Beach (on the Blackpool South Line). Blackpool's airport (Ⓦ www.blackpoolinternational.com) – which handles regular flights to over 25 European destinations – lies two miles south of the centre; there are buses from the bus station or it's a £5 taxi ride. The main tourist office is at 1 Clifton St (Mon–Sat 9am–5pm; Ⓣ01253/478222, Ⓦwww.visitblackpool.com), on the corner of Talbot Road, and sells discounted admission tickets for all major Blackpool attractions (except the Pleasure Beach), as well as Travel Cards (1/3/5/7-day, £5.75/14/20/22) for use on local buses and trams.

Guesthouses and hotels

Bed-and-breakfast prices are generally low (from £20 per person, even less on a room-only basis or out of season), but rise at weekends and during the Illuminations. To avoid the noisy crowds in peak season, make for the peace and quiet (an unusual request in Blackpool, it has to be said) along the North Shore, beyond North Pier (the grid west of Warbreck Hill Road has hundreds of options).

The Big Blue Ocean Blvd, Blackpool Pleasure Beach Ⓣ0845/367 3333, Ⓦwww.bigbluehotel.com. Spacious family rooms with games consoles and separate children's area, plus boutique-style, dark-wood executive rooms. There's a contemporary bar and brasserie, parking and a gym. It's next to the Pleasure Beach (and its train station), and most rooms look out on the rides. Parking. ❺

The Imperial North Promenade Ⓣ01253/623971, Ⓦwww.paramount-hotels.co.uk. The politicians' conference favourite, a four-star hotel with sea-facing rooms, pool and gym, the famous oak-panelled *No. 10 Bar*, *Palm Court restaurant*, and parking. Special online room-only deals from £69. ❼

Number One 1 St Luke's Rd Ⓣ01253/343901, Ⓦwww.numberoneblackpool.com. There's no other B&B quite like it – an extraordinarily lavish boutique experience hosted by the ultra-amiable Mark and Claire. There are just three extravagantly appointed rooms here, though very nearby is their larger seafront outfit, *Number One South Beach* (4 Harrowside West Ⓣ01253/343900, Ⓦwww.numberonesouthbeach.co.uk), whose 14 rooms reflect the new Blackpool – contemporary style, low carbon footprint, Modern British restaurant and bar. There's parking at both, and either is handy for the Pleasure Beach. ❼, South Beach ❽

Raffles 73–77 Hornby Rd Ⓣ01253/294713, Ⓦwww.raffleshotelblackpool.co.uk. Nice place back from Central Pier and away from the bustle, with well-kept rooms, bar, and traditional tearooms attached. Winter rates are a good deal. ❹

Ruskin Albert Rd Ⓣ01253/624063, Ⓦwww.ruskinhotel.com. At the prom end of Albert Rd, the *Ruskin* exudes repro-Victorian style and offers smart rooms with decent bathrooms. Bar and brasserie, and parking available. ❺

The Town

With seven miles of beach – the tide ebb is half a mile, leaving plenty of sand at low tide – and accompanying promenade, you'll want to jump on and off the electric trams if you plan to get up and down much between the piers. Most of the town-centre shops, bars and cafés lie between Central and North piers.

The major draw in town is **Blackpool Pleasure Beach** on the South Promenade (March–Oct daily from 11am though times vary, check website for details; Ⓦwww.blackpoolpleasurebeach.com), just south of South Pier. Entrance to the amusement park is free, but you'll have to fork out for the superb array of "white knuckle" rides including the "Big One", the world's fastest roller coaster (85mph), and the outrageous suspended looping roller coaster that is "Infusion". After these, the wonderful array of antique wooden roller coasters ("woodies" to aficionados) seems like kids' stuff, but each is unique – the original "Big Dipper" was invented at Blackpool in 1923 and still thrills. Recuperate in the park's champagne and oyster bar, which adds a bit of class to the otherwise relentless barrage of fairground noise, shrieking, music and fast food. There are charges for individual rides but best value is to buy an unlimited-ride wristband (£15–28 depending on the season, cheaper if booked online).

Pleasure Beach aside, most of the big-ticket attractions are found near the Central Pier, with its 108-feet-high revolving Big Wheel. You'll need a bulging wallet if you plan to do the lot, from **Sea-Life Centre** (Ⓦ www.sealife.co.uk) to **Doctor Who Museum** (Ⓦ www.doctowhoexhibitions.com), but they are all undeniably slick and entertaining, and open daily for most of the year. Between Central and North piers stands the 518-foot **Blackpool Tower** (June–Oct daily 10am–11pm; Nov–May daily 10am–6pm; £15.95, £9.95 after 7pm; Ⓦ www.theblackpooltower.co.uk), erected in 1894 when it was thought that the northwest really ought not to be outdone by Paris. Paying the hefty entrance fee is the only way to ride up to the top for the stunning view and an unnerving walk on the see-through glass floor. The all-day ticket covers all the other tower attractions, including the gilt Edwardian ballroom, with its Wurlitzer organ tea dances and big band evenings, plus aquarium, children's entertainers, indoor adventure playground, cafés and amusements. From the very early days, there's also been a Moorish-inspired **circus** (2hr shows included in the entry ticket; two daily performances) between the tower's legs.

Eating, nightlife and entertainment

Eating out revolves around the typical British seaside fare of fish and chips, available all over town. You'll have no trouble finding cheap roasts, pizzas, Chinese or Indian food, but might struggle if you're seeking a bit more sophistication. There's a plethora of theme bars, Irish to Australian, and any number of places for karaoke or **dancing** – local opinion favours *The Syndicate*, 120–140 Church St (Ⓦ www.thesyndicate.com), the UK's biggest club, which features star DJs throughout the year. *Funny Girls*, a transvestite-run bar at 5 Dickson

Blackpool – behind the scenes

Down the prom and up Victoria Street leads directly to the **Winter Gardens** (Coronation Street), which opened to fanfares in 1878. Scene of party political conferences over the decades, the Gardens house a motley set of cafés, bars and amusements these days, but don't miss seeing the extraordinary **Spanish Hall Suite** (in the form of a carved galleon) and the Opera House honours board – Lily Langtry, George Formby and Vera Lynn are all present. From in front of the Opera House, follow Abingdon Street to Queen Street and the porticoed Central Library, next to which the **Grundy Art Gallery** (Mon–Sat 10am–5pm; free) might tempt you in to see its Victorian oils and watercolours, contemporary art and special exhibitions. Walking down Queen Street to the promenade you reach **North Pier**, the first pier to be opened (1863) on the Blackpool seafront and now a listed building. At this point, head northbound on the tram, and get off at the **Imperial Hotel**, whose wood-panelled No. 10 Bar is covered with photographs and mementoes of every British prime minister since Lloyd George.

Rd, off Talbot Road (Ⓣ0870/350 2665, Ⓦwww.funnygirlsshowbar.co.uk), has nightly shows that attract long (gay and straight) queues. Otherwise, **entertainment** is based very heavily on family shows, musicals, veteran TV comedians, magicians, ice shows, tribute bands, crooners and stage spectaculars put on at a variety of end-of-pier and Pleasure Beach (Ⓦwww.blackpoolpleasurebeach.com) theatres, or at historic venues such as the Grand Theatre (Ⓣ01253/290190, Ⓦwww.blackpoolgrand.co.uk) and Opera House (Ⓣ0870/380111, Ⓦwww.blackpoollive.com), both on Church Street.

Restaurants

Harry Ramsden's 60–63 The Promenade Ⓣ01253/294386. The celebrated Yorkshire chippie chain has the town's pre-eminent (and priciest) fish and chips. Moderate.

Kwizeen 49 King St Ⓣ01253/290045. Best restaurant in town is this friendly, contemporary bistro with a seasonally changing menu that places a real emphasis on locally sourced produce, from Blackpool tomatoes and Lancashire cheese to Fylde farm ostriches and Goosnargh duck. Mains are £13, though there's a bargain two-course weekday lunch. Closed Sat lunch & Sun, 2 weeks Feb &1 week Aug. Expensive.

Septembers 17 Queen St Ⓣ01253/299200. Sleek champagne bar upstairs, dining room below, for tapas and Spanish-Mediterranean mains, paella to seabass. Closed Mon & Tues, Wed lunch & Sun dinner. Expensive.

White Tower Ocean Blvd, Blackpool Pleasure Beach Ⓣ01253/336365. Blackpool's posh night out and the closest the town gets to Vegas – a lounge-style restaurant with prom views (great for the Illuminations), snappy service and a contemporary bistro-style menu. Tues–Sat dinner only, plus Sun lunch. Expensive.

Lancaster and around

LANCASTER, Lancashire's county town, dates back at least as long ago as the Roman occupation, though only scant remains survive from that period. A Saxon church was later built within the ruined Roman walls as Lancaster became a strategic trading centre, and by medieval times ships were using the River Lune and the coastal routes to Cumbria. A castle on the heights above the river defended the town from attack and provided a focus for the dispensing of regional justice. Lancaster became an important port on the slave trade triangle, and it's the legacy of predominantly Georgian buildings from that time that gives the town its character. Many people choose to spend a night here on the way to the Lakes or Dales to the north; and it's an easy side-trip the few miles west to the resort of Morecambe and to neighbouring Heysham village, with its ancient churches.

The site of **Lancaster Castle** (daily: tours every 30min 10.30am–4pm; £5; Ⓦwww.lancastercastle.com) has been the city's focal point since Roman times. Currently, about a quarter of the battlemented building can be visited on an entertaining hour-long tour, though court sittings sometimes affect the schedules. A two-minute walk down the steps between the castle and the neighbouring **Priory Church of St Mary** brings you to the seventeenth-century **Judges' Lodgings** (Easter–June & Oct Mon–Fri 1–4pm, Sat & Sun noon–4pm; July–Sept Mon–Fri 10am–4pm, Sat & Sun noon–4pm; £3), once used by visiting magistrates. The top floor is given over to a Museum of Childhood, with memory-jogging displays of toys and games, and a period (1900) schoolroom.

Down on the banks of the River Lune – which lent Lancaster its name – one of the eighteenth-century quayside warehouses is taken up by part of the **Maritime Museum** (daily 11am/12.30pm–4/5pm; £3). The museum's ample coverage of life on the sea and inland waterways of Lancashire is complemented

On your bike

Lancaster promotes itself as a **cycling centre**, and miles of canal towpaths, old railway tracks and riverside paths provide excellent traffic-free routes around the Lune estuary, Lancaster Canal and Ribble Valley. Typical is the easy riverside path to the Crook O'Lune beauty spot, where you can reward yourself with a bacon buttie and an Eccles cake at *Woodies*' famous snack bar. Other good routes are down the **Lune estuary** or along the canal to **Carnforth**, all detailed on a useful free map available at the tourist office – or check out ⓦwww.citycoastcountryside.co.uk.

by the City Museum on Market Square back in town (Mon–Sat 10am–5pm; free), which explores the city's history from Neolithic to Georgian times.

For a panorama of the town, Morecambe Bay and the Cumbrian fells, take a bus from the bus station (or a steep 25-minute walk up Moor Lane) to **Williamson Park** (daily 10am–4/5pm; free; ⓦwww.williamsonpark.com), Lancaster's highest point. Funded by local statesman and lino magnate Lord Ashton, the park's centrepiece is the 220-foot-high Ashton Memorial, a Baroque folly raised by his son in memory of his second wife.

Another local trip is out to the seaside at **Morecambe**, five miles to the west – there's a cycle path from Lancaster, while regular buses and trains also make the ten-minute trip. The sweep of the bay is the major attraction, with the Lake District fells visible beyond, while the **Stone Jetty** features bird sculptures, games and motifs – recognizing Morecambe Bay as Britain's most important wintering site for wildfowl and wading birds. A little way along the prom stands the statue of one of Britain's most treasured comedians – Eric Bartholomew, who took the stage name Eric Morecambe when he met his comedy partner, Ernie Wise. Also on the prom, the notable Art Deco *Midland Hotel* (ⓦwww.midlandhotelmorecambe.co.uk) – a crumbling ruin for many years – is due to re-open in 2008 after a stylish refit. Three miles to the southwest – you can walk along the promenade from Morecambe – the shoreside **Heysham Village** is centred on a group of charming seventeenth-century cottages and barns. Proudest relic is the well-preserved Viking hog's-back tombstone in Saxon **St Peter's Church**, set in a romantic churchyard below the headland.

Practicalities

From either the **train station** on Meeting House Lane, or the **bus station** on Cable Street, it's a five-minute walk to the tourist office at 29 Castle Hill (Mon–Sat 10am–4/5pm; ⓣ01524/32878, ⓦwww.citycoastcountryside.co.uk). For **canal cruises**, including the scheduled waterbus service to Carnforth, contact Lancaster Canal Packet Boats (ⓣ01524/389410, ⓦwww.budgietransport.co.uk). The main cultural destination is **Dukes** on Moor Lane (ⓣ0845/344 0642, ⓦwww.dukes-lancaster.org), the city's arts centre, with cinema and theatre (including open-air performances in Williamson Park in summer). Five hundred metres up the hill from here, The **Gregson**, 33 Moorgate (ⓣ01524/849959, ⓦwww.gregson.co.uk), is an enterprising arts and community centre with a good café and bar.

Accommodation

Royal King's Arms 75 Market St ⓣ01524/32451, ⓦwww.oxfordhotelsandinns.com. Fifty pretty rooms with smart bathrooms, plus a bar and brasserie. Ask for a castle view. ⑥

Shakespeare 96 St Leonard's Gate ⓣ01524/841041, ⓔtheshakespearelancaster@talktalk.net. Hard-working hosts maintain seven cosy en-suite rooms (including two singles) in this popular townhouse hotel on a central street near several long-stay car parks. No credit cards. ❹

Sun 63 Church St ⓣ01524/66006, ⓦwww.thesunhotelandbar.co.uk. The city centre's only four-star hotel has eight very handsome rooms (some with king-sized beds, all with fine bathrooms) above a contemporary bar fashioned from a 300-year-old building. Breakfast and meals available in the bar. ❹, superior rooms ❺

Cafés, restaurants and pubs

The Borough 3 Dalton Square ⓣ01524/64170. Great for informal dining, this roomy gastro-pub – in a refurbished 1824 building – has a rigorously sourced local and organic menu. Tapas-style platters offer smoked fish, Lancashire cheese and the like, while mains range from ostrich to salmon. Moderate.

Pizza Margherita 2 Moor Lane ⓣ01524/36333. Long-standing pizza place in an old warehouse conversion, with sixteen choices on the menu, plus a few pastas and some salad-type starters. Inexpensive.

Whale Tail 78a Penny St ⓣ01524/845133. Tucked up a yard on the first floor, this cheery veggie and wholefood café serves good breakfasts, quiche, moussaka and baked potatoes. There's garden seating outside, while dinner (Thurs–Sun night, mains around £9) is more sophisticated. Closes 3pm. Inexpensive.

Ye Olde John O'Gaunt 53 Market St, near the City Museum. Terrific city-centre local that's serious about its drinks, whether real ale or the range of whiskies and vodkas. There's also live jazz and R&B, plus a small beer garden.

The Isle of Man

The **Isle of Man**, almost equidistant from Ireland, England, Wales and Scotland, is one of the most beautiful spots in Britain, a mountainous, cliff-fringed island just thirty-three miles by thirteen. There's peace and quiet in abundance, walks around the unspoilt hundred-mile coastline, rural villages and steam trains straight out of a 1950s picture-book – a yesteryear ensemble if ever there was one.

Many true Manx inhabitants, who comprise a shade under fifty percent of its 80,000 population, insist that the Isle of Man is not part of England, nor even of the UK. Indeed, although a Crown dependency, the island has its own government, **Tynwald**, arguably the world's oldest democratic parliament, which has run continuously since 979 AD. To further complicate matters, the island maintains a unique associate status in the EU, ands also has its own sterling currency (worth the same as the mainland currency), its own laws, an independent postal service, and a Gaelic-based language which is taught in schools and seen on dual-language road signs.

Tourism began to flourish during the late-Victorian and Edwardian eras, but in recent times the real money-spinner has been the offshore finance industry, exploiting the island's low income tax and absence of capital gains tax and death duties. The Isle of Man is also playing a major role in the development of e-banking and e-commerce, while low taxes have provided incentives for the filming of an increasing number of movies. All roads lead to the capital, **Douglas**, the only town of any size on the island. From the summit of **Snaefell**, the island's highest peak, you get an idea of the range of Manx scenery that film directors love, the finest parts of which are to be found in the seventeen officially designated National Glens, most of them linked by the 100-mile **Raad Ny Foillan** (Road of the Gull) coastal footpath, which passes several of the island's numerous hill forts, Viking ship burials and Celtic crosses. Scenery aside, the island's main tourist draw is the **TT (Tourist Trophy) motorcycle races** (held in the two weeks around the late-May bank hol), a frenzy of speed and burning rubber that's shattered the island's peace annually since 1907.

Getting to the island

Most visitors arrive at Douglas on **ferries** or the quicker fastcraft (Sea Cats), both run by the Isle of Man Steam Packet Company (Ⓣ0871/222 1333, Ⓦwww.steam-packet.com), from either Heysham or Liverpool. Heysham (ferry 3hr 30min) has the most frequent service, with two or three sailings a day throughout the year. Liverpool manages one or two fastcraft services a day (2hr 30min) down to one daily at weekends in December. Fares start at £15 one-way for foot passengers, £110 return for drivers.

An increasing number of airlines offer **flights** to the island from around twenty British and Irish regional airports, with regular prices starting from £29 one-way. Services are with A2B (Belfast, Blackpool; Ⓦwww.a2bairways.com); Aer Arran (Dublin; Ⓦwww.aerarran.com); Flybe (Birmingham, London Gatwick, Manchester, Southampton; Ⓦwww.flybe.com); Eastern Airways (Newcastle, Bristol, Birmingham; Ⓦwww.easternairways.com); EuroManx (Belfast City, London City, Manchester, Liverpool; Ⓦwww.euromanx.com); Loganair (Glasgow, Edinburgh; Ⓦwww.loganair.co.uk); and Manx2 (Blackpool, Belfast City, Belfast International, Leeds Bradford, Gloucester M5; Ⓦwww.manx2.com).

Douglas

A mere market town as late as 1850, **DOUGLAS** was a product of Victorian mass tourism and displays many similarities to Blackpool, just across the water. The seafront vista has changed little since Victorian times, and is still trodden by heavy-footed carthorses pulling trams (May–Sept, from 9am; £2 return). On Harris Promenade the opulent **Gaiety Theatre** sports a lush interior that can be seen on fascinating hour-and-a-half-long tours (Sat 10.30am April–Sept only; £6.50; Ⓣ01624/694555). Further up Harris Promenade, approaching Broadway, the spruced-up **Villa Marina gardens** display more Victorian elegance, with their colonnade walk, lawns and bandstand. The main sight, however, is the **Manx Museum**, on the corner of Kingswood Grove and Crellin's Hill (Mon–Sat 10am–5pm; free), which makes a good start for anyone wanting to get to grips with Manx culture and heritage before setting off around the island. Finally, out on **Douglas Head** – the point looming above the southern bay – the town's Victorian camera obscura has been restored for visits (Easter week, plus May–Sept Sat 1–4pm, Sun & bank hols 11am–4pm, weather permitting; £2; Ⓣ01624/686766).

Practicalities

Ronaldsway Airport is ten miles south of Douglas, close to Castletown. Buses connect the airport with Douglas, while a taxi costs around £20. Ferries and Sea Cats dock by the Sea Terminal at the southern end of the Douglas waterfront. Fifty yards beyond the forecourt taxi rank, the Lord Street **bus terminal** is the hub of the island's dozen or so bus routes. North Quay runs 300 yards west from the bus terminal alongside the river and fishing port to Douglas Station, the terminus of the 15-mile **Steam Railway** (April–Oct, regular daily services, 10.15am–4.15pm; £9 return to Port Erin), which connects Douglas to Castletown, Port St Mary and Port Erin. The seafront (progressively Loch, Central and Queen's promenades) runs two miles north to Derby Castle Station for the **Manx Electric Railway** (April–Oct daily 9.40am–4.40pm; some later departures in summer; £8 return to Ramsey), which runs for 17 miles from Douglas to Ramsey via Laxey. You can take the horse-drawn tram along the promenade or bus #24, #24a, #26 or #26a from North Quay.

The **Welcome Centre** in the Sea Terminal building (Mon–Sat 8am–6pm, Sun 9am–2pm; Ⓣ01624/686766 or 01624/662525) has island-wide information and sells the "Island Explorer" ticket, giving one (£12), three (£24), five (£35) or seven (£40) days' unlimited travel on all **public transport** (ⓦwww.iombusandrail.info) on the island. The main websites for information are ⓦwww.gov.im and ⓦwww.visitisleofman.com, while the twelve heritage sites and museums are run under the umbrella of Manx National Heritage (ⓦwww.gov.im/mnh), whose 4 Site Ticket (£11, available from any attraction) will save you some money.

Accommodation

Admiral House Loch Promenade ⓣ01624/629551, ⓦwww.admiralhouse.com. At the ferry terminal end of the prom, this retreat features rooms in bold colours and equipped with elegant bathrooms. The town's most expensive restaurant, *Ciapelli's* (closed Sun) is on the ground floor. 7

Birchfield House York Rd ⓣ01624/673000, ⓦwww.birchfieldhouse.com. The most distinctive of Douglas' guesthouses offers sunny spacious rooms loaded with antiques, all creature comforts, and luxurious bathrooms. 8

Dreem Ard Ballanard Rd, 2 miles west of the centre ⓣ01624/621491. Tranquil, out-of-town B&B with three en-suite rooms, including a family room and large garden suite with its own dressing room and sitting area. No credit cards. 3 suite 4

Regency Queen's Promenade ⓣ01624/680680, ⓦwww.regency.iom-1.net. A contemporary face-lift has retained the decorative oak panelling in the public rooms while kitting out guest quarters in style. Similar rooms also available in the associated *Hotel Penta* further down the prom (book through the *Regency*), plus two-room suites and apartments. 6, suites/apartments 7

Sefton Harris Promenade ⓣ01624/645500, ⓦwww.seftonhotel.co.im. Next to the Gaiety Theatre, this four-star has sleek, spacious rooms offering a sea view or a balcony over the impressive internal water garden. Facilities include pool, gym, Internet access, free bikes, bar and restaurant. 7

Welbeck Mona Drive, off Central Promenade ⓣ01624/675663, ⓦwww.welbeckhotel.com. Mid-sized family-run hotel 100yd up the hill off the seafront. 5, deluxe rooms/apartments 6

Cafés and restaurants

Alpine Café 5 Regent St. This bright and breezy chalet-style café serves a good selection of breakfasts, sandwiches, cakes and daily specials.

Café Tanroagan 9 Ridgeway St ⓣ07624/472411. The best fish and seafood on the island, in a relaxed, contemporary restaurant. Visiting film crews and actors all make a beeline here, for fish (straight off the boat) either given an assured Mediterranean twist or served simply. Dinner reservations essential. Closed Sun. Expensive.

C'est La Vie 28 Victoria St. Good-looking café-bar with dishes ranging from bangers and mash to spicy Indonesian noodles. A busy lunchtime spot, though they serve food until 8.45pm. Closed Sun.

Greens Douglas Station, North Quay. Plant-filled vegetarian café in the ticket office serving drinks and snacks until 5pm, with hot lunches and a veggie buffet noon–2.30pm. Closed Sun.

Paparazzi 26 Loch Promenade ⓣ01624/673222. Locals like this large pizzeria-trattoria with Sicilian beer and a few more unusual specialities alongside the traditional pizzas, pastas and Italian dishes. Moderate.

Spill the Beans 1 Market Hill. Douglas's best coffee house, with a choice of brews plus muffins, croissants, cakes and pastries. Closes at 5pm, and all Sun.

Pubs and bars

Bar George Hill St. A fashionable haunt housed in a converted Sunday School, opposite St George's church. Closed Sun.

Queen's Hotel Queen's Promenade. The best place for an alfresco drink is this old seafront pub at the top end of the promenade, where the picnic tables look out over the sweeping bay.

Rovers Return 11 Church St. Cosy old local where you can try the local Manx beers, including "Old Bushy Tail".

Listings

Airport Ronaldsway Airport, flight enquiries ⓣ01624/821600, ⓦwww.iom-airport.com.

Bicycle rental Eurocycles, 8a Victoria Rd, off Broadway ⓣ01624/624909. Closed Sun.

Car rental Most outfits have offices at the airport or can deliver cars to the Sea Terminal. Contact: Athol ⓣ01624/822481, ⓦwww.athol.co.im; Mylchreests ⓣ01624/823533, ⓦwww.mylchreests.com; or Ocean Ford ⓣ01624/820830, ⓦwww.oceanford.com.

Cruises Seasonal cruises, from Villier steps by the Sea Terminal, Douglas promenade, to Port Soderick or Laxey on the MV *Karina*. Departures daily April–Sept, weather permitting; call ☎01624/861724 or 07624/493592.
Hospital Noble's Hospital, Strang ☎01624/650000.
Pharmacies Boots, 14 Strand St ☎01624/616120; John Atkinson, 2 Granville St ☎01624/673402.
Police Douglas Police Station, Glencrutchery Rd ☎01624/631212.
Post office Main post office is at 6 Regent St ☎01624/686141.
Telephones Using a UK-registered mobile phone in the Isle of Man incurs international call rates for making and receiving calls. Some pay-as-you-go phones may not permit calls from the Isle of Man either.

Laxey

Filling a narrow valley, the straggling village of **LAXEY**, seven miles north of Douglas, spills down from its train station to a small harbour and long, pebbly beach, squeezed between two bulky headlands. The Manx Electric Railway from Douglas drops you at the station used by the Snaefell Mountain Railway (see below). Passengers disembark and then head inland and uphill to Laxey's pride, the **"Lady Isabella" Great Laxey Wheel** (April–Oct daily 10am–5pm; £3.30), smartly painted in red and white. With a diameter of over 72ft it's said to be the largest working water wheel in the world. Otherwise Laxey is at its best down in Old Laxey, around the harbour, half a mile below the station, where large car parks attest to the popularity of the beach and river.

Snaefell

Every thirty minutes, the tramcars of the **Snaefell Mountain Railway** (May–Oct daily 10.15am–3.45pm; £7.80 return) begin their 30min wind from Laxey through increasingly denuded moorland to the island's highest point, the top of **Snaefell** (2036ft) – the Vikings' "Snow Mountain" – from where you can see England, Wales, Scotland and Ireland on a clear day. At the summit, most people are content to pop into the café and bar and then soak up the views for the few minutes until the return journey. But with a decent map and a clear day, you could walk back instead, following trails down the mountain to Laxey (the easiest and most direct route), Sulby Glen or the Peel–Ramsey road.

Maughold

The Manx Electric Railway trains stop within a mile and a half of **MAUGHOLD**, seven miles northeast of Laxey, a tiny hamlet just inland from the cliff-side lighthouse at Maughold Head. It's an isolated spot which only adds to the attraction of Maughold's parish church, in whose grounds is maintained an outstanding collection of early Christian and Norse carved crosses – 44 pieces, dating from the sixth to the thirteenth century, and ranging from fragments of runic carving to a six-foot-high rectangular slab. Bus #16 comes direct to Maughold from Ramsey (not Sun).

St John's

The trans-island A1 (and hourly bus #5 or #6 from Douglas) follows a deep twelve-mile-long furrow between the northern and southern ranges from Douglas to Peel. A hill at the crossroads settlement of **ST JOHN'S**, nine miles along it, is the original site of **Tynwald**, the ancient Manx government, which derives its name from the Norse Thing Völlr, meaning "Assembly Field". Nowadays the word refers to the Douglas-based House of Keys and Legislative Council, but acts passed in the capital only become law once they have been

▲ Mountain biking on the Isle of Man

proclaimed here on July 5 (ancient Midsummer's Day) in an annual open-air parliament that also hears the grievances of the islanders. Until the nineteenth century the local people arrived with their livestock and stayed a week or more – in true Viking fashion – to thrash out local issues, play sports, make marriages and hold a fair. Now **Tynwald Day** begins with a service in the chapel, followed by a procession, after which a fair and concerts begin.

Peel

The main settlement on the west coast, **PEEL** (bus #5 or #6 hourly from Douglas) immediately captivates, with its fine castle rising across the harbour and a popular sandy beach running the length of its eastern promenade. What probably started out as a flint-working village on a naturally protected spot gained significance with the foundation of a **monastery** in the seventh or eighth century, parts of which remain inside the ramparts of the red sandstone Peel Castle (April–Oct daily 10am–5pm; £3.30). The site became the residence of the Kings of Mann until 1220, when they moved to Castle Rushen in Castletown.

It's a fifteen-minute walk from the town around the river harbour and over the bridge to the castle. On the way, you'll have passed the excellent harbourside **House of Manannan** heritage centre (daily 10am–5pm; £5.50, combined ticket with Peel Castle £7.70) named after the island's ancient sea-god. You should allow at least two hours to get around the museum, which concentrates strongly on participatory exhibits – whether it's listening to Celtic legends in a replica roundhouse, examining the contents and occupants of a life-sized Viking ship, walking through a kipper factory or steering a steamer.

If you're looking for something more than the seafront cafés and fish-and-chip shops, then head for the **pub** opposite the House of Manannan: the *Creek Inn* serves a delicious array of specials. The *Marine Hotel* pub, on the seafront, is popular with locals, serving bar meals.

Port Erin

The small resort of **PORT ERIN**, at the southwestern tip of the island, is an hour and a quarter's train ride from Douglas. A wide, fine sand beach backing a deeply indented bay sits beneath green hills, and families relish the sands and nearby coves, and the timewarped atmosphere, which appears to have altered little in forty years. For a stretch of the legs, head up the promenade past the golf club to the entrance of Bradda Glen, where you can follow the path out along the headland to Bradda Head.

The **train station** is on Station Road, a couple of hundred yards above and back from the beach. Buses #1 and #2 from Douglas/Castletown, and #8 from Peel/St John's, stop on Bridson Street, across Station Road and opposite the *Cherry Orchard* hotel. For **accommodation**, the best B&B is *Rowany Cottier* (Ⓣ01624/832287; no credit cards; ❸), a detached house overlooking the bay, opposite the entrance to Bradda Glen.

Port St Mary and around

Two miles east of Port Erin, the fishing harbour still dominates little **PORT ST MARY**, with its houses strung out in a chain above the busy dockside. The best beach is away to the northeast, reached from the harbour along a well-worked Victorian path that clings to the bay's rocky edge.

From Port St Mary, a minor road runs out along the Meayll peninsula towards **Cregneash**, the oldest village on the island, part of which now forms the **Cregneash Village Folk Museum** (April–Oct daily 10am–5pm; £3.30). This picturesque cluster of nineteenth-century thatched crofts is peopled with spinners, weavers, turners and smiths dressed in period costumes; there's a café and information centre, and a chance to walk through the seasonal crops in the field and watch the horses at work. The local views are stunning and it's only a short walk south to **The Chasms**, a headland of gaping rock cliffs swarming with gulls and razorbills.

The footpath continues around Spanish Head, the island's southern tip, to the turf-roofed **Sound Visitor Centre** (daily 10/11am–4/5pm; free), which also marks the end of the road from Port St Mary. There's an excellent café, with windows looking out across The Sound to the **Calf of Man**. It really is worth making the effort to visit this offshore island, where resident wardens monitor the seasonal populations of kittiwakes, puffins, choughs, razorbills, shags, guillemots and others, while grey seals can be seen all year round basking on the rocks. Charter boats leave from Port St Mary, but the most reliable scheduled service (weather permitting) is from the pier at Port Erin (Easter–Sept daily; £10; usually at 10.15am, 11.30am & 1.30pm; Ⓣ01624/832339); call in advance as landing numbers are limited.

Regular **steam trains** run to Port Erin or back to Douglas from Port St Mary, with the station a ten-minute walk from the harbour along High Street, Bay View Road and Station Road; hourly **buses** from the harbour serve the same places. Nicest accommodation is at *Aaron House*, high up on The Promenade (Ⓣ01624/835702, Ⓦwww.aaronhouse.co.uk; ❺), a lovingly recreated Victorian experience combining brass beds and clawfoot slipper baths, with home-made scones and jam in the parlour and splendid breakfasts.

Castletown and around

From the twelfth century until 1869, **CASTLETOWN** was the island's capital, but then the influx of tourists and the increase in trade required a bigger harbour and Douglas took over. Its sleepy harbour and low-roofed cottages are dominated by **Castle Rushen** (April–Oct daily 10am–5pm; £4.80), formerly home to the island's legislature and still the site of the investiture of new lieutenant-governors. Across the central Market Square and down Castle Street in tiny Parliament Square you'll find the **Old House of Keys**. Built in 1821, this was the site of the Manx parliament, the Keys, until 1874 when it was moved to Douglas. The frock-coated Secretary of the House meets you at the door and shows you into the restored debating chamber, where visitors are included in a highly entertaining participatory session of the House, guided by a hologram Speaker. The visits are conducted on the hour (April–Oct daily 10am–noon & 2–5pm; £3.30).

The island's most important medieval religious site, **Rushen Abbey** (April–Oct daily 10am–5pm; £3.30) lies two miles north of Castletown. A Cistercian foundation of 1134, it was abandoned by its "White Monks" in the 1540s and in more recent times the site was used as a school and later a hotel, with tea dances held in the abbey grounds. The excavated remains themselves – low walls, grass-covered banks and a sole church tower from the fifteenth century – would hold only specialist appeal were it not for the excellent interpretation centre, which explains much about daily life in a Cistercian abbey.

Ballasalla is a stop on the Steam Railway, with the abbey a few minutes' walk from the village. Otherwise, Castletown train station is five minutes' walk from the centre, out along Victoria Road from the harbour; buses #8 (from Peel/Port Erin) and #1 (from Douglas) stop in the main square. Best place for food is *The Garrison*, across from the hotel at 5 Castle St (☎01624/824885; closes Sun at 5pm), a tapas bar with a sunny courtyard.

Travel details

Buses

For information on all local and national bus services, contact Traveline ☎0871/200 2233, ⓦwww.traveline.org.uk.

Chester to: Liverpool (every 20min; 1hr 20min); Manchester (3 daily; 1hr).

Lancaster to: Carlisle (4–5 daily; 1hr 10min); Kendal (hourly; 1hr); London (2–3 daily; 5hr 30min); Manchester (2 daily; 2hr); Windermere (hourly; 1hr 45min).

Liverpool to: Chester (hourly; 1hr); London (5 daily; 4hr); Manchester (hourly; 1hr).

Manchester to: Birmingham (6 daily; 3hr); Blackpool (5 daily; 1hr 40min); Chester (3 daily; 1hr); Leeds (6 daily; 2hr); Liverpool (hourly; 40min); London (every 1–2hr; 4hr 30min–6hr 45min); Newcastle (6 daily; 5hr); Sheffield (4 daily; 2hr 40min).

Trains

For information on all local and national rail services, contact National Rail Enquiries ☎0845/748 4950, ⓦwww.rail.co.uk.

Blackpool to: Manchester (hourly; 1hr 10min); Preston (hourly; 30min).

Chester to: Birmingham (5 daily; 2hr); Liverpool (2 hourly; 45min); London (3 daily; 3hr 30min); Manchester (2 hourly; 1hr–1hr 20min).

Lancaster to: Carlisle (every 30min–1hr; 1hr); Manchester (every 30min–1hr; 1hr); Morecambe (every 30min–1hr; 10min); Preston (every 20–30min; 20min).

Liverpool to: Birmingham (hourly; 1hr 40min); Chester (2 hourly; 45min); Leeds (hourly; 2hr); London (hourly; 2hr 40min); Manchester (hourly; 50min); Newcastle (8 daily; 4–5hr); Preston (14 daily; 1hr 5min); Sheffield (hourly; 1hr 45min); York (hourly; 2hr 20min).

Manchester to: Barrow-in-Furness (Mon–Sat 7 daily, Sun 3 daily; 2hr 15min); Birmingham (hourly; 1hr 30min); Blackpool (hourly; 1hr 10min); Buxton (hourly; 50min); Carlisle (8 daily; 1hr 50min); Chester (every 30min; 1hr–1hr 20min); Lancaster (hourly; 1hr); Leeds (hourly; 1hr); Liverpool (every 30min; 50min); London (hourly; 2hr 40min); Newcastle (10 daily; 3hr); Oxenholme (4–6 daily; 40min–1hr 10min); Penrith (2–4 daily; 2hr); Preston (every 20min; 55min); Sheffield (hourly; 1hr); York (hourly; 1hr 35min).

11

Cumbria and the Lakes

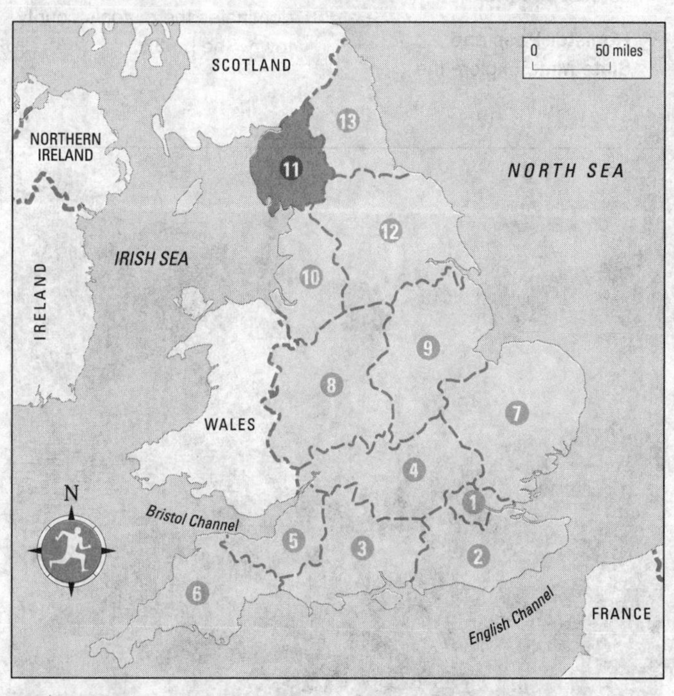

CHAPTER 11 # Highlights

* **Windermere** Take a cruise on England's largest lake. See p.521

* **Brantwood** The home of John Ruskin, beautifully sited on Coniston Water. See p.525

* **Go Ape** Swing through the trees of Grizedale Forest on an aerial high-ropes adventure course. See p.528

* **Honister Pass and Slate Mine** Explore the 300-year-old slate mine and climb the extraordinary Via Ferrata. See p.530

* **Wordsworth House, Cockermouth** Step into the eighteenth century at the birthplace of William Wordsworth. See p.532

* **Carlisle Castle** Cumbria's mightiest fortification dominates the region's county town. See p.537

▲ Lake Windermere

11

Cumbria and the Lakes

The Lake District is England's most hyped scenic area, and for good reasons. Within an area a mere thirty miles across, sixteen major lakes are squeezed between the steeply pitched faces of the country's highest mountains, an almost alpine landscape that's augmented by waterfalls and picturesque stone-built villages packed into the valleys. Most of what people refer to as the Lake District – or simply the Lakes – lies within the **Lake District National Park**. This, in turn, falls entirely within the north-western county of **Cumbria**, formed in 1974 from the historic counties of Cumberland and Westmorland, and the northern part of Lancashire. Consequently Cumbria contains more than just its lakes, stretching south and west to the **coast**, and north to its county town of **Carlisle**, a place that bears traces of a pedigree that stretches back beyond the construction of Hadrian's Wall. To the east, **Penrith** and the **Eden Valley** separate the lakes from the near wilderness of the northern Pennines.

For more **information** about the Lakes, visit Ⓦwww.lake-district.gov.uk; the official site of Cumbria Tourism is Ⓦwww.golakes.co.uk. National Express **coaches** connect London and Manchester with Windermere, Ambleside, Grasmere and Keswick. **Trains** leave the West Coast main line at **Oxenholme**, north of Lancaster, for the branch line service to Kendal and Windermere. The only other places directly accessible by train are Penrith, further north on the West Coast line, and the towns along the Cumbrian coast. The summer-season **Cross Lakes Shuttle** (Ⓣ015394/45161, Ⓦwww.mountain-goat.com, or www.lake-district.gov.uk) – integrating boats and buses – connects Bowness-on-Windermere with Hawkshead, Hill Top (Beatrix Potter house), Coniston Water and Grizedale Forest. The one-day Stagecoach **Explorer Ticket** (£9; Ⓦwww.stagecoachbus.com/northwest) is valid on the entire local bus network, while **Traveline** (Ⓣ0871/200 2233, Ⓦwww.traveline.org.uk) can advise about all the region's bus, coach, rail and ferry services.

The Lake District

Given a week you could easily see most of the famous settlements and lakes – a circuit taking in the towns of Ambleside, Windermere and Bowness, all on

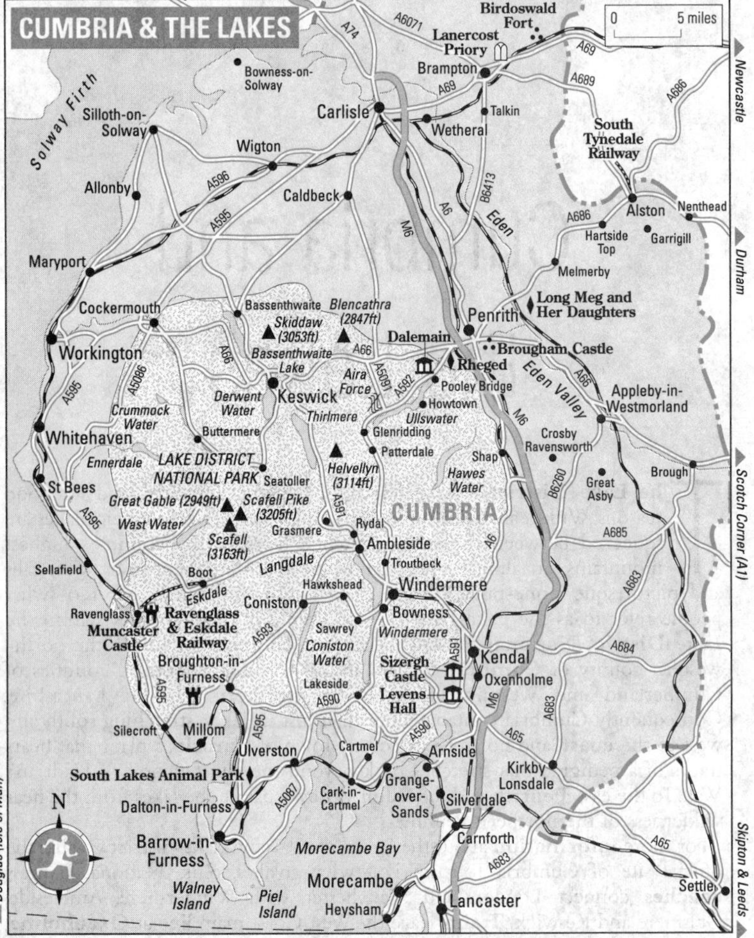

Windermere, the Wordsworth houses and sites in pretty villages such as **Hawkshead** and **Grasmere**, and the more dramatic northern scenery near **Keswick** and **Ullswater** would give you a fair sample of the whole. But it's away from the crowds that the Lakes really begin to pay dividends, in the dramatic valleys of **Langdale** and **Eskdale**, and the lesser-visited lakes of **Wast Water** and **Buttermere**. Four peaks top out at over 3000ft – including **Scafell Pike**, the highest in England – but there are hundreds of other mountains, crags and fells to roam. Bad weather can move in quickly, even in summer, so before a hike always check the **weather forecast** – many hotels and outdoor shops post a daily forecast – or call ⓣ0870/055 0575 (recorded 24-hour line, ⓦwww.lake-district.gov.uk/weatherline).

Kendal

The self-billed "Gateway to the Lakes" (though nearly ten miles from Windermere), **KENDAL** is the largest of the southern Cumbrian towns, with a population of 25,000. It offers rewarding rambles around the "yards" and "ginnels" on both sides of Highgate and Stricklandgate, the main streets, and while the old Market Place long since succumbed to development, traditional stalls still do business outside the Westmorland Shopping Centre every Wednesday and Saturday.

The **Kendal Museum**, on Station Road (hours may vary but currently Thurs–Sat noon–5pm; closed Christmas week; £2.80; Ⓦwww.kendalmuseum.org.uk), holds the district's natural history and archeological finds, and town history displays. These are bolstered by the reconstructed office, pen-and-ink drawings and personal effects of **Alfred Wainwright** (1907–91), Kendal's former borough treasurer (and honorary clerk at the museum). Wainwright moved to Kendal in 1941, and by 1952, dissatisfied with the accuracy of existing maps, he embarked on his series of highly personal walking guides, painstakingly handwritten with mapped routes and delicately drawn views. They have been hugely popular guidebooks ever since, which many treat as gospel in their attempts to "bag" ascents of the 214 fells he recorded.

The town's other two museums are at the Georgian **Abbot Hall** (Mon–Sat 10.30am–4/5pm; closed mid-Dec to mid-Jan; gallery & exhibitions £5, museum £3.75, combined ticket £7.50), by the river near the parish church. The main hall houses the **Art Gallery** (Ⓦwww.abbothall.org.uk), concentrating in particular on the works of the eighteenth-century "Kendal School" of portrait painters, most famously George Romney. Across the way, the former stables contain the **Museum of Lakeland Life and Industry** (Ⓦwww.lakelandmuseum.org.uk), where reconstructed seventeenth-, eighteenth- and nineteenth-century house interiors stand alongside workshops which exhibit rural trades and crafts, from spinning and weaving to shoe-making and tanning. Outside Kendal, the main trips are to the stately homes of **Sizergh Castle** (Ⓦwww.nationaltrust.org.uk) and Levens Hall (Ⓦwww.levenshall.co.uk), only a few miles to the south, both with beautifully kept gardens.

Practicalities

Kendal's **train station** is the first stop on the Windermere branch line, just three minutes from the **Oxenholme** main-line station and a ten-minute walk from the centre. The **bus station** is on Blackhall Road (off Stramongate), while the **tourist office** (Mon–Sat 10am–5pm; Ⓣ01539/725758, Ⓦwww.lakelandgateway.info) is in the town hall on Highgate.

B&Bs are ranged along Milnthorpe Road, a few minutes south of the centre – walk straight down Highgate and Kirkland – while the best hotel in town is the *Riverside* on Stramongate Bridge (Ⓣ01539/734861, Ⓦwww.riversidekendal.co.uk; ⑤), fashioned from one of the old town tanneries. There's a **youth hostel** at 118 Highgate (Ⓣ0870/770 5892, Ⓔkendal@yha.org.uk) attached to the Brewery Arts Centre. Five miles west of town at Crosthwaite, the *Punch Bowl Inn* (Ⓣ015395/68237, Ⓦwww.the-punchbowl.co.uk; ⑧) is a super-stylish restaurant-with-rooms with fine food (meals from around £30).

There are good-value lunches and authentic Spanish tapas, as well as more expensive meals, at *Cortez*, 101 Highgate (Ⓣ01539/723123; closed Sun lunch), while the best restaurant is the *New Moon*, 129 Highgate (Ⓣ01539/729254; closed Sun & Mon), an easy-going, contemporary bistro. For evening entertainment, the **Brewery Arts Centre**, 122 Highgate (Ⓣ01539/725133,

Ⓦ www.breweryarts.co.uk), is the town's central focus, with both a restaurant and lively bar; there's also a cinema, theatre, galleries and concert hall.

Windermere town and Brockhole

WINDERMERE town was all but non-existent until 1847 when a railway terminal was built here, making England's longest lake (after which the town is named) an easily accessible resort. Windermere remains the transport hub for the southern lakes, but there's precious little else to keep you in the slate-grey streets. Instead, all the traffic pours a mile downhill to Windermere's older twin town, Bowness, actually on the lake. However, make time for the **Lake District Visitor Centre at Brockhole** (Easter–Oct daily 10am–5pm; grounds & gardens open all year; free, parking fee charged; Ⓣ015394/46601), a lakeshore mansion three miles northwest of Windermere. It's the headquarters of the Lake District National Park and, besides the permanent natural history and geological displays, the centre hosts a full programme of guided walks, children's trails and activities, special exhibitions and lectures. **Buses** between Windermere and Ambleside run past the visitor centre, or you can get here by Windermere Lake Cruises **launch** (Easter–Oct, hourly service) from either Waterhead, near Ambleside (£6 return) or Bowness (£7.50 return).

Practicalities

All **buses** stop outside Windermere **train station**, with the **tourist office** (daily 9am–5pm; Ⓣ015394/46499, Ⓦ www.lakelandgateway.info) just a hundred yards away at the top of Victoria Street. For **bike rental**, contact Country Lanes at the train station (Ⓣ015394/44544, Ⓦ www.countrylanes.co.uk; from £15), which provides route maps for local rides. Mountain Goat, near the tourist office on Victoria Street (Ⓣ015394/45161, Ⓦ www.mountain-goat.com) offers **minibus tours** (half-day from £21, full-day £34) that get off the beaten track, departing daily from Windermere and other Lakeland towns.

Accommodation

Archway 13 College Rd Ⓣ015394/45613, Ⓦ www.the-archway.com. Four trim rooms in a Victorian house known for its breakfasts – try the great pancakes, kippers, home-made yoghurt and granola. ❸

Brendan Chase 1–3 College Rd Ⓣ015394/45638, Ⓦ www.placetostaywindermere.co.uk. Popular place with a friendly welcome and eight comfortable rooms (some en suite). No credit cards. ❷

Coach House Lake Rd Ⓣ015394/44494, Ⓦ www.lakedistrictbandb.com. Five classy rooms with wrought-iron beds, gleaming bathrooms and elegant touches. ❹

Holbeck Ghyll Holbeck Lane, off A591, 3 miles north Ⓣ015394/32375, Ⓦ www.holbeck-ghyll.co.uk. Luxurious rooms either in the main house or in the lodge or suites in the grounds – sherry decanter in every room, seven acres of gardens, and Michelin-starred Anglo-French food. Price – from around £240 – includes dinner. ❾

Lake District Backpackers' Lodge High St, across from the tourist office Ⓣ015394/46374, Ⓦ www.lakedistrictbackpackers.co.uk. Twenty beds in small dorms (available as private rooms on request). The price includes a tea-and-toast breakfast. No credit cards. Dorm beds from £11.50, or £15.50 per person in a private room.

Miller Howe Rayrigg Rd, A592 Ⓣ015394/42536, Ⓦ www.millerhowe.com. Gorgeous Edwardian house in an elevated position above Windermere, featuring antique- and art-filled rooms and landscaped gardens. Rates (from around £300) include dinner, early-morning tea and lavish breakfast. Closed Jan. ❾

Queen's Head A592, Troutbeck, 3 miles north Ⓣ015394/32174, Ⓦ www.queensheadhotel.com. Although some prefer Troutbeck's traditional *Mortal Man* inn, the style is more contemporary and the food is great at this nearby establishment. ❼

Windermere YHA High Cross, Bridge Lane, 1 mile north of Troutbeck Bridge Ⓣ0870/770 6094, ewindermere@yha.org.uk. Old mansion with lake views and mountain bike rental. A YHA shuttle bus (£2.50) runs from Windermere train station (meeting arriving trains) and Ambleside YHA. Dorm beds £14–16.50, depending on season.

Windermere cruises

Windermere Lake Cruises (Ⓦwww.windermere-lakecruises.co.uk) operates services to Lakeside at the southern tip (£8 return) or to Brockhole and Waterhead (for Ambleside) at the northern end (£7.70 return). There's also a direct service from Ambleside to the Lake District Visitor Centre at Brockhole (£6 return), and a shuttle service across the lake between Pier 3 at Bowness and Ferry House, Sawrey (£3.50 return). The company also operates an enjoyable circular **cruise around the islands** (departs several times daily from Bowness; £6; 45min), while a 24-hour **Freedom-of-the-Lake** ticket costs £14. Services on all routes are frequent between Easter and October (every 30min–1hr at peak times), and reduced during the winter – but there are sailings every day except Christmas Day.

Bowness and the lake

BOWNESS-ON-WINDERMERE – to give it its full title – spills back from its lakeside piers in a series of terraces lined with guesthouses and hotels. There's been a village here since the fifteenth century and a ferry service across the lake for almost as long – these days, though, you could be forgiven for thinking that Bowness begins and ends with **The World of Beatrix Potter** in the Old Laundry on Crag Brow (daily 10am–4.30/5.30pm; £6; Ⓦwww.hop-skip-jump.com). You either like Beatrix Potter or you don't, but it's safe to say that the elaborate 3D story scenes, audiovisual "virtual walks", themed tearoom and gift shop here find more favour with children than the more formal Potter attractions at Hill Top and Hawkshead. The other main attraction is the **Windermere Steamboat Museum** (Ⓦwww.steamboat.co.uk), a fifteen-minute walk north of the centre on Rayrigg Road. This is currently undergoing a major restoration, which will rejuvenate its collection of historic water craft, including the world's oldest mechanically driven boat and the steam-launch that was the inspiration for Captain Flint's houseboat in Arthur Ransome's *Swallows and Amazons*.

The lake itself is the heavyweight of Lake District waters, at ten and a half miles long, a mile wide in parts and a shade over two hundred feet deep. The traditional **ferry service** is the chain-guided contraption from Ferry Nab on the Bowness side (10min walk from the cruise piers) to Ferry House, Sawrey (Mon–Sat 7am–10pm, Sun 9am–10pm; departures every 20min; 50p, cars £3), providing access to Beatrix Potter's former home at Hill Top and to Hawkshead beyond.

Practicalities

The open-top #599 **bus** from Windermere train station stops at the lakeside piers, also the terminus for the #517 (to Troutbeck and Ullswater). The useful **Cross-Lakes Shuttle** (daily Easter–Sept, plus Oct weekends) provides a direct connecting boat-and-minibus service from Bowness Pier 3 to Hill Top (£7.70 return), Hawkshead (£9), Grizedale (£11.40) and Coniston Water (£15.30). **Bowness Bay Information Centre** is near the piers on Glebe Road (daily 9.30/10am–4/5.30pm; Ⓣ015394/42895). Windermere Canoe & Kayak (Ⓣ015394/44451, Ⓦwww.windermerecanoekayak.co.uk), on Ferry Nab Road (on the way to the Sawrey ferry), is the place to **rent bikes, canoes and kayaks**.

Accommodation

Gilpin Lodge Crook Rd, B5284, 2 miles southeast Ⓣ015394/88818, Ⓦwww.gilpin-lodge.co.uk. A renowned country-house retreat with fourteen elegant rooms, plus six more contemporary suites in the grounds with private gardens and hot tubs. Rates (from £250) include breakfast and dinner in the Michelin-starred restaurant. ⑨

Linthwaite House Crook Rd, B5284, 1 mile south ⓣ015394/88600, ⓦwww.linthwaite.com. Contemporary boutique style grafted on to an ivy-covered country house set high above Windermere. Rates vary according to outlook and size (from around £200) and include dinner. ⑨

Montclare House Crag Brow ⓣ015394/42723, ⓦwww.montclareguesthouse.co.uk. Attractive en-suite B&B accommodation above a coffee shop that's about the best value in Bowness. No credit cards. ③

New Hall Bank Fallbarrow Rd ⓣ015394/43558, ⓦwww.newhallbank.com. Detached Victorian house with a lake view (and just a few yards from the *Hole in't Wall* pub). ⑤

Cafés, pubs and restaurants

2 Eggcups 6a Ash St ⓣ015394/45979. Serves the best sandwich in Bowness, plus other blackboard specials. Daytime only, closed Thurs. Inexpensive.

Hole in't Wall Fallbarrow Rd ⓣ015394/43488. For a drink or bar meal you can't beat the town's oldest hostelry, cosy in winter when the fires are lit, and pleasant in summer when you can sit outside. Inexpensive.

Jackson's Bistro St Martin's Square ⓣ015394/46264. The local choice for a family meal or romantic night out – classic bistro dishes, including a good-value three-course *table d'hôte* menu available all night. Dinner only. Moderate.

Around Bowness

Mackay Hugh Baillie Scott's **Blackwell** (daily 10.30am–4/5pm; closed Jan to mid-Feb; £5.45; ⓦwww.blackwell.org.uk) was built in 1900 as a lakeside holiday home, and selected rooms of its superbly restored Arts and Crafts interior can be viewed. There's an informative introductory talk (usually weekdays at 2.30pm), plus tearoom, craft shop and gardens. Parking is available; alternatively, walk from Bowness (about 25 minutes).

From Bowness piers, boats head to the southern reaches of Windermere at Lakeside, which is also the terminus of the **Lakeside and Haverthwaite Railway** (Easter–Oct 6–7 daily; £5.20 return; ⓣ015395/31594, ⓦwww.lakesiderailway.co.uk). The boat arrivals at Lakeside connect with train departures, and you can buy a joint boat-and-train ticket (£12.60 return) at Bowness. Also on the quay at Lakeside is the **Aquarium of the Lakes** (daily 9am–5/6pm; £7.50, joint boat ticket £14.35; ⓦwww.aquariumofthelakes.co.uk), an entertaining natural history exhibit centred on the fish and animals found along a Lakeland river. Alternatively contact Country Lanes bike rental on the quayside for a bike-and-boat day out (ⓦwww.countrylanes.co.uk; from £15).

Ambleside

Five miles northwest of Windermere, **AMBLESIDE** is a first-class base for walkers, who are catered for by a large number of outdoors shops. The town centre consists of a cluster of grey-green stone houses, shops, pubs and B&Bs hugging a circular one-way system, which loops round just south of the narrow gully of stony Stock Ghyll. The tourist office has plenty of local walking leaflets and guides, while for some background on Ambleside's history, stroll a couple of minutes along Rydal Road to the **Armitt Collection** (daily 10am–5pm; £2.50; ⓦwww.armitt.com), which catalogues the very distinct contribution to Lakeland society made by writers and artists from John Ruskin to Beatrix Potter. The rest of town lies a mile south at **Waterhead**, overlooked by the grass banks and spreading trees of Borrans Park.

Walking to Ambleside from the ferry piers at Waterhead takes fifteen minutes, while all **buses** stop on Kelsick Road, opposite the library. The **tourist office** is on Market Cross (daily 9am–5pm; ⓣ015394/32582, ⓦwww.lakelandgateway.info or ⓦwww.amblesideonline.co.uk). There's **bike rental** from Biketreks on Rydal Road (ⓣ015394/31245, ⓦwww.biketreks.net), or Ghyllside Cycles on The Slack (ⓣ015394/33592, ⓦwww.ghyllside.co.uk).

Accommodation

Ambleside YHA Waterhead, A591, 1 mile south ⓣ0870/770 5672, ⓔambleside@yha.org.uk. The YHA's flagship regional hostel, a huge lakeside affair with small dorms, twins, doubles and family rooms, plus bike rental, Internet, licensed café and private jetty. Dorm beds from £20, including breakfast, rooms 3

Compston House Compston Rd ⓣ015394/32305, ⓦwww.compstonhouse.co.uk. There's a breezy New York air in this traditional Lakeland house, with American-style themed rooms and breakfasts of pancakes and maple syrup. 4

Riverside Under Loughrigg ⓣ015394/32395, ⓦwww.riverside-at-ambleside.co.uk. Charming guesthouse, half a mile (10min walk) from town (across Rothay Park). Six large, light country-pine style rooms available, including a river-facing four-poster. 5

Waterhead Waterhead ⓣ015394/32566, ⓦwww.elh.co.uk. Contemporary townhouse-style accommodation provides the Lakes' classiest four-star lodgings. It's very close to the lake, opposite the Waterhead piers. 8

Restaurants

Log House Lake Rd ⓣ015394/31077. An inventive menu – crispy squid to Vietnamese roast duck – in an eye-catching Norwegian log cabin, 5min from the town centre. There are three B&B rooms too. Closed Mon (& also Sun in winter). Expensive.

Lucy's on a Plate Church St ⓣ015394/31191. Really enjoyable bistro offering a daily-changing menu with tons of choice. *Lucy 4* on St Mary's Lane, just over the way, is its moderately priced tapas bar offshoot. Expensive.

Zeffirelli's Compston Rd ⓣ015394/33845, ⓦwww.zeffirellis.com. Famous for its wholemeal-based pizzas, but also serving inventive pastas and veggie food – there's also a great upstairs jazz bar (live music a couple of nights a week), and a dinner with cinema-ticket special for screenings at Zeff's two cinemas in town. Moderate.

Great Langdale

Three miles west of Ambleside along the A593, Skelwith Bridge marks the start of **Great Langdale**, a U-shaped glacial valley overlooked by the prominent rocky summits of the **Langdale Pikes**, the most popular of the central Lakeland fells. The #516 Langdale Rambler **bus** from Ambleside runs to Elterwater (17min) and on up to the *Old Dungeon Ghyll* hotel at the head of the valley (30min).

Pretty **ELTERWATER** is centred on a tiny village green overlooked by the excellent *Britannia Inn* (ⓣ015394/37210, ⓦwww.britinn.co.uk; 6), with comfortable rooms and good food. The local **youth hostel**, *Elterwater YHA* (ⓣ0870/770 5816, ⓔelterwater@yha.org.uk), is just across the bridge from the pub (hiking and activity weekends are held here year-round).

Three miles from Elterwater, at **Stickle Ghyll** car park, Harrison Stickle (2414ft), Pike of Stickle (2326ft) and Pavey Ark (2297ft) form a dramatic backdrop, though many walkers go no further than the hour-long climb to **Stickle Tarn** from Stickle Ghyll. Another car park, a mile further west up the valley road by the **Old Dungeon Ghyll Hotel**, is the starting point for a series of more hardcore hikes to resonant Lakeland peaks like Crinkle Crags (2816ft) or Bowfell (2960ft). The peerless *Old Dungeon Ghyll Hotel* (ⓣ015394/37272, ⓦwww.odg.co.uk; 6) itself is the best-known accommodation in the valley, a traditional mountain inn, at the end of the B5343, seven miles northeast of Ambleside. Dinner is served in the dining room, but all the action is in the stone-flagged **hikers' bar**.

Grasmere and around

Four miles northwest of Ambleside, the village of **GRASMERE** consists of an intimate cluster of grey-stone houses on the old packhorse road that runs beside the babbling River Rothay. It loses some of its charm in high summer thanks to the hordes who descend on the trail of the village's most famous former resident, **William Wordsworth** (1770–1850). The poet, his wife Mary, sister Dorothy and other members of his family are buried beneath the yews in **St Oswald's churchyard**, around which the river makes a sinuous curl. The **lake** is just a ten-minute walk away, down Redbank Road, where tremendous views unfold from **Loughrigg Terrace**, on its southern reaches. A four-mile circuit of Grasmere and adjacent **Rydal Water** takes around two hours, with the route passing Wordsworth haunts Rydal Mount and Dove Cottage.

On Grasmere's southeastern outskirts, just off the A591, stands **Dove Cottage** (daily 9.30am–5.30pm; closed early Jan to early Feb; £6.50; Ⓦ www.wordsworth.org.uk; buses #555 and #599), home to William and Dorothy Wordsworth from 1799 to 1808 and where Wordsworth wrote some of his best poetry. In the adjacent **museum** are paintings, manuscripts (including that of "Daffodils") and mementoes of Southey, Coleridge and Thomas De Quincey.

Another mile and a half southeast along the A591, **Rydal Mount** (March–Oct daily 9.30am–5pm; Nov–Feb daily except Tues 10am–4pm, closed

▲ Dove Cottage

for three weeks in Jan; £5, gardens only £2.50; Ⓦ www.rydalmount.co.uk) was Wordsworth's home from 1813 until his death in 1850. The house is owned by descendants of the poet and you're free to wander around what is essentially still a family home. Buses #555 and #599 pass Rydal Mount and Dove Cottage on the way to Grasmere from Windermere and Ambleside.

Practicalities

Buses stop on the village green in Grasmere. On-street parking is extremely limited, so aim straight for the main **car park** on Redbank Road, by the garden centre. Note that as well as the recommended backpackers' **hostel**, there are two official YHA hostels close to the village (*Butharlyp Howe* and *Thorney How*, details on Ⓦ www.yha.org.uk). For something a bit different contact Full Circle (Ⓣ 01539/821278, Ⓦ www.lake-district-yurts.co.uk; open Easter–Dec), who have three eco-friendly **yurts** in the Rydal Hall grounds, a couple of miles south of the village.

Accommodation

Grasmere Independent Hostel Broadrayne Farm, A591 Ⓣ 015394/35055, Ⓦ www.grasmerehostel.co.uk. Just north of the village, past the *Travellers' Rest* pub, this stylish backpackers' is the top budget choice and the best of its kind in the Lakes. Dorm beds from £16.50.

Harwood Red Lion Sq Ⓣ 015394/35248, Ⓦ www.harwoodhotel.co.uk. Genial family-run hotel with eight smartly furnished rooms, and a coffeehouse and deli below. 4

How Foot Lodge Town End Ⓣ 015394/35366, Ⓦ www.howfoot.co.uk. Spacious Victorian villa, just yards from Dove Cottage, with six rooms, one with its own sun lounge. Closed Jan. 4

Moss Grove Organic Corner of College St, opposite the *Wordsworth Hotel* Ⓣ 015394/35251, Ⓦ www.mossgrove.com. A Victorian-era hotel redesigned on organic, low-impact lines – think reclaimed timber beds, wool carpets and natural wood blinds. The feel is less hotel and more private house party. Two-night minimum stay at weekends. 8

Raise View White Bridge Ⓣ 015394/35215, Ⓦ www.raiseviewhouse.co.uk. There are lovely fell views from every corner of this amiable guest-house. No credit cards. 5

Wordsworth Hotel College St Ⓣ 015394/35592, Ⓦ www.thewordsworthhotel.co.uk. Four-star choice in the village centre, with a heated pool, good bistro and bar (*Dove & Olive Branch*) and excellent restaurant (*Prelude*). 8

Cafés and restaurants

Jumble Room Langdale Rd Ⓣ 015394/35188. Funky café-restaurant with a menu that ranges the world – from Thai prawns to local game pie. Closed Mon & Tues and occasional other days in winter. Expensive.

Rowan Tree Church Bridge, Stock Lane Ⓣ 015394/35528. The main draw here is the outdoor terrace above the river, opposite Grasmere church. A daytime tearoom menu gives way to Med-style dining at night. Moderate.

Villa Colombina Town End Ⓣ 015394/35268. Italian café-restaurant by Dove Cottage, serving pizza, pasta, steak and chicken, plus daily black-board specials. Closed Jan and occasional other days in winter. Moderate.

Coniston and around

Coniston Water is not one of the most immediately imposing of the lakes, yet it has a quiet beauty that sets it apart from the more popular destinations. The nineteenth-century art critic and social reformer John Ruskin made the lake his home, and today his isolated house, **Brantwood**, on the northeastern shore, provides the most obvious target for a day-trip. **Arthur Ransome** was also a frequent visitor, his local memories and experiences providing much of the detail in his famous *Swallows and Amazons* children's books.

The slate-grey village of **CONISTON** hunkers below the craggy and coppermine-riddled bulk of **The Old Man of Coniston** (2628ft), which most fit walkers can climb in under two hours. In the village itself, **John Ruskin's**

Coniston's speed king

On January 4, 1967, **Donald Campbell** set out to better his own world water-speed record (276mph, set three years earlier in Australia) on the glass-like surface of Coniston Water. Just as his jet-powered *Bluebird* hit an estimated 320mph, however, a patch of turbulence sent it into a somersault. Campbell was killed immediately and his body and boat lay undisturbed at the bottom of the lake until both were retrieved in 2001. Campbell's grave is in the small village cemetery behind the *Crown Hotel*, while the reconstructed *Bluebird* is eventually to be displayed in a purpose-built gallery at the local museum, where you can find out more about Campbell and that fateful day.

grave lies in St Andrew's original churchyard beneath a beautifully worked Celtic cross, while just up the road is the excellent **Ruskin Museum** on Yewdale Road (Easter to mid-Nov daily 10am–5.30pm; mid-Nov to Easter Wed–Sun 10am–3.30pm; £4.25; Ⓦwww.ruskinmuseum.com).

Coniston Water is hidden out of sight, half a mile southeast of the village. From the pier, the **Steam Yacht Gondola** (Easter–Oct hourly departures 11am–4pm, weather permitting; £6 round-trip; Ⓣ015394/41288, Ⓦwww.nationaltrust.org.uk/gondola), built in 1859, departs on hour-long circuits of the lake, though you can also stop off at Ruskin's Brantwood. The other lake service is the **Coniston Launch** (Easter–Oct hourly 10.30am–4.30pm; Nov–Easter up to 4 daily depending on the weather; Ⓣ015394/36216, Ⓦwww.conistonlaunch.co.uk), which operates wooden boats on three routes around the lake, north (£5.40 return), south (£7.80) or mid-lake (£6.60), all calling at Brantwood. You can stop off at any pier en route, and local walk leaflets are available, as well as special cruises throughout the year.

Brantwood

Sited on a hillside above the eastern shore of Coniston Water, two and a half miles from Coniston (off B5285), **Brantwood** (mid-March to mid-Nov daily 11am–5.30pm; mid-Nov to mid-March Wed–Sun 11am–4.30pm; £5.95, gardens only £4, combined Coniston Launch ticket available; Ⓦwww.brantwood.org.uk) was home to John Ruskin from 1872 until his death in 1900. Ruskin was the champion of J.M.W. Turner and the Pre-Raphaelites and foremost Victorian proponent of the supremacy of Gothic architecture. His **study** and **dining room** boast superlative lake views, bettered only by those from the **Turret Room** where he used to sit in later life in his bathchair. The surviving Turners from Ruskin's own art collection are on show, and other exhibition rooms and galleries display Ruskin-related arts and crafts, while the excellent *Jumping Jenny Tearooms* – named after Ruskin's boat – has an outdoor terrace with lake views.

Practicalities

Buses stop on the main road through Coniston village. A Ruskin Explorer ticket (from £12) gets you return bus travel on the #505 from Windermere/Ambleside, plus use of the Coniston Launch and entry to Ruskin's house – buy the ticket on the bus. The **Cross-Lakes Shuttle** minibus service from Bowness runs as far as the Coniston Launch pier (for Brantwood and lake services) at the *Waterhead Hotel*, half a mile out of the village. There's a **tourist office** (daily 9.30am–5pm; Ⓣ015394/41533, Ⓦwww.conistontic.org) by the main car park, while best places for a bite to eat are the *Black Bull* **pub**, which brews its own Bluebird beer, and the *Meadowdore Café* (open until late in summer).

Accommodation

Bank Ground Farm Coniston Water, east side ⓣ015394/41264, ⓦwww.bankground.com. Just north of Brantwood, this beautifully set lakeshore farmhouse (the model for Holly Howe Farm in *Swallows and Amazons*) has country-style rooms in the main house, plus self-catering holiday cottages and converted barn. 4

Black Bull Inn Coppermines Rd, by the bridge ⓣ015394/41335, ⓦwww.conistonbrewery.com/blackbull.htm. The village's best pub has a variety of rooms available in the main building or in the renovated cottages attached. Hearty bar meals served. Two-night minimum stay at weekends. 5

Coniston Coppermines YHA ⓣ0870/770 5772, ⓔcoppermines@yha.org.uk. *Holly How* might be closer YHA hostel to the village, but it's *Coppermines* that is the hikers' favourite, set dramatically in the mountains a steep mile or so from the village. Closed Nov–March & some other days in summer season. Dorm beds from £13.

Meadowdore Café Hawkshead Old Rd ⓣ015394/41638, ⓦwww.meadowdore-café-co.uk. High-quality B&B above the café – two en-suite rooms, and one with a lovely private bathroom, all tastefully furnished. 3

Yew Tree Farm A593, 2 miles north ⓣ015394/41433, ⓦwww.yewtree-farm.com. A peaceful seventeenth-century farmhouse with cosy oak-panelled rooms, munching sheep and tearoom – Beatrix Potter once owned the house and furnished its parlour (and you might have seen the house in the Renée Zellweger film, *Miss Potter*, when it doubled as Hill Top). No credit cards. 3

Hawkshead and around

HAWKSHEAD, midway between Coniston and Ambleside, wears its beauty well, its patchwork of cottages and cobbles backed by woods and fells and barely affected by modern intrusions. Huge car parks at the village edge take the strain, and when the crowds of day-trippers leave, Hawkshead regains its natural tranquillity.

The village was an important wool market at the time William Wordsworth was studying at **Hawkshead Grammar School** (Easter–Oct Mon–Sat 10am–12.30pm & 1.30–5pm, Sun 1–5pm; £1), founded in 1585; this is now a small museum. Focus of most visits to Hawkshead, though, is the **Beatrix Potter Gallery** on Main Street (Easter–Oct daily except Fri 10.30am–4.30pm; £4, discount available for Hill Top visitors; NT), where an annually changing selection of her original sketchbooks, drawings, water-colours and manuscripts is displayed. Meanwhile, her beloved house, **Hill Top** (Easter–Oct Mon–Wed, Sat & Sun 10.30am–4.30pm; £5.40; garden entry free on Thurs & Fri when house is closed; NT), lies two miles from Hawkshead, in the hamlet of Near Sawrey. A Londoner by birth, Potter bought the farmhouse here with the proceeds from her first book, *The Tale of Peter Rabbit*, and retained it as her study long after she moved out following her marriage in 1913.

The best local walk from Hawkshead is to **Tarn Hows**, a body of water surrounded by spruce and pine and circled by paths and picnic spots. It's two miles from Hawkshead on country lanes and paths, and once there it takes about an hour to walk around the tarn, or you can always make the half-mile diversion to the tearoom at nearby *Yew Tree Farm*.

Practicalities

The main **bus service** to Hawkshead is the #505 Coniston Rambler between Windermere, Ambleside and Coniston, while the seasonal **Cross-Lakes Shuttle** runs from Hawkshead down to the Beatrix Potter house at Hill Top and on to Sawrey for boat connections back to Bowness.

Accommodation

Drunken Duck Inn Barngates crossroads, 2 miles north, off B5285 ⓣ015394/36347, ⓦwww.drunkenduckinn.co.uk. Superb restaurant-with-rooms in a beautifully located 400-year-old inn. The cuisine is cutting-edge British (dinner around £35 excluding drinks and service; reservations essential), the rooms eminently stylish, the views divine. 7; superior rooms 8

Beatrix Potter, the movie

You'll find it hard to travel around the Lakes and not notice the effect of the 2007 film **Miss Potter** (starring Renée Zellweger and Ewan McGregor), the Beatrix Potter biopic largely filmed in Cumbria. It's bringing in even more tourists than ever to places like **Hill Top** and the **Beatrix Potter Gallery**, while location sites like Yew Tree Farm, Loughrigg Tarn, Loweswater and Derwent Water are making the most of their fleeting fame. See Ⓦwww.visitmisspotter.com for the location and film details; tour guides involved in the filming offer a full-day Miss Potter Film Tour (Ⓦwww.lakedistrictfilmtours.co.uk).

King's Arms Market Square Ⓣ015394/36372, Ⓦwww.kingsarmshawkshead.co.uk. Characterful old inn, with nine rooms retaining their oak beams and idiosyncratic proportions. It's also the best pub in the village, with good-value meals. ⑤

Yewfield Hawkshead Hill, 2 miles west off B5285 Ⓣ015394/36765, Ⓦwww.yewfield.co.uk. Splendid vegetarian guesthouse set amongst organic vegetable gardens and wild-flower meadows. The house is a Victorian Gothic beauty, filled with Oriental artefacts and art from the owners' travels. Closed mid-Nov to Jan. ⑤

Grizedale Forest

Grizedale Forest extends over the fells separating Coniston Water and Hawkshead from Windermere. The best starting point is the **Grizedale Forest Centre** (daily 10/11am–4/5pm; free, parking fee charged; Ⓣ01229/860010, Ⓦwww.forestry.gov.uk/grizedale), three miles southwest of Hawkshead – the Cross-Lakes Shuttle (from Bowness via Hawskhead) runs here in the morning, picking up return visitors later in the day. There's a good café, craft shop, and activity areas at the centre, while **Grizedale Mountain Bikes** (9am–4.30/5pm; Ⓣ01229/860369, Ⓦwww.grizedalemountainbikes.co.uk) has bikes available to explore the waymarked trails through the forest. More adventurous still is the forest high-ropes course known as **Go Ape** (Feb–Oct daily, Nov weekends only, closed Dec & Jan; advance bookings required on Ⓣ0870/444 5562, Ⓦwww.goape.co.uk; £25; minimum age 10), which has you frolicking in the tree canopy for a couple of hours – fantastic fun involving zip-wires, Tarzan-swings, tree platforms and other aerial manoeuvres.

Keswick and Derwent Water

Standing on the shores of **Derwent Water**, the small market town of **KESWICK** makes a good base for exploring the northern Lake District, particularly delightful Borrowdale to the south of town or the heights of Skiddaw (3053ft) and Blencathra (2847ft), which loom over Keswick to the north.

Granted its market charter by Edward I in 1276 – **market day** is Saturday – Keswick was an important wool and leather centre until around 1500, when these trades were supplanted by the discovery of local graphite. Keswick became an important pencil-making town, and the entertaining **Cumberland Pencil Museum** at Greta Bridge (daily 9.30am–5pm; £3; Ⓦwww.pencilmuseum.co.uk) tells the story. In Fitz Park, on Station Road, you'll find the **Keswick Museum and Art Gallery** (Easter–Oct Tues–Sat 10am–4pm; free), a gloriously quirky Victorian collection including (amongst other things) a set of lion's teeth, ancient dental tools, a 600-year-old cat and the famous "musical stones" which sound in tune when you strike them. Meanwhile, **Crosthwaite Church**, a fifteen-minute walk northwest of town over Greta Bridge, is the resting place of the poet Robert Southey.

You also shouldn't miss Keswick's most mysterious landmark, **Castlerigg Stone Circle**, where 38 hunks of volcanic stone, the largest almost eight feet tall, form a circle a hundred feet in diameter, set against a magnificent mountain backdrop. Take the Threlkeld rail line path (signposted by the *Keswick Country House Hotel*) and follow the signs.

Derwent Water

The shores of **Derwent Water** lie five minutes' walk south of the centre. It's among the most attractive of the lakes, ringed by crags and studded with islets, and is most easily seen by hopping on the **Keswick Launch** (regular departures Easter–Nov daily, Dec–Easter weekends only; £8 round-trip, £1.50 per stage; ⓣ017687/72263, ⓦwww.keswick-launch.co.uk), which runs around the lake calling at several points en route. There's also an enjoyable one-hour **evening cruise** (£8.50) from May Day bank holiday until mid-September.

You can jump off the launch at any of the half a dozen piers on Derwent Water for a stroll, but if you've only got time for one hike, make it up **Cat Bells** (take the launch to Hawes End), a superb vantage point (1481ft) above the lake's western shore – allow two and a half hours for the scramble to the top and a return to the pier along the wooded shore.

Practicalities

Buses use the terminal in front of the large Booths supermarket, off Main Street. The **tourist office** is in the Moot Hall on Market Square (daily 9.30am–4.30/5.30pm; ⓣ017687/72645) and there's online information at ⓦwww.keswick.org and ⓦwww.dokeswick.com. **Guided walks** – from lakeside rambles to mountain climbs – depart from the Moot Hall (Easter–Oct daily 10.15am; £8, longer walks £10; ⓦwww.hillwalker.ic24.net); just turn up with a packed lunch. For **bike rental**, there's Keswick Mountain Bikes on Southey Lane (ⓣ017687/75202, ⓦwww.keswickmountainbikes.co.uk; from £17).

There's a fair amount going on in Keswick throughout the year, including the **jazz festival** and **mountain festival** (ⓦwww.keswickmountainfestival.co.uk), both in May, **beer festival** in June, and the traditional **Keswick Agricultural Show** (August bank holiday). The **Theatre by the Lake** on Lake Road (ⓣ017687/74411, ⓦwww.theatrebythelake.com) hosts drama, concerts and exhibitions, as well as a renowned annual literature festival, **Words By The Water** (March, ⓦwww.wayswithwords.co.uk).

Accommodation

Acorn House Ambleside Rd ⓣ017687/72553, ⓦwww.acornhousehotel.co.uk. Handsome eighteenth-century house with nine generously sized rooms, 5min from the centre. Parking. ④

Café-Bar 26 26 Lake Rd ⓣ017687/80863, ⓦwww.cafebar26.co.uk. Three stylish rooms offer a central chintz-free base. Downstairs is the best of the town's café-bars, with good lunches (not Mon). ③, weekends ④

Highfield The Heads ⓣ017687/72508, ⓦwww.highfieldkeswick.co.uk. Beautifully restored Victorian hotel whose stylish "feature rooms" include two turret rooms and even a converted chapel. There's also a decent restaurant with a daily changing menu (dinner included in the price). ⑦

Howe Keld 5–7 The Heads ⓣ017687/72417, ⓦwww.howekeld.co.uk. Welcoming guesthouse with a reputation for great breakfasts (vegetarian specialities included, from rissoles to pancakes and syrup). Parking. ④

Keswick YHA Station Rd ⓣ0870/770 5894, ⓔkeswick@yha.org.uk. Keswick's town YHA, in a converted woollen mill on the river, has a new contemporary look after a major overhaul. Facilities and rooms are bang up to date, while a restaurant and bar offer good-value meals. Dorm beds from £17.50 (May–Sept from £19), breakfast included.

Sweeney's 18–20 Lake Rd ⓣ0500/600725, ⓦwww.lakedistrictinns.co.uk. Four bright en-suite rooms above a contemporary bar-brasserie, with the town's most spacious beer garden out back. ④, weekends ⑤

Cafés, restaurants and pubs

Dog and Gun 2 Lake Rd. Top pub in town, with old slate floors, oak beams, a changing selection of real ales and good food – the house special is a Hungarian goulash with dumplings.

Lakeland Pedlar Henderson's Yard, Bell Close, off Main St ⓣ017687/74492, ⓦwww.lakelandpedlar.co.uk. Keswick's best café serves tasty veggie food – from breakfast burritos to veg crumble or chilli. Daytime only (sometimes until till 9pm in school holidays). Moderate.

Lemon and Lime 31 Lake Rd ⓣ017687/73088. A good choice if you can't decide on a cuisine – there's round-the-world tapas-style starters, followed by mains ranging from burgers and steaks to noodles and Thai curries. Moderate.

Borrowdale

It is difficult to overstate the beauty of **Borrowdale**, with its river flats and yew trees, lying at the head of Derwent Water and overshadowed by Scafell Pike, the highest mountain in England, and Great Gable, reckoned as one of the finest-looking. Climbs up both these peaks start from the head of the valley near Seatoller, accessible from Keswick on **buses** #77A (along the west side of Derwent Water) and #79 Borrowdale Rambler (along the B5289).

The straggling hamlet of **Rosthwaite** is a good place to base yourself for local hikes and mountain climbs. Two or three local B&Bs include *Yew Tree Farm* (ⓣ017687/77675, ⓦwww.borrowdaleherdwick.co.uk; closed Dec & Jan; no credit cards; ❸), favoured on occasion by Prince Charles on incognito walking trips to the Lakes. There are also comfortable **rooms** at the hiker-friendly *Royal Oak Hotel* (ⓣ017687/77214, ⓦwww.royaloakhotel.co.uk; ❻, includes dinner) and the neighbouring *Scafell Hotel* (ⓣ017687/77208, ⓦwww.scafell.co.uk; ❻), though best address is *Hazel Bank* (ⓣ017687/77248, ⓦwww.hazelbankhotel.co.uk; ❽), a country house hotel set in serene gardens just outside the village, where a candlelit dinner is included in the price.

Another mile up the valley, eight from Keswick, the #79 bus route ends its run at Seatoller, where there's a car park and visitor information point (daily 10am–5pm; ⓣ017687/77714). Just opposite is the welcoming *Yew Tree* café-restaurant-bar (ⓣ017687/77634; closed Mon & Jan to mid-Feb), where daytime sandwiches, pies and omelettes give way to African evening specials like Cape Malay curry, grilled ostrich and beef skewers.

It's twenty minutes' walk from Seatoller down the minor road to **Seathwaite**, the base for walks up England's highest peak, **Scafell Pike** (3205ft) – the approach is through the farmyard and up to **Styhead Tarn** via Stockley Bridge; from the tarn the classic ascent is up the thrilling Corridor Route, then descending via Esk Hause – an eight-mile (6hr) loop walk in all from Seathwaite.

Honister Pass and Slate Mine

Overlooked by the steep Borrowdale Fells, the B5289 cuts west at Seatoller, up and over the dramatic **Honister Pass** (bus #77A comes this way). Slate quarrying was well established at Honister by the mid-eighteenth century and though full commercial quarrying ceased in 1986 the mine is now in operation again as a working and heritage enterprise. To get an idea of what traditional slate mining entailed, you can don a hard hat and lamp to join one of the hugely informative guided tours of **Honister Slate Mine** (tours daily at 10.30am, 12.30pm & 3.30pm; £9.75; ⓣ017687/77230, ⓦwww.honister-slate-mine.co.uk), which lead you through narrow tunnels into illuminated, dripping caverns. There's also a dramatic Alpine-style **Via Ferrata** (2 departures daily; £20, all-day pass including mine tour £32; bookings on ⓣ017687/77714) – or "Iron Way" – that allows visitors to be guided to the top of Fleetwith Pike (2126ft), above the mines, by means of a fixed cableway and harness. This requires a strong head for heights, as you'll be following the miners' old route up the exposed face of the mountain.

Buttermere, Crummock Water and Loweswater

From Honister Pass, the B5289 follows Gatesgarthdale Beck for three miles and makes a dramatic descent into the **Buttermere Valley**. The direct bus is the #77 via Whinlatter Pass; the #77A comes the long way around through Borrowdale. At Buttermere village there are no facilities save a seasonal café, a large car park and two **hotels**, while the **youth hostel**, *Buttermere YHA* (ⓣ0870/770 5736, ⓔbuttermere@yha.org.uk), overlooks the lake on the road to Honister Pass. A few hundred yards in the other direction, overlooking Crummock Water, *Wood House* (ⓣ017687/70208, ⓦwww.wdhse.co.uk; no credit cards; ❺) is quite the nicest **B&B** hereabouts, with elegant rooms with views.

There's a particularly easy two-mile hike out along Crummock Water's south-western edge to the 125-foot **Scale Force** falls. The four-mile, round-lake stroll circling Buttermere itself shouldn't take more than a couple of hours; you can always detour up Scarth Gap to **Haystacks** (1900ft) if you want more of a climb and some views.

Wast Water

Nothing prepares you for the first sight of **Wast Water**, England's deepest lake and Lakeland's most remote corner. Awesome screes plunge to its eastern shore, while the highest peaks in the country – Great Gable and the Scafells – frame Wasdale Head, the tiny settlement at its head. The only road (there are no bus services) winds from the main coastal A595, via the hamlet of **Nether Wasdale**, before meeting the lake at its southwestern tip at the *Wasdale Hall* **youth hostel** (ⓣ0870/770 6082, ⓔwastwater@yha.org.uk), a country house set in its own lakeside grounds. The minor road then hugs the shore of the lake, ending three miles away at **Wasdale Head**, a Shangri-La-like clearing between the mountain ranges, where you'll find the marvellous *Wasdale Head Inn* (ⓣ01946/726229, ⓦwww.wasdale.com; ❼), one of the most celebrated of all Lakeland inns, with legendary breakfasts, a great public bar and hearty four-course dinners. Nearby, there's **B&B**, walking advice and packed lunches from hiker-friendly *Lingmell House* (ⓣ019467/26261, ⓦwww.lingmellhouse.co.uk; no credit cards; ❹; closed Jan), on the track to the church.

Eskdale

Eskdale is perhaps the prettiest of the unsung Lakeland valleys, and can be accessed from the Cumbrian coast by the Ravenglass and Eskdale Railway (see p.534), which drops you at Dalegarth Station, right in the heart of superb walking country around the dead-end hamlet of **Boot**. There's a good café and bike rental available at the station, while three miles beyond Boot and 800 feet up, the remains of granaries, bath houses and the commandant's quarters for **Hardknott Roman Fort** (free access) command a strategic and panoramic position.

The traditional accommodation choice in Boot is the *Boot Inn* (ⓣ019467/23224, ⓦwww.bootinn.co.uk; ❺), though it's the first-rate *Woolpack Inn* (ⓣ019467/23230, ⓦwww.woolpack.co.uk; ❺), a mile east of the village on the Hardknott Pass road, that really stands out – cosy rooms, a beer garden with views, ale from the pub's own brewery and excellent food.

Cockermouth

The attractive small town and market centre of **COCKERMOUTH**, midway between the coast and Keswick, is yet another station on the Wordsworth trail: the **Wordsworth House** on Main Street (Easter–Oct Mon–Sat 11am–4.30pm; £4.90, admission by timed ticket; NT) is where William and Dorothy were born and spent their first few years. The building is presented as a functioning eighteenth-century home – with a costumed cook willing to share recipes in the kitchen and a clerk completing the ledger with quill and ink. Afterwards, follow your nose and you're likely to stumble upon **Jennings Brewery**, on Brewery Lane near the river. At Cumbria's best-known beer-maker, the hour-and-a-half-long tour (£4.95; booking advisable; ⓣ0845/129 7190; ⓦwww.jenningsbrewery.co.uk) culminates in a real-ale tasting session.

There's stylish **accommodation** in town at *Six Castlegate*, 6 Castlegate (ⓣ01900/826749, ⓦwww.sixcastlegate.co.uk; ❹), or out of town (two miles southeast) at the *Old Homestead* at Byresteads Farm, Hundrith Hill Rd, off the B5292 (ⓣ01900/822223, ⓦwww.byresteads.co.uk; ❹), a beautifully restored seventeenth-century farmhouse offering quality B&B. *Merienda* **café**, 7A Station St (ⓣ01900/822790, ⓦwww.merienda.co.uk; daytime only, though open Fri night for tapas and music), is the best place for breakfasts, sandwiches and light meals. Vegetarians meanwhile come from far and wide for the fine-dining experience that is the *Quince and Medlar*, 13 Castlegate (ⓣ01900/823579, ⓦwww.quinceandmedlar.co.uk; dinner only, closed Sun & Mon), while the top **pub** is *The Bitter End* on Kirkgate, housing Cumbria's smallest brewery.

Ullswater

At seven miles, serpentine **Ullswater** is Cumbria's second-longest lake. The chief settlements, Glenridding and Patterdale, are less than a mile apart at the southern tip, and are not otherwise notable except as bases for climbing **Helvellyn** (3114ft), the most popular of the four 3000-foot mountains in Cumbria. There are buses here from Penrith (the #108, via Pooley Bridge and Aira Force to Glenridding and Patterdale) and from Bowness (#517 Kirkstone Rambler, via the Kirkstone Pass, daily in summer school hols, weekends and bank hols from Easter–Oct).

The former mining village of **GLENRIDDING** features several inexpensive **B&Bs**, including *Beech House*, on the main road (ⓣ017684/82037, ⓦwww.beechhouse.com; ❹), as well as a couple of grander hotels, and there's **camping** and **bunkhouse** accommodation half a mile away up the valley at *Gillside Caravan & Camping* (ⓣ017684/82346; closed Nov–Feb). It's a seven-mile (5–6hr) circuit to climb the mountain from Glenridding, but hikers wanting an early start on Helvellyn stay at *Helvellyn YHA* (ⓣ0870/770 6110, ⓔhelvellyn@yha.org.uk; from £13), a mile and a half up the valley road from Glenridding. The **tourist office** (Easter–Oct daily 9.30am–5.30pm; Nov–Easter Sat & Sun 9.30am–3.30pm; ⓣ017684/82414) is in the main car park.

At **Gowbarrow Park**, three miles north of Glenridding, the hillside still blazes green and gold in spring, as it was doing when the Wordsworths visited in April 1802; it's thought that Dorothy's recollections of the visit in her diary inspired William to write his famous "Daffodils" poem. The car park and tea-rooms here mark the start of a brief walk up to **Aira Force** (40min round-trip), a seventy-foot fall that's spectacular in spate.

The lake itself is traversed by the **Ullswater Steamers** (ⓣ017684/82229, ⓦwww.ullswater-steamers.co.uk), which have year-round services from Glenridding to Howtown, halfway up the lake's eastern side (£7.90 return;

35min), and from Howtown to the pretty village of Pooley Bridge, at the northern end of the lake (£7.20; 20min).

A minor road from **Howtown** hugs the eastern shore of the lake the four miles to **Pooley Bridge**, passing the incomparable *Sharrow Bay* (ⓣ017684/86301, ⓦwww.sharrowbay.com; ⓽ with dinner) on the way, one of England's finest country-house hotels. Pooley Bridge itself has several local campsites and three pubs, while three miles to the north at **Yanwath**, the welcoming *Gate Inn* (ⓣ01768/862386) is a renowned gastropub.

The Cumbrian coast

The Cumbrian coast attracts much less attention than the spectacular scenery inland, but it would be a mistake to write it off. It splits into two distinct sections, the most accessible being the **Furness peninsulas** area (ⓦwww.lake-district-peninsulas.co.uk), just a few miles from Windermere, where varied attractions include the monastic priory at **Cartmel** and the enjoyable market town of **Ulverston**. The **Cumbrian coast** itself is generally judged to begin at Silecroft near Millom and stretches for more than sixty miles to the small resort of Silloth, on the shores of the Solway Firth. In between lies the estuary village of **Ravenglass**, access point for the **Ravenglass and Eskdale Railway**, though if you had to pick just one coastal destination, the attractive Georgian port of **Whitehaven** would be the clear winner.

Cartmel and Holker Hall

Sheltered several miles inland from Morecambe Bay, **CARTMEL** grew up around its twelfth-century Augustinian priory and is still dominated by the proud **Church of St Mary and St Michael** (daily 9am–3.30/5.30pm; free). Everything else in the village is modest in scale, centred on the attractive **market square**, beyond the church, with its Elizabethan cobbles, water pump and fish slabs. On the square, the **Cartmel Village Shop** is known to aficionados for the quality of its sticky-toffee pudding.

A couple of miles west of the village, one of Cumbria's most interesting country estates, **Holker Hall** (Easter–Oct Mon–Fri & Sun 10am–5.30pm; £9.25, gardens only £5.95; ⓦwww.holker-hall.co.uk) is still in use by the Cavendish family who've owned it since the late seventeenth century. The highly impressive 23-acre **gardens**, both formal and woodland, are the highlight for many, and a celebrated annual garden **festival** (June) is held here, as well as spring and winter markets.

You will need to book in advance for Cartmel's extraordinary *L'Enclume* on Cavendish Street (ⓣ015395/36362, ⓦwww.lenclume.co.uk; ❼; closed first 2 weeks Jan; restaurant closed all Mon, plus Tues & Wed lunch), a highly individual Michelin-starred restaurant-with-rooms. The nearby *Cavendish Arms* (ⓣ015395/36240, ⓦwww.thecavendisharms.co.uk; ❹) is a more traditional sixteenth-century inn, while there's organic farmhouse B&B at genial *Howbarrow Farm* (ⓣ015395/36330, ⓦwww.howbarroworganic.co.uk; ❸), a couple of miles west of the village.

Ulverston

The railway line winds westwards to **ULVERSTON**, a close-knit market town which formerly prospered on the cotton, tanning and iron-ore industries. It's an attractive place, enhanced by its dappled grey limestone cottages and a jumble of cobbled alleys and traditional shops zigzagging off the central **Market Place**. Ulverston's most famous son is Stan Laurel (born Arthur Stanley Jefferson), the whimpering, head-scratching half of the comic duo, celebrated in a mind-boggling collection of memorabilia at the **Laurel and Hardy Museum** (daily 10am–4.30pm, closed Jan; £3; ⓦwww.laurel-and-hardy-museum.co.uk), up an alley at 4c Upper Brook St, near Market Place.

The 70-mile **Cumbria Way** long-distance footpath from Ulverston to Carlisle starts from The Gill, at the top of Upper Brook Street – a waymarker spire marks the start. Ulverston **train station**, serving the Cumbrian coast railway, is only a few minutes' walk from the town centre, while **buses** arrive on nearby Victoria Road, with the **tourist office** in Coronation Hall on County Square (Mon–Sat 9am–5pm; ⓣ01229/587120, ⓦwww.ulverston.net).

Trinity House Hotel, 200 yards downhill from the station, on the corner of Prince's Street and the main A590 (ⓣ01229/588889 ⓦwww.trinityhousehotel.co.uk; ⑤), has spacious **accommodation** in a handsome Georgian building. There's also the terrific *Walker's Hostel* on Oubas Hill (ⓣ01229/585588, ⓦwww.walkershostel.co.uk; no credit cards; from £16), fifteen minutes' walk from the centre on the A590 near Canal Head, at the foot of the Hoad Monument: there are thirty beds in small rooms, with vegetarian breakfasts (included) and evening meals available (£10).

Ravenglass and Muncaster

The single main street of **RAVENGLASS**, twenty miles or so up the coast from Barrow-in-Furness, preserves a row of characterful nineteenth-century cottages facing out across the estuarine mud flats and dunes. Cumbrian coastal line trains stop at Ravenglass, which is also the starting point for the **Ravenglass & Eskdale Railway** (March–Oct, at least 7 trains daily; trains also most winter weekends, plus Christmas, New Year and Feb half-term hols; £10.20 return; ⓣ01229/717171, ⓦwww.ravenglass-railway.co.uk). Opened in 1875 to carry ore from the Eskdale mines to the coastal railway, the 15-inch-gauge track winds seven miles up through the Eskdale Valley to Dalegarth Station near Boot. The full return journey, without a break, takes an hour and forty minutes, though a really good day out is to take your bike up on the train and cycle back from Dalegarth down the traffic-free **Eskdale T-Rail** (8.5 miles, 2hr) – or there's bike rental at Dalegarth station.

A mile east of Ravenglass on the A595 spreads the estate of **Muncaster Castle** (Feb half-term hols to first week of Nov; £9.50, £7 without castle entrance; ⓣ01229/717614, ⓦwww.muncaster.co.uk). Apart from the ghost-ridden rooms of the castle itself (Mon–Fri & Sun noon–5pm), there are also seventy acres of well-kept **grounds and gardens**, as well as an entertaining **owl centre** (daily 10.30am–6pm or dusk; bird displays daily at 2.30pm). The castle is closed in winter, though the grounds remain open for the illuminated **Darkest Muncaster** experience (open until 9pm, not Jan; £5).

The best local **accommodation** is at *The Pennington* (ⓣ01229/717222, ⓦwww.thepennington.co.uk; ⑦), a restored seafront hotel in Ravenglass that belongs to the castle; it also has an excellent restaurant.

Whitehaven and around

Some fine Georgian houses mark out the centre of **WHITEHAVEN**, one of the few grid-planned towns in England. The economic expansion that forced this planning was as much due to the booming slave trade as to the more widely recognized coal traffic, and all the local history is covered entertainingly in **The Beacon** (under refurbishment at time of writing but open for 2008; Ⓦwww.thebeacon-whitehaven.co.uk), an enterprising museum on the harbour. The whole waterfront comes alive during the biennial **maritime festival** in June, held on odd-numbered years.

Whitehaven's Georgian streets and its neatly painted houses make it one of Cumbria's most distinguished towns. Stroll up Lowther Street to the **Rum Story** (daily 10am–4.30pm; £5.45; Ⓦwww.rumstory.co.uk), housed in the eighteenth-century shop, courtyard and warehouses of the Jefferson's rum family, where you can learn about rum, the Navy, temperance and the hideousness of the slaves' Middle Passage, amongst other matters.

The **tourist office** is in the Market Hall on Market Place (Mon–Sat 9.30/10am–4/5pm, plus July & Aug Sun 11am–3pm; Ⓣ01946/598914, Ⓦwww.rediscoverwhitehaven.com), just back from the harbour. Whitehaven is the start of the 140-mile **C2C cycle route** to Sunderland/Newcastle – a metal cut-out at the harbour marks the spot.

Five miles south of Whitehaven, long sands lie a few hundred yards west of the coastal village of St Bees. The steep, sandstone cliffs of **St Bees Head** to the north are good for windy walks and birdwatching, while the headland's lighthouse marks the start of Alfred Wainwright's 190-mile **Coast-to-Coast Walk** to Robin Hood's Bay. There's good **accommodation** at *Fleatham House*, High House Road (Ⓣ01946/822341, Ⓦwww.fleathamhouse.com; ⑤), a lovely retreat with restaurant set in its own grounds just five minutes' walk from the station, or at *Platform 9*, a romantic railway-themed bistro at the old station house (Ⓣ01946/822600, Ⓦwww.platform9.co.uk; ⑤).

East Cumbria: Penrith and the Eden Valley

The Lake District might end abruptly with the market town and transport hub of **Penrith**, ten miles northeast of Ullswater, but Cumbria doesn't. To the east, the **Eden Valley** splits the Pennines from the Lake District fells, and boasts a succession of hardy market towns, prime among which is the former county town of **Appleby-in-Westmorland**. This lies on the magnificent **Settle to Carlisle railway**, connecting Cumbria with the Yorkshire Dales.

Penrith and around

The brisk streets of **PENRITH** have more in common with the towns of the North Pennines than the stone villages of south Cumbria, and even the local building materials emphasize the geographic shift. Its deep-red buildings were erected from the same rust-red sandstone used to construct **Penrith Castle** (daily 7.30am–dusk; free) in the fourteenth century, as a bastion against raids from the north; it's now a romantic, crumbling ruin, opposite the train station. The town itself is at its best in the narrow streets, arcades and alleys off **Market Square**, and around **St Andrew's churchyard**, where the so-called "Giant's Grave" is actually a collection of pre-Norman crosses and "hogsback" tombstones.

Penrith **train station** is five minutes' walk south of Market Square and the main street, Middlegate, while the **bus station** is on Albert Street, behind Middlegate. The **tourist office** is on Middlegate (Mon–Sat 9.30/10am–4/5pm, until 6pm July & Aug, plus Sun 1–4.45pm Easter–Oct; Ⓣ01768/867466,

Ⓦwww.visiteden.co.uk), and shares its seventeenth-century schoolhouse premises with a small local museum. Portland Place, behind the town hall, has a refined row of **guesthouses**, including the excellent *Brooklands*, 2 Portland Place (Ⓣ01768/863395, Ⓦwww.brooklandsguesthouse.com; ❹). Or drive out fifteen miles southeast to *Crake Trees Manor* at Crosby Ravensworth (Ⓣ01931/715205, Ⓦwww.craketreesmanor.co.uk; ❺), a super-stylish barn conversion in the Eden Valley, with quality B&B and local walks.

Three miles southwest of town, the country house of **Dalemain** (Feb half-term hol & Easter–Oct Mon–Thurs & Sun, house 11.15am–4pm, gardens 10.30am–5pm; Nov, Dec & Feb–Easter gardens and tearoom only Mon–Thurs 11am–4pm; £6.50, gardens only £4.50; Ⓦwww.dalemain.com) started life in the twelfth century as a fortified tower, but has subsequently been added to by successive generations.

You also shouldn't miss **Rheged** (daily 10am–5.30pm; Ⓦwww.rheged.com; free) at Redhills on the A66, a couple of minutes' drive from the M6 (junction 40). Billed as Europe's largest earth-covered building, it features a spectacular atrium-lit underground visitor centre, with exhibitions, local art and craft displays, family activities, food hall, restaurant and café. There's also a giant-format cinema screen showing films daily, as well as the separate **National Mountaineering Exhibition**, presenting an entertaining history of mountain-climbers and climbing. Admission to one film or the Mountaineering Exhibition costs £5.95, while seeing each extra film costs £4.

Appleby-in-Westmorland

One-time county town of Westmorland, **APPLEBY-IN-WESTMORLAND** is protected on three sides by a lazy loop in the River Eden. The fourth was defended by the now privately owned **Appleby Castle**, whose Norman keep was restored by Lady Anne Clifford, who, after her father's death in 1605, spent 45 years trying to claim her rightful inheritance. It's currently closed to the public, but you can pursue the Lady Anne trail at the lovely **almshouses** she founded. These are on Boroughgate, the town's backbone, which runs from High Cross, former site of the cheese market outside the castle, down to Low Cross, previously a butter market but now home of the general Saturday market.

The town changes its character completely every June when the **Appleby Horse Fair** takes over nearby Gallows' Hill, as it has done since 1750. Britain's most important gypsy gathering draws thousands of tinkers, New Age travellers and sightseers. Historically, the main day of the fair was the second Wednesday of June (the official day for horse trading), but today most of the action takes place between the previous Thursday and the Tuesday, culminating on the Tuesday evening with the showpiece trotting races.

The Settle to Carlisle railway is the best way to get to Appleby, although **bus services** from Penrith are frequent enough. The **tourist office**, in the Moot Hall on Boroughgate (April–Oct Mon–Sat 9.30am–5pm, Sun 11am–3pm; Nov–March Mon–Thurs 10am–1pm, Fri & Sat 10am–3pm; Ⓣ01768/351177, Ⓦwww.applebytown.org.uk), is ten minutes' walk from the station, across the river, and can help you find somewhere to stay.

Carlisle and around

The county capital of Cumbria and its only city, **CARLISLE** is also the repository of much of the region's history, its strategic location having been fought over for more than 2000 years, since the construction of Hadrian's Wall. The later struggle with the Scots defined the very nature of Carlisle as a border city: William Wallace was repelled in 1297 and Robert the Bruce eighteen years later, but Bonnie Prince Charlie's troops took Carlisle in 1745 after a six-day siege, holding it for six weeks before surrendering to the Duke of Cumberland. It's not surprising, then, that Carlisle still trumpets itself as the "great border city", and it's well worth taking the time to explore its historic centre.

The City

Carlisle Cathedral (Mon–Sat 7.30am–6.15pm, Sun 7.30am–5pm; free, donation requested) dominates the city, founded in 1122 but embracing a considerably older heritage. Christianity was established in sixth-century Carlisle by St Kentigern (often known as St Mungo), who became the first bishop and patron saint of Glasgow. Parliamentarian troops during the Civil War destroyed all but two powerful arches of the original eight bays of the Norman nave, but there's still much to admire in the ornate fifteenth-century choir stalls and the glorious **East Window**, which features some of the finest pieces of fourteenth-century stained glass in the country. Opposite the main entrance, the reconstructed **Fratry**, or monastic building, houses the *Prior's Kitchen*, a daytime café (closed Sun) using space that was once the monks' dining hall.

For more on Carlisle's history, head for the **Tullie House Museum and Art Gallery** (Mon–Sat 10am–4/5pm, Sun noon–4/5pm; £5.50; Ⓦwww.tulliehouse.co.uk), reached up Castle Street or through the cathedral grounds, via Abbey Street. This takes a highly imaginative approach to Carlisle's turbulent past, with special emphasis put on life on the edge of the Roman Empire – climbing a reconstruction of part of Hadrian's Wall, you learn about catapults and stone-throwers, while other sections elaborate on domestic life, work and burial practices. A public walkway from outside Tullie House crosses to **Carlisle Castle** (daily: 9.30/10am–4/6pm; £4; EH), where, in 1568, Elizabeth I kept Mary Queen of Scots as her "guest". **Guided tours** of the castle (Easter–Oct daily; ask at the entrance) help bring the history to life, and don't leave without climbing to the battlements for a view of the Carlisle rooftops.

Practicalities

From either the **train station** or the **bus station**, it's a five-minute walk to the **tourist office** in the old town hall (Mon–Sat 9.30/10am–4/5.30pm, plus May–Aug Sun 10.30am–4pm; Ⓣ01228/625600, Ⓦwww.historic-carlisle.org.uk). Most of the budget **accommodation** is concentrated in a conservation area in the streets between Victoria Place and Warwick Road. Cultural **entertainment** revolves around the concerts, plays, performances, exhibitions and workshops at Tullie House or the associated Stanwix Arts Theatre on Brampton Road (box office Ⓣ01228/534664).

Accommodation

Acorn Bank Wetheral, 4 miles east of Carlisle, off A69 Ⓣ01228/561434, Ⓦwww.acornbank.co.uk. Two lovely rooms available at a country guesthouse in a pretty village. The owners (former restaurateurs) also offer dinner on request (£25). No credit cards. ❻

Langleigh House 6 Howard Place Ⓣ01228/530440, Ⓦwww.langleighhouse.co.uk. Nicely presented Victorian townhouse B&B with eight rooms, including a family room that sleeps four. Parking. No credit cards. ❺

The Weary Castle Carrock, Brampton, 8 miles east of Carlisle Ⓣ01228/670230, Ⓦwww.theweary.com. The inn with the "wow" factor – traditional eighteenth-century outside, utterly contemporary (yet unstuffy and informal) inside. A handsome designer bar-restaurant and conservatory provides classy Modern British meals. 7

Restaurants

Davids 62 Warwick Rd ⓣ01228/523578. Formal restaurant that draws on Mediterranean ingredients for its seasonally changing offerings. Lunch is cheaper and set midweek menus provide value for money. Closed Sun & Mon. Expensive.

The Lemon Lounge 18 Fisher St ⓣ01228/546363. Easy-going cellar bistro with a sun-trap outdoor terrace – eat Thai curry, Mediterranean pasta, salads and the like. Closed Sun & Mon. Moderate.

Number 10 10 Eden Mount ⓣ01228/524183. Agreeable townhouse restaurant, serving a seasonally changing Modern English menu. Dinner only, closed Sun & Tues. Expensive.

Around Carlisle

Eight miles east of Carlisle, the small market town of **Brampton** is at the centre of several outlying attractions, including Talkin Tarn, a pretty lake set within 120 acres of meadow and woodland, and the highly attractive ruins of **Lanercost Priory** (Easter–Sept daily 10am–5pm; Oct Mon & Thurs–Sun 10am–4pm; Nov weekends only 10am–4pm; £3; EH). A little further east, however, is the area's real highlight – **Birdoswald Fort** (Easter–Sept daily 10am–5.30pm, Oct daily 10am–4pm; £4.10; EH), five miles beyond Brampton and fifteen from Carlisle. One of sixteen forts along Hadrian's Wall, it has all tiers of the Roman structure intact, while a drill hall and other buildings have been excavated. There's a tearoom and picnic area at the fort, while its residential study centre is available to overnight hikers and others as a summer-only YHA youth hostel (ⓣ0870/770 6124, ⓔbirdoswald@yha.org.uk). The seasonal Hadrian's Wall Bus (see p.611) connects Carlisle with Brampton (20min), Lanercost (30min) and Birdoswald (40min), before running on to the rest of the Hadrian's Wall sights.

Travel details

Buses

For information on all local and national bus services, contact Traveline ⓣ0871/200 2233, ⓦwww.traveline.org.uk.

Carlisle to: Keswick (3 daily; 1hr 10min); Windermere/Bowness (3 daily; 2hr 20min).

Cross Lake Shuttle (Lake District): up to 9 daily services; launch from Bowness connects with minibus from Sawrey to Hill Top (5min) and Hawkshead (13min) – first and last bus of the day also runs to Grizedale (25min). Service daily Easter–Sept, plus Oct weekends.

Kendal to: Ambleside (hourly; 40min); Cartmel (7 daily; 1hr); Grasmere (hourly; 1hr); Keswick (hourly; 1hr 30min); Lancaster (hourly; 1hr); Windermere/Bowness (hourly; 30min).

Keswick to: Ambleside (hourly; 45min); Buttermere (2 daily; 30min); Carlisle (3 daily; 1hr 10min); Cockermouth (every 30min–1hr; 30min); Grasmere (hourly; 40min); Honister (Easter–Oct 4 daily; 40min); Kendal (hourly; 1hr 30min); Rosthwaite (every 30min–1hr; 25min); Seatoller (every 30min–1hr; 30min); Windermere (hourly; 1hr).

Windermere to: Ambleside (hourly; 15min); Bowness (every 20–30min; 15min); Carlisle (3 daily; 2hr 20min); Grasmere (every 20–30min; 30min); Kendal (hourly; 25min); Keswick (hourly; 1hr).

Trains

For information on all local and national rail services, contact National Rail Enquiries ⓣ08457/484950, ⓦwww.rail.co.uk.

Appleby-in-Westmorland to: Carlisle (6 daily; 40min).

Carlisle to: Appleby (6 daily; 40min); Lancaster (every 30min–1hr; 1hr); Newcastle (hourly; 1hr 20min–1hr 40min); Whitehaven (hourly; 1hr 10min).

Windermere to: Kendal (hourly; 15min) and Oxenholme (hourly; 20min) for onward services to Lancaster and Manchester, or Penrith and Carlisle.

12 Yorkshire

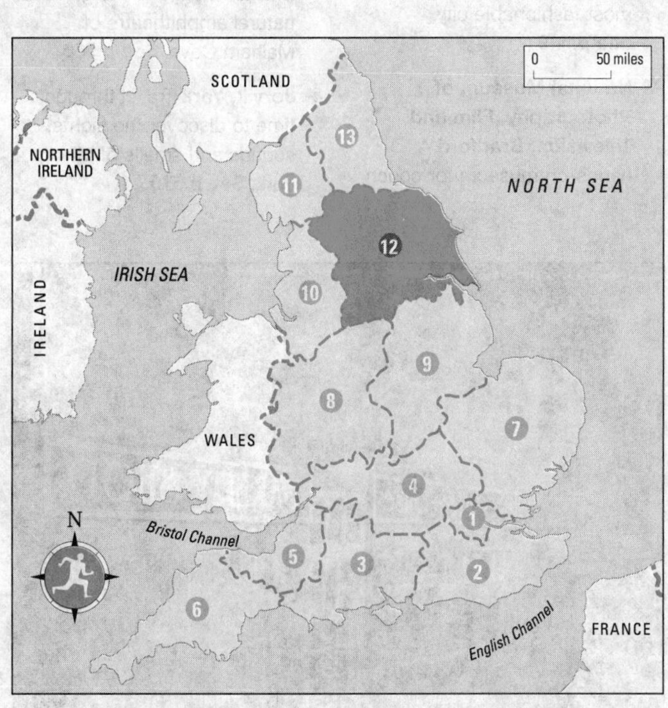

CHAPTER 12 Highlights

* **Millennium Galleries, Sheffield** Centrepiece of revamped Sheffield – terrific exhibitions with hothouse gardens attached. See p.544
* **Shopping in Leeds** Shop till you drop in the markets, malls and arcades of Yorkshire's most fashionable city. See p.549
* **National Museum of Photography, Film and Television, Bradford** A hands-on museum for couch potatoes and film fans of all ages. See p.551
* **Haworth** Visit the bleak moorland home of the Brontë sisters. See p.552
* **Malham** Make the breathtaking hike from Malham village to the glorious natural amphitheatre of Malham Cove. See p.556
* **Jorvik, York** Travel through time to discover the sights, sounds and smells of Viking York. See p.570

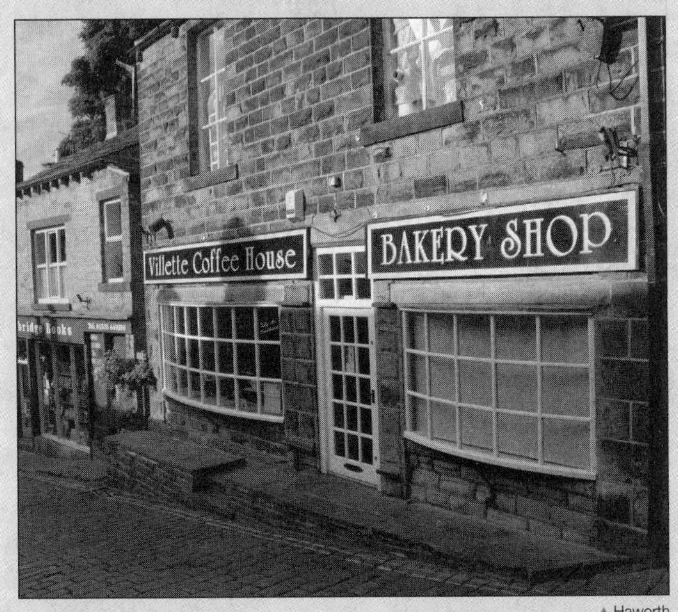

▲ Haworth

12

Yorkshire

It's easy to be glib about **Yorkshire** – for much of the country, England's largest county is shorthand for "up north" and all its clichéd connotations, from flat caps and factories to tightfisted locals. For their part, many Yorkshire born-and-bred are happy to play to the prejudice of southerners, adopting an attitude roughly on a par with that of Texans or Australians in strongly suggesting that there's really nowhere else worth considering. In its sheer size at least, Yorkshire does have a case for primacy, while its most striking characteristics – from dialect to landscape – derive from a long history of settlement, invention and independence that's still a source of pride today. As for Yorkshire's other boasts (the beer's better, the air's cleaner, the people are friendlier than "down south", etc), visitors can make up their own mind.

The number-one destination is undoubtedly history-soaked **York**, for centuries England's second city until the Industrial Revolution created new centres of power and influence. York's mixture of medieval, Georgian and Victorian architecture is mirrored in miniature in towns such as **Beverley**, **Ripon** and **Richmond**, while the Yorkshire coast, too, retains something of its erstwhile grandeur - **Bridlington** and **Scarborough** boomed in the nineteenth century and again in the postwar period, though its in smaller resorts like **Whitby** and **Robin Hood's Bay** that the best of the coast is to be found today.

The engine of growth during the Industrial Revolution was not in the north of the county, but in the south and west, where Leeds, Bradford, Sheffield and their satellites were once the world's mightiest producers of textiles and of steel. Ruthless economic logic devastated the area in the twentieth century, but a new vigour has infused South and West Yorkshire during the last decade, and the city-centre transformations of **Leeds** and **Sheffield** in particular have been remarkable, while **Bradford** waylays people on their way to **Haworth**, home of the Brontë sisters. The **Yorkshire Dales**, to the northwest, form a patchwork of stone-built villages, limestone hills, serene valleys and majestic heights. The county's other National Park, the **North York Moors**, is divided into bleak upland moors and a tremendous rugged coastline between Robin Hood's Bay and Staithes.

Fast **train** services on the East Coast main line link York to London, Newcastle and Edinburgh. Leeds is also served by regular trains from London, and is at the centre of the integrated Metro bus and train system that covers most of West and South Yorkshire. There are also train services to Scarborough (from York) and Whitby (from Middlesbrough), while the **Settle to Carlisle** line, to the southern and western Yorkshire Dales, can be accessed from Leeds. The **North Country Rover** ticket (any four days in eight; £68) covers unlimited train travel north of Leeds, Bradford and Hull and south of Newcastle and Carlisle.

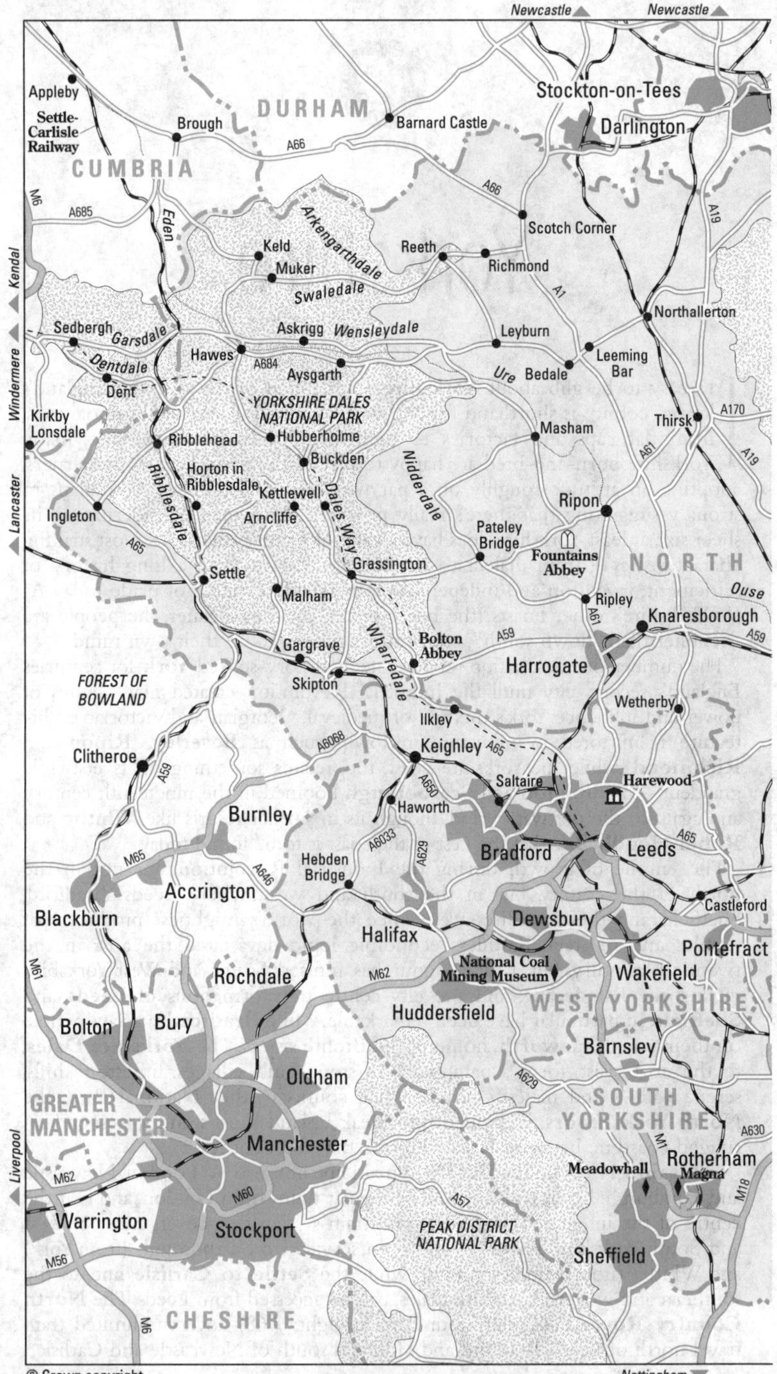

Newcastle
Newcastle
Appleby
Settle-Carlisle Railway
Brough
DURHAM
Barnard Castle
Stockton-on-Tees
Darlington
CUMBRIA
A66
M6
A685
Eden
Arkengarthdale
Scotch Corner
Keld
Reeth
Richmond
Muker
Swaledale
A1
A19
Northallerton
Kendal
Sedbergh
Garsdale
Askrigg
Wensleydale
Leyburn
Windermere
Hawes
A684
Dentdale
Aysgarth
Leeming Bar
Dent
Bedale
Ure
YORKSHIRE DALES NATIONAL PARK
Kirkby Lonsdale
Masham
Thirsk
A170
Ribblehead
Hubberholme
Buckden
Nidderdale
A61
Horton in Ribblesdale
Kettlewell
Dales Way
Ripon
Lancaster
Ingleton
Ribblesdale
Arncliffe
Pateley Bridge
Fountains Abbey
NORTH
A65
Settle
Grassington
Ouse
Malham
Ripley
Knaresborough
Wharfedale
A59
Bolton Abbey
Gargrave
Harrogate
FOREST OF BOWLAND
Skipton
Wetherby
Ilkley
A6068
Keighley
Clitheroe
Saltaire
Harewood
A650
Haworth
Burnley
A6033
A629
Bradford
Leeds
M65
Hebden Bridge
A646
Accrington
Castleford
Blackburn
Halifax
Dewsbury
Pontefract
National Coal Mining Museum
Rochdale
M62
Wakefield
M61
Huddersfield
WEST YORKSHIRE
Bolton
Bury
Barnsley
Oldham
A629
GREATER MANCHESTER
SOUTH YORKSHIRE
A630
M1
Manchester
Liverpool
Meadowhall
Rotherham
Magna
M18
M62
M60
A57
Warrington
Stockport
PEAK DISTRICT NATIONAL PARK
Sheffield
M56
M6
CHESHIRE
Nottingham

YORKSHIRE
N
Saltburn-by-the-Sea
Middlesbrough
Staithes
Runswick Bay
A174
Whitby
Great Ayton
Castleton
Danby
A171
Hawsker
Robin Hood's Bay
Grosmont
Goathland
CLEVELAND HILLS
Ravenscar
A171
NORTH SEA
Rosedale Abbey
NORTH YORK MOORS NATIONAL PARK
B1257
Hutton le Hole
A169
DALBY FOREST
Kirkbymoorside
Scarborough
Rievaulx Abbey
Helmsley
Pickering
Thornton -le-Dale
A170
Filey
Eden Camp
B1363
Castle Howard
Malton
A64
Bempton Cliffs
Flamborough Head
YORKSHIRE
Bridlington
A166
YORKSHIRE WOLDS
A166
Gt. Driffield
York
A1079
A163
A165
A64
EAST YORKSHIRE
Hornsea
Market Weighton
B1242
A63
Beverley
A614
Selby
Kingston upon Hull
Withernsea
A1033
B1445
M62
Goole
Ouse
Humber Bridge
Humber
A15
Easington
Immingham
Scunthorpe
Grimsby
Spurn Head
M180
Cleethorpes
Doncaster
Trent
A159
A46
LINCOLNSHIRE
A16
Gainsborough
Market Rasen
Louth
Worksop
A1
0
20 miles
Newark
Boston

12 YORKSHIRE

Sheffield and around

Yorkshire's second city, **SHEFFIELD** remains inextricably linked with its steel industry, in particular the production of high-quality cutlery. Technological advances in steel production later turned Sheffield into one of the country's foremost centres of heavy and specialist engineering, which meant the city suffered heavy bombing in World War II. However, more damaging than bombs to the city's pre-eminence was the steel industry's subsequent downturn, which by the 1980s had tipped parts of Sheffield into dispiriting decline. The subsequent revival has been rapid, with the centre utterly transformed by flagship architectural projects, from gardens to galleries. Steel, of course, still underpins much of what Sheffield is about: museum collections tend to specialize in the region's industrial heritage, which is complemented by the startling science-and-adventure exhibits at **Magna** built on a disused steel works at nearby **Rotherham**, the former coal and iron town a few miles northeast of the city.

Arrival, information and accommodation

Sheffield's **train station** is on the eastern edge of the city centre, by Sheffield Hallam University, with **Sheffield Interchange** bus and coach station about two hundred yards to the north. The **tourist office** is in the centre at 14 Norfolk Row (Mon–Fri 10am–4pm, Sat 10am–4pm; ⓣ0114/221 1900, ⓦwww.sheffieldtourism.co.uk, ⓦwww.spinsheffield.com). Most local **buses** depart from High Street or Arundel Gate, while the **Supertram** system (ⓦwww.supertram.com) connects the city centre with the flagship shopping mall at Meadowhall. For fare and timetable information, visit the **Mini Interchange** travel centre on Arundel Gate, behind the Crucible Theatre (Mon–Sat 7am–7pm; ⓣ01709/515151 or 0114/201 2675, ⓦwww.sypte.co.uk).

Sheffield has a fair amount of mid-range central **accommodation** – even so, the tourist office's room-booking service can come in handy (ⓣ0871/700 0121). Self-catering **student rooms** (late June to mid-Sept) can be booked through the University of Sheffield (ⓣ0114/289 3500, ⓦwww.victoriahall.com; from £25 per night).

Hotels and guesthouses

Houseboat Hotels Victoria Quays ⓣ0114/232 6556 or 07974/590264, ⓦwww.houseboathotels.com. Something a little bit different – two moored houseboats, available by the night, both with en-suite bathrooms and kitchens. They're rented exclusively, for two people ④ or four people ⑤

Novotel 50 Arundel Gate ⓣ0114/278 1781, ⓦwww.accorhotels.com. A classy refurbishment has made this designer four-star with indoor pool, right by Millennium Square, an attractive option. ⑦

St Paul's 119 Norfolk St ⓣ0114/278 2000, ⓦwww.mercure.com/sheffield. An up-to-the-minute hotel on Millennium Square, with restaurant adjoining the Winter Gardens. Bedrooms are minimalist and neutral in tone. ⑧

Westbourne House 25 Westbourne Rd, Broomhill ⓣ0114/266 0109, ⓦwww.westbournehousehotel.com. Victorian townhouse, a mile out of the centre (and 10min from the bars and restaurants of Ecclesall Rd), with individually furnished light and white rooms. ⑤

The City

A minute's walk east from the Central Peace Gardens is the main symbol of the city regeneration, the stunning **Winter Gardens** (daily 8am–6pm; free), an arched steel-and-wood glasshouse almost 200 feet long and over 60 feet high. Sheffield's **Millennium Galleries** (Mon–Sat 10am–5pm, Sun 11am–5pm; free, visiting exhibitions £4; ⓦwww.sheffieldgalleries.org.uk) back onto the gardens, where, in the **Metalworks Gallery** you can discover why the eighteenth-century city's natural endowments (a fast water supply, forests for charcoal, and gritstone deposits) ensured the rapid development of the cutlery industry. There's also the highly diverting **Ruskin Gallery**, based on the cultural collection founded by John Ruskin in 1875 to "improve" the working people of Sheffield.

Southeast of the Winter Gardens, clubs and galleries exist alongside arts and media businesses in the **Cultural Industries Quarter**. North of the stations, near the River Don, **Castlegate** has a traditional indoor **market** (closed Sun) while spruced-up warehouses and cobbled towpaths line the neighbouring canal basin, **Victoria Quays**. Closer to the Town Hall, at the end of Fargate, the city's **Cathedral of St Peter and St Paul** retains elements of its fifteenth-century origins, and is enhanced by its late twentieth-century lantern tower and colourful glass. **Cutler's Hall**, opposite on Church Street, is an imposing reminder of the importance of the cutlery trade – the Company of Cutlers guild was established here as early as 1624 to regulate the affairs of the industry. South of here, down Fargate and across Peace Gardens, the pedestrianized **Moor Quarter** draws in shoppers, though it's the **Devonshire Quarter**, east of the gardens and centred on Division Street, that is the trendiest shopping area.

Fifteen minutes' walk north of the cathedral, the **Kelham Island Museum** on Alma Street (Mon–Thurs 10am–4pm, Sun 11am–4.45pm; £4; Ⓦwww.simt.co.uk) reveals the breadth of the city's industrial output, where craftspeople demonstrate some of the finer points of cutlery production and other trades. You can then put the city's life and times into perspective a mile or so west at the **Weston Park Museum** (Mon–Sat 10am–5pm, Sun 11am–5pm; free; Ⓦwww.sheffieldgalleries.org.uk) where the imaginatively themed and family friendly galleries draw together the city's extensive archeology, natural history, art and social history collections.

Rotherham: Magna

About six miles northeast of Sheffield, across the M1, **ROTHERHAM**'s major draw is **Magna** (daily 10am–5pm; closed Mon Nov–March; April–Oct £9.95, £9 Nov–March; Ⓦwww.visitmagna.co.uk), the UK's best science adventure centre housed in a former steelworks building on Sheffield Road (A6178), Templeborough, just off the M1 a mile from the Meadowhall shopping complex (bus #69 from either Sheffield or Rotherham Interchanges, or a fifteen-minute taxi ride from Sheffield). The vast internal space comfortably holds four gadget-packed **pavilions**, themed on the basic elements of earth, air, fire and water. In these you're encouraged to get your hands on a huge variety of interactive exhibits, games and machines – operating a real JCB, filling diggers and barrows, blasting a rock face or investigating a twister. On the hour, everyone decamps to the main hall for the **Big Melt** when the original arc furnace is used in a bone-shaking light and sound show that has visitors gripping the railings.

Eating, drinking and nightlife

Sheffield has plenty of great **café-bars** and good-value **restaurants**: just south of the centre, London Road is lined with good, authentic southeast Asian restaurants. For the best insight into what makes Sheffield tick as a party destination take a night-time walk along **Division Street** and **West Street** where competing theme and retro bars go in and out of fashion. Locals and students also frequent the bars and pubs of **Ecclesall Road** (the so-called "golden mile"), out of the centre to the southwest.

Cafés and restaurants

Antibo West:One, Unit 10, Fitzwilliam St ⓣ0114/272 7222. Classy, contemporary Italian restaurant with on-the-mark pizzas and pastas (around £9) and daily fish specials (£16). Expensive.

Blue Moon Café 2 St James St ⓣ0114/276 3443. Relax in the skylit dining room, next to the cathedral, and tuck into home-made vegetarian/vegan food. Closes 8pm; closed Sun. Inexpensive.

The Forum 127–129 Devonshire St ⓣ0114/272 0569, ⓦwww.forumsheffield.co.uk. Long the mainstay of the Devonshire Quarter, the *Forum* has a great menu and laid-back clientele – breakfast from 10am, bar till 1am. Moderate.

Nonna's 535–541 Ecclesall Rd ⓣ0114/268 6166, ⓦwww.nonnas.co.uk. Glam see-and-be-seen Italian bar and restaurant with a great reputation. Restaurant reservations advised. The deli and ice-cream parlour round the corner in Hickmott Rd (closed Mon & Tues) are worth a visit, too. Expensive.

Vietnamese Noodle Bar 200–202 London Rd ⓣ0114/258 3608. Out of the centre, but really worth the trip for terrific Vietnamese and Chinese food. Always busy. Inexpensive.

Pubs, bars and clubs

Crystal 23–32 Carver St. A former scissor factory provides stunning premises for an airy bar-restaurant-patio, good for food, great for a night out, with a bar until 1.30am.

Devonshire Cat 49 Wellington St, Devonshire Green ⓦwww.devonshirecat.co.uk. Renowned ale-house – good cheap food with drinks matched to every selection. For somewhere more traditional, take a walk out (15min from the centre) to the *Fat Cat*, 23 Alma St, the cosier, older sister pub.

Fuel Arundel Gate ⓦwww.fuel-sheffield.co.uk. Sheffield's gay "superclub" – glam décor, resident drag queen, star DJs – is the city's most reliable night out for gay and lesbian visitors.

Leadmill 6–7 Leadmill Rd ⓣ0114/221 2828, ⓦwww.leadmill.co.uk. In the Cultural Industries Quarter, this place hosts live bands and DJs most nights of the week.

The Washington 79 Fitzwilliam St. A favoured hang-out for musicians, just 2min across the green from Division St.

Theatre, cinema and concerts

Crucible, Lyceum & Studio Tudor Square ⓣ0114/249 6000, ⓦwww.sheffieldtheatres.co.uk. Sheffield's theatres put on a full programme of theatre, dance, comedy and concerts. The Crucible, of course, has hosted the World Snooker Championships for 30 years. It also presents the annual Music in the Round festival of chamber music (May), and the Sheffield Children's Festival (late June or July).

Sheffield City Hall Barker's Pool ⓣ0114/278 9789, ⓦwww.sheffieldcityhall.com. Year-round programme of classical music, opera, mainstream concerts, comedy and club nights.

The Showroom 7 Paternoster Row ⓣ0114/275 7727, ⓦwww.showroom.org.uk. The biggest independent cinema outside London also has a relaxed café-restaurant on one side and a great bar on the other.

Leeds and around

Yorkshire's commercial capital, and one of the fastest-growing cities in the country, **LEEDS** has undergone a radical transformation in recent years. There's still a true northern grit to its character, and in many of its dilapidated suburbs, but the grime has been removed from the impressive Victorian buildings and the city is revelling in its persona as a booming financial, commercial and cultural centre. The renowned **shops**, **restaurants**, **bars** and **clubs** provide one focus of a visit to contemporary Leeds – it's certainly Yorkshire's top destination for a day or two of conspicuous consumption and indulgence. Museums include the impressive **Royal Armouries**, which hold the national arms and armour collection, while the **City Art Gallery** has one of the best collections of British twentieth-century art outside London. Outlying attractions range from the fascinating **Thackray Museum** of medicine to the art collection and grounds at **Temple Newsam**, while with more time you can do justice to the region's major draws – the great Georgian country house, **Harewood**, the **National Coal Mining Museum** and the bucolic **Yorkshire Sculpture Park**.

Arrival, transport and information

National and local Metro trains use **Leeds Station** off City Square, which also houses the **Gateway Yorkshire tourist office** in the Arcade (Mon 10am–5.30pm, Tues–Sat 9am–5.30pm, Sun 10am–4pm; ⓣ0113/242 5242, ⓦwww.leeds.gov.uk, ⓦwww.leedsliveitloveit.com). The **bus station** occupies a site to the east, behind Kirkgate Market, on St Peter's Street. The **Metro Travel Centres** at the bus and train stations have up-to-date service details for local transport or call **Metroline** (daily 7am–10pm; ⓣ0113/245 7676, ⓦwww.wymetro.com).

Accommodation

There's a good mix of **accommodation**. Cheaper lodgings lie out to the northwest in the student area of Headingley, though these are a bus or taxi ride away. For **short breaks** and weekends away contact the tourist office's special booking line on ⓣ0800/808050. Rooms in self-catering **student apartments** at Clarence Dock (ⓣ0113/343 6100, ⓦwww.universallyleeds.co.uk), near the Royal Armouries, are available every summer holiday (mid-July to mid-Sept; 2-night minimum stay costs £48, £21 a night thereafter).

42 The Calls 42 The Calls ⓣ0113/244 0099, ⓦwww.42thecalls.co.uk. Converted riverside grain mill, where rooms come with great beds and sharp bathrooms. Weekend rates start from £89. ⑦

Butlers/Boundary Cardigan Rd, Headingley, 1.5 miles northwest. Adjacent, associated hotels in a suburban street: cosy, smart, traditionally furnished en-suite rooms at *Butlers* (ⓣ0113/274 4755, ⓦwww.butlershotel.co.uk) and cheaper lodgings at the *Boundary* (ⓣ0113/275 7700, ⓦwww.boundaryhotel.co.uk). *Boundary* ②, *Butlers* ③, superior rooms ④

Glengarth 162 Woodsley Rd ⓣ0113/245 7940, ⓦwww.glengarthhotel.co.uk. The best of the cheapies on Woodsley Rd, just behind the university, about a mile from the centre. ②

Malmaison 1 Swinegate ⓣ0113/398 1000, ⓦwww.malmaison.com. Classy restored premises with the signature Malmaison style, plus brasserie and bar. Weekend deals from £99. ⑦

Quebecs 9 Quebec St ⓣ0113/244 8989, ⓦwww.theetoncollection.com. The ultimate city-boutique lodgings, boasting glorious Victorian oak panelling and stained glass, offset by chic rooms. Weekend rates from £75. ⑦

Radisson SAS No.1 The Light, The Headrow ⓣ0113/236 6000, ⓦwww.radissonsas.com. The Grade II-listed former HQ of the Leeds Permanent Building Society features snazzy rooms and suites that reflect high-tech, Art Deco or modern Italian design. Weekend rates start at £89. ⑦

Roomzzz 12 Swine Gate; also at 2 & 361 Burley Rd, ⓣ0113/233 0400, ⓦwww.roomzzz.co.uk. Self-catering, one- and two-bedroom apartments in contemporary style, at three locations, Swine Gate being the most central. All come with great kitchens and wide-screen TVs. ⑤

The City

Opposite the train station, a prancing statue of Edward, the Black Prince, welcomes you to **City Square**, a smartened-up space that still retains its bronze nymph gas lamps. It's a short walk to the top of East Parade where you can't miss **Leeds Town Hall**, one of the finest expressions of nineteenth-century civic pride in the country and the masterpiece of local architect Cuthbert Broderick. East from the Town Hall and you're on **The Headrow**, the city's central spine, with the **City Art Gallery** (Mon & Tues 10am–8pm, Wed noon–8pm, Thurs–Sat 10am–5pm, Sun 1–5pm; free; ⓦwww.leeds.gov.uk/artgallery) the major draw. Changing selections from the permanent collection of nineteenth- and twentieth-century art and sculpture are on show, with an understandable bias towards pieces by Henry Moore and Barbara Hepworth, both former students at the Leeds School of Art. The Art Gallery connects to the adjacent **Henry Moore Institute** (daily 10am–5.30pm, Wed until 9pm; free; ⓦwww.henry-moore-fdn.co.uk), devoted to showcasing temporary exhibitions of sculpture from all periods and nationalities.

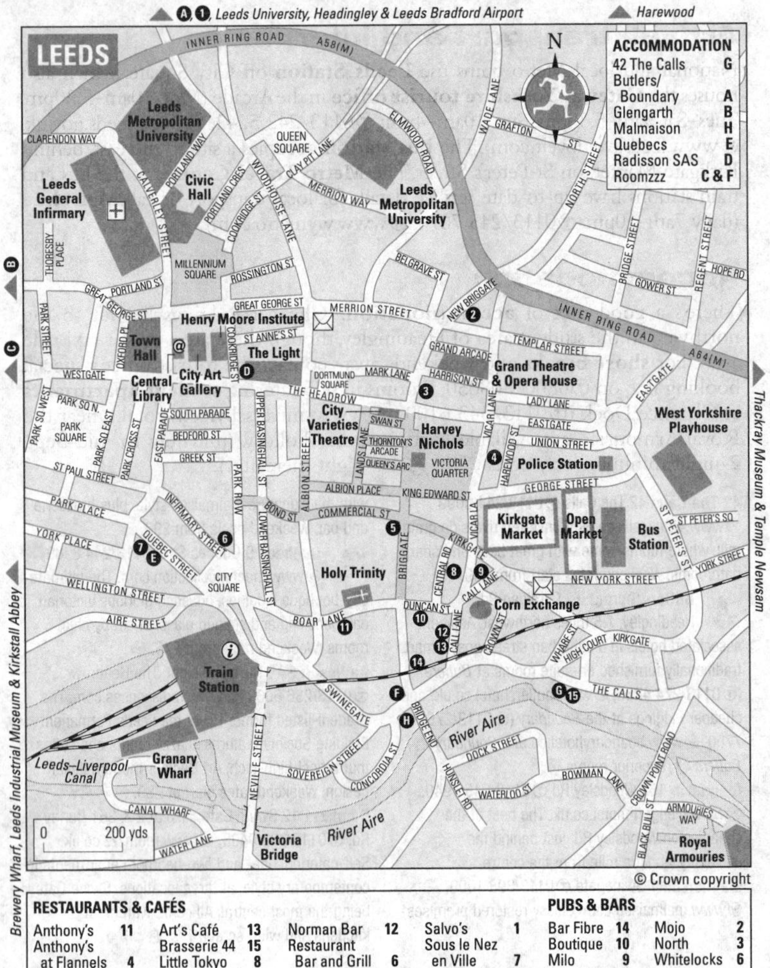

At **Granary Wharf**, a couple of minutes' walk from the train station, specialist shops fill the extensive cobbled, vaulted arches (the "Dark Arches"), while every weekend and bank holiday a market spills out onto the canal basin. **Brewery Wharf**, on the south side (or "Left Bank" as Leeds would like it to be known), sports a welter of bars and brasseries, while further east along the river (10min walk) beckons the glass turret and gunmetal grey-bulk of the **Royal Armouries** (daily 10am–5pm; free; Ⓦ www.armouries.org.uk), purpose-built to house the arms and armour collection from the Tower of London.

Outlying attractions

The **Thackray Museum** on Beckett Street (daily 10am–5pm, last admission 3pm; £5.50; Ⓦ www.thackraymuseum.org; bus #41 or #50 from the Headrow), next to St James' Hospital, is essentially a medical history museum, but a hugely

Shopping in Leeds

Most visitors make a beeline for the shop-filled arcades on either side of pedestrianized **Briggate**. These nineteenth-century palaces of marble, mahogany, stained glass and mosaics have been magnificently restored and perhaps the most splendid of all is the light-flooded **Victoria Quarter** (Ⓦwww.vqleeds.com), with Harvey Nichols (107–111 Briggate) as its designer lodestone. Across Vicar Lane, **Kirkgate Market** (Ⓦwww.leedsmarket.com; closes 2pm Wed & all Sun) is the largest market in the north of England,while the **open market** behind here (closed Wed & Sun) is where Michael Marks set up stall in 1884 with the slogan "don't ask the price, it's a penny" – an enterprise that blossomed into the present-day retail giant Marks & Spencer. At the bottom of the street, on the corner of Vicar Lane and Duncan Street, the elliptical, domed **Corn Exchange** (open daily) is now a hip market for jewellery, retro clothes, furnishings, music and other bits and bobs – extra craft stores open up at weekends.

entertaining one nevertheless, with displays on subjects as diverse as the history of the hearing aid and the workings of the human intestine. It's gruesome, too, with a film of a Victorian limb amputation in a gallery called "Pain, pus and blood". Needless to say, children love it.

Four miles east of the city, the Tudor-Jacobean house of **Temple Newsam** (Tues–Sun 10.30am–4/5pm; £3.50; Ⓣ0113/264 7321, Ⓦwww.leeds.gov.uk/templenewsam) shows many of the paintings and much of the decorative art owned by Leeds City Art Gallery. There are over 1500 acres on the estate (park open daily dawn to dusk; free), which also contains Europe's largest **rare-breeds farm** (closed Mon; £3).

The stately home of **Harewood**, seven miles north of Leeds (mid-March–Oct daily 11am–4.30pm, grounds & bird garden 10am–5pm; July, Aug & bank hol weekends £13.15, otherwise £11.30; grounds & bird garden only £10.90/£8.80; Ⓣ0113/218 1010, Ⓦwww.harewood.org), is still the home of the Earl and Countess of Harewood, who let in the great unwashed in return for nothing more than a sizeable chunk of money. To be fair, there's an enormous amount to see and do, with daily tours, talks and exhibitions included in the entrance fee, while outside in the magnificent **grounds** is an adventure playground and renowned **Bird Garden**. Here, four acres of aviaries cage over 150 species – the penguins get fed at 2pm. There are frequent buses to Harewood from Leeds (including the #36, every 20min, 30min on Sun).

While the gentry enjoyed the comforts of life in grand houses like Harewood, generations of Yorkshiremen sweated out a living underground just a few miles distant. Mining is now little more than a memory in most parts of Yorkshire but visitors can get all too vivid an idea of pit life through the ages at the excellent **National Coal Mining Museum** (daily 10am–5pm; free; Ⓦwww.ncm.org.uk), about ten miles south of Leeds at Overton, halfway between Wakefield and Huddersfield (on A642, signposted from M1). Based in a former pit, Caphouse Colliery, the highlight is an underground mine tour (90min, warm clothes required; arrive early in school hols; last tour 3.15pm) with a former miner as your guide.

Another Yorkshire country estate at West Bretton, outside Wakefield, now serves as the **Yorkshire Sculpture Park** (daily 10am–5/6pm; free, but parking £4; Ⓦwww.ysp.co.uk), a mile from the M1 (junction 38). Trails and paths run across 500 acres of eighteenth-century parkland, past open-air "gallery spaces" for some of Britain's most famous sculptors. The two big local names represented here are Henry Moore (1898–1986), born in nearby Castleford, and his contemporary Barbara Hepworth (1903–75), from Wakefield. The **Visitor Centre** near the car park is the place to check on current exhibitions and pick up a park map – the restaurant here has views over Moore's monumental pieces.

Eating, drinking and nightlife

Many old warehouses and grain mills in Leeds have been converted into up-to-the-minute **restaurants and brasseries**. The best of the city's **pubs** are the ornate Victorian ale-houses in which Leeds specializes, and when these close you can move on to one of the city's DJ bars or **clubs**, many of which have a nationwide reputation – not least because Leeds lets you dance until 5 or 6am most weekends. For information about **what's on**, your best bets are the fortnightly listings magazine *The Leeds Guide* (ⓦwww.leedsguide.co.uk) or the daily *Yorkshire Evening Post*.

Café-bars and restaurants

Anthony's 19 Boar Lane ⓣ0113/245 5922, ⓦwww.anthonysrestaurant.co.uk. Earthy flavours and ingredients dominate in the city's hottest restaurant, so expect squab (baby pigeon), offal and country-style combinations, immaculately presented. At *Anthony's at Flannel's* (68–78 Vicar Lane, ⓣ0113/242 8732; closed Mon) there's moderately priced brunch, lunch and afternoon tea with all the flair of its big brother. Very expensive.

Art's Café 42 Call Lane ⓣ0113/243 8243, ⓦwww.artscafebar.co.uk. A relaxed hang-out for drinks, dinner or a lazy Sun brunch. Mediterranean flavours dominate the well-priced menu, and the wine list is excellent. Moderate.

Brasserie 44 44 The Calls ⓣ0113/234 3232, ⓦwww.brasserie44.com. Informal Modern British bar and brasserie, serving everything from pan-fried mackerel to fancied-up duck confit. Closed Sun. Expensive.

Little Tokyo 24 Central Rd ⓣ0113/243 9090. Leeds' favourite Japanese restaurant has an enormous menu. Main courses around £7, or bento box set meals from £12. Moderate.

Norman Bar 36 Call Lane ⓣ0113/234 3988, ⓦwww.normanbar.co.uk. A boho-chic interior – cast-iron girders to cuckoo clock – plus juice bar, Asian noodle/stir-fry/*dim sum* menu, and varied club nights, add up to one of the city's unique spots. Moderate.

Restaurant Bar and Grill The Old Post Office, 3 City Square ⓣ0113/244 9625. The bank of wine bottles in the huge window draws you in to this classy post office makeover. The menu ranges from Old Spot sausages, calves' liver and grills to Italian, Thai and North African dishes. Expensive.

Salvo's 115 Otley Rd, Headingley ⓣ0113/275 5017, ⓦwww.salvos.co.uk. Pizza in Leeds to a local means *Salvo's* though there's a classy Italian menu as well and a choice list of daily specials. It really is worth the trek out from the centre. Closed Sun. Expensive.

Sous le Nez en Ville Quebec House, 9 Quebec St ⓣ0113/244 0108. Housed in the splendid red-brick building of the former Liberal Club, this basement wine bar/restaurant is particularly strong on fish. Closed Sun. Expensive.

Bars and pubs

Bar Fibre 168 Lower Briggate ⓣ0870/120 0888, ⓦwww.barfibre.com. Leeds' finest gay bar comes has DJs most nights and dancing until midnight, 2am at weekends. It's also the pre-club bar for Leeds' most dramatic club night, Federation (first Sat of month) at *Mission*, 8–13 Heaton's Court.

Boutique 11–5 Hirsts Yard, Briggate ⓣ0113/245 6595, ⓦwww.boutique-leeds.co.uk. Small, perfectly formed venue with outdoor glass-topped tables revealing jelly babies, tennis balls, petals and the like. Closed Sun.

Milo 10–12 Call Lane ⓣ0113/245 7101. Unpretentious, offbeat bar with DJs most evenings, ringing the changes from old soul and reggae to indie and electronica.

Mojo 18 Merrion St ⓣ0113/244 6387, ⓦwww.mojobar.co.uk. A great bar with classic tunes ("music for the people") and a classy drinks menu to match.

North 24 New Briggate ⓣ0113/242 4540, ⓦwww.northbar.com. The city's beer specialist has a massive selection of guest beers (more Belgian than bitter) plus cold meats and cheeses to nibble on.

Whitelocks Turk's Head Yard, off Briggate ⓣ0113/245 3950. Leeds' oldest and most atmospheric pub retains its traditional decor and a good choice of beers.

Clubs and live music

Cockpit Bridge House, Swinegate ⓣ0113/244 1573, ⓦwww.thecockpit.co.uk. The city's best live music venue, plus assorted indie/new wave club nights.

Creation 55 Cookridge St ⓣ0113/242 7272, ⓦwww.creation-leeds.co.uk. Hosts high-profile live bands as well as club nights, chart to cheese, in the city's largest club.

Hifi 2 Central Rd ⓣ0113/242 7353, ⓦwww.thehificlub.co.uk. Small club playing everything from Stax and Motown to hip-hop or drum 'n' bass. Also check out the indie/alternative associate club *Wire* at 2–8 Call Lane (ⓦwww.wireclub.co.uk).

Mint Club 8 Harrison St ⓣ0113/244 3168. Up-to-the-minute beats (there's a "no-cheese" policy), and the best chill-out space in the city.

Oceana 16–18 Woodhouse Lane ⓣ0113/243 8229, ⓦwww.oceanaclubs.com. The choice is dance, chart, R&B and indie in the Venetian Grand Ballroom, 70s and 80s disco on Europe's largest illuminated dance floor, or bars in the style of a Parisian boudoir or Aspen lodge.

The Warehouse 19–21 Somers St ⓣ0113/246 8287. House, electro and techno sounds bring in clubbers from all over the country, especially for Saturday's Technique.

Arts, festivals and entertainment

Temple Newsam hosts numerous concerts and events, from plays to rock gigs and opera, while at **Kirkstall Abbey** every summer there's a Shakespeare Festival (ⓦwww.britishshakespearecompany.com/leeds) with open-air productions of the Bard's works. **Roundhay Park** is the other large outdoor venue for concerts, while Bramham Park, ten miles east of the city, hosts the annual **Leeds Carling Festival** (ⓦwww.leedsfestival.com) at the end of August with rock/indie music on five stages. August bank holiday weekend heralds the **West Indian Carnival** in Chapeltown, only beaten in size by Notting Hill.

City Varieties Swan St, Briggate ⓣ0845/644 1881, ⓦwww.cityvarieties.co.uk. One of the country's last surviving music halls, though these days it's more tribute bands, comedians and cabaret.

Grand Theatre and Opera House 46 New Briggate ⓣ0870/121 4901, ⓦwww.leeds.gov.uk/grandtheatre. The regular base of Opera North (ⓦwww.operanorth.co.uk) and Northern Ballet (ⓦwww.northernballettheatre.co.uk) also puts on a full range of theatrical productions.

Hyde Park Picture House Brudenell Rd, Headingley ⓣ0113/275 2045, ⓦwww.hydeparkpicturehouse.co.uk. The place to come for classic cinema with independent and art-house shows alongside more mainstream films; bus #56.

West Yorkshire Playhouse Quarry Hill ⓣ0113/213 7700, ⓦwww.wyp.org.uk. The city's most innovative theatre has two stages, plus bar, restaurant and café.

Bradford and around

BRADFORD has always been a working town, booming in tandem with the Industrial Revolution, when it changed in decades from a rural seat of woollen manufacture to a polluted metropolis. In its Victorian heyday it was the world's biggest producer of worsted cloth, its skyline etched black with mill chimneys, and its hills clogged with some of the foulest back-to-back houses of any northern city. Contemporary Bradford is valiantly rinsing away its associations with urban decrepitude, and while it can hardly yet be compared with neighbouring Leeds as a visitor attraction it might ultimately succeed on its own distinct terms – plans are in place to restyle the entire city centre as an urban park and cultural quarter.

The main interest in the centre is provided by the superb **National Museum of Photography, Film and Television** (Tues–Sun 10am–6pm; free; ⓣ0870/701 0200; ⓦwww.nationalmediamuseum.org.uk), which wraps itself around one of Britain's largest cinema screens showing daily **IMAX** and 3D film screenings (£6.95). Exhibitions are devoted to every nuance of film and television, including topics like digital imaging, light and optics, and computer animation, while there are detours into the mechanics of advertising and news-gathering.

A walk past the Venetian-Gothic **Wool Exchange** building on Market Street provides ample evidence of the wealth of nineteenth-century Bradford. There's more, too, in the city's extraordinary outlying attraction of **Saltaire**, a model industrial village built by the industrialist Sir Titus Salt, which is three miles out of Bradford towards Keighley; trains to Saltaire run from Bradford Forster Square, or take bus #679 from the Interchange. The village (still lived in today) was built between 1851 and 1876, with **Salt's Mill**, larger than St Paul's Cathedral in London, the biggest factory in the world when it opened in 1853. It was surrounded by schools, hospitals, parks, almshouses and around 850 homes, yet for all Salt's philanthropic vigour the scheme was highly paternalistic: of the village's 22 streets, for example, all – bar Victoria and Albert streets – were named after members of his family. Salt's Mill remains the fulcrum of the village, the focus of which is the **1853 Gallery** (daily 10am–5.30/6pm; free; Ⓦwww.saltsmill.org.uk), three floors given over to the world's largest retrospective collection of the works of Bradford-born **David Hockney**.

Practicalities

Trains and buses both arrive at **Bradford Interchange** off Bridge Street, a little to the south of the city-centre grid. The **tourist office** (Mon 10am–5pm, Tues–Sat 9.30am–5pm; Ⓣ01274/433678, Ⓦwww.visitbradford.com), located in Centenary Square's City Hall, is three minutes' signposted walk from the Interchange. With Haworth, York and the Yorkshire Dales all only an hour away, few stay the night, but you should hang around at least long enough to sample one of Bradford's famous **curry houses** – like the hugely renowned, very inexpensive *Kashmir*, 27 Morley St (Ⓣ01274/726513). Bradford is perhaps the most multi-cultural centre in the UK outside London, with people of South Asian origin accounting for around 18 percent of the conurbation's total population.

Haworth

Of English literary shrines, probably only Stratford sees more visitors than the quarter of a million who swarm annually into the village of **HAWORTH** to tramp the cobbles once trodden by the Brontë sisters. During the summer the village's steep, cobbled Main Street is lost under huge crowds, herded by multi-lingual signs around the various stations on the Brontë trail. Of these, the **Brontë Parsonage Museum** (daily 10/11am–5/5.30pm; £5.50, Ⓦwww.bronte.info), is the obvious focus, a modest Georgian house bought by Patrick Brontë in 1820 to bring up his family. After the tragic early loss of his wife and two eldest daughters, the surviving four children – Anne, Emily, Charlotte and their dissipated brother, Branwell – spent most of their short lives in the place, which is furnished as it was in their day, and filled with the sisters' pictures, books, manuscripts and personal treasures. The **parish church** in front of the parsonage contains the family vault; Charlotte was married here in 1854.

The most popular local walk runs to **Brontë Falls** and **Bridge**, reached via West Lane and a track from the village, and to **Top Withens**, a mile beyond, a ruin fancifully (but erroneously) thought to be the model for Wuthering Heights (allow 3hr for the round trip). The moorland setting, however, beautifully evokes the flavour of the book, and to enjoy it further you could walk on another two and a half miles to **Ponden Hall**, perhaps the Thrushcross Grange of *Wuthering Heights*.

Practicalities

Haworth is eight miles northwest of Bradford. To get here by bus, take the #662 from Bradford Interchange to Keighley (every 10min), and change there for the

Literary Britain

Britain offers the unique experience of following in the footsteps of some of the world's most famous writers. In many cases, this means a visit to a birth- or burial place, or to a dedicated museum, but it's often far more rewarding to immerse yourself in the natural fabric of British literature – tramping the lakeland fells in the company of Wordsworth, say, or exploring the streets of Dickens' Rochester. And for the works themselves, Britain has one essential stop, Hay-on-Wye (p.416), the town on the Anglo-Welsh border entirely devoted to books – its annual literary festival (every May; ⓦwww.hayfestival.co.uk) is the nation's biggest book-related jamboree.

Haworth and the Brontës

Quite why the sheltered life of the **Brontë sisters**, Charlotte, Emily and Anne, should exert such powerful fascination is puzzling, though the contrast of their pinched provincial existence in the Yorkshire village of **Haworth** (p.552) with the brooding moors and tumultuous passions of their novels may well form part of the answer. The mementos, possessions and manuscripts in their old home, and the family vault in the parish church only tell half the story. It's out on the bleak moors above Haworth that inspiration struck, and where works like *Wuthering Heights* progressed from mere parlour entertainments to melodramatic studies of emotion and obsession.

The setting of *Wuthering Heights* ▲

Hamlet and his creator, William Shakespeare ▼

Shakespeare country

Warwickshire in the West Midlands is - as the road signs attest - "**Shakespeare Country**", though to all intents and purposes it's a county with just one destination - the small market town of **Stratford-upon-Avon** (p.407), birthplace of England's greatest writer. So few facts about Shakespeare's life are known that Stratford can be a disappointment for the serious literary pilgrim, its buildings and sights hedged with "reputedlys" and "maybes". Real Shakespeare country could just as easily be London, where his plays were written and performed (there was no theatre in Stratford in Shakespeare's day). But, from the house where he was born to the church in which he's buried, Stratford at least provides a coherent centre for England's Shakespeare industry - and it's certainly the most atmospheric place to see a production by the Royal Shakespeare Company.

Wordsworth's Lake District

William Wordsworth and the Lake District are inextricably linked, and in the streets of Grasmere, Hawkshead and Cockermouth, and the fells surrounding Ullswater and Borrowdale you're never far from a house or sight associated with the poet and his circle. Wordsworth's views on nature and the natural world stood at the very heart of all his poetry, and it's still a jolt to encounter the views that inspired him – from his carefully tended garden at **Rydal Mount** (p.524) to the dancing and reeling daffodils of Gowbarrow Park (p.532). His *Guide to the Lakes* (published in 1810) did much to advertise the charms of his beloved region.

▲ Rydal Mount

The detectives

British contemporary **crime writers** have moved beyond country-house mysteries to serve up realistic depictions of life – and death – in towns, cities and rural areas. Colin Dexter's morose Inspector Morse prowls around Oxford in a cerebral series of whodunnits, while in the novels of PD James it's the remote coast and isolated villages of East Anglia that often provide the backdrop. Britain's urban centres also have their chroniclers: Val McDermid, and her sassy private eye, Kate Brannigan, nail contemporary Manchester, while in the dysfunctional character of John Rebus, Scottish writer Ian Rankin gets to the heart of Edinburgh. Britain's rural areas don't escape the escalating body count either. Peter Robinson's Inspector Banks series is set in the Yorkshire Dales, and for Stephen Booth and his Derbyshire detective Ben Cooper it's the Peak District. See p.1071 for more.

▼ Edinburgh

Thomas Hardy ▲

Jane Austen's writing desk, Chawton ▼

Hardy's Wessex

Thomas Hardy resurrected the old name of Wessex to describe the region in which he set most of his fiction. In his books, the area stretched from Devon and Somerset to Berkshire and Oxfordshire, though its central core was Dorset, the county where Hardy spent most of his years. His books richly depict the life and appearance of the towns and countryside, often thinly disguised – Salisbury as "Melchester", Weymouth as "Budmouth Regis", and Bournemouth as "Sandbourne". But it is **Dorchester** (p.231), county town of Dorset and the "Casterbridge" of his novels, which is portrayed in most detail. Many of the buildings and landmarks that still remain can be identified, especially in *The Mayor of Casterbridge* and *Far From the Madding Crowd*. Hardy was born just outside Dorchester, but went to school in the town, and later moved back to live out the last half of his life.

Five literary diversions

▸▸ **Brantwood**, Cumbria. There's not a more finely sited writer's house in Britain than John Ruskin's Victorian home set high above Coniston Water in the Lake District. See p.526.

▸▸ **Chawton**, Hampshire. Visit the modest house where Jane Austen lived and wrote her most celebrated works. See p.222.

▸▸ **Dumfries**, southwest Scotland. Robbie Burns spent the last five years of his life in the town known as the "Queen of the South". See p.812.

▸▸ **Hill Top**, Cumbria. Join the crowds at Beatrix Potter's beloved lakeland farmhouse. See p.527.

▸▸ **Laugharne**, South Wales. There's a powerful atmosphere at the simple home of Dylan Thomas. See p.661.

stone gate of 1262, that served both as a means of defence for the town and a toll-collection point. To burn off some energy, you could **rent a canoe** for a trip up the Wye from the Monmouth Canoe & Activity Centre (Ⓣ01600/713461, Ⓦwww.monmouthcanoe.com) in Castle Yard, Old Dixton Road.

The **bus station** lies at the bottom of Monnow Street and the **tourist office** is in the Shire Hall, Agincourt Square (daily: April–Oct 10am–5.30pm; Nov–March 9.30am–5pm; Ⓣ01600/713899, Ⓔmonmouth.tic@monmouthshire.gov.uk). **Accommodation** in town is thin on the ground: try the simple but agreeable *Burton House* on St James' Square (Ⓣ01600/714958; ❷), *Tŷ Mawr* at 7 Monk St (Ⓣ01600/714261; ❷), or *Prego* at 7 Church St (Ⓣ01600/712600, Ⓦwww.pregomonmouth.co.uk; ❸). The nearest **campsites** are both on Drybridge Street (over Monnow Bridge then right): the *Monnow Bridge* (Ⓣ01600/714004) is behind the *Three Horseshoes* pub, while the slightly pricier *Monmouth Caravan Park* (Ⓣ01600/714745) is a quarter of a mile beyond.

You can **eat** well at *Cygnet's Kitchen* in White Swan Court, off Church Street, which serves substantial soups and casseroles, or at the wonderful *Prego* (see above), which offers excellent lunches. *Moco's* on Church Street (Ⓣ01600/712001) serves delicious Mexican food, or go for inexpensive pub grub at the *Punch House*, in Agincourt Square, or the *Green Dragon*, in St Thomas Square, down by the Monnow Bridge.

Raglan

Unassuming **RAGLAN** (Rhaglan), seven miles west of Monmouth, is known for its glorious **castle** (June–Sept daily 9.30am–6pm; April, May & Oct daily 9.30am–5pm; Nov–March Mon–Sat 9.30am–4pm, Sun 11am–4pm; £2.90; CADW), whose fussy and comparatively intact style makes it stand out from so many other crumbling Welsh fortresses. The last medieval fortification built in Britain, the design of which combines practical strength with ostentatious style, Raglan was begun on the site of a Norman motte in 1435 by Sir William ap Thomas. The **gatehouse**, still used as the main entrance, houses fantastic examples of the castle's decoration in its heraldic shields, intricate stonework edging and gargoyles. In the mid-fifteenth century, ap Thomas's grandson, William Herbert II, built two inner courts around his grandfather's original gatehouse, hall and keep: the cobbled **Pitched Stone Court** – designed to house the functional rooms like the kitchen, with its two vast, double-flued chimneys, and the servants' quarters – and to the left, **Fountain Court**, a well-proportioned grassy space surrounded by opulent residences that once included grand apartments and state rooms. Separating the two are the original hall, from 1435, the buttery, the remains of the chapel and the dank, cold cellars below.

The Three Castles

The fertile, low-lying land between the Monnow and Usk rivers was important as an easy access route into the agricultural lands of South Wales, and in the eleventh century the Norman invaders built a trio of strongholds here to protect their interests. In 1201, Skenfrith, Grosmont and White castles were presented by King John to Hubert de Burgh, who employed sophisticated new ideas on castle design to replace the earlier, square-keeped castles. In 1260, the advancing army of Llywelyn ap Gruffydd began to threaten the king's supremacy in South Wales, and the three castles were refortified in readiness. Gradually, the castles were adapted as living quarters and royal administration centres, and the only return to military usage came in 1404–05, when Owain Glyndŵr's army pressed down to Grosmont, only to be defeated by the future King Henry V. The castles slipped into disrepair and were finally sold separately in 1902, the first time since 1138 that the three had fallen out of single ownership.

White Castle (Castell Gwyn; Easter–Sept Wed–Sun 10am–5pm; £2.50; all other times free, generally 10am–4pm), eight miles northwest of Monmouth and six miles east of Abergavenny (see p.684), is the most awesome of the three, sited in rolling countryside with some superb views over to the hills surrounding the River Monnow. A few patches of the white rendering that gave the castle its name can be seen on the exterior walls. The grassy Outer Ward is enclosed by a curtain wall with four towers, divided by a moat from the brooding mass of the Inner Ward. A bridge leads to the dual-towered Inner Gatehouse, where you can climb the western tower for its sublime vantage point. At the back of the Inner Ward are the massive foundations of the Norman keep, demolished in about 1260.

Seven miles northeast of White Castle, in the attractive border village of Skenfrith (Ynysgynwraidd), is the thirteenth-century **Skenfrith Castle** (free), dominated by the circular keep that replaced an earlier Norman structure. It's not as impressive as White Castle, but Skenfrith has a pretty riverside setting, with walls built of sturdy red sandstone arranged in an irregular rectangle. In the centre of the ward is a low, round keep, raised slightly on an earth mound, containing the vestiges of the private apartments of the castle's lord on the upper floors.

Five miles upstream of Skenfrith, right on the English border, the most dilapidated of the Three Castles, **Grosmont Castle** (free), sits on a small hill above its village. Entering over the wooden bridge above the dry moat brings you into the small central courtyard, dominated on the right-hand side by the ruins of a large Great Hall dating from the first decade of the thirteenth century.

Newport and Caerleon

Dominating the once industrious valley towns of southern Monmouthshire, **Newport**, Wales's third-largest town, is a downbeat, working-class place that grew up around the docks at the mouth of the River Usk. Its rich history was largely swept away by the twentieth century, but isolated nuggets remain, most notably at Roman **Caerleon** – the "old port" on the River Usk – now a northern suburb of Newport, but predating the town by about a thousand years.

Newport

Newport (Casnewydd), fifteen miles west of Chepstow, is hardly prepossessing, its modern centre strung along the banks of the foul and muddy River Usk. Overlooking these waters stand both the pathetic remains of **Newport Castle**, and Peter Fink's giant red sculpture *Steel Wave*, a nod to one of Newport's great industries. The place does have a tremendous energy, however, and is well worth a night's stopover.

The central High Street leads to Newport and Westgate squares, and the ornate, Victorian **Westgate Hotel** where, in 1839, soldiers sprayed a crowd of Chartist protesters with gunfire (see box, p.635) – the hotel's original pillars still show bullet marks. A hundred yards along Commercial Street, in John Frost Square, the quirky **Newport clock** shudders, shakes, spits smoke and comes near to apparent collapse every hour, usually drawing an appreciative crowd. Situated in front of the clock is the **civic museum** (Mon–Thurs 9.30am–5pm, Fri 9.30am–4.30pm, Sat 9.30am–4pm; free). Starting with the origins of the county of Monmouthshire, the displays examine the county's original occupations and early lifestyles, and include a section on mining, with a roll call of those killed in local pit accidents – 3508 men between 1837 and 1927. Newport's spectacular growth from a thousand townspeople in 1801 to a grimy port town of 70,000 a century later is well charted, but the two most interesting sections deal with the Chartist uprising and a fine Roman mosaic.

Further downstream the skyline is dominated by the spidery legs of the **Transporter Bridge**, not so much a bridge as a dangling platform that glides cars and people across the river, high above the shipping channel.

Practicalities

Newport's **tourist office** is in the museum complex on John Frost Square (Mon–Sat 9.30am–5pm; ⓣ01633/842962, ⓔnewport.tic@newport.gov.uk), a hundred yards from Kingsway **bus station** and five minutes' walk south of the **train station**.

There are some decent **B&Bs**, including the genteel *St Etienne*, 162 Stow Hill (ⓣ01633/262341, ⓔmarilynfanner@yahoo.co.uk; ❸). *Hotel@Walkabout* at 19 Bridge St (ⓣ01633/235990, ⓦwww.walkabout.eu.com; ❸) is a modern and reasonable place, if pretty noisy at times. Alternatively, there's the relaxed and hospitable *Keepe Lodge*, 42 Caerau Rd (ⓣ01633/262351; ❸). A couple of miles west is Tredegar House **campsite** (ⓣ01633/815600) – take bus #30 from the town centre.

For **food**, try *Fratelli's* at 173 Caerleon Rd, easily the finest of the city's many Italian restaurants (closed Sun and Mon) or the trendy *Meze Lounge*, 6 Market St, which turns into a venue for live music and DJs in the evening. Newport has a buoyant **rock and dance music scene** – this is, after all, the city that produced gloriously daft hip-hop outfit Goldie Lookin' Chain. For some night-time amusement, *TJ's* at 14 Clarence Place, over the river from the castle, is worth checking out, or there's *Voodoo* at Bridge Street, and the multi-floored *Zanzibar* on Stow Street for a spot of late-night dancing.

Caerleon

Compact **CAERLEON** (Caerllion), three miles north of central Newport (bus #2; every 15min), but still within the city limits, is peppered with the remnants of the major Roman town of Isca, named after the River Usk (Wysg). The settlement was built to provide administrative and military services for the smaller, outlying camps in the rest of South Wales and grew to a size and importance on a par with the better-known York and Chester in the north of England.

The Chartists

In an era when wealthy landowners bought votes from the enfranchised few, the struggles of the **Chartists** were perhaps a historical inevitability. Thousands gathered around the 1838 People's Charter that called for universal male suffrage and a secret, annual ballot for Parliament. Demonstrations in support of these principles were held all over the country, with some of the bloodiest and most vociferous taking place in the radical heartlands of industrial South Wales. On November 4, 1839, Chartists from all over Monmouthshire marched on Newport where they were gunned down by soldiers hiding in the *Westgate Hotel*; 22 protesters were killed. The leaders of the rebellion were sentenced to death, although the self-righteous and wealthy leaders of the town subsequently commuted their punishment to transportation. Queen Victoria even knighted the mayor who ordered the shooting.

Although time has had an inevitably corrosive effect on the remains since the Roman era, there's a powerful sense of history running through the Roman **fortress baths** (Easter–Oct daily 9.30am–5pm; Nov–Easter Mon–Sat 9.30am–5pm, Sun 11am–4pm; £2.90; CADW). The bathing houses, cold hall and communal pool area are remarkably intact and beautifully presented, using audiovisual equipment, sound commentary and models. On the High Street, a Victorian Neoclassical portico is the sole survivor of the original **Legionary Museum** (Mon–Sat 10am–6pm, Sun 2–6pm; free), now housed in a modern building behind and laden with artefacts unearthed here. Opposite the Legionary Museum, Fosse Lane leads down to the hugely atmospheric Roman **amphitheatre** (free), the only one of its kind preserved in Britain. Hidden under a grassy mound until the 1920s, the amphitheatre was built around 80 AD, at the same time as the Coliseum in Rome. Up to six thousand could watch animal baiting, military exercises or the gory combat of gladiators.

Caerleon's **tourist office** (daily: April–Oct 10am–5pm; Nov–March 10am–4pm; ⓣ01633/422656, ⓔcaerleon.tic@newport.gov.uk) lies next to the Legionary Museum, or there's more esoteric information in the delightful Ffwrrwm craft centre, down the main street. There's central B&B at *Pendragon House*, 18 Cross St (ⓣ01633/430871; ④), and the fractionally pricier *Great House* on Isca Road (ⓣ01633/420216, ⓦwww.visitgreathouse.co.uk; ④). The best place to **eat** is *Oriel*, a bistro in the courtyard of the Ffwrrwm centre.

The Valleys

No other part of Wales is as instantly recognizable as the **Valleys**, a generic name for the string of settlements packed into the narrow gashes in the mountainous terrain to the north of Newport and Cardiff. Each of the Valleys depended almost solely on coal-mining which, although nearly defunct as an industry, has left its mark on the staunchly working-class towns: row upon row of brightly painted terraced housing, tipped along the slopes at some incredible angles, are broken only by austere chapels, the occasional remaining pithead and the dignified memorials to those who died underground.

This is not traditional tourist country, but it's one of the most interesting and distinctive corners of Wales, full of sociological and human interest. Some of the former mines have reopened as gutsy and hard-hitting museums – **Big Pit** at Blaenafon and the **Rhondda Heritage Park** at Trehafod being the best – while other excellent civic museums include those at **Pontypridd**, **Aberdare** and **Merthyr Tydfil**. A few older sites, such as vast **Caerphilly Castle** and the sixteenth-century manor house of **Llancaiach Fawr**, have been attracting visitors for hundreds of years.

Blaenafon and Big Pit

Fourteen miles north of Newport, the valley of the Llwyd opens out at the airy iron and coal town of **BLAENAFON** (sometimes Blaenavon), whose population has shrunk to five thousand, a third of its nineteenth-century size. It's a spirited and evocative place, a fact recognized by UNESCO, who granted it World Heritage Site status in 2000. The town's boom kicked off at the Blaenafon **ironworks**, just off the Brynmawr road (Easter–Oct Mon–Fri 9.30am–4.30pm, Sat 10am–5pm, Sun 10am–4.30pm; £2.50; group tours all year, minimum £20; CADW; ⓣ01495/792615, ⓦwww.blaenavontic.com), founded in 1788. Limestone, coal and iron ore – ingredients for successful charmer's boudoir, this Indian restaurant, patronized by the likes of Shilpa Shetty, has a loyal local following. Dinner only. Moderate.

Bizzie Lizzies 36 Swadford St ⓣ01756/701131. The town's award-winning fish-and-chip shop, with the restaurant side of the operation (dining over the canal) open until 9pm every night. Inexpensive.

The Narrow Boat 38 Victoria St ⓣ01756/797922. All you want from a pub – not just varied cask ales and a multitude of Belgian and German beers, but good food (lunch daily, dinner Tues–Sat until 8.30pm), and no piped music. Inexpensive.

Wharfedale

The best of **Wharfedale** starts just east of Skipton at **Bolton Abbey**, and then continues north in a broad, pastoral sweep scattered with villages as picture-perfect as any in northern England. The popular walking centre of **Grassington** is the main village, and buses run here roughly hourly (not Sun in winter) from Skipton, and then half a dozen times a day on up the B6160 to **Kettlewell**, Starbotton and Buckden in upper Wharfedale.

Bolton Abbey

BOLTON ABBEY, five miles east of Skipton, is the name of a whole village rather than an abbey, a confusion compounded by the fact that the place's main monastic ruin is known as **Bolton Priory** (daily 9am to dusk; free). The priory is the starting point for several popular riverside walks, including a section of the **Dales Way** footpath that follows the river's west bank to take in Bolton Woods and the **Strid** (from "stride"), an extraordinary piece of white water two miles north of the abbey, where softer rock has allowed the river to funnel into a cleft just a few feet wide. Beyond the Strid, the path emerges at **Barden Bridge**, four miles from the priory, where **Barden Tower** shelters a tearoom.

For the loveliest approach to the priory, take the **Embsay and Bolton Abbey Steam Railway** – the Bolton Abbey station is a mile and a half by footpath from the priory ruins. The trains (roughly hourly in summer; rest of year at least at weekends; ⓣ01756/710614 or 795189, ⓦwww.embsayboltonabbeyrailway.org.uk; £7 return) start from Embsay, two miles east of Skipton. There's local **information** from the estate office (ⓣ01756/718009, ⓦwww.boltonabbey.com) and an information point at **Cavendish Pavilion**, a mile north of the priory, where there's also a riverside restaurant and café. At Bolton Abbey the main **hotel** is the sumptuous *Devonshire Arms* (ⓣ01756/718111, ⓦwww.thedevonshirearms.co.uk; ⑨), owned by the Duchess of Devonshire and furnished with antiques from the ancestral pile at Chatsworth; there's a good brasserie and bar open to the public.

Grassington and around

GRASSINGTON is the dale's main village, nine miles from Bolton Abbey. The cobbled **Market Square** is home to several inns, a few gift shops and a small local museum, while the **National Park Centre** is on Hebden Road (April–Oct daily 10am–5pm; Nov–March Fri–Sun 10am–4pm; ⓣ01756/751690), across from the bus stop. There's a fair amount of **accommodation** in the village, but even so, at busy times you may have to look further afield – no hardship since Grassington is surrounded by tiny scenic villages, all connected by minor country roads and footpaths.

Accommodation and food

Angel Barn Lodgings/Angel Inn Hetton, 4 miles southwest ⓣ01756/730263, ⓦwww.angelhetton.co.uk. The Dales' gastropub *par excellence* has five immaculate rooms and suites. Over the road in the inn, Modern British food is served either in the bar-brasserie (lunch & dinner) or more formal restaurant (Mon–Sat dinner & Sun lunch). ❼, Sat night ❽

Ashfield House Summers Fold, Grassington ⓣ01756/752584, ⓦwww.ashfieldhouse.co.uk. Lovely seventeenth-century house, 50yd off the square (behind the *Devonshire Hotel*), boasting a walled garden. ❺

Devonshire Fell Burnsall, 3 miles southeast ⓣ01756/729000, ⓦwww.devonshirefell.co.uk. Rooms here have been given the designer treatment – country house retreat, but definitely not "country" inn feel – while a classy bar and bistro complete the experience. Weekend two-night minimum. ❼

Grassington Lodge 8 Wood Lane, Grassington ⓣ01756/752518, ⓦwww.grassingtonlodge.co.uk. A splash of contemporary style – co-ordinated fabrics, hardwood floors, specially commissioned Dales photography – enhances this comfortable village guesthouse. No credit cards. ❺

Red Lion Burnsall, 3 miles southeast ⓣ01756/720204, ⓦwww.redlion.co.uk. A real old country inn, with log fires, oak beams, a cosy bar, and river views from its comfortable, traditionally furnished rooms. Inventive meals (in the bar or restaurant) use local ingredients (expensive; reservations advised). ❼

Upper Wharfedale

Kettlewell (Norse for "bubbling spring") is the main centre for the upper dale, with plenty of local B&B accommodation plus a youth hostel in the village centre. The pubs, the *Bluebell* and the *King's Head*, are both cosy places for a drink. Incidentally, the village was one of the major locations for *Calendar Girls*, the based-on-a-true-story film of doughty Yorkshire ladies who bared all for a charity calendar. There's also a good pub at **Starbotton**, two miles north, the *Fox & Hounds* (closed Mon & all Jan) which has ancient flagged floors and a huge fire in winter.

Malhamdale

A few miles west of Wharfedale lies **Malhamdale** (ⓦwww.malhamdale.com), one of the National Park's most heavily visited regions, thanks to its three outstanding natural features of Malham Cove, Malham Tarn and Gordale Scar. All three attractions are within easy hiking distance of **Malham village**, reached by bus from Skipton (Mon–Fri year-round) or on the seasonal **Malham Tarn shuttle** which runs between Settle (Easter–Oct, weekends & bank hols only, several daily departures) and the National Park Centre.

Malham village is home to barely a couple of hundred people, who inhabit the huddled stone houses on either side of a bubbling river. Appearing in spectacular fashion a mile to the north, the white-walled limestone amphitheatre of **Malham Cove** rises three hundred feet above its surroundings. After a breath-sapping haul to the top, the rewards are fine views and the famous limestone pavement, an expanse of clints (slabs) and grykes (clefts) created by water seeping through weaker lines in the limestone rock. A simple walk (or summer shuttle bus ride) over the moors abruptly brings **Malham Tarn** into sight, its waterfowl protected by a nature reserve on the west bank. Meanwhile, at **Gordale Scar** (also easily approached direct from Malham village), the cliffs are if anything more spectacular than at Malham Cove. The classic circuit takes in cove, tarn and scar in a clockwise **walk from Malham** (8 miles; 3hr 30min).

The **National Park Centre** is at the southern edge of the village (April–Oct daily 10am–5pm; Nov–March Sat & Sun 10am–4pm; ⓣ01969/652380), while the **Yorkshire Dales Trekking Centre** (ⓣ01729/830352, ⓦwww.ydtc.net; rides from £12) at Holme Farm in the village centre is the place to enquire about saddling up. The two **pubs** in Malham are the best places to eat, either the *Buck Inn* (with its popular walkers' back bar) or the fancier *Lister Arms* over the bridge.

Accommodation

Beck Hall ⓣ01729/830332, ⓦwww.beckhallmalham.com. Extended Dales cottage set in streamside gardens, 200yd from the fork in the village centre. A varied mix of en-suite rooms – some with panelling and four-posters, others with stream and field views – plus a cosy lounge and fire, and all-year daytime café (closed Mon). ④

Malham YHA ⓣ0870/770 5946, ⓔmalham@yha.org.uk. Purpose-built hostel that's well known as a walking and cycling centre. Dorms from £13.95; Nov & Dec usually weekends only; closed Jan.

Miresfield Farm ⓣ01729/830414, ⓦwww.miresfield-farm.com. The first house in the village, by the river, means lovely rural views. Country-pine-style rooms vary in size, and there's also a small campsite with toilet and shower, with breakfast available. ④

Ribblesdale

Ribblesdale, to the west of Malhamdale, is entered from **SETTLE**, starting point of the **Settle to Carlisle Railway** (see box below). The small town has a typical seventeenth-century market square (market day is Tuesday), still sporting its split-level arcaded shambles, which once housed butchers' shops. The **tourist office** in the town hall, just off Market Place (daily 9.30am–4.30pm; ⓣ01729/825192), has hiking maps and pamphlets. The **train station** is less than five signposted minutes' walk from Market Place, down Station Road. Regular **buses** connect Skipton with Settle, from where there are services three or four times daily (not Sun) north to Horton, and northwest to Ingleton in the western Dales. A weekend and bank holiday **shuttle bus** (Easter–Oct) also runs over the tops to Malham in an hour. As for **accommodation**, two old **inns**, the *Royal Oak* on Market Place (ⓣ01729/822561; ④), and the *Golden Lion*, just off Market Place along Duke Street (ⓣ01729/822203, ⓦwww.goldenlionhotel.net; ⑤), are the most atmospheric places to stay. Best of the **B&Bs** is *Settle Lodge* on Duke Street (ⓣ01729/823258, ⓦwww.settlelodge.co.uk; no credit cards; ④), a Victorian house with spacious rooms in contemporary style. Both the inns serve reasonable **food** and decent beer, though during the day it's hard to see anyone resisting the lure of *Ye Olde Naked Man Café* on Market Place (ⓣ01729/823230), serving breakfasts, proper coffee and good home-made food; a former undertaker's, the café's name refers to the old adage that "you bring now't into the world and you take now't out".

The valley's only village of any size is **HORTON IN RIBBLESDALE**, a noted walking centre. The celebrated *Pen-y-ghent Café* in the village has filling meals, and doubles as a **tourist office** (Mon & Wed–Sun 8/9am–5.30pm; ⓣ01729/860333) and an unofficial headquarters for the famous **Three Peaks Walk** – namely the 25-mile, 12-hour circuit of Pen-y-ghent (2273ft), Whernside (2416ft) – Yorkshire's highest point – and Ingleborough (2373ft). The café

The Settle to Carlisle Railway

The 72-mile **Settle to Carlisle** line is a feat of Victorian engineering that has few equals in Britain. In particular, between Horton and Ribblehead, **"England's most scenic railway"** climbs two hundred feet in five miles, before crossing the famous 24-arched **Ribblehead viaduct** and then disappearing into the 2629 yards of the Blea Tunnel. Meanwhile, the station at **Dent Head** is the highest, and bleakest, main-line station in England. The journey from Settle to Carlisle takes an hour and forty minutes, so it's easy to make a **return trip** (day-return £18) along the whole length of the line. If you only have time for a short rail trip, the best section is that between Settle and Garsdale (30min). There are connections to Settle from Skipton (20min) and Leeds (1hr); full **timetable** details are available from National Rail Enquiries, ⓣ0845/748 4950, or ⓦwww.settle-carlisle.co.uk.

operates a "safety service" for walkers, enabling anyone undertaking a long hike to register in and out (not Tues).

The western Dales

The **western Dales** is a term of convenience for a couple of tiny dales running north from **Ingleton**, and for **Dentdale**, one of the loveliest valleys in the National Park. Ingleton has the most accommodation, but **Dent** is by far the best target for a quiet night's retreat, with a cobbled centre barely altered in centuries.

Ingleton and around

The straggling slate-grey village of **INGLETON** sits upon a ridge at the confluence of two streams, the Twiss and the Doe, whose beautifully wooded valleys are easily the area's best features. The four-and-a-half-mile **Falls' Walk** (daily 9am–dusk; entrance fee £4; ⓣ01524/241930, ⓦwww.ingletonwaterfallswalk.co.uk) is a lovely circular walk (2hr 30min) taking in both valleys, and providing viewing points over its waterfalls. Just one and a half miles out of Ingleton on the Ribblehead/Hawes road (B6255) is the entrance to the **White Scar Caves** (daily 10am–5pm; weekends only Nov–Jan, weather permitting; £7.50; ⓣ01524/241244, ⓦwww.whitescarcave.co.uk). It's worth every penny for the eighty-minute tour of dank underground chambers, contorted cave formations and glistening stalactites.

There are a dozen local **B&Bs** and **guesthouses**, most lying along Main Street. *Riverside Lodge*, 24 Main St (ⓣ01524/241359, ⓦwww.riversideingleton.co.uk; ❸), is the pick of them, while the centrally located **youth hostel** (ⓣ0870/770 5880, ⓔingleton@yha.org.uk; from £15) is an old stone house set in its own gardens. The *Inglesport Café* on the first floor of the hiking store on Main Street (daily 9am–6pm) provides hearty soups and potatoes with everything, or drive five miles up the Hawes road (B6255), beyond the hamlet of Chapel-le-Dale, to the *Old Hill Inn* (ⓣ01524/241256; ❹; closed Mon), one of the lonelier pubs in England, but worth the diversion for the cosily restored interior, good beers and posh pub food.

Dentdale

In the seventeenth and eighteenth centuries, **Dentdale** (ⓦwww.dentdale.com) supported a flourishing hand-knitting industry, later ruined by mechanization. These days, the hill-farming community supplements its income through tourism and craft ventures, while in **DENT** village itself the main road soon gives way to grassy cobbles. You can stay at either of the village's two **pubs**, the *Sun Inn* (ⓣ01539/625208; ❶) and the *George & Dragon* (ⓣ01539/625256, ⓦwww.thegeorgeanddragondent.co.uk; ❸), which are virtually next to each other in the centre. There are a handful of **B&Bs**, most notably *Stone Close Guesthouse* (ⓣ01539/625231, ⓔstoneclose@btinternet.com; ❷, en suite ❸, no credit cards), which has a good café (noon–5pm all year; closed Mon & Fri). Dent's **train station** (on the Settle–Carlisle line) is not in Dent at all, but four miles to the east, so be warned.

Wensleydale

Best known of the Dales, if only for its cheese, **Wensleydale** (ⓦwww.wensleydale.org) is the largest and most serene of the National Park's dales. Many of its rural attractions will be familiar to devotees of the **James Herriott** books and TV series, set and filmed in the dale. Year-round **public transport** is provided by a combination of post and service buses from Hawes on varied routes via Bainbridge, Askrigg, Aysgarth and Castle Bolton to Leyburn (for Richmond); and the #159 between Masham, Leyburn and Richmond. There are also summer weekend and bank holiday services connecting Hawes to Wharfedale (#800/805).

Hawes

HAWES is Wensleydale's chief town, main hiking centre, and home to its tourism, cheese and rope-making industries. It also claims to be Yorkshire's highest market town, and received its market charter in 1699; the weekly Tuesday market is still going strong. The cheese trail invariably leads to the **Wensleydale Creamery** on Gayle Lane (Mon–Sat 10am–5pm, Sun 10am–4.30pm; £2.50; ⓣ01969/667664 ⓦwww.wensleydale.co.uk), a few hundred yards south of the centre. The first cheese in Wensleydale was made by medieval Cistercian monks from ewes' milk, and after the Dissolution local farmers made a version from cows' milk which, by the 1840s, was being marketed as "Wensleydale" cheese. The Creamery doesn't make cheese every day, so call first to guarantee a viewing.

The **National Park Centre** (daily 10am–5pm; ⓣ01969/666 210) shares the same building as the Dales Countryside Museum (same hours; £3), which focuses on local trades and handicrafts. **Accommodation** is plentiful in local B&Bs, while all the pubs on and around the market square – the *Board*, *Crown*, *Fountain*, *Bull's Head* and *White Hart* – have rooms, too.

Accommodation and food

Herriot's Main St ⓣ01969/667536, ⓦwww.herriotsinhawes.co.uk. Small hotel, just off Market Place, where a couple of the rooms have fell views. The restaurant here is the best place to eat in town, offering hearty Dales dishes. ④

The Old Dairy Farm Widdale, 3 miles west of Hawes ⓣ01969/667 070, ⓦwww.olddairyfarm.co.uk. Farmhouse accommodation, but of the luxurious and contemporary kind, with fine dining available (dinner, £28). ⑦

Rose & Crown Bainbridge, 5 miles east of Hawes ⓣ01969/650225, ⓦwww.theprideofwensleydale.com. Fifteenth-century coaching inn with restaurant and bar, overlooking an emerald village green. ⑤

Steppe Haugh Town Head ⓣ01969/667645, ⓦwww.steppehaugh.co.uk. Plenty of pine gives a cottagey feel to this traditional B&B, at the Ingleton road turn-off at the top of town. ④

Askrigg, Aysgarth and Castle Bolton

The mantle of "Herriot country" lies heavy on **ASKRIGG**, six miles east of Hawes, as the TV series *All Creatures Great and Small* was filmed in and around the village. Nip into the *King's Arms* – a cosy old haunt with wood panelling, good beer and bar meals – and you can see stills from the TV series. For a rural retreat, you can't beat *Helm* (ⓣ01969/650443, ⓦwww.helmyorkshire.com; ⑤), a seventeenth-century farmhouse a mile west with magnificent views, open fires and oak beams.

Here for the beer

If you're a beer fan, the handsome market town of **Masham** (pronounced Mass'm) is an essential point of pilgrimage, home to **Theakston brewery** (tours daily 11am–3pm; reservations advised; ⓣ01765/680000; £4.95, ⓦwww.theakstons.co.uk), sited here since 1827, where you can learn the arcane intricacies of the brewer's art and become familiar with the legendary Old Peculier ale. In the early 1990s one of the Theakston family brewing team left to set up the **Black Sheep Brewery**, also based in Masham and offering tours (daily 11am–4pm, but call for availability; £5.25; ⓣ01765/680100, ⓦwww.blacksheepbrewery.com). Both breweries are just a few minutes' signposted walk out of the centre.

The ribbon-village of **AYSGARTH**, straggling along and off the A684, is the vortex that sucks in Wensleydale's largest number of visitors, courtesy of the **Aysgarth Falls**, half a mile below the village. A marked nature trail runs through the surrounding woodlands and there's a big car park and excellent **National Park Centre** on the north bank (April–Oct daily 10am–5pm; Nov–March Fri–Sun 10am–4pm; ⓣ01969/662 910).

There's a superb **circular walk** northeast from Aysgarth via Castle Bolton (6 miles; 4hr), which starts at the falls themselves and climbs up through Thoresby, with the foursquare battlements of **Bolton Castle** (March–Nov daily 10am–5pm; restricted winter opening, call for details; ⓣ01969/623981, ⓦwww.boltoncastle.co.uk; £5) a magnetic lure from miles away. The Great Chamber a few adjacent rooms and the castle gardens have been restored, and there's also a café (free to enter) that's a welcome spot if you've just trudged up from Aysgarth.

Swaledale

Narrow and steep-sided in its upper reaches, **Swaledale** emerges rocky and rugged in its central tract before more typically pastoral scenery cuts in at the main village of **Reeth**. From Richmond, **bus** #30 (not Sun) runs up the valley along the B6270 as far as Keld, eight miles north of Hawes and at the **cross-roads** of the **Pennine Way** and the Coast-to-Coast path. The Pennine Way shadows the very minor Stonesdale road for the three or four miles across **Stonesdale Moor** to the *Tan Hill Inn* (ⓣ01833/628246; ④), reputedly the highest pub in Britain (1732ft above sea level). **Thwaite** is the first hamlet south of Keld, just a two-mile walk away, while some of the loveliest scenery follows beyond the little village of **Muker**, a mile or so to the east.

A couple of miles further east lies **REETH**, the dale's main village and market centre – market day is Friday. Its desirable cottages are gathered around

▲ Masham

a triangular green, where you'll find the **National Park Centre** (April–Oct daily 10am–5pm; Nov–March Fri–Sun 10am–4pm; ⓣ01748/884059), the *King's Arms* (ⓣ01748/884259, ⓦwww.thekingsarms.com; ❺; weekend 2-night minimum), or for superior old-fashioned comforts, the *Burgoyne Hotel* (ⓣ01748/884292, ⓦwww.theburgoyne.co.uk; no single Sat night reservations; ❼). *Reeth Bakery* is known for its great chocolate cake; and there's good food at *Overton House Café* (ⓣ01748/884332; open daytime Mon & Wed–Sat, plus Thurs–Sat dinner).

Richmond

RICHMOND is the Dales' single most tempting historical town, thanks mainly to its magnificent castle, whose extensive walls and colossal keep cling to a precipice above the River Swale. Indeed, the entire town is an absolute gem, centred on a huge cobbled market square backed by Georgian buildings, hidden alleys and gardens. Most of medieval Richmond sprouted around its **castle** (April–Sept daily 10am–6pm; Oct–March Mon & Thurs–Sun 10am–4pm; £4; EH), but much of the town now radiates from the **Market Place**, with the Market Hall alongside; market day is Saturday, augmented by a farmers' market on the third Saturday of the month. The defunct **Holy Trinity Church** on the square houses the **Green Howards Museum** (Mon–Sat 10am–4pm; £3.50), honouring North Yorkshire's Green Howards regiment. For the local history, visit the charming **Richmondshire Museum** (April–Oct daily 10.30am–4.30pm; £2.50), down Ryder's Wynd, off King Street on the northern side of the square. The keenest interest of all, however, is in the Georgian **Theatre Royal** (1788), one of England's oldest extant theatres. It's open for both **performances** (box office ⓣ01748/825252, ⓦwww.georgiantheatreroyal.co.uk) and **tours** (mid-Feb to mid-Dec Mon–Sat 10am–4pm, on the hour; £3.50).

A signposted walk runs along the north bank of the **River Swale** out to the the golden stone walls of **Easby Abbey** (dawn to dusk; free; EH), a mile southeast of the town. The evocative ruins are extensive, and in places – notably the thirteenth-century refectory – still remarkably intact.

Practicalities

Buses stop in the Market Place; there are regular services into Wensleydale and Swaledale, and to Darlington, ten miles to the northeast, on the main east-coast train line. The **tourist office**, at Friary Gardens, Victoria Road (daily 9.30am–5.30pm; winter closed Sun; ⓣ01748/850252, ⓦwww.richmond.org.uk), is helpful in finding accommodation, and also organizes free **guided walking tours** around the town in summer.

Accommodation and food

Frenchgate Hotel 59–61 Frenchgate ⓣ01748/822087, ⓦwww.thefrenchgate.co.uk. Georgian townhouse hotel, with eight individually furnished rooms and walled gardens. Its food (meals around £30; restaurant closed Mon) has an excellent reputation. ❻

Frenchgate House 66 Frenchgate ⓣ01748/823421, ⓦwww.66frenchgate.co.uk. The reward for staying in one of the three immaculately presented rooms is breakfast with the best panoramic view in town. ❹

Millgate House Millgate ⓣ01748/823571, ⓦwww.millgatehouse.com. Shut the big green door of this Georgian house and enter a world of books, antiques, embroidered sheets, handmade toiletries, scrumptious breakfasts and the finest (and least precious) hosts you could wish for. No credit cards. ❺, ensuite ❻

Whashton Springs Near Whashton, 3 miles north, Ravensworth Rd ⓣ01748/822884, ⓦwww.whashtonsprings.co.uk. This working Dales farm offers a peaceful night in the country in rooms (in the main house or round the courtyard) filled with family furniture. ❹

Ripon

The attractive market town of **RIPON**, eleven miles north of Harrogate, is centred upon its small **Cathedral** (daily 8am–6.30pm; donation requested, Ⓦ www.riponcathedral.org.uk), which can trace its ancestry back to its foundation by St Wilfrid in 672; the original crypt below the central tower can still be reached down a stone passage. The town's other focus is its **Market Place**, linked by narrow Kirkgate to the cathedral; market day is Thursday, with a farmers' market on the third Sunday of the month. Meanwhile, three restored buildings - prison, courthouse and workhouse - show a different side of the local heritage, under the banner of the Yorkshire Law and Order Museums (all open April–Oct daily: July, Aug & school hols 11am–4pm, other times 1–4pm; combined ticket £6; Ⓦ www.riponmuseums.co.uk).

The **bus station** (#36 from Harrogate, or Leeds) is just off Market Place, while the town's **tourist office** is on Minster Road opposite the cathedral (April–Sept Mon–Sat 9.30/10am–5/5.30pm, Sun 1–4pm; Oct Mon–Sat 10am–4pm; Nov–March Thurs & Sat 10am–4pm; Ⓣ 01765/604625, Ⓦ www.visitripon.org). There's no pressing need to stay the night, though Ripon is the nearest town to Fountains Abbey (see below). Top honours go to *The Old Deanery* on Minster Road (Ⓣ 01765/600003, Ⓦ www.theolddeanery.co.uk; ⑥), just across from the cathedral, completely refurbished in contemporary fashion, with excellent rooms and food (reservations advised for dinner; expensive).

Fountains Abbey and Studley Royal

It's tantalizing to imagine how the English landscape might have appeared had Henry VIII not dissolved the monasteries, with all the artistic ruin precipitated by that act. **Fountains Abbey** (daily 10am–4/5pm; closed Fri Nov–Jan; £6.80; NT), four miles southwest of Ripon off the B6265, gives a good idea of what might have been, and is the one Yorkshire monastic ruin you must see. The estate is owned by the National Trust, which organizes an ambitious range of activities and events – from opera and firework displays to **free guided tours** (April–Oct daily; Ⓣ 01765/608888, Ⓦ www.fountainsabbey.org.uk).

The abbey was founded in 1133 by thirteen dissident Benedictine monks and formally adopted by the Cistercian order two years later. Within a hundred years, Fountains had become the wealthiest Cistercian foundation in England, supporting a magnificent **abbey church**. The **Perpendicular Tower**, almost 180ft high, looms over the whole ensemble, while equally grandiose in scale is the undercroft of the **Lay Brothers' Dormitory** off the cloister, a stunningly vaulted space over 300ft long that was used to store the monastery's annual harvest of fleeces. Its sheer size gives some idea of the abbey's entrepreneurial scope, some thirteen tons of wool a year being turned over, most of it sold to Venetian and Florentine merchants who toured the monasteries.

A riverside walk, marked from the visitor centre car park, takes you through the abbey to a series of ponds and ornamental gardens, harbingers of **Studley Royal** (same times as the abbey; NT), which can also be entered via the village of Studley Roger, where there's a separate car park. This lush medley of lawns, lake, woodland and **Deer Park** was laid out in 1720, and there are some scintillating views of the abbey from the gardens, though it's the cascades and water gardens which command most attention.

Harrogate

HARROGATE – the very picture of genteel Yorkshire respectability – owes its landscaped appearance and early prosperity to the discovery of Tewit Well in 1571. This was the first of over eighty ferrous and sulphurous springs that, by the nineteenth century, were to turn the town into one of the country's leading spas. Tours of Harrogate's spa heritage begin with the **Royal Baths**, facing Crescent Road, first opened in 1897 and now restored to their late-Victorian finery. You can experience the beautiful Moorish-style interior during a session at the **Turkish Baths and Health Spa** (separate sessions for men and women; hours vary; call ⓣ01423/556746; from £14). Just along Crescent Road from the Royal Baths stands the **Royal Pump Room**, built in 1842 over the sulphur well that feeds the baths. The town's earliest surviving spa building, the old Promenade Room of 1806, is just 100 yards from the Pump Room on Swan Road – now housing the **Mercer Art Gallery** (Tues–Sat 10am–5pm, Sun 2–5pm; free), which hosts regularly changing fine-art exhibitions.

To the southwest (entrance opposite the Royal Pump Room), the 120-acre **Valley Gardens** are a delight, while many visitors also make for the botanical gardens at **Harlow Carr** (daily 9.30am–4/6pm; £6; ⓦwww.rhs.org.uk), the northern showpiece of the Royal Horticultural Society. These lie one and a half miles out, on the town's western edge – the nicest approach is to walk (30min) through the Valley Gardens and pine woods, though bus #106 (every 20min) will get you there as well.

Practicalities

Bus and **train** stations are on Station Parade, just a few minutes from all the central sights. Harrogate's **tourist office** (April–Sept Mon–Sat 9am–6pm, Sun 10am–1pm; Oct–March Mon–Fri 9am–5pm, Sat 9am–4pm; ⓣ01423/537300, ⓦwww.enjoyharrogate.com) is in the Royal Baths on Crescent Road. There are scores of **accommodation** options, though it's best to book in advance when major conferences and festivals take place. Of these the most famous are the **flower shows** (late April & mid-Sept, ⓦwww.flowershow.org.uk), but there's also the three-day **Great Yorkshire Show** (second week in July, ⓦwww.greatyorkshireshow.com) and various book and antique fairs, music festivals and craft shows.

Accommodation

The Bijou 17 Ripon Rd ⓣ01423/567974, ⓦwww.thebijou.co.uk. The mellow lounge with wood-burning stove sets the tone for this small family-run boutique hotel, close to the centre. ⑤

Fountains 27 King's Rd ⓣ01423/530483, ⓦwww.thefountainshotel.co.uk. Family-run guesthouse a minute or two from the conference centre. ④

General Tarleton Ferrensby, 5 miles northeast of Harrogate ⓣ01423/340284, ⓦwww.generaltarleton.co.uk. The gastropub with rooms, a couple of miles north of Knaresborough, is well worth the drive for excellent meals in either the restaurant or bar-brasserie. ⑦

Hotel du Vin Prospect Place ⓣ01423/856800, ⓦwww.hotelduvin.com. Beautiful boutique-style rooms overlooking The Stray, featuring trademark enormous beds and lavish bathrooms. The handsome bistro is sensibly priced, while public areas – champagne bar, lounge and snooker room, courtyard garden – are stylishly turned out. ⑦, loft suites ⑨

Restaurants

Betty's 1 Parliament St ⓣ01423/502746, ⓦwww.bettys.co.uk. Very much a Yorkshire institution, established by a Swiss emigrant in the 1920s. The cakes and tarts are to die for (takeaway available), but full meals are also served – Alpine macaroni or *rösti*, say, or changing seasonal specialities. Closes at 9pm. Inexpensive.

Drum and Monkey 5 Montpellier Gardens ⓣ01423/502650, ⓦwww.drumandmonkey.com. Outstanding fish and seafood restaurant, a firm favourite with locals and out-of-towners alike. Choose the best of the daily catch grilled, or go cheaper (sandwich, salad, seafood pie, fish brochette) or more expensive (shellfish platter). Expensive.

Old Bell Tavern 6 Royal Parade ⓣ01423/507930. Bar meals and sandwiches served daily (lunchtime & 6–7pm, Sun from noon) and a brasserie upstairs dispensing braised lamb shank, steaks, smoked haddock, etc. Moderate.

Orchid 28 Swan Rd ⓣ01423/560425. Wok-wielding chefs conjure up specialities from all corners of Southeast Asia, tempura to Shanghai noodles. There's *dim sum* at lunch, and sushi and sashimi sets every Tues. Closed Sat lunch. Moderate.

York

YORK is the north's most compelling city, a place whose history, said George VI, "is the history of England". This is perhaps overstating things a little, but it reflects the significance of a metropolis that stood at the heart of the country's religious and political life for centuries, and until the Industrial Revolution was second only to London in population and importance. These days a more provincial air hangs over the city, except in summer when York feels like a heritage site for the benefit of tourists. That said, no trip to this part of the country is complete without a visit to York, while the city is also well placed for any number of **day-trips**, the most essential being to **Castle Howard**, the gem amongst English stately homes.

A brief history of York

An early Roman fortress of 71 AD in time became a city – Eboracum, capital of the empire's northern European territories and the base for Hadrian's northern campaigns. Later, the city became the fulcrum of Christianity in northern England: on Easter Day in 627, Bishop Paulinus, on a mission to establish the Roman Church, baptized King Edwin of Northumbria in a small timber chapel. Six years later the church became the first minster and Paulinus the first archbishop of York. In 867 the city fell to the **Danes**, who renamed it **Jorvik**, and later made it the capital of eastern England (Danelaw). Later Viking raids culminated in the decisive **Battle of Stamford Bridge** (1066) six miles east of the city, where English King Harold defeated Norse King Harald – a pyrrhic victory in the event, for his weakened army was defeated by the Normans just a few days later at the Battle of Hastings, with well-known consequences for all concerned.

The **Normans** devastated much of York's hinterland in their infamous "Harrying of the North". Stone walls were thrown up during the thirteenth century, when the city became a favoured Plantagenet retreat and commercial capital of the north, its importance reflected in the new title of Duke of York, bestowed ever since on the monarch's second son. Although Henry VIII's Dissolution of the Monasteries took its toll on a city crammed with religious houses, York remained strongly wedded to the Cathoic cause, and the most famous of the Gunpowder Plot conspirators, **Guy Fawkes**, was born here. During the **Civil War** Charles I established his court in the city, which was strongly pro-Royalist, inviting a Parliamentarian siege. Royalist troops, however, were routed by Cromwell and Sir Thomas Fairfax at the **Battle of Marston Moor** in 1644, another seminal battle in England's history, which took place just six miles west of York.

The city's eighteenth-century history was marked by its emergence as a social centre for Yorkshire's landed elite. Whilst the Industrial Revolution largely passed it by, the arrival of the **railways** brought renewed prosperity, thanks to the enterprise of pioneering "Railway King" George Hudson, lord mayor during the 1830s and 1840s. The railway is gradually losing its role as a major employer, as is the traditional but declining confectionery industry; incomes are now generated by new service and bioscience industries – not forgetting, of course, the four million annual tourists.

Arrival, information, transport and tours

Trains arrive at York Station, just outside the city walls, a 750-yard walk from the historic core. National Express **buses** and most other regional bus services drop off and pick up on Rougier Street, 200 yards north of the train station, just before Lendal Bridge. There's a **tourist office** at the train station, though the main office is over Lendal Bridge, 200yd west of the Minster in the De Grey Rooms, on Exhibition Square (Mon–Sat 9am–5/6pm, Sun 10am–4/5pm; Ⓣ01904/550099, Ⓦwww.visityork.org). A **York Pass** (1/2/3 days, £21/27/34; Ⓦwww.yorkpass.com) – available from the tourist office – gets you into thirty different attractions, including Castle Howard.

Bus tours start at around £8.50 per person, but much more interesting are the various **guided walks** (around £5), most famously the evening ghost walks. There's not much to choose between any of these, though one is **free** – the York Association of Voluntary Guides (Ⓣ01904/640780, Ⓦwww.york.touristguides.btinternet.co.uk) offers a two-hour guided tour throughout the year (daily at 10.15am), plus additional tours in summer (April, May & Sept at 2.15pm; June–Aug at 2.15pm & 6.45pm), departing from outside the Art Gallery in Exhibition Square; just turn up. The best river operator is **YorkBoat** (Ⓣ01904/628324, Ⓦwww.yorkboat.co.uk), whose one-hour "cruise on the Ouse" sails daily from King's Staith and Lendal Bridge (Feb–Dec; cruises from £7, evening trips £9).

Accommodation

The main **B&B** concentration is in the side streets off Bootham (immediately west of Exhibition Square), with nothing much more than a ten-minute walk from the centre. Or consider the rooms at the various **budget chains**, like Travelodge, Holiday Inn, Ramada, Novotel, Quality Hotel, and so on, which all have hotels in York. The University of York (Ⓣ01904/432037, Ⓦwww.york.ac.uk) also has overnight B&B accommodation (from £55) available all year round and, for longer stays, self-contained flats/houses (July–Sept).

Hotels and B&Bs

23 St Mary's 23 St Mary's, Bootham Ⓣ01904/622738, Ⓦwww.23stmarys.co.uk. Nine attractive rooms with co-ordinated fabrics and TV/DVDs. Above all, it's peaceful (on a no-through road), but very close to centre and river. 5

Abbey 14 Earlsborough Terrace, Marygate Ⓣ01904/627782, Ⓦwww.abbeyghyork.co.uk. You can't beat the riverside location of this pretty terraced guesthouse, whose five rooms are styled with flair – there are river views at the front. 4, river view 5

Blue Rooms Franklin's Yard Ⓣ01904/673990, Ⓦwww.thebluebicycle.com. The four one- and two-bedroom self-catering "Blue Rooms" apartments (available by the night), behind the fantastic *Blue Bicycle* restaurant, are all furnished in best contemporary style and enhanced by a quiet riverside situation. 7

Four High Petergate 4 High Petergate Ⓣ01904/658516, Ⓦwww.fourhighpetergateyork.co.uk. Townhouse hotel with private garden, just seconds from the Minster. Rooms have been given a classy shot-in-the-arm – teak beds, DVD players, power showers – while the adjacent bistro is one of the best places to eat in York. Parking available nearby. 6

Golden Fleece 16 Pavement Ⓣ01904/625171, Ⓦwww.goldenfleeceyorkwebsites.co.uk. Just four rooms available in this historic pub, but what a collection – one overlooks the Shambles, one has views to the Minster towers and all are haunted (well, maybe). The pub itself is one of the oldest in the city and has a nice beer garden. 5

Guy Fawkes 25 High Petergate Ⓣ01904/671001, Ⓦwww.theguyfawkeshotel.com. You can virtually touch the Minster from the front door of this small townhouse hotel, so no doubting the location (more

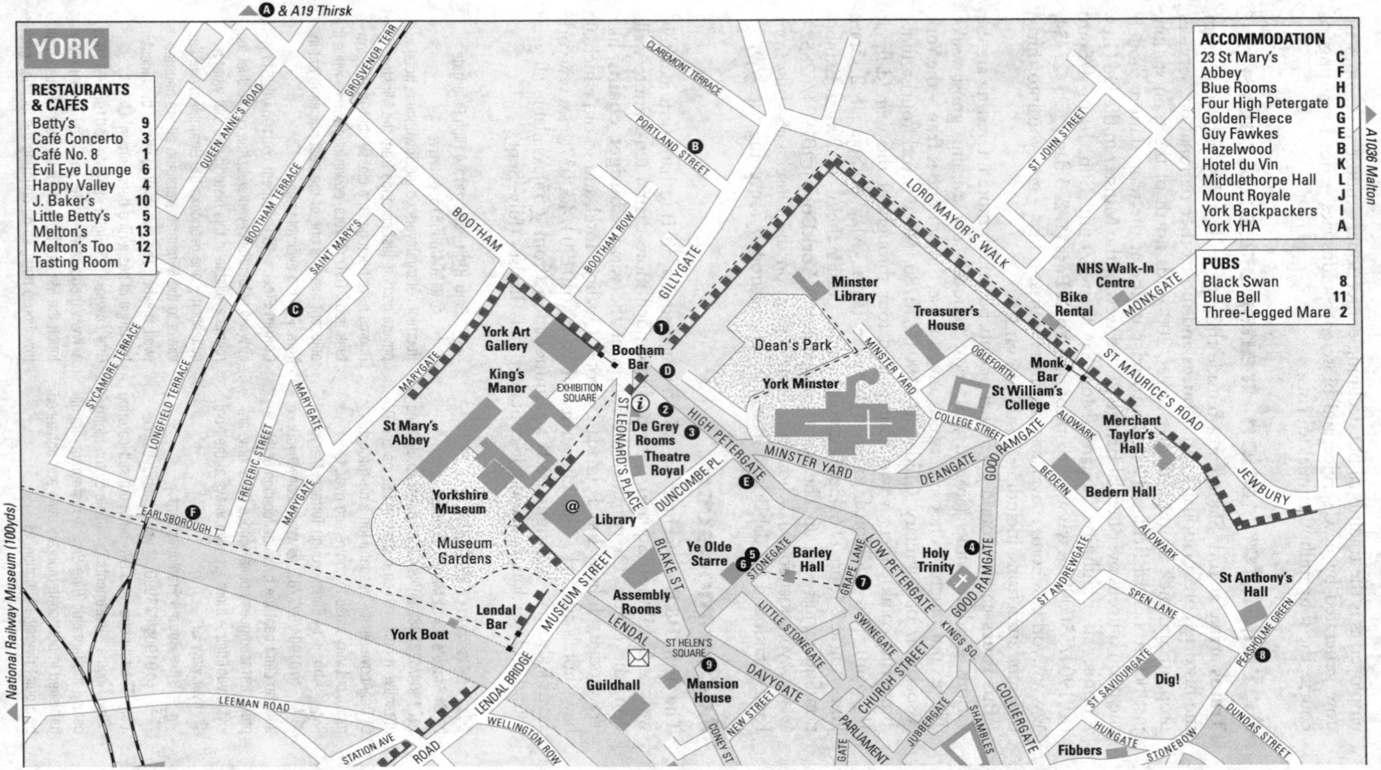

YORK

▲ A & A19 Thirsk

▶ A1036 Malton

◀ National Railway Museum (100yds)

RESTAURANTS & CAFÉS

Betty's	9
Café Concerto	3
Café No. 8	1
Evil Eye Lounge	6
Happy Valley	4
J. Baker's	10
Little Betty's	5
Melton's	13
Melton's Too	12
Tasting Room	7

ACCOMMODATION

23 St Mary's	C
Abbey	F
Blue Rooms	H
Four High Petergate	D
Golden Fleece	G
Guy Fawkes	E
Hazelwood	B
Hotel du Vin	K
Middlethorpe Hall	L
Mount Royale	J
York Backpackers	I
York YHA	A

PUBS

Black Swan	8
Blue Bell	11
Three-Legged Mare	2

Queen Anne's Road
Grosvenor Terr
Bootham Terrace
Saint Mary's
Sycamore Terrace
Longfield Terrace
Marygate
Frederic Street
Earlsborough T
Bootham
Bootham Row
Claremont Terrace
Portland Street
Gillygate
York Art Gallery
King's Manor
Exhibition Square
St Mary's Abbey
Yorkshire Museum
Museum Gardens
Library
Lendal Bar
York Boat
Leeman Road
Station Ave
Road
Lendal Bridge
Wellington Row
Museum Street
Bootham Bar
St Leonard's Place
De Grey Rooms
Theatre Royal
Duncombe Pl.
High Petergate
Blake St
Assembly Rooms
Lendal
St Helen's Square
Guildhall
Mansion House
Coney St
New Street
Davygate
Ye Olde Starre
Stonegate
Barley Hall
Little Stonegate
Grape Lane
Low Petergate
Swinegate
Church Street
Parliament
Gate
Jubbergate
Shambles
Colliergate
Kings Sq.
Holy Trinity
Good Ramgate
Minster Library
Dean's Park
York Minster
Minster Yard
Deangate
Treasurer's House
Ogleforth
College Street
St William's College
Monk Bar
Lord Mayor's Walk
St John Street
Bike Rental
NHS Walk-In Centre
Monkgate
St Maurice's Road
Aldwark
Merchant Taylor's Hall
Bedern
Bedern Hall
Jewbury
St Andrewgate
Spen Lane
St Anthony's Hall
Peasholme Green
St Saviourgate
Dig!
Hungate
Stonebow
Fibbers
Dundas Street

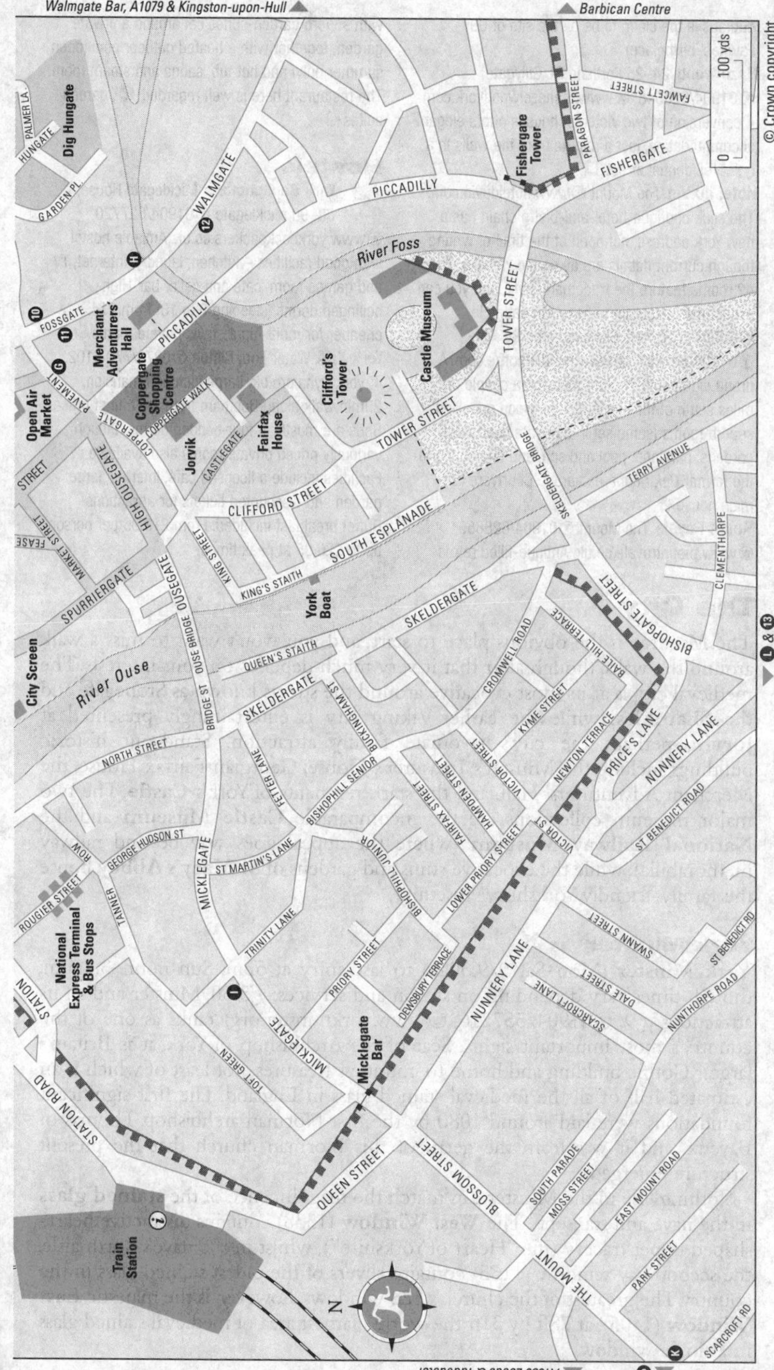
Walmgate Bar, A1079 & Kingston-upon-Hull
Barbican Centre
100 yds
0
© Crown copyright
FAWCETT STREET
PARAGON STREET
Fishergate Tower
FISHERGATE
PICCADILLY
Dig Hungate
PALMER LA.
HUNGATE
GARDEN PL.
WALMGATE
River Foss
FOSSGATE
Merchant Adventurers' Hall
PICCADILLY
Coppergate Shopping Centre
COPPERGATE WALK
Castle Museum
Clifford's Tower
TOWER STREET
TOWER STREET
Open Air Market
PAVEMENT
COPPERGATE
Jorvik
CASTLEGATE
Fairfax House
HIGH OUSEGATE
STREET
TERRY AVENUE
SKELDERGATE BRIDGE
CLIFFORD STREET
SOUTH ESPLANADE
FEASEGATE
MARKET STREET
KING STREET
CLEMENTHORPE
SPURRIERGATE
OUSEGATE
KING'S STAITH
York Boat
SKELDERGATE
BISHOPGATE STREET
BAILE HILL TERRACE
CROMWELL ROAD
City Screen
OUSE BRIDGE
QUEEN'S STAITH
L & 13
River Ouse
BRIDGE ST
SKELDERGATE
BUCKINGHAM ST
KYME STREET
NEWTON TERRACE
PRICE'S LANE
NUNNERY LANE
NORTH STREET
FETTER LANE
BISHOPHILL SENIOR
VICTOR STREET
HAMPDEN STREET
FAIRFAX STREET
ST BENEDICT ROAD
ROW
GEORGE HUDSON ST
MICKLEGATE
ST MARTIN'S LANE
BISHOPHILL JUNIOR
LOWER PRIORY STREET
VICTOR ST
ROUGIER STREET
TANNER
TRINITY LANE
SWANN STREET
ST BENEDICT RD
National Express Terminal & Bus Stops
PRIORY STREET
DEWSBURY TERRACE
NUNNERY LANE
SCARCROFT LANE
DALE STREET
NUNTHORPE ROAD
STATION
MICKLEGATE
TOFT GREEN
Micklegate Bar
STATION ROAD
BLOSSOM STREET
QUEEN STREET
SOUTH PARADE
MOSS STREET
EAST MOUNT ROAD
Train Station
THE MOUNT
PARK STREET
N
SCARCROFT RD
A1036 Leeds & Tadcaster

dubious is the claim to be on the site of Guy Fawkes' birthplace). 5

Hazelwood 24–25 Portland St, Gillygate ⓣ01904/626548, ⓦwww.thehazelwoodyork.com. A conversion of two Victorian houses offers elegant accommodation, just a minute from the walls in a quiet residential street. 5

Hotel du Vin The Mount ⓦwww.hotelduvin.com. The slick boutique-hotel-and-bistro chain has a new York address, not open at the time of writing – though current details are all on the website. The 42 rooms feature the trademark style, and you can expect the restaurant to be worth eating in.

Middlethorpe Hall Bishopsthorpe Rd ⓣ01904/641241, ⓦwww.middlethorpe.com. A grand eighteenth-century mansion a couple of miles south of the city. Antiques, wood panelling, superb rooms (some set in a private courtyard), gardens, parkland, pool and spa, and fine dining in the formal *Oak Room* restaurant. Courtyard 8, main house 9

Mount Royale The Mount ⓣ01904/628856, ⓦwww.mountroyale.co.uk. Antique-filled retreat with superb garden-suites set around a private garden, together with a heated outdoor pool (open summer only) and hot tub, sauna and steam room. The restaurant here is well regarded. 6, garden suites 8

Hostels

York Backpackers Micklegate House, 88–90 Micklegate ⓣ01904/627720, ⓦwww.yorkbackpackers.co.uk. Amiable hostel with good facilities – kitchen, laundry, Internet, TV and games room, café and cellar bar. High-ceilinged dorms (sleeping 8 to 18) from £14, cheaper for multi-night stays, private rooms 1.

York YHA Water End, Clifton ⓣ0870/770 6102, ⓔyork@yha.org.uk. Large Victorian mansion, 20min walk along Bootham from the tourist office. Beds are mostly in four-bedded dorms, though variously priced private rooms also available. Facilities include a licensed café, Internet, large garden and discounted tickets for attractions. Buffet breakfast included. From £13.95 per person, up to £26.95 at peak times.

The City

The **Minster** is the obvious place to start, and you won't want to miss a walk around the walls, though after that it very much depends on your interests. The medieval city is at its most evocative around the streets known as Stonegate and the **Shambles**, while the earlier Viking city is entertainingly presented at **Jorvik**, perhaps the city's favourite family attraction. Stand-out historic buildings include the Minster's Treasurer's House, Georgian Fairfax House, the Merchant Adventurers' Hall, and the stark remnants of York's **Castle**. The two major museum collections are the incomparable **Castle Museum** and the **National Railway Museum** (where the appeal goes way beyond railway memorabilia), while the evocative ruins and gardens of **St Mary's Abbey** house the family-friendly Yorkshire Museum.

York Minster

York Minster (Mon–Sat 9/9.30am to last entry at 5pm, Sun noon–3.45pm, though times vary depending on season and services; £5.50, Minster and all its attractions £9; ⓣ01904/557216, ⓦwww.yorkminster.org) ranks as one of the country's most important sights. Seat of the Archbishop of York, it is Britain's largest Gothic building and home to countless treasures, not least of which is an estimated half of all the medieval stained glass in England. The first significant foundations were laid around 1080 by the first Norman archbishop, Thomas of Bayeux, and it was from the germ of this Norman church that the present structure emerged.

Nothing else in the Minster can match the magnificence of the **stained glass** in the nave and transepts. The **West Window** (1338) contains distinctive heart-shaped upper tracery (the "Heart of Yorkshire"), whilst in the nave's north aisle, the second bay window (1155) contains slivers of the oldest stained glass in the country. The greatest of the church's 128 windows, however, is the majestic **East Window** (1405), at 78ft by 31ft the world's largest area of medieval stained glass in a single window.

The foundations, or **undercroft** (Mon–Sat 9am–5pm, Sun 12.30–5pm; £4, including audioguide), have been turned into a museum, while amongst precious relics in the adjoining **treasury** is the eleventh-century *Horn of Ulf*, presented to the Minster by a relative of the tide-turning King Canute. There's also access from the undercroft to the **crypt**, the spot that transmits the most powerful sense of antiquity, as it contains sections of the original eleventh-century church, including pillars with fine Romanesque capitals. Access to the undercroft, treasury and crypt is from the south transept, also the entrance to the **central tower** (£4), which you can climb for rooftop views over the city.

Around the walls

The city's superb **walls** date mainly from the fourteenth century, though fragments of Norman work survive, particularly in the gates (known as "bars"), whilst the northern sections still follow the line of the Roman ramparts. **Monk Bar** is as good a point of access as any, tallest of the city's four main gates and host to a small **Richard III Museum** (daily 9/9.30am–4/5pm; £2.50; Ⓦ www.richardiiimuseum.co.uk), where you're invited to decide on the guilt or innocence of England's most maligned king. For just a taste of the walls' best section – with great views of the Minster and acres of idyllic-looking gardens – take the ten-minute stroll west from Monk Bar to Exhibition Square and **Bootham Bar**, the only gate on the site of a Roman gateway and marking the traditional northern entrance to the city. A stroll round the walls' entire two-and-a-half-mile length will also take you past the southwestern **Micklegate Bar**, long considered the most important of the gates since it marked the start of the road to London.

York Art Gallery and the Yorkshire Museum

Exhibition Square, outside Bootham Bar, is the site of the refurbished **York Art Gallery** (daily 10am–5pm; free; Ⓦ www.yorkartgallery.org.uk), housing an extensive collection of early Italian, British and northern European paintings. The gallery puts on a year-round series of special exhibitions and events, and is noted for its collections of British studio pottery and twentieth-century British painters. South of here on Museum Street stands the entrance to the **Yorkshire Museum** (daily 10am–5pm; £5; Ⓦ www.yorkshiremuseum.org.uk), which lies within the beautifully laid-out grounds of ruined St Mary's Abbey. It's one of York's better museums, with changing temporary exhibitions aimed largely at families, but otherwise strong on Roman archeological remains. The chief exhibit is the fifteenth-century Middleham Jewel, found in 1985 – a diamond-shaped jewel with an oblong sapphire, acclaimed as the finest piece of Gothic jewellery in England.

Part of the museum basement incorporates the fireplace and chapter house of **St Mary's Abbey** (dawn to dusk; free), the ruins of which lie within the attractive museum gardens. Founded around 1080, the abbey later became an important Benedictine foundation – it was from here that disenchanted monks fled to found Fountains Abbey.

Stonegate and the Shambles

Stonegate is as ancient as the city itself: it was originally the Via Praetoria of Roman York, and is now paved with thick flags of York stone, which were once carried along here to build the Minster, hence the street name. The Tudor buildings retain their considerable charm – **Ye Olde Starre** at no. 40, one of York's original inns, is on every tourist itinerary (you can't miss the sign straddling the street). Step through an alley known as Coffee Yard (by the *Olde*

Starre) to find **Barley Hall** (Tues–Sun 10am/noon–4pm; £3.50, Ⓦwww.barleyhall.org.uk), a fine restoration of a late-medieval townhouse where you can learn about fifteenth-century life by touching the exhibits, playing period games and trying on costumes.

The **Shambles** meanwhile, further to the south, could be taken as the epitome of medieval York. Almost impossibly narrow and lined with perilously leaning timber-framed houses, it was the home of York's butchers (the word "shambles" derives from the Old English for slaughterhouse) – old meat hooks still adorn the odd house.

Jorvik

The city's blockbuster historic exhibit is **Jorvik** (daily 10am–4/5pm; £7.95; Ⓣ01904/543402, Ⓦwww.vikingjorvik.com), located by the Coppergate shopping centre. Propelling visitors in "time capsules" on a ride through the tenth-century city of York, the museum presents not just the sights but the sounds and even the smells of a riverside Viking city. Excavations of Coppergate in 1976 uncovered a real Viking settlement, now largely buried beneath the shopping centre outside. But at Jorvik you can see how the unearthed artefacts were used, complete with live-action domestic scenes on actual Viking-age streets, with constipated villagers, axe-fighting, and other singular attractions.

Where Jorvik shows what was unearthed at Coppergate, the associated attraction that is **Dig!** (daily 10am–4/5pm; £5.50, joint ticket with Jorvik £11.20, pre-booking advised) illustrates the science involved. Housed five minutes' walk away from Jorvik, in the medieval church of St Saviour, on St Savioursgate, a simulated dig allows you to take part in a range of excavations in the company of archeologists, using authentic tools and methods. Tours (£1) to visit **Dig Hungate**, York's latest major archeological excavation, start from here.

York Castle and the Castle Museum

Despite the rich architectural heritage elsewhere in the city, there's precious little left of **York Castle**, one of two established by William the Conqueror. Only the perilously leaning **Clifford's Tower** (daily 10am–4/6pm; £3; EH) remains, a stark stone keep built between 1245 and 1262. Immediately east of the tower lies the outstanding **Castle Museum** (daily 9.30/10am–5pm; £6.50; Ⓦwww.yorkcastlemuseum.org.uk), a remarkable "collection of bygones" instigated by a Dr Kirk of Pickering, who in the 1920s realized that many of the everyday items used in rural areas were in danger of disappearing. A whole range of early craft, folk and agricultural ephemera is complemented by costumes, toys, machinery, domestic implements and show workshops, plus special exhibitions on subjects as diverse as swimming costumes through the ages and fire engines. Two entire reconstructed Victorian and Edwardian streets are perhaps the highlight, though Kirk's fetishistic collections of truncheons and biscuit moulds are surely unsurpassed.

The National Railway Museum

The **National Railway Museum** on Leeman Road (daily 10am–6pm; free; Ⓦwww.nrm.org.uk) is a must if you have even the slightest interest in railways, history, engineering or Victoriana. The Great Hall alone features some fifty restored locomotives dating from 1829 onwards, among them the *Mallard*, at 126mph the world's fastest steam engine. The museum has also acquired the *Flying Scotsman*, the world's most famous locomotive, presently undergoing an overhaul, but due to be taking passengers again in 2009 (check for updates at the museum or call Ⓣ0870/421 4472). There's also the 54-metre-high **Yorkshire Wheel** at the museum (daily 10am–6pm; £6), offering panoramic city and countryside views on a thirteen-minute pod ride. The museum and wheel are ten minutes' walk from the train station, or you can get there on a **road train** (Easter–Oct, every 30min, 11.15am–4.15pm) from Duncombe Place, near the Minster.

Eating and drinking

In keeping with much else in the city, many establishments are self-consciously old-fashioned, though there are some real highlights – truly **historic pubs**, the ultimate **teashop** experience that is *Betty's*, and a scattering of well-regarded **restaurants**. Riverside terraces between the Lendal and Ouse bridges have opened up the city for alfresco drinking, and there's a flourishing **café-bar** scene.

Tearooms, cafés and café-bars

Betty's 6–8 St Helen's Square Ⓣ01904/659142, Ⓦwww.bettys.co.uk. If there are tearooms in heaven they'll be like *Betty's*. Tea, cakes and pastries are the stock-in-trade (pikelets and Yorkshire fat rascals to name just a couple of specials), but there are a dozen or so hot dishes and great puddings too. Open daily until 9pm.

Café Concerto 21 High Petergate Ⓣ01904/610478. Independent bistro with a good reputation and a relaxed atmosphere. Daily until 10pm.

Café No. 8 8 Gillygate Ⓣ01904/653074, Ⓦwww.café8.co.uk. This little café-bar, just outside Bootham Bar, has a great summer garden, while the food ranges from wraps and sandwiches to more substantial mains. No dinner Sun or Mon nights. Closes 10pm.

Evil Eye Lounge 42 Stonegate Ⓣ01904/640002. Colourful café-bar, where cosmopolitan reigns supreme. Tibetan dumplings and Japanese chicken vie with traditional Sun roasts, Peruvian beers with Lindisfarne mead. Closes 11.30pm/12.30am.

Melton's Too 25 Walmgate Ⓣ01904/629222, Ⓦwww.meltonstoo.co.uk. York's best and most relaxed café-bar – superior tapas, pasta, salads, steaks and more, with an emphasis on regional food.

Restaurants

Happy Valley 70 Goodramgate Ⓣ01904/654745. Housed in York's oldest row of houses, this half-timbered café certainly doesn't look like a Chinese restaurant, but pulls in Asian tourists for authentic, homestyle food. Inexpensive.

▲Clifford's Tower

J. Baker's 7 Fossgate ⓣ01904/622688, ⓦwww.jbakers.co.uk. Jeff Baker adds exquisite presentation to his drop-dead-gorgeous food. Experience his take on the best of Yorkshire produce in the seven-course dinner (£35) or the lunchtime grazing menu (a snip at £10). Reservations essential. Closed Sun & Mon. Expensive.

Melton's 7 Scarcroft Rd ⓣ01904/634341, ⓦwww.meltonsrestaurant.co.uk. You're assured of simple, classy cooking, including very good fish dishes, and imaginative vegetarian food. Closed Mon lunch & Sun dinner. Reservations advised. Expensive.

Tasting Room 13 Swinegate Court East, off Grape Lane ⓣ01904/627879. The city's sunniest courtyard makes a great lunch destination; dinner in the pretty pastel restaurant shifts up a gear and the Modern British menu has plenty of choice. Expensive.

Vanilla Black 26 Swinegate ⓣ01904/676750, ⓦwww.vanillablack.co.uk. Sophisticated "vegetable cuisine" in a handsome restaurant – think hickory smoked duchess potato and Wensleydale cheese pudding, and similarly evolved tastes. Closed Sun & Mon, and Tues lunch. Expensive.

Pubs

Black Swan Peasholme Green. York's oldest (sixteenth-century) pub has some superb stone flagging and wood-panelling. The beer's good – you can get the local York Brewery stuff here – and it's also home of the city's folk club (ⓦwww.bsfc.org.uk for details of gigs).

Blue Bell Fossgate. A tiny, no-frills traditional pub – oak-panelling, real ales, no mobile phones, non-tourist clientele.

Three-Legged Mare 15 High Petergate. York Brewery's cosy outlet for its own quality beer and definitely a pub for grown-ups – no juke box, no video games and no kids.

Nightlife, culture and entertainment

Cultural entertainment is wide and varied, with the city supporting several theatres, cinemas and live music venues. Classical music recitals and concerts are often held in the city's churches and York Minster. For what's on listings see the local *Evening Press* (and ⓦwww.thisisyork.co.uk), and the monthly *What's On York* leaflet (ⓦwww.whatsonyork.com), while ⓦwww.yorkfestivals.com gives the lowdown on the annual festivals and events. The famous **York Mystery Plays** are traditionally held every four years, with the next planned for 2010 (ⓦwww.yorkmysteryplays.co.uk). Major annual events include York's **Viking Festival** (ⓦwww.vikingjorvik.com) every February and the **Early Music Festival** (ⓦwww.ncem.co.uk), held in July, perhaps the best of its kind in Britain.

Venues

City Screen 13–17 Coney St ⓣ0870/758 3219, ⓦwww.picturehouses.co.uk. The city's independent cinema is the art-house choice, with three screens, riverside café-bar, and *Basement Bar*.

Grand Opera House Cumberland St, at Clifford St ⓣ0870/606 3595, ⓦwww.grandoperahouseyork.org.uk. Musicals, ballet, pop gigs and family entertainment in all its guises.

The National Centre for Early Music St Margaret's Church, Walmgate ⓣ01904/658338, ⓦwww.ncem.co.uk. Not just early music, but also folk, world and jazz.

Listings

Bike rental Bob Trotter, 13–15 Lord Mayor's Walk, at Monkgate ⓣ01904/622868. Rates from £12 per day, £50 per week.

Bus information National Express ⓣ0870/580 8080; East Yorkshire ⓣ01482/222222 (for Hull, Beverley and Bridlington); Yorkshire Coastliner ⓣ01653/692556 (for Leeds, Castle Howard, Pickering, Scarborough and Whitby).

Hospital York District Hospital, Wigginton Rd (24hr emergency number ⓣ01904/631313); bus #2, #5 or #6. The NHS Walk-in Centre, 31 Monkgate (daily 7am–10pm) offers care, advice and treatment without an appointment.

Pharmacy Boots, Kings Square ⓣ01904/671204.

Police Fulford Rd ⓣ0845/606 0247.

Post office 22 Lendal.

Taxis Ranks at Rougier St, Duncombe Place, Exhibition Square, and the train station; or call Station Taxis ⓣ01904/623332.

Castle Howard

Immersed in the deep countryside of the Howardian Hills, fifteen miles northeast of York off the A64, **Castle Howard** (March–Oct and late Nov to mid-Dec daily 11am–5pm; gardens open at 10am; £10; grounds only £7.50; Ⓦwww.castlehoward.co.uk) is the seat of one of England's leading aristocratic families and among the country's grandest stately homes. It's a pricey visit, but there's no question that it's worth seeing, the grounds especially, and you could easily spend the best part of a day here. The summer Moorsbus (see p.576) comes out here from Helmsley, while some Yorkshire Coastliner buses run from York, Malton or Pickering – it's best to call Traveline (Ⓣ0871/200 2233) to check schedules, or consider taking a bus tour from York.

The colossal main house was designed by **Sir John Vanbrugh** in 1699 and was almost forty years in the making – remarkable enough, even were it not for the fact that Vanbrugh was, at the start of the commission at least, best known as a playwright and had no formal architectural training. Shrewdly, Vanbrugh recognized his limitations and called upon the assistance of **Nicholas Hawksmoor**, who had a major part in the house's structural design – the pair later worked successfully together on Blenheim Palace.

Vanbrugh also turned his attention to the estate's thousand-acre **grounds**, where he could indulge his playful inclinations – the formal gardens, clipped parkland, towers, obelisks and blunt sandstone follies stretch in all directions, sloping gently to two artificial lakes. The whole is a charming artifice of grand, manicured views – an example of what three centuries, skilled gardeners and pots of money can produce. Daily outdoor **tours** (call for times; free) concentrate on aspects of the house and garden. The annual outdoor Proms concert every August is also popular.

Hull

HULL – officially Kingston upon Hull – has a maritime pre-eminence that dates back to 1299, when it was laid out as a seaport by Edward I. It quickly became England's leading harbour, and was still a vital garrison when the gates were closed against Charles I in 1642, the first serious act of rebellion of what was to become the English Civil War. Fishing and seafaring have always been important here, and today's city maintains a firm grip on its heritage while bolstering its attractions for visitors.

The city's maritime legacy is covered in the **Maritime Museum** (Mon–Sat 10am–5pm, Sun 1.30–4.30pm; free), housed in the Neoclassical headquarters of the former Town Docks Offices, on Queen Victoria Square. Over towards the River Hull, you reach the **Museums Quarter** (all attractions Mon–Sat 10am–5pm, Sun 1.30–4.30pm; free) and **High Street**, which has been designated an "Old Town" conservation area thanks to its crop of former merchants' houses and narrow cobbled alleys. At its northern end stands **Wilberforce House**, the former home of William Wilberforce and containing some fascinating exhibits on slavery and its abolition, the cause to which he dedicated much of his life. Next door is **Streetlife**, devoted to the history of transport in the region and centred on a 1930s street scene of reconstructed shops, railway goods yard, and cycle and motor works. The adjoining **Hull and East Riding Museum** is even better, with showpiece attractions including vivid displays of Celtic burials, the unique Bronze Age wooden figures from Roos Carr (complete with appendages the Victorians thought too rude to display) and spectacular Roman mosaics.

Protruding from a promontory overlooking the River Humber looms **The Deep** (daily 10am–6pm, last entry 5pm; £8.50; Ⓦwww.thedeep.co.uk), ten minutes' walk from the old town. Its educational displays and videos wrap around an immense thirty-foot-deep, 2.3-million-gallon viewing tank filled with sharks, rays and octopuses.

Practicalities

There are direct **trains** from London to Hull, while the city is also linked to the main London–York train line via Doncaster. The train station is on the west side of town, on the main drag of Ferensway, with the **bus** station just to the north. The **tourist office** is on Paragon Street at Queen Victoria Square (Mon–Sat 10am–5pm, Sun 11am–3pm; Ⓣ01482/223559, Ⓦwww.hullcc.gov.uk/visithull). They co-ordinate richly anecdotal **guided tours** around the old town (April–Oct Mon–Sat at 2pm, Sun 11am; £3) departing from their office, or you can pick up the entertaining "Fish Trail" leaflet, a self-guided trail that kids will love. The excellent **Hull Truck Theatre Company** (Ⓣ01482/323638, Ⓦwww.hulltruck.co.uk) is where, among others, many of the plays of award-winning John Godber first see the light of day.

Accommodation

Holiday Inn Hull Marina Castle St Ⓣ0870/400 9043, Ⓦwww.holiday-inn.co.uk. Rooms at the city's best central hotel overlook the marina, and there's a restaurant and bar, plus indoor pool, gym and sauna. ⑤

Kingston Theatre Hotel 1–2 Kingston Square Ⓣ01482/225828, Ⓦwww.kingstontheatrehotel.com. Straightforward but good-value hotel rooms on the city's prettiest square, across from Hull New Theatre. ④, suites ⑤

Quality Hotel Royal 170 Ferensway Ⓣ01482/325087, Ⓦwww.hotels-hull.com. Original Victorian hotel, by the station, that has been fully refurbished, and incorporates a good leisure centre and pool. ⑤

Cafés, bars and restaurants

Cerutti's 10 Nelson St Ⓣ01482/328501. Down at the end of the east side of the marina, this leads the way in local seafood. Closed Sun lunch. Expensive.

Mimosa 406–408 Beverley Rd Ⓣ01482/474748. Friendly Turkish restaurant with an open charcoal grill – it's around a mile and a half out of the centre. Moderate.

Studio 10½ King St Ⓣ01482/224625. Take the stairs above the gift shop, opposite Holy Trinity Church, and enter a trompe l'oeil painted walled garden, where a handsome range of lunches and snacks awaits. Daytime only; closed Sun. Inexpensive.

Taman Ria Tropicana 45–47 Princes Ave Ⓣ01482/345640. Sort out your *rendang* from your *laksa* at this agreeable, authentic Malaysian/Indonesian restaurant. Closed Mon. Moderate.

Pubs

George The Land of Green Ginger. Venerable pub found on Hull's most curiously named street – and featuring, if you can find it, England's smallest window.

Minerva Corner of Nelson St and Humber Dock St. Classic marina pub with cosy nooks, outdoor tables and cheap food.

Ye Olde White Harte 25 Silver St. Has a very pleasant courtyard beer garden and a history going back to the seventeenth century.

Beverley

BEVERLEY, nine miles north of Hull, replete with a tangle of old streets, cobbled lanes and elegant Georgian and Victorian terraces, is the very picture of a traditional market town. Approaches are dominated by the fine, Gothic twin towers of **Beverley Minster** (Mon–Sat 9am–4/5.30pm, Sun noon–4/4.30pm; donation requested; Ⓦwww.beverleyminster.org). The **west front**, which crowned the work in 1420, is widely considered without equal, its survival due in large part to architect Nicholas Hawksmoor, who restored much of the church in the eighteenth century. The carving throughout is magnificent, particularly the 68 misericords of the oak **choir** (1520–24), one of the largest and most accomplished in England. Much of the decorative work here and elsewhere is on a musical theme. Beverley had a renowned guild of itinerant minstrels, which provided funds in the sixteenth century for the carvings on the transept aisle capitals, where you'll be able to pick out players of lutes, bagpipes, horns and tambourines.

Cobbled Highgate runs from the minster through town, along the pedestrianized shopping streets and past the main Market Square, to Beverley's other great church, **St Mary's** (Mon–Sat 9.30/10am–noon 4/4.30pm, Sat 10am–4pm; Oct–March closed Sat; free), which nestles alongside the **North Bar**, sole survivor of the town's five medieval gates. Inside, the chancel's painted panelled ceiling (1445) contains portraits of English kings from Sigebert (623–37) to Henry VI (1421–71), while among the carvings, the favourite novelty is the so-called "Pilgrim's Rabbit", said to have been the inspiration for the White Rabbit in Lewis Carroll's *Alice in Wonderland*.

Beverley's **train station** on Station Square is just a couple of minutes' walk from the minster. The **bus station** is at the junction of Walkergate and Sow Hill Road, with the main street just a minute's walk away. The **tourist office** is at 34 Butcher Row in the main shopping area (Mon–Fri 9.30am–5.15pm, Sat 10am–4.45pm, plus Sun in July & Aug 11am–3pm; Ⓣ01482/391672, Ⓦwww.visiteastyorkshire.com). As for local **accommodation**, try *Number One*, 1 Woodlands (Ⓣ01482/862752, Ⓦwww.number-one-bedandbreakfast-beverley.co.uk; no credit cards; ❷), a small B&B in a quiet Victorian house two minutes' walk from the marketplace, or the central *Beverley Arms*, North Bar Within (Ⓣ01482/869241, Ⓦwww.brook-hotels.co.uk; ❻). The **youth hostel** (Ⓣ0870/770 5696, Ⓔbeverleyfriary@yha.org.uk; from £13.95; closed Nov–March) occupies a restored Dominican friary that was mentioned in the *Canterbury Tales*. It's located in Friar's Lane, off Eastgate, just a hundred yards southeast of the minster.

The East Yorkshire coast

The **East Yorkshire coast** curves south in a gentle arc from the mighty cliffs of Flamborough Head to Spurn Head, a hook-shaped promontory formed by the constant erosion and shifting currents. There are few parts of the British coast as dangerous – indeed, the Humber lifeboat station at Spurn Point is the only one in Britain permanently staffed by a professional crew. Between the two points lie a handful of tranquil villages and miles of windswept dunes and mud flats. The two main resorts, **Bridlington** and **Filey** are linked by the regular **train** service between Hull and Scarborough. There's also an hourly bus service between Bridlington, Filey and Scarborough, while the seasonal Sunday **Spurn Ranger** service (Easter–Oct; Ⓣ01482/222222) gives access to the isolated Spurn Head coastline.

The southernmost resort on the Yorkshire coast, **BRIDLINGTON** has maintained its harbour for almost a thousand years. The seafront promenade looks down upon the town's best asset – its sweeping sandy **beach**. It's an out-and-out family resort, which means plenty of candyfloss, fish and chips, rides, boat trips and amusement arcades. The historic core of town is a mile inland, where in largely Georgian Bridlington Old Town the **Bayle Museum** (April–Sept Mon–Fri 10am–4pm, Sun 11am–4pm; £2) presents local history in a building that once served as the gateway to a fourteenth-century priory.

Around fourteen miles of precipitous four-hundred-foot cliffs gird **Flamborough Head**, just to the northeast of Bridlington. From **Bempton**, two miles north of Bridlington, you can follow the grassy cliff-top path all the way round to Flamborough Head or curtail by cutting up paths to Flamborough village. The RSPB sanctuary at **Bempton Cliffs**, reached along a quiet lane from Bempton, is the best single place to see the area's thousands of cliff-nesting birds. It's the only mainland gannetry in England, while Bempton also boasts the second-largest **puffin colony** in the country, with several thousand returning to the cliffs each year. Late March and April is the best time to see the puffins, but the **Visitor Centre** (daily 9.30am/10am–4/5pm; parking £3.50; Ⓣ01262/851179, Ⓦwww.rspb.org.uk) can advise on other breeds' activities.

FILEY, half a dozen miles further north up the coast, is at the very edge of the Yorkshire Wolds (and technically in North Yorkshire). It has a good deal more class as a resort than Bridlington, retaining many of its Edwardian features, including some splendid panoramic gardens. It, too, claims miles of wide sandy beach, stretching most of the way south to Flamborough Head and north the mile or so to the jutting rocks of **Filey Brigg**, where a nature trail wends for a couple of miles through the surroundings.

The North York Moors

Virtually the whole of the **North York Moors**, (Ⓦwww.moors.uk.net), from the Hambleton and Cleveland hills in the west to the cliff-edged coastline to the east, is protected by one of the country's finest National Parks. The heather-covered, flat-topped hills are cut by deep, steep-sided valleys, and views here stretch for miles, interrupted only by giant cultivated forests. Barrows and ancient forts provide memorials of early settlers, mingling on the high moorland with the battered stone crosses of the first Christian inhabitants and the ruins of great monastic houses such as **Rievaulx Abbey**.

Long-distance footpaths cross the park, notably the **Cleveland Way**, which follows the coast and northern moors. The steam trains of the **North York Moors Railway** run between Pickering and Grosmont and on to Whitby (even more popular since being used as the *Hogwarts Express* in the *Harry Potter* films). At Grosmont you can connect with the regular trains on the **Esk Valley** line, running either six miles east to Whitby and the coast, or west through more remote country settlements (and ultimately to Middlesbrough). The main **bus** approaches to the moors are from Scarborough and York to the main towns of **Helmsley** and **Pickering** – pick up the free *Moors Explorer* timetable booklet from tourist offices and park information centres. There are also seasonal **Moorsbus** services (April–Oct; Ⓣ01845/597000, Ⓦwww.moors.uk.net/moorsbus), connecting Pickering and Helmsley to everywhere of interest in the National Park. Departures are several times daily in the school summer holidays, more restricted at other times (at least every Sun & bank hol Mon).

Thirsk and around

The market town of **THIRSK**, 23 miles north of York, made the most of its strategic crossroads position on the ancient drove road between Scotland and

York and on the historic east–west route from dales to coast. Its medieval prosperity is clear from the large, cobbled **Market Place** (market days are Monday and Saturday), while well-to-do citizens later endowed the town with fine Georgian houses and halls. However, Thirsk's main draw is its attachment to the legacy of local vet Alf Wight, better known as James Herriott. Thirsk was the "Darrowby" of the Herriott books, and the vet's former surgery, at 23 Kirkgate, is now the hugely popular **World of James Herriott** (daily 10/11am–4/5pm; £5.20, Ⓦwww.worldofjamesherriot.org), crammed with period pieces and Herriott memorabilia.

Eleven miles north of Thirsk, the little village of **Osmotherley** huddles around its green. The pretty settlement gets by as a hiking centre, since it's a key stop on the **Cleveland Way** as well as starting point for the brutal 42-mile **Lyke Wake Walk** to Ravenscar, south of Robin Hood's Bay. Nearby (an easy two-mile walk, via Chapel Wood Farm) is the fourteenth-century **Mount Grace Priory** (April–Sept Mon & Thurs–Sun 10am–6pm; Oct–March Thurs–Sun 10am–4pm; £4; NT & EH), the most important of England's nine Carthusian ruins. The Carthusians took a vow of silence and lived, ate and prayed alone in their two-storey cells, each separated from its neighbour by a privy, small garden and high walls. The foundations of the cells are still clearly visible, together with one that has been reconstructed to suggest its original layout.

Thirsk is only a half-hour drive from York, making an easy day-trip. **Buses** stop in the Market Place, while the **train station** is a mile west of town on the A61 (Ripon road); minibuses connect the station with the town centre. The **tourist office**, 49 Market Place (daily 10/11am–4/5pm; Ⓣ01845/522755, Ⓦwww.hambleton.gov.uk), can help with **accommodation**. There are B&Bs on Kirkgate, on the road up to the parish church, while the Market Place is ringed by old-fashioned pubs, cafés and tearooms. Four miles to the south, down the A168 at **Asenby**, *Crab Manor* (Ⓣ01845/577286, Ⓦwww.crabandlobster.co.uk; ⑨) is something of a local curiosity – its lavish rooms are all styled in the fashion of famous hotels from around the world, while its *Crab & Lobster* restaurant is a renowned fish place.

Sutton Bank, Kilburn and Coxwold

The main A170 road enters the National Park from Thirsk as it climbs five hundred feet in half a mile to **Sutton Bank** (960ft), a phenomenal viewpoint from where the panorama extends across the Vale of York to the Pennines on the far horizon. At the top of the climb stands a North York Moors **National Park Visitor Centre** (April–Oct daily 10am–5pm; Nov, Dec & March daily 10.30am–3.30pm; Jan & Feb weekends only 10.30am–3.30pm; Ⓣ01845/597426, Ⓦwww.moors.uk.net), full of information on the short walks and off-road bike rides you can make from here.

To the south of the A170, the **White Horse Nature Trail** (2–3 miles; 1hr 30min) skirts the crags of Roulston Scar en route to the **Kilburn White Horse**, northern England's only turf-cut figure, 314 feet long and 228 feet high. You could make a real walk of it by dropping a couple of miles down to pretty **KILBURN** village (a minor road also runs from the A170, passing the White Horse car park) synonymous with woodcarving since the days of "Mouseman" Robert Thompson (1876–1955), whose woodcarvings are marked by his distinctive mouse motif. The **Mouseman Visitor Centre** (daily 10am–5pm; closed Mon in Oct and Mon & Tues in Nov & Dec; £3.50; Ⓦwww.robertthompsons.co.uk) displays examples of Thompson's personal furniture, and you can recuperate in the village's *Forresters Arms*.

Most visitors to the attractive nearby village of **COXWOLD** come to pay homage to the novelist **Laurence Sterne**, who is buried by the south wall (close to the porch) in the churchyard of **St Michael's**, where he was vicar from 1760 until his death in 1768. **Shandy Hall**, 150yd further up the road past the church (May–Sept Wed 2–4.30pm, Sun 2.30–4.30pm; gardens May–Sept Mon–Fri & Sun 11am–4.30pm; also by appointment; house & gardens £4.50, gardens only £2.50; ⓣ01347/868465, ⓦwww.shandean.org), was Sterne's home, now a museum crammed with literary memorabilia. It was here that he wrote *A Sentimental Journey through France and Italy* and the wonderfully eccentric *The Life and Opinions of Tristram Shandy, Gentleman.*

Helmsley

One of the moors' most appealing towns, **HELMSLEY** makes a perfect base for visiting the western moors and Rievaulx Abbey. Local life revolves around a large cobbled market square, dominated by a boastful monument to the second earl of Feversham, whose family was responsible for rebuilding most of the village in the nineteenth century. The old **market cross** now marks the start of the 110-mile Cleveland Way. Signposted from the square, it's easy to find **Helmsley Castle** (March–Oct daily 10am–5/6pm; Nov–Feb Mon & Thurs–Sun 10am–4pm; £4; EH), its unique twelfth-century D-shaped keep ringed by massive earthworks.

Practicalities

Buses all stop on or near the Market Place. The useful **tourist office** is at the castle visitor centre (March–Oct daily 9.30am–5pm; Nov–Feb Fri–Sun 10am–4pm; ⓣ01439/770173, ⓦwww.ryedale.gov.uk), and has information on the **Cleveland Way**, one of England's premier long-distance National Trails, which embraces both wild moorland and the cliff scenery of the North Yorkshire coast. The **Cleveland Way Project** (The Old Vicarage, Bondgate, Helmsley, YO6 5BP; ⓣ01439/770657) produces an annual **accommodation** guide, which you can download on ⓦwww.nationaltrail.co.uk.

Market day in Helmsley is Friday, with the town centre filled with traders. The *Feathers* on the Market Place is the best place for a drink and a **pub** meal, while also on Market Place are two excellent **delis**, Hunters and Perns, the latter associated with the excellent *Star inn* at Harome. At **Helmsley Arts Centre** in the Old Meeting House, off Bridge Street (ⓣ01439/771700, ⓦwww.helmsleyarts.co.uk), there's a full programme of theatre, film and music.

Accommodation and food

Feversham Arms 1 High St, behind the church ⓣ01439/770766, ⓦwww.fevershamarmshotel.com. Combines hip styling with comfort in its spacious rooms and Modern British brasserie. It's favoured by the country pursuits crowd, but there's also an outdoor pool, gym, tennis court and garden terrace, while a spa and new poolside suites will be available in 2008. ⑦

Helmsley YHA ⓣ0870/770 5860, ⓔhelmsley@yha.org.uk. A few hundred yards east of Market Place – follow Bondgate to Carlton Rd and turn left. Open daily April–Sept. Dorm beds from £14.95.

No. 54 54 Bondgate ⓣ01439/771533, ⓦwww.no54.co.uk. A delightful cottage-style B&B offering three superior courtyard rooms just 500 yards from Market Place. Power showers, sheltered terrace and garden add up to a relaxing night. Picnics and evening meals also available. ⑤

Star Inn Harome, 2 miles south of the A170 ⓣ01439/770397, ⓦwww.thestaratharome.co.uk. A thatched pub where Michelin-rated food awaits. Should you wish to make a night of it, eight very nice rooms in the adjacent lodge are individually furnished, some with spa baths, a couple with a private garden. No food Sun eve & Mon. ⑦

Rievaulx Abbey and Terrace

From Helmsley you can easily walk across country to **Rievaulx Abbey** (April–Sept daily 10am–6pm; Oct–March Mon & Thurs–Sun 10am–4/5pm; £4.50; EH). The signposted path takes around an hour and a half. Founded in 1132, the abbey became the mother church of the Cistercians in England, quickly developing into a flourishing community with interests in fishing, mining, agriculture and the woollen industry. At its height, 140 monks and up to 500 lay brothers lived and worked at the abbey, though numbers fell dramatically once the Black Death (1348–49) had done its worst. The end came with the Dissolution, when many of the walls were razed and the roof lead stripped – the beautiful ruins, however, still suggest the abbey's former splendour.

Although they form some sort of ensemble with the abbey, there's no access between the ruins and **Rievaulx Terrace** (daily 11am–5/6pm; £4; NT), a site entered from the B1257, a couple of miles northwest of Helmsley. This half-mile stretch of grass-covered terraces and woodland was laid out as part of Duncombe Park in the 1750s, and was engineered partly to enhance the views of the abbey. The resulting panorama over the ruins and the valley below is superb, and this makes a great spot for a picnic.

Hutton le Hole

Lying eight miles northeast of Helmsley, one of Yorkshire's quaintest villages, **HUTTON LE HOLE**, has become so great a tourist attraction that you'll have to come off-season to get much pleasure from its stream-crossed village green and the sight of sheep wandering freely through the lanes. Apart from the sheer photogenic quality of the place, the big draw is the family-oriented **Ryedale Folk Museum** (daily mid-Jan–mid-Dec 10am–dusk; £4.80; Ⓦwww.ryedalefolkmuseum.co.uk), where local life is explored in a series of reconstructed buildings, notably a sixteenth-century house, a glass furnace, a crofter's cottage and a nineteenth-century blacksmith's shop. The museum also houses a **National Park information centre** (same hours as museum; Ⓣ01751/417367), which has a list of local B&Bs, or make for *Burnley House* (Ⓣ01751/417548, Ⓦwww.burnleyhouse.com; ⑤), a hospitable Georgian house on the green with streamside garden. At **Rosedale Abbey**, four miles northeast of Hutton le Hole, the rooms at the *Milburn Arms* (Ⓣ01751/417312, Ⓦwww.milburnarms.co.uk; ⑤) overlook the small green, and there's a beer garden out front.

Pickering

The biggest centre for miles around, **PICKERING** takes for itself the title "Gateway to the Moors", which is pushing it a bit, though it's certainly a handy halt if you're touring the villages and dales of the **eastern moors**. Its most attractive feature is its motte and bailey **Castle** on the hill north of the Market Place (April–Sept daily 10am–6pm; Oct Mon & Thurs–Sun 10am–5pm; £3; EH), reputedly used by every English monarch up to 1400 as a base for hunting in nearby Blandsby Park. The other spot worth investigating is the **Beck Isle Museum of Rural Life** on Bridge Street (March–Oct daily 10am–5pm; Nov to mid-Dec Fri–Sun 10am–4pm; £3.50; Ⓦwww.beckislemuseum.co.uk), which has reconstructions of a gents' outfitters, and barber's shop, a case full of knickers, and two giant Welsh guardsmen painted by Rex Whistler for a children's party.

Buses stop outside the library and **tourist office** on The Ropery, (March–Oct Mon–Sat 9.30am–5pm, Sun 9.30am–4pm; Nov–Feb Mon–Sat 9.30am–4.30pm;

Ⓣ01751/473791, Ⓦwww.ryedale.gov.uk), opposite the Co-op in the centre of town; the **NYMR train station** (see box below) is less than five minutes' signposted walk away. The tourist office can help with **B&Bs**, though Whitby, only twenty minutes' drive away on the coast, is the better overnight destination (see p.583). A couple of the **pubs** also have rooms, top choice easily being the *White Swan*, on Market Place (Ⓣ01751/472288, Ⓦwww.white-swan.co.uk; ❼), with both contemporary and traditional bedrooms, and fine Modern British food at moderate prices. **Market** day in town is Monday, and there's a farmers' market on the first Thursday of the month.

Along the North Yorkshire Moors Railway

The first stop is Levisham, perfect for walks to the village of **LEVISHAM**, a mile and a half to the east of the station where the *Horseshoe Inn* is a favourite target, especially for Sunday lunch. A steep winding road continues another mile beyond Levisham, down across the beck and then up to **LOCKTON**, where there's a path to the **Hole of Horcum**, a bizarre natural hollow gouged by the glacial meltwaters that carved out Newtondale. The paths run back to Levisham Station from here, and the entire seven-mile circuit is one of the Moors' best short walks – take the short detour halfway round to the *Saltersgate Inn*, on the A169, which has good-value food (and a fire that hasn't been allowed to go out for a couple of centuries).

The third NYMR station is at **GOATHLAND**, a highly attractive village set in open moorland beneath the great expanses of Wheeldale and Goathland moors. If it seems oddly familiar – and if it seems unduly crowded – it's because it's widely known as "Aidensfield", the fictional village at the centre of the *Heartbeat* TV series, while the station doubled as "Hogsmeade" in *Harry Potter and the Philosopher's Stone*. A gentle path from Goathland runs the mile through the fields down to **BECK HOLE**, an idyllic bridgeside hamlet focused on the *Birch Hall Inn*, one of the finest rural pubs in all England – tiny to the point of claustrophobic, and still doubling as a sweet shop and store as it has for a century.

The Esk Valley

The northernmost reaches of the National Park are crossed by the east–west **Esk Valley**, whose pretty river flows into the sea at Whitby. There's not much moorland tramping to be done until you reach the isolated stone village of **DANBY**, one of the finest of all moorland villages. Here, you're within striking distance of some excellent walks, all detailed on trail leaflets available from the

The North Yorkshire Moors Railway

The **North Yorkshire Moors Railway** (NYMR; Ⓣ01751/472508, talking timetables call Ⓣ01751/473535, Ⓦwww.nymr.co.uk) connects **Pickering** with the Esk Valley (Middlesbrough–Whitby) line at **Grosmont**, 18 miles to the north. The line was completed by George Stephenson in 1835, just ten years after the opening of the Stockton and Darlington Railway. Scheduled **services** operate year-round (limited to weekend and school hol service Nov–Feb), and a **day-return ticket** costs £14. Part of the line's attraction are the **steam trains**, though be warned that diesels are pulled into service when the fire risk in the forests is high. Steam services have also been extended from the end of the NYMR line at Grosmont to the nearby seaside resort of Whitby – departures are usually during school and bank holidays, with a return fare from Pickering of £20.

Moors Centre (March–Dec daily 10/10.30am–3.30/5pm; Jan & Feb Sat & Sun only 10.30am–3.30pm; ⓣ01439/772737, ⓦwww.moors.uk.net).

You can reach Danby by road (from Whitby via the A169 through Sleights) or by **train**: the North York Moors Railway (see previous section) connects at **Grosmont**, where you're on the **Esk Valley line**, which runs between Whitby and Middlesbrough, stopping at **GREAT AYTON**. Here, the North York Moors give way to the **Cleveland Hills**, whose scattered peaks provide the buffer between the rural east of the region and the encroaching industry of Teesside to the west. It's Great Ayton's **Captain Cook** connections, though, that draw most visitors: the town was the boyhood home of England's greatest seaman and explorer, James Cook, between 1736 (when he was 8) and 1745. A waymarked path runs northeast out of Great Ayton, up to the summit of **Roseberry Topping** (1050ft), the queerly shaped conical peak visible from all over the locality. It's a reasonably stiff climb, followed by a tramp across Easby Moor to the south to the fifty-foot-high **Cook Monument** (1827) for more amazing views, before circling back to Great Ayton.

The North Yorkshire coast

The **North Yorkshire coast** (ⓦwww.discoveryorkshirecoast.com) is the southernmost stretch of a cliff-edged shore that stretches almost unbroken to the Scottish border. **Scarborough** is the biggest town and resort, with a full set of attractions and a terrific beach. Cute **Robin Hood's Bay** is the most popular of the coastal villages, with fishing and smuggling traditions, while bluff **Staithes** – a fishing harbour on the far edge of North Yorkshire – has yet to tip over into full-blown tourist mode. **Whitby**, in between the two, is the best stopover, its fine sands and resort facilities tempered by its abbey ruins, Georgian buildings and maritime heritage – more than any other local place Whitby celebrates Captain Cook as one of its own. **Walkers** should note that two of the best parts of the **Cleveland Way** depart from Whitby: southeast to Robin Hood's Bay (six miles) and northwest to Staithes (eleven miles), both along thrilling high-cliff sections.

Scarborough

The oldest resort in the country, **SCARBOROUGH** first attracted early seventeenth-century visitors to its newly discovered mineral springs. To the Victorians it was "the Queen of the Watering Places", but Scarborough saw its biggest transformation after World War II, when it became a holiday haven for workers from the industrial heartlands. All the traditional ingredients of a beach resort are still here in force, from superb, clean sands, kitsch amusement arcades to the more refined pleasures of its tight-knit old-town streets and a genteel round of quiet parks and gardens.

There's no better place to acquaint yourself with the local layout than **Scarborough Castle** (April–Sept daily 10am–6pm; Oct–March Mon & Thurs–Sun 10am–4/5pm; £4; EH), mounted on a jutting headland between two golden-sanded bays. Bronze and Iron Age relics have been found on the wooded castle crag, together with fragments of a fourth-century Roman signalling station, Saxon and Norman chapels and a Viking camp, reputedly built by a Viking with the nickname of Scardi (or "harelip"), from which the town's name derives. As you leave the castle, drop into the **Church of St Mary** (1180), immediately below on Castle Road, whose graveyard contains the tomb of Anne Brontë, who died here in 1849.

The town's **museums** are currently undergoing reorganization (latest details on Ⓦwww.scarboroughmuseums.org.uk), but the collections at both the Art Gallery and **Rotunda Museum** (for geological displays) are definitely worth seeing. The miniature **North Bay Railway** (daily Easter–Sept) runs up to the main attraction on the **North Bay** side, namely the **Sea Life Centre and Marine Sanctuary** at Scalby Mills (daily 10am–4.30/5.30pm; £11.95), distinguished by its white pyramids. From the harbourside you'll be able to take one of the short **cruises** and **speedboat trips** that shoot off throughout the day in the summer. For unique entertainment, head for Peasholm Park, where **naval warfare**, in the shape of miniature man-powered naval vessels, battle it out on the lake (Mon, Thurs & Sat in July and August; full details from the tourist office). The **South Bay** is more refined, backed by the pleasant Valley Gardens and the Italianate meanderings of the South Cliff Gardens, and topped by an esplanade from which a **hydraulic lift** (April–Sept daily 10am–5pm) chugs down to the beach.

Practicalities

The **train station** is at the top of town facing Westborough; **buses** pull up outside or in the surrounding streets, though the National Express services (direct from London) stop in the car park behind the station. Scarborough's **tourist offices** are located inside the Brunswick Shopping Centre on Westborough (Mon–Sat 9/9.30am–4.30/5pm, April–Sept Sun 11am–4.30pm; Ⓣ01723/383637) and on Sandside by the harbour (April–Oct daily 9.30/10am–5.30pm; Nov–March Sat & Sun 10am–4.30pm). Open-top **seafront buses** (Easter–Sept daily from 9.30am, March weekends only; £1.60), meanwhile, run from North Bay to the Spa Complex in South Bay.

Accommodation

Helaina 14 Blenheim Terrace Ⓣ01723/375191, Ⓦwww.hotelhelaina.co.uk. Victorian terraced house on North Bay; bedrooms are on the small size, but beautifully furnished in contemporary style. Great sea views, and ample breakfasts. Parking. ③

Interludes 32 Princess St Ⓣ01723/360513, Ⓦwww.interludeshotel.co.uk. Quiet Georgian townhouse in the old-town streets behind the harbour. Bay views from the upper floors, and theatre memorabilia, antiques, fresh flowers and traditional English decor throughout. It's a gay-friendly place, though all (except children) are welcome. ③

Riviera St Nicholas Cliff Ⓣ01723/372277, Ⓦwww.riviera-scarborough.co.uk. Restored Victorian hotel opposite the *Grand* with bay views and refurbished rooms with crisp white bedding and colourful cushions. ⑤

Windmill Mill St, off Victoria Rd Ⓣ01723/372735, Ⓦwww.windmill-hotel.co.uk. Eighteenth-century windmill sited incongruously in the town centre with its country-style rooms (upper-floor ones with veranda) ranged around a cobbled courtyard. Two family rooms available, plus two self-catering flats within the windmill tower. Parking. ③

Cafés and restaurants

Café Fish 19 York Place, at Somerset Terrace Ⓣ01723/500301. For a more sophisticated way with fish than most Scarborough restaurants – like sole Boursin or Cajun-style salmon. Dinner only. Expensive.

Café Italia 36 St Nicholas Cliff Ⓣ01723/501973. Utterly charming, microscopic Italian coffee bar next to the *Grand*, where good coffee, focaccia slices and ice cream keep a battery of regulars happy. Closes 4pm. Closed Sun. Inexpensive.

Golden Grid 4 Sandside Ⓣ01723/360922. The harbourside's choicest fish-and-chip establishment, "catering for the promenader since 1883". Offers grilled fish, crab and lobster, a *fruits-de-mer* platter and a wine list alongside the standard crispy-battered fry-up. Closed Mon–Thurs dinner in winter. Moderate.

Theatre

Stephen Joseph Theatre Westborough Ⓣ01723/370541, Ⓦwww.sjt.uk.com. Housed in a former Art Deco cinema, this premieres every new play of local playwright Alan Ayckbourn and promotes strong seasons of theatre and film; a good café/restaurant (moderate prices) and bar is open daily except Sun.

Robin Hood's Bay

The most heavily visited spot on the coast, **ROBIN HOOD'S BAY** is made up of gorgeous narrow streets and pink-tiled cottages toppling down the cliff-edge site, evoking the romance of a time when this was both a hard-bitten fishing community and smugglers' den *par excellence*. From the upper village, lined with Victorian villas, now mostly B&Bs, it's a very steep walk down the hill to the harbour. The **Old Coastguard Station** (June–Sept Tues–Sun 10am–5pm; Oct–May weekends & school hols only; free; ⓣ01947/885900; NT) has been turned into a visitor centre with displays relating to the area's geology and sealife. When the tide is out, the massive rock beds below are exposed, split by a geological fault line and studded with fossil remains. There's an easy circular walk (2.5 miles) to **Boggle Hole** and its youth hostel, a mile south, returning inland via the path along the old Scarborough–Whitby railway line.

Many people see the village as a day-trip from Whitby, and you can check on accommodation in the tourist office there, or simply stroll the streets of the old part of the village to see if any of the small cottage **B&Bs** has vacancies. There are also three good **pubs** in the lower village, two of which have rooms: the tiny *Laurel*, on Main Street (ⓣ01947/880400; ❸; two-night minimum), whose small self-catering flat sleeps two; and the *Bay Hotel*, right on the harbour (ⓣ01947/880278; ❹), which is the traditional start or end of the Coast-to-Coast Walk. You'll probably end up **eating** in the pubs – food at the *Bay Hotel* is the best – though the *Swell Café* in the Old Chapel, Chapel St (ⓣ01947/880180; closes 4.30pm), serves a good range of dishes and has great coastal views from its terrace tables. Boggle Hole's **youth hostel** is a former mill located in a wooded ravine about a mile south of Robin Hood's Bay at Mill Beck (ⓣ0870/770 5704, ⓔbogglehole@yha.org.uk; from £12.95). A couple of miles northwest of Robin Hood's Bay at Hawsker, on the A171, Trailways (ⓣ01947/820207, ⓦwww.trailways.fsnet.co.uk) is a **bike-rental** outfit based in the old Hawsker train station, perfectly placed for day-trips in either direction along the disused railway line.

Whitby

If there's one essential stop on the North Yorkshire coast it's **WHITBY**, whose historical associations, atmospheric ruins, fishing harbour and intrinsic charm make it many people's favourite northern resort. The seventh-century cliff-top abbey here made Whitby one of the key foundations of the early Christian period, and a centre of great learning. Below, on the harbour banks of the River Esk, for a thousand years the local herring boats landed their catch until the great whaling boom of the eighteenth century transformed the fortunes of the town. Melville's *Moby Dick* makes much of Whitby whalers such as William Scoresby, while James Cook took his first seafaring steps from the town in 1746, on his way to becoming a national hero. All four of Captain Cook's ships of discovery – the *Endeavour*, *Resolution*, *Adventure* and *Discovery* – were built in Whitby.

Divided by the River Esk, the town splits into two distinct halves joined by a swing bridge: the cobbled **old town** to the east, and the newer (though mostly eighteenth- and nineteenth-century) town across the bridge, generally known as **West Cliff**. Cobbled **Church Street** is the old town's main thoroughfare, barely changed in aspect since the eighteenth century, though now lined with tearooms and gift shops. Parallel Sandgate has more of the same, the two streets meeting at the small marketplace where souvenirs and trinkets are sold; there's a farmer's market here every Thursday.

Whitby, understandably, likes to make a fuss of Captain Cook who served an apprenticeship here from 1746–49 under John Walker, a Quaker ship-owner.

The **Captain Cook Memorial Museum** (March–Oct daily 9.45am–3pm; £3; ⓦwww.cookmuseumwhitby.co.uk), housed in Walker's rickety old house in Grape Lane, contains an impressive amount of memorabilia, including ships' models, letters and paintings by artists seconded to Cook's voyages.

At the north end of Church Street, you climb the famous **199 steps** of the Church Stairs – now paved, but originally a wide wooden staircase built for pallbearers carrying coffins to the **church of St Mary** above. This is an architectural amalgam dating back to 1110, boasting a Norman chancel arch, a profusion of eighteenth-century panelling, box pews unequalled in England and a triple-decker pulpit – note the built-in ear trumpets, added for the benefit of a nineteenth-century rector's deaf wife.

Beyond, the cliff-top ruins of **Whitby Abbey** (April–Oct 10am–5/6pm; Nov–Easter Mon & Thurs–Sun 10am–4pm; £4.20; EH) are some of the most evocative in England. Its monastery was founded in 657 by St Hilda of Hartlepool, daughter of King Oswy of Northumberland, and by 664 had become important enough to host the **Synod of Whitby**, an event of seminal importance in the development of English Christianity. It settled once and for all the question of determining the date of Easter, and adopted the rites and authority of the Roman rather than the Celtic Church. You'll discover all this and more in the **Visitor Centre** (hours as above), housed in the shell of the adjacent mansion, built after the Dissolution using material from the plundered abbey.

Final port of call should be the gloriously eclectic **Whitby Museum** in Pannett Park (Tues–Sun 9.30am–4.30pm, plus bank holidays; £3; ⓦwww.whitbymuseum.org.uk), up the hill from the train station on West Cliff. There's more Cook memorabilia, including various objects and stuffed animals brought back as souvenirs by his crew, as well as casefuls of exhibits devoted to Whitby's seafaring tradition, its whaling industry in particular. Some of the best and largest fossils of Jurassic period reptiles unearthed on the east coast are also preserved here.

Practicalities

The **train station** is a couple of hundred yards south of the bridge to the old town. Special school- and bank-holiday steam train services also stop here, departing from the NYMR station at Grosmont. The **bus station** is adjacent and there's a **Travel Centre** (Mon–Fri 8.30am–4pm; ⓣ01947/602146) in the train station for all local transport enquiries. Whitby's **tourist office** (daily; May–Sept 9.30am–6pm; Oct–April 10am–12.30pm & 1–4.30pm;

Bram Stoker and Dracula

The story of Dracula is well known, but it's the exact attention to the geographical detail of Whitby – little changed since Bram Stoker first wrote the words – which has proved a huge attraction to visitors. Using first-hand observation of a town he knew well – he stayed at a house on the West Cliff, now marked by a plaque – Stoker built a story which mixed real locations, legend, myth and historical fact: the grounding of Count Dracula's ship on Tate Hill Sands was based on an actual event reported in the local papers.

With many of the early chapters recognizably set in Whitby, it's hardly surprising that the town has cashed in on its **Dracula Trail**. The various sites – Tate Hill Sands, the abbey, church and steps, the graveyard, Stoker's house – can all be visited, while down on the harbourside the Dracula Experience attempts to pull in punters to its rather lame horror-show antics. Keen interest has also been sparked amongst the **Goth** fraternity, who now come to town en masse a couple of times a year (in late spring and around Halloween) for a vampire's ball, concerts and readings.

Ⓣ01723/383637; Ⓦwww.visitwhitby.com, Ⓦwww.whitbyonline.co.uk), is on the corner of Langborne Road and New Quay Road.

Whitby has a strong local **music scene**, epitomized by the annual **Whitby Folk Week** (Ⓦwww.whitbyfolk.co.uk) in August (the week immediately preceding the bank holiday), when the town is filled day and night with singers, bands, traditional dancers, storytellers and music workshops. Best place to find out more is at *The Port Hole*, 16 Skinner St (Ⓣ01947/603475), a Fair Trade craft shop that's also the HQ of local collective **Musicport** (Ⓦwww.musicport.fsnet.co.uk) who put on gigs from big names in the world/folk scene. Their renowned annual World Music Festival (October) is due to move to Bridlington from 2008.

Accommodation

Dunsley Hall Dunsley Ⓣ01947/893437, Ⓦwww.dunsleyhall.com. This stately oak-panelled pile (the choice of visiting celebs) has fine gardens, pool, sauna and leisure club, and very cosy bar. It's a couple of miles inland (west) of town. ⑦

Estbek House Sandsend Ⓣ01947/893424, Ⓦwww.estbekhouse.co.uk. Georgian house overlooking the stream at Sandsend, 2 miles from Whitby and just yards from the beach. There are four pretty double/twin rooms, while the relaxed restaurant (expensive; reservations recommended) is well known for its meals of fresh fish and seafood. ⑦

Number Five 5 Havelock Place Ⓣ01947/606361. Amiable West Cliff B&B that provides a good breakfast (veggie options available). No credit cards. ②

Shepherd's Purse 95 Church St Ⓣ01947/820228. Popular wholefood store combined with clothes and gift shop, with its best rooms (with brass bedsteads and pine furniture) set around a galleried courtyard. ③

Union Place 9 Upgang Lane Ⓣ01947/605501. The Pottas' elegant Georgian house – featured in *Ideal Home* magazine no less – offers genial B&B in two spacious double rooms, sharing a luxurious bathroom. No credit cards. ②

Whitby YHA Abbey House, East Cliff Ⓣ0870/770 6088, Ⓔwhitby@yha.org.uk. Spanking new flagship hostel, located right next to the Abbey Visitor Centre, with stunning views, Victorian conservatory, tearoom and restaurant. Rates include breakfast and entry to the Abbey. Dorm beds from £16.50, though more expensive in summer, double rooms ③

White Horse & Griffin 87 Church St Ⓣ01947/604857, Ⓦwww.whitehorseandgriffin.co.uk. A welcoming eighteenth-century coaching inn with stylishly decorated en-suite rooms (some have antique panelling, others a rooftop view), open fires and a good bistro restaurant serving local fish, meat and game. ④

White Linen 24 Bagdale Ⓣ01947/603635, Ⓦwww.whitelinenguesthouse.co.uk. Superior B&B in a restored Georgian house – ten individually styled rooms with contemporary colours and furnishings and good shower rooms. Garden at the front, courtyard out back. ⑤

Eating and drinking

Duke of York Church St. Classic Whitby pub, at the bottom of the 199 steps, with harbour views and a mixed clientele of tourists and locals who come for the good-value food and occasional music.

Magpie Café 14 Pier Rd Ⓣ01947/602058. The traditional fish-and-chip choice in town for over forty years, and with a wide-ranging menu if you don't want something battered and fried. In summer you'll have to queue to eat in or even for the takeaways. Closes 9pm. Moderate.

Moon and Sixpence 5 Marine Parade Ⓣ01947/821071. Fish is outstanding here, but this contemporary spot on the quayside dishes up lots more besides, such as local game and champagne cocktails. There's also a luxury room above the restaurant, with Jacuzzi and double shower (with television) from £120. Expensive.

Red Chard 22 Flowergate Ⓣ01947/606660. Relaxed place for coffee or glass of wine, or dig into dishes ranging from prawn cocktail and bubble-and-squeak to saffron pappardelle and the like. Closed Mon, and Sat lunch. Expensive.

Staithes

Beyond the beach at Sandsend, a fine coastal walk through pretty Runswick Bay leads in around four hours to the fishing village of **STAITHES**. At first sight, it's an improbably beautiful grouping of huddled stone houses around a small harbour, backed by the severe outcrop of Cowbar Nab, a sheer cliff face which protects the northern flank of the village. James Cook first worked here in a draper's shop before moving to Whitby and he's remembered in the **Captain Cook and Staithes Heritage Centre**, on the High Street (daily 10am–5pm, weekends only Jan & Feb; £2.75), which recreates an eighteenth-century street among other interesting exhibits. Other than this, you'll have to content yourself with pottering about the rocks near the harbour – there's no beach to speak of – or clambering the nearby cliffs for spectacular views; at **Boulby**, a mile and a half's trudge up the coastal path (45min), you're walking on the highest cliff (670ft) on England's east coast.

You could stay at one of the B&Bs in the houses at the top of the village, but better **accommodation** is available down below, specifically at the *Endeavour Restaurant* (ⓣ01947/840825, ⓦwww.endeavour-restaurant.co.uk; ⑤). This is the best place to eat for miles around, with superb (but pricey) fresh fish meals (dinner only; closed Sun & Mon, except bank holidays).

Travel details

Buses

It's essential to pick up either the *Dales Explorer* or *Moors Explorer* timetable booklets from a local tourist office if visiting those parts of the county. For details of the Moorsbus in the North York Moors National Park see p.576. For information on all other local and national bus services, contact Traveline ⓣ0871/200 2233 (daily 7am–9pm), ⓦwww.yorkshiretravel.net.

Harrogate to: Leeds (every 30–60min; 40min); Ripon (every 30min; 30min).

Helmsley to: Pickering (hourly; 40min); Scarborough (hourly; 1hr 30min); York (Mon–Sat 3–5 daily; 1hr 30min).

Pickering to: Helmsley (hourly; 40min); Scarborough (hourly; 1hr); Whitby (4–6 daily; 55min); York (hourly; 1hr 15min).

Richmond to: Masham (Mon–Sat hourly; 55min); Ripon (Mon–Sat hourly; 1hr 15min).

Scarborough to: Bridlington (hourly; 1hr 15min); Filey (hourly; 30min); Helmsley (hourly; 1hr 30min); Hull (hourly; 2 hr 50min); Leeds (hourly; 2hr 40min); Pickering (hourly; 1hr); Robin Hood's Bay (hourly; 45min); Whitby (hourly; 1hr); York (hourly; 1hr 35min).

Skipton to: Grassington (Mon–Sat hourly; 30min); Malham (4 daily; 40min); Settle (Mon–Sat hourly; 40min).

Whitby to: Robin Hood's Bay (hourly; 25min); Staithes (hourly; 30min); York (4–6 daily; 2hr).

York to: Beverley (Mon–Sat hourly; Sun 7 daily; 30min); Hull (Mon–Sat hourly; Sun 7 daily; 1hr 45min); Pickering (hourly; 1hr 15min); Scarborough (hourly; 1hr 35min); Whitby (4–6 daily; 2hr).

Trains

Main routes and services are given below, and check timetables on ⓦwww.rail.co.uk. For more detailed information about specific lines, see Settle to Carlisle Railway p.557; North Yorkshire Moors Railway p.580; Keighley and Worth Valley Railway p.553.

Harrogate to: Leeds (every 30–60min; 35min); York (hourly; 30min).

Hull to: Beverley (Mon–Sat hourly, Sun 6 daily; 15min); Leeds (hourly; 1hr); London (6 daily; 2hr 45min); Scarborough (every 2hr; 1hr 30min); York (9 daily; 1hr).

Leeds to: Bradford (every 15min; 20min); Carlisle (3–7 daily; 2hr 40min); Harrogate (every 30–60min; 35min); Hull (hourly; 1hr); Lancaster (4 daily; 2hr); Liverpool (hourly; 1hr 50min); London (every 30min; 2hr 20min); Manchester (every 30min; 1hr); Scarborough (every 30–60min; 1hr 20min); Settle (3–8 daily; 1hr); Sheffield (every 30min; 40min–1hr 25min); Skipton (hourly; 40min); York (every 30min; 30min).

Pickering to: Grosmont (April–Oct 5–8 daily, plus limited winter service; 1hr 5min).

Scarborough to: Hull (every 2hr; 1hr 30min); Leeds (hourly; 1hr 20min); York (hourly; 50min).

Sheffield to: Leeds (every 30min; 40min–1hr 25min); London (hourly; 2hr 20min); York (every 30–60min; 1hr).

Whitby to: Danby (4–5 daily; 35min); Great Ayton (4–5 daily; 1hr 5min); Grosmont (4–5 daily; 15min); Middlesbrough (4–5 daily; 1hr 30min).

York to: Bradford (hourly; 1hr); Durham (every 30min; 50min); Harrogate (hourly; 30min); Hull (9 daily; 1hr); Leeds (every 30min; 30min); London (every 30min; 2hr 15min); Manchester (hourly; 1hr 5min 50min); Newcastle (every 30min; 1hr); Scarborough (hourly; 50min); Sheffield (every 30–60min; 1hr).

13

The Northeast

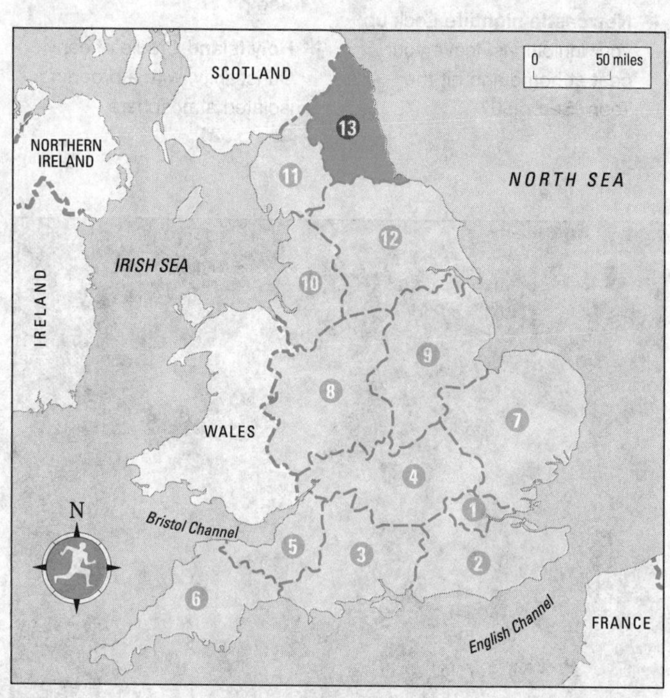

CHAPTER 13 Highlights

* **Durham Cathedral** Awe-inspiring Romanesque church towering above the River Wear. See p.594

* **Killhope Lead-Mining Museum** An excellent family day out – put the kids to work down t'pit. See p.599

* **Newcastle nightlife** Lock up your inhibitions, leave your coat at home and hit the Toon. See p.607

* **Hadrian's Wall Path** Put your walking boots on to make the most of this extraordinary monument. See p.611

* **Chillingham Wild Cattle** Don't get too close – this herd of cows has been seeing off intruders for over 800 years. See p.617

* **Holy Island** Cradle of early Christianity, with a brooding, isolated atmosphere. See p.621

▲ Chillingham Wild Cattle

13

The Northeast

England's **northeast** (principally the counties of Durham and Northumberland) is, in many ways, a land apart from the rest of England – more remote, less affluent, its accents often impenetrable to outsiders. Yet it also has the very stuff of English history etched across its landscapes. Romans, Vikings and Normans all left dramatic evidence of their colonization, while the Industrial Revolution exploited to the limit the northeast's natural resources and its people. The essential sights start with **Hadrian's Wall**, built by the **Romans** to contain the troublesome tribes of the far north. The kings of Northumbria, who dominated the region from 600 until the 870s, nourished the region's early Christian tradition, which achieved its finest flowering with the creation of the **Lindisfarne Gospels** on what is now known as **Holy Island**. The monks abandoned their island in advance of the Vikings' destruction of the Northumbrian kingdom, and only after the Norman Conquest did the northeast again become part of a greater England. The **Norman** kings and their successors repeatedly attempted to subdue Scotland, passing effective regional control to powerful local lords, whose authority is recalled by a sequence of formidable **fortresses** dotted along the coast. Later, the appearance of the northeast was transformed yet again, by the **Industrial Revolution**, as coalfields were established and the **world's first railway** opened, the Darlington and Stockton line (1825), with local coal and ore fuelling the foundries that supplied the shipbuilding and heavy-engineering companies of Tyneside.

Most tourists dodge the industrial areas on the way to **Durham**, a handsome university city dominated by its magnificent twelfth-century cathedral. From Durham it's a short hop to **Newcastle upon Tyne**, distinguished by some fine Victorian buildings, the revitalized Quayside, and a vibrant cultural scene and nightlife. North, past the old colliery villages, the **Northumberland coast** boasts some superb castles as well as a string of superb dune-backed beaches, and a handful of offshore islands. **Holy Island** is the best known, though the **Farne Islands** nature reserve also makes a great day-trip from the small resort of Seahouses. **Alnwick**, four miles inland from the sea, features another stunning castle and northern England's finest new garden, while the extravagant ramparts of **Berwick-upon-Tweed** signal the imminence of the Scottish border. **Hadrian's Wall** is best visited from the appealing abbey-town of **Hexham**, while beyond lie the moorland, plantations and hiking trails of the **Northumberland National Park**.

Useful **train passes** include the Northeast Regional Rover (7 days; £78.50). The **Northeast Explorer Pass** (1 day; £7; Ⓦwww.explorernortheast.co.uk), valid after 9am on weekdays and all day at weekends, gives unlimited travel on

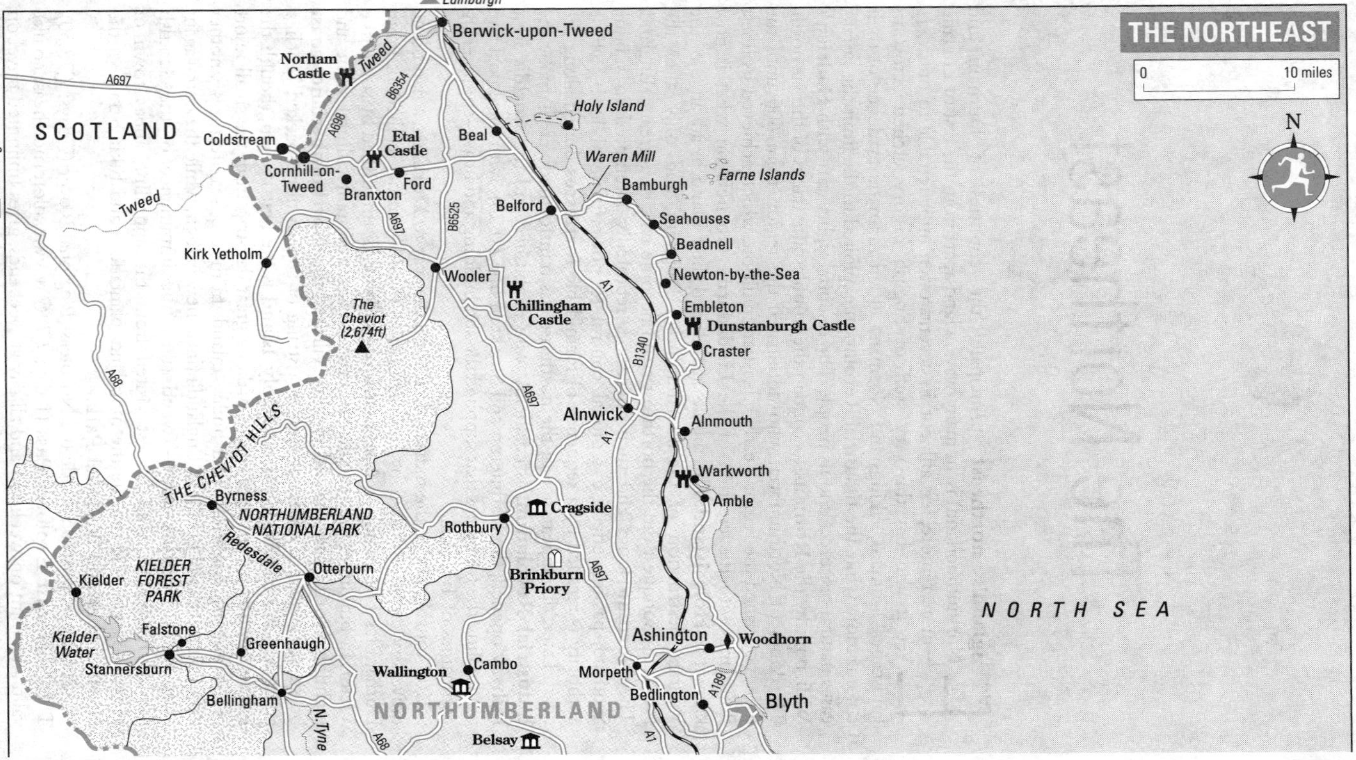

THE NORTHEAST
0
10 miles
N
Edinburgh
Berwick-upon-Tweed
Norham Castle
Tweed
A697
B6354
A698
Holy Island
SCOTLAND
Coldstream
Etal Castle
Beal
Waren Mill
Cornhill-on-Tweed
Ford
Branxton
Farne Islands
Bamburgh
Tweed
Belford
Seahouses
B6525
A697
Beadnell
Kirk Yetholm
Wooler
Newton-by-the-Sea
Chillingham Castle
A1
The Cheviot (2,674ft)
Embleton
Dunstanburgh Castle
Craster
B1340
A68
A697
Alnwick
Alnmouth
THE CHEVIOT HILLS
A1
Warkworth
Byrness
Amble
NORTHUMBERLAND NATIONAL PARK
Cragside
Rothbury
Redesdale
Kielder
KIELDER FOREST PARK
Otterburn
Brinkburn Priory
A697
NORTH SEA
Kielder Water
Falstone
Ashington
Woodhorn
Greenhaugh
Stannersburn
Cambo
Morpeth
Wallington
A189
Bedlington
Blyth
Bellingham
NORTHUMBERLAND
N.Tyne
A68
Belsay
A1

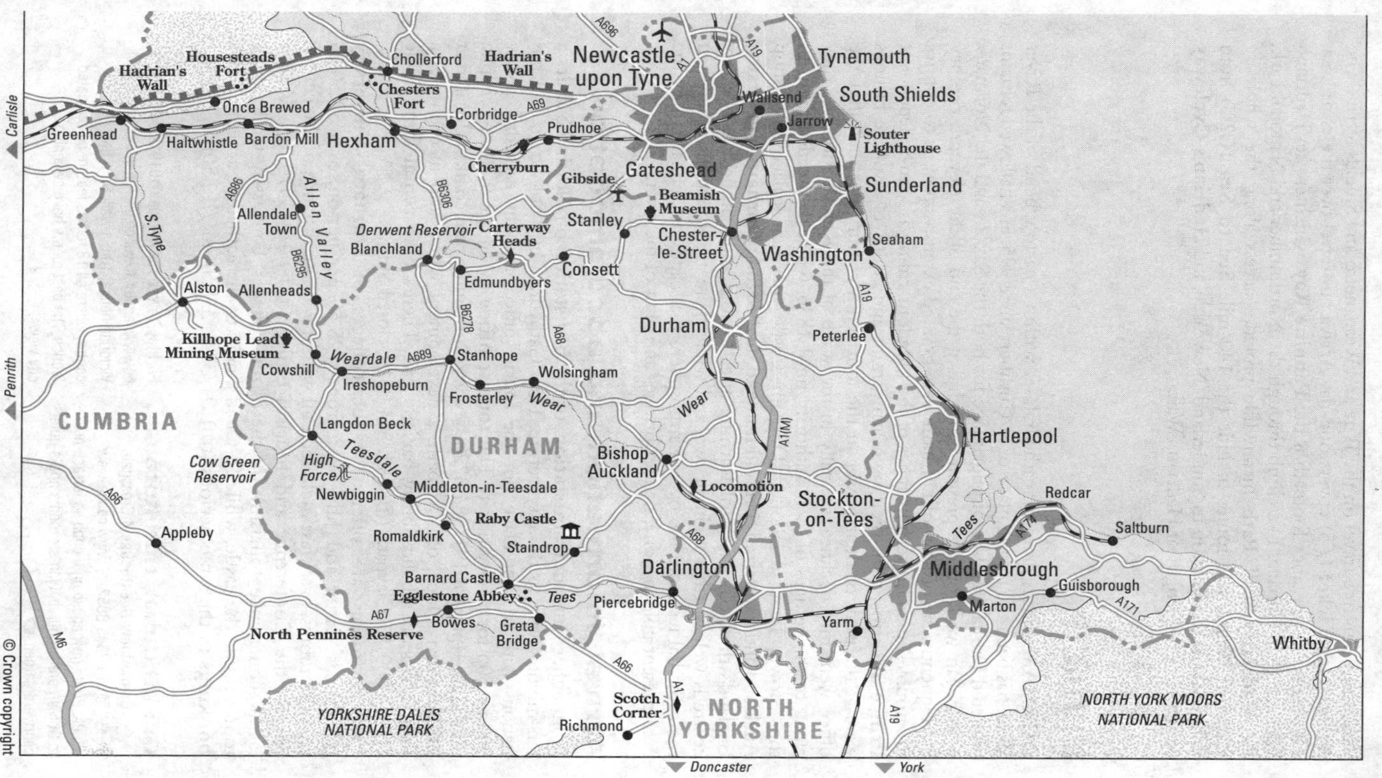

Newcastle upon Tyne
Tynemouth
South Shields
Wallsend
Jarrow
Souter Lighthouse
Gateshead
Sunderland
Gibside
Beamish Museum
Stanley
Chester-le-Street
Washington
Seaham
Hadrian's Wall
Housesteads Fort
Hadrian's Wall
Chollerford
Chesters Fort
Once Brewed
Corbridge
A69
Prudhoe
Greenhead
Haltwhistle
Bardon Mill
Hexham
Cherryburn
A696
A1
A19
A686
B6306
Allendale Town
Allen Valley
S.Tyne
Derwent Reservoir
Carterway Heads
Blanchland
Consett
Edmundbyers
B6295
Alston
Allenheads
Durham
A19
Peterlee
B6278
A68
Killhope Lead Mining Museum
Weardale
A689
Stanhope
Cowshill
Wolsingham
Ireshopeburn
Frosterley
Wear
Wear
CUMBRIA
Langdon Beck
DURHAM
Hartlepool
A1(M)
Bishop Auckland
Cow Green Reservoir
High Force
Teesdale
Locomotion
Newbiggin
Middleton-in-Teesdale
Stockton-on-Tees
Redcar
A66
Raby Castle
Tees
A174
Saltburn
Appleby
Romaldkirk
A68
Staindrop
Darlington
Middlesbrough
Barnard Castle
Guisborough
Egglestone Abbey
Tees
Piercebridge
Marton
A171
A67
Bowes
Yarm
North Pennines Reserve
Greta Bridge
Whitby
M6
A66
A1
Scotch Corner
NORTH YORKSHIRE
A19
YORKSHIRE DALES NATIONAL PARK
Richmond
NORTH YORK MOORS NATIONAL PARK
Carlisle
Penrith
Doncaster
York

local buses, plus free travel on the Tyne and Wear metro and Shields ferries. The **Arriva Day Ticket** (£5) covers one-day Arriva bus travel over the same area. The main long-distance footpath is the **Pennine Way**, which crosses Hadrian's Wall and then climaxes in a climb through the Northumberland National Park; the **Hadrian's Wall Path** meanwhile provides access along the whole of Hadrian's Wall. Cycle routes include the 140-mile **Sea to Sea (C2C)** from Whitehaven/Workington to Sunderland/Newcastle, and **Hadrian's Cycleway** which runs the length of Hadrian's Wall.

Durham

DURHAM and its dramatic cathedral, set within a narrow bend of the River Wear, has been the resting place of St Cuthbert since 995. His hallowed remains rendered Durham a place of pilgrimage for both the Saxons and the Normans, who began work on the present cathedral at the end of the eleventh century. Subsequently, the bishops of Durham were granted extensive powers to control the troublesome northern marches of the kingdom, ruling as semi-independent **Prince Bishops**, with their own army, mint and courts of law. The bishops were at the peak of their power in the fourteenth century, but thereafter the office went into decline, especially in the wake of the Reformation, yet they clung to the vestiges of their authority until 1836, when they ceded them to the Crown. They abandoned Durham Castle for their palace in Bishop Auckland and transferred their old home to the fledgling **Durham University**, England's third-oldest seat of learning after Oxford and Cambridge. The city centre is well worth a night or two, and while there are attractions other than the cathedral it's more the overall atmosphere that captivates, enhanced by the ever-present golden stone, slender bridges and glint of the river.

Arrival, information and accommodation

From either Durham **train station**, or the **bus station** on North Road, it's a ten-minute walk to the city centre. The "Cathedral" **bus** links train and bus stations with Market Place (for the tourist office) and the cathedral (every 20min; 50p for all-day ticket). The **tourist office** (Mon–Sat 9.30am–5.30pm, Sun 11am–4pm; ⓣ0191/384 3720, ⓦwww.durhamtourism.co.uk) is located at **Millennium Place**, off Claypath, a development which also incorporates a theatre, cinema, public library, bar and café. There's **bike rental** from Cycle Force 2000, 87 Claypath (ⓣ0191/384 0319; closed Sun).

Private rooms are offered at the colleges of **Durham University** (Christmas, Easter and July–Sept; from £28.50 per person, or £39.50 in en-suite rooms, breakfast included), all within walking distance of the centre; contact the Conference and Tourism Office (ⓣ0800/289970, ⓦwww.dur.ac.uk/conference_tourism). Of the dozen colleges, University College has rooms inside the castle, while St Chad's, next to the cathedral, accepts **YHA bookings** in the same periods (ⓣ0191/334 3358; from £19.50).

Guesthouses and hotels

Castle View Guesthouse 4 Crossgate ⓣ0191/386 8852, ⓦwww.castle-view.co.uk. Pretty townhouse on a cobbled terrace next to St Margaret's Church, with six rooms and a quiet courtyard garden. ⑤

Farnley Tower The Avenue ⓣ0191/384 2796, ⓦwww.farnley-tower.co.uk. A fine stone Victorian house, 10min walk from the centre, where all 13 rooms feature co-ordinated fabrics. The best rooms have sweeping city views. ⑤

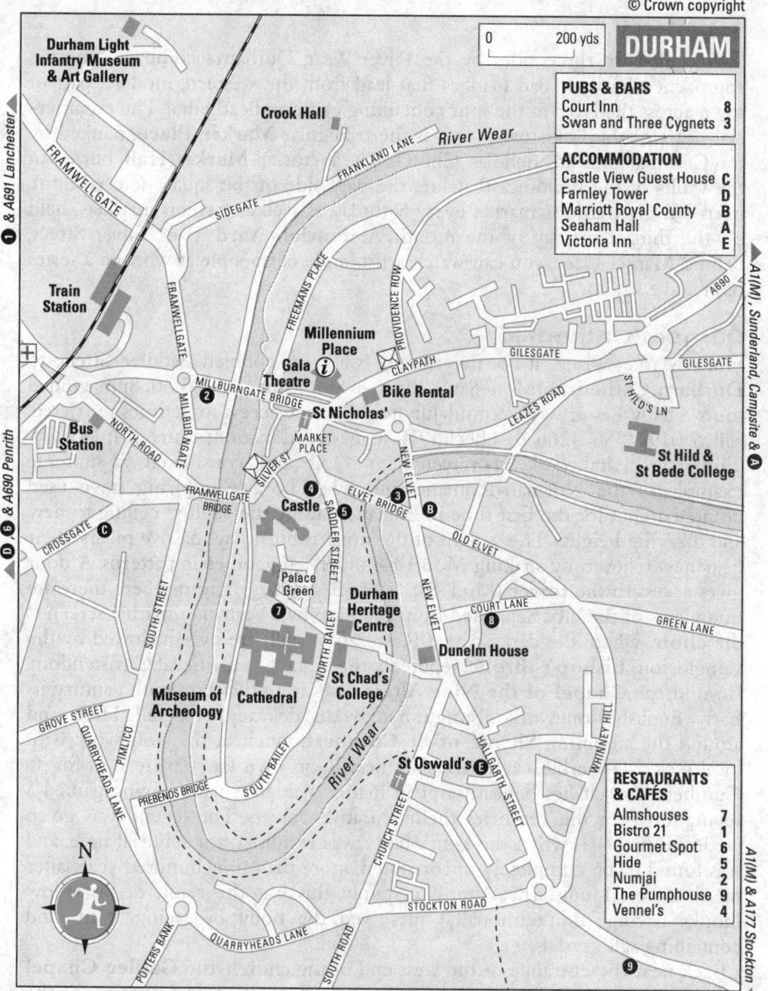

Marriott Royal County Old Elvet ⓣ0191/386 6821, ⓦwww.marriotthotels.com. Durham's top hotel has its own riverside leisure centre with pool, while the rooms have plump beds and marble-trimmed bathrooms. 7

Seaham Hall Lord Byron's Walk, Seaham, 10 miles northeast of Durham ⓣ0191/516 1400, ⓦwww.seaham-hall.com. Hip hotel that makes a great coastal base for city sightseeing – Durham is only a 20min drive away. Breakfast in bed is standard, there are amazing spa facilities, a well-regarded restaurant, and beaches and coastal walks nearby. 9

Victoria Inn 86 Hallgarth St ⓣ0191/386 5269, ⓦwww.victoriainn-durhamcity.co.uk. Six light and pretty rooms with iron bedsteads, above a family-run pub (one of the best in town), just a few minutes from the centre. 4

The City

Surrounded on three sides by the River Wear, Durham's compact centre is approached by two road bridges that lead from the western, modern part of town across the river to the spur containing castle and cathedral. The commercial heart of this "old town" area is the triangular **Market Place**, flanked by the Guildhall and St Nicholas' Church. The Victorian **Market Hall**, buried in the vaults of the buildings that line the west side of the square (closed Sun), hosts a lively outdoor market every Saturday, as well as farmers' markets, held on the third Thursday of the month. At **Fowlers Yard**, Back Silver Street, behind Market Place, you can watch artists and craftspeople at work in a series of creative studios.

Durham Cathedral

From Market Place, it's a five-minute walk up cobbled Saddler Street to **Durham Cathedral** (Mon–Sat 9.30am–6/8pm, Sun 12.30–5.30/8pm; guided tours 3 daily Easter week & mid-July to mid-Sept; access sometimes restricted, call ⓣ0191/386 4266 to check; £4 suggested donation; tours £4; ⓦwww.durhamcathedral.co.uk), completed in 1133 and considered a supreme example of the Norman-Romanesque style. The awe-inspiring **nave** used pointed arches for the first time in England, raising the vaulted ceiling to new and dizzying heights. The weight of the stone is borne by massive pillars, their heaviness relieved by striking Moorish-influenced geometric patterns. A door gives access to the **tower** (Mon–Sat 10am–3/4pm; £3), from where there are fine views of the city. Separated from the nave by a Victorian marble screen is the **choir**, where the dark-stained Restoration stalls are overshadowed by the vainglorious **bishop's throne**, reputedly the highest in medieval Christendom. Beyond, the **Chapel of the Nine Altars** dates from the thirteenth century, its Early English stonework distinguished by its delicacy of detail. Here, and around the adjoining **Shrine of St Cuthbert**, much of the stonework is of local Weardale marble, each dark shaft bearing its own fancy pattern of fossils. Cuthbert himself lies beneath a plain marble slab, his shrine having gained a reputation over the centuries for its curative powers. The legend was given credence in 1104, when the saint's body was exhumed for reburial here, and was found to be completely uncorrupted, more than four hundred years after his death on Lindisfarne. Almost certainly, this was the result of his fellow monks having (unintentionally) preserved the body by laying it in sand containing salt crystals.

Back near the entrance, at the west end of the church, the **Galilee Chapel** was begun in the 1170s, its light and exotic decoration in imitation of the Great Mosque of Córdoba. The chapel contains the simple tombstone of the **Venerable Bede**, the Northumbrian monk credited with being England's first historian. Bede died at the monastery of Jarrow in 735, and his remains were first transferred to the cathedral in 1020. An ancient wooden doorway opposite the main entrance leads into the spacious **cloisters**, which are flanked by what remains of the monastic buildings. These include an oak-beamed **monks' dormitory** (Mon–Sat 10am–4pm, Sun 2–4.30pm; £1) containing fine Anglo-Saxon carved stones, and the **Treasures of St Cuthbert** exhibition in the undercroft (Mon–Sat 10am–4.30pm, Sun 2–4.30pm; £2.50), where you can see some striking relics of St Cuthbert. The cathedral's original twelfth-century lion-head Sanctuary Knocker is displayed here (the one on the main door is a replica), and there's also a splendid facsimile copy of the Lindisfarne Gospels (the originals are in the British Library in London).

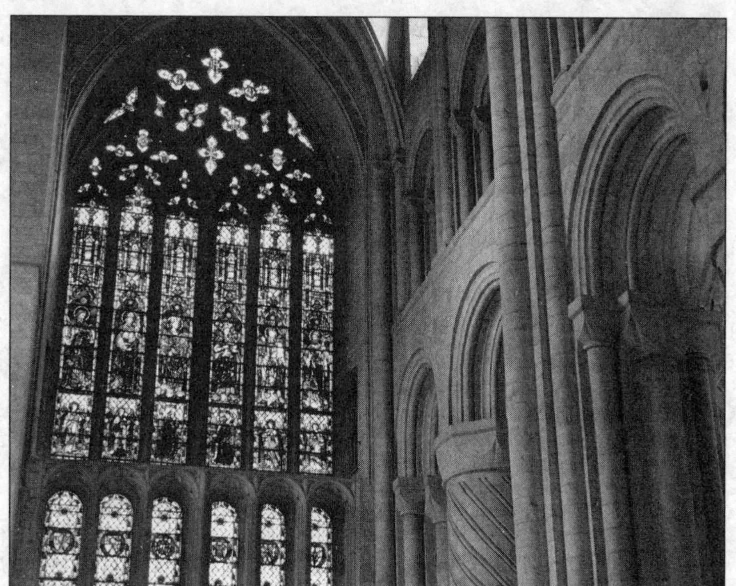

▲ Durham Cathedral

The rest of the city

Across Palace Green from the cathedral, **Durham Castle** (Easter & July–Sept daily 10am–12.30pm & 2–4.30pm; rest of the year Mon, Wed, Sat & Sun 2–4pm; £5; ⓣ0191/334 3800, ⓦwww.durhamcastle.com) lost its medieval appearance long ago, and the university subsequently renovated the old keep as a hall of residence. It's only possible to visit the castle on a 45-minute guided tour, highlights of which include visits to the fifteenth-century kitchen, a climb up the enormous hanging staircase and the jog down to the Norman chapel, notable for its lively Romanesque carved capitals.

Below castle and cathedral are the wooded banks of the **River Wear**, where a pleasant footpath runs right round the peninsula (30min). **Framwellgate Bridge** originally dates from the twelfth century, though it was widened to its present proportions in the mid-nineteenth century. Just along from here on the riverbank the university's **Museum of Archeology** (April–Oct daily 11am–4pm; Nov–March Mon & Fri–Sun 11.30am–3.30pm; £1; ⓦwww.dur.ac.uk/fulling.mill) occupies an old stone fulling mill. Eighteenth-century **Prebends Bridge** boasts celebrated views of the cathedral, and the path then continues round to the handsome **Elvet Bridge**, still retaining traces of both its erstwhile bridge-houses and the chapel, St Andrew's, which once stood at its eastern end.

Heading north of the centre, at **Crook Hall** (Easter weekend & late May to mid-Sept Wed–Sun 11am–5pm; £4.50; ⓦwww.crookhallgardens.co.uk) at Frankland Lane, Sidegate, just above the river, a series of rambling, small enclosed gardens radiate from the medieval hall, a perfect spot for afternoon tea. From here it's a ten-minute walk to the **Durham Light Infantry Museum and Art Gallery**, at Aykley Heads (daily 10am–4/5pm; £3.25; ⓦwww.durham.gov.uk/dli), whose temporary art exhibitions are bolstered by fascinating galleries telling the story of the DLI regiment, from World War I (when it lost 12,000 soldiers) to its last parade in 1968.

Eating, drinking and entertainment

As a student and tourist haven you don't have to look far for inexpensive pizza, pasta or bar meals, and there are plenty of good restaurants to suit all budgets. Check out the Walkergate Complex next to the Gala Theatre, where new bars and restaurants vie with each other for a piece of the action. Regular **classical concerts** are held at venues around the city, including the cathedral, while the **Gala Theatre** on Millennium Place (ⓣ0191/332 4041, ⓦwww.galadurham.co.uk) hosts music of all kinds, plus theatre, cinema, dance and comedy.

Cafés and restaurants

Almshouses Palace Green. Bistro meals for around £5–6, served in a historic building in the shadow of the cathedral. July and Aug open until 8pm. Inexpensive.

Bistro 21 Aykley Heads ⓣ0191/384 4354. Excellent Modern British cuisine, a 10min walk from the DLI Museum and Art Gallery; courtyard seating in summer and good-value set menus at lunchtime. Closed Sun. Expensive.

Gourmet Spot The Avenue ⓣ0191/384 6655. Fun and innovation are the watchwords here. Expect balloons and liquid nitrogen, salmon with cauliflower foam, venison with chocolate paint and sensational puddings. Closed Sun. Expensive.

Hide 39 Saddler St ⓣ0191/384 1999. The best of the café-bars, *Hide* serves a pizza, salad or brunch-style menu during the day, with prices rising at night for a Modern British tour of world cuisine. Moderate.

Numjai 19 Millburngate Centre ⓣ0191/386 2020. Authentic Thai restaurant that dishes up plenty of seafood and veggie options, with a river terrace and cathedral views. Expensive.

The Pumphouse Farm Rd, Houghall ⓣ0191/386 9189. A few minutes' taxi ride southeast of the centre brings you to this Victorian pumphouse, where best use is made of locally sourced produce in imaginative and contemporary dishes. Expensive.

Vennel's Saddler's Yard, Saddler St. Named after the skinny alley or "vennel" where it stands – near the junction with Elvet Bridge – this self-service café dispenses appetizing sandwiches, salads, quiche and pastas in its sixteenth-century courtyard. Closes 5pm.

Pubs

Court Inn Court Lane. Best pub dining in town, a favourite with students and locals, with a classic pub menu and plenty of chips, plus dip-and-share tapas and some intriguing blackboard specials.

Swan & Three Cygnets Elvet Bridge. Town and gown converge in this popular riverside pub with a full-to-the-brim outdoor terrace.

The rest of County Durham

For a taste of the old days, most people visit the open-air **Beamish Museum**, north of Durham, while for the region's considerable railway heritage you shouldn't miss **Locomotion**, south of Durham, near Bishop Auckland – a fascinating outpost of the National Railway Museum. Away from the old coalfields and railway works the rest of County Durham's attractions form a neat triangle. The two main towns are the ecclesiastical residence of **Bishop Auckland** and the well-to-do market town of **Barnard Castle**, beyond which – to the west – lie the isolated Pennine valleys of **Teesdale** and **Weardale**.

Beamish Museum

The open-air **Beamish Museum** (April–Oct daily 10am–5pm; Nov–April Tues–Thurs, Sat & Sun 10am–4pm; last admission 3pm; admission £16, £6 in winter; ⓣ0191/370 4000, ⓦwww.beamish.org.uk) spreads out over 300 acres, about ten miles north of Durham. It's as popular with tourists as it is with local people, who come to chew the fat with the costumed guides, many of whom are recruited for their real-life experience – the collier who takes you down the drift mine may once have been a miner.

Buildings from all over the region have been painstakingly reassembled in six main sections, linked by restored trams and buses. Costumed shopkeepers, workers and householders can answer your questions, and you can walk through many of the buildings and workshops to find out about daily life a century or two ago. Four of the sections show life in 1913, before the upheavals of World War I, including a **colliery village** complete with drift mine (regular tours throughout the day) and a large-scale recreation of the High Street in a market **town**. Two areas date to 1825, at the beginning of the northeast's industrial development: a **manor house**, with horse yard, formal gardens, vegetable plots and orchards; and the **Pockerley Waggonway**, where you can ride behind a replica of George Stephenson's *Locomotion*, the first passenger-carrying steam train in the world. Reckon on at least four hours to get round the lot in summer, two in winter when only certain sections are open.

To **get there**, drivers should follow signs to the museum off the A1(M) Chester-le-Street exit, then follow the signs along the A693 to Stanley. Direct **buses** from Newcastle drop you close to the main entrance, though from Durham you'll need to change at Chester-le-Street – get up-to-date details from Traveline (ⓣ0871/200 2233).

Bishop Auckland

Eleven miles southwest of Durham city, **BISHOP AUCKLAND** has been the country home of the bishops of Durham since the twelfth century and their official residence for more than a hundred years. Their palace, **Auckland Castle** (Easter–June & Sept Sun & Mon 2–5pm; July & Aug Sun 2–5pm, Mon & Wed 11am–5pm; £4; ⓦwww.auckland-castle.co.uk), standing in eight-hundred-acre grounds, is approached through an imposing gatehouse just off the town's large Market Place. Most rooms are rather sparsely furnished, save the splendid seventeenth-century marble and limestone chapel and the long dining room, with its thirteen paintings of Jacob and his sons by Francisco de Zurbarán, commissioned in the 1640s for a monastery in South America. After you've seen the castle, stroll into the adjacent **Bishop's Deer Park** (daily dawn–dusk; free), where an eighteenth-century deer house survives.

The town itself plays second fiddle to the castle, though don't leave until you've followed the mile-long lane from behind the Town Hall (signposted by the *Sportsman Inn*) to the remains of **Binchester Roman Fort** (daily: April–Sept 10/11am–5pm; £2.25). Only a small portion of Roman Vinovia has been excavated, but this includes the country's best example of a **hypocaust**, built to warm the private bath suite of the garrison's commanding officer.

Locomotion

The first passenger train (as opposed to freight) in the world left from the station at Shildon in 1825 – making the small County Durham town, around five miles southeast of Bishop Auckland, the world's oldest railway town. It's a heritage explored in the magnificently realized **Locomotion**, otherwise known as the **National Railway Museum at Shildon** (April–Oct daily 10am–5pm; Nov–March Wed–Sun 10am–4pm; free; ⓣ01388/777999, ⓦwww.locomotion.uk.com); follow the signs off the B6282 (from Bishop Auckland) or the A6072 (from the A68/A1(M)). This regional outpost of York's National Railway Museum traces 200 years of railway history, but it's less a museum and more an experience, spread out around a kilometre-long site, with the attractions linked by free bus from the reception building (where there's parking). Depots, sidings, junctions and coal drops lead ultimately to the heart of the museum, **Collection** – a gargantuan steel hangar containing an extraordinary array of sixty locomotives, dating from the very earliest days of steam. With interactive children's exhibits, summer steam rides, rallies and shows, it makes an excellent family day out.

Barnard Castle and around

Fifteen miles southwest of Bishop Auckland, the attractive market town of **BARNARD CASTLE** is overlooked by the skeletal remains of its **castle** (April–Oct daily 10am–4/6pm; Nov–March Mon & Thurs–Sun 10am–4pm; £4; EH), poking out from a cliff high above the River Tees. Castle aside, the prime attraction in town is the grand French-style chateau that constitutes the **Bowes Museum** (daily 11am–5pm; £6.35; Ⓦwww.bowesmuseum.org.uk), half a mile east of the centre. Begun in 1869, the chateau was commissioned by John and Josephine Bowes, a local businessman and MP and his French actress wife, who spent much of their time in Paris collecting the ostentatious treasures and antiques.

It's a fine mile-and-a-half walk from the castle, southeast (downriver) through the fields above the banks of the Tees, to the glorious shattered ruins of **Egglestone Abbey** (dawn–dusk; free; EH), a minor foundation dating from 1195. Otherwise, seven miles northeast of town, up the A688, beckon the splendid, sprawling battlements of **Raby Castle** (Easter week, May & Sept Wed & Sun 1–5pm; June–Aug Mon–Fri & Sun 1–5pm; gardens same days 11am–5.30pm; £9, park & gardens only £4; Ⓦwww.rabycastle.com), reflecting the power of the Neville family, who ruled the local roost until 1569. The Neville estates were confiscated after the "Rising of the North", the abortive attempt to replace Elizabeth I with Mary Queen of Scots, with Raby subsequently passing to the Vane family in 1626.

Buses to Barnard Castle stop on either side of central Galgate, with the **tourist office** on Flatts Road, at the end of Galgate by the castle (daily 10/11am–4/6pm; Nov–March closed Sun; Ⓣ01833/690909). Among several convenient **B&Bs** along the upper reaches of Galgate, the welcoming *Homelands*, 85 Galgate (Ⓣ01833/638757, Ⓦwww.homelandsguesthouse.co.uk; ③), is the choice pick, offering pretty bedrooms and good breakfasts. The *Old Well Inn*, 21 The Bank, has a beer garden backing on to the castle walls, while Barney's top **restaurant** is *Blagraves House*, 30–32 The Bank (Ⓣ01833/637668; closed Sun & Mon; meals from around £20), sporting low-beamed ceilings and large open fires.

Teesdale

Extending twenty-odd miles northwest from Barnard Castle, **Teesdale** begins calmly enough, though the pastoral landscapes of its lower reaches are soon replaced by wilder Pennine scenery. There's a regular **bus service** as far as Middleton-in-Teesdale, the valley's main settlement, with infrequent (Mon–Sat) services on to the spectacular High Force waterfall.

MIDDLETON-IN-TEESDALE was once the archetypal "company town", owned lock, stock and barrel by the Quaker-run London Lead Company, which began mining here in 1753. The **tourist office** is in the Market Place (restricted hours, though usually daily 10am–1pm; Ⓣ01833/641001) and can help with local accommodation, though the best place to stay hereabouts is three miles back down the road towards Barnard Castle, in the charming village of **Romaldkirk**, where the *Rose & Crown* (Ⓣ01833/650213, Ⓦwww.rose-and-crown.co.uk; ⑦), an ivy-clad eighteenth-century inn, has lovely rooms in dusky colours and highly accomplished Modern British cooking in the bar (moderate) or restaurant (expensive).

Past Middleton, the countryside becomes harsher and the Tees more vigorous as the B6277 travels the three miles on to **Bowlees Visitor Centre** (April–Sept daily 11.30am–4pm; ⓣ01833/622292), the halt for the short walk to the rapids of **Low Force**. A mile further up the road is the altogether more compelling **High Force**, a seventy-foot cascade that rumbles over an outcrop of the Whin Sill ridge. The waterfall is on private Raby land, and visitors must pay £1 to view the falls and £1.50 to use the nearby car park, by the B6277.

Weardale

Weardale is an easy day out in a car from Durham, while bus #101 runs roughly hourly between Bishop Auckland and **STANHOPE**, the main settlement, halfway up the valley. It's an elongated village that makes a useful stop for hikes on the local moors, including the enjoyable five-mile circuit from the town centre, up through the woods of **Stanhope Dene**, after which in summer you can cool off with a splash in its open-air heated swimming pool. The **Durham Dales Centre** – on the main road through Stanhope – houses the **tourist office** (daily 10/11am–4/5pm; ⓣ01388/527650, ⓦwww.durhamdalescentre.co.uk) and a café, while ten miles to the north, over the trans-moorland B6278, it's worth the drive to stay at the the *Lord Crewe Arms Hotel* (ⓣ01434/675251, ⓦwww.crewearms.freeserve.co.uk; ⑥) in Blanchland, an atmospheric hotel that was once a medieval abbot's lodge.

Nine miles upstream of Stanhope at Ireshopeburn, the **Weardale Museum** (Easter, May–July & Sept Wed–Sun 2–5pm, Aug daily 2–5pm; £2) tells the story of the dale, in particular its lead-mining and Methodism (the faith of most of County Durham's lead-miners). In a region dotted with Methodist chapels from the very earliest Wesleyan days, there's something of an unseemly scramble for the title of "world's oldest" – **High House Chapel** (1760), adjacent to the museum (entry included), hedges its bets with a claim to be the world's oldest Methodist chapel in continuous weekly use.

One of the bigger mines, five miles west of Ireshopeburn at the head of the valley, and a windy 1500 feet above sea level, is now the **Killhope Lead Mining Museum** (April–Oct daily 10.30am–5pm; £4.50, £6.50 including mine visit; ⓦwww.durham.gov.uk/killhope), a terrific attraction presenting the nineteenth-century buildings and machinery in a way that really brings home the hardships of a mining life. The highlight is descending Park Level Mine (1hr tour; 01388/537505 call for times) in the company of a guide who expounds entertainingly about the realities of life underground, notably the perils of the "Black Spit", a lung disease which killed many men by their mid-forties. For public transport this far up the valley, call the bus company on ⓣ01388/528235.

The Tees Valley

That the **River Tees** is so far off the contemporary tourist map as to be invisible is hardly the fault of towns whose livelihood largely disappeared once iron- and steel-making and shipbuilding became things of the past in England. But this area was one of the great engines of British economic power in the late nineteenth century. It was from **Darlington**, twenty miles south of Durham city, that George Stephenson's *Locomotion* made its inaugural run and where it is now on permanent display. The railway line ran first to Stockton-on-Tees and was then extended to ports at **Middlesbrough** and **Hartlepool**, to enable ever-increasing amounts of Durham coal to be unloaded and exported.

Darlington

DARLINGTON hit the big time in 1825, when George Stephenson's "Number 1 Engine", later called *Locomotion*, hurtled from here to nearby Stockton-on-Tees at the terrifying speed of fifteen miles per hour. Subsequently, Darlington grew into a rail-engineering centre, and didn't look back till the closure of the works in 1966. It's little surprise, then, that all signs in town point to the **Darlington Railway Centre and Museum** (closed for renovation at time of writing; due to re-open in 2008; Ⓦwww.drcm.org.uk), housed in Darlington's North Road Station, which was completed in 1842. The museum's pride and joy is the original *Locomotion*, which continued in service until 1841, while a special events programme throughout the year offers train rides and other family diversions. The origins of the rest of Darlington lie deep in Saxon times. The monks carrying St Cuthbert's body from Ripon to Durham stopped here, the saint lending his name to the graceful riverside church of **St Cuthbert**. One of England's largest market squares spreads beyond the church up to the restored Victorian covered **market** (Mon–Sat 8am–5pm).

From Darlington's **train station** walk up Victoria Road to the roundabout and turn right down Feethams for the central Market Place. You'll pass the Town Hall on Feethams, opposite which most **buses** stop. The **tourist office** on the south side of Market Place at 13 Horsemarket (Mon–Fri 9am–5pm, Sat 9am–3pm; Ⓣ01325/388666, Ⓦwww.visitdarlington.com) has free **town trail** leaflets (on its railway or Quaker heritage, for example). *Hotel Bannatyne* on Southend Avenue, off the A66 (Ⓣ01325/365858; Ⓦwww.bannatyne.co.uk; ⑤), offers spacious, elegant rooms in a Georgian townhouse, while the eighteenth-century *George Hotel* (Ⓣ01325/374576; ⑤), at **Piercebridge**, five miles west of Darlington, off the A67, has rooms and restaurant looking across the gentle banks of the River Tees. There are several **cafés** on and around Market Place, while the traditional *Hole in the Wall* pub here serves authentic Thai meals (not Sun). *Number Twenty 2*, 22 Coniscliffe Rd, is a self-professed "alehouse" with plenty of guest beers on tap, wine by the glass and pub lunches (not Sun). The enterprising **Arts Centre** (Vane Terrace) and its affiliated **Civic Theatre** (Parkgate, between the Market Place and the train station), together offer a year-round programme of theatre, film, comedy, exhibitions and live music (Ⓣ01325/486555, Ⓦwww.darlingtonarts.co.uk).

Middlesbrough

MIDDLESBROUGH, Teesside's largest town, fifteen miles east of Darlington, is entirely a product of the early industrial age, with nineteenth-century iron and steel barons throwing up factories and housing almost as fast as they could ship their products out of the docks. What was a hamlet at the turn of the nineteenth century was a thriving industrial town of 100,000 people by the turn of the twentieth. For visitors, none of this is as easily celebrated as the "heritage industry" of the coalfields further west, though in the stunning new **Middlesbrough Institute of Modern Art** (Tues–Sat & bank hols 10am–5pm, Sun noon–4pm; free; Ⓦwww.visitmima.com), in Centre Square, the town finally has a major tourist draw. Bringing together its municipal art collections for the first time, changing exhibitions concentrate on fine arts and crafts (ceramics and jewellery in particular) from the early twentieth century to the present day.

The town also considers itself the "Gateway to Captain Cook Country", fair enough given that he was born a mile and a half south of the centre in Marton in 1728. Here, the **Captain Cook Birthplace Museum** in Stewart Park (Tues–Sun 9/10am–4/5.30pm; free; Ⓦ www.captcook-ne.co.uk) entertainingly covers the life and times of Britain's greatest seaman and explorer. Buses run from the bus station every fifteen minutes or so to Marton. For more on the captain and the local area, see Ⓦ www.captaincook.org.uk, or call the town **tourist office** (Ⓣ 01642/729700, Ⓦ www.middlesbrough.gov.uk).

Hartlepool

HARTLEPOOL, ten miles north of Middlesbrough, was England's third-largest port in the nineteenth century and once a noted shipbuilding centre. After years in the doldrums, its image has been transformed by the renaissance of its once decaying dockland area, now spruced up as the family-friendly **Hartlepool's Maritime Experience** (daily 10am–5pm; £7.50; Ⓦ www.hartlepoolsmaritimeexperience.com). The entrance fee gets you on to the bustling eighteenth-century quayside where active attractions based around press gangs, the Royal Navy, seaport life and fighting ships stir the senses. On the edge of the quay in the **Museum of Hartlepool** at Jackson Dock (daily 10am–5pm; free), you can board a restored paddle-steamer and trace the town's history, including its most notorious episode, which to this day earns Hartlepudlians the nickname "monkey hangers": legend has it that when a French ship sank off the coast during the Napoleonic Wars, the locals mistook the sole survivor, a monkey, for a Frenchman, and tried and hanged it as a spy.

Newcastle upon Tyne

At first glance **NEWCASTLE UPON TYNE** – virtual capital of the area between Yorkshire and Scotland – may appear to be just another northern industrial conurbation, but the city has a longer history and a greater breadth of attractions than many of its rivals. The "new castle" appeared as long ago as 1080, while in its nineteenth-century heyday Newcastle's builders gave the city an elegance that has survived today in the impressive buildings of Grainger Town – indeed, only London and Bath have more listed classical buildings. Industrial decline hit Newcastle early, as highlighted by the Jarrow Crusade of 1936, but an extraordinary revival has seen the city shed its dowdy provincial coat and emerge as a vibrant European arts and nightlife destination. Newcastle's city centre has been transformed, particularly along the banks of the River Tyne, where the famous bridges act as a backdrop to the ever-developing cultural and entertainment scene. Both Newcastle and Gateshead sides of the river have seen dramatic change – indeed, these days visitors are encouraged to think of the city not as Newcastle upon Tyne but as "Newcastle Gateshead". On **Gateshead Quays** are the BALTIC contemporary arts centre and Norman Foster's Sage music centre, while Newcastle's **Quayside** is scene of much of the city's contemporary nightlife. Add to these the lure of some impressive museums and galleries and there's a case for taking whatever time you were going to spend in the city and doubling it.

Arrival, information and city transport

Central Station is a five-minute walk from the city centre or Quayside, and has a Metro station. National Express services arrive at the **coach station** on

The Geordie nation

Tyneside and Newcastle's native inhabitants are known as **Geordies**, the word probably derived from a diminutive of the name "George" – there are various explanations of who George was (King George II, railwayman George Stephenson), all plausible, none now verifiable. Geordies speak a largely impenetrable dialect and accent, heavily derived from Old English, and locals can derive hours of innocent amusement by asking tourists for a "tab" (cigarette), requesting directions to the nearest "nettie" (toilet) or confusing a female visitor with a non-gender-specific greeting ("haway man!"). They evince a partisan pride in their city and an endearing, if self-delusional, optimism, most obviously manifested in their fanatical support for the perennially underachieving Newcastle United football team.

St James's Boulevard, not far from Central Station, while most regional bus services use **Haymarket bus station** (Haymarket Metro). Many other city and local bus services use the station in **Eldon Square Shopping Centre**. Newcastle's **airport**, six miles north of the city, is linked by Metro to Central Station (5.50am–11.10pm, every 7–15min; 23min; £2.70) and beyond. Alternatively, take a taxi into the centre (around £15).

There are tourist offices at **Central Arcade**, Market St (Mon–Fri 9.30am–5.30pm, Sat 9am–5.30pm; ⓣ0191/277 8000, ⓦwww.visitnewcastlegateshead.com); in the **Guildhall** on Newcastle Quayside (Mon–Fri 10am–5pm, Sat 9am–5pm, Sun 9am–4pm; same phone); and on the Gateshead side in **St Mary's Church**, Oakwellgate, next to the Sage (Mon–Fri 9am–5pm, Sat 10am–5pm, Sun & bank holidays 11am–5pm; ⓣ0191/478 4222).

Quaylink buses link Newcastle and Gateshead centres (daily 7am–midnight, 80p). The region also has an efficient commuter rail system, the **Metro** (daily 5.15am–11.30pm, services every 3–15min; ⓦwww.tyneandwearmetro.co.uk), and the most useful discount pass is the **Metro Day Saver** for unlimited rides (£3.50 after 9am Mon, Tues, Thurs & Fri, all day Sat & Sun; £2.50 after 9am Wed; or £2 after 6pm any day). For all public transport enquiries, contact **Nexus Traveline** (ⓣ0871/200 2233, ⓦwww.nexus.org.uk), or visit the Nexus Travelshops at the Central Station, Haymarket, Monument or Gateshead Metro stations.

River Escapes Cruises' **sightseeing cruises** (£10/12; ⓣ0167/078 5666, ⓦwww.riverescapes.co.uk) depart most weekends throughout the year, and other days in summer, from Newcastle's Quayside. Finally, a hop-on, hop-off, open-top **sightseeing bus** departs from Central Station (Easter–Dec daily 10am–4/5pm, departures every 30–60min £7; ⓦwww.city-sightseeing.com).

Accommodation

Budget **hotel chains** offer plenty of good-value rooms in the city centre and down by the Quayside, while the biggest concentration of small hotels and **guesthouses** is a mile north of the centre in Jesmond, along and off Osborne Road: take bus #30B, #31B or #80 from Central Station or Haymarket. In addition, both the University of Newcastle (ⓣ0191/222 6318) and University of Northumbria (ⓣ0191/227 4499) have hundreds of **student rooms** available at various locations from July to September, from around £25 per person.

Hotels and guesthouses

Adelphi 63 Fern Ave, off Osborne Rd, Jesmond ⓣ0191/281 3109, ⓦwww.adelphihotelnewcastle.co.uk. Family-run B&B, on a residential street. ④

Copthorne The Close, Quayside ⓣ0191/222 0333, ⓦwww.millenniumhotels.com. This stylish four-star hotel has Tyne views from most of its well-appointed rooms. ⑧, weekend ⑦

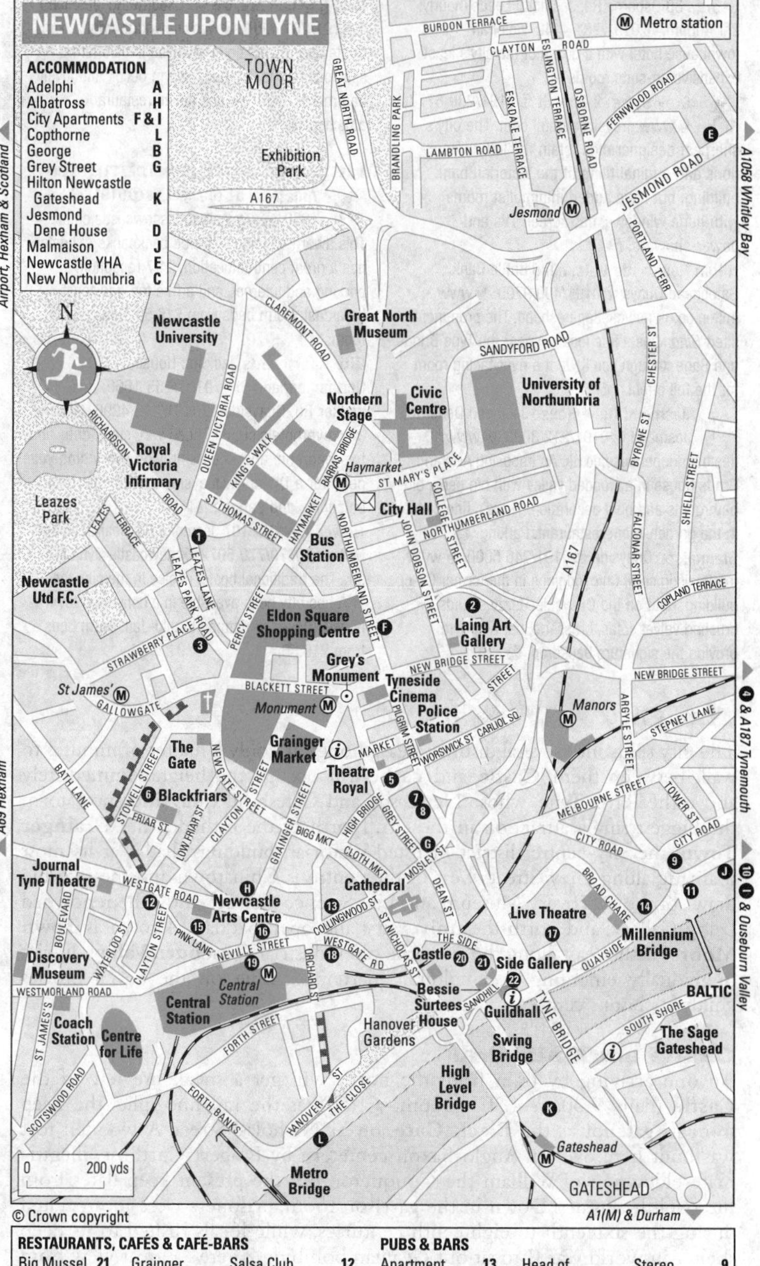

RESTAURANTS, CAFÉS & CAFÉ-BARS

Big Mussel	21	Grainger Rooms	2	Salsa Club	12
Byker Vista Café	4	Mangos	6	Secco Ristorante Salentino	8
Café 21	14	Pani Café	5	Uno's	22
El Coto	3	Paradiso	7	Vujon	17

PUBS & BARS

Apartment	13	Head of Steam	16	Stereo	9
Centurion	19	Pitcher and Piano	11	Tokyo	18
Crown Posada	20	Popolo	7	Trent House	1
Forth Hotel	15				
Free Trade	10				

George 88 Osborne Rd, Jesmond Leeds (hourly; 2hr 40min); ⓣ0191/281 4442. Victorian townhouse hotel with a dozen of the city's least expensive en-suite rooms. ④

Grey Street 2 Grey St ⓣ0191/230 6777, ⓦwww.greystreethotel.com. The city's sharpest designer digs retain the lofty proportions and original tiling of the Victorian bank building, but have added minimalist rooms with huge windows, flat-screen TVs and power-showers. ⑦

Hilton Newcastle Gateshead Bottle Bank, Gateshead Quays ⓣ0191/490 9700, ⓦwww.hilton.co.uk/newcastlegateshead. The prominently sited *Hilton* has a fine location near the Tyne Bridge and Sage, though you'll want a river-facing room for the full effect. ⑦

Jesmond Dene House Jesmond Dene Rd, Jesmond ⓣ0191/212 3000, ⓦwww.jesmonddenehouse.co.uk. An imposing Arts and Crafts house in a wooded valley with big beds, big bathrooms and bold decoration. There's fine dining in the garden-room restaurant. Parking. ⑧

Malmaison Quayside ⓣ0191/245 5000, ⓦwww.malmaison.com. Chic lodgings in the former Co-op building, right on the Quayside. Jazzy sounds, crushed velvet sofas, brasserie, bar and gym provide the signature backdrop. ⑦

New Northumbria 61–69 Osborne Rd, Jesmond ⓣ0191/281 4961, ⓦwww.newnorthumbria.com. Contemporary boutique-style lodgings offering spacious rooms, big beds, warm decor, and lovely bathrooms. Café-bar and Italian restaurant attached. ⑥

Hostels and apartments

Albatross 51 Grainger St ⓣ0191/233 1330, ⓦwww.albatrossnewcastle.co.uk. This award-winning 170-bed backpackers' hostel has a great central location, 24/7 reception, parking and Internet, and a free tea-and-toast breakfast. Dorm beds from £16.50. Double/twin rooms. ③

City Apartments Jackson House, Northumberland St ⓣ0191/255 1660; and Walker Rd, Quayside ⓣ0191/276 4296, ⓦwww.mckeverhotels.co.uk. These very sleek one- and two-bedroom apartments provide everything you need for a DIY stay. Quayside apartments have balconies and parking. ⑤

Newcastle YHA 107 Jesmond Rd, near Jesmond Metro ⓣ0870/770 5972, ⓔnewcastle@yha.org.uk. The traditional hostel choice in the city, the YHA has fifty beds available in a converted townhouse. Closed Christmas to mid-Jan. Dorm beds from £16.50.

The City

The city splits into several distinct areas, though it's only a matter of minutes to walk between them. **Castle** and **cathedral** occupy the heights immediately above the River Tyne, whose Newcastle and Gateshead **quaysides** now form the biggest single attraction in the city. North of the cathedral lies **Grainger Town**, the city-centre district of listed Victorian buildings that is at its most dramatic along Grey Street. West of the centre is Chinatown and the two big draws of the Discovery Museum and Life Science Centre; east is the renowned Laing Gallery; and north the **university** and open parkland known as **Town Moor**. Further east along the river, the old industrial **Ouseburn Valley** district is gradually emerging as a cultural quarter, focusing on the Seven Stories children's books centre.

Castle and Cathedral

Anyone arriving by train from the north will get a sneak preview of the **Castle** (daily 9.30am–4.30/5.30pm; £1.50), as the rail line splits the keep from its gatehouse, the **Black Gate**, on St Nicholas' Street. A wooden fort was built here over an Anglo-Saxon cemetery by Robert Curthose, illegitimate eldest son of William the Conqueror, but the present keep dates from the twelfth century. Down in the garrison room, prisoners were incarcerated during the sixteenth to eighteenth centuries, while locals rushed to its deep shelter in World War II to sit out German bombing. There's a great view from the rooftop over the river and city.

Further along St Nicholas' Street stands the **Cathedral** (Mon–Fri 7am–6pm, Sat 8.30am–4pm, Sun 7.30am–noon & 4–7pm; free), dating mainly from the fourteenth and fifteenth centuries and remarkable chiefly for its tower – erected in 1470, it is topped with a crown-like structure of turrets and arches supporting a lantern. Inside, behind the high altar, is one of the largest funerary brasses in England; it was commissioned by Roger Thornton, the Dick Whittington of Newcastle, who arrived in the city penniless and died its richest merchant in 1430.

Along the River Tyne

From between the castle and the cathedral a road known simply as The Side – formerly the main road out of the city – descends to Newcastle's **Quayside**. The river is spanned by seven bridges in close proximity, the most prominent being the looming **Tyne Bridge** of 1928, symbol of the city. Immediately west is the hydraulic **Swing Bridge**, erected in 1876 by Lord Armstrong so that larger vessels could reach his shipyards upriver, while modern road and rail lines cross the river on the adjacent **High Level Bridge**, built by Robert Stephenson in 1849 – Queen Victoria was one of the first passengers to cross, promoting the railway revolution. Beyond the Tyne Bridge, the modern-day regeneration of the Quayside is in full swing. Riverside apartments, a landscaped promenade, public sculpture and pedestrianized squares have paved the way for a series of fashionable bars and restaurants, centred on the graceful **Gateshead Millennium Bridge**, the world's first tilting span, designed to pivot to allow ships to pass.

The bridge allows pedestrians to cross the Tyne to the **Gateshead Quays**, to visit **BALTIC**, the dramatic Centre for Contemporary Art (Mon–Sun 10am–6pm; free; Ⓦwww.balticmill.com), fashioned from an old brick flour mill. This has been converted into a huge visual "art factory", second only in scale to London's Tate Modern. There's no permanent collection here, though the galleries display specially commissioned or invited art exhibitions and local community projects. Alongside the galleries, the BALTIC accommodates artists' studios, education workshops, an art performance space and cinema, plus a restaurant on the roof with uninterrupted views of the Newcastle skyline. The ground-floor café-bar is a handy spot for a drink, too.

The BALTIC is complemented on the Gateshead side by **The Sage Gateshead** (Ⓦwww.thesagegateshead.org), an extraordinary billowing steel, aluminium and glass concert hall complex, best seen at night when it glows with many colours. It's home to the Northern Sinfonia orchestra and Folkworks, an organization promoting British and international traditional music. The public concourse provides marvellous river and city views, and there's the obligatory café-bar and bistro.

Ouseburn Valley and Seven Stories

Ten minutes' walk up the River Tyne from Millennium Bridge, the now sluggish Ouse Burn tributary was once at the heart of Newcastle's industry. Old Victorian mills and warehouses in the **Ouseburn Valley** are gradually being given a new lease of life by businesses like the Biscuit Factory (Europe's biggest commercial art space), 36 Lime Street (artists' studio group) and The Cluny (innovative music bar), a regeneration cemented by **Seven Stories**, 30 Lime St (Mon–Sat 10am–5pm, Sun 11am–5pm; £5; Ⓣ0845/271 0777, Ⓦwww.sevenstories.org.uk). This national centre for children's literature spreads across seven floors of a beautifully converted riverside mill, showcasing a unique collection of original manuscripts, documents and artwork. Weekends and school holidays see the most activities, and there's also a café and an excellent children's bookshop.

Grainger Town and the city centre

In a few short mid-nineteenth-century years, businessmen-builders and architects such as Richard Grainger, Thomas Oliver and John Dobson fashioned the best-designed Victorian city centre in England, with classical facades of stone lining splendid new streets, most notably **Grey Street**, named for the second Earl Grey (he of the tea), prime minister from 1830 to 1834. In the middle of his term in office he carried the Reform Bill through parliament, an act commemorated by **Grey's Monument** at the top of the street. The restored **Grainger Market** (Mon–Sat 8am–5pm), near Grey's Monument, was Europe's largest undercover market when built in the 1830s.

The **Discovery Museum** in Blandford Square (Mon–Sat 10am–5pm, Sun 2–5pm; free; Ⓦwww.twmuseums.org.uk) puts into context the city's history in a series of impressive displays housed in the former headquarters of the Co-operative Wholesale Society. Stand-out attractions include the "Newcastle Story", a walk through the city's past with tales from animated characters along the way, and the interactive "Science Maze" which focuses on Newcastle's pioneering inventors (including one Joseph Swan who, according to locals at least, beat Edison to the invention of the light bulb).

Heading back towards the Central Station along Westmorland Road, you can't miss the Centre for Life (Mon–Sat 10am–6pm, Sun 11am–6pm, last admission 4pm; £6.95; Ⓣ0191/243 8210, Ⓦwww.lifesciencecentre.org.uk), whose sleek buildings reach around the sweeping expanse of Times Square. This ambitious "science village" project combines bioscience and genetics research centres with a science visitor centre that aims to convey the secrets of life using the latest entertainment technology. Children find the whole thing enormously rewarding – expect to spend a good three hours here, if not more.

The northeast's premier art collection is the **Laing Art Gallery** on New Bridge Street (Mon–Sat 10am–5pm, Sun 2–5pm; free; Ⓦwww.twmuseums.org.uk), off John Dobson Street, behind the library. Local pottery, glassware, costume and sculpture all play their part, while on permanent display is a sweep through British art from Reynolds to John Hoyland, with a smattering of Pre-Raphaelites, so admired by English industrial barons. The other must-see in the gallery is the **Art on Tyneside** exhibition, which romps through the history of art and applied art in the region since the seventeenth century with considerable gusto.

The **Great North Museum** (Ⓦwww.twmuseums.org.uk), due to open in 2009, will bring together the major natural history and archeological collections previously housed in the university's Hancock Museum, Museum of Antiquities, and Shefton (Greek) Museum.

Angel of the North

For over a decade Antony Gormley's **Angel of the North** has stood sentinel over the A1 at Gateshead. Situated on what used to be a colliery's pithead baths, it has become the symbol of Tyneside and the country's most viewed sculpture. The sheer scale of its 175ft wingspan, which inclines slightly forward, makes the most impact and it's even more imposing close up, when the ribbed structure of the body and rough, rusty texture gradually become apparent. The Angel is accessible by car from the A167 (signed Gateshead South; there's a parking lay-by), and by frequent buses (#21 or #21A) that run from Pilgrim Stret in Newcastle and from the Gateshead Interchange bus station.

Eating

At the budget end of the market Italian, Indian and Chinese food dominates the scene, while at the top end of the scale the city has attracted some inventive chefs. The very cheapest places are found around Bigg Market, while in Stowell Street in Chinatown there are plenty of all-you-can-eat buffets as well as more refined Cantonese restaurants.

Café-bars

Byker Vista Café Biscuit Factory, 16 Stoddart St ⓣ0191/261 1103. Best place for a view of the Tyne and landmark Byker Wall, while tucking into soups, salads and sandwiches, or taking a coffee on the terrace. Open daily until 5pm.

Pani Café 61–65 High Bridge St, off Grey St ⓣ0191/232 4366. This buzzy Sardinian café has a loyal clientele, who come day and night (open until 10pm) for good-value sandwiches, pasta and salads. Closed Sun.

Paradiso 1 Market Lane ⓣ0191/221 1240. Mellow café-bar hidden down an alley off Pilgrim St – snacky food during the day, more substantial at night (like home-made pasta or the house special risotto).

Restaurants

Big Mussel 15 The Side ⓣ0191/232 1057. Mussels, chips and mayo served seven ways. A £6 lunch and "clock saver" dinner (5.30–7pm) provide value for money too. Moderate.

Café 21 Trinity Gardens ⓣ0191/222 0755. The Quayside's finest – a stylish Parisian-influenced bistro with a classic menu and slick service. Blackboard specials ring the changes, and the set lunches are a bargain. Expensive.

El Coto 21 Leazes Park Rd ⓣ0191/261 0555. The city's best tapas place makes a good lunch stop (there's a pretty courtyard) or night out – most dishes cost around £4, though you can spend more at the upstairs grill-house (dishes £11–16). Moderate.

Grainger Rooms 7 Higham Place ⓣ0191/232 4949. This place is making a name for itself for its locally sourced, seasonal and organic menu, served in what used to be a gentlemen's club. Expensive.

Mangos 43 Stowell St ⓣ0191/232 6522. A bit more stylish than most Chinatown eateries, *Mangos* offers traditional and new-wave Cantonese dishes, from *dim sum* and country-style hotpots towards sizzling-plate specials. Moderate.

Salsa Club 89 Westgate Rd ⓣ0191/221 1022. A cosy, bare-boards place for a coffee, sandwich and tapas. There's San Mig on draught and DJs some nights. Closed Sun lunch. Inexpensive.

Secco Ristorante Salentino 86 Pilgrim St ⓣ0191/230 0444. The food mixes melt-in-the-mouth southern Italian dishes and Northumbrian ingredients (mains around £15), while the city's beautiful people congregate in the inordinately handsome top-floor bar (until 2am). Closed Sun & Mon. Expensive.

Uno's 18 Sandhill ⓣ0191/261 5264. There are loads of budget Italian places in town but none quite so adept at delivering good food at decent prices (come weekdays before 7pm, or Sat before 5pm, and pizzas or pastas are £4.50). Moderate.

Vujon 29 Queen St ⓣ0191/221 0601. The city's classiest Indian restaurant with dishes a cut above the ordinary, from Rajasthani-style rack of lamb to *bhuna*-style salmon. Moderate.

Drinking, nightlife and music

Newcastle's boisterous pubs, bars and clubs are concentrated in several distinct areas: between Grainger Street and the cathedral in the area called the **Bigg Market** (spiritual home of Sid the Sexist and the Fat Slags from *Viz* magazine); around the **Quayside**, where the bars tend to be slightly more sophisticated; and in the mainstream leisure-and-cinema complex known as **The Gate** (Newgate St). The "**Gay Quarter**" centres on the International Centre for Life, spreading out to Waterloo Street and Westmorland and Scotswood roads. Gigs, club nights and the gay scene are reviewed exhaustively in *The Crack* (monthly; free; ⓦwww.thecrackmagazine.com), a **listings magazine** available in shops, pubs and bars. Top drinking brew is, of course, **Newcastle Brown** – an ale known locally as "Dog" – produced in this city since 1927.

Pubs and bars

Apartment 28–32 Collingwood St. Typical of the latest wave of high-concept city bars is this so-called "luxe bar and diner", divided into spaces where you can variously drink, chat, chill or dine.

Centurion Central Station, Neville St. The station's former first-class waiting rooms, now revived as an extraordinary bar, with Victorian tiling, soaring ceiling and impressive mural.

Crown Posada 31 The Side. Local beers and guest ales in a small wood-and-glass-panelled Victorian pub. Music comes courtesy of the gramophone and a stack of well-worn LPs.

Forth Hotel Pink Lane. Honest city-centre boozer with a fine juke box, a varied crowd, good lunchtime food and a decent range of wines by the glass.

Free Trade St Lawrence Rd. Walk along the Newcastle Quayside past the Millennium Bridge and look for the shabby pub on the hill, where you are invited to "drink beer, smoke tabs" with the city's pub cognoscenti. Superb river views from the beer garden.

Head of Steam 2 Neville St. Relaxed drinking den with good sounds and big sofas. Live gigs every night (not Sun) in the basement from 8pm.

Pitcher & Piano 108 Quayside. The riverfront's most spectacular bar – sinuous roof, huge plate-glass walls, by the Millennium Bridge.

Popolo 82–84 Pilgrim St. This casual American-style bar is a firm city favourite with a slightly older crowd.

Stereo Sandgate, Quayside. Sharp designer style, plus an outdoor deck with Quayside views.

Tokyo 17 Westgate Rd. Follow the tea-lights up the stairs for the outdoor "garden" bar. A pre-club favourite for Shindig (see below).

Trent House 1–2 Leazes Lane. Many people's favourite pub, with a great jukebox – not to mention the surviving Space Invaders machine.

Clubs

Digital International Centre for Life, Times Sq ⓦ www.yourfutureisdigital.com. The city's showpiece dance venue (currently Thurs, Fri & Sat nights) – the big draw is Saturday's Shindig (ⓦ www.shindiguk.com).

Tuxedo Princess Hillgate Quay, Gateshead ⓣ 0191/477 8899. A floating nightclub (aka "The Boat"), on the south side of the river, serving up scantily clad dancers in six bars to a raucous 18- to 25-year-old set. Closed Sun.

World Headquarters Carliol Square ⓣ 0191/261 7007, ⓦ www.theworldheadquarters.com. Newcastle's mellowest bar and club ("no sponsors, no corporates, no sell-out"), playing funk, soul and hip-hop every Fri & Sat.

Live music venues

Black Swan Newcastle Arts Centre, 69 Westgate Rd ⓣ 0191/261 9959. Cellar bar with live music up to five nights a week – rock, folk, world and jazz – and a rollicking Friday-night salsa session. Late bar until 2am.

The Cluny 36 Lime St, Ouseburn Valley ⓣ 0191/230 4474, ⓦ www.theheadofsteam.co.uk. The best small venue in the city is a 20min walk from Quayside, or take the yellow bus, with gigs almost every night from 8pm and a great bar courtesy of the *Head of Steam*.

Jazz Café 23 Pink Lane ⓣ 0191/232 6505. Intimate jazz club with a late licence and live music from 9.30pm; salsa nights Thurs–Sat. Closed Sun.

Trillians Rock Bar Princess Square ⓣ 0191/232 1619, ⓦ www.trilliansrockbar.com. Headbangers of the world unite – local and national rock acts play this pub venue, plus rock DJ nights (Thurs–Sat) until 1am.

Arts, culture and festivals

The Sage and City Hall are the main classical music **concert venues**, but you'll also find performances throughout the year at Newcastle University's King's Hall and in St Nicholas' Cathedral and St Mary's Catholic Cathedral and other churches around town. There's a full **festival calendar** (details from the tourist office), with particular emphasis on outdoor concerts and sports – in October, Europe's biggest half-marathon, the Great North Run, sees 50,000 competitors running across the Tyne Bridge. Undoubted highlight is the New Year's Eve celebration on the Quayside, an exuberantly good-natured rival to the traditional gathering in London.

BALTIC South Shore Rd, Gateshead ⓣ 0191/478 1810, ⓦ www.balticmill.com. As well as the four contemporary art galleries, there are studio sessions and classes, films, artists' talks, community projects, dance and concerts.

Carling Academy Westgate Rd ⓣ 0191/260 2020, ⓦ www.newcastle-academy.co.uk. The city's latest purpose-built music venue hosts big-name bands.

Journal Tyne Theatre 111 Westgate Rd ⓣ 0870/145 1200, ⓦ www.tynetheatre.co.uk. Beautifully restored Victorian theatre with a wide range of shows, comedy and gigs.

Live Theatre 27 Broad Chare ⓣ 0191/232 1232, ⓦ www.live.org.uk. Enterprising theatre company – the attached *Caffe Vivo* is good for coffee by day and pre-theatre meal deals by night.

Tyneside Cinema 10 Pilgrim St ⓣ0191/232 8289, ⓦwww.tynecine.org. The city's premier art-house cinema. There's coffee, light meals and movie talk in the Art Deco cinema café (closes 9pm).
The Sage Gateshead South Shore Rd, Gateshead Quays ⓣ0191/443 4661, ⓦwww.thesagegateshead.org. Stunning international music centre, home of the Northern Sinfonia and Folkworks, hosting a full programme of classical, folk, world and jazz music. Tickets from £6.
Theatre Royal 100 Grey St ⓣ0870/905 5060, ⓦwww.theatreroyal.co.uk. Drama, opera, dance, musicals and comedy; also hosts the annual RSC season in Nov.

Listings

Airport Newcastle International Airport ⓣ0871/882 1121, ⓦwww.newcastleinternational.co.uk.
Bike hire Tyne Bridge Bike Hire ⓣ0191/277 2441, ⓦwww.tynebridgebikehire.co.uk, rents bikes for £15 per day, £60 per week, either for use in the city, or there's a pick-up and drop-off Hadrian's Wall service.
Football Newcastle United play at St James' Park (ticket office ⓣ0191/261 1571, ⓦwww.nufc.co.uk). You're unlikely to get a ticket for the big matches against major rivals, but seats do go on general sale for some games. Don't, under any circumstances, wear anything red (the colour of hated local rivals Sunderland).
Hospital Newcastle General Hospital, Westgate Rd ⓣ0191/233 6161. Has 24hr A&E department, plus non-emergency NHS Walk-In Centre (daily 8am–9pm).
Pharmacy Boots, Eldon Square ⓣ0191/232 4423.
Police Corner of Market and Pilgrim streets ⓣ0191/214 6555.
Post office St Mary's Place, near the Civic Centre, at Haymarket.
Taxis Ranks at Haymarket, Bigg Market and outside Central Station. Weekend nights are the most difficult times to hail a cab. Call Noda Taxis (ⓣ0191/222 1888 or 232 7777) at Central Station for advance bookings.

Around Newcastle

The Metro runs east along both banks of the **River Tyne**, connecting Newcastle with the historic attractions at **Wallsend** and **Jarrow** and with the sandy beaches at Tynemouth and Whitley Bay. The metro also runs southeast to **Sunderland**, twelve miles from Newcastle and its most intense rival: both cities are outraged about being lumped together in the municipal appellation Tyne *and* Wear; while both Geordies (from Newcastle) and Mackems (from Sunderland) remain indignant at being taken for the other by know-nothing southerners.

Wallsend and Segedunum

WALLSEND, four miles east of Newcastle, was the last outpost of Hadrian's great border defence. **Segedunum**, the "strong fort" a couple of minutes' signposted walk from the Metro station (daily 10am–3.30/5.30pm; £3.50; ⓦwww.twmuseums.org.uk/segedunum), has been admirably developed as one of the prime attractions along the Wall. A range of activities takes place year-round (including summer re-enactments of Roman drill and equipment) and the grounds contain a fully reconstructed bathhouse, complete with heated pools and colourful frescoes. The "wall's end" itself is visible at the edge of the site, close to the river and Swan Hunter shipyard, and it's from here that the **Hadrian's Wall Path** (see p.611) runs for 84 miles to Bowness-on-Solway in Cumbria; you can get your walk "passport" stamped inside the museum.

Jarrow

JARROW, five miles east of Newcastle and south of the Tyne, has been ingrained on the national consciousness since the 1936 Jarrow Crusade, a march to London by unemployed protesters, which became the most potent image of the hardships of 1930s Britain. However, the town made a mark rather earlier, as the seventh-century St Paul's church and monastery was one of the region's early cradles of Christianity. It was here that the **Venerable Bede** (673–735 AD) came to live as a boy, growing to become one of Europe's greatest scholars and England's first historian – his *History of the English Church and People*, describing the struggles of the island's early Christians, was completed at Jarrow in 731. Access to the tranquil stone church of **St Paul's** and the adjacent monastery ruins (Mon–Sat 10am–4pm, Sun 2–4.30pm) is free, although they stand within the wider development that is **Bede's World** (Mon–Sat 10am–4.30/5.30pm, Sun noon–4.30/5.30pm; £4.50; Ⓦwww.bedesworld.co.uk), a fascinating exploration of early medieval times, which enterprisingly traces the development of Northumbria and England through the use of extracts from Bede's writings, set alongside archeological finds and vivid recreations of monastic life.

St Paul's and Bede's World are a signposted fifteen-minute walk through an industrial estate from **Bede Metro station**. Alternatively, buses #526 or #527 run roughly every 30 minutes from Neville Street (Central Station) in Newcastle or Jarrow Metro station, and stop in front of the church.

Sunderland and around

SUNDERLAND shares Newcastle's long history, river setting and industrial heritage but cannot match its architectural splendour. Formed from three medieval villages flanking the Wear, it was one of the wealthiest towns in England by 1500, but the twentieth century both made and broke the town: from being the largest shipbuilding centre in the world, Sunderland slumped after ferocious bombing during World War II. Depression and recession did the rest. However, it's worth a trip to visit the **Sunderland Museum** (Mon–Sat 10am–5pm, Sun 2–5pm; free; Ⓦwww.twmuseums.org.uk/sunderland), easily accessible by Metro from Newcastle. It does a very good job of telling the city's history, while its **Winter Gardens** invite a treetop walk to view the impressive polished steel column of a water sculpture. The landscaped **Riverside** is actually the oldest settled part of the city (walk up Fawcett Street and then Bridge Street from the centre and across Wearmouth Bridge, around 20min). Along the north bank of the river, in front of the university buildings, the early Christian **Church of St Peter** (674 AD) is the elder sibling of St Paul's Church at Jarrow and displays fragments of the oldest stained glass in the country. Then walk down to the waterside to find the city's **National Glass Centre** (daily 10am–5pm; free; Ⓦwww.nationalglasscentre.com), which tells the story of British glass and glass-making – there are daily demonstrations in the on-site workshop.

The main stop for **Metros** from Newcastle is in the central **train station** opposite the Bridges Shopping Centre, but get off at the previous stop, St Peter's, to walk along the north side of the river to the National Glass Centre or St Peter's Church. The **tourist office** is behind the central station on the main shopping drag, at 50 Fawcett St (Mon–Sat 9am–5pm, bank hols 10am–4pm; Ⓣ0191/553 2000, Ⓦwww.visitsunderland.com).

Five miles west of Sunderland, the new town of **WASHINGTON** is not an obvious tourist stop, although the original **old village** has been zealously preserved and just off the green stands the ancestral home of the family that spawned the **first US president**. The "de Wessyngtons" – later the Washingtons – originally came over with William the Conqueror and by 1183 were based at the **Old Hall** (April–Oct Mon–Wed & Sun 11am–5pm; £4.65; NT), where they lived until 1613. The other main attraction in the area is the **Washington Wildfowl and Wetlands Centre** (daily 9.30am–4.30/5.30pm; £6, ⓦwww.wwt.org.uk), east of town and north of the River Wear in District 15, its hundred acres designed by Sir Peter Scott and acting as a winter habitat for migratory birds, including geese, ducks, herons and flamingos. It's signposted off most local roads, four miles from the A1(M), one mile from the A19.

Along Hadrian's Wall

Emperor Hadrian, who toured Roman Britain in 122 AD, wanted his empire to live at peace within stable frontiers, but as there was no natural barrier in northern Britain, Hadrian constructed a 76-mile **wall** from the Tyne to the Solway Firth. The wall, its turrets, camps and forts remained in operation until the late fourth century AD, though centralized Roman rule in Britain had broken down by then. Most of Hadrian's Wall disappeared centuries ago, yet walking or cycling its length remains a popular pastime, following the 84-mile **Hadrian's Wall Path** (ⓦwww.nationaltrail.co.uk/hadrianswall), which partly shares its route with Hadrian's Cycleway. Approached from Newcastle along the valley of the Tyne, via the Roman museum and site at **Corbridge**, the prosperous-looking market town of **Hexham** makes a good base. The best-preserved portions of the Wall are concentrated between **Chesters Roman Fort**, four miles north of Hexham, and **Haltwhistle**, sixteen miles to the west, notably the remains of **Housesteads Fort** and the garrison of **Vindolanda**.

A special **Hadrian's Wall bus**, the #AD122, runs from Newcastle to Corbridge, Hexham, and all the wall sites and villages, and then on to Carlisle and Bowness-on-Solway (the end of the Hadrian's Wall Path). This operates between Easter and October, up to five times a day in each direction; **Day Rover** tickets (1/3/7 days, £7/14/28) are available. There's also a year-round hourly service on the #685 bus between Newcastle and Carlisle, and other local services from Carlisle and Hexham, which provide access to various points on the Wall. The nearest **train** stations are on the Newcastle–Carlisle line at Corbridge, Hexham, Bardon Mill and Haltwhistle – a combination Rail Rover ticket with the Hadrian's Wall bus allows travel between Newcastle and Carlisle. The best place to **park and ride** is at Once Brewed visitor centre, where there's all-day parking and a bus stop for the Hadrian's Wall bus. For full local information, contact the **Hadrian's Wall information line** on ⓣ01434/322002, ⓦwww.hadrians-wall.org.

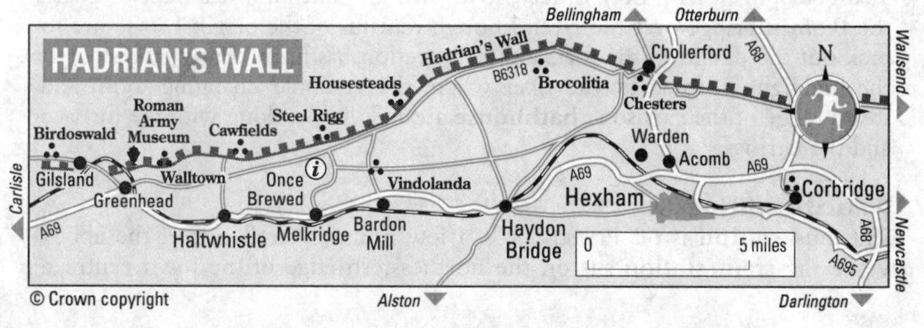

Corbridge

CORBRIDGE is a well-heeled commuter town overlooking the River Tyne from the top of a steep ridge. One mile west of the Market Place, accessible either by road or along the riverside footpath, lies **Corbridge Roman Site** (April–Oct daily 10am–4/5.30pm; Nov–March Sat & Sun 10am–4pm; £4.10; EH), first established as a supply base for the Roman advance into Scotland in 80 AD (and thus predating the Wall itself). It remained in regular military use until the end of the second century, after which it became surrounded by a fast-developing town – most of the extensive archeological remains date from this period, when "Corstopitum" served as the nerve centre of Hadrian's Wall.

Hexham

In 671, on a bluff above the Tyne, St Wilfrid founded a Benedictine monastery whose church was, according to contemporary accounts, the finest north of the Alps. Unfortunately, it proved irresistible to the Vikings, who savaged the place in 876, but the church was rebuilt in the eleventh century as part of an Augustinian priory, and the town of **HEXHAM** grew up in its shadow. The handsome market town is the only significant stop between Newcastle and Carlisle and however focused you are on seeing the Wall, you'd do well to give Hexham a night or even make it your base.

The stately exterior of **Hexham Abbey** (daily 9.30am–5pm; free) still dominates the west side of the Market Place. Entry is through the south transept, where there's a bruised but impressive first-century tombstone honouring Flavinus, a standard-bearer in the Roman cavalry, who's shown riding down his bearded enemy. The memorial lies at the foot of the broad, well-worn steps of the canons' **night stair**, one of the few such staircases – providing access from the monastery to the church – to have survived the Dissolution. The chancel, meanwhile, displays the inconsequential-looking **frith-stool**, an eighth-century stone chair that was once believed to have been used by St Wilfrid, rendering it holy enough to serve as the medieval sanctuary stool.

The rest of Hexham's large **Market Place** (main market day is Tuesday, farmers' market second and fourth Sunday of the month) is peppered with remains of its medieval past. The massive walls of the fourteenth-century **Moot Hall** were built to serve as the gatehouse to "The Hall", a well-protected enclosure that was garrisoned against the Scots. Nearby, the archbishops also built their own prison, a formidable fortified tower dating from 1330 and constructed using stones plundered from the Roman ruins at Corbridge. Known as the **Old Gaol**, this accommodates Hexham's local history museum (March–Oct daily 10am–4.30pm, Feb & Nov Tues & Sat 10am–4.30pm; £3.80).

Four miles north of Hexham, **Chesters Roman Fort** (daily 9.30/10am–4/6pm; £4.10; EH), otherwise known as Cilurnum, was built to guard the Roman bridge over the river. Enough remains of the original structure to pick out the design of the fort, and each section has been clearly labelled, but the highlight is down by the river where the vestibule, changing room and steam range of the garrison's **bathhouse** are still visible, along with the furnace and the latrines.

Practicalities

The **bus station** is off Priestpopple, a few minutes' stroll east of the abbey, while the **train station** sits on the northeastern edge of the town centre, a ten-minute walk from the abbey; the **tourist office** is halfway between the two, in the main Wentworth **car park**, near the supermarket (April–Oct Mon–Sat 9am–6pm, Sun 10am–5pm; Nov–March Mon–Sat 9am–5pm; ⓣ01434/652220, ⓦwww.hadrianswallcountry.org). The main focus of entertainment in town is the **Queen's Hall Arts Centre** on Beaumont Street (ⓣ01434/652477), which puts on a year-round programme of theatre, dance, music and art exhibitions.

Guesthouses and hotels

Hallbank Hallgate, behind the Old Gaol ⓣ01434/605567, ⓦwww.hallbankguesthouse.com. A restored house in a quiet town-centre location, with eight rooms and an associated coffee shop/restaurant. ⑤

Kitty Frisk House Corbridge Rd ⓣ01434/601533, ⓦwww.kittyfriskhouse.co.uk. Welcoming Edwardian retreat, half a mile from the centre down the Corbridge road in a residential area. No credit cards. ④

Matfen Hall Matfen, 10 miles northeast of Hexham ⓣ01661/886500, ⓦwww.matfenhall.com. The northeast's ritziest golf-and-spa hotel presents a stylish take on country-house living. ⑧

Restaurant

The Green Room Station Rd ⓣ01434/608800. There are plenty of daytime cafés, four Indian and a couple of Italian restaurants in town, but the only place that really stands out is this unpretentious Modern British restaurant in the old railway station waiting room. Closed Sun night & Mon. Moderate.

Housesteads and around

Housesteads Roman Fort (daily 10am–4/6pm; £4.10; EH & NT), eight miles west of Chesters, has long been the most popular site on the Wall. The fort is of standard design but for one enforced modification – forts were supposed to straddle the line of the Wall, but here the original stonework tracked along the very edge of the cliff, so Housesteads was built on the steeply sloping ridge to the south. Access is via the tiny **museum**, from where you stroll across to the south gate, beside which lie the remains of the civilian settlement that was dependent on the one thousand infantrymen stationed within. You don't need to pay for entrance to Housesteads if you simply intend to walk west along the Wall from here. The three-mile hike past the lovely wooded **Crag Lough** to **Steel Rigg** (car park) offers the most fantastic views, especially when you spy the course of the Wall as it threads over the crags ahead.

Leaving the Wall at Steel Rigg, it's roughly half a mile south to the main road (B6318) and the very informative **Once Brewed National Park Visitor Centre** (March–Sept daily 9.30am–5/5.30pm; Nov–Feb Sat & Sun 10am–3pm; ⓣ01434/344396), which has exhibitions on both the Wall and the National Park – there's also a nearby youth hostel, pub and access road to the Vindolanda excavations.

Accommodation

Gibbs Hill Farm Once Brewed ⓣ01434/344030, ⓦwww.gibbshillfarm.co.uk. Working farm with great views of the Wall, two miles north of Steel Rigg. Also a hay-barn bunkhouse with shower rooms and kitchen (beds £12, breakfast available). ③

Hadrian's Wall Camping and Caravan Site 2 miles north of Melkridge, just south of B6318 ⓣ01434/320495, ⓦwww.romanwallcamping.co.uk. Family-run site half a mile from the Wall; breakfast available. Open all year.

Langley Castle A686, 2 miles south of Haydon Bridge ⓣ01434/688888, ⓦwww.langleycastle.com. You don't get many chances to spend the night in a genuine medieval castle. The cheaper rooms are in the grounds, looking onto the castle, but all are spacious, some with four-posters, saunas and spa baths. ⑦, castle rooms ⑨

Old Repeater Station Military Rd (B6318), Grindon, 4 miles east of Once Brewed ⓣ01434/688668. ⓦwww.hadrians-wall-bedandbreakfast.co.uk. Remote location close to Hadrian's Wall, with a choice of simple en-suite rooms or rooms with bunk beds. The obliging host cooks breakfasts and dinners, and

offers an airport/rail/bus connection service. Dorm beds £20, rooms ❸
Once Brewed YHA Military Rd, B6318, Once Brewed ⓣ0870/770 5980, ⓔoncebrewed@yha.org.uk. Next to the visitor centre, providing walking leaflets, packed lunches, three-course dinners, kitchen and lounge. Closed Dec & Jan. Dorms from £11.95.

Twice Brewed Inn Military Rd, B6318 ⓣ01434/344534, ⓦwww.twicebrewedinn.co.uk. Friendly community pub, 50yd up from visitor centre and hostel, with simple rooms, food served all day, beer-garden, local beers on tap and Internet access. ❷, en suite ❸

Vindolanda

The excavated garrison fort of **Vindolanda** actually predates the Wall itself, though most of what you see today dates from the second to third century AD, when the fort was a thriving metropolis of five hundred soldiers with its own civilian settlement attached. The site (mid-Feb to mid-Nov daily 10am–5/6pm; winter reduced hours; £4.95, joint admission with Roman Army Museum £7.50; ⓣ01434/344277, ⓦwww.vindolanda.com) is operated by the private Vindolanda Trust, which has done an excellent job of imaginatively presenting its finds. The ongoing **excavations** are spread over a wide area, with civilian houses, guest quarters, administrative building, commander's house and main gates all clearly visible. Beyond lies the **museum** which houses the largest collection of Roman leather items ever discovered on a single site – dozens of shoes, belts, even a pair of baby boots – which were preserved in the black silt of waterlogged ditches. Even more intriguing is the exhibition concerned with an excavated hoard of **writing tablets**, now in the British Museum. These depict graphically the realities of military life in Northumberland: soldiers' requests for more beer, birthday party invitations, court reports, even letters from home containing gifts of underwear for freezing frontline grunts.

Roman Army Museum and Greenhead

Heading west takes you past the remains of **Great Chesters Fort** before reaching a spectacular section of the Wall, known as the **Walltown Crags**. The views from here are marvellous, and there's a handy nearby car park, picnic site and simple tea-and-ice-cream café. Very near the crags, at Carvoran, you can call into the Vindolanda Trust's **Roman Army Museum** (mid-Feb to mid-Nov daily 10am–5/6pm; winter reduced hours; £3.95, ⓣ01697/747485, ⓦwww.vindolanda.com; joint ticket with Vindolanda £7.50), which tells you everything there is to know about life in the Roman army by way of exhibits, dioramas, reconstructions and games.

Push on just a mile southwest and you're soon in minuscule **GREENHEAD**, with a tearoom, pub and **youth hostel** (ⓣ0169/747411, ⓔdougsandragreenh@btconnect.com; £13), the latter located in a converted Methodist chapel. *Holmhead Guesthouse* (ⓣ01697/747402, ⓦwww.holmhead.com; rooms ❹, bunk-barn £12 per person), an old stone farmhouse sporting exposed beams, and partly built with stones taken from the Wall itself, is up a track behind the hostel. Heading west, the next section of Hadrian's Wall worth exploring is at Birdoswald, in Cumbria, a four-mile walk or ten-minute ride on the bus.

Northumberland National Park

Northwest Northumberland, the great triangular chunk of land between Hadrian's Wall and the coastal plain, is dominated by the wide-skied landscapes of the **Northumberland National Park** (Ⓦwww.northumberland-national-park.org.uk), whose four hundred windswept square miles rise to the Cheviot Hills on the Scottish border. These uplands are interrupted by great slabs of forest and a string of river valleys, of which Coquetdale, Tynedale and Redesdale are the longest.

The **Pennine Way** enters the National Park at Hadrian's Wall and runs via **The Cheviot**, the park's highest peak at 2674ft, finishing at Kirk Yetholm, over the border in Scotland. As an introduction, it's hard to beat the lovely moorland scenery of the fifteen-mile stretch from Housesteads at Hadrian's Wall to **Bellingham**, a pleasant town on the banks of the North Tyne. Bellingham is also the gateway to **Kielder Water**, a massive pine-surrounded reservoir, water-sports centre and nature reserve. Further north, Victorian **Rothbury**, in Coquetdale, is convenient for walks in the Simonside Hills and for visits to the country estates of **Cragside** and **Wallington**, whilst at the hiking centre of **Wooler**, footpaths lead into the Cheviot Hills.

Kielder Water and Forest

The road from Bellingham follows the North Tyne River west and skirts the forested edge of **Kielder Water** (Ⓦwww.kielder.org), passing the assorted visitor centres, waterside parks, picnic areas and anchorages that fringe its southern shore. The reservoir – England's largest by volume – makes a good day out, particularly for cyclists and hikers. First stop is the Visitor Centre at **Tower Knowe** (daily April–Oct 10am–4/6pm; Ⓣ0870/240 3549), eight miles from Bellingham, with a café and an exhibition on the history of the valley and reservoir. Another four miles west, at **Leaplish** (opening hours vary; Ⓣ0870/240 3549), the waterside park, bar and restaurant are the focus of most of Kielder's outdoor activities and accommodation: there's also a heated indoor pool and sauna. The **Bird of Prey Centre** here (daily 10.30am–4.30pm; £5; Ⓣ01434/250400) lays on entertaining daily flying displays and "hawk walks". Otherwise, an hour-and-a-half's cruise on the **Osprey ferry** (April–Oct 5 daily; £6) is always a pleasure; departures are from either Tower Knowe or Leaplish.

Five miles from Leaplish at the top of the reservoir, the forestry settlement of **Kielder Village** is dominated by Kielder Castle, built in 1775 as the hunting lodge of the Duke of Northumberland and now the **Kielder Castle Visitor Centre** (April–Oct daily 10am–5pm; Nov Sat & Sun 11am–4pm; Dec daily 11am–4pm; Ⓣ01434/250209). The castle is at the heart of **Kielder Forest Park**, Britain's largest forest, comprising several million spruce trees, criss-crossed by footpaths and bike trails and home to red squirrels, deer, otters and countless birds, including goshawks, merlins and ospreys.

Without a car, you're dependent on the local bus **from Bellingham**, which calls at Tower Knowe, Leaplish and Kielder. There's **mountain bike rental** available from The Bike Place (Ⓣ01434/250457; £20/day), signposted in the village, with advice given on waymarked trails and off-road routes through the forest. As well as the **accommodation** options listed below, the forest also has 14 **backpacking sites** (Ⓣ01434/220242, no facilities, no vehicle access) – bring plenty of midge repellent.

Accommodation and food

Blackcock Inn Falstone Ⓣ01434/240200. Small inn (closed Tues in winter) located in a pretty riverside hamlet. You can eat here, or at the eco-friendly tearooms opposite (summer daily, winter closed Tues & Wed). ③

Kielder Lodges Leaplish Waterside Park Ⓣ0870/240 3549, or Hoseasons Ⓣ01502/502588, Ⓦwww.hoseasons.co.uk. Scandinavian-style self-catering lodges available, £270–725 per week depending on size and season (cheaper 3-night stays available all year) – all have access to the park's pool, sauna, bar and restaurant.

Kielder YHA Kielder village ⓣ0870/770 5898, ⓔkielder@yha.org.uk. Well-equipped activity-based hostel, with some two- and three-bedded rooms plus small dorms, only 200 yards from the pub. Dorm beds from £14.

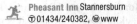

Pheasant Inn Stannersburn ⓣ01434/240382, ⓦwww.thepheasantinn.com. On the road in from Bellingham, this early seventeenth-century inn has eight comfortable rooms and decent meals (seabass to steak, mains £9–13) served in the bar or restaurant. ⑤

Rothbury and around

ROTHBURY, straddling the River Coquet thirty miles northeast of Hexham, prospered as a late-Victorian resort because it gave ready access to the forests, burns and ridges of the Simonside Hills. The small town remains a popular spot for walkers, with several of the best local trails beginning from the **Simonside Hills** car park, a couple of miles southwest of Rothbury. The **Tourist Information and National Park Visitor Centre** is near the cross on Church Street (April–Oct daily 10am–5pm; Nov–March Sat & Sun 10am–5pm; ⓣ01669/620887, ⓦwww.visit-rothbury.co.uk). There's no pressing need to stay, even if you're walking for the day, with Alnwick (12 miles) and the coast so close, but the tourist office does have an informative folder of local **B&Bs**.

Cragside

Victorian Rothbury was dominated by Sir William, later the first **Lord Armstrong**, the wealthy nineteenth-century arms manufacturer, shipbuilder and engineer who built his country home at **Cragside** (April–Oct Tues–Sun, plus bank hols 1–4.30/5.30pm, gardens from 10.30/11am; £10.50, gardens only £7; NT), a mile to the east of the village. He hired Richard Norman Shaw, one of the period's top architects, who produced a grandiose Tudor-style mansion entirely out of place in the Northumbrian countryside. Armstrong was an avid innovator, and in 1880 he managed to make Cragside the first house in the world to be lit by hydroelectric power. The remains of the original pumping system are still visible in the **grounds**, while over at the visitor centre there's a **café/restaurant**, and an explanatory video and other displays in the adjacent Armstrong Energy Centre.

Wallington

Around 13 miles south of Rothbury, down the B6342, stands **Wallington** (April–Oct Mon & Wed–Sun 1–4.30/5.30pm; house and gardens £8; NT), an ostentatious mansion rebuilt in the 1740s by Sir Walter Blackett, the coal- and lead-mine owner. The house is known for its Rococo plasterwork and William Bell Scott's Pre-Raphaelite murals of scenes from Northumbrian history. Children will love the collection of dolls' houses, one of which has thirty-six rooms and was originally fitted with running water and a working lift. However, it's the magnificent **gardens and grounds** (daily all year dawn–dusk; £5.50 without house admission) that are the real delight, with lawns, woods and lakes that are traced by easy-to-follow footpaths. There are events, concerts and activities throughout the year, as well as a café and farm shop on site.

Wooler

Stone-terraced **WOOLER**, a one-street market town twenty miles north of Rothbury, is the best base for climbs up **The Cheviot** (2674ft), seven miles to the southwest, which is the highest point in the Cheviot Hills. From Hawsen Burn, the nearest navigable point, it's two hours walking there and back. Wooler is also a staging-post on **St Cuthbert's Way**, the trans-Cheviot route, which runs west from the town to Kirk Yetholm and beyond or northeast to Holy Island. Frequent buses link Wooler with Berwick-upon-Tweed and Alnwick, the two nearest towns, and the **bus station** is set back off the High Street. At the other end of the High Street, off Burnhouse Road (by the free **car park**), you'll find the **tourist office** in the Cheviot Centre at Padgepool Place (April–Oct Mon–Sat 10am–1.30pm & 2–5pm, Sun 10am–1.30pm & 2–6pm; ⓣ01668/282123), which can provide local walking information.

B&Bs abound – there's a full list posted in the tourist office window – but for complete remoteness, *Hethpool House* (ⓣ01668/216232, ⓦwww.hethpoolhouse.co.uk; ④) at Hethpool, seven miles west of Wooler, fits the bill. The turreted Edwardian manor house offers four charming rooms, dinner using home-grown produce (£15/20), and the Cheviots on the doorstep.

Chillingham

Six miles southeast of Wooler, **Chillingham Castle** (May–Sept daily except Sat 1–5pm, gardens and tearooms from noon; £6.75; ⓦwww.chillingham-castle.com) started life as an eleventh-century tower. The castle was augmented at regular intervals until the nineteenth century, but from 1933 was largely left to the elements for fifty years, until the present owner set about restoring it in his own individualistic – or, eccentric – way: bedrooms, living rooms and even a grisly torture chamber (designed to "cause maximum shock") are decorated with all manner of historical paraphernalia to give an idea of how the place would have looked through the ages.

In 1220, the adjoining 365 acres of parkland were enclosed to protect the local wild cattle for hunting and food. And so the **Chillingham Wild Cattle** (visits April–Oct Mon & Wed–Sat 10am–noon & 2–5pm, Sun 2–5pm; winter by appointment; £4.50; ⓣ01668/215250, ⓦwww.chillingham-wildcattle.org.uk) – a fierce, primeval herd with white coats, black muzzles and black tips to their horns – have remained to this day, cut off from mixing with domesticated breeds. It's possible to visit these unique relics, who number about seventy, but only in the company of a warden, as the animals are potentially dangerous and need to be protected from outside infection. The visit takes up to an hour and a half and involves a short country walk before viewing the cattle at a safe distance – the closest you're likely to get to big game viewing in England. The site is signposted from the A1 and A697; bring strong shoes or walking boots if it's wet.

The Northumberland coast

The low-lying **Northumberland coast**, stretching 64 miles north from Newcastle to the Scottish border, boasts many of the region's principal attractions, most notably the mighty fortresses at **Warkworth**, **Alnwick** and **Bamburgh** and the magnificent Elizabethan ramparts surrounding **Berwick-upon-Tweed**. In between you'll find splendid sandy beaches as well as the site of the Lindisfarne monastery on **Holy Island** and the seabird and nature reserve of the **Farne Islands**, reached by boat from Seahouses.

Warkworth

WARKWORTH, a coastal hamlet set in a loop of the River Coquet a couple of miles from Amble, is best seen from the north, from where the grey stone terraces of the long main street slope up towards the commanding remains of **Warkworth Castle** (April–Oct daily 10am–4/6pm; Nov–March Sat, Sun & Mon 10am–4pm; £3.50; EH). It was here that most of the Percy family, earls of Northumberland, chose to live throughout the fourteenth and fifteenth centuries. The main street sweeps down into the attractive village, flattening out at Dial Place and the Church of St Lawrence before curving right to cross the River Coquet; just over the bridge, a signposted quarter-mile lane leads to the **beach**, which stretches for five miles from Amble to Alnmouth.

Alnmouth

It's three miles north from Warkworth to the seaside resort of **ALNMOUTH**, whose narrow centre is strikingly situated on a steep spur of land between the sea and the estuary of the Aln. It's a lovely setting and has been a low-key holiday spot since Victorian times, while many also come for the golf: the village's nine-hole course, right on the coast, was built in 1869 (it's claimed to be the second oldest in the country) and dune-strollers really do have to heed the "Danger – Flying Golf Balls" signs which adorn Marine Road. There are local **bus services** from Alnwick and Warkworth, while the regular Newcastle to Alnwick bus also passes through Alnmouth and calls at its **train station** at Hipsburn, a mile and a half west of the centre. Most of the **accommodation** lies along or just off the main Northumberland Street. At no. 56, the friendly *Beaches* (Ⓣ01665/830006, Ⓦwww.beachesbyo.co.uk; no credit cards; ④) has a variety of highly individual en-suite rooms attached to a good, moderate **restaurant** (Mon–Sat dinner only).

Alnwick

The appealing market town of **ALNWICK** (pronounced "Annick"), thirty miles north of Newcastle and four miles inland from Alnmouth, is renowned for its castle and gardens – seat of the dukes of Northumberland – which overlook the River Aln. You'll need a full day to do these justice while, as the biggest town between Hadrian's Wall and the Scottish border, Alnwick itself warrants an overnight stop in any case.

The Percys – who were raised to the dukedom of Northumberland in 1750 – have owned **Alnwick Castle** (April–Oct daily 11am–5pm, grounds from 10am; £9; Ⓦwww.alnwickcastle.com) since 1309. In the eighteenth century, the first duke had the interior refurbished by Robert Adam in an extravagant Gothic style – which in turn was supplanted by the gaudy Italianate decoration

The Warkworth hermit

A path from the village churchyard heads along the right bank of the Coquet to the little boat that shuttles visitors (weather permitting, April–Sept Wed, Sun and bank hols 11am–5pm; fee charged) across to **Warkworth Hermitage**, a series of simple rooms and a claustrophobic chapel that were hewn out of the cliff above the river sometime in the fourteenth century, but abandoned by 1567. The last resident hermit, one George Lancaster, was charged by the sixth earl of Northumberland to pray for his noble family, for which lonesome duty he received around £15 a year and a barrel of fish every Sunday.

preferred by the fourth duke in the 1850s. There's plenty to see inside, though the **interior** can be crowded at times – not least with families on the *Harry Potter* trail, since the castle doubled as Hogwarts School in the first two films.

Signs lead you out of the grounds for the short walk to the **Alnwick Garden** (April–Oct 10am–6/7pm; Nov–March 10am–4pm; £6; Ⓦwww.alnwickgarden.com), which draws crowds to marvel at its sheer scale and invention. At its heart is the computerized Grand Cascade, which shoots water jets in a regular synchronized display, while special features include a bamboo labyrinth maze and the popular Poison Garden – filled with the world's deadliest plants. Superior ices, teas and snacks are available from the *Garden Café*, while Europe's biggest **treehouse** that provides the most spectacular location for a meal – it's also open for dinner (Thurs–Sat from 6.30pm; Ⓣ01665/511852; main dishes from £15).

The principal remains of the medieval town walls are on view at the **gatehouses** on Pottergate and Bondgate, while you can't miss the grandiose **Percy Tenantry Column** just to the southeast of the centre along Bondgate Without. A little further on, housed in the Victorian train station, **Barter Books** (Ⓦwww.barterbooks.co.uk), one of the largest second-hand bookshops in England, is definitely worth a call – not just books, but sofas, murals, open fire, coffee and biscuits, and a model railway that runs on top of the stacks.

Practicalities

Alnwick **bus station** is on Clayport Street, a couple of minutes' walk west of the Market Place, where you'll find the **tourist office**, in the arcaded Shambles (April–Oct Mon–Fri 9am–5/6pm, Sat 9/10am–4/5pm, Sun 10am–4pm; Nov–March Mon–Fri 9.30am–4.30pm, Sat 10am–4pm; Ⓣ01665/510665, Ⓦwww.alnwick.gov.uk). Market Place hosts weekly markets (Thurs & Sat) and a farmers' market on the last Friday of the month. **Alnwick Playhouse**, just through the arch on Bondgate Without (Ⓣ01665/510785, Ⓦwww.alnwickplayhouse.co.uk), is a venue for theatre, music and film throughout the year.

Accommodation, eating and drinking

Masons' Arms Rennington, 5 miles northeast of town on the Seahouses (B1340) road Ⓣ01665/577275, Ⓦwww.masonsarms.net. An old coaching inn with good bar food, as well as eleven bedrooms, two with private sitting rooms. ⑤, suites. ⑥

Tower Restaurant & Accommodation 10 Bondgate Within Ⓣ01665/603888, Ⓦwww.tower-alnwick.co.uk. Just inside the gate, this place offers bright, tasteful rooms and hearty breakfasts; the pine-furnished restaurant below serves licensed meals, but closes at 8pm. ④

White Swan Bondgate Within Ⓣ01665/602109, Ⓦwww.classiclodges.co.uk. Alnwick's main hotel – there's a comfortable lounge and restaurant, while the hotel's fine oak-panelled dining room was swiped from an old ocean liner, the *Olympic*, the twin of the *Titanic*. ⑧

Craster, Dunstanburgh, Newton and Beadnell

Heading northeast out of Alnwick along the B1340, it's a six-mile hop to the region's kipper capital, the tiny fishing village of **CRASTER**. The *Jolly Fisherman*, the **pub** above the harbour, features sea views from its back window and garden and famously good crabmeat, whisky and cream soup, crab sandwiches and kipper pâté. Most spectacularly, however, Craster provides access to **Dunstanburgh Castle** (April–Oct daily 10am–4/5m; Nov–March Mon & Thurs–Sun 10am–4pm; £2.90; NT & EH), whose shattered medieval ruins occupy a magnificent promontory about thirty minutes' windy walk up the coast.

Beyond Dunstanburgh, the long sandy beaches backing Embleton and Beadnell bays are windswept and deserted in winter, busier in summer though rarely overly so. At the beachside hamlet of **NEWTON-BY-THE-SEA** the rustic *Ship Inn* (Ⓣ01665/576262; dinner reservations advised) serves terrific fish meals. A couple of miles north around the next bay, **BEADNELL** also has a pub, as well as *Beach Court* (Ⓣ01665/720225, Ⓦwww.beachcourt.com), a distinctive guesthouse right next to the harbour, with glorious bay views, an oak-panelled drawing room and three lovely rooms with big bathrooms (❻ & ❼) – the most expensive of which is a "turret" suite with a crow's nest observatory.

Seahouses and the Farne Islands

From Beadnell, it's three miles north to the fishing port of **SEAHOUSES**, the only place on the local coast that could remotely be described as a resort. It's the embarkation point for boat trips out to the windswept **Farne Islands**, a rocky archipelago lying a few miles offshore. Owned by the National Trust and maintained as a nature reserve, the Farnes are the summer home of hundreds of thousands of migrating sea birds, notably puffins, guillemots, terns, eider ducks and kittiwakes, and home to the only grey seal colony on the English coastline. Weather permitting, several operators run daily **boat trips** (around 2–3hr; from £10) from Seahouses quayside, usually starting at around 10am. You can just wander down to the quayside and pick a departure, or contact either the **National Trust Shop**, 16 Main St (Ⓣ01665/721099), by the Seahouses traffic roundabout, or the **tourist office** (April–Oct daily 10am–5pm; Ⓣ01665/720884, Ⓦwww.seahouses.org), in the nearby main car park. During the bird breeding season (May–July) landings are restricted to morning trips to **Staple Island** and afternoons to **Inner Farne** – landing on either in the breeding season incurs a separate National Trust landing fee of £5.20. At all other times, bird-viewing trips normally land only on Inner Farne (NT fee £4.20), the largest of the Farne Islands. Most operators also offer "sailaround" cruises, which get close to the birds and seals without landing, or you can take a trip to **Longstone Island** (not a bird sanctuary, so no landing fee) whose single attraction is the lighthouse from where Grace Darling (see "Bamburgh" below) launched her daring rescue.

Bamburgh

Flanking a triangular green in the lee of its castle, three miles north of Seahouses, the tiny village of **BAMBURGH** is only a five-minute walk from two splendid sandy beaches, backed by rolling, tufted dunes. From the sands – in fact from everywhere – **Bamburgh Castle** (April–Oct daily 11am–5pm; £6.50; Ⓦwww.bamburghcastle.com) is a spectacular sight, its elongated battlements crowning a formidable basalt crag high above the beach. After a centuries-long decline – rotted by seaspray and buffeted by winter storms – the castle was bought by Lord Armstrong (of Rothbury's Cragside) in 1894, who demolished most of the structure to replace it with a hybrid castle-mansion. The focal point of the new building was the King's Hall, a teak-ceilinged affair of colossal dimensions, whose main redeeming feature is an exquisite collection of Fabergé glass animals.

A regular **bus** service links Alnwick and Berwick-upon-Tweed with Bamburgh, stopping on Front Street by the green. At the top of the village green, the *Victoria Hotel* (Ⓣ01668/214431, Ⓦwww.victoriahotel.net; ❼)

Heroine of the seas

Bamburgh is the burial place of the widely celebrated English heroine **Grace Darling**, who rests beneath a Gothic Revival memorial in the churchyard of thirteenth-century St Aidan's. In September, 1838, a gale dashed the steamship *Forfarshire* against the rocks of the Farne Islands. Nine passengers struggled onto a reef, where they were subsequently saved by Grace and her lighthouseman father, William, who left the safety of the Longstone lighthouse to row out to them. *The Times* trumpeted Grace's bravery, offers of marriage and requests for locks of her hair streamed into the Darlings' lighthouse home and for the rest of her brief life Grace was plagued by unwanted visitors – she died of tuberculosis aged 26 in 1842. The story is told on any Farne Islands boat trip from Seahouses, while a RNLI Grace Darling Museum opposite the church in Bamburgh (under renovation) goes into more detail.

operates a couple of relaxing bars and a more expensive brasserie (dinner only) with a good Modern British menu. *The Greenhouse*, a few doors down at 5 Front St (Ⓣ01668/214513, Ⓦwww.thegreenhouseguesthouse.co.uk; ④) also has rooms, or further down still there's the traditional *Lord Crewe Hotel*, Front St (Ⓣ01668/214243, Ⓦwww.lordcrewe.co.uk; ⑥; closed Jan), a comfortable old inn with oak beams, open fires, public bar and restaurant. Other moderate B&Bs are found on Lucker Road, beyond the top of the village green.

Holy Island

There's something rather menacing about the approach to **Holy Island**, past the barnacle-encrusted marker poles that line the causeway. The danger of drowning is real enough if you ignore the safe crossing times posted at the start of the three-mile trip across the tidal flats. (The island is cut off for about five hours every day, so consult the **tide timetables** at one of the region's tourist offices or in the local newspapers.) Small (just one and a half miles by one), sandy, flat and bare, it's easy to picture the furious Viking hordes sweeping across Holy Island, giving no quarter to the monks at this quiet outpost of early Christianity.

Once known as **Lindisfarne**, it was here that St Aidan of Iona founded a monastery at the invitation of King Oswald of Northumbria in 634. The monks quickly established a reputation for scholarship and artistry, the latter exemplified by the **Lindisfarne Gospels**, the apotheosis of Celtic religious art, now kept in the British Library. The monastery had sixteen bishops in all, the most celebrated being the reluctant **St Cuthbert**, who never settled here – within two years, he was back in his hermit's cell on the Farne Islands, where he died in 687. His colleagues rowed the body back to Lindisfarne, which became a place of pilgrimage until 875, when the monks abandoned the island in fear of marauding Vikings, taking Cuthbert's remains with them.

The **village** consists of a couple of streets radiating out from a small green and church cross; just off the green, the pinkish sandstone ruins of **Lindisfarne Priory** (April–Oct daily 9.30am–4/5pm; Nov–Jan Sat, Sun & Mon 10am–2pm; Feb & March daily 10am–4pm; £3.90; EH) are from the Benedictine foundation. The **museum** (same times as priory; entrance included in priory fee) features a collection of incised stones that constitute all that remains of the first monastery. Stuck on a small pyramid of rock half a mile away from the village, **Lindisfarne Castle** (April–Oct daily except Mon, hours vary according to tide but always include noon–3pm; £5.27; NT; Ⓣ01289/389244) was built in the middle of the sixteenth century to protect the island's harbour from the Scots. It was, however, merely a decaying shell when Edward Hudson, the founder of

▲ Lindisfarne Castle

Country Life magazine, stumbled across it in 1901. Hudson bought the castle and turned it into a holiday home to designs by Edwin Lutyens.

Practicalities

The #477 **bus** from **Berwick-upon-Tweed** to Holy Island is something of a law unto itself given the interfering tides, but basically service is daily in August and twice-weekly the rest of the year. Departure times (and sometimes days) vary with the tides; the journey takes thirty minutes. **Information** is available from Berwick-upon-Tweed tourist office, or consult the local community website, Ⓦwww.lindisfarne.org.uk. A straightforward **B&B** is the *Rose Villa* (Ⓣ01289/389268; Ⓔbarbarakyle2@aol.com; ❸), just by the green, or there are a couple of traditional **hotels**, the *Lindisfarne* (Ⓣ01289/389273; ❺; closed Jan) and the *Manor House* (Ⓣ01289/389207; includes dinner ❻; closed Jan), the latter backing on to the priory. Best pub on the island is the *Ship* on Marygate, down from the green (Ⓣ01289/389311; ❺; closed Nov to early Dec & Jan).

Berwick-upon-Tweed

Before the union of the English and Scottish crowns in 1603, **BERWICK-UPON-TWEED**, twelve miles north of Holy Island, was the quintessential frontier town, changing hands no fewer than fourteen times between 1174 and 1482, when the Scots finally ceded the stronghold to the English. Interminable cross-border warfare ruined Berwick's economy, turning the prosperous Scottish port of the thirteenth century into an impoverished English garrison town. By the late sixteenth century, Berwick's fortifications were in a dreadful state of repair and Elizabeth I, apprehensive of the resurgent alliance between France and Scotland, had the place rebuilt in line with the latest principles of military architecture. Berwick's ramparts – one and a half miles long and still in pristine condition – are no more than twenty feet high but incredibly thick. The ramparts are now the town's major attraction, and warrant a night's stay, especially as Berwick is a useful staging post between England and Scotland.

The Town

Berwick's **walls** – protected by ditches on three sides and the Tweed on the fourth – are strengthened by immense bastions, whose arrowhead-shape ensured that every part of the wall could be covered by fire. The easy mile circuit along the top of the walls and ramparts (about an hour) offers a succession of fine views out to sea, across the Tweed and over the orange-tiled rooftops of a town that's distinguished by its elegant **Georgian mansions**. These, dating from Berwick's resurgence as a seaport between 1750 and 1820, are the town's most attractive feature, with the tapering **Lions' House**, on Windmill Hill, and the daintily decorated facades of **Quay Walls**, beside the river, of particular note.

Within the ramparts, the Berwick skyline is punctured by the stumpy spire of the eighteenth-century **Town Hall** (April–Sept Mon–Fri tours at 10.30am & 2pm; £2) at the bottom of Marygate, right at the heart of the compact centre. This retains its original jailhouse on the upper floor, now housing the **Cell Block Museum**, entertaining tours of which dwell on tales of crime and punishment in Berwick. The town's finely proportioned **Barracks** (April–Sept Wed–Sun 10am–5pm; £3.40; EH), designed by Nicholas Hawksmoor (1717), were in use until 1964, when the King's Own Scottish Borderers regiment decamped. Inside the barracks, there are informative military museums, plus temporary exhibitions of contemporary art in the **Gymnasium Gallery** and the borough museum and art gallery sited in the "**Clock Block**".

Practicalities

From Berwick **train station** it's a 10min walk down Castlegate and Marygate to the town centre. Most regional **buses** stop closer in on Golden Square (where Castlegate meets Marygate), though some may also stop in front of the station. The **tourist office** at 106 Marygate (April–Sept Mon–Sat 10am–5/6pm, Sun 11am–3pm; Oct–March Mon–Sat 10am–noon & 1–4/5pm; Ⓣ01289/330733, Ⓦwww.exploreberwick.co.uk) can book you on to informative one-hour **walking tours** of town (Easter–Oct Mon–Fri, 3 daily; £4). For **bike rental**, contact Wilson Cycles, 17a Bridge St (Ⓣ01289/331476), who also have details of a scenic route to Holy Island (24 miles return).

Local **hotels** and **B&Bs** post pictures and adverts inside the tourist office, or head for Church Street and Ravensdowne (off Woolmarket, the continuation of Marygate), in **Tweedmouth**, just on the other side of the bridge (10min walk), or near the beach at **Spittal** (bus from Golden Square). A plethora of daytime **cafés** and **tearooms** include one on the ground floor of the historic Town Hall, though fine **restaurant** dining is a bit limited – the *Queen's Head* (see below) is the out-and-out winner.

Berwick Backpackers 56–58 Bridge St Ⓣ01289/331481, Ⓦwww.berwickbackpackers.co.uk. Not so much a backpackers' (though there's a small six-bed dorm, beds £14.95) as a self-styled "superior budget B&B". There's a fully equipped kitchen/lounge, plus Internet access; prices include continental breakfast. No credit cards. ❷

Coach House Crookham, 10 miles southwest of Berwick Ⓣ01890/820293, Ⓦwww.coachhousecrookham.com. Has a range of rooms in converted farm buildings sporting exposed beams. Guests are pampered with four-course dinners (£20). ❹

Clovelly House 58 West St Ⓣ01289/302337, Ⓦwww.clovelly53.freeserve.co.uk. A really nice B&B, centrally located on a steep cobbled street by the Arts Centre. Rooms are very smart with lots of little touches – fresh milk, DVD library, fruit and chocolates, posh toiletries – that elevate them out of the ordinary. No credit cards. ❸

No.1 Sallyport Bridge St Ⓣ01289/308827, Ⓦwww.sallyport.co.uk. Berwick's most luxurious B&B, with six sensational rooms in a seventeenth-century house next to the city walls (by the Bridge Street Bookshop). Two rooms and four suites are elegantly furnished, retro to contemporary, and breakfast is terrific. Reservations essential; minimum 2-night weekend stays. ❻, suites ❼

Pot-a-Doodle-Do Wigwam Village Borewell, Scremerston, 3 miles south of Berwick

Ⓣ01289/307107, Ⓦwww.northumbrianwigwams.com. Wooden wigwams sleeping four, with fridge, heating and light, provide a comfortable alternative to camping. In summer, tepees are available too. Closed Mon & Tues Nov–March, and all Jan. Tepees ❷, wigwams ❶

Queen's Head 6 Sandgate Ⓣ01289/307852, Ⓦwww.queensheadberwick.co.uk. Old Berwick inn that's gone for the gastropub look – rooms are good for the price, and it's a handy location, while the daily changing blackboard menu (mains £9–18, crab and seabass to Northumbrian lamb and venison) is the best in town. ❺

Eating and drinking

Amaryllis 7 West St Ⓣ01289/331 711. Contemporary, spacious brasserie with great dishes, like smoked lamb or pesto-stuffed chicken. Closed Sun and dinner Mon–Wed. Dinner reservations advised. Expensive.

Barrels Ale House 59–61 Bridge St Ⓣ01289/308013, Ⓦwww.thebarrelsalehouse.com. Chilled-out independent pub at the foot of the Berwick Bridge with an interesting programme of live music and DJs.

Foxton's 26 Hide Hill Ⓣ01289/303939. This amiable town-centre bar-brasserie serves a varied English and Mediterranean-style menu. Closed Sun. Moderate.

Arts centre

The Maltings Eastern Lane Ⓣ01289/330999, Ⓦwww.maltingsberwick.co.uk. Berwick's arts centre with a year-round programme of music, theatre, comedy, film and dance, and river views from its licensed café.

Travel details

Buses

For more information on all local and national bus services, contact Traveline Ⓣ0871/200 2233, Ⓦwww.traveline.org.uk.

Alnwick to: Bamburgh (Mon–Sat 5 daily; 1hr); Berwick-upon-Tweed (Mon–Sat 5 daily; 1hr).

Bamburgh to: Alnwick (Mon–Sat 5 daily; 1hr); Craster (Mon–Sat 5 daily; 30–40min); Seahouses (Mon–Sat 5 daily, 10min).

Barnard Castle to: Bishop Auckland (Mon–Sat 7 daily, Sun 4 daily; 50min); Darlington (hourly; 40min); Middleton-in-Teesdale (Mon–Sat hourly; Sun 4 daily; 35min); Raby Castle (9 daily; 15min)

Berwick-upon-Tweed to: Holy Island (Aug 2 daily, rest of the year 2 weekly; 35min); Newcastle (Mon–Sat 6 daily, Sun 3 daily; 2hr 15min); Wooler (Mon–Sat 10 daily; 55min).

Darlington to: Barnard Castle (hourly; 40min); Bishop Auckland (Mon–Sat every 30min; Sun hourly; 50min); Durham (every 30min; 1hr 10min); Middleton-in-Teesdale (Mon–Sat 9 daily, Sun 4 daily; 1hr 20min).

Durham to: Bishop Auckland (every 30min; 35min); Chester-le-Street (every 30min; 25min); Darlington (every 30min; 1hr 10 min); Newcastle (Mon–Sat every 30min; Sun 4–6 daily; 50min).

Hexham to: Allendale (Mon–Sat 6 daily; 25min); Allenheads (Mon–Sat 6 daily; 45min); Bellingham (Mon–Sat 8 daily; 45min).

Middlesbrough to: Newcastle (Mon–Sat every 30min; 1hr); Saltburn (Mon–Sat every 30min; 40min).

Newcastle to: Alnmouth (hourly; 1hr 40min); Alnwick (hourly; 1hr 20min–1 hr 50min); Bamburgh (4 daily; 2hr 30min); Beamish (daily every 30min; 1hr); Berwick-upon-Tweed (Mon–Sat 6 daily, Sun 5 daily; 2hr 30min); Carlisle (Mon–Sat hourly; Sun 4 daily; 2hr 10min); Durham (Mon–Sat every 30min; Sun 4–6 daily; 50min); Hexham (hourly; 50min); Middlesbrough (Mon–Sat every 30min; 1hr); Rothbury (Mon–Sat 5 daily; 1hr 20min); Seahouses (4 daily; 2hr 10min); Warkworth (hourly; 1hr 20min).

Wooler to: Alnwick (Mon–Sat 5 daily; 45min); Berwick-upon-Tweed (Mon–Sat 7 daily; 50min).

Trains

For information on all local and national rail services, contact National Rail Enquiries Ⓣ0845/748 4950, Ⓦwww.rail.co.uk.

Darlington to: Bishop Auckland (7 daily; 25min); Durham (every 30min; 20min); Newcastle (every 30min; 35min).

Durham to: Darlington (every 30min; 20min); London (hourly; 3hr); Newcastle (every 30min; 15min); York (every 30min; 50min).

Hexham to: Carlisle (hourly; 50min); Haltwhistle (hourly; 20min); Newcastle (hourly; 40min).

Middlesbrough to: Durham (hourly; 50min); Newcastle (hourly; 1hr 30min); Whitby (5 daily; 1hr 30min).

Newcastle to: Alnmouth (9 daily; 30min); Berwick-upon-Tweed (hourly; 45min); Carlisle (hourly; 1hr 30min); Corbridge (hourly; 35min); Darlington (every 30min; 35min); Durham (every 30min; 15min); Hexham (hourly; 40min); London (hourly; 2hr 45min–3hr 30min); York (hourly; 1hr).

Wales

Wales

South Wales

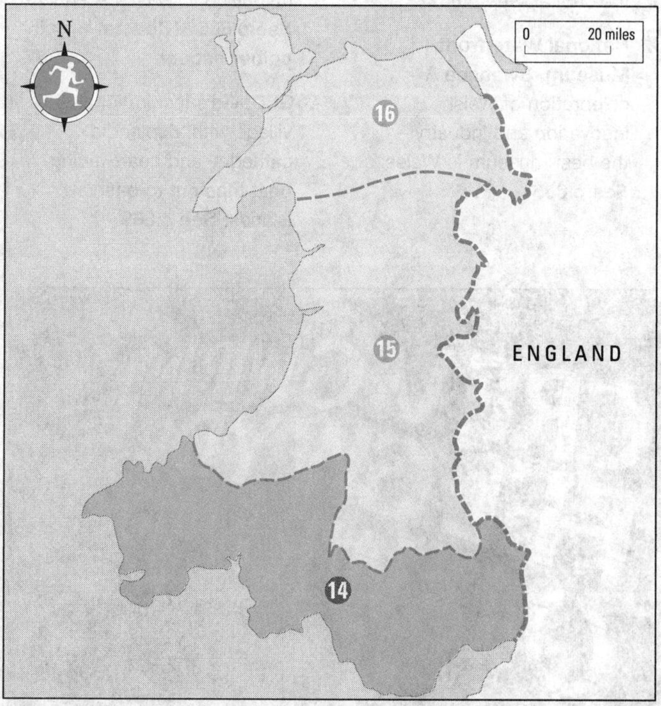

CHAPTER 14

Highlights

* **Blaenafon** Fascinating ironworks town plus deep-mine museum. See p.636

* **Wales Millennium Centre, Cardiff Bay** A symphony of opposites – industry and art, grand and intimate – the WMC is a bold and brilliant asset to the capital. See p.647

* **National Waterfront Museum, Swansea** A celebration of Welsh innovation and industry – the best museum in Wales. See p.655

* **Carreg Cennen Castle** A fantasy fortress, with sublime views and exploration. See p.660

* **The Pembrokeshire Coast Path** A narrow ribbon of mainly clifftop footpath that winds its way through some magnificent coastal scenery. See p.665 & Coastal Britain colour section

* **St David's** Inspirational village with a splendid cathedral and heart-racing boat trips out to offshore islands. See p.669

▲ Wales Millennium Centre

14

South Wales

The most heavily populated, and by far the most anglicized, part of Wales is the **south**. This is a region of distinct character, whether in the resurgent seaport cities of Cardiff and Swansea, the mining-scarred Valleys or the beauty of the Glamorgan, Carmarthenshire and Pembrokeshire coasts. Monmouthshire, the easternmost county in Wales, abuts the English border and contains the full span of South Welsh life, from the bucolic charms of the **River Wye** and **Tintern Abbey** to **Newport**, Wales's third largest conurbation, near the remains of an extensive Roman settlement at **Caerleon**. West and north are the world-famous **Valleys**. Although all but one of the coal mines have closed, the area is still one of tight-knit towns, with a rich working-class heritage that displays itself in some excellent museums and colliery tours, such as **Big Pit** at Blaenafon and the **Rhondda Heritage Park** in Trehafod. The Valleys course down to the great ports of the coast, which once shipped Wales's products all over the world. The greatest of them all was **Cardiff**, now Wales's upbeat capital and an essential stop. Further west is Wales's second city, **Swansea** – rougher, tougher and less anglicized than the capital, it sits on an impressive arc of coast that shelves round to the delightful **Gower Peninsula**, replete with grand beaches, rocky headlands, bracken heaths and ruined castles.

Carmarthenshire, often missed out, is well worth visiting: of all the routes that spoke out of the county town of Carmarthen, the most glorious is the winding road to **Llandeilo** along the **Tywi Valley**, past ruined hilltop forts and two of the country's finest gardens. Immediately west sits Wales's most impressively sited castle at **Carreg Cennen**, high up on a dizzy rock-plug on the edge of the Black Mountain. The wide sands fringing Carmarthen Bay stretch towards the popular seaside resort of **Tenby**, a major stop on the 186-mile **Pembrokeshire Coast Path**. The rutted coastline of **St Bride's Bay** is the most glorious part of the coastal walk, which leads north to brush past the impeccable mini-city of **St David's**, whose exquisite cathedral shelters in its own protective hollow. Nearby are plenty of opportunities for spectacular coast and hill walks, dinghy crossings to local islands, wildlife watching and numerous other outdoor activities.

The main road route into South Wales from England is the M4 motorway, which divides at Junction 21 near Bristol: the old **Severn Bridge** carries the M48 loop, while the M4 itself forms the Second (or **New**) **Severn Crossing** a little downstream. Both impose a **toll** on westbound traffic, payable by cash or cheque only (Ⓦwww.severnbridge.co.uk): a hefty £5.10 for a car, free for a motorbike. Cyclists and pedestrians can follow a dedicated path across the old Severn Bridge for free. The frequent **trains** along the London–Bristol–Cardiff route duck under the water courtesy of the Severn Rail Tunnel.

The Wye Valley

The **Wye Valley** (Ⓦ www.visitwyevalley.com), along with the rest of Monmouthshire, was finally recognized as part of Wales in the local government reorganization of 1974. Before then, the county was officially included as part of neither England nor Wales, so that maps were frequently headlined "Wales and Monmouthshire". Most of the rest of Monmouthshire is firmly and redoubtably Welsh, but the woodlands and hills by the meandering River Wye have more in common with the landscape over the border. The two main centres are **Chepstow**, with its massive castle, and the spruce, old-fashioned town of **Monmouth**, sixteen miles upstream. Six miles north of Chepstow lie the atmospheric ruins of the Cistercian **Tintern Abbey**.

Chepstow and around

Of all the places that call themselves "the gateway to Wales", **CHEPSTOW** (Cas-Gwent) has probably the greatest claim, situated on the western bank of the River Wye. Chepstow is a sturdy place, robbed of the immediate charm of many other Welsh market towns by soulless modern developments. Nonetheless, there's an identifiably medieval street-plan hemmed in by the thirteenth-century **Port Wall**, which encases a tight loop of the River Wye and the strategically sited **Chepstow Castle** (April, May & Oct daily 9.30am–5pm; June–Sept daily 9.30am–6pm; Nov–March Mon–Sat 9.30am–4pm, Sun 11am–4pm; £3.50;

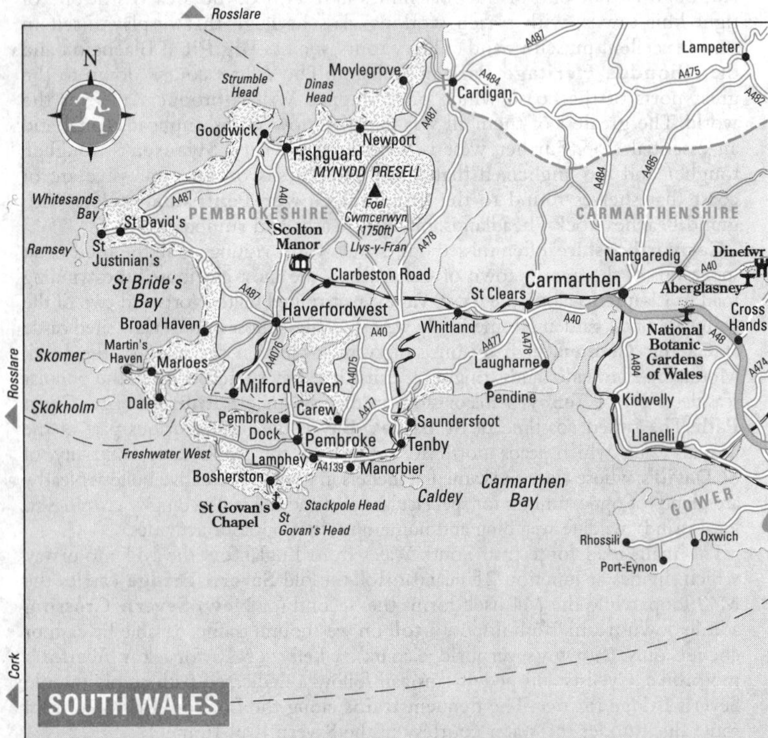

CADW). Guarding one of the most important routes into Wales, Chepstow was the first stone castle to be built in Britain. The Lower Ward was the largest of the three enclosures and dates mainly from the thirteenth century. Here you'll find the **Great Hall**, home to a comprehensive exhibition on the castle's history. Twelfth-century defences separate the Lower Ward from the Middle Ward, which is dominated by the still-imposing ruins of the **Great Tower**, built in 1067. Beyond this is the far narrower Upper Ward, which leads up to the Barbican **watchtower** from where there are superb views looking down the cliff to the river estuary.

Opposite is the **Chepstow Museum** (July–Sept Mon–Sat 10.30am–5.30pm, Sun 2–5pm; Oct–June Mon–Sat 11am–1pm & 2–5pm, Sun 2–5pm; free) containing nostalgic photographs and paintings of the trades supported in the past by the River Wye, and recording Chepstow's brief life in the early twentieth century as a shipbuilding centre.

A mile north of town, **Chepstow Racecourse** (Ⓣ01291/622260, Ⓦwww.chepstow-racecourse.co.uk) is one of the country's premier racing venues, with regular, all-year-round meets. Entrance is off the A466.

Practicalities

Chepstow's **train station** is five minutes' walk to the south of the High Street; its **bus station** is on Thomas Street on the other side of the western Town Gate. The **tourist office** is located in the castle car park, off Bridge Street (daily: Nov–Easter 10am–3.30pm; Easter–Oct 10am–5.30pm;

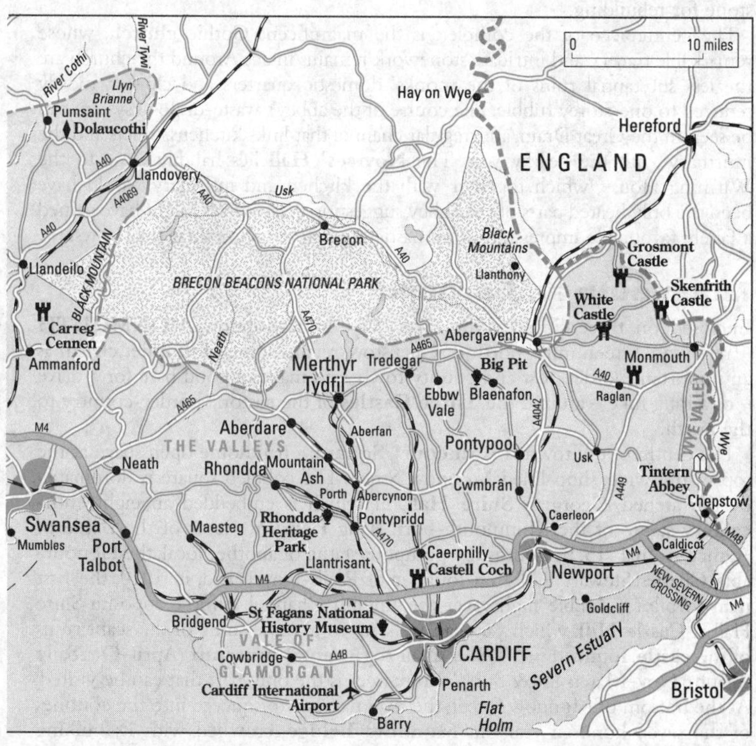

Ⓣ01291/623772, Ⓔchepstow.tic@monmouthshire.gov.uk). There's decent B&B **accommodation** at the *First Hurdle Guesthouse*, 9 Upper Church St (Ⓣ01291/622189; ❸), where the en-suite rooms have firm beds and attractive decor, and, a mile east of town over the Wye, at the wonderful *Upper Sedbury House*, Sedbury Lane (Ⓣ01291/627173, Ⓦwww.smoothhound.co.uk/hotels /uppersed; ❷). *The George Hotel* (Ⓣ01291/625363; ❺) is a grand old coaching inn next to the medieval gate on Moor Street.

For **food and drink**, try the moderately priced *Wye Knot*, on The Back (Ⓣ01291/622929); nearby on the same street is the *Boat Inn*, a waterside tavern with a good veggie-friendly menu. *The Five Alls*, at the bottom of High Street, is an earthy local pub, with a good selection of ales and regular live music.

Tintern Abbey

Six miles north of Chepstow, along one of the River Wye's most spectacular stretches, **Tintern Abbey** (June–Sept daily 9.30am–6pm; April, May & Oct daily 9.30am–5pm; Nov–March Mon–Sat 9.30am–4pm, Sun 11am–4pm; £3.50; CADW) has inspired writers and painters for over two hundred years – Wordsworth and Turner among them. Such is the place's popularity, however, that it's advisable to go out of season or at either end of the day when the hordes have thinned out. The abbey was founded in 1131 by Cistercian monks from Normandy, though most of the remaining buildings date from the massive rebuilding and expansion plan in the fourteenth century, when Tintern was at its mightiest. Its survival after the depredations of the Dissolution is largely thanks to its remoteness, as there were no nearby villages ready to use the abbey stone for rebuilding.

The centrepiece of the complex is the magnificent Gothic **church**, whose remarkable tracery and intricate stonework remains intact. Around the church are the less substantial ruins of the monks' domestic quarters and cloister, mostly reduced to one-storey rubble. The course of the abbey's waste-disposal system can be seen in the Great Drain, an irregular channel that links kitchens, toilets and the infirmary with the nearby Wye. The **Novices' Hall** lies handily close to the Warming House, which together with the kitchen and infirmary would have been the only heated parts of the abbey, suggesting that novices might have gained a falsely favourable impression of monastic life before taking their final vows.

Monmouth and around

Enclosed on three sides by the rivers Wye and Monnow, **MONMOUTH** (Trefynwy), fifteen miles north of Chepstow, retains some of its quiet charm as an important border post and county town, and makes a good base for a drive – or a long hike – around the **Three Castles** of the pastoral border-country to the north.

The centre of the town is **Agincourt Square**, a handsome open space at the top of the wide, shop-lined Monnow Street. The cobbled square is dominated by the arched, Georgian **Shire Hall**, in which is embedded an eighteenth-century statue of the Monmouth-born King Henry V, victor of the Battle of Agincourt in 1415. In front is the pompous statue of another local, the Honourable Charles Stewart Rolls, co-founder of Rolls-Royce and, in 1910, the first man to pilot a double flight over the English Channel. Almost opposite Shire Hall is **Castle Hill**, which you can walk up to glimpse some of the scant ruins of the **castle**, founded in 1068. A small **regimental museum** (April–Oct daily 2–5pm; Nov–March Sat & Sun 2–4pm; free) is the only part that can be visited. At the bottom of Monnow Street, the road narrows to squeeze into the confines of the seven-hundred-year-old **Monnow Bridge**, crowned with its hulking

Working the black seam

The land beneath the inhospitable South Wales Valleys had some of the most abundant and accessible natural seams of **coal and iron ore** to be found, readily milked in the boom years of the nineteenth and early twentieth centuries. Wealthy, predominantly English capitalists came to Wales and ruthlessly stripped the land of its natural assets, while simultaneously exploiting those who risked life and limb underground. The mine owners were in a formidably strong position as thousands flocked to the Valleys in search of work and some sort of sustainable life. By the turn of the twentieth century, the Valleys became packed with pits, chapels and immigrant workers from Ireland, Scotland, Italy and all over Wales.

In 1920, there were 256,000 men working in the 620 mines of the South Wales coalfields, providing one-third of the world's coal. Vast Miners' Institutes jostled for position with the Nonconformist chapels, whose muscular brand of Christianity was matched by the zeal of the region's politics – trade-union-led and avowedly left-wing. Great socialist orators rose to national prominence, cementing the Valleys' reputation as a world apart from the rest of Britain, let alone Wales. Even Britain's pioneering National Health Service, founded by a radical Labour government in the years following World War II, was based on a Valleys' community scheme devised by locally born politician Aneurin Bevan. Over half of the original pits closed in the harsh economic climate of the 1930s, as coal seams became exhausted and the political climate changed. In the 1980s, further closures threatened to bring the number of men employed in the South Wales coalfields down to four figures, and the miners went on strike from 1984–85. Today all of the deep pits – bar one reprieved and taken over in a workers' buyout in 1994 – have closed.

iron-smelting – were abundant locally, and the Blaenafon works was one of the largest in Britain until it closed in 1900. The line of Georgian blast furnaces, the water-balance lift and the **museum** in the workers' cottages offer a thorough picture of both the process and the lifestyle that went with it. The ironworks also contains the town's **tourist office** (same hours and contacts).

At the evocative **Big Pit National Mining Museum** (mid-Feb to Nov daily 9.30am–5pm; last underground tour 3.30pm; free), a mile west of the town and reached by a half-hourly shuttle bus from Blaenafon, you're kitted out with lamp, helmet and very heavy battery pack and lowered three hundred feet into the labyrinth of shafts and coal faces for a guided tour. The guides – most of whom are ex-miners – lead you through explanations and examples of the different types of coal mining, while constant streams of rust-coloured water flow by. The dank and chilly atmosphere must have terrified the small children who were once paid twopence – of which one penny was taken out for the cost of their candles – for a six-day week pulling the coal wagons along the tracks. Back on the surface, the old pithead baths, smithy, miners' canteen and winding engine house have all been preserved and filled with some fascinating displays about the local mining industry.

The Taff and Cynon valleys

The River Taff flows out into the Bristol Channel at Cardiff, after passing through a condensed couple of dozen miles of industry and population. The first town in the Taff vale is **Pontypridd**, one of the most cheerful in the Valleys, and probably the best base. Continuing north, the river splits again at **Abercynon**, where the River Cynon flows in from **Aberdare**, site of Wales's only remaining deep mine. Just outside Abercynon is the enjoyable, sixteenth-century **Llancaiach Fawr** manor house. To the north, the Taff is packed into one of the tightest of all the Valleys, passing Aberfan five miles short of the imposing valley-head town of **Merthyr Tydfil**.

Pontypridd

PONTYPRIDD, twelve miles north of Cardiff, is built up around its quirky arched **bridge** that was once the largest single-span stone bridge in Europe, built in 1775 by local amateur stonemason William Edwards. Across the river is **Ynysangharad Park**, where Sir W. Goscombe John's cloying statue honours Pontypridd weaver Evan James, who composed the stirringly nationalistic song *Hen Wlad fy Nhadau* (*Land of My Fathers*), that became the Welsh national anthem. By the bridge at the end of Taff Street, a lovingly restored church houses the fantastic **Pontypridd Museum** (Mon–Sat 10am–5pm; closed bank holidays; free), a treasure-trove of photographs, videos, models and exhibits that succeeds in painting a warm picture of the town and its outlying valleys, as well as paying homage to the town's famous sons, singer Tom Jones and opera star and actor Sir Geraint Evans.

The **tourist office** (Mon–Sat 10am–5pm; ⓣ01443/490748) is in the museum, on Bridge Street. **Accommodation** is rather scarce: the central and bustling *Market Tavern*, on Market Street (ⓣ01443/485331; ❷) isn't bad. Better bets are a few miles out, notably the well-kept and friendly *Fairmead* guesthouse (ⓣ01443/411174; ❹), almost opposite Llancaiach Fawr (see below), and the very grand *Llechwen Hall* (ⓣ01443/742050, ⓦwww.llechwen.com; ❹), signposted off the A470 a couple of miles north of Pontypridd.

Llancaiach Fawr and the Welsh International Climbing Centre

Five miles north of Pontypridd, the river divides at **Abercynon**, a stark, typical valley town of punishingly steep streets lined with terraced houses that fade out into a coniferous hillside. Two miles east, just north of the village of Nelson, is the sixteenth-century **Llancaiach Fawr** (March–Oct daily 10am–5pm; Nov–Feb closed Mon; £5.50; ⓣ01443/412248), a Tudor house, built around 1530, that has been transformed into a living history museum set in 1645, the time of the Civil War, with all of the guides dressed as house servants, speaking the language of seventeenth-century Britain. Although potentially tacky, it is quite deftly done, with well-researched period authenticity and numerous

Aberfan

North of Abercynon, the Taff Valley contains one sight that's hard to forget. Two neat lines of distant arches mark the graves of 144 people killed in October 1966 by an unsecured slag heap collapsing on Pantglas primary school in the village of **Aberfan**. Thousands of people still make the pilgrimage to the village graveyard, to stand silent and bemused by the enormity of the disaster. Among the dead were 116 children, who died huddled in panic at the beginning of their school day. A humbling and beautiful valediction can be seen on one of the gravestones, that of a 10-year-old boy, who, it simply records, "loved light, freedom and animals". Official enquiries all told the sorry tale that this disaster was almost inevitable, given the cavalier approach to safety so often displayed by the coal bosses. Gwynfor Evans, then newly elected as the first Plaid Cymru (Welsh Nationalist) MP in Westminster, spoke with well-founded bitterness when he said: "Let us suppose that such a monstrous mountain had been built above Hampstead or Eton, where the children of the men of power and wealth are at school...". But that, of course, would never have happened.

fascinating anecdotes from the staff; visitors are even encouraged to try on the master of the household's armour. Regular **buses** from Pontypridd and Cardiff pass the entrance.

A couple of miles north of Llancaiach Fawr, just beyond the village of **Trelewis**, the old Taff Merthyr colliery has been stunningly transformed into the **Welsh International Climbing Centre** (Mon–Fri 10am–10pm, Sat & Sun 10am–7.30pm; ⓣ01443/710749, ⓦwww.e2-adventures.com). As well as vast climbing walls (£5–7), it offers a wide range of adventure options, including potholing and caving; instruction is available. There are also exercise rooms, a sauna, a restaurant and bar open at weekends and evenings, and even B&B (£21.75) in small, clean dorms. Hourly (Mon–Sat) bus #22 from Pontypridd and Nelson will drop you on the doorstep.

Aberdare

Eight miles northwest of Abercynon, towards the top of the Cynon Valley, is the spacious town of **ABERDARE** (Aberdâr), home to one of the Valleys' best museums, the **Cynon Valley Museum & Gallery** (Mon–Sat 9am–4.30pm; free), in an old tram depot next to the Tesco superstore. Exhibits portray the social history of the valley, from the appalling conditions of the mid-nineteenth century, when nearly half of all children born here died by the age of 5, to stirring memories of the 1926 General Strike and the 1984–85 Miners' Strike. Alongside are some fun videos and exhibits on Victorian lantern slides, teenage life through the ages, the miners' jazz bands and Aberdare's role as a prominent centre of early Welsh-language publishing.

Merthyr Tydfil

Downtown **MERTHYR TYDFIL** (or Tudful), ten miles north of Pontypridd, is a robust place whose main glory is its location at the top of the Taff Valley, on the cusp of the industrial coal country to the south and the grand, windy heights of the Brecon Beacons to the north. In the eighteenth century it became the largest iron-producing town in the world, as well as by far the most populous town in Wales, with four massive ironworks exploiting the local abundance of the key ingredients. It became a hotbed for industrial disputes, resulting in occasional riots and eventually the election of Britain's first socialist MP, Keir Hardie, in 1900.

Half a mile northwest of the town centre, just off the A4102 (Bethesda Street), is **Chapel Row**, a line of skilled ironworkers' cottages built in the 1820s, one of which holds composer **Joseph Parry's Birthplace** (April–Sept Thurs–Sun 2–5pm; free). Parry wrote the national favourite, *Myfanwy*, which is now piped into the rooms, some of which are given over to a display on his life and music.

Back across the other side of the river, just beyond the Brecon Road, in absolute contrast to Parry's humble and cramped birthplace, **Cyfartha Castle** (April–Sept daily 10am–5.30pm; Oct–March Tues–Fri 10am–4pm, Sat & Sun noon–4pm; free) was built in 1825 as an ostentatious mock-Gothic castle for William Crawshay II, boss of the town's original ironworks. The castle is set within vast, attractive parkland and contains, in its old wine cellars, an enjoyable and gory walk through the tumultuous history of Merthyr. Upstairs, the castle's grand main rooms house an **art gallery** with an impressive collection of Welsh pieces, including works by Augustus John, Cedric Morris, Vanessa Bell, Jack Yeats and Kyffin Williams.

The **train station** is a minute's walk from the High Street. North from here is Glebeland Street, with the **bus station** and, at no. 14a, the **tourist office** (daily 9.30am–4pm; Ⓣ01685/379884, Ⓔtic@merthyr.gov.uk). **Accommodation** is varied, ranging from the plush *Tregenna Hotel* in Park Terrace, next to Penydarren Park (Ⓣ01685/723627, Ⓦwww.tregennahotel.co.uk; ④), to the less fussy *Chaplin's*, 30–31 High St (Ⓣ01685/387272, Ⓦwww.chaplinshotel.co.uk; ③), and, cheapest of all, the *Penylan* guesthouse, 12 Courtland Terrace (Ⓣ01685/723179; ①). There's a **campsite** four miles north of town in the beautiful surroundings of Grawen Farm, Cwm Taf (Ⓣ01685/723740).

The Rhondda

Pointing northwest from Pontypridd, the **Rhondda Fawr** – sixteen miles long and never as much as a mile wide – is undoubtedly the most famous of all the Welsh Valleys, as well as being the heart of the massive South Wales coal industry. For many it immediately conjures up Richard Llewellyn's 1939 book – and subsequent Oscar-winning weepie – *How Green Was My Valley*, although this was, strictly speaking, based on the author's early life in nearby Gilfach Goch, outside the valley. Between 1841 and 1924 the Rhondda's population grew from less than a thousand to 167,000, squeezed into ranks of houses grouped around sixty or so pitheads. The Rhondda, more than any other of the Valleys, became a self-reliant, hard-living, chapel-going, poor and terrifically spirited breeding-ground for radical religion and firebrand politics. For decades, the Communist Party ran the town of Maerdy (nicknamed "Little Moscow" by Fleet Street in the 1930s). The last pit in the Rhondda closed in 1990, but what was left behind was not some dispiriting ragbag of depressing towns, but a range of new attractions, cleaned-up hillsides and some of the friendliest pubs and communities to be found anywhere in Britain.

The **Rhondda Heritage Park** (April–Sept daily 10am–6pm, last tour 4pm; Oct–March closed Mon; £5.60) at **TREHAFOD** is the best attraction. You can explore the engine-winding houses, lamp room and fan house, and take a simulated "trip underground", with stunning visuals and sound effects, re-creating 1950s' life through the eyes of colliers. Although it's all looking a bit past its best these days, it's a worthwhile trip.

A **train** line from Cardiff, punctuated with stops every mile or so, runs the entire length of the Rhondda, stopping at Trehafod, a few minutes' walk from the Heritage Park. **Buses** also cover the route, continuing up into the mountains and the Brecon Beacons. **Accommodation** in the twin valleys is sparse, but decent places include the business-oriented *Heritage Park Hotel*,

Male voice choirs

Fiercely protective of its reputation as a land of song, Wales demonstrates its fine voice most affectingly in its ranks of **male voice choirs**. Although found all over the country, it is in the southern, industrial heartland that they are loudest and strongest. Their roots lie in the Nonconformist religious traditions of the seventeenth and eighteenth centuries, when Methodism in particular swept the country, and singing was a free and potent way of cherishing the frequently persecuted faith. Classic hymns like *Cwm Rhondda* and the Welsh national anthem, *Hen Wlad Fy Nhadau* (*Land of My Fathers*), are synonymous with the choirs. Each Valleys town still has its own, often depleted choir, most of whom happily accept visitors to sit in on rehearsals. Ask at the local tourist office or library, and take the chance to hear one of the world's most distinctive choral traditions in full, roof-raising splendour.

▲Male voice choir

beside the Rhondda Heritage Park at Trehafod (Ⓣ01443/687057, Ⓦwww.heritageparkhotel.co.uk; ⑥), which has its own pool, and *The Bertie* bar and B&B (Ⓣ01443/688204, Ⓦwww.thebertie.co.uk; ③) at 1–3 Phillips Terrace, not far away. Nearer the top end of the Rhondda Fawr is the reasonable *Baglan Hotel* (Ⓣ01443/776111; ②) on the main road in Treherbert.

Cardiff and around

Official capital of Wales since only 1955 (hence the ubiquitous "Europe's Youngest Capital" slogan), buoyant **CARDIFF** (Caerdydd) has swiftly grown into its new status. A number of massive developments, not least the shiny Welsh National Assembly and Millennium Centre for the arts on the rejuvenated Cardiff Bay waterfront, and a fabulous city-centre sports stadium, give the city the feel of an international capital, if not always with a very Welsh flavour.

The second marquis of Bute built Cardiff's first dock in 1839, opening others in swift succession. The Butes, who owned massive swathes of the rapidly industrializing South Wales Valleys, insisted that all coal and iron exports use the family docks in Cardiff, and it became one of the busiest ports in the world. The twentieth century saw varying fortunes: the dock trade slumped in the 1930s and the city suffered heavy bombing in World War II, but with the creation of Cardiff as capital in 1955, optimism and confidence in the city blossomed. Many government and media institutions have moved here from London, and the development of the dock areas around the new Assembly building in Cardiff Bay has given a largely positive boost to the cityscape.

Arrival and information

The main **bus station** is off Wood Street, on the southwestern side of the city centre. Across the forecourt is Cardiff Central **train station**, for all intercity

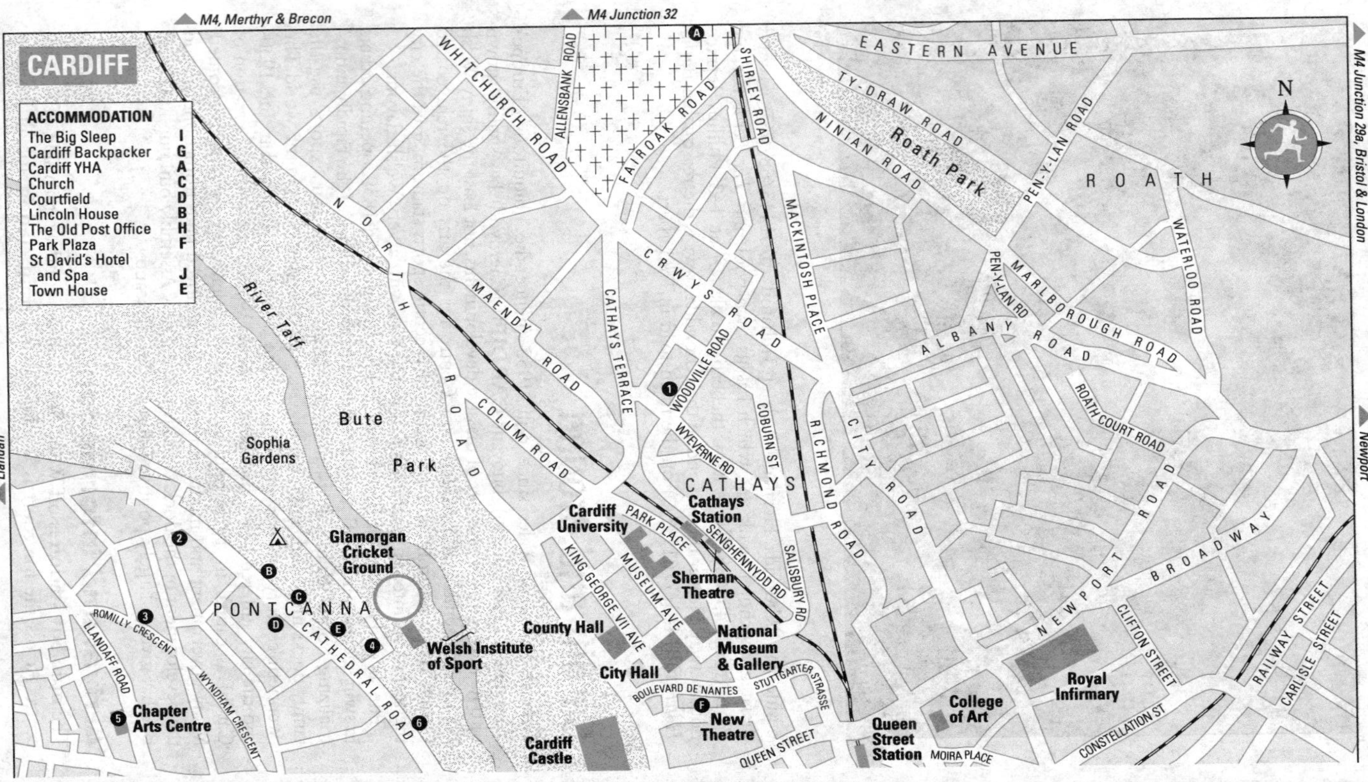
CARDIFF
ACCOMMODATION
The Big Sleep I
Cardiff Backpacker G
Cardiff YHA A
Church C
Courtfield D
Lincoln House B
The Old Post Office H
Park Plaza F
St David's Hotel and Spa J
Town House E
M4, Merthyr & Brecon
M4 Junction 32
M4 Junction 29a, Bristol & London
Newport
Llandaff
N
EASTERN AVENUE
TY-DRAW ROAD
NINIAN ROAD
Roath Park
PEN-Y-LAN ROAD
ROATH
WATERLOO ROAD
MARLBOROUGH ROAD
PEN-Y-LAN RD
ALBANY ROAD
ROATH COURT ROAD
NEWPORT ROAD
BROADWAY
RAILWAY STREET
CARLISLE STREET
CLIFTON STREET
CONSTELLATION ST
Royal Infirmary
College of Art
MOIRA PLACE
Queen Street Station
QUEEN STREET
CITY ROAD
RICHMOND ROAD
MACKINTOSH PLACE
SHIRLEY ROAD
WHITCHURCH ROAD
ALLENSBANK ROAD
FAIROAK ROAD
CRWYS ROAD
CATHAYS TERRACE
WOODVILLE ROAD
COBURN ST
WYEVERNE RD
CATHAYS
Cathays Station
SALISBURY RD
SENGHENNYDD RD
Cardiff University
PARK PLACE
Sherman Theatre
MUSEUM AVE
KING GEORGE VII AVE
National Museum & Gallery
STUTTGARTER STRASSE
County Hall
City Hall
BOULEVARD DE NANTES
New Theatre
Cardiff Castle
NORTH ROAD
MAENDY ROAD
COLUM ROAD
River Taff
Bute Park
Sophia Gardens
Glamorgan Cricket Ground
Welsh Institute of Sport
PONTCANNA
CATHEDRAL ROAD
ROMILLY CRESCENT
LLANDAFF ROAD
WYNDHAM CRESCENT
Chapter Arts Centre

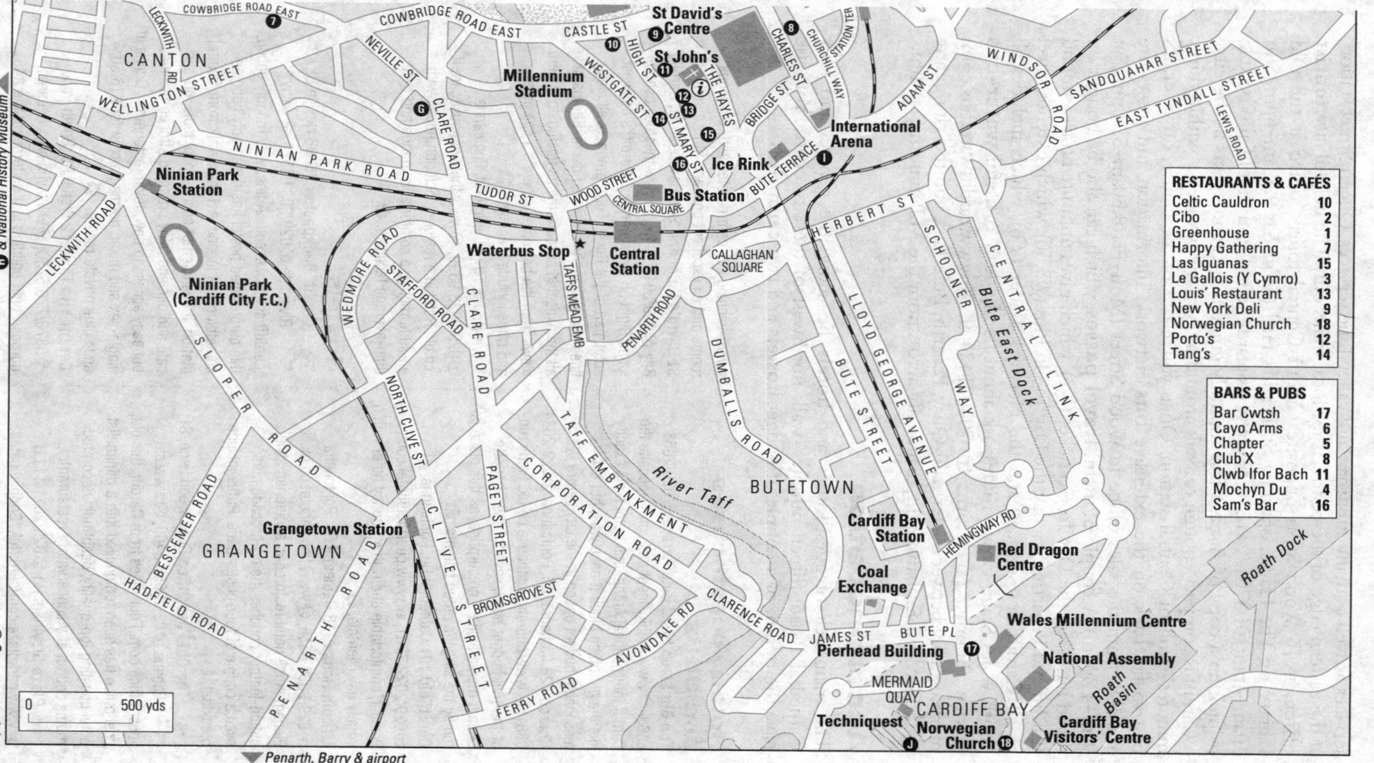
RESTAURANTS & CAFÉS
Celtic Cauldron 10
Cibo 2
Greenhouse 1
Happy Gathering 7
Las Iguanas 15
Le Gallois (Y Cymro) 3
Louis' Restaurant 13
New York Deli 9
Norwegian Church 18
Porto's 12
Tang's 14
BARS & PUBS
Bar Cwtsh 17
Cayo Arms 6
Chapter 5
Club X 8
Clwb Ifor Bach 11
Mochyn Du 4
Sam's Bar 16
CANTON
GRANGETOWN
BUTETOWN
CARDIFF BAY
St David's Centre
St John's
Millennium Stadium
International Arena
Ice Rink
Bus Station
Central Station
Waterbus Stop
Ninian Park Station
Ninian Park (Cardiff City F.C.)
Grangetown Station
Cardiff Bay Station
Red Dragon Centre
Coal Exchange
Wales Millennium Centre
National Assembly
Pierhead Building
Techniquest
Norwegian Church
Cardiff Bay Visitors' Centre
Mermaid Quay
Bute East Dock
Roath Dock
Roath Basin
River Taff
Callaghan Square
Central Square
Cowbridge Road East
Leckwith Rd
Wellington Street
Leckwith Road
Neville St
Clare Road
Ninian Park Road
Tudor St
Wood Street
Westgate St
Castle St
High St
St Mary St
The Hayes
Charles St
Bridge St
Churchill Way
Station Ter
Bute Terrace
Adam St
Windsor Road
Sandquahar Street
East Tyndall Street
Lewis Road
Herbert St
Schooner Way
Central Link
Lloyd George Avenue
Bute Street
Dumballs Road
Penarth Road
Taffs Mead Emb
Wedmore Road
Stafford Road
North Clive St
Clive Street
Paget Street
Bromsgrove St
Taff Embankment
Corporation Road
Clarence Road
Avondale Rd
Ferry Road
Hemingway Rd
James St
Bute Pl
Sloper Road
Bessemer Road
Hadfield Road
Penarth Road
H & National History Museum
Penarth, Barry & airport
0 500 yds
© Crown copyright

services as well as many suburban and Valley Line services. Queen Street station, at the eastern edge of the centre, is for local trains only. The helpful city **tourist office**, at 16 Wood St, is opposite Cardiff Central tourist office at the Old Library on The Hayes, opposite St. David's Hall (Mon–Sat 9.30am–6pm, Sun 10am–4pm; ⓣ08701/211258, ⓦwww.visitcardiff.com). You should also be able to pick up a copy of *Buzz*, a free monthly guide to arts and events in the city.

Cardiff is compact enough to walk around, as even the bay area is within thirty minutes' stroll of Central station. Once you're out of the centre, however, it's best to fall back on the extensive **bus** network. Information and passes are available from the sales office in Wood Street (Mon–Fri 8.30am–5.30pm, Sat 9am–4.30pm). A couple of useful **travel passes**, which can also be bought on board buses, are the Day To Go ticket (£3), which gives unlimited travel around Cardiff and Penarth for a day, the Day To Go Plus (£3.50), which extends travel to all Cardiff bus services; and the Network Rider (£6), which includes all South Wales Stage Coach routes; ask about family deals. A useful **water-bus** service (hourly; £5 return; ⓣ07940/142409, ⓦwww.cardiffwaterbus.com) operates daily between Mermaid Quay, Penarth, Bute Park and the city centre at Taff's Mead Embankment, diagonally across from the Millennium Stadium.

Accommodation

The main belt of guesthouses and **hotels** lies along the genteel and leafy Cathedral Road, fifteen minutes' walk northwest of the city centre. You also have the option of a couple of budget **hostels** and two **campsites**.

Hotels, guesthouses and B&Bs

The Big Sleep Hotel Bute Terrace ⓣ029/2063 6363, ⓦwww.thebigsleephotel.com. Opposite the Cardiff International Arena, this hotel feels exactly like the old office block it once was, but is a reasonable budget option in the city centre. ④

Church 126 Cathedral Rd, Pontcanna ⓣ029/2034 0881, ⓦwww.churchguesthouse.co.uk. Fairly run-of-the-mill budget hotel, save for the Charlotte Church memorabilia – no surprise, as this place is run by the singer's proud parents. ③

Courtfield 101 Cathedral Rd, Pontcanna ⓣ029/2022 7701, ⓦwww.courtfieldhotel.com. Popular, comfortable and rather flouncy hotel with a largely gay clientele. ③

Lincoln House 118 Cathedral Rd, Pontcanna ⓣ029/2039 5558, ⓦwww.lincolnhotel.co.uk. Elegant small hotel restored in a Victorian style: button-leather couches, heavy brocade and even a couple of four-poster beds. Rates include breakfast. ⑤

The Old Post Office Greenwood Lane, St Fagans ⓣ029/2056 5400, ⓦwww.old-post-office.com. Four miles from Cardiff, this old post office has been remodelled into a minimalist hotel boasting top-quality, beautifully decorated rooms and an airy conservatory restaurant. ⑤

Park Plaza Greyfriars Rd ⓣ029/2011 1111, ⓦwww.parkplaza.com/cardiffuk. Sophisticated, award-winning city centre hotel, with gorgeous rooms and an excellent pool and fitness suite. ⑦

St David's Hotel and Spa Havannah St, Cardiff Bay ⓣ029/2045 4045, ⓦwww.thestdavidshotel.com. Right on the waterfront, Cardiff's flashiest hotel, part of the Rocco Forte group, is all clean lines and elegant, understated decor. Rooms have all the expected accoutrements (including superb views from the balconies), there's a spa on site, and rates include breakfast. ⑧

Town House 70 Cathedral Rd, Pontcanna ⓣ029/2023 9399, ⓦwww.thetownhousecardiff.co.uk. Hotel in a restored Victorian house with en-suite rooms, a comfortable lounge and better-than-average facilities. ④

Hostels

Cardiff Backpacker 96–98 Neville St, Riverside ⓣ029/2034 5577, ⓦwww.cardiffbackpacker.com. A fine, very friendly option, this purple-hued hostel has deservedly become something of a legend. A 10min walk from Central station, it has Internet access, pool table, on-site café and bar, and fairly cramped kitchen facilities but easy access to downtown restaurants. Bunks in single-sex and mixed dorms (max 8) for £16.50, and some private rooms. ①

Cardiff YHA Hostel 2 Wedal Rd, Roath Park ⓣ0870/770 5750, ⓦwww.yha.org.uk. Large, purpose-built building just underneath the A48

Eastern Ave flyover at the top of Roath Park, almost two miles from the city centre and reachable via buses #28 or #29 from the central bus station. No curfew. Beds from £12.95 including breakfast. ❶

Campsites

Cardiff Caravan Park Pontcanna Fields ⓣ&ⓕ029/2039 8362. Very good council-run caravan park, with limited tent pitches. Only 25min walk from the city centre. Also offers bike rental to anyone.

Lavernock Point Holiday Estate Lavernock Point, Fort Rd, near Penarth ⓣ029/2070 7310. Back-up option if the *Cardiff Caravan Park* is full. Five miles out of the city, off the B4267; buses #P4, #P5 and #P8 pass within a mile of the site. Also with bungalows.

The City

Cardiff's sights are clustered around fairly small, distinct districts. The compact commercial centre is bounded by the **River Taff**, which flows past the tremendous **Millennium Stadium**; in this rugby-mad city, the atmosphere in the pubs and streets when Wales have a home match – particularly against the old enemy, England – is charged with good-natured, beery fervour. Just upstream, the Taff is flanked by the wall of Cardiff's extraordinary **castle**, an amalgam of Roman remains, Norman keep and Victorian fantasy. North of the castle is a series of white Edwardian buildings grouped around **Cathays Park**: the City Hall, Cardiff University and the superb **National Museum**. A mile south of the commercial centre is the area known as **Cardiff Bay**, once a bustling dock, now a classy waterside development that houses the stunning Welsh National Assembly building, as well as the imposing **Millennium Centre** and some fine bars and eateries. A couple of miles north of the city centre, **Llandaff Cathedral** warrants a visit for its strange clash of Norman and modern styles.

The city centre

Cardiff **city centre** forms a rough square bounded by the castle, Queen Street and Central stations and the Cardiff International Arena. Dominating the skyline, on the other side of Wood Street from Central Station, is the simply magnificent **Millennium Stadium** (daily tours hourly Mon–Sat 10am–5pm, Sun 10am–4pm, subject to events; ⓣ029/2082 2228; £5.50), which has swiftly become an iconic symbol not only of Cardiff but of Wales as a whole. Built in 1999, the stadium – with its trademark retractable roof – can seat 72,500 people and has hosted sporting matches of every description, as well as an array of huge rock gigs and other spectaculars. The tours include walking the players' tunnel, visiting the dressing rooms, VIP areas and a rugby museum. They start from the **stadium shop** at Entrance Gate 3 on Westgate Street. Don't forget to stroll the walkway along the river that was specially built out on ramps to accommodate the huge swell of the stadium walls.

The districts to the east are Cardiff's main shopping areas. **Queen Street**, running from the castle to Queen Street station, is a pedestrianized thoroughfare containing a predictable clutch of big-name chain stores and covered modern malls. Far more interesting are the **Arcades**, a series of Victorian and Edwardian galleries where you'll find all of the city centre's most alluring little independent shops and cafés – great for picking up flyers and information on gigs, club nights and other such events. Particularly impressive are the **High Street and Castle arcades**, either side of the High Street near the castle. A few yards further down towards Central Station is the elegant Edwardian **indoor market** and further still the **Royal and Morgan arcades**, linking St Mary Street with the lower end of The Hayes.

Cardiff Castle

The political, geographical and historical heart of the city is **Cardiff Castle** (daily: March–Oct 9am–6pm, tours every 20min, last tour 5pm; Nov–Feb 9.30am–5pm, 5 tours daily, last tour 4pm; full tour £7.50, grounds only £3.75), an intriguing hotchpotch of remnants of the city's history. The fortress hides inside a vast walled yard corresponding roughly to the outline of the original fort built by the Romans. The neat Norman motte, crowned with its eleventh-century **keep**, looks down onto the turrets and towers of the domestic buildings, which date in part from the fourteenth and fifteenth centuries, but were much extended in Tudor times, when residential needs began to overtake military priorities.

In the late nineteenth century, the third marquis of Bute, one of the richest men in the world, lavished a fortune on upgrading his pile – although he only lived there for six weeks a year – commissioning architect and decorator William Burges to aid him. With their passion for the religious art and the symbolism of the Middle Ages, they systematically overhauled the buildings, adding a spire to the octagonal tower and erecting a clocktower. But it was inside that their imaginations ran free, and they radically transformed the crumbling interiors into palaces of vivid colour and intricate design. These rooms can only be seen as part of the guided tour, making the extra cost well worthwhile. On the **Animal Wall**, visible from Castle Street, outside, stone creatures are frozen in cheeky poses.

Cathays Park and around

On the north side of the city centre is **Cathays Park**, a large rectangle of lawns and flowerbeds that forms the centrepiece for the impressive buildings of the **civic centre**. Dating from the early twentieth century, the gleaming white buildings are arranged with pompous Edwardian precision, and speak volumes about Cardiff's self-confidence, a full half-century before it was officially declared capital of Wales. The dragon-topped, domed **City Hall** is the magnificent centrepiece of the complex, an exercise in every cliché about ostentatious civic self-glory, with a roll call of statues of male Welsh heroes including Llywelyn ap Gruffydd, St David, Giraldus Cambrensis and Owain Glyndŵr.

National Museum and Gallery

The fine **National Museum and Gallery** (Tues–Sun & bank holidays 10am–5pm; free, headset tour £2.50) attempts both to tell the story of Wales and to reflect the nation's place in the wider, international sphere. Start off at the back of the entrance lobby with the epic "Evolution of Wales" exhibition, a fabulous mix of natural history, high-tech gizmos and hugely detailed displays. In the first-floor archeology gallery, don't miss the Bronze Age remains and the comparatively sophisticated **Caergwrle Bowl**, a delicate, 3000-year-old gold-leafed ornament. Nearby is the **Tregwynt Treasure Trove**, an impressive cache of gold and silver coins dating back to the Civil War, uncovered near Fishguard in 1996.

The bulk of the East Wing is given over to **fine art**, with ten galleries on the first floor containing the majority of the museum's extraordinary art collection. The oldest part of the collection starts with the fifteenth- and sixteenth-century **Italian schools**, pushing on to seventeenth-century galleries rich in **Flemish** and **Dutch** work, including Rembrandt's coolly aloof portrait of *Catrina Hooghsaet* and Jacob van Ruisdael's mesmerizing *Waterfall*. The most famous, or perhaps infamous, pieces here are the **Cardiff Cartoons**, four monumental tapestries bought at great expense in 1979 and, at the time, presumed to be the work of Rubens. The first of the great Welsh artists is shown to maximum effect in the **eighteenth-century** galleries, where landscapes by Richard Wilson include *Caernarfon Castle* and *Dolbadarn Castle*. The **nineteenth-century** galleries include a round-up of some of the century's greater painters, including J.M.W. Turner, whose *Thames Backwater, with Windsor Castle* is a characteristic wash of diffuse colour and light.

The most exciting art works are contained in galleries Eleven to Fifteen, kicking off with a wonderful **sculpture collection**, including many by the one-man Victorian Welsh statue industry, Goscombe John, that contrast with the more delicate Rodin pieces nearby. Gallery Thirteen is home to the National Museum's pride, the Davies collection of **Impressionist paintings**. Cézanne, Monet and Degas are here, alongside Corot's legendary *Distant view of Corbeil, morning*, Pissarro's classic views of Rouen and Paris, and Renoir's chirpy portrait of *La Parisienne*. Gallery Fourteen houses a hearty collection of Post-Impressionists, Futurists and Surrealists, while Gallery Fifteen showcases abstract work with a strong Welsh bent.

Cardiff Bay

Although you can get there by water-bus (every hour from Bute Park and Taff's Mead Embankment), train (every 20min from Queen Street station) or bus (#2, #7 or #35 from outside Central station), **Cardiff Bay** is just a half-hour stroll from the city centre along either endearingly tatty Bute Street or the newer but sadly characterless "ceremonial boulevard", **Lloyd George Avenue**.

In years gone by, when the docks were some of the busiest in the world, the area was better known by its evocative name of **Tiger Bay**, immortalized by local lass Shirley Bassey. Today, Cardiff Bay is one of the world's biggest regeneration projects, the downbeat dereliction of the old docks being turned into a designer heaven. It works well in places, though it struggles at times to maintain a life beyond the shifts of the office workers who are the main users of its bars and restaurants; it's deservedly a must-see part of any Cardiff tour.

From Cardiff Bay station, turn left and head down towards the vast open space of **Roald Dahl Plass**, named after the Cardiff-born children's author.

Wales Millennium Centre

The mesmerizing **Wales Millennium Centre** (Ⓣ08700/402000, Ⓦwww.wmc.org.uk) is a vibrant performance space built in 2004 for theatre and music. Likened by critics to a copper-plated armadillo or a great snail, the WMC soars gracefully over the Bay rooftops, its exterior swathed in Welsh building materials, topped with a stainless-steel shell tinted with a bronze oxide to resist salty air. The ground floor houses the main box office, an interactive exhibition, a music shop, souvenir shop, bar and brasserie. Upstairs there's a champagne bar and entrances into the main auditorium, the acoustically sensational Donald Gordon Theatre. The best way to see all this, and other parts of the building that you won't see otherwise, is to take a **guided tour** (times vary, call to check and pre-book on Ⓣ08700/402000; £5). Daily **free performances**, of anything from poetry to hip-hop, take place in the WMC foyer, usually at lunchtime and 6pm.

The Waterfront and around

At the far end of the square, down by the water's edge, is the magnificent red-brick **Pierhead Building**, a typically ornate neo-Gothic terracotta pile that now houses a surprisingly enjoyable **exhibition** (Mon–Thurs 9.30am–4.30pm, Fri 10am–4.30pm; free) about the workings of the **National Assembly for**

Wales, inaugurated in 1999. Next door lies the impressive home of the assembly, the **Senedd** building (various times), where it's possible to witness the decision-making in progress in the giant circular debating chamber. Guided tours need to be pre-booked (Ⓣ0845/010 5500; 1hr; free).

Harbour Drive leads down from the Assembly building towards the startling **Cardiff Bay Visitor Centre**, Harbour Drive (Mon–Fri 9.30am–5pm, Sat & Sun 10.30am–5pm; Ⓣ029/2046 3833), a giant tubular eye peering out over the Bay. Although it's a thinly disguised PR job for the development, there are lots of good exhibits and plenty of information to pick up. In front of the Visitor Centre is the lovely white, stumpy-spired **Norwegian church** (Arts Centre daily 9am–5pm, coffee shop daily 10am–4pm; Ⓣ029/2045 4899 for events), an old seamen's chapel, in which Roald Dahl was christened, now converted into an excellent café (see p.649) and performance and exhibition space.

Central to the whole Bay project is the kilometre-long **Cardiff Bay Barrage** (daily: April–Oct 8am–8pm; Nov–March 8am–4pm; free), built right across the Ely and Taff estuaries, transforming a vast mudflat into a freshwater lake and creating eight miles of useful waterfront. Continuing west along the waterfront brings you straight into **Mermaid Quay**, an airy jumble of shops, bars and restaurants that, on a warm day, is a fine place to hang out and watch the world amble by. The city's water-buses (see p.644) leave from here. Further west, **Techniquest**, on Stuart Street (Mon–Fri 9.30am–4.30pm, Sat & Sun 10.30am–5pm; £6.90), is a fun, hands-on science gallery – perfect for kids; while the five-star **St David's Hotel** (see p.644) acts as a stylish full-stop to the sweep of the Bay. From its car park, a path leads a couple of hundred yards to an eight-hectare **wetland reserve**, created partly to help offset the loss of wading-bird habitats when the barrage was built and the Bay flooded.

Butetown

The area immediately inland from the Bay is the salty old district of **Butetown**, whose inner-city dereliction still peeps through the rampant gentrification. James Street, behind Techniquest, is the main commercial focus, while to its north are the old buildings around **Mount Stuart Square**, the most impressive being the mammoth **Coal Exchange Building** built in the 1880s as Britain's central Coal Exchange. Close by, on the corner of West Bute Street, the old church of St Stephen has been converted into **The Point**, a superb venue for music and, occasionally, drama. A block further east, the **Butetown History & Arts Centre** at 5 Dock Chambers (Tues–Fri 10am–5pm, Sat, Sun & bank holidays 11am–4.30pm; Ⓣ029/2025 6757, Ⓦwww.bhac.org) records and celebrates the multicultural pedigree of the district. A few paces up the street at no. 54b, the cool, contemporary **Bay Art** gallery (Tues–Sat noon–5pm; free) has a varied programme of exhibitions, while a block further east, in an old maritime warehouse, **Craft in the Bay** (daily 10.30am–5.30pm; free) now showcases the work of craft practitioners from all over Wales and has a cute café. Across the way, the sweeping roofline and glass-brick curtain wall of the **Red Dragon Centre** (formerly Atlantic Wharf) make a striking front for what is essentially a big box filled with a twelve-screen multiplex, bowling alley, bars and restaurants. From here it's just a short hop across the road back to Cardiff Bay train station.

Llandaff Cathedral

Two miles northwest of the city centre along Cathedral Road, the small, quiet suburb of **Llandaff** is home to a church that has now grown up into the city's **cathedral** (daily 10am–7pm; free). It's believed to have been founded in the sixth century by St Teilo, but was rebuilt in Norman style in around 1120, and worked on well into the thirteenth century. From the late fourteenth century onwards, it declined into an advanced state of disrepair, and one of the twin towers and the nave roof eventually collapsed. Restoration only began in earnest in the early 1840s, when **Pre-Raphaelite** artists such as Edward Burne-Jones, Dante Gabriel Rossetti and the firm of William Morris were commissioned to make colourful new windows and decorative panels. Their work is best seen in the south aisle.

The fusion of different styles and ages is evident from outside, especially in the mismatched western towers. Inside, the nave is dominated by Jacob Epstein's overwhelming *Christ in Majesty*, a concrete parabola topped with a soaring Christ figure. At the west end of the north aisle, the **St Illtyd Chapel** features Rossetti's cloying triptych *The Seed of David*. In the south presbytery is a tenth-century Celtic cross, the only survivor of the pre-Norman cathedral.

Eating, drinking and nightlife

There are numerous **eateries** right in the centre, most notably in the "café quarter" along Mill Lane, as well as in the cheaper quarters of Cathays and Roath. Cardiff's **pub** life is lively, and there are some wonderful Edwardian palaces of etched, smoky glass and deep red wood, where you'll find Cardiff's very own Brains bitter.

There's plenty of choice when it comes to **nightlife** – from sweaty rock gigs to pumping clubs. **Theatre** encompasses everything from the radical and alternative at The Point and Chapter to big, blowzy productions at the New Theatre or West End spectaculars at the new Wales Millennium Centre, home of the Welsh National Opera (Ⓦwww.wno.org.uk). Classical **music** is best heard at the WMC or St David's Hall. There's no shortage of multiplex **cinemas** for the latest blockbusters, though Chapter is best for art-house movies. Cardiff also has a modest **gay and lesbian scene**, centred on Charles Street, just off Queen Street; the best information source is South Wales Friend (Tues–Thurs 7.30–9.30pm; Ⓣ029/2034 0101).

Cafés and restaurants

Celtic Cauldron Castle Arcade. A friendly daytime café, dedicated to bringing a range of simple Welsh food – soups, stews, laver bread, cakes – to an appreciative public. Inexpensive.

Cibo 83 Pontcanna St, off Cathedral Rd Ⓣ029/2223 2226. A slice of Italy in Cardiff: a small, inexpensive and welcoming trattoria serving ciabatta sandwiches and simple, well-cooked food. No credit cards. Moderate.

Greenhouse 38 Woodville Rd, Cathays Ⓣ029/2023 5731. Quirky and popular restaurant serving fish and vegetarian food with a modern take on traditional dishes. Closed Sun & Mon. Moderate.

Happy Gathering 233 Cowbridge Rd East, Canton Ⓣ029/2039 7531. A true Cardiff phenomenon, the best and most authentic Chinese food in the city.

Las Iguanas 8a Mill Lane Ⓣ029/2022 6373. Wonderful Mexican and Latin American food with pavement tables and a good atmosphere. Can get too lively for intimate meals on weekends.

Le Gallois (Y Cymro) 6–10 Romilly Crescent, Canton Ⓣ029/2034 1264. Sophisticated and fashionable restaurant on a busy suburban road, serving delicious French cuisine with a Welsh twist Expensive.

Louis' Restaurant 32 St Mary St. Wondrously old-fashioned restaurant, serving great dollops of well-cooked, good-value comfort food until around 7.30pm. Moderate.

New York Deli High St Arcade Ⓣ029/2038 8388. Pseudo New York-style deli that serves the biggest and most outrageous sandwich combinations in the capital. Inexpensive.

Norwegian Church Harbour Drive. Cosy spot for Norwegian open sandwiches, salads, some scrumptious cakes and filter coffee. Inexpensive.

Porto's 40 St Mary St Ⓣ029/2022 0060. Authentic restaurant in a dark, wood-beamed room serving massive portions of Portuguese and Madeiran favourites. Moderate.

Tang's 15–23 Westgate St Ⓣ029/2022 7771. Quite pricey, but the best all-round Chinese restaurant in the city centre, whose owners have a long pedigree in Cardiff cuisine. Expensive.

Bars, pubs and clubs

Bar Cwtch at *Jolyon's Hotel*, 5 Bute Crescent, Cardiff Bay. Cosy bar with a wood-burning stove and terrific atmosphere.

Cayo Arms Cathedral Rd, Pontcanna. Great pub a 5min walk up Cathedral Rd from the city centre. Proudly Welsh, with Tomos Watkin beers and decent food every day until 8pm.

Chapter Market Rd, Canton. A trendy bar in the arts centre, with a good choice of real ale, imported lagers and whisky. Frequented by the Canton media and arts crowd.

Club X 39 Charles St. Stylish and popular gay club that manages to span both cheesy and cutting edge. Also has a wonderful roof garden and a great atmosphere. Open Wed till 2am, Fri 3am, Sat 4am & Sun 1am.

Clwb Ifor Bach Womanby St ⓣ029/2023 2199, ⓦwww.clwb.net. A sweaty and enjoyable live-music and DJ club with nightly gigs and sessions, many featuring Welsh-language bands.

Mochyn Du Sophia Close, off Cathedral Rd. Relaxed pub with tables spilling out into the greenery. Good bar menu, great beer, and popular with Welsh speakers.

Sam's Bar 63 St Mary St ⓣ029/2034 5189. Lively club-bar, with everything from live heavy metal, comedy and drag shows to house DJs. A good place to check the pulse of the Mill Lane "café quarter".

Theatre, cinema and classical music

Cardiff International Arena Mary Ann St ⓣ029/2023 4500 (enquiries), ⓣ029/2022 4488 (bookings). Large and imposing venue rising high over the city centre's southern streets and playing host to classical concerts, opera, and major rock and pop gigs.

Chapter Arts Centre Market Rd, Canton ⓣ029/2030 4400, ⓦwww.chapter.org. Multifunctional arts complex that's home to fine British and touring theatre and dance companies.

Glee Club Mermaid Quay, Cardiff Bay ⓣ0870/241 5093, ⓦwww.glee.co.uk. Cardiff's best comedy club, with some of the biggest names of the British stand-up circuit.

New Theatre Park Place ⓣ029/2087 8889, ⓦwww.newtheatrecardiff.co.uk. Splendid Edwardian city-centre theatre that plays host to big shows, musicals and pantos.

St David's Hall The Hayes ⓣ029/2087 8444, ⓦwww.stdavidshallcardiff.co.uk. Part of the massive St David's shopping centre, this large venue is home to visiting orchestras and musicians from jazz to opera to folk, and is frequently used by the excellent BBC National Orchestra of Wales.

Sherman Theatre Senghennydd Rd, Cathays ⓣ029/2064 6900, ⓦwww.shermantheatre.co.uk. An excellent two-auditorium repertory theatre hosting a mixed bag of new and translated classic Welsh-language pieces, stand-up comedy, children's entertainment, drama, music and dance. Many plays on Welsh themes in both English and Welsh.

Wales Millennium Centre Roald Dahl Plass, Cardiff Bay ⓣ029/2040 2000, ⓦwww.wmc.org.uk. Permanent home of the Welsh National Opera, together with a collection of other music and dance companies. Also used for touring mega-productions.

Listings

Airport Cardiff International, out at Rhoose, near Barry ⓣ01446/711111, ⓦwww.cwlfly.co.uk.

Banks and exchange All major banks have branches along High St or Queen St. In addition there's American Express at 3 Queen St (Mon–Fri 9am–5.30pm, Sat 9am–5pm; ⓣ029/2064 9301), and Thomas Cook at 16 Queen St (Mon–Fri 9.30am–5pm, Sat 10am–1pm; ⓣ0845/308 9192).

Bike rental Taff Trail Cycle Hire at the Cardiff Caravan Park, Pontcanna Fields ⓣ029/2039 8362 (see p.645).

Bus enquiries Traveline ⓣ0871/200 2233; National Express ⓣ0870/580 8080.

Dentist For emergency dental work, phone Cardiff NHS Community Dental Service on ⓣ029/2019 0175.

Hospital In the first instance, phone NHS Wales Direct on ⓣ0845/4647.

Laundries Drift In, 104 Salisbury Rd, Cathays Park; Laundry Room, 244 Cowbridge Rd, Canton; Launderama, 58 Caerau Lane.

Pharmacy Boots, 5 Wood St (Mon–Sat 8am–8pm, ⓣ029/2023 4043).

Police Cardiff Central Police Station, King Edward VII Ave, Cathays Park ⓣ029/2022 2111.

Post office The Hayes (Mon–Fri 9am–5.30pm, Sat 9am–12.30pm).

Swimming pools and spas Welsh Institute of Sport, Sophia Gardens ⓣ0845/045 0902.

Around Cardiff

On the edge of the northern Cardiff suburbs, the thirteenth-century fairy-tale castle of **Castell Coch** stands on a hillside in the woods, while just further north is the massive **Caerphilly Castle**. West of the city, the massively popular **National History Museum** at St Fagans tells the country's history through a collection of buildings uprooted from all over Wales.

Castell Coch

Four miles north of Llandaff, the turreted **Castell Coch** (June–Sept daily 9.30am–6pm; April, May & Oct daily 9.30am–5pm; Nov–March Mon–Sat 9.30am–4pm, Sun 11am–4pm; £3.50; CADW) was once a ruined thirteenth-century fortress. Like Cardiff Castle, it was rebuilt and transformed into a fantasy structure in the late 1870s by William Burges for the third marquess of Bute. With its working portcullis and drawbridge, Castell Coch is the ultimate medieval fantasy, isolated on its almost alpine hillside, yet only a few hundred yards from the motorway and Cardiff suburbs. There are many similarities with Cardiff Castle, notably the lavish decor, culled from religious and moral fables, which dazzles in each room. Bus #26A from Central station drops at the castle gates, or the #132 drops in Tongwynlais, from where it's a ten-minute climb.

Caerphilly

Caerphilly (Caerffili), seven miles north of Cardiff, has a particularly staggering town-centre **castle** (Easter–May & Oct daily 9.30am–5pm; June–Sept daily 9.30am–6pm; Nov–March Mon–Sat 9.30am–4pm, Sun 11am–4pm; £3.50; CADW), the first in Britain built concentrically, with an inner system of defences overlooking the outer ring. Looming out of its vast surrounding moat, the medieval fortress with its cock-eyed tower occupies over thirty acres, presenting an awesome promise not entirely fulfilled inside. The castle was begun in 1268 by Gilbert de Clare as a defence against Llywelyn the Last. For the next few hundred years Caerphilly was little more than a decaying toy, given at whim by kings to their favourites. By the turn of the twentieth century, it was in a sorry state, sitting amidst a growing industrial town that saw fit to build in the then-dry moat and castle precincts. Houses and shops were demolished in order to allow the moat to be reflooded in 1958.

The most interesting section of the castle is the massive eastern gatehouse, which includes an impressive upper hall and oratory and, to its left, the wholly restored and re-roofed **Great Hall**.

Caerphilly is also known for its crumbly white **cheese**, made in dairies around the town, and available in a ploughman's lunch at the *Courthouse* pub, on Cardiff Road, right by the castle and a five-minute stroll from the **bus** and **train** stations.

St Fagans National History Museum and Castle

St Fagans (Sain Ffagan), four miles west of Cardiff city centre, has a rural feel that is only partially disturbed by the busloads of tourists that roll in regularly to visit the excellent **National History Museum** (daily 10am–5pm; free), built around **St Fagans Castle**, a country house erected in 1580 and furnished in early nineteenth-century style. Particularly impressive is the fifty-acre outdoor collection of buildings from all corners of Wales that have been carefully dismantled and rebuilt on this site since the museum's inception in 1946. Highlights include the diminutive, whitewashed Pen-Rhiw Chapel, built in Dyfed in 1777; the pristine and evocative St Mary's Board School, built in Lampeter in Victorian times; and the stern mini-fortress of a tollhouse that once guarded the southern approach to Aberystwyth, from 1772. The superb Rhyd-y-car **ironworkers' cottages**, from Merthyr Tydfil, were originally built in around 1800; each of the six houses are furnished in the style of a different period, stretching from 1805 to 1985. **Buses** #32 (hourly) and #320 (variable times) run to the museum from Cardiff Central station.

Swansea and Gower

Dylan Thomas called **SWANSEA** (Abertawe) – his birthplace – an "ugly, lovely town", an epithet which poet Paul Durcan updated to "pretty, shitty city". Both ring true. Large, sprawling and boisterous, with around 200,000 people, Swansea may only be the second city of Wales, but it's the undoubted Welsh capital of attitude, coated in a layer of chunky bling. The city centre was massively rebuilt after devastating bomb attacks in World War II, and a jumble of tower blocks now dot the horizon. But closer inspection reveals Swansea's multifarious charms: some intact old corners of the city centre, the spacious and graceful suburb of Uplands, a wide **seafront** overlooking Swansea Bay and a bold marina development around the old docks. Spread throughout are some of the best-funded **museums** in the country, including the stunning new National Waterfront Museum – itself reason enough to include Swansea on a tour of Wales. Situated on the edge of the **Gower Peninsula**, which holds some of the country's most popular and inspirational coastal and rural scenery, Swansea makes a logical base: transport out into the surrounding areas is good, and beds tend to be less expensive in the city than in the more picturesque parts of Gower.

Swansea's Welsh name, Abertawe, refers to the mouth of the River Tawe, a grimy ditch that is slowly recovering after centuries of abuse by the area's heavy industries. The city itself dates back to the 1099 when William the Conqueror's troops built a castle here. A settlement grew around this, later exploiting its location between the coalfields and the sea to become a shipbuilding centre, and then, by 1700, the largest coal port in Wales. Copper smelting took over as the area's dominant industry in the eighteenth century, and this attracted other metal trades, developing the region into one of the world's most prolific metal-bashing centres.

Arrival, information and accommodation

Swansea is the main interchange station for trains out to the west of Wales, and for the slow line across to Shrewsbury in England. The **train station** is at the top end of the High Street, a ten-minute hike from the **bus station**, which is sandwiched between the Quadrant shopping centre and the Grand Theatre. Nearby, on Plymouth Street, is the **tourist office** (Easter–Sept Mon–Sat 9.30am–5.30pm, Sun 10am–4pm, Oct–Easter closed Sun; ⓣ01792/468321, ⓔtourism@swansea.gov.uk), where you can pick up the comprehensive bimonthly magazine *What's On*. **Ferries** to Cork in Ireland used to leave roughly once a day from the docks, around a mile east of the town centre (ⓣ01792/456116, ⓦhttps://swansea-corkferries.com) but were temporarily suspended at the time of writing.

There are dozens of dirt-cheap **hotels** and **B&Bs** stretched out along the seafront Oystermouth Road. Better places congregate in leafy Uplands, a thirty-minute walk from town. There are no campsites or hostels in the city itself, although nearby places in Gower are easily reached.

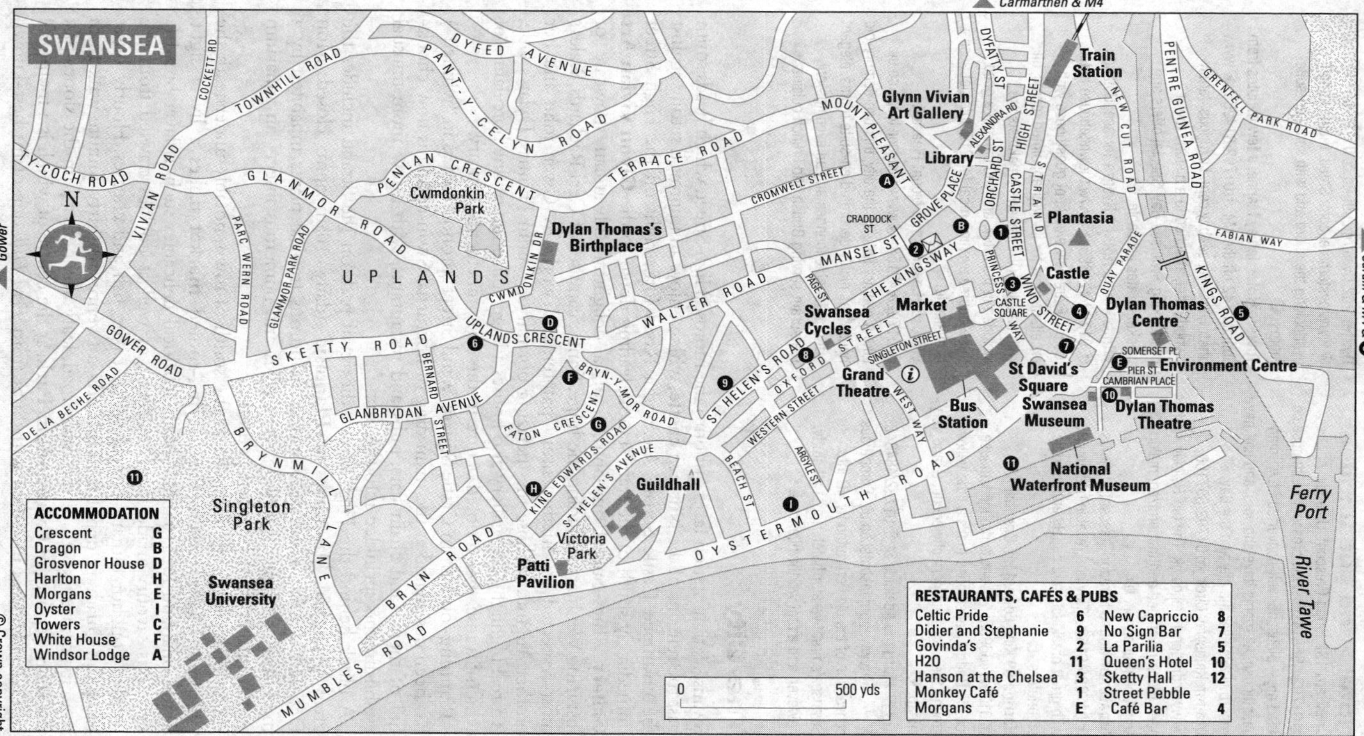
SWANSEA
Carmarthen & M4
Cardiff & M4 & C
Gower
Mumbles
Train Station
Glynn Vivian Art Gallery
Library
Plantasia
Castle
Dylan Thomas Centre
Environment Centre
Market
Swansea Cycles
Grand Theatre
St David's Square
Swansea Museum
Bus Station
Dylan Thomas Theatre
National Waterfront Museum
Dylan Thomas's Birthplace
Cwmdonkin Park
UPLANDS
Guildhall
Victoria Park
Patti Pavilion
Singleton Park
Swansea University
Ferry Port
River Tawe
ACCOMMODATION
Crescent G
Dragon B
Grosvenor House D
Harlton H
Morgans E
Oyster I
Towers C
White House F
Windsor Lodge A
RESTAURANTS, CAFÉS & PUBS
Celtic Pride 6
Didier and Stephanie 9
Govinda's 2
H2O 11
Hanson at the Chelsea 3
Monkey Café 1
Morgans E
New Capriccio 8
No Sign Bar 7
La Parilia 5
Queen's Hotel 10
Skety Hall 12
Street Pebble Café Bar 4
0 500 yds
© Crown copyright

Hotels and guesthouses

Crescent 132 Eaton Crescent, Uplands ⓣ01792/466814, ⓦwww.crescentguesthouse.co.uk. Large, pleasant, well-converted Edwardian guesthouse. All rooms have showers, and half have superb views over the city and the Bay. ③

Dragon Kingsway Circle ⓣ01792/657100, ⓦwww.dragon-hotel.co.uk. The old *Holiday Inn* has been much revamped and modernized, making it a smart central option. ⑤

Grosvenor House Mirador Crescent, Uplands ⓣ01792/461522. Tidy and reliable guesthouse with great breakfasts and hugely enthusiastic proprietors. ④

Harlton 89 King Edward Rd, Brynmill ⓣ01792/466938, ⓦwww.harltonguesthouse.co.uk. Budget guesthouse that's a little yellow around the edges but perfectly adequate and very cheap. ①

Morgans Adelaide St ⓣ01792/484848, ⓦwww.morganshotel.co.uk. Sumptuous conversion of the old Port Authority HQ into Swansea's first five-star hotel. Not at all stuffy, however, and a real worthwhile treat. ⑥

Oyster 262 Oystermouth Rd ⓣ01792/654345, ⓦwww.oysterhotel.com. Small, friendly hotel overlooking the shore and with some en-suite rooms. ②

Towers Hotel Jersey Marine, a few minutes from Junction 42 off the M4 ⓣ01792/814255, ⓦwww.thetowersswanseabay.com. Luxurious, family-owned hotel, attached to a historic tower overlooking Swansea Bay. Special offers and weekend rates available. ⑤

White House Hotel 4 Nyanza Terrace, Uplands ⓣ01792/473856, ⓦwww.thewhitehouse hotel.co.uk. Extremely well-kept guesthouse with excellent rates for its well-appointed rooms, all with satellite TV. Extensive breakfasts are included in the rates, and you can get a good three-course evening meal for £15. Internet access is available. ⑤

Windsor Lodge Hotel Mount Pleasant ⓣ01792/642158, ⓦwww.windsor-lodge.co.uk. Like a country hotel in the city, this two-century-old house has nicely decorated en-suite rooms, elegant but comfortable lounges and an evenings-only restaurant serving British and French cuisine. ④

The City

Swansea's train station faces out onto the morose High Street, which heads south past the remains of the Norman **castle**, which enjoys an improved setting against the revamped Castle Square. Alexandra Road forks right off the High Street immediately south of the train station, leading down to the **Glynn Vivian Art Gallery** (Tues–Sun 10am–5pm; free), a delightful Edwardian showcase of inspiring Welsh art including the huge, frantic canvases of Ceri Richards, Wales's most respected twentieth-century painter, and works by Gwen John and her brother Augustus, whose mesmerizing portrait of Caitlin Thomas, Dylan's wife, is a real highlight. The gallery also houses a large collection of fine porcelain – of which Swansea was a noted centre in the early nineteenth century.

Running south from Castle Square, Wind Street (pronounced as in "whined") has been designated as the main drag of nocturnal Swansea and is now chock-full of theme and chain bars, pubs and restaurants, with a few more unusual establishments sprinkled into the mix.

A block behind the High Street, the retail park on the Strand includes the great pyramidal glasshouse of **Plantasia** (daily 10am–5pm; closed Mon Dec–Jan; £3.50), a sweaty world of wondrous tropical plants inhabited by a mini-zoo of tamarin monkeys, butterflies and numerous insects, an aquarium and a thirteen-foot Burmese python.

The main shopping streets lie to the south of town, notably underneath the Quadrant Centre where the curving-roofed **market** makes a lively sight. Traditional and long-standing stalls sell local delicacies such as laver bread (a delicious savoury made from seaweed), as well as cockles trawled from the nearby Loughor estuary, typical Welsh cakes, fish and cheeses. Hourly buses leave the Quadrant depot for **Uplands**, a twenty- to thirty-minute walk from the city centre. North of the main road, leafy avenues rise up the slopes past the sharp terraces of **Cwmdonkin Park**, at the centre of which is a memorial to Dylan Thomas inscribed with lines from *Fern Hill*, one of his best-known poems. On the eastern side of the park is Cwmdonkin Drive, a sharply rising set of solid Victorian semis, notable only for the blue plaque on no. 5, **birthplace** of the poet in 1914.

The spit of land between Oystermouth Road, the sea and the Tawe estuary has been christened the **Maritime Quarter** – tourist-board-speak for the old docks – built around a vast marina surrounded by legions of modern flats. The city's old South Dock features the enticingly old-fashioned **Swansea Museum** (Tues–Sun & bank holiday Mon; free). A small grid of nineteenth-century streets around the museum houses some enjoyable cafés, pubs and restaurants.

Behind the museum, in Somerset Place, is the airy **Dylan Thomas Centre**, the national literature centre of Wales (daily 10am–4.30pm; free), complete with theatre space, book and craft shops, a great café, and two galleries. One of these is devoted to Dylan Thomas, and includes a mock-up of the shed in which he wrote, where you can see a fascinating video on his life and work.

Burrows Place leads down to the marina and the sublime new **National Waterfront Museum** (daily 10am–5pm; free). Carved out of the shell of the old Industrial and Maritime Museum, the original building has been stunningly extended to accommodate a breathtakingly varied set of exhibitions dealing with Wales's history of innovation and industry. The museum is divided into fifteen zones, looking at topics such as energy, landscape, coal, genealogy, networks and money, and each section is bursting with interactive technology. Within the complex, there are shops, a café and a lovely waterfront balcony. Without doubt, this is the most impressive museum in Wales, and should not be missed.

The museum faces out onto a flotilla of yachts bobbing in the marina. Close by stands John Doubleday's statue of Dylan Thomas, dubbed "A Portrait of the Artist as Someone Else", since it looks nothing like the poet. Just behind the statue, on Gloucester Place, is the mural-splattered warehouse that has now become the **Dylan Thomas Theatre**, which intersperses productions of his work with visiting and local companies' offerings.

Eating, drinking and nightlife

Swansea is a city that knows how to have a good time, and works damn hard at it. Wind Street is the city's main booze artery, with a handful of late-opening club-bars that generally appeal to an older clientele than the brash younger clubs around Kingsway.

The BBC Welsh Symphony Orchestra appears at the **Brangwyn Hall** (Ⓣ01792/635432) in the Art Deco Civic Centre. Thomas's classics get a regular airing at the **Dylan Thomas Theatre** (Ⓣ01792/473238, Ⓦwww.dylanthomastheatre.org.uk), by the marina, while the **Taliesin Arts Centre** (Ⓣ01792/602060, Ⓦwww.taliesinartscentre.co.uk), in the university, is the city's more offbeat venue.

Cafés and restaurants

Didier and Stephanie 56 St Helen's Rd, Uplands Ⓣ01792/655603. Small and lovely French restaurant, specializing in some fairly obscure regional Gallic surprises. Moderate.

Govinda's 8 Craddock St. Vegetarian restaurant in the Hare Krishna tradition, selling very cheap, if somewhat insipid, meals and freshly pressed juices. Inexpensive.

Hanson at the Chelsea Tŷ Castell House, 17 St Mary St Ⓣ01792/464068. Local ingredients served with flair and imagination are the staples of this place, and it's all done extremely well. Moderate.

La Parrilla J Shed, Kings Rd Ⓣ01792/464530. Tasty and original Mediterranean food served in a beautifully converted grain warehouse. Airy yet intimate. Moderate.

Morgans Adelaide St Ⓣ01792/484848. The huge old boardroom of the Port Authority building now houses the excellent restaurant of Swansea's best hotel. Confident modern cooking with sometimes overzealous service. Expensive.

New Capriccio 89 St Helen's Rd ⓣ01792/648804. Popular Italian restaurant with bargain lunch menu. Closed Sun evening & Mon. Inexpensive.

Sketty Hall Singleton Park ⓣ01792/284011. Catering academy in beautiful surroundings, where you can sample the excellent student cuisine for reasonable prices. Booking essential. Moderate.

Street Pebble Café Bar 11 Wind St. Wicker, stones and a candlelit interior provide Wind St's most chilled ambience: great for morning smoothies, daytime paninis or Mediterranean food in the evenings. Inexpensive–moderate.

Pubs and clubs

Celtic Pride 49 Uplands Crescent, Uplands ⓣ01792/645301. Good local pub with almost nightly live music, including jam sessions and Welsh music. The *Uplands Tavern*, opposite, is good for music and studenty rumpus too.

H20 Anchor Court, Victoria Quay, Swansea Marina ⓣ01792/648555. Fairly sterile gay club after dark; pre-club bar offering inexpensive pub food until early evening.

Monkey Café 13 Castle St ⓦwww.monkeycafe.co.uk. Groovy, inexpensive, mosaic-floored café with a relaxed atmosphere and nightly DJs or live music. On a good night, the best in town.

No Sign Bar 56 Wind St. A narrow frontage leads into a long, warm pub interior, one of the oldest in town and easily the best on Wind St. The etymology of the name is explained in depth in the window.

Queen's Hotel Gloucester Place, near the marina. Large old hotel and pub firmly in the Swansea seafaring tradition, with good snack lunches and Sunday roasts, and bags of gritty atmosphere.

Gower

A fifteen-mile-long peninsula of undulating sandstone and limestone, **Gower** (Gŵyr) is a world of its own, pointing down into the Bristol Channel to the west of Swansea. The area is fringed by sweeping yellow bays and precipitous cliffs, with caves and blowholes to the south, and wide, flat marshes and cockle beds to the north. Bracken heaths dotted with prehistoric remains and tiny villages lie between, and there are numerous castle ruins and curious churches lurking about. Out of season, the winding lanes afford wonderful opportunities for exploration, but in the height of summer – July and August especially – they can be horribly congested. Buses from Swansea frequently serve the whole peninsula.

Gower reputedly starts in Swansea's western suburbs, along the coast of Swansea Bay that curves round to a point at the pleasantly old-fashioned resort of **Mumbles** and finishes with **Rhossili Bay**. The southern coast is punctuated by the glorious village of **Port Eynon**, home to an excellent YHA **hostel** (ⓣ0870/770 5998, ⓦwww.yha.org.uk; £14 per bed; closed Nov–March) and a beautiful beach. West of Port Eynon, the coast becomes a wild, frilly series of inlets and cliffs, topped by a five-mile path that stretches all the way to the peninsula's glorious westernmost point, **Worms Head**. The northern coast merges into the tidal flats of the estuary.

Mumbles and Oystermouth

At the far westernmost end of Swansea Bay and on the cusp of Gower, **MUMBLES** (Mwmbwls) is a lively and enjoyable alternative base to Swansea, with a diverse range of seaside entertainment, fine restaurants and the legendary Mumbles Mile of pubs. Derived from the French *mamelles*, or "breasts" (a reference to the twin islets off the end of Mumbles Head), Mumbles is now used to refer to the entire loose sprawl of **OYSTERMOUTH** (Ystumllwynarth) – a term used pretty much interchangeably with Mumbles. Here, the seafront is an unbroken curve of budget hotels, breezy pubs and cafés, leading down to the refurbished pier and the rocky plug of Mumbles Head. Around the headland, reached either by the longer coast road or by a short walk over the hill, is the district of **Langland Bay**, whose sandy beach is popular with surfers.

The hilltop above town is crowned by the ruins of **Oystermouth Castle** (April–Oct daily 11am–5pm; £1), founded as a Norman watchtower. The castle was strengthened to withstand attacks by the Welsh before being converted for more amenable residential purposes during the fourteenth century. Today you can see the remains of a late thirteenth-century keep next to a more ornate three-storey ruin incorporating an impressive banqueting hall and state rooms.

The small **tourist office** (May–July & Sept Mon–Sat 10am–5pm; Aug Mon–Sat 10am–5pm, Sun noon–4pm; Oct–April Mon–Sat 10am–4.30pm; ⓣ01792/361302) is in the Methodist church on Mumbles Road, just beyond the Newton Road junction. Good **accommodation** in Mumbles centres along the shorefront Mumbles Road: the chintzy *Coast House* at no. 708 (ⓣ01792/368702, ⓦwww.thecoasthouse.co.uk; ❸), the elegant *Tides Reach* at no. 388 (ⓣ01792/404877, ⓦwww.tidesreachguesthouse.co.uk; ❹), the tastefully furnished and welcoming *Alexandra House* at no. 366 (ⓣ01792/406406, ⓦwww.alexandra-house.com; ❹) and, best of all, the lovely *Patrick's with Rooms* at no. 638 (ⓣ01792/360199, ⓦwww.patrickswithrooms.com; ❼). Places to **eat** cheaply include *Coffee Denn*, 34 Newton Rd, particularly good for sweet treats, and *Verdi's*, overlooking the sea at Knab Rock near the pier – a Mumbles institution for its lively atmosphere and superb pizzas and ice-cream concoctions. Moving upscale, the moderately priced *P.A.'s Wine Bar*, 95 Newton Rd (ⓣ01792/367723), excels at fish dishes, the pricier *Knight's* at 614–616 Mumbles Rd (ⓣ01792/363184) does fantastic fusion cuisine, and the truly special *698* at 698 Mumbles Rd (ⓣ01792/361616) serves beautifully prepared local beef, lamb and seafood. The scores of pubs along the seafront constitute the Mumbles Mile, one of Wales's most notorious pub crawls. The ones to linger in are the *Antelope*, the *Nag's Head* and the *White Rose*.

Rhossili and Worms Head

The village of **RHOSSILI** (Rhosili), at the western end of Gower, is a centre for walkers and beach loungers alike. Dylan Thomas described the terrain to the west of the village as "rubbery, gull-limed grass, the sheep-pilled stones, the pieces of bones and feathers", and you can tread in his footsteps to **Worms Head**, an isolated string of rocks, accessible for only five hours, at low tide. Be very careful – there are deaths here every year. At the head of the road, near the village, is a well-stocked National Trust **information centre** (Easter–Oct daily 10.30am–5.30pm; Nov–Dec Wed–Sun 11am–4pm; Jan–March Sat & Sun 11am–4pm; ⓣ01792/390707). It posts the tide times outside for those heading for Worms Head, and holds details of local companies renting surfing and hang-gliding equipment.

Below the village, a great curve of white sand stretches away into the distance, a dazzling coastline vast enough to absorb the crowds, especially if you are prepared to head north towards **Burry Holms**, an islet that is cut off at high tide. The northern end of the beach can also be reached along the small lane that runs from Reynoldston, in the middle of the peninsula, to **Llangennith**, on the other side of the towering, 633-foot **Rhossili Down**. In the village, PJ's Surfshop (ⓣ01792/386669, ⓦwww.pjsurfshop.co.uk) rents **surfboards** and boogie boards; a mile away at the *Hillend* campsite (see below) is the Welsh Surf Federation Surf School (ⓣ01792/386426, ⓦwww.wsfsurfschool.co.uk), which runs half-day (£25) and full-day (£45) **surfing courses**.

Accommodation in Rhossili village is pretty scarce: there's only really the average *Worms Head Hotel* (ⓣ01792/390512, ⓦwww.thewormshead.co.uk; ❺), complete with spectacular views. Better is the *King Arthur Hotel* in nearby Reynoldston (Ⓣ01792/390775, Ⓦwww.kingarthurhotel.co.uk; ⑤), which has comfortable rooms and serves good food.

In Llangennith, you could go for the lovely B&B *College House* (Ⓣ01792/386214; ③) in the middle of the village, or the very chilled B&B *Western House* (Ⓣ01792/386620, Ⓦwww.westernhousebandb.co.uk; ③) on the lane towards the beach. Half a mile further, *Hillend* (Ⓣ01792/386204), is a fabulous **campsite** behind the dunes and with direct access to the glorious beach. Back in the village, the *King's Head* is a fine pub for **food** and **drink**.

Carmarthenshire

Frequently overlooked in the stampede towards the resorts of Pembrokeshire, **Carmarthenshire** is a quiet part of the world. **Kidwelly**, with its dramatically sited castle, is the only reason to stop before **Carmarthen**, the unquestioned capital of its region but one which fails to live up to the promise of its status. Better to press on up the bucolic Tywi Valley, visiting the **National Botanic Garden** and the more formal grounds of **Aberglasney** on the way to **Llandeilo** and the wonderfully sited **Carreg Cennen** castle.

On the coast, the village of **Laugharne** has become a place of pilgrimage for Dylan Thomas devotees, while **Tenby** is the quintessential British seaside resort, built high on cliffs and with views across to monastic **Caldey Island**.

Kidwelly

The sleepy little town of **KIDWELLY** (Cydweli) is dominated by its imposing **castle** (June–Sept daily 9.30am–6pm; April, May & Oct daily 9.30am–5pm; Nov–March Mon–Sat 9.30am–4pm, Sun 11am–4pm; £2.90; CADW). Established around 1106 by the bishop of Salisbury as a satellite of Sherborne Abbey in Dorset, the castle is situated at a strategic point overlooking the River Gwendraeth and vast tracts of coast. On entering through the massive fourteenth-century gatehouse, you can still see portcullis slats and murder holes, through which noxious substances could be tipped onto unwelcome visitors. The gatehouse forms the centrepiece of the impressively intact outer-ward walls, which can be climbed for some great views over the grassy courtyard and rectangular inner ward to the river.

There's superb B&B **accommodation** at *Penlan Isaf Farm* (Ⓣ01554/890084, Ⓦwww.penlanisaf.co.uk; ②), on a dairy farm overlooking the town. You can **camp** at the caravan-oriented *Carmarthen Bay Touring & Camp Site*, Tanylan Farm (Ⓣ01267/267306, Ⓦwww.tanylanfarmholidays.co.uk; closed Oct–Easter), which perches alongside the estuary between Kidwelly and Ferryside. Good **food** and **drink** are available at the cosy *Boot & Shoe* at 2 Castle St.

Carmarthen and around

In the early eighteenth century **CARMARTHEN** (Caerfyrddin) was the largest town in the country and it remains the regional hub, a solid, if hardly thrilling place best known as the supposed birthplace of the wizard Merlin.

The most picturesque part of town is around Nott Square, where the handsome eighteenth-century **Guildhall** sits at the base of Edward I's uninspiring **castle**. From the top of Nott Square, King Street heads northeast towards the undistinguished **St Peter's Church** and the Victorian School of Art, which has metamorphosed into **Oriel Myrddin** (Mon–Sat 10am–5pm; free), a craft centre and excellent gallery that acts as an imaginative showcase for local artists.

The severe grey Bishop's Palace at **Abergwili**, a mile east of Carmarthen, was the seat of the Bishop of St David's between 1542 and 1974, and now houses the **Carmarthenshire County Museum** (Mon–Sat 10am–4.30pm; free). This surprisingly interesting exhibition depicts the history of Welsh translations of the New Testament and Book of Common Prayer – both first translated here, in 1567.

Trains between Swansea and Pembrokeshire stop at the **train station**, which lies over the Carmarthen bridge on the south side of the River Tywi. All **buses** terminate at the bus station on Blue Street, north of the river, and many connect with the arrival and departure of trains. The **tourist office** is at 113 Lammas St, near the Crimea Monument (daily: April–Oct 9.30am–5.30pm; Nov–March 10am–4pm; ⓣ01267/231557, ⓦwww.carmarthenshire.gov.uk). For **accommodation** try the *Boar's Head*, 120 Lammas St (ⓣ01267/222789, ⓦwww.boarsheadhotel.com; ④), or *Y Dderwen Fach* B&B, 98 Priory St (ⓣ01267/234193; ①), out along the main road to Llandeilo. The *Café on the Square*, Nott Square, is perhaps the pick of the town's coffee and **snack** spots, while for full meals head for the wonderful *Quayside Brasserie*, on the Tywi quay (ⓣ01267/223000).

The Tywi Valley

The **River Tywi** curves and darts its way east from Carmarthen through some of the most magical scenery in South Wales and a couple of budding gardens: one, the **National Botanic Garden of Wales**, and the other a faithful reconstruction of linked walled gardens around the long-abandoned house of **Aberglasney**. The twenty-mile trip to Llandeilo is punctuated by gentle, impossibly green hills topped with ruined castles, notably the wonderful **Carreg Cennen**: it's not hard to see why the Merlin legend has taken such a hold in these parts.

The National Botanic Garden and around

Though only opened in 2000, the great glass "eye" of the **National Botanic Garden of Wales** (daily: April–Oct 10am–6pm; Nov–March 10am–4.30pm; £8, discounts for groups and those arriving by bike or public transport; ⓦwww.gardenofwales.org.uk), seven miles east of Carmarthen, has quickly become the centrepiece of the Tywi Valley. Its central walkway leads past lakes, sculpture and geological outcrops from all over Wales, with walks down towards slate-bed plantings and different wood and wetland habitats. A double-walled garden has been teased back to life (providing vegetables for the restaurant), and enhanced with the addition of a small but exquisite Japanese garden and a bee garden that's home to a million bees.

At the top of the hill is Norman Foster's stunning oval **glasshouse**, packed with plants from regions with a Mediterranean climate including South Africa, Chile, California and the Mediterranean itself. The whole centre, including the excellent café, has been designed to operate sustainably, using some intriguing technology to achieve this. And in keeping, the surrounding land has been turned over to either organic farming or the restoration of some typical Welsh habitat. The #166 **bus** runs twice daily from Carmarthen train station.

Aberglasney

A much older garden can be found five miles northeast at **Aberglasney** (daily: April–Sept 10am–6pm; Nov–March 10.30am–4pm; £6.50; Ⓦwww.aberglasney.org), half a mile south of the A40 near Broad Oak. While a partly ruined manor house is the estate's centrepiece, interest is focused on the stunning **gardens** where archeological work has peeled back half a century of neglect to reveal a set of interlinking walled gardens mostly constructed between the sixteenth and eighteenth centuries. Once massively overgrown, they have already regained much of their original formal splendour, especially the kitchen garden and what is thought to be the only secular cloister garden in Britain. A walkway leads around the top of the cloister, giving access to a set of six Victorian aviaries from where there are great views over the Jacobean pool garden. The highlight of the garden, however, is the **yew tunnel**, planted around three hundred years ago and trained over to root on the far side. The glassed-in atrium of the manor is now being populated with subtropical plants.

Llandeilo

Fifteen miles east of Carmarthen, the handsome market town of **LLANDEILO** is in a state of transition, with a small kernel of chi-chi cafés and shops set along the main Rhosmaen Street. There's little to see in town, but a mile west is the tumbledown shell of **Dinefwr Castle,** reached through the gorgeous parkland of **Dinefwr Park**. Sited on a wooded bluff above the Tywi, the castle became ill suited to the needs of the landowning Rhys family, who aspired to something a little more luxurious. The "new" castle, now named **Newton House** (mid-March to Oct Mon & Thurs–Sun 11am–5pm; house & park £5.45, park only £3.63; NT), was built in 1523, and has been fully restored with an interpretive centre and tearoom.

Behind the main street are the **tourist office** (Tues–Sat 10.30am–5pm; Ⓣ01558/823960) in the principal car park and, a couple of blocks to the north, the **train station**. **Accommodation** is limited to the chic *Cawdor Arms*, 70 Rhosmaen St (Ⓣ01558/823500, Ⓦwww.thecawdor.com; ④), fashioned from an old coaching inn, and *Penhill* (Ⓣ01558/823060, Ⓦwww.penhill.org.uk; ②), a simple but very pleasant **B&B** a stone's throw from Carreg Cennen castle (see below). For **eating**, try the coffee and cakes at *Barita*, 139 Rhosmaen St, or head across the road for excellent semi-formal dining at the *Cawdor Arms* (three-course lunch £13, dinner £22.50).

Carreg Cennen

Isolated in rural hinterland four miles southeast of Llandeilo, in the far western extremes of the Brecon Beacons National Park (see p.680), is one of the most magnificently sited castles in the whole of Wales, **Carreg Cennen Castle** (daily: April–Oct 9.30am–6.30pm; Nov to mid-March 9.30am–4pm; £3; CADW). Urien, one of King Arthur's knights, is said to have built his fortress on the fearsome rocky outcrop, although the first known construction dates from 1248. Carreg Cennen fell to the English in 1277, during Edward I's initial invasion of Wales, and was finally abandoned after being partially destroyed in 1462 by the Earl of Pembroke, who believed it to be the base of a group of lawless rebels. The most astounding aspect of the castle is its commanding position, 300ft above a sheer drop down into the green valley of the small River Cennen. The highlights of a visit are the views down into the river valley and the long descent down into a watery, pitch-black **cave** that is said to have served as a well. Torches are essential (£1 rental from the excellent tearoom near the car park) – continue as far as possible and then turn them off to experience spooky absolute darkness.

Laugharne

The village of **LAUGHARNE** (Talacharn), on the western side of the Taf estuary, is a delightful spot, with its ragged castle looming over the reeds and tidal flats, and narrow lanes snuggling in behind. Catch it in high season, though, and you're immediately aware that Laugharne is increasingly being taken over by the legend of the poet **Dylan Thomas**.

At the end of a narrow lane is the estuaryside **Dylan Thomas Boathouse** (daily: May–Oct & Easter weekend 10am–5.30pm; Nov–April 10.30am–3.30pm; £3.50; Ⓦ www.dylanthomasboathouse.com), the simple home of the Thomas family from 1949 until Dylan's death in 1953. It's an enchanting museum, with views of the peaceful, ever-changing water and light of the estuary and its "heron-priested shore".

Along the narrow lane, you can peer into the green garage where he wrote: curled photographs of literary heroes, a pen collection and scrunched-up balls of paper suggest that he is about to return at any minute. Thomas is buried in the graveyard of the parish church in the village centre, his grave marked by a simple white cross.

Laugharne plays its Thomas connections with curiously disgruntled aplomb – nowhere more so than his old boozing hole, **Brown's Hotel**, on the main street, where Thomas's cast-iron table still sits in a window alcove in the nicotine-crusted front bar. At the bottom of the main street, the gloomy hulk of **Laugharne Castle** (April–Sept daily 10am–5pm; £2.90; CADW) broods over the estuary. The views from the domed roof over the tight, huddled little town are sublime.

Tiny Laugharne has no tourist office and only limited **accommodation**, so book ahead if you want to stay. The welcoming *Swan Cottage*, 20 Gosport St (Ⓣ 01994/427409; ❷), has just one room, or try *The Boat House Inn*, 1 Gosport St (Ⓣ 01994/427263, Ⓦ www.theboathousebnb.co.uk; ❻). The *New Three Mariners* – also the best **drinking** hole – has comfy rooms (Ⓣ 01994/427426, Ⓦ www.newthreemariners.co.uk; ❸). The nearest **campsite** is *Ants Hill Camping*

▲ Dylan Thomas Boathouse

Dylan Thomas

Dylan Thomas was the stereotypical Celt – fiery, verbose, richly talented and habitually drunk. Born in 1914 into a snugly middle-class family in Swansea's Uplands district, Dylan's first glimmers of literary greatness came when he was posted, as a young reporter, to the *South Wales Evening Post* in Swansea. Some of his most popular tales in the *Portrait of the Artist as a Young Dog* were inspired during this period.

Rejecting what he perceived as the coarse provincialism of Swansea and Welsh life, Thomas arrived in London as a broke 20-year-old in 1934, weeks before the appearance of his first volume of poetry, which was published as the first prize in a *Sunday Referee* competition. Another volume followed shortly afterwards, cementing the engaging young Welshman's reputation in the British literary establishment. He married in 1937, and the newlyweds returned to Wales, settling in the hushed, provincial backwater of Laugharne. Short stories – crackling with rich and melancholy humour – tumbled out as swiftly as poems, further widening his base of admirers, though, like so many other writers, Thomas has only gained star status posthumously. Perhaps better than anyone, he writes in an identifiably Welsh, rhythmic wallow in the language.

Thomas, especially in public, liked to adopt the persona of what he perceived to be an archetypal stage Welshman: sonorous tones, loquacious, romantic and inclined towards a stiff tipple. This role was particularly popular in the United States, where he journeyed on lucrative lecture tours. It was on one of these that he died, in 1953, poisoned by a massive whisky overdose. Just one month earlier, he had put the finishing touches to what many regard as his masterpiece: *Under Milk Wood*, a "play for voices".

Park, a few hundred yards north of Laugharne (Ⓣ01994/427293, Ⓦwww.antshill.co.uk). For **lunches** and Welsh teas make for the *Pea Green Boat*, on the central square, and for something more substantial, go for the *Stable Door*, Market Lane (Ⓣ01994/427777; closed Mon–Wed), a relaxed conservatory tapas and wine bar with a classy menu. There's tasty fish and chips at the *Castle View*.

Tenby and Caldey Island

On a natural promontory of great strategic importance, the beguilingly old-fashioned resort of **TENBY** (Dinbych-y-Pysgod) is everything a seaside resort should be. Narrow streets wind down from the medieval centre to the harbour past miniature gardens fashioned to catch the afternoon sun. Steps lead down the steeper slopes to dockside arches which still house fishmongers selling the morning's catch.

First mentioned in a ninth-century bardic poem, Tenby grew under the twelfth-century Normans, who erected a castle on the headland in their attempt to colonize South Pembrokeshire and create a "**Little England beyond Wales**" – an appellation by which the area is still known today. Three times in the twelfth and thirteenth centuries the town was ransacked by the Welsh. In response, the castle was fortified once more and the stout town walls – largely still intact – were built. Tenby prospered as a major port between the fourteenth and sixteenth centuries, and although decline followed, the arrival of the railway brought renewed wealth as the town became a fashionable resort. Lines of neat, prosperous hotels and expensive shops still stand haughtily along the seafront.

The Town

Tenby is shaped like a triangle, with two sides formed by the coast meeting at Castle Hill. The third side is formed by the remains of the twenty-foot-high town **walls**, first built in the late thirteenth century and massively strengthened by Jasper Tudor in 1457. In the middle of the remaining stretch is the only town gate still standing, **Five Arches**, a semicircular barbican that combined practical day-to-day usage with hidden look-outs and angles acute enough to surprise invaders.

The centre's focal point is the 152-foot spire of the largely fifteenth-century **St Mary's church**, between St George's Street and Tudor Square; its pleasantly light interior shows the elaborate ceiling bosses in the chancel to good effect, and the tombs of local barons demonstrate Tenby's important mercantile tradition.

Wandering the surrounding medieval streets is one of Tenby's delights. **Sun Alley** is a tiny crack between overhanging whitewashed stone houses that connects Crackwell and High streets.

Wedged in a corner of Quay Hill is the fifteenth-century **Tudor Merchant's House** (April–Oct daily except Sat 11am–5pm; £2.20; NT). The compact house with its Flemish-style chimneypieces is on three floors, packed with furniture, either seventeenth- and eighteenth-century originals or Tudor repro made traditionally without glue or nails: notice the superb, inlaid 1753 marriage chest.

Practicalities

Tenby's **train station** is at the western end of the town centre, at the bottom of Warren Street. Some **buses** stop at South Parade, at the top of Trafalgar Road, although most call at the bus shelter on Upper Park Road, just along from the **tourist office** (daily: June & Sept–Oct 10am–5.30pm; July & Aug 10am–6pm; Nov–May 10am–5pm; ⓣ01834/842402).

Tenby has dozens of **hotels** and **guesthouses**, all pressed from pretty much the same mould, though paying more gets you a wider range of facilities and a sea view. The best budget place is the spotless *Boulston Cottage*, 29 Trafalgar Rd (ⓣ01834/843289; ❷). *Glenholme*, Picton Terrace (ⓣ01834/843909, ⓦwww.glenholmetenby.co.uk; ❷), is also agreeable and has en-suite rooms. Stepping up a little try *Lyndale House*, Warren Street (ⓣ01834/842836; ❹), a welcoming B&B near the station, or *Penally Abbey* (ⓣ01834/843033, ⓦwww.penally-abbey.com; ❼), a luxurious country-house hotel a mile west of Tenby in Penally. Four miles west of Tenby, overlooking the cliffs, is the bright and modern *Manorbier* YHA **hostel**, at Skrinkle Haven (ⓣ0870/770 5954, ⓦwww.yha.org.uk; dorms £14; March–Oct). You can **camp** at the small and semi-official *Meadow Farm*, Northcliff, on the northern fringes of town (ⓣ01834/844829; April–Oct).

There are dozens of **cafés** and **restaurants** around town. *Fecci and Sons*, Upper Frog Street, has ice cream and Italian snacks, while *Café 25*, 25 High St, does good coffee and has Internet access. The wood-beamed *Coach and Horses* on Upper Frog Street serves up well-prepared bar meals and tasty Thai dishes as well as good beer. For a splurge, don't miss *Plantagenet House*, Quay Hill (ⓣ01834/842350), offering delicious meals in the congenial surrounds of Tenby's oldest house, complete with massive twelfth-century Flemish chimney breast. For **pubs**, head for the *Lifeboat Tavern*, Tudor Square, or the *Normandie Inn* on Upper Frog Street.

Caldey Island

Celtic monks first settled **Caldey Island** (Ynys Pyr), a couple of miles offshore, in the sixth century. Little is then known of the island until 1136, when it was given to the Benedictine monks who founded their priory here. They lost it with the dissolution of the monasteries in 1536, and it eventually ended up in the hands of Reformed Cistercians who have run the place for the last century.

Boats leave Tenby Harbour (or Castle Beach when the tide is out) every thirty minutes (Easter–Oct Mon–Fri 10.30am–4pm; daily every 20min mid-May to mid-Sept; £10 return; ⓣ01834/844453, ⓦwww.caldey-island.co.uk) for the twenty-minute journey to the island. **Tickets** are sold at the kiosk in Castle Square, directly above the harbour.

The island's village is the main hub of Caldey life. As well as a tiny post office and popular tearoom, there's a **perfume shop** selling the herbal fragrances distilled by the monks from Caldey's abundant flora. The narrow road going to the left leads down to the heavily restored **chapel of St David**, whose most impressive feature is its round-arched Norman door. A lane leads south from the village to the old **priory**, and the remarkable, twelfth-century **St Illtud's church**, which houses one of the most significant pre-Norman finds in Wales, the sandstone **Ogham Cross**, found under the stained-glass window on the south side of the nave. It is carved with an inscription from the sixth century which was added to, in Latin, during the ninth. The lane continues south from the site, climbing up to the gleaming white island **lighthouse**, built in 1828, from which there are memorable views.

Southern Pembrokeshire

The southern zigzag of coast that darts west from Tenby is a strange mix of caravan parks, Ministry of Defence shooting ranges, spectacularly beautiful bays and gull-covered cliffs. From Tenby, the A4139 passes through **Penally**, with its wonderful beach, and continues past idyllic coves, the lily ponds at **Bosherston** and the remarkable and ancient **St Govan's Chapel**, squeezed into a rock cleft above the crashing waves. The ancient town of **Pembroke** really only warrants a visit to its impressive castle before pressing on to neighbouring **Lamphey**, with its fine Bishop's Palace. **Buses** to most corners of the peninsula radiate out from Haverfordwest and Pembroke.

Penally to Bosherston

The coastal path south and west of Tenby skirts the gorgeous long beach of **Penally**, then hugs the cliff top for a couple of miles to **Lydstep Haven** (fee charged for the sands). A mile further west is the cove of Skrinkle Haven, and above it the excellent *Manorbier* YHA hostel (see p.663). A couple of miles further on, the quaint village of **MANORBIER** (Maenorbŷr), pronounced "manner-beer", was birthplace in 1146 of the Welsh-Norman historian, writer and ecclesiastical reformist Giraldus Cambrensis. Manorbier's **castle** (Easter–Sept daily 10.30am–5.30pm; £3.50), founded in the early twelfth century as an impressive baronial residence, sits above the village and its beach on a hill of wild gorse. The strong Norman walls hold a warren of dark passageways to explore, occasionally opening out into little cells with lacklustre wax figures purporting to illustrate the castle's history.

The rocky little harbour at **Stackpole Quay**, reached via the small lane from Freshwater East through East Trewent, is a good starting point for walks along the breathtaking cliffs to the north. Another walk leads half a mile south to one of the finest beaches in Pembrokeshire, **Barafundle Bay**, with its soft beach fringed by wooded cliffs at either end. The path continues around the coast, through the dunes of **Stackpole Warren**, to **BROAD HAVEN**, where a

The Pembrokeshire Coast National Park and Coast Path

The **Pembrokeshire Coast** is Britain's only predominantly sea-based national park (Ⓦwww.pcnpa.org.uk), hugging the rippled coast around the entire western section of Wales. Established in 1952, the park is not one easily identifiable mass, rather a series of occasionally unconnected coastal and inland scenic patches.

Crawling around almost every wriggle of the coastline, the **Pembrokeshire Coast Path** winds 186 miles from Amroth, just east of Tenby, to its northern terminus at St Dogmael's near Cardigan. For the vast majority of the way, the path clings precariously to cliff-top routes, overlooking seal-basking rocks, craggy offshore islands, unexpected gashes of sand and shrieking clouds of sea birds. The most popular and ruggedly inspiring segments of the coast path are the stretch along the southern coast from the castle at Manorbier to the tiny cliff chapel at Bosherston; either side of St Bride's Bay, around St David's Head and the Marloes Peninsula; and the generally quieter northern coast either side of Fishguard, past undulating contours, massive cliffs, bays and old ports.

Spring is perhaps the finest season for walking as the crowds are yet to arrive and the cliff-top flora is at its most vivid. There are numerous publications available about the coast path, of which the best is Brian John's *National Trail Guide* (£13), which includes sections of 1:25,000 maps of the route. The national park publishes an accommodation list on its website Ⓦwww.pcnpa.org.uk.

pleasant small beach overlooks several rocky islets, now managed by the National Trust. Road access is through the village of **BOSHERSTON** where three artificial fingers of water known as **Bosherston Lakes** (free) were beautifully landscaped in the late eighteenth century. The westernmost lake is the most scenic, especially in late spring and early summer when the lilies that form a carpet across its surface are in full bloom.

A lane from Bosherston dips south across the MoD training grounds to a spot overlooking the cliffs where tiny **St Govan's Chapel** is wedged: it's a remarkable building, known to be at least eight hundred years old. Steps descend straight into the sandy-floored chapel, now devoid of any furnishings save for the simple stone altar.

Pembroke and around

The old county town of **PEMBROKE** (Penfro) and its fearsome castle sit on the southern side of Pembroke River. Despite its location, Pembroke is surprisingly dull, with one long main street of attractive Georgian and Victorian houses, some intact stretches of medieval town wall, but little else to catch the eye.

Pembroke's history is inextricably bound up with that of its impregnable **castle** (daily: April–Sept 9.30am–6pm; March & Oct 10am–5pm; Nov–Feb 10am–4pm; £3.50; Ⓦwww.pembrokecastle.co.uk), founded by the Normans as the strongest link in their chain of fortresses across South Wales. During the Civil War, Pembroke was a Parliamentarian stronghold until the town's military governor suddenly switched allegiance to the king, whereupon Cromwell's troops sacked the castle after a 48-day siege. Yet despite Cromwell's battering, and centuries of subsequent neglect, Pembroke Castle still inspires awe at its sheer, bloody-minded bulk. The soaring gatehouse leads into the large, grassy courtyard around the vast, round Norman **keep**, 75ft high and with walls 18ft thick. The intact towers and battlements contain many heavily restored communal rooms; some of them are used to house excellent displays on the history of the castle and the Tudor empire.

▲ Pembrokeshire (standing stones)

Practicalities

Pembroke's **Main Street** stretches from the **train station** in the east to the walls of the castle. The **tourist office** (daily: Easter–June, Sept & Oct 10am–5pm; July & Aug 10am–5.30pm; ⓣ01646/622388), is on Commons Road, parallel to Main Street. If you decide to **stay**, head straight for *Beech House B&B*, 78 Main St (ⓣ01646/683740; ❶), which has shared bathrooms but is fantastic value – one room even boasts a four-poster. If it's full, try *High Noon Guesthouse*, close to the train station on Lower Lamphey Road (ⓣ01646/683736; ⓦwww.highnoon.co.uk; ❷), or stay in Lamphey (see below), a couple of miles east.

Trains continue from Pembroke to Pembroke Dock, two miles northwest, where **Irish Ferries** (ⓣ0870/517 1717, ⓦwww.irishferries.com) operate two daily services to Rosslare in Ireland.

For espresso and light **meals** head for *The Quayside Café in the Cornstore* (closed Sun), down by the river on North Quay, and for something more substantial try the delicious bar and restaurant fodder at the Old *King's Arms Hotel* at 13 Main St. For **drinking** it's hard to beat a summer evening at the *Waterman's Arms*, opposite *The Cornstore*, where you can while away the hours on a veranda overlooking the Mill Pond.

Lamphey

The pleasant village of **LAMPHEY** (Llandyfai), two miles southeast of Pembroke, is best known for the ruined **Bishop's Palace** (daily 10am–5pm; £2.90; CADW), off a quiet lane to the north of the village. A country retreat for the bishops of St David's, the palace dates from around the thirteenth century, but was abandoned following the Reformation. Stout walls surround the ruins, which are scattered over a large area, and many of the palace buildings have long been lost under grassy banks. Most impressive are the remains of the Great Hall, extending across the entire eastern end of the complex.

One of the area's swankiest **hotels** is here, in the shape of the Neoclassical *Lamphey Court Hotel* (ⓣ01646/672273, ⓦwww.lampheycourt.co.uk; ❼), opposite the Bishop's Palace. Otherwise, there's the more modest *Lamphey Hall*

Hotel (Ⓣ01646/672394, Ⓦwww.lampheyhallhotel.co.uk; ⑤) by the church, or the characterful Georgian *Lower Lamphey Park* (Ⓣ01646/672906, Ⓦwww.lowerlampheypark.co.uk; ④), located a few hundred yards north of the delightful and popular *Dial Inn*, The Ridgeway, which offers a reliable menu and good beer.

Carew

Tiny **CAREW**, four miles east of Pembroke, is a pretty place beside the River Carew. Just south of the river crossing stands the village's graceful thirteen-foot **Celtic cross**, the remarkably intact taper of the shaft covered in fine tracery of ancient Welsh designs. A small hut beyond the cross serves as the ticket office for **Carew Castle and Tidal Mill** (Easter–Oct daily 10am–5pm, castle only Mon–Fri Nov–Easter 11am–3pm; £3; Ⓦwww.carewcastle.com). The castle, a hybrid of Elizabethan fancy and earlier defensive necessity, is a few hundred yards to the east of the **Carew French Mill**, used commercially until 1937 and now the only tide-powered mill in Wales. The impressive eighteenth-century exterior belies the rather pedestrian exhibitions and audiovisual displays inside, which describe the milling process.

Mid- and northern Pembrokeshire

The most westerly point of Wales is one of the country's most enchanting. The chief town of the region, **Haverfordwest**, is rather soulless, but it's useful as a jumping-off point for the stunning **St Bride's Bay**. The coast here is broken into rocky outcrops, islands and broad, sweeping beaches curving between two headlands that sit like giant crab pincers facing out into the warm Gulf Stream. The southernmost headland winds around every conceivable angle, offering calm, east-facing sands at **Dale** and sunny expanses of south-facing beach at **Marloes**. At **Martin's Haven**, boats depart for the offshore islands of **Skomer**, **Skokholm** and **Grassholm**. To the north, there's spectacularly lacerated coast around **St David's peninsula**, with towering cliffs interrupted only by occasional strips of sand. The tiny cathedral city of **St David's** is most definitely a highlight: rooks and crows circle above the impressive ruins of the huge Bishop's Palace, sitting beneath the delicate bulk of the cathedral, the most impressive in Wales.

The north-facing coast that forms the very southern tip of Cardigan Bay is wild, rugged and breathtakingly beautiful. It's also noticeably less commercialized and far more Welsh than the touristy shores of south and mid-Pembrokeshire. From the crags and cairns above St David's Head, the coast path perches precariously on the cliffs where only the thousands of sea birds have access. Hidden coves and secluded beaches slice into the rocky headlands, which are at their most magnificent around **Strumble Head,** where a picturesque lighthouse flashes its warning from a tiny islet. From here, there's only wilderness to detain you en route to the charming town of **Newport** – unless you're heading for **Fishguard** and the ferries to Ireland.

Haverfordwest

In the seventeenth and eighteenth centuries, the town of **HAVERFORDWEST** (Hwlffordd), ten miles north of Pembroke, prospered as a port and trading centre. Despite its natural advantages, it is scarcely a place to linger, though as its the main transport hub and shopping centre for western Pembrokeshire, you are likely to pass through.

The **tourist office** (June to mid-July Mon–Sat 9.30am–5pm, mid-July to Aug daily 9.30am–5pm, Sept–April Mon–Sat 10am–4pm; ⓣ01437/763110) is next to the bus terminus, at the end of the Old Bridge. There's low-cost **accommodation** at *College Guesthouse*, 93 Hill St (ⓣ01437/763710, ⓦwww.collegeguesthouse.com; ③), or you could venture three miles west to the lovely *East Hook Farmhouse*, Portfield Gate (ⓣ01437/762211, ⓦwww.easthookfarmhouse.co.uk; ③), which serves delicious breakfasts, and dinner for around £20. There's a cheap **campsite** two miles northwest on the A487, at the *Rising Sun Inn* in Pelcomb Bridge (ⓣ01437/765171).

For **eating**, grab a freshly filled baguette in *Dylan's*, 23 High St, or visit the inexpensive *George's*, 24 Market St (closed Sun), where you can eat in a lovely walled garden if the weather allows, or the cellar bistro if not.

Dale and around

DALE, fourteen miles west of Haverfordwest, can be unbearably crowded in peak season; the east-facing shore makes it excellent for bathing and **water sports** in the lighter seas. West Wales Windsurf and Sailing (ⓣ01646/636642, ⓦwww.surfdale.co.uk) gives instruction in power-boating, windsurfing, surfing, sailing and kayaking (around £65 per half-day), and rents gear. Fast boats leave from here to Skokholm and Grassholm islands (see below).

There's B&B **accommodation** on the Dale waterfront at the comfortable *Richmond House* (ⓣ07974/925009, ⓦwww.richmond-house.com; ③) which also has an upscale bunkhouse with beds for £18, and at *Point Farm B&B* (ⓣ01646/636541, ⓦwww.pointfarm.info; ④; closed Dec & Jan), ten minutes' walk along the shore to the south, with cosy rooms, excellent hospitality and sea views.

Marloes

MARLOES, a mile north of Dale, is an unexciting little place, but the broad, deserted beach is magnificent, and offers a safe place to swim, as well as fine views of the island of Skokholm. From here, the coast path and a narrow road continue for two miles to the National Trust-owned headland of **Deer Park**, the far grassy far tip of the southern peninsula of St Bride's Bay – and **Martin's Haven**, from where you can take a **boat** out to the islands of Skomer, Skokholm and Grassholm. The *Marloes Sands* YHA **hostel** (ⓣ01646/636667, ⓦwww.yha.org.uk; dorms £9.50; April to mid-Sept), consists of a series of converted farm buildings overlooking the northern end of the beach.

Skomer, Skokholm and Grassholm islands

Weather permitting, **boats** (April–Oct Tues–Sun and bank holidays 10am, 11am & noon; £14) run from Martin's Haven to **Skomer Island**, a 722-acre flat-topped island rich in sea birds and spectacular carpets of wild flowers, perfect for birdwatching and walking.

Though no landings are permitted, frequent, fast cruises leave from Dale to **Skokholm Island** (daily 11.30am, 4.30pm & 6.30pm; 2hr; £25), a couple of miles south of Skomer and far smaller, more rugged and remote, noted for its cliffs of warm red sandstone. Britain's first bird observatory was founded here as far back as the seventeenth century, and there are still a huge number of petrels, gulls, puffins, oystercatchers and rare Manx shearwaters. Boat trips also head out even further, to the tiny outpost of **Grassholm Island**, over five miles west of Skomer (daily 12.30pm; 2hr; £25). Visiting the island is an unforgettable experience, largely due to the 70,000 or so screaming gannets who call it home.

No **booking** is required for Skomer trips, but otherwise bookings are made through Dale Sailing (Ⓣ0800/0284090 or 01646/603110, Ⓦwww.dale-sailing.co.uk).

St David's and around

ST DAVID'S (Tyddewi) is one of the most enchanting spots in Britain. This miniature city – really just a large village – sits back from its purple- and gold-flecked cathedral at the very westernmost point of Wales in bleak, treeless countryside. Spiritually, it's the centre of Welsh ecclesiasticism. Traditionally founded by the Welsh patron saint himself in 550 AD, the See of St David's has drawn pilgrims for a millennium and a half – William the Conqueror included – and by 1120, Pope Calixtus II decreed that two journeys to St David's were the spiritual equivalent of one to Rome. Today, with so many historical sites, outdoor-pursuit centres, surf beaches, good cafés, superb walks, bathing and climbing, St David's and its peninsula are a must if you want to experience Wales at its wildest.

The City

From the central **Celtic cross**, the main street runs under the thirteenth-century **Tower Gate**, which forms the entrance to the serene **Cathedral Close**, backed by a windswept landscape of treeless heathland. The cathedral lies down to the right, hidden in a hollow by the River Alun. This apparent modesty is explained by reasons of defence, as a towering cathedral, visible from the sea on all sides, would have been vulnerable to attack. On the other side of the babbling Alun lie the ruins of the Bishop's Palace.

The Cathedral

The **cathedral**'s (donation requested; Ⓦwww.stdavidscathedral.org.uk) 125-foot tower, topped by pert golden pinnacles, has clocks on only three sides – the people of the northern part of the parish couldn't raise enough money for one to be constructed facing them. You enter through the south side of the low, twelfth-century nave in full view of its most striking feature, the intricate latticed oak **roof**. This was added to hide emergency restoration work carried out in the sixteenth century, when the nave was in danger of collapse. The nave floor still has a discernible slope and the support buttresses inserted in the northern aisle look incongruously new and temporary. At the back of the south choir stalls is a unique **monarch's stall**, complete with royal crest, for, unlike any other British cathedral, the Queen is an automatic member of the St David's Cathedral Chapter.

Separating the choir and the presbytery is a finely traced, rare **parclose screen**. The back wall of the **presbytery** was once the eastern extremity of the cathedral, as can be seen from the two lines of windows. The upper row has been left intact, while the lower three were blocked up and filled with delicate gold mosaics in the nineteenth century. The colourful fifteenth-century roof, a deceptively simple repeating medieval pattern, was extensively restored by Gilbert Scott in the mid-nineteenth century. On the south side are the thirteenth-century tombs of bishops Iorwerth and Anselm de la Grace, and opposite is the disappointingly plain tomb of St David, largely destroyed in the Reformation.

The Bishop's Palace

From the cathedral, a path leads to the splendid fourteenth-century **Bishop's Palace** (mid-March to May & Oct daily 9.30am–5pm; June–Sept daily 9.30am–6pm; Nov to mid-March Mon–Sat 9.30am–4pm, Sun 11am–4pm; £2.90; CADW). The huge central quadrangle is fringed by a neat jigsaw of ruined buildings built in extraordinarily richly tinted stone. The **arched parapets** that run along the top of most of the walls were a favourite feature of Bishop Gower. Two ruined but still impressive halls – the **Bishop's Hall** and the enormous **Great Hall**, with its glorious rose window – lie off the main quadrangle, above and around a myriad of rooms adorned by some eerily eroded corbels. Underneath the Great Hall are dank vaults containing an interesting exhibition about the palace and the indulgent lifestyles of its occupants. The destruction of the palace is largely due to sixteenth-century Bishop Barlow, who supposedly stripped the buildings of their lead roofs to provide dowries for his five daughters' marriages to bishops.

Practicalities

The main road from Haverfordwest enters St David's past the National Park **tourist office** (daily 9.30am–5.30pm; ⓣ01437/720392, ⓦwww.stdavids.co.uk), and continues for two hundred yards down High St to the **main bus stop** in New Street. You can **rent bikes** from St. David's Cycle Hire (£10 half-day, £15 full day), tucked behind TYF, 1 High St (ⓣ01437/721611, ⓦwww.tyf.com), which runs various **outdoor courses** and pioneered **coasteering** (£50) – a half-day spent scrambling over rocks, jumping off cliffs and swimming across the narrow bays of St David's peninsula.

Good, inexpensive places to **stay** include the shared-bath *Pen Albro*, 18 Goat St (ⓣ01437/721865; ❶) or *Alandale*, 43 Nun St (ⓣ01437/720404; ❹. *Ramsey House*, Lower Moor (ⓣ01437/720321, ⓦwww.ramseyhouse.co.uk; ❺), is an excellent small hotel a quarter of a mile out on the road to Porth Clais with superb breakfasts; or try *Crug Glas* (ⓣ01348/831302, ⓦwww.crug-glas.co.uk; ❻), four miles northeast at Abereiddy, a luxurious country house on a working farm also serving delicious four-course evening meals for around £20. The nearest **campsite** is at *Caerfai Farm*, Caerfai Bay (ⓣ01437/720548; May–Sept), a fifteen-minute walk south of the city, and there's a YHA **hostel** in a former farmhouse two miles northwest, near the stunning, aptly named Whitesands Bay (ⓣ0870/770 6042, ⓦwww.yha.org.uk; April–Oct).

For inexpensive **eating**, head for *Pebbles Gallery and Café* on Cross Street or *The Bench*, 11 High St, a classy but relaxed restaurant, café and wine bar that's perfect for a quick panini or for lingering over pizza or fresh pasta dishes (£5–9) served inside or out; it also offers Internet access, and Italian ice cream to go. For more of a treat, *Lawton's at No. 16*, 16 Nun St (ⓣ01437/729220), serves delicious meals (mains £14–18) in sleek modern surroundings. **Nightlife** boils down to the lively *Farmers Arms*, Goat Street, the city's only real pub, with a terrace overlooking the cathedral. But be warned: the food and service here can be very average.

The St David's peninsula

Surrounded on three sides by inlets, coves and rocky stacks, St David's is an easy base for some excellent walking around the headland of the same name. A mile due south, the popular **Caerfai Bay** provides a sandy gash in the purple sandstone cliffs, rock which was used in the construction of the cathedral. To the immediate west is the craggy indentation of **St Non's Bay**, reached from Goat Street in St David's. St Non reputedly gave birth to St David at this spot during a tumultuous storm around 500 AD; the bay has received pilgrims for centuries, resulting in the foundation of a tiny, isolated chapel in the pre-Norman age. The ruins of the subsequent thirteenth-century chapel now lie in a field near the sadly dingy well and coy shrine where the nation's patron saint is said to have been born.

Further west, **Porth Clais** is supposedly the place at which St David was baptized. Now a quaint harbour, it was once the city's main harbour, the spruced-up remains of which can still be seen at the bottom of the turquoise river creek.

Northwards from **St. Justinians** – which is two miles west of St David's – the coast path leads over another lowly headland to the magnificent **Whitesands Bay** (Porth-mawr), a narrow arc of dune-backed sand that's popular with both surfers and families alike, and is also accessible by road from St. David's. From here though, there's no further road access to the coast for some distance, giving this section of the coast path a thoroughly wild feel, and making it perfect for wildlife-watching.

The harbour at St Justinian's has a ticket hut for the boats over to **Ramsey Island** (Ⓦwww.ramseyisland.co.uk). This enchanting dual-humped plateau, less than two miles long, has been under the able stewardship of the RSPB since 1992. Birds of prey circle the skies above the island, but it's better known for the tens of thousands of sea birds that noisily crowd the sheer cliffs on its western side and the seals lazing sloppily about.

Boat landings are with Thousand Islands Expeditions (April–Oct daily; Ⓣ01437/721721, Ⓦwww.thousandislands.co.uk; £15) who allow up to six hours on Ramsey. During the springtime nesting season you actually see more from boats which circle the island but don't land: try Voyages of Discovery (daily; Ⓣ01437/720285 or 0800/854367, Ⓦwww.ramseyisland.co.uk; £22).

Fishguard

Back inland, the main road runs northeast, parallel to numerous small and less-commercialized bays, to the wild and windswept **Strumble Head**. This protects **FISHGUARD** (Abergwaun), an attractive, hilltop town seldom seen as anything more than a brief stop-off to or from the Stena Line **ferries** and fast catamarans (Ⓣ08705/707070, Ⓦwww.stenaline.com), which leave four to five times daily for Rosslare in Ireland.

In the centre of town is the **Royal Oak Inn**, where a bizarre Franco-Irish attempt to conquer Britain in 1797 at nearby Carregwastad Point is remembered. The hapless forces arrived to negotiate a cease-fire, which was turned by the assembled British into an unconditional surrender. Part of the invaders' low morale – apart from the drunken farce in which they'd become embroiled – is said to have been sparked off by the sight of a hundred local women marching towards them. The troops mistook their stovepipe hats and red flannel dresses for the outfit of a British infantry troop and instantly capitulated. Even if this is not true, it is an undisputed fact that 47-year-old cobbler Jemima Nicholas, the "Welsh Heroine", single-handedly captured fourteen French soldiers. Her grave can be seen next to the uninspiring Victorian parish church, St Mary's, behind the pub. The fabulous **Fishguard Tapestry**, which tells the story of this ramshackle invasion, is on display in the town hall.

Buses stop in the central Market Square, right outside Fishguard's **tourist office** (July & Aug daily 10am–5pm; April–June, Sept & Oct Mon–Sat 10am–5pm; Nov–March Mon–Sat 10am–4pm; Ⓣ01437/776636, Ⓦwww.abergwaun.com).

The **train station** is next to the ferry terminal on Quay Road. Buses usually meet ferries, though seldom the catamarans; a **taxi** (Ⓣ01348/872088) into town costs around £3.

Accommodation is plentiful and cheap: you'll find comfortable rooms at *Glanmoy Lodge*, on Trefwrgi Road, ten minutes' walk from the port (Ⓣ01348/874333, Ⓦwww.glanmoylodge.co.uk; ❷), and up in Fishguard the peaceful *Plain Dealings* (Ⓣ01348/873655; ❷), half a mile from the centre on Tower Hill. The effortlessly elegant *Cefn-y-Dre* farmhouse (Ⓣ01348/875663, Ⓦwww.cefnydre.co.uk; ❺) is a mile out of Fishguard following Hamilton Street. There are central **dorms** at *Hamilton Backpackers Lodge*, 21–23 Hamilton St (Ⓣ01348/874797; dorms from £14; ❶), and well-appointed **camping** at *Gwaun Vale Caravan Park* (Ⓣ01348/874698, Ⓦwww.gwaunvale.co.uk) on the B4313, a mile and a half southeast of town.

Head to *Three Main Street* for good coffee and **snacks**, then along the street to the *Royal Oak*, Main Square, for a pub meal and good beer.

Newport

Newport (Trefdraeth) is an ancient and proud little town set on a gentle slope that courses down to the estuary of the Afon Nyfer. There's little to do except stroll around, but you'd be hard pressed to find a better place to do it. The footpath that runs along the river either side of the bridge is marked as the Pilgrims' Way; follow it eastwards for a delightful riverbank stroll to Nevern, a couple of miles away. Another popular local walk is up to the craggy and magical peak of **Carn Ingli**, the Hill of Angels, behind the town. On Lower St Mary Street, the old school has metamorphosed into the excellent **West Wales Eco Centre** (Mon–Fri 9.30am–4.30pm; variable extended hours in summer; free), a venue for exhibitions, advice and resources on various aspects of sustainable living.

Newport's nearest beach, the **Parrog**, is complete with sandy stretches at low tide. On the other side of the estuary is the vast dune-backed **Traethmawr beach**, reached over the town bridge down Feidr Pen-y-Bont. Newport also makes a good jumping-off point for **Pentre Ifan**, a couple of miles south of Newport, with its massive, four-thousand-year-old capstone.

The **tourist office** (April–Oct Mon–Sat 9am–5.30pm; Ⓣ01239/820912) is on Long Street, just off the main road. There's plenty of **accommodation**: tucked in behind the Eco Centre on Lower St Mary Street, the *Trefdraeth* YHA **hostel** (Ⓣ0870/7706072, Ⓦwww.yha.org.uk; ❶) is a classy conversion of an old school with bunks and a couple of private rooms; otherwise, *The Globe* B&B (Ⓣ01239/820296, Ⓦwww.theglobepembs.co.uk; ❷) is about the cheapest around and serves continental breakfast. If your budget is a bit bigger, try the superb *Cnapan Country House* on East Street (Ⓣ01239/820575, Ⓦwww.online-holidays.net/cnapan; ❼; closed Jan & Feb). The nearest **campsite** is the *Morawelon* (Ⓣ01239/820565), just west of town, at the Parrog, with nice gardens and its own café.

For **food**, the *Cnapan Country House* (closed Mon & Tues) serves exquisite meals, or there are solid pub classics, including good curries, at the *Royal Oak*, on Bridge Street. *Café Fleur* on Market Street does fantastic sweet and savoury crêpes, panini, smoothies and good coffee.

Travel details

Buses

For information on all local and national bus services, contact Traveline ⓣ0870/608 2608, ⓦwww.traveline-cymru.org.uk.

Cardiff to: Abergavenny (hourly; 1hr 20min); Aberystwyth (2 daily; 4hr); Blaenafon (hourly, 1 change; 1hr 40min); Brecon (6 daily; 1hr 25min); Caerphilly (every 30min; 40min); Cardiff International Airport (every 30min; 30min); Chepstow (hourly; 1hr 20min); London (6 daily; 3hr 10min); Merthyr Tydfil (every 30min; 45min); Newport, Monmouthshire (every 30min; 30min); Swansea (every 30min; 1hr).

Carmarthen to: Aberystwyth (hourly; 2hr 15min); Haverfordwest (3 daily; 1hr); Kidwelly (8 daily; 25min); Laugharne (10 daily; 25min); Llandeilo (12 daily; 30–40min); Swansea (every 30min; 1hr 20min); Tenby (2 daily; 45min).

Chepstow to: Cardiff (every 30min; 1hr 20min); Monmouth (at least hourly; 50min); Newport, Monmouthshire (hourly; 50min); Tintern (8 daily; 20min).

Fishguard to: Cardigan (hourly; 50min); Haverfordwest (hourly; 40min); Newport, Pembrokeshire (hourly; 20min); St David's (7 daily; 50min).

Haverfordwest to: Carmarthen (3 daily; 1hr); Fishguard (hourly; 40min); Manorbier (hourly; 1hr 10min); Newport, Pembrokeshire (hourly; 1hr); Pembroke (hourly; 45min); St David's (hourly; 45min); Tenby (9 daily; 1hr).

Llandovery to: Brecon (4 daily; 45min); Llandeilo (10 daily; 50min).

Merthyr Tydfil to: Abergavenny (every 30min; 1hr 30min); Brecon (9 daily; 40min); Cardiff (every 15min; 45min); Swansea (hourly; 1hr).

Monmouth to: Abergavenny (8 daily; 40min); Chepstow (at least hourly; 50min); Raglan (hourly; 10min); Tintern (hourly; 30min).

Newport (Monmouthshire) to: Abergavenny (hourly; 1hr); Blaenafon (every 15min; 1hr); Brecon (every 2hr; 2hr 20min); Caerphilly (every 30min; 40min); Cardiff (every 30min; 40min); Chepstow (hourly; 50min).

Newport (Pembrokeshire) to: Fishguard (hourly; 20min); Haverfordwest (hourly; 1hr 10min).

Pembroke to: Bosherston (2 daily; 30min); Haverfordwest (hourly; 1hr); Manorbier (every 30min; 20min); Pembroke Dock (every 10min; 10min); Stackpole (2 daily; 20min); Tenby (hourly; 40min).

St David's to: Broad Haven (5 daily; 40min); Fishguard (7 daily; 50min); Haverfordwest (hourly; 45min).

Swansea to: Brecon (3 daily; 1hr 30min); Cardiff (every 30min; 1hr); Carmarthen (every 30min; 1hr 20min); Dan-yr-ogof (2 daily; 1hr); Merthyr Tydfil (hourly; 1hr); Mumbles (every 10min; 15min); Oxwich (7 daily; 1hr); Port Eynon (12 daily; 50min); Rhossili (Mon–Sat 10 daily; 1hr).

Tenby to: Carmarthen (2 daily; 1hr); Haverfordwest (9 daily; 1hr); Manorbier (hourly; 20min); Pembroke (hourly; 40min).

Trains

For information on all local and national rail services, contact National Rail Enquiries ⓣ08457/484950, ⓦwww.nationalrail.co.uk.

Cardiff to: Abergavenny (hourly; 40min); Bristol (every 30min; 50min); Caerphilly (every 15min; 20min); Carmarthen (hourly; 1hr 45min); Chepstow (hourly; 40min); Haverfordwest (9 daily; 2hr 30min); London (hourly; 2hr); Merthyr Tydfil (hourly; 1hr); Newport, Monmouthshire (every 15–30min; 10min); Pontypool (hourly; 30min); Swansea (every 30min; 1hr).

Carmarthen to: Cardiff (hourly; 1hr 30min–2hr); Fishguard (2 daily; 1hr); Haverfordwest (11 daily; 45min); Pembroke (9 daily; 1hr 10min); Swansea (every 30min; 45min); Tenby (9 daily; 50min).

Haverfordwest to: Cardiff (8 daily; 2hr 40min); Carmarthen (10 daily; 55min); Swansea (8 daily; 1hr 30min).

Newport (Monmouthshire) to: Abergavenny (every 30min; 30min); Cardiff (every 15–30min; 15min); Chepstow (hourly; 20min); London (every 30min; 1hr 50min); Swansea (hourly; 1hr 20min).

Pembroke to: Lamphey (9 daily; 3min); Manorbier (9 daily; 10min); Pembroke Dock (9 daily; 10min); Tenby (9aily; 20min).

Swansea to: Cardiff (at least every 30min; 50min); Carmarthen (hourly; 50min); Haverfordwest (9 daily; 1hr 30min); Llandrindod Wells (4 daily; 2hr 20min); London (every 30min; 3hr); Newport, Monmouthshire (at least every 30min; 1hr 20min); Pembroke (8 daily; 2hr); Tenby (8 daily; 1hr 40min).

Tenby to: Carmarthen (7 daily; 50min); Pembroke (7 daily; 20min); Swansea (7 daily; 1hr 40min).

St Davids to Fishguard (5 daily; 40min); Haverfordwest (hourly; 40min).

Mid-Wales

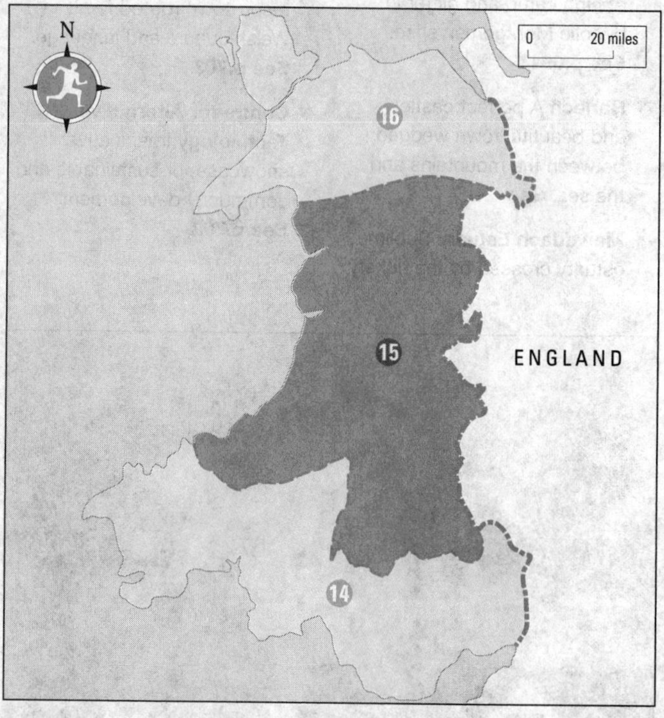

CHAPTER 15

Highlights

* **Abergavenny Food Festival** If food is the new religion, then this lovely town in the Black Mountains is fast becoming a new Jerusalem. See p.686

* **Andrew Logan Museum of Sculpture** A surprising blast of high camp and glitter in bucolic Montgomeryshire. See p.694

* **Harlech** A perfect castle and beautiful town wedged between the mountains and the sea. See p.697

* **Mawddach Estuary** Sublime estuary crossed by the rickety rail bridge to Barmouth. See p.698

* **Ardudwy Beach** Eight miles of one of the best beaches in Wales, with wide sands and a warm sea. See p.698

* **Aberystwyth** Lively, seaside resort town rooted firmly in Welsh culture and language. See p.703

* **Centre for Alternative Technology** Imaginative showcase for sustainable and community development. See p.703

▲ Harlech Castle

15

Mid-Wales

Mid-Wales is a huge, beautiful region, crisscrossed by breathtaking mountain passes, dotted with characterful little towns and never far from water – whether sparkling rivers, great lakes or the sea of the Cambrian coast. This is certainly the least-known part of Wales, which is perhaps to its advantage, for it's here that you'll find Welsh culture at its most natural, folded into the contours of the land, as it has been for centuries.

A quarter of the area of Wales is occupied by the landlocked county of **Powys**, whose name harks back to a fifth-century Welsh kingdom. By far the most popular attraction is **Brecon Beacons National Park**, stretching from the dramatic limestone country of the Black Mountain (singular) in the west through to the English border beyond the Black Mountains. The best bases are the tiny city of **Brecon** or the market town of **Abergavenny**.

North of the Beacons lie the old spa towns of Radnorshire, among them twee **Llandrindod Wells**. The quiet countryside to the north, crossed by spectacular mountain roads such as the **Abergwesyn Pass** from Llanwrtyd, is barely populated, dotted with ancient churches and introspective villages. In the east, the border town of **Knighton** is the home of the flourishing **Offa's Dyke Path** industry. **Montgomeryshire** is the northern portion of Powys, similarly underpopulated and remote. Like many country towns in mid-Wales, beautiful **Llanidloes** has a healthy stock of old hippies among its population, contributing to a thriving arts and crafts community and a relaxed atmosphere.

The enduringly popular **Cambrian coast** stretches from **Harlech** down to **Cardigan**, with some lovely beaches, backed by burbling rivers and stunning mountains, most notably the massif of **Cadair Idris**. South of the great mountain is **Machynlleth**, a great base for beaches, mountains, shopping and the **Centre for Alternative Technology**, a showpiece for community living and renewable energy resources. Back on the coast, the beguiling "capital" of Mid-Wales, **Aberystwyth**, is a great mix of seaside resort, university city and market town. From here, wide sands and beaches give way to cliff-top paths and small sandy coves as the coast heads towards Pembrokeshire. The region's interior here is best seen around two river valleys: the lush and quiet **Teifi**, running through old-fashioned market towns like **Lampeter**, and the dramatic ravines around the **Rheidol**.

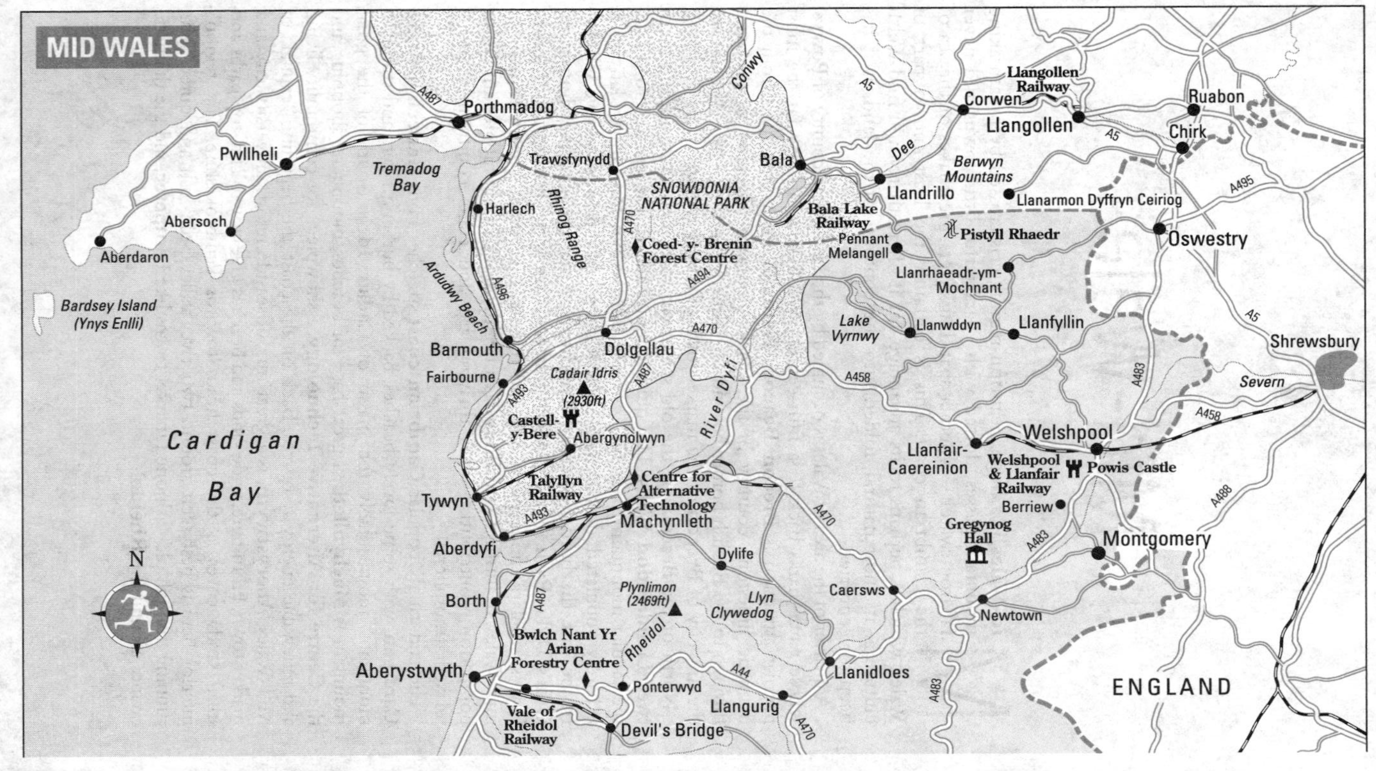
MID WALES
Porthmadog
A487
Pwllheli
Tremadog Bay
Abersoch
Aberdaron
Bardsey Island (Ynys Enlli)
Trawsfynydd
Harlech
Rhinog Range
SNOWDONIA NATIONAL PARK
A470
Coed- y- Brenin Forest Centre
A494
Conwy
Bala
Bala Lake Railway
A5
Corwen
Llangollen Railway
Llangollen
Ruabon
Chirk
Dee
Llandrillo
Berwyn Mountains
Llanarmon Dyffryn Ceiriog
A495
Oswestry
Pistyll Rhaedr
Pennant Melangell
Llanrhaeadr-ym-Mochnant
Lake Vyrnwy
Llanwddyn
Llanfyllin
Shrewsbury
Severn
Ardudwy Beach
A496
Barmouth
Dolgellau
Fairbourne
A493
Cadair Idris (2930ft)
A487
River Dyfi
A458
A483
Castell-y-Bere
Abergynolwyn
Cardigan Bay
Talyllyn Railway
Tywyn
Centre for Alternative Technology
Machynlleth
Aberdyfi
Llanfair-Caereinion
Welshpool
Welshpool & Llanfair Railway
Powis Castle
Berriew
Gregynog Hall
Montgomery
A488
Dylife
Plynlimon (2469ft)
Llyn Clywedog
Caersws
Newtown
Borth
Rheidol
Bwlch Nant Yr Arian Forestry Centre
Aberystwyth
Ponterwyd
A44
Llangurig
Llanidloes
Vale of Rheidol Railway
Devil's Bridge
ENGLAND
N

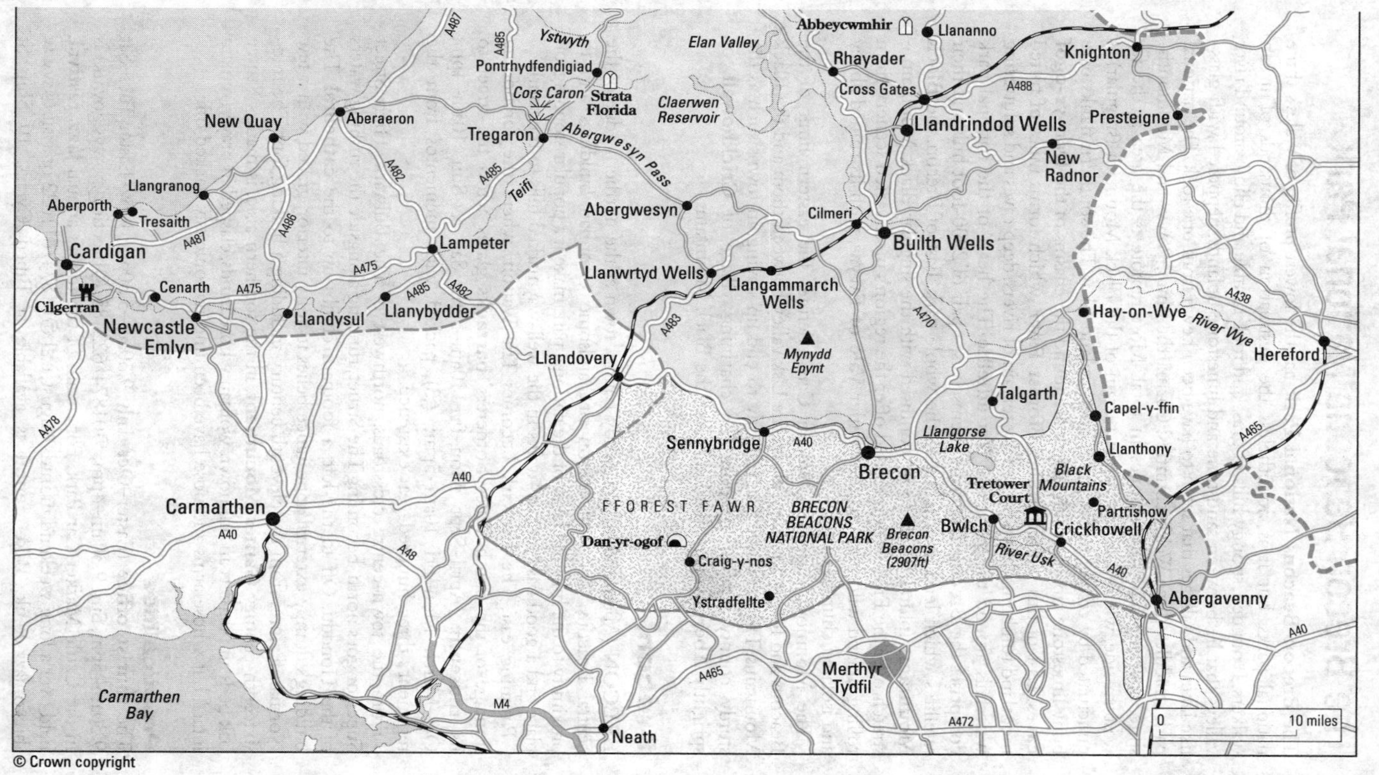

Abbeycwmhir
Llananno
Knighton
Ystwyth
Elan Valley
Rhayader
Pontrhydfendigiad
Cors Caron
Strata Florida
Claerwen Reservoir
Cross Gates
A488
Presteigne
New Quay
Aberaeron
Tregaron
Abergwesyn Pass
Llandrindod Wells
New Radnor
Llangranog
Aberporth
Tresaith
A482
A485
Teifi
Abergwesyn
Cilmeri
A486
A487
Cardigan
Lampeter
Builth Wells
A475
Llanwrtyd Wells
Llangammarch Wells
Cilgerran
Cenarth
Newcastle Emlyn
Llandysul
Llanybydder
A483
A470
A438
Hay-on-Wye
River Wye
Hereford
Mynydd Epynt
Llandovery
Talgarth
Capel-y-ffin
A478
Sennybridge
A40
Llangorse Lake
Llanthony
A465
Brecon
Black Mountains
Tretower Court
Carmarthen
FFOREST FAWR
BRECON BEACONS NATIONAL PARK
Partrishow
Bwlch
Crickhowell
Dan-yr-ogof
Brecon Beacons (2907ft)
Craig-y-nos
River Usk
A48
Ystradfellte
Abergavenny
Merthyr Tydfil
Carmarthen Bay
M4
A472
Neath
0
10 miles

The Brecon Beacons National Park

The **Brecon Beacons National Park** has the lowest profile of Wales's three national parks, but it is nonetheless the destination of thousands of urban walkers. Rounded, spongy hills of grass and rock tumble and climb around river valleys that lie between sandstone and limestone uplands, peppered with glass-like lakes and villages that seem to have been hewn from one rock. The national park straddles three Welsh counties: Carmarthenshire, Powys and Monmouthshire, covering 520 square miles in total. Most remote is the area at the far western side, where the vast, open terrain of the Black Mountain (singular) is punctuated by craggy peaks and hidden upland lakes. The southern flanks bare bony limestone ribs, beneath which are found the chasms of the **Dan-yr-ogof caves**. East of this wilderness lies **Fforest Fawr**, which forms miles of tufted moorland tumbling down to a rocky terrain of rivers, deep caves and spluttering waterfalls around the village of **Ystradfellte**. The heart of the national park comprises the **Brecon Beacons** themselves, a pair of 2900-foot hills and their satellites which lend their name to the whole park. East of Brecon, the **Black Mountains** (plural) – not to be confused with the singular Black Mountain – stretch over the English border, and offer the region's most varied scenery, from rolling upland wilderness to the gentler **Vale of Ewyas**, with its ruined abbey and isolated churches.

The Monmouthshire and Brecon Canal defines the eastern limit of the Beacons and forges a passage along the Usk Valley between them and the Black Mountains. This is where you're likely to end up staying, in towns such as the sturdy county seat of **Brecon**, the charming village of **Crickhowell**, or sprightly **Abergavenny**, nestled below the Black Mountains.

Brecon

BRECON (Aberhonddu) is a sturdy county town at the northern edge of the central Beacons. The proliferation of handsome Georgian buildings and its proximity to the hills and lakes of the national park make it a popular stopping-off place and a good base for day-walks in the well-waymarked hills to the south.

Running east, The Bulwark becomes The Watton, where the foreboding frontage of the South Wales Borderers' **barracks** glares across the street to its **museum** (April–Sept Mon–Fri 10am–5pm, Sat & Sun 10am–4pm; Oct–March Mon–Fri 10am–5pm; £3), packed with mementos from the regiment's three-hundred-year existence.

From the town-centre crossroads, northwest of The Bulwark, High Street Superior goes north, becoming The Struet, running alongside the rushing waters of the Honddu. Off to the left, a footpath climbs up to the **cathedral**. The building's dumpy external appearance belies its lofty interior, graced with a few Norman features from the eleventh century, including a hulking font. The mid-sixteenth-century **Games Monument**, in the southern aisle, is made of three oak beds and depicts an unknown woman whose hands, clasped in prayer, remain intact, but whose arms and nose have been unceremoniously hacked off.

Practicalities

The **tourist office** (Easter–Oct daily 9.30am–5.30pm; Nov–Easter Tues–Sat 9.30am–5pm, Sun 9.30am–4pm; ⓣ01874/622485, ⓔbrectic@powys.gov.uk) is in the Cattle Market Car Park. For details of the town's annual **jazz festival**, held over a long weekend in mid-August, call ⓣ01874/611622 or visit ⓦwww.breconjazz.co.uk. **Bike rental** is available at Biped Cycles, 10 Ship St

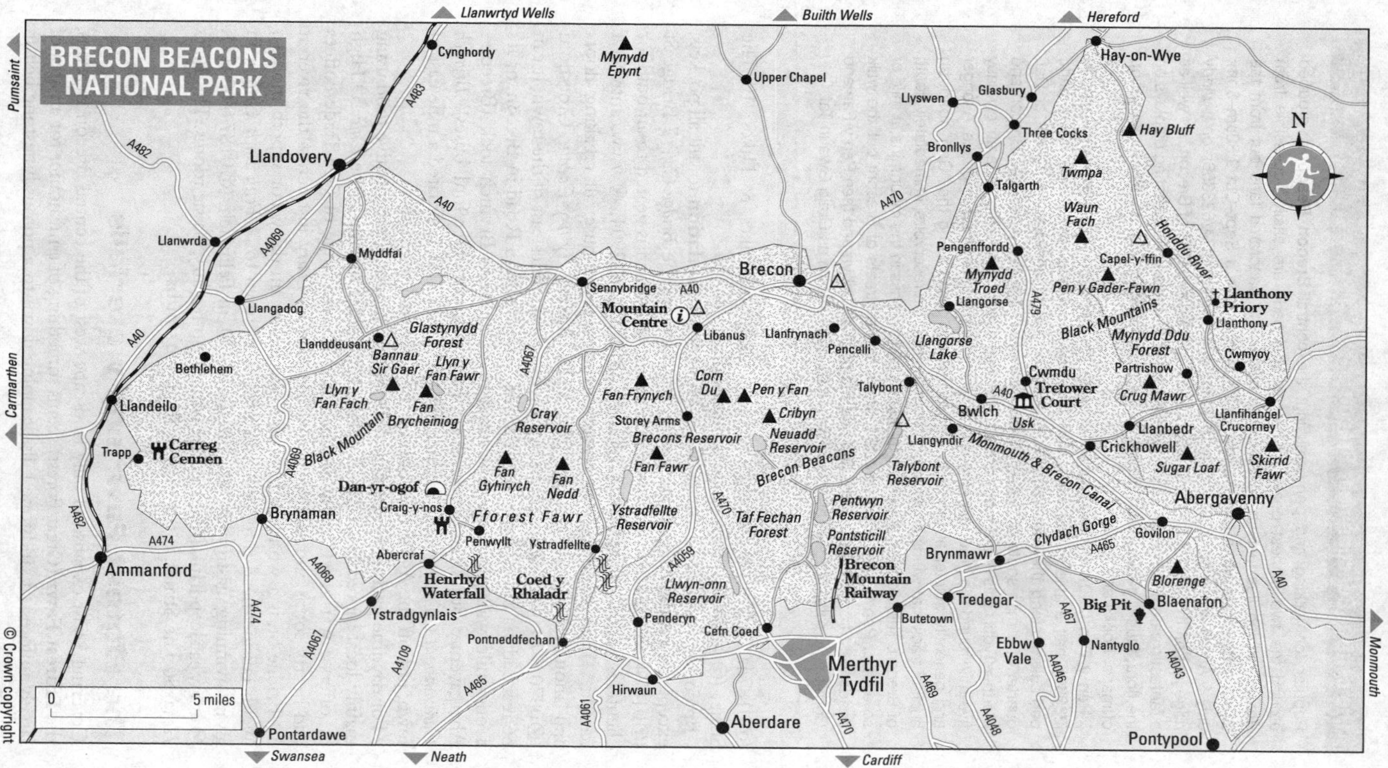
BRECON BEACONS NATIONAL PARK
Llanwrtyd Wells
Builth Wells
Hereford
Pumsaint
Carmarthen
Swansea
Neath
Cardiff
Monmouth
N
Cynghordy
Mynydd Epynt
Upper Chapel
Llyswen
Glasbury
Hay-on-Wye
Three Cocks
Hay Bluff
Bronllys
Twmpa
Talgarth
Waun Fach
Honddu River
Llandovery
A482
A483
A40
A4069
A470
A479
Llanwrda
Myddfai
Pengenffordd
Mynydd Troed
Capel-y-ffin
Pen y Gader-Fawn
Llanthony Priory
Llanthony
Brecon
Sennybridge
Mountain Centre
Libanus
Llangorse
Llangorse Lake
Black Mountains
Mynydd Ddu Forest
Cwmyoy
Partrishow
Llangadog
Llanddeusant
Bannau Sir Gaer
Glastynydd Forest
Llyn y Fan Fawr
Llyn y Fan Fach
Fan Brycheiniog
Bethlehem
Llanfrynach
Pencelli
Corn Du
Pen y Fan
Cribyn
Talybont
Cwmdu
Tretower Court
Crug Mawr
Llandeilo
Fan Frynych
Storey Arms
Brecons Reservoir
Neuadd Reservoir
Bwlch
Usk
Llanbedr
Llanfihangel Crucorney
Trapp
Carreg Cennen
Black Mountain
Cray Reservoir
A4067
Fan Fawr
Brecon Beacons
Llangynidr
Monmouth & Brecon Canal
Crickhowell
Sugar Loaf
Skirrid Fawr
Dan-yr-ogof
Fan Gyhirych
Fan Nedd
Talybont Reservoir
Abergavenny
Craig-y-nos
Fforest Fawr
Ystradfellte Reservoir
Taf Fechan Forest
Pentwyn Reservoir
Brynaman
Penwyllt
Pontsticill Reservoir
Clydach Gorge
Govilon
A474
A465
Ammanford
Abercraf
Ystradfellte
Brynmawr
Henrhyd Waterfall
Coed y Rhaladr
A4068
A4059
Llwyn-onn Reservoir
Brecon Mountain Railway
Blorenge
Tredegar
Big Pit
Blaenafon
Ystradgynlais
Penderyn
A467
Butetown
Cefn Coed
Pontneddfechan
Ebbw Vale
Nantyglo
A4046
A4043
Merthyr Tydfil
A4109
A469
Hirwaun
A4061
0
5 miles
Aberdare
A4048
Pontardawe
Pontypool

The central Beacons near Brecon

Popular for walking and pony trekking, the central **Brecon Beacons**, grouped around the two highest peaks in the national park, are easily accessible from Brecon, which lies just six miles to the north. The panorama fans out from the **Brecon Beacons Mountain Centre** (daily: March–June & Sept–Oct 9.30am–5pm; July & Aug 9.30am–6pm; Nov–Feb 10.30am–4.30pm; ⓣ01874/623366), on a windy ridge just off the A470 turn-off at Libanus, six miles southwest of Brecon. As well as a fantastic café that specializes in local ingredients, there are interesting displays on the flora, fauna, geology and history of the area, together with a well-stocked shop of maps, books and guides.

Pen y Fan (2907ft) is the highest peak in the Beacons. Together with **Corn Du** (2863ft), half a mile to the west, they form the most popular ascents in the park, particularly along the well-trampled muddy red path that starts from Pont ar Daf, quarter of a mile south of Storey Arms, on the A470 midway between Brecon and Merthyr Tydfil. This is the most direct route from a road, where a comparatively easy five-mile round trip gradually climbs up the southern flank of the two peaks. A longer and generally quieter ascent leads up to the two peaks along the "Gap" road, an ancient track that winds its way north from the Neuadd reservoirs, immediately south of Brecon. The old road squeezes through a narrow pass in the mountains, a mile or so east of Pen y Fan, and eventually drops to the streets of Brecon; but the walk heads west from the pass, crossing first the peak of Cribyn and then Pen y Fan and Corn Du, to return to the reservoirs via a lofty ridge known as Graig Gwaun Taf.

(ⓣ01874/622296, ⓦwww.bipedcycles.co.uk), and Bikes & Hikes, 10 The Struet (ⓣ01874/610071, ⓦwww.bikesandhikes.co.uk).

Brecon and adjacent Llanfaes bulge with **accommodation** to suit all pockets, except during the August jazz festival. Best bets are the *Bridge Café*, 7 Bridge St (ⓣ01874/622024, ⓦwww.bridgecafe.co.uk; ❷), which is geared to an outdoor clientele; and *Cantre Selyf*, 5 Lion St (ⓣ01874/622904, ⓦwww.cantreselyf.co.uk; ❹), an imposing seventeenth-century townhouse, all creaking floors and moulded plaster ceilings. The YHA **hostel** *Ty'n-y-Caeau*, Groesffford (ⓣ0870/770 5718, ⓦwww.yha.org.uk; ❶), is two miles east of the town. It can be reached via Slwch Lane, a path from Cerrigcochion Road in Brecon, or it's a one-mile walk from the bus stops at either Cefn Brynich lock (Brecon–Abergavenny buses) or Troedyrharn Farm (Brecon–Hereford buses). *Brynich Caravan and Camping Park*, Brynich (ⓣ01874/623325), is situated a mile east of town, just off the A470, overlooking the town and the river.

For daytime **eating**, *Bridge Café*, 7 Bridge St, produces imaginative food using mainly local ingredients (closed during the winter months). *The Café*, 39 High St, offers a warm, relaxed atmosphere and a good range of Free Trade coffees and hearty soups and sandwiches, while *Llanfaes Dairy*, just across the river at 19 Bridge St, is a wonderful home-made ice-cream dairy. For superb modern Welsh cuisine, head three miles northwest of town to *Felin Fach Griffin*, an award-winning gastropub just off the A470 in Felinfach (ⓣ01874/620111, ⓦwww.eatsleepdrink.ltd.co.uk; ❻) which also has airy, classic rooms. The *Bull's Head*, 86 The Struet, is the pick of the town's **pubs**.

The Fforest Fawr and waterfalls

Covering a vast expanse of hilly landscape west of the central Brecon Beacons, the **Fforest Fawr** (Great Forest) seems something of a misnomer for an area of largely unforested sandstone hills dropping down to a porous limestone belt in the south. The name, however, refers to its former status as a hunting area. The hills rise up to the south of the A40, west of Brecon, with the dramatic A4067 defining the western side of the range and the A470 dividing it from the central Beacons. In the heart of the range, a twisting mountain road crosses a bleak plateau and descends into one of Britain's classic limestone landscapes, around the hamlet of **YSTRADFELLTE**, a place phenomenally popular for its walks over great pavements of bone-white rock next to cradling potholes, disappearing rivers and crashing waterfalls.

A mile to the south, the River Mellte tumbles into the dark mouth of the **Porth-yr-ogof** (White Horse Cave), emerging into daylight a few hundred yards further south. A signposted path heads south from the Porth-yr-ogof car park and into the green gorge of the River Mellte. After little more than a mile, the first of three waterfalls is reached at **Sgwd Clun Gwyn** (White Meadow Fall), where the river crashes fifty feet over two huge, angular steps of rock before hurtling down the course for a few hundred yards to the other two falls – the impressive **Sgwd Isaf Clun Gwyn** (Lower White Meadow Fall) and, around the wooded corner, the **Sgwd y Pannwr** (Fall of the Fuller). The path continues to the confluence of the rivers Mellte and Hepste, half a mile further on. A quarter of a mile along the Hepste is the most popular of the area's falls, the **Sgwd yr Eira** (Fall of Snow), whose rock below the main tumble has eroded back six feet, allowing access behind a dramatic twenty-foot curtain of water, although at the time of writing the paths to this waterfall were closed for safety reasons. You might want to stop off on the main road through Penderyn at the **Welsh Whisky Distillery** (Ⓣ01685/813300, Ⓦwww.welsh-whisky.co.uk), where the long-awaited visitor centre should be up and running by summer 2008.

In the middle of Ystradfellte, you'll find the popular *New Inn*, which serves basic meals, a few yards from *Tŷ-y-Berllan* (Ⓣ01639/722242; ❷), an unfussy **B&B**. Half a mile south is a decent **campsite** at *Penllwyn-Einon Farm* (Ⓣ01639/720542).

Dan-yr-ogof Showcaves

Six miles of upland forest and grass-covered mountains lie between Ystradfellte and the **Dan-yr-ogof Showcaves** (April–Oct daily 10am–3pm; Nov–March call for details; Ⓣ01639/730801, Ⓦwww.showcaves.co.uk; £10.50), off the A4067 to the west. Only discovered in 1912, they are claimed to form the largest system of subterranean caverns in northern Europe, and, although new attractions and relentless marketing have turned them into something of an overdone theme park, the caverns are truly awesome in their size. In a self-guided tour, the path leads you into the **Dan-yr-ogof** showcave – the longest in Britain, and framed by stalactites and frothy limestone deposits. From here, you'll be steered around a circular route of about a mile and a half. Back outside, you pass a tacky dinosaur park and a downbeat recreated Iron Age "village" to get to the **Cathedral Cave**, a hugely impressive 150-foot-long, 70-foot-high cavern, sadly cheapened by a cheesy lightshow. Reachable via a precarious path behind the dinosaur park is the final viewable cavern, **Bone Cave**, known to have been inhabited by prehistoric tribes.

The Black Mountains

The easternmost section of the national park centres on the **Black Mountains**, far quieter than the central belt of the Brecon Beacons and skirted by the wide valley of the River Usk to the south and the Wye to the north. The only exception to the Black Mountains' unremitting sandstone is an isolated outcrop of limestone, long divorced from the southern belt, that peaks due north of Crickhowell at Pen Cerrig-calch (2302ft). The Black Mountains have the feel of a landscape only partly tamed by human habitation: tiny villages, isolated churches and delightful lanes are folded into an undulating green landscape which levels out to the south around the villages of **Tretower** and **Crickhowell**.

Tretower

Rising out of the valley floor, dominating the view from both the A40 and the A479 mountain road, the solid round tower of the **castle and court** (daily: Easter–Sept 10am–5pm; Oct 9am–4pm; Nov–Easter closed; £2.90; CADW) at **TRETOWER** (Tre-tŵr), ten miles southeast of Brecon, was built to guard the pass. The bleak, thirteenth-century round tower replaced an earlier Norman fortification, and in the late fourteenth century was supplemented by a comparatively luxurious manor house, itself being gradually expanded over the ensuing years. An enjoyable audioguide tour takes you around an open-air gallery and wall walk, and explains late medieval building methods using the exposed plaster and beams where work is still under way.

Crickhowell

Compact **CRICKHOWELL** (Crug Hywel) is four miles southeast of Tretower, on the northern bank of the wide and shallow Usk. Apart from a grand seventeenth-century **bridge**, with thirteen arches visible from the eastern end and only twelve from the west, spawning many a local myth, there's not much to see in town. **Table Mountain** (1481ft) provides a spectacular northern backdrop, topped by the remains of the 2500-year-old hill fort (*crug*) of Hywel, accessed on a path past The Wern, off Llanbedr Road. Many walkers follow a route north from Table Mountain, climbing two miles up to the plateau-topped limestone hump of **Pen Cerrig-calch** (2302ft) and on to Pen Allt-mawr from where a circular route can be completed.

The **tourist office** (daily: Easter–Oct 10am–5pm; Nov–March 10am–4pm; ⓣ01873/812105) is situated within the Crickhowell Resource and Information Centre, in a lovely building on Beaufort Street. **Accommodation** is abundant, with a grandiose coaching inn, the *Bear Hotel*, on Beaufort St (ⓣ01873/810408, ⓦwww.bearhotel.co.uk; ❺), and the cheerfully relaxed *Dragon* on the High Street (ⓣ01873/810362, ⓦwww.dragonhotel.co.uk; ❹); for cheaper B&B, try *Greenhill Villas* on Beaufort Street (ⓣ01873/811177, ⓦwww.greenhillvillas.com; ❷). The town-centre *Riverside Park* **campsite** lies on New Road (ⓣ01873/810397).

There's no shortage of places to **eat** and **drink** in and around Crickhowell: try *Number 18*, 18 High St, for daytime sandwiches, paninis and great coffee. Evening food is available in the town's pubs: the *Bear Hotel* (see above) wins legions of awards for its heavenly, pricier-than-average bar and restaurant food. Down by the town bridge, the *Bridge End* pub serves fine food, while a mile along the A40 towards Brecon is the fabulous *Nantyffin Cider Mill Inn* (ⓣ01873/810775), with real ales and ciders as well as tasty food. A mile in the other direction, along the narrow Llangenny Lane, you'll find the unpretentious and rustic *Dragon's Head* (ⓣ01873/810350) dishing up gargantuan portions of extremely tasty food.

Abergavenny and around

Flanking the Brecon Beacons National Park, the lively market town of **ABERGAVENNY** (Y Fenni), seven miles southeast of Crickhowell, is a slick

▲ Crickhowell

and confident town with an ever-growing reputation for its fine cuisine, which reaches something of a zenith during the town's September **Food Festival**. It also makes a great base, with a fine range of places to eat, drink and sleep, and the town is a magnet to walkers bound for the local mountains: **Sugar Loaf**, **the Blorenge**, and the legend-infused **Skirrid Mountain** (Ysgyryd Fawr). Stretching north from town, the **Vale of Ewyas** runs along the foot of the Black Mountains, where the astounding churches at Partrishow and Cwmyoy are lost in rural isolation. Abergavenny also makes a good base for visiting

Monmouthshire's "Three Castles" (see p.633), set in the pastoral border country to the east.

Although only a couple of miles and a few hills away from the iron and coal towns of the Valleys (see p.636), Abergavenny grew on the basis of its weaving and tanning trades, giving it an entirely different feel. These industries prospered alongside a flourishing market, which is still the focal point for a wide area, drawing many people up from the Valleys every Tuesday.

From the train station, Monmouth Road rises gently, eventually becoming High Street, off which you'll find the fragmented remains of the medieval **castle**, whose ugly Victorian keep houses the **town museum** (Easter–Sept daily 11am–5pm, closed 1–2pm outside school summer hols; Oct–Easter Mon–Sat 11am–1pm & 2–4pm; free), which displays ephemera from the town's history and a reconstruction of Basil Jones' grocery shop, once on Main Street. Abergavenny's parish church of **St Mary**, on Monk Street, contains some superb tombs that span the entire medieval period. There are effigies of members of the notorious de Braose family, along with the tomb and figure of Sir William ap Thomas, founder of Raglan Castle (see p.633).

Practicalities

Abergavenny's **train station** lies on the well-used line between Newport and Hereford. Buses depart from Swan Meadow **bus station**, right by the joint **tourist office** (daily: April–Oct 10am–5.30pm; Nov–March 10am–4pm; ⓣ01873/857588, ⓔabergavenny.tic@monmouthshire.gov.uk) and **Brecon Beacons National Park office** (Easter–Sept daily 9.30am–5.30pm; ⓣ01873/853254, ⓦwww.breconbeacons.org). You can **rent bikes** from the *Black Sheep Backpackers* bunkhouse right by the train station (see below).

There's no shortage of **accommodation** in and around the town centre. *Park Guesthouse*, 36 Hereford Rd (ⓣ01873/853715, ⓦwww.parkguesthouse.co.uk; ❷), is among the best of the budget options, while the central *King's Head* pub on Cross Street (ⓣ01873/853575, ⓔkingsheadhotel@hotmail.com; ❸) is very central and has inexpensive, well-appointed rooms. Right by the station, *Black Sheep Backpackers*, *Great Western Hotel*, 24 Station Rd (ⓣ01873/859125, ⓦwww.blacksheepbackpackers.com; ❶), is a welcoming bunkhouse-cum-pub. The nearest place to pitch a **tent** is *Pyscodlyn Farm Caravan and Camping Site* (ⓣ01873/853271), two miles west of town off the A40 – any Brecon or Crickhowell bus will pass by.

In the last fifteen years, **food** has become Abergavenny's main claim to fame – the town's annual **Food Festival** (ⓣ01873/851643, ⓦwww.abergavennyfoodfestival.co.uk), in mid-September, is now one of the most prestigious in Britain. Among the plethora of **places to eat** is the moderately priced *Greyhound Vaults*, Market St, great for a wide range of tasty Welsh and English specialities, including the best vegetarian dishes in town. *Trading Post*, 14 Neville St, is a trendy coffee house and bistro, while the very expensive *Walnut Tree Inn* (ⓣ01873/852797), on the B4521 at Llanddewi Skirrid, two miles north of town, is a legendary foodies' paradise for superb Italian and Mediterranean cuisine. Of Abergavenny's **pubs**, the best is the staunchly traditional *Hen & Chickens*, Flannel Street, just off the High Street.

The Vale of Ewyas

The main A465 Hereford road leads six miles north out of Abergavenny to Llanfihangel Crucorney, where the B4423 diverges off to the north into the beautiful and enchanting **Vale of Ewyas**, along the banks of the Honddu River.

The road winds its way up the valley's western side, past the fork at the *Queen's Head* pub (Ⓣ01873/890241), a great place to **camp**. In the adjacent village of **CWMYOY**, the parish church of St Martin has substantially subsided due to geological twists in the underlying rock. Nothing squares up: the tower leans at a severe angle from the bulging body of the church, and the view inside from the back of the nave towards the sloping altar, askew roof and straining windows is unforgettable.

Four miles further up the valley is the hamlet of **LLANTHONY**, little more than a small cluster of houses, an inn and a few outlying farms around the wide-open ruins of **Llanthony Priory** – a grander setting, and certainly a quieter one, than Tintern, though the buildings are far more modest in scale. It was founded in around 1100 by the Norman knight William de Lacy, who, it is said, was so captivated by the spiritual beauty of the site that he renounced worldly living and founded a hermitage, attracting like-minded recluses and forming Wales's first Augustinian priory. The roofless church, with its pointed transitional arches and squat tower, was constructed in the latter half of the twelfth century and retains a real sense of spirituality and peace. There are two good places to **stay**: the *Abbey Hotel* (Ⓣ01873/890487, Ⓦwww.llanthonyprioryhotel.co.uk; ❹; Nov–March Fri–Sun only), fashioned out of part of the tumbledown priory; and along the road, the *Half Moon Inn* (Ⓣ01873/890611, Ⓦwww.halfmoon-llanthony; ❷), serving superb beer and good-value meals.

From Llanthony, the road slowly climbs four miles alongside the narrowing Honddu River to the isolated hamlet of **CAPEL-Y-FFIN**, which has pony trekking and **camping**, as well as the delightful, tiny St. Mary's Church. The road then weaves a tortuous route up over the **Gospel Pass** close to the popular peak of **Hay Bluff**, on the glorious roof of the Black Mountains, before descending five miles to the border town of Hay-on-Wye (see p.416).

The Wells towns

The **spa towns** of mid-Wales, strung out along the Heart of Wales rail line between Swansea and Shrewsbury, were once all obscure villages, but with the arrival of the great craze for spas in the early eighteenth century, anywhere with a decent supply of apparently healing water joined in on the act. Royalty and nobility spearheaded the fashion, but the arrival of the railways opened them to all.

Today, best of the bunch is undoubtedly the westernmost spa of **Llanwrtyd Wells**, hunkered down beneath stunning mountain scenery. The most famous of the four – **Llandrindod Wells** – attracted the international elite in its Victorian heyday, but it's been a steady slide downhill since then. In between, the larger town of **Builth Wells** was very much the spa of the Welsh working classes and there's no reason to stop, except in mid-July when it hosts the massive and utterly absorbing **Royal Welsh Show**, Britain's biggest rural jamboree. The fourth spa town, Llangammarch Wells, warrants even less attention.

Llanwrtyd Wells and around

Of the four spa towns, **LLANWRTYD WELLS**, twenty miles northwest of Brecon, is the most appealing. This was the spa to which the Welsh – farmers of Dyfed alongside the Nonconformist middle classes from Glamorgan – came to the great eisteddfodau (festivals of Welsh music, dance and poetry) in the valley of the River Irfon. Nowadays, it trades as Britain's smallest town and is the undisputed Welsh capital of wacky events – from the world bog-snorkelling championships to a Man versus Horse race and numerous biking/walking/beer-drinking combination weekends. Call the tourist office for more information or see ⓦwww.green-events.co.uk.

Main Street runs through the centre of town, crossing the Irfon River just below the main square, Y Sgwar, dominated by a stunning sculpture of a red kite. On the opposite side of Main Street, Dolecoed Road winds for half a mile along the river to the *Dolecoed Hotel*, built near the original sulphurous spring. Although the distinctive aroma had been noted in the area for centuries, it was truly "discovered" in 1732 by the local priest, Theophilus Evans, who drank from an evil-smelling spring after seeing a rudely healthy frog pop out of it. The spring, named **Ffynnon Drewllyd** (Stinking Well), bubbles up amongst the dilapidated spa buildings a hundred yards behind the hotel.

Llanwrtyd's **tourist office** is in Tŷ Barcud just off the main square (daily 10am–5pm; ⓣ01591/610666, ⓦwww.llanwrtyd-wells.powys.org.uk). **Accommodation** includes the lively *Neuadd Arms* on the main square (ⓣ01591/610236, ⓦwww.neuaddarmshotel.co.uk; ③), which also does good bar **food**; the lovely *Carlton House* (ⓣ01591/610248, ⓦwww.carltonrestaurant.co.uk; ③), yards away on Dolecoed Road, with cheaper rooms (including two bargain singles) across the street at its brasserie; and the fairly grand *Lasswade* on Station Road (ⓣ01591/610515, ⓦwww.lasswadehotel.co.uk; ⑤). The marvellous *Drover's Rest* **restaurant** by the river bridge (ⓣ01591/610264, ⓦwww.food-food-food.co.uk; ③) serves wholesome, traditional Welsh dishes and snacks, and has some classy, cosy B&B accommodation. Finally, the *Stonecroft Inn* on Dolecoed Road (ⓣ01591/610332, ⓦwww.stonecroft.co.uk) is a superb pub with great food and regular live folk, R&B and rock music as well as beds (£13.50) in a small, self-catering **hostel** annexe. There's very basic tent-only **camping** on the Dolwen Fields, off the main road south from the town square, although 48 hours' notice is required (ⓣ01591/610626, ⓔg.jones@virgin.net).

Bike rental is available at *Cycles Irfon* (ⓣ01591/610710, or 610668 out of hours) on the Maesydre industrial estate off the Beulah Road to the north of town.

▲ A Man versus Horse race

The Abergwesyn Pass

A lane from Llanwrtyd meets up with another road from Beulah at the riverside hamlet of **ABERGWESYN**, five miles north of Llanwrtyd. From here, you can drive the quite magnificent winding thread of an ancient cattle-drovers' road – the **Abergwesyn Pass** – up the perilous **Devil's Staircase** and through dense conifer forests to miles of wide, desolate valleys where sheep graze unhurriedly. At the little bridge over the tiny Tywi River, a track heads south past an isolated, gas-lit **hostel** at **DOLGOCH** (Ⓣ0870/7708868, Ⓦwww.yha.org.uk; closed Oct–April). Remote paths lead from the hostel through the forests and hillsides to the exquisitely isolated chapel at **Soar-y-Mynydd** and over the mountains to the next **hostel** at **TYNCORNEL**, *Tŷ'n-y-cornel* (Ⓣ0870/770 8868, Ⓦwww.yha.org.uk; closed Oct to late March), five miles from Dolgoch. Although the Abergwesyn Pass, which ends in the market square of Tregaron in Ceredigion, is less than twenty miles long, it takes a good hour in a car to negotiate the twisting, narrow road safely.

Llandrindod Wells

Once the most chichi spa resort in Wales, **LLANDRINDOD WELLS** (Llandrindod) is a pale imitation of its former self. Although many of the fine Victorian buildings still stand, the hotels do business and the flower boxes bristle with colour, there's something empty at the town's heart, and it will take more than a lick of paint to sort it out.

It was the railway that made Llandrindod, arriving in 1864 and bringing carriages full of well-to-do Victorians to the fledgling spa. Llandrindod blossomed, new hotels were built, neat parks were laid out and the town came to rival many of the more fashionable spas and resorts over the border. Like so many coastal resorts, however, Llandrindod has been on the slide for years. The hotels have come to rely on ever-ageing visitors, the grand old spa is a mess, and nothing radical or new seems to have been tried in the town for decades. That all said, there is plenty of accommodation here, the surrounding countryside is lovely and transport links are good.

Llandrindod's Victorian opulence is still very much in evidence in the town's grandiose public buildings, even if many are in a sorry state these days. Plans are afoot to restore the lavish **spa pump room** in **Rock Park**, but little has come of this yet and the place continues to crumble. A free chalybeate fountain, in a glade to the front of the pump room, lets you sample more than enough of the town's metallic, salty spa water.

The High Street, running from here to the centre, contains antique, junk and book shops. The tourist office, on Temple Street behind, houses the small **Radnorshire Museum** (April–Sept Tues–Fri 10am–4pm, Sat 10am–5pm, Sun 1–5pm; Oct–March Tues–Fri 10am–4pm, Sat 10am–1pm; non-Powys residents £1), with permanent exhibitions detailing the spa phenomena, and its influence on the region. The **National Cycle Exhibition**, on the corner of Temple Street and Spa Road (March–Oct daily 10am–4pm; call Ⓣ01597/825531 for winter hours; £3), is a nostalgic collection of over 250 bikes, from a reproduction 1818 Hobbyhorse to relatively modern folding bikes and choppers, including styles that look far too uncomfortable to have been a success.

Practicalities

Buses pull in by the **train station** in the heart of town, between High Street and Station Crescent. The **tourist office** is on Temple Street (April–Sept Mon–Fri 9.30am–5.30pm, Sat & Sun 9.30am–5pm; Oct–March Mon–Fri 10am–1pm & 2–5pm; Ⓣ01597/822600, Ⓔllandtic@powys.gov.uk). **Bikes** can be rented from Greenstiles Cyles (Ⓣ01597/824594), in Imperial Buildings, Temple Street: arrange in advance.

As for **accommodation**, there's the smart *Greylands*, High Street (Ⓣ01597/822253, Ⓦwww.greylandsguesthouse.co.uk; ②), or go for the Edwardian elegance of the *Metropole Hotel*, Temple Street (Ⓣ01597/822881, Ⓦwww.bw-metropole.co.uk; ⑤), an old spa hotel with a pool, the centrepiece of the town. Its *Radnor* **restaurant**, open to non-residents, is stuffy and pricey but offers the best local cuisine in town. For reasonably priced food, head for the *Aspidistra*, on Station Crescent, a decent daytime café serving cheap and wholesome sandwiches, snacks and meals, or the *Llanerch Inn*, Llanerch Lane, central Llandrindod's only **pub** – a cosy sixteenth-century inn that predates most of the surrounding town, serving a solid menu of good-value, well-cooked classics.

North and East Radnorshire

Radnorshire has long been one of the most sparsely populated counties in England and Wales, its north and east still being especially remote. In the northwest, Rhayader is the only settlement of any size, a gateway to the four interlocking reservoirs of the **Elan Valley** and the surrounding wild, spartan countryside of waterfalls, bogland and bare peaks. The countryside to the northeast of Rhayader is tamer, and lanes and bridle paths delve in and around the woods and farms, occasionally brushing through minute settlements like the village of **Abbeycwmhir**. The hills roll eastwards towards the handsome town of **Knighton**, perched right on the English border, beside some of the most intact parts of **Offa's Dyke**.

Elan Valley and around

The poet Shelley spent his honeymoon in buildings now submerged by the waters of the **Elan Valley** reservoirs, a nine-mile-long string of four lakes built between 1892 and 1903 to supply water to the rapidly growing industrial city of Birmingham, 75 miles east. Although the lakes enhance an already beautiful and idyllic part of the world, the way in which Welsh valleys, villages and farmsteads were seized and flooded to provide water for English cities is something that Welsh nationalists have long protested. The tourist board prefers to advertise the profusion of rare plants and birds that resulted, notably the red kites.

From the workaday market town of **RHAYADER**, ten miles west of Llandrindod Wells, the B4518 heads southwest four miles to **ELAN** village, a curious collection of stone houses built in 1909 to replace the reservoir constructors' village that had grown up on the site. Just below the bank of Caban Coch, the **Elan Valley Visitor Centre** (mid-March to Oct daily 10am–5.30pm; Ⓣ01597/810898) incorporates a tourist office and a permanent exhibition about the history and ecology of the area. Frequent guided **walks** and even **Land Rover safaris** head off from the centre, and a road tucks in along Caban Coch to the **Garreg Ddu** viaduct, where it winds along for four spectacular miles to the vast, rather chilling 1952 dam on **Claerwen Reservoir**. More remote and less popular than the Elan lakes, Claerwen is a good base for a serious **walk** from the far end of the dam across eight or so harsh but beautiful miles to the monastery of Strata Florida (see p.711). Alternatively, you can follow the path that skirts around the northern shore of Claerwen to the lonely **Teifi Pools**, glacial lakes from which the River Teifi springs.

Back at the Garreg Ddu viaduct, a more popular road continues north along the long, glassy finger of Garreg Ddu reservoir, before doubling back on itself just below the awesome **Pen-y-garreg** dam and reservoir; if the dam is overflowing, the vast wall of foaming water is mesmerizing. At the top of Pen-y-garreg lake, it's possible to drive over the final dam on the system, at **Craig Goch**. Thanks to its gracious curve, elegant Edwardian arches and neat little green cupola, this is the most photographed of all the dams.

A quarter of a mile south of Rhayader, just off the A470, is Gigrin Farm, (Ⓣ01597/810213, Ⓦwww.gigrin.co.uk; £3) a working sheep farm that's become an official RSPB **red kite** feeding station. Every day at 2pm 3pm in summer, they put out meat scraps to attract hundreds of these beautiful birds, which were once close to extinction in the UK. It's a breathtaking spectacle, with the huge animals, swooping down over a well-placed hide, showing their aerial agility and magnificent wingspan.

ABBEYCWMHIR (Abaty Cwm Hir), seven miles northeast of Rhayader, takes its name from the **abbey** whose sombre ruins (free access) lie in a field beneath the village. Cistercian monks founded the site in 1146, planning one of the largest churches in Britain. Destruction by Henry III's troops in 1231 scuppered plans to continue building, but the sparse ruins – a rocky outline of the floor plan – lie in a conifer-carpeted valley alongside a gloomy green lake, lending weight to the site's melancholic associations.

Practicalities

Bus #103 runs to the Elan Valley Visitor Centre from Llandrindod and Rhayader (Mon–Fri). The main **accommodation** base in the area is the *Elan Valley Hotel* (Ⓣ01597/810448, Ⓦwww.elanvalleyhotel.co.uk; ④), an imposing, neocolonial pile on the Rhayader side of Elan village. It's also very good for eating, drinking and entertainment. Otherwise, you may want to make use of Rhayader, where buses stop opposite the **tourist office** (April–Oct daily 9.30am–12.30pm & 1.30–5.30pm; Nov–March Mon, Tues & Thurs–Sat 10am–4pm; Ⓣ01597/810591, Ⓦwww.rhayader.co.uk), housed in the leisure centre. Eighteenth-century coaching inns still line Rhayader's main streets, with more modern **accommodation** at the *Elan Hotel*, West Street (Ⓣ01597/810109, Ⓦwww.elanhotel.co.uk; ③), and the cheerful *Brynteg* B&B on East Street (Ⓣ01597/810052; ②). The cheapest place in town is *Greenfields* on South Street (Ⓣ01597/811101, Ⓦwww.greenfields-hostel.co.uk; ①), which offers B&B and hostel beds (£13.50). There's a **campsite** (Ⓣ01597/810183) at *Wyeside*, off the A44 north of Rhayader. **Bikes** can be

Offa's Dyke

Offa's Dyke has provided a potent symbol of Welsh–English antipathy ever since it was created in the eighth century as a demarcation line by King Offa of Mercia, ruler of central England. George Borrow, in his classic *Wild Wales*, notes that, once, "It was customary for the English to cut off the ears of every Welshman who was found to the east of the dyke, and for the Welsh to hang every Englishman whom they found to the west of it".

The earthwork – up to 20ft high and 60ft wide – made use of natural boundaries like rivers in its run north to south, and is best seen in the sections near **Knighton**. Today's England–Wales border crosses the dyke many times, although the basic boundary has changed little since Offa's day. A glorious, 177-mile **long-distance footpath** runs the length of the dyke from Prestatyn in the north to Chepstow, and is one of the most rewarding walks in Britain.

rented from Clive Powell Mountain Bikes (Ⓣ01597/811343, Ⓦwww.clivepowell-mtb.co.uk) on West Street.

Knighton

A town that straddles King Offa's eighth-century border as well as the modern Wales–England divide, **KNIGHTON** (Tref-y-clawdd, the "Town on the Dyke"), twenty miles northeast of Llandrindod, has developed into the most obvious centre for those walking the **Offa's Dyke Path**. Located almost exactly halfway along the route, it's a lively, attractive place that easily warrants a visit, although it has few specific sights. The town is so close to the border that its **train station** is actually in England. From here, Station Road crosses the River Teme into Wales and climbs a couple of hundred yards to Brookside Square. Further up the hill is the town's alpine-looking Victorian clocktower, at the point where Broad Street becomes West Street and the steep High Street soars off up to the left, past rickety Tudor buildings and up to the mound of the old **castle**.

In West Street, the excellent **Offa's Dyke Centre** (Easter–Oct Thurs–Mon 10am–5pm, Tues & Wed noon–5pm; Oct–Easter Mon & Wed 9.30am–12.30pm, Tues, Thurs & Fri 2–5pm, Ⓣ01547/528753, Ⓦwww.offasdyke.demon.co.uk) also houses the **tourist office** (same hours; Ⓣ01547/529424). **Accommodation** in Knighton is plentiful and generally good value: there's the revamped *Knighton Hotel* right in the middle on Broad Street (Ⓣ01547/520530, Ⓦwww.knightonhotel.co.uk; ⑤), *Fleece House* B&B, at the top of High Street (Ⓣ01547/520168, Ⓦwww.fleecehouse.co.uk; ③), and the bargain *Jenny Stothert's*, behind the imposing parish church at 15 Mill Green (Ⓣ01547/520075; ①), where you can also **camp**. For **eating** and drinking, it's hard to beat the comfortable *Horse & Jockey*, at the town end of Station Road.

Montgomeryshire

The northern part of Powys is made up of the old county of **Montgomeryshire** (Maldwyn), an area of enormously varying landscapes and few inhabitants. The solid little town of **Llanidloes** is a base for ageing hippies on the banks of the infant River Severn (Afon Hafren). To the east, the muted old county town of **Montgomery**, with its fine Georgian architecture, perches amid gentle, green hills above the border and Offa's Dyke. Further north, **Welshpool**, the only major settlement, is packed in above the wide flood plain of the Severn; an excellent local museum, toy rail line, good pubs and reasonable hotels make it a fair stop. On the southern side of Welshpool is Montgomeryshire's one unmissable sight, the sumptuous **Powis Castle** and its exquisite terraced gardens.

Llanidloes

The small market town of **LLANIDLOES**, twelve miles north of Rhayader, has developed from a rural village to a weaving town, and is now a centre for artists, craftspeople and assorted alternative lifestylers. One of mid-Wales's prettiest towns, it has four main streets that meet at the black-and-white **market hall**, built on timber stilts in 1600 to allow the market – which has long since moved – to take place on the cobbles beneath. Running parallel with the length of the market hall are China Street and Long Bridge Street, the latter good for some interesting little shops. Off Long Bridge Street is Church Street, which opens out into a yard surrounding the dumpy parish church of **St Idloes** (daily 10.30am–3.30pm; free), the impressive fifteenth-century hammerbeam roof of which is said to have been poached from Abbeycwmhir. The fantastic **Millennium Window** in the church was designed and built by two local stained-glass artists.

From the market hall, the broad Great Oak Street heads west to the **town hall**, originally built as a temperance hotel to challenge the boozy *Trewythen Arms* opposite. A plaque on the closed hotel commemorates Llanidloes as an unlikely-seeming place of industrial and political unrest, when, in April 1839, Chartists stormed the hotel, dragging out and beating up special constables who had been despatched to the town in a futile attempt to suppress political activism among the town's flannel weavers. In the town hall, you'll also find the wonderfully eclectic **museum** (Easter–Sept daily except Wed 11am–1pm & 2–5pm; Oct–Easter Mon, Tues, Thurs & Fri 11am–1pm & 2–5pm, Sat 10am–1pm; £1), where the diverting collection of old local prints and mementos pales beside the stuffed two-headed lamb, born locally in 1914.

China Street curves down to the car park, from where all **bus** services operate. The **tourist office** (April–Sept daily 9.30am–5pm; Oct–March Mon–Sat 9.30am–5pm; ⓣ01686/412605, ⓔllantic@powys.gov.uk) is at 54 Long Bridge St, near the market hall. **Accommodation** includes the delightful *Red Lion Hotel* (ⓣ01686/412270; ❷) and the more modest *Unicorn* (ⓣ01686/413167; ❶), both on Long Bridge Street. The nicest option is *Lloyds Hotel* (ⓣ01686/412284, ⓦwww.lloydshotel.co.uk; ❹), on Cambrian Place, which also has a superb restaurant – booking is essential. You can **camp** at *Dollly's Farm* (ⓣ01686/412694), on the northern fringe of town. Among the many options for **food**, there's wholesome veggie fare in the laid-back *Great Oak Café*, Great Oak Street, or a few doors down, a great example of that Welsh daytime caff institution, the *National Milk Bar*. For a bit of a treat, go to *Lloyds* (see above). Most of the **pubs** here serve food – the *Unicorn* (see above) and the olde-worlde *Mount Inn* on China Street are the best options.

Montgomery and around

Tiny **MONTGOMERY** (Trefaldwyn), around twenty miles northeast of Llanidloes, is Montgomeryshire at its most anglicized. From the mound of its **castle**, situated just on the Welsh side of Offa's Dyke, there are wonderful views over the lofty church tower and the handsome Georgian streets, notably the impressively symmetrical main street – well-named Broad Street – which swoops up to the perfect little red-brick **town hall**, crowned by a pert clocktower. The rebuilt tower of Montgomery's parish **Church of St Nicholas** dominates the snug proportions of the buildings around it. Largely thirteenth-century, the highlights of its spacious interior include a 1600 monument to local landowner Sir Richard Herbert and his wife. Their eight children – who included prominent Elizabethan poet George Herbert – have been carved in beatific kneeling positions behind them.

Montgomery is within striking distance of one of the best-preserved sections of **Offa's Dyke**, traced by the long-distance footpath (see box, p.691), which runs on either side of the B4386. Ditches almost twenty feet high give one of the best indications of the dyke's original appearance. If you want to **stay** here, the best options are *Brynwylfa* (ⓣ01686/668555; ❷), a beautiful townhouse at 4 Bishops Castle St, or *Little Brompton Farm* (ⓣ01686/668371, ⓦwww.littlebromptonfarm.co.uk; ❸), two miles south of town and handy for the Offa's Dyke path – you can also **camp** there. For **food** and **drink** head for the *Checkers* pub on Broad Street.

Berriew

Three miles northwest of Montgomery, the neat village of **BERRIEW** (Aberrhiw) is more redolent of the Tudor settlements over the English border than anywhere in Wales. Its black-and-white houses are grouped picturesquely around a small church, the shallow waters of the River Rhiw and the posh, half-timbered *Lion Hotel* (ⓣ01686/640452, ⓦwww.thelionhotelberriew.com; ④), which does excellent food. Just over the river bridge, the **Andrew Logan Museum of Sculpture** (Easter weekend & May–Oct Wed–Sun noon–6pm; Nov–Christmas Sat & Sun noon–4pm; ⓦwww.andrewlogan.com; £2) seems an improbably camp addition to the tidy Berriew landscape. In the 1970s, British sculptor Logan inaugurated the great drag-and-grunge ball known as the Alternative Miss World Contest, launchpad of the late Divine's career. A "Divine Shrine" and some dazzling outfits from the contests form a large chunk of the museum's exhibits, sharing space with Logan's oversized horticultural sculptures, gaudy model goddesses and a twelve-foot-high encrusted glass "cosmic egg".

A mile further down the lane from the museum, where it meets the main A493, you'll find **Glansevern Hall Gardens** (May–Sept Thurs–Sat & bank holidays noon–5pm; £4), a beautifully cool collection of plants, trees and follies gathered around a gorgeous Georgian mansion.

Welshpool and around

Eastern Montgomeryshire's chief town of **WELSHPOOL** (Y Trallwng), seven miles north of Montgomery, was formerly known as just Pool, its prefix added in 1835 to distinguish it from the English seaside town of Poole in Dorset. It lies in the valley of the River Severn, just three miles from the English border, and is an attractive place to visit, with a number of fine Tudor, Georgian and Victorian buildings in the centre, and the fabulous Powis Castle nearby.

Along Severn Street from the **train station**, a humpback bridge over the much-restored **Montgomery Canal** hides the canal wharf and a wharfside warehouse that has been carefully restored as the **Powysland Museum** (Mon, Tues, Thurs & Fri 11am–1pm & 2–5pm; May–Sept also Sat & Sun 10am–1pm & 2–5pm; Oct–April also Sat 11am–2pm; £1). The impressive local history collection includes archeological nuggets such as those from an old local woodhenge, and displays medieval remains from the now-obliterated local Cistercian abbey of Strata Marcella.

From the *Royal Oak Hotel*, at the centre of town, follow Broad Street – which changes name five times as it rises up the hill – towards the tiny Raven Square terminus station of the **Welshpool and Llanfair Light Railway** (April to late May, Sept & Oct weekends and bank holidays only; Easter & late May to Aug daily; generally 2–3 trains a day; £10.80 return; ⓣ01938/810441). The eight-mile narrow-gauge rail line was open to passengers for less than thirty years prior to its closure in 1931. Now, scaled-down engines once more chuff their way along to the peaceful little village of **Llanfair Caereinion**, a good base for daytime walks, with good pub food at the *Goat Hotel*. The post office, opposite the church, stocks free leaflets on some good local circular walks.

Practicalities

The pompous neo-Gothic turrets of Welshpool's old Victorian **train station** (its modern replacement is directly behind) sit at the top of Severn Street, which leads down into the town centre – the intersection of Severn, Berriew, Broad and Church streets. The **tourist office** (daily 9.30am–5.30pm; ⓣ01938/552043, ⓔweltic@powys.gov.uk) is fifty yards up Church Street in the Vicarage Gardens car park. There's plenty of **accommodation** in town, including the central *Royal Oak* (ⓣ01938/552217, ⓦwww.royaloakhotel.Info; ⑥), a traditional coaching inn at the main crossroads. Dozens of **B&Bs** line Salop Road; *Montgomery House* (ⓣ01938/552693; ②) is the surest bet. A couple of miles to the north of town is the beautiful *Lower Trelydan Farm* (ⓣ01938/553105, ⓔlowertrelydan@netscapeonline.co.uk; ③). **Camping** is good at the *Green Dragon Inn*, a mile along the Shrewsbury road at Buttington (ⓣ01938/553076). The best **eating** in town is at the *Royal Oak* pub. Cheap and filling breakfasts, lunches and teas are served in the *Buttery*, opposite the town hall on the High Street. Many of the town's **pubs** do lunchtime food, with some, notably the *Raven* (ⓣ01938/553070) up by the narrow-gauge train station, serving decent evening meals as well (booking advised on weekends).

Powis Castle

In a land of ruined castles, the sheer scale and beauty of **Powis Castle** (April–Oct Mon & Thurs–Sun castle 1–5pm, gardens 11am–6pm; July & Aug Tues–Sun, same times; castle £9, gardens and museum only £6.27; NT), a mile from Welshpool up Park Lane, is quite staggering. On the site of an earlier Norman fort, the castle was started in the reign of Edward I by the Gwenwynwyn family; to qualify for the site and the barony of De la Pole, they had to renounce all claims to Welsh princedom. In 1587, Sir Edward Herbert bought the castle and began to transform it into the Elizabethan palace that survives today. Inside, the **Clive Museum** – named after Edward Clive, son of Clive of India, who married into the family in 1784 – forms a lively account of the British in India, through diaries, letters, paintings, tapestries, weapons and jewels. But it is the sumptuous period rooms that impress most, from the vast, kitsch frescoes by Lanscroon above the balustraded staircase, to the mahogany bed, brass and enamel toilets and decorative wall hangings of the state bedroom. The elegant **Long Gallery** has a rich sixteenth-century plasterwork ceiling overlooking winsome busts and marble statuettes of the four elements, placed between the glowering family portraits. The **gardens**, designed by Welsh architect William Winde, are spectacular. Dropping down from the castle in four huge, stepped terraces, the design has barely changed since the seventeenth century, with a charmingly precise orangery and topiary that looks as if it is shaved daily. In summer, outdoor **concerts**, frequently with firework finales, take place in the gardens.

Llanfyllin and around

The hills and plains of northern Montgomeryshire conceal a maze of deserted lanes and farm outposts along the contours that swell up towards the north and the foothills of the Berwyn mountains. The only real settlement of any size is **Llanfyllin**, ten miles northwest of Welshpool, a handsome and friendly hillside town with a Thursday market. There is really nothing to do, though, and you'd do better continuing on to the hiking and nature-communing around **Lake Vyrnwy**, or pressing north to **Pistyll Rhaeadr**, Wales's highest waterfall.

The Rhaeadr Valley

For a place so near the English border, **LLANRHAEADR-YM-MOCHNANT**, six miles north of Llanfyllin, is surprisingly Welsh in its language and appearance. The small, low-roofed village is remembered as the serving parish of Bishop William Morgan, who translated the Bible into Welsh in 1588, but it's mostly visited as a base for **Pistyll Rhaeadr**, Wales's highest waterfall at 240ft. The river tumbles down the crags in two stages, flowing under a natural stone arch known as the Fairy Bridge. Don't miss out on walking to the top of the fall, for vertiginous views down the valley and paths up into the moody Berwyns. Pistyll Rhaeadr is a place rich in legend, which you can gen up on in the cute riverside *Tan-y-Pistyll* licensed café. The owners also offer **B&B** (01691/780392, www.pistyllrhaeadr.co.uk; 4) and **camping**.

The village itself has three great **pubs** – the *Three Tuns*, *Hand Inn* and *Wynnstay Arms* – and a few excellent-value B&Bs, the best of which is the plush *Bron Heulog* on Waterfall Street (01691/780521, www.bronheulog.co.uk; 4).

Lake Vyrnwy

A monument to the self-aggrandizement of the Victorian age, **Lake Vyrnwy** (Llyn Efyrnwy) combines its functional role as a water supply for Liverpool with a touch of architectural genius in the shape of the huge nineteenth-century dam at its southern end and the Disneyesque turreted straining-tower that edges out into the icy waters. It's a magnificent spot, and a popular centre for walking and birdwatching, with nature trails. The village of **LLANWDDYN** was flattened and rebuilt at the eastern end, the inhabitants receiving compensation of just £5 for losing their homes. The story is told, somewhat apologetically, in the RSPB **Vyrnwy Visitor Centre** (April–Dec 24 daily 10.30am–5.30pm; Jan–March Sat & Sun only; free), which is located on the western side of the dam and coexists with an **RSPB Visitor Centre** (same hours). A few yards down the road, there's a **tourist office** (Easter–Oct daily 10am–5pm; Nov–Easter daily except Wed 10am–3pm; 01691/870346) and *Artisans Coffee Shop* (01691/870377), from where you can **rent bikes**.

Lake Vyrnwy's immediate surroundings have some of the best **accommodation** in the region, notably the grand *Lake Vyrnwy Hotel* (01691/870692, www.lakevyrnwy.com; 7), overlooking the waters above the southeastern shore. If you just want a look, the hotel serves a full afternoon tea in a chintzy lounge overlooking the lake. There's a great **B&B** just beyond the visitor centre at *The Oaks* (01691/870250, www.vyrnwyaccommodation.co.uk; 3), and daytime snacks and full evening meals are available at *Lake View* (01691/870286), on the lakeside road beyond the *Lake Vyrnwy Hotel*. There are five **camping** pitches at *Fronheulog* (01691/870662), at the top of the hairpin bends on the road to Llanfyllin, or in Llanwddyn itself at *Bryn Fedwen* (01691/870288).

The Cambrian coast

Cardigan Bay (Bae Ceredigion) takes a huge bite out of the west Wales coast, leaving behind the Pembrokeshire peninsula in the south and the Llŷn in the north. Between them lies the **Cambrian coast**, a loosely defined mountain-backed strip periodically split by tumbling rivers, which stretches from Harlech down to Cardigan. Large sand-fringed sections are peppered with low-key coastal resorts, peopled in the summer by families from the English Midlands. The presence of English-dominated resorts and the influx of rat-race refugees to this staunchly nationalistic part of the country has, on occasion, fuelled local antipathy, although visitors are unlikely to see anything more controversial than the odd piece of graffiti or flyposting.

Coastal highlights include the hilltop fortress of **Harlech**, the bucket-and-spade resort of **Barmouth** and the fabulous stretch of **Ardudwy beach** between them. Barmouth sits at the head of the beautiful **Mawddach estuary**, which snakes its way inland to the old county town of **Dolgellau**, sheltering beneath the northern flank of **Cadair Idris** (2930ft), one of Wales's most inspirational mountains.

To the south, the flat river plain and rolling hills of the **Dyfi Valley** lay justifiable claim to being one of the greenest corners of Europe. Their focal point is the genial town of **Machynlleth**, a candidate for the Welsh capital in the 1950s and site of Owain Glyndŵr's embryonic fifteenth-century Welsh parliament. In the hills to the north, the self-contained **Centre for Alternative Technology** runs on cooperative lines and makes for an interesting day out.

South of Machynlleth is the county of **Ceredigion**, formerly known as Cardiganshire. Lying as it does between the two national parks of the Pembrokeshire coast and Snowdonia, Ceredigion is often overlooked by visitors, but it shouldn't be: it combines the best of both national parks – the stunning mountain scenery of southern Snowdonia with the little ports and sandy coves of Pembrokeshire, and all soaked in a relaxed, upbeat and firmly Welsh culture. The county's main town is ebullient **Aberystwyth**, a top spot for everything from serious study and exhibitions in the National Library to student-oriented raves and bar culture. It's also a great base for the luscious countryside inland, especially the waterfalls and woods of the **Vale of Rheidol** out towards mythical **Devil's Bridge**.

The southern Ceredigion coast is broken by some spirited little ports: most notably Georgian **Aberaeron**, higgledy-piggledy **New Quay** and the old county town of **Cardigan**, where the **River Teifi** flows into the sea. Towns and sights inland along the Teifi are worth exploring, especially the mighty castle at **Cilgerran** and the charming little university town of **Lampeter**. Near the source of the Teifi is the atmospheric **Strata Florida Abbey**.

Harlech

One of the undoubted highlights of the Cambrian coast is charming **HARLECH**, 25 miles due west of Bala, with its time-worn castle dramatically clinging to its rocky outcrop, and the town cloaking the ridge behind, commanding one of Wales's finest views over Cardigan Bay to the Llŷn. There are good beaches nearby, and the town's twisting, narrow streets harbour many places where you can eat and sleep.

Harlech's substantially complete **castle** (June–Sept daily 9.30am–6pm; April, May & Oct daily 9.30am–5pm; Nov–March Mon–Sat 9.30am–4pm, Sun 11am–4pm; £3.50; CADW) sits on its 200-foot-high bluff, a site chosen by Edward I for one more link in his magnificent chain of fortresses. Begun in 1285, it was built of a hard Cambrian rock, known as Harlech grit, hewn from the moat. Harlech withstood a siege in 1295, but was taken by Owain Glyndŵr in 1404. The young Henry VII withstood a seven-year siege at the hands of the Yorkists until 1468, when the castle was again taken. It fell into ruin, but was put back into service for Charles I during the Civil War; in March 1647, it was the last Royalist castle to fall. The first defensive line comprised the three successive pairs of gates and portcullises built between the two massive half-round towers of the **gatehouse**, where an **exhibition** now outlines the castle's history. Much of the castle's outermost ring has been destroyed, leaving only the twelve-foot-thick curtain walls rising up 40ft to the exposed **battlements**. Only the towering gatehouse prevents you from walking the full circuit.

Harlech's **train station** is below the castle on the main A496. Most **buses** call both here and on High Street, a few yards from the **tourist office** (Easter–Oct daily 9.30am–5.30pm; ⓣ01766/780658, ⓔticharlech@hotmail.com). The pick of the local places to **stay** is the cosy, informal *Castle Cottage*, on Pen Llech near the castle (Ⓣ01766/780479, Ⓦwww.castlecottageharlech.co.uk), a "restaurant with rooms" that's often booked well ahead. The best alternative is the *Castle Hotel* on Castle Square, directly opposite the castle (Ⓣ01766/780529, Ⓦwww.harlechcastlehotel.co.uk; ❸). The hardy might prefer a night under canvas at Shell Island (Ⓣ01341/241453, Ⓦwww.shellisland.co.uk), great for camp fires in the dunes and walks on the splendid **Ardudwy Beach** (part of which, near the village of Dyffryn Ardudwy, is officially naturist). If you want to camp in Harlech itself, head for the summer-only *Min y Don* **campsite**, Beach Road (Ⓣ01766/780286), three minutes' walk from the beach; take the first right out of the station. There are some wonderful places to **eat** on High Street, including *Cemlyn Tea Shop* (Ⓣ01766/780425), an excellent upscale licensed café with a lovely sun terrace; the inexpensive but licensed *Plas Café* (Ⓣ01766/780204), with a good range of food and fabulous views from the garden and conservatory; and the bistro-style *Yr Ogof* (Ⓣ01766/780888), where you'll find a good-value range of inventive vegetarian and meat dishes.

Barmouth and around

As you continue along the coast, the best approach to **BARMOUTH** (Abermaw) is from the south, where the Cambrian coast rail line sweeps across the Mawddach Estuary from tiny **Fairbourne**, over 113 rickety-looking wooden spans. Fashioned as a sea-bathing resort in the nineteenth century, Barmouth also offers lovely, breezy rambles on the cliffs of **Dinas Oleu**, above the town, and a great walk around the mouth of the estuary (see box below). Central attractions don't extend beyond the **Tŷ Gwyn Museum** (July–Sept daily 10.30am–5pm; free), a medieval tower house – now a Tudor museum – where Henry VII's uncle, Jasper Tudor, is thought to have plotted Richard III's downfall; and the **Tŷ Crwn Roundhouse**, on the hill behind (same times) which once acted as a lockup for drunken sailors.

Buses from Harlech and Dolgellau stop on Jubilee Road, near the **train station** and just a few yards from the **tourist office**, Station Road (daily: Easter–June, Sept & Oct 10am–5.30pm; July & Aug 10am–6pm; Nov–Easter 9.30am–4.30pm; Ⓣ01341/280787, Ⓔbarmouth.tic@gwynedd.gov.uk). **Accommodation** is plentiful, and best at the *Bae Abermaw Hotel*, Panorama Hill (Ⓣ01341/280550, Ⓦwww.baeabermaw.com; ❼), a former Victorian hotel that has gone all contemporary, or the seafront *Wavecrest Hotel*, 8 Marine Parade (Ⓣ01341/280330, Ⓦwww.barmouthbandb.com; ❸). Two miles north of Barmouth, *Llwyndû Farmhouse* in Llanaber (Ⓣ01341/280144, Ⓦwww.llwyndu-farmhouse.co.uk; ❺) is one of the finest farmhouse B&Bs in Wales.

Walking the Barmouth–Fairbourne Loop

The best lowland walk in the Cambrian coast region, the **Barmouth–Fairbourne Loop** (5 miles; 300ft ascent; 2–3hr) is a fine way to spend an afternoon, with impressive mountain scenery and estuarine and coastal views all the way. The walking component can be virtually eradicated by using both the mainline and Fairbourne railways. The route first crosses the estuary rail bridge (50p) to Morfa Mawddach mainline station, then follows the lane to the main road, crossing it onto a footpath that loops behind a small wooded hill to Pant Einion Hall, then follows another lane back to the main road near Fairbourne. In Fairbourne, turn north, either walking along the beach to the quay at the end of the spit or catching the **Fairbourne Railway** (Easter–Oct; 3–6 daily) to the **passenger ferry** (Easter–Oct; hourly) across the estuary mouth back to Barmouth.

The closest of a long string of **campsites** is *Hendre Mynach*, Llanaber Road (Ⓣ01341/280262, Ⓦwww.hendremynach.cu.uk), a mile north of town and just off the beach.

Basic **cafés** are plentiful, though for just a little more money you can get mammoth French sticks, good pizzas and decent veggie meals at *Isis* on The Quay. Nearby, in Church Street, *The Last Inn*, a fifteenth-century coaching inn in a former cobbler's shop, serves good **pub** meals.

Dolgellau

A former county town, **DOLGELLAU** still maintains an air of unhurried importance, never more so than when all the area's farmers pile into town for market. It's a handsome place indeed, though its dark buildings, seemingly hewn from the one rock, can appear foreboding when gleaming in the frequent downpours. In fine weather, with the lofty crags of **Cadair Idris** framing the grey squares and streets, Dolgellau feels as Welsh and exotic as is possible.

Walks around Dolgellau

Dolgellau is a good base for **walks**, whether fairly easy rambles, like the first two described here, or more strenuous mountain hiking. The OS Explorer 1:25,000 map #OL23, *Cadair Idris & Llyn Tegid*, is recommended, particularly for the ascent of Cadair Idris.

Torrent Walk

The attractive lowland **Torrent Walk** (2 miles; 1hr; 100ft ascent), follows the course of the Clywedog River as it carves its way through the bedrock. Stroll downstream past the cascades and through some gnarled old woodland that drips with antiquity. Bus #32/X32 can take you the 2.5 miles east along the A470, from where it's a couple of hundred yards or so down the B4416 (signposted to Brithdir) to a sign on the left-hand side marking the beginning of the walk.

Precipice Walk and New Precipice Walk

Though the path is narrow in places and there are some steep banks, the **Precipice Walk** (3–4 miles; 2hr; negligible ascent) can hardly be called precipitous. In fact it is very easy going, simple to follow, and has great views to the 1000-foot ramparts of Cadair Idris and along the Mawddach Estuary – best in late afternoon or early morning sun. The path makes a circuit around Foel Cynwch, starting three miles north of Dolgellau from a public car park on the road to Llanfachreth. For those without a vehicle, there's access from a path beside Cymer Abbey. Even less precipitous, the **New Precipice Walk** (4 miles; 2hr; 700ft ascent) combines luscious views of the estuary with a ramble along the old tramways of the Foel Ispri gold mine. Access is easiest from the signed path at the very western end of Llanelltyd village, two miles northwest of Dolgellau.

Cadair Idris ascents

More ambitious Victorians climbed **Cadair Idris** on the since-eroded Fox's Path, now widely ignored in favour of the straightforward, classic **Pony Path** (6–7 miles; 2500ft ascent; 4–5hr), starting three miles up Cadair Road in the car park at Tŷ Nant. As you begin by the sign near the telephone box, the view to the craggy flanks of the massif are tremendous, but they disappear as you climb steeply to the col, where a left turn leads to the summit shelter on **Penygadair** (2930ft). The most impressive ascent of Cadair Idris, however, is up the **Minffordd Path** (6 miles; 2900ft ascent; 5hr), which leads up to and then around the glacial lake of Cwm Cau before reaching the summit. The path starts just west of the *Minffordd Hotel* where the A487 meets the B4405.

Dolgellau has no train station but is well served by **buses**, all of which pull into the central Eldon Square, close to the **tourist office** (Easter–Oct daily 9.30am–5.30pm; Nov–Easter Mon & Thurs–Sun 9.30am–4.30pm; ⓣ01341/422888, ⓔtic.dolgellau@eryri-npa.gov.uk). **Accommodation** is best found at the *Merionnydd*, Smithfield Square (ⓣ01341/422554, ⓦwww.themerionnydd.com; ④), a good-value hotel built in an ex-police station and gaol – the basement cells are used as a restaurant. Outside town, the eighteenth-century *Tyddyn Mawr Farmhouse*, Islawrdref (ⓣ01341/422331, ⓦwww.lokalink.co.uk/dolgellau/tyddynmawr; ④), stands on the slopes of Cadair Idris at the foot of the Pony Path, while the superb seventeenth-century *George III Hotel*, Penmaenpool (ⓣ01341/422525, ⓦwww.georgethethird.co.uk; ⑥), overlooks the Mawddach Estuary, two miles west of Dolgellau. There's a **hostel**, *Kings YHA*, at Penmaenpool, four miles west of Dolgellau (ⓣ0870/770 5900, ⓦwww.yha.org.uk; April–Aug), with six-bed rooms at £12 per person. The tent-only *Bryn-y-Gwyn* **campsite**, Cader Road (ⓣ01341/422733), is less than a mile southeast of town. The best **restaurant** in town is the creative, affordable *Dylanwad Da*, 2 Smithfield St (ⓣ01341/422870), while *Y Sospan* (ⓣ01341/423174), on Queen Square behind the tourist office, is a smart, dependable, central bistro for good lunches and dinners. The *Stag Inn* on Bridge Street is a straightforward town-centre pub with good beer and a garden.

Coed-y-Brenin Forestry Centre

A few miles north of Dolgellau, alongside the A470, the tree-covered valleys and hillsides of **Coed-y-Brenin Forest** conceal some of the best mountain bike trails in the world as well as mile after mile of glorious riverside scenery, numerous way-marked walks, and an innovative **visitor centre** (daily 10am–4pm). Top-quality bikes can be hired from Beics Brenin (open all year 10am–5pm or dusk if earlier; June–Sept daily; March–May, Oct & Nov Thurs–Mon; Dec–Feb Fri–Sun; ⓣ01341/440728, ⓦwww.beicsbrenin.co.uk).

The Talyllyn and Dysynni valleys

From Tywyn, the road runs parallel to the railway, meeting it at **Dolgoch Falls**, a couple of miles short of the valleys' largest settlement, **Abergynolwyn**, which

Mountain biking trails

Wales has some of the best **mountain bike trails** in the world, thanks to the steep hillsides and sumptuous mountain scenery. Hundreds of miles of old trackways, roads and purpose-built trails crisscross the hillsides, offering lungbusting uphill rides, and adrenaline pumping descents. Graded like ski runs – Blacks for experts, Reds and Blues for intermediates and Greens for family riders – the purpose-built trails, which are mainly narrow singletrack, weave through the trees and across open moorland. The early trail development was all in mid Wales, at **Coed-y-Brenin**, near Dolgellau (see p.699), and this remains the spiritual home of Welsh mountain biking. Now, there are also excellent facilities at **Cwm Carn**, near Newport (see p.672); **Afan Argoed**, near Swansea; **Nant-yr-Arian**, near Aberystwyth on the Cambrian coast (see p.703); **Machynlleth** (see p.701) a few miles further north; and **Gwyder Forest and Penmachno**, near Betws-y-Coed (see p.721) to name just the main centres.

Coed-y-Brenin is probably the best place to visit if there's only time to see one centre, but they are all very different, and many mountain bikers devote a whole trip to riding them all, some even biking the miles in between.

For further information, visit ⓦwww.mbwales.com or ⓦwww.mtb-wales.com.

comprises of a few dozen quarry-workers' houses, a shop, a great little café housed in the community centre and a pub, the excellent *Railway Inn*. From here the valley continues northeast to **Tal-y-llyn Lake** (Llyn Mwyngil) and the fifteenth-century **St Mary's**, a fine example of a small Welsh parish church, unusual because of its chancel arch painted with an alternating grid of red and white roses, separated by grotesque bosses.

The **Dysynni Valley** has more to offer in the way of sights, but limited public transport makes access awkward. A mile and a half northwest of Abergynolwyn, a side road cuts northeast to the hamlet of **Llanfihangel-y-Pennant** and the scant, but impressive, ruins of **Castell-y-Bere** (free access; CADW), a fortress built by Llywelyn the Great in 1221 to protect the mountain passes. One of the largest of the Welsh castles, it was besieged twice before being consigned to seven centuries of obscurity and decay. There's plenty to poke around, with large slabs of the main towers still standing. Three miles seaward of the castle stands the impressive **Craig yr Aderyn** (Birds' Rock), a 760-foot-high cliff where breeding cormorants have remained loyal to the spot despite being left landlocked by the receding sea. Also worth seeing is the fabulous three-dimensional patchwork map of the Dysynni Valley in the vestry of Llanfihangel-y-Pennant church.

Good places to **stay** include *Tan-y-Coed-Isaf* (☎01654/782639; ❸; March–Oct), a superb farmhouse B&B close to Dolgoch Falls, and the *Riverside Guesthouse* in Abergynolwyn (☎01654/782235; ❷), which has a limited number of bargain **tent sites**.

Tywyn

TYWYN is primarily of interest as a base for the two valleys, although the town does have miles of sandy beach and the five-foot-high **Ynysmaengwyn**, or St Cadfan's Stone, within the Norman nave of the **Church of St Cadfan** (daily 9am–5pm, later in summer), which actually bears the earliest example of written Welsh, dating back to around 650 AD.

Tywyn's three main roads meet at the joint **train station** and main **bus stop**, a short walk from the **tourist office** on High Street (Easter–Oct daily 10am–5pm; ☎01654/710070, ⓔtywyn.tic@gwynedd.co.uk), and the Tywyn Wharf narrow-gauge railway station, two hundred yards to the south. The Talyllyn Valley is served by the #30 **bus**, running from Tywyn to Abergynolwyn, and continuing to Minffordd (where #32 links with Dolgellau or Machynlleth). The cheapest **accommodation** is the basic *Llys Maldwyn* B&B, opposite the tourist office on High Street (☎01654/711058; ❷), while the *Monfa*, 4 Pier Rd (☎01654/710858, ⓦwww.monfa.co.uk; ❸), between the seafront and the High Street, is a more comfortable alternative. For something smarter, there's the *Corbett Arms Hotel* on Corbett Square, just up the main street from the parish church (☎01654/710264; ❻). The handiest **campsite**, ten minutes' walk from town on the Aberdyfi road, is the *Vaenol Camping Park* (☎01654/710232). The best **eating** in town is upstairs at the moderately priced *Proper Gander* on High Street (☎01654/711270).

Machynlleth and around

Eighteen miles northeast of Aberystwyth, **MACHYNLLETH** (pronounced "ma-hun-thleth") is a bustling little place with a great vibe, as well being the undisputed centre of all things "New Age". The wide main street, **Heol Maengwyn**, is busiest on Wednesdays, when a lively market springs up; **Heol Penrallt** intersects this at the fussy clocktower. Owain Glyndŵr's partly fifteenth-century **Parliament House** (Easter–Sept Mon–Sat 10am–5pm; other times by arrangement on ☎01654/702827; free) sits halfway along Heol

Owain Glyndŵr

No name is more frequently invoked in Wales as that of **Owain Glyndŵr**, a potent figurehead of Welsh nationalism since he rose up against the occupying English in the early fifteenth century. Little is known about the real Glyndŵr, although he was born in the late fourteenth century to an aristocratic family, and had a fairly conventional upbringing, part of it studying English in London, where he became a loyal and distinguished soldier of the English king. When he returned to Wales to take up his claim as Prince of Wales, being directly descended from the princes of Powys and Cyfeiliog, he became the focus of a rebellion born of discontent with the English rulers.

Goaded by a parochial land dispute in which the courts failed to back him, Glyndŵr garnered four thousand supporters and attacked Ruthin, and then Denbigh, Rhuddlan, Flint, Hawarden and Oswestry, before finally encountering English resistance at Welshpool. England's Henry IV dispatched troops, and in a vain attempt to break the spirit of the rebellion, drew up a range of severely punitive anti-Welsh laws, even outlawing Welsh-language bards and singers. But by the end of 1403, Glyndŵr controlled most of Wales.

In 1404, he was crowned king of a free Wales and assembled a parliament at Machynlleth, where he drew up mutual recognition treaties with France and Spain. A second parliament took place in Harlech a year later, with Glyndŵr making plans to carve up England and Wales into three as part of an alliance against the English king. But by now the English were fighting back with increased intensity and Glyndŵr lost battles, ground and castles, before eventually being forced into hiding; dying, it is thought, in Herefordshire. The anti-Welsh laws remained in place until the coronation of Henry VII, who had Welsh origins, in 1485; and Wales was subsequently subsumed into English custom and law. Glyndŵr however remains a national hero and a symbol of Welsh independence.

Maengwyn, a modest-looking black-and-white-fronted building, concealing a large interior. Displays chart the course of Glyndŵr's life, his military campaign, his downfall, and the 1404 parliament, when he controlled almost all of what we now know as Wales.

Opposite the Parliament House, a path leads into the landscaped grounds of **Plas Machynlleth**, the elegant seventeenth-century mansion of the Marquess of Londonderry. Its solitude is entirely intentional: in the 1840s the Marquess bought up all the surrounding buildings and had them demolished, and rerouted the main road away from his grounds. On the other side of the central clocktower, housed in the beautifully serene old chapel Y Tabernacl on Heol Pen'rallt, is the **Museum of Modern Art Wales** (MOMA Cymru: Sat–Mon, Wed & Thurs 10.30am–5.30pm, Fri 10.30am–8pm; free; ⓣ01654/703355, ⓦwww.momawales.org.uk), which hosts an ongoing programme of temporary exhibitions. It is also the place to go for films, theatre, comedy, concerts and the August Gŵyl Machynlleth festival, which combines classical and some folk music with theatre and debate.

Practicalities

The **train station** is a five-minute walk up Heol Pen'rallt from the town's central clocktower, which is the main **bus stop**, though many also call at the train station. The **tourist office** (Easter–Sept Mon–Sat 9.30am–5pm, Sun 10am–4pm; Oct–Easter Mon–Fri 9.30am–5pm, Sat & Sun 10am–4pm; ⓣ01654/702401, ⓔmactic@powys.gov.uk) is next to the Glyndŵr Parliament House on Heol Maengwyn. **Bike rental** is available from The Holey Trail at 31 Heol Maengwyn (ⓣ01654/700411, ⓦwww.holeytrail.com).

B&B **accommodation** includes the *Maenllwyd*, on Newtown Road, the eastern extension of Heol Maengwyn (Ⓣ01654/702928, Ⓦwww.maenllwyd.co.uk; ❸), and *Gwelfryn*, at 6 Greenfields, Bank St (Ⓣ01654/702532; ❷). Hotels include the grand *Wynnstay Arms* on Heol Maengwyn (Ⓣ01654/702941, Ⓦwww.wynnstay-hotel.com; ❹), though if money's no object, the Michelin-starred luxury of *Ynyshir Hall*, near the Ynys-hir Nature Reserve at Eglwysfach, six miles southwest on the A487 (Ⓣ01654/781209, Ⓦwww.ynyshir-hall.co.uk; ❽) is wonderful. There's the *Reditreks* **bunkhouse** off Heol Powys in central Machynlleth (Ⓣ01654/702184, Ⓦwww.reditreks.com), with beds for £15 and basic **camping**; otherwise, the nearest site is three miles north near the Centre for Alternative Technology (CAT) at *Llwyngwern Farm* (Ⓣ01654/702492).

There are plenty of **cafés**, **restaurants** and **pubs** in town, including a popular veggie wholefood café, the CAT-run *Quarry Café*, near the clocktower on Heol Maengwyn. Lunch and dinner are great at the *Wynnstay Arms*, which also has a superb pizzeria in its courtyard bar. The *Skinners Arms* on Heol Pen'rallt is cheaper but cosy and good for food or beer. Liveliest pub is either the *Skinners* or the *White Lion*, by the clocktower.

Centre for Alternative Technology

Since its foundation in the middle of the oil crisis of 1974, the **Centre for Alternative Technology**, or Canolfan y Dechnoleg Amgen (daily: Easter–Sept 10am–5.30pm; Oct–Easter 10am–dusk; £8 summer, £6 winter, £1 discount to those arriving by bike or public transport; Ⓣ01654/705950, Ⓦwww.cat.org.uk) – three miles north of Machynlleth off the A487 – has become one of the biggest attractions in Wales. Over almost three decades, seven acres of a once-derelict slate quarry have been turned into an almost entirely sustainable community, generating eighty percent of its own power from wind, sun and water. But this is no back-to-the-land hippie commune. Right from the start, the idea was to embrace technology – much of the on-site equipment was developed and built here, reflecting the centre's achievements in this field – and, most importantly, to promote its application in urban situations.

CAT's earnest education is leavened with flashes of pizazz, particularly in the water-balanced **cliff railway** (Easter–Oct only), which whisks the visitor 200ft up to the main site from the car park. It is also a beautiful site, sensitively landscaped using local slate and wood, and you can easily spend half a day sauntering around. There's plenty for kids to do, including a children's theatre (mainly mid-July to Aug), the wholefood restaurant turns out delicious food, and the excellent bookshop stocks a wide range of alternative literature along with crafts and intriguing toys.

Primarily, though, this is a working community which exists more to educate by example than entertain, partly facilitated by the new environmental information centre housed in a rammed-earth building.

Aberystwyth and around

The liveliest seaside resort in Wales, **ABERYSTWYTH** is an essential stop. Being rooted in all aspects of Welsh culture, it is possibly the most enjoyable and relaxed place to gain an insight into the national psyche. As the capital of sparsely populated mid-Wales, and with one of the most prestigious university colleges in Wales, there are plenty of cultural and entertainment diversions, as well as an array of Victorian and Edwardian seaside trappings. In 1907, the National Library was inaugurated here, and Cymdeithas yr Iaith (the Welsh Language Society) was founded here in 1963. Aberystwyth's politics are firmly

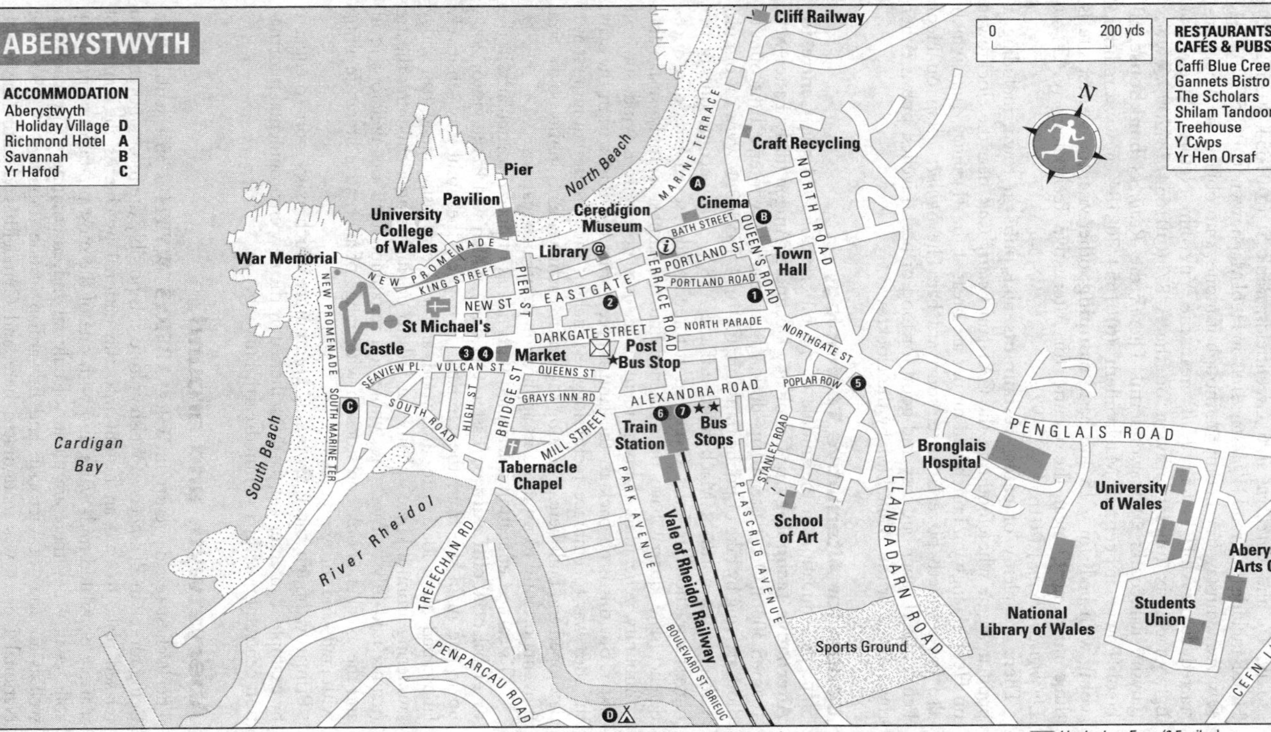
ABERYSTWYTH
ACCOMMODATION
Aberystwyth Holiday Village D
Richmond Hotel A
Savannah B
Yr Hafod C
RESTAURANTS, CAFÉS & PUBS
Caffi Blue Creek 4
Gannets Bistro 3
The Scholars 1
Shilam Tandoori 6
Treehouse 2
Y Cŵps 5
Yr Hen Orsaf 7
0
200 yds
N
Constitution Hill
Glan-y-Mor Leisure Park (3 miles), Borth (5 miles) & Machynlleth (20 miles)
Midfield (1.5 miles) & Cardigan (40 miles)
Llanbadarn Fawr (0.5 miles)
Cliff Railway
Craft Recycling
NORTH ROAD
MARINE TERRACE
North Beach
Pier
Pavilion
Cinema
Ceredigion Museum
BATH STREET
QUEEN'S ROAD
Town Hall
University College of Wales
NEW PROMENADE
KING STREET
Library @
PORTLAND ST
PORTLAND ROAD
TERRACE ROAD
War Memorial
EASTGATE
PIER ST
NEW ST
St Michael's
Castle
DARKGATE STREET
NORTH PARADE
NORTHGATE ST
Market
Post
Bus Stop
SEAVIEW PL.
VULCAN ST
QUEENS ST
POPLAR ROW
ALEXANDRA ROAD
SOUTH MARINE TER.
SOUTH ROAD
HIGH ST
BRIDGE ST
GRAYS INN RD
Train Station
Bus Stops
STANLEY ROAD
Cardigan Bay
South Beach
MILL STREET
Tabernacle Chapel
PARK AVENUE
PLASCRUG AVENUE
School of Art
LLANBADARN ROAD
PENGLAIS ROAD
Bronglais Hospital
University of Wales
River Rheidol
TREFECHAN RD
Vale of Rheidol Railway
Aberystwyth Arts Centre
National Library of Wales
Students Union
Sports Ground
PENPARCAU ROAD
BOULEVARD ST. BRIEUC
CEFN LLAN

radical Welsh, and in a country that still struggles with its inherent conservatism, the town is a blast of fresh air.

The Town

With two long, gentle bays curving around between rocky heads, Aberystwyth's position is hard to beat. **Constitution Hill** (430ft), at the north end of the long Promenade, rises sharply away from the rocky beach. It's a favourite jaunt, crowned with a tatty jumble of amenities – café, picnic area, millennium beacon, telescopes and an octagonal **camera obscura** (Easter–Oct daily 10am–5.30pm; free) – reached on foot or by the clanking 1896 **cliff railway** (April–Oct daily 10am–6pm; Nov–March Wed–Sun 10am–4pm; £2.50 return) from the grand terminus building at the top of Queen's Road, behind the Promenade. South along the Promenade – officially called Marine Terrace – and off to the left on Terrace Road, the **Ceredigion Museum** (Mon–Sat 10am–5pm; free) houses cosy-looking reconstructed cottages, a dairy and a nineteenth-century pharmacy in the atmospherically ornate Edwardian music hall, the Coliseum.

Marine Terrace continues past the spindly **pier** to the dazzling **Old College**, all turrets, friezes and mosaics. Originally a John Nash-designed villa, it was later converted to a hotel to soak up the anticipated masses arriving on the new railway line. When the venture failed, the building was sold to the fledgling university. The Promenade cuts around the front of the building to the ruins of Edward I's thirteenth-century **castle** (free access), a fine place for a picnic, but notable more for its breezy position than for the buildings themselves.

To the east of town, Penglais Road climbs the hill northwards towards the **university**'s main campus and the **National Library of Wales** (Mon–Sat 9.30am–5pm; free; Ⓣ01970/632548, Ⓦwww.llgc.org.uk), which has excellent temporary exhibitions and the **World of the Book**, a well-rounded introduction to the history of the written word and printing in Wales, shown in an absorbing range of old texts, maps, photos, and the Morgan's 1588 Welsh Bible (tours Mon 11am; free; pre-booking essential). Above the National Library is the university campus, which includes the superb **Aberystwyth Arts Centre**, always a sure bet for a couple of decent exhibitions.

Practicalities

Aberystwyth's main line and Vale of Rheidol **train stations** are adjacent on Alexandra Road, a ten-minute walk from the seafront on the southern side of the town centre. Local **buses** stop outside the station, with long-distance ones using the depot immediately next door, by the entrance to the park. The busy **tourist office** (July & Aug daily 10am–6pm; Sept–June Mon–Sat 10am–5pm; Ⓣ01970/612125, Ⓔaberystwythtic@ceredigion.gov.uk) is a ten-minute stroll from the station, straight down Terrace Road towards the seafront. Craft Recycling, in the Old Police Yard, Queens Road (Ⓣ01970/626532), does **bike rental**.

There are hundreds of places to **stay**, mostly in the streets around the station and along South Marine Terrace, where you'll find *Yr Hafod*, at no. 1 (Ⓣ01970/617579, Ⓦwww.yrhafod.co.uk; ❸). The well-priced *Savannah* guesthouse, 27 Queens Rd (Ⓣ01970/615131, Ⓦwww.savannahguesthouse.co.uk; ❷), is another good choice, as is the *Richmond Hotel* at 44–45 Marine Terrace (Ⓣ01970/612201, Ⓦwww.richmondhotel.uk.com; ❻). The nearest place to pitch a **tent** is the *Aberystwyth Holiday Village* (Ⓣ01970/624211), off the main Penparcau Road to the south of town, a twenty-minute walk from the station.

Aberystwyth's cultural and gastronomic life is an ebullient, year-round affair. Just behind the market, *Gannets Bistro*, at 7 St. James Square (Ⓣ01970/617164; Wed–Sat), creates imaginative, inexpensive **meals** from local farm and sea

▲Aberystwyth at night

produce, while *Caffi Blue Creek* is a relaxed small daytime café with comfy sofas and a cheerful vibe. *Shilam Tandoori*, Station Building, Alexandra Rd (Ⓣ01970/615015), is a superb modern Indian restaurant with unusual specialities and good vegetarian choices, or there's the organic, mostly vegetarian *Treehouse* at 14 Baker St (Ⓣ01970/615791; closed Sun). For decent and very reasonable **pub food**, you're best off at *Yr Hen Orsaf*, which is in the old station buildings on Alexandra Road – have a pint or a meal under a stunning glass canopy on the platform. For no-nonsense **drinking**, Aberystwyth has scores of options: try the *Scholars* on Queens Road for good beer, food and atmosphere, as well as occasional live music. *Y Cŵps* (Coopers Arms), Llanbadarn Road, is fun and friendly, with regular Welsh folk and jazz nights. For a slice of Edwardian gentility, take afternoon tea in any of the seafront hotels along the Promenade. The **Aberystwyth Arts Centre**, at the university's Penglais site (Ⓣ01970/623232, Ⓦwww.aber.ac.uk/artscentre), has an art-house **cinema** and **theatre**, while the **Drwm**, at the National Library, Penglais (Ⓣ01970/632548), is a funky centre for film, lectures and concerts.

The Vale of Rheidol

Inland from Aberystwyth, the River Rheidol winds its way up to a secluded, wooded valley, where occasional old industrial workings have moulded themselves into the contours, rising up past waterfalls and hamlets to Devil's Bridge. It's a glorious route, and by far the best way to see it is on board one of the trains of the **Vale of Rheidol railway** (2–4 services daily April–Oct; £13 return; Ⓣ01970/625819, Ⓦwww.rheidolrailway.co.uk), a narrow-gauge steam train that wheezes its way along sheer rock faces from the terminus in Aberystwyth to Devil's Bridge. It was built in 1902, ostensibly for the valley's lead mines but with a canny eye on its tourist potential as well, and has run ever since.

Folk legend, picturesque scenery and travellers' lore combine at **DEVIL'S BRIDGE** (Pontarfynach), twelve miles east of Aberystwyth, a tiny settlement built solely for the growing visitor trade of the last few hundred years. Be warned, however, that Devil's Bridge is a seriously popular day-trip destination: in order to escape some of the inevitable congestion, it's wisest to come here at the beginning or end of the day, or out of season.

The main attraction here is the **bridge** itself, which is actually three stacked bridges spanning the chasm of the churning River Mynach. The road bridge in front of the Alpine *Hafod Arms* **hotel** (Ⓣ01970/890232, Ⓦwww.thehafodhotel.co.uk; ④) is the most modern of the three, dating from 1901. Immediately below it, wedged between the rock faces, are the stone bridge from 1753 and, at the bottom, the original bridge, dating from the eleventh century and reputedly built by the monks of Strata Florida Abbey (see p.711). For a remarkable view of the bridges, you have to enter the turnstile (£1) upstream of the bridge and head down slippery steps to the deep cleft of the **Punch Bowl**, where the water pounds and hurtles through the gap crowned by the bridges. More dramatic still, the **gate** on the other side (Easter–Oct daily 9.30am–5.30pm; £2.50; at other times access through turnstiles; £2) leads west to a path that tumbles down into the valley below the bridges, descending ultimately to the crashing **Mynach Falls**. The scenery here is magnificent: sharp, wooded slopes rise away from the frothing river and distant mountain peaks surface on the horizon. Platforms overlook the series of falls, from where a set of steep steps takes you further down to a footbridge dramatically spanning the river at the bottom of the falls. There's a **campsite** – *Woodlands Caravan Park* (Ⓣ01970/890233) – by the petrol station, just beyond the bridges.

Six miles east from Aberystwyth, the A44 hurdles a high mountain pass close to the entrance of the enchanting **Bwlch Nant yr Arian** Forestry Centre. As well a homely café, and tranquil sun-terrace that offers superb views over the surrounding lakes, there are also some lovely walking trails, some fabulous mountain bike trails (see p.700) and daily red kite feeding at 2pm, 3pm in summer. A mile east of the forest, the road ducks into the village of **Ponterwyd**, which makes an ideal base for the walking and biking trails as well as being a less touristy hub for nearby Devil's Bridge. Best bet for accommodation is the *George Borrow Hotel* (Ⓣ01970/890230, Ⓦwww.thegeorgeborrowhotel.co.uk; ④), which serves excellent food all day.

Aberaeron

ABERAERON, sixteen miles along the coast from Aberystwyth, comes as something of a surprise. Aberaeron's unusual look comes from its odd pedigree, being built in one fell swoop during the early nineteenth century by the Reverend Alban Gwynne. He spent his way through his wife's inheritance by dredging the Aeron Estuary and constructing a formally planned town around it as a new port for mid-Wales.

Georgian planning is most evident around the central **Alban Square**, with graceful terraces of quoin-edged buildings and the odd pedimented porch. From there, the grid of narrow streets stretches away to the sea at **Quay Parade**, the neat line of ordered, colourful houses on the seafront.

Sadly, despite its architectural attractiveness, Aberaeron is almost unique amongst the Ceredigion resorts for its unappealing **beach**. Consequently, the most agreeable activity in Aberaeron is just to amble around the streets and waterfront and graze in its cafés and pubs. Aberaeron's one essential sight lies three miles east along the A482 at **Llanerchaeron** (house and gardens late March to Oct Wed–Sun 11am–5pm; £5.80; parkland all year dawn–dusk; free; NT). Once an integrated smallholding typical of this region, the estate boasts exquisite kitchen gardens and a pristine, Nash-designed main house.

Aberaeron's **tourist office** is on Quay Parade, the seafront road (July & Aug daily 10am–6pm; Easter–June & Sept daily 10am–5pm; Oct–Easter Mon–Sat 10am–5pm; ⓣ01545/570602, ⓔaberaeron@ceredigion.gov.uk). Overlooking the harbour on Cadwgan Place are the *Coedmor*, at no. 2 (ⓣ01545/571615, ⓦwww.coedmorbandb.co.uk; ④), and, better still, the *Arosfa*, at no. 8 (ⓣ01545/570120, ⓦwww.arosfaguesthouse.co.uk; ④). The best place in town, though, is the central *Harbourmaster Hotel*, Pen Cei (ⓣ01545/570755, ⓦwww.harbour-master.com; ⑦), with ultra-modern rooms, great breakfasts, endless creature comforts and a relaxed, informal atmosphere. The nearest local **campsite** is the *Aeron Coast*, on the A487 just north of town (ⓣ01545/570349). For **food**, the best place to eat is the relaxed café/bistro at the *Harbourmaster Hotel* on Pen Cei. Daytime alternatives include the *Hive on the Quay*, Cadwgan Place (April to mid-Sept), which serves fine local seafood in its conservatory, and has scrumptious **honey ice cream** to eat in or take away.

New Quay and around

Along with Laugharne in Carmarthenshire (see p.661), **NEW QUAY** (Cei Newydd), seven miles from Aberaeron, lays claim to being the original Llareggub in Dylan Thomas's *Under Milk Wood*. Certainly, it has the little tumbling streets, prim Victorian terraces, cobbled stone harbour and air of dreamy isolation that Thomas evoked in his play but, in the height of summer, the quiet isolation can be hard to find. Although there is a singular lack of excitement in New Quay, it's a truly pleasant base for good beaches, walking, surfing, eating and drinking.

The pretty **harbour** and small, curving beach are backed by a higgledy-piggledy line of multicoloured shops and houses. The beachfront streets comprise the **lower town** – the more traditionally "seaside" part of New Quay, full of cafés, pubs and beach shops. Tucked away down the slipway above the beach is the recently refurbished **Cardigan Bay Marine Wildlife Centre** (April–Oct daily 10am–5pm; donation requested), which has some excellent interactive and interpretive displays on the dolphins, seals and sea birds of Cardigan Bay. It also organises daily (weather permitting) whale/dolphin watching boat trips on board the survey vessel (2hr £16, 4hr £32, 6hr £48; ⓣ01545/560032 for booking information, ⓦwww.cbmwc.org). Sharply inclined streets lead to the residential **upper town**, with some delightful views over the sweeping shoreline below. The northern beach soon gives way to a rocky headland, **New Quay Head**, where an invigorating path steers along the top of aptly named **Bird Rock**.

Buses stop on Park Street, from where it's a walk down any of the steep streets to the seafront, where you'll find the **tourist office**, centrally located at the junction of Church Street and Wellington Place (April–Sept daily 10am–6pm; ⓣ01545/560865, ⓔnewquay@ceredigion.gov.uk). **Accommodation** includes the *Hungry Trout* on Glanmor Terrace (ⓣ01545/560680, ⓦwww.the hungrytrout .co.uk; ④), a superb seafood restaurant with two pleasant rooms, and the nicely refurbished *Hotel Penwig* (ⓣ01545/560910; ③). The nearest **campsite** is the *Neuadd Farm* (ⓣ01545/560709), fifteen minutes' walk away, behind the *Penrhiwllan Inn*, at the top of the hill on the way to Synod Inn. New Quay contains innumerable cheap **cafés**, among which the *Mariner's Café*, by the harbour wall, is a sure bet. Most of the **pubs** serve food, the best being the *Seahorse* on Margaret Street.

Tresaith and Llangranog

The most popular stopping-off point on the stretch of coast south of New Quay is **Aberporth**, an elderly resort built around two less than appealing bays, easily shown up by the neighbouring hamlet of **TRESAITH**, a mile to the east, which staggers down the tiny valley to a delightful beach. There are **dinghy races** from the beach every Sunday in summer. Around the rocks to the right of the beach, the River Saith plummets over the mossy black rocks in a waterfall. For **accommodation**, there's the superb Georgian *Glandr* (ⓣ01239/811442, ⓦwww.glandwrtresaith.co.uk; ④) at the top of the village on the road to Aberporth, and a little further along, a wonderful tent-only cliff-top **campsite** at the far end of the *Llety Caravan Park* (ⓣ01239/810354), from where a pretty footpath descends straight to the beach.

Three miles north of the A487, **LLANGRANOG** is the most attractive village on the Ceredigion coast, wedged in between bracken and gorse-beaten hills, the main streets winding to the tiny seafront. The beach can become horribly congested in midsummer, when it's better to follow the cliff path to **Cilborth Beach**, and on to the glorious NT-owned headland, **Ynys Lochtyn**. In Llangranog, you can **stay** on the seafront either at the excellent 350-year-old *Ship Inn* (ⓣ01239/654423; ④) or the earthier *Pentre Arms* (ⓣ01239/654345; ③); both do good **food**. Between Penbryn and Llangranog is the *Maesglas* caravan park (ⓣ01239/654268), which takes **tents**.

Cardigan

An ancient borough and former port at the lowest bridging point of the Teifi Estuary, **CARDIGAN** (Aberteifi) was founded by the Norman lord Roger de Montgomery in 1093 around a castle. From the castle mound by the bridge, Bridge Street sweeps through High Street to the turreted oddity of the **Guildhall**. Through the Guildhall courtyard is the town's superb **covered market**, a typically eclectic mix of fresh food, local crafts and secondhand stalls.

The helpful **tourist office** (Easter–Aug daily 10am–6pm; Sept–Easter Mon–Sat 10am–5pm; ⓣ01239/613230, ⓔcardigantic@ceredigion.gov.uk) is in the foyer of Theatr Mwldan, Bath House Road. **Accommodation** includes the old-fashioned *Black Lion* pub on High Street (ⓣ01239/612532, ⓦwww.theblacklioncardigan.com; ③), which also does food, or the basic but decent *Highbury House*, the old county gaol, on Pendre (ⓣ01239/613403, ⓦwww.llety.co.uk/highbury; ①). A mile and a half east of town, the sixteenth-century *Rosehill Farm* in Llangoedmor (ⓣ01239/612019, ⓦwww.rosehillfarm.co.uk; closed Nov–March; ③) offers a gorgeous riverside setting and excellent evening meals. There's a YHA **hostel** four miles away at Poppit Sands, at the end of the Pembrokeshire Coast Path (ⓣ0870/770 5996, ⓦwww.yha.org.uk; closed Nov–Feb; dorms £14); buses connect in July and August, but otherwise terminate half a mile short. For **food**, try the inexpensive *Theatr Mwldan* café or *Food For Thought*, 13 Pendre, which offers a good range of hearty snacks and coffees.

The Teifi Valley

The Teifi is one of Wales's most eulogized rivers, for its rich spawn of fresh fish, its meandering rural charm and the coracles that were a regular feature from pre-Roman times. On the way to its estuary at Cardigan, it flows through some gloriously green and undulating countryside, winding its way over the falls at **Cenarth** and passing the massive ramparts of **Cilgerran Castle**. Further upstream, the river also takes in the proudly Welsh university town of **Lampeter**, and the river's infancy can be seen near the ruins of **Strata Florida Abbey**, beyond which the river emerges from the dark and remote **Teifi Pools**.

Cilgerran Castle

Just a couple of miles up the Teifi River from Cardigan, the attractive village of **CILGERRAN** clusters around its wide main street. Behind is the bulk of the **castle** (daily: April–Oct 9.30am–6.30pm; Nov–March 9.30am–4pm; £2.50; CADW), founded in 1100 at a commanding vantage point on a high wooded bluff above the river, then still navigable for sea-going ships. This is the legendary site of the 1109 abduction of Nest (the "Welsh Helen of Troy") by a love-struck Prince Owain of Powys. Her husband, Gerald of Pembroke, escaped by slithering down a toilet waste chute through the castle walls. The two massive drum towers still dominate the castle, and the outer walls, some four feet thicker than those facing the inner courtyard, are traced by vertiginously high walkways. The outer ward, over which a modern path now runs from the entrance, is a good example of the keepless castle that evolved throughout the thirteenth century.

A footpath runs down from the castle to the river's edge; an exhibition at the quay about local industries – coracles included – also covers the story of America-bound emigrants leaving from Cardigan. Guided two-hour **canoe trips** leave from the quay in summer.

Cenarth

A tourist magnet since it was swooped on by nineteenth-century Romantics and artists, **CENARTH**, five miles east of Cilgerran, is a pleasant spot but hardly merits the mass interest that it receives. The village's main asset, its **waterfalls**, are close to the main road, connected by a path from opposite the *White Hart* pub. This runs past the **National Coracle Centre** (Easter–Oct daily except Sat 10.30am–5.30pm; other times by arrangement ⓣ01239/710980; £3), a small museum with displays of these curiously designed boats from all over the world, before continuing to a restored seventeenth-century flour mill by the falls' edge.

Lampeter

Twenty miles east of Cenarth, **LAMPETER** (Llanbedr Pont Steffan or, popularly, Llambed) is best known as a remote outpost of the British university system. St David's University College was Wales's first university college, founded in 1822 by the bishop of St David's to aid Welsh theological students who couldn't afford to travel to England for their education; it only became part of the University of Wales in the 1970s.

There's not a great deal to see, and what you are able to visit is fairly low-key. A decent heritage trail, with plaques marking out historical places of interest, is accompanied by a leaflet that you can pick up at the library (see below). **Harford Square** forms the hub of the town. The main buildings of the **University College** lie off College Street, and include a quadrangle modelled on an Oxbridge college and the motte of Lampeter's long-vanished castle – a strange sight amidst such order. The High Street is the most architecturally distinguished part of town, its eighteenth-century coaching inn, the *Black Lion*, dominating the streetscape; you can see its old stables and coach house through an archway.

Leaflets in the town library – through the archway of the old town hall and past the supermarket – and the noticeboards in the Mulberry Bush health-food shop at 2 Bridge St are the closest Lampeter get to a tourist office. *Haulfan*, 6 Station Terrace, behind University College (ⓣ01570/422718, ⓦwww.haulfanguesthouse.co.uk; ❷), is the best **B&B**, or you could try the *Black Lion*, High Street (ⓣ01570/422490; ❹). Just off the B4343 is one of the area's best farmhouse B&Bs, at *Pentre Farm*, near Llanfair Clydogau, five miles from Lampeter (ⓣ01570/493313, ⓦwww.pentrefarmholidays.co.uk; ③). The nearest **campsite** is five miles northeast, at Moorlands, near Llangybi (ⓣ01570/493543).

There's decent daytime **eating** at the *Sosban Fach*, 1 Bridge St, opposite the classy chippy *Lloyds*, which stays open until 9pm. In the evenings, *Shapla* on College Street does the best curries for miles around. Stick your head into *Conti's Café*, on Harford Square – the food isn't great, but the decor is wonderfully time-warped, plastered with ageing accolades for the café's home-made ice cream.

Strata Florida Abbey and the Teifi Pools

Twenty miles northeast of Lampeter, the mighty **Strata Florida Abbey** (April–Sept daily 10am–5pm; £2; Oct–April unrestricted entry) dominates the bucolic Ystrad Fflur, the Valley of the Flowers. This Cistercian abbey was founded in 1164, swiftly growing into a centre for milling, farming and weaving, and becoming an important political centre for Wales. In 1238, Llywelyn the Great, whose conquering exploits throughout the rest of Wales had brought him to the peak of the Welsh feudal pyramid, summoned the lesser Welsh princes here. He was near death, and worried that his work of unifying Wales under one ruler would disintegrate, so he commanded the assembled princes to pay homage not just to him but also to his son, Dafydd, so sealing the succession. The church here was vast – larger than the cathedral at St David's – and, although very little survived Henry VIII's dissolution of the monasteries, the huge Norman west doorway gives some idea of its dimensions. Fragments of one-time side chapels include beautifully tiled medieval floors, and there's also a serene cemetery, but it's really the abbey's position that impresses most, in glorious rural solitude amongst wide-open skies and fringed with a scoop of sheep-flecked hills. A yew tree in the neighbouring graveyard shades the spot where Dafydd ap Gwilym, fourteenth-century bard and contemporary of Chaucer, is said to be buried.

The narrow lane running due east from Strata Florida leads to Tyncwm, a farm with bridleways to the drenched grass and craggy outcrops around the **Teifi Pools**, a series of sombre reservoirs where the Teifi River rises, set in stern, but rewarding, walking country.

Travel details

Buses

For information on all local and national bus services, contact Traveline ⓣ0870/608 2608, ⓦwww.traveline.org.uk.

Aberaeron to: Aberystwyth (every 30min; 40min); Cardigan (14 daily; 40min–1hr 20min); Carmarthen (12 daily; 1hr 40min); Lampeter (12 daily; 35min); New Quay (hourly; 20min).

Abergavenny to: Brecon (6 daily Mon–Sat; 1hr); Cardiff (at least hourly; 1hr 30min); Clydach (every 30min; 35min); Crickhowell (7 daily Mon–Sat; 15min); Llanfihangel Crucorney (at least hourly daily; 15min); Merthyr Tydfil (every 30min; 1hr 30min); Monmouth (6 daily; 1hr); Newport (hourly; 1hr 10min); Pontypool (hourly; 25min); Raglan (6 daily; 20min).

Aberystwyth to: Aberaeron (every 30min; 40min); Borth (hourly; 25min); Caernarfon (4 daily; 3hr); Cardigan (11 daily; 1hr 30min–2hr); Carmarthen (mostly hourly; 2hr 20min); Devil's Bridge (1 daily Mon–Sat; 50min); Lampeter (at least hourly; 1hr 15min); Machynlleth (hourly; 45min); New Quay (hourly; 1hr); Ponterwyd (7 daily Mon–Sat; 30min); Pontrhydfendigaid (1 daily Mon–Sat; 40min); Tregaron (10 daily; 1 hr); Ynyslas (hourly; 30min).

Barmouth to: Bala (7 daily; 1hr); Blaenau Ffestiniog (2 daily; 1hr); Dolgellau (hourly; 35min);

Harlech (hourly; 25min); Llangollen (7 daily; 2hr); Wrexham (7 daily; 2hr 30min).
Brecon to: Abergavenny (Mon–Sat 7 daily; 1hr); Cardiff (6 daily; 1hr 30min); Craig-y-nos/Dan-yr-ogof (6 daily; 30min); Crickhowell (Mon–Sat 7 daily 25min); Hay-on-Wye (7 daily; 40min); Libanus (7 daily; 20min); Llandrindod Wells (Mon–Sat 7 daily, 1hr); Merthyr Tydfil (7 daily; 40min); Swansea (3 daily; 1hr 30min).
Cardigan to: Aberaeron (12 daily; 40min–1hr 20min); Aberporth (8 daily; 25min); Aberystwyth (9 daily; 1hr 30min–2hr); Carmarthen (9 daily; 1hr 30min); Cenarth (11 daily; 15min); Cilgerran (6 daily; 10min); Newcastle Emlyn (14 daily; 25min); New Quay (7 daily; 50min).
Dolgellau to: Bala (9 daily; 35min); Barmouth (hourly; 30min); Llangollen (mostly hourly; 1hr 35min); Machynlleth (mostly hourly; 30min); Porthmadog (7 daily; 50min); Tywyn (9 daily; 55min).
Harlech to: Barmouth (hourly; 30min); Blaenau Ffestiniog (2 daily; 40min); Dyffryn Ardudwy (mostly hourly; 15min).
Knighton to: Ludlow (4 daily; 1hr 10min); Presteigne (4 daily; 20min).
Lampeter to: Aberaeron (10 daily; 30min); Aberystwyth (Mon–Sat hourly; 1hr 30min); Carmarthen (mostly hourly; 1hr); Llanddewi Brefi (8 daily Mon–Sat; 25min); Tregaron (Mon–Sat 11 daily; 20–35min).
Llandrindod Wells to: Abbeycwmhir (1 postbus daily Mon–Fri; 2hr); Aberystwyth (6 daily; 3hr with 1 change); Brecon (7 daily Mon–Sat; 1hr); Builth Wells (hourly; 20min); Disserth (16 daily; 45min); Elan Village (1 postbus daily Mon–Fri; 40min); New Radnor (7 daily Mon–Sat; 30min); Newtown (6 daily; 1hr 10min); Rhayader (8 daily; 30min).
Llanfyllin to: Llanwddyn for Lake Vyrnwy (2 daily; 30min); Welshpool (Mon–Sat 1 daily; 40min).
Llanidloes to: Aberystwyth (5 daily; 1hr); Dylife (1 postbus daily; 30min); Newtown (7 daily; 30min); Ponterwyd (5 daily; 40min); Shrewsbury (5 daily; 2hr); Welshpool (6 daily; 1hr 20min).
Llanwrtyd Wells to: Abergwesyn (1 daily postbus; 20min); Builth Wells (7 daily; 20min).
Machynlleth to: Aberdyfi (8 daily; 20min); Aberystwyth (hourly; 45min); Corris (hourly; 15min); Dolgellau (mostly hourly; 35min); Tywyn (8 daily; 35min).
New Quay to: Aberaeron (hourly; 20min); Aberporth (hourly; 30min); Aberystwyth (hourly; 1hr); Cardigan (hourly; 1hr).
Tywyn to: Aberdyfi (9 daily; 10min); Abergynolwyn (6 daily; 18min); Corris (2 daily; 40min); Dolgellau (9 daily; 55min); Fairbourne (9 daily; 35min); Machynlleth (10 daily; 35min).
Welshpool to: Berriew (7 daily Mon–Sat; 20min); Llanidloes (6 daily; 1hr 20min); Llanfyllin (5 daily Mon–Sat; 40min); Llanymynech (6 daily; 30min); Montgomery (3 daily Mon–Sat; 25min); Newtown (10 daily; 35min); Oswestry (4 daily; 50min); Shrewsbury (6 daily; 45min).

Trains

For information on all local and national rail services, contact National Rail Enquiries Ⓣ08457/484950, Ⓦwww.nationalrail.co.uk.
Abergavenny to: Cardiff (hourly at least; 40min); Hereford (hourly; 25min); Newport (hourly at least; 30min); Pontypool (hourly; 10min).
Aberystwyth to: Birmingham (7 daily; 3hr); Machynlleth (10 daily; 30min); Shrewsbury (8 daily; 2hr); Welshpool (9 daily; 1hr 30min).
Barmouth to: Aberdyfi (9 daily; 40min); Harlech (8 daily; 20min); Machynlleth (9 daily; 1hr); Porthmadog (8 daily; 45min).
Harlech to: Barmouth (8 daily; 20min); Birmingham (2 daily; 3hr 45min); Machynlleth (8 daily; 1hr 20min); Porthmadog (8 daily; 20min).
Knighton to: Llandrindod Wells (4 daily; 35min); Llanwrtyd Wells (4 daily; 1hr 10min); Shrewsbury (4 daily; 1hr); Swansea (4 daily; 3hr 10min).
Llandrindod Wells to: Knighton (4 daily; 35min); Llanwrtyd Wells (4 daily; 25min); Shrewsbury (4 daily; 1hr 30min); Swansea (4 daily; 2hr 30min).
Machynlleth to: Aberdyfi (8 daily; 20min); Aberystwyth (10 daily; 30min); Barmouth (8 daily; 50min); Birmingham (7 daily; 2hr 15min); Harlech (8 daily; 1hr 20min); Porthmadog (8 daily; 1hr 45min); Shrewsbury (8 daily; 1hr 20min).
Tywyn to: Aberdyfi (9 daily; 5min); Barmouth (8 daily; 25min); Harlech (8 daily; 50min); Machynlleth (9 daily; 30min); Porthmadog (8 daily; 1hr 10min).
Welshpool to: Aberystwyth (9 daily; 1hr 30min); Birmingham (7 daily; 1hr 30min); Machynlleth (8 daily; 55min); Newtown (8 daily; 15min); Pwllheli (1 daily; 3hr 30min); Shrewsbury (8 daily; 25min).

16

North Wales

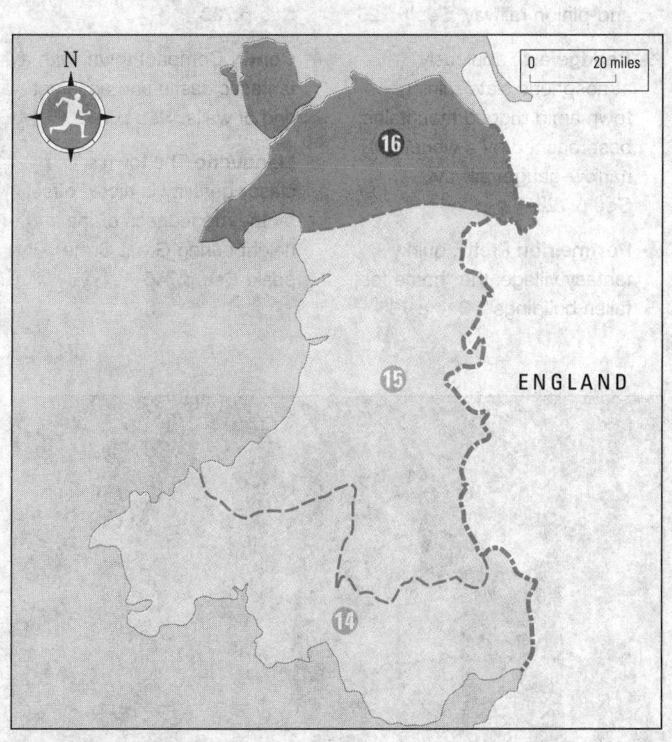

CHAPTER 16

Highlights

* **Llangollen** Robust and enjoyable riverside town, with an internationally famous eisteddfod. See p.718
* **Snowdon** Wales's highest mountain is a stunning hike, or a gentle ascent by rack-and-pinion railway. See p.725
* **Beddgelert** Fabulously atmospheric slate-mining town amid rugged mountains, best reached by a wonderful narrow-gauge railway. See p.728
* **Portmeirion** Pretty, quirky fantasy village, the "home for fallen buildings". See p.733
* **Caernarfon Castle** The mightiest link in Edward I's chain of Norman castles. See p.737
* **Beaumaris** A good base for Anglesey's beaches and Neolithic remains. See p.738
* **Conwy** Compact town, with a fantastic castle and an intact ring of walls. See p.742
* **Llandudno** The town's classy gentility is nicely offset by the ruggedness of the neighbouring Great Orme peak. See p.746

▲Caernarfon Castle

16

North Wales

The fast A55 trunk road has made the North Wales coast considerably more accessible in recent times, but this hasn't tamed the wilder aspects of this stunningly beautiful area. As you walk around most of the brash seaside towns along the eastern section of the coast, only the street signs give any indication that you are in Wales at all; further west, there are places where English is seldom spoken other than to visitors.

Without doubt, **Snowdonia** is the crowning glory of North Wales. This tightly packed bundle of soaring cliff faces, jagged peaks and plunging waterfalls measures little more than ten miles by ten, but packs enough mountain paths to keep even the most jaded walking enthusiast happy for weeks. Even if lakeside ambles and rides on antiquated steam trains are more your style, you can't fail to appreciate the natural grandeur of the scenery, occasionally revealing an atmospheric Welsh castle ruin or decaying piece of quarrying equipment.

Snowdonia is the heart of the massive **Snowdonia National Park** (Parc Cenedlaethol Eryri), which extends north and south, beyond the bounds of Snowdonia itself (and this chapter), to encompass the Rhinogs, Cadair Idris (see p.699) and 23 miles of superb coastal scenery.

One of the best approaches to Snowdonia is along the **Dee Valley**, a fertile landscape much fought over between the English and the Welsh. North Wales's largest town, **Wrexham**, makes the best of its industrial heritage, but there's a more tangibly Welsh feel to fabulous **Llangollen**, a great base for a variety of ruins, rides and rambles, as well as the venue each summer for the colourful International Eisteddfod festival.

Pressing on along the A5 – the region's second, inland main road – you hit the fringes of Snowdonia at **Betws-y-Coed**, great for easy walks but slightly twee. Heading deeper into the park, old mining and quarry towns such as **Beddgelert**, **Llanberis** and **Blaenau Ffestiniog** make arguably better bases – with great hiking on their doorstep and plenty of intrinsic interest. On the eastern fringes of Snowdonia, **Bala** tempts with water sports: either lake sailing or whitewater rafting down the Tryweryn.

To the west of Snowdonia is the former slate port of **Porthmadog**, home to the wonderful **Ffestiniog Railway** and the quirky pretend village of **Portmeirion**. Beyond lies the gentle rockiness of the **Lltn peninsula** where Wales ends in a flourish of small coves and seafaring villages. Roads loop back along the Lltn to **Caernarfon**, which is overshadowed by its stupendous castle, the mightiest link in Edward I's Iron Ring of thirteenth-century fortresses across North Wales.

Across the Menai Strait lies the island of **Anglesey**, a gentle patchwork of beautiful beaches and sites of ancient heritage. Edward's final castle, a masterpiece of design, is sited in **Beaumaris**.

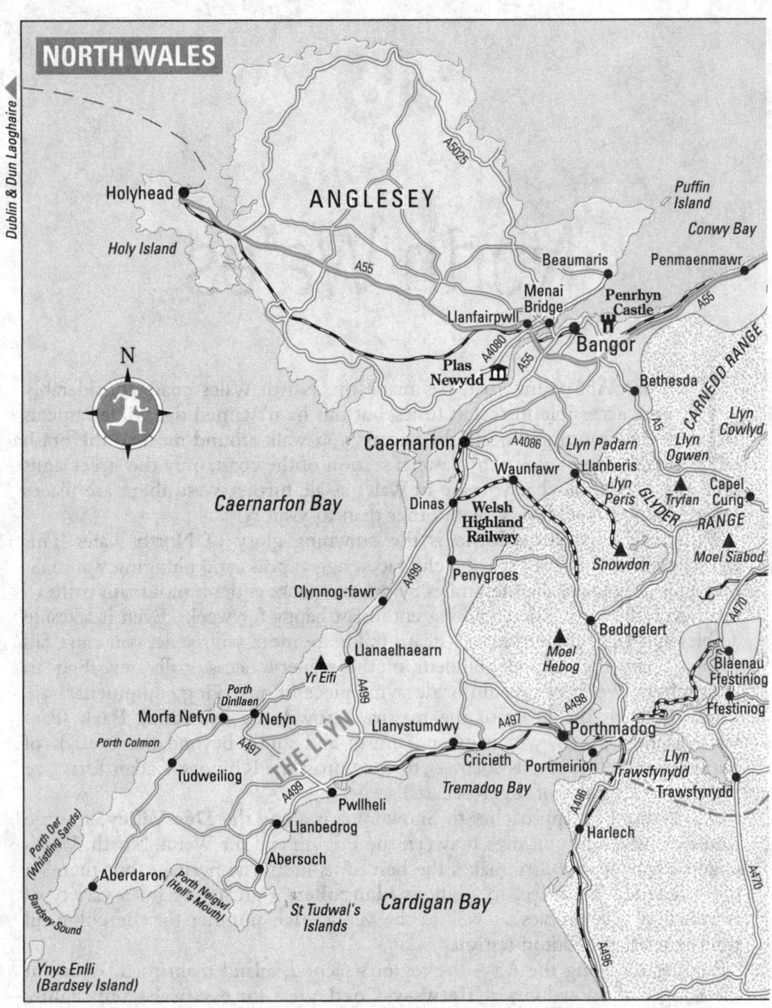

Back on the mainland, the university and cathedral city of **Bangor** is the area's most cosmopolitan haunt, while **Conwy**'s fairytale castle and narrow higgledy-piggledy streets huddle around a scenic quay before a string of Victorian seaside resorts lead eastwards towards the English border – **Llandudno** is a definite cut above the rest, with colourful streets and a striking pier. A couple of highlights in the north include the National Portrait Gallery's collection at **Bodelwyddan**, Britain's smallest cathedral at **St Asaph**, and the allegedly miraculous waters at **Holywell**.

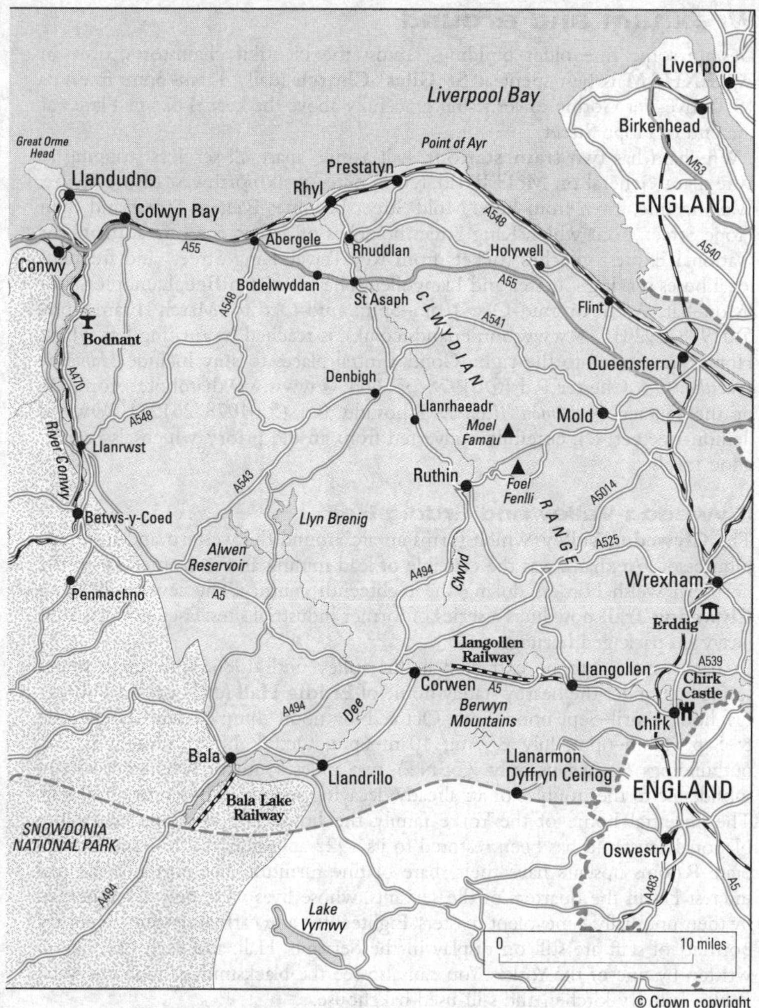

Wrexham and the Dee Valley

Wrexham (Wrecsam) is the largest town in North Wales but, save for its proximity to the **Clywedog Valley** and **Erddig Hall** stately home, offers little reason to linger. If you have your own transport you are better off exploring the local attractions around valley-clad **Llangollen** – the ruins of both a Welsh castle and a Cistercian abbey drew the Romantics to this dramatic gorge naturally blessed with surging rapids.

Wrexham and around

Despite some fine older buildings amidst the identikit chainstores, time in **WREXHAM** is best spent at **St Giles' Church** (daily 11am–3pm; free), its 1520s five-tier Gothic tower rising gracefully above the kernel of small lanes at the end of Hope Street.

Wrexham has two **train stations**, half a mile apart, all services stopping at Wrexham General on Mold Road, ten minutes' walk northwest of the centre. Walking into town from here, Mold Street becomes Regent Street and then Hope Street, from which King Street branches off left to the **bus station**, for National Express coaches (tickets from Key Travel, King Street) and frequent local buses serving Chester and Llangollen. The **tourist office**, Lambpit Street (Mon–Sat: April to mid-Oct 10am–5pm; mid-Oct to March 10am–4pm; ⓣ01978/292015, ⓦwww.borderlands.co.uk), is reached by turning left where Hope Street turns to the right. Good, central places to **stay** include *Hampson Guesthouse*, 6 Chester Rd (ⓣ01978/357665, ⓦwww.wrexhamhotels.com; ❷), or the fancier *Lemon Tree*, 29 Rhosddu Rd (ⓣ01978/261211, ⓦwww.lemon-tree.net; ❹), tastefully converted from an old priory, which also serves good meals.

Clywedog Valley and Erddig Hall

The **Clywedog Valley**, which forms an arc around the western and southern suburbs of Wrexham, was the crucible of lead mining and iron smelting in the northern Welsh borders during the eighteenth century. The seven-mile-long **Clywedog Trail** now links a series of former industrial sites: fascinating, if a bit heavy on packaged heritage.

Coal continued to be extracted in the valley until 1986, with some mines tunnelling under the nearby stately home of **Erddig Hall** (daily except Thurs & Fri: house April–Sept noon–5pm, Oct & Nov noon–4pm; garden March–June & Sept 11am–6pm, July & Aug 10am–6pm, Oct & Nov 11am–5pm; £8, outbuildings & gardens only £5; NT), two miles south of Wrexham, adding subsidence to the troubles of an already decaying seventeenth-century building. The ancestral home of the Yorke family, the house is now managed by the National Trust and has been restored to its 1922 appearance. While the family's State Rooms upstairs have their share of fine furniture and portraits, the real interest lies in the quarters of the servants, whose lives were fully documented by their unusually benevolent masters. Eighteenth- and early nineteenth-century portraits of staff are still on display in the Servants' Hall, and each has a verse written by one of the Yorkes. You can also see the blacksmith's shop, lime yard, stables, laundry, kitchen and still-used bakehouse.

Llangollen and around

LLANGOLLEN, twelve miles southwest of Wrexham, is the embodiment of a Welsh town in both setting and character, clasped tightly in the narrow Dee Valley between the shoulders of the Berwyn and Eglwyseg mountains. Along the valley's floor, the waters of the River Dee run down to the town, licking the angled buttresses of the weighty Gothic bridge, which has spanned the river since the fourteenth century. On its south bank, half a dozen streets form the core of the scattered settlement flung out across the low hills. Every July, the town comes alive for the **International Music Eisteddfod**.

As the only crossing point across the River Dee for miles, Llangollen was an important town long before the early Romantics arrived at the end of the eighteenth century, when they were cut off from their European Grand Tours

The Llangollen International Music Eisteddfod

Llangollen is heaving all summer, and never more so than in early July, when for six days the town explodes in a frenzy of music, dance, poetry and colour. Unlike the National Eisteddfod, which is a purely Welsh affair, the **International Music Eisteddfod** draws amateur performers from fifty countries, all competing for prizes inside the 6000-seat white plastic auditorium and at several other venues around the town.

The eisteddfod has been held in its present form since 1947, when it was started more or less on a whim by one Harold Tudor. Forty choirs from fourteen countries performed at the first event. Today, more than 12,000 participants lure up to 150,000 visitors, and while the whole set-up can seem oppressive, there is an irresistible *joie de vivre* as brightly costumed dancers walk the streets and fill the restaurants. Book **tickets** on ⓣ01978/862001 or ⓦwww.international-eisteddfod.co.uk.

The superbly eclectic **Llangollen Fringe** (ⓣ01978/860600, ⓦwww.llangollenfringe.co.uk) follows with a number of more "alternative" acts – music, dance, comedy and soon – performing in the Town Hall on Castle Street over the last two weeks in July.

by the Napoleonic Wars. Turner came to paint the swollen river and the Cistercian ruin of **Valle Crucis**, a couple of miles up the valley; John Ruskin found the town "entirely lovely in its gentle wildness"; and writer George Borrow made Llangollen his base for the early part of his 1854 tour detailed in *Wild Wales*. The rich and famous came not just for the scenery, but also to visit the "Ladies of Llangollen", an eccentric couple who became the toast of society from their house, Plas Newydd. But by this stage some of the town's rural charm had been eaten up by the works of one of the century's finest engineers, Thomas Telford, who squeezed both his London–Holyhead trunk road and the **Llangollen Canal** alongside the river.

The Town

Standing in twelve acres of formal gardens, half a mile up Hill Street from the southern end of Castle Street, the two-storeyed mock-Tudor **Plas Newydd** (Easter–Oct daily 10am–5pm; £3) was, for almost fifty years, home to the **Ladies of Llangollen**. Lady Eleanor Butler and Sarah Ponsonby were a lesbian couple from Anglo-Irish aristocratic backgrounds, who tried to elope together at the end of the eighteenth century. After two botched attempts dressed in men's clothes, they were grudgingly allowed to leave their family seats in 1778 with an annual allowance of £280, enough to settle in Llangollen, where they became celebrated hosts and legendary local characters. Despite their desire for a "life of sweet and delicious retirement", they didn't seem to mind the constant stream of gentry who called on them. Visitors' gifts of sculpted **wood panelling** formed the basis of the riotous friezes of woodwork that cover the walls of their modest house, visited on a self-guided audio tour (free). It has a wonderful if slightly oppressive effect, set off by a mixed bag of furniture in a style similar to that owned by the ladies. Llangollen takes its name from the **Church of St Collen**, on Bridge Street (May–Sept daily 1.30–6pm; free), outside which is a triangular railed-off monument to the ladies and their devoted maid.

The hills around Llangollen echo to the shrill cry of steam engines easing along the **Llangollen Railway** (April–Oct 3–7 services most days; call ahead at other times; £8 return; ⓣ01978/860979, ⓦwww.llangollen-railway.co.uk), shoehorned into the north side of the valley. From Llangollen's time-warped station it runs along eight miles of the old Ruabon–Barmouth line to Carrog, the belching steam engines creeping west along the riverbank, hauling ancient carriages which proudly sport the liveries of their erstwhile owners.

Across the street is the Llangollen Canal, one of the finest feats of British canal building. Its architect, Thomas Telford, succeeded in building a canal without locks through fourteen miles of hilly terrain, most spectacularly by means of the thousand-foot-long **Pontcysyllte Aqueduct**, passing 127 feet over the River Dee at Froncysyllte, four miles east. **Canal trips** (Easter–Oct daily; £10; ⓣ01978/860702, ⓦwww.horsedrawnboats.co.uk) across the aqueduct leave from Llangollen Wharf, almost opposite the train station.

Practicalities

Buses stop on Market Street, while the nearest **train station** is five miles away at Ruabon, passed by frequent buses on the Llangollen–Wrexham run. The **tourist office** on Castle Street (daily: Easter–Oct 9.30am–5.30pm; Nov–Easter 9.30am–5pm; ⓣ01978/860828, ⓔllangollen@nwtic.com) is fifty yards from the bridge and less than a hundred yards from the bus stop on Market Street. There's **bike rental** from ProAdventure on Parade Street (ⓣ01978/861912, ⓦwww.proadventure.co.uk).

Finding **rooms** in Llangollen can be a chore in summer, especially during the eisteddfod in July. Low-cost, central B&Bs worth checking out include the non-smoking *Hafren*, on Berwyn Street (ⓣ01978/860939; ❸), with shared bathroom and minimal single supplement, and *Hillcrest*, on Hill Street (ⓣ01978/860208, ⓦwww.hillcrest-guesthouse.com; ❸), an appealing licensed Victorian guesthouse up towards Plas Newydd with excellent breakfasts. Moving upmarket, go for *Gales*, 18 Bridge St (ⓣ01978/860089, ⓦwww.galesofllangollen.co.uk; ❹), a comfortable guesthouse above a wine bar; or *Bryn Howel*, two miles east off the A539 (ⓣ01978/860331, ⓦwww.brynhowel.com; ❻), set in beautiful grounds and with good facilities including sauna, solarium, free trout fishing and a top-class restaurant. **Camp** at *Wern Isaf Farm* (ⓣ01978/860632; £4 per person), a simple farmhouse just under a mile up Wern Road: turn right over the canal on Wharf Hill.

Llangollen boasts a fairly good selection of **restaurants** and no shortage of cafés: *The Gallery*, 15 Chapel St (ⓣ01978/860076; closed Sun & Mon), serves moderately priced pizza and pasta dishes while *Gales Wine Bar* (see above) has great old church pews and an extensive cellar, and offers tasty bistro-style food. At the **pub**, *Hand Hotel*, 26 Bridge St, you can listen to a male voice choir in full song (Mon & Fri 7.30pm) or sink a pint in the gorgeous riverside garden. Top no-nonsense boozing haunt is the youthful *Bull Inn* on Castle Street, which also hosts live music.

Around Llangollen

The panoramic view, especially at sunset, justifies the 45-minute slog up to **Castell Dinas Brân** (Crow's Fortress Castle), a few evocative stumps of masonry perched on a hill 800ft above the town, and reached by a path beginning near Llangollen Wharf. This was once the district's largest and most important Welsh fortress, built in the 1230s by the ruler of northern Powys, Prince Madog ap Gruffydd Maelor. Edward I soon captured it as part of his first campaign against Llywelyn ap Gruffydd, but the castle was left to decay.

The gaunt ruin of **Valle Crucis Abbey** (April–Sept daily 10am–5pm; £2.50; all other times free access; CADW), a mile or so west of Llangollen, greets you with its largely intact west wall, pierced by the frame of a rose window. Though one of the last Cistercian foundations in Wales, and the first Gothic abbey in Britain, it is no match for Tintern Abbey (see p.632), but nevertheless stands majestically in a pastoral – and much less-visited – setting. After the Dissolution, in 1535, the church fell into disrepair with the monastic buildings employed as farm buildings. Now they hold displays on monastic life, reached by a detour through the mostly ruined cloister and past the weighty vaulting of the chapterhouse.

Snowdonia

The mountains of **Snowdonia** (Yr Eryri) are widely acclaimed as the most dramatic and alluring of all Welsh scenery, a compact, barren land of tortured ridges dividing glacial valleys, whose sheer faces belie the fact that the tallest peaks only just top three thousand feet. It was to this mountain fastness that Llywelyn ap Gruffydd, the last true prince of Wales, retreated in 1277 after his first war with Edward I; it was also here that Owain Glyndŵr held on most tenaciously to his dream of regaining for the Welsh the title of Prince of Wales. Centuries later, the English came to remove the mountains: slate barons built huge fortunes from Welsh toil and reshaped the patterns of Snowdonian life forever, as men looking for steady work in the quarries left the hills and became town dwellers.

Not surprisingly, the **Snowdon** massif (Eryri) is the focus of the Snowdonia National Park. Thousands of hikers arrive every weekend for some of the country's best walks over steep, exacting and constantly varying terrain. Several of the ascent routes are superb, and you can always take the cog railway up to the summit café from **Llanberis**. But the other mountains are as good or better, often far less busy and giving unsurpassed views of Snowdon. The **Glyderau** and **Tryfan** – best tackled from the **Ogwen Valley** – are particular favourites for more experienced walkers.

If you are serious about doing some **walking** – and some of the walks described here are serious, especially in bad weather (Snowdon gets 200 inches of rain a year) – you need a good map such as the 1:50,000 OS *Landranger* #115 or the 1:25,000 OS *Outdoor Leisure* #17; bear in mind that conditions, especially on higher ground, are notoriously changeable. Weather reports and walking conditions are often posted on the doors or noticeboards of outdoor shops and tourist offices.

But Snowdonia isn't all about walking. Small settlements are dotted in the valleys, usually coinciding with some enormous mine or quarry. Foremost among these are **Blaenau Ffestiniog**, the "Slate Capital of North Wales", where a mine opens its caverns for underground tours, and **Beddgelert**, whose former copper mines are also open to the public. The only place of any size not associated with slate mining is **Betws-y-Coed**, a largely Victorian resort away from the higher peaks.

Betws-y-Coed and around

Sprawled out across a flat plain at the confluence of the Conwy, Llugwy and Lledr valleys, **BETWS-Y-COED** (pronounced "betoos-er-coyd"), the much-vaunted "Gateway to Snowdonia", is hard to avoid. Overlooked by the conifer-clad slopes of the Gwydyr forest, the town is undeniably appealing, and boasts the best selection of hotels and guesthouses in the region, but after an hour mooching around the outdoor equipment shops and drinking tea you may well be twiddling your thumbs. For serious mountain walkers, the best advice is to continue on, but for everyone else there are some delightful and popular easy strolls to the local beauty spots of the **Conwy** and **Swallow** falls.

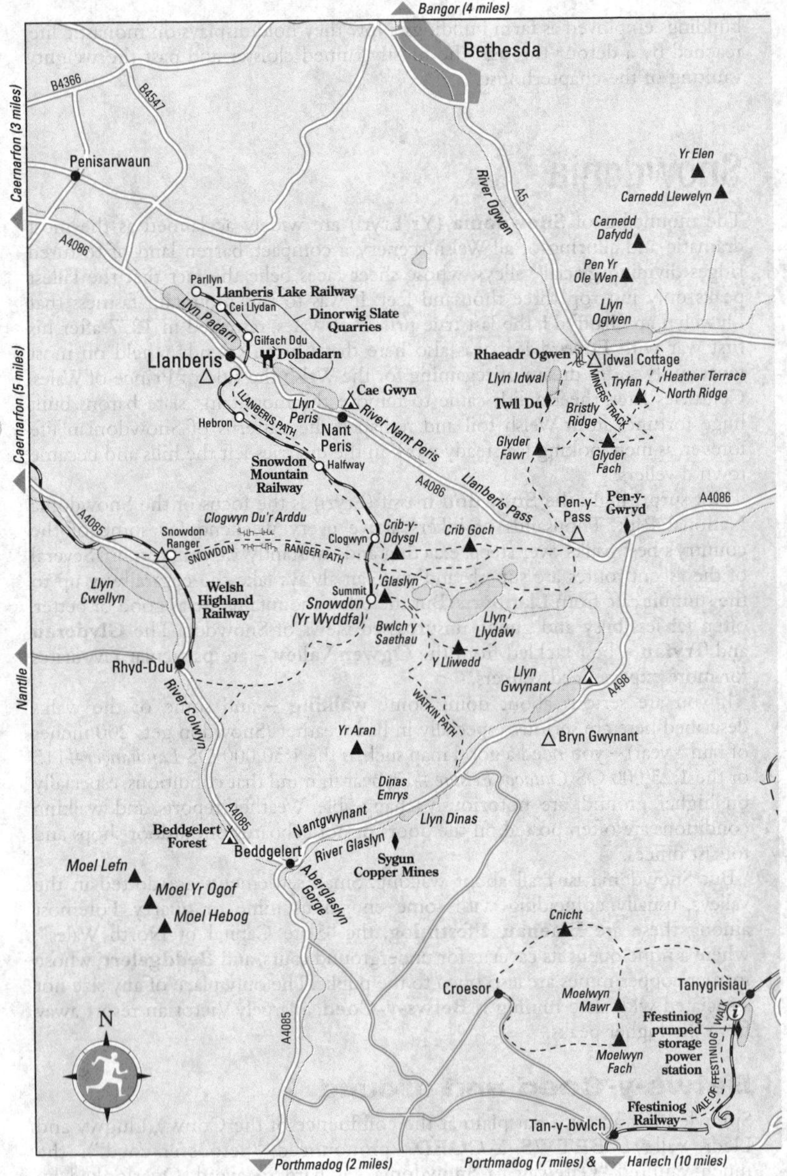

Leisured classes already alerted to the town's beauty by J.M.W. Turner's landscapes arrived when Telford completed the graceful **Waterloo Bridge** (Y Bont Haearn), and the advent of the railway line in 1868 lifted its status from coaching station to genteel resort. By the station, the **Conwy Valley Railway Museum** (daily 10.15am–5pm; £1.50) presents a fairly standard collection of

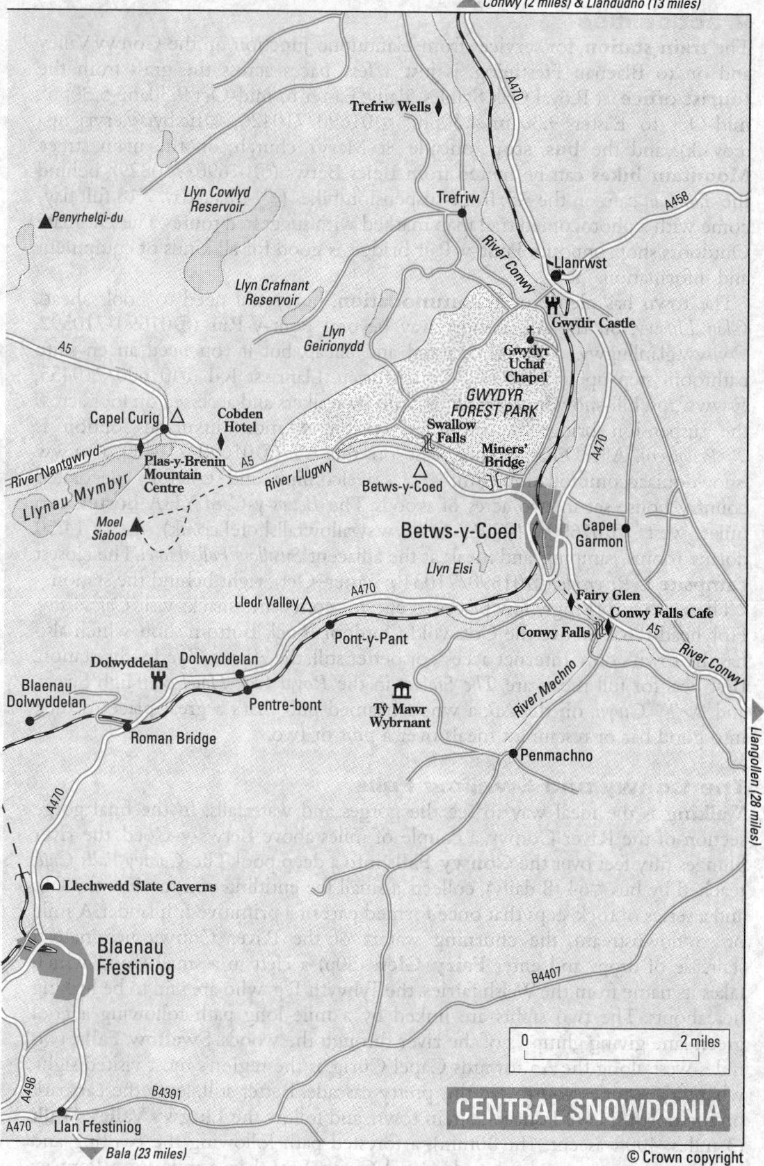

memorabilia and shiny engines, slightly enlivened by the chance of a short ride on a miniature train (£1.50) or tram (£1). The **Motor Museum** (Easter–Oct daily 10am–6pm; £1.50), a couple of hundred yards away behind the tourist office, is little better, with a half-dozen classic bikes and fifteen cars, including a 1934 Bugatti Straight 8 and a Model T Ford.

Practicalities

The **train station**, for services from Llandudno Junction up the Conwy Valley and on to Blaenau Ffestiniog, is just a few paces across the grass from the **tourist office**, at Royal Oak Stables (daily: Easter to mid-Oct 9.30am–5.30pm; mid-Oct to Easter 9.30am–4.30pm; ⓣ01690/710426, ⓔtic.byc@eryri-npa.gov.uk), and the **bus stop**, outside St Mary's church, on the main street. **Mountain bikes** can be rented from Beics Betws (ⓣ01690/710829), behind the *Tan Lan* café on the A5: front-suspension bikes (£14 half-day, £18 full day) come with a photocopied trail map marked with suggested routes. The Ultimate Outdoors shop, opposite Pont-y-Pair bridge, is good for all kinds of equipment and information.

The town has plenty of **accommodation**, but you'll need to book ahead. *Glan Llugwy*, on the A5, a short way beyond Pont-y-Pair (ⓣ01690/710592, ⓦwww.glanllugwy.co.uk; ❷), is good and cheap, but if you need an en-suite bathroom step up to *Rose Hill*, Lôn Muriau, Llanrwst Rd (ⓣ01690/710455, ⓦwww.rosehill-snowdonia.co.uk; ❸), run by walkers and accessed on foot across the suspension bridge by the train station. A more luxurious option is *Pengwern*, Allt Dinas, a mile east on the A5 (ⓣ01690/710480, ⓦwww.snowdoniaaccommodation.com; ❺), a welcoming and tastefully decorated country house set in two acres of woods. The *Betws-y-Coed* YHA **hostel**, two miles west (ⓣ01690/710796, ⓦwww.swallowfallshotel.co.uk) has £14.50 dorms, rooms, camping, and meals at the adjacent *Swallow Falls Hotel*. The closest **campsite** is *Riverside* (ⓣ01690/710310; Easter–Oct), right behind the station.

There are surprisingly few places to **eat**: for coffee and snacks visit *Café Active*, Holyhead Road, above the Cotswold Outdoor Rock Bottom shop, which also has the town's only Internet access, or better still, the *Alpine Café*, by the station. Best bets for full meals are *The Stables* in the *Royal Oak Hotel* on High Street, and *Tŷ Gwyn*, on the A5, a wood-beamed pub that's a great place to tuck into good bar or restaurant meals over a pint or two.

The Conwy and Swallow Falls

Walking is the ideal way to see the gorges and waterfalls. In the final gorge section of the River Conwy, a couple of miles above Betws-y-Coed, the river plunges fifty feet over the **Conwy Falls** into a deep pool. The *Conwy Falls Café*, reached by bus #64 (8 daily), collects a small fee entitling you to view the falls and a series of rock steps that once formed part of a primitive fish ladder. A mile or so downstream, the churning waters of the River Conwy negotiate a staircase of drops and enter **Fairy Glen** (50p) a cleft in a small wood which takes its name from the Welsh fairies, the Tylwyth Teg, who are said to be lurking hereabouts. The two sights are linked by a mile-long path following a cool green lane giving glimpses of the river through the woods. **Swallow Falls**, two miles west along the A5 towards Capel Curig, is the region's most visited sight, where £1 entitles you to see this pretty cascade. Better still, leave the car park on the north side of Pont-y-Pair, in town, and follow the **Llugwy Valley Walk** (3 miles; 400ft ascent; 1hr 30min), a forested path following the twisting and plunging river upstream towards Capel Curig. Less than a mile from Pont-y-Pair you reach the steeply sloping **Miners' Bridge**, which linked miners' homes at Pentre Du, on the south side of the river, to the lead mines in Llanrwst. Just beneath the bridge are a series of idyllic plunge pools, perfect for swimming. The path continues upstream for another mile to the Swallow Falls. Detailed **maps** are available from the tourist office showing numerous routes back through the Gwydyr Forest, or you can continue half a mile to the road bridge from where you can wait for the bus back to Betws-y-Coed.

Capel Curig

Tantalizing flashes of Wales's highest mountains are glimpsed through the forested banks of the Llugwy as you climb west from Betws-y-Coed on the A5, but Snowdon eludes you until the final bend before **CAPEL CURIG**. The tiny, scattered village, six miles west of Betws-y-Coed, is the site of a major centre for outdoor enthusiasts. A quarter of a mile along the A4086 to Llanberis from the main road junction, **Plas-y-Brenin: the National Mountaineering Centre** (Ⓣ01690/720214, Ⓦwww.pyb.co.uk) runs renowned residential courses and offers indoor climbing, lake canoeing and dry-slope skiing sessions (daily 10am–9pm; £10 for 2hr), during July and August. There is also a climbing wall (daily 10am–11pm; £3), and the opportunity to hear talks or watch slide shows of expeditions (usually Mon, Tues & Sat 8pm; free).

There are plenty of places to **stay**: the best is the *Bron Eryri* (Ⓣ01690/720240, Ⓦwww.eryriguesthouse.fsnet.co.uk; ③), a comfortable and welcoming B&B half a mile outside the village towards Betws-y-Coed. The cheapest option in the village is the YHA **hostel** (Ⓣ0870/770 5746, Ⓦwww.yha.org.uk; dorms £16.50; mid-Feb to mid-Dec), five hundred yards along the A5 towards Betws-y-Coed. Two and a half miles west down the Ogwen Valley you can stay for a good deal less in the *Gwern Gof Uchaf* bunkhouse and **campsite** (see below).

During the day, walkers patronize the *Pinnacle Café*, at the intersection of the A5 and the A4086. In the evening they retire to the **bar** of the *Bryn Tyrch Hotel*, which serves good **food** (though service can be poor when it's busy), or the sociable bar at Plas-y-Brenin.

The Ogwen Valley

Northwest of Capel Curig, the A5 forges through the **Ogwen Valley**, which separates the imposing Carneddau massif from the rock-peppered summits of the **Glyderau** range and distinctive triple-peaked **Tryfan**, perhaps Snowdonia's most demanding mountain. West of Tryfan, the road follows the shores of **Llyn Ogwen**, past the YHA hostel and down **Nant Ffrancon**, a perfect example of a U-shaped valley, carved and smoothed by rocks frozen into the undersides of a glacier ten thousand years ago.

The hostel marks the start of some of the UK's most demanding and rewarding hikes but these are best suited to experienced walkers and a little beyond the scope of this book. There are easier walks, too (see box, p.726), the easiest and most rewarding leading up to still waters of Llyn Idwal, which is nestled in the magnificent cirque of **Cwm Idwal**. The area was designated Wales's first nature reserve in 1954, after botanists discovered rare arctic-alpine plants growing here. The **café** in the car park (daily 8.30am–5pm; later on summer weekends) will give you a nature-trail booklet.

Five daily **buses** along the valley provide access to the limited supply of **accommodation**. The most sophisticated is the *Idwal Cottage* YHA **hostel** (Ⓣ0870/770 5874, Ⓦwww.yha.org.uk; dorms £14.95; Feb–Oct), at the western end of Llŷn Ogwen, five miles from Capel Curig. Residents can get meals at the hostel; the valley is otherwise self-catering. The best **camping** is at *Gwern Gof Uchaf*, at the foot of Tryfan (Ⓣ01690/720294, Ⓦwww.tryfanwales.co.uk), which also has a good bunkhouse (£8 per person).

Llanberis and Snowdon

Mention **LLANBERIS**, ten miles west of Capel Curig, to any mountain enthusiast and they will think of **Snowdon**. The two seem inseparable, not

Walks from Ogwen: Llyn Idwal and Llyn Bochlwyd

Tourists hike up Snowdon, but mountain connoisseurs invariably prefer the sharply angled peaks of **Tryfan and the Glyderau**, with their challenging terrain, cantilevered rocks and fantastic views back to Snowdon. But these aren't mountains for the casual visitor, and the walking and scrambling routes that cross the peaks are strictly for experienced climbers. There are a couple of easier options though, and although they omit the summits, they do provide close up views of the magnificent mountain scenery.

The best way to appreciate the spectacle of Cwm Idwal is to follow the well-marked and well-surfaced path up to the shores of Llyn Idwal; it's a walk that can be completed by most people without maps or proper walking clothing. To start, leave the car park next to the hostel at Ogwen; keep the buildings to your right and follow a path that leads to a gate and a bridge. Stay with the path as it continues easily upwards, initially heading towards the distinctive rocky flanks of Tryfan and then swinging around to the right to lead into Cwm Idwal and the lake shores. From here you get a fine view of the precipitous cliffs that make up the head of the valley – often known as the **Twll Du** or **Devil's Kitchen**. Return by the same route – it's around one mile in total.

A circular three-mile walk around Llyn Idwal is possible, but the paths are quite rough and rocky, and there is one very steep section. To follow this, upon arriving at the lake, turn right to cross a footbridge and walk along the pebbly beach to the far end, where a path can be picked up again. Follow the path along the east shore, and climb steeply up rocky steps towards Twll Du. Continue upwards with great views behind you, until the path levels and passes a huge boulder, which is used as a shelter. Here it meets the path coming down from the Devil's Kitchen, and descends steeply. Follow the steps downwards, taking great care, and you'll soon reach an awkward stream crossing. The walk then continues beneath huge sloping cliffs – the **Idwal Slabs** – before hugging the western shore of the lake back to the start.

Another beautiful mountain lake, **Llyn Bochlwyd**, can be reached from Ogwen. It's a fair bit further up the mountain than Llyn Idwal and the paths are more jagged, so wear suitable footwear. Start as for Llyn Idwal but as the path swings right, keep straight ahead to follow a rougher path, easily at first, and then steeply up the banks of a tumbling stream. Eventually the path levels and fords the stream at the outflow of the lake. This is a great viewpoint, right in the heart of the mountains, with the daunting ridges of Tryfan and Glyder Fach towering above. Return by the same route. Guidebooks detailing tougher walks and climbing routes are available in all the outdoor shops in Capel Curig and Betws-y-Coed.

least because of the Llanberis Path to the summit (see p.730) and the five-mile-long umbilical of the **Snowdon Mountain Railway**, Britain's only rack-and-pinion railway, which runs alongside. This is the nearest you'll get to an alpine climbing village in Wales, its single main street thronged with weatherbeaten walkers and climbers. At the same time, Llanberis is very much a Welsh rural community, albeit a depleted one now that slate is no longer being torn from the flanks of Elidir Fawr, the mountain across the town's twin lakes.

Three of the routes up Snowdon start five miles east of Llanberis at the top of the Llanberis Pass, one of the deepest, narrowest and craggiest in Snowdonia. At the summit, a hostel, café and car park comprise the settlement of **PEN-Y-PASS**. Frequent Sherpa #S1 **buses** travel up daily to Pen-y-Pass, the recommended approach even if you have a car, since the Pen-y-Pass car park is expensive and almost always full. Use the "Park and Ride" car park at the bottom of the pass, near the *Vaynol Arms*.

The Town

Scattered remains are all that is left of thirteenth-century **Dolbadarn Castle** (free access; CADW), on the road to **Parc Padarn**, where lakeside oak woods are gradually recolonizing the discarded workings of the defunct Dinorwig Slate Quarries. Here, the **Welsh Slate Museum** (Easter–Oct daily 10am–5pm; Nov–Easter daily except Sat 10am–4pm; free; Ⓦwww.museumwales.ac.uk) occupies the former maintenance workshops; former quarry workers demonstrate their skills at turning an inch-thick slab of slate into six, or even eight, perfectly smooth slivers. The craftsmen here operate an ageing foundry, producing pieces for repairing the trains belonging to the **Llanberis Lake Railway** (July & Aug 4–8 daily; March–June & Sept to early Oct 3–5 daily; £6.50 return; Ⓦwww.lake-railway.co.uk), which once transported slate and workers between the Dinorwig quarries and Port Dinorwig on the Menai Strait, but now carries visitors along part of the old line. It's a tame forty-minute round trip with little to do at the end except come back and explore the old slate workings.

In 1974, five years after the quarry closed, work began on hollowing a monumental chamber out of the mountainside. This was then used to house the **Dinorwig Pumped Storage Power Station**, designed to produce electricity. If you can bear the thinly disguised electricity industry advertisement that precedes it, you can take an hour-long minibus tour around the enormous pipework in the very heart of the mountain. For this, you need to call at **Electric Mountain** (daily: June–Aug 9.30am–5.30pm; Sept–Dec & Feb–May 10am–4.30pm; £7; Ⓦwww.electricmountain.co.uk), by the lake beside the A4086, the town-centre bypass.

Practicalities

All **buses** to Llanberis stop near the **tourist office**, 41b High St (Fri–Mon 10.30am–3.30pm; Ⓣ01286/870765, Ⓔllanberis.tic@gwynedd.gov.uk). For guided hiking, rock climbing and kayaking contact High Trek Snowdonia, Tal y Waen, Deiniolen (Ⓣ01286/871232, Ⓦwww.climbing-wales.co.uk), or Bryn Du Mountain Centre, Ty Du Road (Ⓣ01286/870556, Ⓦwww.boulderadventures.co.uk). The Llanberis Path (see box, p.730), Snowdon Ranger Path and Pitt's Head Track to Rhyd-Ddu are open to **cyclists**, although there's restricted cycle access to and from the summit between 10am and 5pm (May–Sept).

Of the low-cost **accommodation** in or close to town, try *The Heights*, 74 High St (Ⓣ01286/871179, Ⓦwww.heightshotel.co.uk; ❷), a B&B with a good restaurant and a lively bar. Another option on High Street is the lovely *Plas Coch* (Ⓣ01286/872122, Ⓦwww.plas-coch.co.uk; ❹), which has one cheaper attic room. *Llanberis* YHA **hostel**, Llwyn Celyn (Ⓣ0870/770 5928, Ⓦwww.yha.org.uk; dorms £14), is half a mile uphill along Capel Goch Road, signposted off High Street; and there's simple **camping** at *Cae Gwyn* (Ⓣ01286/870718; £3.50 per person, bunkhouse £7) in Nant Peris, two miles southeast of Llanberis.

Out of town, head three miles northwest to *Graianfryn* (Ⓣ01286/871007, Ⓦwww.fastasleep.me.uk; ❸), an exclusively vegetarian and vegan farmhouse in Penisarwaun. Four miles east of town is the *Pen-y-Pass* YHA hostel (Ⓣ0870/770 5990, Ⓦwww.yha.org.uk; dorms £14), well-placed for walks on Snowdon.

For **food** of gut-splitting proportions, climbers and walkers flock to *Pete's Eats*, 40 High St, while *Y Bistro*, 43–45 High St (Ⓣ01286/871278; closed Sun & Mon), is the best restaurant for miles around. The *Vaynol Arms*, two miles east of Llanberis and the only pub before Pen-y-Gwryd, serves good beer and very tasty food in a convivial atmosphere.

Snowdon and the Snowdon Mountain Railway

The highest British mountain outside Scotland, the **Snowdon massif** (3560ft) forms a star of shattered ridges with four major peaks: Crib Goch, Crib-y-ddysgl, Y Lliwedd and the main summit, **Yr Wyddfa**. Snowdon sports some of the finest walking and scrambling in the park. Hardened outdoor enthusiasts dismiss it as overused, and it can certainly be crowded in summer when a thousand visitors a day can be pressed into the postbox-red carriages of the Snowdon Mountain Railway, while another 1500 pound the well-maintained paths.

Opprobrium is chiefly levelled at the **Snowdon Mountain Railway** (mid-March to mid-Nov 6–25 trains daily; £22 return; ⓣ01286/870223, ⓦwww.snowdonrailway.co.uk), completed in 1896, purely for the fact that it exists. Seventy-year-old carriages pushed by equally old steam locos still climb, in just under an hour, from the eastern end of Llanberis opposite the *Royal Victoria Hotel* to the summit café, which is open whenever the trains are running.

A "Railway Stamp" (13p) affixed to your letter – along with the usual Royal Mail one – entitles you to use the highest postbox in the UK and enchant your friends with a "Summit of Snowdon – Copa'r Wyddfa" postmark. Times, type of locomotive and final destination vary with demand and ice conditions at the top: to avoid disappointment, buy your tickets early on clear summer days. If you walk up by one of the routes detailed in the box on p.730, you can take the train down, if there is space (£14).

Beddgelert

A huddle of grey houses, prodigiously brightened with floral displays in summer, makes up **BEDDGELERT**. A sentimental tale fabricated by a wily local publican to lure punters tells how the town got its name: **Gelert's Grave** (*bedd* means burial place), an enclosure just south of town, is supposedly the final resting place of Prince Llywelyn ap Iorwerth's faithful dog, Gelert, who was left in charge of the prince's infant son while he went hunting. On his return, the child was gone and the hound's muzzle was soaked in blood. Jumping to conclusions, the impetuous Llywelyn slew the dog, only to find the child safely asleep beneath its cot and a dead wolf beside him. Llywelyn hurried to his dog, which licked his hand as it died.

Beyond the "grave", the river crashes down the picturesque **Aberglaslyn Gorge** towards Porthmadog. You can walk past Gelert's Grave, then cross over the bridge onto a path which hugs the left bank for a mile, running parallel to the line of the Welsh Highland Railway and affording a closer look at the river's course through chutes and channels in sculpted rocks. Return the same way; the round trip takes around an hour.

A mile in the opposite direction up Nantgwynant, the **Sygun Copper Mine** (daily: Easter–Oct 9.30am–5pm; Nov–Easter 10.30am–4pm; ⓦwww.syguncoppermine.co.uk; £7.95) is the dilapidated remnant of what, until a century ago, had been the valley's prime source of income from Roman times. The multiple levels of tunnels and galleries can now be visited on a 45-minute self-guided tour, accompanied by the disembodied voice of a miner describing his life in the mine.

Buses all stop by the Tŷ Isaf National Trust shop (Easter–Oct Wed, Sat & Sun 1–4pm), by the village bridge and just a few yards from the **tourist office** (Easter–Oct daily 9.30am–5.30pm; Nov–Easter Fri, Sat & Sun 9.30am–4.30pm; ⓣ01766/890615, ⓦwww.beddgelerttourism.com). Good places to **stay** are *Beddgelert Bistro & Antiques*, Waterloo House, directly opposite the bridge (ⓣ01766/890543, ⓦwww.beddgelert-bistro.co.uk; ❷), with three attractive

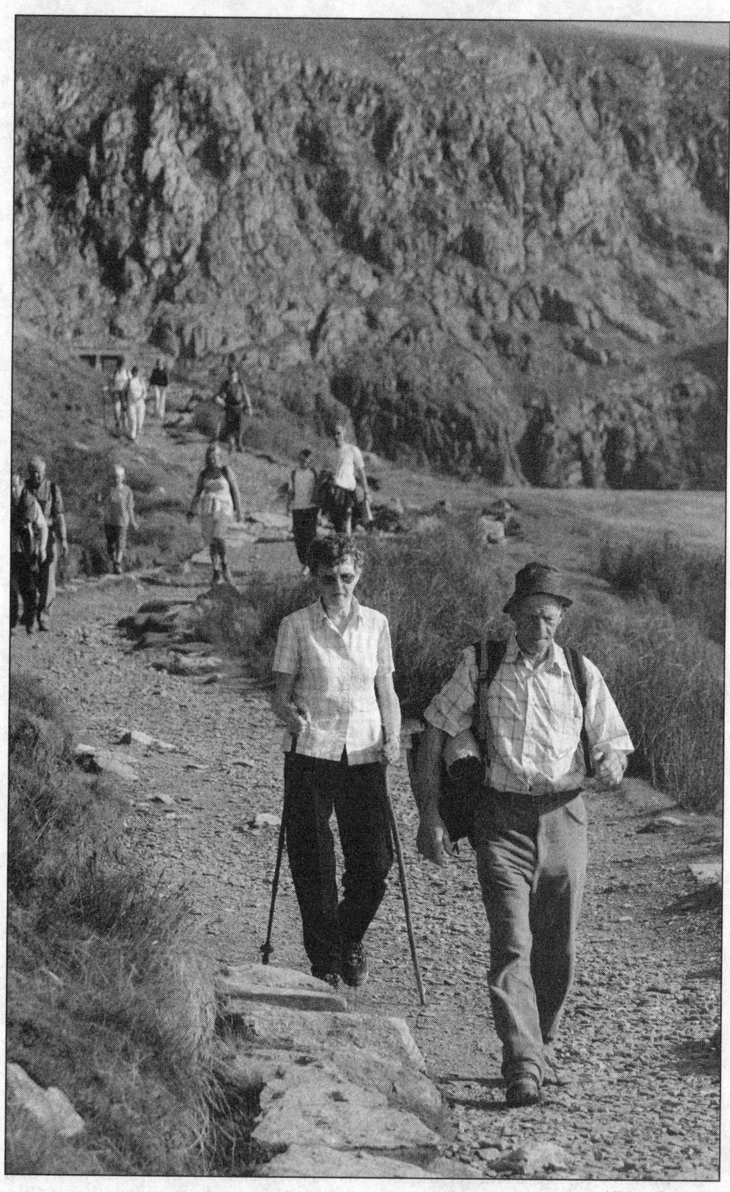

▲Hiking, Snowdon

en-suite rooms above the restaurant; *Plas Tan-y-Graig* (Ⓣ01766/890310, Ⓦwww.plastanygraig.co.uk; ❹), also near the bridge, a comfy B&B aimed at walkers and cyclists; and *Sygun Fawr Country House*, three-quarters of a mile away off the A498 (Ⓣ01766/890258, Ⓦwww.sygunfawr.co.uk; ❺), a sixteenth-century house in its own grounds with a sauna and great four-course evening

Walks up Snowdon

The following are justifiably the most popular of the seven accepted **walking** routes up **Snowdon**. All are easy to follow in good weather but you should still carry the 1:25,000 *OS Explorer* #OL17 map.

Llanberis Path

The easiest, longest and most derided route up Snowdon, the **Llanberis Path** (5 miles to summit; 3200ft ascent; 3hr) follows the rail line, which gets gradually steeper, to the "Finger Stone" at **Bwlch Glas** (Green Pass). This marks the arrival of the Snowdon Ranger Path, and three routes coming up from Pen-y-Pass to join the Llanberis Path for the final ascent to **Yr Wyddfa**, the summit.

The Miners' and Pyg tracks

The **Miners' Track** (4 miles to summit; 2400ft ascent; 2hr 30min) is the easiest of the three routes up from Pen-y-Pass, a broad track leading south then west to the dilapidated remains of the former copper mines in Cwm Dyli. Skirting around the right of a lake, the path climbs more steeply to the lake-filled Cwm Glaslyn, then again to Upper Glaslyn, from where the measured steps of those ahead warn of the impending switchback ascent to the junction with the Llanberis Path.

The stonier **Pyg Track** (3.5 miles to summit; 2400ft ascent; 2hr 30min) is really just a variation on the Miners' Track, leaving from the western end of the Pen-y-Pass car park and climbing up to **Bwlch y Moch** (the Pass of the Pigs) before meeting the Miners' Track prior to the zigzag up to the Llanberis Path.

meals (£22.50). The excellent *Beddgelert Forest Campsite* (ⓣ01766/890288) is a mile out on the Caernarfon road, four miles before the highly rated *Snowdon Ranger* YHA **hostel** (ⓣ0870/770 6038, ⓦwww.yha.org.uk; dorms £12; mid-Feb to Dec). The *Bryn Gwynant* YHA hostel (ⓣ0870/770 5732, ⓦwww.yha.org.uk; Jan–Oct; dorms £12) is beautifully sited in Nantgwynant, four miles northeast of Beddgelert on the A498, and has a **campsite** where you can use the hostel's facilities for half the adult rate. Also at the budget end is *Bryn Dinas* (ⓣ01766/890234, ⓦwww.bryndinasbunkhouse.co.uk; bunks £9), which consists of a number of small but functional sleeping cabins huddled around communal showers and kitchen, also a couple of miles north of Beddgelert.

Blaenau Ffestiniog and around

BLAENAU FFESTINIOG sits at the head of the bucolic Vale of Ffestiniog, hemmed in by stark slopes strewn with heaps of splintered slate. When clouds hunker low in this great cwm and rain sheets the grey roofs, grey walls and grey paving slabs, it can be a terrifically gloomy place. Thousands of tons of slate were once hewn from the labyrinth of underground caverns here each year, but these days the town is only kept alive by its extant slate-cavern tour, and by tourists who change from the Lledr Valley train line onto the wonderful, narrow-gauge **Ffestiniog Railway** (see p.733), which winds up from Porthmadog.

It's difficult to get a real feeling of what slate means to the town without a visit to the **Llechwedd Slate Caverns** (daily: March–Sept 10am–5.15pm; Oct–Feb 10am–4.15pm; single tour £9.25, both tours £14.75; ⓦwww.llechwedd-slate-caverns.co.uk), on the edge of town on the road to Betws-y-Coed. There are two tours available: on the **Miners' Tramway Tour**, a small train takes you a third of a mile along one of the oldest levels to the enormous, awe-inspiring Cathedral Cave and the open-air Chough's Cavern; on the more dramatic **Deep Mine Tour**, a steeply inclined railway takes you down to a labyrinth of tunnels through which you are guided by an irksome taped spiel of a Victorian miner. The long caverns angling back into the gloom are increasingly impressive, culminating in one filled by a beautiful opalescent pool.

Practicalities

The **train station** on the High Street serves both the Ffestiniog line to Porthmadog and mainline train services from Betws-y-Coed, and is a short walk up the main drag from the **tourist office** (Easter–Oct daily 9.30am–5.30pm; ⓣ01766/830360, ⓔtic.Blaenau@eryri-npa.gov.uk), opposite the *Queen's Hotel*. **Buses** stop either in the station car park or along High Street. **Accommodation** is limited, but excellent value: *Isallt Guesthouse* on Church Street (ⓣ01766/832488, ⓦwww.Isallt.com; ❷) is good, or step up to the *Queen's Hotel*, 1 High St (ⓣ01766/830055, ⓦwww.queens-snowdonia.co.uk; ❸), handily sited by the station. Two miles south on the A470 (Manod Rd) is *Cae Du* (ⓣ01766/830847, ⓦwww.caedu.co.uk; ❷), in a sixteenth-century farmhouse, while *Bryn Elltyd* (ⓣ01766/831356, ⓦwww.accommodation-snowdonia.com; ❸), is a fine B&B about a mile from town in Tanygrysiau, which overlooks Llyn Ystradau.

All-day breakfasts and simple lunches are served at *Isallt Café*, near the train station, and the *Lakeside Café* by the information centre at Tanygrisiau. For more substantial **meals**, the *Queen's Hotel* offers tasty, moderately priced dishes, and there's good pub food at *The Commercial* on Commercial Square half a mile north. The chippy across the road from *The Commercial* is the best in town.

Bala

The little water-sports town of **BALA** (Y Bala), twenty miles east of Blaenau Ffestiniog, is set at the northern end of Wales's largest natural lake, **Llyn**

The Welsh slate industry

The Romans recognized the potential of **slate**, roofing the houses of Segontium with it (see p.737), and Edward I used it extensively in his Iron Ring of castles around Snowdonia, but it wasn't until the Industrial Revolution kicked in that the demand for Welsh roofing slates rocketed.

For the 1862 London Exhibition, one skilled craftsman produced a sheet of slate ten feet long, a foot wide and a sixteenth of an inch thick – so thin it could be flexed – firmly establishing Welsh slate as the finest in the world. By 1898, Welsh quarries were producing half a million tons of dressed slate a year, almost all of it from Snowdonia. At Penrhyn and Dinorwig, mountains were hacked away. Workers often slept through the week in damp dormitories on the mountain, and tuberculosis was common, exacerbated by the slate dust. At Blaenau Ffestiniog, the seams required mining underground rather than quarrying, but conditions were no better, with miners even having to buy their own candles, the only light they had. In spite of this, thousands left their hillside smallholdings for the burgeoning quarry towns. Few workers were allowed to join Undeb Chwarelwyr Gogledd Cymru (the North Wales Quarrymen's Union), and in 1900 the workers in Lord Penrhyn's quarry at Bethesda went on strike. They stayed away for three years, but failed to win any concessions. Those who got their jobs back were forced to work for even less money as a recession took hold, and although the two world wars heralded mini-booms as bombed houses were replaced, the industry never recovered its nineteenth-century prosperity, and most quarries and mines closed in the 1950s.

Sadly, what little slate is produced today mostly goes for things besides roofing: floor tiles, road aggregate, and an astonishing array of nasty ashtrays and coasters etched with mountainscapes.

Tegid – perfect for windsurfing due to the winds buffeting up the Talyllyn Valley. Bala Adventure and Watersports Centre (Ⓣ01678/521059, Ⓦwww.balawatersports.com) runs courses and rents equipment for **windsurfing**, **kayaking** and **sailing**.

Around two hundred days a year dam-released water crashes down the whitewater course of the **Afon Tryweryn**, four miles west up the A4212, facilitating commercial **whitewater rafting** trips (Ⓣ01678/521083, Ⓦwww.ukrafting.co.uk), down a mile-and-a-half course. Either go for two runs down (40–60min; £28) or two-hour session (4–7 people for £228 midweek and £259 at weekends). For the intrepid, try the Orca, a two-person inflatable in which you tackle the rapids unguided (half-day £70 per person).

The only public transport access is on **bus** #X94, which runs from Llangollen to Dolgellau, stopping on Bala's High Street. The **tourist office** (Thurs–Mon 10am–5.30pm; Ⓣ01678/521021, Ⓔbala.tic@gwynedd.gov.uk) is on Pensarn Road on the lakeside, five minutes' walk away.

Bala has plenty of good **places to stay**, including the welcoming *Traian*, 95 Tegid St (Ⓣ01678/520059; ❷), with shared bathrooms, and *Abercelyn*, a fine country house half a mile south of Bala on the A494 (Ⓣ01678/521109, Ⓦwww.abercelyn.co.uk; ❹).

The central *Bala Backpackers*, 32 Tegid St (Ⓣ01678/521700, Ⓦwww.bala-backpackers.co.uk; dorms £10–12), is handy, and there's **camping** at *Pen-y-Bont*, just by the lakeside steam-railway station off the B4391 Llandrillo backroad (Ⓣ01678/520549; April–Oct).

For daytime **food**, *Sospan Fach*, 97 High St, provides well-priced, wholesome food, and for dinner, look no further than the cosy *Awel yr Aran*, also on the High Street, which serves up sumptuous dishes made from mainly local produce.

The Llŷn

The most westerly part of north Wales, **the Llŷn** takes its name from an Irish word for peninsula – appropriate, for until the fifth century, it had a significant Irish population. It's a cliff- and cove-lined finger of land that juts out south and west from Snowdonia, separating Cardigan and Caernarfon bays. Its hills taper along its spine, carrying an ancient route to Aberdaron, where pilgrims once sailed for Ynys Enlli (Bardsey Island). Most come to the Llŷn for its beaches, especially those of the south coast family resorts of **Cricieth**, **Pwllheli** and **Abersoch**, but **Aberdaron** is the star around here.

Nowhere in Wales is more remote and staunchly Welsh: road signs are still bilingual but the English is frequently obliterated; Stryd Fawr is used instead of High Street, and in most local shops you'll only hear Welsh spoken.

The Llŷn is reached through one of the two gateway towns: **Porthmadog**, home to the private "dream village" of **Portmeirion** and terminus of the **Ffestiniog Railway**; or **Caernarfon**, where a magnificent fortress guards the mouth of the Menai Strait.

Porthmadog and around

Located at the point where the Llŷn peninsula meets the Cambrian coast, **PORTHMADOG** was once the busiest slate port in North Wales. Nowadays, it's a pleasant enough town to spend a night or two, although it sadly makes little of its situation on the north bank of the vast, mountain-backed estuary. Instead, attention is heaped upon the folly of Portmeirion, almost three miles east of town, and the Ffestiniog Railway that originally carried slate down from Blaenau Ffestiniog through verdant mountain scenery. Porthmadog would never have existed at all without the entrepreneurial ventures of the MP William Alexander Madocks, who named the town after both himself and the Welsh prince Madog, who some say sailed from the nearby Ynys Fadog (Madog's Island) to North America in 1170. Between 1808 and 1812, Madocks fought tides and currents to build the mile-long embankment of The Cob, southeast of present-day Porthmadog, enclosing seven thousand acres of the estuary. A wharf was built and, with the completion of the Ffestiniog Railway in 1836, the town spread along a waterfront thick with orderly heaps of slate and the masts of merchant ships.

The **Ffestiniog Railway** (Easter–Oct 4–8 trains daily; Nov–Easter mainly weekends; return to Blaenau Ffestiniog £16.95, to Tan-y-Bwlch £10.40, discounts on first and last trains of the day; Ⓣ01766/516000, Ⓦwww.festrail.co.uk) ranks as Wales's finest narrow-gauge rail line, twisting and looping up 650ft from the wharf at Porthmadog to the slate mines at Blaenau Ffestiniog, thirteen miles away. It once carried slate from the mines down to the port with the help of gravity, horses riding with the goods then hauling the empty carriages back up again. Steam had to be introduced to cope with the 100,000 tons of slate a year that Blaenau Ffestiniog was churning out by the late nineteenth century, but with the collapse of the slate roofing industry between the wars, the line was abandoned in 1946 and fell into disrepair. Reconstruction of the tracks was complete by 1982. Leaving Porthmadog, trains cross The Cob and then stop at **Minffordd**, a mile from Portmeirion.

Portmeirion

The area's main lure is the unique, Italianate private village of **PORTMEIRION** (daily 9.30am–5.30pm; Ⓦwww.portmeirion-village.com; £6), set on a small rocky peninsula in Tremadog Bay, three miles east near Minffordd. You can walk there in an hour from Porthmadog, or catch the Express #98 bus, which goes right to the gate. By train, take either the main line or Ffestiniog trains to Minffordd, from where it's a signposted 25min walk to Portmeirion.

Best known as "The Village" in the 1960s cult British TV series *The Prisoner*, Portmeirion was the brainchild of eccentric architect Clough Williams-Ellis, and his dream to build an ideal village using a "gay, light-opera sort of approach". The result is certainly theatrical: a stage set with a lucky dip of buildings arranged to distort perspectives and reveal tantalizing glimpses of the seascape behind.

In the 1920s, Williams-Ellis bought the site and turned an existing house into a hotel, the income from this providing funds for his "Home for Fallen Buildings". Endangered structures in every conceivable style from all over Britain and abroad were brought here and arranged around a Mediterranean piazza: a Neoclassical colonnade from Bristol, Siamese figures, a Jacobean town hall, a campanile and a pantheon. Painted in pastel shades of turquoise, ochre and buff yellows, it is continually surprising, with hidden entrances and cherubs popping out of crevices – eclectic yet never quite inappropriate.

More than three thousand visitors a day come to ogle in summer, when it can be a delight; fewer in winter, when it seems just bizarre. Other than buying *Prisoner* memorabilia there's little to actually do, so bring a picnic and spend the afternoon exploring the lovely grounds. In the evening, when the village is closed to the public, patrons at the opulent, waterside *Portmeirion Hotel* (Ⓣ01766/770000, Ⓦwww.portmeirion-village.com; ⑧) and the chic Victorian "castle" *Castell Deudraeth* (same contacts; ⑧) get to see the place at its best – peaceful, even ghostly.

Practicalities

Porthmadog's High Street runs between the mainline **train station**, at the north end, and the **Ffestiniog station**, by the harbour about half a mile to the south. In between the two, National Express **coaches** stop outside the *Royal Sportsman* while local **bus** services stop outside the *Australia Inn*. The helpful **tourist office** (Easter–Oct daily 9.30am–5.30pm; Nov–Easter daily 10am–4pm; ⓣ01766/512981, ⓦwww.porthmadog.co.uk) is by the harbour on High Street.

While limited budgets are well catered for, there's not much really decent **accommodation**, unless you're prepared to splash out for a night at the swanky *Portmeirion Hotel* in Portmeirion (see above). For **B&B** try *Yr Hen Fecws*, 15 Lombard St (ⓣ01766/514625; ④), with comfy, uncluttered rooms, beside a popular restaurant of the same name (see below). Several good options are dotted around the village of Tremadog, a mile north, including the *Snowdon Lodge* on Church Street (ⓣ01766/515354, ⓦwww.snowdonlodge.co.uk; dorms £15 including breakfast), a well-organized and welcoming backpackers' **hostel** in the house where T.E. Lawrence was born. Best of all is *Plas Tan-yr-Allt* (ⓣ01766/514545, ⓦwww.tanyrallt.co.uk; ⑤), a gorgeous, luxury B&B in a house once owned by Shelley, a few hundred yards from Tremadog on the road to Beddgelert. For camping, head for the pleasant, family-oriented *Tyddyn Llwyn* (ⓣ01766/512205), fifteen minutes' walk west along the A497 which spurs off High Street.

For **food** in Porthmadog, there's *Yr Hen Fecws*, at 16 Lombard St (ⓣ01766/514625), a lively bistro with some good veggie options, or *Caffi y Morwr Madog*, Pencei, a small café with pavement tables overlooking the harbour, serving decent espresso and a range of snacks.

If you've got transport or want to walk up an appetite, there's fantastic pub food to be had in nearby Tremadog, less than a mile north, at the *Golden Fleece*. For **drinking**, make for *Y Llong* (The Ship) at 14 Lombard St, a busy pub that sells real ales including those from Porthmadog's new Purple Moose microbrewery.

Criccieth

When sea-bathing became the Victorian fashion, English families descended on the sweeping sand and shingle beach at **CRICCIETH**, five miles west of Porthmadog, a quiet, amiable resort dominated by the battle-worn remains of **Criccieth Castle** (daily: April, May & Oct 10am–5pm, June–Sept 10am–6pm, £2.90; Nov to mid-March Fri & Sat 9.30am–4pm, Sun 11am–4pm, free; CADW), with its twin-towered gatehouse. Started by Llywelyn ap Iorwerth in 1230, it was strengthened by Edward I around 1283, and razed by Owain Glyndŵr in 1404, leaving little besides a plan of broken walls. It's a great spot to sit and look over Cardigan Bay to Harlech, but leave time for the ticket office, where there's a workaday exhibition on Welsh castles and a wonderful animated cartoon about twelfth-century Wales.

Buses and **trains** along the Cambrian coastline stop a couple of hundred yards west of Y Maes, the open square at the centre of Criccieth. **Accommodation** is plentiful, with the *Moelwyn*, 27–29 Mona Terrace (ⓣ01766/522500, ⓔmoelwyn@aol.com; ③; March–Nov), a smart choice with great sea views. For something cheaper head for *Craig-y-Môr*, West Parade (ⓣ01766/522830; ②; March–Oct), a guesthouse with well-appointed rooms, some with fine sea views; or *Tyddyn Morthwyl Farm and Caravan Park*, a mile and a half north on Caernarfon Road (the B4411; ⓣ01766/522115), which has good camping (£7 per tent) and a bunkhouse (£7 per person).

Mynydd Ednyfed (ⓣ01766/523269, ⓦwww.criccieth.net; ❺) is a classy country hotel a mile north on Caernarfon Road.

Good **restaurants** are abundant: make for *Moelwyn* (see above), which has a superb sea-facing restaurant; or head out to *Mynydd Ednyfed* (see above). The *Prince of Wales*, on Stryd Fawr, offers a great **pub** atmosphere and decent bar meals.

Pwllheli and Abersoch

PWLLHELI (pronounced "poolth-heli") is the market town for the peninsula, a role it has maintained since 1355 when it gained its charter, though there's little sign of its history nowadays. Primarily useful as the final stop for Cambrian coast **trains** and the terminus for National Express **coaches** (which stop on Y Maes, the main square), it's a thoroughly Welsh place: even in the tourist season you'll hear far more Welsh spoken here than English. The **tourist office** is on Station Square (April–Oct daily 9am–5pm; Nov–March Mon–Wed, Fri & Sat 10.30am–4.30pm; ⓣ01758/613000, ⓔpwllheli.tic@gwynedd.gov.uk). During the summer you can rent **mountain bikes** at Llŷn Cycle Hire, 2 Ala Rd (ⓣ01758/612414). If you decide to **stay**, try *Llys Gwyrfai*, 14 West End Parade (ⓣ01758/614877; ❷), a comfortable guesthouse with sea views and home-cooked meals.

It is generally better to push seven miles beyond Pwllheli to **ABERSOCH**, a former fishing village pitched in the middle of two golden bays. Over the last century it has become a thoroughly anglicized resort, with a distinctly haughty opinion of itself. Such high self-esteem isn't really justified, but at high tide the harbour is attractive, and the long swathe of the beach-hut-backed Town Beach is a fine spot. A short walk along the beach shakes off most of the crowds, but it's better to make for three-mile-long **Porth Neigwl** (Hell's Mouth), two miles to the southwest, which ranks as one of the country's best **surf beaches**; you'll need your own gear, and beware of the undertow if you're swimming. Back in Abersoch, you can get instruction and **rent windsurfers**, surfboards and wetsuits from West Coast Surf Shop, Lôn Pen Cei (ⓣ01758/713067, ⓦwww.westcoastsurf.co.uk), by the harbour. **Buses** from Pwllheli make a loop through the middle of Abersoch, stopping on Lôn Pen Cei by the **tourist office** (April–Sept daily 10.30am–4.30pm; Oct–March Sat & Sun 11am–1pm; ⓣ01758/712929, ⓦwww.abersochtouristinfo.co.uk). For **accommodation**, try the modest and comfortable *Llwyn Du*, Lôn Sarn Bach (ⓣ01758/712186, ⓦwww.bedandbreakfastabersoch.co.uk; ❷); *Angorfa Guesthouse*, Lôn Sarn Bach (ⓣ01758/712967, ⓦwww.angorfa.com; ❸); and the welcoming *Goslings at the Carisbrooke*, Lôn Sarn Bach (ⓣ01758/712526, ⓦwww.goslingsabersoch.co.uk; ❺), good for families.

Among the decent **places to eat** is *Mañana*, on Lôn Pen Cei, serving Mexican food, while just up the road is *Angelina's* (ⓣ01758/712353), a classy Italian with a broad menu (plus tasty desserts). *The Ship*, out of town in Llanbedrog, near Pwllheli, is excellent.

Aberdaron and Bardsey Island

The small, lime-washed fishing village of **ABERDARON** backs a pebble beach two miles short of the tip of the Llŷn. From the sixth century onwards, it was the last stop for pilgrims to **Bardsey Island** (Ynys Enlli: the Island of the Currents), just offshore, where three visits were proclaimed equivalent to one pilgrimage to Rome. Many pilgrims came to die here, earning the place its epithet "The Isle of Twenty Thousand Saints". For details of the self-catering cottages there, or day-trips, contact the Bardsey Island Trust (Ⓣ01758/112233, Ⓦwww.enlli.org). In olden days, the final gathering place before the treacherous crossing was the fourteenth-century Y Gegin Fawr (Great Kitchen), a stone building which still operates as a **café** in the middle of Aberdaron.

Without your own transport, the only way to get to Aberdaron is to catch bus #17 from Pwllheli (Mon–Sat). **Accommodation** is fairly limited; the least expensive option is *Brynmor* (Ⓣ01758/760344; ❷), overlooking the bay, just up the road to Porth Oer. The beachside *Tŷ Newydd* hotel (Ⓣ01758/760207; ❺) is recommended too; make time for a pint or meal on their beach terrace at sunset. The best and quietest **campsite** around is *Mur Melyn* (Ⓣ01758/760522), just over a mile out from Aberdaron, midway to Porth Oer; take the B4413 west, fork right, then turn left at Pen-y-Bont house.

Caernarfon

It was in **CAERNARFON**, in 1969, that Charles, the current heir to the throne, was invested as Prince of Wales, a ceremony which reaffirmed English sovereignty over Wales in this, one of the most nationalist of Welsh-speaking regions. Since 1282, when the English defeated Llywelyn ap Gruffydd, the last Welsh prince of

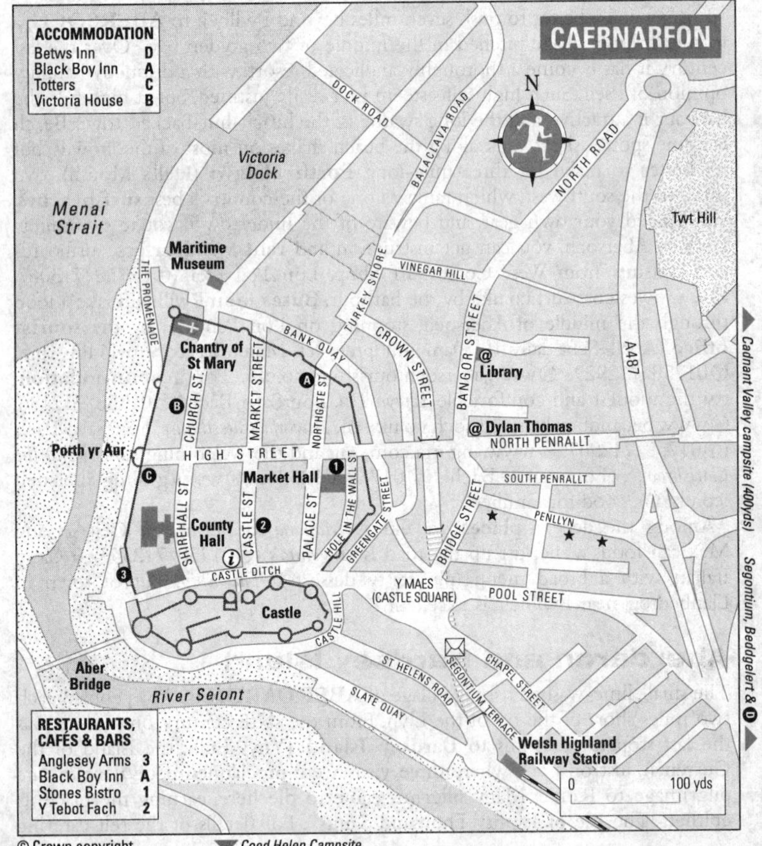

Wales, the title has been bestowed on heirs to the English (and then British) throne, but it wasn't until 1911 that the machinations of David Lloyd George – MP for Caernarfon and future prime minister – brought a theatrical investiture ceremony to the centre of his constituency: an odd move for a proto-nationalist, considering the symbolic implications. Caernarfon's location on the Menai Strait with views across to Anglesey makes it an appealing place, but apart from the vastly imposing **castle** there isn't too much to see. That said, it's a spirited and lively town, and has good bus connections to Llanberis and Snowdonia.

Caernarfon Castle

In 1283, Edward I started work on **Caernarfon Castle** (June–Sept daily 9.30am–6pm; April, May & Oct daily 9.30am–5pm; Nov–Easter Mon–Sat 9.30am–4pm, Sun 11am–4pm; £4.90; CADW), the strongest link in his Iron Ring, a decisive hammer-blow to any Welsh aspirations to autonomy and the ultimate symbol of Anglo-Norman military might. Edward attempted to appease the Welsh by paying tribute to aspects of local legend. The Welsh had long associated their town with the eastern capital of the Roman Empire: Caernarfon's old name, Caer Cystennin, was also the name used for Constantinople, and Constantine himself was believed to have been born at Segontium (see below).

In military terms, the castle is supreme. It was taken once, before building was complete, but then withstood two sieges by Owain Glyndŵr with a garrison of only 28 men-at-arms. As you enters through the **King's Gate**, the castle's strength is immediately apparent. Embrasures and murder holes between the octagonal towers face in on no fewer than five gates and six portcullises, and that's once you have crossed the moat. Inside, the huge lawn gives a misleading impression as the wall dividing the two original wards, and all the buildings that filled them, crumbled away long ago. The towers are in a much better state, and linked by an exhausting honeycomb of wall-walks and tunnels. The tallest is the **King's Tower** whose three slender turrets are adorned with eagle sculptures and give the best views of the town. To the south, the Queen's Tower is entirely taken up by the numbingly thorough **Museum of the Royal Welch Fusiliers**, while the Northeast Tower houses the **Prince of Wales Exhibition**, just outside which is the Dinorwig slate dais used for Charles's investiture.

Segontium Roman Fort

A ten-minute walk along the A4085 Beddgelert road brings you to **Segontium Roman Fort** (fort daily 12.30–4.30pm; museum daily except Mon 12.30–4.30pm; free; CADW), the western end of the Roman road from Chester. The Romans occupied this five-acre site for three centuries from around 78 AD, though most of the remains are from the final rebuilding after 364. The ground plan is seldom more than shin-high and somewhat baffling, making the museum and displays in the ticket office pretty much essential.

Welsh Highland Railway

The narrow-gauge **Welsh Highland Railway** (mid-March to Oct 2–6 trains most days; Ⓣ01766/516000, Ⓦwww.festrail.co.uk) starts in Caernarfon, just near the harbour on St Helen's Road. Ultimately, it will run 25 miles to Porthmadog via Beddgelert, but currently runs to Rhyd-Ddu, starting point for southerly ascents of Snowdon (unlimited one-day travel £16.95), with a stop outside the *Snowdon Ranger* YHA hostel. Joint tickets with the Ffestiniog Railway are available.

Practicalities

The hub of Caernarfon's public transport system is Penllyn, where **buses** stop. The **tourist office** is close by on Castle Street (Easter–Oct daily 9.30am–5pm; Nov–Easter Mon–Sat 10am–4pm; ⓣ01286/672232, ⓔcaernarfon.tic@gwynedd.gov.uk). **Accommodation** options close to the centre include *Victoria House*, 13 Church St (ⓣ01286/678263, ⓦwww.thevictoriahouse.com; ③), a good-value B&B within the town walls, and the characterful *Black Boy Inn* (ⓣ01286/673604; ④) on Northgate Street. Five miles southeast of Caernarfon, the excellent *Betws Inn*, on the A4085 in Betws Garmon (ⓣ01286/650324, ⓦwww.betws-inn.co.uk; ③), occupies a stylishly restored former drovers' inn where wonderful three-course dinners (£15) are served by arrangement. *Totters*, 2 High St (ⓣ01286/672963, ⓦwww.applemaps.co.uk/totters; dorms £14), is a superb and very friendly independent **hostel**. The nearest **campsite** is *Cadnant Valley* (ⓣ01286/673196; £9–12 per tent; closed Nov–Feb), ten minutes' walk east of town near the start of the A4086 to Llanberis.

Caernarfon boasts a number of pleasant, low-key **restaurants**: try the bistro-style fare at *Stones Bistro*, 4 Hole in the Wall St (closed Sun & Mon), or a cream tea at *Y Tebot Bach*, 13 Castle St (closed Sun & Mon), which serves modern food with old-fashioned attention to detail. Cheapest of all are the excellent **bar meals** at the *Black Boy Inn* (see above). For **drinking**, start with a pint on the sea wall outside the *Anglesey Arms*.

The island of Anglesey

Across the Menai Strait from Caernarfon, **Anglesey** (Ynys Môn) welcomes visitors to "Mam Cymru", the Mother of Wales, attesting to the island's former importance as the national breadbasket. The land remains predominantly pastoral, with small fields, stone walls and white houses reminiscent of parts of Ireland or England. Linguistically and politically, though, Anglesey is intensely Welsh, with seventy percent of the islanders being first-language Welsh-speakers. The island was the crucible of pre-Roman druidic activity in Britain, and there are still numerous Neolithic remains at which to soak up the atmosphere of a pagan past. Especially since the advent of the A55 main road, many people charge straight through to **Holyhead** and the Irish ferries, missing out on Anglesey's many charms. There's the ancient town of **Beaumaris**, with its fine castle, the Whistler mural at **Plas Newydd** (not to be confused with Plas Newydd in Llangollen; see p.718) and some superb coastal scenery.

Beaumaris

The original inhabitants of **BEAUMARIS** (Biwmares) were evicted by Edward I to make way for the construction of his new castle and bastide town, dubbed "beautiful marsh" in an attempt to attract English settlers. Today the place can still seem like the small English outpost Edward intended, with its elegant Georgian terrace along the front (designed by Joseph Hansom, of cab fame) and more plummy English accents than you'll have heard for a while.

Beaumaris Castle (June–Sept daily 9.30am–6pm; mid-March to May & Oct daily 9.30am–5pm; Nov to mid-March Mon–Sat 9.30am–4pm, Sun 11am–4pm; £3.50; CADW) might never have been built had Madog ap Llywelyn not captured Caernarfon in 1294. When asked to build the new castle, James of St George abandoned the Caernarfon design in favour of a concentric plan, developing it into a highly evolved symmetrical octagon. Sited on flat land at the edge of town, the castle is denied the domineering majesty of Caernarfon or Harlech, its low outer walls appearing almost welcoming until you begin to appreciate the concentric layout of the defences protected by massive towers, a moat linked to the sea and the Arab-influenced staggered entries through the two gatehouses. Despite more than thirty years' work, the project was never quite finished, leaving most of the inner ward empty and the corbels and fireplaces built into the walls unused. You can explore the internal passages in the walls but the low-parapet wall-walk, from where you get the best idea of the castle's defensive capability, remains off limits. Impressive as they are, none of these defences was able to prevent siege by Owain Glyndŵr, who held the castle for two years from 1403, although they did withhold a Parliamentarian siege during the Civil War.

Almost opposite the castle stands the Jacobean **Beaumaris Court** (Easter–Sept daily 10.30am–5pm; £3, joint ticket with gaol £5.50), built in 1614 and the oldest active court in Britain. It is now used only for the twice-monthly Magistrates Court. On session days you can watch the trials, but won't be able to take the recorded tour or inspect *The Lawsuit*, a plaque in the magistrates' room depicting two farmers pulling the horns and tail of a cow while a lawyer milks it.

Many citizens were transported from the court to the colonies for their misdemeanours; others only made it a couple of blocks to the 1829 **Beaumaris Gaol**, Steeple Lane (same hours; £3.50, joint ticket with court £5.50), which was considered a model prison, with running water and toilets in each cell, and an infirmary. Advanced perhaps, but nonetheless a gloomy place: witness the windowless punishment-cell, the yard for stone-breaking and the treadmill water-pump operated by the prisoners. The least fortunate inmates were publicly hanged – the fate of a certain Richard Rowlands, whose disembodied voice leads the recorded tour of the building and various displays on prison life.

After all this gloom, a good way to lift the spirits is aboard one of the **pleasure cruises** (Ⓣ01248/810251, Ⓦwww.starida.co.uk; £5) out to (but not landing on) Puffin Island. The booking kiosk is at the foot of the pier.

Practicalities

With no trains or tourist office, Beaumaris seems poorly served, but it does have a regular **bus** service to Bangor (#53, #57 & #58). The best of the very limited range of **places to stay** are *Mountfield* B&B, immediately east of the castle (Ⓣ01248/810380; ④), and the ancient and luxurious *Ye Olde Bull's Head Inn*, 18 Castle St (Ⓣ01248/810329, Ⓦwww.bullsheadinn.co.uk; ⑥), used as General Mytton's headquarters during the Civil War. *Kingsbridge* is the nearest **campsite**, two miles north in Llanfaes (Ⓣ01248/490636). *Pier House Café*, Bron Menai, is the best of the daytime **eating** options, while for more substantial fare you can't miss *Ye Olde Bull's Head Inn* (see above), with a chic, modern brasserie, a fine formal restaurant and a great bar. For something simpler visit the wonderfully cosy *Sailor's Return* pub on Church Street.

Llanfairpwllgwyngyllgogerychwyrndrob-wllllandysiliogogogoch

In the 1880s a local tailor invented the longest place-name in Britain in a successful attempt to draw tourists. However, it is an utter disappointment to arrive at **Llanfairpwllgwyngyllgogerychwyrndrobwllllandysiliogo-gogoch**, which translates as "St Mary's Church in the hollow of white hazel near a rapid whirlpool and the Church of St Tysilio near the red cave" – commonly shortened to **LLANFAIRPWLL**. All you'll find here is a train station, a tacky wool shop and a **tourist office** (Mon–Sat 9.30am–5.30pm, Sun

10am–5pm; closes 5pm Oct–Easter; ⓣ01248/713177, ⓔllanfairpwll@nwtic.com), the only one worth its salt on the island.

The marquises of Anglesey still live at **Plas Newydd** (April–Oct Sat–Wed noon–5pm; gardens open an hour earlier; £6.60, garden only £4.60; NT), a mile and a half south of Llanfairpwll, a modest three-storey mansion with incongruous Tudor caps on slender octagonal turrets. Inside, architect James Wyatt was given free stylistic rein, producing a Gothic music room followed by a Neoclassical staircase hall with a cantilevered staircase and deceptively solid-looking Doric columns – actually just painted wood. Corridors of oils and period rooms lead to the highlight, a 58-foot-long wall consumed by a trompe l'oeil painting by **Rex Whistler**, who spent a couple of years here in the 1930s. Walking along his imaginary seascape, your position appears to shift by over a mile as the mountains of Snowdonia and a whimsical composite of elements, culled from Italy as well as Britain, change perspective. Portmeirion (see p.733) is there, as are the Round Tower from Windsor Castle and the steeple from St Martin-in-the-Fields in London. Whistler himself appears as a gondolier, and again as a gardener in one of the two right-angled panels at either end, which appear to extend the room further. The prize exhibit in the **Cavalry Museum**, a few rooms further on, is the world's first articulated false leg, all wood, leather and springs, designed for the first marquis, who lost his leg at Waterloo.

Holyhead and around

Holy Island (Ynys Gybi) is blessed with Anglesey's best scenery and cursed with its most unattractive town. The spectacular sea cliffs around South Stack, and the Stone Age and Roman remains on Holyhead Mountain are just a couple of miles from workaday Holyhead, whose ferry routes to Ireland and good transport links mean you'll probably find your way there at some stage.

The local council's valiant attempts to brighten up **HOLYHEAD** (Caergybi; pronounced in English as "holly-head") somehow make this town of dilapidated shopfronts and high unemployment even more depressing. In 1727, Swift found it "scurvy, ill provided and comfortless", and little seems to have changed. The town is linked by ferries and catamarans run by Stena Line (ⓣ08705/707070, ⓦwww.stenaline.com) and Irish Ferries (ⓣ08705/171717, ⓦwww.irishferries.com) to both Dublin Port and Dun Laoghaire, six miles south of Dublin. The **tourist office** (daily 8.30am–6pm; ⓣ01407/762622, ⓔholyhead@nwtic.com), in the ferry terminal, can point you to the recently upgraded **Holyhead Maritime Museum**, Newry Beach (daily 10am–4pm; £2.50; ⓣ01407/769745), with some interesting displays in the old lifeboat station.

Shun the bunch of poor **B&Bs** along the A5 into the town in favour of those around Walthew Avenue, most easily reached by turning left just before the tourist office onto the beachfront Prince of Wales Road, then left again into Walthew Avenue. While *Orotavia*, at no. 66 (ⓣ01407/760259; ❷), is simple and cosy, the best of the bunch is *Yr Hendre* (ⓣ01407/762929, ⓦwww.yr-hendre.co.uk; ❸), round the corner on Porth-y-Felin Road. Fast **food** is the staple diet in Holyhead, but you can still eat well: the *Castle Bakery*, 83 Market St, is about the best café, and *Raja's*, 8 Newry St, serves the tastiest Bengal curries around.

Holyhead Mountain and South Stack

The northern half of Holy Island is ranged around the skirts of the 700-foot **Holyhead Mountain** (Mynydd Twr), its summit ringed by the seventeen-acre **Caer y Twr** (free access; CADW), one of the largest Iron Age sites in North Wales. The best approach is by car or bus #22 to the car park at **South Stack**

(Ynys Lawd), two miles west of Holyhead, from where a path (30min) leads to the top of Holyhead Mountain. Most visitors only walk the few yards to the cliff-top **Ellin's Tower Seabird Centre** (Easter–Sept daily 10am–5.30pm; free) where, from April until the end of July, binoculars and closed-circuit TV give an unparalleled opportunity to watch up to three thousand birds – razorbills, guillemots and the odd puffin – nesting on the nearby sea cliffs while ravens and peregrine falcons wheel outside the tower's windows. A twisting path leads down from the tower to a suspension bridge over the surging waves, leading over to the now fully automated pepper-pot **South Stack Lighthouse** (April–Sept daily 10.30am–5.30pm; £4). Tickets are issued at the *South Stack Kitchen*, a café-cum-interpretative centre a hundred yards back down the lane. Nearby, nineteen low stone circles make up the **Cytiau'r Gwyddelod** or the "Huts of the Irish", a common name for any ancient settlement – in this case late Neolithic or early Bronze Age.

The north coast

Anglesey connects with the mainland at the university town of **Bangor**, a lively enough place, and best used as base for visiting **Penrhyn Castle** or as a springboard for Snowdonia. Heading east you encounter the **north coast** proper, where the castle town of **Conwy** and elegant **Llandudno** are essential stops. Beyond Llandudno the resorts get tackier, though there's reason enough to stop for the National Portrait Gallery at **Bodelwyddan**, the tiny cathedral at **St Asaph** and the ancient shrine at **Holywell**.

Bangor

BANGOR, across the bridge from Anglesey, is not big, but as the largest town in Gwynedd and home to Bangor University, it passes in these parts for cosmopolitan. Bangor is a hotbed of passionate Welsh nationalism, hardly surprising in such a staunchly Welsh-speaking area, and it's a dramatic contrast from the largely English-speaking north coast resorts.

Bangor's thirteenth- to fifteenth-century **cathedral**, on Deiniol Road (daily 11am–5pm; free), boasts the longest continuous use of any cathedral in Britain, easily predating the town. Pop in if only to see the sixteenth-century wooden **Mostyn Christ**, depicted bound and seated on a rock.

Just over the road, the **Bangor Museum and Art Gallery**, Ffordd Gwynedd (Tues–Fri 12.30–4.30pm, Sat 10.30am–4.30pm; free), offers snippets of local history enlivened by a traditional costume section and an archeology room, containing the most complete Roman sword found in Wales. The art gallery concentrates on predominantly Welsh contemporary works. For a good look down the Menai Strait to Telford's graceful bridge (the world's first large iron suspension bridge, completed in 1826), walk along Garth Road to Bangor's rejuvenated and pristine **Victorian Pier** (25p), which reaches halfway across to Anglesey.

Penrhyn Castle

There can hardly be a more vulgar testament to the Anglo-Welsh landowning gentry's oppression of the rural Welsh than the compelling **Penrhyn Castle** (April–June, Sept & Oct daily except Tues noon–5pm; July & Aug daily except Tues 11am–5pm; £8, £5.40 grounds, kitchens & railway museum only; NT), two miles east of Bangor. This monstrous, nineteenth-century neo-Norman fancy, with over three hundred rooms dripping with luxurious fittings, was funded by the quarry's huge profits. The sugar and slate fortune built by anti-abolitionist Richard Pennant, first Baron Penrhyn, provided the means for his self-aggrandizing great-great-nephew George Dawkins to hire architect Thomas Hopper, who spent thirteen years from 1827 encasing the neo-Gothic hall in a Norman fortress complete with monumental five-storey keep.

Three-foot-thick oak doors separate the rooms, ebony is used to dramatic effect and a slate bed was built for the visit of Queen Victoria. The decoration is glorious, and fairly true to the Romanesque style, with its deeply cut chevrons, billets and double-cone ornamentation. The family amassed Wales's largest private painting collection, including a Gainsborough landscape, Canaletto's *The Thames at Westminster* and a Rembrandt portrait. Also worth a visit are the Victorian kitchen and servants' quarters, something of an antidote to the opulence "above stairs".

Buses #5, #6 and #7 run frequently from Bangor to the gates, from where it is a mile-long walk to the house.

Practicalities

All north coast trains stop at Bangor **train station**, Station Rd, half a mile along Deiniol Road from the **tourist office** (April–Sept Mon, Wed & Fri 9.30am–4pm, Tues, Thurs & Sat 9.30am–5pm; ⓣ01248/352786, ⓔbangor.tic @gwynedd.gov.uk). Bangor doesn't have a huge choice of places to stay. Most of the cheaper **accommodation** is at the northern end of Garth Road (the continuation of Deiniol Road), about twenty minutes' walk from the train station: try *Dilfan* (ⓣ01248/353030; ❷). *Eryl Môr*, 2 Upper Garth Rd (ⓣ01248/353789, ⓦwww.erylmorhotel.co.uk; ❹), is a quiet and comfortable hotel with views over Bangor's pier and the Menai Strait. Five miles southwest of town on the B4366 is *Tŷ Mawr Farm* (ⓣ01286/670147, ⓦwww.tymawrfarm .co.uk; ❸), a working farm with good food and a cosy welcome.

Bangor's YHA **hostel**, *Tan-y-Bryn* (ⓣ0870/770 5686, ⓦwww.yha.org.uk; dorms £12.95), is signposted off the A56, ten minutes' walk east of the centre (bus #6 or #7 along Garth Road). The nearest **campsite** is the very laid-back *Treborth Hall Farm* (ⓣ01248/364399), fifteen minutes' walk (or bus #5) from Upper Bangor, on the road out towards the Menai Bridge.

Bangor offers an enormous selection of **eating** possibilities for north Wales. *Fat Cat Café Bar*, 161 High St, serves huge burgers and pasta at modest prices, while *Herbs*, 162 High St (closed Sun), is a great daytime café with excellent veggie choices and a fantastic salad bar. Put your Welsh language skills to good use at *Tafarn Y Glôb*, a traditional **pub** on Albert Street, where ordering in Welsh is pretty much a house rule. For "a pint of beer, please" try *un peint o gwrw, os gwelwch chi'n dda* (pronounced "een paint o gooroo, os gweloch un tha"). *Y Castell*, on Glanrafon, a street opposite the cathedral, is another very popular student pub.

Conwy and around

Lovely **CONWY**, twenty miles east of Bangor, is backed by a forested fold of Snowdonia. The town boasts a fine castle, a nearly complete belt of town walls and a wonderful setting on the Conwy Estuary. Nowhere in the core of medieval and Victorian buildings is more than two hundred yards from the irregular triangle of protective masonry formed by the town walls. This makes it extremely easy to potter around and though you'll get to see everything you want to in a day, you may well want to stay longer.

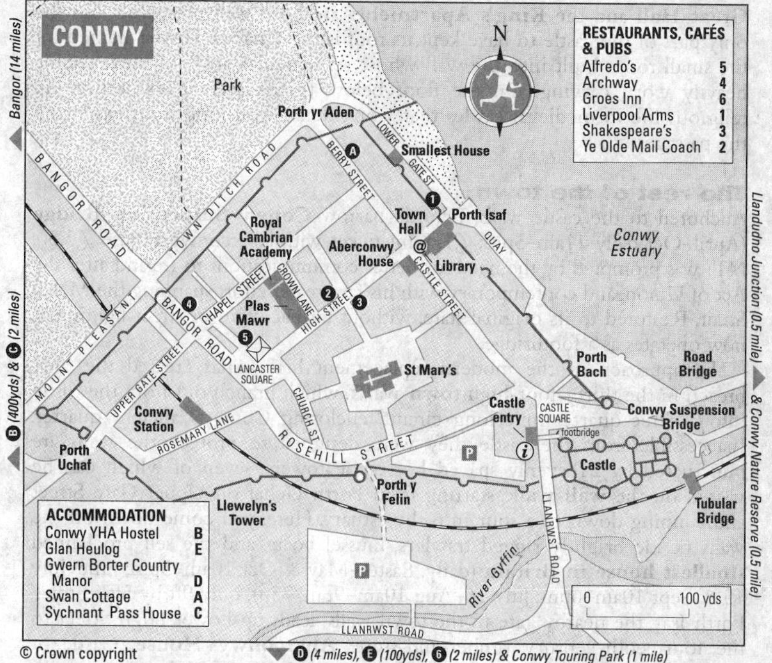

Conwy Castle

Conwy Castle (mid-March to May & Oct daily 9.30am–5pm; June–Sept daily 9.30am–6pm; Nov–March Mon–Sat 9.30am–4pm, Sun 11am–4pm; £4.50, joint ticket with Plas Mawr £7; CADW) is the toughest-looking link in Edward I's Iron Ring of fortresses. After advancing west of the Conwy River in 1283, Edward decided to maintain a bridgehead by establishing another of his bastide towns. He chose a strategic knoll at the mouth of the river and set James of St George to fashion a castle to fit its contours. With the labour of 1500 men it took only five years to build.

Richard II stayed at the castle on his return from an ill-timed trip to Ireland in 1399, until lured from safety by Bolingbroke's vassal, the earl of Northumberland. Northumberland swore in the castle's chapel to grant the king safe passage, but Richard was taken and Bolingbroke became Henry IV. Just two years later, on Good Friday, when the fifteen-strong castle guard were at church, two cousins of Owain Glyndŵr took the castle and razed the town for Glyndŵr's cause. The castle then fell into disuse, and was bought in 1627 for £100 by Charles I's secretary of state, Lord Conway of Ragley, who then had the task of refortifying it for the Civil War. At the restoration of the monarchy, the castle was stripped of all its iron, wood and lead, and was left substantially as it is today.

Being overlooked by a low hill, the castle appears less easily defended than others along the coast, but James constructed eight massive **towers** in a rectangle around the two wards, the inner one separated from the outer by a **drawbridge** and **portcullis**, and further protected by turrets atop the four eastern towers, now the preserve of crows. The outer ward's 130-foot-long

Great Hall and the **King's Apartments** are both well preserved, but the only part of the castle to have kept its roof is the **Chapel Tower**, named for the small room built into the wall whose semicircular apse still shows some heavily worn carving. On the floor below, there's a small exhibition on religious life in medieval castles that won't detain you long from exploring the passages.

The rest of the town

Anchored to the castle walls, Telford's narrow **Conwy Suspension Bridge** (April–Oct daily 11am–5pm; £1, joint ticket with Aberconwy House £3.50; NT) was prompted by the need for better communications to Ireland after the Act of Union, and contemporary with his far greater effort spanning the Menai Strait. Restored to its original state, without tarmac, signs or street lighting, it now operates as a footbridge.

The approach to the modern replacement bridge has created the only breach in the thirty-foot-high **town walls**, which branch out from the castle into a three-quarter-mile-long circuit, enclosing Conwy's ancient quarter. Inaccessible from the castle they were designed to protect, the walls are punctuated by 21 evenly spaced horseshoe towers, seven of which can be visited on the **wall-walk**, starting from Porth Uchaf on Upper Gate Street and running down to a spur into the estuary. Here, you come down off the walls beside brightly rigged trawlers, mussel boats, and the self-proclaimed **smallest house in Britain** (daily: Easter–May & Oct 10am–5pm; June–July 15 & Sept 10am–6pm; July 16–Aug 10am–9pm; 75p), only 9ft by 5ft in total. Porth Isaf, the nearby gate in the town walls, leads up Lower High Street to the fourteenth-century timber-and-stone **Aberconwy House**, Castle St (mid-March to Oct daily except Tues 11am–5pm; £3, joint ticket with suspension bridge £3.50; NT), a former merchant's house. Continue along the High Street to the Dutch-style **Plas Mawr** at no. 20 (Tues–Sun: June–Aug 9.30am–6pm; mid-March to May & Sept 9.30am–5pm; Oct

▲ Conwy Castle

9.30am–4pm; £4.90, joint ticket with castle £7; CADW), a beautifully restored Elizabethan townhouse, built in 1576 for Robert Wynn, one of the first Welsh people to live in the town. Much of the dressed stonework was replaced during renovations in the 1940s and 1950s, but the interior sports more original features, in particular the friezes and superb moulded plaster ceilings depicting fleurs-de-lis, griffons, owls and rams.

Light relief from all the worthy history is on hand at the quay, where regular **river cruises** (30min £4; 45min £5.50) operate on the Conwy Estuary.

Practicalities

Llandudno Junction, less than a mile across the river to the east, serves as the main **train station**; only slow, regional services stop in Conwy itself. National Express **coaches** pull up outside the town walls on Town Ditch Road, while local **buses** use the stops in the centre, mostly on Lancaster Square or Castle Street. The **tourist office** (Ⓣ01492/592248) shares the same building and hours as the castle ticket office.

Accommodation in the centre of town is a bit thin, so booking ahead is advisable in summer. *Swan Cottage*, 18 Berry St (Ⓣ01492/596840; ❶), is the least expensive central B&B with small but attractive rooms. *Glan Heulog*, Llanrwst Road, on the outskirts of town half a mile towards Llanrwst on the B5106 (Ⓣ01492/593845, Ⓦwww.snowdoniabandb.co.uk; ❸), is about the best B&B within easy walking distance of Conwy. Further afield, there's the magnificent *Sychnant Pass House,* towards the top of the Sychnant Pass Road (Ⓣ01492/596868, Ⓦwww.sychnant-pass-house.co.uk; ❻) which oozes class. Dinner in the restaurant is a delight, with traditional dishes such as Welsh lamb served on creamy mashed potato. Bus #19 also goes past the nearest **campsite**, the family-oriented *Conwy Touring Park*, a mile or so south along the B5106 (Ⓣ01492/592856; April–Oct). The YHA **hostel** (Ⓣ0870/770 5774, Ⓦwww.yha.org.uk; dorms £15.50) is on Lark Hill, a ten-minute hike from town up the road to Sychnant Pass, where guests can also hire bikes.

Conwy has relatively few **restaurants**, and on a fine evening you could do worse than fish and chips from *Archway*, 12 Bangor Rd, eaten on The Quay with a pint from the *Liverpool Arms*. Alternatively, eat Italian at *Alfredo's*, Lancaster Square (Ⓣ01492/592381). For something more formal try *Shakespeare's* in the *Castle Hotel* on High Street, easily the finest restaurant in town, with a varied and imaginative a la carte menu, as well as superb Sunday lunch. Good **pubs** are easier to find: try *Ye Olde Mail Coach*, 16 High St, for decent beer and food, or head two miles south on the B5106 to Llanrwst and the fifteenth-century *Groes Inn*, the best pub in the area, which serves excellent bar meals and good cask ales.

Bodnant Garden

Thousands come to Conwy specifically to see **Bodnant Garden** (mid-March to Oct daily 10am–5pm; £7; NT), beside the lower reaches of the Conwy, eight miles to the south. During May and June, the Laburnum Arch flourishes and banks of rhododendrons are in full and glorious bloom all over what ranks as one of the finest formal gardens in Britain. Laid out in 1875 around Bodnant Hall (no public access) by its then-owner, English industrialist Henry Pochin, the garden spreads out over eighty acres of the eastern Conwy Valley. Facing southwest, the bulk of the gardens – divided into an upper terraced garden and lower pinetum and wild garden – catch the late afternoon sun as it sets over the Carneddau range. Though it's arranged so that shrubs and plants provide a blaze of colour throughout the opening season, autumn is a perfect time to be here, with hydrangeas blooming still and fruit trees shedding their leaves. Bus #25 runs here from Llandudno (every 2hr), calling at Llandudno Junction, or it's a two-mile walk from the Tal-y-Cafn train station (request stop) on the Conwy Valley line.

Llandudno

The twin limestone hummocks of the 680-foot **Great Orme** and its southern cousin the Little Orme provide a dramatic frame for the gently curving Victorian frontage of **LLANDUDNO**, four miles north of Conwy. Despite the arrival of more rumbustious fun-seekers to its seaside resort, Llandudno retains an undeniably dignified air while steering clear of retirement-home stagnation.

Llandudno's early history revolves around the Great Orme, where St Tudno, who brought Christianity to the region in the sixth century, built the monastic cell that gives the town its name. In the mid-nineteenth century, local landowner Edward Mostyn exploited the growing craze for sea-bathing and set about a speculative venture to create a seaside resort for the upper-middle classes. Work got under way around 1854 and the town rapidly gained popularity over the next fifty years, becoming synonymous with the Victorian ideal of a respectable resort.

The town and around

First-time visitors are inevitably drawn to Llandudno's nineteenth-century **pier** (open all year; free), one of the few remaining in Wales. It juts out 2220 feet into Llandudno Bay, a leisurely ten-minute stroll along The Promenade from Vaughan Street and the region's premier contemporary art gallery, the **Oriel Mostyn**, 12 Vaughan St (Mon–Sat 10.30am–5.30pm; free; Ⓦwww.mostyn.org), which hosts temporary shows featuring works by artists of international renown. Kids are better entertained at the **Alice in Wonderland Visitor Centre**, 3–4 Trinity Square (April–Oct daily 10am–5pm; Nov–March closed Sun; £3.25; Ⓦwww.wonderland.co.uk), where they are guided through the "Rabbit Hole", full of fibreglass Mad Hatters and March Hares, while a headset treats them to readings of *Jabberwocky* and the like. The *Alice* books were inspired by Lewis Carroll's meeting with one Alice Liddell, the daughter of friends, here in Llandudno.

The view from the top of the **Great Orme** (Pen y Gogarth) ranks with those from the far loftier summits in Snowdonia, combining the seascapes east towards Rhyl and west over the sands of the Conwy Estuary with the brooding, quarry-chewed northern limit of the Carneddau range where Snowdonia crashes into the sea. This huge lump of carboniferous limestone was subject to some of the same stresses that folded Snowdonia, producing fissures filled by molten mineral-bearing rock. A Bronze Age settlement developed around what are now the **Great Orme Copper Mines** (Feb–Oct daily 9.30am–5pm; £6; Ⓣ01492/87047, Ⓦwww.greatormemines.co.uk), accessed via the tramway (see below). Hard hats and miners' lamps are provided for the **guided tour** through just a small portion of the tunnels, enough to get a feel for the cramped working conditions and the dangers of falling rock.

The base of the Great Orme is traditionally circumnavigated on **Marine Drive**, a five-mile anticlockwise circuit from just near Llandudno's pier. The best way to get to the copper mines and the grasslands on top of the Orme is by the San Francisco-style **Great Orme Tramway** (Easter–Oct 10am–6pm; £5.20 return, £3.40 single; Ⓦwww.greatormetramway.com), which creaks up from the bottom of Old Road, much as it has done since 1902.

Practicalities

Llandudno's central **train station** (not to be confused with the mainline Llandudno Junction, three miles south) is at the corner of Augusta and Vaughan streets, five minutes' walk southeast from the **tourist office**, 1–2 Chapel St (Easter–Sept Mon–Sat 9am–5.30pm, Sun 9.30am–4.30pm; Oct–Easter Mon–Sat 9am–5pm; ⓣ01492/876413, ⓦwww.llandudno-tourism.co.uk). Chapel Street runs parallel to Mostyn Street, where local **buses** stop. Less than ten minutes' walk south, National Express **coaches** pull in to the coach park on Mostyn Broadway. **Bike rental** is available from Snowdonia Cycle Hire (ⓣ01492/878771, ⓦwww.snowdoniacyclehire.co.uk) which will deliver and collect bikes within a six-mile radius of Llandudno.

Finding a **place to stay** is not usually a problem, though booking ahead is wise. The cheapest place is the central *Llandudno Hostel*, 14 Charlton St (ⓣ01492/877430; ❶), which has £16 beds and a family room. The greatest concentration of budget places is along St David's Road, just west of the station, where you'll find the excellent-value *Cliffbury Hotel*, 34 St David's Rd (ⓣ01492/877224, ⓔinfo@cliffburyhotel.co.uk; ❷). *No. 9*, 9 Chapel St (ⓣ01492/877251, ⓦwww.no9llandudno.co.uk; ❸), is one of the best-equipped of a string of low-cost hotels just along from the tourist office, while *Plas Madoc*, 60 Church Walks (ⓣ01492/876514, ⓦwww.plasmadocguesthouse.com; ❹), is a superb, tidy guesthouse with great food. The chic, boutique *Escape B&B*, 48 Church Walks (ⓣ01492/877776, ⓦwww.escapebandb.co.uk; ❺), is a classy choice; and there's **camping** at *Dinarth Hall Farm*, Dinarth Hall Road, Rhos-on-Sea (ⓣ01492/548203), three miles east of Llandudno, accessible on buses #14 and #15.

Of the excellent **restaurants**, try *Badgers*, in the Victoria Centre on Mostyn Street, a cut above the average lunch spot, or the basement bistro at *Seahorse*, 7 Church Walks, which dishes up delicious meals, particularly local seafood. For substantial, tasty bar food, there's the *Cottage Loaf*, Market Street, a flag-floored **pub** built from old ships' timbers, or the excellent, lively *King's Head*, on Old Road, the oldest pub in town, where Edward Mostyn and his surveyor mapped out the town. For sheer raucous drinking, the bars along Upper Mostyn Street are generally full and extremely lively.

Bodelwyddan to Holywell

Visitors in a hurry might be tempted to hurtle along the A55 between Llandudno and the English border without stopping. Certainly it is one of the least appealing stretches of Welsh coastline, with its mile upon mile of caravan parks and amusement arcades, but a handful of sights just inland each warrant breaking the journey briefly.

Aficionados of nineteenth-century portraiture won't want to miss the works on display at **Bodelwyddan**, which is just a short hop from **St Asaph**. Castle buffs should then head north to **Rhuddlan**, while those of an ecclesiastical bent will be happier at **Holywell**, a site of pilgrimage since the seventh century.

Bodelwyddan Castle: the National Portrait Gallery

The finest art showcase in North Wales is **Bodelwyddan Castle** (late July to early Sept daily 10.30am–5pm; late March to late July & early Sept to Oct daily except Fri 10.30am–5pm; Nov–March Thurs 9.30am–5pm, Sat & Sun 10.30am–4pm; £5, gardens £2; ⓦwww.bodelwyddan-castle.co.uk), an outpost of the National Portrait Gallery some eighteen miles east of Conwy. The opulent Victorian interiors of what is essentially a nineteenth-century mansion provide a suitable setting for hundreds of paintings by the likes of Millais,

Rossetti, Browning, John Singer Sargent and Landseer. Look out for two sensitive portraits highlighting the Pre-Raphaelite movement's support for social reform: William Holman Hunt's portrayal of the vociferous opponent of slavery and capital punishment, Stephen Lushington; Ford Madox Brown's double portrait of Henry Farell, prime mover in the passing of the 1867 Reform Bill, and suffragette Millicent Garrett.

St Asaph

The tiny city of **ST ASAPH** (Llanelwy), two miles east of Bodelwyddan, is centred on Britain's smallest **cathedral** (Mon–Sat 9am–6.30pm, Sun 7.30am–4.30pm; free), no bigger than many village churches. It was founded around 570 by St Kentigern, the patron saint of Glasgow, and takes its name from the succeeding bishop, St Asaph. Both are commemorated in the easternmost window in the north aisle. From 1601 until his death in 1604, the bishopric was held by **William Morgan**, who was responsible for the translation of the first Welsh-language Bible in 1588. This version replaced the English ones used up until that time and was so successful that the Privy Council decreed that a copy of Y Beibl should be allocated to every Welsh church, thereby setting a standard for prose and codifying the language. Without his efforts, many claim, Welsh would have died out. A thousand Morgan Bibles were printed, of which only nineteen remain, one of them displayed in the south aisle along with notable prayer books and psalters.

The cathedral is perfect for a quick visit between **buses**, which stop outside.

Rhuddlan Castle

Rhuddlan Castle (Easter–Sept daily 10am–5pm; £2.90; CADW) lies two miles north of St Asaph in what is effectively an insignificant suburb of the coastal resort of Rhyl. Built between 1277 and 1282 as a garrison and royal residence for Edward I, the impressive castle commands a canalized section of the river protected by **Gillot's Tower**. Behind, the castle's massive towers were the work of James of St George, who was responsible for the concentric plan that allowed archers on both outer and inner walls to fire simultaneously. Important though the castle was, Rhuddlan earns its position in history as the place where Edward I signed the **Statute of Rhuddlan** on March 19, 1284, consigning Wales to centuries of subjugation by the English. An unintentionally ironic plaque in Rhuddlan's main street details the terms of the statute.

Holywell

A place of pilgrimage for thirteen hundred years, **HOLYWELL** (Treffynnon), just off the A55 ten miles east of St Asaph, comes billed as "The Lourdes of Wales" – but without the tacky souvenir stalls. The cause of all the fuss is **St Winefride's Well** (daily: April–Sept 9am–5.30pm; Oct–March 10am–4pm; 60p), a calm pool capacious enough to accommodate the dozens of the faithful who dutifully wade through the waters three times in the hope of curing their ailments, a relic of the Celtic baptism by triple immersion. The spring was first noted by the Romans, who used the waters to relieve rheumatism and gout. The traditional legend, however, states that in around 660, the virtuous Winefride (Gwenfrewi in Welsh) was decapitated here after resisting the amorous advances of Prince Caradoc; the well is said to have sprung up at the spot where her head fell. Richard I and Henry V provided regal patronage, ensuring a steady flow of believers to what became one of the great shrines of Christendom, and James II came here to pray for a son and heir. **St Winefride's Chapel** (key from the ticket office; CADW), built around 1500, encloses three sides of the well. On St Winefride's Day (the nearest Sunday to June 22), a couple of thousand pilgrims are led through the streets behind a relic, part of Winefride's thumb-bone.

Frequent **buses** between Rhyl and Chester stop at the bus station, from where it is a ten-minute walk along High Street to the well.

Travel details

Buses

For information on all local and national bus services, contact Traveline ⓣ0871/200 2233, ⓦwww.traveline-cymru.org.uk.

Aberdaron to: Pwllheli (3 daily; 40min).
Abersoch to: Pwllheli (1 daily; 15min).
Bala to: Dolgellau (8 daily; 35min); Llangollen (8 daily; 1hr).
Bangor to: Beaumaris (every 30min; 30min); Betws-y-Coed (1 daily; 1hr 25min); Caernarfon (every 20min; 30min); Conwy (every 10min; 40min); Holyhead (every 30min; 1hr 25min); Llanberis (hourly; 30–60min); Llandudno (every 10min; 1hr).
Beaumaris to: Bangor (every 30min; 30min).
Beddgelert to: Caernarfon (10 daily; at least 1hr 30min with one change); Pen-y-Pass (5 daily; 20min); Porthmadog (10 daily; 25min).
Betws-y-Coed to: Bangor (at least hourly; 50min–1hr 25min with one change); Capel Curig (every 30min; 10min); Llanrwst (roughly hourly; 10min); Penmachno (8 daily; 10min); Pen-y-Pass (every 2hr; 20min).
Blaenau Ffestiniog to: Caernarfon (roughly hourly; 1hr 30min); Harlech (4 daily; 40min); Porthmadog (every 15min; 30min).
Caernarfon to: Bangor (every 20min; 20min); Beddgelert (8 daily; 30min); Blaenau Ffestiniog (roughly hourly; 1hr 30min); Criccieth (at least hourly; 45min); Llanberis (every 30min; 25min); Porthmadog (hourly; 50min); Pwllheli (hourly; 45min).
Capel Curig to: Betws-y-Coed (every 30min; 10min); Idwal Cottage (6 daily; 10min); Pen-y-Pass (hourly; 10min).
Conwy to: Bangor (every 15min; 45min); Llandudno (at least every 30min; 20min); Llanrwst (every 30min; 40min).
Criccieth to: Caernarfon (5 daily; 40min); Llanystumdwy (every 30min; 5min); Porthmadog (every 30min; 15min); Pwllheli (every 30min; 25min).
Holyhead to: Bangor (every 30min; 1hr 15min); Llanfairpwll (every 30min; 1hr).
Llanberis to: Bangor (1 daily; 40min); Caernarfon (1 daily; 25min); Pen-y-Pass (every 30min; 15min).
Llandudno to: Bangor (every 30min; 1hr); Conwy (every 30min; 20min); Llanrwst (every 30min; 1hr); Rhyl (every 15min; 1hr).
Llanfairpwll to: Bangor (every 30min; 15min); Holyhead (every 30min; 1hr).
Llangollen to: Bala (8 daily; 1hr); Chirk (8 daily; 20min); Wrexham (every 15min; 30min).
Pen-y-Pass to: Beddgelert (6 daily; 20min); Betws-y-Coed (hourly; 20min); Capel Curig (hourly; 10min); Llanberis (every 30min; 15min).
Porthmadog to: Beddgelert (9 daily; 25min); Blaenau Ffestiniog (hourly; 30min); Caernarfon (at least hourly; 50min); Criccieth (every 30min; 15min); Dolgellau (8 daily; 50min); Pwllheli (every 30min; 35min).
Pwllheli to: Aberdaron (8 daily; 40min); Abersoch (1 daily; 15min); Caernarfon (at least hourly; 45min); Chester (1 daily; 4hr); Cricieth (every 30min; 25min); Nefyn (roughly hourly; 15min); Porthmadog (every 30min; 35min).
Wrexham to: Chester (every 10min; 45min); Chirk (every 30min; 40min); Llangollen (every 15min; 40min).

Trains

For information on all local and national rail services, contact National Rail Enquiries ⓣ08457/484950, ⓦwww.nationalrail.co.uk.

Bangor to: Chester (at least hourly; 1hr 15min); Colwyn Bay (20 daily; 25min); Conwy (14 daily; 20min); Holyhead (20 daily; 30–40min); Llandudno Junction (27 daily; 20min); Llanfairpwll (8 daily; 10min).
Betws-y-Coed to: Blaenau Ffestiniog (6 daily; 25min); Llandudno Junction (6 daily; 30min).
Blaenau Ffestiniog to: Betws-y-Coed (6 daily 25min); Llandudno Junction (6 daily; 1hr); Porthmadog by Ffestiniog Railway (April–Oct 4–8 daily; 1hr).
Conwy to: Bangor (14 daily; 20min); Holyhead (at least hourly; 1hr); Llandudno Junction (14 daily; 3min).

Criccieth to: Barmouth (7 daily; 55min); Machynlleth (7 daily; 1hr 45min); Porthmadog (7 daily; 10min); Pwllheli (7 daily; 15min).
Holyhead to: Bangor (20 daily; 30–40min); Chester (20 daily; 1hr 40min); Llandudno Junction (20 daily; 50min); Llanfairpwll (7 daily; 30min).
Llandudno to: Betws-y-Coed (6 daily; 40min); Blaenau Ffestiniog (6 daily; 1hr 10min); Llandudno Junction (mainly every 30min; 10min).
Llandudno Junction to: Bangor (27 daily; 20min); Betws-y-Coed (6 daily; 30min); Holyhead (17 daily; 1hr).
Llanfairpwll to: Bangor (8 daily; 10min); Holyhead (7 daily; 30min).
Porthmadog to: Barmouth (6 daily; 45min); Blaenau Ffestiniog by Ffestiniog Railway (Easter–Oct 4–8 daily; 1hr); Harlech (8 daily; 30min); Machynlleth (8 daily; 2hr); Pwllheli (8 daily; 25min).
Pwllheli to: Criccieth (7 daily; 15min); Machynlleth (8 daily; 2hr 20min); Porthmadog (8 daily; 25min).
Wrexham to: Liverpool (change at Bidston; every 30min; 1hr 15min).

Scotland

Scotland

Edinburgh and the Lothians

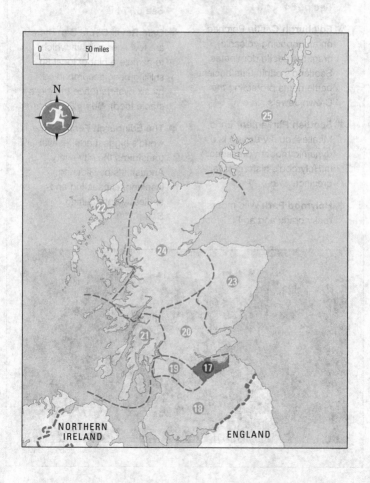

0 50 miles

N

25

22

24

23

21

20

19

17

18

NORTHERN IRELAND

ENGLAND

CHAPTER 17

Highlights

* **The Old Town** The evocative heart of the historic city, with its tenements, closes, courtyards, ghosts and catacombs cheek-by-jowl with many of Scotland's most important buildings. See p.764

* **Edinburgh Castle** Perched on an imposing volcanic crag, the castle dominates Scotland's capital, its ancient battlements protecting the Crown Jewels. See p.764

* **Scottish Parliament** Enric Miralles' quirky design is a dynamic modern presence in Holyrood's historic royal precinct. See p.771

* **Holyrood Park** Wild moors, rocky crags and an 800-foot peak (Arthur's Seat), all slap in the middle of the city. See p.772

* **Museum of Scotland** The treasures of Scotland's past housed in a dynamic and superbly conceived building. See p.774

* **Café Royal Circle Bar** There are few finer pubs in which to sample a pint of local 80 shilling beer, accompanied by six oysters (once the city's staple food). See p.786

* **The Edinburgh Festival** The world's biggest arts festival transforms the city every August: it's bewildering, inspiring, exhausting and endlessly entertaining. See p.789

▲ Edinburgh Castle

Edinburgh and the Lothians

Venerable, dramatic **EDINBURGH**, the showcase capital of Scotland, is a historic, cosmopolitan and cultured city. The setting is wonderfully striking: perched on a series of extinct volcanoes and rocky crags which rise from the generally flat landscape of the Lothians, with the sheltered shoreline of the Firth of Forth to the north. "My own Romantic town", Sir Walter Scott called it, although it was another native author, Robert Louis Stevenson, who perhaps best captured the feel of his "precipitous city", declaring that "No situation could be more commanding for the head of a kingdom; none better chosen for noble prospects".

The centre has two distinct parts, divided by **Princes Street Gardens**, which run roughly east–west under the shadow of **Edinburgh Castle**, in the very heart of the city. To the north, the dignified, Grecian-style **New Town** was laid out in the eighteenth century, after the announcement of a plan to improve conditions in the city. The **Old Town**, on the other hand, with its tortuous alleys and tightly packed closes, is unrelentingly medieval, associated in popular imagination with the city's underworld lore of body snatchers Burke and Hare and of schizophrenic Deacon Brodie, inspiration for Stevenson's *Strange Case of Dr Jekyll and Mr Hyde*. Indeed, Edinburgh's ability to capture the literary imagination has recently seen it dubbed a "World City of Literature" by **UNESCO**, the same organization which previously conferred World Heritage Site status on a large section of the centre covering both Old and New towns.

Set on the hill which sweeps down from the fairy-tale castle to the royal **Palace of Holyroodhouse**, the Old Town preserves all the key reminders of its role as a historic capital, augmented now by the dramatic and unusual new **Scottish Parliament building**, opposite the palace. A few hundred yards away, a tantalizing glimpse of the wild beauty of Scotland's scenery can be had in **Holyrood Park**, an extensive area of open countryside dominated by **Arthur's Seat**, the largest and most impressive of the volcanoes.

In August and early September, around a million visitors flock to the city for the **Edinburgh Festival**, which is in fact a series of separate festivals that make up the largest arts extravaganza in the world. Among Edinburgh's many museums, the exciting **National Museum of Scotland** houses 10,000 of Scotland's most precious artefacts, while the **National Gallery of Scotland**

and its offshoot, the **Scottish National Gallery of Modern Art**, house two of Britain's finest collections of paintings.

Beyond the centre, Edinburgh's liveliest area is **Leith**, the city's medieval port, whose seedy edge is softened by a series of great bars and upmarket seafood restaurants, along with the presence of the former royal yacht **Britannia**, open to visitors. The wider rural surroundings of Edinburgh, known as the **Lothians**, mix rolling countryside and attractive country towns with some impressive historic ruins.

Some history

The name Edinburgh – in its early forms of Dunedin or Din Eidyn ("fort of Eidyn") – first appeared during the **Dark Ages**. A strategic fort atop the Castle Rock volcano served as the nation's **southernmost border post** until 1018, when King Malcolm I established the River Tweed as the permanent frontier. During the reign of Malcolm Canmore in the late eleventh century, the castle became one of the main seats of the court, and the town, which was given privileged status as a **royal burgh**, began to grow. In 1128 King David established Holyrood Abbey at the foot of the slope, later allowing its monks to found a separate burgh, known as **Canongate**.

Under King James IV, the city enjoyed a short but brilliant **Renaissance era**, which saw not only the construction of a new palace alongside Holyrood Abbey, but also the granting of a **royal charter** to the College of Surgeons, the earliest in the city's long line of academic and professional bodies. This period came to an abrupt end in 1513 with the calamitous defeat by the English at the Battle of Flodden leading to several decades of political instability. In the 1540s, King Henry VIII's attempt to force a royal union with Scotland led to the sack of Edinburgh, prompting the Scots to turn to France: French troops arrived to defend the city, while the young queen Mary was dispatched to Paris as the promised bride of the Dauphin, later Francois II of France. While the French occupiers succeeded in removing the English threat, they themselves antagonized the locals, who had become increasingly sympathetic to the ideals of the **Reformation**. When the radical preacher John Knox returned from exile in 1555, he quickly won over the city to his Calvinist message.

James VI's rule saw the foundation of the University of Edinburgh in 1582, but following the **Union of the Crowns** in 1603 the city was totally upstaged by London: although James promised to visit every three years, it was not until 1617 that he made his only return trip. The **Union of the Parliaments** of 1707 dealt a further blow to Edinburgh's political prestige, though the guaranteed preservation of the national church and the legal and educational systems ensured that it was never relegated to a purely provincial role. On the contrary, it was in the second half of the eighteenth century that Edinburgh achieved the height of its intellectual influence. Around the same time, the city began to expand beyond its medieval boundaries, laying out the **New Town**, a masterpiece of the Neoclassical style.

Industrialization affected Edinburgh less than any other major city in the nation, and it never lost its white-collar character. Nevertheless, the city underwent an enormous **urban expansion** in the course of the nineteenth century, annexing, among many other small burghs, the large port of **Leith**.

In 1947 Edinburgh was chosen to host the great **International Festival** which served as a symbol of the new peaceful European order; despite some hiccups, it has flourished ever since, in the process helping to make tourism a mainstay of the local economy. In 1979, an inconclusive referendum on Scottish devolution delayed Edinburgh's revival of its role as a governmental capital, and

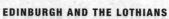

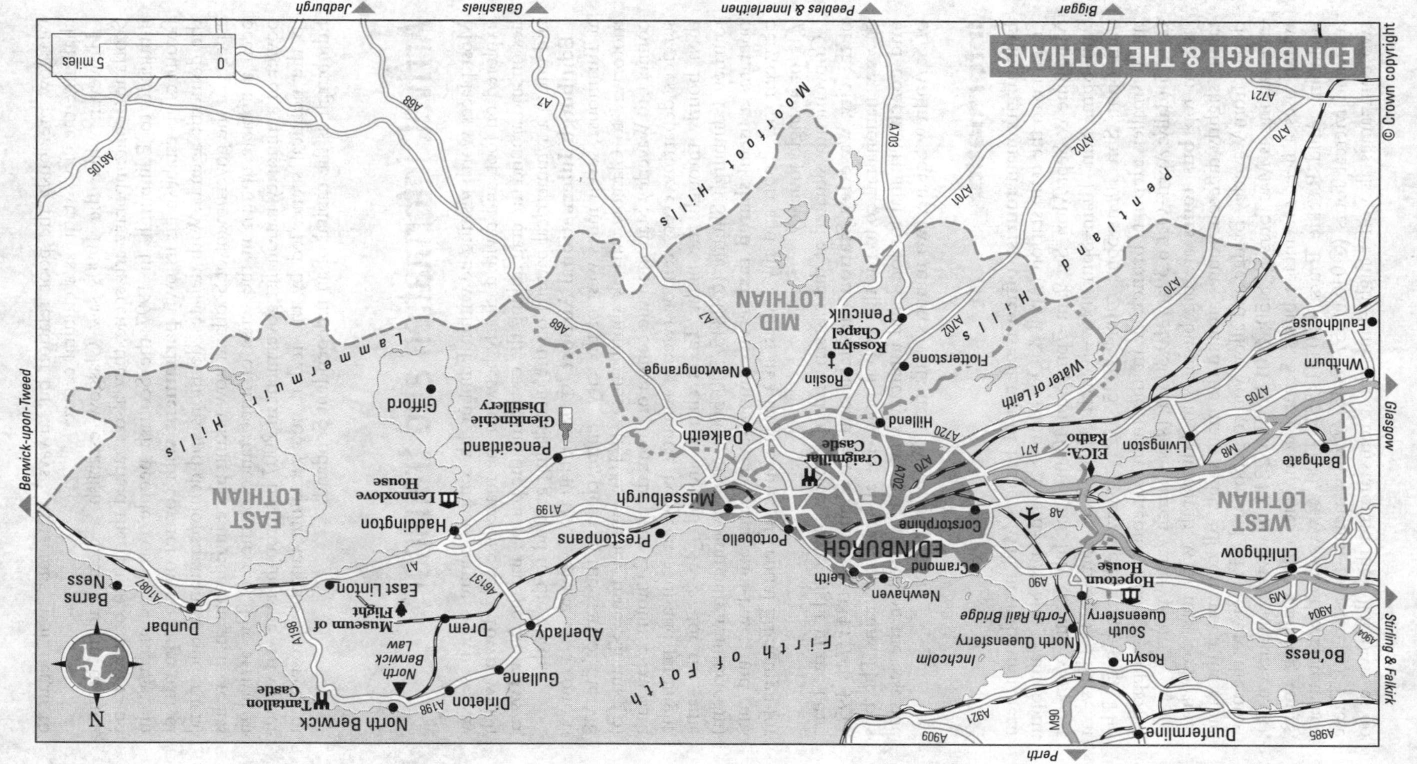
EDINBURGH & THE LOTHIANS
Berwick-upon-Tweed
Jedburgh
Galashiels
Peebles & Innerleithen
Biggar
Glasgow
Stirling & Falkirk
Perth
N
0
5 miles
North Berwick
Tantallon Castle
North Berwick Law
Dirleton
Gullane
Drem
Museum of Flight
East Linton
Dunbar
Barns Ness
Aberlady
Haddington
Lennoxlove House
EAST LOTHIAN
Lammermuir Hills
Gifford
Pencaitland
Glenkinchie Distillery
Prestonpans
Musselburgh
Portobello
Dalkeith
Newtongrange
Moorfoot Hills
MID LOTHIAN
Craigmillar Castle
Roslin
Rosslyn Chapel
Penicuik
Hillend
Flotterstone
Pentland Hills
Water of Leith
Firth of Forth
EDINBURGH
Leith
Newhaven
Cramond
Corstorphine
EICA: Ratho
Inchcolm
North Queensferry
Forth Rail Bridge
South Queensferry
Hopetoun House
Rosyth
Dunfermline
Bo'ness
Linlithgow
WEST LOTHIAN
Livingston
Bathgate
Whitburn
Fauldhouse
A1
A198
A1087
A6137
A199
A68
A7
A6105
A703
A701
A702
A720
A70
A71
A8
A90
A721
A705
M8
M9
A904
A985
A909
A921
M90
© Crown copyright

Glasgow, previously the poor relation but always a tenacious rival, began to challenge the city's status as a cultural centre.

However, while the 1990s saw Glasgow establish a clear lead in driving Scotland's contemporary arts scene, they also marked the return of power and influence to Edinburgh. In 1997 the Scottish people voted resoundingly in favour of re-establishing its own **parliament** with control over a large part of the domestic agenda. With debates, decisions and demonstrations about crucial aspects of the government of Scotland now taking place in Edinburgh, there has been a notable upturn in the sense of importance of the city. The arrival in power of a minority nationalist goverment in 2007 has brought renewed vigour to the political scene, led by the real if not yet quite tangible prospect of Edinburgh as the capital of an independent Scotland.

Arrival, information and transport

Most places worth visiting lie within Edinburgh's compact centre, which is easily explored on foot, and divided clearly between the maze-like **Old Town**, which lies on and around the crag linking the castle and the palace, and the **New Town**, laid out in a symmetrical pattern on the undulating ground to the north.

Edinburgh International Airport (Ⓣ0870/040 0007, Ⓦwww.baa.com) is at Turnhouse, seven miles west of the city centre, close to the start of the M8 motorway to Glasgow. Airlink shuttle buses (#100; journey time 30min; £3) connect to Waverley Station in the centre of town; they run 24 hours a day, with services departing every ten or twenty minutes between 5am and midnight, then hourly through the night. **Taxis** charge around £15-20 for the same journey. Edinburgh Shuttle (Ⓣ0845/500 5000; Ⓦwww.edinburghshuttle.com) operates a useful **shared taxi** service using seven-seater mini-buses, and runs between the airport and any address in a large chunk of central Edinburgh for £8 for a single journey.

Conveniently situated at the eastern end of Princes Street right in the heart of the city, **Waverley Station** (timetable and fare enquiries Ⓣ0845/748 4950, Ⓦwww.nationalrail.co.uk) is the arrival point for all mainline trains. The **bus and coach** terminal for local and intercity services is located on the east side of St Andrew Square, two minutes' walk from Waverley Station.

Information

Edinburgh's main **tourist office** is on top of Princes Mall near the northern entrance to the train station (April & Oct Mon–Sat 9am–6pm, Sun 10am–6pm; May, June & Sept Mon–Sat 9am–7pm, Sun 10am–7pm; July & Aug Mon–Sat 9am–8pm, Sun 10am–8pm; Nov–March Mon–Wed 9am–5pm, Thurs–Sat 9am–6pm, Sun 10am–5pm; Ⓣ0845/225 5121, Ⓦwww.edinburgh.org). The much smaller **airport branch** is in the main concourse, directly opposite Gate 5 (daily: April–Oct 6.30am–10.30pm; Nov–March 7am–9pm).

Open-top **bus tours** are big business in Edinburgh, with four companies taking slightly different routes around the main sights. All cost much the same, depart from Waverley Bridge and allow you to get on and off at leisure: the most entertaining is MacTours (£8.50; Ⓣ0131/556 2244, Ⓦwww.mactours.co.uk), which uses a fleet of vintage buses. Several companies offer **walking tours**, including Auld Reekie Tours (Ⓣ0131/557 4700, Ⓦwww.auldreekietours.co.uk) and Mercat Tours (Ⓣ0131/557 5445, Ⓦwww.mercat-tours.co.uk). These two companies also offer night-time ghost tours around the Old Town, as do the enjoyable Witchery Tours (Ⓣ0131/225 6745, Ⓦwww.witcherytours.com) and the spine-tingling City of the Dead graveyard tour (Ⓣ0131/225 9044, Ⓦwww.blackhart.uk.com).

City transport

Most of Edinburgh's **public transport** services terminate on or near Princes Street. The city is generally well served by **buses**; the white and maroon Lothian Buses provide the most frequent and comprehensive coverage of the city (timetables and passes from offices on Waverley Bridge, Shandwick Place or Hanover Street; Ⓣ0131/555 6363, Ⓦwww.lothianbuses.co.uk), and all buses referred to in the text are run by Lothian unless otherwise stated. Usefully, every bus stop displays diagrams indicating which services pass by and the routes they take; some also have digital displays indicating when buses are next due.

It is emphatically not a good idea to take a **car** into central Edinburgh; despite the presence of several expensive multistorey car parks, finding somewhere to park involves long and often fruitless searches. In addition, Edinburgh's street parking restrictions are famously draconian: illegally parked cars are very likely to be fined £60 by one of the swarms of inspectors who patrol day and night.

Accommodation

Edinburgh has a greater choice of **accommodation** than anywhere else in Britain outside London. **Hotels** (and large backpacker **hostels**) are essentially the only options you'll find right in the heart of the city, but within relatively easy reach of the centre, the selection of **guesthouses**, **B&Bs**, **campus accommodation** and even **campsites** broadens considerably.

Prices are significantly higher than elsewhere in Scotland, with double rooms starting at £60 per night. Budget hotel chains offer the best value for basic accommodation right in the centre. It's worth making advance **reservations** at any time of year, though it's essential for stays during the Festival and around Hogmanay when places often get booked out months ahead. The tourist board operates an accommodation booking service (Ⓣ0845/2255 121, Ⓦwww.visitscotland.com): the £3 fee is waived if you book online.

Hotels and guesthouses

The abundance of hotels in the city centre means that you can often find good deals in quieter periods, and it's always worth looking out for special offers advertised by all the chains. Generally offering much better value for money and a far more homely experience are Edinburgh's vast range of **guesthouses**, **small hotels** and **bed and breakfast** establishments, many located on the edges of the New Town and the inner suburbs of Bruntsfield and the Grange.

Old Town

Ibis Edinburgh Centre 6 Hunter Square Ⓣ0131/240 7000, Ⓦwww.accorhotels.com. Probably the best-located chain hotel cheapie in the Old Town, within sight of the Royal Mile; rooms are modern and inexpensive, but there are few facilities other than a rather plain bar. 6

Point Hotel 34–59 Bread St Ⓣ0131/221 5555, Ⓦwww.point-hotel.co.uk. This former department store is one of Edinburgh's most stylish and individual modern hotels; some rooms have fantastic views of the castle. There's also a popular cocktail bar and a decent restaurant at street level. 6

The Scotsman Hotel 20 North Bridge Ⓣ0131/556 5565, Ⓦwww.thescotsmanhotel.co.uk. Occupying the grand old offices of the *Scotsman* newspaper, this plush but non-stuffy establishment is one of

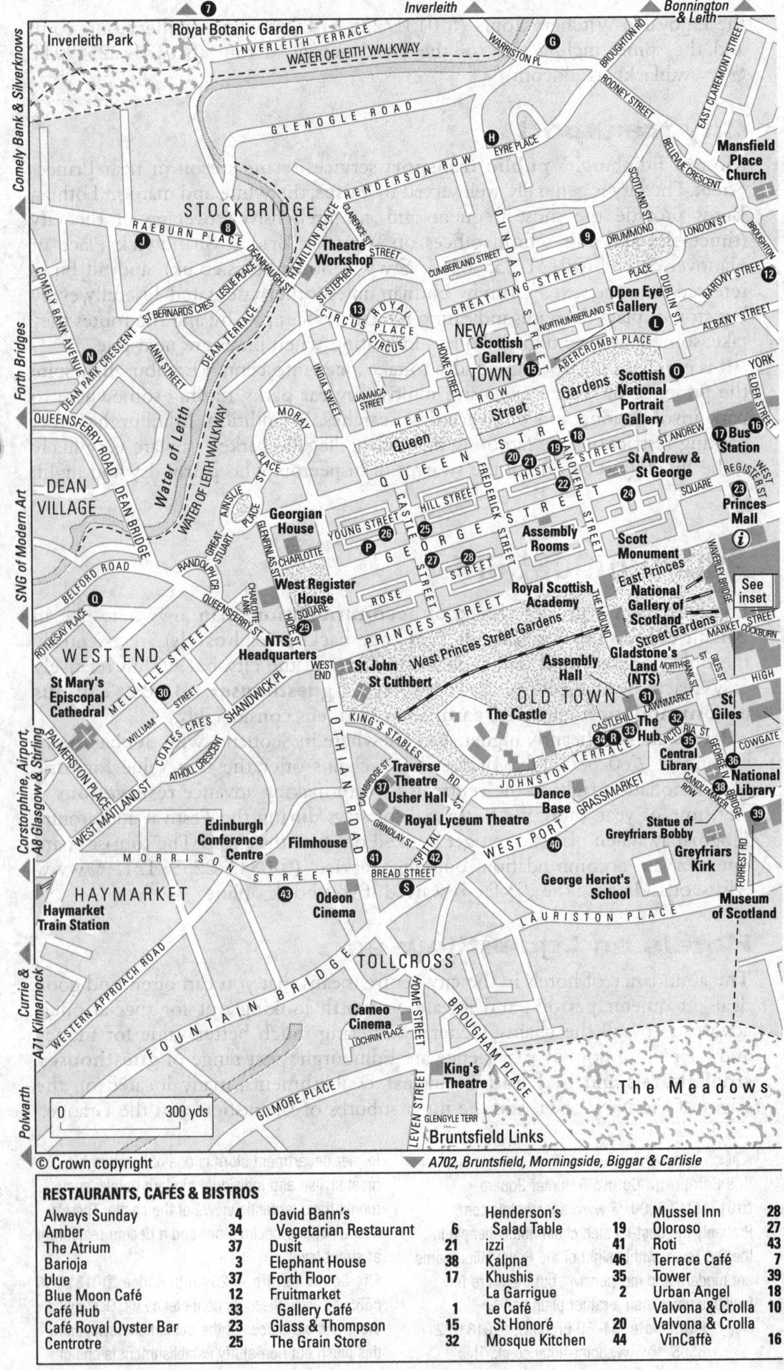

RESTAURANTS, CAFÉS & BISTROS

Always Sunday	4	David Bann's Vegetarian Restaurant	6	Henderson's Salad Table	19	Mussel Inn	28
Amber	34	Dusit	21	izzi	41	Oloroso	27
The Atrium	37	Elephant House	38	Kalpna	46	Roti	43
Barioja	3	Forth Floor	17	Khushis	35	Terrace Café	7
blue	37	Fruitmarket Gallery Café	1	La Garrigue	2	Tower	39
Blue Moon Café	12	Glass & Thompson	15	Le Café St Honoré	20	Urban Angel	18
Café Hub	33	The Grain Store	32	Mosque Kitchen	44	Valvona & Crolla	10
Café Royal Oyster Bar	23					Valvona & Crolla VinCaffè	16
Centrotre	25						

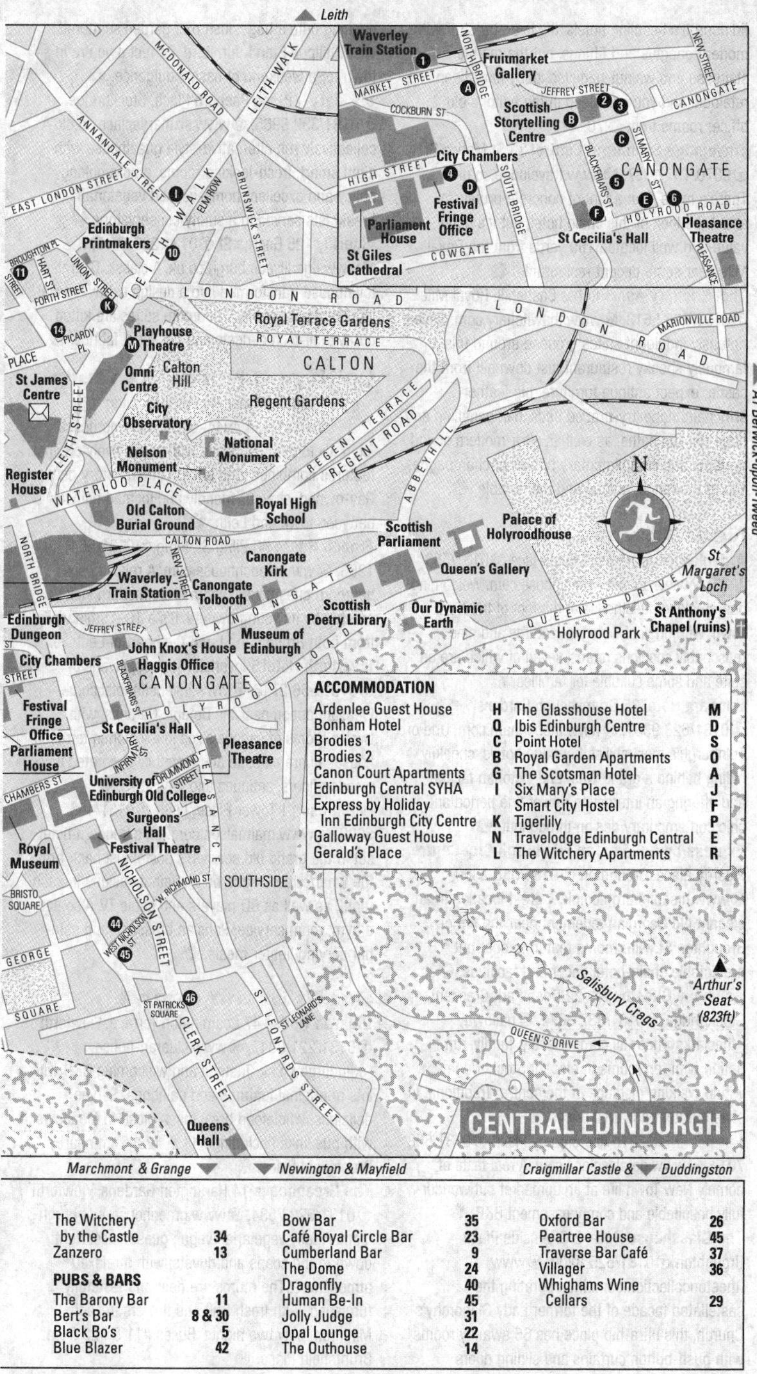

CENTRAL EDINBURGH
Leith
Marchmont & Grange
Newington & Mayfield
Craigmillar Castle & Duddingston
A1 Berwick-upon-Tweed
Waverley Train Station
Fruitmarket Gallery
Scottish Storytelling Centre
City Chambers
Festival Fringe Office
Parliament House
St Giles Cathedral
CANONGATE
Pleasance Theatre
St Cecilia's Hall
Edinburgh Printmakers
Royal Terrace Gardens
Playhouse Theatre
CALTON
St James Centre
Omni Centre
Calton Hill
Regent Gardens
City Observatory
Nelson Monument
National Monument
Register House
Old Calton Burial Ground
Royal High School
Scottish Parliament
Palace of Holyroodhouse
Canongate Kirk
Queen's Gallery
Canongate Tolbooth
St Margaret's Loch
Edinburgh Dungeon
Scottish Poetry Library
Our Dynamic Earth
Holyrood Park
St Anthony's Chapel (ruins)
John Knox's House
Museum of Edinburgh
Haggis Office
University of Edinburgh Old College
Surgeons' Hall
Festival Theatre
Royal Museum
SOUTHSIDE
Salisbury Crags
Arthur's Seat (823ft)
Queens Hall
ACCOMMODATION
Ardenlee Guest House H
Bonham Hotel Q
Brodies 1 C
Brodies 2 B
Canon Court Apartments G
Edinburgh Central SYHA I
Express by Holiday Inn Edinburgh City Centre K
Galloway Guest House N
Gerald's Place L
The Glasshouse Hotel M
Ibis Edinburgh Centre D
Point Hotel S
Royal Garden Apartments O
The Scotsman Hotel A
Six Mary's Place J
Smart City Hostel F
Tigerlily P
Travelodge Edinburgh Central E
The Witchery Apartments R
The Witchery by the Castle 34
Zanzero 13
PUBS & BARS
The Barony Bar 11
Bert's Bar 8 & 30
Black Bo's 5
Blue Blazer 42
Bow Bar 35
Café Royal Circle Bar 23
Cumberland Bar 9
The Dome 24
Dragonfly 40
Human Be-In 45
Jolly Judge 31
Opal Lounge 22
The Outhouse 14
Oxford Bar 26
Peartree House 45
Traverse Bar Café 37
Villager 36
Whighams Wine Cellars 29

Edinburgh's headline hotels. It's five-star stuff with modern gadgets and fittings, but the marble staircase and walnut-panelled lobby have been retained, and you can sleep in the editor's old office; rooms from £270. 9

Travelodge Edinburgh Central 33 St Mary's St ⓣ0870/191 1637, ⓦwww.travelodge.co.uk. There's more than a hint of concrete brutalism about the look of this chain hotel, but it's good value and well located,100 yards from the Royal Mile near some decent restaurants. 5

The Witchery Apartments Castlehill, Royal Mile ⓣ0131/225 5613, ⓦwww.thewitchery.com. Seven riotously indulgent suites grouped around this famously spooky restaurant just downhill from the castle; expect antique furniture, big leather armchairs, tapestry-draped beds, oak panelling and huge roll-top baths, as well as ultra-modern sound systems and complimentary bottles of champagne. Top of the range, unique and memorable. 9

New Town

Ardenlee Guesthouse 9 Eyre Place ⓣ0131/556 2838, ⓦwww.ardenleeguesthouse.com. Welcoming non-smoking guesthouse at the foot of the New Town, with original Victorian features and nine reasonably spacious rooms, seven of which are en suite and some suitable for families. 4

Bonham Hotel 35 Drumsheugh Gardens ⓣ0131/623 9301, ⓦwww.thebonham.com. One of Edinburgh's most stylish boutique hotels, cheekily hiding behind a grand West End Victorian facade and offering an interesting mix of fine period and chic contemporary design throughout. 7

Express by Holiday Inn Edinburgh City Centre Picardy Place, Broughton ⓣ0131/558 2300, ⓦwww.hieedinburgh.co.uk. A great location in an elegant old Georgian tenement near the top of Broughton St, with rooms featuring neat but predictable chain-hotel decor and facilities. 6

Galloway Guesthouse 22 Dean Park Crescent, Stockbridge ⓣ0131/332 3672, ⓔgalloway_theclarks@hotmail.com. Friendly, family-run option with ten rooms in elegant Stockbridge, within walking distance of the centre. Traditional in style but neat and well priced. 3

Gerald's Place 21b Abercromby Place ⓣ0131/558 7017, ⓦwww.geraldsplace.com. A real taste of homely New Town life at an upmarket but wonderfully hospitable and comfy basement B&B. 6

The Glasshouse Hotel 2 Greenside Place, Broughton ⓣ0131/525 8200, ⓦwww.theetoncollection.com. Incorporating the castellated facade of the former Lady Glenorchy's Church, this ultra-hip place has 65 swanky rooms with push-button curtains and sliding doors opening onto a huge, lush roof garden scattered with Philippe Starck furniture. Perfect if you're in town for a weekend of flash indulgence. 8

Six Mary's Place Raeburn Place, Stockbridge ⓣ0131/332 8965, ⓦwww.sixmarysplace.co.uk. A collectively run alternative-style guesthouse with eight smart, fresh-looking rooms, a no-smoking policy and excellent home-cooked vegetarian breakfasts served in a sunny conservatory. 5

Tigerlily 125 George St ⓣ0131 225 5005, ⓦwww.tigerlilyedinburgh.co.uk. A classic Georgian townhouse transformed into a design extravaganza; indulgent pink or black bedroom suites are kitted out with hi-tech gadgets and decadent fabrics. 8

Leith and North Edinburgh

Ardmor House 74 Pilrig St, Pilrig ⓣ0131/554 4944, ⓦwww.ardmorhouse.com. Victorian townhouse with some lovely original features combined with smart contemporary decor. Gay-owned, straight-friendly and located halfway between town and Leith. 5

Fraoch House 66 Pilrig St, Pilrig ⓣ0131/554 1353, ⓦwww.fraochhouse.com. A relaxing six-bedroom guesthouse with a slick, modern look created by its young owners. It's a 10–15min walk from both Broughton St and the heart of Leith. 5

Inverleith Hotel 5 Inverleith Terrace, Inverleith ⓣ0131/556 2745, ⓦwww.inverleithhotel.co.uk. Pleasant option near the Botanic Gardens, with twelve rooms of various sizes in a Victorian terraced house; all are en suite and tastefully decorated with wooden floors, antiques and tapestries. 6

Malmaison 1 Tower Place, Leith ⓣ0131/468 5000, ⓦwww.malmaison.com. Chic, modern hotel set in the grand old seamen's hostel just back from the wharf-side. Bright, bold original designs in each room, as well as CD players and cable TV. Also has a gym, room service, Parisian brasserie and café-bar serving lighter meals. 6

South of the centre

Cluaran House 47 Leamington Terrace, Viewforth ⓣ0131/221 0047, ⓦwww.cluaran-house-edinburgh.co.uk. Tasteful and welcoming B&B with lots of original features and paintings. Serves delicious, wholefood breakfasts. Close to Meadows with bus links (including #11 & #23) from nearby Bruntsfield Place. 5

The Greenhouse 14 Hartington Gardens, Viewforth ⓣ0131/622 7634, ⓦwww.greenhouse-edinburgh.com. A fully vegetarian/vegan guesthouse, right down to the soaps and duvets, with a relaxed atmosphere. The rooms are neat and tastefully furnished, with fresh fruit and flowers in each. Minimum stay two nights. Buses #11 & #23 from Bruntsfield Place. 5

MW Guesthouse 94 Dalkeith Rd, Newington ⓣ0131/662 9265, ⓦwww.mwguesthouse.co.uk. One of only a few guesthouses in town with a fresh, contemporary design – think muted tones and blonde wood. As it's set in a Victorian villa, every room is a bit different: those at the back are quieter. If you're driving, the public parking here is easier than some other Southside choices. ⑤

Prestonfield Priestfield Rd, Mayfield ⓣ0131/225 7800, ⓦwww.prestonfield.com. This seventeenth-century mansion, set in its own park below Arthur's Seat, is run by the *Witchery* team (see opposite), and its extravagant baroque decor has helped make it one of Edinburgh's most lavish and over-the-top places to stay. ⑧

Hostels, self-catering apartments and campus accommodation

Edinburgh is one of the UK's most popular backpacker destinations, and there are a large number of hostels in and around the city centre, ranging in size, atmosphere and quality. Custom-built **self-catering serviced apartments** with no minimum let are popular with business travellers, and make a viable alternative to guesthouses. They're also well worth considering for longer stays, such as during the Festival. **Campus accommodation** is available in the city during the summer months, though it's neither as useful or cheap as might be expected.

Argyle Backpackers Hotel 14 Argyle Place, Marchmont ⓣ0131/667 9991, ⓦwww.argyle-backpackers.com. Quiet, less intense version of the typical backpackers' hostel, pleasantly located in three adjoining townhouses near the Meadows in studenty Marchmont. It's walking distance to town, but you can get bus #41 from the door. There's a pleasant communal conservatory and garden at the back. The small dorms have single beds, and there are a dozen or so double/twin rooms. ①

Brodies 1 12 High St, Old Town ⓣ0131/556 6770, ⓦwww.brodieshostels.co.uk. Tucked down a typical Old Town close, with four simple dorms sleeping up to a dozen and limited communal areas. It's smaller than many hostels, and a little bit more homely as a result. ①

Brodies 2 93 High St, Royal Mile ⓣ0131/556 2223, ⓦwww.brodieshostels.co.uk. The atmosphere at this smart new hostel is even more mellow than in the sister property across the road. Smaller dorms (mostly six- or eight-bed) as well as doubles. ②

Canon Court Apartments 20 Canonmills ⓣ0131/474 7000, ⓦwww.canoncourt.co.uk. A block of smart, comfortable self-catering one- and two-bedroom apartments not far from Canonmills Bridge over the Water of Leith at the northern edge of the New Town. Studio apartments from £74 per night. ⑤

Edinburgh Central SYHA 9 Haddington Place, Leith ⓣ0870 155 3255 ⓦwww.edinburghcentral.org. In a handy location at the top of Leith Walk, this five-star hostel has single, double and eight-bed rooms with en suite facilities. There is a reasonably priced bistro or self-catering kitchen facilities. Dorms, twins ①; family rooms ④

Globetrotter Inn 46 Marine Drive, Cramond ⓣ0131/336 1030, ⓦwww.globetrotterinns.com. A big departure from the buzzy city-centre hostels, in a sylvan parkland setting four miles from the centre with lovely views of the Firth of Forth. The 350-plus beds are mostly bunks with privacy curtains and individual reading lights, but there are also doubles. There's access to a gym and sauna, lots of parking and an hourly shuttle service into town, as well as regular buses (#42). Families and kids are not encouraged. Doubles ②

Royal Garden Apartments York Buildings, Queen St ⓣ0131/625 1234, ⓦwww.royal-garden.co.uk. Superbly equipped, comfortable modern one- and two-bedroom serviced apartments very centrally located opposite the National Portrait Gallery. Prices start at £155 per night. ⑤

Smart City Hostel 50 Blackfriars St, Old Town ⓣ0131 452 9079, ⓦwww.smartcityhostels.com. A five-star hostel just off the Royal Mile, with 620 beds in twin rooms or dorms. Females-only rooms are available. A simple buffet serves good-value pub food and breakfasts and there is a late night bar for residents. Dorms ② and twins ④

University of Edinburgh Pollock Halls of Residence 18 Holyrood Park Rd, Newington ⓣ0131/651 2007, ⓦwww.edinburghfirst.com. Unquestionably the best setting of any of the city's university accommodation, right beside the Royal Commonwealth Pool and Holyrood Park, and with a range of accommodation from single rooms (£29), twins (£69) and en-suite doubles (£74) to self-catering flats (from £340 per week). Available Easter and June to mid-Sept only. Twins ④ and en-suite doubles ⑤

The Old Town

The **OLD TOWN**, although only about a mile long and 300 yards wide, represents the total extent of the twin burghs of Edinburgh and Canongate for the first 650 years of their existence, and its general appearance and character remain indubitably medieval. Containing the majority of the city's most famous tourist sights, it makes by far the best starting point for your explorations. The Old Town is compact enough to see the highlights in a single day, though a thorough visit requires a bit more time. No matter how pressed you are, make sure you spare time for at least a taste of the wonderfully varied scenery and breathtaking vantage points of **Holyrood Park**, an extensive tract of open countryside on the eastern edge of the Old Town that includes Arthur's Seat, the peak of which rises so distinctively in the midst of the city.

Edinburgh Castle

The history of Edinburgh, and indeed of Scotland, is indissolubly bound up with its **castle** (daily: April–Oct 9.30am–6pm; Nov–March 9.30am–5pm, last entry 45min before closing; £11; Ⓦ www.historic-scotland.gov.uk), which dominates the city from its lofty seat atop an extinct volcanic rock. The disparate styles of the fortifications reflect the change in its role from defensive citadel to national monument, and today, as well as attracting more visitors than anywhere else in the country, the castle is still a military barracks and a home to Scotland's crown jewels. The oldest surviving part of the complex is from the twelfth century, while the most recent additions date back to the 1920s.

Though you can easily take in the views and wander round the castle yourself, you might like to join a **guided tour** (every 15min in high season; 25min; free), for stoical talk of war, boiling oil and cannon roar. Alternatively, **audioguides** (£3) are available from a booth just inside the gatehouse.

The Esplanade

The castle is entered via the **Esplanade**, a parade ground laid out in the eighteenth century and enclosed a hundred years later by ornamental walls. For most of the year it acts as a coach park, though huge grandstands are erected for the Edinburgh Military Tattoo (see p.791), which takes place every night during August, coinciding with the Edinburgh Festival. A shameless and spectacular pageant of swinging kilts and massed pipe bands, the tattoo makes full use of its dramatic setting.

Entry to the Esplanade is free, and if you don't want to pay the castle's pricey entry fee, it offers a taste of the precipitous location and eye-stretching views.

The lower defences

The **gatehouse** is a Romantic-style addition to the castle from the 1880s, complete with the last drawbridge ever built in Scotland. Standing guard by the drawbridge are real-life soldiers, members of the regiment in residence at the castle; while their presence in full dress uniform is always a hit with camera-toting tourists, it's also a reminder that the castle is still a working military garrison. Rearing up behind the gatehouse is the most distinctive and impressive feature of the castle's silhouette, the sixteenth-century **Half Moon Battery**, which marks the outer limit of the actual defences. Once through the gatehouse, continue uphill along Lower Ward, passing through the **Portcullis Gate**, a handsome Renaissance gateway.

Beyond this, the wide main path is known as Middle Ward, with the six-gun **Argyle Battery** to the right. Further west on **Mill's Mount Battery**, a well-known Edinburgh ritual takes place – the daily firing of the one o'clock gun. Originally designed for the benefit of ships in the Firth of Forth, these days it's an enjoyable ceremony for visitors and a useful time signal for city-centre office workers. Both batteries offer wonderful panoramas over Princes Street and the New Town to the coastal towns and hills of Fife across the Forth.

National War Museum

Located in the old hospital buildings, down a ramp between the restaurant immediately behind the one o'clock gun and the Governor's House, the **National War Museum** (free) covers the last four hundred years of Scottish military history. Scots have been fighting for much longer than that, of course, but the slant of the museum is very definitely towards the soldiers who fought *for* the Union, rather than against it (or against themselves).

St Margaret's Chapel

Near the highest point of the castle, **St Margaret's Chapel** is the oldest surviving building in the castle, and probably also in Edinburgh itself. Built by King David I as a memorial to his mother, and used as a powder magazine for three hundred years, this tiny Norman church was rediscovered in 1845 and eventually rededicated in 1934, after sympathetic restoration.

The battlements in front of the chapel offer the best of all the castle's extensive views. Here you'll see the famous fifteenth-century siege gun, **Mons Meg**, which could fire a 500-pound stone nearly two miles. Just below the battlements there's a small, immaculately kept **cemetery**, the last resting place of the **soldiers' pets**. Continuing eastwards, you skirt the top of the Forewall and Half Moon batteries, passing the 110-foot **Castle Well** en route

The Stone of Destiny

Legend has it that the **Stone of Destiny** (also called the Stone of Scone) was "Jacob's Pillow", on which he dreamed of the ladder of angels from earth to heaven. Its real history is obscure, but it's known to have been moved from Ireland to Dunadd by missionaries, and thence to Dunstaffnage, from where Kenneth MacAlpine, king of the Dalriada Scots, brought it to the abbey at Scone, near Perth, in 838. There it remained for almost five hundred years, used as a coronation throne on which all kings of Scotland were crowned.

In 1296, an over-eager Edward I stole what he believed to be the Stone and installed it at Westminster Abbey, where, apart from a brief interlude in 1950 when it was removed by Scottish nationalists and hidden in Arbroath for several months, it remained for seven hundred years. All this changed in December 1996 when, after an elaborate ceremony-laden journey from London, the Stone returned to Scotland, in one of the doomed attempts by the Conservative government to convince the Scottish people that the Union was a good thing. Much to the annoyance of the people of Perth and the curators of Scone Palace (see p.884), and to the general indifference of the people of Scotland, the Stone was placed in Edinburgh Castle.

However, speculation surrounds the authenticity of the Stone, for the original is said to have been intricately carved, while the one seen today is a plain block of sandstone. Many believe that the canny monks at Scone palmed this off onto the English king (some say that it's nothing more sacred than the cover for a medieval septic tank), and that the real Stone of Destiny lies hidden in an underground chamber, its whereabouts a mystery to all but the chosen few.

to **Crown Square**, the highest, most important and secure section of the entire complex.

The palace

The eastern side of Crown Square is occupied by the **palace**, a surprisingly unassuming edifice built round an octagonal stair turret heightened in the nineteenth century to bear the castle's main flagpole. Begun in the 1430s, the palace owes its Renaissance appearance to King James IV, though it was remodelled for Mary, Queen of Scots, and her consort Henry, Lord Darnley, whose entwined initials (MAH), together with the date 1566, can be seen above one of the doorways.

Another section of the palace holds a detailed audiovisual presentation on the nation's crown jewels, known as the **Honours of Scotland**, the originals of which are housed in the Crown Room at the end of the display. Despite the slow-moving, claustrophobic queues that shuffle past the displays, the jewels are still impressive, serving as one of the most potent images of Scotland's nationhood. The glass case containing the Honours also holds the **Stone of Destiny** (see box, p.765), a remarkably plain object lying incongruously next to the opulent crown jewels.

The Royal Mile

The **Royal Mile**, the name given to the ridge linking the castle with Holyrood, was described by Daniel Defoe, in 1724, as "the largest, longest and finest street for Buildings and Number of Inhabitants, not in Bretain only, but in the World". Almost exactly a mile in length, it is divided into four separate streets – Castlehill, Lawnmarket, High Street and Canongate. From these, branching out in a herringbone pattern, are a series of tightly packed closes and steep lanes entered via archways known as "pends". After the construction of the New Town, in the eighteenth and nineteenth century, much of the housing along the Royal Mile degenerated into a notorious slum, but has since become once again a highly desirable place to live. Although marred somewhat by tacky tourist shops and the odd misjudged new development, it is still among the most evocative parts of the city, and one that particularly rewards detailed exploration.

Castlehill

The narrow uppermost stretch of the Royal Mile is known as **Castlehill**. Rising up to the north, on the edge of the Castle Esplanade, is **Ramsay Gardens**, among the most picturesque city-centre flats in the world.

A short way downhill, the **Scotch Whisky Experience** (daily: May–Sept 9.30am–6.30pm; Oct–April 10am–6pm; £9.25; Ⓦwww.scotch-whisky-experience.co.uk) mimics the kind of tours offered at distilleries in the Highlands, and while it can't match the authenticity of the real thing, the centre does offer a thorough introduction to the "water of life" (*uisge beatha* in Gaelic). On the ground floor, a well-stocked shop gives an idea of the sheer range and diversity of the drink, while downstairs there's a pleasant whisky bar and restaurant, *Amber* (see p.782).

The imposing black church at the foot of Castlehill is **The Hub** (daily 10am–7pm; Ⓣ0131/473 2015, Ⓦwww.thehub-edinburgh.com), also known as "Edinburgh's Festival Centre". Constructed in 1845 to designs by James Gillespie Graham and Augustus Pugin, one of the co-architects of the Houses of Parliament in London, the Hub is a performance, rehearsal and exhibition space, complete with a ticket centre and café. Permanent works of art have

Robert Louis Stevenson

Born in Edinburgh into a distinguished family of lighthouse engineers, **Robert Louis Stevenson** (1850–94) was a sickly child, with a solitary childhood dominated by his governess, Alison "Cummie" Cunningham, who regaled him with tales drawn from Calvinist folklore. Sent to the university to study engineering, Stevenson rebelled against his upbringing by spending much of his time in the lowlife howffs and brothels of the city.

Stevenson's early successes were two **travelogues**, *An Inland Voyage* and *Travels with a Donkey in the Cevennes*, kaleidoscopic jottings based on his journeys in France, where he went to escape Scotland's weather, which was damaging his health. It was there that he met Fanny Osbourne, an American ten years his senior.

Having married the now-divorced Fanny, Stevenson began an elusive search for an agreeable climate that led to Switzerland, the French Riviera and the Scottish Highlands. He belatedly turned to the novel, achieving immediate acclaim in 1881 for **Treasure Island**, a highly moralistic adventure yarn that began as an entertainment for his stepson and future collaborator, Lloyd Osbourne. In 1886, his most famous short story, **Dr Jekyll and Mr Hyde**, despite its nominal London setting, offered a vivid evocation of Edinburgh's Old Town: an allegory of its dual personality of prosperity and squalor, and an analysis of its Calvinistic preoccupations with guilt and damnation. The same year saw the publication of the historical romance **Kidnapped**, an adventure novel that exemplified Stevenson's view that literature should seek above all to entertain.

In 1887 Stevenson left Britain for good, travelling first to the United States. A year later, he set sail for the South Seas, and eventually settled in **Samoa**. However, Scotland continued to be his main inspiration: he wrote *Catriona* as a sequel to *Kidnapped*, and was at work on two more novels with Scottish settings, *St Ives* and *Weir of Hermiston*, a dark story of father and son confrontation, at the time of his sudden death from a brain haemorrhage in 1894.

been incorporated into the centre, including more than two hundred delightful foot-high sculptures by Scottish sculptor Jill Watson, depicting Festival performers and audiences.

Lawnmarket

Below the Hub, the Royal Mile opens out into the broader expanse of **Lawnmarket**, where you'll find **Gladstone's Land** (daily: April–Oct 10am–5pm, July & Aug 10am–7pm; NTS; £5), the Royal Mile's best surviving example of a typical seventeenth-century tenement. The tall, narrow building – not unlike a canalside house in Amsterdam – would have been home to various families living in cramped conditions. The building is owned by the National Trust for Scotland, who have carefully restored the warren of tight little staircases, tiny rooms, creaking floorboards and peek-hole windows. The upper floors contain apartments, which are rented to visitors.

A few paces further on, steps lead down to Lady Stair's Close and the **Writers' Museum** (Mon–Sat 10am–5pm; also Sun noon–5pm in Aug; free; Ⓦ www.cac.org.uk), housed in Lady Stair's House – a Victorian embellishment of a seventeenth-century residence set to one side of an open courtyard. Dedicated to Scotland's three greatest literary lions, Sir Walter Scott, Robert Louis Stevenson and Robert Burns, the museum has a slightly lacklustre collection of portraits, manuscripts and showcases filled with odd knick-knacks and relics associated with the writers – Scott's walking stick and a plastercast of Burns' skull among them. The house itself holds as much interest as the exhibits, its tight, winding stairs and pokey, wood-panelled rooms offering a flavour of the medieval Old Town.

High Street and the High Kirk of St Giles

Across the junction with George IV Bridge is the third section of the Royal Mile, known as the **High Street**, which occupies two blocks either side of the intersection between North Bridge and South Bridge. The dominant building on the southern side of the street is the **Kirk of St Giles** (May–Sept Mon–Fri 9am–7pm, Sat 9am–5pm, Sun 1–5pm; Oct–April Mon–Sat 9am–5pm, Sun 1–5pm; free; Ⓦwww.stgilescathedral.org.uk), the original parish church of medieval Edinburgh, from where John Knox launched and directed the Scottish Reformation. St Giles is often referred to as a cathedral, although it has only been the seat of a bishop on two brief and unhappy occasions in the seventeenth century. According to one of the city's best-known legends, the attempt in 1637 to introduce the English prayer book, and thus Episcopal government, so incensed a humble stallholder named Jenny Geddes that she hurled her stool at the preacher, prompting the rest of the congregation to chase the offending clergy out of the building. A tablet in the north aisle marks the spot from where she let rip.

The resplendent **crown spire** of the kirk is formed from eight flying buttresses and dates back to 1485, while inside, the four massive piers supporting the tower were part of a Norman church built here around 1120. In the nineteenth century, St Giles was adorned with a whole series of funerary monuments on the model of London's Westminster Abbey; around the same time it acquired several attractive Pre-Raphaelite stained-glass windows designed by Edward Burne-Jones and William Morris.

At the southeastern corner of St Giles, the **Thistle Chapel** was built by Sir Robert Lorimer in 1911 as the private chapel of the sixteen knights of the Most Noble Order of the Thistle, the highest chivalric order in Scotland. Self-consciously derivative of St George's Chapel in Windsor, it's an exquisite piece of craftsmanship, with an elaborate ribbed vault, huge drooping bosses, and extravagantly ornate stalls showing off Lorimer's bold Arts and Crafts styling.

Parliament Square

St Giles is surrounded on three sides by **Parliament Square**, which itself is dominated by the continuous Neoclassical facades of the **Law Courts**, originally planned by Robert Adam (1728–92), one of four brothers in a family of architects whose work helped imbue the New Town with much of its grace and elegance. Because of a shortage of funds and consequent delays, the present exteriors were built to designs by Robert Reid (1776–1856), who faithfully quoted from Adam's architectural vocabulary without matching his flair.

Upper High Street

On the opposite side of the Royal Mile from Parliament Square, the U-shaped **City Chambers** were designed by John Adam, brother of Robert, as the Royal Exchange. Local traders never warmed to the exchange, however, so the town council established its headquarters there instead. Beneath the City Chambers lies **Mary King's Close**, one of Edinburgh's most unusual attractions. When work on the chambers began in 1753, the tops of the existing houses on the site were simply sliced through at the level of the High Street and the new building constructed on top of them. Because the tenements had been built on a steep hillside, this process left parts of the houses, together with the old streets (or closes) that ran alongside them, intact but entirely enclosed among the basement and cellars of the City Chambers. You can visit this rather spooky subterranean "lost city" on **tours** led by costumed actors (daily every 20min: April–Oct 10am–9pm; Nov–March 10am–4pm; 1hr; £8.50; Ⓦwww.realmarykingsclose.com).

Lower High Street

Beyond the intersection of North Bridge and South Bridge and just a little way downhill, jutting out into the street from the main line of buildings, is the fifteenth-century **John Knox's House**, now part of the **Scottish Storytelling Centre** (Mon–Sat 10am–6pm, also Sun noon–6pm in July & Aug; £3.50 entry to John Knox House; Ⓦwww.scottishstorytellingcentre.co.uk). There are two distinct parts to this cultural centre: one half is a stylish contemporary development with an excellent café, the Netherbow Theatre and a small, permanent exhibition about Scottish stories. Conjoined to this is the John Knox House, a fifteenth-century stone and timber building – a classic representation of a Royal Mile dwelling in its medieval heyday. Inside, it contains a series of displays about John Knox, the minister who led the Reformation in Scotland and established Calvinist Presbyterianism as the dominant religious force in the country. Regular performances and events take place in the centre, particularly during the Festival.

Canongate

For over seven hundred years, the **Canongate** district, through which the eastern section of the Royal Mile runs, was a burgh in its own right, officially separate from the capital. A notorious slum area even into the 1960s, it has been the subject of some of the most ambitious **restoration** programmes in the Old Town, though the lack of harmony between the buildings renovated in different decades is fairly obvious. For such a central district, it's interesting to note that most of the buildings here are residential, and by no means are they all bijou apartments. Look out for the eclectic range of shops, which include a gallery of historic maps and sea charts, an old-fashioned whisky bottler and a genuine bagpipe-maker.

Next door to the turreted, late sixteenth-century **Canongate Tolbooth** is **Canongate Kirk** (Mon–Sat 10.30am–4.30pm, depending on volunteer staff and church services; free). It was built in the 1680s to house the congregation expelled from Holyrood Abbey when the latter was commandeered by James VII (James II in England) to serve as the chapel for the Order of the Thistle. The kirk has unusual modesty, with a graceful curved facade, a mixture of arched and round windows and a bow-shaped gable to the rear. The surrounding churchyard is an attractive and tranquil stretch of green in the heart of the Old Town and affords fine views of Calton Hill; it also happens to be one of the city's most exclusive cemeteries – well-known internees include the political economist Adam Smith and Robert Fergusson, regarded by some as Edinburgh's greatest poet, despite his short-lived 24 years. A statue of the young poet striding along the Royal Mile can be seen just outside the gates of the kirk.

Opposite the church, the **Museum of Edinburgh** (Mon–Sat 10am–5pm, also Sun noon–5pm in Aug; free; Ⓦwww.cac.org.uk) is the city's principal collection devoted to local history. The museum is as interesting for the network of wood-panelled rooms within as for its rather quirky array of artefacts, which include a number of items of real historical significance: the National Convention, the petition for religious freedom drawn up on a deerskin parchment in 1638, and the original plans for the layout of the New Town drawn by James Craig, chosen by the city council after a competition in 1767.

Look out for **Dunbar's Close**, on the north side of the street, which has a beautiful seventeenth-century walled garden tucked in behind the tenements. Opposite this is the entry to Crichton's Close, through which you'll find the **Scottish Poetry Library** (Mon–Fri 11am–6pm, Sat 1–5pm; free; Ⓦwww.spl.org.uk), a small island of modern architectural eloquence amid a cacophony of large-scale developments.

Holyrood

At the foot of Canongate lies **Holyrood**, for centuries known as Edinburgh's royal quarter, with its ruined thirteenth-century **abbey** and the **Palace of Holyroodhouse**. The area has been transformed by Enric Miralles' dazzling but highly controversial **Scottish Parliament**, which was deliberately landscaped to blend in with the cliffs and ridges of Edinburgh's most dramatic natural feature, the nearby **Holyrood Park** and its slumbering peak, Arthur's Seat.

The Palace of Holyroodhouse

The **Palace of Holyroodhouse** (daily: April–Oct 9.30am–6pm; Nov–March 9.30am–4.30pm; last admission 1hr before closing; £9.50; Ⓦwww.royal.gov.uk) is largely a seventeenth-century creation, planned for Charles II. Tours of the palace move through a series of royal **reception rooms** featuring some outstanding encrusted plasterwork, each more impressive than the last – an idea Charles II had picked up from his cousin Louis XIV's Versailles – while on the northern side of the internal quadrangle, the **Great Gallery** extends almost the full length of the palace and is dominated by portraits of 96 Scottish kings, painted by Jacob de Wet in 1684 to illustrate the lineage of Stewart royalty: the result is unintentionally hilarious, as it's clear that the artist's imagination was taxed to bursting point in his commission to paint so many different facial types without having an inkling as to what the subjects actually looked like. Leading from this into the oldest part of the palace, known as James V's tower, the formal, ceremonial tone gives way to dark medieval history, with a tight spiral staircase leading to the chambers used by Mary, Queen of Scots. These contain various relics, including jewellery, associated with the queen, though the most compelling room is a tiny supper room, from where in 1566 Mary's Italian secretary, David Rizzio, was dragged by conspirators, who included her jealous husband Lord Darnley, to the outer chamber and stabbed 56 times.

Holyrood Abbey

Immediately adjacent to the palace are the evocative ruins of **Holyrood Abbey** (free as part of Holyroodhouse tour), some of which date from the thirteenth century. The roof tumbled down in 1768, but the melancholy scene has inspired artists down the years, among them Felix Mendelssohn, who in 1829 wrote "Everything is in ruins and mouldering . . . I believe I have found the beginning of my Scottish Symphony there today". Adjacent to the abbey are the formal palace gardens, open to visitors during the summer months and offering some pleasant strolls.

The Queen's Gallery

Essentially an adjunct to Holyrood palace, the **Queen's Gallery** (daily: April–Oct 9.30am–6pm; Nov–March 9.30am–4.30pm; last admission 1hr before closing; £5 or £13 joint ticket with Holyroodhouse; Ⓦwww.royal.gov.uk) is located in the shell of a former church directly between the palace and the parliament. It's used to display changing exhibitions from the Royal

Collection, a vast array of art treasures held by the Queen on behalf of the British nation. Because the pieces are otherwise exhibited only during the limited openings of Buckingham and Windsor palaces, the exhibitions here tend to draw a lot of interest.

The Scottish Parliament

For all its grandeur and size, Holyrood Palace is in danger of being upstaged by the striking buildings that make up the new **Scottish Parliament** (for visiting details, see box below). By far the most controversial public building to be erected in Scotland since World War II, it houses the country's directly elected assembly, which was reintroduced in 1999 – Scotland had had no parliament of its own since 1707, when it joined the English assembly at Westminster as part of the Union of the two nations.

Made up of various linked elements rather than one single building, the complex was designed by Catalan architect **Enric Miralles**, whose death in 2000, halfway through the building process, caused ripples of uncertainty as to whether he had in fact set down his final draft. Initial estimates for the building's cost were tentatively put at £40 million; by the time the Queen cut the ribbon in October 2004, the final bill was over £400 million. A major public inquiry into the overspend blamed costing failures early in the project and criticized the spendthrift attitude of politicians and civil servants alike. Yet the building is still an impressive – if imperfect – testament to the ambition of Miralles. Indeed, it has won over the majority of the architectural community, scooping numerous awards including Britain's prestigious Royal Institute of British Architects (RIBA) Stirling Prize in 2005.

One of the most memorable features of the building are the fanciful motifs and odd architectural signatures running through the design, including the anvil-shaped cladding, and the extraordinary windows of the offices for MSPs (Members of the Scottish Parliament), said to have been inspired by a monk's contemplative cell. The stark concrete of the new building's interior may not be to all tastes, though several of the staircases and passageways remain evocative of the country's medieval castles.

The main **debating chamber** itself is grand yet intimate, with light flooding in through high windows and a complex network of thick oak beams, lights and microphone wires. The European-style layout is a deliberate move away from the confrontational Westminster model, though some have been quick to

Visiting the Scottish Parliament

There's free access into the entrance lobby of the Parliament, entered from Horse Wynd, opposite the palace, where you'll find a small exhibition providing some historical, political and architectural background. If parliament is in session, it's normally possible to watch proceedings in the debating chamber from the public gallery – again, access is free, though you have to get a pass from the front desk in the lobby. To see the rest of the interior properly you'll need to join one of the regular **guided tours** (45min; £5; bookings not essential; ⓣ0131/348 5200), well worth the fee for a more detailed appreciation of the quality and features of the building's design.

There's action in the debating chamber only on "business days" (Tues–Thurs 9am–7pm when Parliament is sitting), but tours don't tend to be as extensive on these days. On "non-business days" (Mon & Fri when parliament is sitting, or Mon–Fri if parliament is in recess), the doors are open April–Oct 10am–6pm, Nov–March 10am–4pm, as well as Sat & Sun 10am–4pm throughout the year. For further details see ⓦwww.scottish.parliament.uk.

point out that while the traditional inter-party insults still fly, the quality of the parliamentarians' rhetoric rarely matches that of the soaring new arena.

Our Dynamic Earth

On the Holyrood Road, beneath a miniature version of London's Millennium Dome, **Our Dynamic Earth** (April–Oct daily 10am–5pm; July & Aug daily 10am–6pm; Nov–March Wed–Sun 10am–5pm; £8.95; Ⓦwww.dynamicearth.co.uk), is a high-tech attraction based on the theme of the wonders of the natural world and aimed at children between 5 and 15. Galleries cover the formation of the earth and continents with crashing sound effects and a shaking floor, while the calmer grandeur of glaciers and oceans are explored through magnificent large-screen landscape footage; further on, the polar regions – complete with a real iceberg – and tropical jungles are imaginatively re-created, with interactive computer screens and special effects at every turn. Outside, the dramatic **amphitheatre**, which incorporates the steps leading up to the main entrance, serves as a great venue for outdoor theatre and music performances, most notably during the Festival.

Holyrood Park, Arthur's Seat and Duddingston

Holyrood Park – or Queen's Park – a natural wilderness in the very heart of the modern city, is unquestionably one of Edinburgh's greatest assets. Packed into an area no more than five miles in diameter is an amazing variety of landscapes – hills, crags, moorland, marshes, glens, lochs and fields – representing something of a microcosm of Scotland's scenery.

Two of the most rewarding walks begin from just outside the palace grounds: one, along a pathway nicknamed the "Radical Road", traverses the ridge immediately below the **Salisbury Crags**, one of the main features of the Edinburgh skyline. This is arguably a finer walk than the sharper climb to the top of Arthur's Seat. For a looped walk of about an hour's duration from Holyrood follow the "Volunteer's Walk" up the glen behind the Crags, then return along the Radical Road.

The usual starting point for the ascent of **Arthur's Seat**, which at 823ft above sea level easily towers over all of Edinburgh's numerous high points, is Dunsapie Loch, reached by following the tarred Queen's Drive in a clockwise direction from the palace gates. Part of a volcano which last saw action 350 million years ago, its connections to the legendary Celtic king are fairly sketchy: the name is likely to be a corruption of the Gaelic *Ard-na-said*, or "height of arrows". From Dunsapie Loch it's a twenty-minute climb up grassy slopes to the rocky summit. On a clear day, the views might just stretch to the English border and the Atlantic Ocean; but you're more likely to see Fife, a few Highland peaks and, of course, Edinburgh laid out on all sides.

Cowgate and the Grassmarket

At the bottom of the valley immediately south of the Royal Mile, and following a roughly parallel course from the Lawnmarket to St Mary's Street, is the **Cowgate**. One of Edinburgh's oldest surviving streets, it was also one of the city's most prestigious addresses. However, the construction of the great **viaducts** of George IV Bridge and South Bridge entombed it below street level, condemning it to decay and neglect. In the last decade or so the Cowgate has experienced something of a revival, with various nightclubs and Festival venues establishing themselves, though few tourists venture here and the contrast with the neighbouring Royal Mile remains stark.

The Grassmarket

At the western end of the Cowgate is an open, partly cobbled area known as the **Grassmarket**, which was used as the city's cattle market from 1477 to 1911. Despite the height of many of the surrounding buildings, it offers an unexpected view up to the precipitous walls of the castle and, come springtime, it's sunny enough for cafés to put tables and chairs along the pavement. However, the Grassmarket is best remembered as the location of Edinburgh's public gallows – the spot is marked by a tiny garden. The notorious body-snatching duo of William Burke and William Hare had their lair in a now-vanished close just off the western end of the Grassmarket, and for a long time before its gentrification over the last two decades it had a seamy edge, with brothels, drinking dens and shelters for down-and-outs. Tucked away in the northwest corner is the award-winning modern architecture of **Dance Base** (Ⓣ0131/225 5525, Ⓦwww.dancebase.co.uk), Scotland's National Centre for Dance, which holds classes, workshops and shows. Elsewhere, the Grassmarket's row of pubs has become a focus for stag and hen parties, and there's also a series of interesting shops, in particular the offbeat, independent boutiques on the unusual, two-tier **Victoria Street**, with arcaded shops below and a pedestrian terrace above.

Greyfriars and around

The **statue of Greyfriars Bobby** at the southwestern corner of **George IV Bridge** must rank as Edinburgh's most sentimental tourist attraction. Bobby was a Skye terrier acquired as a working dog by a police constable named John Gray. When Gray died in 1858, Bobby was found a few days later sitting on his grave, a vigil he maintained until his death fourteen years later. Bobby's legendary dedication was picked up by Disney, whose 1960 feature film of the story ensured that streams of tourists have paid their respects ever since.

The grave Bobby mourned over is in the **Greyfriars Kirkyard**, which has a fine collection of seventeenth-century gravestones and mausoleums, including one to the Adam family of architects. The kirkyard is visited regularly by ghost

▲ The Grassmarket

tours (see p.758) and was known for grave-robbing long before Burke and Hare became the city's most notorious exponents of the crime. Greyfriars Kirk itself was built in 1620 on land that had belonged to a Franciscan convent, though little of the original late-Gothic-style building remains. A fire in the mid-nineteenth century led to significant rebuilding and the installation of the first organ in a Presbyterian church in Scotland; today's magnificent instrument, by Peter Collins, arrived in 1990.

National Museum of Scotland

Immediately opposite *Greyfriars Bobby*, on the south side of Chambers Street, stands the striking honey-coloured sandstone **Museum of Scotland** (Mon–Sun 10am–5pm; free; Ⓦwww.nms.ac.uk). Scotland's premier museum displays many of the nation's most important historical artefacts as a means of telling the country's history from earliest man to the present day. The collection is generally, though not strictly, laid out in chronological order over seven different levels. The labyrinthine feel of the rooms and stairways is a little disorienting at first, though the unexpected views of different parts of the museum above and below are a deliberate effect to emphasize the interconnected layers of Scotland's history.

The main entrance is at the base of the tower (although it is also possible to enter through the neighbouring Royal Museum; see p.775). The information desk is located just before you get to **Hawthornden Court**, the central atrium of the museum and a useful orientation point; on this level you'll also find the shop and access to the Royal Museum café. Free **guided tours** on different themes take place throughout the day, and **audio headsets** (free) give detailed information on the displays.

The first sections, **Beginnings** and **Early People**, are on Level 0. Here, Scotland's story before the arrival of man is presented with audiovisual displays, artistic re-creations, and a selection of rocks and fossils. Among the artefacts on display, highlights are the **Traprain treasure** hoard, 41lb of silver plates, cutlery and goblets found buried in East Lothian; the **Cramond Lioness**, a sculpture from a Roman tombstone found recently in the Firth of Forth; and the beautifully detailed gold, silver and amber **Hunterston brooch**, dating from around 700 AD.

The **Kingdom of the Scots** on Level 1 covers the period between Scotland's development as a single independent nation and the Union with England in 1707. Star exhibits include the **Monymusk reliquary**, an intricately decorated box said to have carried the remains of St Columba, and the **Lewis chessmen**, exquisitely idiosyncratic twelfth-century pieces carved from walrus ivory.

Level 3 shows exhibits under the theme **Scotland Transformed**, covering the century or so following the Union of Parliaments in 1707. This period saw the last of the Highland uprisings under Bonnie Prince Charlie (whose silver travelling-canteen is on display), and also witnessed the expansion of trade links with the Americas and developments in industries such as weaving, and iron and steel production.

Scotland went on to pioneer many aspects of heavy engineering, with ship and locomotive production to the fore. Largest of the exhibits in **Industry and Empire** on Level 4 is the steam locomotive *Ellesmere*. As well as industrial progress, other fields are covered too, including the influence of Scots around the world, both as a result of emigration, and through such luminaries as James Watt, Charles Rennie Mackintosh and Robert Louis Stevenson. Above this the **Modern Scotland** gallery includes the Scottish Sports Hall of Fame.

Royal Museum of Scotland

Interlinked with the Museum of Scotland, though also with its own entrance, is the Royal Museum of Scotland (same hours; free), a dignified Venetian-style palace with a cast-iron interior modelled on that of the former Crystal Palace in London. The Royal Museum is a wonderful example of Victorian Britain's fascination with antiquities and natural history. The wonderfully airy **Great Hall**, framed in cast iron, displays sculpture from Classical Greece and Rome alongside Buddhas from Japan, and the bizarre Millennium Clock, a thirty-two-feet tall, Heath Robinson-style contraption which clicks and whirls into motion at 11am, noon, 2pm and 4pm. Rooms leading off from here hold collections of stuffed animals and birds, though a number of the natural history galleries are under refurbishment.

The University of Edinburgh and around

Immediately alongside the Royal Museum is the earliest surviving part of the **University of Edinburgh**, variously referred to as Old College or Old Quad, although nowadays it houses only a few university departments; the main campus colonizes the streets and squares to the south. The small **Talbot Rice Art Gallery** (Tues–Sat 10am–5pm, also Sun 2–5pm in Aug; free; Ⓦwww.trg.ed.ac.uk) occupies the southwest corner of the Old College, and hosts some excellent touring and temporary avant-garde exhibitions – the show held during the Festival is normally of a high standard.

A little further up Nicolson Street is the stately facade of **Surgeons' Hall**, a handsome Ionic temple built by Playfair as the headquarters of the Royal College of Surgeons. Inside is one of the city's most unusual and morbidly compelling **museums** (Mon–Fri noon–4pm; £5; Ⓦwww.rcsed.ac.uk). In the eighteenth and nineteenth centuries Edinburgh developed as a leading centre for medical and anatomical research, nurturing world-famous figures such as James Young Simpson, pioneer of anaesthesia, and Joseph Lister, the father of modern surgery. The museum's intriguing exhibits range from early surgical tools to a pocketbook covered with the leathered skin of body snatcher William Burke.

The New Town

The **NEW TOWN**, itself well over two hundred years old, stands in total contrast to the Old Town: the layout is symmetrical, the streets are broad and straight, and most of the buildings are Neoclassical. Originally intended to be residential, today the New Town is the bustling hub of the city's professional, commercial and business life, dominated by shops, banks and offices.

The existence of the New Town is chiefly due to the vision of **George Drummond**, who made schemes for the expansion of the city soon after becoming Lord Provost in 1725. Work began on the draining of the Nor' Loch below the Castle in 1759, a job that took some sixty years. The North Bridge, linking the Old Town with the main road leading to the port of Leith, was built between 1763 and 1772 and, in 1766, following a public competition, a plan for the New Town by 22-year-old architect **James Craig** was chosen. Its gridiron pattern was perfectly matched to the site: central **George Street**, flanked by showpiece squares, was laid out along the main ridge, with parallel **Princes Street** and **Queen Street** on either side, built up on one side only, so as not to block the spectacular views of the Old Town and Fife.

The layout of the greater New Town is a remarkable grouping of squares, circuses, terraces, crescents and parks along with **Charlotte Square** and the assemblage of curiosities on and around **Calton Hill**. However, it also contains assorted Victorian additions, notably the **Scott Monument** on Princes Street, the **Royal Botanic Garden** on its northern fringe, as well as two of the city's most important public collections – the **National Gallery of Scotland** and, further afield, the **Scottish National Gallery of Modern Art**.

Princes Street

Although only allocated a subsidiary role in the original plan of the New Town, **Princes Street** had developed into Edinburgh's principal thoroughfare by the middle of the nineteenth century, a role it has retained ever since. Its unobstructed views across to the Castle and the Old Town are undeniably magnificent although its northern side is dominated by ugly department stores, packed with shoppers, and few of the original eighteenth-century buildings remain.

Princes Street Gardens

It's hard to imagine that the **gardens** (dawn to dusk; free) which flank nearly the entire length of Princes Street were once the stagnant, foul-smelling Nor' Loch, into which the effluent of the Old Town flowed for centuries. The railway has since replaced the water and today a sunken cutting carries the main lines out of Waverley Station to the west and north. The gardens, split into East and West sections, were originally the private domain of Princes Street residents and their well-placed acquaintances, only becoming a public park in 1876. These days, the swathes of green lawn, colourful flower beds and mature trees are a green lung for the city centre: on sunny days local office workers descend in their droves at lunchtime, while around Christmas the gardens' eastern section is home to an ice rink (late Nov to early Jan daily 10am–10pm; £7) and a towering Ferris wheel (same times; £2.50). The larger and more verdant western section has a floral clock and the Ross Bandstand, a popular Festival venue.

The Scott Monument

Facing the Victorian shopping emporium Jenners, and set within East Princes Street Gardens, the 200-foot-high **Scott Monument** (April–Sept Mon–Sat 9am–6pm, Sun 10am–6pm; Oct–March Mon–Sat 9am–3pm, Sun 10am–3pm; £3) was erected in memory of prolific author and patriot Sir Walter Scott within a few years of his death. The architecture is closely modelled on Scott's beloved Melrose Abbey (see p.804), while the rich sculptural decoration shows sixteen Scottish writers and 64 characters from Scott's famous *Waverley* novels. On the central plinth at the base of the monument is a **statue** of Scott with his deerhound Maida, carved from a thirty-ton block of Carrara marble. Inside the memorial, a tightly winding spiral staircase climbs to a narrow platform near the top: from here, you can enjoy some inspiring – if vertiginous – vistas of the city below, and hills and firths beyond.

The National Gallery of Scotland

Princes Street Gardens are bisected by the **Mound** – formed in the 1780s by dumping piles of earth and other waste brought from the New Town's building plots. At the foot of the Mound are two Neoclassical buildings on Princes Street level, the **National Gallery of Scotland** and the **Royal Scottish Academy** (daily 10am–5pm, Thurs till 7pm; free, entrance charge for some temporary exhibitions; Ⓦ www.natgalscot.ac.uk), both designed by William Henry Playfair

(1790–1857). The impressive **Weston Link** provides an entrance to both galleries with an underground passageway joining the two buildings.

Built as a "temple to the fine arts" in 1850, the National Gallery houses Scotland's finest array of European and Scottish art from the early 1300s to the late 1800s, with an outstanding clutch of works ranging from High Renaissance to Post-Impressionism. Its modest size makes it a manageable place to visit in a couple of hours and affords a pleasantly unrushed atmosphere.

A gallery highlight is a superb painting by **Botticelli**, *The Virgin Adoring the Sleeping Christ Child*, which has undergone careful restoration to reveal its striking luminosity and depth of colour. Of four mythological scenes by **Titian**, the sensuous *Three Ages of Man* is one of his most accomplished early compositions, while *Diana and Acteon* and its pendant *Diana and Calisto*, painted for Philip II of Spain, illustrate the highly impressionistic freedom of his late style.

Poussin's *Seven Sacraments* are proudly displayed, as well as **Rubens'** meticulously restored *The Feast of Herod*, an archetypal example of his sumptuously grand manner: its gory subject matter is overshadowed by the gaudy depiction of the delights of the table. Among the four canvases by **Rembrandt** is a poignant *Self-Portrait Aged 51*, and the ripely suggestive *Woman in Bed*, which is thought to represent the Biblical figure of Sarah on her wedding night. Saved at the last minute from California's Getty Museum, the gallery houses **Canova's** 1817 statue *The Three Graces*, and there's also a superb group of Impressionist works, such as **Camille Pissarro's** *Kitchen Garden L'Hermitage*, **Degas'** sketches, paintings and bronzes, as well as **Monet's** *Haystacks (Snow)* and **Renoir's** *Woman Nursing Child*. Representing the Post-Impressionists are three exceptional works by **Gauguin**, including *Vision After the Sermon*, set in Brittany, **Van Gogh's** *Olive Trees*, and **Cézanne's** *The Big Trees* – a clear forerunner of modern abstraction.

The gallery's Scottish and English works include some of **Sir Henry Raeburn's** large portraits – the swaggering masculinity of *Sir John Sinclair in Highland Dress* highlights Raeburn's technical mastery, though he was equally confident when working on a smaller scale for one of the gallery's most popular pictures, *The Rev Robert Walker Skating on Duddingston Loch*. The gallery also owns a brilliant array of watercolours by **Turner**, faithfully displayed each January when damaging sunlight is at its weakest.

Contemporary art in Edinburgh

In addition to the contemporary art collections in the city's National Galleries there are a number of fantastic smaller, independent galleries around the city.

Edinburgh Printmakers 23 Union St ⓣ0131/557 2479, ⓦwww.edinburgh-printmakers.co.uk. A highly respected studio and gallery dedicated to contemporary printmaking.

Fruitmarket Gallery 45 Market St ⓣ0131/225 2383, ⓦwww.fruitmarket.co.uk. The stylish modern design of this dynamic and much-admired art space is the capital's first port of call for top-grade international artists.

Open Eye Gallery 34 Abercromby Place ⓣ0131/557 1020, ⓦwww.openeyegallery.co.uk. One of the city's finest commercial galleries features a number of Scotland's best contemporary artists.

Scottish Gallery 16 Dundas St ⓣ0131/558 1200, ⓦwww.scottish-gallery.co.uk. One of a number of small galleries on this New Town street; some of the most striking works here are in the basement area dedicated to applied art.

Charlotte Square

At the western end of George Street, **Charlotte Square** was designed by Robert Adam in 1791, a year before his death. Generally regarded as the epitome of the New Town's elegant simplicity, the square was once the most exclusive residential address in Edinburgh, and though much of it is now occupied by offices, the imperious dignity of the architecture is still evident. Indeed, the north side is once again the city's premier address, with the official residence of the First Minister of the Scottish Executive at no. 6 (Bute House), the Edinburgh equivalent of 10 Downing Street.

The lower floors of no. 7 – the **Georgian House** – are open to the public (daily: March & Nov–Dec 11am–3pm; April–June, Sept & Oct 10am–5pm; July & Aug 10am–7pm; NTS; £5). Restored by the NTS, the interior provides a revealing sense of well-to-do New Town living in the early nineteenth century. The buildings on the south side of the square have also been superbly restored by the NTS to something approaching their Georgian grandeur, and now house the NTS Scottish **headquarters**. Don't miss no. 28, for a peek at the sumptuous interior and its small first-floor **gallery** (Mon–Fri 11am–3pm; free) showing a collection of twentieth-century Scottish art, including a number of attractive works by the Scottish Colourists. In August each year, the gardens in the centre of the square are colonized by the temporary tents of the Edinburgh Book Festival (see p.789).

Scottish National Portrait Gallery

At the eastern end of Queen Street, just to the north of St Andrew Square, is the **Scottish National Portrait Gallery** (Fri–Wed 10am–5pm, Thurs 10am–7pm; free, entrance charge for some temporary exhibitions). A fantastic medieval Gothic palace in red sandstone, the Portrait Gallery makes an extravagant contrast to the New Town's prevailing Neoclassicism. The exterior of the building is encrusted with statues of famous national heroes, a theme reiterated by William Hole's frieze depicting notable figures from Scotland's past, in the stunning two-storey entrance hall. Unlike the more global outlook of its sister National Gallery (see p.776), the Portrait Gallery devotes itself to images of famous Scots – a definition stretched to include anyone with the slightest connection to the country. Taken as a whole, it's an engaging procession through Scottish history, with familiar faces from Bonnie Prince Charlie and Mary, Queen of Scots, to Alex Ferguson and Sean Connery appearing along the way.

Calton Hill

Edinburgh's tag as the "Athens of the North" is nowhere better earned than on **Calton Hill**, the volcanic peak which rises up above the eastern end of Princes Street. The hill and its odd collection of grandiose buildings aren't just for looking *at*: this is also one of the best viewpoints from which to appreciate the whole city and the sea beyond – much closer to Edinburgh than many visitors expect.

Set majestically on the slopes of Calton Hill looking towards Arthur's Seat sits one of Edinburgh's greatest buildings, the **Old Royal High School**. With its bold central portico of Doric columns and graceful symmetrical colonnaded wings, Thomas Hamilton's elegant building of 1829 is regarded by many as the epitome of Edinburgh's Athenian aspirations. The capital's high school was based here between 1829 and 1968, at which point the building was converted to house a debating chamber and became Scotland's parliament-in-waiting.

However, soon after the re-establishment of a Scottish parliament had been confirmed in 1997 the building was controversially rejected as too small for the intended assembly, with a brand-new building at Holyrood favoured instead. Currently used as offices by the city council, the latest plan is to convert it into a museum of the history of photography.

Robert Louis Stevenson reckoned that Calton Hill was the best place to view Edinburgh, "since you can see the Castle, which you lose from the Castle, and Arthur's Seat, which you cannot see from Arthur's Seat". Though the panoramas from ground level are spectacular enough, those from the top of the **Nelson Monument** (April–Sept Mon–Sat 10am–6pm, plus Sun noon–5pm in Aug; Oct–March Mon–Sat 10am–3pm; £3), perched near the summit, are even better. Alongside, the **National Monument** is often referred to as "Edinburgh's Disgrace", yet many locals admire this unfinished and somewhat ungainly attempt to replicate the Parthenon atop Calton Hill. Begun as a memorial to the dead of the Napoleonic Wars, the project's shortage of funds led architect William Playfair to ensure that it would still serve as a striking landmark, despite having only twelve completed columns. With a bit of effort and care you can climb up and around the monument, sit and contemplate from one of the huge steps or meander around the base of the mighty pillars.

Designed by Playfair in 1818, the **City Observatory** is the largest of the buildings at the summit of Calton Hill. Because of pollution and the advent of street lighting, which impaired views of the stars, the observatory proper had to be relocated to Blackford Hill before the end of the nineteenth century. The complex isn't open to the public, but a stroll around its perimeter offers a broad perspective over the city, with views out to the Forth Bridges and Fife.

Mansfield Place Church

The highlight of the Broughton Street area, northwest of Calton, is the neo-Norman **Mansfield Place Church**, on the corner of Broughton and East London streets. It contains a cycle of **murals** by the Dublin-born **Phoebe Anna Traquair**, a leading light in the Scottish Arts and Crafts movement. Covering vast areas of the walls and ceilings of the main nave and side chapels, the wonderfully luminous paintings depict Biblical parables and texts, with rows of angels, cherubs flecked with gold and worshipping figures painted in delicate pastel colours. Viewing of the murals is restricted to one Sunday afternoon each month, although more regular opening is normally arranged during the Festival: for details see Ⓦwww.mansfieldtraquair.org.uk.

The Royal Botanic Garden

Just beyond the northern boundaries of the New Town, with entrances on Inverleith Row and Arboretum Place, is the seventy-acre site of the **Royal Botanic Garden** (daily: March & Oct 10am–6pm; April–Sept 10am–7pm; Nov–Feb 10am–4pm; free; Ⓦwww.rbge.org.uk). Filled with mature trees and a huge variety of native and exotic plants and flowers, the "Botanics" (as they're commonly called) are most popular simply as a place to stroll and lounge around on the grass. The gardens incorporate a series of ten glasshouses (entry £3.50) – including the elegant 1850s Palm House – which show off a steamy array of palms, ferns, orchids, cycads and aquatic plants, and an art gallery showing changing contemporary exhibitions in the attractive eighteenth-century Inverleith House. Scattered all around are a number of outdoor sculptures, and parts of the garden have fabulous great vistas: the busy *Terrace Café* (see p.784) beside Inverleith House offers one of the city's best views of the castle and of Old Town's steeples and monuments. **Guided tours** (£3) leave from the West Gate on Arboretum Place at 11am and 2pm (April–Sept).

The West End

The western extension to the New Town was the last part to be built, deviating from the area's overriding Neoclassicism with a number of Victorian additions. Just over the Water of Leith are two compelling collections of contemporary art, the well-established **Scottish National Gallery of Modern Art** and its newer neighbour, the **Dean Gallery**, both of which regularly host worthwhile seasonal and touring exhibitions.

The most pleasant way of getting to the galleries is on foot along the **Water of Leith walkway**, which can be joined at Stockbridge or the Dean Village. Alternatively, a free **bus** runs there on the hour (daily 10.45am–5pm) from outside the National Gallery on the Mound, via the National Portrait Gallery. Alternatively, bus #13 runs along Belford Road, from the western end of George Street.

The Scottish National Gallery of Modern Art

At the far northwestern fringe of the New Town, the **Scottish National Gallery of Modern Art** on Belford Road (daily 10am–5pm, open till 6pm in Aug; free, entrance charge for some temporary exhibitions; Ⓦwww.natgalscot.ac.uk) was Britain's first collection devoted solely to twentieth-century painting and sculpture, and operates in tandem with Dean Gallery (see p.781). The extensive wooded grounds of the galleries serve as a sculpture park, featuring works by Jacob Epstein, Henry Moore, Barbara Hepworth and, most strikingly, Charles Jencks, whose prize-winning *Landform*, a swirling mix of ponds and grassy mounds, dominates the area in front of the Gallery of Modern Art. The gallery displays temporary exhibitions and a variety of its own works, including early twentieth-century Post-Impressionists, the Fauves, German Expressionism, Cubism and Pop Art. There's a strong section on living British artists, while modern Scottish art ranges from the Colourists – whose works are attracting ever-growing posthumous critical acclaim – to the distinctive styles of contemporary Scots.

The Dean Gallery

Opposite the Modern Art Gallery on the other side of Belford Road is the **Dean Gallery** (same hours; free; Ⓦwww.natgalscot.ac.uk), housed in an equally impressive Neoclassical building completed in 1833. The interior of the gallery, built originally as an orphanage, has been dramatically refurbished specifically to make room for the work of Edinburgh-born sculptor **Sir Eduardo Paolozzi**, described by some as the father of Pop Art. The collection includes some three thousand sculptures, two thousand prints and drawings and three thousand books.

There's an awesome introduction to Paolozzi's work in the form of the huge *Vulcan*, a half-man, half-machine squeezed into the Great Hall immediately opposite the main entrance. In rooms to the right of the main entrance, his London studio has been expertly re-created, right down to the clutter of half-finished casts, toys and empty pots of glue.

The ground floor also holds a world-renowned collection of **Dada** and **Surrealist** art; Marcel Duchamp, Max Ernst and Man Ray are all represented. Look out also for Dalí's *The Signal of Anguish* and Magritte's *Magic Mirror* along with work by Miró and Giacometti – all hung on crowded walls with an assortment of artefacts and ethnic souvenirs.

Out from the centre

Just over a mile northeast of the city centre is **Leith**, a fascinating mix of cobbled streets and new developments, run-down housing and an excellent eating and drinking scene, which focuses on seafood but also includes some of the city's top restaurants side by side with well-worn, friendly pubs. Edinburgh's **zoo** is a perennial favourite with children, who will also enjoy the quiet ruins of **Craigmillar Castle** to the south of the city.

Leith

Although **LEITH** is generally known as the port of Edinburgh, it developed independently of the city up the hill, its history bound up in the hard graft of fishing, shipbuilding and trade. The presence of sailors, merchants and continental traders also gave the place a cosmopolitan – if slightly rough – edge, which is still obvious today.

The best way to absorb Leith's history and seafaring connections is to take a stroll along **The Shore**, a tenement-lined road running alongside the Water of Leith. Until the mid-nineteenth century this was a bustling harbour, visited by ships from all over the world, but as vessels became increasingly large, they moored up instead at custom-built docks beyond the original quays. Nowadays, the spotlight is on the numerous **pubs and restaurants** that line the street, many of which spill tables and chairs out onto the cobbled pavement on sunny days.

A little to the west of The Shore, moored alongside **Ocean Terminal**, a huge shopping and entertainment centre designed by Terence Conran, is one of the world's most famous ships, **Britannia** (daily: April–Sept 9.30am–4.30pm; Oct–March 10am–3.30pm; £9.50; Ⓦwww.royalyachtbritannia.co.uk). Launched in 1953, *Britannia* was used by the royal family for 44 years for state visits, diplomatic functions and royal holidays. Video clips of the ship's most famous moments are shown in the **visitor centre** (within Ocean Terminal) along with royal holiday snaps, and you can roam around the yacht itself, which has been largely kept as she was when in service, with a well-preserved 1950s dowdiness – a far cry from the opulent splendour which many expect.

To get to Ocean Terminal from the city, jump on one of the tour **buses** that leave from Waverley Bridge; otherwise, take buses #11, #22 or #34 from Princes Street, or #35 from the Royal Mile.

Edinburgh Zoo

A couple of miles due west of the city centre is **Edinburgh Zoo** (daily: April–Sept 9am–6pm; March & Oct 9am–5pm; Nov–Feb 9am–4.30pm; £10.50; Ⓦwww.edinburghzoo.org.uk), set on the slopes of Corstorphine Hill (buses #12, #26, #31 & #100 from town). Established in 1913, the zoo has a reputation for preserving rare and endangered species, with the emphasis moving away from bored animals in cages to imaginatively designed habitats and viewing areas. The place is permanently packed with kids, and the zoo's most famous attraction is its **penguin parade** (April–Sept daily 2.15pm, and on sunny days in March & Oct).

Craigmillar Castle

Situated around five miles southeast of Edinburgh's centre, **Craigmillar Castle** (April–Sept daily 9.30am–5.30pm; Oct–March Sat–Wed 9.30am–4.30pm, HS; £4), is one of the best-preserved ruined medieval fortresses in Scotland. Though it's located next to one of Edinburgh's most deprived districts, Craigmillar, the immediate setting feels very rural and the castle enjoys splendid views back to Arthur's Seat and Edinburgh Castle. The oldest part of the complex dates from the early 1400s; surrounded in the 1500s by a quadrangular wall with cylindrical corner towers, it was used on occasion by Mary, Queen of Scots. Abandoned to picturesque decay in the mid-eighteenth century, the peaceful ruins and their adjoining grassy lawns nowadays make a great place to explore, with children in particular loving the run of their very own castle.

Take **bus** #8, #33 or #49, from North Bridge to Edinburgh Royal Infirmary, from where the castle is a ten-minute walk along a footpath.

Eating

Edinburgh has a clutch of original, upmarket and stylish cafés and **restaurants**, serving **contemporary** or **modern Scottish** cuisine and championing top-quality local meat, game and fish. There's also a good selection of mid-market chains and long-established Chinese, Indian and Mexican places, as well as more interesting outposts of Thai, North African and Spanish cuisine.

Royal Mile and around

Cafés and bistros

Always Sunday 170 High St ⓣ0131/622 0667. Proof that there's room for a bit of real food even on the tourist-thronged Royal Mile, this pleasant, independent café serves healthy lunches, home-made cakes, fresh smoothies and Fairtrade coffee. Open daily till 6pm. Inexpensive.

Café Hub Castlehill ⓣ0131/473 2067. Colourful café in the Edinburgh Festival centre, with light modern meals served right through the day and evening. The large terrace is a good spot for watching the world go by on sunny days. Inexpensive.

Elephant House 21 George IV Bridge ⓣ0131/220 5355. Extolled as one of the places where J.K. Rowling, then a hard-up single mum, nursed her cups of coffee while penning the first Harry Potter novel, this is a decent daytime and evening café with a terrific room at the back full of philosophizing students and visitors peering dreamily at the views of the castle. Daily 8am–11pm. Inexpensive.

Fruitmarket Gallery Café 45 Market St ⓣ0131/226 1843. This attractive café feels like an extension of the gallery space, its airy, reflective ambience enhanced by the wall of glass onto the street. Stop in for soups, coffees or a Caesar salad. Mon–Sat 11am–5.30pm, Sun noon–4.30pm. Inexpensive.

Restaurants

Amber Scotch Whisky Heritage Centre, 354 Castlehill ⓣ0131/477 8477, ⓦwww.amber-restaurant.co.uk. Neat, contemporary place serving a good choice of light food such as parsnip and orange tart at lunchtime, and more substantial and expensive dishes in the evenings (Tues–Sat), when there's a "whisky sommelier" on hand to suggest the best drams to accompany your garlic roasted rump of Highland lamb or fillet of Buccleuch beef with truffle oil. Expensive.

Barioja 19 Jeffrey St ⓣ0131/557 3622. Open right through the day and good for a lunchtime *bocadillos* sandwich or late-afternoon drink and snack, this Spanish-owned bar makes a decent stab at tapas in a metropolitan setting. Inexpensive. The more upmarket *Igg's*, a Spanish-Scottish hybrid, is next door.

David Bann's Vegetarian Restaurant 56–58 St Mary's St ⓣ0131/556 5888, ⓦwww.davidbann.com. Thoroughly modern vegetarian restaurant, open long hours and offering a wide choice of interesting, unconventional dishes such as Thai-spiced tofu fritters or goats cheese and roasted sweet potato salad. The prices are very reasonable and the overall design is stylish and classy – not an open-toed sandal in sight. Moderate.

The Grain Store 30 Victoria St ⓣ0131/225 7635, ⓦwww.grainstore-restaurant.co.uk. Often missed by passers-by, this unpretentious restaurant is a relaxing haven amongst the bustle of the Old Town, serving fairly uncomplicated but top-quality modern Scottish food such as Loch Fyne oysters with spinach and hollandaise and matured Aberdeen Angus fillet with lardons.

Reasonable lunchtime and set-price options. Expensive.

Khushi's 9 Victoria St ⓣ0131/220 0057, ⓦwww.khushis.com. The glitzy new premises may perhaps belie its status as one of city's most venerable Punjabi institutions but *Khushi's* remains faithful to a long standing-ethos of serving peerless classics such as lamb bhuna and fish curries, all at extremely affordable prices. No alcohol served, though you can BYO or order one of the excellent fruit lassis. Inexpensive.

La Garrigue 31 Jeffrey St ⓣ0131/557 3032, ⓦwww.lagarrigue.co.uk. Charming, top-quality place, with a menu and wine list dedicated to the produce and traditions of the Languedoc region of France. The care and honesty of the cooking shine through in dishes such as cassoulet or coley with langoustine. Moderate.

Tower Museum of Scotland, Chambers St ⓣ0131/225 3003, ⓦwww.tower-restaurant.com. Unique setting on Level 5 of the Museum of Scotland; at night you are escorted along the empty corridors to the restaurant, where spectacular views to the floodlit castle are revealed. Excellent modern Scottish food such as shellfish and venison haunch in a self-consciously chic setting. Expensive.

The Witchery by the Castle 352 Castlehill ⓣ0131/225 5613, ⓦwww.thewitchery.com. A fine dining restaurant that only Edinburgh could create, set in magnificently over-the-top medieval surroundings full of Gothic panelling, tapestries and heavy stonework, all a mere broomstick-hop from the castle. The rich fish and game dishes are pricey, but you can steal a sense of it all with a lunch or pre- or post-theatre set menu (£12.95). Expensive.

New Town and the West End

Cafés and bistros

Glass & Thompson 2 Dundas St ⓣ0131/557 0909. Tasteful, upmarket café-deli with huge bowls of olives and an irresistible glass counter filled with delicious food; a fine place to linger over a made-to-order sandwich or top-notch cake and coffee. Closed evenings. Inexpensive.

Urban Angel 121 Hanover St ⓣ0131/225 6215. Right-on but easygoing subterranean bistro with a diverse and flexible blackboard menu using lots of organic and Fairtrade produce. Closed Sun eve. Moderate.

Valvona & Crolla VinCaffè 11 Multrees Walk ⓣ0131/557 0088, ⓦwww.valvonacrolla.com. Suave sister venue to the famous Leith Walk deli, with an espresso bar and takeaway downstairs and classy Italian snacks, meals and wines by the glass upstairs. Moderate–expensive.

Restaurants

Café Royal Oyster Bar 17a W Register St ⓣ0131/556 4124. An Edinburgh classic, with its splendidly ornate Victorian interior (featured in *Chariots of Fire*), stained-glass windows, marble floor and Doulton tiling. Time-honoured seafood dishes, including freshly caught oysters, served in a civilized, chatty setting. Very expensive.

Centrotre 103 George St ⓣ0131/225 1550, ⓦwww.centotre.com. Slick but welcoming bar, café and restaurant in an ornate former bank, offering unfussy, top-quality Italian food: fresh pastries and coffee, inventive pizzas, or a simple but blissful plate of gorgonzola served with a ripe pear. All accompanied by a seriously impressive drinks list. Moderate.

Dusit 49a Thistle St ⓣ0131/220 6846, ⓦwww.dusit.co.uk. The bold but effective blend of Thai flavours and well-sourced Scottish ingredients here brings a bit of originality and refinement to the often predictable Thai dining scene. Specialities include guinea fowl with red curry sauce or vegetables stir-fried with a dash of whisky. Moderate.

Forth Floor Harvey Nichols, 30–34 St Andrew Square ⓣ0131/524 8350, ⓦwww.harveynichols.com. While the rooftop views don't quite match those of its rivals *Oloroso* and the *Tower*, *Forth Floor's* restaurant and brasserie still possesses that quality to make it a real contender among the city's fine modern Scottish establishments. Dishes include seared scallops with foie gras, perhaps, or spiced monkfish. Closed Sun & Mon eve. Moderate to expensive.

Henderson's Salad Table 94 Hanover St ⓣ0131/225 2131, ⓦwww.hendersonsofedinburgh.co.uk. A much-loved Edinburgh institution, this self-service basement vegetarian restaurant offers freshly prepared hot dishes plus a decent choice of salads, soups and cakes. The slightly antiquated cafeteria feel can be off-putting, but the food is honest, reliable and always tasty. Light live jazz every evening. Mon–Sat 8am–10.30pm. Inexpensive–moderate.

Le Café St Honoré 34 Thistle St Lane ⓣ0131/226 2211, ⓦwww.cafesthonore.com. A little piece of Paris discreetly tucked away in a New Town back lane. Fairly traditional top-quality French fare – grilled oysters, warm duck salad and tarte tatin. Closed Sun. Moderate.

Mussel Inn 61–65 Rose St ⓣ0131/225 5979, ⓦwww.mussel-inn.com. After feasting on a kilo of mussels and a basket of chips for under £10 you'll realize why there's a demand to get in here. Owned by two west coast shellfish farmers, which ensures that the oyster's journey from sea to stomach is speedy. Closed Sun. Moderate.

Oloroso 33 Castle St ⓣ0131/226 7614, ⓦwww.oloroso.co.uk. Edinburgh's most glamorous upmarket dining space, with a rooftop location giving views to the castle and the Forth. The menu features strong flavours such as chump of lamb or halibut in a mussel and sorrel broth. Eating (or drinking) from the more convivial bar is the cost-effective way to enjoy the setting, but the best views are from the balcony. Expensive.

Broughton and Leith Walk

Cafés and bistros

Blue Moon Café 1 Barony St ⓣ0131/557 0911. One of the best-known beacons of Edinburgh's gay scene, this easygoing, straight-friendly café-bar serves decent coffee, hearty breakfasts and light meals right through to 11pm. Moderate.

Valvona & Crolla 19 Elm Row, Leith Walk ⓣ0131/556 6066, ⓦwww.valvonacrolla.com. The café at the back of this Italian deli – arguably Britain's finest – serves authentic and delicious breakfasts, lunches and snacks. The best advert for the café is the walk through the shop – which has food stacked from floor to ceiling, with display cabinets full of sublime olives, meats and cheeses. *V&C* also has a wine bar and restaurant in the New Town (p.775). Mon–Sat 8am–5pm. Moderate.

Stockbridge and around

Cafés and bistros

The Gallery Café Scottish National Gallery of Modern Art, Belford Rd, Dean Village ⓣ0131/332 8600. Far more than a standard refreshment stop for gallery visitors, the cultured setting (which includes a lovely outside eating area) and appealing menu of hearty soups, healthy salads and filled croissants pulls in crowds of locals. Daily 10am–4.30pm. Moderate.

Terrace Café Royal Botanic Garden, Inverleith ⓣ0131/552 0616. A great location right in the middle of the garden, with outside tables offering stunning views of the city skyline, but the food isn't that memorable and it can be busy (and noisy) with families. Inexpensive.

Zanzero 15 North West Circus Place ⓣ0131/220 0333, ⓦwww.zanzero.com. Upbeat, fresh café-bistro from the same stable as *Centotre* (see p.783), serving lighter, healthier food including pizzas, salads and fish. Moderate.

Lothian Road and Tollcross

Cafés and bistros

blue 10 Cambridge St ⓣ0131/221 1222. With minimalist modern decor, this impressive café/bistro hits the spot in terms of standards of food and service. It's handy for a quality pre- or post-theatre bite, with tasty modern dishes such as sea bass and baby onion tatin or confit duck leg with black pudding mash for under £10, and is one of the city's more sophisticated child-friendly options. Closed Sun. Moderate.

Restaurants

The Atrium 10 Cambridge St ⓣ0131/228 8882, ⓦwww.atriumrestaurant.co.uk. One of the most consistently striking of Edinburgh's top-end restaurants. Quirky, arty design including features such as railway-sleeper tables, while the food focuses on high-quality Scottish produce, some of it sourced from the nearby farmers' market. Closed Sun. Expensive.

izzi 119 Lothian Rd ⓣ0131/466 9888, ⓦwww.izzi-restaurant.co.uk. Set among the bright lights and late-night revelry of Lothian Rd, this is a slick, contemporary restaurant offering both Chinese and Japanese cuisine, including some of the better sushi around. Moderate.

Roti 73 Morrison St ⓣ0131/221 9998, ⓦwww.roti.uk.com. A refreshing take on contemporary Indian dining, moving towards the more sophisticated end of the market, but free of many of Britain's standard subcontinental clichés. Lunch menu includes a tiffin box selection. Closed Sun & Mon. Moderate.

Southside

Cafés and bistros

The Apartment 7–13 Barclay Place, Bruntsfield ☎0131/228 6456. Hugely popular, highly fashionable diner, with sleek, modern furniture, sisal flooring and abstract contemporary art on the walls. Their "Chunky, Healthy Lines" feature wholesome kebabs of meat, fish or vegetables. Closed lunch Mon–Fri. Moderate.

Mosque Kitchen Edinburgh Central Mosque, 50 Potterrow, Newington. Very cheap, filing curries served from a tiny kitchen behind the mosque; the only seating is outside under a large awning. Popular with students and on sunny days. Inexpensive.

Restaurants

Celadon 49–51 Causewayside, Newington ☎0131/667 1110. There are now dozens of Thai restaurants in Edinburgh; this is one of the more reliable bets with original, fresh cooking. Moderate.

Hanedan 41 W Preston St, Newington ☎0131/667 4242. Small and relatively simple BYOB. The authentic kebabs, *moussaka* and *dolmates* make this Turkish place an interesting alternative to cheaper Italian or bistro fare. Closed Mon. Moderate.

Kalpna 2–3 St Patrick's Square, Newington ☎0131/667 9890. Outstanding vegetarian restaurant serving authentic Gujarati dishes. Four set meals, including a vegan option, stand alongside the main menu. Moderate.

Sweet Melinda's 11 Roseneath St, Marchmont ☎0131/229 7953. A smart seafood restaurant in a single, timber-panelled room with a friendly neighbourhood feel. It's edging towards the expensive side, but it's worth shelling out for dishes such as grilled mackerel in a broth of ginger and chillies or roast cod with capers and Puy lentils. Closed Sun & lunchtime Mon. Moderate–expensive.

Leith and Newhaven

Restaurants

The Kitchin 78 Commercial Quay ☎0131/555 1755, ⓦwww.thekitchin.com. Opened in 2006 by young Scottish chef Tom Kitchin – holder of a Michelin star little more than six months later – the restaurant puts itself at the more relaxed end of the fine-dining bracket and offers some tantalizing dishes including rolled pig's head with crispy ear salad, or duck cooked whole. Closed Sun & Mon. Expensive.

Loch Fyne Restaurant 25 Pier Place, Newhaven Harbour ☎0131/559 3900, ⓦwww.lochfyne.com. In a fantastic location by the fish market and old stone harbour at Newhaven. Best for simple oysters and fish with a glass of wine. Moderate.

Restaurant Martin Wishart 52 The Shore ☎0131/553 3557, ⓦwww.martin-wishart.co.uk. The eponymous chef is one of the leading lights of the Scottish culinary scene, and was the first Michelin star holder in Edinburgh. Though relatively modest in size and demure in atmosphere, this place wows the gourmets with highly accomplished and exquisitely presented French-influenced dishes. A two-course lunch is £22.50, a seven-course evening tasting menu £60. Reservations recommended. Closed Sun & Mon. Very expensive.

The Shore 3–4 The Shore ☎0131/553 5080. A well-lived-in bar/restaurant with huge mirrors, wood panelling and aproned waiters who serve up good fish dishes and decent wines. Live jazz, folk and hubbub floats through from the adjoining bar. Moderate.

The Vintner's Rooms 87 Giles St ☎0131/554 6767, ⓦwww.thevintnersrooms.com. Splendid restaurant in a seventeenth-century warehouse; the small but ornate Rococo dining room is a marvel and the food – from seafood to game – isn't bad either. Closed Sun eve & Mon. Expensive.

The Waterfront 1c Dock Place ☎0131/554 7427, ⓦwww.waterfrontwinebar.co.uk. Housed in the former lock-keeper's cottage, with dining space in the wonderfully characterful wine bar or waterside conservatory. Fish dishes dominate. Moderate.

Pubs and bars

Many of Edinburgh's **pubs**, especially in the Old Town, have histories that stretch back centuries, while others, particularly in the New Town, are unaltered Victorian or Edwardian period pieces. Add a plentiful supply of trendy modern **bars**, and there's enough to cater for all tastes. The standard licensing hours are 11am to11pm

A fun way to explore Edinburgh's pubs is to take the **Edinburgh Literary Pub Tour**, a pub crawl with culture around Old and New Town watering holes. Starting from the *Beehive Inn*, 18–20 Grassmarket (Ⓣ0131/226 6665, Ⓦwww.edinburghliterarypubtour.co.uk), and led by professional actors, the tour introduces you to the scenes, characters and words of the major figures of Scottish literature, including Burns, Scott and MacDiarmid.

(12.30–11pm on Sun), but many honest howffs stay open later and, during the Festival especially, it's no problem to find bars open until at least 1am.

The Royal Mile and around

Black Bo's 55 Blackfriars St. No music and no decent ales, but a good example of how to stay trendy without going minimalist, with church pews and candles alongside original art and DJ decks. Just fifty yards from the Royal Mile, but well off the tourist trail.

Bow Bar 80 West Bow. Wonderful, award-winning old wood-panelled bar. Choose from among nearly 150 whiskies or a changing selection of first-rate Scottish and English cask beers.

Dragonfly 52 West Port. Among the hippest of the city's style bars, with chandeliers, faux-regal wallpaper, a display of designer trainers and a wide range of ingenious cocktails.

Jolly Judge 7a James Court. Atmospheric, low-ceilinged bar in a close just down from the castle. Cosy in winter and pleasant outside in summer.

Villager 49–50 George IV Bridge. One of the hippest bars in this part of town, so expect the local glitterati and lots of designer clothing lurking in and amongst the chocolate-brown sofas and teetering bar stools.

New Town and West End

Café Royal Circle Bar 17 W Register St. As notable as the *Oyster Bar* restaurant next door, the *Café Royal* is worth a visit for its Victorian decor alone, notably the huge elliptical island bar and the tiled portraits of renowned inventors. More than that, the beer and food are good, too.

Cumberland Bar 1 Cumberland St. One of the few pubs in this part of the New Town, this mellow, cultured, old-fashioned place full of wood panelling and cosy nooks is a delightful find, and serves excellent cask-conditioned ales.

The Dome 14 George St. Opulent conversion of a massive New Town bank, thronging with well-dressed locals. Probably the most impressive bar interior in Edinburgh, though the ultra-chic atmosphere can be a bit intense. Sun–Thurs open till 11.30pm, Fri & Sat till 1am.

Opal Lounge 51 George St. A much-talked about, intimate bar with a faintly oriental theme, loud music and a long cocktail list. Over-dressed twentysomethings flock here for a glimpse of local celebrities, but usually have to stand in a queue and squeeze past the bouncers to get in.

Oxford Bar 8 Young St. An unpretentious, unspoilt, no-nonsense city bar – which is why local crime writer Ian Rankin and his Inspector Rebus like it so much. Fans duly make the pilgrimage, but fortunately not all the regulars have been scared off. Open tlil 1am.

Whighams Wine Cellars 13 Hope St, Charlotte Square. One of the more sophisticated venues in the city centre, with an impressive wine list and some gloomy subterranean cubby holes. There's good seafood available, too.

Broughton and Leith Walk

The Barony Bar 81–85 Broughton St. A fine old-fashioned bar which manages to be big and lively without being spoilt. Chainification has blunted a bit of its appeal, but there's still real ale and a blazing fire.

The Outhouse 12a Broughton St Lane. Busy pre-club bar tucked away down a cobbled lane off Broughton St, with a lively beer garden and funky music. Open till 1am.

Stockbridge

Bert's Bar 2–4 Raeburn Place (also 29 William St, West End). Popular locals' pubs with a lived-in feel, despite their relatively recent arrival. Both serve excellent beer, tasty pies and strive to be authentic, non-theme-oriented venues, though the telly rarely misses any sporting action.

Lothian Road and Tollcross

Blue Blazer 2 Spittal St. This traditional Edinburgh howff with an oak-clad bar and church pews serves as good a selection of real ales as you'll find anywhere in the city. Open till 1am.

Traverse Bar Café Traverse Theatre, 10 Cambridge St. Much more than just a theatre bar, attracting a lively, sophisticated crowd who dispel any notion of a quiet interval drink. Good food available. One of the places to be during the Festival.

Southside

Human Be-In 2–8 West Crosscauseway, Newington. One of the trendiest student bars around, with huge plate-glass windows to admire the beautiful people and tables outside for summer posing. Good food too. Open till 1am.

Peartree House 36 W Nicolson St, Newington. Fine bar in an eighteenth-century house with old sofas and a large courtyard – one of central Edinburgh's very few beer gardens. Serves budget bar lunches. Open Mon–Wed & Sun till midnight, Thurs–Sat till 1am.

Leith

Cruz 14 The Shore. Situated right on the Water of Leith in a ship that has served as a minesweeper, luxury yacht, and night club in previous incarnations, this floating style-bar is sleek and elegant inside and includes a sun terrace for classy alfresco cocktails during the summer months. Daily noon–1am.

Kings Wark 36 The Shore. Real ale in an atmospheric restored eighteenth-century pub right in the heart of Leith, with bar meals chalked up on the rafters. Open till midnight Fri & Sat.

The Shore 3–4 The Shore. Traditional bar with an adjacent restaurant (see p.785). There's regular live jazz or folk music as well as real ales and good bar snacks.

Elsewhere in the city

Athletic Arms (The Diggers) 1–3 Angle Park Terrace, Polwarth. Known to all as *Diggers* after the spade-wielding employees of the cemetery across the road, this is a place of pilgrimage if you're into sport (Murrayfield and Hearts' Tyncastle ground are just along the road) and real ale, with the Caledonian Brewery's beers well represented. Open Mon–Thurs till midnight, Fri & Sat till 1am, Sun till 6pm.

Canny Man's (Volunteer Arms) 237 Morningside Rd, Morningside. Atmospheric and idiosyncratic pub-cum-museum adorned with anything that can be hung on the walls or from the ceiling. Local ales and over 200 whiskies on offer, as well as snacks.

Sheep Heid Inn 43 The Causeway, Duddingston. One of Edinburgh's best-known historic pubs, the building has barely survived various predictable makeovers, but despite this, remains an attractive spot. Decent meals are available at the bar, and there's an old-fashioned skittle alley out the back.

Nightlife and entertainment

Inevitably, Edinburgh's **nightlife** is at its best during the Festival (see p.789), which can make the other 49 weeks of the year seem like an anticlimax. However, at any time the city has plenty to offer, especially in the realm of **theatre** and **music**.

The **nightclub** scene is lively, and you can normally hear **live jazz**, **folk** and **rock** every evening in one or other of the city's pubs. There are also permanent venues large enough to host large touring **orchestras** and **ballet** companies.

Hogmanay

Edinburgh hosts Europe's largest **New Year's Eve street party**, with around 100,000 people on the streets of the city enjoying the culmination of a week-long series of events. On the night itself, stages are set up in different parts of the city centre, with big-name rock groups and local ceilidh bands playing to the increasingly inebriated masses. The high point of the evening is, of course, midnight, when hundreds of tons of fireworks are let off into the night sky above the castle, and Edinburgh joins the rest of the world singing **"Auld Lang Syne"**, an old Scottish tune with lyrics by Robert Burns, Scotland's national poet. For information about celebrations in Edinburgh, and how to get hold of tickets for the street party, go to ⓦwww.edinburghshogmanay.org.

Out of the capital, the best way to celebrate **Hogmanay** is to join one of the street parties that are held in the middle of towns and cities, often centred around a prominent clockface which rings out "the bells" at midnight. For more details about the background to Hogmanay, see the *Festivals* colour section.

The city boasts a couple of excellent art-house **cinemas**, and its top **comedy** club, The Stand, 5 York Place (ⓣ0131/558 7272, ⓦwww.thestand.co.uk), has a different act every night with some of the UK's top comics headlining at the weekends: the bar is worth a visit in itself.

Edinburgh also has a dynamic **gay** culture, centred round the top of Leith Walk and Broughton Street; more and more gay enterprises, especially cafés and nightclubs, have sprung up in this area, dubbed the "Pink Triangle".

The best way to find out **what's on** is to pick up a copy of *The List*, a fortnightly listings magazine covering both Edinburgh and Glasgow (£2.20).

Nightclubs

Cabaret Voltaire 36–38 Blair St ⓣ0131/220 6176, ⓦwww.thecabaretvoltaire.com. A nightclub in the atmospheric setting of the Old Town's underground vaults. The venue plays host to some of city's best clubs such as deep-house favourite Ultragroove and Taste, an evening of frenetic hard-house that has long been a favourite with the city's gay community.

Ego 14 Picardy Place ⓣ0131/478 7434, ⓦwww.clubego.co.uk. A former casino, this big venue is the monthly home for acclaimed Glasgow club *Optimo* and the epic party night *Vegas*. The smaller *Cocteau Lounge* downstairs is occasionally in use for more intimate alternative and retro club nights.

The Liquid Room 9c Victoria St ⓣ0131/225 2564, ⓦwww.liquidroom.com. One of the best of the larger venues, with nights such as the indie *Evol*, and *Lively*, a popular gay-friendly house night.

Lulu's 125b George St ⓣ0131/225 5005, ⓦwww.luluedinburgh.co.uk. Sultry subterranean nightspot beneath *OTT* bar and restaurant *Tigerlily*. A place to see and be seen, with its fair share of Travolta-wannabes striding to the sound-responsive disco lightfloor.

Gay clubs and bars

CC Bloom's 23–24 Greenside Place ⓣ0131/556 9331. Edinburgh's only uniquely gay club, with a big dance floor, stonking rhythms and a young, friendly crowd.

Sala Café Bar 60 Broughton St ⓣ0131/478 7069. Fresh food, light Spanish snacks and drinks in a relaxed atmosphere at the Edinburgh Gay, Lesbian and Bisexual Centre.

The Street 2 Picardy Place ⓣ0131/556 4272. Located at the top of Broughton St, and therefore at the "gateway" to the Pink Triangle, this mainstream, gay-friendly bar is a sociable spot and good for watching the world (and talent) pass by.

Live music

Corn Exchange 11 Newmarket Rd, Slateford ⓣ0131/477 3500, ⓦwww.ece.uk.com. Once a slaughterhouse, now it's a 3000-capacity venue for big-name contemporary pop and rock acts, though the location, three miles west of the centre, is a bit off-putting.

The Liquid Room 9c Victoria St ⓣ0131/225 2564, ⓦwww.liquidroom.com. Good-sized venue frequented by visiting indie and local R&B bands.

Queen's Hall 89 Clerk St ⓣ0131/668 2019, ⓦwww.queenshalledinburgh.net. Converted Georgian church which now operates as a concert hall; it's used principally by the Scottish Chamber Orchestra and Scottish Ensemble, and much favoured by jazz, blues and folk groups.

Royal Oak 1 Infirmary St ⓣ0131/557 2976, ⓦwww.royal-oak-folk.com. A traditional pub hosting regular informal folk sessions and the "Wee Folk Club" on Sun.

Usher Hall cnr Lothian Rd and Grindlay St ⓣ0131/228 1155, ⓦwww.usherhall.co.uk. Edinburgh's main civic concert hall, seating over 2500. Excellent for choral and symphony concerts, but less suitable for solo vocalists. The upper circle seats are cheapest and have the best acoustics. Closed until Aug 2008 for refurbishment.

Theatre and dance

Festival Theatre Nicolson St ⓣ0131/529 6000, ⓦwww.eft.co.uk. The largest stage in Britain, principally used for Scottish Opera and Scottish Ballet's appearances in the capital, but also for everything from the children's show *The Snowman* to the Glenn Miller Orchestra.

King's Theatre 2 Leven St ⓣ0131/529 6000, ⓦwww.eft.co.uk. Stately Edwardian civic theatre that majors in pantomime, touring West End plays and the occasional major drama or opera performance.

Playhouse Theatre 18–22 Greenside Place ⓣ0870/606 3424, ⓦwww.edinburgh-playhouse.co.uk. The most capacious theatre in Britain, formerly a cinema. Used largely for extended runs of popular musicals and occasional rock concerts.

Royal Lyceum Theatre 30 Grindlay St ⓣ0131/248 4848, ⓦwww.lyceum.org.uk. Fine Victorian civic theatre with a compact auditorium. The leading year-round venue for mainstream drama.

Traverse Theatre 10 Cambridge St ⓣ0131/228 1404, ⓦwww.traverse.co.uk. Unquestionably one of Britain's premier venues for new plays and avant-garde drama from around the world. Going from strength to strength in its custom-built home beside the Usher Hall, with a great bar downstairs and the popular *blue* café-bar (see p.784) upstairs.

Art-house cinemas

Cameo 38 Home St, Tollcross ⓣ0131/228 2800, ⓦwww.picturehouses.co.uk; bookings ⓣ0131/228 4141. A treasure of an art-house cinema screening more challenging mainstream releases and cult late-nighters. Tarantino's been here and thinks it's great.

Filmhouse 88 Lothian Rd ⓣ0131/228 2688, ⓦwww.filmhousecinema.com. Three screens showing an eclectic programme of independent, art-house and classic films. The café is a hangout for the city's dedicated film buffs.

Shopping

Princes Street, one of Britain's most famous shopping streets, is all but dominated by standard chain outlets, though no serious shopper should miss out on a visit to Edinburgh's venerable department store, Jenners, at no. 48 opposite the Scott Monument. More fashionable upmarket shops and boutiques are to be found on and around parallel **George Street**, including the shopping area on the east side of St Andrew Square. There's nothing compelling about central Edinburgh's two big shopping malls, **Princes Mall** and the **St James Centre**, which are dominated by the big names.

For more original outlets, head for **Cockburn Street**, south of Waverley Station, a hub for trendy clothes and record shops, while on **Victoria Street** and in and around the **Grassmarket** you'll find an eclectic range of antique, crafts, food and book shops. Along and around the **Royal Mile** there are several distinctly offbeat places among the tacky-souvenir sellers.

The Edinburgh Festival

The **Edinburgh Festival** is an umbrella term that encompasses different festivals taking place at around the same time in the city. The principal events are the **Edinburgh International Festival** and the much larger **Edinburgh Festival Fringe**, but there are also **Book**, **Jazz and Blues** and **Television** festivals, as well as the **Military Tattoo** on the Castle Esplanade.

For the visitor, the sheer volume of the Festival's output can be bewildering: virtually every branch of arts and entertainment is represented somewhere, and world-famous stars mix with pub singers in the daily line-up. It can be a struggle to find accommodation, get hold of the tickets you want, book a table in a restaurant or simply get from one side of town to another; you can end up seeing something truly dire, or something mind-blowing; you'll inevitably try to do too much, stay out too late or spend too much money – but then again, most Festival veterans will tell you that if you don't experience these things then you haven't really done the Festival. Dates, venues, names, star acts, happening bars and burning issues change from one year to the next. This unpredictability is one of the Festival's greatest charms, so while the following information will help you get to grips with it, be prepared for – indeed, enjoy – the unexpected.

For up-to-the-minute **information** at any time of year, ⓦwww.edinburghfestivals.co.uk has links to the home pages of most of Edinburgh's main festivals. In addition to each festival's own programme, various publications give information about what's on day by day during the Festival. *The Guide* is published daily and gives a chronological listing of virtually every show scheduled for that day. It's available free from the Office (see below) and hundreds of other spots around Edinburgh, along with *The Guardian* newspaper's Scottish edition. Of the local newspapers, the best coverage is in *The Scotsman*, which issues a dedicated daily Festival supplement.

The Edinburgh International Festival

The **Edinburgh International Festival** (Ⓦwww.eif.co.uk), sometimes called the "Official Festival", was the original Edinburgh Festival, conceived in 1947 as a celebration of pan-European culture in the postwar era. Initially dominated by opera, other elements such as top-grade theatre, ballet, dance and classical music were gradually introduced, and it's still very much a highbrow event, with forays into populist territory rare.

The festival generally runs over the second two weeks of **August** and the first week of September, culminating in a **Fireworks Concert** based in Princes Street Gardens but visible from all over the city. Performances take place at the city's larger venues such as the Usher Hall and the Festival Theatre and, while ticket **prices** run to over £40, it is possible to see shows for £10 or less if you're prepared to queue for the handful of tickets kept back until the day. The International Festival's year-round headquarters are located at **The Hub** (see p.766), where there's a booking office.

The Edinburgh Festival Fringe

Even standing alone from its sister festivals, the **Edinburgh Festival Fringe** is easily the world's largest arts gathering. Each year sees around 15,000 performances from over 700 companies, with more than 12,000 participants from all over the world. There are something in the region of 1500 shows every day, round the clock, in 200 venues around the city. While the headlining names at the International Festival reinforce the Festival's cultural credibility, it is the dynamism, spontaneity and sheer exuberance of the Fringe that dominates Edinburgh every August, giving the city its unique atmosphere.

Crucially, no artistic control is imposed on those who want to produce a show, a defining element of the Fringe. This means that the shows range from the inspired to the diabolical, and ensures a highly competitive atmosphere, in which one bad review in a prominent publication means box-office disaster. Many unknowns rely on self-publicity, taking to the streets to perform highlights from their show, or pressing leaflets into the hands of every passer-by. Performances go on round the clock: if so inclined, you could sit through twenty shows in a day.

The full Fringe programme is usually available in June from the **Festival Fringe Office** (Ⓣ0131/226 0000, Ⓦwww.edfringe.com). Postal and telephone bookings for shows can be made immediately after its release, while during the Festival, tickets are sold at the Fringe Office, on the Royal Mile at no. 180 (daily 10am–9pm), as well as online or at venues. Ticket **prices** for most Fringe shows start at £5, and average from £8 to £12 at the main venues, with the better-known acts going for even more.

The Fringe starts a week earlier than the International Festival and culminates on the last weekend in August, traditionally an English (but, confusingly, not a Scottish) Bank Holiday weekend.

The smaller festivals

The **Edinburgh International Book Festival** (Ⓣ0845/373 5888, Ⓦwww.edbookfest.co.uk) takes place in the last two weeks of August, and is the largest celebration of the written word worldwide. It's held in a tented village in

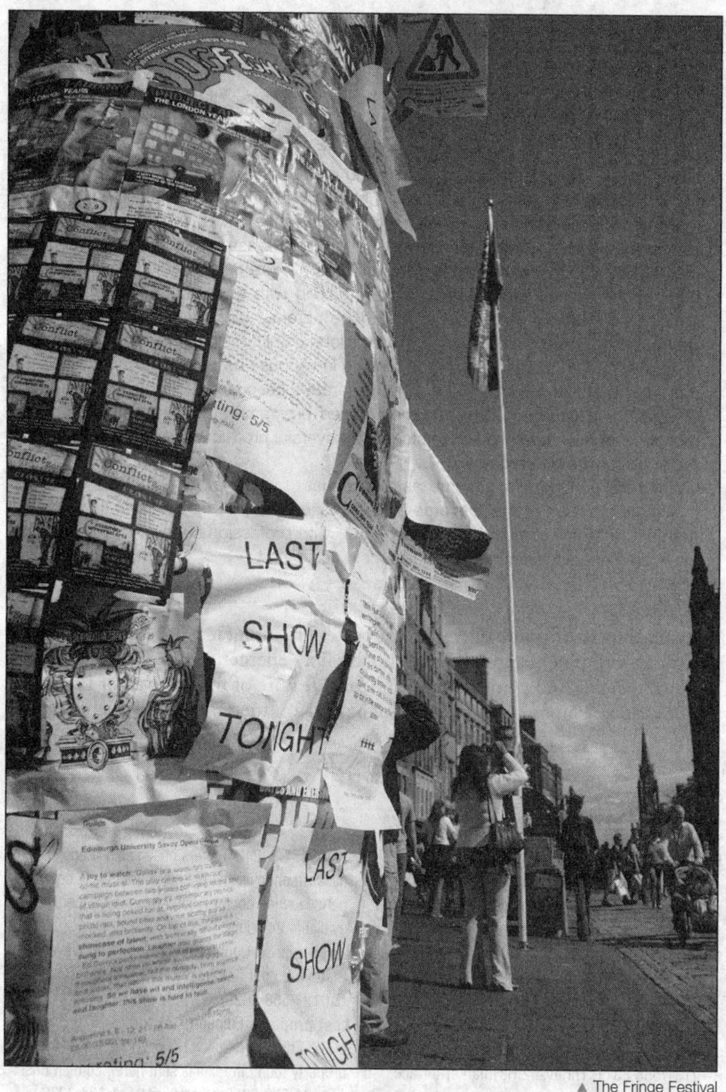

▲ The Fringe Festival

Charlotte Square, with talks, readings and signings by a star-studded line-up of visiting authors, as well as panel discussions and workshops. The **Edinburgh International Jazz and Blues Festival** (Ⓣ0131/473 2000, Ⓦwww.edinburghjazzfestival.co.uk) runs immediately prior to the Fringe in the first week in August, easing the city into the festival spirit. Highlights include **Jazz On A Summer's Day**, a musical extravaganza in Princes Street Gardens, and a colourful New Orleans-style **street parade**.

Staged in the spectacular stadium of the Edinburgh Castle Esplanade throughout August, the **Military Tattoo** (Ⓣ0131/225 1188, Ⓦwww.edintattoo.co.uk) is a

Fringe venues

In addition to the many tiny and unexpected auditoriums, the four **main Fringe venues** are The Assembly Rooms, The Pleasance, The Gilded Balloon and "C". Venue complexes rather than single spaces, the last three colonize clusters of different-sized spaces for the duration of the Festival. If you're new to the Fringe, these are all safe bets for decent shows and a bit of star-spotting.

The **Assembly Rooms** (50 George St ⓣ0131/623 3000, ⓦwww.assemblyrooms.com) provide a slick, grand setting for top-of-the-range drama and big-name music and comedy acts, while the atmosphere at the **Pleasance** (60 The Pleasance ⓣ0131/556 6550, ⓦwww.pleasance.co.uk) has a more raucous feel, thanks to its busy courtyard bar, with off-beat comedy mixing with whimsical appearances by panellists on Radio 4 game shows. The Fringe's premier comedy venue, **The Gilded Balloon** (ⓣ0131/622 6555, ⓦwww.gildedballoon.co.uk), lost its long-standing home in a fire in late 2002, but was up and running in various new venues around town by the time the Festival came along. The disparate locations of **C** (ⓣ0870/701 5105, ⓦwww.cthefestival.com) have the most varied programme of the big four, and in recent years have been known to stage controversial productions that other venues might be too wary to promote.

While it's nothing like as large as the venues above, you shouldn't ignore the programme put on at the **Traverse Theatre** (see p.788). Long a champion of new drama, the "Trav" combines the avant-garde with professional presentation and its plays are generally among the Fringe's most acclaimed.

fantastic display of pomp and military pride. The programme of choreographed drills, massed pipe bands, historical tableaux, energetic battle re-enactments, national dancing and pyrotechnics has been a feature of the Festival for fifty years, the emotional climax provided by a lone piper on the Castle battlements.

Listings

Bike rental Biketrax, 11 Lochrin Place ⓣ0131/228 6633, ⓦwww.biketrax.co.uk; Edinburgh Cycle Hire, 29 Blackfriars St ⓣ0131/556 5560, ⓦwww.cyclescotland.co.uk.

Car rental Arnold Clark, 38 Seafield Rd East ⓣ0844/8443817; Avis, 5 West Park Place ⓣ0870/1539103; Budget, Edinburgh Airport ⓣ0131/333 1926; Europcar, 24 East London St ⓣ0131/557 3456; Hertz, 10 Picardy Place ⓣ0131/556 8311; Thrifty, 42 Haymarket Terrace ⓣ0131/337 1319.

Genealogical research General Register Office for Scotland ⓣ0131/334 0380, ⓦwww.scotlandspeople.gov.uk; Scottish Genealogy Society, 15 Victoria Terrace ⓣ0131/220 3677, ⓦwww.scotsgenealogy.com; Scottish Roots, 22 Forth St ⓣ0131/477 8214, ⓦwww.scottishroots.com.

Hospital Royal Infirmary, Little France (ⓣ0131/536 1000), has a 24hr casualty department. There's also a casualty department for children at the Sick Kid's hospital, Sciennes Rd (ⓣ0131/536 0000). NHS24 (ⓣ08454/242424) offers health advice and clinical assessment over the phone; it essentially covers periods when doctors' surgeries aren't open, but is available 24 hours.

Left luggage Counter by platform 1 at Waverley Station; £5 per item (daily 7am–11pm; ⓣ0131/558 3829).

Lost property Edinburgh Airport ⓣ0870/040 0007; Edinburgh Police HQ ⓣ0131/311 3141 (lost property found in taxis is sent here); Lothian Buses ⓣ0131/558 8858; Scotrail ⓣ0141/335 3276.

Pharmacy Boots, 48 Shandwick Place (Mon–Fri 8am–8pm, Sat 8am–6pm, Sun 10.30am–4.30pm; ⓣ0131/225 6757) has the longest opening hours.

Police In an emergency call 999. Otherwise contact Lothian and Borders Police HQ, Fettes Ave ⓣ0131/311 3131.

Post office 8–10 St James Centre (Mon–Sat 9am–5.30pm; ⓣ0845/722 3344).

Taxis Central Radio Taxis ⓣ0131/229 2468; City Cabs ⓣ0131/228 1211.

East Lothian

East Lothian consists of the coastal strip and hinterland immediately east of Edinburgh, bounded by the Firth of Forth to the north and the Lammermuir Hills to the south. All of it is within easy day-trip range from the capital, though there are places you can stay overnight if you're keen to explore it properly. Often mocked as the "home counties" of Edinburgh, there's no denying its well-ordered feel, with prosperous farms and large estate houses dominating the scenery. There's something for most tastes here, including the wide sandy beaches by **Aberlady**, famous golf courses of **Gullane**, the enjoyable Seabird Centre at **North Berwick**, dramatic cliff-top ruins at **Tantallon** and the supersonic draw of **Concorde** at the Museum of Flight.

North Berwick and around

NORTH BERWICK has a great deal of charm and a somewhat faded, old-fashioned air, its guesthouses and hotels extending along the shore in all their Victorian and Edwardian sobriety. Two nearby volcanic heaps, the **Bass Rock** and **North Berwick Law**, are the town's defining physical features. The former can be observed closely from North Berwick's principal attraction, the **Scottish Seabird Centre** (April–Oct daily 10am–6pm; Nov–March Mon–Fri 10am–4pm, Sat & Sun 10am–5.30pm; till 5pm Mon–Fri Feb & March; £6.95; ⓣ01620/890202, ⓦwww.seabird.org), by the harbour. It offers an introduction to all the sea birds found around the Scottish coast, particularly the 100,000-plus gannets and puffins which nest on the Bass Rock every summer and there's even a live link to cameras mounted on the volcanic island, showing close-up pictures of the birds in their nesting grounds. Weather permitting, there are also **boat trips** around the rock from North Berwick harbour, though only a few have landing rights on the rock.

North Berwick is served by a regular **train** from Edinburgh Waverley (30min), with discount deals for those heading for the Seabird Centre (ask at Waverley ticket office or call ⓣ08457/550033). From the station it's a ten-minute walk east to the town centre, and the **tourist office** (April–Sept Mon–Sat 9am–6/8pm, Sun 11am–4/6pm, April & May closed Tues; Oct Mon–Sat 9am–5pm; ⓣ01620/892197) on Quality Street. One of the best **cafés** in town is at the Seabird Centre, with panoramic views over the beach. Among the town's **restaurants**, *Bass Rock Bistro* (ⓣ01620/890875, ⓦwww.bassrockbistro.co.uk; closed Sun & Mon), at 37–39 Quality St, serves Scottish seafood and meat sourced from the excellent local butcher, while *Osteria Cosmo & Angelo* at 71 High St (ⓣ01620/890589, ⓦwww.osteria-no1.co.uk; closed Sun) offers a pricey but classy menu of classical Italian cooking – booking recommended.

Tantallon Castle

The melodramatic ruins of **Tantallon Castle** (April–Sept daily 9.30am–5.30pm; Oct–March Mon–Wed, Sat & Sun 9.30am–4.30pm; HS; £4.50), three miles east of North Berwick on the A198, stand on precipitous cliffs facing the Bass Rock. With a sheer drop down to the sea on three sides and a sequence of moats and ditches on the fourth, the castle's desolate invincibility is daunting, especially when the wind howls over the remaining battlements and the surf crashes on the rocks far below. You can reach Tantallon Castle from North Berwick by the Dunbar **bus** (Eves Coaches #120; Mon–Sat 6 daily, Sun 2 daily), which takes fifteen minutes, or you can walk there from town along the cliffs in around an hour.

National Museum of Flight

A few miles southwest of North Berwick, on an old military airfield by East Fortune, the **National Museum of Flight** (April–Oct daily 10am–5pm; Nov–March Sat & Sun 10am–4pm; £5.50, Concorde boarding pass £3 extra, pre-booking essential; ⓣ0870/421 4299, ⓦwww.nms.ac.uk/flight) is now home to *Alpha Alpha*, British Airways' first **Concorde**. The supersonic passenger jet, one of only twenty such planes built, has been reassembled to show how she looked when decommissioned in 2003. A visit onboard is restricted to a slightly stooped wander through the forward half of the aircraft, with the chance to look at the cockpit through a perspex partition; elsewhere, a short film tells the story of *Alpha Alpha*, while a display follows the Concorde project as a whole, from the early days of Anglo-French bickering to the tragic Paris crash of 2000. In and around the older hangars on the site, you can see over fifty vintage aircraft including a Vulcan bomber, a Comet airliner, a Spitfire and a Tigermoth. To get to the museum by public transport, catch **First Bus** #121 from North Berwick or Haddington, both of which have connections from Edinburgh.

Dunbar

Twelve miles along the coast from North Berwick lies **DUNBAR** and the **John Muir Birthplace** at 126 High St (April–Oct Mon–Sat 10am–5pm, Sun 1–5pm; Nov–March Wed–Sat 10am–5pm, Sun 1–5pm; free; ⓦwww.jmbt.org.uk). Birthplace of the explorer and naturalist who created the United States national-park system, it's an engaging interpretative and education centre about the pioneer's life and legacy. Dunbar's delightfully intricate double **harbour** also merits a stroll, with its narrow channels, cobbled quays and roughened rocks, set beside the shattered remains of the castle.

The town's **tourist office** is at 143a High St (April, May, Sept & Oct Mon–Sat 9am–5pm; June–Aug Mon–Sat 9am–6/8pm, Sun 11am–4/6pm; ⓣ01368/863353). For **food**, the best place is the hotel, *The Rocks* on Marine Road (ⓣ01368/862287, ⓦwww.experiencetherocks.co.uk), which also has a dozen decent rooms (❺), or try the *Creel* (ⓣ01368/863279, ⓦwww.creelrestaurant.co.uk), located near the old harbour, which serves local fish dishes served in a simple Mediterranean style.

Haddington

Inland, East Lothian's main town, **HADDINGTON**, preserves an intriguing ensemble of seventeenth- to nineteenth-century architectural styles with everything of any interest labelled and plaqued. Heading east from the town centre along High Street, it's a brief walk down Church Street – past the hooped arches of **Nungate Bridge** – to the hulking mass of **St Mary's Church** (Easter–Sept Mon–Sat 11am–4pm, Sun 2–4.30pm; free), Scotland's largest parish church. Built close to the reedy River Tyne, the church dates from the fourteenth century, but it's a real hotchpotch of styles, the squat grey tower uneasy above clumsy buttressing and pinkish-ochre stone walls. Inside, on the **Lauderdale Aisle**, a munificent tomb features the best of Elizabethan alabaster carving, moustached knights and their ruffed ladies lying beneath a finely ornamented canopy.

Fast and frequent **buses** connect Haddington with Edinburgh, fifteen miles to the west, and with North Berwick on the east coast, with all services stopping on High Street. There's no **tourist office**, but orientation is easy and *A Walk Around Haddington* (£1), detailing every building of any conceivable consequence, is available from local newsagents. For daytime **snacks** the place to seek out is *Jaques & Lawrence* at 37 Court St, opposite the post office. For an **evening meal**, try the restaurant in the *Maitlandfield Hotel* (Ⓣ01620/826513, Ⓦwww.maitlandfieldhouse.co.uk) or the pleasant *Bonars Brasserie* (Ⓣ01620/822100) in nearby Poldrate on the southeastern fringes of Haddington.

Glenkinchie Distillery

Six miles west of Haddington along the A6093, the village of Pencaitland is the closest place to Edinburgh where malt whisky is made. Set in a peaceful dip in the rolling countryside about two miles outside Pencaitland, the **Glenkinchie Distillery** (Easter–Oct Mon–Sat 10am–5pm, Sun noon–5pm; Nov daily noon–4pm; Dec–Easter Mon–Fri noon–4pm; last tour 1hr before closing; £5) is one of only a handful found in the Lowlands of Scotland. Here, of course, they emphasize the qualities that set Glenkinchie, a lighter, drier malt, apart from the peaty, smoky whiskies of the north and west.

Midlothian

Immediately south of Edinburgh lies the old county of **MIDLOTHIAN**, once called Edinburghshire. It's one of the hilliest parts of the Central Lowlands, with the Pentland chain running down its western side, and the Moorfoots defining its boundary with the Borders to the south. Midlothian's main town is **Dalkeith**, eight miles southeast of central Edinburgh.

Newtongrange and Roslin

A mile or so south of Dalkeith, the Lady Victoria Colliery at **NEWTONGRANGE** is open to the public as the **Scottish Mining Museum** (daily: Feb–Oct 10am–5pm; Nov–Jan 11am–3pm; £5.95; Ⓦwww.scottishminingmuseum.com). Staffed in large part by former miners, the museum mixes coal-mining heritage and artefacts with hands-on exhibits for children and the chance to see some of the key working parts of the colliery.

The tranquil village of **ROSLIN** lies seven miles south of the centre of Edinburgh, from where it can be reached by bus #15 or First Bus #62A from St Andrew Square. An otherwise nondescript place, the village has two unusual claims to fame: it was near here, at the Roslin Institute, that the world's first cloned sheep, Dolly, was created in 1997, and it's also home to the mysterious, richly decorated late-Gothic **Rosslyn Chapel** (Mon–Sat 9am–6pm, Sun noon–4.45pm; £7; Ⓦwww.rosslynchapel.org.uk). Construction of the chapel halted soon after its founder's death in 1484, and the vestry built onto the facade nearly four hundred years later is the sole subsequent addition. After a long period of neglect, the chapel is currently undergoing a massive restoration, though it's still open to the public.

Rosslyn's exterior bristles with pinnacles, gargoyles, flying buttresses and canopies, while inside the stonework is even more intricate. The foliage carving is particularly outstanding, with botanically accurate depictions of over a dozen different leaves and plants. The rich and subtle figurative sculptures have given Rosslyn the nickname of "a Bible in stone", though they're more allegorical than literal. The greatest and most original carving of all is the extraordinary knotted **Apprentice Pillar**. According to local legend, the pillar was made by an apprentice during the absence of the master mason, who killed him in a fit of jealousy on seeing the finished work. A tiny head of a man with a slashed forehead, set at the apex of the ceiling at the far northwestern corner of the building, is popularly supposed to represent the apprentice, his murderer the corresponding head at the opposite side.

The imagery of carvings such as the floriated cross and five-pointed star, together with the history of the family, the St Clairs of Rosslyn, which owns the chapel, leave little doubt about its links to the Knights Templar and freemasonry. More intriguing still are claims that, because of such connections, Rosslyn Chapel has been the repository for items such as the lost Scrolls of Solomon's Temple in Jerusalem, the true Stone of Scone and, most famously, the Holy Grail. The chapel is regularly drawn into conspiracy theories on these themes, most prominently recently in Dan Brown's bestseller *The Da Vinci Code*.

West Lothian

To many, West Lothian is a poor relative to the rolling, rich farmland of East and Midlothian, with a landscape dominated by motorways, industrial estates and giant hillocks of ochre-coloured mine waste called "bings". However, in the royal palace at **Linlithgow**, the area boasts one of Scotland's more magnificent ruins. Nearby, the village of **South Queensferry** lies under the considerable shadow of the **Forth rail and road bridges**, though it's an interesting enough place in its own right, with a historic high street and the notable stately home of **Hopetoun** nearby.

Linlithgow

Roughly equidistant (fifteen miles) from Falkirk, to the west, and Edinburgh is the ancient royal burgh of **LINLITHGOW**. The town itself has largely kept its medieval layout, but development since the 1960s has sadly stripped it of some fine buildings, notably around the **Town Hall** and **Cross** – the former market-place – on the long High Street.

Though hidden from the main road, **Linlithgow Palace** (daily: April–Sept 9.30am–5.30pm; Oct–March 9.30am–4.30pm; HS; £5) is a splendid fifteenth-century ruin romantically set on the edge of Linlithgow Loch. The palace's royal connections are strong: from the top of the northwest tower, Queen Margaret looked out in vain for the return of James IV from the field of Flodden in 1513 (indeed, the views from her bower, six storeys up from the ground, are exceptional), and Mary, Queen of Scots, was born here in on 8 December 1542 and became queen six days later. The ornate octagonal **fountain** in the inner courtyard, with its wonderfully intricate figures and medallion heads, flowed with wine for the wedding of James V and Mary of Guise.

This is a great place to take children: the elegant, bare rooms echo with footsteps and there's a labyrinthine network of spiral staircases and endless nooks and crannies. The galleried **Great Hall** is magnificent, as is the adjoining kitchen, which has a hugely cavernous fireplace.

There are a few decent places to **eat** in Linlithgow: for pub grub try *The Four Marys*, opposite the Cross on High Street, which also has real ales; *Marynka* (Ⓣ01506/840123, Ⓦwww.marynka.com), also on the High Street at no. 57, is a brighter, more modern bistro-style place.

EICA:Ratho

EICA:Ratho, or Edinburgh International Climbing Arena (Mon–Fri 10am–10pm, Sat & Sun 10am–7pm; free, times and charges for activities vary; ⓣ0131/333 6333, ⓦwww.eica-ratho.com), is the world's largest indoor climbing facility, incorporating a remarkable artificial climbing wall. The spectacular vision of its architect founders was to enclose (and roof) a disused quarry, creating a giant arena that's now used for inter-national climbing competitions as well as classes (from £20 for an hour-long taster session) for climbers of all levels, including beginners and kids. Above the arena, just under the glass roof, "Aerial Assault" (£8) is a stomach-churning, suspended obstacle course 100 feet off the ground – thankfully, you are safely attached via a sliding harness.

South Queensferry and around

Eight miles northwest of Edinburgh city centre is the small town of **SOUTH QUEENSFERRY**, located at the southern end of the two mighty Forth Bridges. It's an attractive old settlement, with a narrow, cobbled High Street lined with tightly packed buildings, most of which date from the seventeenth and eighteenth centuries. The town's small **museum**, 53 High St (Mon & Thurs–Sat 10am–1pm & 2.15–5pm, Sun noon–5pm; free), contains historical relics and information on the building of the two bridges that loom overhead.

South Queensferry has a couple of excellent spots to **eat**. *The Boathouse* (ⓣ0131/331 5429) at 19b High St, houses a moderately expensive restaurant serving classy local seafood as well as a wine bar and deli; a few doors away at no. 17, *Orocco Pier* (ⓣ0131/331 1298, ⓦwww.oroccopier.co.uk) is more ostentatiously slick and contemporary, but is a good spot for a drink, some pleasant bistro food or a comfy bed for the night (6). Both spots have great views over the water to the bridges.

Hopetoun House

Sitting in its own extensive estate on the south shore of the Forth, just to the west of South Queensferry, **Hopetoun House** (April–Sept daily 10am–5.30pm; £8 house and grounds, £3.70 grounds only; ⓦwww.hopetounhouse.com) ranks as one of the most impressive stately homes in Scotland. The original house was built at the turn of the eighteenth century for the first Earl of Hopetoun by Sir William Bruce, the architect of Holyroodhouse. A couple of decades later, William Adam carried out an enormous extension, engulfing the structure with a curvaceous main facade and two projecting wings – superb examples of Roman Baroque pomp and swagger. Hopetoun's architecture is undoubtedly its most compelling feature, but the furnishings aren't completely overwhelmed, with some impressive seventeenth-century tapestries, Meissen porcelain and a distinguished collection of paintings. The house's grounds include a long, regal driveway and lovely walks along woodland trails and the banks of the Forth, as well as plenty of places for a picnic.

Inchcolm

From South Queensferry's Hawes Pier, just west of the rail bridge, a couple of ferry services head out in the direction of the island of **Inchcolm**, located about five miles northeast of South Queensferry near the Fife shore. The island is home to the best-preserved medieval **abbey** in Scotland, founded in 1235 after King Alexander I was stormbound on the island and took refuge in a hermit's cell. Although the structure as a whole is half-ruined today, the tower, octagonal chapterhouse and echoing cloisters are intact and well worth exploring. The hour and a half you're given ashore by the boat timetables also allows time for a picnic on the abbey's lawns or the chance to explore Inchcolm's old military fortifications and its extensive bird-nesting grounds. If you're lucky, dolphins and porpoises are sometimes sighted from the boat crossing to the island, which are run by *Maid of the Forth* (Ⓣ0131/331 4857, Ⓦwww.maidoftheforth.co.uk; April–Oct 2–3 trips daily; £13.50 including landing fee) and *Forth Belle* (Ⓣ0870/118 1866, Ⓦwww.forthtours.com; £19.50 including bus from Edinburgh and landing fee). *Maid of the Forth* also run a high-speed RIB to the island from Newhaven harbour (see p.781) beside Leith (£20).

Travel details

Buses

For information on all local and national bus services, contact Traveline Ⓣ0870/608 2608 (daily 7am–10pm), Ⓦwww.travelinescotland.com.

Edinburgh (St Andrew Square) to: Aberdeen (hourly; 3hr 50min); Dundee (hourly; 1hr 45min–2hr); Glasgow (every 15min; 1hr 10min); Inverness (hourly; 3hr 30min–4hr 30min); London (8 daily; 7hr 50min); Newcastle-upon-Tyne (5 daily; 2hr 45min); Perth (hourly; 1hr 20min).

Trains

For information on all local and national rail services, contact National Rail Enquiries Ⓣ08457/484950, Ⓦwww.nationalrail.co.uk or Ⓦwww.firstscotrail.com.

Edinburgh to: Aberdeen (hourly; 2hr 20min); Dunbar (8 daily; 30min); Dundee (hourly; 1hr 45min); Glasgow (2–4 hourly; 50min); Inverness (6 daily direct; 3hr 50min); London (hourly; 4hr 30min); Newcastle-upon-Tyne (hourly; 1hr 30min); North Berwick (hourly; 30 min); Perth (6 daily; 1hr 15min); Stirling (every 30min; 45min).

Flights

For information on flights to and from Edinburgh, contact BAA Edinburgh Ⓣ0870/040 0007, Ⓦwww.edinburghairport.com or Ⓦwww.travelinescotland.com.

Edinburgh to: Belfast (Mon–Fri 8 daily; Sat & Sun 4 daily; 55min); Cardiff (2 daily; 1hr 10min); Dublin (Mon–Fri 3 daily, Sat & Sun 3 daily; 1hr); Kirkwall (Mon–Fri 2 daily, Sat & Sun 1 daily; 1hr 55min); London City (Mon–Fri 12 daily, Sat 1, Sun 4 daily; 1hr 15min); London Gatwick (Mon–Fri 14 daily, Sat & Sun 6 daily; 1hr 15min); London Heathrow (Mon–Fri 18 daily, Sat & Sun 11–15 daily; 1hr); London Luton (Mon–Fri 6 daily, Sat & Sun 4 daily; 1hr 20min); London Stansted (Mon–Fri 6 daily, Sat & Sun 4–6 daily; 1hr 10min); Stornoway (Mon–Fri 3 daily, Sat 2, Sun 1; 1hr 10 min); Sumburgh (Shetland) (2 daily; 1hr 30min); Wick (Mon–Fri 1 daily; 1hr 10min).

18

Southern Scotland

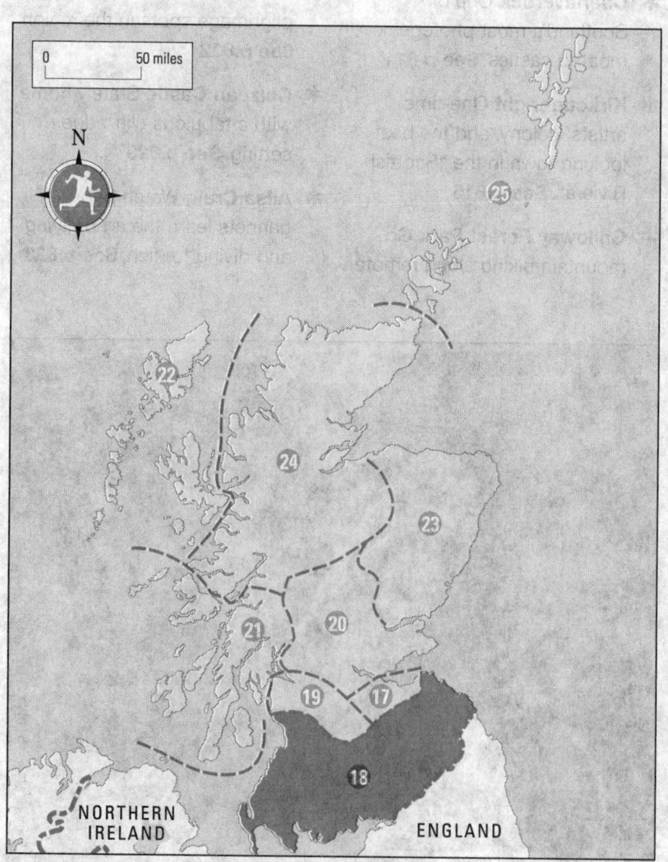

CHAPTER 18

Highlights

* **Melrose Abbey** Border abbey with the best-preserved sculptural detail, set in a charming town. See p.804

* **Caerlaverock** One of Scotland's most photogenic moated castles. See p.814

* **Kirkcudbright** One-time artists' colony, and the best-looking town in the "Scottish Riviera". See p.816

* **Galloway Forest Park** Go mountain biking along remote forest tracks, or hiking on the Southern Upland Way. See p.818

* **Alloway** The village where poet Robert Burns was born, and the best of many Burns pilgrimage spots in the region. See p.822

* **Culzean Castle** Stately home with a fabulous cliff-edge setting. See p.823

* **Ailsa Craig** Watch baby gannets learn the art of flying and diving for fish. See p.823

▲ Mountain biking in Galloway Forest

18

Southern Scotland

Southern Scotland divides neatly into three distinct regions: the Borders, Dumfries and Galloway, and Ayrshire. Although none of the regions has the highest of tourist profiles, those visitors who whizz past on their way to Edinburgh, Glasgow or the Highlands are missing out on a huge swathe of Scotland that is in many ways the very heart of the country. Its inhabitants, particularly in the Borders, bore the brunt of long wars with the English, its farms have fed Scotland's cities since industrialization, and two of the country's literary icons, Sir Walter Scott and Robbie Burns, lived and died here.

Geographically, the region is dominated by the **Southern Uplands**, a chain of bulging round-topped hills and weather-beaten moorland, punctuated by narrow glens, fast-flowing rivers and blue-black lochs. This region is at its most dramatic in the **Galloway Forest Park** to the southwest, with peaks reaching to over 2000ft, crisscrossed by numerous popular walking trails. Back in the valleys, and down by the coast, the landscape is fairly lush – farming country for the most part, with tourism an important, but secondary, industry. On the coast, you'll find enormous variety: the east coast is fairly bleak, with dramatic cliffs interspersed with tiny fishing villages; the **Solway coast**, in the southwest, is much gentler, indented by sandy coves and estuaries; while the Ayrshire coast, by contrast, is much more heavily populated, and in parts an almost continuous stretch of seaside resorts and industrial centres.

Lying north of the inhospitable Cheviot Hills, which separate Scotland from England, the **Borders** region is dominated by the meanderings of the **River Tweed**. None of the towns along the Tweed is of any great size, yet they have provided inspiration for countless folkloric ballads telling of bloody battles with the English and clashes between the notorious warring families, the Border Reivers. The small but delightful town of **Melrose**, in the heart of the Borders, is the most obvious base for exploring the region, and has the most impressive of the four **Border abbeys** founded by the medieval Canmore kings, all of which are now reduced to romantic ruins.

Dumfries and Galloway, occupying the southwestern corner of Scotland, gets even more overlooked than the Borders, though the region remains popular with Lowland Scots and folk from the north of England. If you do make the effort to get off the main north–south highway to Glasgow, you'll find several more ruined abbeys, medieval castles, forested hills and dramatic tidal flats and sea cliffs ideal for birdwatching. The key resort is the modest, but charming town of **Kirkcudbright**, halfway along the marshy Solway coast, well placed for exploring the rest of the county.

Ayrshire is rich farming country, and not an obvious destination for first-time visitors to Scotland. It has fewer sights than its neighbours, with almost everything of interest confined to the coast. However, the **golf courses** along its gentle coastline are among the finest links courses in the country, and golfers can buy three- and five-day passes from tourist offices allowing free or reduced-fee access to many of the region's golf courses. Fans of **Robert Burns** could happily spend several days exploring the author's old haunts, especially at **Ayr**, the county town, and the nearby village of Alloway, the poet's birthplace.

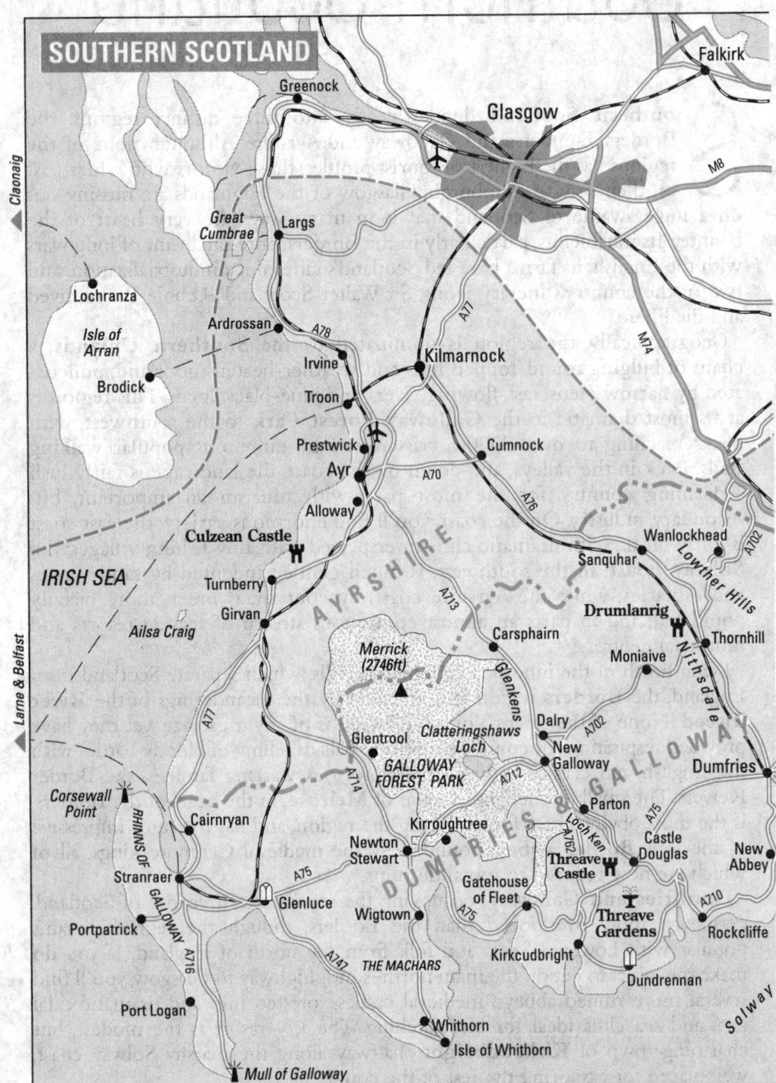

The Borders

Sandwiched between the Cheviot Hills on the English border and the Pentland and Moorfoot ranges to the south of Edinburgh, is the **Borders** region (Ⓦwww.scot-borders.co.uk). The finest section of the lush **Tweed valley** lies between **Melrose** and **Peebles**, where you'll find a string of attractions, from the eccentricities of Sir Walter Scott's mansion at **Abbotsford** to the intriguing Jacobite past of **Traquair House**, along with the region's famous abbeys, founded in the reign of King David I (1124–53).

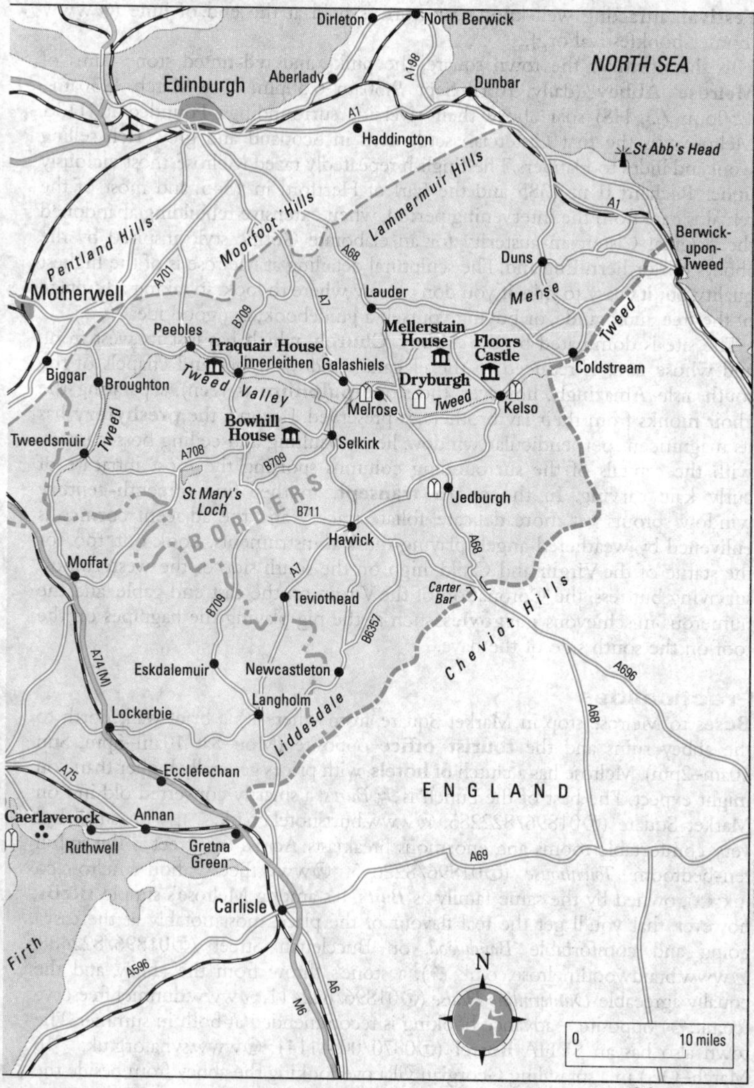

Melrose and around

Minuscule **MELROSE**, tucked in between the Tweed and the gorse-backed Eildon Hills, is the most beguiling of towns, its narrow streets trimmed by a harmonious ensemble of styles, from pretty little cottages and tweedy shops to high-standing Georgian and Victorian facades. Its chief draw is its ruined abbey, but it's also perfectly positioned for exploring the Tweed Valley. Most of the year it's a sleepy little place, but as the birthplace in 1883 of the **Rugby Sevens** (seven-a-side games), it swarms during Sevens Week (second week in April), and again in early September when it hosts the **Melrose Music Festival**, a popular weekend of traditional music attracting folkies from afar. The **Book Festival**, attracting well-known authors, is held at the end of June (Ⓦwww.bordersbookfestival.org).

To the north of the town square, the pink- and red-tinted stone ruins of **Melrose Abbey** (daily: April–Sept 9.30am–6.30pm; Oct–March 9.30am–4.30pm; £5; HS) soar above their riverside surroundings. Founded in 1136, Melrose was the first Cistercian settlement in Scotland and grew rich selling wool and hides to Flanders. The English repeatedly razed Melrose, most viciously under Richard II in 1385 and the Earl of Hertford in 1545, and most of the remains date from the intervening period, when extensive rebuilding abandoned the original Cistercian austerity for an elaborate Gothic style inspired by the abbeys of northern England. The sculptural detailing at Melrose is of the highest quality, but it's easy to miss if you don't know where to look, so taking advantage of the free audioguide, or buying yourself a guidebook, is a good idea.

The site is dominated by the **Abbey Church**, which has lost its west front, and whose nave is reduced to the elegant window arches and chapels of the south aisle. Amazingly, however, the stone **pulpitum** (screen), separating the choir monks from their lay brothers, is preserved. Beyond, the **presbytery** has its magnificent perpendicular window, lierne vaulting and ceiling bosses intact, with the capitals of the surrounding columns sporting the most intricate of curly kale carving. In the **south transept**, another fine fifteenth-century window sprouts yet more delicate, foliate tracery and the adjacent cornice is enlivened by weathered angels playing musical instruments. Look out, too, for the statue of the Virgin and Child, high on the south side of the westernmost surviving buttress, the Coronation of the Virgin on the east end gable, and the numerous mischievous **gargoyles**, such as the pig playing the bagpipes on the roof on the south side of the nave.

Practicalities

Buses to Melrose stop in Market Square, from where it's a brief walk north to the abbey ruins and the **tourist office** opposite (Mon–Sat 10am–5pm, Sun 10am–2pm). Melrose has a clutch of **hotels**, with prices generally higher than you might expect. The best of the bunch is *Burt's*, a smartly converted old inn on Market Square (Ⓣ01896/822285, Ⓦwww.burtshotel.co.uk; ⑥), with small but very comfortable rooms and enormous breakfasts. Across the street is the stylish ten-bedroom *Townhouse* (Ⓣ01896/822645, Ⓦwww.thetownhousemelrose.co.uk; ⑥), owned by the same family as *Burt's*. It's among Melrose's simple **B&Bs**, however, that you'll get the real flavour of the place, most notably at the easy-going and comfortable *Braidwood*, on Buccleuch Street (Ⓣ01896/822488, Ⓦwww.braidwoodmelrose.co.uk; ②), a stone's throw from the abbey, and the equally agreeable *Dunfermline House* (Ⓣ01896/822411, Ⓦwww.dunmel.freeserve.co.uk; ②) opposite – advance booking is recommended at both in summer. The town also has an SYHA **hostel** (Ⓣ0870/004 1141, Ⓦwww.syha.org.uk; £16 March–Oct) in a sprawling Georgian villa overlooking the abbey from beside the access road into the bypass. The *Gibson Caravan Park* **campsite** (ⓣ01896/822969; mid-May to mid-Sept) is in the town centre, just off the High Street, opposite the Greenyards rugby grounds.

For a light **lunch** or **snack**, head to *Russell's* (closed Thurs), a popular, very traditional tearoom on Market Square; or *Haldane's Fish & Chip Shop* (closed Wed), next door. **Dinner** options are plentiful: *Marmion's Brasserie* (ⓣ01896/822245), Buccleuch St, serves well-prepared imaginative meals, as does the award-winning restaurant run by Gary Moore in the *Station Hotel* on the square. *Burt's* does excellent bar meals and, if you're feeling energetic, walk 500 yards past the abbey and across the old suspension bridge to the *Hoebridge Inn* (ⓣ01896/823082; closed Mon), one of the Borders' best restaurants, serving home-made Scottish food in relaxed, low-key surroundings. **Pubs** include the popular *King's Arms* on the High Street, or the *Ship Inn*, on East Port at the top of the square, the liveliest in town, especially during the Folk Festival and on Saturday afternoons when the Melrose rugby team have played at home. Check out what's on at The Wynd (ⓣ01896/823854, ⓦwww.thewynd.com), Melrose's very own pint-sized **theatre**, tucked away down the alleyway, north off the main square, which shows films and puts on gigs as well as live drama.

Abbotsford

The stately home of **Abbotsford** (mid-March to Oct Mon–Sat 9.30am–5pm, March, April, May & Oct Sun 2–5pm; June–Sept Sun 9.30am–5pm; £6), three miles up the Tweed from Melrose, was designed to satisfy the Romantic inclinations of **Sir Walter Scott**, who lived here from 1812 until his death. Abbotsford (as Scott chose to call it) took twelve years to evolve, with the fanciful turrets and castellations of the Scots Baronial exterior incorporating copies of medieval originals. Despite all the exterior pomp, the interior is surprisingly small and poky, with just six rooms open for viewing on the upper floor. Visitors start in the wood-panelled study, with its small writing desk made of salvage from the Spanish Armada, at which Scott banged out the Waverley novels at a furious rate. The heavy wood-panelled library boasts Scott's collection of more than nine thousand rare books and an extraordinary assortment of memorabilia, the centrepiece of which is Napoleon's pen case and blotting book, but which also includes Rob Roy's purse and *skene dhu* (knife), and the inlaid pearl crucifix that accompanied Mary, Queen of Scots, to the scaffold. You can also see Henry Raeburn's famous portrait of Scott hanging in the drawing room, and all sorts of weapons – notably Rob Roy's sword, dagger and gun – in the armoury.

The fast and frequent Melrose–Galashiels **bus** provides easy access to Abbotsford: ask for the Tweedbank island on the A6091, from where the house is a ten-minute walk up the road.

Dryburgh Abbey

Hidden away in a U-bend in the Tweed, three or four miles east of Melrose, the remains of **Dryburgh Abbey** (Easter–Sept daily 9.30am–6.30pm; Oct–Easter Mon–Sat 9.30am–4.30pm, Sun 2–4.30pm; £4.50; HS) occupy an idyllic position against a hilly backdrop. The Premonstratensians founded the abbey in the twelfth century, but they were never as successful as their Cistercian neighbours in Melrose. The ruins of the **Abbey Church** are less substantial than Melrose or Jedburgh, and virtually nothing survives of the nave, though the transepts have fared better, their chapels now serving as private burial grounds for, among others, Sir Walter Scott and Field Marshal Haig, the World War I commander whose ineptitude cost thousands of soldiers' lives. The night stairs, down which the monks stumbled in the early hours of the morning, survive in the south transept,

Sir Walter Scott

As a child, **Walter Scott** (1771–1832) was left disabled by polio and his anxious parents sent him to recuperate at his grandfather's farm in Smailholm, where his imagination was fuelled by his relative's tales of the old, violent troubles in the Borders. Scott returned to Edinburgh to resume his education and take up a career in law. Throughout the 1790s he transcribed hundreds of old Border ballads, publishing a three-volume collection entitled *Minstrelsy of the Scottish Borders* in 1802. An instant success, *Minstrelsy* was followed by Scott's own *Lay of the Last Minstrel*, a narrative poem whose strong story and rose-tinted regionalism proved very popular.

More **poetry** was to come, most successfully *Marmion* (1808) and *The Lady of the Lake* (1810), not to mention an eighteen-volume edition of the works of John Dryden and nineteen volumes of Jonathan Swift. However, despite having two paid jobs, his finances remained shaky. He had become a partner in a printing firm, which put him deeply into debt, not helped by the enormous sums he spent on his mansion, Abbotsford. From 1813, Scott was writing to pay the bills and thumped out a veritable flood of historical novels using his extensive knowledge of Scottish history and folklore. He produced his best work within the space of ten years: *Waverley* (1814), *The Antiquary* (1816), *Rob Roy* and *The Heart of Midlothian* (both 1818), as well as two notable novels set in England, *Ivanhoe* (1819) and *Kenilworth* (1821). In 1824 he returned to Scottish tales with *Redgauntlet*, the last of his quality work.

A year later Scott's money problems reached crisis proportions after an economic crash bankrupted his printing business. Attempting to pay his creditors in full, he found the quality of his writing deteriorating with its increased speed and the effort broke his health. His last years were plagued by illness, and in 1832 he died at Abbotsford and was buried within the ruins of Dryburgh Abbey.

and lead even today to the monks' dormitory. Leaving the church via the east processional door in the south aisle, with its dog-tooth decoration, you enter the cloisters, the highlight of which is the barrel-vaulted **Chapter House**, complete with low stone benches and blind interlaced arcading.

Next door to the abbey is the sprawling red-sandstone *Dryburgh Abbey Hotel* (Ⓣ01835/822261, Ⓦwww.dryburgh.co.uk; ⑦), a hunting, shooting, fishing kind of place. Dryburgh is not easy to get to by **public transport**, though it's only a mile's walk north of St Boswell's on the A68, and a pleasant three or four miles from Melrose. Drivers and cyclists should approach the abbey via the much-visited **Scott's View**, to the north on the B6356, overlooking the Tweed valley, where the writer and his friends often picnicked and where Scott's horse stopped out of habit during the writer's own funeral procession. The scene inspired Joseph Turner's *Melrose 1831*, now on display in the National Gallery of Scotland (see box above).

Kelso and around

KELSO, ten miles or so downstream from Melrose, grew up in the shadow of its now-ruined Benedictine **abbey** (April–Dec daily; free), once the richest and most powerful of the Border abbeys. The English savaged Kelso three times in the first half of the sixteenth century, and such was the extent of the devastation – compounded by the Reformation – that less survives of Kelso than any of the Border abbeys. Nevertheless, at first sight, it looks pretty impressive, with the heavy Norman west end of the abbey church almost entirely intact. Beyond, little remains, though it is possible to make out the two transepts and towers that gave the abbey the shape of a double cross, unique in Scotland.

Kelso town managed to rebuild itself and is now centred on **The Square**, a large cobbled expanse presided over by the honey-hued Ionic columns, pediment and oversized clock belltower of the elegant **Town Hall**. Leaving the Square along Roxburgh Street, take the alley down to the **Cobby Riverside Walk**, where a brief stroll leads to Floors Castle (see below). En route, but hidden from view by the islet in the middle of the river, is the spot where the Teviot meets the Tweed. This bit of river, known as The Junction, has long been famous for its **salmon fishing**, with permits – costing thousands – booked years in advance. Permits for fishing other, less expensive reaches of the Tweed and Teviot are available from Tweedside Tackle, 36 Bridge St (ⓣ01573/225306, ⓦwww.tweedsidetackle.co.uk).

Practicalities

Kelso **bus station** on Roxburgh Street is a brief walk from The Square, where you'll find the **tourist office** in the Town Hall (April–Nov Mon–Sat 10am–5pm, Sun 10am–2pm; Jan–March Mon, Fri & Sat 10am–2pm). **Accommodation** is rarely a problem: one of the best B&Bs in town is *Abbey Bank*, near Kelso Pottery on The Knowes (ⓣ01573/226550, ⓔdiah@abbeybank.freeserve.co.uk; ③), a Georgian house with large double beds and a lovely south-facing garden. Another good choice is the *Ednam House Hotel* (ⓣ01573/224168, ⓦwww.ednamhouse.com; ⑥), a splendid Georgian mansion set back off Bridge Street, with antique furnishings and gardens that abut the Tweed; make sure you're not put in the modern extension. Lastly, there's the *Roxburghe Hotel* (ⓣ01573/450331, ⓦwww.roxburghe.net; ⑧), a luxury hotel two miles south of Kelso on the A698 at Heiton, owned by the Duke and Duchess of Roxburghe, which also boasts an eighteen-hole championship golf course.

Most **eating** places are just off The Square: the *Cobbles Inn* restaurant is housed in a former pub just up Bowmont Street – check the specials menu for the best dishes – while the *Cross Keys* in the square specializes in local produce. *Oscar's Wine Bar* in Horsemarket is popular in the evenings (open daily) or try the excellent *Queen's Bistro* in the *Queen's Head Hotel* on Bridge Street for more gourmet fare. For a snack, there's *Le Jardin*, next to Kelso Pottery (closed Mon).

Floors Castle

If you stand on Kelso's handsome bridge over the Tweed, you can easily make out the pepperpot turrets and castellations of **Floors Castle** (Easter & May–Oct daily 11am–5pm; £6.50, grounds & garden only £3; ⓦwww.floorscastle.com), a vast, pompous mansion a mile or so northwest of the town. The bulk of the building was designed by William Adam in the 1720s, and, picking through the Victorian modifications, the interior still demonstrates his uncluttered style. However, you won't see much of it, as Floors is still privately owned and just ten rooms and a basement are open to the public. Highlights include paintings by Matisse, Augustus John and Odilon Redon, and some fine Brussels and Gobelin tapestries.

Mellerstain House

Six miles northwest of Kelso off the A6089, **Mellerstain House** (guided tours: Easter–June & Sept Wed & Sun 12.30–5pm; July & Aug Mon, Wed, Thurs & Sun; Oct Sun only; £6, gardens only £3.50; ⓦwww.mellerstain.com) represents the very best of the Adam brothers' work – William designed the wings in 1725, and his son Robert the castellated centre fifty years later. Robert's love of columns, roundels and friezes culminates in a stunning sequence of plaster-moulded, pastel-shaded ceilings: the **library** is the high-point of the tour for Adam lovers, with four unusual long panels in plaster relief of classical scenes that relegate the books to second place. The art collection, which includes works by Constable, Gainsborough, Ramsay and Veronese, is also noteworthy. After a visit you can wander the formal Edwardian gardens, which slope down to the lake.

Jedburgh

Ten miles south of Melrose, **JEDBURGH** nestles in the lush valley of the Jed Water. During the interminable Anglo-Scottish Wars, Jedburgh was the quintessential frontier town, a heavily garrisoned royal burgh incorporating a mighty castle and abbey. Though the castle was destroyed by the Scots in 1409 to keep it out of the hands of the English, the abbey survived, albeit in ruins. Today, Jedburgh is the first place of any size that you come to on the A68, having crossed over Carter Bar from England, and as such gets quite a bit of passing tourist trade.

Founded in the twelfth century as an Augustinian priory, **Jedburgh Abbey** (May–Sept daily 9.30am–6.30pm; Oct–April Mon–Sat 9.30am–4.30pm, Sun 2–4.30pm; £5: HS) is the best preserved of all the Border abbeys, its vast church towering over a sloping site right in the centre of town, beside the Jed Water. Entry is through the bright **visitor centre** at the bottom of the hill, where you can view Jedburgh's most treasured archeological find, the **Jedburgh Comb**, carved around 1100 from walrus ivory and decorated with a griffin and a dragon. Enter the **Abbey Church** itself via the west door to appreciate fully the three-storey nave's perfectly proportioned parade of columns and arches. Be sure you climb up the narrow staircase in the west front to the balcony overlooking the nave, where you can contemplate how the place must have looked all decked out for the marriage of Alexander III to Yolande de Dreux in 1285.

It's a couple of minutes' walk from the abbey to the small, square **Market Place**, up the hill from which, at the top of Castlegate, stands **Jedburgh Castle Jail** (Easter–Oct Mon–Sat 10am–4.30pm, Sun 1–4.30pm; £2), an impressive castellated nineteenth-century pile built on the site of the old royal castle, with displays on prison life throughout the ages. Back down near the Market Place, signs will guide you to **Mary, Queen of Scots' House** (March–Nov Mon–Sat 10am–4.30pm, Sun 11am–4.30pm; £3). Despite the name, it seems unlikely that Mary ever actually stayed in this particular sixteenth-century house. The house's highlights are a copy of Mary's death mask and one of the few surviving portraits of the Earl of Bothwell.

Practicalities

Buses pick up and drop off at Canongate near the town centre. Close by, on Murray's Green, is the **tourist office** (Mon–Sat 9.30am–5pm, Sun 10am–5pm). For **accommodation**, try *Meadhon House*, 48 Castlegate (Ⓣ01835/862504, Ⓦwww.meadhon.com; ❷), with a conservatory round the back overlooking a pretty sloping garden, or the Georgian *Glenbank House Hotel* in Castlegate (Ⓣ01835/862258, Ⓦwww.glenbankhotel.co.uk; ❸). Another great choice is *Hundalee House* (Ⓣ01835/863011, Ⓦwww.accommodation-scotland.org; March–Oct; ❷), a seventeenth-century mansion house in open grounds, a mile south of town on the A68. Of the two **campsites** nearby, the *Jedwater Caravan Park* (Ⓣ01835/840219; March–Oct) is cheaper and more secluded, in a pleasant riverside site four miles south of town on the A68.

There's a shortage of good **eating** places, but probably the best place is *Simply Scottish*, 6–8 High St (Ⓣ01835/864696), a smart but relaxed bistro-style café/restaurant serving inexpensive Scottish meals, as well as pasta dishes and the usual snacks. You should also try the local speciality **Jethart Snails**, sticky boiled sweets invented by a French POW in the 1700s and on sale everywhere.

Selkirk and around

Just south of the River Tweed, some five miles southwest of Melrose, lies the royal burgh of **SELKIRK**. The old town sits high up above Ettrick Water; down in the valley by the riverside, the town's imposing grey-stone woollen mills are mostly boarded up now, an eerie reminder of a once prosperous era. There's precious little reason to linger in Selkirk itself, though the town sits on the edge of some lovely countryside, and serves as the gateway to the picturesque, sparsely populated valleys of Yarrow Water and Ettrick Water, to the west.

At the centre of Selkirk, at one end of the High Street, you'll find the tiny **Market Square**, overlooked by a statue of Sir Walter Scott, behind which stands the former Town House, now dubbed **Sir Walter Scott's Courtroom** (April–Sept Mon–Fri 10am–4pm, Sat 10am–2pm, May–Aug also Sun 10am–2pm; Oct Mon–Sat 1–4pm; free), where he served as sheriff for 33 years. Just off Market Square to the south is **Halliwell's House Museum** (April–Sept Mon–Sat 10am–5pm, Sun 10am–noon; July & Aug Mon–Sat 10am–5.30pm, Sun 10am–1pm; Oct Mon–Sat 10am–4pm, Sun 10am–noon; free), an old-style hardware shop with an informative exhibit on the industrialization of the Tweed valley.

The **tourist office** is in Halliwell's House (same hours) off Market Square, and can help with **accommodation**. First choice for those with an unlimited budget is the upmarket *Philipburn House Hotel* (ⓣ01750/720747, ⓦwww.philipburnhousehotel.co.uk; ❻), an unusual eighteenth-century house set in its own grounds a mile west of the town centre; the hotel offers expensive, but excellent Scottish cuisine. Slightly more modest in price, but still full of character is the *Heatherlie House Hotel* (ⓣ01750/721200, ⓦwww.heatherlie.freeserve.co.uk; ❺), a Victorian mansion a sharp left turn up from the road to Ettrick at Heatherlie Park.

Bowhill House

Three miles west of Selkirk off the A708, **Bowhill House** (July daily 1–5pm; £7) is the property of the seriously wealthy Duke of Buccleuch and Queensberry. Beyond the grandiose mid-nineteenth-century mansion's facade of dark whinstone is an outstanding collection of French antiques and European **paintings**: in the dining room, for example, there are portraits by Reynolds and Gainsborough, and a Canaletto cityscape, while the drawing room boasts Boulle furniture, Meissen tableware, paintings by Ruysdael, Leandro Bassano and Claude Lorraine, as well as two more family portraits by Reynolds. Look out also for the Scott Room, which features a splendid portrait of Sir Walter by Henry Raeburn, and the Duke of Monmouth's execution shirt.

The wooded hills of **Bowhill Country Park** adjoining the house (dawn–dusk: Easter, May & June Sat & Sun; July & Aug daily; £3) are crisscrossed by scenic footpaths and cycle trails. The park also shelters a 72-seat **Bowhill Theatre** (ⓣ01750/22204, ⓦwww.bowhilltheatre.co.uk), in the house's former game larder, which hosts the occasional production. Getting to Bowhill by **public transport** is difficult. The Peebles bus, leaving Selkirk daily at 2pm, will drop you at General's Bridge (10min), from where it's a mile or so walk through the grounds to the house.

Peebles and around

Fast, wide, tree-lined and fringed with grassy banks, the Tweed looks at its best at **PEEBLES**, a handsome royal burgh that sits on the north bank, about fifteen miles northwest of Selkirk. The town itself has a genteel, relaxed air, its wide, handsome High Street bordered by houses in a medley of architectural styles, mostly dating from Victorian times, and ending in the soaring crown spire of the **Old Parish Church** (daily 10am–4pm; free) at the western end.

Halfway down the High Street is the **Tweedale Museum & Gallery** (Mon–Fri 10am–noon & 2–5pm, April–Oct also Sat 10am–1pm & 2–4pm; free), housed in the Chambers Institute, and complete with an art gallery dedicated to the enlightenment of his neighbours. The place is stuffed with casts of the world's most famous sculptures and, although most were lost long ago, today's "Secret Room", once the Museum Room, boasts two handsome friezes: one a copy of the Elgin marbles taken from the Parthenon; the other of the **Triumph of Alexander**, originally cast in 1812 to honour Napoleon.

Of the various walks through the hills surrounding Peebles, the five-mile **Sware Trail** is one of the easiest and most scenic, weaving west along the north bank of the river and looping back to the south. On the way, it passes **Neidpath Castle** (Easter & May–Sept Wed–Sat 10.30am–5pm, Sun 12.30–5pm; £3), a gaunt medieval tower-house perched high above the river on a rocky bluff. It's a superb setting, and the interior possesses a pit prison and a great hall bedecked with stunning batik wall hangings depicting the life of Mary, Queen of Scots.

Practicalities

Buses stop outside Peebles' post office, a few doors down from the well-stocked **tourist office** on the High Street (Mon–Sat 9am–5pm, Sun 11am–4pm). For **B&Bs**, try *Rowanbrae,* a trim, pint-sized Victorian place on a quiet cul-de-sac on Northgate, off the east end of High Street (Ⓣ01721/721630, Ⓔjohn@rowanbrae.freeserve.co.uk; ❷), or *Viewfield*, 1 Rosetta Rd (Ⓣ01721/721232, Ⓔmmitchell38@yahoo.com; ❷), an attractive detached Victorian house a 10min walk west of the bridge, with rooms overlooking a lovely garden. For upmarket **hotels** you have to head out of town: *Castle Venlaw Hotel* (Ⓣ01721/720384, Ⓦwww.venlaw.co.uk; ❼) is an impressive Scots Baronial house set in its own grounds on the edge of town up the Edinburgh Road, while the *Cringletie House* (Ⓣ01721/730233, Ⓦwww.cringletie.com; ❽) is a still more splendid Baronial pile a couple of miles further up the Edinburgh Road. Of the two **campsites** on the edge of town, the *Rosetta Caravan Park* (Ⓣ01721/720770; April–Oct) is the quieter, set in fields surrounded by mature woods, a fifteen-minute walk north of the High Street.

The best place to **eat** is the *Sunflower* (Ⓣ017221/722420), a tiny, brightly coloured restaurant at 4 Bridgegate, just off Northgate, which does sandwiches at lunch, and more adventurous (and slightly pricier) evening meals. You can munch on a baguette and get a good coffee at the **café** in the Eastgate Theatre, a state-of-the-art church conversion (Ⓦwww.eastgatearts.com). *The Halcyon Restaurant*, 39 Eastgate (Ⓦhalcyonrestaurant.com; closed Mon & Sun) has an smart designer menu in formal, elegant surroundings; try the off-peak fixed three-course menu for £17.50. As for **pubs**, the *Crown Hotel* on the High Street is a cosy place to hunker down; the *Tontine Hotel*, opposite, is a grander place with views south over the Tweed, and a standard hotel menu. For really good pub food, try one of the bar meals at the *Castle Venlaw Hotel*.

Traquair House

Six miles east of Peebles, a mile or so south of the A72, **Traquair House** (daily: April, May & Sept noon–5pm; June–Aug 10.30am–5pm; Oct 11am–4pm; Nov Sat & Sun 11am–3pm; £6.30, grounds only £2.50; Ⓦ www.traquair.co.uk) is the oldest continuously inhabited house in Scotland, with the present owners – the Maxwell Stuarts – having lived here since 1491. Persistently Catholic, the family paid for its principles: the fifth earl got two years in the Tower of London for his support of Bonnie Prince Charlie, Protestant millworkers repeatedly attacked their property, and by 1800 little remained of the family's once enormous estates – certainly not enough to fund any major rebuilding.

Consequently, Traquair's main appeal is its ancient shape and structure. The whitewashed facade is strikingly handsome, with narrow windows and trim turrets surrounding the tiniest of front doors – an organic, homogeneous edifice that's a welcome change from other grandiose stately homes. Inside, you can see original vaulted cellars, where locals once hid their cattle from raiders; the twisting main staircase as well as the earlier medieval version, later a secret escape route for persecuted Catholics; a carefully camouflaged priest's hole; and even a **priest's room** where a string of resident chaplains lived in hiding. In the **museum room** there is a wealth of treasures, including a fine example of a Jacobite Amen glass, a rosary and crucifix owned by Mary, Queen of Scots, and the cloak worn by the Earl of Nithsdale during his dramatic escape from the Tower of London.

It's worth sparing time for the surrounding **gardens**, where you'll find a **hedge maze**, several craft workshops and the **Traquair House Brewery** dating back to 1566, which was revived in 1965, and claims to be the only British brewery that still ferments totally in oak. You can learn about the brewery and taste the ales in the Brewery Shop, as well as buy them. There's an attractive café serving snacks in an estate cottage on the redundant avenue which leads to the locked **Bear Gates**; Bonnie Prince Charlie departed the house through the gates, and the then owner promised to keep them locked till a Stuart should ascend the throne.

If you're really taken by the place, you can stay in one of its three guest **rooms** (Ⓣ01896/830323; ⑧), decked out with antiques and four-posters, on a bed-and-breakfast basis only.

Dumfries and Galloway

The southwest corner of Scotland, known as **Dumfries and Galloway** (Ⓦ www.visitdumfriesandgalloway.co.uk), has stately homes, deserted hills and ruined abbeys to compete with the best of the Borders. It also has the **Solway coast**, a long, indented coastline of sheltered sandy coves that's been dubbed the "Scottish Riviera" – an exaggeration perhaps, but it's certainly Scotland's warmest, southernmost stretch of coastline.

Dumfries is the obvious gateway to the region, a pleasant enough town that's only really a must for those on the trail of **Robert Burns**, who spent the last part of his life here. Further west, and more attractive is **Kirkcudbright**, once a bustling port thronged with sailing ships, later an artists' retreat, and now a tranquil, well-preserved little eighteenth- and early nineteenth-century town. Contrasting with the essentially gentle landscape of the Solway coast, is the brooding presence of the **Galloway Hills** to the north, their beautiful moors, mountains, lakes and rivers centred on the 150,000-acre

Galloway Forest Park, a seriously underused hill-walking and mountain-biking paradise.

Dumfries and around

Situated on the wide banks of the River Nith a short distance inland from the Solway Firth, **DUMFRIES** is by far the largest town in southwest Scotland. Long known as the "Queen of the South" (as is its football club), the town flourished as a medieval seaport and trading centre. Enough remains of the original, warm red-sandstone buildings to distinguish Dumfries from other towns in the southwest. A worthwhile stop, it also acts as a convenient base for exploring the Solway coast, to the east and west, and is second only to Ayr for its associations with Robbie Burns.

The Town

Dumfries' pedestrianized **High Street** runs roughly parallel to the Nith; at its northern end, presiding over a floral roundabout, is the **Burns Statue**, a sentimental piece of Victorian frippery in white Carrara marble, featuring the great man holding a posy in one hand while the other clutches at his heart. His faithful hound, Luath, lies curled around his feet – though it doesn't look much like a Scots collie (as Luath was). Further down the High Street, Burns' body lay in state at the town's most singular building, the **Midsteeple**, an appealingly wonky hotchpotch of a place, built in 1707 to fulfil the multiple functions of town prison, clocktower, courthouse and arsenal.

If you're on Burns' trail, make sure you duck down the alleyway to the whitewashed **Globe Inn**, a little further down the High Street, which was Burns' favourite *howff* (pub). Southeast of the High Street, in Burns Street, stands

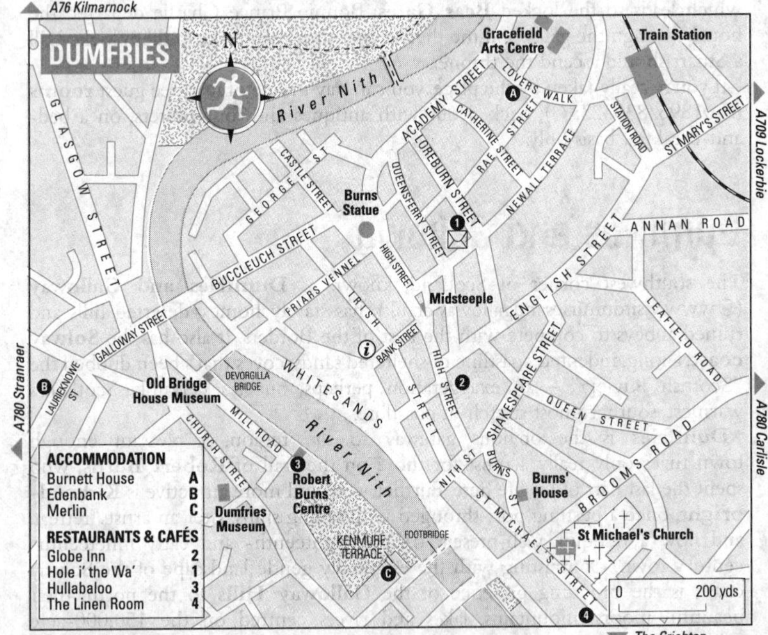

Burns' House (April–Sept Mon–Sat 10am–5pm, Sun 2–5pm; Oct–March Tues–Sat 10am–1pm & 2–5pm; free), a simple sandstone building where the poet died of rheumatic heart disease in 1796, a few days before the birth of his last son, Maxwell. Inside, along with the usual collection of Burns memorabilia, one of the bedroom windows bears his signature, scratched with his diamond ring. Burns was buried nearby in a simple grave by **St Michael's Church** (Mon–Fri 10am–4pm; free), but in 1815, he was dug up and moved across the graveyard to a purpose-built **Mausoleum**, a bright white Neoclassical eyesore, which houses a slightly ludicrous statue of Burns being accosted by the Poetic Muse.

From the church, head down to the shallow and fast-running Nith, and cross over to the old water mill which houses the **Robert Burns Centre**, or RBC (April–Sept Mon–Sat 10am–8pm, Sun 2–5pm; Oct–March Tues–Sat 10am–1pm & 2–5pm; free), with a simple exhibition on the poet's years in Dumfries and an optional twenty-minute slide show (£1.55). On the hill above the RBC stands the **Dumfries Museum** (April–Sept Mon–Sat 10am–5pm, Sun 2–5pm; Oct–March Tues–Sat 10am–1pm & 2–5pm; free), from which there are great views over the town. The museum is housed partly in an eighteenth-century windmill, which was converted into the town's observatory in the 1830s, and features a **camera obscura** on its top floor (£2), well worth a visit on a clear day.

A little upstream from the RBC is the pedestrian-only **Devorgilla Bridge**, built in 1431 and one of the oldest bridges in Scotland. Attached to its south-western end is the town's oldest house, built in 1660, now home to the tiny **Old Bridge House Museum** (April–Sept Mon–Sat 10am–5pm, Sun 2–5pm; free), stuffed full of Victorian domestic bric-a-brac, including a teeth-chattering range of Victorian dental gear.

Practicalities

Dumfries **train** station is five minutes' walk east of the town centre, while **buses** drop you off at Whitesands beside the River Nith, where you'll also find the **tourist office** (Mon–Sat 9am–5.30pm; June–Sept also Sun 10am–3.30pm). Dumfries abounds in handsome sandstone villas, several of which have been turned into **guesthouses** and **B&Bs**. For value and convenience, you can't beat *Burnett House*, 4 Lovers Walk (ⓣ01387/263164, ⓦwww.burnetthouse.co.uk; ❸), a Victorian house near the station. For a more distinctive setting, try *The Merlin*, 2 Kenmure Terrace (ⓣ01387/261002; ❷), overlooking the Nith near the RBC. If you're looking for a **hotel**, head for Laurieknowe Street, a five- to ten-minute walk west of Devorgilla Bridge, where you'll find the welcoming, family-run *Edenbank* (ⓣ01387/252759, ⓦwww.edenbankhotel.co.uk; ❺) at no. 17.

Dumfries top foodie **restaurant** is *The Linen Room* (ⓣ01387/255689, ⓦwww.linenroom.com; closed all day Mon & Tues lunch), at 53 St Michael's St, a very smart place run by one of Scotland's most garlanded and adventurous young chefs. A more relaxed option is *Hullabaloo* (ⓣ01387/259679; ⓦwww.hullabaloorestaurant.co.uk; closed Mon & Sun eve), a cosy restaurant on the top floor of the RBC, with a summer terrace overlooking the river. Lunchtimes are for wraps, bagels and ciabatta sandwiches; in the evening, there are more adventurous global dishes on offer.

Two of Burns' favourite drinking places are still in operation: the *Hole i' the Wa'* **pub**, down an alley opposite Woolworth's on High Street, serves the usual bar food; but for somewhere with a bit more atmosphere, make for the smoky, oak-panelled *Globe Inn* on the High Street, which is crammed with memorabilia connected with the poet but is otherwise little changed since his time. **Films** are regularly shown at the RBC (ⓣ01387/264808, ⓦwww.rbcft.co.uk;

Tues–Sat). Grierson and Graham, 10 Academy St (Ⓣ01387/259483), offer **bike rental**, useful for reaching the nearby Solway coast.

Drumlanrig Castle

Seventeen miles north of Dumfries, **Drumlanrig Castle** (May–Aug daily 11am–5pm; May & June closed Fri; Ⓦwww.drumlanrig.co.uk; £7) is not a castle at all, but the grandiose stately home of the Duke of Buccleuch and Queensberry. The highlights of the richly furnished interior are the **paintings**, in particular, Rembrandt's *Old Woman Reading*, and Hans Holbein's formal portrait of Sir Nicholas Carew, Master of the Horse to Henry VIII. Also be sure to check out the striking 1950s portrait of the present duchess, all debutante coiffure and high-society décolletage, by John Merton in the morning room, and, in the serving room, John Ainslie's *Joseph Florence, Chef*, a sharply observed and dynamic portrait much admired by Walter Scott. As well as the house, Drumlanrig offers a host of other attractions, including formal **gardens** and a forested **country park** (April–Sept daily 11am–5pm; £3). The old stableyard beside the castle contains a visitor centre, a few shops, the inevitable tearoom, and also a useful **bike rental** outlet – the park is crisscrossed by footpaths and cycle routes. There's also a **cycle museum** filled with every type of bike from MTBs to a replica of the first-ever pedal bike. If you're heading here by bus from Dumfries or Ayr, bear in mind it's a one-and-a-half-mile walk from the road to the house.

Caerlaverock

Caerlaverock Castle (daily: April–Sept 9.30am–5.30pm; Oct–March 9.30am–4.30pm; £5; HS), eight miles southeast of Dumfries, is a picture-perfect ruined castle. Not only is it moated, it's built from the rich local red sandstone, is triangular in shape and has preserved its mighty double-towered gatehouse. The most surprising addition, however, lies inside, where you're confronted by the ornate Renaissance facade of the **Nithsdale Lodging**, erected in the 1630s by the first earl of Nithsdale. The decorated tympana above the windows feature lively mythological and heraldic scenes in what was clearly the latest style. Sadly, Nithsdale didn't get much value for money: just six years later he and his royal garrison were forced to surrender after a thirteen-week siege and bombardment by the Covenanters, who proceeded to wreck the place. It was never inhabited again.

Three miles further east, at Eastpark, is the **Caerlaverock Wildfowl and Wetlands Trust (WWT) Centre** (daily 10am–5pm; Ⓦwww.wwt.org.uk; £5.50), more than a thousand acres of protected salt marsh and mud flat edging the Solway Firth. It's famous for the 25,000 or so barnacle geese that winter here between September and April. Throughout the year, though, the wild whooper swans have a daily feeding time and the wardens run free wildlife safaris; call Ⓣ01387/770200 for details. You can **camp** or stay in one of the **rooms** in the centre's converted farmhouse (Ⓔinfo.caerlaverock@wwt.org.uk; ❸), which has its own observation tower, plus a kitchen and washing machine for guests' use. Both the castle and the centre are reached along the B725; this is the route the bus takes, mostly terminating at the castle but sometimes continuing to the start of the two-mile lane leading off the B725 to the centre.

New Abbey and Sweetheart Abbey

NEW ABBEY is a tidy little one-street village, eight miles south of Dumfries, which evolved in order to service its giant neighbour, **Sweetheart Abbey** (April–Sept daily 9.30am–5.30pm; Oct–March Mon–Wed, Sat & Sun

9.30am–4.30pm; £3; HS). Lying romantically ruined to the east of the village, the abbey takes its unusual name from its founder, Devorgilla de Balliol, Lady of Galloway, who carried the embalmed heart of her husband, John Balliol (of Oxford college fame) around with her for the last 22 years of her life – she is buried with the casket, in the presbytery. The last of the Cistercian abbeys to be founded in Scotland – in 1273 – Sweetheart is dominated by the red-sandstone abbey church, which remains intact, albeit minus its roof. Its grassy nave is flanked by giant compound piers supporting early Gothic arches, and above them a triforium. The other great survivor is the precinct wall, to the north and east of the abbey, a massive structure – up to ten feet high and four feet wide in places – made from rough granite boulders.

The *Abbey Cottage* **tearoom** is renowned for its good coffee, teas and home-made cakes, and enjoys an unrivalled view over the abbey. At the centre of the village, two **pubs** face one another across a cobbled square: the *Abbey Arms* (Ⓣ01387/850489, Ⓔenquiries@abbeyarms.netlineuk.net; ③) and the *Criffel Inn* (Ⓣ01387/850244, Ⓦwww.criffelinn.com; ③); both have seats outside, serve pub food and do B&B.

The Colvend coast

The **Colvend coast**, twenty miles or so southwest of Dumfries, is probably one of the finest stretches of coastline along the so-called "Scottish Riviera". The best approach is via the A710, which heads south through New Abbey, before cutting across a handsome landscape of rolling farmland to **ROCKCLIFFE**, a beguiling little place of comfortable villas sheltered beneath wooded hills and nestled around a beautiful, rocky sand and shell bay. Excellent B&B **accommodation** is available at *Millbrae House* (Ⓣ01556/630217; March–Oct; ②), a whitewashed cottage a short stroll from the bay. For **camping**, the *Castle Point Caravan Site* (Ⓣ01556/630248; March–Oct) is in a secluded spot, just south of the village, a stone's throw from the seashore. The *Garden House* tearoom (closed Mon & Tues), at the entrance to the village, provides simple sustenance and has a garden at the back.

For vehicles, Rockcliffe is a dead end, but it's the start of a pleasant half-hour's walk along the Jubilee Path to neighbouring **KIPPFORD**, a tiny, lively yachting centre strung out along the east bank of the Urr estuary. At low tide you can walk over the Rough Firth causeway from the shore below across the mud flats to **Rough Island**, a humpy twenty-acre bird sanctuary owned by the National Trust for Scotland – it's out of bounds in May and June during the nesting season. The reward for your gentle stroll is a drink and a bite to eat at the ever-popular *Anchor Hotel* (Ⓣ01556/620205), on Kippford's waterfront, which serves tasty **bar meals**. If you need to stay the night, head for the *Rosemount* (Ⓣ01556/620214, Ⓦwww.rosemountguesthouse.com; Feb–Nov; ②), an excellent **guesthouse** close by on the seafront, or the stylish *Roughfirth House* B&B (Ⓣ01556620 330; Ⓦwww.roughfirth.com; ⑤), a whitewashed villa in the woods, with wonderful views over the estuary.

Castle Douglas and around

Most folk come to **CASTLE DOUGLAS** (Ⓦwww.castledouglas.net), eighteen miles southwest of Dumfries, in order to visit the nearby attractions of Threave Garden and Castle. **Threave Garden** (daily 9.30am–5.30pm; £6; NTS) is a pleasant mile or so's walk south of Castle Douglas, along the shores of Loch Carlingwark. The garden features a magnificent spread of flowers and woodland, sixty acres subdivided into more than a dozen areas, from the bright, old-fashioned blooms of the Rose Garden to the brilliant banks of rhododendrons in the Woodland Garden and the ranks of primula, astilbe and gentian in the Peat Garden. In springtime, thousands of visitors turn up for the flowering of more than two hundred types of daffodil and, from late May onwards, the herbaceous beds are the main attraction, with most of them arranged like islets in a sea of lawn (so that they can be viewed from all sides).

The best way of reaching **Threave Castle** (April–Sept daily 9.30am–6.30pm; £4; HS), a mile or so north of the gardens, is to walk through the estate. However you decide to get there, you should follow the signs to the Open Farm, from where it's a lovely fifteen-minute walk down to the River Dee. Here you ring a brass bell for the boat to take you over to the flat and grassy island on which the stern-looking tower house stands. Built for one of the Black Douglases, Archibald the Grim, the sturdy, rectangular fortress was completed shortly after the War of Independence, in around 1370. The rickety curtain-wall to the south and east is all that remains of the artillery fortifications, hurriedly constructed in the 1450s in a desperate – and unsuccessful – attempt to defend the castle against James II's newfangled cannon. The place was wrecked in 1640 after a thirteen-week siege, but enough remains of the interior to make it worth exploring.

Practicalities

Castle Douglas **tourist office** (April–June, Sept & Oct Mon–Sat 10am–4.30pm, Sun 11am–4pm; July & Aug Mon–Sat 10am–6pm, Sun 11am–5pm) is at the top end of King Street. All the old coaching inns on King Street offer **accommodation**, but you're better off trying one of the well-built Victorian guesthouses out on Ernespie Road, such as *Albion House* (Ⓣ01556/502360, Ⓔpikoe007@aol.com; March–Nov; ③), at no. 49. Alternatively, just south of Castle Douglas, the *Smithy House* (Ⓣ01556/503841, Ⓦwww.smithyhouse.co.uk; ④) is a nicely converted *smiddy* overlooking Loch Carlinwark. Campers should make for the *Lochside* **campsite** (Ⓣ01556/502949; Easter–Oct), beside Loch Carlingwark, a short walk from the bottom of King Street down Marle Street. The best place to grab a bite to **eat** is *Designs* (closed Sun), a daytime café at the back of an arts and crafts shop at 179 King St, with a lovely conservatory and garden, serving great ciabattas and decent coffee. **Bike rental** – useful for getting out to Threave – is available from the Castle Douglas Cycle Centre on Church Street (Ⓣ01556/504542, Ⓦwww.cdbikes.co.uk; closed Sun).

Kirkcudbright and around

KIRKCUDBRIGHT – pronounced "kir-coo-bree" – hugging the muddy banks of the River Dee ten miles southwest of Castle Douglas, is the only major town along the Solway coast to have retained a working harbour. In addition, it has a ruined castle and an attractive town centre, a charming medley of simple two-storey cottages with medieval pends, Georgian villas and Victorian townhouses, all built in a mixture of sandstone, granite and brick, and painted, with their windows and quoins picked out.

The most surprising sight in Kirkcudbright is **MacLellan's Castle** (April–Sept daily 9.30am–5.30pm; £3.50; HS), a pink-flecked sixteenth-century tower house that sits at one end of the High Street by the harbourside. Part fortified keep and part spacious mansion, the castle was built in the 1570s for the then Provost of Kirkcudbright, Sir Thomas MacLellan of Bombie. Its interior is well preserved, from the kitchen (complete with bread oven) to the spyhole known as the "**laird's lug**", behind the fireplace of the Great Hall. Sir Thomas MacLellan is buried in the neighbouring **Greyfriars Church**, where his tomb is an eccentrically crude attempt at Neoclassicism; it even incorporates parts of someone else's gravestone.

Near the castle, on the L-shaped High Street, is **Broughton House** (April–June, Sept & Oct Mon & Thurs–Sun noon–5pm; July & Aug daily noon–5pm; also Feb & March garden only daily 11am–4pm; £8; NTS), a smart Georgian townhouse and former home of the artist **Edward Hornel** (1863–1933). Hornel was an important member of the late nineteenth-century Scottish art scene, who spent his childhood a few doors down the street, and returned in 1900 to establish an artists' colony in Kirkcudbright with some of the "Glasgow Boys" (see p.842). At the back of the house Hornel added a studio and a vast, glass-roofed, mahogany-panelled gallery, now filled with the mannered, vibrantly coloured paintings of girls at play, which he churned out in the latter part of his career. Hornel's trip to Japan in 1893 imbued him with a lifelong affection for the country, and his surprisingly large, densely packed, wonderful, rambling **gardens** have a strong Japanese influence.

For background information on Kirkcudbright, visit the imposing, church-like **Tolbooth**, with its stone-built clocktower and spire. Built in the 1620s, the building now houses the **Tolbooth Art Centre** (May, June & Sept Mon–Sat 11am–5pm, Sun 2–5pm; July & Aug Mon–Sat 10am–5pm, Sun 2–5pm; Oct Mon–Sat 11am–4pm, Sun 2–5pm; Nov–April Mon–Sat 11am–4pm; free), which has, on the upper floor, a small permanent display of works by some of Kirkcudbright's erstwhile resident artists, including Hornel's striking *Japanese Girl*, and S.J. Peploe's Colourist view of the Tolbooth. Don't miss the **Stewartry Museum** (times as above), an extraordinary collection of local exhibits packed into a purpose-built Victorian building on St Mary Street.

Practicalities

Buses to Kirkcudbright stop by the harbour car park, next to the **tourist office** (mid-Feb to March & Nov Mon–Sat 10am–4pm, Sun 11am–4pm; April–June, Sept & Oct Mon–Sat 10am–5pm, Sun 11am–4pm; July & Aug Mon–Sat 9.30am–6pm, Sun 11am–5pm), where you can get help finding **accommodation**. One of the best options is *Number* 3 (Ⓣ01557/330881,

▲ Kirkcudbright

Galloway Forest Park

Galloway Forest Park (Ⓦwww.forestry.gov.uk/gallowayforestpark) has three **visitor centres** (times vary but are basically April–Oct daily 10.30am–4.30pm) in the forest park: by Clatteringshaws Loch, at Glentrool and at Kirroughtree. Each visitor centre has a tearoom, several waymarked walks and lots of information on activities and events. In addition, both Glentrool and **Kirroughtree** have **mountain bike trails**, which form part of southern Scotland's outstanding mountain-biking facilities, known as the 7 Stanes (Ⓦwww.7stanes.co.uk). Of the two, **Kirroughtree**, three miles east of the town of Newton Stewart, is by far the most varied and fun, with lots of exciting single track trails for all abilities and good bike-rental facilities.

Hikers are better off heading for **Glentrool**, at the western edge of the park, about ten miles north of Newton Stewart, where a narrow lane twists the five miles over to Loch Trool. From here, you can follow the Gariland Burn to Loch Neldricken and Loch Enoch, with their silver granite sands, and then on to the Devil's Bowling Green, strewn with hundreds of erratic boulders left by the retreating glaciers. Alternatively, you can head for the Range of the Awful Hand, whose five peaks include the **Merrick** (2746ft), the highest hill in southern Scotland.

The only tarmacked road to cross the park is the desolate twenty-mile stretch of the A712 between Newton Stewart and New Galloway, known as the **Queen's Way**. About seven miles east of Newton Stewart, at the **Grey Mare's Tail Bridge**, there are various forest trails, all delving into the pine forests beside the road, crossing gorges, waterfalls and burns. There's also a **Wild Goat Park** and, a mile or so further up the road, a **Red Deer Range**, A few more miles on, you'll come to **Clatteringshaws Loch**, a reservoir surrounded by pine forest, with a fourteen-mile footpath running right round the loch.

Ⓦwww.number3-bandb.co.uk; ④), a Georgian house opposite Broughton House with comfortable rooms, good cooking and a beautiful garden with sundeck, followed by *Gladstone House* (Ⓣ01557/331734, Ⓦwww.kirkcudbrightgladstone.com; ④), another excellent Georgian B&B set back slightly from the street. The *Silvercraigs* caravan and **campsite** (Ⓣ01557/330123; Easter to late Oct) is five minutes' walk down St Mary's Street and Place, on a bluff overlooking town.

Top choice for **restaurants** is the *Auld Alliance*, 5 Castle St (Ⓣ01557/330569), a superior, if pricey, restaurant offering a fusion of French and Scottish cuisine, where you need to book ahead. Otherwise, there's the usual bar food at the *Best Western*-run *Selkirk Arms Hotel* on the High Street, which boasts a large garden out the back. Alternatively, there's *Solway Tide*, an attractive tearoom on Castle Street (closed Sun), which serves good coffee, smoothies, paninis, bagels and home-made scones. For a **drink**, the busy *Masonic Arms*, on Castle Street, pulls a reasonable pint of real ale.

Wigtown

Seven miles south of Newton Stewart (see box above), **WIGTOWN** (Ⓦwww.wigtown-booktown.co.uk) is a tiny place, considering it was once the county town of Wigtownshire. Despite its modest size, it has a remarkable main square, a vast, triangular-shaped affair, its layout unchanged since medieval times. Overlooking and dominating the square and its central bowling green are the gargantuan **County Buildings**, built in French Gothic style, and now home, on the top floor, to a CCTV link to a local osprey nest (May–Sept Mon, Thurs & Sat 10am–5pm, Tues, Wed & Fri 10am–7.30pm, Sun 2–5pm; free). Wigtown styles itself as "Scotland's National Book Town", with a highly rated **literary**

festival in late September and over twenty **bookshops** occupying some of the modest houses that line the square, and more elsewhere in the vicinity. The Bookshop, on the north side of the square, is the largest second-hand bookshop in Scotland, a wonderful, rambling affair, while *Readinglasses*, on the opposite side of the square, boasts a small **café**.

Whithorn and around

Fifteen miles south of Wigtown is **WHITHORN** (Ⓦwww.whithorn.com), a one-street town. It's here, in 397, that **St Ninian** is thought to have founded the first Christian church north of Hadrian's Wall. No one can be sure where Ninian's church actually stood, and very little is known about Ninian's life, but his tomb at Whithorn soon became a popular place of pilgrimage. These days, it takes a serious leap of the imagination to envisage Whithorn as a medieval pilgrimage centre. For this reason, it's a good idea to start by watching the audiovisual show at the **Whithorn Dig** (Whithorn Story; Easter–Oct daily 10.30am–5pm; £3.50) on the main street. Heading outside, the dig site is pretty uninspiring, as are the nearby ruins of the nave of **Whithorn Priory**. More compelling are the early Christian standing crosses and headstones housed in the on-site **Whithorn Museum**.

The pilgrims who crossed the Solway to visit St Ninian's shrine landed at the **ISLE OF WHITHORN**, four miles south of Whithorn, no longer an island, but an antique and picturesque little seaport. If you continue to the end of the harbour, you'll pick up signs to the minuscule remains of the thirteenth-century **St Ninian's Chapel**, which some believe was the site of the original Candida Casa. If you want to **stay**, try the unassuming *Steam Packet Inn* (Ⓣ01988/500334, Ⓦwww.steampacketinn.com; ③), right on the quay in Isle of Whithorn; it does pub food that's above average in quality and price, and has a moderately expensive **restaurant**.

The Rhinns of Galloway

The hilly, hammer-shaped peninsula at the western end of the Solway coast is known as the **Rhinns of Galloway.** The main town is **STRANRAER** (Ⓦwww.stranraer.org) but unless you're heading to (or coming from) Northern Ireland, there's really no reason to go there. For the moment Stena Line still use Stranraer, which has rail links with Ayr and Glasgow, but they are threatening to move five miles north to **CAIRNRYAN**, where P&O have their base.

The nicest place to stay on the peninsula is the old seafaring port of **PORTPATRICK** which has an attractive pastel-painted seafront that wraps itself round a small rocky bay, sheltered by equally rocky cliffs. Portpatrick has several good **hotels** and **guesthouses**, the best of which is the lilac-painted *Waterfront Hotel* (Ⓣ01776/810800, Ⓦwww.waterfronthotel.co.uk; ⑤). For something a bit cheaper, the *Rickwood House Hotel* (Ⓣ01776/810270, Ⓦwww.portpatrick.me.uk; ③) is an excellent option, set back from the harbour on Heugh Road, near the golf club, and run by a very welcoming couple. There are several caravan and **campsites** in a row on the hill overlooking Portpatrick and Dunskey Castle, quite a distance from town (and the sea), but accessed by a pleasant walk along the disused railway and cliff-top trail; *Sunnymeade* (Ⓣ01776/810293; March–Oct) has the better facilities, but *Castle Bay* (Ⓣ01776/810462; March–Oct) has the more informal atmosphere. For **pubs** and **grub**, *The Crown* on the seafront is probably the cosiest, though the adjacent *Harbour House Hotel* has real ale. For something more formal and slightly pricier, head to the *Waterfront Bistro* next door.

It's twenty miles south from Portpatrick to the **Mull of Galloway** (Ⓦwww.mull-of-galloway.co.uk), but it's well worth the ride. This precipitous headland, crowned by a classic whitewashed Stevenson lighthouse, from which you can see the Isle of Man, as well as the coasts of Ireland and England, really feels like the end of the road. It is, in fact, the southernmost point in Scotland, and a favourite nesting spot for guillemots, razorbills and kittiwakes. The headland has a **visitor centre** (Easter–Sept daily 10.30am–5pm) in a building near the **lighthouse**, which can be climbed on summer weekends (April–Sept Sat & Sun 10am–3.30pm; £2). Just below the car park, perched on the cliff edge, is an excellent *Gallie Craig* **café**, serving hot meals and snacks (Nov–March closed Wed & Thurs), with a terrace that provides armchair birdwatching.

Ayrshire

The rolling hills and rich soil of **Ayrshire** (Ⓦwww.ayrshire-arran.com) make for prime farming country, and as such are not really top of most visitors' Scottish itinerary. **Ayr**, the county town and birthplace of Robert Burns, is handsome enough, but won't distract you for long. Most folk wisely stick to the coastline, attracted by the wide, flat sandy **beaches** and the region's vast number of **golf** courses. South of Ayr, the most obvious points of interest are **Culzean Castle**, with its Robert Adam interior and extensive wooded grounds, and the offshore islands of **Ailsa Craig**, home to the world's second largest gannetry. North of Ayr, where the towns benefited from the industrialization of Glasgow, there are even fewer places to detain you, with the exception of **Irvine**, home to the Scottish Maritime Museum.

Ayr and around

AYR is by far the largest town on the Firth of Clyde coast. It was an important seaport and trading centre for many centuries, and rivalled Glasgow in size and significance right up until the late seventeenth century. Nowadays, the town won't keep you long, though it pulls in the crowds for the Scottish Grand National and the Scottish Derby (Ⓦwww.ayr-racecourse.co.uk), and the local tourist industry continues to do steady business out of the fact that Robbie Burns was born in the neighbouring village of **Alloway** (see p.822).

Ayr's town centre, wedged between Sandgate and the south bank of the River Ayr, is busy most days with shoppers from all over the county. The town's most venerable sight is the medieval **Auld Brig**, east off the High Street. It survived the threat of demolition in the early twentieth century thanks largely to its featuring in a Burns poem, and is now one of the oldest stone bridges in Scotland, having been built during the reign of James IV (1488–1513). A short stroll upstream from the bridge stands the much-restored **Auld Kirk**, the church funded by Cromwell as recompense for the one he incorporated into the town's fortress. The church's dark and gloomy interior retains the original pulpit (ask at the tourist office about access).

All you can see of Cromwell's zigzag **Citadel**, built to the west of the town centre in the 1650s, is a small section of the old walls – the area is still known locally as "the Fort". To the south of the citadel are the wide, gridiron streets of Ayr's main Georgian and Regency residential development. **Wellington Square** is the area's showpiece, its trim gardens and terraces overlooked by the **County Buildings**, a vast, imposing Palladian pile from 1820. The opening of the Glasgow–Ayr train line in 1840 brought the first major influx

Robert Burns

The eldest of seven children, **Robert Burns** (Ⓦwww.robertburns.org), the national poet of Scotland, was born in Alloway on January 25, 1759. His father, William, was employed as a gardener until 1766 when he became a tenant farmer at Mount Oliphant, near Alloway, moving to Lochlie farm, Tarbolton, eleven years later. A series of bad harvests and the demands of the landlord's estate manager bankrupted the family, and William died almost penniless in 1784. These events had a profound effect on Robert, leaving him with an antipathy towards political authority and a hatred of the land-owning classes.

With the death of his father, Robert became head of the family and they moved again, this time to a farm at Mossgiel, near Mauchline. Burns had already begun writing **poetry** and **prose** at Lochlie, recording incidental thoughts in his *First Commonplace Book*, but it was here at Mossgiel that he began to write in earnest, and his first volume, *Poems Chiefly in the Scottish Dialect*, was published in Kilmarnock in 1786. The book proved immensely popular, celebrated by ordinary Scots and Edinburgh literati alike, with the satirical trilogy *Holy Willie's Prayer*, *The Holy Fair* and *Address to the Devil* attracting particular attention. The object of Burns' poetic scorn was the kirk, whose ministers had obliged him to appear in church to be publicly condemned for fornication – a commonplace punishment in those days.

Burns spent the winter of 1786–87 in the capital, lionized by the literary establishment. Despite his success, however, he felt trapped, unable to make enough money from writing to leave farming. He was also in a political snare, fraternizing with the elite, but with radical views and pseudo-Jacobite nationalism that constantly landed him in trouble. His frequent recourse was to play the part of the unlettered ploughman-poet, the noble savage who might be excused his impetuous outbursts and hectic womanizing.

He had, however, made useful contacts in Edinburgh and as a consequence was recruited to collect, write and rearrange two volumes of songs set to traditional Scottish tunes. These volumes, James Johnson's *Scots Musical Museum* and George Thomson's *Select Scottish Airs*, contain the bulk of his **songwriting**, and it's on them that Burns' international reputation rests, with works like *Auld Lang Syne*, *Scots Wha Hae*, *Coming Through the Rye* and *Green Grow the Rushes, O*. At this time, too, though poetry now took second place, he produced two excellent poems: *Tam o' Shanter* and a republican tract, *A Man's a Man for a' That*.

Burns often boasted of his sexual conquests, and he fathered several illegitimate children; but in 1788, he eventually married **Jean Armour**, a stonemason's daughter from Mauchline, with whom he already had two children, and moved to Ellisland Farm, near Dumfries. The following year he was appointed excise officer and could at last leave farming, moving to Dumfries in 1791. Burns' years of comfort were short-lived, however. His years of labour on the farm, allied to a rheumatic fever, damaged his heart, and he died in Dumfries on July 21, 1796, aged 37.

Burns' work, inspired by a romantic nationalism and tinged with a wry wit, has made him a potent symbol of "Scottishness". Ignoring the anglophile preferences of the Edinburgh elite, he wrote in Scots vernacular about the country he loved, an exuberant celebration that filled a need in a nation culturally colonized by England. Today, Burns Clubs all over the world mark every anniversary of the poet's birthday with the Burns' Supper, complete with Scottish totems – haggis, piper, and whisky bottle – and a ritual recital of Burns' *Ode to a Haggis*.

of holiday-makers to the town, but today, only a few hardy visitors and local dog-walkers take a stroll along Ayr's bleak, long **Esplanade** and beach, which look out to the Isle of Arran. The one building of note is the distinctive whitewashed **Ayr Pavilion**, built in 1911 with four tall corner towers – it now houses the suitably tacky Pirate Pete's indoor adventure playground.

Practicalities

Ayr is the nearest large town to **Glasgow Prestwick airport** (Ⓣ0871/223 0700, Ⓦwww.gpia.co.uk), which lies three miles north and has regular trains to Ayr and Glasgow. Ayr **train** station is ten minutes' walk southeast of the town centre; the **bus** station is in the centre at the foot of Sandgate, near the **tourist office**, at 22 Sandgate (July & Aug Mon–Sat 9am–6pm, Sun 10am–5pm; Oct–June Mon–Sat 9am–1pm & 2–5pm), which can help with **accommodation**. Of the numerous choices on Queen's Terrace, head for *Craggallan* (Ⓣ01292/264998, Ⓦwww.craggallan.com; ④), a friendly little guesthouse with a dining table that converts into a billiards table. In the leafy streets to the south of the town centre, *The Dunn Thing*, 13 Park Circus (Ⓣ01292/284531, Ⓦwww.thedunnthing.co.uk; ②) is a smartly decorated B&B that lets out rooms with or without breakfast, and *The Crescent* is a lovely spacious Victorian house with a four-poster suite, at 26 Bellevue Crescent (Ⓣ01292/287329, Ⓦwww.26crescent.freeserve.co.uk; ⑤). Campers should head for the *Heads of Ayr* caravan and **campsite** (Ⓣ01292/442269; March–Oct), three miles south of town along the coastal A719, beside the popular activity centre, **Heads of Ayr Farm Park** (Easter–Oct daily 10am–5pm; Ⓦwww.headsofayrfarmpark.com).

Arguably the town's best **restaurant** is *Fouters*, 2a Academy St, a cellar bistro off Sandgate (Ⓣ01292/261391, Ⓦwww.fouters.co.uk; closed Mon & Sun), or try one of the town's good Italian places, such as the long-established *Bonfanti* (Ⓣ01292/266577), at the top of Sandgate. On the eastern side of Wellington Square is the *Rupee Room* (Ⓣ01292/283002), a popular and welcoming Indian restaurant, decked out with modern minimalist furnishings. You can have eat-in or takeaway fish and chips from the chippie, *Wellington*, at the corner of Sandgate and Fort Street, while *Renaldo's* next door is renowned for its authentic Italian ice cream and Ayr rock. A mixed crowd packs out the *West Kirk*, a **pub** in a converted church on Sandgate; but the most historic drinking den in town is the thatched *Tam o' Shanter*, on the High Street.

Alloway

ALLOWAY, formerly a small village but now on the outskirts of Ayr, is the birthplace of Robert Burns (1759–96), Scotland's national poet. The first port of call is the **Burns Cottage and Museum** (daily: April–Sept 9.30am–5.30pm; Oct–March 10am–5pm; £4), the poet's birthplace, a low, whitewashed, thatched cottage where animals and people lived under the same roof. Although much altered over the years, it nevertheless gives a good impression of what the place must have been like when Burns was born in the box bed in the only room in the house. The nearby two-room museum boasts all sorts of Burnsiana.

Ten minutes' walk down the road from the cottage are the plain, roofless ruins of **Alloway Kirk**, where Robert's father William is buried, and where Burns set much of *Tam o' Shanter*. Down the road from the church, the **Brig o' Doon**, the picturesque thirteenth-century humpback bridge over which Tam is forced to flee for his life, still stands, curving gracefully over the river. High above the river and bridge, towers the **Burns Monument** (daily: April–Sept 9am–5pm; Oct–March 10am–4pm; free), a striking Neoclassical temple in a small, carefully manicured garden. To enter the garden, you need to approach via the nearby **Tam o' Shanter Experience** (daily: April–Sept 10am–5.30pm; Oct–March 10am–5pm; £2), on the opposite side of the road from Alloway Kirk. Don't bother with the "Experience" itself, however, as its low-budget audiovisual presentation of *Tam o' Shanter* fails to do justice to Burns' poem.

To reach Alloway from Ayr town centre, **buses** #1 and #57 set off from Sandgate (Mon–Sat hourly) and go right to the Tam o' Shanter Experience; otherwise, catch bus #58 or #60 from the bus station to Alloway.

Culzean Castle

Sitting on the edge of a sheer cliff, looking out over the Firth of Clyde to Arran, **Culzean Castle** (pronounced "Cullane"; Easter–Oct daily 10.30am–5pm; £12; NTS), ten miles south of Ayr, couldn't want for a more impressive situation. The current castle is actually a grand, late eighteenth-century stately home, designed by highly successful Scottish Neoclassical architect **Robert Adam**, for the tenth earl of Cassillis (pronounced "cassles"). The most brilliantly conceived work by Adam is the Oval Staircase, where tiers of classical columns lead up to a huge glazed cupola. Other highlights include a portrait of Napoleon by Lefèvre, a superb Chippendale four-poster bed, a great book-shaped tin bath and a boat-shaped cradle. Many folk come here purely to stroll and picnic in the castle's 500-acre **country park** (daily 9.30am to dusk; £8), mess about by the beach, or simply have tea and cakes.

You can **stay** at Culzean (ⓣ01655/884455, April–Oct; ⑨), on the top floor, where six double bedrooms have been done out in a comfortable, genteel style. A less grand option is the popular *Culzean Castle* **campsite** (ⓣ01655/760627; March–Oct), in the woods by the castle entrance, with great views across to Arran.

Irvine

IRVINE, twelve miles north of Ayr, was once the principal port for trade between Glasgow and Ireland, and later for coal from Kilmarnock, its halcyon days recalled in the enjoyable **Scottish Maritime Museum** (April–Oct daily 10am–5pm; ⓦwww.scottishmaritimemuseum.org; £3), which is spread across several locations around the town's beautifully restored old harbour. The best place to start is in the late nineteenth-century **Linthouse Engine Shop**, on Harbour Road, a hangar-like building housing everything from old sailing dinghies and canoes to giant ship's turbines. Free guided tours set off regularly

Ailsa Craig

If the weather's half decent, it's impossible to miss the views of the island of **Ailsa Craig**, which lies ten miles off the south Ayrshire coast in the middle of the Firth of Clyde. The island's name means "Fairy Rock" in Gaelic, though the island looks more like an enormous muffin than a place of enchantment. It would certainly have been less than enchanting for the persecuted Catholics who escaped to the island during the Reformation. The island's granite has long been used for making what many consider to be the finest curling stones, and in the late nineteenth century, 29 people lived on the island, either working in the quarry or at the Stevenson lighthouse. With its volcanic, columnar cliffs and 1114ft summit, Ailsa Craig is now a **bird sanctuary** – home to some 40,000 gannets. The best time to make the trip is at the end of May and in June when the fledglings are learning to fly.

Several companies in Girvan offer **cruises** round the island, but only Mark McCrindle, who also organizes sea-angling trips, is licensed to land (May to late Sept 1–2 daily; ⓣ01465/713219, ⓦwww.ailsacraig.org.uk). It takes about an hour to reach the island, after which you get enough time to walk up to the summit of the rock and watch the birds, weather permitting. The exact timings and prices depend on the length of trip, tides and weather; booking ahead is essential.

for the nearby **Shipyard Worker's Tenement Flat**, which has been restored to something like its appearance in 1910, when a family of six to eight would have occupied its two rooms and scullery (and rented one of them out to a lodger). Moored at the **pontoons** on Harbour Street is an assortment of craft, which you can board, including a tug, a trawler, a "puffer" boat and the oldest seagoing steam yacht in the country.

Arriving at Irvine's adjacent **train** or **bus stations**, you'll find yourself exactly halfway between the harbour, to the west, and the Riverfront shopping complex and old town, to the east. Kilwinning Road, heading north out of Irvine, has several inexpensive **B&Bs** such as *Laurelbank Guesthouse*, at no. 3 (Ⓣ01294/277153, Ⓔlaurelbankguesthouse@hotmail.com; ❷); should you wish to pamper yourself a bit more, head for *Annfield House*, 6 Castle St (Ⓣ01294/278903, Ⓦwww.annfieldhousehotel.co.uk; ❺), a big Victorian mansion overlooking the river at the end of Sandgate, that has spacious bedrooms.

Travel details

Buses

For information on all local and national bus services, contact Traveline Ⓣ0870/608 2608 (daily 7am–10pm), Ⓦwww.travelinescotland.com.

Ayr to: Ardrossan (Mon–Sat every 30min, Sun every 2hr; 55min); Culzean Castle (Mon–Sat hourly, Sun every 2hr; 30min); Dumfries (Mon–Sat every 2hr; 2hr 10min); Glasgow (hourly; 55min); Portpatrick (Mon–Sat 6 daily; 2hr 25min); Stranraer (4–6 daily; 2hr).

Castle Douglas to: Dumfries (Mon–Sat hourly, 4 on Sun; 45min); Kirkcudbright (Mon–Sat hourly, Sun every 2hr; 20min).

Dumfries to: Ayr (Mon–Sat every 2hr; 2hr 10min); Caerlaverock (Mon–Sat every 2hr, 2 on Sun; 30min); Carlisle (Mon–Sat hourly, Sun every 2hr; 1hr 35min); Castle Douglas (Mon–Sat hourly, Sun every 2hr; 45min); Kirkcudbright (Mon–Sat hourly, 6 on Sun; 1hr 10min); New Abbey (Mon–Sat hourly, 4 on Sun; 15min); Newton Stewart (Mon–Sat every 2hr, 2 on Sun; 1hr 30min); Rockcliffe (5 daily; 1hr); Stranraer (Mon–Sat every 2hr, 2 on Sun; 2hr 10min).

Edinburgh to: Dumfries (Mon–Sat 4 daily, 2 on Sun; 2hr 40min); Jedburgh (3–4 daily; 1hr 50min); Kelso (4–6 daily; 2hr); Melrose (hourly; 2hr 15min); Peebles (hourly; 1hr); Selkirk (hourly; 1hr 40min).

Jedburgh to: Kelso (Mon–Sat 5–7 daily; 25min); Melrose (Mon–Sat 1–2 hourly, 7 on Sun; 30min).

Kelso to: Melrose (Mon–Sat 7–9 daily, 5 on Sun; 30–40min).

Melrose to: Jedburgh (Mon–Sat 1–2 hourly, 7 on Sun; 30min); Kelso (Mon–Sat 7–9 daily, 5 on Sun; 30–40min); Peebles (Mon–Sat hourly, 6 on Sun; 1hr 10min); Selkirk (Mon–Sat hourly, 2 on Sun; 20min).

Newton Stewart to: Glentrool (Mon–Sat 7–8 daily, 4 on Sun; 25min); Stranraer (Mon–Sat 15 daily, 5 on Sun; 45min); Isle of Whithorn (Mon–Sat hourly, 4 on Sun; 1hr); Whithorn (Mon–Sat hourly, 4 on Sun; 50min).

Trains

For information on all local and national rail services, contact National Rail Enquiries Ⓣ08457/484950, Ⓦwww.nationalrail.co.uk.

Ayr to: Glasgow Central (every 30min; 50min); Irvine (every 30min; 15–20min); Prestwick Airport (every 30min; 7min); Stranraer (Mon–Sat 7 daily, 2 on Sun; 1hr 20min).

Dumfries to: Carlisle (Mon–Sat 14 daily, 5 on Sun; 40min); Glasgow Central (Mon–Sat 8 daily, 2 on Sun; 1hr 50min); Stranraer (Mon–Sat 2 daily; 3hr).

Glasgow Central to: Ayr (every 30min; 50min); Dumfries (Mon–Sat 8 daily, 2 on Sun; 1hr 50min); Irvine (every 30min; 35min); Prestwick Airport (every 30min; 45min); Stranraer (2 daily; 2hr 10min; 2hr).

Stranraer to: Ayr (Mon–Sat 7 daily, 2 on Sun; 1hr 20min); Dumfries (Mon–Sat 2 daily; 3hr); Glasgow Central (Mon–Sat 4 daily, Sun 2 daily; 2hr).

Ferries (summer timetable)

Ardrossan to: Brodick, Isle of Arran (4–6 daily; 55min).

Cairnryan to: Larne (7–9 daily; 1hr–1hr 45min).

Stranraer to: Belfast (7–8 daily; 1hr 45min–3hr 15min).

Troon to: Larne (2 daily; 1hr 50min).

19

Glasgow and the Clyde

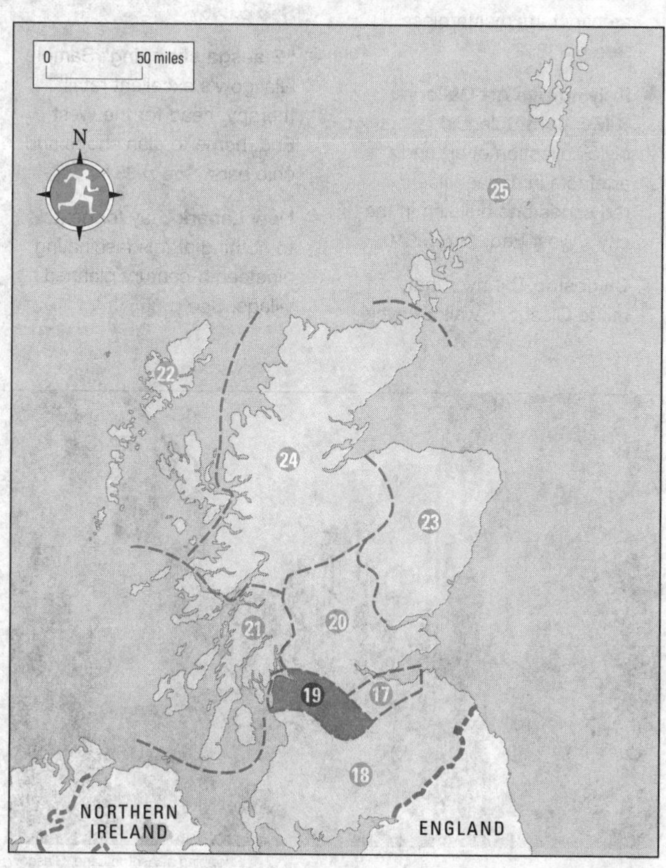

CHAPTER 19

Highlights

* **Necropolis** Elegantly crumbling graveyard on a city-centre hill behind the ancient cathedral, with great views. See p.834

* **Glasgow School of Art** Take a student-led tour of Charles Rennie Mackintosh's architectural masterpiece. See p.838

* **Kelvingrove Art Gallery & Museum** Splendid civic collection of art and artefacts in a magnificent red sandstone building in the city's West End. See p.840

* **Clydeside** The river that made Glasgow: walk or cycle along it, take a boat on it, cross a bridge over it, or get a view of it from the futuristic Science Centre. See p.843

* **Burrell Collection** An inspired and eclectic art collection displayed in a purpose-built museum in Pollok Park. See p.845

* **"Glaesga shopping"** Sample Glasgow's excellent retail therapy: head for the West End, home to glan shops and chic bars. See p.851

* **New Lanark** Stay for next to nothing at this fascinating nineteenth-century planned village. See p.855

▲ Shopping at Ashton Lane, Glasgow

Glasgow and the Clyde

Rejuvenated, upbeat **Glasgow**, Scotland's largest city, has not traditionally enjoyed the best of reputations. Set on the banks of the mighty River Clyde, this former industrial giant can still initially seem a grey and depressing place, with the M8 motorway screeching through the centre and dilapidated housing estates on its outskirts. However, the effects of Glasgow's remarkable overhaul, set in motion in the 1980s by the "Glasgow's Miles Better" campaign, are still much in evidence, the most recent feather in its cap being the award of the right to host the Commonwealth Games in 2014. Glasgow's image of itself has changed irrevocably and few visitors will be left in any doubt that the city is, in its own idiosyncratic way, a cultured and dynamic place well worth getting to know.

The city has much to offer, including some of the best-financed and most imaginative museums and galleries in Britain – among them the showcase **Burrell Collection** and popular **Kelvingrove Art Gallery and Museum** – nearly all of which are free. Glasgow's **architecture** is some of the most striking in the UK, from the restored eighteenth-century warehouses of the **Merchant City** to the hulking Victorian prosperity of George Square. Most distinctive of all is the work of local luminary Charles Rennie Mackintosh, whose elegantly streamlined Art Nouveau designs appear all over the city, reaching their apotheosis in the stunning **School of Art**. Development of the old shipyards of the Clyde, notably in the space-age shapes of the **Glasgow Science Centre**, hint at yet another string to the city's bow: combining design with innovation. The metropolis boasts thriving live-music venues, distinctive places to eat and drink, busy theatres, concert halls and an opera house. Above all, the feature that best defines the individualism and peculiar attraction of the city is its **people**, whether rough-edged comedians on the football terraces or bright young things dressed to the nines in the trendiest of bars.

Despite all the upbeat hype, Glasgow's gentrification has passed by deprived inner-city areas such as the **East End**, home of the **Barras market** and some staunchly change-resistant pubs. Indeed, even in the more stylish quarters of Glasgow, there's a gritty edge that's never far away, reinforcing its peculiar mix of grime and glitz.

Glasgow makes an excellent base from which to explore the **Clyde valley and coast**, made easily accessible by a reliable train service. Chief among the

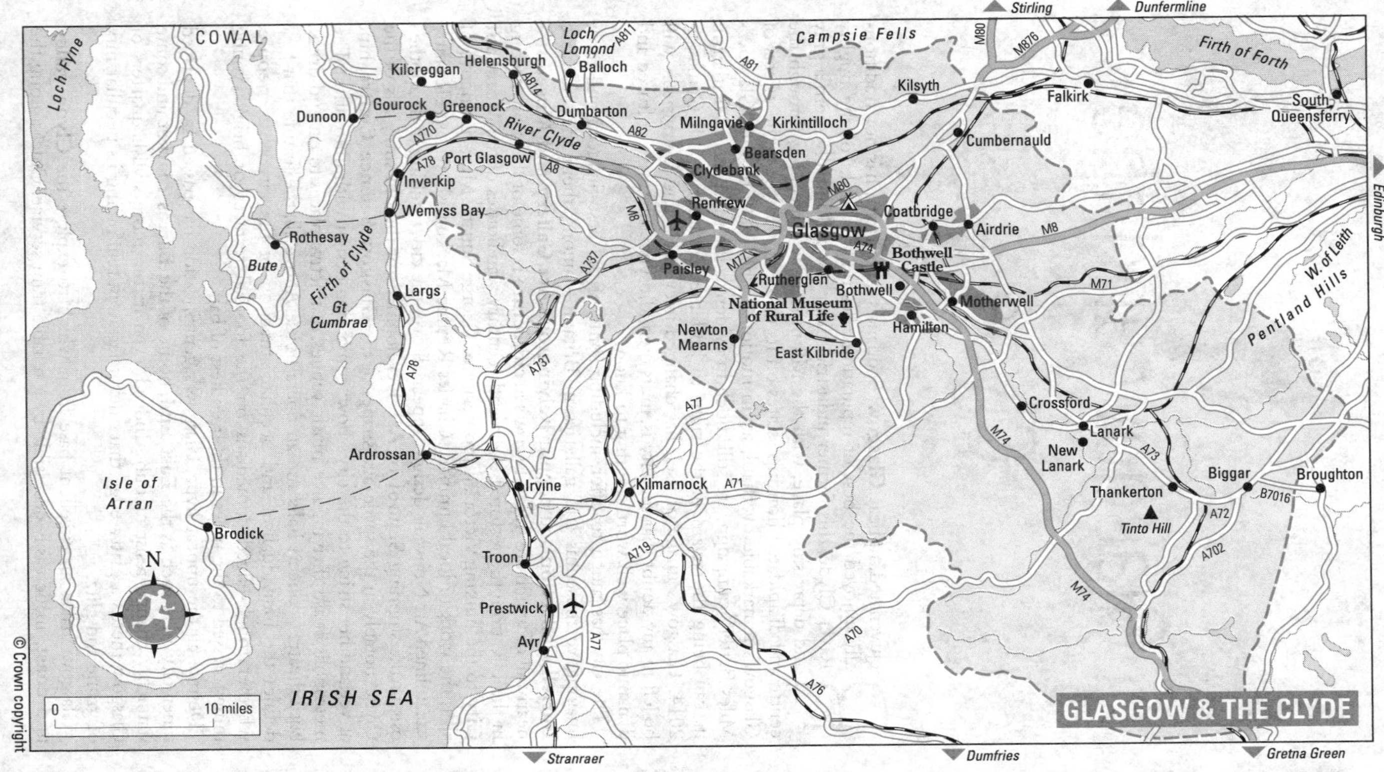

© Crown copyright

draws is the remarkable eighteenth-century **New Lanark** mills and workers' village, a World Heritage Site, while other day-trips might take you towards the scenic Argyll sea lochs, past the old shipbuilding centres on the Clyde estuary.

Some history

GLASGOW's earliest history, like so much else in this surprisingly romantic city, is obscured in a swirl of myth. Its name is said to derive from the Celtic *Glas-cu*, which loosely translates as "the dear, green place" – a tag that the tourist board is keen to exploit as an antidote to the sooty images of popular imagination. It is generally agreed that the first settlers arrived in the sixth century to join Christian missionary **Kentigern** – later to become St Mungo – in his newly founded monastery on the banks of the tiny Molendinar Burn.

William the Lionheart granted the town an official charter in 1175, after which it continued to grow in importance, peaking in the mid-fifteenth century when the **university** was founded on Kentigern's site – the second in Scotland after St Andrews. This led to the establishment of an archbishopric, and hence city status, in 1492, and, due to its situation on a large, navigable river, Glasgow soon expanded into a major industrial **port**. The first cargo of tobacco from Virginia offloaded in Glasgow in 1674, and the 1707 Act of Union between Scotland and England – despite demonstrations against it in Glasgow – led to a boom in trade with the colonies. Following the **Industrial Revolution** and James Watt's innovations in steam power, coal from the abundant seams of Lanarkshire fuelled the ironworks all around the Clyde, worked by the cheap hands of the Highlanders and, later, those fleeing the Irish potato famine of the 1840s.

The **Victorian** age transformed Glasgow beyond recognition. The population boomed from 77,000 in 1801 to nearly 800,000 at the end of the century, and new tenement blocks swept into the suburbs in an attempt to cope with the choking influxes of people. By the turn of the twentieth century, Glasgow's industries had been honed into one massive **shipbuilding** culture. Everything from tugboats to transatlantic liners were fashioned out of sheet metal in the yards that straddled the Clyde. In the harsh economic climate of the 1930s, however, unemployment spiralled, and Glasgow could do little to counter its popular image as a city dominated by inebriate violence and (having absorbed vast numbers of Irish emigrants) sectarian tensions. The **Gorbals** area in particular became notorious as one of the worst slums in Europe. The city's image has never been helped by the depth of animosity between its two great rival football teams, Catholic **Celtic** and Protestant **Rangers**.

Shipbuilding, and many associated industries, died away almost completely in the 1960s and 1970s, leaving the city depressed, jobless and directionless. Then, in the 1980s, the self-promotion campaign began, snowballing towards the 1988 Garden Festival and year-long party as European City of Culture in 1990. Glasgow then beat off competition from Edinburgh and Liverpool to become **UK City of Architecture and Design** in 1999, and in 2007 won the right to host the Commonwealth Games of 2014. These various titles have helped to reinforce the impression that Glasgow, despite its many problems, has successfully broken the industrial shackles of the past and evolved into a city of stature and confidence.

Arrival and information

Glasgow International airport (Ⓣ0870/040 0008, Ⓦwww.glasgowairport.com) is at Abbotsinch, eight miles southwest of the city. From here, the 24-hour

Glasgow Flyer bus (£3.95) runs from bus stop 1 into the central Buchanan Street bus station every ten minutes during the day; the journey takes 25 minutes. Airport taxis charge around £18–20.

Glasgow Prestwick airport (Ⓣ0871/223 0700, Ⓦwww.gpia.co.uk) is thirty miles south of Glasgow, near Ayr. From here the simplest way to get to the city is by train: there's a station right by the terminal (alight at the airport, not Prestwick Town), with trains taking 45 minutes to reach Glasgow Central station (Mon–Sat every 30min, Sun hourly).

Nearly all **trains** from England come into **Central station**, which sits over Argyle Street, one of the city's main shopping thoroughfares. Bus #398 from the front entrance on Gordon Street shuttles every ten minutes to **Queen Street station**, at the corner of George Square, terminus for trains serving Edinburgh and the north. The walk between the two stations is about ten minutes. Bus #398 also stops at **Buchanan Street bus station**, arrival point for regional and intercity **coaches**.

The **tourist office** is at 11 George Square (April & May Mon–Sat 9am–6pm, Sun 10am–6pm; June & Sept Mon–Sat 10am–7pm, Sun 10am–6pm; July & Aug Mon–Sat 9am–8pm, Sun 10am–6pm; Oct–March Mon–Sat 9am–6pm; Ⓣ0141/204 4400, Ⓦwww.seeglasgow.com); there's also one in Glasgow **airport's** international arrivals hall (daily 7.30am–5pm, except Oct–April Sun 8am–5pm; Ⓣ0141/848 4440).

City transport

Although it can be tough negotiating Glasgow's steep hills, **walking** is the best way of exploring any one part of the city. However, as the main sights are scattered – the West End, for example, is a good thirty-minute walk from the centre – you'll probably need to use the comprehensive **public transport** system.

The best way to get between the city centre and the West End is to use the **Underground** (Mon–Sat 6.30am–11pm, Sun 10am–6.30pm), whose stations are marked with a large orange U. If you're travelling beyond the city centre or the West End, or to the main sights on the Southside, you may need to use the bus and train networks. The array of different **bus** companies and the various routes they take is perplexing even to locals, and there's no easy guide to using them other than picking up individual timetables at the Travel Centre on St Enoch's Square.

The suburban **train** network is swift and convenient. Suburbs south of the Clyde are connected to Central station, either at the mainline station or the subterranean low-level station. The trains are an excellent way to link to points west and northwest of Glasgow, including Milngavie (for the start of the West Highland Way), Balloch (for Loch Lomond) and Helensburgh.

City tours

An alternative way to get round the sights of the city is to take a **city tour**: City Sightseeing (April–Oct daily 9.30am–4.30pm; £9) runs **open-top bus** tours, which leave every thirty minutes from George Square on a continuous circuit of all the major attractions in the city centre and West End, allowing you to get on and off as you please.

Accommodation

There's a good range of **accommodation** in Glasgow, from a large, well-run SYHA hostel through to some highly fashionable (and not overpriced) designer hotels in the centre. In general, prices are significantly lower than in Edinburgh, and given that many hotels are business-oriented, you can often negotiate good deals at weekends. If you're prepared to sacrifice character and ambience, you'll often find the cheapest rooms at the **budget chain hotels** dotted throughout the city centre. Big players include *Ibis* (ⓣ0141/225 6000, ⓦwww.ibishotel.com), *Premier Inn* (ⓣ0870/242 8000, ⓦwww.premierinn.co.uk), and *Express by Holiday Inn* (ⓣ0141/548 5000, ⓦwww.hiexpressglasgow.co.uk) – the latter two also have hotels in a handy position near Glasgow Airport.

Hotels

City centre

The Brunswick 106 Brunswick St ⓣ0141/552 0001, ⓦwww.brunswickhotel.co.uk. A small, independent and individual designer hotel in the heart of the Merchant City; fashionable but good value with minimalist furniture and a smart bar and restaurant. ❸

Langs 2 Port Dundas Place ⓣ0141/333 1500, ⓦwww.langshotels.co.uk. Big, sassy, classy but refreshingly independent modern hotel with a spa, trendy restaurants and lots of mod cons. ❻

Malmaison 278 West George St ⓣ0141/572 1000, ⓦwww.malmaison.com. Glasgow's version of the sleek, chic mini-chain, an austere Grecian-temple frontage masking a superbly comfortable designer hotel. ❼

Mark's Hotel 110 Bath St ⓣ0141/353 0800, ⓦwww.markshotels.com. Angular, glass-fronted central hotel, with rooftop views from the upper floors and smartly appointed rooms. Double, triple and family rooms available. ❺

West End and Clydeside

Alamo Guesthouse 46 Gray St ⓣ0141/339 2395, ⓦwww.alamoguesthouse.com. Good-value, family-run boarding house next to Kelvingrove Park. Small but comfortable rooms. ❷

City Inn Finnieston Quay ⓣ0141/240 1002, ⓦwww.cityinn.com. One of the better of the chain hotels made interesting by its riverside location right under the Finnieston crane; stylish rooms and competitive rates. ❺

Hotel du Vin at One Devonshire Gardens 1 Devonshire Gardens, Great Western Rd ⓣ0141/339 2001, ⓦwww.onedevonshiregardens.com. Glasgow's most exclusive and exquisite small hotel, a 10min walk up the Great Western Rd from the Botanic Gardens. There's good chance it's where visiting pop and film stars will stay. ❼

Kirklee 11 Kensington Gate ⓣ0141/334 5555, ⓦwww.kirkleehotel.co.uk. Characterful West End B&B in an Edwardian townhouse, with antique furniture and walls crammed with paintings and etchings. ❺

Number 36 36 St Vincent Crescent ⓣ0141/248 2086, ⓦwww.no36.co.uk. Neat, comfortable guesthouse in a lovely crescent well located for Kelvingrove, the SECC and transport links to the city centre. ❹

Hostels and self-catering

Glasgow isn't short of bed space, thanks to the bright-pink liveried, seven-storey *Euro Hostel* smack in the centre of the city at 318 Clyde St (ⓣ0141/222 2828, ⓦwww.euro-hostels.co.uk), which tries to bridge the gap between **backpacker hostel** and budget hotel. Its 360 beds are all bunks, but they're in smart en-suite rooms sleeping two, four, six or more – some of which have great views. Bed and continental breakfast costs from £14.75. The popular and recently upgraded **SYHA hostel**, 7–8 Park Terrace (ⓣ0870/004 1119, ⓦwww.syha.org.uk), is located in a large townhouse in one of the West End's grandest terraces. It's a ten-minute walk south of Kelvinbridge underground station; bus #44 from the city centre leaves you with a short stroll west up Woodlands Road.

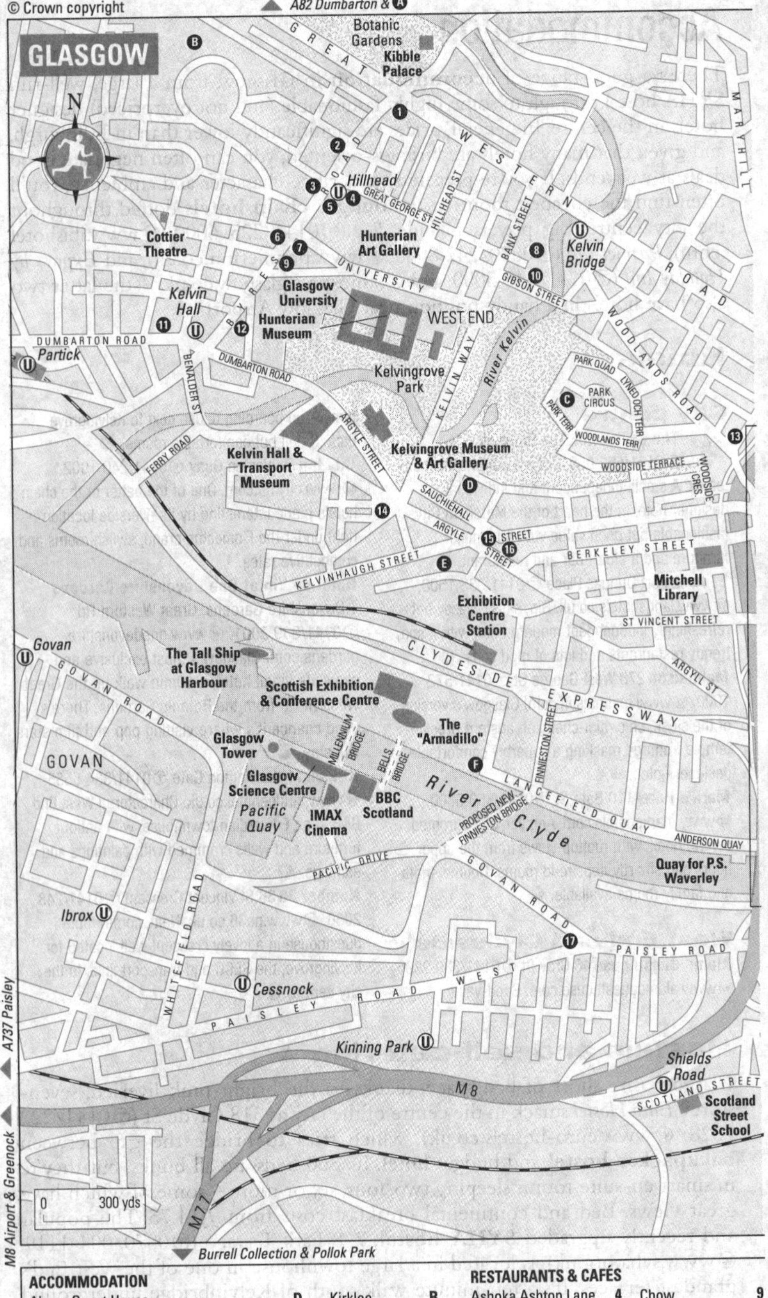

ACCOMMODATION				RESTAURANTS & CAFÉS			
Alamo Guest House	D	Kirklee	B	Ashoka Ashton Lane	4	Chow	9
City Inn	F	SYHA hostel	C	Café Antipasti	2	La Fiorentina	17
Hotel du Vin at One Devonshire Gardens	A	Number 36	E	Café Source	18	Grassroots Café	13

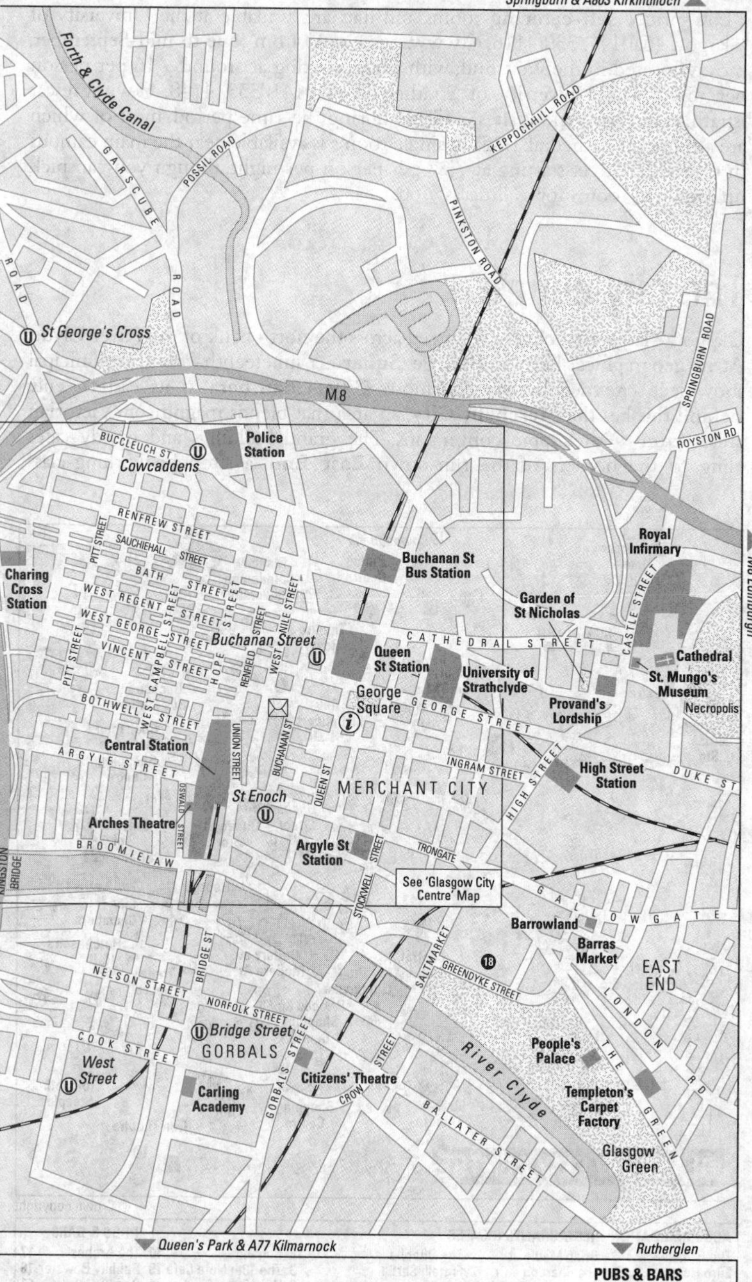

						PUBS & BARS	
Kember & Jones	7	No. Sixteen	12	Tchai Ovna	8	Firebird	14
Kokuryo	16	Stravaigin	10	Tinderbox	6	Lismore Lounge	11
Mother India	15	Stravaigin 2	3	The Ubiquitous Chip	5	Oran Mor	1

Low-priced **self-catering** rooms and flats are available at the University of Glasgow (Ⓣ0141/330 4116, Ⓦwww.cvso.co.uk) from June to mid-September, mostly located in the West End, with prices starting at around £16 per person per night. The University of Strathclyde (Ⓣ0141/553 4148, Ⓦwww.rescat.strath.ac.uk) has various sites available during the same period, most of which are around the cathedral: B&B in single rooms is available near the main campus in Cathedral Street starting at £27 per person per night, though you can pick up four-bed rooms for as little as £60.

The city centre

Glasgow's large **city centre** is ranged across the north bank of the River Clyde. At its geographical heart is **George Square**, a nineteenth-century municipal showpiece crowned by the enormous **City Chambers** at its eastern end. Behind this lies the **Merchant City**, an area that blends magnificent Victorian architecture with yuppie conversions. The grand buildings and trendy cafés cling to the borders of the run-down **East End**, a strongly working-class

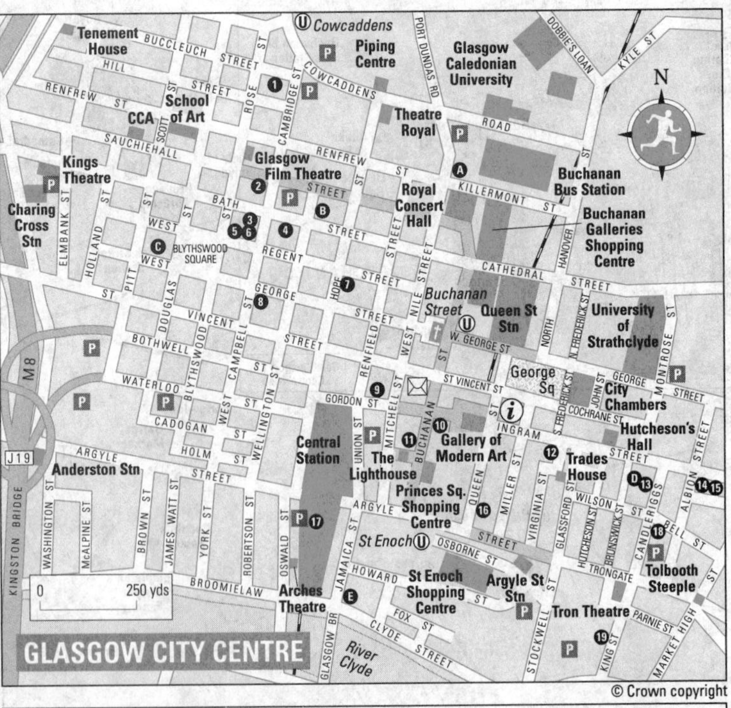

ACCOMMODATION

- The Brunswick D
- Euro Hostel E
- Langs A
- Malmaison C
- Mark's Hotel B

RESTAURANTS & CAFÉS

- Brian Maule at Le Chardon d'Or 6
- Café Gandolfi and Bar Gandolfi 14
- City Merchant 13
- Dakhin 13
- The Dhabba 18
- Fratelli Sarti 3
- Gamba 8
- Ichiban Japanese Noodle Café 15
- Michael Caines @ Abode 4
- Rogano 10
- The 13th Note Café 19
- Wee Curry Shop 1
- Where the Monkey Sleeps 5
- Willow Tea Rooms 2

PUBS & BARS

- The Arches 17
- Babbity Bowster 16
- Bar 10 11
- Corinthian 12
- Horseshoe Bar 9
- Pot Still 7

▲ The GOMA

district that chooses to ignore its rather showy neighbour. The oldest part of Glasgow, around the **Cathedral**, lies immediately north of the East End.

George Square and around

Now hemmed in by the city's grinding traffic, the imposing architecture of **George Square** reflects the confidence of Glasgow's Victorian age. The wide-open plaza almost has a continental airiness about it, although there isn't much subtlety about the eighty-foot column rising up at its centre. It's topped by a statue of Sir Walter Scott, even though his links with Glasgow are, at best, sketchy. Haphazardly dotted around the great writer's plinth are a number of dignified statues of assorted luminaries, ranging from Queen Victoria to Scots heroes such as James Watt and wee Robbie Burns. The florid splendour of the **City Chambers**, opened by Queen Victoria in 1888, occupies the entire eastern end of the square. Built from wealth gained by colonial trade and heavy industry, it epitomizes the aspirations and optimism of late-Victorian city elders. Inside, you can wander around the ground floor, with its domed mosaic ceilings and two mighty Italian marble stairwells; but to get any further join in one of the free **guided tours** of the labyrinthine interior (Mon–Fri 10.30am & 2.30pm).

The Gallery of Modern Art

Queen Street leads south from George Square to **Royal Exchange Square**, whose focal point is a graceful mansion built in 1775 for tobacco lord William Cunninghame. The most ostentatious of the Glasgow merchants' homes, it now houses the **Gallery of Modern Art** (**GOMA**; Mon–Wed & Sat 10am–5pm, Thurs 10am–8pm, Fri & Sun 11am–5pm; free). Relatively small in size, certainly compared to some of the country's grander art collections, it has few airs and graces and for that reason has proved enduringly popular with the Glasgow public. At any time, you should be able to find a good selection of work by the foremost contemporary artists based in Scotland.

Glasgow's architecture

Founded on religion, built on trade and now well established as a cultural centre, Glasgow is known for its architectural riches, from its medieval cathedral to the modern glass-lined galleries of the Burrell Collection. Most dominant is the legacy of the **Victorian age**, when booming trade and industry allowed merchants to commission the finest architects of the day. The celebrated work of **Charles Rennie Mackintosh** (see box, p.840) took Glasgow's architecture to the forefront of early twentieth-century design, with a last flowering of homespun genius before economic conditions effectively stopped the architectural trade in its tracks, its revival only really taking hold in the 1980s and 1990s.

The city's expansion: 1750–1850

Glasgow's great expansion was initiated in the eighteenth century by wealthy tobacco merchants who built the grand edifices of public and municipal importance that still make up much of the **Merchant City**. One of the finest Merchant City views is down Garth Street, which frames the Venetian windows and Ionic columns of the **Trades Hall**, designed by Robert Adam in 1791. Further west, **Royal Exchange Square** is one of the best examples of a typical Glasgow square: treeless, bare and centred around a building of importance, the 1829 **Royal Exchange**, now housing the Gallery of Modern Art. As workers piled into the centre of Glasgow in the early nineteenth century, wealthy residents began moving west to the gridded streets that line **Blythswood Hill** (mostly developed after 1820) with two- or three-storey terraces, their porches and heavy cornices providing textural relief to the endless sandstone monotony. Above all, the long streets provide a beautiful selection of open-ended views, one moment leading into the heart of the city, the next filled with distant hills and sky.

"Greek" Thomson and the Victorians

Long since overshadowed by Charles Rennie Mackintosh, the design of **Alexander "Greek" Thomson**, in the latter half of the nineteenth century, though well respected in its time, has been sadly neglected. Energetic and talented, he designed buildings from lowly tenements to grand suburban villas. The 1857 **St Vincent Street Church**, his best work, has a massive simplicity and serenity lightened by the use of exotic Egyptian and Hindu motifs, particularly in the tower with its decorated egg-shaped dome.

West from Park Circus lies **Glasgow University** (1866–86), its Gothic Revivalism – the work of Sir George Gilbert Scott – representing everything that Greek Thomson despised. Scottish features abound, such as crow-stepped gables, round turrets with conical caps and the top-heavy central tower. Inside, cloisters and quadrants sum up a suitably scholastic severity.

Originally conceived as a convenient way to house the influx of workers in the late 1800s, the Glasgow **tenement** design became more refined as the wealthy middle classes began to realize its potential. Mainly constructed between 1860 and 1910, tenements are decked out with bay windows, turrets and domes. A fascinating example of the style of these buildings, as well as the typical life inside them, can be seen at the **Tenement House** (see p.839).

The present

The 1980s onwards have seen the return of the grand public building as inheritor of architectural innovation. Beginning with the imaginative **Burrell Collection**, the theme has been taken up by the titanium-clad behemoths of Clydeside: the unmistakeable Clyde Auditorium, better known as the "**Armadillo**", the curvaceous **Science Centre** and its new neighbour, the glass shoe-box of BBC Scotland's new HQ. Not to ignore the poverty of artistry which went into great works such as the Kingston Bridge and Royal Concert Hall, but few could argue that Glasgow has failed to open itself to innovation and ideas.

The spacious ground-floor gallery is principally used for temporary exhibitions, though large-scale socially committed works by the "New Glasgow Boys" – Peter Howson, Adrian Wiszniewski, Ken Currie and Steven Campbell – are often included. Down in the basement there's an art library and café, while the smaller galleries on the two upper floors are either linked together for larger exhibitions or used to show smaller themed shows by contemporary artists from around the world.

Along Buchanan Street

Buchanan Street runs north–south one block west of George Square, defining Glasgow's main shopping district. At the southern end of the street is **Princes Square**, one of the most stylish and imaginative shopping centres in the country, hollowed out of the innards of a soft sandstone building. The interior, all recherché Art Deco and ornate ironwork, holds lots of pricey, highly fashionable shops.

At 11 Mitchell Lane, an otherwise nondescript alleyway between Buchanan Street and Union Street, is **The Lighthouse** (Mon & Wed–Sat 10.30am–5pm, Tues 11am–5pm, Sun noon–5pm; £3; Ⓦ www.thelighthouse.co.uk), a spectacularly converted Charles Rennie Mackintosh building which has found new life as Scotland's Centre for Architecture, Design and the City. The 1895 building was Mackintosh's first public commission, and housed the offices of the *Glasgow Herald* newspaper; it mounts temporary exhibitions on design and architecture alongside the permanent **Mackintosh Interpretation Centre**, a great place to learn more about the man and his work.

The Merchant City

The grid of streets that lies immediately east of the City Chambers is known as the **Merchant City**, an area of eighteenth-century warehouses and homes that has been sandblasted and swabbed clean with greater enthusiasm and municipal money than any other part of Glasgow in an attempt to bring residents back into the city centre. The expected flood of yuppies, however, was more like a trickle, yet the expensive designer shops, style bars and bijou cafés continue to flock here, giving the area a pervasive air of sophistication. A Merchant City Trail leaflet, which guides you around a dozen of the most interesting buildings in the area, is available at the tourist office.

The East End

East of Glasgow Cross, down Gallowgate beyond the train lines, lies the **East End**, the district that perhaps most closely corresponds to the old perception of Glasgow. Hemmed in by Glasgow Green to the south and the old university to the west, this densely packed industrial area essentially created the city's wealth. Today isolated pubs, tatty shops and cafés sit amidst this dereliction, in sharp contrast to the gloss of the Merchant City only a few blocks west. Walking around here you definitely get the sense that you're off the tourist trail, and there's no doubt that the area offers a rich flavour of working-class Glasgow, though unless you're here after dark it's not as threatening as it may feel.

Between London Road and the River Clyde are the wide and tree-lined spaces of **Glasgow Green**. Reputedly Britain's oldest public park, the Green has been common land since at least 1178, and has been a popular spot for Sunday-afternoon strolls for centuries. It's also home to the **People's Palace** (Mon–Thurs & Sat 10am–5pm, Fri & Sun 11am–5pm; free), a wonderfully haphazard evocation of the city's history. This squat, red sandstone Victorian building was purpose-built as a museum back in 1898 – almost a century before the rest of the country caught on to the fashion for social-history collections. Many of the displays are designed to instill a warm glow in the memories of older locals: the museum is refreshingly unpretentious, with visitors almost always outnumbered by Glaswegian families.

Glasgow Cathedral and around

Built in 1136, destroyed in 1192 and rebuilt soon after, stumpy-spired **Glasgow Cathedral** (April–Sept Mon–Sat 9.30am–5.30pm, Sun 1–5pm; Oct–March Mon–Sat 9.30am–4pm, Sun 1–4pm; free; Ⓦ www.glasgowcathedral.org.uk) was not completed until the late fifteenth century. Dedicated to the city's patron saint and reputed founder, St Mungo, the cathedral is effectively on two levels, the crypt being part of the lower church. On entering, you arrive in the impressively lofty nave of the **upper church**, with the lower church entirely hidden from view. Beyond the nave, the **choir** is concealed by the curtained stone pulpit, making the interior feel a great deal smaller than might be expected from outside. In the choir's northeastern corner, a small door leads into the gloomy **sacristy**, in which Glasgow University was first founded over five hundred years ago. Two sets of steps from the nave lead down into the **lower church**, where you'll find the dark and musty **chapel** surrounding the tomb of St Mungo. The saint's relics were removed in the late Middle Ages, although the tomb still forms the centrepiece. The chapel itself is one of the most glorious examples of medieval architecture in Scotland, best seen in the delicate fan vaulting rising up from the thicket of cool stone columns.

The Necropolis

Rising up behind the Cathedral and inspired by the Père Lachaise cemetery in Paris, the atmospheric **Necropolis** is a grassy mound covered in a fantastic assortment of crumbling and tumbling gravestones, ornate urns, gloomy catacombs and Neoclassical temples. Various paths lead through the rows of eroding, neglected graves, and from the summit, next to the column topped with an indignant John Knox, there are superb **views** of the city and its trademark mix of grit and grace – the steaming chimneys of the Tennants brewery, the traffic on the M8 motorway, the crowded city-centre offices, the serene cathedral itself, and a wide cityscape of spires and high-rise blocks to the south and east.

Sauchiehall Street and around

Glasgow's most famous street, **Sauchiehall Street**, runs in a straight line west from the northern end of Buchanan Street, past some unexciting shopping malls to a few of the city's most interesting sights. Charles Rennie Mackintosh fans should head for the **Willow Tea Rooms** (Ⓦ www.willowtearooms.co.uk), above Henderson the Jeweller at 217 Sauchiehall St. This is a faithful reconstruction (opened in 1980 after more than fifty years of closure) on the site of the 1904 original, which was created for Kate Cranston, one of Mackintosh's few contemporary supporters in the city. Taking inspiration from the word *Sauchiehall*, which means "avenue of willow", he chose the willow leaf as a theme to unify the whole structure from the tables to the mirrors and the ironwork.

The Glasgow School of Art

Rising above Sauchiehall Street to the north is one of the city centre's steepest hills, with Dalhousie and Scott streets veering up to Renfrew Street, where you'll find Charles Rennie Mackintosh's **Glasgow School of Art** at no. 167 (guided tours April–Sept daily on the hour 10am–4pm; Oct–March Mon–Sat 11am, 2pm & 3pm; booking advised; £6.50; ⓣ0141/353 4526, ⓦwww.gsa.ac.uk). Widely considered to be the pinnacle of Mackintosh's work, the school is a characteristically angular building of warm sandstone which, due to financial constraints, had to be constructed in two sections (1897–99 and 1907–09). There's a clear change in the architect's style from the earlier severity of the mock-Baronial east wing to the softer lines of the western half.

The only way to see the school is to take one of the student-led **guided tours** (dependent on curricular activities), which show off key examples of Mackintosh's dynamic and inspired touch and a handful of the most impressive rooms. All over the school, from the roof to the stairwells, Mackintosh's unique touches recur – light Oriental reliefs, tall-backed chairs and stylized Celtic illuminations.

The Tenement House

Just a few hundred yards north of the School of Art – on the other side of a sheer hill – is the **Tenement House**, 145 Buccleuch St (March–Oct daily 1–5pm; £5; NTS). In a typical tenement block still lived in on most floors, the first floor holds the perfectly preserved home of Agnes Toward, who moved here with her mother in 1911, changing nothing and throwing very little out until she was hospitalized in 1965. The flat gives every impression of still being inhabited, with a cluttered hearth and range, kitchen utensils, recess beds, framed religious tracts and sewing machine all untouched. Tenement flats were home to the vast majority of Glaswegians for much of the twentieth century, and as such developed a culture and vocabulary all of their own: the "hurley", for example, was the bed on castors which was kept below the box bed in an alcove off the kitchen.

The West End

The urbane **West End** seems a world away from Glasgow's industrial image and the hustle and bustle of the city centre. In the 1800s, the city's wealthy merchants established huge estates away from the soot and grime of city life, and in 1870 the ancient university was moved from its cramped home near the cathedral to a spacious new site overlooking the River Kelvin. Elegant housing swiftly followed, the Kelvingrove Museum and Art Gallery was built to house the 1888 International Exhibition and, in 1896, the Glasgow District Subway – today's Underground – started its circuitous shuffle from here to the city centre.

The hub of life in this part of Glasgow is **Byres Road**, running between Great Western Road and Dumbarton Road past Hillhead underground station. Shops, restaurants, cafés, some enticing pubs and hordes of students give the area a sense of style and vitality. Glowing red sandstone tenements and graceful terraces provide a suitably upmarket backdrop to this cosmopolitan district.

The main sights straddle the banks of the cleaned-up River Kelvin, which meanders through the gracious acres of the **Botanic Gardens** and the slopes, trees and statues of **Kelvingrove Park**. Overlooked by the Gothic towers and turrets of **Glasgow University**, Kelvingrove Park is home to the pride of Glasgow's civic collection of art and artefacts, **Kelvingrove Museum and Art Gallery**, off Argyle Street.

Charles Rennie Mackintosh

The work of the architect **Charles Rennie Mackintosh** (1868–1928) is synonymous with the image of Glasgow. Historians may disagree over whether his work was a forerunner of the Modernist movement or merely the sunset of Victorianism, but he undoubtedly created buildings of great beauty, idiosyncratically fusing Scots Baronial with Gothic, Art Nouveau and modern design. Though the bulk of his work was conceived at the turn of the twentieth century, since the postwar years Mackintosh's ideas have become particularly fashionable, giving rise to a certain amount of ersatz **"Mockintosh"** in his home city, with his distinctive lettering and small design features used time and again by shops, pubs and businesses. Fortunately, there are also plenty of examples of the genuine article, making the city something of a pilgrimage centre for art and design students from all over the world. A one-day **Mackintosh Trail Ticket** (£12) includes entry to twelve principal Mackintosh buildings as well as unlimited Underground and bus travel. It can be bought from the tourist office, from any of the attractions on the trail or from Ⓦwww.crmsociety.com.

Although his family did little to encourage his artistic ambitions, as a young child Mackintosh began to cultivate his interest in drawing from nature during walks in the countryside, taken to improve his health. This talent was to flourish when he joined the Glasgow School of Art in 1884, whose vibrant new director, Francis Newberry, encouraged his pupils to create original and individual work. Here he met Herbert MacNair and the sisters Margaret and Frances MacDonald, whose work seemed to be sympathetic with his, fusing the organic forms of nature with a linear, symbolic Art Nouveau style. Nicknamed **"The Spook School"**, the four created a new artistic language, using extended vertical design, stylized abstract organic forms and muted colours, reflecting their interest in Japanese design and the work of Whistler and Beardsley. However, it was architecture that truly challenged Mackintosh, allowing him to use his creative artistic impulse in a three-dimensional and cohesive manner.

His big break came in 1896, when he won the competition to design a new home for the **Glasgow School of Art** (see p.838). This is his most famous work, but a number of smaller buildings created during his tenure with the architects Honeyman and Keppie, which began in 1889, document the development of his style. One of his earliest commissions was for a new building to house the *Glasgow Herald* on Mitchell Lane, off Argyle Street. A massive tower rises up from the corner, giving the building its popular name of **The Lighthouse**; it now houses the Mackintosh Interpretation Centre (see p.837).

Kelvingrove Art Gallery and Museum

Founded on donations from the city's industrialists Victorian and opened at an international fair held in 1901, the huge, red sandstone fantasy castle of **Kelvingrove Art Gallery and Museum** (Mon–Thurs & Sat 10am–5pm, Fri & Sun 11am–5pm; Ⓦwww.glasgowmuseums.com; free) is a brash statement of Glasgow's nineteenth-century self-confidence. Intricate and ambitious both in its riotous outside detailing and within, where a superb galleried main hall running the depth of the building gives way to attractive upper balconies and small, interlinked display galleries, Kelvingrove (as it's popularly known) offers an impressive and inviting setting for the engaging display of art and artefacts within.

Following a massive, three-year refurbishment, the art gallery and museum reopened in the summer of 2006. Kelvingrove lost little time re-establishing itself as the most popular museum in the UK outside London. The wide and

In the 1890s Glasgow went wild for tearooms, where the middle classes could play billiards and chess, read in the library or merely chat. The imposing Miss Cranston, who dominated the Glasgow teashop scene and ran the most elegant establishments, gave Mackintosh great freedom of design, and in 1896 he started to plan the interiors for her growing business. Over the next twenty years he designed articles from teaspoons to furniture and, finally, as in the case of the **Willow Tea Rooms** (see p.847), the structure itself.

Mackintosh designed few **religious buildings**: Queens Cross Church of 1896, at the junction of Garscube and Maryhill roads in the northwest of the city, is the only completed example standing. Hallmarks include a sturdy box-shaped tower and asymmetrical exterior with complex heart-shaped floral motifs in the large chancel window. To give height to the small and peaceful interior, Mackintosh used an open-arched timber ceiling, enhanced by carved detail and an oak pulpit decorated with tulip-form relief. It isn't the most unified of structures, but shows the flexibility of his distinctive style. It is now home to the **Charles Rennie Mackintosh Society** (Mon–Fri 10am–5pm; March–Oct also Sun 2–5pm; £2; ⓣ0141/946 6600, ⓦwww.crmsociety.com).

The spectre of limited budgets was to haunt Mackintosh throughout his career, and he never had the chance to design and construct with complete freedom. However, these constraints didn't manage to dull his creativity, as demonstrated by the **Scotland Street School** of 1904, just south of the river opposite Shields Road underground station (Mon–Thurs & Sat 10am–5pm, Fri & Sun 11am–5pm; free). Here, the two main stairways that frame the entrance are lit by glass-filled bays that protrude from the building. It is his most symmetrical work, with a whimsical nod to history in the Scots Baronial conical tower roofs and sandstone building material. Mackintosh's forceful personality and originality did not endear him to construction workers: he would frequently change his mind or add details at the last minute, often overstretching budgets. This lost him the support of local builders and architects, despite his being admired on the continent, and prompted him to move to Suffolk in 1914 to escape the "philistines" of Glasgow and to re-evaluate his achievements. Indeed, the building which arguably displays Mackintosh at his most flamboyant was one he never saw built, the **House for an Art Lover** (April–Sept Mon–Wed 10am–4pm, Thurs–Sun 10am–1pm; Oct–March Sat & Sun 10am–1pm; call for weekday opening during winter; £3.50; ⓣ0141/353 4770, ⓦwww.houseforanartlover.co.uk), constructed in Bellahouston Park in 1996, 95 years after plans for it were submitted to a German architectural competition.

sometimes bizarre range of exhibits, from a World War II Spitfire suspended from the roof of the West Court to suits of armour, ancient Egyptian relics and priceless paintings by Rembrandt, Whistler and Raeburn, has led to accusations that the museum is somewhat ill-defined. In contradi-ction to this argument though, Kelvingrove holds an undeniably rich and deliberately varied civic collection, gathered from legacies, astute purchases and serendipitous good fortune, which principally aims to educate, enlighten and entertain the people of Glasgow.

Most visitors will be drawn to the **paintings**, most famous of which is Salvador Dalí's stunning *St John of the Cross*, located on the West Balcony. You can also acquaint yourself with significant **Scottish art** including works by the Glasgow Boys and the Scottish Colourists. There's a special section of paintings, furniture and murals devoted to Charles Rennie Mackintosh and the "**Glasgow Style**" he and his contemporaries inspired.

Glasgow University and the Hunterian bequests

Dominating the West End skyline, the gloomy turreted tower of **Glasgow University** (Ⓦ www.gla.ac.uk), designed by Sir George Gilbert Scott in the mid-nineteenth century, overlooks the glades edging the River Kelvin. In the dark neo-Gothic pile under the tower you'll find the **University Visitor**

Scotland's artistic avant-garde: the Glasgow Boys and the Colourists

In the 1870s a group of Glasgow-based painters formed a loose association that was to imbue Scottish art with a contemporary European flavour far ahead of the rest of Britain. Dominated by five men – Guthrie, Lavery, Henry, Hornel and Crawhall – **"The Glasgow Boys"** came from very different backgrounds, but all rejected the eighteenth-century conservatism which spawned little other than sentimental, anecdotal renditions of Scottish history peopled by "poor but happy" families.

Sir James Guthrie, taking inspiration from the *plein air* painting of the Impressionists, spent his summers in the countryside, observing and painting everyday life. Instead of happy peasants, his work shows individuals staring out of the canvas, detached and unrepentant, painted with rich tones but without undue attention to detail or the play of light. Typical of his finest work during the 1880s, *A Highland Funeral* (in the Kelvingrove collection; see p.840) was hugely influential for the rest of the group, who found inspiration in its restrained emotional content, colour and unaffected realism. Seeing it persuaded **Sir John Lavery**, then studying in France, to return to Glasgow. Lavery was eventually to become an internationally popular society portraitist, his subtle use of paint revealing his debt to Whistler, but his earlier work, depicting the middle class at play, is filled with light and motion.

An interest in colour and decoration united the work of friends **George Henry** and **E.A. Hornel**. The predominance of pattern, colour and design in Henry's *Galloway Landscape*, for example, is remarkable, while their joint work *The Druids* (both part of the Kelvingrove collection; see p.840), in thickly applied impasto, is full of Celtic symbolism. In 1893 both artists set off for Japan, funded by Alexander Reid and later William Burrell, where their work used vibrant tone and texture for expressive effect and took Scottish painting to the forefront of European trends.

Newcastle-born **Joseph Crawhall** was a reserved and quiet individual who combined superb draughtsmanship and simplicity of line with a photographic memory to create watercolours of an outstanding naturalism and originality. Again, William Burrell was an important patron, and a number of Crawhall's works reside at the Burrell Collection (see p.845).

The Glasgow Boys school reached its height by 1900 and did not outlast World War I, but the influence of their work cannot be underestimated, shaking the foundations of the artistic elite and inspiring the next generation of Edinburgh painters, who became known as the "**Colourists**". Samuel John Peploe, John Duncan Fergusson, George Leslie Hunter and Francis Cadell shared an understanding that the manipulation of colour was the heart and soul of a good painting. All experienced and took inspiration from the avant-garde of late nineteenth-century Paris as well as the landscapes of southern France. **J.D. Fergusson**, in particular, immersed himself in the bohemian, progressive Parisian scene, rubbing shoulders with writers and artists including Picasso. Some of his most dynamic work, which can be seen in the Fergusson Gallery in Perth (see p.884), displays elements of Cubism, yet is still clearly in touch with the Celtic imagery of Henry, Hornel and, indeed, Charles Rennie Mackintosh. The work of the Scottish Colourists has become highly fashionable and valuable over the last couple of decades, with galleries and civic collections throughout the country featuring their work prominently.

Centre & Shop (Mon–Sat 9.30am–5pm, also Sun 11am–3pm June–Sept). From April to September **guided tours** of the campus are run from here (Wed–Sat 11am; bookings advised on ☎0141/330 5511; £3.50).

Beside the Visitor Centre is the **Hunterian Museum** (Mon–Sat 9.30am–5pm; free), Scotland's oldest public museum, dating back to 1807. Opposite, across University Avenue, is Hunter's more frequently visited bequest, the **Hunterian Art Gallery** (Mon–Sat 9.30am–5pm; free), best known for its wonderful works by James Abbott McNeill Whistler: only Washington, DC, has a larger collection. The gallery's other major collection is of nineteenth- and twentieth-century Scottish art, including the quasi-Impressionist Scottish landscapes of William McTaggart, a forerunner of the Glasgow Boys movement, itself represented here by Guthrie and Hornel. Finally, the monumental dancing figures of J.D. Fergusson's *Les Eus* preside over a small collection of work by the Scottish Colourists.

A side gallery leads to the **Mackintosh House** (£3, free after 2pm Wed), a re-creation of the interior of the now-demolished Glasgow home of Margaret MacDonald and Charles Rennie Mackintosh. Its exquisitely cool interior contains over sixty pieces of Mackintosh furniture on three floors. In addition, a permanent Mackintosh exhibition gallery shows a selection of his two-dimensional work, from watercolours to architectural drawings.

The Botanic Gardens

At the northern, top end of Byres Road, where it meets the Great Western Road, is the main entrance to the **Botanic Gardens** (daily 7am–dusk; free). The best-known glasshouse here, the hulking, domed **Kibble Palace** (10am–4.45pm or 4.15pm in winter; free), houses a damp, musty collection of swaying palms from around the world. Nearby, the **Main Range Glasshouse** is home to lurid flowers and plants luxuriating in the humidity, including stunning orchids, cacti, ferns and tropical fruit.

In addition to the area around the main glasshouses, there are some beautifully remote paths in the gardens that weave along the closely wooded banks of the deep-set River Kelvin, linking up with the walkway running alongside the river all the way down to Dumbarton Road, near its confluence with the Clyde.

Clydeside

"The **Clyde** made Glasgow and Glasgow made the Clyde" runs an old saying, full of sentimentality for the days when the river was the world's premier shipbuilding centre, and when its industry lent an innovation and confidence that made Glasgow the second city of the British Empire. Despite the hardships heavy industry brought, every Glaswegian would follow the progress of the skeleton ships under construction in the riverside yards, cheering them on their way down the Clyde as they were launched. The last of the great liners to be built on **Clydeside** was the *QE2* in 1967, yet such events are hard to visualize today, with the banks of the river all but devoid of any industry: shipbuilding is now restricted to a couple of barely viable yards, as derelict warehouses, crumbling docks and overgrown wastelands crowd the river's flanks.

Glasgow is often accused of failing to capitalize on its river, and it's only in the last few years, with a flurry of construction, that it's once again becoming a focus of attention. Striking riverside buildings including the titanium-clad **Armadillo** concert hall and **Glasgow Science Centre** have become icons of the city's forward-thinking image.

The Waverley

One of Glasgow's best-loved treasures is the **Waverley**, the last seagoing paddle steamer in the world, which spends the summer cruising "doon the watter" to various ports on the Firth of Clyde and the Ayrshire coast from its base at Glasgow Science Centre. Built on Clydeside in 1947, she's an elegant vessel to look at, not least when she's thrashing away at full steam with the hills of Argyll or Arran in the background. Contact ⓣ0845/130 4647 or ⓦwww.waverleyexcursions.co.uk for sailing times and itinerary.

The Glasgow Science Centre

On the south bank of the river, linked to the SECC by pedestrian Bell's Bridge, are the three space-age, titanium-clad constructions which make up the **Glasgow Science Centre** (daily 10am–6pm; one attraction £6.95, two for £9.95; ⓦwww.gsc.org.uk). Of the three buildings, the largest is the curvaceous, wedge-shaped **Science Mall**. Behind the vast glass wall facing the river are four floors of interactive exhibits, ranging from lift-your-own-weight pulleys to high-tech thermograms. The centre covers almost every aspect of science, from simple optical illusions to cutting-edge computer technology, including a section on moral and environmental issues – lots of good fun, although weekends and school holidays are busy and noisy.

Alongside the Science Mall is the bubble-like **IMAX theatre**, which shows a range of mostly science- and nature-based documentaries on its giant screen. Also on the site is the enormous **Glasgow Tower**, built with an aerofoil-like construction to allow it to rotate to face into the prevailing wind. Glass lifts ascend to the viewing cabin at the top, offering suitably panoramic views of central Glasgow.

The Southside

The section of Glasgow south of the Clyde is generally described as the **Southside**, though within this area there are a number of recognizable districts, including the notoriously deprived Gorbals and Govan, which are sprinkled with new developments but still derelict and tatty in many parts. There's little reason to venture here unless you're making your way to the Science Centre (see above), or the famously innovative Citizens' Theatre (see p.850). Further south, inner-city decay fades into altogether gentler and more salubrious suburbs, including Queen's Park, home to Scotland's national football stadium, **Hampden Park**, Pollokshaws and the rural landscape of Pollok Park, which contains one of Glasgow's major museums, the **Burrell Collection**.

Southside attractions are fairly widely spread. A **train** from Central station is best for Hampden Park (Mount Florida station), and for Pollok Park either take the train to Pollokshaws West station (not to be confused with Pollokshields West), or **bus** #45, #47, #48 or #57 to Pollokshaws Road, or a **taxi** (around £10 from the centre). From the park gates a **free minibus** runs every half-hour between 10am and 4.30pm to the Burrell Collection.

Hampden Park and the Scottish Football Museum

Two and a half miles due south of the city centre, just to the west of the tree-filled Queen's Park, the floodlights and giant stands of Scotland's national football stadium, **Hampden Park**, loom over the surrounding suburban tenements and terraces. It's home to the engaging **Scottish Football Museum** (Mon–Sat 10am–5pm, Sun 11am–5pm; £5.50), with extensive collections of memorabilia, video clips and displays covering almost every aspect of the game. On view is the Scottish Cup, the world's oldest football trophy and a re-creation of the old changing room at Hampden, as well as a bizarre life-sized reconstruction of the most famous goal in Scottish footballing history, scored during the 1978 World Cup in Argentina.

The Burrell Collection

Located in Pollok Park some six miles southwest of the city centre, the outstanding **Burrell Collection** (Mon–Thurs & Sat 10am–5pm, Fri & Sun 11am–5pm; free), the lifetime collection of shipping magnate Sir William Burrell (1861–1958), is, for some, the principal reason for visiting Glasgow. Unlike many other art collectors, Sir William's only real criterion for buying a piece was whether he liked it or not, enabling him to buy many "unfashionable" works, which cost comparatively little but subsequently proved their worth.

The simplicity and clean lines of the Burrell building are its greatest assets, with large picture windows giving sweeping views over woodland and serving as a tranquil backdrop to the objects inside. An airy covered **courtyard** includes the **Warwick Vase**, a huge bowl containing fragments of a second-century AD vase from Emperor Hadrian's villa in Tivoli. On three sides of the courtyard, a trio of dark and sombre panelled rooms have been re-erected in faithful detail from the Burrells' Hutton Castle home, their heavy tapestries, antique furniture and fireplaces displaying the same eclectic taste as the rest of the museum.

Elsewhere on the ground floor are Greek, Roman and earlier artefacts, including an exquisite mosaic Roman cockerel from the first century BC and a 4000-year-old Mesopotamian lion's head. Nearby, also illuminated by enormous windows, the **Oriental Art** collection forms nearly a quarter of the whole display, ranging from Neolithic jades through bronze vessels and Tang funerary horses to cloisonné. Burrell considered his **medieval and post-medieval European art**, which encompasses silverware, glass, textiles and sculpture, to be the most valuable part of his collection: these are ranged across a maze of small galleries.

▲ Glasgow Science Centre

Football in Glasgow

Football, or *fitba'* as it's pronounced locally, is one of Glasgow's great passions – and one of its great blights. While the city can claim to be one of Europe's premier footballing centres, it's known above all for one of the most bitter rivalries in any sport, that between **Celtic** and **Rangers**. Two of the largest clubs in Britain, with weekly crowds regularly topping 60,000, the Old Firm, as they're collectively known, have dominated Scottish football for a century, most notably in the last fifteen years as they have lavished vast sums of money on foreign talent in an often frantic effort both to outdo each other and to stay in touch with the standards of the top English and European teams.

The roots of Celtic, who play at Celtic Park in the eastern district of Parkhead (Ⓣ0871/226 1888, Ⓦwww.celticfc.co.uk), lie in the city's immigrant Irish and **Catholic** population, while Rangers, based at Ibrox Park in Govan on the Southside (Ⓣ0871/702 1972, Ⓦwww.rangers.co.uk), have traditionally drawn support from local **Protestants**: as a result, sporting rivalries have been enmeshed in a sectarian divide, and although Catholics do play for Rangers, and Protestants for Celtic, sections of supporters of both clubs seem intent on perpetuating the feud. While large-scale violence on the terraces and streets has not been seen for some time – thanks in large measure to canny policing – Old Firm matches often seethe with bitter passions, and sectarian-related assaults do still occur in parts of the city.

However, there is a less intense side to the game, found not just in the fun-loving "Tartan Army" which follows the (often rollercoaster) fortunes of the Scottish national team, but also in Glasgow's smaller clubs, who actively distance themselves from the distasteful aspects of the Old Firm and plod along with home-grown talent in the lower reaches of the Scottish league. **Queen's Park**, residents of Hampden (Ⓣ0141/632 1275, Ⓦwww.queensparkfc.co.uk), **St Mirren**, the Paisley team (Ⓣ0141/840 4100, Ⓦwww.stmirren.net), and the much-maligned **Partick Thistle**, who play at Firhill Stadium in the West End (Ⓣ0141/579 1971, Ⓦwww.ptfc.co.uk), offer the best chances of experiencing the more down-to-earth side of Glaswegian football – along with all-important reminders that it is, in the end, only a game.

Upstairs, the cramped and comparatively gloomy **mezzanine** is probably the least satisfactory section of the gallery, not the best setting for its sparkling array of paintings by the likes of Degas, Pissarro, Manet, Cézanne and Boudin.

Eating

Glasgow's **restaurant scene** is reasonably dynamic, with new places replacing old (and sometimes not very old) every year. Most places to eat are concentrated in the commercial hub and Merchant City district of the city centre, as well as in the trendy West End.

City centre and the Merchant City

All the cafés and restaurants in this section are marked on the Glasgow City Centre map on p.834, unless otherwise stated.

Cafés, diners and café-bars

Café Gandolfi and Bar Gandolfi 64 Albion St Ⓣ0141/552 6813, Ⓦwww.cafegandolfi.com. *Gandolfi* was one of the first to test the waters in the revived Merchant City in the 1980s and today it's a landmark. Designed with distinctive wooden furniture from the Tim Stead workshop, the café serves up Scottish staples (including great black pudding), soups, salads, fish dishes and Continental cuisine. The bar upstairs is more contemporary in feel but the food's equally good. New to the scene, just up the street, is *Gandolfi Fish* (Ⓣ0141/552 9475). Moderate.

Café Source 1 St Andrew's Square Ⓣ0141/548 6020, Ⓦwww.cafesource.co.uk. See map, p.834. In the basement of St Andrew's, an eighteenth-century church, patterned on London's St Martin in the Fields, and now a folk music and Scottish dance centre. The café serves up Scottish favourites featuring local produce. Frequent live jam sessions. Inexpensive.

Where the Monkey Sleeps 182 West Regent St Ⓣ0141/226 3406, Ⓦwww.wherethemonkeysleeps.com. Owned by graduates of the nearby Glasgow School of Art who acquired their barista skills between classes, this hip home-grown café features freshly prepared sandwiches and salads, and the espresso is superb. Usually closes at 5pm. Inexpensive.

Willow Tea Rooms 217 Sauchiehall St Ⓣ0141/332 0521, Ⓦwww.willowtearooms.co.uk. An authentic bit of architectural heritage on the Charles Rennie Mackintosh trail, the first-floor dining room here offers tea with scones and midday meals. A similarly themed branch is at 97 Buchanan St (Ⓣ0141/204 5242). Closes before 5pm. Moderate.

Restaurants

Brian Maule at Le Chardon d'Or 176 West Regent St Ⓣ0141/248 3801, Ⓦwww.brianmaule.com. Owner/chef Maule once worked with the Roux brothers at *Le Gavroche* restaurant in London. Fancy but not pretentious French-influenced food along the lines of grilled sea bass with fennel and broad beans in a Pernod cream. Closed Sun. Expensive.

City Merchant 97 Candleriggs Ⓣ0141/553 1577, Ⓦwww.citymerchant.co.uk. Popular brasserie that blazed the Merchant City trail, which plenty of others have followed. Fresh Scottish produce from Ayrshire lamb to the house speciality: west coast seafood. Closed Sun. Expensive.

Dakhin 89 Candleriggs Ⓣ0141/553 2585, Ⓦwww.dakhin.com. Opened in 2004 and owned by the same people as *The Dhabba* (see below), this first-floor restaurant (above *Bar 91*) specializes in South Indian cuisine. Be sure and try a rice dosa. Moderate–expensive.

The Dhabba 44 Candleriggs Ⓣ0141/553 1249, Ⓦwww.thedhabba.com. This is not your typical Glasgow curry house. Prices are higher, portions are smaller but the menu has some truly interesting options – such as chicken with spinach, pistachio and cashew nuts and spiced vegetable dumplings – and fresh ingredients that place it steps above most others. Moderate–expensive.

Fratelli Sarti 133 Wellington St or 121 Bath St Ⓣ0141/204 0440, Ⓦwww.fratellisarti.com. The Sarti brothers' flagship Italian café and restaurant: authentic and popular. The slightly more formal dining space is accessed from the Bath St entrance; the atmospheric café round the corner opens in the mornings Mon–Sat. Moderate.

Gamba 225a West George St Ⓣ0141/572 0899, Ⓦwww.gamba.co.uk. This modern basement restaurant offers one of the best meals in Glasgow. Continental contemporary sophistication prevails, with dishes such as mussel and oyster stew or grilled halibut served with scallop cream. If you love fish, come here. Closed Sun. Expensive.

Ichiban Japanese Noodle Café 50 Queen St Ⓣ0141/204 4200, Ⓦwww.ichiban.co.uk. Japanese-style informal eating, with long benches and tables shared by diners. Bowls (or plates) of noodles are specialities here; service is efficient. There's a second branch in the West End. Inexpensive.

Michael Caines @ Abode 129 Bath St Ⓣ0141/572 6011, Ⓦwww.michaelcaines.com. At the time of writing, this is the closest that Glasgow gets to a Michelin star. Although this restaurant has not yet secured one, Caines earned two at his restaurant in southwest England. Here he has hired a staff who are ambitious, with modern French-inspired recipes using local produce such as roast partridge with quince purée and braised chicory. Expensive.

Rogano 11 Exchange Place Ⓣ0141/248 4055, Ⓦwww.rogano.co.uk. An Art Deco fish restaurant and Glasgow institution since 1935, decked out in the style of the *Queen Mary* ocean liner. *Café Rogano*, in the basement, is cheaper. Or just have some oysters at the bar. Expensive.

The 13th Note Café 50–60 King St Ⓣ0141/553 1638, Ⓦwww.13thnote.co.uk. Vegetarian and vegan fare with Greek and other Mediterranean influences in one of Glasgow's hipper drinking and indie/experimental music haunts on arty King St. Inexpensive.

Wee Curry Shop 7 Buccleuch St Ⓣ0141/353 0777. Tiny but welcoming place near the Glasgow Film Theatre and Sauchiehall St shops, serving home-made bargain meals to compete with the best in town. BYOB. Inexpensive.

West End

All the cafés and restaurants in this section are marked on the Glasgow map on pp.832–833.

Cafés, diners and café-bars

Grassroots Café 93 St George's Rd ⓣ0141/333 0534, ⓦwww.grassrootsorganic.com. Although the competition is not especially stiff, this vegetarian outlet (just cross the M8 motorway from the city centre) has the best reputation for meat-free fare in Glasgow. Fresh, creative cooking and a relaxed atmosphere. Inexpensive–moderate.

Kember & Jones 134 Byres Rd ⓣ0141/337 3851, ⓦwww.kemberandjones.co.uk. This café and deli is a popular spot in the competitive Byres Rd market. There is not much hot food per se, but freshly made salads and sandwiches are excellent. Inexpensive.

Stravaigin 2 8 Ruthven Lane ⓣ0141/334 7165, ⓦwww.stravaigin.com. A popular diner/bistro just off busy Byres Rd that serves excellent burgers alongside an innovative menu similar to the award-winning modern Scottish *Stravaigin* restaurant. Moderate.

Tchai Ovna 42 Otago Lane ⓣ0141/357 4524, ⓦwww.tchaiovna.com. A low-key bohemian hangout that overlooks the Kelvin River, serving savoury vegetarian options, cakes, snacks and a selection of teas from around the world. Inexpensive.

Tinderbox 189 Byres Rd ⓣ0141/339 3108. A modern espresso café-bar offering an array of lattes, cappuccinos and the like, as well as designer looks. Even in trendy Glasgow, it remains amazingly successful. Inexpensive.

Restaurants

Ashoka Ashton Lane 19 Ashton Lane ⓣ0141/337 1115, ⓦwww.harlequingroup.net. Lively curry house in the Harlequin chain, which has franchises across the west of Scotland; all offer consistent quality. Moderate.

Café Antipasti 337 Byres Rd ⓣ0141/337 2737. A busy Italian bistro serving tasty and well-priced pastas and salads. No bookings are taken, so expect a queue on busy nights. Inexpensive.

Chow 98 Byres Rd ⓣ0141/334 9818. Proof that Chinese restaurants can be modern and non-kitsch. This bijou diner with extra tables upstairs offers excellent value-for-money meals. Moderate.

Kokuryo 1138 Argyle St ⓣ0141/334 5566. Korean restaurant in a tiny space but with lots of big flavours on your plate, whether spiced *kimchi* or sizzling pork and beef. Inexpensive–moderate.

Mother India 28 Westminster Terrace, off Sauchiehall St ⓣ0141/221 1663. This is one of the best Indian restaurants in Glasgow. Home cooking with some original specials as well as the old favourites at affordable prices in laid-back surroundings. Moderate. Also very much worth trying if you're on a budget is the nearby spin-off: *Mother India's Café* at 1355 Argyle St (ⓣ0141/339 9145). Inexpensive.

No. Sixteen 16 Byres Rd ⓣ0141/339 2544. A local favourite, with daily menus of Scottish produce, from pigeon to fillet of sea bream. Moderate.

Stravaigin 28–30 Gibson St ⓣ0141/334 2665, ⓦwww.stravaigin.com. Scottish meat and fish are given an international make-over using a host of unexpected ingredients, offering unusual flavour combinations such as Thai-spiced Aberdeen Angus beef carpaccio or ham and pistachio terrine. Adventurous fine dining in the basement restaurant and an exceptional-value menu in the street-level bar-café. Restaurant closed Mon. Moderate upstairs, expensive downstairs.

The Ubiquitous Chip 12 Ashton Lane ⓣ0141/334 5007, ⓦwww.ubiquitouschip.co.uk. Opened in 1971, *The Chip* led the way in headlining Scotland's quality fresh produce at the heart of a contemporary, upmarket dining experience. Come for a dish of organic salmon with lime and vanilla mash or wood pigeon in a wild mushroom sauce. Some say it's living on its reputation, but it's still up there. Expensive, but less pricey options upstairs in the bistro.

Southside

Cafés, diners and café-bars

1901 1534 Pollokshaws Rd ⓣ0141/632 0161. Once known as the *Stoat & Ferret*, this French-influenced bistro/pub near Pollok Country Park is a lesser-known gem serving hearty Mediterranean food. Moderate.

Art Lovers' Café In House for an Art Lover, Bellahouston Park, 10 Dumbreck Rd ⓣ0141/353 4779. The dining room, looking onto a charming garden in this showcase house based on unfinished Mackintosh designs, offers sublime cooking at lunch with dishes such as topside of lamb with lentil and bacon stew. Closed evenings. Moderate.

Restaurants

La Fiorentina 2 Paisley Rd West ⓣ0141/420 1585, ⓦwww.la-fiorentina.com. A critical favourite that also tops popular surveys, this Tuscan-oriented restaurant has become an institution. Not far from the Glasgow Science Centre in Govan. Moderate.

Urban Grill 61 Kilmarnock Rd ⓣ0141/649 2745, ⓦwww.urbangrill.co.uk. In the heart of the Shawlands district, this sophisticated combo of modern restaurant and champagne/oyster bar offers arguably the best dining option on the Southside of the city – try a black pudding and chorizo salad or fish soup with prawn dumplings. Moderate–expensive.

Drinking

Glasgow's mythical tough-guy image has been linked with its **pubs**, mistakenly believed by a few to be no-go areas for visitors. Today, however, the city is much changed and many of the once windowless, nicotine-stained working-men's taverns have been converted into airy modern bars. Most drinking dens in the **city centre**, the adjoining **Merchant City** and the fashionable **West End** are places to experience real Glaswegian bonhomie.

From Sunday to Thursday, many pubs and bars will serve until midnight, although some outside the centre close at 11pm during the week. On Friday and Saturday, bars usually open until 1am – and occasionally later.

Pubs and bars

City centre and Merchant City

All the pubs and bars in this section are marked on the Glasgow city centre map on p.834.

The Arches 253 Argyle St. The basement bar is a focal point in this contemporary arts centre under Central station. Decent pub grub and an arty clientele.

Babbity Bowster 16–18 Blackfriars St, off the High St. Lively place with an unforced and kitsch-free Scottish feel that features spontaneous folk sessions at the weekend. Good beer and wine, tasty food and some outdoor seating.

Bar 10 10 Mitchell St. Across from the Lighthouse architecture centre, and considered the granddaddy of Glasgow style bars. Still popular and suitably chic.

Corinthian 191 Ingram St. A remarkable renovation of a florid, early Victorian Italianate bank. Three distinct bars, one restaurant and a private club: dress smartly.

Horseshoe Bar 17 Drury St. A must for pub aficionados. An original "Gin Palace" with the longest continuous bar in the UK, this is reputedly Glasgow's busiest drinking hole; karaoke upstairs.

Pot Still 154 Hope St. Whisky galore – at least 500 different single malts are found in this traditional pub, which has a decent ale selection as well.

West End

All the pubs and bars in this section are marked on the Glasgow map on pp.832–833.

Firebird 1321 Argyle St. Airy modern drinking spot near the Kelvingrove Art Gallery, with a wood-stoked pizza oven producing some tasty snacks, plus DJs to keep the pre-clubbing crowd entertained.

Lismore Lounge 206 Dumbarton Rd. Decorated with specially commissioned stained-glass panels depicting the Highland Clearances, this bar is a meeting point for the local Gaels, who come here to chat, relax and listen to the impromptu music sessions.

Oran Mor Byres Rd at corner of Great Western Rd ⓣ0141/357 6200. An impressive member of Glasgow's nightlife scene, with a big bar, club venue and performance space/auditorium (plus two different dining rooms) all within a tastefully – and expensively – restored Kelvinside parish church.

Nightlife and entertainment

Glasgow offers a thriving **contemporary music** scene, with loads of new bands emerging every year, The Fratellis being the best-known recently. There's a clutch of venues, from the famous *Barrowland* to *King Tut's Wah Wah Hut*, where you've a good chance of catching a live act, while the city's **clubbing scene** has long been the best in the UK. Opening hours hover between 11pm to 3am, though some places stay open until 5am. Cover charges are variable: expect to pay around £5 during the week and up to £20 at the weekend. Drinks are usually about thirty percent more expensive than in the pubs.

On the **performing arts** scene, Glasgow is no slouch either: it's home to Scottish Opera, Scottish Ballet and the Royal Scottish National Orchestra. Most of the larger theatres, cinema multiplexes and concert halls are in the city centre; the West End is home to just one or two venues, while the Southside can boast two theatres noted for cutting-edge drama, the Citizens' and Tramway.

For detailed **listings** of what's on, pick up the comprehensive fortnightly magazine *The List* (£2.20), which also covers Edinburgh, or consult Glasgow's *Herald* or *Evening Times* newspapers.

Clubs

The Arches 30 Midland St, off Jamaica St ⓣ0141/221 4001, ⓦwww.thearches.co.uk. In converted railway arches under Central station, the club portion of this huge arts venue offers an eclectic array of music: hard house, trance, techno and funk. One of *DJ* magazine's top 10 clubs in the world.

Sub Club 22 Jamaica St ⓣ0141/248 4600, ⓦwww.subclub.co.uk. Near-legendary venue, home to quality underground house and techno nights, as well as the brilliantly entertaining Sun night mash-up Optimo (Espacio).

The Tunnel 84 Mitchell St ⓣ0141/204 1000. Contemporary and progressive house music club with arty decor (have a look at the gents' cascading waterfall walls) and fairly strict dress codes.

Gay clubs and bars

Bennets 90 Glassford St, Merchant City ⓣ0141/552 5761, Glasgow's longest-running gay club: predominantly male, fairly traditional with MOR music. Open Wed–Sun.

Polo Lounge 84 Wilson St, off Glassford St ⓣ0141/553 1221. Original Victorian decor – marble tiles and open fires – and gentleman's-club atmosphere upstairs, with dark, pounding nightclub underneath; attracts a gay and gay-friendly crowd.

Revolver 6a John St ⓣ0141/553 2456. Geared more towards the art of conversation than dance, although the (free) jukebox is fantastic; welcomes men and women.

Live music venues

Barrowland 244 Gallowgate ⓣ0141/552 4601, ⓦwww.glasgow-barrowland.com. Legendary East End ballroom that hosts some of the sweatiest and best gigs you may ever encounter. With room for a couple of thousand, it mostly books bands securely on the rise but still hosts some big-time acts who return to it as their favourite venue in Scotland.

Carling Academy 121 Eglington St ⓣ0870/771 2000, ⓦwww.glasgow-academy.co.uk. Owned by the same people behind London's *Brixton Academy*, and with a capacity for 2500, this is the city's principal mid-sized venue. Less atmosphere than the *Barrowland*, but gets reliably big names.

King Tut's Wah Wah Hut 272a St Vincent St ⓣ0141/221 5279, ⓦwww.kingtuts.co.uk. Famous as the place where Oasis were discovered, and still presenting one of the city's best live music programmes. Also has a good bar, with an excellent jukebox.

Theatres and comedy venues

Arches Theatre 253 Argyle St ⓣ0141/565 1023, ⓦwww.thearches.co.uk. Home to its own avant-garde theatre company, reviving old classics and introducing new talent in this hip subterranean venue.

Citizens' Theatre 119 Gorbals St ⓣ0141/429 0022, ⓦwww.citz.co.uk. The "Citz" has evolved from its 1960s working-class roots into one of Britain's most respected and innovative contemporary theatres. Three stages, concession rates for students and free preview nights.

The Stand 333 Woodlands Rd ⓣ0870/600 6055, ⓦwww.thestand.co.uk. Sister to the first-rate comedy club in Edinburgh, booking local, national and international acts.

Theatre Royal 282 Hope St ⓣ0141/332 9000, ⓦwww.theatreroyalglasgow.com. This late nineteenth-century playhouse was revived in the mid-1970s as the opulent home of Scottish Opera, whose repetoire features large-scale but still adventurous productions of the likes of *Madam Butterfly* and *Der Rosenkavalier*. It also plays regular host to visiting theatre groups, including the Royal Shakespeare Company, as well as orchestras.

Tron Theatre 63 Trongate ⓣ0141/552 4267, ⓦwww.tron.co.uk. Varied repertoire of some mainstream and, more importantly, challenging productions from itinerant companies, such as Glasgow's Vanishing Point. Folk music performances in theatre bar.

Concert halls

City Halls Candleriggs ⓣ0141/353 8000, ⓦwww.glasgowcityhalls.com. Completely renovated old fruitmarket, this Merchant City performance space is home to the BBC Scottish Symphony and hosts many of the annual Celtic Connections concerts.

Glasgow Royal Concert Hall 2 Sauchiehall St ⓣ0141/353 8000, ⓦwww.grch.com. One of Glasgow's less memorable modern buildings, this is the venue for big-name touring orchestras and the home of the Royal Scottish National Orchestra. Also features major rock and R&B stars, and middle-of-the-road music-hall acts.

Scottish Exhibition and Conference Centre and **Clyde Auditorium** Finnieston Quay ⓣ0870/040 4000, ⓦwww.secc.co.uk. The SECC is a gigantic airplane-hangar-like space with dreadful acoustics that, unfortunately, is Scotland's only indoor venue for world-touring megastars from Bob Dylan to 50 Cent. The adjacent Clyde Auditorium – better known as the Armadillo – is smaller but more melodic.

Art-house cinemas

Glasgow Film Theatre 12 Rose St ⓣ0141/332 8128, ⓦwww.gft.org.uk. Dedicated art, independent and repertory cinema house. Its in-house *Café Cosmo* is an excellent place for pre-show drinks.

Grosvenor Ashton Lane ⓣ0141/339 8444, ⓦwww.grosvenorcinema.co.uk. Renovated two-screen neighbourhood film house with bar and sofas you can reserve for screenings of mostly mainstream films.

Shopping

Glasgow's **shopping** is reckoned to be the second-best in the UK – after London, of course. The main area for spending in the city centre is formed by the Z-shaped and mostly pedestrianized route of **Argyle, Buchanan and Sauchiehall streets**. Along the way you'll find Princes Square, the city's poshest malls, plus major department stores such as M&S, Debenhams and John Lewis and branches of high-street chains including Hugo Boss, Gap, Karen Millen and Urban Outfitters. The Buchanan Galleries, a bland complex built around John Lewis, features some high-fashion budget stores.

Otherwise, make for the **West End** – or the **Merchant City**, with its chichi and pricey Italian Centre for some imported glamour or home-grown Cruise for designerwear on Ingram Street. In general the Merchant City and West End have more eccentric and individual offerings – the latter being the place to head for secondhand and antiquarian **book shops**.

Listings

Bike rental and routes West End Cycles, 16 Chancellor St (ⓣ0141/357 1344) has a good selection and is located close to the start of the Glasgow to Loch Lomond route, one of a number of cycle routes that radiate out from the city. For further details, check ⓦwww.sustrans.co.uk.

Car rental Arnold Clark, multiple branches (ⓣ0845/607 4500); Avis, 70 Lancefield St (ⓣ0141/221 2827); Budget, 101 Waterloo St (ⓣ0141/243 2047). Car hire at the airport includes Budget (ⓣ0141/889 1479) and Hertz (ⓣ0870/846 0007).

Gay and lesbian contacts Strathclyde Lesbian and Gay Switchboard (ⓣ0141/847 0447); Glasgow Lesbian, Gay, Bisexual and Transgender (LGBT) Centre, 84 Bell St (ⓣ0141/552 4958, ⓦwww.glgbt.org.uk).

Hospital 24hr casualty department at the Royal Infirmary, 84 Castle St near Glasgow Cathedral (ⓣ0141/211 4000).

Left luggage Buchanan St bus station and lockers at Central or Queen St train stations (depending on current security restrictions).

Police Strathclyde Police HQ, Pitt St (ⓣ0141/532 2000). For emergencies, dial 999.

Post office General information (ⓣ0845/722 3344). Main office at 47 St Vincent St (Mon–Fri 8.30am–5.45pm, Sat 9am–5.30pm); city centre office at 87–91 Bothwell St.

Taxis Glasgow Taxi Ltd for Fast Black (ⓣ0141/429 7070); Glasgow Private Hire (ⓣ0141/774 3000).

The Clyde

The **River Clyde** is the dominant physical feature of Glasgow and its environs, an area that comprises the largest urban concentration in Scotland, with almost two million people living in the city and satellite towns. Little of this immediate hinterland can be described as beautiful, with crisscrossing motorways and relentlessly grim housing estates dominating much of the landscape. Beyond the urban sprawl, rolling green hills, open expanses of water and attractive countryside eventually begin to dominate, not always captivating initially, but holding promises of wilder country beyond.

West of the city, regular trains and the M8 motorway dip down from the southern bank of the Clyde to **Paisley**, where the distinctive cloth pattern gained its name, before heading back up to the edge of the river again as it broadens into the **Firth of Clyde**. North of Glasgow trains terminate at tiny Milngavie (pronounced "Mill-guy"), which acts as the start of Scotland's best-known long-distance footpath, the **West Highland Way** (see p.869).

Southeast of Glasgow, the industrial landscape of the **Clyde valley** eventually gives way to a far more attractive scenery of gorges and towering castles. Here lie the stoic town of **Lanark**, where eighteenth-century philanthropists built their model workers' community around the mills of **New Lanark**, and the spectacular **Falls of Clyde**, a mile upstream.

The Firth of Clyde – south bank

The swift journey from Glasgow along the M8, coupled with the proximity of the international airport, can belie the fact that **Paisley** is not a suburb of Glasgow but a town in its own right, with a long and distinctive history, particularly in the textile trade. Further west, the former shipbuilding centres of Port Glasgow and **Greenock** crowd the riverbank, followed by the old-fashioned resort of **Gourock**, and eventually Wemyss Bay, where thousands of Glaswegians used to alight for their steamer trip "doon the watter", but today of note only for its CalMac **ferry** connection to Rothesay on Bute (see p.896).

Paisley

Founded in the twelfth century as a monastic settlement around an abbey, **PAISLEY** expanded after the eighteenth century as a linen-manufacturing town, specializing in the production of highly fashionable imitation Kashmiri shawls. It quickly eclipsed other British centres producing the cloth, eventually lending its name to the swirling pine-cone design. Inside the **Museum and Art Gallery,** opposite the university (Tues–Sat 10am–5pm, Sun 2–5pm; free), the Shawl Gallery deals with the growth and development of the Paisley pattern, from its simple beginnings to elaborate later incarnations.

Opposite the town hall, Paisley's **Abbey** (Mon–Sat 10am–3.30pm; free) was built on the site of the town's original settlement and was massively overhauled in the Victorian age. The unattractive, fat grey facade of the church does little justice to its renovated interior, which is tall, spacious and ornately decorated; the elongated choir, rebuilt extensively throughout the last two centuries, is illuminated by jewel-coloured stained glass from a variety of ages and styles.

Practicalities

Regular **trains** from Glasgow Central connect with Paisley's Gilmour Street station in the centre of town. Buses leave its forecourt every ten minutes for Glasgow International airport, two miles north of the town. The **tourist office** is right in the centre at 9a Gilmour St (Mon–Sat 9am–5pm; ⓣ0141/889 0711).

For **food** the Paisley Arts Centre has a small bar, daytime café and outside seating, while *Aroma Room* is a more modern spot right opposite the Museum and Art Gallery, which serves coffees, snacks and lunches. Both *Cardosi's* on Storie Street and *Raeburn's Bistro and Grill* on New Street have decent evening menus.

Greenock

GREENOCK, west of Glasgow, was the site of the first dock on the Clyde, founded in 1711, and the community has grown on the back of shipping ever since. From Greenock's Central train station (also served by hourly Citylink buses from Glasgow's Buchanan Street station), it's a short walk to the dockside, where the Neoclassical **Custom House** is Greenock's finest building, splendidly located looking out over the river. Now the principal office for HM Customs & Excise in Scotland, it has an informative **museum** inside (Mon–Fri 10am–4pm; free), which covers the work of the Customs and Excise departments, with displays on illicit whisky distilleries as well as more modern contraband.

Greenock's town centre has been disfigured by astonishingly unsympathetic developments. More attractive, and indicative of the town's wealthy past, is the western side of town, with its mock-Baronial houses, graceful churches and quiet, tree-lined avenues. Here the **McLean Museum and Art Gallery** on Union Street (Mon–Sat 10am–5pm; free) contains pictures and contemporary records of the life and achievements of Greenock-born James Watt, prominent eighteenth-century industrialist and pioneer of steam power, as well as featuring a small art gallery with work by Glasgow Boys Hornel and Guthrie plus Colourists Fergusson, Cadell and Peploe.

On the train line west of Greenock, Fort Matilda station perches below **Lyle Hill**, an invigorating 450-foot climb that is well worth the effort for the astounding views over the purple mountains of Argyll and the creeks and lochs spilling off the Firth of Clyde.

Gourock

West of Lyle Hill lies the dowdy old resort of **GOUROCK**, once a holiday destination for generations of Glaswegians, but today only of real significance as a **ferry** terminal: both CalMac (enquiries ⓣ08000/665400, sales ⓣ08000/665000, ⓦwww.calmac.co.uk) and the more frequent Western Ferries (ⓣ01369/704452, ⓦwww.western-ferries.co.uk) ply the twenty-minute route across the Firth of Clyde to Dunoon on the Cowal peninsula, while a passenger-only ferry runs year-round to Kilcreggan and Helensburgh on the north bank of the Clyde (Mon–Sat 12 daily, also Sun 5 daily in summer; £2.20 single; ⓦwww.spt.co.uk/ferry).

The Firth of Clyde – north bank

Heading west out of Glasgow, the A82 road and the train tracks both follow the north bank of the river, passing through Clydebank, another ex-shipbuilding centre, and Bowling, the western entry point of the Forth & Clyde canal. Three miles beyond Bowling, they reach the town of **DUMBARTON**, founded in the fifth century, but today for the most part a brutal concrete sprawl. Only **Dumbarton Castle** (April–Sept daily 9.30am–5.30pm; Oct–March Sat–Wed 9.30am–4.30pm; HS; £4), which sits atop a twin outcrop of volcanic rock surrounded by water on three sides, is worth stopping to see. First founded as a Roman fort, the castle became a royal seat, from which Mary, Queen of Scots, sailed for France to marry Henri II's son in 1548. Since the 1600s, the castle has been used as a garrison and artillery fortress to guard the approaches to Glasgow; most of the current buildings date from this period.

Helensburgh

HELENSBURGH, twenty miles or so northwest of Glasgow, is a smart, Georgian grid-plan settlement overlooking the Clyde estuary. The inventor of TV, John Logie Baird, was born here, as was Charles Rennie Mackintosh, who in 1902 was commissioned by the Glaswegian publisher Walter Blackie to design **Hill House** on Upper Colquhoun Street (April–Oct daily 1.30–5.30pm; NTS; £8). Without doubt the best surviving example of Mackintosh's domestic architecture, the house is stamped with his very personal, elegant interpretation of Art Nouveau – right down to the light fittings and fire irons – characterized by his sparing use of colour and stylized floral patterns. Various upstairs rooms are given over to interpretative displays on the architect's use of light, colour, form and texture, while changing exhibitions on contemporary domestic design from around Britain are a testament to Mackintosh's ongoing influence and inspiration. After exploring the house, head for the **tearoom** in the kitchen quarters, or wander round the beautifully laid-out **gardens**.

The Clyde valley

Mostly following the course of the Clyde upstream, the journey southeast of Glasgow into Lanarkshire is dominated by endless suburbs, industrial parks and wide strips of concrete highway. The principal road here is the M74, though you'll have to get off the motorway to find the main points of interest, which tend to lie on or near the banks of the river. On the outskirts of the new town of East Kilbride, the **National Museum of Rural Life**, set on a historic farm, offers an in-depth look at the history of agriculture in Scotland. Further south, **New Lanark** is a remarkable eighteenth-century planned village.

National Museum of Rural Life

On the edge of **EAST KILBRIDE** new town, seven miles southeast of Glasgow centre, the **National Museum of Rural Life** (daily 10am–5pm; £5; NTS) is an unexpected union of historic farm and modern museum. The site of the museum, **Kittochside**, is a 170-acre farm which avoided the intensive farming that came to dominate agriculture in Britain after World War II, and it has been retained as a working model farm showcasing traditional methods of farming.

The custom-built, £6million museum building on the edge of the farm uses space and light creatively to show displays about the Scots' relationship with the land over centuries and the farm equipment they have used, from early ploughs to the combine harvester. A tractor and trailer shuttles visitors the half-mile up to the eighteenth-century **farmhouse**, which is furnished much as it would have been in the 1950s, the crucial decade just before traditional methods using horses and hand-tools were replaced by tractors and mechanization.

Transport isn't straightforward if you don't have your own vehicle. Bus #31 from Glasgow's St Enoch Centre to East Kilbride takes you past the museum (Stewartfield Way), or you can get the train from Glasgow Central, and then take a taxi for the final three miles to the museum.

Lanark and New Lanark

The neat little market town of **LANARK** is an old and distinguished burgh, sitting in the purple hills high above the River Clyde, its rooftops and spires visible for miles around. There's little to see in town unless you are around during the lively **Lanimer** celebrations in early June, one of Scotland's oldest ceremonies of riding the marches or boundaries, which goes back to 1140. Most people head straight on to the village of **NEW LANARK** (Ⓦwww.newlanark.org), a mile below the main town on Braxfield Road, whose importance as a centre of social and industrial innovation has recently been recognized by UNESCO, who include it on their list of World Heritage Sites.

The first sight of the village, hidden away down in the gorge, is unforgettable: large, broken, curving walls of honeyed warehouses and tenements, built in Palladian style, are lined up along the turbulent river's edge. The community was founded by David Dale and Richard Arkwright in 1785 to harness the power of the Clyde waterfalls in their cotton-spinning industry, but it was Dale's son-in-law, Robert Owen, who revolutionized the social side of the experiment in 1798, creating a "village of unity". Believing the welfare of the workers to be crucial to industrial success, Owen built adult educational facilities, the world's first day nursery and playground, and schools in which dancing and music were obligatory and there was no punishment or reward.

While you're free to wander around the village, which rather unexpectedly for such a historic site is still partially residential, to get into any of the **exhibitions** (all daily 11am–5pm) you need to buy a passport ticket (£5.95; various discount tickets are available, including an all-in ticket covering admission and the return train and bus trip from Glasgow). The Neoclassical building that now houses the visitor reception was opened by Owen in 1816 under the utopian title of **The Institute for the Formation of Character**. These days, it houses the **New Millennium Experience**, which whisks visitors on a chairlift through a social history of the village, conveying Robert Owen's vision not just for the idealized life at New Lanark, but also what he predicted for the year 2000.

Other parts of New Lanark village prove just as fascinating: everything, from the co-operative store to the workers' tenements and workshops, was built in an attempt to prove that industrialism need not be unaesthetic. Situated in the Old Dyeworks, the **Scottish Wildlife Trust Visitor Centre** (daily: Jan & Feb noon–4pm; March–Dec 11am–5pm; £2) provides information about the history and wildlife of the area. Beyond the visitor centre, a riverside path leads you the mile or so to the major **Falls of the Clyde**, where at the stunning tree-fringed Cora Linn the river plunges 90ft in three tumultuous stages.

Practicalities

Lanark is the terminus of **trains** from Glasgow Central. The town's **tourist office** (May–Sept daily 10am–5pm; Oct–April Mon–Sat 10am–5pm; Ⓣ01555/661661) is housed in the Horsemarket, next to Somerfields supermarket, one hundred yards west of the station.

By far the most original **accommodation** options in the area, at both ends of the market, make use of reconstructed mill buildings in New Lanark: the SYHA **hostel** (ⓣ0870/004 1143, ⓦwww.syha.org.uk) has two-, four- and five-bed rooms in the cutely named Wee Row on Rosedale Street, while the *New Lanark Mill* (ⓣ01555/667200, ⓦwww.newlanarkhotel.co.uk; ⑥) is a four-star **hotel** with good views and lots of character.

Travel details

Buses

For information on all local and national bus services, contact Traveline ⓣ0870/608 2608 (daily 7am–10pm), ⓦwww.travelinescotland.com.

Glasgow Buchanan Street to: Aberdeen (hourly; 3hr 15min); Campbeltown (3 daily; 4–5hr); Dundee (every 30min; 1hr 50min); Edinburgh (every 15min; 1hr 10min); Fort William (4 daily; 3hr); Glen Coe (4 daily; 2hr 30min); Inverness (1 direct daily; 4–5hr); Kyle of Lochalsh (3 daily; 5–6hr); Loch Lomond (hourly; 45min); London (5 daily; 8–9hr); Oban (3 daily; 2hr 50min); Perth (hourly; 1hr 35min); Portree (3 daily; 6–7hr); Stirling (hourly; 45min).

Trains

For information on all local and national rail services, contact National Rail Enquiries ⓣ08457/484950, ⓦwww.nationalrail.co.uk or ⓦwww.firstscotrail.com.

Glasgow Central to: Ardrossan for Arran ferry (every 30min; 45min); Ayr (every 30min; 50min); East Kilbride (every 30min; 30min); Gourock (every 30min; 50min); Greenock (every 30min; 40min); Lanark (every 30min; 50min); London (hourly; 5–6hr); Paisley (every 10min; 10min); Queen's Park (every 15min; 6min); Stranraer (4 daily direct; 2hr 15min); Wemyss Bay (every 30min; 50min).

Glasgow Queen Street to: Aberdeen (hourly; 2hr 30min); Balloch (every 30min; 45min); Dumbarton (every 20min; 30min); Dundee (hourly; 1hr 20min); Edinburgh (every 15min; 50min); Fort William (1–3 daily; 3hr 40min); Helensburgh (every 30min; 45min); Inverness (3 daily direct; 3hr 25min); Milngavie (every 30min; 25min); Oban (1–3 daily; 3hr); Perth (hourly; 1hr); Stirling (hourly; 30min).

Flights

Glasgow International to: Barra (2 daily; 1hr 10min); Belfast (Mon–Fri 7 daily; Sat & Sun 3 daily; 45min); Benbecula (Mon–Sat 2 daily; Sun 1 daily; 1hr); Campbeltown (Mon–Fri 2 daily; 40min); Dublin (3 daily; 55min); Islay (Mon–Fri 2 daily, Sat 1 daily; 40min); Kirkwall (1 daily; 1hr 20min); London City (Mon–Fri 4 daily, Sun 1 daily; 1hr 35min); London Gatwick (Mon–Fri 11 daily, Sat & Sun 4 daily; 1hr 30min); London Heathrow (Mon–Fri 18 daily, Sat & Sun 10 daily; 1hr 20min); London Luton (Mon–Fri 5 daily, Sat 2 daily, Sun 3 daily; 1hr 15min); London Stansted (Mon–Fri 5 daily, Sat 3 daily, Sun 4 daily; 1hr 20min); Shetland (Mon–Fri 2 daily, Sat & Sun 1 daily; 1hr 30min); Stornoway (Mon–Fri 4 daily, Sat & Sun 2 daily; 1hr 10min); Tiree (Mon–Sat 1 daily; 50min).

Glasgow Prestwick to: Dublin (Mon–Fri 3 daily, Sat & Sun 2 daily; 45min); London Stansted (4 daily; 1hr 10min).

Central Scotland

CHAPTER 20 Highlights

* **Stirling Castle** Impregnable, impressive and resonant with history. If you see only one castle in Scotland, make it this one. See p.864

* **The Trossachs** Pocket Highlands with shining lochs, wooded glens and noble peaks. Great for hiking and mountain biking. See p.870

* **Himalayas putting green, St Andrews** The world's finest putting course right beside the world's finest golf course; a snip at £1.50 a round. See p.876

* **The East Neuk** Buy freshly cooked lobster from the wooden shack at Crail's historic stone harbour or dine in style at *The Cellar* restaurant in the fishing town of Anstruther. See p.877

* **Forth Rail Bridge** An icon of Victorian engineering spanning the Firth of Forth, floodlit to stunning effect at night. See p.881

* **Rannoch Moor** One of the most inaccessible places in Scotland, where hikers can discover a true sense of remote emptiness. See p.888

▲Forth Rail Bridge

20

Central Scotland

Central Scotland, the strip of mainland north of the densely populated Glasgow–Edinburgh axis and south of the main swathe of Highlands, has been the main stage for some of the most important events in Scottish history. **Stirling**, its imposing castle perched high above the town, was historically the most important bridging point across the River Forth. From the castle battlements you can see the peaks of the forested **Trossachs** region, filled with archetypal Scottish scenery. Popular for walking and, in particular, cycling, much of the Trossachs, together with the attractive islands and "bonnie banks" of **Loch Lomond**, form the core of Scotland's first national park.

To the east, between the firths of Forth and Tay, lies the county of **Fife**, a Pictish kingdom that boasts a fascinating coastline sprinkled with historic fishing villages and sandy beaches, as well as the historic university town of **St Andrews**, famous worldwide for its venerable golf courses. A little to the north, the ancient town of **Perth** has as much claim as anywhere to be the gateway to the Highlands. Spectacular **Highland Perthshire** begins north and west of Perth – an area of glorious wooded mountainsides and inviting walks, particularly around Rannoch Moor.

Stirling, Loch Lomond and the Trossachs

The central lowlands of Scotland were, for several centuries, the most strategically important area in Scotland. In 1250, a map of Britain was compiled by Matthew Paris, a monk of St Albans, which depicted Scotland as two separate land masses connected only by the thin band of Stirling Bridge; although this was a figurative interpretation, Stirling was once the only **gateway** from the fertile central belt to the rugged, mountainous north.

As a result, **Stirling** and its fine castle, from where you can see both snowcapped Highland peaks and Edinburgh, is essential for anyone wanting

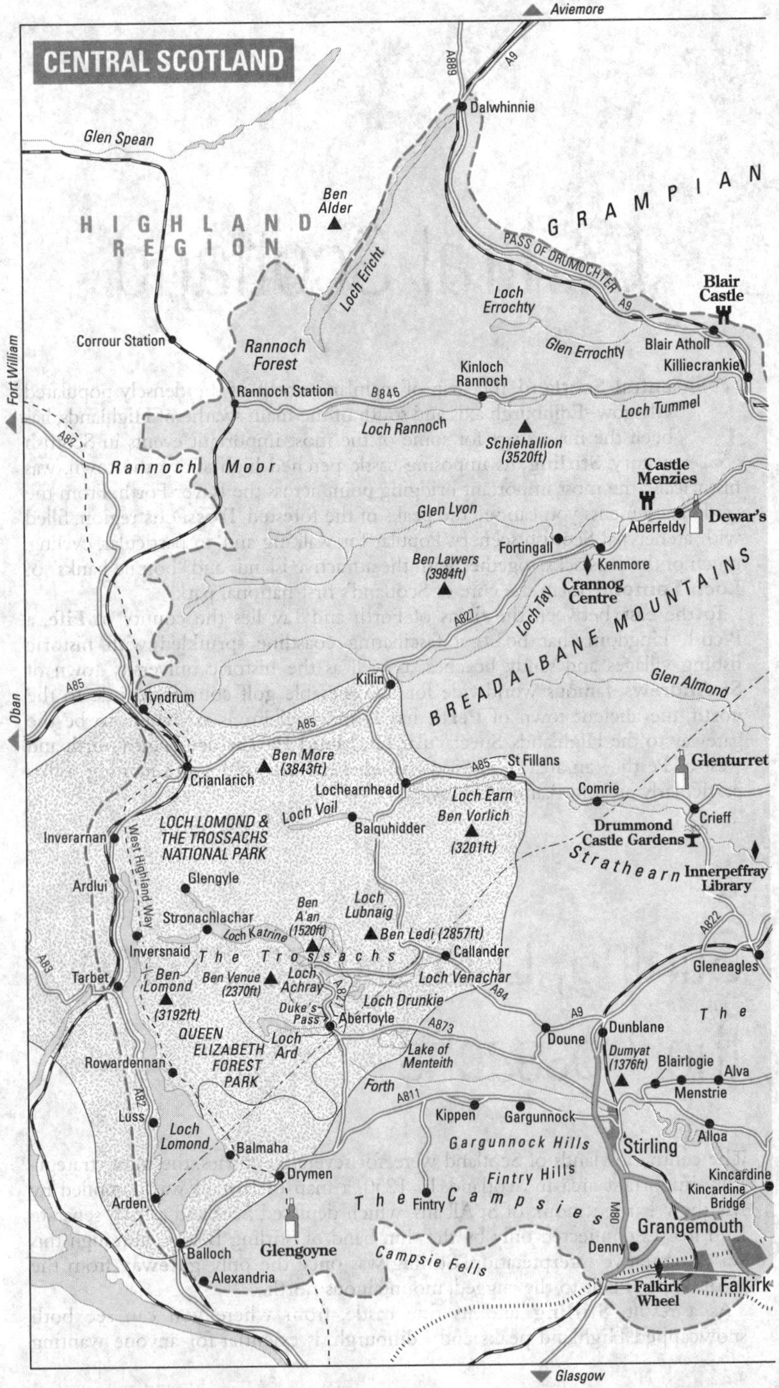
CENTRAL SCOTLAND
Aviemore
A889
A9
Dalwhinnie
Glen Spean
HIGHLAND REGION
Ben Alder
GRAMPIAN
PASS OF DRUMOCHTER
Loch Ericht
Loch Errochty
Blair Castle
A9
Corrour Station
Rannoch Forest
Glen Errochty
Blair Atholl
Killiecrankie
Fort William
Kinloch Rannoch
Rannoch Station
B846
Loch Tummel
Loch Rannoch
A82
Schiehallion (3520ft)
Rannoch Moor
Castle Menzies
Glen Lyon
Aberfeldy
Dewar's
Fortingall
Kenmore
Ben Lawers (3984ft)
Crannog Centre
BREADALBANE MOUNTAINS
Loch Tay
A827
Glen Almond
A85
Killin
Tyndrum
Oban
A85
Ben More (3843ft)
A85
St Fillans
Glenturret
Crianlarich
Lochearnhead
Loch Earn
Comrie
Loch Voil
Ben Vorlich
Crieff
LOCH LOMOND & THE TROSSACHS NATIONAL PARK
Balquhidder
(3201ft)
Drummond Castle Gardens
Inverarnan
West Highland Way
Strathearn
Innerpeffray Library
Ardlui
Glengyle
Loch Lubnaig
Ben A'an (1520ft)
Stronachlachar
Loch Katrine
Ben Ledi (2857ft)
A822
Inversnaid
The Trossachs
Callander
A83
Gleneagles
Tarbet
Ben Lomond (3192ft)
Ben Venue (2370ft)
Loch Achray
A821
Loch Venachar
A84
Loch Drunkie
Duke's Pass
Aberfoyle
A873
A9
Dunblane
The
QUEEN ELIZABETH FOREST PARK
Loch Ard
Lake of Menteith
Doune
Dumyat (1376ft)
Rowardennan
Blairlogie
Alva
Menstrie
Forth
A82
A811
Luss
Kippen
Gargunnock
Loch Lomond
Gargunnock Hills
Stirling
Alloa
Balmaha
Drymen
Fintry Hills
Kincardine
Kincardine Bridge
The Campsies
Fintry
Arden
M80
Grangemouth
Balloch
Glengoyne
Denny
Campsie Fells
Alexandria
Falkirk Wheel
Falkirk
Glasgow

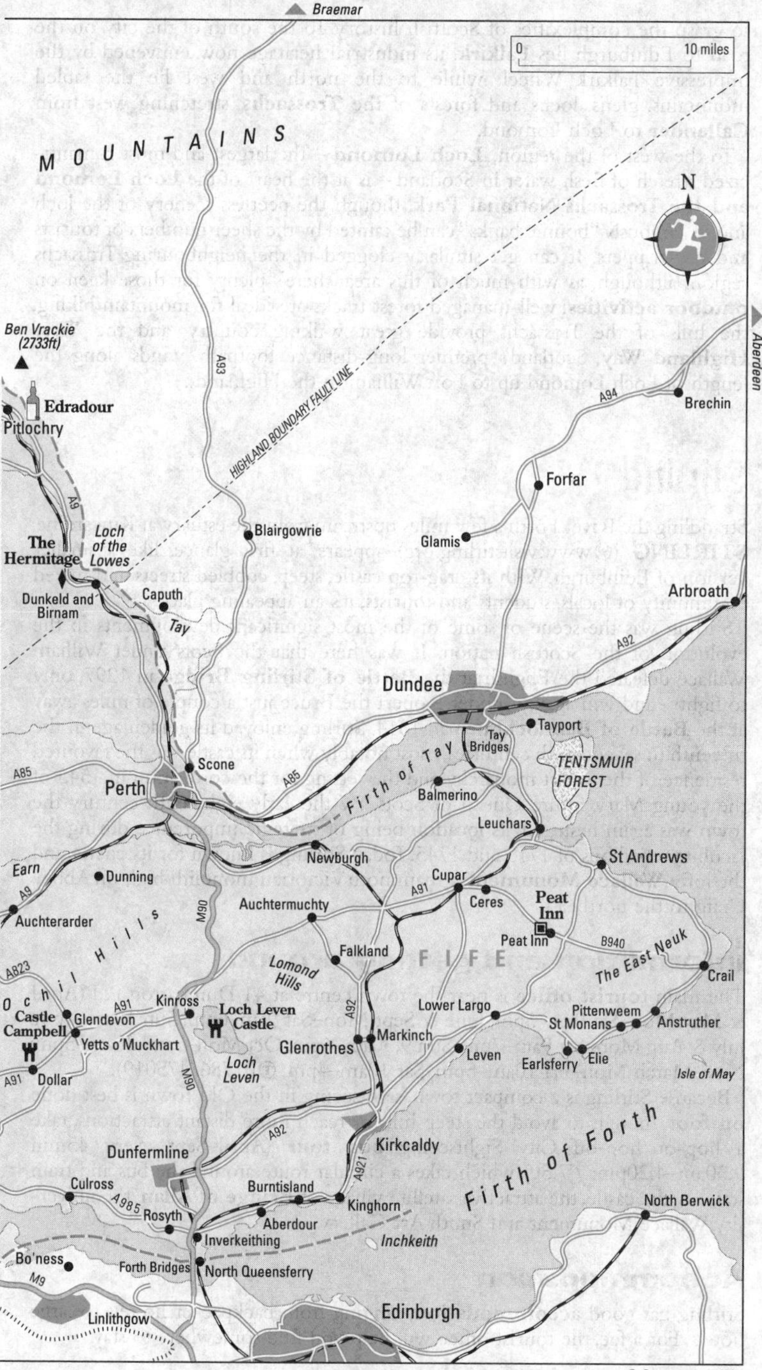

Braemar
0
10 miles
MOUNTAINS
N
Ben Vrackie (2733ft)
Edradour
Pitlochry
A93
HIGHLAND BOUNDARY FAULT LINE
Aberdeen
A94
Brechin
Forfar
A9
The Hermitage
Loch of the Lowes
Blairgowrie
Glamis
Dunkeld and Birnam
Caputh
Tay
Arbroath
A92
Dundee
Tayport
Tay Bridges
TENTSMUIR FOREST
A85
Scone
Perth
A85
Firth of Tay
Balmerino
Leuchars
Newburgh
St Andrews
Earn
Dunning
A9
Cupar
A91
Ceres
Peat Inn
Auchterarder
Auchtermuchty
M90
Peat Inn
B940
Ochil Hills
Falkland
FIFE
The East Neuk
A823
Lomond Hills
Crail
A92
Castle Campbell
A91
Glendevon
Kinross
Loch Leven Castle
Lower Largo
Pittenweem
Anstruther
St Monans
Yetts o'Muckhart
Markinch
Glenrothes
Leven
Earlsferry
Elie
A91
Dollar
Loch Leven
M90
Isle of May
A92
Kirkcaldy
A921
Firth of Forth
Dunfermline
Culross
Burntisland
A985
Rosyth
Kinghorn
North Berwick
Aberdour
Inverkeithing
Inchkeith
Bo'ness
Forth Bridges
North Queensferry
M9
Linlithgow
Edinburgh

to grasp the complexities of Scottish history. To the south of the city on the road to Edinburgh lies **Falkirk**, its industrial heritage now enlivened by the impressive Falkirk Wheel, while to the north and west lie the fabled mountains, glens, lochs and forests of the **Trossachs**, stretching west from **Callander** to Loch Lomond.

To the west of the region, **Loch Lomond** – the largest and most romanticized stretch of fresh water in Scotland – is at the heart of the **Loch Lomond and the Trossachs National Park**, though the peerless scenery of the loch and its famously "bonnie banks" can be tainted by the sheer numbers of tourists and day-trippers. It can get similarly clogged in the neighbouring Trossachs region, although, as with much of this area, there's plenty for those keen on **outdoor activities**: well-managed forest tracks are ideal for mountain biking; the hills of the Trossachs provide great walking country; and the **West Highland Way**, Scotland's premier long-distance footpath, winds along the length of Loch Lomond up to Fort William in the Highlands.

Stirling

Straddling the River Forth a few miles upstream from the estuary at Kincardine, **STIRLING** (Ⓦwww.visitstirling.org) appears, at first glance, like a smaller version of Edinburgh. With its crag-top castle, steep, cobbled streets and mixed community of locals, students and tourists, it's an appealing place.

Stirling was the scene of some of the most significant developments in the evolution of the Scottish nation. It was here that the Scots under William Wallace defeated the English at the **Battle of Stirling Bridge** in 1297, only to fight – and win again – under Robert the Bruce just a couple of miles away at the **Battle of Bannockburn** in 1314. Stirling enjoyed its golden age in the fifteenth to seventeenth centuries, most notably when its castle was the favoured residence of the Stuart monarchy and the setting for the coronation in 1543 of the young Mary, future Queen of Scots. By the early eighteenth century the town was again besieged, its location being of strategic importance during the Jacobite rebellions of 1715 and 1745. Today Stirling is known for its **castle** and the lofty **Wallace Monument**, a mammoth Victorian monolith high on Abbey Craig to the northeast.

Information and getting around

The main **tourist office** is near the town centre at 41 Dumbarton Rd (April & May Mon–Sat 9am–5pm; June & Sept Mon–Sat 9am–6pm, Sun 10am–4pm; July & Aug Mon–Sat 9am–7pm, Sun 9.30am–6pm; Oct Mon–Sat 9.30am–5pm; Nov–March Mon–Fri 10am–5pm, Sat 10am–4pm; Ⓣ01786/475019).

Because Stirling is a compact town, sightseeing in the Old Town is best done **on foot**, though to avoid the steep hills or reach more distant attractions, take a hop-on/hop-off City Sightseeing **bus tour** (April–Sept every 45min 9.30am–4.20pm; £7.50) which takes a circular route around the bus and train stations, the castle, the attractive satellite village of **Bridge of Allan**, the university, Wallace Monument and Smith Art Gallery.

Accommodation

Stirling has good **accommodation**, ranging from backpacker hostels to large hotels. For a fee, the tourist office will help you find somewhere to stay.

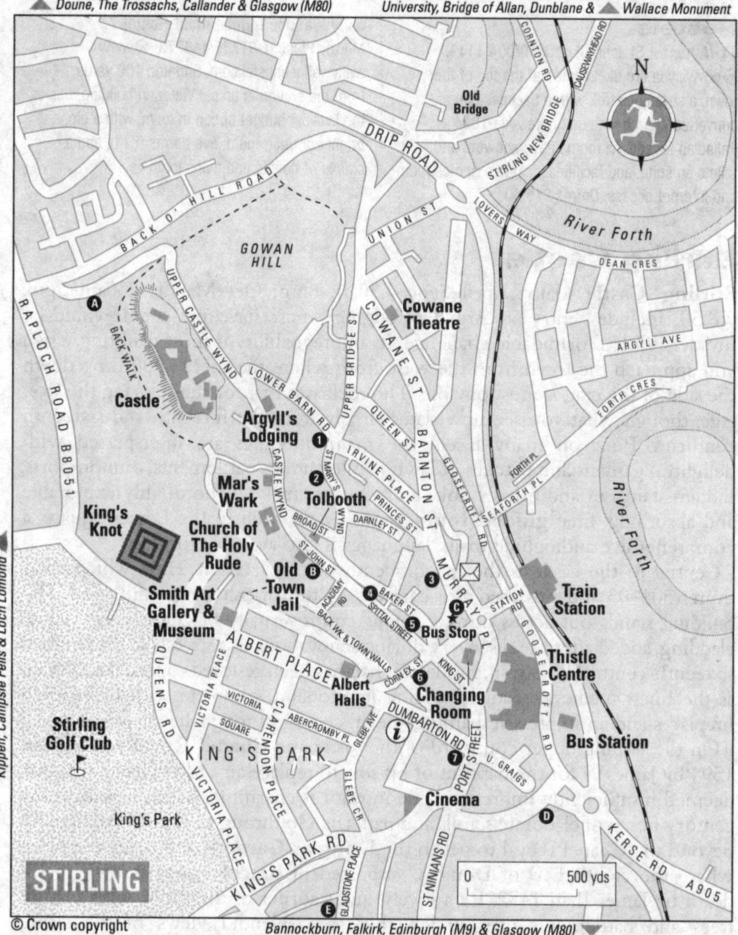

ACCOMMODATION				RESTAURANTS & CAFÉS		PUBS & BARS	
Castlecroft	A	SYHA Hostel	B	Barnton Bar and Bistro	3	Drouthy Neebors	5
No. 10	E	Willy Wallace Independent Hostel	C	L'Angevine	4	Pivo	6
Osta	D			Osta	D	Settle Inn	1
				Peckham's	7	Whistlebinkies	2

Hotels and B&Bs

Castlecroft Ballengeich Rd ⓣ01786/474933, ⓦwww.castlecroft.uk.com. Modern guesthouse with six en-suite rooms on the site of the King's Stables just beneath the castle rock, with terrific views north and west. 4

Kilronan House 15 Kenilworth Rd, Bridge of Allan ⓣ01786/831054, ⓦwww.kilronan.co.uk. A grand Victorian family house built in 1853 with spacious en-suite B&B rooms in the Bridge of Allan, just a couple of miles north of Stirling and easily reached by regular buses. 3

No. 10 10 Gladstone Place ⓣ01786/472681, ⓦwww.cameron-10.co.uk. Modernized Victorian home with neat, uncluttered decor providing friendly and pleasant B&B accommodation close to the city centre. 3

Osta 78 Upper Craigs ⓣ01786/430890, ⓦwww.osta.uk.com. Stirling's only real boutique hotel with lots of purple and black contemporary styling inside a sturdy stone mansion close to the city centre. Mod cons in the rooms and an all-day menu in the relaxed restaurant. 6

Hostels

SYHA hostel St John St ⓣ0870/004 1149, ⓦwww.syha.org.uk. Located at the top of the town, a strenuous trek with a backpack, in a converted church with an impressive 1824 Palladian facade. All rooms have showers and toilets en suite, and facilities include a games room and Internet access. Dorms £15.50.

Willy Wallace Independent Hostel 77 Murray Place ⓣ01786/446773, ⓦwww.willywallacehostel.com. Situated 100 yards from the station in an old Victorian building, this is the liveliest budget option in town, with a big, bright common room, five dorms (£14), and a couple of double and twins (both ❶).

Stirling Castle

Stirling Castle (daily: April–Sept 9.30am–6pm; Oct–March 9.30am–5pm; £8.50, includes entry to Argyll's Lodging) must have presented would-be invaders with a formidable challenge. Its impregnability is most daunting when you approach the town from the west, from where the sheer 250ft drop down the side of the crag is most obvious. The rock was first fortified during the Iron Age, though what you see now dates largely from the fifteenth and sixteenth centuries. Built on many levels, the main buildings are interspersed with delightful gardens and patches of lawn, while endless battlements, cannon ports, hidden staircases and other nooks and crannies make it thoroughly explorable and absorbing. Free **guided tours** begin by the well in the Lower Square; a comprehensive audioguide in six languages is also available for £2.

Central to the castle is the magnificently restored **Great Hall**, which dates from 1501–03 and was used as a barracks by the British army until 1964. The building stands out across Stirling for its controversially bright, creamy yellow cladding, added after the discovery during renovations of a stretch of the original sixteenth-century limewash. Inside, the hall has been restored to its original state as the finest medieval secular building in Scotland, complete with five gaping fireplaces and an impressive hammer-beam ceiling of rough-hewn wood.

On the sloping upper courtyard of the castle, the **Chapel Royal** was built in 1594 by James VI for the baptism of his son, to replace an earlier chapel that was deemed insufficiently impressive. The interior is charming, with a seventeenth-century fresco of elaborate scrolls and patterns. Go through a narrow passageway beyond the Chapel Royal to get to the **Douglas Gardens**, reputedly the place where the eighth Earl of Douglas, suspected of treachery, was thrown to his death by James II in 1452. It's a lovely, quiet corner of the castle, with mature trees and battlements over which there are splendid views of the rising Highlands beyond, as well as a bird's-eye view down to the **King's Knot**, a series of grassed octagonal mounds which, in the seventeenth century, were planted with box trees and ornamental hedges.

The Old Town

Stirling evolved from the top down, starting with its castle and gradually spreading south and east onto the low-lying flood plain. In the eighteenth and nineteenth centuries, as the threat of attack decreased, the centre of commercial life crept down towards the River Forth, with the modern town growing on the edge of the plain over which the castle has traditionally stood guard.

Leaving the castle, head downhill into the old centre of Stirling, fortified behind the massive, whinstone boulders of the **town walls**, built in the mid-sixteenth century and intended to ward off the advances of Henry VIII, who had set his sights on the young Mary, Queen of Scots, as a wife for his son, Edward. The walls now constitute some of the best-preserved town defences in Scotland, and can be traced by following the path known as **Back Walk**, which leads right under the castle, taut along the edge of the crag. Though a little overgrown in places, it's a great way to take in the castle's setting, and in various places you'll catch panoramic views of the surrounding countryside.

A short walk down St John Street, a sweeping driveway leads up to the impressive **Old Town Jail** (daily: April & May 9.30am–5.30pm; June–Sept 9am–6pm; Oct 9.30am–5pm; Nov–March 10am–4pm; ⓣ01786/450050, ⓦwww.oldtownjail.com). Built by Victorian prison reformers, it was rescued from dereliction in 1994, with part of the building turned into offices and a substantial section used to create an entertaining visitor attraction. Telling the history of the building and prisons in general, tours are either self-led using an audio handset (£5) or led by actors (April–Sept daily; Oct–March Sat & Sun; £5.75), who enthusiastically change costumes and character a number of times. Take the glass lift up to the prison roof for spectacular views across Stirling and the Forth Valley.

Directly opposite the Old Town Jail, between St John Street and Broad Street, is the original medieval prison, the **Tolbooth**, now the city's main music and arts centre (daily from 9am; ⓣ01786/274000, ⓦwww.stirling.gov.uk/tolbooth).

The Lower Town and around

The further downhill you go in Stirling's Lower Town, the newer the buildings become. The main **shopping** area is down here, along Port Street and Murray Place. The only sight of note is the **Smith Art Gallery and Museum** on Dumbarton Road, near the King's Knot (Tues–Sat 10.30am–5pm, Sun 2–5pm; ⓦwww.smithartgallery.demon.co.uk; free). Founded in 1874 with a legacy from local painter and collector Thomas Stuart Smith, it houses "The Stirling Story", a reasonably entertaining whirl through the history of the town, balancing out the stories of kings and queens with more social and domestic history.

The National Wallace Monument

A mile and a half north of the Old Town over the new bridge, the prominent **National Wallace Monument** (daily: March–May & Oct 10am–5pm; June 10am–6pm; July & Aug 9am–6pm; Sept 9.30am–5.30pm; Nov–Feb 10.30am–4pm; £6.50, including a free audio tour handset; ⓣ01786/472140, ⓦwww.nationalwallacemonument.com) is a freestanding, five-storey tower built in the 1860s as a tribute to Sir William Wallace, the freedom fighter who led Scottish resistance to Edward I, the "Hammer of the Scots", in the late thirteenth century. A hero to generations of Scots, Wallace shot to international fame with the epic movie *Braveheart*. The crag on which the monument is set was the scene of Wallace's greatest victory, when he sent his troops charging down the hillside onto the plain to defeat the English at the Battle of Stirling Bridge in 1297. Exhibits inside the tower include Wallace's long steel sword and a life-sized "talking" model of Wallace, who tells visitors about his preparations for the battle. If you can manage the climb – up 246 spiral steps – to the top of the 220-foot tower, you'll be rewarded with superb views across to Fife and Ben Lomond. The City Sightseeing tour bus or various local buses including First's #63 will get you here.

Bannockburn

A couple of miles south of Stirling centre, on the A872, all but surrounded by suburban housing, the **Bannockburn Heritage Centre** (daily: April–Oct 10am–5.30pm; rest of the year 10.30am–4pm, closed Jan; £5; NTS) commemorates the most famous battle in Scottish history, when King Robert the Bruce won his mighty victory over the English at the **Battle of Bannockburn** on June 24, 1314. It was this battle, the climax of the Wars of Independence, which united the Scots under Bruce and led to independence from England.

Inside the centre there's an audiovisual presentation on the battle, highlighting the brilliantly innovative tactics Bruce employed in mustering his army to defeat a much larger English force. The actual site of the main battle is still a matter of debate: most agree that it didn't take place near the present visitor centre, but on a boggy carse a mile or so to the west. Get to Bannockburn on the City Sightseeing tour bus or local services #24, #52 or #57 from Stirling bus station or Murray Place.

Restaurants and cafés

A few **restaurants** serve quality contemporary Scottish cuisine and lighter bistro-style food, and there's a range of tearooms, cafés and pubs. In **Bridge of Allan**, foodies head straight for *Clive Ramsay*'s delicatessen at 28 Henderson St (the main street), one of the best delis in Scotland with a **café**-restaurant next door.

Barnton Bar and Bistro Barnton St. Popular local bar with a hearty menu of pub staples, great coffee and an upbeat attitude. Moderate.

L'Angevine 52 Spittal St ⓣ01786/446124. One of only a few good places to eat in the Old Town, this pleasant mid-priced bistro serves French-influenced food and decent wine. Moderate.

Osta 78 Upper Craigs ⓣ01786/430890, ⓦwww.osta.uk.com. Well-presented, varied and contemporary food, served from morning to night. Sleek dining room, bar and outside terrace are all pleasant places to dine. Moderate–expensive.

Peckham's 52 Port St ⓣ01786/463222. Tasty international dishes served at the back of the popular deli in a slightly subdued restaurant space with dominating high-backed booths. Moderate.

Nightlife and entertainment

Nightlife in Stirling revolves around **pubs** and **bars** and is dominated by the student population. The *Settle Inn*, 91 St Mary's Wynd, serves a wide range of Scottish real ales to an eclectic crowd and is Stirling's oldest alehouse. The hipper modern bars in town include *Pivo*, a popular hangout with DJs playing regularly. *Drouthy Neebors* on Baker Street, with its slate-clad bar, is another popular nightspot.

For **live music**, head for the Tolbooth (see p.865), where you can see local and touring folk, rock and jazz acts, or to a pub such as *Whistlebinkies*. **Theatre** and **film**, both art-house and mainstream, takes place in the excellent MacRobert Arts Centre (ⓣ01786/466666, ⓦwww.macrobert.org) on the university campus.

Around Stirling

To the north and west of Stirling, the historic element of the region is reflected in the cathedral at **Dunblane** and the imposing castle at **Doune**, while to the south, the area around **Falkirk** tells of a rich industrial heritage. An undoubted highlight of this hinterland is the massive **Falkirk Wheel**, a spectacular feat of modern engineering at the interchange of the newly restored Forth & Clyde and Union canals.

Dunblane and Doune

Five miles north of Stirling, **DUNBLANE** is a small, attractive place that's been an important ecclesiastical centre since the seventh century, when the Celts founded the Church of St Blane here. **Dunblane Cathedral** (April–Sept Mon–Sat 9.30am–5pm, Sun 2–5pm; Oct–March Mon–Sat 9.30am–4pm, Sun 2–4pm; free; HS) dates mainly from the thirteenth century, and restoration work carried out a century ago has returned it to its Gothic splendour. Various memorials within the cathedral include a tenth-century Celtic cross-slab standing stone and a modern, four-sided standing stone by Richard Kindersley

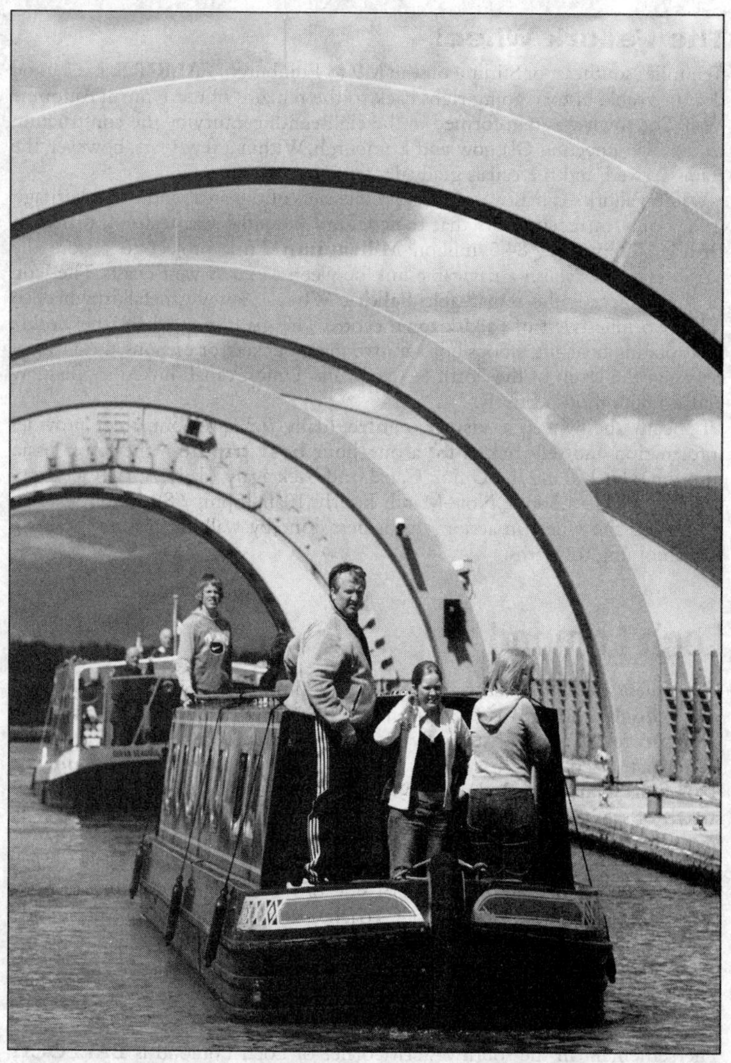

▲Narrow boats at the Falkirk Wheel

commemorating the tragic shooting in 1996 of sixteen Dunblane schoolchildren and their teacher by a local man, Thomas Hamilton.

Three miles west of Dunblane, **DOUNE** is a sleepy village surrounding a stern-looking, fourteenth-century **castle** (April–Sept daily 9.30am–6.30pm; Oct–March Mon–Wed & Sat 9.30am–4.30pm, Sun 2–4.30pm; £3; HS). A marvellous semi-ruin standing on a small hill in a bend of the River Teith, the castle's greatest claim to fame is as the setting for the 1970s movie *Monty Python and the Holy Grail*; the shop by the gatehouse keeps a scrapbook of stills from the film, as well as a selection of souvenirs including bottles of the locally brewed Holy Grail Ale.

The Falkirk Wheel

Ten miles southeast of Stirling on the M9 to Edinburgh, **FALKIRK** has a good deal of visible history, going right back to the remains of the Roman Antonine Wall. The town was transformed in the eighteenth century by the construction of canals connecting Glasgow and Edinburgh. Within a few years, however, the trains arrived, and the canals gradually fell into disuse.

While Falkirk's canals were a very visible sign of the area's industrial heritage, it was only in recent years that their leisure potential was realized, thanks to British Waterway's £84.5 million **Millennium Link** project to restore the canals and re-establish a navigable link between east and west coasts. The icon of this project is the remarkable **Falkirk Wheel** (Ⓦwww.thefalkirkwheel.co.uk), two miles west of Falkirk town centre. The giant grey wheel, the world's first rotating boat-lift, scoops boats in two giant buckets, or caissons, the 115 feet between the levels of the Forth & Clyde and Union canals linked to Glasgow and Edinburgh respectively.

Beneath the wheel, a **visitor centre** (daily 9.30am–6pm; free) provides information and sells tickets for a one-hour **boat trip** from the lower basin into the wheel, along the Union Canal, and back again (daily: April–Oct every 30min 9.30am–4.30pm; Nov–March hourly 10am–3pm; £8). If you want to simply see the wheel in action, this is best done by walking around the basin and adjoining towpaths.

Loch Lomond

The largest stretch of fresh water in Britain (23 miles long and up to five miles wide), **Loch Lomond** is the epitome of Scottish scenic splendour, thanks in large part to the ballad that fondly recalls its "bonnie, bonnie banks".

Designated Scotland's first national park in 2002, the **Loch Lomond and the Trossachs National Park** (Ⓦwww.lochlomond-trossachs.org) covers a large stretch of scenic territory from the lochs of the Clyde Estuary to Loch Tay in Perthshire, with the centrepiece being Loch Lomond. The most popular gateway into the park is the town of **Balloch**, just nineteen miles from Glasgow city centre. Both Balloch and the western side of the loch around **Luss** are often packed with day-trippers and tour coaches, though the loch's eastern side, abutting the Trossachs, is very different in tone, with wooden ferryboats puttering out to a scattering of tree-covered islands off the village of **Balmaha**.

Balloch

The settlement in the southwestern corner of Loch Lomond is **BALLOCH**. The town has few redeeming features, and is little more than a suburb of the

The West Highland Way

Opened in 1980, the spectacular **West Highland Way** was Scotland's first long-distance footpath, stretching some 95 miles from Milngavie (pronounced "mill-guy") six miles north of central Glasgow, to Fort William, where it reaches the foot of Ben Nevis, Britain's highest mountain. Today, it is by far the most popular such footpath in Scotland, and while for many the range of scenery, relative ease of walking and nearby facilities make it a classic route, others find it a little too busy in high season.

The route runs along the eastern shores of Loch Lomond, over the Highland Boundary Fault Line, then round Crianlarich, crossing the open heather wilderness of **Rannoch Moor**. It passes close to **Glen Coe**, notorious for the massacre of the MacDonald clan, before reaching **Fort William**. Apart from one stretch halfway along when the path is within earshot of the main road, this is wild, remote country, and you should be well-prepared for sudden and extreme weather changes.

Though this is emphatically not the most strenuous of Britain's long-distance walks, a moderate degree of fitness is required as there are some steep ascents. If you're looking for an added challenge, you could work a climb of Ben Lomond or Ben Nevis into your schedule. You might choose to walk individual sections of the Way (the eight-mile climb from Glen Coe up the Devil's Staircase is particularly spectacular), but to tackle the whole thing you need to set aside at least seven days; avoid a Saturday start from Milngavie and you'll be less likely to be walking with hordes of people, and there'll be less pressure on accommodation. Most walkers tackle the route from south to north, and manage between ten and fourteen miles a day, staying at hotels, B&Bs and bunkhouses en route. Camping is permitted at recognized sites.

Although the path is clearly waymarked, you may want to check one of the many maps or guidebooks published: the **official guide**, published by Mercat Press (£16.99), includes a foldout map as well as descriptions of the route, with detailed cultural, historical, archeological and wildlife information. For further details on the Way, including a comprehensive accommodation list and various tour options, check out Ⓦwww.west-highland-way.co.uk.

much larger factory-town of Alexandria, to the south. However, its accessibility from Glasgow by both car and train ensured that it was chosen as the focal point of the national park: the location for the huge **Loch Lomond Shores** complex (Ⓦwww.lochlomondshores.com). Signposted from miles around, it contains the **National Park Gateway Centre** (daily 9.30am–6pm, extended hours in the summer; Ⓣ08707/200631), which has background on the park, **tourist information** and a leaflet outlining all transport links within the park, as well as Internet access and a "retail crescent" including a branch of Jenners. Alongside, **Drumkinnon Tower** is a striking cylindrical building housing an aquarium (daily 10am–5pm; £9.95; Ⓣ01389/721000).

Beside Drumkinnon Tower, Can You Experience (Ⓣ01389/602576, Ⓦwww.canyouexperience.com) organizes a number of **activities**, including nature walks and canoe-, bike- and pedalo-rental. Loch **cruises** (including a 2–3hr trip to Luss) leave from the nearby slipway with Sweeney's Cruises (Ⓣ01389/752376, Ⓦwww.sweeney.uk.com).

Few folk bother staying in Balloch: instead, head two miles northwest of the train station to one of Scotland's most impressive SYHA **hostels** (Ⓣ0870/004 1136, Ⓦwww.syha.org.uk; April–Oct), just off the A82. A grand country house with turrets, stained-glass windows and walled gardens, it has dorms sleeping five to ten for £16.75 per person.

Balmaha and the islands

The tranquil eastern shore is far better for walking and appreciating the loch's natural beauty than the overcrowded western side. The dead-end B837 from Drymen will take you halfway up the east bank, as far as you can get by car or bus (#309 from Balloch and Drymen runs to Balmaha every 2hr), while the West Highland Way sticks close to the shores for the entire length of the loch, beginning at the tiny lochside settlement of **BALMAHA**, which stands on the Highland Boundary Fault, the geological fault that separates the Highlands from the Lowlands. If you stand on the viewpoint above the pier, you can see the fault line clearly marked by a series of woody islands that form giant stepping-stones across the loch. Many of the loch's 37 **islands** are privately owned, and, rather quaintly, an old wooden mail-boat still delivers post to four of them. It's possible to join the **mail-boat cruise**, which is run by MacFarlane & Son from the jetty at Balmaha (May, June & Sept Mon, Thurs & Sat 11.30am returns 2pm; July & Aug Mon–Sat 11.30am returns 2pm; Oct–April Mon & Thurs 10.50am returns 12.50pm; £8; Ⓣ01360/870214, Ⓦwww.balmahaboatyard.co.uk). In summer the timetable allows a one-hour stop on Inchmurrin Island, the largest and most southerly of the islands inhabited by just ten permanent residents; if you're looking for an island to explore, however, a better bet is **Inchailloch**, the closest to Balmaha. Owned by Scottish Natural Heritage, it has a two-mile, signposted nature trail round the island. It's possible to row here yourself using a boat hired from MacFarlane & Son (from £10/hr), or you can use their on-demand ferry service (£4 return).

Beside the large car park is a **National Park Centre** (April–Sept daily 10am–5.30pm) for information on local forest walks, and you can **stay** at the well-run *Oak Tree Inn*, set back from the boatyard (Ⓣ01360/870357, Ⓦwww.oak-tree-inn.co.uk), with en-suite double rooms (④) and bunk-bed quads (③). It's also a convivial pub that serves **food** all day. **Camping** is available two miles north, on the lochside at Milarrochy Bay (Ⓣ01360/870236; March–Oct), or, a couple of miles or so further up the road, at *Cashel*, a lovely secluded Forestry Commission campsite (Ⓣ01360/870234, Ⓦwww.forestholidays.co.uk; March to mid-Jan).

The Trossachs

Often described as the Highlands in miniature, the **Trossachs** area boasts a magnificent diversity of scenery, with dramatic peaks and mysterious, forest-covered slopes that live up to all the images ever produced of Scotland's wild land. It is country ripe for stirring tales of brave kilted clansmen, a role fulfilled by Rob Roy Macgregor (see box, p.871), the seventeenth-century outlaw whose name seems to attach to every second waterfall, cave and barely discernible path. The Trossachs' high tourist profile was largely attributable in the early days to the novels of Sir Walter Scott, set in the area. Since then, neither the popularity nor beauty of the region have waned, and in high season the place is jam-packed with coaches full of tourists as well as walkers and mountain-bikers taking advantage of the easily accessed scenery. Autumn is a better time to come, when the hills are blanketed in rich, rusty colours and the crowds are thinner.

The **Trossachs Trundler** is a useful minibus service which loops round the main focal points in central Trossachs: **Callander**, **Loch Katrine** and **Aberfoyle**. The bus runs four times a day (9.50am–4.20pm; no service Wed)

Rob Roy

A member of the outlawed Macgregor clan, **Rob Roy** (meaning "Red Robert" in Gaelic) was born in 1671 in Glengyle, just north of Loch Katrine, and lived for some time as a respectable cattle-farmer and trader, supported by the powerful Duke of Montrose. In 1712, finding himself in a tight spot when a cattle deal fell through, Rob Roy absconded with £1000, some of it belonging to the duke. He took to the hills to live as a brigand, his feud with Montrose escalating after the duke repossessed Rob Roy's land and drove his wife from their house. He was present at the Battle of Sheriffmuir during the Jacobite uprising of 1715, ostensibly supporting the Jacobites but probably as an opportunist: the chaos would have made cattle-raiding easier. Eventually captured and sentenced to transportation, Rob Roy was pardoned and returned to **Balquhidder**, northeast of Glengyle, where he remained until his death in 1734.

Rob Roy's status as a local hero in the mould of Robin Hood should be tempered with the fact that he was without doubt a notorious bandit and blackmailer. His life has been much romanticized, from Sir Walter Scott's 1818 novel *Rob Roy* to the 1995 film starring Liam Neeson, although the tale does serve well to dramatize the clash between the doomed clan culture of the Gaelic-speaking Highlanders and the organized feudal culture of lowland Scots, which effectively ended with the defeat of the Jacobites at Culloden in 1746.

from late June to mid October; helpfully for walkers, it stops on demand and can also cope with two bikes and wheelchairs. The bus is timed to connect with sailings of the SS *Sir Walter Scott* on Loch Katrine (see p.872), and costs £5 for a day pass or £12 for two adults and four children (for further details call ⓣ01786/451200).

Hiking and biking in the Trossachs

Despite the steady flow of coach tours taking in the scenic highlights of the area, the Trossachs is ideal for exploring **on foot** or on a **mountain bike**. This is partly because the terrain is slightly more benign than the Highlands proper, but much is due to the excellent management of the **Queen Elizabeth Forest Park**, a huge chunk of the national park between Loch Lomond and Loch Lubnaig. The main visitor centre for the area, David Marshall Lodge, is just outside Aberfoyle (see p.872).

For **hill-walkers**, the prize peak is Ben Lomond (3192ft), best accessed from Rowardennan on Loch Lomond's east shore. Other highlights include Ben Venue (2370ft) and Ben A'an (1520ft) on the shores of Loch Katrine, as well as Ben Ledi (2857ft), just northwest of Callander, which all offer relatively straightforward but very rewarding climbs and, on clear days, stunning views. Walkers can also choose from any number of waymarked routes through the forests and along lochsides; pick up a map of these at the visitor centre.

The area is also a popular spot for **mountain biking**, with a number of useful rental shops, a network of forest paths and one of the more impressive stretches of the National Cycle Network cutting through the region from Loch Lomond to Killin. You can **rent** bikes from Wheels Cycling Centre (ⓣ01877/331100, ⓦwww.scottish-cycling.co.uk), next to *Trossachs Tryst* (see p.872) a mile and a half southwest of Callander, the best rental place in the area, with front- or full-suspension models available, as well as baby seats and children's cycles. Also well set up is Trossachs Cycles (ⓣ01877/382614; ⓦwww.trossachscycles.co.uk), at the *Trossachs Holiday Park* on the A81 two miles south of Aberfoyle, while Mounter Bikes (ⓣ01877/331052; ⓦwww.callandercyclehire.co.uk) is handily located in the centre of Callander (see p.872).

Aberfoyle

Each summer the sleepy little town of **ABERFOYLE**, twenty miles west of Stirling, dusts itself down for its annual influx of tourists. Though of little appeal itself, Aberfoyle's position in the heart of the Trossachs is ideal. From here, the A821 road to **Loch Katrine** winds its way into the Queen Elizabeth Forest, snaking up **Duke's Pass** (so called because it once belonged to the Duke of Montrose). You can walk or drive the short distance to the park's excellent **visitor centre** at David Marshall Lodge (Jan Sat & Sun 10am–4pm; Feb Thurs–Sun 10am–4pm; March–Dec daily 10am–4/6pm; car park £2), where you can pick up maps of the walks and cycle routes in the forest, get background information on the flora and fauna of the area, which includes roe deer and birds of prey, or settle into the café with its splendid views over the tree tops.

Loch Katrine

Heading down the northern side of the Duke's Pass you come first to **Loch Achray**, tucked under Ben A'an. At the head of the loch, a road leads the short distance through to the southern end of **Loch Katrine** at the foot of Ben Venue (2370ft). Here, an elegant Victorian passenger **steamer**, the SS *Sir Walter Scott*, has been plying the waters since 1900, chugging up to the wild country of Glengyle. It makes various cruises each day, but only the first (departing at 10.30am) stops off at Stronachlachar every day; on Wednesdays and weekends there's a second tip to Stronachlachar departing at 2.30pm (April–Oct daily; £8 return; ⓣ01877/376315, ⓦwww.lochkatrine.co.uk); the shorter 45min cruises don't make any stops (April–Oct daily; £7). A popular combination is to **rent a bike** from the Katrinewheels (ⓣ01877/376316) hut by the pier, take the steamer up to Stronachlachar, then cycle back by way of the road around the north side of the loch.

From Loch Katrine, the A821 heads due east past the tiny village of **Brig o'Turk**, where it's worth looking in on the *Byre Inn*, a tiny pub and restaurant set in an old stone barn with wooden pews and a welcoming open fire. If you fancy staying here, the historic *Burnt Inn House* (ⓣ01877/376212, ⓦwww.burntinnhouse.co.uk; ③) offers simple, farmhouse-style B&B.

Callander

CALLANDER, on the eastern edge of the Trossachs, sits on the banks of the River Teith at the southern end of the **Pass of Leny**, one of the key routes into the Highlands. Significantly larger than Aberfoyle, eleven miles west, it is a popular summer holiday base and suffers in high season for being on the main tourist trail from Stirling through to the west Highlands. There are no attractions as such in the town itself.

Callander's best central **accommodation** is at *Callander Meadows*, 24 Main St (ⓣ01877/330181, ⓦwww.callandermeadows.co.uk; ③), an attractive townhouse with three comfortable en-suite rooms and a decent restaurant. Alternatively, *Arden House* on Bracklinn Road (ⓣ01877/330235, ⓦwww.ardenhouse.org.uk; April–Oct; ⑤), is a grand Victorian guesthouse in its own gardens with good views and woodland walks from the back door, while *Trossachs Tryst*, Invertrossachs Road (ⓣ01877/331200, ⓦwww.trossachstryst.com), is a friendly, well-equipped and comfortable 32-bed hostel and activity centre, with self-catering dorms (£15) and family rooms. **Bike rental** is available at Wheels Cycling Centre (see p.871).

Callander has few **restaurants** worth recommending: *Callander Meadows* (see above; restaurant closed Mon & Tues) dishes up delicious, freshly cooked lunches and dinners. Also on the main drag, the *Ben Ledi Café* is one of a new breed of fish and chip shops trying to offer more discerning fare with a sustainable fish policy, daily specials and a varied menu. For good **pub food** try the convivial *Lade Inn* in Kilmahog, a mile west of Callander. For fresh sandwiches, decent coffee and other deli items head for *Deli Ecosse* on Ancaster Square.

Fife

The ancient Kingdom of **Fife** is a small area, barely fifty miles at its widest point, but one which has a definite identity, inextricably linked with the waters that surround it on three sides – the Tay to the north, the Forth to the south, and the cold North Sea to the east. Despite its small size, Fife encompasses several different regions, with a marked difference between the rural north and the semi-industrial south. Fishing still has a role, but ultimately it is to **St Andrews**, the home of the world-famous Royal and Ancient Golf Club, that most visitors are drawn. South of St Andrews, the tiny stone harbours of the **East Neuk** fishing villages are an appealing extension to any visit to this part of Fife.

Inland from St Andrews is the absorbing village of **Falkland** with its impressive ruined palace. To the **south**, the perfectly preserved town of **Culross** is the most obvious draw with its cobbled streets and collection of historic buildings.

St Andrews and the East Neuk

Confident, poised and well groomed, if a little snooty, **ST ANDREWS**, Scotland's oldest **university town** and a pilgrimage centre for **golfers** from all over the world, is situated on a wide bay on the northeastern coast of Fife. Of all Scotland's universities, St Andrews is the most often compared to Oxford or Cambridge, both for the dominance of gown over town, and for the intimate, collegiate feel of the place. In fact, the university attracts a significant proportion of English undergraduates, among them, famously, Prince William, who spent four years studying here.

According to legend, the town was founded, pretty much by accident, in the fourth century. **St Rule** – or Regulus – a custodian of the bones of St Andrew in Patras in southern Greece, had a vision in which an angel ordered him to carry five of the saint's bones to the western edge of the world, where he was to build a city in his honour. The conscientious courier set off, but was shipwrecked on the rocks close to the present harbour. Struggling ashore with his precious burden, he built a shrine to the saint on what subsequently became the site of the **cathedral**; St Andrew became Scotland's patron saint and the town its ecclesiastical capital.

From St Andrews, the attractive beaches and little fishing villages of the **East Neuk** (*neuk* is Scots for "corner") are within easy reach, although the area can also be approached from the Kirkcaldy side. Though golf and coastal walks are a shared characteristic, the East Neuk villages have few of the grand buildings and important bustle of St Andrews, with old cottages and merchants' houses huddling round stone-built harbours in scenes fallen upon with joy by artists and photographers.

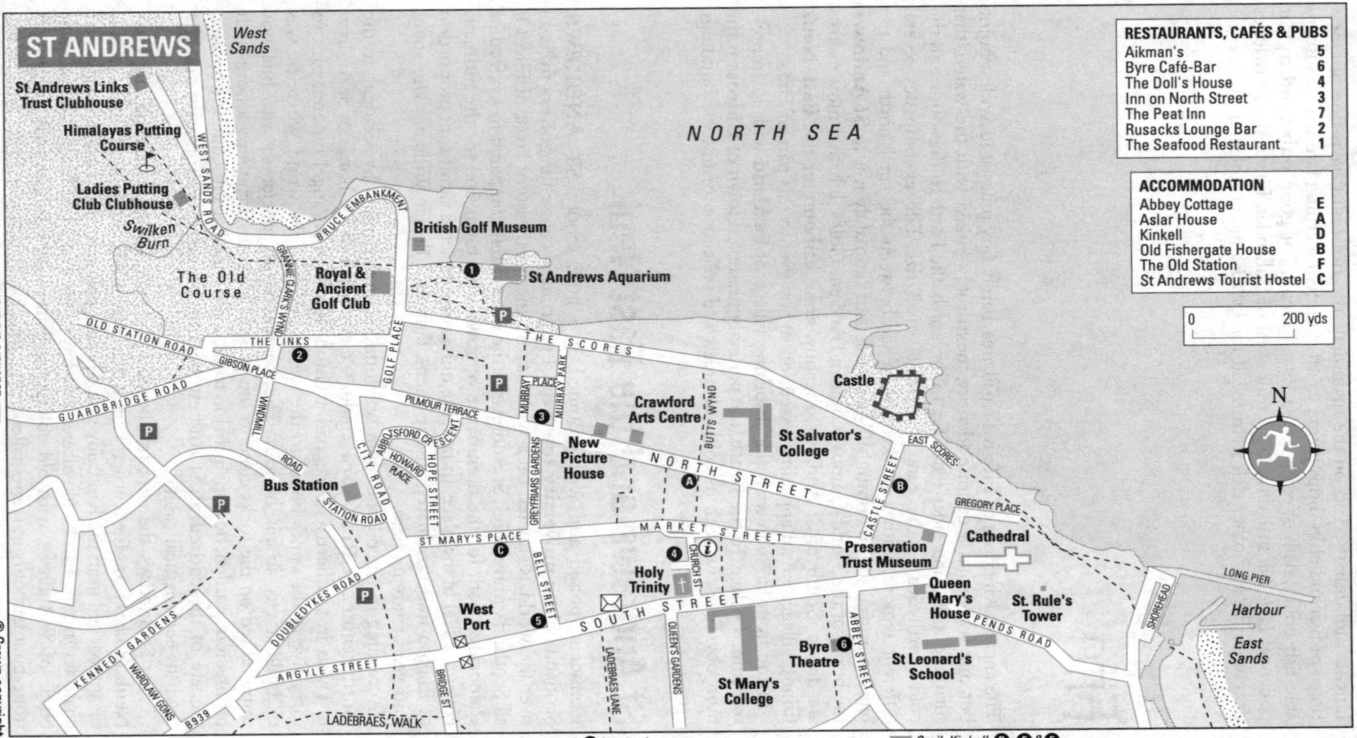

ST ANDREWS

RESTAURANTS, CAFÉS & PUBS

Aikman's	5
Byre Café-Bar	6
The Doll's House	4
Inn on North Street	3
The Peat Inn	7
Rusacks Lounge Bar	2
The Seafood Restaurant	1

ACCOMMODATION

Abbey Cottage	E
Aslar House	A
Kinkell	D
Old Fishergate House	B
The Old Station	F
St Andrews Tourist Hostel	C

0 200 yds

NORTH SEA
West Sands
East Sands
Harbour
LONG PIER
St Andrews Links Trust Clubhouse
Himalayas Putting Course
Ladies Putting Club Clubhouse
Swilken Burn
The Old Course
Royal & Ancient Golf Club
British Golf Museum
St Andrews Aquarium
Castle
Crawford Arts Centre
St Salvator's College
New Picture House
Bus Station
Preservation Trust Museum
Cathedral
Queen Mary's House
St. Rule's Tower
Holy Trinity
West Port
Byre Theatre
St Mary's College
St Leonard's School
WEST SANDS ROAD
BRUCE EMBANKMENT
GRANNIE CLARK'S WYND
THE LINKS
OLD STATION ROAD
GIBSON PLACE
GUARDBRIDGE ROAD
GOLF PLACE
THE SCORES
MURRAY PLACE
MURRAY PARK
PILMOUR TERRACE
WINDMILL ROAD
ABBOTSFORD CRESCENT
HOWARD PLACE
HOPE STREET
CITY ROAD
STATION ROAD
GREYFRIARS GARDENS
BUTTS WYND
NORTH STREET
EAST SCORES
CASTLE STREET
GREGORY PLACE
MARKET STREET
ST MARY'S PLACE
CHURCH ST
BELL STREET
SOUTH STREET
SHOREHEAD
PENDS ROAD
DOUBLEDYKES ROAD
KENNEDY GARDENS
WARDLAW GDNS
B939
ARGYLE STREET
BRIDGE ST
LADEBRAES LANE
QUEEN'S GARDENS
ABBEY STREET
LADEBRAES WALK

Leuchars & Dundee
Botanic Gardens & 7 (6 miles)
Crail, Kinkell, D, E & F

Arrival, information and getting around

St Andrews' nearest **train station** (on the Edinburgh–Dundee line) is five miles northwest at Leuchars, across the River Eden, from where regular buses make the fifteen-minute trip into town. When you buy your rail ticket to Leuchars, ask for a St Andrews rail-bus ticket which includes the bus fare. The **tourist office**, 70 Market St (April–June Mon–Sat 9.30am–5.30pm, Sun 11am–4pm; July & Aug Mon–Sat 9.30am–7pm, Sun 10am–5pm; Sept & Oct Mon–Sat 9.30am–6pm, Sun 11am–4pm; Nov–March Mon–Sat 9.30am–5pm; ⓣ01334/472021), holds comprehensive information about St Andrews and northeast Fife.

An open-top hop-on/hop-off **bus tour** (July & Aug daily 11am–3pm; £6) takes a one-hour spin around the main sights, although the town is compact enough to explore thoroughly on foot. Offering a bracing introduction to the importance of **golf** to the town, St Andrews Links Trust runs walking tours of the Old Course, starting from the Golf Shop just behind the 18th green (June Sat & Sun 11am–4pm; July & Aug daily 11am–4pm; ⓣ01334/466666, ⓦwww.standrews.org.uk; £2.50).

The town's fiendish **parking** system requires vouchers (Mon–Sat 9am–5pm; 70p/hr) which you can get from the tourist office and some local shops – you may find it easier leaving your car in one of the free car parks fringing the centre. Spokes, at 37 South St (ⓣ01334/477835), offers **bike rental**.

Accommodation

With St Andrews' wide-ranging appeal to visitors, there's no shortage of **accommodation** both in town and around, although average prices in all categories vie with Edinburgh's as the highest in Scotland. There are plenty of **guesthouses**, though rooms often get booked up in the summer, when you should definitely book in advance.

Abbey Cottage Abbey Walk ⓣ01334/473727, ⓦwww.abbeycottage.co.uk. Inexpensive B&B in a cottage with a pretty garden, south of the cathedral, near the harbour. ③

Aslar House 120 North St ⓣ01334/473460, ⓦwww.aslar.com. A smart guesthouse in a three-storey townhouse with an unusual round tower at the back. ⑤

Kinkell By Brownhills ⓣ01334/472003, ⓦwww.kinkell.com. Countryside B&B in a lovely family farmhouse near the beach, about two miles south of town off the A917. ⑤

Old Fishergate House North Castle St ⓣ01334/470874, ⓦwww.oldfishergatehouse.co.uk. Seventeenth-century townhouse in the oldest part of St Andews, with two spacious twin rooms full of period features. ⑤

The Old Station Stravithie Bridge ⓣ01334/880505, ⓦwww.theoldstation.co.uk. A couple of miles south of town on the B9131 to Anstruther, with tasteful rooms in the main house (based around a former station waiting-room). Alternatively, you can stay in the imaginatively designed suite in an old railway carriage parked alongside. Main house ⑤, carriage ⑦

St Andrews Tourist Hostel St Mary's Place ⓣ01334/479911, ⓦwww.hostelsaccommodation.com. Superbly located backpacker hostel in a pleasant converted townhouse above *The Grill House* restaurant, with plenty of dorm beds (£16), but no doubles.

The Town

On the three main thoroughfares, **North Street**, **Market Street** and **South Street** – which run west to east towards the ruined Gothic cathedral – are several of the original university buildings from the fifteenth century. Narrow alleys connect the cobbled streets, attic windows and gable ends shape the rooftops, and here and there you'll see the old wooden doors with heavy knockers and black iron hinges. Housed in a picturesque sixteenth-century cottage with a low wooden door on North Street near the cathedral, the

St Andrews Preservation Trust Museum and Garden (June–Sept daily 2–5pm; at other times of year open at same time when exhibitions run; Ⓦwww.standrewspreservationtrust.co.uk) presents an intimate picture of the town's history and glamorous golf connections.

St Andrews Cathedral and Castle

The ruin of the great **cathedral** (visitor centre April–Sept daily 9.30am–5.30pm; Oct–March 9.30am–4.30pm; £4, joint ticket with castle £7; grounds year-round 9am–5.30pm; free; HS), at the east end of town, gives only an idea of the importance of what was once Scotland's largest cathedral. Founded in 1160, the cathedral was plundered and left to ruin during the Reformation by supporters of John Knox, fresh from a rousing meeting.

In front of the cathedral window a slab is all that remains of the high altar, where the relics of St Andrew were once enshrined. Previously, it is believed that they were kept in **St Rule's Tower**, the austere Romanesque monolith next to the cathedral, which was built as part of an abbey in 1130. From the top

Golf in St Andrews

St Andrews **Royal and Ancient Golf Club** (or "R&A") has been the international governing body for golf since 1754, when a meeting of 22 of the local gentry founded the Society of St Andrews Golfers, being "admirers of the ancient and healthful exercise of golf". The game itself has been played here since the fifteenth century. Those early days were instrumental in establishing Scotland as the home of golf, for the rules were distinguished from those of the French game by the fact that participants had to manoeuvre the ball into a hole, rather than hit an above-ground target. It was not without its opponents, however – particularly James II who, in 1457, banned his subjects from playing since it was distracting them from archery practice.

The approach to St Andrews from the west runs adjacent to the famous **Old Course**, one of seven courses in the immediate vicinity of the town. The R&A's strictly private **clubhouse**, a stolid, square building dating from 1854, is at the eastern end of the Old Course overlooking both the 18th green and the long strand of the West Sands. The British Open Championship was first held here in 1873, having been inaugurated in 1860 at Prestwick in Ayrshire, and since then it has been held at St Andrews regularly, pulling in enormous crowds. Pictures of golfing greats from Tom Morris to Tiger Woods, along with clubs and a variety of memorabilia donated by famous players, are displayed in the admirable **British Golf Museum** on Bruce Embankment, along the waterfront below the clubhouse (April–Oct Mon–Sat 9.30am–5.30pm, Sun 10am–5pm; Nov–March Mon–Sat 10am–4.30pm; £5.25).

Where to play

It is possible to **play** any of the town's courses, ranging from the nine-hole Balgove course (from £8 per round) to the venerated Old Course itself – though for the latter you'll need a valid handicap certificate and must enter a daily ballot for tee times; if you're successful the green fees are £130 in summer. All this and more is explained at the clubhouse of the **St Andrews Links Trust** (Ⓦwww.standrews.org.uk), the organization which looks after all the courses in town, located alongside the fairway of the first hole of the Old Course. Arguably the best golfing experience in St Andrews, even if you can't tell a birdie from a bogey, is the **Himalayas** (April–Sept Mon–Sat 10.30am–6.30pm, Sun noon–6.30pm; £1.50), a fantastically lumpy eighteen-hole putting course in an ideal setting next to the Old Course and the sea. Officially the Ladies Putting Club, founded in 1867, with its own clubhouse, it has grass as perfectly manicured as the championship course, and you can have all the thrill of sinking a six-footer in golf's most famous location, at a bargain price.

of the tower (a climb of 157 steps) there's a good view of the town and surroundings, and of the remains of the monastic buildings that made up the priory. Around the entire complex is a sturdy wall dating from the sixteenth century, over half a mile long and with three gateways.

Not far north of the cathedral, the rocky coastline curves inland to the ruined **castle** (same hours as cathedral; £5, joint ticket with cathedral £7; HS), with a drop to the sea on two sides and a moat on its inland side. Founded around 1200 and extended over the centuries, it was built as part of the Palace of the Bishops and Archbishops of St Andrews. There's not a great deal left of the castle, since it fell into ruin in the seventeenth century, and most of what can be seen dates from the sixteenth century, apart from the fourteenth-century Fore Tower.

The beaches

St Andrews has two great **beaches**: the West Sands, which stretch for two miles from just below the R&A Clubhouse, and the shorter, more compact, East Sands that curve round from the harbour beyond the cathedral. The West Sands are best known from the opening sequences of the Oscar-winning film *Chariots of Fire*. The blustery winds, which are the scourge of golfers and walkers alike, do at least make the beach a great place to **fly kites**.

Eating, drinking and entertainment

The town has a number of blow-out **restaurants**, but given the local student population, there's plenty of cheaper establishments as well as lots of good **pubs**. There's also a healthy cultural scene: the **Byre Theatre** (Ⓣ01334/475000, Ⓦwww.byretheatre.com) occupies a stylish modern building on Abbey Street, with a pleasant café/bistro (see below). There's also a small **cinema**, the New Picture House (Ⓣ01334/473509, Ⓦwww.nphcinema.co.uk).

Restaurants and cafés

Byre Café-Bar Abbey St Ⓦwww.byretheatre.com. One of the nicer spots in town for a leisurely coffee or light meal; a good spot for eating with kids. Moderate.

The Doll's House 3 Church Square Ⓣ01334/477422, Ⓦwww.dolls-house.co.uk. Stylish modern dishes based around top Scottish produce, with a continental feel to the outdoor tables. Moderate–expensive.

The Peat Inn Cupar, six miles southwest of town Ⓣ01334/840206, Ⓦwww.thepeatinn.co.uk. With a reputation as one of Scotland's gourmet hot spots for the past 25 years, its high standards of cuisine and hospitality have been retained by chef-proprietors Geoffrey and Katherine Smeddle. Fine dining featuring top local produce is served in an intimate dining room, with menus ranging from a three-course set lunch at £16 to a six-course tasting menu for £48. Also has eight plush, if pricey, suites attached (8). Closed Sun & Mon. Very expensive.

The Seafood Restaurant The Scores Ⓣ01334/479475, Ⓦwww.theseafoodrestaurant.com. This venue has as much wow-factor as its fish-dominated menu: an amazing location in a custom-built glass building on the beach between the Aquarium and the Old Course. Expensive.

Pubs and bars

Aikman's 32 Bell St, Ⓦwww.cellarbar.co.uk. Long-established live music bar also serving real ale and home-made grub.

Inn on North Street 127 North St. Tends to attract slightly older students, but houses the popular *Lizard* basement nightclub on Fri & Sat.

Rusacks Lounge Bar 16 Pilmour Links. Hotel bar with the best views of the Old Course; settle into one of their comfy chairs and watch golfers through huge windows as you sip pricey drinks.

The East Neuk

Extending south of St Andrews as far as Largo Bay, the **East Neuk** is famous for its series of quaint fishing villages replete with crow-stepped gables and red

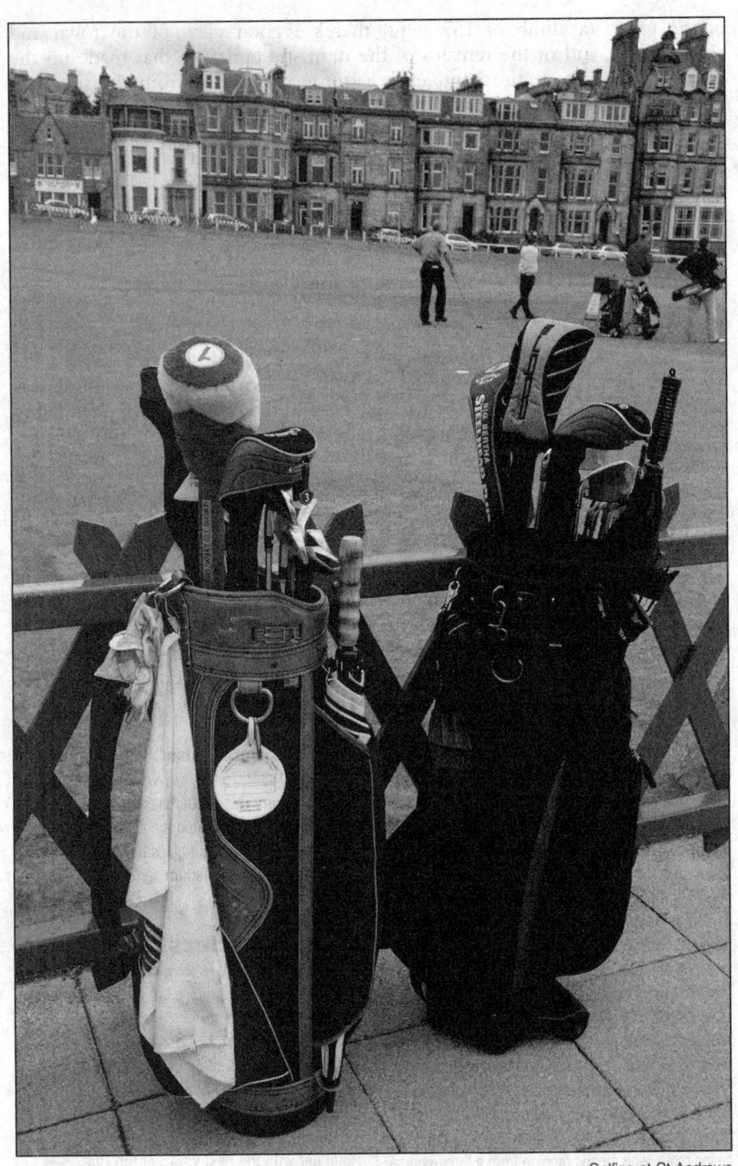

▲ Golfing at St Andrews

pan-tiled roofs, the Flemish influence in the architecture indicating a history of strong trading links with the Low Countries. The area is dotted with windy **golf courses**, and there are also plenty of bracing coastal paths, including the waymarked **Fife Coastal Path**: tracing the shoreline between St Andrews and the Forth Rail Bridge, it's at its most scenic in the East Neuk stretch. **Bus** #95 runs from Leven around the coast to St Andrews.

Crail

CRAIL is the archetypally charming East Neuk fishing village, its maze of rough cobbled streets leading steeply down to a tiny stone-built harbour surrounded by piles of lobster creels, and with fishermen's cottages tucked into every nook and cranny in the cliff. Though often populated by artists at their easels and camera-toting tourists, it is still a working harbour, and if the boats have been out you can buy fresh lobster and crab cooked to order from a small wooden shack on the harbour edge (see below). The **tourist office** is at the **Crail Museum and Heritage Centre**, 62 Marketgate (April Sat 10am–5pm, Sun noon–5pm; May–Sept Mon–Sat 10am–5pm, Sun noon–5pm; free), where you can trace the history of the town. The **Crail Pottery**, 75 Nethergate (Mon–Fri 9am–5pm, Sat & Sun 10am–5pm), is worth a visit for its wide range of locally made pottery.

The best places to sit down and **eat** are at *Mrs Riley's* lobster and crab shack at the harbour (mid-April to early Oct Tues–Sun noon–4pm), or at *Crail Harbour Gallery and Tearoom* (daily 11am–5pm), tucked into a wee cottage on the way down to the harbour: it serves fresh coffee and toasted panini and has a terrace overlooking the Isle of May.

Anstruther and around

ANSTRUTHER is the largest of the East Neuk fishing harbours, but it too has an attractively old-fashioned air and no shortage of character in its houses and narrow streets. It's home to the wonderfully unpretentious **Scottish Fisheries Museum** (April–Oct Mon–Sat 10am–5.30pm, Sun 11am–5pm; Nov–March Mon–Sat 10am–4.30pm, Sun noon–4.30pm; £5). Set in an atmospheric complex of sixteenth- to nineteenth-century buildings with timber ceilings and wooden floors, it chronicles the history of the Scottish fishing and whaling industries with ingenious displays, including a whole series of exquisite ships' models built on site by a resident model-maker. Anstruther's helpful **tourist office** (April–Sept Mon–Sat 10am–5pm, Sun 11am–4pm; Oct Mon–Sat 10am–4pm, Sun noon–4pm; ⓣ01333/311073) is next to the museum.

Located on the rugged **Isle of May**, several miles offshore from Anstruther, is a lighthouse erected in 1816 by Robert Louis Stevenson's grandfather, as well as the remains of Scotland's first lighthouse, built in 1636. The island is now a nature reserve and bird sanctuary, and can be reached by boat from Anstruther (May–Sept 1 daily; May & June no sailing on Tues; £16; ⓣ01333/310103, ⓦwww.isleofmayferry.com). Check in advance for departure times, as crossings vary according to weather and tide, and allow between four and five hours for a round trip.

Tucked in beside the museum in one of the village's oldest buildings, once a cooperage and smokehouse, is a fantastic fish **restaurant**, *The Cellar*, at 24 East Green (ⓣ01333/310378; booking recommended). For decent fish and chips, head for the *Anstruther Fish Bar*, at 44 The Shore, a regular award-winner.

Central Fife

The main A92 road cuts right through **Central Fife**, ultimately connecting the Forth Road Bridge on the southern coast of Fife with the Tay Road Bridge on the northern coast. The main settlement of this inland region is **Glenrothes**, a new town created after World War II in old coal-mining territory. Generally the scenery in this part of the county is pleasant rather than startling, though it's worth making a detour to **Falkland** and its magnificent ruined palace.

Falkland

The **Howe of Fife**, north of Glenrothes, is a low-lying stretch of ground (or "howe") at the foot of the twin peaks of the heather-swathed **Lomond Hills** – West Lomond (1696ft) and East Lomond (1378ft). Nestling in the lower slopes of East Lomond, the narrow streets of **FALKLAND** are lined with fine and well-preserved seventeenth- and eighteenth-century buildings. The village grew up around **Falkland Palace** (March–Oct Mon–Sat 10am–5pm, Sun 1–5pm; £10, gardens only £5; NTS), which stands on the site of an earlier castle, home to the Macduffs, the earls of Fife. James IV began the construction of the present palace in 1500; it was completed and embellished by James V, and became a favoured country retreat for the royal court. The palace was completely restored by the third Marquess of Bute, and today it is a stunning piece of architecture, complete with parapets, mullioned windows, round towers and massive walls. Free audioguides lead you round a cross section of public and private rooms in the south and east wings. Outside, the **gardens** are also worth a look, their well-stocked herbaceous borders lining a pristine lawn. Don't miss the high walls of the oldest real (or Royal) tennis court in Britain – built in 1539 for James V and still used.

The concentration of charming old cottages and historic buildings in the heart of Falkland also make it a particularly pleasant place to wander around. The *Covenanter Hotel* (Ⓣ01337/857224, Ⓦwww.covenanterhotel.co.uk; ❸ in separate cottage, ❹ in hotel) is a comfortable traditional **inn** with a great pub; attached to the hotel, a small restaurant serves pizzas cooked in a wood-fired oven. Not far out of the village on the A912 there's a great little farm **shop** and **café** (Ⓣ01337/857749, Ⓦwww.pillars.co.uk; daily 10am–6pm), *Pillars of Hercules Organic Farm*.

Southern Fife

Although the coast of **southern Fife** is predominantly industrial – with everything from cottage industries to the refitting of nuclear submarines – mercifully only a small part has been blighted by insensitive development. Thanks to its proximity to the early coal mines, the charming village of **Culross** was once a lively port which enjoyed a thriving trade with Holland, the Dutch influence obvious in its lovely gabled houses. It was from nearby **Dunfermline** that Queen Margaret ousted the Celtic Church from Scotland in the eleventh century; her son, David I, founded an abbey here in the twelfth century. Southern Fife is linked to Edinburgh by the two **Forth bridges**, the red-painted girders of the Rail Bridge representing one of Britain's great engineering spectacles.

Culross

CULROSS (pronounced "Coorus") is one of Scotland's most picturesque settlements, owing to the work of the National Trust for Scotland, which has been renovating its whitewashed, pan-tiled buildings since 1932. For an excellent introduction to the burgh's history, head to the **National Trust Visitor Centre** (April, May & Sept Thurs–Mon noon–5pm; June–Aug daily noon–5pm; Oct Thurs–Mon noon–4pm; joint ticket for Town House, Palace and Study £8; NTS), located in the **Town House** facing Sandhaven, where goods were once unloaded from ships. The most impressive building in the village is the nearby ochre-coloured **Culross Palace** (same hours), built by wealthy coal merchant George Bruce in the late sixteenth century; it's not a palace at all but a grand and impressive house, with lots of small rooms and connecting passageways. Inside, well-informed staff point out the wonderful painted ceilings, pine panelling, antique furniture and curios; outside, dormer windows and crow-stepped gables dominate the walled court in which the house stands.

The charm of Culross is evident simply by wandering through its narrow streets looking for old inscriptions above windows or investigating crooked passageways with names such as "Wee Causeway" and "Stinking Wynd". Leading uphill from the Town House, a cobbled alleyway known as **Back Causeway** leads up to the **Study** (same hours as visitor centre), a restored house that takes its name from the small room at the top of the corbelled projecting tower, reached by a turnpike stair. Further up the hill from the Study lie the remains of **Culross Abbey**, founded by Cistercian monks on land given to the church in 1217 by the Earl of Fife.

Dunfermline

Scotland's capital until the Union of the Crowns in 1603, **DUNFERMLINE** lies inland seven miles east of Culross, north of the Forth bridges. The oldest part of **Dunfermline Abbey** (April–Sept daily 9.30am–5.30pm; Oct–March Mon–Wed & Sat 9.30am–4.30pm, Thurs 9.30am–12.30pm, Sun 2–4.30pm Ⓦ www.dunfermlineabbey.co.uk; £3.50; HS) is attributable to Queen Margaret, who began building a Benedictine priory in 1072, the remains of which can still be seen beneath the nave of the present church; her son, **David I**, raised the priory to the rank of abbey in the following century. In 1303, during the first of the **Wars of Independence**, the English king Edward I occupied the palace and ordered the destruction of most of the monastery buildings. **Robert the Bruce** helped rebuild the abbey, and when he died of leprosy 25 years later he was buried here, although his body went undiscovered until building began on a new parish church in 1821. Inside, the stained glass is impressive, and the columns are artfully carved into chevrons, spirals and arrowheads.

The Forth Bridges

The highlight of Fife's **south coast** is one of Scotland's largest man-made structures, the impressive Forth Rail Bridge, which joins Fife at **NORTH QUEENSFERRY**. Until the opening of the road bridge, this small fishing village was the northern landing point of the ferry from South Queensferry (see p.797), but today everything in the village is quite literally overshadowed by the two great bridges, each about a mile and a half in length, which traverse the Firth of Forth at its narrowest point.

The cantilevered **Forth Rail Bridge**, built from 1883 to 1890 by Sir John Fowler and Benjamin Baker, ranks among the supreme achievements of Victorian engineering, with some 50,000 tons of steel used in the construction of a design that manages to express grace as well as might. The only way to cross the rail bridge is aboard a train heading to or from Edinburgh, though inevitably this doesn't allow much of a perspective of the spectacle itself. For the best **panorama** of it, make use of the pedestrian and cycle lane on the east side of the road bridge.

Derived from American models, the suspension format chosen for the **Forth Road Bridge** alongside makes an interesting modern complement to the older structure. Erected between 1958 and 1964, it finally killed off the 900-year-old ferry, and now attracts such a heavy volume of traffic that a second road crossing is being considered.

Tucked beneath the mighty rail bridge is **Deep Sea World** (Mon–Fri 10am–5pm, Sat & Sun 10am–6pm; £10; ⓣ01383/411880, ⓦwww.deepseaworld.com), one of Scotland's most popular family attractions. Full of weird and wonderful creatures from sea horses to piranhas, the highlight is a huge aquarium that boasts the world's largest underwater viewing tunnel, through which you glide on a moving walkway while sharks, conger eels and all manner of fish from the deep swim nonchalantly past.

Perthshire

Genteel, attractive **Perthshire** is, in many ways, the epitome of well-groomed rural Scotland. An area of gentle glens, mature woodland, rushing rivers and peaceful lochs, it's the long-established domain of Scotland's well-to-do country set. First settled over eight thousand years ago, it was ruled by the Romans and then the Picts before Celtic missionaries established themselves.

The ancient town of Perth occupies a strategic position at the mouth of the River Tay; salmon, wool and, by the sixteenth century, whisky, were exported, while a major import was Bordeaux claret. At nearby **Scone**, Kenneth MacAlpine established the capital of the kingdom of the Scots and the Picts in 846. When this settlement was washed away by floods in 1210, William the Lion founded Perth as a royal burgh.

North and west of Perth, **Highland Perthshire** is made up of gorgeous and mighty woodlands, particularly along the banks of the River Tay. The area is dotted with neat, confident towns and villages like **Dunkeld** and **Birnam**, with its mature trees and lovely ruined cathedral, and **Aberfeldy** set deep amongst

Outdoor activities in Perthshire

To many, Perthshire is a celebration of the great outdoors, with **activities** ranging from gentle strolls through ancient oak forests to white-knuckle rides down frothing waterfalls. The variety of landscapes and relative accessibility from the central belt has led to a significant number of **outdoor operators** being based in the area: the tourist board's **Activity Line** (ⓣ01577/861186, ⓦwww.adventureperthshire.co.uk) can give advice and contacts for over thirty companies who comply with the Adventure Perthshire Operators' Charter. For canyoning, cliff-jumping and sphere-ing (which involves tumbling down a hillside inside a giant plastic ball), contact adrenalin junkies Nae Limits (ⓣ01796/482600, ⓦwww.naelimits.co.uk), based in Dunkeld and Ballinluig. For rafting on larger craft through the best rapids on the Tay at Grandtully, try Splash (ⓣ01887/829706, ⓦwww.rafting.co.uk) or Freespirits (ⓣ01887/840400, ⓦwww.freespirits-online.co.uk), both based in or near Aberfeldy. Also in Aberfeldy is the National Kayak School (ⓦwww.nationalkayakschool.com), and the rather more sedate Highland Adventure Safaris (ⓣ01887/820071, ⓦwww.highlandadventuresafaris.co.uk), which offers an inspiring introduction to wild Scotland in which you're taken by four-wheel-drive vehicle to search for golden eagle eyries, stags and pine martens.

farmland east of Loch Tay. Further north, the countryside becomes more sparsely populated and spectacular, with some wonderful walking country, especially around **Pitlochry**, **Blair Atholl** and the wild expanses of **Rannoch Moor** to the west.

Perth and around

Surrounded by fertile agricultural land and beautiful scenery, the bustling market town of **PERTH** was Scotland's capital in the fifteenth century. The town expanded in the eighteenth and has prospered ever since; today the whisky and insurance trades employ significant numbers, and Perth remains an important town.

The City

Two large areas of green parkland, known as the North and South Inch, flank the **centre**; the city's main shopping areas are **High Street** and **South Street**, as well as St John's shopping centre on King Edward Street. Perth is at its most attractive along **Tay Street**, with a succession of grander buildings along one side and the attractively landscaped riverside embankment on the other.

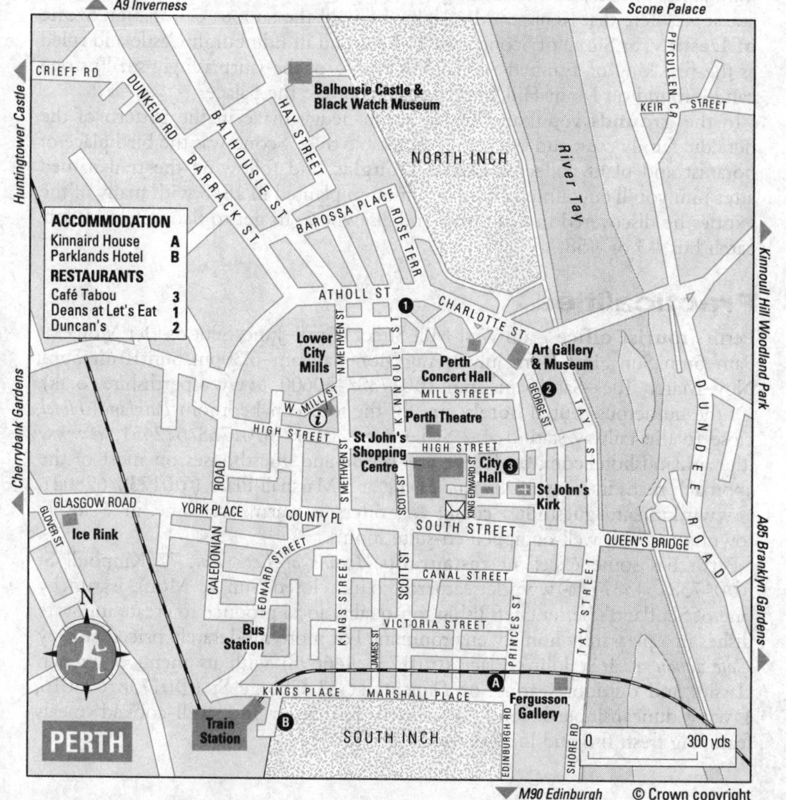

On the corner of Tay Street and Marshall Place, Perth's highlight is the **Fergusson Gallery** (Mon–Sat 10am–5pm, plus Sun 1–4.30pm May–Aug; free), located in a striking round Victorian sandstone water tower, and home to an extensive collection of work by J.D. Fergusson, foremost artist of the Scottish Colourist movement (see p.842). He was greatly influenced by Impressionist and Post-Impressionist artists, creating a distinctive approach which marries both movements' freedom of style with bold use of colour and lighting – shown, for example, in his portrait of Elizabeth Dryden entitled *The Hat with the Pink Scarf*. As well as oils, the collection includes sketches, notebooks and sculpture: among the latter, look out for *Eastre: Hymn to the Sun*, an exotic, radiant, and almost sexy brass head dating from 1924.

Scone Palace

Just a couple of miles north of Perth on the A93, **Scone Palace** (pronounced "skoon"; April–Oct daily 9.30am–5.30pm; £7.50, grounds only £4; Ⓦwww.scone-palace.co.uk) is one of Scotland's finest historical country homes. Owned and occupied by the Earl and Countess of Mansfield, the two-storey building on the eastern side of the Tay is stately but not overpowering, far more a home than an untouchable monument. The rooms, although full of priceless antiques and lavish furnishings, feel lived-in and used.

The abbey that stood here in the sixteenth century was where all Scottish kings until James IV were crowned. Long before that, Scone was the capital of Pictavia, and it was here that Kenneth MacAlpine brought the famous Coronation **Stone of Destiny**, or Stone of Scone, now to be found in Edinburgh Castle and ruled as the first king of a united Scotland. A replica of the (surprisingly small) stone can be found on Moot Hill, immediately opposite the palace.

In the **grounds** you'll also find a beech-hedge maze in the pattern of the heraldic family crest and avenues of venerable trees. Scone was the birthplace of botanist and plant collector **David Douglas**, and following the trail named after him you'll encounter a fragrant pinetum planted in 1848 with many of the exotics he discovered in California and elsewhere. To get to Scone from Perth, catch bus #3 or #58.

Practicalities

Perth's **tourist office** is on West Mill Street (April–June, Sept & Oct Mon–Sat 9am–5pm, Sun 11am–4pm; July & Aug Mon–Sat 9am–6.30pm, Sun 10am–5pm; Nov–March Tues–Sat 10am–4pm; Ⓣ01738/450600, Ⓦwww.perthshire.co.uk). Of the numerous central **hotels**, aim for the fourteen-bedroom *Parklands Hotel*, close to the railway station at 2 St Leonards Bank (Ⓣ01738/622451, Ⓦwww.theparklandshotel.com; ❻). There are **B&Bs** and guesthouses on most of the approach roads into town; *Kinnaird House*, at 5 Marshall Place (Ⓣ01738/628021, Ⓦwww.kinnaird-guesthouse.co.uk; ❹), offers a warm welcome in a lovely townhouse with well-equipped en-suite rooms.

Perth has some excellent **restaurants**. *Deans at Let's Eat*, 77 Kinnoull St (Ⓣ01738/643377, Ⓦwww.letseatperth.co.uk; closed Sun & Mon), is run by one of Scotland's better chefs using top-quality local produce to create innovate dishes in a pleasantly homely environment. For more moderately priced fare try *Café Tabou* at 4 St John's Place (Ⓣ01738/446698) with its menu of French classics and outdoor seating, or *Duncan's* at 33 George St (Ⓣ01738/626016, Ⓦwww.duncansinperth.com), a relaxed bistro serving well-cooked meals featuring fresh fish and local game.

Strath Tay to Loch Tay

Due north of Perth, both the railway and main A9 trunk road speed through some of Perthshire's most attractive countryside before heading into the bleaker Highlands. Perthshire has been dubbed "**Big Tree Country**" in recognition of its magnificent woodland, much of which is found around the valley – or "strath" – of the River Tay, as it heads towards the sea from attractive **Loch Tay**. On the eastern side of the loch, the Tay calmly glides past the attractive country town of **Aberfeldy**. The loch itself, meanwhile, is set up among the high Breadalbane mountains, which include the striking peak of **Ben Lawers**, Perthshire's highest, and the hills that enclose the long, enchanting **Glen Lyon**.

Dunkeld and Birnam

Twelve miles north of Perth on the A9, **DUNKELD** was proclaimed Scotland's ecclesiastical capital by Kenneth MacAlpine in 850. The town is one of the area's most pleasant communities, with handsome whitewashed houses, appealing arts and crafts shops and a charming cathedral. The **tourist office** is at The Cross in the town centre (April–June, Sept & Oct Mon–Sat 10am–4.30pm, Sun 10.30am–3.30pm; July & Aug Mon–Sat 9.30am–6.30pm, Sun 10am–4pm; ⓣ01350/727688). Dunkeld's partly ruined **cathedral** (daily: May–Sept 9.30am–6.30pm; Oct–April 9.30am–4pm; ⓦwww.dunkeldcathedral.org.uk; free) is on the northern side of town, in an idyllic setting amid lawns and trees on the east bank of the Tay. The present structure consists of the fourteenth-century choir and the fifteenth-century nave; the choir, restored in 1600 (and several times since), now serves as the parish church, while the nave remains roofless apart from the clocktower.

Dunkeld is linked to its sister community, **BIRNAM**, by Thomas Telford's seven-arched bridge of 1809. This little village has a place in history thanks to Shakespeare, for it was on Dunsinane Hill, to the southeast of the village, that Macbeth declared: "I will not be afraid of death and bane/Till Birnam Forest come to Dunsinane", only to be told later by a messenger "I look'd toward Birnam, and anon me thought/The Wood began to move. . .".

The **Birnam Oak**, a gnarly old character propped up by crutches on the waymarked riverside walk, is inevitably claimed to be a survivor of the infamous mobile forest. Several centuries after Shakespeare, another literary personality, Beatrix Potter, drew inspiration from the area: a Potter-themed exhibition and garden, aimed at both children and adults, can be found on the main road in the impressive barrel-fronted **Birnam Institute** (daily 10am–5pm; ⓦwww.birnaminstitute.com; free), a busy, modern theatre, arts and community centre.

Practicalities

There are several large **hotels** in Dunkeld and Birnam, such as the *Dunkeld House Hilton* (ⓣ01350/727771, ⓦwww.hilton.co.uk/dunkeld; ❽ including dinner), a vast country-estate house on the banks of the Tay to the north of Dunkeld, which incorporates a spa, swimming pool and excellent outdoor-pursuits facilities. Much less grand, but full of personality, is the central *Taybank Hotel*, Tay Terrace (ⓣ01350/727340, ⓦwww.taybank.com; ❷), a real beacon for music fans who come for the regular live sessions in the convivial bar; the rooms are simple and inexpensive, and the rate includes a continental breakfast. Alternatively, there's the pleasant *Waterbury Guesthouse* (ⓣ01350/727324, ⓦwww.waterbury-guesthouse.co.uk; ❹) on Murthly Terrace in Birnam. For

food, try the decent bar meals at the *Taybank* (the stovies are particularly filling); during the day the *Foyer Café* in the Birnam Institute (see above) serves coffee, cakes and light meals, or you can pick up delicious snacks and sandwiches at the Robert Menzies deli in Dunkeld.

Around Dunkeld

Dunkeld and Birnam are surrounded by some lovely countryside: a mile and a half from Birnam is **The Hermitage**, set in a grandly wooded gorge of the plunging River Braan. Here you'll find a pretty eighteenth-century folly, known as Ossian's Hall, which neatly frames a dramatic waterfall. Nearby, you can see a Douglas fir, claimed to be the tallest tree in Britain. Two miles east of Dunkeld, the **Loch of the Lowes** is a nature reserve that offers a rare chance to see breeding ospreys, among other wildfowl; its **visitor centre** (April–Sept 10am–5pm; ⓣ01350/727337; £3) has video relay screens and will point you in the direction of the best vantage points.

Aberfeldy and around

From Dunkeld the A9 runs north alongside the Tay for eight miles to Ballinluig, and the turn-off along the A827 to **ABERFELDY**. A generally prosperous settlement of large stone houses and 4WDs, Aberfeldy acts as a service centre for the wider Loch Tay area, with an enthusiastic **tourist office** at The Square (April–June, Sept & Oct Mon–Sat 9.30am–5pm, Sun 11am–3pm; July & Aug Mon–Sat 9.30am–6.30pm, Sun 10am–4pm; Nov–March Mon–Sat 10am–4pm; ⓣ01887/820276) providing advice on local accommodation and details of nearby walking trails.

The town's main attraction is **Dewar's World of Whisky** at the Aberfeldy Distillery (April–Oct Mon–Sat 10am–6pm, Sun noon–4pm; Nov–March Mon–Sat 10am–4pm; ⓦwww.dewarswow.com; £5), which puts on an impressive show of describing the making of whisky. The rest of the small town centre is a busy mixture of craft and tourist shops, the most interesting being **The Watermill** on Mill Street (Mon–Sat 10am–5pm, Sun noon–5pm; ⓦwww.aberfeldywatermill.com), an inspiring book shop, art gallery and café located in a restored early nineteenth-century mill.

Accommodation in and around Aberfeldy includes *Guinach House*, by The Birks (ⓣ01887/820251, ⓦwww.guinachhouse.co.uk; ❻), a tastefully decorated guesthouse in well-tended grounds, and *Balnearn Guesthouse* on Crieff Road (ⓣ01887/820431, ⓦwww.balnearnhouse.com; ❸). The closest bunkhouse is *Adventurer's Escape* (ⓣ01887/820498, ⓦwww.adventurers-escape.co.uk), a brightly painted lodge right next to the *Weem Hotel* on the road to Castle Menzies.

Your best bet for a good cup of coffee or a lunchtime **snack** is the relaxed café in *The Watermill*. Decent **bar meals** can be found at the *Ailean Chraggan Inn* in Weem, half a mile from Aberfeldy on the north side of the Tay, while the dining room at the *Weem Hotel* is good for hearty Scottish fare.

Loch Tay

Aberfeldy grew up around a crossing point on the River Tay, which leaves it oddly six miles adrift of **Loch Tay**, a fourteen-mile-long stretch of fresh water that virtually hooks together the western and eastern Highlands. Guarding the northern end of the loch is **KENMORE**, a cluster of whitewashed estate houses and well-tended gardens. The main attraction here is the fantastic heritage museum, **Scottish Crannog Centre** (mid-March to Oct daily 10am–5.30pm;

Nov Sat & Sun 10am–4pm; £5.25; Ⓦwww.crannog.co.uk). **Crannogs** are Iron Age loch dwellings built on stilts over the water, with a gangway to the shore which could be lifted up to defy a hostile intruder, whether animal or human. Here, visitors can walk out over the loch to a superbly reconstructed, thatched, wooden crannog, complete with sheepskin rugs, wooden bowls and other evidence of the way life was lived 2500 years ago.

Dominating the northern side of Loch Tay is moody **Ben Lawers** (3984ft), Perthshire's highest mountain; from the top there are incredible views towards both the Atlantic and the North Sea. The ascent – which should not be tackled unless you're properly equipped for Scottish hill-walking – takes around three hours from the NTS visitor centre (April–Sept daily 10am–5pm), located at 1300ft and reached by a winding hill road off the A827.

Glen Lyon

North of Breadalbane, the mountains tumble down into **Glen Lyon** – at 34 miles long, the longest enclosed glen in Scotland. The narrow single-track road through the glen starts at **Keltneyburn**, near Kenmore at the northern end of the loch; a few miles on, the village of **FORTINGALL** is little more than a handful of pretty thatched cottages, although locals make much of their 5000-year-old yew tree, believed (by them at least) to be the oldest living thing in Europe. The venerable tree can be found in the churchyard, showing its age a little but well looked after, with a timeline nearby listing some of the events the yew has lived through. One of these, bizarrely, is the birth of Pontius Pilate, reputedly the son of a Roman officer stationed near Fortingall in the last years BC.

Highland Perthshire

North of the Tay valley, Perthshire doesn't discard its lush richness immediately, but there are clear indications of the more rugged, barren influences of the Highlands proper. The principal settlements of **Pitlochry** and **Blair Atholl**, both just off the A9, are separated by the narrow gorge of Killiecrankie, a crucial strategic spot in times past for anyone seeking to control movement of cattle or armies from the Highlands to the Lowlands. Greater rewards, however, are to be found further from the main drag, most notably in the winding westward road along the shores of **Loch Tummel** and **Loch Rannoch** past the distinctive peak of **Schiehallion**, which eventually leads to the remote wilderness of **Rannoch Moor**.

Pitlochry

PITLOCHRY has, on the face of it, a lot going for it, not least the backdrop of Ben Vrackie and the River Tummel slipping by. However, there's little charm to be found on the main street, filled with crawling traffic and endless shops selling cut-price woollens, knobbly walking sticks and glass baubles. Its one nearby attraction is Scotland's smallest distillery, the **Edradour Distillery** (March–Dec Mon–Sat 9.30am–5/6pm, Sun 11.30am–4/5pm; Jan & Feb Mon–Sat 10am–4pm, Sun noon–4pm; free; Ⓦwww.edradour.co.uk), set in an idyllic position tucked into the hills a couple of miles east of Pitlochry on the A924.

On the western edge of Pitlochry, just across the river, lies Scotland's renowned "Theatre in the Hills", the **Pitlochry Festival Theatre** (Ⓣ01796/484626, Ⓦwww.pitlochry.org.uk). A variety of productions – mostly mainstream theatre from the resident repertoire company, along with regular music events – are staged in the summer season (May–Oct) and on ad hoc dates the rest of the year. Part of the theatre site is the absorbing **Explorers: the Scottish Plant Hunters' Garden** (daily: April–Oct 10am–5pm; £4; tours £1 extra; Ⓦwww.explorersgarden.com), an extended garden and forest area which pays tribute to Scottish botanists and collectors who roamed the world in the eighteenth and nineteenth centuries in search of new plant species. This is very much a modern rather than traditional garden, made up of carefully constructed, sinuous trails.

Pitlochry's **tourist office** is at 22 Atholl Rd (April–June & Oct Mon–Sat 9am–5pm, Sun 10am–5pm; July–Sept Mon–Sat 9am–6pm, Sun 10am–6pm; Nov–March Mon–Sat 10am–4pm; Ⓣ01796/472215). For **bike rental**, advice on local cycling routes, as well as general outdoor gear, try Escape Route at 3 Atholl Rd (Ⓣ01796/473859, Ⓦwww.escape-route.biz).

Pitlochry is packed with grand houses converted into large- and medium-sized **hotels**: The *Moulin Hotel* (Ⓣ01796/472196, Ⓦwww.moulinhotel.co.uk; ❹), at Moulin on the outskirts of Pitlochry along the A924, is a pleasant and popular old travellers' inn with a great bar and its own brewery, while *Craigatin House and Courtyard* (Ⓣ01796/472478, Ⓦwww.craigatinhouse.co.uk; ❺) on the northern stretch of the main road through town, is an attractive, contemporary **B&B** with large beds, soothing decor and an agreeable garden. Right in the centre at 134 Atholl Rd, *Pitlochry Backpackers Hotel*, (Ⓣ01796/470044, Ⓦwww.pitlochrybackpackershotel.com) is a **hostel** based in a former hotel with dorms (£13) as well as ten twin and double rooms (❶).

Pitlochry is the domain of the tearoom and you have to hunt to find decent places for a full **meal**: *The Old Armoury* (Ⓣ01796/474281, Ⓦwww.theoldarmouryrestaurant.com), on a back road between the train station and dam, is a civilized restaurant, while the best bet for traditional pub grub is the *Moulin Inn*, handily placed at the foot of Ben Vrackie. There's a good **deli** serving sandwiches and coffee called *Food for Thought* at 8 West Moulin Rd.

Loch Tummel and Loch Rannoch

West of Pitlochry, the B8019/B846 makes a memorably scenic, if tortuous, traverse of the shores of **Loch Tummel** and then **Loch Rannoch**. These two lochs and their adjoining rivers were much changed by massive hydroelectric

Rannoch Moor

Rannoch Moor occupies roughly 150 square miles of uninhabited and uninhabitable peat bogs, lochs, heather hillocks, strewn lumps of granite and a few gnarled Caledonian pine, all of it over 1000ft above sea level. Perhaps the most striking thing about the moor is its inaccessibility: one road, between Crianlarich and Glen Coe, skirts its western side, while another struggles west from Pitlochry to reach its eastern edge at Rannoch Station. The only regular form of transport is the West Highland railway, which stops at Rannoch and, a little to the north, Corrour Station, which has no road access at all. There's a SYHA **hostel** a mile away on the shores of Loch Ossian (Ⓣ0870/004 1139, Ⓦwww.syha.org.uk; April–Oct), making the area a great place for hikers seeking somewhere genuinely off the beaten track. From Rannoch Station it's possible to catch the train to Corrour and walk the nine miles back; it's a longer slog west to the eastern end of Glen Coe (see p.993), the dramatic peaks of which poke up above the moor's western horizon. Determined hill-walkers will find a clutch of Munros around Corrour, including remote Ben Alder (3765ft), high above the forbidding shores of Loch Ericht.

schemes built in the 1940s and 1950s, yet this is still a spectacular stretch of countryside and one which deserves leisurely exploration. **Queen's View** at the eastern end of Loch Tummel is an obvious vantage point, looking down the loch to the misty peak of **Schiehallion** (3520ft), whose name comes from the Gaelic meaning "Fairy Mountain". One of Scotland's few freestanding hills, it's a popular, fairly easy and inspiring climb, with views on a good day to both sides of the country and north to the massed ranks of Highland peaks. The path up starts at Braes of Foss, just off the B846, which links Aberfeldy with Kinloch Rannoch: allow three to four hours to the top and back.

Beyond Loch Tummel, at the eastern end of Loch Rannoch, the small community of **KINLOCH RANNOCH** doesn't see a lot of passing trade – fishermen and hill-walkers are the most common visitors. Otherwise, the only real destination here is **Rannoch Station**, a lonely outpost on the Glasgow–Fort William West Highland train line, sixteen miles further on at the end of the road. There is a simple tearoom in the station building, as well as a pleasant small hotel, the *Moor of Rannoch* (Ⓣ01882/633238, Ⓦwww.moorofrannoch.co.uk; mid-Feb to Oct; ❺), but even these struggle to diminish the feeling of isolation. A local **bus** (Broons Bus #85) from Kinloch Rannoch and a postbus from Pitlochry (#223; departs 8am, Mon–Sat) provide connections to the railway station.

North of Pitlochry

Four miles north of Pitlochry, the A9 cuts through the **Pass of Killiecrankie**, a breathtaking wooded gorge which falls away to the River Garry below. This dramatic setting was the site of the **Battle of Killiecrankie** in 1689, when the Jacobites quashed the forces of General Mackay. Legend has it that one soldier of the Crown, fleeing for his life, made a miraculous jump across the 18-foot **Soldier's Leap**, an impossibly wide chasm halfway up the gorge. Exhibits at the slick NTS **visitor centre** (April–Oct daily 10am–5.30pm; parking £2) recall the battle and examine the gorge in detail.

Blair Atholl

Three miles north of Killiecrankie, the village of **BLAIR ATHOLL** makes for a much quieter and more idiosyncratic stop than Pitlochry. The **Atholl Estates Information Centre** (April–Oct daily 9am–4.45pm; Ⓣ01796/481646, Ⓦwww.athollestatesrangerservice.co.uk) provides details of the extensive network of local walks and bike rides as well as interesting information on surrounding flora and fauna. Nearby, you can wander round the **Water Mill** on Ford Road (April–Oct daily 10.30am–5.30pm; Ⓦwww.blairathollwatermill.co.uk; £1.50), which dates from 1613, and witness flour being milled; better still, you can enjoy home-baked scones and light lunches in its pleasant timber-beamed tearoom.

By far the most important and eye-catching building in these parts, however, is **Blair Castle** (April–Oct daily 9.30am–last admission 4.30pm; Nov–March Tues & Sat 9.30am–12.30pm; £7.90, grounds only £2.70; Ⓦwww.blair-castle.co.uk), seat of the Atholl dukedom. This whitewashed, turreted castle looks particularly impressive as you drive up the driveway leading from the centre of Blair Atholl village, especially if a piper is playing. The pipers belong to the Atholl Highlanders, a select group retained by the duke as his private army – a unique privilege afforded to him by Queen Victoria, who stayed here in 1844. Highlights are the soaring **entrance hall**, with every spare inch of wood panelling covered in weapons of some description, and the vast **ballroom**, with its timber roof, antlers, and mixture of portraits.

Travel details

Buses

For information on all local and national bus services, contact Traveline ⓣ0870/608 2608 (daily 7am–10pm), ⓦwww.travelinescotland.com.

Aberfeldy to: Perth (6 daily; 1hr 20min).
Aberfoyle to: Callander (late June to mid-Oct 4 daily; Thurs–Tues; 25min); Port of Menteith (late June to mid-Oct 4 daily; Thurs–Tues; 10min).
Balloch to: Balmaha (every 2hr; 25min); Luss (hourly; 15min).
Callander to: Loch Katrine (late June to mid-Oct 4 daily; Thurs–Tues; 55min).
Dunfermline to: Culross (hourly; 20min); Edinburgh (every 30min; 40min); Glasgow (every 30min; 1hr 10min); Kirkcaldy (hourly; 30min); Stirling (every 2hr; 1hr 15min).
Kinloch Rannoch to: Pitlochry (3 daily; 50min); Rannoch Station (4 daily; 40min).
Perth to: Aberfeldy (10 daily; 1hr 15min); Crieff (hourly; 45min); Dundee (hourly; 45min); Dunkeld (hourly; 30min); Edinburgh (hourly; 1hr 20min); Glasgow (hourly; 1hr 35min); Gleneagles (hourly; 25min); Inverness (hourly; 2hr 45min); Pitlochry (hourly; 45min); Stirling (hourly; 50min).
St Andrews to: Dundee (every 15min; 35min); Dunfermline (hourly; 1hr 15min); Edinburgh (every 30min; 1hr 50min); Glasgow (every 30min; 2hr 25min); Glenrothes (hourly; 40min); Kirkcaldy (every 30min; 1hr); Stirling (every 2hr; 1hr 55min).
Stirling to: Aberfoyle (4 daily; 45min); Callander (1–2hr; 45min); Dollar (every 2hr; 30min); Doune (1–2hr; 25min); Dunblane (hourly; 20min); Dundee (hourly; 1hr 30min); Edinburgh (hourly; 1hr); Falkirk (hourly; 30min); Glasgow (hourly; 50min); Inverness (every 2hr; 3hr 20min); Perth (hourly; 40min); St Andrews (every 2hr; 1hr 55min).

Trains

For information on all local and national rail services, contact National Rail Enquiries ⓣ08457/484950, ⓦwww.nationalrail.co.uk or ⓦwww.firstscotrail.com.

Balloch to: Glasgow (every 30min; 40min).
Crianlarich to: Fort William (3–4 daily; 1hr 50min); Glasgow Queen St (6–8 daily; Mon–Sat; 1–3hr; Sun; 1hr 50min); Oban (3–4 daily; Mon–Sat; 1–3hr; Sun; 1hr 10min).
Dunfermline to: Edinburgh (every 30min; 35min); Kirkcaldy (hourly; 40min).
Falkirk to: Edinburgh (every 15–30min; 30min); Glasgow Queen St (every 15–30min; 25min); Stirling (every 30min; 15min).
Leuchars (for St Andrews) to: Aberdeen (1–2hr; 1hr 30min); Dundee (1–2hr; 15min); Edinburgh (1–2hr; 1hr).
Perth to: Aberdeen (hourly; 1hr 40min); Blair Atholl (3–7 daily; 45min); Dundee (hourly; 25min); Dunkeld (3–7 daily; 20min); Edinburgh (every 1–2hr; 1hr 25min); Glasgow Queen St (hourly; 1hr); Inverness (4–9 daily; 2hr); Pitlochry (4–9 daily; 30min); Stirling (hourly; 30min).
Rannoch to: Corrour (3–4 daily; 12min); Fort William (3–4 daily; 1hr); Glasgow Queen St (3–4 daily; 2hr 45min); London Euston (sleeper service; Sun–Fri daily; 11hr).
Stirling to: Aberdeen (hourly; 2hr 5min); Dundee (hourly; 55min); Edinburgh (every 30min; 1hr); Falkirk Grahamston (every 30min; 15min); Glasgow Queen St (every 20min; 30min); Inverness (3–5 daily; 2hr 55min); Perth (hourly; 30min).

Argyll

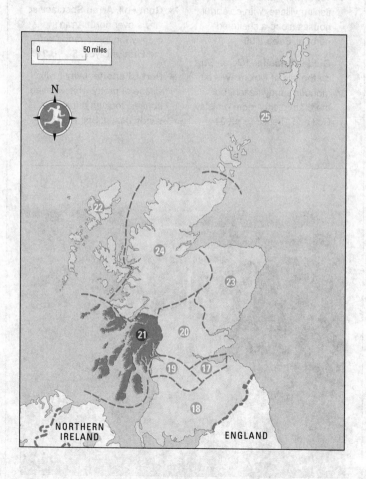

CHAPTER 21

Highlights

* **Mount Stuart, Bute** Overblown aristocratic mansion, set in beautiful grounds. See p.896
* **Tobermory, Mull** Picturesque fishing village, with colourful houses along a sheltered harbour. See p.899
* **Golden beaches** Kiloran Bay on the Isle of Colonsay is a glorious sandy beach, but there are plenty more on Islay, Coll and Tiree. See p.904
* **Isle of Gigha** The perfect island escape: sandy beaches, friendly folk, decent hotel and lovely gardens. See p.907
* **Goat Fell, Arran** Spectacular views over north Arran's craggy mountain range and the Firth of Clyde. See p.910
* **Port Charlotte, Islay** Idyllic village of pretty whitewashed houses, looking out over a sandy beach. See p.913

▲ Arran

21

Argyll

Cut off for centuries from the rest of Scotland by the mountains and sea lochs that characterize the region, **Argyll** remains remote, its scatter of offshore islands forming part of the Inner Hebridean archipelago (the remaining Hebrides are dealt with in the next chapter). Geographically as well as culturally, this is a transitional area between Highland and Lowland, boasting a rich variety of scenery, from lush, subtropical gardens warmed by the Gulf Stream to flat and treeless islands on the edge of the Atlantic. It's in the folds and twists of the countryside, the interplay of land and water and the views out to the islands that the strengths and beauties of mainland Argyll lie. The one area of man-made sights you shouldn't miss, however, is the cluster of **Celtic** and **prehistoric sites** near Kilmartin. Overall, the population is tiny; even **Oban**, Argyll's chief ferry port, has just seven thousand inhabitants, while the prettiest town, **Inveraray**, boasts less than eight hundred.

The eastern duo of **Bute** and **Arran** are the most popular of Scotland's more southerly islands, the latter – now, strictly speaking, part of Ayrshire – justifiably so, with spectacular scenery ranging from the granite peaks of the north to the Lowland pasture of the south. Of the Hebridean islands covered in this chapter, mountainous **Mull** is the most visited, though it is large enough to absorb the crowds, many of whom are only passing through en route to the tiny isle of **Iona**, a centre of Christian culture since the sixth century. **Islay**, best known for its distinctive malt whiskies, is fairly quiet even in the height of summer, as is neighbouring **Jura**, which offers excellent walking opportunities. And, for those seeking further solitude, there are the more remote islands of **Tiree** and **Coll**, which, although swept with fierce winds, boast more sunny days than anywhere else in Scotland.

Public transport throughout Argyll is minimal, though buses do serve most major settlements, and the train line reaches Oban. In the remoter parts and on the islands, you'll have to rely on a combination of walking, shared taxis and the postbus. If you're planning to take a **car** across to one of the islands, it's essential that you reserve both your outward and return journeys as early as possible, as the ferries get very booked up.

Isle of Bute

The island of **BUTE** is in many ways simply an extension of the Cowal peninsula, from which it is separated by the narrow Kyles of Bute. Thanks to its

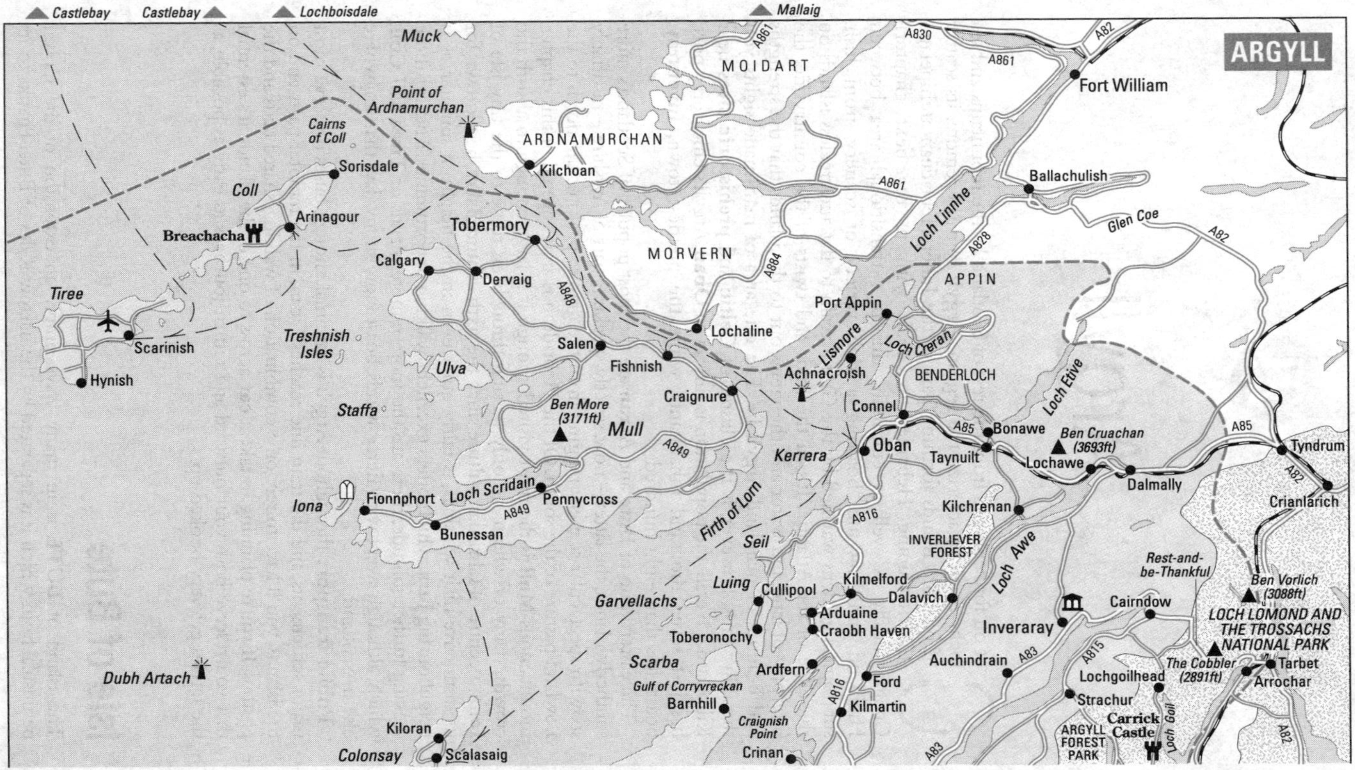

ARGYLL

Castlebay
Castlebay
Lochboisdale
Mallaig

Muck
MOIDART
A861
A830
A82
Fort William
Point of Ardnamurchan
Cairns of Coll
ARDNAMURCHAN
Kilchoan
Sorisdale
Coll
Arinagour
Breachacha
Tobermory
Ballachulish
Glen Coe
A82
Loch Linnhe
A828
MORVERN
A884
Calgary
Dervaig
A848
Tiree
Scarinish
Hynish
Treshnish Isles
Ulva
Salen
Fishnish
Lochaline
Port Appin
APPIN
Lismore
Loch Creran
Achnacroish
BENDERLOCH
Loch Etive
Craignure
Connel
Staffa
Ben More (3171ft)
Mull
A849
Kerrera
Oban
A85
Bonawe
Taynuilt
Ben Cruachan (3693ft)
Lochawe
Dalmally
A85
Tyndrum
A82
Crianlarich
Iona
Fionnphort
Loch Scridain
Pennycross
A849
Bunessan
Firth of Lorn
A816
Seil
Kilchrenan
INVERLIEVER FOREST
Loch Awe
Rest-and-be-Thankful
Ben Vorlich (3088ft)
Luing
Cullipool
Kilmelford
Dalavich
Garvellachs
Arduaine
Craobh Haven
Inveraray
Cairndow
LOCH LOMOND AND THE TROSSACHS NATIONAL PARK
Toberonochy
Scarba
Ardfern
Auchindrain
A83
A815
Lochgoilhead
The Cobbler (2891ft)
Tarbet
Arrochar
Dubh Artach
Gulf of Corryvreckan
Barnhill
Ford
A816
Kilmartin
Strachur
Kiloran
Colonsay
Scalasaig
Craignish Point
Crinan
A83
ARGYLL FOREST PARK
Carrick Castle
Loch Goil
A82

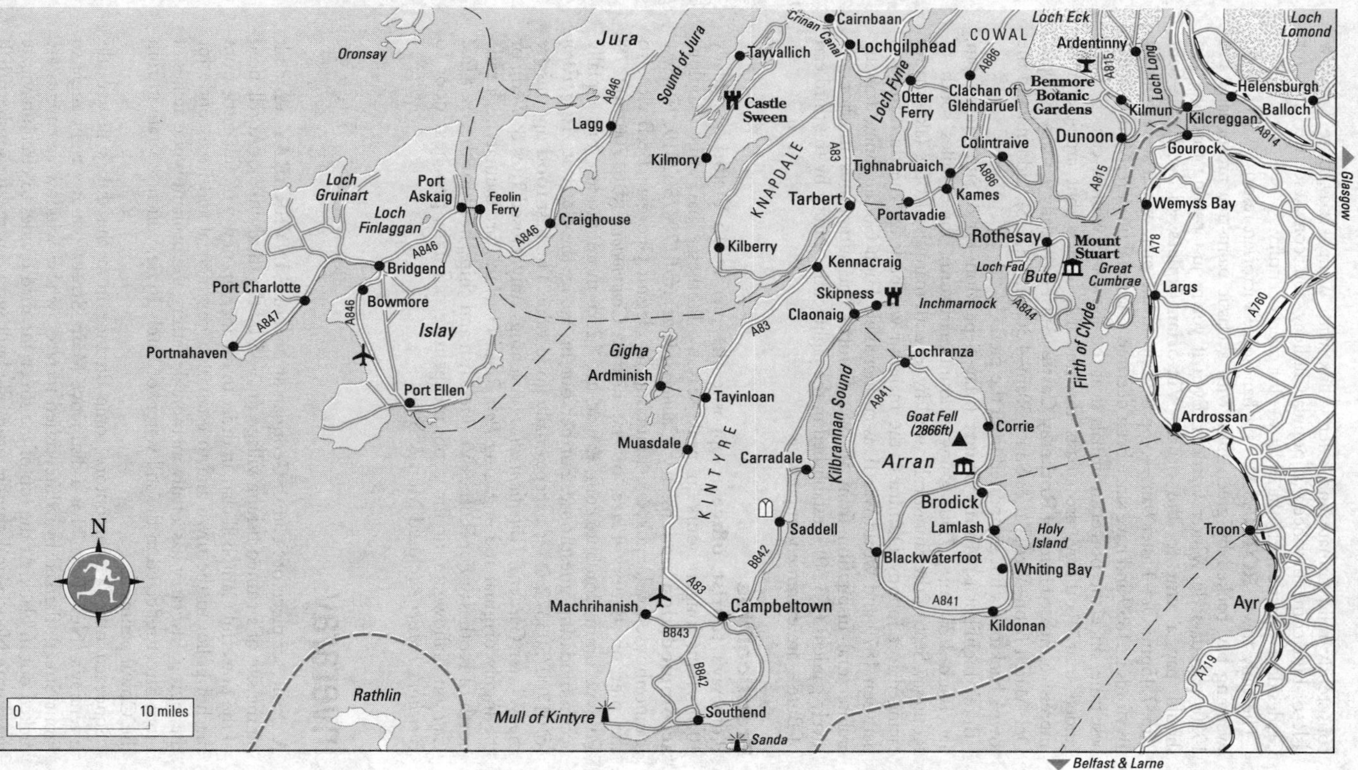
Glasgow
Loch Lomond
Helensburgh
Balloch
Kilcreggan
A814
Gourock
Loch Long
Kilmun
Ardentinny
A815
Loch Eck
Benmore Botanic Gardens
Dunoon
COWAL
A886
Clachan of Glendaruel
Colintraive
Otter Ferry
Loch Fyne
Lochgilphead
Cairnbaan
Crinan Canal
Tayvallich
Castle Sween
Sound of Jura
Jura
Oronsay
A846
Lagg
Kilmory
KNAPDALE
A83
Tighnabruaich
Kames
Portavadie
Tarbert
Kilberry
Craighouse
Feolin Ferry
Port Askaig
Loch Gruinart
Loch Finlaggan
Bridgend
Bowmore
Port Charlotte
A847
Portnahaven
Islay
Port Ellen
Wemyss Bay
A78
Rothesay
Mount Stuart
Loch Fad
Bute
Great Cumbrae
A844
Largs
A760
Kennacraig
Skipness
Inchmarnock
Claonaig
Firth of Clyde
Lochranza
Gigha
Ardminish
Tayinloan
Kilbrannan Sound
A841
Goat Fell (2866ft)
Corrie
Ardrossan
Arran
Muasdale
KINTYRE
Carradale
Brodick
Lamlash
Holy Island
Saddell
Troon
Blackwaterfoot
Whiting Bay
B842
Machrihanish
Campbeltown
Kildonan
Ayr
B843
A719
Rathlin
Mull of Kintyre
Southend
Sanda
N
0
10 miles
Belfast & Larne

consistently mild climate and a ferry link with Wemyss Bay, Bute (Ⓦwww.isle-of-bute.com) has been a popular holiday and convalescence spot for Clydesiders – particularly the elderly – for over a century.

The only town, **ROTHESAY** is a handsome Victorian resort set in a wide sweeping bay, backed by green hills, with a classic palm-tree promenade and 1920s pagoda-style Winter Gardens. Even if you're just passing through, you should pay a visit to the ornate **Victorian toilets** (daily: Easter–Sept 8am–7.45pm; Oct–Easter 9am–4.45pm; 20p) on the pier, which were built by Twyfords in 1899 and have since been declared a national treasure. Men have the best time, since the porcelain urinals steal the show, but women can ask for a guided tour. Rothesay also boasts the militarily useless, but architecturally impressive, moated ruins of **Rothesay Castle** (April–Sept daily 9.30am–5.30pm; Oct–March Mon–Wed, Sat & Sun 9.30am–4.30pm; £4; HS), hidden amid the town's backstreets but signposted from the pier.

Bute's highlight is **Mount Stuart** (May–Sept Mon–Fri & Sun 11am–5pm, Sat 10am–1.30pm; £7.50; Ⓦwww.mountstuart.com), three miles south of Rothesay. Seat of the fantastically wealthy seventh marquis of Bute (aka former racing driver Johnny Dumfries), the mansion was built for the third marquis between 1879 and World War II, as an incredible High Gothic fancy, drawing architectural inspiration from all over Europe. The sumptuous interior and lovely gardens (£3.50) – established in the eighteenth century by the third earl of Bute – are extremely impressive.

Practicalities

Rothesay's **tourist office** is opposite the pier at 15 Victoria St (daily 10am–4pm; longer hours in peak season). Rothesay has some fabulous **accommodation** options: try *Cannon House* (Ⓣ01700/502819, Ⓦwww.cannonhousehotel.co.uk; ❹), a fantastically elegant Georgian B&B close to the pier on Battery Place, or the nearby *Commodore* (Ⓣ01700/502178, Ⓦwww.commodorebute.com; ❷) at no. 12, a more modest but equally accommodating guesthouse. Further out in Ascog, the B&B at *Ascog Farm* (Ⓣ01700/503372; ❷) is exceptionally good value. The best **food** options are the Winter Gardens' *Waterfront Bistro* (evenings only; closed Tues & Wed), or the highly original and engaging *Port Royal Hotel* in Port Bannatyne, a mile north of Rothesay. For Rothesay's finest fish and chips, head for the *West End Café* on Gallowgate, or for good, inexpensive café fare, pop next door to *Brerchin's Brasserie* (closed Mon & Sun).

Inveraray

A classic, set piece of Scottish Georgian architecture, **INVERARAY** was built on the site of a ruined fishing village in 1745 by the third duke of Argyll, head of the powerful Campbell clan, in order to distance his newly rebuilt castle from the hoi polloi in the town and to establish a commercial and legal centre for the region, Inveraray has a truly memorable setting, the brilliant white arches of Front Street reflected in the still waters of **Loch Fyne**, which separate it from the Cowal peninsula.

Squeezed onto a promontory some distance from the duke's new castle, Inveraray's "New Town" has a distinctive **Main Street** (set at a right angle to Front Street), flanked by whitewashed terraces, whose window casements are picked out in black. At the top of the street, the road divides to circumnavigate the town's Neoclassical church, originally built in two parts: the southern half served the Gaelic-speaking community, while the northern half served those who spoke English.

East of the church is **Inveraray Jail** (daily: April–Oct 9.30am–6pm; Nov–March 10am–5pm; £6.50), whose attractive Georgian courthouse and grim prison blocks ceased to function in the 1930s. The jail is now an imaginative and thoroughly enjoyable museum, which graphically recounts prison conditions from medieval times.

A ten-minute walk north of the New Town, the neo-Gothic **Inveraray Castle** (April, May & Oct Mon–Thurs & Sat 10am–1pm & 2–5.45pm, Sun 1–5.45pm; June–Sept Mon–Sat 10am–5.45pm, Sun 1–5.45pm; £5.90) remains the family home of the Duke of Argyll. Built in 1745, its most startling feature is the armoury hall, whose displays of weaponry – supplied to the Campbells by the British government to put down the Jacobites – rise through several storeys; look out for Rob Roy's rather sad-looking sporran and dirk handle (a "dirk" being a dagger, traditionally worn in Highland dress).

Practicalities

Inveraray's **tourist office** is on Front Street (April–Oct Mon–Sat 9am–5pm, Sun noon–5pm; Nov–March Mon–Fri 10am–3pm, Sat & Sun 11am–3pm), by the town's landmark *Argyll Hotel*. For intimate, well-appointed **accommodation**, try the *Fernpoint Hotel* (ⓣ01499/302170, ⓦwww.fernpointhotel.co.uk; ❺), a Georgian house round by the pier, with a good restaurant and a nice pub garden; a cheaper alternative is *Creag Dhubh* (ⓣ01499/302430, ⓦwww.creagdhubh.com; Feb–Nov; ❸), set in a large garden overlooking Loch Fyne, further down the A83 to Lochgilphead. The SYHA **hostel** (ⓣ0870/004 1125, ⓦwww.syha.org.uk; mid-March to Oct; dorm beds £15) is in a modern building a short distance north on the A819 Dalmally road. The best place to sample Loch Fyne's delicious fresh fish and seafood is the *Loch Fyne Oyster Bar* (ⓣ01499/600236, ⓦwww.loch-fyne.com), six miles up the A83 towards Glasgow. This place sells more oysters than anywhere else in the country, plus lots of other fish and seafood treats; you can stock up on provisions or eat at the moderately expensive restaurant. The **bar** of the central *George Hotel* is the town's liveliest spot.

Oban

The solidly Victorian resort of **OBAN** (ⓦwww.oban.org.uk) enjoys a superb setting distinguished by a bizarre granite amphitheatre, dramatically lit at night, on the hilltop above the town. Despite a small population, it's by far the largest port in northwest Scotland, and the main departure point for ferries to the Hebrides. If you arrive late, or are catching an early boat, you may have to spend the night here; if you're staying elsewhere, it's a useful base for wet-weather activities and shopping.

The only truly remarkable sight in Oban is the town's landmark, **McCaig's Tower**, a stiff ten-minute climb from the quayside. Built in imitation of Rome's Colosseum, it was the brainchild of a local businessman a century ago, who had the twin aims of alleviating off-season unemployment among the local stonemasons and creating a museum, art gallery and chapel. In his will, McCaig gave instructions for the lancet windows to be filled with bronze statues of the family, though no such work was ever undertaken. Instead, the folly has been turned into a sort of walled garden, and provides a wonderful seaward panorama, particularly at sunset.

Practicalities

The CalMac **ferry terminal** (Ⓣ01631/566688, Ⓦwww.calmac.co.uk) for the islands is on Railway Pier, a stone's throw from the **train station**, which is itself adjacent to the **bus station** on Station Square. The **tourist office** (April–Oct daily 10am–5pm; longer hours in peak season; Nov–March Mon–Sat 10am–5pm, Sun noon–5pm; Ⓣ01631/563122) is housed in a converted church on Argyll Square.

Top choices for **accommodation** include the hospitable *Kilchrenan House* (Ⓣ01631/562663, Ⓦwww.kilchrenanhouse.co.uk; ④), a tasteful place on the Corran Esplanade, or *Hawthornbank* (Ⓣ01631/562041, Ⓦwww.oban.org.uk; ③), a traditional Victorian guesthouse in the backstreets. There are also three **hostels**, the friendliest, cheapest and most central of which is the *Oban Backpackers*, Breadalbane St (Ⓣ01631/562107, Ⓦwww.hostel-scotland.co.uk; March–Oct; dorm beds £12). **Campers** should head for *Oban Caravan & Camping Park* on Gallanach Road (Ⓣ01631/562425, Ⓦwww. obancaravanpark.com; April–Oct), a mile and a half from Oban up a pretty glen.

Oban has several great fish and seafood **restaurants**: the swanky designer *Ee-usk* (Ⓣ01631/565666), on the North Pier, the less glamorous *Waterfront* (Ⓣ01631/563110), on the CalMac pier, which uses the best of the daily catch. Alternatively, head 750 yards down Gallanach Road, where you'll find the *Seafood Temple* (Ⓣ01631/566000; closed Tues & Wed), a small restaurant supplied and run by local fishermen. *Oban Fish & Chip Shop & Restaurant*, is at 116 George Street, and the **café** above the impressive *Kitchen Garden* deli, is good for sit-down snacks. Oban's half-decent **pub** is the *Oban Inn* opposite the North Pier, with a classic dark-wood-flagstone-and-brass bar downstairs and lounge bar with stained glass upstairs. Oban has a **cinema**, confusingly known as the Highland Theatre (Ⓣ01631/562444), at the north end of George Street.

Isle of Mull

Mull (Ⓦwww.holidaymull.co.uk) is by far the most accessible of the Hebrides: just forty minutes from Oban by ferry. As so often, first impressions largely depend on the weather – it's the wettest of the Hebrides (and that's saying something) – as without the sun the large tracts of moorland, particularly around the island's highest peak, Ben More (3196ft), can appear bleak and unwelcoming. There are, however, areas of more gentle pastoral scenery around **Dervaig** in the north and the indented west coast varies from the sandy beaches around **Calgary** to the cliffs of Loch na Keal. The most common mistake is to try and "do" the island in a day or two: flogging up the main road to the picturesque capital of **Tobermory**, then covering the fifty-odd miles between there and Fionnphort, in order to visit **Iona**. Mull is a place that will grow on you only if you have the time and patience to explore.

Craignure and around

CRAIGNURE is the main arrival point, linked by frequent daily **car ferry** to Oban (booking advised). It's little more than a scattering of cottages with a small shop, a bar, some toilets and a CalMac and **tourist office** situated opposite the pier (April to mid-Oct Mon–Fri 8.30am–5.15pm, Sat 9am–5pm, Sun 10.30am–5.15pm; longer hours in summer; mid-Oct to March Mon–Sat 9am–5pm, Sun 10.30am–noon & 3.30–5pm). The *Craignure Inn* (Ⓣ01680/812305, Ⓦwww.craignure-inn.co.uk; ⑤), just a minute's stroll

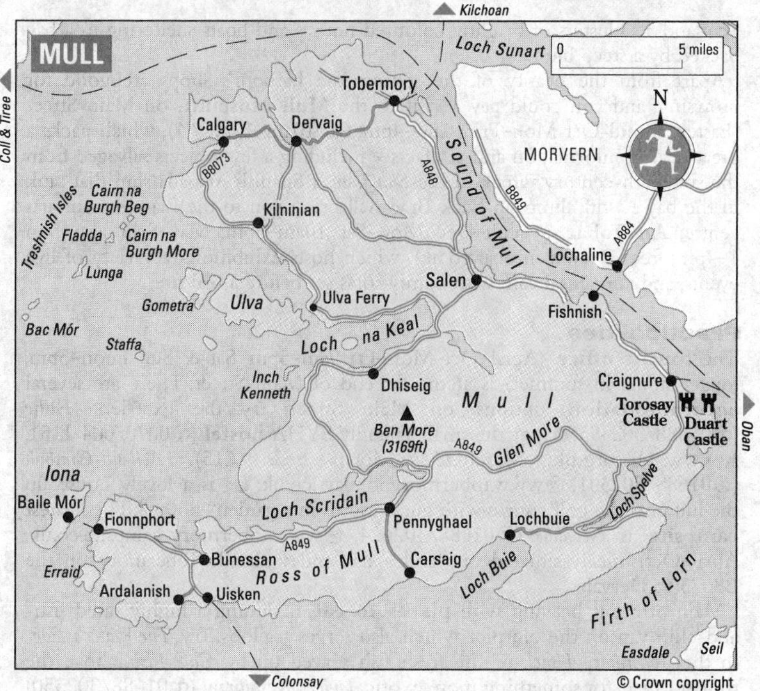

up the road towards Fionnphort, is a snug **pub** to hole up in. There's also a well-equipped **campsite** (Ⓣ01680/812496, Ⓦwww.shielingholidays.co.uk; April–Oct) on the south side of Craignure Bay, behind the village hall.

Two castles lie immediately southeast of Craignure. **Torosay Castle** (Easter–Oct daily 10.30am–5pm; £5.50), a full-blown Scots Baronial creation, is linked to Craignure by the narrow-gauge **Mull Rail** (Easter–Oct; £4.50 return). Its magnificent **gardens** (daily: April–Oct 9am–7pm, Nov–March 9am to dusk; £2.50) include an avenue of eighteenth-century Venetian statues, a Japanese section and views over to neighbouring Duart. The house itself, in the mid-nineteenth-century style, is stuffed with junk relating to the present owners, the little-known Guthries.

Lacking the gardens, but perched on a picturesque spit of rock a couple of miles east of Torosay, **Duart Castle** (April Mon–Thurs & Sun 11am–4pm; May–Oct daily 10.30am–5.30pm; £5) is clearly visible from the Oban–Craignure ferry. Headquarters of the once-powerful MacLean clan from the thirteenth century, it was burnt down by the Campbells and confiscated after the 1745 rebellion. Finally in 1911, the 26th clan chief, Fitzroy MacLean (1835–1936), managed to buy it back and restore it. You can peek at the dungeons, climb up to the ramparts, study the family photos, and learn about the world scout movement – the 27th clan chief became Chief Scout in 1959. After your visit, you can enjoy home-made cakes and tea at the castle's excellent tearoom (May–Sept).

Tobermory

Mull's chief town, **TOBERMORY** (Ⓦwww.tobermory.co.uk), at the northern tip of the island, is easily the most attractive fishing port on the west coast of

Scotland, its clusters of brightly coloured houses and boats sheltering in a bay backed by a steep bluff.

Apart from the beauty of the setting, the harbour's shops are good for browsing, and you could pay a visit to the **Mull Museum,** on Main Street (Easter to mid-Oct Mon–Fri 10am–4pm, Sat 10am–1pm; £1), which packs a great deal of information and artefacts – including a few objects salvaged from the sixteenth-century wreck of the *San Juan*, a Spanish Armada ship that sank in the bay. A stiff climb up Back Brae will bring you to the island's main arts centre, **An Tobar** (March–Dec Mon–Sat 10am–5pm; May–Sept also Sun 1–4pm; free; Ⓦwww.antobar.co.uk), which hosts exhibitions, a variety of live events, and contains a café with comfy sofas set before a real fire.

Practicalities

The **tourist office** (April–Oct Mon–Fri 9am–5pm, Sat & Sun noon–5pm; longer hours in summer) is at the far end of Main Street. There are several **accommodation** options on Main Street: try the excellent *Fàilte* (Ⓣ01688/302495; ④), or the small, friendly SYHA **hostel** (Ⓣ0870/004 1151, Ⓦwww.syha.org.uk; March–Oct; dorm beds £15). *Ach-na-Craiboh* (Ⓣ01688/302301, Ⓦwww.tobermoryholidays.co.uk; ③) is a lovely house up the hill near the golf course with guest rooms in a garden "bothy". The nearest **campsite** is *Newdale* (Ⓣ01688/302624, Ⓦwww.tobermory-campsite.co.uk; April–Oct), nicely situated one and a half miles outside Tobermory on the B8073 to Dervaig.

Main Street is heaving with **places to eat**, including a highly rated fish-and-chip van on the old pier which also serves scallops. Try *The Water's Edge* in the *Tobermory Hotel*, or the fresh fish served up by *Café Fish*, above the tourist office; for something more exotic, *Javier's Restaurant* (Ⓣ01688/302350) above *MacGochan's* (on the opposite side of the harbour near the distillery) serves authentic ArgentinianHispanic cuisine. The *Mishnish*, on Main Street, has been the most popular local **pub** for many years, and features live music at the weekend.

The Isle of Staffa

Seven miles off the west coast of Mull, **Staffa** is the most romantic and dramatic of Scotland's many uninhabited islands. On its south side, the perpendicular rock face features an imposing series of black basalt columns, known as the Colonnade, which have been cut by the sea into cathedralesque caverns, most notably **Fingal's Cave**. The Vikings knew about the island – the name derives from their word for "Island of Pillars" – but it wasn't until 1772 that it was "discovered" by the world. Turner painted it, Wordsworth explored it, but Mendelssohn's *Die Fingalshöhle*, inspired by the sounds of the sea-wracked caves he heard on a visit here in 1829, did most to popularize the place – after which Queen Victoria gave her blessing, too. The geological explanation for these polygonal basalt organ-pipes is that they were created by a massive subterranean explosion some sixty million years ago. A huge mass of molten basalt burst forth onto land and, as it cooled, solidified into what are, essentially, crystals. From April to October several operators offer **boat trips to Staffa**: long-established Turus Mara (Ⓣ0800/085 8786, Ⓦwww.turusmara.com) is a classy outfit, setting out from Ulva Ferry and charging around £45 return, as does Gordon Grant Marine (Ⓣ01681/700338, Ⓦwww.staffatours.com), departing from Fionnphort. If you just want to go to Staffa, try Iolaire (Ⓣ01681/700358, Ⓦwww.staffatrips.f9.co.uk), who charge around £20 for passage from Fionnphort.

Ben More and the Ross of Mull

From the southern shores of Loch na Keal, which almost splits Mull in two, rise the terraced slopes of **Ben More** (3169ft) – literally "big mountain" – a mighty extinct volcano. Stretching for twenty miles west of Ben More as far as Iona is Mull's rocky southernmost peninsula, the **Ross of Mull**, which, like much of Scotland, appears blissfully tranquil in good weather, and desolate and bleak in bad.

The road ends at **FIONNPHORT**, facing Iona, probably the least attractive place to stay on the Ross, though it has a nice sandy bay backed by pink, granite rocks to the north of the ferry slipway. Partly to ease congestion on Iona, and to give their neighbours a slice of the tourist pound, Fionnphort was chosen as the site for the little-visited **St Columba Centre** (Easter–Sept daily 10.30am–1pm & 2–5.30pm; free); inside, a small exhibition outlines Iona's history, tells a little of Columba's life, and has a few facsimiles of the illuminated manuscripts produced by the island's monks.

The Isle of Iona

Less than a mile off the southwest tip of Mull, **IONA** (ⓦ www.isle-of-iona.com) – just three miles long and not much more than a mile wide – has been a place of pilgrimage for several centuries, and a place of Christian worship for more than 1400 years. It was to this flat Hebridean island that **St Columba** fled from Ireland in 563 and established a monastery, compiling a vast library of illuminated manuscripts and converting more or less all of pagan Scotland as well as much of northern England. This history and the island's splendid isolation have lent it a peculiar religiosity; in the much-quoted words of Dr Johnson, who visited in 1773, "That man is little to be envied . . . whose piety would not grow warmer among the ruins of Iona." Today, however, the island can barely cope with the constant flood of day-trippers, and charges visitors entry to its abbey, so to appreciate the special atmosphere and to have time to see the whole island, including the often-overlooked west coast, you should plan on staying at least one night.

The passenger ferry from Fionnphort drops you off at the island's main village, **BAILE MÓR** (literally "large village"), which is in fact little more than a single terrace of cottages facing the sea. Just inland lie the extensive pink-granite ruins of the **Augustinian nunnery**, built around 1200 but disused since the Reformation – if nothing else, it gives you an idea of the state of the present-day abbey before it was restored. Across the road to the north is the **Iona Heritage Centre** (Easter–Oct Mon–Sat 10.30am–4.30pm; £2), with displays on the social history of the island over the last two hundred years, including the Clearances, which nearly halved the island's population of five hundred in the mid-nineteenth century. At a bend in the road, just south of the manse and church, stands the fifteenth-century **MacLean's Cross**, a fine, late-medieval example of the distinctive, flowing, three-leaved foliage of the Iona school.

No buildings remain from Columba's time: the present **abbey** (daily: April–Sept 9.30am–5.30pm; Oct–March 9.30am–4.30pm; £4.50; HS) dates from the arrival of the Benedictines in around 1200, was extensively rebuilt in the fifteenth and sixteenth centuries, and restored virtually wholesale early last century. Adjoining the facade is a small steep-roofed chamber, believed to be St Columba's grave, now a small chapel. The three high crosses in front of the abbey date from the eighth to tenth centuries, and are decorated with the

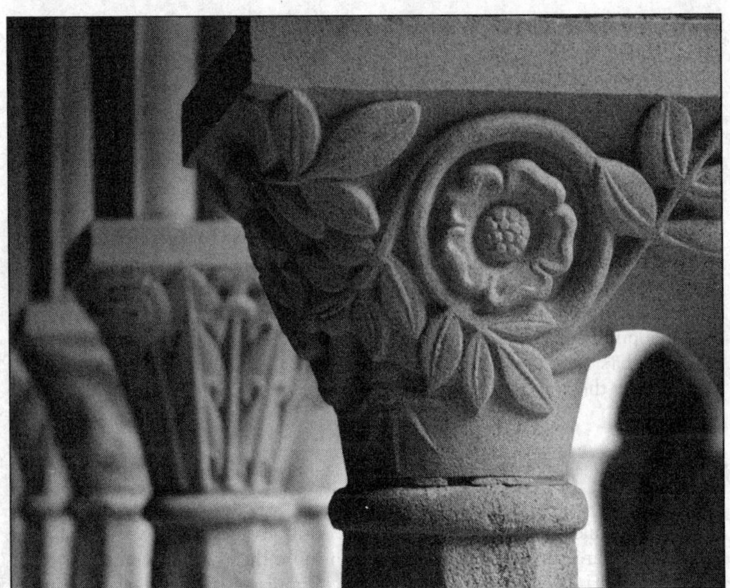

▲ Decorated stone in Iona Abbey

Pictish serpent and boss and Celtic spirals for which Iona's early Christian masons were renowned. For reasons of sanitation, the cloisters were placed, contrary to the norm, on the north side of the church (where running water was available); entirely reconstructed in the late 1950s, they now shelter a useful historical account of the abbey's development.

Iona's oldest building, the plain-looking **St Oran's Chapel**, lies south of the abbey, and boasts an eleventh-century door. Oran's Chapel stands at the centre of Iona's sacred burial ground, **Reilig Odhráin** (Oran's Cemetery), which is said to contain the graves of sixty kings of Norway, Ireland, France and Scotland, including Duncan and Macbeth. The best of the early Christian gravestones and medieval effigies that once lay in the Reilig Odhráin have unfortunately been removed to the Infirmary Museum, behind the abbey.

Practicalities

There's no **tourist office** on Iona, and as demand far exceeds supply you should organize **accommodation** well in advance. Of the island's two **hotels**, the stone-built *Argyll* (Ⓣ01681/700334, Ⓦwww.argyllhoteliona.co.uk; Feb–Nov; ❻), in the terrace of cottages overlooking the Sound of Iona, is by far the nicer. As for **B&Bs**, try *Shore Cottage* (Ⓣ01681/700744, Ⓦwww.shorecottage.co.uk; Jan–Oct; ❷), a short walk south. **Camping** is not permitted on Iona, but there is a terrific **hostel** (Ⓣ01681/700781, Ⓦwww.ionahostel.co.uk; dorm beds £17.50) in the north of the island. If you want to stay with the **Iona Community**, contact the MacLeod Centre (Ⓣ01681/700404, Ⓦwww.iona.org.uk), popularly known as the "Mac". The **restaurant** at the *Argyll* isn't bad, and the grub at the *Martyrs' Bay Restaurant* by the jetty is reasonable too; for even more convivial surroundings you can eat from the same menu in the adjoining bar. For something lighter during the day, there's a **tearoom** beside the Heritage Centre.

Coll, Tiree and Colonsay

Coll and **Tiree** are among the most isolated of the Inner Hebrides, and if anything have more in common with the outlying Western Isles than with their closest neighbour, Mull. Each is roughly twelve miles long and three miles wide, both are low-lying, treeless and exceptionally windy, with white sandy beaches and the highest sunshine records in Scotland. Isolated between Mull and Islay, **Colonsay** – eight miles by three at its widest – is nothing like as bleak and windswept as Coll or Tiree. All three islands are served by CalMac ferries from Oban.

Isle of Coll

The fish-shaped rocky island of **Coll** (Ⓦwww.visitcoll.co.uk), with a population of around a hundred, lies less than seven miles off the coast of Mull. The CalMac ferry drops off at Coll's only real village, **ARINAGOUR**, whose whitewashed cottages dot the western shore of Loch Eatharna. Half the island's population lives in the village, and it's here you'll find the hotel and pub, post office, churches and a couple of shops.

On the southwest coast there are two edifices, both confusingly known as **Breachacha Castle**. The older is a restored fifteenth-century tower house, and now a training centre for overseas aid volunteers. The less attractive "new castle", to the northwest, is made up of a central block built around 1750 and two side pavilions added a century later, and is currently being restored. Much of the area around the castles is now owned by the RSPB, with the aim of protecting the island's small corncrake population. A vast area of **giant sand dunes** lies to the west of the castles, with two glorious golden sandy bays stretching for over a mile on either side.

Aside from self-catering cottages, **accommodation** options are very limited. In Arinagour, the small, family-run *Coll Hotel* (Ⓣ01879/230334, Ⓦwww.collhotel.com; ❺) is excellent, or else there's *Tigh-na-Mara* (Ⓣ01879/230354, Ⓦwww.sturgeon.dircon.co.uk; ❸), a purpose-built guesthouse near the pier. *Garden House* (Ⓣ01879/230374), down a track on the left before the turn-off for the castles, runs a **campsite** in the shelter of an old walled garden. The *Coll Hotel* doubles as the island's social centre, and does delicious **meals.**

Isle of Tiree

Tiree (Ⓦwww.isleoftiree.com), as its Gaelic name *tir-iodh* ("land of corn") suggests, was once known as the breadbasket of the Inner Hebrides, thanks to its acres of rich machair (sandy, grassy, lime-rich land). Nowadays crofting and tourism are the main sources of income for the small resident population. One of the most distinctive features of Tiree is its architecture, in particular the large numbers of "pudding" or "spotty" houses, where only the mortar is painted white. Tiree's sandy beaches also attract large numbers of windsurfers for the Tiree Wave Classic (Ⓦwww.tireewaveclassic.com) every October.

The ferry calls at Gott Bay Pier, now best known for **An Turas** (The Journey), Tiree's award-winning artistic "shelter". Just up the road from the pier is the village of **SCARINISH**, home to a post office, some public toilets, a supermarket, a butcher's and a bank, with a petrol pump back at the pier. Also in Scarinish you'll find **An Iodhlann** (June–Sept Tues–Fri noon–5pm; Oct–May Mon–Fri 10.30am–3.30pm; £3) – meaning "haystack" in Gaelic – the island's two-roomed archive which puts on occasional exhibitions.

The most intriguing sights lie in the bulging western half of the island, where Tiree's two landmark hills rise up. Below the higher of the two is **HYNISH**, with its restored **harbour**, designed by Alan Stevenson in the 1830s to transport building materials for the magnificent 140-foot-tall **Skerryvore Lighthouse**, which lies on a sea-swept reef some twelve miles southwest of Tiree. Up on the hill behind the harbour, a stumpy granite signal tower, whose signals used to be the only contact the lighthouse keepers had with civilization, now houses a **museum** telling the history of the Herculean effort required to erect the lighthouse; weather permitting, you can see the lighthouse from the tower's viewing platform.

As well as a daily **ferry** connection from Oban, Tiree has **flights** (Mon–Sat) to and from Glasgow. The best way to get around is on the Ring'n'Ride **minibus** service (Mon–Sat 7am–6pm, Tues until 10pm; ⓣ01879/220419), which will take you anywhere on the island. The island has two **hotels**, but the best accommodation is available from the *Kirkapol House* (ⓣ01879/220729, ⓦwww.kirkapoltiree.co.uk; ④), a friendly **B&B** in a tastefully converted kirk, a mile or so east of Scarinish along Gott Bay, and *Glebe House* (ⓣ01879/220758, ⓦwww.glebehousetiree.co.uk; ⑤), the renovated former manse overlooking the pier in Scarinish. Good **hostel** accommodation is available at the *Millhouse* (ⓣ01879/220435, ⓦwww.tireemillhouse.co.uk; dorm beds £13), near Loch Bhasapol, in the northwest of the island. There's no official campsite, but **camping** is allowed with the local crofter's permission. As for **eating**, the bar meals at both hotels are good, and there are unpretentious snacks and meals available at the pine-clad *Rural Centre* café by the airport.

Isle of Colonsay

Isolated between Mull and Islay, **Colonsay** (ⓦwww.colonsay.org.uk) is not as bleak and windswept as Coll or Tiree. Its craggy, heather-backed hills even support the occasional patch of woodland, plus a bewildering array of plant and birdlife, wild goats and rabbits, and one of the finest quasi-tropical gardens in Scotland. The population is currently around a hundred, down from a pre-Clearance peak of just under a thousand. CalMac **ferries** call daily except Tuesday and Saturday from Oban (2hr 15min), and once a week from Kennacraig via Islay (Wed; 3hr 35min), when a day-trip is possible, giving you around six hours on the island.

The ferry docks at **SCALASAIG**, on the east coast, where there's a post office/shop, a petrol pump, a restaurant and the island's hotel. Right by the pier, the old waiting room now serves as the island's heritage centre and is usually open when the ferry docks. Two miles north of Scalasaig is **Colonsay House**, built in 1722 by Malcolm MacNeil. In 1904, the island and house were bought by Lord Strathcona, who made his fortune building the Canadian Pacific Railway and who was responsible for the house's lovely woodland **gardens** (April–Sept Wed & Fri), which are slowly being restored to their former glory. To the north of Colonsay House, where the road ends, you'll find the island's finest sandy beach, the breathtaking **Kiloran Bay**, where the breakers roll in from the Atlantic.

The **Isle of Oronsay**, half a mile to the south, is only an island when the tide is in, and, as you can't stay overnight, it can only be visited as a day-trip from Colonsay. The two are separated by "The Strand", a mile of tidal mud flats which act as a causeway for two hours either side of low tide; check locally for current timings. The ruins of the **Oronsay Priory** date back to the fourteenth century, and it still has the original church and cloisters. The highlight, however, is the Oronsay Cross, a superb example of late-medieval artistry from Iona, and the numerous finely carved grave slabs that lie within the Prior's House.

Colonsay's only **hotel**, *The Colonsay* (Ⓣ01951/200316, Ⓦwww.thecolonsay.com; ❼), is within easy walking distance of the pier in Scalasaig and serves very decent bar snacks. Alternatively there's the superb *Seaview* **B&B** (Ⓣ01951/200315; April–Oct; ❹), or the budget *Keepers' Lodge*, in Kiloran (Ⓣ01951/200312; dorm beds £12), a very comfortable **hostel** with a real fire. An alternative to hotel bar **food** is the *Pantry*, above the pier in Scalasaig, which offers simple home-cooking as well as teas and cakes (ring ahead for evening meals; Ⓣ01951/200325).

Mid-Argyll

Mid-Argyll is a vague term that loosely describes the central wedge of land south of Oban and north of Kintyre. The highlights of this gently undulating scenery lie along the sharply indented west coast, in particular the rich Bronze Age and Neolithic remains in the **Kilmartin** valley, one of the most important prehistoric sites in Scotland.

Kilmartin Glen

The **Kilmartin Glen** is the most important prehistoric site on the Scottish mainland, whose most remarkable relic is the **linear cemetery**, where several cairns are aligned for more than two miles, to the south of the village of Kilmartin. These are thought to represent the successive burials of a ruling family or chieftains, but nobody can be sure. The best view of the cemetery's configuration is from the Bronze Age **Mid-Cairn**, but the Neolithic **South Cairn**, dating from around 3000 BC, is by far the oldest and the most impressive, with its large chambered tomb roofed by giant slabs. Close to the Mid-Cairn, the two **Temple Wood stone circles** appear to have been the architectural focus of burials in the area from Neolithic times to the Bronze Age. Visible to the south are the impressively cup-marked **Nether Largie standing stones** (no public access), the largest of which looms over 10ft high.

Situated on high ground to the north of the cairns is the tiny village of **KILMARTIN**, where the old manse adjacent to the village church now houses an enlightening **Museum of Ancient Culture** (daily 10am–5.30pm; Ⓦwww.kilmartin.org; £4.60). The **café** is equally enticing, with local home-baked produce on offer, which you can wash down with heather beer (also open early evening Thurs–Sat). The nearby church is worth a brief reconnoitre, as it shelters the badly damaged and weathered **Kilmartin crosses**, while a separate enclosure in the graveyard houses a large collection of medieval grave slabs of the Malcolms of Poltalloch.

To the south of Kilmartin, beyond the linear cemetery, lies the raised peat bog of Mòine Mhór (Great Moss), best known as home to the Iron Age fort of **Dunadd**, one of Scotland's most important Celtic sites, occupying a distinctive 176-foot-high rocky knoll once surrounded by the sea but currently stranded beside the winding River Add. It was here that Fergus, the first king of Dalriada, established his royal seat, having arrived from Ireland in around 500 AD. Its strategic position, the craggy defences and the view from the top are all impressive, but it's the **stone carvings** between the twin summits which make Dunadd so remarkable: several lines of inscription in *ogam* (an ancient alphabet of Irish origin), the faint outline of a boar, a hollowed-out footprint and a small basin. The boar and the inscriptions are probably Pictish, since the fort was clearly occupied long before Fergus got there, but the footprint and basin have been interpreted as being part of the royal coronation rituals of the kings of Dalriada. It's thought that the Stone of Destiny was used at Dunadd before being moved to Scone Palace (see p.884), then to Westminster Abbey in London, where it languished until it was returned to Edinburgh in 1996.

The nearest **B&B** is at *Dunchraigaig House* (Ⓣ01546/605209, Ⓦwww.dunchraigaig.co.uk; ❸), a large detached Victorian house situated opposite the Ballymeanoch standing stones, where you get home-made clootie dumpling for breakfast.

Crinan Canal

In 1801 the nine-mile-long **Crinan Canal** opened, linking Loch Fyne, at Ardrishaig south of Lochgilphead, with the Sound of Jura, thus cutting out the long and treacherous journey around the Mull of Kintyre. The canal runs parallel to the sea for quite some way before hitting a flight of locks either side of **CAIRNBAAN** (there are fifteen in total); a walk along the towpath is both picturesque and pleasantly unstrenuous. A useful pit stop can be made at the *Cairnbaan Hotel* (Ⓣ01546/603668; ❻), an eighteenth-century coaching inn overlooking the canal, with a decent restaurant and bar meals featuring locally caught seafood.

There are usually one or two yachts passing through the locks, but the most relaxing place from which to view the canal in action is **CRINAN**, a pretty little fishing port at its western end. For **accommodation**, try the secluded *Tigh-na-Glaic* (Ⓣ01546/830245; ❸), a modern B&B perched above the harbour, also with views out to sea, or the superb *Bellanoch House* (Ⓣ01546/830149, Ⓦwww.bellanochhouse.co.uk; ❺), a grand, old schoolhouse with stripped pine floors and lots of character, right on the canal, a mile or so before Crinan. It's worth having a pint or one of the excellent **bar meals** at the *Crinan Hotel*, which has lovely views out to sea. Down on the lockside there's a cheaper, cheerful **café** called the *Coffee Shop* (Easter–Oct), serving mouthwatering home-made cakes and wonderful clootie dumplings.

Kintyre

But for the mile-long isthmus between West Loch Tarbert and the much smaller East Loch Tarbert, the little-visited peninsula of **KINTYRE** (Ⓦwww.kintyre.org) – from the Gaelic *Ceann Tire*, "land's end" – would be an island. Indeed, in the eleventh century, when the Scottish king, Malcolm Canmore, allowed Magnus Barefoot, king of Norway, to lay claim to any island he could circumnavigate by boat, Magnus succeeded in dragging his boat across the Tarbert isthmus and added the peninsula to his Hebridean kingdom. During the Wars of the Covenant, the vast majority of the population and property were wiped out by a combination of the 1646 potato blight and the destructive attentions of the earl of Argyll. Kintyre remained a virtual desert until the earl began his policy of transplanting Gaelic-speaking Lowlanders to the region. They probably felt quite at home here, as the southern half of the peninsula lies on the Lowland side of the Highland Boundary Fault.

Tarbert

A distinctive rocket-like church steeple heralds the fishing village of **TARBERT** (in Gaelic *An Tairbeart*, meaning "isthmus"), sheltering an attractive little bay backed by rugged hills. Tarbert's harbourfront is pretty, and is best appreciated from the rubble of Robert the Bruce's fourteenth-century **castle** above the town to the south.

Tarbert's **tourist office** (April–Oct Mon–Sat 10am–5pm, Sun 10am–noon; longer hours in summer) is on the harbour. The *Ca'Dora* is the caff to head for on the seafront, while *The Anchor* pub, also overlooking the harbour, is a good option for a seafood lunch. The best **food** is to be had at the evening-only *Corner House Bistro* (ⓣ01880/820263), just by the side of the *Corner House* pub, or at the more expensive, but equally excellent *Anchorage* (ⓣ01880/820881; Oct–March Tues–Sun eve only), on the south side of the harbour.

Isle of Gigha

Gigha (ⓦwww.gigha.co.uk) – pronounced "geeya" – is a low-lying, fertile island three miles off the west coast of Kintyre, reputedly occupied for five thousand years. Like many of the smaller Hebrides, Gigha was bought and sold numerous times after its original lairds, the MacNeils, sold up, and was finally bought by the islanders themselves in 2002.

The ferry from Tayinloan, 23 miles south of Tarbert, deposits you at the island's only village, **ARDMINISH**, where you'll find the post office and shop. The main attraction on the island is the **Achamore Gardens** (daily 9am–dusk; £4), a mile and a half south of Ardminish. Established by the first postwar owner, Sir James Horlick of hot drink fame, their spectacularly colourful display of azaleas is best seen in early summer. The real draw of Gigha, however, apart from the peace and quiet, is the white sandy beaches – including one at Ardminish itself – that dot the coastline.

Gigha is so small – six miles by one mile – that most visitors come here just for the day. It is, however, possible **to stay** either at the *Post Office House* (ⓣ01583/505251, ⓦwww.gighastores.co.uk; ❷) or at the beautiful *Achamore House* (ⓣ01583/505400, ⓦwww.achamorehouse.com; ❻), in the midst of Achamore Gardens. The licensed *Boathouse* (ⓦwww. boathouse-bar.com), by the pier, is the place to go for delicious **food**, while the shop offers **bike rental**.

Campbeltown

CAMPBELTOWN's best feature is its setting, in a deep bay sheltered by Davaar Island and the surrounding hills. With a population of around five thousand, it's also one of the largest towns in Argyll and, if you're staying in the southern half of Kintyre, its shops are by far the best place to stock up on supplies. Campbeltown's heyday was the Victorian era, when shipbuilding was going strong, coal was shipped by canal from Drumlemble, the fishing fleet was vast and Campbeltown had no fewer than 34 whisky distilleries – today only a few remain. If you're interested in visiting one of the distilleries, pop into **Cadenhead's** whisky shop at 7 Bolgam St (ⓣ01586/554258, ⓦwww.wmcadenhead.com), which runs parallel with Longrow. Here you can sign up for a guided tour (£5) of the deeply traditional, family-owned **Springbank**, the only distillery in Scotland that does absolutely everything – from malting to bottling – on its own premises.

On the town's palm-tree-dotted waterfront you'll find the **Wee Pictures**, a little Art Deco cinema on Hall Street, built in 1913 and still going strong (daily except Fri; ⓣ01586/533657, ⓦwww.weepictures.co.uk). Campbeltown's most popular attraction is the **Scottish Owl Centre** (April to early Oct daily except Tues 1.30–4.30pm; Ⓦwww.scottishowlcentre.tk; £5), signposted off the B842 to Machrihanish, five minutes' walk out of town. The centre has a huge collection of owls spread out in terraced aviaries, ranging from the tiny Scops Owl to the world's largest, the Eurasian Eagle Owl. Try and time your visit with the daily flight display at 2.30pm.

Campbeltown's **tourist office** is on the Old Quay (May–Oct Mon–Fri 10am–5pm, Sun noon–4pm; Nov–April Mon–Fri 10am–4pm). The best **accommodation** in Campbeltown itself is *Craigard House* (Ⓣ01586/554242, Ⓦwww.craigard-house.co.uk; ⑤), a former whisky distiller's grandiose sandstone mansion with a hint of the Italian Renaissance, on Low Askomill, on the north side of the bay. For an inexpensive, central B&B, head for *Westbank Guesthouse*, on Dell Road (Ⓣ01586/553660; ②), off the B842 to Southend. As for **places to eat**, the *Gallery 10,* on Longrow South (closed Mon & Sun), is the best café in town; the *Mussel Ebb*, in Aqualibrium, on the Esplanade, also serves up decent bistro fare. The best bar meals are to be found at the *Ardshiel Hotel*, situated on a lovely leafy square, just a block or so back from the harbourfront.

Mull of Kintyre

The bulbous, hilly end of Kintyre, to the south of Campbeltown, features some of the most spectacular scenery on the whole peninsula, mixed with large swathes of Lowland-style farmland. Most people venture west of Campbeltown to make a pilgrimage to the **Mull of Kintyre**, made famous by the mawkish number-one hit by Paul McCartney, with the help of the Campbeltown Pipe Band. The nearest Britain gets to Ireland, whose coastline, just twelve miles away, appears remarkably close on fine days, there's nothing specifically to see in this godforsaken storm-wracked spot but the view and a memorial to the 29 military personnel who died in 1994 when an RAF helicopter crashed into the hillside. The roads up to the "**Gap**" (1150ft) – where you must leave your car – and particularly down to the lighthouse, itself 300ft above the ocean waves, are terrifyingly tortuous.

Isle of Arran

Shaped like a kidney bean and occupying centre stage in the Firth of Clyde, **Arran** (Ⓦwww.visitarran.net) is the most southerly (and therefore the most accessible) of all the Scottish islands. The Highland–Lowland dividing line passes right through its centre – hence the cliché about it being like "Scotland in miniature" – leaving the northern half sparsely populated, mountainous and bleak, while the lush southern half enjoys a much milder climate. The tourists, like the population of around five thousand – many of whom are in-comers – tend to stick to the southeastern quarter of the island, leaving the west and the north relatively undisturbed.

Transport on Arran itself is pretty good: daily **buses** circle the island (Brodick tourist office has timetables and an Arran Rural Rover day-ticket costs just over £4).

Brodick

Although the resort of **BRODICK** (from the Norse *breidr vik*, "broad bay") is a place of only moderate charm, it does at least have a grand setting in a

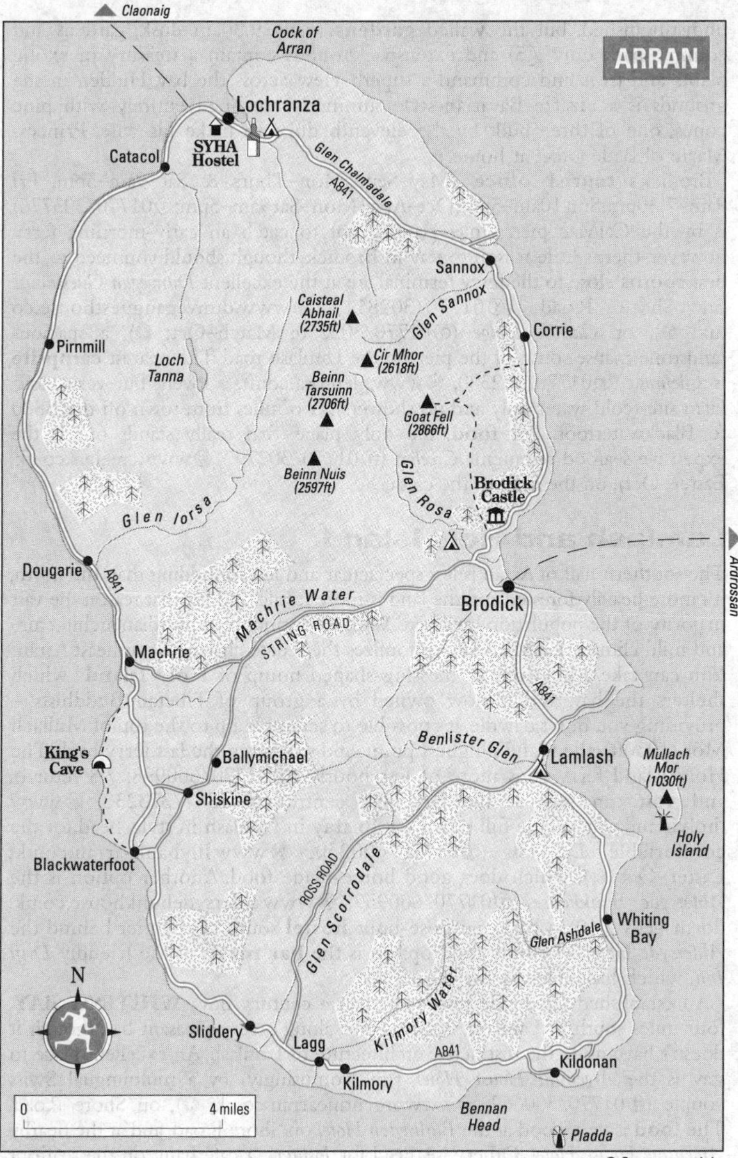

wide, sandy bay set against a backdrop of granite mountains. As the island's capital and main communication hub, Brodick is by far the busiest town on Arran.

The local dukes of Hamilton used to rule over the town from **Brodick Castle** (daily: April–Sept 11am–4.30pm; Oct 11am–3.30pm; £10; NTS), on a steep bank on the north side of the bay. The interior is comfortable if undistinguished, but the walled **gardens** (daily 9.30am–dusk; gardens and country park only £5) and extensive grounds contain a treasury of exotic plants and trees and command a superb view across the bay. Hidden in the grounds is a bizarre Bavarian-style summerhouse lined entirely with pine cones, one of three built by the eleventh duke to make his wife, Princess Marie of Baden, feel at home.

Brodick's **tourist office** (May–Sept Mon–Thurs & Sat 9am–5pm, Fri 9am–7.30pm, Sun 10am–5pm; Oct–April Mon–Sat 9am–5pm; ⓣ01770/303776) is by the CalMac pier. Unless you've got to catch an early-morning ferry, however, there's little reason to stay in Brodick, though should you need to, the best **rooms** close to the ferry terminal are at the excellent *Dunvegan Guesthouse* on Shore Road (ⓣ01770/302811, ⓦwww.dunveganguesthouse.co.uk; ③), or *Carrick Lodge* (ⓣ01770/302550; March–Oct; ④), a spacious sandstone manse south of the pier on the Lamlash road. The nearest **campsite** is *Glenrosa* (ⓣ01770/302380, ⓦwww.glenrosa.com), a lovely, but very basic, farm site (cold water only and no showers), two miles from town off the B880 to Blackwaterfoot. For **food**, the only place that really stands out is the expensive seafood restaurant *Creelers* (ⓣ01770/302797, ⓦwww.creelers.co.uk; Easter–Oct), on the road to the castle.

Lamlash and Holy Island

The southern half of Arran is less spectacular and less forbidding than the north; it's more heavily forested and the land is more fertile, and for that reason the vast majority of the population lives here. With its distinctive Edwardian architecture and mild climate, **LAMLASH** epitomizes the sedate charm of southeast Arran. You can take a boat out to the slug-shaped hump of **Holy Island**, which shelters the bay, and is now owned by a group of Tibetan Buddhists – providing you don't dawdle, it's possible to scramble up to the top of Mullach Mór (1030ft), the island's highest point, and still catch the last ferry back. The Holy Island ferry runs more or less hourly (ⓣ01770/600998; £8 return), and you can stay at the Buddhist centre (ⓣ01387/373232, ⓦwww.holyisland.org; veggie full board ④). To **stay** in Lamlash in style, head for the comfortable *Lilybank* (ⓣ01770/600230, ⓦwww.lilybank-arran.co.uk; Easter–Oct; ③), which does good home-made food. Another option is the *Aldersyde Bunkhouse* (ⓣ01770/600959, ⓦwww.aldersydebunkhouse.co.uk; dorm beds £10), a basic, purpose-built **hostel** south of the pier behind the *Aldersyde Hotel*. The only food option is the **bar meals** at the friendly *Drift Inn*, which has tables by the shore.

An established Clydeside resort for over a century now, **WHITING BAY**, four miles south of Lamlash, is spread out along a very pleasant bay, though it doesn't have quite the distinctive architecture of Lamlash. An excellent place to stay is the *Argentine House Hotel*, run (confusingly) by a multilingual Swiss couple (ⓣ01770/700662, ⓦwww.argentinearran.co.uk; ④), on Shore Road. The **food** is very good at the *Burlington Hotel* on Shore Road, and at the nearby *Argentine House Hotel*. Otherwise, head for *Joshua's*, a café bang on the seafront offering excellent home-made cakes and snacks, along with great views.

Goat Fell and Lochranza

The desolate north half of Arran – effectively the Highland part – features bare granite peaks, the occasional golden eagle and miles of unspoilt scenery, within reach only to those prepared to do some serious hiking. Arran's most accessible peak is also the island's highest, **Goat Fell** (2866ft), which can be ascended in just three hours from Brodick, though it's a strenuous hike. You can also hike up Goat Fell from **CORRIE**, Arran's prettiest little seaside village, six miles north of Brodick, where a procession of pristine cottages lines the road to Lochranza and wraps itself around an exquisite little harbour and pier.

The ruined castle which occupies the mud flats of the bay, and the brooding north-facing slopes of the mountains which frame it provide **LOCHRANZA** with one of the most spectacular settings on the island. Despite being the only place of any size in this sparsely populated area, Lochranza attracts far fewer visitors than other Arran resorts, and its main sight is the modern **distillery** (mid-March to Oct daily 10am–6pm; Nov & Dec phone ⓣ01770/830264, ⓦwww.arranwhisky.com; £3.50), at the south end of the village. The best **accommodation** is to be had at the superb *Apple Lodge* (ⓣ01770/830229; ⑤), the old village manse where you'll get excellent home-cooking, or at the equally welcoming *Lochranza Hotel* (ⓣ01770/830223, ⓦwww.lochranza.co.uk; ③), whose bar is the centre of the local social scene. Lochranza also has an SYHA **hostel** (ⓣ0870/004 1140; March–Oct; dorm beds £15), situated halfway between the distillery and the castle, and a well-equipped **campsite** (ⓣ01770/830273, ⓦwww.arran.net/lochranza; April–Oct), beautifully placed by the golf course on the Brodick road, where red deer come to graze in the early evening. The campsite has a friendly **tearoom** serving all-day breakfasts and light snacks; in the evening, head for the *Lochranza* whose **bar meals** are very popular.

Islay and Jura

The fertile, largely treeless island of **ISLAY** (ⓦwww.isle-of-islay.com) is famous for one thing – single malt **whisky**. The smoky, peaty, pungent quality of Islay whisky is unique, recognizable even to the untutored palate, and all the island's distilleries will happily take visitors on a guided tour, ending with the customary complimentary tipple. In medieval times, Islay was the political centre of the Hebrides, with **Finlaggan**, near Port Askaig, the seat of the MacDonalds, lords of the Isles. The picturesque, whitewashed villages you see on Islay today, however, date from the planned settlements founded by the Campbells in the late eighteenth and early nineteenth centuries. Apart from whisky and solitude, the other great draw is the **bird life** – there's a real possibility of spotting a golden eagle, or the rare crow-like chough, and no possibility at all of missing the scores of white-fronted and barnacle geese who winter here in their thousands. The long, whale-shaped neighbouring island of **Jura** is one of the wildest and most mountainous of the Inner Hebrides, its entire west coast uninhabited and inaccessible except to the dedicated walker.

Port Ellen and around

Laid out as a planned village in 1821 by Walter Frederick Campbell, and named after his wife, **PORT ELLEN** is the chief port on Islay, with the island's largest fishing fleet, and main CalMac ferry terminal. The neat whitewashed terraces which overlook the town's bay of golden sand, are pretty enough, but the view is dominated by the village's modern maltings, whose powerful odours waft across the town.

The only reason to pause in this part of the island is to head off east along a dead-end road that passes three **distilleries** in as many miles (see box, p.912).

Islay whisky

Islay has woken up to the fact that its whisky distilleries are a major tourist attraction. Nowadays, every distillery offers guided tours, traditionally ending with a generous dram, and a refund for your entrance fee if you buy a bottle in the shop. Phone ahead to make sure there's a tour running, as times do change frequently.

Ardbeg ⓣ01496/302244, ⓦwww.ardbeg.com. Ardbeg is traditionally considered the saltiest, peatiest malt on Islay (and that's saying something). Bought by Glenmorangie in 1997, the distillery has been thoroughly overhauled and restored, yet it still has bags of character inside. The *Old Kiln Café* is excellent (Mon–Fri 10am–4pm; June–Aug daily 10am–5pm). Guided tours regularly 11.30am–2.30pm; £2.

Bowmore ⓣ01496/810671, ⓦwww.bowmore.co.uk. The most touristy and most central of the Islay distilleries, it's also one of the few still doing its own malting and kilning. Daily guided tours (Easter–June Mon–Sat 9am–5pm; July to mid-Sept daily 9am–5pm; mid-Sept to Easter Mon–Fri 9am–5pm, Sat 9am–noon; £2).

Bruichladdich ⓣ01496/850190, ⓦwww.bruichladdich.com. Rescued in 2001 by a group of whisky fanatics, this independent distillery offers regular guided tours (Easter–Oct Mon–Fri 10.30am, 11.30am & 2.30pm, Sat 11.30am & 2.30pm; Nov–Easter Mon–Fri 11.30am & 2.30pm, Sat 11.30am; £4).

Kilchoman ⓣ01496/850011, ⓦwww.kilchomandistillery.com. Established in 2005 as the first new distillery on Islay for over a century, Kilchoman is farm-based and aims to grow the barley, malt, distil, mature and even bottle its whisky on site. The distillery welcomes visitors, and there are regular guided tours (by appointment; £3).

Lagavulin ⓣ01496/302730, ⓦwww.discovering-distilleries.com. Lagavulin probably is the classic, all-round Islay malt, with lots of smoke and peat. The distillery enjoys a fabulous setting and is extremely busy all year round. Phone ahead for details of the guided tours (Mon–Fri by appointment at 9.30am, 11.15am & 2.30pm; £3), at the end of which you'll get a taste of the best-selling 16-year-old malt.

Laphroaig ⓣ01496/302418, ⓦwww.laphroaig.com. Another classic smoky, peaty Islay malt, and another great setting. One bonus at Laphroaig is that you get to see the malting and see and smell the peat kilns. There are regular guided tours (Mon–Fri by appointment).

Another six miles down the track and you eventually come to the simple thirteenth-century **Kildalton Chapel**, which boasts a wonderful eighth-century Celtic ringed cross made from the local "bluestone". The quality of the scenes matches any to be found on the crosses carved by the monks in Iona: the Virgin and Child are on the east face, with Cain murdering Abel to the left, David fighting the lion on the top, and Abraham sacrificing Isaac on the right; on the west side amidst the serpent-and-boss work are four elephant-like beasts.

For **accommodation** in Port Ellen itself, the best place is *Caladh Sona* (ⓣ01496/302694, ⓔhamish.scott@lineone.net; ③), a detached house at 53 Frederick Crescent; alternatively, head a few miles up the road to Ardbeg and stay at the peaceful *Tigh-na-Suil* (ⓣ01496/302483, ⓔtighnasuilagav@onetel.com; ②). For something really special, though, opt for the *Glenegedale House Hotel* (ⓣ01496/300400, ⓦwww.glenegedalehouse.co.uk; ⑥), the whitewashed guesthouse opposite the airport, for superb home cooking and fantastic breakfasts. There's also a **campsite**, three miles northwest of Port Ellen, at the southern tip of Laggan Bay, at *Kintra Farm* B&B (ⓣ01496/302051, ⓦwww.kintrafarm.co.uk; April–Sept; ③).

Bowmore

On the other side of the monotonous peat bog of Duich Moss, on the southern shores of the tidal Loch Indaal, lies **BOWMORE**, Islay's administrative capital. It's a striking place, laid out in 1768 on a grid plan rather like Inveraray, with the whitewashed terraces of Main Street climbing up the hill in a straight line from the pier on Loch Indaal to the town's crowning landmark, the **Round Church**. Built in the round, so that the devil would have no corners in which to hide, it has a plain, wood-panelled interior, with a lovely tiered balcony and a big central mushroom pillar.

Islay's only **tourist office** is in Bowmore (April–Oct Mon–Sat 10am–5pm; April–Aug also Sun 2–5pm; Nov–March Mon–Fri 10am–3pm; ⓣ0870/720 0617); it can help you find **accommodation** anywhere on Islay or Jura. In Bowmore itself, head for one of the town's better B&Bs, such as *Lambeth House* (ⓣ01496/810597, ⓔlambethguesthouse@tiscali.co.uk; ❺), centrally located on Jamieson Street. For reliable hotel accommodation, go for the *Bridgend Hotel* (ⓣ01496/810212, ⓦwww.bridgend-hotel.com; ❻), a couple of miles further round the bay.

If you're visiting Islay between mid-September and the third week of April, it's impossible to miss the island's staggeringly large wintering population of **barnacle and white-fronted geese**. During this period, the geese dominate the landscape, feeding incessantly off the rich pasture, strolling by the shores, and flying in formation across the winter skies. You can see the geese just about anywhere on the island – there are an estimated 15,000 white-fronted and 40,000 barnacles here (and rising) – though in the evening, they tend to congregate in the tidal mud flats and fields around **Loch Gruinart**.

Port Charlotte

PORT CHARLOTTE, named after the founder's mother, is generally agreed to be Islay's prettiest village, its immaculate whitewashed cottages clustered around a sandy cove overlooking Loch Indaal. On the northern fringe of the village, in a whitewashed former chapel, the imaginative **Museum of Islay Life** (Easter–Oct Mon–Sat 10am–5pm, Sun 2–5pm; Nov–Easter Mon–Sat; £3), has a children's corner, quizzes, a good library of books about the island, and tantalizing snippets about eighteenth-century illegal whisky distillers. The **Wildlife Information Centre** (Easter–Oct daily except Sat 10am–3pm; July & Aug daily 10am–5pm; £2.50), housed in the former distillery warehouse, is also worth a visit for anyone interested in the island's fauna and flora.

The welcoming *Port Charlotte Hotel* (ⓣ01496/850360, ⓦwww.portcharlottehotel.co.uk; ❼) has the best **accommodation** – the seafood lunches served in the bar are very popular, and there's a good, though expensive restaurant. For B&B, you're actually better off going for the excellent *Octofad Farm* (ⓣ01496/850594, ⓦwww.octofadfarm.com; April–Oct; ❸), a few miles down the road beyond Nerabus. Port Charlotte itself is also home to Islay's SYHA **hostel** (ⓣ0870/004 1128, ⓦwww.syha.org.uk; April–Sept; dorm beds £14), housed in an old bonded warehouse next door to the Wildlife Information Centre. In addition, there's a **campsite** at the new Port Mòr Centre (ⓣ01496/850441, ⓦwww.islandofislay.co.uk), situated outside on the village on the road to Portnahaven. For inexpensive food, there's a choice between the *Croft Kitchen* (ⓣ01496/850230; April–Oct), opposite the museum, and the café in the Port Mòr Centre. The **bar** of the *Port Charlotte* is very easy-going, while the fun (and occasional live music) goes on at the *Lochindaal Inn*, down the road, where you can also tuck into a very good local-bred steak.

Finlaggan and Port Askaig

Just beyond Ballygrant, on the road to Port Askaig, a narrow road leads off north to **Loch Finlaggan**, site of a number of prehistoric crannogs (artificial islands) and, for four hundred years from the twelfth century, headquarters of the lords of the Isles, semi-autonomous rulers over the Hebrides and Kintyre. You can happily skip the **information centre** (Easter & Oct Tues, Thurs & Sun 2–4pm; May–Sept daily except Sat 2.30–5pm; £2), to the northeast of the loch, and simply head on down to the site itself (access at any time), which is dotted with interpretive panels. Duckboards allow you to walk out across the reed beds of the loch and explore the main crannog, **Eilean Mor**, where several carved gravestones are displayed under cover in the chapel, which seem to support the theory that the lords of the Isles buried their wives and children here, while having themselves interred on Iona.

Easily the most comfortable **place to stay** in the vicinity is the lovely whitewashed *Kilmeny Farmhouse* (Ⓣ01496/840668, Ⓦwww.kilmeny.co.uk; ❻), southwest of Ballygrant, a place which richly deserves all the superlatives it regularly receives, its rooms furnished with antiques and its dinners (Mon–Fri only) worth the extra £30 a head. The *Ballygrant Inn* is a good **pub** in which to grab a pint (and a bar meal), while the *Port Askaig Hotel* enjoys a wonderful position by the pier, with views over to the Paps of Jura.

Isle of Jura

Jura's distinctive Paps – so called because of their smooth breast-like shape, though there are in fact three of them – seem to dominate every view off the west coast of Argyll, their glacial rounded tops covered in a light dusting of quartzite scree. The island's name is commonly thought to derive from the Norse *dyr-oe* (deer island) and, appropriately enough, the current deer population of six thousand far outnumbers the 180 humans. With just one road, which sticks to the more sheltered eastern coast of the island, and only one hotel and a smattering of B&Bs, Jura is an ideal place to go for peace and quiet and some great walking.

If you're just coming over for the day from Islay, and don't fancy climbing the Paps, you could happily spend the day in the lovely wooded grounds of **Jura House** (daily 9am–5pm; £2.50), five miles up the road from Feolin Ferry, where the car ferry from Port Askaig arrives. Pick up a booklet at the entrance to the grounds, and follow the path down to the sandy shore, a perfect picnic spot in fine weather. Closer to the house itself, there's an idyllic **walled garden**, divided in two by a natural rushing burn that tumbles down in steps.

Anything that happens on Jura happens in the island's only real village, **CRAIGHOUSE**, eight miles up the road from Feolin Ferry. The village enjoys a sheltered setting, overlooking Knapdale on the mainland – so sheltered, in fact, that there are even a few palm trees thriving on the seafront. There's a shop, a post office, the island hotel and a tearoom, plus the tiny **Isle of Jura distillery** (Ⓣ01496/820240, Ⓦwww.isleofjura.com), which is very welcoming to visitors.

The family-run *Jura Hotel* in Craighouse is the island's one and only **hotel** (Ⓣ01496/820243, Ⓦwww.jurahotel.co.uk; ❺), not much to look at from the outside, but warm and friendly within, and centre of the island's social scene. The hotel does moderately expensive bar meals, and has a shower block and laundry facilities round the back for those who wish **to camp** in the hotel gardens. For **B&B**, contact George McBride at 8 Woodside (Ⓣ01496/706600; ❸). Very occasionally a **minibus** (☎01496/820314) meets the **car ferry** (☎01496/840681) from Port Askaig – phone ahead to check times.

In April 1946, Eric Blair (better known by his pen name of **George Orwell**), suffering badly from TB and intending to give himself "six months' quiet" in which to write his novel *1984*, moved to a remote farmhouse called Barnhill, on the northern tip of Jura. He lived out a spartan existence there for two years but was forced to return to London shortly before his death. The house, 23 miles north of Craighouse up an increasingly poor road, is as remote today as it was in Orwell's day, and is now let out as a self-catering cottage (☎01786/850274). If you're planning to explore the north end of the island, it's worth knowing about the **bunkhouse** at Kinuachdrachd (☎07899/912116).

Travel details

Trains

Glasgow (Queen Street) to: Arrochar and Tarbert (Mon–Sat 3–4 daily, Sun 1–3 daily; 1hr 20min); Oban (Mon–Sat 3–4 daily, Sun 1–3 daily; 3hr).

Mainland buses (excluding postbuses)

Arrochar to: Inveraray (Mon–Sat 3 daily, Sun 2 daily; 35min).
Campbeltown to: Glasgow (2–3 daily; 4hr 25min).
Dunoon to: Inveraray (Mon–Sat 3 daily, Sun 0–3 daily; 1hr 10min).
Glasgow to: Arrochar (3–5 daily; 1hr 10min); Campbeltown (2–3 daily; 4hr 25min); Inveraray (4–6 daily; 1hr 45min); Kennacraig (Mon–Sat 2 daily, Sun 1 daily; 3hr 30min); Lochgilphead (2–3 daily; 2hr 40min); Oban (Mon–Sat 4 daily, Sun 2 daily; 3hr); Tarbert (2–3 daily; 3hr 15min).
Inveraray to: Dunoon (Mon–Sat 3 daily, Sun 0–3 daily; 1hr 10min); Oban (Mon–Sat 3 daily, Sun 2 daily; 1hr 5min); Tarbert (2–3 daily; 1hr 30min).
Kennacraig to: Claonaig (Mon–Sat 3 daily; 15min).
Lochgilphead to: Campbeltown (3–5 daily; 1hr 45min); Crinan (Mon–Sat 3–4 daily; 20min); Oban (Mon–Sat 2–4 daily; 1hr 30min); Tarbert (3–4 daily; 30min).
Oban to: Mallaig (1 daily; 2hr 30min).
Tarbert to: Campbeltown (Mon–Sat 4 daily, Sun 2 daily; 1hr 15min); Claonaig (Mon–Sat 3 daily; 30min); Kennacraig (3–6 daily; 15min).

Island buses

Arran

Brodick to: Blackwaterfoot (Mon–Sat 12 daily, Sun 6 daily; 30min); Corrie (4–6 daily; 20min); Lamlash (Mon–Sat 14–16 daily, Sun 4 daily; 10–15min); Lochranza (Mon–Sat 6 daily, Sun 3 daily; 45min).

Bute

Rothesay to: Kilchattan Bay (Mon–Sat 4 daily, Sun 3 daily; 30min); Mount Stuart (every 45min; 15min); Rhubodach (Mon–Fri 1–2 daily; 20min).

Colonsay

Scalasaig to: Kilchattan (Mon–Fri 2–4 daily; 30min); Kiloran Bay (Mon–Fri 2–3 daily; 12min); The Strand (Mon–Fri 1 daily; 15min).

Islay

Bowmore to: Port Askaig (Mon–Sat 8–10 daily, Sun 1 daily; 30–40min); Port Charlotte (Mon–Sat 5–6 daily; 25min); Port Ellen (Mon–Sat 9–12 daily, Sun 1 daily; 20–30min); Portnahaven (Mon–Sat 5–7 daily; 50min).

Mull

Craignure to: Fionnphort (Mon–Sat 3–4 daily, Sun 1 daily; 1hr 10min); Fishnish (3 daily; 10min); Tobermory (4–6 daily; 45min).
Tobermory to: Calgary (Mon–Sat 2 daily; 45min); Dervaig (Mon–Fri 3 daily, Sat 2 daily; 30min); Fishnish (2–4 daily; 40min).

Car ferries (summer timetable)

To Arran: Ardrossan–Brodick (4–6 daily; 55min); Claonaig–Lochranza (8–9 daily; 30min).
To Bute: Colintraive–Rhubodach (frequently; 5min); Wemyss Bay–Rothesay (every 45min; 30min).
To Coll: Oban–Coll (1 daily; 2hr 40min).
To Colonsay: Kennacraig–Colonsay (Wed 1 daily; 3hr 35min); Oban–Colonsay (daily except Tues & Sat; 2hr 15min); Port Askaig–Colonsay (Wed 2 daily; 1hr 15min).
To Dunoon: Gourock–Dunoon (hourly; 20min); McInroy's Point–Hunter's Quay (every 30min; 20min).
To Gigha: Tayinloan–Gigha (hourly; 20min).
To Islay: Colonsay–Port Askaig (Wed 2 daily; 1hr 15min); Kennacraig–Port Askaig (1–3 daily;

2hr); Kennacraig–Port Ellen (1–3 daily; 2hr 10min).
To Jura: Port Askaig–Feolin Ferry (Mon–Sat hourly, Sun 3 daily; 10min).
To Kintyre: Portavadie–Tarbert (hourly; 25min).
To Mull: Kilchoan–Tobermory (Mon–Sat 7 daily; June–Aug also Sun 5 daily; 35min); Lochaline–Fishnish (Mon–Sat every 50min, Sun hourly; 15min); Oban–Craignure (Mon–Sat 6–7 daily, Sun 4–5 daily; 45min).
To Tiree: Barra–Tiree (Wed 1 daily; 3hr 5min); Oban–Tiree (daily; 3hr 40min).

Passenger-only ferries (summer timetable)

To Iona: Fionnphort–Iona (Mon–Sat frequently, Sun hourly; 5min).

Flights

Glasgow to: Campbeltown (Mon–Fri 2 daily; 35min); Islay (Mon–Fri 2 daily, Sat 1 daily; 40min); Tiree (Mon–Sat 1 daily; 45min).

22 Skye and the Western Isles

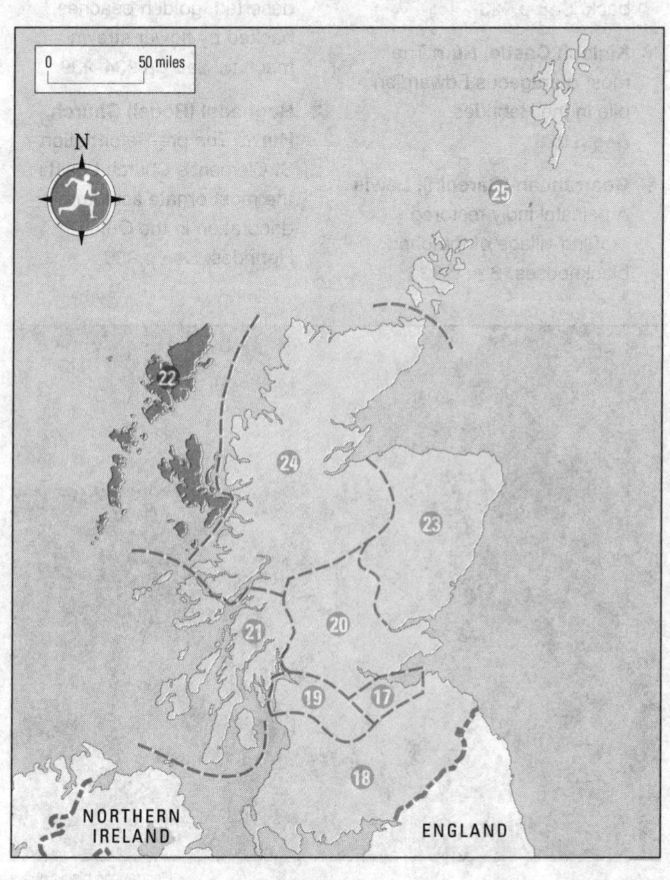

CHAPTER 22

Highlights

* **Skye Cuillin** These jagged peaks make Skye a great place to visit. See p.923
* **Loch Coruisk boat trip, Skye** Take the boat from Elgol to the beautiful, remote, glacial Loch Coruisk in the midst of the Skye Cuillin, and walk back. See p.923
* **Kinloch Castle, Rùm** The most outrageous Edwardian pile in the Hebrides. See p.928
* **Gearrannan (Garenin), Lewis** A painstakingly restored crofting village of thatched blackhouses. See p.933
* **Calanais (Callanish), Lewis** Scotland's finest standing stones are set in a serene lochside setting. See p.934
* **Golden sandy beaches** Harris and the Uists have some stunning, mostly deserted, golden beaches, backed by flower-strewn machair. See pp.934–939
* **Roghadal (Rodel) Church, Harris** The pre-Reformation St Clement's Church boasts the most ornate sculptural decoration in the Outer Hebrides. See p.936

▲ Gearrannan blackhouses

22

Skye and the Western Isles

A procession of Hebridean islands, islets and reefs off the northwest shore of Scotland, **Skye and the Western Isles** between them boast some of the country's most alluring scenery. It's here that the turbulent seas of the Atlantic smash up against an extravagant shoreline hundreds of miles long, a geologically complex terrain whose rough rocks and mighty sea cliffs are interrupted by a thousand sheltered bays and, in the far west, a long line of sweeping sandy beaches. The islands' interiors are equally dramatic, a series of formidable mountain ranges soaring high above great chunks of boggy peat moor, a barren wilderness enclosing a host of lochans, or tiny lakes.

Each island has its own distinct character, though the grouping splits quite neatly into two. **Skye** and the **Small Isles** – the improbably named **Rùm**, **Eigg**, **Muck** and **Canna** – are part of the Inner Hebrides, which also include the islands of Argyll (see p.893). Beyond Skye, across the unpredictable waters of the Minch, lie the Outer Hebrides or Outer Isles, nowadays known as the **Western Isles**, a 130-mile-long archipelago stretching from **Lewis** and **Harris** in the north to **Barra** in the south. The whole region has four obvious areas of outstanding natural beauty to aim for: on Skye, the harsh peaks of the **Cuillin** and the bizarre rock formations of the **Trotternish** peninsula; on the Western Isles, the mountains of **North Harris** and the splendid sandy beaches that string along the Atlantic seaboard of **South Harris** and the **Uists**.

Skye and the Western Isles were first settled by Neolithic farming peoples in around 4000 BC. They lived along the coast, where they are remembered by scores of remains, from passage graves through to stone circles, most famously at **Calanais** (Callanish) on Lewis. Viking colonization gathered pace from 700 AD onwards – on Lewis four out of every five place-names is of Norse origin – and it was only in 1266 that the islands were returned to the Scottish crown. James VI (James I of England), a Stuart and a Scot, though no Gaelic-speaker, was the first to put forward the idea of clearing the Hebrides. However, it wasn't until after the Jacobite uprisings, in which many Highland clans disastrously backed the wrong side, that the **Clearances** began in earnest.

The isolation of the Hebrides exposed them to the whims and fancies of the various merchants and aristocrats who bought them up. Time and again, from the mid-eighteenth century to the present day, both the land and its people were sold to the highest bidder. Some proprietors were well-meaning, but others simply forced the inhabitants onto ships bound for North America at gunpoint. Always the islanders were powerless and almost everywhere they were driven from their ancestral homes. However, their language survived, ensuring a degree of cultural continuity, especially in the Western Isles, where even today the first language of the vast majority is **Gaelic** (pronounced "gallic").

Skye

Jutting out from the mainland like a giant butterfly, the bare and bony promontories of **Skye** (Ⓦ www.skye.co.uk) fringe a deeply indented coastline. Despite the unpredictability of the weather, **tourism** has been an important part of the

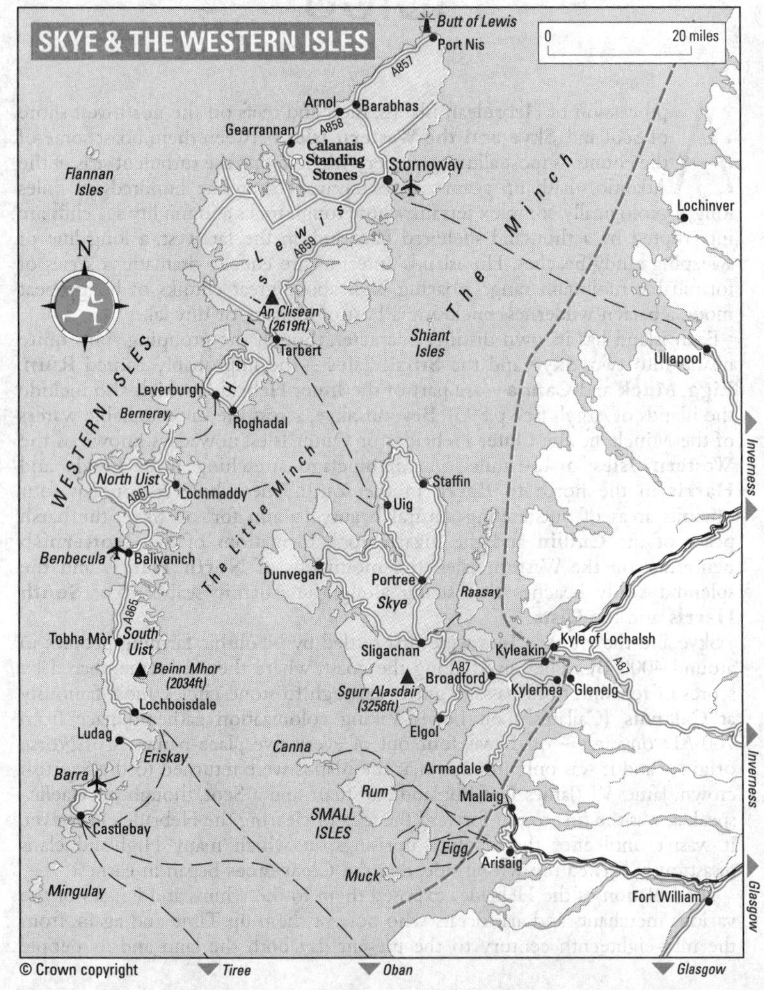

island's economy for a hundred years, since the train line pushed through to **Kyle of Lochalsh** in the western Highlands in 1897. From Kyle, it was the briefest of boat trips across to Skye, and the Edwardian bourgeoisie was soon swarming over to walk its mountains, whose beauty had been proclaimed by an earlier generation of Victorian climbers.

Though some estimate that today only half the island's population are indigenous *Sgiathanachs* (pronounced "Ski-anaks"), Skye remains the most important centre for **Gaelic culture** and language outside the Western Isles. For a taste of Gaelic culture, don't miss the Skye and Lochalsh Festival, *Feis an Eilein* (Ⓦwww.feisaneilein.com), which takes place over two weeks in mid-July.

Skye's most popular destination is the **Cuillin** ridge, whose jagged peaks dominate the island during clear weather. More easily accessible and equally dramatic in their own way are the rock formations of the **Trotternish** peninsula, in the north, from where there are inspirational views across to the Western Isles. If you want to escape the summer crush, head for the **Isle of Raasay**, off Skye's east coast. Of the island's two main settlements, **Portree** is the only one with any charm, and a useful base for exploring the Trotternish.

Most visitors still reach Skye via Kyle of Lochalsh, which is linked to Inverness by **train** and to Kyleakin, on the eastern tip of the island, by the **Skye Bridge**. The more scenic approach is by **ferry** from Mallaig, further south, crossing to Armadale. A third option is the privately operated summer-only car ferry that leaves the mainland at Glenelg, south of Kyle of Lochalsh, to arrive at Kylerhea. **Bus** services, while adequate between the villages, virtually close down on Sundays.

Sleat

Ferries from Mallaig connect with the **Sleat** (pronounced "Slate") **peninsula**, Skye's southern tip, an uncharacteristically fertile area known as "The Garden of Skye". The CalMac ferry terminal is at **ARMADALE** (Armadal), an elongated hamlet stretching along the wooded shoreline. If you need to stay near Armadale, your best bet is one of the peninsula's **hostels**: Armadale SYHA hostel (Ⓣ0870/004 1103, Ⓦwww.syha.org.uk; mid-April to mid-Sept; dorm beds £12) is a convenient ten-minute walk up the A851 towards Broadford and has a good position overlooking the bay; the *Flora MacDonald Hostel* (Ⓣ01471/844272, Ⓦwww.skye-hostel.co.uk; dorm beds £11), two miles further up the same road, beyond Sabhal Mòr Ostaig, is a converted barn with bunkbeds and private rooms (③); run by locals who will fetch you from the ferry. For a **hotel**, head a mile southwest towards neighbouring Ardvasar, for the traditional, whitewashed *Ardvasar Hotel* (Ⓣ01471/844223, Ⓦwww.ardvasarhotel.com; ⑤), which has a good restaurant specializing in local seafood and a lively bar. **Bike rental** is available from the SYHA hostel or the local petrol station (Ⓣ01471/844249), close to the pier.

On the A851, past the SYHA hostel, you'll find the handsome forty-acre **Armadale Castle Gardens** (April–Oct daily 9.30am–5.30pm; £5; Ⓦwww.clandonald.com). Within the gardens lies the shell of the MacDonalds' neo-Gothic castle, a café and a library for those who want to chase up their ancestral Donald connections. The gardens' slick, purpose-built **Clan Donald Museum** has a good section on the Jacobite period and its aftermath and one or two topnotch works of art by Angelika Kaufmann, and Raeburn.

Continuing northeast, it's another eight miles to **ISLEORNSAY** (Eilean Iarmain), a secluded little village of whitewashed cottages that was once Skye's main fishing port. You can **stay** at the mid-nineteenth-century *Hotel Eilean Iarmain*, a pricey place whose **restaurant** serves great seafood (Ⓣ01471/833332,

ⓦwww.eilean-iarmain.com; ❼), but where you can also just have a good bar meal by an open fire.

Kyleakin and Broadford

The **Skye Bridge** links the tidy hamlet of **KYLEAKIN** (Caol Acain – pronounced "Ka*la*kin") with the Kyle of Lochalsh on the mainland. The bridge rests on an island in the middle, **Eilean Bàn**, whose lighthouse cottages were once the home of author and naturalist Gavin Maxwell. The house has been turned into a museum, but can only be visited on a guided tour (£6); numbers are limited and tours must be booked in advance through the **Bright Water Visitor Centre** in Kyleakin (April–Oct Mon–Fri 10am–5pm; free; ⓣ01599/530040, ⓦwww.eileanban.org). The centre itself is well worth a visit, as it's full of hands-on things for children of all ages.

With its ferry now defunct, Kyleakin has reinvented itself as something of a backpackers' hang-out and in summer, the population more than doubles. For a decent, reliable **hostel**, go for either the cosy *Dun Caan Hostel* (ⓣ01599/534087, ⓦwww.skyerover.co.uk; dorm beds £13), or nearby *Skye Backpackers* (ⓣ01599/534510, ⓦwww.scotlands-top-hostels.com), part of the MacBackpackers' circuit of hostels. **Bike rental** is available from *Dun Caan* and Skye Bikes (ⓣ01599/534795) on the pier.

Skye's second-largest village is the charmless **BROADFORD** (An t-Ath Leathann), where you'll find a **tourist office** (Easter–Oct Mon–Fri 10am–5pm; Sat 11am–4pm) by the 24-hour garage on the main road, as well as a laundry, small shop and bureau de change. There's a surfeit of **B&Bs**, but one stands out of the crowd: *Berabhaigh*, 3 Lime Park (ⓣ01471/822372, ⓦwww.isleofskye.net/berabhaigh; March–Oct; ❸), a whitewashed crofthouse close to the centre of the village. If you want a bite **to eat**, try the justifiably popular *Creelers Seafood Restaurant* (ⓣ01471/822281, ⓦwww.skye-seafood-restaurant.co.uk) at the south end of the bay.

Isle of Raasay

Travelling west from Broadford, with the Skye Cuillin to your left and the sea to your right, it's thirteen miles to Sconsor, where a CalMac car ferry (Mon–Sat only) leaves for the lovely **Isle of Raasay**, which, with its bleak and barren hills, remains well off the tourist trail. Raasay's population stands around two hundred, and the Free Presbyterian Church has a strong following here – the island keeps a strict observance of the Sabbath.

The ferry docks at the southern tip of the island, an easy fifteen-minute walk from **INVERARISH**, a tiny village set within thick woods on the island's southwest coast. The grand Georgian mansion of **Raasay House**, built by the MacLeods in the late 1740s, on the western edge of the village, is now an outdoor centre offering comfortable **accommodation** in pleasantly casual rooms (ⓣ01478/660266, ⓦwww.raasay-house.co.uk; ❶). You can also **camp** in the grounds or stay in the bunkhouse, and they'll happily collect you from the ferry terminal. In addition, you can join the centre's **activity programme**, which includes anything from sailing, windsurfing and canoeing, to climbing and hill-walking. Close by is the welcoming *Isle of Raasay Hotel* (ⓣ01478/660222, ⓦwww.isleofraasayhotel.co.uk; ❺), which serves traditional Scottish food and has views of the Cuillin that surpass any other.

A rough track cuts up the steep hillside from the village to Raasay's isolated but beautifully placed SYHA **hostel** (ⓣ0870/004 1146, ⓦwww.syha.org.uk; mid-May to mid-Sept; dorm beds £15). Most of the rest of Raasay is starkly barren, a rugged and rocky terrain of sandstone in the south and gneiss in the north, with the most obvious feature being the curiously truncated basalt cap on top of **Dun Caan** (1456ft), where Boswell "danced a Highland dance" on his visit to the island with Dr Johnson in 1773.

The Cuillin and the Red Hills

For many people, the **Cuillin**, whose sharp snowcapped peaks rise mirage-like from the flatness of the surrounding terrain, are the *raison d'être* for a visit to Skye. When the clouds finally disperse, they are the dominating feature of the island, visible from every other peninsula. There are basically three approaches to the Cuillin: from the south, by foot or by boat from Elgol; from the *Sligachan Hotel* to the north; or from Glen Brittle to the west of the mountains. The second is one of the most popular routes, dividing as it does the granite of the round-topped **Red Hills** (sometimes known as the Red Cuillin) to the east from the dark, coarse-grained jagged-edged gabbro of the real Cuillin (also known as the Black Cuillin) to the west. With some twenty Munros between them, these are mountains to be taken seriously, and many routes through the Cuillin are for experienced climbers only.

Elgol and Loch Coruisk

The road to **ELGOL** (Ealaghol), fourteen miles southwest of Broadford at the tip of the Strathaird peninsula, is one of the most dramatic on the island, leading right into the heart of the Red Hills and then down a precipitous slope, with a stunning view from the top down to Elgol pier. The chief reason for visiting Elgol is, weather permitting, to take a **boat** across Loch Scavaig, past a seal colony, to a jetty near the entrance of **Loch Coruisk** (from *coire uish*, "cauldron of water"). An isolated, glacial loch, this needle-like shaft of water, nearly two miles long but only a couple of hundred yards wide, lies in the shadow of the highest peaks of the Black Cuillin, a wonderfully overpowering landscape. The journey takes about an hour and passengers are dropped to spend time ashore. From Easter to October, two boats currently offer the trip: the *Bella Jane* (Ⓣ0800/731 3089, Ⓦwww.bellajane.co.uk), and the *Misty Isle* (Ⓣ01471/866288, Ⓦwww.mistyisleboattrips.co.uk; Mon–Sat only).

If you want a bite to eat, Elgol has a coffee shop and the excellent seafood **restaurant** at *Coruisk House* (Ⓣ01471/866330, Ⓦwww.seafood-skye.co.uk; April–Oct; ⑤), which also offers **B&B** in its bright and cheerful rooms. Alternatively, try *Rowan Cottage* (Ⓣ01471/866287, Ⓦwww.rowancottage-skye.co.uk; March–Oct; ④), a lovely **B&B** a mile or so east in Glasnakille. By far the most popular place to stay is the **campsite** and **bunkhouse** (Ⓣ01478/650204, Ⓦwww.sligachan.co.uk; April–Oct; dorm beds £10) by the *Sligachan Hotel* on the A87, at the northern end of Glen Sligachan. The hotel's huge *Seamus Bar* serves food for weary walkers until 11pm, and quenches their thirst with its own real ales, and often has live bands.

Glen Brittle

Six miles along the A863 to Dunvegan from the *Sligachan Hotel*, a turning signed "Carbost and Portnalong" quickly leads to the entrance to stony **Glen Brittle**, edging the most spectacular peaks of the Cuillin; at the end of the glen, idyllically situated by the sea, is the village of **GLENBRITTLE**. Climbers and serious walkers tend to congregate at the SYHA **hostel** (Ⓣ0870/004 1121, Ⓦwww.syha.org.uk; April–Sept; dorm beds £14) or the beautifully situated **campsite** (Ⓣ01478/640404; April–Oct), a mile or so further south behind the wide sandy beach at the foot of the glen. At the time of writing, there was no bus service to Glenbrittle; both the hostel and the campsite have grocery stores, the only ones for miles.

From the valley a score of difficult and strenuous trails lead east into the **Black Cuillin**, a rough semicircle of peaks rising to about 3000ft, which surround Loch Coruisk. One of the easiest walks is the five-mile round-trip from the campsite up **Coire Lagan**, to a crystal-cold lochan squeezed in among the sternest of rock faces. Above the lochan is Skye's highest peak, **Sgurr Alasdair** (3258ft), one of the more difficult Munros, while Sgurr na Banachdich (3166ft), to the northwest, is considered the most easily accessible Munro in the Cuillin.

Dunvegan

After the Portnalong and Glen Brittle turning, the A863 slips north across bare rounded hills to skirt the bony sea cliffs and stacks of the west coast. After twenty miles or so, it reaches **DUNVEGAN** (Dùn Bheagain), an unimpressive place, but a good base for exploring the interesting Duirinish peninsula. The main tourist trap in the village is **Dunvegan Castle** (daily: mid-March to Oct 10am–5pm; Nov to mid-March 11am–4pm; £7.50, gardens only £5.50; Ⓦ www.dunvegancastle.com) which sprawls on top of a rocky outcrop, sandwiched between the sea and several acres of beautifully maintained gardens. Seat of the Clan MacLeod since the thirteenth century, the present greying, rectangular fortress dates from the 1840s. Inside, you don't get a lot of castle for your money and the contents are far from stunning, the most intriguing being the battered remnants of the **Fairy Flag** which was allegedly carried back to Skye by Norwegian king Harald Hardrada's Gaelic boatmen after the Battle of Stamford Bridge in 1066.

Dunvegan has a **tourist office** (April & May Mon–Fri 10am–5pm; June–Oct Mon–Sat 10am–5pm; July & Aug also Sun 10am–4pm; Nov–March Mon–Fri 10am–1.30pm) and several good **hotels** and **B&Bs** in the vicinity: try the converted traditional croft *Roskhill House* (Ⓣ 01470/521317, Ⓦ www.roskhillhouse.co.uk; ❺), or the excellent **campsite** (Ⓣ 01470/521210, Ⓦ www.kinloch-campsite.co.uk; April–Oct), at the southern end of Loch Dunvegan.

The area's culinary highlight is the expensive *Three Chimneys* **restaurant** (Ⓣ 01470/511258, Ⓦ www.threechimneys.co.uk), on the road to Colbost, which serves sublime three-course meals at just under £50 a head (lunch is around £30); there are also six fabulous rooms at the restaurant's adjacent *House Over-By* (❾). Much more reasonable is the sixteenth-century *Stein Inn* (Ⓣ 01470/592362, Ⓦ www.steininn.co.uk; ❸), in Stein, with welcoming fires and good **pub food**; next door is the pricier *Lochbay Seafood Restaurant* (Ⓣ 01470/592235; Easter–Oct closed Sat & Sun; Aug closed Sun), where you'll need to book ahead.

Portree

Although referred to by the locals as "the village", **PORTREE** is Skye's only real town, and is one of the most attractive fishing ports in northwest Scotland, its deep, cliff-edged harbour filled with fishing boats and circled by multi-coloured restaurants and guesthouses. Up above the harbour is the spick-and-span town centre, spreading out from **Somerled Square**, built in the late eighteenth century as the island's administrative and commercial centre, and now housing the bus station and car park. The **Royal Hotel** on Bank Street occupies the site of *McNab's Inn* where Bonnie Prince Charlie took leave of Flora MacDonald (see p.926), and where, 27 years later, Boswell and Johnson had "a very good dinner, porter, port and punch".

A mile or so out of town on the Sligachan road is the **Aros Centre** (daily 9am–6pm; open later in summer; Ⓦwww.aros.co.uk), one of Skye's most successful tourist attractions despite the fact that it's little more than an enormous souvenir shop. If it's wet, you can watch a live RSPB webcam centred on sea eagles' nests and an audiovisual roam around the island (£4). Aros also hosts gigs and contains a **cinema**, an exhibition space, a licensed bar and a popular café, and there's a play area for small kids.

Practicalities

Hours vary enormously at Portree's **tourist office**, just off Bridge Street, so the ones here are just a guideline (April–Oct Mon–Sat 9am–8pm, Sun 10am–4pm; Nov–March Mon–Sat 9am–5.30pm); the office will, for a small fee, book **accommodation**. Probably the best hotel is the comfortable *Cuillin Hills* (Ⓣ01478/612003, Ⓦwww.cuillinhills-hotel-skye.co.uk; ❽), ten minutes' walk out of town along the northern shore of the bay, though *Viewfield House Hotel* (Ⓣ01478/612217, Ⓦwww.viewfieldhouse.com; ❺; mid-April to mid-Oct), on the southern outskirts of town, is also worth investigating for its Victorian atmosphere, stuffed polecats and antiques. For B&Bs, try *Medina* (Ⓣ01478/612821, Ⓦwww.medinaskye.co.uk; ❸), a well-run B&B in a quiet spot by the *Cuillin Hills Hotel*, or *Balloch*, Viewfield Rd (Ⓣ01478/612093, Ⓦwww.balloch-skye.co.uk; ❸; Easter–Oct). The best **hostel** is the small, but clean *Bayfield Backpackers* (Ⓣ01478/612231, Ⓦwww.skyehostel.co.uk; dorm beds £13), just by the main car park. *Torvaig* **campsite** (Ⓣ01478/612209; April–Oct) is well-kept, with a friendly owner, and lies a mile and a half north of town off the A855 Staffin road.

Portree has a surfeit of **eating** options, but for somewhere relaxed, try *Café Arriba*, at the top of road down to the harbour, which offers reasonably priced Mediterranean dishes, or else there's an excellent chippy on the harbour. The most popular evening venue is the *Isles Inn* on Somerled Square, with excellent bar meals as well as live music.

Trotternish

Protruding twenty miles north from Portree, the **Trotternish peninsula** boasts some of the island's most bizarre scenery, particularly on the east coast, where volcanic basalt has pressed down on the softer sandstone and limestone underneath, causing massive landslides. These, in turn, have created pinnacles and pillars that are at their most eccentric in the Quiraing, above Staffin Bay, on the east coast. An occasional bus service (Mon–Sat 2–4 daily) along the road encircling the peninsula gives access to almost all the peninsula.

The east coast

The first geological eccentricity on the **Trotternish** peninsula, six miles north of Portree along the A855, is the **Old Man of Storr**, a distinctive 165ft column of rock, shaped like a willow leaf, which, along with its neighbours, is part of a massive landslip. Huge blocks of stone still occasionally break off the cliff face of the Storr (2358ft) above and slide downhill. It's a half-hour trek up a footpath to the foot of the column from the woods beside the car park. Further north, **Staffin Bay** is spread out before you, dotted with whitewashed and "spotty" houses. A single-track road cuts across the peninsula from the north end of the bay, allowing access to the **Quiraing**, a spectacular forest of mighty pinnacles and savage rock formations. There are two car parks: from the first, beside a cemetery, it's a steep half-hour climb to the rocks; from the second, on the saddle, it's a longer but more gentle traverse.

Most **accommodation** choices on the east coast enjoy fantastic views out over the sea. Just beyond the Lealt Falls there's the very welcoming and comfortable *Glenview Inn* (ⓣ01470/562248, ⓦwww.glenview-skye.co.uk; ⑥), with an excellent restaurant, and a **campsite** (ⓣ01470/562213; April–Sept) south of Staffin Bay. Good bar snacks are served on the castellated terrace of the stylish *Flodigarry Country House Hotel*, three miles up the coast from Staffin. Behind the hotel (and now part of it) is the cottage where local heroine Flora MacDonald lived, and had six of her seven children, from 1751 to 1759. You can **camp** or stay at the neat and attractive *Dun Flodigarry* **hostel** (ⓣ01470/552212, ⓦwww.hostelflodigarry.co.uk; dorm beds £12.50), a couple of minutes' walk away.

The west coast

Heading down the west shore of the Trotternish, two miles beyond Duntulm is the **Skye Museum of Island Life** (Easter–Oct Mon–Sat 9.30am–5pm; £2.50; ⓦwww.skyemuseum.co.uk), an impressive cluster of thatched blackhouses on an exposed hill overlooking Harris. The museum gives a fascinating insight into a way of life that was commonplace on Skye a hundred years ago. The blackhouse, now home to the ticket office, is much as it was when it was

Bonnie Prince Charlie

Prince Charles Edward Stewart – better known as **Bonnie Prince Charlie** or "The Young Pretender" – was born in Rome in 1720, where his father, "The Old Pretender", claimant to the British throne, was living in exile. At the age of 25, having little military experience, no knowledge of Gaelic, an imperfect grasp of English and a strong attachment to the Catholic faith, the prince set out for Scotland on a French ship, disguised as a seminarist from the Scots College in Paris. He arrived on the Outer Hebridean island of **Eriskay** on July 23, 1745, and was immediately implored to return to France by the clan chiefs, who were singularly unimpressed by his lack of army. Charles was unmoved and went on to raise the royal standard at Glenfinnan, gather together a Highland army, win the Battle of Prestonpans, march south into England and reach Derby before finally (and foolishly) agreeing to retreat. Back in Scotland, he won one last victory, at Falkirk, before the final disaster at **Culloden** in April 1746.

The prince spent the following five months in hiding, with a price of £30,000 on his head, and thousands of government troops searching for him. He certainly endured his fair share of cold and hunger whilst on the run, but the real price was paid by the Highlanders themselves, who risked and sometimes lost their lives by aiding and abetting the prince. The most famous of these was 23-year-old **Flora MacDonald**, whom Charles met on South Uist in June 1746. Flora was persuaded – either by his beauty or her relatives, depending on which account you believe – to convey Charles "over the sea to Skye", disguised as an Irish servant girl by the name of Betty Burke. She was arrested just seven days after parting with the prince in Portree, and held in the Tower of London until July 1747. She went on to marry a local man, had seven children, and in 1774 emigrated to America, where her husband was taken prisoner during the American War of Independence. Flora returned to Scotland and was reunited with her husband on his release; they resettled in Skye and she died at the age of 68.

Charles eventually boarded a ship back to France in September 1746, but, despite his promises – "for all that has happened, Madam, I hope we shall meet in St James's yet" – never returned to Scotland, nor did he ever see Flora again. After mistreating a string of mistresses, he eventually got married at the age of 52 to the 19-year-old Princess of Stolberg, in an effort to produce a Stewart heir. They had no children, and she eventually fled from his violent drunkenness; in 1788, a none-too-"bonnie" Prince Charles died in the arms of his illegitimate daughter in Rome.

last inhabited in 1957, while the two houses to the east contain interesting snippets of local history. Behind the museum in the cemetery up the hill are the graves of **Flora MacDonald** and her husband. Thousands turned out for her funeral in 1790, creating a funeral procession a mile long – indeed, so widespread was her fame that the original family mausoleum fell victim to souvenir hunters and had to be replaced. The Celtic cross headstone is inscribed with a simple tribute by Dr Johnson, who visited her in 1773: "Her name will be mentioned in history, if courage and fidelity be virtues, mentioned with honour."

Skye's chief ferry port for the Western Isles is **UIG** (Uige), which curves its way round a dramatic, horseshoe-shaped bay. Most folk are just passing through Uig, but if you need to stay near the ferry terminal, *Orasay*, 14 Idrigill (Ⓣ01470/542316, Ⓦwww.holiday-skye.co.uk; ❷), is an inexpensive **B&B**, a minute's walk from the pier, while *Braigh-uige* (Ⓣ01470/542228, Ⓦwww.uig-skye.co.uk; April–Oct; ❷), is on the other side of the bay near the church. There's also the attractive *Kilmuir House* (Ⓣ01470/542262, Ⓦwww.kilmuir-skye.co.uk; ❷), an old manse, a couple of miles up the road to Kilmuir. Uig's **campsite**, on a sloping field very close to the pier (Ⓣ01470/542714, Ⓦwww.uig-camping-skye.co.uk), is open all year and also offers **bike rental**. By contrast, the SYHA **hostel** (Ⓣ0870/004 1155; April–Oct; dorm beds £14) is a fifteen-minute walk away, high up on the south side of the village, with exhilarating views over the bay. The *Pub at the Pier* offers basic **pub food**, and serves beers from the nearby **brewery** (Mon–Fri tours by appointment; Ⓣ01470/542477, Ⓦwww.skyebrewery.co.uk).

The Small Isles

The history of the **Small Isles**, which lie to the south of Skye, is typical of the Hebrides: early Christianization, followed by a period of Norwegian rule that ended in 1266 when the islands fell into Scottish hands. The Scots support for the Jacobite cause resulted in hard times after the failed rebellion of 1745, but the biggest problems came with the introduction of the **potato** in the mid-eighteenth century, which prompted a population explosion. At first, the problem of overcrowding was lessened by the **kelp** boom, in which the islanders were employed. But the economic bubble burst with the end of the Napoleonic Wars and most owners eventually resorted to forced Clearances.

Since then, each of the islands has been bought and sold several times, though only **Muck** is now privately owned by the benevolent laird, Lawrence MacEwen. **Eigg** was bought by the islanders themselves in 1997. The other islands were bequeathed to national agencies: **Rùm**, by far the largest and most-visited of the group, possessing a cluster of formidable volcanic peaks and the architecturally remarkable Kinloch Castle, belongs to Scottish Natural Heritage; while **Canna**, in many ways the prettiest of the isles with its high basalt cliffs, is owned by the National Trust for Scotland.

Accommodation on the Small Isles is limited and every establishment requires **booking** at all times of year. CalMac ferries run to the Small Isles from Mallaig (Ⓣ01687/462403, Ⓦwww.calmac.co.uk; Mon–Sat only). In addition, the **Sheerwater** (Ⓣ01687/450224, Ⓦwww.arisaig.co.uk; May–Sept), operates a daily service from Arisaig to Rùm, Eigg or Muck. Day-trips are possible to each of the islands on certain days.

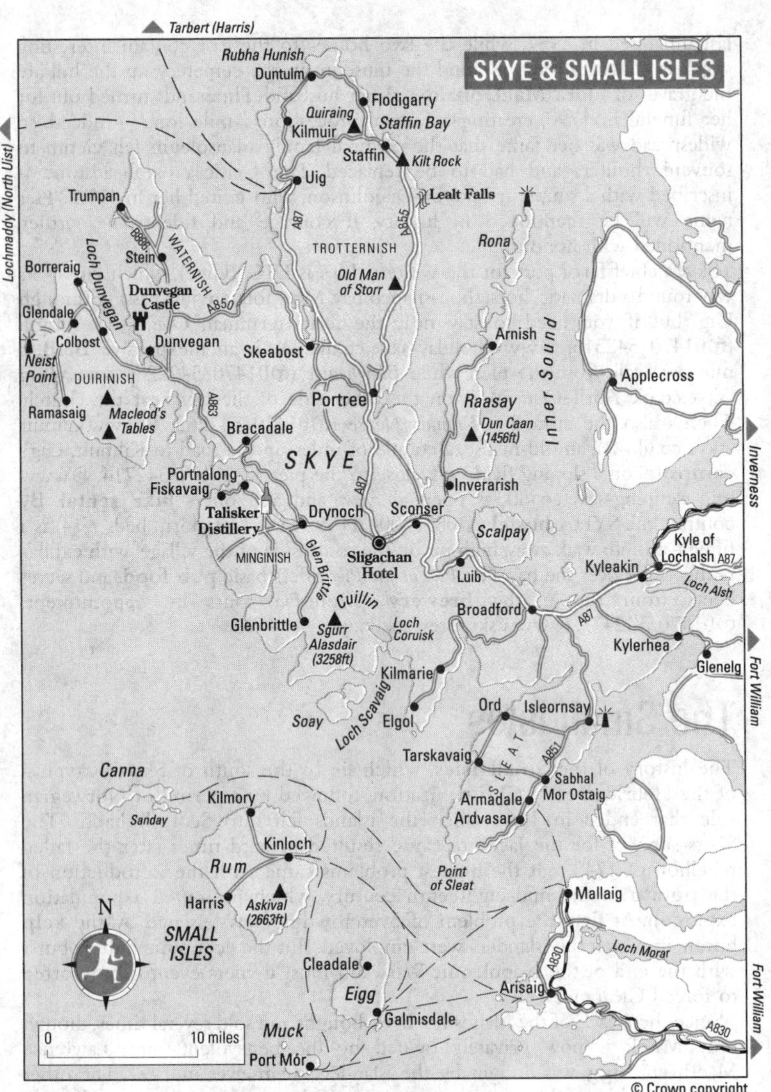

Rùm

Like Skye, **Rùm** (Ⓦwww.isleofrum.com) is dominated by its Cuillin, which, though only reaching a height of 2663ft at the summit of Askival, rises up with comparable drama straight up from the sea in the south of the island. Rùm's chief formal attraction is **Kinloch Castle** (guided tours most days at around 2pm; £6; Ⓦwww.kinlochcastle.co.uk), a squat red-sandstone edifice fronted by colonnades and topped by crenellations and turrets, that overshadows the village of Kinloch. From the galleried hall, with its tiger rugs, stags' heads and giant Japanese incense-burners, to the "Extra Low Fast Cushion" of the Soho snooker table in the Billiard Room, the interior is packed with knick-knacks and technical gizmos accumulated by **Sir George Bullough** (1870–1939), the spendthrift son of self-made millionaire Sir John Bullough, who bought the island as a sporting estate in 1888. One of Bullough's prize possessions was his orchestrion, an electrically driven barrel organ (originally destined for Balmoral) crammed in under the stairs, that would grind out an eccentric mixture of pre-dinner tunes – *The Ride of the Valkyries* and *Ma Blushin' Rosie* among others; a demo is included in the tour.

Two gentle waymarked **heritage trails** start from Kinloch, both taking around two hours. The island's best beach is at **KILMORY**, to the north (5hr return), though check with the reserve manager about public access (Ⓣ01687/462026). The hamlet of **HARRIS** on the southwest coast (6hr return) once housed a large crofting community; all that remains now are several ruined blackhouses and the extravagant **Bullough Mausoleum**, built by Sir George to house the remains of his father in the style of a Greek Doric temple, overlooking the sea.

Kinloch Castle lets a few of its (non en-suite) four-poster rooms (❺), but it's basically run as an independent **hostel** (Ⓣ01687/462037; dorm beds £14), with dormitories in the old servants' quarters. There are also two simple mountain **bothies** (maximum stay 3 nights), in Dibidil and Guirdil, and basic **camping** near the old pier – book ahead for both with the White House (Ⓣ01687/462026). Wherever you're staying, you can use the hostel kitchen, or eat the unpretentious **food** offered in the hostel's licensed bistro, which serves full breakfasts, offers packed lunches and charges just under £15 a head for a three-course evening meal. There is also a small shop/off-licence/post office in Kinloch. Bear in mind that Rùm is the wettest of the Small Isles, and is known for having some of the worst **midges** in Scotland – come prepared for both.

Eigg

Eigg (Ⓦwww.isleofeigg.org) is without doubt the most easily distinguishable of the Small Isles from a distance, since the island is mostly made up of a basalt plateau 1000ft above sea level, and a great stump of columnar pitchstone lava, known as An Sgurr, rising out of the plateau another 290ft. It's also by far the most vibrant, populous and welcoming of the Small Isles, with a strong sense of community.

Ferries arrive at the causeway, which juts out into **Galmisdale Bay** at the southeast corner of the island where **An Laimhrig** (The Anchorage), the island's community centre, stands, housing a shop, post office, tearoom and information centre. Davie's minibus meets incoming ferries, and will take you to wherever you need to go on the island (Ⓣ01687/482494; £2). With the island's great landmark, **An Sgurr** (1292ft), watching over you wherever you go, many folk feel duty-bound to climb it, and enjoy the wonderful views over to Muck and Rùm (3–4hr return).

The nicest place **to stay** on Eigg is *Kildonan House* (Ⓣ01687/482446; full board ❹), an eighteenth-century wood-panelled house beautifully situated on the north side of Galmisdale Bay, with good home-cooking. The island has a very comfortable **bunkhouse**, *Glebe Barn* (Ⓣ01687/482417; dorm beds £14), while basic **camping** is possible at Galmisdale Bay.

Muck

Smallest and most southerly of the Small Isles, **Muck** (Ⓦwww.isleofmuck.com; dorm beds £11.50) is low-lying, mostly treeless and extremely fertile, and as such shares more characteristics with the likes of Coll and Tiree than its nearest neighbours. **PORT MÓR**, the village on the southeast corner of the island, is where visitors arrive. A road, just over a mile in length, connects Port Mór with the island's main farm, **Gallanch**, which overlooks the rocky seal-strewn skerries on the north side of the island. The nicest sandy beach is Camas na Cairidh, to the east of Gallanach. Despite being only 452ft above sea level, it really is worth climbing **Beinn Airein**, in the southwest corner of the island, for the 360-degree panoramic view; the return journey from Port Mór takes around two hours.

You can **stay** with one of the MacEwen family, who have owned the island since 1896, at *Port Mór House* (ⓣ01687/462365; full board ⑤); the rooms are pine-clad and enjoy great views, and the food is delicious. Alternatively, you can stay at the island's seven-bed **bunkhouse** (ⓣ01687/462042), a characterful, wood-panelled bothy heated by a Raeburn stove. You can also hire the island **yurt** (ⓣ01687/462362), or **camp rough** – ask at the craft shop (April–Sept), in Port Mór, which springs into life when day-trippers arrive, and serves evening meals on request. Bring supplies with you, as there is no shop.

Canna

Measuring five miles by one, and with a population of less than twenty, **Canna** is run as a single farm and bird sanctuary by the National Trust for Scotland. For visitors, the chief pastime is walking: from the dock it's about a mile across a grassy basalt plateau to the bony sea cliffs of the north shore, which rise to a peak around **Compass Hill** (458ft) – so called because its high metal content distorts compasses – in the northeastern corner of the island, from where you get great views across to Rùm and Skye. The cliffs of the buffeted western half of the island are a breeding ground for both Manx shearwater and puffin. Some seven miles offshore stands the **Heiskeir of Canna**, a curious mass of stone columns sticking up thirty feet above the water.

With permission from the NTS, you may **camp rough** on Canna, though you need to bring your own supplies, as there's no real shop to speak of. *Tighard*, a Victorian house half a mile from the jetty, is the island's only **guesthouse** (ⓣ01687/462474). Wendy MacKinnon can help answer most queries (ⓣ01687/462465, ⓦwww.harbourview-canna.co.uk) and runs the *Harbour View* licensed **tearoom** (March–Oct), which serves lunch and dinner (advance booking essential).

The Western Isles

Beyond Skye, across the unpredictable waters of the Minch, lie the wild and windy Outer Hebrides or Outer Isles, also known as the **Western Isles** (ⓦwww.visithebrides.com), a 130-mile-long archipelago stretching from Lewis and Harris in the north to the Uists and Barra in the south. An elemental beauty pervades the more than two hundred islands that make up the Long Isle, as it's sometimes known; only a handful are inhabited, by a total population of just under 27,000 people.

The Outer Hebrides remain the heartland of **Gaelic** culture, with the language spoken by the vast majority of islanders, though its everyday usage remains under constant threat from the national dominance of English. Its survival is, in no small part, due to the efforts of the Western Islands Council and the Scottish Executive, and down to the influence of the church in the

Gaelic in the Western Isles

Except in Stornoway, and Balivanich on North Uist, **road signs** in the Western Isles are almost exclusively in **Gaelic**, a difficult language to the English-speaker's eye, with complex pronunciation, though the English names can often provide a rough pronunciation guide. Particularly if you're driving, it's a good idea to buy the bilingual Western Isles **map**, *Bord Turasachd nan Eilean*, available at most tourist offices.

region: the Free Church and its various Presbyterian offshoots in Lewis, Harris and North Uist, and the Roman Catholic Church in South Uist and Barra.

The interior of the northernmost island, **Lewis**, is mostly peat moor, a barren and marshy tract that gives way abruptly to the bare peaks of **North Harris**. Across a narrow isthmus lies **South Harris**, presenting some of the finest scenery in Scotland, with wide beaches of golden sand trimming the Atlantic in full view of a rough boulder-strewn interior. Across the Sound of Harris, to the south, a string of tiny, flatter isles – **North Uist**, **Benbecula**, **South Uist** – linked by causeways, offer breezy beaches, whose fine sands front a narrow band of boggy farmland, which, in turn, is mostly bordered by a lower range of hills to the east. Finally, tiny **Barra** contains all these landscapes in one small Hebridean package, and is a great introduction to the region.

In direct contrast to their wonderful landscapes, villages in the Western Isles are rarely very picturesque in themselves, and are usually made up of scattered, relatively modern croft houses dotted about the elementary road system. **Stornoway**, the only real town in the Outer Hebrides, is eminently unappealing. Many visitors, walkers and nature watchers forsake the settlements altogether and retreat to secluded cottages and B&Bs.

Transport practicalities

Several airlines operate fast and frequent daily **flights** from Glasgow, Edinburgh and Inverness to Stornoway on Lewis, and from Glasgow to Barra and Benbecula (Mon–Sat). CalMac **car ferries** run from Ullapool in the Highlands to Stornoway (Mon–Sat); from Uig, on Skye, to Tarbert (Mon–Sat) and Lochmaddy; and from Oban to South Uist and Barra, via Tiree (Thurs only). There's also an **inter-island ferry** from Leverburgh, on Harris, to Berneray, and thence to the Uists, and between Eriskay, at the foot of the Uists, and Barra. For more on ferry services, see "Travel details" on p.942.

Lewis (Leodhas)

The northernmost island in the Hebridean archipelago, **Lewis** is the largest and most populous of the Western Isles. Most of its 20,000 inhabitants live in the crofting and fishing villages strung out along the northwest coast, between **Calanais** and **Port Nis**, in one of Scotland's most densely populated rural areas. On this coast you'll find the islands' best-preserved **prehistoric remains** – Dùn Charlabhaigh broch and Calanais standing stones – as well as a smattering of ancient crofters' houses in various stages of abandonment. The landscape is mostly flat peat bog, but the shoreline is more dramatic especially around Rubha Robhanais (Butt of Lewis), a group of rough rocks on the island's northernmost tip, near Port Nis. To the south, where Lewis is physically joined with Harris, the land rises to just over 1800ft, providing a more exhilarating backdrop for the excellent beaches that pepper the isolated west coast. **Stornoway**, on the east coast, is the only substantial town in the Western Isles, but it's really only useful for stocking up on provisions or catching the bus.

Stornoway (Steornabhagh)

In these parts, **STORNOWAY** is a buzzing metropolis, with over six thouand inhabitants. It's the social hub of the island and, perhaps most importantly of all, home to the Western Isles Council or **Comhairle nan Eilean Siar**, which has done much to promote Gaelic language and culture, and stem the tide of anglicization. For the visitor, however, the town is unlikely to win any great praise – aesthetics are not its strong point, and the urban pleasures on offer are limited.

Stornoway's best-looking building is the old **Town Hall** on South Beach, a splendid Scots Baronial building, its rooftop interspersed with conical towers, above which a central clocktower rises. One block east along South Beach, you'll find **An Lanntair** (Mon–Sat 10am–10pm; free; Ⓦwww.lanntair.com) – Gaelic for "lantern" – Stornoway's state-of-the-art cultural centre, which houses a 250-seat auditorium and cinema, and gallery space for temporary exhibitions, plus a decent café-bar. Continuing up the pedestrian precinct into Francis Street, you'll eventually reach the **Museum nan Eilean** (April–Sept Mon–Sat 10am–5.30pm; Oct–March Tues–Fri 10am–5pm, Sat 10am–1pm; free; Ⓦwww.cne-siar.gov.uk), with lots of information about the island's history and its herring and weaving industries.

To the northwest of the town centre stands **Lews Castle** (Ⓦwww.lews-castle.com), a nineteenth-century Gothic pomposity built by Sir James Matheson in 1863 after resettling the crofters who used to live here. Its chief attraction is its mature wooded grounds, a unique sight on the Western Isles, and its **Woodland Centre** (Mon–Sat 10am–5pm; free), which has a straightforward exhibition on the history of the castle and the island upstairs, and a respectable **café** serving soup, salads and cakes downstairs.

Practicalities

The island's **airport** (Ⓣ01851/707400, Ⓦwww.hial.co.uk) is four miles east of the town centre: the hourly bus takes fifteen minutes, or else it's £5 by taxi. The CalMac **ferry terminal** is on South Beach, close to the **bus station**, and the **tourist office** is near North Beach at 26 Cromwell St (April to mid-Oct Mon–Fri 9am–6pm, Sat 9am–5pm, plus open to meet the evening ferry; mid-Oct to March Mon–Fri 9am–5pm).

As for **accommodation**, the *County Hotel* on Cromwell Street (Ⓣ01851/703250; ④) is the best of the hotels. Alternatively, there's the *Park Guesthouse* on James Street (Ⓣ01851/702485; ④), whose public areas have bags of lugubrious late-Victorian character, the bedrooms less so, or *Fernlea*, a Victorian B&B, along leafy Matheson Road, at no. 9 (Ⓣ01851/702125, Ⓔfernlea_guesthouse@hotmail.co.uk; ③). There's also the *Heb Hostel* (Ⓣ01851/709889, Ⓦwww.hebhostel.co.uk; dorm beds £15), a newly converted place at 25 Kenneth St.

For **food**, the first choice is *Thai Café*, 27 Church St (Ⓣ01851/701811; closed Sun), which serves inexpensive authentic Thai food. The café-restaurant in An Lanntair does nicely presented and reasonably priced sandwiches, pasta, burgers and the like, as well as more adventurous stuff in the evening. The *Royal Hotel*'s café-bar *HS-1*, is a stylish, modern place offering simple fare like baked potatoes to stir-fries and curries. *MacNeills* on Cromwell Street is the liveliest central **pub**, or there's the tiny *Criterion*, on Point Street.

The road to Port Nis (Port of Ness)

Northwest of Stornoway, the A857 crosses the vast, barren **peat bog** of the interior, an empty undulating wilderness riddled with stretchmarks formed by peat cuttings and pockmarked with freshwater lochans. For the people of Lewis the peat continues to serve as a valuable energy resource, its pungent smoke one of the most characteristic smells of the Western Isles. Plans are afoot to build Europe's largest **wind farm** (Ⓦwww.lewiswind.com) here, with some 180 wind turbines, each standing 400ft high, harnessing a vast renewable resource that the Western Isles has.

Twelve miles across the peat bog the road approaches the west coast of Lewis near Barabhas and divides, heading southwest towards Calanais (see p.934), or northeast through a string of scattered settlements to the fishing village of **PORT NIS** (Port of Ness). Shortly before Port Nis, a minor road heads two miles northwest to the hamlet of **EOROPAIDH** (Europie) – pronounced "yor-erpee". Here, by the road junction that leads to the Butt of Lewis, stands the simple stone structure of **Teampull Mholuaidh** (St Moluag's Church), thought to date from the twelfth century. From Eoropaidh, a narrow road twists to the bleak and blustery northern tip of the island, Rubha Robhanais – known to devotees of the BBC shipping forecast as the **Butt of Lewis** – where a lighthouse sticks up above a series of sheer cliffs and stacks, alive with sea birds and a great place for marine mammal-spotting.

Four to six buses a day run from Stornoway to Port Nis (Mon–Sat). The best **accommodation** in the area is at *Galson Farm Guesthouse* (Ⓣ01851/850492, Ⓦwww.galsonfarm.freeserve.co.uk; ④), an eighteenth-century farmhouse in Gabhsann Bho Dheas (South Galson), halfway between Barabhas and Port Nis, with a **bunkhouse** close by (phone number as above; dorm beds £9). The only **pub** is the *Cross Inn* in Cros, and there are only a few shops (supplemented by mobile ones) in these parts, so stock up in Stornoway before you set out.

Arnol and around

Heading southwest from the crossroads near Barabhas brings you to several villages that meander down towards the sea. In **ARNOL**, the remains of numerous blackhouses lie abandoned by the roadside; at the north end of the village, no. 42 has been preserved as the **Arnol Blackhouse** (Mon–Sat: April–Sept 9.30am–5.30pm; Oct–March 9.30am–4.30pm; £5; HS) to show exactly how a true blackhouse (*taigh dubh*) would have been. The dark interior is lit and heated by a small peat fire, which is kept alight in the central hearth of bare earth, and is usually fairly smoky as there's no chimney; instead, smoke drifts through the thatch, helping to kill any creepy-crawlies, keep out the midges and turn the heathery sods and oat-straw thatch itself into next year's fertilizer. The *Eilean Fraoich* **campsite** (Ⓣ01851/710504, Ⓦwww.eileanfraoich.co.uk; April–Oct) is located behind the old church in Siabost (Shawbost), and you can grab a bite to **eat** at the *Shawbost Inn*.

Five miles on at Carlabhagh (Carloway), a mile-long road leads off north to the beautifully remote coastal settlement of **GEARRANNAN** (Garenin), with its nine thatched crofters' houses – the last of which was abandoned in 1974 – restored to appear like an old **Baile Tughaidh** or blackhouse village (May–Sept Mon–Sat 9.30am–5.30pm; £2.50). The first house you come to is the ticket office and **café**; the second has been restored to its condition at the time of abandonment; while the third house tells the history of the village and the folk who lived there. Opposite, another house has been renovated to contain a basic GHHT **hostel** (Ⓦwww.gatliff.org.uk; dorm beds £8), and several others have been converted into **self-catering** houses (Ⓦwww.gearrannan.com).

Just beyond Carlabhagh, about 400 yards from the road, the two-thousand-year-old **Dùn Charlabhaigh Broch** perches on top of a conspicuous rocky outcrop overlooking the sea. This is one of Scotland's best-preserved brochs (a circular, prehistoric stone fort), its dry-stone circular walls reaching a height of more than 30ft on one side. The **Doune Broch Centre** (May–Sept Mon–Sat 10am–5pm; free) is situated at a discreet distance, stone-built and sporting a turf roof. It's a good wet-weather retreat, and fun for kids, who can walk through a hay-strewn mock-up of the broch.

Calanais (Callanish)

Five miles south of Carlabhagh lies **CALANAIS** (Callanish), site of the islands' most dramatic prehistoric ruins, the **Calanais standing stones**, which occupy a serene lochside setting. These monoliths – nearly fifty slabs of gnarled and finely grained gneiss up to 15ft high – were transported here between 3000 and 1500 BC, but there have been years of heated debate about the origin and function of the stones, although it's obvious that the planning and construction of the site – as well as several other lesser circles nearby – were spread over many generations. Such an endeavour could, it's been argued, only be prompted by the desire to predict the seasonal cycle upon which these early farmers were entirely dependent, and indeed many of the stones are aligned with the positions of the sun and the stars. This rational explanation, based on clear evidence that this part of Lewis was once a fertile farming area, dismisses as coincidence the ground plan of the site, which resembles a colossal Celtic cross, and explains away the central burial chamber as a later addition of no special significance. These two features have fuelled a plethora of theories ranging from alien intervention to human sacrifice.

A blackhouse adjacent to the main stone circle serves as a **tearoom** offering limited snacks. On the other side of the stones, the **Calanais Visitor Centre** (April–Sept Mon–Sat 10am–6pm; Oct–March Wed–Sat 10am–4pm; museum £1.85; Ⓦwww.calanaisvisitorcentre.co.uk) has a slightly longer (though no more imaginative) menu and a small museum on the site, but with so much information on the panels beside the stones there's little reason to visit it.

There are several good **places to stay** in Calanais: try the modern *Eshcol Guesthouse* (Ⓣ01851/621357, Ⓦwww.eshcol.com; ④), no beauty from the outside, but very well-run and comfortable within, or the newly built *Leumadair Guesthouse* (Ⓣ01851/612706, Ⓦwww.leumadair.co.uk; ④).

Harris (Na Hearadh)

Harris, to the south of Lewis, is much hillier, more dramatic and much more appealing than its neighbour, its boulder-strewn slopes descending to aquamarine bays of dazzling, white sand. The island is clearly divided by a minuscule isthmus, into the wild, inhospitable mountains of **North Harris** and the gentler landscape and sandy shores of **South Harris**. Crofting continues on Harris on a small scale, supplemented by the tweed industry, and shellfish fishing continues on Scalpay, while the rest of the population gets by on whatever employment is available: roadworks, crafts and, of course, tourism. There's a regular **bus** connection between Stornoway and **Tarbert**, and an occasional service that circumnavigates South Harris.

Tarbert (An Tairbeart)

The largest place on Harris is the ferry port of **TARBERT**, sheltered in a green valley on the narrow neck of land that marks the border between North and South Harris. Its mountainous backdrop is impressive, and the town is attractively laid out on steep terraces sloping up from the dock. It boasts Harris's only **tourist office** (April to mid-Oct Mon–Sat 9am–5pm; also open to greet the evening ferry), close to the ferry terminal.

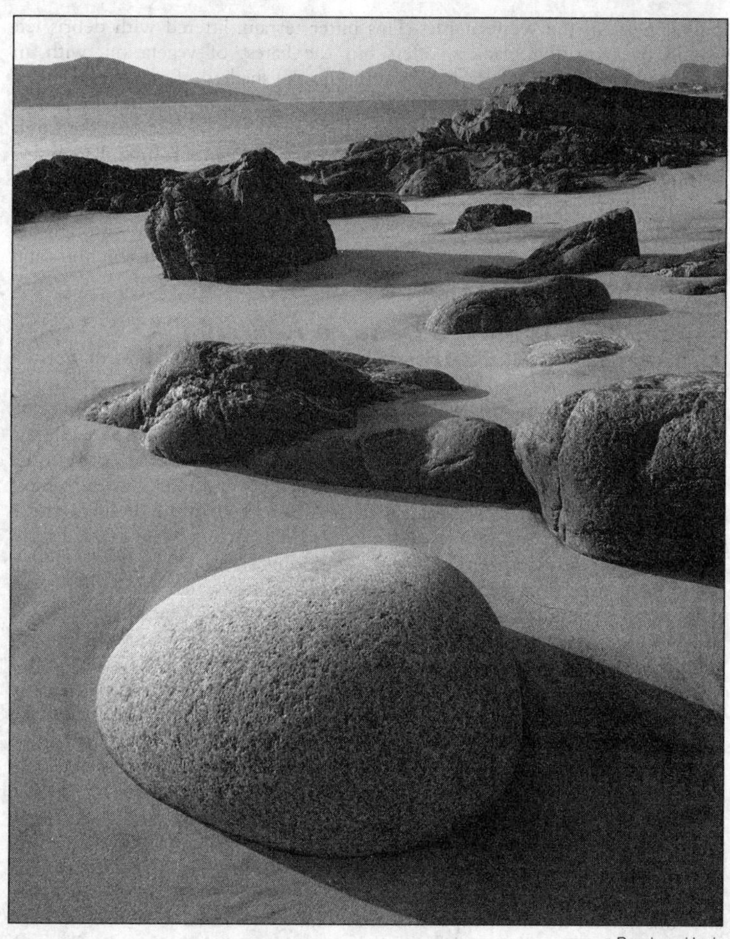

▲Beach on Harris

In Tarbert itself, there's an excellent **hostel** called the *Rockview Bunkhouse* (Ⓣ01859/502081; dorm beds £10), on Main Street, which has laundry facilities and also offers **bike rental**. If you're looking for **accommodation** close to the ferry terminal, there's a very good **B&B**, *Tigh na Mara* (Ⓣ01859/502270, Ⓦwww.tigh-na-mara.co.uk; ③), or the long-established *Harris Hotel* (Ⓣ01859/502154, Ⓦwww.harrishotel.com; ⑤), five minutes' walk away. The best **fish and chips** are dispensed by *Ad's Take-Away* (April–Oct; closed Sun), next to the hostel. Otherwise, head for the very pleasant *First Fruits* **tearoom** (April–Sept; closed Sun), behind the tourist office, housed in an old stone-built cottage and serving real coffee, home-made cakes, toasties and so forth, plus evening meals (Ⓣ01859/502439; Tues–Sat; booking advisable).

North Harris (Ceann a Tuath na Hearadh)

The A859 north to Stornoway takes you over a boulder-strewn saddle between mighty **Sgaoth Aird** (1829ft) and An Cliseam or the **Clisham** (2619ft), the highest peak in the Western Isles. This bitter terrain, littered with debris left behind by retreating glaciers, offers but the barest of vegetation, with an occasional cluster of crofters' houses sitting in the shadow of a host of pointed peaks, anywhere between 1000ft and 2500ft high. These bulging, pyramidal mountains reach their climax around the dramatic shores of the fjord-like **Loch Seaforth**. The only place to stay in this area is the GHHT **hostel** (Ⓦwww.gatliff.org.uk; dorm beds £8) in the lonely coastal hamlet of **REINIGEADAL** (Rhenigdale). To reach the hostel on foot from Tarbert (3hr one-way), take the path from Caolas Scalpaigh (Kyles Scalpay), which threads its way through the peaks of the craggy promontory that lies trapped between Loch Shìphoirt and Loch an Tairbeart.

South Harris (Ceann a Deas na Hearadh)

The mountains of **South Harris** are less dramatic than in the north, but the scenery is equally breathtaking. There's a choice of routes from Tarbert to the ferry port of **Leverburgh**, which connects with North Uist: the east coast, known as Na Baigh (The Bays), is rugged and seemingly inhospitable, while the **west coast** is endowed with some of the finest stretches of golden sand in the whole of the archipelago, buffeted by the Atlantic winds. Paradoxically, most people on South Harris live along the harsh eastern coastline of **Bays** rather than the more fertile west side. But not by choice – they were evicted from their original crofts to make way for sheep-grazing.

The main road from Tarbert into South Harris snakes its way west for ten miles across the boulder-strewn interior to reach the coast. Once there, you get a view of the most stunning **beach, Tràigh Losgaintir**. The road continues to ride above a chain of sweeping sands, backed by rich **machair** that stretches for nine miles along the Atlantic coast. In good weather, the scenery is particularly impressive, with foaming breakers rolling along the golden sands set against the rounded peaks of the mountains to the north and the islet-studded turquoise sea to the west – and even on the dullest day the sand manages to glow beneath the waves. *Beul-na-Mara* (Ⓣ01859/550205, Ⓦwww.beulnamara.co.uk; ❺) is a very good modern **B&B** in Seilebost, overlooking the sands of Tràigh Losgaintir. Five miles further south lies *Scarista House* (Ⓣ01859/550238, Ⓦwww.scaristahouse.com; ❽) whose rooms are beautifully furnished, though quite small for the price; the **restaurant** is one of the best on the Western Isles, and thus among the most expensive, at around £40 a head.

From Taobh Tuath the road veers to the southeast to trim the island's south shore, eventually reaching the sprawling settlement of **LEVERBURGH** (An t-Ob), named after Lord Leverhulme, who planned to turn the place into the largest fishing port on the west coast of Scotland. It's a place that has languished for quite some time, but has picked up quite a bit since the establishment of the CalMac **car ferry** service to Berneray and the Uists. For **accommodation**, head for *Sorrel Cottage* (Ⓣ01859/520319, Ⓦwww.sorrelcottage.co.uk; ❷), a converted crofthouse a mile or so back towards Taobh Tuath from Leverburgh, that also offers **bike rental**. A cheaper alternative is the quirky, timber-clad *Am Bothan* (Ⓣ01859/520251, Ⓦwww.ambothan.com; dorm beds £12), a luxurious, very welcoming **bunkhouse** that's only a few minutes' walk from the ferry. On the north side of the bay is the *An Clachan* Co-op store which houses a small **information office**. For some local langoustines, home-made cakes and the usual comfort **food**, head for *The Anchorage* (closed Sun), over by the ferry slipway, and look out for the occasional live music night.

Three miles southeast of Leverburgh and a mile or so from Renish Point, the southern tip of Harris, is the old port of **ROGHADAL** (Rodel), where a

Harris Tweed

Far from being a picturesque cottage industry, as it's sometimes presented, the production of **Harris Tweed** is vital to the local economy, with a well-organized and unionized workforce. Traditionally, the tweed was made by women from the wool of their own sheep, to provide clothing for their families, using a 2500-year-old process. Each woman was responsible for plucking the wool by hand, washing and scouring it, dyeing it with lichen, heather flowers or ragwort, carding (smoothing and straightening the wool, often adding butter to grease it), spinning and weaving. Finally the cloth was dipped in urine and "waulked" by a group of women, who beat the cloth on a table to soften and shrink it whilst singing Gaelic waulking songs. Harris Tweed was originally made all over the islands, and was known simply as *clò mór* (big cloth).

In the mid-nineteenth century, the Countess of Dunmore, who owned a large part of Harris, started to sell surplus cloth to her aristocratic friends; she then sent two sisters from Srannda (Strond) to Paisley to learn the trade. On their return, they formed the genesis of the modern industry, which serves as a vital source of employment, though demand (and therefore employment levels) can fluctuate wildly as fashions change. To earn the official Harris Tweed Association trademark of the Orb and the Maltese Cross – taken from the Countess of Dunmore's coat of arms – the fabric has to be hand-woven on the Outer Hebrides from 100 percent pure new Scottish wool, with other parts of the manufacturing process taking place only in local mills.

The main centre of production is now Lewis, where the wool is dyed, carded and spun. In the last few decades, there has been a revival of traditional tweed-making techniques, with several small producers following old methods, using indigenous plants and bushes to dye the cloth: yellow comes from rocket and broom; green from heather; grey and black from iris and oak; and, most popular of all, reddish brown from crotal, a flat grey lichen scraped off rocks.

smattering of ancient stone houses lies among the hillocks surrounding the dilapidated harbour where the ferry from Skye used to arrive. On top of one of these grassy humps is **St Clement's Church** (Tur Chliamainn), burial place of the MacLeods of Harris and Dunvegan in Skye. Dating from the 1520s, the church's bare interior is distinguished by its wall tombs, notably that of the founder, Alasdair Crotach (also known as Alexander MacLeod), whose heavily weathered effigy lies beneath an intriguing backdrop and canopy of sculpted reliefs depicting vernacular and religious scenes. Look out, too, for the *sheila-na-gig* (a naked pre-Christian fertility goddess) halfway up the south side of the church tower; unusually, she has a brother displaying his genitalia too, below a carving of St Clement on the west face.

North Uist (Uibhist a Tuath)

Compared to the mountainous scenery of Harris, **North Uist** – seventeen miles long and thirteen miles wide – is much flatter and for some comes as something of an anticlimax. Over half the surface area is covered by water, creating a distinctive peaty-brown lochan-studded "drowned landscape". Most visitors come here for the trout and salmon fishing and the deerstalking, both of which (along with poaching) are critical to the survival of the island's economy. Others come for the smattering of prehistoric sites, the birds, or the sheer peace of this windy isle, and the solitude of North Uist's vast sandy beaches, which extend – almost without interruption – along the north and west coasts.

Despite being situated on the east coast, some distance away from any beach, the ferry port of **LOCHMADDY** (Loch nam Madadh, or "Loch of the Dogs") makes a good base for exploring the island. The village itself, occupying a narrow, bumpy promontory, is nothing special, but it does have a **tourist office** (April to mid-Oct Mon–Sat 9am–5pm; also open to greet the evening ferry), and the nearby **Taigh Chearsabhagh** (Mon–Sat 10am–5pm; free Ⓦwww.taigh-chearsabhagh.org), a converted eighteenth-century merchant's house. Now home to a community arts centre, with a simple airy café, post office and shop, it also has an excellent museum which puts on some seriously innovative exhibitions. Taigh Chearsabhagh was one of the prime movers behind the Uist Sculpture Trail that starts outside the arts centre on the shore, and takes visitors to some remote corners of the Uists. The first and most popular of the sculptures, **Both nam Faileas** ("Hut of the Shadow"), is a short walk past the Uist Outdoor Centre, across a footbridge.

The best **accommodation** on North Uist is at *Langass Lodge* (Ⓣ01876/580285, Ⓦwww.langasslodge.co.uk; ❻), a venerable **hotel** with a stylish modern extension, whose restaurant and bar serves excellent local seafood. Back in Lochmaddy itself, there's *Redburn House* (Ⓣ01876/500301, Ⓦwww.redburnhouse.com; ❹), a nicely renovated Victorian house, and in the opposite direction, the *Uist Outdoor Centre* (Ⓣ01876/500480, Ⓦwww.uistoutdoorcentre.co.uk; Feb to mid-Dec; dorm beds £12), which has **hostel** accommodation and offers activities, ranging from sea-kayaking to "rubber tubing".

Several prehistoric sights lie within easy cycling distance of Lochmaddy, the most significant being the **Barpa Langass**, a large, mostly intact, chambered cairn seven barren miles to the southwest along the A867. North Uist's other main draw is the **Balranald RSPB Reserve**, on the western tip of the island and best known for its population of corncrakes: there are usually one or two making a loud noise right outside the RSPB **visitor centre**, from which you can pick up a leaflet outlining a two-hour walk along the headland, marked by posts. A wonderful carpet of flowers covers the machair in summer, and there are usually corn buntings and arctic terns inland, and gannets, Manx shearwater and skuas out to sea. On a clear day you can see the unmistakeable shape of the remote archipelago of St Kilda, looking miraculously near on the western horizon.

Bhearnaraigh (Berneray)

The ferry connection with Harris leaves from the very southeastern point of **Berneray** (Ⓦwww.isleofberneray.com), a low-lying island immediately to the north of North Uist and connected to the latter via a causeway. Two miles by three, with a population of just over a hundred, the island has a superb three-mile-long sandy beach on the west and north coast, backed by rabbit-free dunes and machair. The island boasts a wonderful GHHT **hostel** (Ⓦwww.gatliff.org.uk; dorm beds £8), which occupies a pair of thatched blackhouses in a lovely spot by a beach, beyond Loch a Bhàigh and the main village. Alternatively you can follow in Prince Charles's footsteps and stay (and help out) at "Splash" MacKillop's *Burnside Croft* **B&B** (Ⓣ01876/540235, Ⓦwww.burnsidecroft.fsnet.co.uk; Feb–Nov; ❷), in Borgh (Borve), overlooking the machair and dunes, and enjoy "storytelling evenings"; bike rental is also available. There's a **tearoom** called *The Lobster Pot* in the shop on the main road, near the junction, and a **bus** connection with Lochmaddy.

Benbecula (Beinn na Faoghla)

Blink and you could miss the pancake-flat island of **Benbecula** (put the stress on the second syllable), sandwiched between Protestant North Uist and Catholic South Uist. Most visitors simply trundle along the main road that cuts across the middle of the island in less than five miles – not such a bad idea, since the island is scarred from the postwar presence of the Royal Artillery who until recently made up half the local population.

The legacy of Benbecula's military past is only too evident in barracks-like **BALIVANICH** (Baile a Mhanaich), the grim, grey island capital in the northwest. The only reason to come here at all is if you happen to be flying into or out of **Benbecula airport** (direct flights to Glasgow, Barra and Stornoway), need an ATM, the laundrette (behind the bank) or a supermarket. There's no tourist office and no need to stay here, but if you need a bite to eat, there's *Stepping Stone* (closed Mon eve), a purpose-built **café/restaurant** that serves chips with everything during the day and more adventurous fare in the evening.

South Uist (Uibhist a Deas)

To the south of Benbecula, the island of **South Uist** (Ⓦwww.southuist.com) is arguably the most appealing of the southern chain of islands. The west coast is blessed with some of the region's finest machair and beaches – a necklace of gold and grey sand strung twenty miles from one end to the other – while the east coast features a ridge of high mountains rising to 2034ft at the summit of Beinn Mhor.

One of the best places to gain access to the sandy shoreline is at **TOBHA MÒR** (Howmore), a pretty little crofting settlement with a fair number of restored houses, many still thatched, including one distinctively roofed in brown heather. A GHHT **hostel** (Ⓦwww.gatliff.org.uk; dorm beds £8) occupies one such house near the village church, from where it's an easy walk across the flower-infested machair to the gorgeous beach. Close by the hostel are the shattered, lichen-encrusted remains of no fewer than four medieval churches and chapels, and a burial ground now harbouring just a few scattered graves.

Five miles south of Tobha Mòr, on the main road, the **Kildonan Museum** (April–Oct Mon–Sat 10am–5pm, Sun 2–5pm; £2; Ⓦwww.kildonanmuseum.co.uk) includes mock-ups of Hebridean kitchens through the ages, two lovely box beds and an impressive selection of old photos, accompanied by a firmly unsentimental yet poetic written text on crofting life in the last two centuries. Pride of place goes to the sixteenth-century **Clanranald Stone**, carved with the arms of the clan who ruled over South Uist from 1370 to 1839, which used to lie in the church at Tobha Mòr. The museum also runs a café serving sandwiches and home-made cakes.

Apart from the aforementioned hostel, there's the *Orasay Inn* (Ⓣ01870/610298, Ⓦwww.orasayinn.co.uk; ❺), a modern **hotel** off the road to Loch a Charnain (Lochcarnan); the rooms are pretty standard, but the location is wonderfully peaceful and the breakfasts are good. South Uist's chief settlement and ferry port, **LOCHBOISDALE**, occupying a narrow, bumpy promontory on the east coast, has much less to offer than Lochmaddy. There's a **tourist office** (Easter to mid-Oct Mon–Sat 9am–5pm; open to meet the ferry) and the refurbished *Lochboisdale Hotel* (Ⓣ01878/700332, Ⓦwww.lochboisdale.com; ❻), which does decent bar meals, including succulent local cockles. There are also several small, perfectly friendly **B&Bs** within comfortable walking distance of the dock, one of the best (and nearest) being *Brae Lea House* (Ⓣ01878/700497, Ⓦwww.braelea.co.uk; ❸).

Eriskay (Eiriosgaigh)

Famous for its patterned jerseys (on sale at the community centre) and a peculiar breed of pony, the barren, hilly island of **Eriskay** is connected to the south of South Uist by a causeway. The island, which measures just over two miles by one, and shelters a small fishing community of about 150, makes a great day-trip from South Uist. The walk up to the island's highest point, **Beinn Sciathan** (607ft; 2hr return), is well worth the effort on a clear day, as you can see the whole island, plus Barra, South Uist, and across the sea to Skye, Rùm, Coll and Tiree. On the way up or down, look out for the diminutive Eriskay ponies, originally used for carrying peat and seaweed, and who now roam free on the hills but tend to graze around Loch Crakavaig, the island's freshwater source. CalMac runs a **car ferry** to **Barra** (4–5 daily; 40min) from the southwest coast of Eriskay.

For a small island, Eriskay has had more than its fair share of historical headlines. The island's main beach on the west coast, Coilleag a Phrionnsa (Prince's Cockle Strand), was where **Bonnie Prince Charlie** landed on Scottish soil on July 23, 1745 – the sea bindweed that grows there to this day is said to have sprung from the seeds Charles brought with him from France. Eriskay's other claim to fame came in 1941 when the 8000-ton **SS Politician** or *Polly* as it's fondly known, sank on its way from Liverpool to Jamaica, along with its cargo of bicycle parts, £3 million in Jamaican currency and 264,000 bottles of whisky, inspiring Compton MacKenzie's book – and the Ealing comedy (filmed here in 1948) – *Whisky Galore!* (released in the US as *Tight Little Island*). The ship's stern can still be seen to the northwest of the Isle of Calvey at low tide, and one of the original bottles (and lots of other related memorabilia) is on show in the island's purpose-built pub, *Am Politician*, on the west coast.

Barra (Barraigh)

Just four miles wide and eight miles long, **Barra** (Ⓦ www.isleofbarra.com) is like the Western Isles in miniature. It has sandy beaches, backed by machair, glacial mountains, prehistoric ruins, Gaelic culture, and a welcoming Catholic population of just over 1300. The only settlement of any size is **CASTLEBAY** (Bàgh a Chaisteil), which curves around the barren rocky hills of a wide bay on the south side of the island. It's difficult to imagine it now, but Castlebay was a herring port of some significance back in the nineteenth century, with up to four hundred boats in the harbour, and curing and packing factories ashore. Barra's religious allegiance is immediately announced by the large Catholic church, Our Lady, Star of the Sea, which overlooks the bay; to underline the point, there's a Madonna and Child on the slopes of **Sheabhal** (1260ft), the largest peak on Barra, and a fairly easy hike from the bay.

As its name suggests, Castlebay has a castle in its bay, the medieval islet-fortress of Caisteal Chiosmuil or **Kisimul Castle** (April–Sept daily 9.30am–5.30pm; £4.50; HS), ancestral home of the MacNeil clan. The castle burnt down in the eighteenth century, but in 1937 the 45th MacNeil chief bought the island back and set about restoring Kisimul. There's nothing much to see inside, but the whole experience is fun – head down to the slipway at the bottom of Main Street, where the ferryman will take you over (weather permitting; Ⓣ 01871/810313). To learn more about the history of the island, and about the postal system of the Western Isles, it's worth paying a visit to Barra Heritage Centre, known as **Dualchas** (March, April & Sept Mon, Wed & Fri 11am–4pm; May–Aug Mon–Sat 11am–4pm; £2; Ⓦ www.barraheritage.com), on the road that leads west out of town; the museum also has a handy **café** serving soup, toasties and cakes.

One of Barra's most interesting sights is its **airport**, on the north side of the island, where planes land and take off from the crunchy shell sands of Tràigh Mhór, better known as **Cockle Strand**; the exact timing of the flights depends on the tides, since at high tide the beach (and therefore the runway) is covered in water.

There are two **ferry terminals** on Barra: from Eriskay, you arrive in the northeast of the island; from Oban, Lochboisdale or Tiree, you arrive in Castlebay itself. Barra Car Hire (Ⓣ01871/810243) will deliver **cars** to either terminal, and Barra Cycle Hire (Ⓣ01871/810284) will do the same with **bikes**. Barra's **tourist office** (April–Oct Mon–Sat 9am–1pm & 2–5pm; also open to greet the Oban ferry) is on Main Street in Castlebay just round from the pier. In Castlebay itself, the *Castlebay Hotel* (Ⓣ01871/810223, Ⓦwww.castlebay-hotel.co.uk; ❺) is the more welcoming of the town's two **hotels**, followed by *Tigh-na-Mara* (Ⓣ01871/810304, Ⓔighnamara@aol.com; ❷), a Victorian guesthouse a couple of minutes' walk from the pier, overlooking the sea. Alternatively, there's *Dunard Hostel* (Ⓣ01871/810443, Ⓦwww.dunardhostel.co.uk; dorm beds £12), a relaxed, family-run place just west of the ferry terminal. The best options outside Castlebay are in Bagh a Tuath (Northbay): the old church is home to the *Heathbank Hotel* (Ⓣ01871/890266, Ⓦwww.barrahotel.co.uk; ❺), now a comfortable hotel and local watering hole, and the old school is now the equally good *Northbay House* (Ⓣ01871/890255, Ⓦwww.barraholidays.co.uk; April–Oct; ❹). Places to **eat** in Castlebay include the *Kisimul* **café** (closed Sun) that specializes in cheap-and-cheerful Scottish fry-ups, or, for fancier fare, the *Castlebay Hotel*'s cosy **bar**, which regularly has cockles, crabs and scallops on its menu, and good views out over the bay.

Travel details

Trains

Fort William to: Mallaig (4–5 daily; 1hr 20min).
Glasgow Queen Street to: Mallaig (Mon–Sat 3 daily, 1 on Sun; 5hr 10min).
Inverness to: Kyle of Lochalsh (Mon–Sat 3–4 daily, 1–2 on Sun; 2hr 30min).

Buses

Mainland

Glasgow to: Broadford (3 daily; 5hr 30min); Portree (3 daily; 6hr 15min); Uig (2 daily; 6hr 50min).
Inverness to: Broadford (2 daily; 2hr 50min); Portree (2 daily; 3hr 15min).
Kyle of Lochalsh to: Broadford (Mon–Sat every 30min–1hr; 25min); Kyleakin (Mon–Sat every 30min–1hr; 10min); Portree (Mon–Sat 6–8 daily; 1hr).

Skye

Armadale to: Broadford (Mon–Sat 5–7 daily, 3 on Sun; 35min); Portree (Mon–Sat 5–7 daily, 3 on Sun; 1hr 20min); Sligachan (Mon–Sat 5–7 daily, 3 on Sun; 1hr).
Broadford to: Elgol (Mon–Sat 2–3 daily; 40min); Portree (Mon–Sat 5–10 daily; 40min).
Kyleakin to: Broadford (Mon–Sat 4–10 daily, 3–5 on Sun; 15min); Portree (Mon–Sat 4 daily, 3–5 on Sun; 1hr); Sligachan (Mon–Sat 7–8 daily, 5 on Sun; 45min); Uig (Mon–Sat 2 daily; 1hr 20min).
Portree to: Duntulm (Mon–Sat 4 daily; 55min); Dunvegan (Mon–Sat 3–4 daily; 45min); Staffin (Mon–Sat 4–5 daily; 35min); Uig (Mon–Sat 7–8 daily, 3 on Sun; 30min).

Lewis/Harris

Stornoway to: Arnol (Mon–Sat 4–6 daily; 35min); Barabhas (Mon–Sat 8–12 daily; 25min); Calanais (Mon–Sat 4–6 daily; 40min); Carlabhagh (Mon–Sat 4–6 daily; 1hr); Leverburgh (Mon–Sat 4–5 daily; 1hr 55min); Port Nis (Mon–Sat 4–6 daily; 1hr); Siabost (Mon–Sat 4–6 daily; 45min); Tarbert (Mon–Sat 4–5 daily; 1hr).
Tarbert to: Leverburgh (Mon–Sat 5-7 daily; 45min–1hr).

The Uists and Benbecula

Berneray to: Balivanich (Mon–Sat 2–3 daily; 1hr 15min); Lochmaddy (Mon–Sat 6–7 daily; 20–30min).
Lochboisdale to: Eriskay (Mon–Sat 6–7 daily; 35min).

Lochmaddy to: Balivanich (Mon–Sat 5–6 daily; 45min–2hr); Balranald (Mon–Sat 3 daily; 50min); Lochboisdale (Mon–Sat 5–6 daily; 2hr).

Barra

Castlebay to: Airport/Ferry for Eriskay (Mon–Sat 4–6 daily; 35–45min).

CalMac ferries (summer timetable)

To Barra: Eriskay–Barra (5 daily; 40min); Lochboisdale–Castlebay (Mon & Tues; 1hr 30min); Oban–Castlebay (1 daily; 4hr 50min); Tiree–Castlebay (Thurs; 3hr).
To Canna: Eigg–Canna (Mon & Sat; 2hr 30min); Mallaig–Canna (Mon, Wed, Fri & Sat; 2hr 30min–3hr 50min); Muck–Canna (Sat; 1hr 35min); Rùm–Canna (Mon, Wed, Fri & Sat; 55min).
To Eigg: Canna–Eigg (Mon & Sat; 2hr 15min); Mallaig–Eigg (Mon, Tues & Thurs–Sat; 1hr 15min–2hr 25min); Muck–Eigg (Tues & Thurs–Sat; 35min); Rùm–Eigg (Mon & Sat; 1hr–3hr 30min).
To Harris: Berneray–Leverburgh (3–4 daily; 1hr); Uig–Tarbert (Mon–Sat 2 daily; 1hr 45min).
To Lewis: Ullapool–Stornoway (Mon–Sat 2–3 daily; 2hr 45min).
To Muck: Canna–Muck (Sat; 1hr 35min); Eigg–Muck (Tues, Thurs & Sat; 35min); Mallaig–Muck (Tues, Thurs, Fri & Sat; 1hr 40min–4hr 20min); Rùm–Muck (Sat; 2hr 45min).
To North Uist: Leverburgh–Berneray (3–4 daily; 1hr); Uig–Lochmaddy (1–2 daily; 1hr 45min).
To Raasay: Sconser–Raasay (Mon–Sat 9–11 daily, Sun 2 daily; 15min).
To Rùm: Canna–Rùm (Mon, Wed, Fri & Sat; 55min); Eigg–Rùm (Mon & Sat; 1hr–3hr 30min); Mallaig–Rùm (Mon, Wed, Fri & Sat; 1hr 20min–2hr 30min); Muck–Rùm (Sat; 1hr 10min).
To Skye: Glenelg–Kylerhea (daily frequently; 15min); Mallaig–Armadale (Mon–Sat 8 daily, Sun 4–6 daily; 30min).
To South Uist: Castlebay–Lochboisdale (Mon, Wed, Fri & Sun; 1hr 40min); Oban–Lochboisdale (Tues, Thurs, Sat & Sun; 5hr 20min–6hr 30min).

Flights

Benbecula to: Barra (Mon–Fri 1 daily; 25min); Stornoway (Mon–Fri 2 daily; 30min).
Edinburgh to: Stornoway (Mon–Fri 3 daily, Sat & Sun 1–2 daily; 1hr 1hr 10min).
Glasgow to: Barra (Mon–Sat 1 daily; 1hr 10min); Benbecula (Mon–Fri 2 daily, Sat & Sun 1 daily; 1hr); Stornoway (daily; 1hr 10min).
Inverness to: Stornoway (Mon–Fri 4 daily, Sat & Sun 1–2 daily; 35–40min).

23 Northeast Scotland

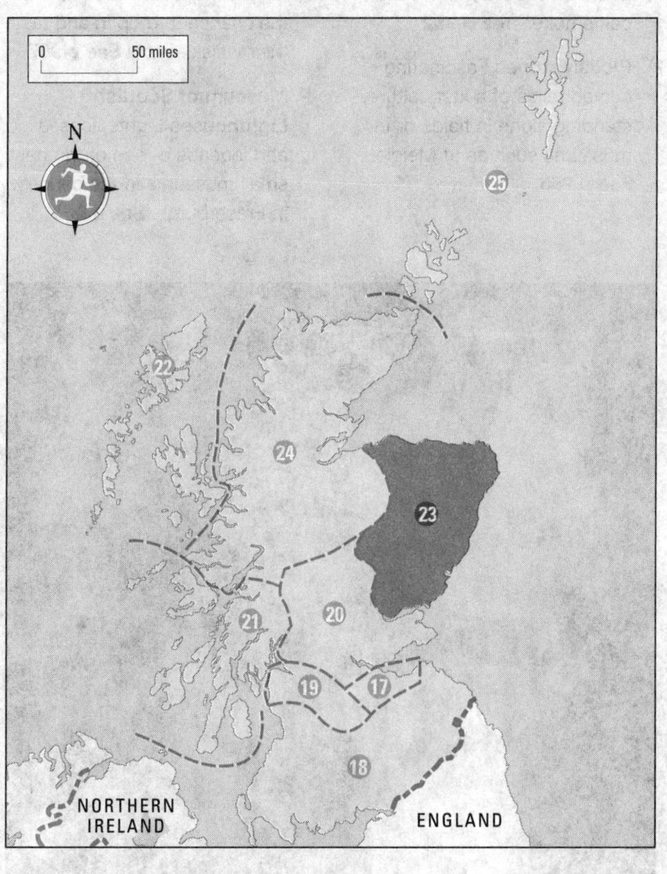

CHAPTER 23 Highlights

* **DCA** Arts centre/cinema/ café at the hip heart of Dundee's up-and-coming cultural scene. See p.951
* **Arbroath smokie** A true Scottish delicacy: succulent haddock still warm from the oak smoker. See p.952
* **Pictish stones** Fascinating carved relics of a lost culture, standing alone in fields or in museums such as at Meigle. See p.955
* **Dunnottar Castle** The moodiest cliff-top ruin in the country. See p.963
* **Speyside's Whiskies** See the distilleries and landscapes of places such as Glenfiddich, Glenlivet and Glen Grant, with the chance to drop in and taste their whiskies too. See p.967
* **Museum of Scottish Lighthouses** Lights, lenses and legends at one of the best small museums in the country, in Fraserburgh. See p.968

▲ Drying haddock

23

Northeast Scotland

A large triangle of land thrusting into the North Sea, **northeast Scotland** comprises the area east of a line drawn roughly from Perth north to the fringe of the Moray Firth at Forres. The area takes in the county of Angus and the city of Dundee to the south and, beyond the Grampian Mountains, the counties of Aberdeenshire and Moray and the city of Aberdeen. Geographically diverse, the landscape in the south of the region is comprised predominantly of undulating farmland, but as you travel further north of the Firth of Tay, this gives way to wooded glens, mountains and increasingly harsh land fringed by a dramatic coast of cliffs and long sandy beaches.

The northeast was the southern kingdom of the **Picts**, reminders of whom are scattered throughout the region in the form of numerous beautifully carved, symbolic stones found in fields, churchyards and museums, such as the one at **Meigle**. The area never grew particularly prosperous, and a handful of feuding and intermarrying families, such as the Gordons, the Keiths and the Irvines, grew to wield disproportionate influence, building many of the region's **castles** and religious buildings and developing and planning its towns.

Many of the most appealing settlements are along the coast, but while the fishing industry is but a fondly held memory in many parts, a number of the northeast's ports were transformed by the discovery of **oil** in the North Sea in the 1960s – particularly **Aberdeen**, Scotland's third-largest city. The northeast's next-largest metropolis, **Dundee**, is valiantly trying to shed its depressed post-industrial image with a reinvigorated cultural scene and some heavily marketed tourist attractions.

North of the glens and west of Aberdeen, **Deeside** is a fertile yet ruggedly attractive area made famous by the Royal Family. Beyond Deeside are the eastern sections of the **Cairngorm National Park**, while travelling north into Moray brings you to Scotland's most productive whisky-making area, Speyside. The northeast coast, meanwhile, offers yet another aspect of a diverse region, with rugged cliffs, empty beaches and historic fishing villages tucked into coves and bays.

Dundee and Angus

The predominantly agricultural county of **Angus**, east of the A9 and north of the Firth of Tay, holds some of the northeast's greatest scenery and is relatively

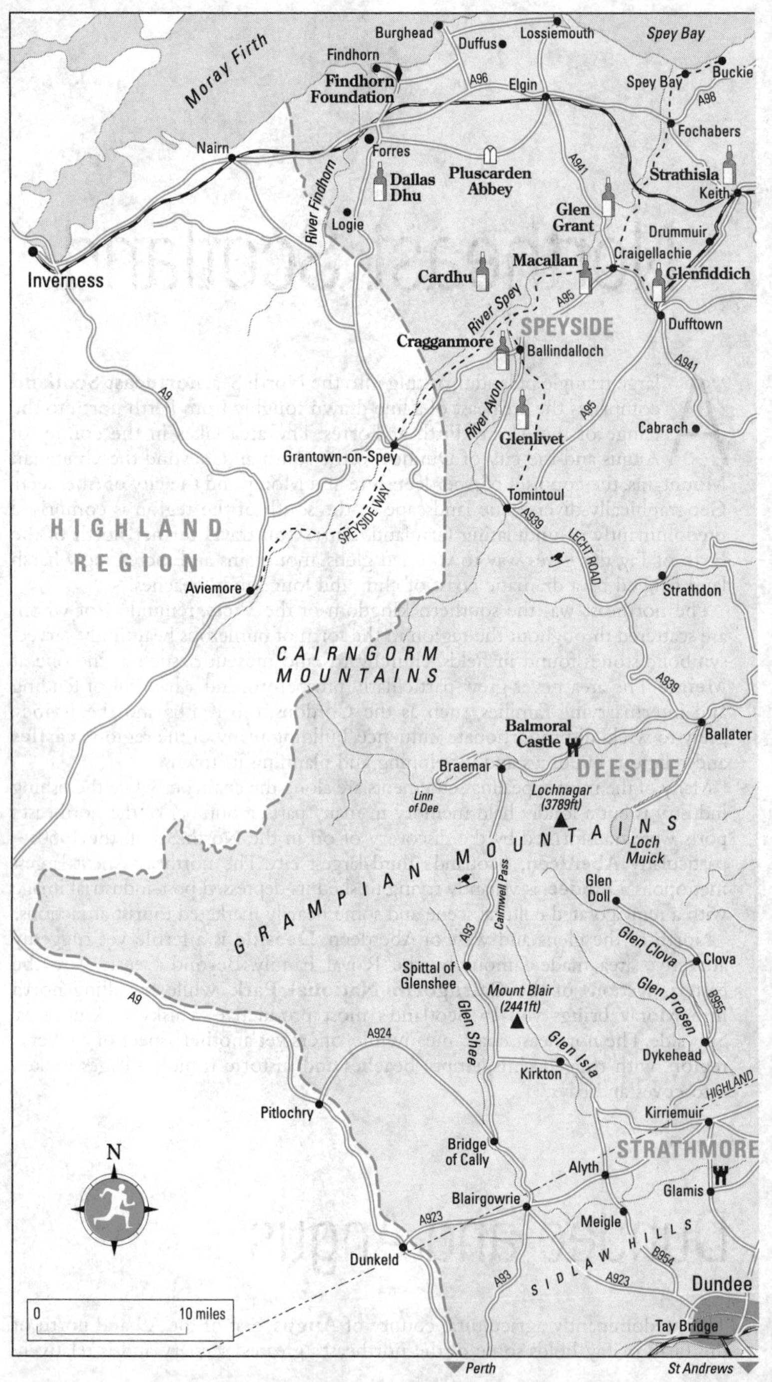
Moray Firth
Burghead
Duffus
Lossiemouth
Spey Bay
Findhorn
Findhorn Foundation
A96
Elgin
Spey Bay
Buckie
A98
Fochabers
Nairn
Forres
River Findhorn
Dallas Dhu
Pluscarden Abbey
A941
Strathisla
Keith
Logie
Glen Grant
Drummuir
Inverness
Craigellachie
Macallan
Glenfiddich
Cardhu
A95
River Spey
SPEYSIDE
Dufftown
Cragganmore
Ballindalloch
A941
A9
River Avon
A95
Glenlivet
Cabrach
Grantown-on-Spey
SPEYSIDE WAY
Tomintoul
A939
LECHT ROAD
HIGHLAND REGION
Aviemore
Strathdon
CAIRNGORM MOUNTAINS
A939
Balmoral Castle
Ballater
Braemar
DEESIDE
Linn of Dee
Lochnagar (3789ft)
Loch Muick
GRAMPIAN MOUNTAINS
Cairnwell Pass
Glen Doll
A93
Glen Clova
Clova
Spittal of Glenshee
Glen Prosen
B955
A9
Mount Blair (2441ft)
Glen Shee
A924
Glen Isla
Dykehead
Kirkton
HIGHLAND
Pitlochry
Kirriemuir
Bridge of Cally
STRATHMORE
N
Alyth
Glamis
Blairgowrie
A923
Meigle
SIDLAW HILLS
B954
Dunkeld
A93
A923
Dundee
0
10 miles
Tay Bridge
Perth
St Andrews

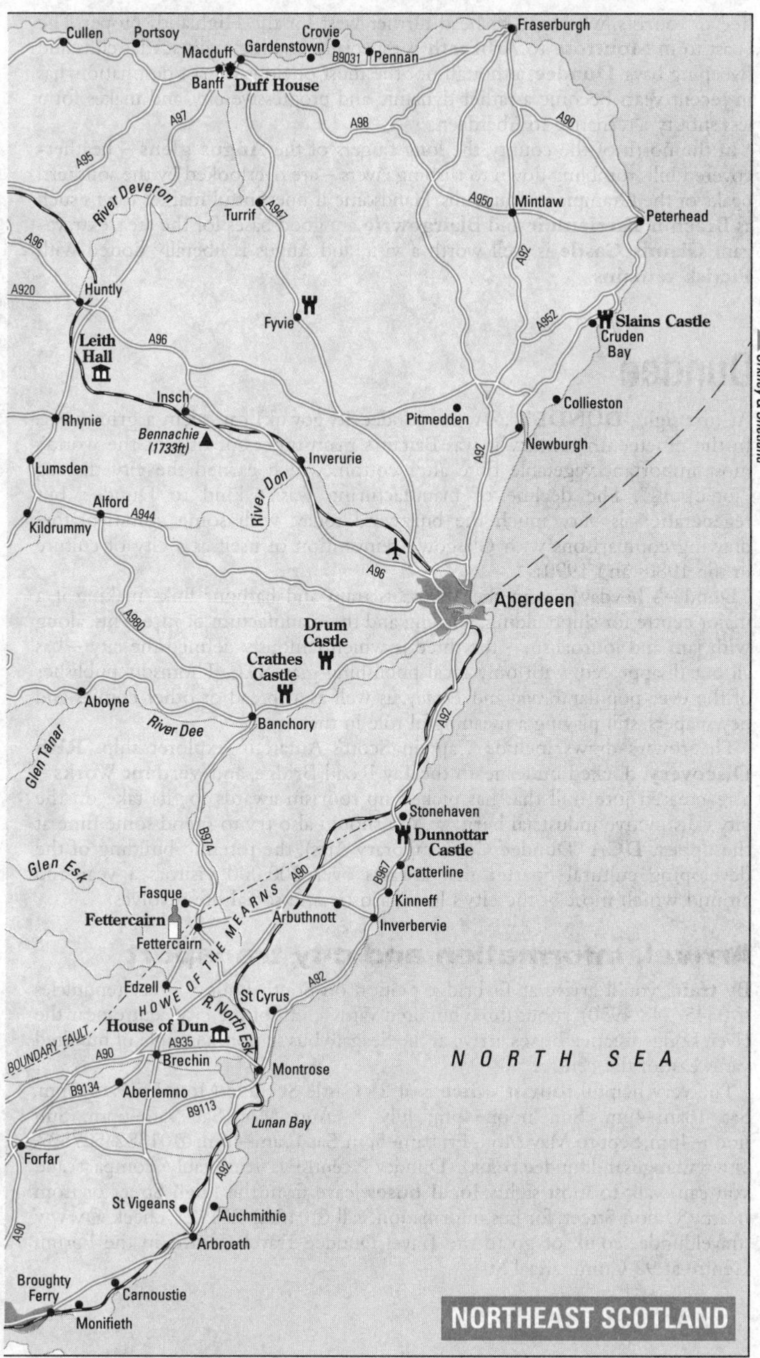
Cullen
Portsoy
Crovie
Fraserburgh
Macduff
Gardenstown
B9031
Pennan
Banff
Duff House
A97
A98
A90
A95
River Deveron
Turrif
A947
A950
Mintlaw
Peterhead
A96
A92
A920
Huntly
Fyvie
A952
Slains Castle
Cruden Bay
Leith Hall
A96
Orkney & Shetland
Insch
Collieston
Rhynie
Pitmedden
Bennachie (1733ft)
Newburgh
Lumsden
Inverurie
A92
River Don
Alford
A944
Kildrummy
A96
Aberdeen
A980
Drum Castle
Crathes Castle
Aboyne
River Dee
Banchory
A92
Glen Tanar
Stonehaven
Dunnottar Castle
B974
Glen Esk
A90
Catterline
B967
Kinneff
Fasque
Fettercairn
Arbuthnott
Inverbervie
Fettercairn
HOWE OF THE MEARNS
Edzell
A92
St Cyrus
House of Dun
R. North Esk
BOUNDARY FAULT
A935
A90
Brechin
Montrose
NORTH SEA
B9134
Aberlemno
B9113
Lunan Bay
Forfar
A92
St Vigeans
Auchmithie
A90
Arbroath
Broughty Ferry
Carnoustie
Monifieth
NORTHEAST SCOTLAND

free of tourists, who tend to head further west for the Highlands proper. The coast from **Montrose** to **Arbroath** is especially inviting, with scarlet cliffs and sweeping bays. **Dundee**, although not the most obvious tourist destination, has in recent years become a rather dynamic and progressive city, and makes for a less snooty alternative to Aberdeen.

In the north of the county, the long fingers of the **Angus glens** – heather-covered hills tumbling down to rushing rivers – are overlooked by the southern peaks of the Grampian Mountains. Handsome if uneventful market towns such as **Brechin**, **Kirriemuir** and **Blairgowrie** are good bases for the area, extravagant **Glamis Castle** is well worth a visit, and Angus is liberally dotted with **Pictish remains**.

Dundee

At first sight, **DUNDEE** (Ⓦwww.dundeecity.gov.uk) can seem a grim place. In the nineteenth century it was Britain's main processor of jute, the world's most important vegetable fibre after cotton, which earned the city the tag "Juteopolis". The decline of manufacturing wasn't kind to Dundee, but regeneration is very much the buzzword today, with some commentators drawing comparisons with Glasgow's reinvention of itself as a city of culture in the 1980s and 1990s.

Dundee's heyday was in the 1800s, its train and harbour links making it a major centre for shipbuilding, whaling and the manufacture of **jute**. This, along with jam and journalism – the three Js which famously defined the city – has all but disappeared, with only local publishing giant D.C. Thomson, publisher of the ever-popular *Beano* and *Dandy*, as well as a spread of other comics and newspapers, still playing a meaningful role in the city.

The town's draws include Captain Scott's Antarctic explorer ship, **RRS Discovery**, docked underneath the Tay Road Bridge, and **Verdant Works** – a re-created jute mill that has picked up tourism awards for its take on the city's distinctive industrial heritage. You should also try to spend some time at the upbeat **DCA** (Dundee Contemporary Arts), the totemic building of the developing cultural quarter that attracts over 300,000 visitors a year and around which most of the city's lively artistic and social life revolves.

Arrival, information and city transport

By **train**, you'll arrive at Taybridge Station on South Union Street (enquiries Ⓣ0845/748 4950), about three hundred yards south of the city centre near the river. Long-distance **buses** arrive at the Seagate bus station, a couple of hundred yards east of the centre.

The very helpful **tourist office** is at 21 Castle St (June Mon–Fri 9am–5pm, Sat 10am–4pm, Sun noon–4pm; July & Aug Mon–Sat 9am–6pm, Sun noon–4pm; Sept to May Mon–Fri 9am–5pm, Sat 10am–4pm; Ⓣ01382/527527, Ⓦwww.angusanddundee.co.uk). Dundee's centre is reasonably compact and you can walk to most sights; **local buses** leave from the High Street or from nearby Union Street; for bus information, call Ⓣ01382/201121, check Ⓦwww.traveldundee.co.uk or go to the Travel Dundee Travel Centre, in the Forum Centre at 92 Commercial St.

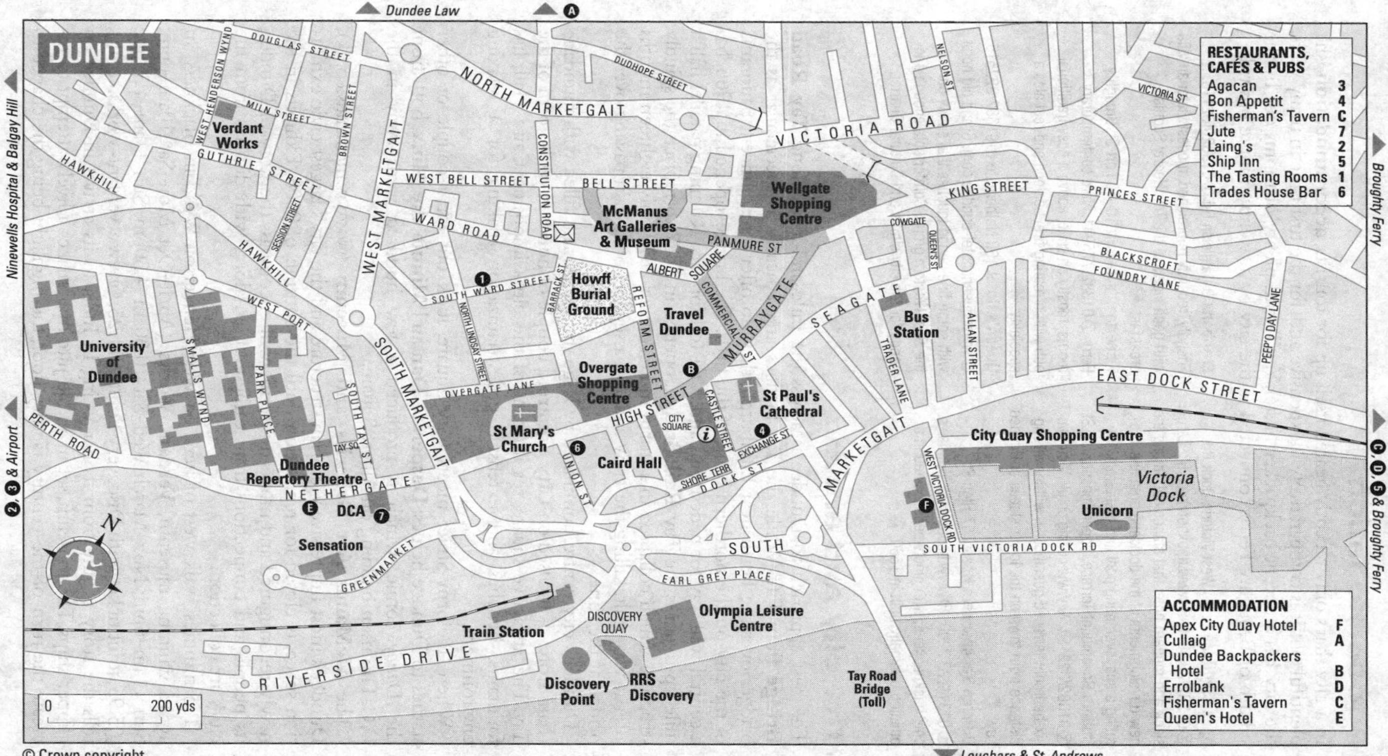

DUNDEE
Dundee Law
A
Ninewells Hospital & Balgay Hill
2, 3 & Airport
Broughty Ferry
C, D, 5 & Broughty Ferry
Leuchars & St. Andrews
RESTAURANTS, CAFÉS & PUBS
Agacan 3
Bon Appetit 4
Fisherman's Tavern C
Jute 7
Laing's 2
Ship Inn 5
The Tasting Rooms 1
Trades House Bar 6
ACCOMMODATION
Apex City Quay Hotel F
Cullaig A
Dundee Backpackers Hotel B
Errolbank D
Fisherman's Tavern C
Queen's Hotel E
DOUGLAS STREET
WEST HENDERSON WYND
MILN STREET
BROWN STREET
Verdant Works
GUTHRIE STREET
HAWKHILL
SESSION STREET
WEST MARKETGAIT
NORTH MARKETGAIT
DUDHOPE STREET
NELSON ST
VICTORIA ST
VICTORIA ROAD
CONSTITUTION ROAD
WEST BELL STREET
BELL STREET
WARD ROAD
McManus Art Galleries & Museum
PANMURE ST
Wellgate Shopping Centre
KING STREET
PRINCES STREET
COWGATE
QUEEN'S ST
BLACKSCROFT
FOUNDRY LANE
PEEP O' DAY LANE
ALLAN STREET
TRADER LANE
Bus Station
SEAGATE
MURRAYGATE
COMMERCIAL ST
ALBERT SQUARE
Howff Burial Ground
BARRACK ST
SOUTH WARD STREET
NORTH LINDSAY STREET
REFORM STREET
Travel Dundee
WEST PORT
University of Dundee
SMALLS WYND
PARK PLACE
SOUTH TAY ST
TAY SQ
SOUTH MARKETGAIT
OVERGATE LANE
Overgate Shopping Centre
HIGH STREET
CITY SQUARE
CASTLE STREET
St Paul's Cathedral
EXCHANGE ST
St Mary's Church
UNION ST
Caird Hall
SHORE TERR
DOCK ST
EAST DOCK STREET
MARKETGAIT
City Quay Shopping Centre
Victoria Dock
Unicorn
WEST VICTORIA DOCK RD
SOUTH VICTORIA DOCK RD
PERTH ROAD
Dundee Repertory Theatre
NETHERGATE
DCA
Sensation
GREENMARKET
SOUTH
EARL GREY PLACE
Olympia Leisure Centre
DISCOVERY QUAY
Train Station
RIVERSIDE DRIVE
Discovery Point
RRS Discovery
Tay Road Bridge (Toll)
0 200 yds
N

Accommodation

In a city that's only recently geared itself up for tourists, **accommodation** isn't plentiful, but it is comparatively inexpensive and, for the first time in many years, the city has a decent backpacker hostel. You'll find plenty of rooms out by the suburb of Broughty Ferry, connected to the city by a twenty-minute bus ride.

Apex City Quay Hotel West Victoria Dock Rd ⓣ01382/202404, ⓦwww.apexhotels.co.uk. Large, sleek and modern hotel that stands out among the new developments of the dockland area, incorporating a spa, swimming pool and restaurant. ❻

Cullaig Rosemount Terrace, Upper Constitution St ⓣ01382/322154, ⓦwww.cullaig.co.uk. Victorian six-bedroom terraced guesthouse, within walking distance from town on the lower slopes of Dundee Law. ❸

Dundee Backpackers Hostel 57 High St ⓣ0131/220 2200, ⓦwww.hoppo.com. Dundee's only backpacker's, with ninety beds located in a building originally built in 1560. ❶

Errolbank 9 Dalgleish Rd ⓣ01382/462118. Friendly, recently refurbished, modest Victorian villa with good views of the Tay. Hearty Scottish breakfast. ❸

Fisherman's Tavern 10–16 Fort St, Broughty Ferry ⓣ01382/775941. Neat contemporary rooms, mostly en suite, above a cosy traditional pub with a roaring fire. Seafood and real ales a speciality. ❹

Queen's Hotel 160 Nethergate ⓣ01382/322515, ⓦwww.queenshotel-dundee.com. Grand old hotel with some fine period touches that's now part of the *Best Western* group. Comfortable enough and handy for the city sights and Cultural Quarter. ❹

The city and around

The best approach to Dundee is across the mile-and-a-half-long **Tay Road Bridge** from Fife. While the Tay bridges aren't nearly as spectacular as the bridges over the Forth near Edinburgh, they do offer a magnificent panorama of the city on the northern bank of the firth. The bridge, opened in 1966, has a central walkway for pedestrians and a £1 toll for cars. Running parallel half a mile upstream is the **Tay Rail Bridge**, opened in 1887 to replace the spindly structure which collapsed in a storm in December 1879 only eighteen months after it was built, killing the crew and 75 passengers on a train passing over the bridge at the time.

Dundee's city centre, dominated by large shopping malls filled with mundane chain stores, is focused on **City Square**, a couple of hundred yards north of the Tay. The attractive square, set in front of the city's imposing Caird Hall, has fountains, benches and extensive pedestrianization making for a relaxing environment.

Where Reform Street meets City Square, look out for a couple of other statues to Dundee heroes: **Desperate Dan** and **Minnie the Minx**, both from the *Dandy* comic, which is produced a few hundred yards away in the D.C. Thomson building on Albert Square.

The **McManus Art Galleries and Museum** (ⓦwww.mcmanus.co.uk), Dundee's most impressive Victorian structure and the city's largest civic exhibition space, is closed for renovation until the autumn of 2008. Exhibits in the newly reconfigured and modern interior will encompass the story of Dundee, its people and connections from earliest times, along with displays from the city's art collection.

Ten minutes' walk west of here, on West Henderson Wynd in Blackness, an award-winning museum, **Verdant Works** (April–Oct Mon–Sat 10am–6pm, Sun 11am–6pm; Nov–March Wed–Sat 10.30am–4.30pm, Sun 11am–4.30pm; £5.95, joint ticket with Discovery Point £11.25; ⓦwww.verdant-works.co.uk), tells the story of jute from its harvesting in India to its arrival in Dundee on clipper ships. The museum, set in an old jute mill, makes a lively attempt to re-create the turn-of-the-century factory floor, the highlight being the chance to watch jute being processed on fully operational quarter-size machines originally used for training workers.

The Cultural Quarter

Immediately west of the city centre, High Street becomes Nethergate and passes into what has been dubbed, with a fair amount of justification, Dundee's "**Cultural Quarter**". As well as the university and the highly respected Rep Theatre, the area is also home to the best concentration of pubs and cafés in the city. Principal among the many arts venues is the hip and exciting **DCA**, or Dundee Contemporary Arts, at 152 Nethergate (Mon–Sat 10.30am–midnight, Sun noon–midnight; galleries Tues–Sat 10.30am–5.30pm, until 8.30pm Thurs, Sun noon–5.30pm; ⓣ01382/909900, ⓦwww.dca.org.uk), a stunningly designed five-floor complex which incorporates galleries, a print studio, a classy design shop and an airy café-bar (see below). The centre, opened in 1999, was designed by Richard Murphy, who converted an old brick building which had been a garage and car showroom into an inspiring new space, given energy and confidence by its bright, sleek interior and distinctive ship-like exterior. It's worth visiting for the stimulating temporary and touring exhibitions of contemporary art, as well as an eclectic programme of art-house films and cult classics.

The waterfront

Just south of the city centre, at the water's edge alongside the Tay Road Bridge, the domed **Discovery Point** is an impressive development centring on the Royal Research Ship *Discovery* (April–Oct Mon–Sat 10am–6pm, Sun 11am–6pm; Nov–March Mon–Sat 10am–5pm, Sun 11am–5pm; £6.95, joint ticket with Verdant Works £11.25; ⓦwww.rrs-discovery.co.uk). Something of an icon for Dundee's renaissance, *Discovery* is a three-mast steam-assisted vessel built in Dundee in 1901 to take Captain Robert Falcon Scott on his polar expeditions. A combination of brute strength and elegance, she has been beautifully restored, with polished wood panels and brass trimmings giving scant indication of the privations suffered by the crew.

Eating, drinking and nightlife

The west end of Dundee, around the main university campus and Perth Road, is the best area for **eating and drinking**; the city centre has a few good pubs and one or two decent restaurants tucked away. Broughty Ferry is a pleasant alternative, with a good selection of pubs and restaurants that get particularly busy on summer evenings.

Restaurants and cafés

Agacan 113 Perth Rd ⓣ01382/644227. Tiny Turkish restaurant with a colourful exterior, and rough-hewn walls inside; they serve up decent kebabs and stuffed pittas, and also do takeaways. Moderate. Closed lunchtimes & all day Mon.

Bon Appetit 22–26 Exchange St ⓣ01382/809000, ⓦwww.bonappetit-dundee.com. Probably the most reliable (if not necessarily glamorous) spot for well-sourced, confidently cooked food in the city. Friendly service and tasty, good-value French cuisine. Moderate. Closed Sun.

Jute Café-Bar DCA, 152 Nethergate. ⓣ01382/809000. An airy café, popular as a coffee haunt with trendy students and offering good-value pre-theatre dining. Moderate.

Ship Inn 121 Fisher St, Broughty Ferry ⓣ01382/779176. A narrow pub with a warm atmosphere and nautical feel right on the waterfront with good views over the Tay. Good seafood dishes with fine selection of beers. Moderate.

The Tasting Rooms 5 South Ward Rd ⓣ01382/224188, ⓦwww.thetastingrooms.com. A smart and justifiably popular café-restaurant and wine bar in an old jute factory shell, incorporating a contemporary deli and wine store on the ground floor. Good for breakfast, snacks and lunches, but only open occasionally in the evening. Moderate.

Pubs

Fisherman's Tavern 10–16 Fort St, Broughty Ferry. Just off the shore in a busy traditional cottage, this pub serves a variety of real ales and is a popular weekend haunt for seafood lunches including Arbroath Smokie Pie. Moderate.

Laing's 8 Roseangle, off Perth Rd. Packed on warm summer nights, thanks to its beer garden and great river views. Lively student haunt.

Trades House Bar 40 Nethergate. In the heart of the city, a converted bank fronted with stained-glass windows and a convivial atmosphere.

Nightlife

Right at the heart of the Cultural Quarter on Tay Square, north of Nethergate, is the prodigious Dundee Repertory Theatre (Ⓣ01382/223530, Ⓦwww.dundeereptheatre.co.uk), home to an indigenously produced contemporary **theatre** and the only permanent repertory company in Scotland. For **movies**, DCA (Ⓣ01382/909900, Ⓦwww.dca.org.uk) has two comfy auditoriums showing an appealing range of foreign and art-house movies alongside the more challenging mainstream releases.

Listings

Bike rental Easy Ride Cycles, off Wm Fitzgerald Way, Barns of Claverhouse Ⓣ01382/505683 (from £6 per day).

Books Black Hole Comic Shop (second-hand comics), 5 Victoria Rd; Waterstone's, 35 Commercial St.

Bus information Scottish Citylink Ⓣ0870/550 5050; Stagecoach Strathtay for regional buses Ⓣ01382/228345; Traveline Scotland Ⓣ0871/2002233.

Car rental Alamo, 45–53 Gellatly St Ⓣ0870/4004562; Arnold Clark, East Dock St Ⓣ01382/225382; Hertz, 18 West Marketgate Ⓣ01382/223711.

Medical facilities Ninewells Hospital in the west of the city has an Accident and Emergency department (Ⓣ01382/660111). Dundee Dental Hospital (Ⓣ01382/425791). Boots pharmacy is at 108 High St (Ⓣ01382/611144, Mon–Sat 8.30am–6pm, Tues opens 9am, Thurs closes 7pm, Sun 12.30–5pm).

Police Tayside Police HQ, West Bell St Ⓣ01382/223200.

Post office 4 Meadowside (Mon–Fri 9am–5.30pm, Sat 9am–12.30pm).

Taxis There are taxi ranks on Nethergate, or call Dundee Private Hire Ⓣ01382/203020; Handy Taxis Ⓣ01382/225825; or 505050 Taxis Ⓣ01382/505050.

The Angus coast

Two roads link Dundee to Aberdeen and the northeast coast of Scotland. By far the more pleasant option is the slightly longer A92 coast road, which joins the inland A90 at Stonehaven, just south of Aberdeen. Intercity **buses** follow both roads, while the coast-hugging train line from Dundee is one of the most picturesque in Scotland, passing attractive beaches and impressive cliffs, and stopping in the old seaports of **Arbroath** and **Montrose**.

Arbroath and around

Since it was settled in the twelfth century, local fishermen have been landing their catches at **ARBROATH**, about fifteen miles northeast of Dundee. The town's most famous product is the **Arbroath smokie** – line-caught haddock, smoke-cured over smouldering oak chips and still made here in a number of family-run smokehouses tucked in around the harbour. One of the most approachable and atmospheric is M&M Spink's tiny whitewashed premises at 10 Marketgate (Ⓣ01241/875287); chef and cookery writer Rick Stein described the fish here, warm from the smoke, as "a world-class delicacy".

The town's real glory days came with the completion in 1233 of **Arbroath Abbey** (daily April–Sept 9.30am–5.30pm; Oct–March 9.30am–4.30pm; £4.50; HS), whose rose-pink sandstone ruins, described by Dr Johnson as "fragments of magnificence", stand on Abbey Street. Founded in 1178 but not granted abbey status until 1285, it was the scene of one of the most significant events in Scotland's history when, on April 6, 1320, a group of Scottish barons drew up the **Declaration of Arbroath**, asking the pope to reverse his excommunication of Robert the Bruce and recognize him as king of a Scottish nation independent from England. The wonderfully resonant language of the document still makes for a stirring expression of Scottish nationhood: "For so long as one hundred of us remain alive, we will never in any degree be subject to the dominion of the English, since it is not for glory, riches or honour that we do fight, but for freedom alone, which no honest man loses but with his life." It was duly dispatched to Pope John XXII in Avignon, who in 1324 agreed to Robert's claim. A radically designed **visitor centre** at the Abbey Street entrance offers some in-depth background on these events and other aspects of the history of the building.

Arbroath's helpful **tourist office** enjoys views over the sea from the Fishmarket Quay in the revamped harbour area (April, May & Sept Mon–Fri 9am–5pm, Sat 10am–5pm; June–Aug Mon–Sat 9.30am–5.30pm, July–Aug also Sun 10am–3pm; Oct–March Mon–Fri 9am–5pm, Sat 10am–3pm; ⓣ01241/872609). For somewhere **to stay**, the central and friendly *Old Vicarage* (ⓣ01241/430475; ④) offers a breakfast table that includes smokies, a freshly baked loaf and home-made preserves.

Montrose and around

A seaport and market town since the thirteenth century, **MONTROSE** sits on the edge of a virtually landlocked two-mile-square lagoon of mud known as the Basin. On the south side of the Basin, a mile out of Montrose along the A92, the **Montrose Basin Wildlife Centre** (mid-March to mid-Nov daily 10.30am–5pm; mid-Nov to mid-March Fri–Sun 10.30am–4pm; £3; ⓦwww.montrosebasin.org.uk) has binoculars, high-powered telescopes, bird hides and remote-control video cameras. In addition, the centre's resident ranger leads regular guided walks around the reserve.

For B&B **accommodation** in Montrose, try *36 The Mall*, in the northern section of the town (ⓣ01674/673464, ⓦwww.36themall.co.uk; ④) or, if you don't mind heading out of Montrose, make for *Woodston Fishing Station* (ⓣ01674/850226, ⓦwww.woodstonfishingstation.co.uk; ⑤), a neat, antique-filled house on the cliff-top at St Cyrus, a couple of miles north of town.

The House of Dun

Across the Basin, four miles west of Montrose, is the Palladian **House of Dun** (April–June & Sept–Oct Wed–Sun 12.30–5.30pm; July & Aug daily 11.30am–5.30pm; £8; NTS), accessible on the hourly Montrose–Brechin Strathtay Scottish bus #30; ask the driver to let you off outside. Built in 1730 for David Erskine, Laird of Dun, to designs by William Adam, the house was opened to the public in 1989 after extensive restoration, and is crammed full of period furniture and objets d'art. Inside, the ornate relief plasterwork is the most impressive feature, extravagantly emblazoned with Jacobite symbolism. The buildings in the courtyard – a hen house, gamekeeper's workshop and potting shed – have been renovated, and include a tearoom and a craft shop. Bikes can be hired from the shop.

Strathmore and the Angus glens

Immediately north of Dundee, the low-lying Sidlaw Hills divide the city from the rich agricultural region of **Strathmore**, whose string of tidy market towns lies on a fertile strip along the southernmost edge of the heather-covered lower slopes of the Grampian Mountains. These towns act as gateways to the **Angus glens** (Ⓦwww.angusglens.co.uk), a series of tranquil valleys penetrated by single-track roads and offering some of the most rugged and majestic landscapes in northeast Scotland. It's a rain-swept, wind-blown, sparsely populated area, whose roads become impassable with the first snows, sometimes as early as October, and where the summers see clouds of ferocious midges. The most useful road through the glens is the A93, which cuts through **Glen Shee**, linking Blairgowrie to Braemar on Deeside (see p.964). It's pretty dramatic stuff, threading its way over Britain's highest main-road, the **Cairnwell Pass** (2199ft).

Glen Shee and Blairgowrie

The upper reaches of **Glen Shee**, the most dramatic and best known of the Angus glens, are dominated by its **ski fields**, ranged over four mountains above the Cairnwell mountain pass. To get to Glen Shee from the south you'll pass through the well-heeled little town of **BLAIRGOWRIE**, set among raspberry fields on the glen's southernmost tip and a good place to pick up information and plan your activities. Blairgowrie's friendly **tourist office** (April–June & Sept–Oct Mon–Sat 10am–4pm, Sun 10am–2pm; July & Aug Mon–Sat 9.30am–5.30pm, Sun 10.30am–3.30pm; Nov–March Tues–Sat 10am–3pm; Ⓣ01250/872960, Ⓦwww.perthshire.co.uk) is on the high side of Wellmeadow. A number of Blairgowrie's grand houses offer B&B, among them the attractive *Duncraggan* (Ⓣ01250/872082; ③) on Perth Road and *Heathpark House* (Ⓣ01250/870700, Ⓦwww.heathparkhouse.com; ⑤) on the Coupar Angus Road. **Camping** is available at the year-round *Blairgowrie Holiday Park* on Rattray's Hatton Road (Ⓣ01250/876666), within walking distance of Wellmeadow.

Blairgowrie boasts plenty of places to **eat**: *Cargills* (Ⓣ01250/876735) by the river on Lower Mill Street serves inexpensive formal meals and civilized coffee and cakes; while the inexpensive *Dome Restaurant*, just behind the tourist office, is a cheery place serving hearty platefuls of traditional grub.

Skiing at Glen Shee

Scotland's **ski resorts** make for a fun day out for anyone from beginners to experienced skiers interested in experiencing the conditions and, given that **Glen Shee** is both the most extensive and the most accessible of Scotland's ski areas, just over two hours from both Glasgow and Edinburgh, it's as good an introduction as any to the sport in Scotland.

For information, contact Ski Glenshee (Ⓣ013397/41320, Ⓦwww.ski-glenshee.co.uk), which also offers ski rental and lessons. In addition, lessons, skis and boards are available from Cairnwell Mountain Sports (Ⓣ01250/885255, Ⓦwww.cairnwell mountainsports.co.uk), at the Spittal of Glenshee. **Ski rental** starts at around £16 a day, whilst a 90min lesson is around £15. **Lift passes** cost £24 per day or £96 for a five-day (Mon–Fri) ticket. For the latest snow and **weather conditions**, phone the centre itself or check out the Ski Scotland website (Ⓦski.visitscotland.com). Should you be more interested in **cross-country** skiing, there are some good touring areas in the vicinity; contact Cairnwell Mountain Sports (see above) or Braemar Mountain Sports (Ⓣ013397/41242, Ⓦwww.braemarmountainsports.com) for information and equipment rental.

Meigle and Glen Isla

Fifteen miles north of Dundee on the B954 lies the tiny settlement of **MEIGLE**, home to Scotland's most important collection of early Christian and Pictish inscribed stones. Housed in a modest former schoolhouse, the **Meigle Museum** (April–Sept daily 9.30am–6.30pm; £2.20; HS) displays some thirty pieces dating from the seventh to the tenth centuries, all found in and around the nearby churchyard. The majority are either gravestones that would have lain flat, or cross slabs inscribed with the sign of the cross, usually standing. Most impressive is the seven-foot-tall great cross slab, said to be the gravestone of Guinevere, wife of King Arthur. The exact meaning and purpose of the stones and their enigmatic symbols is obscure, as is the reason why so many of them were found at Meigle. The most likely theory suggests that Meigle was once an important ecclesiastical centre that attracted secular burials of prominent Picts.

Three miles north of Meigle is **Alyth**, near which, legend has it, Guinevere was held captive by Mordred. The sleepy village lies at the south end of **Glen Isla**, which runs parallel to Glen Shee and is linked to it by the A926. Ten miles or so up the glen is the tiny hamlet of **KIRKTON OF GLENISLA**, where the cosy *Glenisla Hotel* (ⓣ01575/582223, ⓦwww.glenisla-hotel.com; ③) is great for classy home-made bar food and convivial drinking.

Glamis Castle

The wondrously over-the-top, five-storey pink-sandstone **Glamis Castle** (mid-March to Oct daily 10am–6pm; Nov & Dec 11am–5pm; £7.50, grounds only £3.70; ⓦwww.glamis-castle.co.uk) is set in an extensive landscaped park complete with highland cattle and pheasants beside the picturesque village of **GLAMIS** (pronounced "glahms"). One of Scotland's most famous castles, Shakespeare chose it as a central location in *Macbeth*, and its **royal connections** (as the childhood home of the late Queen Mother and birthplace of the late Princess Margaret) make it one of the essential stops on every coach tour of Scotland.

Obligatory guided tours take in the fifteenth-century **crypt**, where the 12ft-thick walls enclose a haunted "lost" room, the family **chapel** and **Duncan's Hall**, a fifteenth-century guardroom, the traditional – but inaccurate – setting for Duncan's murder by Macbeth. Glamis' **grounds,** including the Italian Gardens, are worth a few hours in their own right, with verdant walks out to Earl John's Bridge and through the woodland.

Kirriemuir

The sandstone town of **KIRRIEMUIR**, known locally as Kirrie, is set on a hill six miles northwest of Forfar on the cusp of **glens Clova** and **Prosen**. The main cluster of streets have all the appeal of an old film set, with their old-fashioned bars, tiled butcher's shop, tartan outlets and haberdasheries somehow managing to avoid being contrived and quaint – although the re-cobbling of the town centre around a twee statue of Peter Pan undermines this somewhat. Peter's presence is justified, however, since Kirrie was the birthplace of his creator, **J.M. Barrie**. A local handloom-weaver's son, Barrie first came to notice with his series of novels about "Thrums", a village based on his home town, in particular *A Window in Thrums* and his third novel, *The Little Minister*. The story of Peter Pan, the little boy who never grew up, was penned by Barrie in 1904 – some say as a response to a strange upbringing dominated by the memory of his older brother, who died as a child. **Barrie's**

birthplace, a plain little whitewashed cottage at 9 Brechin Rd (April–June & Sept Mon–Wed & Sat noon–5pm, Sun 1–5pm; July & Aug Mon–Sat 11am–5pm, Sun 1–5pm; £5; NTS, includes entrance to the camera obscura), has been opened up as a visitor attraction, with a series of small rooms decorated as they would have been during Barrie's childhood, as well as displays about his life and works.

Reasonable **accommodation** is available at the attractive, inn-styled *Airlie Arms*, St Malcolm's Wynd (Ⓣ01575/572847, Ⓦwww.airliearms-hotel.co.uk; ❹) while on the edge of town, and offering a taste of the rolling countryside, is the working *Muirhouses Farm* (Ⓣ01575/573128, Ⓦwww.muirhousesfarm.co.uk; ❹).

Glen Clova and Glen Doll

With its stunning cliffs, heather slopes and valley meadows, **Glen Clova** – which in the north becomes **Glen Doll** – is one of the loveliest of the Angus glens. Although it can get unpleasantly congested in peak season, the area is still remote enough to enable you to leave the crowds with little effort. Wildlife is abundant, with deer on the mountains, wild hare and even grouse and the occasional buzzard. The meadow flowers on the valley floor and arctic plants (including great splashes of white and purple saxifrage) on the rocks also make it something of a botanist's paradise.

The hamlet of **CLOVA** consists of little more than the hearty *Glen Clova Hotel* (Ⓣ01575/550350, Ⓦwww.clova.com; ❺), which also runs a bunkhouse (£18 B&B) and a private fishing loch. Meals and real ale are available in the lively *Climbers' Bar* at the side of the hotel.

Aberdeenshire and Moray

Aberdeenshire and Moray cover a large chunk of northern Scotland – some 3500 square miles, much of it open and varied country dotted with historic and archeological sights, from neat NTS properties and eerie prehistoric rings of standing stones to quiet kirkyards and a rash of dramatic castles. Geographically, the counties break down into two distinct areas: the **hinterland**, once barren and now a patchwork of fertile farms, rising towards high mountains, sparkling rivers and gentle valleys; and the **coast**, a classic stretch of rocky cliffs, remote fishing villages and long, sandy beaches.

For visitors, the large city of **Aberdeen** is the obvious focal point of the region, and while it's not a place to keep you engrossed for long, it does boast some intriguing architecture, attractive museums and a lively social scene. From here, it's a short hop west to **Deeside**, visited annually by the Royal Family, where the trim villages of **Ballater** and **Braemar** act as a gateway to the spectacular mountain scenery of the Cairngorms National Park, which covers much of the upland areas in the west of this region. Further north, the "Malt Whisky Country" of Speyside has less impressive scenery but no shortage of diversions in its numerous whisky distilleries, while the **coast** beyond has dramatic cliffs and long beaches punctuated by picturesque fishing villages.

Aberdeen

The third-largest city in Scotland, **ABERDEEN** (Ⓦwww.aberdeen-grampian.com), commonly known as the "Granite City", lies 120 miles northeast of Edinburgh on the banks of the rivers Dee and Don, smack in the middle of the northeast coast. Based around a working harbour, it's a place that people either love or hate. Certainly, while some extol the many tones and colours of Aberdeen's **granite** buildings, others see only uniform grey and find the city grim and cold. The weather doesn't help: Aberdeen lies on a latitude north of Moscow and the cutting wind and driving rain (even if it does transform the buildings into sparkling silver) can be tiresome.

In the twelfth century, Alexander I noted "Aberdon" as one of his principal towns, and by the thirteenth century it had become a centre for **trade and fishing**. A century or so later Bishop Elphinstone founded the Catholic university in the area north of town known today as **Old Aberdeen**, while the rest of the city developed as a mercantile centre and important port. By the mid-twentieth century, Aberdeen's traditional industries were in decline, but the discovery of **oil** in the North Sea transformed the place from a depressed port into a boom town. Since the 1970s, oil has made Aberdeen a hugely wealthy and self-confident place. Despite (or perhaps because of) this, it can seem a soulless city; there's a feeling of corporate sterility and sometimes Aberdeen seems to exist only as a departure point for the transient population of some ten to fifteen thousand who live on the 130 oil platforms out to sea.

Arrival, information and city transport

Aberdeen's Dyce **airport**, seven miles northwest of town, is served by flights from 37 UK and European destinations. The main **train station** is on Guild Street, in the centre of the city, with the **bus** terminal right beside. Aberdeen also has **ferry** links to Lerwick in Shetland and Kirkwall in Orkney, with regular crossings from Jamieson's Quay in the harbour; see p.971 for details.

Oil and Aberdeen

When **oil** was discovered in BP's Forties Field in 1970, Aberdonians rightly viewed it as a massive financial opportunity, and – despite fierce competition from other British ports, Scandinavia and Germany – the city succeeded in persuading the oil companies to base their headquarters here. In a decade the city's **population** swelled by sixty thousand, and earnings escalated from fifteen percent below the national average to well above it. At the peak of production in the **mid-1980s**, 2.6 million barrels a day were being turned out, and the price had reached $80 a barrel. The effect of the 1986 slump – when oil prices dropped to $10 a barrel – was devastating: jobs vanished at the rate of a thousand a month, house prices dropped and Aberdeen soon discovered just how dependent on oil it was. The moment oil prices began to rise, crisis struck again with the loss of 167 lives when the **Piper Alpha oil rig** exploded, precipitating an array of much-needed but very expensive safety measures.

Oil remains the cornerstone of Aberdeen's **economy**, keeping unemployment down to one of the lowest levels in Britain and driving up house prices in the city itself and an increasingly wide area of its rural hinterland. Predictions of the imminent decline in oil reserves and the end of Aberdeen's economic boom are frequently voiced, but reliable indicators suggest that the black gold will be flowing for decades to come. Even so, business leaders are already looking to refocus existing expertise and make Aberdeen just as famous for the new game in town – renewable energy.

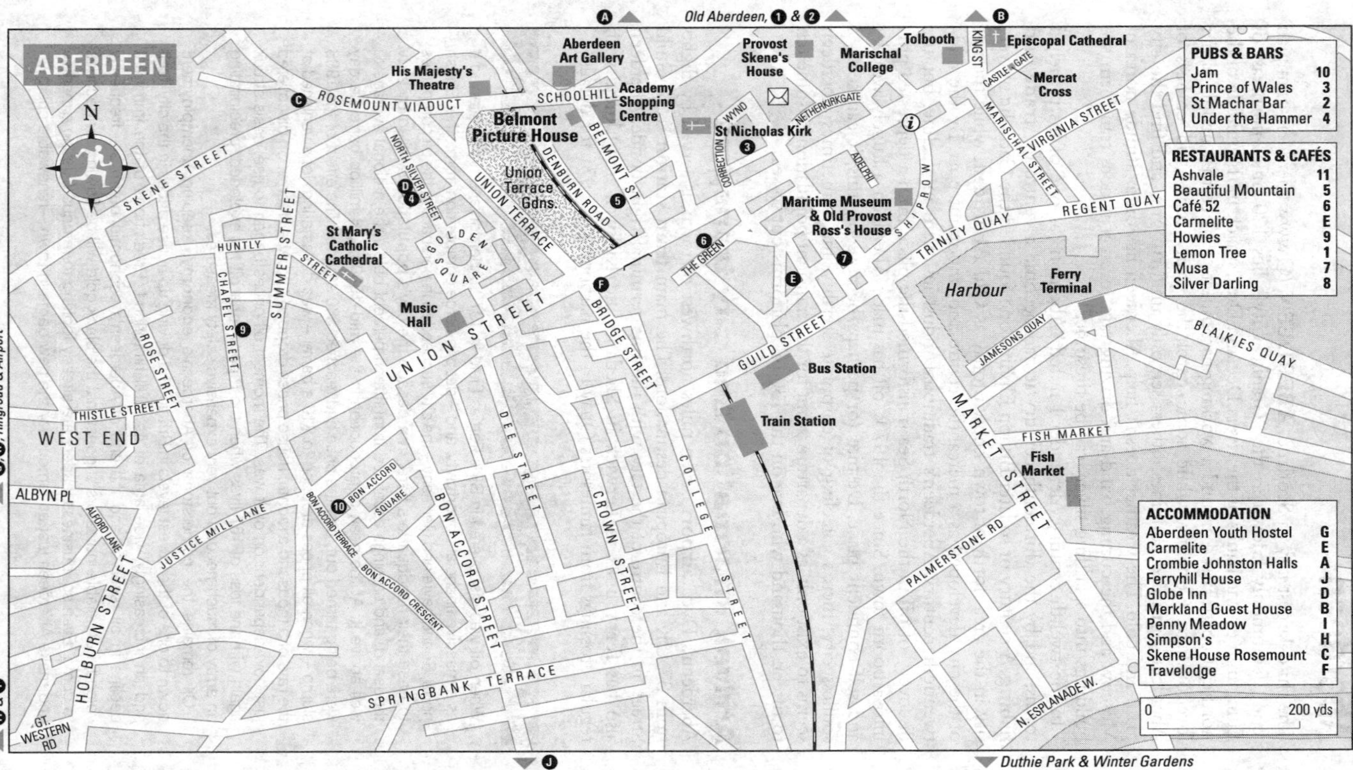
ABERDEEN
PUBS & BARS
Jam 10
Prince of Wales 3
St Machar Bar 2
Under the Hammer 4
RESTAURANTS & CAFÉS
Ashvale 11
Beautiful Mountain 5
Café 52 6
Carmelite E
Howies 9
Lemon Tree 1
Musa 7
Silver Darling 8
ACCOMMODATION
Aberdeen Youth Hostel G
Carmelite E
Crombie Johnston Halls A
Ferryhill House J
Globe Inn D
Merkland Guest House B
Penny Meadow I
Simpson's H
Skene House Rosemount C
Travelodge F
0 200 yds
© Crown copyright
Old Aberdeen, 1 & 2
Beach
Footdee & 8
Duthie Park & Winter Gardens
G, H, Ringroad & Airport
11 & I
J
Aberdeen Art Gallery
His Majesty's Theatre
Academy Shopping Centre
Provost Skene's House
Marischal College
Tolbooth
Episcopal Cathedral
Mercat Cross
Belmont Picture House
Union Terrace Gdns.
St Nicholas Kirk
Maritime Museum & Old Provost Ross's House
St Mary's Catholic Cathedral
Music Hall
Harbour
Ferry Terminal
Bus Station
Train Station
Fish Market
WEST END
ROSEMOUNT VIADUCT
SCHOOLHILL
BELMONT ST
DENBURN ROAD
UNION TERRACE
SKENE STREET
NORTH SILVER STREET
GOLDEN SQUARE
HUNTLY STREET
SUMMER STREET
CHAPEL STREET
ROSE STREET
THISTLE STREET
UNION STREET
BRIDGE STREET
THE GREEN
CORRECTION WYND
NETHERKIRKGATE
ADELPHI
SHIPROW
KING ST
CASTLE GATE
MARISCHAL STREET
VIRGINIA STREET
REGENT QUAY
TRINITY QUAY
GUILD STREET
JAMESONS QUAY
BLAIKIES QUAY
MARKET STREET
FISH MARKET
DEE STREET
CROWN STREET
COLLEGE STREET
BON ACCORD SQUARE
BON ACCORD TERRACE
BON ACCORD CRESCENT
BON ACCORD STREET
JUSTICE MILL LANE
ALFORD LANE
ALBYN PL
HOLBURN STREET
GT. WESTERN RD
SPRINGBANK TERRACE
PALMERSTONE RD
N. ESPLANADE W.

From the train and bus station it's a five-minute uphill walk to Union Street, Aberdeen's main thoroughfare. The **tourist office** is at the east end at number 23 (July & Aug Mon–Sat 9am–6.30pm, Sun 10am–4pm; April–June, Sept & Oct Mon–Sat 9.30am–5pm; Nov–June Mon–Sat 9.30am–5pm; ⓣ01224/288828).

Aberdeen's centre is best explored on foot, but you might need to use **buses**, most of which pass along Union Street, to reach some sights. For information on city bus services, call the Busline (ⓣ01224/650065, ⓦwww.firstgroup.com).

Accommodation

Aberdeen has a large choice of **accommodation**. Despite some characterless and expensive chain hotels targeting the business trade, there are also now a number of boutique hotels. Cheapest of all are the **hostel** and **student halls** left vacant for visitors in the summer.

Aberdeen Youth Hostel 8 Queen's Rd ⓣ0870/0041100, ⓦwww.syha.org.uk. Hostel in a historic building a mile from the train station, equipped with dorms and private rooms. Doors close at 2am but you can arrange to get in later. Bus #14 or #15 from Union St. Dorm bed £15. ❶

Carmelite Stirling St ⓣ01224/589101 ⓦwww.carmelitehotels.com. This boutique hotel will delight the style conscious with its fusion of antiquity and modern in a revamped 1820s hotel. Plans for a spa are in the offing, whilst the kitchen serves up a surprisingly modestly priced taste of Scotland. ❼

Crombie Johnston Halls College Bounds, Old Aberdeen ⓣ01224/273444, ⓦwww.abdn.ac.uk/hospitality. Private rooms in the city's best student halls, in one of the most interesting parts of town. Available from early July to Sept, though some year-round accommodation also available. ❶

Ferryhill House 169 Bon Accord St ⓣ01224/590867, ⓦwww.ferryhillhousehotel.co.uk. A mansion set in its own grounds within walking distance of Union St. Good-value lunches and great Malt Room for guests to sample real ales and whisky by a roaring fire. Beer garden. ❹

Globe Inn 13–15 North Silver St ⓣ01224/624258. Easy-going city-centre inn with seven en-suite rooms above a bar that hosts live jazz and blues Thurs–Sun. Rate includes continental breakfast. ❸

Merkland Guesthouse 12 Merkland Rd East ⓣ01224/634451. Standard but comfortable B&B handy for beach. Will cater for vegan and vegetarian guests. ❷

Penny Meadow 189 Great Western Rd ⓣ01224/588037. Very friendly guesthouse 10min walk from Union St. Guests can use immaculately kept back garden. ❹

Simpson's 59–63 Queen's Rd ⓣ01224/327777, ⓦwww.simpsonshotel.co.uk. Boutique hotel in a former granite terrace house, offering style and space, with an excellent brasserie that serves good-value midweek lunches. Good weekend room rates. ❻

Skene House Rosemount 96 Rosemount Viaduct ⓣ01224/645971, ⓦwww.skene-house.co.uk. There are 98 self-catering apartments here with one to three rooms, all with continental breakfast and TVs, and some with Internet. Good central location. ❺

Travelodge 9 Bridge St ⓣ0870/1911617, ⓦwww.travelodge.co.uk. Typically bland budget option – but you can't beat the convenient location, right next to Union St and minutes from the stations. It's worth enquiring about weekend deals. ❹

The City

The centre of Aberdeen is dominated by mile-long **Union Street**, still the grandest and most ambitious single thoroughfare in Scotland – although these days its impressive architecture is sometimes lost among the shoppers and chain stores.

Any exploration of the **city centre** should begin at the open, cobbled **Castlegate**, where Aberdeen's long-gone castle once stood. At its centre is the late seventeenth-century **Mercat Cross**, carved with a unique gallery of Stewart sovereigns alongside some fierce gargoyles. Castlegate was once the focus of city life but nowadays seems rather lifeless, though the view up gently rising Union Street – a jumble of grey spires, turrets and jostling double-decker buses – is quintessential Aberdeen.

Marischal College and museum

On Broad Street stands Aberdeen's most imposing edifice, and the world's second-largest granite building after the Escorial in Madrid – exuberant **Marischal College**, whose tall, steel-grey pinnacled neo-Gothic facade is in absolute contrast to the hideously utilitarian concrete office blocks opposite. This spectacular building, with all its soaring, surging lines, was once described by a minor art historian as "a wedding cake covered in indigestible grey icing". The college was founded in 1593 by the fourth Earl Marischal, and coexisted as a separate Protestant university from Catholic King's, just up the road, for over two centuries – it wasn't until 1860 that the two were united as the University of Aberdeen.

The university has all but moved from the college, and the building is largely closed to the public. What you can see is the **Marischal Museum** (Mon–Fri 10am–5pm, Sun 2–5pm; free) and its wealth of weird exhibits, many gathered by Victorian anthropologists and other collectors who roamed the world filling their luggage with objects.

The Aberdeen Art Gallery and around

A little further west up Schoolhill is Aberdeen's engrossing **Art Gallery** (Mon–Sat 10am–5pm, Sun 2–5pm; free), purpose-built in 1884 to a Neoclassical design by Mackenzie. You enter via the airy **Centre Court**, dominated by Barbara Hepworth's central fountain and thick pillars running down from the upper balcony, each hewn from a different local marble. Nearby are a number of the gallery's recent acquisitions of contemporary art, with British work to the fore. The **Memorial Court**, a calming, white-walled circular room under a skylit dome, serves as the city's principal war memorial. It also houses the Lord Provost's book of condolence for the 167 people who died in the 1988 Piper Alpha oil rig disaster.

The **upstairs** rooms house the main body of the gallery's painting collection. This includes a superb collection of Victorian narrative art, some decent twentieth-century British painting and a collection of Impressionist art, including works by Boudin, Courbet, Sisley, Monet, Pissarro and Renoir.

Opposite the gallery is a designer shopping arcade called **The Academy**, a gateway to Aberdeen's answer to a Bohemian quarter: cobbled Belmont and Little Belmont streets feature a number of the city's more interesting bars, shops and restaurants, and farmers' markets take place on the first and last Saturday of each month.

The harbour

Old, cobbled Shiprow winds down from Castlegate at the east end of Union Street to the north side of the **harbour**. Just off this steep road, peering towards the harbour through a striking glass facade, is the **Maritime Museum** (Mon–Sat 10am–5pm, Sun noon–3pm; free), which combines a modern, airy museum with the aged labyrinthine corridors of **Provost Ross's House**. The museum is a thoroughly engrossing, imaginative tribute to Aberdeen's maritime traditions.

Just inside the front entrance you'll see a blackboard updated every day with the price of a barrel of crude oil, and suspended above the foyer, visible from five different levels, is a spectacular 27ft-high model of an oil rig, which, along with terrific views over the bustling harbour, serves as a constant reminder that Aberdeen's maritime links remain very much alive. The older industries of herring fishing, whaling, shipbuilding and lighthouses also have their place, with well-designed displays and audiovisual presentations, many drawing heavily on personal reminiscences.

At the north end of Market Street, Trinity Quay runs past industrial yards and down York Street towards **Footdee**, or Fittie (an easy walk or bus #14 or #15 from Union Street), a quaint nineteenth-century fishermen's village of higgledy-piggledy cottages backing onto the sea.

Old Aberdeen

An independent burgh until 1891, tranquil **Old Aberdeen**, a ten-minute ride north of the city centre on bus #20 from Marischal College on Littlejohn Street, has maintained a village-like identity. Dominated by King's College and St Machar's Cathedral, its medieval cobbled streets, wynds and little lanes are beautifully preserved. The southern half of cobbled High Street is overlooked by **King's College Chapel** (Mon–Fri 8am–4pm; free), the first and finest of the college buildings, completed in 1495, with a chunky Renaissance spire. The highlights of the interior, which, unusually, has no central aisle, are the ribbed arched wooden ceiling and the rare and lovely examples of medieval Scottish woodcarving in the screen and the stalls. From the college, High Street leads a short way north to **St Machar's Cathedral** on the leafy Chanonry (daily 9am–5pm, except during services; free), overlooking Seaton Park and the River Don. The site was reputedly founded in 580 AD by Machar, a follower of Columba, when he was sent by the latter to find a grassy platform near the sea, overlooking a river shaped like the crook on a bishop's crozier. This setting fitted the bill perfectly, and the cathedral, a huge fifteenth-century fortified building, became one of the city's first great granite edifices.

The beach

Aberdeen can surely claim to have the best sandy **beach** of all Britain's large cities. Less than a mile east of Union Street is a great two-mile sweep of clean sand, broken by groynes and lined all along with an esplanade, where most of the city's population seems to gather on sunny days. The massive **Beach Leisure Centre** includes flumes and a wave machine, and a ten-minute walk south will take you to sprawling **Codona's amusement park** complete with its new roller coaster, slides and restaurant areas. Further north, most of the beach's hinterland is devoted to golf links.

Eating, drinking and nightlife

Most of Aberdeen's **cafés** and **restaurants** are clustered around Union and Belmont streets, though you'll find them pricier than elsewhere in northeast Scotland. Although you'll find no shortage of loud, flashy **bars** , there are still a number of more traditional **pubs** that, though usually packed, are well worth a visit.

Cafés and restaurants

Ashvale 42–48 Great Western Rd ⓣ01224 596981 ⓦwww.theashvale.co.uk. Diners who finish the "Ashvale Whale", a 1lb cod fillet (£9.95) receive another for free at this renowned northeast chippy and family-oriented restaurant. Moderate.

Beautiful Mountain 11 Belmont St ⓣ01224/645353. Welcoming daytime café and takeaway with a staggering range of good-value sandwiches, including ample vegetarian and organic options. Inexpensive.

Café 52 52 The Green ⓣ01224/590094, ⓦwww.cafe52.net. Cosy, bohemian hang-out by day that turns into a hip restaurant by night with Cullen skink soup, game and vegetarian meals among the tasty options. Closed Sun eve & Mon daytime. Moderate.

Carmelite Stirling St ⓣ01224/589101 ⓦwww.carmelitehotels.com. One of Aberdeen's newer dining experiences with a stylish interior and tasty Scottish-influenced cuisine served with simplicity. Moderate–expensive.

Howies 50 Chapel St ⓣ01224/639500, ⓦwww.howies.uk.com. Aberdeen outpost of an Edinburgh institution, serving Scottish cooking in a stylish environment. Well-priced set meals and house wine. Moderate.

Lemon Tree 5 West North St ⓣ01224/642694, ⓦwww.lemontree.org/café. Easy-going daytime café inside the arts centre, serving snacks and meals – including good vegetarian and vegan options – to live music. Open Thurs–Sun noon–2.30pm (bar open until 4pm). Inexpensive.

Musa Exchange St ⓣ01224/571771. Based in an old church and banana warehouse, the terrific daytime vibe in the good-value art music café continues into the evening with live music and mouthwatering dining on the likes of Thai stockpot. Tues–Sat 8.30am–11pm, Sun 10am–4.30pm. Moderate–expensive.

Silver Darling Pocra Quay, North Pier ⓣ01224/576229. Attractively located at the harbour in Footdee, the French owner specializes in tickling your taste buds with delicious, freshly caught seafood. Closed Sat lunchtime & Sun. Expensive.

Pubs and bars

Jam 67 Langside Place. This trendy watering hole is where to find DJ's putting out a nightly beat of Indie and party anthem tunes. Noon–midnight.

Prince of Wales 7 St Nicholas Lane. Opened in 1850, the quintessential Aberdeen pub has a six-metre-long bar and flagstone floor. With fine pub grub, renowned real ales and a Sun eve folk session, it's little wonder that it's often crowded.

St Machar Bar 97 High St, Old Aberdeen. The medieval quarter's only pub, a poky, old-fashioned bar attracting an intriguing mix of King's College students and workers.

Under the Hammer 11 North Silver St. This snug little basement wine bar has a continental vibe and is a popular refuge when icy winter winds hit the city. Relax in the knowledge there's no TV to drown out your convivial evening chat.

Clubs, live music venues and concert halls

Babylon 9 Alford Place ⓣ01224/595001. Bills itself as one of Aberdeen's coolest and hippest nightspots, the Gothic-styled interior here reverberates to the beat of latest dance tunes. Tends to attract a thirty-something crowd. Fri & Sat 10pm–3am.

The Globe Inn 13–15 North Silver St ⓣ01224/624258. Pleasant city-centre inn with traditional folk music on Tues and a variety of musical genres on weekend evenings.

Lemon Tree 5 West North St ⓣ01224/642230, ⓦwww.lemontree.org. The fulcrum of the city's arts scene, with a great buzz and regular live music, club nights and comedy, as well as decent theatre.

The Tunnels Carnegies Brae ⓣ01224/211121. One of Aberdeen's most popular live music venues, established within old tunnels under Union St. Live bands and a different musical genre every evening including reggae, hip-hop, ska and Northern Soul.

Theatres and cinemas

Belmont Picture House 9 Belmont St ⓣ01224/343536, ⓦwww.picturehouses.co.uk. Art-house cinema showing the more cerebral new releases alongside classic, cult and foreign-language films. There's a comfortable café-bar inside and some good places nearby for a bite before or after.

His Majesty's Rosemount Viaduct ⓣ01224/641122, ⓦwww.hmtaberdeen.com. The city's recently refurbished main theatre resides in a beautiful Edwardian building, and its extensive programme ranges from highbrow drama and opera to pantomime.

Listings

Airport ⓣ0870/0400006.

Bike rental Alpine Bikes, 66–70 Holburn St ⓣ01224/211455 (£20 a day).

Bookshops The largest is Waterstone's, 269–271 Union St and there are various WH Smith outlets including in the St Nicholas Centre. Winram's, 32–36 Rosemount Place and The Old Aberdeen Bookshop, 140 Spital, are best for second-hand, while Books and Beans, 22 Belmont St, offers a more populist selection.

Bus information First Aberdeen Busline ⓣ01224/650065.

Car rental Arnold Clark, Girdleness Rd ⓣ01224/249159, Lang Stracht (airport pick-ups) ⓣ01224/663723; Budget, Wellheads Drive (airport pick-ups) ⓣ01224/793333; National, 16 Broomhill Rd ⓣ01224 595366 and airport ⓣ0870/400 4502.

Ferry information ⓣ0845/6000449, ⓦwww.northlinkferries.co.uk.

Medical facilities The Royal Infirmary, on Foresterhill, northeast of the town centre, has a 24hr casualty department (ⓣ01224/681818). Boots pharmacy is at 161 Union St (Mon–Wed &

Dunnottar Castle and Stonehaven

Two miles south of Stonehaven, the stunningly capricious **Dunnottar Castle** (Easter–Oct Mon–Sat 9am–6pm, Sun 2–5pm; Oct–Easter Fri–Mon 9am–sunset; £5) is one of Scotland's finest ruined castles, a huge ninth-century fortress set on a three-sided sheer cliff jutting into the sea – a setting striking enough to be chosen as the backdrop for Zeffirelli's movie version of *Hamlet*. Once the principal fortress of the northeast, the ruins are worth a good root around, and there are many dramatic views out to the crashing sea.

Stonehaven itself is a pretty little harbour town, split into two parts, the picturesque working harbour most likely to detain you. On one side of the harbour, Stonehaven's oldest building, the **Tolbooth** (June–Sept Mon & Wed–Sun 1.30–4.30pm; free), built as a storehouse during the construction of Dunnottar Castle, is now a museum of local history and fishing. In the northern part of the new town is Stonehaven's wonderful open-air Art Deco **swimming pool** (June & Sept Mon–Fri 1–7.30pm, Sat & Sun 10am–6pm; July & Aug Mon–Fri 10am–7.30pm, & Wed 10pm–midnight, Sat & Sun 10am–6pm; £3.50; ⓦwww.stonehavenopenairpool.co.uk), opened in 1934 and always packed with locals on a sunny day. The **tourist office** is at 66 Allardice St, the main street past the square (April–June, Sept & Oct Mon–Sat 10am–1pm & 2–5pm; July & Aug Mon–Sat 10am–7pm, Sun 1–5.30pm; ⓣ01569/762806).

▲ Dunnottar Castle

Fri 7.45am–6pm, Thurs 7.45am–8pm, Sat 8.30am–6pm, Sun noon–5pm; ⓣ01224/211592). For late-night pharmacies, Tesco's at Bridge of Don until 9pm or Morrisons supermarket on King St (ⓣ01224/624404) until 8pm.

Police Main station is on Queen St (ⓣ0845/6005700), including the lost property office.

Post office The central office is in the St Nicholas Centre, between Union St and Upperkirkgate (Mon–Sat 9am–5.30pm), with other branches at 371 George St (Mon–Fri 9am–5.30pm, Sat 9am–12.30pm) and 489 Union St (hours same as George St).

Taxis Rainbow Taxis ⓣ01224 725500.

Deeside

More commonly known as **Royal Deeside**, the land stretching west from Aberdeen along the River Dee revels in its connections with the Royal Family, who have regularly holidayed here, at **Balmoral**, since Queen Victoria bought the estate. Eighty thousand Scots turned out to welcome her on her first visit in 1848, but some weren't so charmed: one local journalist remarked that the area was about to be "desolated by cockneys and other horrible reptiles". Today, most locals are fiercely protective of the royal connection.

Deeside is undoubtedly handsome in a fierce, craggy, Scottish way, and the royal presence has helped keep a lid on any unattractive mass development. The villages strung along the A93, the main route through the area, are well-heeled and have something of an old-fashioned air. Facilities for visitors hereabouts are first-class, with a number of bunkhouses and hostels, some decent hotels and plenty of castles and grounds to snoop around. It's also an excellent area for **outdoor activities**, with hiking routes into both the Grampian and Cairngorm mountains, alongside good mountain biking, horse riding and skiing.

West of Aberdeen

Fourteen miles west of Aberdeen, **Crathes Castle** (daily: April–Sept 10.30am–5.30pm; Oct 10.30am–4.30pm; Nov–March Wed–Sun 10.30am–3.45pm; £10; NTS) is a splendid sixteenth-century granite tower house adorned with flourishes such as overhanging turrets, gargoyles and conical roofs. Its thick walls, narrow windows and tiny rooms loaded with heavy old furniture make Crathes rather claustrophobic, but it is still worth visiting for some wonderful painted ceilings, either still in their original form or sensitively restored; the earliest dates from 1602. The grounds include an impressive walled garden complete with yew hedges subjected to a spot of topiary.

Another dozen or so miles west on the A93, **ABOYNE** is a typically well-mannered Deeside village at the mouth of **Glen Tanar**, which runs southwest from here for ten miles or so deep into the Grampian hills. The glen, with few steep gradients and some glorious stands of mature Caledonian pine, is ideal for walking, mountain biking or horse riding; the ranger information point two miles into the glen off the B976 has details of suitable routes, while the Glen Tanar Equestrian Centre (☎01339/886448) offers one- and two-hour **horse rides**.

Ballater and Balmoral

Ten miles west of Aboyne is the neat and ordered town of **BALLATER**, attractively hemmed in by the river and fir-covered mountains. It was in Ballater that Queen Victoria first arrived in Deeside by train from Aberdeen back in 1848; she wouldn't allow a station to be built any closer to Balmoral, eight miles further west. Although the line has long been closed, the town's rather self-important royalism is much in evidence with oversized "By Appointment" crests sported above the doorways of most businesses from the butcher to the newsagent.

Ballater is an excellent base for local **walks** and **outdoor activities**. There are numerous hikes from Loch Muik (pronounced "mick"), including the well-worn but strenuous all-day trek up and around Lochnagar (3789ft), the mountain much painted and written about by the current Prince of Wales. Good-quality **bikes** can be rented from Cabin Fever (☎013397/54004; £15 a day), beside the station on Station Square, or Cycle Highlands (Ⓣ013397/55864; £15 a day, or £35 a day for full suspension) at 16 Bridge St.

Ballater's **tourist office** is in the renovated train station (daily: July & Aug 9am–6pm; rest of year 10am–5pm; Ⓣ013397/55306). Good-quality **bunkhouse** accommodation with breakfast is available at the *Schoolhouse*, Anderson Rd (Ⓣ013397/56333, Ⓦwww.theschool-house.com; ❶), complete with ghost walks and storytelling, and there are plenty of reasonable **B&Bs** in town, including *Inverdeen House* on Bridge Square (Ⓣ013397/55759, Ⓦwww.inverdeen.com; ❸), which offers a wide choice of breakfasts, most involving local produce and home baking.

There are numerous **places to eat**, from smart hotel restaurants to bakers and coffee shops: the *Green Inn* (Ⓣ013397/55701, Ⓦwww.green-inn.com; ❹) is pricey but excellent with locally sourced game on the menu, while a couple of miles east of Ballater at Cambus O'May the *Crannach Coffee Shop and Gallery* (closed Mon) has good coffees, snacks and light meals, as well as superb cakes and bread from their in-house organic bakery.

Balmoral Estate

Originally a sixteenth-century tower house built for the powerful Gordon family, **Balmoral Castle** (April–July daily 10am–5pm; £7 or £8 for optional guided tour; Ⓣ013397/42534, Ⓦwww.balmoralcastle.com) has been a royal residence since 1852. The Royal Family traditionally spend their summer holidays here each August, but despite its fame it can be something of a disappointment even for a dedicated royalist. For the three months when the doors are nudged open, the general riffraff are permitted to view only the ballroom, an exhibition room and the grounds.

Braemar

Continuing westwards for another few miles, the road rises to 1100ft above sea level in the upper part of Deeside and the village of **BRAEMAR**, situated where three passes meet. It's an invigorating, outdoor kind of place, well patronized by committed hikers, but probably best known for its Highland Games, the annual **Braemar Gathering**, on the first Saturday of September (Ⓦwww.braemargathering.org). Since Queen Victoria's day, successive generations of royals have attended and the world's most famous Highland Games have become rather an overcrowded, overblown event. You're not guaranteed to get in if you just turn up; the website has details of how to book tickets in advance.

Braemar's **tourist office** is in the modern building known as the Mews, in the middle of the village on Mar Road (June & Sept daily 9am–5pm; July & Aug daily 9am–6pm; Oct Mon–Sat 9am–5pm, Sun 1–5pm; Nov–May Mon–Sat 10.30am–1.30pm & 2–5pm, Sun 1–4pm; Ⓣ013397/41600). *Clunie Lodge Guesthouse*, Clunie Bank Rd (Ⓣ013397/41330, Ⓦwww.clunielodge.com; ❷), on the edge of town, is a good **B&B** with lovely views up Clunie Glen, while cheery *Rucksacks*, an easygoing bunkhouse that's well equipped for walkers and backpackers, is just behind the Mews complex (Ⓣ013397/41517).

For **food**, avoid the large hotels, which tend to be filled with coach parties, and try either *Taste*, a coffee shop and moderately priced contemporary restaurant on the road out to the Linn of Dee, or *The Gathering Place* in the heart of the village (by Braemar Mountain Sports) where you'll find mouthwatering, though pricey, freshly prepared Scottish-based cuisine.

Speyside

Strictly speaking, the term **Speyside** refers to the entire region surrounding the River Spey, but to most people the name is synonymous with the **whisky triangle**, stretching from just north of Craigellachie, down towards Tomintoul in the south and east to Huntly. Indeed, there are more whisky distilleries and famous brands concentrated in this small area (including Glenfiddich and Glenlivet) than in any other part of the country. Running through the heart of the region is the River Spey, whose clean, clear, fast-running waters not only play such a vital part in the whisky industry, but also make it one of Scotland's finest angling locations. At the centre of Speyside is the quiet market town of **Dufftown** and, along with the well-kept nearby villages of **Craigellachie** and **Aberlour**, it makes the best base for a tour of whisky country, whether on the official Malt Whisky Trail or more independent explorations.

Dufftown

The cheery community of **DUFFTOWN**, founded in 1817 by James Duff, the fourth Earl of Fife, proudly proclaims itself "Malt Whisky Capital of the World" with good reason – it produces more of the stuff than any other town in Britain. There are nine distilleries around Dufftown (not all of them still working), as well as a cooperage and a coppersmith, and an extended stroll around the outskirts of the town gives a good idea of the density of whisky distilling going on, with glimpses of giant warehouses filled with barrels of the heady liquid, and whiffs of fermenting barley or peat smoke lingering on the breeze.

There isn't a great deal to do in town, but it's a useful starting point for orienting yourself towards the whisky trail. On the edge of town along the A941 is the town's largest working distillery, **Glenfiddich** (see p.967), as well as the old Dufftown train station, which has been restored by enthusiasts in recent years and is now the departure point for the **Keith & Dufftown Railway** (April–Sept Sat & Sun 3 trips daily, June–Aug also runs Fri; 40min; ⓣ01340/821181, ⓦwww.keith-dufftown.org.uk for journey times and fares), which uses restored diesel locomotives to chug through whisky country to Keith, home of the Strathisla distillery (see p.967).

Dufftown's official **tourist office** is located inside the handsome clocktower at the centre of the square (July & Aug Mon–Sat 10am–1pm & 2–5.30pm, Sun 11am–3pm; April–June, Sept & Oct Mon–Sat 10am–1pm & 2–5pm, Sun 11am–3pm; ⓣ01340/820501), though there's also an information and accommodation booking service at The Whisky Shop (ⓣ01340/821097) across the road.

There's a handful of places to stay in Dufftown itself, although you may prefer to stay elsewhere on Speyside, closer to the attractive countryside. For **B&B**, *Tannochbrae*, 22 Fife St (ⓣ01340/820541, ⓦwww.tannochbrae.co.uk; ❸), is a pleasant, enthusiastically run place with a small restaurant on the ground floor. You can also rent **bikes** from here.

Craigellachie

Four miles north of Dufftown, the small settlement of **CRAIGELLACHIE** (pronounced "Craig-*ell*-ach-ee") sits above the confluence of the sparkling waters of the Fiddich and the Spey, spanned by a beautiful iron bridge built by Thomas Telford in 1815. For an unusual alternative to a distillery tour, the **Speyside Cooperage** (Mon–Fri 9.30am–4pm; £3.20) is worth a visit: after

Touring Malt Whisky Country

Speyside is the heart of Scotland's **whisky** industry, with over fifty distilleries testimony to a unique combination of clear, clean water, benign climate and gentle upland terrain. Yet it's worth keeping in mind that in these parts whisky is a hard-edged, multimillion-pound business dominated by huge corporations, and it sometimes comes as a surprise to visitors that a lot of distilleries are unglamorous industrial units, not all open to the public. Having said that, there are plenty located in attractive historic buildings which now go to some lengths to provide an engaging experience for visitors. Mostly this involves a tour around the essential stages in the whisky-making process, though for real enthusiasts a number of distilleries now offer pricier connoisseur tours.

There are eight distilleries on the official **Malt Whisky Trail** (Ⓦwww.maltwhiskytrail.com). Unless you're seriously interested in whisky, it's best to just pick out a couple that appeal: we've highlighted some below. All offer a guided tour (some are free, others charge but then give you a voucher which is redeemable against a bottle of whisky from the distillery shop), with a tasting to round it off. Most people travel the route by car, though you could cycle parts of it, or even walk using the Speyside Way long-distance footpath.

Glen Grant, Rothes (April–Oct Mon–Sat 9.30am–5pm, Sun noon–5pm; £3.50 including voucher). A well-known, floral whisky aggressively marketed to a younger market. A regular, well-informed tour, but the highlight here is the attractive Victorian gardens, a mix of well-tended lawns and mixed, mature trees which include a tumbling waterfall and a hidden whisky-safe.

Glenfiddich, on the A941 just north of Dufftown (April to mid-Oct Mon–Sat 9.30am–4.30pm, Sun noon–4.30pm; mid-Oct to March Mon–Fri 9.30am–4.30pm; free). The biggest and slickest of all the Speyside distilleries, and the first to offer regular tours to visitors, despite the fact that it's still owned by the same Grant family who founded it in 1887. It's a light, sweet whisky packaged in triangular-shaped bottles – unusually, the bottling is still done on the premises and is part of the tour (offered in various languages).

Glenlivet, on the B9008 to Tomintoul (April–Oct Mon–Sat 9.30am–4pm, Sun noon–4pm; free). A famous name in a lonely hillside setting. This was the first licensed distillery in the Highlands, following the 1823 Act of Parliament that aimed to reduce illicit distilling and smuggling. The Glenlivet 12-year-old malt is a floral, fragrant medium-bodied whisky.

Strathisla, Keith (April–Oct Mon–Sat 9.30am–4pm, Sun noon–4pm; £5). A small, old-fashioned distillery claiming to be Scotland's oldest (1786); it's certainly one of the most attractive, with classic pagoda-shaped buildings and the River Isla rushing by. Inside are some impressive and interesting bits of equipment such as an old-fashioned mashtun and brass-bound spirit safes. The malt itself has a rich almost fruity taste and is pretty rare, but is used as the heart of the better-known Chivas Regal blend. You can arrive here on board one of the restored trains of the Keith & Dufftown Railway (see p.966).

A number of other distilleries, not on the official trail, can also be visited:

Aberlour, on the outskirts of the village (April–Oct daily 10.30am & 2pm; £7.50; booking essential ⓣ01340/881249). The twice-daily tours are quite specialized, with a tutored nosing and the chance to buy and fill your own bottle of cask-strength single malt.

Macallan, near Craigellachie (April–Oct Mon–Sat 9.30am–4.30pm, Nov–March Mon–Fri 11am–3pm; ⓣ01340/872280), can only take ten people on its tours, and therefore doesn't attract coach parties.

the exhibition explaining the ancient and skilled art of cooperage, you're shown onto a balcony overlooking the workshop where the oak casks for whisky are made and repaired by fast-working, highly skilled coopers.

For somewhere **to stay** in the village there's an extremely welcoming and tasteful B&B attached to the *Green Hall Gallery* on Victoria Street (Ⓣ01340/871010, Ⓦwww.aboutscotland.com/greenhall; ④); in Archiestown, a few miles west of Craigellachie, the pleasant, traditional *Archiestown Hotel* (Ⓣ01340/810218, Ⓦwww.archiestownhotel.co.uk; ⑦) caters for fishermen and outdoor types, and serves good evening **meals**.

The coast

The **coast** of northeast Scotland from Aberdeen to Inverness has a rugged, sometimes bleak fringe with pleasant if undramatic farmland rolling inland. Still, if the weather is good, it's well worth spending a couple of days meandering through the various little fishing villages and along the miles of deserted, unspoilt beaches.

The largest coastal towns are **Peterhead** and **Fraserburgh**, both dominated by sizeable fishing fleets; while neither has much to offer, the latter's Museum of Scottish Lighthouses is one of the most attractive small museums in Scotland. More appealing to most visitors are the quieter spots along the Moray coast, including the charming villages of **Pennan**, **Gardenstown**, **Portsoy** and nearby **Cullen**. The other main attractions are **Duff House** in Banff, a branch of the National Gallery of Scotland; the working abbey at **Pluscarden** by Elgin; and the **Findhorn Foundation**, near Forres.

Fraserburgh and the north coast

Large and severe-looking **FRASERBURGH** (Ⓦwww.visitfraserburgh.com) is home of the excellent **Museum of Scottish Lighthouses** (April–June, Sept & Oct Mon–Sat 11am–5pm, Sun noon–5pm; July & Aug Mon–Sat 10am–6pm, Sun 11am–6pm; Nov–March Mon–Sat 11am–4pm, Sun noon–4pm; £5), where you can see a collection of huge lenses and prisms gathered from decommissioned lighthouses, and a display on various members of the famous "Lighthouse" Stevenson family (including the father and grandfather of author Robert Louis Stevenson), who designed many of them. Highlight of the museum is the tour of Kinnaird Head lighthouse itself, preserved as it was when the last keeper left in 1991, with its century-old equipment still in perfect working order.

PENNAN, twelve miles west of Fraserburgh, is a tiny fishing hamlet consisting of little more than a single row of whitewashed stone cottages tucked between a cliff and the sea. The movie *Local Hero* was filmed here in 1982 and you can stay at one of the landmarks from the film, the *Pennan Inn* (Ⓣ01346/561201, Ⓦwww.thepennaninn.com; ②–⑤), where you can also grab a drink or a bite to eat. A serious landslip here during the wet summer of 2007 caused an evacuation of the village and forced the *Inn* to close pending reconstruction.

In tiny and equally appealing **CROVIE** (pronounced "crivie"), on the other side of Troup Head from Pennan, residents have to park their cars at one end of the village and continue to their houses on foot. **GARDENSTOWN**, a short way west, is a little larger and supports the *Garden Arms Hotel* (Ⓣ01261/851260, Ⓦwww.gardenarms.co.uk; ③), as well as the Gallery 83 art space and the excellent *Harbour Restaurant and Café* (Ⓣ01261/851690;

Festivals and events

From a Scottish Highland Games gathering to the pyrotechnics of Bonfire Night, Britain's annual events and festivals illustrate the richness of the region's history and depth of its diversity. Some, of course are no more than an excuse for a bizarre day out and a booze-up – the sight of the entire population of a village following a burning tar barrel or chasing a cheese downhill is not easily forgotten. May and August bank holiday weekends and the summer school holidays (July and Aug) are the favoured times for events to be held: contact local tourist offices for exact dates. For a full list of Britain's festivals and events, see p.51.

Street dancing, Llangollen International Music Festival ▲

Glorious Glastonbury ▼

Llangollen International Music Eisteddfod

During the first week of July the town of Llangollen in the Dee Valley explodes in a frenzy of music, dance and poetry. The **International Music Eisteddfod** comes billed as the "world's greatest folk festival" but unlike the National Eisteddfod, which is a purely Welsh affair, the Llangollen draws more than 12,000 amateur performers from countries around the world, all competing for prizes in their chosen disciplines. There's an irresistible *joie de vivre* as brightly costumed dancers fill the streets, while the Fringe Festival offers rock and comedy gigs and performance events. For ticket details, see p.719.

Glastonbury

When Michael Eavis held a rock festival on his Somerset farm in 1970 (audience of two thousand, ticket price a quid, headliners T-Rex), he had no idea that it would eventually turn into England's biggest summer music and arts bash. Four decades on, the annual **Glastonbury Festival** of Performing Arts (to give it its full title) sees Worthy Farm inundated by 100,000 revellers, hellbent on enjoying themselves whatever the weather – just as well, since late June downpours are notorious for turning the three-day festival into a mudbath. Many complain that Glasto has moved away from its hippy roots, as high ticket prices, state-of-the-art security and even proper toilets have become the norm. But despite the contemporary buzz and headlining superstars, the "alternative" Glastonbury spirit is never far away – in the vast campsite village, organic cafés, circus fields, healing areas or performance tents. For more details, see p.304.

Highland Games

Despite their name, the summer **Highland Games** are held all over Scotland, not just in the Highlands. The most famous games take place at Braemar (p.965) and Cowal (Dunoon), though smaller events are often more fun. The most distinctive events are known as the "**heavies**" – tossing the caber, putting the stone, and tossing the weight over the bar – all of which require prodigious strength and skill and the wearing of a kilt. Tossing the caber is the most spectacular, when the athlete must lift an entire tree trunk cupping it in his hands, before running with it and attempting to heave it end over end in a perfect, elegant throw. Just as important as the sporting events are the **piping** and **dancing** competitions, where you'll see girls as young as three tripping the intricate steps of the Highland Fling.

▲ A "heavy" event

▼ Notting Hill

Notting Hill Carnival

Europe's greatest street party takes place over the last weekend of August (Sun and bank holiday Mon). Born out of despair following the **Notting Hill** race riots of 1958, it started out as a few church-hall events and a carnival parade, inspired by the Caribbean roots of many of the area's residents. Today, hundreds of thousands of revellers turn up, following a three-mile procession around the neighbourhood. At its heart are the truck-borne sound systems and *mas* (masquerade) bands, behind which the masqueraders dance in outrageous costumes. There are also live music stages and numerous sound systems, with the partying fuelled by cans of Red Stripe, curried goat and Jamaican patties. It's not quite Rio, but it's certainly not staid old England either.

Fireworks ▲

Bog-snorkelling ▼

Bonfire Night

"Remember, remember, the fifth of November", goes the old rhyme, "gunpowder, treason and plot" – and remember it the English certainly do, with fireworks and fires across the country, commemorating the foiling of the 1605 Gunpowder Plot to blow up Parliament. Atop every bonfire is hoisted an effigy known as the "guy", after Guy Fawkes, one of the failed conspirators; an anonymous concoction of sticks and old clothes stuffed with newspaper suffices for most fires, but some effigies might represent resented contemporary or local figures (at Lewes in East Sussex, which puts on the most dramatic show in the country – see p.191). Although November 5 is technically **Bonfire Night** or Guy Fawkes' Night, many prefer to hold their bonfire on the nearest weekend.

The weird and wonderful

For a taste of Britain at its most idiosyncratic, steer towards one of the numerous local celebrations that perpetuate **ancient customs**. The May Day frolics of the **Padstow Obby Oss**, in Cornwall, can be traced back to fertility rites in the distant past, while other events are grounded in ceremony, like **Swan Upping** (third week in July), the traditional registering of cygnets on the River Thames. Some do nothing more than celebrate British regional eccentricity: witness Gloucestershire's **Brockworth Cheese Rolling** contest, Cheshire's annual **World Worm-Charming Championships**, or the **Bog-Snorkelling Competition** held every August in Llanwrtyd Wells (Mid-Wales). See p.51 for more.

booking recommended), which overlooks the collection of small local boats tied up to the quayside.

Banff

Heading west along the coast from Pennan brings you, after ten miles, to **Macduff** and its neighbour **BANFF**, separated by the beautiful seven-arch bridge over the River Deveron. Banff has a mix of characterful old buildings and boarded-up shops, which give little clue to the extravagance of **Duff House** (generally April–Oct daily 11am–5pm; Nov–March Thurs–Sun 11am–4pm; Ⓦwww.duffhouse.org.uk; £6; HS), the town's main attraction. Built to William Adam's design in 1730, this elegant four-floor Georgian Baroque house has been painstakingly restored and reopened as an outpost of the **National Gallery of Scotland**'s extensive collection, and while the emphasis is on displaying period artwork rather than any broader selection of the Gallery's paintings, temporary exhibitions of work from the collections are mounted regularly. Banff's **tourist office** (April–Oct Mon–Sat 10am–1pm & 2–5pm; Ⓣ01261/812419) is housed in the old gatehouse of Duff House in St Mary Square.

Cullen to Spey Bay

Twelve miles west of Banff is **CULLEN**, strikingly situated beneath a superb series of arched viaducts. The town is made up of two sections: Seatown, by the harbour, and the new town on the hillside. The local delicacy, **Cullen skink** – a soup made from milk (or cream), potato and smoked haddock – is available at local hotels and bars

West of Cullen, the scruffy working fishing town of **BUCKIE** marks one end of the **Speyside Way** long-distance footpath, which follows the coast west for five miles to windy **Spey Bay**, at the mouth of the river of the same name (which can also be reached by a small coastal road from Buckie). It's a remote spot bounded by sea, river and sky; there's a small but dedicated **wildlife centre** (April–Oct daily 10.30am–5pm; Nov–March Sat & Sun 10.30am–5pm; Ⓦwww.wdcs.org/wildlifecentre; free), whose main mission is researching the Moray Firth dolphin population (for more on which, see p.983).

Elgin and around

The lively market town of **ELGIN**, just inland about fifteen miles west of Cullen, grew up around the River Lossie in the thirteenth century. On North College Street is the lovely ruin of **Elgin Cathedral** (April–Sept daily 9.30am–5.30pm; Oct–March Mon–Wed, Sat & Sun 9.30am–4.30pm; £4.50; HS, joint ticket with Spynie Palace £6), once considered Scotland's most beautiful cathedral, though it's little more than a shell today. Founded in 1224, the three-towered building stood as the region's highest religious house until 1390 when the inimical Wolf of Badenoch (Alexander Stewart, Earl of Buchan and illegitimate son of Robert II) burned the place down, along with the rest of the town, in retaliation for having been excommunicated by the bishop of Moray when he left his wife.

Elgin's **tourist office** is at 17 High St (April–June & Sept Mon–Sat 10am–5pm, Sun 11am–3pm; July & Aug Mon–Sat 9am–6pm, Sun 11am–4pm; Oct–March Mon–Sat 10am–4pm; Ⓣ01343/542666). Five miles east of town, the *Old Church of Urquhart* (Ⓣ01343/843063, Ⓦwww.oldkirk.co.uk; ❸) is the most appealing place to stay in the area, an unusual and comfortable B&B in an imaginatively converted church on Meft Road.

Pluscarden Abbey

Seven miles southwest of Elgin, **Pluscarden Abbey** (daily 9am–5pm; free; Ⓦ www.pluscardenabbey.org), looms impressively large in a peaceful clearing off an unmarked road. One of only two abbeys in Scotland with a permanent community of monks, it was founded in 1230 for a French order. In 1948 a small group of Benedictine monks from Gloucester established the present community. They are an active bunch, running stained-glass workshops, making honey and even recording Gregorian chants on CDs, all of which is detailed on the website. The abbey itself is airy and tranquil, with the monks' singing often eerily floating through from the connecting chapel.

Findhorn

Northwest of Elgin, at one end of a wide sweep of sandy beach, **FINDHORN** is a tidy village with some neat fishermen's cottages and a delightful harbour dotted with moored yachts. Findhorn is best known, however, for the controversial **Findhorn Foundation**, based beside the town's caravan park about a mile before you reach the village itself. Visitors are generally free to stroll around the community, but the **guided tour** is worthwhile (April–Nov Mon, Wed & Fri–Sun 2pm; no Sun tour in April, Oct & Nov; £3); you can also guide yourself via a booklet (£3) available from the shop or visitor centre (Mon–Fri 10am–5pm, also open Sat & Sun 1–4pm in summer; Ⓣ 01309/690311, Ⓦ www.findhorn.org), which also has information on staying within the community.

The Findhorn Foundation

In 1962, with little money and no employment, Eileen and Peter Caddy, their three children and friend Dorothy Maclean, settled on a caravan site at Findhorn. Dorothy believed she had a special relationship with what she called the "devas…the archetypal formative forces of light or energy that underlie all forms in nature – plants, trees, rivers", and from the uncompromising sandy soil they built a remarkable garden filled with plants and vegetables, far larger than had ever been seen in the area.

A few of those who came to see the phenomenon stayed to help out and tune into the spiritual aspect of the daily life of the nascent community. With its emphasis on inner discovery and development, but unattached to any particular doctrine or creed, the **Findhorn Foundation** (Ⓦ www.findhorn.org) has today blossomed into a permanent community of a couple of hundred people, with a well-developed series of courses and retreats on subjects ranging from astroshamanic healing to organic gardening, drawing another eight thousand or so visitors each year. The original caravan still stands, surrounded by a whole host of newer timber buildings and other caravans employing solar power, earth roofs and other green initiatives. The most intriguing of these are a group of round houses made from huge barrels reclaimed from a Speyside whisky distillery, while elsewhere you can see an ecological sewage treatment centre, a huge wind generator and various community businesses including a café, pottery and weaving studio.

The foundation is not without controversy: a community leader once declared that "behind the benign and apparently religious front lies a hard core of New Agers experimenting with hallucinatory techniques marketed as spirituality". Whatever the truth, Findhorn can be accused of being overly well-heeled, as betrayed by a glance into the shop or a tally of the smart cars parked outside the well-appointed eco-houses. However, there's little doubt that the community continues to prosper (its latest venture is a café/restaurant) and it is well known around the world. The reputation of the place is such that it attracts visitors both sympathetic and cynical – and both find something to feed their impressions.

Travel details

Trains

For information on all local and national rail services, contact National Rail Enquiries ⓣ08457/484950, ⓦwww.nationalrail.co.uk or ⓦwww.firstscotrail.com.

Aberdeen to: Arbroath (every 30min; 1hr); Dundee (every 30min; 1hr 15min); Edinburgh (1–2 hourly; 2hr 35min); Elgin (Mon–Sat 10 daily, Sun 5 daily; 1hr 30min); Glasgow (hourly; 2hr 35min); Inverness (Mon–Sat 10 daily, Sun 5 daily; 2hr 15min); London (Sun–Fri sleeper service; 10hr); Montrose (every 30min; 45min); Nairn (Mon–Sat 10 daily, Sun 5 daily; 1hr 50min); Stonehaven (every 30min; 15min).

Dundee to: Aberdeen (every 30min; 1hr 15min); Arbroath (every 30min; 20min); Edinburgh (1–2 hourly; 1hr 15min); Glasgow (1–2 hourly; 1hr 30min); Montrose (1–2 hourly; 30min).

Buses

For information on all local and national bus services, contact Traveline ⓣ0870/608 2608 (daily 7am–10pm), ⓦwww.travelinescotland.com.

Aberdeen to: Ballater (hourly; 1hr 45min); Banff (hourly; 1hr 55min); Braemar (at least once every 2hr; 2hr 10min); Cullen (hourly; 2hr 30min); Dundee (hourly; 2hr); Elgin (hourly; 3hr 20min); Fraserburgh (hourly; 1hr 30min); Macduff (hourly; 1hr 50min); Stonehaven (every 15min; 50min).

Dufftown to: Aberlour (Mon–Sat hourly; 15min; Sun every two hours); Elgin (Mon–Sat hourly; Sun every two hours; 50min).

Dundee to: Aberdeen (hourly; 1hr 20min); Arbroath (hourly; 50min); Blairgowrie (7 daily; 50min); Forfar (hourly; 30min); Glamis (5 daily; 35min); Kirriemuir (5 daily; 55min); Meigle (hourly; 40min); Montrose (hourly; 1hr 10min).

Elgin to: Aberdeen (hourly; 3hr 30min); Forres (hourly; 25min); Nairn (hourly; 45min); Pluscarden (1 daily schooldays only; 20min).

Forres to: Elgin (hourly; 25min); Findhorn (hourly; 20min).

Fraserburgh to: Banff (2 daily; 55min); Macduff (2 daily; 45min).

Montrose to: Brechin (every 30min; 20min).

Ferries

Aberdeen to: Kirkwall, Orkney (Thurs, Sat & Sun plus Tues in summer; 6hr); Lerwick, Shetland (daily; 10–12hr overnight).

Flights

Aberdeen to: Kirkwall, Orkney (1 daily; 55min); London Gatwick (min 3 daily; 1hr 35min); London Heathrow (Mon–Fri, min 7 daily, Sat–Sun min 2; 1hr 30min); Sumburgh, Shetland (Mon–Fri 5 daily, Sat & Sun 2 daily; 1hr).

Dundee to: London City (Mon–Fri 4 daily, Sat 1 daily, Sun 2 daily; 1hr 25min).

24

The Highland region

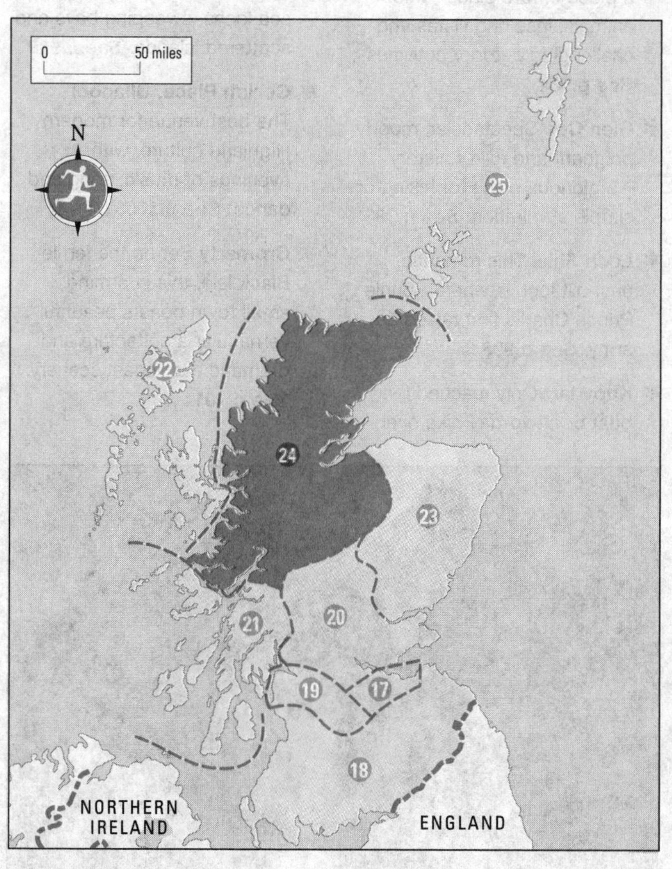

CHAPTER 24

Highlights

* **West Highland Railway** From Glasgow to Mallaig via Fort William: the further north you travel, the more spectacular it gets. See p.978

* **The Cairngorms** Scotland's grandest mountain massif, a place of rare plants, wild animals, inspiring vistas and challenging outdoor activities. See p.984

* **Glen Coe** Spectacular, moody, poignant and full of history – a glorious place for hiking or simple admiration. See p.993

* **Loch Shiel** This romantic, unspoilt loch is where Bonnie Prince Charlie first raised an army. See p.996

* **Knoydart** Only reached by boat or a two-day hike over the mountains, this peninsula also boasts mainland Britain's most isolated pub, the welcoming *Old Forge*. See p.997

* **Wester Ross** Scotland's finest scenery – a heady mix of dramatic mountains, rugged sea lochs, sweeping bays and scattered islands. See p.999

* **Ceilidh Place, Ullapool** The best venue for modern Highland culture, with evenings of music, song and dance. See p.1003

* **Cromarty** Set on the fertile Black Isle, this charming small town boasts beautiful vernacular architecture and dramatic east-coast scenery. See p.1011

▲ Glen Coe

24

The Highland region

The **Highland region** of Scotland, covering the northern two-thirds of the country, holds much of the mainland's most spectacular scenery: a classic combination of mountains, glens, lochs and rivers surrounded on three sides by a magnificently pitted and rugged coastline. You may be surprised at just how remote much of it still is: the vast peat bogs in the north, for example, are among the most extensive and unspoilt wilderness areas in Europe, while a handful of the west coast's isolated crofting villages can still be reached only by boat.

Capital of the Highlands and the only major urban centre in the region, **Inverness** is an obvious springboard for more remote areas, with its good transport links and facilities, and while there are some engaging historic sites nearby, the city itself is of limited appeal. South of Inverness, the **Strathspey** region, with a string of villages lying along the River Spey, is dominated by the dramatic **Cairngorm mountains**, an area brimming with attractive scenery and opportunities for outdoor activity.

The Monadhliath mountains lie between Strathspey and **Loch Ness**, the largest and most famous of the necklace of lochs which make up the **Great Glen**, an ancient geological fault line which cuts southwest across the region from Inverness to the town of **Fort William**. From Fort William, located beneath Scotland's highest peak, Ben Nevis, it's possible to branch out to some fine scenery – most conveniently the beautiful expanses of **Glen Coe**, but also in the direction of the appealing **west coast**, notably the remote and tranquil **Ardnamurchan peninsula**, the "Road to the Isles" to **Mallaig**, and the lochs and glens that lead to **Kyle of Lochalsh** on the most direct route to Skye. Between Kyle of Lochalsh and **Ullapool**, the main settlement in the northwest, lies **Wester Ross**, home to quintessentially west-coast scenes of sparkling sea lochs, rocky headlands and sandy beaches set against some of Scotland's most dramatic mountains, with Skye and the Western Isles on the horizon.

The little-visited **north coast** stretching from wind-lashed **Cape Wrath**, at the very northwest tip of the mainland, east to **John O'Groats** is even more rugged, with sheer cliffs and sand-filled bays bearing the brunt of frequently fierce Atlantic storms. The main settlement on this coast is **Thurso**, jumping-off point for the main ferry service to Orkney.

On the fertile **east coast**, stretching north from Inverness to the old herring port of **Wick**, green fields and woodland run down to the sweeping sandy beaches of the **Black Isle** and the **Cromarty** and **Dornoch firths**. This region is rich with historical sites, including the **Sutherland Monument** by Golspie, **Dornoch**'s fourteenth-century sandstone cathedral, and a number of places linked to the Clearances (see p.1014), a poignantly remembered chapter in the Highland story.

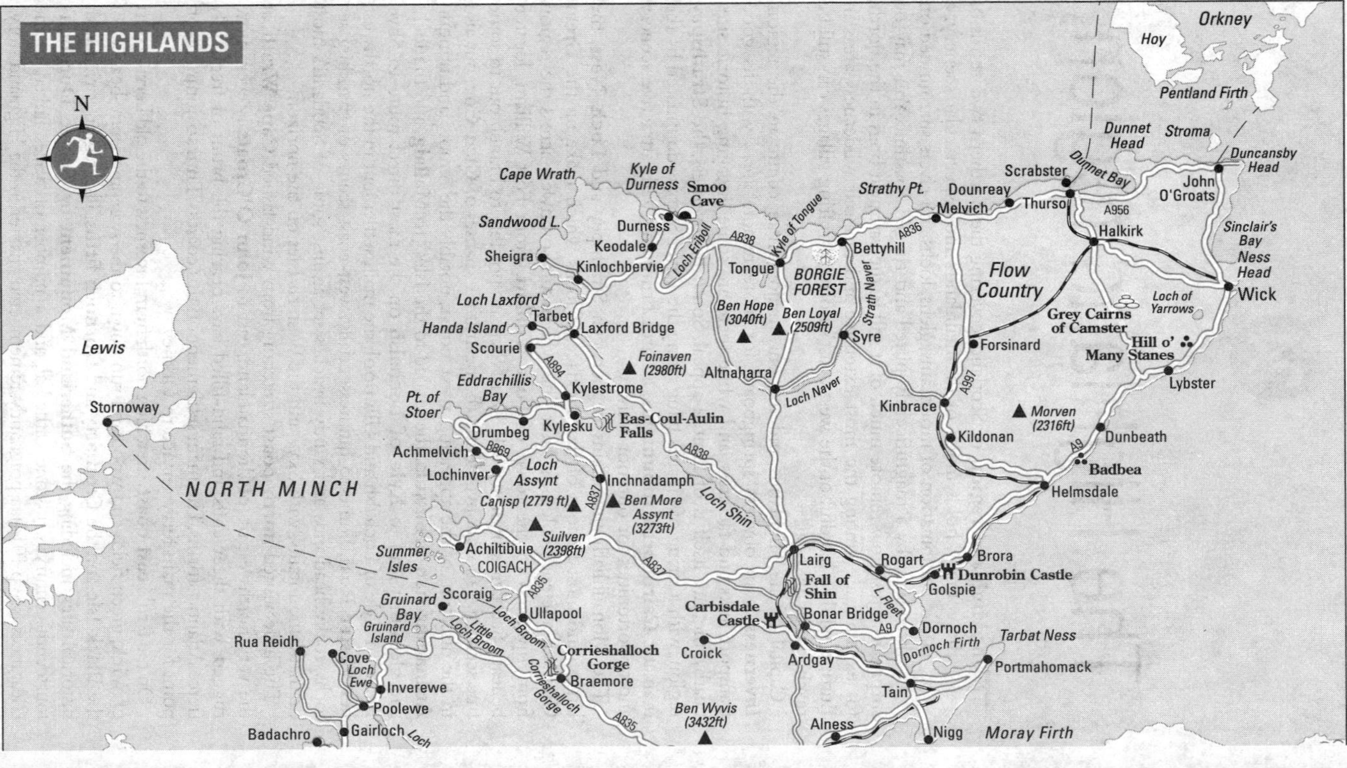
THE HIGHLANDS
N
Orkney
Hoy
Pentland Firth
Dunnet Head
Stroma
Duncansby Head
Dunnet Bay
Scrabster
Thurso
John O'Groats
A956
Halkirk
Sinclair's Bay
Ness Head
Wick
Dounreay
Melvich
Strathy Pt.
A836
Bettyhill
Flow Country
Loch of Yarrows
Grey Cairns of Camster
Hill o' Many Stanes
Lybster
Forsinard
A997
Kinbrace
Morven (2316ft)
Kildonan
Dunbeath
A9
Badbea
Helmsdale
Cape Wrath
Kyle of Durness
Smoo Cave
Durness
Sandwood L.
Keodale
Sheigra
Kinlochbervie
Loch Eriboll
A838
Kyle of Tongue
Tongue
BORGIE FOREST
Strath Naver
Ben Hope (3040ft)
Ben Loyal (2509ft)
Syre
Altnaharra
Loch Naver
Loch Laxford
Tarbet
Handa Island
Laxford Bridge
Scourie
A894
Foinaven (2980ft)
Eddrachillis Bay
Kylestrome
Pt. of Stoer
Drumbeg
Kylesku
Eas-Coul-Aulin Falls
Achmelvich
B869
Lochinver
Loch Assynt
Inchnadamph
A838
Loch Shin
Canisp (2779 ft)
A837
Ben More Assynt (3273ft)
Suilven (2398ft)
Lewis
Stornoway
NORTH MINCH
Summer Isles
Achiltibuie
COIGACH
A837
Lairg
Rogart
Brora
Dunrobin Castle
Golspie
Fall of Shin
L. Fleet
Scoraig
A835
Gruinard Bay
Gruinard Island
Ullapool
Loch Broom
Little Loch Broom
Carbisdale Castle
Bonar Bridge
A9
Dornoch
Dornoch Firth
Tarbat Ness
Rua Reidh
Cove
Loch Ewe
Inverewe
Poolewe
Corrieshalloch Gorge
Braemore
Croick
Ardgay
Portmahomack
Corrieshalloch Gorge
A835
Tain
Ben Wyvis (3432ft)
Alness
Nigg
Moray Firth
Badachro
Gairloch
Loch

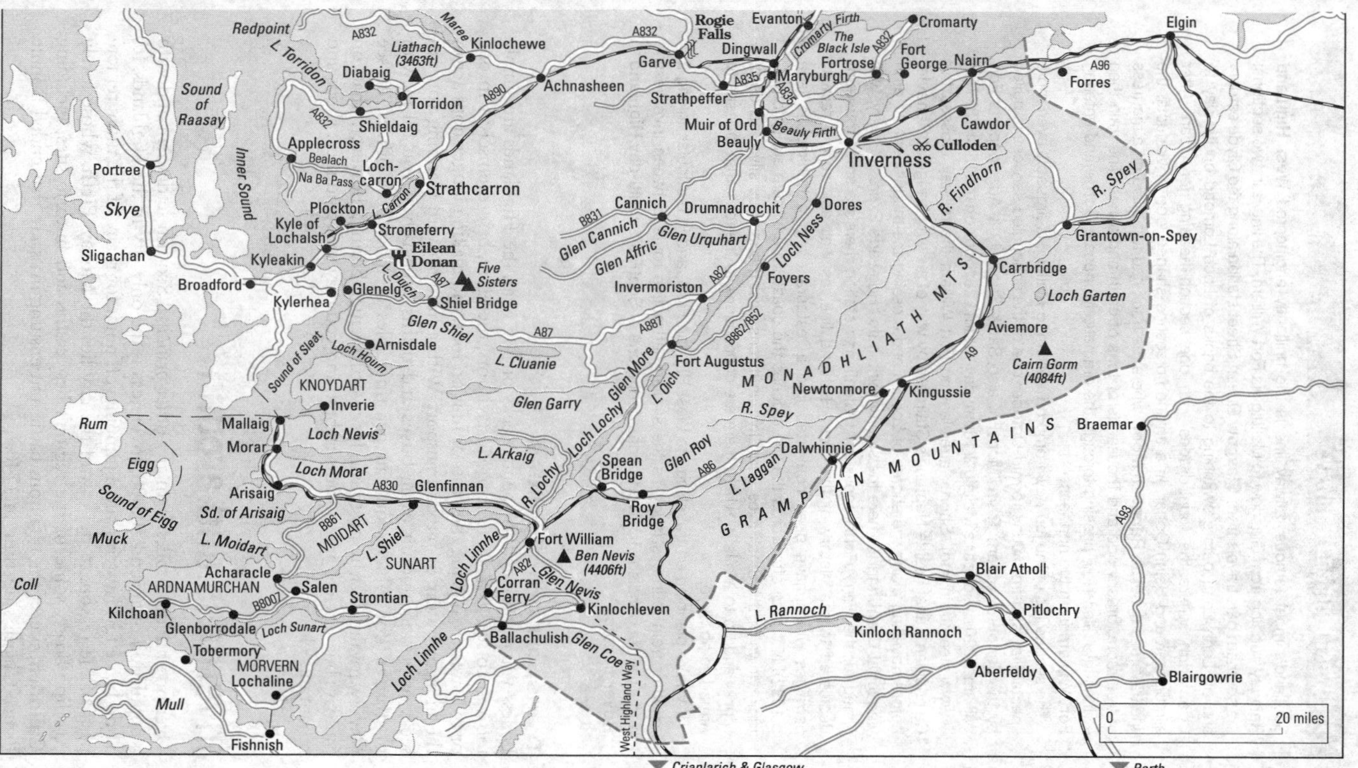
Elgin
Redpoint
L. Torridon
Liathach (3463ft)
Maree
Kinlochewe
A832
Rogie Falls
Evanton
Cromarty Firth
Cromarty
The Black Isle
Dingwall
Garve
Fortrose
Fort George
Nairn
A96
Forres
Diabaig
Torridon
Achnasheen
A890
Sound of Raasay
Maryburgh
A835
Strathpeffer
Shieldaig
Muir of Ord
Beauly
Beauly Firth
Cawdor
Culloden
Inverness
Applecross
Bealach Na Ba Pass
Lochcarron
Strathcarron
L. Carron
Portree
Inner Sound
R. Findhorn
R. Spey
Skye
Plockton
Kyle of Lochalsh
Stromeferry
Cannich
Drumnadrochit
Dores
B831
Glen Cannich
Glen Affric
Glen Urquhart
Loch Ness
Grantown-on-Spey
Sligachan
Kyleakin
Eilean Donan
Five Sisters
Foyers
Carrbridge
Broadford
Kylerhea
Glenelg
L. Duich
A87
Shiel Bridge
Invermoriston
A82
Loch Garten
Glen Shiel
A887
B862/852
Aviemore
Arnisdale
Loch Hourn
L. Cluanie
Fort Augustus
MONADHLIATH MTS
A9
Cairn Gorm (4084ft)
Sound of Sleat
KNOYDART
Inverie
Glen More
L. Oich
Newtonmore
Kingussie
Glen Garry
Loch Lochy
R. Spey
Rum
Mallaig
Loch Nevis
Braemar
Morar
L. Arkaig
Glen Roy
Dalwhinnie
GRAMPIAN MOUNTAINS
Eigg
Loch Morar
Spean Bridge
A86
L. Laggan
Glenfinnan
A830
R. Lochy
Sound of Eigg
Arisaig
Sd. of Arisaig
B861
MOIDART
Roy Bridge
A93
Muck
L. Moidart
L. Shiel
Loch Linnhe
Fort William
Ben Nevis (4406ft)
SUNART
A82
Acharacle
Coll
ARDNAMURCHAN
Salen
Corran Ferry
Glen Nevis
Blair Atholl
Strontian
Kinlochleven
Kilchoan
B8007
L. Rannoch
Pitlochry
Glenborrodale
Loch Sunart
Kinloch Rannoch
Ballachulish
Glen Coe
Tobermory
MORVERN
Lochaline
Aberfeldy
Blairgowrie
Mull
West Highland Way
0
20 miles
Fishnish
Crianlarich & Glasgow
Perth

The West Highland Railway

Scotland's most famous railway line is the brilliantly engineered **West Highland Railway**, running from Glasgow to Mallaig via Fort William. The line is in two sections: the southern part travels from **Glasgow** Queen Street station along the Clyde estuary and up Loch Long before switching to the banks of Loch Lomond on its way to **Crianlarich**, where the train divides with one section heading for Oban. After climbing around Beinn Odhar on a unique horseshoe-shaped loop of viaducts, the line traverses desolate **Rannoch Moor**, where the track had to be laid on a mattress of tree roots, brushwood and thousands of tons of earth and ashes. The train then swings into Glen Roy, passing through the dramatic **Monessie Gorge** and entering **Fort William** from the northeast.

The second leg of the journey, from Fort William to Mallaig, is arguably even more spectacular, and from June to mid-October one of the scheduled services is pulled by the **Jacobite Steam Train** (Mon–Fri, also Sat & Sun July & Aug; departs Fort William 10.20am, departs Mallaig 2.10pm; day-return £28; book on ⓣ01524/737751; ⓦwww.steamtrain.info). Shortly after leaving Fort William the railway crosses the Caledonian Canal beside Neptune's Staircase by way of a swing bridge at **Benavie**, before travelling along the shores of Locheil and crossing the magnificent 21-arch viaduct at **Glenfinnan**, where the steam train, in its "Hogwarts Express" livery, was filmed for the *Harry Potter* movies. At Glenfinnan station there's a small **museum** dedicated to the history of the West Highland line, as well as two old railway carraiges which have been converted into a restaurant and a bunkhouse (see p.1082). Not long afterwards the line reaches the coast, where there are unforgettable views of the Small Isles and Skye as it runs past the famous silver sands of **Morar** and up to **Mallaig**, where there are connections to the ferry that crosses to Armadale on Skye.

If you're planning on travelling the West Highland line, and in particular linking it to other train journeys (such as the similarly attractive route between Inverness and Kyle of Lochalsh), it's worth considering one of ScotRail's multi-day **Highland Rover tickets**.

Transport practicalities

Unless you're prepared to spend weeks on the road, the Highlands are simply too vast to see in a single trip. Most visitors, therefore, base themselves in one or two areas, exploring the coast or hills on foot, and making longer hops across the interior by car or public transport. With a little forward planning you can see a surprising amount using **buses** and **trains**, especially if you fill in with **postbuses** (for which you can get timetables at most post offices, or see ⓦwww.royalmail.com/postbus). It's worth remembering, however, that on Sundays bus services are sporadic at best, and you may well find most shops and restaurants closed.

Inverness and around

Over one hundred miles from any other principal Scottish settlement and with a population of around 50,000, **Inverness** is the only city in the Highlands. It's a good base for day-trips and a jumping-off point for many of the more remote parts of the region: to the east of the city lies the **Moray Firth**, whose lovely coastline boasts some of the region's best castles and historic sites, including **Culloden**, site of the infamous battle and ensuing massacre that ended Bonnie Prince Charlie's uprising in 1746.

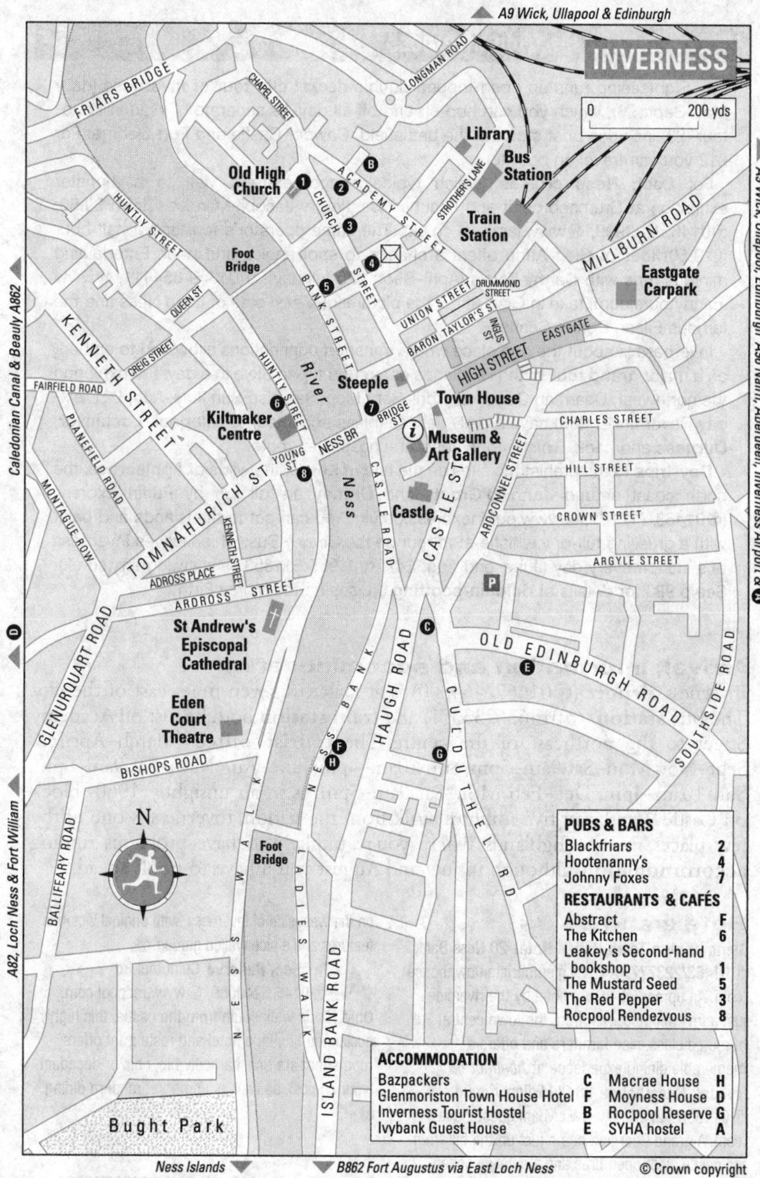

Inverness

Straddling a nexus of road and rail routes, **INVERNESS** is the busy and prosperous hub of the Highlands, and an inevitable port of call if you're exploring the region by public transport: **buses** and **trains** leave for communities right across the far north of Scotland. Though boasting few conventional sights, the city's setting on the banks of the River Ness is appealing.

Tours and cruises from Inverness

City Sightseeing runs an open-topped double-decker **city tour** of **Inverness** (daily May–Sept; £6), which you can hop on and off all day. Its separate "Culloden Loop" tour (£8) includes brief stops at the battlefield, Cawdor Castle and Fort George. For £12 you can travel on both tours.

For **Loch Ness cruises**, which typically incorporate a visit to a monster exhibition at Drumnadrochit and Urquhart Castle, try Jacobite Cruises (from £9.50; ⓣ01463/233999, ⓦwww.jacobite.co.uk). The same operator's four-and-a-half-hour (£19.50) tour of Glen Affric offers a chance to spot eagles and deer. Entertaining minibus trips with **Canny Tours** (April–Sept; £25 full day; ⓣ01349/854411, ⓦwww.cannytours.com) take in Glen Affric, the picturesque east side of Loch Ness and the famous Eilean Donan Castle.

Inverness is about the one place where transport connections allow you to embark on a major **grand tour** of the Highlands or a round trip to Skye in a day. For exploring the northwest, Dearman Coaches (April–Sept Mon–Sat; also Sun July–Aug; £21, six-day Rover ticket £36) have a daily service (bikes accepted) to **Ullapool**, **Lochinver**, **Durness** and back, which stops at several hostels en route.

Day-trips to the prehistoric sites on the **Isle of Lewis**, the wilds of **Applecross**, the north coast around **John O'Groats** and **Orkney** are all run by Puffin Express (ⓣ01463/717181, ⓦwww.puffinexpress.co.uk). You can get to the islands and back with a gruelling full-day whistle-stop tour on the Orkney Bus, which leaves Inverness bus station every day (June–end Aug; £47; ⓣ01955/611353, ⓦwww.jogferry.co.uk). See p.983 for details of **dolphin-spotting** cruises on the Moray Firth.

Arrival, information and accommodation

Inverness **airport** (ⓣ01667/464000) is at Dalcross, seven miles east of the city. The **bus station** (ⓣ01463/233371) and **train station** both lie just off Academy Street to the northeast of the centre. The **tourist office** (March–April & Sept–Nov Mon–Sat 9am–5pm, Sun 10am–4pm; June–Aug Mon–Sat 9am–6pm, Sun 10am–4pm, Dec–Feb Mon–Sat 9am–5pm) is in an unsightly 1960s block on Castle Wynd, just five minutes' walk from the station. Inverness is one of the few places in the Highlands where you're unlikely to have problems finding **accommodation**, although in July and August you'll have to book ahead.

Hotels and B&Bs

Glenmoriston Town House Hotel 20 Ness Bank ⓣ01463/223777, ⓦwww.glenmoristontownhouse.com. An upmarket, luxury hotel by the riverside just a few minutes walk from the town centre. Full of muted class, nice furniture and offers a memorable dining experience at *Abstract*. ❼

Ivybank Guesthouse 28 Old Edinburgh Rd ⓣ01463/232796, ⓦwww.ivybankguesthouse.com. A grand Georgian home just up the hill from the castle, with open fires and a lovely wooden interior. ❷

Macrae House 24 Ness Bank ⓣ01463/243658, ⓦwww.macraehouse.co.uk. Very friendly B&B in a house that dates back to 1842, with large, comfortable rooms and views of the river. Serves a substantial continental breakfast. ❷

Moyness House 6 Bruce Gardens ⓣ01463/233836, ⓦwww.moyness.co.uk. Warm and welcoming B&B on the west side of Inverness, with original Victorian features and a nice walled garden. ❺

Rocpool Reserve Culduthel Rd ⓣ01463/240089, ⓦwww.rocpool.com. Only 10min walk south from the castle, this highly acclaimed boutique hotel and restaurant offers rooms that are unashamedly hip, chic or decadent (your choice), as well as upmarket modern dining. ❼–❾

Hostels

Bazpackers Top of Castle St ⓣ01463/717663. The most cosy and relaxed of the city's hostels, with over thirty beds including two double rooms and a twin (❶); some dorms are mixed (£14). Has good views and a garden, which is used for barbecues, as well as the usual cooking facilities.

Inverness Tourist Hostel 24 Rose St ⓣ01463/241962, ⓦwww.invernesshostel.com. A central, clean, well-equipped 60-bed hostel offering topnotch amenities including wide-screen TVs and Internet access. Dorms £12.50.

SYHA hostel Victoria Drive, off Millburn Rd, about three-quarters of a mile east of the centre ⓣ0870/004 1127, ⓦwww.syha.org.uk. One of SYHA's flagship hostels, though hardly central: it's fully equipped with large kitchens and communal areas, eco-friendly facilities and ten four-bed family rooms among the 166-bed total (dorm beds £15.75).

The Town

Looming above the Town House and dominating the horizon is **Inverness Castle**, a predominantly nineteenth-century red-sandstone edifice perched picturesquely above the river. It houses the Sheriff Court and and is not open to the general public. However, there are good views down the River Ness and various plaques and statues in the grounds including a small plinth marking the start of the 73-mile Great Glen Way.

Below the castle, the **Inverness Museum and Art Gallery** on Castle Wynd (Mon–Sat 9am–5pm; free; ⓦwww.invernessmuseum.com) offers an insight into the social history of the Highlands, with treasures from the times of the Picts and Vikings, taxidermy exhibits such as "Felicity" the puma, caught in Cannich in 1980, and interactive features including an introduction to the Gaelic language.

Rising from the west bank directly opposite the castle, **St Andrew's Episcopal Cathedral** was intended by its Victorian architects to be one of the grandest buildings in Scotland. However, funds ran out before the giant twin spires of the original design could be completed. The interior is pretty ordinary, too, though it does claim an unusual octagonal chapter house. Alongside the

The truth about tartan

Originally called **Helande**, the first form of tartan was a fine, hard and almost shower-proof cloth spun in Highland villages from the wool of the native sheep, dyed with preparations of local plants and with patterns woven by artist-weavers. It was worn as a huge single piece of cloth, or **plaid**, which was belted around the waist and draped over the upper body, rather like a knee-length toga. The natural colours of old tartans were clear but soft, and the broken pattern gave superb camouflage, unlike modern versions, where garish, clashing colours are often used to create impact.

The myth-makers were about four centuries ahead of themselves in dressing up the warriors of the film *Braveheart* in plaid: in fact tartan did not become popular in the Lowlands until the beginning of the eighteenth century, when it was adopted as the anti-Union badge of the **Jacobites**. After Culloden, a ban on the wearing of tartan in the Highlands lasted some 25 years; in that time it became a fondly held emblem for emigrant Highlanders in the colonies and was incorporated into the uniforms of the new Highland regiments in the British Army. Then Sir Walter Scott set to work glamorizing the clans, dressing George IV in a kilt (and, just as controversially, flesh-coloured tights) for his visit to Edinburgh in 1822. By the time Queen Victoria set the royal seal of approval on both the Highlands and tartan with her extended annual holidays at Balmoral, the concept of tartan as formal dress rather than rough Highland wear was assured.

Scotsmen today will commonly wear the **kilt** for weddings and other formal occasions; properly made kilts, however – comprising some four yards of 100 percent wool – are likely to set you back £300 or more, with the rest of the regalia at least doubling that figure. If the contents of your sporran don't stretch that far, most places selling kilts will rent outfits on a daily basis. The best place to find better-quality material is a recognized Highland outfitter rather than a souvenir shop: in Inverness, try the Scottish Kiltmaker Centre at the Highland House of Fraser shop (daily 9am–5pm, open later in summer months; £2).

cathedral, **Eden Court Theatre** (Ⓦwww.eden-court.co.uk) is a major multi-arts venue in Scotland and hub for theatrical performances in the Highlands. From here, you can wander a mile or so upriver to the peaceful **Ness Islands**, an attractive, informal public park linked by footbridges.

Eating, drinking and nightlife

Inverness has a few excellent-quality **gourmet** options. The far end of Academy Street has a cluster of good **pubs**; there's a good atmosphere at *Blackfriars*, where you can enjoy folk and ceilidh music five nights a week – the same can be found at *Hootananny's*, Church St. Over on Bank Street, *Johnny Foxes* is a fine local watering hole with a terrific atmosphere, outdoor seating and good-value bar food.

Cafés and restaurants

Abstract *Glenmoriston Town House Hotel* 20 Ness Bank Ⓣ01463/223777, Ⓦwww.abstractrestaurant.com. This award-winning French restaurant continues to tempt discerning diners with delicious creations served with panache. Closed Mon. Expensive. The adjacent *Contrast Brasserie* (Ⓣ01463/227889) is more affordable and relaxed but still good quality.

Leakey's Second-Hand Bookshop Church St Ⓣ01463/239947. Prise yourself away from the old books and maps for delicious soup and open sandwiches. Inexpensive.

The Kitchen 15 Huntly St Ⓣ01463/259119. Beneath a distinctive wavy roof, this stylish sister restaurant of *The Mustard Seed* (see below) has riverside views and thoughtfully prepared seafood and meat dishes. Expensive.

The Mustard Seed 16 Fraser St Ⓣ01463/220220. Airy, welcoming restaurant with Mediterranean-style, great-value lunches and tasty a la carte dining. Moderate.

The Red Pepper 74 Church St. Ever popular and hip coffee-bar hang-out with lots of freshly made sandwiches. Takeaway available. Inexpensive.

Rocpool Rendezvous 1 Ness Walk Ⓣ01463/717274. Another of the city's excellent middle-to upper-end dining options, with a smart contemporary setting, attentive staff and delicious bistro food. Moderate–expensive.

Listings

Bike rental Fancy a Ride? (Ⓣ07902 242301, Ⓦwww.tickettoridehighlands.co.uk; from £18 a day), will deliver bikes to you and also offer tours. For cycle kit try Bikes of Inverness, 39 Grant St Ⓣ01463/225965.

Book shops Leakey's, Scotland's largest used bookshop, is located in a former church in Greyfriars Hall, Church St and filled with almost 100,000 second-hand books. Great spot to browse with a warming wood stove in winter and a cosy, inexpensive café (see above). There's also Waterstones at 50–52 High St.

Car rental Budget, Railway Terrace, behind the train station (Ⓣ01463/713333); Turner Hire Drive, Lotland St (Ⓣ01463/716058); Focus Vehicle Rental, 36 Shore St (Ⓣ01463/709517); Aberdeen 4x4 Self-Drive,15b Harbour Rd (Ⓣ01463/871083).

Cinemas VUE, Inverness Retail Park, Eastfield Way Ⓣ08712/240240; Eden Court Theatre and Cinema, Bishop's Rd Ⓣ01463/234234.

Hospital Raigmore Hospital (Ⓣ01463/704000) on the southeastern outskirts of town close to the A9.

Post office 14–16 Queensgate (Mon–Thurs 9am–5.30pm, Fri 9.30am–5.30pm, Sat 9am–1pm Ⓣ01463/234111); also noon–5pm at Tesco's.

Taxis Tartan Taxis Ⓣ01463/719719. Expect to pay £11 from city centre to airport.

Culloden

Five miles east of Inverness, the windswept moorland of **CULLODEN** (site open all year; free), witnessed the last-ever battle on British soil when, on April 16, 1746, the Jacobite cause was finally subdued – a turning point in the history of the Scottish nation.

The second Jacobite rebellion had begun on August 19, 1745, with the raising of the Stuarts' standard at **Glenfinnan** on the west coast (see p.996). Shortly after, Edinburgh fell into Jacobite hands, and Bonnie Prince Charlie began his march on London. The English had appointed the ambitious young Duke of Cumberland to command their forces, and his pursuit, together with bad weather and lack of funds, eventually forced the Jacobites to retreat north. They ended up at Culloden, where, ill-fed and exhausted, they were hopelessly outnumbered by the English. After the battle, in which 1500 Highlanders were slaughtered (many of them as they lay wounded on the battlefield), Bonnie Prince Charlie fled west to the hills and islands. He eventually escaped to France, leaving his erstwhile supporters to their fate – the clans were disarmed, the wearing of tartan and playing of bagpipes forbidden, and the chiefs became landlords greedy for higher and higher rents. Within a century, the Highland way of life had changed out of all recognition.

Your first stop should be the eco-friendly **visitor centre** (daily: April–Oct 9am–6pm; Nov–March 10am–4pm; £10; NTS). The sleek building hosts actors, state-of-the-art audiovisual and interactive technology, all employed to tell the tragedy of Culloden. The *pièce de résistance* is the "battle immersion theatre" where visitors are surrounded on all sides by lifelike cinematography and the sounds of the raging, bloody scenes of the fight. Go up to the rooftop platform to enjoy the elevated view across the actual battlefield before, armed with a nifty audioguide, walking around the battle site on twenty-, forty-five- and sixty-minute routes. Flags mark out the positions of the two armies while simple headstones mark the **clan graves**.

Fort George

Eight miles or so of undulating coastal farmland separate Culloden from **Fort George** (daily: April–Sept 9.30am–5.30pm; Oct–March 9.30am–4.30pm;

The dolphins of the Moray Firth

The **Moray Firth**, a great wedge-shaped bay forming the eastern coastline of the Highlands, is one of only three areas of UK waters that supports a resident population of **dolphins**. Over a hundred of these beautiful, intelligent marine mammals live in the estuary, the most northerly breeding ground for this particular species – the bottle-nosed dolphin (*Tursiops truncatus*) – in Europe, and you stand a good chance of spotting a few, either from the shore or a boat.

One of the best places to look for them is **Chanonry Point**, on the Black Isle (see p.1011) – a spit of sand protruding into a narrow, deep channel, where converging currents bring fish close to the surface, and thus the dolphins close to shore; a rising tide is the most likely time to see them. **Kessock Bridge**, one mile north of Inverness, is another prime dolphin-spotting location. You can go all the way down to the beach at the small village of North Kessock, underneath the road bridge, where there's a decent place to have a drink at the pub in the *North Kessock Hotel*, or you can stop above the village in a car park just off the A9 at the Dolphin Visitor Centre and listening post (June–Sept daily 9.30am–12.30pm 1–4.30pm; free). Set up by a team of zoologists from Aberdeen University, the centre has hydrophones that allow you to eavesdrop on the clicks and whistles of the dolphins' underwater conversations.

Several companies run dolphin-spotting **boat trips** around the Moray Firth from £10 for one hour. Operators currently accredited by the Dolphin Space Programme (see Ⓦwww.morayfirth-partnership.org and Ⓦwww.wdcs.org) include Phoenix, based in Nairn (Ⓣ01667/456078), Moray Firth Cruises, Inverness (Ⓣ01463/717900), and the WDCS Wildlife Centre, Spey Bay (Ⓣ01343/820339). Also, on the Black Isle, on the northern side of the Firth, try Dolphin Trips Avoch (Ⓣ01381/622383, Ⓦwww.dolphintripsavoch.co.uk) and the highly regarded Ecoventures, Cromarty (Ⓣ01381/600323, Ⓦwww.ecoventures.co.uk).

£6.50; HS), an old Hanoverian bastion with walls a mile long, considered by military architectural historians to be one of the finest fortifications in Europe. Crowning a sandy spit that juts into the middle of the Moray Firth, it was built between 1747 and 1769 as a base for George II's army, in case the Highlanders should attempt to rekindle the Jacobite flame.

Apart from the sweeping panoramic views across the Firth from its ramparts, the main incentive to visit Fort George is the **Regimental Museum** of the Queen's Own Highlanders. Displayed in polished glass cases is a predictable array of regimental silver, coins, moth-eaten uniforms and medals, along with some macabre war trophies, ranging from blood-stained nineteenth-century Sudanese battle robes to Iraqi gas masks gleaned in the First Gulf War.

The Cairngorms and Strathspey

Rising high in the heather-clad hills above remote Loch Laggan, forty miles due south of Inverness, the **River Spey**, Scotland's second longest river, drains northeast towards the Moray Firth through one of the Highlands' most spell-binding valleys. Famous for its ancient forests, salmon fishing and ospreys, the area around the upper section of the river, known as **Strathspey**, is dominated by the sculpted **Cairngorms**, Britain's most extensive mountain massif, unique in supporting subarctic tundra on its high plateau. Outdoor enthusiasts flock to the area to take advantage of the superb hiking, water sports and winter snows, aided by the fact that the area is easily accessible by road and rail from both the Central Belt and Inverness. A string of villages along the river provide useful bases for setting out into the wilder country, principal among them **Aviemore**. The area boasts a wide choice of good-quality accommodation, particularly in the budget market, with various easy-going hostels run by and for outdoor enthusiasts.

Note that Strathspey is distinct from Speyside, located further downstream to the north and famous for its whiskies, described on p.967.

Cairngorms National Park

The **Cairngorms National Park** (Ⓦwww.cairngorms.co.uk) covers some 1500 square miles and incorporates the **Cairngorms massif**, the UK's largest mountain-scape and only sizeable plateau over 2500ft. While Aviemore and the surrounding area is the main point of entry, particularly for those planning outdoor activities, it's also possible to access the eastern side of the park from both Deeside and Donside in Aberdeenshire (see p.964).

The name Cairngorm comes from the Gaelic *An Carm Gorm*, meaning "the blue hill" after the blueish-tinged stones found in the area, and within the park there are 52 summits over 2953ft, as well as a quarter of Scotland's native woodland, and a quarter of the UK's threatened wildlife species. The conservation of the landscape's unique flora and fauna is, of course, one of the principal reasons national-park status was conferred. However, an important role for the park is to incorporate the communities living within it and integrate the array of outdoor activities enjoyed by visitors.

Vegetation in the area ranges from one of the largest tracts of ancient **Caledonian pine and birch forest** remaining in Scotland, at Rothiemurchus, to subarctic tundra on the high plateau, where **alpine flora** such as starry saxifrage and the star-shaped pink flowers of moss campion peek out of the pink granite in the few months of summer that the ground is free of snow. **Birds of prey** you're most likely to see are the **osprey**, especially at Loch Garten's osprey observation centre (see p.987), or fishing on the lochs around Aviemore.

▲ Sailing at Aviemore

Aviemore and around

AVIEMORE was first developed as a ski and tourism resort in the mid-1960s and, over the years, it fell victim to profiteering developers with scant regard for the needs of the local community. Although a large-scale face-lift has removed some of the architectural eyesores of that era, the settlement remains dominated by a string of soulless shopping centres and sprawling housing estates surrounding a Victorian railway station. That said, Aviemore is well equipped with services and facilities for visitors, and is the most convenient base for the Cairngorms, benefits which for most folk far outweigh its lack of aesthetic appeal.

Summer activities

Walking (see box, p.986) and **water sports** are the main summer activities. Two centres offer sailing, windsurfing and canoeing including equipment rental and tuition: the Loch Morlich Watersports Centre (Ⓣ01479/861221, Ⓦwww.lochmorlich.com), five miles or so east of Aviemore on the way to Cairn Gorm mountain, in a lovely setting with a sandy beach; and the Loch Insh Watersports Centre (Ⓣ01540/651272, Ⓦwww.lochinsh.com) is six miles up-valley near Kincraig, in equally beautiful surroundings. Here you can find basic but practical en-suite B&B rooms (❷) as well as a decent waterfront café/restaurant (Ⓣ01540/651394).

The area is also great for **mountain biking**, with both Rothiemurchus and Glenmore estates providing waymarked routes. The Rothiemurchus Visitor Centre at Inverdruie has route maps, and you can also rent bikes from Bothy Bikes (Ⓣ01479/810111, Ⓦwww.bothybikes.co.uk), located beside the tennis courts at Inverdruie.

Winter activities

Scottish **skiing** on a commercial level first really took off in Aviemore. By continental European and North American standards it's all on a tiny scale, but occasionally snow, sun and lack of crowds coincide and you can have a great day. February and March are usually the best times, but there's a chance of decent snow at any time between mid-November and April. Lots of places – not just

Walks around Aviemore

Walking is a highlight of the Aviemore area, though before setting out you should heed the usual safety guidelines. These are particularly important if you want to climb to the high tops, which include a number of Scotland's loftiest peaks. However, as well as the high mountain trails, there are some lovely and well-signposted **low-level walks** in the area. It takes an hour or so to complete the gentle circular walk around pretty **Loch an Eilean** (with its ruined castle) in the Rothiemurchus Estate, beginning at the end of the back road that turns east off the B970 a mile south of Inverdruie. The helpful estate **visitor centres** at the lochside and by the roadside at Inverdruie provide more information on the many woodland trails that crisscross this area.

Another good shortish (half-day) walk leads along a well-surfaced forestry track from *Glenmore Lodge* up towards the **Ryvoan Pass**, taking in An Lochan Uaine, known as the "Green Loch" because of its amazing colours that range from turquoise to slate grey depending on the weather. The **Glenmore Forest Park Visitor Centre** by the roadside at the turn-off to *Glenmore Lodge* has information on other trails in this section of the forest.

A pleasant day-trip involves walking along the Speyside Way from Aviemore to Boat of Garten, on to the RSPB osprey sanctuary at Loch Garten, and then returning on the **Strathspey Steam Railway** (June–Sept 4 daily; less regular service at other times; ⓣ01479/810725, ⓦwww.strathspeyrailway.co.uk for details).

Ordnance Survey Explorer Maps nos. 402 & 403 or *OS Outdoor Leisure Map* no. 3 are the best maps to use.

in Aviemore itself – sell or rent equipment; for a rundown of ski schools and rental facilities in the area, check out the tourist office's *Ski Scotland* brochure or visit ⓦski.visitscotland.com.

The **Cairngorm Ski Area** (ⓦwww.cairngormmountain.com), nine miles southeast of Aviemore, above Loch Morlich in Glenmore Forest Park, is well served in winter by buses from Aviemore. Several places sell or rent standard **equipment** though The Ski School (ⓦwww.theskischool.co.uk) in the Day Lodge at Corie Cas on Cairngorm mountain is your best bet for ski/board hire and lessons. A **funicular railway** is the principal means of getting to the top of the ski slopes. The facilities include a ski school, cafés at three different levels and a separate terrain park for skiers and boarders. If there's lots of snow, the area around **Loch Morlich** and into the **Rothiemurchus Estate** provides enjoyable cross-country skiing through lovely woods, beside rushing burns and even over frozen lochs.

Practicalities

Aviemore's **tourist office** is in the heart of things at 7 The Parade, Grampian Rd (April–Oct Mon–Sat 9am–5pm, Sun 10am–4pm; Nov–March Mon–Fri 9am–5pm, Sat 10am–4pm). For **accommodation**, try *Ravenscraig Guesthouse* (ⓣ01479/810278; ③), on the Grampian Road, which has twelve rooms and is welcoming and family-friendly. Alternatively, there's the secluded *Corrour House Hotel* at Inverdruie, two miles southeast of Aviemore (ⓣ01479/810220, ⓦwww.corrourhousehotel.co.uk; ⑤). Aviemore's large SYHA **hostel** (ⓣ0870/004 1104, ⓦwww.syha.org.uk; dorm beds £16) is well placed within walking distance of the centre of the village, while the *Aviemore Bunkhouse* (ⓣ01479/811181, ⓦwww.aviemore-bunkhouse.com; dorm beds £15) is a large, modern place beside the *Old Bridge Inn* on Dalfaber Road, again within walking distance from the station. Towards the Cairngorms, there's another SYHA hostel at Loch Morlich (Christmas–Oct; ⓣ0870/004 1137), as well as excellent accommodation in twin rooms (with shared facilities) just up the road at *Glenmore Lodge* (Ⓣ01479/861256, Ⓦwww.glenmorelodge.org.uk; ❷) – full use of their superb facilities, which include a pool, weights room and indoor climbing-wall, is included.

All along Aviemore's main drag are bistros, hotels and takeaways serving fairly predictable, run-of-the-mill **food**. One exception is the reasonably priced *Mountain Café* (Ⓣ01479/812473), above Cairngorm Mountain Sports, which serves an all-day menu of wholesome snacks and freshly prepared meals. Alternatively, *The Old Bridge Inn* on the east side of the railway on Dalfaber Road, dishes up decent pub grub and real ales in a mellow, cosy setting, while *Café Mambo*, in Aviemore Shopping Centre on Grampian Road, matches its bright, funky decor with a cheerful burger'n'chips-style menu.

Cairn Gorm mountain

From Aviemore, a road leads past Rothiemurchus and Loch Morlich and winds its way up into the Cairngorms, reaching the Coire Cas car park at a height of 2150ft. Here is the base station for the ski area with a **ranger office** (daily: April–Oct 9am–5pm; Nov–March 8.30am–4.30pm) where you can find out about the area's various trails. It's also the departure point for the **Cairn Gorm Mountain Railway** (daily 10am–5pm; last train up 4.20pm; trains run every 15min; £8.95; Ⓦwww.cairngormmountain.com), a two-car funicular railway that whisks skiers in winter, and tourists at any time of year, along a mile and a half of track to the top station at an altitude of 3600ft, not far from the summit of Cairn Gorm mountain.

Loch Garten and around

The **Abernethy Forest RSPB Reserve** on the shore of **LOCH GARTEN**, seven miles northeast of Aviemore and eight miles south of Grantown-on-Spey, is famous as the nesting site of one of Britain's rarest birds. A little over fifty years ago, the **osprey**, known in North America as the fish hawk, had completely disappeared from the British Isles. Then, in 1954, a single pair of these exquisite white-and-brown raptors mysteriously reappeared and built a nest in a tree half a mile or so from the loch. Thereafter the area became the centre of an effective high-security operation, though now the birds are well established not only here but elsewhere across the Highlands. The best time to visit is between April and August, when the RSPB opens an **observation centre** (daily 10am–6pm; £3; Ⓣ01479/831476), complete with powerful telescopes and CCTV monitoring of the nest. This is the place to get a glimpse of osprey chicks in their nest; you'll be luckier to see the birds perform their trademark swoop over water to pluck a fish out with their talons. The reserve is also home to several other species of rare birds and animals, including the Scottish crossbill, capercaillie, whooper swan and red squirrel; once-weekly **guided walks** leave from the observation centre (Wed 9.30am).

The Great Glen

The **Great Glen**, a major geological fault line cutting diagonally across the Highlands from Fort William to Inverness, is the defining geographic feature of the north of Scotland. A huge rift valley was formed when the northwestern and southeastern sides of the fault slid in opposite directions for more than sixty miles, while the present landscape was shaped by glaciers that retreated only around 8000 BC. The glen is impressive more for its sheer scale than its beauty, but the imposing barrier of loch and mountain means that no one can travel into the northern Highlands without passing through it. With the two major service centres of the Highlands at either end it makes an obvious and rewarding route between the west and east coasts.

Of the Great Glen's four elongated lochs, the most famous is **Loch Ness**, home to the mythical monster; lochs **Oich**, **Lochy** and **Linnhe** (the last of these a sea loch) are less renowned though no less attractive. All four are linked by the Caledonian Canal. The southwestern end of the Great Glen is dominated by **Fort William**, the second-largest town in the Highland region. Situated at the heart of the Lochaber area, it's a useful base with plenty of places to stay and eat, and an excellent hub for accessing a host of outdoor activities. Dominating the scene to the south is **Ben Nevis**, Britain's highest peak, best approached from scenic Glen Nevis. The most famous glen of all, **Glen Coe**, lies on the main A82 road half an hour's drive south of Fort William. Nowadays the whole area is unashamedly given over to tourism, and Fort William is swamped by bus tours throughout the summer, but, as ever in the Highlands, within a thirty-minute drive you can be totally alone.

Loch Ness and around

Twenty-three miles long, unfathomably deep, cold and often moody, **Loch Ness** is bounded by rugged heather-clad mountains rising steeply from a wooded shoreline with attractive glens opening up on either side. Its fame,

Nessie

The world-famous **Loch Ness monster**, affectionately known as **Nessie** (and by serious aficionados as *Nessiteras rhombopteryx*), has been a local celebrity for some time. The first mention of a mystery creature crops up in St Adamnan's seventh-century biography of **St Columba**, who allegedly calmed an aquatic animal that had attacked one of his monks. In 1934, the *Daily Mail* published London surgeon R.K. Wilson's sensational photograph of the head and neck of the monster peering up out of the loch, and the hype has hardly diminished since. Encounters range from glimpses of ripples by anglers to the famous occasion in 1961 when thirty hotel guests saw a pair of humps break the water's surface and cruise for about half a mile before submerging.

Photographic evidence is showcased in the two "Monster Exhibitions" at Drumnadrochit, but the most impressive of these exhibits – including the renowned black-and-white movie footage of Nessie's humps moving across the water, and Wilson's original head and shoulders shot – have now been exposed as fakes. Indeed, in few other places on earth has watching a rather lifeless and often grey expanse of water seemed so compelling, or have floating logs, otters and boat wakes been photographed so often and with such excitement. Yet while even high-tech sonar surveys carried out over the past two decades have failed to come up with conclusive evidence, it's hard to dismiss Nessie as pure myth. After all, no one yet knows where the unknown layers of silt and mud at the bottom of the loch begin and end: best estimates say the loch is over 750 feet deep, deeper than much of the North Sea, while others point to the possibilities of underwater caves and undiscovered channels connected to the sea. Technological advances have also expanded the scope for Nessie-watching: ⓦwww.lochness.co.uk offers round-the-clock **webcams** for views across the loch, while ⓦwww.lochnessinvestigation.org is packed with research information. The local tourist industry's worst fear – a dwindling of the speculation – is about as unlikely as an appearance of the mysterious monster herself.

however, is based overwhelmingly on its legendary inhabitant Nessie, the "Loch Ness monster", who ensures a steady flow of hopeful visitors to the settlements dotted along the loch, in particular **Drumnadrochit**. Nearby, the impressive ruins of **Castle Urquhart** – a favourite monster-spotting location – perch atop a rock on the lochside and attract a deluge of bus parties during the summer. Almost as busy in high season is the village of **Fort Augustus**, at the more scenic southwest tip of Loch Ness, where you can watch queues of boats tackling one of the Caledonian Canal's longest flights of locks.

Drumnadrochit and Castle Urquhart

Situated above a verdant, sheltered bay of Loch Ness fifteen miles southwest of Inverness, **DRUMNADROCHIT** is the southern gateway to remote Glen Affric and the epicentre of Nessie-hype complete with a rash of tacky souvenir shops and two rival monster exhibitions. Of the pair, the **Loch Ness 2000 Exhibition** (daily: Easter–May 9.30am–5pm; June & Sept 9am–6pm; July & Aug 9am–8pm; Oct 9.30am–5.30pm; Nov–Easter 10am–3.30pm; £5.95), though more expensive, is the better bet, offering an in-depth rundown of eyewitness accounts and information on various research projects that have attempted to shed further light on the mysteries of the loch. The **Original Loch Ness Monster Visitor Centre and Lodge Hotel** (daily: April–June & Sept–Nov 9am–5pm; July & Aug 9am–9pm; Dec–March 9am–4pm; £5) has a less impressive exhibition, though it's worth stopping for the delicious array of home-baked goods offered at the adjacent comfortable **hotel** (ⓣ01456/450429, ⓦwww.lochness-hotel.com; ❻), and to go in search of the resident ghost within its tartan interior.

Cruises on the loch aboard *DeepScan Cruises* run from the Loch Ness 2000 Exhibition (hourly 10am–6pm, Easter–end Sept; 1hr; £10; ⓣ01456/450218), while the *Nessie Hunter* (hourly: Easter–Dec 9am–6pm; 50min; £10; ⓣ01456/450395) can be booked at the Original Loch Ness Visitor Centre.

Most photographs allegedly showing the monster have been taken a couple of miles east of Drumnadrochit, around the thirteenth-century ruined lochside **Castle Urquhart** (daily: April–Sept 9.30am–5.30pm; Oct–March 9.30am–4.30pm; £6.50; HS). It's one of Scotland's classic picture-postcard ruins, crawling with tourists by day but particularly splendid floodlit at night when all the crowds have gone.

Drumnadrochit's **tourist office** (April, May, Sept & Oct, Mon–Sat 9am–5pm & Sun 10am–4pm; June to end Aug Mon–Sat 9am–6pm, Sun 10am–4pm; Nov–March closed; ⓣ01456/459086) is in the middle of the main car park in the village. Between here and Castle Urquhart, *Gillyflowers* (ⓣ01456/450641, ⓦwww.cali.co.uk/freeway/gillyflowers; ❷) is a very welcoming **B&B** in a renovated 1780s farmhouse, while **hotels** include the friendly *Benleva* in the Lewiston area of the village (ⓣ01456/450080, ⓦwww.benleva.co.uk; ❹). For **hostel** beds (£12.50) there's the immaculate and friendly *Loch Ness Backpackers Lodge* in Lewiston (ⓣ01456/450807, ⓦwww.lochness-backpackers.com).

Most of the hotels in the area – the *Benleva* in particular – serve good bar **food**; in Drumnadrochit the *Glen Café* on the village green has a short and simple menu with basic grills, while the slightly more upmarket *Fiddlers' Café Bar* next door offers local steaks, salmon and hearty lunches.

Glen Affric

Due west of Drumnadrochit is a vast area of high peaks, remote glens and few roads, including **Glen Affric**, generally held as one of Scotland's most beautiful landscapes and heaven for walkers, climbers and mountain-bikers. The approach to the glen is through the small settlement of **CANNICH**, fourteen miles west of Drumnadrochit on the A831. A quiet, uninspiring village, Cannich has an excellent **campsite** (☎01456/415364) where mountain bikes can be rented, as well as the friendly *Glen Affric Backpackers Hostel* (☎01456/415263; all beds £10), which offers inexpensive twin or four-bed rooms.

Hemmed in by a string of Munros, Glen Affric is great for picnics and pottering, particularly on a calm and sunny day, when the still water reflects the islands and surrounding hills. From the car park at the head of the single-track road along the glen, ten miles southwest of Cannich, there's a selection of **walks**: the trip around Loch Affric will take you a good five hours but captures the glen, its wildlife and Caledonian pine and birch woods in all their remote splendour.

Fort Augustus

FORT AUGUSTUS, a tiny, busy village at the scenic southwestern tip of Loch Ness, was named after George II's son, the chubby lad who later became the "Butcher" Duke of Cumberland of Culloden fame; today, the village is dominated by comings and goings along the Caledonian Canal, which leaves Loch Ness here. The *Loch Ness Express* (Easter–Oct; 1hr 20min one way/2hr 30min return; £13 one-way, £25 return; ☎0800/3286426, Ⓦwww.lochnessexpress.com) makes speedy daily trips up the length of Loch Ness and will carry bikes for free. From its berth by the Clansman Centre, *Cruise Loch Ness* (March–Oct; 1hr; £9; ☎01320/366277, Ⓦwww.cruiselochness.com) sails five miles up Loch Ness, using sonar technology to provide passengers with impressive live 3D imagery of the deep.

The **tourist office** (May–Sept daily 9.30am–5pm; Oct–Dec & mid-Feb to March Sat & Sun 11am–3pm; ☎01320/366779) hands out useful free walking leaflets. There's **hostel** accommodation at *Morag's Lodge* to the east of the village (☎01320/366289; dorm beds £16), while the *Old Pier* (☎01320/366418, Ⓔjenny@oldpierhouse.com; ❹) is a particularly appealing **B&B** right on the loch at the north side of the village, with two roaring log fires and the option of renting two-person Canadian canoes (£15 per day) and horse riding (min £50 for two people) in the mountains.

Fort William

With its stunning position on Loch Linnhe, tucked in below the snow-streaked bulk of Ben Nevis, **FORT WILLIAM** (often known as "Fort Bill"), should be a gem. Sadly, the same lack of taste that nearly saw the town renamed "Abernevis" in the 1950s is evident in the ribbon bungalow development and ill-advised dual carriageway – complete with grubby pedestrian underpass – which have wrecked the waterfront. The main street and the little squares off it are more appealing, though occupied by some decidedly tacky tourist gift shops. Ultimately, however, Fort William is an important regional centre, with facilities including a cinema, swimming pool and a large supermarket.

Practicalities

The **tourist office** is on Cameron Square, just off High Street (April, May & Sept Mon–Sat 9am–5pm, Sun 10am–4pm; July & Aug Mon–Sat 9am–6pm, Sun 10am–5pm; Oct Mon–Sat 10am–5pm; Nov–March Mon–Sat 10am–4pm; ☎01397/701801, Ⓦwww.visithighlands.com). **Mountain bikes** are available for rent at Off Beat Bikes, 117 High St (☎01397/704008, Ⓦwww.offbeatbikes.co.uk); they know the best routes, issue free maps and also have a branch at the Nevis Range gondola base station (June–Sept; ☎01397/705825), with forest

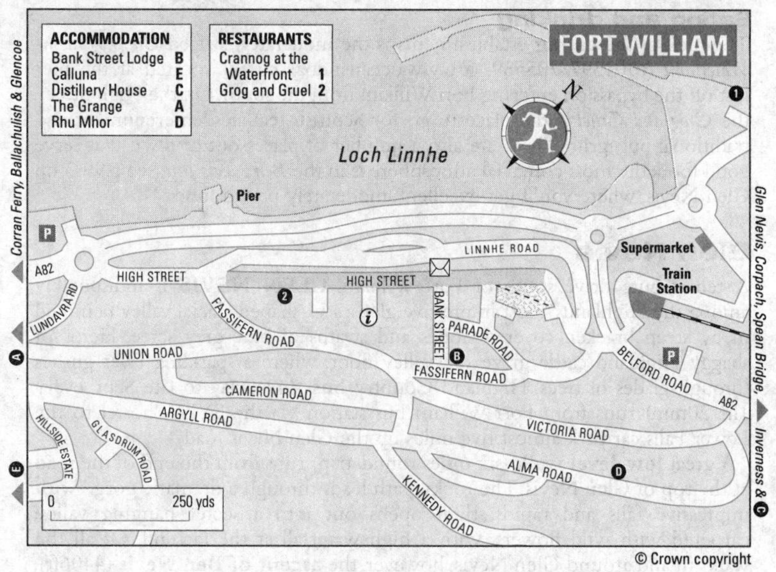

© Crown copyright

rides and a world-championship-standard downhill track. Local **mountain guides** include Alan Kimber of *Calluna* (see below), or contact the Snowgoose Mountain Centre (ⓣ01397/772467, ⓦwww.highland-mountain-guides.co.uk), which also offers instruction and residential courses on activities such as mountaineering.

Accommodation in town

Bank Street Lodge Bank St ⓣ01397/700070, ⓦwww.bankstreetlodge.co.uk. A 43-bed centrally located lodge-cum-hostel that's handy for transport and the town centre; dorm beds from £13.

Calluna Heathercroft, Connachie Rd ⓣ01397/700451, ⓦwww.fortwilliamholiday.co.uk. Well-run self-catering and hostel accommodation ten minutes' walk from the centre of town. Free pick-up from town available, along with on-site laundry and mountain guiding services (see ⓦwestcoast-mountainguides.co.uk); dorm beds from £12.

The Grange Grange Rd ⓣ01397/705516, ⓦwww.thegrange-scotland.co.uk. Top-grade accommodation in a striking old stone house, with log fires, views towards Loch Linnhe and luxurious en-suite doubles. Vegetarian breakfasts on request. April–Oct. 7

Rhu Mhor Alma Rd ⓣ01397/702213, ⓦwww.rhumhor.co.uk. Congenial and characterful B&B, ten minutes' walk from the town centre, offering good breakfasts; vegetarians and vegans are catered for by arrangement. 3

Accommodation out of town

Achintee Farm Guesthouse Glen Nevis ⓣ01397/702240, ⓦwww.achinteefarm.com. Friendly B&B with adjoining hostel (the *Ben Nevis Bunkhouse*; £14 per dorm) right by the *Ben Nevis Inn* (see below), at the start of the Ben Nevis footpath. 4

The Ben Nevis Inn Achintee, Glen Nevis ⓣ01397/701227. A basic and cosy 20-bed bunkhouse housed within the rustic and lively pub just north of the *Achintee Farm Guesthouse* (see above). Dorm beds from £12.50.

Farr Cottage Lodge Corpach, on the main A830 ⓣ01397/772315, ⓦwww.farrcottage.co.uk. Well-equipped, lively hostel. Offers a multitude of outdoor activities with evening entertainment including whisky tastings. Has a range of dorms (£13) and double/twin rooms 1

Rhiw Goch Banavie ⓣ01397/772373, ⓦwww.rhiwgoch.co.uk. Comfortable and welcoming B&B overlooking Neptune's Staircase with great views to Ben Nevis. For a super-healthy breakfast, try the great fresh fruit platter. Bike and canoe hire also available. 3

Eating and drinking

The pick of the **eating** establishments is the moderately priced *Crannog at the Waterfront* (ⓣ01397/705589, ⓦwww.oceanandoak.co.uk), located at the pier just off the bypass on entering Fort William from the south. On the High Street, the *Grog and Gruel* is the place to go for Scottish real ales, entertainment and traditional pub grub. There are also a number of places out of town that serve good food: the most convivial atmosphere is in the *Ben Nevis Inn* (see p.991) up Glen Nevis, where you'll get excellent, moderately priced food.

Glen Nevis

A ten-minute drive south of Fort William, **GLEN NEVIS** is indisputably among the Highlands' most impressive glens: a U-shaped glacial valley hemmed in by steep bracken-covered slopes and swaths of blue-grey scree. Herds of shaggy Highland cattle graze the valley floor, where a sparkling river gushes through glades of trees. Highland Country **bus** #42 (May to late Sept; every 1hr 20min) runs from Fort William bus station via the SYHA hostel to the Lower Falls car park almost five miles up the Glen Nevis road

A great **low-level walk** (six miles round-trip) runs from the end of the road at the top of Glen Nevis. The rocky path leads through a dramatic gorge with impressive falls and rapids, then opens out into a secret hanging valley, carpeted with wild flowers, with a high waterfall at the far end. Of all the walks in and around Glen Nevis, however, the **ascent of Ben Nevis** (4406ft), Britain's highest summit, inevitably attracts the most attention. Despite the fact that it's quite a slog up to the summit, and it's by no means the most attractive mountain in Scotland, in high summer the trail is teeming with hikers, whatever the weather. It can snow round the summit any day of the year, so take the necessary precautions; in winter, of course, the mountain should be left to the experts. The most obvious **route** to the summit, a Victorian pony path up the whaleback south side of the mountain, built to service the observatory that once stood on the top, starts from the helpful **Glen Nevis visitor centre**, a mile and a half along the Glen Nevis road

The Nevis Range

Seven miles northeast of Fort William by the A82, on the slopes of **Aonach Mhor**, one of the high mountains abutting Ben Nevis, the **Nevis Range** (ⓣ01397/705825, ⓦwww.nevis-range.co.uk) is Scotland's highest winter ski area. Highland Country bus #42 runs from Fort William (year-round; Mon–Sat 5 daily, 3 on Sun) to the base station of the country's only **gondola** system (daily: 10am–5pm; July & Aug 9.30am–6pm; closed mid-Nov to mid-Dec for maintenance; £8.50 return). The one-and-a-half-mile gondola trip (15min), rising 2000ft, gives an easy approach to some high-level walking as well as spectacular views from the terrace of the self-service restaurant at the top station. From the top of the gondola station, you can experience Britain's only World-Cup-standard **downhill mountain-bike course** (mid-May to mid-Sept 11am–3pm; £10.25 includes gondola one way; £19 multitrip), a hair-raising 3km route, that's not for the faint-hearted. There's also 25 miles of waymarked off-road bike routes, known as the Witch's Trails, on the mountainside and in the Leanachan Forest, ranging from gentle paths to cross-country scrambles. Off Beat Bikes (ⓣ01397/704008, ⓦwww.offbeatbikes.co.uk) rents mountain bikes as well as full-suspension bikes for the downhill course from their shops in Fort William and at the gondola base station (mid-May to mid-Sept). The base station area also has a café and there's a play area and nature trail nearby.

(daily: Easter to mid-May & Oct 9am–5pm; mid-May to end Sept 9am–6pm): allow a full day for the climb (8hr).

Glen Coe

Sixteen miles south of Fort William on the A82, breathtakingly beautiful **Glen Coe** (literally "Valley of Weeping") is justifiably the best known of the Highland glens: a spectacular mountain valley between velvety-green conical peaks, their tops often wreathed in cloud, their flanks streaked by cascades of rock and scree. In 1692 it was the site of a notorious massacre, in which the MacDonalds were victims of a long-standing government desire to suppress the clans. When clan chief **Alastair MacDonald** missed the deadline of January 1, 1692, to sign an oath of allegiance to William III, a plot was hatched to make an example of "that damnable sept". **Campbell of Glenlyon** was ordered to billet his soldiers in the homes of the MacDonalds, who for ten days entertained them with traditional Highland hospitality. In the early morning of February 13, the soldiers turned on their hosts, slaying between 38 and 45, and causing more than three hundred to flee.

Beyond the small village of **GLENCOE** at the western end of the glen, the glen itself (a property of the National Trust for Scotland since the 1930s) is virtually uninhabited, and provides outstanding climbing and walking. A mile south of the village is the NTS **visitor centre** (March daily 10am–4pm; April–Aug daily 9.30am–5.30pm; Sept & Oct daily 10am–5pm; Nov to mid-Dec, Jan & Feb Thurs–Sun 10am–4pm; NTS; £5) where you'll find a informative exhibition with a balanced account of the massacre alongside some entertaining material on rock and hill-climbing down the years. Enlightening ranger-led **guided walks** (Easter & June–Sept) leave from the centre, while a cabin area provides information on the local weather and wildlife, and a café sells good cakes.

There's a good selection of **accommodation** in Glen Coe and the surrounding area: the lively *Clachaig Inn* (Ⓣ01855/811252, Ⓦwww.clachaig.com; ❺) is a great place to swap stories with fellow climbers and to reward your exertions with cask-conditioned ales and heaped platefuls of food; it's three miles south of Glencoe village on the minor road off the A82. More basic options include a SYHA **hostel** (Ⓣ0870/004 1122, Ⓦwww.syha.org.uk; dorm beds £14.50) on a back road halfway between Glencoe village and the *Clachaig Inn*; the year-round *Red Squirrel* **campsite** (Ⓣ01855/811256) nearby; and a grassier Caravanning and Camping Club site (Ⓣ01855/811397; April–Oct) on the main road.

Kinlochleven

At the easternmost end of Loch Leven, the settlement of **KINLOCHLEVEN** was best known for many years as the site of a huge, unsightly aluminium smelter built in 1904. The disused smelter is now home to an innovative indoor mountaineering centre called **The Ice Factor** (Ⓣ01855/831100, Ⓦwww.ice-factor.co.uk). This impressive facility includes the world's largest artificial ice-climbing wall (13.5m) as well as a range of more traditional climbing walls and other facilities such as steam room, sauna and an inexpensive café. Another part of the aluminium smelter has been transformed into the **Atlas Brewery**, which you can tour on summer evenings (groups can phone to arrange tours at other times; Ⓣ01855/831111, Ⓦwww.atlasbrewery.com). Kinlochleven stands at the foot of the spectacular Mamore hills, and is a day's walk from Fort William on the **West Highland Way**.

Walks around Glen Coe

A good introduction to the splendours of Glen Coe is the half-day hike over the **Devil's Staircase**, which follows part of the old military road that once ran between Fort William and Stirling. The trail, part of the West Highland Way (see p.869), starts at the village of **Kinlochleven** and is marked by thistle signs, which lead uphill to the 1804ft pass and down the other side into Glen Coe.

Set right in the heart of the glen, the half-day **Allt Coire Gabhail** hike starts at the car park opposite the distinctive Three Sisters massif on the main A82. This explores the so-called "Lost Valley" where the Clan MacDonald fled and hid their cattle when attacked. Once in the valley, there are superb views of the upper slopes of Bidean nan Bian, Gearr Aonach and Beinn Fhada, which improve as you continue on to its head, another twenty- to thirty-minute walk.

Undoubtedly one of the finest walks in the Glen Coe area that doesn't entail the ascent of a Munro is the **Buachaille Etive Beag** circuit, which follows the textbook glacial valleys of Lairig Eilde and Lairig Gartain, ascending 1968ft in only nine miles of rough trail. Park near the waterfall at **The Study** – the gorge part of the A82 through Glen Coe – and walk up the road until you see a sign pointing south to "Loch Etiveside". Refer to the **map**, *Ordnance Survey Explorer Map* no. 384.

The west coast

The Highlands' starkly beautiful **west coast** – stretching from the **Morvern peninsula** (opposite Mull) in the south to wind-lashed **Cape Wrath** in the far north – is arguably the finest part of Scotland. Serrated by fjord-like sea lochs, the long coastline is scattered with windswept white-sand beaches, cliff-girt headlands, and rugged mountains sweeping up from the shoreline. When the sun shines, the sparkle of the sea, the richness of colour and the clarity of the views out to the scattered Hebrides are simply irresistible. This is the least populated part of Britain, with just two small towns, and yawning tracts of moorland and desolate peat bog between crofting settlements.

The most visited part of the west coast is the stretch between Kyle of Lochalsh and Ullapool. Lying within easy reach of Inverness, this sector boasts the region's more obvious highlights: the awesome mountainscape of **Torridon**, **Gairloch**'s sandy beaches, the famous botanic gardens at **Inverewe**, and **Ullapool** itself, a picturesque and bustling fishing town from where ferries leave for the Outer Hebrides. However, press on further north, or south, and you'll get a truer sense of the isolation that makes the west coast so special. Traversed by few roads, the remote northwest corner of Scotland is wild and bleak, receiving the full force of the North Atlantic's frequently ferocious weather. The scattered settlements of the far southwest, meanwhile, tend to be more sheltered, but they are separated by some of the most extensive wilderness areas in Britain – lonely peninsulas with evocative Gaelic names like **Ardnamurchan**, **Knoydart** and **Glenelg**.

Without your own vehicle, **transport** can be a problem. There's a reasonable **train** service from Inverness to Kyle of Lochalsh and from Fort William to Mallaig, and a useful **summer bus** service connects Inverness to Ullapool, Lochinver, Scourie and Durness. **Driving** is a much simpler option: the roads aren't busy, though they are frequently single-track and scattered with sheep.

Morvern to Knoydart: the "Rough Bounds"

The remote and sparsely populated southwest corner of the Highlands, from the empty district of **Morvern** to the isolated peninsula of **Knoydart**, is a dramatic, lonely region of mountain and moorland fringed by a rocky, indented coast whose stunning white beaches enjoy wonderful views to Mull, Skye and other islands. Its Gaelic name, *Garbh-chiochan*, translates as the "**Rough Bounds**", implying a region geographically and spiritually apart. Even if you have a car, you should spend some time here exploring on foot; there are so few roads that some determined hiking is almost inevitable.

The Ardnamurchan peninsula

A nine-mile drive south of Fort William down Loch Linnhe, the five-minute ferry crossing at **Corran Ferry** (every 20–30min; Mon–Sat 6.30am–9.20pm, Sun 8.45am–9.20pm; car and passengers £5.20; foot passengers and bicycles go free) provides the most direct point of entry for Morvern and the rugged **Ardnamurchan peninsula**. The most westerly point on the British mainland, the peninsula lost most of its inhabitants during the infamous Clearances (see p.1014) and is now sparsely populated with only a handful of tiny crofting settlements clinging to its jagged coastline. Ardnamurchan, however, can be an inspiring place for its pristine, empty beaches, wonderful vistas of sea and island, and the sense of nature all around. A variety of **walking** routes, from hill climbs to coastal scrambles, are detailed in a guide produced annually by the local community (available from tourist offices and most shops on the peninsula, priced around £4).

The coastal hamlet of **SALEN** marks the turn-off for Ardnamurchan Point: from here it's a further 25 miles of slow but scenic driving along the single-track road which follows the northern shore of Loch Sunart. Along this road, just west of the hamlet of **GLENBORRODALE**, look out for the engaging **Glenmore Natural History Centre** (April–Oct Mon–Sat 10.30am–5.30pm, Sun noon–5.30pm; Ⓦwww.ardnamurchan.com; £4), which provides an inspiring introduction to the diverse flora, fauna and geology of Ardnamurchan: CCTV cameras relay pictures of the comings and goings of heron, a pine marten's nest and sea and golden eagles feeding nearby.

Nine miles west of the Glenmore Centre, **KILCHOAN** is Ardnamurchan's main village – a straggling but appealing crofting township overlooking the Sound of Mull. A **car ferry** runs from here to Tobermory (Mon–Sat 8am–6.40pm 7 daily; May–Aug also Sun 10.15am–4.45pm 5 daily; 35min). The community centre in the village houses a **tourist office** (Easter–Oct daily 9am–5pm; Ⓣ01972/510222, Ⓦwww.ardnamurchan.com), who can book accommodation; the community centre (and its simple tearoom) are open year-round and can provide informal local advice. **Accommodation** isn't plentiful in Kilchoan, and in summer you're advised to book well ahead. Try the very friendly B&B *Doirlinn House* (Ⓣ01972/510209, Ⓔdoirlinnhouse@ardnamurchan-holidays.com; ③; March–Oct) or the nearby two-bedroom *Torrsolais* (Ⓣ01972/510389, ⒺTorrsolais@ardnamurchan-holidays.com; ③). There's a good campsite with lovely coastal views by the Ardnamurchan Study Centre (Ⓣ07787 812084, Ⓦwww.ardnamurchanstudycentre.co.uk), about half a mile past the Ferry Stores.

The road continues beyond Kilchoan to the rocky, windy **Ardnamurchan Point** and its famous **lighthouse**. The lighthouse buildings house a small café and an absorbing **exhibition** (April–Oct daily 10am–5pm; £5; Ⓣ01972/510210), with well-assembled displays about lighthouses, their construction and the people who lived in them. Best of all is the chance to climb up the inside of the Egyptian-style lighthouse tower; at the top, a guide is on hand to tell some of the tall tales relating to the lighthouse and show you around the lighting mechanism.

Also worth exploring around the peninsula are the myriad coves, beaches and headlands along the long coastline. The finest of the sandy beaches is about three miles north of the lighthouse at **Sanna Bay**, a shell-strewn strand and series of dunes which offers truly unforgettable vistas of the Small Isles to the north, circled by gulls, terns and guillemots.

The Road to the Isles

The "**Road to the Isles**" (ⓦwww.road-to-the-isles.org.uk) from Fort William to Mallaig, followed by the West Highland Railway and the narrow, winding A830, traverses the mountains and glens of the Rough Bounds before breaking out onto a spectacularly scenic coast of sheltered inlets, stunning white beaches and wonderful views to the islands of Rùm, Eigg, Muck and Skye. This is country commonly associated with **Bonnie Prince Charlie**, whose adventures of 1745–46 began and ended on this stretch of coast, with his first, defiant gathering of the clans at **GLENFINNAN**, nineteen miles west of Fort William at the head of lovely Loch Shiel. The spot is marked by a column (now a little lopsided), crowned with a clansman in full battle dress, erected in 1815.

Glenfinnan is a poignant place, a beautiful stage for the opening scene in a brutal drama that was to change the Highlands for ever. The **visitor centre** and café (daily: April, May, June, Sept & Oct 10am–5pm; July & Aug 9.30am–5.30pm; £3; NTS), opposite the monument, gives an account of the '45 uprising through to the rout at **Culloden** eight months later (see p.982). Loch Shiel Cruises (ⓣ01687/470322, ⓦwww.highlandcruises.co.uk) run a number of **boat trips** on the loch, all offering a worthwhile opportunity to view the remote, captivating scenery and occasionally a golden eagle.

This area is the most spectacular section of the **West Highland Railway** line (see box, p.978), offering glimpses of the graceful Loch Shiel. You can learn more about the history of this segment of the railway at the **Glenfinnan Station Museum** (June–Sept Mon–Fri 9.30am–5pm, Sat & Sun 10am–5pm; 50p), set in the old booking office of the station. Next door, two old railway carriages have been converted into a highly original **restaurant** and **bunkhouse**: the *Dining Car* (June–Sept daily 10am–5pm; ⓣ01397/722300) is open for light lunches and home-baking (phone ahead to make arrangments for evening meals), while the *Sleeping Car* (ⓣ01397/722295; year-round), a converted 1958 camping coach, sleeps ten in bunk beds.

West of Glenfinnan, the A830 runs alongside captivating Loch Eilt and onto a coast marked by acres of white sands, turquoise seas and rocky islets draped with orange seaweed. **ARISAIG**, scattered round a sandy bay at the west end of the Morar peninsula, makes a good base for exploring the vicinity. A **bypass** whizzes cars (and, more importantly, fish lorries) on their way to Mallaig, but you shouldn't miss the slower coast road, which enjoys the best of the scenery.

Stretching north of Arisaig is a string of stunning **beaches** backed by flowery machair, with barren granite hills and moorland rising up behind, and wonderful seaward views of Eigg and Rùm. Of the string of **campsites** along the coast road try the popular, eco-friendly *Camusdarach* (ⓣ01687/450221, ⓦwww.road-to-the-isles.org.uk/camusdarach), four miles north of Arisaig and just three minutes walk from the beach where scenes from *Local Hero* were shot.

Mallaig

A cluttered, noisy port whose pebble-dashed houses struggle for space with great lumps of exposed granite strewn over the hillsides sloping down to the sea, **MALLAIG**, 47 miles west of Fort William, isn't pretty. As the main ferry stop for

Skye, the Small Isles and Knoydart, it's always full of visitors, though the continuing source of the village's wealth is its **fishing** industry: on the quayside, piles of nets, tackle and ice crates lie scattered around a bustling modern market. When the fleet is in, trawlers encircled by flocks of raucous gulls choke the harbour, and the pubs, among the liveliest on the west coast, host bouts of serious drinking.

The **tourist office** (April–Oct Mon–Sat 10am–5pm; call ⓣ01687/462064 for winter opening hours) is by the harbour, with the CalMac ticket office (ⓣ01687/462403), serving passengers for Skye and the Small Isles, nearby. For transport to Knoydart, Bruce Watt Cruises (ⓣ01687/462320, ⓦwww.knoydart-ferry.co.uk) sails to Inverie, on the Knoydart peninsula, every morning and afternoon (mid-May to mid-Sept Mon–Fri; mid-Sept to mid-May Mon, Wed & Fri).

For **B&B**, head around the harbour to East Bay, where you'll find the cheery *Western Isles Guesthouse* (ⓣ01687/462320, ⓦwww.road-to-the-isles.org.uk/western-isles.html; ④), or there's *Sheena's Backpackers' Lodge* (ⓣ01687/462764), a laid-back independent **hostel** overlooking the harbour, with mixed dorms (£13) and a modest seafood restaurant (Easter to end Oct). Alternatively, the *Fishmarket Restaurant*, facing *Sheena's*, serves up lots of fresh seafood, while the *Cornerstone*, across the road from the tourist office, does the freshest of fish and chips – or a portion of scallops and chips if you're feeling decadent.

The Knoydart peninsula

Flanked by **Loch Nevis** ("Loch of Heaven") in the south and the fjord-like inlet of **Loch Hourn** ("Loch of Hell") to the north, **Knoydart peninsula**'s knobbly green peaks – three of them Munros – sweep straight out of the sea, shrouded for much of the time in a pall of grey mist. To get to the heart of the peninsula, you must catch a **boat** from Mallaig or Glenelg, or else **hike** for a couple of days across rugged moorland and mountains and sleep rough in old stone bothies (most of which are marked on Ordnance Survey maps).

At the end of the eighteenth century, around a thousand people eked out a living from this inhospitable terrain through crofting and fishing. These days the peninsula supports around seventy people, most of whom live in the hamlet of **INVERIE**. Nestled beside a sheltered bay on the south side of the peninsula, it has a pint-sized post office, a shop, and mainland Britain's most remote pub.

Three-quarters of a mile east of the village on the side of the mountain, there's an upmarket independent **hostel**, *Torrie Shieling* (ⓣ01687/462669, ⓔtorrie@knoydart.org; £16), while the Knoydart Foundation runs a simple **bunkhouse** (ⓣ01687/462242, ⓦwww.knoydart-foundation.com; £14) nearby in some old steadings. In Inverie itself there are a couple of guesthouses, the cosy *Pier House* (ⓣ01687/462347, ⓦwww.thepierhouseknoydart.co.uk; ⑥ for dinner, B&B), and *The Gathering* (ⓣ01687/460051, ⓦwww.thegatheringknoydart.co.uk; ⑤), which has some bunk beds and beautiful wood furnishings. The *Old Forge* is one of Scotland's finer pubs, with a convivial atmosphere where visitors and locals mix happily, generous bar meals often feature freshly caught seafood, real ales, an open fire, and a good chance of live music of an evening. You can rent **mountain bikes** from *Pier House*. Your best source of information for walking and wildlife in the area (including guided walks) is from the ranger post (ⓣ01687/462242) beside the *Old Forge*.

Kyle of Lochalsh and around

As the main gateway to Skye, **Kyle of Lochalsh** used to be an important transit point for tourists, locals and services. However, with the building of the **Skye Bridge** in 1995, Kyle was left as merely the terminus for the train route from

Inverness, with little else to offer. Of much more interest is nearby **Eilean Donan Castle**, one of Scotland's most famous and popular sights, perched at the end of a stone causeway on the shores of **Loch Duich**. A few miles north of Kyle of Lochalsh, the delightful village of **Plockton** is a refreshing alternative to its utilitarian neighbour, with cottages grouped around a yacht-filled bay and Highland cattle wandering the streets.

Kyle of Lochalsh

KYLE OF LOCHALSH is not particularly attractive and is ideally somewhere to pass through rather than linger. The **tourist office** (April–Oct Mon–Fri 9.30am–5pm; Sat & Sun 10am–4pm) is on top of the small hill near the old ferry jetty. The best **hotel** is the welcoming *Kyle Hotel* in Main Street, with a menu including fresh seafood and game (Ⓣ01599/534204, Ⓦwww.kylehotel.co.uk; ❺). The spacious and comfortable *Ardenlea* on Church Street (Ⓣ01599/534630 ❸) is a good central B&B. There's a simple bunkhouse in town, *Cúchulainn's* (Ⓣ01599/534492), above a pub across the main street from the tourist office. To **eat**, sample the steak and home-made puddings at the *Waverley Restaurant* (5.30–9.30pm, closed Thurs; Ⓣ01599/534337), or for a snack visit *Sheila's Café* opposite the tourist office.

Buses run to Kyle of Lochalsh from Glasgow via Fort William and Invergarry and from Inverness via Invermoriston, and all continue at least as far as Portree on Skye: book in advance for all of them (Ⓣ0870/550 5050, Ⓦwww.citylink.co.uk; see "Travel Details" for times and journey duration). Buses also shuttle across the bridge to Kyleakin on Skye every thirty minutes or so.

Eilean Donan Castle

Eilean Donan Castle (April–end Oct daily 10am–5pm; from 9am July–Aug; £4.95), ten miles north of Shiel Bridge on the A87, has to be one of Scotland's most photographed monuments. The forbidding crenellated tower rises from the water's edge, joined to the shore by a narrow stone bridge and with sheer mountains as a backdrop. The original castle was established in 1230 by Alexander II to protect the area from the Vikings. Later, during a Jacobite uprising in 1719, it was occupied by troops dispatched by the king of Spain to help the "**Old Pretender**", James Stuart. However, when King George heard of their whereabouts, he sent frigates to take the Spaniards out, and the castle was blown up with their stocks of gunpowder. Thereafter, it lay in ruins until John Macrae-Gilstrap had it rebuilt between 1912 and 1932. Eilean Donan has since featured in several major **films**, including *Highlander*, *Entrapment*, and the James Bond adventure *The World is Not Enough*. Three floors, including the banqueting hall, the bedrooms and the troops' quarters are open to the public, with various Jacobite and clan relics also on display, though like many of the region's most popular castles, the large numbers of people passing through make it hard to appreciate the real charm of the place.

Plockton

A fifteen-minute train ride north of Kyle at the seaward end of islet-studded Loch Carron lies the unbelievably picturesque village of **PLOCKTON**: a chocolate-box row of neatly painted cottages ranged around the curve of a tiny harbour and backed by a craggy landscape of heather and pine. The unique brilliance of Plockton's light has also made it something of an artists' hang-out, and during the summer the waterfront, with its row of shaggy palm trees, even shaggier Highland cattle, flower gardens and pleasure boats, is invariably dotted with painters dabbing at their easels.

The *Haven Hotel*, on Innes Street (Ⓣ01599/544223; ⑥), the almost adjacent family-run *Plockton Inn* (Ⓣ01599/544222, Ⓦwww.plocktoninn.co.uk; ⑤) and the *Plockton Hotel* on Harbour Street (Ⓣ01599/544274, Ⓦwww.plocktonhotel.co.uk; ⑥) all offer comfortable accommodation within their respective atmospheric walls, though the latter also offers terrific harbour and loch views. Of the fifteen or so **B&Bs**, *The Shieling* (Ⓣ01599/544282; ③) has a great location on a tiny headland at the top of the harbour.

For a small village, Plockton offers a number of good places to **eat**. *Plockton Seafood Restaurant* (Ⓣ01559/544423) at the train station serves tasty cakes, moderately priced lunches (noon–3pm) and delicious if pricier evening meals of seafood and game (6–9pm) in a delightful wood-panelled restaurant. Fresh seafood is also a staple on the (moderately expensive) evening menus at *The Haven*, the *Plockton Inn* and the *Plockton Hotel*. The latter two sell the locally brewed Crags real ale and it's hard to beat the views over the bay from the hotel.

Wester Ross

The western seaboard of the old county of Ross-shire, **Wester Ross**, blends all the classic elements of Scotland's **coastal scenery** – dramatic mountains, sandy beaches, whitewashed crofting cottages and shimmering island views – in spectacular fashion. Though popular with generations of adventurous Scottish holiday-makers, only one or two places feel blighted by tourist numbers, with places such as **Applecross** and the peninsulas north and south of **Gairloch** maintaining an endearing simplicity and sense of isolation. There's some tough but wonderful **hiking** to be enjoyed in the mountains around **Torridon** and **Coigach**, while **boat trips** out among the islands and the prolific sea- and birdlife of the coast are another draw. The main settlement is the attractive fishing town of **Ullapool**, port for ferry services to Stornoway in the Western Isles, but a pleasant enough place to use as a base, not least for its active social and cultural scene.

The Applecross peninsula

The most dramatic approach to the **Applecross peninsula** (the English-sounding name is a corruption of the Gaelic *Apor Crosan*, meaning "estuary") is from the south, up a glacial U-shaped valley and over the infamous **Bealach na Bà** (literally "Pass of the Cattle"). Crossing the forbidding hills behind Kishorn and rising to 2053ft, with a gradient and switchback bends worthy of the Alps, this route – a popular cycling piste – is hair-raising in places, and the panoramic views across the Minch to Raasay and Skye augment the experience.

The sheltered, fertile coast around **APPLECROSS** village (Ⓦwww.applecross.info), where the Irish missionary monk Maelrhuba founded a monastery in 673 AD, comes as a surprise after the bleakness of the moorland approach. Maybe it's the journey, but Applecross feels like an idyllic place: you can wander along lanes banked with wild iris and orchids, and explore beaches and rock pools on the shore. There's a small **Heritage Centre** (April–Oct Mon–Sat noon–4pm; Ⓦwww.applecrossheritage.org.uk) overlooking Clachan church and graveyard, and a number of short **waymarked trails** along the shore – great for walking off a pub lunch.

The old, family-run *Applecross Inn* (Ⓣ01520/744262; ⑥), right beside the sea, is the focal point of the community, with **rooms** upstairs, and a lively bar that serves delicious local seafood and produce (noon–9pm). The inn is the first stop for most folk coming here, though just a mile down the road the excellent *Walled Garden Café and Restaurant*, (Ⓣ01520/744440; March to end-Oct Mon–Sat 11am–8.30pm, Sun 11am–4pm; book ahead) is a culinary delight; the

Walks around Torridon

There can be difficult conditions on virtually all hiking routes around Torridon, and the weather can change very rapidly. If you're relatively inexperienced but want to do the magnificent ridge walk along the **Liathach** (pronounced "lee-ach") massif, or the strenuous traverse of **Beinn Eighe** (pronounced "ben ay"), you can join a National Trust Ranger Service guided hike (July & Aug; Torridon Countryside Centre; ⓣ01445/791221).

For those confident to go it alone, one of many possible routes takes you behind Liathach and down the pass, **Coire Dubh**, to the main road in Glen Torridon. This is a great, straightforward, full-day walk, covering thirteen miles and taking in superb landscapes.

A rewarding walk even in rough weather is the seven-mile hike up the coast from **Lower Diabaig**, ten miles northwest of Torridon village, to **Redpoint**. On a clear day, the views across to Raasay and Applecross from this gentle undulating path are superlative, but you'll have to return along the same trail, or else make your way back via Loch Maree on the A832. If you're staying in Shieldaig, the track that winds up the peninsula running north from the village makes a pleasant 90min round walk. The *Ordnance Survey Explorer Map* no. 433 **map** is particularly useful.

garden, woods and sea provide fresh, rich pickings for the chefs, who serve up delectable platefuls in a laid-back atmosphere.

Loch Torridon

Loch Torridon marks the northern boundary of the Applecross peninsula, its awe-inspiring setting enhanced by the appealingly rugged mountains of **Liathach** and **Beinn Eighe**, hulks of reddish 750-million-year-old Torridonian sandstone tipped by streaks of white quartzite. Some 15,000 acres of the massif are under the protection of the National Trust for Scotland, which runs a **Countryside Centre**, by Torridon Village by the head of the loch (Easter–Sept Mon–Sat 10am–5pm; £3), where you can learn about the local geology, flora and fauna. On the south side of the loch stands one of the area's grandest **hotels**, the smart, rambling Victorian *Loch Torridon Hotel* (ⓣ01445/791242, ⓦwww.lochtorridonhotel.com; ⑧), set amid well-tended grounds. The hotel also runs the adjacent *Ben Damph Lodge* (March–Oct; ⑤), a cyclist- and walker-friendly conversion of an old farmstead, with neat twins and doubles and a bistro-bar. Close to the Countryside Centre is a rather unsightly SYHA **hostel** (ⓣ0870/004 1154, ⓦwww.syha.org.uk; March–Oct; dorm beds £13.50) and a council-run **campsite**.

Loch Maree

About eight miles north of Loch Torridon, **Loch Maree**, dotted with Caledonian pine-covered islands, is one of the west's scenic highlights, best viewed from the A832 road that skirts the loch's southern shore, passing the **Beinn Eighe Nature Reserve**, the UK's oldest wildlife sanctuary. Parts of the reserve are forested with Caledonian pinewood, which once covered the whole of the country, and it is home to wildlife including pine marten, wildcat, buzzards and golden eagles.

A mile north of Kinlochewe, the well-run **Beinn Eighe Visitor Centre** (Easter & May–Oct daily 10am–5pm) on the A832, uses excellent audiovisual presentations and child-friendly displays to inform visitors about the area's rare species. Outside, the "talking trails" provide an easy walk through the vicinity, while several longer **walks** start from the car park, a mile north of the visitor centre.

Gairloch and around

GAIRLOCH spreads itself around the northeastern corner of the wide sheltered bay of Loch Gairloch. During the summer, Gairloch thrives as a low-key holiday resort with several tempting sandy beaches and some excellent coastal walks within easy reach. The main supermarket and **tourist office** (June–Sept daily 9am–5.30pm; Oct Mon–Sat 9am–5.30pm; Nov–May Mon–Sat 10am–4pm) are in Achtercairn, right by the **Gairloch Heritage Museum** (March–Sept daily 10am–5pm; Oct Mon–Sat 10am–1.30pm); £3), which has eclectic, appealing displays covering geology, archeology, fishing and farming that range from a mock-up of a croft house to an early knitting machine.

There's a good choice of **accommodation** around Gairloch: opposite the post office, the *Mountain Lodge* (Ⓣ01445/712316; March–Nov; ❷) has rooms, and you can get good coffee and fresh scones at the laid-back *Mountain Café* next door, with views over the bay. There are also some very good **B&Bs** in the section of the village known as Strath, including Miss Mackenzie's *Duisary* (Ⓣ01445/712252, Ⓦwww.duisary.freeserve.co.uk; April–Oct; ❷) or *Stratford House* (Ⓣ01445/712183, Ⓦwww.stratfordhouse.btinternet.co.uk; ❷) on Mihol Road.

For **food**, head for the pier, where the *Old Inn* (Ⓦwww.theoldinn.co.uk) offers moderately priced seafood on its bar menu and a very good range of Scottish real ales. There's also good-value lunch and evening fare at the *Harbour Lights Café*. For **snacks**, try the *Mountain Lodge* or the bistro-style *Café Blueprint* across the road – where you'll also find the chip shop.

The Gairloch coast

The area's main attraction is its beautiful coastline, easily explored on a wildlife-spotting **cruise**: several operators, including Gairloch Marine Life Centre & Cruises (Easter–Oct; Ⓣ01445/712636; Ⓦwww.porpoise-gairloch.co.uk; from £10), run informative and enjoyable boat trips across the bay in search of dolphins, seals and even the odd whale. One of the most impressive stretches of **coastline** is around the north side of the bay, along the single-track B8021, at **BIG SAND**, which has a cleaner and quieter beach than Gairloch, with an excellent **campsite** above it (Ⓣ01445/712152). Just before Big Sand, there's an SYHA **hostel** at Carn Dearg (Ⓣ0870/004 1110, Ⓦwww.syha.org.uk; April–Sept; dorm beds £12.50), spectacularly set on the edge of a cliff with views to Skye. Three miles beyond at **Rubha Reidh** (pronounced "roo-a-ray"), you can stay at the headland's still operational *Rua Reidh Lighthouse* (Ⓣ01445/771263, Ⓦwww.ruareidh.co.uk; ❷), which looks out to the Outer Hebrides. Comfortable accommodation includes a bunkhouse (£10), double and family rooms (meals extra; book ahead in high season). Fran, the cheerful owner, can provide breakfast (£5.50) and a pre-booked evening meal (£13.50). Guided walking and climbing courses are also offered.

Three miles south of Gairloch, a narrow single-track lane winds west to **BADACHRO**, a sleepy former fishing village in a very attractive setting with a wonderful pub, the *Badachro Inn* (Ⓦwww.badachroinn.com), right by the water's edge, where you can sit in the beer garden watching the boats come and go and tuck into deliciously fresh seafood with a real ale. Beyond Badachro, the road winds for five more miles along the shore to **REDPOINT**, a straggling hamlet with beautiful beaches of peach-coloured sand and great views to Raasay, Skye and the Western Isles.

Inverewe Gardens

It's a 15min hop by bus over the headland from Gairloch to the trim little village of **Poolewe**, which sits by a small bay at the sheltered southern end of

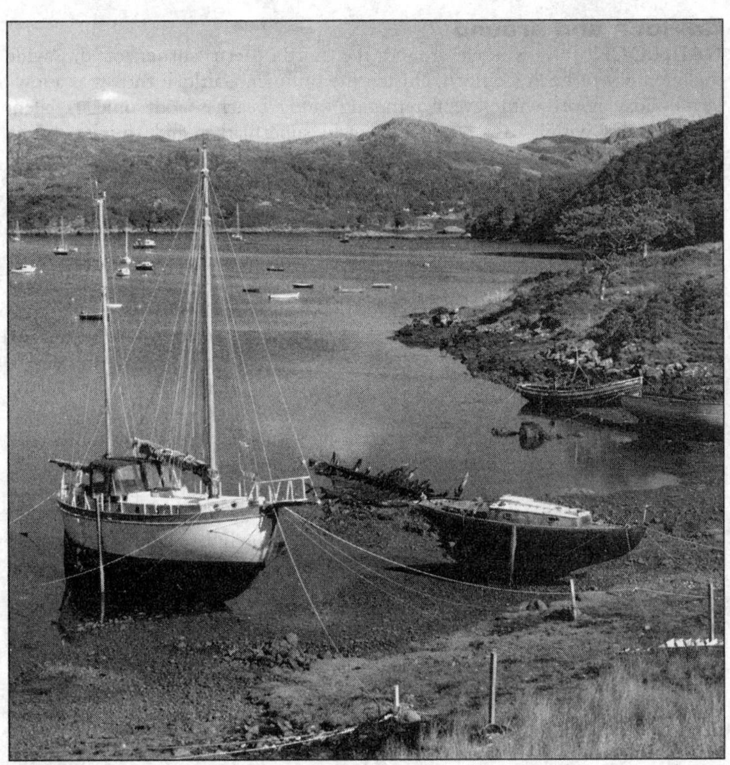

▲ Gairloch

Loch Ewe. Half a mile across the bay from Poolewe on the A832, **Inverewe Gardens** (daily: April–Oct 9.30am–9pm or dusk; Nov–March 9.30am–4pm; £8; NTS), a verdant oasis of foliage and riotously colourful flower collections, forms a vivid contrast to the wild, heathery crags of the adjoining coast. Taking advantage of the area's famously temperate climate (a consequence of the Gulf Stream, which draws a warm sea current from Mexico to within a stone's throw of these shores), plants from all over the world grow here, flourishing on rich soil brought here as ballast on Irish ships to overlay the previously infertile beach gravel and sea grass. Strolling around the lotus ponds, palm trees and borders ablaze with exotic blooms, it's amazing to think you're at the same latitude as Hudson's Bay. The **visitor centre** (April–Sept daily 9.30am–5pm) houses an informative display on the history of the garden and is the starting point for **guided walks**.

Ullapool

ULLAPOOL (Ⓦwww.ullapool.co.uk), the northwest's principal centre of population, was founded at the height of the herring boom in 1788 by the British Fisheries Society, on a sheltered arm of land jutting into Loch Broom. The grid-plan town is still an important fishing centre, though the **ferry** link to Stornoway on Lewis (see p.1003) ensures that in high season it's swamped with visitors. Though busy, Ullapool remains a hugely appealing place and a good base for exploring the northwest Highlands. Regular **buses** run from here to Inverness and Durness, as well as an early-morning run through to the remote train station at Lairg. **Day-trips** to **Lewis** by ferry and bus can be organized through Caledonian MacBrayne (☎0870/565 0000; £27.95). **Accommodation** is plentiful and Ullapool is an obvious hideaway if the weather is bad, with cosy pubs, a swimming pool and a lively **arts centre**, the Ceilidh Place.

Information and accommodation

The well-run **tourist office** (April–May Mon–Sat 9am–4.30pm; June–Aug Mon–Sat 9am–5pm, Sun 10am–4pm; Oct Mon–Fri 10am–5pm; call ☎01854/612486 for winter opening hours) is on Argyle Street.

Accommodation

The Ceilidh Place West Argyle St ☎01854/612103. Tasteful and popular hotel, with the west coast's best bookshop, a relaxing first-floor lounge, a great bar-restaurant, sea views and a laid-back atmosphere. 7

Dromnan Garve Rd ☎01854/612333, ⓦwww.dromnan.co.uk. Excellent B&B run by welcoming hosts, who serve up a hearty breakfast. Lovely sea views and from the dining area you can walk onto the patio or down to the shore. 4

Point Cottage 22 West Shore St ☎01854/612494, ⓦwww.pointcottage.co.uk. Rustic, very well-equipped B&B at the quieter end of the seafront. Guests can borrow OS maps that have been already marked up with walking routes. 3

SYHA hostel Shore St ☎0870/004 1156, ⓦwww.syha.org.uk. Busy hostel on the front, with Internet access, laundry, and lots of good information about local walks. March–Oct. Dorm beds £14.

West House West Argyle St ☎01854/613126, ⓦwww.scotpackers-hostels.co.uk. Friendly 22-bed hostel; some dorms en suite. Internet access and bike rental available (£12 per day). Dorm beds £15.

The Town

By day, Ullapool's attention focuses on the comings and goings of the ferry, fishing boats and smaller craft, while in the evening, yachts swing on the current, the shops stay open late, and customers from the *Ferry Boat Inn* line the sea wall. During summer, booths advertise trips to the **Summer Isles** – a cluster of uninhabited islets two to three miles offshore – to view seabird colonies, dolphins and porpoises.

The only conventional attraction in town is the award-winning **museum**, in the old parish church on West Argyle Street (April–Oct Mon–Sat 10am–5pm; by prior arrangement in winter; ☎01854/612987; £3), where photographs, audiovisual and touch-screen displays provide an insight into life in a Highland community, including crofting, fishing, local religion and emigration.

Eating, drinking and entertainment

The busy *Seaforth Inn* on Quay Street serves terrific value **meals**, including a scrumptious fish pie – it also hosts regular live music performances. If you've no time to wait, its adjacent chip shop, overlooking the pier, also serves hearty portions of fast food from the sea. Though pricier, the *Ceilidh Place* hotel is another popular destination for lunch, snacks and dinners in a pleasant bistro area. The best **pub** is *Ferry Boat Inn* (or "FBI"), where you can enjoy a pint of real ale at the lochside – midges permitting. **Live Scottish folk music** is a special feature at The Ceilidh Place and often at the *FBI*.

Assynt

If you've come as far as Ullapool it really is worth continuing further north into the ever more dramatic, remote and highly distinctive hills of **Assynt** (ⓦwww.assynt.co.uk), which marks the transition from Wester Ross into Sutherland.

One of the least populated areas in Europe, this is a landscape not of mountain ranges but of extraordinary peaks rising individually from the moorland.

Coigach peninsula

Immediately to the north of Loch Broom and accessible via a slow, winding single-track road that leaves the A835 ten miles north of Ullapool, **Coigach's** (Ⓦwww.coigach.com) main settlement is **ACHILTIBUIE**, an old crofting village scattered across the hillside above a series of white-sand coves and rocks, from where a fleet of small fishing boats carries sheep, and tourists, to the enticing pastures of the **Summer Isles**, lying a little way offshore. For **boat** trips round the isles, including some time ashore on the largest, Tanera Mor, *Hectoria* (Ⓣ01854/622200) usually runs twice a day from the pier (Easter–Oct; £18, 3hr 30min). The village attracts gardening enthusiasts, thanks to the unlikely presence of the **Hydroponicum** (April–Sept daily 11am–4pm; Oct Mon–Fri 11am–4pm; Ⓦwww.thehydroponicum.com; £4.50), a cross between a giant greenhouse and a scientific research station, and, it has to be said, something of an eyesore. Dubbed "The Garden of the Future", all kinds of flowers, fruits and vegetables are grown without using soil in conditions that concentrate the sun's heat while protecting the plants from winter (and summer) chill. You can taste whatever's being harvested in the subtropical setting of the functional *Lilypond Café*, which serves snacks and lunches. Five miles northwest of the Hydroponicum at Altandhu, the **Achiltibuie Smokehouse** (Ⓣ01854/622353; Ⓦwww.summerislesfoods.co.uk; free) is also worth a visit, to see meat, fish and game being cured in the traditional way and to buy some afterwards.

For **accommodation**, the *Summer Isles Hotel* (Ⓣ01854/622282, Ⓔinfo@summerisleshotel.co.uk; Easter–Oct; ❼), just up the road from the Hydroponicum, enjoys a perfect setting with views over the islands. It's also a memorable, if pricey, spot for a seafood lunch or dinner. Of Achiltibuie's several **B&Bs**, *Dornie House* (Ⓣ01854/622271, Ⓔdorniehousebandb@aol.com; Easter–Nov; ❸), halfway to Altandhu, is welcoming and provides huge breakfasts. There's also a beautifully situated twenty-bed SYHA **hostel** (Ⓣ0870/004 1101, Ⓦwww.syha.org.uk; May–Sept; dorms £13.50), three miles southeast of Achiltibuie down the coast at Achininver.

Lochinver and around

The potholed and narrow road north from Achiltibuie through Inverkirkaig is unremittingly spectacular, threading its way through a tumultuous landscape of heaving valleys, moorland and bare rock, past the distinctive sugar-loaf **Suilven** (2398ft). Sixteen miles due north of Ullapool (although more than thirty by road), **LOCHINVER** is one of the busiest fishing harbours in Scotland, from where large trucks head off for the continent. The **tourist office** (April–Oct Mon–Sat 10am–5pm, June–Sept also Sun 10am–4pm), within the excellent **Assynt Visitor Centre**, gives an interesting rundown on the area's geology, wildlife and history and has a CCTV link to a nearby heronry. A handy leaflet, *Walks around Assynt*, is available from the tourist office, depicting thirty-one walks.

The first village worthy of a detour on the road north is **ACHMELVICH**, three miles northwest of Lochinver, where a tiny bay cradles a stunning white-sand beach lapped by startlingly turquoise water. There's a **campsite** and a basic 36-bed SYHA **hostel** (Ⓣ0870/004 1102, Ⓦwww.syha.org.uk; April–Sept; dorms £13.50) just behind the largest beach. However, for total peace and quiet, head to other, equally seductive beaches beyond the headlands.

Kylesku and around

At **KYLESKU**, 33 miles north of Ullapool on the main A894 road, a long, curving road bridge sweeps over the mouth of lochs Glencoul and Glendhu. Here, the congenial *Kylesku Hotel* (Ⓣ01971/502231; March–Oct; ⑤) by the water's edge above the old ferry slipway, has a welcoming **bar** where guests can feast on reasonably priced dishes, including fresh seafood. Statesman Cruises runs entertaining **boat trips** (March–Oct twice daily except Sat; round trip 2hr; £15; Ⓣ01971/502345) from the jetty below the *Kylesku Hotel* to the 650ft **Eas-Coul-Aulin**, Britain's highest waterfall, located at the head of Loch Glencoul; otters, seals, porpoises and minke whales can occasionally be spotted along the way. The boat also makes regular trips out to **Kerracher Gardens** (mid-May to mid-Sept Tues, Thurs & Sun at 1pm; £15), which are only accessible from the sea; this remarkable plot created on a disused croft harnesses the Gulf Stream weather to create a riot of colour and exotic vegetation in the rugged Highland scenery.

The far northwest coast

The Sutherland coastline north of Kylesku is a bridge too far for some, yet for others the stark, elemental beauty of the Highlands is to be found on the **far northwest coast** as nowhere else. Here, the peaks become more widely spaced and settlements smaller and fewer, linked by twisting single-track roads and shoreside footpaths that make excellent hiking trails. Places to stay and eat can be thin on the ground, particularly out of season, but the lack of infrastructure is testimony to the isolation which this corner of Scotland delivers in such sweeping style.

Scourie and Handa Island

Ten miles north of Kylesku, the widely scattered crofting community of **SCOURIE**, on a bluff above the main road, surrounds a beautiful sandy beach. Scourie has some good **accommodation** including the charming *Scourie Lodge* (Ⓣ01971/502248; March–Oct; ⑤), an old three-bedroomed shooting retreat surrounded by trees on the north side of the sandy bay. Visible just offshore to the north of Scourie is **HANDA ISLAND**, a huge chunk of red Torridon sandstone surrounded by sheer cliffs, carpeted with machair and purple-tinged moorland, and teeming with sea birds. A **wildlife reserve** administered by the Scottish Wildlife Trust (Ⓦwww.swt.org.uk), Handa Island supports one of the largest seabird colonies in northwest Europe. It's a real treat for ornithologists, with razorbills and guillemots breeding on its guano-covered cliffs during summer. From late May to mid-July, large numbers of puffins waddle comically over the turf-covered cliff-tops where they dig their burrows. You'll need about three hours to follow the **footpath** around the island. Camping is not allowed. Weather permitting, **boats** (Ⓣ01971/502347) leave for Handa throughout the day (Easter to Sept Mon–Sat 9.30am–2pm outbound; £10) from the tiny cove of **TARBET**, three miles northwest of the main road and accessible by postbus from Scourie.

The north coast

Though a constant stream of sponsored walkers, caravans and tour groups makes it to the dull town of **John O'Groats**, surprisingly few visitors travel the whole length of the Highlands' wild **north coast**. Those that do, however, rarely return disappointed. Pounded by one of the world's most ferocious seaways, Scotland's rugged northern shore is backed by barren mountains in the west, and in the east by lochs and open rolling grasslands. Between its far ends, mile upon mile of crumbling cliffs and sheer rocky headlands shelter bays whose perfect white beaches are nearly always deserted, even in the height of summer – though, somewhat incongruously, they're also home to Scotland's best **surfing** waves.

Durness is a good jumping-off point for nearby Balnakiel beach, one of the area's most beautiful sandy strands, and for rugged **Cape Wrath**, the windswept promontory at Scotland's northwest tip. **Thurso**, the largest town on the north coast, is really only visited by those en route to Orkney. More enticing are the huge seabird colonies clustered in clefts and on remote stacks at **Dunnet Head** and **Duncansby Head**, to the east of Thurso.

Durness and around

Scattered around a string of sheltered sandy coves and grassy cliff-tops, **DURNESS** (Ⓦwww.durness.org) is the most northwesterly village on the British mainland. It straddles the turning point on the main A838 road as it swings east from the inland peat bogs of the interior to the north coast's fertile strip of limestone machair. Durness village sits above its own sandy bay, Sango Sands, while half a mile to the east is **SMOO**, formerly a RAF station. In between Durness and Smoo is the village hall, whose windblown and rather forlorn community garden harbours a memorial commemorating the Beatle **John Lennon**, who used to come to Durness on family holidays as a kid (and revisited the place in the 1960s with Yoko). It's worth pausing at Smoo to see the 200ft-long **Smoo Cave**, a gaping hole in a sheer limestone cliff formed partly by the action of the sea and partly by the small burn that flows through it.

A narrow road winds a mile or so northwest of Durness to **BALNAKIEL Craft Village**. Housed in a grim 1940s military base, it was transformed in the 1960s into a sort of industrial estate for arts and crafts, thanks to the carrot of cheap rents for studio and living quarters. A dozen or so eclectic businesses (generally Mon–Sun 10am–5.30pm) continue to function, including a print-makers and woodcarving studio and a pottery. The Loch Croispol bookshop runs a modest daytime **café** (Ⓣ01971/511777) whilst the nearby *Balnakeil Bistro* (March–Oct; Ⓣ01971/511232) serves reasonably priced lunches and evening meals. At *Cocoa Mountain*, you can watch chocolates and truffles being made before sitting down over a coffee or hot chocolate to sample some (Ⓣ01971/511233).

Practicalities

Public transport to Durness is sparse; the key service is the Dearman Coaches link (May–Sept Mon–Sat 1 daily; also Sun in July & Aug) from Inverness via Ullapool and Lochinver. Postbuses provide a more complicated year-round alternative and meet trains at Lairg; check schedules at the post office or tourist office. The helpful Durness **tourist office** (March–April & Oct Mon–Sat 10am–5pm; May–Sept Mon–Sat 10am–5pm, Sun 10am–4pm; Nov–Feb Mon–Fri, 10am–1.30pm) has a small **visitor centre** that features excellent interpretive panels detailing the area's history, geology, flora and fauna, with insights into the daily life of the community.

In terms of **accommodation**, *Mackays Room and Restaurant*, at the western edge of the village, stands out for its welcoming personal touches and a daily-changing dinner menu (from 7pm) featuring locally sourced seafood, lamb and beef (Ⓣ01971/511202, Ⓦwww.visitmackays.com ❺). The proprietor also runs the clean and popular *Lazy Crofter Bunkhouse* (Ⓣ01971/511202,

Ⓦwww.durnesshostel.com; £12) next door. Alternatively, *Glengolly B&B* in the village has two en-suite rooms in a working croft (Ⓣ01971/511255, Ⓦwww.glengolly.com; ③), and there's also a basic SYHA **hostel** (Ⓣ0870/004 1113, Ⓦwww.syha.org.uk; March–Oct; £12.50), beside the Smoo Cave car park half a mile east of the village. In addition to *Mackays*, the *Seafood Platter* (May–Sept; Ⓣ01971/511215) on the eastern fringe of the village is simple, tasty and moderately priced.

Cape Wrath

An excellent day-trip begins two miles southwest of Durness at **KEOLDALE**, where (tides and MOD permitting) a foot-passenger **ferry** (daily: May, June & Sept 11am & 1.30pm; July & Aug 4 trips between 9.30am and 6.30pm; Ⓣ01971/511376 for ferry; £4.70 return) crosses the spectacular Kyle of Durness estuary to link with a **minibus** (Ⓣ01971/511343; May–Sept; £7.50 return) that runs the eleven miles out to **Cape Wrath**, mainland Britain's most northwesterly point. Note that Garvie Island (An Garbh-eilean) is an air bombing range, and the military regularly close the road to Cape Wrath, so check first with Durness tourist office or the MOD advisory line (Ⓣ0800/833300 or 01971/511242). The headland takes its name not from the stormy seas that crash against it for most of the year, but from the Norse word *hvarf*, meaning "turning place" – a throwback to the days when Viking warships used it as a navigation point during raids on the Scottish coast.

Tongue to Thurso

There's great drama in the landscape between Tongue and Thurso, as the A836 – still single-track for much of the way – wends its way over bleak and often totally uninhabited rocky moorland, intercut with sandy sea lochs. Tiny little **Tongue** is pleasant enough, as is the equally small settlement of **Bettyhill**, to the east, but the real reason to venture this far is to explore the countryside: **Ben Hope** (3040ft), the most northerly Munro, and the fascinating blanket bog of the **Flow Country** even further inland.

Tongue and around

The road takes a wonderfully slow and circuitous route around Loch Eriboll and east over the top of A' Mhoine moor to the pretty crofting township of **TONGUE**. Dominated by the ruins of **Castle Varrich** (Caisteal Bharraich), a medieval stronghold of the Mackays (three-mile return walk), the village is strewn above the east shore of the **Kyle of Tongue**, which you can either cross via a new causeway, or by following the longer and more scenic single-track road around its southern side. When the tide recedes, this shallow estuary becomes a mass of golden sand flats, superb on sunny days, with the sharp profiles of **Ben Hope** (3040ft) and **Ben Loyal** (2509ft) looming like twin sentinels to the south.

The best **accommodation** in Tongue is the nineteen-bedroom *Tongue Hotel* (Ⓣ01847/611206, Ⓦwww.tonguehotel.co.uk; April–Oct; ⑥), the plush, former hunting lodge of the Duke of Sutherland, which serves delicious food, and has a cosy downstairs bar. The SYHA **hostel** (Ⓣ0870/155 3255, Ⓦwww.syha.org.uk; dorm beds £12.50) is right beside the causeway a mile north of the village centre on the Kyle's east shore. Over on the western side of the Kyle, five miles away at **Talmine**, a converted nineteenth-century church with great views towards the Orkney Islands is home to the popular *Cloisters* B&B (Ⓣ01847/601286, Ⓦwww.cloistertal.demon.co.uk; ②). There is also a very basic **campsite** opposite the sandy beach.

Bettyhill and around

Twelve miles east of Tongue, **BETTYHILL** is a major crofting village, set among rocky green hills. The village's splendid, sheltered **Farr beach** forms an unbroken arc of pure white sand between the Naver and Borgie rivers. Even more visually impressive is the River Naver's narrow tidal estuary, to the west of Bettyhill, and **Torrisdale beach**, which ends in a smooth white spit that forms part of the **Invernaver Nature Reserve**.

As you move east from Bettyhill, the north coast changes dramatically as the hills on the horizon recede to be replaced by fields fringed with flagstone walls. It provides an incongruous setting for **Dounreay Nuclear Power Station** (Ⓦwww.ukaea.org.ukDounreay), a surreal collection of chimney stacks and box-like buildings, including the famous golf-ball-shaped DFR (Dounreay Fast Reactor). Established back in 1955, Dounreay pioneered the development of fast reactor technology and was the first reactor in the world to provide mains electricity. The reactors themselves have long since closed, though Dounreay remains by far the biggest employer on the north coast, with decommissioning estimated to last until 2033 and cost £2.9 billion. The helpful **visitor centre** (Easter–Nov daily 10am–4pm; free) details the processes (and, unsurprisingly, the benefits) of nuclear power, and seeks to offer explanations for a range of issues such as the area's "leukaemia cluster" and the radioactive particles that continue to be found on the nearby beaches.

The Flow Country

At a junction six miles before Dounreay, you can head forty miles or so south towards Helmsdale on the A897, through the **Flow Country**, whose name comes from *flói*, an Old Norse word meaning "marshy ground". At the train station at **FORSINARD**, fourteen miles south of Melvich and easily accessible from Thurso, Wick and the south, there is an RSPB **visitor centre** (April–Oct daily 9am–6pm; Ⓣ01641/571225), with CCTV coverage of hen harriers nesting, as well as a **Peatland Centre**, which explains the wonders of peat. To get to grips with the whole concept of blanket bog, take a leaflet and follow the short **Dubh Lochan Trail** that's been laid out over the flagstones, through peat banks to some nearby black lochans.

Thurso

Approached from the isolation of the west, **THURSO** feels like a metropolis. In reality, it's a relatively small service centre visited mostly by people passing through to the adjoining port of **Scrabster** to catch the ferry to Orkney, or by increasing numbers of surfers attracted to the waves on the north coast. Thurso's grid-plan streets boast some rather handsome Victorian architecture in the local, greyish sandstone, though there's nothing really specific to detain you. The Victorian Town Hall on the High Street is due to reopen in the autumn of 2008 as **Caithness Horizons** (Ⓦwww.caithnesshorizons.co.uk), a museum and interactive exhibition space. The exhibition space will include information panels about Dounreay, a café and new tourist office.

The **Scrabster ferry terminal** is a mile or so northwest of town, with regular buses from the train station in the morning, and from Olrig Street in the afternoon. The **tourist office** (April–June, Sept & Oct Mon–Sat 10am–5pm; July & Aug Mon–Sat 9.30am–5.30pm & Sun 10am–4pm) is currently by the riverside. **Accommodation** includes the central, comfortable and friendly *Murray House*, 1 Campbell St (Ⓣ01847/895759, Ⓦwww.murrayhousebb.com; ❹), and *Tigh na Abhainn*, an old house by the river (Ⓣ01847/893443; ❷). The best hostel is *Sandra's*, 24/26 Princes St

(Ⓣ01847/894575, Ⓦwww.sandras-backpackers.co.uk; from £9), a clean and well-run place owned by the popular chippie downstairs; it also offers free use of **bikes** and **Internet** access. By far the best place **to eat** locally is *The Captain's Galley* at the Harbour in Scrabster (Ⓣ01847/894999, Ⓦwww.captainsgalley.co.uk; Tues–Sat) A former ice house and salmon bothy; each day the menu details the boats that day's fish has come from. In Thurso itself, the popular *Le Bistro*, 2 Traill St (Ⓣ01847/893737; Tues–Sat) serves reasonably priced traditional fare, such as Cullen skink (haddock and potato soup). If you're coming to **surf**, want a lesson, need to hire a board (£10 per day) or simply fancy a coffee and home-made cake before hitting the waves, head for Tempest Surf on Riverside Road by Thurso harbour (Ⓣ01847/892500).

Dunnet Head and the Castle of Mey

Thurso doesn't have much of a beach, so if you want to sink your toes into sand, head five miles east along the A836 to **Dunnet Bay**, a vast golden beach backed by huge dunes. The bay is enormously popular with surfers – even in the winter you can usually spot intrepid figures far out in the Pentland Firth's breakers. At the northeast end of the bay, there's a **Ranger Centre** (April, May & Sept, 2–5.30pm; July & Aug 10.30am–5.30pm, closed Sat; free) beside the excellent campsite, where you can pick up information on local history and nature walks.

Despite the publicity that John O'Groats customarily receives, mainland Britain's most northerly point is in fact **Dunnet Head**, north of Dunnet along the B855, which runs for four miles over bleak heather and bog to the tip of the headland, crowned with a Stevenson lighthouse, at 105m above sea-level. On a clear day you can see the whole northern coastline from Cape Wrath to Duncansby Head, and across the treacherous Pentland Firth to Orkney.

Roughly fifteen miles east of Thurso, just off the A836, lies the Queen Mother's former Scottish home and the most northerly castle on the UK mainland, the **Castle of Mey** (daily: May to end July & mid-Aug to end Sept; 10.30am–4pm; Ⓦwww.castleofmey.org.uk; £7.50). It's a modest little place, hidden behind high flagstone walls, with great views north to Orkney, and a herd of the Queen Mother's beloved Aberdeen Angus grazing out front. She used to spend every August here, and unusually for a royal palace, it's remarkably unstuffy inside, the walls hung with works by local amateur artists (and watercolours by Prince Charles). There's a reasonable tearoom at the castle, or try the nearby *Simply Unique* in Mey for traditional home-baking and coffee.

John O'Groats and around

Romantics expecting to find a magical meeting of land and water at **JOHN O'GROATS** (Ⓦwww.visitjohnogroats.com) are invariably disenchanted – sadly it remains an uninspiring tourist trap. The views north to Orkney are fine enough, but the village offers little more than a string of souvenir and craft shops, and cafés thronged with coach parties. The village gets its name from the Dutchman, Jan de Groot, who obtained the ferry contract for the hazardous crossing to Orkney in 1496. The eight-sided house he built for his eight quarrelling sons (so that each one could enter by his own door) is echoed in the octagonal tower of the much-photographed but now vacant *John O'Groats Hotel*.

There are several **boat trips** offered: John O'Groats Ferries (Ⓣ01955/611353, Ⓦwww.jogferry.co.uk) does leisurely afternoon cruises round the seabird colonies and stacks of Duncansby Head or the seal colonies of Stroma (mid-June to Aug daily at 2.30pm; 1hr 30min; £15). North Coast Marine Adventures (Easter–Oct daily; Ⓣ01955/611797, Ⓦwww.northcoast.fsnet.co.uk) has rather

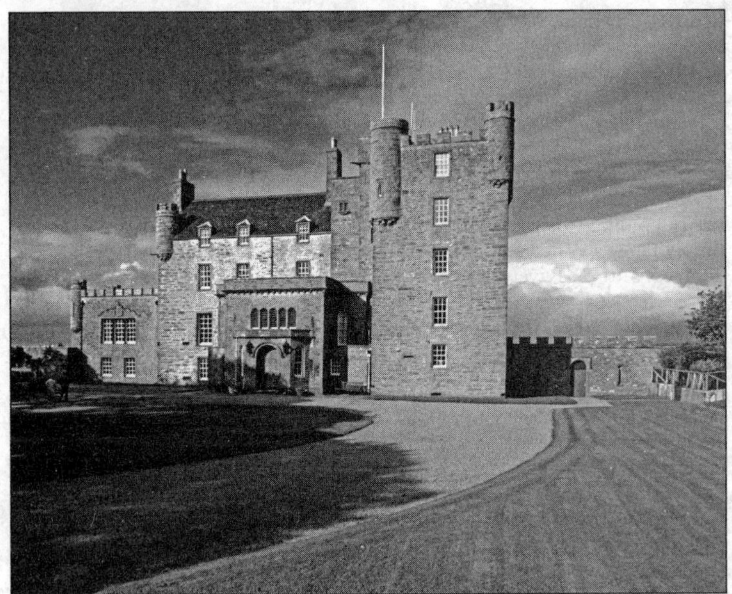

▲Castle of Mey

more energetic 30min trips in a rigid inflatable (£15), and a 1hr scenic wildlife tour (£20).

If you're disappointed by John O'Groats, press on a couple of miles further east to **Duncansby Head**, which, with its lighthouse, dramatic cliffs and well-worn coastal path, is much more stimulating. The birdlife here is prolific, and south of the headland lie some spectacular 200ft cliffs, cut by sheer-sided clefts known locally as *geos*, and several impressive sea-stacks, including a very photogenic triangular one.

The east coast

The **east coast** of the Highlands, between Inverness and Wick, is nowhere near as spectacular as the west, with gently undulating moors, grassland and low cliffs where you might otherwise expect to find sea lochs and mountains. While many visitors speed up the main A9 road through this region in a headlong rush to the Orkneys' prehistoric sites, those who choose to dally will find a wealth of brochs, cairns and standing stones, many in remarkable condition. The area around the Black Isle and the Tain was a Pictish heartland, and has yielded many important finds. Further north, from around the ninth century AD onwards, the **Norse** influence was more keenly felt than in any other part of mainland Britain, and dozens of Scandinavian-sounding names recall the era when this was a Viking kingdom.

The fishing heritage is a recurring theme along this coast, though there are only a handful of working boats scattered around the harbours today; the area therefore remains one of the country's poorest, reliant on relatively thin pickings from sheep farming, fishing and tourism. The one stretch of the east coast that's always been relatively rich, however, is the **Black Isle** just over the Kessock Bridge heading north out of Inverness, whose main village, **Cromarty**, is the region's undisputed highlight, with a crop of elegant mansions and appealing fishermen's cottages clustered near the entrance to the Cromarty Firth. Beyond the well-known golfing resort of **Dornoch**, the ersatz-Loire chateau **Dunrobin Castle** is the main tourist attraction, a monument as much to the iniquities of the Clearances (see p.1014) as to the eccentricities of Victorian taste. **Wick**, the largest town on this section of coast, has an interesting past inevitably entwined with the fishing industry, but is otherwise uninspiring.

The Black Isle and around

Sandwiched between the Cromarty Firth to the north and, to the south, the Moray and Beauly firths which separate it from Inverness, the **Black Isle** is not an island at all, but a fertile peninsula whose rolling hills, prosperous farms and stands of deciduous woodland make it more reminiscent of Dorset or Sussex than the Highlands. It probably gained its name because of its mild climate: there's rarely frost, which leaves the fields "black" all winter; another explanation is that the name derives from the Gaelic word for black, *dubh* – a possible corruption of St Duthus. On the south side of the Black Isle, near Fortrose, **Chanonry Point** juts into a narrow channel in the Moray Firth and is an excellent place to look for **dolphins** (see p.983).

Cromarty

An ancient legend recalls that the twin headlands flanking the entrance to the **Cromarty Firth**, known as The Sutors (from the Gaelic word for shoemaker), were once a pair of giant cobblers who used to protect the Black Isle from pirates. Nowadays, however, the only giants in the area are the colossal oil rigs marooned in the estuary off Nigg and Invergordon like metal monsters marching out to sea. They form a surreal counterpoint to the web of tiny streets and charming workers' cottages of **CROMARTY**. The Black Isle's main settlement, Cromarty was an ancient ferry-crossing point on the pilgrimage trail to St Duthus's shrine in Tain, but lost much of its trade during the nineteenth century to places served by the railway; a branch line to the town was begun but never completed. Cromarty became a prominent port in 1772 when an entrepreneurial local landlord, George Ross, founded a hemp mill here, fuelling a period of prosperity during which Cromarty acquired some of Scotland's finest Georgian houses: these, together with the terraced fishers' cottages of the nineteenth-century herring boom, have left the town with a wonderfully well-preserved concentration of Scottish domestic architecture.

To get a sense of Cromarty's past, wander through the town's pretty streets to the **museum** housed in the old **Courthouse** on Church Street (daily: April–Oct 10am–5pm; £5), which tells the history of the town using audiovisuals and animated figures. Dolphin- and other wildlife-spotting trips are offered locally by Ecoventures (Ⓣ01381/600323, Ⓦwww.ecoventures.co.uk; £20; 2hr), who blast out through the Soutars to the Moray Firth in a powerful RIB. The tiny two-car Nigg–Cromarty **ferry** (June–Sept daily 8am–6.15pm; until 7.15pm July-Aug; £2.50) is Scotland's smallest. Embark from the jetty near the lighthouse.

For **B&B**, try the modest but friendly traditional abode in the Little Vennel area, run by Mrs Watson (Ⓣ01381/600430; ❷) or *Gisborne B&B* (Ⓣ01381/600376, ❸) on Marine Terrace, which was once the cottage hospital. For something **to eat**, there are few more down-to-earth restaurants in the Highlands than *Sutor Creek* at 21 Bank St (Ⓣ01381/600855, Ⓦwww.sutorcreek.co.uk; Wed–Sun 11am–late). An intimate place, it serves organic wines, delicious seafood and fresh pizza cooked in a wood-fired oven – the imaginative toppings (and the daily blackboard specials) are local and seasonal rather than conventionally Italian. In the nearby *Cromarty Bakery*, you'll find tasty fresh breads such as spinach and walnut, and whisky cake.

The Dornoch Firth and around

North of the Cromarty Firth, the hammer-shaped **Fearn peninsula** can still be approached from the south by the ancient ferry-crossing from Cromarty to Nigg, though to the north the link is a causeway over the **Dornoch Firth**, the inlet which marks the northern boundary of the peninsula. On the southern edge of the Dornoch Firth the A9 bypasses the quiet town of **TAIN**, an attractive, old-fashioned small town of grand whisky-coloured sandstone buildings that was the birthplace of **St Duthus**, an eleventh-century missionary who inspired great devotion in the Middle Ages. Tain's main attraction is the **Glenmorangie whisky distillery** where the highly rated malt is produced (Ⓣ01862/892477; shop Mon–Fri 9am–5pm, April–Oct also Sat 10am–4pm, June–Aug also Sun noon–4pm; tours Mon–Fri 10.30am–3.30pm, Sat 10.30am–2.30pm, Sun 12.30–2.30pm; £2.50 including discount voucher); it lies beside the A9 on the north side of town. Booking is recommended for the tours.

Carbisdale Castle

Towering high above the River Shin, around twenty miles northwest of Tain, the daunting neo-Gothic profile of **Carbisdale Castle** overlooks the Kyle of Sutherland. The castle was erected between 1906 and 1917 for the dowager Duchess of Sutherland, following a protracted family feud. Designed in three distinct styles (to give the impression it was added to over a long period of time), Carbisdale was eventually acquired by a Norwegian shipping magnate in 1933, and finally gifted, along with its entire contents and estate, to the Scottish Youth Hostels Association, which has turned it into what must be one of the most opulent **hostels** in the world, full of white Italian marble sculptures, huge gilt-framed portraits, sweeping staircases and magnificent drawing rooms alongside standard facilities such as self-catering kitchens, games and TV rooms and thirty dorms, including some four-bed family rooms (Ⓣ0870/004 1109, Ⓦwww.carbisdale.org; March–Oct; £16). You can tuck into a hearty three-course dinner at the hostel's restaurant before wandering the supposedly haunted corridors in search of ghosts. Bike rental is available from the hostel for £12 per day, allowing you to take advantage of the several miles of **mountain-biking trails** in the nearby Balblair and Carbisdale woods. The best way to get here by public transport is to take a **train from Inverness** to nearby Culrain station, which lies within half a mile of the castle. Citylink buses (minimum 4 daily) stop in Tain, from where Macleod's Coaches (Mon–Sat 3 daily; 20min; Ⓣ01408/641354) go as far as **Ardgay**, three miles from Carbisdale Castle.

Dornoch

DORNOCH, a genteel and appealing town eight miles north of Tain, lies on a flattish headland overlooking the **Dornoch Firth**. It's something of a middle-class holiday resort, with solid Edwardian hotels, trees and flowers in profusion, and miles of sandy beaches giving good views across the estuary to the Fearn peninsula. The town is renowned for its championship **golf course**, Scotland's most northerly first-class course. Nearby Skibo Castle was made famous as the scene of the marriage of pop mogul Madonna to Guy Ritchie; she also had her son baptized in Dornoch **cathedral**.

The **tourist information** office (☎01862/810594; Easter to end Sept Mon–Fri 9am–5pm; June–Sept also Sat 9.30am–5pm; July & Aug also Sun 10am–4pm) is located in the sheriff courthouse right next to the *Dornoch Castle Hotel*, which in turn is in the Bishop's Palace on the Square. The *Castle Hotel* (☎01862/810216, Ⓦwww.dornochcastlehotel.com; ⑦) has a decent **restaurant** and a cosy old-fashioned bar with a roaring, 11-foot-wide log fire. The *Caravan Park* (☎01862/810423, Ⓦwww.dornochcaravans.co.uk; April–Oct) is attractively set between the manicured golf course and the uncombed vegetation of the sand dunes which fringe the beach; it also offers **camping**, although the site is caravan-heavy in July and August.

North to Wick

North of Dornoch, the A9 hugs the coastline for most of the sixty or so miles to **Wick**, the principal settlement in the far north of the mainland. Perhaps the most important landmark in the whole stretch is the **Sutherland Monument** near Golspie, erected in memory of the first Duke of Sutherland, the landowner who oversaw the eviction of thousands of his tenants in a process known as the Clearances. The bitter memory of those times resonates through most of the small towns and villages on this stretch, including **Badbea**, the gold-prospecting village of **Helmsdale**, **Dunbeath** and **Lybster**.

Golspie and Dunrobin Castle

Ten miles north of Dornoch on the A9 lies the straggling red-sandstone town of **GOLSPIE**, whose status as an administrative centre does little to relieve its dullness. It is, however, the jumping-off point for some brilliant **mountain biking**: the fabulous Highland Wildcat Trails (Ⓦwww.highlandwildcat.com) are within the forested hills just half a mile to the west. The easy to severe (colour-coded) trails include a huge descent from the summit of Ben Bhraggie to sea-level and a ride past the **monument** to the Duke of Sutherland.

Mountain-bikers aside, the main reason to stop here is to look around **Dunrobin Castle** (April, May, Sept & early Oct Mon–Sat 10.30am–4.30pm, Sun noon–4.30pm; June–Aug daily 10.30am–5.30pm; £7), overlooking the sea a mile north of town. This fairy-tale confection of turrets and pointed roofs – modelled by the architect Sir Charles Barry (designer of the Houses of Parliament) on a Loire chateau – is the seat of the infamous Sutherland family, at one time Europe's biggest landowners, with a staggering 1.3 million acres, and the principal driving force behind the Clearances in this area. The castle is on a correspondingly vast scale, boasting 189 furnished rooms, of which the tour takes in only seventeen. Staring up at the pile from the midst of its elaborate **formal gardens**, it's worth remembering that such extravagance was paid for by uprooting literally thousands of crofters from the surrounding glens.

Sutherland Monument

Immediately behind Golspie, you can't miss the 100ft **monument** to the first Duke of Sutherland, which peers proprietorially down from the summit of the 1293ft **Beinn a'Bhragaidh** (Ben Bhraggie). An inscription cut into its base recalls that the statue was erected in 1834 by "a mourning and grateful tenantry [to] a judicious, kind and liberal landlord [who would] open his hands to the distress of the widow, the sick and the traveller". Unsurprisingly, there's no reference to the fact that the duke, widely regarded as Scotland's own Josef Stalin, forcibly evicted 15,000 crofters from his million-acre estate. It's worth the stiff **climb** to the top of the hill (round trip 1hr 30min) for the wonderful views south along the coast past Dornoch to the Moray Firth and west towards Lairg and Loch Shin. The path is steep and strenuous in places, however, and there's no view until you're out of the trees, about twenty minutes from the top. Head up Fountain Road about halfway along Golspie's main street; after crossing the railway line and passing through Rhives farm steading, follow the Beinn a'Bhragaidh footpath (BBFP) signs along the path into the woods.

Helmsdale

Eleven scenic miles north along the A9 from Golspie, **HELMSDALE** is an old herring port, founded in the nineteenth century to house the evicted inhabitants of Strath Kildonan, which lies behind it. The Strath was the unlikely location of a gold rush in the 1860s, and a few determined prospectors still pan the Kildonan Burn. The full story of the area's gold hunters is told in the **Timespan Heritage Centre**, beside the river (Easter–Oct Mon–Sat 10am–5pm, Sun noon–5pm; £4), along with tales of Viking raids, witch-burning, Clearances and fishing. The centre also has an art gallery, café and geology garden.

Just north of Helmsdale, the A9 begins its long haul up the **Ord of Caithness**. Once over the pass, the landscape changes dramatically as heather-clad moors give way to miles of treeless green grazing lands, peppered with derelict crofts and latticed by long dry-stone walls. As you come over the pass, look out for

The Highland Clearances

Once the clan chiefs had been forbidden their own armies after the defeat at Culloden, they had no need of the large tenantry that had previously been a vital military asset – and yet the second half of the eighteenth century saw the Highland population double after the introduction of the easy-to-grow and nutritious potato. The clan chiefs adopted different policies to deal with the new situation: some encouraged emigration, and as many as six thousand Highlanders left for the Americas between 1800 and 1803 alone. Other landowners developed alternative forms of employment for their tenants, mainly fishing and the gathering of kelp, used to manufacture soap, glass and explosives. Other landowners developed sheep runs on the Highland pastures, introducing hardy breeds like the black-faced Linton and the Cheviot. But extensive sheep farming proved incompatible with a high peasant population, and many landowners decided to clear their estates of tenants, some of whom were forcibly moved to tiny plots of marginal land, where they were to farm as crofters.

The pace of these **Highland Clearances** accelerated after the end of the Napoleonic Wars in 1815, when the market price for kelp, fish and cattle declined, leaving sheep as the only profitable Highland product. As the dispossessed Highlanders scratched a living from the acid soils of some tiny croft, they learnt through bitter experience the limitations of the clan. Famine followed, forcing large-scale emigration and leaving huge uninhabited areas found in the region today. The crofters eked out a precarious existence, but they hung on throughout the nineteenth century, often by taking seasonal employment away from home.

In the 1880s, however, a sharp downturn in agricultural prices made it difficult for many crofters to pay their rent. This time, inspired by the example of the Irish Land League, they resisted eviction, forming the **Highland Land Reform Association** and the **Crofters' Party**. In 1886, in response to the social unrest, Gladstone's Liberal government passed the **Crofters' Holdings Act**, which conceded three of the crofters' demands: security of tenure, fair rents to be decided independently, and the right to pass on crofts by inheritance. But Gladstone did not attempt to increase the amount of land available for crofting and shortage of land remained a major problem until the **Land Settlement Act** of 1919 made provision for the creation of new crofts. Nevertheless, the population of the Highlands continued to decline during the twentieth century, with many of the region's young people finding city life more appealing.

signs to the ruined village of **Badbea**, reached via a ten-minute walk from the car park at the side of the A9. Built by tenants cleared from nearby Ousdale, the settlement now lies deserted, although its ruined hovels show what hardship the crofters had to endure: the cottages stood so near the windy cliff edge that children had to be tethered to prevent them from being blown into the sea.

Lybster

Nineteen miles north of the Ord of Caithness, the planned village of **LYBSTER** (pronounced "libe-ster") was established at the height of the nineteenth-century herring boom, when 200-odd boats worked out of its harbour; now there are just one or two. The **Water Lines** heritage centre by the harbour (May–mid-Oct daily 11am–5pm; £2.50) is an attractive modern display about the "silver darlings" and the fishermen that pursued them; there's a snug café downstairs. There's not much else to see here apart from the harbour area: the upper town is a grim collection of grey pebble-dashed bungalows centred on a broad main street.

Wick

Originally a Viking settlement named *Vik* (meaning "bay"), **WICK** has been a royal burgh since 1589. It's actually two towns: Wick proper, and **Pultneytown**, immediately south across the river, a messy, rather run-down community planned by Thomas Telford in 1806 to encourage evicted crofters to take up fishing. Wick's heyday was in the mid-nineteenth century, when it was the busiest herring port in Europe, with a fleet of over 1100 boats, exporting tons of fish to Russia, Scandinavia and the West Indian slave plantations. Though redevelopment of the harbour is underway, including the installation of pontoons and facilities for yachts, the town still possesses a down-at-heel atmosphere. If you're here for a few hours, the area around the harbour in Pultneytown, lined with rows of fishermen's cottages, is most worth a wander, with acres of largely derelict net-mending sheds, stores and cooperages around the harbour giving some idea of the former scale of the fishing trade. The town's story is told in the **Wick Heritage Centre** in Bank Row, Pultneytown (Easter–Oct Mon–Sat 10am–5pm; £3), and the only other visitor attraction is the fairly simple **Pulteney Distillery** (Mon–Fri 10am–1pm & 2–4pm; tours at 11am & 2pm or by arrangement ⓣ01955/602371; £4) on nearby Huddart Street, a few blocks back from the sea.

The best of the **hotels** is *Mackay's*, on the south side of the river in the town centre (ⓣ01955/602323, ⓦwww.mackayshotel.co.uk; ❻), while reasonable **B&B** options include *Quayside*, 25 Harbour Quay (ⓣ01955/603229, ⓦwww.quaysidewick.co.uk; ❸), and seventeenth-century *Bilbster House* (ⓣ01955/621212, ⓦwww.accommodationbilbster.com; April–Oct, in winter by prior arrangement; ❷), a lovely manor house five miles towards Thurso.

Good **eating** options don't abound, though the moderately priced *Bord de l'Eau* (ⓣ01955/604400; closed Mon) on Market Street, which runs along the north side of the river, offers a reasonable menu of classic French standards.

Travel details

Buses

For information on all local and national bus services, contact Traveline ⓣ0870/608 2608 (daily 7am–10pm), ⓦwww.travelinescotland.com.

Aviemore to: Cairngorm ski area (hourly; 30min); Edinburgh (5 daily; 2hr 30min–3hr 30min); Glasgow (7 daily; 3hr 30min); Grantown-on-Spey

(Mon–Sat twice hourly; 35min); Inverness (Mon–Sat 6 daily, 5 on Sun; 45min).
Fort William to: Acharacle (Mon–Sat 1–2 daily; 1hr 30min); Drumnadrochit (8 daily; 1hr 30min); Edinburgh (4 daily; 4hr); Fort Augustus (5 daily; 1hr); Glasgow (4 daily; 3hr); Inverness (5 daily; 2hr 15min); Kilchoan (1–2 daily on request only from Acharacle; 3hr 35); Kyle of Lochalsh (3 daily; 4hr 20min–5hr); Mallaig (Mon–Fri 3 daily; 1hr 20min); Oban (Mon–Sat 4 daily; 1hr 30min); Portree, Skye (2 daily; 3hr).
Gairloch to: Inverness (Mon–Sat 1 daily; also ScotBus 1 daily Mon–Sat, June–Sept only; 2hr 45min); Ullapool (1 daily Mon, Wed, Thu & Sat). To Redpoint and Melvaig only Dial-a-bus service ⓣ01445/712255.
Inverness to: Aberdeen (hourly; 3hr 40min); Aviemore (6 Mon–Sat, 5 Sun; 45min); Drumnadrochit (8 daily; 25min); Durness (Mon–Sat 1 daily; 2hr 40min; also bike bus, May to end Sept Mon–Sat 1 daily, also July–Aug Sun 1 daily); Fort Augustus (5 daily; 1hr); Fort William (6 daily; 2hr); Glasgow (6 daily direct; 3hr 35min–4hr 25min); Kyle of Lochalsh (3 daily; 2hr 10min); Nairn (hourly; 50min); Perth (10 daily; 2hr 35min); Portree (3 daily; 3hr); Thurso (Mon–Sat 5 daily, Sun 2 daily; 3hr 30min); Ullapool (2 Mon, Tues, Thurs & Sat; 3 Wed & Fri; 2hr 25min); Wick (Mon–Sat 3 daily, Sun 2 daily; 3hr).
Kyle of Lochalsh to: Fort William (3 daily; 1hr 50min); Glasgow (3 daily; 5hr); Inverness (3 daily; 2hr).
Lochinver to: Inverness (May to end Sept 1 daily; plus July–Aug Sun 1 daily, 3hr 10min); Ullapool (Mon–Sat 2 daily,1hr).
Thurso to: Inverness (4–5 daily; 3hr 30min); John O' Groats (Mon–Fri 4 daily, Sat 3 daily; 1hr); Wick (Mon–Sun 4 daily; 35min).
Ullapool to: Durness (May to end Sept Mon–Sat 1 daily; also July–Aug Sun 1 daily; 3hr); Inverness (Mon–Sat 2 daily; 1hr 30min).
Wick to: John O' Groats (4 daily Mon–Sat; 50min).

Trains

For information on all local and national rail services, contact National Rail Enquiries ⓣ08457/484950, ⓦwww.nationalrail.co.uk or ⓦwww.firstscotrail.com.
Aviemore to: Edinburgh (Mon–Sat 9 daily, 5 on Sun; 2hr 30min); Glasgow (9 daily, 5 on Sun; 2hr 30min); Inverness (Mon–Sat 9 daily, 5 on Sun; 1hr).
Fort William to: Arisaig (Mon–Sat 3–4 daily, Sun 1–2 daily; 1hr 10min); Crianlarich (Mon–Sat 5 daily, 2 on Sun; 1hr 50min); Glasgow (Mon–Sat 4 daily, 2 on Sun; 3hr 45min); Glenfinnan (Mon–Sat 3–4 daily, Sun 2–4 daily; 35min); London (Sun–Fri 1 nightly; 12hr); Mallaig (Mon–Sat 3–4 daily, Sun 2–4 daily; 1hr 25min).
Inverness to: Aberdeen (Mon–Sat 10 daily; 5 on Sun; 2hr 15min); Aviemore (Mon–Sat 9 daily, 5 on Sun; 40min); Edinburgh (Mon–Sat 5 daily, 3 on Sun; 3hr 30min); Glasgow (Mon–Sat 3 daily; 3 on Sun; 3hr 20min); Kyle of Lochalsh (Mon–Sat 2–3 daily, 2 on Sun; 3hrs); London (Mon–Fri & Sun 1 nightly; 11hr); Thurso (Mon–Sat 2 daily, 1 on Sun; 3hr 25min); Wick (Mon–Sat 2 daily, 1 on Sun; 3hr 45min).
Kyle of Lochalsh to: Dingwall (Mon–Sat 3–4 daily, Sun 1–2 daily; 2hr); Inverness (Mon–Sat 3–4 daily, Sun 1–2 daily; 2hr 40min); Plockton (Mon–Sat 3–4 daily, Sun 1–2 daily; 15min).
Thurso to: Dingwall (Mon–Sat 4 daily, Sun 2 daily; 3hr); Inverness (Mon–Sat 4 daily, Sun 2 daily; 3hr 20min); Lairg (Mon–Sat 4 daily, Sun 2 daily; 1hr 50min); Wick (Mon–Sat 3 daily, Sun 2 daily; 35min).
Wick to: Dingwall (Mon–Sat 4 daily, Sun 2 daily; 3hr 30min); Inverness (Mon–Sat 4 daily, Sun 2 daily; 4hr); Lairg (Mon–Sat 4 daily, Sun 2 daily; 2hr 20min).

Ferries

To Lewis: Ullapool–Stornoway (Mon–Sat 2 daily; 2hr 45min).
To Mull: Kilchoan–Tobermory (Mon–Sat 7 daily; also May–Aug Sun 5 daily; 35min); Lochaline–Fishnish (Mon–Sat every 50min, Sun hourly; 15min).
To Orkney: Gill's Bay–St Margaret's Hope (3 daily; 45min); John O'Groats–Burwick (passengers only; 2–4 daily; 40min); Scrabster–Stromness (2–3 daily; 90min).
To Skye: Glenelg–Kylerhea (every 15–30min; 15min); Mallaig–Armadale (Mon–Sat 8 daily; also mid-May to mid-Sept Sun at least 4 daily; 30min).
Mallaig to the Small Isles: Eigg (Mon, Thurs, Sat 1 daily; 1hr 15min); Rùm (Mon, Wed, Fri, Sat 1 daily, 1hr 20min); Muck (Tues, Thurs, Fri, Sat 1 daily; 2hr 5min); Canna (Mon, Wed, Fri and Sat 1 daily; 2hr 30min).
To Nigg from Cromarty: May–Oct, daily from 8am and every 30min until 6pm.

Flights

Inverness to: Edinburgh (Mon–Fri 2 daily, 1 Sat; 45min); Kirkwall (Mon–Fri 2 daily, 1 Sat & Sun; 45min); London (Gatwick 4 daily Mon–Fri; 3 Sat & Sun; Heathrow 1 daily; Luton Mon–Fri 1 daily; 2 daily Sat & Sun; 1hr 30min); Shetland (Mon–Fri 2 daily; 1 daily Sat & Sun; 1hr 40min); Stornoway (Mon–Fri 4 daily, Sat 2 daily, Sun 1 daily; 40min).
Wick to: Edinburgh (Mon–Fri 1 daily; 1hr 10min); Aberdeen (Mon–Fri 4 daily; 35min).

25

Orkney and Shetland

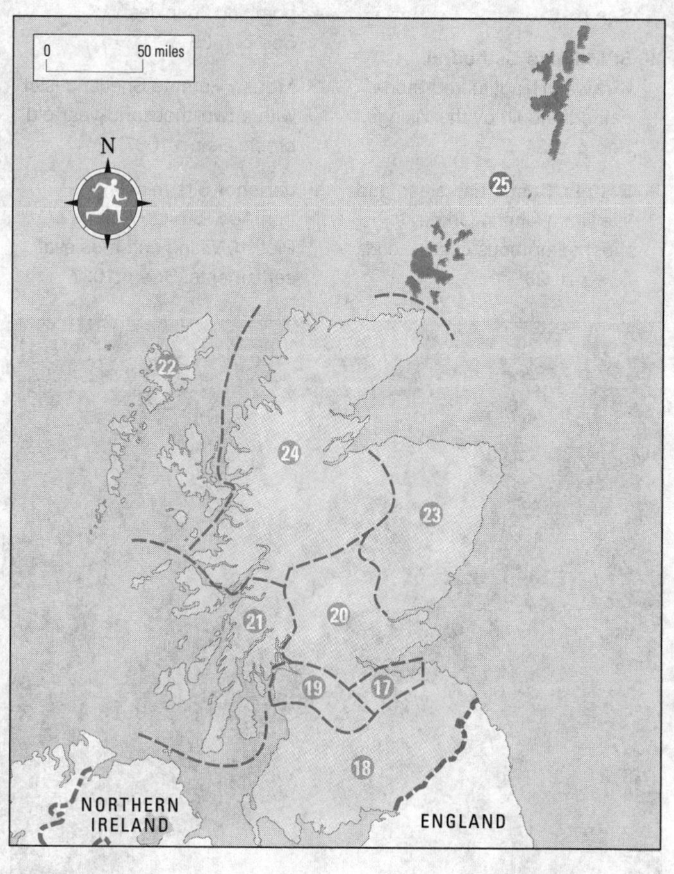

CHAPTER 25

Highlights

* **Maes Howe** Orkney's, and Europe's, finest Neolithic chambered tomb. See p.1023
* **Skara Brae** Neolithic village giving a fascinating insight into prehistoric life. See p.1023
* **St Magnus Cathedral, Kirkwall** Beautiful red-stone cathedral built by the Vikings. See p.1024
* **Balfour Castle** Eat, sleep and live like a king in Orkney's most sumptuous castle hotel. See p.1028
* **Westray** Thriving Orkney island with seabird colonies, sandy beaches and a ruined castle. See p.1029
* **Isle of Noss** Guaranteed seals, puffins and dive-bombing "bonxies". See p.1036
* **Mousa** Remote Shetland islet with a two-thousand-year-old broch. See p.1037
* **Jarlshof** Site mingling Iron Age, Bronze Age, Pictish, Viking and medieval settlements. See p.1037

▲ Isle of Noss puffin

25

Orkney and Shetland

Reaching up towards the Arctic Circle, and totally exposed to turbulent Atlantic weather systems, the **Orkney** and **Shetland** islands gather neatly into two distinct and very different clusters. The seventy or so **Orkney Islands** lie just a short step north of the Scottish mainland. With the major exception of **Hoy**, which is high and rugged, these islands are mostly low-lying, gently sloping and richly fertile, and for centuries have provided a reasonably secure living for their inhabitants from farming and, to a much lesser extent, fishing. There's a peaceful continuity to Orcadian life reflected not only in the well-preserved treasury of Stone Age settlements, such as **Skara Brae**, and standing stones, most notably the **Stones of Stenness**, but also in the rather conservative nature of society here today.

Sixty miles further north, the **Shetland Islands** are in nearly all respects a complete contrast. Ice-sculpted sea inlets cut deep into the land that rises straight out of the water to rugged, heather-coated hills. With little fertile ground, Shetlanders have traditionally been crofters rather than farmers, often looking to the sea for an uncertain living in fishing and whaling or the naval and merchant services. The Norse heritage is clear in every road sign and there are many well-preserved prehistoric sites, such as **Mousa Broch** and **Jarlshof**.

It's impossible to underestimate the influence of the **weather** up here. More often than not, it will be windy and rainy, though you can have all four seasons in one day. The wind-chill factor is not to be taken lightly, and there's frequently a dampness or drizzle in the air, even when it's not actually raining. Even in late spring and summer, when there can be dry spells and long days with lots of sunshine, you still need to come prepared for wind, rain and, most frustrating of all, the occasional sea fog. The one good thing is that midges are less of a problem, except on Hoy.

Orkney

Just a short step from John O'Groats, **Orkney** is a unique and fiercely independent archipelago. For an Orcadian, the "Mainland" invariably means the largest island in Orkney rather than the rest of Scotland, and throughout their history they've been linked to lands much further afield, principally Scandinavia.

Orkney Mainland has two chief settlements: the old port of **Stromness**, an attractive old fishing town on the far southwestern shore, and the central capital of **Kirkwall**, which stands at the dividing point between East and West Mainland. The whole of Mainland is relatively heavily populated and farmed

Getting to and around Orkney

Orkney is connected to the Scottish mainland by several **ferry** routes. Pentland Ferries (Ⓣ0800/6888998, Ⓦwww.pentlandferries.co.uk) operates the shortest car ferry crossing, from **Gill's Bay**, on the north coast near John O'Groats (and linked by bus to Wick and Thurso) to **St Margaret's Hope** on South Ronaldsay (3–4 daily; 1hr). Services to **Stromness** from **Scrabster** (2–3 daily; 1hr 30min), which is connected to nearby Thurso by a shuttle bus, are run by NorthLink Ferries (Ⓣ0845/600 0449, Ⓦwww.northlinkferries.co.uk), who also operate ferries to **Kirkwall** from **Aberdeen** (4 weekly; 6hr) and from **Lerwick** in Shetland (3 weekly; 5hr 30min). John O'Groats Ferries (Ⓣ01955/611353, Ⓦwww.jogferry.co.uk) runs a passenger ferry from **John O'Groats** to **Burwick** on South Ronaldsay (May & Sept 2 daily; June–Aug 4 daily; 40min), its departure timed to connect with the arrival of the Orkney Bus from Inverness; there's also a free taxi service from Thurso train station. Direct **flights** serve Kirkwall airport from Sumburgh in Shetland, Wick, Inverness and Aberdeen, and there are good connections from Edinburgh, Glasgow, Manchester, Birmingham and London. All can be booked through British Airways (Ⓣ0870/850 9850, Ⓦwww.ba.com).

Bus services on the Orkney Mainland are infrequent, and skeletal on Sundays, making a Day Rover (£6) or Three-Day Rover (£15) of limited value (see Ⓦwww.rapsons.co.uk for more). On the smaller islands, a minibus usually meets the ferry and will take you to your destination; in addition, folk are very friendly and it's easy enough to hitch a lift. **Cycling** is not a bad option, though the wind can make it hard going. Instead of bringing your car, **renting a car** locally will save you the steep ferry fares. If time is limited, you may want to consider one of the informative bus or minibus **tours** on offer: Wildabout Orkney Tours (Ⓣ01856/851011, Ⓦwww.wildaboutorkney.com; March–Oct) has good-value tours of the chief sights on the Mainland and Hoy.

Getting to the other islands from the Mainland isn't difficult, though it is expensive: Orkney Ferries (Ⓣ01856/872044, Ⓦwww.orkneyferries.co.uk) operates daily **ferries** to all the islands except North Ronaldsay, which has a weekly boat on Fridays. If you're taking a car on any of the ferries, it's essential to book your ticket well in advance. There are also **flights** from Kirkwall to some of the islands, operated by Loganair (Ⓣ01856/872494, Ⓦwww.loganair.co.uk), using a tiny eight-seater plane. Loganair also offers a number of discounted packages in the summer, plus special £12 fares on return flights to North Ronaldsay or Papa Westray if you stay over.

throughout, and is joined by causeways to a string of southern islands, the largest of which is **South Ronaldsay**. The island of **Hoy**, the second largest in the archipelago, to the south of Mainland, presents a superbly dramatic landscape, with some of the highest sea cliffs in the country. Hoy, however, is atypical: Orkney's smaller, much quieter **northern islands** are low-lying, elemental but fertile outcrops of rock and sand, scattered across the ocean.

Small communities began to settle in the islands around 4000 BC, and the village at **Skara Brae** on the Mainland is one of the best-preserved Stone Age settlements in Europe, and just one of numerous archeological sites in Orkney. From the ninth century, the islands became a **Norse earldom** and although the last of the Norse earls was killed in 1231, the Vikings had a lasting cultural and linguistic impact on the islands. With the end of Norse rule, the islands became the preserve of **Scottish earls**, who exploited and abused the islanders, although a steady increase in sea trade did offer some chance of escape. The **Hudson Bay Company** recruited hundreds of Orcadians to work in the Canadian fur trade and the islands remained an important staging post in the **whaling industry** and the herring boom until the early twentieth century. Later, the choice of **Scapa Flow**, Orkney's natural harbour, as the Royal Navy's main base brought plenty of money and activity during both world wars, and left the seabed scattered with wrecks – which these days make for wonderful diving opportunities. Since the mid-1970s the large **oil terminal** on the island of Flotta, combined with EU development grants, have brought surprise windfalls, stemming the exodus of young people.

Stromness

STROMNESS has to be one of the most enchanting ports at which to arrive by boat, its picturesque waterfront a procession of tiny sandstone jetties and slate roofs. Stromness is well worth a day's exploration, or for use as a base in preference to Kirkwall. Its natural sheltered harbour must have been used in Viking times, but the town itself only really took off in the eighteenth century when the Hudson Bay Company made Stromness its main base from which to make the long journey across the North Atlantic: crews from Stromness were also hired for herring and whaling expeditions – and, of course, press-ganged into the Royal Navy. Today Stromness remains an important harbour town and is the focus of the popular four-day **Orkney Folk Festival** (Ⓦwww.orkneyfolkfestival.com), held in May.

The Town

The old town of Stromness hugs the shoreline, its one and only street a narrow, winding affair paved with great flagstones and fed by a tight network of alleyways or closes. The central section, which begins at the *Stromness Hotel*, is known as **Victoria Street**, though it has several other names as it heads southwards. On the east side the houses are gable-end-on to the waterfront, and originally each would have had its own pier, from which merchants would trade with passing ships.

The first of the old jetties, south of the modern harbour, houses the **Pier Arts Centre** (Mon–Sat 10.30am–5pm; May–Sept also Sun 1–5pm; free). The art gallery hosts temporary exhibitions, often featuring works by local artists, as well as having a remarkable permanent display of twentieth-century British art. Ten minutes' walk further down the main street is the **Stromness Museum** (May–Sept daily 10am–5pm; Oct–April Mon–Sat 11am–3.30pm; £3), which boasts an early inflatable boat, the Halkett cloth boat. There are also numerous salty artefacts gathered from shipwrecks, including some barnacle-encrusted crockery from the German High Seas Fleet that sank in Scapa Flow.

Practicalities

Arriving by ferry, you disembark at the modern ferry terminal, which also houses the **tourist office** (April–Oct Mon–Fri 8am–5pm, Sat 9am–4pm, Sun 10am–3pm; Nov–March Mon–Fri 9am–5pm; Ⓣ01856/850716). As far as **hotels** go, the venerable Victorian *Stromness Hotel* (Ⓣ01856/850298, Ⓦwww.stromnesshotel.com; ❻) – the town's first – is probably your best bet. For something with more character, head for *Miller's House* and *Harbourside Guesthouse*, at 7 & 13 John St (Ⓣ01856/851969, Ⓦwww.orkneyisles.co.uk/millershouse; ❸), in the town's oldest property. *Brown's* is a laid-back family-run **hostel** at 45–47 Victoria St (Ⓣ01856/850661, Ⓦwww.brownshostel.co.uk; £12); there's also a well-equipped **campsite** (Ⓣ01856/873535; May to mid-Sept) in a superb (but exposed) setting a mile south of the ferry terminal at Point of Ness.

Stromness has only a few **places to eat**, starting with the daytime-only *Julia's Café and Bistro*, opposite the ferry terminal, with a sunny conservatory, tasty meals and delicious cakes. The moderately expensive, evening-only *Hamnavoe*, at 35 Graham Place (Ⓣ01856/850606; April–Sept; closed Mon), offers the town's most ambitious cooking. For **takeaways**, head for the *Chip Shop* on the

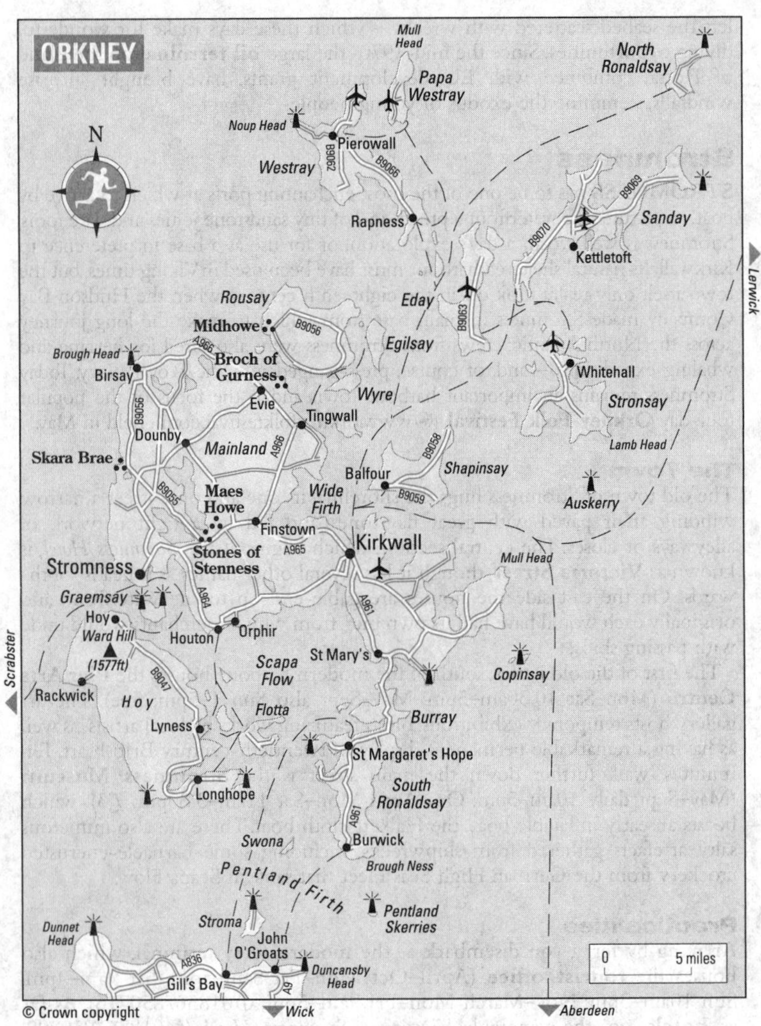

main street (closed Thurs eve, Sat lunch & Sun). The downstairs *Flattie Bar* of the *Stromness Hotel* is a congenial place to warm yourself by a real fire (or, depending on the season, sit outside) with a **drink**.

West Mainland

The great bulk of the **West Mainland** is fertile, productive farmland, fenced off into a patchwork of fields used either to produce crops or for cattle grazing. It's fringed by some spectacular coastline, particularly in the west, and littered with some of the island's most impressive prehistoric sites, such as the village of **Skara Brae**, the standing **Stones of Stenness** and the chambered tomb of **Maes Howe**.

The Stones of Stenness

The parish of **Stenness** lies along the main road from Stromness to Kirkwall, south of the twin lochs of Stenness and Harray, which are separated by a couple of promontories, that once stood at the heart of Orkney's most important Neolithic ceremonial complex. The most visible part of the complex are the **Stones of Stenness**, originally a circle of twelve rock slabs, now just four, the tallest of which is over 16ft and remarkable for its incredible thinness. A broken table-top lies within the circle, which is surrounded by a much-diminished henge (a circular bank of earth and a ditch) with a couple of entrance causeways. Less than a mile to the northwest, you reach another stone circle, the **Ring of Brodgar**, a much wider circle dramatically sited on raised ground. Here there were originally sixty stones, 27 of which now stand; of the henge, only the ditch survives.

Maes Howe

There are several quite large burial mounds visible to the south of the Ring of Brodgar, but these are entirely eclipsed by one of the most impressive Neolithic burial chambers in the whole of Europe, **Maes Howe** (April–Sept guided tours daily every 45min 9.45am–5.15pm; Oct–March Mon–Sat 9.45am–4.30pm, Sun 2–4.30pm; ⓣ01856/761606; £5; HS), which lies less than a mile northeast of the Stones of Stenness. Dating from around 3000 BC, Maes Howe is in an excellent state of preservation, partly due to the massive slabs of sandstone it was constructed from, the largest of which weighs over thirty tons. Perhaps its most extraordinary aspect is that the tomb is aligned so that the rays of the winter solstice sun reach right down the passage to the ledge of one of the three cells built into the walls of the tomb. The Vikings entered in the twelfth century, leaving large amounts of runic graffiti, cut into the walls of the main chamber and still clearly visible today. When Maes Howe was opened in 1861, it was found to be virtually empty, thanks to the work of generations of grave-robbers who had left behind only a handful of human bones. In summer, to visit the tomb, you must buy a **timed ticket** for a specific guided tour, either over the phone or direct from the nearby converted nineteenth-century Tormiston Mill, by the main road, which houses the ticket office; in winter, you can wander around the site freely.

Skara Brae

Around seven miles north of Stromness, the beautiful white curve of the Bay of Skaill is home to **Skara Brae** (April–Sept daily 9.30am–6.30pm; Oct–March Mon–Sat 9.30am–4.30pm, Sun 2–4.30pm; £6.50; HS), where the extensive remains of a small Neolithic fishing and farming village, dating back to 3000 BC, were discovered in 1850 after a fierce storm. The village is very well preserved, its houses huddled together and connected by narrow passages which would originally have been covered over with turf. The houses themselves consist of a single, spacious living room, filled with domestic detail, including fireplaces, cupboards, beds and boxes, all ingeniously constructed from slabs of stone.

Unfortunately, the sheer numbers now visiting Skara Brae mean that you can no longer explore the site itself properly, but only look down from the outer walls. Before you reach the site you must buy a ticket from the **visitor centre**, which houses an excellent **café-restaurant**. After a short video, you pass through a small introductory **exhibition**, with a few replica finds, before proceeding to a full-scale replica of House 7 (the best-preserved house); it's all a tad neat and tidy, but it'll give you the general idea.

Birsay and Evie

Occupying the northwest corner of the Mainland, the parish of **BIRSAY** was the centre of Norse power in Orkney for several centuries before the earls moved to Kirkwall. Today a tiny cluster of homes is gathered around the sandstone ruins of the **Earl's Palace**, which was built in the second half of the sixteenth century by Robert Stewart, Earl of Orkney, using the forced labour of the islanders. The palace appears to have lasted barely a century before falling into rack and ruin, though the crumbling walls and turrets retain much of their grandeur.

Just over half a mile northwest of the palace is the **Brough of Birsay**, a substantial Pictish settlement on a small tidal island only accessible during the two hours each side of low tide. Once you reach the island, there's a small ticket office, where you must pay your **entrance fee** (mid-June to Sept daily; £3). The focus of the village was – and still is – the sandstone-built twelfth-century **St Peter's Church**. Close by is a large complex of Viking-era buildings, including several houses, a sauna and some sophisticated stone drains.

On the north coast, the village and parish of **EVIE** looks out across the turbulent waters of Eynhallow Sound towards the island of Rousay. Its chief draw is the **Broch of Gurness** (9.30am–12.30pm & 1.30–6.30pm; £3.30; HS), the best-preserved broch on an archipelago replete with them, and one which is still surrounded by a remarkable complex of later buildings. As at Birsay, the sea has eaten away half the site, but the broch itself, dating from around 100 BC, still stands, its walls reaching a height of 12ft in places, its inner cells still intact. The compact group of homes huddled around the broch have also survived amazingly well, with much of their original and ingenious stone shelving and fireplaces still in place.

Practicalities

The best **B&B** in the West Mainland is a lovingly converted water mill, the *Mill of Eyrland* (Ⓣ01856/850136, Ⓦwww.millofeyrland.com; ③), set in a delightful spot by a trout-filled stream, off the A964 to Orphir, whilst *Woodwick House* (Ⓣ01856/751330, Ⓦwww.woodwickhouse.co.uk; ④) is situated in a beautiful, secluded position southeast of Evie. The simple *Eviedale* **campsite**, run by Dale Farm (Ⓣ01856/751270, Ⓦwww.creviedale.orknet.co.uk; April–Oct) in Evie, also rents out cottages.

Kirkwall

Initial impressions of **KIRKWALL**, Orkney's capital, are not always favourable. However, it does have one great redeeming feature – its sandstone **cathedral**, without doubt the finest medieval building in the north of Scotland. Nowadays, the town is very much divided into two main focal points: the old **harbour**, at the north end of the town, where inter-island ferries come and go all year round, and the flagstoned **main street**, which changes its name four times as it twists its way south from the harbour past the cathedral.

The Town

Standing at the very heart of Kirkwall, **St Magnus Cathedral** (Mon–Sat 9am–5pm, Sun 2–5pm) is the town's most compelling sight. This beautiful red-sandstone building was begun in 1137 by the Orkney Earl Rognvald, who built the cathedral in honour of his uncle Magnus, killed on the orders of his cousin Haakon in 1117. The first version of the cathedral was somewhat smaller than today's structure, which has been added to over the centuries. Today much of the detail in the soft sandstone has worn away – the capitals around the main doors are reduced to gnarled stumps – but it's still an immensely impressive building, its shape and style echoing the great cathedrals of Europe. Inside, the atmosphere is surprisingly intimate, the bulky sandstone columns drawing your eye up to the exposed brickwork arches, while around the walls is a series of mostly seventeenth-century tombstones, many carved with a skull and cross-bones and other emblems of mortality.

To the south of the cathedral are the ruined remains of the **Bishop's Palace** (April–Sept daily 9.30am–5.30pm; £3.50; HS), residence of the Bishop of Orkney since the twelfth century. Most of what you see now, however, dates from the time of Bishop Robert Reid, sixteenth-century founder of Edinburgh University. A narrow spiral staircase takes you to the top of the palace for a good view over the cathedral and Kirkwall's rooftops. The ticket for the Bishop's Palace also covers entry to the neighbouring **Earl's Palace**, built by the infamous Earl Patrick Stewart around 1600, using forced labour. With its grand entrance, fancy oriel windows, dank dungeons, massive fireplaces and magnificent central hall, it is reckoned to be one of the finest examples of Renaissance architecture in Scotland. The roof may be missing, but many domestic details remain, including a set of toilets and the stone shelves used by the clerk to do his filing.

Opposite the cathedral stands the sixteenth-century Tankerness House, now home to the **Orkney Museum** (Mon–Sat 10.30am–5pm; May–Sept also Sun 2–5pm; free). Among the more unusual artefacts to look out for are a witch's spell box, and a lovely whalebone plaque from a Viking boat grave discovered on Sanday.

Practicalities

NorthLink **ferries** from Shetland and Aberdeen (and all cruise ships) dock at the Hatston terminal, a mile or so northwest of town; the buses waiting at Hatston will take you to Stromness or Kirkwall. Kirkwall **airport** is about three miles southeast of town on the A960; a bus (Mon–Sat 7–8 daily; 15min) will take you to the **bus station,** a few minutes' walk west of the centre. The helpful **tourist office** is in the travel centre by the bus station (April–Sept daily 8.30am–8pm; Oct–March Mon–Sat 9.30am–5pm; ⓣ01856/872856).

The waterfront *Ayre Hotel* on Ayre Road (ⓣ01856/873001, ⓦwww.ayrehotel.co.uk; ⑥) offers the smartest **accommodation** in town; equally central is the more lively and contemporary *Albert* on Mounthoolie Lane (ⓣ01856/876000, ⓦwww.alberthotel.co.uk; ⑥). Try *Peter McKinley's* B&B (ⓣ01856/872249; ③) at 13 Palace Rd, right by the cathedral. The SYHA **hostel** (ⓣ0870/004 1133; April–Sept; £15) is ten minutes' walk out of the centre on the road to Orphir. More central is the small, privately run *Peedie Hostel* (ⓣ01856/875477; £10) on the waterfront beside the *Ayre Hotel*. There's also a **campsite** (ⓣ01856/879900; mid-May to mid-Sept) behind the Pickaquoy Leisure Centre, five minutes' walk west of the bus station.

The best **café** in town is the venerable *Trenabies* on Albert Street, which does high teas, but is very busy. Opposite is the well-stocked *Peppermill Deli* for takeaway coffee and **picnic** fodder. *The Reel Coffee Shop*, above the Wrigley Sisters Music Shop, on Castle Street, offers an excellent range of sandwiches, toasties and home-made cakes. Otherwise, you'll have to head for one of the town's hotels: the *Kirkwall*, on Harbour Street, is probably the best option, as it offers both **bar meals** and good a la carte.

Kirkwall has its very own state-of-the-art **nightclub**, *Fusion* (Fri & Sat; ⓦwww.fusionclub.co.uk), which occasionally attracts top-name DJs and also stages live gigs. The liveliest **pub** is the *Torvhaug Inn* at the harbour end of Bridge Street; another good place to try is the *Bothy Bar* in the *Albert Hotel*, which sometimes has live music. The Pickaquoy Leisure Centre (Ⓦwww.pickaquoy.com) – known locally as the "Picky" – contains the New Phoenix **cinema** (Ⓣ01856/879900).

South Ronaldsay

At the southern end of the Churchill Barriers (see box below) is low-lying **South Ronaldsay**, the largest of the islands linked to the Mainland. Its main settlement is **ST MARGARET'S HOPE** – or "The Hope", as it's known locally – a pleasing little gathering of stone-built houses overlooking a sheltered bay. The Hope was once a thriving port, but nowadays, despite the presence of the Pentland Ferries terminal, it remains a very peaceful place.

One of the most enjoyable archeological sights on Orkney is the ancient chambered burial cairn at the southeastern corner of South Ronaldsay, known as the **Tomb of the Eagles** (daily: March 10am–noon; April–Oct 9.30am–6pm; Nov–March by appointment; £5.50; Ⓣ01856/831339, Ⓦwww.tomboftheeagles.co.uk). Discovered, excavated and still owned by local farmer Ronald Simpson, the tomb makes a refreshing change from the usual interpretative centre. First, you get to look round the family's private museum of prehistoric artefacts; then, you get a brief guided tour of a nearby Bronze Age **burnt mound**, which is basically a Neolithic rubbish dump; and finally you can walk out to the **chambered cairn**, by the cliff's edge, where human remains were found alongside talons and carcasses of sea eagles. To enter the cairn, you must lie on a trolley and pull yourself in using an overhead rope.

If you want **to stay** in St Margaret's Hope itself you should head for *The Creel* (Ⓣ01856/831311, Ⓦwww.thecreel.co.uk; ⑥) on the harbourfront, with a view over the bay and one of Scotland's best, award-winning **restaurants**. More modest bar meals are available from the *Murray Arms Hotel* (Ⓣ01856/831205, Ⓦwww.murrayarmshotel.com; ④), on Back Road, which has rooms above the

Scapa Flow and the Churchill Barriers

The presence of a huge naval base in **Scapa Flow** during both world wars presented an irresistible target to the Germans, and protecting the fleet was always a nagging problem for the Allies. During World War I, blockships were sunk to guard the eastern approaches, but in October 1939, just weeks after the outbreak of World War II, a German U-boat managed to manoeuvre past the blockships and torpedo the battleship HMS *Royal Oak*, which sank with the loss of 833 lives. The U-boat captain claimed to have acquired local knowledge while fishing in the islands before the war. Today the wreck of the *Royal Oak*, marked by a green buoy off the Gaitnip Cliffs, is an official war grave.

The sinking of the *Royal Oak* convinced the First Lord of the Admiralty, Winston Churchill, that Scapa Flow needed better protection, and in 1940 work began on a series of barriers – known as the **Churchill Barriers** – to seal the waters between the Mainland and the string of islands to the south. Special camps were built to accommodate the 1700 men involved in the project; their numbers were boosted by the surrender of Italy in 1942, when Italian prisoners of war were sent to work here.

Besides the barriers, which are an astonishing feat of engineering when you bear in mind the strength of Orkney tides, the Italians also left behind the beautiful **Italian Chapel** (daily dawn–dusk; free) on the first of the islands, Lamb Holm. This, the so-called "miracle of Camp 60", must be one of the greatest adaptations ever, made from two Nissen huts, concrete, barbed wire and parts of a rusting blockship. It has a great false facade, and colourful trompe l'oeil decor, lovingly restored by the chapel's principal architect, Domenico Chiocchetti.

pub and a backpackers' **hostel** round the side. For a **hostel** and **campsite** with some character, head for *Wheems* (☎01856/831537; April–Oct; dorm bed £10), on the eastern side of South Ronaldsay, a mile and a half from the war memorial on the main road outside The Hope.

Hoy

Hoy, Orkney's second-largest island, rises sharply out of the sea to the southwest of the Mainland. Its dramatic landscape is made up of great glacial valleys and mountainous moorland rising to over 1500ft, dropping into the sea off the red-sandstone cliffs of St John's Head.

Walkers arriving by passenger ferry from Stromness at Moaness Pier, near the tiny village of **HOY**, and heading for Rackwick (four miles southwest), can either take the well-marked footpath that passes Sandy Loch or catch the minibus via the single-track road. From the road, duckboards head across the heather to the **Dwarfie Stane**, Orkney's most unusual chambered tomb, cut from a solid block of sandstone and dating back to 3000 BC.

Rackwick

RACKWICK is an old crofting and fishing village squeezed between towering sandstone cliffs on the west coast. A small farm building beside the hostel (see below) serves as a tiny **museum** (open any time; free), with a few old photos and a brief rundown of Rackwick's rough history. Despite its isolation, Rackwick has a steady stream of walkers and climbers passing through it en route to the **Old Man of Hoy**, a great sandstone column some 450ft high, perched on an old lava flow which protects it from the erosive power of the sea. The well-trodden footpath from Rackwick is an easy three-mile walk (3hr return).

Lyness

Hoy defines the western boundary of Scapa Flow (see box opposite), and **LYNESS** played a major role for the Royal Navy during both world wars. Many of the old wartime buildings have been cleared away over the last few decades, but the harbour and hills around Lyness are still scarred with the scattered remains of concrete structures that once served as hangars and store-houses during World War II, and are now used as barns and cowsheds. The old oil pump house, which still stands opposite the Lyness ferry terminal, has been turned into the **Scapa Flow Visitor Centre & Museum** (April–Oct Mon–Sat 9am–4.30pm, Sun 10.30am–4pm; July–Sept Sun until 6.15pm; Nov–March Mon–Fri only; free), a fascinating insight into wartime Orkney. The pump house itself retains much of its old equipment – you can even ask for a working demo of one of the oil-fired boilers – used to pump oil off tankers moored at Lyness into sixteen tanks, and from there into underground reservoirs cut into the neighbouring hillside. On request, an audiovisual show on the history of Scapa Flow is screened in the sole surviving tank, which has incredible acoustics. Even the café has an old NAAFI feel about it.

Practicalities

Two **ferry services** run to Hoy: a passenger ferry from Stromness to Moaness pier, by Hoy village (☎01856/850624), which also serves the small island of Graemsay; and the roll-on/roll-off car ferry from Houton on the Mainland to Lyness (☎01856/811397), which sometimes calls in at the oil terminal island of Flotta, and begins and ends its daily schedule at Longhope. There's no bus service on Hoy, but those arriving on the passenger ferry from Stromness should find a **minibus** waiting to take them to Rackwick. **Bike rental** is available from Moaness Pier (ⓣ01856/791225).

There are only a few places **to stay** in North Hoy. Luckily one of them is *The Glen* (ⓣ01856/791262; ⓦwww.rackwick-orkney.com; ❷), in Rackwick, run by a friendly local couple; they also offer dinner and will collect guests from Hoy. There are two council-run, SYHA-affiliated **hostels**, housed in converted schools (bookings are made through the education department at the Orkney Islands Council; ⓣ01856/873535 ext 2404): the *Hoy Centre* (open all year) in Hoy village is large and modern, with all rooms en suite; *Rackwick Hostel* (mid-March to mid-Sept; £13) has just eight beds, but is in Rackwick village itself. You can **camp** in Rackwick, either behind the hostel or beside the heather-thatched *Burnside Bothy* (ⓣ01856/791316). There's no shop in Rackwick, so take all your supplies with you; the post-office shop in Hoy only sells chocolate, but the *Hoy Inn*, near the post office, serves very good **bar meals** in season. South Hoy has a handful of good accommodation options, including the small, welcoming *Stromabank Hotel*, a nicely converted old schoolhouse (ⓣ01856/701494, ⓦwww.stromabank.co.uk; ❹), which also does good bar **food** in the evening (closed Thurs).

Shapinsay

Just a few miles northeast of Kirkwall, **Shapinsay** is the most accessible of Orkney's northern isles. A gently undulating grid-plan patchwork of rich farmland, the island's chief attraction for visitors is **Balfour Castle** (May–Sept guided tours Sun 3pm; see below for details of the all-inclusive ticket), the imposing Baronial pile designed by David Bryce and completed in 1848 by the Balfour family of Westray, who had made a small fortune in India the previous century. The Balfours died out in 1960 and the castle was bought by a Polish cavalry officer, Captain Tadeusz Zawadski, whose family now runs the place as a hotel. The guided tours are great fun, finishing off with complimentary tea and cakes in the servants' quarters.

Less than thirty minutes from Kirkwall by **ferry**, Shapinsay is an easy day-trip. If you want to visit the castle (Sun only), you should phone ahead and book an **all-inclusive ticket** from Balfour Castle (£20), which includes a return ferry ticket. The ferry for the guided tour leaves at 2.15pm, but you can catch an earlier ferry if you want to have some time to explore the rest of the island. It's also possible **to stay** for dinner, bed and breakfast in lord-of-the-manor style at the *Balfour Castle Hotel* (ⓣ01856/711282, ⓦwww.balfourcastle.co.uk; ❾); the rooms are vast and beautifully furnished, and you can also use the library and the other public rooms. More modest **B&B** is available at *Girnigoe* (ⓣ01856/711256, ⓦwww.girnigoe.net; ❷), a comfortable croft close to the north shore of Veantro Bay. Even if you're just coming for the day, it's worth popping into *The Smithy* (May–Sept; ⓣ01856/711722, ⓦwww.shapinsaysmithy.com), the wonderfully cosy licensed **café** below the island's heritage centre, which serves delicious food (daily lunchtime plus Fri & Sat eve) and also offers **bike rental**.

Rousay

Just over half a mile from the Mainland's northern shore, the hilly island of **Rousay** is home to a number of intriguing prehistoric sites. The first trio of sights is spread out over a couple of miles, on and off the road that leads west from the ferry terminal. **Taversoe Tuick**, the nearest chambered cairn, is unusual in that it exploits its sloping site by having two storeys, one entered from the upper side and one from the lower. A little further west is the

Blackhammar Cairn, which is divided into "stalls" by large flagstones, rather like the more famous cairn at Midhowe (see below). Finally, there's the **Knowe of Yarso**, another stalled cairn dating from the same period that's a stiff climb up the hill from the road, worth it if only for the magnificent view.

The mile-long **Westness Walk** heritage trail begins at Westness Farm, four miles west of the ferry terminal, and passes several archeological sites. **Midhowe Cairn**, about a mile on from the farm, comes as something of a surprise, both for its immense size – it's known as "the great ship of death", and measures nearly 100ft in length – and for the fact that it's now entirely surrounded by a stone-walled barn with a corrugated roof. Unfortunately, you can't actually explore the roofless communal burial chamber, dating back to 3500 BC, but only look down from the overhead walkway. A couple of hundred yards beyond Midhowe Cairn is **Midhowe Broch**, built as a sort of fortified family house, surrounded by a complex series of ditches and ramparts. The interior of the broch is divided into two separate rooms, each with their own hearth, water tank and quernstone, all of which date from the final phase of occupation around the second century AD.

Practicalities

Rousay makes a good day-trip from the Mainland, with regular **car ferry** sailings from Tingwall (30min), linked to Kirkwall by buses. In season, join one of the very informative **minibus tours** run by Rousay Traveller (June–Aug Tues–Fri; £16.50; ⓣ01856/821234). **Accommodation** on Rousay is limited: try the hostel at *Trumland Farm* (ⓣ01856/821252; £12), half a mile or so west of the terminal, with a couple of dorms, camping and **bike rental**. The *Taversoe Inn*, further along the road, offers unpretentious accommodation (ⓣ01856/821325, ⓦwww.taversoehotel.co.uk; ③) and good bar **meals**. The *Pier* **pub**, right beside the terminal, serves bar meals at lunchtime and will make up fresh crab sandwiches if you phone in advance (ⓣ01856/821359).

Westray

Although exposed to the full force of the Atlantic weather in the far northwest of Orkney, **Westray** shelters one of the most tightly knit and prosperous island communities. Old Orcadian families still dominate every aspect of life, giving the island a strong individual character.

The main village and harbour is **PIEROWALL** in the north, a good eight miles from the Rapness ferry terminal on the southernmost tip of the island. The island's most impressive ruin is the colossal sandstone hulk of **Noltland Castle**, which stands above the village half a mile west up the road to Noup Head. This Z-plan castle, which is pockmarked with over seventy gun loops, was begun around 1560 by Gilbert Balfour, a shady character from Fife, who was Master of the Household to Mary, Queen of Scots, and was implicated in the murder of her husband Lord Darnley.

The northwestern tip of Westray rises up sharply, culminating in the dramatic sea cliffs of **Noup Head**. During the summer months the guano-covered rock ledges are packed with over 100,000 nesting sea birds, primarily guillemots, razorbills, kittiwakes and fulmars, with puffins as well – a truly awesome sight, sound and smell. For a close view of the puffins, head for **Castle o' Burrian**, a sea stack in the southeast of the island.

Practicalities

Westray is served by car **ferry** from Kirkwall (ⓣ01856/872044), or you can **fly** from Kirkwall (Mon–Sat only). **Guided tours** of the island by minibus or bike can also be arranged with Westraak (ⓣ01857/677777, ⓦwww.westraak.co.uk). A **minibus service** meets the ferry (May–Sept) at Rapness and connects with the Papa Westray ferry at Gill Pier; you can book a seat on the bus when on board the ferry or ring ahead ⓣ01857/67758 or 07789034289. For **bike rental**, contact either of the hostels (see below).

Westray's finest **accommodation** is at the *Cleaton House Hotel* (ⓣ01857/677508, ⓦwww.cleatonhouse.com; ❺), a whitewashed Victorian manse about two miles southeast of Pierowall, with great views. This is also the best place on the island to sample Westray's organic salmon, either in the expensive **restaurant** or the congenial **bar**. The *Pierowall Hotel* (ⓣ01857/677472, ⓦwww.orknet.co.uk/pierowall; ❷), in Pierowall itself, is less stylish and less expensive, but equally welcoming, with a popular bar and excellent fish and chips, fresh off the boats. **B&B** is available at *No. 1 Broughton* (ⓣ01857/677726, ⓦwww.no1broughton.co.uk; ❸), a renovated mid-nineteenth-century house on the edge of Pierowall. Westray is positively spoilt for **hostels**: the hostel and cottages of *Bis Geos* (ⓣ01857/677420, ⓦwww.bisgeos.co.uk; £13), on the road to Noup Head, has unbeatable views along the cliffs and out to sea, while the luxurious *Barn* (ⓣ01857/677214, ⓦwww.thebarnwestray.co.uk; £13) is situated in an old farm at the southern edge of Pierowall; it's easier to get to, has a small **campsite** adjacent to it, and lovely hosts.

Papa Westray

Across the short Papa Sound from Westray is the island of **Papa Westray**, known locally as "Papay". With a population hovering precariously around seventy, Papay has had to fight hard to keep itself viable over the last couple of decades, helped by a hefty influx of outsiders. To get an idea how life used to be when the Traill family ruled over the island, visit the small **museum** (free access) in an old bothy opposite Holland House, at the centre of the island.

A road leads down from Holland House to the western shore, where the **Knap of Howar** stands. Dating from around 3500 BC, this Neolithic farm building makes a fair claim to being the oldest standing house in Europe. Half a mile north along the coast is **St Boniface Kirk**, a restored pre-Reformation church, with a bare flagstone floor, dry-stone walls, a little wooden gallery and just a couple of surviving box pews.

Papay is an easy day-trip from Westray, with a daily **passenger ferry** service from Pierowall. On Tuesdays and Fridays, the **car ferry** from Kirkwall to Westray continues on to Papa Westray; at other times, a bus (which accepts a limited number of bicycles) from Rapness connects with the Pierowall passenger ferry. Papay is also connected to Westray by the **world's shortest scheduled flight** – two minutes in duration, or less with a following wind. You can also fly direct from Kirkwall to Papa Westray (Mon–Sat 2–3 daily, 1 on Sun) for a special return fare of £12 if you stay overnight. Papay's Community Co-operative has a **minibus**, which will take you from the pier to wherever you want on the island, and can arrange a Papay Peedie Package Tour (mid-May to mid-Sept Tues, Thurs & Sat; £35; ⓣ01857/644321). It also runs a shop, a sixteen-bed SYHA-affiliated **hostel** (ⓦwww.syha.org.uk; £11) and the *Beltane House* **B&B** (ⓣ01857/644267, ⓔpapaybeltane2@hotmail.com; ❸), all housed within the old estate-workers' cottages at Beltane, east of Holland House.

Eday

A long, thin island at the centre of Orkney's northern isles, **Eday** is dominated by a great block of heather-covered upland, with farmland confined to a narrow strip of coastal ground. The chief points of interest are all in the northern half of the island, beyond the community shop on the main road. This marks the beginning of the signposted **Eday Heritage Walk**, which covers all the main sights (about 3hr). The walk initially follows the road heading northwest, past the hide overlooking **Mill Loch**, where several pairs of red-throated divers regularly breed. Clearly visible to the north of the road is the fifteen-foot **Stone of Setter**, weathered into three thick, lichen-encrusted fingers. From here, you can climb the hill to reach the **Vinquoy Chambered Cairn**: you can crawl into the tomb through the narrow entrance – a skylight inside lets light into the main, beehive chamber, but not into the four side-cells.

Eday's terminal for **ferries** is at Backaland pier in the south. Car rental and taxis can be organized through Mr A. Stewart by the pier (Ⓣ01857/622206), who also runs **minibus tours** (May–Aug Mon, Wed, Fri & Sun). It's also possible to do a day-trip **flight** on Wednesdays from Kirkwall to Eday (Ⓣ01856/872494 or 873457). Friendly **B&B** with full board is available at *Skaill Farm*, a traditional farmhouse just south of the airport (Ⓣ01857/622271; ③). The basic SYHA-affiliated **hostel** occupies an exposed spot just north of the airport; it's run by Eday Community Association (Ⓣ01857/622206, Ⓦwww.syha.org.uk; April–Sept; £9), who will also advise on **camping**.

Stronsay

A wonderful combination of green pastures, white sands and clear turquoise bays, **Stronsay** was one of the main Scottish centres for the curing of herring until the 1930s. **WHITEHALL** is the island's only real village, made up of rows of stone-built fishermen's cottages set between two large piers. Wandering along the tranquil, rather forlorn harbourfront today, you'll find it hard to believe that the village once supported five thousand people in the fishing industry during the summer season, as well as a small army of coopers, coal merchants, butchers, bakers, several Italian ice-cream parlours and a cinema. The old fish market by the pier houses a **museum**, with a few photos and artefacts from the herring days; ask at the adjacent café.

Stronsay is linked to Kirkwall by a regular car **ferry** service, and **flights** (Mon–Sat only). There's no bus service, but D.S. Peace (Ⓣ01857/616335) operates taxis and **rents cars**. Of the few **accommodation** options, the *Stronsay Fish Mart* **hostel** (Ⓣ01857/616386; £14) in the old fish market by the pier, and the refurbished *Stronsay Hotel* (Ⓣ01857/616213, Ⓦwww.stronsay.co.uk/stronsayhotel; ③) opposite, are both good choices. A cheaper alternative is the *Stronsay Bird Reserve* (Ⓣ01857/616363; ②), a nicely positioned **B&B** in a lovely old crofthouse, which also allows **camping** on the shores of Mill Bay. The *Stronsay Hotel* does good pub **food**.

Sanday

Sanday, though the largest of the northern isles, is also the least substantial, a great low-lying, drifting dune strung out between several rocky points. The island's sweeping aquamarine bays and vast stretches of clean white sand are the finest in Orkney, and in dry, clear weather it's a superb place to spend a day or two. The entire coastline presents the opportunity for superb walks, with particularly spectacular sand dunes to the south of Cata Sand. The most impressive archeological sight is **Quoyness Chambered Cairn**, on the fertile farmland of Els Ness peninsula, dating from before 2000 BC, and partially reconstructed to a height of around 13ft.

Ferries arrive at the southern tip of the island and are met by a **minibus** (book on ⓣ01857/600284). The airfield is in the centre of the island, with regular **flights** to Kirkwall (Mon–Sat only). The fishing port of **Kettletoft**, where the ferry used to dock, is where you'll find the island's two **hotels**: of the two, *The Belsair* (ⓣ01857/600206; ③) has the slightly more adventurous restaurant menu, while the *Kettletoft* has a lively bar that's popular with the locals. Of the numerous **B&Bs**, try the *Marygarth Manse* (ⓣ01857/600284; ②), in Broughtown, who can also organize car and **bike rental**. If you're on a budget, head for nearby *Ayre's Rock* (ⓣ01857/600410, ⓦwww.ayres-rock-sanday-orkney.co.uk), a well-equipped **hostel** and **campsite** by the Bay of Brough with washing and laundry facilities, a chip shop (Sat only), and bike rental.

North Ronaldsay

Measuring just three miles by one and rising only 66ft above sea level, **North Ronaldsay** is almost overwhelmed by the enormity of the sky, the strength of wind and the ferocity of the sea – so much so that its very existence seems an act of tenacious defiance. Despite these adverse conditions, North Ronaldsay has been inhabited for centuries, and continues to be heavily farmed, from old-style crofts whose roofs are made from huge local flagstones.

The island's **sheep** are a unique, tough, goat-like breed, who feed mostly on seaweed, giving their flesh a dark tone and a rich, gamey taste, and making their thick wool highly prized. A high **dry-stone dyke**, completed in the mid-nineteenth century and running the thirteen miles around the edge of the island, keeps them off the farmland, except during lambing season. The most frequent visitors are ornithologists, who come to catch a glimpse of the rare migrants who land here briefly on their spring and autumn migrations. The only features to interrupt the island's flat horizon are two lighthouses: the stone-built **Old Beacon**, first lit in 1789, but topped by a huge bauble of masonry since 1809; and, half a mile to the north and rising to a height of over 100ft, the **New Lighthouse** (May–Sept Sun 12.30–5.30pm; at other times by appointment; £3; ⓣ01857/633257), built in 1854.

The **ferry** from Kirkwall runs only once a week (usually Fri), though day-trips are possible on occasional summer Sundays (ⓣ01856/872044). Your best bet is to catch one of the daily **flights** from Kirkwall: if you stay the night on the island, you're eligible for a £12 return fare. A **minibus** usually meets the ferries and planes (ⓣ01857/633244) and will take you to the lighthouse. You can **stay** at the eco-friendly *Bird Observatory* (ⓣ01857/633200, ⓦwww.nrbo.f2s.com), which offers full board either in private guest rooms (③) or in a **bunkhouse**; the observatory's *Obscafé* is a sort of pub-restaurant and serves decent **meals**. Full-board accommodation is also available at *Garso*, in the northeast (ⓣ01857/633244, ⓔmuir886@btinternet.com; ③). The *Burrian Inn*, to the southeast of the war memorial, is the island's small **pub**, and does hot food.

Shetland

In nearly all respects **Shetland** is a complete contrast with Orkney. Orkney lies within sight of the Scottish mainland, whereas Shetland lies beyond the horizon. Many maps plonk the islands in a box somewhere off Aberdeen, but in fact they're a lot closer to Bergen in Norway than Edinburgh. Shetland endures the most violent weather experienced in the British Isles: in winter, gales are routine and Shetlanders take the occasional hurricane in their stride, marking a

Getting to Shetland

NorthLink Ferries (☎0845/600 0449, Ⓦwww.northlinkferries.co.uk) operates a daily overnight **car ferry** to Lerwick **from Aberdeen**, either direct (12hr) or via Kirkwall (13hr). British Airways (☎0870/850 9850) has nonstop **flights** to Shetland from several airports in Scotland. Atlantic Airways (☎0870/199 9440, Ⓦwww.flyshetland.com) also run a service (mid-June to mid-Sept) from London Stansted. Shetland's main airport is at **Sumburgh** (☎01950/461000), from where buses make short work of the 25-mile journey north to Lerwick.

calm fine day as "a day atween weathers". There are some good spells of dry, sunny weather from May to September, but it's the "**simmer dim**", the twilight which lingers through the small hours at this latitude, that makes Shetland summers so memorable.

The islands' capital, **Lerwick**, is a busy little port and the only town of any size. Many parts of Shetland can be reached from here on a day-trip. **South Mainland** is a narrow finger of land that runs some 25 miles from Lerwick to **Sumburgh Head**, an area particularly rich in archeological remains, including the Iron Age **Mousa Broch** and the ancient settlement of **Jarlshof**. A further 25 miles south of Sumburgh Head is the remote but thriving **Fair Isle**, synonymous with knitwear and exceptional birdlife. Even more remote are the distinctive peaks and precipitous cliffs of the island of **Foula**, 14 miles west of Mainland. Shetland's three **North Isles** bring Britain to a dramatic, windswept end: **Yell** has the largest population of otters in Shetland; **Fetlar** is home to the rare red-necked phalarope; north of **Unst**, there's nothing until you reach the North Pole.

People have lived in Shetland since **prehistoric times** (from about 3500 BC), and the islands display spectacular remains. For six centuries they were part of the **Norse empire**, which brought together Sweden, Denmark and Norway. The Scottish king annexed Shetland in 1472 and Scottish **mainland lairds** set about grabbing what land and power they could, controlling the fish trade and the tenants who supplied it through a system of truck, or forced barter. During the two world wars, Shetland's role as gatekeeper between the North Sea and North Atlantic meant that the defence of the islands and control of the seas around them were critical. Careful negotiation in the 1970s, backed up by pioneering local legislation, produced a substantial income from North Sea **oil**, which has been reinvested in the community. The oil boom days are over, though, and **tourism** is slowly beginning to play a more important role in the economy.

Lerwick

Very much the focus of Shetland's commercial life, **LERWICK** is home to about 6600 people, just less than a third of the islands' population. All year, its sheltered **harbour** at the heart of the town is busy with ferries, fishing boats, oil-rig supply vessels and in summer, the quaysides come alive with local pleasure craft, visiting yachts and cruise liners. Behind the old harbour is the compact town centre, made up of one long main street, Commercial Street; from here, narrow lanes, known as "**closses**", rise westwards to the late-Victorian new town.

Arrival, information and accommodation

The **ferry terminal** lies in the north harbour, about a mile from the town centre. **Flying** into Sumburgh Airport, you can take one of the regular buses to Lerwick; taxis (around £25) and car rental are also available. Buses stop on the Esplanade,

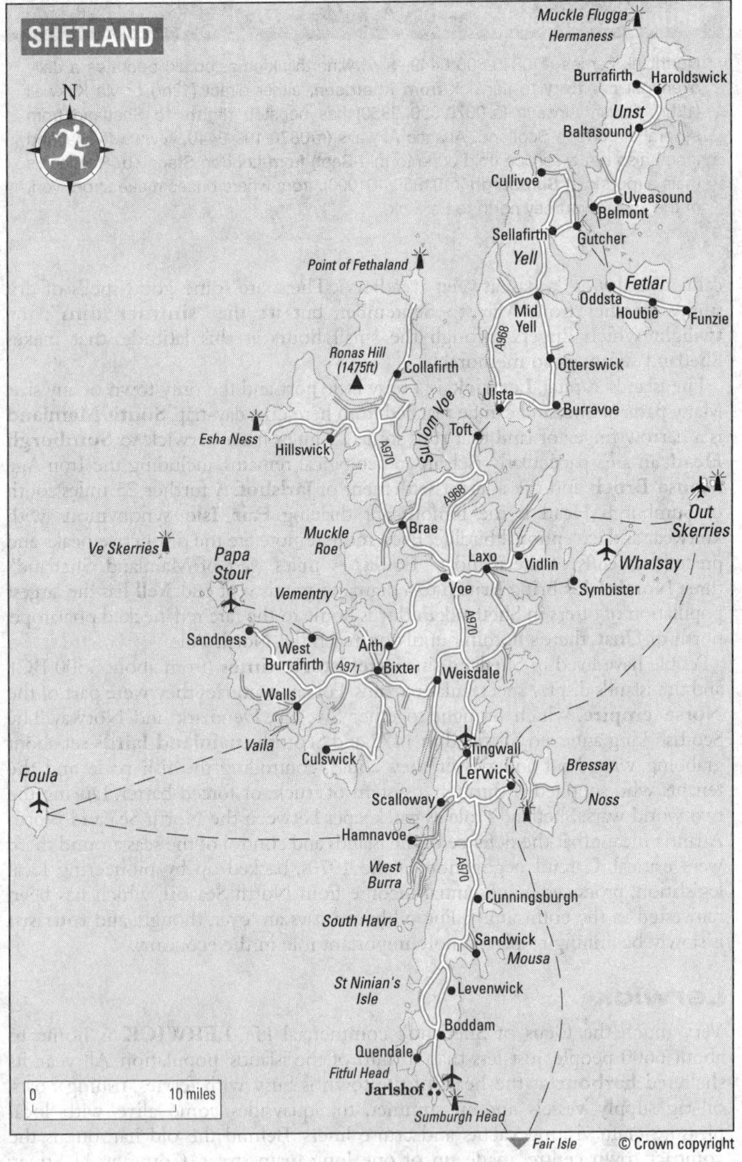

very close to the old harbour, or at the Viking bus station on Commercial Road, north of the town centre. The **tourist office** (April–Oct Mon–Fri 8am–6pm, Sat & Sun 8am–4pm; Nov–March Mon–Fri 9am–5pm; ⓣ0870/199 9440, ⓦwww.visitshetland.com) is at the Market Cross on Commercial Street.

There are spacious **rooms** at *Brentham House* (ⓣ01595/460201, ⓦwww.brenthamhouse.co.uk; ⑤), 7 Harbour St; there's no reception, so you pick up the keys from *Baroc* bar a few doors down. *Alder Lodge Guesthouse*, 6 Clairmont Place (Ⓣ01595/695705; ❸), is the best middle-range B&B choice. The SYHA **hostel** (Ⓣ01595/692114; April–Sept; £13) at *Islesburgh House* on King Harald Street, offers unusually comfortable surroundings, with useful laundry facilities. The *Clickimin* **campsite** (Ⓣ01595/741000, May–Sept) enjoys the excellent facilities of the neighbouring Clickimin leisure centre, but no idyllic locale.

The Town

Lerwick's attractive, flagstone-clad **Commercial Street** is still very much the core of the town, with its narrow, winding form, set back one block from the Esplanade, providing shelter from the elements even on the worst days. The street's northern end is marked by the towering walls of **Fort Charlotte** (daily: June–Sept 9am–10pm; Oct–May 9am–4pm; free), begun for Charles II in 1665 during the wars with the Dutch, burnt down by the Dutch fleet in August 1673, and repaired and named in honour of George III's queen in the 1780s.

Although the **closses** that connect the Street to Hillhead are now a desirable place to live, it's not so long ago that they were regarded as slum-like dens of iniquity. Hillhead, up in the Victorian new town, is dominated by the splendid **Town Hall** (Mon–Thurs 9am–5pm, Fri 9am–4pm; free), a Scottish Baronial monument to civic pride, built by public subscription. Lerwick's chief tourist sight, however, is the excellent **Shetland Museum** (Mon–Wed, Fri & Sat 10am–5pm, Thurs 10am–7pm, Sun noon–5pm; Ⓦwww.shetland-museum.org.uk; free), housed in a wonderful waterfront building at Hay's Dock, off Commercial Road, filled with historical artefacts and nauticalia and a great café.

A mile or so southwest of the town centre on the road leading to Sumburgh, the much-restored **Clickimin Broch** stands on what was once a small island in Loch Clickimin. The settlement here began as a small farmstead around 700 BC and was later enclosed by a defensive wall. The main tower served as a castle and probably rose to around 40ft, though the remains are now not much more than 10ft high.

Just beyond Lerwick's main ferry terminal, a mile and a half north of the town centre, stands the **Böd of Gremista** (May to mid-Sept Wed–Sun 10am–1pm & 2–5pm; free), the birthplace of **Arthur Anderson** (1792–1868). The displays explore Anderson's life as beach boy (helping to cure and dry fish), naval seaman, businessman, philanthropist, Shetland's first native MP and founder of Shetland's first newspaper, the *Shetland Journal*.

Eating, drinking and entertainment

Lerwick's best **restaurant** is *Monty's Bistro* on Mounthooly Street (Ⓣ01595/696555; closed Mon & Sun), serving inexpensive and delicious meals at lunchtimes, and more accomplished cooking in the evening. Shetland Museum's bright, modern *Hay's Dock* café-restaurant (closed Sun eve) is also

Böds

With only one official SYHA hostel in Shetland, it's worth knowing about the islands' unique network of **camping böds**, which are open from April to September, and are similar to English camping barns. All the camping böds have some form of (primitive) heating system, cold water, toilets and bunk beds (but no mattresses), so a sleeping bag and mat are pretty much essential. In order to stay at a böd, you must **book in advance** through Shetland Amenity Trust (Ⓣ01595/693434, Ⓦwww.camping-bods.com), as there are no live-in wardens; expect to pay around £6–8 a person.

great, offering a short and imaginative menu. Other places to try include the very good Indian *Raba*, 26 Commercial Rd, and the Chinese/Thai *Great Wall*, located above the Viking Bus Station. The *Peerie Café* (closed Sun), on the Esplanade, is a fantastic café, serving cakes, soup and sandwiches. The *Fort Café* (closed Sun lunch), situated below Fort Charlotte at 2 Commercial St, is Lerwick's best fish-and-chip shop.

The friendliest **pub** in town is the upstairs bar in the *Lounge*, up Mounthooly Street, where local musicians often play sessions. The Garrison Theatre (Ⓣ01595/692114), by the Town Hall, shows occasional **films** as well as putting on theatre productions, comedy acts and live gigs. The Islesburgh Community Centre has introduced regular **crafts and culture evenings** (mid-June to mid-Aug Mon, Wed & Thurs 7–9.30pm; £4), where you can buy local knitwear, meet the locals and listen to traditional music.

Bressay and Noss

Shielding Lerwick from the full force of the North Sea is the island of **Bressay**, dominated at its southern end by the conical Ward Hill (744ft) – "da Wart" – and accessible on an hourly car and passenger ferry from Lerwick (takes 5min). The chief reason most visitors pass through Bressay is in order to visit the tiny but spectacular island of **Noss**, just off Bressay's eastern shore. The island was inhabited until World War II but is now given over to sheep farming and is also a National Nature Reserve. Scottish Natural Heritage operates an inflatable as a ferry from the landing stage below the car park on the east side of Bressay (May–Aug Tues, Wed & Fri–Sun; £3 return; Ⓣ0800/107 7818). On the island, the old farmhouse of Gungstie contains a small **visitor centre** where the warden will give you a free map and guide. Behind the house is an old stud farm for **Shetland ponies**, which were sent to work in the mines of County Durham in northeast England. The most memorable feature of Noss is its cliffed coastline rising to a peak at the massive 500-foot **Noup**, home to vast colonies of cliff-nesting gannets, puffins, guillemots, shags, razorbills and fulmars. Be warned: if you stray off the marked path, the great skuas will do their best to intimidate with alarming dive-bombing raids.

Scalloway

Once the capital of Shetland, **SCALLOWAY**'s importance waned throughout the eighteenth century as Lerwick grew in trading success and status. Nowadays, Scalloway is fairly sleepy, its prosperity still closely linked to the fluctuations of the fishing industry. The town is dominated by the imposing shell of **Scalloway Castle**, a classic fortified tower house built with forced labour in 1600 by the infamous Earl Patrick Stewart, who held court in the castle and gained a reputation for cruelty and corruption. On Main Street, the small **Scalloway Museum** (May–Sept Mon 9.30–11.30am & 2–4.30pm, Tues–Fri 10am–noon & 2–4.30pm, Sat 10am–12.30pm & 2–4.30pm; free) attempts to tell the story of the Shetland Bus, the link between Shetland and Norway which helped to sustain the Norwegian resistance in World War II.

Scalloway has very little **accommodation** apart from the *Scalloway Hotel* (Ⓣ01595/880444, Ⓦwww.scalloway-hotel.co.uk; ⑤), on the harbourfront, whose bar acts as the local pub, and the wood-clad *Windward* B&B (Ⓣ01595/880769; ②), at the far western end of the bay. For **food**, head for *Da Haaf* (Ⓣ01595/880747; closed Sat & Sun), the unpretentious licensed restaurant in the North Atlantic Fisheries College, which serves a wide range of fresh fish.

South Mainland

Shetland's **South Mainland** is a long, thin finger of land, only three or four miles wide, but 25 miles long, ending in the cliffs of Sumburgh Head and Fitful Head. It's a beautiful area with wild landscapes but also good farmland, and has yielded some of Shetland's most impressive archeological treasures – in particular, **Jarlshof** and **Mousa Broch**, on the Isle of Mousa.

The main road leads to Sumburgh airport, to the west of which is **Old Scatness Broch & Iron Age Village** (May–Oct Mon–Thurs 10am–5pm, Sun 10.30am–5.30pm; £4), where a vast Iron Age settlement is being excavated. First, you get a guided tour of the site from a viewing platform, followed by a taste of Norse and Pictish life in a restored wheelhouse, and a weaving demonstration. South of the airport lies **Jarlshof** (April–Sept daily 9.30am–5.30pm; £4.50; HS), the largest and most impressive of Shetland's archeological sites. The best-preserved buildings are the Pictish wheelhouses surrounding a Neolithic broch, and also the Norse longhouses. Towering over the whole complex is the laird's house, originally built by Robert Stewart, Earl of Orkney, in the late sixteenth century.

The Mainland comes to a dramatic end at **Sumburgh Head**, about two miles from Jarlshof. The lighthouse, designed by Robert Stevenson, was built in 1821; although not open to the public, its grounds offer great views to Noss in the north and Fair Isle to the south. This is also the easiest place in Shetland to get close to **puffins**. During the nesting season, you simply need to look over the western wall by the lighthouse gate to see them arriving at their burrows with beakfuls of fish or giving flying lessons to their offspring; on no account should you try to climb over the wall.

Practicalities

The best **accommodation** in the South Mainland is at *Setterbrae* (Ⓣ01950/440468, Ⓦwww.setterbrae.co.uk; ❸), a comfortable B&B a stone's throw from the *Spiggie Hotel* (Ⓣ01950/460409, Ⓦwww.thespiggiehotel.co.uk; ❺), which has a lively bar serving real ales, and a **restaurant** with great views over the Loch of Spiggie. There's also a **camping böd** in *Betty Mouat's Cottage* (book on Ⓣ01595/693434; April–Sept), in Scatness, at the tip of the peninsula, close to the airport. At Levenwick, around eighteen miles south of Lerwick, there's a small, terraced **campsite** (Ⓣ01950/422207; May–Sept), with hot showers, a tennis court and a superb view over the east coast.

Mousa Broch

From Leebitton, in the district of Sandwick, halfway to Sumburgh Head, you can take a small passenger **ferry** (mid-April to mid-Sept 1–2 daily; 15min; £10 return; Ⓣ01950/431367, Ⓦwww.mousaboattrips.co.uk) to the small **Isle of Mousa**, on which stands Scotland's best-preserved broch. Rising to more than 40ft, and looking rather like a Stone Age cooling tower, **Mousa Broch** has a remarkable presence, and features in both *Egil's Saga* and the *Orkneyinga Saga*, contemporary chronicles of Norse exploration and settlement. The low entrance passage leads through two concentric walls to a central courtyard, divided into separate beehive chambers. Between the walls, a rough (very dark) staircase leads to the top parapet (torch provided). From late May to late July, a large colony of around six thousand **storm petrels** breeds in and around the broch walls, fishing out at sea during the day, and only returning to the nests after dark. The ferry also runs late-night trips (Wed & Sat weather permitting), setting off in the "simmer dim" twilight around 11pm.

Fair Isle

Tiny **Fair Isle** is marooned in the sea halfway between Shetland and Orkney. At one time Fair Isle's population was not far short of four hundred, but by the 1950s, the population had shrunk to just 44, a point at which evacuation and abandonment of the island was seriously considered. George Waterston, who'd bought the island and set up a bird observatory in 1948, passed it into the care of the National Trust for Scotland in 1954 and rejuvenation began.

The croft land and the island's scattered houses are concentrated in the south, but the focus for many visitors is the **Bird Observatory**, built just above the sandy bay of North Haven where the ferry from Shetland Mainland arrives. It's one of Europe's major centres for ornithology and its work in watching, trapping, recording and ringing resident and migrant birds goes on all year. Fair Isle is even better known for its **knitting** patterns, still produced with great skill by the local knitwear co-operative. There are a few samples on display at the island's **museum** (Mon 2–5pm, Wed 10am–noon, Fri 2–4.30pm; free; ⓣ01595/760244), situated next door to the Methodist chapel.

The passenger **ferry** (ⓣ01595/760222) connects Fair Isle with either Lerwick (Sat & alternate Thurs; 4–5hr) or Grutness in Sumburgh (Tues & alternate Thurs; 3hr); **flights** go from Tingwall (Mon, Wed, Fri & Sat) or Sumburgh (Sat). Camping is not permitted, but there is full-board **accommodation** at the *Fair Isle Lodge & Bird Observatory* (ⓣ01595/760258, ⓦwww.fairislebirdobs.co.uk; ❺) in twins and singles or hostel-style dorms. A good alternative is *Upper Leogh* in the south of the island (ⓣ01595/760248; ❸) or the *Auld Haa* (ⓣ01595/760349; ❸).

25

ORKNEY AND SHETLAND | Shetland

The Westside

The western Mainland of Shetland – known as the **Westside** – boasts outstanding **coastal scenery**, with dramatic cliffs, intimate coves and some fine beaches. The finest Neolithic structure in the Westside is the **Staneydale Temple**, so called by the archeologist who excavated it because it resembled one on Malta. Whatever its true function, it was twice as large as the surrounding oval-shaped houses (now in ruins) and was certainly of great importance, perhaps as some kind of community centre. The foundations measure more than 40ft by 20ft internally with immensely thick walls, still around 4ft high, whose roof would have been supported by spruce posts (two post holes can still be clearly seen).

The best **accommodation** and **eating** options on the Westside are in and around Walls, 24 miles northwest of Lerwick. In Walls itself, *Voe House* (ⓣ01595/693434; April–Sept) is the largest **camping böd** on Shetland, with its own peat fire, while the wonderfully welcoming *Skeoverick* (ⓣ01595/809349; ❷) is a lovely modern crofthouse B&B a mile or so north of Walls. The only guesthouse in the area is *Burrastow House* (ⓣ01595/809307, ⓦwww.users.zetnet.co.uk/burrastow-house-hotel; April–Oct; ❺), beautifully situated three miles southwest of Walls; with fresh Shetland ingredients and a French chef, the cooking is superb, though dinner is available to non-residents only at the weekend.

Foula

Southwest of Walls, at "the edge of the world", **Foula** is without a doubt the most isolated inhabited island in the British Isles, separated from the nearest point on Mainland Shetland by about fourteen miles of often turbulent ocean.

Its western **cliffs**, the second highest in Britain after those of St Kilda, rise at **The Kame** to some 1220ft above sea level; a clear day at The Kame offers a magnificent panorama stretching from Unst to Fair Isle. On a bad day, the exposure is complete and the cliffs generate blasts of wind known as "flans", which rip through the hills with tremendous force. In addition to its forty human inhabitants, the island is home for a quarter of a million **birds**, including a colony of **great skuas** or "bonxies" which you can't fail to notice in the breeding season.

It's essential to book and reconfirm the summer passenger **ferry** from Walls or Scalloway (ⓣ01595/840880, ⓦwww.atlanticferries.co.uk) to Ham, in the middle of Foula's east coast. There are also regular **flights** from Tingwall (Mon–Wed & Fri; ⓣ01595/753226); tickets cost around £25 one way and day-trips are possible on Wednesdays (mid-Feb to mid-Oct) and Fridays all year. Foula's only **B&B** is *Leraback* (ⓣ01595/753226, ⓦwww.originart.com; ❸), near Ham, which does full board only.

North Mainland

The **North Mainland**, stretching more than thirty miles north from the central belt around Lerwick, is wilder than much of Shetland, with almost relentlessly bleak moorland and some rugged and dramatic coastal scenery. You're bound to pass by **VOE**, as it sits at the main crossroads of the area, but it's easy to miss the picturesque old village, a tight huddle of homes and workshops down below the road around the pier (and signposted Lower Voe). Set at the head of a deep, sheltered sea loch, Voe has a Scandinavian appearance, helped by the presence of the **Sail Loft**, now a large **camping böd** (ⓣ01595/693434; April–Sept). Across the road, the old butcher's is now the *Pierhead Restaurant & Bar* (ⓣ01806/588332): the cosy wood-panelled **pub** has a real fire, occasional live music and offers a good bar menu, a longer version of which is on offer in the upstairs restaurant, featuring local mussels and the odd catch from the fishing boats.

Eight miles northeast of Voe down the B9071, *Lunna House* (ⓣ01806/577311, ⓦwww.lunnahouse.co.uk; ❸), built in 1660, is a wonderful **place to stay**, with spacious bedrooms, lovely views and a top-class breakfast. North of Voe the main road divides: the northern leg leads to Toft, the ferry terminal for the island of Yell (see p.1040), while the other branch cuts northwest to **BRAE**, a sprawling settlement expanded in some haste in the 1970s to accommodate the workforce for the huge **Sullom Voe Oil Terminal** nearby. Brae boasts one of Shetland's finest **hotels**, *Busta House* (ⓣ01806/522506, ⓦwww.bustahouse.com; ❻), a lovely laird's house which sits across the bay of Busta Voe from modern Brae. It's worth coming here for a drink or an excellent meal in the hotel's pub-like bar.

Northmavine, the northwest peninsula of North Mainland, begins a mile west of Brae at **Mavis Grind**, a narrow isthmus at which it's said you can throw a stone from the Atlantic to the North Sea, or at least to Sullom Voe. **HILLSWICK**, the main settlement, boasts **Da Böd**, once the oldest pub in Shetland, said to have been founded by a German merchant in 1684, now an alternative veggie café called *The Booth* (ⓣ01806/503348; May–Sept).

Just outside Hillswick, a side road leads west to the exposed headland of **Esha Ness** (pronounced "*Ay*sha Ness"), celebrated for its splendid coastline views. A mile or so south off the main road is the **Tangwick Haa Museum** (Easter–Sept daily 11am–5pm; free), which tells the moving story of this remote corner of Shetland and its role in the dangerous trade of deep-sea fishing and whaling. To the north the road ends at the **Esha Ness Lighthouse**, a great place to view the cliffs, stacks and, in rough weather, blowholes of this stretch of coast, and the starting point for an excellent three-hour walk. One of the few places to stay in Esha Ness is *Johnnie Notions* **camping böd** (Ⓣ01595/693434; April–Sept; no electricity), up a turning north off the main road, in Hamnavoe.

The North Isles

Many visitors never make it out to Shetland's trio of remote **North Isles**, which is a shame, as the ferry links are frequent and inexpensive, and the roads fast. Certainly, there is no dramatic shift in scenery: much of what awaits you is familiar undulating peat moorland, dramatic coastal cliffs and silent glacial voes. However, with Lerwick that much further away, the spirit of independence and self-sufficiency in the North Isles is much more keenly felt. **Yell**, the largest of the three, is best known for its vast otter population. **Fetlar**, the smallest, is home to the rare red-necked phalarope. **Unst**, though, probably has the widest appeal, partly as the most northerly landmass in the British Isles, but also for its nesting seabird population.

Yell

The interior of **Yell** features a lot of peat moorland, but the coastline is gentler and greener and provides an ideal habitat for a large population of **otters**. At **BURRAVOE**, in the southeast corner, there's also a lovely whitewashed laird's house that now houses the **Old Haa Museum** (late April to Sept Tues–Thurs & Sat 10am–4pm, Sun 2–5pm; free), which is stuffed with artefacts, and has lots of material on the history of the local herring and whaling industries; there's a very pleasant wood-panelled café on the ground floor. In the north, the area around **CULLIVOE** has relatively gentle, but attractive, coastal scenery. The **Sands of Brekken** are made from crushed shells, and are beautifully sheltered in a cove a mile or two north of Cullivoe.

Ferries to Yell from Toft on the Mainland are very frequent (20min). You can **stay** with the very welcoming, storytelling Tullochs at *Gutcher Post Office* (Ⓣ01957/744201, Ⓔmargaret.tulloch@btopenworld.com; ❷) by the Unst ferry terminal, or in the *Windhouse Lodge* **camping böd** (Ⓣ01595/693434; April–Sept), the gatehouse on the main road near Mid Yell; it has a wood- and peat-fired heater and hot showers. **Food** options are limited: the aforementioned museum café in Burravoe (closed Mon & Fri) has soup, snacks and delicious home baking; the only other decent option is the funky, camp *Wind Dog Café* (Ⓣ01957/744321, Ⓦwww.winddogcafe.co.uk), opposite the post office at Gutcher, which offers evening meals (if you book ahead), provides Internet access, as well as hosting the odd event including storytelling from the inimitable Tullochs and other events.

Fetlar

Fetlar is the most fertile of the North Isles, much of it grassy moorland and lush green meadows with masses of summer flowers. At the main settlement, **HOUBIE**, you can learn more about the island from the nearby welcoming **Fetlar Interpretive Centre** (May–Sept Mon–Fri 11am–3pm, Sat & Sun 1–4pm; £2; Ⓦwww.fetlar.com). Fetlar is also one of the very few places in the UK where you'll see graceful **red-necked phalarope** (late May to early Aug): a hide has been provided overlooking the marshes (or mires) to the east of the **Loch of Funzie** (pronounced "finny"). **Ferries** depart daily from both

Gutcher on Yell and Belmont on Unst, docking at Hamar's Ness, three miles northwest of Houbie. The only public transport is an infrequent and small postcar (Mon, Wed & Fri 2 daily). **Accommodation** boils down to *Gord* (Ⓣ01957/733227, Ⓔnicboxall@btinternet.com; ③), a comfortable modern house attached to the island shop in Houbie, and the **camping böd** in Aithbank (Ⓣ01595/693434, April–Sept), a cosy wood-panelled cottage, a mile east of Houbie. There's also *Garths* **campsite** (Ⓣ01957/733227; May–Sept), a simple field just to the west of Houbie, with toilets, showers and drying facilities.

Unst

Much of **Unst** (Ⓦwww.unst.org) is rolling grassland but the coast is more dramatic: a fringe of cliffs relieved by some beautiful sandy beaches. As Britain's most northerly inhabited island, there is a surfeit of "most northerly" sights, which is fair enough, given that many visitors only come here in order to head straight for Hermaness, to see the sea birds and look out over Muckle Flugga and the northernmost tip of Britain, to the North Pole beyond. The island has been badly affected by the recent closure of the local RAF radar base at Saxa Vord: it used to employ a third of the island's population, which has now fallen to around six hundred.

On the south coast, not far from the ferry terminal, is **UYEASOUND**, east of which lie the ruins of **Muness Castle**, a diminutive defensive structure, built in 1598 with matching bulging bastions and corbelled turrets at opposite corners (keys and torch from the house nearby). Unst's main settlement is **BALTASOUND**, an old herring port, where the excellent **Unst Heritage Centre** (May–Sept daily 11am–5pm; free) occupies the old school building by the main crossroads. From Baltasound, the main road crosses a giant boulder field of serpentine, a greyish green, occasionally turquoise rock that weathers to a rusty orange. The **Keen of Hamar**, east of Baltasound, and clearly signposted from the main road, is one of the largest expanses of serpentine debris in Europe, and is home to an extraordinary array of plantlife.

Beyond the Keen of Hamar, the road drops down into **HAROLDSWICK**, where near the shore you'll find the **Unst Boat Haven** (May–Sept daily 11am–5pm; free), displaying a beautifully presented collection of historic boats with many tools of the trade and information on fishing. The road that heads off northwest leads to the bleak headland of **Hermaness**, home to more than 100,000 nesting sea birds (May–Aug). There's an excellent **visitor centre** in the former lighthouse-keeper's shore station, where you can pick up a leaflet showing the marked routes across the heather to the view over to **Muckle Flugga** lighthouse and **Out Stack**, the most northerly bit of Britain. The views from here are inevitably marvellous, as is the birdlife; there's a huge gannetry on one of the stacks, and puffins burrow all along the cliff-tops.

Ferries shuttle regularly from Gutcher on Yell over to **BELMONT** on Unst (Ⓣ01957/722259; 10min). The best and most unusual **accommodation** is the family-owned *Buness House* (Ⓣ01957/711315, Ⓦwww.users.zetnet.co.uk.Buness-house; ⑥), a seventeenth-century Haa in Baltasound. Another very good bet is *Prestagaard* (Ⓣ01957/755234, Ⓦwww.prestegaard.shetland.co.uk; ②), a modest Victorian B&B in Uyeasound, where you'll also find the clean and modern *Gardiesfauld Hostel* (Ⓣ01957/755240, Ⓦwww.gardiesfauld.shetland.co.uk; April–Sept; £11), near the pier, which allows **camping** and offers **bike rental**.

Travel details

Orkney

Ferries to Orkney (summer only)

Aberdeen to: Kirkwall (4 weekly; 6hr).
Gill's Bay to: St Margaret's Hope (3–4 daily; 1hr).
John O'Groats to: Burwick (passengers only; 2–4 daily; 40min).
Lerwick to: Kirkwall (3 weekly; 5hr 30min).
Scrabster to: Stromness (2–3 daily; 1hr 30min).

Inter-island ferries (summer only)

To Eday: Kirkwall–Eday (2–3 daily; 1hr 15min–2hr).
To Hoy: Houton–Lyness (Mon–Fri 6 daily, Sat & Sun 2–4 daily; 45min–1hr 25min); Stromness–Hoy (passengers only; Mon–Fri 4–5 daily, Sat & Sun 2 daily; 25min).
To North Ronaldsay: Kirkwall–North Ronaldsay (Fri; 2hr 40min–3hr).
To Papa Westray: Kirkwall–Papa Westray (Tues & Fri; 2hr 15min); Pierowall (Westray)–Papa Westray (passengers only; 2–5 daily; 25min).
To Rousay: Tingwall–Rousay (5–6 daily; 30min).
To Sanday: Kirkwall–Sanday (2 daily; 1hr 25min).
To Shapinsay: Kirkwall–Shapinsay (4–5 daily; 45min).
To Stronsay: Kirkwall–Whitehall (2 daily; 1hr 40min–2hr).
To Westray: Kirkwall–Westray (2–3 daily; 1hr 25min).

Inter-island flights (Mon–Sat only)

Kirkwall to: Eday (Wed; 8–26min); North Ronaldsay (2–3 daily; 15min); Papa Westray (Mon–Sat 2–3 daily, 1 on Sun; 12–19min); Sanday (Mon–Sat 2 daily; 10min); Stronsay (Mon–Sat 2 daily; 25min); Westray (Mon–Sat 2 daily, 1 on Sun; 12min).

Buses on Orkney Mainland

Kirkwall to: Burwick (5 daily; 40–55min); Birsay (Mon–Fri 2 daily; 45min); Evie (Mon–Sat 4–5 daily; 30min); Houton (Mon–Fri 5 daily, 3 on Sat; 20–25min); St Margaret's Hope (Mon–Fri 6 daily, 3 on Sat; 30min); Skara Brae (June–Aug Mon–Fri 2 daily; 1hr 15min); Stromness (Mon–Fri hourly, 8 on Sat, 4 on Sun; 30min); Tingwall (Mon–Fri 5 daily, Sat 3 daily; 35min–1hr).
Stromness to: Skara Brae (Mon–Fri & Sun 3–4 daily; 20min); Tingwall (Wed & Fri 2 daily; 1hr).

Shetland

Ferries to Shetland (summer only)

Aberdeen to: Lerwick (daily; 12hr).
Kirkwall (Orkney) to: Lerwick (3–4 weekly; 6hr).

Inter-island ferries (summer only)

To Bressay: Lerwick–Bressay (every 30min–1hr; 7min).
To Fair Isle: Lerwick–Fair Isle (Sat & alternate Thurs; 4–5hr); Grutness–Fair Isle (Tues & alternate Thurs; 3hr).
To Fetlar: Belmont (Unst) and Gutcher (Yell)–Hamar's Ness (Mon–Sat 7–9 daily, 5 on Sun; 25–40min).
To Foula: Scalloway–Foula (Sat & alternate Thurs; 3hr 30min); Walls–Foula (Tues & alternate Thurs; 2hr).
To Unst: Gutcher (Yell)–Belmont (every 30–45min; 10min).
To Yell: Toft–Ulsta (every 30–45min; 20min).

Inter-island flights (summer only)

Sumburgh to: Fair Isle (Sat; 15min).
Tingwall to: Fair Isle (Mon, Wed & Fri 2 daily, 1 on Sat; 25min); Foula (Mon & Tues 1 daily, Wed & Fri 2 daily; 15min); Out Skerries, calling at Whalsay on request (Mon & Wed 1 daily, Thurs 2 daily; 20min); Papa Stour (Tues 2 daily; 10min).

Buses on Shetland Mainland

Lerwick to: Brae (Mon–Sat 4–6 daily; 45min); Hamnavoe (Mon–Sat 2 daily; 30min); Hillswick (Mon–Sat 1 daily; 1hr 40min); Scalloway (Mon–Sat hourly; 25min); Sumburgh (Mon–Sat 6–8 daily, 4 on Sun; 45min); Toft (Mon–Sat 3–5 daily; 50min); Vidlin (Mon–Sat 2 daily; 45min); Voe (Mon–Sat 5–6 daily; 35min); Walls (Mon–Sat 1–3 daily; 45min).

Buses on Unst

Baltasound to: Haroldswick (Mon–Sat 3–4 daily; 10min).
Belmont to: Baltasound (Mon–Sat 2–3 daily; 20min); Uyeasound (Mon–Sat 1–2 daily; 5min).

Buses on Yell

Mid Yell to: Gutcher (Mon–Sat 1–5 daily, Sun 1 daily in school term; 20min).
Ulsta to: Burravoe (Mon–Sat 1 daily; 15min); Gutcher (Mon–Sat 1–3 daily, 1 on Sun in school term; 25min).

Contexts

Contexts

History

Off and on, **Britain** has been inhabited for the best part of half a million years, though the earliest archeological evidence of human life dates from about **250,000 BC**. These meagre remains, found near Swanscombe, east of London across the Thames from Tilbury, belong to one of the migrant communities whose comings and goings depended on the fluctuations of the Ice Ages. Renewed glaciation then made the area uninhabitable once more, and the next traces – mainly roughly worked flint implements – were left around 40,000 BC by cave-dwellers at Creswell Crags in Derbyshire, Kents Cavern near Torquay and Cheddar Caves in Somerset. The last spell of intense cold began about 17,000 years ago, and it was the final thawing of this last **Ice Age** around 5000 BC that caused the British Isles to separate from the European mainland.

The sea barrier did nothing to stop further migrations of nomadic hunting communities, drawn by the rich forests that covered ancient Britain. In about 3500 BC a new wave of colonists arrived from the continent, probably via Ireland, bringing with them a **Neolithic** culture based on farming and the rearing of livestock. These tribes were the first to make some impact on the British environment, clearing forests, enclosing fields, constructing defensive ditches around their villages and digging mines to obtain flint used for tools and weapons. Fragments of Neolithic pottery have been found near Peterborough and at Windmill Hill, near Avebury in Wiltshire; other settlements – like the well-preserved village of Skara Brae in Orkney – were near the sea, enabling them to supplement their diet by fishing and to develop their skills as boat builders. The most profuse relics of this culture are their graves, usually stone-chambered, turf-covered mounds (called long barrows, cairns or cromlechs), which are scattered throughout the country; the most impressive ones are at Belas Knap in Gloucestershire, Barclodiad y Gawres in Anglesey, and Maes Howe on Orkney.

The transition from the Neolithic to the Bronze Age began around 2000 BC, with the immigration from northern Europe of the so-called **Beaker Folk** – named from the distinctive cups found at their burial sites. Originating in the Iberian peninsula and bringing with them bronze-workers from the Rhineland, these newcomers had a well-organized social structure with an established aristocracy, and quickly intermixed with the native tribes. Many of Britain's **stone circles** were completed at this time, including Stonehenge in Wiltshire, and Calanais on the Isle of Lewis, while many others belong entirely to the Bronze Age – for example, the Hurlers and the Nine Maidens on Cornwall's Bodmin Moor. Large numbers of earthwork forts were also built in this period, suggesting a high level of tribal warfare, but none were able to withstand the waves of Celtic invaders who, spreading from a homeland in central Europe, began settling in Britain around 600 BC.

The Celts

Highly skilled in battle, the **Celts** soon displaced the local inhabitants from one end of Britain to the other, establishing a sophisticated farming economy and a social hierarchy that was headed by **Druids**, a priesthood with attendant poets, seers and warriors. Through a deep knowledge of ritual, legend and the mechanics of the heavens, the Druids maintained their position between the people and a pantheon of over four thousand gods. Familiar with Mediterranean artefacts through their far-flung trade routes, they introduced a superior method of metalworking that favoured iron rather than bronze, from which they forged not just weapons but also coins.

The principal Celtic contribution to the landscape was a network of hillforts or brochs, and other defensive works stretching over the entire country, the greatest of them at **Maiden Castle** in Dorset, a site first fortified almost 3000 years earlier, and **Mousa** in the Shetland Islands. The original Celtic tongue – the basis of modern Welsh and Scottish Gaelic – was spoken over a wide area, gradually dividing into Goidelic (or Q-Celtic) now spoken in Ireland and Scotland, and Brythonic (P-Celtic) spoken in Wales and Cornwall, and later exported to Brittany in France. Great though the Celtic technological and artistic achievements were, the people and their pan-European cousins were unable to maintain an organized civic society to match that of their successors, the Romans.

The Romans

The **Roman** invasion began hesitantly, with small cross-Channel incursions by **Julius Caesar** in 55 and 54 BC. Britain's rumoured mineral wealth was a primary motive behind these raids, but the immediate spur to the eventual conquest nearly a century later was the dangerous collaboration between British Celts and the fiercely anti-Roman tribesmen in France, and the need of the emperor **Claudius**, for a great military triumph. The death of the British king Cunobelin (the original of Shakespeare's Cymbeline), ruler of southeast England, offered the opportunity Claudius required, and in August 43 AD, a substantial force landed in Kent, from where it fanned out, soon establishing a base along the estuary of the Thames. Joined by Claudius and a menagerie of elephants and camels for the major battles of the campaign, the Romans soon reached Camulodunum (Colchester), and within four years were dug in on the frontier of south Wales, though Wales itself and the north of England were not subdued for another thirty years.

By 80 AD the Roman governor, **Agricola**, felt secure enough in the south of Britain to begin an invasion of the north, building a string of forts across the Clyde–Forth line and defeating a large force of Scottish tribes at Mons Graupius. The long-term effect of his campaign, however, was slight. In 123 AD the emperor Hadrian decided to seal the frontier against the northern tribes and built **Hadrian's Wall**, which stretched from the Solway Firth to the Tyne and was the first formal division of the island of Britain. Twenty years later, the Romans again ventured north and built the **Antonine Wall** between the Clyde and the Forth. This was occupied for about forty years, but thereafter the Romans, frustrated by the inhospitable terrain of the Highlands, largely gave up their attempt to subjugate the north, and instead adopted a policy of containment.

The written history of Britain begins with the Romans, whose rule lasted nearly four centuries. For the first time most of England was absorbed into a unified and peaceful political structure, in which commerce flourished and cities prospered, particularly **Londinium**, which immediately assumed a pivotal role in the commercial and administrative life of the province. Although Latin became the language of the Romano-British ruling elite, local traditions were allowed to coexist alongside Roman customs, so that Celtic gods were often worshipped at the same time as Rome's, and sometimes indeed merged with them. Perhaps the most important legacy of the Roman occupation, however, was the introduction of **Christianity** from the third century on, becoming firmly entrenched after its official recognition across the empire by Constantine in 313.

The Anglo-Saxons

As early as the reign of Constantine, Roman England suffered raids by Germanic Saxon pirates. As economic life declined and rural areas became depopulated, so individual military leaders began to usurp local authority and by the start of the fifth century England had become irrevocably detached from what remained of the Roman Empire. Within fifty years the **Saxons** were settling on the island, the start of a gradual conquest that – despite bitter resistance led by such semi-mythical figures as King Arthur, who is alleged to have held court at Caerleon in Wales – culminated in the defeat of the native Britons in 577 at the **Battle of Dyrham** (near Bath). Driving the recalcitrant Celtic tribes west, the invaders eliminated the Romano-British culture and by the end of the sixth century the bulk of England was divided into the Anglo-Saxon kingdoms of Northumbria, Mercia, East Anglia, Kent and Wessex, and only in Scotland, Wales and the far southwest of England did the ancient Celtic traditions survive. In the fifth century, Irish-Celtic invaders formed distinct colonies in parts of Wales and in the northwest of Scotland, and between the fifth and the eighth centuries ascetic evangelical missionaries from Celtic Ireland spread the gospel around western Britain, promoting the eremitical tradition of living a reclusive life. In south Wales, **St David** was the most popular (and subsequently Wales's patron saint), while in northwest Scotland, **St Columba** founded several Christian outposts, the most famous of which was on the island of Iona.

Elsewhere, the revival of Christianity in England was driven mainly by the arrival of **St Augustine**, who was dispatched by Pope Gregory I and landed on the Kent coast in 597, accompanied by forty monks. The missionaries were received by Ethelbert, who gave Augustine permission to found a monastery at **Canterbury**. Despite some reversals in the years that followed, the Christianization of England proceeded quickly, so that by the middle of the seventh century all the Anglo-Saxon kings had at least nominally adopted the faith. Tensions and clashes between the Augustinian missionaries and the more freebooting Celtic monks inevitably arose, to be resolved by the **Synod of Whitby** in 663, when it was settled that the English church should follow the rule of Rome, thereby ensuring a realignment with the European cultural mainstream.

The central English region of **Mercia** became the dominant Anglo-Saxon kingdom in the eighth century under kings Ethelbald and Offa, the latter being responsible for the greatest public work of the Anglo-Saxon period, **Offa's Dyke**, an earthwork stretching from the River Dee to the Severn, marking the border with Wales. After Offa's death **Wessex** gained the upper hand, and by 825 King Egbert had conquered or taken allegiance from all the other English kingdoms. The supremacy of Wessex coincided with the first large-scale Norse or **Viking** invasions, which began with coastal pirate raids, such as the one that destroyed the great monastery of Lindisfarne in 793, but gradually grew into a migration, initially concentrated in the Scottish islands of Orkney, Shetland and the Hebrides.

In 865, a substantial Danish army landed in East Anglia, and within six years they had conquered Northumbria, Mercia and East Anglia. The Danes then set their sights on Wessex, whose new king was the formidable and talented **Alfred the Great** (reigned 871–899). Despite the odds, Alfred successfully resisted the Danes and eventually the two warring parties signed a truce, which fixed an uneasy border between Wessex and Danish territory – the **Danelaw** – to the north. Ensconced in northern England and what is today the East Midlands, the Danes soon succumbed to Christianity and internal warfare, while Alfred modernized his kingdom and strengthened its defences.

Alfred's successor, **Edward the Elder** (899–925), capitalized on his efforts, establishing Saxon supremacy over the Danelaw to become the de facto overlord of all England. The relative calm continued under Edward's son, **Athelstan** (925–40), who extended his overlordship over much of Scotland and Wales, and his son, **Edgar** (959–75), who became the first ruler to be crowned **king of England** in 973. However, this was but a lull in the Viking storm. Returning in force, the Vikings milked Edgar's son **Ethelred the Unready** (978–1016) for all the money they could, but the ransom (the Danegeld) paid brought only temporary relief and Ethelred hot-footed it to Normandy, leaving the Danes in command.

The first Danish king of England was **Canute** (1016–35), a shrewd and gifted ruler, but his two disreputable sons quickly dismantled his carefully constructed Anglo-Scandinavian empire. Thereafter, the Saxons regained the initiative, restoring Ethelred's son, **Edward the Confessor** (1042–66), to the throne in 1042. It was a poor choice. Edward was more suited to be a priest than a king and he allowed power to drift into the hands of his most powerful subject, Godwin, Earl of Wessex, and his son Harold. On Edward's death, the Witan – a sort of council of elders – confirmed **Harold** (1066) as king, ignoring several rival claims including that of William, Duke of Normandy. William's claim was a curious affair, but he always insisted – however improbable it may seem – that the childless Edward the Confessor had promised him his crown. Unluckily for Harold, his two main rivals struck at the same time. First up was his alienated brother **Tostig** and his ally King Harald of Norway, a giant of a man reliably reckoned to be seven feet tall. They landed with a Viking army in Yorkshire and Harold hurriedly marched north to meet them. Harold won a crushing victory at the Battle of Stamford Bridge, but then he heard that William of Normandy had invaded the south. Rashly, Harold did not pause to muster more men, but dashed south, where William famously routed the Saxons – and killed Harold – at the **Battle of Hastings** in 1066. On Christmas Day, William the Conqueror was installed as king in Westminster Abbey.

England: Normans and Plantagenets (1066–1399)

Making little attempt to reach any understanding with his new subjects, **William I** (1066–87) imposed a Norman aristocracy, reinforcing his rule with a series of strongholds, the grandest of which was the Tower of London. Perhaps the single most effective controlling measure was the compilation of the **Domesday Book** between 1085 and 1086. Recording land ownership, type of cultivation, the number of inhabitants and their social status, it afforded William an unprecedented body of information about his subjects, providing the framework for the administration of taxation, the judicial structure and feudal obligations.

William was succeeded by his son **William Rufus** (1087–1100), an ineffectual ruler who died in mysterious circumstances – killed by an unknown assailant's arrow while hunting in the New Forest – and the throne passed to **Henry I** (1100–35), William I's youngest son. Henry spent much of his time struggling with his unruly barons, but at least he proved to be more conciliatory in his dealings with the Saxons, even marrying into one of their leading families. On his death in 1135, William I's grandson Stephen of Blois (1135–54) contested the accession of Henry's daughter Mathilda and the result was a long-winded civil war. Matters were eventually resolved when both factions accepted Mathilda's son as **Henry II** (1154–1189), the first of the **Plantagenets**, so called after this branch of the family. Energetic and far-sighted, Henry kept his barons firmly in check and instigated profound administrative reforms, including the introduction of trial by jury. England was not Henry's only concern, as his inheritance had bequeathed him great chunks of France, though his downfall was his attempt to subordinate Church to Crown. This went terribly awry in 1170, when Henry sanctioned the murder in Canterbury Cathedral of his erstwhile drinking companion **Thomas à Becket**, whose canonization just three years later created an enduring Europe-wide cult.

The last years of Henry's reign were riven by quarrels with his sons, the eldest of whom, **Richard I** (or Lionheart; 1189–99), spent most of his ten-year reign crusading in the Holy Land. Neglected, England fell prey to the scheming of Richard's brother **John** (1199–1216), the villain of the Robin Hood tales, who became king in his own right after Richard died of a battle wound in France in 1199. But John's inability to hold on to his French possessions and his rumbling dispute with the Vatican alienated the English barons, who eventually forced him to consent to a charter guaranteeing their rights and privileges, the **Magna Carta**, which was signed in 1215 at Runnymede, on the Thames.

The power struggle with the barons continued into the reign of **Henry III** (1216–72), but Henry's successor, **Edward I** (1272–1307), was much more in control of his kingdom than his predecessor. Edward was also a great law-maker, but he became obsessed by military matters, spending years subduing Wales and imposing English jurisdiction over Scotland. Fortunately for the Scots – it was too late for Wales – the next king of England, **Edward II** (1307–27), proved to be completely hopeless and in 1314 Robert the Bruce inflicted a huge defeat on his guileless army at the Battle of Bannockburn (see below). This spelt the beginning of the end for Edward, who was subsequently murdered by his wife Isabella and her lover Roger Mortimer in 1327.

Edward III (1327–77) began by sorting out the Scottish imbroglio before getting stuck into his main preoccupation – his (essentially specious) claim to the throne of France. Starting in 1337, the resultant **Hundred Years War** kicked off with several famous English victories, principally Crécy in 1346 and Poitiers in 1356, but was interrupted by the outbreak of the **Black Death** in 1349. The plague claimed about one and a half million English souls – some one-third of the population – and the scarcity of labour that followed gave the peasantry more economic clout than they had ever had before. Predictably, the landowners attempted to restrict the concomitant rise in wages, thereby provoking widespread rioting that culminated in the **Peasants' Revolt** of 1381. The rebels marched on London hoping to appeal to the king – now **Richard II** (1377–99) – for fair treatment. The monarch agreed to meet the spokesperson, **Wat Tyler**. However, Richard's aristocratic bodyguards, offended by Wat's conduct, killed **Tyler**. The murder acted as a prelude to the enforced dispersal of the crowds and mass slaughter.

The conquest of Wales (1272–1415)

William the Conqueror did not attempt to conquer Wales, but instead installed a huge retinue of barons, the **Lords Marcher**, along the border: in so doing, he kept an eye on the Welsh and secured the frontier. At the end of the thirteenth century, **Edward I**, prompted by the actions of a Welsh chief, **Llywelyn the Last**, decided to conquer Wales: the chief had failed to attend Edward's coronation and refused to pay him homage. With effective use of sea power, Edward had little trouble in forcing Llywelyn into Snowdonia and when peace was restored with the **Treaty of Aberconwy**, Llywelyn was left with the hollow title of "Prince of Wales, and deprived of almost all his land. Shortly afterwards,

Llywelyn's brother **Dafydd** rose against Edward, dragging Llywelyn along with him. Edward crushed the revolt, captured Llywelyn, and executed him. The **Treaty of Rhuddlan** in 1284 set down the terms by which the English monarch was to rule Wales: much of it was given to the Lords Marcher, the rest was divided into administrative and legal districts similar to those in England. Though the treaty is often seen as a symbol of English subjugation, it respected much of Welsh law and provided a basis for civil rights and privileges. Many Welsh were content to accept Edward's rule, but in 1294 a rebellion led by **Madog ap Llywelyn** spread across Wales and was only halted by Edward's swift and brutal response. Most of the privileges enshrined in the Treaty of Rhuddlan were now rescinded and the Welsh were brought firmly under the English heel.

Defeated but not broken, the Welsh were ultimately rallied by the charismatic Welsh hero **Owain Glyndŵr**, who declared himself "Prince of Wales" in 1400, and with a posse of local supporters attacked the English. The English king **Henry IV**, in an effort to quell the disturbance, imposed restrictions on Welsh landownership, thereby swelling the ranks of Glyndŵr's supporters. The key fortress of Conwy Castle (while the garrison was at church) was captured in 1401, and in 1404, Glyndŵr summoned a parliament in Machynlleth, and had himself crowned Prince of Wales. He then demanded independence for the Welsh Church from Canterbury and set about securing alliances with those English noblemen who had grievances with Henry IV. However, a succession of defeats soon prompted Glyndŵr's allies to desert him and the rebellion fizzled out, though Glyndŵr was never captured and, ignoring English offers of a royal pardon, disappeared into the mountains, where he died in 1415 or 1416.

Scotland in the Middle Ages (1057–1320)

In the post-Roman period, the petty chieftains of the **Picts** and **Scotti** – followed later by the Vikings – battled for control of Scotland, but by the ninth century **Kenneth MacAlpine**, king of the Scotti and son of a Pictish princess, was able to create a united kingdom known as Alba, later as Scotia. His successors extended MacAlpine's frontiers by marriage and conquest until, by 1034, almost all of modern Scotland was under their rule.

In 1040, **Macbeth** famously killed King Duncan and usurped the Scottish throne, but in 1057 Duncan's son, **Malcolm III**, returned to Scotland, where he defeated Macbeth and began a long reign which was to transform Scottish society. Malcolm established a secure dynasty – the Canmores ("Bighead") – based on succession through the male line, and replaced the old Gaelic system of blood ties with **feudalism**: the followers of a Gaelic king were his kindred, whereas the followers of a feudal king were his vassals. The Canmores successfully feudalized much of southern and eastern Scotland by making grants to their Norman, Breton and Flemish followers, but beyond that, traditional clan-based forms of social relations persisted, a division which was to define much of Scotland's later history.

The Canmores also began to reform the **Church**. Malcolm III's English wife **Margaret** brought Scottish religious practices into line with those of the rest of Europe – and was eventually canonized – while **David I** (1124–53) imported monks to found a series of monasteries, principally in the Borders at Kelso, Melrose, Jedburgh and Dryburgh. By 1200 the country was covered by a network of eleven bishoprics, although church organization remained weak within the Highlands. Similarly, the dynasty founded a series of **royal burghs**, towns such as Edinburgh, Stirling and Berwick, and bestowed upon them charters recognizing them as centres of trade. The charters usually granted a measure of self-government, vested in the town corporation or guild, and the monarchy hoped this arrangement would both encourage loyalty and increase the prosperity of the kingdom. Scotland's Gaelic-speaking clans had little influence within the burghs, and by 1550 Scots – a northern version of Anglo-Saxon – had become the main language throughout the Lowlands.

Progress as an independent nation, however, was threatened after 1286, when **Alexander III** died, leaving a hotly disputed succession. Edward I, the king of England, muscled in on the action, presiding over a conference in which the rival claimants to the Scottish throne presented their cases. Edward chose John Balliol, in preference to **Robert the Bruce**, and obliged John to pay him homage, thus turning Scotland into a vassal kingdom. Bruce refused to accept this decision, thereby continuing the conflict, and in 1295 Balliol renounced his allegiance to Edward and formed an alliance with **France** – the beginning of what is known as the "Auld Alliance". In the conflict that followed, Balliol was defeated and imprisoned, and Edward seized control of almost all of Scotland.

Edward had shown little mercy during his conquest of Scotland and his cruelty seems to have provoked a truly national resistance. This focused on **William Wallace**, a man of relatively lowly origins who forged an army of peasants, lesser knights and townsmen that was fundamentally different from the armies raised by the nobility: he led proto-nationalist forces determined to expel the English from their country. Wallace never received the support of the nobility, and, after a bitter ten-year campaign, he was betrayed, captured and then executed in London in 1305.

With Wallace out of the way, feudal intrigue resumed. In 1306 **Robert the Bruce**, the erstwhile ally of the English, defied Edward and had himself crowned king of Scotland. Edward died the following year, but the turbulence dragged on until 1314, when Bruce decisively defeated a huge English army under Edward II at the battle of **Bannockburn**. At last Bruce was firmly in control of his kingdom, and in 1320 the Scots asserted their right to independence in a successful petition to the pope, now known as the **Arbroath Declaration**.

England: the houses of Lancaster and York

In 1399, **Henry IV** (1399–1413), the first of the **Lancastrian** kings, supplanted the weak and indecisive Richard II, and was then succeeded by his own son, the bellicose **Henry V** (1413–22), who promptly renewed the Hundred Years War. A comprehensive victory over the French at **Agincourt** forced the French king to acknowledge Henry as his heir in the Treaty of Troyes of 1420. However, Henry died just two years later and his son, **Henry VI** (1422–61 & 1470–1471) – or rather his regents – all too easily succumbed to a French counterattack inspired by **Joan of Arc** (1412–1431); by 1454, only Calais was left in English hands.

It was soon obvious that Henry VI was mentally unstable, and consequently two aristocratic factions attempted to wrest control. These were the Yorkists, whose emblem was the white rose, and the Lancastrians, represented by the red rose – hence the **Wars of the Roses**. At first, the Lancastrians had the better of things, but the Yorkist **Edward IV** seized the crown in 1461. Imprudently, Edward then attempted to shrug off his most powerful backer, Richard Neville, Earl of Warwick – aka "Warwick the Kingmaker" – and Warwick returned the favour by switching sides. Edward was driven into exile and Henry VI came back for a second term as king – but not for long. In 1471, Edward IV returned, Warwick was killed and Henry captured – and subsequently dispatched – when the Yorkists crushed the Lancastrians at the Battle of Tewkesbury.

Edward IV (1461–70 & 1471–83) proved to be a precursor of the great Tudor princes – licentious, cruel and despotic, but also a patron of Renaissance learning. In 1483, his 12-year-old son succeeded as **Edward V** (1483), but his reign was cut short after only two months, when he and his younger brother were murdered in the Tower of London – probably by their uncle, the Duke of Gloucester, who was crowned **Richard III** (1483–85). Richard was toppled at Bosworth Field in 1485 by Henry Tudor, Earl of Richmond, who took the throne as **Henry VII** (1485–1509).

England: the Tudors (1485–1603)

The start of the **Tudor** period brought radical transformations. A Lancastrian through his mother's line, **Henry VII** promptly reconciled the Yorkists by marrying Edward IV's daughter Elizabeth, ending the Wars of the Roses at a stroke. It was a shrewd gambit and others followed. Henry married his daughter off to James IV of Scotland and his son to Catherine, the daughter of Ferdinand and Isabella of Spain – and by these means England began to assume the status of a major European power.

Henry's son, **Henry VIII** (1509–47) is best remembered for his separation of the English Church from Rome and his establishment of an independent Protestant church – the **Church of England**. The schism between Henry and the pope was triggered not by doctrinal issues but by the failure of his wife **Catherine of Aragon** – widow of his elder brother – to provide Henry with male offspring. Since Pope Clement VII refused to grant him a decree of nullity, Henry dismissed his longtime chancellor Thomas Wolsey and turned instead to Thomas Cromwell, who helped make the English Church recognize Henry as its head. One of the consequences was the **Dissolution of the Monasteries**, giving both king and nobles the chance to get their hands on valuable monastic property. In his later years Henry became a corpulent, syphilitic wreck, six times married but at last furnished with an heir, **Edward VI** (1547–53), who was only nine years old when he ascended the throne. His short reign saw Protestantism established on a firm footing, with churches stripped of their images and Catholic services banned, yet on Edward's death most of the country readily accepted his half-sister **Mary** (1553–58), daughter of Catherine of Aragon and a fervent Catholic, as queen. She returned England to the papacy and married the future Philip II of Spain, forging an alliance whose immediate consequence was war with France and the loss of Calais, the last of England's French possessions. The marriage was unpopular and so was Mary's persecution of Protestants: the leading lights of the English Reformation, Hugh Latimer, Nicholas Ridley and Thomas Cranmer, the archbishop of Canterbury, who was largely responsible for the first **English prayer book**, published in 1549, were all executed.

When she came to the throne in 1558 on the death of her half-sister, **Elizabeth I** (1558–1603) looked very vulnerable. The country was divided by religion – Catholic against Protestant – and threatened from abroad by Philip II of Spain, the most powerful man in Europe. Famously, Elizabeth eschewed marriage and, although a Protestant herself, steered a delicate course between the two religious groupings. Her prudence rested well with the increasingly powerful English merchant class, who were mostly opposed to foreign military entanglements. An exception was, however, made for the piratical activities of the great English seafarers of the day, sea captains like Walter Raleigh, Martin Frobisher, John Hawkins and Francis Drake, who made a fortune raiding Spain's American colonies. Inevitably, Philip II's irritation took a warlike turn, but the **Spanish Armada** he sent in 1588 was defeated, and England was established as a major European sea power. Elizabeth's reign also saw the efflorescence of a specifically English Renaissance, especially in the field of literature with such major talents as **William Shakespeare** (1564–1616).

Wales under the Tudors (1485–1603)

Welsh allegiance during the Wars of the Roses lay broadly with the Lancastrians, who had the support of the ascendant north Welsh Tewdwr (or Tudor) family. Welsh expectations of the first Tudor monarch, Henry VII, were high and though Henry lived up to some of them – removing many of the restrictions on land ownership imposed at the start of Glyndŵr's uprising, and promoting many Welshmen to high office – administration remained piecemeal. Control was still shared between the Crown and largely independent Marcher lords until a uniform administrative structure was achieved under Henry VIII.

Wales had been largely controlled by the English monarch since the Treaty of Rhuddlan in 1284, but the **Acts of Union** in 1536 and 1543 formalized English sovereignty over the country. At the same time the Marches were replaced by shires (the equivalent of modern counties), the Welsh laws codified by Hywel Dda were made void and partible inheritance gave way to primogeniture. For the first time the Welsh and English enjoyed legal equality, but the break with native traditions wasn't well received. Most of the people remained poor, the gentry became increasingly anglicized and the use of Welsh was banned.

As for the **church**, Christianity had always been a ritual way of life rather than a philosophical code in Wales, and consequently Protestantism soon supplanted Catholicism during the religious upheavals of Henry VIII's reign. What the Reformation did promote was a more studied approach to religion and learning in general. Under the reign of Elizabeth I, Jesus College was founded in Oxford for Welsh scholars, and the Bible was translated into Welsh for the first time by a team led by Bishop **William Morgan**.

With new landownership laws enshrined in the Acts of Union, the stimulus provided by the Dissolution hastened the emergence of the Anglo-Welsh gentry, a group eager to claim a Welsh pedigree while promoting the English language and the legal system, which helped to perpetuate their hegemony. Meanwhile, landless peasants remained poor, only gaining slightly from the increase in cattle trade with England and the development of mining and ore smelting.

The Stewarts in Scotland (1371–1603)

In the decades following the death of Bruce in 1329, the Scottish monarchy gradually declined. The last of the Bruce dynasty died in 1371, to be succeeded by the "Stewards", hence **Stewarts** (known as Stuarts in England). However, a series of them came to the throne while still children, so the power vacuum was filled by the nobility, whose key members exercised control as Scotland's regents while carving out territories that they ruled with the power, if not the title, of kings. **James IV** (1488–1513), the most talented of the early Stewarts, might have restored the authority of the Crown, but his invasion of England ended in a terrible defeat for the Scots – and his own death – at the **Battle of Flodden Field**.

The reign of **Mary, Queen of Scots** (1542–87), typified the problems of the Scottish monarchy. Mary came to the throne when just one week old, and immediately caught the attention of the English king, Henry VIII, who sought, first by persuasion and then by military might, to secure her hand in marriage for his 5-year-old son, Edward. Beginning in 1544, the English launched a series of devastating attacks on Scotland, until, in the face of another English invasion in 1548, the Scots – or at least those not supporting Henry – turned to the "Auld Alliance". The French king proposed marriage between Mary and the Dauphin Francis, promising in return military assistance against the English. The 6-year-old queen sailed for France in 1548, leaving her loyal nobles and their French allies in control, and her husband succeeded to the French throne in 1559. When she returned thirteen years later, following the death of Francis, she had to deal with something entirely new – the religious Reformation.

The **Reformation** in Scotland was a complex social process, whose threads are hard to unravel. Nevertheless, it's quite clear that by the middle of the sixteenth century the established Church was held in general contempt. Protestantism became associated with anti-French feeling brought on, in no small measure, by Mary of Guise, the French mother of the absent Queen Mary, who had become regent of Scotland in 1554: Mary of Guise had alienated the Scottish nobility by appointing Frenchmen to high office rather than Scots. In 1557, a group of Scottish nobles banded together to form the **Lords of the Congregation**, with a dual purpose to oppose French influence and promote the reformed religion. With English military backing, the Protestant lords succeeded in deposing Mary of Guise in 1559, and, when the Scottish Parliament assembled shortly afterwards, it asserted the primacy of Protestantism.

Mary tried to avoid an open breach with her Protestant subjects, but her difficulties were exacerbated by a disastrous second marriage to **Lord Darnley**. A cruel character, his jealousy led to his involvement in the murder of Mary's favourite, **David Rizzio**, who was dragged from the queen's chambers at Holyrood and stabbed 56 times. The incident caused Scottish Protestants more than a little unease, though they were even more horrified when, in 1567, Darnley himself was murdered and Mary promptly married the **Earl of Bothwell**, widely believed to be the murderer. This was too much to bear, and the Scots rose in rebellion, driving Mary into exile in England at the age of just 25. The queen's illegitimate half-brother, the Earl of Moray, became regent and her son, the infant James, was left behind to be raised a Protestant prince. Mary, meanwhile, was seen as such a threat to the English throne that Queen Elizabeth I had little choice but to imprison and ultimately execute her in 1587.

With Mary gone, Protestant reformer **John Knox** could concentrate on the organization of the reformed Church, or **Kirk**, which he envisaged as a body empowered to intervene in the daily lives of the people. Andrew Melville, another leading reformer, proposed the abolition of all traces of episcopacy – the rule of the bishops in the Church – and suggested instead a **presbyterian** structure, administered by a hierarchy of assemblies, part elected and part appointed. At the bottom of the chain, beneath the General Assembly, Synod and Presbytery, would be the Kirk session, responsible for church affairs, the performance of the minister and the morals of the parish. In 1592, the Melvillian party achieved a measure of success when presbyteries and synods were accepted as legal church courts and the office of bishop was suspended.

United Kingdom: 1603–1660

The son of Mary, Queen of Scots, **James VI of Scotland** succeeded Elizabeth as **James I of England** (1603–1625), thereby **uniting the English and Scottish crowns**. James quickly moved to end hostilities with Spain and adopted a policy of toleration to the country's Catholics. Inevitably, both initiatives offended many Protestants, whose worst fears were confirmed in 1605 when **Guy Fawkes** and a group of Catholic conspirators were discovered preparing to blow up the king and Houses of Parliament in London in the foiled **Gunpowder Plot**: Fawkes was hung, drawn and quartered. **Puritan** fundamentalism and commercial interests converged with the founding of the first permanent **colony in North America** in Virginia in 1608. Twelve years later, the Pilgrim Fathers landed in New England, establishing a colony that would absorb about a hundred thousand Puritan immigrants by the middle of the century.

Meanwhile, James restored the Scottish bishops, much to the fury of the Presbyterians and assorted Protestants, and in England succeeded in alienating his landed gentry. He clung to an absolutist vision of the monarchy – the divine right of kings – that was totally out of step with the Protestant leanings of the majority of his subjects and he also relied heavily on court favourites, especially the much reviled George Villiers, Duke of Buckingham. It was a recipe for disaster, but it was to be his successor, **Charles I** (1625–49), who reaped the whirlwind. Charles inherited James's dislike of the Protestants and approval of absolutism, ruling without Parliament from 1629 to 1640. However, he overreached himself when he tried to impose a new Anglican prayer book on the Kirk. Scottish reformers denounced these changes as "popery" and organized the **National Covenant**, a religious pledge that committed the signatories to "Labour by all means lawful to recover the purity and liberty of the Gospel as it was established and professed." Charles declared all the "**Covenanters**" to be rebels, a proclamation endorsed by his Scottish bishops. Consequently, when the king backed down from military action and called a General Assembly of the Kirk, the assembly promptly abolished the episcopacy. Charles pronounced the proceedings illegal, but lack of finance stopped him from mounting an effective military campaign – whereas the Covenanters, well financed by the Kirk, assembled a proficient army under Alexander Leslie. In desperation, Charles summoned the English Parliament hoping it would pay for an army, but – like the calling of the General Assembly in Scotland – the decision was a disaster and Parliament refused to support Charles. Indeed, the **Long Parliament**, as it became known, impeached several of Charles's allies, and compiled its grievances in the Grand Remonstrance of 1641.

Confronted by this concerted hostility, the king withdrew to Nottingham where he raised his standard, the opening act of the **Civil War**. The Royalist forces ("Cavaliers") were initially successful, winning the Battle of Edgehill. In response, **Oliver Cromwell** overhauled the Parliamentarian army ("Roundheads"), to create the formidable **New Model Army**, which won the battles of Naseby and Marston Moor. Charles surrendered to the Scots, who handed him over to the English Parliament, by whom he was ultimately executed in January 1649. The following year, at the invitation of the Earl of Argyll, Charles's son, the future Charles II, returned from exile to Scotland. In order to secure his royal inheritance, Charles was obliged to renounce his father and sign the Covenant, two bitter pills taken to impress the Scots. In the event, however, the "Presbyterian Restoration" was short-lived: Cromwell invaded, defeated the Scots at Dunbar and forced Charles into exile.

For the next eleven years the whole of Britain was a **Commonwealth** – at first a true republic, then, after 1653, a **Protectorate** with Cromwell as Lord Protector and commander-in-chief. He reformed the government, secured commercial treaties with foreign nations and used his New Model Army to put the fear of God into his various enemies. The turmoil of the Civil War and the pre-eminence of the army spawned a host of leftist sects, the most notable of whom were the **Levellers**, who demanded wholesale constitutional reform. **Nonconformist** religious groups also flourished, prominent among them the pacifist **Quakers**, led by George Fox (1624–91), and the **Dissenters**, to whom the most famous writers of the day, John Milton (1608–74) and John Bunyan (1628–88), both belonged. Cromwell died in 1658 to be succeeded by his son **Richard**, who ruled briefly and ineffectually, and in May 1660, Parliament voted to restore the monarchy and **Charles II** (1660–85), the exiled son of the previous king, was crowned.

The Restoration and the later Stuarts (1660–1714)

The terms of the **Restoration** included a general amnesty for all those who had fought against the Stuarts, except those who had signed Charles I's death warrant. With the re-establishment of a royal court came a new exuberance in art, literature and theatre, and the foundation of the **Royal Society**, whose scientific endeavours were furthered by Isaac Newton (1642–1727). However this period also saw the **Great Plague** of 1665 and the **Great Fire of London** (1666). Politically, there were still underlying tensions between the monarchy and Parliament, though the latter was more concerned with the struggle between the **Whigs** and **Tories**, political factions representing, respectively, the low-church gentry and the high-church aristocracy. There was a degree of religious toleration too, but its brittleness was all too apparent in the anti-Catholic riots of 1678.

The succession of the Catholic **James II** (1685–88), brother of Charles II, provoked much opposition, though there was still an indifferent response when the Protestant **Duke of Monmouth**, the favourite among Charles II's illegitimate sons, raised a rebellion in the West Country. Monmouth was defeated at Sedgemoor, in Somerset, in July 1685; nine days later he was beheaded at Tower Hill, and in the subsequent **Bloody Assizes** of Judge Jeffreys, hundreds of rebels and suspected sympathizers were executed or deported. James's unpopularity increased with his **Declaration of Indulgence**, which removed anti-Catholic restrictions, and further when the birth of his son secured a Catholic succession. Alarmed, the country's most powerful Protestants sent for **William of Orange**, the Dutch husband of Mary, the Protestant daughter of James II, to save them from Catholic tyranny. William landed in Devon and, as James's forces simply melted away, he speedily took control of London in the **Glorious Revolution** of 1688. This was the final postscript to the Civil War – although it was another three years before James and his Jacobite forces were finally defeated in Ireland.

William and Mary (1688–94) were made joint sovereigns after they agreed to a **Bill of Rights** defining the limitations of the monarchy's power and the rights of its subjects, thereby making Britain a **constitutional monarchy**, in which the roles of legislature and executive were separate and interdependent. The model was broadly consistent with that outlined by the philosopher and political thinker **John Locke** (1632–1704), whose essentially Whig doctrines of toleration and social contract were gradually embraced as the new orthodoxy.

After Mary's death, William (1694–1702) ruled alone; during his reign the **Act of Settlement of 1701** was passed, barring Catholics, or anyone married to one, from succession to the English throne. This Act did not, however, apply in Scotland, and the English feared that the Scots would invite James II's son, James Edward Stuart, back from France to be their king. These fears were allayed when Scotland passed the **Act of Union** uniting the English and Scottish parliaments in 1707, though neither the Scottish legal system nor the Presbyterian Kirk were merged with their English equivalents.

After William's death the crown passed to Mary's sister **Anne** (1702–14), whose reign saw British armies winning a string of remarkable victories on the continent, beginning with the Duke of Marlborough's triumph at Blenheim in

1704, followed the next year by the capture of Gibraltar, establishing a British presence in the Mediterranean. These military escapades were part of the Europe-wide **War of the Spanish Succession**, which rumbled on until the Treaty of Utrecht in 1713 – a treaty which all but settled the European balance of power for the rest of the eighteenth century.

The Hanoverians (1714–1815)

On Anne's death, the succession passed to the Protestant Elector of Hanover, who became **George I** (1714–27) of England. This prompted the first major **Jacobite uprising** in support of James Edward Stuart, the "Old Pretender" (Pretender in the sense of having pretensions to the throne, Old to distinguish him from his son Charles, the "Young Pretender"). Its timing appeared perfect: Scottish opinion was moving against the Union, which had failed to bring Scotland any tangible economic benefits. Moreover, Jacobite sentiments were not confined to Scotland – there were many in England who toasted the "king across the water". In 1715, the Earl of Mar raised the Stuart standard at Braemar Castle in Scotland and just eight days later he captured Perth, where he gathered an army of over 10,000 men. Mar's rebellion took the government by surprise. They had only 4000 soldiers in Scotland, under the command of the Duke of Argyll, but Mar dithered until he lost the military advantage. There was an indecisive battle at Sheriffmuir, but by the time the Old Pretender landed in Scotland in December 1715, 6000 veteran Dutch troops had reinforced Argyll. The rebellion disintegrated rapidly and James slunk back to exile in France.

Back in London, power slowly leaked away from the monarchy into the hands of the Whig oligarchy; the king ceased to attend Cabinet meetings, his place being taken by his chief minister. Most prominent of these ministers was **Robert Walpole** (1676–1745), regarded as the UK's **first prime minister**.

Peace ended in the reign of **George II** (1727–60), when England declared war on Spain in 1739 at the start of yet another dynastic squabble, the eight-year War of the Austrian Succession. Then, in 1745, came the second and most dangerous of the Jacobite rebellions, with the **Young Pretender**, **Charles Stuart** (aka Bonnie Prince Charlie) and his Highland army reaching as far south as Derby, just 120 miles from London, and creating pandemonium in the capital. However, their lines of supply were over-extended, and they failed to rally the Lowland Scots – never mind the English – to their cause, so were obliged to retreat north. A Hanoverian army under the brutal Duke of Cumberland caught up with them at Culloden Moor near Inverness, in April 1746, and hacked them to pieces. Jacobite hopes died at Culloden and the prince lived out the rest of his life in drunken exile. In the aftermath of the uprising, the wearing of tartan, the bearing of arms and the playing of bagpipes were all banned. Most significantly, the government prohibited the private armies of the chiefs, thereby effectively destroying the clan system.

Meanwhile, the **Seven Years War** (1756–1763) harvested England yet more overseas territory in India and Canada at the expense of France and, in 1768, **Captain James Cook** sailed to New Zealand and Australia, thereby netting another chunk of the globe. In 1760, **George III** (1760–1820) succeeded his father. The early years of his sixty-year reign saw a revived political struggle between king and Parliament, enlivened by the intervention of John Wilkes, first of a long and increasingly vociferous line of parliamentary radicals. The contest was exacerbated by the deteriorating relationship with the thirteen colonies of North America, a situation brought to a head by the **American Declaration of Independence** and Britain's subsequent defeat in the Revolutionary War.

Chastened by this disaster, Britain chose not to interfere in the momentous events taking place across the Channel, where France, long its most consistent foe, was convulsed by revolution. Out of the turmoil emerged the most daunting of enemies, **Napoleon** (1769–1821), whose stunning military progress was interrupted by Nelson at **Trafalgar** in 1805 and finally halted ten years later by the Duke of Wellington at **Waterloo**.

The Industrial Revolution

Britain's triumph over Napoleon was largely due to the country's financial strength, born out of the **Industrial Revolution**. This switch from an agricultural to a manufacturing economy transformed Britain in the space of a hundred years. The earliest mechanized production lines were in the Lancashire **cotton mills**, where cotton spinning went from a cottage industry to a highly productive factory-based system. James Watt's **steam engine**, patented in 1781, ended the use of water to power the mills: Watt's engines needed **coal**, which made it important to locate mills and factories near coal mines. Accordingly, there was a shift of population towards the Midlands, central Scotland and the north of England, where the great coal reserves were located, and as the industrial economy boomed and diversified, so these regions' towns mushroomed at an extraordinary rate. Steel towns like Sheffield grew up, huge cotton warehouses were built in Manchester and vast dock facilities in Liverpool, where raw materials from India and the Americas came in and manufactured goods went out. Commerce and industry were also served by improving transport facilities, such as the building of a network of **canals**, but the great leap forward came with the arrival of the **railway**, heralded by the Stockton–Darlington line in 1825, followed five years later by the Liverpool–Manchester railway, where George Stephenson's *Rocket* made its first outing.

Boosted by a vast influx of Jewish, Irish, French and Dutch workers, the country's population rose from about eight and a half million at the beginning of George III's reign to more than fifteen million at its end. And as the factories and their attendant towns expanded, so the rural settlements of England declined, inspiring the elegiac pastoral yearnings of Samuel Taylor Coleridge and William Wordsworth, the first great names of the **Romantic** movement, though later Romantic poets such as Percy Bysshe Shelley and Lord Byron took a more socially engaged position. Meanwhile discontent was rising among the nation's factory workers when machines put thousands of them out of work, and the **Chartist** movement was born to demand parliamentary reform – the most important of the industrial boom towns were still unrepresented in Parliament – and the repeal of the **Corn Laws**, which kept the price of bread artificially high. In 1819, during a mass demonstration in support of parliamentary reform in Manchester, protestors were hacked down by troops in what became known as the **Peterloo Massacre**.

The following year, a weak, blind and insane George III died to be succeeded, in fairly rapid succession, by two of his sons, **George IV** (1820–30) and then **William IV** (1830–37). Tensions continued to run high throughout the 1820s, until a series of judicious parliamentary acts were passed: the **Reform Act** of 1832 established the principle (if not always the practice) of popular representation; the **Poor Law** of 1834 improved the condition of the most destitute; and the repeal of the Corn Laws in 1846 reduced the price of bread. Significant sections of the middle classes supported progressive reform, as evidenced by the immense popularity of **Charles Dickens** (1812–70), whose novels railed against poverty and injustice. John Wesley (1703–91) and his **Methodists** had preempted these social concerns by leading the anti-slavery campaign. As a result of their efforts, slavery was banned in Britain in 1772 and throughout the British Empire in 1833.

Victorian Britain

William IV was succeeded by his niece, **Victoria** (1837–1901), whose long reign witnessed the zenith of British power. For much of the period, the economy boomed, and the British trading fleet was easily the mightiest in the world, with Victoria becoming the symbol of both the nation's success and the imperial ideal. There were extraordinary intellectual achievements too – as typified by the publication of Charles Darwin's *On the Origin of Species* in 1859. Britain's industrial and commercial prowess was best embodied by the great engineering feats of **Isambard Kingdom Brunel** (1806–1859) and by the **Great Exhibition** of 1851, a display of manufacturing achievements without compare.

During the last third of the century, Parliament was dominated by the duel between Disraeli and the Liberal leader **Gladstone**. It was Disraeli who eventually passed the Second Reform Bill in 1867, further extending the electoral franchise, but it was Gladstone's first ministry of 1868–74 that created some of the century's most far-reaching legislation, including compulsory education, and the full legalization of trade unions.

There were foreign entanglements, too. In 1854 troops were sent to protect the Ottoman Empire against the Russians in the **Crimea**, an inglorious debacle whose horrors were relayed to the public by the first-ever press coverage of a military campaign and by the revelations of **Florence Nightingale** (1820–1910), who was appalled by the lack of medical care for soldiers. The fragility of Britain's hold over the Asian subcontinent was exposed during the **Indian Mutiny** of 1857, though the imperial status quo was eventually restored and Victoria took the title Empress of India after 1876. Thereafter, the British army fought a series of minor wars against poorly armed Asian and African opponents, but promptly came unstuck when it faced the Dutch settlers of South Africa in the **Boer War** (1899–1902). The British ultimately fought their way to a sort of victory, but the discreditable conduct of the war prompted a military shake-up at home that was to be of significance in the coming European war.

The two World Wars (1914–1945)

Victoria was succeeded by her son, **Edward VII** (1901–10), whose leisurely lifestyle could be seen as the epitome of the complacent era to which he gave his name. This complacency came to an end with the accession of **George V** (1910–36) and more specifically on August 4, 1914, when the Liberal government, honouring the Entente Cordiale signed with France in 1904, declared war on Germany. Hundreds of thousands volunteered for the army, but their enthusiastic nationalism was not enough to ensure a quick victory and **World War I** dragged on for four miserable years. Britain and her allies eventually prevailed, but the number of dead beggared belief, undermining the British people's respect for their ruling class, whose generals had displayed a startling combination of incompetence and indifference to the plight of their men. Many looked admiringly towards the Soviet Union, where Communists had rid themselves of the Tsar and seized control in 1917.

At the war's end in 1918 the political fabric of Britain was changed dramatically when the sheer weight of public opinion pushed Parliament into extending the **vote** to all men over 21 and to women over 30. The liberalization of women's rights owed much to the efforts of the radical **Suffragettes**, led by

Emmeline Pankhurst and her daughters Sylvia and Christabel, but the process was only completed in 1929 when women were at last granted the vote at 21, on equal terms with men.

During this period, the **Labour Party** supplanted the Liberals as the main force on the left wing of British politics, its strength built on an alliance between the working-class trade unions and middle-class radicals. Labour formed its first government in 1923 under **Ramsay MacDonald** (1866–1937), but the publication of the **Zinoviev Letter**, a forged document that purported to be a letter from the Soviets urging British leftists to promote revolution, undermined MacDonald's position and the Conservatives were returned with a large parliamentary majority in 1924. Two years later, a bitter dispute between the nation's colliers and the owners of the coal mines escalated into a **General Strike**, quickly spreading from the coal mines to the railways, the newspapers and the iron and steel industries. The strike lasted nine days and involved half a million workers, provoking the government into draconian action – the army was called in, and the strike was broken. The economic situation deteriorated further after the crash of the New York Stock Exchange in 1929, precipitating a worldwide depression. Unemployment reached over 2.8 million in 1931, generating a series of mass demonstrations, which peaked with the **Jarrow March** from the Northeast to London in 1936. The same year, economist John Maynard Keynes argued in his *General Theory of Employment, Interest and Money* for a greater degree of state intervention in the management of the economy, though the whole question soon became overshadowed by international events.

Abroad, the structure of the **British Empire** had undergone profound changes since World War I. The status of **Ireland** had been partly resolved following the electoral gains of the nationalist Sinn Féin in 1918. Their success led to the establishment of the Irish Free State in 1922, though (and this was to cause endless problems thereafter) the six counties of the mainly Protestant North (Ulster) chose to stay part of the United Kingdom. Four years later, the **Imperial Conference** recognized the autonomy of the British dominions, comprising all the major countries that had previously been part of the Empire. This agreement was formalized in the 1931 Statute of Westminster; each dominion was given an equal footing in a **Commonwealth of Nations**, though each still recognized the British monarch. The royal family itself was shaken in 1936 by the **abdication of Edward VIII** (1936), following his decision to marry a twice-divorced American, Wallis Simpson. In the event, the succession passed smoothly to his brother **George VI** (1936–52), though the royals had a hard job regaining their popularity among the population as a whole.

Non-intervention in both the Spanish Civil War and the Sino-Japanese War was paralleled by a policy of appeasement towards **Adolf Hitler**, who began to rearm Germany in earnest in the mid-1930s, so when **World War II** broke out in September 1939, Britain was seriously unprepared. In May 1940, a national coalition government headed by the charismatic **Winston Churchill** (1874–1965) took over from Neville Chamberlain. Partly through Churchill's manoeuvrings, the United States became a supplier of foodstuffs and munitions to Britain, then broke trade links with Japan in June in protest at their attacks on China. In response to the Japanese bombing of Pearl Harbour on December 7, 1941, the US joined the war, declaring against both Japan and Germany, and its intervention, combined with the stirring efforts of the Soviet Red Army, swung the military balance. In terms of the number of casualties, World War II was not as calamitous as World War I, but its impact upon the civilian population of Britain was much greater. In its first wave of **bombing** on the UK, the Luftwaffe caused massive damage to industrial and supply centres such as

London, Glasgow, Swansea, Coventry, Manchester, Liverpool, Southampton and Plymouth. In later raids, intended to shatter morale rather than factories and docks, the cathedral cities of Canterbury, Exeter, Bath, Norwich and York all took a battering too.

Postwar Britain: from Attlee to Thatcher: 1945–1990

The end of the war in 1945 was quickly followed by a general election. Hungry for change (and demobilization), the electorate replaced Churchill with the Labour Party under **Clement Attlee** (1883–1967), who, with a large parliamentary majority, set about a radical programme to **nationalize** the coal, gas, electricity, iron and steel industries, as well as the inland transport services. The **National Insurance Act** and the **National Health Service Act** were both passed early in the Labour administration, giving birth to what became known as the **welfare state**. But despite substantial American aid, the huge problems of rebuilding the economy made austerity the keynote, with the rationing of food and fuel remaining in force long after 1945.

In April 1949, Britain, the United States, Canada, France and the Benelux countries signed the **North Atlantic Treaty** as a counterbalance to Soviet power in Eastern Europe. Yet confusion regarding Britain's post-imperial role was shown up by the **Suez Crisis** of 1956, when Anglo-French and Israeli forces invaded Egypt to secure control of the Suez Canal, only to be hastily recalled following international (American) condemnation. Revealing severe limitations on the country's capacity for independent action, the Suez incident resulted in the resignation of the Conservative prime minister Anthony Eden, who was replaced by the more pragmatic **Harold Macmillan** (1894–1986). Nonetheless, Macmillan maintained a nuclear policy that suggested a continued desire for an international role, and nuclear testing went on against a background of widespread marches under the auspices of the Campaign for Nuclear Disarmament.

The 1960s, dominated by the Labour premiership of **Harold Wilson** (1916–1995), saw a boom in consumer spending, some pioneering social legislation (primarily on the legalization of homosexuality and abortion), and a corresponding cultural upswing, with London becoming the hippest city on the planet. The good times lasted barely a decade. Though Tory prime minister Edward Heath led Britain into the brave new world of the **European Economic Community** (ECC), the 1970s were a decade of recession and industrial strife. A succession of public-sector strikes and mistimed decisions by James Callaghan's Labour government handed the 1979 general election to the Conservatives, led by **Margaret Thatcher**, Britain's first female prime minister.

Thatcher went on to win three general elections, steering the UK into a period of sharp social polarization. While taxation policies and easy credit fuelled a consumer boom for the professional classes, the erosion of manufacturing industry and the weakening of the welfare state impoverished a great swathe of the population. However, Thatcher won an increased majority in the 1983 election, largely thanks to the successful recapture of the **Falkland Islands**, a remote British dependency in the south Atlantic, retrieved from the occupying Argentine army in 1982. Her electoral domination was also assisted by the fragmentation of the Labour opposition.

Social and political tensions surfaced in sporadic urban rioting and the year-long **miners' strike** (1984–85) against colliery closures, a bitter industrial dispute in which the police were given unprecedented powers to restrict the movement of citizens. The violence in Northern Ireland also intensified, and in 1984 the bombing campaign of the IRA came close to killing the entire Cabinet when they blew up the Brighton hotel where the Conservatives were staying during their annual conference.

The 1990s to today

The divisive politics of Thatcherism reached their apogee with the introduction of the **Poll Tax**, a desperately unpopular tax that led ultimately to Thatcher's overthrow by Conservative colleagues who feared defeat should she lead them into another general election. The uninspiring new leader was **John Major**, who nonetheless managed to win the Conservatives a fourth term of office in 1992, albeit with a much reduced Parliamentary majority. While his government presided over steady economic growth, they gained little credit amid allegations of mismanagement, incompetence, corruption and feckless leadership. The Conservatives were also divided over Europe, with the pro-European Union (formerly EEC) faction pitted against the vocal right-wing Eurosceptics, who were vehemently against the EU in general and the proposed common currency – the euro – in particular.

The early 1990s saw further difficulties for the **Royal Family**, with the messy break-up of the marriage of Prince Charles and Diana. Revelations about the cruel treatment of Diana by both the prince and his family badly damaged the royals' reputation, including that of **Queen Elizabeth II**. In contrast with her in-laws, **Diana**, who was formally divorced from Charles in 1994, appeared warm-hearted and glamorous; her death in a car accident in Paris in 1997 had a very profound impact on the British, leading to unprecedented public grieving.

Meanwhile, the **Labour Party**, which had been wracked by factionalism in the 1980s, regrouped under Neil Kinnock and then John Smith, though neither reaped the political rewards. These dropped into the lap of a new and dynamic young leader, **Tony Blair**, who soon began to move the party away from traditional left-wing socialism. Blair's mantle of idealistic, media-friendly populism swept the Labour Party to power in the **general election of May 1997** on a wave of genuine popular optimism. There were immediate rewards in enhanced relations with Europe and progress in the Irish peace talks, and Blair's electoral touch was soon repeated in Labour-sponsored **devolution referenda**, whose results semi-detached Scotland and Wales from their larger neighbour. The Scots got a Parliament, the Welsh an Assembly, reflecting different levels of devolution – the first has more powers than the second. There was also much Labourite tub-thumping about the need to improve **public services**, but Blair only set about the task in earnest after the **general election of June 2001**, which Labour won with another parliamentary landslide. This second victory, however, reflected little of the optimism of before and voter turnout was lower than any time since World War II. Few voters fully trusted Blair and his administration, which developed a reputation for "spin" – laundering events to present the government in the best possible light.

Blair's second term saw massive and much-needed investment in public services, with education and health being the prime beneficiaries, and a concerted attempt to lift the country's poorer citizens out of poverty. However, the focus was torn abruptly away from the domestic agenda with the bombing of New York's World Trade Center on **September 11, 2001**. Blair's rush to support President Bush in his attack on Afghanistan and, in 2003, **Iraq**, permanently alienated a large section of Labour's support. Although Saddam Hussein was deposed with relative ease, neither Bush nor Blair seemed to have a coherent exit strategy, and back home Blair was widely seen as having spun Britain into the war by exaggerating the danger Hussein presented with his alleged Weapons of Mass Destruction – none of which were ever found.

Nonetheless, Blair's political opponents failed to deliver the *coup de grâce* and he managed to win a **third general election in May 2005** – though with the promise of stepping down before the end of the term. This bizarre situation was apparently the result of an agreement between Blair and his longtime ally and rival in the Labour Party, **Gordon Brown**. Finally, in June 2007, Blair did indeed move on, and was succeeded by Brown without any contest. Born in Glasgow and brought up in Fife, where he is an MP, Brown has so far shown little of Blair's surefootedness, and it remains to be seen whether he can persuade a rather Labour-weary electorate to stick with him in the years to come. One of the main challenges ahead will be in the regions, most of all in Scotland itself, where Labour has a declining presence. Moreover, the First Minister, Scottish Nationalist Alex Salmond, has promised to pursue his agenda for ever greater devolution and ultimately independence for Scotland – probably, he thinks, by 2017.

Books

Most of the books listed below are paperbacks in print – those that are out of print should be easy to track down either in second-hand book shops or through Amazon's used and secondhand book service (@www.amazon.co.uk, @www.amazon.com). Note also that while we recommend all the books we've listed below, we do have our favourites, however partial and partisan – and these have been marked with a ★.

Travel and journals

★ **Bill Bryson** *Notes from a Small Island*. Bryson's best-selling and highly amusing account of an extended journey round Britain.

William Cobbett *Rural Rides*. First published in 1830, Cobbett's account of his various fact-finding tours bemoaned the death of the old rural England and its customs, while decrying both the growth of cities and the iniquities suffered by the exploited urban poor.

David Craig *On the Crofter's Trail*. Using anecdotes and interviews with descendants, Craig conveys the hardship and tragedy of the Highland Clearances without being mawkish.

Daniel Defoe *Tour through the Whole Island of Great Britain*. Defoe, the son of a London butcher, was a novelist, pamphleteer, journalist and sometime spy. This classic travelogue opens a fascinating window onto 1720s Britain.

Charles Jennings *Up North*. A provocative, but very readable account of a mid-1990s journey round the north of England, by a self-confessed southerner.

Jan Morris *The Matter of Wales*. Prolific half-Welsh travel writer Jan Morris immerses herself in the country that she evidently loves. Highly partisan and fiercely nationalistic, the book combs over the origins of the Welsh character, and describes the people and places of Wales with precision and affection.

Samuel Pepys *The Diary of Samuel Pepys*. Pepys kept a voluminous diary from 1660 until 1669, recording the fall of the Commonwealth, the Restoration, the Great Plague and the Great Fire, as well as describing the daily life of the nation's capital. The unabridged version is published in eleven weighty tomes; there's also an abridged version.

J.B. Priestley *English Journey*. Quirky account of the Bradford-born author's travels around England in the 1930s.

Paul Theroux *The Kingdom by the Sea*. Thoroughly bad-tempered critique of a depressed and drizzly nation.

Dorothy Wordsworth *Journals*. The engaging diaries of William's sister, with whom he shared Dove Cottage in the Lake District, provide a vivid account of walks and visits, and reflect Dorothy's fascination with the natural world.

History, society and politics

Asa Briggs *Social History of England*. Immensely accessible overview of English life from Roman times to the 1980s.

Beatrix Campbell *Diana, Princess of Wales: How sexual politics shook the monarchy*. A little hastily written perhaps, but still the most penetrating insight into the life and times of Diana. Also her *Goliath: Britain's Dangerous Places* explores the decline of traditional working-class culture and the rise of the English yob – the young, violent male.

Alan Clark *Diaries: In Power*. Candid, conceited and often cutting account of the inner sanctum of Thatcher's government by this controversial former minister. Easily the most interesting of the barrow-loads of political memoirs churned out in the 1980s and 1990s.

Linda Colley *Britons: Forging the Nation 1707–1837*. Successful and immaculately researched book that offers all sorts of fresh insights into eighteenth-century Britain and the evolution of a national identity.

David Daiches (ed) *The New Companion to Scottish Culture*. More than 300 articles interpreting Scottish culture in its widest sense, from eating to marriage customs, the Scottish Enlightenment to children's street games.

Friedrich Engels *The Conditions of the Working Class in England*. Portrait of life in England's hellish industrial towns, written in 1844 when Engels was only 24.

Mark Girouard *Life in the English Country House*. Fascinating documentation of the day-to-day existence of the landed gentry; packed with the sort of facts that get left out by tour guides.

Christopher Hill *The English Revolution* and *The World Turned Upside-Down*. Britain's foremost Marxist historian, Hill was without doubt the most interesting writer on the Civil War and Commonwealth period.

Eric Hobsbawm *Industry and Empire*. Ostensibly an economic history of Britain from 1750 to the late 1960s charting Britain's decline and fall as a world power, this book's great skill lies in its detailed analysis of the effects on ordinary people. By the same author, *Captain Swing* focuses on the labourers' uprisings of nineteenth-century England, while his magnificent trilogy, *The Age of Revolution 1789–1848*, *The Age of Capital 1848–1875* and *The Age of Extremes 1914–1991* can't be beaten.

Philip Jenkins *A History of Modern Wales 1536–1990*. Magnificently thorough book, placing Welsh history in its British and European contexts. Unbiased and rational appraisal of events and the struggle to preserve Welsh consciousness.

Michael Lynch (ed) *The Oxford Companion to Scottish History*. A copious collection, covering two thousand years and subjects as varied as climate, archeology, folklore and national identity.

A.J.P. Taylor *The First World War: An Illustrated History*. Penetrating analysis of how the war started and why it went on for so long; first published in 1963, but still unsurpassed. Similarly unrivalled is *The Origins of the Second World War*, also published in the 1960s.

E.P. Thompson *The Making of the English Working Class*. A seminal text – essential reading for anyone who wants to understand the fabric of English society.

Wynford Vaughan-Thomas *Wales – a History*. This masterpiece is a warm and spirited history of Wales. Working chronologically from the pre-Celtic dawn to the aftermath of the 1979 devolution vote, the book offers perhaps the clearest explanation of the evolution of Welsh culture.

Regional guides

Paul Bailey (ed) *Oxford Book of London*. Authoritative anthology of writings, observations and opinions about the capital. Published in 1995

Joe Fisher *The Glasgow Encyclopedia*. The essential Glasgow reference book, covering nearly every facet of this complex urban society.

Simon Jenkins *England's Thousand Best Churches* and *England's Thousand Best Houses*. Jenkins is a well-known UK journalist and these two superb books describe the pick of England's churches and houses in lucid detail. Wittily written, the books are divided into counties with a star system to indicate the best. For the houses book, Jenkins adopts a wide brief, including all sorts of curiosities from caves in Nottingham to prefabs in Buckinghamshire.

Jan Morris *Oxford*. Adulatory but inspiring collection on Oxford by the famous travel writer.

Pathfinder Walks Series of practical guides with maps and route descriptions to popular outdoor spots such as the Yorkshire Dales, the Chilterns, Cornwall and the Cotswolds. Produced by the Ordnance Survey.

A. Wainwright *A Coast to Coast Walk*. Beautiful palm-sized guide by acclaimed English hiker and Lake District expert. Printed from his handwritten notes and sketched maps. Also in the series are seven authoritative books covering a variety of walks and climbs in the Lake District.

Ben Weinreb and Christopher Hibbert *The London Encyclopaedia*. More than a thousand pages of concisely presented and well-illustrated information on London past and present – the most fascinating single book on the capital.

Art, architecture and archeology

John Betjeman *Ghastly Good Taste, Or, A Depressing Story of the Rise and Fall of English Architecture*. Classy – and classic – one-hundred page account of England's architecture written by one of the country's shrewdest poet-commentators. First published in 1970.

William Gaunt *English Painting*. This succinct and excellently illustrated book provides a useful introduction to its subject, covering the Middle Ages to the twentieth century in just 260 pages.

Samantha Hardingham *London: A guide to recent architecture*. A handy pocket-sized book detailing the best of the capital's modern buildings.

Andrew Hayes *Archaeology of the British Isles*. Useful introduction to the subject from Stone Age caves to early medieval settlements.

Duncan MacMillan *Scottish Art 1460–2000* and *Scottish Art in the Twentieth Century*. The former is a lavish overview of Scottish painting with good sections on landscape, portraiture and the Glasgow Boys, while the latter covers the last hundred years in splendid detail.

Thomas Pakenham *Meetings With Remarkable Trees*. Unusual and intriguing large-format picture book about the author's favourite sixty trees, delving into their character as much as the botany.

Nikolaus Pevsner *The Englishness of English Art*. Wide-ranging romp through English art concentrating on Hogarth, Reynolds, Blake and

Constable, including a section on the Perpendicular style and landscape gardening.

Pevsner and others *The Buildings of England, Scotland and Wales*. Magisterial series, at least one volume per county, covering just about every inhabitable structure in the country. This project was initially a one-man show, but later authors have revised Pevsner's text, inserting newer buildings but generally respecting the founder's personal tone.

Fiction before 1900

Jane Austen *Pride and Prejudice*; *Sense and Sensibility*; *Emma*; *Persuasion*. All-time classics on manners, society and provincial life; all laced with bathos and subtly ironic plot twists.

R.D. Blackmore *Lorna Doone*. Blackmore's swashbuckling, melodramatic romance, set on Exmoor, has done more for West Country tourism than any other book.

James Boswell *The Life of Samuel Johnson*. England's most famous man of letters and pioneer dictionary-maker has his engagingly low-life Scottish biographer to thank for the longevity of his reputation.

Charlotte Brontë *Jane Eyre*. Deep, harrowing and quietly feminist story of a much put-upon governess.

Emily Brontë *Wuthering Heights*. Set on the Yorkshire Moors, this is the ultimate English melodrama, complete with volcanic passions, craggy landscapes, ghostly presences and gloomy villagers.

John Bunyan *Pilgrim's Progress*. Simple, allegorical tale of hero Christian's struggle to achieve salvation.

Geoffrey Chaucer *Canterbury Tales*. Fourteenth-century collection of bawdy tales told in verse during a pilgrimage to Canterbury. If you don't fancy struggling with the Old English of the original, there are lots of translations – into blank verse, prose and even rhyming couplets.

Daniel Defoe *Journal of a Plague Year*. An account of the Great Plague seen through the eyes of an East End saddler and written some sixty years after the event.

Thomas De Quincey *Confessions of an English Opium Eater*. Tripping out with the most famous literary drug-taker after Coleridge – *Fear and Loathing in Las Vegas* it isn't, but neither is this a simple cautionary tale.

Charles Dickens *Bleak House*; *David Copperfield*; *Little Dorrit*; *Oliver Twist*; *Hard Times*. Many of Dickens' novels are set in London, including *Bleak House*, *Oliver Twist* and *Little Dorrit*, and these contain some of his most trenchant pieces of social analysis; *Hard Times*, however, is set in a Lancashire mill town, while *David Copperfield* draws on Dickens' own unhappy experiences as a boy, with much of the action taking place in Kent and Norfolk.

George Eliot *Scenes of Clerical Life*; *Middlemarch*; *Mill on the Floss*. Eliot (real name Mary Ann Evans) wrote mostly about the county of her birth, Warwickshire, the setting for the three depressing tales that comprise her fictional debut, *Scenes of Clerical Life*. *Middlemarch* is a gargantuan portrayal of English provincial life prior to the Reform Act of 1832, while *Mill on the Floss* is based on her own childhood experiences.

Henry Fielding *Tom Jones*. Mock-epic comic novel detailing the exploits of its lusty orphan-hero; set in Somerset and London.

Thomas Hardy *Far from the Madding Crowd; The Mayor of Casterbridge; Tess of the D'Urbervilles; Jude the Obscure.* Hardy's novels contain some famously evocative descriptions of his native Dorset, but at the time of their publication it was Hardy's defiance of conventional pieties that attracted most attention: *Tess*, in which the heroine has a baby out of wedlock and commits murder, shocked his contemporaries, while his bleakest novel, the Oxford-set *Jude the Obscure*, provoked such a violent response that Hardy gave up novel-writing altogether.

Sir Walter Scott *Waverley*. The first of the books that did much to create the romanticized version of Scottish life and history. Others include *Rob Roy*, a rich and ripping yarn that transformed the diminutive brigand into a national hero.

William Shakespeare *Complete Works*. The entire output can usually be picked up at a bargain price. For individual plays, you can't beat the Arden Shakespeare series, each volume containing illuminating notes and good introductory essays.

Lawrence Sterne *Tristram Shandy*. Anarchic, picaresque eighteenth-century ramblings based on life in a small English village; full of bizarre textual devices – like an all-black page in mourning for one of the characters.

Robert Louis Stevenson *Dr Jekyll and Mr Hyde; Kidnapped; The Master of Ballantrae; Treasure Island; Weir of Hermiston.* Superbly imagined and pacily written nineteenth-century tales of intrigue and adventure.

William Makepeace Thackeray *Vanity Fair*. A sceptical but compassionate overview of English capitalist society by one of the leading realists of the mid-nineteenth century.

Anthony Trollope *Barchester Towers*. Trollope was an astonishingly prolific novelist who also, in his capacity as a postal surveyor, found time to invent the letter box. The "Barsetshire" novels, of which *Barchester Towers* is the best known, are set in and around a fictional version of Salisbury.

Izaak Walton *Compleat Angler*. Light-hearted, seventeenth-century fishing guide set on London's River Lea. Sprinkled with poems and songs, it has gone through more reprints than any other comparable book in the English language.

Contemporary fiction

Peter Ackroyd *English Music*. A typical Ackroyd novel, constructing parallels between interwar London and distant epochs to conjure a kaleidoscopic vision of English culture. His other novels, such as *Chatterton, Hawksmoor* and *The House of Doctor Dee*, are variations on his preoccupation with the English psyche's darker depths.

Julian Barnes *England, England; Metroland*. One of the UK's most versatile writers, Barnes seems to be able to turn his hand to just about anything. His controversial *England, England* is a satire on the role of tourism in England with the country being re-created as a theme park on the Isle of Wight, while *Metroland* tells the story of two boys growing up in London's suburbs.

George Mackay Brown *Beside the Ocean of Time*. A child's journey through the history of an Orkney island, and an adult's effort to make sense of the place's secrets in the late twentieth century.

John Buchan *The Complete Richard Hannay*. This one volume includes *The 39 Steps, Greenmantle, Mr Standfast, The Three Hostages* and *The Island of Sheep*. Good gung-ho stories with a great feel for Scottish landscape.

Joseph Conrad *The Secret Agent*. Spy story based on the 1906 anarchist bombing of Greenwich Observatory, exposing the hypocrisies of both the police and anarchists.

Daphne du Maurier *Frenchman's Creek*; *Jamaica Inn*; *Rebecca*. Nail-biting, swashbuckling romantic novels set in the author's adopted home of Cornwall.

Helen Fielding *Bridget Jones's Diary*. Originating as a newspaper column, Fielding's fictional account of contemporary female "neuroses" proved to be the literary phenomenon of the late 1990s, spawning a host of lesser imitators.

E.M. Forster *Howards End*. Bourgeois angst in Hertfordshire and Shropshire, by one of the country's best-loved modern novelists.

John Fowles *The Collector*; *The French Lieutenant's Woman*; *Daniel Martin*. *The Collector*, Fowles' first novel, is a psychological thriller in which the heroine is kidnapped by a psychotic pools-winner, the story being told once by each protagonist. *The French Lieutenant's Woman*, set in Lyme Regis on the Dorset coast, is a tricksy neo-Victorian novel with a famous DIY ending, while *Daniel Martin* is a dense, realistic novel set in postwar Britain.

Lewis Grassic Gibbon *A Scots Quair*. A landmark trilogy, set in northeast Scotland during and after World War I, the events are seen through the eyes of Chris Guthrie, "torn between her love for the land and her desire to escape a peasant culture". Strong, seminal work.

William Golding *The Spire*; *Rites of Passage*. Atmospheric novel centred on the building of a cathedral spire, taking place in a thinly disguised medieval Salisbury. Also, if you ever wondered what it was like to be at sea in an early nineteenth-century British ship, try the splendid *Rites of Passage* trilogy.

Robert Graves *Goodbye to All That*. Horrific and humorous memoirs of public school and World War I trenches, followed by postwar trauma and life in Wales, Oxford and Egypt.

Alasdair Gray *Lanark*. Gray's first novel was twenty-five years in the writing and remains his most influential, leading Anthony Burgess to hail him as "the most important Scottish writer since Sir Walter Scott". This challenging, loosely autobiographical work – part science fiction, part *bildungsroman* – relates in sometimes hallucinatory style the journey of a man who longs to create great art.

Graham Greene *Brighton Rock*; *The Human Factor*; *The Heart of the Matter*. Three of the best from the prolific Greene: *Brighton Rock* is a melancholic thriller with heavy Catholic overtones, set in the criminal underworld of a seaside resort; *The Human Factor*, written some forty years later, probes the underworld of London's spies; while *The Heart of the Matter* is a searching and very English novel exploring the Anglo-Catholic mindset.

James Kelman *The Busconductor Hines*; *How Late It Was*. The first is a wildly funny story of a young Glasgow bus conductor with an intensely boring job and a limitless imagination. *How Late It Was* is Kelman's award-winning and controversial look at life from the perspective of a blind Glaswegian drunk. A disturbing study of personal and political violence, with language to match.

D.H. Lawrence *Sons and Lovers; Lady Chatterley's Lover; Selected Short Stories*. Lawrence's magnificent prose on working-class life in Nottinghamshire's pit villages never went down well with the locals. His early short stories contain some of his finest writing, as does *Sons and Lovers*, a fraught, autobiographical novel, and the infamous *Lady Chatterley's Lover*, which brings together sex and class.

Laurie Lee *Cider with Rosie*. Beautifully written reminiscences of adolescent frolics in the rural Cotswolds of the 1920s.

Richard Llewellyn *How Green Was My Valley; Up into the Singing Mountain; Down Where the Moon is Small; Green, Green My Valley Now*. Vital tetralogy in eloquent and passionate prose, following the life of Huw Morgan from his youth in a South Wales mining valley through emigration to the Welsh community in Patagonia and back to 1970s Wales. A bestseller during World War II and still the best introduction to the vast canon of "valleys novels", *How Green Was My Valley* captured a longing for a simple if tough life, steering clear of cloying sentimentality.

Ian McEwan *Atonement; Saturday*. Many reckon McEwan to be England's finest contemporary novelist, his dark and brooding works punctuated by the unforeseen and the accidental. *Atonement* is possibly his most masterful book, tracing the course of three lives from a sweltering country garden in 1935 to absolution in the new century, while *Saturday* provides an evocative (and controversial) insight into contemporary London and responses to the "war on terror".

Alan Sillitoe *Saturday Night and Sunday Morning*. Gritty account of factory life and sexual shenanigans in Nottingham in the late 1950s.

Dylan Thomas *Under Milk Wood; Collected Stories; Collected Poems: 1934–1953*. *Under Milk Wood* is Thomas's most popular play, telling the story of a microcosmic Welsh seaside town over a 24-hour period. *Collected Stories* contains all of Thomas's classic prose pieces: *Quite Early One Morning*, which metamorphosed into *Under Milk Wood*, the magical *A Child's Christmas in Wales* and the compulsive, crackling autobiography, *Portrait of the Artist as a Young Dog*. Thomas's beautifully wrought and inventive poems carry a deep, pained concern with mortality and the nature of humanity.

Evelyn Waugh The *Sword of Honour* Trilogy is a brilliant satire of the World War I officer class laced with some of Waugh's funniest set pieces. The best-selling *Brideshead Revisited* is possibly his worst book, rank with snobbery, nostalgia and money-worship.

PG Wodehouse *Thank You, Jeeves; A Damsel in Distress*. For many, Wodehouse (1881–1975) is the quintessential English humorist and his deftly crafted tales – with their familiar cast of characters, primarily Bertie Wooster and Jeeves – have remained popular for decades.

Virginia Woolf *Orlando; Mrs Dalloway*. Woolf's lover, Vita Sackville-West, is the model for *Orlando*, whose life spans four centuries and both genders. *Mrs Dalloway*, which relates the thoughts of a London society hostess and a shell-shocked war veteran, sees Woolf's "stream of consciousness" style in full flow.

Contemporary crime fiction

Stephen Booth *Black Dog*; *Scared to Live*. The Derbyshire Peak District, its locations and traditions are the backdrop for Booth's effective thrillers, in which detective Ben Cooper pursues the truth.

Ian Rankin *Knots and Crosses*; *The Falls*. Britain's best-selling crime author introduced John Rebus in 1987 and since then the hard-drinking, anti-authoritarian, emotionally scarred detective has featured in almost twenty novels. He inhabits the mean streets of Edinburgh that the tourists rarely see, though in cherished locations like the *Oxford Bar* pub visitors can rub shoulders with Rebus.

Ruth Rendell/Barbara Vine *From Doon With Death*; *Gallowglass*; *King Solomon's Carpet*; *Grasshopper*. Rendell writes brilliantly and disturbingly of contemporary dysfunction in all its guises. Her longstanding Inspector Wexford series is set in the fictional West Sussex town of Kingsmarkham, but it's writing as Barbara Vine that Rendell excels in a sense of place, namely London, creating serious, memorable fictions from unsung locales like Kilburn and Cricklewood, the London tube, and the streets and rooftops of Maida Vale.

Peter Robinson *Gallows View*; *A Piece of My Heart*. Robinson's lauded Inspector Banks series has used the bleak corners and beauty spots of the Yorkshire Dales to dramatic effect. His gritty novels featuring the troubled, music-loving detective show a sophistication gleaned from studying creative writing under Joyce Carol Oates.

Poetry before 1900

William Blake *The Complete Poems*. Blake ranges from the limpid wisdom of *Songs of Innocence and Experience* to the mystical complexities of the prophetic books. He is unique among major poets in illustrating his own work, most of which is set in, or has a significant relationship to, London.

Robert Burns *Selected Poems*. Comprises the best-known work of Scotland's greatest bard, who employed vigorous vernacular language. Immensely popular all over the world, his famous early poems include *Auld Lang Syne* and *My Love Is Like A Red, Red Rose*.

Lord Byron *Selected Poems*. Byron was a best-seller in his day celebrated for his exotic poems of adventure such as *The Corsair*, and he is also a master of the Romantic lyric; but the core of his achievement lies in his unfailingly inventive satire on all aspects of early nineteenth-century life, *Don Juan*.

Samuel Taylor Coleridge Coleridge wrote little, but to the highest quality. *Kubla Khan* and *The Rime of the Ancient Mariner* are amongst the strangest products of the Romantic period, but equally noteworthy are the quieter "conversation" poems such as *Frost at Midnight*.

John Donne *The Complete English Poems*. Donne (1572–1631), the greatest of the "metaphysical poets", brought passionate physicality and brilliant intellectual rigour to both his love poetry and religious verse.

John Keats *Selected Poems*. Keats was potentially one of the greatest writers who ever lived. Even given his early death – he was only 25 – his achievements in poems such as the *Ode to Autumn* are extraordinary.

Percy Bysshe Shelley *Selected Poems*. Shelley's poetry moves from swooning Romantic intensity to a vigorously expressed hatred of the establishment of his day. He is a seminal figure in the pantheon of English radical dissent.

Alfred Tennyson *Selected Poems*. Tennyson's is perhaps the most purely musical poetry in English, filled with sensuous detail and dreamy evocations of natural beauty and the past. *In Memoriam* shows him to be the great poet of Victorian doubt and faith.

William Wordworth *Selected Poetry*. It's impossible to exaggerate Wordsworth's originality and his influence on the future direction of English culture; his presence is clearly felt in the novels of Dickens and George Eliot as well as in the work of later poets. His understanding of what it means to be human can only be described as profound.

Contemporary poetry

W.H. Auden *Collected Poems*. Auden combines the themes of history, politics and love in poems that are definitive expressions of his times. The politically committed work of the 1930s gives way to a later religious commitment, but all his work is marked by stylistic virtuosity.

John Betjeman *Collected Poems*. Betjeman's humorous and often nostalgic work dissected England and the English in satirical light verse, homing in on provincial and suburban manners.

T.S. Eliot *The Waste Land*. Published in 1922, this is considered one of the cornerstones of Modernist writing, offering a revolutionary vision of Western civilization imbued with resonant images of contemporary and ancient London.

Ted Hughes *Collected Poems*. Best known for his brooding, sometimes brutal portrayals of nature, Hughes set much of his verse in his native Yorkshire. *Birthday Letters*, published just before his death in 1998, was a moving account of his complex relationship with the poet Sylvia Plath.

Philip Larkin *Collected Poems*. Larkin used plain language in his work, the subject of which is often the insignificance of human life. Many of the poems achieve an apparently unstudied beauty, though in fact Larkin published very little, preferring to refine his verse to its basic elements.

Hugh MacDiarmid *Selected Poems*. A poet and nationalist who sought, through his fine lyrical verse, to reinvigorate the use of Scottish literary language.

Roger McGough *Blazing Fruit: Selected Poems*. A contemporary Liverpool poet, whose witty rhetorical verse is instantly recognizable. Some of McGough's earlier work, alongside Adrien Henri and Brian Patten, can be found in the influential 1960s collection *The Mersey Sound*.

Wilfred Owen *The Poems of Wilfred Owen*. As with Keats, Owen's early death was a tragedy for English literature. His war poetry is at its best in the likes of *Strange Meeting*, with its strikingly original use of half-rhymes.

Film

For much of its history the British **film industry** has largely been an English affair, with its major studios (Ealing, Pinewood and Shepperton) not far from central London and its stars drawn from the ranks of the capital's stage. However, unlike the Hollywood star system, the English film industry tended – and still significantly relies on – strong ensemble playing. While **Ealing's** films were a byword for social comedy, other significant elements have included the **Hammer horror series** (usually featuring either or both Christopher Lee and Peter Cushing), costume dramas typified by the **Gainsborough** company's productions and the **James Bond** films, while the cheeky, cheap-and-cheerful **Carry On** series kept a generation of comedy actors in work long past their sell-by dates. In the 1960s, British films developed a justifiable reputation for social realism, which has been maintained in more recent times by directors such as **Ken Loach** and **Mike Leigh**.

For the most part, however, Britain's film industry is still in thrall to Hollywood values, though without Hollywood's commercial nous. The few international successes tend to be drawn from adaptations of literary works, costume dramas and a rather stale concoction of easily exportable, largely class-based stereotypes. All too often, the influence of television means that many productions are essentially unambitious and parochial small-screen ventures, though occasionally something genuinely original breaks the mould.

The films listed below are all set in the UK. They are not exclusively greats – though some rank amongst the best movies ever made – but all depict a particular aspect of British life, whether reflecting the experience of immigrant communities, exploring the country's history, or depicting its richly varied landscapes.

The 1930s and 1940s

Brief Encounter (David Lean, 1945). Wonderful weepie as Trevor Howard and Celia Johnson teeter on the edge of adultery at a commuter railway station. Noël Coward was responsible for the clipped dialogue, Rachmaninov for the flushed, dreamy score.

Brighton Rock (John Boulting, 1947). A fine adaptation of Graham Greene's novel, featuring a young, genuinely scary Richard Attenborough as the psychopathic hood Pinkie, who marries a witness to one of his crimes to ensure her silence. Beautiful cinematography and good performances, with a real sense of *film noir* menace.

Fires Were Started (Humphrey Jennings, 1943). One of the best films to come out of the British documentary tradition, this is the story of the experiences of a group of firemen through one night of bombing during the Blitz. The use of real firemen as performers rather than professional actors, and the avoidance of formulaic heroics, gives the film great power as an account of the courage of ordinary people who fought, often uncelebrated, on the home front.

Great Expectations (David Lean, 1946). Early film by one of England's finest directors – *Lawrence of Arabia*, *Bridge on the River Kwai* – this superb rendition of the Dickens novel features magnificent performances by John Mills (as Pip) and Finlay Currie (as Abel Magwitch). The scene in the graveyard is nothing short of wonderful.

Henry V (Laurence Olivier, 1944). Featuring glowing Technicolor backdrops, this wonderful piece of wartime propaganda is emphatically "theatrical", the action spiralling out from the Globe Theatre itself. Olivier is a brilliantly charismatic king, the pre-battle scene where he goes disguised amongst his men being delicately muted and atmospheric.

Jane Eyre (Robert Stevenson, 1943). Joan Fontaine does a fine job of portraying Jane, and Orson Welles is a suavely sardonic Rochester – the scene where he is thrown from his horse in the mist hits the perfect melodramatic pitch. With the unlikely tagline "A Love Story Every Woman Would Die a Thousand Deaths to Live!", it briefly features a young Elizabeth Taylor as a dying Helen Burns.

Kind Hearts and Coronets (Robert Hamer, 1949). As with the best of the Ealing movies, this is a savage comedy on the cruel absurdities of the British class system. With increasing ingenuity, Dennis Price's suave and ruthless anti-hero murders his way through the d'Ascoyne clan (all brilliantly played by Alec Guinness) to claim the family title.

The Life and Death of Colonel Blimp (Michael Powell and Emeric Pressburger, 1943). An epic celebration of the oft-ridiculed romantic spirit of the English, personified by the wonderful Roger Livesey. We follow him through the actual and emotional duels of his youth, against his equally dashing German foe, to crusty old age in World War II. A daring and visually stunning story of love and friendship, it was hated by Churchill for supposedly being unpatriotic, which is surely recommendation enough.

The Private Life of Henry VIII (Alexander Korda, 1933). The catalyst for a boom in British film-making – thanks to the success of the gargantuan Charles Laughton in the title role – this film has little now to commend it other than some superb cinematography and Laughton's own sometimes grotesque performance.

Rebecca (Alfred Hitchock, 1940). Hitchcock does Du Maurier: Laurence Olivier is wonderfully enigmatic as Maxim de Winter, and Joan Fontaine glows as his meek second wife, living in the shadow of her mysterious predecessor. Perfectly paced and beautifully shot, Hitch's first Hollywood picture is a true classic.

The Thirty-Nine Steps (Alfred Hitchcock, 1935). Hitchcock's best-loved British movie, full of wit and bold acts of derring-do. Robert Donat stars as innocent Richard Hannay, inadvertently caught up in a mysterious spy ring and forced to flee both the spies and Scotland Yard. In a typically perverse Hitchcock touch, he spends a generous amount of time handcuffed to Madeleine Carroll, fleeing across the Scottish countryside, before the action returns to London for the film's great music-hall conclusion.

Whisky Galore! (Alexander Mackendrick, 1949). When a shipwrecked stock of the water of life is washed ashore on a remote Scottish island, the locals contrive all manner of cunning ruses to conceal its presence from the pursuing authorities. A beautiful Ealing comedy, with real sympathy for its eccentric little community as they battle the forces of dull authority in the entirely laudable ambition of having a good time at no expense.

The Wicked Lady (Leslie Arliss, 1945). One of the best of Gainsborough Studios' series of escapist romances, this features a magnificently amoral and headstrong Margaret Lockwood, wooed into a criminal double life by James Mason's quintessentially dashing highwayman.

Its opulent re-creation of eighteenth-century England is terribly appealing, as are the tempestuous entanglements of its two wayward stars.

Wuthering Heights (William Wyler, 1939). The version of Emily Brontë's novel that everyone remembers, with Laurence Olivier as the dysfunctional Heathcliff and Merle Oberon as Cathy. It's tense, passionate and wild, and lays proper emphasis on the Yorkshire landscape, the only place where the doomed lovers can belong.

1950 to 1970

Billy Liar! (John Schlesinger, 1963). Tom Courtenay is stuck in a dire job as an undertaker's clerk in a northern town, and spends his time creating extravagant fantasies. His life is lit up by the appearance of Julie Christie, who holds out the glamour and promise of swinging London. Touching and amusing.

Far From the Madding Crowd (John Schlesinger, 1967). A largely successful and imaginative adaptation of Hardy's doom-laden tale of the desires and ambitions of wilful Bathsheba Everdene. Julie Christie is a radiant and spirited Bathsheba, Terence Stamp flashes his blade to dynamic effect, Alan Bates is quietly charismatic as dependable Gabriel Oak, and the West Country setting is sparsely beautiful.

Kes (Kenneth Loach, 1969). The unforgettable story of a neglected Yorkshire schoolboy who finds solace and liberation in training his kestrel. As a still-pertinent commentary on poverty and an impoverished school system, it's bleak but idealistic. Pale and pinched David Bradley, who plays Billy Casper, is hugely affecting.

The Ladykillers (Alexander Mackendrick, 1955). Alec Guinness is fabulously toothy and malevolent as "Professor Marcus", a murderous con man who lodges with a sweet little old lady, Mrs Wilberforce. The professor and his ragbag of criminal accomplices – their sinister intent a hilarious counterpoint to Mrs Wilberforce's genteel tea parties – try to pass themselves off as musicians, while, thanks to her innocent interventions, the body count inexorably mounts.

A Man for All Seasons (Fred Zinnemann, 1966). Sir Thomas More versus Henry VIII in one of British history's great moral confrontations. However, tedium intrudes, largely due to the film's stage-bound, talky origins in Robert Bolt's play, though there's a heavenly host of theatrical talent (including a cheering appearance by Orson Welles as Cardinal Wolsey).

Night and the City (Jules Dassin, 1950). Great *film noir*, with Richard Widmark as an anxious nightclub hustler on the run. Gripping and convincingly sleazy, the London streetscapes have an expressionist edge of horror.

Performance (Nicolas Roeg/Donald Cammell, 1970). Credited with precipitating James Fox's breakdown and subsequent retirement from the movies, this shape-shifting tale of gangsters and pop culture is the best account of the hedonistic end to Britain's psychedelic 1960s. The film also starred Mick Jagger, and, despite scenes of brutal violence, is brilliantly funny in parts.

Saturday Night and Sunday Morning (Karel Reisz, 1960). Reisz's monochrome captures all the grit and dead-end grind of Albert Finney's life working in a Nottingham bicycle factory and his attempts to find excitement and romance in the city.

This Sporting Life (Lindsay Anderson, 1963). One of the key British films of the 1960s, *This Sporting Life* tells the story of a northern miner turned star player for his local rugby team. The young Richard Harris gives a great performance as the inarticulate anti-hero, able only to express himself through physical violence, and the film is one of the best examples of the gritty "kitchen sink" genre it helped to usher in.

The War Game (Peter Watkins, 1965). Watkins' astonishing documentary approach to the effects of a Russian nuclear attack on southeast England, using both local people and various official "talking heads", shocked its commissioner, the BBC, into refusing to show it. Although dated, it still retains the power to alarm.

The 1970s and 1980s

Akenfield (Peter Hall, 1974). A powerfully involving evocation of English rural life whose ingredients include glowing cinematography and Michael Tippett's wonderful music. Past and present are skilfully contrasted, but the heart of the film lies in its sometimes ecstatic, but also harsh, rendering of the past.

Babylon (Franco Rosso, 1980). A moving account of black working-class London life. We follow the experiences of young Blue through a series of encounters that reveal the insidious forces of racism at work in Britain. Good performances and a great reggae soundtrack: an all too rare example of Black Britain taking centre stage in British movies.

A Clockwork Orange (Stanley Kubrick, 1971). Famously banned in the UK by director Kubrick, this is a genuinely disturbing if now slightly dated depiction of violence and society's reaction to it, in which young droog Alex – played with charm and menace by Malcolm McDowell – finds himself first the perpetrator and then the victim, to a rousing soundtrack of Beethoven classics.

Comrades (Bill Douglas, 1986). In 1830s England, a group of farm workers decide to stand up to the exploitative tactics of the local landowner, and find themselves prosecuted and transported to Australia. Based on the true story of the Tolpuddle Martyrs, this combines political education (the founding of the modern union movement) with a moving and visually stunning celebration of working lives.

Distant Voices, Still Lives (Terence Davies, 1988). Beautifully realized autobiographical tale of growing up in Forties and Fifties Liverpool. The mesmeric pace is punctuated by astonishing moments of drama, and the whole is a very moving account of how a family survives and triumphs, in small ways, against the odds.

Get Carter (Mike Hodges, 1971). One of the most vivid and interesting British gangster movies, featuring a monumentally evil outing for Michael Caine as the eponymous villain, returning to his native Newcastle to avenge his brother's death. Great use of its northeast locations and a fine turn by playwright John Osborne as the local godfather don't quite, however, compensate for its now faintly ridiculous misogyny.

Hope and Glory (John Boorman, 1987). A glorious autobiographical feature about the Blitz seen through the eyes of 9-year-old Bill, who revels in the liberating chaos of bomb-site playgrounds, tumbling barrage balloons and shrapnel collections. His older sister's romps with a Canadian soldier and the adults' privation and occasional despair are an additional source of amusement for Bill and his tiny sister.

The Last of England (Derek Jarman, 1987). Derek Jarman was a genuine maverick presence in Eighties Britain; this is his most abstract account of the state of the nation. Composed of apparently unrelated shots of decaying London landscapes, rent boys, and references to emblematic national events such as the Falklands War, this may not be to all tastes, but it is a fitting testament to Jarman's unique talent.

Mona Lisa (Neil Jordan, 1986). This fine London-based thriller has powerful performances from Bob Hoskins, Michael Caine and then-newcomer Cathy Tyson, the latter playing a high-class prostitute who recruits Hoskins to help find her lost friend. This takes him, and us, on a nightmarish exploration of the dark side of Eighties London, lightened only slightly as Bob begins to fall for his beautiful employer.

My Beautiful Laundrette (Stephen Frears, 1985). A slice of Thatcher's Britain, with a young Asian, Omar, on the make, opening a ritzy laundrette, where he employs his lover (Daniel Day-Lewis), an ex-National Front glamour boy. The racial, sexual and class dynamics of their relationship are closely observed.

On the Black Hill (Andrew Grieve, 1987). A visually absorbing adaptation of Bruce Chatwin's rather slight novel of Welsh farming folk. Hardyesque characterization and a similar predilection for doom, with a strong performance by Bob Peck as stubborn Amos Jones, trapped in an unhappy marriage to a middle-class woman.

Withnail and I (Bruce Robinson, 1986). Richard E. Grant is superb as the raddled, drunken Withnail, an out-of-work actor with a penchant for drinking lighter fluid. Paul McGann is the "I" of the title – a bemused and beautiful spectator of Withnail's wild excesses, as they abandon an astonishingly grotty London flat for the wilds of a remote cottage, and the attentions of Withnail's randy Uncle Monty. A rare look at the 1960s that avoids nostalgia, and opts instead for emotional truth.

The 1990s

Bhaji on the Beach (Gurinder Chadha, 1993). An Asian women's group takes a day-trip to Blackpool in this issue-laden but enjoyable picture. A lot of fun is had contrasting the seamier side of British life with the mores of the Asian aunties, though the male characters are cartoon villains all.

Braveheart (Mel Gibson, 1995). Cod-Highland high camp, with a shaggy-haired Mel Gibson wielding his claymore as thirteenth-century Scottish nationalist William Wallace. The English are thieving effete scum, the Scots all warm-blooded noble savages, and history takes a firm back seat. Filmed largely in Ireland.

Breaking the Waves (Lars von Trier, 1996). A lyrical, moving drama set in a devout community in the north of Scotland. An innocent young woman, Bess (Emily Watson), falls in love with Danish oil-rig worker Jan (Stellan Skarsgaard). Blaming herself for the injury which cripples him, she embarks on a masochistic sexual odyssey, which rapidly takes her into uncharted waters.

East Is East (Damien O'Donnell, 1999). Seventies Salford is the setting for this lively comedy, with a Pakistani chip-shop owner struggling to keep control of his seven children as they rail against the strictures of Islam and arranged marriages. Inventively made, and with some pleasing performances.

Elizabeth (Shekhar Kapur, 1998). Charismatic Cate Blanchett is, thankfully, the still heart of this history-lite and madly over-blown production, where all political and emotional nuance is lost in an orgy of decapitations, swirling cloaks and stagy thunderstorms.

Four Weddings and a Funeral (Richard Curtis, 1994). Standard rom-com that used an American actress and gags based on English eccentricities to pull in big audiences worldwide. Unrepresentative of contemporary England with its Hugh Grant-led cast of middle-class whites, it still manages some very funny – and quite moving – set pieces.

The Full Monty (Peter Cattaneo, 1997). Six Sheffield ex-steel workers throw caution to the wind and become male strippers, their boast being that all will be revealed: the "full monty". Unpromising physical specimens all, they score an unlikely hit with the local lasses. The film was itself an unlikely hit worldwide: the theme of manhood in crisis is sensitively explored, and the long-awaited striptease is a joy to behold.

Ratcatcher (Lynne Ramsay, 1999). Set in 1970s Glasgow during a refuse-workers' strike, Ramsay's striking first feature follows 12-year-old James, who accidentally drowns his friend as the rubbish around the tenement blocks mounts. Weaving rich humour into the gloomy narrative, Ramsay layers poetic images of the city, rejecting realism for a lyrical, symbolic approach.

The Remains of the Day (James Ivory, 1993). Kazuo Ishiguro's masterly study of social and personal repression translates beautifully to the big screen. Anthony Hopkins is the overly decorous butler who gradually becomes aware of his master's fascist connections, Emma Thompson the housekeeper who struggles to bring his real, deeply suppressed feelings to the surface.

Richard III (Richard Loncraine, 1995). A splendid film version of a renowned National Theatre production, which brilliantly transposed the action to a fascist state in the 1930s. The infernal political machinations of a snarling Ian McKellen as Richard are heightened by Nazi associations, and the style of the period imbues the film with the requisite glamour, as does languorously drugged Kristin Scott-Thomas as Lady Anne.

Secrets and Lies (Mike Leigh, 1995). Much-loved Mike Leigh slice-of-life drama, with wonderful Timothy Spall at the head of a spectacularly dysfunctional London family. His sister Cynthia (Brenda Blethyn), her heart of gold buried in boozy, cloying unhappiness, is reunited with the black daughter she gave up for adoption at birth. Over-long improvised sequences, and a depiction of suburban vulgarity which comes close to parody, are lifted by stunning ensemble performances.

Shakespeare in Love (John Madden, 1998). Shakespeare is sexed up for Hollywood, but it works fine, full of humour and genuine wit, teetering on the edge of – and occasionally plunging into – unabashed absurdity. Joseph Fiennes, as the young Bard, struggles with his new play, Romeo and Ethel, but it all comes right after he meets Viola (Gwyneth Paltrow) – enough said.

Small Faces (Gillies MacKinnon, 1995). A moving little saga about the lives of three brothers growing up in 1960s Glasgow amid feuding gangs of local teenagers. We follow the rough education of young Lex, torn between the excitement and real danger of a life of fighting, and the alternative artistic ambitions of his older brother. A convincing and occasionally very funny re-creation of the period.

Trainspotting (Danny Boyle, 1996). High-octane dip into the heroin world of a group of young Scotsmen, including what might be the best cinematic representation of a heroin fix ever.

2000s

24-hour Party People (Michael Winterbottom, 2002). Steve Coogan plays the entrepreneurial and inspirational Tony Wilson in this fast-moving re-creation of the early days of Manchester's Factory Records. Stunning soundtrack too.

Atonement (Joe Wright, 2007). This adaptation of Ian McEwan's highly literary novel of misunderstanding and regret might well have fallen flat, but in fact works very well. The performances by Keira Knightley and James McAvoy are convincing and the plotting is fluent, though the set-piece Dunkirk scene looks overly contrived.

Bend It Like Beckham (Gurinder Chadha, 2003). Immensely successful film focusing on the coming of age of a football-loving Punjabi girl in a suburb of London. Both socially acute and comic.

Bridget Jones's Diary (Sharon Maguire, 2001). American Renée Zellweger put on a plummy English accent and several pounds to play the lead in this *Pride and Prejudice* for the new millennium. Ably assisted by deliciously nasty love-interest Hugh Grant, the film stands out as one of the better British romantic comedies of the last few years.

Dirty Pretty Things (Stephen Frears, 2003). A tumbling mix of melodrama, social criticism and black comedy, this forceful, thought-provoking film explores the world of Britain's illegal migrants.

Eastern Promises (David Cronenberg, 2007). With London as a rather underplayed setting, this violent thriller shows Cronenberg on top form, though following the more mainstream path he mined in his *History of Violence*. As in that film, the great Viggo Mortensen plays the lead, menacing and dark, embroiled in a web of Russian gangsters, prostitution and human vulnerability.

Gosford Park (Robert Altman, 2001). Astutely observed upstairs-downstairs murder mystery set in class-ridden 1930s England. The multi-layered plot is typical of the director while the who's who of great British actors is led by the superb Maggie Smith – and only let down by Stephen Fry's bumbling police inspector who looks like he's wandered in from an entirely different film.

Harry Potter and the Philosopher's Stone (Chris Colombus, 2001). The first film in a series about hero Harry Potter's life at wizard school did wonders for the English tourist industry with its use of places such as Alnwick Castle as locations. The subsequent films are also darkly enjoyable, with excellent ensemble casts – Spall, Gambon, Rickman, Thompson et al.

London to Brighton (Paul Andrew Williams, 2006). Shot on a minimal budget with an unknown writer/director and actors, this thriller that follows a prostitute and a twelve-year-old runaway fleeing from the criminal underworld has a raw charm. The sordid storyline and bleak settings are quintessentially British, making even Brighton look like hell.

Pride and Prejudice (Joe Wright, 2005). Despite the pouting of Keira Knightley in the leading role and the strange casting of Donald Sutherland as Mr Bennet, this version of Jane Austen's classic romance is a corker, with a great performance by Matthew MacFadyen as Darcy, superb cinematography and gorgeous music.

This is England (Shane Meadows, 2007). A review of 1980s skinhead culture, based on the director's own experiences. Period detail abounds in this volatile stew of masculinity, violence, race and class, set in Thatcher's Britain.

Glossary of architectural terms

Aisle Clear space parallel to the nave, usually with lower ceiling than the nave.

Altar Table at which the Eucharist is celebrated, at the east end of the church. (When the church is not aligned to the geographical east, the altar end is still referred to as the "east" end.)

Ambulatory Passage behind the chancel.

Apse The curved or polygonal east end of a church.

Arcade Row of arches on top of columns or piers, supporting a wall.

Ashlar Dressed building stone worked to a smooth finish.

Bailey Area enclosed by castle walls.

Barbican Defensive structure built in front of main gate.

Barrel vault Continuous rounded vault, like a semi-cylinder.

Boss A decorative carving at the meeting point of the lines of a vault.

Box pew Form of church seating in which each row is enclosed by high, thin wooden panels.

Broach spire Octagonal spire rising straight out of a square tower.

Broch A Scottish, circular, dry-stone fort, dating from the Iron Age.

Buttress Stone support for a wall; some buttresses are wholly attached to the wall, others take the form of an outer support with a connecting half-arch, known as a "flying buttress".

Capital Upper section of a column, usually carved.

Chancel Section of the church where the altar is located.

Chantry Small chapel in which mass was said for the soul of the person who financed its construction; none built after the Reformation as Protestants rejected the doctrine of prayers for the dead.

Choir Area in which the church service is conducted; next to or same as chancel.

Clerestory Upper storey of nave, containing a line of windows.

Coffering Regular recessed spaces set into a ceiling.

Crenellations Battlements with square indentations.

Crossing (church) The intersection of the nave, choir and transepts.

Decorated Middle Gothic style; about 1280–1380.

Dogtooth Form of early Gothic decorative stonework, looking like raised "X"s.

Dormer Window raised out of the main roof.

Early English First phase of Gothic architecture in England, about 1150–1280.

Fan vault Late Gothic form of vaulting, in which the area between walls and ceiling is covered with stone ribs in the shape of an open fan.

Finial Any decorated tip of an architectural feature.

Flushwork Kind of surface decoration in which tablets of white stone alternate with pieces of flint; very common in East Anglia.

Gargoyle Grotesque exterior carving, usually a decorative form of water spout.

Hammer beam Type of ceiling in which horizontal brackets support vertical struts that connect to the roof timbers.

Jesse Tree Christian legend asserts that Jesse, the father of King David, was the ancestor of Jesus, and Jesse windows trace the genealogical tree by means of their stained-glass pictures.

Keep Main structure of a castle.

Lady Chapel Chapel dedicated to the Virgin, often found at the east end of major churches.

Lancet Tall, narrow and plain window.

Lantern Upper part of a dome or tower, often glazed.

Misericord Carved ledge below a tip-up seat, usually in choir stalls, as support when occupant stands.

Motte Mound on which a castle keep stands.

Mullion Vertical post between the panes of a window.

Nave The main part of the church usually to the west of the central crossing.

Ogee Double curve; distinctive feature of Decorated style.

Oriel Projecting window.

Palladian Seventeenth- and eighteenth-century classical style adhering to the principles of Andrea Palladio.

Pediment Triangular space above a window or doorway.

Perpendicular Late Gothic style, about 1380–1550.

Pier A massive column, often consisting of several fused smaller columns.

Pilaster Flat column set against a wall.

Reredos Painted or carved panel behind an altar.

Rood screen Wooden screen supporting a crucifix (or rood), separating the choir from the nave; few survived the Reformation.

Rose window Large circular window, divided into vaguely petal-shaped sections.

Sedilia Seats for the participants in the church service, usually on the south side of the choir.

Stalls Seating for clergy in the choir area of a church.

Tracery Pattern formed by narrow bands of stone in a window or on a wall surface.

Transept Section of the main body of the church at right angles to the choir and nave.

Triforium Arcade above the nave or transept in a church.

Tympanum Panel over a doorway, often carved in medieval churches.

Vault Arched ceiling.

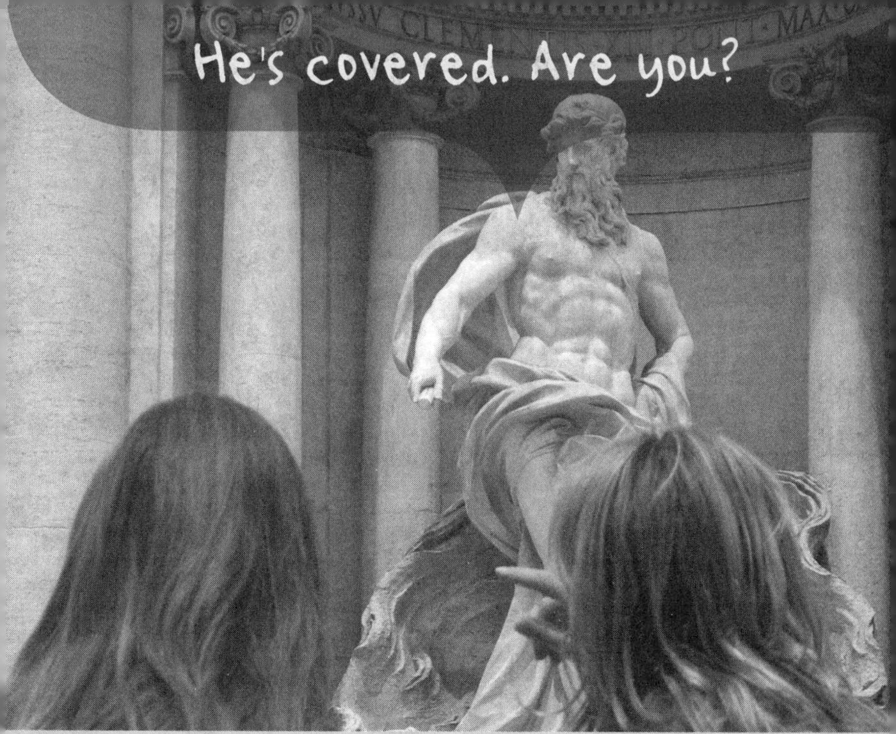

Small print and

Index

A Rough Guide to Rough Guides

Published in 1982, the first Rough Guide – to Greece – was a student scheme that became a publishing phenomenon. Mark Ellingham, a recent graduate in English from Bristol University, had been travelling in Greece the previous summer and couldn't find the right guidebook. With a small group of friends he wrote his own guide, combining a highly contemporary, journalistic style with a thoroughly practical approach to travellers' needs.

The immediate success of the book spawned a series that rapidly covered dozens of destinations. And, in addition to impecunious backpackers, Rough Guides soon acquired a much broader and older readership that relished the guides' wit and inquisitiveness as much as their enthusiastic, critical approach and value-for-money ethos.

These days, Rough Guides include recommendations from shoestring to luxury and cover more than 200 destinations around the globe, including almost every country in the Americas and Europe, more than half of Africa and most of Asia and Australasia. Our ever-growing team of authors and photographers is spread all over the world, particularly in Europe, the USA and Australia.

In the early 1990s, Rough Guides branched out of travel, with the publication of Rough Guides to World Music, Classical Music and the Internet. All three have become benchmark titles in their fields, spearheading the publication of a wide range of books under the Rough Guide name.

Including the travel series, Rough Guides now number more than 350 titles, covering: phrasebooks, waterproof maps, music guides from Opera to Heavy Metal, reference works as diverse as Conspiracy Theories and Shakespeare, and popular culture books from iPods to Poker. Rough Guides also produce a series of more than 120 World Music CDs in partnership with World Music Network.

Visit www.roughguides.com to see our latest publications.

Rough Guide travel images are available for commercial licensing at www.roughguidespictures.com

Rough Guide credits

Text editor: Lucy White
Layout: Jessica Subramanian
Cartography: Amod Singh
Picture editors: Sarah Cummins and Emily Taylor
Production: Rebecca Short
Proofreader: Samantha Cook and Karen Parker
Cover design: Chloë Roberts
Editorial: **London** Ruth Blackmore, Alison Murchie, Karoline Thomas, Andy Turner, Keith Drew, Edward Aves, Alice Park, Jo Kirby, James Smart, Natasha Foges, Róisín Cameron, Emma Traynor, Emma Gibbs, James Rice, Kathryn Lane, Christina Valhouli, Monica Woods, Mani Ramaswamy, Joe Staines, Peter Buckley, Matthew Milton, Tracy Hopkins, Ruth Tidball; **New York** Andrew Rosenberg, Steven Horak, AnneLise Sorensen, April Isaacs, Ella Steim, Anna Owens, Sean Mahoney, Paula Neudorf, Courtney Miller; **Delhi** Madhavi Singh, Karen D'Souza
Design & Pictures: **London** Scott Stickland, Dan May, Diana Jarvis, Nicole Newman, Mark Thomas; **Delhi** Umesh Aggarwal, Ajay Verma, Ankur Guha, Pradeep Thapliyal, Sachin Tanwar, Anita Singh, Nikhil Agarwal
Production: Vicky Baldwin
Cartography: **London** Maxine Repath, Ed Wright, Katie Lloyd-Jones; **Delhi** Jai Prakash Mishra, Rajesh Chhibber, Ashutosh Bharti, Rajesh Mishra, Animesh Pathak, Jasbir Sandhu, Karobi Gogoi, Alakananda Bhattacharya, Swati Handoo
Online: Narender Kumar, Rakesh Kumar, Amit Verma, Rahul Kumar, Ganesh Sharma, Debojit Borah, Saurabh Sati, Ravi Yadav
Marketing & Publicity: **London** Liz Statham, Niki Hanmer, Louise Maher, Jess Carter, Vanessa Godden, Vivienne Watton, Anna Paynton, Rachel Sprackett, Libby Jellie, Jayne McPherson, Holly Dudley; **New York** Geoff Colquitt, Katy Ball; **Delhi** Ragini Govind
Manager India: Punita Singh
Reference Director: Andrew Lockett
Operations Manager: Helen Phillips
PA to Publishing Director: Nicola Henderson
Publishing Director: Martin Dunford
Commercial Manager: Gino Magnotta
Managing Director: John Duhigg

Publishing information

This seventh edition published June 2008 by
Rough Guides Ltd,
80 Strand, London WC2R 0RL
345 Hudson St, 4th Floor,
New York, NY 10014, USA
14 Local Shopping Centre, Panchsheel Park,
New Delhi 110017, India
Distributed by the Penguin Group
Penguin Books Ltd,
80 Strand, London WC2R 0RL
Penguin Group (USA)
375 Hudson Street, NY 10014, USA
Penguin Group (Australia)
250 Camberwell Road, Camberwell,
Victoria 3124, Australia
Penguin Books Canada Ltd,
10 Alcorn Avenue, Toronto, Ontario,
Canada M4V 1E4
Penguin Group (NZ)
67 Apollo Drive, Mairangi Bay, Auckland 1310,
New Zealand

Cover concept by Peter Dyer.

Typeset in Bembo and Helvetica to an original design by Henry Iles.

Printed in Italy by LegoPrint S.p.A.

1112pp includes index

A catalogue record for this book is available from the British Library

ISBN: 978-1-85828-549-8

1 3 5 7 9 8 6 4 2

Help us update

We've gone to a lot of effort to ensure that the seventh edition of **The Rough Guide to Britain** is accurate and up to date. However, things change – places get "discovered", opening hours are notoriously fickle, restaurants and rooms raise prices or lower standards. If you feel we've got it wrong or left something out, we'd like to know, and if you can remember the address, the price, the hours, the phone number, so much the better.

Please send your comments with the subject line "**Rough Guide Britain Update**" to ⓔmail@roughguides.com. We'll credit all contributions and send a copy of the next edition (or any other Rough Guide if you prefer) for the very best emails.

Have your questions answered and tell others about your trip at ⓦcommunity.roughguides.com

Acknowledgements

Robert Andrews would like to thank heartily Jo Morgan and Quinn Andrews, for excellent contributions, and Lucy White for thorough and sympathetic editing.

Donald Reid would like to thank Colin Hutchison, Barry Shelby, Duncan Forgan and Claire Sawers for their contributions.

Tom Hutton would like to thank friends and family for accompanying him on numerous research trips. And also his partner, Steph, for her constant support and coping with life with a workaholic.

Readers' letters

Thanks to all the readers who have taken the time to write in with comments and suggestions (and apologies if we've inadvertently omitted or misspelt anyone's name):

GM Ackroyd, Mrs CB Allen, Julia Atkinson, Andy Bennetts, James Carron, Peter Cormack, Leslie Croce, Don Dennis, June Fillmore, Christian Fletcher, Anita R George, Steve Gillon, Sarah Hague, Godfrey Hall, Colin Hood, Rosalind Jarvis, Lesley Kew, Simon Kings, B Koo, Catherine Mackie, Donald J MacLeod, Andrew Moncrieff, Stephen & Sheilah Moore, Liz Mullen, Tim Newman, Mark C O'Connor, Vicki Ong, Richard and Barbara Siddall, Amanda Townley, Jenny Walmsley, WF White, S Whailin, Brenda Wickham, Dr A Young.

Photo credits

All photos © Rough Guides except the following:

Title page
Blustery day on Brighton seafront © Roger Bamber/Alamy

Introduction
Merry-go-round, Brighton © Mark Thomas/Axiom
Piccadilly underground © Photolibrary.com
Red telephone box in the snow © Realimage /Alamy
Tintern Abbey © The Photolibrary Wales/Alamy
Wild Red deer, Scottish highlands © John Morgan/Alamy
English pub © Photolibrary.com
Seafront fish and chips sign © Naki Kouyioumtzis/Axiom
Mug of tea © Photolibrary.com

Things not to miss
01 Steam train on the West Highland Line © Scottish Viewpoint/Alamy
02 Greek sculpture, British Museum © Mark Thomas/Axiom
07 Bottle-nosed dolphins © Blickwinkel/Alamy
08 Iona Abbey © David Ball/Alamy
09 Path beside Loch Lee, Glen Esk © Navin Mistry/Alamy
10 Whitby fish and chips © Mike Kipling/Alamy
13 Kinloch Castle © Michael Jenner/Alamy
15 Glenfinnan Monument © David Robertson /Digital Railroad
16 Cyclists in Wales © Tom Hutton
17 Edinburgh Castle © Lucy Cooke
18 Boat on Ullswater © Chris Coe/Axiom
21 National Museum of Wales, Cardiff © David Lyons/Alamy
27 Bath Spa © courtesy of Bath Spa
28 Harlech castle © Rolf Richardson/Alamy
30 County Arcade, Leeds © Diana Jarvis
31 Conwy Castle © Tom Hutton

Colour section: Coastal Britain
Windsurfing lessons in Sandbanks, Dorset © Buzz Pictures/Alamy
Par Beach, St Martins, Isles of Scilly © Sarah Cummins
Lobster pots, St Martins, Isles of Scilly © Sarah Cummins
Esha Ness © LOOK Die Bildagentur der Fotografen GmbH/Alamy

Colour section: Festivals and events

Detail of legs of two young girls © Scottish Viewpoint/Alamy

Girl dancing in the mud at Glastonbury Music Festival, England © Mark Thomas/Axiom

Children Dancing at Llangollen International Eisteddfod © The Photolibrary Wales/Alamy

Bog snorkelling © Jeff Morgan Llanwrtyd Wells/Alamy

Colour section: Literary Britain

Rydal Mount, home of the poet William Wordsworth, Ambleside, Lake District © Geoff Renner/Jupiter

Statue of Hamlet with a statue of William Shakespeare in the background, Stratford-upon-Avon © Sigrid Dauth/Digital Railroad

The writing desk Jane Austen used at her house at Chawton, Hampshire © Jeremy Hoare/Alamy

Thomas Hardy © Bettman/Corbis

Ruins of Top Withins Farmhouse © John Heseltine/Corbis

Black and whites

p.218 Isle of Wight © Worldwide Picture Library /Alamy

p.279 Pump Room, Cheltenham © nagelestock .com/Alamy

p.302 Glastonbury Festival © Mark Thomas/Axiom

p.310 Sign advertising fresh fish © Fergus Kennedy/Alamy

p.358 Boscastle Harbour © Stephen Bond/Alamy

p.364 Stall, Norwich Market © Simon Pocklington /Alamy

p.382 Castle Mall shopping centre, Norwich © geogphotos/Alamy

p.476 Chester City Walls © Graham Light/Alamy

p.502 Liverpool nightlife © imagebroker/Alamy

p.512 Mountain bikers on the Isle of Man © Seb Rogers/Alamy

p.571 Cliffords Castle © Rolf Richardson/Alamy

p.588 Chillingham cows © Gary Cook/Alamy

p.628 Millennium Centre, Cardiff © Courtesy of Millennium centre

p.641 Welsh Male Voice Choir © Jeff Morgan /Alamy

p.685 Town and Bridge Crickhowell, Powys © Colin Underhill/Alamy

p.688 Competitors in Man and Horse race © The Photolibrary Wales/Alamy

p.773 Grassmarket © Lucy Cooke

p.791 Flyers for shows during the Edinburgh Fringe Festival © Lucy Cooke

p.800 Mountain biking in Galloway © South West Images Scotland/Alamy

p.817 The River Dee looking across to marina, MacLellans Castle and Kirkcudbright © South West Images Scotland/Alamy

p.826 Night scene, Glasgow © Axiom

p.835 The Glasgow Royal Exchange and Museum of Art © Ian Arthur/Alamy

p.867 Holiday narrow boats exiting the Falkirk wheel © Iain Masterton/Alamy

p.892 Arran © Scott Stickland

p.918 Gearrannan blackhouse village © Neil McAllister/Alamy

p.935 The beach at Seilebost on the Isle of Harris © nagelestock.com/Alamy

p.944 A string of Arbroath smokies © Louisa Macdonell/Alamy

p.974 The Three Sisters, Glen Coe © South West Images Scotland/Alamy

p.985 Sailing at Loch Morlich © David Gowans /Alamy

p.1002 Loch Gairloch at Badachro © David Gowans/Alamy

p.1010 Castle of Mey © John Peter Photography /Alamy

p.1018 Puffin © f1 online/Alamy

Index

Map entries are in colour.

A

B

INDEX

INDEX

F

G

INDEX

L

M

N

INDEX

Q

R

INDEX

S

INDEX

INDEX

Y

Z